DICTIONARY

OF

NATIONAL BIOGRAPHY

1961–1970

THE
DICTIONARY
OF
NATIONAL BIOGRAPHY

1961–1970

EDITED BY

E. T. WILLIAMS

AND

C. S. NICHOLLS

With an Index covering the years 1901–1970
in one alphabetical series

OXFORD UNIVERSITY PRESS
1981

Oxford University Press, Walton Street, Oxford OX2 6DP

London Glasgow New York Toronto
Delhi Bombay Calcutta Madras Karachi
Kuala Lumpur Singapore Hong Kong Tokyo
Nairobi Dar es Salaam Cape Town Salisbury
Melbourne Auckland

and associate companies in
Beirut Berlin Ibadan Mexico City

Published in the United States by
Oxford University Press, New York

British Library Cataloguing in Publication Data

Dictionary of national biography
1961–1970
1. Great Britain—Biography
I. Title   II. Williams, *Sir* Edgar
III. Nicholls, Christine
920'.041   CT774   80–41902
ISBN 0–19–865207–0

Typeset by the University Press, Oxford
Printed in Great Britain
by Richard Clay & Co. Ltd.,
Bungay, Suffolk

PREFATORY NOTE

THE individuals noticed in this Supplement were British subjects who died between 1 January 1961 and 31 December 1970.

Winston Churchill, the most famous of them, is joined here by other prime ministers: amongst them Clement Attlee, who succeeded him, Jawaharlal Nehru, W. T. Cosgrave, Stanley Bruce, Walter Nash, Norman Manley, and Abu Bakar Tafawa Balewa, who was assassinated. Churchill shared, too, membership of the Order of Merit with others to be discovered here, amongst them three presidents of the Royal Society each himself also a Nobel prizeman: Henry Dale, Howard Florey, and Cyril Hinshelwood; as well as another Nobel prizeman in J. D. Cockcroft, the first master of the College which bears Churchill's name.

Within the Order we may remark here sailors, soldiers, and airmen in Ernle Chatfield and Andrew Cunningham, Alanbrooke and Alexander, Cyril Newall and Arthur Tedder; or public servants of the stature of Malcolm Hailey, Edward Bridges, and Alexander Cadogan. The Order also encompassed T. S. Eliot, G. M. Trevelyan, John Masefield, Geoffrey de Havilland, the wayward genius of Augustus John and Bertrand Russell, as well as the more circumspect talents of Herbert Samuel or G. P. Gooch. As one strolls through the volume, one may notice too more than thirty Companions of Honour: amongst them Nancy Astor, J. D. Beazley, Thomas Beecham, John Barbirolli, Edward Gordon Craig, J. C. C. Davidson, John Dover Wilson, General Ismay, Walter Layton, Megan Lloyd George, Herbert Morrison, Lord Nuffield, Vita Sackville-West, Osbert Sitwell, and Arthur Waley.

Those who held the defence portfolios under Churchill are here: Margesson, then P. J. Grigg in the War Office, A. V. Alexander in the Admiralty, and Archibald Sinclair at the Air Ministry. And Maurice Hankey, who invented the role of secretary to the Cabinet, was followed by Bridges and by Normanbrook, who served alongside Ismay and Hollis in a central secretariat with a galaxy of remarkable civil servants in the various ministries and ambassadors and proconsuls beyond Whitehall itself.

It is all too easy for an editor who has lived so long with them to go on listing these various groupings. As well as the prime ministers with whom we began we may discover home secretaries from Churchill himself and Herbert Samuel to Herbert Morrison, Chuter-Ede, and Maxwell Fyfe, as it happens the sole lord chancellor in this volume. Or, if we sample another category, we may note amongst university chancellors not only Churchill himself at Bristol or Tedder at Cambridge, but Woolton in Manchester, Trevelyan and Scarbrough in Durham, Thomas Johnston in Aberdeen, Alanbrooke in Belfast, Iveagh and Edward Bridges at Reading, Florey and Cockcroft in Canberra, Beaverbrook in New Brunswick, Albert Centlivres in Cape Town, or Richard Feetham in the Witwatersrand. Amongst the newer universities in this country we may observe amongst their chancellors Walter Monckton in Brighton, Princess Marina at Canterbury, and two who died on the eve of becoming chancellor, Rootes of Warwick at Coventry, and Mackintosh of East Anglia at Norwich. Vice-chancellors may of course be remarked here too: most notably John Stopford at Manchester; Hector Hetherington, finally, in Glasgow; at Edinburgh Edward Appleton, another Nobel prizeman—there are seven such scientists in this Supplement—or Lillian Penson, the first woman vice-chancellor in London. And one cannot but notice too the striking links with the London School of Economics not only with one of the prime ministers but also in providing two chancellors of the Exchequer, Hugh Dalton and Hugh Gaitskell (but not Iain Macleod), as well as directors of the School itself such as Beveridge or Carr-Saunders. LSE boasted, too, R. H. Tawney, Morris Ginsberg, and Ivor Jennings, yet another vice-chancellor.

Whereas there are, one supposes, as many Etonians as in previous Supplements, it would be difficult for any school to match a half dozen as remarkable as Harrow's Churchill, Nehru, Alexander, G. M. Trevelyan, Walter Monckton, and R. A. Fisher.

Some have written lovingly of places—Percy Lubbock of Earlham, Wyndham Ketton-Cremer of Felbrigg, or Vita Sackville-West of Knole. Others have made places where they lived or worked abbreviations or household names. Readers may care to seek for themselves the links with, for example, Farnborough or Cranfield, Babraham or East Malling, Bloomsbury or Dartington. Or they may remark the influence of periodicals which crop up in these pages: the *Criterion*, *Medium Aevum*, the *New Statesman*, the *Political Quarterly*, the *Contemporary Review*, the *Illustrated London News*, the *Week-end Review*, *The Economist*, and, of course, *The Times*. Or of cartoonists, like David Low, 'Vicky', H. M. Bateman, 'Fougasse', 'Tom' Webster, or J. F. Horrabin. One notices too contributive publishers in Allen Lane, Victor Gollancz, Geoffrey Faber, and Stanley Unwin, or shopkeepers of the calibre of Simon Marks, Hugh Fraser, J. Spedan Lewis, and William Foyle. And children and sometimes parents must have been grateful to Richmal Crompton, 'Frank Richards', Enid Blyton, Captain W. E. Johns, John Wyndham, C. S. Lewis, or Arthur Ransome.

Since this is the third of the ten-year Supplements in the preparation of which the present editor has found it most agreeable to collaborate, it will be scarcely surprising that it follows the pattern of its predecessors. We are as grateful to and as dependent as ever upon our contributors for what you see here. On many of them we have relied too, most acceptably, for further advice most willingly afforded. Some have been especially helpful when others have fallen by the wayside. Many, alas, themselves are dead. Our job has been to check the facts so far as we are able. Opinions are another matter. We have tried to be neither too grasping nor too rigid in the choice of those included: there would seem, in the end, room for about the same total in each Supplement. There are 745 in this one. With the publication of a DNB in both Canada and Australia we have thought it apt to begin gradually to include fewer of their citizens in our pages; but not to have found space here for Vincent Massey, say, or Stanley Bruce, high commissioners in London throughout the war of 1939–45, would have seemed to draw the line too fiercely.

Two unrelated topics virtually excluded from earlier Supplements by taste or statute are now alluded to with less circumspection: 'Ultra' and homosexuality. As the admirable official histories of the war of 1939–45 begin to include their volumes on intelligence, the life-saving expertise of Bletchley may now be discussed more freely and the contribution of A. G. Denniston or Stewart Menzies acclaimed more fully. Less reticence today about homosexuality may make more intelligible the career of E. M. Forster or W. Somerset Maugham.

As well as thanking our contributors, we would wish to acknowledge most gratefully our continued reliance on obituaries furnished by learned societies, the Royal Society and the British Academy in particular. Without *The Times* we would have been bereft. As one tries to encompass a whole decade one acknowledges thankfully too the ready convenience of *Who Was Who*.

In the past the editor has attempted a conspectus by way of preface. This time in thanking those who have given him help so generously he has preferred instead just to express a very personal pleasure that, in addition to some of those mentioned in this note already (such as R. H. Tawney or T. S. Eliot), his last volume should include notices of Slim, Freyberg, J. B. Hobbs, Siegfried Sassoon, Myra Hess, and E. R. Peacock to whom he is surely not alone in feeling very much indebted indeed.

PREFATORY NOTE

In the acknowledgement which follows, contributors have not been thanked again individually but we would wish to express gratitude for advice from: Sir George Abell, Mr J. M. Bruce, Professor J. H. Burnett, Mr Andrew Carden, Sir Hugh Casson, the Very Revd Henry Chadwick, Professor J. F. Coales, the late Lord Cohen of Birkenhead, Dr Alexander Cooke, Sir Frederick Dainton, Sir Samuel Edwards, Sir Percival Griffiths, Sir Ewart Jones, Mr J. F. Kerslake, Professor Arthur J. Marder, Sir William Paton, Professor R. R. Porter, Sir Rex Richards, Sir Folliott Sandford, Mr Colin Watson, the late Sir Kenneth Wheare, and Sir David Willcocks. We hope that nobody who has helped, and there have been many, should go, by the editor's negligence, unthanked. Miss Helen Palmer, who worked with such effective devotion upon previous Supplements, set the standard for this one, in the earlier stages of which Mrs Anna Baidoun was then of great assistance. That this volume appears at all is due to the persistent and scholarly dedication of Mrs Christine S. Nicholls, the assistant editor whose name accordingly appears alongside a most grateful editor's on the title page. Both of us have been greatly aided by Mrs Pamela Coote and all three of us are most grateful for the help of the staffs of the Bodleian and its associated libraries. Finally, the editor has been given tremendous support throughout the compilation of all three Supplements by his wife, whom he would like to thank here most sincerely as he leaves a task which he has greatly enjoyed since 1949.

E. T. W.

Rhodes House, Oxford
30 September 1980

LIST OF CONTRIBUTORS

ABEL SMITH, Sir Henry:
Clifford.
ABRAHAM, Sir Edward Penley:
Colebrook.
ADDISON, Paul:
Sinclair (Thurso).
ALDERSON, Brian Wouldhave:
Attwell.
ALDISS, Brian Wilson:
Harris (John Wyndham).
ALLEN, Sir Peter Christopher:
Freeth.
ALLEN, William Alexander:
De Soissons.
AMIS, Kingsley:
Fleming.
AMOS, (Dennis) Bernard:
Gorer.
ANDREWES, Sir Christopher Howard:
Isaacs.
†ANDREWS, Sir (William) Linton:
Swaffer.
ANNAN, Noël Gilroy Annan, Baron:
Forster.
ARDWICK. See Beavan.
ARMSTRONG, Sir Robert Temple:
Eady.
ARMSTRONG, Sir Thomas Henry Wait:
Ley; Sargent (H. M. W.).
AVERY, Gillian Elise (Mrs A. O. J. Cockshut):
Ransome.

BAKER, Peter James:
Round.
BARNES, Christopher Henry George Bartlett:
Lachmann; Page.
BARR, James:
Rowley.
BARRETT, Anthony Gerard Martin:
Linstead.
BARRETT, Edwin Cyril Geddes:
Winstedt.
BARTON, Sir Derek Harold Richard:
Linstead.
BAWN, Cecil Edwin Henry:
Travers.
BAXANDALL, David Kighley:
Redpath.
BEAGLEHOLE, Timothy Holmes:
Nehru.
BEAMENT, Sir James William Longman:
Pantin.
†BEATON, Sir Cecil Walter Hardy:
Elsie.
BEAVAN, John Cowburn, Baron Ardwick:
Bone; Connor.
BECKINGHAM, Charles Fraser:
Cheesman.
BELL, (Anne) Olivier:
Bell (V.).
BELL, John Frederick:
Farjeon.

BELL, Quentin Claudian Stephen:
Woolf.
†BENNETT, Jack Arthur Walter:
Lewis (C. S.); Onions.
BENNETT, Richard Lawrence:
Kennedy (M. M.).
BERRESFORD ELLIS, Peter:
Johns.
BIRKINSHAW, Douglas Crosbie:
Shoenberg.
BIRLEY, Eric:
Richmond (I. A.).
BISHOP, James:
Ingram.
BLACKMAN, Moses:
Finch.
BLACKWELL, Sir Basil Henry:
Wilson (J. G.).
BLAKE, Robert Norman William Blake, Baron:
Ball; Davidson.
BLISS, Kathleen Mary:
Oldham.
BLUNT, Anthony Frederick:
Harris (T.).
BLUNT, Wilfrid Jasper Walter:
Cockerell.
BOND, Brian James:
Gough (H. de la P.); Morgan; Pownall.
BOULTER, Eric Thomas:
Whitfield (Kenswood).
BOWLE, John Edward:
Turner (G. C.).
BOYD, Sir (John) Francis:
Davies (C. E.).
BOYD, Sir John Smith Knox:
Fairley; MacArthur.
BRADSHAW, Maurice Bernard:
Orde; Salisbury.
BRETT-JAMES, (Eliot) Antony:
Giffard.
BRIGGS, Asa Briggs, Baron:
Mallon; Tawney.
BROADBENT, Donald Eric:
Bartlett.
BROCK, Patrick Willet:
Meade-Fetherstonhaugh; Oliver.
BROTHERSTON, Sir John Howie Flint:
Mackintosh.
BROWN, Sir (Ernest) Henry Phelps:
Carr-Saunders.
BROWN, John:
Jackson (Jackson of Burnley).
BROWN, John:
McNeill.
BRUCE, Gordon:
Short.
BRUNT, Peter Astbury:
Jones (A. H. M.).
BRYMER, Jack:
Beecham.
BUCKLEY, Sir Denys Burton:
Harman; Jenkins.

†BULMAN, George Purvis:
  Buchanan.
BULMER-THOMAS, Ivor:
  Fletcher (Winster).
BURCHFIELD, Robert William:
  Gowers.
BURKILL, John Charles:
  Besicovitch; Ingham.
†BUTLER, Sir James Ramsay Montagu:
  Trevelyan.
BUTLER OF SAFFRON WALDEN, Richard Austen
  Butler, Baron:
  Fox (L. W.).
†BUTTERFIELD, Sir Herbert:
  Gooch.
BUTTERWORTH, John Blackstock:
  Rootes.
BYAM SHAW, (John) James:
  Popham.

CADOGAN, John Ivan George:
  Read (J.).
CADOGAN, Mary:
  Lamburn (Richmal Crompton).
CAIRD, George Bradford:
  Hooke.
CAIRNCROSS, Sir Alexander Kirkland:
  Devons; Gray (A.).
CAMPBELL, Eila Muriel Joice:
  Taylor (E. G. R.).
CAMPBELL, Marian Laura:
  Lindsay.
†CAMPS, Francis Edward:
  Smith (S. A.).
CARNWATH, Sir Andrew Hunter:
  Peacock.
CAROE, Sir Olaf Kirkpatrick:
  Cunningham (G.).
CARTER, Harry Graham:
  Morison.
CARTWRIGHT, Dame Mary Lucy:
  Collingwood; Titchmarsh.
CARTWRIGHT, (William) Frederick:
  Pode.
CARVER, (Richard) Michael (Power) Carver, Baron:
  Fuller.
†ČERNÝ, Jaroslav:
  Gardiner (A. H.).
CHADWICK, (William) Owen:
  Raven.
†CHANDOS, Oliver Lyttelton, Viscount:
  Crookshank.
CHARLESTON, Robert Jesse:
  Rackham.
CHARLTON, Evan:
  Reed.
CHARNOCK, Henry:
  Doodson.
CHESTER, Sir (Daniel) Norman:
  Morris (Nuffield).
CHIBNALL, Albert Charles:
  Bailey (K.).
CHILTON, Sir (Charles) Edward:
  Joubert de la Ferté.
CHRISTIE, Walter Henry John:
  Menon.
CLAPHAM, Arthur Roy:
  Pearsall.

CLAPP, Brian William:
  Murray (J.).
†CLARK, Sir George Norman:
  Webster (C. K.).
CLARKSON, Richard Milroy:
  De Havilland.
COCKBURN, Sir Robert:
  Cawood.
COHEN, Richard Henry Lionel:
  Lucas.
COLDSTREAM, Sir William Menzies:
  Wellington.
†COLE, Dame Margaret Isabel:
  Horrabin, Middleton.
COLEMAN, Donald Cuthbert:
  Ashton (T. S.).
COLIN, Sidney:
  Flanagan.
COLLAR, (Arthur) Roderick:
  Relf.
COOPER, Bertram Samuel:
  Ryde.
COOPER, Leslie Hugh Norman:
  Harvey (H. W.).
†COOTE, Sir Colin Reith:
  Morrison (Dunrossil).
COOTE, Pamela Joy:
  Turrill.
†CORBISHLEY, Thomas:
  Martindale.
CORK, Richard Graham:
  Stephenson (J. C.).
CORNFORTH, John Lawley:
  Hussey.
†COURT, William Henry Bassano:
  Hindley (Hyndley).
COWLING, Thomas George:
  Chapman.
COWPER, Francis Henry:
  Evershed; Hilbery.
Cox, Anthony David Machell:
  Noyce.
Cox, Anthony Wakefield:
  De Syllas.
Cox, Sir (Ernest) Gordon:
  Slater.
CRIPPS, Sir John Stafford:
  Robertson Scott.
CRITCHLEY, Thomas Alan:
  Dixon (A. L.).
CRITTALL, John Francis:
  Webb.
CROMARTY, Roger Anthony:
  Spencer.
CROMBIE, Ian MacHattie:
  Farrer.
CROOK, John Anthony:
  Adcock.
CROSS, Lionel Lesley:
  Lawson (Burnham).
CUNNINGHAM, Daniel John Chapman:
  Douglas (C. G.).
CURREY, Ralph Nixon:
  Gibson.

DANIEL, Reginald Jack:
  Lillicrap.

†DARLINGTON, William Aubrey:
Ashton (Clemence Dane); Clunes; Hardwicke; Malleson; O'Casey; Sherek; Wynyard.

†DAVENPORT, Nicholas Ernest Harold:
Dalton.

DAVIDSON, John Frank:
Fox (T. R. C.).

DAVIN, Daniel Marcus:
Freyberg; MacNeice.

†DEAN, Sir Maurice Joseph:
Garrod; Newall; Worboys.

DENNISTON, Robin Alastair:
Unwin.

DEVLIN, Patrick Arthur Devlin, Baron:
Birkett; Wright (R. A.).

DITCHBURN, Robert William:
Smith (T.).

DOGGART, George Hubert Graham:
Altham.

DOLL, Sir (William) Richard (Shaboe):
Brown (W. M. C.).

DOUGLAS, Sir Donald Macleod:
Learmonth.

DOUGLAS, Ronald Walter:
Turner (W. E. S.).

DOWNIE, Allan Watt:
Bedson.

DRUETT, Henry Arthur:
Henderson.

DRURY, Paul Dalou:
Anderson.

DRYDEN, Colin John:
Clark (J.).

DUFF, Patrick William:
Gater.

DUKE, Cecil Howard Armitage:
Fergusson.

DUNBAR, Janet (Mrs Clifford Webb):
Knight (H. and L.).

DUNHAM, Sir Kingsley Charles:
Hollingworth; Holmes (A.); Richey; Taylor (James Hayward).

EDWARDS, David Lawrence:
Shirley.

EDWARDS, Joseph:
Hammond (J.).

ELLIOT, Sir John:
Aitken (Beaverbrook).

ELLIOT OF HARWOOD, Katherine Elliot, Baroness:
Horsbrugh.

ELLMANN, Richard:
Eliot.

ENTHOVEN, Roderick Eustace:
Robertson (H. M.).

EVANS, Sir David Gwynne:
Glenny.

EVANS, Sir David Lewis:
Flower.

EVANS, Sir (Robert) Charles:
Brown (T. G.).

EVELYN, (John) Michael:
Mathew.

FAIRN, (Richard) Duncan:
Maxwell (A.).

FALCON, Norman Leslie:
Fearnsides; Illing.

FALKNER, Sir (Donald) Keith:
Dyson.

FARMER, Bertram Hughes:
Wordie.

FARR, Dennis Larry Ashwell:
Wilde (J.).

FARRAR-HOCKLEY, Sir Anthony Heritage:
Nye.

FARRER, David:
Dunne.

†FEATHER, Norman:
Whiddington.

FELDBERG, Wilhelm Siegmund:
Dale; Gaddum.

FENTON, Colin:
Hodgson.

FERGUSON, Howard:
Hess.

FLEMING, Sir Charles Alexander:
Marsden.

FLETCHER, Hans Duncan:
Charoux; Dobson (F. O.); Lambert.

FLETCHER-COOKE, Sir Charles Fletcher:
Hobson.

FLETCHER-COOKE, Sir John:
Twining.

FOOT, Michael Richard Daniell:
Browning; Hambro.

FOX, Hazel Mary Fox, Lady:
Williams (I.).

FOYLE, Christina Agnes Lilian (Mrs Ronald Batty):
Foyle.

FRANK, Sir (Frederick) Charles:
Powell.

FRANKFORT, Enriqueta Eva:
Bing.

FRASER, Sir David William:
Brooke (Alanbrooke).

FREEDLAND, Mark Robert:
Macassey.

FRERE, Richard Burchmore:
Maxwell (G.).

GALE, Ernest Frederick:
Woods (D. D.).

GARDINER, Richard Aylmer:
Hotine.

GARDNER, Dame Helen Louise:
Simpson (P.).

GARLICK, Kenneth John:
Bodkin.

GARNETT, Alice:
Fleure.

GARNETT, (William) John (Poulton Maxwell):
Hyde.

GAYE, Freda:
Leigh.

GILES, Frank Thomas Robertson:
Knollys.

GILMOUR, Sir Ian Hedworth John Little, Bart.:
Macleod.

GILSON, John Cary:
Morant.

GLADWYN, Hubert Miles Gladwyn Jebb, Baron:
Sargent (H. O. G.).

GLASGOW, Mary Cecilia:
Wilson (J. S.).

GLUBB, Sir John Bagot:
Peake (F. G.).
GODBER, Sir George Edward:
Jameson; MacNalty.
GOLDIE, Grace Wyndham:
Somerville.
†GOLDSMITH, William Noel:
Gray (A. M. H.).
GOODBODY, Douglas Maurice:
Lawrence.
†GOODEVE, Sir Charles Frederick:
Smith (F. E.).
†GOODHART, Arthur Lehman:
Nathan.
†GORDON-WALKER, Patrick Chrestien Gordon
Walker, Baron:
Gaitskell.
GORE-BOOTH, Paul Henry Gore-Booth, Baron:
Cadogan.
GOULDEN, Gontran Iceton:
Cross.
GOWING, Margaret Mary:
Darwin (C. G.).
GRANT, Patrick Thomas:
Kermack.
GRAY, Basil:
Waley (A. D.).
GREANY, Hugh Wingate:
Snedden.
†GREAVES, Robert William:
Penson.
GREEN, David Mitchell:
Tulloch.
GREEN, John:
Fox (H. M.).
GREENE, Sir Hugh Carleton:
Gedye.
GREENFIELD, George Charles:
Blyton.
GREENHAM, Peter George:
Gunn.
GRENFELL, Harry St. Leger:
Robins.
†GRENFELL, Joyce Irene:
Potter.
GRETTON, Sir Peter William:
Le Fanu; North (D. B. N.); Plunkett-Ernle-Erle-Drax; Vian.
GRIBBLE, Leonard Reginald:
Hatry.
GRIGG, John Edward Poynder:
Astor.
†GRIMSDITCH, Herbert Borthwick:
Flint.
GUEST, John:
Hassall.
GULLICK, John Michael:
MacGillivray.
GUNSTONE, Frank Denby:
Hilditch.

HACKETT, Sir John Winthrop:
Wilson (H. M.).
HACKMANN, Willem Dirk:
Burney.
HAIR, Paul Edward Hedley:
Edwards (E.).

HALBERSTAM, Heini:
Davenport.
†HALE, Sir Edward:
Hancock (H. D.).
HALEY, Sir William John:
Barry (G. R.); Bonham Carter (Asquith of Yarnbury); Jones (G. R.); Walter.
HALL, Sir Arnold Alexander:
Dobson (R. H.).
HALL, Harry Syre:
Hosier.
HALLIWELL, Leslie:
Karloff.
HALSBURY, John Anthony Hardinge Giffard, Earl of:
Mills.
HALSEY, Albert Henry:
Ginsberg.
HAMILTON, Sir (Charles) Denis:
Berry (Kemsley).
HAMILTON, (John) Alan:
Smart.
HAMILTON, Walter:
Duff.
HAMILTON-EDWARDS, Gerald Kenneth Savery:
Marina (Kent); Victoria Alexandra Alice Mary (Princess Royal); Victoria Eugénie (Queen of Spain); Wrench.
HAMMOND, Percy:
Moullin.
HANCE, Betty Kathleen:
Round.
HARDIE, Frank Martin:
Angell; Martin (B. K.).
HARKNESS, David William:
Cosgrave.
HARRIS, José Ferial:
Beveridge.
HARRIS, Thomas Maxwell:
Thomas (H. H.).
HARRIS, Sir William Gordon:
Whitaker.
HART-DAVIS, Sir Rupert Charles:
Sassoon.
†HARTLEY, Sir Harold:
Hinshelwood; Livens; McKie; Merton.
HARTREE, Edward Francis:
Keilin.
†HASKELL, Arnold Lionel:
Turner (H.).
HASLAM, Edward Brooke:
Dowding.
HAWTHORNE, Sir William Rede:
Constant.
HAYNES, Sir George Ernest:
Adams.
HAYTER, Sir William Goodenough:
Harvey (Harvey of Tasburgh).
HEAL, Anthony Standerwick:
Coatalen.
HENDERSON, Kenneth David Druitt:
Creed.
†HERBAGE, Julian Livingston-:
Ireland.
HEUSTON, Robert Francis Vere:
Fyfe (Kilmuir).
HICKS, Sir John Richard:
Robertson (D. H.).

HILL, John Edward Bernard:
Margesson.
HILL, (Richard) Desmond:
Barry (E. J.); Burnell.
HILL, Robert:
Mapson.
HIMSWORTH, Sir Harold Percival:
Elliott; Jefferson.
HINSLEY, Francis Harry:
Denniston.
HOBSON, Anthony Robert Alwyn:
Abbey.
HODSON, Francis Lord Charlton Hodson, Baron:
Merriman.
HODSON, Frank:
Hawkins.
HOLLAND, Thomas, Bishop of Salford (R.C.):
Godfrey (W.).
HOLLINGSWORTH, Dorothy Frances:
Wright (N. C.).
†HOLME, Thea:
Thirkell.
HOLT, James Clarke:
Stenton.
†HONE, Sir Evelyn Dennison:
Gore-Browne.
HOPKINS, Kenneth:
Powys.
HORNBY, Sir (Roger) Antony:
Drayton.
HORNE, Ronald Cozens-Hardy:
Holland (E. M.).
HUDSON, Norman Harry:
Hanbury-Williams.
HUMPHREY, Arthur Hugh Peters:
Thomas (T. S. W.).
HUNT, Sir David Wathen Stather:
Alexander (Alexander of Tunis).
HUSSEY, Joan Mervyn:
Baynes.
†HUTCHISON, Sir James Riley Holt, Bart.:
Yeo-Thomas.
HUTCHISON, Robert Edward:
Hutchison.
HUTCHISON, Sidney Charles:
Dick; Rushbury.
HUTTON, (David) Graham:
Layton.
HUXTABLE, (William) John (Fairchild):
Franks; Watson (J. A.).
HUXTER, Neil Ellison Wilkie:
Forester.

IGNATIEFF, George:
Massey.
INCHCAPE, Kenneth James William Mackay, Earl of:
Currie.
†INMAN, Philip Albert Inman, Baron:
Mackintosh (Mackintosh of Halifax).

JACKSON, John Semple:
Hudson.
JACOB, Sir (Edward) Ian (Claud):
Hollis.
JARRETT, Sir Clifford George:
Alexander (Alexander of Hillsborough).
JENKINS, Gilbert Kenneth:
Walker.

JENKINS, Harold:
Wilson (J. D.).
JENSEN, John Paisley:
Bateman.
JEPSON, Selwyn:
Peulevé.
†JOHNSON, Harold Cottam:
Jenkinson; Johnson (C.).
JOHNSTON, Douglas Harold Johnston, Lord:
Thomson (G. R.).
JOPE, Edward Martyn:
Fox (C. F.).

KARMEL, David:
Monckton (Monckton of Brenchley).
KEATING, Henry Reymond Fitzwalter:
Allingham.
KEENLYSIDE, Francis Hugh:
Leathers.
KELLY, Anthony:
Gough (H. J.).
KEMP, Peter Kemp:
Boyle (Cork and Orrery); Chatfield; Cunningham (J. H. D.).
KENNEDY, (George) Michael (Sinclair):
Barbirolli.
KINGSFORD, Peter Wilfred:
Lanchester.
KINGS NORTON, Harold Roxbee Cox, Baron:
Griffith; Hives; Lombard; North (J. D.).
KINROSS, John Blythe:
Piercy.
†KIPPING, Sir Norman Victor:
Beaver; Costain; Woods (J. H. E.).
KIRK, Harry:
Peppiatt.
KIRK-GREENE, Anthony Hamilton Millard:
Arden-Clarke; Meek.
KNIGHT, Robert:
Bowater.
†KNOX, Sir (Thomas) Malcolm:
Fraser (Fraser of Allander); Taylor (T. M.).

LAITHWAITE, Sir (John) Gilbert:
Dundas (Zetland); Lumley (Scarbrough); Maffey (Rugby).
LAUTERPACHT, Elihu:
Hurst.
LEAKE, Bernard Elgey:
Whittard.
LEE, Sir David John Pryer:
Longmore; Salmond.
†LEE, David Thomas:
Griffiths.
LEES-MILNE, James:
Nicolson.
LEHMANN, John Frederick:
Sitwell (E. L.); Sitwell (F. O. S.).
LE MAY, Godfrey Hugh Lancelot:
Feetham.
LENNOX-SHORT, Alan:
Centlivres.
LESLIE, Anita (Mrs W. Leslie-King):
Sheridan.
LEWIN, (George) Ronald:
Dimbleby; Ismay; Liddell Hart.
LIDDERDALE, Sir David William Shuckburgh:
Fellowes.

NICHOLLS, Christine Stephanie:
   Martin (W. K.); Nelson (Nelson of Stafford).
NICHOLSON, Sir John Norris, Bart.:
   Hobhouse.
†NICOLSON, Lionel Benedict:
   Bell (A. C. H.).
NIVEN, Sir (Cecil) Rex:
   Bello.
NOCK, Oswald Stevens:
   Stanier.
NORMAN, (Alexander) Vesey (Bethune):
   Mann.
NORMAN, Kathleen Mary:
   Jarvis.
NORMAN, Mark Richard:
   De Stein.
NORRINGTON, Sir Arthur Lionel Pugh:
   Williams (A. T. P.).
NORTHCOTT, (William) Cecil:
   Berry (S. M.); Martin (H.).
NOWELL-SMITH, Simon Harcourt:
   Richmond (B. L.).

†OAKLEY, Cyril Leslie:
   Cameron.
ODD, Gilbert Edward Scott:
   Wilde (W. J.).
O'LEARY, Cornelius:
   O'Kelly.
O'NEILL, Hon. Sir Con Douglas Walter:
   Kirkpatrick.
ONSLOW, Richard Arthur Michael:
   Webster (G. T.).
OWEN, (Reginald) John:
   Paget.
OXBURY, Harold Frederick:
   Grigg; Pethick-Lawrence; Samuel; Warner.

†PACK, Stanley Walter Croucher:
   Brind; Cunningham (Cunningham of Hyndhope).
†PARKER, Sir Harold:
   Leith-Ross.
PARKER, Herbert Thomas:
   Clark (A. G.).
PARKER, Kenneth Alfred Lamport:
   Game.
PARKES, Sir Alan Sterling:
   Brambell; Folley.
†PARSONS, Ian Macnaghten:
   Huxley.
PATON, Sir Leonard Cecil:
   Macfadyen.
PATTERSON, Alfred Temple:
   Wood.
PATTINSON, John Mellor:
   Fraser (Strathalmond).
PAYNTER, (Thomas) William:
   Horner.
PEARCE, Solomon:
   Milner (Milner of Leeds).
PEART, (Thomas) Frederick Peart, Baron:
   Williams (Williams of Barnburgh).
PEEL, Sir John Harold:
   Holland (E. L.).
PEEL, John Hugh Brignal:
   Street.
†PENFIELD, Wilder Graves:
   Holmes (G. M.).

PENNEY, William George Penney, Baron:
   Cockcroft; Kronberger.
PENROSE, Harold James:
   Petter.
PEPYS-WHITELEY, Derek:
   Low; Lubbock.
PEROWNE, Stewart Henry:
   Luke.
PETERSON, Sir Arthur William:
   Chuter-Ede.
†PETRIE, Sir Charles Alexander, Bart.:
   Jerrold.
PHILLIPS, Patrick Laurence:
   Brown (O. F. G.).
PICKERING, Sir Edward Davies:
   Christiansen.
†PICKERING, Sir George White:
   Brain; Pickles.
PICKFORD, (Lillian) Mary:
   Verney.
PIMLOTT, Benjamin John:
   Wilmot.
PIRIE, Norman Wingate:
   Russell (E. J.).
PLATT, Sir Harry, Bart.:
   Stopford.
POLLOCK, John Charles:
   Aylward.
PORTER, Helen Kemp:
   Blackman; Gregory; Richards.
POSNETTE, Adrian Frank:
   Hatton.
POUND, Reginald:
   Gibbs.
POWELL, (Elizabeth) Dilys:
   Field; Mackworth-Young.
POYNTON, Sir (Arthur) Hilton:
   Lloyd (T. I. K.); Parkinson.
PRAIN, Sir Ronald Lindsay:
   Beatty.
PRESTON, Reginald Dawson:
   Astbury.
†PRICE, Morgan Philips:
   Carruthers.
PRINGLE, John William Sutton:
   Pumphrey.
PRITCHARD, Sir Fred Eills:
   Hawke.
PROCHASKA, Alice Marjorie Sheila:
   Crowdy; Gwynne-Vaughan.
PUGH, Lewis Owain:
   Tuker.
PUGH, Patricia Marie:
   Jones (A. C.).
PUGSLEY, Sir Alfred Grenvile:
   Southwell.
PYKE, Magnus:
   Bacharach.

QUINN, David Beers:
   Skelton.
QUINTON, Anthony Meredith:
   Russell (B. A. W.).

RANKINE, Sir John Dalzell:
   Mitchell.

RAPHAEL, Frederic Michael:
  Maugham.
RATCLIFFE, John Ashworth:
  Appleton; Eccles.
RAYNOR, Geoffrey Vincent:
  Hume-Rothery.
READER, William Joseph:
  McGowan.
REASON, John:
  Davies (W. J. A.).
REDCLIFFE-MAUD, John Primatt Redcliffe Redcliffe-
  Maud, Baron:
  Marquis (Woolton).
REESE, Max Meredith:
  *Barnes (S. F.); Hammond; Hardy; Hobbes;
  Worrell.*
REID, John Kelman Sutherland:
  Duncan.
REILLY, Paul Reilly, Baron:
  Yerbury.
RICHARDS, Paul Westmacott:
  Thoday.
RITCHIE-CALDER, Peter Ritchie Ritchie-Calder,
  Baron:
  Weisz (Vicky); Williams (Francis-Williams).
ROBERTS, Colin Henderson:
  Bell (H. I.).
ROBERTS, John Alexander Fraser:
  Gates.
†ROBERTS, Michael Rookherst:
  Slim.
ROBERTS, Paul Harry:
  Havelock.
ROBERTSON, Charles Martin:
  Beazley.
ROBERTSON, Sir James Wilson:
  Symes; Tafawa Balewa.
ROBERTSON, Jean (Mrs Jean Bromley):
  Wilson (F. P.).
†ROBIESON, Sir William:
  Johnston.
ROBINSON, Kenneth Ernest:
  Ormsby-Gore (Harlech).
ROBINSON, Ronald Edward:
  Cohen (A. B.).
ROBSON, William Alexander:
  Jennings.
ROCHESTER, George Dixon:
  Curtis.
ROLO, Paul Jacques Victor:
  Harari (M.); Harari, (R.A.)
ROSE, Kenneth Vivian:
  *Brabazon (Brabazon of Tara); Hooper; Turnour
  (Winterton).*
ROTHENSTEIN, Sir John Knewstub Maurice:
  Ironside; John.
ROTHMAN, Nathan:
  Campbell.
RUSSELL, Arthur Colin:
  Danquah.
†RUSSELL, Sir (Sydney) Gordon:
  Barlow (T. D.).
RUST, Brian Arthur Lovell:
  Hylton; Payne.
†RYAN, Alfred Patrick:
  Brown (A. E.).
RYDE, Peter Leighton:
  Darwin (B.); Taylor (John Henry).

†SACHS, Sir Eric, Lord Justice Sachs:
  Littlewood.
SAMUELS, Albert Edward:
  Latham.
SARGENT, Sir Donald:
  Gardiner (T. R.).
SAVILLE, John:
  Myrddin-Evans; Phillips.
SAWER, Geoffrey:
  Evatt.
SCHMOLLER, Hans Peter:
  Lane.
SCHOFIELD, Andrew Noel:
  Roscoe.
SCOTT-JAMES, Anne Eleanor (Lady Lancaster):
  Sackville-West (V. M.).
SCOTT-SUTHERLAND, Colin:
  Scott.
SEALY, Theodore Eustace:
  Manley.
SEARLE, Humphrey:
  Goossens.
SELLORS, Sir Thomas Holmes:
  Souttar.
SEWARD, John Richard Gowing:
  Worthington.
†SHAKESPEARE, Sir Geoffrey Hithersay, Bart.:
  Bellman.
SHEPPARD, Richard:
  Yorke.
†SHIPTON, Eric Earle:
  Longstaff.
SHOCK, Maurice:
  Attlee.
SHOENBERG, David:
  London.
SHONE, Richard Noël:
  Le Bas.
SHONE, Sir Robert Minshull:
  Hunter.
SHOPPEE, Charles William:
  Ingold.
SHORTT, Henry Edward:
  Leiper.
SHOTTON, Frederick William:
  King (W. B. R.).
SHUCKBURGH, Sir (Charles Arthur) Evelyn:
  Dixon (P. J.).
†SIEFF, Israel Moses Sieff, Baron:
  Marks (Marks of Broughton).
SILK, Dennis Raoul Whitehall:
  Masefield.
SIMKINS, Charles Anthony Goodall:
  Petrie; Sillitoe.
SINCLAIR, Keith:
  Nash.
SKEMPTON, Alec Westley:
  Pippard.
SKIPWITH, Peyton Stephen:
  Wolmark.
SLATER, August Henry Klie:
  Fyfe (W. H.).
SMEATON, William Arthur:
  Partington.
SMITH, Sir (James) Eric:
  Cannon.
SMITH, Thomas Broun:
  Keith (Keith of Avonholm); Normand.

†SMYTH, David Henry:
Evans (C. A. L.).
SMYTH, Sir John George, Bart.:
Sterry.
SNOW, Philip Albert:
Spens.
SOUTHERN, Sir Richard William:
Powicke.
†SPEAIGHT, Robert William:
Bridges-Adams; Read (H. B.); Sackville-West
(Sackville).
SPEED, Sir Robert William Arney:
Barnes (T. J.).
†SPRING, Marion Ursula Howard:
Spring.
STEERS, James Alfred:
Debenham.
STEPHENSON, Alan Malcolm George:
Major.
STEVENSON, Derek Paul:
Dain.
†STEWART, Alexander Bernard:
Daley.
STIRLING, Alfred Thorpe:
Bruce (Bruce of Melbourne).
STOCKWOOD, Arthur Mervyn:
Johnson (H.).
†STOW HILL, Frank Soskice, Baron:
Hall.
STRAWSON, John Michael:
Dempsey; McCreery.
†STRUTT, Sir (Henry) Austin:
Barlow (J. A. N.); Newsam; Sheepshanks.
STUBBLEFIELD, Sir (Cyril) James:
Bailey (E. B.).
SUMMERSON, Sir John Newenham:
Godfrey (W. H.); Richardson.
SUTCLIFFE, Reginald Cockcroft:
Brunt.
SUTHERLAND, James Runcieman:
Smith (D. N.).
SUTTON, John:
Read (H. H.).
SWEET-ESCOTT, Bickham Aldred Cowan:
Nelson (F.).
SYKES, Christopher Hugh:
Laycock.
SYMONS, Eleanor Dale Putnam:
Franklin.

TABOR, David:
Bowden.
TAPLIN, Walter:
Howitt.
TAYLOR, Sir George:
Bailey (F. M.).
TAYLOR, William Hodge:
James.
TEMPLE, George:
Bairstow; Wilson (W.).
THOMAS, Brian Dick Lauder:
Easton.
THOMAS, Hugh Swynnerton:
Strachey.
THOMPSON, Edwin Reynolds:
King-Hall.
THOMPSON, Sir Harold Warris:
Raman.

THOMPSON, Kenneth Douglas:
Dawtry.
THOMSON, George Malcolm:
Cudlipp.
†TILLOTSON, GEOFFREY:
Williams (H. H.).
TILLOTSON, Kathleen Mary:
Darbishire.
TOMLIN, Eric Walter Frederick:
Ferguson; Hayward.
TOMPKINS, Frederick Clifford:
Guggenheim.
TOMPKINS, James Charles Harrison:
Wilson (J. L.).
TREND, Burke St. John Trend, Baron:
Bridges; Brook (Normanbrook); Waley (S. D.).
TREVOR-ROPER, Patrick Dacre:
Holland (H. T.).
TREWIN, John Courtenay:
Craig; Jackson (B. V.).
TURNER, Ernest Sackville:
Hamilton (Frank Richards).
TURNOCK, Benjamin Joseph Wesley:
Warrington.
TURVEY, James Robert:
Peat.

URQUHART, Brian Edward:
Owen.

VEVERS, (Henry) Gwynne:
Fisher (J. M. M.).
VICARY, Douglas Reginald:
Chavasse.
VINCENT, Ewart Albert:
Wager.

WALKER, Stella Archer:
Edwards (L. D. R.).
†WALL, John Edward Wall, Baron:
French; Lloyd (E. M. H.).
WALLS, Henry James:
Holden.
WALSH, Patrick Gerard:
Waddell.
WARDLE, (John) Irving:
Devine.
WARMINGTON, Eric Herbert:
Lockwood.
WATT, David:
Brand.
WENDEN, David John:
Asquith (A.).
†WEST, Harry:
Bailey (G. E.).
WHALLEY, William Basil:
Robertson (A.).
WHITE, Eirene Lloyd White, Baroness:
Brittain.
WHITE, Errol Ivor:
Cox.
WHITTAKER, John Macnaghten:
Aitken (A. C. A.); Watson (G. N.).
WIGGLESWORTH, Sir Vincent Brian:
Uvarov.
WILKINSON, (Lancelot) Patrick:
Ord.
WILLETT, Archibald Anthony:
Wilshaw.

WILLIAMS, Alwyn:
Jones (O. T.).
WILLIAMS, Sir Edgar Trevor:
Allen (C. K.); Carton de Wiart; Churchill.
WILLIAMS, Gareth Howel:
Kenyon; Turner (E. E.).
WILLIAMS, Piers:
Johns.
†WILLIAMS, Sir William Emrys:
Pooley.
WILSON, Clifford:
Ellis; Evans (H.).
WISE, Michael John:
Stamp; Wooldridge.
WOHLFARTH, Erich Peter:
Stoner.
WOOD, Frederick Lloyd Whitfield:
Holland (S. G.).
†WOODRUFF, (John) Douglas:
Waugh.
WOODWARD, David:
Thomson (G. P.).
WOOLNER, Frank Thomas:
Pollitt.
WOOTTON, Ian David Phimester:
King (E. J.).
WORTHINGTON, Edgar Barton:
Sewell.
WRIGHT, (Arthur Robert) Donald:
Coade.

WRIGHT, Cyril Maynard:
Fleck.
†WRIGHT, Sir Michael Robert:
Lampson (Killearn).
WRIGHT, Peter:
McNaughton.
WRIGHT, Ronald William Vernon Selby:
Warr.
WYKEHAM, Sir Peter:
Atcherley; Camm; Douglas (Douglas of Kirtleside); Tedder.
WYKES, Nigel Gordon:
Christie.

YATES, Anne:
Luthuli.
YATES, Frank:
Fisher (R. A.).
YONGE, Sir (Charles) Maurice:
Stephenson (T. A.).
YOUNG, Sir Frank George:
Frazer.
YOXALL, Harry Waldo:
Allen (H. W.).

ZIMAN, Herbert David:
Watson (A. E.).
ZUCKERMAN, Solly Zuckerman, Baron:
Cotton.

DICTIONARY

OF

NATIONAL BIOGRAPHY

(TWENTIETH CENTURY)

PERSONS WHO DIED 1961-1970

ABBEY, JOHN ROLAND (1894-1969), book collector, was born in Brighton 23 November 1894, the eldest of three sons of William Henry Abbey, brewer, of Sedgwick Park, Horsham, and his wife, Florence, daughter of Henry Belcher, of Hove, Sussex. He was named John Rowland, but later dropped the 'w'.

In consequence of an accident which caused lasting damage to one elbow, he was educated by a private tutor, Mr Möens, at Rottingdean, instead of at school. In November 1914 he was commissioned in the Rifle Brigade and served as a regimental officer on the western front for two years from September 1915. The 13th and 8th battalions, to which he was posted in succession, saw severe fighting and both suffered heavy casualties. During the capture of Flers on 15 September 1916, when he was temporarily in reserve, the 8th battalion lost all its officers except one. He spent five months in hospital and on sick leave after being gassed in November 1916, the only interval in this long term of active service. He was invalided home in October 1917 and demobilized in August 1919. His war experiences in France and Flanders, especially during the third battle of Ypres, remained a vivid memory even in old age. His younger brother, Lt. Noel Roland Abbey, was killed in action in France in 1918 serving with the Grenadier Guards.

Abbey became a director of the Kemp Town Brewery, Brighton, after leaving the army, and succeeded his father as chairman after the latter's death in 1943. The brewery was sold to Charrington's in 1954. He rejoined the Rifle Brigade in November 1939 and served for two years from 1941 as staff officer to the admiral-superintendent, Great Yarmouth, until his release in October 1943. In 1946 he was granted the honorary rank of major.

He started to collect in 1929, buying initially the productions of the modern private presses, and eventually formed complete collections of books from the Kelmscott, Ashendene, and Gregynog presses. His Kelmscott books included the Bible in pigskin blind-tooled by the Doves Bindery after a design by William Morris [q.v.]; the Gregynog books were all bound by the press bindery. Meanwhile he had become interested in modern bindings and in 1931 commissioned examples from Sybil Pye and R. de Coverley & Sons. The latter, on a copy of *Memoirs of an Infantry Officer* by Siegfried Sassoon [q.v.], bore Abbey's arms and was decorated to his design. His first antiquarian bindings were some modestly priced armorial examples from the Rosebery sale of 1933 but this part of the collection was rapidly built up between 1936 and 1938 with purchases from the Mensing, Moss, Aldenham, Schiff, and Cortlandt F. Bishop sales and ultimately numbered over 1,300 works, including seven Groliers. Contemporary French binding, with its faultless technique, its air of luxury, and its bold colouring, gave him particular pleasure. In 1937 he ordered his first specimen from Paul Bonet, whom he regarded as the greatest living master of the craft, and eventually he owned a hundred modern illustrated books, mostly in polychrome bindings by Bonet, Creuzevault, Martin, and other members of the Société de la Reliure Originale, acquired or commissioned on post-war visits to Paris.

Bindings, however, did not monopolize his interest or resources. From 1935, with the help of two booksellers, George Stephenson of Messrs Rimell, and later George Bates, of Hove, he collected English colour-plate books of the eighteenth and nineteenth centuries. Here he broke new ground by paying attention to many neglected minor works, to copies in the wrappered parts in which they were issued, and to original condition. The collection, eventually consisting of 1,914 items, represented the most creative side of his connoisseurship.

In 1946 he entered a new field by buying for £40,000 the collection of illuminated manuscripts, mostly written in gothic or humanistic scripts, formed by C. H. St. John Hornby [q.v.], the founder of the Ashendene Press. With the help of a small but distinguished group from Sir Sydney Cockerell [q.v.], of the fourteenth-century *Ruskin Hours* and the late and lavish *Monypenny Breviary* bought from a Hove collector, D. M. Colman, and of single purchases from booksellers and at auction, Abbey finally acquired 143 medieval and Renaissance manuscripts. This collection, however, although including many outstanding volumes, remained a somewhat heterogeneous assemblage, owing its excellence more to the taste of Hornby and Cockerell than to its owner's discrimination. The library reached its maximum size at Greyfriars, Storrington, in the mid 1950s, with the addition of many bibliographical works and private library catalogues—bought in part at the suggestion of A. N. L. Munby—and an almost complete set of Roxburghe Club publications.

Abbey made no pretensions to scholarship and knew no language except English. It was the appearance, not the contents, of books which appealed to him. He was, however, a keen reader and a tireless visitor to libraries and bookshops; he had an excellent visual memory and a flair for quality in bindings; and he was fortunate in being advised by distinguished scholars notably G. D. Hobson [q.v.] and A. N. L. Munby. He admired bibliographical scholarship and wanted his collections to be of service to bibliographers. For this purpose he commissioned a series of handsomely produced catalogues; G. D. Hobson, *English Bindings, 1490–1940, in the Library of J. R. Abbey* (1940); A. R. A. Hobson, *French and Italian Collectors and their Bindings, illustrated from examples in the library of J. R. Abbey* (1953); J. J. G. Alexander and A. C. de la Mare, *The Italian Manuscripts in the Library of Major J. R. Abbey* (1969). The bindings he had commissioned both in England and on the Continent were exhibited at the Arts Council in 1949 and 1965, and described in the exhibition catalogues. In early days he bought many damages or over-restored specimens. But a post-war visit to Sir Robert Abdy's eighteenth-century morocco library at Newton Ferrers, in a room permanently curtained to prevent sunlight fading the spines, converted him to the French attitude to book collecting, in which quality and fine condition are the predominant considerations.

Having bought extensively in the buyer's market of the 1930s Abbey was not always able to resist the temptation of a profit when prices rose after the war. Through John Carter of Charles Scribner & Sons he sold the colour-plate collection to Paul Mellon before the last two volumes of the catalogue had appeared. It is now at Yale University. A small group of fine books went to H. P. Kraus, of New York, and his German bindings to the Württembergische Landesbibliothek, Stuttgart. The other bindings and the bibliography were auctioned in a

series of four sales in 1965–7 for £378,313. In 1967 Abbey moved from Redlynch House Salisbury (his residence since he left Storrington in Sussex in 1957) to a flat at 12 Hill Street, Mayfair. Here the medieval manuscripts, French illustrated books, and modern bindings were shelved. He died in London 24 December 1969. With the exception of a select group of manuscripts retained by his family, the Kelmscott Press books, which he had given to Eton College library, and a choice of six French bindings bequeathed to the British Museum, the remainder of the collection was dispersed in five further sales in 1970–5 for £993,509.

If not the most learned, Abbey was certainly the largest English book collector of his time. His colour-plate collection showed genuine originality and his catalogues represented real advances of knowledge. Although sometimes too ready to take offence in matters affecting his collection, he was of a naturally amiable disposition and a generous and charming host, always glad to welcome scholars or fellow collectors. He was responsible for the publication of three books, compiled by E. Jutro and other collaborators: *Scenery of Great Britain and Ireland in Aquatint and Lithography, 1770–1860* (1952); *Life in England, in Aquatint and Lithography 1770–1860* (1953); and *Travel in Aquatint and Lithography* (1956/7, 2 vols.). His favourite pastime, next to book collecting, was croquet, a game he played with skill and enthusiasm. In 1921 he married Lady Ursula Helen, second daughter of the fourth Earl Cairns. There were two daughters of the marriage. Abbey was appointed high sheriff of Sussex in 1945.

A portrait of Abbey riding on the Sussex Downs was painted by Edward Seago and is in the possession of the family.

[J. F. Hayward, 'Silver bindings from the collection of J. R. Abbey', *The Connoisseur*, October 1952; *The Book Collector*, vol. x, 1961, 40–8; *The Times*, 29 December 1969 and 3 January 1970; private information; personal knowledge.]   A. R. A. HOBSON

ABELL, SIR WESTCOTT STILE (1877–1961), naval architect and surveyor, was born 16 January 1877 at Littleham in Devon, the first of the four sons of Thomas Abell (MBE and JP), house painter and, later, builder and member of Exmouth Council for over fifty years, and of his wife, Mary Ann Stile. He also had a half-sister. He was educated at West Buckland and Devon County schools and the Royal Naval Engineering College, Keyham (1892–7), before proceeding in 1897 to the Royal Naval College, Greenwich. At the age of twenty he lost his right hand and suffered serious throat injuries while lighting fireworks to celebrate the Diamond

Jubilee. Despite this handicap, he taught himself to write with his left hand and recovered to such good purpose that he passed out head of his year (1900) at Greenwich with a level of marks unsurpassed for many years.

He entered the Royal Corps of Naval Constructors in 1900, was attached to the staff of the chief constructor at Devonport dockyard, and was shortly afterwards transferred temporarily to the Admiralty to assist at the inquiry into the stability of the Royal Yacht *Victoria and Albert*. After a further short spell at Devonport, he was posted to the Admiralty, and from 1904 to 1907 he was professional private secretary to Sir Philip Watts [q.v.], director of naval construction. During this period he was closely involved with the committee on designs which had been appointed by Sir John (later Lord) Fisher [q.v.].

In 1907 Abell became junior lecturer on naval architecture at the Royal Naval College until his selection in December 1909 to be professor of naval architecture in the newly founded chair at Liverpool. In 1909 he also became a member of the Institution of Naval Architects. In 1913 he was appointed a member of the committee of the Board of Trade to examine the application of the Merchant Shipping Act to the internationalization of load lines. It was for this work that he was awarded the James Watt gold medal in 1919. He was chairman of the technical subcommittee, and his lifelong interest and association with the solution of the problems of safety of life at sea probably dated from this period. His outstanding contributions to the Institution of Naval Architects on these subjects must certainly have earned him recognition by the committee of Lloyd's Register of Shipping, and in 1914 he was invited to fill the post of chief ship surveyor, a position which he occupied with distinction for the next fourteen years. On vacating the chair at Liverpool, he was succeeded by his brother, Thomas Bertrand Abell.

During the war of 1914-18 he made a significant contribution in the field of merchant shipbuilding and was also closely associated with the Admiralty in the construction of great numbers of naval auxiliary craft. He also served on a special Admiralty committee to determine the feasibility of submarine merchant vessels to thwart the growing U-boat menace, and in 1917 was also appointed technical adviser to the controller of shipping. Among his many other commitments he was a member of a war committee on the distribution of steel and of the advisory committee on the merchant shipbuilding programme.

In recognition of his outstanding services he was created KBE in 1920, and now turned his attention to the peacetime problems of ship classification and safety. Fully aware that the war had stimulated technological advance, Abell directed a complete revision of the structural requirements of Lloyd's rules and effected major amendments to their philosophy, which resulted in an increase of structural efficiency and, as a corollary, the reduction of steel weights. For the first time longitudinal framing was recognized as a valid form of construction. He also recruited many young graduates of attainment who were later to rise to eminence in the service of Lloyd's.

Abell served on the Board of Trade load-line committee in 1927, but in 1928 he resigned his appointment with Lloyd's Register to take up the chair of naval architecture at the Armstrong College of Durham University at Newcastle upon Tyne; and, shortly after his return to academic affairs, he was a British delegate at the international Safety of Life at Sea Conference in 1929. It was he who designed the Channel train ferry, for which special docks had to be built at Dover and Dunkirk. Three ships were built, one of which was launched by Abell's wife. They were used for mine-laying during the war of 1939-45.

Abell made many important contributions to technical institutions. His publications included *The Ship and her Work* (1932), *The Safe Sea* (1932), and *The Shipwright's Trade* (1948), the last of which exhibited a profound understanding of ships and shipbuilding. It was he who was responsible for getting the *Cutty Sark* dry-docked at Greenwich, and his worry about the condition of the *Victory* at Portsmouth caused Lord Louis Mountbatten to get the woodwork restored.

He was a member of the executive committee of the National Physical Laboratory and chairman of the Froude ship research subcommittee of the ship division of the Laboratory. It was in large measure due to his resource and initiative that the new Ship Hydrodynamics Laboratory at Feltham was completed in 1959.

He was a source of help and encouragement to the younger men of his profession, particularly during his tenure of office in the Worshipful Company of Shipwrights. On public occasions his experience, shrewd understanding, and wit were inestimable assets.

Abell was president of the Institute of Marine Engineers (1924-5), master of the Worshipful Company of Shipwrights (1931-2), and president of the Smeatonian Society of Civil Engineers (1941). At the time of his death he was senior honorary vice-president of the Royal Institution of Naval Architects. Both he and his wife held the freedom of the City of London. He did much for the Institute of Marine Engineers and Shipbuilders in Newcastle, which awarded him a gold medal and placed a gold plaque in his honour in Bolbec Hall, Newcastle.

In 1902 he married Beatrice Gertrude (died 1953), daughter of Joseph Wyld Davenport, dentist, of Devonport, by whom he had one son, who adopted his father's profession (T. W. D. Abell, FRINA), and three daughters, one of whom married D. W. W. Henderson [q.v.]. Abell died 29 July 1961 at Kenton, Newcastle upon Tyne. There is a portrait in crayon by Frank Humphris (1945) in the possession of the family.

[*The Times*, 31 July 1961; personal knowledge.]   J. McCallum

ABU BAKAR TAFAWA BALEWA, Alhaji Sir (1912–1966), prime minister of the Federation of Nigeria. [See Tafewa Balewa.].

ADAMS, WILLIAM BRIDGES- (1889–1965), theatrical producer. [See Bridges-Adams.]

ADAMS, WILLIAM GEORGE STEWART (1874–1966), public servant, was born 8 November 1874 at Hamilton, Lanarkshire, the second son and youngest of the four children of John Adams, for many years headmaster of St. John's Grammar School, Hamilton, and his wife, Margaret, of Appin, daughter of John Stewart of Glasgow, cotton manufacturer. His father came of Aberdonian farming ancestors and was a close friend of David Livingstone [q.v.]. He was educated at his father's school and the university of Glasgow, where he obtained a first class in classics (1897). From there he won a Snell exhibition to Balliol College, Oxford (1896), where he had a distinguished academic record, was president of the Arnold Society, and obtained second class honours in classical moderations (1898) and first classes in *literae humaniores* (1900) and modern history (1901). He was a contemporary at Balliol of (Sir) W. D. Ross and (Sir) R. C. K. Ensor [q.v.]. He then became a tutor at Borough Road Training College, Isleworth (1901–2).

In 1902 Adams went as lecturer in economics to the graduate school of the university of Chicago—the beginning of a lifelong interest in the United States, which he frequently revisited, and of many friendships with Americans. He returned to England in 1903, to become lecturer in economics and secretary of university extension at the university of Manchester.

In 1905 he was invited to the post of superintendent of statistics and intelligence in the Irish Department of Agriculture and Technical Instruction in Dublin under Sir Horace Plunkett [q.v.], whose friendship was a source of lasting inspiration to Adams and greatly influenced his life and work.

In 1910 Adams was appointed to the newly created readership in political theory and institutions, with a fellowship at All Souls College, Oxford, which in 1912 became the Gladstone professorship, a chair which he held until he was elected warden of the college in 1933. He lectured on representative government and the theory of the modern state. In 1911 Adams's specialized knowledge of Ireland was recognized by his appointment as a member of the committee set up to advise the Cabinet on Irish finance. In 1914 he made, for the Carnegie United Kingdom Trust, a comprehensive survey of library services in the United Kingdom, which greatly influenced the Trust's pioneering activities. In the same year he founded and edited the *Political Quarterly* but this ceased publication in 1916 when his wartime appointment made its continuance impossible. In 1915 he had joined the staff of the Ministry of Munitions and at the end of 1916 Lloyd George invited him and others, including Philip Kerr (later Marquess of Lothian) and David (later Lord) Davies [q.v.] to his personal secretariat not long after he became prime minister.

For the two ensuing years Adams served as one of the prime minister's private secretaries and edited the reports of the War Cabinet of 1917 and 1918. At the centre of Lloyd George's dynamic direction of the nation's wartime efforts, Adams developed a high regard for his leader's decisiveness in critical situations, for his boundless courage and energy in confronting crisis after crisis, and for the loyalty he displayed towards his staff. There were, however, other aspects of this leadership which came strangely to one of Adams's training and character. In later years he steadfastly refused to write any memoir of his own wartime services, believing that this would be a break of the confidential trust under which he had worked. In 1918 Adams was made a member of the committee on examinations for the Civil Service.

After the war he returned to Oxford where he made an important contribution to the development of the school of 'modern greats' (philosophy, politics, and economics). As a teacher his scholarly standards were of a high order, and to these he added a sensitive understanding of human problems and situations which brought his lectures vividly alive for his audiences. The care which he devoted to the preparation of his lectures was matched by the helpful relationship he quickly established with those whose studies came under his supervision. An American Rhodes scholar of the time has described the Adams lectures as models of clarity free from any touch of pedantry, filling the halls in which they were delivered. He made his themes live dramatically in terms of persons, and they were faultlessly delivered. Adams's influence was truly pervasive and made a lasting impression on students who were privileged to hear and know him. From 1919 to 1922 he was a member of the royal commission on the universities of Oxford and Cambridge. He entered fully into the life of All Souls and of the university. He was a pro-vice-chancellor from 1939 to 1945. His personal qualities and wide experience of men and public affairs won him the trust and deep respect of his colleagues.

In 1933 Adams was elected warden of All Souls, in succession to Lord Chelmsford [q.v.]. Sir Arthur (later Lord) Salter, his distinguished contemporary, paid tribute to the qualities which Adams brought to bear on the tasks which confronted him as head of the college—his simple modesty and absence of personal ambition, his firm grasp of issues of policy which called for practical decisions, all contributed to a personal authority which marked his service to the college. He strengthened its links with the outside world, and until he retired in 1945, the warden's lodgings became a meeting-place for leaders and workers from public and voluntary institutions. He conceived the idea of forming a group of educationists to meet from time to time for the study and discussion of current educational policy and practice. This took shape in 1941 when he brought together some leading directors of education and others with comparable responsibilities. This group, which became known as the 'All Souls Group', subsequently continued as an influential circle of discussion, although, with Adams's own retirement, the direct link with the college ended.

His deep concern for the countryside and country people progressively became a dominating interest. In 1920, with the support of a group of friends, he formed a Preservation Trust to acquire some country east of Cumnor Hurst, beloved of Matthew Arnold [q.v.], to prevent its despoliation by industrial development and to secure for posterity the preservation of its most beautiful areas. Through this private initiative they were able to preserve a beautiful open space of some 700 acres. For some years he owned a farm on Boars Hill, where he raised pigs on the open-range basis and grew potatoes and cereals. He was alert to the need for new methods and was very interested in crop drying and other farming innovations. He kept in touch with agricultural co-operatives and sought to keep alive the spirit of co-operation as Horace Plunkett had conceived it, 'in better farming, better business and better living'. He took a leading part in the establishment of the National Federation of Young Farmers' Clubs in 1932 and became its first chairman. Adams was a member of the Development Commission (1923–49). He became keenly involved in its measures to further the provision of village halls, of training schemes

for rural craftsmen, in the introduction of new industries, and in research projects designed to enlarge the boundaries of enterprise in the countryside. His knowledge of rural conditions and zeal for their improvement were a valuable asset to the commission, and were highly esteemed by his colleagues.

He played a leading part in the founding of the National Council of Social Service in 1919 and was its chairman for thirty years and of its rural committee for nearly as long. His kindly and humorous disposition, and infectious faith in co-operative action in social affairs, made him an ideal chairman of the council with its diverse and wide-ranging membership. He exercised an inspiring influence on the council's promotion of social amenities, and the rural community councils, which it sponsored in England and Wales, looked to him as their leader.

In 1923–4 he gave the Stevenson lectures on citizenship in Glasgow and in 1924 the Lowell lectures in Boston, USA. In 1931–2 he was one of a three-man delegation to China from the universities' China committee.

On his retirement from All Souls he and his wife went to live in Donegal and from there he was able to take an active interest in the affairs of Magee University College, Londonderry.

His manifold activities left him with little time and, perhaps, inclination for writing about his life's work or his personal philosophy. So there is a considerable gap in his record which he might have filled had he allowed himself more leisure. Those who knew him best, however, recognized that his outlook and convictions were best expressed by the encouragement he could give to others through personal contacts and his priceless gift of making lasting friendships with all sorts and conditions of people. His most natural medium of communication was through the spoken word, and that is perhaps why so many persons, eminent or unknown, came to him for help and advice.

In his private life and public work George Adams was sustained by a serene and firmly held religious faith. He was liberal minded and unsectarian in outlook. Brought up a Scots Presbyterian, he found a spiritual home in the Church of England and, in later life, in the Church of Ireland.

He was appointed CH in 1936 and was an honorary DCL of Oxford and an honorary LLD of the universities of Glasgow and Manchester. Upon his retirement in 1945 he was elected an honorary fellow of All Souls.

In 1908 he married Muriel, daughter of William Lane, a Treasury solicitor, of Stonehurst, Killiney, county Dublin. It was a devoted and happy marriage until his wife died in 1956. There was one son. Adams died at Fahan House, county Donegal, 30 January 1966.

There are two portraits (1942) by Alexander Christie; one is at All Souls and the other was lent to the National Council of Social Service, and hung in the Adams Room, 99 Great Russell Street.

[John Turner, *Lloyd George's Secretariat*, 1980; private information; personal knowledge.]   GEORGE HAYNES

ADCOCK, SIR FRANK EZRA (1886–1968), historian of Greece and Rome, was born 15 April 1886 at Desford, Leicestershire, the fourth of the five children of Thomas Draper Adcock, schoolmaster, head of the Desford Industrial School, and his wife, Mary Esther Coltman. He was educated at the Wyggeston Grammar School, Leicester, and as a scholar of King's College, Cambridge, where he obtained first class honours in both parts of the classical tripos (1908–9) and won the Craven scholarship (1908), a Chancellor's medal (1909), and the Craven studentship (1910). As was then the custom at the beginning of a professional career in classical studies, he attended the seminars of Wilamowitz in Berlin and Eduard Meyer in Munich in 1910–11. He was elected a fellow of his college and appointed to a university lectureship in classics in 1911; his early research and first publications concerned the problems of source-criticism relating to the statesman Solon. From 1913 to 1919 he was lay dean of King's.

Adcock's service in the war of 1914–18 was armchair but distinguished: he went into the intelligence division of the Admiralty as an interpreter of codes and ciphers, and in 1917 was appointed OBE. The crucial determinant of his academic career was that as soon as the war was over J. B. Bury [q.v.] decided to launch the previously projected *Cambridge Ancient History*, and chose Adcock to join himself and S. A. Cook [q.v.] in the editorship. Volume i was published in 1923; from the death of Bury in 1927 Adcock was in effect chief editor of the great undertaking, of which the last volume, thanks to his energy and constancy, came out in the nick of time in 1939. In 1925 he was promoted to the chair of ancient history at Cambridge. From 1929 to 1931 he was president of the Roman Society; and already in 1929 academic honours began to accrue to him, with an honorary D.Litt. of Durham University, followed in 1936 by fellowship of the British Academy.

In 1939 Adcock reverted to wartime duties in a branch of the Foreign Office, and stayed until 1943, when he was released to his college and his chair. In 1947–8 he was president of the Classical Association. He retired from his chair in 1951, and served as vice-provost of King's from 1951 to 1955. In 1954 he was knighted, and further academic distinctions followed: the

honorary Litt.D. of Dublin (1955) and Manchester (1955) and honorary D.Litt. of Leicester (1961).

Adcock was a small round man, who lost his hair early; he had a rosy colour, twinkling, intent eyes that peered from behind strong spectacles, a Leicestershire accent, and an 'r'-lisp. Having been brought up a Methodist he remained sympathetic and helpful to Methodism all his life. He was a very competitive golfer and a cricket enthusiast, but he had no gift for the arts, and indeed, although very clever and learned, was not an intellectual. Nevertheless, Cambridge accepted him as one of the notable personalities of his age, celebrated for his wit in conversation and in lectures. He was perhaps the last of the studied wits: his sallies were strategically prepared, and part of the fun of his famous lectures in the flat-accented, high-pitched, maiden-auntish voice was to detect the build-up of forces, feel the imminence of the 'punch-line', observe the dawning of the tiny smirk on the bland face, and savour the release of tension when the *bon mot* came.

The writings of Adcock apart from his contributions to the *Cambridge Ancient History* are not extensive: eight or nine good papers mostly related to the *Cambridge Ancient History* chapters, and the short books and brochures which arose from his visiting lectures—*The Roman Art of War under the Republic* (1940, the Martin classical lectures, Oberlin); *The Greek and Macedonian Art of War* (1957, the Sather classical lectures, California); and *Roman Political Ideas and Practice* (1959, Jerome lectures, Michigan). The Raleigh lecture to the British Academy (1953) was entitled 'Greek and Macedonian Kingship', the Todd memorial lecture (Sydney, 1961), 'The Character of the Romans'. In addition, three independent short books were published at Cambridge: *Caesar as Man of Letters* (1956), *Thucydides and his History* (1963), and *Marcus Crassus, Millionaire* (1966). But essentially Adcock's monument is the *Cambridge Ancient History*, and in two ways—in his vigorous and determined editorship that brought it to fruition (and as part of a scholar's monument that achievement must not be underestimated), and in his own chapters. There are ten in all, and in them he made the central periods of both Greek and Roman political history his own: the archaic age and the Thucydidean age of Athens, and the late Roman Republic, with Julius Caesar and, as a summing up, the achievement of Augustus. What they contain is political history entirely (with war as an extension of policy)—a conception against which the fashion of Adcock's age was turning, but which faithfully reflected his own ideal of history. It was a Thucydidean ideal, both in being political and in being magisterial: the historian tells the reader what he thinks is fit for the reader to know. It was also a tribute to Clio as a muse, for Adcock wrote with a poise and style which never lapsed into idiosyncracy, and had the rare gift of being able to transfer the twinkle in the eye to the printed page.

Adcock was still musing and writing about the Greek and Roman political past to the end of his life. To King's, as undergraduate and bachelor don, he had been devoted (not short of partisanship) for sixty years; and he gave a paper to the King's College Classical Society only three days before his death, which came peacefully, in Cambridge, 22 February 1968.

[A. H. McDonald in *Journal of Roman Studies*, vol. lvi, 1966, with bibliography of the published writings; memoir by L. P. Wilkinson, privately printed for King's College, Cambridge, 1969; N. G. L. Hammond in *Proceedings* of the British Academy, vol. liv, 1968; private information; personal knowledge.]   J. A. Crook

AITKEN, ALEXANDER CRAIG (1895-1967), mathematician, was born at Dunedin, New Zealand, 1 April 1895, the eldest of the seven children of William Aitken and his wife, Elizabeth Towers. His grandfather, Alexander Aitken, had emigrated from Lanarkshire to Otago in 1868 and farmed in the neighbourhood of Dunedin. However, Aitken's father, one of fourteen children, left the farm to work as a grocer in Dunedin. He was successful and acquired the business. Aitken's mother was born in Wolverhampton and went to New Zealand at the age of eight.

Aitken became head boy of Otago Boys' High School in 1912 and won first place in the entrance scholarship examination to Otago University. His most striking characteristic at this stage was a phenomenal memory, and he had not shown any special bent for mathematics. He decided on a course combining languages with mathematics, but this was soon interrupted by the outbreak of war in 1914. He enlisted as a private soldier in the New Zealand Expeditionary Force and reached Gallipoli in November 1915 with the 6th Infantry reinforcements, five weeks before the evacuation. Subsequently he served in France and was commissioned on the field of battle. He was badly wounded in a raid during the battle of the Somme and in March 1917 was invalided home to New Zealand after three months in hospital at Chelsea. It was thus possible for him to resume his interrupted university career. The months preceding the start of term were spent in writing an account of his experiences in the war. His continuing anguish about those experiences caused him, forty-five years later, with but little revision, to publish the work as *Gallipoli to the Somme, Recollections of a New Zealand Infantryman* (1963), and it was awarded the Hawthornden prize.

Mathematics was at a low ebb in Otago because there was no professor until R. J. T. Bell arrived from Glasgow in 1920. This may explain why in 1920 Aitken gained only a second class in mathematics, although he achieved a first class in languages and literature (Latin and French). Nevertheless it was in mathematics that he chose to proceed. After spending three years as a master at his old school, in 1923 he was awarded a postgraduate scholarship and went to Edinburgh University to work under (Sir) E. T. Whittaker [q.v.] who was greatly interested in numerical mathematics and in 1913 had founded the only mathematical laboratory in the country. Since one of Whittaker's closest friends was G. J. Lidstone, the leading actuary of his time, problems of actuarial interest received particular attention. Aitken was given one of these problems as his doctoral subject: the graduation or the fitting of a smooth curve to a set of points subject to statistical error. Whittaker had taken the first step towards providing the subject with a rational basis but his formula was unsuited to numerical calculation. Aitken overcame the difficulty, an achievement for which he was awarded a D.Sc. in 1926. His course was then set. The rest of his life, all of which was spent in Edinburgh, was devoted to the closely linked disciplines of numerical mathematics, statistics, and the algebra of matrices.

Numerical mathematics is a difficult subject to appraise since it is dependent on the characteristics of the machines or tables in use at the time. Mechanical calculating machines were in common use in industry and commerce but their cost, and not less their noise, precluded their use in a class of fifty students. Whittaker considered that a properly trained student could do nearly as well with tables. It was on this basis that Aitken took over the conduct of the laboratory. He discovered two new devices which have passed into general use: 'Aitken's δ-process', by which a sequence may be transformed into one more rapidly convergent; and the Neville-Aitken method in finite difference theory, by which the values of the interpolating polynomial at a series of equidistant points can be discovered without having to find the polynomial explicitly.

In 1925 Aitken was appointed as lecturer in actuarial mathematics at Edinburgh and in 1936 he became a reader in statistics. Much of his later work belongs to the discipline of statistics, and more particularly to the mathematics to which it gives rise. Aitken was also interested in decimal coinage, and broadcast on the subject. He succeeded Whittaker in the Edinburgh chair of mathematics when the latter retired in 1946. He himself retired in 1965.

Aitken was renowned for his powers of mental calculation. They were the subject of a paper by the psychologist I. M. L. Hunter, who concluded that his skill 'possibly exceeds that of any other person for whom precise authenticated records exist'. Professor A. R. Collar wrote that 'he had also in large measure the kind of mystical insight into problems which characterized, for example, Isaac Newton' [q.v.]. Aitken, who was a close friend of the musician, Sir D. F. Tovey [q.v.], said that he gave roughly four times as much thought to music as to mathematics. A violin which accompanied him on his war service is preserved at Otago Boys' High School and for a time he was leader of the Edinburgh University orchestra. Physically he was short and slight, a leading high-jumper in his youth and a keen hill walker in his Edinburgh days.

He was elected FRS in 1936 and for several terms was a vice-president of the Royal Society of Edinburgh, to which he had been elected in 1925. The universities of Glasgow and New Zealand awarded him honorary degrees. He was also FRSL (1964), Hon. FRSNZ, and an honorary fellow of the Faculty of Actuaries.

In 1920 Aitken married Mary Winifred, daughter of Alfred Betts, of Nelson, New Zealand. She was a lecturer in botany at Otago University from 1916 to 1923. They had two children, a boy and a girl. Aitken died at Edinburgh 3 November 1967.

[J. M. Whittaker and M. S. Bartlett in *Biographical Memoirs of Fellows of the Royal Society*, vol. xiv, 1968; obituary in *Proc. Edin. Math. Soc.*, vol. xvi, 1968; personal knowledge.]   J. M. WHITTAKER

AITKEN, WILLIAM MAXWELL, first BARON BEAVERBROOK (1879-1964), newspaper proprietor, was born 25 May 1879 at Vaughan, Maple, Ontario, the third son in the family of ten children of a Presbyterian minister, William Cuthbert Aitken, who had emigrated to Canada from Torpichen, West Lothian. The mother was Jane, daughter of Joseph Noble, storekeeper and farmer in Vaughan. The year after 'Max' Aitken was born, his father received a call from St. James's church at Newcastle, a township on the Miramichi river in New Brunswick where the boy spent a happy and adventurous childhood and attended the local school until he was sixteen, but failed in Latin in the entrance examination to Dalhousie University. Instead, he entered a law firm in Chatham, down river from Newcastle, but soon began to sell insurance, then switched successfully to selling bonds at the right moment in the Canadian boom. He found a patron in John F.

Stairs, the leading financier and Conservative in Halifax, Nova Scotia, who helped to set him up in a finance company, Royal Securities Corporation.

One of the talents Max Aitken exhibited throughout his life lay in confecting combines and alliances. He used his knowledge of local banking to negotiate the sale of the Commercial Bank of Windsor to Stairs's Union Bank of Halifax, a merger which brought him a personal profit of 10,000 dollars. He was soon venturing too in the West Indies. On 30 January 1906 he married Gladys Henderson, the beautiful nineteen-year-old daughter of Colonel (later General) Charles William Drury, the first Canadian to command the Halifax garrison, Nova Scotia. They moved to Montreal where Aitken acquired a set on the Stock Exchange. By 1907 'the little fellow with the big head' was a dollar millionaire. In 1909 he formed the Canada Cement Company, a controversial amalgamation much criticized in some quarters, the echoes of which, much to his righteous indignation, were to reverberate about his ears for years to come.

In the following year the Aitkens came to England. Aided by Andrew Bonar Law, himself the son of a New Brunswick manse, Max Aitken stood as a Conservative in the Liberal-held Lancashire seat of Ashton-under-Lyne and, after a whirlwind campaign, he won by 196 votes, one of the few Unionist gains in the general elections of that December.

He had bounced into the political limelight, but he spoke rarely in the House where he was regarded as a 'Canadian adventurer'; however, he had the friendship of Bonar Law, as well as financial links, and he soon gained the support of F. E. Smith (later the Earl of Birkenhead, q.v.) through whom he came to know (Sir) Winston Churchill. In 1911 Aitken's name appeared in the coronation honours; his knighthood was not universally well received. When Bonar Law, whose resolution Aitken had helped to stiffen (and this was but the first instance in their close friendship), came to succeed Arthur Balfour as Conservative leader, Aitken's political stock, as his intimate, was correspondingly strengthened. He bought a large Victorian country house in Surrey, Cherkley Court, near Leatherhead, where he would entertain friends and leading politicians whilst he continued to expand his Canadian business interests. He refused to eat in other people's houses: he preferred to be the focus of attention from the middle of his own dinner table. After the war he was to acquire The Vineyard, a tiny Tudor house with a tennis court at Hurlingham Road, Fulham, more intimate than Cherkley.

In July 1914 it was 'Max Aitken, Bonar Law's financier and jackal', as one of Asquith's Cabinet described him, who was the intermediary through whom the abortive Buckingham Palace conference over the Ulster question came to be held: the silhouette of a future political merger.

When war broke out Sir Max Aitken soon became the Canadian Government representative at British GHQ at St. Omer with the rank of lieutenant-colonel in the Canadian Militia—as 'Canadian eyewitness'. He initiated the *Canadian Daily Record*, which lasted until 31 July 1919, for Canadian troops in Europe, and published a historical narrative, *Canada in Flanders*, the first two volumes of which he wrote himself. He created the Canadian War Records Office, set up a war memorial fund, and was the first to commission war artists. Impatient at the muddles of the military men, he soon came to spend much of his time in Whitehall. Living in the Hyde Park Hotel, not far from Bonar Law's house in Edwardes Square, by July 1916 he had acquired a room in the War Office, two doors down the corridor from Lloyd George's.

Aitken was to play a special part in the downfall of Asquith, who disdained him, and in the manœuvring which made Lloyd George war minister and then, in December 1916, prime minister. The details of the struggle to overthrow Asquith and to replace him by Bonar Law or Lloyd George, in which Aitken acted as spur and go-between, he was to record in his incomparable *Politicians and the War* (2 vols. 1928–32) which will remain, despite all carping, the authoritative narrative; nor does the story want in the telling thereof.

Confident, according to his own account, that he would be recompensed with office for the decisive part he believed himself to have played in the new arrangements, Aitken awaited a call from the new prime minister. Instead, since a seat in the Commons was required for Sir Albert Stanley (later Lord Ashfield, q.v.), the incoming president of the Board of Trade, the very post which he himself had his eye on, Aitken hesitated before reluctantly accepting Lloyd George's offer of a peerage, vacating his seat at Ashton-under-Lyne (to which Stanley was promptly elected), and becoming—he was already a baronet (January, 1916)—Lord Beaverbrook, an elevation which he claimed to regret to the end of his days.

Whilst the war lasted Beaverbrook gave what help he could to the Government in his own idiosyncratic way on becoming chancellor of the Duchy of Lancaster, despite the King's objection, then, from February to November 1918, minister of information. In March 1918 he was sworn of the Privy Council. He was still entertaining freely: 'It was during Duff's time in France' (from May 1918), Lady Diana Duff Cooper (later Lady Norwich) was to write, 'that the Montagus and I saw almost daily this strange attractive gnome with an odour of genius about him. He was an impact and a great excitement to me, with his humour, his accent, his James the First language, his fantastic stories of his Canadian past, his poetry and his power to excoriate or heal' (*The Rainbow Comes and Goes*, 1958).

Since 1910 Beaverbrook had been a close friend of R. D. Blumenfeld [q.v.], who had been editor of the *Daily Express* since 1904. Although a lively, well-written, and politically influential newspaper, it was losing money and in danger of closing. In December 1916 Blumenfeld on Bonar Law's advice turned to Aitken (who had been interested in the paper at least as early as May), who bought the paper—and its debts—for £17,500 and so acquired not only a platform for his views and additional political leverage, but what was to prove his dominant interest for the rest of his life.

The partnership with R. D. B., who remained as editor-in-chief until 1929 and paterfamilias until he died in 1948, was faithful, fruitful, and at times explosive. 'Blum', Beaverbrook once remarked, 'taught me the business of journalism.' Beaverbrook for his part taught his editor how to make a newspaper pay. He introduced 'more money, better management', and, above all, he made the paper controversial. Advertisements became a major source of revenue. Beaverbrook personally sold space to Gordon Selfridge [q.v.]. Blumenfeld said that Max was the most gifted natural journalist he had ever met, not excluding Lord Northcliffe [q.v.]. Together, they gathered a remarkable team of writers, cartoonists, and business managers into the building in Shoe Lane and set off after the circulation leadership of the *Daily Mail*. Foremost among them was John Gordon, together with two Canadians, (Sir) Beverley Baxter and, on the management side, E. J. Robertson. After Northcliffe's death in 1922 the struggle for circulation amongst the popular dailies became intense, but eventually by 1936, with Arthur Christiansen as editor (since 1934), the *Daily Express*, with a two and a quarter million sale, achieved the largest circulation in the world and Beaverbrook by then was the unchallenged leader. By 1954 the circulation was exceeding four million a day. Meanwhile the *Sunday Express* had been launched in December 1918, and in 1923 Beaverbrook acquired from Sir Edward Hulton [q.v.] control of the *Evening Standard*, in which the cartoons of (Sir) David Low [q.v.] achieved their uncensored popularity. Beaverbrook impishly liked to pretend that he left his newspapers to run themselves, but it is evident that the chief shareholder's telephonic interventions were menacingly perpetual and his flair for informed gossip—and malice—unexampled. For good or ill, his newspapers were the extension of Beaverbrook's complex personality and friendships. Amongst those who wrote for them were men as varied as Arnold Bennett, Dean Inge, (Sir) Robert Bruce Lockhart, and Harold Nicolson [qq.v.], Lord Castlerosse, and, later, Michael Foot. 'Vicky' [q.v.] in his day was allowed as much freedom as Low had had when he would portray Beaverbrook's characteristic features with the huge urchin grin lurking in the corner of many of his cartoons. Timothy Healy, the Duff Coopers, H. G. Wells, and subsequently Brendan Bracken, and much later the Aneurin Bevans, Stanley Morrison [qq.v.], and A. J. P. Taylor, who was to write his biography (1972), were among Beaverbrook's intimates; but nobody could ever replace Bonar Law in his heart. After the war of 1939-45 he eventually resumed his highly personal account of affairs in *Men and Power 1917-1918* (1956) and *The Decline and Fall of Lloyd George* (1963). It was he, for example, who had seen to it that Bonar Law attended the Carlton Club meeting in October 1922 which brought about the downfall of the very wartime coalition which Beaverbrook himself had helped to initiate, a meeting which enabled Stanley Baldwin to reveal those unexpected qualities which were to deprive Beaverbrook—and Churchill—of the influence each, very independently, sought to exert upon Conservative policy between the wars. Years passed before he and Churchill came to work together again—they had crossed tempers during the general strike—and then once again, those ten years later, it was Baldwin who won the day. In 1936 King Edward VIII sought Beaverbrook's advice on the public handling of his decision to marry Mrs Simpson. Beaverbrook, joined by Churchill, strove mightily to delay the issue, advising the King to wait rather than precipitate a clash with Church and Cabinet with an inevitable outcome. It was in vain. After Beaverbrook's death his version of the struggle behind the scenes, *The Abdication of King Edward VIII*, was published (1966). It is perhaps significant that, whereas both Baldwin and Churchill were most distressed by what took place, Beaverbrook, for his part, had 'never had so much fun in my life'.

Bonar Law's death in 1923 had left Beaverbrook outside the innermost circles of power, and he threw himself into battle after battle with Baldwin over the issue of imperial preferences, which Beaverbrook chose to call 'Empire Free Trade', or, again, his 'Empire Crusade'. He campaigned in by-elections; he wrote at length week after week on a theme which he had made his own, and he used his three papers relentlessly to press his ideas on imperial preferences; the iniquity, in Beaverbrook's view, of Baldwin's settlement of the British war debt to the United States; and the neglect of the Empire, about which Beaverbrook himself knew very little outside Canada. Beaverbrook frankly admitted that 'S. B.' defeated him every time and he was intensely irritated by the public image of Baldwin as 'a quiet, honest country gentleman', to him a successful travesty. Starting as admirers of Bonar Law, they had soon parted company and they were never reconciled. It was probably Beaverbrook whom Baldwin chiefly had in mind rather than Lord Rothermere [q.v.] when, deeply wounded by the press campaigns against him, he spoke (24 June 1930) in the words of his cousin Rudyard Kipling [q.v.] (who had earlier parted from Beaverbrook over the Irish treaty) of newspaper proprietors who exercised 'power without responsibility, the prerogative of the harlot throughout the ages'.

The political merger of 1931 might seem to have been 'made' for Beaverbrook, yet he was not involved in the formation of the 'national' Government: he seemed to have shot his political bolt. It appeared that Churchill was not the only 'busted flush'. It was noteworthy, as his biography was to reveal, that 'no Prime Minister came to Cherkley between 1922 and 1941'.

During the rise of Hitler Beaverbrook used his newspapers to damp down the threat of war. He accompanied Lord Vansittart to Paris in December 1935 and sustained him and Sir Samuel Hoare (later Viscount Templewood) [qq.v.] at the time of the Hoare-Laval pact. From 1938 Beaverbrook made Hoare (who had served with him in the Commons before 1914) an allowance of £2,000 a year. He supported Neville Chamberlain over Munich and as late as mid 1939 the *Daily Express* was busily informing its public that 'there will be no war this year'. During the 'phoney war' he visited President Roosevelt, a kindred spirit, a visit which was to bear fruit. When Churchill became prime minister, Beaverbrook re-entered the *arcana imperii* and the old intimacy was renewed. In November 1940 he became minister of aircraft production and a member of the War Cabinet. He accompanied Churchill to Tours whilst France was collapsing, because the premier knew that 'in trouble' Beaverbrook was 'always buoyant'. Beaverbrook's contribution to victory in the Battle of Britain was immense and unique: Churchill and Dowding [q.v.] paid public tribute to it. The hour and the man proved a fit match. By the most ruthless methods Beaverbrook burst through the entrenched conventions of the Air Ministry and long-term plans of 'the bloody Air Marshals', as he called them, and demanded successfully that every ounce of the war effort be thrown into producing the fighter aircraft which the Royal Air Force (in which his son and heir was gallantly serving) needed to deny the Luftwaffe control of the narrow seas, without which the invasion of Britain was impossible. His torrential, piratical energy was centred in Stornoway House in St. James's which he had acquired in the 1920s. He made plenty of enemies not only in the Air Staff, but also, for example, Lord Nuffield and Ernest Bevin [qq.v.], but he carried the day. The story of his tempestuous handling of the new Ministry remains an epic. He gave a new and primal urgency to the cycle: production, cannibalization, repair, and dispersal. Beaverbrook, said Churchill, was 'at his very best when things are at their worst.' Nothing that he did in his long life was as important as the part Beaverbrook played in winning the Battle of Britain.

Typically, when the battle in the air was won, the man who had done most to make it possible tired of the burden, and in May 1941 he became simple minister of state; in June he succeeded Sir Andrew Duncan [q.v.] as minister of supply—'he believes in orderly advance,' he announced, 'I am given to immediate methods.' In August he visited Washington; in September Moscow, with Averell Harriman, to bargain with Stalin over war supplies. He returned to Washington with Churchill after Pearl Harbor to press for more tanks, aircraft, and—his own significant contribution to the debate—landing craft. In February 1942 he became minister of production, again in succession to Duncan, but a couple of weeks later ill health—which was never far away and his asthma may have been partly psychosomatic—gave him the excuse to leave the Government. He loathed committees. His letters of resignation had become as frequent as those of Gladstone of John Morley. In September 1943, however, he agreed to become lord privy seal and so remained until the war ended. Beaverbrook was never a team man but he was a very present help in time of trouble, especially to Churchill. It was Harry Hopkins who spotted that Beaverbrook was a member of that inner cabinet 'of the men who saw Churchill after midnight'. They might not always agree. Beaverbrook pressed for an early Second Front, especially after his return from Moscow, just as from 1940 onwards he continued to stress the strategic ineffectiveness of massive bombing. But the court favourite no longer had quite the same influence. Yet it was he who arrived at Marrakesh in December 1943 when Churchill was taken ill there after the Big Three meeting at Tehran, just as it had been Beaverbrook who had been summoned to Chequers when Germany declared war on Russia in June 1941.

Beaverbrook took a leading—and, in some people's view, a disastrous—part in Churchill's 1945 election campaign. With 393 Labour seats compared with 189 Conservative, the Carlton Club, which Beaverbrook rarely visited, and the Tory backbenchers whom he derided, turned their wrath on him. He bore it as he always did (with irritated interruptions) with buoyancy,

and his friendship with Churchill survived undamaged. Indeed, it was the 'best of foul weather friends' who realized that Churchill would feel especially deprived in his moment of defeat and saw to it that a motor car and chauffeur were at his door when the familiar government perquisites had abruptly disappeared. It was typical—a point which Lord Rosebery was to make at the memorial service at St. Paul's—of Beaverbrook's many secret acts of kindness when people were down on their luck—to the Asquiths, or the Snowdens, or, until she died in 1952, Lady Brade, the widow of Sir Reginald, who had befriended him in far-off days as secretary to the War Office. More formally, in 1954 he set up the Beaverbrook Foundation.

Two more campaigns remained for the happiest of warriors: he opposed Maynard Keynes [q.v.] over the American loan in 1947 and Harold Macmillan's attempt in 1961 to put Britain into 'that blasted Common Market'. Much of his old resilient fire returned and, at the age of eighty-two, with most of his friends long since dead, he waged a tremendous fight against what he believed would mark the end of British independence. He had never really liked allies. When the Common Market proposal temporarily foundered, his headline was a characteristic 'Hallelujah Hallelujah'.

In his last years, although Maurice Woods who had furnished the first drafts for his political memoirs had died as long ago as 1929, Beaverbrook resumed his career as political historian, a special talent about which he was curiously modest. He was able to draw upon his extensive collection of political papers (now in the House of Lords Library), from those left to him by Bonar Law, Lord Wargrave's papers which he had acquired, and the Lloyd George papers, which he had purchased from the widow together with her diaries. He had already made use of Asquith's letters to Mrs Edwin Montagu and Mrs Reginald McKenna in his *Politicians and the War*. He had published further books in the series of memoirs, but *The Age of Baldwin*, the final volume, long-plotted, somehow never seemed to get written.

At the end of his long life Canada came to give him full recognition as one of her foremost sons. Since the war of 1939-45 he had endowed the university of New Brunswick, of which he had become chancellor in 1953, with impatient generosity. He founded scholarships there and provided new buildings, notably the library and the Beaverbrook Art Gallery, which he ensured was filled with masterpieces of every age, few of which he himself appreciated.

On 9 June 1964, at the age of eighty-five, he died at Cherkley of cancer. But a fortnight earlier he had attended a mammoth dinner in his honour given in London by his fellow Canadian,

Lord Thompson of Fleet. At the end 'the Beaver' rose, old and frail, and held his audience spellbound. He spoke for half an hour, in the inimitable Canadian twang he never lost, of his successes and his failures, what he had hoped for and what he had lived for. 'And now', he said, 'I am to become an apprentice again, somewhere, soon.' As he walked steadfastly out the six hundred guests, men of all ages, stood and cheered him. It was his farewell, wholly typical of the man, full of wisdom, rich in humour, glowing with courage.

Beaverbrook achieved eminence in three worlds—finance, politics, and journalism. (Some, perhaps a minority, might add a fourth, as an annalist, of the school of John Aubrey.) In the first and last of these three he was pre-eminent. He made a vast fortune and he owed no man a penny, making money for others as well as himself. He helped to make and unmake prime ministers, yet never succeeded in winning the trust and confidence of the Conservative Party to which, almost by accident, he belonged. He was a radical by temperament, yet he could never have fitted with any comfort into the ranks of radicals or liberals, and certainly not of socialists: he was a lone fighter, in politics as in everything else.

His influence on popular journalism was great, founded as it was on an inborn sense of news values and an unfailing gift for knowing what would interest ordinary men and women. Moreover, the mass circulations he achieved were built on sheer efficiency in a difficult art, and he accepted nothing less than the best of its kind; smut was an anathema to him. His papers sparkled with controversy, and it was his particular genius that made them appeal to all classes of reader, whether or not they agreed with his point of view. The man who read *The Times* was likely to read the *Daily Express* as well. Beaverbrook's tendency at times to indulge in personal vendettas, such as that against Earl Mountbatten whom he blamed for the Canadian losses at Dieppe, or his running feud against the British Council, perhaps contradicted the high standards by which he judged himself and other people. The secrets of his long and at times fantastic career were the brilliance and shrewdness of his intellect, the restless energy which only left him in his last year, and the courage and ruthlessness with which he attacked his every objective. In private life he had friends everywhere who throughout the years remained as devoted to him as he to them. His loves and his hatreds came all alike to him, and once generated they seldom changed. Once dropped, a friend remained unforgiven. Not everybody who came under his patronage was improved by the contact. He had an original and at times hilarious wit, stuffed shirts his instinctive target.

The son of a Christian minister, he retained from first to last a vocabulary based on the Bible and a strong religious faith, unorthodox, sporadic, but real, to which his little book *The Divine Propagandist* (1962) bears witness. For his father and mother, for whom from 1902 until their deaths he ensured every comfort, he had a deep love and respect. He himself believed, towards the end of his life, that he had failed in the things he had sought most; if so, it was perhaps because of an impish streak which he enjoyed, and also because, despite his half-century of life in England, he remained at heart a Canadian. Although he loved and admired the British people, he ever fully understood their mental processes or the traditions in which their lives were rooted, and in 1956 he wrote: 'My last home will be where my heart has always been.'

His first wife, who bore him two sons and a daughter, died at Cherkley in 1927. Beaverbrook had often been a neglectful husband. For twenty years, until she died in 1945, Mrs Jean Norton was his most intimate woman friend. In 1963 he married Marcia Anastasia, daughter of John Christopher and widow of his friend Sir James Dunn, first baronet. Beaverbrook's eldest son, John William Max (born 1910) succeeded to the baronetcy created in 1916 but disclaimed the barony, maintaining that 'there will be only one Lord Beaverbrook'.

There is a portrait by Sickert and another (1950) by Graham Sutherland which Beaverbrook bequeathed to his widow. There are also two busts: one by Oscar Nemon on the plinth in the town square, Newcastle, New Brunswick, above Beaverbrook's ashes; the other by Epstein.

[A. J. P. Taylor, *Beaverbrook*, 1972; Beaverbrook's own writings; private information; personal knowledge.]   JOHN ELLIOT

ALANBROOKE, first VISCOUNT (1883-1963), field-marshal. [See BROOKE, ALAN FRANCIS.]

ALDINGTON, EDWARD GODFREE ('RICHARD') (1892-1962), writer, was born at Portsea, Portsmouth, 8 July 1892, the eldest of the two sons and two daughters of Albert Edward Aldington, a clerk articled to a solicitor, and his wife, Jessie May Godfrey. Educated at Dover College and at University College, London, which he was forced to leave, for financial reasons, before taking his degree, he rapidly established for himself a reputation as an avant-garde poet. Although for a while he became a sports journalist he decided to concentrate upon a literary career when, having had some poems accepted, he was introduced to influential writers such as Ford Madox (Hueffer) Ford, W. B. Yeats [qq.v.], Harold Monro, and Ezra Pound.

Through Pound, Aldington also met his future wife, H. D. (Hilda Doolittle, 1886–1961), an American poet. H. D., daughter of Charles Doolittle, mathematician and later professor of astronomy at the university of Pennsylvania, shared Aldington's love of the classics and of European language and literature. In the autumn of 1912, Aldington, H. D., and Ezra Pound became the original 'Imagists': poets who consciously broke with current diction and prosody in order to present 'an intellectual and emotional complex in an instant of time'. Aldington's verse, through the influence of Pound, was soon being published on both sides of the Atlantic and, on the strength of his growing reputation, he spent most of the following year travelling in Italy with H. D., whom he married in London 18 October 1913.

By now, and again through Pound's influence, Aldington had become literary editor of *The New Freewoman*, to be renamed in 1914 *The Egoist*. Moreover, between 1914 and 1917 the Aldingtons contributed to *Des Imagistes*, edited by Pound, and to three anthologies, *Some Imagist Poets* edited by Aldington and Amy Lowell (1915, 1916, and 1917), while Harold Monro's Poetry Bookshop in 1915 published Aldington's first book of verse, *Images 1910–1915*. During 1914, as a European war threatened, Aldington also worked for a while as secretary to Ford and took down by dictation in longhand the first draft of *The Good Soldier* (1915). However, although Aldington volunteered as soon as war began in 1914, for medical reasons he was not allowed to begin his service until mid 1916 when he enlisted as a private in the Royal Sussex Regiment. He was later commissioned, as a lieutenant and subsequently an acting captain, and saw front-line service in France and Flanders. The war marked a permanent change in Aldington's life. Not only did it cause him physical damage—he suffered for some time from the effects of gassing and shell-shock—but undoubtedly there were other reactions of an emotional nature that affected his personal and creative life. By the autumn of 1919 Aldington, now staying in a cottage at Hermitage, Berkshire, lent to him by D. H. Lawrence (whose notice he was to write for this Dictionary), had agreed to live apart from his wife. He had become attached to another resident at their lodgings at 44 Mecklenburgh Square, Dorothy Yorke, who was called Arabella and who joined him in Berkshire. He was also trying to concentrate upon a career as a writer and editor, which exposed him to increasingly varied literary experiences. In addition to publishing poetry and articles he became a regular reviewer of French books for the *Times Literary Supplement* and in 1921 assistant editor of T. S. Eliot's [q.v.] *Criterion*. During this period of renewed interest in French and Italian literature Aldington began to blossom not only as a critic but also as a translator. These activities were to continue throughout his life and he was ultimately to produce over twenty works of criticism and biography and thirty books of translation.

By 1926, despite his growing success (he had been expected to succeed (Sir) Bruce L. Richmond [q.v.] as editor of the *Times Literary Supplement*), Aldington seems to have become disenchanted with the life he was leading and though for the next two years he retained a cottage in Berkshire his thoughts and travels took him increasingly abroad. In 1928 he left England for France and, although he returned periodically until 1939, he never again regarded England as his home. Indeed, Aldington considered 1928 as 'a watershed'. That autumn, while with D. H. Lawrence and his wife on the Mediterranean island of Port Cros, Aldington was writing his first novel *Death of a Hero* (1929), the anti-war book which made him almost overnight a best-selling and internationally known author. During the next ten years he published seven novels, some books of short stories, three long poems, four editions of poetry, and many critical works.

It has frequently been said, especially by critics of his later biographical work, that Aldington's writing became possessed, even obsessed, with a bitterness which, however obscure in origin, was directed against the British literary establishment, which included many of his former colleagues and associates. It is true that *Death of a Hero* and 'Stepping Heavenward' (a satirical short story in *Soft Answers*, 1932), contain harsh lampoons—the latter is about T. S. Eliot and his wife—and it seems undeniable that Aldington's departure from England in 1928 occasioned, and was perhaps caused by, an expatriate resentment (the militantly satirical tone is particularly apparent in *The Colonel's Daughter*, 1931, although here it is directed at English village life). However, Aldington retained throughout his life the affection of friends and relatives who say that he had great personal warmth and generosity. None the less, the undoubted sharpness and anger of some of his writing—most notable perhaps in his well-known war novel—may show evidence both of literary power and of a kind of hard honesty: a quality which comparatively few writers possess.

Between 1935 and 1947 Aldington regarded the United States as his headquarters though until 1939 he still made frequent visits to Europe. In 1936 Aldington met Netta Patmore

(1911–77), daughter-in-law of his mistress Brigit Patmore and the daughter of James McCulloch, a lawyer, of Pinner, Middlesex. Having obtained their divorces, Aldington and Netta were married in London on 25 June 1938; they had one daughter, Catherine, who was born a week after the marriage and who was educated primarily in France where she married and practised as a child psychiatrist. Following the adverse publicity about his marriage, Aldington found a new publisher in America and in 1941 his autobiography, *Life for Life's Sake*, appeared. In that year he edited *The Viking Book of Poetry of the English-Speaking World*. Between 1942 and 1946 he worked as a freelance film writer in Hollywood, where he had sold the rights to his novel *All Men Are Enemies* (1933) ten years earlier for a film which was never made. He also wrote during this period a good deal of biography (including *Wellington*, 1946, which won the James Tait Black memorial prize of 1947) and editions and anthologies of verse and prose. Although Aldington had said that he would 'never return to Europe' he finally tired of Hollywood and returned to France. By 1947 they were at Le Lavandou, and Aldington declared himself 'home after a long absence'.

The next few years, in which his work reflected a renewed zest and energy, were to prove crucial to his literary and personal life. He produced the major biographies, *Portrait of a Genius, But . . ., a Life of D. H. Lawrence* (1950), *Pinorman, Personal Recollections of Norman Douglas, Orioli, and Prentice* (1954), and *Lawrence of Arabia* (1955). These books mark a progression in the extent of controversy which they aroused. The frankness and honesty that had already made Aldington enemies in the writing and publishing world were now directed, with perhaps a certain relish, at these important figures—two of whom had become internationally admired, even idolized. If open discussion of, for example, (George) Norman Douglas's [q.v.] homosexuality caused wild hostility, such a reaction was utterly mild compared to that which his biography of T. E. Lawrence [q.v.] received. It is ironical that only in the latter case was the individual discussed not known personally, that as always Aldington was meticulous in checking his facts, and that he had initially set out to write a book confirming his belief in a justified national hero. His conclusion, however, that Lawrence was a liar and a fraud, attracted to Aldington a quite extraordinary wrath—and it was a wrath that could hurt. Indeed, it appears that there was a plot by powerful members of the British literary establishment to discredit the book before its publication in an attempt to keep it unpublished, and that the net effect of *Lawrence of Arabia* and *Pinorman* was to cause

Aldington's life's work, 'some seventy titles in all', to go out of print.

This was a time when, perhaps as never before, Aldington needed the support of his friends. In 1950 his wife returned to live in England but he still had a daughter, who remained with him, to support. He had, however, in 1947 met Alister Kershaw, an Australian writer, who was to remain for the rest of Aldington's life his loyal friend. And despite all his problems—in particular the war waged against him as a controversial author which soon occasioned acute financial difficulties—he continued to write and to publish, notably his biography of the French poet Frederic Mistral (1956) which was awarded the *Prix de Gratitude Mistralienne* in 1959. From 1957, and for the last five years of his life, Aldington's situation became increasingly happy and secure. Alister Kershaw made available a house near Sury-en-Vaux in the Loire Valley; Aldington's books began to come back into print; he helped to translate the *Larousse Encyclopaedia of Mythology*; he contributed his significant knowledge of D. H. Lawrence to a new work on that author. The last years were especially contented because of the continued friendship and loyalty of those whom he had known for half a century. For example, in 1959 he visited Zurich to see H. D., his first wife, and Annie Winifred Ellerman, who wrote under the pseudonym 'W. Bryher', and whom he had first known as a soldier in the war of 1914–18. One of the most remarkable events of this time was an invitation for him and his daughter to spend three weeks in Russia as guests of the Soviet Writers' Union to honour his seventieth birthday. He had become well known there ever since the publication of *Death of a Hero*. This was his final journey for he died suddenly 27 July 1962 in Maison Sallé near Sury-en-Vaux only ten days or so after returning from Russia.

Aldington lived through, and was intimately associated with, the development of modernism in English literature. Moreover, few other writers have covered such a wide range of literary activity, published in some 200 titles. Indeed, Aldington's versatility has given rise to criticisms of superficiality and plagiarism (such as the claim that his long poem 'A Fool i' the Forest', 1925, is derivative of T. S. Eliot's 'The Waste Land'). He had two major assets. One was his passion for truth which, when threatened by hypocrisy or suppression, burst into formidably explosive utterance. The other was a sensitivity to beauty, especially of shape and colour as revealed in classical and Mediterranean art, and in the natural beauty of the human form, animals, and plants. It was a combination of these talents which created the first Imagist poet just as they were later to produce the angry novelist and biographer. When he saw beauty and truth attacked Aldington combined all his resources to create his most memorable and potent work.

[Richard Aldington, *Life for Life's Sake*, 1941; Brigit Patmore, *My Friends when Young*, 1968; Norman Timmins Gates, *A Checklist of the Letters of Richard Aldington*, 1977; Alister Kershaw and Frédéric-Jacques Temple, *Richard Aldington; an Intimate Portrait*, 1965; private information.]

J. A. MORRIS

ALEXANDER, ALBERT VICTOR, EARL ALEXANDER OF HILLSBOROUGH (1885-1965), politician, was born 1 May 1885 at Weston-super-Mare, the fourth child and only son of Albert Alexander, blacksmith and artisan engineer, and his wife, Eliza Jane Thatcher. After the death of his father in 1886, his mother, a woman of great determination and energy, moved with her young family to her parents' house in Bristol and set out to provide for herself and her children by returning to her trade of surgical belt and corset-making. Although she ultimately built up a thriving business, the early years were a hard struggle and when Alexander was only thirteen he decided, for himself, to give up full-time schooling and start contributing to the family income.

He left his first job after a few months to become a boy clerk in the office of the Bristol school board, to begin a career in educational administration which was to last until 1920. In 1903 he transferred to the school management department of the Somerset County Council and returned to Weston-super-Mare to live. By his natural abilities he rose to become in 1919 chief clerk of the higher education department.

In 1908 Alexander married a schoolteacher, Esther Ellen, daughter of George Chapple, of Tiverton, Devon. Influenced by her he joined the Baptist Church and became a lay preacher, thus following in the footsteps of his maternal grandfather, who had been a highly individual evangelist of some note. During this period as a local government official he not only continued his education at evening classes, but also took an active interest in the National Association of Local Government Officers, eventually becoming secretary of the Somerset County Council branch. He also joined in the affairs of his local Co-operative Society and in time became its vice-president. On the outbreak of war in 1914 he joined the Artists' Rifles; he served throughout the war and was demobilized with the rank of captain.

His activities as a lay preacher, trade-union branch secretary, and Co-operative Society committee member all provided Alexander with experience which was to prove valuable in his subsequent political career; but his entry into politics at the national level was quite fortuitous. After returning from the army, life as a local government officer ceased to satisfy him and, on a sudden impulse, he applied in 1920 for the post of secretary to the parliamentary committee of the Co-operative Congress, which he happened to see advertised. To his surprise he got it. At first it proved less exciting than he had hoped but when he complained that the work was insufficiently demanding, his chief suggested that he should set about defeating the Lloyd George Government's proposal in the finance Bill of 1921 to introduce a corporation profits tax applicable to Co-operative Societies. After an intensive lobbying campaign the measure was in fact defeated by a narrow margin, and Alexander's contribution to this success caused him to be immediately recognized as a rising star in the Co-operative movement and he was invited to stand as Labour and Co-operative Party candidate in the Hillsborough division of Sheffield, for which he was returned in the general election of 1922. He held the seat, except for a break between 1931 and 1935, until 1950. In the Commons he quickly gained a reputation as a forceful and knowledgeable debater on matters of trade and industry, so that when the Labour Party formed a minority Government in 1924 he became parliamentary secretary to the Board of Trade, under Sidney Webb [q.v.].

His first term of office lasted only a few months, but when Labour won the general election in 1929 he was judged ready for promotion. On the strength, it is said, of the acquaintance with Merchant Navy affairs which he had gained in 1924, he was appointed first lord of the Admiralty. Although MacDonald's choice was perhaps surprising, it was a happy one. Alexander took to naval affairs as if by instinct and he rapidly developed an enduring admiration and affection for the navy. During this first term of office his most important work lay in the negotiation of the London Naval Treaty signed in 1930. Although the policy of agreed numerical and qualitative limitations enshrined in the treaty provided less than he or the naval staff would have wished, Alexander welcomed the fact that agreement of some kind had been achieved; he was later to take particular pride in the achievements in the battle of the River Plate of two of the cruisers, *Achilles* and *Ajax*, built in conformity with the treaty.

In the crisis of 1931 Alexander was among those who were not prepared to support a reduction in unemployment payments and he did not join the 'national' Government. At the general election he stood once more as an orthodox Labour-Co-operative candidate. He lost his seat and returned to his work for the parliamentary committee of the Co-operative Congress. In 1935, however, he was once more returned for Hillsborough and became the principal Opposition spokesman on naval affairs. In this role his understanding and support of the needs of naval defence were unwavering, although he did not hesitate to attack the Government with great vigour if he thought that any particular aspect of policy was unsound.

By now Alexander had become a recognized master of naval affairs, so that there was nothing surprising in his second appointment as first lord in May 1940, when Churchill formed his wartime Government. Not only was he the only Labour minister with experience in charge of a Service ministry, but it was also an appointment in a field in which the prime minister, who had also twice been first lord, would brook no interference. It may be significant of the prime minister's attitude to Alexander, and perhaps also that of the Service chiefs, that the first lord was not allowed access to the most secret materials and did not have entry to the most secret war room. Alexander remained in this post for the whole of the war. The direction of operations was of course concentrated in the hands of the prime minister and the chiefs of staff; but what was left to the first lord Alexander tackled with unflagging energy and solid competence. He enjoyed the support of the sea lords and worked in full harmony with them, especially with the first sea lords, Sir Dudley Pound [q.v.] and Sir Andrew Cunningham (later Viscount Cunningham of Hyndhope, q.v.). With Pound he made a hazardous journey to Bordeaux in June 1940 in an effort to secure assurances from the French authorities that the French Fleet would not be allowed to fall into enemy hands. The failure of this mission faced him and his colleagues with a cruel dilemma: whether to use force to immobilize the French ships at Oran in July 1940. Neither on this occasion nor any other did he falter in his judgement of naval needs or his resolve to see that, if possible, they were met. He represented with skill and persistence the naval case in the crucial discussions which went on continually about the allocation of scarce resources between the Services; and he found time somehow to speak up and down the country during the 'Warship Weeks' which were designed in part to sustain public enthusiasm for the war effort and in part to stimulate investment in national savings. His sense of identity with the navy was, indeed, so marked that he occasionally caused raised eyebrows by talking of 'my navy', when all he meant to signify was his own devotion to the Service of which he was immensely proud to be the political head.

The war over, Alexander was replaced as first lord during the short caretaker Government which preceded the general election of 1945; but he returned to the Admiralty for his third term of office as first lord when the Labour Party emerged victorious. Alexander's long experience of naval administration served him in good stead in the difficult task of guiding the navy through the transition from a war to a peace footing. He also served as a member of the Cabinet delegation, with Sir Stafford Cripps and Lord Pethick-Lawrence [qq.v.], which went to India in 1946. Lord Wavell [q.v.] recorded in his journal that 'Alexander was straight, sensible and honest, the very best type of British Labour, the best we breed. At the beginning he knew nothing of India and the ways of Indian politicians, and sat back. At the end he really had a surer and more realistic grasp of the situation than either of the other two.'

In December 1946 Alexander moved, after a brief interval as minister without portfolio, to a yet higher office in the defence field, when he was appointed as the first defence minister of the new Department of Defence created to reorganize the higher direction of defence policy. His term of office was both less successful and less satisfying than his time at the Admiralty. The chiefs of staff tended as before to pursue the interests of their separate Services and there was no Service chairman to co-ordinate their views from an independent standpoint. The task of adjudicating between conflicting claims came less naturally to Alexander's particular talents than the advocacy of a single case. Nor were his relations with some of his Service colleagues, and Field-Marshal Montgomery in particular, as uniformly harmonious as they had been with the sea lords. Furthermore he faced political difficulties over conscription as a result of the conflict between the military needs as assessed by his advisers and the widespread dislike of conscription among Labour backbenchers. The opposing pressures thus engendered caused him first to propose a period of eighteen months, then to reduce it to twelve during the passage of the national service Bill, only to restore an eighteen-month period a few months later. Whereas his policy on this central issue appeared vacillating, in the international sphere he played a consistently constructive role in the Western Defence Union through his ability to get on well with the defence ministers of the other countries in the alliance.

The general election of 1950 signalled the end of Alexander's career as a departmental minister. The Labour Party had so narrow a majority that it was felt essential that the minister of defence should be in the House of Commons. Alexander, who had been raised to the peerage in the New Year honours, became chancellor of the Duchy of Lancaster. When Labour went out of office in 1951 he became deputy leader of the Opposition in the House of Lords; and even though he was by then seventy, in 1955 he was unanimously elected to succeed Lord Jowitt [q.v.] as leader. In spite of increasing physical disability from an arthritic hip he insisted on performing the duties of leader with great conscientiousness until late in 1964. To the end he made well-informed, hard-hitting contributions to debate, especially on defence matters.

In the Co-operative movement Alexander was a leading figure, for many years by far the best-known and most effective advocate of its ideals and policies. From time to time he also played a significant part in shaping the movement's internal organization. He was, for example, one of the prime movers in the creation of a new national Co-operative authority in 1932. A few years later, when the probability of war became apparent, he joined with other representatives of the food industry in pressing for the creation of a large reserve of stocks of wheat.

As a Baptist lay preacher it was natural that Alexander should be a staunch defender of the Protestant faith. Both before his energies were absorbed by high ministerial duties and after he moved into the calmer atmosphere of the House of Lords, he campaigned actively for the right of every man to worship God in his own way, and, if he so desired, without the intervention of priesthood or hierarchy. He was fond of quoting the dictum of his favourite author, Emerson, that 'whosoever would be a free man must first be a non-conformist'. In 1956 he was president of the Council of Protestant Churches.

When Alexander died, Attlee paid a moving tribute to 'this loyal, strong man'. Loyal he certainly was, with an unshakeable devotion to the national interest, as he saw it, and to his party; but 'strong' was not strictly accurate if taken to mean inflexible in the pursuit of his own policies. Certainly Alexander held a few fundamental principles on which he was unyielding, but in what to him were secondary matters his approach was pragmatic and his way to a solution the search for a consensus. Similarly, as a political figure, he was trenchant and forthright in debate; but generous in his personal relations with friends and opponents alike. He declined to publish his memoirs because he saw so many others draw into backbiting criticism in the pursuit of self-justification. This innate magnanimity earned him the respect and friendship of so many colleagues. Indeed, behind an often gruff exterior he had a gift for conviviality and friendship. The circle of his friends extended far beyond politics and the Co-operative movement and included men and women in industry, in the City, in medicine, in the theatre, and in sport. He was particularly proud, as a lifelong soccer enthusiast, to be vice-president of the Chelsea football club. He was a member of the Bakers' Company and served his turn as master. A keen self-taught musician, he was never happier than when seated at the piano, leading a ward-room gathering, a group of European defence ministers, or even a viceroy in a sing-song.

Although he wrote a good number of articles on political and Co-operative subjects and at least one short religious tract, Alexander exerted his public influence as a speaker. When himself deeply moved, his speeches, and still more his sermons, were fired by an equally moving fervour; but his normal parliamentary manner was different. It was well summed up by Harold Laski [q.v.] who described him as 'a good debater without being a great orator' and went on 'what he says is always made with point and directness. He is never at a loss for a phrase or an idea. He puts his views with a hale honesty that is a real index to his character.'

But if Laski caught Aledxander's normal speaking style accurately he exaggerated his commitment to socialist ideology. In fact there was nothing of the dogmatist about him and his social-political philosophy was essentially that of a nonconformist radical, concerned to work pragmatically for the freedom and welfare of those whose lives, like his own when young, were cramped by circumstances outside their own control.

Alexander was a man of medium height; broad in the shoulder and deep in the chest, with a square jaw to match. His features were well marked but the most readily noticeable was his wide mouth, sometimes set in a very firm line, but often relaxed in a good-humoured smile. His voice had a warm resonance about it in which his west-country origins could often be detected and his manner had an engaging, if occasionally blistering, spontaneity about it. Nature had endowed him with the enormous stamina for the long hours which he had to accept throughout his ministerial career and he had the invaluable gift of being able to sleep at will and managing on only a few hours rest during the night.

He was sworn of the Privy Council in 1929 and appointed CH in 1941. In the same year he became an elder brother of Trinity House. In 1950 he was created a viscount and in 1963 an earl. In 1964 not long before his death he was appointed KG. He was an honorary freeman of Sheffield and Weston-super-Mare, and an honorary LLD of Bristol (1945) and Sheffield (1947). He had a son, who died in infancy, and a daughter. The title therefore became extinct when he died in London 11 January 1965. His widow died in 1969.

Of two portraits by Ernest Moore, one is in the possession of the family and the other went on indefinite loan to the Admiralty. He was also painted by Flora Lion.

[*The Times*, 12 January 1965; private information; personal knowledge.]

CLIFFORD JARRETT

ALEXANDER, HAROLD RUPERT LEOFRIC GEORGE, first EARL ALEXANDER OF TUNIS (1891-1969), field-marshal, was born in London 10 December 1891, the third son of James Alexander, fourth Earl of Caledon, and his wife, Lady Elizabeth Graham-Toler, daughter of the third Earl of Norbury. His youth was spent at the family estate, Caledon Castle, in the county Tyrone. His father, who had served briefly in the Life Guards but was better known as an adventurous deep-water yachtsman, died when Alexander was six; his mother, eccentric and imperious, held aloof from her children; but their four sons were perfectly happy in their own company. It was in Northern Ireland that Alexander developed both the athletic and the aesthetic sides of his character; he trained himself as a runner and enjoyed all the usual country sports, but he also taught himself to carve in wood and stone and began what was to prove one of the main passions of his life, painting. After reading Reynolds's *Discourses on Art* he decided that the thing he wanted most in the world was to be president of the Royal Academy. At Harrow he worked well enough to rise smoothly up the school. His games were cricket, athletics, rackets, rugger, boxing, fencing, and gymnastics and he won distinction at all of them; he is best remembered as nearly saving the game for Harrow in what *Wisden* called the most extraordinary cricket match ever played, at Lord's in 1910. He also won a school prize for drawing.

He went on to the Royal Military College, Sandhurst, and was commissioned in the Irish Guards in 1911. Although he was pleased at the idea of spending a few years in a Guards battalion, he intended to retire before long and make a living as an artist. These plans were upset by the outbreak of war in 1914. Alexander's battalion went to France in August and he served there continuously until early 1919, being in action throughout except when recovering from wounds or on courses. He was twice wounded, awarded the MC (1915), and appointed to the DSO (1916). Promotion was rapid. A lieutenant when he arrived, he became a captain in February 1915, a major, one of the youngest in the army, eight months later, with the acting command of the 1st battalion of his own regiment, and a lieutenant-colonel, commanding the 2nd battalion, in October 1917. During the retreat from Arras in March 1918 he was acting brigadier-general in command of the 4th Guards brigade.

The war was a turning-point in Alexander's character and career. He had painted in the trenches, and he continued to paint throughout his life, reaching at times a standard only just short of the professional; but in the course of the war he had come to realize the fascination of the profession of arms, and had proved to himself, and demonstrated to others, that he was outstandingly competent at it. His reputation stood very high for courage but also for a cheerful imperturbability in all circumstances. For four years he lived the life of a regimental officer, without any staff service; he later criticized senior commanders of that war for never seeking personal experience of the conditions of the fighting troops.

Not wishing to go back to barracks or to the army of occupation in Germany, he applied in 1919 for an appointment to one of the many military missions in Eastern Europe. He was first posted as a member of the Allied Relief Commission in Poland under (Sir) Stephen Tallents [q.v.] and later went with Tallents to Latvia which was in danger of falling either to Russia or to Germany. The Allies had no troops in the Baltic and only a small naval detachment under Sir Walter Cowan [q.v.]. Tallents placed the *Landwehr*, composed of Baltic Germans, under Alexander's command. At the age of twenty-seven he found himself at the head of a brigade-sized formation with mainly German officers. He was good at languages and had taught himself German and Russian; his authority derived from his charm and sincerity and his obvious professionalism. He kept his men steady and resistant to the attractions of the German expeditionary force under von der Goltz and led them to victory in the campaign which drove the Red Army from Latvia.

Alexander retained all his life a keen interest in Russia. During the war of 1914-18 he designed a new uniform cap for himself with a high visor and flat peak, on the model of one he had seen a Russian officer wearing. He always wore the Order of St. Anne with swords which Yudenitch awarded him in 1919; when he met Rokossovsky in 1945 the Russian general muttered to him in an aside that he had once had it too. In the second war, like Churchill, he admired Stalin and was enthusiastic about the Soviet Army.

After the Soviet Union recognized the independence of Latvia in 1920 Alexander returned to England to become second-in-command of his regiment. In 1922 he was given command and took it to Constantinople as part of the army of occupation. In 1923, after the treaty of Lausanne, the regiment went to Gibraltar and thence in 1924 to England. In 1926-7 he was at the Staff College. He was very senior in rank, a full colonel, but for the duration of the course he was temporarily reduced to the rank of major. After commanding the regiment and regimental district of the Irish Guards (1928-30), he attended the Imperial Defence College. This was followed by the only two staff appointments in his career, as GSO 2 at the War Office (1931-2) and as GSO 1 at Northern Command (1932-4). He was already widely regarded as likely to make the outstanding fighting commander of a future war; the other name mentioned, from the Indian Army, was that of (Sir) Claude Auchinleck.

In 1934 Alexander was appointed to command the Nowshera brigade on the North-West Frontier, one of the most coveted in India. Auchinleck commanded the next brigade, in Peshawar. Alexander surprised and delighted his Indian troops by learning Urdu as rapidly and fluently as he had Russian and German. Next year he commanded the brigade in the Loc Agra campaign (called after a small village north of the Malakand pass) against invading tribesmen; and not long after, under Auchinleck's command as the senior brigadier, in the Mohmand campaign. Both operations were successful; roads were built, large regions pacified; Alexander was appointed CSI (1936). It was noted not only that he had mastered the difficult techniques of fighting in mountainous country but also that he was always to be seen with the foremost troops. This was both a revulsion from the behaviour he had condemned in his senior commanders in France and a natural result of his personal courage; it remained to the end a characteristic of his style of leadership.

His promotion to major-general in 1937, at the age of forty-five, made him the youngest general in the British Army; in 1938 he was given command of the 1st division at Aldershot. In 1939 he took the division to France as one of the two in I Corps under Sir John Dill [q.v.]. In the retreat to Dunkirk his division only once fought a serious if brief battle, when he successfully defended the Scheldt for two days, throwing back all German penetrations; for the rest of the time he was obliged to fall back to conform to the movement of other divisions. It was Dunkirk which first brought his name prominently before the public notice. I Corps was to form the final rearguard and Lord Gort [q.v.] superseded the corps commander and put Alexander in command. His orders were definite: to withdraw all the British troops who could be saved. A different interpretation of the military necessities of the moment was held by the French commander, Admiral Abrial, and Alexander confessed that to carry out his orders while leaving the French still fighting made him feel that he 'had never been in such a terrible situation'. During the three days in which he commanded, 20,000 British and 98,000 French were evacuated: Alexander left on the last motor launch in which he toured the beaches to see that there were no British troops remaining.

On his return to England he was confirmed in command of I Corps which was responsible for the defence of the east coast from Scarborough to the Wash. Promoted lieutenant-general, in December 1940 he succeeded Auchinleck at Southern Command. He showed himself an admirable trainer of troops and was the first to introduce the realistic 'battleschools' which became so prominent a feature of military life from 1940 to 1944. He was also put in command of a nominal 'Force 110' which was to be used for amphibious operations; he and his staff planned a number which never came off, such as the invasion of the Canaries and of Sicily.

In February 1942 Alexander was suddenly informed that he was to take command of the army in Burma where the situation was already desperate. The key battle had been lost before Alexander arrived; the Japanese were across the Sittang river, in a position to encircle and capture Rangoon. It was by the greatest good fortune, and the oversight of a Japanese divisional commander in leaving open one narrow escape route, that Alexander himself and the bulk of his forces were able to escape from Rangoon which, in obedience to ill-considered orders from Sir A. P. (later Earl) Wavell [q.v.], he had tried to hold almost beyond the last reasonable moment. After its fall Burma had no future military value except as a glacis for the defence of India. Alexander decided that the only success he could snatch from the jaws of unmitigated defeat was to rescue the army under his command by withdrawing it to India. It was a campaign of which he always spoke with compunction and distaste, except for his admiration for General (later Viscount) Slim [q.v.]. Left entirely without guidance after the fall of Rangoon—not that the guidance he had received previously had been of any value—Alexander did the best he could. As a further sign of the gifts he was to display as an Allied commander, it should be recorded that he got on the best of terms not only with Chiang Kai Chek but also with General J. W. Stilwell.

It might be thought that two defeats in succession would have meant the end to Alexander's hopes of high command. Churchill had shown no mercy to Gort or Wavell and was to show none to Auchinleck. But as he wrote in *The Hinge of Fate* (1951), in sending Alexander to Burma 'never have I taken the responsibility for sending a general on a more forlorn hope'. He had formed so high an appreciation of Alexander's ability that he immediately confirmed his designation as commander-in-chief of the First Army which was to invade North Africa, under Eisenhower's command, in November 1942 when the Allies for the first time seized the strategic initiative. But before that could take effect, Churchill felt impelled in early August to visit Egypt. Auchinleck was more impressive in the field than in conversation in his caravan; Churchill decided to replace him with Alexander. It is ironical that one of the main reasons why Auchinleck was replaced was that he declared himself unable to take the offensive until September: Churchill was to accept from Alexander, with but little remonstrance, a postponement until late October.

Alexander took over as commander-in-chief, Middle East, on 15 August 1942. For the first time he found himself in a position which was not only not desperate but full of promise. He had a numerical superiority, and at last equality of equipment, against an army fighting at the end of a long and precarious line of communication with its bases and debilitated by sickness. General Gott [q.v.], who was to have been his army commander, was killed; but he was replaced immediately by General Montgomery (later Viscount Montgomery of Alamein) who had been one of Alexander's corps commanders in Southern Command and whose capacities as a trainer and inspirer of men were well known to him. He had a sound defensive position, strongly manned, and plans had been prepared for the expected enemy assault; they were based on a partial refusal of the left flank while holding the strong position of Alam Halfa, fortified and prepared by Auchinleck to block an advance on Alexandria. Reinforcements in men and tanks continued to arrive. Nevertheless there was a problem of morale, since the Eighth Army had been fighting in retreat since May and had lost one position after another; it was natural for the troops to wonder whether they might not find themselves retreating once more. The first step towards victory in Egypt was when Alexander made it known, as soon as he assumed command, that there was to be no further retreat; the decisive battle was to be fought on the Alamein line.

The defensive battle of Alam Halfa and the offensive battle of Alamein were, as Alexander always insisted, Montgomery's victories. He had always had the gift of delegating and no one was more generous in acknowledging the merits of his subordinates. There is reason for

argument whether, after the failure of the first plan at Alamein, *Lightfoot*, part of the credit for *Supercharge*, the modified version, should go to suggestions from Alexander. In truth the two generals, the commander-in-chief and the army commander, were aptly suited to their respective roles and played them well. The successful campaign in Egypt, won at almost the lowest point in the Allied fortunes, marked the beginning of a period in which British and Allied armies knew scarcely anything but success.

The invasion of North Africa in November meant that after two months a British Army, the First, with a French and an American corps, was fighting in northern and central Tunisia against a mixed German–Italian army and meanwhile the German–Italian Armoured Army of Africa, defeated at Alamein, was withdrawing towards southern Tunisia pursued by the Eighth Army. It was evident that a headquarters was required to command and co-ordinate the two Allied armies. Alexander was summoned to the Casablanca conference of January 1943. He made a great impression on President Roosevelt, General Marshall, and the United States chiefs of staff; his reputation at home had never been higher. The conference decided to appoint him deputy commander-in-chief to General Eisenhower with command over all the forces actually fighting the enemy. He set up a very small headquarters, called the 18th Army Group from the numbers of the two British armies which made up the bulk of his command; this was originally located in the town of Constantine, but as soon as he could Alexander moved out into the field and operated from a tented camp, moved frequently.

The Tunisian campaign provides a convincing proof of Alexander's capacity as a strategist. It also demonstrates his great gift of inspiring and elevating the morale of the troops he commanded, as well as his skill in welding together the efforts of different nationalities. At the beginning he faced a difficult task. The southern flank of his western front had been driven in by a bold enemy thrust which threatened to come in upon the communications of the whole deployment. Alexander was on the spot, even before the date at which he was officially to assume command (20 February 1943); he was seen directing the siting of gun positions at the approaches to the Kasserine pass. This was a flash of his old style but it was not long before he took a firm grip on higher things and reorganized the whole direction of the campaign. He sorted out the confusion into which the First Army had been thrown by the rapid vicissitudes of the past, brought into play the ponderous but skilful thrust of the Eighth Army, and directed the efforts of both in the final victory of Tunis. In this last battle in Africa he employed an elaborate and successful plan of deception, based on an accurate knowledge of enemy dispositions and intentions, and broke through their strong defensive front with a powerful and well-concealed offensive blow. In two days all was over. A quarter of a million enemy were captured. On 13 May he was able to make his historic signal to the prime minister: 'Sir, it is my duty to report that the Tunisian campaign is over. All enemy resistance has ceased. We are masters of the North African shores.'

Sicily was the next objective on which the Casablanca conference had decided. The forces commanded by Alexander, as commander-in-chief 15th Army Group, consisted of the United States Seventh and British Eighth armies. The principal interest in the campaign lies in the immense size of the amphibious effort required, larger in the assault phase even than for the invasion of Normandy, and in the elaborate planning which preceded it. It fell to Alexander to decide on the final form of the plan, a concentrated assault on the south-eastern corner of the island, rather than, as originally proposed by the planning staff, two separate attacks in the south-east and the north-west. In this decision he was vindicated, mainly because of his correct assessment of the new possibilities of beach maintenance produced by recently acquired amphibious equipment. In the course of the first few days, however, he made one of his few strategic errors in yielding to Montgomery's insistence that the Eighth Army could finish off the campaign by itself if the United States Seventh Army were kept out of its way; admittedly Alexander was deceived by inaccurate reports of the progress that the Eighth Army was making. As a result the reduction of the island took rather longer than expected and a high proportion of the German defenders managed to withdraw into Calabria. Nevertheless, the capture of Sicily in thirty-eight days was not only a notable strategic gain but also brought encouraging confirmation of the validity of the methods of amphibious warfare of which so much was expected in the next year's invasion of France.

That invasion was the principal factor affecting the last two years of Alexander's career as a commander in the field, during which he was engaged on the mainland of Italy. His troops were now no longer the spearhead of the Allied military effort in Europe. He was required to give up, for the benefit of the western front, many divisions of his best troops on three occasions and his task was defined as to eliminate Italy from the war and to contain the maximum number of German divisions. The

first part of this directive was rapidly achieved. In his second task also, which from September 1943 onwards represented the sole object of the campaign, he was strikingly successful. So far from diverting troops from Italy to the decisive front, the Germans continuously reinforced it, not only robbing the Russian front but even sending divisions from the west. To obtain this success, however, in a terrain always favouring the defence, Alexander was obliged to maintain the offensive and to compensate for the lack of superior force by using all the arts of generalship.

'The campaign in Italy was a great holding attack', Alexander states in his dispatch. As is the nature of holding attacks, it was directed against a secondary theatre. Nevertheless it gave scope for daring strategic planning in spite of the odds and of the forbidding and mountainous nature of the ground. The initial assault at Salerno, simultaneous with the announcement of the Italian surrender, was a good example; a force of only three divisions, all that could be carried in the landing craft allotted to the theatre, was thrown on shore at the extreme limit of air cover. The landing at Anzio was a masterpiece of deception which caught the enemy off balance and forced him to send reinforcements to Italy. It made a vital contribution to the offensive of May and June 1944 in which the Germans were driven north of Rome, with disproportionately heavy losses in men and equipment. For this offensive Alexander made a secret redeployment of his two armies and mounted a most ingenious plan of deception; his opponent, Field-Marshal Kesselring, was unable to react in time, for all that his defensive positions were strong both by nature and artificially. The capture of Rome just before the landing in Normandy was a fillip to Allied morale. A more important result from the point of view of Allied grand strategy was that this crushing defeat obliged the Germans to reinforce Italy with eight fresh divisions, some taken from their western garrisons; a month later, in contrast, Alexander was ordered to surrender seven of his divisions for the campaign in France. The final battle, in April 1945, was another example of Alexander's skill in deployment and in deception; by 2 May he had routed the most coherent enemy group of armies still resisting; all Italy had been overrun and a million Germans had laid down their arms in the first big surrender of the war.

The Italian campaign showed Alexander at the height of his powers. These included besides the skill of a strategist a thorough grasp of the principles of administration. As an Allied commander he was supreme; there were no instances of friction anywhere in his command in spite of its varied composition, including at one time or another troops from Britain, the United States, India, Canada, New Zealand, South Africa, France, Poland, Italy, Brazil, and Greece. For the greater part of the campaign, as commander-in-chief of 15th Army Group, later renamed Allied Armies in Italy, he acted as an independent commander, since it had been agreed that the commander-in-chief, Mediterranean, Sir Maitland (later Lord) Wilson [q.v.], should concern himself primarily with the general maintenance of the Italian campaign and with the security of the other areas of the command.

On 12 December 1944 Alexander succeeded Wilson. He was appointed to the rank of field-marshal to date from 4 June 1944, on which day the Allied armies entered Rome. But for all his high rank and heavy responsibilities he remembered his criticism of the commanders in the war of 1914–18. He always spent more time with the forward troops than in his headquarters. His popularity was immense, and his strategic planning benefited because he knew what the war was like at the point that counted.

After the war it was expected by some that Alexander would become chief of the imperial general staff. But W. L. Mackenzie King [q.v.] invited him to be governor-general of Canada, and Churchill pressed him to accept. His sense of duty was reinforced by a strong attraction to the idea of serving Canada. His extended tenure of office ran from 1946 to 1952. He was the last British governor-general and his popularity was as great as that of any of his predecessors. He was comparatively young and brought a young family with him; he toured the whole country, played games, skied, and painted. To his dignity as the representative of the King of Canada and his reputation as a war leader he added an informal friendliness and charm. While in Canada he produced his official dispatches on his campaigns published in the London Gazette; they have been described by his biographer as 'among the great state papers of our military history'.

In January 1952 Churchill visited Ottawa and offered Alexander the post of minister of defence in his Government. When a friend remonstrated he replied: 'Of course I accepted. It's my duty.' To another friend he said, 'I simply can't refuse Winston.' As he entered on his first political post in that frame of mind it is not surprising that he did not much enjoy his period of office. He was not temperamentally suited to political life and in any case he had few real powers to exercise. Churchill continued to behave as though it was he who was the minister of defence and Alexander his spokesman in the Lords. Nevertheless, Alexander had the assets of his great personal popularity,

his charm, and the fact that he numbered so many personal friends among foreign statesmen and military men, especially in the United States, and especially after the election of President Eisenhower. He made no particular mark as minister of defence because he preferred to rely on discreet persuasion and guidance; but he led a good team and suffered no diminution of his reputation. After two and a half years he resigned at his own request, in the autumn of 1954.

In the last fifteen years of his life he accepted a number of directorates. He was most active as director of Alcan and also served on the boards of Barclay's Bank and Phoenix Assurance. He travelled extensively on business for Alcan. He continued to paint and devoted more and more time to it. In 1960 he was persuaded by the Sunday Times to allow his memoirs to be ghosted. They were edited by John North and published in 1962, but were not very favourably received because of the curiously disorganized and anecdotal form. His motive in agreeing to publication was the desire to see that justice was done to the armies in Italy; for himself he preferred to be judged on the basis of his dispatches. For the rest he devoted himself to his garden and to reunions with old comrades. He died suddenly after a heart attack on 16 July 1969, in hospital in Slough. His funeral service was held in St. George's Chapel, Windsor, and he was buried in the churchyard of Ridge, near Tyttenhanger, his family's Hertfordshire home. The headstone of his grave bears at the top the single word ALEX, the name by which he was known to his friends and his soldiers.

He married in 1931 Lady Margaret Diana Bingham (died 1977), younger daughter of the fifth earl of Lucan; she was appointed GBE in 1954. They had two sons, one daughter, and an adopted daughter. He was succeeded by his elder son, Shane William Desmond (born 1935).

Alexander was created a viscount in 1946 and an earl in 1952 on his return from Canada. He was appointed CB (1938), KCB and GCB (1942), GCMG on his appointment to Canada, and in the same year (1946) KG. He was sworn of the Privy Council in 1952 and also of the Canadian Privy Council. In 1959 he was admitted to the Order of Merit. He was colonel of the Irish Guards from 1946 to his death, constable of the Tower of London from 1960 to 1965. From 1957 to 1965 he was lieutenant of the county of London, and for a further year of Greater London. He was chancellor and then grand master of the Order of St. Michael and St. George, an elder brother of Trinity House, and in 1955 president of the MCC. He was a freeman of the City of London and of many other cities. His numerous foreign decorations included the grand cross of the Legion of Honour and the Legion of Merit and Distinguished Service Medal of the United States.

Alexander was 5 feet 10 inches tall, slim, muscular, and handsome. His features were regular in the style which when he was young was regarded as typical of the army officer; he wore a trim Guardsman's moustache all his life. He dressed with careful and unaffected elegance on all occasions; his Russian-style cap was only the precursor of a number of variations on uniform regulations whereas in plain clothes he favoured neatness, fashion, and the avoidance of the elaborate.

There are two portraits of him at the National Portrait Gallery, by Edward Seago (a close personal friend) and by Maurice Codner; and two at the Imperial War Museum, by R. G. Eves and Harry Carr. The Irish guards have two, by John Gilroy and Richard Jack; another version of the Gilroy portrait is in McGill University, Montreal. White's Club has a portrait by Sir Oswald Birley. The National Portrait Gallery has a sculptured bust by Donald Gilbert. A bronze bust by Oscar Nemon, in the Old Radcliffe Observatory at Oxford, was unveiled by Queen Elizabeth the Queen Mother in 1973 to mark the endowment of a chair of cardio-vascular medicine at the university in Alexander's memory. In the possession of the family is a bronze bust by Anthony Gray.

[Nigel Nicolson, *Alex*, 1973; dispatches in *London Gazette*, 5 and 12 February 1948, 12 June 1950; I. S. O. Playfair and C. J. C. Molony, and others, (Official) *History of the Second World War. The Mediterranean and Middle East*, vol. iv, 1966, and C. J. C. Molony and others, vol. v, 1973; personal knowledge.]   DAVID HUNT

ALGERANOFF, HARCOURT (1903-1967), dancer and ballet master, was born in London 18 April 1903, the son of Thomas Richard Essex, a sculptor, and his wife, Alice Kendall. He was named Harcourt Algernon Leighton. He dropped his original name and assumed that of Algeranoff when he joined Anna Pavlova's company in 1921. It was as though he had not only taken on a Russian stage-name—as was usual enough at the time when, in the world of ballet, to be British was to be nothing much whereas to be Russian was to be in the height of fashion—but had largely assumed a Russian identity; Algeranoff, it seemed, became the most persistent of the many character roles in which he excelled. He studied at one time or another under the Russians Nicholas Legat and Lubov Tchernicheva, but his most formative period was that of the far-ranging tours which

he undertook as 'character-soloist' with Pavlova. It was then that he became interested in Indian and Japanese dance, about which he subsequently lectured. His experiences of that period, remembered with nostalgia, were eventually put into a book, *My Years with Pavlova* (1957).

Algeranoff was a founder-member of the Markova-Dolin Company in 1935, joined the De Basil Ballet Russe, the company with the best claim to be the successor to the great Diaghilev Ballet, in 1936, and the International Ballet, under Mona Inglesby, in 1943. It was with De Basil and the International that chiefly made, and consolidated, his considerable reputation as a character-dancer or, more specifically, as a character-actor; for the roles with which he was memorably associated were those in which dancing counted for less than acting. Algeranoff learnt the traditional character roles (Carabosse, Rothbart, Hilarion) from a colleague of his in the International, Nicholas Sergeyev, the one-time regisseur of the Maryinsky Ballet in St. Petersburg. Sergeyev's notation of the nineteenth-century classics, which he brought with him when he left the USSR, had enabled the Sadler's Wells (subsequently the Royal) Ballet to present exceptionally authentic versions of those basic works. He had then transferred his allegiance from the Sadler's Wells Ballet to the International. Among the character roles in which Algeranoff excelled were the astrologer in *Le Coq d'Or*, the magician Kastchei in *Firebird*, Pierrot in *Carnaval*, Dr. Coppélius in *Coppélia*, the master of ceremonies in *Gaîté Parisienne*, Carabosse in *The Sleeping Beauty*, and Death in Mona Inglesby's choreographic version of *Everyman*.

Algeranoff also conducted outstanding classes in character and national dancing at the International Ballet. However, the ballet *For Love or Money*, which he made for the company in 1951, is remembered only as indicating that, for all his stage-craft, his ability as a teacher, and his exceptional skill as a performer, he lacked the inventiveness of movement which bespeaks a true choreographer.

After the International Ballet ceased to exist, Algeranoff went to Australia in 1954. There he worked at first in the Australian Children's Theatre. He then became ballet master to the Borovansky Ballet (1959) and a guest artist (1962-3) in the Australian Ballet which at that time was beginning to take shape under the guidance of (Dame) Peggy van Praagh. For a time Algeranoff returned to Europe, becoming director of the Norwegian State Opera and Ballet Company. But in 1959 he decided to settle in Australia, making his home in Mildura, where he opened a dance studio. In contemporary Australia there was scarcely the opportunity for Algeranoff's career to prosper conspicuously; but he was one of the pioneers whose example and influence contributed to the growth of an indigenous company in that country where ballet had been previously an intermittent import only. Algeranoff became ballet master for Australia's North Western Ballet Society.

Algeranoff did not belong to the native and nascent British ballet which, young though it was, sent its missionaries, such as Peggy van Praagh, to the Dominions. He was one of the last of those few British dancers who made their way in a world of cosmopolitan ballet still dominated by expatriate Russians. But they too have their place in the story of the widening popularity of ballet in the mid-twentieth century.

Algeranoff was dapper, talented, youthfully handsome, and took himself very seriously. He played his Russian character role with zest, in public at least, and loved to tell stories about Pavlova. Algeranoff married the French dancer Claudie Leonard; by her he had a son, Noel, who, following in parental footsteps, became a mime. Claudie Algeranova later became ballet mistress at the Bavarian State Opera in Munich. Algeranoff died in a road accident in Robinvale, Australia, 7 April 1967.

[Algeranoff, *My Years with Pavlova*, 1957; *The Times*, 19 April 1967; private information.]   JAMES MONAHAN

ALLEN, SIR CARLETON KEMP (1887–1966), legal scholar, was born 7 September 1887 in Carlton, Melbourne, the youngest of the three sons of the Revd William Allen, Nonconformist minister, whose own father, a civil engineer, had emigrated from England in the 1850s. Allen's mother, Martha Jane Holdsworth, of Yorkshire stock, was born in Australia at Maryborough, Victoria. The family moved to New South Wales in 1900 where Allen's father was for many years the minister of the flourishing Congregational church in the Sydney suburb of Petersham. The two elder sons were to spend their lives in the academic profession in Australia. 'C. K.'—he was always known by his initials—came to England. He had been educated at Newington College, Sydney, and in the University of Sydney where he obtained honours and prizes in classics and English. In 1909 he went up with a travelling scholarship to New College, Oxford, with a contemporary group of exceptionally able young lawyers, pupils of Francis de Zulueta [q.v.].

Allen gained a first in jurisprudence in 1912, his sound Australian training in classics standing him in good stead in his Roman law papers. In 1913 he was elected Eldon law scholar. His main outside interests were music and acting. In the Oxford University Dramatic Society production he was a memorable Julius Caesar to the Mark Antony of Philip Guedalla [q.v.] and in 1913 he produced and played a leading part in Thomas Dekker's *The Shoemaker's Holiday*. He long retained an interest in the OUDS through which he met his wife, and after the war he became its senior treasurer, producing and playing Jaques in *As You Like It* in 1912 which inaugurated the summer productions which became a feature of the Oxford Trinity term. He was also a member of the founding committee of the Oxford Playhouse with J. B. Fagan [q.v.]. Before the war he had resisted several offers to go on the stage professionally. At the time, he was intending to go to the bar and supported himself by freelance journalism. He also acted as secretary and assistant to Sir Paul Vinogradoff [q.v.] whose *Outlines of Historical Jurisprudence* (1920–2) he helped to see through the press. He was commissioned in January 1915 in the 13th battalion of the Middlesex Regiment and almost immediately was thrown into the battle of Loos in which the battalion had severe losses. He was badly wounded during the attack on the Hohenzollern redoubt. On sick leave he revisited Australia, as it turned out for the last time. He rejoined his battalion in February 1916 and in it was almost continuously engaged in battle. He was wounded again on the Somme in July 1916, before becoming captain and adjutant. In the March 1918 retreat he was awarded the Military Cross. These savage experiences left a deep imprint upon a stoical nature.

On demobilization Allen was appointed lecturer in law at University College, Oxford. He was called to the bar (Lincoln's Inn) in 1919 but elected not to practise, for in 1920 he was elected Stowell Civil Law fellow of the college where he became dean (1922–6). In 1924–5 he was junior proctor, with Austin Lane Poole of St. John's as his senior colleague. Allen also reviewed novels, and for fifteen years wrote under a pseudonym regular columns in the *Illustrated London News* and the *Sketch*. In 1925 he wrote a light comedy, *The Judgement of Paris*, which was accepted for a London production but was never staged, so he converted it to a novel which was published by the Bodley Head and sold reasonably well in Britain and the United States. He never wrote another.

In 1926 Allen went to India for six months to deliver the Tagore lectures in Calcutta. These formed the core of *Law in the Making*, published by the Clarendon Press (1927). Over the years in later editions this grew from 377 to 632 pages, embodying new and discarding older ideas. Throughout its changes the brief introduction remained a remarkable analysis of the various schools of thought in legal philosophy in this country and abroad. *Law in the Making*, indispensable to the law student, received the Swiney prize of the Royal Society of Arts in 1944. It had led in 1929 to Allen's election as professor of jurisprudence in succession to Walter Ashburner, in the chair which Vinogradoff had held. At the same time Allen was elected to a professorial fellowship at University College, with which he remained closely associated for the rest of his life, becoming an honorary fellow in 1963. Like Ashburner's, Allen's tenure of the chair was brief but, whereas his predecessor left for the more amiable climate of Italy, C. K. was to stay in Oxford until his death.

It was a great surprise when in 1931 he resigned the chair to accept the invitation of the Rhodes trustees to succeed Sir Francis Wylie, whose notice he was afterwards to write for this Dictionary, a characteristic piece, as Oxford secretary to the Rhodes trustees and thus the second warden of Rhodes House, Oxford. It was thought at the time that this would mean a great loss to legal science since he had been an admirable teacher, and the most lucid of lecturers, his exposition combining that lightness of touch and seriousness of thought notable in his published work. In fact administration did not take up too much of his time. As Oxford secretary he was not primarily concerned with the Rhodes Trust's activities overseas, although he made it his dutiful concern to be in touch with selection committees in the various constituencies from which the Rhodes scholars were drawn and he and his wife travelled widely in consequence. The administration of the Trust itself, however, was in the charge of two successive secretaries—Philip Kerr, Marquess of Lothian [q.v.] (1925–39), and Godfrey, Lord Elton (1939–59), whereas the investment portfolio was diversified by (Sir) Edward Peacock [q.v.], of Baring Bros.

Hospitality at Rhodes House was in the capable hands of Allen's wife, whom he had married in 1922: Dorothy Frances, youngest daughter of Edward Halford, retired Customs and Excise official, of Oxford. She was the dominant member of a very happy partnership as is manifest in her *Sunlight and Shadow* (1960), which she scribbled for her grandchildren just before her death in 1959 and which Allen subsequently edited for publication.

Allen's own experience of the difficulties of the young arrival at Oxford from overseas qualified him to an unusual degree to guide the Rhodes scholars with the keenest sympathy in their hopes and disappointments allied to a shrewdly dispassionate common sense. To the Rhodes scholars Allen extended an imaginative fair mindedness with a quite exceptional gift for staying outside his own firm prejudices.

The Allens saw three distinct phases of the brief history of Rhodes House: the spacious and well staffed hospitality of the pre-war epoch; the exhilarating improvisations (with C. K. himself sometimes at the piano) of wartime Oxford with the leave courses for which Dorothy Allen was awarded a British Empire Medal; then, the return of the ex-servicemen with their wives, while rationing still continued. To each period the Allens brought a note of quiet enjoyment and, particularly on Dorothy Allen's part, a gift of greeting the unexpected which was combined with a shared sense of continuity and subdued adventure.

Allen's own account of his twenty-one-year stewardship of Rhodes House may be found in his contribution to *The First Fifty Years of the Rhodes Scholarships* (1955), edited by Lord Elton. It was typical of C. K. that when he came to hand over Rhodes House to his successor in 1952 he should have secured for him those advantages of which he had felt himself deprived throughout his own tenure and that no man could have eased another's path with a quieter understanding.

Allen's strength as a legal scholar was noteworthy, as his successor in the chair of jurisprudence was to emphasize, in his insistent relation of theory and practice. Whatever he wrote was very readable. His *Law and Orders* (1945) was at the time an important contribution to administrative law. *Bureaucracy Triumphant* had appeared in 1931, and in the same year, *Legal Duties. Law and Disorders* and *Legal Indiscretions* both appeared in 1954, *Administrative Jurisdiction* in 1956, and *Aspects of Justice* in 1958. In 1953 he delivered his Hamlyn lectures which were published under the title *The Queen's Peace* (1953).

In World War II Allen undertook Civil Defence duties and was a member of the appellate tribunal for conscientious objectors. He was appointed a JP for Oxford late in 1941, took silk in 1945, and was chairman of the bench (1952–6) at a time when its reputation was high. His appearance and his learning lent him much authority. He was elected FBA in 1944 and was awarded an honorary LLD by Glasgow University. He received an Oxford DCL in 1932. He was knighted in 1952.

Allen was essentially a believer in the individual, with the deep distrust of the good lawyer—and the good Australian—for the increasing power of the State. If in later years he came to modify his extreme distaste for some of the aspects of delegated legislation to which he was uneasily reconciled, he maintained his eagle-eyed readiness to expose often in the correspondence columns of *The Times*, both the absurdities and the tendency to overbear to which he felt public servants were liable. *Democracy and the Individual* (1943) was a good example of the flavour of his view and manner. His club was the Reform.

Allen was of short, stocky build but impressive appearance. His strong eyes, striking nose, clipped moustache, and magnificent crop of lint-white hair (he greyed early) reminded one that he had been a soldier. That he was an Australian might be remarked by the way he wore his hat.

If he came to absorb some, more, maybe, than he was aware, of the prejudices of the English with whom he spent most of his life, he retained his quizzical right to poke his own sort of fun at them. An increasing deafness made him harder to convince but he continued to make his point with the same courteous clarity and the same deliberation with which he would tap away the ash from his ever-present cigarette as emphasis. He gave up smoking, however, at the age of seventy-five, but he continued to enjoy his bridge (at which he did not greatly like losing) and his wine (of which he was a good judge) and until his last illness he took not too much notice of the regimen which his physicians recommended. Austere in appearance, jaunty in carriage, he was a charming companion and a staunch colleague. A good judge of Oxford— and Surrey—cricket, the essence of integrity, Allen was a man of great determination. Beneath a tolerantly wry scepticism there was a solid core of stern, almost puritanical, devotion to truth and justice. He was busy to the end, still contributing to the *Law Quarterly Review* (1965).

The stoical way in which Allen set about coping with a new existence after Dorothy Allen's death, for they had been a most devoted pair, was impressive. They were survived by a daughter and a son. To the delight of their many friends C. K. remarried in 1962. His second wife, Hilda Mary (died 1969), daughter of Arthur Grose, had been Dorothy Allen's closest friend. The second marriage was also exceptionally contented and 114 Banbury Road, Oxford, warm in its welcome. Allen died in Oxford 11 December 1966. There is a portrait by (Sir) James Gunn (1953), which hangs in Rhodes House.

[A. L. Goodhart in *Proceedings of the British Academy*, vol. liii, 1967; private information; personal knowledge.]   E. T. WILLIAMS

ALLEN, (HERBERT) WARNER (1881–1968), journalist and author, was born at Godalming 8 March 1881, the elder son of Captain George Woronzow Allen, RN, and his wife, Ethel Harriet, daughter of the Revd

(Canon) John Manuel Echalaz, rector of Appleby in Derbyshire and fellow of Trinity College, Oxford. He was educated at Charterhouse, where he came under the influence of the classicist T. E. Page [q.v.]. He won a scholarship to University College, Oxford, and obtained a first class in classical honour moderations in 1902, and a third in *literae humaniores* in 1904. Having had some disinclination towards metaphysics, and a leaning towards a literary career, he had meanwhile taken up modern languages and won the Taylorian Spanish scholarship in 1903.

When writing his first book, an edition of the translation by James Mabbe [q.v.] of the Spanish *Celestina* (1908), he supported himself by journalism, and in 1908 was appointed to the position of Paris correspondent of the *Morning Post*. He thus became immersed in French life at the end of the *belle époque*, and reported the sensational trial of Mme Caillaux.

Shortly after the outbreak of war in 1914 he was made an official representative of the British press at the French front. In 1917 he accompanied the British divisions diverted to support the Italians, and remained in Italy until the following year, when he was transferred to the American Expeditionary Force in France, and accompanied it in its occupation of Germany, where he stayed until March 1919. Out of these experiences he published *The Unbroken Line* (1916) and, with the paintings of Captain Martin Hardie [q.v.], *Our Italian Front* (1920). He was made CBE (1920) and chevalier of the Legion of Honour for his war services.

As an extramural obligation to his proprietor he participated in the cross-Channel flight of the *Morning Post* dirigible, which ended in disaster; but he fortunately escaped almost unscathed. He was foreign editor of the *Morning Post* (1925–8), and London editor of the *Yorkshire Post* (1928–30), while at the same time he made many contributions to the *Saturday Review*. He then retired to Sotwell, in Berkshire (now Oxon.), to concentrate on writing books. A succession of his books appeared, only to be interrupted by the outbreak of war in 1939. Although fifty-eight years old, he was then gazetted acting wing commander, RAFVR, and he served as assistant deputy director in the foreign division of the Ministry of Information from 1940–1.

As a writer he was best known for his books on wine, beginning with, *The Wines of France* (1924) and continuing with, notably, *The Romance of Wine* (1931), *Sherry* (1933), *A Contemplation of Wine* and *Natural Red Wines* (1951), *White Wines and Cognac* and *Sherry and Port* (1952), and ending with his *A History of Wine: Great Vintage Wines from the Homeric*

Age to the Present Day (1961), in all of which vinous information was nicely interwoven with literary and historical allusions. He travelled widely among the European vineyards; his accurate judgement of wine was recognized by all amateurs qualified to assess this, while, at the same time, he was greatly respected by the leaders of the wine trade. But perhaps his name came most to the attention of the general public through his collaboration with his friend E. C. Bentley [q.v.] in the latter's famous sequel to *Trent's Last Case—Trent's Own Case* (1936). To this Dictionary he contributed the notice of H. A. Gwynne.

He himself, however, set greatest value on a series of mystical writings such as *The Uncounted Hour* (1936), *The Timeless Moment* (1946), and *The Uncurtained Throne* (1951). As a youth Allen had abandoned formal Anglicanism, but T. E. Page had imbued him with the spirit of Plato, and later reading of Plotinus and acquaintance with, among others, T. S. Eliot and Dean W. R. Inge [qq.v.] evoked in him a perception of transcendental values and a faith in the immortality of the soul—attuned to an ethic that was certainly Christian. This gave him great personal serenity and an outward gentleness of address which made him deeply loved, particularly by the young.

Warner, as everyone called him, was a man of rather above average height, with kindly features and, as the French politely put it, a *léger embonpoint* of the true gourmet. He was a keen Savage in the heyday of the Savage Club, and was naturally elected to the Saintsbury Club, founded in oenophilist memory of Professor George Saintsbury [q.v.] with its limited membership and precious cellar. At home and at his club he went to great pains to select food and wines that would gratify his guests, who were usually considerable connoisseurs. Although he lived long as a countryman and had a fine garden, he was not addicted to field sports. But with his vast reading, undimmed memory, and facility with words, he had a quick draw and a flawless aim for the clues of *The Times* crossword puzzles.

In 1908 he married Ethel, daughter of Warwick Pemberton. They had one son. He died at Sotwell 12 January 1968, and was mourned by a large circle of friends, and a school of young disciples who were perhaps more attracted by his philosophy of the table than by his spiritual intimations.

[An unpublished autobiography; private information; personal knowledge.]

H. W. YOXALL

ALLINGHAM, MARGERY LOUISE (1904–1966), crime novelist, was born in Ealing 20 May 1904, the eldest child of Herbert John Allingham, editor of the *London Journal* and the *Christian Globe* and prolific writer of serial fiction, by his wife, Emily Jane Hughes. John Till Allingham [q.v.] was among her forebears. She was born to be a writer and wrote all her life. 'My father wrote,' she said, 'my mother wrote, all the weekend visitors wrote and, as soon as I could master the appallingly difficult business of making the initial marks, so did I.'

She was educated at a private school in Colchester and at the Perse High School, Cambridge, where she wrote and acted in her own play, but left at fifteen determined to earn by her pen. She wrote a great deal of fiction for magazines such as *Sexton Blake* and *Girls' Cinema* and in 1923 *Blackkerchief Dick*, a swashbuckling romance. Before long she turned to crime as her theme with a serial for the *Daily Express* in 1926 and *The Crime at Black Dudley* (1929), into which stepped her running-hero Albert Campion. It was followed by *Mystery Mile* (1930), her first considerable success, into which she introduced Campion's manservant, Lugg, the truculent ex-burglar. In the next ten years she wrote many stories for periodicals like the *Strand* and another ten mysteries, among them *Sweet Danger* (1933) and *The Fashion in Shrouds* (1938).

In 1940 she was asked by her American publisher for a factual book on wartime England: *The Oaken Heart* appeared in 1941. During the war years, which were heavily occupied with ARP and first-aid duties, she produced a 'mainstream' novel, *Dance of the Years* (1943), but it had to be finished too hastily and is only a shadow. With peace, however, a new writer emerged, more conscious of evil and the great issues, although she had as early as *Flowers for the Judge* (1936) produced a murder story which kept the dull bits a whodunit writer normally omits, infusing them with a novelist's life-giving art. The change is interestingly reflected in her treatment of Albert Campion. Originally a caricature in the mode of the Scarlet Pimpernel of Baroness Orczy [q.v.], he was soon found a considerable hindrance as such and was skilfully turned into little more than a pair of eyes. With the wartime break his creator seized the opportunity to make him yet more mature. In *More Work for the Undertaker* (1949) she introduced in addition the 'pile-driver personality' of Charles Luke of the CID.

The post-war books contain her best work, among it *The Beckoning Lady* (1955), her own favourite. Freed of urgent commercial pressures, she was able to write a first draft, dictate a second, rewrite that, and finally dictate all again at speed to restore colloquial raciness. The qualities which had developed over a writing lifetime came to ripeness. There was first a remarkable energy of expression and thought. She had the gift of seeing with a passion which plucked from their everyday context into a startling and rich light things and ideas, people and places, particularly here both the salt-marshes of Essex, where she had grown up, and where from 1934 she lived in the attractive agglomerated D'Arcy House at Tolleshunt D'Arcy, and a romantic yet real London of fog 'like a saffron blanket soaked in ice-water'.

The energy expressed itself as a splendid certainty in everything she wrote. Pen in hand, she was afraid of no one. She could cheerfully label a county family as 'frightful females who smell like puppies' breath' and she could at the end create a figure of true evil like the criminal Jack Havoc of *The Tiger in the Smoke* (1952). Thus armed, she could write without strain of love and of death. She could if necessary compose a poem for one of her characters and a string of genuine *bons mots* for another. With it she brought distinction to the detective story and it enabled her to celebrate an unlikely but entirely harmonious shotgun marriage between truth and romance. Increasingly it permitted her to give rein to a strong intuitive intelligence and say much both penetrating and wise about men and especially women. This in turn gave her pictures of her day a universality which, often forty years after writing, made them still eagerly read in reissued editions in the libraries and as ubiquitous paperbacks.

Margaret Allingham married in 1927 Philip Youngman Carter (died 1969), artist, whom she described as 'a lank youth', a physique the very opposite of her own 'figure designed for great endurance at a desk'. He was the son of the late William Robert Carter, headmaster of Watford Grammar School (1884–1914). He provided dust-jacket illustrations for many of her books, completed her last, *Cargo of Eagles* (1968), and wrote a short memoir which well conveys her 'infectious exhilarating charm'. She died at Colchester 30 June 1966.

[P. Youngman Carter, memoir in the collection *Mr. Campton's Clowns*, 1967; private information.]   H. R. F. KEATING

ALTHAM, HARRY SURTEES (1888–1965), schoolmaster, cricket historian and administrator, was born at Camberley 30 November 1888, the younger son of (Sir) Edward Altham Altham and his wife, Georgina Emily, daughter of W. Macpherson Nicol, of Inverness. His father was the first university candidate for the army, in 1876, and retired with the rank of lieutenant-general, having served as quartermaster-general in India (1917–19). Altham

was educated at Repton, where he showed himself a gifted cricketer and natural leader, and he remained devoted to the school for the rest of his life. In the opinion of a number of good judges, the side which he captained in 1908 challenges that of 1905 as the best school cricket eleven there has ever been. He made his début in first-class cricket, for Surrey against Leicestershire, at the Oval in August 1908, and played also for Hampshire after the war. Going up to Trinity College, Oxford, where he obtained a second class in *literae humaniores* in 1912, he gained his blue in 1911 and 1912. In May 1913 he became an assistant master at Winchester, and apart from war service with the 5th King's Royal Rifle Corps, during which he was appointed to the DSO, awarded the MC, and three times mentioned in dispatches, he lived in Winchester for the rest of his life.

In his chosen profession as schoolmaster Altham found supreme happiness and complete fulfilment. He felt an instinctive sympathy for the young, for over fifty years infecting young Wykehamists with his own vitality and optimism, and with his simple belief that life was there to be lived with zest, humanity, courage, and conviction. He had, too, the priceless gift of all great teachers of being able to communicate to others his delight in the things he valued—a play by Shakespeare, maybe, or a poem by Browning or Housman, or a trifid spoon, an illuminated capital, a well-executed on-drive, or a well-loved feature in the cathedral at Winchester, which he served as editor of its *Record* from 1948 onwards. When Altham was 'on form' and involved his eyes would light up and his hands move, as he caught the humour or the happiness of the moment with an allusive comment, a warm reflection, or a lively quip.

He was, perhaps, most at home, apart from home itself, in the classroom, on the cricket field—cricket was only *primus inter pares* of several games that he enjoyed and excelled at—and in Chernocke House, or Furley's, as it is known colloquially, of which, wonderfully supported by his wife, he was housemaster between 1927 and 1947. This was for him an extremely happy period, when a whole set of shared assumptions had yet to be questioned and when those under him could react instinctively to his concern both for them and for the values he hoped they would accept.

Altham's influence on cricket was profound. On returning to Winchester after the war in 1919 he quickly showed that that influence would not be parochial, for he found time, while teaching in term and playing for Hampshire in the summer holidays, to write a *History of Cricket* (1926) 'remarkable for its scope, perception and mature style'. Subsequent editions were published in collaboration with E. W. Swanton. Altham's other writings included editorship, anonymously, of *The M.C.C. Cricket Coaching Book* (1952), joint-authorship of *Hampshire County Cricket* (1957), and contributions to *Wisden*, the *Cricketer* (in which his *History of Cricket* first appeared in serial form in 1922), the *Observer*, *The World of Cricket* (1966), County Cricket Club handbooks, and various publications in England and abroad.

In addition Altham made a notable contribution to the cricketing scene as an administrator, an after-dinner speaker of real distinction, and an unrepentant advocate of what cricket could do for the young in terms of character and enjoyment. He served the MCC as president in 1959-60, as treasurer from 1950 until 1963, and as a member of the committee for close on a quarter of a century; he was chairman of the MCC cricket inquiry committee in 1949; and although not himself a test player, he was chairman of the test selection committee in 1954. He helped to found the MCC Youth Cricket Association and became its first chairman (1952-65), being the 'head and right arm' of the coaching courses at Lilleshall, where he was in his element as coach, conversationalist, and companion. He was the first president of the English Schools Cricket Association (1951-7); and what, perhaps, in his later days meant as much to him as anything, he was president of the Hampshire County Cricket Club from 1947 until his death. Few men can have given back to a game so much of what they have taken from it.

In 1917 Altham married Alison, daughter of Somerville Reid Livingstone-Learmonth, sheepfarmer in Australia; they had one son and two daughters. Altham died suddenly in Sheffield 11 March 1965, some two hours after addressing the Sheffield Cricket Lovers Society. He was appointed CBE in 1957. There is a tablet to his memory in the Memorial Gallery at Lord's; and a portrait by Peggy Bell (1959) in the Committee Room.

[*The Heart of Cricket, a Memoir of H. S. Altham*, ed. Hubert Doggart, 1967; personal knowledge.]   G. H. G. DOGGART

ANDERSON, STANLEY ARTHUR CHARLES (1884-1966), engraver, etcher, and water-colour painter, was born in Bristol 11 May 1884, the son of Alfred Ernest Anderson, of Heavitree, Devon, who started his own business as a skilled general and heraldic engraver, and his wife, Emma Bessie Mitchell. Stanley Anderson had a twin sister and another sister. He was educated at the Merchant Venturers' Technical College, Bristol, where he became a great reader, developed a love for music, and determined to become a professional artist. His mother had less precarious ambitions for him and persuaded him against his will at the age of fifteen to be apprenticed to his father. During this apprenticeship he learned to engrave on metal with exacting precision on, for example, salvers, tankards, and cutlery. While earning only six shillings a week (then the normal rate), he paid for an evening's weekly tuition at the Bristol School of Art. In 1909 he won the British Institution open etching scholarship of £50 a year, with the etched portrait stipulated.

Receiving neither encouragement nor money from his parents, Anderson arrived in London on 10 January 1909 to study at the Royal College of Art, under the expert technical instruction of (Sir) Francis (Frank) Short [q.v.] in the wider freedoms of etching and drypoint, with general drawing. To these Anderson applied himself diligently, while also attending classes at the Goldsmiths' College, New Cross. But he had a dislike for schools and averred that he did his most rewarding study in the print rooms of the British and the Victoria and Albert museums where a bona fide student might closely examine original prints, drawings, and, in a few cases, surviving plates. There he formed an abiding love for Dürer (whose line-engraving, 'St. Jerome, in his study with lion', was ever to influence his pictorial attitude and technique), and for Rembrandt, Goya, and the later masters J. F. Millet and C. Meryon. Anderson exhibited two works in the Royal Academy in 1909, the first of the 214 he was eventually to show there. Sir Frank Short, always on the look-out for 'likely men' for the Royal Society of Painter-Etchers (and Engravers), of which he was president, welcomed Anderson as associate in 1910, and as fellow in 1923.

Although he was encouraged by artists and was able to get a deal of small hackwork to eke out his resources, Anderson's life was hard; but the habit of work, dedication to his calling, and tenacity of purpose helped him to surmount difficulties of finance and health and to maintain himself until the outbreak of war in 1914. While returning on the eve of hostilities from a topographical visit to France, where he had made many studies, he lost both them and all his belongings in the panic at the port.

In 1910 Anderson had married Lilian Phelps (died 1967), daughter of a master-builder in Essex. A woman of fine character who had been a nurse at St. Thomas's Hospital, she was calm, practical, and entirely selfless in all her relationships. Throughout their married life she provided a confidence in her husband's talents and a well-ordered home. After the war she returned at times to private nursing in order to augment their income while bringing up their two sons, the younger of whom, Maxim, was to earn a considerable reputation as a director of documentary films before his early death in 1959. Anderson engraved a dignified portrait of Lilian, his wife, in nursing uniform, 'The Sister', 1931.

During the war of 1914-18 the Andersons moved to Eltham, near Woolwich where Anderson was engaged on munitions work, having been rejected as unfit for active service by several army medical boards because he had severely strained his heart in youth. In Chelsea again after the war, Anderson resumed his uphill struggle, aided by small graphic jobs from publishers. He became one of a formidable quarter of etchers and drypointists who were to achieve fame, the others being (Sir) Henry Rushbury [q.v.], Gerald Brockhurst, and Malcolm Osborne, all young men of common purpose and enthusiasm. They were inspired by (Sir) Muirhead Bone, Francis Dodd, and William Strang [qq.v.], who were to the fore in the renascence of British etching. Anderson admired Strang's wide range of subject and media, composed with well-realized emphasis on the human content (in the Millet–Legros tradition), which he found helpful and affinitive.

Since there was a growing market for contemporary topographical prints, these artists often visited France and Spain, with this in mind and by natural inclination. By the age of thirty-five Anderson had already set his course, with self-imposed disciplines through which to exploit his talents. He had always felt and now saw life as a whole: not for him was the stylized object *mise en page* as an isolated image, or the 'brilliant first state'—with everything to lose by its gains', but, rather, a composition of contiguous relationships between man and his surroundings, with objects made and used by man, such as tools, implements for agriculture, buildings, and places of worship. Consequently Anderson's predominantly architectural motifs—townscape, market, harbour, or even landscape—are animated by people in appropriate groups or activities. And, conversely, predominantly figure-subjects include their authentic setting. From earlier days he had acutely observed people's actions, attitudes, and peculiarities, and had recorded these in sketch-books. He had great sympathy with the underdog, from the going-down to the down-and-out, the aged, or the blind. But, although many of his subjects show his social sympathies, a certain wry, humorous irony creeps in. Even more ironic, almost in caricature, are his oil paintings, few in number, which depict 'types'—those who, for example, frequented the Farringdon Road bookstalls.

At first Anderson worked more often in boldly designed drypoint, using its full richness of 'burr'—through luminous half-tones to silvery greys. Notable examples are 'Tortoni's, Le Havre', 'The Goose Fair, Albi', 'Dürer's House, Nürnberg', and 'St. Nicholas, Prague', which Campbell Dodgson [q.v.] pronounced to be 'the finest drypoint executed in this century'. But Anderson became convinced when he pushed the burin with his early acquired mastery, that only in line-engraving, with its incised clarity, could he truly express his well-premeditated designs. That this formal method might deaden movement or atmosphere is immediately belied by such examples as 'The Fallen Star' (1929), and 'Morning on the Seine' (both of *clochards* by the river bank), though it suits the quiet inaction of timeless mental activity as in 'The Reading Room', which was awarded the medal 'for the best print in the exhibition' at the Chicago Society of Etchers International Exhibition in 1931. All Anderson's subsequent line-engravings maintained his consistently high standards and intensity of understanding.

In 1925 Anderson succeeded Malcolm Osborne as visiting instructor in the etching department of Goldsmiths' College School of Art, then directed by the well-known Clive Gardiner. There he found a small band of students who were already seriously attracted to etching, among whom were Graham Sutherland, Edward Bouverie-Hoyton, Robin Tanner, and Paul Drury. To quote one of their number, 'As a teacher Anderson was always anxious to help in any way, but never sought to divert us from our own predilections. He was diffident in general criticism, but demonstrably exact about technical matters. His highest words of praise (behind anyone's back) were "sterling, probity, and guts". They were his own qualities, and his students held him in high esteem and affection.' He was warmly regarded for his sympathetic and tirelessly helpful teaching, patience, and goodwill. Until 1940 he continued on the visiting staff of Goldsmiths', where he also taught wood-engraving, a medium which he admired.

In 1940 Anderson moved to Towersey, near Thame, an agricultural region useful for his water-colour drawings, to which he turned even more after being afflicted by worsening arthritis which was soon to put an end to his engraving. The luminous evocative landscapes, eagerly sought by collectors, were to be his mainstay while he added to a series of plates of country seasonal activities with a set depicting still-practising rural craftsmen. Anderson was never so happy and relaxed than when making exhaustive studies of these craftsmen pursuing their callings—for example, those of chairmaker, smith, and wheelwright—surrounded by their tools and handwork in its typical stages. These plates, which provide lasting records of English rural life and its crafts before their disappearance, may well be considered among his most important.

In 1938 he was the sole representative of British line-engraving and drypoint at the Venice Biennial International Art Exhibition. He was a member of the engraving faculty of the British School at Rome from 1930 to 1952. In 1934 he was made ARA and in 1941 RA. He was appointed CBE in 1951.

Anderson's work was widely exhibited and is represented in numerous public and private collections in Britain, the USA, and Europe. There are works in the British, Victoria and Albert, Fitzwilliam, and Ashmolean museums. It is in the Ashmolean Museum's Department of Prints and Drawings that the most comprehensive collection of Anderson's print-making is to be found; it is the most instructive collection because of its many 'states', working proofs, artist's notes, and studies which are available, together with a complete explanatory catalogue compiled in the department by Ian Lowe with the co-operation of the artist. Also available are many prints of English etchers of the period referred to in this notice.

Anderson's elder son, Ivan Phelps, often read to his father from English translations of the Russian novelists during meals, acted as disc-jockey with classical music while he worked at bench or press, and posed as model in well-worn clothes for numerous studies. Anderson was shy, reticent, and vulnerable, but in the company of fellow artists and craftsmen he could be relaxed and expansive. Affectionate and generous in disposition, he could be a stern critic of the meretricious or slovenly of mind or manners—although his self-criticism was harsher. He was of middle height, quietly eager, and brisk in mind and movement. Anderson died in Chersley, near Thame, 4 March 1966.

There are three self-portraits by Anderson: the first in 1913 was an experiment in sand-ground process of which only six prints were taken; the second, in the line-etching boldly bitten and directly executed by artificial light which emphasizes his intent eye and craggy determination, is reproduced in E. L. Allhusen's 'Self-portraiture in Etching, some living artists', *Print Collectors Quarterly*, July 1931; the third, of 1933/4, is in line-engraving and shows Anderson holding a graver and looking up from his work—a true likeness in a sculptural sense.

[James Laver, *The Work of Stanley Anderson* (printed lecture given at the opening of the Stanley Anderson exhibition at Cheltenham Art Gallery, 1949); Martin Hardie,

'Etchings and Engravings of Stanley Anderson', *Print Collectors Quarterly*, vol. iii, 1933; private information; personal knowledge.]
         PAUL DRURY

ANGELL, SIR (RALPH) NORMAN (1872–1967), publicist, was born in the Mansion House, Holbeach, 26 December 1872, the seventh and youngest child of Thomas Angell Lane, draper and grocer, by his wife, Mary Ann Brittain. He went to a local preparatory school and then to the *lycée* in St. Omer. He read J. S. Mill [q.v.], *On Liberty*, in its sick-bay at the age of twelve and, as precocious practically as intellectually, edited a bi-weekly English paper at fifteen whilst attending classes at Geneva University. Teenage rebellion took the form of wanting, at seventeen, to be a manual labourer in America rather than a Cambridge undergraduate. An understanding father gave him £50 to make this possible. Angell spent the following seven years in America, mainly in a variety of ranching jobs in the south-west, but ending up as a newspaper man, principally in San Francisco. He returned to Europe in 1898, settling in Paris, writing for one French and a group of American papers, and editing an English-medium paper, the *Daily Messenger*. This brought him to the attention of the future Lord Northcliffe [q.v.] and thereby to the editorship of the *Continental Daily Mail* in 1904.

Angell's first book, *Patriotism Under Three Flags*, was published in 1903 under his original name of Lane, but this he thereafter dropped. Its sub-title, *A plea for rationalism in politics*, proved to be his 'life-job description'; he was fascinated by the extent to which 'illusions' made groups act contrary to their own best interests. In 1909 he published the book, *Europe's Optical Illusion*, with which his name will always be primarily associated. It was republished, enlarged, in 1910 as *The Great Illusion*, translated into many languages, and—appearing in many and revised editions—sold over a million copies; it was republished as a Penguin Special as late as 1938. The book narrowly missed, however, being a complete flop. Rejected by every publisher approached, Angell published it himself, but publication passed unnoticed. Rather than remainder casually, he sent copies to a number of public men in Britain, France, and Germany. The book began to be discussed and then had its first full notice, in the *Nation* (18 December 1909), written by H. N. Brailsford [q.v.]. Lord Esher [q.v.] became interested in it and in 1912 helped to create the Garton Foundation to propagate Angell's doctrines.

The Great Illusion was one of the most influential books of the first half of the twentieth century; it is very much a period piece. Angell's gospel was essentially addressed to the Germany of William II; its basic doctrine was that, in contemporary Europe, successful armed aggression by one economically advanced state against another would not benefit the aggressor economically. In 1909 this was a new and startling idea. Pacifists read the book, said that the author had proved that wat did not pay, and added this somewhat misleading summation of it to their own doctrinal corpus. (Angell held that 'war might pay very handsome dividends in terms of defence'.) Militarists, who for the most part did not read the book, tied to the author the tag of having said that war was impossible. (He subsequently wasted much time and energy in a vain attempt to rebut this complete misrepresentation.) Marxists tended, wrongly, to see him as a convert to the idea that the causes of war were primarily economic. In truth Angell was far from being a Marxist or a pacifist. His belief in democracy was profound; his challenge to Communism continuous; his main interest in defence rather than peace. What he had done was to provide middle ground between pacifists, who thought war an absolute evil, and militarists who thought it at best beneficial and at worst inescapable.

The Great Illusion was the first practical discussion of the possibility of preventing war, but it suffered from the defects of its qualities. Because it was pamphleteering in size and spirit, it attracted attention and provoked controversy; because it was not a deeply considered treatise the controversy was confused. The real tragedy, however, was that only two years were given for the effective discussion of its ideas.

Angell gave up his editorship in 1912 and for the rest of his career defended, developed, and propagated his doctrines whilst keeping up a running commentary on international affairs. He lectured and wrote prodigiously. His style, whether with his pen or on the platform, was lucid and trenchant, his content invariably informed by a passionate rationality. He worked almost as much in the United States, where he spent some twenty-five years in all, as in England. Some of his most important journalism appeared, especially in 1916, in the New Republic.

Angell was one of the pioneers of the idea of a League of Nations. In America he was one of the inspirers of the League of Free Nations Association out of which grew both the Foreign Policy Association and ex-President Taft's League to Enforce Peace. From the creation of the League of Nations onwards Angell's main doctrinal emphasis was on the putting of force in international affairs behind the law rather than the litigants. By this emphasis he hoped, but failed, to merge the ranks of 'internationalists' and pacifists.

Next to his interest in international affairs came his interest in the problems of securing a free and fair press in a democracy and in the simplified exposition of economics, especially banking and currency problems. He took a lot of trouble in inventing the Money Game, a card game designed to give instruction in those subjects, but it did not really catch on.

He made three unsuccessful attempts to enter Parliament, and from 1929 to 1931 was Labour member for North Bradford. He was, however, unhappy with parliamentary life and party politics and came to regret his involvement in both activities. In 1931 he was knighted and in 1933 was awarded the Nobel peace prize.

Angell had a short and spare figure with sharp-cut features, conspicuous brow, and a pale complexion. The Barber Institute of Fine Arts at Birmingham University has a portrait of him by Edmund Kapp. He was frail-looking but, to judge by his favourite recreation, small-boat sailing, his output, and his longevity, must have been exceedingly tough. In Britain he published, on the lowest computation, twenty-seven books; others were published only in the United States. He was a considerate and modest man, for all his public appearances a natural solitary. A brief marriage was ended by separation. He died at Croydon 7 October 1967.

[Sir Norman Angell, *After All*, 1951; *The Times*, 9 October 1967; Mary Agnes Hamilton, *Remembering My Good Friends*, 1944; L. R. Bisceglia, *Norman Angell and the 'pacifist' muddle*, in *Bulletin* of Institute of Historical Research, May 1962; private information; personal knowledge.]

FRANK HARDIE

APPLETON, SIR EDWARD VICTOR (1892–1965), physicist, was born in Bradford, Yorkshire, 6 September 1892, the eldest child of Peter Appleton, of Eccleshall, Bradford, a warehouseman on the staff of Charles Senior & Co., and his wife, Mary Wilcock. In 1903 he won a scholarship to Hanson School, Bradford, where, it is said, 'he was brilliant in every way . . . He not only learnt with ease and rapidity everything that his teachers put before him, but he also seemed to have anticipated the next lesson. This was due to his remarkable talent, very rare in schoolboys, for grasping the significance of a school subject as a whole.' He obtained a first class in the London matriculation examination at the minimum allowable age of sixteen, and he passed the London intermediate examination the next year, again at the minimum age.

Realizing the unusual ability of the young

Vic (as his family always called him) his parents nobly helped him in every way to continue at school as long as possible. In 1910 he was awarded the Isaac Holton scholarship tenable at Cambridge and in 1911 he was also awarded an exhibition at St. John's College, Cambridge, where he started to read for the natural sciences tripos. He once wrote: 'Music in the home, and sport outside—notably cricket—were my main interests beyond school until I reached the age of sixteen. At that age I suddenly became interested in physics and mathematics . . . I think it must have been largely the influence of my school physics master, J. A. Verity . . . which made me specially fascinated with physics. By then, the fame of the Cavendish laboratory as a centre for modern physical research, under Sir J. J. Thomson, was even reaching the schools and I recall that, in my schoolboy mind, I was firmly determined to go to Cambridge.'

He gained first classes in part i of the tripos in 1913 when he received the Wiltshire prize, and in part ii (physics) in 1914, when he also received the Hutchinson research studentship in mineralogy and the Hicken prize in physics. He immediately began research with (Sir) W. L. Bragg [q.v.] and helped in the unravelling of the structure of one or two metallic crystals. Soon, however, war broke out in 1914 and he joined the army (the 6th West Yorkshire battalion) as a signals officer. He then trained with the Royal Engineers where his duties introduced him to the thermionic valve (then a new device which was little understood) and to problems of radio-wave propagation.

In 1919 he returned to Cambridge as a fellow of St. John's College and, in 1920, he became an assistant demonstrator in physics at the Cavendish Laboratory. At first, together with Balth van der Pol, he investigated the behaviour of thermionic valves. But in 1924 he was joined by Miles Barnett, a young research student from New Zealand, and together they started the series of investigations for which Appleton is best known. They began by studying the fading of the radio waves received at Cambridge from the recently installed broadcasting station in London, and in December 1924 they performed a crucial experiment, which demonstrated, for the first time, that radio waves were reflected when they fell steeply on the ionized part of the upper atmosphere (later called the ionosphere). This experiment initiated Appleton's long series of researches that led, in 1947, to his being awarded the Nobel prize.

Appleton had already been appointed, in October 1924, to the Wheatstone chair of physics at King's College, London, and from there he set up an experimental field station at a suitable site near Peterborough where Barnett and others conducted researches under his direction. In 1932 much of the work was moved to a more convenient site in Hampstead. In a house that had been given to King's College by Sir Halley Stewart [q.v.] there were laboratories on the ground floor, and a residence for Appleton and his family on the upper floors; since many of the experiments had to be made during the night this arrangement proved particularly convenient.

In 1936 Appleton returned to Cambridge to the Jacksonian chair of natural philosophy; this was attached to the Cavendish Laboratory under Lord Rutherford [q.v.], who, however, soon died suddenly and unexpectedly. Appleton then found himself acting, for a short time, as head of the laboratory, but later, in 1939, when Bragg was appointed as the new director, Appleton took the crucial step of leaving active scientific work to become secretary of the Department of Scientific and Industrial Research. Almost his first task was to turn the attention of the Department from peacetime to wartime activities. He firmly believed that some of the work, for example on fuel, roads, buildings, engineering, and the like, would continue to be necessary, and he emphasized that it was not in the national interest to drain off all the best of the Department's staff to Service laboratories. Some of his teams were turned to work, for example, on the protection of stored foodstuffs from insect attack, on the design of Civil Defence protection of buildings, and on studies with models for bombing attacks on enemy objectives. He was closely concerned with the development of radar and with the secret work on the atomic bomb.

When the war was over, Appleton returned, in 1949, to academic work as principal and vice-chancellor of the university of Edinburgh. There he proved to be 'an inspiring guide and an imaginative leader. His enthusiasm, particularly for the doings of the young, seemed to increase as his years advanced and he was both a source of ideas in himself and a ready recipient of ideas and new projects which emanated from others. But it is particularly as a wise chairman of capacious and incredibly retentive memory, of great patience, and of real shrewdness that all those who served on the University Court will best remember him . . . . Throughout his busy life, without in any degree losing that human touch and capacity for enjoyment which so endeared him to all his friends, he maintained a feeling for the importance and dignity of the university rather than of himself, and never for one moment lost sight of the fact that he held a position of the most sacred trust.' However, at Edinburgh he faced much criticism of his handling of the university building programme, and he failed to mollify the opposition.

In the crucial experiment of 1924 Appleton and Barnett established clearly the existence of ionized regions of the upper atmosphere (the ionosphere), capable of reflecting radio waves. As early as 1902 it had been suggested, by Oliver Heaviside [q.v.] and others, that these regions probably existed, but it was not until 1924 that their existence was clearly established. Thereafter Appleton devoted all his scientific activities to understanding the ionosphere. He used radio waves to probe and investigate it; he showed that it consisted predominantly of two layers, a lower 'Heaviside' layer and an upper one, later called the 'Appleton' layer; he showed how these layers varied with the time of the day, the year, and the sunspot cycle; and he developed theories to explain their behaviour.

Up to 1939 Appleton was pre-eminently the leader in ionospheric research: in practically every point of importance his was the leading paper and it is fair to say that what was known about the ionosphere up to that time was almost entirely due to him, or to the research schools which he started and inspired. Since the war of 1939-45, able and enthusiastic schools of ionosphere research have grown up in several different parts of the world quite independent of Appleton and they have added very considerably to what was known of the ionosphere in 1939, but although some of Appleton's ideas have been revised, most of them still remain sound.

In 1950 Appleton started the *Journal of Atmospheric and Terrestrial Physics* and he remained its editor-in-chief for the rest of his life. He took a very personal interest in this journal, which he used to encourage publication by workers in remoter parts of the world; it became known everywhere as 'Appleton's Journal'.

Realizing that the observed behaviour of the ionosphere would depend on the position of the observer, Appleton played an important part in encouraging its study on a world-wide basis. He used the International Union of Scientific Radio (known as URSI after the initial letters of its name in French) for this purpose, and he was its president for eighteen years, from 1934 to 1952. It was at the 1927 meeting in Washington that he first announced his 'magneto-ionic theory' describing the travel of radio waves through the ionosphere.

Those who remember Appleton recall in common several outstanding characteristics: his wide humanity, his ability as a public speaker, and his continuing dedication to his scientific researches. His humanity showed itself in all he did. He was invariably considerate to everyone and especially to those in humble positions. He never failed to pass the time of day with the servitors and the cleaners and to discuss with them the latest football match or anything he thought would interest them.

He was a skilled public speaker with a happy knack of combining penetrating observations with amusing anecdotes. His ability in this respect was never so well demonstrated as at international conferences where he seemed able to convey the point of his very English stories to a wide variety of people from other countries. Perhaps his custom of repeating the essential point, slowly and with a pause just at the right place, helped him here. But it was his beautifully modulated voice which finally added charm to what would otherwise have been merely clever and competent speeches. His father was an accomplished singer and, for thirty-eight years, had been choirmaster at a Wesleyan chapel in Bradford. The young Appleton inherited the tenor voice and sang in his father's choir for some time—surely a good training for any gifted speaker. With his easy manner of delivery he often gave the impression that his speeches were made without effort, but those who knew him best realized what great care he lavished on them. His notebooks contained numerous phrases which might be turned to use on some suitable occasion, and the typescripts of his speeches frequently had the most telling words inserted at the last minute in manuscript. His gifts as a speaker were equally evident in his lectures to students. In these he was never afraid of showing how simple a matter was and, like all the best lecturers, he never tried to blind the audience with the extent of his knowledge. It was only those who knew the subject well who appreciated how penetrating his account in simple terms could really be.

Appleton never lost his deep interest in the ionosphere. Until the end of his life the little notebooks that he carried around with him contained ideas and suggestions about it, interspersed with suggestions and stories for his speeches. Until the day of his death he was discussing the details of his researches through regular correspondence with other investigators. When an ionosphere worker visited him in his office some new results would probably be produced from a drawer and, forgetting the worries of the principal of a great university, Appleton would discuss and argue again, just as he had once done with members of his research teams.

Appleton became a fellow of the Royal Society in 1927 and, for his work on the ionosphere, he received the Nobel prize in 1947. He was appointed KCB in 1941 and GBE in

1946, and received decorations from France, the United States, Norway, and Iceland. He held honorary degrees from ten British and six foreign universities, and was honorary member or honorary fellow of several British and foreign scientific and engineering societies; he received medals from seven British and five foreign institutions. He published widely in the major scientific journals, and wrote *Thermionic Vacuum Tubes, and their Applications* (1932). In 1956 he gave the Reith lectures on the subject 'Science and the Nation'.

In 1915 Appleton married Jessie, daughter of the Revd John Longson, sometime of Huddersfield, later of Canada; they had two daughters. His wife died in 1964 and in 1965 he married Mrs Helen F. Allison, daughter of John Gordon Lennie. She was his secretary for thirteen years, and had helped him to keep a little time for his own researches during the pressure of his other work. He died suddenly at home 21 April 1965, just one month after his second marriage. There is a portrait by Bernard Hailstone in the Imperial War Museum and another, by Sir William O. Hutchison (1959), in the Court Room of Edinburgh University.

[J. A. Ratcliffe in *Biographical Memoirs of Fellows of the Royal Society*, vol. xii, 1966; private information; personal knowledge.]   J. A. RATCLIFFE

ARBERRY, ARTHUR JOHN (1905-1969), orientalist, was born at Buckland, Portsmouth, 12 May 1905, fourth of the five children of William Arberry, signal boatswain in the Royal Navy, by his wife, Sarah Ann Bailey. Arberry won a scholarship to Portsmouth Grammar School and in 1924 went up as a scholar to Pembroke College, Cambridge. At school he had shown a talent for mathematics, but he decided to specialize in classics, having, as he wrote, 'read everything worth reading in Greek and Latin'. At Cambridge he attended the lectures of A. E. Housman [q.v.]—'prodigiously erudite and prodigiously dull'—and took a first in both parts of the classical tripos (1925-7).

As an undergraduate, Arberry coincided at Pembroke with the great Islamic scholar, E. G. Browne [q.v.], who died in 1926, and it was Browne's friend, (Sir) Ellis Minns, who suggested that Arberry should apply for the newly established Browne studentship in Arabic and Persian. Financed by this and additional scholarship awards, he took a first in both parts of the oriental languages tripos simultaneously in 1929, and, after two years' work supported by Wright and Goldsmiths' studentships, in 1931 he was elected to a research fellowship at Pembroke. In 1932 he married Sarina Simons of Braila, Romania, and

left Cambridge as he 'could not hope to support a wife on the slender dividend of a junior research fellow'. For two years he acted as head of the department of classics at the university of Cairo, where his only daughter was born. On their return to England in 1934 he took the post of assistant librarian at the India Office, where he remained until the outbreak of war in 1939. For most of the war he served in the Ministry of Information, but in 1944 he returned to academic life on being appointed to the chair of Persian at London University. In 1946 he became professor of Arabic and head of the Near and Middle East department, and in 1947 he left London to return to his old college at Cambridge, as Sir Thomas Adams's professor of Arabic, a post which he held for the remainder of his life.

Arberry was an immensely prolific, as well as a versatile, writer, covering Maltese as well as a wide range of topics in Arabic and Persian studies, on which he published over sixty works. In addition, he produced catalogues of manuscripts and books in the India Office Library, the University Library of Cambridge, and the Chester Beatty Collection. An early enthusiasm for neo-Platonism developed into a general interest in mystical philosophy under the guidance of his 'beloved master', R. A. Nicholson [q.v.], who had perhaps the deepest influence on his career. It was Nicholson's failing eyesight which convinced Arberry that textual editions in Arabic and Persian was a young man's task, and after some early work in this field, notably an edition on the *Mawāqif and Mukhāṭabāt* of Niffarī (1935), he turned to more general subjects and to translation in both poetry and prose, with the intention of rounding off his research with a work on Nicholson's favourite author, Jalāl al Dīn Rūmī, planned for his retirement.

Arberry had a perspicuous view of the problems of his subject and was fond of drawing a comparison with classical studies at the start of the Renaissance. Manuscripts were uncatalogued, texts unedited and untranslated. As far as western scholarship was concerned, the magnitude of the task put it out of the range of the handful of professional academics who were being produced in each generation, and to Arberry the answer lay in a broadening of the appeal of the subject to attract interest and, eventually, recruits. He wrote: 'The most abiding lesson taught me by my four years under Brendan Bracken' (later Viscount Bracken, q.v.—in the Ministry of Information) 'was the relevance of publicity, in the broadest sense of the word, to oriental studies.' As a result, although he disclaimed any liking for administration, he threw himself into the work of planning and development which followed the acceptance by Parliament in 1947 of the report of the committee headed by Lord Scarbrough [q.v.]. Here his motives were not merely academic. Although he was a complex man, he had a number of simple principles and emotions, amongst them patriotism, and he felt that it must be in Britain's interests to strengthen her links with the Islamic world. He was responsible for the introduction of Turkish and modern Arabic into the Cambridge tripos, and he fought a long battle for the establishment at Cambridge of a Middle East Centre, which he saw as a focal point both of academic research and of cultural interest.

He could not have covered the ground he did without a remarkable capacity for assimilating information quickly and a love of hard work. Ambition was a powerful factor here, but the exact blend of personal ambition and ambition for his subject was hard to determine. He would count on finishing what he was writing with a single revision of the original draft, and set himself a twelve-hour working day. In time this proved too great a strain for his constitution and he later traced the deterioration in his health to his work on the translation of the Koran (published 1955). He was forced to shelve some of his plans and, in particular he was never able to tackle Rūmī as he had wished, but he refused to surrender to progressive weakness and he continued to work almost until his death.

For undergraduates he kept something of the 'quiet and reserved air' which he attributed to Nicholson, and he required wholehearted enthusiasm for his subject. With bushy moustache and eyebrows, thick spectacles, and broad, full face, with his considerable presence, he was in his lectures a Leviathan amongst minnows. As his health failed he was inclined to see ingratitude and plots, but for the most part with friends and colleagues his relations were governed by the agility of his brain and, at times, by a mischievous sense of humour. He loved quick-moving argument and the development of paradox, in attitude as well as logic. He refused to read J. R. R. Tolkien, who, he said, had too Celtic an imagination, but he enjoyed describing in matter-of-fact terms the ghosts he claimed to see. He liked watching football because of the speed of the game, and it was only as a stamp collector and a gardener that he slowed his pace. Arberry obtained the degree of Litt.D. at Cambridge (1936), and was elected FBA in 1949; he was awarded an honorary D.Litt. by the Royal University of Malta (1963). His services to Islam brought him recognition in the form of the Persian Nīshān-i Dānish, first class, in 1964. Even more significantly, numbers of research students from the Middle East were attracted to Cambridge by his reputation: they found in him a profound and inspiring teacher, and their affection was perhaps his most immediately fruitful memorial.

Arberry died in Cambridge 2 October 1969. His widow died in 1973.

[*The Times*, 4 October 1969; A. J. Arberry, *Oriental Essays*, 1960, and other works; G. M. Wickens in *Proceedings* of the British Academy, vol. lviii, 1972; personal knowledge.]
       M. C. LYONS

ARDEN-CLARKE, SIR CHARLES NOBLE (1898-1962), colonial governor, was born in India, 25 July 1898, the eldest son of the Revd Charles William Arden Clarke, an India missionary and the principal of Noble College, Masulipatam (the hyphen was added by deed poll). Educated at Rossall School, he was just old enough to serve in the war of 1914-18, enlisting in the Machine-Gun Corps in 1917. By the time he was twenty, he was already a captain and had earned a mention in dispatches. A breach of discipline while stationed in post-war Germany led him to volunteer for the South Russia expeditionary force mounted by the Allies in support of the White Russian Army. But coming to the conclusion that the army was not the career for him, he set aside the classical scholarship he had won at Emmanuel College, Cambridge (his father's college), and joined the Colonial Service in 1920. He attributed this decision partly to the inspiration of Sir F. J. D. (later Lord) Lugard [q.v.], also an old Rossallian.

After a sustained spell as a district officer in the northern provinces of Nigeria, where he earned recognition as an able and authoritarian administrator, in 1934 Arden-Clarke was transferred to the secretariat in Lagos. There in the native affairs department he quickly improved on his growing reputation as a skilled specialist in local government institutions and in 1936 was offered the post of assistant resident commissioner of Bechuanaland. A year later he was promoted resident commissioner. In 1942 he became resident commissioner of Basutoland.

At the end of World War II, when the Labour Government decided to assume responsibility for Sarawak from Sir Charles Vyner Brooke, the last of the so-called white rajas, it was Arden-Clarke whom the Colonial Office chose for this pioneer governorship in 1946. To set the seal on its status, he was immediately knighted. To the problems of rebuilding an economy ravaged during the Japanese occupation of the East Indian archipelago was added a measure of local resentment against a Crown presence. Arden-Clarke survived an attempt on his life only because he was out of the country;

his successor as governor, D. G. Stewart, was assassinated in the same year.

Appointed to the class i governorship of the Gold Coast in June 1949, it was in his uninterrupted eight years of guiding the Gold Coast from dependent territory to independent Ghana that Arden-Clarke reached the summit of his reputation as an outstanding modern colonial administrator. His brief to channel rather than check the vigorous nationalist spirit was a turning-point in the annals of Britain's colonial administration in Africa. Arriving in Accra in the aftermath of the 1948 riots, which had shaken the Colonial Office both by the threat they posed to the new, liberal policies of Arthur Creech Jones and his right-hand official in the Africa Division, (Sir) Andrew Cohen [qq.v.], and by the outspoken tenor of the ensuing commission of inquiry chaired by Aitken Watson, Arden-Clarke soon found himself confronted by the proconsular nightmare of a vociferous political party (in his case the Convention Peoples' Party) under a demagogic leader (the charismatic Kwame Nkrumah) gathering strength in support of a campaign for 'Full Self-Government NOW' through 'Positive Action'—violent if need be. In the strikes which followed, violence was indeed used, and Nkrumah was imprisoned for sedition. However, despite his leadership, at one remove, the mass party CPP triumphed in the Gold Coast's first general election. On his own initiative, Arden-Clarke released Nkrumah and, summoning him from gaol to Government House, invited him to form a Government. Although their first meeting was characterized by mutual suspicion and mistrust, they soon developed a real feeling of friendship and partnership.

Arden-Clarke was the first, and one of the most effective, of that small group of final or penultimate governors who, by establishing close personal links with the nationalist leadership, were as much part of the successful transfer of power as the African prime ministers themselves (Sir James Robertson in Nigeria, Sir Maurice Dorman in Sierra Leone, and Sir Richard Turnbull in Tanganyika were others). On Arden-Clarke's death, the arch-nationalist Nkrumah testified to this relationship in exceptional terms: 'It can be truly said that independence for Ghana might have been seriously delayed but for Sir Charles's readiness to co-operate with the forces of nationalism' (quoted in West Africa, 22 December 1962).

Arden-Clarke's governorship of the decolonizing Gold Coast remains a monument to the new style of colonial administrator which was in such great demand, yet at the very top initially in such short supply, in the immediate post-war years of British rule in Africa. In recognition of Arden-Clarke's role in helping Ghana to become, in March 1957, Britain's first African colony to attain independence, Arden-Clarke was invited to stay on as its inaugural governor-general. He left, however, within two months.

In retirement Arden-Clarke remained active in African affairs. In 1958 he acted as chairman of the UN good offices committee on Namibia; the recommendation for partition was not accepted. In 1959 he became chairman of the Royal African Society and of the Royal Commonwealth Society for the Blind, and a year later accepted the challenging chairmanship of the important National Council for the Supply of Teachers Overseas. Wisely, Whitehall did not part with his skills and experience. He was a member of the 1960 advisory commission on Central Africa chaired by Lord Monckton of Brenchley [q.v.], and in 1961 was invited to return to the High Commission territories, where he had first served twenty-five years earlier, to act as constitutional adviser to Swaziland on its final stages towards independence.

Arden-Clarke was appointed CMG in 1941, KCMG in 1948, and GCMG in 1952. Philately and gardening were among his hobbies. In appearance he was tall, well-built, and imposing.

In 1924 Arden-Clarke married Georgina Dora, daughter of Robert N. H. Reid, civil engineer. They had one son and two daughters. He died at his home, Syleham House, Diss, 16 December 1962, having spent thirty-seven years in the Colonial Service, more than half of them in a gubernatorial capacity.

There is a portrait by Helena Urszenyi in the Ambassador Hotel, Accra, and another at Syleham House, Diss, Norfolk.

[The Times, 18 December 1962; West Africa, 13 August 1949; Journal of the Royal African Society, January 1958; private information including that from D. Rooney.]

                              A. H. M. KIRK-GREENE

ASHTON, THOMAS SOUTHCLIFFE (1889-1968), economic historian, was born at Ashton-under-Lyne 11 January 1889, the second son and third child of Thomas Ashton, manager of the local Trustee Savings Bank, and his wife, Susan Sutcliffe. From Ashton-under-Lyne secondary school he won a scholarship to Manchester University where he read history and political economy and obtained his MA in 1910. After a brief and inappropriate spell as a schoolteacher in Dublin, he returned to England to lecture to trade-unionists on economic topics, continuing to do so until 1912, when he was appointed to lecture in economics at Sheffield University. Unfit for military service, he remained at Sheffield throughout the war but moved to Birmingham University in 1919 where, however, he found the dominating figure of Sir William Ashley [q.v.] wholly uncongenial. In 1921 at the instigation of a man to whom Ashton was devoted and whose influence on him was powerful—George Unwin, professor of economic history at Manchester and still, then, the sole professor of that subject in Britain—Ashton became senior lecturer in economics at Manchester.

There he stayed for twenty-three years, lecturing mainly on public finance (he became reader in public finance and currency in 1927), but researching and writing on economic history. His most important early works were written during this period. They included two important studies in industrial history: *Iron and Steel in the Industrial Revolution* (1924) and *The Coal Industry of the Eighteenth Century* (with Joseph Sykes, 1929); an entertainingly written centenary history of the Manchester Statistical Society: *Economic and Social Investigations in Manchester, 1833-1933* (1934); and a small but illuminating piece of business history, *An Eighteenth Century Industrialist: Peter Stubs of Warrington* (1939). In 1944 he was persuaded by R. H. Tawney [q.v.] to move to the chair of economic history at the London School of Economics which he occupied until his retirement in 1954. During that time he published two books of a notably more general nature than those of his Manchester period: *The Industrial Revolution* (1948) and *An Economic History of England: the Eighteenth Century* (1955). In 1953 he was Ford's lecturer at Oxford and from those lectures emerged his last major work. *Economic Fluctuations in England 1700-1800* (1959).

In his own upbringing and in his intellectual approach, Ashton seemed to reflect some of the qualities of the men who had been associated with the very industrial revolution on which he became the most notable authority of his day. He was something of a Manchester radical; his faith was in economic liberalism. Reared in a thrifty Nonconformist household, he was practical and pragmatic, not overtly brilliant nor given to flights of intellectual fancy. His range was limited but he brought to his subject what it then badly needed: an insistence on asking economic questions of historical sources. His concern was always to find the typical and representative characteristics of the phenomena he investigated, using quantitative data wherever possible. Such a path could easily have led to history of a very arid sort. That it did not do so in Ashton's books

was a consequence of his warmth of personal character, his concern for the role of the individual in history, and his great lucidity in writing. These qualities were probably best exhibited in the brief compass of *The Industrial Revolution*, which was a superb compression of his learning, experience, and technique; it deservedly enjoyed substantial sales and was translated into French, Italian, Japanese, Portuguese, Spanish, and Swedish.

Short in stature and wiry in build, Ashton was one of the kindest of men, utterly devoid of self-importance and pretentiousness, friendly, and immensely helpful to many students and colleagues. He was at his best in seminars, and those who attended them soon became familiar with the penetrating and pertinent questions gently delivered in a Lancashire accent and through a fog of cigarette smoke. His long labours, in a field of enquiry which orthodox British historians had too easily regarded with a suspicion and contempt born of ignorance, were eventually rewarded with due honours: elected FBA in 1951 and an honorary vice-president of the Royal Historical Society in 1961, he received the honorary degrees of D.Litt. from Nottingham in 1963, Litt.D. from Manchester in 1964, and D.Phil. from Stockholm in the same year. He declined honours other than those of the academic variety. He was the recipient of a *Festschrift*, entitled *Studies in the Industrial Revolution* (ed. L. S. Pressnell), on the occasion of his seventieth birthday.

In 1915 Ashton married Marion Hague, daughter of Joseph Slater, of Ashton-under-Lyne; they had one son. Shortly after his retirement Ashton and his wife went to live in Blockley in the Cotswolds. He died in hospital in Oxford 22 September 1968, only a few months short of his eightieth birthday. Amongst his bequests were £500 to a local school, Campden Grammar School, and £500 to the Economic History Society, which was used in helping to endow a T. S. Ashton prize in his memory.

[R. S. Sayers in *Proceedings* of the British Academy, vol. lvi, 1970; private information; personal knowledge.]

D. C. COLEMAN

ASHTON, WINIFRED (1888-1965), playwright and novelist under the name of CLEMENCE DANE, was born in Greenwich 21 February 1888, the daughter of Arthur Charles Ashton, commission merchant, and his wife, Florence Bentley. She was educated in England, Germany, and Switzerland. Intending at first to make painting her profession, she studied in Dresden and at the

Slade School; but in 1913, finding that the theatre had won her deepest love, she went on the stage under the name of Diana Cortis. Tall and beautiful, and at that time slim, she had some success; but war broke out, conditions were difficult, her health gave trouble, and she ceased to act. After teaching for a time in a girls' school she found that her true bent was for writing and, under the name with which she was soon to become famous, she started out as a novelist.

This name she adapted from that of the church in the Strand, St. Clement Danes, and it symbolized her love of the Covent Garden district of London, in which she was to live for the greater part of her life, which became, as it were, her village, and of which she wroite in *London Has a Garden* (1964). She knew everybody, and commanded the respect and affection of all. She kept open house for the friends who flocked about her from every rank, kind, or calling, and when she died her loss was felt by her neighbours as a personal bereavement.

By 1919 she had written three novels of which the first, *Regiment of Women* (1917), had been hailed as the work of a new writer of distinction. Her new name had already acquired lustre, and she was about to take the step which was to give it popularity. Her passion for the theatre had not abated. She decided to try her hand at writing plays, and on 14 March 1921 the first of these, *A Bill of Divorcement*, was produced at the St. Martin's Theatre. It had an instant triumph, both artistic and commercial, and ran for 401 performances.

The central situation of the play was strongly theatrical, concerning as it did a girl who, finding that the father she had believed dead was in fact still alive and a discharged lunatic, decided that she had a taint in her blood and must not marry. Fearing that her promised husband might not want to take the risk if he knew the truth, she deliberately set herself to provoke him into breaking the engagement— and succeeded, at the cost of her hopes of happiness. Artificially contrived though this scene was, it was written with great sincerity and emotional insight and, receiving similar treatment from a brilliantly promising, but unhappily short-lived, actress, Meggie Albanesi, it swept its first audience to wild enthusiasm.

Clemence Dane's next play was eagerly awaited, and her public did not have to wait long, for in November of the same year *Will Shakespeare*—written in admirable blank verse, no doubt from a sense of its suitability—was produced at the Shaftesbury Theatre, and was a resounding failure. 'Resounding' is literally correct, for the play's distinction had made a deep impression on the reading public, and its instant rejection by the drama critics caused a public controversy of extreme violence. A certain armchair critic from Wales, who had not visited the play, stated categorically that '*Will Shakespeare*' was 'beyond comparison the greatest and most beautiful play of our time'. Another commentator, facing the issue less one-sidedly but expressing himself no less strongly said that the piece was 'a masterpiece in the study, a travesty on the stage'.

The truth, as it was to reveal itself during the rest of Clemence Dane's career as a writer of original plays, was that she could write magnificent parts for women to act, but not for men. In her first play the whole weight had been carried by the two women, mother and daughter. In the second, the central character was inescapably Shakespeare himself; and the Bard of Miss Dane's imagination proved in action to be a trivial nonentity, quite unacceptable as the author of any of the great tragedies. The only characters of importance seemed to be the neglected wife, Anne Hathaway, and Queen Elizabeth; and in spite of a remarkable performance by Haidée Wright as the Queen, the play sagged and collapsed.

Some defeats are as honourable as victories. Clemence Dane's reputation now stood higher than ever; and among the friends she made about this time were (Dame) Sybil Thorndike and her husband (Sir) Lewis Casson and the composer Richard Addinsell, all of whom call for particular mention because they were destined to be not only her lifelong intimates but also her professional colleagues and collaborators. Addinsell, indeed, besides writing background music for every work of hers which needed it, became her close, and often fiercely admonitory, adviser on other matters. As for the Cassons, they showed their admiration in a practical way by staging two more of her series of distinguished failures—*Granite* (1926) and *Mariners* (1927). She also became a lifelong friend of (Sir) Noel Coward and taught him painting.

Year by year frustration continued: while her reputation as a writer remained high and she enjoyed success in other fields of authorship such as novels and film-scripts, her dearest ambition, to bring the play-going public once again to her feet, remained unfulfilled. *Adam's Opera* (1928), in which she and Addinsell collaborated at the Old Vic, did moderately well, and a later collaboration with him in a new version of the Alice books, in which Sybil Thorndike did a remarkable 'double' as the Queen of Hearts and the White Queen, made its mark. But neither *Wild Decembers* (1932), a play about the Brontës with Diana Wynyard [q.v.] as Charlotte, nor *The Happy Hypocrite* (1936), an adaptation of the story by (Sir) Max Beerbohm [q.v.], with Ivor Novello and Vivien Leigh [qq.v.], attracted the public attention they might have been thought to deserve.

Perhaps the worst of her disappointments came in 1951. During the forties she had written many plays for radio, and one of these, dealing with Elizabeth I and Essex, she had considered strong enough to be rewritten as a stage play for Sybil Thorndike. It was thought that in the character of Essex she had at last succeeded in creating a role which a star actor would be pleased to play. Sir Charles Cochran [q.v.] accepted the piece, and (Sir) John Mills was cast for Essex. But on 31 January 1951 Cochran died and the play went on to the shelf. After this, her only play was *Eighty in the Shade* (1959) especially written for Sybil Thorndike.

Always a tireless worker, Clemence Dane found time and energy during her theatrical vicissitudes to write a number of novels. The best of these, *Broome Stages* (1931), had a curious origin. She found her story in the history books and planned to tell it as a true-to-life account of the doings and relationships of several generations of the House of Plantagenet. Addinsell hotly argued against such waste of effort, maintaining there was no public for a long historical novel; so she transformed the Plantagenets to a modern theatrical family and translated their surname, and found a satisfactorily responsive public.

She kept up her painting all her life for the pleasure and relaxation it gave her, and from time to time turned to sculpture also. With her varied talents, her wide experience, and her gift for friendship, she was one of the outstanding personalities of her chosen world. She was appointed CBE in 1953 and died in London 28 March 1965. The National Portrait Gallery has a pastel by Fred Yates.

[*The Times*, 29 March 1965; private information.]   W. A. DARLINGTON

ASQUITH, ANTHONY (1902-1968), film director, was born 9 November 1902 in London, the youngest son of Herbert Henry Asquith (later Earl of Oxford and Asquith), the Liberal statesman and future prime minister, and his second wife, Margaret (Margot), daughter of Sir Charles Tennant, merchant and art patron [q.v.]. There were five children of this second marriage, two of whom survived. Of these two, Elizabeth was six years older than Anthony (who was universally known by his childhood name of 'Puffin'). There were also five children of H. H. Asquith's first marriage.

Anthony Asquith was educated at Summer Fields, Oxford, Winchester, and Balliol College, Oxford, where he obtained second classes in both classical moderations (1923) and *literae humaniores* (1925). He had a passionate love of music from an early age, but deciding that he was not talented enough for a professional career, concentrated on his other great interest, the cinema. After leaving Oxford in 1925, Asquith, a founder-member of the Film Society in London, was invited to study the American industry in Hollywood, as a guest of Douglas Fairbanks and Mary Pickford.

Returning home after six months he joined H. Bruce Woolfe's British Instructional Film Company in 1926. Thereafter, unlike Alfred J. Hitchcock and many other leading figures in British cinema, Asquith never left London to work in Hollywood. He was essentially English in his tastes and his style, a characteristic that was his greatest strength but also, owing to the restricted nature of the native industry, one that imposed technical and financial limitations on his work. Most of his best films were screen adaptations of West End plays, opened out for the cinema, but with a limited conventional use of the flexibility that technical developments brought to film-makers in his lifetime. His artistic and personal integrity, coupled with a sensitive literary and visual imagination, won the respect of all his studio associates from the leading international film stars to the humblest technicians, and enabled him to create a whole-hearted devotion for any feature he made. In an industry whose outstanding directors were often flamboyant hectoring egotists, Asquith was modest and undemonstrative, getting his way by persuasion and attention to his craft. It was not surprising that when the Association of Cinematographic Technicians was created in 1937, Asquith was invited to become the first president and retained this position until his death in 1968, a fitting tribute to the 'technicians' director'.

Shooting Stars (1927), for which he was scriptwriter and assistant director, began a decade in which Asquith was a film *auteur*, directing from his own scripts. His first independent success was *A Cottage On Dartmoor* (1929)—one of the last, and best, British silent films. A growing reputation was enhanced by *Tell England* (1930-1), based on the 1915 Gallipoli campaign, but this was unfortunately followed by six years of making less distinguished films for uncongenial company producers. Asquith's service in (Sir) Alexander Korda's [q.v.] studio at Denham ended after one film, *Moscow Nights* (1935), remarkable only for an early screen appearance by Laurence (later Lord) Olivier. Few men could have been more unalike than the gentle Asquith and the overbearing Korda.

This frustrating period ended with *Pygmalion* (1938), probably his greatest achievement. Asquith wrote the script, in consultation with G. Bernard Shaw [q.v.], and encouraged the experienced Leslie Howard [q.v.] and the comparatively unknown (Dame) Wendy Hiller to give outstanding performances as Professor Higgins and Eliza Doolittle. Asquith had discovered his *métier*, the transformation of plays written for middle-class London theatre audiences into films that would appeal to the much wider cinema-going public. He managed to popularize the material without debasing its quality.

Pygmalion was followed by *French Without Tears* (1939) with (Sir) Terence Rattigan, the author of many of his films over the next twenty years. One of the few breaks in this partnership linked Asquith with a very different playwright, Samuel Beckett, in the creation of a short film *Zero* (1960). During the war Asquith directed two documentaries, one an introduction to Britain for American servicemen *Welcome to Britain* (1943), successful feature films such as *Quiet Wedding* (1940) and *Fanny by Gaslight* (1944), and films with a political or war interest —*The Demi-Paradise* (1943) and *The Way to the Stars* (1945). After 1945 Asquith formed a company with Terence Rattigan to film the latter's stage successes, *While the Sun Shines* (1947), *The Winslow Boy* (1948), *The Browning Version* (1950), and a tribute to English cricket, *The Final Test* (1952). He also supervised brilliant screen versions of Oscar Wilde's [q.v.] *The Importance of Being Earnest* (1951) and Shaw's *The Doctor's Dilemma* (1958).

Surprisingly, and sadly, Asquith's one professional excursion into the musical world which he loved so much, as producer of *Carmen* for Covent Garden in 1953, was not very successful. Asquith was more at ease with films that combined a fictional story with shots of stage performances of ballet, as in *The Young Lovers* (1945) and the earlier *Dance Pretty Lady* (1931), and of opera, with *On Such a Night* (1955)—devoted to an evening of Mozart at Glyndebourne. In the mid 1950s he directed several successful television films of ballets danced by Dame Margot Fonteyn and Rudolf Nureyev. The greater appreciation of ballet and opera by British television audiences in the 1960s and 1970s came unfortunately too late for Asquith, who would have been exceptionally well suited to make such productions.

In the last years of his career he was employed by the big international companies who dominated the industry to direct expensive films for the world market, such as *The VIPs* (1963) and *The Yellow Rolls-Royce* (1964), very different from the restrained, essentially English works with which he had made his name. In December 1963 he had a serious automobile accident. Although he recovered,

and within four months was directing the last film he was able to complete, he was never again fully fit. Working in Italy on a film of *The Shoes of the Fisherman* he was taken ill and died in London of cancer 21 February 1968.

He will be best remembered for his early contributions to British cinema when it was seeking to evolve a distinctive style to compete with the American domination of the market. Although he helped to achieve this in the 1930s and 1940s, the British industry, like Asquith himself, was too delicate to flourish long in the face of the superior resources of the United States. He will be remembered also for his modesty, charm, and sincere concern for all who worked with him and for him. His dress was casual, wayward at times, and endeared him to his many friends who ranged from distinguished figures in public affairs, banking, and the arts, to working men and women. Brought up in 10 Downing Street he was at home and happy in stately homes or in lorry drivers' cafés. Asquith's outstanding physical features were the long delicate fingers of a pianist, always gesticulating, as though they were trying to keep up with the quickness of his thought and speed. His strong finely cut features seemed sometimes at odds with his careless dress, and suggested that he was in too much of a hurry to meet and help people to waste much time on external appearances. Lord David Cecil wrote 'There are people in this confused and distracted age who question the possibility of human goodness. No one could do so who knew Anthony Asquith.'

There is, in private hands, a drawing of Asquith as a child by John Singer Sargent (1909); a head-and-shoulders drawing by D. B. Wyndham Lewis (1932), and a portrait in oils by Allan Gwynne-Jones in the Asquith Room, Association of Cinematographic, Television, and Allied Technicians in Soho Square, London.

[R. J. Minney, *'Puffin' Asquith*, 1973; private information.]   D. J. WENDEN

ASQUITH OF YARNBURY, BARONESS (1887–1969), political figure. [See BONHAM CARTER, (HELEN) VIOLET.]

ASTBURY, WILLIAM THOMAS (1898–1961), physicist, crystallographer, and molecular biologist, was born 25 February 1898 at Longton in the Stoke district, the fourth of seven children and the eldest son of William Edwin Astbury, potter's turner, of Longton, and his wife, Clara Dean. Astbury was educated at Longton High School and at Jesus College, Cambridge. He went up in 1917 but his education was interrupted for two years by war service in the RAMC in Cork where he met his future wife. After graduation with first classes in both part i (physics, chemistry, mineralogy, 1920) and part ii (physics, 1921) of the natural sciences tripos, he joined Professor Sir William H. Bragg [q.v.] first at University College, London (1921), and then at the Royal Institution (1923). He first signalled his life's work by accepting an invitation as lecturer at the university of Leeds (1928) where he set up the textile physics laboratory in the Department of Textile Industries, based in the first instance on X-ray diffraction studies of keratin, the wool protein. Subsequently, in 1937, Astbury was appointed reader in textile physics and, in 1945, professor and head of a new department, the Department of Biomolecular Structure. After Astbury's death the university replaced this department by a new one (1962) entitled in his honour the Astbury Department of Biophysics.

Astbury was throughout a pioneer attempting solution of structural problems, with brilliant intuition, long before the appropriate techniques had been developed. His first papers dealt with small molecules but nevertheless more complicated than any other crystal structure solved at the time. His greatest contribution came, however, after his transfer to Leeds. In three key papers, published between 1931 and 1935, with improved diagrams obtained by X-ray cameras of his own careful design, he showed that the diagram of unstretched wool fibres was interpretable in terms of a folded molecular chain which by stretching could be converted reversibly into another form with straight chains substantially as in silk. These structures he named respectively the α-form and the β-form. This was the first example of a mechanical polymorph. Astbury favoured an α-structure in which the long chain of the protein was folded in a sequence of flat hexagons. When, later, accurate atomic models proved that such a fold could not accommodate the bulky side chains of the protein, he developed another, orthogonal fold consonant with all the properties of the protein known at that time. This folding and unfolding of protein chains, and Astbury's observation that single crystals of globular proteins such as edestin could be turned by denaturation into a set of parallel fibres, led him directly to the profound conclusion that a protein could exhibit different properties and activities simply through differences in the folding pattern.

In the meantime, Astbury had extended his interests to othe proteins: the myosin of muscle which he studied extensively, the epidermin of skin, and the fibrinogen and fibrin of blood. These formed a choerent group, the k-m-e-f group, all of which showed a keratin-like structure. The keratin of bird feathers and reptile scales he found to be slightly different so that he could separate these from mammals on a molecular basis. All these proteins differed sharply from collagen, the inextensible protein of connective tissue, which he regarded as an entirely different protein. In the first Procter memorial lecture (1939), based on a wide selection of collagens, he deduced that the molecular chain of collagen was not quite fully extended; in the ninth (1960) he gave the correct, Ramachandran, structure. Astbury was a man who delighted in the success of others as much as he did in his own and, when Linus Pauling announced the α-helical structure of proteins he fully accepted it.

Perhaps Astbury's greatest contribution to molecular biology was with nucleic acids. He was early convinced of the importance of these acids. Again he reached a structure long before anyone else had one, but again he missed the real structure of a double helix because the necessary techniques and information were not yet available.

His work had a profound effect on the textile industry, on the development of molecular biology, and in the medical field. He received many honours. He was elected a fellow of the Royal Society (1940), gave the Croonian lecture (1945), and was a member of the council (1946-7). He was elected honorary life member of the New York Academy of Sciences (1950), corresponding member of the Istituto Lombardo de Scienze (1951), foreign member of the Swedish Royal Academy of Sciences (1956), and honorary founder-member of the British Biophysical Society (1961). He was Sc.D. (Cantab.) and doctor honoris causa of the university of Strasbourg (1946). He also achieved many other distinctions.

Astbury was a man of the Potteries who retained a bluff, hearty, simple style and a traditional extreme independence. A sturdy figure with a somewhat rolling gait, he was welcomed the world over and loved by the thousands who knew him. He found his relaxation in music; he was an accomplished pianist and learned to play the violin late in life.

In 1922 Astbury married, in London, Frances Hannah Mary, daughter of Daniel Gould, horticulturalist, of Cork in Ireland. They had two children, a son and a daughter to whom, and subsequently to his grandchildren, he was devoted in happy family surroundings. Astbury died at the Leeds General Infirmary 4 June 1961.

Astbury's portrait in oils by Gavin Stuart (1956) hangs in the Royal Institution.

[J. D. Bernal in *Biographical Memoirs of Fellows of the Royal Society*, vol. ix, 1963; R. D. Preston in *Proceedings* of the 26th Symposium of the Coston Research Society (eds. E. D. T. Atkins, A Keller).]

R. D. PRESTON

ASTOR, NANCY WITCHER, VISCOUNTESS ASTOR (1879-1964), politician and hostess, was born 19 May 1879 at Danville, Virginia, the eighth, and fifth surviving, child of Chiswell Dabney Langhorne, Southern gentleman and Civil War veteran, who later made a fortune in railway development and bought an estate at Mirador near Charlottesville. Her mother, Nancy Witcher Keene, was of Irish extraction. The beauty of the second daughter, Irene, was immortalized by Charles Dana Gibson, the artist, whom she married.

Nancy herself was gifted with beauty, as well as wit and a good—although inadequately schooled—intelligence. In 1897 she was married, at the age of eighteen, to Robert Gould Shaw, by whom she had one son, but whom she divorced in 1903. This was a source of considerable embarrassment to her in her later career, when she was a vigorous opponent of divorce. In 1904 she came to England for the social and hunting seasons, and in 1906, after rejecting other suitors, married Waldorf (later second Viscount) Astor [q.v.], who brought her immense wealth and lifelong devotion. They had four sons and one daughter.

Naturally religious, Nancy was converted in 1914 to Christian Science, which she thereafter practised and preached with missionary fervour, and to which she soon converted her friend Philip Kerr [q.v.], later eleventh Marquess of Lothian. Her friendship with Kerr (always regarded as platonic) remained, until his death in 1940, the closest of her many friendships; and, since he was a fugitive from Roman Catholicism, it was probably under his influence that her natural Protestantism assumed an obsessively anti-Popish form.

In 1919 Waldorf Astor had to vacate his parliamentary seat—the Sutton division of Plymouth—on inheriting the peerage which he had not wanted his father to accept. In the resulting by-election Nancy, now Lady Astor, stood in his place and was returned as a Conservative supporter of the Lloyd George coalition. When she took her seat, 1 December 1919, she was the first woman to do so, since the Sinn Fein Countess Markievicz, elected in 1918, had disqualified herself by refusal to take the oath. To mark the historic occasion, Lady Astor was introduced by Lloyd George and Arthur Balfour, the only two members who had attained the rank of prime minister.

A more conventional woman might have shown her reverence for the ancient and illustrious men's club to which she had gained admittance by conforming very punctiliously to its rules and customs. But Lady Astor did not seek to prove herself the equal of her male colleagues, since it was her line that women were the superior sex. 'I married beneath me,'

she used to say, 'all women do'—and in that spirit she made her presence felt in the House of Commons. Partly because she hated pomposity of any kind, and partly because her mind was rather disorderly, she was never a good parliamentarian in the traditional sense. Her interruptions, although often witty, were too frequent, and once, when she claimed to have been listening for hours before interrupting, a member exclaimed: 'Yes, we *heard* you listening!

Yet her service in the House of Commons was by no means barren of achievement, and her best work was done during the early years. In 1923 she introduced and carried through all its stages her own private member's Bill raising, in principle, to eighteen the age qualification for the purchase of alcoholic drinks. Her husband then took charge of it in the Lords, and it became law. Her maiden speech had been in favour of Temperance, and her Bill gave practical, if limited, effect to her convictions. In addition, she championed a variety of women's causes: for instance, votes for women at twenty-one, equal rights in the Civil Service, and the preservation of the women's police force. She was also active on behalf of children, especially as a strong supporter and benefactress of the nursery schools of Margaret McMillan [q.v.].

In 1931 she and her husband visited the Soviet Union with G. B. Shaw [q.v.]. Shaw returned an ecstatic admirer of Stalin, but the Astors were not blind to the atrocity of the Soviet regime. At home Lady Astor was one of those who vainly demanded more generous treatment of the unemployed.

She was instinctively anti-Nazi, never visited Hitler, and was, later, on his black list. All the same, she believed that the policy of appeasement was right and became one of its most conspicuous partisans—conspicuous mainly through the influence of the 'Cliveden set' myth. Cliveden was the Astors' magnificent home overlooking the Thames near Taplow, where they entertained liberally. The idea of a conspiratorial set meeting there to promote appeasement and a sell-out to Nazi Germany was a journalistic invention. It was demonstrably mythical since the outstanding feature of the Astors' hospitality was its open-endedness: no country house of the period had a more comprehensive clientele. Moreover, even among the Astors' intimate friends (naturally their most frequent guests) there were deep differences of opinion on foreign policy.

Churchill, however, was not one of their friends. Between him and Lady Astor relations were never good, although in 1940 she helped to make him prime minister by voting against the Government in the Norway division.

During the war of 1939–45 the Astors dedicated themselves to Plymouth, she as one of the city's members of Parliament, he as its lord mayor for five successive years. They spent a lot of time at their house on the Hoe, which—with them in it—was damaged by high explosive and incendiary bombs. Lady Astor did much to sustain morale, not least by performing, for the benefit of people in air-raid shelters, the cartwheels with which she had amazed Edwardian house-parties when she was nearly forty years younger.

It is a virtual certainty, however, that she would have lost her seat in the Labour tide had she stood again in 1945, and it is possible that she would not have been asked to stand, for her parliamentary performance had deteriorated over the years. Her husband wisely persuaded her not to seek re-election. Resentful at being out of Parliament, she turned her resentment against him, with the sad result that their partnership was clouded during the years before he died in 1952. Surviving him by more than a decade, she died at her daughter's house, Grimsthorpe in Lincolnshire, 2 May 1964, and was buried with her husband at Cliveden.

Lady Astor was short and neat, but her air of alertness and challenge made her seem taller. Her eyes were blue, her colouring was fair, her nose and chin were strong and finely shaped, but without undue prominence. Her clothes were expensive, but she never wore bright colours, and in the House of Commons unfailingly wore a black coat and skirt with a white blouse and a black tricorn hat. A gardenia or sprig of verbena was usually in her lapel. Her finest qualities were courage, generosity, and zest; her principal defects insensitivity, prejudice, and a streak of cruelty. She was a curious mixture of religious maniac and clown, oscillating between the extremes of earnestness and levity. Moderation never came easily to her, yet paradoxically she always supported moderates in politics.

An oil painting of her by J. S. Sargent (1923) is in the National Portrait Gallery. There are three charcoal drawings of her by the same artist, two belonging to the fourth Viscount Astor, and one presented to the National Portrait Gallery by her son, Michael Astor. A picture by Charles Sims of her taking her seat in the House of Commons is on loan to the university of Virginia at Charlottesville, and a copy of this painting is in the Plymouth Art Gallery. A bust of her by K. de Strobl was presented by Shaw to the Palace of Westminster.

Lady Astor was appointed CH in 1937 and made an honorary freeman of Plymouth in 1959.

[Maurice Collis, *Nancy Astor*, 1960; Michael Astor, *Tribal Feeling*, 1963; Christopher Sykes, *Nancy: the Life of Lady Astor*, 1972; private information; personal knowledge.]

JOHN GRIGG

ATCHERLEY, SIR RICHARD LLEWELLYN ROGER (1904–1970), air marshal, was born in York 12 January 1904, one of twin sons of Major (later Major-General Sir) Llewellyn William Atcherley, and his wife, Eleanor Frances, younger daughter of Richard Micklethwait. His father who divided his career between the army and the police served in 1919–36 as an inspector of constabulary. The family had lived in Shropshire for many years, tracing their ancestry to the sixteenth century, when a Sir Richard Atcherley was mayor of London. Atcherley was educated at Oundle School, leaving without any special distinction, but with a burning interest in flying. He and his twin brother David were guided towards commerce, but applied on their own initiative for cadetships at the Royal Air Force College. Dick was accepted, but for medical reasons David was turned down. He went instead into the army, but managed to transfer later to the Royal Air Force and rejoin his twin.

From childhood until the end of their lives Atcherley and his twin brother were extraordinarily identical in appearance; and their voices, movements, and mannerisms were indistinguishable, while they had an uncanny mental affinity even when far apart. If one was posted abroad they would exchange the dog they owned in common, which was said to be unable to tell one from the other. In this remarkable partnership Dick just tended to be the dominant twin, and his career was the more spectacular. Serving first in fighter squadrons he quickly proved his worth as an exceptional pilot, and was selected as an instructor at the Central Flying School in 1926, where he brought aerobatic flying to a new degree of excellence. From this already élite assembly he was chosen as a member of the Royal Air Force High Speed Flight then being assembled for the 1929 Schneider Trophy contest. Although disqualified during the competition, he set up a new world speed record, and also a record for the course, flying a Supermarine seaplane of the type which formed the basis of the design of the Spitfire. In the same year, with Flight-Lieutenant Stainforth, he won the King's Cup air race. When he returned to squadron duty he was established as one of the world's foremost practical high speed pilots, and a master of the art of exhibition flying. For the next few years he was invited to American aviation meetings at Chicago and Cleveland, where his flying performances became increasingly entertaining and hair-raising, including such feats as flying an aircraft while riding it pick-a-back dressed as a huntsman, or disguising himself as an elderly eccentric with no knowledge of flying and then giving a display whose terrifying craziness concealed his underlying mastery of the machine. It is not surprising that his universal nickname was 'Batchy'.

A period in the Middle East was followed by a posting as a Service test pilot, which found him in his ideal medium. He next attended the Staff College and some less welcome staff duty brought him to 1939 and war. He soon gained the command of a night fighter squadron, a new branch of operations, and one beset with every possible problem, both human and technical. From there he was snatched away to command the air element of the British Expeditionary Force to north Norway. This short, desperate, and finally disastrous campaign gave full play for his energy, imagination, and powers of improvisation, but chiefly showed his ability to inspire those he commanded to efforts beyond anything they had thought possible. When the last of the British forces was withdrawn he was promoted to group captain and appointed to the command of a night fighter training airfield at Drem in Scotland, where he applied all the lessons so bitterly learned in Norway, and for good measure invented a new system of airfield lighting which was subsequently standardized throughout the Service. With his brother commanding another Scottish airfield his creative spirit was at its highest, for the twins reacted on one another like spark and tinder, but their effervescence, unthinkable to most officers of their rank, never diverted them from the relentless pursuit of improvements in every aspect of flying which could lead to greater success in air operations.

In 1942 Atcherley was made sector commander first of Fairwood Common and then of Kenley. From there, while flying a Spitfire, he was shot down into the Channel and wounded. In 1943 he was sent to North Africa to command a Group in the Desert Air Force, and then returned to the staff of Allied Expeditionary Air Forces. There he invented the concept of a Central Fighter Establishment, designed the organization, and when the war ended he was serving as its first commandant. He followed this by commanding the Royal Air Force Cadet College (1946-8), and in 1949 was appointed commander-in-chief of the new air force of a new country—Pakistan; whose pilots regarded with mingled awe and hilarity a commander-in-chief who could fly any aircraft they possessed as well as they could, and whose sense of humour still remained outrageous and unpredictable.

In 1951 Atcherley was given the command of No. 12 Fighter Group, then in 1954 sent to the United States as commander RAF staff, British Joint Services Mission. His last appointment (1955-8) was as commander-in-chief Flying Training Command. The years had in no way modified his character, and to the end of his career he managed successfully to combine a uniquely flippant style with an underlying sense of duty so strong that he was unhappy during weekends and holidays, and truly at ease only when working. This made his retirement exceptionally hard to bear, but far worse was the loss of his brother David, posted missing on a jet flight over the Mediterranean in 1952. Although outwardly unaffected, it was the heaviest blow of his life.

Atcherley was awarded the AFC in 1940 and bar in 1942. He was promoted air vice-marshal in 1951 and air marshal in 1956. He was appointed OBE (1941), CBE (1945), and KBE (1956), and CB in 1950.

What made Atcherley memorable was his character rather than his deeds, and particularly his power to combine brilliance and irreverence so that they became indistinguishable. He and his twin were a type of man whose ability, devotion to duty, and intensity of purpose allowed them to survive and prosper through careers studded with crashes, courts martial, and the type of gaffe which offended the more pompous heads of military and civil life. The great majority of their Service loved them deeply; a minority, and a great many civilian officials, heaved a sigh of relief when there were no more Atcherleys in uniform. Dick Atcherley set a style which played a major part in determining the traditions of the youngest fighting Service, and created a legend which continues to influence it far beyond his actual impact upon events. Thus the future inspiration of the Royal Air Force will always include something of the influence of the Atcherley brothers, far more than that of greater and more important men.

From 1959 to 1961 Atcherley was coordinator of Anglo-American Community Relations, and from 1959 to 1965 sales director of the Folland Aircraft Company. He was an early member of the British Interplanetary Society.

There is a portrait at the Royal Air Force College, Cranwell, by Herbert Holt, and another much better one of his brother David by Eric Kennington at RAF West Raynham, which serves as well. He died in hospital in Aldershot 18 April 1970. Neither brother married.

[John Pudney, *A Pride of Unicorns*, 1960; *The Times*, 20 April 1970; Air Historical Branch (RAF); private information; personal knowledge.]

PETER WYKEHAM

ATTLEE, CLEMENT RICHARD, first EARL ATTLEE (1883–1967), statesman, was born in London 3 January 1883, the fourth son and seventh child of Henry Attlee, a leading solicitor in the City, and his wife, Ellen, daughter of T. S. Watson, secretary of the Art Union of London. The Attlee family had lived near Dorking for generations as farmers, millers, and merchants, but by the middle of the nineteenth century were in the main solid and prosperous members of the professional class.

The Attlee house was in Putney; a country house in Essex was added in 1896. Attlee always said that his was 'a typical family of the professional class brought up in the atmosphere of Victorian England'. He was taught at home until he was nine, acquiring an abiding love of literature from his mother. Other teaching was done by a succession of governesses engaged for his sisters, one of whom had previously had (Sir) Winston Churchill in her charge. A preparatory school at Northam Place, Potters Bar, was then followed by Haileybury College. His record at both was undistinguished. When he left Haileybury he was still immature and painfully shy, having made a mark only as an outstandingly good cadet.

He went up to University College, Oxford, in 1901 and spent three happy years there. He emerged with a deep love of literature and history (he obtained second class honours in modern history in 1904), a half blue for billiards, the sole game for which he had skill, and a lasting affection for his college and Oxford. Otherwise he was as conventional in general outlook and as Conservative in politics as he had been at Haileybury. He had already begun to eat dinners' at the Inner Temple and was called to the bar in 1905.

In October 1905 Attlee's life took what proved to be a decisive turn when he paid his first visit to Haileybury House, a boy's club in Stepney, supported by his old school. He soon began to help regularly in the club and took a commission in its cadet corps. In 1907 he agreed to become manager of the club and went to live there. His home was in the East End for the next fourteen years.

By the end of 1907 he was a socialist, converted by his experience of life in Stepney and his reading of the works of John Ruskin, William Morris, Sidney and Beatrice Webb [qq.v.], and other apostles of socialism. In 1908 he joined the tiny Stepney branch of the Independent Labour Party. There was nothing unusual in such a conversion to socialism. Two of his brothers and several of his friends took the same path. What marked out Attlee was that he abandoned any idea of a regular career which might be combined with political agitation and social work on the side. His father's death in

1908 assured him of an income of £400 a year. It enabled him to abandon the law and was enough for his spartan tastes. He took a succession of ill-paid jobs connected with social work or politics: lecture secretary of the Webbs' campaign for the minority report of the Poor Law Commission, secretary of Toynbee Hall, lecturer at Ruskin College, Oxford, in 1911, and official explainer of the National Insurance Act of that year. At the instigation of Sidney Webb (later Lord Passfield), he became a lecturer in social administration at the London School of Economics in 1913. The other candidate was E. Hugh (later Lord) Dalton [q.v.].

He thus had plenty of time for social work and socialist propaganda. As secretary of the Stepney branch of the ILP he was active in Labour's London organization and, his early shyness conquered, became an experienced, if not very effective, street-corner orator. By 1914, without any abandonment of his old friends and connections, his roots were deep in the East End and the growing Labour movement.

He had not, however, given up his voluntary commission in the cadets and within a few weeks of the outbreak of war, at the age of thirty-one, was a lieutenant in the 6th South Lancashire Regiment. He went with his battalion to Gallipoli and had two spells there, the second ending with command of the rearguard at the evacuation of Suvla Bay. He was in Mesopotamia in 1916, where he was badly wounded by a British shell and invalided home. After recovery he served with the Tank Corps for a year and was promoted to major in 1917. By the summer of 1918 he was back with the South Lancashires in France. During the advance to Lille he was injured and sent home, celebrating the armistice in hospital.

Attlee was unusual among the coming Labour leaders in having served as an active officer throughout the war. For many years he was most commonly known as 'Major Attlee', his vaguely military bearing and appearance, and the clipped anachronisms of his conversation, setting him somewhat apart from his contemporaries in the Labour Party. The war also gave rise to a keen interest in the theory of warfare; he was, for example, convinced that Churchill's strategic conception at Gallipoli had been sound.

Attlee returned to the London School of Economics and to political activity in the East End immediately after demobilization. In 1919 he was co-opted by Stepney Borough Council as mayor. Apart from the routine work of the Council his main concern was the high level of unemployment in Stepney. He helped to form an association of the Labour mayors of London boroughs and became its first chairman, leading a deputation to 10 Downing Street to appeal to Lloyd George for stronger measures to deal with unemployment in London.

Attlee continued, as an alderman, to be active in the affairs of Stepney until 1927. But marriage in 1922, the purchase of a house in an Essex suburb, and election as an MP brought to an end the years of absorption in the life of the East End. His main role became that of representing Stepney on many of the organizations set up to co-ordinate the work of the London borough councils; for some years he served as vice-president of the Municipal Electricity Authorities of Greater London.

When he was elected to the House of Commons in 1922 Attlee gave up his post at the London School of Economics and became, in effect, a full-time politician. His constituency, Limehouse, was one of the few safe Labour seats outside the mining districts. It was a fitting reward for all that he had done in the East End since 1907. Elsewhere, he was virtually unknown. Platform oratory was the route to reputation in the Labour Party and he had little talent for it.

He did, however, have some long-run advantages over the other middle-class and professional men who became Labour MPs in the elections of 1922 and 1923. His experience of working-class life was both extensive and first-hand and he had started at the bottom of the Labour movement. He had already begun to show, too, unusual effectiveness at the hard slog of committee work. His views were well to the left of his party's official policy. He was a member of a small 'ginger group' in the ILP in company with A. Fenner (later Lord) Brockway and R. Clifford Allen (later Lord Allen of Hurtwood, q.v.), and also attracted by the guild socialism advocated by G. D. H. Cole [q.v.].

Ramsay MacDonald was elected leader of the Labour Party after the election of 1922 and invited Attlee to be one of his parliamentary private secretaries. But the Parliament was short-lived. Stanley Baldwin (later Earl Baldwin of Bewdley) decided to seek a mandate for tariff reform and went to the country at the end of 1923. The upshot was a minority Labour Government which held office for ten uneasy months. Attlee served as under-secretary of state for war, under Stephen Walsh [q.v.], a post which he found congenial.

Back in opposition, Attlee's contribution was largely confined to putting his party's case on the Electricity Bill (1926) and a Rating and Valuation Bill (1925) which was one of Neville Chamberlain's key reforms as minister of health. Attlee's growing reputation for competence at the detailed work of committees must have played some part in MacDonald's invitation in 1927 to serve as one of the two Labour members on a statutory commission for India, chaired by Sir John (later Viscount) Simon [q.v.]. For the next two years Attlee devoted himself to the political problems of India. The commission met considerable obstruction on its two visits to India and its report in 1930 was rejected by the leaders of the Congress and denigrated by their supporters in the Labour Party. Attlee himself always defended the commission's proposals for an extension of self-government in the provinces as going as far as was realistic at the time. Certainly his service on the Simon commission gave him a valuable insight into the problems of India.

After the election of 1929 MacDonald broke a promise that serving on the Simon commission would not affect Attlee's chance of a post in the event of Labour coming to power. His opportunity did not come until the spring of 1930 when Sir Oswald Mosley resigned from the chancellorship of the Duchy of Lancaster. Attlee succeeded him but with a considerably reduced brief. He assisted Addison with his Agricultural Marketing Bill, one of the Government's few parliamentary successes, and wrote a major memorandum on 'The Problems of British Industry' which, although it went unheeded by the Cabinet, was the first indication of his ability to analyse a problem and distil a course of action. In March 1931 Attlee was transferred to the Post Office which had gone to seed under Sir G. E. P. Murray [q.v.], who had ruled it with an autocratic hand since 1914. Attlee set to with a will and inaugurated a number of reforms, the benefits of which largely accrued to Sir H. Kingsley Wood [q.v.] in the succeeding Government.

He was on holiday with his family in August 1931 when he was summoned to Downing Street and told, with the other non-Cabinet ministers, that the Labour Government was at an end and that MacDonald was forming a coalition Government. Attlee was never in any doubt about his own course of action in spite of his past association with MacDonald and a growing reputation for being not only middle-class but also middle-of-the-road. He had become increasingly disillusioned with MacDonald since joining the Government but the reasons for his staying with the Labour Party lay deeper, in the strength of his personal beliefs and his roots in the movement. He never changed his view that MacDonald had perpetrated 'the greatest betrayal in the political history of the country'.

Attlee survived the landslide of the 1931 election but with a majority at Limehouse of only 551. Labour, including the rump of the ILP, was reduced to 52 members. George Lansbury [q.v.], the sole survivor of those who had sat in Cabinet, was elected leader of the parliamentary party and Attlee became his deputy. Sir R. Stafford-Cripps [q.v.] completed a triumvirate; although solicitor-general in the Labour Government he had been in the Commons for little more than a year. The team of three worked harmoniously. Cripps provided the driving force and for a time Attlee was' considerably influenced by him. But as Cripps moved further to the left, neither his views nor his crusade against Transport House were to Attlee's liking. Attlee was the last man to wish to split the Labour Party and his own ideas about policy were becoming increasingly balanced and eclectic. He expressed them in *The Will and the Way to Socialism* published shortly before the election of 1935.

The years from 1931 to 1935 were the making of Attlee. He was no longer confined to occasional parliamentary speeches on specialist topics but, as deputy leader, was called upon to cover the whole range of debate. In 1932 he filled more columns of *Hansard* than any other member and led the party for several months in 1934 when Lansbury fell ill. His own parliamentary style was steadily developing. His speeches lacked flourish to the point of being laconic but they were thorough and spiced with an occasional waspish sting. But none of this was enough to suggest that he was a potential leader of the party.

Lansbury resigned the leadership after his defeat at the Brighton conference in October 1935, a bare three weeks before the start of the election campaign. The parliamentary party had little choice but to appoint Attlee as leader. The *Manchester Guardian* reflected universal opinion; it observed, 'This is hardly more than an interim appointment'. Attlee worked hard in the campaign but made little personal impact on the electorate and the result, 154 seats to Labour, was a disappointment. In the contest for the leadership that followed the election the loyalty of his old colleagues, particularly the miners, from the previous Parliament and his reputation for rectitude were enough to ensure the defeat of Herbert Morrison (later Lord Morrison of Lambeth) and Arthur Greenwood [qq.v.], his rivals for the leadership. Even his modesty helped, for his approach to the tasks of leadership was the antithesis of the style which MacDonald had made suspect.

There was a full testing of Attlee in the years that followed. Few leaders have had a more difficult baptism. The Labour Party struggled to cope with its own divisions in the face of Hitler's challenge to the country's security and the seeming impregnability of the 'national' Government. Attlee largely concentrated on his role in Parliament. He recognized that he had no talent for the more flambouyant arts of leader-

ship in opposition and that the constitution of the Labour Party provided little scope for the imposition of his views on others. In so far as he gave a lead it was, as he said, 'from slightly left of centre'.

With political passions running high his gift, as Dalton noted, was that he 'lowered the temperature'. This low-key approach was denounced as colourless and uninspiring by the militants of both Left and Right in the party. Nor did it make Attlee appear to the electorate at large as being of the stuff of which prime ministers are made. But if he did not inspire the Labour Party, he did nothing to divide it and it was this preservation of Labour's fragile unity which made it possible to seize the opportunity of 1940.

Attlee's approach stemmed from his deep understanding of the Labour Party as a loose alliance of divergent views and interests. He was fortunate in one respect. The shock of 1931 and the depth of the economic depression combined to remove most of the ambiguities that had characterized the party's domestic programme in the MacDonald era. By 1935 the Labour Party was firmly pledged to policies of socialist planning and public ownership. This measure of agreement was, however, obscured by a more fundamental debate, stirred by the political and economic crisis of the thirties, in which the defenders of parliamentary democracy came under increasingly heavy Marxist fire.

Attlee put his own views in *The Labour Party in Perspective* which he was invited to write for the Left Book Club in 1937. His intention, he wrote in the introduction, was 'to show the Labour Party in its historical setting as an expression in place and time of the urge for socialism, to show it as a characteristic example of British methods and as an outcome of British political instincts'. This belief in parliamentary institutions and the traditional ways of government was also exemplified in his support for Stanley Baldwin, for whom he had a lasting admiration, during the abdication crisis. They found themselves of one mind on the issue. Nor did Attlee doubt that he was expressing the views of the ordinary supporters of the Labour Party although not, as he noted later, 'of a few of the intelligentsia who can be trusted to take the wrong view on any subject'.

But as Germany grew more menacing, domestic questions gave way to the problem of how the challenge was to be met. Chamberlain, who became prime minister in May 1937, quickly dispelled the hesitations of the Baldwin Government by a forceful combination of policies of positive appeasement and moderate rearmament. The Labour Party found if difficult to make a coherent response. It had previously paid little attention to foreign policy. The split in World War I had been healed with the slogan, 'No more war' and the pull of the pacifists remained powerful. In May 1935 Attlee stated views to which the majority of Labour Party members would have subscribed: 'We stand for Collective Security through the League of Nations. We reject the use of force as an instrument of policy. We stand for the reduction of armaments and pooled security . . . Our policy is not one of seeking security through rearmament but through disarmament.' These policies of disarmament and collective security, tinged with pacifism, were slowly abandoned under the pressure of events. The occupation of the Rhineland, the Spanish civil war, and the Anschluss added substance to the arguments which Ernest Bevin [q.v.] and Dalton, in particular, had been advancing since Hitler's early days in power. Attlee himself denounced Chamberlain with vigour. When (Sir) Anthony Eden (later the Earl of Avon) resigned from the Foreign Office in February 1938 Attlee argued that the Government's policy was one of 'abject surrender to the dictators'. He attacked the Munich agreement as 'a tremendous victory for Herr Hitler' and pressed Chamberlain hard in the summer of 1939 to come to terms with the Soviet Union.

The key issue, however, was rearmament. In July 1937 the Parliamentary Labour Party finally decided to abandon its traditional vote against the defence estimates and to confine itself to abstention. Attlee voted against the change. It was not until after Munich that he began to accept the case for rearmament and when Chamberlain announced the introduction of conscription for military service in April 1939 Attlee attacked the measure as useless and divisive.

The Labour Party was so divided in its views that Attlee, as leader, was in a difficult position. Urged on by Bevin, the leaders of the unions were able to ensure, after 1937, that the official line was in support of rearmament. But the main movement of opinion among the rank and file was sharply to the left and looked to the Soviet Union for salvation. The middle path followed by Attlee sprang as much from conviction as from his conception of his role as leader. The conclusions that he had arrived at after World War I were not readily discarded and his hostility to Chamberlain and his policies ran deep. In later years Attlee came close to admitting that the Labour Party had been in blinkers. His own comment on the vote against conscription is perhaps the best epitaph: 'Well, it probably wasn't awfully wise.'

Attlee was ill when war broke out. Two operations for prostate trouble kept him out of action for several months and Arthur Greenwood took over the leadership. It was not until the fiasco of the Norwegian campaign in April 1940 that the opportunity arose to topple Chamberlain.

After the debate on 7 and 8 May 1940 it was evident that he could not carry on without Labour support. When Attlee and Greenwood saw Chamberlain on 9 May, Attlee said that he would put two questions to the Labour National Executive Committee: (1) Are you prepared to serve under Chamberlain? (2) Are you prepared to serve under someone else? He telephoned the replies on the following afternoon: 'The answer to the first question is, no. To the second question, yes.' Chamberlain resigned within the hour. Churchill was summoned to the Palace and during the night he and Attlee agreed on the distribution of posts in a coalition government.

Attlee served in the War Cabinet as lord privy seal until February 1942. He then became secretary for the Dominions and, from September 1943, lord president of the Council. He was also deputy prime minister, at first *de facto*, but, from February 1942, with the formal title. At the highest level the war was run by the War Cabinet and two subsidiary bodies; military matters were dealt with by the Defence Committee, civil by the Lord President's Committee. Attlee alone served on all three bodies and did so for the life of the Government. But although he played his part on the Defence Committee, his main responsibility lay on the civil side where, by 1944, he was very much the committee workhorse of the coalition. Most of the key committees were chaired by him and by the end of the war he had earned a high reputation for the efficient and business-like dispatch of business.

The day-to-day care of Government business in the House of Commons also fell mainly on Attlee and as deputy prime minister he took the chair at the War Cabinet and the Defence Committee when Churchill was absent from the country, as he increasingly was during the last two years of the war. These arrangements rested on a confidence and trust that lay at the heart of the coalition's high degree of harmony. Attlee's loyalty to Churchill never wavered for an instant, even in the dark days of 1941 and 1942.

From his central position in the machinery of government, Attlee was called upon to preside over much of the discussion of social reform that not only made the coalition one of the most considerable of all reforming governments but led to a consensus of view between the two parties and laid the framework for much of the work of Attlee's own administration. The war was fought on the home front with the weapons of economic control and social amelioration advocated by the Labour Party and it was evident by the end of 1943 that peace would bring further reforms: the implementation of the report of the committee on social insurance and allied services chaired by Sir W. H. (later Lord) Beveridge [q.v.], the establishment of a National Health Service, and the carrying out of economic policies aimed at full employment.

Attlee was well suited by temperament and experience to soothe such strains as these great changes brought to the coalition. In backing proposals for reform he eschewed the socialist arguments and socialist labels which would have antagonized his Tory colleagues. The case was put in terms of national unity and what was needed to win the war. But it was not easy for Attlee to avoid offending Tories without outraging many of his own supporters who wished Labour to use its leverage in the coalition for more socialist purposes. Attlee's reply was that 'we cannot dictate to others the acceptance of our Socialist programme', but this realism was usually tempered with emphasis on how much had been gained by participation: 'The acceptance', as he said at West Hartlepool in January 1944, 'of so much of what our party has preached in the last thirty years.'

Attlee's wider responsibilities included the chairmanship of the committee on India and of committees dealing with the details of the post-war settlement in Europe. He opposed the Morgenthau plan to destroy Germany's industrial capacity although convinced of the need to enforce fundamental changes in its economic and social structure. He found himself very much in sympathy with Eden on more general questions and they combined on occasion to restrain Churchill, particularly when they thought him too influenced by Roosevelt. But the disagreements were minor and the bi-partisan policy of the post-war years was forged during the coalition. No member of the Government was more hostile to Stalin than Attlee and he fully agreed with Churchill that long-term American participation in the peace settlement and the maintenance of the British Commonwealth were essential to counter the Russians and ensure stability.

Attlee's record during the war earned him little public reputation compared, for example, with Bevin and Morrison whose departments covered much of the home front. Within Whitehall, however, his standing grew as a chairman and conciliator of unusual quality. Churchill and he made an effective combination, of leader and chairman, which echoed that of Lloyd George and Bonar Law in the previous war. It also became increasingly clear that Attlee could not be lightly crossed; he could be devastating in his criticisms and his judgement,

if sparsely offered, lacked neither crispness nor authority. It was an appreciation of these qualities, as he had seen them emerge during the war, that led Bevin to compare Attlee with Campbell-Bannerman as possessing 'that gift of character which enabled him to hold a team of clever men together'.

One of his Tory colleagues in the War Cabinet said subsequently that he could not remember Attlee 'ever making a point which I felt came from him as leader of the Labour Party' as distinct from his pressing for improvements in the lot of the working class and for effective preparation for the post-war period. It was this non-partisan approach to the coalition which led Aneurin Bevan [q.v.] to accuse Attlee of bringing 'to the fierce struggle of politics the tepid enthusiasm of a lazy summer afternoon at a cricket match'. Attlee's own view was that his biggest achievement had been 'to take a party intact into a coalition, to keep it intact for five years and to bring it out intact'.

In May 1945 Attlee accompanied Eden to the foundation conference of the United Nations in San Francisco. The prospect of a general election forced them to return early, but, on his way back, Attlee was able to meet Truman and found to his pleasure that they 'talked the same language'.

Churchill and Attlee would have preferred to continue the coalition until Japan had been defeated but opinion in both parties, especially on the Labour side, was in favour of a quick end. Churchill formed a caretaker Government and a general election followed immediately.

During the campaign Attlee established himself for the first time in the public eye. His broadcast in reply to Churchill's 'Gestapo' speech was a model of effective restraint and his campaign, for which he was driven about by his wife in their small family car, was in telling contrast to his opponent's almost regal style. He also emerged with credit from the one testing episode of the campaign, an attempt by Churchill and Beaverbrook to take advantage of some tiresome interventions by Harold Laski [q.v.], the chairman of the Labour Party's National Executive Committee.

The result of the election, much to Attlee's surprise, was a Labour landslide with a majority over the Tories of 170. But he did not become prime minister without some exchanges in which, in Emanuel (later Lord) Shinwell's words, 'the brotherly love advocated by the movement was conspicuous by its absence'. Bevin's unwavering support ensured the defeat of a challenge by Morrison for the leadership and Attlee proceeded to form a strong and experienced Government. His first task, once the principal posts had been filled, was to return to the Potsdam conference with the new foreign secretary, Ernest Bevin.

Conservatives feared and socialists hoped that the election of 1945 presaged fundamental changes. The Labour Party's manifesto had declared, 'The Labour Party is a Socialist Party. Its ultimate aim is the establishment of the Socialist Commonwealth of Great Britain.' Attlee's own horizon was more restricted: to the implementation of the manifesto's specific proposals and the tackling of the problems which the post-war period would bring, particularly in economic policy and foreign affairs. During the war he and all his leading colleagues had participated in a gigantic exercise in planning and economic control so that, to a considerable extent, the election of 1945 signified not change but continuity. Nor, in spite of the dismay of defeat, did the Conservative Party lag far behind Labour. It was by 1945 already well on the way to embracing both the managed economy and the Welfare State. If Attlee presided over a revolution, therefore, it was, as he himself stressed, an extraordinarily quiet and peaceful revolution which had begun well before 1945 and was to lead more to consensus between the parties than to conflict.

The leading figures in the Government, Bevin, Morrison, Cripps, Dalton, and Bevan, formed an exceptionally able but difficult team, managed by Attlee with great skill. He was at his best when he could delegate substantial control of major areas of policy to ministers in whom he had complete confidence, as with Bevin at the Foreign Office and Cripps at the Treasury, and so be free to concentrate his own efforts on one or two key political problems and the general tasks of co-ordination and management. 'If you have a good dog, don't bark yourself' was a favourite Attlee proverb.

The backing of Bevin was proof against all intrigues but Attlee's authority over his principal colleagues and his more general mastery of the Cabinet sprang from his own qualities. He was a good judge of men and adept at managing them, rarely allowing his judgement to be clouded by personal prejudice. His integrity was accepted as being beyond question.

From the beginning Attlee succeeded in enforcing his own style on the working of his Government. He put high value on the bureaucratic virtues of formality, order, and regularity and in structure and method the Government conformed to them to an unusual degree. His own strong preference was for working through paper. Even at the highest level the circulation of boxes was the medium by which the work of the Attlee Government was mainly done. There was little of the informal and speculative discussion typical of Churchill's methods. The same

puritanical concentration on the matter in hand characterized Attlee's running of the Cabinet and its committees. As he later remarked, 'I was always for getting on with the job.' Some indulgence was shown to senior ministers but short shrift was usually dealt out to anyone who had failed to master his brief or who attempted to read it. In summing up Attlee was invariably precise and succinct. Otherwise he said little and rarely took a vote. His aim was to make the Cabinet and its committees efficient machines for the dispatch of well-prepared business and to cut to the minimum their tendency to become talking shops.

The main defect of such methods was that Attlee remained remote from his party and the general public, and even from ministers who were not privy to the inner circle. The impression that he gave of a Victorian headmaster keeping his school under strict control was compounded by an inability to participate in the complimentary small-talk of politics, a consequence doubtless of his innate shyness. His considerable kindliness was invariably expressed by letter.

'The little man', as Bevin affectionately called him, had few of the attributes normally looked for in a political leader but this was of little significance while Bevin was attempting to forge a Western alliance or Cripps was embarking on his austere crusade. But when ill health compelled them to resign and Morrison proved a palpable failure at the Foreign Office, it was beyond Attlee's power to fill the gap. The Labour Party respected him to an unsurpassed degree but could not rise to him. Nor had he the gift, possessed by Bevin and Cripps, of rallying those outside the ranks of his own party even though his lack of partisan spite and devotion to the broad national interest came to be increasingly recognized. But as a catalyst among politicians engaged in the business of government Attlee has few rivals.

In domestic politics the first eighteen months or so of his office were almost untarnished honeymoon. The Opposition showed few signs of recovery and major legislation poured from Parliament at an unprecedented rate. Attlee was determined to push ahead and by the end of 1946, an *annus mirabilis*, acts had been passed nationalizing the Bank of England, the coal industry, civil aviation, and Cable and Wireless; there had also been a National Insurance Act, a New Towns Act, a Trade Disputes Act, an Act for the establishment of a National Health Service, and a host of minor measures. The legislation remains as a permanent memorial. It was passed in a period of optimism in politics and cheap money in the economy. The Japanese war ended with unexpected speed, taxation was cut, demobilization went smoothly with none of the unemployment that had been feared, and industry was turning over to peacetime production with remarkably little friction. The Welfare State was in an advanced state of construction and the nation was still proud of its rationing system and its sense of social discipline.

At this stage there was little public consciousness that there would be tight physical constraints on what could be done. J. M. (later lord) Keynes [q.v.], for example, wrote to Dalton about the latter's National Land Fund to say that he should have 'acquired for the nation all the coastline round the island at one stroke'. It was a time when anything seemed possible.

Attlee did not share this euphoria. He was shocked by the sudden ending of Lend-Lease in August 1945 and, while adamant that there was no alternative but to accept the terms on which the American loan was subsequently made, knew that the most severe difficulties would be likely to arise from the requirement to make sterling convertible within a year of the commencement of the loan.

In foreign affairs events at first appeared to match the fears that Churchill and Attlee had shared in the last months of the war. Stalin cemented his hold on Eastern Europe and was obstructive in Germany. Large Communist parties in France and Italy awaited his bidding. It was, however, the uncertainty engendered by American policy which most disturbed the Government.

Attlee did not doubt Truman's own goodwill but the negotiation of the loan and the passing of the McMahon Act by Congress in 1946 were jolting experiences and the American reaction to Russia seemed ambivalent and at times naïve. Relations between the two countries were further strained by Bevin's policy in Palestine, fully backed by Attlee, which American opinion thought pro-Arab and anti-Zionist.

A transformation of American policy began with the arrival of General Marshall at the State Department in January 1947. The Truman Doctrine which secured aid to Greece and Turkey, previously British responsibilities, was declared in March. A year later the Marshall Plan was launched and followed in 1949 by the setting up of the North Atlantic Treaty Organization. Together they ensured the economic recovery and political security of Western Europe. If the main influence bringing about the change was the effect of Stalin's obduracy on American opinion, the patient persuasion of Bevin and Attlee should not be discounted. In a relationship which Attlee called 'the closest of my political life' they were of one mind on the necessity of involving the United States in the defence of Western Europe.

Attlee's own most important contribution, and one with which his name will always be associated, was, however, the granting of independence to India. He acted in effect as his own secretary of state and all the major decisions bear his unmistakable stamp. He began with the intention of modifying the plan which Cripps had proposed to the Indians in 1942 but the failure of the Cabinet mission in 1946 convinced him of the need to take full account of the strength of the Muslim League and its determination to establish Pakistan. Viscount (later Earl) Wavell [q.v.], who had been viceroy since 1943, was dismissed and replaced by Attlee's personal choice, Lord Louis Mountbatten, who was charged with the negotiation of independence within a time limit. The new viceroy arrived in India in March 1947 and acted with great speed and decisiveness. On the day of the declaration of Indian independence he wrote to Attlee, 'The man who made it possible was you yourself. Without your original guidance and your unwavering support nothing could have been accomplished out here.'

Attlee was also mainly responsible for the decision that Britain should manufacture her own atomic bomb. Concern at the narrowness with which American officials were interpreting the Quebec agreement for the exchange of atomic information led him to fly to Washington in November 1945. His discussions with Truman were cordial but the President was in the event unable to deliver even the little that he offered. The *coup de grâce* was delivered by Congress a few months later with the passage of the McMahon Bill. Attlee had no hesitation in deciding that Britain should make her own bomb: 'It had become essential. We had to hold up our position *vis-à-vis* the Americans. We couldn't allow ourselves to be wholly in their hands, and their position wasn't awfully clear always.' He also insisted on the maximum of secrecy. All but a few members of the Cabinet were kept in the dark, questions in Parliament discouraged, and large sums concealed in the estimates. 'The project', as Attlee put it, 'was never hampered by lack of money.'

The Government ran into its first major trouble early in 1947 when fuel supplies broke down in savage weather. For a time two and a half million men were out of work. During the following months the Cabinet was further shaken by a dispute over the nationalization of iron and steel and by an economic crisis. The nationalization of iron and steel was the only major item of the 1945 programme on which there had been no progress. Morrison, whose responsibilities included the co-ordination of economic policy, had always been lukewarm. With some encouragement from Attlee, he succeeded in negotiating an agreement with the leaders of the industry which fell well short of nationalization. But the compromise ran into trouble in the Cabinet, with Bevin, Cripps, and Dalton in opposition, and raised a storm in the party. Although Attlee took care to leave the running to Morrison, it was evident that he had made an error of judgement.

A growing exchange crisis came to a head in July when sterling became freely convertible, under the terms of the American loan. The Cabinet dithered for five weeks before suspending convertibility. His critics were confirmed in their view that Attlee, never at his best in discussions about finance, was losing his grip.

Foremost among these critics was Cripps who had some success in persuading one or two of his leading colleagues that Bevin should replace Attlee, with the latter taking the Exchequer. The attempt was doomed from the start by Bevin's response: 'What has the little man ever done to me?' But Cripps persisted. Although deserted by his fellow conspirators he went to see Attlee on 9 September. The interview began with Cripps suggesting that Attlee should give way to Bevin. It ended with Cripps agreeing to take on the new post of minister for economic affairs. Whatever the summer might have disclosed of Attlee's failings, his touch with men had not deserted him.

Dalton was compelled to resign in November as a consequence of a few indiscreet words to a journalist immediately before his budget speech. He was succeeded at the Exchequer by Cripps who thus came to dominate economic affairs and, to Attlee's immense relief, soon brought authority and purpose to domestic policy. Cripps's policies were hard and austere. Rations were, for a time, lower than they had been in the war. The housing programme was cut and the building of hospitals and roads brought almost to a halt. The bombed wastes at the centre of cities became even more derelict. But the aim was clear: to bring the balance of payments into equilibrium and, in particular, to solve the problem of the dollar shortage while maintaining the benefits which the Government had earlier secured for the working class.

Attlee was content to leave the lead to Bevin and Cripps. In foreign affairs, the early work began to bear fruit. The Organization for European Economic Co-operation was set up and the Marshall Plan implemented in 1948, so providing the underpinning for Cripps's policies. The Russian challenge at Berlin was successfully met by the Anglo-American airlift and the North Atlantic Treaty Organization was established in 1949. But the growing movement in favour of a federal Western Europe was met by Bevin with a mixture of hostility and scepticism. Attlee was of the same mind. As he later wrote, 'Britain has never regarded itself as just a European power. Her interests are world-wide. She is the heart of a great Commonwealth and tends to look outwards from Europe.'

By the end of 1949, ten years of continuous office had taken its toll of the leading members of Attlee's Government. They had all suffered bouts of serious illness and Bevin and Cripps were soon to be forced to resign. It was also evident that the Government had little to offer by way of new ideas and policies once it had exhausted the capital of the 1945 manifesto. Cripps had successfully completed the transition from a war economy by marrying Keynesian techniques of budgetary manipulation to the system of rationing and controls inherited from the Churchill coalition but it could scarcely be argued that this was more than a temporary solution to the problem of how the economy should be run.

The inevitable consequence was an intensification of the ancient dispute between the left and right wings of the Labour Party. Attlee offered no lead, took no initiative. He increasingly concentrated his energies on contriving to achieve agreement in Cabinet and became even less disposed than before to contemplate crossing his bridges before he came to them.

Nevertheless, Attlee and his colleagues approached the general election in February 1950 with some confidence in spite of having been forced to devalue sterling in the previous autumn. No other industrial country in Europe had made a comparable recovery, the promises of 1945 had been broadly kept, and the working class, in particular, had much to be greatful for. The result was a disappointment, a majority of ten for Labour. Attlee, who had represented Limehouse since 1922, stood at West Walthamstow. He remained in office although no one expected that his Government would last more than a few weeks. In the event it survived for twenty difficult months. Few governments have achieved so little, been so battered by external circumstances, or suffered so much from internal disharmony. The Korean war, which began in June 1950 and brought in its train a massive rearmament programme, inflation, and a disruption of the balance of payments, was the main catalyst of disaster. Much of the ground that had been so painfully gained during the previous three years was lost. When Attlee's Government was defeated at the polls in October 1951, it ended as it had begun, running a war economy.

The strain on Attlee was considerable. The two mainstays of his Cabinet were forced to resign after long periods of ill health, Cripps in October 1950 and Bevin in March 1951. But he enjoyed something of a Roman triumph in December 1950 when, with Bevin too ill to fly, he decided suddenly to go to Washington because of a general worry that the Americans were intending to extend the Korean war and a particular fear, based on a misunderstanding, that Truman was contemplating the use of the atomic bomb. Morrison, who took Bevin's place, was a disaster at the Foreign Office; 'the worst appointment I ever made', was Attlee's conclusion. He was of necessity drawn into direct intervention in the conduct of foreign policy and it was largely due to his steadying hand that there was such a muted response to Musaddeq's expropriation of the Anglo-Iranian Oil Company.

Hugh Gaitskell [q.v.] succeeded Cripps at the Exchequer. There was no doubt about his competence but his promotion roused the resentment of Bevan who stood high in the party and had done well as minister of health. Attlee thought highly of Bevan's talents but had always found him difficult, in respect both of temperament and opinions, and had usually tried to deal with him through an intermediary. What he now had to face was not just personal animosity between the two men but a conflict between the standard bearers of the right and left wings of the party.

Matters came to a head with the preparation of the budget in April 1951. Gaitskell was determined to impose charges for a number of services which had previously been provided free in the National Health Service. Attlee was in hospital with a duodenal ulcer and Morrison, his deputy, made little attempt to confine the resulting conflict. When Attlee returned to duty, the breach was beyond repair. Bevan, (Sir) Harold Wilson, and John Freeman had already resigned and were soon leading a wide-ranging attack on the Government's policies.

A spurious unity was patched up for the election in October but the Labour Party entered it with considerable handicaps. Attlee was its sole leader with a reputation that still counted with the electorate and he campaigned with his wife in what had become his familiar style. He lost and Churchill took office but the total Labour vote was greater than that of the Conservatives and indeed the highest achieved by any party in any election.

The size of the vote was a remarkable indication of the loyalty which the Attlee Government aroused in its supporters. Labour's straightforward mixture of social concern and sensible pragmatism, exemplified by Attlee's own views, may not have been socialist enough to satisfy the Left or been a reliable pointer to the party's future but it satisfied its supporters. The main legacies of the Attlee Government

were that it ensured the country's safety and initiated policies of welfare, full employment, and the budgetary control of the economy to such effect that Governments for the next twenty years had no alternative but to attempt to follow in its wake.

Attlee remained leader of the party for four more years. But they were years of frustration and anticlimax. In the House of Commons he continued to speak at a high level of statesmanship, particularly in support of the bipartisan policies in defence and foreign affairs of which he and Bevin had been the principal architects. But it was as leader of the Labour Party that he was judged and for much of this period the leadership was virtually in commission. The broad consensus of the 1940s had disappeared and divisions of opinion had inexorably hardened into faction. Attlee, bereft of the authority of a prime minister, found it hard to cope with the dissensions of Opposition and failed to regain his old touch with backbenchers and the rank and file of the party.

His aim, as it had been before 1939, was to hold the party together. Although unwilling to make any policy concessions to the left wing, he consistently opposed the hounding of Bevan and its other leaders which was enthusiastically led by Arthur Deakin, Bevin's successor at the Transport and General Workers' Union. But passions were too high and the division of opinion too deep for there to be a chance of more than a passing reconciliation. Attlee increasingly withdrew into silence and the anonymity of committee membership. As one of his colleagues put it, 'At the National Executive, he doodled where he should have led'.

The election of May 1955 was a dull affair. The result was a comfortable Conservative victory and it was evident that Attlee's retirement could not be long delayed. The candidates for the succession were Morrison, Bevan, and Gaitskell and by the autumn they were all in the field. But Attlee held on. The consequence, and almost certainly the intention, was that the prize went to Gaitskell. Attlee announced his retirement in a brief and unheralded speech at a regular meeting of the Parliamentary Labour Party on 7 December 1955. The Queen conferred an earldom on him; he had already been admitted to the Order of Merit in 1951.

Attlee was sworn of the privy council in 1935, was made CH in 1945, and KG in 1956. He became an honorary bencher (Inner Temple) in 1946 and FRS in 1947. He was awarded honorary degrees by many universities, and was made an honorary fellow of University College, Oxford (1942), Queen Mary College, London (1948), and LSE (1958).

Attlee's retirement was happy and busy. He travelled widely and wrote and lectured about politics with a frankness that surprised many of his former colleagues. To this Dictionary he contributed the notice of William Whiteley, Labour chief whip. His own stock rose as his virtues of integrity, fairness, and coolness in adversity came to be more widely appreciated. Even his habitual restraint and understatement, which had so often offended his supporters by making him appear remote and almost disinterested, appealed to a generation over-fed on political hyperbole.

Attlee is the leading example in modern times of a politician who achieves high office against all expectations, only then to reveal unsuspected talents. Before 1940 it was assumed that he held a short lease on the leadership of the Labour Party. Many of his colleagues still thought him unfitted for the premiership in 1945. Five years later there would have been little disagreement with Bevin's reported verdict, 'By God, he's the only man who could have kept us together'. Attlee's contribution doubtless lacked the ideas, stimulation, and flair, which are usually thought of as the stuff of leadership. He could act decisively, as he did with India, but he was in general content to wait until opinion had formed before he moved out to express it.

The qualities that made him indispensable and gained him the respect and loyalty of his colleagues were his sense of justice, his imperturbability in a crisis, his skill at the business of administration, and, above all, his adroitness in choosing and managing men. In the main, these are qualities not for opposition, but for office. They enabled Attlee to play a significant part during the war of 1939-45 and then to harness men of inherently greater ability and imagination into a team which effectively laid the foundations of post-war politics both at home and abroad.

Attlee was a solitary man but only in the sense that he had no political cronies. 'It's very dangerous', he said, 'to be the centre of a small circle.' His gregariousness was expressed in other ways. He liked formal dinners and kept in close touch with the ramified Attlee family. The fortunes of his old friends of school, university, and army were followed in *The Times*; his daily recreation was then to solve the crossword. But his wife, to whom he remained devoted until her death in 1964, and his family, provided all the ordinary company and relaxation that he needed.

He married in 1922 Violet Helen, daughter of H. E. Millar, of Hampstead. They had three daughters and a son, Martin Richard (born 1927), who succeeded his father in the earldom. Attlee died in Westminster Hospital 8 October 1967.

There are portraits of Attlee by Flora Lion (1941); Rodrigo Moynihan (1948) in the Oxford and Cambridge Universities Club; G. Harcourt (1946) in the National Portrait Gallery; Cowan Dobson (1956); Lawrence Gowing (1963); and Derek Fowler, at Haileybury. There is also a bronze presentation medallion (1953), a bronze head by David McFall (1965) in the National Portrait Gallery, and a statue by Ivor Roberts-Jones in the lobby of the House of Commons (1979).

[Attlee's own writings, principally *As It Happened*, 1954; Kenneth Harris, a biography of Attlee in draft; Francis Williams, *A Prime Minister Remembers*, 1961; *The Times*, 9 October 1964; personal knowledge.]
MAURICE SHOCK

ATTWELL, MABEL LUCIE (1879-1964), illustrator, was born in Mile End, London, 4 June 1879, the sixth child of Augustus Attwell, a butcher, of Mile End, and his wife, (Emily) Ann, daughter of George Harris, a coach builder. She was educated privately and at the Coopers' Company School, where she showed a bent for art. She later attended classes at Regent Street and Heatherley's art schools, but disliked the heavy emphasis placed on still-life drawing and copying classical casts and she did not remain there long. Her preference lay in making sketches and drawings of imaginary subjects, arising out of her enjoyment of fairy stories, and it was through these that she came to be known. The acceptance of drawings for publication in such magazines as the *Tatler* and the *Bystander* led her to show her work to the agents Francis & Mills, and although they held out little hope of success they found that her sketches sold readily at twenty guineas each. From that time on, almost to the end of her life, they played an important part in gaining commissions for her and encouraging her to apply her art to a variety of purposes.

In 1908 Mabel Lucie Attwell married the painter and illustrator Harold Earnshaw (died 1937) by whom she had a daughter in 1909 and two sons in 1911 and 1914. One of her sons died in 1935. The appearance of one, two, or three of these children in drawings on the preliminary pages of her early illustrated gift-books can serve as a rough guide to the sequence of publication of volumes which are always undated. During the war of 1914-18 Harold Earnshaw was badly wounded, losing his right arm, and much of the task of running family and business affairs thus devolved upon his wife. It was a responsibility which accorded well with her temperament, for this handsome woman was strong-willed and dedicated to her work, and she continued to develop and exploit an illustrative mode which brought her national fame. She had few interests outside her pre-occupation with her family and her work, and she remained active as an artist to the end of her life.

Mabel Lucie Attwell's career as an illustrator began with work done for magazines, which was always to be her stand-by. Around the turn of the century, however, she started to receive commissions from the publishing firm of W. & R. Chambers and this led her into the field of book illustration. Initially she provided colour designs for trade bindings (for example, in M. Howitt, *The Steadfast Gabriel, c.* 1900) and sets of monochrome plates for children's stories (for example, in May Baldwin, *That Little Limb*, 1905). Before long, however, she was asked to undertake more ambitious work for the 'Raphael House Library of Gift Books', published by Messrs Raphael Tuck. Her earliest volumes in the series were *Mother Goose* (*c.* 1909) and *Alice in Wonderland* (1910). In these books she was required to provide line drawings printed in the text and colour work for twelve full-page halftone plates, a formula which was followed in later additions to the series: *Hans Andersen's Fairy Tales* (1913), an abridged *The Water Babies* (1915), *Children's Stories from French Fairy Tales* by Doris Ashley (1917), and *Grimms Fairy Tales* (1925).

Her illustrations for these gift-books won the admiration of Queen Mary of Romania, a prolific writer (in English) of books and short stories for children. In 1922 Mabel Lucie Attwell was invited to spend several weeks at the royal palace in Bucharest, and she also illustrated two long stories by the Queen which were published in a large gift-book format: *Peeping Pansy* (1919) and *The Lost Princess* (1924). The publisher of these, Messrs Hodder & Stoughton, also commissioned a set of illustrations for Sir J. M. Barrie's *Peter Pan and Wendy*, which was issued in a gift-book edition in 1921 and remained in print in various less ornate styles of production until the 1970s.

Almost all Mabel Lucie Attwell's early book illustration was derivative. The early work for Chambers echoed that of Hilda Cowham (a personal friend) and Jessie Willcox Smith, and the gift-book illustrations were modelled on the work of other contemporary exponents of that genre: John Hassall and the brothers Charles and William Heath Robinson [qq.v.]. A poster which she designed for London Transport, and which may be numbered among the first of their very successful 'Travel by Underground' series (*c.* 1918) owes a considerable debt to the work of John Hassall.

Perhaps the most successful book of her whole career—the 1910 *Alice*—is the one in which she was able to combine the linear strength of such artists with her own feeling for child gesture and homely detail, but before long she began to exploit the latter in a way which, while leading to wide commercial success, was at the cost of compositional values and the integrity of illustration and text to be illustrated. In such books as *The Water Babies*, *Peter Pan*, and *Grimms Fairy Tales* the graphic design was weakened through the introduction of too many extraneous elves and gauzy fairies, while the content of the portraiture in the pictures often ran counter to the intentions of the text.

At the heart of this decline in the character of her book illustrations lay Mabel Lucie Attwell's growing reputation as an artist who could gratify adult susceptibilities towards the 'cuteness' of children. Rotund and cuddly infants had appeared in her early gift-books, but they were also to be found in her magazine illustrations and in the long series of picture postcards which she designed for Messrs Valentine & Sons of Dundee from about 1914 onwards. Here she met the needs of a period when childhood was widely sentimentalized (as shown by the success of other artists like Margaret Tarrant, and writers like Marion St. John Webb), and during the 1920s and 1930s Mabel Lucie Attwell children were ubiquitous. They figured on all kinds of nursery equipment, from calendars and nursury pictures to crockery and Chad Valley dolls, which were made from models which Miss Attwell prepared in plasticine. They appeared regularly in the *Lucie Attwell Annual*, which ran from 1922 to 1974— and the fact that this serial continued for ten years after her death shows how her stories or pictures might be reused. From 1924 a complex series of 'Lucie Attwell Picture Books', and books like the *Lucie Attwell Rainy Day Tales* (1931), were published, where previously published tales and pictures might be 'bulked' (that is, selected promiscuously from the annuals or from other picture books and reproduced as they first appeared, or even with the pictures in reduced sizes or uncoloured, as in *Lucie Attwell's Great Big Midget Book*, 1934). Play books such as the doll-dressing album *Peggy* (1921) and painting books (1934 onwards) were also published.

Probably the happiest form in which Mabel Lucie Attwell's distinctive child pictures are to be found, is in individual pictures in some of her annuals, and in her postcards, where the opportunity for cartoonist's wit, or even for self-parody, gives life to the subject. However, her delicate drawing in line and water-colour was often sadly coarsened by mass-production printing methods. Like Kate Greenaway [q.v.] before her, she also exerted a considerable influence in adult reactions to children, which was not just to be found in her idealization of childhood as a time of dimpled, if cheeky, innocence, but also—for small girls anyway—in her creation, rather than reflection, of new fashions in dress and in the bobbing of hair. There was a centenary exhibition in her honour at the Brighton Museum, December 1979–January 1980. She died at her home at Fowey, Cornwall, 5 November 1964. Her business was carried on by her daughter, who had helped her in her later years and is herself a talented portrait artist. Portraits by her grandson, Mark Wickham, and her daughter, Peggy (c. 1930 are in the possession of the family.

[*The Times*, 14 November 1964; private information.]   BRIAN ALDERSON

AYLWARD, GLADYS MAY (1902–1970), missionary, was born 24 February 1902 in Edmonton, Middlesex, the eldest of the three children of Thomas John Aylward, postman, and his wife, Rosina Florence Whiskin, daughter of a surgical bootmaker. After receiving an elementary education, at the age of fourteen she became a shopgirl, then a children's nanny, settling finally to be a parlourmaid. She was efficient and pleasant, liked frequent moves, and served in several well-known households in the West End of London.

Her father, who had been vicar's warden of St. Aldhelm's Church, Edmonton, had joined a near-by gospel mission when Gladys was nine; the Aylwards were brought up as active Christians, and in London a youth movement soon absorbed her free evenings to the exclusion of an earlier interest in the stage. In December 1929 she was accepted for missionary training by the China Inland Mission, which had been founded in 1865, partly to provide opportunity for men and women of strong faith but indifferent education; however, she was soon rejected as a willing yet hopeless student. Still intent on China, Gladys Aylward worked in the slums of Bristol and Swansea until she nearly died of double pneumonia. Back in Edmonton for convalescence, depressed by her failure to reach China, she went reluctantly with her mother to a Primitive Methodist meeting at Wood Green. Here she heard that a widowed Mrs Jeannie Lawson, an elderly member of a small independent mission in North China, needed a helper who must find her own way out.

Gladys Aylward returned home that evening a different woman. She became a parlourmaid again to save money for the cheapest fare, by Trans-Siberian railway. In an incident, afterwards made famous on film, she sat in an attic room in the South Kensington home of the daughter of Sir Francis Younghusband [q.v.] and put her few coppers on the bed and prayed: 'Oh God! Here's me. Here's my Bible, here's my money! Use us, God! Use us!'

On 15 October 1932 she left Liverpool Street station for China. She needed all her Cockney wit and pluck to survive the passage through the Soviet Union, and reached North China via Japan to join Mrs Lawson, a prickly, unpredictable Scot, in the country town of Yangsheng, Shansi province.

They opened an inn for muleteers as a means of evangelism. There Gladys Aylward learned Chinese by ear rather than by book. After her patron's death the mandarin made her inspector of feet, in the campaign against female footbinding, a post which gave her openings everywhere. With her tiny size (she was but five feet tall) and very dark brown hair, her humour and entire lack of colour or cultural prejudice, she became a greatly loved and masterly story-teller of simple Christianity: the Jesus of Gladys Aylward was real and alive, to be talked to and consulted at every turn.

Known as 'Ai Weh-te'—the nearest the Chinese could get to 'Aylward' and which meant, felicitously, 'the virtuous one', she became a Chinese citizen in 1936. Her best-known exploit, during the Japanese war, was in 1940 to lead a hundred children through hardships and dangers to safety across the Yellow River. At Fufeng she fell dangerously ill, and on partial recovery worked as a Bible-woman and among lepers. In 1949 she was given passage money and returned to England after seventeen years.

Gladys Aylward, whose adventures and achievements in China could be equalled by other missionaries, might have remained unknown had not her mother alerted Hugh Redwood, the celebrated religious journalist, who sent reporters to meet her. This led a BBC writer, Alan Burgess, to contact Gladys Aylward and dramatize her story on radio. In 1952 a publisher heard a report and suggested that Burgess should write a popular biography. His fictionalized *The Small Woman* (1957) became a bestseller and later a memorable and moving film, *The Inn of the Sixth Happiness* (1959). This she tried to stop and refused to see, because of the fictional love interest and her portrayal by a divorcee, Ingrid Bergmann.

Book and film together made her eminent, the archetype of the selfless, dedicated woman of faith, brushing away hardships and danger as she had once brushed crumbs from her employer's tables. Gladys Aylward, more than many of her generation, brought the Christian missionary ideal before the general public.

Her last twelve years, apart from speaking tours, were spent in Taiwan. There her trusting nature made her the victim of embezzlement by the husband of an adopted daughter who helped her run an orphanage. She saved him from execution but attracted much unpopularity for putting temptation in his way. None the less, she lived it down, still the same uninhibited woman, intensely concerned about the poor and sinful, making Christianity vividly alive, with complete contempt for all she thought was wrong.

Gladys Aylward died in Taipei after a few hours' illness, 1 January 1970. The Chinese buried her in a marble tomb in the hilltop garden of Christ's College, Tamshui, overlooking the estuary and facing mainland China. There are no portraits or busts.

[Alan Burgess, *The Small Woman*, 1957, revised edition 1971; Phyllis Thompson, *A London Sparrow*, 1971; *Gladys Aylward, Her Personal Story, as told to Christine Hunter*, 1970; private information.]

JOHN POLLOCK

B

BACHARACH, ALFRED LOUIS (1891-1966), food scientist, publicist, and musician, was born in Hampstead, London, 11 August 1891, the son of Otto Leonhard Bacharach, a businessman, of Hampstead, and his wife, Alice Eva Wagner. He lived for the remainder of his life in Hampstead. Bacharach was educated at St. Paul's School, where he was a foundation scholar, and at Clare College, Cambridge, where he gained a second class in part i (1911) and a third class in part ii (1913) of the natural sciences tripos. It was at Cambridge that the first of his interests became apparent: an intellectual commitment to left-wing political views. He involved himself with the Independent Labour Party, joined the Fabian Society, and developed a concern that continued for nearly forty years with the affairs of the Working Men's College in North London. His commitment to socialist ideas was recognized during the tenure of the Labour Government of 1924 by his appointment to the controlling bodies of a number of educational establishments including the Borough Polytechnic and Kynaston School. However, although he was deeply concerned with political theory and widely admired for his intellectual stature in this field, this was only one of his interests. Many of those with whom his other activities brought him into contact were only dimly aware of his enthusiasm for socialism. The second thread of which the fabric of his life was woven was music. He himself was an accomplished pianist and he gathered other musicians about him to play and talk. Out of this came the four books for which, as editor and author, his name became widely known. *The Musical Companion*, of which there was also a later edition, was first published in 1934, *Lives of the Great Composers* in 1935, *British Music of our Time* in 1946, and *The Music Masters* appeared in instalments between 1948 and 1954. Thus, in another field, Bacharach built for himself a considerable reputation as a knowledgeable connoisseur of music, an aspect of his life of which many of his political friends, and more of his scientific colleagues, were virtually unaware.

On leaving university in 1915 Bacharach worked for three years in the Wellcome Chemical Research Laboratories and then, for a further year, in the Wellcome Chemical Works. In 1920 he was employed by the firm of Joseph Nathan & Co. Ltd., later to become the Glaxo Laboratories, where he remained for thirty-five years. In 1920 there were problems with artificial baby-foods: even when dried cow's milk, which was imported from New Zealand, was mixed with other ingredients in order to make it resemble human milk as closely as possible, it was not uniformly satisfactory as an artificial substitute There was, for example, the danger of rickets, caused by a lack of vitamin D. Bacharach threw himself into the study of that vitamin, one form of which, as was demonstrated by research, could be manufactured by irradiation. Bacharach attacked the problem of measuring the amount of the vitamin present both in concentrated preparations and in the mixtures in which the concentrates were incorporated. At that time the only way to do this was to administer the test substance to young rachitic rats and examine the degree to which their rickets were ameliorated. Bacharach was among the first to apply rigorous statistical techniques to improve the precision of such assays. He also introduced, at least in British practice, the use of pure-bred rats in the tests.

Without being a profound scientific thinker, any more than he was a great musician or a major political figure, Bacharach was a keen observer of the passing scene and an expert commentator. His agile mind was at its most sparkling in discussion, suggestion, and debate. Whether it was on the council of the Royal Institute of Chemistry, of which he became a fellow and a vice-president, as chairman of the Food Group of the Society of Chemical Industry, as a member of the Chemical Council or of the council of the Society of Analytical Chemistry, or as president of the Nutrition Society which he played a part in founding and of which he was the first honorary treasurer, Bacharach could be found debating and discussing, stimulating more pedestrian colleagues to delight, despair, admiration, or exasperation. He was invariably urbane, never dull, often the catalyst bringing about the collision of ideas from which something new emerged. In 1938 he published *Science and Nutrition*; in 1941, jointly with F. A. Robinson, he produced an English translation of Lazlo Zechmeister's *Principles and Practice of Chromatography;* and in 1946 he edited *The Nation's Food*.

There was yet a fourth strand in Bacharach's disparate interests—the complement to his virtuosity as a talker. This was his passion for words and the grammatical rules which he belived should apply to them. Scientific writers, as much as any other people, may from time to time benefit if their attention is drawn to syntactical order. And so unflaggingly (and in violet ink) Bacharach dealt out deserved, and good-humoured, reproof. In his later years he would visit outlying branches of the learned scientific societies to which he belonged and deliver his lecture, 'Writing Wrongs', the principles of which guided his actions while meting out his judgements as a member of their publications committees. In 1950 he ceased to control the nutritional laboratories at Glaxo and, as head of the Publicity Services Group, corrected the grammar and improved the sense of the written words of the firm.

There are some scientists who advance knowledge by working silently in their laboratories, there are others who found businesses or build machines. Bacharach was more than a man of science, he was an outstandingly eclectic man of his time. His major contribution was to make his contemporaries think.

In 1931 he married Elizabeth Owen and they had two sons. He died at his home in Hampstead 16 July 1966.

[*The Times*, 18, 21, and 29 July 1966; *Chemistry and Industry*, October 1966; personal knowledge.]   MAGNUS PYKE

BAILEY, SIR EDWARD BATTERSBY (1881-1965), geologist, was born in Marsden, Kent, 1 July 1881, the third of six sons of James Battersby Bailey, a medical practitioner, and his wife, Louise Florence, daughter of Isaac Carr, a Cumberland farmer. One of the best-known and colourful geologists of his time, he excelled in unravelling the geological complexities of the Grampian Mountains.

He went to Kendal Grammar School and by open scholarship from there to Clare College, Cambridge. He gained first class honours in both parts i (1901) and ii (1902, geology and physics) of the natural sciences tripos and gained the Harkness scholarship (1902). His subsequent career covered four periods. From 1902 to 1929 he was a field geologist with the Scottish branch of the Geological Survey of Great Britain. This period was interrupted by service with the Royal Garrison Artillery. Twice wounded in France, losing his left eye and much use of his left arm, he was awarded the MC and the French croix de guerre with palms; also he was made a chevalier of the Legion of Honour, and retired from the army with the rank of lieutenant. The second period (1929-37) saw him professor of geology in Glasgow University. Then came eight years as director of the Geological Survey of Great Britain and the Museum of Practical Geology. In retirement he was still actively involved with geological pursuits.

He had joined the Geological Survey enthusiastically; he wrote that he was 'among a jostling crowd of problems awaiting solution'. His studies of igneous rocks in the Scottish Lowlands soon identified him as a skilled interpreter of the composition and history of ancient volcanoes. He enjoyed writing, and

with C. T. Clough and H. B. Maufe he described the geological mapping of Glencoe, demonstrating the relics of a large sunken volcano, called a cauldron subsidence, surrounded by ring fractures, some occupied by igneous rocks later termed ring dykes. This fostered the recognition and study of ring dykes elsewhere in the world. In 1910 came his revolutionary description of the general geological structure of the western Grampians as strata, some transported great distances, bent into recumbent folds of which the limbs were partly replaced by low-angled faults or slides. Bailey was uncertain of the depositional order of the strata within the folds but in 1930, after other workers had demonstrated the significance of current-bedding and graded bedding, he showed that the Ballachulish Slide was developed in the lower limb of a syncline. Later it was realized that the concept of recumbent folding applied to the whole of the Grampians.

Bailey's fertile brain and courage were unaffected by his war wounds and in 1919 he was given charge of west Highland fieldwork and he saw through the press the geological map of Mull (1923) which he had helped to construct. One of the most complex and beautiful maps produced by Ordnance Survey for the Geological Survey, it depicts the results of two great cauldron subsidences and of gravitational differentiation of Tertiary magma; also there are crater lakes, pillow lavas, and ring dykes. When mapping sedimentary rocks, Bailey in 1922 studied a very pure white sandstone by Loch Aline, on the mainland opposite Mull; this, he inferred, formed the desert shores of the same sea that deposited the Chalk of the English downs. In World War II, when normal shipments of optical glass from overseas ceased, the purity of the Loch Aline sands was recalled and they were extensively mined and used.

Some of Bailey's lectures to his Glasgow undergraduates were incorporated into his *Introduction to Geology* (1939) written with his colleagues J. Weir and W. J. McCallien, and his book, *Tectonic Essays, mainly Alpine* (1935), still proves good reading. Among his researches were inferences concerning ancient submarine earthquakes and the accompanying tidal waves affecting sedimentation. These led other workers subsequently to develop the concept of turbidity-currents of high density and their effects on present-day ocean configuration.

Bailey's stay in Glasgow ended in 1937 when he was offered the directorship of the Geological Survey and its newly sited museum at South Kensington. The war, which occupied six of the eight years of his directorate, caused a change in his plans for the Survey; these are outlined in his book, *Geological Survey of*

Great Britain (1952), as are the activities of his staff, diverted from regional geological mapping to successful work on minerals associated with the war effort. The museum was evacuated and became the headquarters of London Region Civil Defence; from 1940 to 1942 Bailey was lieutenant commanding the Geological Survey and London Region section of the Home Guard. In 1943 he visited Malta to advise on water resources there. He also worked extensively on the production of the two sheets of the ten-mile-to-one-inch geological map of Great Britain, which, however, was not published until 1948, whereas he retired in 1945, the year in which he was knighted.

In collaboration with W. J. McCallien, he then took up the origin of associated serpentine, pillow lava, and radiolarian chert (his Steinmann trinity) in Scotland, Turkey, and Italy. He also prepared a second edition of the *Geology of Ben Nevis and Glen Coe* (1960) and he wrote biographies of Sir Charles Lyell (1962) and of James Hutton (1967) [q.v.].

Bailey was a tallish man of excellent physique; he had gained a freshman's heavyweight boxing medal at Cambridge. Always a keen walker, he had Spartan habits and a strong personality. Dedicated to his work, he inspired others but at times he was over-enthusiastic or even intolerant, thus antagonizing some. Honorary doctorates were given him by the universities of Belfast, Birmingham, Cambridge, Edinburgh, Glasgow, and Harvard. He was elected FRS in 1930 and awarded a Royal medal in 1943. A foreign member of the national academies of Belgium, India, Norway, Switzerland, and Washington, he was also an honorary member of many geological societies and received several prestigious medals.

Bailey married in 1914 Alice, daughter of David Meason, of Kirkwall, and a sister of the wife of (Sir) John S. Flett [q.v.]; they had a son and a daughter. The first Lady Bailey died in 1956 and in December 1962 Bailey married Miss Mary M. W. Young, who with the children of the first marriage survived him. He died in Middlesex Hospital 19 March 1965 and was cremated at Golder's Green.

C. J. Stubblefield in *Biographical Memoirs of Fellows of the Royal Society*, vol. xi, 1965; *Bulletin Geological Society of America*, vol. lxxvii, 1966; personal knowledge.]

C. JAMES STUBBLEFIELD

BAILEY, FREDERICK MARSHMAN (1882–1967), explorer and naturalist, elder son of Major (later Lieutenant-Colonel) Frederick Bailey, Royal Engineers, was born 3 February 1882 at Lahore where his father served in the Indian Army for a few years. Later his father became head of the Indian Forestry Survey Department and, on retirement from the army on health grounds, lecturer in forestry at Edinburgh University. His mother was Florence, daughter of John Clark Marshman, who had landed with his missionary parents in India in 1799. Marshman became *The Times* correspondent and was one of the founders of the newspaper the *Pioneer of India*. F. M. Bailey was educated at Edinburgh Academy where, to his disappointment, he spent only three years before going to the Wellington and the Royal Military College, Sandhurst.

His first commissioned posting was in 1900 to the Middlesex Regiment, which was then in the Nilgiri hills in India. There he became interested in birds, butterflies, and plants, an interest which he maintained throughout his travels and which produced valuable material and many new species for museums in India and Britain. He transferred to the Durham Light Infantry, in which he developed proficiency in polo. His horsemanship, and the influence of Lord Roberts [q.v.], a family friend, led to his posting to the 17th Bengal Lancers. Hoping to see active service, in 1903 he asked to be transferred to the 32nd Sikh Pioneers, whom he accompanied to Sikkim. This introduced him to Tibet, a country which intrigued him for the rest of his life and brought him a high reputation as an explorer. He was a member of the mission to Lhasa in 1903–4 led by (Sir) Francis Younghusband [q.v.] to resolve the intransigence of the Tibetan Government in implementing the Anglo-Chinese convention of 1890. On the successful completion of this mission Bailey, now proficient in Tibetan, was given his first opportunity to explore when he was sent to report on the trade and trade routes between India and Gartok, in western Tibet. He travelled hundreds of miles, living for weeks at at a time at a height of over 14,000 feet. Although only twenty-two, he gave a most detailed report on this assignment, which was published by the Government of India (Simla, 1905).

In 1905 he applied to be transferred to the political department and later that year went to Gyantse as trade agent to relieve the official due for leave. After the official's return, Bailey was for two years in the Chumbi Valley, a wedge of Tibet which thrusts south of the Himalayas between Sikkim and Bhutan. It was a suitable area in which to pursue his interest in natural history. In 1911, accompanied y his young Tibetan servant, he embarked on an expedition to explore the Tsangpo river, discover its source from the Tibetan plateau, and find out whether, as previously reported, it had falls of some 150 feet in height. Since an approach from the south was barred by unfriendly hill tribes and totally discouraged by the Indian Government, Bailey decided to enter in the east from China and therefore obtained a passport in Peking which allowed him to travel through Szechwan and Yunnan. He travelled to Ichang on the Yangtze by steamer and from there hired a small boat to take him through the Yangtze gorges. He trekked through this most difficult mountainous area to Tatsienlu and eventually to Batang on the Tibetan frontier. He did not, however, manage to reach the Tsangpo but returned to India through Mishmi country. In his book *China—Tibet—Assam* (1945) Bailey gave a fine account of this journey.

Hoping to solve the mystery of the Tsangpo gorges, he set out in 1913 with Captain Henry Treise Morshead, Royal Engineers, who worked on the Survey of India and, in defiance of official orders, they entered Tibet from Assam. Their three-and-a-half-month journey has been described as one of the longest and most remarkable journeys of exploration completed on foot in this century. It proved that the Tsangpo broke through the Himalayan range to emerge on the plains of India as the Brahmaputra. In Bailey's opinion the chief results of this expedition were the mapping of some 380 miles of the Tsangpo, the discovery of the two portals of the Tsangpo gorge, the high mountains Gyala Peri and Namcha Barwa, and the knowledge that the Subansiri was another river which had its source in Tibet and pierced the main Himalayan range. On this expedition he discovered the renowned blue poppy and collected fragmentary flowering specimens on which the species *meconopsis baileyi* was based. It was Kingdon Ward [q.v.] who introduced the plant to Britain in 1924 from seeds from the same locality. *No Passport to Tibet* (1957) was Bailey's account of the journey. As a result of his discoveries, Bailey was appointed CIE in 1915.

In 1915 Bailey was sent to France with the 31st Sikh Pioneers. Wounded at Ypres, he returned to England. On recovery he was dispatched to Gallipoli with the Gurkhas, only to be wounded again by a bullet which passed through both his legs. Pronounced unfit for active service, he returned to the political department of the India Office. Posted to India in 1916, he worked for two years as political officer in Kohat and then Charsada.

In March 1917 Bailey was sent as a political officer to Shustar, Persia. Early in 1918 he was ordered to Kashgar in Chinese Turkestan and then to Tashkent in Russian territory to report on the conditions in the region following the revolution of 1917 and the collapse of the Eastern front under German pressure. It was feared that there were subversive movements likely to affect the equilibrium on the North-West frontier of India. Bailey was to endeavour to establish good relations and influence the Tashkent authorities in favour of the Allies. Because of the hostility of the Bolshevik Government in Russian Turkestan, Bailey was compelled to go underground. Since he understood and could speak limited Russian, he was able repeatedly to change his identity. Despite a price on his head, he succeeded in securing his own recruitment into the Russian counter-espionage service, with the task, among other duties, of tracking a foreign agent named Bailey! He was thus able to reach Bokhara and finally Meshed in Persia. His *Mission to Tashkent* (1946) tells the fascinating story of these dangerous adventures.

In 1921 he was appointed political officer in Sikkim and, living in Gangtok for seven years, he was able to travel into Tibet and Bhutan. He became a personal friend of the Dalai Lama with whom he could converse freely. He next spent some months as a political officer in central India before going to Srinagar, Kashmir, as resident, and eventually to Nepal as British minister. He retired in 1938. After the outbreak of war in 1939 he joined the Home Guard and was in charge of the North Norfolk auxiliary units. For almost two years he was a King's messenger based at Miami and Washington.

Bailey was an unassuming man of handsome appearance and military bearing a spoke in a soft voice. He was modest and gentle mannered, with immense charm and persuasiveness, and a fine sense of humour which earned him the nickname 'Hatter'. Although he sometimes defied authority his results usually justified his resolve. In 1912 the Royal Geographical Society granted him the Gill memorial award and in 1916 its gold medal. He also received the premier award of the Royal Scottish Geographical Society in 1920, the Livingstone gold medal.

In natural history Bailey's major interest was butterflies, which he collected in all his travels. His specimens were given to the British Museum (Natural History) and his cabinets of duplicates went to the Metropolitan Museum in New York. His fine collection of birds, mostly from Nepal, and his collection of mammals, were donated to the British Museum. He published a number of papers on many aspects of natural history.

In 1921 Bailey married Irma, only child of William Hepburn, second Lord Cozens-Hardy, a barrister and secretary to his father, the first Lord Cozens-Hardy [q.v.] when master of the Rolls. There were no children of the marriage. Bailey died at his home in Stiffkey, Norfolk, 17 April 1967.

[*The Times*, 19 April 1967; Arthur Swinson, *Beyond the Frontiers*, 1971; personal knowledge.]   GEORGE TAYLOR

BAILEY, SIR GEORGE EDWIN (1879 1965), mechanical engineer and industrialist, was born in Loughborough 19 October 1879, the tenth child of Thomas W. Bailey, master tailor, and his second wife, Ann Wilmot. He was educated at Loughborough Grammar School, and entered the works of the Brush Electrical Engineering Company, Loughborough, as an apprentice, continuing his technical education at the University College, Nottingham. Completing his works training as a draughtsman he left the Brush Company in 1907 and joined the British Westinghouse Company at Trafford Park as a draughtsman in the engine department. In 1909 he was appointed chief draughtsman, and in 1913 he became superintendent responsible for manufacture, thus determining his future career and interest in production and manufacture. In 1919 the British Westinghouse Company ceased to exist, and became Metropolitan-Vickers Electrical Company, a name which was to become known throughout the world. Bailey was chosen as works manager, until a rearrangement of the board became necessary in 1927, when he took a seat on the board, becoming director and general manager of manufacture.

In 1929 Metropolitan-Vickers was merged with the British Thomson Houston Company and the Ediswan Electric Company to form the Associated Electrical Industries Limited. Although the individual companies retained their own identities, Bailey was made responsible for the co-ordination of production in the group. In 1944 he was appointed chairman of Metropolitan-Vickers Electrical Company, and in the following two years he became managing director and then deputy chairman of Associated Electrical Industries. In 1951 Oliver Lyttleton (later Lord Chandos) entered the Government as secretary of state for the colonies and Bailey took his place as chairman of the company until 1954, when Chandos returned, after which he continued as director, retiring in 1957.

Bailey was a man of strong character, and it was undoubtedly his great energy and single-mindedness that caused him to be chosen for heavy responsibility in his early years. He was notable for his ability to handle men, and despite his critical outlook and sometimes more than trenchant comments, he left no rancour. He was adept at devising various ways of maintaining good communications with his employees. The company had probably the first works committee in the country, anticipating the Whitley councils by nine months. Although Bailey regarded himself as a very hard man, he was far more sympathetic and sentimental about other people's misfortunes than he cared to admit, and often arranged for help to be given anonymously. He was assiduous in encouraging extra-mural activities for the company's employees, and a school for evening tuition for women and girls in cookery, sewing, and dressmaking, and in his unremitting support for a wide range of activities, such as choral singing, amateur dramatics, and boxing.

Despite heavy involvement in the armament programme during the war of 1914–18, Bailey became a captain in the Local Defence Volunteers, but it was in the war of 1939–45 that he was to make his greatest contribution. In 1938 the company was involved with (Sir) Robert Watson-Watt in producing the first radar sets, and George Bailey was proud to be involved with many technical developments in heavy-bomber production, with the first axial flow gas turbine to fly (the forerunner of the jet), and with much equipment for the navy and air force, including the first thousand radar sets ordered by the Government. His relations with the trade unions, though rugged, were always sincere and left no ill feelings.

During the war he served as a member of the Engineering and Industrial Panel of the Ministry of Labour and National Service, and as a member of the committee which considered the position of skilled men in industry, led by Sir W. H. (later Lord) Beveridge [q.v.], and on the Industrial Panel of the Ministry of Production. At various times he was president of the British Electrical and Allied Manufacturers' Association, the Engineering and Allied Employers' National Federation, the Manchester District Engineering Employers' Association, the Manchester Engineering Council, and the Institute of Production Engineers. His skill and wide experience were used to the full after the 'blitz' on Manchester, in supervising the restoration of the badly damaged factories in the district. His contribution to the Manchester Defence scheme earned him the appointment as CBE in 1941. For his services to production of armaments he was knighted in 1944.

Despite his heavy responsibilities and the many calls on his time, Bailey never lost interest in golf, fishing, and gardening. Like his father before him he was a good gardener and his chief interest was in the cultivation of carnations in which he specialized.

He married in 1910 Margaret Fanny (died 1971), daughter of Thomas Bolesworth, farmer of Loughborough; they had one daughter, Lady Bailey was appointed MBE. Bailey died at his home at Compton, Berkshire, 14 October 1965.

[Private information; personal knowledge.]   H. WEST

BAILEY, KENNETH (1909–1963), biochemist, was born 18 August 1909 at Alsagers Bank, near Stoke-on-Trent, the fourth child and elder son of Bertram Bailey, a colliery clerk, and his wife, (Elizabeth) Florence Buckley. He received his early education at the Orme Boys' School, Newcastle under Lyme, on leaving which he enrolled with a major county scholarship at the university of Birmingham, where he achieved a first class honours B.Sc. in 1931, and took his Ph.D. degree under R. H. Hopkins in the department of industrial fermentation in 1933. The award of a Beit fellowship in 1933 took him to the Royal College of Science, Imperial College, London, where A. C. Chibnall was, *inter alia*, studying the structure of proteins. There he came under the influence of W. T. Astbury [q.v.] of Leeds University, who was visiting the laboratory periodically to discuss the analysis and denaturation of proteins. This led to a scientific collaboration and the development between these two very different personalities of a happy friendship based on mutual respect, a love of music, and common origin in the Potteries.

Bailey's work soon showed a remarkable understanding of the physical, chemical, and biological facets of protein structure and in 1939 the Rockefeller Foundation awarded him a travelling grant to join E. J. Cohn and J. T. Edsall at Harvard. In December 1939, however, he returned home, to work first at Porton and then at the Low Temperature Research Station in Cambridge. Later he joined a team investigating organo-phosphorous compounds in the university biochemical laboratory at Cambridge. He obtained a Cambridge Ph.D. in 1944. After the war he was granted an ICI fellowship, which released him to do research on the chemistry of muscle and the coagulation of blood, both projects which brought him once again into contact with Astbury. In 1948 he became an assistant director of research in the university and was elected a fellow of Trinity College. He enjoyed the society there and found supervision of keen young minds stimulating; he also took pleasure in sharing with the younger members his love of music (he was himself a competent pianist), of gardening, and of modern art. In 1953 he obtained a Cambridge Sc.D., was elected FRS, and spent a few months as visiting professor at Washington University, Seattle, where he finished editing, with Hans Neurath, their monumental book, *The Proteins* (1954), which was the first to treat the subject comprehensively. In 1961 he became a reader in biochemistry.

Although he was master of many aspects of protein chemistry Bailey made no attempt to build up a research school of his own: he firmly believed that worthwhile discoveries were made only by those who 'played about' at the bench and he never wanted more than one or two junior workers with him, which explains why he always refused offers of chairs at home and abroad. As time has shown, his researches are notable for their impact on the development of biological science. One was his clear demonstration with F. R. Bettelheim (now Jevons) in 1951 and, independently of the Leeds group under Lorand, of the nature of the action of thrombin on fibrinogen. This work led to the isolation of the fibrinopeptides and for the first time to an understanding of the molecular mechanisms involved in the formation of the fibrin clot.

Bailey's other great achievement, which may be of more general significance, was his discovery in 1946 of the protein tropomyosin, which although originally isolated from skeletal muscle has now been shown to be present in most eucaryotic cells. With remarkable flair he purified, crystallized, and characterized the protein in a way which could not be faulted even with the much more sophisticated methods of protein fractionation later available. Tropomyosin was the first fibrous protein to be crystallized and Bailey immediately recognized the uniqueness of the properties of this remarkable protein with 100% α-helical content. It was not until after his death, however, that the importance of tropomyosin for the function of all contractile systems depending on actomyosin was appreciated. In vertebrate skeletal muscle, in association with the troponin complex, tropomyosin is concerned with the regulation of the interaction of actin with myosin and hence contraction itself.

Bailey also made another less direct, but nevertheless important, contribution to the understanding of the regulation of contraction in muscle through his research student, B. B. Marsh. Marsh's investigation, under Bailey's direction, of the changes which occur in postmortem minced muscle tissue resulted in the discovery of the Marsh factor, the further study of which by other investigators subsequently led to the discovery of the calcium pump of the sarcoplasmic reticulum.

Unlike his colleague Astbury, who was openhearted and never tried to hide his feelings, Bailey was always somewhat reserved, and his gentle demeanour could often mask a deep intuitive understanding of people and affairs. He had, moreover, the rare gift of being able to express himself in lucid and, when needed, in vivid language. He was unmarried. His later years were marred by severe recurrent depressive illness and he committed suicide in Cambridge 22 May 1963.

[R. R. Porter, *Nature*, vol. cc, pp. 520–1; A. C. Chibnall in *Biographical Memoirs of*

Fellows of the Royal Society, vol. x, 1964; *The Times*, 31 June 1963; private information; personal knowledge.]

A. C. CHIBNALL

BAIRSTOW, SIR LEONARD (1880–1963), professor of aviation, was born 25 June 1880 at Halifax in Yorkshire, the son of Uriah Bairstow, a commercial clerk, and his wife, Elizabeth Lister. He was educated in the elementary and secondary schools of Halifax, from which he obtained, in 1898, a scholarship at the Royal College of Science, London. There he became a Whitworth scholar in 1902. In 1904 he entered the Engineering Department of the National Physical Laboratory, where he worked under (Sir) T. E. Stanton on the problems of fatigue and of aerodynamics. In 1909 he moved to the new section of aerodynamics and became the principal in charge. There he carried out pioneer investigations into wind tunnel design and aircraft stability, using small mica models and making the measurements of aerodynamic derivatives in a wind tunnel. One of his assistants at the time was E. F. Relf [q.v.].

In 1917 he was appointed to the Air Board where he worked for Sir David Henderson [q.v.] on aircraft design and aerodynamics research. As deputy to Alex. Ogilvie he co-ordinated the departmental work on structural strength, aerodynamics, performance, and air screws. In 1920 he was appointed professor of aerodynamics at the Imperial College, London, and in 1923 he became Zaharoff professor of aviation and head of the Department of Aeronautics until his retirement in 1945.

He was a member of the Aeronautical Research Committee (later called the Aeronautical Research Council) from 1921 to 1955 and was its chairman from 1949 to 1952. He served on over fifty committees and had an unequalled record of service. In 1917 he was elected a fellow of the Royal Society and appointed CBE. He gave the seventh Wilbur Wright memorial lecture in 1919—an event well remembered for the subsequent controversy in which Bairstow's references to S. P. Langley's 'heavier than air' aircraft were ultimately justified. He was chairman of the council of the Royal Aeronautical Society in the year 1922–3, was made an honorary fellow in 1945, and received the society's gold medal in 1946. He was knighted in 1952.

The outstanding feature of Bairstow's scientific career was the great controversies in which he was engaged—controversies which ultimately had considerable effect on the development of aeronautical research. Bairstow was a doughty fighter, always well equipped with extensive knowledge and powerful arguments, and it required considerable new experimental work and most careful theoretical exposition to convince him of his mistakes.

The first controversy arose from the discrepancies between the measurements of aerodynamic derivatives made in an aeroplane in flight at the Royal Aircraft Establishment by (Sir) W. S. Farren [q.v.] and (Sir) G. P. Thomson with the measurements made in wind tunnels at the National Physical Laboratory. Bairstow maintained, in an argument which seemed most reasonable and convincing, that measurements made in a wind tunnel, by skilled observers, with accurate instruments, under ideal conditions, must be more reliable and were undoubtedly more reproducible than observations made by a pilot distracted by the problems of manœuvring an aircraft.

Nor was the situation clarified when (Sir) R. V. Southwell [q.v.] obtained the co-operation of a number of foreign laboratories to test a standard 'international' aerofoil. The measurements so obtained unfortunately differed among themselves. To resolve this difficulty (Sir) G. I. Taylor suggested that the differences were due to different levels of turbulence in the tunnels and in the atmosphere. This happy suggestion was later confirmed and has been of the utmost importance in the design of wind tunnels and the use of models. The controversy had produced the 'scale effect subcommittee' of the Advisory Committee for Aeronautics in 1917 and its successor, the aerodynamics subcommittee of the Aeronautical Research Council. Bairstow himself was finally convinced of the effects of turbulence in wind tunnels and must be praised for sustaining a controversy which ultimately led to results of such consequence for aerodynamic research.

The second controversy was over the validity of the theory of the 'boundary layer' advanced by Ludwig Prandtl in 1904. Previously in aerodynamic theory the air had been treated as an incompressible non-conducting and inviscid gas. The effects of compressibility and thermal conduction were indeed of negligible importance at the low aircraft speeds attainable before 1920, but Prandtl made the first step to allow for the effects of viscosity. Prandtl's theory was that the effects of viscosity are confined to a thin 'boundary layer' on the surface of an aerofoil or wing, and he advanced a much simplified mathematical theory to represent these effects. It must be confessed that Prandtl's arguments may be found unconvincing to a mathematician, although they are readily accepted by aerodynamicists.

For a long time Prandtl's theory was ignored in England, and, even when Bairstow became acquainted with it, he rejected it as mathematically unsound. He did not remain content with this negative reaction but proceeded to solve the full and exact equations of a viscous fluid as advanced much earlier by Navier and Sir G. G. Stokes [q.v.]. Wisely he contented himself with the flow past a circular cylinder in a tunnel of finite and uniform width, and by a laborious arithmetical process obtained a satisfactory solution. Later he considered the similar problem for a cylinder in an infinite fluid using the conditions at infinity suggested by Oseen, and, indeed, he attempted to discuss the resistance of a flat plate of infinite span but finite chord.

Bairstow was eventually persuaded to adopt Prandtl's theory and when he did so he invented the most rapid and precise method of solving the famous Blasius equation for a semi-infinite flat plate. His criticism of Prandtl's theory was undoubtedly justified and it was not until (Sir) M. J. Lighthill had developed the theory of differential equations with singular perturbations that an adequate theory could be constructed. Bairstow should be remembered not only for his part in these controversies but also for his considerable contributions to our knowledge of the stability of aircraft.

The mathematical theory of stability had been established by G. H. Bryan in his *Stability in Aviation* (1911) but the theory lacked two important aspects—the actual numerical values of the aerodynamic forces and couples acting on real aircraft, and experimental studies of the behaviour of aircraft.

Bairstow and his colleague, J. L. Nayler, considerably generalized the work of Bryan, and expressed the theory in a compact and elegant form. Bryan's investigations were restricted to the study of small oscillations about steady level flight with no side-slip. Bairstow studied the general case of aeroplane stability in which longitudinal and lateral motions were coupled, together with the effects of pitching, rolling, and yawing, and of the spiral dive. He and Nayler developed the general equations for stability, which led to a determinantal equation of the eighth degree, for which they provided an iterative method of solution.

In order to illustrate the general theory and to obtain qualitative measurements of aerodynamic forces, Bairstow made a number of small gliding models from mica sheets and aluminium foil. He also applied the model method to the design of wind tunnels and in later papers he studied the stability of balloons and airships. His researches on the tail oscillations which occur in an aeroplane represent the first attempt to understand the important problem of flutter.

The great experience gained by Bairstow and his staff naturally led to his appointment to two government committees which investigated the accidents to the airships, R.38 and R.101. Unfortunately Bairstow's earlier work, which

would have permitted calculations of the structural stresses due to aerodynamic forces on the R.38, had not been consulted and it was not until after the accident that the accidents investigation subcommittee (in 1922) called attention to the dangerously low factor of safety.

In the case of the R.101 the Airworthiness of Airships Panel, under the chairmanship of Bairstow, was intimately associated with the airship's design and construction and would have made the complete re-examination of the aerodynamic calculations necessitated by modifications to the original design. Unfortunately the refusal of a Cabinet minister to postpone the date of the projected flight to India made this impossible. The immediate cause of the R.101's crash in 1930 was the stormy weather over northern France which caused a substantial loss of gas from the balloons, which fretted against the metal structure.

Bairstow's earlier researches were concerned with the inflammability of mixtures of coal gas and air and with metallic fatigue, but far more important were his numerous investigations into the numerical solution of partial differential equations. He devised powerful methods for the solution of the biharmonic equation and of the potential equation (in two dimensions) and he applied these methods to problems of elasticity and of fluid flow. Although Bairstow paid little attention to formal mathematical theory he was extremely successful in devising practical techniques which gave good approximate solutions. It should also be emphasized that his calculations were all made on desk machines, which by modern standards were frustratingly slow.

The considerable debt which aerodynamics owes to Bairstow was fittingly expressed by Sir Harold Roxbee Cox (later Lord Kings Norton) who made the jocular suggestion that the roof of the large wind tunnel at Farnborough should be decorated with statues of all the great pioneers of aviation from Leonardo da Vinci to Leonardo da Bairstow.

He married, first, Eleanor Mary Hamer (died 1926), by whom he had one son and one daughter. In 1930 he married Florence Katharine, the eldest daughter of D. J. Stephens, of Llandaff, who survived him with the children of the first marriage.

[G. Temple in *Biographical Memoirs of Fellows of the Royal Society*, vol. xi, 1965; J. Lawrence Pritchard and J. L. Nayler, *Journal of the Royal Aeronautical Society*, vol. lxviii, 1964; personal knowledge.]   G. TEMPLE

BALEWA, ALHAJI SIR ABU BAKAR TAFAWA (1912-1966), prime minister of the Federation of Nigeria. [See TAFAWA BALEWA.]

BALFOUR-BROWNE, WILLIAM ALEXANDER FRANCIS (1874-1967), entomologist, who used the single forename Frank when writing, was born at 16 Ebury St., London, 27 December 1874, the eldest of the two sons and two daughters of John Hatton Balfour-Browne, KC, later of Goldielea, Dumfries, an authority on railway law and compensation, and his wife, Caroline, daughter of Sir Robert Lush, lord justice [q.v.]. Balfour-Browne showed an interest in natural history as a child, and at St. Paul's School won a prize for a collection of beetles. At Magdalen College, Oxford, he was frustrated to find that he had already covered at school the first two years of the botany course, and the deepest impression of his undergraduate days was left by the field excursions from Edinburgh University where he was granted permission to spend a term. He represented Oxford against Cambridge at hockey in 1894 and 1895, and achieved a half blue for cycling in 1894. While at Edinburgh he used to cycle home to Dumfries for week-ends. In 1896 he gained a second class honours degree in natural science (botany).

After graduating he yielded to his father's pressure and was called to the bar in 1898, but natural inclination overcame filial piety and he returned to Oxford to take a course in zoology. His first employment was in the marine field, but after two years he moved, in 1902, to become director of the Sutton Broad Laboratory.

From 1906 he taught biology at Queen's College, Belfast (from 1908 Queen's University), and in 1913, to his delight, he was invited to Cambridge to teach entomology. In 1915 he went to France as a lieutenant, RAMC, but his active service was terminated the following year by a shell which, bursting near by, buried him. In 1925 he decided to retire, and soon afterwards turned down an invitation to the chair of entomology at Imperial College, London University. However, he was the man the college wanted, and a compromise was reached that Balfour-Browne should come to London on Mondays and return to his new home in Somerset on Thursdays. In 1930 he did retire and settled down to the work which really interested him.

Unlike most of his contemporaries, Balfour-Browne, widely referred to as B.-B., was inspired less by Darwin that by the other great Victorian naturalist, A. R. Wallace [q.v.], and his ideas about geographical distribution. This influence, his early interest in beetles, and a taste for studying organisms in their natural environment, led Balfour-Browne, after a restless start, to a lifelong study of the distribution of British water beetles.

He sifted the earlier records for reliable data,

an arduous task in the study of a group that had been popular for a long time, and mastered the taxonomy. In the course of this he frequently found himself in disagreement with the International Commission on Zoological Nomenclature, and his numerous papers are peppered with pungent comments which, cogent if common sense were more common, did not always take account of the price which must be paid for international agreement in an imperfect world.

His own collecting was extensive, and many a coleopterist, both professional and amateur, remembered with gratitude his readiness to put names to collections which contained widespread and common species. He brought sound sense and reliable information to a field where speculation had been wild and rife, even among the eminent, who had erected theories on the assumption that distribution had not changed since the Ice Age and had postulated land bridges unsupported by geological evidence.

Balfour-Browne wrote three Ray Society monographs on British water beetles (1940, 1950, 1958), which were primarily aids to identification but which also contained much information on distribution and natural history. His last book, entitled *Water Beetles and Other Things* (1964), which was partly autobiographical, summarizes his life's work. In the year of its publication he gave his collections, notebooks, and card indexes to the Royal Scottish Museum. Thereafter he retained much of his mental vigour but rheumatism curtailed outdoor activities. He died suddenly 28 September 1967 while on a visit to Edinburgh from his home, Brocklehirst, Collin, Dumfries.

Balfour-Browne's spruce figure, forthright comments, and genial personality were familiar in many scientific societies, and he was a keen supporter, often generous with money as well as time, of any organization promoting studies in the field. He was particularly interested in the foundation of the Nature Conservancy, for his main work had been to provide the basis from which conservation must start.

He was a fellow of the Royal Society of Edinburgh but perhaps the recognition that would have pleased him most was the decision of those interested in water beetles to come together as the Balfour-Browne Club. He was president of many societies in his field.

Balfour-Browne was a small man but possessed great stamina. In 1902 he married Elizabeth Lochhead (died 1947), daughter of the Revd William Henderson Carslaw, of Helensburgh, Dunbartonshire. They had one son and two daughters.

[Frank Balfour-Browne, *Water Beetles and Other Things, Half a Century's Work*, 1964;

R. B. Angus in the *Entomologist's Monthly Magazine*, vol. ciii, p. 286, 1967; private information; personal knowledge.]

T. T. MACAN

BALL, SIR (GEORGE) JOSEPH (1885–1961), intelligence officer, party administrator, and business man, was born in Luton 21 September 1885, the son of George Ball, bookstall clerk, of Salisbury, and his wife, Sarah Ann Headey. He was educated at King's College School, Strand, and at King's College, London. After leaving college he worked as a civilian official in Scotland Yard, and he was called to the bar with first class honours by Gray's Inn in 1913. He was a keen footballer, playing centre-half for the Casuals till an injury prevented him. He was a good shot and an expert fly fisher. On the outbreak of war he joined MI5, and was appointed OBE in 1919. He remained in the service until 1927 when he was persuaded by J. C. C. (later Viscount) Davidson [q.v.], chairman of the Conservative Party, to join the party organization as director of publicity. Major Joseph Ball, as he then was, proved to be a notable asset, along with Sir Patrick Gower, also diverted by Davidson from government employment. Years later in 1955 Davidson said 'he is undoubtedly tough and has looked after his own interests . . . On the other hand he is steeped in the Service tradition, and has had as much experience as anyone I know in the seamy side of life and the handling of crooks.' One of Ball's successful clandestine efforts was to insert agents in the Labour Party headquarters and in Odham's Press which did most of the party's printing. In this way he managed to secure both Labour reports of political feeling in the country and also advance 'pulls' of their leaflets and pamphlets; it was thus possible for the Conservatives to reply suspiciously instantaneously to their opponents' propaganda. Not surprisingly Ball was closely involved in assisting Stanley Baldwin to deal with the parliamentary debate in 1928 on the affair of the Zinoviev letter which had occurred four years earlier. Baldwin was able to emerge triumphantly. It is not known whether Ball played any part in the original episode.

In 1930 in the aftermath of the loss of the general election, Davidson created the Conservative Research Department and made Ball its director under the chairmanship first (briefly) of Lord Eustace Percy and then of Neville Chamberlain [qq.v.] to whom Ball is said to have taught the art of fly-fishing. Chamberlain respected Ball's knowledge, discretion, and reliability, later using him in 1938 as an intermediary with Count Grandi, Italian ambassador in London, in order to bypass the foreign secretary, Anthony Eden (later the Earl of Avon). Ball was appointed KBE in 1936.

Ball was a very able director. He did much to lay the foundations for the success of the Conservative Party's Research Department after World War II and he recruited for it many young men of high calibre, among others Henry Brooke (later Lord Brooke of Cumnor) and Frank Pakenham (later the Earl of Longford) who, however, later moved to the Labour Party. Ball retired in 1939. From 1940 to 1942, reverting to his earlier profession as an intelligence officer, he served as deputy chairman of the Security Executive.

After the end of the war Ball entered the world of business, becoming chairman of Henderson's Transvaal Estates and five subsidiary companies, and also of Lake View & Star. He was a director of Consolidated Goldfields of South Africa and of the Beaumont Property Trust. He was chairman of the Hampshire Rivers Catchment Board 1947–53. He died in London 10 July 1961.

Moving for most of his life in the shadow of events and deeply averse to publicity of any sort he gave very little away, and the formal accounts of his career, whether written by himself or others, are curt and uninformative. He was, however, a quintessential *eminence grise*, and his influence on affairs cannot be measured by the brevity of the printed references to him. Alan Hugh Ball, his son by his wife, Mary Caroline, became a director of Lonrho Ltd.

[*The Times*, 12 July 1961; Robert Rhodes James, *Memoirs of a Conservative*, 1969; L. Chester, S. Fay, and H. Young, *The Zinoviev Letter*, 1967; John Ramsden, *A History of the Conservative Party*, vol. iii, *The Age of Balfour and Baldwin 1902–48*, 1978.]

BLAKE

BARBIROLLI, SIR JOHN (GIOVANNI BATTISTA) (1899–1970), conductor and cellist, was born in London 2 December 1899, the elder son and second of the three children of an *émigré* Italian violinist, Lorenzo Barbirolli, and his French wife, Louise Marie Ribeyrol, of Paris. He began to play the violin when he was four, but a year later changed to the cello. He was educated at St. Clement Dane's school and, at the same time, from 1910, was a scholar at the Trinity College of Music. He made his public début in a cello concerto in the Queen's Hall in 1911. In 1912 he won a scholarship to the Royal Academy of Music, which he attended from 1912 to 1916. He was elected an associate of the Academy at the age of thirteen. From 1916 to 1918 he was a freelance cellist in London, playing in the Queen's Hall Orchestra, in opera under Sir Thomas Beecham [q.v.], and in theatre and cinema orchestras.

He served in the Suffolk Regiment 1918-19 and, on demobilization, resumed his orchestral career, although he was gifted enough to be soloist in Sir Edward Elgar's [q.v.] Cello Concerto at Bournemouth in 1921. In 1924 he became the cellist in both the Music Society and Samuel Kutcher string quartets. However, his ambition since childhood had been to conduct and later that year he formed his own string orchestra. He gradually attracted attention and in 1925 was invited to conduct for the British National Opera Company, making his début in C. F. Gounod's *Romeo and Juliet* in Newcastle upon Tyne in 1926.

When the BNOC foundered financially in 1929, Barbirolli was appointed conductor of the Covent Garden Opera touring company and also became a regular conductor at the Royal Opera House, Covent Garden, in the Grand Opera season. In 1931 the company staged thirteen operas, including the revival of Dame Ethel Smyth's [q.v.] *The Wreckers*. In 1933 he became conductor of the Scottish Orchestra, rejuvenating the playing and the programmes and winning most favourable opinions. Even so, no one was prepared for the sensation in 1936 when the Philharmonic-Symphony Society of New York, having been forced by public protests to withdraw their invitation to Wilhelm Furtwängler to succeed Arturo Toscanini as conductor, asked Barbirolli for the first ten weeks of the 1936-7 season. He conducted in Carnegie Hall for the first time 5 November 1936 and a month later was offered a three-year contract.

The years in New York were both rewarding and scarring for Barbirolli. Working with a great orchestra, with whom he was always on excellent terms, and with the most talented of the world's soloists, matured him musically; but the handicap imposed upon him by having succeeded Toscanini, who was idolized in New York and for whom a rival orchestra was created, was almost insurmountable. The critics, whose power and influence in New York at that time were notorious, were savage in their attacks on Barbirolli's interpretations. Nevertheless, in 1940 his contract was renewed for a further two years. When in April 1943 he was invited to become permanent conductor of the Hallé Orchestra at a time of crisis in its history, he accepted without hesitation, not wishing to avoid Britain's wartime privations.

Barbirolli arrived in Manchester to find that he had a month in which to recruit forty players to add to the thirty-five under contract. He scoured the country for talent, no easy task in 1943, and launched a virtually new orchestra which was soon acclaimed as the best in the country. This period, when he recreated the orchestra, bound him emotionally and indis-solubly to the Hallé, so that despite lucrative offers from elsewhere and despite his own exasperation with its post-war financial problems, he could not be lured away. He was knighted in 1949 and was awarded the Royal Philharmonic Society's gold medal in 1950. In 1959 he accepted engagements in America and returned to a rapturous welcome from public and critics in New York. From 1961 he was a regular and much-admired guest conductor of the Berlin Philharmonic, and from 1961 to 1967 was conductor-in-chief of the Houston Symphony Orchestra. But the Hallé was still his principal concern and, after twenty-five years with it, in 1968 he was appointed conductor laureate for life. He was made a Companion of Honour in 1969. For some years he had suffered from heart disease and he died in London 29 July 1970 after a day of rehearsal in preparation for concerts with the New Philharmonia Orchestra in Japan.

Barbirolli was a complete musician. His magnetism as a conductor was exemplified by his ability to obtain quickly the special quality of sound which he liked from an orchestra. His aim was to lead players and listeners into the composer's world: this power of commitment was his strength, as his recordings testify. If concentration on broad lines and expressive phrasing meant some loss of rhythmical impulse, that was a weakness which was usually outweighed. In the music of Mahler, Elgar, Sibelius, Brahms, and Vaughan Williams he was at his greatest, combining power and poetry, but his excellent Haydn was underrated and it was most unfortunate that after 1936 he conducted comparatively little opera. No one who saw him—dynamic, with a touch of arrogance in his demeanour on the rostrum, small of stature but big in every other way—would have guessed that after a concert he would often lapse into deep depression. He was prey to an insecurity which partly stemmed from experiences during his rise to fame, was partly the result of his years in New York, and was also due to his own genuine humility in the face of great music. But with his sardonic humour, his courage, and his gift for friendship, he concealed these human failings from all but his intimates. His capacity for work was prodigious and he demanded most from himself.

In 1932 Barbirolli married Marjorie Parry, a soprano. The marriage was not a success and they were divorced in 1939, when he married a celebrated oboist, Evelyn, daughter of R. H. Rothwell, a tea-dealer, of Wallingford, Berkshire. There were no children of either marriage. Barbirolli was a fellow of the Royal Academy of Music (1928), and an honorary freeman of Manchester, King's Lynn, and Houston, Texas. Honorary degrees were conferred on him by the universities of Manchester

(1950), Dublin (1952), Sheffield (1957), London (1961), Leicester (1964), and Keele (1969). He received the Bruckner (1959) and Mahler (1965) medals and was decorated by the governments of Italy, Finland, and France. There are drawings of him by Augustus John and Harold Riley, and a triptych sculpture by Byron Howard is in Manchester Town Hall.

[Michael Kennedy, *Barbirolli, Conductor Laureate*, 1971; Charles Reid, *John Barbirolli*, 1971; Charles Rigby, *John Barbirolli*, 1948; personal knowledge.]   MICHAEL KENNEDY

BARLOW, SIR (JAMES) ALAN (NOEL), second baronet (1881-1968), public servant, was born in London 25 December 1881, the eldest of the three sons and two daughters of (Sir) Thomas Barlow [q.v.], physician extraordinary to Queen Victoria, Edward VII and George V, and president of the Royal College of Physicians, who was created a baronet in 1901 and died in his hundredth year in 1945, and his wife, Ada Helen, daughter of Patrick Dalmahoy, writer to the signet, of Edinburgh. One of Alan's brothers was (Sir) Thomas Barlow, industrialist and public servant, whose notice appears below.

He was educated at Marlborough and at Corpus Christi College, Oxford, of which he was a scholar and later an honorary fellow, and took a first in *literae humaniores* (1904). In 1906 he was appointed to a clerkship in the House of Commons but in 1907 Sir Robert Morant [q.v.], who among his many outstanding qualities had a remarkable flair for choosing young men of promise, selected him to be a junior examiner in the Board of Education. Appointed private secretary to the parliamentary secretary to the Board in 1914 Barlow was in 1915 transferred to the Ministry of Munitions where in 1916 he became private secretary to the minister, Edwin Samuel Montagu [q.v.]. During his time in that department he had been deputy controller of the Labour Supply Department and had acquired valuable experience in the handling of labour problems and disputes. So it was not surprising that after the end of the war of 1914-18 he was transferred to the new Ministry of Labour as principal assistant secretary in charge of the Training Department. In that post it became clear that the blood of his forebears, who had been Manchester cotton spinners, made a fortune during the industrial revolution, and set up as landed gentry in Buckinghamshire, ran in his veins. In successfully pioneering the establishment of training centres all over the country he showed initiative, the capacity for getting to the core of a problem, the ability of quickly deciding what wanted doing, and the executive drive to get it done.

In 1933 he was selected to be principal private secretary to the prime minister, Ramsay Macdonald, a surprising choice for Barlow was then fifty-one years of age, relatively old for such a post. It was not a happy time for Barlow whose temperament was not suited to that of the prime minister, but it only lasted until 1934 when he was appointed an under-secretary at the Treasury, where he remained until his retirement in 1948. In 1938 he became joint second secretary.

Barlow was much more than a distinguished civil servant: he was a man of wide-ranging culture with interests in a variety of fields and hosts of friends in differet spheres, artistic, scientific, and academic. This knowledge was invaluable to the Treasury which provided funds for these activities and to all these interests which knew that there was somebody at the top where the money came from who knew about them and cared for them. His range of information and contacts was such that if any of his colleagues wanted advice which he himself could not give he almost always knew the source to go to, and if he did not, he would find out. And because of his specialized knowledge he was naturally consulted about the constitution of commissions and committees: the first thing to be done was to 'ask Alan for names'.

He was chairman of the Barlow committee which was set up after the war to consider the policy which should govern the use and development of Britain's scientific manpower resources over the forthcoming decade, and recommended that the scientific output of the universities should be doubled. He was a member of the Iron and Steel Board in 1946-8 and for several years he served on the Advisory Council on Scientific Policy. From 1948 to 1955 he was a trustee of the National Gallery, serving as chairman in 1949-51. He was on the court of the university of London from 1949 to 1956. For many years he was president of the Oriental Ceramic Society: he had started collecting oriental porcelain when he was eighteen. Ceramics were his special interest: his collection of Islamic pottery and Chinese porcelain was of national importance: in his later years he made many generous gifts to the Ashmolean, Fitzwilliam, Victoria and Albert and British Museums and to the university of Sussex. He was also interested in both old books and modern printing. In Buckinghamshire he found scope for his interest in archaeology and was from 1945 to 1962 president of the Buckinghamshire Archaeological Society during which period he succeeded, after years of negotiation, in securing the leasing of the society's museum to the County Council, leaving the society, whose resources were inadequate to maintain the museum in the post-war world, to develop its other activities. He was practically interested in these—he made a generous contribution towards financing the Ivinghoe dig. As if these activities were not enough he served as chairman of the executive committee of the Athenaeum, chairman of the Savile Club, was a justice of the peace for Buckinghamshire, successfully farmed several hundred acres near Wendover, and found time to be a keen gardener.

With his heavy and lined face he could, peering through his glasses, appear a forbidding person, especially to the young man meeting him for the first time. But that impression was misleading. In normal dealings he was conciliatory and good tempered and those who worked with him in any capacity paid tribute to his tact and wisdom and the firmness with which he was prepared to express his views in the face of opposition; these qualities, as well as his very able and direct mind, ensured for him the confidence of successive chancellors of the Exchequer.

He married in 1911 Emma Nora, daughter of (Sir) Horace Darwin [q.v.], herself the editor of the Beagle diary and the autobiography of Charles Darwin, her grandfather. Barlow would have been the first to acknowledge that it was his wife who fostered that undertanding of and sympathy with scientists which, conjoined with his strong interests in artistic matters, made him such a widely cultured man. They had four sons, three of whom became doctors, and two daughters. He died 28 February 1968 at home in Wendover, Buckinghamshire, and was succeeded in the baronetcy by his eldest son, Thomas Erasmus (born 1914).

[*The Times*, 29 February 1968; private information; personal knowledge.]

AUSTIN STRUTT

BARLOW, SIR THOMAS DALMAHOY (1883-1964), industrialist and public servant, was born in London, 23 February 1883, the second son in the family of three sons and two daughters of (Sir) Thomas Barlow [q.v.], physician extraordinary to Queen Victoria and Kings Edward VII and George V, and his wife, Ada Helen, daughter of Patrick Dalmahoy, writer to the signet, of Edinburgh. Thomas's elder brother was (Sir) J. Alan Barlow, whose notice appears above.

He was educated at Marlborough (1897-1900) and Trinity College, Cambridge, where he obtained an ordinary degree in four parts (parts i–iii, 1901–3, and part iv in mechanism, 1904). He then entered the century-old family textile business, Barlow and Jones Ltd., of Bolton and Manchester, and over the years was to become one of the most prominent figures in the cotton spinning and weaving industry. He also became a distinguished banker, joining the board of the District Bank in 1922 and becoming its chairman in 1947.

The interests of Lancashire industry were close to Barlow's heart. He became chairman of the Lancashire Industrial Development Council and from 1931 to 1933 was president of the Manchester Chamber of Commerce. This experience fitted him for the post of director-general of civilian clothing which he held from 1941 to 1945. Shortly after the outbreak of war he went to work at the Board of Trade when Sir Cecil Weir [q.v.] and (Dame) Alix Kilroy (later Meynell) were setting up the Control of Factory and Storage Premises, in order to close down factories not required by the war effort or for essential civilian production, thus releasing both employees for essential work and premises which could be used for the replacement of essential factories which had been bombed or for storage, the latter of which was particularly important for the housing of American materials sent to Britain before the United States entered the war. Barlow was controller of factory premises and indeed cleared one of his own factories of spinning and weaving machinery. As director-general of civilian clothing Barlow had to cope with thousands of small businesses. Despite his outspoken and forthright manner and his vigorously held opinions, Barlow won the affection and co-operation of these businesses. Having gained their confidence, he was able to control them with a firm hand. He was an unassuming and courteous man of great integrity and transparent honesty, with the strongest sense of public service. If he found in wartime that not everyon lived up to his high standards, he had no hesitation in telling them so, whosoever they might be.

Barlow cannot have relished spending the whole week in London but he had strong sense of duty and must have known that he was at the top of a very short list of people who could do this job. Perhaps what finally decided him was the thought that he would be able to wear his oldest clothes in London as a duty and boast of his resolve not to buy a new suit until the end of the war. For among his many remarkable qualities masochism held an honoured place. He was known to catch a late, slow train to Manchester in order to avoid a public dinner in that city and a cocktail party in London. People were apt to wonder at his dislike of the latter curious form of entertaining which, it was argued, was entirely suited to his temperament, but certainly not to his tastes. For he was an excellent judge of food and wine, especially Moselle, and liked to invite a couple of friends to a small dinner at his house at Strand-on-the-Green. He would carefully choose a simple dinner to match the qualities of the wines, on which his running commentary was an education. Perhaps, if the next morning were Saturday, he would catch a train to Manchester, where his wife had promised to meet him and escort him to a British Restaurant, just completed in a disused factory. She was a great public worker and felt it was essential for him, a well-known personality, not only to visit such an institution but to be seen to lunch there and, if possible, enjoy the novel experience. As he stood with his wife outside in the rain waiting to hail a taxi he may have remembered being chaffed by fellow members of the Savile Club when he walked out in a cloudburst refusing all offers of a lift.

Despite his robust views Barlow was tolerant of those who disagreed with him. From disagreement there often developed respect and friendship. His annual statements to the District Bank shareholders, until his retirement in 1960, had the typical Barlow stamp of outspoken practicality, sound industrial and trade experience, and an understanding of financial affairs. His financial knowledge led him to be appointed a member of the Capital Issues Committee in post-war years.

Barlow's practical knowledge went hand in hand with artistic appreciation. He was a member of the Council for the Encouragement of Art in Industry and was chairman of its successor, the Council of Industrial Design, which was set up in 1944. The latter arose from the wish of Sir Stafford Cripps and Hugh (later Lord) Dalton [qq.v.] to establish a body to improve industrial design in order to enhance the attractiveness of exports. It was natural that 'Tommy Barlow', as he was known to everyone, should be called in for the preliminary discussions of the project and should emerge as the chairman. In the early days of the Council of Industrial Design his valuable, down-to-earth comments were accepted by the well-known manufacturers who were invited to sit on the Council but had not the advantage of his wide interests. It was certainly unfortunate that in 1947 he reluctantly gave up the chairmanship on the strong advice of his doctors to avoid so much travelling. It was typical of him that almost immediately he took on the chairmanship of the District Bank in Manchester where, as a consolation, he was known to walk about with a book of Greek poems in his pocket. With his deep interest in the arts and his rare wish to influence his great textile business, he had started up before the war a small subsidiary, Helios, inside Barlow & Jones, to produce the finest individual weaving and for this purpose had appointed a distinguished Swiss designer, Marianne Straub. Barlow also became a member of the council of the Royal College of Art.

Barlow's interest in beautiful things originated in his youth. He became a successful collector of early books and manuscripts, and gathered, over forty years, a fine collection of Dürer woodcuts, engravings, and illustrated books. This collection was sold in 1956 to the National Gallery of Victoria, in Melbourne, to which Barlow had previously given important items. Barlow also lent pictures to the Art Treasures Centenary Exhibition (1957) of the Manchester Art Gallery, of which he was for some years chairman of the council. He was created KBE in 1934 and GBE in 1946.

In 1911 Barlow married Esther Sophia (died 1956), daughter of Henry Gaselee, barrister-at-law; they had one son and two daughters. Barlow died at his London home 22 November 1964.

[*The Times*, 24 and 27 November 1964; personal knowledge.]   GORDON RUSSELL

BARNES, SYDNEY FRANCIS (1873-1967), cricketer, was born at Smethwick 19 April 1873, second of the three sons of Richard Barnes, metal tester, who worked for a Birmingham firm for sixty-three years, and his wife, Ann Wood. When Barnes first played in a test match he had taken only 13 wickets in first-class cricket. In a few games for Warwickshire (1893-5) he achieved so little that he was not offered a professional engagement, but 411 wickets in five seasons with Rishton in the Lancashire League brought invitations to join the staff at Old Trafford. These he refused, and he went to Burnley until A. C. MacLaren [q.v.] persuaded him to play in the last match of the 1901 season, in which he took 6-70 against Leicestershire. MCC having refused, MacLaren had undertaken to lead a team to Australia, and he chose Barnes to join it on condition that he played for Lancashire on his return.

Barnes justified his surprising selection with 19 wickets in the first two tests, and if his knee had not broken down early in the third, England might have won the rubber. The injury still troubled him in 1902, when he played in only one test, and it was five years before he played for England again. He had the reputation of being difficult and undependable, and he was in frequent dispute with the Lancashire committee over financial terms. After two seasons, in which he took 213 wickets, he left the county because they would not find him employment in the winter. In 1904 he returned to league cricket and also began to play for Staffordshire in the Minor Counties championship.

Other players having refused terms, Barnes went to Australia in 1907-8 in an unrepresentative side which lost the rubber 4-1. But his bowling was one of the successes of the tour, and he was now approaching the fullness of his remarkable powers. He could bowl almost anything, and his high action, off a short springing run, dug the ball into the pitch and made it lift dangerously. But his unique asset was the strength and suppleness of his fingers, which enabled him to spin the ball above medium pace in either direction. On this tour, by diligent practice under the friendly tuition of M. A. Noble, he cultivated a lethal ball which swung into the batsman's legs and spun away towards the off-stump. He also had some success as a batsman. His 93 against Western Australia was his highest score in first-class cricket, and at Melbourne he came in at 198-7, when 84 were still needed, and with 38 not out helped England to an exciting victory, adding 39 with A. Fielder for the last wicket.

When the Australians won again in England in 1909, Barnes was unfit for the first two tests, but he took 17 wickets in the remaining three, and with F. R. Foster he was largely responsible for the recovery of the Ashes in the tour of 1911-12. In the first test he was uncooperative because he was not allowed to open the bowling, and his record for the match, which was lost, was 4-179. But at Melbourne he achieved one of the historic performances of test cricket, taking the first 4 wickets for 1 run in 5 overs. When on a fast and perfect pitch the sixth wicket fell at 38, his analysis was 11-7-6-5. With (Sir) Jack Hobbs [q.v.] mastering Hordern's spin, this game and the next three were all won and in the series Barnes took 34 wickets at 22.88.

1912 was the year of the triangular tournament. Barnes took 5 wickets in the only game with Australia not ruined by rain, and in three tests against South Africa 34 for 282. In the same wet season he had 70 of 128 wickets taken by Staffordshire at an average of 5.37, including 17-59 against Monmouthshire, and in league cricket for Porthill 66 at 6.98. He put the South Africans to renewed devastation in 1913-14 with 125 wickets on the tour and in four tests 49 at 10.93, his 17-159 at Johannesburg standing as a test record until 1956. In the final test he was 'not available', on the ground that his financial sponsors had not fulfilled their undertakings. War came and this was the end of his test career, although he was asked to go to Australia in 1920, at the age of forty-seven, declining because his family expenses were not guaranteed. In twenty-seven tests he took 189 wickets at 16.43, 83 against South Africa at 9.85.

With odd games for the MCC, the Players, the Minor Counties, and Wales, where he achieved a residential qualification through taking a business at Colwyn Bay after the war, Barnes continued to play spasmodically in first-class cricket until 1930, and at the age of fifty-six he took 8-41 against the South African tourists in 32 consecutive overs. His complete record in first-class cricket was 719 wickets at 17.09, and in 173 innings he made 1,563 runs at 12.70.

In twenty-three seasons for Staffordshire between 1904 and 1935 his total was 1,441 wickets at 8.15, easily a record for the competition. In the short minor-county programme he twice took more than 100 wickets in a season. Some of his feats were astonishing. In 1909 he took 14-13 against Cheshire in a single day, and in 1932, when he was fifty-nine, 13-50 against Lancashire II. Although by now heavily reliant on embrocation, bandages, and other supports, he played in league cricket until 1940, and in forty-six seasons he had 4,069 wickets at 6.08. In all grades of cricket more than a quarter of his 23,509 overs were maidens, and he took 6,229 wickets at 8.33. Ten times he had all 10 wickets in an innings. At the lower levels he was also a useful batsman, making a number of centuries.

It has been severely said of Barnes that 'practically all his cricket days were confined to intimidating poor Saturday afternoon working-men who were out before they got to the wicket'. It is true that much of his career cannot be measured by the highest standards, and he was seldom even playing in the strongest leagues, but his reputation is secure. In the great seasons before 1914 it was the opinion of nearly all the cricketers who played with him that he was the finest bowler they had known. The technical perfection was made more formidable by an unsmiling hostility towards the batsman. He bowled fast and straight with a positive intent, allowing no relaxation as he probed for weakness and laid it bare. Even when playing under authoritarians like MacLaren he would set his own field and pursue his own tactical plan. 'Whenever I have been bowling', he once said, 'I have been captain.'

In his dedication to the task of removing the batsman Barnes was sometimes an uneasy colleague, but to some extent his attitudes have been misunderstood. In an age when professional cricketers tended to be feckless or subservient he insisted on a proper rate for the job. He preferred league cricket because it allowed him the security of regular employment outside the game, and even in the glamour of international cricket he would not be exploited. Many of the principles for which he contended have become commonplaces of the professional's life.

From 1940 to 1967 Barnes was employed in the clerk's department of the Staffordshire County Council, being mainly concerned with the engrossing of agreements and the preparation of indictments for quarter-sessions. Even at his retirement at the age of ninety-four his handwriting had a remarkable strength and clarity. He died at Chadsmoor, Staffordshire, 26 December 1967. A portrait by Harry Rutherford was commissioned by the Staffordshire club in 1952 and presented to the MCC, of which Barnes had been made an honorary member in 1949.

In 1903 Barnes married Alice Maud, daughter of Charles Pearce, jeweller, and divorced wife of George Taylor; they had one son.

[W. S. White, *Sydney Barnes*, 1935; Leslie Duckworth, *S. F. Barnes—Master Bowler*, 1967; *Wisden's Cricketers' Almanack*, 1963, 1968.]
                                           M. M. REESE

BARNES, SIR THOMAS JAMES (1888–1964), Treasury solicitor, was born 21 March 1888 at Wilmslow, Cheshire, the only son of Thomas Barnes and his wife, Esther Mary Pither. His father was a clerk attached to the Chancery division of the High Court of Justice. After education at Mercers School, Barnes was articled for five years to Robert John Ball, a partner in the firm of H. C. Coote & Ball, solicitors in the City of London, which specialized in shipping matters. He was admitted a solicitor in 1911. He did not take out a practising certificate, but just before his admission he followed his father into the lord chancellor's department. He joined as a temporary clerk and later became a principal clerk in the Chancery Registrars' Office. Shortly after the outbreak of war in 1914 he joined the Royal Naval Volunteer Reserve. He became chief petty officer in 1915 and sublieutenant in 1916, serving in the Dover Patrol. His ship was blown up in 1916 and as a result of this experience he developed a lasting form of neurosis and was discharged in May 1917. In the following month he was lent by the lord chancellor's department to the Ministry of Shipping legal adviser's department; within two years he had become the legal adviser. In 1920 he was appointed solicitor to the Board of Trade at the early age of thirty-two.

In 1934 Barnes was appointed procurator-general and Treasury solicitor, a position which he retained for nearly twenty years. He was the first solicitor ever to be appointed to these offices and he proved to be the outstanding government lawyer of his generation. During his time there was an enormous increase in the work of his office. At the beginning of the war new departments were set up for which the Treasury solicitor acted; many of them remained for the rest of his term of office.

As a general rule Barnes was content to let his staff get on with their allotted work with the minimum of supervision. He did, however, take personal and active charge over a number of matters of special importance and difficulty. He directed a number of inquiries under the Tribunals of Inquiry (Evidence) Act, 1921, the best known being the budget leak in 1936 and the Lynskey tribunal in 1948. During the war he was particularly successful in settling difficult problems of compensation arising from the requisitioning of land and other property by the armed forces and government departments. Towards the end of the war he was actively concerned in the arrangements for setting up the Nuremberg tribunal to try the major war criminals.

After the war, although Barnes had always been a formidable champion of the Crown's position in the courts, he played a leading part in the Crown Proceedings Act, 1947, which made the Crown liable to all the ordinary forms of action. The proposals for this reform had languished for twenty years or more, but he realized that the time had arrived for a big step forward, and he threw himself wholeheartedly into the preparation of the legislation, and later into the task of making it work smoothly.

While Treasury solicitor, Barnes served on a number of important committees, including the Evershed committee on Supreme Court practice and procedure (1947–53). To all these problems he brought a lively intelligence. He worked very quickly and had an astonishing resource in finding solutions to intractable problems. He never dwelt on difficulties, but turned his acute and practical mind to the task of finding a solution. He had a real talent for negotiation. He always disclaimed an academic knowledge of the law, but he had an extremely tenacious memory and acquired a fund of legal wisdom and experience which was always available and to the point. It was a delight to work with him. He was always accessible and informal. If a colleague brought him a problem, he would listen intently, pick up the problem quickly, and then make some helpful suggestions, often referring to some decided case which on examination proved to be exactly in point or to a precedent in the office. It was all done quickly and decisively and with charm and humour. He was generous in his encouragement of others. He had a good political sense and his advice was essentially practical. All these qualities endeared him to the ministers and departmental officials for whom he worked, and to his own staff.

Barnes retired in 1953 and became a part-time director of the Prudential Assurance Company. But the work did not appeal to him and he soon resigned. In 1954 he was appointed a member of the Monopolies Restrictive Practices Commission and remained a member until the end of 1959 when he retired on the grounds of ill health. While Treasury solicitor he had frequently been called upon to advise on ecclesiastical matters. After his retirement, right up to the time of his death, he took a leading part in revising the Canon Law of the Church of England.

His main recreation was golf, which he much enjoyed. He had been brought up at Sunningdale, and for most of his life he was a leading member of Sunningdale and Swinley Forest golf clubs. In between the wars he played to a single-figure handicap, and was a difficult man to beat.

In 1924 he married Elsie Margaret Clover, a widow, daughter of John Alexander, formerly chief clerk, Bow Street police court; they had no children. He was knighted in 1927, appointed KCB in 1938 and promoted GCB in 1948. He died in London 4 February 1964 and his widow later in the same year.

[*The Times*, 6 February 1964; private information; personal knowledge.]

ROBERT SPEED

BARRY, ERNEST JAMES (1882–1968), professional sculler, was born 13 February 1882 at Canning Town, the son of Henry Barry, lighterman, and his wife, Elizabeth Spall.

While still an apprentice in 1902, Barry was entered for the Newcastle Handicap, a sculling race on which considerable betting took place, and reached the final. He started favourite but lost by a length to Jack Dodds of Hexham who, according to the local press, 'got five cuts at the water before Barry left the stakeboat'. There is little doubt that Barry was held back at the word 'Go'. Coming out of his time, Barry won the 1903 Doggett's Coat and Badge 'pretty easily' but there are no further records until 1908. Then, still a virtual novice, he raced the Australian, George Towns, who had already won the world championship four times and held the British championship since 1899. Towns led the lighter Barry as far as Chiswick church but was beaten by two lengths in 21 minutes 12⅖ seconds, a time for the Putney to Mortlake course which has only once been bettered.

Barry challenged Dick Arnst of New Zealand for the world championship in August 1910 and the pair raced over 3¼ miles on the Zambesi river, five miles above Victoria Falls. Fearing the effects of the altitude, Barry delayed his effort until the last quarter-mile but both scullers stopped 300 yards from the finish. The huge New Zealander recovered first and paddled home alone.

In 1911 and 1912 Barry successfully defended the *Sportsman* Challenge Cup for the British championship against W. Albany of Lea Bridge and W. H. Fogwell of Australia and in July 1912, in appalling conditions, took his revenge on Arnst over the Putney to Mortlake course to become the first English world champion for thirty-six years. Starting at three to one on, Arnst led by two lengths at Harrods, where Barry closed the gap and with superior watermanship drew level above Hammersmith. The lead changed hands several times before Chiswick Steps and at the crossing to Duke's Meadows Barry, mastering the rough water better, gained two lengths within 150 yards. Arnst was six lengths behind at Barnes Bridge

but with a final effort closed to within two lengths. But he could do no more and stopped 80 yards from the post. The race was described as the finest professional sculling race ever seen in England. Three months later Barry easily retained his title against the Canadian, Edward Durnan, over the same course, winning the *Sportsman* Cup outright and £1,000.

In 1913 there followed a second defence of his world title for £500 a side against Harry Pearce of Australia, father of the 1928 Olympic winner and subsequent world champion, Bob Pearce. Pearce led to Hammersmith but was six lengths down by Chiswick Steps. One month after the outbreak of World War I, in which he spent four years in the army, Barry beat another Australian, J. Paddon, and there were no further challengers until Felton in 1919.

The Zambesi river race of 1910 was Barry's sole defeat until, at the age of thirty-seven, in 1919, he lost to F. Felton of Australia, who was fitter and two stones heavier, when it was so rough at Putney it was possible to see under the bottom of the boats. This reverse was avenged by Barry a year later in 1920, before an estimated 150,000 spectators, on the Parramatta river, when he won by twelve lengths, to gain his fifth world championship. He was, with some justice, known as 'The Incomparable'.

On his retirement as a sculler, Barry spent the rest of his working life as a professional coach in Denmark and Germany, enjoying such success that it is remarkable, and even sad, that he was never employed by British clubs. He was appointed King's Bargemaster, a position from which he retired in 1952 because of ill health.

Over six feet in height, Barry still weighed no more than 11 stone 9 lbs for his last race. Though a sufferer from asthma in old age, he retained full mental alertness and an upright, soldierly bearing.

Barry married Lottie Hammerton, of Twickenham; there were two sons and three daughters of the marriage. Later in his life Barry had to sell all but two of his trophies to support himself and his daughter, Thelma, who contracted poliomyelitis. Barry died at West Middlesex Hospital, Isleworth, 21 July 1968.

[*British Rowing Almanacks*; Hylton Cleaver, *A History of Rowing*, 1957; private information; personal knowledge.] DESMOND HILL

BARRY, SIR GERALD REID (1898–1968), journalist and administrator, was born in Surbiton, Surrey, 20 November 1898, the fourth of six children and the second of four sons of the Revd George Duncan Barry, a clerk in holy orders, and his wife, Edith Geraldine Reid. He was educated at Marlborough College, and in 1916 was elected to an exhibition at Corpus Christi,

Cambridge, where he proposed to study history, but from 1917 to 1919 he served in the RFC and RAF, being demobilized with the rank of captain.

He became a journalist, wrote leading articles for the *Daily Express*, and then joined the staff of the *Saturday Review* in 1921, becoming editor 1 January 1925. He was twenty-six. He sought to make the periodical 'an organ of the most persuasive kind of Conservatism', but his politics concerned principles not Party. Throughout his journalistic career he was equally interested in literature and the arts. The *Saturday Review* regained its distinction under his leadership. When in February 1930 its owner committed the journal, without Barry's knowledge, to support the United Empire Party of Lord Beaverbrook [q.v.], he resigned. His editorial staff went with him.

The next two weeks saw a remarkable feat of journalism. Barry left the *Saturday Review* on 28 February. Six days later the creation of the *Week-end Review* was announced with Barry as editor. With his old colleagues he produced its first number on 14 March. The *Week-end Review* (of politics, books, the theatre, art, and music), as its full title ran, got off to a resounding start. Barry's refusal to accept proprietorial dictation had aroused powerful interest. His first number carried messages from the prime minister, Ramsay MacDonald, Stanley Baldwin, Herbert (later Viscount) Samuel, Augustine Birrell, (Sir) Max Beerbohm, Sir Ronald Ross, Sir Edwin Lutyens [qq.v.], and others.

It might have been expected that after such euphoria there would be anticlimax. But the next four years were Barry's journalistic heyday. In 1932 he edited *A Week-end Calendar* and in 1933 he published *This England*, extracts from a *Week-end Review* column to which readers had sent absurdities from the English Press. That the *Week-end Review* was 'independent with a Conservative background' was subordinate to the fact that it was lively, well written, and always interesting. This could not compensate for its lack of funds. In January 1934 it was merged into the *New Statesman*. Barry held his seat on the board of the combined journals until his death, and the *New Statesman* continued the 'This England' feature.

He had been gradually moving leftwards and in 1934 became features editor of the *News Chronicle*, becoming managing editor in February 1936. He resigned at the end of 1947, but stayed on that board also. Memories of his previous resignation aroused rumours of new conflict, but the truth was that Barry had reached a climacteric and needed new pastures. On 10 March 1948 Herbert Morrison (later Lord Morrison of Lambeth, q.v.), lord president of the Council, announced in the House of Commons that Lord Ismay [q.v.] had agreed to be chairman of the council for the Festival of Britain, with Barry as its salaried director-general. The Festival gave Barry new life. He impressed his character on it and made it, in the words of a later tribute, 'a manifestation of gaiety and ordered imagination in a world that he knew to be short of both'. His influence extended to the Festival's architecture. In *Who's Who* he listed his interests as 'people, places, and buildings'.

The success of the Festival was his second great triumph. It was also his last. *The Times* (22 November 1968) said he had become a much sought-after figure. In fact he never found another post to challenge his qualities. Morrison had assured him such a post would be forthcoming when the Festival ended, but by then the Labour Government was out of office, and although Morrison strove to keep his promise, he was powerless to do so. The remaining sixteen years of Barry's life were filled with various appointments—adviser on public policy to the National Farmers' Union, consultant to the London County Council on the development of the Crystal Palace and park, chairman of the Barbican committee, from 1958 editor in charge of Granada Television's plans for educational broadcasting, chairman of a theatre censorship reform committee, and others. He was said to revel in presiding over committees—he was a founder member of PEP (Political and Economic Planning)—but it was *faute de mieux*. Probably the time in later years that he was happiest was when in 1955 he returned temporarily to the *News Chronicle* as literary editor. For some years he wrote leaders for the *Sunday Times*. In 1945 he had written *Report on Greece*, and in 1965 he edited, together with J. Bronowski, James Fisher [q.v.], and Sir Julian Huxley, *Health and Wealth*. To this Dictionary Barry contributed the notices of Robert James Cruikshank and Gerald Aylmer Vallance. He died in London 21 November 1968.

Barry was a good talker, with a lively mind. He was knighted in 1951, was made an honorary ARIBA (1940), and a FRSA. He was four times married, three marriages ending in divorce. In 1920 he married Gladys, daughter of G. Chishom Williams, a surgeon; they had one son. In 1932 he married Mrs Helen Edith Selwyn Jepson, daughter of Richard Rigg, a barrister and former MP, who later became mayor of the city of Westminster. In 1944 he married Mrs Vera Burton, daughter of Vladimir Poliakoff, and they had one son. His fourth marriage in 1959 was to Mrs Diana Wooton Schlumberger. A plaque commemorating Barry was unveiled outside the Royal Festival Hall in 1971.

[*The Times*, 22, 25, and 28 November 1968; private information; personal knowledge.]

WILLIAM HALEY

BARSTOW, SIR GEORGE LEWIS (1874-1966), civil servant and chairman of the Prudential Assurance Company, was born in India 20 May 1874, the second son of Henry Clements Barstow, ICS, and his wife, Cecilia Clementina, daughter of the Hon. and Revd John Baillie, canon of York. His grandfather was Thomas Barstow of Fulford Park and Garrow Hill, York, of which city members of the family had been prominent merchant adventurers since the early seventeenth century.

Barstow was a scholar of Clifton College and Emmanuel College, Cambridge, where he obtained first classes in both parts of the classical tripos (1895-6). He entered the Home Civil Service in the Local Government Board in 1896 and transferred to the Treasury in 1898. He became a principal clerk in 1909 and was appointed CB in 1913. During the war of 1914-18 Barstow was primarily involved in the problems of supply to the armed forces. In the unprecedented circumstances of a world war he earned the gratitude and respect of many of the chiefs of the Services for the positive and helpful way in which he dealt with their requirements.

In 1919 Barstow was appointed an assistant secretary in control of one of the major functions of the Treasury, the supply services, where he served until 1927 and was notable not only for his efficiency but also for the humour he brought to his job. It fell to him to approve on behalf of the Treasury the settlement of the numerous points, some trivial in terms of money but some serious, and many of them highly technical, arising out of the financial control of the railways during the war. It was not always easy to see those points which it would ultimately be to the interest of the Treasury to press against a particular company—and there were then over a hundred of them covered by the agreement. But Barstow's acumen in discerning what to challenge and where to compromise impressed the highly skilled railway accountants with his almost instinctive ability to combine a sense of equity with instant insistence of what was due to the public purse. He was promoted KCB in 1920.

During the transition of the British navy from coal- to oil-firing before the war Barstow had been concerned in the Treasury with the negotiations whereby the British Government took a substantial share in the Anglo-Persian Oil Company. When he left the Treasury in 1927 he was appointed to be the government director of the Anglo-Persian (later Anglo-Iranian) Oil Company in succession to Lord Bradbury [q.v.] and he so remained until 1946. He was for many years also a director of the Midland Bank and other companies, but undoubtedly his most significant work after leaving the public service was on the board of the Prudential Assurance

Company. He joined as a director in 1928, became deputy chairman in 1935, and was chairman from 1941 until his retirement from the board in 1953. He bore the heavy responsibility of chairman during the war years in London after 1941 and after the war he served the Prudential during a period of vigorous growth and reorganization. The board exchanged much of its earlier formal routine for a more lively and informed participation by all the directors who, under Barstow's chairmanship, learned to work in close intimacy with the management: the change had lasting effect.

At the Prudential, as in the Civil Service, Barstow was long remembered for his wit. He was a man of erudition and wide reading with catholic tastes both in literature and in the arts and a most retentive memory. He had a capacity which never left him for being interested in any person or subject. A member of the Society of Dilettanti, he also possessed a marked talent for the writing of light verse which he employed for the pleasure of his family and friends; his verses were always infused with his kindly wit and gentle humour and were treasured by their recipients. In the Confrères, a well-known dining club, he excelled most in the cut and thrust of conversation across the table rather than in the more formal statements of points of view which followed dinner.

Barstow married in 1904 Enid Lilian, only daughter of Sir A. T. Lawrence (later first Baron Trevethin, q.v.). They had a daughter and two sons, the elder of whom won the DSO, and the younger was killed in action, in the war of 1939-45. The Barstows were devoted to their home, Chapel House, Builth, Breconshire, where Barstow died 29 January 1966. While still at the Prudential and after his retirement he reorganized the finances of the Welsh Church, as chairman of the finance committee at an important time. He took a great interest in the university of Wales and, in particular, Swansea University College, of which he was president from 1929 to 1955. He was also deputy chairman of the court of the university of London and a governor of Christ College, Brecon.

His portrait, painted by his daughter, Lady Caccia, is included in a comprehensive collection of Prudential portraits at Holborn Bars, and another, by Allan Gwynne-Jones, hangs at Swansea University College.

[Private information; personal knowledge.]

JOHN MELLOR

BARTLETT, SIR FREDERIC CHARLES (1886-1969), psychologist, was born in Stow-on-the-Wold 20 October 1886, the second son of William Bartlett, master boot-maker, and his wife, Temperance Matilda Howman. In his teens he was eductaed at home, his health being thought too poor, following an attack of pleurisy, for him to go away to school. This apparent handicap allowed him to read very widely, and to spend time walking about the Gloucestershire countryside. He preserved throughout his life a tendency to observe human everyday activity and to base psychological thought upon that observation, rather than upon academic thinking.

As an external student of London University, Bartlett obtained first class honours in philosophy in 1910 and an MA with special distinction in 1912. He moved next to Cambridge: he had by this time strong interests in sociological questions, and was attracted to St. John's College where W. H. R. Rivers was active. The anthropological interests of the latter were, however, combined with a firm belief in the importance of experimental measurements of the performance of individual people. Bartlett thus worked in the new laboratory of experimental psychology under C. S. Myers (whose notice he subsequently contributed to this Dictionary), and obtained another first in part i of the moral sciences tripos in 1914. He then became assistant director of the laboratory, and with the coming of war was thrust into major responsibility for it. His health made him unfit for military service, whereas Myers and Rivers left Cambridge for the duration. Even when they returned to Cambridge, Myers soon left again, and Rivers died: thus from 1922 Bartlett became director of the psychological laboratory and reader in experimental psychology. In 1931 he was made the first professor of experimental psychology in Cambridge, the post which he retained until his retirement in 1952. During the thirty-year period of directing the laboratory he had developed it from one assistant to over seventy staff and research workers, and had trained a remarkable galaxy of students. In the post-war years, the chairs at Oxford, Cambridge, and London were for a substantial time all occupied simultaneously by Bartlett students, as were a very large number of other chairs both in the United Kingdom and overseas.

This remarkable achievement within the university was accompanied after 1939 by a great deal of public service. The new technology of the war created a need for more information about resistance to stress by human beings, their sensory abilities, or their performance as a gunnery control system. Without such information it was difficult to design radar screens, target indicators, or tank gunnery controls. Bartlett served on the flying personnel research committee of the Air Ministry, and also on the Medical Research Council, as well as making his laboratory in Cambridge a centre for investigations of his kind. After the war, industrial

problems were added to military ones. From 1944 onwards the Medical Research Council maintained an applied psychology research unit within Bartlett's department, and after his retirement he continued to act as a consultant to it, as well as taking part energetically in committee work on the problem of improving efficiency in the individual person at work. His services were recognized by the CBE in 1941 and by his knighthood in 1948. His pre-eminence in his field was unchallenged.

Throughout this period his scientific thought was highly original and unconventional, and yet has since been widely accepted. His best-known book was *Remembering*, published in 1932. In it he reported a lengthy series of experiments on perception and on memory, which showed that human awareness of events was both selective and constructive: much which struck the eye was never seen or remembered, and conversely a great deal was thought to have been perceived or recalled which had not in fact occurred. These importations, as well as the choice of the items which were correctly reported, showed that perception and remembering were controlled by some process sensitive to the purposes and interests of the man concerned. This line of thought departed from the orthodoxy of the day, which whether behaviourist or *gestaltist* tended to see human awareness as passively determined by the pattern of present events or of past experience. Some intellectual origins for Bartlett's views can be found not only in Rivers and Myers, but also in James Ward [q.v.] whom he had known in Cambridge, and from the neurologist Sir Henry Head [q.v.]. The greater part of Bartlett's ideas, however, must have originated with his own observation of human behaviour, and *Remembering* is copiously illustrated with cases in which Africans had selectively remembered events of little importance to an Englishman or vice versa.

This tendency to observe naturally occurring behaviour was given a fresh thrust by wartime problems. In dealing with them, he was assisted by K. J. W. Craik, a brilliant young investigator who was one of the first to see the possible use in psychology of explanations derived from cybernetics and control engineering. Bartlett actively encouraged Craik's ideas, and following Craik's tragic accidental death in 1945, Bartlett continued to inspire and administer a group of research workers developing similar theories. Characteristically, his interest in control processes was stimulated not only by abstract intellectual influences, but also by his keen interest in cricket and tennis. He would frequently discuss the ways in which the everyday behaviour of the player making a stroke required the psychologist to suppose that each action was controlled by a computed model of future events, a process far more complex than the simple theories of classical psychology.

Bartlett's personal style of leadership was kindly, encouraging, and informal. He possessed pre-eminently the gift for inspiring enthusiasm, and for bringing out the value in any contribution no matter how humble. His influence was probably spread most effectively through discussion classes and informal meetings, with his exciting lectures as a second string. He did, however, write a number of other books besides *Remembering*, as well as many papers.

From 1924 to 1948, an unenviably long tour of office, Bartlett was editor of the *British Journal of Psychology*. He was president of Section J (psychology) of the British Association in 1929, was elected FRS in 1932, was president (1950) and honorary fellow (1954) of the British Psychological Society, and was an honorary member of the Experimental Psychology Society of the UK (1960). He was a foreign member or associate of the Société Française de Psychologie, of the American Philosophical Society of Philadelphia, of the US National Academy of Sciences, and of the American Academy of Arts and Sciences, and an honorary member of a number of foreign psychological societies. He received honorary degrees from Athens, Princeton, Louvain, London, Edinburgh, Oxford, and Padua. He also received the Baly and the Huxley medals (1943), the Royal medal of the Royal Society (1952), the Longacre award of the Aero Medical Association (1952), and the gold medal of the International Academy of Aviation and Space Medicine (1964).

To the end of his life Bartlett continued to take an active interest in new developments, corresponding and discussing personally with a world-wide network of leading investigators who found his comments to the last invaluable and worth seeking. He died in Cambridge 30 September 1969.

Bartlett married in 1920 Emily Mary (died 1974), daughter of William Henry Smith, JP, of Helmshore, Lancashire, herself a psychologist from the early days in Cambridge; they had two sons. A portrait of Bartlett by Peter Greenham is in the Psychological Laboratory, university of Cambridge.

[*The Times*, 1 October 1969; D. E. Broadbent in *Biographical Memoirs of Fellows of the Royal Society*, vol. xvi, 1970; private information; personal knowledge.]

D. E. BROADBENT

BATEMAN, HENRY MAYO (1887-1970), cartoonist, was born 15 February 1887, of English parents, in Sutton Forest, New South Wales, Australia, the only son and elder of two children of Henry Charles Bateman, then a farmer and later a business man, and his wife, Rose Mayo. The family returned to England in 1888.

Bateman was educated at Forest Hill House, in south-east London, but left school at the age of sixteen. He then studied drawing and painting at Westminster School of Art and the Goldsmith's Institute at New Cross. Afterwards he worked for three years in the London studio of the Dutch painter, Charles van Havenmaet.

In 1903 Bateman's first published drawings appeared in *Scraps* 'for a few shillings each'. The year 1904 saw the tentative beginnings of his long association with the *Tatler* magazine. These early essays in humour were drawn before the artist had decided upon the true course of his career. A gifted draughtsman, he could not decide between a career as a fine artist or one as a caricaturist. Ultimately he chose to fulfil a childhood ambition 'to make people laugh'.

In 1919 the shy, diffident, moody young artist, in his own words, 'went mad on paper'. He began drawing people not as they looked, which was the traditional manner, but as they *felt*, which was not. Influenced by two artists of originality and comic genius, Emmanuel Poiré ('Caran d'Ache'), a Russian-born Frenchman, and another Russian, the caricaturist Henry Ospovat, his new-found freedom of expression injected a refreshing liveliness and spirit into English comic art. His humour rarely depended upon a caption but was, instead, an intrinsic part of the drawing, while his subject matter reflected 'the very holy of holies of suburbia'.

Bateman's first one-man exhibition, 'Satires and Caricatures', was held in the Brook Street Art Gallery, London, in 1911. In spite of some acidity and youthful cynicism, Bateman was never a satirist; his was the humour of (sometimes grudging) acceptance rather than rebellion. In appearance he neither looked nor acted the part of the Bohemian artist of popular imagination. In *The Art of the Illustrator* (1917) is reproduced a photograph of the 'triumphantly funny' artist standing sternly by his drawing board, wearing a stiff white collar and a pin-stripe suit.

In 1912, while producing a series of acutely observed theatrical caricatures for the *Tatler* under the heading 'By Our Untamed Artist', he drew 'The Missed Putt', a golfing drama which he considered to be the first of 'The Man Who . . .' cartoons, a long-running series illustrating social gaffes based on middle-class aspirations and snobbery. The drawings usually depicted a crushed, embarrassed figure having just committed a flagrant breach of convention—'The Man Who Threw a Snowball at St. Moritz' for example—surrounded by a writhing assembly, apoplectic with outrage and contempt. The humour was strengthened by accurate recording of costume, architecture, and background. The appeal of 'The Man Who . . .' is summed up in the words of the philosopher Thomas Hobbes [q.v.]: 'The passion of laughter is nothing else but sudden glory, arising from sudden conception of some eminency in ourselves, by comparison with the infirmity of others, or with our own formerly.' In *Punch*, which began publishing his work in 1915, Bateman brought to perfection the strip without words of which 'The Boy Who Breathed on the Glass at the British Museum' is a good example.

Reviewing Bateman's second one-man show at the Leicester Galleries in 1919 an art critic from *The Times* declared that the drawings had 'a comic beauty of line, a rhythmical extravagance like that of the Ingoldsby Legends and the choruses of Offenbach'. This exhibition was perhaps Bateman's artistic high-water mark although his public popularity continued to flourish and grow.

As a young man he attempted to overcome shyness and to release pent-up energies by taking boxing lessons and tap-dancing instruction. But he was not a robust man. In 1915, after volunteering for military service, he was swiftly returned to civilian life. For many years he was an active member of the Chelsea Arts Club and London Sketch Club. After World War I he moved from London to Reigate, Surrey, where he lived quietly but industriously for fourteen years.

As his popularity grew, Bateman's cartoons were published throughout the world, providing him with an international reputation and an income which made him the most highly paid cartoonist in Britain. His drawings inspired countless imitators.

Several collections of Bateman's drawings were published during his lifetime. Apart from the two already mentioned, his exhibitions included: 'Exhibition of Drawings', Leicester Galleries, London (1921); 'Paintings of Spain', Leicester Galleries, London (1936); 'Retrospective Exhibition of Drawings', the Fine Art Society, London (1962); 'Caricatures by H. M. Bateman', Leicester Galleries, London (1974); 'More Caricatures by H. M. Bateman', Leicester Galleries, London (1974); and 'H. M. Bateman', The Langton Gallery, London (1978).

Shortly after the outbreak of World War II Bateman decided upon semi-retirement. He moved to Devon where he indulged his lifelong recreation of trout fishing with the fly. In old age he remained an upright figure, as clipped and neat, and as peppery, as the 'Colonels' (another of his cartoon series) which he drew with relish and affection. He visited London only rarely but managed to travel extensively abroad.

In 1926 Bateman married Brenda Mary Collison, the daughter of Octavius Weir, a country gentleman, of Stratford St. Mary. There were two daughters. Bateman died on the Maltese island of Gozo 11 February 1970. Some of his best self-caricatures are reproduced in the book edited by Jensen listed in the bibliography below.

[*H. M. Bateman by Himself*, 1937; Percy V. Bradshaw, *The Art of the Illustrator*, 1917; John Jensen (ed.), *The Man Who . . . and Other Drawings*, 1975; Michael Bateman, *The Man Who Drew the Twentieth Century*, 1969; *The Times*, 13 February 1970; private information; personal knowledge.]

JOHN P. JENSEN

BAYNES, NORMAN HEPBURN (1877–1961), historian, was born at Putney 29 May 1877, the elder child and only son of Alfred Henry Baynes, the general secretary of the Baptist Missionary Society, and his wife, Emma Katherine Bigwood. He lived in London, then in Eastbourne, moving to Northwood on his father's retirement in 1906. He never married and after his father's death in 1914 he continued to live in Northwood with his mother until she died in 1935, when he eventually settled in London. Brought up in a close-knit and devoted family circle he enjoyed a sheltered and happy childhood and at the same time had instilled into him a strong sense of public duty and Christian purpose. He went to Eastbourne College for which, despite his intense dislike of organized games, he retained throughout his life a strong affection, although his surviving papers and later personal recollections indicated that the formative influence in his life was his family circle.

His diaries contain a wealth of factual detail on family holidays and later, as a young man, travel abroad, particularly a visit to Istanbul where he and his father met Sir Edwin Pears [q.v.]. He spent some months in Tübingen gaining considerable mastery of the German language. At New College, Oxford, he took a first class in classical honour moderations (1898), but a second in *literae humaniores* (1900). He was bitterly disappointed at not getting a first, although the more mature judgement of later years admitted that this had been a fair assessment, for he recognized that he was no philosopher. His powers as a historian were, however, shown by his success in winning the Lothian prize (1901) and the Arnold essay prize (1903). In both cases the subject (Heraclius, and then the military reforms of Diocletian and Constantine), as well as entries in his diaries, indicated his growing interest in East Rome. But he first chose as his profession the bar, studying in the chambers of R. J. Parker (later Lord Parker of Waddington, q.v.); he was called to the bar by Lincoln's Inn in 1903; and until 1916 he was a tutor under the Law Society.

During the war of 1914-18 Baynes worked on intelligence matters at Watergate House. It was at this time that he finally decided to abandon the law and turn to the teaching of history. He had already refused an invitation to stand for a Liberal seat in the London area, and in 1913 he had forged his first link with University College, London, when he was appointed assistant in the department of history. After the war he refused an invitation to return as a don to his Oxford college. Indeed he always prided himself on being a cockney and the member of a cockney university. In 1919 he became a reader in the history of the Roman Empire in the university of London and from 1931 he held a personal chair of Byzantine history; in 1936 he was elected a fellow of University College; from 1937 he gave up all duties in ancient history and was reappointed to an honorary professorship of Byzantine history and institutions. On his retirement in 1942 he was given the title of emeritus professor by the university and was presented by his friends with an *Address* and Bibliography of his writings (privately printed).

During the last years of his academic career Baynes worked in Oxford in the Foreign Research and Press Service, for he found it impossible to concentrate on academic work during a time of world crisis. Therefore from 1939 to 1945 he used his historical training in the field of modern German history and produced two large fully annotated volumes of Hitler's pre-war speeches (1942). The depth of his involvement in the national struggle was demonstrated by his choice of subject for his Romanes lecture in Oxford in June 1942: 'Intellectual Liberty and Totalitarian Claims'; its delivery was said to have been a brilliant caricature of the oratory of the Führer on whose speeches he had been working. In 1945 he returned to London and to Byzantine studies. On his seventieth birthday the *Journal of Roman Studies* (vol. xxxvii, 1947, with a bibliography of his writings) was dedicated to him. He spent much time editing in his own impeccable way a volume of essays on Byzantium (1948), planned more than twenty years earlier, and he collaborated with E. A. S. Dawes to translate the lives of three early Byzantine saints (1948). But he did little of the major work planned, notably a social history of East Rome, because of increasing illness, finally culminating in several years of complete helplessness.

Baynes's interests as a scholar covered a wide range from biblical history to the early middle ages, but he came increasingly to concentrate on the late Roman and early Byzantine periods and is perhaps best known for his work on Constantine I (Raleigh lecture, 1929) and the *Historia Augusta* (1926). He contributed chapters on the sixth- and seventh-century Byzantine emperors to the *Cambridge Medieval History* (vols. i and ii) and was one of the editors of the *Cambridge Ancient History* (vol. xii), as well as a contributor on Constantine. Much of his work took the form of reviews or bibliographical notes (many for the *Byzantinische Zeitschrift*, often subjected to ruthless editorial pruning. He was never afraid to combine his exact scholarship with imaginative reconstruction, unlike J. B. Bury (whose notice he contributed to this Dictionary), whom he knew and admired, although he realized Bury's inadequacies, as he showed in the perceptive appraisal in his Memoir of him (1929). In contrast to Bury, Baynes had the power of vivid reconstruction, bringing Byzantium to life for the uninitiated, as his masterly short study of the *Byzantine Empire* (1925) well illustrates. His published work in the academic field was often controversial, but always stimulating and marked by intellectual integrity. The full extent of his activities can best be realized from his continuous stream of correspondence with contemporary scholars, including names such as Delehaye, Ensslin, Stein, Bidez, Grégoire, and Dölger. He was almost overfastidious in his approach and often put as much work into his letters, or his reviews and biographical notes, as others put into an article or chapter of a book. But in all he did or said he remained essentially a Victorian individualist to whom the elimination of 'alternatives' was unthinkable.

But Baynes's influence can never be fully assessed. Above all he valued friendship and he had a genius for making contacts in every walk of life. He had an extensive circle of friends ranging from his non-graduate evening students and his Ancient History Circle to the more severely academic dons invited to the week-end meetings of his Near East Group. Surviving correspondence and press cuttings illustrate the range of lectures, social evenings, discussions, play readings, which flourished in the stimulating atmosphere he created. From an early age he had been a gifted performer as a comedian and he was always ready to improvise his unrivalled comic turns, whether in his family circle, or in aid of charities, or to amuse soldiers in wartime hospitals. He had a magnificent presence and was a master of Victorian oratory as well as of exact scholarship. In later years he rarely left England, but on his infrequent visits to congresses abroad he created such an impression that he was long remembered not only as a scholar but as a splendid critic and fierce opponent in debate who could yet remain 'an English gentleman'.

Baynes was elected FBA in 1930, an honorary

fellow of Westfield College, London (1937), and of New College, Oxford (1947), a corresponding member of the Bavarian Academy of Sciences (1937), and later of the Belgian (1952) and Serbian (1959) Academies. He was doctor *honoris causa* of the universities of St. Andrews (1934), Oxford (1942), Durham (1946), Cambridge (1949), and London (1951). He died in London 12 February 1961.

[An *Address presented to Norman Hepburn Baynes*, privately printed, 1942; J. M. Hussey in *Proceedings* of the British Academy, vol. xlix, 1963, and in the *Bulletin* of Dr Williams's Library, no. 72, 1967; private information; personal knowledge.]   J. M. HUSSEY

BEATTY, SIR (ALFRED) CHESTER (1875–1968), mining engineer, art collector, and philanthropist, was born 7 February 1875 in New York City, the youngest of the three sons of John Cuming Beatty, banker, of New York City, and his wife, Hetty, daughter of William Gedney Bull. He was educated at Westminster School, Dobbs Ferry, New York, at Columbia University (School of Mines) from which he graduated as a mining engineer, and at Princeton University. At Columbia School of Mines he came top in every subject except geology, where he came second. At the age of twenty-eight he became consulting engineer and assistant general manager of the Guggenheim Exploration Company, where he worked with the equally renowned engineer John Hays Hammond. Together they acquired and developed many of Guggenheim's best mines, including silver mines in Mexico, copper mines in the western states of the USA, and prospecting concessions in the Belgian Congo (later Zaïre).

In 1913 Beatty settled in England where he founded Selection Trust Limited. This remained a small company until after World War I when Beatty embarked on the development, finance, and administration of mining businesses throughout the world. In this way he developed zinc/lead mines at Tetiuhe in Siberia, diamond mines on the west coast of Africa, and lead and zinc mines in Serbia. His greatest achievement, however, was the part he played in the development of the Copperbelt, in Northern Rhodesia (later Zambia). He formed the great mines of Road Antelope and Mufulira.

The extraordinary feature of Beatty's work in these territories is that, as far as is known, he never visited any of these countries. He built round himself a team of expert geologists and mining engineers whom he sent to these places with very specific instructions where they should explore. With his great knowledge of

geology and mining, and his unerring flair for potential mining areas, his judgement was seldom proved wrong, and in these four areas great and successful mining enterprises were established. In the subsequent fifty years one by one these were nationalized, first in Siberia and then in Yugoslavia. The last of the nationalizations was in Zambia in 1970. In the meantime, however, Selection Trust had acquired valuable interests in other mines around the world including Australia, Canada, South Africa, South West Africa (Namibia), and interests in the North Sea and the UK.

In 1933 Beatty became a British subject and during the war of 1939–45 he gave valuable service to government departments active in his own field. He retired in 1950 and left England to live in Dublin. His son, Alfred Chester Beatty, took control of Selection Trust until he in turn retired in 1978.

Between the time that he retired from Guggenheim and came to Britain, Beatty spent much time in the Middle and Near East exploring the art treasures of that part of the world. He built up a unique collection of Indian and Persian miniatures and manuscripts and early Bibles, one of which was two centuries older than the *Codex Sinaiticus*, and he acquired the earliest known copy of the *Rubáiyát* of Omar Khayyam. Later he turned his attention to the Impressionist school of art where he built up one of the most valuable private collections in the world. He also collected French and Russian gold snuff boxes, watches from the eighteenth century, clocks, stamps, and a library of rare books which were said to number 9,000 and which weighed 35 tons. On retiring to Ireland he gave more than eighty of his Impressionist pictures to the National Gallery in Dublin and in 1955 he handed over to the Irish nation a thirteenth-century *Book of Hours* which had previously been on loan to the British Museum.

In the philanthropic field he is best known for his interest in cancer research. In the 1930s he purchased the old Freemansons' Hospital in the Fulham Road and converted it into the Chester Beatty Research Institute (later the Institute of Cancer Research: Royal Cancer Hospital).

Beatty was a man of great and bountiful disposition, generous to a fault not only in his national benefactions but to individuals as well. Cast in a heroic mould, he had a Churchillian sweep and a supreme contempt of every kind of socialist bureaucracy. His endearing mannerisms included a total dislike of smoking in any room in which he was present, and a horror of draughts and cold, which was obvious from the impressive cloak which he wore, often on the warmest days.

In his professional life he received many

honours including the gold medal of the Institution of Mining and Metallurgy which he was awarded in 1935, and the *grand cordon* of the Order of St. Sava which he received in recognition of his services to Yugoslavia in developing its mineral resources. He was knighted in 1954, and later became the first honorary citizen of the Irish Republic under the Irish Nationality and Citizenship Act of 1956.

He married first, in 1900, Grace Madeline (died 1911), daughter of Alfred Rickard, mining engineer, of Denver, Colorado; they had a son and a daughter. In 1913 Beatty married Edith (died 1952), daughter of John Dunn of New York City. Beatty died in Monaco 19 January 1968 and was buried in Ireland.

There is a portrait in oils by Colin Colahan (1940) and a pencil sketch by E. Newling (1934).

[*The Times*, 22 and 27 January 1968; private information; personal knowledge.]

RONALD LINDSAY PRAIN

BEAVER, SIR HUGH EYRE CAMPBELL (1890-1967). industrialist and engineer, was born in Johannesburg 4 May 1890, the oldest of three sons of Hugh Edward Campbell Beaver, a landowner of Montgomeryshire, and his wife, Cerise, daughter of John Eyre, who was of Anglo-Irish extraction. His father died when he was only two years old and the family returned to England to settle in modest style in Penn Street, Buckinghamshire. He won a scholarship to Wellington College, where for his final year he was head boy and was awarded the King's medal in 1910. He became a governor in 1948 and was vice-president in 1956-60.

Beaver tried unsuccessfully for an open scholarship to Oxford, but came out first in the examination for entry to the Indian Police. In India he showed outstanding administrative talent and was engaged increasingly on administrative and intelligence work. Feeling insufficient scope for his sparkling intellect and restless personality, he returned finally to England in 1922. At Penn Street he met his mother's neighbour, Sir Alexander Gibb [q.v.], a well-known contractor and engineer, who was engaged in the audacious experiment of setting up as a consulting engineer in a new mould, very different from the traditional practice of his profession. He proposed to offer his services to expanding productive industries, covering all the engineering problems of the modern factory. Gibb saw in Beaver just the man to become his personal assistant. And so Beaver, a great worker, became steeped in engineering problems. He obtained a mastery of the principles and an understanding of the engineering profession, and was involved in detail in a number of industrial projects on which Gibb was engaged. In 1931 the Canadian Government awarded

Gibb's firm a commission to undertake a national ports survey of Canada, which was to cover not only the technical and constructional problems, but also the organization and administration of the national ports. Gibb appointed Beaver to lead the team as he himself could spare time for a brief visit only. While this work was proceeding, a disastrous fire occurred at the port of St. John, New Brunswick. The Canadian Government commissioned Beaver to get the port working again for the winter season, when the ports of Quebec and Montreal would be ice-bound. This was achieved, five berths being constructed in five months. A year later the report on the Canadian national ports was published, and was later implemented. Thus Beaver proved himself as leader of a gigantic engineering and planning project. In 1932 he was made secretary and a partner in Gibb's firm. In the next year he suffered the great grief of the loss of his wife, and as an anodyne plunged himself even more deeply into work.

Among Gibb's many commissions during the next few years, two were of special importance to Beaver. The first was the new Guinness brewery on the outskirts of London which involved land acquisition, the planning and designing of every detail, and the construction itself. Beaver was put in charge. The other was a report for the Special Areas Commission, followed by a series of reports in 1936 and later which were the foundation of the industrial estates which formed the basis of the Government's attack on the problems of the distressed areas.

As the threat of war loomed, the Government asked Beaver to design and commission three filling factories. In 1940, under pressure from Lord Reith, he became director-general of the Ministry of Works, where he continued throughout the war, with responsibilities which included the building and construction of the entire wartime programme of works and the supply of building materials. On reaching the age of fifty he was elected a member of the Institution of Civil Engineers, under an 'eminence clause'. In 1943 he was knighted.

With the war ended, Beaver was an automatic choice for appointment to the Reith New Towns committee, and to Stafford Cripps's working party on the building industry, but his problem of choice of career was solved by an invitation from Lord Iveagh [q.v.] to go to Guinness's, of which in 1946 he became managing director.

It was about five years before Beaver felt he was on top of the Guinness problem. He introduced modern management methods, inspired more effective research, introduced a policy of diversification, saw through a notable growth of exports, encouraged the development of young managers, and, incidentally, initiated the *Guinness Book of Records*.

Eventually there came a time when he wanted to develop his ideas in a wider sphere, and in 1951 he accepted the chairmanship of the British Institute of Management, and the deputy chairmanship of the Colonial Development Corporation. A year later he was chairman of the committee on power stations. But these were not enough for a man of his restless energy. He joined the governing body of the Lister Institute of Preventive Medicine, and continued as its honorary treasurer until 1966. He took a particular interest in the Tavistock Institute of Human Relations, joining its council in 1956, and serving as chairman from 1957 until 1966.

In 1953 the Government appointed Beaver chairman of the committee on air pollution, whose recommendations were later embodied in the Clean Air Act of 1956, one of the most beneficial pieces of amenity legislation in his time. For this work he was appointed KBE (1956).

In 1954-6 Beaver was chairman of the Advisory Council of the Department of Scientific and Industrial Research. Then came the presidency of the Federation of British Industries from 1957 to 1959. It was during his presidency that the first big studies were made of the Treaty of Rome, and Beaver is remembered for the meticulous care with which he conducted the critical council meetings at which the reaction of British industry had to be determined. The same was true of the talks in Paris, Stockholm, and London which preceded the formation of EFTA—the 'outer seven'.

While he was in the thick of this, a group of industrialists were working on the problem of the serious shortage of pure and applied scientists. They considered that a contributory cause was the poor quality of science teaching in schools, in many of which the laboratory facilities had not been revised for many decades. They raised a Fund of £3¼ million, expressly to make capital grants to independent and direct grant boys' and girls' schools for building, expanding, modernizing, and equipping school laboratories. It was to Beaver that the fund-raisers turned as chairman of their executive committee. Between 1958 and 1963 he chaired 18 meetings of the executive and 32 meetings of the grants committee, and visited a large number of the 210 schools that received grants.

Yet Beaver still had time and energy to accept the chairmanship of Ashridge College and the presidency of the Institution of Chemical Engineers. He received honorary degrees from Cambridge, Trinity College, Dublin, and the National University of Ireland.

Retiring from Guinness in 1960, it may be that Beaver had a little more time for his leisure pursuits. He loved his garden and his pictures. He was a keen amateur archaeologist, a voracious reader, and a fine shot. But still there was no sitting back. He hated waste, particularly of brains, including his own. He undertook the treasurership of the university of Sussex, and the chairmanship of the British Council for the Rehabilitation of the Disabled. His very active work in the Federation of British Industries continued long past his presidency, and in 1960-1 he played a leading part in the studies and discussions which led to the formation of the National Economic Development Council. Thus he continued to the end of his life to make a great personal contribution. He had an unflagging capacity for work and extraordinary ability to absorb and understand new problems. He died at Luxford, his home in Sussex, 16 January 1967. He had married in 1925 his second cousin Jean Atwood, daughter of Major Robert Atwood Beaver, MD; they had two daughters.

A portrait of Beaver by John Gilroy hangs in the Guinness boardroom, and one by Middleton Todd hangs at his old home. The CBI have a charming pencil-drawing by Sir James Gunn.

[The Guinness house magazines: *Guinness Time* and *The Harp*; private information; personal knowledge.]   NORMAN KIPPING

BEAVERBROOK, first BARON (1879-1964), newspaper proprietor. [See AITKEN, WILLIAM MAXWELL.]

BEAZLEY, SIR JOHN DAVIDSON (1885-1970), classical archaeologist, was born in Glasgow 13 September 1885, the elder son of Mark John Murray Beazley, interior decorator, of London, and his wife, Mary Catherine, daughter of John Davidson, of Glasgow. He went to King Edward VI School, Southampton, and as a scholar to Christ's Hospital and Balliol College, Oxford, where he took firsts in both classical moderations (1905) and *literae humaniores* (1907), and was Ireland scholar and Craven scholar (1904), Hertford scholar (1905), and Derby scholar in 1907. His Gaisford prize for Greek prose (1907), 'Herodotus at the Zoo', an enchanting work, was reprinted in 1911 and in a collection of classical parodies produced in Switzerland in 1968. He became a close friend of James Elroy Flecker [q.v.] and himself at this time wrote poetry, but abandoned it with the growth of his total dedication to scholarship. In 1908 he was made student of Christ Church and tutor in classics, a position he held until in 1925 he succeeded Percy Gardner [q.v.] as Lincoln professor of classical archaeology. Long before this, however, although a fine classical scholar and an able and conscientious tutor, he had established his life's work as devoted to Greek art and in particular to Attic vase-painting. Greek vase-painting, by virtue of its quality and in the all but total loss of other painting from

Greece, is of peculiar importance in the history of art. Its study is now on an entirely different footing from what it was seventy years ago; and that is Beazley's work.

His first article, published in the year of his appointment to Christ Church, is on vases, but is untypical, being concerned mainly with iconography and hardly at all with style. He was already beginning, however, the minute stylistic study of individual vases in all the museums he could visit, the first-fruits of which were the seminal articles which appeared from 1910 in the *Journal of Hellenic Studies* and elsewhere, on individual painters of Attic red-figure. Essays in this direction had already been made by the great German scholars whom Beazley always revered as his masters, Hartwig, Hauser, and Furtwängler; but their work had two serious limitations. They tended to start from signatures, haphazard in application and still more so in survival; and they only concerned themselves with good work. Beazley never underestimated the master and the masterpiece, but he saw that for the study to be properly based he must survey the whole field. He loved and knew well painting of many times and places, and he took his method from Morelli's studies of the Italian masters: minute observation of individual mannerisms of drawing, controlled by a deep sensitivity to style. The Berlin Painter, to whom he devoted the first of many studies in 1911, is a great draughtsman whose style is now as familiar as Dürer's or Utamaro's. Most of the vases first grouped under the name had long been known, but their relation had not been observed and the artistic personality was lost. By recognizing a whole range of such personalities, from the best to the worst, colleagues or rivals, masters and pupils over many generations, Beazley left the subject, which he had found more or less chaotic, an organized field of study comparable to a school of painting in a documented age.

He began by concentrating on red-figure (and the related white-ground) in the first hundred years or so of its existence, from the later sixth century. Afterwards he pushed forward to the fourth century and backward to black-figure. The first phase of his work is summed up in *Attic Red-figure Vases in American Museums* (1918), where a history of the art is given through an account of artists and their relations, lists of their works being interspersed in the text. *Attische Vasemaler des rotfigurigen Stils* (1925) is lists alone, greatly expanded in number and length. He continued to build up these lists throughout his life: in *Attic Red-figure Vase-painters* (1942) and its second (three-volume) edition (1963), the parallel *Attic Black-figure Vase-painters* (1956), and *Paralipomena* which supplements and corrects these and was posthumously published (1971). These are the backbone of his work; but it is fleshed out in innumerable articles and many books, wide-ranging and beautifully written: *Greek Vases in Poland* (1928); *Der Berliner Maler* (1930), *Der Panmaler* (1931), and *Der Kleophradesmaler* (1933; the English texts of these three monographs were published in 1974); *Attic Vase-paintings in Boston* (with L. D. Caskey, 1931–63); *Campana Fragments in Florence* (1933; the most spectacular display of Beazley's astounding visual memory, a gift basic to his work); *Attic White Lekythoi* (1938); *La Raccolta Guglielmi* (with F. Magi, 1939); *Potter and Painter in Ancient Athens* (1945); *The Development of Attic Black-figure* (1951; lectures given as Sather professor at the university of California, 1949); *The Berlin Painter* (1964); as well as two Oxford fascicles for the *Corpus Vasorum Antiquorum* (1927 and 1931, the second with E. R. Price and Humfry Payne, his best pupil, whose notice he contributed to this Dictionary). *Greek Sculpture and Painting* (with B. Ashmole, 1932) remains the best short introduction to the subject, and he did important work in other fields: *The Lewes House Collection of Ancient Gems* (1920) and *Etruscan Vase-painting* (1947); but it is his work on Attic vase-painters which is, in the historiography of Greek art, strictly epoch-making.

In 1919 Beazley married Marie, daughter of Bernard Bloomfield and widow of David Ezra, by whom he had a daughter who married Louis MacNeice [q.v.]. Marie devoted her powerful personality entirely to serving Beazley and his work. She learned to photograph vases, took over the practical side of his life completely, and was his guardian dragon. He could not have done what he did without her, and he adored her, never recovering from her death in 1967. He had retired from the chair in 1956 and died in Oxford 6 May 1970. They had no children.

He was elected FBA in 1927, knighted in 1949, appointed CH in 1959, and held honorary degrees from Oxford, Cambridge, Glasgow, Durham, Reading, Paris, Lyon, Marburg, and Thessalonika. He was an honorary fellow of Balliol and Lincoln, and honorary student of Christ Church and the British School at Athens. He was honorary vice-president of the Greek Archaeological Society, honorary fellow of the Metropolitan Museum, New York, and a foreign member of many learned societies. He was awarded the Petrie medal in 1937, the British Academy's Kenyon medal in 1957 (the first award), and the Antonio Feltrinelli Foundation prize in 1965.

Beazley was a person of wide culture, interested in and knowledgeable about the arts (and several of the literatures) of Europe, though he did not care to look much beyond those bounds. He had great charm, and could be an amusing and delightful companion; but as he grew older his total deafness and his increasing absorption in his work combined to cut him off to some degree from other people. He was modest, and took immense trouble with the guidance of his pupils, treating them as equals and winning their devoted affection. He was completely generous in communicating his knowledge, not only to these but to all who consulted him, as in increasing numbers scholars, collectors, and dealers constantly did. In appearance he was somewhat under medium height, slight but well made, with striking blue eyes and fair hair (white in age), and fine rather ascetic features which suggested to many a fifteenth-century Flemish portrait, a Van Eyck or a van der Weyden. He was never professionally painted, but his wife, a talented untaught artist, drew several heads of him in coloured chalks which are preserved in Oxford, at Balliol, Christ Church, and Lincoln.

[*The Times*, 7 May 1970; Bernard Ashmole in *Proceedings* of the British Academy, vol. lvi, 1970; D. von Bothmer in *Oxford Magazine*, 12 June 1970; personal knowledge.]

MARTIN ROBERTSON

BEDSON, Sir SAMUEL PHILLIPS (1886–1969), experimental pathologist and virologist, was born 1 December 1886 at Newcastle upon Tyne, the second son of Peter Phillips Bedson, professor of chemistry in the Durham College of Science, and his wife, Annie, daughter of Samuel Hodgkinson, cotton spinner, of Marple, Cheshire. He was educated at Abbotsholme School in Derbyshire and the university of Durham. Before he left school he had decided on a medical career, but was persuaded by his father to take a degree in science first. He graduated B.Sc. with distinction in 1907, his chief subject being zoology with botany and chemistry as subsidiary subjects. From 1907 to 1912 he studied medicine at Durham University College of Medicine and graduated with honours in 1912. Influenced by the stimulating teaching of H. J. Hutchens, the professor of bacteriology, he decided to specialize in this branch of pathology. He therefore went to the Pasteur Institute in Paris where he studied under brilliant French microbiologists, among them Roux, Borrel, Laveran, Besredka, and Metchnikoff. The research work which he carried out in Weinberg's laboratory at this time on the toxic substances obtained from parasitic worms was embodied in a thesis which gained the MD (1914) with gold medal of Durham University.

In 1913 Bedson returned to London where he worked as British medical scholar at the Lister Institute under the supervision of (Sir) John Ledingham [q.v.], who later succeeded Sir Charles Martin [q.v.] as director of the Institute. Bedson regarded this as another valuable period in his research training. The experimental work

on blood platelets and purpura in which he collaborated with Ledingham was interrupted by the outbreak of war in 1914. As his application for a commission in the Royal Army Medical Corps was turned down on the grounds that there were no vacancies for doctors trained in research, he joined the Northumberland Fusiliers as a combatant officer and went with the 8th battalion to Gallipoli in 1915. In August of that year he suffered a severe chest wound and was evacuated to England. He was later sent to France where in 1916 he was transferred to the RAMC, largely through the influence of the future Lord Dawson of Penn [q.v.], then serving in the Medical Corps. From then until his demobilization in 1919 Bedson served as pathologist in various laboratories in France and became adviser in pathology to the Fifth Army (France). After the war he was for two years lecturer in bacteriology in the medical school in Durham before returning in 1921 to the Lister Institute where he continued his valuable work on the origin and disposal of blood platelets and their role in the production of purpura. The conclusions reached on the basis of his experimental studies have been confirmed by the subsequent work of others.

In 1924 Bedson was seconded to work on foot-and-mouth disease at the Lister Institute under the general supervision of (Sir) Joseph Arkwright [q.v.] who was a member of the committee formed by the Ministry of Agriculture to advise on research on this important disease of farm animals. Thus Bedson began his research on virus disease, then largely an unexplored field. The facts relating to the causal virus of foot-and-mouth disease and immunity to it, discovered by Bedson and his colleagues, provided a sound basis for subsequent advance in the knowledge of virus diseases. In 1926 he was appointed to one of two newly created Freedom research fellowships at the London Hospital, the future Lord Florey [q.v.] being appointed to the other. Thus began a close friendship with (Sir) Philip Panton, who had been responsible for the creation of the fellowships, which continued until Panton's death in 1950. The eight years of Bedson's tenure of the fellowship were the most productive of his scientific career. He published several important papers on the nature of viruses, using the viruses of vaccinia and herpes simplex in his experiments. In 1929 there occurred the pandemic of human psittacosis infection caused by the commercial distribution of psittacine birds from South America and Australia. Bedson's previous training had equipped him admirably for the investigation of this disease. He discovered and described the causal agent of the disease and much of his subsequent work was devoted to the study of this and related micro-organisms. Because of the importance of his discoveries, this group of infective agents are commonly referred to as the Bedsoniae. Bedson was a pioneer investigator in the young science of virology but his international reputation was associated mainly with his brilliant work on the micro-organisms of the psittacosis-lymphogranuloma group, which was summarized in his Harben lectures (1959). He was elected FRS in 1935. In 1934 Bedson succeeded William Bulloch [q.v.] as professor of bacteriology at the London Hospital Medical College. Although the teaching and administrative duties inseparable from the professorship lessened the time he could spend in the laboratory he enjoyed contact with the students. He was a good lecturer and took a keen interest in the welfare and subsequent careers of his pupils. From 1939 to 1944 he was pathologist to Metropolitan Region 5 of the Emergency Medical Service with his headquarters at Billericay in Essex. He returned to the London Hospital in 1944 and in 1946 succeeded Panton as director of the division of pathology, thus adding to his responsibilities in the Medical College. In 1949 he followed Panton as consultant adviser in pathology to the Ministry of Health, an office which he held until 1960. When he retired from the chair at the London Hospital in 1952 he was invited to take charge of the British Empire Campaign Virus Unit in the Middlesex Hospital where he continued his research for the next ten years.

Bedson's experience and wise counsel in matters of medical research made involvement in outside committee work inevitable. He was a member of the governing body of the Foot-and-Mouth Disease Research Institute at Pirbright (1950-5), the council of the Imperial Cancer Research Fund (1942-55), the Army Pathological Advisory Committee (1937-62), the governing body of the Lister Institute (1944-54), the Public Health Laboratory Service Board (1950-7), the Medical Research Council (1941-5), and the council of the Royal Society (1937-8 and 1941-2). He was awarded the Conway Evans prize in 1952. The honorary degree of D.Sc. was conferred on him by Queen's University, Belfast, in 1937 and by the university of Durham in 1946. He was elected FRCP in 1945 and knighted in 1956.

Bedson was slim and under average height. He almost invariably wore a bow tie. He was neat and orderly in all he did. He was a very skilful technician and preferred to do all his own experiments which were devised with care and precision. His opinions were tenaciously held and would be abandoned only if convincing evidence were forthcoming. He was regarded with great affection and respect by his colleagues and pupils and in private life he was a delightful companion and host. He was a competent

golfer and a keen gardner, but the hobby which gave him greatest pleasure was trout fishing. For many years he enjoyed an annual holiday with his sons, fishing the streams of Westmorland and Yorkshire. At school and university he played cricket and rugby and in later years followed the fortunes of Sussex at cricket and England at rugby with strongly partisan enthusiasm.

In 1926 Bedson married a research assistant at the Lister Institute, Dorothea Annie, the elder daughter of Henry Herman Hoffert, a senior inspector of schools for the Board of Education. There were three sons, the second of whom, Henry Samuel Bedson, became reader in virology in Birmingham University. Bedson died in Hove 11 May 1969, and his widow died later in the same year.

[A. W. Downie in *Biographical Memoirs of Fellows of the Royal Society*, vol. xvi, 1970; personal knowledge.]   A. W. DOWNIE

BEECHAM, SIR THOMAS, second baronet (1879-1961), conductor, was born 29 April 1879 at St. Helens, Lancashire, the elder son and second child of (Sir) Joseph Beecham, chemist, of St. Helens and later Huyton, and Josephine Burnett. His family background was that of the very prosperous business started by his grandfather, Thomas Beecham [q.v.], a famous name in the world of digestive pills, which were sold at first personally by their inventor, and later marketed and advertised in vast quantities. There was good personal rapport between Beecham and his grandfather, better than that between him and his father.

At an early age Beecham showed two personal gifts—a good memory for words, and a passion for music. He was taught the piano from the age of six. He was also interested in sport, and in spite of his short stature, played football and cricket for Rossall School, Lancashire, which he attended from 1892 to 1897 and where he was a house-captain. He later went for eighteen months to Wadham College, Oxford (1897/8), where he practised the piano, played football, and indulged in bouts of foreign travel to hear his favourite operas. It soon became obvious that music was to be his chosen life's work. He was given, at twenty, and obviously by family influence, the opportunity to conduct his first professional orchestra—the Hallé, upon a visit to St. Helens, who were faced with an empty podium because Dr Hans Richter, who had been asked to conduct, had other engagements. Previously Beecham had learnt something about conducting with his own St. Helens Orchestral Society—which he had founded two years previously—and seemed to find no difficulty in leading the Hallé orchestra through an almost unrehearsed performance, a capacity he was to

demonstrate superbly with a succession of
orchestras over the next sixty years.

Having left Oxford without taking a degree,
Beecham went to live in London in 1900, where
he studied musical composition with Charles
Wood [q.v.], Frederic Austin, and other
teachers. In 1902, aged twenty-two, Beecham
joined, as one of its conductors, a small London
touring opera company directed by Kelson
Trueman, and soon had committed its repertory
to memory. In 1903 he married Utica ('Utie')
Celestia, daughter of Charles Stuart Welles, of
New York, an American diplomat, at a time of
serious discord in his own family. There were
two sons of his marriage. It was a short-lived
union of which he rarely spoke in later years,
although the separation which soon followed
seemed sad rather than bitter. They were
divorced in 1943 and Utica, Lady Beecham,
died in 1977.

An injury to his wrist in 1904 destroyed
Beecham's ambition to be a concert pianist.
Most of that year he spent travelling on the
Continent with his wife, attending perfor-
ances and collecting musical scores. In December 1905 he gave his first public orchestral
concert in London, with players of the Queen's
Hall orchestra. Press notices were poor, and
Beecham himself far from satisfied. In 1906,
helped by the clarinettist Charles Draper, he
founded the New Symphony Orchestra, which
expanded to sixty-five players in 1907, all of whom
were carefully selected. This time Beecham's
arresting style triumphed, and it was obvious
that Britain had an important young conductor.
It was at this stage that he met Frederick Delius
[q.v.], whose music was to be such an important
part of Beecham's work. In 1908 he presented
several works by his new friend, with whom he
went to Norway on holiday. In 1910, backed by
his father, whose friendship he had now regained, Beecham mounted the first of his many
Covent Garden opera seasons, a mammoth affair
with thirty-four works represented, many of
them very grand in scale and quite unknown in
Britain. There were works by Richard Strauss
(*Elektra* and *Feuersnot*); Wagner (*Tristan and
Isolde*); Debussy (*L'Enfant Prodigue*); four
of the less familiar Mozart operas; and many
works by lesser composers. This did not prevent
—indeed it inevitably produced—very heavy
financial losses; but it could well be taken as a
pattern for many of Beecham's finest achievements in the years which followed. In 1911
he presented Diaghilev's Russian Ballet with
Nijinsky and in 1913 he introduced Chaliapin in
a season of Russian opera, as well as giving the
first London performance of Richard Strauss's
Der Rosenkavalier. The tragic international
events which followed in 1914 cut short
Beecham's operatic activities, but he remained

indefatigable in his fight to keep music going,
and sustained both the Hallé Society and the
London Symphony Orchestra with financial
and artistic help. His greatest achievement at
this time was the touring of his opera company,
working in theatres large and small up and down
the country, performing more than thirty different operas, including such works as *The
Boatswain's Mate* by (Dame) Ethel Smyth [q.v.]
and Isidore de Lara's *Naïl*, all at prices so low as
to put them within reach of everyone. In 1916
Beecham succeeded to his father's baronetcy,
having been knighted earlier in the same year.
A final financial disastrous Covent Garden
season in 1920 left him fighting to stave off
bankruptcy, and until 1923 he was almost absent
from the musical scene. From then until 1929 his
life seems to have been a gradual climb back to
the pinnacle he had achieved so early. In that
year he presented the first Delius Festival in
London, which was attended by the now blind
and paralysed composer, who for the first time
began to receive the public appreciation he
deserved.

In 1932, after heated negotiations, lasting
some years, with the BBC and the London
Symphony Orchestra for the foundation of a
full-time permanent symphony orchestra in
London, Beecham founded, with the assistance
of Courtaulds, the excellent London Philharmonic Orchestra, which still exists (1979).
With them he was to present many excellent
concert and opera seasons until 1939, when war
once again changed the London scene. In 1934
Delius died and the Delius Trust, planned by
Beecham, took over the task of presenting his
music on records and in concert-halls. In 1936
Beecham took his orchestra to Nazi Germany,
and had the audacity to include in his party
his secretary Berta Geissmar, the expatriate
German who travelled safely and openly with
him. Two occasions are remembered from this
tour—the evening when Beecham refused to
precede Adolf Hitler into the concert-hall, thus
avoiding having to salute the arrival of the
Führer, and the concert at Ludwigshaven, in the
concert-hall of BASF, manufacturers of recording equipment, which marked the first recording
ever made on tape of any orchestra. From 1939
to 1944 Beecham travelled constantly abroad, in
the USA and Australia, and his reputation as a
wit and a raconteur grew as rapidly as his stature
as a conductor.

Upon his return to London in 1944, and after
trials and arguments with both the London
Philharmonic Orchestra and what was soon to
be the Philharmonia under Walter Legge's
direction, in 1946 he formed the Royal Philharmonic Orchestra, which was to be his last
orchestra and the one with which he was to be
longest in association. In 1946 he gave an im-

portant series of concerts in the second Delius Festival; and in 1947, in the presence of the eighty-three-year-old composer, a Richard Strauss Festival.

In 1950 he presented his orchestra in a lengthy tour of North America—an enterprise which somehow supported itself without government help and with Beecham's own generous donation of his services to balance a precarious budget. In the years which followed, Beecham busied himself with almost every possible aspect of orchestral and operatic activity at the very highest level. His recordings were among the finest produced anywhere. He conducted extensively in Britain, America, and Paris. He was made a Companion of Honour in 1957, an event which was clouded for him by the death of his second wife, Betty, daughter of Daniel Morgan Humby, a surgeon, of London. She was a pianist who was formerly the wife of the Revd H. C. Thomas, of London, and they had been married in 1943, after Beecham terminated his long association with Lady Cunard. Beecham's publications included an early autobiography, *A Mingled Chime* (1944), which described his life only until 1924, and should have been augmented by a later volume; and a biography of Frederick Delius (1958). In 1956 he gave the Romanes lecture at Oxford.

In 1959 he married his personal secretary, Shirley Hudson, who was with him in the United States in 1960, when illness forced him to return to London, where he died 8 March 1961. He was succeeded in the baronetcy by his elder son, Adrian Welles Beecham, born in 1904.

Beecham was often a harsh taskmaster and could sometimes be inconsiderate to those working for him. Punctuality was not among his most noticeable virtues. Nevertheless, such peccadilloes were easily overlooked in view of his effervescent enthusiasm which communicated itself to musicians and public alike. Orchestral players will long remember him as not only a great conductor, but a witty and stimulating person who could inspire them to produce their best and showed obvious pleasure in what he heard. He was a man of wide reading, which informed and enlivened his conversation, and he was renowned for his wit. Sometimes his interpretations of the music he conducted were controversial—for example, it was felt that he failed to bring out the heroic nature in some passages by Beethoven. But he succeeded in giving a freshness of outlook to performances and often astonished the public by his vitality, his flamboyance of manner, and his deep musical understanding. His own favourite composer was Mozart.

In appearance Beecham, although invariably an impressive figure, changed considerably over the years. In youth he was, judging from the many photographs and cartoons of the time, slim, elegant, dark-haired, and something of a dandy. The famous story of his summer evening walk along Piccadilly when he is said to have hailed a cab, thrown in his redundant overcoat, and said 'Follow me' as he continued his stroll is probably exaggerated, but contains a germ of the truth about the Beech of the time. By his fifties he had already become a more sturdy character, but by no means rotund; now white-haired and with his famous 'goatee' beard jutting formidably (especially if he were arguing or directing a more dramatic musical work), he took on a more pinkish hue and a somewhat more benign aspect in moments of repose. With the passing years the figure became stouter, but Beecham was never anything like a fat man, and to the very end he presented an impressive pair of shoulders to orchestras the world over. Sitting down at this time he seemed gigantic; it was when he stood that he was revealed as a very short man—his legs were surprisingly short, belying every other physical aspect of this remarkable man. One feature remained constant through the years— the large and lustrous eyes, at once the agents of fear and confidence in the hearts of the players who faced him, and possibly the most important tool in his conducting equipment.

Apart from photographs and cartoons, portraits of Beecham seem to be few and rarely successful. Simon Elwes painted a portrait in 1951, but it is generally regarded as not a good likeness. In the Royal Festival Hall there is an excellent if somewhat skeletal bust in bronze which catches the mercureal conductor very much in action with a typical sideways cut-off which was extremely characteristic of his technique. There is a portrait of Beecham in oils by Gordon Thomas Stuart (1953) and a drawing by Guy Passet (1950), both in the possession of Alan Denson. One of six bronze bust casts by David Wynne (1957) is at the National Portrait Gallery, and others are at the Festival Hall, Bristol, and Aberdeen. Several caricatures were drawn by Edmund Dulac. There is also a portrait by Dorothy E. F. Cowen (1952). Skeches made at the Queen's Hall, London, during the Delius Festival of 1929, by Ernest Procter, are in the National Portrait Gallery, and the Royal Philharmonic Orchestra has a sculpture by Muriel Liddle (1979).

[Charles Reid, *Thomas Beecham*, 1961; Neville Cardus, *Sir Thomas Beecham*, 1961; Humphrey Proctor-Gregg, *Beecham Remembered*, 1976; Ethel Smyth, *Beecham and Pharaoh*, 1935; Sir Thomas Beecham, *A Mingled Chime, Leaves from an Autobiography*, 1944; Harold Atkins and Archie

Newman, *Beecham Stories: Anecdotes, Sayings and Impressions*, 1978; Alan Jefferson, *Sir Thomas Beecham: A Centenary Tribute*, 1979; personal knowledge.]

JACK BRYMER

BELL, (ARTHUR) CLIVE (HEWARD) (1881-1964), art critic, the second son of William Heward Bell, civil engineer, and his wife, Hannah Taylor Cory, was born 16 September 1881 at East Shefford, Berkshire. In the words of his son, Quentin (*Bloomsbury*, 1968), he came from a 'family which drew its wealth from Welsh mines and expended it upon the destruction of wild animals'. He was educated at Marlborough and at Trinity College, Cambridge, where he was an exhibitioner and Earl of Derby student. He became at once associated with a remarkable group of fellow undergraduates, Leonard Woolf, Thoby Stephen, Lytton Strachey [qq.v.], and others. The philosopher G. E. Moore [q.v.] of King's, of an older generation, wrote Bell in *Old Friends—Personal Recollections* (1956), was 'the dominant influence in all our lives'. Bell obtained a second class in both parts of the historical tripos (1901-2), went down in 1903, and spent the following year in Paris, where he studied the Old Masters in the Louvre and wasted his time most profitably in the company of painters. His Cambridge group was reinforced on his return to London by Thoby's two sisters Vanessa and Virginia [qq.v.], the children of Sir Leslie Stephen [q.v.], the eminent Victorian man of letters and editor of this Dictionary. In 1907 Bell married Vanessa (died 1961) and in 1912 Virginia became the wife of Leonard Woolf. This was the nucleus of the so-called Bloomsbury group. Clive and Vanessa Bell had two sons: Julian, who was killed in 1937 in the Spanish civil war, and Quentin who became professor of fine art at Sussex University. In 1918 Vanessa Bell and Duncan Grant had a daughter, who was always known as Bell, and who married David Garnett.

The most important intellectual event of Bell's life was a chance meeting in 1910, in a railway carriage between Cambridge and London, with the considerably older Roger Fry [q.v.], a painter and art critic steeped in a more austere nineteenth-century tradition. Together and in the company of (Sir) Desmond MacCarthy [q.v.], in the late summer of that year, they searched Paris for suitable exhibits for the historic first Post-Impressionist exhibition which opened at the Grafton Galleries that autumn. Bell wrote the introduction to the catalogue of the 'English Group' which exhibited at the second Post-Impressionist show (October 1912). The book for which he is chiefly remembered, *Art*, was published in February 1914 but was based on articles which had already appeared in periodicals. During the war of 1914-18 he was a conscientious objector, attacking the war courageously in a pamphlet, *Peace at Once* (1915). Another famous publication was *Civilization, an Essay* (1928). Bell's definition of that difficult word 'civilization' was maliciously described by Virginia Woolf as 'a lunch party at No. 50 Gordon Square' (his Bloomsbury house). Other books included *Potboilers* (1918), *Landmarks in Nineteenth-Century Painting* (1927), a sympathetic study of *Proust* (1928), and *Enjoying Pictures* (1934). Appropriately he was made a chevalier of the Legion of Honour by France, but he received no comparable distinction from his own country.

There can be no question that *Art* was his most notable achievement: in an introductory chapter entitled 'The Aesthetic Hypothesis' he formulated his theory of 'Significant Form'. He became convinced that this was the most important element in works of art and common to all of them, from the earliest times to the Cubists, consisting in 'relations and combinations of lines and colours'. He did not deny that there were other pleasures to be derived from them, such as recognition of the subject represented, what he called the representational or descriptive element, but these were subsidiary to the ecstatic delight which forms and colours provided for those privileged to experience it. The theory was not startlingly original: it was derived partly from the philosophy of G. E. Moore, who believed in the value of states of mind for their own sake—and Bell indeed went on to extol the state of mind which the apprehension of significant form induces; and partly from a published essay by Roger Fry, 'Essay in Aesthetics' (1909), in which an attempt had been made to isolate this quality of disinterested contemplation, separating style from content. Bell's contribution consisted in driving the theory to its logical conclusion, a conclusion Fry could never quite accept, because for him it was too schematic, and excluded some of the greatest artists such as Rembrandt and Michelangelo. To the later twentieth century also, the theory is hard to stomach. In the first place Bell never got down to explaining in what sense one form or combination of forms was more significant than another, in the second, most people believe that form and content are indivisible, that content actually determines form. Fry has remained acceptable because he was always correcting a theory by his reactions to what he saw (and often in the process making nonsense of the theory). Bell, after this early essay, went further, in abandoning theory altogether in order to leave himself free to express his feelings about individual works of art.

His great loves were the Byzantines and modern art since Cézanne where in his view the illustrative element was at its feeblest. This bias led him to some absurd statements, such as: 'The bulk . . . of those who flourished between the high Renaissance the the contemporary movement may be divided into two classes, virtuosi and dunces'; or 'Giotto could be intentionally second-rate' (when the artist wished to describe some too human emotion); or 'since the Byzantine primitives set their mosaics at Ravenna no artist in Europe has created forms of greater significance unless it be Cézanne'. But one has to read such statements in the context of the time; it was the triumphant epoch of the avant-garde, when Futurists and Vorticists were making statements even more bewildering. Bell was as courageous as they were. His book may not have stood the test of time, but it has fervour and is never dull.

Bell was the most charming man; not only a genial host but a guest who could be relied on to apply oil to a sticky evening. Lord Keynes [q.v.] described him when an undergraduate as a 'gay and amiable dog', and this he remained until old age. He enjoyed most of the best things in life; and so infectious was his delight that it was impossible not to be happy in his company. He died in London 17 September 1964. A cartoon by Beerbohm of Bell and Fry was reproduced in Old Friends. There is also a portrait in oils by Roger Fry, c. 1924, in the National Portrait Gallery.

[Private information; personal knowledge.]
BENEDICT NICOLSON

BELL, SIR (HAROLD) IDRIS (1879-1967), scholar, was born 2 October 1879 at Epworth, Lincolnshire, the son of Charles Christopher Bell, chemist, and his wife, Rachel Hughes. His father's family had been yeoman farmers in the north Midlands and had marked literary leanings, his father not least; but the Welsh inheritance from his mother meant more to Bell and was a determining factor in his life. He was educated at Nottingham High School and Oriel College, Oxford, which he entered as an Adam de Brome scholar in 1897; he was placed in the first class in classical moderations in 1899 and two years later narrowly missed a first in *literae humaniores*. More significant for his future career was the year he subsequently spent in Hanover, Halle, and Berlin learning German and studying Hellenistic history; classical scholarship in Germany was then in its heyday and among the lecturers he heard were Friedrich Blass, Eduard Meyer, and

U. von Wilamowitz-Moellendorf. This experience both deepened his knowledge of the classical world and introduced him to the most rigorous methods of contemporary scholarship, reinforcing a native tendency to painstaking accuracy and objectivity.

If his ancestry and his period of study in Germany were decisive factors in his development, a third was his appointment as an assistant in the department of manuscripts in the British Museum in 1903. Here, more by chance than design, he found himself working before long on Greek papyri with (Sir) F. G. Kenyon (whose notice he contributed to this Dictionary). After collaborating with him for the third volume of the museum catalogue on documents of an earlier period, chance again directed him to the department's large holdings of Byzantine papyri. Verbose, complex, and often illiterate and lacking the obvious attractions of many Ptolemaic and Roman texts, documents of this period had been largely ignored both in England and on the Continent. Bell's edition of these papyri in volumes iv and v of the catalogue, two massive volumes with an ample commentary (1910 and 1917), which provided a striking picture of the Byzantine empire seen from a provincial standpoint and one to which in an article in the *Journal of Egyptian Archaeology* (vol. iv, 1917) he supplied the title 'The Byzantine Servile State', both set a new standard for the museum's publications in accuracy of decipherment and in interpretation, and established him as the leading authority on Byzantine and early Arab Egypt.

While he always retained his interest in Byzantine studies, Roman Egypt later became his main field of study. Both his *Jews and Christians in Egypt* (1924), an elaborate edition of some remarkable and important documents, and *Fragments of an Unknown Gospel and Other Early Christian Papyri* (1935), jointly edited by him and his colleague T. C. Skeat, are still indispensable in spite of the numerous re-editions and discussion they have occasioned. Bell's achievement was due in part to his technical expertise and capacity for hard work, and in part to the fact that he rightly saw papyrology as a *Hilfsdisziplin* to be pursued in the wider perspective of the historian; he demonstrated this belief most clearly in the chapters he contributed on Roman Egypt to the *Cambridge Ancient History* (in vols. x and xi), which remain a definitive statement of their subject. His work as editor, writer, and contributor of numerous articles in learned journals was done against the background of, and largely in the intervals from, steadily increasing departmental duties; in 1927 he was promoted to deputy keeper, and on the death of J. P. Gilson [q.v.] in 1929 he became keeper, a post he held until his retirement in 1944. In these years the much-debated Codex Sinaiticus was acquired, as well as the Luttrell Psalter and some of the missing Paston letters; the department also became the centre of international papyrology from which, thanks mainly to Bell's activities, an understanding of Greek papyri extended to an ever wider circle of studies and in which many younger scholars received an invaluable if informal training. In 1935 he was made an honorary reader in papyrology at Oxford where until 1950 he did much to secure the continuity of papyrological studies; in 1936 he became an honorary fellow of Oriel College.

His training and long practice in the school of severely objective scholarship controlled but did not inhibit a mercurial temperament and lively imagination. This found scope in his translations from Welsh poetry in which a lifelong devotion to poetry (especially for that in the tradition of Swinburne) joined with a no less deep and lasting enthusiasm for Welsh language and literature. *Poems from the Welsh*, a work of collaboration between Bell and his father, had appeared in 1913 and was followed in 1925 by *Welsh Poems of the Twentieth Century in English Verse*, again by father and son. The pattern was continued in a more ambitious venture, an edition of fifty poems of the greatest Welsh poet of the later middle ages, Dafydd (David) ap Gwilym [q.v.], consisting of text, translation, and introduction, in which Bell collaborated with his son David. Here scholarship had its part to play too, as it did in his admirable *The Development of Welsh Poetry* (1936) and in his translation of Dr Thomas Parry's history of Welsh literature down to 1900, to which Bell added an appendix of his own, amounting to a quarter of the whole, on the twentieth century. In this book, which appeared in 1955, and in its predecessors, he was concerned to introduce the English reader to the often unsuspected riches of Welsh literature, just as in much of his papyrological work he was intent on making available to scholars generally the information lurking in the technical publications of papyrologists. For his services to Welsh literature he was awarded the Cymmrodorion medal in 1946 and was president of this society in 1947; he was also admitted to the Gorsedd as a druid in 1949.

Unassuming, courteous, kindly, always accessible, a man of wide sympathies and considerable power of enjoyment, Bell had many friends at all levels. He was a lifelong supporter of the Labour Party and in matters of religion an agnostic for most of his working life. Shortly after the war of 1939—45, however, for reasons he made clear in a volume of essays, *The Crisis of Our Time* (1954), he returned to the Christian faith. On leaving the British Museum in 1944 he retired to Wales where he had always spent his holidays, and in his later years played an active part in the intellectual life of the principality and in that of the Church in Wales, of whose governing body he became a member. He died 22 January 1967 in Aberystwyth.

He was appointed OBE in 1920, CB in 1936, and knighted in 1946. Elected a fellow of the British Academy in 1932, he served as its president from 1946 to 1950, helping to renew the ties with Continental scholarship, a task much after his own heart. He received honorary degrees from the universities of Liverpool, Brussels, Michigan, and Wales, and he was a member of many foreign academies; he was vice-president of several learned societies, and president of the Society for the Promotion of Roman Studies from 1937 to 1945, of the International Association of Papyrologists from 1947 to 1955, and of the Classical Association in 1955.

He married Mabel Winifred, daughter of Ernest Ayling, in 1911; there were three sons of the marriage, of whom the eldest and the youngest survived him; his wife died a week before he did. There is a portrait in chalk by Powys Evans in the National Museum of Wales, and a pencil drawing by his second son is in the possession of the family.

[C. H. Roberts in *Proceedings* of the British Academy, vol. liii, 1967; E. G. Turner and T. C. Skeat in *Journal of Egyptian Archaeology*, vol. liii, 1967; personal knowledge.]

C. H. Roberts

BELL, VANESSA (1879-1961), painter, was born at 22 Hyde Park Gate, London, 30 May 1879, the eldest in the family of two sons and two daughters of (Sir) Leslie Stephen [q.v.], first editor of this Dictionary, by his second wife Julia Jackson (1846-95), the widow of Herbert Duckworth. (Sir) Leslie Stephen also had a daughter from his previous marriage, and Julia had two sons and a daughter from her marriage to Herbert Duckworth. From an early age Vanessa and her sister Virginia (Woolf, q.v.) determined the one to be a painter, the other a writer. The sisters were educated at home; in 1896 Vanessa began to attend Sir Arthur Cope's School of Art and in 1901 she gained admission to the Royal Academy Schools, where she was much influenced by the teaching of J. S. Sargent [q.v.]. By the time she left in 1904 it is clear that she had moved far from the artistic dominion of her mother's family which had been on familiar terms with the Pre-Raphaelites and which venerated G. F. Watts [q.v.].

The domestic and social pressures which fell upon Vanessa Stephen as the eldest daughter of an eminent widower and the protégée of her more socially ambitious relations were eased on the death of Sir Leslie in 1904, and later that year she moved with her sister and two brothers from Kensington to Bloomsbury, a respectable but unfashionable district, where they set out to follow their own pursuits without undue regard to the conventionalities and constrictions of formal London society. Increasingly they found themselves in the company of the Cambridge contemporaries of the elder brother, Thoby Stephen. In 1905 Vanessa founded the Friday Club in order to provide a meeting place for artists and persons interested in art, and this led to a closer friendship with (Arthur) Clive (Heward) Bell [q.v.], the most visually educated and aware of Thoby's friends, and following the latter's untimely death in 1906, to their marriage in 1907. The Bells' home at 46 Gordon Square was thereafter one of the focal points of what has come to be referred to as the Bloomsbury circle, which included such friends as (Giles) Lytton Strachey, (Sir) C. O. Desmond MacCarthy, and, somewhat later, (John) Maynard Keynes, Leonard Woolf (who married Virginia in 1912), Roger Fry [qq.v.], and Duncan Grant.

Although Vanessa Bell shared her husband's interest in the developments of contemporary French art, her own painting remained essentially sober and tonal, having much in it of J. A. McN. Whistler [q.v.] and of the New English Art Club, with which she sometimes exhibited. However, early in 1910 began the Bells' close and lasting friendship with Roger Fry; this had a profound influence, both personal and intellectual, particularly upon Vanessa, with whom Fry was to fall deeply and enduringly in love. In November of that year, with their enthusiastic co-operation, Fry promoted the notorious exhibition 'Manet and the Post-Impressionists', which was to give the British public its first opportunity to see the work of such painters as Cézanne, Gauguin, and Van Gogh. In its successor of 1912, the 'Second Post-Impressionist Exhibition', four of Vanessa Bell's paintings were hung, with other British and Russian examples, among the Picassos, Matisses, Derains, and other representatives of the School of Paris. Liberated from the English tradition of direct representation by the intoxicating example of the French and the stimulating theorizing of Bell and Fry, Vanessa's work grew increasingly bold, with a simplification of design and form and a free and joyous use of colour, a progression which was to lead her, before 1916, to paint some of the first totally abstract pictures in this country; but under-

lying the audacious innovations of this period, her passion for order, serenity, and harmony was always evident.

In 1913 Roger Fry founded the Omega workshops to enable artists fired by Post-Impressionism to apply their gifts to the decorative arts. Although it failed in 1919, Vanessa Bell was from the outset a wholehearted collaborator in this venture from which she derived, besides a number of commissions, a permanent interest in the use of ornament and decoration. Textiles, embroideries, ceramics, mosaics, painted furniture, and the many book-jackets designed for the Hogarth Press remain to show her remarkable and felicitous talent as a decorator; but changes of taste and the disasters of war have all but obliterated her larger decorative schemes, which were usually undertaken in conjunction with Duncan Grant. The mural decorations of Berwick Church, Sussex (1940-2) and rooms at nearby Charleston, Firle (which became her country home in 1916) survive from among the considerable body of work which they carried out together, mainly for private patrons; but she herself seldom lived in a house, studio, or flat without feeling impelled to decorate its walls and furnishings. This partnership with Duncan Grant was one of the happiest in the history of art, and from 1913—while remaining always on terms of amity with Clive Bell—they lived virtually as man and wife.

In the 1914-18 war Vanessa Bell, like most of her circle, held pacifist views; she lived in the country with Duncan Grant and her children, and the difficulties of domestic life in wartime left little time for painting. But she appears during this period to have come to feel that in abstraction she approached a dead end, and that, as she put it, 'Nature was more interesting'. She turned to the form of representational art which she felt best suited her. Her method, which allowed her to explore and to celebrate the solidity and brilliance of the natural world, was not radically changed for the rest of her life. Although she had a considerable gift for portraiture and used her friends and family as subjects when she could prevail upon them to sit, she painted few formal portraits and, from necessity as much as choice, applied herself to still life, landscape, interiors with figures, and, from time to time, translations from the Old Masters. She contributed regularly to group exhibitions (particularly the London group, of which she became a member in 1919); the first exhibition consisting solely of her own works was held at the Independent Gallery in 1922, and others followed in 1930 (Cooling Gallery), in 1934 and 1937 (Lefevre Gallery), in 1941 (Leicester Galleries), and in 1956 (Adams Gallery); in 1964 a memorial exhibition organized by the Arts Council was shown in six English cities. She gave generous encouragement to fellow-artists, particularly the young, and was a sponsor of, and taught in, the so-called Euston Road School when it opened in 1937.

Between the wars Vanessa Bell lived very privately, mainly in London, devoted to her painting, her family, and her close friends. She travelled in Spain, Germany, and Austria, and made extended stays in Provence, Italy, and Paris. The death of Roger Fry in 1934 was a severe loss to her; but that of her elder son Julian, killed in the Spanish civil war in 1937, was a shattering blow from which she never fully recovered. The suicide of her sister Virginia Woolf four years later was a further calamity. With the outbreak of World War II she again began to live almost wholly in the country, with Duncan Grant and Clive Bell, painting industriously to the last; she died at Charleston, after a brief illness, 7 April 1961.

Vanessa Bell was a woman of grave and distinguished beauty, with a low and beautiful speaking voice—characteristics which tended to mask her wit and humour and capacity for laughter. Her affections when given were strong and enduring; she was a powerful centripetal force in the small group of friends whom she thought of as 'old Bloomsbury', and amongst such often difficult and egotistical people she was a conciliator and a peacemaker. As an artist she may be accounted one of the most gifted of her time in this country, blessed with an instinctive sense of colour and design. She had the intelligence and self-awareness not to be seduced by the pioneering experimentalism of her brilliant Post-Impressionist period into a sterile extremism; her integrity and sincerity of purpose, her workmanlike discipline and total lack of affectation led her, during the last four decades of her life, to produce a body of work which affirmed her belief in the simpler pleasures and beauties of the visible world. Her own humility and her unwavering confidence in the superiority of his genius may have encouraged critics to regard Vanessa Bell as a follower of Duncan Grant, and thus to undervalue her real originality. Their community of interest was indeed close, but in fact the influences were reciprocal.

Portraits of Vanessa Bell (1942 and 1916) by Duncan Grant are in the Tate and National Portrait Galleries, London; the latter also has a head by the French sculptor Marcel Gimond (c. 1922–6), and a portrait by Dame Ethel Walker (1937); a late self-portrait (1958) is in the possession of Lord Clark.

Of Vanessa Bell's two sons, the elder, Julian (1908–1937), poet, was for a time professor of English literature at the university of Wuhan,

China; the younger, Quentin (b. 1910), is an artist, teacher, and writer; her daughter by Duncan Grant, born in 1918, became the wife of the writer David Garnett.

[Introductions to catalogues of the above-mentioned exhibitions; and to one held at the Anthony d'Offay Gallery, London, in 1973; Quentin Bell, *Virginia Woolf, a Biography* (2 vols., 1972); Richard Shone, *Bloomsbury Portraits*, 1976; private information.]

ANNE OLIVIER BELL

BELLMAN, SIR (CHARLES) HAROLD (1886–1963), a pioneer of the building society movement, was born in Paddington 16 February 1886, the second son of Charles Henry Bellman, coachbuilder, and his wife, Ellen Clemens. Both his parents came from Cornwall where for some 300 years the Bellmans had been master builders or seamen; his father had moved to London and settling in Paddington had begun to buy his house through the Abbey Road Building Society. Bellman left his higher-grade school in Beethoven Street before he was fourteen to spend another six months receiving special coaching from a Scottish dominie before entering the Railway Clearing House near Euston in 1900; but he continued his education and broadened his outlook by selective reading all his life. For the next fifteen years he ploughed his way through dreary railway accounts. He relieved the monotony by joining the 'Sharpshooters'—the 3rd County of London Imperial Yeomanry, with whom he learnt to ride the hard way. He served for ten years and as a sergeant commanded his own troop.

When war came in 1914 Bellman tried to rejoin his regiment but was rejected on medical grounds. Instead he was lent to the Ministry of Munitions where he became principal assistant in the establishment department. His talent for organization found full scope in a ministry which was driven at breakneck speed, first by Lloyd George and finally by Winston Churchill. He also joined the special constabulary and ended the war as assistant commandant of the London headquarters central detachment.

Having by this time some savings to invest, Bellman went to the Abbey Road Building Society where he made friends with Gilbert Lane, the secretary, and some of the directors. In 1918 he was invited to join the board and in 1920 to become asssistant to Lane, with the promise of the succession, which came to him in 1921 when Lane died. In 1927 Bellman became general manager, in 1930 managing director, and in 1937 chairman.

When Bellman joined the Society it was little

known outside the borough in which it was situated. Bellman studied minutely every aspect of the work—the processes of borrowing and lending, the duties of clerks, cashiers, and surveyors—and made many innovations and improvements. He appointed agents and started on a policy of opening branches. He overhauled the publicity, wrote the prospectus himself, and advertised in the national press. Home-ownership through thrift became for him a conviction, certainly a dedication, almost a religion. The assets which in 1919 were £750,000 rose to £8 million in eight years and advances had risen from about £150,000 to over £3 million. The board was strengthened by new directors; Sir Josiah (later Lord) Stamp [q.v.] became president. Bellman took great trouble to make the annual meeting a memorable occasion, inviting a prominent person, usually a Cabinet minister, to be the chief speaker. In 1932 the Society's new building, with the lofty belled tower, in Upper Baker Street, was opened by the prime minister. In 1944 the Society merged with the National Society to form the Abbey National, with assets of £80 million and Bellman as chairman and joint managing director. After four years he gave up his executive post, but he remained chairman until his death.

Bellman's activities were not confined to his own Society. As early as 1922 he formed the Metropolitan Building Societies Association, composed of some fifty societies, and became its first honorary secretary, then its chairman. In 1923 he was elected to the council of the central organization, the National Association of Building Societies. Of this he was elected chairman in the years 1933 to 1936. In 1934 the Building Societies' Institute for training building society staff was founded, with Bellman as the first president. Apart from this, his years of chairmanship were stormy: he tried to secure the co-operation of the 374 societies for the common purpose of adopting a new code of ethics and procedure, but was frustrated by the obstinate individuality and independence of the old-established societies. Consequently those societies assenting to the new code dissolved the National Association in 1936 and formed the new Building Societies Association. Bellman remained its chairman for another year. Some fifty societies, however, splintered off and founded their own national organization. The split was only healed in 1940 after public anxiety about alleged irregularity by a Yorkshire society in the 'Borders' case' had led to the passing of the Building Societies Act of 1939. This embodied in the main the code of ethics and procedure which the dissenting societies had rejected and which all societies now had to accept. The Building Societies Association then became the authoritative voice of the whole movement, consulted on all building society matters by the Treasury, the Bank of England, and the department which deals with housing, for building societies are now among the leading financial institutions of the country, and the foremost media for savings, with assets comparable to those of the London Clearing Banks. Bellman retired from the chair in 1937 but remained on the council until 1956 when he was made a vice-president.

In 1934-8 Bellman was president of the International Union of Building Societies and he presided with great distinction over two conferences: at Salzburg in 1935 and at Zurich in 1938. His influence in the building society movement had become world-wide. It spread throughout the dominions and the United States and those countries of Europe where the movement had a foothold. He kept the closest contacts with America and gave many lectures there on housing and the economic state of Britain to universities and institutions.

Bellman had a dignified presence. His articulation was perfect and his voice pleasing and mellow and pitched in an audible key. At times he was capable of real oratory. He had first learnt to speak in the Sunday School and the guild attached to the Wesleyan chapel in Fernhead Road, Paddington, which he claimed had been the strongest influence in his life as a boy, both in culture and character building. He remained always faithful to the Methodist connection which he served in various capacities open to the layman. He was chairman of Clayesmore, the boys', and Queenswood, the girls', public schools. He was chairman and treasurer of the National Children's Home; chairman of several hospitals, and a member of the Ministry of Health's central housing advisory committee and of numerous departmental committees. He was president of the Aldwych Club (1935-6) and of the Advertising Association (1939); and as a member of the court of governors of the London School of Economics took a special interest in its department of business management. He was chairman of the Hampstead and Marylebone bench of magistrates and a vice-lieutenant of Middlesex. In the war of 1939-45 he served as a major in the 22nd Middlesex battalion Home Guard. He wrote some dozen books—four of which became standard works in the building society world: *The Building Society Movement* (1927), *The Silent Revolution* (1928), *The Thrifty Three Millions* (1935), and *Bricks and Mortals* (1949). He was appointed MBE in 1920 and knighted in 1932. He was a chevalier of the Legion of Honour, an officer of the Australian Order of Merit, and an honorary

LLD of the American University, Washington (1939).

After 1956 Bellman had more leisure to cultivate his azaleas and his prize blooms of roses and chrysanthemums, for gardening was his chief relaxation and hobby, with Kasta, his long-haired dachshund, at his side.

In 1911 Bellman married Kate, daughter of Edwin George Peacock, of Brondesbury Park. They had been at school together, but it was their common interest in the choir and the social life of the chapel which ripened their friendship. When she died in 1959 Bellman presented a window to the new Fernhead Road chapel in her memory. They had two sons and a daughter. Bellman died in London 1 June 1963. There is a portrait by Sir James Gunn in the boardroom of the Abbey National Building Society.

[Sir Harold Bellman, *Cornish Cockney*, 1947; personal knowledge.]

GEOFFREY SHAKESPEARE

BELLO, SIR AHMADU, SARDAUNA OF SOKOTO (1910-1966), prime minister of Northern Nigeria, was born in 1910 in the small town of Rabah, twenty miles upstream of Sokoto, where his father, Ibrahim, a member of the Sokoto ruling house, was district head in charge of some sixty villages; his mother was a Sokoto woman. Ahmadu was brought up in rustic simplicity and received his first instruction from a Koranic teacher sitting under a big tree. When he was ten he was sent off to the new provincial school at Sokoto. At sixteen he went on to the new Moslem Katsina Training College, 170 miles away, where most of the future leaders of the North were educated.

At the college he took a prominent part in games, especially cricket and the Eton fives which became his lifelong passion—'quick exercise for stiff Ministers' he used to say. But it was to the academic side that he devoted himself in the wholehearted manner so typical of the young African and so gratifying to the teacher. He himself, on completion of the five-year course, went back to Sokoto to teach in the new Middle School. In 1934 at the early age of twenty-four he was appointed to Rabah as district head. He devoted himself to improving primitive agricultural methods, to introducing new crops, and to teaching those children who were near at hand, for there were then no schools in the districts. He kept up his English by reading the *Illustrated London News* and other English papers given him by the district officer.

Four years later he was posted to Gusau on the new railway from Zaria. He was made a member of the Sultan's council and was given supervision not only of a number of districts but also of the sub-offices of the Sultan's administration there. After 1939 he found himself deeply involved in 'war work' including the purchase of grain on a huge scale, recruiting of labour, organizing frontier patrols, and the maintenance of airfields and the like. He had been given the title of Sardauna in 1938 and it was perhaps not surprising that backstair intrigue caught up with him: he was accused and convicted of keeping back taxes paid over to him. But he was cleared on appeal to the Supreme Court and went back to Sokoto as Sultan's councillor for police and prisons.

In 1948 he visited England under British Council aegis to study local government. In the following year a vacancy permitted his election as second Sokoto member in the new Northern House of Assembly. At first he seldom took part in debates, but he made his mark with a new public. It was at this time that the NPC (Northern Peoples Congress) was set up: of this he became president, with the majority support of all classes of people in the region. Under the 1951 constitution, ministries, albeit rather nebulous, were created and the Sardauna became first minister of works for the North, adding thereto, before long, community development and local government.

Although he was a 'Northern' member of the Nigerian House of Representatives he never held office in Lagos; this he left to his extremely able friend and lieutenant (Sir) Abu Bakar Tafawa Balewa [q.v.]. The Sardauna handled the 1953 crisis, when the Southern parties tried to force a date for independence, with vigour and initiative, although it brought the North to the verge of secession. Under the consequent 1954 constitution, which gave more power to the Regions, he became first premier of the Northern Region, and caused some astonishment by describing his party as modified socialist in policy.

The Sardauna continued in office after Nigerian independence in 1960; but when the five majors attempted to seize control in January 1966 Bello and his wife were assassinated, as were the premier of the Western Region and the prime minister of Nigeria, Tafawa Balewa.

The Sardauna was a tall man, very distinguished in appearance and conspicuously well dressed in the many-coloured splendour of the Northern robes. He spoke faultless English. His natural language was Hausa but classical Arabic was a close second. He was quick-tempered and suffered no fools, but laughter came easily to him. He could not tolerate any kind of presumption, especially in Europeans, but appreciated good honest service. He had an enormous popularity in the Region, for everyone knew that he worked continuously and selflessly for his people. He was a dynamic and inspiring leader. Religion played a great part in his life and he carried out the pilgrimage to Mecca at least seven times. He was the founder and first chancellor of the Ahmadu Bello University.

The Sardauna was appointed CBE in 1953 and KBE in 1959 when he assumed as a family name that of his revered ancestor Sultan Bello who had known the explorer Hugh Clapperton [q.v.]. He married in 1932 and had two daughters.

[Sir Ahmadu Bello, *My Life*, 1962; personal knowledge.]

REX NIVEN

BENSON, SIR REGINALD LINDSAY (REX) (1889–1968), merchant banker, was born at South Street, London, 20 August 1889, the second son of Robert Henry Benson, of Buckhurst Park, Sussex, banker, and his wife, Evelyn, daughter of Robert Stayner Holford, for seventeen years member of Parliament for East Gloucestershire. At Eton Benson was captain of cricket, excelled also at rackets and athletics, and was president of 'Pop' (1908). After a year at Balliol he was in 1910 gazetted a subaltern in the 9th Lancers in South Africa. From 1913 to 1914 he served in India as aide-de-camp to the viceroy, Lord Hardinge of Penshurst [q.v.]. He joined his regiment in France in August 1914 and took part in the retreat from Mons, winning one of the first MCs and being wounded and gassed. After attachment to the French Sûreté and service in Ireland during the 1916 uprising he became liaison officer with General Franchet d'Espérey of the Groupe des Armées du Nord and later at French headquarters with Marshal Pétain. After the armistice he became chief of the British mission and was attached to the staff of Sir Henry Wilson [q.v.] at the peace conference. Whilst in France he was appointed to the DSO, awarded the croix de guerre and the Legion of Honour and was four times mentioned in dispatches. He was promoted major in 1920 and in 1921 became military secretary to Sir George (later Lord) Lloyd [q.v.], governor of Bombay, and organized the official tour of the Prince of Wales in the presidency in November 1921, for which he was awarded the MVO.

Benson resigned his commission in 1922 and was sent by Lloyd George to Batum on a special mission to try to reopen trade with post-revolutionary Russia. He travelled to Tiflis, Baku, and Moscow. A Russian-speaking American colleague was flung into jail but Rex Benson, secreting some £10,000 of the proceeds of his sales inside his socks, eventually escaped by canoe through the Polish lakes.

In 1924 he joined his father in the firm of Robert Benson & Co., and in 1926 he converted it to a private limited company, of which he became chairman in the mid thirties. He made many business trips to the United States and Canada. He vigorously exploited the company's long-standing connections in the United States, developed underwriting and new issue business in Canada and South Africa, and increased the firm's involvement in investment trust management.

During the inter-war years Benson was deeply involved in polo, both as player (in his heyday he was accorded a 7 handicap), and as organizer and manager of two British international polo expeditions; he also hunted enthusiastically, played golf, fished at his beloved Grogarry, South Uist, shot, and in his younger days flew his·own aeroplane. He was also active in other varied fields, for example financing (and sometimes participating in) the Savoy Orpheans band of Debroy Somers and using his considerable artistic experience to arrange as executor the sale of the great collection of pictures, silver, china, and works of art owned by his uncle, Sir George Holford of Dorchester House and Westonbirt, Gloucester, who had died in 1926.

In September 1939, although aged fifty, Benson resumed uniform and served as liaison officer to the First French Army until Dunkirk. After short spells as staff officer to the inspector of foreign contingents and as chairman of the Inter-Allied Timber Commission he became, with the rank of colonel, military attaché to Lord Halifax [q.v.] in Washington in June 1941, six months prior to the United States' entry into the war, and during the next three years his great knowledge and understanding of the States were most useful.

In 1944 he returned to Robert Benson & Co. Ltd. and took the lead in rebuilding the business. In 1947 the company merged with Lonsdale Investment Trust (a quoted public company) to form Robert Benson, Lonsdale & Co. under his chairmanship, and thereafter continued its expansion until it joined with Kleinwort, Sons & Co. to form Kleinwort, Benson, Lonsdale Ltd., registered in January 1961—a holding company for Kleinwort, Benson Ltd., the merchant bank, and of Lonsdale Investment Trust Ltd. Rex Benson had retired as chairman of Robert Benson, Lonsdale & Co. in 1959 but remained on the board of the new company until his death. Apart from the welfare of those in the company, his main interest lay in the fields of investment trust management and of company finances, particularly for new projects and developing companies; he was especially attracted by the investment opportunities in smaller companies in Canada and the United States and to the last year of his life got much pleasure from finding such 'situations' and the talent to run them.

In the post-war years Benson devoted much time to the promotion of Anglo-American understanding and for this he was knighted in 1958. The English-Speaking Union, founded by Sir Evelyn Wrench [q.v.], in particular owed much to his enthusiastic support and financial guidance as honorary treasurer from 1935, as joint deputy chairman from 1957, and as vice-president in 1968. He was one of the organizers of the Winston Churchill Memorial Trust and became a trustee, and he was also one of the original trustees of the World Wild-life Fund. He became interested in sheep farm-ing and from 1954 worked with typical energy at improving the stock at his farm in Singleton, Sussex, to the effect that his sheep won two championships at the Royal Show in 1960 and 1968.

Benson had panache, zest, and great charm. To travel with him abroad was an exhilarating, if exhausting, experience; his many friends were so unaffectedly glad to see him. His bright blue eyes would sparkle with high spirits and a wide smile crease his bronzed aquiline features. His warmth, gaiety, and enthusiasm were supported by great pertinacity and purposefulness; he was methodical and thorough, direct and forthright in argument, and would not tolerate anything he considered mean or shabby. He disliked any 'non-possumus' attitude and responded to a challenge, sometimes almost to the point of quixotry, and he was receptive of new notions. He was generous, hospitable, and wonderful company.

In 1932 Benson married Leslie, formerly wife of the publisher Condé Nast, and daughter of Albert Volney Foster, investment banker, of Lake Forest, Illinois; they had two sons. Benson died 26 September 1968 as he was returning from holiday in Italy.

He was painted by (Sir) Oswald Birley in 1937, by Simon Elwes in 1959, and by Edward I. Halliday in 1968. The first two portraits are in the possession of the family and the last is in the offices of Kleinwort, Benson Ltd.

[Private information; personal knowledge.]

G. P. S. MACPHERSON

BERRY, (JAMES) GOMER, first VISCOUNT KEMSLEY (1883-1968), newspaper proprietor, was born at Merthyr Tydfil 7 May 1883, the son of Alderman John Mathias Berry, estate agent, and his wife, Mary Ann, daughter of Thomas Rowe, of Pembroke Dock. He was the youngest brother of (Henry) Seymour Berry (later Lord Buckland, q.v.) and of William

Ewart Berry (later Lord Camrose, q.v.). He was educated at Merthyr Tydfil and, after appren-ticeship on the *Merthyr Tydfil Times*, was invited at eighteen to join his brother William in a newspaper partnership in London which lasted thirty-five years. Gomer Berry's career until 1937 may be studied in the notice of his brother, William.

When the brothers, who had been joined by Sir E. M. (later Lord) Iliffe [q.v.] in 1924, divided their business in 1937 because of their growing families, Kemsley became chairman of Allied Newspapers (renamed Kemsley News-papers in 1943). The group owned the *Daily Sketch*, later renamed the *Daily Graphic*, *Sunday Graphic*, and *Sunday Times* in London, and in the rest of Britain six morning, seven evening, six weekly, and four Sunday papers. This holding, maintained for twenty-two years at much the same size, made him the largest newspaper owner in the kingdom. By 1947 he was selling 26½ million newspapers a week.

From the start, Kemsley concentrated his energies on the *Sunday Times*, which he had retained on the last-minute intervention of Lady Kemsley. In 1937 its circulation was already 263,000; by 1959 the figure was 885,000. As a benevolently autocratic editor-in-chief he held, in matters of politics and morals, to an unreflective conservatism. Near the begin-ning of his rule he supported Neville Chamber-lain's pacific approach to Hitler, mainly out of a belief that Hitler offered the best hope for the containment of international Communism; an attempt to bring about an exchange of articles between Kemsley papers and the German press culminated on 27 July 1939 (six weeks before the outbreak of war) in a fruit-less visit to Hitler at Bayreuth. When (Sir) Anthony Eden (later the Earl of Avon) identified a new Hitler in Colonel Nasser and British troops joined Israel and France in an attack on the Suez Canal, Kemsley was the simple patriot aligning his newspapers behind his Govern-ment. 'As a nation', declared the *Sunday Times* of 4 November 1956, 'we are in this together.'

Because of the uncomplicated appeal of the *Graphic* papers and parts of his provincial holding (including the *Daily Dispatch*, *Sunday Empire News*, and *Sunday Chronicle* in Man-chester, the *Daily Record* and *Sunday Mail* in Glasgow, and the *Sunday Sun* in Newcastle), Kemsley found it necessary to fight a number of libel actions against the charge that he ran a 'gutter press'. In August 1946 he obliged Sir Hartley (later Lord) Shawcross, Labour's attorney-general, to apologize for having used that very phrase in by-election speeches. The extent, and the political colour, of Kemsley's empire made him the chief target for Labour MPs during the Commons debate in October

1946 which resulted in the setting up of the 1947-9 royal commission on the press. He gave robust evidence before it—'In its freedom, its honesty and its sense of responsibility the British press is unsurpassed'—and took the opportunity to explain the Kemsley Plan for the training of journalists, forerunner of the National Council for the Training of Journalists. The commission report concluded that ownership was not so concentrated as to threaten press freedom, and that 'an industry that lives by the sale of its products must give the public what the public will buy'.

It was in the 1950s that the gradual lifting of wartime restrictions on competition made the ownership of popular newspapers an increasingly hazardous business. Kemsley now made a crucial error of judgement. When commercial television began in Britain in 1955 he could have had a share in it. With Maurice Winnick, an impresario, and (Sir) Isaac Wolfson he had formed a consortium to which the Independent Television Authority awarded the franchise for week-end broadcasting in the midlands and the north. But Kemsley's sons (to whom the conduct of the new company would in part have fallen) were cool, Kemsley and Wolfson pulled out, and the consortium collapsed. Kemsley lost an insurance that his newspapers badly needed. He had already sold the *Daily Graphic* to Lord Rothermere in 1952. Late in 1955 he merged his two Sunday papers in Manchester and sold his morning paper there. In 1957 he parted with his Glasgow holding

By 1959 he was in no mood to go on. He and his immediate family—always influential in his calculations—had spent heavily to increase their shareholding, yet they still felt vulnerable to a take-over bid. A recent strike had been expensive. Taxation was heavy; death duties would be crushing. The sons, all directors, were not averse to selling and Lady Kemsley was ill. At first Kemsley sought to retain the *Sunday Times*: but in August 1959 he sold the family shareholding for £5 million to the Canadian newspaper owner and proprietor of the *Scotsman*, Roy H. Thompson (later Lord Thomson of Fleet)—who could find the money on the strength of his commercial-television franchise in Scotland. Kemsley had first approached a surprised Thomson, who some years before had tried to purchase one of his Scottish newspapers.

Kemsley's withdrawal from the newspaper world was total, and his sons kept no connection with either the firm or the newspapers. They were his children by his first wife. In 1907 he married Mary Lilian, daughter of Horace George Holmes of Brondesbury Park, London. She had died in 1928, after having borne him

six sons, four of whom survived him, and a daughter. In 1931 he married Edith (died 1976), daughter of E. N. Merandon du Plessis, of Constance, Flacq, Mauritius, who had been divorced from a Dutch diplomat, Cornelius Dresselhuys. She was appointed OBE in 1953 and was a commander of the Legion of Honour. Kemsley sold Chandos House, scene of his London entertaining, but kept Dropmore, his country estate.

With Northcliffe, Rothermere, Beaverbrook, and Camrise [qq.v.] gone, Kemsley was the last survivor of the old-style self-made newspaper barons. His air of being a man out of his time was heightened by his chosen trappings—his great London house and the Buckinghamshire mansion, the high-bodied Rolls Royce, the striped black silk tie and pearl tie-pin, the private lift at Kemsley House with the gates opened five minutes before he arrived, the office atmosphere like a medieval court. Though his role was limited to advertising and finance until 1937, the fact remains that once he was in sole command the circulation of one good newspaper, the *Sunday Times*, more than trebled. Certainly he was aided by an advance in public taste, and by a staff of able journalists under W. W. Hadley [q.v.] and H. V. Hodson. But he contrived, by supporting them and encouraging the young, to draw from them loyalty and enthusiasm; and although he reserved to himself 'final authority in all matters of policy', he allowed them in practice substantial liberty.

Berry became a baronet in 1928, a baron in 1936, a viscount in 1945, and was appointed GBE in 1959. He died in Monte Carlo 6 February 1968 and was succeeded in the viscountcy by his eldest son, (Geoffrey) Lionel (born 1909). His portrait by Sir Oswald Birley hangs in the offices of Times Newspapers. A portrait by Henry Carr was exhibited at the Royal Academy in 1960.

[Viscount Kemsley, the *Kemsley Manual of Journalism*, 1950; Viscount Camrose, *British Newspapers and their Controllers*, 1947; Harold Hobson, Phillip Knightley, and Leonard Russell, *The Pearl of Days: An Intimate Memoir of The Sunday Times, 1922-1972*, 1972; evidence to the royal commission on the press, 27 May 1948, cmnd. 7503; commission *Report*, 1949, cmnd. 7700; Peter Black, *The Mirror in the Corner: People's Television*, 1971; Lord Thomson of Fleet, *After I was Sixty*, 1975; *The Times*, 7 February 1968; *Sunday Times*, 11 February 1968; personal knowledge.]

C. D. HAMILTON

BERRY, SIDNEY MALCOLM (1881-1961), Congregational Church leader, the younger son of the Revd Charles Albert Berry and his wife, Mary Agnes Martin, was born at Southport, Lancashire, 25 July 1881, and was always proud to think of himself as a Lancastrian. His father (1852-99) was then becoming widely known as a minister to large and flourishing Congregational churches in Bolton then at Queen Street, Wolverhampton, and a preacher of great power. His fame crossed the Atlantic where the Plymouth Church, Brooklyn, invited him to succeed Henry Ward Beecher, an honour he declined, and in later years Sidney himself also declined a similar invitation.

Charles Berry's early death at forty-seven at Wolverhampton (1899), while in the high tide of his ministry, greatly affected his young son, then eighteen. Berry determined to follow him into the Congregational ministry, and from Tettenhall College, Wolverhampton, went up to Clare College, Cambridge, to read history, in which he received second classes in both parts i (1902) and ii (1903). He then went on to Mansfield College, Oxford (1903), then under the principalship of Andrew Martin Fairbairn [q.v.]. Mansfield College and its welfare always had a prime place in Berry's affections. He was chairman of the college council for twenty-five years.

He was ordained at the Oxted Congregational church in Surrey in 1906, and in 1909 was called to Chorlton-cum-Hardy, Manchester, and then in 1912 to Carr's Lane chapel, Birmingham, a pastorate made famous by R. W. Dale [q.v.]. There Berry succeeded John Henry Jowett (1863-1922) in a strong church in the heart of Birmingham, with large regular congregations.

Sidney Berry was now launched on a civic and national career in addition to the pastoral cares of his large congregation. In Birmingham he had his initiation into public life while in the country his personal charm and wit as a preacher made him much sought after for the notable occasions of Church life. To take him away from a great pastorate, as the Congregational Union of England and Wales successfully did in 1923, was thought by some to be a disservice to Congregationalism as a whole. But Berry was persuaded—perhaps in loyalty to his father's memory, who had declined a similar invitation in 1893—that he had a duty to serve as the Union's secretary and so he went to the Memorial Hall in London, where he stayed until 1948. For Congregationalism it was a revolutionary period. The independency of the Congregational churches was gradually reshaping itself into a more centralized fellowship, which carried responsibility for one another's churches and for their ministers. The moderational system,

started in 1919, had proved its worth and the £500,000 given through the Forward Movement (1925) helped to raise the standards of stipends, as did the later creation of the Home Churches Fund (1948) which made the regular income for ministerial maintenance a responsibility of the local county unions. Berry also took his share in raising the post-war Reconstruction Fund of £500,000.

Sidney Berry saw his task mainly as a *pastor pastorum* welcoming his fellow churchmen for consultation to the Memorial Hall as members of a family. In return he was welcomed in local churches with enthusiasm. He tended to gird under the routine of committee work and administration but he had the gift of discerning the leadership of other people, and was adroit in using it.

Berry gave considerable study to the art and style of preaching, and his Warrack lectures, entitled *Vital Preaching* (1936), delivered to theological students in the universities of Aberdeen and Glasgow are a fine exposition of his methods, and one of the best examples of homiletical skill at work. He also wrote religious meditations for the London *Sunday Times*. Glasgow made him an honorary DD in 1936.

In public as well as Church affairs Sidney Berry was the national leader of English Congregationalism from 1923 to 1948. He was moderator of the Free Church Federal Council (1934-7), chairman of the Congregational Union (1947), supported the moves for a British Council of Churches (1942), and was present at the Lausanne Faith and Order meeting (1927) and at the World Assemblies at Amsterdam (1948) and Evanston (1954).

But Berry was no over-zealous ecumenist. He believed that his best service for the cause of Church unity was to nurture the life and witness of the Congregational churches and, if possible, to foster their union with the Presbyterian Church of England. It was this union he worked for through all its set-backs over fifteen years from 1932 to 1947, and he would have rejoiced in the eventual union of the two Churches as the United Reformed Church in 1972.

Berry's secretaryship of the Congregational Union coincided with the economic and political crises which preceded the war of 1939-45. The grave unemployment in the industrial areas of the north, and south Wales where the strength of Congregationalism lay, threatened Church stability and from the Memorial Hall Berry organized much private relief in money and goods.

As a League of Nations man and a convinced supporter of collective security he had to face strong pacifist opposition from the younger generation of both ministers and laymen, who accused him of supporting 'the establishment' rather than the Christian pacifist view. At the Union Assembly in Norwich in 1929 the whole three days' agenda was devoted almost entirely to disarmament and the problems raised by pacifism in the Church. The dropping of the atomic bomb on Hiroshima in 1945 produced a further period of frustration and helplessness for the Churches whose only activity could be resolutions of protest.

A fresh career opened before him on his retirement in 1948 when Berry was elected minister-secretary of the reorganized International Congregational Council (1949) which, under him, became a well-organized body for consultation and fellowship. Until 1956 he roamed the world as an ambassador of good will to the Congregational churches, and their immense affection for him was shown at a banquet in his honour at the Hartford (Connecticut) Assembly in 1958.

Berry married in 1907 Helen, daughter of John Logan, JP, of Cambridge and had two daughters. His portrait (1938) by Frank O. Salisbury hangs in the Congregational Library at the Memorial Hall, London. He died in London 2 August 1961.

[R. Tudor Jones, *Congregationalism in England*, 1962; Albert Peel, *These Hundred Years*, 1931; *Congregational Year Book*, 1900 and 1962; private information; personal knowledge.]   CECIL NORTHCOTT

BESICOVITCH, ABRAM SAMOILO-VITCH (1891–1970), mathematician, was born at Berdyansk, on the Sea of Azov, 24 January 1891, the fourth child of the family of four sons and two daughters of Samoil Abramovitch Besicovitch and his wife, Eva Ilinichna Sauskan. By descent the family belonged to the Karaim people, whose ancestors were the Khazans. Their language was originally Turkish of the Qipchaq group but is now mostly Russian. Samoil Besicovitch was a jeweller but, after losses by theft, he gave up his shop and became a cashier. All the children were talented and studied at the university of St. Petersburg, the older ones in turn earning money and helping to support the younger. Abram Besicovitch graduated in 1912, one of his teachers having been A. A. Markov, who encouraged him to research in probability. In 1917 he became a professor of mathematics in the university of Perm, which was established in 1916 and developed rapidly until it was overrun in the civil war of 1919. From 1920 to 1924 Besicovitch was in Leningrad as professor in the Pedagogical Institute and lecturer in the university.

The duties of a university teacher were then subject to political constraints. He was obliged to teach classes of workers deficient in knowledge and ability. Besicovitch's reputation brought him the offer of a Rockefeller fellowship to work abroad, but the authorities refused him leave to accept. Ultimately, in 1924, in company with another mathematician, J. D. Tamarkin, he crossed the border under cover of darkness and made his way to Copenhagen, where the fellowship enabled him to work for a year with Harald Bohr, who was then investigating almost periodic functions. Besicovitch visited Oxford, staying for some months in New College with G. H. Hardy [q.v.] who was quick to see his great analytical powers and secured for him a lectureship in the university of Liverpool for 1926. At the earliest opportunity in 1927 Cambridge appointed him a lecturer in the university, conferring on him in 1928 the title of Cayley lecturer, and in 1930 he was elected a fellow of Trinity College. This fellowship he retained to the end of his life. He was naturalized in 1931.

In 1916 Besicovitch had married a mathematician, Valentina Vitaliyevna Doynikova, daughter of Vitaliy Doynikov, an administrator. She remained in Russia when he left. There were no children and the marriage was dissolved in 1926. A friend from Perm days, Maria Ivanovna Denisova, widow of a mathematician Alexander Denisov, came to live in England and in 1928 Besicovitch married her elder daughter, Valentina Alexandrovna, then aged sixteen. They had no family and it was the children of his friends who, throughout his life, enjoyed his affection. He would invite these children into his rooms in Trinity, where he provided them with coloured pencils and paper and cream cakes.

Besicovitch's book, *Almost Periodic Functions* (1955), originated in his work with Harald Bohr in 1924–5. He wrote more than 120 papers, shedding new and bright light on many questions in analysis and the classical theory of functions. He was more likely than many to solve problems which seemed intractable. Few mathematicians, facing such problems, can rid themselves of preconceived ideas about the nature of the solution and possible methods of obtaining it. Besicovitch could keep an open mind and envisage unexpected results. He was a master of intricate construction which could reveal paradoxical truths. He did not strive after abstractions and generalities; he was a problem-solver, not a system-builder. His formal statements had to be in the notation of analysis; the underlying mental pictures were geometrical, often expressible in simple language, as the following illustrations show.

A point having no magnitude (Euclid) is of

dimension o. A straight segment is of dimension 1; so is the circumference of a circle. The inside of a circle or the surface of a sphere has dimension 2. In 1918 Hausdorff defined dimensions of fractional order. A suitably sparse set of points on a line could have a measure of dimension (say) $\frac{1}{2}$. This notion has been abundantly fruitful. Besicovitch and his pupils added to our knowledge.

In a similar line of thought, the area of a curved surface was a concept needing analysis. Lebesgue and Fréchet defined it as a limit of the areas of polyhedra fitting closely to the surface, and Hausdorff had a definition in his scheme of two-dimensional measure. Besicovitch expected to prove the equivalence of the two definitions. He found instead paradoxical incompatibilities; 'I came to results very different from ones I was hoping for'.

An earlier paradox is easy to state, but not to prove. In 1917, S. Kakeya had asked: what is the smallest plane area within which a segment of unit length can turn through 360°? Trials with a pencil on a table suggested a three-cusped hypocycloid, of area $\pi/8$. Besicovitch constructed a complicated figure of arbitrarily small area which would serve to answer the question.

It is possible only to list other investigations undertaken by Besicovitch and his pupils—density and tangential properties of sets in a plane, covering theorems, convexity, and complex function theory.

In 1950 Besicovitch was elected to the Rouse Ball chair of mathematics at Cambridge University, succeeding the first holder, J. E. Littlewood. After his retirement in 1958 he remained active in teaching and research and spent eight successive years as visiting professor in the United States. He then returned to live in Trinity College. Towards his eightieth year his health failed and he died in Cambridge 2 November 1970.

Besicovitch's intellectual gifts were matched by his generous sympathy which endeared him to pupils, colleagues, and a wide circle of friends. He usually spoke Russian with his wife and his English accent and idiom remained foreign all his days. For him the definite article was superfluous. He became one of the characters of Cambridge.

He had been elected FRS in 1934 and was Sylvester medallist of the Royal Society in 1952. He received in 1930 the Adams prize of the university of Cambridge for his work on almost periodic functions, and in 1950 the De Morgan medal of the London Mathematical Society.

In Trinity College there is an oil portrait (1956) by E. Coxeter and a drawing (1952) by H. A. Freeth.

[J. C. Burkill in *Biographical Memoirs of Fellows of the Royal Society*, vol. xvii, 1971; S. J. Taylor in *Bulletin of the London Mathematical Society*, vol. vii, 1975; personal knowledge.]   J. C. BURKILL

BEVERIDGE, WILLIAM HENRY, BARON BEVERIDGE (1879-1963), social reformer and economist, was born at Rangpur in Bengal, 5 March 1879. He was the second child and elder son of Henry Beveridge, a district sessions judge in the Indian Civil Service, and his second wife, Annette Susannah Ackroyd, daughter of a Worcestershire business man. Henry Beveridge's father was David Beveridge of Dunfermline, a Scots Presbyterian bookseller and publisher who had written a radical history of British rule in India. The Beveridge parents were rather unusual figures in the Victorian raj, for Henry was a passionate advocate of Indian nationalism and home rule, and Annette had originally travelled to India before her marriage as a pioneer of secondary education for Hindu women. Both parents were deeply attached to Indian culture, and both became distinguished amateur oriental scholars and translators of Hindi and Persian texts. Of their four children only one apart from William survived childhood—their second daughter Annette Jeanie, or Jeannette, who married R. H. Tawney [q.v.], Beveridge's Balliol contemporary.

Throughout his life Beveridge idealized family relationships and tended to portray his own childhood as uniquely happy. Yet he privately admitted that he had few adult recollections of childhood before his late teens; and evidence of family correspondence suggests that this ideal childhood was almost entirely imaginary. At the age of five he was sent to a Squeers-like Unitarian boarding-school in Worcestershire, and saw nothing of his parents for the next two years. Although intellectually precocious he was a sickly and solitary child with few friends. His mother, perhaps the main influence on his early life, was by turns domineering, neglectful, and violently possessive. In 1882 he won a scholarship to Charterhouse, where he was bullied for being bad at games and discouraged from pursuing his passionate interest in natural science and astronomy. He excelled in both classics and mathematics, but neither of these subjects captured his imagination, and he afterwards complained that both intellectually and emotionally his life at Charterhouse had been almost entirely barren. Later in life he frequently felt himself to be a natural scientist *manqué* and blamed his early education for blocking the possibility of a scientific career. These childhood experiences may perhaps help to explain certain characteristics that many people found puzzling about the adult Beveridge—that he was a man of powerful and at times dazzling intellect, who yet never seemed to have developed his creative faculties nor to have discovered his true intellectual *métier*.

In 1897 Beveridge went as an exhibitioner to Balliol College, Oxford, where he gained first class honours in mathematical moderations (1898), classical moderations (1899), and *literae humaniores* (1901). He then studied for several terms in the chambers of a London commercial barrister, and was awarded a prize fellowship at University College, Oxford, in 1902. The following year he became a Bachelor of Civil Law. A brilliant career seemed to lie before him, in academic life or at the bar. At this point, however, in the face of fierce parental opposition, he decided to abandon the law and to devote himself to the study and cure of social problems. He accepted an invitation from Samuel Barnett [q.v.] to become sub-warden of the well-known Oxford settlement in the East End of London, Toynbee Hall. This decision was denounced by his father as 'sentimental philanthropy', but in fact Beveridge's motives were the reverse of sentimental. After reading T. H. Huxley [q.v.] he had become convinced that social problems could be studied with the same rigour and exactitude as natural phenomena, and that social policies should be grounded not in spontaneous charity but in applied social science.

Beveridge's commitment to social reform came at a crucial moment in the history of social policy in Britain. The statistics of mass poverty published by Charles Booth and Benjamin Seebohm Rowntree [qq.v.], the 'physical deterioration' scare at the end of the Boer War, and the debate on tariff reform all conspired to thrust social problems into the forefront of high politics. At Toynbee Hall Beveridge soon found himself in contact with reformers of all parties—progressive Liberals, 'national efficiency' Conservatives, and Fabian socialists—who were pressing for more positive government action on the 'social question'. In particular he fell under the spell of Sidney and Beatrice Webb [qq.v.], and while rejecting their socialist economic policies, was strongly influenced by their concept of a 'national minimum' and their theories of administrative reform. He became active in the old age pensions movement, the free school meals campaign, and in pressure for government action on behalf of the unemployed. In 1904 he began to collect material for what eventually became *Unemployment: a Problem of Industry* (1909)— a pioneering study which explored the structural complexity of the market for labour. During the depression of 1904-5 he helped to

set up the London Unemployed Fund; and in 1905 he became a leading member of the Central (Unemployed) Body—a semi-official committee set up under the Unemployed Workmen Act to harmonize relief works provided by local authorities, boards of guardians, and private charities. It was as a member of the CUB that Beveridge first began to campaign for a national system of labour exchanges—bodies which he claimed would streamline the market for labour, eliminate casual unemployment, and enable social welfare agencies to distinguish between the 'loafer' and the 'genuinely unemployed'.

Toynbee Hall soon became too narrow a base for Beveridge's ambitions, and at the end of 1905 he accepted a post as a leader-writer on 'social problems' with the Conservative daily newspaper, the *Morning Post*. During the next three years he produced nearly a thousand articles on such socio-economic questions as unemployment and casual labour, eugenics and the environment, progressive taxation and social insurance, rating reform and 'back to the land'. He argued not merely for specific social policies but for the development of a strong, centralized, bureaucratic state and for a far-reaching programme of 'social organization'— claiming, like the Benthamites eighty years earlier, that regulation of society through social administration would strengthen rather than weaken the free market economy. Beveridge's commitment to an interventionist state was reinforced by a visit to Germany, where he inspected the system of labour exchanges and contributory social insurance set up by the Prussian Government. He returned to England convinced that a dual policy of labour exchanges and state insurance offered the best practical solution to the unemployment problem; and he argued strongly for both these policies in evidence to the royal commission on the poor laws in the autumn of 1907. A few months later he was introduced by the Webbs to (Sir) Winston Churchill, the newly appointed Liberal president of the Board of Trade. Churchill at this stage of his career was strongly influenced by the claim of the 'national efficiency' school that social reform was an urgent strategic and imperial necessity; and as a result of this meeting he invited Beveridge to join the Board of Trade as his personal assistant in preparing legislation on unemployment.

Beveridge entered Whitehall as a non-established civil servant in July 1908, at a time when the Liberal Government was embarking upon the most active and ambitious phase of its social legislation programme. He spent the next three years working closely with the Board of Trade's permanent secretary, Sir Hubert

Llewellyn Smith [q.v.], in drawing up the Labour Exchanges Act of 1909 and part ii of the National Insurance Act of 1911. Under these acts labour exchanges under Board of Trade control were established in all parts of the country, and unemployment insurance was provided for two and a quarter million workers in heavy industries. Beveridge himself became a permanent civil servant in 1909, with administrative responsibility for the labour exchanges system, and by 1913 he had reached the rank of assistant secretary. During this period he was convinced that he was within reach of a 'final solution for the unemployment problem' and was anxious to extend unemployment insurance and compulsory decasualization of the whole of the nation's labour force.

These ambitions were frustrated, however, by the outbreak of World War I. In 1915 Beveridge together with Llewellyn Smith was temporarily drafted to the new Ministry of Munitions, set up under Lloyd George to deal with the crisis in production of shells. Beveridge fully supported Lloyd George's view that fighting the war required a total commitment of national resources, even if this involved a suspension of civil liberties; and with Llewellyn Smith he drafted the Munitions of War Act, which severely limited wartime collective bargaining and imposed a system of quasi-military discipline upon civilian workers in munitions. This Act, which met with fierce resistance from the engineering unions and from the militant shop stewards' movement, was largely responsible for the prolonged mutual hostility that prevailed between Beveridge and the trade union movement for the next twenty-five years. In the summer of 1916 he returned to the Board of Trade where he drafted a new Unemployment Insurance Act, which extended insurance to all workers employed in war production. This Act was designed to take advantage of wartime full employment to insure workers against the probable onset of depression at the end of the war. It was opposed, however, by both sides of industry and further soured Beveridge's relations with the trade unions. His unpopularity with the labour movement was largely responsible for Beveridge's exclusion from the new Ministry of Labour, set up to co-ordinate all labour and employment policies at the end of 1916. In after years Beveridge looked back on this exclusion as the death-blow to his dream of solving the unemployment problem, and as the main cause of the futility of government unemployment policies in the inter-war years. He was moved instead to the new Ministry of Food, where as second secretary he was made responsible for rationing and control of prices. Throughout 1917 domestic food supplies were

severely hit by the German submarine campaign and by diversion of the mercantile marine to the transport of American troops. There were severe food shortages and long queues in many parts of the country, and in spite of some opposition from food traders a general rationing scheme drawn up by Beveridge was introduced at the end of the year. When the war came to an end in 1918 Beveridge was sent as British representative on an Inter-Allied Food Mission to central and eastern Europe—where he pressed unsuccessfully for instant and unconditional famine relief to the defeated powers. Early in 1919 he was appointed KCB and became permanent secretary to the Ministry of Food, at thirty-nine one of the youngest men ever to reach that rank in Whitehall.

Beveridge throughout the war had been involved in prolonged discussions with the Webbs, Llewellyn Smith, and other administrative experts about the advance planning of post-war social and economic reforms. Nevertheless, his wartime experiences—and particularly the resistance to state regulation that he had met from both trade unions and employers—had gradually undermined his pre-war faith in the virtues of a strong paternalist administrative state. The failure of co-operation between Allied Governments in the relief of Germany and Austria convinced him that European prosperity could be restored only by a revival of business confidence and restoration of the gold standard and international free trade. Thus Beveridge emerged from the war considerably more sympathetic to traditional views of *laissez-faire* and considerably less enthusiastic for state intervention than he had been in 1914. He was highly critical of the view that food controls should be retained in peacetime; and in June 1919 he resigned from the Civil Service to take up the directorship of the London School of Economics—a post offered him by his old friend and mentor, Sidney Webb.

The LSE had been founded by the Webbs in the 1890s as a college of London University, and had been closely involved in the Edwardian 'national efficiency' movement. In 1919 it was still a small college, catering mainly for part-time students; but Sidney Webb was convinced that the time was ripe for expansion in all areas of the social sciences. He looked to Beveridge as an ambitious and imaginative administrator to be the dynamo for that expansion. Over the next eighteen years Beveridge devoted himself to raising massive funds from such bodies as the Rockefeller Foundation, to a large-scale building programme, and to attracting a range of distinguished scholars in all branches of the social sciences—Tawney,

H. J. Laski, L. T. Hobhouse [qq.v.], L. C. (later Lord) Robbins, F. A. Hayek, and Bronislaw Malinowski, to name but a few. In the early 1930s he was personally responsible for bringing to the School many distinguished academic refugees expelled from Hitler's Germany—and he helped to find posts for many other refugee scholars in universities in both England and America. As vice-chancellor of London University from 1926 to 1928 he laid the foundations for a new centralized university, and was responsible for acquiring and raising funds for the university's Bloomsbury site. By the early 1930s the LSE was recognized as one of the world's leading centres of the social sciences, and Beveridge himself was seen as mainly responsible for its prodigious growth. Yet, as in the Civil Service, many of Beveridge's activities attracted controversy and conflict. His day-to-day administrative methods were seen as despotic and high-handed by many of his staff. On matters of politics he held the view that academics should abstain from open commitment to ideologies and parties—a standpoint that brought him into recurrent conflict with the controversial professor of political science, Harold Laski. Beveridge had, moreover, very fixed ideas about how the social sciences should be properly conducted. Since his days in Oxford he had been strongly attached to the empirically based scientific positivism expounded by T. H. Huxley; and he was highly critical of those of his colleagues—including a majority of the School's economists and sociologists—who preferred a more deductive or analytical approach. To counteract such an approach Beveridge established in 1930 a social biology department under Professor Lancelot Hogben, to carry out empirical research into problems of the 'real world'; but the department was never integrated with the rest of the School and folded up after Hogben's resignation at the end of 1936.

Beveridge's relations with his colleagues were further hampered by his increasing intimacy with the School's academic secretary, his second cousin-by-marriage, Mrs Janet ('Jessy') Mair, wife of David Beveridge Mair and daughter of William Philip, business man and philanthropist, of Newport, Fife. David and Jessy Mair had a son and three daughters, one of whom, Lucy, became professor of applied anthropology at LSE. An overbearing and temperamental Scotswoman, Mrs Mair had come to the School with Beveridge in 1919 (having been his secretary and aide during the war) and was highly unpopular with many of the School's professors. Throughout the 1930s there were complaints about the 'Beveridge-Mair dictatorship' and a general sense of relief when Beveridge decided to leave the School to accept the mastership of University College, Oxford, in 1937.

Beveridge returned to Oxford with the avowed intention of devoting himself to the study of unemployment and to a statistical study of the history of prices which he had started nearly twenty years before. In 1937 he was elected a fellow of the British Academy—an honour that he accepted with some hesitation, fearing that it would identify him as a student of the humanities rather than a practitioner of science. His studies of both unemployment and prices were intended to demonstrate the superiority of empirical methods over abstract speculation, and both were designed to support the academic position that Beveridge had adopted at the LSE—namely, that the problems of society would only be solved by discovering objective socio-economic laws rather than by ill-informed subjective political action. Yet it may be doubted how profound was Beveridge's inner commitment to this latter principle. Throughout his time at LSE he had periodically engaged in various kinds of public or political activity—as a participant in the Liberal summer school movement in 1922-4, as a member of the royal commission on the coal industry of 1925-6, as a campaigner for the family allowances scheme of Eleanor Rathbone [q.v.] in the late 1920s, and as chairman of the Unemployment Insurance Statutory Committee from 1934. From the mid 1930s onwards it seems clear that Beveridge was increasingly anxious to return to some more central role in public administration. Since Hitler's invasion of the Rhineland in 1936 he had become convinced that another war with Germany was virtually inevitable—and he was equally convinced that Whitehall was making no preparations whatsoever for such an emergency. At the same time his earlier faith in the capacities of enlightened public administration appears to have revived; he abandoned the rather exaggerated belief in an economic free market that he had adopted in the 1920s, and by 1939 had become committed to far-reaching state planning in both social and economic affairs. At the outbreak of war his ambition was to be given the task that he thought should have been his during the war of 1914-18—that of controlling and directing both civilian manpower and military recruitment.

Not for the first time in his life, however, Beveridge's hopes were doomed to disappointment. No summons came from Whitehall. Throughout the winter of 1939-40 Beveridge kicked his heels in frustration—occasionally meeting together with other neglected veterans of World War I such as J. Arthur (later Lord) Salter and J. M. (later Lord) Keynes [q.v.]. During these months Beveridge published numerous articles and made several broadcasts, arguing that the times required a totally new kind of socio-economic policy, both to mobilize resources for fighting the war and to lay the foundations of a more just and equal society after the return of peace. Not until a year after the outbreak of war was he invited by Ernest Bevin [q.v.] to carry out a survey of the Government's manpower requirements; and in December 1940 he was appointed under-secretary in the Ministry of Labour with the special task of drawing up a list of 'reserved' occupations. Beveridge's new career in Whitehall, however, ended almost before it had begun. From the start he made it clear that he was determined to take control of the wartime manpower programme. Ernest Bevin, possibly remembering Beveridge's clashes with the unions in the war of 1914-1918, was equally determined that he should not do so. The result was that Beveridge was hived off into the chairmanship of an obscure interdepartmental inquiry into the co-ordination of social services—an inquiry that was not expected to report until after the war was over. Beveridge, who was under no illusions about what was happening to him, accepted his new appointment with tears in his eyes. Yet it was to prove in many ways the most important commission and the major drama of his life.

Beveridge started work on his social services inquiry in June 1941 and within a few days had convinced himself that it offered the opportunity he had been looking for to determine the shape of British society after the war. Over the next eighteen months he carried out a detailed survey of the deficiencies of Britain's social services—focusing particularly on the long-term unemployed, on inadequate provision for health care, and the widespread problem of poverty in childhood and old age. With the help of a committee of Civil Service advisers he interviewed hundreds of witnesses and consulted with economic experts like Keynes, Robbins, and James Meade. His proposals were drawn up in close consultation with representatives of the Trades Union Congress, with whom Beveridge at last found himself in close harmony. For perhaps the first time in his life he became fired with an abstract ideal of 'social justice'; and in numerous articles and broadcasts he argued passionately for the forging of an ideal new society out of the ashes of war. His conception of how such a society should be organized was spelt out in the report on *Social Insurance and Allied Services* in December 1942. In it he outlined a Bunyan-esque vision of society's battle against the five giants of idleness, ignorance, disease, squalor, and want; and he put forward a programme for overcoming them which consisted of a free national health service, family allowances,

government policies to maintain full employment, and universal subsistence-level social insurance to include all classes in society and to cover all social contingencies from the cradle to the grave. Such a programme, Beveridge maintained, could eliminate poverty without in any way impairing the civil and personal freedom that was central to the British political tradition. The lynch-pin of his programme he believed to be the maintenance of full employment, and his views on how this might be attained were spelt out in a second report, *Full Employment in a Free Society*, published privately in 1944. In this second report Beveridge argued that full employment could be achieved in a variety of ways—either by Keynesian-style fiscal regulation, or by direct control and deployment of manpower, or by total state control of the means of production. Beveridge's private papers suggest that at this stage in his career he had little objection to this latter policy, nor did he think it incompatible with personal freedom: 'private ownership of the means of production', he wrote, was 'not one of the essential British liberties' and could not be allowed to stand in the way of rebuilding British society after the war.

Beveridge's report of 1942 met with a cool response in Whitehall and from the Churchill Government, but it proved overwhelmingly popular with the British public, and over 70,000 copies were sold in the space of a few days. Early in 1943 the only major parliamentary revolt of the war forced the Government to commit itself to the Beveridge proposals—with the result that Beveridge's plan eventually became the blueprint for the welfare state legislation of 1944 to 1948. Shortly after his report appeared Beveridge married, on 15 December 1942, his recently widowed cousin, Jessy Mair, and with his new wife he travelled about the country canvassing his proposals and addressing large public audiences. His curiously prophetic figure, with its straight white hair, sharp, bird-like profile and high-pitched, meticulous Oxford voice, was flashed by Pathé News into every cinema in the country. Dazzled by this success, and disappointed by the Government's lack of enthusiasm, Beveridge was tempted by the suggestion that he should promote his Plan by going into politics. He had previously had no formal connection with any political party, but in 1944 he resigned the mastership of University College and entered Parliament as Liberal MP for Berwick-upon-Tweed, at the same time setting up home with Lady Beveridge in a Northumbrian country house, Tuggal Hall. Almost certainly he hoped that the first post-war election would bring about the long-awaited 'Liberal revival' and that he would find himself in charge of post-war reconstruction. In 1945, however, he lost his seat and went to the House of Lords as a Liberal peer.

His old age was employed in a series of rather peripheral public roles—leader of the Liberals in the Lords, chairman of the Newton Aycliffe New Town Corporation from 1947 to 1952, and chairman of the committee that opposed commercial broadcasting in 1949–51. As a private individual much of his time was spent in writing his autobiography (*Power and Influence*, 1953) and a memoir of his parents (*India Called Them*, 1947). To this Dictionary he contributed the notice of Lord Stamp. He did not hesitate to attack the shortcomings of the social legislation that emerged after 1945. He was highly critical of the Labour Government for excluding the voluntary friendly societies from state insurance and for rejecting the principle of subsistence-level pensions. His book on *Voluntary Action* (1948) was a passionate defence of the role of the voluntary sector in provision of social welfare—and, perhaps, an admission of doubt about the increasing bureaucratization of welfare that his own ideas on social policy had done much to bring about. In the mid 1950s he was highly critical of the erosion of pension values by continuous inflation, and spoke frequently on this subject in the House of Lords. Increasingly, however, he devoted himself to his unfinished history of prices, still hoping that this would unravel the mysteries of the economic system; and to his dying day he believed that his history of prices (in 1939 had been published the first volume of his *Prices and Wages in England from the Twelfth to the Nineteenth Century*) rather than his much acclaimed report on social insurance would be his 'main contribution to the understanding of the modern world'.

Beveridge's life and personality may be, and indeed have been, interpreted in a number of different ways. Some people regarded him as a mechanistic bureaucrat with little feeling for the infinite subtleties and complexities of human life. Others saw him as a tireless if sometimes tactless campaigner for a more efficient, just, and compassionate social order. Throughout his life he continually clashed with colleagues who resented his autocratic ways and his chronic inability to suffer fools gladly. Yet in private life he is remembered by people who knew him well as gentle, humorous, quixotic, and humane. He was perceived by many, and indeed described himself, as a 'self-centred' person; yet he could devote himself with utter selflessness to a cause which fired his moral imagination. In middle life he had a reputation for hardness and harshness; but this was belied by the loving and unflagging care that he bestowed on his aged parents, both of whom

lived with him almost continuously from 1918 until their deaths in 1929. It was belied also by the fact that he secretly gave away more than a third of his income to charitable causes, needy relatives, and friends. The abrasiveness of Beveridge's character may be partly ascribed to the unsatisfactory nature of his personal life: in youth and middle age he deeply regretted his failure to find a suitable wife, and one of the attractions of Mrs Mair was undoubtedly that she provided him with the kind of close-knit family circle that he always cherished as the highest social ideal. Yet Beveridge had certain unusual characteristics that cannot be explained away simply in terms of personal unhappiness. For a man of such keen intellect he showed little interest in general philosophical ideas, and he sometimes admitted rather regretfully that many of the main intellectual currents of his generation had simply passed him by. He was curiously unconscious of many of the glaring paradoxes and contradictions contained in his own beliefs—such as the view implicit in his writings of the early 1940s that one could indefinitely expand the powers of the state without thereby modifying any of the basic structures of political, social, and family life. Beveridge's intellectual blind-spots may perhaps have been linked with the fact that from early childhood he had been cut off from the kind of scientific studies that might have been his true vocation. A more speculative conclusion is that such blind-spots may be a necessary part of the mental equipment of all effective social reformers. 'I really do think', he wrote at the age of nineteen, 'that no man can do really progressive work who had not one idea carried to excess . . . The man must have one great ideal to aim at, to a certain extent excluding all else, and his convictions must be very strong.' In this early statement of faith lies the clue to many aspects of Beveridge's inner personality and of his public career.

Beveridge received many honours. In 1916 he was appointed CB and in 1919 KCB. In 1946 C. R. (later Earl) Attlee created him first Baron Beveridge. He became honorary LLD at the universities of London, Aberdeen, Birmingham, Chicago, Columbia, Melbourne, Paris, and Oslo; honorary D.Litt. at New Zealand and McGill; honorary D.Litt.Hum. at Pennsylvania; honorary Dr of Social Sciences at Brussels; and honorary Dr.Econ. at Rotterdam. He was made an honorary fellow of Balliol, Nuffield, and University Colleges, Oxford.

Beveridge and his wife retired to Oxford in 1954. She died in 1959, he surviving her for four years until he died at home in Oxford 16 March 1963. They were buried together in Throckington churchyard, high on the

Northumbrian moors. Upon Beveridge's death the barony became extinct.

There is a portrait in oils by (Sir) William Nicholson (1927) in the London School of Economics, a photographic portrait in the National Portrait Gallery, a portrait in oils by Allan Gwynne-Jones (1959) at University College, Oxford, and a bronze bust by Benno Elkan at Balliol College, Oxford.

[Beveridge correspondence in the British Library of Political Science; Lord Beveridge, *Power and Influence*, 1953; José Harris, *William Beveridge: a Biography*, 1977; Janet Beveridge, *Beveridge and his Plan*, 1954; Lord Salter in *Proceedings* of the British Academy, vol. xlix, 1963; J. Harold Wilson, *Beveridge Memorial Lecture*, Institute of Statisticians, 1966; private information.]   JOSÉ HARRIS

BING, GERTRUD (1892-1964), scholar, was born in Hamburg 7 June 1892, the third child of Moritz Bing, merchant, and his wife, Emma Jonas. She was educated in Hamburg, where she qualified as a schoolteacher and taught for eighteen months. In 1916 she entered the university of Munich to read philosophy, German literature, and psychology. After returning to teaching for a year in 1918, she resumed her studies at the newly founded university of Hamburg, under Ernst Cassirer whose philosophy of symbolic forms pre-occupied her throughout her life. She took her Ph.D. degree in 1921 and in 1922 joined the Kulturwissenschaftliche Bibliothek Warburg, a private foundation in Hamburg, in which she was successively librarian and personal assistant to Aby Warburg. After Warburg's death in 1929 she took a major part, as assistant to Fritz Saxl (whose notice she contributed to this Dictionary), in the activities of the Bibliothek Warburg and in its removal to England in 1933. After 1944, when the Warburg Institute was incorporated in the university of London, Gertrud Bing, as assistant director, took on the work of administrator, first for Saxl, then for Henri Frankfort, whom she had herself proposed should succeed him. In 1955 she in her turn was appointed director of the Institute and professor of the history of the classical tradition in the university of London. By 1959 when she retired, and was elected as honorary fellow of the Institute, it had been lodged in its new premises in the Bloomsbury precinct of the university. In the same year she received an honorary D.Litt. from the university of Reading.

Gertrud Bing's career was one of devotion to scholarship and to the principles on which Warburg had founded his library. She came to accept wholeheartedly Warburg's approach to history, especially the history of the classical tradition and its influence on European civilization. As Warburg's literary executor she edited his *Gesammelte Schriften* (1932), in which her own learning and her gift of understanding and interpreting the ideas of others were fully evident. These talents she was to develop still further in the criticism and editing of scholarly books and articles during her whole life. Saxl's *Lectures*, which she brought out in 1957, was one example among many. One of her last acts was to arrange for the publication of a selection of Warburg's writings in Italian translation (*La Rinascita del paganesimo antico*, Florence, 1966) and to contribute to it a study of Warburg.

Short, dark, and spectacled, with a serious expression which easily changed to a friendly smile, Gertrud Bing impressed all by her strength of purpose, courage, and humanity. The scholarly concerns of others rapidly became her own. Discussion of them, by telephone or letter, was as much a pleasure to her as it was benefit to those whose work was being discussed. Her standards were high, her range of competence large. As a critic she was often formidable, never solemn or unfair, always firm and patient, sympathetic and tactful, always willing to bring her retentive, scrupulous, and orderly mind to bear on the drafts of friends and colleagues all over the world. She knew how established scholars and beginners alike needed encouragement, but she was never over-indulgent: in the end, she believed, she could only help so far and the final responsibility was the author's.

Gertrud Bing's willingness to devote her time to others was only one reason why she published so little herself. Her masterly memoir of Saxl, in the volume of memorial essays edited by D. J. Gordon in 1957, made no mention of the part she played in the evacuation of the Warburg Institute, its staff, and library, from Nazi Germany to England. English and Continental scholars were attracted to the 'new' Institute in London as much by the personal interest and stimulus offered by Bing (neither she nor her friends used her forename), Saxl, and their colleagues as they were by the novel approaches to historical studies which the Library invited. To refugee scholars, among many others who came for practical help and counsel as well as for their own research, Bing was as remarkable for her understanding of human problems and help in resolving them as for her intellectual guidance. Throughout her career and in retirement, she made the Institute the centre of her interest and of her studies.

Like Warburg, whom she accompanied on his last visits between 1927 and 1928, and like Saxl, Bing had a lifelong attachment to Italy, especially to Florence. Her knowledge of the country, in the Renaissance and the present, was deep and instinctive. Nothing pleased her more about the Warburg Institute than its traditional associations, continually renewed and fostered, with Italian scholars and scholarship. But England had become her home; she was naturalized in 1946; and her house in Dulwich, where she lived for nearly thirty years, with a garden which she herself planted and cultivated, was a meeting-place for friends and scholars from all over the world. She died in London 3 July 1964.

[The Warburg Institute, *Annual Report*, 1963–4; *Gertrud Bing, 1892–1964*. (*In memoriam*), privately printed, with bibliography, 1965; private information; personal knowledge.]   ENRIQUETA FRANKFORT

BIRD, (CYRIL) KENNETH (1887–1965), the cartoonist FOUGASSE, was born 17 December 1887 in London, the younger son of Arthur Bird, iron merchant of London, who was known as a prominent cricketer and a first-class shot, and his wife, Mary Wheen. He was educated at Farnborough Park School, Hampshire, from 1898 to 1902, and in 1902 went to Cheltenham College. At Cheltenham Bird set up an outstanding record, becoming head boy at the age of sixteen. In 1904 he proceeded to King's College, London, where he studied engineering and was president of the University Union Society and of the King's College Engineering Society. He suggested that he would like to be an artist, but his father had felt that art was a rather flighty profession. However, while at King's, Bird attended evening art classes at the Regent Street Polytechnic and at the School of Photo-Engraving and Lithography in Bolt Court. Bird graduated B.Sc. in civil engineering in 1908, and qualified as AMICE. By this time he had developed into a good rugby player and boxer.

In 1909 he started work at the naval dockyard at Rosyth. He continued his rugby and in 1913 was invited to play in the final international trials and scored the only try. He would have been certain of his cap for Scotland had he not got concussion and remained unconscious until after the match was over. At King's College he had joined the Artists' Rifles and in August 1914 he applied urgently for release from the dockyard, a 'reserved occupation', in order to join the army, and in September joined the Royal Engineers. In the same year he married Mary ('Mollie') Holden, daughter of William Hay Caldwell of Morar Lodge, Morar, former zoology fellow of Gonville and Caius College, Cambridge. Mollie was a painter in watercolours and oils, and an etcher under the name of Mary Holden Bird. They had no children. Later they both became Christian Scientists.

Bird's military career was tragic and brief. In 1915 he was blown up by a shell at Gallipoli, and was home in 1916 with a shattered back and little hope of survival. For three years he lay helpless. After five years he was just able to walk. But during these years he had an opportunity to return to his old hobby. Encouraged by his artist wife he started to draw. He also took a course in art from Percy V. Bradshaw. His first drawing was accepted by the editor of *Punch* in 1916. It was entitled 'War's Brutalising Influence' and was signed 'Fougasse' (a French mine which might or might not go off). By 1917 he was contributing regularly to *Punch* and after the war he started to publish his drawings in book form. In 1921 appeared *A Gallery of Games*, and in 1922 *Drawn at a Venture*, with a preface by A. A. Milne [q.v.], a close friend. He ran a series of exhibitions and did some brilliant commercial work. His contributions to the Austin Reed [q.v.] advertisements 'For Men about Regent Street' and for Pyramid handkerchiefs were most successful. In 1936 Bird became a fellow of King's College, London.

In 1937 he became art editor of *Punch* in succession to George Morrow and was appointed editor in 1949, on the retirement of his friend E. V. Knox. Meanwhile he visited the United States, coming back just in time for the war. From 1939 he was an air-raid warden in Kensington. He was actively engaged throughout the blitz dealing with incendiary bombs and rescue work. In 1940 he visited France, shortly before Dunkirk, at the request of the War Office. On his return he did over a thousand drawings and posters for various Ministries. One of his earliest was a series of posters on security—superb cartoons of Hitler, Goering, and Goebbels listening to indiscreet conversations, illustrating the phrase 'Careless Talk Costs Lives'. These were displayed all over the country and reproduced throughout the world. Later he did illustrations and posters for the army on the subjects of gas drill, concealment, maintenance of equipment, physical fitness, and recruiting parachute troops. For the Royal Air Force he did a most dramatic and entertaining series of instructional posters—a typical example was an airman doing a dive out of a machine that has piled up on its nose, with the caption, 'I'm afraid this is going to cure me permanently of jamming my brakes on'. For the Royal Navy he did hundreds of drawings for secret manuals—so secret that he said he had to draw them with his eyes shut. He also drew a most appealing series of posters for the Royal Navy Libraries.

For the Treasury he did many posters for National Savings. Outstanding was the drawing of a Churchill tank, the big gun being shown as a large cigar stuck in the turret—giving a ferocious impression of the prime minister going into action. A tender masterpiece was a Christmas card, a present for the Civil Defence —two wardens standing beside an ambulance looking out into a sea of fire and saying, 'It is a bit quieter tonight, isn't it?' For the Ministry of Aircraft Production he produced several series of posters emphasizing the vital importance of speedy, high-quality workmanship. For the Ministry of Supply his posters made a cheerful appeal for old iron to make tanks, and old bones for Spitfires. He did many more drawings for the Ministry of Fuel and Power, the Ministry of Food, and the Ministry of Agriculture, including posters for the Women's Land Army. But it is probably with the Ministry of War Transport that he was most at home. He scored great successes with his posters giving advice to down-trodden travellers in wartime—superb examples of works of art that attract, inform, and cheer. The crowd of bewildered people, huddled together in a corner of a platform with the caption 'The more we are together the more uncomfortable we'll be', is still remembered.

It is not surprising that Fougasse was at home with work for the Ministry of War Transport, because in 1935 one of the bestsellers in England was his little book—written with W. D. H. McCullough—*You Have Been Warned*, a hilarious attack on the misdemeanours of road-users. This was so popular that the Ministry of War Transport ultimately decided to distribute with every driving licence a small concentrated volume of good advice by the same authors called *Many Happy Returns* (1937).

It would be difficult to find anything more persuasive than the work of this artist who imparted so much official information so quickly, efficiently, and humorously to almost every section of Britain's fighting and working forces by means of a few simple lines, all created as an extra, entirely unpaid honorary war job in addition to his own professional work as an art editor and his amateur work as an air-raid warden. He was also a member of the BBC Brains Trust. Bird was appointed CBE in 1946.

He died in London, 11 June 1965. A memorial exhibition of his work was held in the following year at the Fine Art Society.

[*Fougasse*, ed. Bevis Hillier, 1977; private information; personal knowledge.]

W. D. H. McCULLOUGH

BIRKETT, WILLIAM NORMAN, first Baron Birkett (1883-1962), barrister and judge, was born at Ulverston, Lancashire, 6 September 1883, the fourth of the five children of Thomas Birkett and his first wife, Agnes, daughter of Moses Tyson, butcher. His mother died when he was three. His father was a draper with a substantial business at Ulverston, a prominent Wesleyan, active in the UDC and the Liberal Club. Norman Birkett was educated at the Wesleyan day school at Ulverston until he was eleven, and then at the higher-grade school at Barrow. He left school at fifteen and started in one of his father's shops as an apprentice. It was not long before he became a local preacher on the Ulverston Methodist circuit. His success was such that his father, who had decided that his son would never make a good draper, allowed him to leave the business when he was twenty-one and to study at home for the Wesleyan ministry. After about a year, the Methodist minister who was coaching him suggested he should go to Cambridge and read for a degree in history and theology.

So in 1907 at the age of twenty-four Birkett went up to Emmanuel College where he spent four years. He became president of the Union in 1910 and obtained a second class in history in part i of his tripos (1909) and a second in law in part ii (1911). He also obtained a first class in the theological special examination in 1910. Birkett did not find the change from theology to law an easy one to make, since he knew that it would be a disappointment to his father. But he had blossomed out in Cambridge and felt, as he told his father, that he would 'find the ministry rather cramping'. His confidence that he could get to the bar without being a further burden on his father was justified. He was lucky enough to get a job as private secretary to one of the Cadburys at Birmingham; this paid him £200 a year with time to work for his bar examinations. He was called to the bar by the Inner Temple in June 1913 and in the following September he started practice as a local at Birmingham where obviously his prospects were best.

Birkett was thirty when he went to the bar but, like many who start practising at that age, he soon made up for lost time. His progress was naturally hastened by the fact that, when war broke out in 1914, most of his competitors went into the Services while Birkett himself was twice rejected as medically unfit. It was unusual, but not unheard of, for a junior barrister who had made a success at a local bar to move to London to spread his wings. In 1920 Birkett made the move and entered the chambers of Sir Edward Marshall Hall [q.v.], then at the height of his fame and fashion; he acquired also the services of Edgar Bowker, Hall's clerk and one of the most successful of his time. In the same year (1920) Birkett married Ruth (died 1969), daughter of Emil Nilsson, of Sweden; this brought him lifelong happiness and a son and a daughter. The move to London was of course intended to lead to a silk gown; and after four years, when his earnings were over £4,000, Birkett felt justified in taking the step; he was made KC in 1924.

From then on until the outbreak of war in 1939 Birkett led a glorious life. The speed of his success was due in some measure to the talent of his clerk and to the ill health of Marshall Hall which gave Birkett unexpected chances. But these aids did no more than hasten his recognition as one of the foremost advocates of his time. In his first year as a silk he doubled the earnings of his last as a junior; and thereafter, although some of the sensational murderers he defended cannot have been sensational payers, his earnings averaged around £25,000 a year. Speaking thirty-five years later of Marshall Hall, Birkett said: 'The age that produced and gloried in his spectacular triumphs in the courts, has passed away for ever. The advocate no longer plays the part in our public life that he once did. The fashionable divorce suit, the sensational libel action, the great murder trial—they are no longer the dramatic events that once occupied public attention to the exclusion of almost everything else.'

Hall died in 1927, but the great age continued until the second war; when that was over the special jury list perished and advocacy changed its bright apparel for a sober suit. Birkett had not the grandiose appearance of Hall—he was lanky, had untidy red hair, angular features, and spectacles—but he had the golden voice. In all the forensic gifts he was highly skilled but in chief he was an orator. Oratory itself was changing: tawdriness was more easily detected and men were beginning to look for earnestness and sincerity; these were Birkett's qualities, founded on his great integrity. He gave all he had to all his cases, often to the point of nervous exhaustion. At the bar he was universally liked; there can hardly have been anyone who knew him who did not receive from him some piece, great or small, of kindness or of courtesy. Of the many famous cases with which he was connected may be mentioned his defence in the Gladstone libel case (1927), of Clarence Hatry [q.v.] (1930), of Maundy Gregory in the 'honours case' (1933), of the murderers Mancini (1934) and Dr. Ruxton (1936), as well as his prosecution of another murderer A. A. Rouse in the 'blazing car case' (1931).

During this time Birkett was also in politics. He first stood for Parliament in the post-war election of 1918 when, like many other Liberals without the 'coupon', he was at the bottom of the poll. Thereafter he shared the vicissitudes of the Liberal Party with the result that he was in the House only briefly, in the Parliaments of 1923–4 and 1929–31. He wanted very much to hold one of the law offices; but while many of his contemporaries, despairing otherwise of a political future, moved either to the left or to the right, he would not swerve.

Birkett held his last brief on the first day of the Michaelmas term in 1939 after the war broke out. Then he accepted the chairmanship of a committee to advise the home secretary on cases of detention under the emergency powers. The work was unpaid and in June 1941 he was knighted in recognition of his services. In 1928 Birkett had refused a seat on the High Court bench: 'I wasn't really drawn to the judicial office', he said later, 'I loved the Bar so much.' When the offer was made again in November 1941, he was fifty-eight and must have sensed that, if ever he went back to the bar, things would be very different. He accepted, and went to the King's Bench.

It is rare for an impassioned advocate to be made a judge, for fear that he will be lacking in judicial restraint and unable not to take sides. Birkett proved the contrary. Greatly helped by an innate diffidence, he made himself an excellent judge of first instance. But he had to school himself rigorously as his diary shows. 'The truth is I like the limelight, and cannot bear now to be in obscurity,' he recorded after three months on the bench. Ill health troubled him and he was often depressed. He was at the bottom of the judicial ladder, junior to many whom he had led to the bar. A great chance came and went in 1945 when the prime minister and the lord chancellor selected him to be the British judge at the projected trial of German war criminals with the likelihood of presiding over the international tribunal. But the men of protocol thought that someone higher in the judicial hierarchy was required. So in the end Birkett went to Nuremberg only as the alternate to Lord Justice Lawrence. When at the end of the proceedings Lawrence was made a baron, as Lord Oaksey, and Birkett's work went unrecognized, he was dreadfully upset; he was consoled in 1947 by a privy councillorship. He yearned for promotion to the Court of Appeal for which he was unsuited, since he was not an especially acute lawyer nor a profound one. When eventually it came in 1950, he found the work dull and it became duller. At the end of 1956, as soon as he had served the fifteen years on the bench which entitled him to a pension, he retired.

Thereafter he lived for five reviving years. In 1958 he went to the House of Lords. In the same year Cambridge gave him an honorary LLD; he had been an honorary fellow of his college since

1946 and already had honorary degrees from London (where he was chairman of the university court), Birmingham, and Hull. His interests had always been wide—cricket, literature, especially Dickens, the City of London (he was four times master of the Company of Curriers), the preservation of the English countryside, especially the Lakes from which he came. He revelled in speech and excelled in every form of speechmaking and on the radio and television. He was asked everywhere, from prizegivings to the great Bar Association meetings of America where he was as popular as in Britain; he became president of the Pilgrims in 1958 in succession to Lord Halifax [q.v.]. He did not speak much in the House of Lords, but in 1962 he was stirred by a private Bill (but one which had the blessing of the Government) to secure Manchester's water supply by, its opponents said, the despoiling of Ullswater. On 8 February he moved the rejection of the Bill and with a speech which once again plucked the strings of advocacy he carried the House by 70 votes against 36. His life thus rounded, two days later he died, in London, 10 February 1962, and was succeeded by his son, Michael (born 1929).

The Imperial War Museum has a portrait by Dame Laura Knight and the National Portrait Gallery a working drawing by Sir David Low. A portrait by Maurice Codner is privately owned.

[H. Montgomery Hyde, *Norman Birkett*, 1964; personal knowledge.]   DEVLIN

BLACKER, (LATHAM VALENTINE) STEWART (1887-1964), soldier, inventor, and explorer, was born 1 October 1887, the son of Major Latham Charles Miller Blacker, who came of a family of soldiers. One of his ancestors was Valentine Blacker (1778-1823, q.v.), who was instrumental in the mapping of Mount Everest. He was educated at Cheltenham College (1899-1900) and at Bedford School. From there he went to the Royal Military College at Sandhurst, and then entered the Indian Army, following his father's footsteps. He served first in India, and later in Afghanistan, Turkistan, and Russia. Although he had had no special engineering training, Blacker early on showed an aptitude for armaments design, and in 1905 was associated with the development of the 3.5 inch infantry mortar. He became keen on flying, and in 1911 obtained his flying certificate No. 121. During his service abroad he was awarded many medals and clasps, and was frequently mentioned in dispatches.

When war broke out in 1914 he succeeded in getting himself transferred from the Indian Army to the Royal Flying Corps. As an RFC pilot he was first shot down in France in 1915 and severely wounded. He was again seriously wounded in 1916 and 1917. After the war he decided to devote his energies to the development at his own expense of special weapons without any assistance from the Services, and it was his proud boast that he was the only private inventor of armaments in the country.

In 1920 he was appointed OBE, and from 1924-8 was a member of the Imperial General Staff. In 1927 he married Lady Doris, eldest daughter of the first Earl Peel, whose notice she wrote for this Dictionary. He became in due course the father of twin sons and two daughters. At his mansion in Liss, Hampshire, he was able to set up a modern workshop for the manufacture of his devices and a firing range for trying them out.

In 1933 he was a member of the first expedition to fly over Mount Everest. This led to his writing *First over Everest* (1933), the last of his three books, and to the award of the Paris Geographical Society's gold medal.

The war of 1939-45 found Blacker with the rank of lieutenant-colonel in the Territorial Army, but obviously unfit for further service overseas. He therefore concentrated on his weapon development projects. His first interest had been in trying to devise an anti-tank weapon for use by the infantry. What was needed was a projector for a bomb containing high explosive of the plastic variety, which would plaster on to the tank so that the comparatively large area of contact required to blow a hole on detonation could be obtained. Such a bomb was much too large to be fired through any barrel, so Blacker adopted the simple solution of making the barrel a part of the bomb and firing the entire unit from a spigot.

Before the war neither the anti-tank Blacker Bombard, as he called it, nor any of his other weapons had been adopted by the army. However, when the war had started Blacker, complete with eyeglass and leggings, approached everyone he knew at the War Office to do something about them. A new section of Military Intelligence Research (MIRc) had recently been formed there for the express purpose of developing special weapons, and Blacker was referred to the head of it, Major (later Major-General Sir) R. Millis Jefferis. Jefferis, always receptive to new ideas, welcomed Blacker's invention and arranged for his bombard to be perfected and put into production. It was modified for the Royal Navy as the anti-submarine Hedgehog.

The PIAT, based on one of Blacker's experimental guns, became one of the most successful of our anti-tank weapons, and was responsible for the destruction of many German tanks. Carrying on with his spigot principle. Blacker had developed a spigot gun which could be fired from the shoulder, a spring taking up the recoil so that it did not affect the firer. Jefferis was experimenting with what were known as hollow-charge rounds. A high-explosive charge carried in a bomb would be focused by a cone so that on contact with the target and detonation a small hole would be driven through heavy armour plate. This hollow charge weighed 2 lbs, and Jefferis wanted means whereby an infantry-man could fire it from the shoulder. The PIAT, based on Blacker's spring gun, proved to be the answer. Blacker later received an inventor's award of £25,000.

Blacker was the perfect example of an Irish gentleman. He was always courteous and understanding. In addition, he had a remarkable brain, was very persuasive, had acquired a vast fund of knowledge concerning the development of armaments, and was an ingenious inventor. He died at Cold Hayes, Liss, Hampshire, 19 April 1964.

[Stuart Macrae, *Winston Churchill's Toy-shop*, 1971; personal knowledge.]

STUART MACRAE

BLACKMAN, VERNON HERBERT (1872-1967), plant physiologist, was born 8 January 1872 at York Road, Lambeth, London, the sixth child and third son in a family of ten. His father, Frederick Blackman, was a general medical practitioner; his mother, Catherine Elizabeth, was the daughter of Charles Maynard Frost, medical superintendent of Portland prison. His eldest brother, F. F. Blackman, FRS [q.v.], reader in botany in the university of Cambridge, achieved international renown.

Blackman was educated at the City of London and King's College Schools. In 1889, with an open scholarship, he entered St. Bartholomew's Hospital Medical School where he won a second open scholarship. The pre-clinical classes introduced him to the biological sciences and stimulated a lifelong interest in the processes of living organisms. As a result, and influenced by his brother, he interrupted his medical course and proceeded to St. John's College, Cambridge, with an entrance exhibition. From 1893 to 1895 he was a foundation scholar and Hutchinson student. He achieved first classes in both parts of the natural sciences tripos (1894 and 1895, specializing in botany) and later became a fellow of St. John's (1898-1904). He received the Walsingham medal in 1897 and the Sc.D. (Cambridge) in 1906.

As an undergraduate he began cytological research on nuclear fusion in *Pinus sylvestris* and so became familiar with the great current advances in this field in Germany. He abandoned medicine and went to Strasburger's laboratory in Bonn after graduation. On his return in 1896 he became an assistant in the Department of Botany at the British Museum (Natural History) where his function was to look after the fungal collections. Most of his time was, however, spent doing research on the nucleus in fungi. He was also a lecturer at Birkbeck, University, and East London Colleges, university of London.

In 1907 Blackman was appointed to the first chair of botany at Leeds University where he developed an active department and initiated some mycological research. He returned to London in 1911 as professor of plant physiology and pathology at Imperial College. By now he was recognized as an outstanding botanist and was elected a fellow of the Royal Society in 1913. His cytological work, spread over twenty years, 1895 to 1915, includes many original observations on the behaviour of the nucleus in *Pinus sylvestris* and in the *Uredineae*, for example the demonstration of alternation of generations in the rust fungi.

At Imperial College Blackman joined Professor (Sir) J. B. Farmer [q.v.], whose notice he later contributed in this Dictionary, with the expressed purpose of promoting training and research in 'those aspects of plant life from which economic benefits may be expected to flow'. This unique opportunity arose because for the first time public money was available for such a project through the Development Commission. Blackman persuaded the Board of Agriculture to set up, under his direction, a research Institute of Plant Physiology with its headquarters at Imperial College and its staff located, in addition, at research stations, with the dual aim of relating research directly to agricultural science and of providing facilities for field experiments. He had long maintained that progress in the understanding of plant processes demanded the application of chemistry and physics to biological problems. From then on he bent his energies to encouraging the quantitative analytical approach to the study of crop plants.

The outbreak of World War I delayed the implementation of his plans, and, at the request of the Board of Agriculture, he examined claims that overhead electric discharges increased plant growth. By numerous carefully executed experiments both in the laboratory and in the field he demonstrated a small beneficial effect on cereal growth. The increase was, however, too small and too variable in the field to warrant practical application of the method. He also considered the formulation of a mathematical equation to describe the growth history of a plant and in 1919 published an important paper in which he set out a correct expression for relative growth rate, which he termed the 'efficiency index'. His work provided a remarkable impetus to measurements of the expansion of plants, and studies of the control of growth.

After the war agricultural research greatly expanded and Blackman assumed responsibility for an ever-increasing number of people and projects. Financed by the Food Investigation Board of the Department of Scientific and Industrial Research, he supervised, at Imperial College, research on chemical changes in stored apples, and he was a member of the Department's Advisory Council from 1926 to 1930. He was also particularly concerned with the development of the Fruit Research Station at East Malling, Kent, as a state-aided institute, serving for thirty-five years on its committee, twenty of them as vice-chairman. He is commemorated there by the Blackman scholarship for applied botany. During these post-war years Farmer and Blackman built up a Botany Department for teaching and research in plant physiology and pathology, which soon became the most advanced centre in the United Kingdom, and within which developed the research schools in these subjects associated with the names of F. G. Gregory [q.v.], and William Brown, FRS. Trained men went to many parts of the world and many Commonwealth students came to the college for postgraduate training. Numerous publications appeared, dealing in the main with problems of transpiration, nutrition, and growth characteristics of plants, and of parasitism by fungi. Many of the students and staff achieved distinction as professors, heads of research establishments, and fellows of the Royal Society, and Blackman became a dominant figure of his time in the development in Britain of experimental botany.

He succeeded Farmer as head of department in 1929 and in 1937 retired from his college appointments, but he remained as head of the Research Institute until 1942. He became in this last decade a rather remote figure absorbed in manifold administrative duties and committee work.

He was a member of the Imperial College board of governors (1931 to 1937), of the Water Pollution Research Board (1927 to 1947), of the governing bodies of Rothamsted Experimental Station, the John Innes Horticultural Institute, Long Ashton Research Station, and the Forest Products Research Board. He edited the *Annals of Botany* for twenty-five years (1922–47) and

was on the first editorial board of the *Biochemical Journal*. In 1937 he received honorary doctorates of the universities of Allahabad and Benares while on a visit to India.

Blackman was a fastidious and somewhat shy man always impeccably neat and courteous. He was extremely conscientious and meticulous over detail in all he undertook, and was renowned for his insistence on clarity of expression and correct grammar in scientific writing. He held together a large group of research workers and teachers with a quiet assurance and the exercise of a benign and unchallenged authority. He was greatly respected for both his foresight and his wisdom. In his long years of retirement he maintained his interest in botanical affairs and also joined the English Association to continue his crusade on the correct use of words.

In 1901 Blackman married Edith Delta, daughter of Joseph Emett, accountant. She was skilled in the making of wax models of biological specimens for teaching purposes. She died in 1940 and in 1941 he married Thérèse Elizabeth, daughter of S. G. S. Panisset, a research director at Associated Portland Cement. She was his former student and secretary. There were two sons and a daughter of the first marriage. The elder son, G. E. Blackman, FRS, became Sibthorpian professor of rural economy at Oxford and director of the Agricultural Research Council's Unit of Plant Agronomy. The younger son died at the early age of twenty-four. Blackman himself died 1 October 1967 at 17 Berkeley Place, Wimbledon, where he had lived for over fifty years. A portrait by Reginald Lewis (1957) is at East Malling Research Station in Kent, and there is a bronze bust by his daughter-in-law, Audrey Blackman (1953).

[Archives of Imperial College; H. K. Porter in *Biographical Memoirs of the Fellows of the Royal Society*, vol. xiv, 1968; private information; personal knowledge.]

H. K. PORTER

BLOOD, Sir HILARY RUDOLPH ROBERT (1893–1967), colonial administrator, was born in Glasgow 28 May 1893, the eldest son of the Revd (later Canon) Alban Francis Blood, rector of Holy Trinity church, Kilmarnock, and his wife, Adelaide Thérèse Feldtmann. He was educated at the Irvine Royal Academy and at Glasgow University where he obtained his MA in 1914. In the war of 1914–18 he served in the Royal Scots Fusiliers and was wounded in the Gallipoli campaign.

In 1920 Blood entered the Ceylon Civil Service as a cadet, and served there for the next ten years. He was colonial secretary in Grenada (1930-4) and in Sierra Leone (1934-42). He was governor of the Gambia (1942-7), of Barbados (1947-9), and of Mauritius (1949-54). As a governor, Blood was highly regarded. He was a shrewd administrator, and his friendly nature, his genuine interest in people and their individual problems made him a sympathetic and popular ruler. He had the dignity and presence for ceremonial occasions but none of the vanity and pretence which sometimes afflict men in these elevated positions. Perhaps the happiest moment in his career was in Barbados when he went into the commentator's box during a test match between the West Indies and the MCC and took over anonymously from the official commentator. He did it very well, and when the public learnt that the new commentator was none other than their own governor, he became more popular than ever.

His wide experience in so many of the smaller territories in the British Empire gave him a particular interest in the very difficult problem of their advance to some form of self-government or independence. In 1958 he wrote a pamphlet for the Conservative Commonwealth Council in which he tried to identify the complex factors, varying from colony to colony, which affected this advance and to put forward tentative solutions. He was able to give some practical shape to his ideas by service as a constitutional commissioner in British Honduras (1959) and in Zanzibar (1960). In the same year he became chairman of the constitutional commission for Malta. There his work was of great importance and in the opinion of good judges it facilitated a smooth transition from the period of direct rule to the grant of independence in 1964.

In his later years Blood was active in the service of the Royal Commonwealth Society, the Royal Commonwealth Society for the Blind (of which he was chairman in 1962-5), and as chairman of the Royal Society of Arts from 1963 to 1965. During this period of active retirement he worked frequently for the Civil Service Commission, both as a group chairman at the Civil Service selection board testing candidates for the administrative class of the Home Civil Service and the senior branch of the Foreign Service, and as a member of the final selection boards in the same class of competition.

Blood was a burly man, standing about six feet tall, with broad brow, square jaw, and lively hazel eyes. He walked with a pronounced limp, the result of his wound in Gallipoli. To all his activities throughout his life he gave his undeflected attention and performed all his tasks with complete integrity. A deeply religious man, his chief distinction was his humanity and his sympathetic understanding of all those who worked for him and with him. His whole bearing, his friendly smiles, and the deep tones of his voice gave people, young and old, confidence in him and brought him innumerable friends and a devoted family.

Appointed CMG in 1934, Blood was advanced to KCMG in 1944 and appointed GBE in 1953. The honour which gave him the most pride and pleasure was the honorary LLD which his old university at Glasgow conferred on him in 1944.

In 1919 he married Alison Farie (died 1972), youngest daughter of William Boyd Anderson, a lawyer in Glasgow; they had one son and two daughters. Blood died at Ashford, Kent, 20 June 1967.

[*The Times*, 21 June 1967; Royal Commonwealth Society *Journal*, August 1967; private information; personal knowledge.]

GEORGE MALLABY

BLYTON, ENID MARY (1897-1968), writer for children, was born 11 August 1897 at Lordship Lane, East Dulwich, London, the eldest child in a family of one girl and two boys of Thomas Carey Blyton, a businessman of modest means, formerly of Sheffield and then of London, and his wife, Theresa Mary Harrison. He was ambitious for her to be a concert pianist and she studied hard for many years, taking her LRAM at an early age. But after he had left the family house to live with another woman—an event that must have psychologically affected Enid who was then thirteen and loved him deeply—she gradually dropped her studies and took to writing poems and stories. Educated at St. Christopher's School for Girls (1907-15), where she became head girl in 1913, she subsequently spent some months studying music, and in 1916 she began to train as a teacher at Ipswich, where she studied the Froebel and Montessori methods for teaching the young—a training that influenced her writing techniques in later years. Having completed the course by December 1918, in 1919 she went to teach at Bickley Park School in Kent and the following year became nursery governess in Surbiton to a family of four young boys and the children of neighbours.

In the last decade of her life, she often claimed to have papered her bedroom with rejection slips from magazine and book publishers but her surviving diaries of those formative writing years tell a story of early and ever-growing success. At the age of fourteen she had published a poem in one of the children's papers of Arthur Mee [q.v.], and in March 1917 *Nash's Magazine* published one of her poems. In 1921 and 1922 various short stories and poems appeared in the *Saturday Westminster Review*, the *Bystander*, the *Londoner*, *Passing Show*, and other magazines of the period. Her first book, *Child Whispers*, a collection of poems, was published in 1922 and in the next year she earned well over £300 from her published work. In 1924 the total exceeded £500 and in 1925 over £1,200— a substantial income for any contemporary author. By then she had given up her teaching work.

In 1924 she married Major Hugh Alexander Pollock, DSO, the son of an antique bookseller in Ayr. After a distinguished army career in the war of 1914-18, in 1923 Pollock had become editor of the book department at Newnes, the magazine and book publishers. Pollock had been married before, but his wife had left him during the war. He submitted Enid's books to his employers and also arranged for her to write and edit *Sunny Stories*, a new weekly publication with which she was to be associated for nearly a quarter of a century. They had two daughters, Gillian, born in 1931, and Imogen, born in 1937. But by the outbreak of war in 1939 the relationship was already under strain and Hugh Pollock's later absences on military duties increased the pressures. In 1942 they were divorced and six months later, in 1943, Enid married a middleaged London surgeon, Kenneth Fraser Darrell Waters (died 1967). The second marriage was a happy and harmonious one. Darrell Waters, whose first marriage had been childless, looked on Enid's daughters as his own; their names were eventually changed to Darrell Waters by deed poll.

By the mid 1930s, Enid Blyton had got into the prolific stride which she maintained for a further thirty years. In 1935 she published six different titles and in 1940 eleven titles and two under the pseudonym 'Mary Pollock' emerged from her facile pen: or rather, from her portable typewriter. She had the habit of typing on a sunny veranda at her home, Green Hedges, in Beaconsfield, Buckinghamshire, with a portable typewriter on her knees and a shawl around her shoulders. Ten thousand words a day was a good cruising speed and she was known to complete a full-length book for children between a Monday and a Friday of the same week. So vast was her output that her books were rumoured to be created by a team of ghostwriters. The rumours were baseless. With the help of her immense energy, years of practice, and a vast if quiet self-confidence, she would tell close friends that she could sit down with the typewriter on her knees, think of a compelling opening sentence, and then go off into a trance-like state while the story

flowed from her imagination through her nimble fingers on to the page. When this became public knowledge, unkind critics maintained that the resulting story read as though the author had indeed been in a trance at the time of writing.

Because of paper-rationing during the war of 1939-45, Enid Blyton's output was too prolific to be confined to one publisher. By the early fifties, she had close on forty British publishers. At the end of her active writing career around 1965, she had published over four hundred different titles, many of which had also appeared in translation in about twenty different languages or dialects—from Afrikaans to Swahili, as she was proud to claim. The English-speaking sales alone (1977) were in excess of two hundred million copies and, nearly ten years after her death, were increasing at the rate of about five million copies per year. She was the first major children's author to appear in paperback editions and in 1977 over one hundred of her individual titles were continually in print. She deliberately wrote, in the language of every age-group, for children from five to fifteen, so that those who discovered her works when very young would remain faithful for the next decade.

She became a well-known author in the 1940s with her *Famous Five* and *Secret Seven* stories, and her *Adventure* series, but in 1949 she became a major public figure with the creation of Little Noddy. One day she called on a publisher and was shown some original line and colour drawings depicting puppet figures by a Dutch artist named Harmsen van der Beek. At once she began to weave names, stories, and a continuing background for the characters depicted—Little Noddy, Big Ears, Mr Plod the policeman, and the other characters of Toyland Village. Noddy and his friends were not only immensely successful in book form— the sales ran into several million copies—but manufacturers rushed to produce Noddy dolls, Noddy toothpaste, Noddy pyjamas, and Noddy drawings on cereal packets. There was a very popular 'Noddy in Toyland' pantomime for children each Christmas and fifty-two Noddy puppet films shown weekly on commercial television.

Such a huge popular success was bound to create an adverse reaction in certain quarters. Literary articles were published which criticized the moral qualities inherent in Enid Blyton's work. Some librarians banned her works from public libraries on the grounds that the simple prose style and black-and-white moralizing in the plots deterred young children from reading books with more subtle literary values. The simple and incontrovertible answer was that the children themselves *wanted* to read her books and continued to do so in ever-increasing numbers.

Although she produced several hundred thousand words every year, conducted an immense correspondence by postcard with her many young fans, edited and wrote the *Enid Blyton Magazine*, actively supported charities for children, and ran the domestic household at Green Hedges, up to the last fifteen years of her life Enid Blyton did not use the services of a literary agent for her voluminous and intricate publishing affairs. She dealt with a variety of British and foreign publishers and with her incisive business mind always drove a good bargain. She would never accept an advance payment on account of royalties but insisted that the minimum printing of each book should be twenty-five thousand copies. She also insisted on having complete control over the choice of artist for the dust-jacket and illustrations: the publisher who erred once in presenting indifferent art-work to her never did so twice.

As a famous writer who for many years enjoyed an annual income of well over £100,000, Enid Blyton was quiet and unostentatious in her private life. She shunned publicity and often wrote to literary editors asking them not to review her books but to devote the space to up-and-coming authors. Once her legal advisers took action because of a humorous remark about her in 1952 on the *Take it From Here* radio programme on the BBC. She saw life in simple, unshaded terms and sensed from her early teaching days that young children prefer certainty and the familiar in their reading tastes. Her monument remains on the shelves of bookshops and libraries.

In her prime, Enid Blyton was a woman of striking appearance—somewhat above average in height, with dark, curly hair and eloquent dark eyes, a longish nose, and ruddy complexion. She was handsome in a Spanish gypsy style rather than conventionally pretty and, although she was not well versed in social small talk, she would light up and become the focus of any conversation that settled on her favourite topics—children, her books for and about them, and the publishers who helped to introduce the former to the latter. She died in a Hampstead nursing home, 28 November 1968. There is a portrait in oils by Derek Houston, which is in the possession of the family.

[Barbara Stoney, *Enid Blyton*, 1974; Enid Blyton, *The Story of My Life*, 1952; personal knowledge.]   GEORGE GREENFIELD

BODKIN, THOMAS PATRICK (1887–1961), museum director and art critic, was born in Dublin 21 July 1887, the eldest of the family of two sons and four daughters of Matthias McDonnell Bodkin, a journalist who was later county court judge of Clare and MP for North Roscommon, and his wife, Arabella, daughter of Francis Norman, of Dublin. He was educated at Belvedere College, Clongowes Wood College, and the Royal University of Ireland, from which he graduated in 1908, having won medals and prizes for oratory, among them the Lord Chancellor's prize. He was called to the bar (King's Inn) in 1911 and practised for five years. He was a fluent speaker and a ready wit, a man who enjoyed debate and argument, and these characteristics, perhaps exaggerated by his legal training, were to affect his attitudes in the very different career he was later to adopt.

Bodkin had a great love of beautiful things. He began to collect for himself early in life and there is no doubt that a major influence on his development in this and other respects was Sir Hugh Lane [q.v.]. His fastidious care for personal appearance both in himself and others, his conviction that taste and flair were more important than scholarship, perhaps even his addiction to playing bridge, all owed something to Lane's example. Bodkin came to know him well and in one of the codicils to Lane's controversial will, the wish is expressed that he should advise in the matter of setting up a Gallery of Modern Art in Dublin. The disputes on the interpretation of the will following Lane's death in the sinking of the *Lusitania* in 1915, and the consequent legal uncertainties, were well set out by Bodkin in *Hugh Lane and his Pictures* (Verona, 1932).

On leaving the bar Bodkin became increasingly involved in public affairs. He acted as commissioner and secretary to the Commission of Charitable Donations and Bequests in the Irish Free State and in 1926 served as a member of the commission to advise the Irish Government on the coinage design, being mainly responsible for the choice of animal and bird designs by Percy Metcalfe. His appointment to succeed Lucius O'Callaghan as director of the National Gallery of Ireland followed in 1927. During his term of office perhaps the most notable acquisition was the Perugino *Pietà* once in the celebrated Orleans collection.

In 1935 Bodkin left Ireland to take up the dual appointment as director of the newly founded Barber Institute and professor of fine arts in the university of Birmingham. At that time the funds of the Institute compared favourably even with those of some of the national museums and Bodkin was given an enviable opportunity to build up a major new public collection. One of the terms of the Barber Trust was that all works of art purchased on its behalf should be among the best of their kind. It would have been impossible for any director to live up to this demand consistently, but Bodkin began well, his early acquisitions ranging from Egyptian, Greek, and Chinese sculpture, medieval ivories, and Italian Renaissance bronzes, to paintings by Simone Martini, Mabuse, Poussin, and Gainsborough [q.v.]. Perhaps with Lane in mind, and perhaps instinctively, he bought as if for his own private enjoyment and thereby gave the gallery the stamp of a connoisseur's collection which it still retains. This character was emphasized in the actual design of the picture galleries—each one having a succession of bays which create a semi-private atmosphere for the group of paintings they contain. Bodkin was proud of the fact that he had some influence on the plans of the architect, Robert Atkinson.

Bodkin became a colourful if sometimes disputatious personality in the university of Birmingham, for some years acting as public orator, an office well suited to his gifts and temperament. He also responded to the rapidly developing media of radio and television. His Irish voice and bearded features, not unlike those of George Bernard Shaw [q.v.], became popular in such programmes as 'Animal, Vegetable, and Mineral'. This, however, was not quite the true Bodkin. There was a more serious and basically simple side to him which is best appreciated in his writings, in particular *The Approach to Painting* (1927), a book which has always 'told' with the young, and in personal reminiscences like *My Uncle Frank* (1941), a spontaneous piece of unabashed and natural writing. His other books include *May it Please Your Lordships* (1917), which contains his translations of modern French poetry, *Four Irish Landscape Painters* (1920), and *Dismembered Masterpieces* (1945). To this Dictionary he contributed the notice of Sir John Lavery.

Bodkin could never quite appreciate the fact that the English are not very Irish, a failure of understanding which frequently landed him and others in situations of embarrassment and sometimes fury. He was quite unlike any other museum director in this country. In many ways he belonged to the generation just before his own, the silk and velvet world of the Edwardian dealer and private collector, and as a midnight raconteur he evoked this society with complete success. He received honorary degrees from the National University of Ireland and the university of Dublin, was a trustee of the National Library of Ireland, a governor and guardian of the National Gallery of Ireland, and honorary professor of the history of fine arts at Trinity College, Dublin. He was an honorary ARIBA, an officer of the Legion of Honour, and a Knight of St. Gregory to the Holy See.

In 1917 Bodkin married Aileen Patricia, third daughter of Joseph Richard Cox, Nationalist MP for North Clare. They had five daughters. He died in Birmingham 24 April 1961.

The figure of Bodkin is included in the group portrait, 'Homage to Hugh Lane' (*c.* 1919) by John Keating, in the Municipal Gallery of Modern Art, Dublin. There is a portrait in oils by Bernard Fleetwood-Walker (1956) in the City Museum and Art Gallery, Birmingham, and another by James Sleator (1949) in the possession of the family. A bronze bust by (Sir) Charles Wheeler (1956) is in the Barber Institute, and a terracotta bust by the same sculptor is in the National Portrait Gallery.

[Alan Denson, *Thomas Bodkin, a Bio-bibliographical Survey*, Dublin, the Bodkin Trustees, 1966; *The Times* and the *Birmingham Post*, 25 April 1961; personal knowledge.]
K. J. GARLICK

BONE, JAMES (1872–1962), journalist, was born in Glasgow 16 May 1872, the second of the six sons among the eight children of the journalist David Drummond Bone and his wife, Elizabeth Millar Crawford. Among his brothers were Sir Muirhead Bone, artist [q.v.], Sir David Bone, of the Anchor Line, and Alex Bone, writer of seafaring reminiscences. 'We were born', said James Bone, 'With a pencil in our mouths.' Bone, like his brothers, left school in Glasgow early. At the age of fourteen he went to work in the waterfront office of the Laird Line until he could join the *North British Daily Mail*, the paper his father served. By the time it closed in 1901 Bone's gifts as a descriptive writer were well developed and he and (Professor) A. M. Charteris [q.v.] wrote the text, under the pseudonym James Hamilton Muir, for a book *Glasgow in 1901* (1901), which was illustrated by his brother, Muirhead. While freelancing, Bone met a man from the *Manchester Guardian* and in 1902 its editor, C. P. Scott [q.v.], was persuaded to give him a trial at the London office. His appointment was confirmed at what was then a respectable salary of £280 a year. Bone served under two London editors, J. B. Atkins and R. H. Gretton. In 1912, after ten years' service, Bone was made London editor. However, command was incomplete, for he was not given charge of the parliamentary lobby work. Scott told him: 'You have no great political knowledge or interest'— which was true. Bone, although fanatically loyal to the paper and its Liberal policies, was conservative by temperament and not radical; nor was he an intellectual, but rather an artist with a painter's vision and a poetic pen.

Indeed Bone was a very good art critic and

if he could not bring himself to accept the Post-Impressionist revolution when Roger Fry [q.v.] presented it to London in 1910, he grappled hard with the problem. He was not blind to the decorative charm of Gauguin and of Van Gogh's iris. Of the latter he wrote: 'They are painted with a fierce, arid skill which seems to rob the iris of its floweriness. In one way the identity of the iris is heightened . . . but the flower, all the same, has been wronged.'

Bone's life work was the London Letter of the *Manchester Guardian*, headed: 'Our London Correspondence. By Private Wire.' Most provincial morning papers carried a London Letter and the *Guardian*'s was acknowledged to be easily the best of them. Bone inherited a Letter which had been much improved by Atkins and strengthened by contributions from G. W. E. Russell, a former secretary of Gladstone. The feature was supposed to be a letter to the editor who was addressed, sometimes to the mystification of the reader, as 'you'. To preserve the atmosphere of a letter all titles were informal. Clergymen, for example, were always 'Mr' and never 'The Reverend'. The Letter could describe events in home and foreign politics as they were seen from London (sometimes important news was buried in it). Most of the paragraphs were written by Bone, two general reporters, and their colleagues on the political staff. A miscellany of paragraphs told of sales and exhibitions of paintings and sculptures, the arrival of interesting visitors from abroad, what was happening at Court, buildings going up and coming down, the fashions, new Christmas party games, and even the weather. Bone excelled at writing what was known as 'the mood paragraph' which might be about a political scandal, a strike inconveniencing the capital, or a spell of exceptional weather. Stuck for a lead paragraph, Bone would write, 'People are saying tonight that . . .', and the inspiration would come. The Letter was the only collective feature in the paper. Bone sub-edited severely, but creatively, and made the copy, as it were, his own.

He drew on a number of outside contributors, a band of scholarly, decayed gentlemen, who eked out their private incomes by hawking erudite paragraphs around the London offices of provincial papers, about coins, stamps, curios, and visiting Ruritanian royalty. Bone's London Letter, never sour or malicious, was invested with his own blithe spirit and unquenchable Victorian optimism. He filled the London office with his own zest for the event of the hour, be it a test match, an abdication, or a fog. He would invent a series of paragraphs prescribing mottoes for London clubs or telling 'short, short' stories: '"Drive me to the Caledonian Club"; the cabby's face fell.'

Yet admirable miniaturist though Bone was, he was still better on a broader canvas, writing glowing descriptive pieces about royal occasions, or going to the Derby, in the news columns of the paper where the London editor enjoyed the exclusive title of 'Our London Correspondent'. On 31 December each year he published his 'Londoner's Retrospect', a social history of the past year. But Bone was best of all when his frame was a book containing his brother's illustrations. His *The London Perambulator* (1925) is a small masterpiece, a description and an obituary of the London of the first twenty-five years of the twentieth century, the London that had lost Nash's Regent Street and Rennie's Waterloo Bridge. Anyone who read the chapter on Portland stone saw London with new eyes. That, and a chapter in *The Perambulator in Edinburgh* (1926) on the 'lands', the decayed and elegant mansions where the aristocracy lived when Edinburgh was indeed a capital, was Bone's writing at its best.

Yet what Bone did was in his day perhaps less important than what Bone was. He moved in a group which might be described as 'the higher Bohemia'—a circle of writers and painters with style, wit, and a fondness of one another's society. Bone, plump, dapper, in dark suit, bow-tie, and bowler hat, would appear each night in three or four Fleet Street taverns, staying for fifteen minutes only and having one small drink. He was a good listener but his Glasgow accent and a slight stammer handicapped his stories in a noisy environment. His rooms in the Temple and his cat Arthur were known to writers in many parts of the English-speaking world. When his home in King's Bench Walk was bombed in the war of 1939–45, he settled into the Strand Palace Hotel to keep an eye on wartime London. Bone also became well known in Mencken's Baltimore. The *Baltimore Sun* employed the *Guardian* editorial service and Bone took its London correspondents into his pastoral care.

In 1903 he married Annie, daughter of John McGavigan, of Lenzie; there were no children. She died in 1950, and yet she might well have survived him, for in December 1940 Bone was returning from the United States in the *Western Prince* when it was torpedoed. He was then sixty-eight and had undergone an operation in Baltimore. Nevertheless, he survived hours in an open boat and, on landing, filed a long descriptive piece. 'The line between wives and widows', he wrote, 'was very close that Saturday night.' He was made a companion of honour in 1947, after he had retired from the London editorship of the *Manchester Guardian* in 1945. For a while he continued as one of its directors, which he had become in 1919. He was made an honorary ARIBA (1927). Bone lived to celebrate his ninetieth birthday and received messages from the Queen, President Kennedy, the prime minister, and Hugh Gaitskell [q.v.]. He died at his home in Tilford, Surrey, a few months later, 23 November 1962.

[David Ayerst, *Guardian: Biography of a Newspaper*, 1971; *The Times*, 24 November 1962; private information; personal knowledge.]   JOHN BEAVAN

BONHAM CARTER, (HELEN) VIOLET, BARONESS ASQUITH OF YARNBURY (1887–1969), political figure, was born in Hampstead, London, 15 April 1887, the fourth of the five children and the only daughter of Herbert Henry Asquith (later first Earl of Oxford and Asquith) and his wife, Helen Kelsall, daughter of Frederick Melland, a well-known Manchester physician. The youngest child, Cyril, became Lord Asquith of Bishopstone [qq.v.].

Her mother died of typhoid fever in 1891, when Violet was four. In 1894 her father married Margaret (Margot), daughter of Sir Charles Tennant [q.v.]. There were two surviving children of this second marriage, one of whom, Anthony [q.v.], achieved prominence in the film world. In 1892 Asquith became home secretary in Gladstone's last administration. Violet Bonham Carter often said she could not remember a time when she did not hear talk of politics. Her devotion to her father, and after his death in 1928 to his memory, was absolute. Some of the fiercest battles she fought in later years were in defence of his conduct as wartime prime minister. She would not let even trivialities go unchallenged. A powerful controversialist with a biting wit, she excelled in curt ridicule. As with all other causes she took up, she would never compromise or give up a battle.

Violet Asquith had no English schooling. Educated privately and unsystematically by a series of governesses, she read English literature widely and was taught French and German. Finished, as the term was, in Dresden and Paris, she returned to England with a full knowledge of both languages and of their literatures. However politically busy, she always made time for reading. Some of her warmest friendships were based on a shared love of the classics.

But her overriding interest was in public affairs. From the time of her mother's death her father treated her as an adult. She could remember how on his return from the House she would ask him 'Did Mr Gladstone speak?' and 'What did the Irish do?'. He gave her careful answers. When she was eighteen he was appointed chancellor of the Exchequer in Sir

Henry Campbell-Bannerman's Government. He became prime minister (1908) in the month of her coming of age. She was with her father when the suffragettes stopped his car and lashed at both of them with dog whips. She had been also with him throughout the 1906 general election that produced the Liberal landslide. She won her own political spurs in the Paisley by-election of 1920 that returned Asquith to Parliament after his defeat at East Fife in the 'khaki election' of 1918. She was his most effective platform supporter.

Fourteen years earlier she had met the other immortal 'whom I was blessed to call my friend'. In the first volume of *Winston Churchill as I Knew Him* (1965), a work which, alas, she never finished, she described how at a dinner party in the early summer of 1906 she found herself seated next to a 'young man who seemed to me quite different from any other young man I had ever met'. She was nineteen, Churchill was thirty-one. These were the years when she made her early contacts with famous men—Grey, Balfour, Morley, Lloyd George, Kitchener [qq.v.], and others. But the relationship with Churchill became a thing apart. She had too strong a mind to follow him blindly. There were periods of disagreement which Churchill resented. But throughout almost sixty years the friendship held to the day of Churchill's death.

Violet Bonham Carter—she married in 1915 (Sir) Maurice Bonham Carter (died 1960), her father's principal private secretary; they had two sons and two daughters (one of whom, Laura, married Joseph Grimond, who became the leader of the Liberal Party)—must, however, be seen in her own right, not merely as an accompanist to others more famous. She was the last Asquithian Liberal. Her bitterness towards Lloyd George never diminished. But her father's death closed for her the aftermath of the Edwardian age. Soon thereafter Britain was faced with problems and menaces which the first three decades of the century were thought to have banished. In October 1931 she declared in favour of the 'national' Government brought into being by the perilous state of the nation's finances. Inherently against both Conservatives and Socialists she regarded this as merely an emergency measure. She was president of the Women's Liberal Federation twice (1923–5 and 1939–45). In 1945 she accepted an invitation to succeed Lord Meston [q.v.], who had died in 1943, as president of the Liberal Party Organization, an office which she held until 1947—the first woman to do so.

In the general election of 1945 she gave one of the Liberal Party's broadcasts, ridiculing Churchill's efforts to panic people with 'the threat of Mr Attlee and the Gestapo'. She stood for Wells in that election, coming bottom of the poll, behind Lt.-Col. D. Boles, a Conservative who had won the seat unopposed in a by-election in 1939, and C. Morgan, the Labour candidate. She tried again in 1951, standing as Liberal candidate for Colne Valley. This time she had Conservative support, the local Conservative association being split. Unfortunately for her her opponent was one of the most attractive members of the Labour Party, William Glenvil Hall [q.v.]. He won by a majority of 2,189 in a poll of over 58,000. Finally she entered Parliament as a life peeress, Baroness Asquith of Yarnbury, in 1964. Although she had never sat in the Commons and was then seventy-seven, she immediately engaged in the work of the House of Lords, her last speech being about Biafra.

This was highly characteristic. Violet Bonham Carter's horizon was never insular. She knew Europe well; moreover, she had visited Egypt in her twenties and the Middle and Far East in her seventies. She also crusaded for the League of Nations from its conception, and was a member of the executive of the League of Nations Union until 1941. In May 1933 she vigorously attacked Franz von Papen who, having made a deal with Hitler, had forced Hindenburg to appoint the Führer chancellor, and had himself taken office as vice-chancellor. She was an active supporter of Churchill's anti-Nazism in the 1930s, joining him and Sir A. Sinclair (later Viscount Thurso, q.v.) in their campaign to create a Ministry of Supply. She became a vice-chairman of the United Europe Movement in 1947. She was, in addition, a delegate to the Commonwealth Relations Conference in Canada in 1949, and president of the Royal Institute of International Affairs 1964–9. Letters to *The Times* concerning international as well as domestic causes often had her as one of their signatories, and unfriendly fun was sometimes made of this. But if occasionally her zeal did outrun her discretion, of her passionate care for fundamental freedoms and her sympathy for suffering people in all nations there was no doubt.

The general election of 1945 briefly interrupted one of Violet's most fruitful services to the nation. When Churchill, on becoming prime minister in 1940, restored to the BBC its full muster of seven governors—at the outbreak of war Neville Chamberlain had left only Sir (George) Allan Powell [q.v.], the chairman, and C. H. G. Millis, the vice-chairman, in office—he appointed Violet Bonham Carter as one of them. Under the stresses of war, a novel situation for every broadcasting organization, the BBC had become apprehensive, narrow, and inhibiting to the point of intolerance. With (Sir) Harold Nicolson and J. J. Mallon [qq.v.]

as her supporters, Violet Bonham Carter swung a hesitant board behind a new director-general committed to freeing the BBC from its political and psychological straitjacket and to enlarging its provision for information and culture. She had to resign from the board to fight the Wells seat in 1945, was reappointed on her defeat, and finished her term of office in 1946. She was also a member of the royal commission on the press (1947–9), a governor of the Old Vic from 1945, and a trustee of the Glyndebourne Arts Trust from 1955.

In 1963 she became the first woman to give the Romanes lecture at Oxford; she spoke on 'The Impact of Personality on Politics'. It was a historic and memorable occasion. Starting with her personal experiences, she ended with a denunciation of 'the fallacy of Historic Fatalism'. 'In all ages great human beings have overcome material odds by the inspiration they have breathed into their fellow men.' She was also a speaker at the Royal Academy dinner in 1967, the first time in over a century and a half that women had attended. She had a pure carrying voice, which she was able to modulate with thrilling effect. She depended on gestures hardly at all, and indeed, she seemed frail to carry such a load of conviction. When she died, the tribute to her from Jeremy Thorpe, the Liberal leader—'The Party has lost its greatest orator'—was valid beyond politics.

Violet Bonham Carter never thought of herself as an orator. Her voice was a minor weapon in her lifelong battle for her beliefs. Her major one was the alliance of cogency and passion. She exemplified the dictum of William Hazlitt [q.v.]: 'The seat of knowledge is in the head, of wisdom, in the heart.' Her lifetime covered the rise, zenith, and nadir of the Liberal Party of her youth. Her first reported speech was in aid of funds for Liberalism when she was twenty-two. Never did she lower her flag. She was still fighting gallantly, if rather forlornly, at the end. She was appointed DBE in 1953, and received an honorary LLD from Sussex University in 1963. She died in London 19 February 1969.

A portrait of her by (Sir) William Orpen, the gift of the House of Commons on her marriage in 1915, is in the possession of her son, Raymond. Her elder son, Mark, has a watercolour portrait by E. Barnard (1910). A bust by Oscar Nemon (1960–9) is in the National Portrait Gallery.

[Violet Bonham Carter, *Winston Churchill as I Knew Him*, 1965; *The Times*, 20 February 1969; personal knowledge.]

WILLIAM HALEY

BOWATER, SIR ERIC VANSITTART (1895–1962), industrialist, was born in London

16 January 1895, the third child and only son of (Sir) Frederick William Bowater, paper merchant, of London, and his wife, Alice Emily, daughter of Joseph Sharp, of Bognor, Sussex. He was educated at Charterhouse, leaving there with ambitions of becoming a professional soldier. He was commissioned in the Royal Artillery, serving from 1913 to 1917, but suffered wounds at Ypres in 1915 of such severity that he was later invalided out. Thus ended all possibility of following a military career.

During his lengthy and enforced convalescence he gave thought to a new career and eventually joined his father and two uncles in the family business, W. V. Bowater & Sons, in the City of London. At that time the company operated purely as paper merchants, having been founded by Eric Bowater's grandfather in 1881. Although Eric had no background technical knowledge of the paper industry he soon realized that the true potential of the business was not in marketing other firms' products but in manufacturing the goods oneself. With this end in view and in the face of some opposition, but with his father's backing, he planned the first Bowater paper mill at Northfleet in Kent. This was opened in 1926 with Bowater as managing director of the Company. His father had died two years before.

It was during this stage of his career that he learned to back his own judgement to the limit and, having enlisted the financial support of Lord Rothermere [q.v.], he bought out his uncles in 1927. Thereafter he took full command of the company as its chairman, a position he continued to hold in the expanding Bowater Organization for thirty-five years until his death in 1962 when the total assets were close on £200 million.

It was characteristic of Eric Bowater that he would never accept a negative attitude towards plans for future developments and his persistence in questioning every objection proved its worth in the success of his enterprises. It was a mark of the confidence which he inspired in others, as well as his own confidence in the future, that at this period, in spite of severe financial stringency within the company, he decided to double the capacity of the Northfleet mill, a project completed in 1928. He thus correctly foreshadowed the need for the supply of newsprint to keep abreast of the accelerating pace of newspaper circulation. In 1929 he opened another newsprint mill at Ellesmere Port in Cheshire. This was designed to supply the press rooms in Manchester which printed northern editions of the London national dailies and the growing markets for provincial newspapers of the north.

In spite of industrial depression, Eric Bowater's confidence in the future ensured for him the support of Lord Beaverbrook [q.v.] as well as of Lord Rothermere in the venture at Ellesmere Port and by the end of 1930 the mill was in production. Only two years later its capacity was doubled and subsequently both Rothermere and Beaverbrook's interests in the mill were acquired by Bowater.

Eric Bowater took further steps towards his eventual goal of making Bowater one of the largest newsprint manufacturers in the world by acquiring in 1936 the Edward Lloyd paper mills at Sittingbourne and Kemsley in Kent and, setting his sights across the Atlantic, by purchasing in 1938 the newsprint and pulp mills at Corner Brook in Newfoundland. Although Bowater had had a sales office in New York for many years, this was its first major industrial venture in North America. Soon afterwards World War II intervened and further development was temporarily halted.

In 1940, having been invited by Beaverbrook to join him in the Ministry of Aircraft Production, Eric Bowater became its director-general. In 1945 he became controller. It was in recognition of his services in this field that a knighthood was bestowed upon Bowater in 1944. During his five years at the Ministry, Bowater continued to control and plan for his firm. When he eventually returned after the war he began to diversify.

To begin with, he entered the packaging industry. A factory in Croydon, manufacturing corrugated containers, was acquired and extended, as were installations in various parts of the United Kingdom making many types of packaging based mainly on paper but also on plastics and foil. The range of papers made in addition to newsprint was considerably widened and the road transport fleet and other auxiliary services were expanded. By the mid fifties Bowater were also handling by sea over a million tons of raw materials and finished products. So that the organization might be self-sufficient to the extent of at least one half of its shipping needs, nine news ships were built in British yards.

In 1956 a highly successful partnership was entered into with Scott Paper Company, one of the largest United States manufacturers of domestic tissues. The joint company, called the Bowater-Scott Corporation, with Bowater as its chairman, was set up to manufacture soft tissues in Britain; new mills were built, first at Northfleet and later at Barrow in Furness. A parallel and equally successful development in tissues was embarked upon in Australia. Plans for expansion in North America, which had been interrupted by the war, were also resumed. In 1953, at a time when post-war restrictions and difficulties seemed to make such confidence a thing of the past, Bowater began what was probably his most outstanding enterprise, namely the conception, planning, and construction of a newsprint mill in the state of Tennessee, designed to serve the rapidly growing market in the southern United States. At a cost of $60 million, this was the largest newsprint mill in the United States, and represented the largest investment of British capital in that country since the war. Despite the shortage of dollars, the necessary consents for the equity investment were granted by the Bank of England. The Tennessee mill was extended in 1957 and in 1959, and in 1959 a large new pulp mill was built in South Carolina. Meanwhile Bowater established his company in the Common Market area long in advance of Britain's eventual entry into the EEC.

Bowater was so preoccupied with his business that his inner personality is difficult to assess. His appearance was well known; there could have been few readers of the financial press, and fewer Bowater employees and shareholders, who did not come to know and admire the clean-cut, commanding features. His tall, straight, military bearing and his colouring together combined to present a most distinguished appearance. He gave away little of his true self, however, and whilst always courteous to all who came into contact with him he remained aloof, though friendly—always a little remote and, to most people, perhaps impenetrable in his reserve, but these mannerisms were the instinctive defences of a fundamentally shy man.

Those who knew him well, however, and were close to him will remember him for his sudden smile, the unexpected gesture of generosity, things which would break through the reserve. To those who were proud of his great organization, like himself, he was their leader who by his personal magnetism had welded them together into a family throughout the world, and to whom they owed their complete loyalty and allegiance. These they gave in full measure, holding him always in the highest esteem and affection and, it must be said, some awe. Bowater welcomed change as an ally; he never became comfortable or complacent nor did he condone cosy half-efficiency, demanding much of those who served him.

Bowater was an officer of the Legion of Honour and in 1948 was made FRSA. He was twice married. By his first marriage to Blanche Currie, née de Ville, in 1915, he had one daughter and by his second marriage, in 1937, to Margaret Vivian, daughter of Charles Perkins, of Toronto, Canada, he had one daughter and one son. He lived on a 300-acre estate in West Horsley, Surrey, where, although international travel on his business took up much time, he was still able to follow his country pursuits of farming, with a highly prized herd of pedigree Guernsey cattle, and shooting. He died at his Surrey home, 30 August 1962.

A portrait of Eric Bowater hangs in the boardroom at Bowater House and was painted by Anna Zinkeisen shortly after his death, from one of his favourite official photographs by Douglas Glass taken in 1952.

[An address by Sir Frank Lee at St. Paul's Cathedral, October 1962; personal knowledge.]   ROBERT KNIGHT

BOWDEN, FRANK PHILIP (1903-1968), experimental physicist, was born in Hobart, Tasmania, 2 May 1903, the fifth of the six children of Frank Prosser Bowden, telegraph and telephone manager for Tasmania, and his wife, Grace Elizabeth Hill. Both his parents were Tasmanian. He was educated at the Hutchins School, Hobart, and, in spite of difficulties with mathematics, having failed at his first attempt, in 1921 he matriculated successfully, entering the university of Tasmania as a science student. He was never good at mathematics and this influenced all his later researches in which he always chose an approach which provided answers without the need for mathematical analysis. In his second year as a student he fell ill and spent six months in the back blocks of New South Wales, returning completely recovered to continue his university studies (B.Sc., 1924), with the strong encouragement of A. I. McAuley, later professor of physics. His first researches with McAuley on electrochemistry were published in 1925 and later that year he became the first recipient of a scholarship provided by the Electrolytic Zinc Company of Australia. In 1925 he also obtained his M.Sc. degree with first class honours. In 1926 he was awarded an 1851 scholarship and left to work under (Sir) Eric Rideal in Cambridge.

Bowden was admitted as a research student at Gonville and Caius College in 1927 and began research with Rideal on electrode potentials. This, like the earlier work with McAuley, was concerned with the processes occurring at the surface of the electrode during electrolysis and was the precursor of a sustained and broader interest in the general field of surface science. He became a fellow of Caius in 1929. In the 1930s he was involved in a collaborative research project with C. P. (later Lord) Snow on the photochemistry of vitamins and, although the conclusions proved to be faulty, this phase marked the beginning of a lifelong friendship. In his later novels on Cambridge life, Snow drew on Bowden as the prototype of Getliffe, the gifted, wise, and sensitive scientist.

Bowden soon moved on to a study of surface phenomena related to friction and lubrication. In this field he pioneered a scientific approach to an applied problem and established for himself and his research group a world-wide reputation in the field. It was during this period that he developed his ideas of the physics of skiing, combining scientific research with pleasurable field experiments. In 1933 he was awarded the Tasmanian D.Sc. degree, and in 1938 the Cambridge Sc.D.

In 1939, after a lecture tour in America, Bowden decided to return via Australia where his wife and first child had meanwhile arrived direct from England. World War II broke out and he was asked to establish a research laboratory under the Council for Scientific and Industrial Research (forerunner of the Commonwealth Scientific and Industrial Research Organization) to deal with friction, lubrication, wear, and bearing problems associated with the Australian war effort. The laboratory, later known as the Division of Tribophysics, also became involved in studies of the initiation and growth of explosions, a field in which Bowden again made original contributions of outstanding importance.

After the war Bowden returned to Cambridge and, with support from the Ministry of Supply (Air), set up a research group to continue his work on explosives and friction. The high-speed photographic techniques which he acquired for his explosive studies were later applied to the study of impact, erosion, and fracture, and this area of research again proved fruitful and original. It is a reflection of Bowden's catholic interests that he was called upon to organize three Royal Society discussions—on friction, on explosives, and on deformation by impact. Other areas of work included the direct study of surface forces and the mechanical and structural properties of high-temperature solids such as the carbides and borides of transition metals. It was characteristic of his attitude to research that he recruited his students from several fields so that, long before it became fashionable, his group was in practice an interdisciplinary entity. He showed a keen interest in applying fundamental science to practical problems, recognizing that applied science could be as intellectually challenging and rewarding as pure science: and, although his experiments were basically simple in concept, he recognized the need for sophisticated and specialized equipment, the development of which he did much to foster.

Bowden had been made a director of studies in natural sciences in 1933 and a reader in physical chemistry in 1946. Ten years later, when the Physical Chemistry Department began to move into new accommodation, he changed his affiliations and became a reader in physics (1957). His laboratory became a sub-department of the Cavendish and in 1966 he was appointed to a personal chair (ad hominem) in surface physics, an appointment which gave him great pleasure.

Apart from his university commitments Bowden showed a keen interest in co-operating with industry. In 1953 he was appointed adviser to Tube Investments Ltd., and in 1954 established for them a research laboratory at Hinxton with a view to contributing to the general pool of fundamental scientific knowledge and to the commercial needs and benefit of TI. The laboratory proved itself and four of its leading members became fellows of the Royal Society. In 1958 he was elected a director of the English Electric Company and played an important part in stimulating and co-ordinating its research efforts. He also served on a number of government scientific and technical committees, his most long-term involvement being that as chairman of the Executive Committee of the National Physical Laboratory (1955-62). He greatly enjoyed his contacts with industry and the broader world of affairs as well as the rewards that these contacts provided. Yet he refused several important appointments which would have meant leaving his laboratory in Cambridge. Indeed his deepest and most sustained interest throughout his life was his laboratory and the challenge and excitement of scientific work.

Bowden served as president of the Cambridge Philosophical Society (1957) as president of the Cambridge Alpine Club (from 1965) and as vice-president of the Faraday Society (1953-6). In later years Bowden was something of an elder statesman, bringing his wisdom and equanimity to bear on complex college problems. He was elected a fellow of the Royal Society in 1948 and awarded its Rumford medal in 1956. He received the Redwood medal of the Institute of Petroleum in 1953, the Elliott Cresson medal of the Franklin Institute in 1955, and the medal of the Société Française de Métallurgie in 1957. In 1954 he delivered the Hawkesley lecture of the Institution of Mechanical Engineers and in 1967 the Kelvin lecture of the Institution of Electrical Engineers. In 1968 he was awarded the Glazebrook medal and prize of the Institute of Physics and the Physical Society and in the same year the Bernard Lewis gold medal of the Combustion Institute of America. He received the CBE in 1956.

Bowden's researches were characterized by simplicity and elegance. His approach was direct and his conclusions clear and uncomplicated. He was recognized as an experimental scientist of great originality and in almost every field which he touched he provided some germinal idea of value and importance. Although his approach was highly individual he was able to establish a research school not once but thrice: at Melbourne in Tribophysics, at Hinxton for Tube Investments, and at the Cavendish. Apart from his gifts as a scientific leader Bowden showed a great personal interest in the well-being of his staff who recognized that he could be relied upon in times of need. Consequently, all the laboratories in which he was involved were happy institutions. Bowden was a lightly built man with fine features, a certain measure of reserve, and considerable charm. All his life he showed a capacity for hard work and was possessed of outstanding stamina and reserves of intellectual energy. He had a sensitive and discerning taste in literature and art and an aesthetic sense which was discernible in his science as well as in his broader cultural interests. His hobbies included skiing, mountaineering, and tennis. He died at his home in Cambridge after a protracted illness 3 September 1968.

In 1931 he married Margot Grace, daughter of Robert Hutchison, architect and engineer, of Hobart, Tasmania. They had three sons and one daughter. His eldest son, Piers (1937-74), was a gifted polymer scientist in his own right.

[D. Tabor in *Biographical Memoirs of Fellows of the Royal Society*, vol. xv, 1969.]

DAVID TABOR

BOYLE, WILLIAM HENRY DUDLEY, twelfth EARL OF CORK AND ORRERY (1873-1967), admiral of the fleet, was born, together with a twin sister, at Hale, Farnham, 30 November 1873, the second of the four sons in a family of nine of Colonel Gerald Edmund Boyle and his wife, Lady (Elizabeth) Theresa Pepys, daughter of the first Earl of Cottenham. He entered the *Britannia* as a naval cadet in 1887 and two years later went to sea as a midshipman in the *Monarch* of the Channel Squadron, later transferring to the *Colossus* in the Mediterranean. In later life he used to claim that it was his service in this ship which was responsible for his future career in the navy, since it brought him into contact in very early life with officers of outstanding ability and dedication, and in fact no fewer than six of the seven lieutenants serving in the *Colossus* later reached flag rank.

As a commander Boyle served in the Naval Intelligence Department in the Admiralty in 1909-11, and on promotion to captain in 1913 was appointed naval attaché in Rome, a post in which he was still serving when Italy joined

the Allies during the war of 1914-18. In 1915 he returned to sea in command of the *Fox*, serving in the Red Sea and Indian Ocean. At the same time he was senior officer of the Red Sea Patrol, and as such was called upon to support some of the irregular operations of T. E. Lawrence [q.v.], with whom he worked in close and cordial cooperation. He returned home in 1917 to command the *Repulse* in the Grand Fleet, serving as flag captain to Rear-Admiral Richard Phillimore and subsequently to Rear-Admiral Sir Henry Oliver [qq.v.]. In 1918 he transferred to the *Lion*, where he was flag captain and chief of staff to Vice-Admiral Sir William Pakenham [q.v.], serving in the rank of commodore, 2nd class. At the end of the war he was appointed C.B.

Boyle was promoted rear-admiral in 1923 and served as second-in-command of the first battle squadron in the Atlantic Fleet, and later as rear-admiral commanding the first cruiser squadron in the Mediterranean. On promotion to vice-admiral in 1928 he commanded the Reserve Fleet, and followed that appointment as president of the Royal Naval College, Greenwich, and vice-admiral commanding the Royal Naval War College in charge of the senior officers' war course. Having been appointed KCB in 1931, in 1932 he reached the rank of admiral and in the following year became commander-in-chief, Home Fleet, flying his flag in the *Nelson*. During this appointment he succeeded his kinsman as Earl of Cork and Orrery (1934).

In normal circumstances Lord Cork's command of the Home Fleet would have been his last appointment and he would have been placed on the retired list on its completion, but the unexpected death of Admiral Sir William Fisher in 1937 left a vacancy in the Portsmouth Command and Lord Cork was appointed to the post. He remained as commander-in-chief Portsmouth for the normal period of two years, during which a vacancy occurred in the list of admirals of the fleet and he was selected to fill it (January 1938).

He had left Portsmouth by the start of the war of 1939-45 and was unemployed, but being exceedingly fit physically and full of energy and drive, he offered his services to the Admiralty for an active employment. An early opportunity arose with the command of the force provisionally arranged by the War Cabinet to assist Finland, then under unprovoked attack by Russia, but it foundered on the rock of Norwegian and Swedish neutrality which effectively barred all means of access. But before that expedition was finally cancelled, the German attack on Norway was launched on 8 April 1940 and he was given the appointment of flag officer, Narvik, with the force originally destined for Finland being switched to the capture of Narvik and the destruction of the iron ore trade from that port to Germany. His joint military commander was Major-General P. J. Mackesy, who had preceded him to Norway, and the two men met for the first time at Harstad, a small port north of Narvik, which had been selected as the main base for the operation, to discover, as Lord Cork described in his official dispatch, that they had left London with 'diametrically opposed views'. This was hardly surprising in view of Lord Cork's naval reputation as a fiery leader, and the expedition began on a sour note. It was not eased by the failure in England to load the transports tactically, so that the weapons most urgently needed on arrival were stowed at the bottoms of the holds and were therefore the last to be unloaded. The impasse between naval and military theories of attack on Narvik were partially solved five days later when the War Cabinet gave Lord Cork supreme command of the expedition, but by then the over-all effect of the campaign of Norway was becoming academic in relation to the European war as a whole. In the event, Narvik was eventually captured by Lord Cork's expedition and the iron ore loading installations in the port destroyed, but the force had to be withdrawn and Narvik abandoned to the Germans the following week. During this operation Lord Cork had the unusual distinction of flying his Union flag at sea as an admiral of the fleet, which officially made him senior to the commander-in-chief, Home Fleet, Admiral Sir Charles Forbes [q.v.], who was in over-all command of the naval side of the whole campaign, but this anomaly passed without incident.

The Narvik operation was the final episode of Lord Cork's active career, although in 1941 he was sent to Gibraltar to inquire into the circumstances of the indecisive naval action off Spartivento, in which the pursuit of a fleeing Italian fleet had been called off by Admiral Sir James Somerville [q.v.], commanding Force H, in the belief that they were too fast to be caught and that no good purpose could be saved by chasing the enemy to within range of shore-based aircraft. The result of Lord Cork's inquiry completely vindicated Somerville's decision.

Lord Cork had no further naval employment. He was now sixty-nine years old, and in his now exalted rank there was no avenue of active service left open to him. He became president of the Shaftesbury Homes and Arethusa Training Ship in 1942 and served in that position until 1953.

Lord Cork was small in stature with fiery red hair, and was familiarly known as 'Ginger' throughout the navy. He always wore a monocle which perhaps enhanced his aristocratic appearance, and right up to the end of his very long life he had a commanding presence, walking very upright with his shoulders back. Although a strict disciplinarian, he was regarded with affection by officers and men who served with him. He married in 1902 Lady Florence Cecilia Keppel (died 1963), daughter of William, seventh Earl of Albemarle, but there were no children of the marriage. He died in London at the age of ninety-three, 19 April 1967, and was succeeded, as thirteenth Earl of Cork and Orrery, by his nephew, Patrick Reginald Boyle.

[Admiralty records; official dispatches of the war of 1939–45; the Earl of Cork and Orrery, *My Naval Life*, 1942; personal knowledge.]

PETER KEMP

BRABAZON, JOHN THEODORE, CUTHBERT MOORE-, first BARON BRABAZON of TARA (1884–1964), aviator and politician, was born in London 8 February 1884, the younger son of Lt.-Col. John Arthur Henry Moore-Brabazon, of Tara Hall, county Meath, Ireland, and his wife, Emma Sophia, daughter of Alfred Richards, of Forest Hill. He was educated at Harrow (1898–1901) and at Trinity College, Cambridge, where he read engineering but did not take a degree. Attracted to the mysteries of the early internal combustion engine even while at school, he spent his university vacations as unpaid mechanic to Charles S. Rolls [q.v.], the pioneer of motor cars. On leaving Cambridge, Moore-Brabazon became an apprentice in the Darracq works in Paris from which he graduated as an international racing driver. In 1907 he won the *Circuit des Ardennes* in a Minerva.

As an aviator he soon exchanged the tranquil pleasures of the balloon for a Voisin aircraft resembling a huge box kite. In it he became the first Englishman to pilot a heavier-than-air machine under power in England. The flight took place over the Isle of Sheppey in May 1909, lasted rather more than a minute, and ended in a crash which nearly cost him his life. This courageous enterprise brought him, in March 1910, the first pilot's certificate to be issued by the Royal Aero Club. Some years later he set a whimsical fashion among motorists by acquiring the number plate FLY 1. In October 1909, piloting a machine made by the Short brothers, he won a prize of £1,000 offered by the *Daily Mail* for the first English aircraft to fly one mile. But after witnessing the death of his friend Rolls in an air crash nine months later, he was persuaded by his wife to abandon flying until the outbreak of war in 1914. Moore-Brabazon served with the Royal

Flying Corps on the western front, specializing in the development of aerial reconnaissance and photography. His qualities of leadership and mechanical flair brought him the regard and friendship of that exacting commander (Sir) Hugh (later Viscount) Trenchard [q.v.]. He rose to the rank of lieutenant-colonel, was awarded the MC, received three mentions in dispatches, and became a commander of the Legion of Honour.

In 1918 his brother officer Lord Hugh Cecil (later Baron Quickwood, q.v.) encouraged him to stand for Parliament as a Conservative. He was elected for the Chatham division of Rochester, a seat which he held until his defeat in 1929. From 1931 to 1942, when he was created a peer, he sat for Wallasey. Fearlessly ebullient, he delivered his maiden speech within two days of entering the House and in 1919 was rewarded by an invitation to become parliamentary private secretary to (Sir) Winston Churchill, the newly appointed secretary of state for war and air. From 1923 to 1924 and 1924 to 1927 he was parliamentary secretary to the Ministry of Transport. Under his direction the London docks remained open to receive shipments of food during the general strike of 1926. In the same year he steered through the Commons a Bill to rationalize the electricity industry. He supported Churchill's pleas for a more spirited policy of rearmament throughout the era of appeasement. His loyalty was recognized when in October 1940 he replaced Lord Reith as minister of transport in the wartime coalition and was sworn of the Privy Council. After seven months largely spent in making good the dislocation caused by enemy air raids he became minister of aircraft production. He had many friends in the industry and both in and out of office kept abreast of its technical developments, particularly the jet engine invented by (Sir) Frank Whittle. He also restored a more orderly regime in the Ministry after the inspired piracy by which his predecessor Lord Beaverbrook [q.v.] had ensured a desperately needed flow of fighter planes. In February 1942, however, when a speech at a private luncheon leaked into the newspapers, he was alleged to have expressed the hope that the German and Russian armies would annihilate each other. Although he had done as much as any minister to keep our Russian allies supplied with British aircraft, whatever the cost to our own war effort, Churchill asked for his resignation. He accepted his dismissal with characteristic good humour and was consoled with a peerage.

That was the end of Moore-Brabazon's political career but not of his influence on aviation. He became chairman of the committee that planned the construction of civil aircraft in the post-war years, not least the huge and beautiful machine that bore his name but never flew commercially. He was also elected president of the Royal Aero Club, president of the Royal Institution, and chairman of the Air Registration Board. As a father figure of aeronautical enterprise he never ceased to insist that speed should if necessary be sacrificed to safety, comfort, economy, and prestige. In 1953 he was appointed GBE.

It is unlikely that Moore-Brabazon would have achieved Cabinet rank except in a wartime administration led by Churchill. Although he brought an inventive and industrious mind to his ministerial duties, he had no great regard for the niceties of procedure or administration; and his genial presence, heralded by a cigarette in its holder and sustained by the humour of an after-dinner speaker, failed to inspire confidence in staider colleagues. With characteristic panache he was one of the last to wear a top hat in the House of Commons. He could be endearingly irreverent. In youth he had flown with a pig as his passenger in order to confound a familiar adage; and the speech that caused his downfall in 1942 echoed in tone his retort to the major who in the early days of the war of 1914–18 had ordered him to obey his superior officer: '*Superior* officer? Senior, if you please, sir.'

Tall, muscular, and deceptively ponderous, he excelled at several sports well into his eighth decade. Except during the two world wars he braved the Cresta Run at St. Moritz every year from 1907 until his death. Three times he won the Curzon Cup, the blue riband of tobogganing. He was a member of the Royal Yacht Squadron and in 1952 captain of the Royal and Ancient Gold Club of St. Andrews.

He married in 1906 Hilda Mary (died 1977), only daughter of Charles Henry Krabbe, who farmed an estate in Buenos Aires; they had two sons, the younger of whom died in 1950. He died at Chersey 17 May 1964 and was succeeded by his elder son, Derek Charles (born 1910). The second baron died in 1974 and was succeeded by his only son Ivon Anthony (born 1946).

There is a portrait of Moore-Brabazon by Sir Oswald Birley in the possession of the third baron; a pastel drawing by A. Egerton Cooper is in the National Portrait Gallery; and a bronze by David McFall was exhibited in the Royal Academy in 1964.

[Lord Brabazon of Tara, *The Brabazon Story*, 1956; *The Times*, 18 May 1964; private information.]   Kenneth Rose

BRAIN, WALTER RUSSELL, first Baron Brain (1895–1966), physician and medical statesman, was born in Reading 23 October 1895, the only son and elder child of Walter John Brain, solicitor, and his wife, Edith Alice, daughter of Charles Smith, architect. At Mill Hill School he studied classics, since he was intended for the law. His hobbies were English literature, writing, and natural history. He wanted to do science, but this was not allowed by his parents. In 1914 he entered New College, Oxford, as a commoner to read history, which he disliked. Disapproving strongly of war, he joined the Friends' Ambulance Unit in 1915 and was sent to work in York; moving later·to the King George Hospital, London, he became attached to the X-ray department, where he met Stella, daughter of a physician, Reginald Langdon Langdon-Down. She later became his wife. He attended evening classes at Birkbeck College and in 1919 went back to New College to read medicine. He was taught by J. B. S. Haldane, (Sir) Charles Scott Sherrington [qq.v.], (Sir) Julian Huxley, and H. C. Bazett. He took a shortened course for the BA (1919) and obtained the Theodore Williams scholarship in physiology (1920). He married in September 1920 and entered the London Hospital in October. He qualified BM, B.Ch. (Oxon.) in 1922, proceeded DM in 1925, and was elected FRCP in 1931.

Brain joined the newly formed medical unit at the London Hospital. Through the influence of (Sir) Henry Head [q.v.] and Dr George Riddoch, he took up neurology. He was appointed physician to Maida Vale Hospital in 1925, assistant physician to the London Hospital in 1927, and he was physician to Moorfields Hospital in 1930-7. Brain made four important contributions to neurology. With A. Dickson Wright and Marcia Wilkinson he showed that the median nerve could be paralysed by compression at the wrist in the carpal tunnel; surgical relief of this would restore function. With D. W. C. Northfield and M. Wilkinson he demonstrated the importance of backward protrusion of the intervertebral disc in the cervical spine as a cause of paralysis of the legs; this has since been recognized as a very common neurological disturbance. He described damage to the brain and peripheral nerves in cancer, particularly cancer of the lung. As a consequence, the British Empire Cancer Campaign established at the London Hospital a unit for the investigation of carcinomatous neuropathies, of which Brain was the director until his death. And he showed that the great protrusion of the eyes which is usually associated with an overactive thyroid gland could occur in its absence; he called this endocrine exophthalmos. He was an excellent and scholarly physician; not an experimentalist.

Brain had originally considered making a career in psychiatry. He never lost his interest in affairs of the mind, and particularly the problem of perception. *Mind, Perception and Science* (1951), the Riddell lectures on *The Nature of Experience* (1959), and a book on *Speech Disorders* (1961) were the outcome. From the time he was elected to the London Hospital, Brain earned his livelihood as a physician in consulting practice, in which he was very successful. He had a remarkable memory and a flair for exposition, resulting in a book *Diseases of the Nervous System*, first published in 1933 and reaching its sixth edition in 1962. His book with E. B. Strauss, *Recent Advances in Neurology*, was first published in 1929 and had gone into seven editions by 1962. He also wrote *Some Reflections on Genius, and other Essays* (1960), *Doctors Past and Present* (1964), *Science and Man* (1966), *Tea with Walter de la Mare* (1957), and *Poems and Verses* (1961). He edited *Brain* from 1954. Eighteen books and over one hundred and fifty papers was a remarkable output for a busy Harley Street physician, especially when his public service is considered. He achieved it by interest, industry, and a remarkable capacity for using every minute, particularly those spent in the back of his motor car. It was thus that he wrote *Dialogues of Today*, published anonymously in the *Lancet* during 1959 and reprinted as *Socrates on the Health Service* (1960), which had a profound effect on the ethos of the new service.

In public Brain was a shy, silent man. He once wrote: 'There are two international languages of religion: the Latin of the Roman Catholic Church, and the silence of the Quakers.' His elegant after-dinner speeches, full of wit and learning, came as a surprise to the uninitiated.

Russell and Stella Brain were a partnership from their meeting in the X-ray department until Brain's death. They had two sons and a daughter, to whom they were devoted. The Brains joined the Society of Friends in 1931 and were subsequently regular attenders at the Meeting Houses on Sundays. He gave the Swarthmore lecture in 1944 on *Man, Society and Religion*, in which he stressed the importance of a social conscience. This conscience of his led him to take on a variety of public services. He became chairman of the medical council of the London Hospital during the war, defending the interests of those who were away on active service. He became a member of King Edward's Hospital Fund for London and chairman of its Hospital Service Plan. In 1950 he succeeded Lord Moran as president of the Royal College of Physicians of London, retaining this office until 1957. His wide interests, experience, and sympathy, and his lucid mind earned him the respect and admiration of the profession, the administrators, and the lawmakers. He proved a medical statesman of wisdom, insight, and stature. He was a member of the royal commission on marriage and divorce in 1952, of the royal commission in mental certification and detention in 1954; chairman of the distinction awards committee from 1962, of the interdepartmental committee on drug addiction in 1958, and of the standing committee on drug addiction in 1966. He was president of the British Association for the Advancement of Science in 1963–4.

Brain was knighted in 1952, created a baronet in 1954, and a baron in 1962. He was elected FRS in 1964 and an honorary fellow of New College, Oxford, in 1952. He received honorary degrees from Oxford, Manchester, Southampton, Wales, Belfast, and Durham. He was an honorary fellow of the Royal Colleges of Physicians of Edinburgh and of Ireland, the Royal Colleges of Surgeons of England, of Obstetricians and Gynaecologists, and of Physicians and Surgeons of Glasgow, the Royal Australasian College of Physicians, the American and South African Colleges of Physicians, and the Faculty of Radiologists. He was president of the Association of Physicians (1956), of the Association of British Neurologists (1960), of the International Society of Internal Medicine (1958), of the Family Planning Association from 1956, and of the Migraine Trust which, as one who had been a sufferer, he was active in founding in 1966. Brain was an honorary member of American, French, German, and Spanish neurological societies, and of the Swiss Academy of Medicine. He gave the Rede, Eddington, and Linacre lectures at Cambridge, the Riddell lectures at Durham, the Bryce lecture at Oxford, and the Osler oration in Canada. He was awarded the Osler medal for 1960 at Oxford.

Brain died in London 29 December 1966, working to the end; his last working day was devoted to arranging a new issue of *Brain*. He was succeeded by his elder son, Christopher Langdon (born 1926). His younger son, Michael, became assistant professor of medicine at McMaster University, Ontario, in 1969. The Royal College of Physicians has a bust of Brain by Sir Jacob Epstein.

[Sir George Pickering in *Biographical Memoirs of Fellows of the Royal Society*, vol. xiv, 1968; private information; personal knowledge.]   GEORGE PICKERING

BRAMBELL, FRANCIS WILLIAM ROGERS (1901–1970), zoologist, was born 25 February 1901 at Combridge House, Sandy-cove, Dublin, the eldest of three sons (one of whom died in infancy) of Louis Alfred Brambell, an accountant in Guinness Brewery in Dublin, and his wife, Amelia Jane Mary Rogers. His paternal ancestry was known for three generations back, when, it seems, the name was Bramble.

Brambell recorded that as long as he could remember he had been interested in natural history. When eleven years old he was introduced to R. M. Barrington whose influence was probably decisive in developing the urge and by the age of thirteen years he was systematically collecting bird skins. He had no encouragement from school (Aravon School, 1911–14), where science was not taught and from which, being bad at languages and mediocre in other subjects, he obtained little benefit. In spite of a very adverse report from the headmaster, his parents had him coached privately for matriculation and he entered Trinity College, Dublin, with an entrance prize in natural science. He was awarded a foundation scholarship in 1920 and graduated BA in 1922 with a gold medal in natural sciences. He then worked with Professor James Brontë Gatenby, whose notice he later wrote for this Dictionary, and obtained a Ph.D. (Dublin) in 1924.

Brambell was next awarded a science research scholarship of the royal commission for the Exhibition of 1851 and chose to hold it in Professor J. P. Hill's department in University College, London, where he arrived in October 1924. In UCL he met (Sir) Alan S. Parkes with whom he collaborated extensively during the next three years on the effects of X-irradiation on the gonads and the sexual cycles of mammals, as well as carrying out his own work on the development of the reproductive system. In 1926 Brambell was awarded a fellowship of the International Education Board. A year later he obtained a London D.Sc., and accepted a lectureship in zoology at King's College, London, under Professor Doris McKinnon, though at the expense of having to decline a Beit memorial fellowship. Very soon afterwards, on 27 December 1927, he married Margaret Lilian, daughter of William Adgie, an accountant in Leeds; she was then studying at the London School of Economics. There were two children of the marriage, a girl and a boy, Michael Rogers, who became a well-known zoologist. During his three years at King's College Brambell became a much-valued member of the department, and his departure in 1930 to take up the Lloyd Roberts chair of zoology at the University College of North Wales, Bangor, in succession to P. J. White, was much regretted by his colleagues. During the King's College period his research was naturally less intense but he found time to write his book on *The Development of Sex in Vertebrates* (1930).

Brambell remained in Bangor until he retired in 1968, during which time he became a father figure in the department and an elder statesman of the College. Early in his time at Bangor a course of marine biology was started with the enthusiastic co-operation of L. H. Jackson and H. A. Cole and from this initiative grew the Marine Sciences Laboratory at Menai Bridge. Later, in 1953, Brambell was instrumental in having the Agricultural Research Council set up in Bangor a Unit of Embryology, of which he was director until he retired. Brambell also initiated a postgraduate M.Sc. course in animal reproduction, held each year in his department. During the war of 1939–45 the department of zoology at University College, London, was evacuated to the department of zoology in Bangor and made very welcome.

In Bangor, Brambell's value to the College soon became obvious. He was dean of the faculty of science from 1939 to 1943 and vice-principal (1948–50 and 1956–8). After his death the new zoology building was named after him. He held many scientific and public offices. In addition to being a member and sometime councillor of many scientific societies, he was a member of the Agricultural Research Council standing committee on animals and of the editorial board of the *Journal of Embryology and Experimental Morphology*. He was elected a fellow of the Royal Society in 1949 and served on its council (1954–6). He was created CBE in 1966. Brambell's two most important public appointments were as a member of the University Grants Committee from 1960 to 1968 and latterly chairman of its biology subcommittee, and as chairman of the so-called Brambell committee, set up to investigate the methods used in intensive animal husbandry with a view to recommending a code of practice which would combine humane with economic considerations. Brambell felt very strongly on the subject, paradoxically so perhaps for one addicted to shooting and fishing, and the impact of the committee's report was lessened by the fact that recommendations were made for which there was little factual basis.

Brambell's personal research covered many fields of experimental and observational biology. The one for which he is best known and for which he was awarded a Royal medal in 1964 concerned the transfer of passive immunity from mother to young. This work, like many major researches, arose in a curious way. In his early days at King's College his facilities for experimental work were not extensive and with Alan Parkes at University College, with whom he was still in touch, he planned a programme of research on reproduction in British mammals. This work continued at Bangor and led early in the war to an investigation by Brambell and his colleagues of reproduction in the wild rabbit, designed to assist in the control of rabbit populations. The resulting observations indicated a high pre-natal mortality, mainly accounted for by the loss of whole litters at an early stage of gestation. In seeking microscopically for an explanation of this mortality Brambell and his collaborators discovered the presence of fibrinogen and fibrin in the yolk-sac cavity of the blastocyst and suggested that this must be of maternal origin. From this small beginning, which showed that proteins could pass from mother to embryo, was developed the massive work fully described in his book *The Transmission of Passive Immunity from Mother to Young* (1970).

Brambell was a generous, warm-hearted man and a most understanding colleague with whom it was a real pleasure to be associated. His sense of humour, though occasionally misunderstood by lesser mortals, was a delight to the initiated. His work was unhurried and careful in the extreme and his refusal to be rushed into a quick decision saved at least one of his colleagues, and on a later occasion himself, from serious error. He ran his department with a firm but benevolent hand and, in the words of the principal of University College, Bangor, 'those who worked with Brambell in College or University will remember his wisdom, his perfect courtesy and above all his loyalty to the staff and to the College, to which he had given his heart'. Brambell died in Bangor 6 June 1970.

There is a portrait in oils by Fiona Campbell Blair (*c*.1965) in the possession of the family. A copy of it hangs in the Brambell Laboratory, University College of North Wales, Bangor.

[C. L. Oakley in *Biographical Memoirs of Fellows of the Royal Society*, vol. xix, 1973; personal knowledge.]   ALAN S. PARKES

BRAND, ROBERT HENRY, BARON BRAND (1878–1963), banker and public servant, was born in Kensington 30 October 1878, the fourth son in the family of six sons and three daughters of Henry Robert Brand (later second Viscount Hampden, q.v.), a Liberal MP, and his second wife, Susan Henrietta, daughter of Lord George Henry Cavendish. Educated at Marlborough and New College, Oxford, where he obtained a first class in modern history in 1901, he was elected to an All Souls fellowship in the same year, but although that college subsequently claimed an important part of his affections and time, his practical bent and the Liberal imperialist traditions of his family drew him rapidly to South Africa. Through the intervention of his father he joined Lord

Milner's [q.v.] staff in Johannesburg in December 1902 and thus became a member of the remarkable band of young Oxford aides known as 'Milner's Kindergarten'. The friendships formed at this time between Brand and other members such as Lionel Curtis, (George) Geoffrey Dawson, (Sir) Patrick Duncan, (William) Lionel Hichens, Philip Kerr (later the Marquess of Lothian), John Buchan (later first Baron Tweedsmuir), and Richard Feetham [qq.v.] were lifelong, intimate, and influential in the careers of all of them.

Milner quickly recognized Brand's quality and made him successively assistant secretary, acting secretary, and, in March 1904, permanent secretary to the Intercolonial Council of the Transvaal and the Orange River Colony, the body formally charged with the administration of the main reconstruction loan guaranteed by the British Government. At first much of Brand's work was concerned with the running of the newly merged Central South African Railways system whose expansion and modification was essential to the prosperity of the Witwatersrand. But, being forced to deal with the constant and growing friction between the four South African colonies over freight rates and tariffs and to act as secretary to two abortive inter-colonial railway conferences and a Railways Commission, Brand was one of the first to become convinced that nothing short of the political unification of the country would solve the practical problems.

Brand's part in the campaign for a South African Union was less flamboyant than that of some other Kindergarten members. His temperament did not lean towards public propaganda and he decided to remain an employee of the Transvaal Government even after the Afrikaners gained power in the 1907 election. But in the Kindergarten's secret preparation of the seminal Selborne Memorandum on unification, Brand exerted an important restraint on the wilder theoretical enthusiasms of Curtis. More importantly, he gained the trust of the Afrikaner leaders, particularly J. C. Smuts [q.v.], and having been appointed secretary to the powerful Transvaal delegation to the 1908–9 constitutional conventions he was able to underpin Smuts's vision and tactical skill with a firm basis of theoretical rigour and practical foresight. Much to his disappointment his own most distinctive contribution to the balance of the Union constitution—a form of proportional representation—fell a victim at the last moment to the electoral calculations of the Cape Government. But, as Smuts later acknowledged Brand was the 'most outstanding member of a very able team'.

Having come to London in 1909 to help steer the South Africa Act through the Westminster Parliament, he intended to return to South Africa permanently, but influenza caused him to miss his boat and while waiting for the next he was introduced to R. M. (later Lord) Kindersley [q.v.] who persuaded him to join Lazard Brothers, then in process of reorganization. 'Bob' Brand's connection with that banking house, of which he was for many years managing director, lasted for fifty years. He devoted the six years after this move to banking but was also deeply involved in the attempt by Curtis and a number of other Kindergarten members to give new impetus to the idea of imperial federation. The project ultimately foundered but resulted in the establishment under Kerr's editorship of the *Round Table*, a quarterly review, which for some years exerted real influence. As a member of the editorial board Brand's role, as in South Africa, was to contribute an important element of sanity to the enterprise as well as a number of extensive articles on the financial and economic aspects of the imperial problem. He later edited the letters of John Dove [q.v.], a subsequent editor of *Round Table*; they were published in 1938. He also wrote for this Dictionary the notices of Lionel Curtis, Robert Kindersley, and Philip Kerr.

A weak heart prevented Brand enlisting in 1914 but in September 1915 a crisis in the supply of shells caused Lloyd George, then minister of munitions, to send him with Hichens to Canada to sort out the chaotic purchasing arrangements there. Having set up an Imperial Munitions Board in Ottawa under (Sir) Joseph Flavelle, Brand became permanently responsible in London for the new body's liaison with the Ministry of Munitions. By the end of the war the IMB had bought sixty million shells in Canada and spent £240 million, but the administrative complexities of the operation called for diplomacy of a very high order from Brand. The financial arrangements, always on the point of collapse, involved the Americans and took him to Washington in 1917 as deputy chairman of Lord Northcliffe's [q.v.] mission. Here he married Phyllis, daughter of a Virginian auctioneer and landowner, Chiswell Dabney Langhorne, and sister of Nancy (Lady) Astor [q.v.] of whose circle at Cliveden Brand was already an intimate. She bore him two daughters and a son who was killed in action in 1945. She died herself, to his great distress, in 1937.

Brand attended the Paris peace conference as a frustrated adviser to Lord Robert Cecil (later Viscount Cecil of Chelwood, q.v.) who was chairman of the Supreme Economic Council in 1919 and whom, as Brand said later, he 'never ceased to tell that reparations would not work'. In 1920 Brand was the initiator in convening the important League of Nations financial conference in Brussels. Smuts recruited him in 1922 to be financial representative of South Africa at the Genoa conference and the same year saw the development of a long and fruitful friendship with J. M. (later Lord) Keynes [q.v.]. The two men had been in agreement at Versailles and were now together in the panel of four experts called in to advise on the stabilization of the German Mark. Though they were of utterly different temperaments and often held widely differing views, on the many occasions their professional paths crossed in the next twenty-five years they proved superb foils to each other—Keynes stimulating the liberal, imaginative side of the banker, Brand providing a tough, though sympathetic, resistance which brought out Keynes's most fertile genius. A verbatim example of this creative tension fortunately survives in the minutes of the historic Committee on Finance and Industry (1929-31), chaired by Hugh (later Lord) Macmillan [q.v.], on which both he and Keynes served.

The war of 1939-45 brought Brand back to the public service—first as deputy chairman of Lord Willingdon's mission to promote British exports to Latin America and then, in 1941, as head of the British Food Mission in Washington. From 1941 to 1944 he was the senior British member of the British American Combined Food Board which was set up to establish how much food was available and how it could be most efficiently and equitably distributed between the many rival claimants, military and civilian, within the alliance. This machine, upon which Brand exerted a stabilizing and often guiding hand, on the whole managed to extract steady supplies, stable prices, and equitable rationing from the conflicting interests of the US Department of Agriculture, the British Food Ministry, and third-country suppliers. Brand's single most valuable contribution was probably given between April and November 1942 when, called in as acting chairman, he successfully reconstructed the whole British Supply Council in Washington, which was threatening to break down under the stress of personal and departmental jealousies. In 1944 he was transferred to the post of chief Treasury representative in Washington. In the central events of that period—the Bretton Woods conference, the abrupt ending of Lend-Lease, and the negotiation of the American loan—he appeared somewhat overshadowed by the major actors, notably Keynes, but there is no doubt that his unrivalled knowledge of the American political and financial worlds, his authority with the British Treasury, and the universal trust he inspired, not least with Keynes himself, helped to turn many difficult corners.

In 1946 he returned to England. The peerage, which while his son was alive he had refused, he now accepted. He had already been appointed CMG (1910) and had received an honorary DCL from Oxford (1937). He divided the rest of his life between Lazards, All Souls, the House of Lords, and his house at Eydon in Northamptonshire. He died at the Old Vicarage, Firle, Sussex, 23 August 1963.

Brand is one of those figures, puzzling to historians, whose influence with their contemporaries can be sensed but not easily charted. His books, *The Union of South Africa* (1909), *War and National Finance* (1921), and *Why I am not a Socialist* (1923) are, like his frequent occasional articles, clear statements of a middle-of-the-road position, but they are a little dull. His judgement of the major issues of the day, though acute, often lacked cutting edge; and the perception which does him most credit—his opposition to the appeasement of Hitler—had little practical effect on influential friends of the opposite persuasion like Dawson, Lothian, and the Astors. Yet Brand's reputation for wisdom was very great and, as his voluminous papers, now in the Bodleian Library, testify, it was legitimately earned by the successful application of a quiet, slightly austere common sense not only to many national and international economic problems but also to the practical concerns of a vast number of contacts and interests, ranging from the Royal Economic Society, of which he was a governor, to the Oxford Historic Buildings Fund. His authority rested even more on what he was than what he did. The combination of a beautifully lucid brain, a natural open-mindedness, and a formidable toughness of will on matters he judged to be questions of principle produced a personality of great integrity. He was also a man of the utmost charm, with a soft voice and a mild, short-sighted appearance. Felix Frankfurter wrote after Brand's death that his was one of the sweetest natures he had ever encountered.

An oil painting (1963) by the Hon. George Bruce is in the possession of the artist. A pencil drawing by Arnold Mason (1956) and a pencil and chalk drawing by Jane de Glehn (1935) are at Eydon Hall.

[Brand papers, Bodleian Library, Oxford; private knowledge.]   DAVID WATT

BRIDGES, EDWARD ETTINGDENE, first BARON BRIDGES (1892-1969), public servant, was born at Yattendon Manor in Berkshire, 4 August 1892, the third of the three children and the only son of Robert Seymour Bridges [q.v.], later poet laureate, and his wife, (Mary) Monica, daughter of the architect Alfred Waterhouse [q.v.]. His education followed a classical pattern, which equipped him admirably for the career which he was to adopt in later life. In 1906 he went to Eton; and in 1911 he entered Magdalen College, Oxford, where he gained a first class in *literae humaniores* three years later. He had intended to read history after his first degree; and, to the end of his life, the interests and concerns of scholarship claimed a large part of his affection. But the war abruptly ended any thought of an academic career. He joined the 4th battalion of the Oxfordshire and Buckinghamshire Light Infantry and served as adjutant and captain until he was wounded on the Somme in March 1917; and, after being awarded the MC, he held a temporary post in the Treasury until he was fit to return to active service.

At the end of the war he passed the Civil Service examination and returned to the Treasury as an assistant principal. Although he was a fellow of All Souls from 1920 to 1927, he seems finally to have decided to resist Aristotle's injunction that the contemplative life should be rated more highly than the practical; and the next twenty years were spent in learning the ways of Whitehall and acquiring that expert knowledge of the machinery of government which was to serve him so well during the culminating years of his career. At that date the Treasury was responsible not merely for budgetary and financial policy but also for the administration of the public service; and Bridges' early years in Whitehall were devoted to learning the intricacies of principle and practice which governed the control of numbers, grading, and conditions of service in the increasingly complex machine of modern government. The skill which he acquired in these matters was reinforced by successive appointments to several departmental inquiries and royal commissions (including the royal commissions on police powers, 1928-9; the Civil Service, 1929-31; and lotteries and betting, 1932-3); and by a subsequent period of attachment to the Estimates Committee of the House of Commons.

In 1934 he became an assistant secretary; and in 1935 he was appointed to be head of the Treasury division which controlled expenditure on the supply and equipment of the armed forces. It was in the following three years that his powers of organization first became fully apparent. The need for greatly enlarged expenditure on rearmament had at last been acknowledged; and the normal criteria implied by orthodox Treasury doctrine were required increasingly to defer to that need. But economic solvency was no less vital to the nation's survival; and in so reshaping the machinery of Treasury control as to maintain a reasonable balance between those conflicting claims on national resources Bridges showed a pragmatic flexibility of judgement which was to become his most outstanding characteristic.

In 1938 he succeeded Sir Maurice (later Lord) Hankey [q.v.] as secretary to the Cabinet, the Committee of Imperial Defence, the Economic Advisory Council, and the Ministry for the Co-ordination of Defence. The cumulative burden of these appointments was eased when (Sir) Winston Churchill became prime minister and the responsibilities which Bridges had inherited from Hankey were divided. Sir H. L. (later Lord) Ismay [q.v.], who had been deputy secretary of the Committee of Imperial Defence under Hankey, was appointed an additional member of the Chiefs of Staff Committee in 1940 and became, in effect, the prime minister's principal staff officer when Churchill succeeded Neville Chamberlain. It was Ismay, therefore, who carried, throughout the war, the immense burden of acting as the unique link between Churchill and the chiefs of staff, both in the formulation of global strategy and in the conduct of major military operations. To Bridges fell the less glamorous, but no less vital, task of harnessing the whole of the intricate machinery of government to serve the war effort. The conflict was so different from the war of 1914-18, both in nature and scope, that he had little in the way of precedent to guide him. But to each task—whether the concise recording of the discussions and decisions of a Cabinet which would meet at any hour of the day or night; or the creation of new and unorthodox administrative machinery to deal with the wholly unforeseen problems which the war created; or the mobilization of the morale of a public service required to work for long periods under almost intolerable conditions of strain—he brought the same indomitable energy, the same fixed determination to master the odds against him. It was typical of this quiet but resolute confidence that, at an early stage in the war, he should have found time to arrange for the commissioning of its official history, a work which, as he realized, would not be finished until many years after the war had ended. And the same concern for the longer term was evident, on a larger scale, in the care which he brought to the creation of machinery, notably the Ministry of Reconstruction, to prepare for the eventual transition from war to peace.

Initially, Bridges' relations with Churchill were not wholly easy. The prime minister was wary of an official recruited from the ranks of the Treasury, which he regarded as at least partly responsible for the pre-war procrastination in mobilizing the country to meet the growing Nazi menace. But he quickly came to realize the superb administrative ability of his Cabinet secretary. And he would surely have agreed that his success in guiding the nation to ultimate victory owed not a little to the untiring service of Bridges and Ismay, who, although men of very different temperaments, shared a common devotion to their great leader and shouldered, between them, the immense responsibility of translating the inspired poetry of his directives into the plain prose of effective action. Bridges has left his own testimony to the great prime minister in his contribution to *Action This Day* (a collection of memoirs by six public servants who worked closely with Churchill during the war, edited by Sir John Wheeler-Bennett, 1968); and it is matched by Churchill's generous, and illuminating, tribute to Bridges in *Their Finest Hour* (volume ii of *The Second World War*, 1949), where he describes him as 'a man of exceptional force, ability, and personal charm, without a trace of jealousy in his nature. All that mattered to him was that the War Cabinet Secretariat as a whole should serve the prime minister and War Cabinet to the very best of their ability. No thought of his own personal position ever entered his mind, and never a cross word passed between the civil and military officers of the Secretariat.'

But Bridges did not serve only on the home front. His concerns and responsibilities extended to the oversight of the whole of the intricate network of international relationships which sustained the British war effort after the United States and the Soviet Union entered the war. The negotiation of the Lend-Lease agreements, the organization of supplies to the Russian theatre, the creation of such novel posts as British ministers resident in North and West Africa, the preparation of complex and sensitive briefs for the British teams at the critical Allied conferences at Yalta and Potsdam—all these required his attention; and all benefited from his experience of brigading diverse, and not always harmonious, interests into a common purpose.

As a result, when Sir Richard Hopkins [q.v.] retired as secretary to the Treasury in 1945 and Bridges was appointed by Attlee to succeed him, he brought to the post an unrivalled knowledge of the changed position which Britain would henceforward occupy in an international community which had itself changed, in some ways beyond recognition, since 1939. This was particularly true of British relations with the United States. Bridges never had any doubt about the primacy of this relationship in any realistic inventory of British interests; and it was he who, at the turning point in the negotiation of the vital post-war American loan

to Britain, was dispatched to Washington to break the deadlock which had developed between the two parties about its precise terms and conditions. Two years later, when it became necessary for the United Kingdom to suspend the convertibility of sterling which it had been one of the main purposes of the loan to promote, it was again Bridges who finally persuaded a reluctant chancellor of the Exchequer that this step was inevitable. In each case he achieved his end not by any display of economic or financial expertise, which he gladly left to others, but by a genuine comprehension and acceptance of the altered status of Britain in the world, combined with the kind of irresistible common sense best exemplified by the question which was, for him, the acid test of any decision—'Have you a better alternative?' It was a test before which, more often than not, the experts fell silent.

He brought a second category of experience from his wartime service to the administration of post-war Britain—a knowledge, acquired at first hand, of the resourceful flexibility of the British administrative machine under pressure, coupled with a shrewd appreciation of the constitutional and practical limits to that flexibility. In 1945 new prophets were abroad in the land, J. M. (later Lord) Keynes, Sir W. H. (later Lord) Beveridge [qq.v.], and a whole generation of scientists and technologists, to whom the war had given enhanced status. These prophets preached novel, and not always consistent, doctrines. But they had a willing audience in a public which was anxious to end the austerity of the past six years and had been encouraged to believe that the new doctrine of economic growth would enable them to move forward into a world of full employment and a rising standard of living. By one means or another the Government of the day was expected to realize these aspirations as rapidly as possible; and it fell to Bridges to devise the machinery which would enable it to discharge this task. As early as 1942 he had subscribed to the view that, if the machinery of government was to match the problems of the post-war world, it would need to be overhauled well before the war ended. But his approach to the problem was essentially pragmatic—difficult questions, he once wrote, are solved 'by good sense, not by definition'; and he had no enthusiasm for an inquiry on the model of the committee on the machinery of government chaired by Lord Haldane [q.v.] at the end of World War I, purporting to be based on logical principles of administrative methodology, which, if correctly applied, would impose order and coherence on the most intractable administrative confusion. He was concerned to produce a machine which would work effectively in the actual conditions of a post-war world as he foresaw them;

and his contribution to the deliberations of the committee chaired by Sir John Anderson (later Viscount Waverley, q.v.), which was established in 1942 to review the machinery of government against the day when peace would return, was determined largely by his realization of the unprecedented scope and nature of the problems which the war would bequeath to the years thereafter. When Bridges took charge of the Government Organization Committee towards the end of 1946, he knew that one of its most urgent tasks would be the construction of integrated administrative machinery capable of formulating the national economic plan proposed by the Labour Government and operating the controls required by that plan within the constraints of Britain's post-war balance of payments and the novel disciplines imposed by the new international economic and commercial order. He brought to the task a fund of massive common sense, combined with an unrivalled knowledge of what the machinery of Whitehall could, and could not, do. And, as he led the public service through the successive economic crises of 1947, it was very clear that he had no equal in promoting the kind of interdepartmental collaboration which was to play an increasingly important part in post-war administrative history.

But, although he was inevitably concerned with immediate problems for some years after the war, the longer-term future of the public service had its fair share of his attention and concern. He realized, almost instinctively, what needed to be done. Professional economists and statisticians were introduced into the Treasury for the first time; departments were encouraged to draw more readily on scientific advice and to include scientists and technologists among their regular staffs; following on the recommendations of the committee chaired by Ralph Assheton (later Lord Clitheroe), systematic schemes of training for civil servants were introduced and their pay and conditions of service were progressively improved; and, within the necessary limits of financial prudence, the Treasury was encouraged to adopt a liberal attitude to its functions of financing the universities and exercising the State's new patronage of the arts. By the time of his retirement in 1956 Bridges had laid the foundations of the public service as it was to be in the second half of the twentieth century; and the achievements of later reforms, notably those recommended by the committee on the Civil Service chaired by Lord Fulton (1966-8), would have been impossible without his pioneering work. In 1964 he published a book on the workings of the Treasury.

If, untypically, Bridges had looked back and tried to evaluate the result of his years in Whitehall, he would certainly have disclaimed any pretension to radical greatness. He was essentially an unassuming man, who disliked the affectation of importance in others as intensely as he would have despised it in himself. He had a great sense of fun and a keen sense of the ridiculous; and he often took an impish delight in deflating the more pompous members of the official community. But it was always done without malice or rancour; and it reflected an impatience with anything that was superficial or irrelevant to the task in hand rather than any assumption of moral or intellectual superiority. His own principles were high and strongly maintained; and the habit of his daily life was simple and unaffected. But he made no attempt to impose his personal views on others; and he ruled Whitehall by example rather than by precept. It was essentially an example of strenuous endeavour. He was a tireless worker, who brought to every task an intense concentration of effort to establish the facts of a situation, to judge the direction in which they pointed, and to ensure that the conclusion of the debate which they had occasioned was promptly and effectively translated into action. His style of administration did not conform with the conventional ideal of an effortless superiority which transacts business from a clear desk by vigorous delegation with the minimum of personal intervention. He was an artist rather than a craftsman; and he established his mastery over his material by immersing himself in it and moulding it to his purpose rather than by subordinating it to any specific technique or expertise. This did not always make for economy of effort; and his light would often be burning in Whitehall long after all others had been extinguished. But he set an example of sustained expenditure of strength and stamina which evoked an instant response from all who worked for him; and the unfaltering leadership which he provided during the darkest days of the war attracted a respect and affection transcending the normal loyalties of Whitehall.

He remained, however, an essentially private individual, who had few close friends outside his family and guarded the intimacy of his personal life very jealously. He retained a devoted memory of his father and spent much of his spare time ordering his letters and papers. But he seldom spoke of him and made no attempt to claim any share in his reputation. The integrity of his own character was his sufficient reward; and the homespun virtue, which he wore like a piece of honest, durable, worsted cloth, was his surest cloak against the wind and weather of the world of public affairs.

Retirement in 1956 brought a change in the pattern of his life but no relaxation in his service to the public interest. He was chairman of the National Institute for Research into Nuclear Energy from 1957, of the Fine Arts Commission from 1957 to 1968, of the British Council from 1959 to 1967, and of the Pilgrim Trust from 1965 to 1968. In 1963 he was appointed to preside over the commission on training in public administration for overseas countries. From 1945 to 1965 he was a member of the governing body of Eton; and he was also much concerned with higher education, being chairman of the board of governors of the London School of Economics and Political Science from 1957 to 1968, chancellor of Reading University in 1959, chairman of the Oxford Historic Buildings Fund in 1957, and from 1960 to 1962 chairman of the commission appointed at Cambridge to study the relationship between the colleges and the university.

Bridges' work was rewarded by many honours. He was appointed GCB (1944), GCVO (1946), privy councillor (1953), baron (1957), and KG (1965). He received honorary degrees from the universities of Oxford, Cambridge, London, Bristol, Leicester, Liverpool, Reading, and Hong Kong; he was elected to a fellowship of the Royal Society in 1952, an honour which gave him particular pleasure; and he was an honorary fellow of All Souls and Magdalen Colleges at Oxford, of the London School of Economics and Political Science, and of the Royal Institution of British Architects.

In 1922 Bridges married Katherine ('Kitty') Dianthe Farrer, daughter of the second Baron Farrer. They had two sons and two daughters. Bridges died at the Royal Surrey County Hospital, Guildford, 27 August 1969, and was succeeded by his elder son, Thomas Edward (born 1927).

A portrait of Bridges by Allan Gwynne-Jones was exhibited at the Royal Academy Summer Exhibition in 1963.

[Lord Bridges in *Action This Day*, ed. Sir John Wheeler-Bennett, 1968; Sir John Winnifrith in *Biographical Memoirs of Fellows of the Royal Society*, vol. xvi, 1970; personal knowledge.]   TREND

BRIDGES-ADAMS, WILLIAM (1889-1965), theatrical producer, was born 1 March 1889 in Wealdstone, Harrow, the only son of Walter Bridges Adams, tutor, and his wife, Mary Jane Daltry. Nothing in his background suggested a theatrical career, and he remained to the end of his days a quite untheatrical person. But he was brought up on Shakespeare, Dickens, and Wagner—and this helped to counteract the seriously, although not smugly, socialist ambience of his home. He was educated

at Bedales, and Worcester College, Oxford, where he played Leontes in *The Winter's Tale* and Prospero in *The Tempest* for the OUDS. At the same time he had friends in Cambridge, and was associated with the production of Marlowe's *Dr. Faustus* by the ADC in 1907. At Oxford he staged two operas for (Sir) Hugh Allen [q.v.], and directed the Oxford millenary pageant. His visual sense, always very acute, was quickened by the Post-Impressionists and personal contacts with Charles Ricketts and Charles Shannon [qq.v.]. On leaving Oxford he assisted Nugent Monck in the stage-management of the production of *The Two Gentlemen of Verona* by William Poel for Sir Herbert Beerbohm Tree [qq.v.] at His Majesty's Theatre. He admired the character and, to some extent, the genius of Poel, but kept his distance from what he liked to call 'Elizabethan Methodism'.

After further experience in Shakespeare repertory, with Lena Ashwell [q.v.], and the Stage Society, he appeared in 1916 with Sir George Alexander [q.v.] at the St. James's, learning the difference between what Oscar Wilde [q.v.] had described as Alexander's 'behaviour' and the 'throw it away' school of naturalism. His next move was to Liverpool where in 1916-17 he directed in repertory at the Playhouse, giving it the name by which it became well known.

In 1919 the control of the annual Shakespeare Festival at Stratford-upon-Avon passed into the hands of the Stratford governors and London's 'Shakespeare Memorial National Theatre Committee'. Bridges-Adams was appointed to direct the festivals, inheriting a number of players who had previously worked with Sir Frank Benson [q.v.] and a certain local disappointment that Benson was no longer there to direct them himself. The Memorial Theatre was not well adapted to the methods of production advocated by Harley Granville-Barker [q.v.] and Poel, and Bridges-Adams himself hankered a little after the romanticism of Irving's Lyceum, of which he knew only by hearsay. But his own productions—which he designed himself—were scenically effective in their simple way, and he secured swift and clear performances of six plays rehearsed in only five weeks. They were given virtually unabridged (except for Christopher Sly in *The Taming of the Shrew*, for whom he had conceived an irrational dislike); and this earned him the sobriquet of 'Mr Unabridges-Adams'. He was not afraid of sensible innovation, putting Richard II into black armour inherited from the Black Prince, interpreting the apparitions in *Macbeth* as the sovereigns of the Stuart dynasty, and making Banquo's ghost re-enter as the murdered Duncan. In contrast to Poel's archaism and Barker's hygienic tidiness, there was a sense of bustling 'boot and saddle' about these early productions. He preserved the footlights, and live musicians in the well of the orchestra.

On 6 March 1926 the Memorial Theatre was burnt down—greatly to the relief of G. B. Shaw [q.v.]. Within hours of the mysterious conflagration Bridges-Adams was on the spot, tracing in the mud with his umbrella the plan for an enlarged stage. The spring Festival went forward in the local cinema, with costumes lent from America by Julia Marlowe and E. H. Sothern; and American generosity, activated by three American tours, made it possible for the new Memorial Theatre to be opened by the Prince of Wales on 23 April 1932. Bridges-Adams was happily at home at the drawing-board, and the stage was very much as he had planned it. He had insisted on 'absolute flexibility—a box of tricks out of which the childlike mind of the producer may create whatever shape it pleases'. This disappointed the 'Elizabethan Methodists', but not the guest directors—(Sir) Tyrone Guthrie and Theodore Komisarjevsky [q.v.]—or the guest designers—Aubrey Hammond and Norman Wilkinson—who were now invited to use it. Stratford seemed in a fair way of becoming the 'British Bayreuth' of Bridges-Adams's dreams.

The governors, however, were still content with more limited horizons. They were unwilling to pay the larger salaries which would attract a stronger company, although players like Randle Ayrton, George Hayes, and Fabia Drake continued to give exemplary performances. In 1934 Bridges-Adams resigned—'not without due thought', as he told the governors, 'and not without reluctance'. He wanted an easier schedule of rehearsals and opening nights, and a closer liaison with other bodies working in the same field, giving him larger resources in personnel, for which he was prepared to forgo a certain degree of independence. He wanted an international status for the theatre, and more guest directors of international repute. When he found little backing for these policies, he felt that it was time for him to go.

He had directed at Stratford twenty-nine out of the thirty-six plays in the First Folio, *The Merry Wives of Windsor* at the Lyric, Hammersmith, in 1923, and *Much Ado about Nothing* at the New Theatre in 1926. But he was not an ambitious man, and he was among the few who had not begrudged Granville-Barker his early retirement. He had married in 1929 Marguerite Doris, formerly the wife of (Sir) Colin Reith Coote and daughter of the late William Henry Wellsted, architect. She had comfortable private means, and he now settled down with her at Badingham in Suffolk; they

had one son. His earlier marriage, in 1915, to Muriel Edith Amy, daughter of William Dymock Pratt, architect, had been annulled. In 1936 he directed *Oedipus Rex* at Covent Garden; and was appointed to the Council of the Royal Academy of Dramatic Art and the building advisory committee for the National Theatre; and in 1937 became honorary dramatic adviser for the British Council, with special responsibility for their foreign tours. From 1939 to 1944 he worked as a full-time member of their staff. After the war he moved with his wife to Ireland, building a house to his own design at Castletownbere in county Cork. There he completed the first volume of *The Irresistible Theatre* (1957) which promised to be a classic of its kind, and contributed the chapter on the Edwardian theatre to Simon Nowell-Smith's symposium, *Edwardian England* (1964). He maintained, at the same time, a close and fascinating correspondence with his friends.

Bridges-Adams was at once sociable and solitary. At Stratford he had kept somewhat aloof from his company, but he delighted in his membership of the Garrick and Savile Clubs. A brilliant conversationalist—for he could listen as well as talk—he was free with illuminating comment on the theatre which he had never ceased to love, although he had left it when he was still so young. He was appointed CBE in 1960, a welcome, if belated, recognition of the foundations he had laid, on which others were to build with the means that had been denied him. No one since Granville-Barker had shown a surer grasp of Shakespearian stage-craft, or a clearer mind on the essential content of the plays. His wife died, very suddenly, in 1963; Bridges-Adams died 17 August 1965 at Bantry, county Cork, after recovering gradually a little of his former zest for a life which he had endured, at need, as a stoic and otherwise enjoyed as an epicurean.

A portrait by G. R. Schelderup is in the possession of the family.

[Private information; personal knowledge.]

ROBERT SPEAIGHT

BRIND, SIR (ERIC JAMES) PATRICK (1892-1963), admiral, was born at Paignton 12 May 1892, the third son of Colonel Edward Agincourt Brind of the 88th Connaught Rangers, and his wife, Florence Lund. Brind's father settled in Dorchester after retiring from the army.

Brind entered the Royal Navy as a cadet in 1905, passing through Osborne and Dartmouth Colleges before joining his first sea-going ship as a midshipman on 5 September 1909. In May 1916, as a young lieutenant, he was at the

Battle of Jutland in the new 15-inch battleship *Malaya* which suffered damage.

Early promotion to commander on 30 June 1927 indicated that he was well thought of, and this was further substantiated when he was promoted captain on 31 December 1933, at the age of forty-one, at a time when the number of promotions had been much reduced.

Brind's appointment to the Admiralty Tactical Division in May 1934 gave further indication of a promising future, and offered scope for his insistence that the new aircraft carriers of the Formidable class should be fitted with armoured flight decks, an indispensable benefit in the war that followed.

As a captain, Brind commanded the cruiser *Orion*, and later the cruiser *Birmingham*. He took the latter to Tsingtao in 1939, at a time when China and Japan were at war, to investigate the arrest of a British merchant ship by the Japanese. He called on the Japanese admiral and announced his intention of rescuing the British ship despite the presence of Japanese heavy cruisers and a carrier, and the threat to blow the *Birmingham* out of the water. Brind insisted on the release of the merchant ship and sailed the next day, escorting her to safety.

In December 1940 Brind became chief of staff to Admiral (Sir) John Tovey, C.-in-C. Home Fleet, and was thus involved in the long chase and the destruction of the *Bismarck* on 27 May 1941. He was created CBE for his part in the action.

Having been promoted rear-admiral on 6 February 1942, Brind was appointed assistant chief of naval staff in May 1942, and served in the Admiralty until August 1944, taking a large part in the planning for Operation Neptune (the Normandy landings). In July 1944 he was made CB in recognition of this work. From October 1944 until January 1946 Brind had command of a squadron of ships of the British Pacific Fleet, and was engaged in offensive operations in the long task of defeating the Japanese. He was present at the conclusion of the war with the Japanese in August 1945 and attended the act of surrender in Tokyo.

Brind was promoted vice-admiral on 16 October 1945, and was advanced to KCB in June 1946. In October 1946 he was appointed president of the Royal Naval College at Greenwich, and held this appointment until he assumed the naval command C.-in-C. Far East Station in January 1949. He retained the latter, perhaps his most important job, until 1951, the year in which he was created GBE. He was promoted full admiral on 20 March 1949. It was in 1949 that the *Amethyst* was held hostage by Communists 150 miles up the River Yangtze for three months.

Realizing that negotiations were fruitless, Brind turned a blind eye to official policy, and initiated and organized the *Amethyst*'s spectacular withdrawal from the Yangtze—a triumphant success.

When the Korean war broke out in June 1950, Brind was ready to oppose the North Korean assault. He at once ordered his ships to be placed under American command, without waiting to learn the official policy. The whole area was in turmoil, with Communist aggression in China and Korea, the threat to Taiwan, an emergency in Malaya, and piracy. A false move might have had major international repercussions, but Brind, who was on the spot, seemed instinctively to sense the right moves. With a sizeable fleet involved in continuous operations 2,000 miles from its main base, Brind had to improvise rapidly. Thanks to enthusiastic support his efforts were highly successful. His staff officer operations, Captain P. Dickens, thought that Brind's performance at this time was the peak of his career: 'To his patience, charm, and kindness I would add an indefatigable capacity for work, and a sense of duty, directed towards God and what he believed to be right.' Brind's final appointment was as C.-in-C. Allied Forces Northern Europe (1951-3), a new NATO command. He retired in 1953 and was succeeded in the NATO appointment by his deputy, General Sir Robert Mansergh.

Brind was known throughout the navy as 'Daddy'. When his secretary, Captain S. A. B. Morant, was asked about the derivation of the nickname, he replied that doubtless it was because he had white hair, a paternal air, and was one of the kindest and most charming men one could ever hope to meet. His widow said that the nickname 'Daddy' was given to him when he was a lieutenant doing courses. His hair was prematurely white and he had a benign appearance.

Brind died 4 October 1963 at Withyham near Crowborough at the age of seventy-one. His memorial in Withyham church has the appropriate inscription: 'Write me as one that loves his fellow men.'

Brind married, in 1918, Eileen Margaret, daughter of the Revd Josiah Marling Apperly, the rector of Tonge, Sittingbourne, Kent, by whom he had one daughter, born in 1919. Brind's first wife died in 1940. In 1948 he married Edith Gordon (died 1979), daughter of William Duncan Lowe, Writer to the Signet, Edinburgh, and widow of Rear-Admiral H. E. C. Blagrove who was lost in the sinking of the *Royal Oak* in 1939.

[*The Times*, 5 and 10 September, 1963, private information.]

S. W. C. PACK

BRITTAIN, VERA MARY (1893-1970), writer, pacifist, and feminist, was born at Newcastle under Lyme 29 December 1893, the only daughter of Thomas Arthur Brittain, paper manufacturer, and his wife, Edith Mary Bervon. Her only surviving brother, Edward, less than two years her junior, a cherished companion, was killed in action in 1918. Vera Brittain grew up in Macclesfield and then in Buxton in Derbyshire, amidst provincial restrictions against which she increasingly chafed. Her intellectual powers were stimulated by her brother and his Uppingham friends and at St. Monica's, Kingswood, a school which afforded unusual scope for extra-curricular reading and discussion. When she left, she was already set on one of the paths which she followed to the end of her days, the cause of feminism.

That her awakened mind should seek deeper and more disciplined experience would never have occurred to her kind but conventional parents had not chance brought to their Buxton home a distinguished university extension lecturer in the person of (Sir) John Marriott [q.v.]. With his encouragement, she won an open exhibition to Somerville College and went up to Oxford in 1914. There followed the nightmare years of war. University life became insupportable and she enrolled as a VAD, among the young women who were not trained nurses, but who worked and suffered side by side with them. She served in France and Malta as well as London. In the carnage of trench warfare one by one her gifted fiancé, Roland Leighton (brother of the artist Clare Leighton), their closest friends, and finally her beloved brother were killed or died of wounds.

Post-war Oxford (where she obtained a second in history in 1921) brought frustrations but it enabled her to establish a friendship of remarkable quality with a fellow student from Yorkshire, Winifred Holtby, author of *South Riding*, whose untimely death in 1935 led Vera Brittain to commemorate her in *Testament of Friendship* (1940). Meanwhile, another Oxford graduate had noticed the talented young woman who was beginning to make her way in her chosen career as a lecturer and writer. (Sir) George Catlin (died 1979), of New College, became professor of politics at Cornell University in 1924 at the age of twenty-eight. In 1925 he and Vera Brittain were married at St. James's, Spanish Place. She herself never embraced the Roman Catholic faith, although Roland Leighton, her husband, and her daughter did so.

Marriage posed for Vera Brittain in its sharpest form the dilemma of home and career. She had no doubt that, for her, a career as writer and speaker was essential. Transatlantic correspondence on this necessity preceded mar-

riage. One winter at Cornell convinced her that she could not work there. There followed a long period of what she termed 'semi-detached marriage', with Catlin going each winter to Cornell and later to other universities, while she and their son and daughter remained at home. Despite much physical separation, the bond of affection remained strong and when, in her last years, her strength began to fail, nothing could have exceeded the devotion with which her husband tended her.

It was in 1933 that the book which brought her fame was published. *Testament of Youth* spoke with the most moving eloquence for a whole generation. There had been other war books and much war poetry. But this autobiographical narrative, based on diaries and the letters of a group of exceptionally intelligent, sensitive, and articulate young people, was the first book of note to view the horror and heartbreak of war through the eyes of a woman: 'The world was mad and we were all victims . . .'. The book's controlled poignancy brought immediate and overwhelming response: Vera Brittain awoke to find herself famous. The impression made on the post-war generation as well as on her contemporaries was intense.

She wrote the book to release her deeply felt obligations to the dead, but also with the conviction that, for those who had survived, nothing mattered so much as to persuade the world of the criminal futility of war. Already a socialist, in 1936 she joined the Peace Pledge Union of Canon Dick Sheppard [q.v.] and spoke widely at pacifist meetings. During the war of 1939-45 her courageous denunciation of the saturation bombing of Germany brought much public criticism in the United States as well as Britain.

As a publicist for feminist and pacifist causes, Vera Brittain achieved a fair measure of success. As a novelist, she lacked the humour and skill in characterization of her friend Winifred Holtby. The special interest of a further autobiographical instalment, *Testament of Experience* (1957), lies in the references to her children, especially her daughter who, as Mrs Shirley Williams, was destined to become a leading Labour politician and Cabinet minister, thus fulfilling both her mother's feminist aspirations and her father's unrealized personal political ambitions.

In youth, Vera Brittain's slight figure and 'large, melting dark eyes' were clearly very attractive, although she frequently lamented her lack of stature and 'immature appearance' as handicaps on public platforms. She took a lively interest in clothes. Always reticent and a little formal, within her own circle she could arouse intense devotion. She received an honorary

D.Litt. from Mills College, California, in 1940. She died in London 29 March 1970. A drawing and a portrait by Sir William Rothenstein are in the possession of her daughter.

[Vera Brittain, *Testament of Youth*, 1933, and *Testament of Experience*, 1957; private papers; personal knowledge.]   EIRENE WHITE

BROOK, NORMAN CRAVEN, BARON NORMANBROOK (1902-1967), secretary of the Cabinet, was born in Bristol 29 April 1902, the son of Frederick Charles Brook, assessor of taxes, and his wife, Annie Smith. He was educated at Wolverhampton Grammar School and Wadham College, Oxford, where he obtained a first in honour moderations in 1923 and a second in *literae humaniores* in 1925; he became an honorary fellow in 1949.

He chose the Civil Service as his career; and from the moment of his entry into the Home Office in 1925 it was clear that he possessed exceptional administrative ability. It was almost inevitable that he should be selected, in 1938, to become principal private secretary to Sir John Anderson (later Viscount Waverley, q.v.), who was then lord privy seal and later home secretary; the link between the two men which was thus established remained a firm bond in the subsequent years when Brook continued to serve Anderson as his personal assistant when he was lord president of the Council from 1940 to 1942.

The next steps followed logically when Brook became successively one of the deputy secretaries of the Cabinet, with special responsibility for the co-ordination of the civil aspects of the war effort, and (1943-5) permanent secretary of the Ministry of Reconstruction, which was concerned with elaborating, in anticipation of the end of the war, detailed plans for the eventual restoration of the civil life of the country. When Brook became secretary of the Cabinet at the beginning of 1947 in succession to Sir Edward (later Lord) Bridges [q.v.] he was thus in a unique position to observe, for the next sixteen years, the extent to which those plans were brought to fulfilment or were forcibly modified by the series of economic crises which confronted Britain in the post-war years. In 1956 he became joint permanent secretary of the Treasury and head of the Home Civil Service, an office which he combined with that of secretary of the Cabinet until he retired from the public service at the end of 1962.

This bare recital of the successive stages of Brook's career illustrates the common thread which links all of them in a continuous and consistent experience. Each of them was essentially regulatory, rather than innovative, in character; each entailed the reconciliation of multiple and differing views rather than the pursuit of a single, undivided, purpose. It was in the exercise of a function of this kind that Brook excelled. His natural disposition was that of the co-ordinator, seeking to transcend departmental boundaries and to elicit from the conflict of disparate purposes the measure of agreement which would most nearly accord with the basic policy of the government of the day and would be most likely to promote the interests of the country as a whole. All that survives of such work is the final product—the memorandum of proposals as finally submitted to the Cabinet and the record of the Cabinet's subsequent discussion and decision. There is little, if any, evidence of the earlier stages, often difficult and protracted, in which differences of departmental view were laboriously argued out and the conflict of competing claims was gradually reduced, even if not completely resolved. But it was in this area of management that Brook's penetrating intellect and cool judgement were unequalled and commanded a respect which was not accorded to any of his contemporaries.

The skill and patience which he brought to this daily round of painstaking and unspectacular administration sprang from a twofold root. By temperament, he was disciplined and austere; and his classical education reinforced an instinctive belief that dispassionate reason should be capable of reducing the most intractable conflict and confusion to an orderly and acceptable solution. But at a deeper level of conviction he was concerned to defend the concepts of Cabinet government and collective ministerial responsibility as he interpreted them in the context of a system of parliamentary democracy. In such a system a government must so manage its affairs that the Cabinet must be able to present to Parliament, at any moment, a united front against any challenge, whether to their policies as a whole or to the actions of only one of their number. So, and only so, can the liberty of the subject be defended against attack, whether by external aggression or by domestic tyranny. If so, however, the apparatus of central administration must clearly be devised to serve this purpose as efficiently as possible. The refinement of the machinery of government was one of Brook's most dominant concerns. His approach was essentially that of a pragmatist, whose period of office as secretary of the Cabinet covered a time of momentous changes. The great programmes of social and economic reform which were introduced in the years immediately after the war; the construction of the post-war partnership between Europe and the United States of America which found its most significant expression in the North Atlantic Treaty Organization; and the gradual replacement of a colonial Empire by a Commonwealth of independent nations united only by a common acceptance of the British sovereign as its head—all of these carried far-reaching implications for Britain. In each case the major decisions of policy involved were necessarily reserved to the Cabinet as a whole. But a mutiplicity of more detailed questions had inevitably to be delegated to a rather lower level, to a body of committees designed to relieve the Cabinet of as much as possible of the burden of discussion and analysis.

Brook brought clear and concise ideas to the elaboration of the committee system, derived from his experience of its very successful operation during the war, when speed was of the essence of decision. He maintained that a Cabinet committee was invested with executive authority by implied devolution from the Cabinet; and it could, and should, take firm decisions on that basis. But its proceedings should conform to certain principles designed both to protect the Cabinet's own supremacy and to maintain the doctrine of collective responsibility. Its chairman should always, if possible, be a minister who was himself a member of the Cabinet and could judge the point at which the committee should report to senior colleagues, whether for approval or for further instructions. Its membership should be carefully chosen in order to ensure that those departments whose interests were directly engaged should be fully represented but that the committee as a whole should remain sufficiently compact to deal with its business with dispatch. Its discussions should be as thoroughly prepared, as efficiently conducted, and as accurately recorded as those of the Cabinet itself.

To serve the Cabinet and its committees there had to be an effective administrative apparatus, responsible for circulating the relevant papers in good time, for arranging and recording discussions, and for ensuring the prompt and efficient implementation of decisions. The Cabinet Secretariat owed much to the care and time which Brook devoted to these purposes. Always an economical administrator, he was concerned that it should remain small and compact and that its members should be encouraged to work quickly and—as he himself worked—with the minimum expenditure of words. He wrote well and easily, but without great colour or emphasis. His prose was lean and muscular; eschewing rhetoric and emotion; and designed to reduce the most heated and confused exchanges to a record of orderly, logical, objective discussion. This was what was required for the efficient dispatch of government business; and this overriding purpose should not be obscured or obstructed by undue consideration for individual views and personal preferences which were of merely ephemeral interest and of no relevance to the final decision.

It was a severe process of redaction; and when the official records are opened future historians and biographers may regret that they are so spare and undramatic in their descriptions of the nature of the major crises of government and the reactions of those who took part in the momentous discussions involved. But in other respects their profession owes Brook a considerable debt. Although the monumental *Official History of the Second World War* was not finally complete when he retired, the great bulk of it was published during his period of office; and each of its successive volumes, whether in the military or the civil series, passed under his watchful and exacting scrutiny before it was released. Authors and editors alike paid tribute to the generous spirit in which he made time, among many weightier preoccupations, to deal with their problems, to help them with their researches, and to ensure, so far as he could, that their work measured up to his own high standards of historical accuracy.

He was no less helpful to former ministers who wished to publish their memoirs. It was consistent with his basic conviction about the true nature of responsibility in a democratic society that he should vigorously defend the right of those who had been personally and publicly accountable to Parliament to publish their own version of affairs while no less firmly deprecating any corresponding claim by civil servants who had discharged only an advisory function and were constitutionally entitled to expect their ministers to shoulder the blame for failure no less than to accept the credit for success. The criterion of propriety in such matters was already changing in Brook's last years; but however much fashions of literary discretion may change, Brook would certainly have held that the maintenance of a proper balance between public order and personal liberty in a democratic society requires both a generous measure of freedom of speech for those who carry ultimate political responsibility and a reasonable degree of reticence on the part of those whose function is essentially non-political in any party sense.

He brought this concept with him when, in 1956, he became the official head of the Home Civil Service; and in the following years, until his retirement, he was well placed to affirm throughout the whole public service the high standards of professional efficiency and personal integrity which he had maintained when he was the secretary of the Cabinet.

But he continued to hold the latter office as well; and the combination of two such exacting responsibilities prevented him from giving to the public service as much attention as he would have wished. He introduced no major reforms in public administration; and when he retired the radical review of the public service which was eventually undertaken by the Fulton commission still lay several years ahead. But he foresaw the tendencies very clearly and he did much, within the existing framework of the Service, to improve its processes of recruitment and training and to modernize its methods of work.

Perhaps his most significant, although also least definable, contribution to the development of the machinery of government was made in a wider field, which was always very close to his heart. For sixteen years he acted as secretary to successive meetings of Commonwealth heads of government and served their members with the same loyalty and efficiency with which he served the members of British governments. He watched the development and enlargement of the modern Commonwealth with keen interest, wasting no time or tears on sentimental regrets for a fading imperial past but seeking strenuously to ensure that the basic community of purpose which had animated the Commonwealth from the outset, together with the relationship of easy and informal friendliness among its members, should not be diluted or destroyed by its progressive enlargement. It was the essence of the Commonwealth, as he envisaged it, that it should have neither constitution nor rules of procedure, that it should take no formal decisions and reach no necessary conclusions. This unique forbearance enabled it, against all reasonable expectations in an age of increasing self-determination, to ventilate differences of view, and not infrequently to reach broad agreement, on issues which would have proved intractable by a more self-conscious and organized procedure; and Brook, as he marshalled its agenda and recorded its debates, could rightly claim that the continuing allegiance which it commanded was perhaps the most eloquent tribute to the principle of free and rational discussion between equal partners to which his own professional life had been dedicated.

His last years were overshadowed by illness; and, although he found that his duties as chairman of governors of the BBC (1964-7) presented administrative problems which to him were novel and intensely interesting, the oversight of an independent corporation, inevitably and rightly concerned with debatable issues, was liable from time to time to take him closer to the area of public controversy than his naturally reticent temperament found wholly congenial. But he strove unremittingly to uphold the standards of propriety and impartiality which his years in Whitehall had instilled so deeply in him.

His appearance reflected his character: correct, sober, and unostentatious, even in moments of leisure and relaxation. He discouraged informality in greeting and address; and his manner was one of rather intimidating reserve. But, as acquaintance deepened into friendship, he revealed himself as a kindly and generous host, with a ready wit and a keen sense of social enjoyment. At home, as at his office, he was essentially the craftsman; and the woodwork which was his favourite hobby was the occasion of many simple jokes about his skill as a Cabinet maker. These he endured with the same slightly impatient tolerance with which he observed the other frailties of mankind.

Brook married in 1929 (Ida) Mary ('Goss'), daughter of Edwyn Alfred Goshawk. She died in 1981. He was appointed CB (1942), KCB (1946), GCB (1951), and was sworn of the Privy Council in 1953. He was created a baron in 1963. He had no children and the title became extinct when he died in London 15 June 1967.

[Private information; personal knowledge.]

TREND

BROOKE, ALAN FRANCIS, first VISCOUNT ALANBROOKE (1883-1963), field-marshal, was born at Bagnères de Bigorre, France, 23 July 1883, the ninth and youngest child and sixth son of Sir Victor Alexander Brooke, third baronet, of Colebrooke in county Fermanagh, and his wife, Alice Sophia Bellingham, second daughter of Sir Alan Edward Bellingham, third baronet, of Castle Bellingham in County Louth. On both sides of the family his roots lay deep in the Irish Protestant ascendancy. The first Brooke of Colebrooke, Sir Henry Brooke of Donegal, was the son of an Elizabethan captain of Cheshire origin, and had been rewarded for his part in suppressing the native rising of 1641 by the grant of Colebrooke and 30,000 acres of Fermanagh. From that time until Alan Brooke's the natural tastes and aptitudes of the men of the family were for the soldier's life. They fought campaign after campaign, often achieving high rank and distinction in the service of the Crown. Twenty-six Brookes of Colebrooke served in the war of 1914-18; twenty-seven in that of 1939-45.

Alan Brooke was born and brought up at or near Pau in the south of France where his family owned a villa and periodically took a small house in the neighbouring hills in the heat of summer. His mother preferred life at Pau, where there was a flourishing and fashionable English society, excellent hunting and shooting, and an agreeable climate, to the rigours of Colebrooke; one consequence was that Alan Brooke spoke French—and German—before he spoke English, never underwent a conventional English schooling, and, although he was an excellent horseman, shot, and fisherman, he first entered communal British life on joining the Royal Military Academy at Woolwich at the age of eighteen, largely ignorant of the team games and the usual *mores* of the English schoolboy. From so comparatively solitary an upbringing—he had been to a small local school in Pau, was by some years the youngest of the family, and his father had died when he was eight—he was, by his own account, shy and unsure of himself. He was also delicate and introspective. Nevertheless, he passed out of Woolwich well—not high enough to become a Royal Engineer, but sufficiently well to join a battery of Royal Field Artillery in Ireland and to be earmarked early as a likely candidate for the coveted jacket of the Royal Horse Artillery.

Brooke's first four years of army life were spent in Ireland; then, from 1906, in India where he entered with enthusiasm into every aspect of his profession, caring for his men and his horses and his guns with a meticulous throughness and an eye for detail which were his abiding hallmark. He was a noted big-game hunter in India, just as he was a noted race rider there and in Ireland. If early he had thought of himself as uncertain and hesitant, diffidence dissolved in the warmth of regimental life. He became the best of companions, quick-witted and amusing, an excellent draughtsman and caricaturist, and a skilled mimic. He early showed, however, a deep vein of seriousness about both life and his profession which found expression in long letters to the mother he adored. He was highly efficient, very incise, and received outstanding reports at every step. In 1909 he joined N battery, Royal Horse Artillery, in India, and in 1914 found himself commanding the Artillery brigade ammunition column in France.

The 1914-18 war saw Brooke's progress from lieutenant to lieutenant-colonel, at all times on the western front and in artillery appointments. In each he shone, and his name as an intelligent, thoughtful, and, in some respects, innovatory, gunner came to stand very high. He was brigade major, Royal Artillery, in the 18th division (Ivor Maxse, q.v.) during the Somme battle, and was credited with the production of the first 'creeping barrage' to ensure that the ground between the enemy's trench lines was covered and the exposure of our advancing infantry to unsilenced machine-gun fire was minimized. He himself attributed the idea to the French; whatever its provenance, it was highly successful and both in the 18th division battles and in the great Canadian attacks of 1917—he was posted as chief artillery staff officer to the Canadian Corps (Julian Byng, q.v.) in 1917—ground was gained with fewer casualties than in other engagements in the same period. The artillery support in all formations in which Brooke served and where his ideas accordingly prevailed was widely praised and trusted absolutely.

It was natural that he should be selected for the first post-war course at the Staff College at Camberley where he met the best of his contemporaries in the army, men like Gort, Dill, Freyberg, Fuller [qq.v.], and others whose careers or ideas were to coincide with or cross his own. He was an outstanding student and after a few years on the staff of a Northumbrian division of the Territorial Army he was brought back to Camberley as an instructor in 1923. There he distilled his experience of artillery in the recent war and drew lessons which found expression in a series of lectures and published articles. He believed, unequivocally, that firepower dominated movement, which was itself impossible in modern war without the production of massive and effective supporting fire. He also believed that the effect of firepower tended to be underestimated in peacetime, because of the difficulties of simulation and therefore to be extruded from men's calculations; whereas movements, because they could actually be performed, were practised with inadequate regard to the dominant effect of fire. This was the period when the British prophets of armoured warfare were singing different songs—that mechanization would restore mobility to the battlefield in a way which even the major tank battles of the recent war had not demonstrated because of inadequate comprehension and therefore inadequate exploitation of opportunity; and that deep penetration and great operational movements would again become possible, the tactical stalemate apparently imposed by machine-gun, cannon, and barbed wire having been potentially nullified by the tank. Nevertheless, the tank was not yet reliable and its limited operational effectiveness had probably owed as much to mechanical factors as to unimaginative handling. Brooke pondered the matter deeply. He was initially unconvinced and he was certainly not one of the pioneers of armoured warfare such as Hobart, Lindsay, and Martel, who looked to Fuller as in some ways their most original mind and to Liddell Hart [qq.v.] as their most articulate spokesman. Nevertheless, Brooke's ideas moved a great deal between 1926 when he left the Staff College as instructor and 1937 when, to the surprise of some and the displeasure of those who felt that the appointment should go to a tank expert rather than to a gunner, he became the first commander of the Mobile division—prototype of the later armoured divisions—on Salisbury Plain.

Meanwhile, however, Brooke went in 1927 as one of the first students to the new Imperial Defence College, to which he returned in 1932 for two years as an instructor. There he first studied in depth questions of imperial strategy, joint service co-operation, and the higher politico-military direction of war—and of preparations for or prevention of war—with which his life was to be so intimately concerned. He was, by now, a man who inspired no little awe. As at the Staff College he made a profound impact through the speed and incisiveness of his mind, the clarity and brevity of his speech, and—not least—the gift of friendship all the more profound because never lightly given. He was a generous and delightful companion to those who got to know him. He was invariably thoughtful and a good listener. He retained his wide interests, his capacity to amuse and for repartee, and his immense knowledge and love of all things connected with nature. Sport, at which he was invariably skilful, had to some extent yielded to ornithology among his loves. He was passionately interested in all sorts of birds, particularly waders; loved photographing them at which he made himself an expert; and started to collect books and pictures connected therewith. As an ornithologist he has been placed by the highest experts as 'of the very first rank of non-professionals'. Brooke retained this enthusiasm to the end, and it provided solace in many dark hours of the war which was to come.

Before his time as instructor at the IDC, Brooke, now a brigadier, commanded the School of Artillery at Larkhill between 1929 and 1932. He made his usual mark as a meticulous and absolutely determined superior, a man of clear and original ideas, and a dedicated gunner. He commanded an infantry brigade from 1934—a widening experience he greatly enjoyed and was the first to say found highly educative. After a short spell as inspector, Royal Artillery, in the rank of major-general in 1935, he had an equally brief tour as director of military training. It was from that post that he was selected to command the Mobile division.

Two contentious issues lay at the heart of policy. First was the principle and the pace of mechanization and the whole future of horsed cavalry. Second was the proper operational employment—and thus the size and shape—of armoured formations. This second question contained another, whether such formations should be virtually 'all tank' or whether the needs of the tactical battle, whatever the scale of the operational movement, would require the combination—and therefore the mobility and the protection—of all arms. Brooke was by now a convinced supporter of rapid mechanization, and his tact and understanding did much to reconcile the sentiment of the dedicated cavalrymen to the stubborn facts of technology. On the operational and tactical issues he stood four-square behind those who believed that future battle would, as before, demand the co-operation of all arms and that therefore all arms must have appropriate equipments in the armoured formations of the future.

From 1938 until shortly before the outbreak of World War II Brooke was moved to a completely different but no less vital sphere. He was taken from the Mobile division, promoted to lieutenant-general, and placed in command first of a newly reshaped Anti-Aircraft Corps and then of the whole Anti-Aircraft command. Our air defences were in a state of inadequacy which the European situation and the rate of growth of the Luftwaffe forced upon the Government's tardy attention. The first necessity was a sufficiency of fighter aircraft, a requirement supervised by the chief of Fighter Command, Air Marshal Sir Hugh (later Lord) Dowding [q.v.], alongside whose headquarters Brooke established his own and with whom he developed a warm rapport. Next was the need for a great increase in the number of searchlights and anti-aircraft guns—and the volunteers to man them. A huge expansion was under way, and it fell to Brooke to organize this, to ensure that manning kept pace with production and that organization and operational requirements matched the need of the hour. This was in harmony with RAF doctrine and pursued as expeditiously as the familiar constraints of finance and bureaucracy permitted. Brooke achieved much and laid foundations on which others successfully built for the test to come.

In August 1939 Brooke was made commander-in-chief, Southern Command, and nominated to command the II Corps of a British expeditionary force on mobilization. It was not long delayed. In September he moved with his largely untrained and ill-equipped corps to France, taking over a part of the line on the Franco-Belgian frontier and profiting by the unexpected pause before the Germans attacked in the west to get his corps into as good shape as conditions permitted. After much debate it had been agreed (plan 'D') that in case of German attack through Belgium and Holland—the repetition of Schlieffen's 'giant wheel' of 1914 which the Allies anticipated albeit at a mechanized rate—the Allied left wing, including the British Expeditionary Force under Gort, would advance into Belgium and prolong the French Maginot line defences northwards on the line of the Meuse and thence from Namur, Wavre, to Antwerp, meeting and following the river Dyle.

From the first Brooke disliked the concept of moving from prepared positions and meeting the German Army in open warfare for which he believed neither the Allied left wing's equipment nor its tactical expertise to be adequate. He had two further doubts. He knew the French well and had not only seen much of them in the war of 1914-18 but had grown up among them and loved them. He saw enough of them in 1939 now to have profound misgivings about their quality and morale. Secondly, although he deeply respected the courage and energetic character which Gort as a leader radiated throughout the army, Brooke did not believe he had the strategic vision required in a commander-in-chief. For his part Gort regarded Brooke as showing pessimism where duty demanded the reverse whether or not it was justified. The two men were too different to do justice to each other, and throughout the war after Dunkirk Gort felt that Brooke was unfair in his apparent determination to keep him from another field command. Others, including Alexander but not Montgomery (and both were protégés of Brooke) were disposed to feel with Gort on that issue. Brooke was sharp and ruthless in judgements: however, he had what he certainly believed was a sound nose for success.

When the German attack came in May 1940 Brooke's corps took part in the series of withdrawals forced on the BEF by the disintegration of the front in the French sector around Sedan and the rapid advance of the German spearheads. The surrender of the Belgian Army soon left his left wing in the air—a gap which he closed by a series of hazardous manœuvres of great ingenuity and boldness—while in the south the deep flank of the British Army had already been bypassed by the virtually unopposed westward advance of the German armoured forces. Gort, on his own initiative and (at the time) contrary to the instructions of the British Government, cancelled a joint counter-attack with the French which he rightly saw would be futile and withdrew his army and as many French troops as possible to Dunkirk whence the majority were safely embarked. On 29 May Brooke himself was recalled to England and after a few days' rest was sent to Cherbourg to make contact with General Weygand who had assumed the Sypreme Command from General Gamelin, and to build a new British Army in France on the foundations of the numerous line-of-communication troops between Normandy and the Loire.

Brooke soon saw that any plan to hold an Allied bridgehead in Brittany, as was the declared intention, was impracticable for lack of troops. He was also certain that French will to continue fighting was exhausted. He therefore urgently persuaded the British authorities to cancel plans for sending new formations to the Continent. Meanwhile he organized the evacuation of the many remaining troops from the various northern and western ports still available. On his second return to England on 19 June he reverted to his previous post at Southern Command. After a brief interval there, organizing his sector of the English coast against invasion, he became commander-in-chief, Home Forces.

Invasion was expected daily, and throughout the last two months of 1940 and the early part of 1941, counter-invasion measures and the reorganization and re-equipment of the army were pursued with the greatest energy. Brooke believed that invasion should meet light beach defences, then be dealt with by the strongest and most concentrated counter-attack by mobile troops which could be mounted. Meanwhile, however, the battle for air supremacy, the winning of which Hitler had laid down as a prerequisite for invasion, was won by the Royal Air Force. Operation 'Sea Lion'—the German invasion project—was postponed, and finally abandoned. In June 1941 the German Army invaded Russia. British isolation was over.

Thereafter it was clear that the function of the British Army would be to prepare for overseas operations, a task upon which Brooke had directed increasing emphasis through the early months of 1941. He was untiring in his visits and unsparing in his scrutiny of every part of the expanding army which would soon again, it became clear, be able to go over to the offensive. In December the Japanese attacked Pearl Harbor. The Axis Powers thereafter declared war on America. Japanese forces invaded British possessions or treaty states in Hong Kong and Malaya, and the war became global. In December 1941, also, Brooke assumed the appointment of chief of the imperial general staff in place of Dill who had been no match for Winston Churchill. Soon thereafter Brooke became, in addition, chairman of the chiefs of staff committee and effectively the principal strategic adviser to the War Cabinet as well as the professional head of the army.

The issue which dominated the early part of Brooke's tenure of office was to obtain agreement on an Allied strategy—co-ordinated between very disparate allies—one of which (the Soviet Union) was unconcealedly hostile and about whose ultimate intentions he had few illusions. The Red Army had been very nearly extinguished by the brilliance and rapidity of the initial German operations and great sacrifices by Britain were regarded as imperative to keep Russia combatant. These sacrifices took the form of huge quantities of British and American war *materiel*, and a series of hazardous convoys in northern waters, expensive in ships and casualties with no gratitude from the recipient, Stalin's sole concern being to procure the earliest possible offensive against Germany in the west to take the pressure off Russia—and later to ensure that no western Allied theatre of operations would be opened in the Balkans where the advance of Allied armies might interfere with long-term Soviet plans when the German tide ultimately ebbed.

With the United States—and in the early years of Brooke's chairmanship the United States had comparatively small forces engaged and the Americans were not yet the senior partners—the first issue was to agree over-all priorities: it was determined that the war against Germany would be treated as paramount. Next the question of theatres of engagement. Against Germany and Italy the Americans, with some reluctance, were persuaded to co-operate in a Mediterranean campaign, including landings in North Africa, linking up with the British Eighth Army which would take the offensive and advance westwards along the North African coast, and a subsequent invasion of Italy. This strategy inevitably postponed the cross-Channel invasion of France which the Americans regarded as the most expeditious route to Germany and to victory. They were persuaded that it could be successfully contemplated only after German strength had been drawn off by a Mediterranean campaign with consequent release of shipping resources, and after the further prosecution of an intensive strategic air offensive.

In the event this strategy was carried out. North Africda was cleared, Italy was invaded and made independent peace, the Anglo-American armies invaded France in June 1944, and Germany capitulated unconditionally eleven months later. Meanwhile the campaign against Japan was conducted by a successful defence of India followed by a counter-offensive in Burma; and by a maritime and 'island-hopping' Pacific strategy progressively reconquering territory taken by Japanese armies, culminating in the surrender of Japan in August 1945 after the dropping of two atomic bombs. All this was accompanied by a savage Russian war of attrition on Germany's eastern front which ultimately bled her white.

If the course of events appeared rational, if not inevitable, in retrospect, at the time they were highly debatable. 1942, Brooke's first year as CIGS, started with Allied fortunes at a low ebb. The key to strategy lay in shipping resources and their provision and protection were necessary in support of every existing or projected Anglo-American front. Because of their shortage offensive plans were inevitably delayed and preliminary steps had to be taken to lessen the strain on and threat to shipping without which even direct defence on land would be inadequate. Meanwhile the British Empire overseas, with the entry of Japan into the war, was increasingly menaced. Hong Kong and Singapore fell, the latter the greatest single blow to the British arms and prestige for centuries. India was directly threatened by land and sea, communications with Asia equally threatened by Japanese maritime concentration in the Indian Ocean. In North Africa there were serious and profoundly disappointing reverses. Promising Allied offensives would peter out and be turned by the ever-resourceful German command into what too easily appeared triumphs of German boldness and professionalism over British infirmity of purpose and uncertain grasp of the principles of war. In June Tobruk fell to Rommel's forces. In Russia the Germans advanced to the Volga and invaded the Caucasus. Throughout all this the amount of work Brooke got through astonished his staff, yet he always found time to think, and think ahead.

Ahead the tide would undoubtedly turn, since the material resources of the Western Allies and the geographic extent of Russia would, after the first shocks and reverses, lead to overstretch by the Axis Powers. In the summer of 1942 Brooke agreed with Churchill to certain changes in the high command in Egypt which brought Alexander and Montgomery to the direction of affairs in the desert and which immediately preceded the great victory of El Alamein in November. In North Africa in the same month took place the Allied landings under General Eisenhower which were to culminate in the surrender of the German forces in Africa, the invasion of Sicily and Italy, and Italian capitulation in 1943. In February 1943, the German Sixth Army surrendered at Stalingrad, the Germans began to extricate their army from the Caucasus and seek to shorten their front. The long withdrawal in the east began.

Brooke had himself been offered high command instead of Alexander. The temptation was sore but he believed, certainly with justice, that he could best serve his country and the

Allied cause as CIGS and that he must remain in Whitehall.

Meanwhile the battle of the Atlantic was still the overwhelming anxiety of the British Government and chiefs of staff. At the conference held with the Americans at Casablanca in February 1943 defeat of the German submarine offensive was agreed as the first Allied operational priority, followed by the invasion of Sicily, the clearance of the Mediterranean, and any step which might bring Turkey into the war. Yet another priority was to be the remorseless bombing of Germany, creating a new front in a third dimension.

The first six months of 1943 were probably the most critical in the battle of the Atlantic. By the second half of the year the menace had been largely mastered by a brilliant combination of maritime and aerial operations. By the end of the year everywhere the enemy was withdrawing. For Brooke the year was dominated by inter-Allied conferences. Casablanca, Washington in May, Quebec in August, Moscow in October, and Cairo followed by Teheran at the end of the year. At each of these hard talking and hard bargaining took place, and at each Brooke's business was to ensure that, from the British point of view, plans were realistic in scope and in timing, that resources matched aspirations, and—not least, and with increasing difficulty—that British strategic and military interests were safeguarded. In all this, and by universal consent, no military man at Churchill's elbow could have been more intelligent, more robust, more zealous, or more loyal.

In 1944 the Allied triumphs began which were to end in the total rout of those who had attacked them in 1939 and 1941. France was successfully invaded in June, and by September had been completely liberated. From that point the only serious setbacks were the remarkably (albeit temporarily) successful German offensive in the Ardennes in December 1944, and the Allied airborne operation at Arnhem. In May 1945 the German armed forces surrendered unconditionally, and in August so did those of Japan.

In his chairmanship of the chiefs of staff committee and in his dealings therein with his naval and RAF colleagues, Brooke combined personal charm and sufficient tact with the vigorous conviction that on no account should there be compromise on essentials unless as the result of genuine conviction. If the chiefs could not agree—and he spent long and patient hours seeking honest agreement on the many contentious issues which arose from simultaneous demands on scarce resources—then he was invariably sure that the matter could be resolved only at the political level and by the prime minister himself who should hear all the arguments in the case. He never wavered in this belief and practice, just as he never wavered in his certainty that no 'neutral' military chairman should preside over the chiefs of staff committee, and that the votes should be those and only those of the men personally and individually responsible for the Armed Services whose chiefs they were (although he supported the concept of a joint commander-in-chief of an operational theatre). Brooke's colleagues during this time as chairman were first Dudley Pound (who died in October 1943), then Andrew (Lord) Cunningham [qq.v.], first sea lords, and 'Peter' (later Lord) Portal, chief of the air staff; and the system worked the better for the fact that, sharp though professional disagreement often was, these men had deep personal affection for each other. They shared many tastes as well as qualities. Portal like Brooke was a dedicated ornithologist and like both Brooke and Cunningham, a keen and skilful fisherman.

Brooke's chief concerns throughout were to procure and maintain (but only at the appropriate price) sufficient Allied harmony to achieve the great design; to ensure that the British Army in its various war theatres—Far Eastern, North African, Italian, and Northwest European—was properly organized, equipped, reinforced, and, above all, commanded; to achieve consensus in the chiefs of staff committee between the three British Services about the right operational policy to follow, particularly over such matters as the appropriate application of air power; and, often above all, to contrive that the indispensable and magnificent energies of the prime minister were not misdirected towards unsound and erratic strategic schemes for which, at least in the view of his professional advisers, he had a pronounced and idiosyncratic penchant.

In his dealings with the War Cabinet, and with Churchill in particular, Brooke succeeded magnificently, although not without many sharp exchanges and a good deal of passing acrimony. He always said exactly what he thought, and, in the face of even the most unremitting determination by Churchill to hear something palatable rather than true, he stuck to his guns. Brooke, as chairman of the committee, was its spokesman on joint matters and it fell to him to enforce in stubborn argument the compulsion of strategic facts upon Churchill's restless genius without sacrifice of its astonishing impetus and fertility. Churchill never overruled the chiefs of staff, when united, on a profesional matter. He goaded them and girded at their constraints but he respected their robust integrity. Neither Churchill or Brooke could have done so much without the other—yet each found the other abrasive as well as stimulating and indispensable. That they were able to work together—Brooke wrote of the prime minister as someone whom he 'would not have missed working with for anything on earth', Churchill firmly rejected the idea that he ever contemplated replacing Brooke—was a tribute at once to Churchill's perspicacity as to Brooke's strength of mind, character, and physique. It was a high-spirited, high-tempered, exhausting, and astonishingly successful partnership. An indispensable figure in all this was 'Pug' Ismay [q.v.], chief staff officer to the minister of defence, capable as few have been of softening obduracy and interpreting strong men to each other.

Brooke was not an easy man—his brain moved too fast for him to suffer fools gladly and he was impatient, sometimes to a fault, with slower wits than his own. In his dealings with ministers, with colleagues and with subordinates alike he could appear intolerant. Junior officers were always struck by the considerable awe in which their seniors held the CIGS—the man, not just the office. Clearly they recognized 'Brookie' as the best soldier of them all, straight as a die, uncompromising and unambiguous and entirely devoid of pomposity or self-seeking. In his demanding and abrupt efficiency he knew when to scold, when to encourage, when to protect. He was admired, feared, and liked: perhaps in that order. He became, in particular, the conscience of the army: a dark, incisive, round-shouldered Irish eagle. To those who worked for him he was a tower of strength, a man whose own inner power radiated confidence. All were grateful he was where he was. Only to his diary, intended for the eyes of his wife alone, did he confide the irritations, anxieties, self-questionings, and uncertainties of a deeply sensitive mind and heart. To all others he was calm, energetic, and indomitable. Those who knew the man rather than just the soldier were to discover an almost unexpected gentleness within the undoubted authority. He had unfailing power to interest and amuse and he was intensely sympathetic to those with whom he had real affinity.

At first Brooke's rapidity of thought and speech, his abrupt, staccato, and very positive method of expression led the Americans to regard him with some reserve, in succession to the exceptionally popular and courteous Dill. Soon, however, they appreciated Brooke's worth for what it was—that of a first-class and utterly professional mind. Even the redoubtable Admiral King came to recognize that he was biting on granite. The British and American Combined Chiefs of Staff became a remarkable, indeed unique, example of Allied co-operation. With the Russians it was inevitably different. As the war drew closer to its obvious end Russian intransigence grew as their fears receded and their ambitions loomed more naked. Churchill and Brooke saw with unwilling clarity what President Roosevelt and the American chiefs of staff chose to ignore or treat as a distraction—the shape of post-war Europe and the new tyranny by which Allied victory would be succeeded.

In his second responsibility, the professional leadership of the British Army, Brooke's influence and effectiveness lay largely in his selection of commanders; he delegated to Sir Archibald Nye [q.v.], vice-chief, much of the running of the general staff in the War Office, concentrating only on major issues and on senior personalities. He trusted, and brought to high positions, Alexander, Montgomery, and Slim, amongst others. They, in turn, respected him as one whose opinion was almost invariably justified in the event and whose word, once given, was law.

After the war Brooke handed over office as soon as could be arranged, only ensuring that Montgomery did not appoint his own favourites. He had been promoted field-marshal in 1944. Now additional honours were conferred upon him. He became master gunner of St. James's Park in 1946, an exacting chancellor of Queen's University, Belfast, in 1949, lord lieutenant of the county of London and constable of the Tower in 1950. At the coronation of Queen Elizabeth II in 1953 he was nominated lord high constable of England and commander of the Parade. He was created Baron Alanbrooke, of Brookeborough, in September 1945 and Viscount Alanbrooke in January 1946. In 1946 too he received the freedom of Belfast and of London.

Alanbrooke had been appointed to the DSO and had received the bar and six mentions in dispatches in the war of 1914-18. Appointed KCB in 1940, he later received the grand cross of both the Bath (1942) and the Victorian Order (1953). In 1946 he was created KG and admitted to the Order of Merit. After giving up active service he became a director of the Midland Bank and numerous companies, engaged in a number of philanthropic activities, and pursued his beloved ornithology. From 1950 to 1954 he was president of the Zoological Society. He died 17 June 1963 at his Hampshire home, Ferney Close, Hartley Wintney, shortly before his eightieth birthday.

Alanbrooke was twice married: first, in 1914, to Jane Mary (died 1925), the daughter of Colonel John Mercyn Ashdall Carleton Richardson, of Rossfad in Fermanagh. They had a daughter and a son, the second viscount, who died without issue. The first Mrs Brooke died tragically after a car accident in which her husband was driving. In 1939 he married, secondly, Benita Blanche (died 1968), daughter of Sir Harold Pelly, fourth baronet of Gillingham in Dorset, and widow of Sir Thomas Evan Keith Lees, second baronet, of Lytchet Manor. There were born to them a daughter, who died as a result of a riding accident in 1961, and a son Victor, who became the third Viscount Alanbrooke in 1972.

Portraits of Alanbrooke by Sir Oswald Birley, Anthony Devas, and (Sir) James Gunn (1957) are held by the Royal Regiment, and an unfinished portrait by R. G. Eves is in the possession of the Honourable Artillery Company. There is also a small portrait, by R. G. Eves (1941), at the Staff College, Camberley. A stained-glass memorial window by Lawrence Lee was unveiled at the Royal Military Academy, Sandhurst, in 1965. There is a portrait chalk drawing by Juliet Pannett (1961-3) in the National Portrait Gallery.

[The Alanbrooke Papers in the Liddell Hart Centre, King's College, London; Arthur Bryant, *The Turn of the Tide*, 1957, and *Triumph in the West*, 1959, both of which include edited extracts from Alanbrooke's wartime diaries; *The Economist*, 23 February 1957; private information; personal knowledge.]   D. W. FRASER

BROWN, (ALFRED) ERNEST (1881-1962), politician, was born in Torquay 27 August 1881, the eldest son of William Henry Browne, fisherman, and his wife, Anna Badcock. His father was a prominent Baptist and he early joined with the zeal of a Spurgeon in his father's religious work, being helped in expressing deeply felt faith by a stentorian voice and a torrential eloquence. These assets he put at the disposal of the Liberal Party, becoming a much sought-after political platform orator at a time when loudspeakers had not yet been invented.

Brown was educated locally and became a clerk before in 1914 he joined the Sportsman's battalion and in 1916 was commissioned in the Somerset Light Infantry. He won the Military Medal as a private and the Military Cross and the Italian silver star for valour as an officer. After the war he made unsuccessful attempts in 1918 and 1922 to be elected as Liberal member for Salisbury and he failed again at Mitcham in February 1923. He got in for Rugby in November of the same year, but was defeated in 1924. Three years later he gained Leith for the Liberals, with the help of some Conservative votes, by a narrow majority. Dissatisfied with the attitude of his party towards the Labour Government of the day he joined Sir John (later Viscount) Simon

[q.v.] and Sir Robert Hutchison (later Lord Hutchison of Montrose) in 1931 and became a Liberal National. This move was approved by his constituents in Leith and he retained the seat until defeated at the general election of 1945.

Between 1931 and the end of the war he held a number of ministerial posts. In 1931-2 he was parliamentary secretary to the Ministry of Health and also chairman of the select committee on procedure. Next, he moved to the Mines Department where he threw himself with vigour into attempts to further export trade with the Continent. The Gresford mine disaster happened while he was in office and he was in his element speaking up for his department against its critics on that sombre occasion. As minister of labour, the post to which he was appointed in 1935, he had charge of the Unemployment Insurance (Agriculture) Act of 1936 which brought in nearly all workers in agriculture, horticulture, and forestry. Frequently attacked, he stoutly defended himself, declaring on one occasion that, if any Labour minister had done as much as he had to benefit the unemployed, he would have deserved three haloes round his head. He was proud when in 1937 the Trades Union Congress passed without a dissentient voice a vote of thanks to him for the part he had played in organizing the workers in the distributive trades. The growing need to prepare for war occupied much of his time and in 1939 the Ministry of National Service was added to his own.

When Churchill formed his Cabinet in May 1940 Brown became, an unusual figure, an English secretary of state for Scotland. While in that office he visited the Highlands, concerned himself with hill-sheep farming, and secured a subsidy for breeding ewes. Early in 1941 he took over the Ministry of Health, a transfer which made him responsible for evacuating people to safer areas and finding accommodation for workers at a period of severe housing shortage. In his nineteen months in that office he visited every region of the country and every bombed town and city. He claimed in the summer of 1941 that the policy of taking a million and a half women and children away from their homes and families and mixing them with strangers had proved an 80 per cent success; what had been done had kept nearly a million children away from the most dangerous areas and saved thousands of lives. This was the most testing and controversial period of his career and he came under fire in the House of Commons, but his strongest critics allowed that his devotion to duty and capacity for working long hours were beyond dispute. It was said of him that what he preached on Sundays in

Bloomsbury he sought to put into practice on Mondays in Whitehall. In November 1943 he became chancellor of the Duchy of Lancaster and then from May to July 1945 minister of aircraft production in Churchill's caretaker Government before the general election. During 1944 and the early part of 1945 he acted as chairman of the European committee of UNRRA.

Brown was president of the Baptist Union of Great Britain and Ireland in 1948-9 and a leader in the Baptist Men's Movement. He went as a delegate in 1948 to the Amsterdam assembly of the World Council of Churches and served from 1948 to 1954 as a member of the Central Committee, visiting India in 1952-3 for its meetings in Lucknow. In 1950-1 he toured Australia as guest of the Federal Government addressing religious meetings up and down the Commonwealth. For many years he was an officer of the Free Church Federal Council. A dedicated temperance worker, he energetically supported a miscellany of social causes. His youthful enthusiasm for rugby football was kept up long after he had ceased to play and he was a keen yachtsman. The large and wide-ranging library which he collected was a main source of his leisure. His later years were clouded by a seizure from which he never fully recovered his physical powers; but he fought against disability and gallantly kept as active as possible. The ebullience which made him a more than life-size figure in Parliament sometimes led to his being a target for affectionate amusement. Baldwin is said to have remarked on seeing him in a House of Commons call-box that he never knew Brown needed a telephone to speak to his constituents in Leith.

He was sworn of the Privy Council in 1935 and ten years later appointed CH. He married in 1907 Isabel Eva, daughter of Richard Bonstow Narracott, master plumber, of Torquay, whom he had first met when they were children at Sunday school. There were no children. He died in London 16 February 1962. The National Portrait Gallery has a working drawing of him by Sir David Low; and the Imperial War Museum a pencil drawing by William P. Roberts.

[*The Times, passim*; personal knowledge.]

A. P. RYAN

BROWN, OLIVER FRANK GUSTAVE (1885-1966), fine art dealer, was born at Dulwich 4 October 1885, the only son and elder child of Ernest George Brown, fine art dealer, and his wife, Elsie Taylor. Educated at St. Paul's School, he left late in 1902 when he went to Tours to learn French.

His father, who had been managing the

exhibitions at the Fine Art Society, Bond Street, for some twenty-five years, was an old friend of Lawrence B. Phillips, inventor and artist, whose sons, Wilfred and Cecil Phillips, had in 1902 opened the Leicester Galleries, Leicester Square—an unfashionable address. Ernest Brown boldly decided to join the new firm in 1903. Thereafter, it became known as Ernest Brown & Phillips.

In the autumn of 1903 Brown joined the Leicester Galleries and thenceforth devoted his life to them. In his father's lifetime Brown appeared to be dominated by his taste and interests. During this period the Leicester Galleries displayed the Mortimer Menpes collections of the prints of J. A. McN. Whistler [q.v.] and mounted exhibitions of works by Charles Conder [q.v.], J. F. Millet, William Holman Hunt [q.v.], Ford Madox Brown, and the illustrators Philip William ('Phil') May, (Edward) Gordon Craig, Arthur Rackham, Edmund Dulac, and 'the incomparable Max' Beerbohm [qq.v.].

Brown constantly visited art schools, observing developments and enjoying social occasions, especially at the Slade. However, in 1912, rheumatic fever seriously affected his heart and caused a deafness which was to burden him for the rest of his life and which barred him from enlistment in the forces during the war. After a year's absence, he returned to work in 1913 and became a partner in the firm in 1914 when his father became ill. His father died in 1915. During the war of 1914-18, when many younger artists were making their reputation, Brown and his partners actively supported them, adding new names to the Galleries' repertoire. Among them were Gaudier-Brzeska, (Sir) Jacob Epstein [q.v.], and three official war artists—C. R. W. Nevinson, Paul Nash, and Eric Kennington [qq.v.].

In 1918 Brown married Monica Mary (Mona), daughter of Dr Charles MacCormack, medical inspector of the Prisons Board of Ireland. They had two sons and one daughter, Nicholas, the eldest, joined the Leicester Galleries in 1938 but war service caused his absence until 1946, when he became a director. Roland, who was called to the bar in 1949, was in Tanzania as attorney-general from 1961 to 1965.

Between the wars, Brown and Cecil Phillips produced a series of important shows by foreign artists. These included the first 'one man' exhibition in England of Henri Matisse (1919), Camille Pissarro (1920), Picasso (1921), the whole of the sculpture of Degas (1923), Vincent Van Gogh (1923), Paul Gauguin (1924), Paul Cézanne (1925), P. A. Renoir (1926), and Marc Chagall (1935). Monumental displays of sculpture by Epstein, Rodin, and Henry Moore were also arranged. In 1937, anticipating for some twenty years the vogue for Victorian artists, and on the centenary of Queen Victoria's accession, Brown gathered a collection of works of Victorian artists and produced a large-scale exhibition with the title 'Victorian Life'.

Brown, a man of short stature with an infectious enthusiasm which he was able to communicate to an academic or a casual visitor, was interested in all the arts, except perhaps music. His main associates were painters, sculptors, and writers, and he was at his happiest in their company—be it at the old Café Royal, the pubs and haunts they frequented, the Alhambra, the 'old' Empire, or in the studios of Hampstead, Chelsea, or 'Fitzrovia'. His encouragement to newcomers was unstinting, and, however preoccupied he was, he always aimed to examine their work. Walter Sickert [q.v.], to whom he endeared himself and with whom he shared a love of music-hall, was amongst his earliest acquaintants. Many others followed, especially (Sir) William Nicholson, Paul Nash, Nevinson, (Sir) Osbert Sitwell [qq.v.], Ethelbert White, Henry Moore, and Reginald Wilenski.

Brown had an obsessional interest in mounting exhibitions, as many as three, and sometimes four, being held monthly. It is not surprising that the title of his autobiography is *Exhibition* (1968). His experience made him invaluable to the Arts Council in its earlier days. He was on the arts panel for two periods of three years, from January 1949 to December 1954. In 1960 he was appointed to the OBE.

His last visits to the Continent were in 1951 —to Paris to acquire paintings by Sickert from the heirs of André Gide, and to Rapallo to see Sir Max Beerbohm. A comprehensive exhibition of Beerbohm's work, 'Max in Retrospect', was mounted in 1952.

Having spent the greater part of his life in London, in 1960 Brown decided to live in Rye, of which he had many early memories. He visited London several times a week. Whilst in Rye he began to write his memoirs, which were only completed shortly before his death there 20 December 1966. The address given by Sir Kenneth (later Lord) Clark at a memorial service held 27 January 1967 at St. Martin-in-the-Fields was reprinted in *Exhibition* to which Brown's lifelong friend, Sir Alec Martin, contributed a foreword. In the possession of the family there are an oil painting of Oliver Brown standing in the Leicester Galleries by Bernard Dunstan (1957), a pencil drawing by William Roberts (1924), and a posthumous oil painting by Lawrence Toynbee (1967).

[*Exhibition, The Memoirs of Oliver Brown*, 1968; private information; personal knowledge.]   PATRICK L. PHILLIPS

BROWN, THOMAS GRAHAM (1882–1965), neurophysiologist and mountaineer, was born 27 March 1882 in Edinburgh, the eldest child of the three sons and one daughter of John James Graham Brown, sometime president of the Royal College of Physicians of Edinburgh, and his wife, Jane Pasley Hay Thorburn. He was educated at Edinburgh Academy and the university of Edinburgh, where he studied medicine. His fellow students appointed him president of the Royal Medical Society, he gained a B.Sc. 'summa cum laude' in 1903, and graduated with honours in medicine in 1906. Awarded a travelling scholarship, he went to Strasburg to work in Professor Ewald's laboratory and on his return in 1907 had determined to make physiology his career.

He was Muirhead demonstrator in physiology at Glasgow until 1910 when he was awarded a Carnegie fellowship to work on neurophysiology with (Sir) Charles Sherrington [q.v.] at Liverpool. During the busy and productive period which followed he published a series of papers on aspects of 'experimental epilepsy' in guinea-pigs, and a further series dealing with general aspects of the reflex activity of the central nervous system and with factors influencing that reflex activity, topics which were at that time the chief concern of Sherrington's laboratory. In 1912 he was awarded an MD and gold medal, and in 1914 a D.Sc.

In 1913 Graham Brown became a lecturer in experimental physiology at the university of Manchester, but left in 1915 to join the Royal Army Medical Corps with which, from 1916 onwards, he served on the Salonika front. Among those dreary scenes, he tells us, he diverted himself with imaginative day-dreams of direct routes on Alpine faces of which he had read but which he did not yet know, the faces of Mont Blanc on which he was later to make his reputation as a mountaineer.

His health suffered in Salonika and it was not until November 1919 that he was demobilized. In 1920 he was appointed professor of physiology in the university of Wales, a chair tenable at University College, Cardiff, and one which he occupied until his retirement. He was burdened, in the difficult post-war years, with the cares of building up his department; nevertheless he continued to research actively. He was a 'skilful and tireless experimenter', but one whose work was rather outside the main stream of advance in neurophysiology at that time; he became MRCP (Edinburgh) in 1921 and was elected FRS in 1927.

An independent and determined man, Graham Brown was not averse, when he thought it in the interest of his department, from crossing swords with the university and college authorities. He never married, and at

Cardiff he lived a rather solitary life, lodging in a hotel. After his retirement in 1947 he continued to occupy his old laboratory, a large room filled with stacks of books, periodicals, and papers, some of them physiological, most of them Alpine. Behind the stacks his camp bed and his belongings were invisible, and he himself (for he was short of stature) hardly to be seen until a visitor was close upon him.

In early middle life his attention moved more and more to mountaineering and to his dream of a new route on the Brenva face of Mont Blanc, which he first saw in 1926. In 1927, with F. S. Smythe [q.v.], he made his first route on the face, the Sentinelle route, and a year later, again with Smythe, climbed the more demanding Route Major; five years later his long obsession with the Brenva face culminated in the climbing of the Via della Pera, the last of the great routes described in his book *Brenva*, published in 1944; his companions now were the guides Alexander Graven and Adolf Aufdenblatten. The Brenva climbs were joint achievements, and Graham Brown's contribution probably lay chiefly in the imaginative conception, in the calm appraisal of risks, and in meticulous planning and timing. He may be regarded as the last representative of an earlier epoch when the amateur planned the expedition and guides supplied much of the technical expertise.

Graham Brown's mountaineering extended far beyond the Alps: to Alaska (Mt. Foraker), to the Himalayas (Nanda Devi), and to the Karakoram (Masherbrum); but his chief interest was Alpine, and in the thirties he was one of the few British mountaineers whose Alpine reputation was internationally recognized as outstanding.

In the series of his Alpine seasons one was remarkable by any standards: 1933. That year, in addition to eight major expeditions in other parts of the Alps, he climbed Mont Blanc by six separate routes: the Chamonix face, the Bionnassay ridge (descending by Mont Maudit and Mont Blanc du Tacul), the Brouillard ridge, the Innominata, Route Major, and the Pear (first ascent).

On his last visit to the Alps in 1952, in his seventieth year, he made his only ascent of the Matterhorn—by the Hörnli ridge, an expedition put off in earlier years when hopes of climbing the mountain by the more elegant Zmutt or Italian ridge were thwarted by weather.

From 1949 to 1953 Graham Brown was editor of the *Alpine Journal* and he retained into his seventies his keen interest in mountaineering. He was, however, physically less active now and turned to an old love, the sea. He bought and converted the former Cromer lifeboat

which took part in the Dunkirk evacuation, named her *Thekla*, and in her cruised widely in Scottish and Norwegian waters, one year going as far north as Tromsö.

As well as *Brenva* Graham Brown wrote numerous scholarly articles on mountaineering subjects and in 1957, jointly with Sir Gavin de Beer, published *The First Ascent of Mont Blanc*.

He returned to Edinburgh for the last years of life and died there 28 October 1965, leaving to the National Library of Scotland his rare and valuable library of Alpine books.

[Lord Adrian in *Biographical Memoirs of Fellows of the Royal Society*, vol. xii, 1966.]

CHARLES EVANS

BROWN, WILLIAM MICHAEL COURT (1918-1968), medical research worker, was born at Scotby near Carlisle 17 April 1918, the only son of James Court Brown, market gardener, and his wife, Jessie Buchanan Hayes. He was educated at Fettes College, Edinburgh, and St. Andrews University and soon showed that he had inherited his father's interest in chemistry. He graduated B.Sc. in 1939 and completed his medical degree three years later. An interest in radiotherapy led him to take the diploma of medical radiology a year after he qualified and to join the department of radiotherapy at the Edinburgh Royal Infirmary, under Professor Robert McWhirter. In 1950 he was elected a fellow of the Faculty of Radiologists and made deputy director of the department. By this time, however, he had developed an overriding interest in research; a career as a consultant radiotherapist no longer attracted him, and he resigned his clinical appointments to become a member of the scientific staff of the Medical Research Council in the department of medicine at the Postgraduate Medical School in London. In 1956 he was made director of the clinical effects of radiation research unit, which had been newly created by the Medical Research Council, and he and the group of people working with him moved to new laboratories in the Western General Hospital, Edinburgh, where he continued to work until his death.

Court Brown was one of the most productive medical research workers of his generation. Interested at first in the acute effects of radiation, he sought to find a biochemical explanation for the sickness and vomiting which was often a distressing complication of radiotherapy. This, however, was not a fruitful field and he soon began to study the long-term effects as well. Reports from the Atomic Bomb Casualty Commission provided evidence of an increased mortality from leukaemia among the survivors of the atomic bomb explosions at

Hiroshima and Nagasaki and Court Brown showed that a similar increase followed the use of X-rays for the treatment of ankylosing spondylitis. At that time most scientists thought that the production of leukaemia and other forms of cancer required exposure to large amounts of radiation and that there was a minimum dose below which serious effects were not produced. There was, however, no real evidence that this was so, and it became increasingly important to be sure, as first one nation and then another added to the radioactivity of the environment by exploding hydrogen bombs. At the request of the Medical Research Council, he and (Sir) Richard Doll tackled the problem as a matter of urgency. Information collected from 15,000 patients showed that the incidence of leukaemia was approximately proportional to the dose of radiation and a quantitative relationship was deduced which was used internationally as a basis for determining the acceptable levels of industrial and medical exposure.

Court Brown was not satisfied with this result, which depended on extrapolation from the effect of high doses, and he sought to confirm it by studying the effect of radiation on individual cells. Methods for displaying chromosomes were just being developed and he immediately introduced them into his unit, choosing as his colleague for this purpose Miss Patricia Jacobs, a young botanist from St. Andrews. From then on discoveries followed one another with astonishing rapidity, the most notable being that Klinefelter's syndrome was due to the presence of three sex chromosomes in each cell (X, X, and Y) instead of two (X and X, or X and Y). This discovery showed for the first time that human disease could be due to an abnormal complement of chromosomes. In 1960, when it became possible to examine chromosomes from small samples of human blood, the way was open for large scale surveys. Court Brown saw that it would be necessary to determine the incidence of chromosomal abnormalities both in the newborn and in the general adult population in order to assess the significance of the findings obtained in selected groups, such as the mentally retarded or disturbed, the congenitally handicapped, the infertile, or groups of people exposed to particular hazards. His work in this field established the study of human population cytogenetics on a firm basis and led to many discoveries, including the observation that a substantial proportion of recidivists imprisoned for senseless crimes had an XYY chromosomal constitution, that chromosomal abnormalities increased in incidence with age differently in men and women, and that abnormalities in the circulating blood cells could be used to measure the extent of past irradiation down to levels experienced in the course of occupational exposure. His principal findings were presented and discussed critically in the short monograph *Chromosome Studies on Adults* (1966), in his book *Human Population Cytogenetics* (North-Holland, 1967), and in a review in the *British Medical Bulletin* (xxv, no. 1, 1969). Much of the research which he initiated, however, was of a long-term nature and the main harvest remained to be reaped after his death, including, in particular, the results of automated chromosomal analysis, which began to be attempted in the United Kingdom as a result of his energy and imagination.

Court Brown saw medicine in the wider context of biology and was one of those rare people who could take an idea from one field and apply it in another. He had few interests outside science, and conversation with him was almost entirely limited to the subject of his current enthusiasm; but he was never dull. New ideas erupted continually and what is more unusual they frequently led to early action. He did not have the gift of suffering fools gladly, but was always ready to listen to criticism and, if presented with a good case, would set about building a new hypothesis on fresh foundations. He was unusually free from scientific jealousy and was delighted when his juniors were praised for work which had been his in origin. Outside the circle of his immediate colleagues he had a reputation for being difficult, but that was because he allowed nothing to stand in the way of what he believed was needed for research. Within the circle he inspired intense loyalty and affection.

He was appointed OBE in 1957 following his work on the leukaemogenic effects of radiation for the Medical Research Council's committee which produced the first white paper on the hazards to man of nuclear and allied radiation; and, in the following year, he was awarded (jointly) the Anderson-Berry prize of the Royal Society of Edinburgh for the same work. In 1965 he was elected FRCPE and in 1967 the university of Edinburgh conferred on him the title of honorary professor.

In 1946 Court Brown married Caroline, daughter of William Thom, of Edinburgh; they had a son and two daughters. He expected to die young and cannot have been surprised when he had a serious coronary thrombosis in early 1968. He returned to work at the first opportunity but soon had a recurrence and died in Edinburgh 16 December 1968.

[*The Times*, 27 December 1968; *British Medical Journal* and *Lancet*, 4 January 1969; private information; personal knowledge.]

RICHARD DOLL

BROWNE, SIR STEWART GORE- (1883-1967), soldier, and settler and politician in Northern Rhodesia (Zambia). [See GORE-BROWNE.]

BROWNE, WILLIAM ALEXANDER FRANCIS BALFOUR- (1874-1967), entomologist. [See BALFOUR-BROWNE.]

BROWNING, SIR FREDERICK ARTHUR MONTAGUE (1896-1965), soldier and courtier, was born in Brompton, London, 20 December 1896, the son of (Colonel) Frederick Henry Browning—then a general merchant, later of Flaxley Abbey, Gloucestershire, who was appointed CBE for work in War Office Intelligence in 1916-18—and his wife, Anne Alt. Browning went to (Sir) A. A. Somerville's house at Eton in 1910, and left in 1914 for the Royal Military College, Sandhurst; whence he arrived in France, as a second lieutenant in the 2nd battalion, the Grenadier Guards, on 19 October 1915. Courses and leave apart, he spent the rest of the war of 1914-18 with this élite unit, became a specialist in trench raids, and served successively as adjutant and as company commander before he came of age. He looked even younger than he was; hence his nickname, 'Boy'. For conspicuous courage, especially during the capture of Gauche Wood, near Gouzeaucourt, 1 December 1917, he was appointed to the DSO. He also received a French croix de guerre and was mentioned in dispatches. He became acting captain in 1918, captain in 1920, and major in 1928 on concluding four years as adjutant at Sandhurst, where he was known as the best-turned-out officer in the army and as a steely disciplinarian. From 1935 to 1939 he commanded his old battalion, mainly on ceremonial duties. In 1939-40 he held a succession of brigadier's appointments, commanding the Small Arms School, Netheravon, 128th Infantry brigade, and 24th Guards brigade group, a training formation. Late in 1940 he was chosen to head an experimental airborne formation, which early in 1941 became 1st Airborne division. He had been a bobsleigh rider, and a high hurdler of Olympic class (he had thrice been English champion and once represented England at the Olympic Games), so that the then still dangerous business of parachuting came to him easily. Having been so far strictly orthodox, he now had charge of an unconventional body. He managed to infuse it with the best elements of Guards panache and discipline while maintaining a spirit of enterprise, vindicated in several actions—such as the raids at the Tragino aqueduct (10-11 February 1941) and Bruneval (February 1942), and the invasions of Algeria and Sicily—in none of which he took combatant

part himself. Airborne troops felt under his leadership that they formed a new *corps d'élite*.

He was promoted lieutenant-general in January 1944 to command the newly created 1st Airborne Corps (composed of 1st and 6th Airborne divisions and the Special Air Service brigade), and supervised 6th Airborne division's critical landing on the left flank of the Normandy invasion of 5-6 June. The SAS troops were also committed to battle, with decisive local effect, during the next ten weeks. 1st Airborne division was repeatedly alerted for a drop, and then stood down, as developments in the tactical situation in France and Belgium imposed changes of plan.

Browning took a leading part in planning Operation 'Market Garden', which was designed by Field-Marshal Montgomery (later first Viscount Montgomery of Alamein) to secure bridges in order to facilitate the advance of the armies to the northward. This plan was hurriedly prepared in early September 1944 and executed on the 17th by the 1st Allied Airborne army, of which in August he had become deputy commander under the American General Lewis Brereton. Two American airborne divisions, the 82nd and the 101st, seized the bridges over four major water obstacles between Eindhoven and Nijmegen. Browning himself landed, with his Corps headquarters, just south of Nijmegen alongside the 82nd US division. 'I think', he had said on 10 September to Montgomery, his army group commander, 'we might be going a bridge too far.' The last four words of this comment were borrowed for the title of a film on the Arnhem operation which was released in 1977. 1st Airborne division, under Major-General R. E. Urquhart, landed close to Arnhem, still further north; elements of it reached the Rhine road bridge there, but could not hold it against superior German armoured forces, reports of the presence of which Browning had discounted. Bad weather hindered reinforcement and air supply, and signals were inadequate: neither Urquhart nor Browning was able to exercise any close control of the battle, and although only fifteen miles apart, they were unable to communicate directly with each other, because the Arnhem troops lacked the more powerful equipment essential for communications over more than three miles. The remnant of the division, about a quarter of its strength, was withdrawn overland southwards on 25-6 September.

Shortly thereafter Browning was transferred to the Far East as chief of staff to Admiral Lord Louis Mountbatten (later first Viscount Mountbatten of Burma), the supreme allied commander, whom he impressed as 'a man of very high principles, immense courage', and 'most loyal'. The two made a powerful combination. Browning's lack of staff training hardly affected his efficiency. It even helped him not to be hidebound, when he had to deal with naval, air-force, Chinese, French, American, Indian Army, and clandestine staffs as well as the home authorities. The still formidable Japanese effort ended in surrender on 14 August 1945. An awkward year followed, most of it spent by Browning at Singapore, while he wrestled under Mountbatten with demobilizing their hundreds of thousands of men and with satisfying as best they could the political aspirations of so many Asian peoples.

Browning was withdrawn late in 1946 to London, to the post of military secretary to the secretary of state for war. He resigned from the army in January 1948. He then became comptroller of the household of the newly married Princess Elizabeth and her husband, the Duke of Edinburgh. He set up their establishment at Clarence House with complete success. When Princess Elizabeth became Queen in 1952, Browning moved to Buckingham Palace as treasurer and comptroller to the duke. In this less independent post his health began to trouble him; and he retired in July 1959 to his house at Menabilly, beyond Fowey in Cornwall, where he died of heart disease on 14 March 1965. He had been appointed CB in 1943, KBE in 1946, and KCVO in 1953, and was advanced to GCVO on retirement.

He had married in 1932 the novelist (Dame) Daphne, second daughter of (Sir) Gerald du Maurier [q.v.], the actor-manager. They had a son and two daughters, one of whom married the son of the first Viscount Montgomery of Alamein. There are two portraits; one, by (Sir) Gerald Kelly (1925) is in the possession of the widow, and the other, of the early 1950s, by Denis Fildes, is in the Airborne Forces Museum, Browning Barracks, Aldershot.

[Army lists; Sir Frederick Ponsonby, *The Grenadier Guards in the Great War*, 3 vols., 1920; Christopher Hibbert, *The Battle of Arnhem*, 1962; Cornelius Ryan, *A Bridge too Far*, 1974; Major-General B. E. Urquhart, *Arnhem*, 1958; Brian Horrocks, *Corps Commander*, 1977; *The Times*, 15 March 1965; private information.]   M. R. D. FOOT

BRUCE, STANLEY MELBOURNE, VISCOUNT BRUCE OF MELBOURNE (1883–1967), Australian prime minister and diplomatist, was born in Melbourne 15 April 1883, the youngest of the four sons and one daughter of John Munro Bruce and his wife, Mary Ann Henderson, who both came from Ireland. His father was born in county Leitrim of an old Scottish family, and was schooled at Madras College,

St. Andrews, Scotland. After experience in Belfast he went to Melbourne at the age of nineteen and soon became the head of Paterson, Laing & Bruce, a softgoods firm with branches in Sydney and Queensland. He introduced golf to Australia in 1891. His son was to be the first Australian captain of the Royal and Ancient, at St. Andrews, Scotland.

Bruce was educated at Melbourne Grammar School, where he was captain of rowing, cricket, football, athletics, and of the school. The family firm suffered in the bank crash of 1893 and his father died in 1901. After a year in the warehouse, Bruce entered Trinity Hall, Cambridge, in 1903. He read law and rowed in the winning Cambridge crew of 1904. He coached college crews (and the Cambridge crew in 1911) until the war of 1914–18 and again in 1919. He wrote an excellent treatise, *Rowing, Notes on Coaching* (1936, written in 1919), which could serve as a guide to his Cabinet-formation. He was president of the Leander Club 1948–52.

Called to the bar by the Middle Temple in 1907, he practised in the equity jurisdiction, specializing in company law. At the age of twenty-three he became chairman of the London board of his firm. Early briefs took him, for evidence on commission, to Mexico and Colombia and introduced him to Latin America, to diplomacy, and to the Spanish language. These cases brought him the approval and friendship of Sir Edward (later Lord) Carson [q.v.]. He returned to Australia on business in 1911 and in 1913, at the age of thirty, married a Melbourne schooldays friend, Ethel (died 1967), daughter of Andrew Anderson. The marriage brought over fifty years of mutual happiness. His wife, quiet, elegant, and attractive, devoted herself to his career. Early in the war of 1914–18 he enlisted and served at Gallipoli with the Royal Fusiliers. Twice badly wounded he was invalided to England. He won an MC and croix de guerre *avec palme*.

Still on crutches Captain Bruce returned to Australia in 1917, after the death of his eldest brother, also a war casualty, to run the family firm. He pioneered in profit-sharing. Early in 1918, at a by-election, he won the seat of Flinders, close to Melbourne, then the federal capital. A reluctant politician, he intended soon to return to London and the bar. In 1919 the Nationalist Government of W. M. Hughes [q.v.] fought its second general election. While in London, in 1921, Hughes suddenly nominated Bruce as Australian delegate to the League of Nations. One of the few delegates who had fought in the front line, he made a deeply moving speech on disarmament. Hughes at once offered him the Cabinet post of Customs, an offer refused and quickly raised to one of the Treasury which Bruce, after a while, accepted.

On taking office Bruce at once shed all his business commitments. He soon presented his only budget which included a revolutionary reform of the Post Office, importing an expert from England as its head. Following the 'Chanak' crisis with Turkey late in 1922 and the narrow avoidance of renewed war, Hughes's Government lost heavily at a general election. To avoid a Labour Government the Nationalists coalesced with the new Country Party, led by a surgeon, (Sir) Earle Page [q.v.], which was strongly anti-Hughes and refused to co-operate with him. Bruce warned: 'If you get rid of the prime minister against his will he could wreck you tomorrow'—a prophecy fulfilled seven years later. Hughes, enigmatic and often devious, advised the governor-general to send for Bruce, but always maintained that he had been 'stabbed in the back'. Bruce and Page formed a Cabinet of six to five. Page became treasurer and Bruce—at thirty-nine the youngest in his Cabinet—prime minister (the first businessman to hold the post) and also minister for external affairs. His first speech as prime minister demanded a voice in the foreign policy of the British Empire. Almost at once he left for England for the 1923 Imperial Conference. While there he borrowed an Australian in the Foreign Office, (Sir) R. W. Allen Leeper, to advise how best to ensure full briefing on foreign affairs. Baldwin promised to accept an Australian liaison officer in the Foreign Office. Richard (later Lord) Casey was the first appointee and Bruce had him installed in the British Cabinet Secretariat under Sir Maurice (later Lord) Hankey [q.v.], himself half Australian. Forty years later Bruce claimed that from 1924, until he himself ceased to be high commissioner in London in 1945, 'Australia was invariably better informed on international affairs and had far more influence on the United Kingdom Government and its policy than all the rest of the Empire together'.

On his way home in 1923 Bruce went to Turkey, met Atatürk, and visited Gallipoli. Bruce attacked the MacDonald Government's decision to abandon the provision of the Singapore naval base, and he strengthened the depleted Australian navy with two cruisers built in Scotland. To apply science to industry in Australia he set up the Council for Scientific and Industrial Research. (For this he became a fellow of the Royal Society in 1944.) He also set up the Development and Migration Commission in 1926. He did much to harmonize Commonwealth and State relationships with a Financial Agreement, a Loan Council, and States Grants Commission. He set about linking the vast continent with more and better highways. One major concern was the extension of Empire trade and preference. At the 1923 conference, constantly advised and encouraged by Lord Milner [q.v.] he urged that Britain limit her imports of agricultural produce to what British and Dominions farmers could not supply. Empire preference won the day. Trade treaties were concluded between Britain, Canada, Australia, and New Zealand with guarantees of quality at special prices, preferential tariff duties, and reduction of freights. At home Bruce introduced a lost orderliness in the conduct of public business. He soon persuaded Sir (Cyril) Brudenell White, then chief of staff, to head the Commonwealth Public Service Board for five years. He fulfilled the pre-federation pledge to create a new national capital and by 1927 the Government had moved to Canberra which the Duke of York (later George VI) inaugurated. Bruce was appointed CH in the same year.

For his first four years Bruce seemed to dominate, firmly and politically, a difficult Parliament. Widely respected rather than popular he was untarnished by the political quarrels of the war years. The press found him punctilious and courteous. He won his first election, that of 1925, by a big majority. After the 1926 Imperial Conference, the main outcome of which was the Balfour Declaration, he paid his first official visit to the United States where he succeeded in having long talks with the normally silent President Coolidge.

But about 1927 his luck seemed to turn. He and Page were charged with extravagance and he ran into much industrial trouble. With his able attorney-general, (Sir) John Latham (later chief justice, q.v.), he tried to secure new arbitration powers for the Commonwealth, and to solve the vexed problem of the overlapping between States and Commonwealth. At the general election of 1928 there were large Labour gains. Rumbles of the depression were heard and there was continuing unrest on waterfronts and coalfields. In mid 1929, Bruce, reversing his former policy, proposed to hand over industrial powers to the States, to stop overlapping and duplication. Hughes, who had recommended Bruce as his successor, now led five other rebels to defeat the Government. Bruce invited Latham to take over but Latham declined. There was a dissolution and Bruce not only lost the election but his own blue-riband seat. Labour took over under James H. Scullin. Bruce in after years characteristically spoke of his own 'perfect preparedness to get thrown out of politics'. The morning after his fall he quietly returned to his desk at Paterson, Laing & Bruce which once again was facing crises. He was still only forty-six.

In 1930 and 1931 Bruce made world tours on business for his firm, but with Scullin's defeat in 1931 he easily regained his seat in absentia, and agreed to serve under J. A. Lyons [q.v.] as minister without portfolio. In 1932 he led the Australian delegation to the Ottawa conference and played a major role working on all the committees, to safeguard Australian economic interests, and wrestling with Baldwin and Chamberlain. The conference was a victory for the British Commonwealth as a whole and worked out the pattern of trade which was to survive for thirty years, until the development of the European Common Market. After a visit to President Hoover, Bruce went on to London with the status of resident minister. Experienced in finance, and with a personality which created confidence, he negotiated the conversion of nearly $300 million of Australian Government Loans in London which came due, and $73 million of new loans. This was against a background of great financial difficulties in Australia, but Bruce was patient and persuasive in his wrangles with the chancellor of the Exchequer, Chamberlain. He had long enjoyed great support from the governor of the Bank of England, M. C. (later Lord) Norman [q.v.]. In 1931 was published Bruce's *The Imperial Economic Situation*.

After a year as resident minister Bruce resigned from Cabinet and Parliament and began a record term of twelve years as high commissioner. From 1932 until its demise he regularly led the Australian delegation to the League of Nations. Early in 1933 he headed a mission to Germany, still economically weak, and he visited France twice-yearly—Paris, and Le Touquet or Monte Carlo. In 1934 he was rapporteur for a League of Nations committee on world agriculture, trade, and nutrition, which he believed was a key to world peace. (This work was in close co-operation with Frank McDougall, his economic adviser at the Imperial Conference and later his economic counsellor at Australia House, and with Sir John (later Lord) Boyd Orr [q.v.], the Scottish nutrition expert.) By 1935 he always had in mind the fear that Germany would draw Italy and Japan into alliance and he constantly strove to warn against this threat. He deplored the United States' non-adhesion to the League and warned that Great Britain's closest ally, France, could prove a broken reed. Bruce was president of the League Council at its London meeting during the time of the Rhineland crisis in 1936. He chaired the Montreux conference on the future of the vital 'Straits of Constantinople'. He was an admirable chairman, not least because of his fluent, and constantly repolished, French. In 1936 he played a role at the abdication crisis, notably because of his close association with both Baldwin and King Edward's private secretary Lord Hardinge [q.v.], and he clarified Baldwin's confused attitudes. This period has been described as the high point of Australian influence on British policy. From 1937 to 1939 his association with Chamberlain, a friendship born of fights in earlier years, was very close. Bruce was desperately worried about the pace of British rearmament, before and after the Munich crisis. He always believed that the year's respite gained at Munich was all-important. Early in 1939 he returned to Australia for consultation, and visited President Roosevelt on the way. During his return journey Lyons died suddenly and Page, prime minister for nineteen days, urged Bruce to return as prime minister, which would have proved politically impossible. Bruce continued on to London, to serve the new Menzies Government and later, after 1941 and Japan's entry into the war, the Labour Government of John Curtin [q.v.] with complete loyalty and immense energy, until the war ended. He promoted the Empire Air Training Scheme. His work was endless, despite his personal difficulties from clashes with Churchill as prime minister and from the fact that the consultation once given freely now had sometimes to be fought for, despite his membership from 1942 of the British War Cabinet. He remained patient and tactful and his uniquely wide range of contacts in London enabled him to make Australia's views known and respected. He devoted increasing time to international relations, keeping up bridges with Japan almost to the end, using his exceptional prestige with the Turks, from Atatürk onwards, to strengthen their neutrality and keep Germany out of the Middle East. He kept himself briefed on another important neutral buffer, Spain, through his friendship with Sir Samuel Hoare (later Viscount Templewood, q.v.). He carefully cultivated relations with the Russians. From 1941 he was Australian minister to the Netherlands Government in exile. He was convinced of the vital importance of Australian relations with the United States and never missed an opportunity of consultation with visiting Americans, from Harry Hopkins and Eisenhower down. He continually pressed, in London and Washington, for consideration of war aims and a new world organization to replace the League.

John Curtin died just as the war ended and his successor J. B. Chifley [q.v.] did not renew Bruce's appointment. The British Labour Government under Attlee at once offered him a seat in the House of Lords. He declined and returned to Australia, but accepted the offer two years later (1947) in order to have a forum on Australian questions and to promote his old dream of a World Food and Agriculture Organization. Returning to London Bruce became director of the London boards of Australian companies and of the P&O. Later he became, for ten years until he was seventy-four, chairman of the Finance Corporation for Industry. He presided over the commission in Washington which set up FAO and was chairman of the World Food Council for four years, but left it, as did Boyd Orr, disillusioned with its powerlessness. He spoke forcefully in the House of Lords on Commonwealth and international affairs, notably on the Suez crisis, until he feared that deafness was impeding him. Active to the end—and driving his own car in London traffic at over eighty years of age—he revisited Australia yearly as first chancellor of the Australian National University at Canberra. He died in his London flat 25 August 1967, surviving his wife by only five months. They had no children and his viscountcy lapsed. His funeral was private and by direction his ashes were scattered by the Royal Australian Air Force—after a service in Canberra—over the Australian Capital Territory.

Bruce was six feet tall, dark, with well-cut aquiline features. From his father he inherited a proud tradition. The Bruce clan motto 'Fuimus' guided him—not '"we're have-beens", but "we have been kings"'. With the new Bruce peerage he conformed to heraldry by adding 'fideles'; loyalty was ingrained in him. A well-trained and successful lawyer, a brave soldier, an experienced and common-sense businessman, he was equipped not with oratory but great clarity in speech and writing and a flawless Celtic memory. Not scholastic, the one art which he cultivated was drama and its techniques. In the best sense he was a splendid actor with a sense of occasion and gift of stage-management, well hidden by his casualness but evident in all his activities. He combined insistence on essentials with a capacity for taking infinite pains. He served Australia well for nearly seven years as prime minister, and perhaps even more successfully for twice as long as her first and best diplomatist. As each of his many roles ended he turned dutifully to the next. He was a man of high personal standards and Gallipoli had given him a deep faith. He was cool, imperturbable, good-tempered, and persuasive. Some found him cold or even arrogant. For long the legend lingered that he was 'an Englishman in Australia', but in England he was regarded as very much an Australian. He was in fact a Scottish-Irish blend, common among Australians. His whole career was devoted both to Australia and the strengthening of Anglo-Australian and British Commonwealth relations. He received honorary degrees from Cambridge, Oxford, St. Andrews, Glasgow, Edinburgh, Leeds, Toronto, and all the Australian universities of his time.

There is a portrait of him by W. B. McInnes

(1932) in King's Hall, Parliament House, Canberra.

[Cecil Edwards, *Bruce of Melbourne, Man of two Worlds*, 1965; Alfred Stirling, *Lord Bruce: the London Years*, 1974; Sir Robert Menzies in *Biographical Memoirs of Fellows of the Royal Society*, vol. xvi, 1970; private information; personal knowledge.]

ALFRED STIRLING

BRUCE LOCKHART, SIR ROBERT HAMILTON (1887-1970), diplomatist and writer. [See LOCKHART.]

BRUNT, SIR DAVID (1886-1965), meteorologist, was born 17 June 1886 at Staylittle, a remote village in mid Wales, the youngest of the five sons and four daughters of the Welsh-speaking family of John Brunt, farmworker, later coalminer, and his wife, Mary Jones. He was educated at Abertillery Intermediate (later County) School (1899-1904), and, with a scholarship, at the University College of Wales at Aberystwyth, from which he graduated in 1907 with first class honours in mathematics. He was then awarded a sizarship (later converted to a scholarship) at Trinity College, Cambridge. There he obtained first classes in parts i (1909) and ii (1910) in the mathematical tripos. Awarded the Isaac Newton studentship in 1911, he remained in Cambridge for research in astronomy under H. F. Newall [q.v.], but in 1913 he took a lectureship in the university of Birmingham. From 1914 to 1916 he was lecturer in mathematics at the Teachers' Training College, Caerleon.

Brunt was then commissioned in the Royal Engineers in the meteorological section, a wartime creation to meet the needs of the army in France, and in due course he became meteorologist at the Independent Air Force headquarters. The RE section had been formed around a nucleus of staff recruited from the civilian Meteorological Office and, when he was demobilized in 1919, Captain Brunt, as he had become, accepted a permanent post in that Office as superintendent of the Army Services Division, which in 1921 became part of the Air Ministry. At that time and for many years to come the expanding needs of aviation were to dominate meteorological services whereas the peacetime needs of the army were limited. Brunt was therefore able to find time to indulge his bent for scholarship and research, activities beyond the call of duty. He had published a few papers before the war and had had an early success with a textbook on mathematical statistics, *Combination of Observations* (1917), and now, turning his attention to his newly adopted science, he was soon publishing original contributions to meteorological theory. His published researches were never voluminous but always lucid, cogent, and significant. At the same time he was putting together his renowned textbook *Physical and Dynamical Meteorology*, a pioneer work first published in 1934, which became a standard text.

Brunt's duties in the Meteorological Office did, however, have one special feature of far-reaching importance. Experience in the war of the use of poisonous gases had shown the need for comprehensive research and in 1921 the Chemical Warfare Experimental Station was set up at Porton. Brunt became chairman of the Meteorological Sub-Committee of the Chemical Warfare (later Defence) Committee, an office which he held for the following twenty-one years. He created at Porton a meteorological group to study the problems of diffusion and turbulence about which almost nothing was known on the quantitative scientific plane. Although arising in the context of chemical warfare, the problems were fundamental to meteorology and the advances made founded the scientific reputations of two future heads of the Meteorological Office—(Sir) Nelson K. Johnson and (Sir) (Oliver) Graham Sutton—and put at least three others on their path to fellowships of the Royal Society. No comparable effort in meteorological research was initiated for another generation, not indeed until the great expansion after World War II, and Brunt's enterprise in seizing the unique opportunity offered by chemical warfare cannot be over-estimated.

The Meteorological Office of that time, pre-occupied with weather services and with no research programme, was not the ideal environment for a theoretician of Brunt's calibre, and his appointment in 1934, in succession to Sir Gilbert T. Walker [q.v.], to the chair of meteorology at Imperial College, was wholly advantageous. Expanded both before and after the 1939–45 war, mostly for postgraduate work, Brunt's department of meteorology earned great repute; his former students were later to be found in responsible positions all over the world.

Brunt was secretary of the Royal Society from 1948 to 1957, having been elected to a fellowship in 1939. He performed his duties with zest and distinction. He was knighted in 1949 and appointed KBE ten years later. He was president of the Royal Meteorological Society 1942–4 and of the Physical Society 1945–7. He became Sc.D. of Cambridge in 1940 and had honorary doctorates of Wales (1951) and London (1960). He was awarded a Royal medal of the Royal Society (1944), the Buchan prize (1933), and the Symons gold medal of the Royal Meteorological Society (1947). From 1952, when he retired from his chair at Imperial Col-

lege, he became chairman of the Electricity Supply Research Council of the Central Electricity Authority.

Smart in appearance and alert in manner, Brunt had an admitted liking for influence, not to say intrigue, a ready wit in ordinary conversation, but a direct and unequivocal approach to scientific discussion. Occasionally he seemed to take dislikes for little reason and to be less than fair in his judgements, but with his students and those who worked smoothly with him he was open and friendly and widely regarded with warm affection.

In 1915 he married Claudia Mary Elizabeth, an arts graduate of Aberystwyth, daughter of William Roberts, schoolmaster, of Nantyglo, Monmouthshire. It was a happy marriage but Brunt's last years were saddened by his wife's long illness and later by the death of their only child, an unmarried son. He himself died in Ashtead, Surrey, 5 February 1965.

[O. G. Sutton in *Biographical Memoirs of Fellows of the Royal Society*, vol. xi, 1965; personal knowledge.]   R. C. SUTCLIFFE

BUCHANAN. SIR JOHN SCOULAR (1883–1966), aeronautical engineer, was born at Cambuslang, Lanarkshire, 23 November 1883, son of Joseph Buchanan, a steel smelter, and his wife, Janet M. Scoular Hogg. They also had another son and a daughter who emigrated to Canada. He was educated at Allan Glen's School, and served a marine engineering apprenticeship at G. & J. Weir of Glasgow before going on to the Royal Technical College after winning a Whitworth exhibition in 1906. In 1908 he became a temporary civil servant, as an inspector of factories in the Newcastle district until 1914 when he joined the RNVR as a technical officer attached to the Royal Naval Air Service.

The merging under the Air Ministry of the Royal Flying Corps and RNAS in the Royal Air Force on 1 April 1918 brought together the former military and naval personnel. Buchanan was posted to the Royal Aircraft Establishment (RAE) at Farnborough which had been set up by the War Office in 1909 for aeronautical research, and which had inspired the design of most of the early war aircraft ordered by the War Office for the RFC, until the nascent British industry began to take over.

The armistice caused an immediate-break clause in all aircraft contracts and within six months reduced the number of RAF squadrons from ninety-six to twenty-three of which only ten were fully serviceable owing to drastic demobilization. (Sir) Winston Churchill, then war and air minister, informed the air staff that no war planning was necessary for ten years, an instruction which was extended for the same period in 1925, and cancelled only in 1929; and that the RAF budget would be kept down to £15 million.

At the end of the war Buchanan joined the Air Ministry Research and Development Department, but in the early 1920s little money was left for new government contracts, and the meagre funds were devoted to research, the building of the new RAF College at Cranwell, and mechanics' schools. Although the RAE continued its fundamental research and testing, analysing in the greatest detail all established aspects of flying, aviation had perforce to be left to private enthusiasm, and sporting contests had to be stimulated by the Royal Aero Club.

In December 1924 Buchanan presented to the Royal Aeronautical Society a paper analysing the light-aeroplane trials at Lympne, for aircraft fitted in 1923 with motor-cycle engines not exceeding 750 cc (followed in 1924 with 1,100 cc engines), at which he had been an official observer. Both trials were extraordinarily successful in stunt flying, but revealed clearly that such engine limitation was not really as practicable as had been hoped 'by the enthusiast in the back street' until engines of 60 hp appeared a few years later—for example in the Gypsy Moth.

In July 1926 Buchanan presented a similar paper on the Schneider Trophy seaplane race in Baltimore, USA, at which he was the Air Ministry observer, won by the American entrant at an average speed of 234 mph. Buchanan proved convincingly that although the British had bad luck, America had slipped ahead in high-speed flying in what had been a sporting event but had become a fiercely international contest increasingly used by Mussolini to vaunt his Italian Air Force. He pinpointed the need for an RAF team to be formed for high-speed flight; and concluded that body drag of United States planes had been improved by increasing efficiency and reducing size, by the use of wing radiators, and a better type of propeller.

The outcome was that an RAF high-speed flight was set up; increasing government money was devoted to the development of the design of the seaplanes, and a Rolls Royce engine was specially developed. The subsequent contests at Venice in 1927, Cowes in 1929, and again at Cowes in 1931 were won by Britain and the trophy finally secured for British possession.

In 1930 Buchanan became assistant director, research and development (aircraft), at the Air Ministry under the direct responsibility of Air Chief Marshal Hugh (later Lord) Dowding [q.v.], the air member for research and development for the Air Council, in common with similar permanent Civil Service officers for engines and instruments. These civil servants were almost autonomous in their powers for the detailed supervision and encouragement of the industry in meeting the progressive specifications of the air staff for new fighters, bombers, reconnaissance, and naval aircraft; and for their respective budget estimates and expenditure, which involved them in close contact both with the Treasury, and with the Service commands in the elimination of defects arising from Service experience and changing conditions. The 'professional' civilians had the advantage of permanence in their appointment, unlike the frequently shifted Services personnel; and, being civilians, suffered no disadvantage of rank and could speak frankly to their Service colleagues. In the Air Ministry both categories shared the same *esprit de corps*, *élan*, and mutual good will.

In 1936 Dowding moved on to create the new Fighter Command, and was succeeded by (Sir) Wilfrid R. Freeman [q.v.], who became air member for research and development, and later for 'development and production' as production planning became of greater importance no less to the civilian organization.

Throughout these years Buchanan was held in the highest regard by all he met, for his utmost integrity and unswerving impartiality. He was short in height, with a charming Scots accent, and a face like that of an ancient Greek philosopher. He was essentially conservative in disposition, and when faced with a new suggestion from the industry or foreign competition he would first ponder on the possible disadvantage it would have, rather than the potential benefits it might offer. He would often say reflectively, 'No I don't think I would do that. No I wouldn't agree with that', and so won himself a reputation for immense sagacity.

When the entire technical staff of the Air Ministry was transferred overnight to the new Ministry of Aircraft Production, on 10 May 1940, after sowing the seed for over five years of immense effort, to provide a harvest which was to be gathered by Lord Beaverbrook [q.v.], it was inevitable that the utter dissimilarity save in height between the new minister and the wee Scot would shroud the latter in some obscurity, despite his apparent rise in titular rank. However, Buchanan's inherent knowledge and wisdom were not lost by the industry which perhaps surreptitiously sought him out.

It was not until 1942, when Sir R. Stafford Cripps [q.v.] had become minister after J. T. C. Moore-Brabazon (later Lord Brabazon of Tara, q.v.) and J. J. (later Lord) Llewellin [q.v.] had reigned for short intervals, that Buchanan emerged from eclipse as assistant chief executive, and gave great personal service in introducing Cripps to the industry and the understanding of its aeronautical intricacies. For his services Buchanan was knighted in 1944, having been appointed CBE in 1934.

After serving some years on the council of the Royal Aeronautical Society Buchanan became president in 1949–50 and led the Society's deputation to the USA to meet its opposite number, the Institute of Aeronautical Sciences, for the first of what has become a biennial gathering alternately held in Britain and America, with valuable results.

From 1945, after retirement, he was appointed until 1948 a technical director of Short Bros. & Harland, flying-boat builders. From 1949 until 1960 he was chairman of the London and South-Eastern Regional Board for Industry, a government appointment.

In 1910 in Cathcart he married Helen, daughter of Walter Parker, a cotton operative. They had one son, Ian Scoular Buchanan, MD, MRCP. Buchanan died 5 April 1966 in Edgbaston, Birmingham.

There is a portrait in oils by Eastwood at the Royal Aeronautical Society (of which Buchanan was a fellow), 4 Hamilton Place, London, W.1.

[Private information; personal knowledge.]
G. P. Bulman

BURNELL, CHARLES DESBOROUGH (1876–1969), oarsman, was born at Notting Hill, London, 13 January 1876, the only child of George Edward Burnell, stockbroker, of Notting Hill, and his wife, Harriet Desborough. He was educated at Eton and Magdalen College, Oxford, later becoming senior partner in the stockbroking firm of Wise & Burnell.

A giant of a man, he showed exceptional promise as a schoolboy oarsman, winning the Ladies' Plate at Henley Royal Regatta in 1894, and on arrival at Oxford was a member of four consecutive winning crews in the Oxford/ Cambridge boat race from 1895 to 1898.

In 1896 conditions for the race were appalling and Oxford, having lost the toss, chose to tuck in behind Cambridge rather than attempt to race alongside them on the outside of the Hammersmith bend. Though they were at one time a length and a half behind, they overlapped at Barnes Bridge and then, forcing Cambridge out into the rougher water, won by two-fifths of a length, at that time the closest finish in the history of the race except for the 1877 dead heat.

Burnell won the Grand Challenge Cup each year from 1898 to 1901, rowing for his college in 1899 and for Leander on the other occasions. In all but the last of those four years he also won the Stewards' Challenge Cup, the premier prize for Coxless IVs. Still in Leander colours, he

won the Cork International VIIIs in 1902 and 1903. He was persuaded to come out of retirement to join the Leander VIII which represented Great Britain in the 1908 Olympic Regatta at Henley-on-Thames, beating Belgium in the final to win the gold medal—a feat equalled by his son, Richard, also at Henley, in the 1948 Olympics.

'Don' (as he was called by rowing men) used to say that in the fully forward position he rubbed the outside of his shoulders against the inside of his knees, an extraordinary illustration of how widely styles differ. 'Steve' Fairbairn [q.v.], the ultimate advocate of the unorthodox, once described Burnell as the best oarsman he had ever seen.

After World War I, in 1919 Burnell was elected a steward of the Royal Regatta, joining the committee of management the following year and umpiring at the Regatta for over forty years. He umpired the university boat race from 1927 to 1930 and was president of Leander and of the Henley Rowing Club, holding the latter office until his death.

Burnell joined the London Rifle Brigade as a territorial in 1894 and retired with the rank of major in 1913. Rejoining the army on the outbreak of war, as a captain, he commanded a company in France and was wounded at the second battle of Ypres and on other occasions. He commanded the 1st battalion of the regiment between 1917 and 1919, was twice mentioned in dispatches, and appointed to the DSO (1919) for services in France and Flanders. He played a major part in local government, initially as vice-chairman of Walton and Weybridge Urban District Council and for over thirty years as chairman of the Wokingham Rural District Council. He became a JP in 1934 and was deputy lieutenant of the county of Berkshire in 1936. He was appointed OBE in 1954 for services in Berkshire.

During World War II Burnell served as a major in the Upper Thames Patrol of the Home Guard.

Burnell married in 1903 Jessie Backhouse (died 1966), daughter of Dr Frederick Thomas Hulke. They had two sons and two daughters. One daughter, Mary Balding, was appointed MBE in 1978. One of Burnell's grandsons (Peter, the son of Richard) gained an Oxford blue in 1962. The family was only the fourth to have had a father, son, and grandson row in the university boat race, all coincidentally for Oxford.

A special parade was held in the Guildhall in 1964 'to mark the seventieth anniversary of his entry into the London Rifle Brigade and as a token of the universal esteem in which he is held'. Burnell died at Blewbury 3 October 1969.

[Private information; personal knowledge.]
Desmond Hill

BURNETT, DAME IVY COMPTON- (1884-1969), novelist. [See COMPTON-BURNETT.]

BURNEY, SIR [CHARLES] DENNISTOUN, second baronet (1888-1968), naval inventor, was born in Bermuda, 28 December 1888, the only son among the three children of (Admiral Sir) Cecil Burney [q.v.], later second in command of the Grand Fleet at Jutland, and his wife, Lucinda Marion, second daughter of George Richards Burnett, of London. He received a formal naval education, starting his training at the *Britannia* in 1903, and joining the battleship *Exmouth* as midshipman in early 1905.

He joined the destroyer *Afridi* in 1909, and soon afterwards, the *Crusader*, used for experimental work by the Anti-Submarine Committee, of which his father was the first president. Burney became very interested in the experiments then in progress for destroying this, then novel, craft by towing explosive charges. He was also quick to see the potential of another recent invention, the aeroplane, as a means of spotting submarines, and this sparked off his interest in aeronautics. In September 1911, he went on half pay so that he could continue his researches at the Bristol aviation works of Sir George White. His work there was interrupted by appointments to the battleship *Venerable* and the cruiser *Black Prince*, but in each ship he remained only long enough to apply for half pay and return to Bristol. In August 1912, he commenced a one-year gunnery course, and on its completion the Admiralty allowed him to continue his anti-submarine work and seaplane construction. At this time Burney made the far-reaching suggestion that aircraft fitted with wireless for hunting and attacking submarines should be carried by ships. For this purpose, he and F. S. Barnwell developed at Bristol a seaplane which the Admiralty afforded facilities for trials at Burney's expense, but the outbreak of war in 1914 halted this work. Seaplanes were indeed used during the war for tracking down submarines. They were fitted with hydrophones (a form of underwater microphone), which allowed them to listen for submerged submarines underway. However, these flimsy craft could be used only in calm weather.

When World War I broke out, Burney was given command of the destroyer *Velox*, but soon afterwards he joined the *Vernon*, the Portsmouth Torpedo School, where up to that time much of the navy's scientific research and development had taken place. At *Vernon*, he was primarily responsible for the development of the explosive paravane. He was able to make good use of his knowledge of aircraft design, as this device, towed astern, was essentially a small underwater aeroplane, consisting of a torpedo-shaped body fitted with fins and a rudder to keep it at any depth. He described its basic uses in a secret patent taken out in 1915. These included destroying submarines on impact, and cutting the moorings of underwater mines by means of serrated cutters attached to the nose, allowing the mines to be destroyed on the surface. Trials with this device started in the spring of 1915, and in June Burney was appointed to organize a new paravane department at *Vernon*. In the following year he took out another ten patents dealing with paravanes and associated gear, such as davits and towing cables. In 1920 the royal commission on awards to inventors gave Burney the main credit for this invention, but recommended that, as he had received some £350,000 for patent rights for its use by merchant vessels and abroad, no further payments should be made to him. He had received no payment for the navy's wartime use of this device, but he had been rewarded in the 1917 birthday honours by his appointment as CMG, an honour rarely given to a lieutenant. In 1920 Burney retired from the navy as a lieutenant-commander, and on reaching the age of forty, he was promoted on the retired list to commander. He succeeded his father in the baronetcy in 1929.

After the war, Burney took out a series of patents relating to precast concrete as a building material, and he joined Vickers Ltd. as a consultant. He realized that the new developments in aviation held both economic and political implications. Communications in the British Empire would be greatly improved by a comprehensive system of air travel: airships to operate the main trunk routes over the oceans, large flying boats for the Eastern routes, serving Egypt, India, and the Far East, feeding the trunk routes, and smaller land planes for shorter routes, feeding the flying boats. These ideas were set out in his *The World, the Air and the Future* (1929), and to further them he entered Parliament as a Unionist member for Uxbridge in 1922, and held his seat until 1929. Burney was keen to start his airship service with the German Zeppelins surrendered to Britain at the cessation of hostilities, but these were found to be too corroded. After lengthy negotiations with Vickers and the Government, Burney formed the Airship Guarantee Company, appointing (Sir) Barnes Wallis as chief designer in 1923, and soon thereafter Nevil Shute Norway [q.v.], who became a novelist, as chief calculator. An order for a new airship, the R.100, was placed with Burney's firm, but the Government decided that competition was healthy and put together its own design team at the Air Ministry (consisting mainly of members already discarded by Burney for his board on the advice of Barnes Wallis), to develop the R.101 at the Royal Airship Works at Cardington. This resulted in an unhealthy race between the two projects that eventually ended with the crashing of the R.101 on 5 October 1930 at Beauvais in France, killing 48 of the 54 people on board, including Lord Thomson [q.v.], the secretary of state for air who had instituted this project, and the design team. This destroyed the British rigid airship programme for all time. The R.100, which had made a successful acceptance flight to Canada and back in July–August 1930, on which both Burney and Nevil Shute Norway were present, was dismantled in 1931, its valuable remains crushed by a steam-roller.

In the late 1920s Burney designed a stream-lined rear-engined saloon car, the prototype of which is in the Montagu motor car museum at Beaulieu. Its novel features were the subject of a number of patents taken out in 1929–33, and included independent suspension and hydraulic brakes. It was supplied with either a six-cylinder Crossley or an eight-cylinder Beverley Barnes engine. The Prince of Wales bought one, but at £1,500 it was not an economic proposition and very few were sold. In 1933, this unconventional design was taken up by Crossley but they, too, could not make it a commercial success.

During the war of 1939–45 Burney was employed by the War Office on secret experimental work, the scope of which can be surmised by a large number of patents that began to appear in the early 1950s relating to, among other matters, aerial gliding bombs and marine torpedoes with gyroscopically con-trolled aerofoils, gun-fired rocket projectiles, and a non-recoil gun. After the war, he became interested in improving fishing trawlers. He designed a catamaran trawler, apparatus to facilitate trawling and landing the catch, an otter or 'porpoise' (a kind of paravane) incorporating sonar to detect fish shoals, and plants for freezing fish either on board or ashore. In all, Burney took out more than 100 patents during the period 1915 to 1962. Amongst these were six with Barnes Wallis and one with Wallis and Nevil Norway on aspects of airship design. In 1947, acting for British iron and steel interests, he secured a concession in Northern Rhodesia for iron and coal prospecting, and consequently maintained two homes: one in Rhodesia and the other in Bermuda.

Burney could be a difficult taskmaster and his relations with his colleagues were sometimes uneasy. One of them described him as 'a man of whom one could believe that no situation could be so awful as actually to daunt him'. In 1921 he married Gladys, the younger daughter of George Henry High, of Chicago. He died 11 November 1968 in Hamilton, Bermuda. His only son, Cecil Denniston Burney (born 1923), succeeded to the title.

[*The Times* and *Guardian*, 14 November 1968; Nevil Shute, *Slide Rule*, 1954; J. E. Morpurgo, *Barnes Wallis, A Biography*, 1972; patents literature; private information.]   W. D. HACKMAN

BURNHAM, fourth BARON (1890-1963), newspaper proprietor and soldier. [see LAWSON, EDWARD FREDERICK,]

C

CADOGAN, SIR ALEXANDER GEORGE MONTAGU (1884-1968), diplomatist, was born in London 24 November 1884, the seventh son of the fifth Earl Cadogan [q.v.] and the youngest of nine children by his first wife, Lady Beatrix Jane, daughter of the second Earl of Craven. Cadogan grew up in surroundings of what can only be called grandeur. Life alternated between Chelsea House at the corner of Cadogan Square, a residence termed by Harold Macmillan 'a kind of baronial castle', and a family estate of 11,000 acres near Bury St. Edmunds in Suffolk. As was not unusual, however, the grandeur was tempered by a strict routine and the cultivation of a high sense of obligation. Cadogan went, as seemed natural, to Eton, to the house of A. C. Benson [q.v.], an outstanding and versatile master in an outstanding Eton period. His all-round ability brought him to be captain of the Oppidans, president of the Eton Society ('Pop'), and an editor of the *Eton College Chronicle*. He also showed at Eton early signs of that satirical sense of humour which never left him nor ever descended into wounding sarcasm or bad taste. A. F. Scholfield, librarian of Cambridge University (1923-49), a contemporary of Cadogan, used to recall the pleasure with which the back row of sixth form awaited the next cartoon or caricature to be handed down from Cadogan further in front.

Like his next brother Edward, Cadogan went on to Balliol College, Oxford, where he read history, gaining, to his and other people's disappointment, second class honours (1906). The result was perhaps not surprising. The life led by undergraduates of Cadogan's background and attainments had the intellectually distinguished gaiety of that distinguished generation, so many of whom went bravely to their death in the war of 1914-18. The solitary grind required by scholarship was hardly to be expected.

Cadogan spent 1906 to 1908 studying languages for the competitive examinations for the Diplomatic Service. He headed the list in October 1908. In January 1909 he was posted as attaché to Constantinople. There he was granted an allowance for knowledge of Turkish which he is unlikely to have used later. In the summer of 1912, coinciding with a transfer back to London, he married Lady Theodosia Louisa Augusta Acheson (died 1977), daughter of the fourth earl of Gosford. She was a lady of highly individual character who exercised great influence in family matters without intrusion into official business, and the

marriage was extremely happy. They had one son and three daughters.

In April 1913, less than a year after his marriage, Cadogan was transferred to Vienna. He left again on 14 August 1914, two days after the British declaration of war on Austria-Hungary. There followed a period of nearly twenty years in the Foreign Office. During this period Cadogan went steadily up the promotion ladder, obtaining some experience of nearness to political life while private secretary in 1919-20 to Cecil (later Lord) Harmsworth, parliamentary secretary of state for foreign affairs. But his most important assignment was head of the League of Nations section for which the head of the Office, Sir Eyre Crowe [q.v.], recommended him as 'the best man in the Office'. He discharged this task not only with the great technical competence which was by now taken for granted, but with something more than a hope that the League itself and, above all, the pursuit of disarmament could lead to real and permanent results.

In this uphill, pioneering work there were periods of progress under Sir Austen Chamberlain (1924-9), and Arthur Henderson (1929-31) [qq.v.]. But the Japanese invasion of Manchuria in 1930, in response to which the League proved powerless, was an irretrievable setback. Cadogan derived renewed hope from the fresh approach initiated by Anthony Eden (later the Earl of Avon) who, as parliamentary under-secretary at the Foreign Office and with experience of work with Austen Chamberlain, gave new life to British presentation of policy. But once Hitler had assumed power in Germany in 1933, there was no further hope of reconciling German claims and French insistence on security (and Cadogan attached much weight to security). The task now seemed hopeless. Cadogan was appointed minister in Peking in January 1934 and confided to his diary his pleasure at 'going 11,000 miles away'.

The two years in China were pleasant, and he established a good relationship with Chiang Kai-Shek. But beneath this surface he experienced, as did his successors, the British Far Eastern dilemma of the time—how to preserve friendship with China and protect British interests there while keeping relationships with Japan as friendly as possible in the hope that Japanese military and political ambitions might have limits.

In 1936 Eden, now foreign secretary, appointed Cadogan a deputy under-secretary of state in the Foreign Office. On 1 January 1938 he succeeded Sir Robert (later Lord)

Vansittart [q.v.] as permanent under-secretary, a position which he held until 1946. His position was rendered difficult by the retention of his predecessor as 'chief diplomatic adviser', a position which carried no authority but was not interpreted by Vansittart as a sinecure. The two men were totally different in temperament, Vansittart seeing the worsening European situation with intellectual clarity, Cadogan seeing it without illusions but with a sensitive eye to what the country and its leaders would in fact be prepared to do.

In the trauma of Munich in September 1938 Cadogan took a characteristically middle position. Knowing the Anglo-French weakness in defence (notably the weakness of the French Air Force), he felt that nearly but not absolutely every effort should be made to reach a compromise with Hitler. But when at one moment it appeared that the British Government might positively encourage Hitler to march into Czechoslovakia, he wrote a strong minute urging the foreign secretary, Lord Halifax [q.v.], to try to dissuade Neville Chamberlain from going as far as that; Halifax was persuaded—and successful.

By the time war broke out in 1939 Cadogan enjoyed the complete confidence of Halifax, with whom he shared background and, to a great degree, views. When Eden returned to the Foreign Office in 1940, this confidence was continued, if in a somewhat different mode, and he soon acquired that of Churchill. There is little more to be said of Cadogan's wartime experiences in administration, policies, and performance in London or at inter-Allied conferences than to quote Professor Dilks: 'No one else occupied a position in the British Government comparable with Cadogan's in the years 1938 to 1950.' From July 1954 Cadogan received from Ernest Bevin [q.v.] and Attlee the same confidence accorded to him by Churchill. But in that year the Labour Government, after debating whether to appoint a politician or a diplomat as the first United Kingdom resident representative at United Nations headquarters in New York, appointed Cadogan. He seems himself to have wanted the embassy in Washington, but, given his unique knowledge of world affairs as a whole in contrast to his lack of specialized knowledge of the United States, the Government chose rightly. This was his final post. In it he displayed an authority, in all senses of the word, which maintained at a precarious time the standing of the United Kingdom in the world organization, and so proved a worthy culmination to his career.

Cadogan's diplomatic career had been remarkable in its 'parallelism'. He was in the Foreign Office for the duration of two world wars, and he took a direct part after each of these wars in the efforts to make international organization work. For all his quietly ironic humour, he was never a cynic and he believed that, despite human frailties and incompetences, it was better to strive after workable international institutions than to do nothing.

One cannot sum up Cadogan's professional quality better than in the words of Sir Llewellyn Woodward in his preface to *British Foreign Policy in the Second World War* (vol. i, 1970): 'Sir Alexander Cadogan had remarkable powers of judgement and lucid expression. His minutes on paper after paper deal with almost every aspect of foreign affairs. They stood out at the time, and are likely to stand out in retrospect, as models of open-mindedness and sound conclusion. They bear no signs of haste or half-finished reasoning even when the writer gives a warning that he needs more time for reflection. They often have a certain irony, never any rancour or prejudice. Only their modesty is delusive; the reader of these short notes written (they are very rarely typed) in a firm, quiet hand may not realize at once how great a mastery they show.'

This description of Cadogan's style does not cover one other side of his professional talent, his instinct for consulting or informing the right person in the right way at the right time. He was discriminatingly discreet rather than self-importantly secretive and this was invaluable to the diplomatic machine as a whole. In his relations with ministers he did not officiously push advice, but everybody knew that it was indispensable. In an age requiring innovation, change of style, and the concept of planning he might have been less happy; the period in which wartime diplomacy had to do its best with what it had rendered his techniques ideal.

Two years after Cadogan's retirement in 1950 Churchill appointed him chairman of the BBC. This was in one way surprising; he had no liking for radio and television and took a poor view of the journalistic profession. But he interpreted his job as that of presiding over policy and not interfering in daily administration. This suited his director-general, Sir Ian Jacob. During the long Suez crisis of 1956, several proposals were made for limiting the independence of the BBC, which was widely listened to in the Middle East. Cadogan aligned himself firmly with the BBC in resisting all such pressures. At the end of his term with the BBC in 1957 Cadogan retired completely from public life.

The record shows Cadogan as a man of outstanding professional skill and standards, of consistent calm, reticent about personal and family matters, and eschewing conventional affability. His naturally grave face, long in proportion to his height, made him at first sight a little forbidding unless one knew about the humorous corner to his mouth or provoked a sudden smile, reminiscent perhaps of young and gayer days. When younger he had been skilful at woodwork and oil painting; in later life he returned to the latter and added keenness for gardening and the open air. Throughout his life he played golf regularly, vehemently, and rather badly.

What was only known to very few was that he kept a diary. The publication of this diary in 1971 revealed a side of Cadogan which surprised the world. It showed him to have had sudden reactions of fury about the conduct of individuals and groups with whom he had to deal. He was careful not to give voice to these reactions or to let them develop into feuds (he maintained a magnanimous peace with Sir Horace Wilson, Neville Chamberlain's special adviser). But in the pre-war and wartime high-level tensions he had to let himself go somehow. The diary may have started as a convenience for reference; it undoubtedly became a safety valve.

Cadogan thus emerges as a man who, as part of his professional equipment, practised a truly prodigious self-control. Colleagues who worked close to him testified to a 'passion for work', in which some, but not all, found a trace of melancholy, alleviated in his last two years at the United Nations by an easing of the strains of recurring crisis. What all could agree is that he was, as one colleague put it, 'a most distinguished civil servant'—provided that the emphasis is laid on the 'distinguished'.

Cadogan died in London 9 July 1968. He had been appointed CB (1932), KCB (1941), CMG (1926), KCMG (1934), GCMG (1939); he was sworn of the Privy Council in 1946, admitted to the Order of Merit in 1951; and elected an honorary fellow of Balliol in 1950. Portraits by Duncan Grant and Frank Eastman are in the possession of the family.

[*The Diaries of Sir Alexander Cadogan, 1938-45*, ed. David Dilks, 1971; Harman Grisewood, *One Thing at a Time*, 1968; private information; personal knowledge.]

GORE-BOOTH

CAM, HELEN MAUD (1885-1968), historian, fourth of the nine children of the Revd William Herbert Cam and his wife, Katherine, daughter of George Erving Scott, was born at Abingdon 22 August 1885. Her early life was spent there and at Birchanger, Essex, where her father became rector when he retired from the headmastership of Roysse's Grammar School in Abingdon. She and three sisters were educated at home by their parents,

an education which she delightfully described in a broadcast 'Eating and drinking Greek' in 1964. With this grounding she won a scholarship to the Royal Holloway College in 1904 and took a first in history at London University (1907). In 1908 a fellowship in history took her for a year to Bryn Mawr College in the United States, where she worked on Anglo-Saxon and Frankish studies; the results were presented as a thesis for the MA degree at London University in 1909, and published in 1912 as *Local Government in Francia and England 768-1034*.

For three years she taught with great success at Cheltenham Ladies' College and in 1912 returned to Royal Holloway, first as assistant lecturer until 1919, then as staff lecturer. In 1921 she went to Girton College, Cambridge, where she became successively Pfeiffer research fellow (until 1926), lecturer in history for the college, and for the university from 1929; she was also director of studies in history and law, and vice-mistress from 1944. In 1948 she left one Cambridge for the other on appointment as the first Zemurray Radcliffe professor at Harvard. This chair she held for six years with much enjoyment, greatly appreciated by the academic world of Harvard and other centres of medieval study in the United States. Retirement in 1954 brought increased opportunity to research, write, and lecture as well as to contribute to historical studies as a member of councils of learned societies, especially as president of the International Commission for the History of Assemblies of Estates from 1949 to 1960—in which capacity she was described as 'a great abbess'. She was editing the records of the eyre of London 1321 for the Selden Society up to the time of her death, and a memoir by Professor S. F. C. Milsom, who completed the edition and saw the volumes through the press, gives a vivid picture of her at eighty-two, as enthralled by her subject as if she had been fifty years younger.

When Helen Cam began historical research the principal interests of the great teachers of the day and of the immediate past were constitutional, legal, and administrative. To Stubbs, Maitland, and Vinogradoff [qq.v.] she gave a lifetime's allegiance. With the exception of the papers 'Suitors and *Scabini*' read at Warsaw in 1933, her published work after 1912 was confined to English history, but was enriched by her continual contact with Continental scholars and their work.

After the publication in the *English Historical Review* (1916) of a surprising short article on 'The Legend of the Incendiary Birds', she produced an impressive series of articles and books on counties and boroughs based on the hundred rolls, with which her name will always be especially connected, on the *quo warranto* rolls, and on the records of the general eyres. Her appreciation of the importance of topography as a key to some local problems was illustrated by the sub-title of the first group of her collected papers, *Liberties and Communities in Medieval England: collected studies in administration and topography* (1944). Her feeling for the continuity of English institutions was brilliantly expounded in the John Coffin lecture of 1960, 'What of the middle ages is alive in England to-day?' Her second collection, *Law Finders and Law Makers in Medieval England* (1962), included her inaugural lecture at Harvard in 1948 when she reviewed the study of medieval history at the time, surveying also the contribution of Harvard's first professor of medieval history, Henry Adams, and the graduate school he founded, with tributes to and reminiscences of the historians who had been her teachers, guides, and colleagues.

As a teacher she herself gave her pupils contact with a great range of learning and an interest in them as marked as in the subjects of her own studies. As one said, 'Judgement might be severe but it was impersonal: no-one was more ready to respect the personalities of students'. To those past their undergraduate days and to those who consulted her she gave unstinted help in their fields of research.

Nor were her interests and sympathies solely academic. A lecture to which she went as a student, impelled thereto by a tutor rather than of her own volition, converted her to the cause of women's suffrage though not to its militancy. She was also much concerned with the YWCA, and the provision of education for women who had to start earning their living after very limited schooling, and she gave every possible help to the residential centre which later became Hillcroft College, in conjunction with her contemporary at Royal Holloway, Miss Fanny Street. For some years she contributed a monthly page on novels, plays, and questions of the day to *The Torch*, a paper for those beginning to make increasing use of the free libraries. She was also as active member of the Cambridge Labour Party and Trades Council.

Historical novels she had always greatly enjoyed, considering them a 'standing reminder that history is about human beings', and lectures on them resulted in the pamphlet *Historical Novels* (1961). Nothing roused her wrath more than the attempted whitewashing of certain historical characters, especially Richard III. Among her other recreations was watercolour sketching in which she had considerable talent. She is described in her thirties, as 'of serious and matronly mien', and during vacations spent at Oxford (whither, to Keble

Road, her parents retired in 1926) she was to be seen in the Bodleian, 'sitting squarely by a window' in one of the carrels in Duke Humfrey's library—'sharp eyes, sharp nose, heavy eyebrows—intent on her books, looking like a broody hen in a nesting box, placid and comfortable, but ready to peck if the occasion demanded. Some of her best articles must have been hatched there.'

She was a woman who by her learning, integrity, and warmth of personality contributed much to any group of which she was a member. Her importance as a historian was recognized by election to the British Academy in 1945, in which year she was the first woman to deliver the Raleigh lecture of the Academy. She also received honorary doctorates at Smith College, Mount Holyoke College, the university of North Carolina and, in 1962, Oxford; she became an honorary fellow of Somerville College in 1964. She was one of the first women to join the council of the Selden Society, of which she was vice-president in 1962-5. In 1958 she became a vice-president of the Royal Historical Society, and in 1963 honorary vice-president; she was also corresponding fellow of the Medieval Academy of America and a fellow of the American Academy of Arts and Sciences. Her work for the International Commission of Assemblies and Estates was commemorated by the *Album Helen Maud Cam* (1960), two volumes presented to her for her seventy-fifth birthday, containing essays by scholars of many nations, a bibliography of her works to 1957, and an appreciation by an American colleague, Professor Caroline Robbins. Her public as well as her historical services were recognized by her appointment as CBE in 1957. She died in hospital at Orpington, Kent, 9 February 1968. A pencil drawing of her by Malcolm Osborne, 1948, hangs in a corridor at Girton College.

[*The Times*, 12 February 1968; letters and papers of Helen Cam in the possession of the mistress and fellows of Girton College, Cambridge; C. R. Cheney in *Proceedings of the British Academy*, vol. lv, 1969 (which contains an excellent photograph of her, as also does *Album Helen Maud Cam*); Janet Sondheimer in the *Girton Review*, centenary number 1969; memorial minute by Giles Constable adopted by the Faculty of Arts and Sciences, Harvard University, in *Harvard University Gazette*, December 1968; private information; personal knowledge.]

KATHLEEN MAJOR

CAMERON, Sir (GORDON) ROY (1899-1966), pathologist, was born at Echuca, Victoria, Australia, 30 June 1899. His paternal grandparents, who came of farmer stock in Dyce, Aberdeenshire, emigrated to Australia in the early 1870s. Their son George, the eldest of their eleven children, took part with his father in opening up the Mallee area in northern Victoria, later became a Methodist preacher, and married Emily Pascoe, who had herself emigrated from Cornwall with her parents at the age of eleven. Cameron was their elder child; his younger brother died in infancy; and because his father, like most Methodist preachers, went on circuit, Cameron was mainly brought up by the women of the family.

All his early schooling was in the state schools of the villages—Mitiamo, Lancefield, Dunkeld, and finally Kyneton, where he lived from 1911 to 1917, and was able to read extensively and to listen to music. From 1913 to 1917 he did his compulsory military training, and reached the rank of second-lieutenant. The teaching at Kyneton was none too good, but he had a good deal of encouragement from a few teachers, and finally obtained a senior scholarship and a major scholarship at Queen's College, Melbourne University, which he joined in February 1916.

He had already decided on medicine; but it was not easy to make up for his ignorance of physics and chemistry, and he did only fairly well until his fourth year; in 1922 he graduated with second class honours. After first hearing Sir Harry Allen lecture on pathology he had decided on this as his subject, and after a year as resident medical officer at Melbourne Hospital, during which he did some research work in the pathology of pancreatitis, he was appointed Stewart lecturer in pathology in the university department, where he pioneered experimental work by setting up a small animal house and a colony of guinea-pigs.

Early in 1925 he was invited by C. H. Kellaway [q.v.] to succeed (Sir) F. M. Burnet as his first assistant and deputy director of Walter and Eliza Hall Institute in Melbourne. Two years later, encouraged by others, he left on leave to work under Ludwig Aschoff in Freiburg im Breisgau and later under A. E. Boycott [q.v.] in University College Hospital medical school, London. It was intended that he should in time return to Melbourne to succeed Allen as professor; but when his time was up, he found, to his great consternation, that he did not wish to return. Encouraged by his father, he went to live with Boycott's chief technician, Fred Crew, who with his wife Alice made him welcome; indeed they almost gave up their private lives, apart from a few short intervals, to look after him until he died.

Cameron became Graham scholar in pathology in 1928 and was Beit fellow from 1930 to 1933; after a rather unhappy year as

pathologist at Queen Mary's Hospital, Stratford, London, he returned to University College medical school as reader in morbid anatomy (1934). In 1937, after Boycott's retirement, he was appointed professor, and in 1946 director of the Graham department, both of which posts he held until he retired in 1964. In the war years 1939–45 he was seconded to the Chemical Defence Experimental Station at Porton.

Over the years he received many honours and was always in demand for more and more work. From 1935 to 1955 he was an assistant editor of the *Journal of Pathology and Bacteriology* under Matthew Stewart. In 1941 he became an honorary FRCP. He was elected FRS in 1946, served on its council in 1948–9, and was one of its Royal medallists in 1960. He became honorary LLD of Edinburgh in 1956 and of Melbourne in 1962. He received the gold medal of the Graham Research Fund and the Crawford Mollison research prize of the British Medical Association in Australia, and was honorary member of many pathological societies. From 1947 to 1956 he was a member of the Agricultural Research Council and from 1952 to 1956 a member of the Medical Research Council. He was knighted in 1957. But the honour which gave him the greatest pleasure was undoubtedly his unanimous election in 1962 to be founder-president of the College of Pathologists.

Cameron's research work covered a very wide field, but he is most likely to be remembered for his work on the pathology of liver disease and of oedema of the lung, and for his willingness to encourage those who could bring biochemical concepts into pathology. By working out the pathological changes in the liver associated with poisoning by pure substances he was able to provide others with tools that would produce well-defined limited lesions in the liver, and thus to show how biliary obstruction, liver necrosis, vascular changes, and poisons affected it. Though no biochemist himself, he had little difficulty in understanding biochemical concepts, and gave every help to those who wished to introduce them. Similar comment applies to his work on pulmonary oedema; he introduced new methods of producing it, and made a number of valuable suggestions to account for its development and for the remarkable species-specific response to some lung irritants. He was in the main an experimental pathologist, according to some not so expert, indeed not so interested, in morbid anatomy. In practice, however, he used anything that came to hand—casual findings at necropsy, the results of surgery, intended or unintended, accidental experimental results, morbid anatomy—to stimulate experimental inquiry.

Cameron was universally regarded as an entirely honest, kindly man, whose judgements were invariably based on wide learning, vast experience, and natural impartiality. He had a sparkling sense of humour, and could tell a tale against himself, or about other pathologists, or about human foibles, with the greatest delight in human absurdity. Moreover, he had interests outside science: he loved music, was a good pianist, and a goodish mathematician; he had a profound knowledge of the history of the Renaissance popes, and of the Renaissance in Italy—a country he greatly loved. From his early years he liked walking, even mountaineering; he had little personal interest in games, though later on the Crews got him interested in watching football. Most subjects interested him, except perhaps politics, in which he remained a benevolent Conservative, with considerable attachment to the idea of the British Empire. This conservatism he brought into his work, mainly by working with the simplest available techniques, and refusing, sometimes perhaps unreasonably, to buy apparatus by which newer techniques might have been introduced. The vast amount that he did with these simple means is perhaps his best justification.

In his early days Cameron was a somewhat dull lecturer, and his papers were rather heavy; later he became a brilliant lecturer, whose papers were models of clarity and conciseness. He was the author of several books, notably *The Pathology of the Cell* (1952). He carried on a vast correspondence with former students and colleagues; some people said that 'all Cameron's geese were swans', but as one of them said 'he expected you to become a swan and, to your amazement, under his tutelage you showed signs of becoming one'.

Cameron, who never married, died in London 7 October 1966.

There is no portrait, but the Royal College of Pathologists possesses a fine bust by R. B. Claughton, a copy of which is in University College Hospital medical school.

[C. L. Oakley in *Biographical Memoirs of Fellows of the Royal Society*, vol. xiv, 1968; private information; personal knowledge.]

C. L. OAKLEY

CAMM, SIR SYDNEY (1893-1966), aircraft designer, was born in Windsor 5 August 1893, the eldest of twelve children of Frederick Camm, journeyman carpenter and joiner, and his wife, Mary Smith. He attended the Royal Free School at Windsor, where his interest in aviation was awakened at an early age through the construction of elementary flying models. Soon after he left school Camm became an apprentice woodworker, helped to set up the Windsor Model Aeroplane Club, and became its secretary at the age of nineteen. Stimulated by his efforts, the club rapidly progressed from models to the design and building of a man-carrying glider which flew as early as December 1912. It was followed by a powered aircraft project, and Camm's leading role in these activities was cut short only by the outbreak of war in 1914.

With his knowledge of practical woodworking and theoretical aerodynamics he had no difficulty in joining the Martinsyde aeroplane company at Brooklands. There he remained throughout the war, rising through the practical working levels to first minor and then major design tasks on Martinsyde aircraft. It was during this period that he learnt his profession, taking every opportunity to study and write articles about all available types of British and even captured enemy aircraft. Thus, when he was elected an associate fellow of the Royal Aeronautical Society in 1918, he was able to describe himself as a technical journalist.

After the war, Martinsyde declined from lack of orders and closed in 1921, but G. H. Handasyde, continuing as an independent designer, took on Camm as his assistant, and together they designed an advanced glider. R. P. Raynham, the Martinsyde test pilot, took Camm with him as mechanic when he competed in the first King's Cup race in 1922 with a Martinsyde F4.

In the same year Raynham joined the Hawker Engineering Company at Kingston, and when Camm's work with Handasyde finished, in 1923, he followed his friend into this famous firm, in which he was to work with the greatest distinction for the next forty-three years. He was already an expert in detail design and practical workmanship, and much preoccupied with the aeronautical virtues of simplicity, symmetry, and lightness. He joined as a senior draughtsman; such was his ability that he became chief designer only two years later. At this period aircraft could still be designed and built cheaply and quickly, and Camm was charged with the supervision of the design of a light biplane, the Cygnet. This remarkable little two-seater won many light-aircraft competitions in 1925 and 1926, and clearly showed his gifts for imaginative conception, excellence of detail, and careful weight control. However, the market was not at this time favourable to light aircraft, and it never went into large-scale production. Instead, with the background provided by the Sopwith range of aircraft which had founded the fortunes of the Hawker Company, Camm was directed, from 1925 onwards, to the development of future military types.

Progressing by the stages possible at that time he produced two biplane aircraft, the Heron in 1925, which used metal for the main structure, and the Hornbill in 1926, the basic design from which his future bomber and fighter types were developed.

In 1928 the emergence of the Hawker Hart day bomber with a Rolls-Royce Kestrel engine produced the first complete picture of a characteristically Camm aircraft. It was notable for grace, balance of design, and for the complete integration of the engine within the aircraft, thus contrasting strongly with most contemporary aeroplanes, whose engines often appeared to have been added as an afterthought. The Hart was adopted by the Royal Air Force, and with its variants the Hind, Audax, Osprey, and Nimrod was also sold to a large number of foreign air forces, so that finally some 3,000 were built. A single-seater redesign of the Hart produced a high performance fighter named the Fury, which was similarly sold all over the world, and is widely held to have been the most beautiful biplane ever flown. The Hart and Fury put the Hawker Company back on the map.

The Supermarine and Gloster companies were engaged in the monoplanes associated with the Schneider Trophy, but Hawkers had not been drawn in. Camm, and Hawkers, decided, however, that the firm's future lay in the construction of fast fighter aircraft. By 1933 Camm realized that he could go no further with biplane designs, and he began the study of a fighter monoplane to be built round the new Rolls-Royce Merlin. In 1934 the Air Ministry issued specification F. 36/34 for a monoplane eight-gun fighter, and the new Hawker design was thereafter produced to this specification, in close co-operation with Air Ministry operational requirements branch. It was named the Hurricane.

The story of the Hurricane is well known. It was the first monoplane fighter supplied to the Royal Air Force, 100 miles an hour faster than anything previously flown, and it went into production under the shadow of impending war. This urgency caused Camm to allow some compromises in design which he would not otherwise have permitted, but the aircraft was fast, manœuvrable, and sturdy. In the event it was in full production by the outbreak of war in 1939, formed the major part of the strength of Fighter Command during the Battle of Britain, and so earned the major credit in the winning of that decisive battle. Hurricanes also fought in Europe, Africa, Burma, and over the oceans, first armed with eight machine-guns, later carrying bombs, rockets, and cannons. Some thousands were supplied to Russia, and a total of some 14,500 were finally built. As for the pilots of Fighter Command, 1940 provided Camm's finest hour. But by the outbreak of war he was already well into the design of the Hurricane's successor, the Typhoon. When the Normandy invasion was launched in 1944 Typhoon fighter-bombers were present in large quantities, and Camm, driving himself and his team relentlessly through years of continual and intensive work, was producing the Tempest. This very powerful fighter, derived from the Typhoon and itself the parent of the Sea Fury, achieved the ultimate in the exploitation of propeller-driven monoplanes, and indeed the Tempest and Sea Fury were so fast and robust that they served on until the fifties, well into the jet era.

The advent of the jet engine in 1942 was a powerful stimulant to a designer with Camm's special interests, and before the war was over his team was directed on to studies using the new engine. Others were ahead of him, and due to the post-war relaxation his new jet-driven design was not needed until 1948, when the navy ordered it for carrier work and named it the Sea Hawk. This too was a successful project for peacetime military sales, 500 being built and supplied to a number of navies. The well-marked line of his design progress was continued with its successor, the Hunter. In this aircraft Camm pushed performance to the limit possible with subsonic aircraft, and once more he brought forth an outstanding aircraft, carrying all the distinctive marks of his design genius. Two thousand were built and sold, in 1953 it gained the world air speed record, and the Hunter was still in operational service twenty years after its first flight.

Camm's next logical step was to design a supersonic fighter, and this he did in a number of variants, but due to chance and government policy none were built, a denial which he resented greatly. Instead, he embarked on studies with Bristol Siddeley Engines of a possible combination of a special engine and air-frame, which would give the flying characteristics of a high-performance fighter together with the landing and take off of a helicopter. This concept, VTOL (vertical take-off and landing) permitted a number of different solutions, but the gifted Bristol Siddeley engine designer, Dr Hooker, favoured a single engine with vectored thrust, giving the ability to swivel the thrust of the engine downwards under the control of the pilot. Such a system required a completely new control system based on reaction jets, for that phase of flight in which the aircraft had insufficient speed for normal control. It is a proof of Camm's persistent character in design that though revolutionary in concept the resulting fighter looked much like the others of its line. It was, however, a completely new aspect of aviation, releasing military aircraft from the prepared bases on which they had always been at their most vulnerable, and bringing them nearer to the areas where they needed to fight. Such a radical step took much time to evolve, mainly due to timidity by the customers, and its development exercised him from 1958 until his death.

Camm was an aircraft designer pre-eminent during the exciting early years of aviation, specializing in military aircraft, and particularly in fighters. Circumstances placed him in a position in which, by his undoubted design genius, he could make a major contribution to the decision of one of the great battles of history. Self-taught, he worked so hard for most of his life that, though not without other interests, his history is inseparable from the aircraft projects he fathered and carried through. He was a tall, lean man, of quick speech and mercurial disposition. As his success and prestige grew, the same self-confidence which displayed his signature on each one of his aircraft showed also in a growing intolerance of questioning or opposition. He fiercely resented criticism of any of his projects, and persistent overwork brought this quality at times to the borderline of eccentricity, although his angriest outbursts, after a subsequent period of brooding solitude, might be succeeded by a reasonable assimilation of the criticism into his own opinion. He drove his staffs hard, and his opinions of officialdom were more often than not unprintable. However, although not himself a pilot, he was always sympathetic to those who had to test and fly his aircraft. In an era when individual design was possible he could be regarded as one of the last of the great individual designers, whose personality and name could never be submerged in any committee or project team.

He was elected a fellow of the Royal Aeronautical Society in 1932, received the society's gold medal in 1958, served as president in 1954-5, and was elected honorary fellow in 1961. From 1951 to 1953 he was chairman of the technical board of the Society of British Aircraft Constructors. He was appointed CBE in 1941 and knighted in 1953. He received a number of foreign professional honours, of which the chief was the Daniel Guggenheim medal, which he received in 1965. He was elected to the board of Hawker Siddeley Aviation in 1935 and served until his death at Richmond, Surrey, 12 March 1966. He was survived by his wife, Hilda Rose Starnes, whom he married in 1915 and who died in 1977, and by one daughter. There is a portrait of Camm at the Royal Aeronautical Society's premises in London, by Frank Eastman.

[Private information; personal knowledge.]
PETER WYKEHAM

CAMPBELL, (RENTON) STUART (1908-1966), journalist, was born in Kensal Rise, London, 4 June 1908, the third child of John Campbell, a printer's manager from Scotland, and his wife, Florence Harmsworth. He was educated at Lavender Hill School and Wandsworth Technical Institute Secondary School. Encouraged by his father, he quickly embarked on a career in newspapers, starting as a junior reporter on the *Hendon and Finchley Times* and going on to the *Woking Gazette* and the *Nottingham Guardian*. He was still a reporter when in 1933 he moved to the Manchester office of the *News Chronicle* and then, in 1935, to the *Daily Mirror* in London. In 1937 he was appointed assistant editor of the *Sunday Pictorial* under Hugh (later Lord) Cudlipp. From then on he was a Sunday newspaperman of the watchdog breed.

When Cudlipp joined the forces early in the war of 1939-45, Campbell became editor of the *Sunday Pictorial*. The paper was already making a name as a campaigner for populist causes, and Campbell developed the reputation. The *Pictorial* took up many issues on behalf of soldiers and their families and investigated numerous complaints of profiteering. Campbell trained his reporters in the art of detecting, trapping, and exposing ration dodgers, oppressive landlords, petrol thieves, and other 'villains' of the home front. It was a role he relished as an ardent, although undogmatic, socialist and passionate believer in the journalist as crusader. Libel actions were an inevitable hazard and in the course of fighting them Campbell acquired considerable legal agility.

Cudlipp's return to the *Pictorial* in 1946 meant that Campbell was an editor without a newspaper. But he was quickly promised the editorship of the *People*, a Sunday newspaper owned by Odhams Press. The paper was then edited by Harry Ainsworth, who was soon due to retire. In the meantime Campbell became managing editor, running the paper without interference save for timid occasional grumbles from Ainsworth. The grumbles arose because Campbell systematically removed or transformed editorial features which he regarded as almost criminally soporific and out of date, replacing them with his own brand of sharp, topical, combative reporting and comment. Within two years, having also completely redesigned the *People*'s layout and typography, Campbell had a newspaper which, in his view, would appeal to a new post-war generation far more demanding than their parents of entertainment, sensation, and information. He retained one highly successful feature of the old *People*, its 'confession' series written by, or ghosted for, the famous and the notorious. But Campbell's confessionals were often those of obscure people, whose experiences somehow reflected the unacknowledged hopes or fears of his readers. He was a master of the telling headline that 'sold' these articles, for example: 'I Took a Lorry Ride to Shame', 'I was a G.I.'s Slave Bride', and 'Because My Skin is Black'.

It was, however, in the investigation and exposure of criminal and social wrongdoing that Campbell put his distinctive stamp on popular journalism. Disclosure has always been the business of newspapers. Campbell went a stage further, for he not only printed the results of his reporters' inquiries, but he also produced the evidence on which those conclusions were based. Thus, when in 1950 the *People* disclosed that the Messina brothers were running an empire of prostitution in London, his reporter, Duncan Webb, set out the whole course of his investigation, showing how he had traced the women to their various addresses and had established their links with the gang exploiting them. It was a pattern which Campbell followed with equal success in exposures of bribery among footballers, slum landlordism, fake religions, and numerous other social scandals. His techniques were adopted by other newspapers, especially the 'quality Sundays'. All of them, like the *People* itself, gained in circulation as a result.

The *People*'s success was also due to its highly personal flavour. It spoke with one voice, Campbell's. He wrote or rewrote a great part of the paper himself. Reporters', and even columnists', copy was often no more to him than raw material for moulding by the master. His immediate assistants caught Campbell's tone and articles which he did not have time to edit himself came out with his accent. The note was often strident, especially when evil was being denounced. Articles usually carried black and white moral judgements; as a journalist Campbell knew no greys and, as a stern Caledonian by upbringing, he tended to hark back to hell-fire. Campbell did not even leave sport to the experts. He often edited sporting features and constantly briefed sports columnists. His own regular contribution to the paper was the 'Man o' the People' column, for a time written by Gilbert Harding [q.v.]. In it he and Harding produced miniature exposés of the type carried on other pages, often campaigning on behalf of victims of officialdom. Campbell encouraged Harding to start an annual Christmas appeal for charities which was remarkably successful and remained a feature of the paper which Campbell always cherished.

In 1957 Campbell succeeded Ainsworth as editor. The change meant little. He had been in effective command of the paper for years and remained so until his death. But his elevation did, for the first time in his professional life, give him an uneasy place in the journalists' establishment. From 1961 to 1964 he was a member of the Press Council, whose occasional strictures on his editorial methods he had often scorned. He believed in getting 'the story' even if in the getting he sometimes violated the Press Council canon. But he did come to realize, under his colleagues' influence, the need to improve standards of taste and responsibility in popular newspapers.

Accused more than once as an editor of invasion of privacy, away from his newspaper Campbell was himself a very private man. In 1935 he married Joan Mary Algernon (died 1977), of Nottingham; they had one daughter. When he went home to them at Stella Cottage, near Farnham, where the Stella of Jonathan Swift [q.v.] once lived, he practised family seclusion. Always approachable in office hours by staff and visitors alike, he discouraged callers to his home. Once, when acquaintances were walking around the house in the hope of finding him in, he lay prone on the kitchen floor for half an hour to avoid detection, reading a book. He read, gardened, and fished enthusiastically. But his passion was newspapers. He died at his home near Farnham, 1 February 1966.

[*The Times*, 3 February 1966; private information; personal knowledge.]

NAT ROTHMAN

CANNON, HERBERT GRAHAM (1897-1963), zoologist, was born at Wimbledon, London, 14 April 1897, the third of the four children of David William Cannon, a compositor in the firm of Eyre and Spottiswoode who was for several years engaged in the preparation of maps for the India Office, and his wife, Alice, the daughter of Charles Graham who owned and drove one of the first horse buses to run on a regular service in south London. When Cannon was about five years old his parents moved to Brixton and it was from the local council school that he won a scholarship to Wilson's Grammar School in Camberwell, where he studied, in the higher forms, science subjects in preparation for entry into a university. He took little interest in games and an accident at the age of sixteen when he fell from a window while sleep-walking caused compound fractures of both wrists and damage to the lumbar vertebrae and pelvis which made strenuous or sustained exercise painful and often impossible for the rest of his life. His energies found compensation in a variety of hobbies and interests. As a boy he had a good singing voice; he played chess, liked making gadgets and finding out how things worked, and he was a skilful artist with pencil and crayon. In 1916, at the age of nineteen, and being unfit because of his physical disabilities for war service, he went up to Cambridge as a choral scholar of Christ's College to read for the natural sciences tripos. In 1918 he passed part i with first class honours in zoology, chemistry, and physiology. Instead of continuing with part ii he obtained leave of absence to take up a temporary post as naturalist in the Board of Fisheries laboratory at Conway, returning to Cambridge in January 1919 to complete the three years of residence necessary for the BA degree.

For a while Cannon thought of taking up research in experimental zoology which appealed to him for a number of reasons. He was well qualified to do so; had a feeling for apparatus and gadgetry; and, largely through the example of (Sir) James Gray, lately returned from war service, would have found himself in the mainstream of the exciting developments of the newly emerging experimental school. However, Cannon was unable to get a post in Cambridge and, encouraged by his experiences at Conway with a variety of living marine animals, he turned his attention to the problems of interpreting animal structure and the nature of their developmental processes in terms of their functional significance and adaptational value. In 1920 he was appointed a demonstrator in the department of zoology in Imperial College, London, under Professor E. W. MacBride, a powerful and provocative advocate of the Lamarckian view of the evolution of organisms through the inheritance of acquired characters. MacBride's 'tea parties' were a regular meeting-place for zoologists from the London colleges and the Natural History Museum. Cannon became friendly with W. T. Calman [q.v.], deputy keeper of zoology in the museum and an authority on the Crustacea which, through the number, variety, and range of function of their limbs and systems of movable parts, and a diversity of form expressed in animals as different as lobsters and barnacles, appealed strongly to Cannon as material for research; and in 1922 he began the long series of skilful investigations of the embryology, feeding mechanisms, and general anatomy of the Crustacea which were to establish his reputation as a zoologist of high distinction.

In 1926, at the age of twenty-nine, he was appointed to the chair of zoology at Sheffield University where, in the space of five years and in spite of a full teaching programme, he published several important papers, three in collaboration with Dr Sidnie M. Manton. It had long been known that many crustaceans can feed by filtering small organisms from the surrounding water. Particles are drawn towards the body in currents generated by limb movements, enmeshed by limb setae, combed out by other setae, and carried to the mouth. Cannon and Manton studied in detail the structure, shapes, changing postures, and relative motion of the limbs in relation to feeding currents made visible through the movements of particles and dyes. Limb movements were analysed by stroboscopic viewing and the sites of filtration and particle transfer traced by microscopic examination of sections of animals with their limbs carefully preserved in their natural relationships.

Cannon was a fine teacher and lecturer. He used plain language delivered with an actor's generous use of gestures and emphasis, and he was watchful of the responses of his audience. His drawings, whether in illustration of a paper or on a blackboard, were beautifully executed, and he wrote clearly and concisely. Forthright and uncompromising in the defence of his beliefs, and quick to react to criticism, he was nevertheless by nature warm-hearted and generous. He took an especial pleasure in beautiful things whether they were natural or artefacts. His main hobby was the collection and annotation of elegantly worked swords and furnishings on which he was an authority. In his later years his thoughts turned to evolutionary topics and he wrote *The Evolution of Living Things* (1958) and *Lamarck and Modern Genetics* (1959).

Cannon was elected a fellow of the Royal Society of Edinburgh in 1927 and a fellow of the Royal Society in 1935. His marriage in 1927 to Annie Helen ('Nannie'), a zoologist and graduate of Edinburgh, the daughter of Edwin J. Fyfe, of Edinburgh, was a singularly happy one. Their family life was enriched by four children. Cannon died in a London hospital 6 January 1963 shortly after being flown home from Las Palmas where he had become seriously ill while on a recuperative voyage.

[J. E. Smith, in *Biographical Memoirs of Fellows of the Royal Society*, vol. ix, 1963; private information; personal knowledge.]

ERIC SMITH

CARR, SIR CECIL THOMAS (1878–1966), public lawyer, was born 4 August 1878, the younger son in the family of two sons and two daughters of Thomas Carr, a woollen manufacturer of Twerton, near Bath, and his wife, Susan Arnell Creed. Educated first at Bath College under T. W. Dunn, who made boys enjoy working to their limits and gained their lasting devotion, Carr kept alive an association of old boys more than fifty years after the school closed. In 1897 he went to Trinity College, Cambridge, with an exhibition soon converted into a scholarship. He was placed in the second division of the first class of part i of the classical tripos in 1899—and the classics remained a resource throughout his life—and in the third class of part ii of the law tripos in 1901. Called to the bar by the Inner Temple in 1902, he practised on the Western Circuit; and although his practice was still small when war broke out, private means had enabled him in 1911 to contract his happy marriage with Norah, daughter of the civil engineer, Sir Alexander R. Binnie, whose notice Carr contributed to this Dictionary, as he did that of Sir W. M. Montagu Graham-Harrison. There were no children of the marriage.

The briefless days were filled. Carr twice won the Cambridge Yorke prize (in 1902 and 1905) with books published as *The General Principles of the Law of Corporations* (1905) and *Collective Ownership* (1907); and F. W. Maitland [q.v.] entrusted him with a Selden Society volume, which appeared in 1913 as *Select Charters of Trading Companies*. More light-heartedly Carr regularly entered for literary competitions, developing the lugubrious wit characteristic of his letters and speeches. He was good enough at various games to be an occasional recruit for county sides, and organized a cricket team for west country tours which inspired a series in *Punch* by A. A. Milne [q.v.], one of his regular players: a tall, awkward character seems to be based upon Carr.

Carr joined the 2/4th Wiltshire Regiment in September 1914, and spent the war in staff appointments in India. A year before he proceeded to the degree of LLD, Cambridge, in 1919 he became assistant to the editor and in 1923 editor of the Revised Statutes and of the Statutory Rules and Orders (later called Statutory Instruments). His appointment followed from the chance recollection of his qualities by a former member of his chambers; and his main quality was a determination to make something of whatever engaged him. His duties lay in the edition and consolidation of the growing mass of delegated legislation, and in the consolidation of the statute book; and without the staff which Carr was later instrumental in securing for his successors most men would have been proud just to keep up with the work. But not Carr: with delegated legislation he made it his business to understand each item, and caught many flaws which had passed departmental muster; and with the Revised Statutes he hunted down suspect enactments, verified that they were obsolete, and himself drafted Statute Law Revision Bills.

Ultimately more important than his official duties was Carr's work in focusing thought on the problems of delegated legislation. He was one of the founders of administrative law in England, and played some part in the United States. This originated with three lectures given in Cambridge in 1921, subsequently published as *Delegated Legislation* (1921). When a Congressional committee was considering the systematic notification of administrative regulations in the United States, a travelling fellowship was arranged which took Carr in 1935 to Washington, where he advised on techniques for the *Federal Register*, first published in 1936. This journey took him also to universities in the east and mid-west, where talks enhanced his reputation and gained him many friendships. In 1940 he gave the Carpentier lectures at Columbia University, published on both sides of the Atlantic in 1941 as *Concerning English Administrative Law*. Paradoxically this book was influential in England precisely because it was not addressed to English lawyers. Its historical detachment showed them the point they had reached after Lord (Gordon) Hewart's [q.v.] *The New Despotism* (1929) and the *Report of the Committee on Ministers' Powers* (1932). Ignoring slogans for and against the inevitable, Carr addressed the actual problems. It is the spirit in which the subject has since grown; though one might wish that Carr's imagination and values could also have been perpetuated.

In 1943, at an age when most men retire, Carr became counsel to the Speaker, an office largely concerned with private Bills. In securing procedural improvements generally, and in the passage of individual Bills, Carr's resourceful helpfulness was widely appreciated. It was also extensively used. From 1944 to 1947 he headed a committee considering the law about parliamentary and local elections. From 1943 to 1965 he served on the Statute Law Committee, and helped initiate more radical consolidation of the statute book. And in 1944 his experience with delegated legislation was again enlisted: the 'watchdog' select committee then set up was granted the assistance of Speaker's counsel, and Carr did much to settle the principles upon which it was to act.

Carr retired in 1955 at the age of seventy-seven. He was knighted in 1939, becoming KCB in 1947. He became bencher of the Inner Temple in 1944 and KC in 1945. He received honorary degrees from Columbia in 1940, London in 1952, and the Queen's University of Belfast in 1954; and he became fellow of the British Academy in 1952, and honorary fellow of Trinity College, Cambridge, in 1963. From 1943 to 1956 he was election secretary, then chairman, of the Athenaeum. From 1958 to

1961 he was president of the Selden Society, editing for it after almost fifty years a second volume, *Pension Book of Clement's Inn* (1960), and travelling to Washington in 1960 to address American members. A year earlier he had captained a team sent to the United States by the Senior Golfers' Society, of which he later became president, to compete with their North American counterparts; and at the age of eighty-two he combined this with addresses to the American Philosophical Society and two law schools.

He played golf, on the course beside which he lived at Rock in Cornwall, almost to the end. No less energetic was his reading, also kept up to the end. As in his Westminster offices, everything was digested into untidy piles of clear notes which he could always find but rarely needed: what mattered remained in his head. He was offered an academic post when the first war ended; and had he accepted, the problems of English public law might have been identified more clearly, more quickly, and much more quietly. But there is no saying what would have been lost without the practical authority exercised during a critical period by a shy man whose few words were always so compelling.

Carr died 12 May 1966 in a nursing home in Exeter.

[H. A. Hollond, 'Cecil Thomas Carr, 1878–1966' in *Proceedings* of the British Academy, vol. lii, 1966; *The Times*, 14 May 1966.]

S. F. C. MILSOM

CARR-SAUNDERS, SIR ALEXANDER MORRIS (1886–1966), biologist, sociologist, and academic administrator, was born at Reigate 14 January 1886, by some fifteen years the youngest child of James Carr-Saunders, a wealthy underwriter, and his wife, Flora Anne Tower. He was proud of his descent from the architect Robert Morris [q.v.], and conscious of his affinity with two other relatives, W. W. and Edward Saunders [q.v.], both entomologists and fellows of the Royal Society. In childhood he was lonely, and at Eton intensely unhappy. He left at sixteen, to spend two years in Paris and the French Alps. In this period he came to believe that it was in biology that the greatest advancement of learning would be made in the years ahead, and it was to read this subject that he went up to Magdalen College, Oxford. He took a first in 1908 in zoology, was elected to the biological scholarship at Naples for a year, then returned to Oxford as a demonstrator in comparative anatomy.

But it became clear to him that his interests extended beyond the laboratory. His imagination had been fired by the prospects for human betterment opened by Mendel's rediscovered paper of 1865 and the work of William Bateson [q.v.] on heredity. In 1910 he moved to London, where he studied biometrics under Karl Pearson [q.v.], became secretary of the research committee of the Eugenics Education Society, and served as sub-warden of Toynbee Hall. He was elected to the Stepney Borough Council, and in 1914 was called to the bar by the Inner Temple.

At the outbreak of war he enlisted in the ranks of the infantry, but was commissioned in the Army Service Corps, and after a year in France was posted to a depot at Suez, where he remained, against his will, for the rest of the war. His duties left him leisure to plan a work on population that would 'view the whole problem . . . from an historical and evolutionary standpoint'. He came back in a state of depression and indecision, and accepted an offer to return to Oxford as a demonstrator in zoology. Here, however, he accomplished his grand design rapidly; his book *The Population Problem* (1922) did much to establish his reputation among his contemporaries, although it did not attract wide attention at the time. Forty years later it was claimed as having anticipated later developments in ethology by its stress on behaviour that contributes to the survival of the group, and on the practices by which groups are secured of their territory. His concern for the problems of population was to lead him to serve as chairman of the Population Investigation Committee from 1936, and of the statistics committee of the royal commission on population from 1944 to 1949; he was instrumental in establishing the study of demography, and unflagging in his leadership of the Eugenics Society, which awarded him its first Galton medal in 1946.

In 1923 he was called to Liverpool as the first holder of the Charles Booth chair of social science. The task of directing a department proved highly congenial to him. The air of detachment that his colleagues felt in him did not prevent him from entering fully into the life of a civic university. His own publications meanwhile added to his reputation, especially the pioneering account of the history and structure of *The Professions* (with P. A. Wilson, 1933).

The appointment to Liverpool had been quite unforeseen. Equally unforeseen, but readily accepted, was the call to him in 1937 to succeed Sir William (later Lord) Beveridge [q.v.] as director of the London School of Economics. In the next nineteen years he held the School together through its exile during the war, and presided over its ensuing expansion of numbers and activities. When he joined it he found an academic community agitated and divided by his predecessor's style of administration: he himself established his authority and restored harmony in the community by a style that was an absence of style. His simple and quiet approach to business flowed from his self-image: he saw himself as no more thart a scholar among scholars animated by a common devotion. He was vigorous, even combative when necessary, and was able to transact business in the office rapidly. But in council his touch was as light as it was deft: where sectional interests were latent his own selflessness diffused disinterest; discussions in which he never forcibly intervened served their therapeutic purpose, and moved to generally accepted conclusions that seldom ran contrary to his own judgement.

When in 1943 he joined the commission under Sir Cyril Asquith (later Lord Asquith of Bishopstone, q.v.) on higher education in the colonies he took up a task to which he was drawn alike by his scholarly and his humanitarian concern for its object. He created and became chairman both of the university of London senate committee which guided the development of university colleges in East Africa, Sudan, Central Africa, Nigeria, the Gold Coast, and the West Indies; and of the Inter-University Council through which the help of all the British universities was given to the colleges and universities of the dependent territories. He was chairman in 1947 of the commission which promoted the university of Malaya, and in 1952-3 of the commission which led to the foundation of the multi-racial University College of Rhodesia and Nyasaland. On his retirement from LSE in December 1965 he devoted himself to this work more than ever, travelling continually to maintain personal contacts with the new colleges. He carried out the survey of the manpower requirements of the African universities presented to the Tananarive conference of 1962. His book *New Universities Overseas* (1961) gives an account of these developments.

Two interests formed in early years remained with him throughout life. In the French Alps he had learned the craft of the mountaineer; he had a special knowledge of the Aiguilles Rouges, and while he was at Liverpool he climbed Tryfan more than a hundred times. His first sight of Raphael's frescoes in the Vatican had opened a new world to him, and he continued to find a lively pleasure in paintings and to collect them. He also had a lifelong interest in farming and country pursuits, finding happiness in their practical and creative aspects. He once remarked that

the farmer is 'the man who does the only job that really matters'. Seemingly withdrawn and remote, he was keenly observant, and warm in his attachments. In his private judgement of men he made sharp distinctions, but in his dealings with them he was uniformly tolerant. His lean frame and ascetic, somewhat melancholy, mien concealed great energy; the strength of his hands marked the tenacity which enabled him to carry through on his retirement a task that would have extended most men fully in the prime of life. His exertions responded to the breadth of his intellectual interests and his deep sense of social responsibility. As a young man he had been a sceptic in the tradition of the Victorian rationalists, but his philosophic bent and concern for right action drew him insistently towards theology, and he found a faith within the Anglican fold.

He married in 1929 a former Oxford pupil, Teresa, daughter of Major Edmund Harington Molyneux-Seel, a professional soldier and Lancashire landowner. They had two sons and a daughter. He was knighted in 1946, in which year he also became a fellow of the British Academy, and was appointed KBE in 1957. He received honorary doctorates from the universities of Glasgow, Columbia, Natal, Dublin, Liverpool, Cambridge, Grenoble, Malaya, and London; he was also honorary fellow of Peterhouse, Cambridge, of the University College of East Africa, and of the London School of Economics. He died near Grasmere 6 October 1966. His portrait by Sir William Coldstream hangs in the London School of Economics.

[E. H. Phelps Brown in *Proceedings* of the British Academy, vol. liii, 1967; private information; personal knowledge.]

HENRY PHELPS BROWN

CARRUTHERS, (ALEXANDER) DOUGLAS (MITCHELL) (1882-1962), explorer and naturalist, was born in London 4 October 1882, the eldest son of William Mitchell-Carruthers, who took orders in 1886, and his wife, Antonia, daughter of the Revd Atkinson Alexander Holden, who had been rector of Hawton, Newark-on-Trent. Educated at Haileybury and Trinity College, Cambridge, Carruthers started in quite a humble way as secretary to different people who were working at the Royal Geographical Society, and underwent training in land survey work. He also learnt how to skin animals and became an expert taxidermist. This enabled him to take part in expeditions which advanced his career. On the British Museum expedition to Ruwenzori and the Congo (1905-6) he sent home remarkable specimens of birds and mammals. In 1907-8 a German businessman who was also a natural historian, made it possible for Carruthers to travel in Russian Turkestan and the borders of Afghanistan. There he did research work in the various kinds of wild sheep in the Tian-shan range of mountains. He established the territories inhabited by the *Ovis ammon* and *Ovis poli* and found another specimen of sheep, new to natural history, which was later named *Ovis karolini*. He supplied many museums in Europe and America with specimens of these sheep at a time when very little was known about them. He then explored by himself the countries south-east of Syria and shot certain rare deer, among them the Arabian Oryx, one species of which was hitherto unknown. He also made a collection of Marmots, one of which was new.

His next most important work was undertaken in collaboration with the big-game hunter John H. Miller and Morgan Philips Price. In 1910 they decided to explore the stony desert of Outer Mongolia, then part of the old Chinese empire, during the last years of the Manchu dynasty. The expedition took eleven months, crossed Siberia, and went up the Yenesei river to the source. The explorers had some difficulty in crossing the Sayansk mountains on the Russo-Chinese frontier as they entered Outer Mongolia, but Carruthers was expert in dealing with obstructive officials.

The country of the Upper Yenesei basin was largely unknown. Only two Russian explorers had been there before and virtually no mapping had been done. Carruthers was able to do some surveying and made some maps of the country watered by the Japsa river which flows into the Upper Yenesei north of the Tannu-ola mountains. This was difficult forested and mountainous country which had never been worked at before. Carruthers and his colleagues were real pioneers and the expedition owed much to his capacity for organization and leadership and his knowledge of human nature. His two volumes on *Unknown Mongolia* were published in 1913 and in the meantime he had been awarded the Gill memorial (1910) and the Patron's gold medal (1912) of the Royal Geographical Society which he was to serve as honorary secretary in 1916-21.

During the war years after 1914 Carruthers was employed mainly at the War Office compiling maps of the Middle East. He settled in the countryside of East Anglia and his later career consisted largely in working at map making and with explorers and travellers. He published some articles and memoranda on various aspects of geography, and further books, among them *Arabian Adventure* (1935) and *Beyond the Caspian, a Naturalist in Central Asia* (1949). One feature of his work

was his consciousness of the effects of climatic and physical variations on the nature of all forms of life: a thought which ran through most of his lecturing and writing. He did some work on climatic conditions in Central Asia and continued some of the work started by Ellsworth Huntington and other geographers and explorers. He was interested in the idea that in the course of centuries a process of desiccation had been going on in the centre of the continent. This induced him to work in getting information about the old civilizations which had arisen and disappeared in Central Asia, thereby adding to what had been done by Sven Hedin, Sir Aurel Stein [q.v.], and others. He was awarded the Sykes medal of the Royal Central Asian Society in 1956.

In 1915 Carruthers married Mary, daughter of the first Lord Trevor and divorced wife of Major James Archibald Morrison. The marriage was dissolved in 1948 and in that year he married Rosemary Arden, daughter of Lieutenant-Colonel Ernest Charles Clay. Carruthers died in a London hospital 23 May 1962.

[Personal knowledge.]

M. PHILIPS PRICE

CARTER, (HELEN) VIOLET BONHAM, BARONESS ASQUITH OF YARNBURY (1887-1969), political figure. [See BONHAM CARTER.]

CARTON DE WIART, SIR ADRIAN (1880-1963), lieutenant-general, was born in Brussels 5 May 1880, the son of Léon Carton de Wiart, lawyer, who moved to Cairo, and his first wife, who died when the boy was six. He was educated at the Oratory School, Edgbaston, from 1891 and went up to Balliol College, Oxford, in January 1899, having failed 'Smalls' at the first attempt. He proceeded to fail the preliminary examination in law but returned to an indulgent college for Michaelmas term. He ran away and under an assumed name and age joined Paget's Horse, a yeomanry unit off to fight the Boers. He was severely wounded, his identity was revealed, and he returned to Balliol to be treated as the college hero for whom his friend, Auberon Herbert (later eighth Baron Lucas, q.v.) subsequently coined the description 'genius in courage'. He returned to South Africa and enlisted in the Imperial Light Horse. The war ending, he obtained a regular commission in the 4th Dragoon Guards, then stationed in Rawalpindi. Pigsticking and polo began to pall and he became ADC to Sir Henry Hildyard, C.-in-C. South Africa. Three years later, in 1908, he rejoined his regiment in England and was seconded as adjutant to the Royal Gloucestershire Hussars. In July 1914 he sailed for Somaliland to join the Camel Corps to fight the 'Mad Mullah'. Shortly after the outbreak of war in Europe, he used an eye injury sustained while storming a fort to get himself back to England. His eye was removed and he was appointed to the DSO.

His heroic career in the war of 1914-18 was spent in the trenches or in hospital. He was severely wounded eight times and lost his left hand. He was awarded the Victoria Cross after the battle of the Somme, in which he led the 8th battalion of the Gloucestershire Regiment in the capture of La Boiselle, in the first week of July 1916. He subsequently commanded a series of infantry brigades—the 12th, and at Arras the 105th and 113th. After the armistice he was appointed second in command to General Louis Botha [q.v.], who was to lead the British Military Mission to Poland. When Botha died in 1919 Carton de Wiart took over. In 1924 he resigned his commission when Prince Charles Radziwill, who had been his last Polish ADC, lent him a house in the Pripet marshes where he spent the inter-war years happily shooting duck. He was summoned back to England and asked to resume his old mission to Poland in July 1939 but he had strong disagreements with Marshal Smigly-Rydz, the Polish C-in-C. When the Germans invaded Poland Carton de Wiart returned to England by way of Romania and was given command of the 61st division, a Midland Territorial formation with its headquarters in Oxford. In the spring he left his division to command a force bound for Namsos in Norway, whose capture was a forlorn hope and from which •he. skilfully extricated his forces. In April 1941 he was dispatched to form a British military mission in Yugoslavia but his aircraft was shot down in the sea and he became an Italian prisoner. He joined a group of senior officers held prisoner at Sulmona and the Castello di Vincigliati at Fiesole and was at once busy with plans to escape. The Italians eventually found a role for their restless captive as an intermediary, dispatched to Lisbon in August 1943, in the arrangements which led to Italy's withdrawal from the war in September 1943.

Less than a month after his return to England, (Sir) Winston Churchill sent him, as a lieutenant-general, as his personal representative to Generalissimo Chiang Kai-shek in China. The rest of the war he spent in Chungking where he made a great impression. He attended the Cairo conference and in December 1944 made a personal report to the Cabinet, at the prime minister's insistence, on the situation in the Far East. He also managed to be involved in the naval bombardment of Sabang. He was invited by Attlee to continue in his post after the British general election of 1945 and eventually retired to England in 1946, having broken his back in Rangoon *en route*.

In 1908 he had married Countess Frederica, eldest daughter of Prince Fugger Babenhausen; they had two daughters. His wife died in 1949 and two years later he married Mrs. Joan Sutherland. They settled in county Cork where he continued the tireless pursuit of snipe and salmon. There he died 5 June 1963.

With his black eye-patch and empty sleeve, Carton de Wiart looked like an elegant pirate and he became a figure of legend, an 'absolute non-ducker', utterly without sentimentality but full of fine-drawn sentiments. His pleasures were simple, his contempts obvious. His *Happy Odyssey* gives something of the flavour. He might have ridden out with Prince Rupert over Magdalen Bridge on May morning in the sunshine. He was unusually quick and so was his temper. He bore himself magnificently, loathed humbug, and detested meanness. He taught himself to manage with one hand—and one eye—more neatly than most ever achieve with two. He was elected an honorary fellow of Balliol in 1947 and held an honorary doctorate from Aberdeen. He was appointed CMG in 1918, CB in 1919, and KBE in 1945, and he held several Belgian, French, and Polish decorations. It was said of him that in the world of action he occupied the sort of niche which Sir Max Beerbohm [q.v.] occupied in the world of letters.

The National Portrait Gallery owns a portrait in oils by Sir William Orpen (1919). A portrait in oils by Simon Elwes was exhibited at the Royal Academy Summer Exhibition in 1972.

[Sir Adrian Carton de Wiart, *Happy Odyssey*, 1950; *The Times*, 6 June 1963; *Balliol Record*, July 1964; personal knowledge.]

E. T. WILLIAMS

CAWOOD, SIR WALTER (1907-1967), scientist and civil servant, was born 28 April 1907 in York, the son of Walter Cawood, civil servant, of New Earswick, York, and his wife, Elizabeth McSall, the daughter of a Lincolnshire farmer. He had one sister. He was educated at Archbishop Holgate's Grammar School, York, and at the university of Leeds, where he took his Ph.D. degree in chemistry (1932), having obtained a B.Sc. (London) in 1929. He was a Cohen prizeman (1931), a Ramsey memorial fellow (1931-3), and a Moseley scholar of the Royal Society (1933-8). His research during this period was concerned with the properties of aerosols and the theory of coagulation; and despite his widening experience, particularly of aeronautical matters, he always maintained his original interest in physical chemistry. In 1938, as the international situation worsened, he joined an Air Ministry team engaged on chemical warfare. This involved him in the design of proximity fuses, and from 1942 his most valuable work was in instrumentation. He was responsible for the development of bomb and torpedo sights and for synthetic training aids, particularly for night flying. He improvised a simple pre-set rangefinder for use in aircraft attacking the flying bomb; and to improve this device he flew in operations as an honorary wing commander.

He was deputy director at the Royal Aircraft Establishment, Farnborough, from 1947 to 1953 and it was during this time that he acquired an abiding interest in aviation and in ground and airborne avionics. In 1954, when Theodor von Karman was creating the Advisory Group for Aerospace Research and Development, a unique organization which did so much to restore European aeronautical collaboration, Cawood gave enthusiastic support and as a national delegate spent a great deal of his time during the critical early stages. From 1953 to 1959 he was at the headquarters of the Ministry of Aviation, where he was responsible for the aeronautical research programme. He believed in identifying the few important growth points from a wide range of promising alternatives; and once he had made his choice he was single-minded in his support. He foresaw the potential of vertical take-off and as early as 1958 provided support for Sir Sydney Camm's [q.v.] deflected thrust aircraft, the forerunner of the Harrier in service with the Royal Air Force. He understood the need to supplement wind-tunnel measurements with actual flight trials. He encouraged the investigation of light weight-lifting engines in the 'flying bedstead' and later with Oswald Short's [q.v.] SC 1, and of the low-speed handling properties of the slender wing with the Fairey Delta which did so much to validate the design of the Concorde.

In 1959, when responsibility for research and development in the munitions field was transferred from the Ministry of Supply to the War Office, Cawood became the first chief scientist of that department and later, in 1964, the first scientist to be a member of the Army Board. He had already in 1955 brought together armament research and development into one establishment at Fort Halstead. His wide experience was invaluable in welding into one team the various scientific and engineering organizations within the War Office, and in building up confidence between the scientists and their military colleagues. His own personal knowledge of aviation technology was particularly useful to the army, which was beginning to invest heavily in helicopters and in air trans-

portability; and his earlier training as a chemist found new application in the affairs of the Chemical Defence Establishment at Porton and the ordnance factories.

In 1964 he returned to the Ministry of Aviation as chief scientist and became involved in the redeployment of effort after the defence reviews, which led to the integration of the Ministry of Aviation into the new Ministry of Technology. His particular concern was to extend the mandate of the defence establishments so that their unique resources would be more directly available to civil industry. He was not in good health during his last year, but he continued to carry his heavy responsibilities and at the last he was among his colleagues and friends at the Royal Aircraft Establishment where he had so many active years. He died at the Royal Cambridge Hospital in Farnborough 6 March 1967.

Cawood was an enthusiastic yachtsman and crewed in many off-shore races as well as sailing single-handed in his own boat, *Cobber*. He was an active member of the Royal Ocean Racing Club, of the Royal Southern, and of the Royal Aeronautical Society, of which he was a fellow. He was appointed CBE in 1953, CB in 1956, and KBE in 1965.

In 1934 he married Molly, daughter of Fred Johnson, a schoolmaster, of York. They had one son and one daughter.

[*Nature*, 8 April 1967; *New Scientist*, 16 March 1967; *Journal of the Royal Aeronautical Society*, April 1967; personal knowledge.]   ROBERT COCKBURN

CAWTHORNE, SIR TERENCE EDWARD (1902–1970), ear specialist, was born in Aberdeen 29 September 1902, the only child of William Cawthorne, a customs official, and his wife, Annie England. Cawthorne was educated at Denstone College and at the medical school of King's College Hospital, London. He qualified MRCS, LRCP in 1924 and obtained the FRCS in 1930. He held a number of junior appointments at King's, including house-anaesthetist and house-surgeon to the ear and throat departments, before becoming registrar to the latter. He was appointed to the honorary consultant staff of the hospital as assistant surgeon to the now united ear, nose, and throat department in 1932, becoming full surgeon in 1939. For a time he was also a consultant at the Metropolitan Hospital, the Royal Hospital, Richmond, and the East Surrey Hospital. In 1936 he became aural surgeon to the National Hospital for Nervous Diseases. In 1948 he was appointed consulting adviser in otolaryngology to the Ministry of Health, and held this position until 1967.

Early after his staff appointment at King's, Cawthorne began to find the problems of aural disease more absorbing than those of the nose and throat, and the close relationship between some forms of deafness and vertigo with neurology made his appointment at the National Hospital peculiarly appropriate. He was fascinated with the possibility of being able to restore hearing by means of making a new fenestra for the entry of sound waves to the internal ear in certain types of deafness, and he visited the pioneers in this field in various countries. He became convinced that Lempert, of New York, had made a valuable contribution and he did much to import Lempert's fenestration operation to Europe. He went further than Lempert, however, and was the first in this country to recognize the value of the operating microscope in ear surgery. It was a natural step for Cawthorne to become interested in the form of vertigo known as Ménière's disease, and with C. S. Hallpike he did much to further the understanding, diagnosis, and treatment of this condition. His third great neuro-otological interest was in the anatomically neighbouring facial nerve and in the various forms of paralysis of this. These matters, of which he made himself an authority, brought a constant stream of visitors, which must have been very wearing, but he received them all with characteristic patience and courtesy.

Although fully appreciative of the value of laboratory and clinical research and of the need to be closely associated with the research workers, Cawthorne was essentially a clinical diagnostician and accurate technical surgeon. His influence attracted the Wernher research unit on deafness to King's and he was clinical director of this in 1958-64. He was an excellent teacher of students and graduates, and even found time to be dean of the medical school at King's (1946-8). He was president of the Royal Society of Medicine (1962-4) and received its Dalby (1953) and W. J. Harrison (1961) prizes; and he was master of the second British Academic Conference in Otolaryngology in 1967.

As early as 1938 Cawthorne determined that he would 'have something to say' at meetings and in the learned journals, and inevitably he had numerous invitations to meetings all over the world. He delivered various endowed lectures and was awarded medals in the United Kingdom and other countries. He was particularly well known in the United States and Canada. He was given an honorary MD of Uppsala in 1963, an honorary LLD of Syracuse, New York, in 1964, and the honorary FRCS Ireland in 1966. He was knighted in 1964.

Cawthorne was tall, dark, and handsome and he combined a calm reassuring manner with being a good listener. These were traits which made easy his approaches to patients. In his later years he was often thought unduly solemn and portentous—magnificent might be a more suitable adjective—but this covered an innate diffidence and schoolboyish sense of humour. As a graduate student he had worked for a time in an endowed dispensary in Drury Lane and there had met many of the odd characters connected with the stage and Covent Garden. No doubt these contacts stimulated his lifelong interest in the arts and led to his membership of the Garrick Club.

Like many medical men of academic inclination he became interested in the history of his speciality and its relationship with famous figures. He wrote papers for instance to show that Julius Caesar and Dean Swift suffered from Ménière's disease.

In 1929 Cawthorne met Lilian (died 1975), daughter of William Southworth, at the King's College Hospital annual ball, and they were married in 1930. They had one son and one daughter.

In 1964 Cawthorne had his first warning of the heart trouble of which ultimately he died, and the necessity to diminish his commitments caused his premature retirement from King's. But he found it hard not to remain involved with people, and he continued to travel. He died in London 22 January 1970. There is a portrait of him by Robert Swan in Chandos House, the Domus Medica of the Royal Society of Medicine.

[Personal knowledge.]   RONALD MACBETH

CENTLIVRES, ALBERT VAN DE SANDT (1887-1966), chief justice of South Africa and chancellor of the university of Cape Town, was born at Newlands, Cape Town, 13 January 1887, the third son and seventh of the eleven children of Frederick James Centlivres, director of companies and mayor of Rondebosch, and his wife, Albertina de Villiers. Matriculating with distinction at the South African College School in 1903, he went on, at the South African College, to academic achievements which included honours in classics and a Rhodes scholarship. At New College, Oxford, he took his BA (with second class honours in jurisprudence) in 1909, and the following year, with third class honours, his BCL. He had joined the Middle Temple and was called to the bar in 1910. In 1911 he was admitted as an advocate of the Cape Provincial division, South Africa.

At first his was the usual fate of the young advocate and he had the time in which to edit

Juta's Daily Reporter and so consolidate and extend his knowledge of procedure. His practice began to prosper after two interruptions: a brief interlude in Southern Rhodesia and the eruption of the war of 1914–18, in which he served in German South-West Africa as a private and returned to civil life with, it is believed, a military discharge recording his education as 'fair'. In 1927 he became a KC. It was as a lawyer rather than an advocate that he was achieving a reputation. His preparation was as comprehensive as it was thorough, his arguments were closely packed, yet precise, and he was considered an expert on the law of wills. He took part in a number of important cases, among them being the 'heresy trial', *Du Plessis* v. *Synod of the Dutch Reformed Church*, and *Hofmeyr* v. *Badenhorst*, a defamation case resulting from an election at Riversdale. It was perhaps a portent that in 1920 he had been appointed parliamentary draftsman, a post which, during fourteen years, gave him a special insight into statute law. After acting as a judge of the High Court of South-West Africa in 1922 and of the Cape Provincial division in 1932, 1933, and 1934, he was appointed a puisne judge of the Cape Provincial division in February 1935. Four years later, in 1939, he was elevated to the Appellate division. Appointed chairman of the public service inquiry commission in 1944, his investigations into the salaries and conditions of service of civil servants were notable for their effective celerity. In 1950 he succeeded E. F. Watermeyer as chief justice and in 1957 he retired after a period in the Appellate division which, in length, had been exceeded only by Sir William Solomon.

While, in other legal fields, Centlivres was responsible for a number of notable judgements, as he was in the celebrated case *R.* v. *Milne and Erleigh* (1951), it is his pronouncements in the three most important constitutional cases in the history of South Africa which, in particular, have ensured for him the attention of posterity. These, *Harris* v. *Minister of the Interior* (1952), *Minister of the Interior* v. *Harris* (1952), and *Collins* v. *Minister of the Interior* (1956), represent a collision between Cabinet and judiciary, and were the culmination of a government attempt to remove the Coloured population from the common roll. Of the three cases the second is perhaps the most remarkable. Frustrated by the Appellate division's insistence that the requirements for amending the entrenched clauses of the South Africa Act be respected, the House of Assembly and the Senate constituted themselves a superior High Court of Parliament. This was unanimously declared unconstitutional by the Appellate division, the chief justice rejecting

the contention that Parliament could decide bicamerally that no previous court had the right finally to decide whether an Act conformed with the requirements of the South Africa Act. His judgement in the first case was described by Professor E. N. Griswold, then dean of the Harvard Law School, as 'a great judgement, deserving to rank with the best work of the judges who have contributed to the field of constitutional law'. In the end the Senate was 'packed' and the number of judges of the Appellate division was increased from five to eleven without consultation with the chief justice, who endured political attacks with dignified restraint. It was during this turbulent period that the chief justice represented South Africa at, for instance, the seventh legal convention of the Law Council of Australia (1952) and the conference on 'Government under Law' at Harvard (1955). In his address at Harvard, 'The South African Constitution and the Rule of Law', he forcibly reaffirmed his faith in the rule of law and the rights and dignity of the individual, causes for which he fought unceasingly after his retirement.

In 1951 he had succeeded J. C. Smuts [q.v.] as chancellor of the university of Cape Town and, after his retirement as chief justice, was unremitting, through word and action, symbol, meeting, and procession, in his refusal to accept government insistence that, wherever possible, the university should be restricted to Whites only. On his installation as chancellor he had emphasized his attitude: 'To put it positively, academic freedom, as I understood it, means the unrestricted right on the part of a University to decide for itself what it shall teach, how it shall teach it and whom it shall admit to be taught, as well as the unrestricted right to select as its teachers the best men and women available, whether they happen to have been born in South Africa or elsewhere.'

Sociable, unaffected, accessible, Albert Centlivres was typical of the English-speaking South African at his best. In action as well as word he was a democrat. Like Smuts, whom he knew well, he was happy climbing Table Mountain, and, when those days were over, his tall, craggy figure, with pipe, stick, and dog, could be seen ranging the walks of his neighbourhood. Honours burdened him little. He was an honorary DCL of Oxford, and an honorary LLD of the universities of Melbourne, Cape Town, and the Witwatersrand, and of Rhodes University. He was also an honorary fellow of New College and an honorary bencher of the Middle Temple.

In 1916 he married Isabel, daughter of George Short, accountant and merchant of Cape Town, and had one son who predeceased him and three daughters. He died at Claremont,

Cape Town, 19 September 1966. There is a portrait in oils by Neville Lewis in the Jameson Hall, university of Cape Town, and a bust in bronze by Laura Rautenbach in the Jagger Library, university of Cape Town.

[*South African Law Journal*, vols. lii (1935) and lxxiv, part i (1957); *Inaugural Address*, university of Cape Town, 6 April 1951; *Cape Argus*, 19 September 1966; *The Times* and *Cape Times*, 20 September 1966; *Albert Centlivres, 1887–1966* (university of Cape Town memorial ceremony, Jameson Hall, 13 October 1966); private information; personal knowledge.]

A. LENNOX-SHORT

CHAPMAN, SYDNEY (1888–1970), mathematician and geophysicist, was born 29 January 1888 in Eccles, Lancashire, the second son of Joseph Chapman, chief cashier at Rylands, a Manchester textiles firm, and his wife, Sarah Gray. When he left elementary school at the age of fourteen he was advised to have two years at the Royal Technical Institute, Salford, before entering industry; there he was encouraged to try for a county scholarship to Manchester University, and he was the lowest successful candidate. At the age of sixteen he embarked on an engineering course at the university. Finding that he had a flair for mathematics, after this course he spent a further year taking a mathematics degree, during which he won a sizarship to Trinity College, Cambridge (1908). He was promoted to a full scholarship after one year.

During his third Cambridge year, when he had already taken his final examinations and become a wrangler in the mathematical tripos (part ii, 1910) and was starting research, the astronomer royal, (Sir) Frank Dyson [q.v.], offered him a post as senior assistant at the Greenwich Observatory, which he accepted. He was set to work supervising the installation of instruments for a new magnetic observatory. He found that magneticians were unduly devoted to collecting data, spending too little time trying to interpret them. Encouraged by Dyson and (Sir) Arthur Schuster [q.v.] he set to work to rectify this. Thus began the study of the influences of the Sun and Moon on terrestrial phenomena which was to be a prime ingredient of his later work. In 1913 Chapman won the first Smith's prize.

Not relishing the prospect of becoming an administrator, and wishing to complete work on gas theory begun earlier at the suggestion of Sir Joseph Larmor [q.v.], Chapman left Greenwich in 1914 and returned to Trinity College, Cambridge, as a college lecturer. His return coincided with the outbreak of the 1914–18 war, during which his religious principles made him a pacifist. He was granted exemption from military service, but was asked in 1916 to return to Greenwich in an honorary capacity, remaining there until December 1918. However, he felt the strain of maintaining unpopular views, and after the war he went through a period of agonized reappraisal.

Chapman's scientific achievements during the years 1912–19 were remarkable. In gas theory he, and independently David Enskog in Sweden, gave an exact solution to the problem of gas viscosity, heat conduction, and diffusion; this problem, posed much earlier by (James) Clerk Maxwell [q.v.] and Ludwig Boltzmann, had until then defied attempts at a general solution. Chapman and Enskog identified a hitherto overlooked phenomenon—thermal diffusion. After having had to overcome doubts as to its reality forcefully expressed by (Sir) James Jeans, whose notice, as well as that of Sir Horace Lamb, he wrote for this Dictionary, Chapman felt paternal pride when in 1939 Clusius used it in developing a powerful method of separating gases in mixtures.

In four massive papers (1913–19) Chapman examined the regular variations in the geomagnetic field arising from tidal flows in the ionosphere, excited by the Sun and Moon. He was able (following Schuster) to estimate the electrical conductivity of the ionosphere, and to show how it depends on the Sun's radiation. In 1918 he identified a lunar atmospheric tide from sixty years of Greenwich barometer records; this was a remarkable achievement, both because the effect detected was smaller than the limit of accuracy of an individual measurement, and because of the very considerable amount of computation which had to be done without mechanical aids. He followed this up during the next thirty years with determinations of the lunar tide at numerous stations over the surface of the globe.

Finally, in 1919 he made a first attempt at a theory of magnetic storms—sudden irregular changes in the geomagnetic field. Although this theory was soon abandoned as unsound, the accompanying analysis of storm morphology was to prove invaluable.

In 1919 his scientific achievements were recognized in his election as a fellow of the Royal Society and his appointment to succeed (Sir) Horace Lamb as professor of natural philosophy at Manchester. He was there until 1924, when he accepted an invitation to become chief professor of mathematics at the Imperial College, London. During the period up to 1928 he was much involved in reorganizing and modernizing student courses, though finding time to win the Adams prize for 1928 with an essay on geomagnetism, and to develop earlier ideas further, often in collaboration with younger men—for example, E. A. Milne [q.v.].

The years 1928–32 were another period of intense intellectual activity. Chapman extended his gas-theory methods to cover Brownian motions and the electrical conductivity of plasmas (ionized gases). He introduced a junior colleague, A. T. Price, to study what could be learnt about the Earth's interior from surface magnetic variations. With a research student, V. C. A. Ferraro, he produced the first satisfactory explanation of the initial phase of magnetic storms as due to compression of the geomagnetic field by plasma streams emanating from the Sun. Chapman and Ferraro explained only one feature of magnetic storms; their theory was later strongly criticized by Hannes Alfvén, who in 1939–40 produced a rival partial theory. The most significant feature of the Chapman—Ferraro theory was its recognition, twenty years before the post-war explosion of interest in plasmas, that plasma behaviour was essentially different from that of single charged particles, so that solar plasma streams could pen the geomagnetic field within a bounded 'magnetosphere'.

In the 1931 Royal Society Bakerian lecture Chapman gave a trail-breaking discussion of the effects of the Sun's ultraviolet radiation on the Earth's upper atmosphere. He provided a standard theory of layer formation in the lower ionosphere against which later experiments could be compared; he also gave an enlightening account of photochemical reactions in the upper atmosphere. In this, as in the discussion of solar streams which accompanied the Chapman–Ferraro theory, many, though not all, of his ideas have stood the test of time. Working in a period when experimental facts were at best only partially available, his achievement was to enable later observers to direct their efforts in the most profitable directions.

1932 to 1940 were years of expanding horizons. Always an internationalist, in 1934 Chapman spent three months in Cairo as visiting professor. He regularly attended international conferences, often cycling across Europe to do so. He made no secret of his distaste for Hitler, a feeling the more profound because of discussions with young Germans whom he met on his cycling trips. He did all he could, personally and through committees, to get refugee scientists settled in suitable posts. However, he maintained friendly relations with German scientists; from 1929 onwards he worked sporadically with Julius Bartels on a treatise, *Geomagnetism*,

finally published in 1940 after the outbreak of war. He had a copy of this book transmitted via America to Adolf Schmidt in Germany, which led him into temporary trouble with officials concerned with stopping trade with the enemy.

A second book on which Chapman began to work much earlier, *The Mathematical Theory of Non-Uniform Gases*, was published in 1939, this time with T. G. Cowling as co-author. The war put an end to such pursuits. Chapman was now no longer a pacifist and undertook civilian war work, finally (1943–5) working for the Army Council on problems of military operational research. His methodical nature and capacity for marshalling facts made him a valued leader in his group, whose members could rely on his firm support even against the wrath of generals. He strove to maintain his contacts with science, but the papers he published during this time were mainly minor ones. However, in 1943 he stimulated the Gassiot committee of the Royal Society to sponsor a group of researches on radiation and its effects in the upper atmosphere.

In 1946, after the war, Chapman accepted an invitation to become Sedleian professor of natural philosophy at Oxford, and became a fellow of the Queen's College. He appreciated the gracious living there, but not the relatively secondary status he found allotted to science. He tried to improve that status by giving general science lectures to non-scientists. He also supervised research students who were later to make their mark, like F. D. Kahn and K. C. Westfold. However, this time at Oxford was marked by no exciting new advance; his scientific role was becoming that of an elder statesman and counsellor.

He spent the year 1950–1 at the California Institute of Technology, also visiting the new Geophysical Institute at College, Alaska. Then, determined not to let himself be retired when he reached the official age, in 1953 he resigned his Oxford chair to take up a research post in Alaska, helping to establish the research school there. In 1955 he added a similar post at the High Altitude Observatory, Boulder, Colorado, officially dividing his time between the two. In practice, however, the two were used as bases for sorties throughout the world. He was visiting professor at many places, among them Istanbul (1954) and Ibadan (1964). He also made numerous visits to secure the co-operation of groups in many countries in the work of the International Geophysical Year (IGY) of 1957–8, of whose organizing committee he was an indefatigable president. His especial care during the actual IGY was as reporter of the results on aurorae, which he had had ample opportunity to study in Alaska.

Soon after the IGY Chapman was joined by S.-I. Akasofu, a young geophysicist who had already begun good work in his native Japan. Their co-operation over the next few years was remarkably fruitful; even though Chapman was now over seventy, his intellectual powers were unabated, and his great experience was admirably complemented by Akasofu's freshness of approach. They worked together on the completion of the theory of magnetic storms and the explanation of aurorae in the light of recent discoveries about the van Allen belts, the magnetosphere, and the surrounding plasma from the Sun. Another collaborator during this period was P. C. Kendall, with whom Chapman produced a theory of noctilucent clouds.

During the last years of his life Chapman tried, through review papers, to make generally available the wide knowledge he had accumulated over the years. Two of his longer papers were republished as books, *Solar Plasma, Geomagnetism and Aurora* (1964), and (written jointly with R. S. Lindzen) *Atmospheric Tides* (1970). In addition, at the time of his death he had largely completed the manuscript of a new and comprehensive book with Akasofu, entitled *Solar-Terrestrial Physics*; this was published posthumously in 1972. He was working hard on a variety of other projects up to the time of his death, which occurred at Boulder, 16 June 1970, after only a few days' illness.

Chapman's most distinctive personal characteristics were his kindliness, persistence, integrity, and simplicity. Those who saw through his surface reserves always found him ready to help. He was never afraid to tackle massive problems, though sometimes he surveyed them for years before the final assault; also he tried to give complete solutions, often returning time and again to particular topics. His strength of principle was manifested both by his pacifism during the war of 1914-18 and his war work in 1939-45; each was motivated by his opposition to violations of humanity. He had a strong sense of duty (including scientific duty) and encouraged high standards in others. If satisfied that a course of action was reasonable he would take it, even if it meant defying convention. When convinced of an error he was ready to acknowledge it. A simple directness pervaded both his writings and his way of life. He knew the value of his own work, but succeeded in making the many who collaborated with him feel that they too had increased in stature.

His distinctions and honours were many. He was in turn president of five British scientific societies, and of four international bodies, including the International Union of Geodesy and Geophysics (1951-4). He received Royal

and Copley medals from the Royal Society, and eight other medals and awards from societies in Britain and abroad, and was elected honorary member of six national academies. He was given honorary doctorates by ten universities, six British and four foreign.

He married in 1922 Katharine Nora (died 1967), daughter of Alfred E. Steinthal, barrister and honorary treasurer of Manchester University. His wife shared many of his peregrinations. They had three sons and one daughter.

[*Sydney Chapman, eighty, from his friends* (privately printed for the universities of Alaska and Colorado and UCAR, 1968, ed. by S-I. Akasofu, B. Fogle, and B. Haurwitz); T. G. Cowling in *Biographical Memoirs of Fellows of the Royal Society*, vol. xvii, 1971; personal knowledge.]

T. G. COWLING

CHAROUX, SIEGFRIED JOSEPH (1896-1967), sculptor, was born in Vienna 15 October 1896, the only son of Joseph Charoux, a captain in the Austrian Army, and his wife, Anna Kinich, a peasant from Czechoslovakia. He attended elementary and secondary schools in Vienna. He was called up to serve in the Austro-Hungarian Army at the beginning of 1915, but after being wounded three times, he was invalided out at the end of 1917. In 1919 Charoux was admitted to the master class of the Vienna School of Fine Arts where he remained until 1924; he then studied for four years at the Vienna Academy under Professor Hans Bitterlich. At the same time he worked as a political cartoonist. In 1925 he married Margarete Treibl: they had no children.

Charoux began work in the optical concern of Goerz where he had to affix lenses to telescopes with wax and this led to his making figures in wax. He was a man of extreme political sensitivity which had a vehicle in his cartoons for the *Arbeiter-Zeitung*. His first exhibition was in 1925; he created the Robert Blum Memorial (Vienna, 1928), the Matteotti Memorial (Vienna, 1930), the Professor Herz Memorial (university of Vienna, 1932), and he undertook various commissions for municipal buildings in Vienna (1930-5).

In 1933 he won an international competition, which had eighty-three entrants, for a monument to Lessing. This statue, completed in 1935, was destroyed by the Nazis and melted down for armaments because of their hatred of any unusual or unconventional art. After the war Charoux returned to make another. During the preparation of the first monument he exhibited works in Austria, Germany, Belgium, and Italy.

Charoux came to settle in England in September 1935. His early preference for the art of Auguste Rodin expressed in his bronze group 'Man with Lamb' (Chicago Art Museum) gave way to his enthusiasm for the more tranquil quality of Greek and Gothic sculpture at about the time of his arrival in England, where he seems to have undergone a spiritual rebirth which is clearly apparent in his work. England freed him as an artist and a human being and he was able to explore and develop his art without fear of political persecution. The increased monumentality and the tranquillity in appearance is visible in the terracotta figure of 'Youth: Standing Boy' which was acquired under the terms of the Chantrey Bequest in 1948 for the Tate Gallery. This work was carried out in a technique, once used by the Etruscans, of building up a hollow shell in terracotta without the reinforcement of an armature.

As in his technique, Charoux was apostolically and artistically catholic about his ideas: 'My tolerance knows no limit,' he once wrote to a friend, 'the fruits painted may be square, and so can be the arses, but they must be alive and carry a message.'

The significant commission of a terracotta figure for novelist Hannah Cohen's garden at Durford Heath, Petersfield, in Hampshire, set his career. He was naturalized a British subject in November 1946 following his showing of a bronze bust of Sir Stafford Cripps [q.v.] in the Royal Academy Summer Exhibition of that year.

In 1938 he executed stone carvings for the new School of Anatomy and the Engineering Laboratory at Cambridge. He contributed a monumental group, 'The Islanders', to the South Bank Festival of Britain exhibition in 1951, after which he completed nine figures, eight feet tall, for Salters' Hall, London, representing Manual and Spiritual Labour. His best-known work is the cycle of sculptures entitled 'Civilization': 'The Judge' for the Law Courts, 'Motor Cyclist' for the Shell Building, and 'The Cellist' outside the Royal Festival Hall, London. He contributed to open-air exhibitions of sculptures in Battersea Park, London, in 1948, 1951, 1954, and 1960, and in Holland Park in 1957.

Charoux was elected an associate of the Royal Academy of Arts in 1949 and an academician in 1956. In 1948 he received the highest award for sculpture of the city of Vienna and in 1958 was made an honorary professor of the Republic of Austria.

He was described as a typical Austrian in appearance, fair-haired and blue-eyed, heroic in build, and with a magnificent head like a much more amiable edition of Beethoven. Almost always he wore a faded old sculptor's smock, the rolled-up sleeves revealing a massive pair of forearms and hands. He seemed happy so long as he was making something—sculpture, pictures, pots, a new kiln, bread. Jugged hare was one of his special accomplishments. He loved a good argument among friends and could be devastatingly funny, manipulating his enormous fingers to emphasize a point and wielding a shaky knowledge of English with more wit and wisdom than most of us who have spoken the language all our lives. Charoux died in London 26 April 1967.

A self-portrait in oils, painted during the 1960s, is in the possession of the family.

[Ashgate Gallery, Farnham, exhibition catalogue, 1975; Piccadilly Gallery, London, exhibition catalogue, 1958; *The Times*, 28 April, 3 and 5 May 1967; private information.]   HANS FLETCHER

CHATFIELD, ALFRED ERNLE MONTACUTE, first BARON CHATFIELD (1873-1967), admiral of the fleet, was born in Southsea 27 September 1873, the fourth child and only son of Admiral Alfred John Chatfield and his wife, Louisa, eldest daughter of Thomas Faulconer, of Hampstead. Much of his early childhood was spent in naval circles, first in Malta when his father commanded *Thunderer* in the Mediterranean Fleet and later at Devonport and Pembroke Dock during the years that his father held shore appointments in those establishments. He was educated at St. Andrew's School, Tenby, and in 1886 passed the examination for entry into the *Britannia*, joining her at Dartmouth a few days before his thirteenth birthday. On passing out in 1888 he joined the *Iron Duke*, a barque-rigged battleship in the Channel Fleet, and a few months later was appointed to the *Cleopatra*, a new corvette bound for the South American station. She also was square-rigged with auxiliary steam engines and during the young Chatfield's early years in the navy he had much experience of sail and sail drill. Fortunately it did not last long enough to indoctrinate him into the diehard resistance to change which so dominated the Royal Navy of the late nineteenth century.

As a lieutenant Chatfield specialized in gunnery during a period when the need for developing a modern navy suitable to the times was widely recognized as paramount, and when the specialist, particularly in gunnery and torpedoes, was usually starred for advancement. In 1899, when he took up his first sea-going appointment as a gunnery specialist in the *Caesar*, the navy was undergoing a long overdue surge of feeling towards modern appliances and modern techniques. Stimulated by the advanced naval doctrines of Sir John (later Lord) Fisher and, particularly in the art and practice of gunnery by Captain (later Admiral Sir) Percy Scott [qq.v.], Chatfield was swept up in this surge and became an enthusiastic and, in his specialization, a brilliant supporter of any and every technical advance which could add to the efficiency of the navy. These were the years of the naval building competition with Germany, and the knowledge of a new navy building and training hard on the other side of the North Sea acted as a spur to most of the younger naval officers to dedicate themselves to their profession. Chatfield was undoubtedly one of these.

In 1909 he was promoted captain and appointed to command the *Albemarle* in the Atlantic Fleet, in which one of his fellow captains was David (later Admiral of the Fleet first Earl) Beatty [q.v.]. He first became Beatty's flag captain in the *Aboukir* for six weeks during the manœuvres of 1912, and when Beatty was appointed in 1913 to command the battle-cruiser squadron, flying his flag in the *Lion*, he again took Chatfield with him as his flag captain with the additional responsibility of organizing and training the squadron in gunnery. Thus he took part in the three principal actions fought in the North Sea, those of Heligoland Bight (28 August 1914), Dogger Bank (24 January 1915), and Jutland (31 May 1916). The *Lion* was heavily hit both at the Dogger Bank and Jutland battles, sustaining considerable damage, due in part to the faulty distribution of fire of the battle-cruisers which in each action left a German opponent unengaged, a surprising lapse in a gunnery officer of Chatfield's calibre. Chatfield remained in the *Lion* until November 1916, when Beatty relieved Sir John (later Admiral of the Fleet first Earl) Jellicoe [q.v.] as commander-in-chief, Grand Fleet, and again Chatfield went with him as flag captain and chief of staff first in the *Iron Duke* and later in the *Queen Elizabeth*.

After the war, in June 1919, Chatfield went to the Admiralty as fourth sea lord, becoming assistant chief of staff in February 1920, shortly after Beatty had taken up his appointment as first sea lord in November 1919. As such he had an important part to play in the negotiations for the Treaty for the Limitation of Naval Armaments, the end result of the Washington conference of 1921–2. He had been promoted rear-admiral in August 1920 and, when Beatty left the conference in November 1921 to look after naval affairs at home, Chatfield became the senior naval delegate in Washington, a position which involved him in long technical discussions on the levels of armament and displacement of the

future naval ships of all the maritime nations. This introduction to international and political negotiations on naval affairs, allied to his extensive experience of senior command at sea and of the administrative machine in the Admiralty, gave him an unrivalled background against which to build his future career. Already he had very clear views of the future shape and organization of the navy, and was clearly marked for promotion to high office.

After two years in command of the third cruiser squadron in the Mediterranean, Chatfield returned to the Admiralty in 1925 as third sea lord and controller of the navy, a position which he did not relish. As controller he was responsible for the material development and supply of the navy, whereas his chief interest lay more in organization and in tactical and strategical thought. At the same time it was a particularly difficult period, hedged in as it was by the limitations on size and armament agreed at the Washington conference, by the 'ten year rule' laid down by the Treasury, on which all service estimates were to be based, and also hindered by various Treasury committees set up to enforce the deflationary fiscal policies of those years, and by severe disagreement with the United States over the number of cruisers required by Britain for the defence of the Empire. Chatfield was the main driving force in resisting American demands for a reduction in British cruiser strength, and it was his insistence, against strong Treasury and, indeed, Cabinet, opposition to his views, which finally won the day. He was, at the same time, brought into the unhappy dispute with the Air Ministry over control of the Fleet Air Arm, and also had to concern himself with the decision to build up Singapore as a defended naval base in the Far East. He remained controller for three and a half years, being promoted vice-admiral in 1926.

On leaving the Admiralty he hoisted his flag in 1929 in the *Nelson* as commander-in-chief, Atlantic Fleet, and a year later was transferred to the Mediterranean Fleet, having in the meantime been promoted admiral (1930). He flew his flag in the *Queen Elizabeth*, the same ship in which he had ended the war of 1914–18 as Beatty's flag captain. During his two years in the Mediterranean as commander-in-chief he exercised the fleet many times in night fighting, filling a large gap in naval training, the need for which had been demonstrated in 1916, when the German High Seas Fleet had been allowed to escape from possible destruction in the Battle of Jutland. Night fighting exercises had been first instituted in 1921, but in a desultory fashion, and it was largely as a result of Chatfield's enthusiasm in the Mediterranean that it took its proper and overdue place in fleet training. He also experimented with carriers and naval aircraft in an attempt to introduce a viable tactical doctrine for their use in battle; this had little success partly because of the low priority which was given to the development of the aircraft carrier and to naval aircraft under Air Ministry control.

In 1933, on the expiration of his term of command, Chatfield realized his great ambition by returning to the Admiralty as first sea lord. Since the limitations on naval shipbuilding imposed by the Washington and London (1930) treaties were due to expire in 1936, he set about preparing a new building programme which would restore the navy to something like the power it had formerly enjoyed before the cuts imposed on it had reduced its operational strength. At the same time, determined to rectify the weakness which his Mediterranean experiences in carrier and aircraft exercises had revealed, he renewed the battle with the Air Ministry for naval control of the Fleet Air Arm. In this he was successful when, in 1937, the Cabinet upheld the Admiralty's case.

As a gunnery specialist, Chatfield had always been a firm supporter of the battleship as the dominant weapon at sea, and there were those who feared, on his appointment as first sea lord, that too great a proportion of the money voted for naval rearmament would be spent on the construction of these expensive ships to the detriment of cruisers and, particularly, of destroyers and escort vessels. The experience gained in the U-boat campaign of the war of 1914-18, and the technical advances made in submarine construction and torpedoes since then, meant that there were many naval officers who considered that in the next war (a war which, during Chatfield's term of office, seemed increasingly likely to be fought against Hitler's Germany), the decisive battle would be fought against submarines in the Atlantic. Because of this, they felt that during naval rearmament priority should be given to the building of an adequate convoy escort force for anti-submarine warfare. In the event, a large programme of new battleship construction was authorized, and it was only after four years of war, and grievous losses of merchant tonnage, that the escort forces were at last able to assert a mastery over the U-boats. Nevertheless, the fact that the navy, throughout the first three years of the war, was able to meet and discharge the heavy commitments which it was called upon to undertake, though with very little to spare, was due largely to Chatfield's drive. His term of office as first sea lord was twice extended, and he left the Admiralty in August 1938, having been promoted admiral of the fleet in 1935 and raised to the peerage as first

Baron Chatfield in the coronation honour list of 1937.

After leaving the Admiralty Chatfield served as chairman of the expert committee on Indian defence, and while still in India received an invitation from the prime minister, Neville Chamberlain, to join the Cabinet as minister for co-ordination of defence, in succession to T. W. H. Inskip (later Viscount Caldecote, q.v.). He started this work in Whitehall in February 1939 at a time when it was certain that war with a rearmed Germany could not be long delayed. He was sworn of the Privy Council on taking up the appointment, having been admitted to the Order of Merit in the previous month. But the essential pragmatism of politics was entirely foreign to one who had been brought up since youth to the decision-taking character of naval life, and he was constantly irked by his lack of power to press ahead in his own way with the rapid build-up, which war demanded, of the navy, army, and air force. As he himself wrote in his memoirs, when he found himself after the declaration of war a member of the War Cabinet, he was little more than 'a fifth wheel to the coach', but his malaise in political life went deeper than that. He was apt to be intolerant of politicians, perhaps not understanding that they, like him, also had their particular spheres of responsibility for which they were answerable to Parliament. His disillusionment with the political side of service life was also exacerbated by the fact that, although he was an admiral of the fleet, he now had no say in the chiefs of staff committee which, as first sea lord, he had grown used to dominate. He was asked to resign in March 1940 and his office was abolished. He then turned his undoubted abilities into less irksome occupations, of which the most important was the chairmanship of the committee on evacuation of casualties in London region hospitals.

Chatfield was one of the most able and dedicated naval officers of his generation, a man of great intellect, force of character, and complete integrity. In stature he was small, with little of the traditional look of an admiral about him, and he was austere with little sense of humour. He reached the top of his profession, deservedly, through hard work, an intense devotion to duty, and an unbending resolution to carry into effect the policies he considered necessary to transform the hidebound Grand Fleet of 1914-18 into the flexible instrument so ably used by the fleet commanders of 1939-45, a transformation as successful as it was necessary. He received many decorations and honours in his life, both British and foreign, which included honorary degrees from both Oxford and Cambridge universities.

He married, in 1909, Lillian Emma St. John (died 1977), daughter of Major George L. Matthews, and had two daughters, one of whom died in 1943, and one son. He died at home at Farnham Common 15 November 1967 and was succeeded in the barony by his son, Ernle David Lewis (born 1917). There is a portrait of him by R. G. Eves in the National Portrait Gallery.

[Lord Chatfield, *The Navy and Defence*, 1942, and *It Might Happen Again*, 1947 (these are two autobiographical volumes); Lord Chatfield, *Defence After the War*, 1944 (a pamphlet); official dispatches; Cabinet Office papers; family papers.]

PETER KEMP

CHAVASSE, CHRISTOPHER MAUDE (1884-1962), bishop of Rochester, was born at Oxford 9 November 1884, the eldest (and twin) son of the Revd Francis James Chavasse [q.v.], then rector of St. Peter le Bailey, Oxford, and later bishop of Liverpool, and his wife, Edith Maude. He had an elder sister, twin younger sisters, and two younger brothers. Educated at Magdalen College School, Oxford, and Liverpool College, he went up to Trinity College, Oxford, in 1905, where he distinguished himself as an athlete, gaining blues for lacrosse and athletics. Both he and his twin brother represented England at the Olympic Games of 1908. In the same year Chavasse failed his history schools, whereupon he sat pass moderations and a group.

Chavasse was ordained to a curacy at St. Helens, Lancashire, where his gifts of leadership among men and his initiative in tackling social problems were immediately apparent. He enlisted as a chaplain in the forces in 1914 and served throughout the war of 1914-18, being awarded the MC and the croix de guerre. In 1917 his twin brother Noel, who had won the VC, was killed in France. One of his younger brothers was also killed. He was promoted deputy assistant chaplain general in IX Corps in 1918. On demobilization in 1919, he was appointed vicar of St. George's, Barrow in Furness.

In 1922 Chavasse returned to Oxford as rector of St. Aldates where he built up a vigorous congregation of undergraduates and established a reputation as a gifted preacher and a leader among younger evangelicals. He became known outside Oxford as a tenacious and well-informed opponent of the proposals for the revision of the Prayer Book, at the risk, he was told by the archbishop of Canterbury, Randall Davidson (later Lord Davidson of Lambeth, q.v.), of any chance of preferment. In 1928 it fell to him to initiate the fulfilment of the vision of his father who had died that year, namely the founding in Oxford of a new and evangelical college which would attract men of modest means and provide bursaries for ordination candidates. He left St. Aldates for St. Peter le Bailey, a living which he had held in plurality for six months, and round St. Peter le Bailey and the buildings associated with it he began the first stage as a hostel for non-collegiate students. A petition was presented to the Convocation of the university for the licensing of St. Peter's as a permanent private hall, with Chavasse as its first master. Permission was granted in 1929 but not without some opposition, partly from Anglo-Catholic opinion and partly provoked by the impetuousness and enthusiasm of the young master in his dealings with the Delegacy of Lodgings. Chavasse recruited an able body of tutors and the early years were marked by a steady growth in numbers and reputation. Behind the scenes there was a constant struggle to establish the Hall on a sound financial footing; but from the impact that Chavasse made on the first generation of men in the Hall, no one could have guessed the stress of financial worry. It was typical of Chavasse that he was able to enlist the support of W. R. Morris (later Viscount Nuffield, q.v.) on the basis of a friendship formed through his pastoral ministry at the death of Morris's mother. With Morris's support and the personal sacrifice of Chavasse and some of his friends, the finances of the Hall were secured. During this period his interests were not confined to Oxford. He served as proctor in Convocation for the university, 1936-9, and continued as chaplain to the Territorial Army.

In July 1939 Chavasse was nominated to the see of Rochester, but his consecration had to be delayed until St. Mark's Day, 25 April 1940, owing to injuries sustained in a boating accident, as a result of which he lost the use of a leg, which was amputated in 1942. His episcopate of over twenty years fell into two periods. The first decade was devoted to the problems of wartime and post-war reconstruction. He had a deep understanding of the pastoral needs of men and women in the forces, and a concern for their homes and churches, so badly damaged by enemy action. The figure of the bishop with an artificial leg, worn with great fortitude, was an inspiration to many in what he used to call his 'bomb-alley' diocese. In preparing for peace he launched, in 1944, a great appeal for one million pounds for rebuilding and augmentation. He was concerned for 'diocesan consciousness' in an area where all roads lead towards London, and to achieve this he appointed a 'mobile force of diocesan officers' and held regular clergy conferences. Early in his episcopate he was faced with a problem of discipline which attracted widespread attention. It concerned the Reservation of the Sacrament in the parish of St. Mary's, Swanley. He insisted on loyalty to the policy laid down by both Houses of Convocation, which permitted Reservation in the manner allowed in the 1928 Prayer Book. His action was misrepresented by some Anglo-Catholics, but he was later able to claim that his stand, which was upheld in the Consistory Court, had smoothed the path for his episcopal brethren. His most distinguished service to the Church at this time was his chairmanship of the commission which produced the report, *Towards the Conversion of England* (1945), which created much discussion in the post-war period and inspired evangelistic campaigning, but the bishop was disappointed in the subsequent attitude of the Church Assembly. Chavasse also produced many other books and pamphlets.

The second decade of his episcopate was devoted to further advance. A church extension campaign was launched to provide churches in the new housing estates arising from the overspill of London's population. Chavasse had a great sense of occasion and in 1954 used the 1,350th anniversary of the founding of the diocese as a focus of effort. His last years saw the creation of a third archdeaconry at Bromley (1954), the suffragan bishopric of Tonbridge, and a diocesan centre at Chislehurst. He also founded at Rochester a theological college for older men.

Chavasse was more than a diocesan figure. He had a rare combination of great moral and physical courage which led him to be outspoken on a number of issues such as on the element of gambling in premium bonds and on the Wolfenden Report. As an evangelical churchman he had an independent position for, although he was their undoubted leader, he was distrustful of liberals on grounds of vague theology and he opposed extreme conservative fundamentalism.

In 1936 Chavasse was appointed OBE, in 1940 TD, in 1959 DL, and he was also DD (Lambeth). In 1960 he retired to Oxford where he had become an honorary fellow of Trinity College (1955) and of St. Peter's (1949). He lived to see the fulfilment of his earlier ambitions when St. Peter's became fully incorporated as a college of the university in 1961.

He married in 1919 Beatrice Cropper (died 1977), daughter of William Edward Willink, JP, of Dingle Bank, Liverpool. He had three sons and two daughters. The eldest son, Noel, gained the MC in World War II and the second son, Michael, became a QC and a circuit judge. Chavasse died at Oxford 10 March 1962. He is commemorated in St. Peter's College by a portrait in the hall by (Sir) Oswald

Birley (1938), and in the chapel, where the east window by John Hayward is his memorial.

[Selwyn Gummer, *The Chavasse Twins*, 1963; Eric H. F. Smith, *St. Peter's—the Founding of an Oxford College*, 1978; *The Times*, 12, 14, and 30 March 1962; personal knowledge.]   DOUGLAS R. VICARY

CHEESMAN, ROBERT ERNEST (1878-1962), explorer and naturalist, was born at Westwell, Kent, 18 October 1878, the eldest son and second of five children of Robert Cheesman, farmer, and his wife, Florence Maud Tassell. His younger sister, Lucy Evelyn (1881-1969), became a well-known entomologist, traveller, writer, and broadcaster. Cheesman was educated at Merchant Taylors' School and Wye Agricultural College. He then worked for Sharpe and Winch, brewers, of Cranbrook, Kent. He was a keen ornithologist. As a boy he tried to rear wood-pigeon squabs by swallowing and regurgitating clover leaves, like the mother bird. He was elected to the British Ornithologists' Union in 1908, and in 1912-14 contributed notes to *British Birds*.

In 1914 Cheesman enlisted in the Buffs, misrepresenting his age. He served in India and in the attempted relief of Kut. In 1916 he met Sir Percy Cox [q.v.], then political officer to the Mesopotamian Expeditionary Force, who shared his enthusiasm for birds. Together they undertook to collect the avifauna of Iraq. Cox wanted to organize the growing of vegetables for the troops and persuaded Cheesman to take a commission (1916) in the Indian Army reserve of officers. Cheesman then became assistant to the deputy director of agriculture. His pamphlet *Notes on Vegetable Growing in Mesopotamia in 1917* was published officially in 1918. While Cox was high commissioner in Iraq, Cheesman was his private secretary (1920-3). He was elected to the British Ornithologists' Club in 1919, a fellow of the Royal Geographical Society in 1920, and a corresponding member of the Zoological Society of London in 1921.

In 1921 Cheesman mapped the Arabian coast from 'Uqair to the head of the Gulf of Salwa. He was appointed OBE in 1923. In 1923-4 he spent eleven weeks at Hufuf and then travelled to Jabrin; he fixed its position, mapped 150 miles of the desert, identified the site of ancient Gerra, and corrected serious mistakes about the wadi system. He received the Royal Geographical Society's Gill memorial award in 1925 for this journey, which he described in *In Unknown Arabia* (1926). In 1925 he became consul for North-West Ethiopia, resident at Dangila, as a member of the Sudan Political Service. Officially he was much concerned with preventing elephant poachers from entering the Sudan, but he used every opportunity for exploration. He visited the source of the Blue Nile several times, first in March 1926. He mapped the river from Tisisat to Wanbera in January-April 1927, returning. to Dangila through little-known country. He completed the map from Wanbera to the frontier in February-April 1929. He explored the river from its source to Lake Tana, correcting many cartographical errors, in 1932. He circumnavigated the lake, landing on all the bigger islands and making a compass traverse of the coast, in November 1932-April 1933. He retired in 1934, was made a commander of the Star of Ethiopia, and was appointed CBE (1935). He received the Royal Geographical Society's Patron's medal in 1936 for his explorations, which he described in *Lake Tana and the Blue Nile* (1936).

Cheesman married, in 1927, Catherine, daughter of William Francis Winch, estate agent and brewer, of Cranbrook, and resigned from the reserve as major in 1928. After he retired in 1934 he and his wife lived at her fifteenth-century house, Tilsden, outside Cranbrook, where they farmed together. In 1940, at the request of the governor-general of the Sudan, Cheesman became head of the Ethiopian section of intelligence, Sudan Defence Force, first as bimbashi, then as colonel. Notes and bearings he had taken previously now proved valuable. It was largely on his recommendation that O. C. Wingate [q.v.] selected his first objective in the invasion of Ethiopia. In 1942 Cheesman became oriental counsellor at the legation, Addis Ababa. In 1944 he retired finally to Cranbrook, having been mentioned in dispatches in both wars. The farm was sold after his wife's death in 1958, but he continued to live quietly at Tilsden. He died 13 February 1962 in Tunbridge Wells. He had no children.

On all his travels Cheesman assiduously collected specimens of fauna, flora, and minerals, nearly all of which he presented to the British Museum. They included several new species of mammals and insects. He described them in articles in which he collaborated with professional taxonomists in *Annals and Magazine of Natural History* in 1919-28, *Journal of the Bombay Natural History Society* in 1920-6, and *Ibis* in 1923-36. He contributed occasionally to the *Geographical Journal* in 1923-60. His books are both readable and authoritative, characterized by modesty, a sense of humour, and accurate observation, especially of topography and wildlife. In temperament and tastes he was a countryman, deliberate, patient, thorough, kind, and personally frugal. Never pretending to expertise he did not possess, he did whatever was possible

to ensure that his travels should benefit every branch of knowledge.

[Cheesman's own writing; *The Times*, 15 February 1962; P. P. Graves, *The Life of Sir Percy Cox*, 1941; Evelyn Cheesman, *Things Worth While*, 1957; private information.]   C. F. BECKINGHAM

CHRISTIANSEN, ARTHUR (1904-1963), editor, was born in Wallasey, Cheshire, 27 July 1904, the only son and second of the three children of Louis Niels Christiansen, a master shipwright of Danish descent, and his wife, Ellen Miller. From the age of fourteen, at Wallasey Grammar School, he was producing a magazine, reporting school events, writing the short stories, drawing the illustrations, and stitching the pages together on his mother's sewing machine. He had fallen in love with the printed word; and he never fell out of it. Soon after his sixteenth birthday he joined the *Wallasey and Wirral Chronicle* as a reporter. From there, three and a half years later, he moved to the *Liverpool Evening Express* and *Daily Courier*, and became the *Evening Express*'s London editor in 1925. Within a year he had become news editor of the *Sunday Express* and in 1928 assistant editor. He took charge of the office on the Sunday morning in 1930 when the airship R.101 crashed in flames at Beauvais on its maiden voyage to India, bringing out a special late-morning edition which won the admiration of Fleet Street and, more importantly, brought him to the attention of the proprietor, Lord Beaverbrook [q.v.].

In 1932 Beaverbrook sent Christiansen to Manchester to edit the northern edition of the *Daily Express* and brought him back to London in 1933 first as assistant editor and then in the same year as editor of the *Daily Express*. He was only twenty-nine. It was the beginning of a remarkable association which was to last nearly twenty-five years and to lift the *Daily Express* from a sale of 1,700,000 to 4,000,000. Christiansen described their association thus: 'I was a journalist not a political animal. My proprietor was a journalist and a political animal. The policies were Lord Beaverbrook's the presentation mine.' This was a frank and truthful piece of self-analysis but it conveys no flavour of the battles, the tensions, the coolnesses, the moments of warm affection which made up the association of the two men.

Christiansen's presentation was not simply a matter of making headlines bigger and bolder; by the brilliant and highly personal use of type and illustration he combined legibility with dramatic appearance in a harmony new to popular journalism. His best work represented a revolution in newspaper design—not always acceptable to the typographical purists but much copied by other newspapers and overwhelming in its appeal to the public. At the very outset of his editorship Christiansen—who had the support and understanding of Beaverbrook's able manager, E. J. Robertson—surrounded himself with forceful, energetic men of his own generation, many of whom stayed with him throughout his career. A constant flow of talent was recruited into the paper's columns.

In a particularly turbulent period of a turbulent calling, Christiansen inspired loyalty not only by the exercise of a considerable personal charm, but by his daily staff conferences and his daily bulletins. His conferences were conducted with a high-spirited, shirt-sleeved exuberance which not only expressed his own jovial, generous nature, but also set the tone for the next day's paper. Dullness was banished; optimism shone through. What was good for the executives turned out to be a formula which had an intense appeal for those millions of readers whose struggles, ambitions, and aspirations Christiansen instinctively understood. Immediately the morning conference ended, he wrote his daily bulletin, in which he analysed the paper, gave praise or blame, stated general principles, produced such much-quoted phrases as 'The Man in the Back Streets of Derby' (a character who grew into the prototype *Express* reader), and developed his ideas on 'presentation' of news.

Yet policy and presentation could not be wholly divorced; in the printed word, the medium can also be the message. An example of this occurred when in 1938 the *Express* published the headline 'There will be no war' with the later addition of 'this year, or next year either'. Authorship remains doubtful; what is certain is that Christiansen projected the slogan so prominently and so vigorously that the headline subsequently became a convenient weapon for critics to employ in attacking everything they found hateful about *Express* political policies. Criticism of political policies, however, did nothing to halt the rising sales of the *Express* and for many years, until the post-war rise of the *Daily Mirror*, it had the highest sale of any newspaper in Britain.

In July 1956, after twenty-three years of editorship, Christiansen had a heart attack while staying with Beaverbrook in the South of France. He was no longer able to edit in the pattern of vigorous leadership which he had established, and after an unhappy period when he tried, and failed, to adjust himself to new jobs and to a new relationship with Beaverbrook, he resigned in May 1958 and finally severed his connection with the Beaverbrook press in 1959.

Christiansen switched his energies to work in television and films, but he never found there the satisfaction which newspapers brought him. On 27 September 1963 he collapsed and died in a television studio in Norwich.

In 1926 Christiansen married Brenda Winifred Wray (otherwise Shepherd). There were two sons and two daughters of the marriage. The elder son, Michael Robin, edited the *Sunday Mirror* from 1964 to 1972.

A portrait head of Christiansen, by Vasco Lazzolo, the sculptor, is in the possession of the family.

[Arthur Christiansen, *Headlines all my Life*, 1961; Tom Driberg, *Beaverbrook*, 1956; A. J. P. Taylor, *Beaverbrook*, 1972; personal knowledge.]   EDWARD PICKERING

CHRISTIE, JOHN (1882–1962), founder of Glyndebourne Opera, was born 14 December 1882, at Eggesford, Devon, the only child of Augustus Langham Christie, a country squire, and his wife, (Alicia) Rosamond Wallop, third daughter of the fifth Earl of Portsmouth. His family had acquired large estates over the past hundred years since their ancestor came from Switzerland to settle in England, and now owned the manor house at Glyndebourne and some ten thousand acres, as well as an extensive property in north Devon. Unfortunately Augustus Christie suffered from a nervous instability verging upon insanity, and the early life of the son was spent away from his father. His childhood was unhappy, which had the effect of making him fiercely independent and often rebellious; so that at the age of six, being strong and well able to look after himself, he was sent away to school, where he quickly earned a reputation for indiscipline. In 1896 he went to Eton, like his father and grandfather, where, despite his small stature, he made his mark by unconventional behaviour and by the capricious use of his intelligence according to whether he liked or disliked his masters. From there he was sent in 1900 to the Royal Military Academy, Woolwich, but he injured his foot in a riding accident, and, much to his satisfaction he abandoned a military career and in 1902 passed into Trinity College, Cambridge. Here he spent three years reading natural sciences, which he liked, and developed a keen interest in music and the motor car. After getting a second class degree (1905) he became a master at Eton in 1906 and spent sixteen years there (apart from two years on war service), which proved, as he often said, to be the happiest of his life. At that time Eton masters were allowed very considerable freedom, and he was conspicuous among a somewhat eccentric community for a novel approach to his duties and methods. But he enjoyed teaching and had the gift of inspiring loyalty among his pupils and made many friends among his colleagues. The years 1914–16 saw him in France, where, as a captain in the King's Royal Rifle Corps he showed absolute fearlessness in action, which won him the Military Cross and the admiration of his men. But trench warfare proved too severe a strain on his injured foot and he returned to Eton, staying there another six years, until he decided to give up teaching in order to pay more attention to the development of his inherited assets. In 1913 his father had let him have virtual control of Glyndebourne, which he made his own home and used for entertaining his friends. In 1920, when he gained legal ownership of the estate, he at once set about improving the amenities of the house. He had already built on a large room which was to become the centre of his musical activities. Here he had installed a cathedral organ, buying up an organ company for the purpose, and developed the estate workyard, which later grew into a most successful commercial enterprise. He also acquired a controlling interest in various other businesses; for he felt strongly that a landlord should do something constructive with his money and property, and he had no use for the idle and parasitic rich. As yet he confined his musical interests to performances in the Organ Room, but in 1930 he became engaged to (Grace) Audrey Laura St. John-Mildmay (died 1953) daughter of the Revd Aubrey Neville St. John-Mildmay (later tenth baronet) a gifted soprano with the Carl Rosa Opera Company, and they were married the next year. Almost at once he made plans to give complete operas at Glyndebourne, but his wife saw that this would not be practicable unless it were done 'properly' (as she put it). Therefore her husband, who trusted her professional judgement implicitly, decided to build a theatre on to the back of his country house. So Glyndebourne Opera was founded.

When this announcement was made, the music world was incredulous, the press derisive, and even his closest friends thought that such a wild scheme could not possibly succeed. But he went ahead, and by summer 1934 the opera house had been built with a large and excellently equipped stage but a relatively small auditorium holding about three hundred people. A first-rate team was assembled under the leadership of the conductor Fritz Busch and the producer Carl Ebert, with John Christie himself and his wife at hand to keep things under control. Recent visits to Salzburg and elsewhere had made them both ardent Mozartians, and the first season opened with Le nozze di Figaro.

It was immediately pronounced a triumphant success both by the musical intelligentsia and by the lay public, and an equally good reception was given to Cosi fan tutte which followed. During the next four years the repertoire was extended to the other three best-known Mozart operas and to Verdi's Macbeth and Donizetti's Don Pasquale. In five productions of three of these operas Audrey Mildmay sang with great charm and distinction, while in the same period managing to have a daughter and a son and to act as an exemplary hostess to her many guests. She was indeed a person of rare quality. The first three seasons had cost John Christie about £100,000, of which £21,000 had been lost on the running costs of the Opera, but in 1937 he was able to make a small profit and thus to prove that such a thing could be done. Then war started, and Glyndebourne became a home for London children. Audrey Christie, much against her will, took her own children to Canada, where she eked out a precarious existence by giving concerts, but was able to return home in 1944. At once Christie set about considering means of reviving the Opera, but financial problems were acute, since he did not feel it reasonable to spend more of his private fortune for the benefit of the public. A few concerts with Sir Thomas Beecham [q.v.] and opera performances (the world premières of Benjamin Britten's The Rape of Lucretia and Albert Herring, and Gluck's Orpheus with Kathleen Ferrier, q.v.) were given in 1946–7, while Glyndebourne was engaged in creating the Edinburgh Festival, where it performed opera exclusively from 1947 to 1949. But it was not until 1950 that support from the John Lewis Partnership enabled Glyndebourne to put on its own festival again. Then in 1952 the Hungarian textile manufacturer, Nicholas Sekers (later knighted for his services to music) organized the supporters of Glyndebourne into a group known as 'The Glyndebourne Festival Society' (the first scheme of its kind in Britain), and this substantially assisted the opera to remain solvent. Shortly afterwards the decision was taken to place it under a charitable Trust, the first to be registered for the benefit of the performing arts, and now the normal procedure in this field. But before this could come into effect Glyndebourne suffered a tragic blow with the death in 1953 of Audrey Mildmay at the age of fifty-two. Fortunately she had lived to see the Opera on its way to permanent existence, and her principles and ideals are alive to this day. The year after, John Christie became a Companion of Honour as a reward for his work and the Trust was set up. Thenceforth he played a less active part, and his son George took over most of the executive control. Christie lived another seven years, mentally as alert as ever but physically much handicapped by failing eyesight. In the last months of his life he became almost completely blind in his one remaining eye (he had lost the use of the other some fifty years before and had eventually had it removed), but even now, bearded and confined to a wheelchair, he was still the same genial host and stimulating company that he had always been. At last in 1962 he was no longer well enough to attend the opening night of the season, and on 4 July he died at Glyndebourne, aged seventy-nine.

In any estimate of the character and achievement of this remarkable man, perhaps the most obvious conclusion would be that he had to an extraordinary degree the ability to reconcile the ideal with the practical. Most people who knew him well would agree that among his many qualities the most vital were a highly original and creative mind, dynamic and inexhaustible energy, and unfailing and unbounded optimism. He was fifty when he established a new and challenging objective in his life, and from that moment he pursued this purpose with a ruthless and unflagging singleness of aim. Many thought of him as impossibly eccentric, but a closer acquaintance with the man himself showed that most of his decisions were amply justified in the event, even if he sometimes gave curious reasons for making them. Cast in a mould somewhat larger than life, it was not surprising that he should advise others to 'think big' (to use his own phrase) and to ignore and despise littleness of mind and action. Above all he believed that life was not worth living without what he called 'amusement'. By this he did not mean that a man should show a shallow or frivolous attitude to his problems, but rather that he must be capable of sifting out whatever grains of humour might be found in the chaff of experience. All through his life John Christie applied this philosophy in handling difficult situations and people, and he had the rare gift of settling disputes by making them appear ridiculous. He did not suffer fools gladly, and he had no time for those who bored him or did not try to see his point of view; nor was he particularly ready to see their own. Nevertheless he did what no man has ever done before in producing opera at his own country house and persuading people to come from all over the world to hear it. As he often said, the object of Glyndebourne was not just to put on good performances of opera but to aim at perfection, and, in the opinion of many, he came nearer to realizing this ideal than anyone else in the history of opera.

There is a portrait of Christie by Kenneth Green (1937) which hangs in the dining room at Glyndebourne, and a bronze bust by Oscar Nemon (1960) in the garden surrounding the opera house.

[Wilfrid Blunt, *John Christie of Glyndebourne*, 1968; Spike Hughes, *Glyndebourne*, 1965; Glyndebourne Festival programmes; private information; personal knowledge.

NIGEL WYKES

CHURCHILL, SIR WINSTON LEONARD SPENCER (1874-1965), statesman, was born, prematurely, at Blenheim Palace, his grandfather's Oxfordshire seat, 30 November 1874, the elder of the two sons of Lord Randolph Spencer Churchill, third son of the seventh Duke of Marlborough [qq.v.], and his wife, Jennie, daughter of Leonard Jerome, of New York. After a not particularly happy childhood, he was packed off to Harrow where, after a year, he found himself in the army class. Thence, at the third attempt, he passed into Sandhurst, but he passed out twentieth of 130 and was commissioned, 20 February 1895, in the 4th Queen's Own Hussars, a financial strain on his extravagant and recently widowed mother. In October he set off with a fellow subaltern, via New York, to Cuba to survey the rebellion there. He first saw action on his twenty-first birthday and reported it for the *Daily Graphic*. For the rest of his life he was able to keep himself by his journalism, took a siesta in the afternoon, and smoked cigars.

The two young officers were awarded the Spanish Order of the Red Cross, then, after a spell of London life and polo, left with their regiment for India. His mother sent Churchill books which he 'devoured', Gibbon and Macaulay becoming the anvil of an intensely idiosyncratic literary style. 'A few months in South Africa', he told her, 'would earn me the S.A. medal and in all probability the Company's Star. Thence hot-foot to Egypt—to return with two more decorations in a year or two—and beat my sword into an iron despatch box' (Randolph Churchill, *Winston S. Churchill*, companion vol. i, 1967, p. 676).

In August 1897, on returning to Bangalore from leave, he hurried north after arranging to cover the campaign for two newspapers, to join Sir Bindon Blood [q.v.] for reprisals upon the Pathans on the frontier. Barely a couple of months later he had completed his enthralling *The Story of the Malakand Field Force*, which came out in March 1898, and resumed *Savrola*, his only novel, which was published in 1900.

'It is a pushing age and we must shove with the best', he told his mother (10 January 1898: Randolph Churchill, op. cit., p. 856). Through her influence with the prime minister, he was attached by a reluctant sirdar, the future Lord

Kitchener [q.v.], to the 21st Lancers as they moved on Khartoum. They engaged the Dervishes at Omdurman (2 September 1898), an earlier shoulder injury compelling Churchill to carry a pistol instead of a lance: which may have saved his life in that last cavalry charge of the dying century.

Back in Bangalore he helped the 4th Hussars to win the inter-regimental polo tournament, scoring, despite the strapped shoulder, three of their four goals in the final. Meanwhile he had completed his superb *The River War*, which appeared, nearly a thousand pages long, in the autumn of 1899, by when he had already resigned his commission and had been narrowly defeated in the Oldham by-election in July.

With an arrangement with the *Morning Post*, he set sail 14 October 1899 for South Africa alongside J. B. Atkins of the *Manchester Guardian* who recalled him as 'slim, slightly reddish-haired, pale, lively, frequently plunging along the deck "with neck out-thrust" as Browning fancied Napoleon' (*Incidents and Reflections*, 1947, p. 122). Churchill himself would not have found the comparison incongruous.

He got himself to Durban, thence was swiftly involved in the Boer ambush of an armoured train. He was taken prisoner, but escaped from Pretoria, with a price on his head, and made his way back to Durban, to be carried shoulder-high. He attached himself to the South Africa Light Horse, in which his brother 'Jack' soon joined him, but by June 1900 he was ready for home once more. There he published (1900) a couple of books based on his *Morning Post* dispatches, *London to Ladysmith, via Pretoria* and *Ian Hamilton's March*, and, with his accumulated royalties and the proceeds of lecture tours in England and North America, he had by now accumulated £10,000, which Sir Ernest Cassel [q.v.], his father's friend, agreed to invest for him.

He was elected Unionist MP for Oldham in the 'khaki' election of October 1900 and had barely been sworn in before he rose, 18 February 1901, from the corner-seat above the gangway which his father had occupied in 1886 after his sensational resignation, to make a maiden speech in which Winston Churchill informed the House that 'If I were a Boer, I hope I should be fighting in the field'.

He was evidently in the wrong party and soon the tariff reform proposals of Joseph Chamberlain [q.v.], which electrified the political world in May 1903, convinced Churchill of this and of his own free trade credo. By December 1903 the Oldham Unionists had disowned him and in January 1904 he was refused the Conservative whip. At the end of

May he crossed the floor and took his seat on the Liberal benches.

Conservatives never forgave him: Tories have always placed a high premium upon loyalty. Joseph Chamberlain, himself a party renegade, misread his Balfour in maintaining that 'Winston is the cleverest of all the young men and the mistake Arthur made was letting him go' (Margot Asquith, *Autobiography*, vol. ii, 1922, p. 134).

For Churchill January 1906 was momentous. Already in office since 15 December 1905 in Campbell-Bannerman's new administration, he issued his election address as Liberal candidate for North-West Manchester, which was followed next day by the publication of the two masterly volumes of his *Lord Randolph Churchill*. 'Few fathers have done less for their sons', his cousin was to aver. 'Few sons have done more for their fathers . . . perhaps the greatest filial tribute in the English language' (Sir) Shane Leslie, *The End of a Chapter*, 1916, p. 110).

Churchill's exciting election meetings were crowded to the doors; refusing to be 'henpecked' by the suffragettes, he was elected (15 January), whilst, in another part of Manchester, Balfour had lost his seat and the 'Stupid Party' had been routed.

John Burns [q.v.] having preferred to remain at the Local Government Board, Churchill was relieved of his dread of being 'shut up in a soupkitchen with Mrs Sidney Webb' [q.v.], but to the prime minister's surprise he refused the post of financial secretary to the Treasury, choosing instead to become parliamentary undersecretary for the colonies, his chief Lord Elgin [q.v.], the former viceroy of India, being in the Lords. In the Colonial Office Churchill discovered (Sir) Edward Marsh [q.v.] as his private secretary and signed him on for life. In his first important state paper (2 January 1906) Churchill persuaded Elgin to abandon the new Transvaal constitution proposed by his predecessor Alfred Lyttelton [q.v.], in favour of fully responsible government: to make another friend for life in Jan Christian Smuts [q.v.]. But Churchill's vivid brain raced ahead of the Opposition's unforgiving prejudice which rejected the turncoat's eloquent appeal (31 July) to make the new dispensation 'the gift of England'. Chinese labour on the Rand was another stumbling block, even though Churchill had already explained to the House in February that it might not be termed slavery without 'some risk of terminological inexactitude'; and he badly misjudged the mood of the Commons in a carefully prepared speech about Lord Milner [q.v.]. Nor was his relationship with Elgin invariably plain sailing. 'These are my views', one of his exhaustive memoranda concluded; 'but not mine', the colonial secretary subjoined (Sir Austen Chamberlain, *Politics From Inside*, 1936, p. 459).

Churchill was sworn of the Privy Council, 1 May 1907. Intent on seeing for himself more than public funds or criticism might allow, he arranged to write for the *Strand Magazine* to pay for an extended—and voluble—visit to East Africa which inevitably became an official progress. In *My African Journey* (1908), the final text of which he was to complete on his honeymoon, he visualized harnessing the Nile waters and the industrial development of colonial Africa.

From the industrialization of the Empire his soaring imagination and compulsive reading were already turning to social reform at home and a growing emphasis on the minimum wage began to suggest far less reluctance to sup with Mrs. Webb. In April 1908, when Asquith succeeded Campbell-Bannerman as Liberal prime minister, he offered Churchill the presidency of the Board of Trade in succession to David Lloyd George who was about to replace Asquith himself at the Exchequer. A by-election was accordingly necessary in the case of the youngest Cabinet minister since 1866 and, to unbridled Tory jubilation, Churchill was narrowly defeated in North-West Manchester. He was, however, promptly re-elected to Parliament, at Dundee, and 'settled down to enjoy the Board of Trade'.

His engagement was announced, 15 August 1908, to Clementine Ogilvy, younger daughter of Lady Blanche Hozier, eldest daughter of the seventh Earl of Airlie and widow since 1907 of Colonel Sir Henry Hozier, secretary of Lloyd's. They were married, 12 September 1908, at St. Margaret's, Westminster, with Lord Hugh Cecil (later Lord Quickswood, q.v.) as best man, the bridegroom busily discussing the political situation with Lloyd George in the vestry during the signing of the register.

The elegant, accomplished, but dowerless twenty-three-year-old bride was to devote the rest of her very able life to helping her extraordinary husband in his career. The extent of her self-sacrifice was revealed after her death, 12 December 1977, in *Clementine Churchill* (1979), by her youngest daughter, Lady Soames. Marriage to a genius can never have been easy. Her invariably sound advice was always cheerfully received but rarely taken. Since 'Clemmie' was primarily interested in Winston and so was Winston, their relationship to each other was always closer than that with their five children. They had four daughters: Diana (1909–63); Sarah (born 1914); Marigold (1918–21); and Mary (born 1922) who grew up beloved by both her parents. They had one son: Randolph (1911–68), the godson of F. E. Smith (later the

Earl of Birkenhead, q.v.), the Tory *sabreur* into whose high-living company Churchill had plunged in the summer of 1907, to forge a steadfast friendship with perhaps the only man he recognized, warily, to be his intellectual superior.

From 1908, whilst both men readily acknowledged allegiance to Asquith's chairmanship over the next seven years, to the exasperated incomprehension of less gifted souls, Churchill with Lloyd George as his senior partner comprised a political alliance from which much of modern Britain stems. Each in his own very different way was a self-made man, the one the grandson of a duke, the other brought up by the village cobbler. Each, like the prime minister, discovered in himself the power to sway the mass meetings then still popular in a sermon-tasting age before the advent of radio. If Lloyd George told people what he sensed they wanted to listen to, Churchill told them what he, Churchill, wanted them to hear. A prodigious amount of preparation preceded his every speech which, because he had once 'dried' in the House (22 April 1904), was always learned by heart after extensive dictation. A sheaf of notes in his right hand, shoulders hunched forward, Churchill exhibited a studied oratory in the grand manner with a highly personal vocabulary and humour, the lisp which the Boers had noted in their prisoner being turned to advantage. Because they were so assiduously rehearsed, his speeches still read well today, whereas Lloyd George's, with a few glowing exceptions, have blown away with the atmosphere which went to create them.

From Lloyd George Churchill 'was to learn the language of Radicalism', the prime minister's daughter came to explain [Lady Violet Bonham Carter (Lady Asquith, q.v.), *Winston Churchill as I Knew Him*, 1965, p. 161]. 'It was Lloyd George's native tongue', but it was not Churchill's and he spoke it, as it were, in translation. 'Lloyd George was saturated with class-consciousness. Winston accepted class distinction without thought.' Churchill's main preoccupation at this period was the alleviation of distress, whereas Lloyd George purposed to refashion the State itself. Believing, because of his own escapes from death already, that he was to die early like his father, Churchill was 'full of the poor whom he has just discovered. He thinks he is called by providence—to do something for them' (Lucy Masterman, *C. F. G. Masterman*, 1939, p. 97). The study of socialism had been amongst Churchill's manifold activities on his East African journeyings, and on his return he had favoured an unimpressed Asquith with one of his strenuous memoranda on future policy. At the Home Office Herbert (later Viscount) Gladstone [q.v.] was to discover in Churchill the only colleague to go out of his way to support him over the Coal Mines Regulation (Eight Hours) Bill which became law in 1908.

The Board of Trade, with Sir Hubert Llewellyn Smith as the permanent secretary and because of the existence since 1886 of the Labour Department which he had built up there and which was shortly to be joined by George (later Lord) Askwith [qq.v.], was peculiarly geared to undertake the reforms which Churchill had in mind. Throughout his long career he had the knack of galvanizing and enthusing exceptionally able civil servants and deploying the figures with which they furnished him to buttress his most uncommon powers of persuasion.

He made a beginning with 'sweated labour', a problem which the Home Office had neglected. The Trade Boards Act of 1909 concerned in the first instance four trades only, but empowered the Board of Trade to extend their number. And, whilst at the Local Government Board John Burns was failing to tackle unemployment, Churchill brought William Henry (later Lord) Beveridge [q.v.] into the Board of Trade to establish labour exchanges as 'the Intelligence Department' of labour. Then, with Asquith's concurrence, he introduced an insurance Bill against unemployment which Lloyd George himself had been planning to include in his own legislative proposals and which eventually became law as part ii of the National Insurance Act of 1911.

To pay for their welfare programme Lloyd George and Churchill caballed to cut back on defence expenditure (in Churchill's case a hereditary posture), and an exasperated prime minister found himself compelled to resort to the formula by which Reginald McKenna [q.v.], the first lord of the Admiralty, was vouchsafed an immediate four of the eight Dreadnoughts he was seeking to have laid down, the rest to come later. To pay for them as well as social insurance—for old-age pensions were to be non-contributory—Lloyd George came to formulate his 'People's Budget'. In the consequent controversies over the powers of the House of Lords, if Churchill did not resort to Lloyd George's brand of 'Limehouse' demagogy, his own inborn pugnacity, together with a convert's over-reaction, led him into 'teasing goldfish'—and, of course, reinforced Tory hatred of the renegade grandson. Lloyd George even suggested that Churchill was, in fact, 'opposed to pretty nearly every item in the Budget except the "Brat"' (children's allowances against income tax). Nevertheless, Churchill was chairman of the Budget League and one of the most effective Liberal campaigners. He was rewarded in 1910 by the ap-

pointment of home secretary, Gladstone going out to South Africa as governor-general.

Recalling his own imprisonment, Churchill was eager to improve the lot of the prisoner and, with the aid of Sir Evelyn Ruggles-Brise [q.v.], chairman of the Prison Commission, books and entertainment were introduced into prisons and the sentences of all child prisoners were reviewed. The principal piece of Home Office legislation during Churchill's secretaryship was the Mines Act of 1911 affecting safety in the pits, with a substantial increase in the inspectorate. A Shops Bill to improve the lot of shop assistants did little (because of the shopkeepers' obduracy) to improve conditions, but at least a weekly half-holiday became compulsory. Churchill became president of the Early Closing Association (1911–39).

Much of the home secretary's time came to be occupied by questions of law and order. Churchill was, of course, suspect already as a firebrand, and two episodes in his tenure at the Home Office, the one eternally distorted, the other too much in character, cast doubts especially amongst 'Lib-Labs' about how genuinely naturalized as a Radical this young reformist aristocrat was at bottom. In November 1910 rioting miners on strike at Tonypandy in the Rhondda Valley were dispersed by metropolitan policemen using rolled-up mackintoshes as truncheons, but the soldiery arrived as the riot was ending. For the rest of his life Churchill was branded as having used troops against the miners at Tonypandy whereas in truth, as the relevant general (Sir) Nevil Macready [q.v.] recorded, 'it was entirely due to Mr. Churchill's forethought . . . that bloodshed was avoided' (*Annals of an Active Life*, 2 vols., 1924).

Not long after Tonypandy, in January 1911, Churchill rushed from his bath to superintend 'the battle of Sidney Street' in which he was photographed apparently directing troops who were assisting police in the ambush of a gang in a house off the Mile End Road. Arthur Balfour drew acid attention in the House to the incongruity of the home secretary's presence. 'Now Charlie. Don't be croth. It was such fun', Churchill reassured Charles Masterman [q.v.], his remonstrating parliamentary under-secretary. Churchill lent credence to malicious criticism by his obvious enjoyment of moving bodies of troops about the country for use in emergency—'mistaking a coffee-stall row for the social revolution', John Burns called it—and his flamboyant ever-readiness throughout his life never to mind his own business did little to widen his friendships. 'His future is the most interesting problem of personal speculation in English politics', wrote A. G. Gardiner [q.v.] in the *Daily News*. 'At thirty-four he stands before the country one of the two most arresting figures in politics, his life a crowded drama of action, his courage high, his vision unclouded, his boats burned. . . . But don't forget that the aristocrat is still there—latent and submerged, but there nevertheless. The occasion may arise when the two Churchills will come into sharp conflict' (*Prophets, Priests and Kings*, 2nd edn., 1914, pp. 233-4).

With a major responsibility for national security as home secretary Churchill began to take a close interest in the Committee of Imperial Defence. Returning from being the guest of the Kaiser at the German manœuvres, 'I can only thank God', he remarked, 'that there is a sea between England and that Army.'

The Agadir crisis (July/August 1911) led Churchill to contemplate at length what might happen if it came to war with that army. He foresaw the Germans crossing the Meuse on the twentieth, but the tide of battle turning by the fortieth, day. The Admiralty, he pointed out to Asquith, had no proper plans for an emergency, nor an appropriate staff such as Lord Haldane [q.v.] had created in the War Office.

Whilst they were on a golfing holiday together at Archerfield, on the Firth of Forth, Asquith abruptly invited Churchill to exchange places with McKenna. Churchill became first lord of the Admiralty (25 October 1911), McKenna departing stiffly to the Home Office.

Churchill's immediate task was to impose a staff system upon the navy, most hierarchical of Services, which had survived the reforms of Lord Fisher [q.v.], first sea lord in 1904-10, without one. Churchill was the last man to concur in a structure which left the war plan in the undisclosed possession not of the first lord of the Admiralty but of the first sea lord. So, Sir Arthur Knyvet Wilson [q.v.], who had succeeded 'Jacky' Fisher as first sea lord, departed for Norfolk in October 1911. (He was to come back in 1915.) Fisher, not wanting to return to become 'second fiddle', stayed in the wings advising Churchill from the Continent. Since Asquith, on Lloyd George's advice, opposed the promotion of Prince Louis of Battenberg beyond second sea lord at this juncture, Sir Francis Bridgeman [qq.v.] arrived from the Home Fleet as first sea lord when Churchill, a month after taking office, announced his Navy Board, 28 November 1911.

Left behind by Churchill's intellectual pace and physical stamina, Bridgeman lasted precisely a year, his dismissal enabling the Opposition to raise a political storm in which Lord Charles Beresford [q.v.] was able to renew his feud with Fisher in the Commons, where the leader of the Opposition was by then Andrew Bonar Law, who distrusted Churchill profoundly despite his own close friendship with Max Aitken (later Lord Beaverbrook, q.v.), who

had been introduced to Churchill by F. E. Smith. Even so, Bonar Law was an early member of 'The Other Club', which Churchill and F. E. Smith had invented to straddle the benches.

On arriving at the Admiralty Churchill had immediately appointed as his naval secretary David (later Earl) Beatty [q.v.], by far the youngest flag officer in the navy. They had not encountered one another since the eve of Omdurman when the wealthy young sailor had lobbed a bottle of champagne from his gunboat to the impecunious 4th Hussar on the Nile bank.

Churchill and Beatty got along famously, Beatty at once spotting Churchill's proclivity to be utterly engrossed in the immediate. He had now discovered the navy just as three years earlier he had discovered the poor. 'He talks about nothing but the Sea', Beatty told his wife, 27 May 1912, 'and the Navy and the wonderful things he is going to do.' Lloyd George was soon complaining that he could no longer catch Churchill's political attention since he would 'only talk of boilers'. With the powerful support of the Committee of Imperial Defence and the Cabinet, Churchill at once, January 1912, reorganized the Navy Board into an Admiralty War Staff of three divisions, Operations, Intelligence, and Mobilization, under a chief of staff. Churchill evidently wanted this officer to be answerable to himself as first lord of the Admiralty, but, as ever, he was rushing his fences and, with Haldane's support, Prince Louis, as second sea lord, successfully resisted the proposal. In the first instance the Staff was advisory only. Moreover, there were no trained staff officers. Accordingly, a staff course was instituted at the Naval War College, Portsmouth, the cost being met by suppressing the private yachts of the three shore-based commanders-in-chief. Naval tradition stood in the way of the ablest young officers being posted there, since sea service, gunnery, and navigation were the paths to promotion.

'Tug' Wilson had warned Churchill that responsibility uncertainly divided between the first sea lord and a chief of war staff was unlikely to be viable and Prince Louis, when he succeeded Bridgeman in December 1912, evidently held it *infra dig.* for the first sea lord to become chief of staff to a civilian. Not until quite long after war had broken out, and then only after a minor disaster, did the roles of first sea lord and chief of staff become fused. Until then the former remained responsible not only for operations but also for manifold administrative tasks. An additional civil lord was introduced to lessen the burden by transferring Sir Francis Hopwood (later Lord Southborough, q.v.), whom Churchill had known in the Colonial Office, to take charge especially of contracts.

But this only became another point of friction between Bridgeman and Churchill. Although Churchill did not manage to have matters all his own way, at least he had achieved the major change: war plans were no longer locked in the immaculate bosom of the first sea lord, and effective co-ordination with the War Office, via the Committee of Imperial Defence, had at last become feasible. An Expeditionary Force might now be conveyed across the English Channel.

Churchill's task was as speedily as possible to modernize and strengthen the Royal Navy which he soon held to be quintessential to Great Britain, whereas, as he incautiously pointed out in Glasgow (February 1912), Germany's fleet was 'more in the nature of a luxury', an observation not advancing hopes of a 'naval holiday'. He worked incredibly long hours in wielding an intensely busy and often impulsive new broom. He visited every naval dockyard and establishment at home and in the Mediterranean in his first eighteen months in the Admiralty, during which he spent 182 days at sea, often in the Admiralty yacht *Enchantress*. Senior officers were scandalized by what Sir John (later Earl) Jellicoe [q.v.], the second sea lord, termed his 'meddling', all taking exception especially to his direct dealings with junior officers and even the lower deck in these ceaseless tours of inspection. In July 1912 Rear-Admiral (Sir) Lewis Bayly [q.v.] informed him on the bridge of the *Lion* in Weymouth that 'on any repetition of his inquisitorial methods he would turn him off the ship. Winston took his drubbing very well' (*Inside Asquith's Cabinet*, the diaries of Charles Hobhouse, ed. Edward David, 1977, p. 117). A year later à more serious instance arose when Sir Richard Poore, at the Nore, complained to the second sea lord, whose province was naval discipline, and the second, third, and fourth sea lords threatened resignation (Sir Peter Gretton, *Former Naval Person*, 1968, pp. 89–92).

Anyone who attempted naval reform was likely to find opposition among the more senior officers. The more junior found Churchill's ways exciting and in the lower deck he was popular as the only first lord to pay attention to their pay and punishments or to devise a slender promotion channel for exceptional seamen to reach commissioned rank.

The most revolutionary change lay in the field of *matériel*. It was decided, on Fisher's advice, to build a new fast division of battleships—the Queen Elizabeth class—armed with 15-inch guns and faster because driven by oil instead of coal: which necessitated the acquisition of distant oilfields and of the Anglo-Persian Oil Company and was clearly unpopular with MPs from mining constituencies. Churchill also went out of his way to encourage the Royal Naval Air Service which was experimenting with various types of aircraft, frequently flying himself and taking lessons as a pilot.

War inevitably revealed untackled weaknesses: insufficient attention had been paid to protection of the Fleet's bases from submarine attack; ammunition supply to gun turrets was poorly designed, and so were shells. Churchill had rubbed a lot of people up the wrong way, from the King downwards, by his impulsive, opinionated, and constant interference, and he had strained his relationship with his Cabinet colleagues, especially Lloyd George, because of the cost of his revolutionary changes (F. W. Wiemann in *Lloyd George: Twelve Essays*, ed. A. J. P. Taylor, 1971); yet the German naval attaché could report to Admiral Tirpitz (4 June 1914): 'On the whole the Navy is satisfied with Mr. Churchill, because it recognizes that he has done and accomplished more for them than the majority of his predecessors in office. There is no doubt that there has been friction between Mr. Churchill and the officers at the Admiralty as well as those at sea. That is not surprising with such a stubborn and tyrannical character as Mr. Churchill. The intensive co-operation of all forces for an increase in the power and tactical readiness of the English Navy has under Mr. Churchill's guidance not only not suffered but has experienced rather energetic impulses and inspiration. The English Navy is very much aware of it' (Arthur J. Marder, *From The Dreadnought to Scapa Flow*, vol. i, 1961, pp. 263–4). As Kitchener was to tell Churchill when they parted in May 1915: 'There is one thing, at least, they can never take away from you. When the war began, you had the Fleet ready.'

Engrossed as Churchill was during his four years in the Admiralty in getting the navy expensively readied for war, he could never ignore the obligations of party in a Liberal Cabinet. Nor did he forget—and this was characteristic of him throughout his life—the calls of friendship, as Lloyd George had cause to remember over the Marconi affair (1912–13). He found it needful, too, for party reasons, 'to mingle actively in the Irish controversy'. With typical courage the Churchills, for his wife went with him, had fulfilled a speaking engagement in Belfast in February 1912. Two years later he was involved, once more, as a member of the Cabinet committee from which the 'Curragh incident' emerged. Characteristic ardour led him to overplay his hand both in demanding at Bradford (14 March 1914) to 'put these grave matters to the proof' and in directing the third battle squadron (under the self-same Lewis Bayly) to Lamlash on 19 March, to overawe Belfast: a flamboyant order which Asquith countermanded. In this episode the vindictive distrust of the Opposition, Bonar Law's especially, was intensified by their suspicion of Churchill.

In July 1914 the trial mobilization of the fleets, which had been decided on as less expensive than manœuvres, was in train and, in view of the Austrian ultimatum to Serbia, Prince Louis took the decision to cancel their dispersal. Churchill returned from a family holiday in Cromer to confirm this. When Austria declared war on 30 July, with Asquith's concurrence Churchill ordered the fleets to their battle stations. Unlike some of his Cabinet colleagues, he housed no doubts but was 'geared up and happy' and 'the splendid *condottiere* at the Admiralty' (as Viscount Morley of Blackburn [q.v.] affectionately called him in his *Memorandum on Resignation*, 1928) influenced Lloyd George towards the arbitrament of war. On the evening of 1 August 1914 Churchill 'went straight out like a man going to a well-accustomed job' (Lord Beaverbrook, *Politicians and the War*, 2 vols., 1928 and 1932, vol. i, p. 36).

Churchill's brief popularity from having the fleet ready on the outbreak was dissolved by his intervention in Antwerp in early October 1914. He went there post-haste, at the request of his Cabinet colleagues, and, with complete disregard for his own safety, personally superintended the defence of the city. A week was gained and the Channel ports (Dunkirk, Calais, and Boulogne) saved before the Allied line was stabilized—till March, 1918. But some of the newly formed Naval Division perished or were interned and Churchill, who clearly enjoyed the whole affair, was accused of having neglected his primary duties at the Admiralty for a characteristically impulsive adventure. So enthralled had he been by being in action once more that he offered to take military command, a suggestion which his colleagues, Kitchener apart, treated with incredulous laughter. Not for the first time Asquith came to question Churchill's priorities.

Not long afterwards Churchill was to make the mistake which led to his political downfall. Prejudice having forced the resignation (29 October 1914) of Prince Louis as first sea lord, Churchill, against advice (the King's especially), brought in Fisher to succeed him. Those who knew them both, Beatty, for example, or Admiral R. E. Wemyss (later Lord Wester Wemyss, q.v.), realized that the arrangement involving such domineering characters, each used to having his own way, fond as they were of each other, would not work; it was only a matter of time before an irreconcilable clash. Moreover, their timetables, like their age-groups (for Fisher was seventy-three and Churchill not yet forty) were too incompatible. Fisher got up early and finished his work in the

daytime to be off to bed by 9 p.m., by when Churchill, having slept in the afternoon, was just getting his second wind.

After a series of setbacks and a defeat at Coronel (2 November 1914) the navy badly needed a success. Moreover, the British Expeditionary Force was bogged down in Flanders. Trench warfare evoked Churchill's two most signal contributions. 'Impatient, resourceful and undismayed', as Asquith noted 27 October 1914, Churchill saw clearly that the alternatives were to break through by new methods or to outflank: hence his part in the evolution of the tank by establishing the Admiralty landship committee under (Sir) E. H. W. Tennyson-d'Eyncourt [q.v.] in February 1915; and his initiation of the Dardanelles campaign.

'Are there not other alternatives', he had asked Asquith (29 December 1914) 'than sending out armies to chew barbed wire in Flanders? Further, cannot the power of the Navy be brought more directly to bear upon the enemy?'

His first preoccupation lay in the Baltic and Fisher was enthusiastic about seizing the island of Borkum, to block the German Navy's exit. On the far-off opposite flank, Churchill envisaged opening up the passage to the sea of Marmora where the fleet might turn its guns on Constantinople and help to relieve the hard-pressed Russians. In early January 1915 the Grand Duke Nicholas asked for a demonstration to relieve Turkish pressure in the Caucasus. Fisher was willing to use obsolete pre-Dreadnought battleships unfit for service in the North Sea but Kitchener was reluctant at this stage to provide military support in the Mediterranean. As a result, an exasperated Churchill contemplated forcing the Dardanelles by naval forces alone. Admiral (Sir) S. H. Carden [q.v.], commanding in the Eastern Mediterranean, replied: 'I do not think that the Dardanelles can be rushed but they might be forced by extended operations.' This was enough for Churchill, whose ardour was whetted by Fisher's suggestion that the *Queen Elizabeth* should conduct her trials by demolishing the Dardanelles forts.

'The idea caught on at once', reported Maurice (later Lord) Hankey [q.v.], who was secretary of the War Council. 'The whole atmosphere changed. Fatigue was forgotten. The War Council turned eagerly from .the dreary vista of a "slogging match" on the Western Front to brighter prospects, as they seemed, in the Mediterranean. The Navy, in whom everyone had implicit confidence and whose opportunities had so far been few and far between, was to come into the front line. . . . Churchill had secured approval in principle to the naval attack on the Dardanelles on which he had set his heart. Fisher alone, whose silence had not meant consent as was generally assumed, was beginning to brood on the difficulties of his position which were eventually to lead to his resignation' (*The Supreme Command 1914-1918*, vol. i, 1961, pp. 265-7). At the end of January 1915 Asquith saw Churchill and Fisher together before the War Council assembled. 'I am the arbitrator', he told them (28 January 1915), 'I have heard Mr Winston Churchill and I have heard you and now I am going to give my decision. . . . The Dardanelles will go on' (Henry Pelling, *Winston Churchill*, 1977, p. 192).

Should the naval demonstration appear successful, military action would be called for and Kitchener agreed in mid-February that a regular division, the 29th, should be available to stiffen the proposed expeditionary force of Australians and New Zealanders, to whom Churchill added his own favourite Naval Division. Delay compounded delay. Churchill grew tempestuously impatient. The Turkish guns could not be silenced until the mines were swept; the mines could not be swept until the guns were silenced. By mid-March Admiral (Sir) John De Robeck, who had succeeded Carden, paused to co-ordinate his activities with Sir Ian Hamilton [qq.v.], the military commander. There were muddles too about the transports and it was not until 25 April that the military assault began: by then the enemy was ready.

Fisher insisted on the return of the *Queen Elizabeth* to safer waters and by mid-May it was evident that he was in a highly nervous state. Arriving at the Admiralty on Saturday, 15 May, he was met with an overnight draft list from Churchill of the naval vessels they had agreed to send to the Mediterranean, but which now included two submarines which had not been part of the previous day's bargain between them. Unwilling to face Churchill's relentless persuasiveness any longer, Fisher resigned and left the Admiralty. Attempts to get him to withdraw led him to lay down impossible terms for his return. Sir Arthur Wilson, who had been serving with Fisher and Churchill on the War Council, persuaded the other sea lords not to resign with Fisher and showed himself most generously willing to serve as first sea lord under Churchill. Asquith, who was facing an additional crisis over an attack in *The Times* on the shell shortage in France, seized the opportunity to form a coalition. Amongst Bonar Law's conditions for Opposition adherence was that Haldane should leave the Government and Churchill the Admiralty. Dumbfounded, Churchill went on begging to stay on, but on 20 May 1915 Asquith told him in writing: You must take it as settled that you are not to remain

at the Admiralty.' Mrs Churchill joined his pleas. 'Winston may in your eyes', she wrote to the prime minister, '& in those with whom he has to work have faults but he has the supreme quality which I venture to say very few of your present or future Cabinet possess—the power, the imagination, the deadliness, to fight Germany' (Roy Jenkins, *Asquith*, 1964, p. 361). On 22 May her husband took his dignified leave of the departmental heads in the Admiralty where Balfour succeeded him. He became chancellor of the Duchy of Lancaster but with continued membership of the War Council, now to be renamed the Dardanelles Committee. 'If he could do things over again, he said without rancour (27 May 1915), he would do just the same with regard to appointing Fisher, as . . . he has done really great organising work' (Lady Cynthia Asquith, *Diaries 1915-18*, 1968, p. 31).

The Dardanelles Commission, which a reluctant Asquith was obliged to set up in September 1916 was eventually in its report of March 1917 to exonerate Churchill from the widely held suspicion that he had wilfully persisted in the enterprise without the concurrence of his naval experts or the co-operation of the War Office and more blame came to be laid at Asquith's door for his failure in timely and effective co-ordination and, by implication, on Kitchener who by this time had perished in the *Hampshire* (June 1916).

Meanwhile Churchill, not knowing quite what to do with himself—'my veins threatened to burst from the fall in pressure'—took refuge in the silent recreation of painting.

His Conservative colleagues vetoed a personal visit to the Dardanelles and when Sir Edward (later Lord) Carson [q.v.] joined the Dardanelles Committee, Churchill's support of Hamilton's continued operations was outweighed. He urged yet another naval attempt to force a way through, but by the end of October 1915 Sir Charles C. Monro [q.v.] replaced Hamilton and recommended evacuation.

Churchill, who had again asked Asquith for a military command on the western front, was not included in the smaller War Committee which replaced the Dardanelles Committee. He now faced no alternative but to resign from a post of 'well-paid inactivity'. On 18 November 1915 Major Churchill crossed to France to rejoin his yeomanry regiment, the Oxfordshire Hussars. After a brief attachment to the reluctant 2nd battalion, Grenadier Guards, to experience trench warfare, and disappointed, as a result of Asquith's intervention, of his hope of a brigade, he was posted in January 1916 to command the 6th battalion of the Royal Scots Fusiliers in the 9th (Scottish) division and was allowed Sir Archibald Sinclair (later Viscount

Thurso, q.v.) as his second-in-command. Churchill was a fearless and well-liked commanding officer.

Perforce out of touch, Churchill baffled the House of Commons, when on leave in March 1916, by calling for Fisher's recall. Pressed by Beaverbrook to return to politics, Churchill, deprived of seniority when the 6th battalion had to be merged with the 7th because of manpower shortage, took the opportunity to resume his parliamentary and political duties. He returned to England in May 1916.

His family had to be provided for and he began a series of well-paid articles, first for the *Sunday Pictorial*, then for the *London Magazine*.

When Lloyd George formed his Government in December 1916 Churchill was still awaiting his exoneration. The new prime minister, using the two newspaper proprietors, Beaverbrook and Sir George (later Lord) Riddell [q.v.] as intermediaries, tried to propitiate Churchill in his frustrated loneliness. After the second session in May 1917 Lloyd George and Churchill met behind the Speaker's chair and 'he assured me of his determination to have me at his side. From that day, although holding no office, I became to a large extent his colleague. He repeatedly discussed with me every aspect of the war and many of his secret hopes and fears' (Winston S. Churchill, *The World Crisis*, 5 vols., 1923–31, vol. ii, p. 1144). But it was not until July 1917 that Lloyd George felt himself strong enough to ride off organized Conservative opposition to Churchill's reinstatement in high office and, even then, Bonar Law had difficulty with his back-benchers. Only then did a chastened Churchill himself come to appreciate the problem posed by the firm Tory prejudice against him: political alignments made Lloyd George's attitude unavoidably ambivalent. It was a measure of Churchill's stature that, despite the personal unpopularity of his old ministerial ally, the prime minister sought opportunity to risk the reabsorption of his unique energy into the war effort.

Churchill resumed office as minister of munitions (17 July 1917), but was outside the War Cabinet. He swiftly took grip of the sprawling empire in the Hotel Metropole by establishing a Munitions Council of business men already enrolled in the ministry, Lloyd George's 'men of push and go': to be served by a proper secretariat organized by Sir W. Graham Greene [q.v.] and (Sir) James E. Masterton-Smith, whom he had known in the Admiralty. Because he was at last happy again himself, he could assure the prime minister, early in September, that 'this is a very happy Department' (Pelling, op. cit., p. 232). There were frontier incidents with Sir Eric C. Geddes [q.v.], the new first

lord, since the Admiralty retained control of its own supply, and with Lord Derby (seventeenth Earl, q.v.) at the War Office. A War Priorities Committee was established by the prime minister under J. C. Smuts's chairmanship—it had been at Churchill's suggestion that Lloyd George had taken General Smuts into his Cabinet—and if squabbles over munition workers, leaving certificates, wage rates, and differentials continued to arise, stoppages, because of Churchill's imaginative approach, were rarely serious or extensive. Churchill proved himself a quite exceptional departmental head in successfully imposing coherence upon a vast organization. He kept closely in touch with his French and American counterparts and was at pains as 'a shopman at the orders of the War Cabinet' to serve the needs of his customers. He gradually wore down Sir Douglas (later Earl) Haig's [q.v.] suspicion of him; indeed, the commander-in-chief arranged to put the Château Verchocq in the Pas de Calais at his disposal.

Although Churchill was not a member of the War Cabinet, Lloyd George was increasingly glad to avail himself in private of Churchill's courage and resourcefulness as well as his first-hand reports. When Churchill returned from a visit to his old division in Third Army when the German March offensive began, Lloyd George and Sir Henry H. Wilson [q.v.], the new CIGS, dined with the Churchills at 33 Eccleston Square (24 March). Churchill was the prime minister's chosen emissary to Clemenceau (who shared Churchill's love of danger) following the appointment of Foch to the Supreme Command. In August he flew over to Amiens to witness a British tank attack and Haig went out of his way to refer to 'the energy and foresight which you have displayed as Minister of Munitions' (Pelling, op. cit., p. 241).

Mollified by the implied offer of post-war Cabinet membership, Churchill agreed to fight the general election of December 1918 as a Coalition Liberal and was again returned for Dundee. Lloyd George had evidently been impressed by his departmental ability and asked him to move to the War Office (with which he combined responsibility for the Air Ministry) to deal with the frictions arising from demobilization. With Haig's agreement, he scrapped the existing scheme and substituted one based on age, length of service, and wounds, 'to let three men out of four go, and to pay the fourth double to finish the job'. His decisive formula was successful and more than two and a half million men were released, leaving under a million for garrisons abroad whilst the peace treaties were being negotiated.

Whereas Lloyd George was anxious to terminate British aid to the anti-Bolshevik forces in

Russia as soon as possible, Churchill, not without some Conservative support, gave the impression of being himself far from averse to much more positive action. Happily (though not in his view), war weariness undermined further crusades and, somewhat ignominiously, Allied intervention dribbled away leaving Churchill worsted. 'So ends in disaster', wrote Sir Henry Wilson savagely in his diary, March 1920, 'another of Winston's military attempts—Antwerp, Dardanelles, Denikin' (Major-General Sir C. E. Callwell, *Field Marshal Sir Henry Wilson*, vol. ii, 1927, p. 231).

Impressed by the inexpensive intervention of the Royal Air Force in Somaliland, Churchill supported Sir Hugh (later Viscount) Trenchard [q.v.] in his struggle for an independent air force as imperial policeman, particularly in view of the tasks created by the new territories falling under British control in the eastern Mediterranean. Lloyd George seized upon Churchill's suggestion that the Colonial Office should take charge of new territories, with the RAF keeping the peace. At the end of an inconclusive 1920 he sent Churchill to the Colonial Office, from which Milner was retiring, and by 1 March Churchill had brought a new Middle Eastern Department into existence and, to the envy of George Nathaniel Curzon (later Marquess Curzon of Kedleston, q.v.), a grandiose conference, which T. E. Lawrence [q.v.] was to attend, was arranged at the Semiramis Hotel in Cairo to determine the future, especially of Iraq. 'First, we would repair the injury done to the Arabs and to the House of the Sherifs of Mecca by placing the Emir Feisal upon the throne of Iraq as King, and by entrusting the Emir Abdulla with the government of Trans-Jordania. Secondly, we would remove practically all the troops from Iraq and entrust its defence to the Royal Air Force. Thirdly, we suggested an adjustment of the immediate difficulties between the Jews and Arabs in Palestine which would serve as a foundation for the future' (Churchill, *Great Contemporaries*, 1937, p. 134).

Churchill's economical dispositions lasted longer than many expected and even in Palestine, where Sir Herbert (later Viscount) Samuel [q.v.], his old, pre-war, Cabinet colleague, was by now the high commissioner, there was a period of comparative quiet. Churchill reasserted the Balfour Declaration in Jerusalem but received Arab delegates to assure them that Great Britain, as 'the greatest Moslem state in the world', cherished Arab friendship. Whilst he was still at the War Office Churchill had attempted to reassert British control in Ireland but Lloyd George had come to realize that some sort of political settlement was called for. The dominant figures on the

Government side in the negotiations with the Sinn Fein representatives were Lloyd George himself and Birkenhead but Churchill's personal rapport with Michael Collins [q.v.], the leader of the Irish Republican Army, was a significant factor. 'Tell Winston', Collins said, 'we could never have done anything without him.' Fighting continued after a treaty which left the Tories most unhappy and it was General Sir Nevil Macready, commanding in Ireland, whose blind eye enabled the Provisional Government to survive.

At Chanak (15 September 1922), the episode which brought the Government down, Sir Charles Harington [q.v.] was the general whose blind eye saved the Government from head-on collision with Mustapha Kemal in the Dardanelles. Churchill himself had been trying to dissuade a too euphoric prime minister who was increasingly rude to him—theirs was 'the relationship of master and servant', he was to tell Robert (later Lord) Boothby years afterwards (Robert Boothby, *I Fight to Live*, 1947, p. 45)—from over-enthusiastic support of the Greeks, but in the event joined him in a solemn warning to Kemal. Churchill's request, as colonial secretary, for Dominion support unluckily became public; and so was the rebuff (J. G. Darwin, 'The Chanak Crisis', *History*, vol. 65, 1980). The Tories in the coalition had been made to take too much from the Liberals. The Carlton Club meeting ensued, 19 October 1922, and Lloyd George resigned. At the subsequent general election, 15 November 1922, Churchill, himself recovering from acute appendicitis, was beaten into fourth place at Dundee and found himself 'without a seat, without a party, and without an appendix'. He was appointed a Companion of Honour in the resignation honours list, 1922.

By February 1923 serialization of his *World Crisis* began in *The Times*, the whole torrential book (save the *Aftermath* some years later, 1931) appearing by the end of October. It was 'a brilliant autobiography disguised', as Balfour told a friend, 'as a history of the universe', a staggering performance from a man who for most of the time when he was dictating the huge volumes had been still busy in high office. Rhetorical as it inevitably is, for it is an orator's autobiography, there are magnificent passages in it which Churchill himself scarcely ever bettered.

He was by now politically isolated. He fought his last election as a Liberal and free trader in Leicester West, where he was defeated by F. W. (later Lord) Pethick-Lawrence [q.v.], the Labour candidate (6 December 1923). Repulsed by Asquith's acquiescence in suffering the Labour Party to take minority office in January 1924, Churchill stood as an 'Independent anti-

Socialist', with the young Brendan (later Viscount) Bracken [q.v.] among his supporters, in a by-election for the Abbey division of Westminster, only to be defeated by 43 votes in March 1924 by a Conservative.

A lifeline back to the Conservatism of his youth was uncoiled by Sir Archibald Salvidge [q.v.], his father's old Liverpool henchman. Free trade, the issue on which he had left the party twenty years before, no longer seemed quite the same shibboleth. He swallowed the McKenna duties and a form of imperial preference, which had been dividing him from Stanley Baldwin, in a speech at Liverpool in May 1924, after which he remarked of his wife at supper in the Adelphi: 'She's a Liberal, and always has been. It's all very strange for her. But to me, of course, it's just like coming home' (Stanley Salvidge, *Salvidge of Liverpool*, 1934, p. 275).

He was adopted at Epping in September and a month later was elected as a 'Constitutionalist' by a majority of nearly 10,000 in a high poll. Baldwin, like Lloyd George before him (and both were advised by Thomas Jones, q.v.), preferred Churchill on the inside looking out rather than sniping from the flank, but there was considerable surprise when, Neville Chamberlain having somewhat unexpectedly chosen to go to the Ministry of Health, the prime minister invited Churchill (8 November 1924) to become chancellor. 'Of the Duchy?' Churchill asked. 'No, the Exchequer', replied Baldwin. Tears came to Churchill's eyes (G. M. Young, *Stanley Baldwin*, 1952, p. 88): 'You have done more for me than Lloyd George ever did' (Thomas Jones, *Whitehall Diary*, ed. Keith Middlemas, vol. i, 1969, p. 303). Lord Randolph's robe, kept for thirty years in tissue paper and camphor by his widow, who had died not long before, lay ready. Birkenhead (with whom Churchill and Beaverbrook dined that night) and (Sir) Austen Chamberlain [q.v.], the other coalitionists, were also included in Baldwin's encompassing administration in which Churchill himself, in Asquith's phrase, towered like 'a Chimborazo or Everest amongst the sandhills' (H. H. Asquith, *Letters to a Friend*, 1934, p. 123).

Eventually it became fashionable in retrospect to deplore what J. M. (later Lord) Keynes [q.v.] called at the time *The Economic Consequences of Mr. Churchill* (1925) and Churchill's decision in his first, superbly introduced, budget to return to the gold standard: a cautious and reluctant decision, made after taking considerable advice, to return to such orthodoxy as could be had. All his five bravura budgets, each brilliantly stage-managed, were ingenious rather than fundamental in their thinking and could do little to alter the country's changed position in the post-war international economy. With Neville Chamberlain's assistance, he was able to resume both his own pre-war preoccupation with pensions and an even earlier reluctance to concede increases in defence expenditure: an issue which led to brushes with Beatty, by now first sea lord, and William C. (later Viscount) Bridgeman, the first lord of the Admiralty and perhaps Baldwin's closest ally. It also led to the consequent extension of the 'ten years rule'—that war was unlikely for ten years—from a more recent starting-point than 1919 when it had first made its appearance. Income tax was reduced to 4s. in the £ by the substitution of indirect taxation, such as the revival of the McKenna duties or duties on silk, real and artificial.

Churchill always went all out for victory; and, having achieved it, showed magnanimity towards the defeated. So it was over the Great War, over the Irish Treaty, and in the general strike of 1926. But if Churchill did not in this particular case want a fight to the finish, his handling of the *British Gazette*, which became under his strenuous editorship an anti-strikers pamphlet, served to inflame rather than to inform, since Churchill characteristically refused 'to be impartial between the fire brigade and the fire'. He strove hard, after the strike folded, to find a settlement in the coal industry but, in the main, despite his constructive interventions, when the miners had to return to work, it was on the owners' terms. Churchill chose to close the resultant deficit, £32 million of which was attributable to strikes, by a series of juggling expedients until he 'reached the end of (his) . . . adventitious resources'. In the following year, again in not always easy collaboration with Neville Chamberlain, he introduced his de-rating scheme for industry, which was coupled with Chamberlain's Local Government Act (1929), transferring the powers of the old Poor Law Unions and Boards of Guardians to the counties and boroughs; and he felt able to abolish the tax on tea. Abroad, bad 'dun' as he was—this was what (Sir) P. J. Grigg [q.v.], then his private secretary, called him (*Prejudice and Judgment*, 1948, p. 208)—he could claim that British war debt repayments to the United States were just about balanced by the receipts from German reparations and other foreign debtors to this country.

In September 1922 he had bought Chartwell manor, an estate of 300 acres near Westerham in Kent and proceeded to rebuild it with the assistance of Philip Tilden, the architect who had redesigned Churt for Lloyd George. Although he continued to play polo—his last game was in Malta in 1927, when he was fifty-two—and his painting was assiduously practised, much of his time when he was not staying with friends was devoted to the development, surrounded by his family, of Chartwell, to which his wife, although she made it delightful, was less devoted than he was, and to working on and dictating his books. In 1928 he told a less assiduous Baldwin that he had spent the whole of August 'building a cottage & dictating a book: 200 bricks and 2,000 words per day' (Pelling, op. cit., p. 335). He lived very well but he worked very hard to live very well. His stamina, his assiduity, his fertility of mind, and his sense of enjoyment were prodigious, his conversation a unique delight.

Totally at odds with Baldwin's mildly liberal policy towards India, Churchill resigned his membership of the Conservative shadow Cabinet (January 1931) and, with minimal support, fought the Government's India Bill clause by clause, to the bitter end. He had never seemed so isolated and he found solace in preparing a huge four-volume (1933-8) life of his ancestor, the first Duke of Marlborough [q.v.] (Maurice Ashley, *Churchill as Historian*, 1968). In the thirties he also published *My Early Life* (1930), his most delightful book, followed by *Thoughts and Adventures* (1932), and the almost unexpectedly perceptive *Great Contemporaries* (1937). His political isolation made it all the harder to recover an attentive audience for a growing series of warnings about the threat of a revived and rearming Germany, about which he made sure that he was remarkably well informed. An extraneous occurrence in December 1936 cast him further into the wilderness when the abdication of King Edward VIII restored Baldwin's popularity, whereas the romantically loyal Churchill for the first time in his life was shouted down in the House of Commons. He had gathered round him a small 'Focus' group which challenged the Government's foreign policy but Neville Chamberlain, who had become prime minister, was determinedly pursuing his own course, deliberately impervious to Churchill's eloquent prophecies.

When the brief popularity of the Munich agreement abated, Churchill's consistency gathered more appreciation outside the Cabinet but it was not until the German invasion of Poland (1 September 1939) that he was reluctantly invited to take office once again. He returned to his room in the Admiralty. 'Winston is back', the Fleet was informed (Arthur Marder, *Winston is back: Churchill at the Admiralty 1939-40*, 1972). There were a few exciting successes: the *Graf Spee* sank itself in the River Plate to avoid capture; and a British ship rescued our prisoners from the *Altmark* in a Norwegian fjord; but in April 1940 an ill-prepared incursion into Norway, from which British forces were forced to withdraw, led to a debate in the House which revealed the strength of the opposition to Chamberlain. It was ironical that Churchill, who was the responsible minister, should emerge victorious. Two days after the debate Hitler's armour invaded France and the Netherlands and the Labour Party demanded a coalition, refusing to serve under Chamberlain, who resigned (10 May 1940). Churchill became prime minister. 'At last I had authority to give directions over the whole scene. I felt as if I were walking with destiny . . .' (*The Second World War*, vol. i, 1948, pp. 526-7).

Churchill's first task was to formulate an administration. He was determined from the outset so to construct it as, by integration under the prime minister, to avoid and render impossible the sort of clash between 'frocks' and 'brass hats' which had bedevilled Lloyd George. 'Winston's concrete contribution to the war effort,' Lord Attlee was to recall in the *Observer* (in 1965), '. . . the setting up of the intragovernmental machine that dealt with the war, was most important. Winston, on becoming prime minister, also became minister of defence. Within the Cabinet he formed a Defence Committee, which, of course, he dominated in his twin capacity as prime minister and minister of defence. The committee had a nucleus of permanent members: myself as deputy chairman, the service ministers, and the three chiefs of staff. Other ministers attended as required. . . . Given Winston's knowledge of military men, his own military experience and flair, his personal dynamism, and the sweeping powers that any prime minister in wartime can have if he chooses to use them, the deadly problem of civilians-versus-generals in wartime was solved. Everybody involved should get some credit for this. But Winston's role has only to be described for its over-riding importance to be clear' (reprinted in *Churchill: a Profile*, ed. Peter Stansky, 1973, pp. 189-90).

'When we heard he was to be Prime Minister,' Sir Ian Jacob explained, '. . . I well remember the misgivings . . . in the War Cabinet Office. We had not the experience or the imagination to realise the difference between a human dynamo when humming on the periphery and when driving at the centre . . . the lack of administrative understanding displayed by Mr. Churchill would hardly have been counterbalanced by the other qualities he possessed, if he had not been quickly harnessed to a most effective machine. . . . It was in achieving this that General Ismay made . . . his greatest contribution. . . . He had to jostle the friends and adherents of Churchill who were at first like bees round a honey pot. He had to ensure that the Prime Minister received from the military machine rapid and effective service . . . and . . . in spite of occasional disagreements and temporary estrangements, the Prime Minister and the Chiefs of Staff came increasingly together as parts of a well-designed team. . . . As the Prime Minister's Chief Staff Officer, and as an additional member of the Chiefs of Staff Committee, Ismay took the knocks from above and below . . . to ensure that misunderstandings were smoothed out, and that the often exasperating vagaries of the Prime Minister and the sometimes mulish obstinacy of the Chiefs of Staff did not break up the association' (*Action This Day: Working with Churchill*, ed. Sir John Wheeler-Bennett, 1968, pp. 162 and 164–5).

Churchill gave himself to the task completely. To avoid misunderstandings, everything had to be submitted on paper. He began his long day with a secretary on one side of his bed providing him with the papers and a shorthand writer on the other side taking down the answers or any other observation which might occur to him. Copies of minutes on civil topics went to the secretary of the War Cabinet, Sir Edward (later Lord) Bridges [q.v.], to be followed up by him and the civil side of the War Cabinet Office. Those on military topics were fielded by Sir Ian Jacob and duly processed.

If Churchill retained as a potential point of friction the private evaluation with which 'the Prof' (F. A. Lindemann, later Viscount Cherwell, q.v.) and his statistical office supplied him, he shared with the chiefs of staff an incredible flow of information from Bletchley of the enemy's decrypted wireless traffic. Rarely has a wartime organization become so rapidly coherent and never so well informed. This did not mean, however, that, in galvanizing the swiftly adjusted central machinery into a new intensity of activity which was palpable throughout Whitehall, Churchill's own dominant part in it all was impeccably clear-headed and far-sighted, with long- and short-term objectives unwaveringly tuned into strategic coherence. His brain was too active, his interests too all-embracing, his urge to leave unplucked no benefit, covenanted or uncovenanted, too strong, his energy too unremitting, for this to be straightforwardly accomplished. 'Winston was always in a hurry', said Attlee. 'He didn't like to wait for the pot to boil, you know' (Marder, *From the Dreadnought to Scapa Flow*, vol. ii, p. 261). He could and did waste the time of busy experts by harebrained interventions, impatient short cuts, and chimerical projects so that the central machinery operated betimes in a series of judders. Yet within it might be detected—at least in retrospect—a corrective mechanism, Ismay [q.v.] on the military and Bridges on the civilian side as governors, which managed to prevent disaster without subduing the incredible impetus which Churchill's genius elicited.

'What Winston did, in my view, was to keep us all on our toes', wrote Attlee. 'He did very little work in the Cabinet. Churchill's Cabinets, frankly, were not good for business, but they were great fun. He kept us on our toes partly by just being Winston, and partly because he was always throwing out ideas. Some of them were not very good, and some of them were downright dangerous. But they kept coming, and they kept one going, and a lot of them were excellent . . . the best were those that came out of his gift of immediate compassion for people who were suffering. . . . If Winston's greatest virtue was his compassion, his greatest weakness was his impatience. He never understood that a certain time was always bound to elapse between when you ask for something to be done and when it can be effected. He worked people terribly hard, and was inconsiderate. On the whole, he did not vent his impatience on people in bursts of temper or in bullying. But . . . he kept people working impossible hours' (Stansky, op. cit., pp. 191–3). Such was the force of his personality, his charm as well as his purposefulness that none of the 'secret circle' whom he took into his family resented this: there was a war on and this was their dutiful and bewitched contribution.

'He lived well and ate everything', wrote Beaverbrook. 'He exaggerated his drinking habits by his own remarks in praise of wine and brandy' (*Men and Power*, 1956, p. xiv). He could never remember the time when he 'could not order a bottle of champagne for myself and offer another to a friend' (Lady Violet Bonham Carter, op. cit., p. 135). He invariably drank champagne at lunch and dinner followed by brandy. After his afternoon sleep and during the long evening he would sip weak whisky and water. 'None of this affected him in the least and he was as alert and active-minded at 8 a.m. as at midnight or midday. As for his cigars he didn't really smoke them. He never inhaled and simply lit and re-lit the cigar was half done when he threw it away' (Sir Ian Jacob in *The Listener*, 25 October 1979). 'His use of matches', Beaverbrook noted, 'outstripped his consumption of cigars.' His working day suited himself; a routine which he also maintained throughout his travels. It fell into two: from when he awoke, when a secretary brought him the papers, until he withdrew after luncheon for his afternoon sleep; and from when that sleep ended until the early hours of the following morning. Many night meetings, beginning at 10 or 10.30 p.m., continued until after midnight, after which Churchill conversed with his cronies whilst the Secretariat worked through the night to have ready the minutes for the breakfast tables of all who should receive them.

Having urgently forced the central

machinery to his will, he then had to inspire the British people with his own uncomplicated belief in ultimate victory and the recognition that life would be extremely unpleasant before it came. He would offer them nothing but 'blood, toil, tears, and sweat', and the impossibility of surrender. To inspire the French, too, was beyond him but even he was surprised to discover how bad their case was. Five abortive, even dangerous, visits, including an offer of 'union' of the two states, were accompanied by the eventual decision to send to France no more metropolitan fighter aircraft. His aim, if France dropped out of the struggle, was to guarantee that the minimum of gain should accrue to the enemy and the minimum of loss to the British. And he had shown the Americans that he would not desert an ally. At them his eye was cocked from the outset since, unflagging as was his belief in ultimate victory, he was far from certain how to achieve it, but he was quite clear in his own mind that it would not come about without American assistance 'until, in God's good time, the New World, with all its power and might, steps forth to the rescue' (speech in the Commons, 4 June 1940). His first success in the systematic wooing of the Americans away from neutrality was to begin a sustained correspondence with President Roosevelt from a 'Former Naval Person' with a shopping list (15 May 1940) of British needs from what he already envisaged as the arsenal of democracy (*Roosevelt and Churchill: their Secret Wartime Correspondence*, ed. F. L. Loewenheim et al., 1975). American subventions began to be dispatched in June 1940. Political devices such as Lend-Lease kept the flow of munitions going across the Atlantic while America was still neutral, and it never ceased till the war itself ended.

On 3 July 1940 he informed the Russian ambassador cheerfully that his 'general strategy at present is to last out the next three months'. On the same day he personally supervised the plan to seize French warships in British ports and immobilize those elsewhere, which entailed Admiral Sir James F. Somerville [q.v.] destroying three French battleships which refused an ultimatum at Oran in French North Africa. For the first time Churchill received a warm ovation from the Conservative benches in the House.

On 19 July 1940 Churchill chose Sir Alan Brooke (later Viscount Alanbrooke) to succeed Sir W. Edmund (later Lord) Ironside [qq.v.] as C.-in-C. Home Forces, a significantly personal choice of the best man to deal with invasion. Convinced that invasion would not be attempted until the enemy had gained air supremacy over the British Isles, Churchill threw himself characteristically into measures which would defeat that enterprise, supporting to the hilt

Lord Beaverbrook's frenetic acceleration of fighter aircraft production and giving urgent attention to such technical countermeasures for which, with Lindemann as interpreter, he could help to ensure priority. Persuaded by a young scientist that the Germans were bombing on a navigational beam, Churchill insisted that it should be 'bent' (R. V. Jones, *Most Secret War*, 1978). And with that unique capacity to combine fierce concentration on the immediate with awareness of the more distant problem, he sent Sir Henry Tizard [q.v.] to Washington armed with the unrestricted gift of every technical secret the British possessed, whilst at the same time he was inaugurating what were to become the airborne divisions and the commandos of the future. He had asked the President in May to send obsolete destroyers to supplement the Royal Navy and eventually achieved an arrangement by which they were exchanged for long leases for American bases in British islands in the West Indies, in Bermuda, and in Newfoundland. The affairs of the British Empire and the United States, he reported contentedly to the Commons, 20 August 1940, 'will have to be somewhat mixed up together'.

Of the Battle of Britain itself, he was, like the rest of his fellow countrymen, an amazed spectator but, unlike them, entirely articulate and able on their behalf to voice their relief with a singularly heartening felicity. 'Never', he recorded, 'has so much been owed by so many to so few.'

By 15 September 1940 he had realized that the threat of the invasion of Britain would ease (indeed, Hitler postponed Operation Sea Lion on 17 September) and Churchill's reaction was typical — to hasten a supply of tanks, which were therefore to his mind no longer needed at home, straight through the Mediterranean to Egypt instead of by safer route via the Cape; also, to strengthen the Mediterranean Fleet under Admiral Sir A. B. Cunningham (later Viscount Cunningham of Hyndhope, q.v.).

General Sir Archibald (later Earl) Wavell [q.v.], whose vigour Churchill came to doubt, launched an offensive in the Western Desert which culminated in February 1941 in the annihilation of the Italian land forces there. But the German threat to Greece prevented successful exploitation towards Tripoli.

Meanwhile at home the blitz (from September 1940) had been withstood without undue loss of production or morale which Churchill's personal example, as he stumped about amidst the debris, did much to sustain. He had become a legend in his lifetime. Babies were all said to resemble him. Many of the population in the temporarily classless society could produce their own parody of his accents and what he might have said. Moreover, the blitz convinced the Americans that Britain could 'take it', and was worth support. By December 1940 Roosevelt was willing to help to put his neighbour's fire out without haggling over the price of the hose.

Chamberlain's death (9 November 1940), which Churchill himself deeply regretted, for their relations had shown both men at their best (David Dilks, 'The Twilight War and the Fall of France', *Transactions of the Royal Historical Society*, 5th series, vol. xxviii, 1978), nevertheless eased the political situation. Churchill was elected to succeed him as leader of the Conservative Party and his parliamentary majority was now assured. In September Sir John Anderson (later Viscount Waverley, q.v.) had already succeeded Chamberlain as lord president.

The sudden death of Lord Lothian [q.v.], the British ambassador in Washington, 12 December 1940, led to other ministerial changes. Lord Halifax [q.v.] was persuaded to succeed him and (Sir) Anthony Eden (later Earl of Avon) replaced Halifax as foreign secretary. Captain David (later Viscount) Margesson [q.v.], the Conservative whip, succeeded Eden at the War Office.

In January 1941 Harry Hopkins, President Roosevelt's trusted confidant, arrived at Claridge's and Churchill's conquest of him ratified the link with Roosevelt (Robert Sherwood, *The White House Papers of Harry L. Hopkins*, 2 vols., 1948 and 1949).

Eden, accompanied by the CIGS (Sir John Dill, q.v.), set off for Cairo, Athens, and Ankara to attempt some sort of barrier to German expansion in the Balkans but Yugoslavia swiftly capitulated and the Allied forces sent to Greece had rapidly to withdraw some to Crete, which was quickly lost, the rest to Egypt.

The decision to support Greece with troops will always remain controversial. No aid had gone to Poland; efforts to buttress France had proved of no avail. Was Greece to be denied succour? Churchill was at pains to allow those on the spot to make the decision which he hoped they would make. It was needful to show Roosevelt that the British meant business. The President's response to what he told Churchill was a 'wholly justified delaying action' in Greece was to dispatch across the Atlantic seventy-four ships bearing further munitions for Egypt.

In May 1941 Churchill easily survived a vote of confidence in the House but, as became his technique, he subsequently conceded some ministerial changes and on 1 July Beaverbrook became minister of supply, responsible for the production of tanks as previously of aircraft. Fearful that the Germans would leap-frog

into Iraq, Churchill asked the Indian Government to send troops to Basra. Sir Claude Auchinleck's rapid response as C.-in-C. India impressed Churchill in sharp contrast to Wavell's lack of immediacy. In early June Wavell had to be prodded into the invasion of Syria, where the regime was still loyal to the Vichy Government. The failure of Operation Battleaxe in the Western Desert, upon which Churchill set much store and which began on 15 June 1941, led to Auchinleck and Wavell being made to change places. When Auchinleck became C.-in-C. Middle East, at the suggestion of Randolph Churchill, who was serving in GHQ Middle East, he was joined in Cairo as minister of state by Captain Oliver Lyttelton (later Viscount Chandos), who had been until then president of the Board of Trade.

Churchill had become convinced that Russia was Hitler's next target and he personally warned Stalin of his suspicion without response. When Russia was invaded (22 June 1941) his reaction was immediate. In a strategic instant, his anti-Bolshevik past went overboard. 'If Hitler invaded Hell,' he had told his secretary the day before, 'I would at least make a favourable reference to the Devil in the House of Commons.' In July an Anglo-Soviet agreement was signed that neither country would make a separate peace with Germany; and two squadrons of Hurricanes were sent to Murmansk to protect the northern shipping route. A supply route via Iran was also opened and in September 1941 an Anglo-American Supply Conference in London allocated to Russia what had previously been destined for Britain.

Throughout this whole period the Battle of the Atlantic was a constant anxiety. American willingness to help was useless unless the help could be delivered successfully. None knew better than Churchill that Britain could not survive if she lost command of the sea. In February 1941, through his intervention, the Western Approaches Command was moved from Plymouth to Liverpool and on 18 March a Battle of the Atlantic Committee was set up with Churchill in the chair. The Canadian and American governments extended the range of their naval activities and the sinkings by U-boats and Focke-Wulfs were brought under control. In May Churchill, remembering Frederick Leathers [q.v.] from when he himself had held a peacetime directorship in the P & O Company in 1930, combined the Ministries of Shipping and Transport, put Leathers in charge of a new Ministry of War Transport and, to avoid his being badgered in the House of Commons, sent him to the Lords as Lord Leathers (8 May). There was grave worry too in May when the *Bismarck*, the new German battleship, moved into the North

Atlantic and sank the cruiser *Hood*. On 27 May the *Bismarck*, after an anxious hunt, was sunk in its turn.

Auchinleck was summoned home to explain why he could not resume the attack in the desert before 1 November and 'Pug' Ismay took 'the Auk' aside at Chequers to brief his old Indian Army friend about the prime minister. 'Here is the gist of what I said. Churchill could not be judged by ordinary standards; he was different from anyone we had ever met before, or were ever likely to meet again. As a war leader, he was head and shoulders above anyone that the British or any other nation could produce. He was indispensable and completely irreplaceable. The idea that he was rude, arrogant and self-seeking was entirely wrong. He was none of these things. He was certainly frank in speech and writing, but he expected others to be equally frank with him. . . . He was a child of nature. He venerated tradition, but ridiculed convention. When the occasion demanded, he could be the personification of dignity; when the spirit moved him, he could be a *gamin*. His courage, enthusiasm and industry were boundless, and his loyalty was absolute. No commander who engaged the enemy need ever fear that he would not be supported. His knowledge of military history was encyclopaedic, and his grasp of the broad sweep of strategy unrivalled. At the same time, he did not fully realise the extent to which mechanisation had complicated administrative arrangements and revolutionised the problems of time and space; and he never ceased to cry out against the inordinate "tail" which modern armies required . . . [and] refused to subscribe to the idea that generals were infallible or had any monopoly of the military art. He was not a gambler, but never shrank from taking a calculated risk if the situation so demanded. His whole heart and soul were in the battle, and he was an apostle of the offensive. . . . He made a practice of bombarding commanders with telegrams on every kind of topic, many of which might seem irrelevant and superfluous. I begged Auchinleck not to allow himself to be irritated by these never-ending messages, but to remember that Churchill, as Prime Minister and Minister of Defence, bore the primary responsibility for ensuring that all available resources in shipping, man-power, equipment, oil, and the rest were apportioned between the Home Front and the various theatres of war, in the best interests of the war effort as a whole. Was it not reasonable that he should wish to know exactly how all these resources were being used before deciding on the allotment to be given to this or that theatre? He was not prone to harbouring grievances, and it was a mistake to take lasting umbrage if his criticisms were sometimes unduly harsh or even

unjust. . . . The way of life of the Politician was very different from that of the soldier' (*The Memoirs of Lord Ismay*, 1960, pp. 269-71).

In August 1941 Churchill and Roosevelt had their long-postponed meeting at Argentia in Placentia Bay off the Newfoundland coast. Churchill arrived in the *Prince of Wales*, the newest battleship, just refitted after the successful sinking of the *Bismarck*. The upshot was the Atlantic Charter, but more important than this statement of principles was the assumption by the American navy of the task of convoying fast merchant ships as far east as Iceland, which Churchill visited on his way back to England.

Whereas it was the cardinal doctrine of the chiefs of staff that the defence of Singapore was more important than that of the Suez Canal, Churchill in his heart of hearts never adhered to this priority. He knew that he could not hope to be strong everywhere. In the Anglo-American staff talks of February and March 1941 the British had hoped that the Americans would commit themselves to the defence of Singapore, but they refused. Advice from the CIGS to reinforce the Far East found Churchill dragging his feet. He believed, mistakenly, that Singapore was capable of all-round defence. 'I ought to have known. My advisers ought to have known, and I ought to have been told and I ought to have asked' (*The Second World War*, vol. iv, p. 43). He sent out Alfred Duff Cooper (later Viscount Norwich, q.v.) to report and he arranged that the *Prince of Wales* and the *Repulse* should be sent to the Far East, under the command of Sir Tom Phillips [q.v.], whom he had known as vice-chief of the naval staff and who shared his exaggerated view of the efficacy of battleships. They were to have been accompanied by the aircraft-carrier *Indomitable* but it had run aground and no substitute was forthcoming. Unprotected they proved a purposeless and expensive sacrifice.

On Sunday 7 December Churchill heard on the wireless of the Japanese attack on the American battleships in Pearl Harbor and immediately recognized that this must result in American entry into the war. 'So we had won after all' was his reaction, and that night he slept 'the sleep of the saved and thankful' (*The Second World War*, vol. iii, pp. 539-40). He also realized that what he had been visualizing primarily as a European struggle was now world-wide. Hitler's declaration of war against the United States helped him to keep the Americans to their agreed plan to defeat Germany first despite Pearl Harbor. He set off for the United States with a party of about eighty in the *Duke of York*, working over three clear-headed strategic papers with the staff on the uncomfortable voyage. He argued for American intervention in French North Africa to free the Mediterranean for Allied shipping. He hoped, too, for American troops to relieve the British in Northern Ireland and that American aircraft would begin to bomb Germany from bases in the United Kingdom. The invasion of mainland Europe he did not envisage until 1943. Throughout he was determined that that invasion should not begin until its success was as certain as it could be.

On Boxing Day 1941 he successfully addressed both Houses of Congress noting that had his father been American and his mother British 'instead of the other way round, I might have got here on my own'. On his return to the White House he had what his accompanying physician, Sir Charles Wilson (later Lord Moran), realized had been a slight heart attack.

He accepted Roosevelt's proposal for a united Allied command in the south-west Pacific under Wavell, agreed to the establishment as a consequence of a Combined Chiefs of Staff Committee in Washington (perhaps the most important piece of administrative machinery devised in the war), and left Sir John Dill, who had just been succeeded as CIGS by Brooke, as the senior British representative there.

Before he left Washington he and Roosevelt signed the declaration which led to the creation of the United Nations Organization.

On his return to Britain he found opinion very uneasy not only about the losses of the *Prince of Wales* and the *Repulse* to Japanese aircraft but also because of German success in Cyrenaica. A three-day debate on a vote of confidence at the end of January 1942 resulted in a vote of 464 to 1 in his favour but the news continued to worsen: the Germans recaptured Benghazi and the Japanese took Singapore: 'the worst disaster and largest capitulation in British history'; the German cruisers *Scharnhorst*, *Gneisenau*, and *Prinz Eugen* passed apparently unscathed through the English Channel from Brest.

Again he decided to reconstruct his ministry. Sir R. Stafford Cripps [q.v.] had returned from his embassy in Moscow and, as the symbol of strong pro-Russian sentiment, was an obvious candidate for office. After some jostling, he became lord privy seal and leader of the House. Attlee was restyled deputy prime minister and also took over the Dominions Office. Beaverbrook set off for the United States and was succeeded by Oliver Lyttelton as minister of production. A surprised Sir James Grigg replaced Margesson as secretary of state for war and was found a seat in the Commons.

In April 1942 Churchill proposed a visit to Roosevelt because he felt that the President was exhibiting too lively an interest in the future of India and that Colonel Louis Johnson, the President's representative in New Delhi ostensibly dealing with war *matériel*, was dipping too intrusive a finger in the Indian political pie. The War Cabinet, which included several members with considerable Indian experience, was not at one in the matter and it was eventually agreed to send Sir Stafford Cripps, a friend of both Nehru and Gandhi [qq.v.], to discuss Dominion status after the war. Churchill seemed determined to stymie whatever Cripps came up with and the mission petered out largely because Churchill preferred it that way; moreover, through American success in the Pacific war, the threat to India receded.

In May 1942 Molotov, the Russian foreign minister, began to press for a 'Second Front' in Europe together with recognition of the Russian frontiers of 1941. Churchill could not agree without repudiating the British guarantee to Poland. He was himself still toying with an assault on Norway (Operation Jupiter) to 'roll the map of Hitler's Europe down from the top'. The chiefs of staff successfully frustrated this proposal and when he went to the United States in mid-June with Brooke and Ismay his plan was to revert to a joint Anglo-American assault on French North Africa. During the visit to the President's family home at Hyde Park, New York State, he agreed with Roosevelt in the strictest privacy on the manufacture of the atomic bomb in the United States instead of in Britain. On 21 June in the White House he received the news that Tobruk (which he had made symbolic of British resistance in North Africa) had capitulated with the loss of 25,000 men taken prisoner. It was a singular tribute to their relationship that Roosevelt immediately proffered help. The Americans sent 300 Sherman tanks together with 100 self-propelled guns: a gift which was to turn the tide in North Africa.

Churchill returned home to learn that a by-election at Maldon had gone against the Government and to face a motion in the House expressing dissatisfaction with the central direction of the war. His critics, headed by a long forgotten figure, Sir James Wardlaw-Milne, produced contradictory remedies and Churchill rode off the last parliamentary criticism of his wartime coalition by 475 votes to 25.

Roosevelt sent Harry Hopkins, General Marshall, and Admiral King to London to discuss future strategy. The British chiefs of staff strongly opposed invasion of Europe in 1942 and Roosevelt agreed 25 July upon an American assault on French North Africa. Churchill then set off with Brooke for Cairo to consider the Middle East Command with Smuts's help. General Sir Harold Alexander (later Earl Alexander of Tunis, q.v.), Churchill's favourite field commander, was appointed to succeed Auchinleck, Brooke recognizing that he himself should remain as CIGS and, after Churchill's choice to command the Eighth Army—Lt.-Gen. W. H. E. Gott [q.v.]—almost at once was killed, Lt.-Gen. B. L. Montgomery (later Viscount Montgomery of Alamein), Brooke's choice, was summoned from England to take command at El Alamein.

Churchill then flew to Moscow to tell Stalin to his face (12 August 1942) that there could be no Second Front in 1942. He went on to explain, as Averill Harriman told the President, the advantages of attacking the 'underbelly' of a crocodile which he drew for Stalin, in telling him of the proposed Anglo-American assault (Operation Torch) on French North Africa. The difficult visit seemed to end amicably enough. Churchill promised a Second Front in Europe in 1943. Stalin 'now knew the worst and yet we parted in an atmosphere of goodwill' (Churchill, *The Second World War*, vol. iv, p. 430).

Back in England he instituted a weekly luncheon in 10 Downing Street with the American General Dwight D. Eisenhower, the commander designate for North Africa. Eighth Army attacked on 23 October at El Alamein with the aim of capturing the Martuba airfields in time for air cover to be furnished for the last convoy to reprovision Malta. Churchill now felt confident enough to allow church bells, silent since 1940, to be rung again (15 November 1942). A few days before, he had gone out of his way at the Mansion House to emphasize that he had 'not become the King's First Minister in order to preside over the liquidation of the British Empire'.

With the conquest of North Africa on the strategic horizon it was time to meet with Roosevelt again. Stalin was unable to join them and the President and premier met (January 1943) in a curious atmosphere of picnic on the Moroccan coast at Casablanca. Churchill had been persuaded, at least temporarily, by Brooke that the cross-Channel invasion which he had promised Stalin and which General Marshall continued to demand from the American side, was not feasible in 1943 and Marshall was eventually argued into a reluctant agreement to invade Sicily. The two political leaders attempted also to effect a political settlement of French North Africa by reconciling General de Gaulle with General Giraud and Roosevelt introduced in the final stages of the meeting the concept of 'unconditional surrender', in which Churchill, after consulting the War Cabinet, concurred.

At Casablanca command arrangements were changed and Alexander took over 18 Army Group, under Eisenhower's over-all command, to co-ordinate what were hoped to be the rapid final stages of the North African campaign which lasted, in fact, until mid-May.

By mid-April Churchill had realized that,

because of the Pacific war, shortage of shipping and landing-craft would rule out a cross-Channel invasion in 1943. Already he had had to tell Stalin of delays in polishing off North Africa and of the need to interrupt the Arctic convoys in order to mount the invasion of Sicily. The disturbing discoveries at Katyn made for further friction with the Russians.

Churchill felt that he must see Roosevelt once more. Feeling confident that the next stage should be the collapse of Italy, he travelled with the chiefs of staff in the *Queen Mary*, which had become a troop carrier. The American chiefs of staff remained adamant about a cross-Channel attack and it was agreed that General Marshall and the prime minister should go together to Algiers to consult Eisenhower and Alexander about the question of invading Italy. Since Eisenhower would not commit himself until he knew the fate of the invasion of Sicily, which was not due till 10 July, Churchill, who had been joined by Eden, had to face the question of what to tell Stalin. He was dissuaded because of his recent illness—he had had pneumonia in February—from going in person; the news by telegram was ill received.

Churchill had hoped that landing-craft, which had 'all our strategy in the tightest ligature', would not have to be switched too early from the Mediterranean to be available for the cross-Channel invasion (Operation Overlord), so as to imperil the development of the Italian campaign on which he had set his heart. His very eloquence served to make the Americans suspicious of his arguments, some of which were better than others. He was genuinely anxious to bring such pressure on the Germans as might relieve their pressure on the Russians and was successful to the extent that Hitler called off his Kursk offensive on 13 July 1943 to reinforce Italy. The combined chiefs of staff came round to the decision for a direct amphibious landing at Salerno Bay.

In the middle of the excitement over the collapse of Italy Churchill and Roosevelt met in Quebec in mid-August 1943 and sharp disagreements ensued. Churchill's advocacy of the development of the Italian campaign was coupled incongruously with his raising the question of Norway once more, which served to arouse suspicion of his genuine support for a cross-Channel invasion.

The Americans were also anxious to clear the Burma road to sustain China and build up air bases for an assault on Japan. Churchill sought to propitiate them by agreeing to a forward move in Burma under the newly appointed Lord Louis Mountbatten (later Earl Mountbatten of Burma) as supreme commander of a new South-East Asia Command, Churchill's own choice.

After a few days' holiday, Churchill returned as the President's guest to the White House during which visit, in the course of receiving an honorary degree at Harvard, he proposed a common citzenship for Britain and the United States.

Events in Italy led to some diminution of the German pressure on the Eastern Front and, despite his insulting remarks about Arctic convoys, Stalin let it be known that he was willing to have a meeting in Tehran with Roosevelt and Churchill. The president and prime minister conferred beforehand in Cairo where, to Churchill's discomfort, they were joined by Chiang Kai-shek. Churchill failed to get American agreement to keep enough landing-craft in the Mediterranean to allow for not only the capture of Rome but also the seizure of Rhodes and the opening up of supply routes in Yugoslavia for the partisans under Tito. Roosevelt was opposed to an attack on Rhodes unless Turkey first entered the war—Churchill's persistent and unfulfilled hope. On their return to Cairo after meeting with Stalin in Tehran at the end of November, Roosevelt agreed to two supreme commanders being appointed, an American for Overlord, the European invasion (he chose Eisenhower in order to retain Marshall in Washington), and a British general for the Mediterranean, where the bulk of the forces would be British. Churchill chose General Sir Henry Maitland (later Lord) Wilson [q.v.], who thus became responsible for an abortive Dodecanese expedition under Churchill's pressure.

On 12 December 1943 Churchill flew to Tunis as Eisenhower's guest before a proposed visit to the Italian front, but he fell gravely ill and his wife flew out to join him. His recovery at Marrakesh was aided by the news of the sinking of the *Scharnhorst* while attacking an Arctic convoy, and the American agreement to delay the return of the landing-craft from the Mediterranean in order to mount an amphibious assault on Anzio. Owing to American tardiness to exploit, the result was deeply disappointing to him, and instead of the 'wild cat' Churchill was hoping to hurl ashore, the result was 'a stranded whale'. The main forces, attempting to break out from the south, were held up by ferocious fighting at Monte Cassino. Churchill reassured the House of Commons: 'We must fight the Germans somewhere, unless we are to stand still and watch the Russians. This wearing battle in Italy occupies troops who could not be employed in other greater operations, and it is an effective prelude to them.' Not until mid-May 1944 was Alexander, deprived of troops who had returned to England to prepare for Overlord, able to renew his offensive. Rome was taken on 5 June.

On returning home from Marrakesh in January 1944, Churchill decided at last to give the invasion of Normandy priority in his attention even over the struggle with the U-boats. He instituted a weekly committee, over which he presided, to keep careful watch on how preparations were proceeding—in the production of artificial harbours ('Mulberry'), perhaps his own most personal contribution to the invasion, and the plans for both the airborne drop and the naval bombardment. By March he felt able to tell General Marshall in Washington that he was 'hardening very much on this operation'.

The role of the air forces in the proposed cross-Channel invasion was in dispute and it was Churchill who furnished the working formula in his proposal that they should be co-ordinated by Eisenhower's deputy as supreme allied commander, Sir Arthur (later Lord) Tedder [q.v.], in consultation with the commanders of Bomber Command and the American Eighth Air Force. By now Churchill, who had allowed considerable independence to Sir Arthur Harris at Bomber Command when he could see no other way to assist Russia than by the bombing of Germany, was less willing to accept its effectiveness and Tedder was able to pursue an interdiction programme aimed to isolate the invasion area from early reinforcement. Churchill, however, had second thoughts when he contemplated the potential casualties which might be inflicted upon the French population. However, in the upshot, Roosevelt refused 'to impose from this distance any restriction on military action by the responsible commanders' and Churchill gave in.

On 15 May the King and the prime minister attended General Montgomery's presentation of his assault plans at St. Paul's School in Hammersmith. It was agreed reluctantly between them that neither should have his wish and go to sea on D-day. Churchill had to content himself with having his special train, in which he was accompanied by Smuts and Ernest Bevin [q.v.], near Eisenhower's headquarters outside Portsmouth, where de Gaulle raised last minute difficulties which led to Churchill's exasperated observation that if forced to choose between France and the United States he would always choose the latter.

Accompanied by Brooke and Smuts, Churchill paid his first visit to Normandy on 12 June, but, as the American effort in France began to bulk larger and the British contribution lessened, his influence (like Montgomery's) diminished notably and, when on 1 September Eisenhower assumed direct command of the land forces, it abated further. He was unable to persuade Eisenhower to reconsider the decision taken at Tehran to reinforce the invasion of France from the

Mediterranean by landings on the Riviera, at the expense of the Italian campaign. Having failed in this, he tried at almost the last perverse moment to have the operation switched from the Riviera to Brittany instead. He had to content himself with witnessing, from the destroyer *Kimberley*, the invasion he had attempted to divert.

The dispute over Montgomery's criticism of how the campaign should develop left Churchill out on a limb since Eisenhower did not welcome his interference or his suggested recipe.

In Italy, where the command was predominantly British, Churchill was more welcome. He was also preoccupied with the situation in Greece, where he wished to avoid a Communist *coup* in Athens as the Germans began to withdraw. He agreed with Roosevelt in mid-August that a British force should be sent there. Russian behaviour over the Warsaw rising upset him deeply and he grew more sombre about the post-war world.

In September, accompanied by a large staff in the *Queen Mary*, he went to see Roosevelt again, and he was persuaded to agree to the Morgenthau plan to 'pastoralize' Germany after the war, a decision he quickly repented. He insisted that there should be a substantive British contribution to the Pacific war and Mountbatten was instructed to recapture Burma. It was, however, very evident that Admiral King, the American chief of naval staff, was reluctant to receive the assistance of the Royal Navy.

Meanwhile German resistance in the West was stiffening and the failure of the Arnhem operation presaged a harsh winter. Churchill decided to visit Stalin again to achieve some sort of agreement about Poland and Greece. Roosevelt could not go. Churchill reached a paper agreement with Stalin about spheres of influence taking no account of American views and not really tackling the Polish question. On his return he managed to secure Roosevelt's agreement to American recognition of de Gaulle's Government in France. The path was clear at last for Churchill to visit Paris, where he had a triumphant reception on 11 November 1944.

Greece was not so simple nor was it improved by a press leakage of Churchill's signal to Lt.-Gen. (Sir) R. M. Scobie, the commander of the British force sent to Athens: 'Do not however hesitate to act as if you were in a conquered city where a local rebellion is in progress.' He gained Roosevelt's agreement to the appointment of a regency pending elections and the return of the Greek king, and, with his customary disregard of danger, decided to go with Eden to Athens to settle the situation on the spot. About Damaskinos he inquired, 'This Archbishop, is he a cunning, scheming prelate more interested in temporal power than celestial glory?' and, on being told that he was, decided 'Then, he's our man'.

In replying to Smuts's message for his seventieth birthday (30 November 1944) Churchill admitted that 'it is not so easy as it used to be for me to get things done'. This was not only because he was influencing the Americans increasingly less and the Russians not at all, but also because he himself was tired and, through playing too many away matches, losing his grip over an increasingly irritated Cabinet. Attlee sent him a long letter, 19 January 1945, criticizing his 'method or rather lack of method of dealing with matters requiring Cabinet decisions' and of paying too much attention to the views of his cronies Bracken and Beaverbrook, neither of whom was in the War Cabinet.

The last meeting of the 'Big Three' took place in February in the Crimea. It was a sign of the times that, although Roosevelt agreed to staff talks in Malta *en route*, he did not wish for long discussions with Churchill himself lest they appeared to be 'ganging up' on Stalin. The atmosphere at Yalta was apparently cordial and agreement was reached on the establishment of the United Nations and the occupation of Germany, but the Polish question remained unsolved. Stalin was at this time still trusted by Churchill, who none the less felt that too many concessions were made to him because of Americans' anxiety for Russian participation in the war against Japan.

After a visit to Balaclava (13 February 1945) Churchill flew to Athens, and thence to Egypt before leaving for home again.

He was determined to see for himself the closing stages of the campaign in the West and flew to Venlo (23 March) to watch the Rhine crossing with Montgomery and Eisenhower. He crossed the Rhine himself at Wesel. Eisenhower, who had already told Stalin direct, much to Churchill's annoyance, how he proposed to move into Germany, refused Churchill's advice to forestall the Russians by capturing Berlin first. Since Roosevelt supported Eisenhower, Churchill perforce dropped the matter (5 April).

On 12 April Roosevelt died suddenly and Churchill felt bereft. His first instinct was to go to Washington, but Eden, in any case due to go to the San Francisco conference later in the month, went instead. On 8 May Churchill declared the war in Europe finally at an end. On 12 May he wrote to President Harry S. Truman of his concern at the proposed early withdrawal of American forces from Europe and was reassured by the new President's swift and determined reaction to Yugoslav intransigence over Trieste.

He proposed formally to Attlee the continuation of the wartime coalition until Japan had been defeated. The Labour Party refused and Churchill formally resigned (23 May 1945) and was invited by the King to form what was to be a caretaker government until the election, which was settled for 5 July. On 28 May he took an unashamedly tearful farewell of his wartime senior ministers. It was assumed that the war against Japan might last another eighteen months.

With a contested election in prospect it would have been out of character if Churchill had not reverted to partisanship. His reference to Labour introducing some sort of Gestapo was counter-productive. Churchill and Attlee fought very different campaigns, Churchill inevitably on the grand scale, Attlee in an old car driven, none too well, by his wife. Churchill and Attlee met again at Potsdam, as had been agreed, and were told by the Americans of the successful experiment with an atomic bomb in New Mexico. There was no argument about using such a bomb against Japan. The three Englishmen, Churchill, Eden, and Attlee, returned to England on 25 July and next day it was clear that Churchill had been heavily defeated in the election. The Labour Party won a total of 393 seats whereas Churchill's supporters barely exceeded 200. Churchill at once visited the Palace to submit his resignation and advised the King to send for Attlee. He was offered the garter but felt, as did Eden, who was also offered it, that the moment was inappropriate.

'God knows where we should be without him', Brooke told himself (4 December 1941), 'but God knows where we shall go with him' (Arthur Bryant, *The Turn of the Tide*, 1957). Brooke was not alone in both the realization and the conjecture. It had rested with the chiefs of staff, with Brooke himself, as their eventual chairman, and with Ismay, to frustrate and divert the minister of defence when he was for striking out everywhere and anywhere and to be prepared to argue with him till far into the night without forfeiting the urgency which Churchill brought to every matter, good, bad, or indifferent.

The availability from Bletchley of information about the enemy compounded his impatience and made life intolerable for Wavell, then Auchinleck in the Middle East, wore out Pound, then Dill in Whitehall. There was scarcely an admiral but had been threatened with dismissal in his time (Stephen Roskill, *Churchill and the Admirals*, 1977). Unable to perceive how best he might help Russia, save by expensive and most hazardous convoys of munitions, Churchill was perforce committed, though with reluctant and increasingly disillusioned wrestling about its effectiveness, to

strategic bombing until it was possible to hazard a Continental invasion.

Home affairs he had in the main to leave to others though not without bombarding them with queries and injunctions, 'Action this Day', which reflected an underlying recognition of the importance of domestic morale, particularly over rationing, and of achieving a proper balance between civilian and military needs, especially in the allocation of shipping. There were as a result only two backbench revolts, by the Tories against Ernest Bevin's catering wages Act in February 1943 and shortly afterwards by Labour supporters against the Government's apparently tepid attitude to the Beveridge Report. In March 1944 the Government lost a Labour amendment (which concerned the pay of women teachers) on its Education Bill (Paul Addison in *British Prime Ministers*, ed. J. P. Mackintosh, vol. ii, 1978, p. 25). Churchill compelled the House to reverse itself but on the whole he relied on Anderson and Attlee to cope with the Home Front for him and sensed that the size of Ernest Bevin warranted the minimum of his intrusion where manpower was concerned. Bevin for his part backed him to the hilt (Alan Bullock, *Bevin*, vol. ii, 1967, p. 108). Moreover, the prime minister came increasingly to spend less time in England.

As the war developed, he moved from his initial task of keeping Britain at war to trying to direct a war in which his country was to play a diminishing part. Up to September 1944 his was the most powerful voice. The last (the sixth) volume of his war memoirs exhibits his saddened recognition that his influence in Allied counsels had gone over the crest and that his voice was no longer·as effective. He had come to confide in Smuts instead of Roosevelt, who was no longer listening. For five years the architect of the 'Grand Alliance' had done most to hold it together. The huge and welcome responsibility of war leadership did not abate the fertility of his monologue, the range of his interests and vocabulary, or his willingness to interfere in anything which crossed his path or stimulated his abundant fancy. Never readily persuaded, he became, thanks to his position at the top, less persuadable than ever before and the vastness of the work-load he set himself meant that he was ever liable to emphasize matters less important to busy chiefs of staff than they seemed to him. The chiefs of staff who with Ismay survived the war were men of considerable physical resilience and extraordinary technical competence in their own professions; Cunningham, who had succeeded Pound [q.v.] as first sea lord, in October 1943, was impervious to Churchill's spell. Brooke, Portal, and Cunningham had to be prepared to return to arguments on issues which the three of them had hoped were regarded as settled when the whim of their political master swung his searchlight once again in that direction. It was claimed at the war's end that on no matter of real import did Churchill eventually overrule them: some decisions were in any case overtaken by events. He could be petulant and unfair to individuals, and he could side-track decisions he was reluctant to take, but in the big things—'matters of great moment', as he would call them—he and the chiefs of staff, after some wrestling, had usually achieved an eventual concurrence.

Churchill took some time to adjust himself to the leadership of the Opposition. Much of the parliamentary battle he left to others and he devoted much of his time to the production of his very personal *The Second World War*. The theme running through his public speeches was the need for European unity in a cold war. He set the tone at Fulton, Missouri (March 1946), and at Zurich (September 1946). Again and again he harked back to the notion of 'summit' talks between the Americans, the British, and the Russians, which the Americans, more conscious than he appeared to be of the change in British power, were reluctant to undertake.

He returned to office in 1951 with a majority of seventeen. He resumed his old post of minister of defence for a while but the load proved too much. Earl Alexander of Tunis was brought back from Canada, where he was happily governor-general, to take over the defence portfolio, but this scarcely proved an apt appointment. Ismay was brought back from retirement to become Commonwealth secretary and an experiment with three 'overlord' ministers—Lords Woolton [q.v.], Leathers, and Cherwell—did not last long, since political responsibilities remained with the individual departments over which they were supervisory. Eden, of course, resumed as foreign secretary, and other wartime ministers came back to new offices: R. A. Butler (later Lord Butler of Saffron Walden) as chancellor of the Exchequer, Oliver Lyttelton as colonial secretary, and Harold Macmillan to deal with housing. Sir Walter Monckton (later Lord Monckton of Brenchley, q.v.) was brought in to charm the trade unions into inactivity.

If Churchill was still vigorous in Cabinet he showed less willingness to interfere and less zeal in furthering business. Colleagues in the European movement came to feel that Churchill's hankering after a 'special' relationship with the United States caused him to drag his feet with regard to Europe. He himself realized that he was no longer the man he had been. He was increasingly deaf. 'In the midst of the war', he said, 'I could always see how to do it. Today's problems are elusive and intangible' (*Memoirs of Lord Chandos*, 1962, p. 343).

In April 1953 he accepted the garter, which he had refused at the end of the war, and was able to wear it at the coronation in June. He suffered a stroke on 23 June but forced himself to complete his four-volumed *A History of the English-Speaking Peoples* (1956-8), which he had begun before the war. In December he attended a meeting with President Eisenhower in Bermuda which postponed the sort of summit which he had been advocating for so long. A minor Cabinet reshuffle preceded his eightieth birthday and it became clear that he could not fight another election as prime minister. On 4 April 1955 he gave a dinner party for the Queen and the Duke of Edinburgh at 10 Downing Street and next day made his formal resignation at the Palace. He toyed with becoming Duke of London but was dissuaded by his son who had no wish to go to the Lords. Eden, who had waited so long, was summoned to succeed him. Churchill was returned for the Woodford division at yet another election (26 May 1955). When Eden's health gave way after Suez Churchill was amongst those whom the Queen consulted about his successor. He recommended Harold Macmillan, who like himself had fought in World War I. He visited the House of Commons for the last time on 27 July 1964 and celebrated his ninetieth birthday later in the year. On 24 January 1965 he died at his home at 28 Hyde Park Gate. After the lying-in-state at Westminster Hall the funeral service was at St. Paul's Cathedral in the presence of the Queen. The final journey was by train to a station near Blenheim Palace. He was buried beside his parents in the nearby Bladon churchyard.

Chancellor of Bristol University from 1929, Churchill held honorary degrees from more than twenty universities, was an honorary freeman of more than fifty cities, and was an honorary fellow of many learned societies. He was lord warden of the Cinque Ports from 1941 and was admitted to the Order of Merit in 1946. In 1953 he won the Nobel prize for literature. He was decorated by General de Gaulle with the Cross of Liberation in 1958 and was proclaimed an honorary citizen of the United States 9 April 1963. An honour which he relished particularly was honorary Royal Academician Extraordinary (1948), and his speeches at the annual banquet were one of its features. But he was most at ease in Zion at the Harrow songs which he tried to attend every year. Churchill College, Cambridge, was founded in 1960 as a memorial, and in 1964 Churchill became its first honorary fellow. In 1965 the Winston Churchill Memorial Trust was established to provide for 100 travel scholarships a year.

'Half-American but all British', Winston

Churchill may have changed parties, or his rig, or his head-gear, readily enough, but he scarcely changed his basic concepts. 'If anyone wishes to discover his views on the large and lasting issue of our time, he need only set himself to discover what Mr. Churchill has said or written on the subject at any period in his long and exceptionally articulate public life, in particular during the years before the First World War: [Churchill] . . . knows with an unshakeable certainty what he considers to be big, handsome, noble, and worthy of pursuit by someone in high station, and what, on the contrary, he abhors as being dim, gray, thin, likely to lower or destroy the play of colour and movement in the universe . . . Mr Churchill is one of the diminishing number of those who genuinely believe in a specific world order' (Sir Isaiah Berlin, *Mr. Churchill in 1940*, 1949, pp. 16-17).

This most extraordinary human being, with a lifetime in politics, seemed to have an intuitive comprehension of what might irk the ordinary man whose way of life was so conspicuously different from his own. Beneath his torrential impatience there lay an almost unexpected core of compassion. From the magniloquence peeped an impish sense of humour, Abreast as he was of modern inventions and devices, nevertheless he was impelled by an old-fashioned patriotism nourished by a sense of history and an awareness that he himself was one and not the least distinguished of a line of historical figures.

'Churchill on top of the wave', Beaverbrook once wrote, 'has in him the stuff of which tyrants are made' (*Politicians and the War*, vol. ii, p. 82). But he had been brought up or had brought himself up to oppose tyranny wherever he might discern it: as the duty of an Englishman; tyranny was for foreigners. Overbearing in counsel, often intolerably difficult to persuade, nevertheless he elected to be surrounded by men of great ability who could stand up to him and speak frankly—'we are not here to exchange compliments'. 'All I wanted', he would maintain, 'was compliance with my wishes after reasonable discussion.' Incapable of sustained rancour and too open-hearted to stoop to intrigue, in the long run, at the end of the argument, he had succeeded for the main part of the war in enforcing his own grand strategy twice over: at the time; then, in six majestic volumes, how it should come to be remembered. The 'central sanity of his character', the constraints imposed by having to operate within an ill-assorted alliance, and the quality of those with whom he came to work as a war leader—all these stood in the path of tyranny. Above all, he was most happily married to someone who did not fear him in the least and could never have been a tyrant's wife.

Of the many portraits of Churchill, the National Portrait Gallery holds those by Walter Sickert (1927), Juliet Pannett (1964), and Bernard Hailstone (1965). Oscar Nemon sculpted Churchill frequently. Examples of his work are the 1946 bronze head, the 1955 study of Churchill seated (commissioned by the Guildhall), the bust in Churchill College, Cambridge, and the 1968 bust in the Conservative Central Office. Nemon also sculpted Churchill and his wife 'in informal mood' (1978, Blenheim Palace), and provided the House of Commons with the Churchill statue (1969). Many museums have a copy of the bronze head by (Sir) Jacob Epstein (1946). The portrait by (Sir) William Orpen (1916), a copy of which (by John Leigh Pemberton) is at Churchill College, is a good depiction of Churchill as a young Cabinet minister. A portrait by Graham Sutherland, a gift to Churchill on his eightieth birthday by both Houses of Parliament, is believed to have been destroyed.

[See F. B. Woods, *A Bibliography of the Works of Sir Winston Churchill* (1963, 2nd revised edn. 1975). The official life was begun by Churchill's son, Randolph, and then continued, more ably and most exhaustively, by Martin Gilbert (5 volumes, with companion volumes of documents 1966-76). Robert Rhodes James, *Churchill, a Study in Failure, 1900-1939* (1970), is useful as is his *Gallipoli* (1965). The most comprehensive biography in a single volume is Henry Pelling, *Winston Churchill* (1974), to which this notice is greatly indebted. Chester Wilmot's *The Struggle for Europe* (1952) appeared before Churchill's own final volumes v and vi came out. The admirable *Grand Strategy* volumes of the official war history are most helpful, especially Michael Howard's volume iv (1972). John Ehrman, author of volumes v and vi (1956) also compared 'Lloyd George and Churchill as War Ministers' in *Transactions of the Royal Historical Society*, 5th series, vol. ii, 1961. See also Ronald Lewin, *Churchill as Warlord* (1973) and his *Ultra Goes to War* (1978). There is a perceptive essay on the Statistical Office by Sir Donald MacDougall in *Policy and Politics*, edited by David Butler and A. H. Halsey (1978). Elisabeth Barker, *Churchill and Eden at War* (1978) is helpful. A distasteful book by Churchill's physician, Lord Moran— *Churchill, the Struggle for Survival, 1940-65* (1966)—provoked members of Churchill's personal staff to write an attractive collection of essays entitled *Action this Day: Working with Churchill*, edited by Sir John Wheeler-Bennett (1968). See also Sir George Mallaby, *From my Level* (1965); Sir David Hunt,

On the Spot (1975); Sir John Colville (a contributor to *Action this Day*), *Footprints in Time* (1976). Other relevant publications are cited in the text above.] E. T. WILLIAMS

CHUTER-EDE, JAMES CHUTER, BARON CHUTER-EDE (1882-1965), parliamentarian, was born 11 September 1882 in Epsom, Surrey, the son of James Ede, a grocer, and his wife, Agnes Mary Chuter. He had one sister. He was educated at Epsom National Schools, Dorking High School, Battersea Pupil Teachers' Centre, and (with a scholarship) at Christ's College, Cambridge. However, the scholarship was insufficient to maintain himself, and he left without a degree. He became an assistant master in Surrey elementary schools until 1914. He was elected to the Epsom Urban District Council in 1908, becoming chairman of its electricity undertaking, and in 1914 he was elected to the Surrey County Council.

When war broke out in 1914 Ede enlisted in the armed forces, becoming a sergeant in the East Surreys and Royal Engineers. During the war his political views encouraged him to join the Labour Party; in 1918 he stood as Labour candidate for the newly formed division of Epsom. He was defeated, but five years later he became, briefly, MP for Mitcham, losing his seat the same year. He returned to Parliament in 1929, as Labour member for South Shields, a seat which he held until 1931, and thereafter from 1935 to 1964.

His first ministerial appointment was in the 1940-5 coalition Government, as parliamentary secretary in the Ministry of Education, a post for which he had unique qualifications. R. A. Butler (later Lord Butler of Saffron Walden), the minister of education, and Ede made a highly successful partnership during the passage of the Education Act of 1944. Ede, who changed his name by deed poll to Chuter-Ede in 1964, played a major part in the delicate negotiations during the preparation of the Bill, and in piloting it through the committee stages.

Yet it is as home secretary that he will be chiefly remembered. He held that office for over five years (1945-51), longer than anyone for many years, and at a time when much needed to be done to revise wartime legislation and to catch up with necessary reforms in many areas of Home Office business. He was thus faced with a programme of legislation formidable both in size and variety; in 1947-8 alone he sponsored six major Bills—a British nationality Bill; a Bill to make better provision for deprived children; legislation adapting wartime defence regulations; a police pensions Bill; a large and controversial Bill on parliamentary representation; and the most substantial criminal justice Bill for many years, which made important changes in court powers and in the prison regime. In other sessions he dealt with the denationalization of the fire service; the peacetime organization of Civil Defence; the re-settlement of Polish forces; major changes in magistrates' courts; and reform of the licensing laws. To this unprecedented burden of legislation was added the day-to-day administration of the Home Office, which presented special problems at a time of rapid social change. Among his most important tasks was the modernization of the police service. Endurance and versatility are qualities which home secretaries need, but few in such measure as those required at such a time.

The difficulty of the criminal justice Bill was greatly increased by the controversy which arose about capital punishment. The Cabinet had decided to allow a free vote on a new clause put down by a private member, providing for the abolition of capital punishment for an experimental period of five years. Ede, giving the Government's advice, argued against accepting the clause on the grounds that public opinion was against any change, that there had been a marked increase in violent crime, and that careful consideration by the home secretary of every case ensured that the death penalty was exacted only when it was absolutely necessary. But after one of the most dramatic debates in recent years the clause was passed by a small majority.

When the Bill reached the House of Lords the new clause was decisively rejected, and Ede then tabled a compromise clause limiting capital punishment to a number of specific offences. This also was rejected by the Lords and Ede then advised the Commons not to insist on the new clause, which would have meant the loss of the whole Bill for that session.

Shortly afterwards the Government set up the royal commission on capital punishment, whose report was debated in 1955. By then Ede's views had changed; he was much influenced by the controversy about the execution, during his time as home secretary, of Timothy John Evans, for whom he had denied a reprieve and later came to believe was innocent, and he had also come to the conclusion that the case for capital punishment as a deterrent could not be proved either way. Of public opinion, to which he had attached so much importance in 1947, he said, 'I doubt very much whether, at the moment, public opinion is in favour of this change but I doubt also whether, at any time during the past hundred years, a plebiscite would have carried any of the great penal reforms which have been made'. He voted for a motion to suspend capital punishment, but it was not carried.

In 1956 there was yet another debate, in

which Ede himself moved an amendment urging the Government to abolish or suspend the death penalty. This was carried by 293 votes to 262 on a free vote. This led to the passage of the Homicide Act which restricted capital punishment to specific types of murder (the compromise rejected in 1947), and before long to the abolition of the death penalty.

Capital punishment is a particularly emotive example of the conflict between the protection of society and concern for the individual which is central to so much of a home secretary's responsibilities. Chuter-Ede's part in this long controversy showed his integrity of character and his parliamentary skills in a dramatic light. Although he found his duties in dealing with individual capital cases profoundly distasteful, he carried them out with scrupulous and impartial judgement; and while he still believed in the need for the death penalty, he put the case for retention forcibly, but without exaggeration. But when he changed his point of view he had the courage to explain why he had done so, even if this exposed him to the charge of inconsistency. It is a tribute to the respect in which he was held by the House that his sincerity was never doubted.

To those who did not know him well Chuter-Ede often appeared austere and they may have been reminded of his early training as a schoolmaster. He was a radical of the old school and a puritan in the sense of a phrase used by one of his favourite poets, James Russell Lowell, in that 'the home-spun dignity of man he thought it worth defending'. It was this respect for human nature, coupled with a natural tolerance and good humour, that were the essence of his character.

He became PC (1944), CH (1953), DL (Surrey), and an honorary freeman of several boroughs. He received an honorary MA from Cambridge (1943), and honorary doctorates from Bristol (1951), Sheffield (1960), and Durham (1954). He served on many public bodies, including the BBC advisory council, of which he was chairman for seven years.

His personal tastes were simple. Among his pleasures were horse-racing (he always had a box at the Epsom Derby meeting, and recalled with pride that his father had had the contract for painting the course railings); excursions on the Thames in a small motor-cruiser; and a yearly Christmas visit to the circus, to which he used to invite a party of children from a Surrey orphanage.

Ede married in 1917 Lilian Mary Stephens (died 1948), daughter of Richard Williams, of Plymouth. She was a fellow member of the Surrey County Council. In her latter years she became crippled and he was often to be seen pushing her about the House of Commons in a wheelchair. They were a devoted couple, and he was much affected by her unexpected death. There were no children. On ceasing to be home secretary in 1951, Chuter-Ede was for a few months leader of the House of Commons, having been deputy-leader in 1947. He became a life peer in 1964 and died in a Ewell nursing home 11 November 1965.

[*The Times*, 12 November 1965; private information; personal knowledge.]

ARTHUR PETERSON

CLARK, SIR ALLEN GEORGE (1898-1962), entrepreneur and industrialist, was born 24 August 1898 in Brookline, Massachusetts, in the United States of America, the elder child and only son of Byron George Clark, a business man who travelled extensively in Europe on behalf of the United Shoe Machinery Corporation, and his wife, Helen Peirce. Coming to the UK with his parents and younger sister Marion in 1905, A. G. Clark was educated at Felsted School (1913-15) and subsequently served in the British Army (with the London Scottish) until he was wounded at Cambrai in 1917. After recovery he was commissioned in the Royal Flying Corps and served in Egypt until the armistice. After the war he purchased, with the aid of his father, a share in the struggling engineering company 'Plessey' which then had six employees. With his co-managing director, W. O. Heyne, he was to build Plessey into a major international company.

The first important step towards success for Clark, Heyne, and Plessey was an order—in 1922—from Marconi for domestic radio receivers. This took the company into the rapidly developing electronics business and Clark into his lifelong involvement with this industry. Subsequently, the company designed and built the first portable radio sets made in Britain. A few years later it manufactured the first commercially produced television set in the world, on behalf of Baird.

Clark and Heyne concentrated on making the company a supplier to other manufacturers, rather than on selling direct to the public, and in those pioneering days they achieved major advances in the rationalization of the production of electronic components. Clark's talents were particularly suited to selling; he was very much an extrovert, with complete confidence in the abilities of himself and the company, regarding business as a challenge and having high ambitions for the company's growth. A major factor in the company's success was Clark's talent for getting on to good personal terms with potential customers—he was the commercial driving force behind the company, while Heyne was the engineer. 'AG', as Clark was generally known, believed strongly in management involvement with the work-force, and was a familiar and distinctive figure on the shop-floor.

Clark believed that the right way for his company to remain technically up to date in the early days was to buy the neccessary technology. The very significant contribution that the company made to the British effort during the war of 1939-45 resulted partly from this policy. In particular, Clark took out licences—from America—to manufacture both the fuel pumps which fed the Merlin engines for Spitfires and the electrical connectors which were also for use in aircraft. By allowing aircraft wiring to be prefabricated and built-in at an early stage of airframe construction, these connectors helped to make possible the very high production rates of aircraft which Britain achieved. Clark was also responsible for the purchase, immediately before the outbreak of war, of machinery that made possible the company's large output of munitions during the war—ironically enough, this was bought from Germany, and Clark himself brought back some vital components in his personal baggage as late as 1 September 1939.

During the war years Clark was able to build up the company's expertise in electronic systems—for example, Plessey supplied more than 160,000 complete radio and electrical installations for many famous fighters and bombers. At the same time important pioneer developments in such areas as direction-finding receivers (including specially designed cathode-ray direction-finding equipment for the detection of U-boats) took place under Clark's control.

Immediately after the war Clark had to supervise a period of retrenchment as Plessey geared itself to peacetime markets. From a wartime peak of nearly 11,500, the number employed dropped to less than 5,250. Under his direction, the company again prospered, growing very rapidly through both internal growth and acquisitions. By 1953 the number employed had grown far beyond the wartime peak.

At this time the expertise in electronics that Clark had built within the company really came into its own, while additionally Clark now sanctioned far greater expenditure on internal research and development, rather than on buying technology through licensing agreements as had been his previous policy. As early as 1952, for example, the company was deeply involved in silicon technology. In the last years of Clark's life the move into systems was accelerated by the acquisition of the telephone companies Automatic Telephone and Electric, and the British Ericsson's.

Clark's hobbies were fishing, golf, and shooting; he was a member of the team representing Great Britain at the clay-pigeon shooting world championship held in Berlin in 1936 in conjunction with the Olympic Games. He shot for England in the eight Home International matches held between 1935 and 1950.

In 1925 Clark married Jocelyn Anina Marie-Louise Emerson, daughter of Percy Culverhouse, then chief architect to the Great Western Railway. The couple were subsequently divorced but neither remarried. They had a daughter, and two sons who took over the running of Plessey following their father's death. Both sons achieved distinction, with John Allen Clark being knighted in 1971 for services to exports and Michael William Clark being appointed CBE in 1977, again for services to exports. Clark, who was American by birth and naturalized in 1927, was knighted in 1961; he was a council member of both the Society of British Aircraft Constructors and the Telecommunication Engineering and Manufacturing Association.

Clark died at his home in St. James's, London (on 30 June 1962, the last day of the company's financial year), after some months of illness. By the time of his death he had seen Plessey grow from a struggling company employing a handful of people to a multi-million pound organization with some 50,000 employees.

There is a portrait in bas-relief by David McFall at the Allen Clark Research Centre, Towcester, Northamptonshire. Another portrait, by R. Norman Hepple, is in the company's boardroom, Millbank Tower, London SW1.

[Private information; personal knowledge.]

H. T. PARKER

CLARK, JAMES (JIM) (1936-1968), racing motorist, was born in Kilmany, Fife, 4 March 1936, the only son and fifth child of James Clark, farmer, and his wife, Helen Rorie Niven. Educated at Loretto School, Edinburgh, he left at sixteen and went to work on the family sheep farm on the Borders. Like many farmers' sons he was at home with machinery and handling cars off the road long before he was old enough to take a driving test.

Another Border farmer, his older brother-in-law, Alec Calder, brought motor racing into the Clark family through driving a Brooklands Riley on Scottish circuits in the early 1950s. The young Jim Clark would go and watch and it was not long before he was taking part in local motor-club events with a Sunbeam Talbot Mark III which he would drive with great style.

Écurie Écosse, Le Mans winners in 1956 and

1957, were the heroes of Scottish motor racing and it was Ian Scott Watson's revival of the Border Reivers racing team in opposition to them that was to set his friend, Jim Clark, on the road to two World Drivers' championships.

Clark's intended role had been that of mechanic to Scott Watson but his natural driving genius was soon so apparent that a second-hand D-Type Jaguar was bought to do it justice. In winning with the car at Full Sutton on 5 April 1958, Clark became, at twenty-two, the first post-war sports-car driver to lap a British circuit at over 100 mph. With his innate natural driving ability he had started as he was to continue during a decade that saw him become the greatest driver of his own time.

Success with the Border Reivers led to wider recognition and Clark's connection with Colin Chapman's Lotus team which was to last throughout his career in top-class motor racing. In 1960 he had his first race in a Lotus Grand Prix car at Zandvoort and contested fourth place with Graham Hill's BRM before retiring with a seized gearbox on the forty-third lap.

Resisting offers from other Grand Prix teams, including Ferrari, Clark stayed with Lotus for 1961, the first year of the new 1½-litre engine formula. During the Italian Grand Prix at Monza, Clark's Lotus and Wolfgang von Trip's Ferrari touched at the Vedano curve. The German driver was killed with fourteen spectators when his car crashed into the crowd. Clark was numbed with horror but physically unhurt.

A winter trip to South Africa where he won three races out of four restored Clark's morale and he was able to look forward to the 1962 season with confidence. Lotus now had the Coventry Climax V-8 engine and, with BRM, were in a better position to do battle with the Ferraris.

In only his third season in Grand Prix racing Clark was established as a contender for the world championship which he was destined to lose to Graham Hill's BRM during the last race of the season in South Africa. Clark was leading as usual when a bolt failed on the sixty-third lap causing the engine oil to leak away.

It was a different story in 1963 and the combination of Clark and the Climax-engined Lotus 25 achieved seven Grand Prix victories in a season—a record which was still unbeaten in 1979. Clark also nearly won the American Indianapolis 500 classic.

In 1964 the pattern of 'Clark wins' or 'Clark retires' was well established, but in that year he had more than his fair share of mechanical problems. Despite this it was again the last race of the season that was to decide between Clark, Graham Hill, and John Surtees (Ferrari).

This time a fractured oil pipe ended Clark's chances and Surtees became world champion.

The year 1965 was Clark's greatest with a second world championship and victory at a new record speed at Indianapolis. At the Nürburgring, the most difficult circuit of all, he set race and lap records and there was another feat not since equalled—five consecutive Grand Prix wins.

Twice world champion and just missing the title twice more, Clark had dominated the 1½-litre formula which was superseded by 3 litres in 1966. Only Jack Brabham was properly prepared with his Repco engine and he took the title. In an unhappy season with unsuitable engines Clark won only one Grand Prix race.

The year 1967 saw the arrival of the most successful Grand Prix engine ever, the Cosworth-Ford DFV which went first to Lotus. Clark won his fifth British Grand Prix at Silverstone and four others but the world championship went to Denis Hulme (Brabham).

Clark won the first Grand Prix of 1968 in South Africa to bring his total to twenty-five, a figure only passed in 1973 by his friend and fellow Scot, Jackie Stewart. He seemed set for another championship year until his death on 7 April 1968 in a minor Formula 2 race at Hockenheim. The Lotus swerved off the track at high speed into trees killing Clark instantly. The most likely explanation is thought to be a puncture.

Clark's death stunned the motor-racing world. In the most competitive of sports he was admitted to be master by those who raced against him. Juan Manuel Fangio, five times world champion, described Clark as 'the greatest driver in the world'. His incredible car control, race craft, and ability to nurse an ailing car to victory was matched by his sportsmanship.

Of medium height with dark hair and a flashing smile which could light up his whole face, Clark was a true representative of his Border farming stock. Modest, unassuming, and shy of the fame his racing exploits attracted he was never happier than relaxing at home. Reserved with strangers, only his friends knew the impish, practical joker side to his nature.

Had he survived the 1968 season, Clark might have retired from motor racing and combined farming with his new love of flying light aircraft. Believing that racing drivers should not marry he was a bachelor.

Appointed OBE in 1964, he became first honorary burgess of Duns the following year. The Jim Clark Memorial Room at Duns contains many of his trophies and a painting in oils by Gordon Ellis.

[Jim Clark, *Jim Clark at the Wheel*, 1964; Graham Gauld and others, *Jim Clark,*

Portrait of a Great Driver, 1968; Graham
Gauld, Jim Clark Remembered, 1975; private
information; personal knowledge.]

COLIN DRYDEN

CLARKE, SIR CHARLES NOBLE ARDEN-
(1898-1962), colonial governor. [See ARDEN-
CLARKE.]

CLIFFORD, SIR BEDE EDMUND HUGH
(1890-1969), colonial governor, was born 3
July 1890 on his father's sheep farm in the
South Island of New Zealand. He was the third
and youngest son of William Hugh Clifford,
later tenth Baron Clifford of Chudleigh, and
his wife, Catherine Mary, daughter of
R. Bassett, a New Zealander. Losing his mother
when he was very young, he moved with his
father from one unsuccessful farm to another.
At an early age he displayed outstanding intelligence with an unorthodox bent. Although he
entered a Melbourne boarding school at the
age of ten without having the ABC, he became
the star pupil. After a brief spell at Melbourne
University he joined a firm of surveyors in
Western Australia, but eventually signed on as
fourth officer on a tramp steamer, of which his
brother was the navigating officer, in order
to reach England. He took the opportunity to
master the use of the sextant for solar and stellar
observations.

On the outbreak of war in 1914 Clifford
enlisted in the Royal Fusiliers and soon gained
his commission. He was gassed and invalided
and in 1917 was appointed aide-de-camp to
Sir Ronald Munro-Ferguson (later Viscount
Novar, q.v.), governor-general of Australia.
He was quickly promoted to the more congenial
position of private secretary (1918-20) and was
therefore privileged to meet with many famous
figures. He accompanied Admiral Jellicoe [q.v.]
on an inspection of the outlying defences of
Australia, and for his services during the visit
of the Prince of Wales was appointed MVO.
In 1921 Clifford was selected by Lord Milner
[q.v.] as secretary to Prince Arthur of
Connaught [q.v.], governor-general of South
Africa. J. C. Smuts [q.v.], the prime minister,
quickly appreciated Clifford's ability and consulted him on imperial problems.

In 1924 Clifford was appointed secretary to
Prince Arthur's successor, the Earl of Athlone
(whose notice he subsequently contributed to
this Dictionary). But in the same year he
became imperial secretary to the South
African High Commission. The protectorates
of Bechuanaland, Swaziland, and Basutoland
being under his jurisdiction, he immediately
carried out a detailed tour. In 1928 he became
the first white man to cross the Kalahari
Desert, a fine feat of navigation. In 1929 and

1931 he surveyed the boundaries and determined the size of the Great Makarikari Salt
Lake for a possible railway route from Southern
Rhodesia to Walvis Bay. In the meantime
J. B. M. Hertzog [q.v.] had applied for Clifford
to be appointed (1928) first representative of the
United Kingdom to the Union of South Africa.
He was able to persuade Hertzog to defer
constitutional changes until after he had
attended the prime ministers' conference; and
by subtle argument he persuaded the Govern-
ment to join in financing the Imperial Airways
link with South Africa in spite of strong
German competition. For his services in South
Africa Clifford was appointed CMG (1923) and
CB (1931).

At the end of 1931 he was appointed governor
of the Bahamas, the youngest governor in the
Colonial Service. Due to his imagination and
initiative in encouraging the development of the
tourist industry the prosperity of the islands
was greatly increased. He was promoted
KCMG in 1933. In 1937 a visit to Germany
convinced Clifford that war was inevitable. In
the same year he was appointed governor of
Mauritius, and during a visit to Diego Suarez
en route, he was able to make a careful study
of the harbour defences which was a great
help in its eventual capture.

On arrival in Mauritius he stimulated
research for the improvement of the sugar and
pineapple industries. In case of war, he laid
in large stocks of coal, so that the railways
could be maintained. He developed the hydro-
electric and irrigation resources: a lasting contribution. He provided machinery for the
regulation of wages and working conditions. His
handling of industrial disputes was unorthodox
but effective. When the docks were picketed to
prevent the loading of sugar for export Clifford
had a labour force recruited from the planta-
tions. The men were transported in closed
railway wagons into the port area with sufficient
equipment and supplies to be self-supporting,
and the strike was broken.

In 1942 Clifford was appointed governor of
Trinidad, a very sensitive area in the U-boat
campaign. His principal task was to resolve
friction which had arisen between the British
and American admirals, and this he was able to
do with tact and firmness. In appreciation he
was awarded the Legion of Merit by the
United States Government. He was able also to
negotiate a most satisfactory agreement with
Venezuela over the demarcation of the sea
bed of the gulf between the two countries for
oil exploration and exploitation. Clifford was
most solicitous for the large numbers of
survivors from vessels sunk by U-boats and at
times up to four and five hundred were in the
clearing stations.

Clifford was appointed GCMG in 1945 and in the next year his medical advisers told him that he should cease to work in the tropics. In his retirement he loved travelling. He enjoyed being his own builder and electrician and designed and partly built the small house in which he and his wife lived. He was an insatiable reader, his favourite author Herodotus. In 1964 his autobiography *Proconsul* was published. He advised and edited *For My Grandchildren* by Princess Alice, Countess of Athlone (1966). He was writing a radio play, 'Cyrus the Great', and a history of the Clifford family at the time of his death. An excellent portrait in oils was painted by his daughter, the Viscountess Norwich.

In 1925 Clifford married Alice Devin (died 1980), daughter of John Murton Gundry, an eminent banker, of Cleveland, Ohio. His very beautiful and highly talented wife played a most important role in helping him in their arduous public life. They had three daughters famous for their beauty and wit. Clifford died at Queen Anne Farm, Jacob's Well, Guildford, 6 October 1969 and was buried in the family vault at Ugbrooke Park, Chudleigh.

[Sir Bede Clifford, *Proconsul*, 1964; private information; personal knowledge.]

HENRY ABEL SMITH

CLUNES, ALEXANDER DE MORO SHERRIFF (ALEC) (1912-1970), actor, stage director, and theatre manager, was born in Brixton 17 May 1912, the son of Alexander Sherriff Clunes, actor, and his wife, Georgina Ada Sumner. He was educated at Cliftonville, Margate. Although he came of stage stock on both sides, he did not originally intend to adopt his parents' profession, but earned his living in advertising and journalism while keeping his inherited acting talent to enliven his leisure time. He was, however, an exceptionally well-graced natural player and after considerable and valuable experience with leading amateur groups he found the urge to turn professional too strong for him. By 1934 he was touring with Sir P. Ben Greet [q.v.] and later in the same year joined the Old Vic Company. His progress thereafter was steady, and the parts he was called upon to play, both in the classics and contemporary drama, grew in importance until in 1939 he was one of the leaders of the company at the Shakespeare Memorial Theatre at Stratford-upon-Avon playing Petruchio, Richmond, Iago, Benedick, and Coriolanus. He was now firmly established and what was more his work during the Malvern festival of 1938 had caught the eye and ear of G. B. Shaw [q.v.] who in 1940 gave him the part of Godfrey Kneller in *In Good King*

Charles's Golden Days at the New Theatre in London. In 1941 Clunes toured with the Old Vic Company, during its wartime exile, playing Young Marlow, Malvolio, and Taffy in *Trilby*; but he left them in order to embark, in the following year, upon a project of his own which was to prove his most important contribution to the theatre and carry him to the peak of his career.

This was the foundation, in May 1942, of the Arts Theatre Group of Actors, a body which he served as leading spirit, manager, director, and actor for the next ten or eleven years. Some movement of the kind was badly needed at the time; for though in a general way the theatre was prosperous during and after the last years of the war, the taste of the emergent new playgoing public was for revivals of established favourite plays rather than for new work. One of Clunes's best claims to respect during his time at the Arts Theatre Club was his readiness to help high-aspiring new dramatists. He subsidized Christopher Fry during the writing of *The Lady's Not for Burning*, and then staged the play (1948) with himself in the lead. And he accepted John Whiting's obscure *Saint's Day* (1951) at a time when it was unlikely that any of the regular theatre-managers would have taken the risk. In all, he was responsible for the production of more than a hundred plays at this little theatre, and the artistic standard at which he aimed was always impressively high.

Clunes's work at the Arts Theatre was very much to his credit and might well have carried him to the topmost rank in his profession; but this did not quite happen. The reason was not easy to see, for in every technical respect he was an exceptionally well-graced actor. He had a good stage presence, a fine voice which he knew very well how to use, an impressive sense of character, and a lively intelligence. All these qualities were well in evidence when in 1945 he played Hamlet; while the performance was going on it was possible for a critic to rate it among the best Hamlets of the day. Yet somehow when the final curtain was down there was a feeling that his Hamlet had been addressed to the intellect rather than the emotion of its audience; and in the event it proved not to have much hold upon the memory.

So, the later years of Clunes's stage career seemed to be tinged with disappointment: his varied natural talent and intensive experience had not availed to put him among those leaders of his profession whom the public acclaimed. He lacked, perhaps, that personal magnetism popularly known as 'star quality'. For instance, when he succeeded Rex Harrison as Professor Higgins in *My Fair Lady*, his performance was strikingly excellent; yet it was Harrison's image which lived more vividly in the memory. Luckily for him, Clunes had other interests. He collected prints and drawings and owned and ran a bookshop. In 1964 he published a handsomely produced volume on *The British Theatre*.

In 1956 Clunes married Daphne Acott by whom he had one son and one daughter. An earlier marriage, in 1949, to Stella Richman, had been dissolved in 1954. Clunes died in London 13 March 1970.

[J. C. Trewin, *Alec Clunes*, 1958; *The Times* and *Daily Telegraph*, 14 March 1970; personal knowledge.]   W. A. DARLINGTON

COADE, THOROLD FRANCIS (1896-1963), headmaster of Bryanston School, was born in Dublin 3 July 1896, the only son of the Revd Charles Edward Coade and his wife, Jessie Wilhelmine Spencer. He was educated at Glebe House School, Hunstanton, and at Harrow (1910-15), where he became head of the Headmaster's House. He then went to the Royal Military College, Sandhurst, and in 1916 to France with the Loyal North Lancashire Regiment. There he was wounded on the Somme, losing an ear-drum when a bomb exploded in the trench, and on leaving hospital he was transferred to East Anglia.

On demobilization Coade went up to Christ Church, Oxford, on the shortened degree course in English. In 1921 he passed with distinction. Meanwhile, following in her father's line, his only sister Eileen went up to Oxford to read theology, in which she gained a first class in 1924. While at Oxford Coade rekindled his youthful interest in drama, especially production, and also played golf for the university. In 1922, having been introduced to her by his sister, he married Kathleen Eleanor, daughter of Harold Hugh Hardy, a business man. They had two daughters. In 1922 he returned as an assistant master to Harrow, for which he always retained a romantic attachment. But his experience there gave insufficient scope for his widening vision.

In those ten years at Harrow, however, his imagination was released through his wife's affection and rapport. They both loved poetry and the arts, and she was always to share deeply in his thoughts. In 1931 he began residential conferences for schoolmasters at Harrow.

By 1932 he was restive for change and looking for opportunity, and in that year he was appointed to Bryanston. The school had been founded only four years before and its founding headmaster had resigned. It was a time of crisis when institutions of all kinds were at grave financial risk. Perhaps only the school's

governors detected beneath Coade's shy unpretentious exterior his unswerving determination and purpose, supported by his Christian faith. With him at its centre, often almost hidden, the school passed from its troubled though exciting, seemingly eccentric, beginnings to its acceptance at large as an interesting experiment until, after about twenty years, it became recognized nationally as a remarkable creation.

Bryanston offered him an almost clear field. An appreciable number of ideas he inherited from his predecessor, some he borrowed from others, but their management and interaction were his creative own. Private study was encouraged as a method of work, after a modified Dalton plan, the competitive spirit was reduced, there was no corporal punishment, nor private fagging, prefects being given responsibility not privilege. Relationships between masters and boys were less inhibited, more relaxed, than elsewhere. There was much opportunity for self-expression in the visual arts, in music, and for other creative uses of leisure. Estate work replaced the conventional training corps (except during World War II), and boys were deliberately given more free time than at other schools. When Coade was taunted as headmaster of a school where 'the boys do what they like', he replied that 'they like what they do'. A merry debunker, and his witty asides often devastating, he could nevertheless be stern, even adamant. Compassion and tenderness were, however, his signal qualities.

Coade produced many school plays. One of his finest achievements was in the summer of 1954 when he produced the Chester mystery plays in the Greek theatre at Bryanston with over a hundred boys and girls from the sister school of Cranborne Chase taking part.

Coade shunned the limelight and was rarely prominent, for instance in the Headmasters' Conference. However, he was much in demand at conferences because of his wise and witty interventions. He could seldom meet strangers (or parents) half-way. His personality was complex, yet his presence gave reassurance, inspiring trust and confidence. He drew staff and others to him, leading them into strong partnership. For him wholeness, the balance and harmony of a boy's entire person, was the purpose of education, as is recognized so widely today. Over-specialization and narrowness of any kind was an intrusion into adolescence. Through creative encounters and relationships, a boy's imagination and talent can be captured for life itself. For Coade, therefore, the use of leisure, and through it self-discovery and realization, rang truer than the pursuit of outer objectives.

A man of ideas but still more of ideals, it was as if they came elusively to use him as their interpreter. His sight was more intuitive than observing, and his love of others grounded in the faith which shaped his personality. The unifying thread was for him the awakening of mind, body, and spirit in each unique adolescent boy and their harnessing to the purposes of God, the Spirit moving where it will. 'You cannot teach boys to be religious,' he said, 'for they are religious already.' *God with Us* by S. L. Frank, translated by N. Duddington (1946), was of central importance to him.

After twenty-six years the governors of Bryanston invited Coade to remain for a further five, but ill health compelled him to retire a year later, in 1959. Although one of the less well known, he was amongst the greatest headmasters of his time. He died at his cottage at East Knoyle, not far from the school, 1 February 1963.

Coade's published work included 'Education for Leisure' in E. D. Laborde (ed.), *Education of Today* (1935), and 'The New Term' (*Spectator*, 1937). He edited *Harrow Lectures in Education* (1931), and *Manhood in the Making* (1939), to which he contributed an essay entitled 'Maturity'. A posthumous selection of his papers forms *The Burning Bow* (1966). Portraits of Thorold Coade by Claud Rogers (1958) and Robert Tollast (1978) are at Bryanston, as is also a bronze head by Titus Lesser (1958).

[M. C. Morgan, *Bryanston 1928-78*, published by Bryanston School, 1978; personal knowledge.]   A. R. DONALD WRIGHT

COATALEN, LOUIS HERVÉ (1879-1962), automobile engineer and aero-engine designer, was born 11 September 1879 at Concarneau, Finisterre, the second son of a hotelier François Marie Coatalen, and his wife, Louise Le Bris. After three years at the École des Arts et Métiers at Cluny he started as a draughtsman with De Dion-Bouton et Cie and then with Clement et Cie and Panhard et Levassor. Seeing greater opportunities in the motor industry in England, in 1900 he joined the Crowden Motor Car Company at Leamington Spa and then at the age of twenty-one he became chief engineer with Humber Limited at Coventry. For them he designed two models which restored the company's fortunes. He drove a Coventry Humber in the 1906 Tourist Trophy race, finishing sixth.

In partnership with William Hillman of Coventry from 1907, he designed the 24-hp Hillman-Coatalen car with which he put up the fastest lap in the 1907 Tourist Trophy race before crashing at Quarter Bridge.

Thomas Cureton, managing director of the Sunbeam Motor Car Company, Wolverhampton, engaged Coatalen as chief engineer in February 1909 and his first product, the 16/20-hp Sunbeam, distinguished itself in the Scottish Six Days Trial in the same year. Encouraged by this, a smaller 12/16-hp model was produced which proved an even greater success.

It was this model and its subsequent development which established Coatalen's reputation as an automobile engineer and put the Sunbeam Motor Car Company in the forefront of motor manufacturers. During the next twenty-one years Coatalen produced a succession of touring cars, luxury cars, racing cars, record-breaking cars, and aero-engines which won international fame for Sunbeam and its associated marques Talbot and Darracq.

In 1910 Coatalen married Olive Mary, daughter of Henry James Bath, director of the Sunbeam Company; they had two sons. Coatalen acquired British nationality during World War I. He was divorced in 1922 and in 1923 he married Mrs Enid Florence van Raalte (née Graham); they had one daughter. This second marriage lasted until 1935 when he married Emily Bridson who remained with him until his death.

Coatalen wrote in 1924: 'Racing car practice accelerates development. Racing stimulates designers and engineers and raises the morale of the factory workpeople.' He drove Sunbeams in races at Brooklands and entered them in the Coupe de 'L'Auto' *voiturette* races in France. They competed in international Grand Prix races and set up many world records. They held the Brooklands lap record five times and the land-speed record in 1922, 1924, 1925, 1926, and 1927.

Sunbeam cars won the Coupe de 'L'Auto' in 1912, the Tourist Trophy in 1914 and 1922, the French Grand Prix in 1923, and the Spanish Grand Prix in 1924. The 1½-litre Talbot-Darracqs were invincible in *voiturette* races from 1921 until 1925.

Coatalen was not only a competent engineer but also a skilled impresario, quick to spot and use the abilities of others. He engaged the design talents of Ernest Henry, Vincent Bertarione, Captain J. S. Irving, and others. The racing cars were handled by the leading drivers of their time: Sir Henry Segrave, K. Lee Guinness, Sir Algernon Guinness, Dario Resta, Jean Chassagne, Albert Divo, Réné Thomas, Sir Malcolm Campbell [q.v.], André Boillot, J. Moriceau, George Duller, Count Masetti, and Kaye Don.

The Sunbeam Company was amongst the first to standardize overhead valve engines and four-wheel brakes and in 1925 produced a twin overhead camshaft 3-litre sporting model.

The company also played an important role

in the development of aero-engines. The
'Crusader' 150-hp V.8 was already in production before the outbreak of war in 1914. Lessons
learned in racing were applied to meet the ever-
increasing demands from the Services for more
power. Over twenty types of Sunbeam aero-
engines were designed and produced and power
output rose from 150 to 900 hp. Sunbeam-
Coatalen engines were fitted to the British
airship R.34 which made the first out and home
flight across the Atlantic in 1919. The French
Government nominated Coatalen commander
of the Legion of Honour.

The development of a Sunbeam-Coatalen
diesel aero-engine was undertaken in 1930 but
economic conditions and Coatalen's ill health
held it back. He was then living and working
in Paris and Capri. With his stimulating
influence removed, the fortunes of the Sunbeam Talbot Darracq Group declined and in
1935 they were taken over by the Rootes Group
under W. E. R. (later Lord) Rootes [q.v.].

Meanwhile Coatalen became chairman and
managing director of Freins Hydrauliques
Lockheed in Paris and chairman of S. A.
Bougies KLG. He continued his work on diesel
aero-engines using an Hispano-Suiza engine
which he converted using very high pressure
injection. In 1953 the Société des Ingenieurs
de l'Automobile elected him their president.
He was still actively engaged in his work until
his death in Paris 23 May 1962. In 1974 the
French mint struck a commemorative medal,
bearing a bas-relief portrait by Lhoste.

[The Times, 25 May and 1 June 1962; Auto-
motor Journal, 2 December 1911; Autocar,
March 1924 et seq.; Ian Nickols and Kent
Karslake, Motoring Entente, 1956; A Sou-
venir of Sunbeam Service 1899-1919, 1919, and
The History and Development of the Sunbeam
Car 1899-1924, 1924, both published by
Sunbeam Motor Car Co. Ltd; Motor Sport,
September 1979; Autocar, 5 September
1979.]   ANTHONY S. HEAL

COCKCROFT, SIR JOHN DOUGLAS
(1897-1967), physicist, was born 27 May 1897 at
Todmorden, the first of five sons in his parents
family. The Cockcrofts had been involved in
the weaving industry for generations and
Cockcroft's father, John Arthur, and mother,
Annie Maud Fielden, moved from a mill at
Todmorden to Birks Mill, Walsden, in 1899
where a water-wheel and steam-engine were
used as a source of power for spinning and
weaving machinery. The training given by the
father in the mill, and the machinery there,
gave Cockcroft an interest in technology which
affected his whole life.

Cockcroft was educated at Todmorden

Secondary School and went with a scholarship
to the Victoria University of Manchester in
1914. He volunteered for war service in 1915
and spent three years as a signaller in the
Royal Field Artillery, and was twice mentioned
in dispatches. After the war, Cockcroft returned
to Manchester University, at the College of
Technology, and then became a college apprentice at Metropolitan Vickers for a short time. He
obtained his M.Sc. Tech. degree in 1922.
In the same year he entered as a sizar St.
John's College, Cambridge, where he graduated
as a B* wrangler in part ii of the mathematical tripos in 1924. Then began a fifteen-
year period when he worked as a creative
scientist. He was one of the outstanding group
of people attracted by Sir Ernest (later Lord)
Rutherford [q.v.], as a research student in the
Cavendish Laboratory, to explore the physics
of atomic nuclei. Cockcroft's theoretical and
practical skills in electrical engineering found
many outlets. He helped with the engineering
aspects of some of Peter L. Kapitza's major
devices, such as magnetic coils and helium
liquifiers; and then, with E. T. S. Walton,
he developed the high-voltage particle accelerator machine which bears their name. In 1931
a high-energy proton beam (500-600 keV)
was directed on a lithium target and bright
scintillations were observed. Cockcroft's understanding of G. Gamow's idea that bombarding
energies of millions of electron volts was not
necessary to penetrate the nuclei of light
elements, because of the quantum mechanical
effect of 'tunnelling', was confirmed and the
experiment at once created world-wide interest.
Experiments with deuterons followed, and in
1933 Cockcroft began to persuade a somewhat
unwilling Rutherford that the Cavendish
Laboratory should have a cyclotron. By the
time work started in 1937, based on E. O.
Lawrence's 36-inch machine, Cockcroft had
taken over in 1935 the supervision of the
Mond Laboratory from Kapitza and was
becoming increasingly involved with efforts
being made in technical fields to prepare for
war with Hitler's Germany.

Sir H. T. Tizard [q.v.] spoke confidentially
to Cockcroft early in 1938 about RDF—the
highly secret radio technique for finding aircraft: 'These devices would be troublesome,
and would require a team of nurses.' Cockcroft
played a major role in persuading about eighty
physicists to spend a month at various coastal
radar defence stations, and he also persuaded
a number of leading physicists to participate.
Some of these scientists made some of the
major advances in radar and Cockcroft's part
was one of his greatest contributions to the
war effort. In August 1940 Cockcroft joined
Tizard as his deputy on a mission to the

United States to establish an exchange of defence-science information. The disclosure to the Americans of the British microwave magnetron was to be of immense importance.

Cockcroft became chief superintendent of the Air Defence Research and Development Establishment at Christchurch in late 1940. Radar was then being applied to direct anti-aircraft gunnery upon unseen targets. Coastal defence radar, and radar for combat use by the army to detect moving vehicles and tanks in the darkness, were other major projects. Attempts to produce a proximity fuse for use against aircraft was nearly successful. The failure was a frustrating experience for Cockcroft.

Part of the history of the war of 1939-45 relates to a few men in the world-wide scientific community, men at the forefront of nuclear physics who perceived, when the war was beginning, the possibility of a nuclear explosive device of orders of magnitude greater than any military weapons using conventional high explosives. Cockcroft knew about these ideas and thought that Britain should make an effort to produce a nuclear explosive; but for most of the war period he was so completely engaged in radar that his contributions were mainly advisory, until late in 1943, when his involvement sharply increased. Cockcroft's assignment was to go to Canada in 1944 and to take charge of the Montreal laboratory, and then to build the NRX heavy-water reactor at Chalk River, together with associated facilities. His calm but energetic direction gave the laboratory, with its mixed British, Canadian, and French staff, a firm sense of purpose. The nuclear explosions at Hiroshima and Nagasaki brought the war to an abrupt end but the nuclear work continued. The Canadians wanted Cockcroft to stay but he was wanted at home to direct the new establishment which was being built at Harwell for atomic energy research. Cockcroft commuted for a while and did both jobs but, as a result of high-level discussions, he moved full-time to Harwell in 1946. By this time the NRX reactor was almost complete, the laboratories were fully occupied, and the new township at Deep River was becoming a settled community.

Cockcroft's name and the excitement of atomic energy attracted many able people of all ages to work at Harwell, especially the young. Rapid progress was made, in spite of the shortages resulting from the war. The engineering side of atomic energy, under Christopher Hinton (later Lord Hinton of Bankside), and a little later the weapons side, under W. G. (later Lord) Penney, were also being developed at the greatest possible speed. Among many other activities, a great deal of technology and

design work on pressurized gas-cooled reactors made it possible in 1953 to base the production of additional plutonium on dual-purpose reactors to be built at Calder Hall. The justification was primarily military, but for the first time the vision of cheap nuclear power, so prominent in Cockcroft's mind, began to have a practical endorsement. The Government decided in 1954 to take the responsibility for atomic energy from the Ministry of Supply and create the Atomic Energy Authority (AEA). Cockcroft became the first member for research, while also remaining director of Harwell.

Cockcroft always attached great importance to travel and to making personal contacts with scientists in other countries. When President Eisenhower addressed the General Assembly of the United Nations in December 1953 he spoke about the 'atomic dilemma'. He suggested forming the International Atomic Energy Agency. The General Assembly unanimously resolved in December 1954 to hold a technical conference under the auspices of the United Nations on the peaceful uses of atomic energy. An advisory committee from seven countries was formed to help the secretary-general, Dag Hammarskjöld, and Cockcroft was chosen as the British representative. This extra-ordinary conference, held at Geneva in August 1955, was a political event of outstanding importance which might have heralded the end of the cold war. Scientifically, it was an enormous success. Cockcroft was able to invite I. Kurchatov, of the Soviet Union, to give a lecture at Harwell on a subject (fusion research) which only a few months earlier was regarded as extremely secret. The second Geneva conference was held in 1958, and Cockcroft gave what was widely considered to be a masterly summary of the proceedings.

Meanwhile, at Harwell and elsewhere, ideas about possible new reactor systems were proliferating. Cockcroft persuaded the AEA to set up a site at Winfrith to test experimental or small prototype reactors. He obtained European support for a joint project on a high-temperature reactor (HTR) and the Organization for Economic Co-operation and Development Dragon project was agreed and put at Winfrith. Technically, the helium gas cooling and the coated particle fuel behaved well and internationally the project gained a good reputation. Ultimately, however, the project came to an end because of the great cost of engineering full-scale commercial nuclear power stations.

One of the special research projects in atomic energy was called CTR (controlled thermonuclear reactions) or, more briefly, fusion research. Cockcroft gathered much of the British work to Harwell and the major project was the torroidal discharge machine called ZETA. The work, and particularly the work with this machine, had its ups and downs but, in retrospect, ZETA was a major step forward in fusion research. Cockcroft was able to give a great deal of help and encouragement to the Medical Research Council in their work on radiological protection. Radio-isotopes for biological and industrial uses became an important and profitable part of the work of the Research Group. His influence led to the creation of the Rutherford High Energy Laboratory. He was also closely concerned with the early years of CERN.

Cockcroft resigned as a full-time member of the AEA in 1959 but remained a part-time member, and moved to Cambridge to become the first master of Churchill College, having been nominated by Sir Winston Churchill himself. No better person could have been chosen. The Cockcrofts' hospitality, their international friendships among scientists, and Cockcroft's interests in all sides of industry exactly matched the purposes for which the college was formed.

There were many other activities in Cockcroft's busy life, such as science policy and education, defence policy, university matters, and international science. He received many honorary degrees, awards, and honours, the three principal being the Order of Merit (1957), the Nobel prize for physics, jointly with E. T. S. Walton (1951), and the Atoms for Peace award (1961). He was appointed CBE in 1944, knight bachelor in 1948, and KCB in 1953. Further details will be found in the Royal Society memoir listed in the bibliography below.

In 1925 Cockcroft married (Eunice) Elizabeth, daughter of Herbert Crabtree, JP, of Stansfield Hall. The Crabtrees were cotton manufacturers and John and Elizabeth had known each other from childhood. Their first child, a boy, died at two years. Subsequently they had four daughters and then a son. Cockcroft was deeply interested in architecture and music. He was a man of few words and his writing was minute. He never lost his temper. He and his family enjoyed relaxing at their holiday home at Cley, walking and sailing in the crisp Norfolk air. Cockcroft died 18 September 1967, at Churchill College. On 17 October 1967, at noon, a service of memorial and thanksgiving was held in Westminster Abbey.

There are portraits in oils of Cockcroft by W. A. Dargie (1956) in the Cockcroft Hall at the Atomic Energy Research Establishment, Harwell; by R. M. Tollast (1962) in the Cockcroft Room at Churchill College; by H. A. Freeth (1957), in chalk, in the National Portrait Gallery; and by R. Moynihan at the Imperial War Museum.

[M. L. E. Oliphant and Lord Penney in *Biographical Memoirs of Fellows of the Royal Society*, vol. xiv, 1968; Margaret Gowing, *Britain and Atomic Energy 1939-45*, 1964; M. Gowing and L. Arnold, *Independence and Deterrence, Britain and Atomic Energy 1945-52*, 2 vols., 1974; personal knowledge.]
PENNEY

COCKERELL, SIR SYDNEY CARLYLE (1867-1962), museum director and bibliophile, was born at Brighton 16 July 1867, the second in the family of four sons and two daughters of Sydney John Cockerell, coal merchant of London, and his wife, Alice Elizabeth, elder daughter of Sir John Bennett, sheriff of London and Middlesex [q.v.].

In May 1882 'Carlie' (as his family called him) won a scholarship to St. Paul's, which he entered as a day-boy and where he remained until Christmas 1884, when he joined the family firm of George J. Cockerell & Co. as a clerk. An admiration of the works of John Ruskin [q.v.] and an interest in conchology led to his wooing his hero with a gift of shells and in 1887 visiting him at Brantwood; in the previous year he had already made contact with the man who was to become the second greatest influence in his life, William Morris [q.v.]. On a holiday in France in 1888 he chanced to run into Ruskin in Abbeville and accompanied him to Beauvais.

Cockerell's father had died in 1877, leaving the family business in the hands of his two brothers, and his widow and six young children none too well provided for. Young Cockerell dutifully remained in his uncongenial job, after 1889 as a partner, until the last day of 1891, after which he accepted an offer from Morris to catalogue his books and manuscripts. This led to his becoming secretary to the Kelmscott Press. After Morris's death in 1896 and the winding up of the Press he divided his time between acting as secretary and factotum to Wilfrid Scawen Blunt and as adviser to the bibliophile and collector of manuscripts, Henry Yates Thompson [qq.v.]. In 1900 he joined as a partner the process-engraver (Sir) Emery Walker [q.v.], with whom he remained for four years. In 1903 came a memorable visit to Tolstoy at Yasnaya Polyana.

Cockerell continued to be variously employed in the fields of manuscripts and bibliography until 1907, when his marriage to (Florence) Kate, daughter of Charles Tomson Kingsford, of Canterbury, and a talented artist, bookbinder, and illuminator, made it essential for him to find a steady job. On the retirement in the following year of Montague Rhodes James [q.v.] as director of the Fitzwilliam Museum at Cambridge, Cockerell, although not a university man, successfully applied for the post. During the twenty-nine years he remained at Cambridge he transformed a dreary and ill-hung provincial gallery into one which set a new standard of excellence which was to influence museums all over the world. This he achieved by the skilful and uncrowded display of its pictures against suitable backgrounds, and by the introduction of fine pieces of furniture, Persian rugs, and flowers provided and arranged by lady admirers fired by his enthusiasm. By methods that have been described as 'brutally direct', this 'scrounger of genius' extracted the equivalent of a quarter of a million pounds from generous donors whose resistance soon crumbled before his importunity. The money was allotted to many shrewd purchases and to the building of the Marlay Galleries (1922) and Courtauld Galleries (1931). In 1936 Cockerell was appointed European adviser to the Felton trustees of the National Gallery of Victoria, Melbourne, and in this capacity visited Australia with his younger daughter, Katharine.

Soon after her marriage, Cockerell's wife developed disseminated sclerosis and eventually became bedridden until her death in 1949: he grieved, but did not allow this personal tragedy to interfere with his work. They had two daughters and a son, (Sir) Christopher, who as a boy had shown more interest in mechanics than in the arts, and whom Cockerell had once dismissed as 'no better than a garage hand'. He invented the hovercraft, and it is ironic that several obituary notices of the father referred to him principally as the 'grandfather of the hovercraft'. Cockerell's elder brother, Theodore Dru Alison (1866-1948), and a younger brother, Douglas Bennett [q.v.], also achieved distinction, the former as a biologist and the latter as a bookbinder.

On his retirement from the Fitzwilliam in 1937, Cockerell settled at Kew, Surrey. 'People will come to see the Gardens, and look in on me afterwards if they have time,' he said with uncharacteristic modesty; in the event, an ever widening circle of friends, both old and young, preferred to make his house their first port of call. In his seventies he remained immensely active, but after a fall in 1951 he took to his bed, never to leave it. Here, devotedly tended by women friends and, in due course, professional nurses, the 'sage of Kew' continued to hold court almost until his death, at his Kew home, 1 May 1962, in his ninety-fifth year.

Few men have made more friends, or cultivated the art of friendship more assiduously, than did Cockerell in the course of his long life. But there were enemies also, quarrels always resulting (he believed) from the wrongheadedness and obstinacy of others. Some of the letters he received from the famous, among them Ruskin, Octavia Hill (for whom he had at one time worked), Bernard Shaw, T. E. Lawrence, Thomas Hardy (whose joint literary executor he was) [qq.v.], were edited by Viola Meynell and published under the titles *Friends of a Lifetime* (1940) and *The Best of Friends* (1956); those from the most devoted but less distinguished friends were not included. Cockerell published little else beyond several scholarly monographs for the Roxburghe Club, but a remarkable uninterrupted series of diaries from 1886 to 1962, written in a minute and exquisite hand, are now in the British Library. He did much to encourage better handwriting and the revival of the italic script.

Cockerell was short and stockily built, pugnacious and somewhat alarming on first acquaintance but soon revealing, to those who won his approval, innate kindness and a warm heart. His enthusiasms were infectious, and his zest for life remained undiminished to the end; as a firm agnostic he had no belief in a future existence. He was a fellow of Jesus College, Cambridge, from 1910 to 1916, and, after sixteen angry years 'in the wilderness', of Downing College from 1932 to 1937 after which he was made an honorary fellow; he received an honorary Litt.D. from Cambridge University in 1930, and was knighted in 1934. In the National Portrait Gallery are portraits in pencil (1952) and in water-colour (1960) by his friend Dorothy Hawksley, and there is a chalk drawing (1937) by Francis Dodd in the Fitzwilliam Museum.

[Wilfrid Blunt, *Cockerell*, 1964; personal knowledge.]   WILFRID BLUNT

COHEN, Sir ANDREW BENJAMIN (1909-1968), colonial administrator, was born 7 October 1909 at Berkhamsted, Hertfordshire, the twin son of Walter Samuel Cohen, financier and company director, and his wife, Lucy Margaret Cobb. On his father's side, Andrew Cohen stemmed from the *haute juiverie* of business, and on his mother's, from a radical Unitarian family; the two strains combined in the son to produce an élitist with a social conscience. His elder sister, Ruth Louisa, was principal of Newnham College, Cambridge, 1954-72. Andrew Cohen won a scholarship to Malvern College, and another to Trinity College, Cambridge, where, although his spiritual home was King's, he obtained a double first in the classical tripos (1930-1). In 1932 he entered the Civil Service, where he spent a year as an assistant principal at the Board of Inland Revenue, before transferring to the Colonial Office to join the other classical scholars under (Sir) Charles Jeffries.

For the next few years Cohen inhaled trusteeship with the dust on the African files; and he came to sympathize with the black rather than the white. Contemptuous of colour bars, he was shocked by how little the colonial trustees seemed to him to have done for Africans in Rhodesia. For a time he was private secretary to Sir John Maffey (later Lord Rugby, q.v.), and visited Central Africa as secretary to a financial commission. As an acting principal in 1939, he was chosen for a Commonwealth Fund Fellowship to visit America, but his schedule was cut short by the outbreak of war. In 1940 he was sent to organize supplies during the siege of Malta, deputizing at times for the lieutenant-governor. It was his first taste of power (for which he was voracious), in an embattled Government organizing a society to meet an emergency; the experience left him with a Fabian socialist's view of the State's duty to reorganize the social order. In 1943 he returned to the Colonial Office as an assistant secretary, to take part in post-war African planning.

By 1947, when he was appointed assistant under-secretary of state for the Colonial Office's African division, Cohen's vision for Africa was sharply defined. It seemed to him vital, in the interests of both Britain and Africa, to turn the colonies into self-governing nations within 'the next generation'. As head of the division and *alter ego* of his minister, Arthur Creech Jones [q.v.], he helped to prepare a report for tropical Africa, in which he was able to give this meaning to the colonial shibboleths of the Labour Party. There were many in the euphoria of peace who wished to make colonies into modern welfare states and bring them into production to repair the ravaged United Kingdom economy. Cohen was one of the few who realized that colonial rule would have to be nationalized if those aims were to be fulfilled. Alien officials could never do so, he insisted, through petty chiefs; to achieve them, the excluded but educated African who understood modern ideas must be brought into partnership, and his price would be the most rapid possible transfer of power. As a realist, Cohen discerned that the age of empire was ended; as a moralist, he resolved to end it constructively.

African nationalists seemed a derisory band at the time, and some governors objected bitterly to the new course; to educate the African service, Creech Jones and Cohen began the *Journal of African Administration*, and the annual conferences at Cambridge. They were prepared to concede power to progressive nationalist movements, but as a result of the Accra riots of 1948, the ballot box and a quasi-ministerial system were introduced in the Gold Coast earlier than intended; the extreme nationalists won the election and Kwame Nkrumah left gaol to become leader of government. What had been conceded in Ghana could not then be denied to Nigeria, and a 'domino effect' spread throughout British West Africa. Thus Cohen's plan, designed to educate the national movements gradually into responsibility, provoked them into swift action. By 1951 West Africa at least was set on course to self-government, although fifteen years later, contemplating the one-party states and military coups, Cohen was depressed by the outcome. Like many of Africa's friends, he had over-estimated the power of the nationalists to transcend ethnic divisions and behave democratically in the Westminster tradition.

For Central Africa, Cohen's construct in 1948–51 was more realistic if the outcome was less fortunate. Fearful of a white unilateral declaration of independence, and of apartheid spreading from South Africa, he advocated a confederation of the Rhodesias and Nyasaland: power was to be transferred to the white minority on condition that it was shared with the African majority. A version of the plan was carried out in 1953 after he had left the Colonial Office; but the offer of 'half a loaf' so angered the Africans that Kenneth Kaunda and Hastings Banda could organize nationalist movements strong enough to break the association ten years later and achieve majority rule, save in Rhodesia itself.

In September 1951, after James Griffiths had replaced Creech Jones as colonial secretary following the general election of 1950, Cohen was appointed governor of Uganda and sworn in early in 1952. Although he disliked the ceremonial, he gladly practised in the field what he had preached in Whitehall; Africans and Asians were invited to Government House and advanced in central government; Makerere was developed into a university to strengthen the educated cadre; local authorities were made more democratic, which encouraged political parties and national consciousness. But in underestimating the strength of traditional loyalty and deporting the Kabaka of Buganda in 1953, only to restore him later on constitutional conditions, Cohen was strongly criticized on all sides, although when he finally left Uganda early in 1957 the foundations for independence were securely laid, and indeed the Ugandans themselves petitioned for his term of office to be extended.

Disappointed in his hope of a Labour seat in Parliament, and despite being an unlikely choice as a diplomat, he was appointed permanent representative (1957-60) on the Trusteeship Council at the United Nations. But he seemed to have been put on the shelf, and he did not always find it easy to square the representations which the Foreign Office instructed him to make with his personal convictions. In 1959 he published *British Policy in Changing Africa*, and, given his natural affinity with liberal Americans and his candid and widespread working relations with African and Asian leaders, he discovered another way to serve African independence: the idea of international and Commonwealth co-operation in aid of modernizing Africa captured his mind. In helping to link American aid to British schemes for developing East Africa, especially in university education, he took up the concepts of the United Nations 'Development Decade'. It was fitting, therefore, that he was recalled to Whitehall in 1961 to set up a Department of Technical Co-operation, which took over most of the old Colonial Office's non-political functions. In 1964 the Department was transformed into a Ministry of Overseas Development, with Cohen as its permanent secretary; he carried out the organization of first one establishment and then the other with his usual dynamic enthusiasm.

He was cut out to be a planner, even a philosopher king, and if reading lyric verse on an antique Mediterranean island may have been his private Elysium, he admired intellect most; arrogantly intellectual, and avid for original ideas, if they were to engage his excellent mind they had to be practical in shaping better things to come. With a heroic image of himself as idea in action, compounded of Carlyle and Euripides, Cambridge and Malta combined to make him unflinchingly realistic in finding means to achieve a passionately speculative vision of ultimate ends. Of giant stature, appetite, and energy, boyish in charm and enthusiasm, the intellectual dreamer of the Colonial Office was one of the most anti-colonial and unofficial of the imperial officials who finally dismantled the tropical African empire. In one way or another his measures helped to awaken the slumbering genius of African nationalism, and, wittingly or unwittingly, he did more to bring about the fall of empire and the rise of the nationalists than most African politicians were able to achieve between them.

He was appointed OBE in 1942, CMG in 1948, and was advanced to KCMG in 1952; he was also appointed KCVO (1954), and received the honorary degree of LLD from the Queen's University, Belfast, in 1960. In 1949 he married Mrs Helen Phoebe Donington (died 1978), JP, commander of the Order of St. John of Jerusalem, only daughter of George Hope

Stevenson, praelector in ancient history, University College, Oxford (1907-49); Cohen was as affectionate towards his three step-children as towards their own son (born 1950). His marriage brought him closer to Bloomsbury and the political Left.

Cohen died suddenly in London 17 June 1968. A portrait by Robert Buhler was exhibited at the Royal Academy in 1957.

[*The Times*, 19 June 1968; government records; private information; personal knowledge.]   R. E. ROBINSON

COHEN, HARRIET (1896-1967), pianist, was born 2 December 1896, the eldest of the three daughters and one son of Joseph Verney Cohen, a composer and business man, of London and Aldershot, and his wife, Florence, daughter of Benjamin White, a dental surgeon, of Ludgate Hill, London. Harriet Cohen's paternal grandfather had emigrated from Lithuania; her father was an amateur cellist and an amateur military historian who combined his two hobbies by writing music for military bands.

The young Harriet Cohen, known to family and friends as 'Tania', was educated at the Royal Academy of Music, which she entered in 1909 as the youngest student ever to hold the Ada Lewis scholarship; she was booked in the register as Harriette Pearl Alice Cohen. Her scholarship, originally awarded for three years, was extended to keep her at the Royal Academy until 1915, and as a student she won the Sterndale Bennett prize, the Edward Nicholls prize, the Hine prize, the RAM prize, the medal of the Worshipful Company of Musicians, and the Chappell pianoforte prize. Having worked as a piano pupil of Felix Swinstead and a harmony pupil of Frederick Corder, she left the Royal Academy of Music for further study under Tobias Matthay, becoming the third of a trio of outstanding pianists—its other members were (Dame) Myra Hess [q.v.] and Irene Scharrer—who much enhanced the reputation of Tobias Matthay and the Matthay method of piano teaching. Already occupied as a pupil teacher, in 1922 Harriet Cohen joined the staff of the Matthay School as a professor. Her combination of beauty and elegance with real musicianship quickly established her on the concert platform, and the unusual programmes she offered made her recitals lively musical events. She was devoted to the music of J. S. Bach, whose works she played in a style perhaps more overtly expressive than would be approved by some modern critics; she did all she could to popularize the works of the Tudor composers represented in the *Fitzwilliam Virginal Book*, and she took many an opportunity of playing new music; her performances of the standard classics were no less popular. Manuel de Falla's *Nights in the Gardens of Spain*, Prokofiev's concertos and sonatas, and the piano music of Shostakovich, were music she did all she could to popularize, and she became the first pianist outside the Soviet Union to learn the *Twenty-Four Preludes* which Shostakovich composed in 1932 and 1933. Modern British music, in particular, won her allegiance, and (Sir) Arnold E. T. Bax, Ralph Vaughan Williams, John Ireland, and Constant Lambert [qq.v.] all wrote works for her as, in a later generation, did Peter Racine Fricker. Her devotion to the music of Bach led a group of grateful composers (it included Sir G. R. Bantock and Bax among her seniors, and (Sir) William T. Walton among her contemporaries) to compile *A Bach Book for Harriet Cohen* (1932), which consisted of piano transcriptions of choral preludes and cantata movements. When, in 1936, she published *Music's Handmaid*, a book principally concerned with her ideas about interpretation, she wrote particularly of Bach, Mozart, Chopin, Brahms, de Falla, Debussy, Bartok, Vaughan Williams, and Arnold Bax. Bax, a close friend of Harriet Cohen since their student days, owed a great deal to the unswerving loyalty with which she played his music wherever she was heard in Europe and across the Atlantic.

Despite the inexhaustible energy which took her from end to end of the British Isles, across Europe, and over the Atlantic on frequent concert tours, Harriet Cohen's health was never strong. In 1925 a course of treatment enabled her to keep tuberculosis at bay, although it forced a lengthy interruption in her career. In 1948, at the Cheltenham Festival, an accident robbed her of the use of her right hand, but two years later she gave the first performance of the *Concertino for Left Hand* which Sir Arnold Bax had written for her. Despite failing sight and two major eye operations, she continued to act as vice-chairman of the Harriet Cohen International Music Awards, which she instituted under the presidency of Jean Sibelius and of which Bax was chairman. In 1938 she was created CBE for services to British music. Among many foreign honours bestowed upon her, she was commander of the Order of the Crown of Belgium (1947), and a member (first class) of the Order of the White Lion of Czechoslovakia; in 1950 she became an officer de l'Académie Française and in 1954 a cavalière of the Order of the Southern Cross of Brazil. She was also a freeman of the City of London (1954) and received an honorary doctorate from the National University of Ireland (1960).

She was energetic, widely read, and gifted with endless enthusiasm for literature as well as for music, and her continuous musical activities did not prevent her from leading a vigorous social life. She remained unmarried. Her friends, an impressive and international body of celebrities, included Sir Edward W. Elgar [q.v.] and those most prominent in the world of music; such literary eminences as G. Bernard Shaw, H. G. Wells, and E. Arnold Bennett; J. Ramsay Macdonald, the first Labour prime minister [qq.v.]; and a glittering array of European and American intellectuals, Albert Einstein among them. They were great figures not only in music but in many branches of politics, learning, and the arts. Her autobiography, *A Bundle of Time*, (published posthumously in 1969 after her sudden death at University College Hospital, London, 13 November 1967) quotes extensively from the letters of the many celebrities who regularly corresponded with her. If her autobiography shows that she delighted in the eminence of her friends, the letters they wrote to her show that her beauty, intelligence, and vivacity delighted her friends as surely as their achievements delighted her.

There is a pen, ink, and wash drawing by Dame Laura Knight, and a drawing by Edmond X. Kapp (1921), entitled 'Harriet Cohen and Debussy'. There are also three portraits of her at the Royal Academy of Music by Stochell, Somorov, and an unknown painter.

[*A Bundle of Time: The Memoirs of Harriet Cohen*, 1969; Harriet Cohen, *Music's Handmaid*, 1936; *The Times*, 14 November 1967; personal knowledge.]

IVOR NEWTON

COLEBROOK, LEONARD (1883-1967), bacteriologist, was born in Guildford, Surrey, 2 March 1883, the fifth child and third son of six children born to May Colebrook, a prosperous farmer and Nonconformist preacher, and his second wife, Mary Gower. He was educated from 1891 to 1896 at Guildford Grammar School, from 1896 to 1899 at Westbourne High School, Bournemouth, and from then for one year at Christ's College, Blackheath, Kent. In 1900 he began pre-medical studies at the London Hospital Medical College, from which he won an entrance scholarship to St. Mary's Hospital, where he graduated MB, BS (London) in 1906.

His decision to go into medicine was apparently prompted by the Nonconformist social conscience of the Colebrook family. Indeed, he first intended to become a medical missionary. But he was much impressed by the lectures in pathology and bacteriology of

Sir Almroth E. Wright (whose notice Colebrook later wrote for this Dictionary), and one year after graduation he accepted an appointment as assistant in the Inoculation Department of St. Mary's Hospital Medical School. There he worked partly on the vaccine therapy pursued by Wright, but his second publication, in 1911, was with (Sir) Alexander Fleming [q.v.] on the treatment of syphilis with the arsenical, salvarsan, of Paul Ehrlich. On the outbreak of war in 1914 he became a captain in the RAMC and worked on wound infections, first at St. Mary's Hospital and later in Wright's laboratory at No. 13 General Hospital in Boulogne. In 1919 he was appointed a member of the scientific staff of the Medical Research Council and worked on dental caries but early in 1922 he was seconded to work again with Wright at St. Mary's Hospital. It was under Almroth Wright that he developed his skill as a bacteriologist. Despite the contrast in their personalities and beliefs, the two men became close friends and Colebrook's loyalty and admiration for his old teacher lasted throughout his life. He published a biography of Wright in 1954.

In the mid 1920s Colebrook began the study of puerperal fever for which he is probably best known. Vera Colebrook has written that he was set on this course by the death of the wife of a close friend from a streptococcal infection in childbirth and by the suffering which followed. Wright's vaccine therapy was ineffective against these dangerous infections, which at that time contributed to many cases of maternal mortality, and treatment with arsenicals was of relatively little value. When, in 1930, Colebrook became honorary director of the research laboratories of Queen Charlotte's Maternity Hospital, he undertook a thorough investigation of the origins of infection in the labour wards and became a vigorous proponent of an aseptic regimen by which it would be reduced. In 1935 his attention was drawn to a German paper by Gerhard Domagk, reporting that a red dye, prontosil, could cure infection with virulent haemolytic streptococci. By the following year Colebrook and his colleagues had confirmed these findings and shown that the drug was effective in a number of cases of puerperal fever. After subsequent use of sulphanilamide, the active fragment of prontosil which was produced from it *in vivo*, and then of other sulphonamides, the death rate in the isolation block of the hospital fell from 30 to 4 per cent. The life-saving power of the sulphonamides in human medicine was thus established.

In 1939 Colebrook went to France as a colonel in the RAMC and bacteriological consultant to the British Expeditionary Force.

There he became aware of the distressing prevalence of infected burns in mechanized warfare. After his return to England in 1940 he began work on the infection and treatment of burns, and showed that infection could be controlled by sulphonamides and, in a later study, by penicillin. He renewed a much earlier interest in skin grafting and consulted (Sir) Peter Medawar in Oxford, to whom he introduced the problems of tissue rejection. From 1942 to 1948 he was director of the Burns Investigation Unit of the Medical Research Council, which was first based in Glasgow Royal Infirmary, and then at the Birmingham Accident Hospital. Thus he developed ideas on the airborne transfer of infection and procedures for asepsis during dressing. The unit had acquired an outstanding reputation when he retired in 1948.

From the time when he first directed a burns unit, Colebrook fought doggedly for changes in handling the problems of sepsis and for other causes in which he believed. Many of his burned patients were young children. For more than ten years after 1946, with the support of his wife, he was a persistent propagandist of measures to prevent burns to both children and old people in the home. The campaign was not without success, for the Fireguards Act was passed in 1952 and safety regulations for nightdresses were introduced in 1964 and 1967.

In the last phase of his life Colebrook was a supporter of the Euthanasia Society. He felt that there were situations in which men had the right to dispose of their own lives, and also that the first duty of a doctor was to relieve suffering, even if life were thereby curtailed.

He was elected an honorary fellow of the Royal College of Obstetricians and Gynaecologists in 1944 and a fellow of the Royal Society in 1945. He received an honorary D.Sc. from the university of Birmingham in 1950 and became an honorary fellow of the Royal College of Surgeons of England in the same year. A variety of other honours came to him, including the Blair Bell medal of the Royal Society of Medicine (1954) and the Jenner medal in 1962. Nevertheless, he was a man of true modesty. He insisted that he deserved no special recognition and that what had been achieved had come from the work of a team of people; and he made special mention of the contributions of his younger sister, Dora, herself a bacteriologist, and of Ronald Hare.

Colebrook, known as 'Coli' to his friends and colleagues, was impelled by compassion for the sick. During his working life there were major discoveries in chemotherapy and he dedicated himself to their application in the treatment of life-threatening bacterial infections for which no effective remedy previously had been known.

Colebrook was a small slim man with outdoor recreations which included skiing and tending the large garden of his cottage, 'Silverwood', at Farnham Common. He could sometimes give the impression of severity, but the enduring memories of his friends were of his transparent honesty, his sense of humour, his humanity, and his generosity. He was not outstanding as a scientist, or an originator, and certainly never thought of himself in this light, but he was a man who unremittingly used his energy and ability to confer great medical benefits on those of his generation.

In 1914 he married Dorothy Scarlett, daughter of John Scarlett Campbell, of the Indian Civil Service, judge of the High Court at Lahore. She died in 1941 and five years later he married Vera Scovell, daughter of Thomas James Locke, a civil servant. She was a war widow working as a freelance broadcaster. There were no children of either marriage. He died at Farnham Common, Buckinghamshire, 29 September 1967.

There is an oil portrait of Colebrook, painted in 1967 by Gyula Sajö, at the Royal College of Pathologists in London.

[C. L. Oakley in *Biographical Memoirs of Fellows of the Royal Society*, vol. xvii, 1971; Vera Colebrook, 'Injury', *The British Journal of Accident Surgery*, vol. ii, 1971; Ronald Hare, *The Birth of Penicillin*, 1970; W. C. Noble, *Coli: Great Healer of Men*, 1974.]   E. P. ABRAHAM

COLLINGWOOD, SIR EDWARD FOYLE (1900–1970), mathematician, medical administrator, and university leader, was born at Lilburn Tower, near Wooler, Northumberland, 17 January 1900, the eldest of the four sons of Colonel Cuthbert George Collingwood, landowner, of Glanton Pyke, and his wife, Dorothy, daughter of the Revd William Fawcett of Somerford Keynes, Gloucestershire. Fawcett's wife was one of the co-heiresses of the Foyle estate at Somerford Keynes. Col. Collingwood was the grandson of John, brother of Vice-Admiral Collingwood [q.v.]. Col. Collingwood, who commanded the Lancashire Fusiliers at the battle of Omdurman in 1893, had retired in 1899, and died in 1933. Collingwood and his brothers all enjoyed shooting and fishing and the social life of the country. Collingwood's mother, who survived him, was always a strong influence in the family.

Collingwood went to Osborne in 1913, Dartmouth in 1914, and a year later joined the Royal Navy as a midshipman in the *Collingwood* (by special arrangement). Before experiencing any action, he fell down a hatchway, sustaining serious injuries, and was in a hospital ship which followed the battle of Jutland. He was invalided out of the navy. After passing twelfth for Woolwich he failed the medical examination owing to his nervous condition at that time, whereupon he went up to Trinity College, Cambridge, in 1918 to read mathematics. At Lilburn there were letters of the vice-admiral showing his interest in the teaching of mathematics to the young, and Edward was much interested in these and other papers showing his great-grandfather's attention to details, as also in the small observatory built by his grandfather and in biology, bacteria, and photographic techniques.

At Cambridge Collingwood's director of studies, G. H. Hardy [q.v.], who was for many years the most outstanding personality in English pure mathematics, inspired him to aim at mathematical research, to the dismay of his father and uncle. He obtained a third class in part i of the mathematical tripos in 1919 and in political specials i and ii in the Michaelmas term of 1920, and then took his degree (1921). This unorthodox course left him free to study those parts of mathematics which interested him at his own pace and omit large parts of the heavy course for part ii of the mathematical tripos.

As an undergraduate he kept somewhat aloof from his mathematical contemporaries, and had a full, but entirely separate, social life among a group, most of whom had served in the forces and distinguished themselves both as undergraduates and in later life. He used his private means to entertain well, but never ostentatiously. He was unable to drink alcohol without getting hay fever (later this was rectified with antihistamines).

When Hardy went to Oxford in 1920, J. E. Littlewood, Hardy's most important collaborator, advised Collingwood on research. He obtained a Rayleigh prize in 1923, but failed in his one attempt to obtain a Trinity research fellowship. At the invitation of W. H. Young [q.v.] he went, to Aberystwyth in 1922. There Professor G. Valiron of Strasbourg was lecturing in French on integral functions, and Collingwood made translations which eventually formed a book. In 1924–5 he held a Rouse Ball travelling studentship, mainly at the Sorbonne, and thus became the only one of the Hardy–Littlewood school to have close relationships with French mathematicians.

He took his MA degree in 1925 and, returning to Cambridge, read for a Ph.D. degree (which he obtained in 1929) for a dissertation which included material from some already published papers on integral and meromorphic functions. He was made a member of the high table at Trinity, and in 1930 steward. Most unusually for a non-fellow, he was elected to the council of Trinity College. He was also treasurer of the Third Trinity Boat Club and made a number of friends who became well known later. He still entertained well. He also regularly gave two advanced courses for the mathematical faculty, but did no regular undergraduate teaching. The six mathematicians, Littlewood, Collingwood, Macintyre, Clunie, Rahman, and Joyal, constituted a sequence, each the Ph.D. student of the one before. Collingwood's lectures on Ahlfor's Distortion Theorem had an important influence on the work of the author.

In the 1930s Collingwood became interested in pictures, and, when a family trust fell in on the death of an aunt, he bought some fine contemporary and eighteenth-century pictures through (Sir) Geoffrey Agnew, one of his earlier Cambridge friends. He also made a collection of Chinese porcelain, becoming quite an expert on the subject.

He was lieutenant in the Northumberland Hussars (Yeomanry) in 1923-7 and became a JP in 1935. He was chairman of the bench for many years and deputy lieutenant (1959). He gave much time and thought to the management of the Lilburn estate, even during university terms. When in 1937 he became high sheriff of Northumberland he gave up his Cambridge obligations, but continued to visit, in particular for the college commemoration feast at the end of the Lent term on his way to join his mother on holiday at Menton.

In the war of 1939-45 he joined the Admiralty minesweeping division as an officer of the RNVR, reaching the rank of acting captain. He served as director of scientific research with the Admiralty delegation in Washington in 1942, as officer in charge of the sweeping division in 1943, chief scientist, Admiralty Mine Design Department in 1943-5, and as one of a delegation to Moscow on a special scientific mission. His all-round ability and wide experience, backed by his determination, were effective in getting the money needed for the scientists' work; he also impressed the scientists as having a sound grasp of physical principles. In 1946 he was appointed CBE, and became an officer of the Legion of Merit.

Collingwood's first paper in 1924 generalized Nevanlinna's second fundamental theorem from 2 to p exceptional values, a result which Littlewood had, independently, stated in a letter to Nevanlinna. Collingwood's second paper, also in 1924, developed the idea of deficient values, questioning whether they were asymptotic. During the war this was proved false. After a gap from 1932 to 1948 Collingwood

returned to this subject and discussed the islands in which $|f(z)-a| < \sigma$ and $f(z)$ takes no value more than p times, where σ and p may tend to infinity with $|a|$. These later papers seem less effective than the first two but led to fruitful discussions with Weitsman in June 1970. Collingwood's wide knowledge of the literature of mathematics enabled himself and the writer to develop the theory of cluster sets in a joint paper in *Acta Math.* lxxxvii (1952) which Professor W. K. Hayman described as the beginning of the modern subject. If $f(z)$ takes values on the Riemann sphere in $|z| < 1$, and there exists a sequence $z_n \rightarrow e^{i\theta}$ such that $f(z_n) \rightarrow w$, then w belongs to the cluster set $C(f, e^{i\theta})$ of $f(z)$ at $e^{i\theta}$. Their relationship to the range of values taken by $f(z)$ near $e^{i\theta}$, and to neighbouring Fatou points, $e^{i\theta_n}$, $\theta_n \rightarrow \theta$ at which $f(z)$ tends to a limit in any angle, etc., formed the subject-matter of the rest of Collingwood's mathematical papers. The standard textbook, written by Collingwood and A. J. Lohwater (1966) includes Collingwood's important applications to prime ends.

After 1945 Collingwood actively sought mathematical contacts, attending international congresses and specialized colloquia, and in particular, the new British Mathematical Colloquium, where he helped to organize special sessions on the theory of functions, and thus soon became a well-known figure. In 1959 he obtained a Cambridge Sc.D., in 1962 he was knighted, and in 1965 he was elected FRS and made an honorary LLD of Glasgow University where in 1961 he had given the seventh Gibson lecture. He joined the council of the London Mathematical Society (LMS) in April 1959 and was treasurer from 1960 to 1969, when he became president. The benefaction from G. H. Hardy on the death of his sister in 1963 was the largest ever received by the LMS, and Collingwood made the fullest use of it to strengthen and widen the activities of the society—including the founding of the Applied Probability Trust for the publication of the *Journal of Applied Probability*, edited by J. Gani, which began in 1964. Collingwood took a large part in drafting the petition, draft charter, and statutes for a royal charter (approved by the Privy Council in 1964) for the LMS to mark its centenary in 1965.

His early interest in bacteria, as well as in local affairs, and perhaps the influence of a Cambridge friend of the 1930s, led Collingwood into medical affairs. He was a founder member, and in 1953-68 chairman, of the Newcastle Regional Hospital Board, vice-chairman of the board of governors of the United Newcastle Hospitals from 1955, vice-chairman of the Central Health Services

Council (1959-63), vice-president of the International Hospital Federation (1959-67), a member of the Medical Research Council (1960-8) and treasurer (1960-7), and a member of the royal commission on medical education (1965-8). He was made an officer of l'Ordre de la Santé Publique, France, in 1963. Although himself not medically qualified, he had a great effect on medicine, largely through his wisdom, good sense, and attention to detail when visiting medical institutions, but also by contributing to the technical development of the use of computers in medicine. He spoke at the annual congress of the British Institute of Radiology in 1967 and at that of the British Dental Association in 1970.

His friend of undergraduate days, Sir James Duff [q.v.], was alternately vice-chancellor and pro-vice-chancellor of Durham University until it was separated from Newcastle in 1963, and then vice-chancellor. Collingwood was made an honorary D.Sc. of Durham in 1950, a member of the council of the Durham Colleges, a member of the court of the university in 1955, and chairman of the council of Durham University from 1963 until his death at home at Lilburn Tower 25 October 1970. His large mathematical library and many manuscripts were left to the Department of Mathematics at Durham. As in other spheres his foresight and wisdom benefited both Durham and Newcastle universities.

In appearance Collingwood was short and fair and walked with long strides. He early became very bald. He was unmarried.

[*The Times*, 27 and 30 October and 3 November 1970; *Lancet*, 31 October 1970; M. L. Cartwright in *Biographical Memoirs of the Fellows of the Royal Society*, vol. xvii, 1971; private information; personal knowledge.]   M. L. CARTWRIGHT

COLQUHOUN, ROBERT (1914-1962), painter, was born at Kilmarnock, Ayrshire, 20 December 1914, the son of Robert Colquhoun, an engineering fitter whose pleasure was in caged birds, and his wife, Janet Candlish. He was educated at the local primary school and, from 1926, at the Kilmarnock Academy to the age of fourteen. He had already begun to show talent in drawing and painting, but the economic depression of those years sharpened the need for him to leave school and contribute to the family income. His art master, James Lyle, took the case to two local patrons, and with their help Colquhoun was able to leave an engineering apprenticeship and return to the Academy. He won a scholarship to the Glasgow School of Art in 1932, and went there in 1933.

At the School he met MacBryde, and the

Roberts—as they were generally known—became tender and inseparable companions. Hereafter their careers are jointly described. MACBRYDE, ROBERT (1913-1966), painter, was born at Maybole, also in Ayrshire, 5 December 1913, the son of John McBride, general labourer, and his wife, Agnes Kennedy McKay. His schooling ended at fourteen and he worked in a factory before entering the Glasgow School of Art a year ahead of Colquhoun. The older man was 'the one who washed the socks and things in their digs in Renfrew Street'. At the School they were respected as a serious, hardworking, and lonely couple. Their teachers, Hugh Crawford and Ian Fleming, turned their attention to the Impressionist, Post-Impressionist, and even more recent French painting to be seen in Glasgow—Colquhoun seeming particularly responsive towards Degas and Gauguin. The Roberts won prizes for drawing, and then post-diploma awards which allowed them to spend a year under the wardenship of James Cowie at the Patrick Allan-Frazer School of Art at Hospitalfield, near Arbroath. Finally, in 1938, Colquhoun was awarded a travelling scholarship from the Glasgow School of Art and, because there was concern within the School that this would divide the partnership, an equal sum was found from a private patron to give a scholarship to MacBryde.

As students the Roberts had been to Paris in 1937 and 1938 on visits arranged by the School of Art, partly recorded in their first joint exhibition at Kilmarnock in September 1938. In 1938-9 they went to Italy, the south of France, Belgium, and Holland, but it was again in Paris that they were most nourished. They were working at Pontoise in August 1939 when the international crisis enforced their return to Ayrshire. Colquhoun trained as a teacher until he was conscripted into the Royal Army Medical Corps in the spring of 1940. Not many months later he collapsed on duty in Leeds and was invalided out of the army. MacBryde, who was tubercular and so exempt from service, had followed him and in 1941 they were in Ayrshire together again, facing an uncertain future. Prompted by the hope that they would find commissions under the War Artists' scheme, and with further support from their earlier patrons, they decided that London must be their sphere.

In London, Colquhoun joined the ambulance service of the Civil Defence Corps (1941-4), painting between shifts and much at night. Late in 1941 the Roberts moved into a studio at 77 Bedford Gardens, shared for a short time with F. John Minton [q.v.]. This was their home until 1947, and for Colquhoun the years there were the period of his most intense and essential achievement. The studio soon became a hospitable, if noisy, point of intersection between circles which included Michael Ayrton, Prunella Clough, John Craxton, and J. Keith Vaughan, among the younger painters who shared some stylistic kinship with the Roberts through their reactions to John Piper and Graham Sutherland of an older generation —who were also visitors. Painters of different inclinations, Francis Bacon, Ian Hamilton Finlay, and Lucian Freud among them, met there. Writers who frequented them were J. Maclaren-Ross, Dylan Thomas [q.v.], Ruthven Todd and, from 1943, George Barker and W. S. Graham; Peter Watson, the publisher of *Horizon*, and (Sir) Colin Anderson were their first patrons.

The Roberts continued to make occasional visits to Ayrshire, where their deportment made something of a stir; Colquhoun's last visit was in 1946. He stayed with W. S. Graham in Cornwall in 1943, visited an army cloth factory in the Hebrides on a belated commission from the War Artists' Advisory Committee at the end of 1944, stayed frequently with Denis Wirth-Miller and Richard Chopping at Wivenhoe, Essex, in 1945, and spent two months in county Cork in 1946. In their earlier London years, the Roberts also kept links with Glasgow which brought Jankel Adler to occupy a studio in the same building as their own in November 1942. Adler (1895–1949), a Polish refugee who had worked with S. W. Hayter in Paris, was a stimulating example of French professionalism in the wartime isolation of Scotland and London, bringing with him influential mannerisms derived from the Picasso of the earlier 1930s. For Colquhoun, earlier understandings of the authority of Picasso were confirmed by the exhibition of Picasso's wartime work at the Victoria and Albert Museum in 1945.

The first group of paintings exhibited by the Roberts in London were at the Lefevre Gallery in 1942, in a mixed gathering of 'Six Scottish Painters'. Colquhoun's principal exhibitions were held in the same gallery in 1943, 1944, 1947, 1949, and 1950; MacBryde exhibited with him there in 1943, 1944, and 1949. Colquhoun's exhibitions were successful but for the last, from which little was sold. By 1951 he was stagnating, from several causes. With other painters of his generation whose achievement was grounded in a neo-romanticism highly tuned to the stresses of the war years, he was particularly vulnerable to the change in taste brought about by renewed, first-hand awareness of painting in France, and by the radical shift in pictorical ambition being wrought in the United States. MacBryde, having dared less as an artist, had to that extent less to lose. At a private level, the constructive nervous constriction imposed by the

war had begun to relax, and their circle was beginning to disintegrate; one of their most perceptive supporters, Duncan Macdonald of the Lefevre Gallery, had died in 1949, and from then on they had no regular income from a dealer; even earlier, and more fundamentally unsettling, they had been put out of their studio to make way for the demolishers, at a time when critical esteem for Colquhoun, and expectation for his future, were at their highest. They never had a permanent home and workplace again, and drink, formerly a vehicle of boisterous conviviality, now began to isolate them. By many who came to know them in the 1950s they came to be remembered as frequently tiresome drifters in the pubs and drinking clubs on the beat from Charlotte Street to Dean Street.

Frances Byng Stamper who, with her sister, Caroline Lucas, ran Miller's Press, befriended the Roberts in 1947 and gave them a studio at Lewes, Sussex, which was their base for two years. Both spent much of their time on lithography. In 1948 they began designs for the costumes and scenery for Léonide Massine's ballet *Donald of the Burthens*, produced at Covent Garden in 1951; the designs were exhibited at the Redfern Gallery in 1952. (Colquhoun, alone, made designs for *King Lear*, presented at Stratford in 1953.) In 1949 the Roberts went with George Barker to Italy, where the puppet plays at Modena and the Palio at Siena provided Colquhoun with the subjects for his exhibition at Lefevre's in 1950. After their return they lived at Tilty Mill House, Duton Hill, Essex, owned by Ruthven Todd and also used by Barker and Elizabeth Smart. Tension, but not a break in friendship with Barker, led to their return to London in 1954. During the 1950s much of Colquhoun's work consisted of drawings, water-colours, and a noteworthy body of monotypes—a medium he had begun to use by 1946. Exhibitions of his drawings and prints were held at the Redfern Gallery in 1954, and at the Parton Gallery in 1957.

A brave effort to bring vitality back to Colquhoun was made by Bryan Robertson, who assembled an important retrospective exhibition of his work at the Whitechapel Gallery in 1958. Respectfully received, it failed in its essential purpose. Certainly the works of Colquhoun painted for the occasion, in the early months of the year, betrayed a lack of concentration, and the attempt to paint on a fashionably larger scale was mistaken. Colquhoun reverted to making monotypes. The exhibition allowed the Roberts to visit Spain; in London thereafter they shifted from one dismal lodging to another. Their last joint exhibition was at the Kaplan Gallery in 1960.

Colquhoun's health had been weakening, and he died in London suddenly in the early hours of 20 September 1962 while working for an exhibition at the Museum Street Galleries—which was held a fortnight later. He was buried at Kilmarnock. A memorial exhibition was held at the Establishment Club in December, and at the Douglas & Foulis Gallery, Edinburgh, the following spring. A Robert Colquhoun Memorial Art Competition was inaugurated at the Dick Institute, Kilmarnock, in 1972.

After Colquhoun's death, the rudderless MacBryde drank more than ever. He stayed for a while in Spain with Anthony Cronin, returned to unhappiness in London, became the foredoomed instructor at a painting summer school in county Cork, then disappeared to Dublin. There he lived aimlessly, latterly sharing a flat with Patrick Kavanagh. On the night of 6 May 1966 he was killed in Dublin by a car. He was buried at Maybole. In 1972 there was a memorial exhibition at the New 57 Gallery, Edinburgh.

Although Colquhoun was not significantly influential, his work of the 1940s had a dogmatic, puritan passion which remains impressive. It was without illustrative intention and was formed from imagination and memory. His figures—often of women, alone but for some enigmatic animal or bird—are anxious and vulnerable, yet exhausted of sentiment; their action is abruptly fixed in what seems the enactment of a private, existential ritual. His use of colour was forceful without being strident. P. Wyndham Lewis [q.v.] saw the work of the Roberts as 'almost identical'; rather, the art—as the life—of each was complementary to that of the other. MacBryde's work, which was dependent on Braque, is largely concerned with clear, rhythmic patterns of line and colour which are decorative rather than analytic in character.

The Roberts are represented in many public collections in Great Britain, and in some galleries in Australia, Canada, and the United States. Portrait drawings of each other are in the Scottish National Portrait Gallery. There is also a self-portrait in pencil of Colquhoun (1940) in the National Portrait Gallery, London.

[Exhibition catalogues; private information.]
HAMISH MILES

COMPTON-BURNETT, DAME IVY (1884-1969), novelist, was born at Pinner, Middlesex, 5 June 1884, the fourth daughter of Dr James Compton Burnett, and the eldest of the seven children of his second wife, Katharine, daughter of Rowland Rees, a cantankerous mayor of Dover. She was educated at Addiscombe College in Hove where the family moved in 1892 and briefly at Howard College, Bedford. In 1902 she went to the Royal Holloway College, Egham, where she read classics. The influence of the classics on her writing is debated, but the overwhelming influences are certainly not from literature but life. Her father was a crusading homoeopathic doctor, who wrote many books and pamphlets on medical subjects. The five surviving children of his first wife who had died in 1882 did not get on with their stepmother, and she made no attempt to get on with them. The large, frequently divided families in the novels are clearly modelled on the Compton Burnetts. Even within the second family there were distinct groupings, Ivy herself forming a very strong attachment to her brother Guy, born in 1885. And after Dr James's death in 1901, Mrs Compton-Burnett (who added the hyphen herself) became a most difficult and emotionally demanding head of the family, like one of the many tyrants in her daughter's books.

The first two decades of the century brought a number of severe psychological blows. The greatest of these was the death of Guy from pneumonia in 1905. The following year, having left Holloway with second class honours, Ivy was required by her mother to act as governess to her four younger sisters. It was in these monotonous years at Hove that she wrote her first novel, *Dolores* (1911), a turgid work, heavily influenced by George Eliot [q.v.]. Later she disowned it, claiming that much of it had been written by her brother Noel (born in 1887) who had to an important extent taken Guy's place in her life. Her next novel, *Pastors and Masters*, the first of those unmistakably her own, was not published until 1925.

Meanwhile, following her mother's painful and lingering death in 1911, she became head of what remained of her family. She ruled it with so little kindness or understanding that her sisters finally rebelled. Although they were very musical, they were forbidden to play the piano as it got on Ivy's nerves. In 1915 the family home was finally broken up, the sisters refusing to allow Ivy even to share the new London home into which they moved with (Dame) Myra Hess [q.v.]. In 1916 Noel was killed on the western front and his young wife tried to commit suicide. In December 1917 the two youngest Compton-Burnett sisters were found in their locked bedroom, dead from overdoses of veronal. In 1918 Ivy herself nearly died in the influenza epidemic. In 1919, however, Ivy invited the writer and art historian, Margaret Jourdain, to share her flat, and the two friends lived together until Miss Jourdain's death in 1951. About the same time Ivy began to write again. From 1929

I. Compton-Burnett produced a new novel nearly every two years.

Ivy once said 'I do not feel that I have any real or organic knowledge of life later than about 1910' and almost all her books are set before that date. They concern large upper-class families who live in the country, and who struggle ferociously for power amongst themselves. The twenty novels (apart from *Dolores*) have very similar titles, for instance, *Brothers and Sisters* (1929), *Daughters and Sons* (1937), *Parents and Children* (1941), and *Mother and Son* (1955) which was awarded the James Tait Black memorial prize. They are also all written in a markedly individual style. Each character is given a brief description on first appearance, and the action, often melodramatic, is passed over in a few rapid sentences. The heart of the books is the conversation, epigrammatic, stylized, witty, and brilliantly revealing of character and motive. Servants and children, although beautifully individualized, speak in the same formal style as their masters and parents. The novels require concentration until the reader is familiar with the style: after that, they are wonderfully rewarding. Immensely funny, they are also profound studies of family life. For many years they were admired only by a small circle, but they came to be widely read and enjoyed. Comparisons have been made with Jane Austen, Oscar Wilde, and Henry James [qq.v.] but they are unhelpful. The novels are genuinely original.

She was appointed CBE in 1951, DBE in 1967, and C.Lit. in 1968, and received the honorary D.Litt. of Leeds in 1960. She died unmarried in London 27 August 1969.

[Hilary Spurling, *Ivy When Young*, 1974; Elizabeth Sprigge, *The Life of Ivy Compton-Burnett*, 1973; Robert Liddell, *The Novels of I. Compton-Burnett*, 1955; Charles Burkhart, *I. Compton-Burnett*, 1965; personal knowledge.]

JULIAN MITCHELL

CONNOR, SIR WILLIAM NEIL (1909–1967), journalist, was born in London 26 April 1909, a twin son of William Henry Connor, a Protestant Ulsterman and Admiralty clerk, and his wife, Isobella Littlejohn, a telegraphist, from Aberdeenshire. Connor went to a primary Board-school, then to a local private school, and finally to Glendale Grammar School in Wood Green. He left at sixteen, attended a crammers in the hope of getting into the navy, only to be rejected because his eyesight was not good enough. He then did one or two clerical jobs which did not appear to be leading him anywhere until he became book-keeper at Arks Publicity, a small firm which helped to nourish the talent of (Sir) Alec Guinness the actor and Phil Zec the cartoonist. There Connor found himself writing odd bits of advertising copy and discovered that he had some gift for the pen.

At the age of twenty-three he got a job as a copywriter with a leading advertising agency, J. Walter Thompson, where he met Basil Nicholson, inventor of the remarkable concept of 'night starvation' and the strip-cartoon used to advertise the particular milky beverage which would relieve it. Connor and Zec then collaborated with Nicholson on a general-knowledge strip plagiarizing Ripley's eternal 'Believe it or not?' series. All three eventually found their way to employment on the *Daily Mirror*.

At that time H. G. Bartholomew had begun to convert the *Mirror* from a respectful servants'-hall picture paper to a brash demagogic tabloid. (Sir) Hugh Cudlipp who was also to play a leading part in the revolution joined the paper on the same day as Connor in August 1935.

Bartholomew asked Connor to try his hand at a column. When the pen name 'Cassandra' was suggested, Connor looked it up, and he later wrote: 'I was a bit surprised to discover that I had changed my sex; was the daughter of the King of Troy; that I could foretell in the stars when the news was going to be bad; . . . and that I was going to come to a sticky end by being efficiently murdered by Clytaemnestra . . .'.

The column appeared two or three times a week as and when there was room. Connor soon showed a talent for robust invective and his column became what has been called 'the whipping post, stocks and ducking stool for jacks-in-office, muddling magistrates, indiscreet politicians and erring judges'. The column varied. It could contain hard-hitting political comment, attacks on government departments and individuals; lavish praise of individuals and dithyrambic essays on cats or on homely dishes such as cabbage and herring cooked in a particular way. Whatever it was, it was always Connor and it had a tremendous audience.

In Connor's denunciation of the wicked and praise of the virtuous, it was often possible to catch echoes of the Presbyterian pulpit beneath which Connor had regularly sat throughout his youth. About his religion he was publicly ambiguous although he was a deeply spiritual man and regularly read his Bible and Prayer Book. Arnold's 'Dover Beach' was never far from his thoughts.

The youthful Connor, a tall slender young man, was effaced by the later man, who was plump and red-faced, with thinning hair. It was remarked that he belonged to a Bohemian race of journalists which had almost disappeared, a generation which read prodigiously, drank heartily, and argued endless hours away at the bar counter. Connor at this period did not suffer fools gladly either in his column or in his personal encounters. He participated in a brief revival in London of a fashion for contrived rudeness as an antidote to the smoothness and alleged effeteness of the Establishment. It was all pose. Connor was basically a kindly man as his colleagues with troubles found out.

Cassandra was an early critic of Nazism and was convinced that Hitler meant war. But when war came he and the *Mirror* aroused Churchill's anger. In a letter to Cecil King, already a director of the *Mirror*, the prime minister complained of the work of a writer 'dominated by malevolence'. Cassandra had in fact described a government reshuffle as a game of musical chairs 'being played to a funeral march . . . Ours'. King replied that Cassandra was not malevolent but was known as 'a hard hitting journalist with a vitriolic style'. Throwing vitriol, Churchill observed, was one of the worst of crimes.

Churchill expressed an opinion that the *Mirror* papers generally were written in a spirit of hatred and malice against the 'national' Government. Then Zec did a cartoon showing a torpedoed sailor, his face blackened with oil, lying on a raft in an empty ocean. The draft caption had been 'Petrol is dearer now'. Connor said it could be better dramatized by bringing in the penny rise. The caption as printed was: 'The price of petrol has been raised by a penny (Official).'

This aroused more wrath. The *Mirror* argued that the object of the cartoon was to show that petrol cost lives as well as money and should not be wasted. The Government's interpretation was that it suggested the sailor's life had been put at risk to raise the profits of the oil companies. There was a serious threat from Herbert Morrison (later Lord Morrison of Lambeth, q.v.) to close the *Mirror* down, even an investigation of its ownership. The paper weathered the storm but tempered its criticism.

On 27 March 1942 Connor wrote: 'This is the last wartime column you will read by Cassandra . . . I campaigned for Churchill and my support was early and violent. But since he came to power I have distrusted many of his lieutenants—and I have said so with scant respect for either their position or their feelings . . . [The Government] . . . are far too glib with the shameful rejoinder that those who do not agree with them are subversive— and even traitors. . . . I cannot and will not change my policy . . .'

Connor concluded grandiloquently: 'I propose to see whether the rifle is a better weapon than the printed word. Mr. Morrison can have my pen—but not my conscience. Mr. Morrison can have my silence—but not my self-respect.' Connor then joined the army. He spent a good deal of the war with Cudlipp in Italy producing the forces paper *Union Jack*, in spirit not unlike a miniature *Daily Mirror*.

On his return to the *Mirror* in September 1946 Connor's journalism became deeper and more mature. He drove himself hard, travelled widely, went regularly to the United States, and covered in his highly personal style some historic events: the trials of Eichmann, General Salan, and Jack Ruby who shot Kennedy's assassin; the enthronement of Pope John, Churchill's funeral, the Korean war. He interviewed, amongst many others, President Kennedy, Senator McCarthy, Billy Graham, Charles Chaplin, Adlai Stevenson, Ben-Gurion, Archbishop Makarios, and Marilyn Monroe. Of course the writing had to have more splashes of melodrama and sentiment than the fastidious writer of later years would have wished. But that was the limitation of popular journalism. He only once ran into serious trouble, when he was successfully sued for libel by Liberace in 1959.

In his last years Connor, who had developed diabetes, suffered much ill health. His knighthood in 1966, an inspiration of (Sir) Harold Wilson, gave him and all his friends great delight; and he enjoyed the irony of its bestowal on a lifelong professional critic of the Establishment.

In 1936 Connor married Gwynfil Mair Morgan; they had two sons and one daughter. He died in London 6 April 1967.

[*The Times*, 7 April 1967; Robert Connor, *Cassandra: Reflections in a Mirror*, 1969; *Daily Mirror* library; personal knowledge.]

JOHN BEAVAN

CONSTANT, HAYNE (1904-1968), mechanical and aeronautical engineer, was born at Gravesend, Kent, 26 September 1904, the second son of the family of six children of Frederick Charles Constant, dental surgeon, of Gravesend and later Folkestone, and his wife, (Mary) Theresa Hayne, of Northfleet, Kent. At the age of eleven he went to King's College Choir School, Cambridge, and then to King's School, Canterbury, the Technical Institute in Folkestone, and Sir Roger Manwood's School in Sandwich. In the higher school certificate examination he obtained distinctions in mathematics and physics and was awarded a state scholarship. He entered Queens' College, Cambridge, in 1924 as an open exhibitioner where he took a second class in part i of the mathematical tripos (1925) followed by a first class in the mechanical sciences tripos (1927). He was awarded a college scholarship. After taking his degree in 1927 Constant stayed in Cambridge for a postgraduate year to work on the torsional vibration of crankshafts which he reported in his first publication. For the next six years he was a member of the engine department of the Royal Aircraft Establishment, Farnborough, working on carburettors, dynamometers, torsional vibration, and on the modes of vibration of aircraft when forced by engine dynamics. A paper to the Royal Aeronautical Society describing and analysing tests on a biplane suspended upside down and vibrated by rotating masses mounted on the aircraft won him the Busk memorial prize in 1932.

From 1934 to 1936 he held the post of lecturer at Imperial College, but found it not to his liking and returned to RAE where, in July 1936, he was put in charge of the Supercharger Section under Dr A. A. Griffith [q.v.], who was then head of the Engine Department. Constant attributed his return to RAE partly to a discussion with (Sir) Henry T. Tizard [q.v.], who suggested that the gas turbine had a great future in aircraft propulsion. He was also influenced by Griffith's ideas, put forward in 1928, on axial flow compressors and gas turbine engines for driving propellers. After a few months, in March 1937 Constant presented a case to the Aeronautical Research Council for the development of the aircraft gas turbine engine. Working almost alone he had designed a small axial flow compressor and various gas turbine engine schemes which were described in his report. The report was well received and authority was given to start a programme, mainly in collaboration with Metropolitan-Vickers, for the development of gas turbine engines. This work resulted in the design, building, and testing of some six axial flow compressors and several parts of gas turbine engines.

Meanwhile a prototype of (Air Commodore Sir) Frank Whittle's turbojet engine made by Power Jets Ltd. was tested in 1937 and from then on its further development was supported by the Air Ministry. Constant's programme at the RAE had initially favoured the development of a gas turbine engine for driving a propeller or a ducted fan and saw the Whittle scheme as applicable only to short-range high-altitude fighter aircraft. But with the outbreak of war in 1939 Constant suggested to Power Jets that a jet engine with the flow passing straight through an axial compressor, an annular combustion chamber, and axial flow turbine should be jointly developed. In the

event Constant's scheme was developed and built by Messrs Metropolitan-Vickers. It was flight-tested in 1943 and became the prototype of the modern jet engine. It was Constant's most important individual contribution to aircraft propulsion. His other contributions ranged from his rule for determining the flow angle leaving a cascade of compressor blades, the specification and layout of other axial flow jet engines, and his leadership of the research and development programme which continued at RAE after he became head of the Engine Department in 1941, and then later at Pyestock after the end of the war.

Apart from the problems of combustion, compressor design, materials, and thermal expansion, the problem of starting an axial compressor loomed so large that, just before the war, RAE bought a large-scale Brown Boveri gas turbine for starting tests. Accounts of much of this important research and development work were given to the Institution of Mechanical Engineers after the war by Constant and his team in 1945, 1948, and 1950.

From 1941 the team in the Turbine Division of the RAE Engine Department grew in numbers and facilities, but in 1944, much to Constant's dismay, the Turbine Division of the Engine Department was transferred from RAE to merge with Air Commodore Sir Frank Whittle's organization, Power Jets Ltd., into a nationalized company: Power Jets (Research and Development) Ltd. Two years later this became the National Gas Turbine Establishment based at Pyestock with Constant as deputy director. After another two years he succeeded Harold Roxbee Cox (later Lord Kings Norton) as director and further built up the facilities and activities to make the Establishment the foremost centre for gas turbine testing and research in the world. In 1948 Constant was made a fellow of the Royal Society and won the James Clayton prize of the Institution of Mechanical Engineers. In 1951 he was appointed CBE and in 1958 CB. In 1963 he was awarded the gold medal of the Royal Aeronautical Society. He published twenty-three papers, ten patent specifications, and an unpretentious book, Gas Turbines and their Problems, which appeared in 1948 and was revised and enlarged in 1953.

In 1960 Constant reluctantly left Pyestock to become scientific adviser to the Air Ministry and then chief scientist (RAF), Ministry of Defence (1964). His friends thought he was not very happy in the Whitehall atmosphere with its discussions and debates about weapons, resources, and budgets and that he obviously would have preferred to remain in research and inventive activities.

Constant was a man of austere habit and

thought with a self-contained reserve, but with a keen mind delighting in logical argument about technical matters. He would question the facts and objectives, almost arrogantly, behind any proposed design or development and would sharpen each point of decision by arguments based on facts and fundamental physical principles. This approach, which only acknowledged the thought processes behind most engineering decisions when they could be made explicit, did not always endear him to his superiors, but greatly encouraged the younger engineers on his staff. In committee his speech was precise and economical. He was not only concerned about the professional development and rewards of his staff, but also their housing and sports. He was unmarried and his relaxations included tennis, ski-ing, amateur dramatics, motor cycles, sailing and boat building, listening to records of some American musicals, and, finally, building his unique bachelor's house. It was typical of him to tackle each of them with zest and enjoy them with others and then to proceed to the next interest. He retired in 1962 to live in the bungalow of his own design in Hindhead, Surrey, where he died 12 January 1968.

[Sir William Hawthorne, H. Cohen, and A. R. Howell in *Biographical Memoirs of Fellows of the Royal Society*, vol. xix, 1973; Sir Frank Whittle, *Jet, The Story of a Pioneer*, 1953; W. R. Hawthorne, 'Aircraft Propulsion from the Back Room' in *Journal of the Royal Aeronautical Society*, March 1978; private information; personal knowledge.]

W. R. Hawthorne

COOPER, CHARLOTTE (1870–1966), lawn tennis champion. [See STERRY.]

CORK AND ORRERY, twelfth EARL OF (1873–1967), admiral of the fleet. [See BOYLE, WILLIAM HENRY DUDLEY.]

COSGRAVE, WILLIAM THOMAS (1880–1965), first president of the Executive Council of the Irish Free State, was born in Dublin 5 June 1880, the second son and second child of Thomas Cosgrave, licensed vintner, of 174 James St., Dublin, and his wife, Bridget Nixon. After schooling with the Christian Brothers, he entered his father's business, soon turning also to share his father's interest in local politics.

In 1905 he participated with Arthur Griffith [q.v.] in the founding of Sinn Fein and in 1909 was elected a Sinn Fein representative to Dublin Corporation. He served this body for thirteen years, being elected chairman of its estates and finance committee in 1915, and being returned as an alderman in 1920. In 1916, as a lieutenant in the Irish Volunteers, he fought under Eamon Ceannt in the South Dublin Union, was captured and condemned to death, a sentence later commuted to life imprisonment. After one year in Portland prison he was released in the general amnesty of 1917.

Cosgrave entered national politics as a Sinn Fein abstentionist, winning a two-to-one victory over the Parliamentary Party candidate, John Magennis, in the Kilkenny City by-election of August 1917. In October 1917 he became one of the honorary treasurers of Sinn Fein, and in December 1918 was returned unopposed in the general election, for Kilkenny North. At the meeting of the first Dáil Eireann on 2 April 1919 he was appointed minister for local government. In the subsequent elections of 1921, 1922, 1923, and June 1927 he represented the Carlow-Kilkenny constituency. In the election for the sixth Dáil, in September 1927, he was returned for both Carlow-Kilkenny and Cork Borough, topping the poll in each. He chose to sit for the Cork seat and in the elections of February 1932, January 1933, July 1937, June 1938, and June 1943 he topped the poll there on all occasions except 1938. He retired from Dáil Eireann in 1944.

After his important management of a Local Government Ministry which did much to disrupt British administration in Ireland in 1919–21, Cosgrave was thrust to greater prominence upon the acceptance of the Anglo-Irish treaty of December 1921. A determined advocate of this agreement, which he felt represented the best settlement available, he accepted membership of the Provisional Government, established to receive power from Britain, in January 1922, becoming its chairman in August after the death of Griffith and Michael Collins, both of whose notices he contributed to this Dictionary. He added the office of president of Dáil Eireann in September 1922, finally becoming the first elected president of the Executive Council of the Irish Free State 6 December 1922. He held also the Ministry of Finance, 1922–3, and for a short time the Ministry of Defence, in 1924, and the Ministry of External Affairs, in 1927. Having steered the country through civil war during 1922–3, it was his responsibility to establish the domestic administration and the international reputation of his country, which had assumed a somewhat ambiguous 'dominion status' by the 1921 treaty.

Under his wise chairmanship, an able Cabinet team established full parliamentary, legal, and administrative processes on a foundation of probity and wide acceptance. Orthodox financial management and cautious economic development secured an equally sound reputation for integrity in these spheres. The Government's main economic initiative, the harnessing of the River Shannon to generate electricity, also proved a resounding success, while the body established to control it, the Electricity Supply Board (established in 1927), set a pattern of semi-state authorities widely emulated in the future. The failure of the Boundary Commission to advance Irish unity provided both crisis and disappointment for the Government in 1925, but the ensuing agreement with Britain in December of that year was, Cosgrave felt, 'a damned good bargain'. His subsequent policy of co-operation with Belfast and of promoting Irish unity through the attraction of good government set a realistic course all too soon interrupted.

Surviving other crises such as the army mutiny in 1924 and the assassination of his vice-president, Kevin O'Higgins [q.v.], in 1927, Cosgrave enjoyed a personal triumph when he visited the United States and Canada in 1928. Already he had led his country into the League of Nations, in 1923, while at successive Imperial Conferences, notably 1926 and 1930, his ministers helped expand 'dominion status' into full sovereignty, a position given legal force in the 1931 Statute of Westminster.

With the state firmly founded at home and abroad, and successfully weathering the world depression, Cosgrave suffered defeat in February 1932, but watched with satisfaction the ensuing peaceful change from his administration to that of Eamon de Valera. Apart from a period of political confusion in 1933-4, he spearheaded parliamentary opposition as leader of Fine Gael (established in 1933) until his retirement in January 1944. His interest in horse-racing was then reflected in his chairmanship of the Irish Racing Board, 1946-56, and again from 1957. He died at his home in Dublin 16 November 1965.

In 1919 Cosgrave married Louise (died 1959), daughter of Alderman Flanagan, a farmer of Dublin. Of their two sons, Liam and Michael, the former became leader of Fine Gael in 1965, and subsequently prime minister of a Coalition Government in 1973.

Cosgrave received a number of honours during his lifetime, becoming a Knight Grand Cross, 1st class, of the Pian Order, in 1925, and gaining honorary doctorates from the Catholic University of Washington; Columbia, Cambridge, and Dublin universities; and the National University of Ireland.

Regarded by Sir Winston Churchill as 'a chief of higher quality than any who had yet appeared', Cosgrave was throughout his life an unpretentious and modest man. Short in stature, with a shock of hair he retained into old age, he had a lively eye and a ready wit, with gifts of common sense, courage and coolness, good humour and humanity, which won the respect and affection of opponents as well as supporters. A deeply religious man, courteous and considerate and a reconciler, he proved more successful in office than as an Opposition leader, his greatest work being done in the decade 1922-32. The parliamentary democracy then established against daunting odds remains his most fitting monument.

Portraits of Cosgrave were painted by Sir John Lavery (Municipal Gallery of Modern Art, Dublin) and Leo Whelan. There is also a charcoal drawing by Sean O'Sullivan in the National Gallery of Ireland, Dublin).

[The *Irish Times*, and *The Times*, 17 November 1965; personal knowledge.]

D. W. HARKNESS

COSTAIN, SIR RICHARD RYLANDES (1902-1966), industrialist and builder, was born in Crosby, Liverpool, 20 November 1902, the elder son of William Percy Costain, builder, and his wife, Maud May Smith. W. P. Costain was one of the five sons of Richard Costain (1839-1902), a Manxman who had founded and developed a small but well-equipped and successful building and contracting business in Crosby, into which he took three of his sons.

Costain was sent first to Merchant Taylors at Crosby, then to Rydal School at Colwyn Bay. By the time he left school in 1920 the family firm, Richard Costain & Sons, had grown to considerable stature on Merseyside. It had built many thousands of houses for sale, artisans' flats for Liverpool Corporation, houses and cottages for steelworks and other industries; army camps, munitions factories, churches, theatres, and college extensions. Costain automatically entered the family firm, first learning the trades of the joiner and the bricklayer. He took also a short architectural course in Rome. In 1922 W. P. Costain decided on a move to London, leaving his brothers to continue with the activities in Liverpool, so it was in London that Richard Costain cut his teeth as a builder, notably by working on the firm's large venture on the Kingswood housing estate in Surrey.

By 1927 he was made joint managing director, and on the death of his father in 1929 'R. R.' as he was then widely known, became sole managing director. Speculative house-building was at that period the firm's main activity, some 10,000 houses being built on eight estates. The London end of the business was floated as a public company in 1933.

This marked a policy change, the company determining to be less dependent on house-building, and many building contracts were won for important public and industrial buildings and for blocks of flats. In 1934 important civil engineering contracts were won for the first time for sewage disposal works, and in 1935 for a variety of works in Persia.

A unique opportunity occurred in 1935 when proposals were made to build a huge block of flats, known as Dolphin Square, on the Embankment on the site of the former army clothing depot. 'R. R.' took a personal decision in a matter of hours to seize the opportunity of purchasing this site and constructing what was not only the biggest block of flats in Europe, but was the pioneer as a self-contained city community with its own shops and social amenities. He remarked to a colleague 'In two or three years we'll either drive up to this spot in a Rolls-Royce, or we'll be standing here selling matches'.

Not only was this decision a demonstration of the spontaneity and courage of 'R. R.', but also of the reputation and liking he had earned, for he was able in a few hours to gather the financial backing which this undertaking involved. His ability to size up a project was matched by his quick assessment of men. He was an inspired picker of staff, and a natural leader. He was short but sturdy in stature, with a forthright manner and a ready smile. He was good company, especially on the golf course, where he was an exceptional club golfer who twice reached the second round of the amateur championship; and at the bridge table, where he was brilliant.

On the outbreak of war in 1939 Costain offered his services to the Government and was appointed deputy director of emergency works, later deputy director of works, in the Ministry of Works.

After the war, when he was appointed CBE (1946), he returned to his company, which had become thoroughly experienced and well-equipped contractors, as chairman. Seeing clearly the national need to earn foreign exchange, he set himself the objective of obtaining a half of the company turnover abroad. Indeed it was no longer possible to speak of 'the company' for with the launching or absorption of specialist activities, association with other companies in joint ventures, and the formation of subsidiaries and branches in many countries, it became the Costain Group.

Among many domestic contracts in the early post-war years, Costain's built the Festival of Britain, and was involved in very large building and civil engineering works in many different countries. Chairman 'Dick', as he became affectionately known throughout the company, did not hesitate in 1950 to replace the centralized control which had been characteristic of a family business by a system of operating divisions, which led progressively to the structure of something like eighty autonomous companies of which the Costain Group came to be comprised.

However, Costain did not keep himself exclusively to company affairs. In 1950 he was elected president of the London Master Builders' Association, and in the same year the Government appointed him chairman of Harlow Development Corporation. This was the piece of public work which gave him the greatest satisfaction, and he devoted great efforts to seeing that the town was a well-balanced community. His work there was rewarded in 1954 by a knighthood.

From 1955 to 1957 Costain was president of the Export Group for the Construction Industries. Both for this group, and for his own company, he travelled extensively, for he believed in personal knowledge of his customer as well as his staff, and travel was necessitated also by the forming of international consortia for specialist construction work in many countries. He took a particular interest and pleasure in Southern Rhodesia, where his contract for the construction of the Kariba Dam township frequently took him.

In 1927 Costain married Gertrude, daughter of William John Minto, by whom he had one son and two daughters. He died at his home in Farnham, Surrey, 26 March 1966. A portrait in oils by Maurice Codner hangs in the chairman's suite at 111 Westminster Bridge Road, London, SE 1.

[Private information; *Bulletin*, Staff Journal of the Costain Group, centenary number, June 1965; personal knowledge.]

NORMAN KIPPING

COTTON, JACK (1903-1964), property developer, was born in Birmingham, 1 January 1903, the third son of Benjamin Marcus Cotton who had founded a flourishing export business, mainly with South Africa, and his wife, Caroline Josephine Rudelsheim. Jack Cotton was educated first at the King Edward VI Grammar School, then at Cheltenham College, which he left at the age of eighteen to become an articled clerk in a firm of estate agents and surveyors. In 1924, on his twenty-first birthday, he set up his own firm in Birmingham. From then on he was to become the dominant figure in the world of property development, and the man whose methods of operation provided a model for others involved in the property boom in the years following the war of 1939-45.

Cotton learnt about the business when acting as an agent; but he was dealing on his own account by the thirties, buying farmland which he then sold to speculative builders of housing estates. These operations turned over rapidly, and were financed by bank loans and loans from private backers. In 1932 Cotton began the first of his purely urban developments, starting with blocks of flats and moving on to commercial property. His first major development was in 1937, when he built King Edward House on the site of the King Edward VI School in New Street, his old school, and which was rebuilt in Edgbaston close to the university of Birmingham. The finance for this development was provided by a public institution, as well as by private backers. This venture was followed by the redevelopment of the site of the Midland Conservative Club in a transaction which allowed the club to occupy the top floors of the new building at a peppercorn rent. Other office blocks in the centre of Birmingham followed.

During the war, when Cotton was employed by the Government in building shadow-factories, he realized how insatiable the demand would be for new building once the fighting stopped. He then went to live in London, and as a base for his operations bought an old but small property company called Mansion House Chambers Ltd., which he then absorbed into another existing company called Chesham House (Regent Street) Ltd., the name of which was changed in 1955 to City Centre Properties. Each of these changes was associated with an extension of the business.

Finance was the only constraint on Cotton's operations. Beginning with the banks and private backers, he soon conceived of the idea of giving the big institutions or the companies which owned the land he wanted to develop a share in the development in return for their financial support. In this way the Pearl and the Legal and General Insurance Companies became partners in his ventures, as did Barclays Bank in his overseas operations. In 1960 City Centre Properties merged with two other big property companies, 'City and Central' and 'Murrayfield', to create the biggest property company in the world.

The most important of Cotton's developments were the Big Top three and a half acre site in Birmingham, the Notting Hill complex in London, and the Pan Am building over the Grand Central station in New York City, a development in which he was associated with an American developer. The biggest of Cotton's disappointments was the obstruction of his plans to develop the Piccadilly area in London in 1960. In order to meet the critics of his designs, Cotton then called in first one and then another of the world's most distinguished architects. None of his later plans was approved, nor were several others put forward in the ten years following his death.

Shortly after the final mergers of 1960, City Centre Properties started to break up, partly as a result of internal dissensions and partly because of Cotton's ill health. After his death, the company which had been developed with such brilliance was sold to, and absorbed in, another vast property business.

A few months before his death early in 1964, Cotton divested himself of all his interests in his company. His meteoric career may have closed sadly, but during its course he had added a new dimension to the business of development and building. Until the last six years of his life he was almost an unknown character, having preferred not to be a director of the companies of which he was the main shareholder and driving force. But even if he was almost unknown to the press before his final years, he was none the less widely known in the business world where he was recognized as a man whose word was his bond, and as a man of decisive and quick action.

Cotton was a highly respected member of the Jewish community in Birmingham, of whose main synagogue he had been vice-president and treasurer, following his father and grandfather, who was president. He was also a generous contributor to charities. His name is commemorated in the Cotton Terraces of the Zoological Gardens in Regent's Park, to whose redevelopment after the war he contributed greatly. He also founded a chair of architecture and fine arts at the Hebrew University of Jerusalem and chairs of biochemistry at the Royal College of Surgeons and the Weizmann Institute in Israel.

In 1928 Cotton married Marjorie Rachel, daughter of Moss Mindelsohn, company director; they had three sons and one daughter. He died at Nassau 21 March 1964. The National Portrait Gallery has working drawings of him by Sir David Low.

[Private information; personal knowledge.]
ZUCKERMAN

COURT BROWN, WILLIAM MICHAEL (1918–1968), medical research worker. [See BROWN.]

COX, LESLIE REGINALD (1897–1965), palaeontologist, was born 22 November 1897 in Islington, North London, the son of Walter Cox and his wife, Jessie Lucy Witte, both from Dorset. Walter Cox was employed in the Post Office telephone engineers' department and there he met his wife. Leslie Cox was educated at Owen's School, Islington, where he had a quite remarkable scholastic record and showed an agreeable proficiency at games. In

1916 he won an open scholarship to Queens' College, Cambridge, but his war service began that August. He joined the Royal Naval Air Service in the Experimental Section, and two years later, when he was in charge of flame-throwing apparatus on *Iris II*, took part in the memorable attempt to block the German submarine base at Zeebrugge. But, as he related on the only occasion on which the writer ever heard him refer to his war experiences in an acquaintanceship of more than forty years, the flame-thrower was put out of action long before getting within range of the mole; but what he did not mention was that he himself was wounded in three places. Later he also took part in smoke-laying off Dunkirk.

On leaving the navy the following year (1919) Cox went up to Queen's College, Cambridge. He read chemistry, physics, and geology for part i of the natural sciences tripos, with geology as main subject in part ii, and obtained a first class in both parts (1920 and 1921) and also a college prize. He later took his Cambridge Sc.D. in 1937.

Like other geologists, Cox had been attracted to the subject by studying the cliffs of Dorset during numerous holidays spent at Charmouth; he had made a considerable collection from the readily accessible and highly productive strata there. In his final year at Cambridge he applied for a vacant post in the department of geology (now palaeontology) in the British Museum (Natural History) at South Kensington, and in 1922 he was appointed an assistant keeper (second class) and put in charge of all the fossil Mollusca except the ammonites. Thus without previous experience he was required to curate two of the largest groups of macro-fossils with by far the most considerable annual intake—the Gastropoda and the Bivalvia (Lamellibranchia). He was therefore responsible for virtually all the 'sea-shells', snails, and mussels throughout geological time—groups, moreover, which were not generally esteemed for philosophical content nor for evolutionary interest.

However, from the very start of his career at the Museum Cox always had in mind the work and methods of certain specialists on other groups of fossils, particularly the erratic genius of S. S. Buckman and the more sober L. F. Spath, whose studies on the long-extinct ammonites had shown that these remarkable molluscs were invaluable for dating and so correlating strata over wide distances by reason of their rapid evolution, even at generic level, and relative mobility, being free-swimming. But the molluscs with which Cox had to deal had no such distinctive characteristics, being slow to show distinctive changes and generally sedentary in habit. Furthermore, their usually small size and often poor state of preservation made them anything but easy material for study.

In spite of these apparent drawbacks, Cox, who had an excellent memory and an enviable capacity for work even of the least stimulating kind, quietly set himself to acquire a sound working knowledge of the huge collections already in the Museum, which even then may well have numbered over a million specimens, and to come to terms with the correspondingly extensive literature, making in the process detailed card indexes of 'staggering size' and permanent usefulness. At the same time he seems to have kept pace with the ceaseless flow of specimens, information, and queries from all over the world.

Cox's chief interest was in the Mesozoic and Tertiary faunas, on which he wrote a number of important papers, chiefly on faunas from British and Continental localities; but he also did much valuable work on more distant regions, particularly for the Geological Surveys of the former colonies. His coverage and his influence was indeed world-wide.

Latterly he had been much involved in the great *Treatise on Invertebrate Palaeontology*, published by the Geological Society of America, in which he played a significant part, not only in the contribution of those sections where he was the accepted authority but in the influence which he had on the supra-generic classifications. He was also the general editor of the volume on the gastropods (1960).

Apart from his scientific publications (his bibliography runs to some 160 titles of which more than half refer to substantial works), Cox wrote an important memoir on William Smith (1769-1835, q.v.), 'the father of English geology', whom Cox held in great esteem, and the discovery of an important unedited collection of manuscripts in the University Museum at Oxford gave Cox the opportunity to pay a lasting tribute to a man whose work he had so long admired ('New light on William Smith and his work', *Proc. Yorks. Geol. Soc.*, vol. xxv, 1942, pp. 1-99). Cox also contributed the notices of Henry Woods and W. J. Arkell to this Dictionary.

Cox was essentially a quiet man, who minded his own business and got on with it: he was indeed a tireless worker. Although he never gave advice unasked for, if approached, he was generous with his help, both verbal and practical. A man of simple integrity, he knew neither malice nor envy, and had a neat sense of humour.

Cox travelled extensively in England to study and collect from Mesozoic strata in particular, often with his wife, who had been a keen amateur geologist, and he knew many of the classical localities on the Continent; but he went further afield only once—to Mexico to attend the International Geological Congress in 1956.

Although so heavily engaged with his work at the Museum, Cox nevertheless played a full part in the affairs of the rather numerous societies concerned with his special interests, serving on the councils and in special capacities in all of them: the Geological Society of London (vice-president 1952-4; awarded Lyell medal 1956); the Palaeontographical Society (vice-president 1957 onwards); the Geologists' Association (president 1954-6); the Palaeontological Association (president 1964-5); the Malacological Society (treasurer 1926-51; president 1957-60). Cox was elected FRS in 1950 and was honoured by the membership of a number of foreign institutions. He was appointed OBE in 1958.

In 1925 Cox married Hilda Cecilia, ARCA, daughter of the Revd William John Lewis, of Mountsorrel, Leicestershire, and they had a son and a daughter, both of whom read geology at Cambridge, and another daughter who died in infancy. Cox died suddenly at his home in Hendon 5 August 1965.

[Andrew Rothstein, E. I. White, and C. P. Nuttall in *Biographical Memoirs of Fellows of the Royal Society*, vol. xii, 1966; personal knowledge.]   E. I. WHITE

CRAIG, (EDWARD HENRY) GORDON (1872-1966), artist and stage designer, was born 16 January 1872 at Stevenage, the only son and second child of Edward William Godwin, architect, and (Dame) (Alice) Ellen Terry, actress [qq.v.]. His parents were unmarried; Ellen Terry had been separated but not divorced from her first husband, the artist George Frederic Watts [q.v.]. Godwin left her in 1875; free by then from Watts, she married an actor, Charles Clavering Wardell, whose stage name was Charles Kelly, from whom she was judicially separated in 1881.

'Teddy' and his sister Edith were brought up by their mother who in 1878 became (Sir) Henry Irving's [q.v.] leading lady at the Lyceum Theatre, London. The boy, known first as Edward Wardell, entered a preparatory school near Tunbridge Wells in 1883; just before his thirteenth birthday (1885), and during a Christmas holiday with his mother, then touring in the United States, he acted at Chicago the small part of a gardener's boy in Irving's production of *Eugene Aram*. At fourteen he went to Bradfield College, and later to a school at Heidelberg from which in 1888 he was expelled for breaches of discipline: Irving ('as kind as a father', said Craig) engaged the tall, good-looking youth for the Lyceum where he played Arthur in *The Dead Heart* (28 September 1889) and remained, off and on,

until 1896. He adopted Craig as a stage name, afterwards legalized by deed poll. Christened when he was sixteen, 'Teddy' had received the additional names of Henry and Gordon from his godfather and godmother, Henry Irving and Lady Gordon. He chose Craig from the island named Ailsa Craig.

Besides minor work at the Lyceum he made various summer repertory tours where he could play such leading parts as Hamlet (1894) and Macbeth. In 1893 he married an actress, May, daughter of Robert Gibson, of St. Albans. Ellen Terry said of him as an actor: 'I have never known anyone with so much natural gift.' Some of his later antagonists would forget that, never simply an unattached theorist, he was bred to the stage.

Ceasing to act after 1897, he started a magazine, *The Page*, in which he published many of his earliest wood-engravings; though now he had four children—three sons and a daughter— he was on bad terms with his wife and conducting one of the many liaisons familiar throughout his career, relationships which frequently resulted in the birth of a child. Already, as actor and artist, he had radical views on the theatre. Encouraged by Martin Shaw, in 1900 he designed and directed at the Hampstead Conservatoire of Music Henry Purcell's [q.v.] *Dido and Aeneas*, for its time a startlingly original production in terms of light and colour, with an oblong stage opening and lit from above: a break with popular pictorial realism that foreshadowed later experiment as 'a supreme master of the theatre of the clouds' (H. Granville-Barker's [q.v.] phrase).

By 1902 he was in love with Elena Meo, a twenty-two-year-old violinist, daughter of Gaetano Meo, a Hampstead painter. That year, at the Great Queen Street Theatre, his production of Purcell's *Acis and Galatea* was 'an ever-shifting maze of colour, form, and motion'. Living now with Elena, he turned to other theatre work, particularly for his mother, newly in management (1903) at the Imperial in Tothill Street and preparing to do Henrik Ibsen's *The Vikings at Helgeland* and Shakespeare's *Much Ado About Nothing*.

An American critic, James Huneker, wrote of the first: 'Abolishing foot and border lights, sending shafts . . . from above, Mr Craig secures unexpected and bizarre effects.' The second, equally a commercial failure, contained a well-known scene in which Craig indicated the church by a widening, many-coloured light that streamed through an unseen stained-glass window to illuminate a huge crucifix. His fame had developed among artists but not with the established theatre; he left for Berlin and produced contentious designs of two scenes for *Venice Preserved* at the Lessing (1905). Thereafter he rarely returned to England for any sustained visit. His wife May had divorced him; Elena's first child had died but she had a second daughter and in 1905 gave birth to a son, Edward.

Craig began in 1905 his association with the extravagantly temperamental dancer Isadora Duncan. This was at the heart of a complex period, rich in his visionary ideas of a unified theatre experience under one master-mind. During the autumn of 1906 (shortly after Isadora had given birth to a daughter) he was contemplating his designs for Ibsen's *Rosmersholm*, staged by Eleonora Duse at the Teatro della Pergola in Florence: an extraordinary visual conception that the Italian designer, Enrico Corradini, described as 'a new architecture of great height, ranging in colour from green to blue . . .; it portrayed a *state of mind*'. Parting from Isadora in 1907, the unbiddable Craig settled for seven years in Florence; he brought over Elena (to whom he was never married) and the children, and began a theatre magazine, *The Mask*, which (except for a gap in World War I) lasted until 1929. European managers, even Sir Herbert Beerbohm Tree [q.v.], London's high priest of naturalism, were anxious for his work, but a proposed *Macbeth* for Tree got no further; in spite of Craig's imaginative mastery he could ignore simple practical problems and minimize the actor.

His most influential book, *On the Art of the Theatre*, which grew from an earlier one, appeared in 1911, about the time that he designed *Hamlet* for Constantin Stanislavsky at the Art Theatre, Moscow; this was a triumph, especially its first court scene with Claudius and Gertrude enthroned at the back of the stage in a glittering sea of gold, and Hamlet, a lonely black-clad figure, sitting far downstage, a silhouette under a great shadow. A school for the art of the theatre, founded by Craig in Florence, had to close when war came. Craig lived temporarily in Rome; there in 1917 Elena and the children joined him from England, and they went to live at Rapallo where steadily he wrote, drew, and engraved. *The Theatre Advancing* appeared in England during 1921; his etchings, *Scene*, in 1923; *Woodcuts, and Some Words*—(Sir Max Beerbohm's [q.v.] title—in 1924. For an elaborate final venture, the staging of Ibsen's *The Pretenders* in Copenhagen (1926), he received the Order of the Knights of Dannebrog in 1930, the year in which the designs were published by the Oxford University Press. In 1938 he was appointed RDI of the Royal College of Art.

After 1930 he concentrated on his books. The Cranach Press, Weimar, had published in 1929 *Hamlet*, with his superb woodcuts. He wrote an acutely detailed study of his idol, *Henry Irving* (1930), and in the following year one of his mother, *Ellen Terry and Her Secret Self*. Presently, still a handsome amorist, he left Elena and moved to Paris to live with his secretary and their daughter. Squalidly interned for a period during the German occupation, they were released and Craig continued his work. He travelled, alone, after the war, settling finally at Vence where he was living in 1957 at the publication of the only volume of his memoirs, *Index to the Story of My Days* (1872–1907). It contained an affectionate tribute to Elena. Just before Christmas 1957 she died suddenly in her English home, and her daughter Nelly went out to Vence to live with Craig.

Many devotees visited him during the last years of his self-exile. In 1958 he was made a Companion of Honour, and in 1964 became president of the Mermaid Theatre, London. He lived on, quietly but zestfully, remembering the high days of his youth, until two disastrous strokes, one in the winter of 1965 and a second in the ensuing summer. On 29 July 1966 he died at Vence aged ninety-four, having seen the best of his former revolutionary ideas pass into general theatre practice.

A wood-cut self-portrait is at the university of Hull, a drawing by Sir Max Beerbohm in the Victoria and Albert Museum, London, and a drawing by Sir William Rothenstein in the Manchester City Art Gallery.

[Edith Craig and Christopher St. John (eds.), *Ellen Terry's Memoirs*, 1933; Janet Leeper, *Edward Gordon Craig: Designs for the Theatre*, 1948; Edward Gordon Craig, *Index to the Story of My Days, 1872–1907*, 1957; Marguerite Steen, *A Pride of Terrys*, 1962; Denis Bablet, *Edward Gordon Craig*, Paris 1962, London 1966; Edward A. Craig, *Gordon Craig: The Story of His Life*, 1968; personal knowledge.] J. C. TREWIN

CREECH JONES, ARTHUR (1891–1964), politician. [See JONES, A. C.]

CREED, SIR THOMAS PERCIVAL (1897–1969), lawyer and educationist, was born in Leicester 29 January 1897, the third son in the family of five children of the Revd Colin John Creed, curate of St. Peter's, Leicester, and later rector of Farthinghoe, Northamptonshire, and his wife, Etheldreda Wright, daughter of Frederic Robert Spackman, MD, of Harpenden, Hertfordshire. He was educated at Wyggeston School, Leicester, joined the Artists' Rifles in 1915, and served in France with the Leicestershire Regiment, being twice wounded and winning the MC (1917).

After demobilization in 1919 he was awarded

a classical scholarship at Pembroke College, Oxford, taking third class honours in *literae humaniores* in 1922. He then entered the Sudan Political Service, and read for the bar while serving as assistant district commissioner in Berber Province (1923) and Darfur (1925). After being called to the bar (Lincoln's Inn) in 1925, in 1926 he was seconded to the legal department of the Sudan Government as district judge of the first grade and permanently transferred to this post in 1929. Two years later he was seconded to the Iraqi Government under the Anglo-Iraqi Judicial Agreement. There, after a short period as additional judge in Baghdad, he served as president of the courts in Kirkuk (1932) and Mosul (1934) before returning to the Sudan as a judge of the High Court, Khartoum, in 1935. He was appointed chief justice of the Sudan in 1936, and legal secretary, with a seat on the governor-general's council, in 1941. He was awarded the Order of the Nile, second class, in 1939, appointed CBE in 1943, and KBE in 1946. In 1947 he was chief representative of the Sudan Government at the hearing of the Anglo-Egyptian dispute by the Security Council at Lake Success.

Shortly before his retirement from the Sudan in 1948 he took silk, but preferred to seek a career in the world of education, like other members of his family. One of his brothers, John Martin Creed [q.v.] had been Ely professor of divinity at Cambridge, and another, (Richard) Stephen, a fellow of New College, Oxford. Their sister, Mary, was a lecturer at Aberystwyth College (university of Wales), and the fourth brother, Edward, a senior pathologist at King's College Hospital. Thomas Creed became secretary to King's College, London, in 1948, and principal of Queen Mary College in 1952, a post he was to hold for fifteen years. From 1964 to 1967 he was vice-chancellor of London University.

During this period he also served as chairman of the Medical Appeal Tribunal under the National Insurance (Industrial Injuries) Act, chairman of the committee of inquiry into the administration of the Forest of Dean (1955), chairman of the Burnham committee for the assessment of pay scales for teachers (1958-64), and chairman of Oxford House social settlement in Bethnal Green. He was made an honorary fellow of Pembroke in 1950, a freeman of the Drapers' Company (with which Queen Mary College had close ties) in 1963, an honorary LLD of Leicester in 1965, and an honorary bencher of Lincoln's Inn, a distinction which he prized especially highly, in 1967. He was also a member of the education committee of the Goldsmiths' Company.

The key to Creed's character lay in his unswerving integrity. As chief justice he could forgive an error of judgement but admit no excuse for careless or slipshod behaviour in a magistrate, however hard-worked he might be. As legal secretary he regarded himself as a watchdog for the Sudanese people, ensuring that their constitutional rights were not infringed and firmly refusing to agree to any project, however well-intentioned, for which no clear legal authority existed. As adviser to the governor-general, and as his representative from time to time in his absence, he would not tolerate evasion, or failure to clarify the true nature and purpose of every proposed act or policy. He would have disliked being a professional diplomat or a politician, and to the end of his life he was accustomed to use the correspondence columns of *The Times* to convey trenchant and uninhibited criticism of the policy of the British Government in Middle Eastern affairs.

His headship of Queen Mary's College happily coincided with a period of expansion of which he took full advantage, trebling the size of the student body and providing the college with a whole range of new buildings.

He resisted for some time pressure to let his name go forward for the vice-chancellorship, although he served as deputy vice-chancellor from 1958 to 1961, but his supporters finally convinced him, in 1963, that his leadership and wisdom were needed at a time when the future of London University had become a live issue. Creed firmly believed that the particular excellence of the university lay in the retention of its broadly based federal structure. He was one of those who feared that the threat of an independent commission of inquiry into the future of the university might lead to its premature dismemberment or to a regrouping which would result in a loss of the identity of some of its smaller institutions. The threat was not averted, but Creed's work, in close accord with the officers of the Senate House, did not go unrewarded, for the outcome of the independent inquiry left the federation intact.

As *The Times* said on his death, Creed 'seemed to embody everything that is excellent in the law . . . He was the embodiment of impartiality; he had a deep and abiding concern for the rights of individuals; yet he was determined that decisions, once taken, should be strictly and honourably carried out.' He seldom minced his words. His strictures were devastating, without respect of persons, but where he considered praise to be due, he bestowed it unstintingly. Recognition of this capacity, which is not so common, heightened for the recipient the value of both experiences.

In 1928 Creed married (Agnes) Margaret, elder daughter of Arthur Brewis, solicitor, of

St. Helens in Lancashire. They had one son (also in practice as a solicitor) and two daughters. Creed died at home in London 11 May 1969.

At Queen Mary College there is a portrait in oils by Peter Greenham (1967), which does not commend itself to his family or his friends.

[*The Times*, 13 May 1969; personal knowledge.]   K. D. D. HENDERSON

CREMER, ROBERT WYNDHAM KETTON- (1906-1969), biographer and historian. [See KETTON-CREMER.]

CROMPTON, RICHMAL (1890-1969), author. [See LAMBURN, RICHMAL CROMPTON.]

CROOKSHANK, HARRY FREDERICK COMFORT, VISCOUNT CROOKSHANK (1893-1961), politician, came of an old Ulster family and was born in Cairo 27 May 1893, the only son and elder child of Harry Maule Crookshank, physician and surgeon, inspector-general of Egyptian prisons, and his wife, Emma Walraven, daughter of Major Samuel Comfort, of New York. He was a King's scholar at Eton, was in the Newcastle select in 1911 and 1912 and edited the *Eton College Chronicle* in 1912. Although at Magdalen College, Oxford, he obtained only a second class in honour moderations in 1914, he might have secured higher honours in *literae humaniores* had his academic career not been cut short by the outbreak of war. He joined the Hampshire Regiment and in 1915 transferred to the Grenadier Guards (Special Reserve). He served with distinction both in France, with the regiment, and in Salonika. He was twice wounded, once very severely, and received the Order of the White Eagle and the Serbian gold medal for valour.

After the war he joined the Foreign Office with the rank of third, then second, secretary, served from 1921 in Constantinople, and in 1923 was appointed to Washington. In September 1924 he resigned and in October was elected to Parliament as Conservative member for Gainsborough, a seat which he held for thirty-two years. He was parliamentary under-secretary to the Home Office (1934-5), secretary for mines (1935-9), and financial secretary to the Treasury (1939-43). He was sworn of the Privy Council in 1939. He was postmaster-general from 1943 until the advent of the Labour Government in 1945. With the return of the Conservatives in 1951 he was appointed minister of health with a seat in the Cabinet and became leader of the House of Commons. In May 1952 he resigned from the Ministry of Health to become lord privy seal to enable him to devote more time to the leadership of the House in which he continued in Churchill's Government and for a time in Eden's. He was appointed CH in 1955, resigned towards the end of the year, and was created a viscount in January 1956.

To Crookshank '*pas trop de zèle*' would have been an unnecessary warning. His methods of conducting a controversy often concealed the more profound sources of his argument. He liked to pick upon some small points, perhaps of procedure, which at first glance appeared petty: he deployed them as Napoleon deployed his sharpshooters: to harass and throw the enemy a little bit off balance, rather than to inflict major casualties at the outset. Behind this screen were masked batteries and well-drilled battalions, planned to be the real and penetrating assault upon the enemy defences. Or, to change the image, he liked to point out a thread showing in the lapel of an opponent's coat, and to pull it out. It could then be seen that the thread ran up the lapel into the shoulder, the shoulder into the sleeve, and suddenly the whole garment began to look threadbare.

This method concealed from many, and particularly from Churchill, the logical power of his mind; and perhaps too it was the reason why his progress to the top was slow. He did not attain Cabinet rank until 1951. The wait no doubt distressed him and gave a disenchanted twist to his mind. He was not in sympathy with Chamberlain's foreign policy, and considered resigning at the time of Munich. That he did not do so was doubtless because the office which he held did not carry Cabinet responsibility. Nor, as a confirmed Tory, did he get on particularly well with the ex-Liberal Churchill, until one day in the House of Commons he tore the Labour Government apart by a speech of great dialectical skill, supported by a comprehensive knowledge of the facts. From his bent he was a master of the intricacies of parliamentary procedure, and could have edited Erskine May with the same facility with which he could have edited Horace. When he became leader of the House of Commons it was obvious that he filled the position and mastered its responsibilities to everyone's satisfaction, and perhaps even to his own exacting standards. Success banished his disappointment, and added sparkle and warmth to his personality. Brave in battle, uncomplaining in suffering, devoted to the public interest, formidable in debate, urbane in conversation, he might have risen even higher had chance made it necessary for him to earn his living in the market-place or to rub shoulders with more of those who were his intellectual inferiors. He was well off, even rich, and lived in Pont Street, with his mother until she died in 1954, in a house which was adorned in the Victorian mode and in which a shrine to Norman Shaw would have been more in harmony with its surroundings than one to Christopher Wren. His Rolls-Royce appeared quite in keeping. He was unlike the usual idea of a Guardsman: rather short in stature, and his head seemingly a little big for his body. His grievous wounds prevented him from living a full private life: he was a bachelor; and possibly because of his physical disabilities took no part in sport or games. His interests were not confined to politics: he was an active churchman and in 1956 became chairman of the Historic Churches Preservation Trust. He was no less assiduous in the service of his regiment and he was a keen freemason. A good charitable cause could always enlist his support and his money.

In 1958 he was appointed chairman of the Political Honours Scrutiny Committee. He became high steward of Westminster in 1960 and in the same year received an honorary DCL from Oxford. He died at his home in London 17 October 1961 when the title became extinct.

[*The Times*, 18, 20, and 25 October 1961; *Burke's Landed Gentry*; private information; personal knowledge.]   CHANDOS

CROSS, KENNETH MERVYN BASKER-VILLE (1890–1968), architect, was born in Hampstead, London, 8 December 1890, the eldest son of Alfred William Stephen Cross, architect, of London and Hastings, and his wife, Emily Thursfield. A. W. S. Cross was himself the son of an architect, Alfred Cross, of Greenwich. Kenneth Cross was educated at Felsted School (1902–9), where he captained the cricket XI. He then went up to Gonville and Caius College, Cambridge. He obtained a third class in both parts of the historical tripos (1911 and 1912) and studied at the university school of architecture, in the founding of which his father had played an important part. He completed his professional training in articles to his father, setting up in private practice in 1919, and becoming his father's partner in 1922.

In a wide-ranging general practice he acted as architect for a number of local authorities including Westminster City Council, Newcastle upon Tyne Council, and Bournemouth Council. He also carried out commissions for the Barbers' and Grocers' companies, the London Hospital, and Barclays Bank. By the late 1930s Cross had, like his father before him, earned a reputation as a specialist in the design and construction of swimming baths, and, with his father, had written a book on the subject: *Modern Public Baths and Wash-Houses* (1930),

of which a new edition appeared in 1938. He had previously revised his father's *Practical Notes for Architectural Draughtsmen*, series 2 and 3 (1922, 1923), a useful guide for the young, in whom he was always interested. In architecture he was a solid traditionalist with a good appreciation of modern structural techniques. Cross was best known for his devoted work for the Royal Institute of British Architects, of which he became a fellow in 1931 and was president from 1956 to 1958, having previously served as honorary secretary (1952–5) and as vice-president (1955–6). He was chairman of the Board of Architectural Education from 1950 to 1952, chairman of the Competitions Committee from 1937 to 1949, and served on a number of the Royal Institute's other committees. He was chairman of the committee on the constitution of the council, and also of the committee on the architects' registration acts.

Kenneth Cross was a quiet, soft-spoken, and unassuming man of friendly aspect. In private life he was interested in English literature, gardening, and walking. Always correctly and modestly dressed, he seemed to come from a generation older than himself, and, although somewhat diffident in conversation, below the surface his standards were high and his opinions firmly based. These qualities showed most clearly when he was in charge of a meeting. He became president of the RIBA at a time when the senior members, who had seen the Royal Institute through the war of 1939–45, attempted to re-establish it as it had been, predominantly a learned society, inward looking and comfortably unaware of the changes taking place in architecture and the building industry. They were, above all, unaware of, or perhaps just not interested in, the aspirations of the generation of architects trained after the war, which felt that the older generation was essentially out of date and that the profession needed total reorganization within an efficient and aggressive Institute. It fell to Cross as honorary secretary to attend, and afterwards as president to preside over, meetings at which these views were forcefully made known. The annual general meeting of the RIBA changed during Cross's time from a peaceful, badly attended, and unquestioning affair to a crowded battle-field where officers of the Institute were attacked and received little support from the floor. Few regretted the passing of the old order and the introduction of important electoral, educational, and administrative reforms which followed. The importance of Kenneth Cross's part in these reforms should not be underestimated. His manner in the chair was impeccable. He was urbane but firm, tolerant, even-tempered, and procedurally correct. He could be witty but sometimes there was a glint of steel in his remarks. He retained control at all times, and his wisdom ensured the introduction of constructive change. Whatever his personal feelings were he met the storms graciously and with understanding. During his presidency and largely on his own initiative, he made a world tour of the Royal Institute's allied societies which much improved relations between the RIBA and its overseas members.

Cross was an honorary DCL of Durham University and an honorary fellow of the Royal Architectural Institute of Canada, the American Institute of Architects, and the New Zealand Institute of Architects. There is a portrait of Cross by A. R. Middleton Todd (1958) at the RIBA. It is a fair likeness. Cross died at Chelmsford Hospital 16 January 1968. He was unmarried.

[*The Times*, 18 January 1968; RIBA *Journal*, March 1968; *Builder*, 6 January 1933; private information; personal knowledge.]

GONTRAN GOULDEN

CROWDY, DAME RACHEL ELEANOR (1884–1964), social reformer, was born 3 March 1884, the daughter of James Crowdy, solicitor, of Kensington, and his wife, Mary Isabel Ann Fuidge. One of four sisters who were all to develop an active interest in social service in their adult lives, she was educated at Hyde Park New College in London, and at Guy's Hospital where she completed her training as a nurse in 1908. In 1911 she joined the newly formed Voluntary Aid Detachments, volunteer nursing units attached to the Territorial Army. With characteristic thoroughness, she immediately began to study at Apothecaries' Hall for a certificate to serve as dispenser to her unit, VAD 22, London. Between 1912 and 1914 she was also a lecturer and demonstrator at the National Health Society.

It was through her work for the VADs during the war of 1914–18 that Rachel Crowdy made her name. With her friend (Dame) Katharine Furse [q.v.] she broke down the prejudices of both male administrators and professional nurses, setting up first-aid and home-nursing classes all over the country. The VADs had been trained for the eventuality of invasion, but they managed to send a small group to Boulogne, where they set up a rest station for wounded soldiers in a railway siding. There, during the first battle of Ypres, about twenty nurses ministered to 30,000 men. At the end of 1914 Katharine Furse returned to London and for the rest of the war Rachel Crowdy was in charge of the VADs on the Continent. She set up rest stations along the lines of communication in France and Belgium, established ambulance depots, hostels for nurses and for

relatives of the sick and wounded, and hospitals and sick bays wherever they were needed. Before long the VADs had proved themselves so well that the two Crowdy sisters, Rachel and Mary, could set up an office in the Joint War Committee centre in the Hôtel Crystol in Boulogne.

Rachel Crowdy was mentioned in dispatches several times, receiving the Royal Red Cross 2nd class in 1916 and 1st class in 1917; in 1919 she was created DBE. Her experiences had tested her courage to the full. They had also helped to make her into an exceptionally firm and determined administrator. In 1919 she became chief of the Social Questions and Opium Traffic Section at the League of Nations, the only woman to head a section at the League. During her twelve years there she considered a wide range of social problems, becoming best known for her inquiries into the traffic in women and children and into the opium trade. Her work won international acclaim. In 1920–1 she went with the International Typhus Commission to Poland when the epidemic was at its height, and in 1922 she was made a commander of the Order of Polonia Restituta. In 1926 Smith College in the United States made her an honorary doctor of laws, and in 1931, at the end of her work for the League of Nations, the Spanish Government made her a commander of the Order of Alphonso XII 'for services of outstanding value in the international field of social reform'.

During the 1930s Dame Rachel's career as a 'social worker' (her own description) continued unabated. She was a member of the British delegation to the Conference on Pacific Relations at Shanghai in 1931, having attended the Conference on Pacific Affairs in Honolulu the previous year. She travelled alone to Shanghai, as she did again in 1936, when she returned to Manchuria. She revelled in the freedom to go where she wished and see what she pleased. In 1935–6 she was a member of the royal commission on the private manufacture of and trading in arms. The commission's report concluded that nationalization was impracticable, but recommended some far-reaching British and international regulations, which were not implemented. In 1937 Dame Rachel went with a parliamentary commission to observe the war in Spain. In 1938–9 she served on the West Indies Royal Commission whose recommendations included the establishment of a West Indian Welfare Fund. From 1939 to 1946 she served as regions' adviser to the Ministry of Information, her last major appointment in a long and remarkably varied career.

Dame Rachel Crowdy belonged to a generation when women had to possess very obvious strength of character if they were to attain recognition. She certainly could have been described as 'formidable', but those who knew her found much more besides. Strikingly good-looking and always well turned out, she impressed her colleagues with her incisive mind and quick wit. Her orderliness and other administrative talents tempered an abiding zest for life, a curiosity about people and places which seemed to be insatiable, and a feeling for poetry and visual beauty which was reflected in the vivid and graceful language of her many lectures to audiences all over the world. In 1939 she married Colonel Cudbert John Massy Thornhill, CMG, DSO (died 1952) the son of Lt.-Col. Sir Henry Beaufoy Thornhill. Dame Rachel died at her home at Outwood, Surrey, 10 October 1964, at the age of eighty.

In the Imperial War Museum is a portrait (1919) in pastel and water-colour by Austin O. Spare.

[Thekla Bowser, *The Story of British V.A.D. Work in the Great War*, 1918; Foreign Office General Correspondence in the Public Record Office; *The Times*, 12 October 1964; Katharine Furse, *Hearts and Pomegranates*, 1940; Philip Gibbs, *Ordeal in England*, 1937; private information.]   ALICE PROCHASKA

CUDLIPP, PERCIVAL THOMAS JAMES (1905-1962), journalist, eldest son of William Christopher Cudlipp, commercial clerk, and his wife, Bessie Amelia Kinsman, was born in Cardiff 10 November 1905. Cudlipp's mother, educated at an elementary school, was a woman of strong personality and considerable intelligence, very ambitious for her children. In addition to Percy and a daughter, there were two younger sons, both of whom were to become editors of national newspapers. Cudlipp said that his mother chose the names Percival, Hubert, and Reginald for her sons because they would sound well with knighthoods. The story was probably one of Cudlipp's fabrications but it fairly represents his mother's confidence in her sons. Sir Hugh Cudlipp became a life peer in 1974.

Brought up in the Welsh Nonconformist tradition, the Cudlipp family attended the Wesleyan Chapel at Crwys Street, Cardiff, although it seems that for Percy the most powerful magnet there was not religion but the chapel's flourishing dramatic society for which, having a natural histrionic gift inherited from his mother, he played the part of Shylock in *The Merchant of Venice*. He was educated at Howard Gardens Secondary School which he left at the age of thirteen. His mother paid a fine so that before reaching school-leaving

age the boy could begin work in the office of the *South Wales Echo* where an opening had occurred which Cudlipp was determined to fill. He had a precocious talent for rhyme and had already contributed a great deal of verse to the paper which advertised him as the boy poet of Cardiff. His facility for dexterous and witty verse remained with him through his career.

After six years of apprenticeship, during which he assimilated the techniques of the profession, while he was assiduous in attendance at the local night school, Cudlipp went in 1924 to Manchester as a reporter on the *Evening Chronicle*. At the same time he was contributing articles and light verse to London newspapers. Cudlipp's next move was predictable, and predictably early. In 1925 he moved to London as dramatic critic and humorous columnist on the *Sunday News*.

That would have been enough for most journalists but it was not enough for Cudlipp. Through a publicity agent he became a purveyor of topical lyrics to the Co-optimists revue running in a London theatre. Every afternoon he went to the theatre with the latest edition of the evening newspaper which provided him with the material for a few verses to add to the lyric. The show ran so long that Cudlipp was compelled to cancel his honeymoon so that the supply of topical rhymes could continue. He needed the money.

By that time it was becoming known in Fleet Street that a brilliant and versatile talent had descended on it. In consequence, Cudlipp in 1929 became a special writer on the *Evening Standard*. He had arrived, at the age of twenty-four, where every ambitious young journalist of the time wished to be, not indeed at 'the top of the tree', but within earshot of Lord Beaverbrook [q.v.]. By this time Cudlipp's free-ranging talent was in full flower. One morning he interviewed (Sir) Noël Coward; in the later editions of the *Evening Standard* that day there appeared a half-page interview with Coward by Cudlipp in verse which was a parody of Coward's style and which astonished even Coward.

In 1931 Cudlipp was appointed assistant editor of the *Standard* and two years later editor. He was then twenty-seven, the youngest editor of a British national newspaper. In becoming an editor Cudlipp turned his back on the particular talent which had marked him out among popular journalists: his ability to write smooth and witty English. From now on he was to be an executive journalist, an editor. If this involved the sacrifice of something which he valued, Cudlipp never showed it. At the *Evening Standard*, however, he was not completely happy because of a temperamental clash between himself and the manager of the paper, Michael Wardell, who combined a strong personality with highly conservative views about the *Evening Standard*. In 1938 Cudlipp joined the *Daily Herald* as editorial manager. In 1940 when Francis Williams (later Lord Francis-Williams, q.v.) resigned, Cudlipp became editor in defiance of the veto of the *New Statesman* which thought that the paper should have a socialist editor. In fact Cudlipp had always been a convinced socialist. The change of newspaper disconcerted those of Cudlipp's associates who had not realized how heavy had been the strain of his editorship at the *Standard*. At the *Daily Herald* he found working conditions far more complicated and demanding all his very considerable powers of diplomacy.

The trade unions, the Labour Party, Odhams Press—co-proprietors of the newspaper—each had different views about how a Labour newspaper should be run. There were, too, personal rivalries to consider. Cudlipp was on friendly terms with Herbert Morrison (later Lord Morrison of Lambeth, q.v.) and incurred the dislike of Ernest Bevin [q.v.] who wished to dominate the newspaper. When Cudlipp left the editorship in November 1953, it seemed that his editorial career was ending in something like frustration. Nothing could have been further from the truth. After a period as columnist in the *News Chronicle*, he became founder-editor in 1956 of the *New Scientist*, a weekly which sought to convey accurate, authoritative scientific information in language which the layman could understand. In inspiring scientists to become comprehensible, Cudlipp performed a notable service and made a brilliant success of the journal. His last years were, therefore, years of triumph.

Cudlipp was a gregarious man of great charm, good-natured and lively minded, a master in speech as in writing of precise and elegant English. After journalism, music was the passion of his life. His wit was sharp and exuberant. Beaverbrook once said of him 'Percy's spear knows no brother'. But, in fact, his tongue was without malice. His most celebrated remark was made about one of Beaverbrook's lieutenants who, in describing a ride with Beaverbrook over a snow-covered terrain in Surrey, said incautiously, 'It was like the retreat from Moscow. Beaverbrook was Napoleon; I was Marshal Ney.' 'You mean Marshal Yea!', said Cudlipp. It was, however, the victim of the remark who spread its fame.

In 1927 Cudlipp married Gwendoline James who was through life his source of companionship and counsel. They had one son, Michael, who also became a journalist.

Cudlipp died in London 5 November 1962.

The National Portrait Gallery has a pencil drawing by Sir David Low.

[Private information; personal knowledge.]
GEORGE MALCOLM THOMSON

CUNNINGHAM, ANDREW BROWNE, VISCOUNT CUNNINGHAM OF HYNDHOPE (1883-1963), admiral of the fleet, was born in Dublin 7 January 1883, the third of the five children—three sons and two daughters—of Daniel John Cunningham [q.v.], then professor of anatomy at Trinity College, Dublin, by his wife, Elizabeth Cumming, daughter of the Revd Andrew Browne, of Beith, Ayrshire. 'A. B. C.', as he was generally known, was not related to Sir John Henry Dacres Cunningham, who succeeded him in 1943 in the Mediterranean command and again in 1946 as first sea lord, and a notice of whom appears below. Andrew Cunningham's elder brother, John, had reached the rank of lieutenant-colonel by 1924 as a doctor in the Indian Medical Service, and later practised in Edinburgh. His younger brother became General Sir Alan Cunningham during a long and striking career as a professional soldier.

Although none of his forebears had served at sea, Cunningham was always interested in boats, and throughout his life he took more interest in sailing than in any other sport. He was educated first at Edinburgh Academy, followed by three years at Stubbington House, Fareham, preparing for the Royal Navy; in January 1897 he entered the *Britannia* fourteenth in order of merit among sixty-five cadets and was tenth upon passing out in May 1898 when he earned first class passes in mathematics and seamanship.

Having stated a preference for service on the Cape station, Cunningham was serving there as midshipman in the *Doris* when the South African war broke out in 1899; by February 1900 he had winkled his way into the Naval Brigade which promised opportunities for brave deeds and distinction in action. Lord Roberts [q.v.], who knew his father, used his influence to get Cunningham to the front line, to the annoyance of his commanding officer who resented such nepotism. Thus in spite of front line service with mobile naval guns, Cunningham was the only midshipman to be omitted from a list of those 'noted for early promotion'. This upset him, but he bore it philosophically. About the same time he met and was impressed by (Sir) Walter Cowan [q.v.], then a lieutenant and naval aide-de-camp to Lord Kitchener [q.v.] and who at twenty-nine had seen more action than many admirals.

In 1902-3 Cunningham took sub-lieutenant courses at Portsmouth and Greenwich, obtaining first class passes in seamanship and torpedo. As a sub-lieutenant, Cunningham's first six months were in the battleship *Implacable* in the Mediterranean; but his most rewarding time took place when he was transferred to the destroyer *Locust*, September 1903, to serve as second-in-command under a young lieutenant, a 'taut hand' renowned for efficiency and ability, with the reputation for getting rid of sub-lieutenants who failed to come up to his requirements. Cunningham passed the test well and developed a great fondness for destroyers. He was promoted lieutenant in 1904, but it was not until 1908, after service in the cruisers *Northampton*, *Hawke*, and *Suffolk*, and as a result of repeated requests, that he found himself back in his beloved 'boats', in command of torpedo-boat no. 14.

His persistent importuning, together with the advent of war, and the increasing number of vessels becoming available, were responsible for keeping Cunningham in the 'boats'. He was given command of the destroyer *Scorpion* in 1911 and was destined to serve in her until 1918. At the Dardanelles the *Scorpion* seemed to be always at the forefront of action; he witnessed the tragic losses of British capital ships and the failure of naval bombardment undertaken without the follow-up of troops, until too late—an experience he never forgot. He was promoted commander in 1915, and was appointed to the DSO in the same year. Meanwhile his reputation as a first-class destroyer commander and man of action was growing, and it was not long before he was regarded as a rising star by various influential senior officers such as (Sir) John De Robeck, Roger (later Lord) Keyes, and Sir Reginald (later Lord) Tyrwhitt [qq.v.] with whom he had served. He was known as an effectual leader, aggressive fighter, and highly competent seaman. But beneath that redoubtability lay the sense of fun which in his *Britannia* days had led to records of 'laughing in study', and 'skylarking at muster': a quality which endeared him to those who really knew him, and which during the war of 1939-45 would be responsible for such remarks as 'I hope the old man is coming with us . . . we shall be all right if his is'.

Throughout most of 1918 he took part in numerous engagements in the Dover Patrol under Keyes (including the Zeebrugge raid), for which he was awarded a bar to his DSO the following year; he was promoted captain in December 1919, and a second bar was awarded in 1920 for service the previous year with a force in the Baltic under the command of Cowan (by then a rear-admiral), where Cunningham had taken firm but diplomatic individual action against the encroachment of German troops in Latvia. Post-war international problems and demobilization reduced the number of sea-going appointments: never-

theless, after taking the senior officers' technical course at Portsmouth, Cunningham found himself back in destroyers early in 1922, first as captain (D) of the 6th flotilla, and in January 1923 as captain (D) of the 1st flotilla, then temporarily in the Mediterranean to support British ships based on Istanbul. He gave considerable thought to exercises using destroyers in an offensive role with torpedoes in mass attacks against heavy ships, and also in the underwater detection and destruction of submarines.

After a spell ashore in command of the destroyer base at Port Edgar in the Firth of Forth during 1924-6, Cunningham became flag captain and chief staff officer to Cowan, who had become vice-admiral and commander-in-chief North America and West Indies station: an appointment to gladden any captain's heart, although Cunningham deplored what he called 'the mysteries' of red tape and paperwork involved in administration, and took a certain humorous pride in the fact that he never did a staff course. He admired Cowan's courage and dedication, owning that Cowan had taught him a lot.

In December 1929, at the end of a year at the Imperial Defence College, he was given command of the battleship *Rodney*—an appointment marking him as a captain of great promise. Eighteen months later he was appointed commodore of the Royal Naval Barracks at Chatham. Promotion to flag rank in September 1932, in which year he was also naval aide-de-camp to the King, was followed (December 1933) by his appointment as rear-admiral (destroyers) in the Mediterranean, a job he said he would have chosen above all others. He was appointed CB in 1934. The period was one of increasing naval training, with much attention to night exercises as well as to all-round readiness in case of war with Italy.

On his promotion to vice-admiral in July 1936, prospects for further active employment seemed remote. However, a year later there occurred a vacancy suddenly caused by the illness of Sir Geoffrey Blake and Cunningham assumed his combined appointment of commander of the Battle Cruiser Squadron and second-in-command of the Mediterranean Fleet, hoisting his flag in the *Hood*. This important command he retained until September 1938, when he was appointed to the Admiralty as deputy chief of the naval staff, a post he took up in December. He accepted a shore job with reluctance, maintaining that he was no good at paperwork; but the appointment was clear proof of the Board of Admiralty's high regard for him, and for six months he acted as deputy, on the Committee of Imperial Defence and Admiralty Board, to the first sea lord, Sir Roger Backhouse [q.v.], during the latter's illness. However, in June 1939 Cunningham was appointed commander-in-chief Mediterranean station with the acting rank of admiral. Hoisting his flag in the battleship *Warspite*, he took over from Sir Dudley Pound [q.v.] (who was to succeed Backhouse). In the same year he was promoted KCB.

Italy's attitude remained uncertain both before and after the outbreak of war until the collapse of France in June 1940, when she threw in her lot with Germany. Cunningham's immediate aim was to restore and maintain British supremacy in the Mediterranean with the policy of 'seek out and destroy'. He unequivocally deprecated suggestions of withdrawal from the Mediterranean, and insisted that both Alexandria and Malta must be maintained as British naval bases to sustain communications and to provide support for the army and the RAF. When ordered (from London) to seize the French fleet, which under Admiral Godfroy at Alexandria had hitherto co-operated fully against the Axis, Cunningham instead entered into friendly but firm negotiation with Godfroy and obtained a clear agreement whereby the French warships would remain permanently immobilized in Alexandria harbour, safe from misappropriation by the Axis. This was a masterly achievement, especially when viewed against the considerable bloodshed and national hatred engendered by the British naval attack ordered against the French fleet at Oran at the same time. Cunningham no longer had the French as an ally, however, and was also faced with an Italian fleet of considerable strength.

The Italians adopted a policy of maintaining a 'fleet in being', best achieved by withdrawing to harbour whenever their material superiority was threatened. Cunningham's first encounter with the Italian navy occurred 9 July 1940, when a powerful fleet was returning to Italy after covering the passage to North Africa of a large military convoy bound for Libya. Cunningham also was at sea, covering an important convoy from Malta to Alexandria. Neither knew of the other's presence. Upon receiving a submarine report of an enemy fleet at sea, Cunningham aimed to intercept the Italians off Calabria before they could reach port. In numbers of capital ships his fleet was superior to that of the Italians, but in effect the latter were so modern that they could outrun and outrange all his battleships except the modernized *Warspite*. With the *Warspite* were the old battleships *Malaya* and *Royal Sovereign*, both unable to keep up with the fleet at full speed. Moreover, although Cunningham had the benefit of reconnaissance from the carrier *Eagle*, the latter lacked suitable aircraft and experienced crews to provide a strike which would effectively slow down the Italians. The great moment came, however, when the *Warspite* brought the leading enemy battleship, the fast and powerful *Cesare*, within range of her guns. Until that moment, five light British cruisers had been having a rough time from the enemy's six heavy and ten light cruisers firing at a range of thirteen miles. It was at 4.00 p.m. that the *Warspite*, her fifteen-inch guns elevated to maximum range, scored a direct hit on the *Cesare*, causing a heavy explosion and fires. The Italians immediately withdrew for home under a heavy smoke-screen, hoping to lure the British fleet into waters close to Italian shore-based bombers. In the face of heavy attacks from the latter, and the danger also of submarines in the smoke-laden sea, Cunningham was forced to relinquish pursuit.

His audacity in closing the Italian coast at Calabria with three veteran battleships and an old and vulnerable carrier, in the presence of a powerful modern enemy fleet and air force, established a moral ascendancy which set the pattern of aggressive action for the next eighteen months, during times of both triumph and adversity. Cunningham's strategy and daring received support in August 1940 with the arrival of the new carrier *Illustrious* and the old but modernized battleship *Valiant* on the Mediterranean station, together with two anti-aircraft cruisers. Both sides continued the covering of convoys: the British, east–west; the Italian, north–south. But in general the Italian battleships were safely confined in the harbour of Taranto, and although Cunningham's ships never relaxed their offensive role, the prospect of a main fleet action appeared remote. Cunningham, however, scored a dramatic success in November 1940 with a night attack on Taranto harbour, using naval Swordfish aircraft armed with torpedoes. Half the Italian battleships were put out of action, and since the remaining three were promptly removed to Naples for safety, the threat to British convoys bound for Greece and Crete was greatly diminished.

On 3 January 1941 Cunningham was confirmed in the rank of admiral. His reputation was high, for British convoys were now passing both ways through the Mediterranean and his fleet was exacting an increasing toll of the enemy's convoys to Tripoli. There was also no appearance of the Italian battle fleet. He celebrated promotion with a bombardment of Bardia to give support to the inshore squadron which worked in co-operation with the British army in the desert. The presence of the *Illustrious* gave him local control of the air whenever he took his fleet to sea. But already a shadow lay over the scene: Mussolini's fiasco in Greece had provoked German in-

tervention in the Mediterranean, the Luftwaffe arrived in Sicily in January 1941, and
Germany's campaigns in Greece and Libya
were already in preparation. The *Illustrious* was
put out of action when her flight-deck was
wrecked by Junkers 87 and 88 on 10 January:
Cunningham was once again without fighter
defence at sea, and until the new carrier
Formidable arrived in the Mediterranean two
months later, he suffered some loss and damage
to his ships.

But that spring Cunningham gained a major
victory over the Italian fleet off Cape
Matapan—the first large-scale naval action
for twenty-five years. He sailed from Alexandria after dark, 27 March, with the battleships
Warspite, *Valiant*, and *Barham* (all of which
had fought at Jutland), the *Formidable*, and nine
destroyers, having received a report earlier that
day that a force of three Italian cruisers had
been sighted heading towards Crete. A light
force of four British cruisers which was already
operating in the Aegean sea, covering British
military convoys proceeding to Greece, was
ordered to rendezvous south of Crete with
Cunningham at dawn 28 March. Cunningham
believed that the Italian battle fleet might be
at sea, and at first light reconnaissance aircraft from the *Formidable* reported the presence
of two groups of Italian heavy cruisers, eight
in all. One of these groups sighted the British
light cruiser force and engaged them from
8.12 a.m. to 8.55 a.m. at a range which was
beyond that of three of the British light
cruisers. The latter began leading the Italian
ships to the south-east, where it was hoped
they would meet Cunningham's battle fleet
head on.

Unknown to Cunnningham was the presence
of the *Vittorio Veneto*, one of Italy's newest
battleships flying the flag of Admiral Iachino,
the Italian commander-in-chief. It was the latter,
then only a few miles to the west of his own
cruisers, who had ordered them to cease fire
at 8.55 a.m. and to steam north-west, unwilling
as he was that his forces should be drawn
further into the unknown. The British light
force then turned to shadow the Italian cruisers,
and at 10.58 a.m. unexpectedly sighted the
Vittorio Veneto to the northward. She immediately opened fire on the British light cruisers,
whose survival seemed remote as they altered
course to the southward at full speed. But at
least the presence of the *Vittorio Veneto* was
known, and Cunningham immediately increased to full speed in his advance north-
westward. Meanwhile Iachino, still unaware of
Cunningham's presence only eighty miles to
the south-east, experienced no difficulty in
keeping up with the British light cruisers
and finding the range. Moreover, he had dis-

persed his fleet so that the division of Italian
heavy cruisers which had attacked the British
light cruisers earlier should be in a position
to supplement the *Vittorio Veneto*'s fire.
Annihilation of the four British ships would
have certainly followed but for a tactical
surprise: the providential torpedo strike at
11.27 a.m. by the *Formidable*'s aircraft, which
had been dispatched from the carrier by
Cunningham at 9.39 a.m. Their arrival at this
critical moment saved the British light cruisers.
No hits were scored, however, and the Italians
began to hasten home at twenty-eight knots,
with Cunningham doing his utmost, only
forty-five miles astern, at a speed which would
be quite insufficient to catch them unless the
Italian fleet could be slowed down. An afternoon strike from the *Formidable* succeeded in
hitting the *Vittorio Veneto*, but she was able
to maintain a speed of nineteen knots after
some repair, and later to increase it.

With the approach of twilight it appeared
that the Italians—who had had no effective air
protection the whole day—would be able to
reach home under cover of darkness. However,
a dusk strike from the *Formidable* successfully
slowed down the heavy cruiser *Pola*; Iachino
thereupon sent back two heavy cruisers, the
Zara and *Fiume*, together with four destroyers,
to stand by her. These were seen on the
Valiant's radar screen and reported, and
Cunningham decided on a night attack with
his battle fleet, despite the risk from enemy
torpedoes. At 10.20 p.m. the *Pola* was only four
miles away according to the radar screen, and
at that very moment the massive shapes of
darkened ships could be seen by eye, crossing
the path of Cunningham's battle fleet: seven
enemy ships, all unsuspecting and unready.
Almost simultaneously the *Warspite*, *Valiant*,
and *Barham* opened fire with fifteen-inch
broadsides at a range of two miles. At 10.31
Cunningham made an emergency turn to avoid
possible enemy torpedoes and ordered his
destroyers to finish off the enemy. The loss to
the Italians was three heavy cruisers and two
destroyers, against Cunningham's loss of one
aircraft, although Iachino himself had escaped
with the remains of his fleet. The results were
substantial, but there were to be lean months
ahead for Cunningham as for the army,
during the withdrawal from Greece and Crete
and the reverses in North Africa, while the
growing local Axis strength in the air was
to create a position calling for the greatest
defiance and supreme leadership—qualities in
which Cunningham excelled.

The immobilization of the *Formidable* from
damage in the attack on Scarpanto, May 1941,
and the fall of Crete itself shortly afterwards,
left Cunningham virtually without air pro-

tection in the 'Narrows' around Malta and in 'Bomb Alley' south of Crete, and the forces under his command suffered increasingly grievous losses right through to the end of 1941. But his inspiring attitude at Crete was typical of his steadfast refusal to give up: 'it takes the navy three years to build a ship but three hundred years to build a tradition', and 'we must not let the army down'.

From June to October 1942, however, Cunningham was with the combined chiefs of staff in Washington, as head of the British Admiralty delegation, where he made a profound impression. His contribution to Allied harmony was considerable, and his selection as 'Allied naval commander Expeditionary Force', under General Eisenhower, was highly acceptable to all, especially to the Americans who admired his integrity and the resolute manner in which he had maintained a presence in the Mediterranean through times of dire shortage and adversity, and who, in fact, were not prepared to accept any other naval commander.

There followed the covering of the successful 'Torch' landings in North Africa, November 1942; the convoying of the Allied armies for the invasion of Sicily, July 1943, and Salerno landings, September 1943; and the Italian collapse which enabled Cunningham to make his historic signal: 'be pleased to inform their lordships that the Italian battle fleet now lies at anchor beneath the guns of the fortress of Malta.' Admiral Iachino generously acknowledged Cunningham's humanity in victory.

In January 1943, resuming his title of commander-in-chief Mediterranean, he was promoted admiral of the fleet, and in October the same year, on the death in harness of Sir Dudley Pound, he was selected for the highest post, that of first sea lord and chief of naval staff, in which he remained for the rest of the war. Apart from his earlier honours and decorations, Cunningham had been promoted GCB in March 1941, and was created a baronet in July 1942; in January 1945 he was created KT, an honour which he prized more than any other. Further laurels followed the conclusion of the war, when he was raised to the peerage in September 1945 as Baron Cunningham of Hyndhope, of Kirkhope, county Selkirk. In 1946 he was advanced to a viscountcy, and in the same year he was appointed to the OM on relinquishing his office as first sea lord. His retirement was quiet but not inactive, for in addition to publishing a lengthy volume of memoirs, *A Sailor's Odyssey* (1951), he was lord high commissioner to the General Assembly of the Church in Scotland in 1950 and 1952, lord rector of Edinburgh University in 1945-8, and president of the Institu-

tion of Naval Architects in 1948-51, besides other honorary posts and memberships. He received many foreign orders and decorations, as well as honorary degrees from the universities of Oxford, Cambridge, Birmingham, Leeds, Edinburgh, Glasgow, St. Andrews, and Sheffield. He also received the freedom of the cities of London, Edinburgh, Manchester, and Hove, and was an elder brother of Trinity House from 1943.

Cunningham was of medium stature, compact, and with a rosy, weatherbeaten complexion; his implacable and resolute spirit was expressed in steely blue eyes which could—and frequently did—twinkle with humour and optimism. He was a man of human warmth, sympathy, and generosity, although he did not suffer fools gladly, and had no use for slackers. He drove himself to the limit of excellence and endurance, and expected his men to do the same. Some could not stand up to his thrusting and testing: (Sir) Richard Symonds-Tayler claimed to have been Cunningham's thirteenth first lieutenant in the *Scorpion*—all his predecessors having been 'flung out'. 'The Old Man of the Sea', as soldiers came to call him, was forthright and would truckle to nobody: this sometimes led to strained relationships with authority, notably (Sir) Winston Churchill, who at times attempted—always unsuccessfully—to force him to an action which he considered unsound.

In 1929 Cunningham married Nona Christine (died 1978), third daughter and ninth child of Horace Byatt, schoolmaster, of Midhurst, Sussex, and sister of Sir Horace Byatt, GCMG, then governor of Trinidad and Tobago. The marriage was a very happy one, although there were no children. Cunningham died suddenly in London 12 June 1963 and was buried at sea off Portsmouth.

Lord Alexander of Tunis [q.v.] referred to him as one of 'the great sea commanders of our island race': by holding the Mediterranean with a handful of ships while Britain fought alone, Cunningham prevented the certain disaster which would have followed withdrawal from the Mediterranean, the loss of Malta, and probably also of Egypt and the Suez. It was fitting, therefore, that he should be commemorated close to the Nelson monument in Trafalgar Square, his bust (by Franta Belsky) alongside those of Jellicoe and Beatty, the naval leaders of the war of 1914-18. At his memorial service in St. Paul's Cathedral 12 July 1963, the bishop of Norwich, an old shipmate, thanked God for 'giving our people and nation such a man at such a time'.

There is a portrait in oils of him by (Sir) Oswald Birley (1947) in the Royal Naval College at Greenwich; a copy of it hangs in the

Britannia Royal Naval College at Dartmouth, and another is in the Imperial War Museum, together with portraits of him by Henry Carr (1943) and John Worsley (1945); a painting by David S. Ewart was exhibited at the Royal Academy in 1944.

[S. W. C. Pack, *The Battle of Matapan*, 1961, and *Cunningham the Commander*, 1974; *The Times*, 13 June 1963.]   S. W. C. PACK

CUNNINGHAM, SIR GEORGE (1888-1963), Indian civil servant, was born 23 March 1888 at Broughty Ferry, Forfarshire, the third son of James Cunningham, jute merchant, and his wife, Anna Sandeman. She died in 1892 and later the family moved to St. Andrews. Cunningham won an open scholarship to Fettes, and as a classical demy of Magdalen College, Oxford, was pre-eminent among those who were both athlete and scholar. He obtained a first class in honour moderations; and for three successive years played for the Oxford rugby team, captaining the side which in 1909 defeated Cambridge by a record score. He also played as an international for Scotland eight times and was captain in the last year before he went to India. He obtained a third class in *literae humaniores* in 1910 and in the same year passed into the Indian Civil Service.

Cunningham departed for India leaving a memory still green at Magdalen where dons and undergraduates alike spoke of him as having almost run the college when president of the junior common room. He went first for three years to the Punjab; then to the North West Frontier in the Indian Political Service. He served for some years as personal assistant to Sir George Roos-Keppel [q.v.] who was head of the province during the difficult days of the war of 1914-18. Cunningham soon learned the way to the heart of the Pathan; in the Pathan scene he detected in some sense the realization in practice of a way of life which touched some inner spring of conviction, even of passion. Dealing with a volatile people, he was able to turn in a moment from dignity to geniality, from argument to threat, from command to appeal.

In 1922-3 Cunningham was political agent in North Waziristan; and in 1925-6 counsellor at the British legation in Kabul. In 1926-31 he served as private secretary to Lord Irwin (later the Earl of Halifax, q.v.) who wrote to Cunningham on his way home from India: 'I have loved our association together; and I cannot count the times when I have owed very much to your steadiness and wisdom.' Cunningham returned to the North-West Frontier to serve in 1932-6 as a member of the executive council in charge of the portfolios

known as the reserved subjects. When he became governor of the province in 1937 he had the task of implementing the reformed constitution under which the Congress Party took office under Khan Sahib [q.v.] with whom Cunningham was able to establish cordial relations. The bonds of affection and respect in which Cunningham held the province kept the peace during the uneasy years of the war of 1939-45. Cunningham retired in 1946, only to be recalled at the request of M. A. Jinnah [q.v.] to serve again in 1947-8 in the difficult days when the province became part of Pakistan.

In the meantime Cunningham had been elected rector of St. Andrews in 1946; and when he was living in St. Andrews after his final retirement he was elected also captain of the Royal and Ancient, on whose greens he completed a round in 79 when over the age of seventy.

Cunningham was appointed CIE (1925), CSI (1931), KCIE (1935), KCSI (1937), and GCIE (1946). He received an honorary LLD from St. Andrews and from Edinburgh in 1946 and was elected an honorary fellow of Magdalen in 1948.

In 1929 Cunningham married Kathleen Mary Adair, an Irishwoman from county Carlow, always known as Robin, who gave him devoted support and help. They had no children. Cunningham died suddenly 8 December 1963 while talking to Lady Halifax in her London home when on his yearly pilgrimage to watch the university match at Twickenham.

There was something rock-like and imperturbable about Cunningham, so that those who looked on him were compelled into liking. Then—on a solemn, somewhat priest-like face—there would break the most enchanting smile, turning anger and obstinacy away. Jon Stallworthy in 'Here Comes Sir George' (*Out of Bounds*, 1963), might have had him in mind:

They do not know or, if they know, forget
The old fool held a province down larger
Than England; not as a Maharaja
Prodigal with silver and bayonet;

But with cool sense, authority and charm
That still attend him, crossing a room
With the *Odes of Horace* under his arm
And in his button-hole a fresh-cut bloom.

[Norval Mitchell, *Sir George Cunningham*, 1968; personal knowledge.]   OLAF CAROE

CUNNINGHAM, SIR JOHN HENRY DACRES (1885-1962), admiral of the fleet, was born 13 April 1885 at Demerara, British Guiana (now the independent state of Guyana), the son of Henry Hutt Cunningham, a barrister, and his wife, Elizabeth Park. He passed into the *Britannia* in 1900 and, after the initial naval training there, served as a midshipman in the *Gibraltar*, flagship on the Cape of Good Hope Station. For this service he was awarded the South African medal. Returning to England in 1904, he obtained the maximum seniority possible by gaining five first class certificates in his sub-lieutenant's courses, and was promoted lieutenant in October 1905. In the following year he decided to specialize in navigation and, after qualifying at the navigation school, had a number of appointments as assistant navigator and navigator in various ships. He passed the first class ship course in 1910 and became an instructor at the Navigation School. When war broke out in August 1914, he was navigator in the cruiser *Berwick* on the West Indies station, and in 1915 was appointed as navigating officer of the battleship *Russell* in the Mediterranean. Surviving her sinking by a mine in Maltese waters in April 1916, he was appointed to the *Renown*, and later, in 1918, to the *Lion*, and served in the Grand Fleet for the remainder of the war. He was promoted commander in 1917.

When the new battle-cruiser *Hood* was commissioned in 1920 Cunningham was appointed to her as navigator and as squadron navigator of the battle-cruiser squadron, then commanded by Sir Roger (later Lord) Keyes [q.v.]. Two years later he served as commander of the Navigation School, following which he was appointed in 1923 master of the fleet in the *Queen Elizabeth*, flagship of Admiral Sir John de Robeck [q.v.]. He was promoted captain in 1924.

For the next twelve years he served in a variety of posts, generally alternating staff appointments with periods of command at sea, the classical steps towards high command. He served on the staff of the Naval War College and as deputy director and director of plans at the Admiralty, and his commands at sea included the cruiser-minelayer *Adventure* and the battleship *Resolution*, in which he was flag captain to Admiral Sir William Fisher [q.v.], commanding the Mediterranean Fleet. This was the period of the Abyssinian crisis, and much of the contingency planning of that time equipped Cunningham with an intimate knowledge of the waters in which he was to exercise the chief command a few years later. He was promoted rear-admiral in 1936 and in October of that year was brought back to the Admiralty as assistant chief of naval staff to Admiral Sir A. Ernle (later Lord) Chatfield [q.v.] the first sea lord. When, after long and painful argument, the administration of the Fleet Air Arm was transferred from the Air Ministry to the Admiralty in 1937, Cunningham was made assistant chief of naval staff (air), a title which was changed in 1938 to that of fifth sea lord and chief of naval air services, bringing Cunningham a seat on the Admiralty Board.

On his promotion to vice-admiral in June 1939 he went to sea in command of the first cruiser squadron in the Mediterranean, flying his flag in the *Devonshire*. The squadron was ordered home shortly after the outbreak of war in 1939 to reinforce the Home Fleet, and took an active part in the Norwegian campaign of 1940 in which the evacuation of Namsos and the bringing to Britain of King Olaf of Norway and his Government from Tromsö fell to Cunningham to conduct. Later in that year he was selected as one of the two joint commanders for Operation 'Menace', the ill-fated expedition to Dakar, his co-commander being Major-General N. M. S. Irwin. The operation was dogged by ill fortune from the outset, and relations with General de Gaulle, who insisted on committing his Free French forces to the expedition and leading them himself, were far from friendly and did not add to the chances of success. The expedition was a failure and Cunningham was perhaps fortunate that it was not held against him in his future career. In the early months of 1941 he was back in the Admiralty as fourth sea lord and chief of supplies and transport, remaining in that post for over two years. It was an especially gruelling appointment at that period of the war, particularly with the entry of Japan on the side of Germany and Italy in December 1941. He was appointed KCB in 1941, having been appointed CB in the coronation honours of 1937.

In June 1943, with the Mediterranean station divided into two separate naval commands following the Allied assault on North Africa in November 1942, Cunningham was appointed commander-in-chief, Levant, with the acting rank of admiral. He was promoted admiral two months later and, at the end of 1943, when Admiral Sir Andrew Cunningham (later Viscount Cunningham of Hyndhope, q.v.) was brought home to serve as first sea lord after the death of Sir (Alfred) Dudley Pound [q.v.], the two Mediterranean commands were amalgamated and Sir John Cunningham appointed commander-in-chief. By this time, with the whole of the North African coast firmly in Allied hands, the difficulties and anxieties of naval command in those waters had eased considerably. Nevertheless, Cunningham had the responsibility of several important operations, the main ones being the amphibious assaults at Anzio and the south of France. In addition to being the British commander-in-chief, Cunningham was also Allied naval commander, with ships of the United

States, France, and Greece under his direct orders, in addition to the Italian ships lately surrendered.

. Lord Cunningham of Hyndhope completed his term of office in May 1946 and John Cunningham, who was not related to him, came to the Admiralty to take over as first sea lord. He was the first navigating officer to reach the top of his profession in this post. During his term of office he was called on to preside over a drastic reduction of the wartime fleet, including the scrapping of some warships still with many years of useful life ahead of them. He was promoted admiral of the fleet in January 1948 and in September of that year left the Admiralty on completion of his term of office. He then went into business as chairman of the Iraq Petroleum Company, retiring from that post in 1958.

Cunningham was a man of considerable intellectual attainment and was credited among his contemporaries with having the quickest brain in the navy. He was a dour man with a sarcastic tongue and with a reputation for not suffering fools gladly, and these were to him some 95 per cent of human beings. He was a strict disciplinarian and rarely, if ever, bestowed praise either verbally or by signal. Although never a popular officer, he was widely respected and trusted by those who served with him as a sound, practical officer of the highest professional skill and competence. He received, deservedly, a number of foreign orders and decorations, from Norway, Greece, France, and the United States, but the one which perhaps gave him the greatest pleasure was the rank of corporal in the French Foreign Legion, given to him 'for carrying the Legion from the Arctic (Norwegian campaign) to the Equator (the assault on Dakar)'. He became a freeman of the City of London in 1947. He married, in 1910, Dorothy, daughter of C. K. Hannay, of Ulverston, Lancashire. They had two sons, of whom one was lost in 1941 while serving in submarines. Cunningham died in the Middlesex Hospital 13 December 1962. There is a portrait of him by Sir Oswald Birley in the Greenwich Collection.

[Admiralty papers in Public Records Office; official dispatches of the war of 1939-45; personal knowledge.]　　　　PETER KEMP

CURRIE, Sir WILLIAM CRAWFORD (1884-1961), shipowner and director of the Peninsular and Oriental Steam Navigation Company and of the British India Steam Navigation Company, was born in Calcutta, India, 4 May 1884, the elder son of William Currie, East India merchant, of Glasgow and Calcutta, and his wife, Jessie, also of Scotland. He also had a half-brother and half-sister from his father's second marriage. Currie may be said to have been born into the P&O Group, as his father was at that time a partner of Mackinnon, Mackenzie & Co., the managing agents of the BISN Company, which had been founded by his kinsman (Sir) William Mackinnon [q.v.], and which was in 1914 merged into the P&O SN Company.

As soon as he was old enough Currie was sent home to school in Scotland, attending first the Glasgow Academy, and then Fettes College in Edinburgh, and finally in 1902 Trinity College, Cambridge, where he gained his rugby blue and graduated BA in history in 1905. Going down from Cambridge in 1906 Currie joined David Strathie, a firm of Glasgow chartered accountants, qualifying as a chartered accountant in 1910, when he left England for an appointment in Calcutta as assistant in Mackinnon, Mackenzie & Co.

Currie became a partner in Mackinnon's in 1918 and began to take a prominent part in public life in India. Sheriff of Calcutta in 1921-2, he was also elected to the Bengal Legislative Council in 1921, where he remained until he left India in 1925. In 1924 he was elected president of the Bengal Chamber of Commerce and also president of the Associated Chambers of Commerce of India, Burma, and Ceylon. During his last year in India he was appointed a member of the Council of State for India and received a knighthood for his services.

On his return to Britain, Currie became a partner in the Inchcape family firm of Gray, Dawes & Co., London agents of the BISN Company, and was soon immersed in shipping affairs centred in London, being appointed in the following year to the Imperial Shipping Committee on which he served for four years, and in 1929-30 was elected president of the Chamber of Shipping of the United Kingdom.

In 1932 Alexander Shaw (later Lord Craigmyle), who had become chairman of the P&O and BI Companies as a result of the serious illness and subsequent death of James L. Mackay, the first Earl of Inchcape [q.v.], invited Currie to join the Company as deputy chairman and managing director, and in 1938 he was elected chairman to succeed Lord Craigmyle.

World War II brought many additional and onerous duties to all engaged in the shipping business and Currie was no exception. Throughout the war he was a member of the Advisory Council of the Ministry of War Transport and became director of the Liner Division at the Ministry in 1942, a position he held until 1945. During his time at the Ministry of Transport he kept in close touch with the P&O Group's affairs and all major decisions were still very much his concern. For his services during the war he was invested with the GBE in 1947. He became a commander of the Legion of Honour in 1953.

Back at his desk in Leadenhall Street, after the war, Currie, along with other chairmen of shipping companies, faced the major task of repairing the damage to the group's fleets from war losses under conditions becoming rapidly more difficult, and this was successfully achieved in this period.

Subsequently, Currie had to deal with all the revolutionary changes in the structure of the P&O Group brought about by the transfer of power in India. During and after the war Currie also played a major part as a trustee and partner in the control and direction of the Inchcape family's associated Eastern merchanting and shipping agency business, and in 1958 became one of the first directors of Inchcape & Co. Ltd.

Despite such anxious and worrying years, Currie found time to become president of the Institute of Marine Engineers (1945-6), high sheriff of Buckinghamshire in 1947, and in 1949 prime warden of the Worshipful Company of Shipwrights. Amongst a multitude of business interests he was deputy chairman of Williams Deacon's Bank; extraordinary director of the Royal Bank of Scotland; chairman of the Marine and General Mutual Life Assurance Society; and a director of the Suez Finance Company, of the Southern Railway, and of William Cory & Son Ltd.

Among Currie's other activities were the membership of the Commonwealth Shipping Committee; president of the Seafarers' Education Service; chairman of the hon. committee of management of the training ship *Worcester*; a trustee of the National Maritime Museum at Greenwich; member of the council of King George's Fund for Sailors; and an honorary member of the Company of Master Mariners. A singular honour was conferred on Currie when he was appointed honorary captain, Royal Naval Reserve, a distinction which recognized the good work he had done for the RNR over many years. An earlier award was the Royal Humane Society's certificate in 1904 (when he was at Cambridge) for saving a child in danger of drowning in the River Ouse.

A man of great modesty and of immense charm, with an innate kindliness, Currie had the power and ability to lead by persuasion and example. Nobody could have been less of the typical shipping magnate he might have become by his long tenure of the chairmanship of the largest shipping company in the world for over twenty years. He was held in a high degree of respect, devotion, and affection throughout

the P&O Company, and the key to his outstanding success in his shipping career was largely because he made friends in every office, every ship, every dock, and every agency in the world.

In 1914 Currie married Ruth Forrest Dods, of Edinburgh. They had two sons, the elder of whom was killed in action in Burma in 1944. Currie's was a very united family and Lady Currie was a tower of strength to her husband during the whole of his business career. As befitted a Scotsman who had been brought up in and lived for many years in India, Currie was a keen sportsman and, when time allowed (mostly before the war), he hunted and shot from his beautiful country home, Dinton Hall in Buckinghamshire. He died 3 July 1961 at Aylesbury, Buckinghamshire.

A portrait in oils of Currie painted by Edward Halliday is in the City offices of the General Council of British Shipping and a copy of the same portrait by Robert Swan is in the P&O offices in London.

[P&O records; private information; personal knowledge.]   INCHCAPE

CURTIS, WILLIAM EDWARD (1889-1969), experimental physicist, was born in Islington, North London, 23 October 1889, the younger child and only son of Charles Curtis, a gilder, originally of Horsham in Sussex, and his wife, Emily Sarah Haward, from Ipswich. Curtis was outstanding at school (Owen's, Islington), and at university (Imperial College, 1907-10), where he graduated with a first class in physics in 1910. He was awarded the Governor's scholarship in 1908 and 1909 and shared the Tyndall prize in 1908. Later he took the newly instituted London University honours degree in astronomy, being the first student ever to take it, and again obtained a first. A college demonstratorship followed and research under the supervision of (Professor) Alfred Fowler [q.v.], a spectroscopist of international repute. Fowler introduced Curtis to some of the major problems in spectroscopy and in particular to the strange fact that certain stellar spectra have lines with wavelengths close to some of the Balmer lines of hydrogen and yet apparently are emitted by helium. Niels Bohr solved this problem in 1913 as an extension to his now famous theoretical treatment of the hydrogen atom, when he showed that these lines are due to ionized helium; contemporaneous experimental work by Fowler and Curtis proved that the lines are definitely due to helium and not to a new form of hydrogen as certain scientists had assumed. In the course of this work Curtis discovered a unique band spectrum, emitted by excited helium, which was to become his main research interest throughout his scientific career. Unfortunately, after such a promising start, the war intervened in 1914 and temporarily put an end to his researches. Indeed, at the outbreak of war Curtis was in Riga waiting to go to Kiev to observe a solar eclipse. The expedition was called off; Curtis returned to England by a devious route, and enlisted as a sapper in the Royal Naval Division. After initial training he was sent to Gallipoli where he served during the whole campaign, being twice mentioned in dispatches. For the rest of the war he was an instructor in the Wireless Training Centre at Malvern.

On demobilization Curtis returned to Imperial College and to his study of spectra. From the College he moved in 1919 to a lectureship at the university of Sheffield, then to a readership at King's College, London, and finally to a professorship at Armstrong College at Newcastle upon Tyne in the university of Durham. In each of these posts he made his mark, gradually blossoming on the research side into a world specialist on band spectra and on the teaching side into a gifted lecturer noted for his skill in demonstration. Many scientific papers were published by him in this period, but perhaps the most important were those in the decade 1922–32 on the band spectrum of the helium molecule for which accurate wavelength measurements could be made and the theoretical predictions of the new quantum mechanics tested with great precision.

Curtis took up his professorship at Newcastle upon Tyne in 1926 and for more than forty years he took a leading part in the educational life of Armstrong College, the university, and the city. As the head of the physics department he built up strong research schools in spectroscopy and acoustics. Later, a School of Theoretical Physics was created. For his contributions to spectroscopy he was elected a fellow of the Royal Society in 1934.

Apart from research, Curtis played an active part in the life of the College, taking his full share of administrative work. In 1931 there began a serious constitutional upheaval involving Armstrong College and the Medical College and Curtis, as a senior science professor, reluctantly, but inevitably, became much involved. The outcome was a royal commission and the creation of one large college named King's College under a rector.

Curtis's contributions to the war of 1939–45 were varied. After chairmanship of the Durham University Recruiting Board he moved in 1940 to Leamington as director of camouflage and decoy, and when air attacks diminished became successively a scientific adviser at the Ministry of Home Security, with Solly (later Lord) Zuckerman and Professor J. D. Bernal, and then, in 1943, superintendent of applied explosives at Fort Halstead.

On returning to Newcastle Curtis became more and more involved in college and public affairs. He was sub-rector of King's for three years (1947–50), president of the Institute of Physics (1950–2), and senior adviser in Civil Defence for the North-Eastern Region. For his work for Civil Defence he was appointed CBE in 1967, and in 1969 the university of Newcastle named its largest theatre the Curtis Auditorium.

He retired in 1955 but continued to be very active, especially in lectures whose purpose was to stimulate interest in science in young people by showing demonstrations for which school facilities were inadequate. They succeeded admirably and drew huge audiences for many years.

Outside his professional life Curtis was impressive as a man of many parts. He had boundless physical energy and played many games well, especially cricket. He liked music and was a modest performer. He died at Newcastle upon Tyne 6 May 1969.

He married in 1918 (Adeline Mary) Grace, the only daughter of Charles Mitchell, of the War Office, and they had two children: a son, who became a physicist, and a daughter, who became a doctor and the wife of Professor R. L. Plackett.

[G. D. Rochester in *Biographical Memoirs of Fellows of the Royal Society*, vol. xvi, 1970; personal knowledge.]   G. D. ROCHESTER

D

DAIN, SIR (HARRY) GUY (1870-1966), general medical practitioner, was born in Birmingham 5 November 1870, the eldest of six children of Major Dain, draper, and his wife, Diana Weaver. He was educated at King Edward's Grammar School, Five Ways, and Mason College, to which in 1892 the medical department of Queen's College, Birmingham, was transferred. He qualified MRCS, LRCP in 1893 and took the MB, BS, London, in the following year. After holding appointments as resident medical officer at the Children's Hospital, Birmingham, and assistant house-surgeon at the General Hospital, he settled in general practice to become later the head of a large partnership in the residential area of Selly Oak, Birmingham.

The introduction of national health insurance occasioned his interest in medico politics, an interest which was sustained throughout his professional life. Starting in his native city of Birmingham, he was a member of the first Insurance Committee and of the first Panel Committee. Very soon he became its chairman, and in 1917 he became a member of the Insurance Acts Committee in London where his knowledge of the working of the Act and his skill as a negotiator rapidly marked him out as a leader. His qualities were soon recognized by his colleagues, and for six years he presided over the Annual Conference of Local Medical and Panel Committees (1919-24) and for twelve years (1924-36) he was chairman of the Insurance Acts Committee itself. During this period it was said that his name was suggested for every subcommittee or deputation to the Government. It seemed that only if he were present would a case be well presented and successful. He had the gift of clear and persuasive speech, and an enviable ability to disentangle complicated matters. Whilst everyone was afforded a full part in the process of decision making, it was made all the easier by the way in which he presented the essential facts, and drew attention to the root of a problem.

In 1934 Dain was elected to the General Medical Council on which he remained until 1961. In 1937 he was elected chairman of the Representative Body of the British Medical Association, and was able to widen his knowledge and embrace the problems of the whole profession. This was to stand him in good stead when in 1943-9, having been a member since 1921, he served as chairman of council of the BMA. This was a testing time for his profession which included the introduction of a comprehensive National Health Service. Throughout this time Dain was the leader and spokesman for the profession. Whether he was negotiating at

the Ministry, in the chair of council, at mass meetings of the profession, or holding press conferences, he was steadfast and persuasive, never departing from the principles he held to be essential. He was now well on through his seventies, but his clarity of thought and unbounded energy became the admiration of all. It was he more than anyone else who was able to keep the profession united in the face of the most severe pressures.

In recognition of his service to his profession Dain received the honorary LLD from Aberdeen in 1939, and the honorary MD from Birmingham in 1944. He was elected FRCS in 1945, having served for some years on the council, and awarded the gold medal of the British Medical Association in 1936. It was with special pleasure that in 1957 he became the first recipient of the Claire Wand award for outstanding services to general practice. He was knighted in 1961.

Dain's life was not devoted solely to the troubles and difficulties which beset his section of the profession in the first half of the century. His interests in medicine were wide and throughout his association with the British Medical Association he nevertheless devoted a great deal of his time to his busy practice in Birmingham, where he was loved by all his patients.

Dain was twice married: in 1898 to Flora Elizabeth Lewis who died in 1934; and secondly in 1939 to Alice Muriel Hague. There were two daughters and two sons of the first marriage, of whom one son was killed in the war of 1939-45 and the other became a member of the medical profession.

Dain died at Aberdovey 26 February 1966. A portrait by Sir James Gunn is in the Hastings Room at BMA House.

[Private information; personal knowledge.]

DEREK STEVENSON

DALE, SIR HENRY HALLETT (1875-1968), physiologist-pharmacologist, was born in London 9 June 1875, the third son and third of the seven children of Charles James Dale, manager of a manufacturing firm, and his wife, Frances Ann, daughter of Frederick Hallett, a furniture-maker in Clerkenwell. Dale's younger brother, Benjamin James Dale, who died in 1943, was a composer of some distinction and warden of the Royal Academy of Music. At each stage of his education Dale had to face financial problems. To continue school at sixteen he had to win a scholarship, and so went to The Leys School in Cambridge.

Three years later he entered Trinity College, Cambridge, on a minor scholarship and a subsizarship in natural sciences; he was soon awarded a sizarship and then won a major foundation scholarship in 1896. In his natural sciences tripos, parts i (1896) and ii (1898), he was placed in the first class.

He stayed up for another two years to work, in J. N. Langley's [q.v.] department, for a college fellowship before going to hospital to finish his medical studies. His college scholarship of £100 per annum was not sufficient to keep him even in those days, and as he failed to obtain a Coutts-Trotter studentship at Trinity, which had gone to Ernest Rutherford (later Lord Rutherford of Nelson, q.v.) the previous year, Dale set about collecting whatever demonstratorships and private coaching he could. But soon afterwards with Rutherford's appointment as professor at McGill, the studentship fell vacant again, and this time the college divided it between Dale and another candidate, and allowed them to retain their scholarships as well. A similar condition of competition arose again when Dale eventually presented his thesis for the college fellowship. But this time he was not successful, though the thesis was highly commended. Before leaving Cambridge Dale devoted a few weeks to 'shameless cramming' of descriptive anatomy and then sat for a Schuster scholarship at St. Bartholomew's Hospital, London—awarded on examination in anatomy and physiology—and he was elected. Whilst at Bart's Dale lived with his parents for reasons of economy. A few months before he qualified B.Ch., Cambridge, in 1902, he applied for a George Henry Lewes studentship, founded by George Eliot [q.v.], was successful, and made arrangements with Professor E. H. Starling [q.v.] to work in his department at University College, London. During the tenure of this studentship, in October 1903, he went for four months to Frankfurt-am-Main to work under Paul Ehrlich. On returning to London Dale applied for the Sharpey studentship and was appointed in March 1904, but later in that year he accepted a research post in physiology at the Wellcome Research Laboratories offered to him by (Sir) Henry S. Wellcome [q.v.]. Dale spent ten extremely fruitful years in these laboratories, the first eighteen months as their pharmacologist and the remainder of the time as director. Here he met George Barger [q.v.] and engaged two youngsters who started their scientific career with Dale: (Sir) P. P. Laidlaw [q.v.] and J. H. Burn. In 1914 Dale became director of the Department of Biochemistry and Pharmacology of the projected Institute for Medical Researches, which in 1920 became the National Institute for Medical Research at Hampstead.

In 1923 Dale was made chairman of the committee of departmental directors and, in 1928, the first director of the Institute, a position he held until his retirement in 1942, when he accepted the directorship of the Royal Institution, whereby he became at the same time Fullerian professor of chemistry. He retired from this position in 1946.

In 1936, when Sir Henry Wellcome died, Dale found himself nominated as trustee of the Wellcome Trust, became its chairman from 1938 to 1960, and continued as scientific adviser until 1968, but in fact he gave scientific and other advice until a week before he died at the age of ninety-three. To commemorate his unique services as chairman, the Trust in 1961 endowed a Royal Society professorship, the Henry Dale research professorship.

Dale was secretary of the Royal Society from 1925 to 1935 and its president from 1940 to 1945. During his secretaryship the form of publication of the obituary notices of the fellows of the Society was changed so that they were published collectively in a single volume each year. During his presidency a meeting of the Society was held outside Britain for the first time, in India; the number of fellows to be elected each year was increased from twenty to twenty-five and, a more revolutionary change, in 1945 women were admitted to the fellowship for the first time. Dale's years as president were years of war, which created special responsibilities. To ensure the widest scientific co-operation within the British Commonwealth, Dale set up the British Commonwealth Science Committee, the natural outcome of which was the Royal Society Empire Scientific Conference in 1946. His presidency brought him advisory duties of a secret nature, including service from 1942 as chairman of a small, highly confidential, scientific advisory committee to the War Cabinet, and later to the post-war Cabinet, until 1947.

His last two years as director of the National Institute for Medical Research were largely devoted to the detailed planning of the new building at Mill Hill. After his retirement Dale became a member of the Medical Research Council (1942-6), chairman of its important post-war committee on the medical and biological application of nuclear physics (1945-9), member of the advisory committee on atomic energy (1945-7), chairman of the radioactive substances advisory committee (1949-52), of the governing body of the Lister Institute, and of the scientific committee of the British Council. He was president of the Royal Society of Medicine (1948-50) and of the British Council (1950-5), and in 1947 presided over the British Association at its Dundee meeting and over the 17th International Physiological Congress at Oxford. He was a trustee of the National Central Library and a member of the Standing Commission on Museums and Galleries. Before and after his retirement he found time for the spoken and written word. During the twenty years at Hampstead, before his retirement, he gave on average two lectures per annum and prepared them for publication, and during the twenty years following his retirement he gave over thirty lectures and addresses.

In the field of research, in 1906 Dale provided the first example of an adrenergic blocking agent by showing that ergotoxin reversed the blood pressure raising effect of sympathetic stimulation and of adrenaline; in 1909 he discovered the uterus contracting (oxytocic) action of posterior pituitary extract. In 1910 he and Barger introduced into pharmacology the term 'sympathomimetic', now in general use, with their important paper on 'Chemical structure and sympathomimetic actions of amines'. The year 1913 saw a fundamental discovery by Dale which changed our views about the mechanisms of anaphylaxis, allergy, and immunity: his finding that the anaphylactic contraction of plain muscle resulted from the formation of cell-fixed antibodies. Between 1914 and 1929 Dale's investigations, with a number of co-workers, were concerned mainly with histamine and acetylcholine. Both substances were shown to be natural constituents of animal tissue and their pharmacology was established. A beautiful analysis was made of the vascular effects of histamine and of the mechanism of histamine shock. Acetylcholine was shown to have an atropine-sensitive, muscarinic action on smooth muscles, gland cells, and heart, and a nicotine-sensitive, nicotinic action on autonomic ganglion cells and the medullary cells of the adrenals. To these actions was later added the action on motor endplates. This distinction, made in 1914, enabled Dale about twenty years later to envisage, and with a number of co-workers to establish, the physiological role of the nicotinic action of acetylcholine, its role as a synaptic transmitter of nerve effects to autonomic ganglia, to the medullary cells of the adrenals, and to the motor endplates of striated muscle fibres. He coined the term 'cholinergic' and 'adrenergic' nerve fibres and showed their distribution in the efferent nervous system. This work earned him the Nobel prize in 1936 together with Otto Loewi. When trying to assess Dale's scientific achievements, not least was the immense contribution he made, in the twenties, to therapeutics throughout the world by the work he did for the acceptance of international standards for hormones, vitamins, and drugs, he himself providing the first international standard for insulin.

Dale published numerous articles and two books. To this Dictionary he contributed the notices of Sir F. W. Andrewes, Sir F. G. Hopkins, Sir H. G. Lyons, H. D. Dakin, A. J. Ewins, Sir L. E. Hill, and C. H. Kellaway.

Dale's work was recognized by his appointment as a fellow of the Royal Society (1914); CBE (1919); knight (1932); GBE (1943); and by his admission to the OM (1944). Dale shared the unique position of being holder of two orders of merit—the second one being the pour le mérite of the German Bundesrepublik (1955)—with only one other person in Britain, T. S. Eliot [q.v.]. In 1949 Dale received the grand croix de l'ordre de la couronne, Belgium. In 1900 Dale won the Gedge prize, Cambridge University; in 1909 the Raymond Horton Smith prize; in 1926 the Cameron prize, university of Edinburgh; and in 1936 the Nobel prize for physiology and medicine which he shared with O. Loewi, of Graz. A research professorship of the Royal Society bears his name and in 1959 a Dale medal was struck in his honour by the Society of Endocrinology. It is awarded annually and the recipient delivers the Sir Henry Dale lecture. Dale was an honorary fellow of Trinity College, Cambridge, of University College, London, and of the Chemical Society. He received honorary degrees from twenty-five universities, including eleven in Britain; he was the recipient of seventeen medals, an honorary member of the Physiological Society, British Pharmacological Society, Pharmaceutical Society, Royal Society of Medicine, the Royal Society, Edinburgh, the Royal Society, New Zealand, an honorary associate of the Royal College of Veterinary Surgeons, and an honorary, foreign, corresponding, or associate member of thirty-seven foreign scientific societies.

Dale married in 1904 his first cousin Ellen Harriet, daughter of F. W. Hallett. She died in 1967. They had three children, all of whom studied either physiology or medicine. Their elder daughter, Alison Sarah, married Alexander Robertus (later Lord) Todd, FRS, professor of organic chemistry at Cambridge. Their second daughter, Eleanor Mary, married Robert Edgar Hope Simpson, a medical practitioner. Their third child, a son, Robert Henry, became a plastic surgeon in Saskatoon, Canada. He died in 1957. Dale himself died in the Evelyn Nursing Home, Cambridge, 23 July 1968.

A painting of Dale by Francis Dodd (1944) hangs at the National Institute for Medical Research, Mill Hill, London; another by (Sir) James Gunn, at the Royal Society, London; a third, by A. R. Middleton Todd (1967), at the Hall of the Salters' Company, Fore Street, London EC; a fourth, by John Ward, at The Leys School, Cambridge; and there is a profile by Mary Gillick (1956) at the Royal Society of Medicine.

[W. Feldberg in *Biographical Memoirs of Fellows of the Royal Society*, vol. xvi, 1970; private information; personal knowledge.]

W. FELDBERG

DALEY, SIR (WILLIAM) ALLEN (1887-1969), medical officer of health, was born at Bootle 19 February 1887, the elder son of William Daley, medical officer of health of Bootle, and his wife, Mary Allen. He was educated at Merchant Taylors' School, Crosby, and at the university of Liverpool. He graduated B.Sc. London in chemistry in 1906, then MB, Ch.B. Liverpool, 1909, with first class honours, and MB, BS London, 1910, with distinction in medicine, obtained the Cambridge DPH in 1911 with distinction, and his London MD in 1912. After holding resident posts in Liverpool he became resident medical officer at the London Fever Hospital in 1911. In May that year his father was drowned at the age of forty-seven in a yachting accident and Daley was recalled to Bootle to succeed him as medical officer of health at the early age of twenty-four.

For the next forty-one years Daley held posts of increasing responsibility and importance in the field of preventive medicine. The early work at Bootle showed energy and promise leading to similar appointments successively in Blackburn (1920-5) and Hull (1925-9). He was appointed in 1928 to serve on a departmental committee of the Ministry of Health on the recruitment and training of midwives and his work there was noticed by the medical officer of health of the London County Council, (Sir) Frederick Menzies (whose notice Daley subsequently contributed to this Dictionary). In 1929 Daley was appointed a principal medical officer of the London County Council and in 1938 deputy to Menzies. In the nine years before the outbreak of war in 1939 the hospitals of the Metropolitan Asylums Board and metropolitan Boards of Guardians were being integrated into a single service by the London County Council. Menzies had chosen well: Daley's apparently unlimited energy and industry had found an appropriate task. Within a short time he had a complete grasp of the complexities of the service down to the smallest detail. He recorded and reported on all his activities and copies were distributed widely so that staff were made aware of progress or delay in all projects. It was a commonplace to hear from staff that at no other time or place in their careers were they so well informed about their work. He chaired many departmental committees dealing with such diverse subjects as pathological services, hospital standards and staffing, district medical

service, ambulance service, and the tuberculosis scheme. He was demonstrably a master of the committee method: well informed, affable, urbane.

In 1939 Daley succeeded Menzies as county medical officer; in the same year he was elected FRCP. During the war of 1939-45 he had the difficult task of guiding the hospital service during a time when it acquired a reputation of never refusing a casualty a bed although many buildings were badly damaged. His work was recognized by a knighthood in 1944 and by an honorary physicianship to the King. He took a special pride in his election to the council of the Royal College of Physicians while a practising medical officer of health, a rare honour.

The National Health Service Act of 1946 led to a further period of great activity during which the London County Council hospitals were transferred to the newly formed regional hospital boards and simultaneously steps were taken to absorb the personal health services previously in the care of the metropolitan boroughs which made up the County Council area. This was accomplished with Daley's accustomed skill in 1948 and four years later he reached the official retiring age. This had no perceptible effect on his activities; he transferred his personal files to his home and continued to serve on the many committees to which he had been appointed in a personal capacity.

Daley was president of the Central Council for Health Education, having been a founder-member and the author of a paper in the twenties which played a considerable part in the thinking which led to the formation of the Council. He was chairman of the Chadwick trustees and president of the National Association for Maternal and Child Welfare. These were appointments which he continued to the end of his life, but in addition he held appointments on boards of governors of hospitals and other bodies concerned with health. Age limits removed him from many, but to the end he retained the vice-chairmanship of the academic board of the Royal Postgraduate Hospital at Hammersmith.

At the time of his retirement from his official post, Daley had written or spoken on subjects varying from addresses for learned societies to speeches at prizegivings to the number of 250. Some fifteen years later this had been increased to more than 450. He delivered the Croonian lectures to the Royal College of Physicians, the De Lamar lecture at Johns Hopkins School of Hygiene and Public Health, Baltimore, and a report to the World Health Organization and Rockefeller Foundation on health and social workers in England and France. On retirement he visited Australia on behalf of the Nuffield

Foundation, lecturing on the British National Health Service, and lectured also in North America, where for several months he was associate health officer of the city of Baltimore.

Although in the last five years of his life physical afflictions slowed him down, there was no lack of mental power and he continued by correspondence and conversation to be one of the best-informed, as also one of the best-known, figures in public health circles. He died 21 February 1969 at Tenerife during a winter holiday.

In 1913 Daley married Mary (Marie) (died 1962), daughter of Edward Toomey, of Liverpool; they had a daughter who became a consultant obstetrician and gynaecologist in London and a son who became a consultant physician at St. Thomas's Hospital. There is a portrait of Daley by William Sibbons (1967) in the possession of the family.

[*The Times*, 24 February 1969; *British Medical Journal*, 1 March 1969; *Lancet*, 8 March 1969; private information; personal knowledge.]   A. B. STEWART

DALTON, (EDWARD) HUGH (JOHN NEALE), BARON DALTON (1887-1962), Labour politician, was born at Neath, Glamorganshire, 26 August 1887, the eldest child of Canon John Neale Dalton by his wife, Catharine Alicia, elder daughter of Charles Evan-Thomas, JP, DL, of the Gnoll House, Neath, and sister of Sir Hugh Evan-Thomas [q.v.]; there was also a daughter, and another son who died at birth. Hugh Dalton's father had been tutor to Prince Edward, and to Prince George, afterwards King George V, whose friend and counsellor he remained throughout his life, serving as his domestic chaplain from 1892. He was a canon of St. George's Chapel, Windsor, from 1885 until his death in 1931; chaplain-in-ordinary to the sovereign in 1891-7, and thereafter deputy clerk of the closet. He was appointed KCVO in 1911.

Hugh Dalton was educated at Summer Fields, Oxford, and Eton, where he became captain of his house. He went up to King's College, Cambridge, where he won the Winchester reading prize and was classed junior optime in part i of the mathematical tripos (1909); he went on to read economics in his fourth year, studying under A. C. Pigou and J. M. (later Lord) Keynes [qq.v.], and obtained a good second in part ii of the economics tripos (1910). At Cambridge he became a close friend of Rupert Brooke [q.v.], and a somewhat romantic socialist through his strong adolescent dislike of unfair privilege; his socialism was fermented by a visit of Keir Hardie [q.v.] shortly after Dalton had joined the Fabian Society. In 1911 he won the Hutchinson research studentship to the London School of Economics and began to work on a thesis on 'Some aspects of the inequality of incomes in modern communities'. He also joined the Middle Temple, and was called to the bar in 1914. On the outbreak of war in that year he joined the Inns of Court OTC; he served in France in 1916-17, and was then transferred to an artillery regiment on the Italian front for a year and a half. He was demobilized early in 1919 and in the same year published his first book, *With British Guns in Italy*.

He then returned to the London School of Economics, where he lectured on economics under Professor Edwin Cannan [q.v.], completed his thesis, which was published in 1920, and obtained his D.Sc. (1921). He also took tutorial classes in economics for the Workers' Educational Association. He was Sir Ernest Cassel reader in commerce (1920-5) and reader in economics (1925-36) at London University, and was a member of the Cambridge University statutory commission in 1923-5. In 1923 he published his classic, *Principles of Public Finance*, based on orthodox pre-Keynesian economics; there followed the publication of *Towards the Peace of Nations* (1928) and *Practical Socialism for Britain* (1935). It was not until after 1937 that he became an ardent Keynesian.

Dalton entered politics in 1922 equipped for his way through life, as he said, with 'good physical health ... great stamina, a strong voice, a strong temper, strong views, some obstinacy ... a capacity for friendship on equal terms ... and an abiding loyalty to firm friends'. By 1924 he had fought three general elections and two by-elections as Labour candidate, winning a seat at Peckham in that year. He was chosen as prospective candidate for Bishop Auckland in 1928, but the sitting member died in December while Dalton was still member for Peckham; so his wife stood in his stead and won the seat in February 1929 to 'keep it warm' for him. In the general election later that year Dalton won Bishop Auckland himself with an over-all majority for Labour of 3,700. On the formation of a Labour Government by Ramsay MacDonald, Dalton was delighted at his appointment as parliamentary under-secretary to Arthur Henderson [q.v.] at the Foreign Office; he was devoted to Henderson, and glad of the opportunity to advance the cause of disarmament and the League of Nations.

However, Dalton declined to serve in MacDonald's 'national' Government of 1931, and lost his seat in the ensuing general election. He travelled extensively during the next four years, visiting Russia, Italy (where he had a cordial interview with Mussolini, claiming to have been a soldier of the Italian 'unconquered army'), France, and Germany, where he was appalled by the Nazi treatment of his Jewish academic friends. Later he visited Australia and New Zealand, which he loved.

In the general election of 1935 Dalton regained Bishop Auckland with a Labour majority of 8,086. As Opposition spokesman for foreign affairs in the House of Commons he spoke frequently and, convinced of Hitler's menace, fought hard to stop his party's voting against all Service estimates, in which he succeeded in 1937. By that time he had gained stature in the Labour Party, of which he was chairman in 1936-7. In 1935 he had been top of the constituency votes for the national executive, to which he was first elected in 1926 and on which he served without a break from 1928 to 1952.

When war broke out in 1939 Dalton was prominent in support of policies which (Sir) Winston Churchill also advocated; in 1940 he was appointed minister of economic warfare in the coalition Government, and was sworn of the Privy Council: he chose Hugh Gaitskell [q.v.] to be his principal private secretary, and John Wilmot (later Lord Wilmot of Selmeston, q.v.) as parliamentary private secretary. In addition, Dalton had the task of setting up the Special Operations Executive—the secret organization for subversion and sabotage and the strengthening of guerrilla and resistance movements in occupied countries—with which Churchill invited him to 'set Europe ablaze'. He appointed (Sir) Frank Nelson [q.v.] to 'build up the new machine', and battled—often successfully—against suspicion and even hostility from the Foreign Office and the Services.

His organizational abilities were recognized by Churchill who promoted him to the presidency of the Board of Trade in February 1942, although, as Dalton said, 'Handing over S.O.E. twanged my heart-strings'. The Board of Trade was at that time 'a rag-bag of problems with no connecting thread', containing, among others, the Department of Overseas Trade, the Mines Department, and the Petroleum Department. At first Dalton's main preoccupation was with the fuel shortage, and after four months' intense and patient consultation his recommendations were finally adopted and a Ministry of Fuel and Power was set up, to which those responsibilities were transferred. In that short time he had done much for the coal industry, especially in regard to miners' wages and in ensuring government control (with owners, miners, and others) through a National Coal Board. His major achievement was to forearm against post-war unemployment by steering new factories into the 'distressed' (renamed 'development') areas. He used the allocation of building licences and compulsory consultation with industrialists to 'take the work to the worker'; his white paper also included important provisions for powers of compulsory purchase, and financial aid. These

measures were embodied in the distribution of industry Bill, which Churchill's caretaker Government saw through its final stages, the royal assent being received on the very day the wartime Parliament was dissolved.

In the 1945 general election Dalton held Bishop Auckland with an increased majority of 8,860. In the ensuing Labour Government, the prime minister, Clement (later Earl) Attlee, gave Dalton the Treasury, Ernest Bevin [q.v.] the Foreign Office, and Herbert Morrison (later Lord Morrison of Lambeth, q.v.) the lord presidency of the Council with leadership of the House of Commons.

Dalton's first act as chancellor of the Exchequer was to appoint Keynes as his personal adviser and give him the arduous job of negotiating an American loan to replace 'lease-lend', which he believed could save the country from mass unemployment and starvation. Dalton steered both the loan agreement and the Bretton Woods agreement through the House of Commons in December 1945. In his first budget—October 1945—he cut income tax by a shilling in the pound, raised surtax, and cut excess profits tax. In his second budget, April 1946, he remitted purchase tax on some household necessities, made a start in the repayment of post-war credits, substantially raised estate duties, making provision for the transfer of land and historic houses to the National Trust and similar bodies, and carried £50 million from the sale of war stores to a National Land Fund for the purchase of beautiful tracts of land on behalf of the nation, an issue on which, as an inveterate hiker, he felt strongly. He also allocated generous sums for the 'development' areas, for many forms of welfare, and for education, especially the universities. In the nationalization programme to which the Labour Government was committed, he was responsible for the nationalization of the Bank of England (1946)—which made it a public board independent of the Treasury in most monetary affairs—and for the Borrowing (Control and Guarantees) Act of 1946, which regulated new issues. On Treasury advice he did not set up a National Investment Board, as he had intended, but only a consultative National Investment Council, which had no powers at all.

But Dalton's popularity as chancellor did not last long. Trouble came in 1947, which he described as 'annus horrendus' as compared with the 'annus mirabilis' of 1946. He had been encouraged by Keynes to pursue cheap money —dear money would have added to inflation— and with the continuation of strict rationing, cheap money was a tenable policy. But Keynes was no longer there to help, and Dalton carried cheap money too far: it was a great achievement to have financed the floating debt at $\frac{1}{2}\%$, but he put too much faith in the official control of the gilt-edged market through the government broker. Advised by the Treasury and Bank of England, he decided to call 3% Local Loans stock and replace it with an undated $2\frac{1}{2}\%$ Treasury stock (thereafter called 'Daltons'). This proved more than the market was prepared to accept, having just digested a $2\frac{1}{2}\%$ savings bond issue redeemable in eighteen to twenty-one years. The new $2\frac{1}{2}\%$ Treasury undated stock only held its issue price for a very short time in February 1947 and was then heavily sold, falling to a substantial discount.

After this market disaster came the coal fuel crisis (when electricity was cut off for several hours a day), and a worsening balance of payments. To no avail Dalton had begged his ministerial colleagues to reduce their expenditure. In April 1947 he introduced his third budget, which did little to help, since it still adhered to cheap money. In July-August a sterling crisis broke, and the convertibility clause of the American loan agreement had to be suspended. By now overworked and overstrained with worry, Dalton prepared his fourth budget in November 1947. On his way into the chamber of the House of Commons to deliver it, he was questioned by a well-known lobby correspondent of the *Star*. Thinking that he spoke in confidence and that his questioner would continue on his way to the press gallery to listen to his speech, Dalton briefly outlined his proposals. They appeared prematurely in the guise of a forecast in an edition of the paper on sale before the proposals were announced just after 4 o'clock by Dalton. On discovering his error of judgement next morning, Dalton immediately offered his resignation which Attlee reluctantly felt obliged to accept. His place at the Treasury was taken by Sir Stafford Cripps [q.v.].

Dalton rejoined the Cabinet in June 1948 as chancellor of the Duchy of Lancaster, and went to Paris in November as head of the British delegation to the conference which in the following year provided the constitution for the new Council of Europe. He served on its Consultative Assembly in 1949 as deputy leader of the Labour section under Morrison, and as leader in 1950. He was well equipped for the task, as he was fluent in French and Italian (an unusual accomplishment for a Labour minister), but he did not disguise his dislike of the Germans, and his love of the Poles and of all Slavs and Latins. After the general election of 1950 he was made minister of town and country planning (in 1951 enlarged into local government and planning), an office he accepted because of his interest in the new towns and parks; but his ministerial career came to an end—although he retained his seat in the Commons—after Labour's defeat in the general election of October 1951. He won

Bishop Auckland yet again in the general election of 1955 (with a reduced majority), but withdrew from the shadow Cabinet and urged other veterans in the party to do the same; in 1957, shortly after his seventieth birthday, he announced that he would not stand at the next election, which took place in 1959. He received a life peerage in 1960. He published the last of the three volumes of his memoirs, *High Tide and After*, in 1962; the earlier volumes were *Call Back Yesterday* (1953) and *The Fateful Years (1931-1945)* (1957).

Dalton was master of the Drapers' Company in 1958-9, as his father and other members of his family had also been, taking much interest in its affairs. He was an honorary fellow of LSE, and the universities of Sydney, Manchester, and Durham awarded him honorary degrees; he had also been elected an honorary bencher of the Middle Temple in 1946.

Dalton was for many years one of the 'big five' in the Labour Party with Attlee, Bevin, Morrison, and Cripps; he did much to help transform the party by attracting and promoting the talent of younger men such as James Callaghan, Hugh Gaitskell, Anthony Crosland, Denis Healey, and Douglas Jay, who gave it a non-Marxist egalitarian but pragmatic socialism. He was essentially patriotic, rooting out pacifism from the party before 1939 and, with Bevin, steadily opposing Marxist infiltration. He was one of the few Labour leaders who had actually fought for his country on the battlefields of Europe, and he loved the virile young men who had done the same and had voted Labour. Apart from the miners of Bishop Auckland, whom he represented for twenty-six years in all, many others were grateful to him too, not least for extending the national parks and forests which he loved. He was perhaps too emotional, but there were many who valued his loyal friendship and generosity, especially the young; tributes were also paid to his buoyant optimism and exuberance of spirits—not to say panache—with matching drive and decision and a 'big booming voice' which, as Queen Victoria had remarked when he was only four years old, was 'just like his father's'. He excelled as a teacher, being scrupulously fair, and wrote good English easily, with brevity and clarity—an advantage to any politician. In appearance he was rather ungainly: over six feet tall, with long legs and short arms; he had piercing light-blue eyes, which he turned up to heaven when he talked, and a great bald domed head; but his smile was warm and friendly, his expression one of cheerful benevolence, and in youth he had been decidedly handsome.

In 1914 Dalton married Ruth (died 1966), daughter of Thomas Hamilton-Fox, a business man; they had one daughter who died in 1922, aged four and a half. Dalton died in London 13 February 1962, after a lengthy illness.

[*The Times*, 14 and 20 February 1962; *Manchester Guardian Weekly*, 15 February 1962; Hugh Dalton, *Memoirs*, op. cit.; Nicholas Davenport, *Memoirs of a City Radical*, 1974; personal knowledge.]

NICHOLAS DAVENPORT

DANE, CLEMENCE (pseudonym), playwright and novelist. [See ASHTON, WINIFRED.]

DANQUAH, JOSEPH BOAKYE (1895-1965), lawyer and politician in the Gold Coast (Ghana), was born 21 December 1895 at Bepong in Kwahu, not far from his native state of Akyem Abuakwa, in the Eastern Region of the Gold Coast. He was the son of Emmanuel Yaw Boakye Danquah, an evangelist of the Basel Mission (later to become the Church of Scotland Mission, then the Presbyterian Church of Ghana). He attended the local schools and at the age of seventeen became a clerk in a solicitor's office, later transferring to government service as a clerk in the Supreme Court. When he was twenty-one he was taken under the wing of his elder half-brother (Sir) Nana Ofori Atta, paramount chief of Akyem Abuakwa, soon to become probably the most influential African in the Legislative Council.

After some five years as secretary to Ofori Atta, during which time he made a careful study of the religions, laws, and customs of his people (which later resulted in various publications), he moved to London in 1921 and entered University College. In 1926 he obtained the degrees of BA and LLB of London University, was awarded the John Stuart Mill scholarship in the philosophy of mind and logic, and was called to the bar by the Inner Temple. He proceeded Ph.D. in 1927.

Danquah then travelled extensively on the Continent, and returned to the Gold Coast later in the same year to set up in legal practice, his heart set on politics and law, in that order. In 1930 he attended the first meeting of the 'Youth Conference', and as its secretary used this body as a means of publicizing his views on constitutional reform, on which he became the recognized leader when in 1931 he established the *Times of West Africa*, the first Gold Coast daily newspaper. In London he had been a foundation member of the West African Students Union and editor of its magazine in 1923-7.

In view of his interest in the customs of the Akans, his relationship with Ofori Atta, and his constitutional rather than revolutionary approach to problems, Danquah always had the backing of the chiefs and elders and professional classes: almost the total vocal element in the Gold Coast at that time. In 1940 he put forward the idea of making use of the colony's Council of Chiefs as an Upper House in a two-tier Parliament, the Legislative Council to be reconstituted as the Lower House. He also put forward ideas for the inclusion of Ashanti and, later, of the Northern Territories, both then administered by the governor in person and not subject to the Legislative Council. When the secretary of state for the colonies visited the Gold Coast in 1943, Danquah, then at the zenith of his career, submitted a memorandum on constitutional reform.

In 1947 Danquah formed the United Gold Coast Convention (UGCC), more as a political movement than a party; in December of that year, on Danquah's invitation, Dr Kwame Nkrumah, who had been out of the country for some years, arrived to be its secretary. In 1948 occurred the Accra riots, engineered largely by a prepared boycott of European stores by disillusioned ex-servicemen; but also by the leaders of the UGCC. Danquah cabled to the secretary of state that law and order had broken down and asked for a new government to be formed under himself and other persons he named. Instead, Danquah, with Nkrumah and four others, was taken into preventive detention, the first of several such incarcerations. They were soon released, but friction in the UGCC between Danquah and Nkrumah was soon only too obvious and while Danquah had the support of all the maturer elements in the country, Nkrumah was rallying the masses to his side. By 1949 Nkrumah was winning the fight for leadership and policy-making; in June he broke away from the UGCC and formed the Convention People's Party (CPP). While the UGCC's platform was 'self-government in the shortest possible time', Nkrumah chose 'self-government now', which had a far greater appeal.

In 1950 there were further riots and again Danquah and Nkrumah were arrested, and again soon released. General elections under a new constitution were held in 1951; the CPP won a great victory and Danquah found himself leader of the Opposition. In 1954 there was another general election and Danquah lost his seat. He had stood in a constituency amongst his own people, the Akim Abuakwas, where he was undoubtedly popular, and the loss of his seat was a great blow to Danquah and an indication that Nkrumah's programme was the more popular.

When the Gold Coast was granted independence in 1957 it changed its name to Ghana, the name of an ancient kingdom in the Sahara which had a connection with the Gold Coast according to Danquah, who was the first to advocate its use.

After independence, opposition parties based on regions or tribes were forbidden, so a United

Party was formed with Danquah as its leader. In 1960 Ghana became a republic and Danquah stood as a candidate for the presidency, but received only some 120,000 votes to a million cast for Nkrumah. In 1961 Danquah was again imprisoned, but released in 1962. In 1963 he was elected president of the Ghana Bar Association. In that year the chief justice was dismissed from office and amendments to the constitution proposed to make the country a one-party state. Neither of these events was agreeable to Danquah who was imprisoned again in January 1964. While in prison he addressed numerous petitions to President Nkrumah, pleading for detainees to be tried, for parliamentary democracy to be restored, and for the law to be respected. But all to no avail and he died in prison 4 February 1965. He was twice married.

[*The Times*, 5 February 1965; Martin Wight, *The Gold Coast Legislative Council*, 1947; K. Kesse-Adu, *The Politics of Political Detention*, 1971; personal knowledge.]

A. C. RUSSELL

D'ARANYI, JELLY (1893-1966), violinist. [See under FACHIRI, ADILA (1886-1962).]

DARBISHIRE, HELEN (1881-1961), scholar, critic, and principal of Somerville College, Oxford, was born in Oxford 26 February 1881, the second child and elder daughter of Samuel Dukinfield Darbishire, a Balliol man who had stroked Oxford's winning eight in 1868 and 1869 and who was physician to the Radcliffe Infirmary and coroner to the university, by his wife, Florence Eckersley. Both her parents were natives of Manchester, where the Darbishires' home in the mid nineteenth century was a centre of liberal and Unitarian society, including the Gaskells and Martineaus; her grandfather, the elder Samuel Darbishire, befriended J. A. Froude [q.v.] and employed him as tutor to his daughters in 1849. Helen Darbishire was educated at first privately with her cousins in North Wales, where the family lived during her father's long illness, and then, after his death, at the Oxford High School. In 1900 she entered Somerville as a Pfeiffer scholar, and took a first class in the recently instituted honour school of English in 1903. One of her teachers was Ernest de Selincourt (whose notice she contributed to this Dictionary), the first university lecturer in the subject and a cousin by marriage of her mother; he became, as she wrote later, 'a lifelong friend ... I owe more to his mind and spirit than can be said.' After a few years' lecturing at the Royal Holloway College, university of London, she returned to Somerville in 1908 as English tutor and remained for thirty-seven years, becoming a fellow in 1922, university lecturer in

1927-31, principal in 1931-45, and honorary fellow in 1946. Her only absence of more than a few months was as visiting professor at Wellesley College, Mass., in 1925-6.

As a tutor, she was quick to recognize and foster any genuine response to literature, however immature; and if her teaching was not always immediately stimulating (some pupils found her remote), it was felt as a slow-growing, durable influence, sustained by the continuing example of her own disciplined and disinterested scholarship. One of the future directions of her own studies is seen in an early publication, the exemplary edition of *Wordsworth's Poems published in 1807* (1914), which already shows her characteristic power of combining close attention to textual matters with sensitive interpretation; revised in 1952 in the light of later discoveries, it has held its own as the standard edition of the greatest of Wordsworth's shorter poems. For the ensuing thirty years most of her work on Wordsworth was selflessly merged with de Selincourt's, on whose death in 1943 she took over and completed the five-volume Clarendon edition.

Meanwhile she was laying the foundations of her own monumental text of Milton, with *The Manuscript of Paradise Lost, Book I* (1931), which broke new ground by demonstrating Milton's minute care for spelling and punctuation in the service of his meaning and the movement of his verse. But after *The Early Lives of Milton* (1932), publication, apart from articles and reviews, was long intermitted by her duties as principal—an office unsought, and even unwelcome to her modesty and reserve, but fulfilled with conscience and devotion in a period of change both unexpected and foreseen. In the troubled years before and during the war she was active in assistance and hospitality to displaced foreign scholars. Her tenure of office saw new developments in the college's constitution and additions to its buildings, including the east quadrangle (now named after her) and the college chapel. A selection of her regular addresses was posthumously published in 1962; their keynote, as of her life and her teaching, was Wordsworth's 'We live by admiration, hope, and love; | And even as these are well and wisely fixed, | In dignity of being we ascend.'

In retirement, after completing the Clarendon Wordsworth, she returned to Milton. Believing that 'an editor must take his courage in his hands and exercise his critical judgment', she set herself to offer a text of *Paradise Lost* 'as near as possible to that which Milton himself would have given us, if he had had his sight'. No one was better equipped for this formidable task. The new text (published in 1952) invited and received criticism, some of it constructive, but has remained a basic work for subsequent editors. The second, less controversial volume, containing the rest of Milton's poems, appeared in 1955, and the complete poems in the Oxford Standard Authors series in 1958.

The garnered wisdom and undiminished ardour implicit in her long editorial labours on these two great poets found direct and moving expression in the Clark lectures on *The Poet Wordsworth* (1949; published 1950) and the James Bryce memorial lecture on *Paradise Lost* (1950; published 1951). Further work on the MSS of *The Prelude* led to the revision of de Selincourt's great edition in 1959; and fittingly, her own last publication was a new edition in 1958 of the Journals of Dorothy Wordsworth, with whom she felt a particular sympathy.

The completion of her own large designs meant less to her than the promotion of good or better work by others after her. Constantly resorted to by Wordsworth scholars and eager amateur inquirers from all parts of the world, she was generous with the fruits of her own researches and with the resources of the Wordsworth library at Grasmere; as trustee and, from 1943 to her death, chairman of Dove Cottage, she greatly developed its facilities as a centre of study by her initiative and practical efficiency. For the last seven years, Shepherds How, overlooking the vale of Grasmere, was the 'quiet heart's selected home', shared with one friend and visited by many. Age hardly affected her singular powers of steady unhurried work, but released her reserve, and the dry humour and gifts as a raconteur, long known to intimates, were more freely exercised. She died at home after a short illness 11 March 1961.

She was twice awarded the Rose Mary Crawshay prize of the British Academy, in 1932 and 1950, and was elected a fellow in 1947. Honorary degrees of D.Litt. were conferred on her by Durham and London, and in 1955 she was appointed CBE.

Helen Darbishire was of middle height, fair, with candid blue eyes and a look of serenity and determination. A portrait by (Sir) William Coldstream (1939) is at Somerville and one by Bernard Meninsky (1923) in private hands.

[Basil Willey, in *Proceedings* of the British Academy, vol. xlvii, 1961; private information; personal knowledge.]

KATHLEEN TILLOTSON

DARWIN, BERNARD RICHARD MEIRION (1876-1961), essayist and sports writer, was born at Downe in Kent 7 September 1876, the only son of (Sir) Francis Darwin [q.v.], botanist, and his first wife, Amy, daughter of Lawrence Ruck, of Pantlludw, Machynlleth, North Wales. Amy died in childbirth in 1876. Bernard was the grandson of Charles

Darwin [q.v.], a piece of information with which he sometimes greeted strangers, so often had he been asked his relationship to the author of *Origin of Species*.

He was educated at Summer Fields (Oxford), at Eton (1889-94), to which he won a scholarship, and at Trinity College, Cambridge. He played for three years in the university golf team, captaining it in his third year, 1897. In the law tripos he took third class honours in part i (1896) and second class honours in part ii (1897). In 1903 he was called to the bar of the Inner Temple but his heart was not in law. In 1908, a year after being engaged to contribute occasional articles to the *Evening Standard*, *Country Life*, and *The Times*, he began to devote himself full-time to the world of golf. It was almost as though he had deliberately turned his back on the scholarship and literary talent by which he was surrounded in his family, including two relatives, Berta Ruck and Gwen Raverat [q.v.], who became established literary figures.

The links that were forged with Fleet Street that year endured. He continued to write about golf for *The Times* until 1953 and for *Country Life* until shortly before his death. The only time his weekly article for *The Times* failed to appear was on his first visit to the United States in 1913 when the *Mauretania* containing his dispatch was held up by fog in New York harbour.

War intervened between what were for Darwin two important visits to the United States. That first one in 1913 enabled him to cover for *The Times* the appearance of Harry Vardon and Edward Ray in the United States open championship. The contest resulted in victory for an unknown American youth, Francis Ouimet, a historic event since it marked the turning of the tide in the direction of American ascendancy in the game. Darwin was the only daily British correspondent present and marked the card for the winner in the three-way play-off.

In the war of 1914-18 Darwin served in the Royal Army Ordnance Corps as a lieutenant (acting major). He spent two and a half years in Macedonia. For some time he was deputy assistant director of Ordnance Services for the 26th division.

His second visit to the United States was in 1922 when he accompanied the British amateur team which played in the first Walker Cup match against the United States. The British captain fell ill and Darwin replaced him. The match was lost but Darwin won his single.

He was well qualified to fill that gap for he had just reached the semi-finals of the British amateur championship for the second time (1921 and 1909). He had also to his credit achievements which today may sound trivial but which in his time ranked second in importance only to the amateur championship: eight England caps against Scotland, victory in the *Golf Illustrated* golf vase (1919) and in the President's Putter (1924). In 1934 he received golf's greatest honour when he was elected captain of the Royal and Ancient Golf Club. He continued writing through the war of 1939-45, both golf articles and fourth leaders, his supply of raw material coming from his own personal experience and from the letters of friends who wrote to him from all corners of the world. Because of the restrictions on newsprint he was never given full rein after the war, and in 1953 he retired from *The Times*. His departure was marked by a dinner given to him not by *The Times*, whose staff scarcely knew him apart from his writings, but by a host of golfing friends which included not only golfers and writers but a governor-general, members of Parliament, and judges.

Golf has always had its eloquent apologists but nobody before had attempted to submit his thoughts on the subject to the glare of daily journalism. Blandly expressing ignorance of the workings of Fleet Street Darwin succeeded in making his reports acceptable to a wide public through the milder qualities of scholarship, humour, and urbanity. When he began to write, golf reporting was little more in the daily press than a list of figures at the bottom of a column; by the time of his retirement he had turned it into a branch of literary journalism.

That Darwin was something of a snob few would deny, but this seldom showed in his writings, and when it did the point was so delicately made that it was almost impossible to take offence. More important from the golfing point of view was the fact that whereas his keen, experienced eye could instantly detect a weakness he was uniformly kind to the perpetrators of it. Because he himself had suffered at the highest level, not perhaps from a lack of nerve but from an overheated temperament, he was long-suffering in print about all except bores.

Partisanship was the key to his outlook on life. A taste for murder trials, to which he readily confessed, might be attributed to his legal background, but what fascinated him most was the contest between the accuser and the accused, and the insight which such trials gave him into the lives of others. He was fascinated by prize-fighting to the extent of writing a book on it, and this pugnacious streak in his temperament may have accounted for his love of Dickens and his battling characters. Darwin quoted freely and without affectation from his favourite authors Stevenson, Thackeray, Hazlitt, Borrow, and Trollope, but in the case of Dickens he seemed hardly able to help

himself; quotations spilled over from his abundant knowledge of and deep affection for his characters. He was an entirely suitable choice for the formidable task of writing a foreword to the *Oxford Dictionary of Quotations* (1941), and it occasioned little surprise when the citation for the CBE which he was appointed in 1937 spoke of his contribution to both literature and sport. In a thousand small ways he must have kindled in others an appreciation of the joys of good reading. To this Dictionary Darwin contributed the notices of John Ball, H. G. Hutchinson, and James Braid.

Darwin married in 1906 Elinor Mary (died 1954), daughter of William Thomas Monsell; they had one son and two daughters. His son, Robin, became principal of the Royal College of Art (1948-67) and was knighted in 1964. Darwin's wife provided the illustrations for some children's books he wrote, the first of which, *The Tale of Mr. Tootleoo*, appeared in 1926. Outside the realm of golf his writings reflected his own interests—a book on the English public school (1929), on London clubs, and on W. G. Grace (1934). It was in his autobiographical writing that he scored most heavily. In *Green Memories* (1928), *Pack Clouds Away* (1941), and *The World that Fred Made* (1955), his style was nostalgic without becoming sentimental. It brought vividly to life the gentle pleasures of childhood and family life. Darwin died at Denton in Sussex 18 October 1961.

There is a pen-and-ink portrait of Darwin by Powys Evans (*c*.1930) in the National Portrait Gallery.

[Bernard Darwin, *Green Memories*, 1928, *Pack Clouds Away*, 1941, and *The World that Fred Made*, 1955; Peter Ryde (ed.), *Mostly Golf*, 1976; *The Times*, 19, 24, and 25 October 1961; private information; personal knowledge.]   PETER RYDE

DARWIN, SIR CHARLES GALTON (1887-1962), physicist, was born 19 December 1887 at Newnham Grange, Cambridge, the eldest of the two sons and two daughters of (Sir) George Darwin, FRS [q.v.], and his wife, Maud, daughter of Charles du Puy, of Huguenot descent, from Philadelphia. George, originally a lawyer then mathematician, astronomer, and Plumian professor of astronomy at Cambridge, also had a deep interest in history and languages. Through him Charles belonged to the extraordinary Darwin-Wedgwood family described by N. G. Annan in 'The Intellectual Aristocracy' in *Studies in Social History*, edited by J. H. Plumb (1955). His grandfather, Charles Robert Darwin [q.v.], who wrote *Origin of Species*

(1859), his great-grandfather, and his two great-great-grandfathers (Erasmus Darwin and Josiah Wedgwood of Etruria, qq.v.) were all fellows of the Royal Society. So were two of C. G. Darwin's four Darwin uncles: Sir Francis (naturalist and biographer, q.v.) and Sir Horace (engineer and manufacturer, q.v.). One sister, Margaret, married (Sir) Geoffrey Keynes, surgeon and writer, and the other, Gwen Raverat [q.v.], described in *Period Piece* (1952) the family's happy early life when five Darwin first cousins, including Frances (later) Cornford [q.v.], the poet, were especially close Cambridge companions. A notice of Bernard Darwin, C. G. Darwin's cousin, precedes this essay.

Darwin was a scholar at Marlborough College (1901–6) and at Trinity College, Cambridge (1906–10), where he read for the unreformed mathematical tripos, becoming fourth wrangler in part i in 1909 and obtaining a first class in part ii in 1910. He joined Ernest (later Lord) Rutherford in Manchester as Schuster lecturer in mathematical physics in 1910, the period of the discovery of the nucleus. Niels Bohr joined the talented Manchester team in 1912. Darwin wrote, *inter alia*, a paper on the collision of alpha particles with light nuclei which helped Rutherford in work which led to the discovery of artificial nuclear disintegration. He then worked with H. G. J. Moseley [q.v.] on the diffraction of X-rays and in 1914 published two papers which were 'landmarks in the history of X-ray analysis of crystals' (Sir Lawrence Bragg, quoted in the Royal Society memoir listed below).

In the war of 1914–18 Darwin commanded a section in one of the Royal Engineer units organized to detect enemy guns by sound ranging and won the MC. Late in 1917 he was attached to the Royal Flying Corps for work on aircraft noise.

From 1919 to 1922 he was fellow and lecturer at Christ's College, Cambridge, and in this period he and (Sir) R. H. Fowler [q.v.] wrote joint papers about the basis of classical atomic statistics and their relation to thermodynamics, introducing the useful concept of 'the partition function'. In 1922 he was elected a fellow of the Royal Society. In the same year, while a visiting professor at the California Institute of Technology, he began work on optical properties, especially those involving magnetic fields.

In 1924 Darwin was appointed first Tait professor of natural philosophy at Edinburgh University, but, although an outstanding lecturer, he did not establish a school of theoretical physics. He himself worked on the applications to magneto optics of the then new Bohr–Sommerfeld quantum theory of atomic structure. When he spent short periods at Niels Bohr's Institute in Copenhagen in 1927 and 1928 he was excited by the ferment of ideas there and

returned to write important papers. The first, in 1927, usefully suggested the way free electrons behave. Then on 1 February 1928 Paul A. M. Dirac's first paper on his new relativistic electron appeared. Darwin immediately realized its significance and a month later had produced a paper which made Dirac's theory accessible to ordinary physicists and greatly hastened its general acceptance. He also used the theory to derive for the first time the correct explanation of the fine structure of the hydrogen spectrum. Two further papers analysed the magnetic moment, and the diffraction, of the relativistic electron. Subsequently he worked out in detail for non-relativistic Schrödinger electrons the very important case of a collision between two electrons and then considered other examples of the uncertainty principle. At intervals over the years he continued to spend time on a purely classical problem concerning the effective electric field acting on an electron in an ionized medium.

Darwin returned to Cambridge in 1936 as master of Christ's College but in 1938 he became director of the National Physical Laboratory. He successfully reorganized the NPL for urgent war work and in 1941 was seconded to Washington for a year as first director of the British office set up to improve Anglo-American scientific war co-operation—a crucial post which he filled with energy, sound scientific judgement, and diplomatic skill. Involved in liaison over the atomic bomb, he was one of the few to realize that it presented problems different in kind, as well as in explosive power, from conventional weapons. On returning to Britain he became scientific adviser to the War Office. When he went back full time to the NPL he was concerned with the reconversion for peace and with reorganization and new creations among the laboratories of the Department of Scientific and Industrial Research. Foreseeing the great potentialities of electronic computers, he created in the NPL two new divisions, namely mathematics and electronics. The successful collaboration of these divisions produced Pilot ACE, the first electronic digital computer available to British industry. Darwin retired from the NPL in 1949. Thereafter he continued to write some scientific papers but his chief interest was now in population problems and eugenics. In his book *The Next Million Years* (1952) he considered the long-term future of mankind. To this Dictionary he contributed the notices of Sir W. H. Bragg and D. R. Hartree.

Before and after retirement he was in demand for committee work. For example, he was a member of the University Grants Committee for a double term, from 1943 to 1953. From 1941 to 1944 he was president of the Physical Society and from 1953 to 1959 president of the Eugenics

Society. He and his wife enjoyed foreign travel and among his missions was a visit as scientific adviser to Thailand in 1953 on behalf of UNESCO.

Darwin was made a KBE in 1942. He received honorary degrees from Bristol, Manchester, St. Andrews, Trinity College (Dublin), Delhi, Edinburgh, Chicago, and California. He was an honorary fellow of Christ's College (1939) and of Trinity College, Cambridge (1953). He received the Royal medal of the Royal Society in 1935 and was a vice-president in 1939. He also received the MacDugal Brisbane prize from the Royal Society of Edinburgh. He was a foreign member of the Hollandsche Matsch. Wet. of Haarlem, and an honorary member of the French Physical Society and of the American Philosophical Society.

Sir George P. Thomson, who wrote the Royal Society memoir of Darwin listed below, describes him therein as an 'applied mathematician' rather than a theoretical physicist, saying that 'his ideas were derived from experiments or from other men's work. He used his mathematics on them rather than to suggest them.' Thomson and others conclude that Darwin's most useful work was as an interpreter of the new quantum theory to experimental physicists and that he was especially fitted for this because of his exceptionally wide range of understanding and a most unusual capacity for seeing the essential idea in a maze of complicated mathematics or conflicting experiments. This capacity of seeing essentials equally helped him at the National Physical Laboratory and in his work in the two wars.

Darwin was physically large, cheerful, and tolerant. He was warm and sympathetic to those who knew him well but students and some of his staff at the National Physical Laboratory felt awe as well as admiration for him. He had wide curiosity. He was proud of his family connections and devoted to his immediate family. In 1925 he married Katharine, daughter of Francis William Pember, a lawyer, who was the warden of All Souls College, Oxford, from 1914 to 1932. She was the granddaughter of Edward Henry Pember [q.v.] and was herself a mathematician. They had one daughter (a crystallographer) and four sons (an electronic engineer, a civil engineer, a Foreign Office lawyer, and a zoologist). Darwin died 31 December 1962 at Cambridge in the house where he was born, which subsequently became part of Darwin College. There are two similar portraits, painted by his cousin (Sir) Robin Darwin soon after Darwin's retirement from the NPL in 1949. One is at Darwin College, Cambridge, and the other belongs to the Royal Society.

[G. P. Thomson, in *Biographical Memoirs of Fellows of the Royal Society*, vol. ix, 1963; N. G. Annan, 'The Intellectual Aristocracy', *Studies in Social History*, ed. J. H. Plumb, 1955; Gwen Raverat, *Period Piece*, 1952; private information.]   MARGARET GOWING

DAVENPORT, HAROLD (1907-1969), mathematician, was born 30 October 1907, in Huncoat, near Accrington, Lancashire, the elder child and only son of Percy Davenport, a clerk at Perseverance Mill and, later, the company secretary, and his wife, Nancy, daughter of John Barnes, the owner of the mill. From Accrington Grammar School Davenport won scholarships to Manchester University, where, in 1927, at the age of nineteen he graduated with first class honours in mathematics. In Manchester he came to the notice of E. A. Milne [q.v.], who encouraged him to enter for a scholarship at Trinity College, Cambridge. He was successful and in 1929 was classed as wrangler in part ii of the mathematical tripos and was declared by the examiners to have deserved special credit in the subjects of Schedule B (which represented the most advanced part of the examination).

When Davenport first went to Manchester he had an interest in the history of mathematics, but there were no signs of an early commitment to arithmetical questions; indeed, at this time he even considered seriously a career in chemistry. But in 1929 all doubts had vanished, and Davenport became Professor J. E. Littlewood's research student, with number theory as his chosen field. Littlewood was then at the height of his fame and Cambridge was soon to become, thanks to his celebrated partnership with G. H. Hardy [q.v.], a world centre for mathematics. It was a wonderful time, in the ideal place, to embark on studies in the subject which C. F. Gauss has termed the queen of mathematics, and Davenport used his opportunity to the full. His first investigations, into the distribution of quadratic residues, involved pioneering studies of character sums and exponential sums; the skills he acquired then he put to good use in many subsequent researches. Indeed, it was a significant feature of Davenport's genius that he assimilated his mathematical experiences so well that they were always readily available for his own use and, later, for that of his students. By the summer of 1930 his first two papers were in the course of publication, in 1931 he was Rayleigh prizeman, and in 1932 he was elected to a Trinity fellowship. These and the next few years were of decisive importance in Davenport's development.

A long visit to Helmut Hasse in Marburg in 1931 taught Davenport the power of modern algebra in the study of arithmetical questions, as well as giving him a fluent command of German, and their joint work proved to be notably influential. In the course of his stay in Germany, Davenport met (Professor) H. Heilbronn, Landau's last 'Assistent' in Göttingen, and by the time Heilbronn arrived in Cambridge as a refugee in 1933, the two had become firm friends. Each the product of a famous school of number theory, it is hardly surprising that the friendship of these gifted young men led to a successful and, as it turned out, lifelong collaboration; their last two joint papers appeared in 1969 and 1971. Several of their earliest papers were skilful applications of the celebrated circle method of Hardy and Littlewood to novel additive problems; and Davenport himself at this time made several highly original contributions to Waring's problem (Edward Waring, q.v.). He was, for example, the first to prove the best possible result that every sufficiently large integer is representable as the sum of sixteen fourth powers of integers. Years later the mastery he thus gained in all aspects of the circle method was to stand him in good stead in his work on values taken by quadratic and cubic forms in many variables. This work, whether done alone, in association with collaborators such as B. J. Birch and D. J. Lewis, or by students under his direction, is perhaps the most enduring part of Davenport's mathematical testament, a witness alike to his mental powers and his matchless ability to inspire others.

However, that was still in the future; in 1937, after the expiry of his fellowship, Davenport joined L. J. Mordell as an assistant lecturer in Manchester and set himself to study the geometry of numbers. Although Davenport was by now a scholar of international renown—in 1938 he received the Cambridge Sc.D., in 1940 he was elected to a fellowship of the Royal Society, and in the same year he won the Adams prize of the university of Cambridge—it is probably fair to say that the Manchester period completed his mathematical education. In 1941 he went to the chair of mathematics at the University College of North Wales in Bangor, and in 1945 he became Astor professor of mathematics in University College, London.

The greater stage of London, the growth of education in the post-war period, as well as the renewed freedom to travel, now gave Davenport the opportunity to reveal his extraordinary powers as a director of research. His presence in London was a magnet, and drew to him scholars and students from all parts of the world; and when, in 1958, he moved to the Rouse Ball chair of mathematics at Cambridge in succession to A. S. Besicovitch [q.v.] he recreated there the vitality of his London seminar. The list of mathematicians who are his former students or consider themselves such in some measure, is of an awe-inspiring quality—C. A. Rogers, F. J. Dyson, K. F. Roth, B. J. Birch, D. A. Burgess,

G. L. Watson, Alan Baker, E. Bombieri, J. Conway, H. L. Montgomery (three of these winners of Fields medals, 'the Nobel prize of mathematics') constitute only the beginning of the list and Davenport was proud of them all; but he had many other students, less richly endowed, whose studies he planned and supervised with no less care, and some of these he nursed to achievements which were a greater surprise to them than to their teacher. And beyond these there were many more again, with whom he corresponded tirelessly (in his beautiful handwriting), giving freely of his enthusiasm, wisdom, and patience.

In 1956 he embarked on his important researches on quadratic forms and the success which attended him in this seemed to release a new vitality. From now on until the end, and especially after his return to Cambridge, the scale of his mathematical activities continued to increase, as did his range of interests. At the time of his death in Cambridge, 9 June 1969, he was the unquestioned leader of the important British school of number theory.

In person Davenport was shy and reserved and in later years could put a slight deafness to good use. He was very conservative by temperament, and one of his favourite sayings was that all change was for the worse! In mathematical contacts he was always accessible, entirely without arrogance, and genuinely modest. While he admired talent enormously, it was characteristic of him that he tended to think of his own achievements as having been more the result of tenacious study and perseverance.

An outstanding lecturer, he was also an exceptionally lucid writer, and his little book, *The Higher Arithmetic* (1952), is a minor classic. He wrote two other books, each the outcome of a lecture course given at the university of Michigan, both influential but now sadly out of print.

Davenport was awarded the senior Berwick prize of the London Mathematical Society in 1954, and in 1957-9 he was president of the Society. He received the Sylvester medal of the Royal Society in 1967. In 1964 he had been elected an ordinary member of the Royal Society of Science in Uppsala, and in 1968 he received an honorary D.Sc. from the university of Nottingham. He spent the summer term of 1966 at the university of Göttingen, as Gauss professor; he was the first Englishman to hold this distinguished visiting appointment.

In 1944, when Davenport was professor in Bangor, he married a colleague from the modern languages department, Anne, daughter of James J. Lofthouse, engineer, and there were two sons of the marriage.

H. Halberstam and D. A. Burgess in *Biographical Memoirs of Fellows of the Royal*

Society, vol. xvii, 1971; private information; personal knowledge.]   HEINI HALBERSTAM

DAVIDSON, JOHN COLIN CAMPBELL, first VISCOUNT DAVIDSON (1889-1970), politician, was born 23 February 1889 at Aberdeen, the younger child and only son of (Sir) James Mackenzie Davidson, a distinguished surgeon, and his wife, Georgina Barbara Watt, daughter of the Revd William Henderson, of Aberdeen. Davidson's grandfather, John Davidson, in 1825 had emigrated to the Argentine where he carved out a substantial fortune of which his grandson eventually inherited a half share. Davidson was educated at Fretherne House preparatory school, Westminster, and Pembroke College, Cambridge, where he obtained a third class in part i of the law tripos in 1909. He was called to the bar by the Middle Temple in 1913.

In May 1910 Davidson left Cambridge and joined the Colonial Office as unpaid private secretary to the secretary of state, Lord Crewe [q.v.]. He continued in that capacity under Crewe's successor, Lewis (later Viscount) Harcourt [q.v.], from the end of 1910. On the outbreak of war in 1914 Davidson was anxious to serve in the armed forces, but his tact, zeal, and efficiency had become indispensable to Harcourt whose reiterated pleas prevailed on him to stay at the Colonial Office, despite receiving the white feather on one occasion. In May 1915 Bonar Law replaced Harcourt who strongly urged him to retain Davidson. The two men soon struck up a warm friendship: Bonar Law treated him as a member of the family and relied on him as heavily as Harcourt had done.

With the accession of Lloyd George as prime minister in December 1916, Bonar Law became chancellor of the Exchequer, leader of the House, and second man in the Government. He insisted on taking Davidson with him to the Treasury. There Davidson was to some extent responsible for an appointment which had far-reaching effects on his own career and the history of Britain. He persuaded Bonar Law to take on as his parliamentary private secretary Stanley Baldwin, a hitherto obscure backbencher who thus made his first step in the ladder of promotion. Davidson and Baldwin found that they had much in common. Their close personal and political friendship ended only with Baldwin's death some thirty years later. There was, however, one intimate of Law's whom Davidson kept at arm's length. He did not doubt the sincere affection with which Lord Beaverbrook [q.v.] regarded Bonar Law, but he sensed dangers. Nor did he like the slightly raffish atmosphere of Beaverbrook's house, Cherkley Court. 'I dined, I lunched there,' he wrote,

'but I never slept there. . . . Perhaps I was puritanical, but I also wanted to be independent . . .'

Davidson was responsible for the final draft of the famous 'coupon' for the election in 1918, and on behalf of the leader of the House reported the political scene in the new Parliament to the King's secretary, Lord Stamfordham [q.v.], who came to have a high respect for his judgement. In November 1920 Davidson was elected unopposed as Conservative member for Hemel Hempstead at a by-election and became parliamentary private secretary to Bonar Law who had become lord privy seal in 1919 while continuing as leader of the House. In March 1921, because of ill health, Bonar Law resigned. Davidson then became parliamentary private secretary to Baldwin, the new president of the Board of Trade. The coalition by now was beginning to lose its glitter. Davidson distrusted Lloyd George and his closest confidants, Churchill and Lord Birkenhead [q.v.]. In October 1922 he was among the many influences causing Bonar Law to return and agree to accept the leadership of the Conservative Party if it voted to end the coalition. As he walked up the steps of the Carlton Club to the famous meeting on 19 October a lobby correspondent called out 'What is going to happen?' Davidson prophetically replied 'A slice off the top'.

On becoming prime minister, Bonar Law promptly invited Davidson to return as his parliamentary private secretary and reassume his old position as unpaid, unofficial secretary. Davidson was thus closely involved in the formation of the new Cabinet. His next assignment was to wind up Lloyd George's 'garden suburb'—a task he performed with cool ruthlessness. Bonar Law's premiership ended with the collapse of his health in May 1923. The succession lay between Lord Curzon [q.v.] and Baldwin. Davidson's part in influencing a decision remains something of a puzzle.

Bonar Law himself was ill and undecided. He personally preferred Baldwin but he did not see how Curzon's claims could be set aside. He asked to be excused from giving advice; but his true opinion was understandably of interest to Stamfordham who had the task of making 'soundings'. In 1954 there was discovered in the royal archives a typed memorandum (unsigned but admittedly dictated by Davidson) in which the case for Baldwin against Curzon was most cogently argued. (Sir) Ronald Waterhouse, another of Law's secretaries, had handed it to Stamfordham when he and Sir Frederick Sykes [q.v.] conveyed Law's official letter of resignation to the King. Stamfordham minuted at the head of the document that Waterhouse had stated that it 'practically expressed the views of Mr. Bonar Law'.

There is nothing in the memorandum to corroborate this statement, and all the evidence suggests that Waterhouse had no right to make it. Davidson himself, in conversation long after the event, said that he had dictated it in response to a request from Stamfordham for a note 'written from the point of view of the average backbencher in the House of Commons'. There is nothing in the memorandum (or any contemporary papers which have come to light) to corroborate that statement either. Davidson, who doubted whether Waterhouse had even read the memorandum, was certain that he had no authority to pass it off as Law's opinion. Nevertheless he considered that it did not in fact misrepresent Law, although its forceful clearcut arguments for Baldwin and against Curzon can scarcely be regarded as an accurate picture of a dying man's mind torn by misgivings, hesitation, and doubt. In any case, the result was affected only marginally. The King's decision was firmly based on his own good sense and the powerful arguments of Balfour against the choice of a peer as prime minister.

Davidson became chancellor of the Duchy of Lancaster in Baldwin's Government, in effect continuing as the prime minister's private secretary. He lost his seat at the general election of December 1923, the timing of which he regarded as disastrous, but he recovered it in the election of 1924. In Baldwin's second administration he became parliamentary and financial secretary to the Admiralty where he had to circumvent Churchill's determination to force economies upon the Service, especially in regard to the building of new cruisers. During the general strike he played an important part as deputy chief civil commissioner, responsible for publicity. He managed the *British Gazette* and showed some skill in controlling the more intemperate outpourings of its turbulent editor, Churchill. He also arranged for the broadcasting of official bulletins whilst taking care to safeguard in principle if not in practice the independence of the BBC.

At the end of 1926 Davidson left office to take up the post of chairman of the Conservative Party. His main tasks were to clean up the honours system and simultaneously raise a great deal of money. He succeeded in both (ruining incidentally in the process that most notorious of honours touts, Maundy Gregory). The foundation of Ashridge, in memory of Bonar Law, as a Conservative adult education college was due almost entirely to Davidson's enthusiasm and he was now able to set about establishing its finances on a firm basis. He presided over its opening in 1929. Into the Central Office he introduced new blood: (Sir) Joseph Ball [q.v.] from the secret service and Sir Patrick Gower from the Civil Service. He left a lasting imprint

on the organization of the party and many of the changes attributed to his successor, Neville Chamberlain, were in fact his. He recognized the importance of the women who worked for the party; and he saw the need for a research department financially independent of Central Office. He and Ball also managed to 'penetrate' the Labour Party headquarters and secure advance information about its policies and plans. But the loss of the election in 1929 counted against him, as did the personal link with Baldwin who, himself under heavy fire from Beaverbrook, Lord Rothermere [q.v.], and other malcontents, felt obliged to accept Davidson's resignation in May 1930. Davidson considered that he had been let down but he did not allow this to mar his friendship with Baldwin.

After the election of 1931, Davidson again became chancellor of the Duchy of Lancaster. He went to India in 1932 as chairman of the Indian States inquiry committee and in 1933 became a member of the joint select committee whose proposals preceded the Government of India Act of 1935. He was offered, but refused, the governorship of Bombay. When Baldwin finally retired from politics in 1937 Davidson, who had little sympathy with Neville Chamberlain, retired too, and was made a viscount. Although he maintained his interest in Ashridge, he took no further active part in politics, but devoted himself to business interests and the promotion of good relations between Britain and South America. In 1940-1 he served in the Ministry of Information and in 1942 he made an official tour of South America.

A man of much charm and geniality, bespectacled and ruddy complexioned, Davidson could be very tough. He was essentially one who operated behind the scenes rather than on the front of the stage. A streak of Scottish puritanism put him emphatically on the side of the 'respectable'. He had no sympathy with the buccaneers—Lloyd George, Churchill, Birkenhead, Beaverbrook. He was deeply devoted to Baldwin who owed a great debt to his advice, companionship, and support.

Davidson was appointed CB in 1919, CH in 1923, and GCVO in 1935. He was sworn of the Privy Council in 1928.

In 1919 Davidson married a friend of Baldwin's family, Frances Joan, daughter of Sir Willoughby (later Lord) Dickinson. They had two sons and two daughters. His wife succeeded him as member of Parliament for Hemel Hempstead from 1937 until 1959. She was created a life peeress in 1963 as Baroness Northchurch. Davidson died at his London home 11 December 1970 and was succeeded by his elder son, John Andrew (born 1928).

[Robert Blake, *The Unknown Prime Minister: the Life and Times of Andrew Bonar Law*,

1955; Robert Rhodes James, *Memoirs of a Conservative: J. C. C. Davidson's Memoirs and Papers 1910-37*, 1969; Keith Middlemas and John Barnes, *Baldwin*, 1969; A. J. P. Taylor, *Beaverbrook*, 1972; H. Montgomery Hyde, *Baldwin, the Unexpected Prime Minister*, 1973; private information; personal knowledge.]   BLAKE

DAVIES, CLEMENT EDWARD (1884-1962), lawyer and politician, was born 19 February 1884 at Llanfyllin, Montgomeryshire, the youngest of the seven children of Moses Davies, auctioneer, and his wife, Elizabeth Margaret Jones, of Llanerfyl, Montgomeryshire. Clement Davies was sent to the local English school, but won a scholarship to Llanfyllin county school when it was founded in 1897. He went on to Trinity Hall, Cambridge, where he was a senior foundation scholar, obtained first class honours in both parts of the law tripos (1906-7), and was law student (1907-11). He won prizes in criminal law, constitutional law, and the law of real property, and was awarded the bar prize and certificate of honour in the bar finals in 1909 when he was called by Lincoln's Inn. Shortly before this he had been a lecturer at Aberystwyth University College, but in 1909 he joined the North Wales circuit before transferring in 1910 to the Northern circuit. In that year he moved to London and rapidly developed a successful commercial practice. He had the capacity to read quickly and accurately, once mastering twenty-five briefs in a morning. He also published works on agricultural law and the law of auctions and auctioneers.

On the outbreak of war in 1914 Clement Davies volunteered for military service, but was posted instead to the office of the procurator-general as adviser on enemy activities in neutral countries and on the high seas. It was he, it is believed, who recommended the interception of the ship on which von Papen, German military attaché to Washington, was returning home. Among his papers, seized at Falmouth, an important code was found.

Davies was later seconded to the Board of Trade's department concerned with trading with the enemy. After the war he was successively secretary to the president of the Probate, Divorce, and Admiralty division (1918-19) and to the master of the Rolls (1919-23). From 1919 to 1925 he was a junior counsel to the Treasury. He took silk in 1926 and in 1935 he was appointed chairman of the Montgomeryshire quarter-sessions, a post which he was most assiduous in filling until his death. In the meantime he had given up practice in 1930 when he joined the board of Unilever upon which he remained until 1941 when he resigned in order to concentrate on his political work, although his legal advice remained available to the firm.

From his youth onwards Clement Davies had been fascinated by radical politics. One of his forebears had voted for the Reform Bill of 1832. Politics were in the air he breathed as a young barrister when he worked as junior counsel with John (later Viscount) Simon and F. E. Smith (later Earl of Birkenhead) [qq.v.], both destined to become lord chancellor; and quite late in life Davies would speak of the Asquith Government as though he had been in Parliament at the time. But it was not until 1929 that he felt able to contest a seat and was returned at the general election as a Liberal for Montgomeryshire which he represented for the rest of his life. He was rooted in the county of his birth and made his home there at Meifod. Inevitably, he became entangled in the party disputes which followed the formation of MacDonald's 'national' Government in 1931. At the general election of that year he held his seat unopposed as a Liberal National. He did so again at the election of 1935, although by this time the Liberal Party, led by Sir Herbert (later Viscount) Samuel [q.v.], had withdrawn its support of the Government and was in opposition.

It was in his Liberal National phase that Davies did his most valuable work as a back-bencher, serving on a number of committees, and especially as chairman of an inquiry into the incidence of tuberculosis in Wales. Between 1937 and 1938 he made the most searching inquiries and found grave inadequacies in the provision of public health services and housing. His legal training and political sense here complemented each other perfectly. His report was not published until 1939 and most of the remedies had to await the post-war period.

At the beginning of the war in 1939 Clement Davies became the chairman of an action committee in the House of Commons which sought the most effective prosecution of the war and which was supported by members of the three main parties in the House. Davies had become convinced that there must be a coalition Government in which all three parties should be represented. In the critical debate on the Norwegian campaign which led to the downfall of the Chamberlain Government, it was Clement Davies who, on the second day, persuaded Lloyd George to speak—a speech which Churchill described as Lloyd George's 'last decisive intervention in the House of Commons'. The vote on 8 May was a moral defeat for the Government and on 10 May 1940 Churchill became prime minister. Lord Boothby, who worked closely with Davies in the action committee as its secretary, has described him as 'one of the architects—some may judge the principal architect' of the Churchill coalition Government.

In 1942 Clement Davies rejoined the independent Liberal Party, but when the normal party battle was resumed after the war the Liberals could not all forgive him for having dallied for so long with the Liberal Nationals. Even when he became the leader of the Liberal Party in 1945, in succession to Sir Archibald Sinclair (later Viscount Thurso, q.v.) who had been defeated in Caithness and Sutherland, Davies was not given the full trust of his party. When Churchill formed his Conservative Government in 1951 with only a small majority and offered Davies the post of minister of education, the Liberal Party managers advised him to refuse— as he did. They did not want the party, in the post-war political atmosphere, to be thought to be doing a deal with the Conservatives.

As leader of the Liberals until 1956, when he made way for Joseph Grimond, Clement Davies spent all his energy and gifts in trying to bring strength back to the party. He had an appalling political task, and he was working under a severe personal strain of which the public knew nothing—the effects of excessive indulgence in alcohol. He secured meagre results for his party; but at least he held it together in independence and provided a much-needed focus at a time when the energies of radicals tended to become diffused. He was a kindly man who made friends in all parties in the House of Commons. He was devoted to Parliament as an institution and his respect for it, with his awareness of the chafings of poverty, made him a sturdy advocate of a decent standard of pay for all members. Liberal organization during his leadership was not taut. But he would spread the gospel of Liberalism anywhere with zeal. He had an agreeable voice and spoke frequently in the country, liking particularly to talk to students at the universities. He was a radical evangelist by temperament rather than a party boss. The ease with which he found himself in his public speeches developing Patrick Henry's theme 'Give me liberty, or give me death!' almost endeared him to his critics. Such causes as social reform, collective security, and world government warmed his heart, and towards the end of his career he found deep satisfaction in his work as president of the Parliamentary Association for World Government. He was nominated, unsuccessfully, in 1955 for a Nobel peace prize.

Davies was sworn of the Privy Council in 1947. He was elected an honorary fellow of Trinity Hall in 1950 and a bencher of Lincoln's Inn in 1953. In that year he received the freedom of Welshpool and in 1955 an honorary LLD from the university of Wales. He died in London 23 March 1962.

In 1913 Davies married Jano Elizabeth, daughter of Morgan Davies, a Welsh surgeon with a practice in London. They had three sons and one daughter; three of the children each died at the age of twenty-four; one son and the daughter were both accidentally killed while on active service. Mrs Clement Davies was herself a graduate of the university of Wales and had been the youngest head teacher of her time in London. She was a linguist and an excellent public speaker and brought valuable support to her husband's political work. A portrait of Clement Davies by Sir Gerald Kelly, and a bronze bust by John Harvey are in the possession of the family.

[Lord Boothby, *My Yesterday, Your Tomorrow*, 1962; Frank Owen, *Tempestuous Journey*, 1954; J. C. Rasmussen, *The Liberal Party*, 1965; private information; personal knowledge.]   FRANCIS BOYD

DAVIES, WILLIAM JOHN ABBOTT (1890–1967), rugby footballer, was born 21 June 1890 in Pembroke, the eldest of the four children and only son of William George Davies, a shopkeeper, of Pembroke, and his wife, Florence Meyrick. Davies, who was known by the nickname of 'Dave', was educated at Pembroke Dock Grammar School, the Royal Naval College, Keyham, and the Royal Naval College, Greenwich. He was a Pembroke dockyard apprentice in 1905 and went to Greenwich College in 1910. He proved himself to be a gifted athlete and games player at Greenwich, but he did not take up rugby football seriously until he was nearly twenty years old. As a boy, he played more soccer than rugby, and he was about to play a game of hockey when he was pressed into service to play a game of rugby instead. His playing career quickly developed with the United Services Club, Portsmouth, and, within three years, he was capped for England as a fly-half.

He played a full international season for England in 1913, winning five caps, before the outbreak of World War I, in which he served in the Grand Fleet, first in the *Iron Duke*, and then in *Queen Elizabeth*. After the war he returned to Admiralty work in Portsmouth as assistant constructor and was appointed OBE in 1919.

Davies resumed playing rugby football for the United Services Club, Portsmouth, and began his club and international half-back partnership with C. A. Kershaw. They played together for England for four seasons after World War I, and were so successful that England never lost a match when they were in the team. Indeed, when Davies retired from regular first-class rugby at the end of the 1922–3 season, he had never appeared in a losing

England team in the international championship, even though he had won twenty-two caps over a period of eleven years spanning the war. England's only defeat in that time in a match in which Davies played was against South Africa in 1913.

Lord Wakefield of Kendal (formerly W. Wavell Wakefield), one of England's greatest rugby forwards, who played half his distinguished international career in the same team as Davies, has said of him: 'As "Dave" was born in Wales, I am pretty sure he was qualified to play for Wales, even though I believe his parents came originally from the West Country. However, he chose to play for England instead, and that was a happy decision for us, because no international team can function properly without a sound partnership at half-back, and Kershaw and Davies were wonderfully effective. . . . "Dave" was always immaculate. He was always calm, and always appeared to be in control of the situation. He never had a hair out of place, his boots shone, and his playing kit was impeccable. It was an enduring ambition of his opponents, particularly the forwards, to disturb that calm by dumping him unceremoniously on his backside in the mud, but I cannot remember that they ever succeeded! Some of Kershaw's passes were pretty erratic, but "Dave" had such a fantastic pair of hands that he picked them up without any fuss. He was perfectly happy to do so, because the length of "K's" pass enabled him to stand so far away from the forwards that he had great flexibility of operation. "Dave" had the ability to wait for his chance, too, and by doing so, he often lulled the opposition into a false sense of security. He usually made only one break in each half, but when he did so, it was decisive. He and Kershaw were both in the Navy and they were firmly established as the best half-backs in England when I won my first cap in 1920. I have often thought since how much easier it made the game for the rest of us.'

In 1923 Davies married Margaret Bleecker, daughter of Major Ernest Glanville Waymouth, of the Royal Artillery. They had a son and a daughter, both of whom became medical doctors. Davies's widow, who in 1979 was still living only two miles from the Rugby Union's ground at Twickenham, recalled that her husband used to practise with C. A. Kershaw almost every day when they were playing for US Portsmouth. 'What they did may have looked easy, but it was born of long and hard practice', she said.

Davies captained the Royal Navy and Hampshire and he became an England selector for three years when he retired. In the year of his retirement, in 1923, he played in the centenary match at Rugby School, exactly 100 years after

William Webb Ellis had supposedly first picked up the ball and ran with it, 'thus originating the distinctive feature of the Rugby game'. This assertion is open to some doubt, but few would dispute that Davies was one of the best fly-halves who played for England.

When his playing days were over, Davies continued his work at the Admiralty. He was attached to the staff of the commander-in-chief of the Mediterranean Fleet at Malta between 1935 and 1938, and in 1939 was appointed by the Admiralty as chief constructor. He was assistant director of warship production in 1942, superintendent of warship production on the Clyde in 1946, and director of merchant shipbuilding and repairs between 1949 and 1950.

He was president of the Civil Service Football Club between 1937 and 1966. In 1951 he became a liveryman of the Royal Company of Shipwrights. He wrote two books on rugby football: *Rugby Football* (1923) and *How to Play Rugby Football* (1933). He died at home in Teddington 26 April 1967.

[Rugby Union records; private information.]
JOHN REASON

DAWTRY, FRANK DALMENY (1902–1968), secretary of the National Association of Probation Officers, was born 17 January 1901 at 54 Cromwell Street, Walkley, Sheffield. His father, Wycliffe Bright Dawtry, a Unitarian and keen Liberal, was a cabinet maker, who had been apprenticed as a pattern maker by his father, a renowned foundry foreman, when the use of cast iron was at its height. His mother was Alice Jackson Ross. Frank Dawtry was the youngest and most delicate of four brothers. He won a scholarship to the Sheffield Central Secondary School, but left at fifteen owing to a breakdown in health. After a period as office boy and later junior clerk in a Sheffield steelworks, he was thrown out of work for almost two years after the trade recession of 1921. This early experience of unemployment made him familiar with the problems faced by the less fortunate members of the community and at this time he became a member of the Independent Labour Party.

In 1923 chance led him to the field of work to which he was to devote his energies for the next forty years. He was appointed clerk/bookkeeper to the Sheffield Council of Social Service and within four years became secretary of its Personal Services Committee. At the same time, after a brief apprenticeship with the Wakefield Discharged Prisoners' Aid Society, he was appointed secretary and thus began his close co-operation with the Probation Service.

On 19 October 1931 at Port Erin, Isle of Man, Dawtry married Dora Anna, a schoolteacher, whose father, James Robinson Corrin, a local builder and a member of the House of Keys, was appointed MBE 29 October 1957, the same day as Dawtry, who was advanced to OBE in 1967. They had no children.

Dawtry worked hard to co-ordinate the work of the other local Discharged Prisoners' Aid Societies and during this time made weekly visits to both Leeds and Wakefield prisons, where he organized discharge committees and was responsible for the welfare of the prisoners. On the foundation of the National Association of Discharged Prisoners' Aid Societies in 1937 Dawtry was the first to be appointed resident DPA secretary and welfare officer at HM Prison Wakefield. Additionally he was involved with the first local open prison and the training centre for prison staff. He found a ready acceptance from both prisoners and staff at Wakefield and spent much time visiting and helping prisoners' families. He also travelled extensively, lecturing about prisoners and their needs and enlisting financial support for what was still a voluntary society.

Revised methods of training prisoners were developed and when the new system was extended to Maidstone prison in 1944 Dawtry was appointed organizer there. However, two years later, feeling that the continued existence of capital punishment in this country could not be reconciled with his view of the good society, Dawtry resigned and became secretary of the National Council for the Abolition of the Death Penalty. Almost at once he initiated a misleadingly successful campaign, for no sooner had the death penalty been suspended for a trial period than public pressure caused the question to be reconsidered, and it had to be reimposed by the home secretary. However, the number of executions was subsequently substantially reduced until the eventual abolition of the death penalty in 1965.

In 1948 Dawtry became general secretary to the National Association of Probation Officers, for which cause he worked untiringly until his retirement in January 1967. He commenced long-overdue negotiations on the pay and conditions of service of probation officers. Largely due to his personal influence and his wise and dedicated efforts, the voice of the Service was increasingly heard in matters of policy relating to its duties and the prevention and treatment of delinquency. During those years of almost constant change in the scope and nature of its functions, he focused and expressed the view of the Service in a way which enabled it to contribute increasingly, from its wealth of practical experience, to the many legislative and other decisions which led to the creation of the modern Probation and After-Care Service.

For many years, and up to the time of his death, he was on the executive of the Howard League for Penal Reform and an active member of the Institute for the Study and Treatment of Delinquency. He was a founder-member of the National Association for the Care and Resettlement of Offenders, was equally involved with the National Association for Mental Health, and was on the council of the National Citizens Advice Bureaux. He was a convinced pacifist and founded the Sheffield No More War movement, serving as secretary until it amalgamated with the Peace Pledge Union, of whose council he was a member. He was also a fellow of the Royal Society of Arts as well as belonging to many other bodies which reflected his concern for peace, justice, and beauty. In May 1963 the university of Leeds conferred on him the degree of Master of Arts, *honoris causa*.

After his death at his home in Weybridge 5 October 1968 a Frank Dawtry Memorial was established whereby a public seminar on a subject within the field of the treatment of offenders, the prevention of crime, and the administration of justice is held regularly in the university of Leeds.

His warmth of personality and love of people, particularly the underdog and the victim of inequality in society, were translated into a life of service without thought of personal reward. To care was to do. He fully understood the importance of political action in furthering the causes for which he was concerned and had a close association with the House of Commons, where the lord chancellor honoured him with a retirement dinner to express the appreciation of his parliamentary and Civil Service friends.

He had an intense love of cricket and for forty years was a keen member of the Yorkshire Cricket Club. His slight figure was familiar and respected on the international scene as well as at the smallest probation branch conference, where his lively mind and imagination were alert to the impact and potential of new ideas. Modest and dedicated, with a keen sense of humour, he was a visionary who translated his visions into achievements, not only for the Probation Service but in the whole field of penology.

[*The Times*, 7 and 9 October 1968; private information; personal knowledge.]

KENNETH THOMPSON

DEBENHAM, FRANK (1883-1965), geographer, was born at Bowral, New South Wales, 26 December 1883, the second son of the Revd John Willmott Debenham and his wife, Edith Cleveland. He went to the King's School, Parramatta, and Sydney University where he read English and philosophy. He then taught for three years at Armidale School, and during this time taught himself—as well as his pupils—some science. He then re-entered Sydney University and majored in geology. (Sir) Edgeworth David [q.v.] who was then professor had been with Sir Ernest Shackleton [q.v.] in the Antarctic. When Captain Scott [q.v.] was recruiting for his second expedition in 1910 he wished to associate Australia with it and having secured Griffith Taylor in London, when in Sydney asked Debenham to join him.

In the Antarctic, Debenham's work, geological and cartographical, was done first on the western side of McMurdo Sound. He visited the Koettlitz glacier, the Ferrar glacier, and other features in the foothills of the Royal Society range. In the following season—having recovered from an injury to his knee whilst playing football—he went to Granite harbour and the Mackay glacier. One of his most significant contributions to the work of the expedition, and subsequently to his pupils at Cambridge, was his expertise in plane-table mapping. He convinced Scott and other members of the expedition of its value not only at base camps but also on sledge journeys. Scott in his diary recorded that Debenham was 'a well-trained, sturdy worker, with a quiet meaning that carries conviction; he realizes the conceptions of thoroughness and conscientiousness'.

After leaving the Antarctic Debenham went, with other members of the expedition, to Cambridge to work up his results. This was interrupted by the outbreak of war in 1914. He joined the Oxfordshire and Buckinghamshire Light Infantry, and after service in Salonika, where he was severely wounded and shell-shocked, he was demobilized as a major and returned to Cambridge.

In 1919 he was appointed to the Royal Geographical Society's lectureship in surveying and cartography at Cambridge. In 1920 he was elected into a fellowship at Gonville and Caius College where he was a tutor in 1923–8. It was in the immediate post-war years that the geographical tripos was founded, and the first examination for part i was in 1920. Debenham at once became closely associated with Philip Lake, the head of the new department, and in addition to continuing his Antarctic work he gave himself wholeheartedly to the building up of the department, which before he retired in 1949, and largely through his own drive and energy, had become one of the leading schools of geography in the world.

But in 1919 the university had not begun to build its new departments and laboratories. Debenham continued his Antarctic work in a large attic in the Sedgwick Museum of Geology; there, too, he taught many of his pupils. The department of geography consisted of two rooms on the ground floor, and shared lecture rooms with the geologists. Debenham had suggested that some of the Scott Mansion House Fund should be used to build an institute for polar research. This was accepted and he was appointed director in 1926. A year previously he had, for his polar work, moved into Lensfield House which stood at the corner of Lensfield Road and Panton Street. In 1934 the Scott Polar Research Institute was opened, and it owed much to the enterprise and planning of Debenham who was perhaps happiest in this kind of work. The Institute took on its later enlarged form after his death, but he knew of the gift from the Ford Foundation for the great addition to the original building.

The department of geography expanded continuously from its foundation. Lake retired in 1927 and was succeeded by Debenham who became a reader. He was primarily responsible for the move from the Sedgwick Museum to the building in Downing Place previously known as the Balfour Laboratory. For a few years this was fairly satisfactory; but when the School of Forestry was closed, the building was handed over to geography in 1933 and provision was also made for a new and larger addition to it. Once again Debenham's skill and interest as a planner were invoked.

In 1928 the twelfth International Geographical Congress was held in part in Cambridge and Debenham acted as secretary of the executive committee. In 1931 he was elected to the chair of geography and so became the first professor of that subject in Cambridge. The new department was in full use by 1936, and during the war of 1939–45 its activities were numerous. Debenham had a great gift of teaching practical survey methods and how to make and record astronomical and other observations. Apart from his normal teaching which still continued, he was notably successful in training a large number of Service cadets who were attached for six-month courses. Two of the London departments were also billeted in Cambridge and with Debenham's help and encouragement found a welcome and temporary home in it. Meanwhile, the Scott Polar Research Institute, still under his direction, housed a section of the Naval Intelligence Division of the Admiralty. He retired as director in 1946.

The sudden influx of numbers after the war strained the accommodation of the department of geography to the limit. These years, until his retirement in 1949, were perhaps the most satisfying of all, because they showed so clearly that what he had done for both geography and polar research was fully and sincerely appreciated.

After retirement Debenham for some years was very active. He travelled extensively in Central Africa and made an interesting study of the water resources of the Bangweulu swamp. He had written reports on survey and geology for the *Terra Nova* expedition; and during his association with the department and the Institute, and also in his retirement, he published numerous papers and books, including *The Polar Regions* (1930), *In the Antarctic* (1952), *Antarctica; the Story of a Continent* (1959), and he edited Bellingshausen's *Antarctic Narrative* for the Hakluyt Society in 1945. For some years he edited the *Polar Record*.

Lord McNair said that Debenham 'was one of the most modest and unselfregarding persons that I have ever known. He was in his true element as a member of a group, be it an expedition, a college, a faculty or his family. He had a very warm heart under the control of a sound judgement. He was a good organizer and knew how to get the best out of those working with him—mainly because he was generous in giving credit to others and because he inspired their affection and confidence.' The writer of this notice worked with him for thirty years. In the war of 1939–45 when Debenham lost his elder son he was under great strain but was always in control of himself. Even if he disagreed with a colleague he never bore the slightest resentment and was never out of temper. He was pre-eminently an ingenious man and his own approach to university work was perhaps more practical than strictly academic. Nevertheless he respected and encouraged scholarship in others.

He had an extremely happy domestic life. He married in 1917 Dorothy Lucy, daughter of J. T. Lempriere of Melbourne, and had six children. He and his wife were most hospitable and gave a memorable welcome to former colleagues and students. In the last years of his life he suffered from heart trouble and deafness and spent much of his time at his desk, but was always glad to talk to friends for a short time.

In 1919 Debenham was appointed OBE. He received the Victoria medal of the Royal Geographical Society in 1948 and the David Livingstone centenary medal of the American Geographical Society in the same year. In 1965 he was made an honorary fellow of the Royal Geographical Society; and he received honorary degrees from Sydney, Perth, and Durham. He died in Cambridge 23 November 1965. The Scott Polar Research Institute has two portraits (one in crayon) by H. A. Freeth.

[Private information; personal knowledge.]

J. A. STEERS

DE HAVILLAND, Sir GEOFFREY (1882–1965), aircraft designer and manufacturer, was born at Wooburn, Buckinghamshire, 27 July 1882, the second son in a family of three sons and two daughters of the Revd Charles de Havilland, curate at Hazlemere, and Alice Jeannette, daughter of Jason Saunders. Charles de Havilland's half-brother was the father of the actresses Olivia de Havilland and Joan Fontaine.

At an early age de Havilland had engineering ability. After attending St. Edward's School, Oxford, in 1900 he took a three-year course in mechanical engineering at the Crystal Palace Engineering School, followed by an apprenticeship with Willans and Robinson, Rugby. In 1905 he obtained his first job as draughtsman with the Wolseley Tool and Motor Car Co., Birmingham. He then moved to the design office of the Vanguard Omnibus Company in Walthamstow. During this period he designed and built a quite revolutionary motor cycle which subsequently became the well-known Blackburn motor cycle. In 1908–9, inspired by the Wright brothers' exploits, he designed his own aeroplane and engine, and in 1910 taught himself to fly a second version of it. This aeroplane was one of the first half dozen British-built machines which really got off the ground. In December 1910 the government aeronautical establishment bought the successful aeroplane and employed him to develop it. From 1912–14 de Havilland evolved an important range of generic aeroplanes.

In May 1914 de Havilland, at the age of thirty-one, was engaged by the Aircraft Manufacturing Company to create and lead a design team. In the war of 1914–18 he designed and flew eight military aeroplanes, five going into war service in large production; the most important—and fastest—the DH4, can still be seen in the Smithsonian Institution, Washington DC. The number of 'DH' aeroplanes built in Britain and the United States was approximately 30 per cent of the total output of these two Allies.

In 1920 de Havilland founded the de Havilland Aircraft Company with a staff of fifty. His heart was in the civil application of the aeroplane, and during the next five years of precarious expansion, airliners were supplied to three airlines. In 1925 he pioneered the light-aeroplane movement with the Moth; the next twelve years saw the production of over 2,500 Moths and derivatives, in which thousands of civilians learnt to fly. Many long-distance flights were made in them by Amy Johnson [q.v.] and others. The Tiger Moth trainer appeared in 1931 and became the standard Royal Air Force primary trainer throughout the war of 1939–45, 8,300 being built. The first de Havilland aero-engine came in 1927. In 1927–8 were formed companies in Australia and Canada.

In the 1930s the Dragon, Express, and Dragon Rapide airliners appeared, all with de Havilland engines: 862 were built in Britain. In 1934 the de Havilland Comet racer won the MacRobertson International England to Australia air race and made seven world records. In 1935 de Havilland pioneered the manufacture in Britain of American controllable pitch propellers, which subsequently played a crucial role in winning the Battle of Britain.

In the war of 1939-45 de Havillands' prime contribution was the Mosquito, perhaps the most versatile warplane ever built, and for most of the war, the fastest aircraft. Over 14,000 de Havilland aircraft were produced in the Commonwealth, about half of them Mosquitoes.

After the war de Havillands returned to civil markets with the Dove and Heron feederliners and entered the jet age with the Vampire fighter powered by the first British production (DH) jet engine, subsequently used by a dozen air forces. Rocket engines followed in 1947 and guided weapons in 1951. During the 1950s de Havillands supplied many Venom, Hornet, and Sea Vixen fighters to the navy and air force. In this period civil (and ultimately military) aeroplane design began in de Havilland, Canada.

The de Havilland Comet, which first flew in 1949, pioneered the jet age of civil airliners when few accepted their economic viability. It was the first jet airliner to cross the Atlantic with fare-paying passengers: 110 Comets were built. In 1959 the Elmer A. Sperry award, 'for outstanding achievement in the field of transport' and one of America's most coveted engineering honours, was given 'to the de Havilland Aircraft Company for the vision, courage and skills displayed in conceiving, developing and producing the world's first jet-propelled passenger transport aircraft, the de Havilland Comet, powered by de Havilland Ghost jet engines'. The de Havilland Trident jetliner (first flight 1962, 117 built) followed the Comet.

De Havilland retired from active involvement in his company in 1955, thereafter remaining as president. In 1959, in the national rationalization of the aircraft industry, his companies offered themselves to and were taken over by Hawker Siddeley Aviation Ltd. During de Havilland's lifetime over 45,000 aeroplanes bearing his name were produced.

As a designer de Havilland saw clearly the right direction to go and unerringly judged the right step forward; he was often unorthodox, yet acted within the bounds of existing knowledge. Outlandish ideas had no place in his thinking, but, working within sound principles, he was first in the field with many revolutionary ideas, and probably unique among the pioneers in flying his own creations. He won the King's Cup air race in 1933 and continued flying until his seventieth year.

Retiring and self-effacing, he shrank from being an important figure in any official or public activity; at the same time he was no recluse and was a good companion among friends. With employees he was the same at all levels—courtly, unaffected, and disarming. His remarkable quality of leadership became legendary. C. C. Walker, his chief engineer and lifelong friend, wrote: 'As a leader, Geoffrey de Havilland had some rare qualities. He was a selfless man, a magnet that subconsciously drew together the same sort of people and inspired them. He was completely unpretentious and always discussed the current problems with those around him with open-minded candour, with the result that they had a feeling of being partners in any enterprise in which he was engaged.'

Natural history was de Havilland's leisure interest; he was a good mechanic and keen photographer, had an extensive collection of moths and butterflies, and made some excellent nature films, which were shown on television. A member of the Zoological Society and council member of the Fauna Preservation Society, he took some remarkable photographs of African wildlife, which were exhibited in a one-man show in London. He also designed an anaesthetizing rocket, which became indispensable equipment in ecology.

He received the following awards and decorations: OBE (1918), Air Force Cross (1919), CBE (1934), OM (1962), and many national and international gold and silver medals and honorary fellowships of learned and engineering societies. He was knighted in 1944.

De Havilland married in 1909 Louie (died 1949), daughter of Richard Thomas, of Chepstow. There were three sons: the eldest, Geoffrey Raoul [q.v.], was killed in 1946 after a brilliant eight-year career as chief test pilot to the de Havilland Aircraft Company, being responsible for the entire flight development of the Mosquito in all its variants throughout the war, and of the first DH jet fighter; the youngest son died in an air collision. De Havilland married in 1951 Joan Mary (died 1974), widow of Geoffrey Mordaunt and daughter of E. P. Frith. He died 21 May 1965 at Stanmore, Middlesex. A portrait (1940) by (Sir) Oswald Birley hangs in the boardroom at Hawker Siddeley Aviation, Hatfield, and another (1953) by Frank Eastman in the de Havilland suite, London airport.

[Sir Geoffrey de Havilland, *Sky Fever*, an autobiography, 1961; C. Martin Sharp, *D.H. An Outline of de Havilland History*, 1960; R. M. Clarkson, the first de Havilland memorial lecture—*Journal of the Royal Aeronautical Society*, vol. lxxi, no. 674; personal knowledge.]   R. M. CLARKSON

DEMPSEY, Sir MILES CHRISTOPHER (1896-1969), general, was born in New Brighton, Cheshire, 15 December 1896, son of Arthur

Francis Dempsey, a marine insurance broker, and his wife, Margaret Maud de la Fosse. He was educated at Shrewsbury and the Royal Military College, Sandhurst, and was commissioned into the Royal Berkshire Regiment in 1915. He served with his regiment in France from 1916, when he commanded a company at the age of nineteen, to 1918; he was wounded, mentioned in dispatches, and awarded the MC. He subsequently took part in operations in Iraq (1919–20). Between the wars he served both with his regiment and on the staff, at one time with Archibald (later Earl) Wavell [q.v.] as his divisional commander. At the outbreak of war in 1939, Dempsey was lieutenant-colonel in command of the 1st battalion of his regiment. During the battle for France he took command of 13th Infantry brigade, which played a major part in the British counter-attack at Arras in May 1940; as a result of its contribution in a three-day battle in the Ypres–Comines canal area, the British Expeditionary Force gained time for its withdrawal to Dunkirk. Dempsey was appointed to the DSO.

The next action which Dempsey saw was in the Middle East. Promoted to lieutenant-general, he took command of XIII Corps of the Eighth Army after the battle of Alamein, and aided Sir Bernard Montgomery (later Viscount Montgomery of Alamein) in planning the invasion of Sicily. His corps landed at Syracuse 10 July 1943 and took part in the hard battle for Catania. During the descent on Italy itself, 3 September 1943, his corps was in the spearhead, and Dempsey conducted the winter battles in southern Italy in a masterly fashion. But he was not to remain there for long. Montgomery needed him for the coming invasion of Western Europe, and in January 1944 he returned home to command the Second Army. His part in the battle for Normandy and the subsequent breakout, closing up to the Rhine and finally advancing to the Elbe, was a model of how to conduct operations soundly and successfully. He was in many ways the ideal subordinate to Montgomery: never seeking the limelight, nor able (from the nature of Montgomery's directives) to indulge in bold strokes of initiative, he always fully understood what Montgomery's purpose was, and quietly and steadily got on with it. He would spend much of his time visiting his subordinate commanders and their troops, assessing the situation, listening to their problems, and giving instructions clearly and succinctly. He had profound understanding of the soldiers under his command and firm control over operations, which inspired both subordinates and superior commanders with confidence in his judgement and leadership. Yet he remained relatively unknown to the public.

Dempsey was very good at understanding a battlefield; a map became a relief map in his hand. His sound, albeit cautious, establishment of the initial bridgehead was followed by the application of ever-growing pressure in the Caen sector. His conduct of the battle was governed by the knowledge that the breakout was to be by the Americans in the western flank of the bridgehead; he therefore went on hitting away at the Germans, drawing more and more of their strength against his own army. He was determined to take Caen, since its capture would, as he put it, 'loosen the enemy's hinge and provide us with a firm hinge'. During the subsequent operations in the latter part of July 1944, which led to the American breakout and the subsequent Falaise and Argentan battles which broke the German positions in Normandy, Dempsey was always ready to take advantage of the opportunity to exploit success, but never tried to reinforce stalemate. He would also wholeheartedly accept responsibility for taking critical decisions, without worrying if the efforts of the army were misinterpreted by the press or senior Allied commanders. He was quite unperturbed when there were suggestions of 'failure' after Operation 'Goodwood' (which was designed to draw more German panzers away from General Omar Bradley's First Army), and he merely pointed out that such misunderstandings would help with the deception plan. After the breakout in Normandy, Dempsey's army conducted difficult and deliberate winter operations in Belgium (it was during a visit to the front at this time that King George VI dubbed him KCB, an appointment which had been gazetted in June 1944), and established itself at the Rhine by March 1945; in the subsequent advance to the Elbe, his army was in the forefront, and he himself received the surrender of Hamburg 3 May 1945.

When the European war was over, Dempsey was appointed commander of the Fourteenth Army for the reoccupation of Singapore and Malaya, in succession to Sir William (later Viscount) Slim [q.v.], whom he also followed as commander-in-chief Allied Land Forces South East Asia until 1946 when he was promoted to the rank of general. He was appointed KBE in 1945. In 1946–7 he was commander-in-chief Middle East, and he retired in July 1947 at his own request.

After his retirement Dempsey joined a number of companies: he was a director of H. & G. Simonds, and chairman in 1953–63; he was also chairman of Green, King & Sons in 1955–67, and deputy chairman of Courage, Barclay, and Simonds in 1961–6. But he derived especial pleasure from his chairmanship of the Racecourse Betting Control Board (1947–51). He had always been an excellent horseman, and was very fond of hunting and racing; he bred and raced his own horses, and once commented that his position on the Betting Control Board enabled him to savour the enjoyment of racing more than ever by the reflection that it was also his duty to be there. Nor did he sever his connection with the army: he was colonel commandant of the Corps of Royal Military Police in 1947–57, and of the Special Air Service in 1951–60. He was also colonel of his regiment, the Royal Berkshires, in 1946–56, and a deputy lieutenant for Berkshire from 1950. He became commander-in-chief (designate) UK Land Forces in 1951–6, and was appointed GBE on his retirement from this post.

In 1948 he married Viola Mary Vivien, youngest daughter of Captain Percy O'Reilly, of Colamber, Westmeath; they had no children. He died at his home in Yattendon, Berkshire, 5 June 1969.

Among his many interests, 'Bimbo' Dempsey was a student of military history with a remarkable memory, and he loved music, both playing the piano and singing. At Shrewsbury he captained the first eleven, and later at Staff College he played cricket—he was left-handed —with (Sir) Thomas Troubridge [q.v.], who was afterwards his naval colleague for the invasion of Sicily. Tall, lean, and tough, a man of considerable charm and modesty, young-looking and always immaculately turned out, he radiated confidence and authority. There is a portrait of him by Bernard Hailstone (1946) in the Imperial War Museum.

[*The Times*, 7 June 1969; L. F. Ellis, (Official) *History of the Second World War. Victory in the West*, vols. i and ii, 1962–8; personal knowledge.]   JOHN STRAWSON

DENNISTON, ALEXANDER GUTHRIE (ALASTAIR) (1881–1961), public servant (intelligence), was born 1 December 1881 at Greenock, the eldest child of James Denniston, a medical practitioner, and his wife, Agnes Guthrie. He was educated at Bowdon College, Cheshire, and at the universities of Bonn and Paris.

From 1906 to 1909 Denniston taught at Merchiston Castle School. He then went to teach foreign languages at Osborne, the pre-Dartmouth naval college. A considerable athlete, he played hockey for Scotland in the pre-war Olympic Games. When war broke out in 1914, as one of the few men in the service of the Admiralty who were fluent in German, he played a leading part in the hasty establishment of Room 40 OB. Taking its name from the office in which it operated (Room 40, Old Buildings, Admiralty), this organization intercepted, decrypted, and interpreted, on behalf of the naval staff, German and other enemy wireless and cable communications. For its wartime exploits—and most of all, perhaps, for its success in decrypting the notorious Zimmermann telegram—Room 40 OB subsequently became internationally known. The fame did not extend to Denniston, nor (though he was at the centre of the cryptanalytical process) did he contribute to the publicity on which it rested: he was by nature reticent, and in 1919 he had been selected to lead the country's peacetime cryptanalytical effort as head of the Government Code and Cypher School (GC and CS).

In this capacity he served from 1919 to February 1942. He supervised the formation of GC and CS as a small interdepartmental organization of twenty-five people recruited from Room 40 OB and its equivalent section in the War Office. It included defectors from Russia, linguists, and talented amateurs of all kinds. Denniston, appointed CBE in 1933, presided over its slow expansion during the inter-war years—a period in which it had to cope with the continuously increasing sophistication of cipher security and a decline in wireless communications, as well as against a shortage of funds, but nevertheless succeeded in the important task of preserving a continuity of expertise and experience—and also over its rapid expansion and transfer to Bletchley Park on the outbreak of World War II in 1939. In the first half of 1940 he had the satisfaction of knowing that, reinforced by wartime staff which he had recruited (many having served with him in Room 40 OB), and assisted by the change to wartime conditions, it was beginning to solve the problem which had most stubbornly defied all its efforts, the problem posed by the adoption by Germany since the late 1920s, for the secret communications of the armed forces, the railways, the secret service, the police, and other government organizations, of the Enigma cipher machine.

GC and CS achieved virtually complete mastery of the Enigma machine in the second half of 1941, reading from then till the end of the war most of the many ciphers based on it. In the course of doing so, it increased its staff further to some 5,000, it encountered new administrative requirements, and to an ever greater extent it came to rely for its operation on specialized apparatus and machinery. Although Denniston recognized that these developments called for a major reorganization, he was not himself the man to carry it out: he had always been a reluctant administrator, preferring to concentrate on technical matters. The reorganization adopted in February 1942 divided GC and CS into a military and a civil, and much smaller, wing. As head of the military division Denniston was succeeded by

Commander (Sir) Edward W. Travis; he himself, having been appointed CMG in 1941, remained the head of the civil division, moving to London (to Madame Riché, couturier des dames in Berkeley St.) where, on seven floors, he and his team worked on intercepts dealing with German diplomatic and Abwehr activity. The department worked eighteen hours a day, seven days a week, and achieved many successes. Although Denniston was bitterly disappointed at what had occurred, he headed the Berkeley St. section most effectively. He retired in 1945 and thereafter taught French and Latin at a Leatherhead preparatory school.

Throughout his long period of office as head of an undivided GC and CS, directly responsible to the chief of the Secret Service, Denniston brought unusual distinction and expertise, as well as devotion, to his work. If he had little liking for questions of administration, he had even less for the ways of bureaucracy and the demands of hierarchy. By his willingness to delegate, his trust in subordinates, his informality and his charm he set his stamp on the character of the place, particularly in the early war years in Bletchley Park. More than any other man, he helped it to maintain both the creative atmosphere which underlay its great contribution to British intelligence during World War II, and the complete security which was a no less important precondition of its achievement.

In 1917 Denniston married Dorothy Mary, who worked at the time with him in Room 40 OB. She was the daughter of Arthur Gilliat, a business man; they had one son and one daughter. Their son, Robin, made his career in publishing, and became the academic publisher at the Oxford University Press. Alastair Denniston was a small man, with a strong, craggy-featured face—indeed, he was known to his colleagues as 'the little man'. With his athletic figure, he was always very neatly turned out. Denniston died at Lymington Hospital 1 January 1961.

[F. H. Hinsley, with others, *British Intelligence in the Second World War*, vol. i, 1979 (official history); Patrick Seale and Maureen McConville, *Philby: The Long Road to Moscow*, 1973.]　　　　　　F. H. HINSLEY

D'ERLANGER, SIR GERARD JOHN REGIS LEO (1906-1962), investment banker, company director, and airman, was born at Stratton House, Stratton Street, London, 1 June 1906, the only son and the elder of the two children of Baron Émile Beaumont d'Erlanger, international banker and chairman of Erlanger Ltd., and his wife, Marie Rose Antoinette Catherine de Robert d'Aqueria, daughter of the

Marquis de Rochegude of Bollène in Vaucluse, France.

D'Erlanger was educated at Eton where he acquired the nickname 'Pops' by which he was known to his friends for the rest of his life. As a member of a family which had as many links with France as with England, d'Erlanger completed his education in Paris and then qualified in London as a chartered accountant in 1933. At the same time he took up private flying with enthusiasm and gained a pilot's 'A licence' (Royal Aero Club aviator's certificate No. 9730) at the Airwork Flying School at Heston on 11 March 1931. In company with Gordon Selfridge the younger and Whitney Straight he acquired a taste for Continental touring by air and, on a business visit to Argentina in 1932, flew himself around in a single-seat Comper Swift owned locally.

D'Erlanger started a career in the family tradition when he joined Myers and Company in 1934 and, in the following year, became a member of the London Stock Exchange.

Already his flying interests had begun to extend beyond the sporting field. In 1934 he joined the board of the privately owned Hillman's Airways. No more incongruous—or successful—association could be imagined than that of the tough, self-made businessman, Edward Hillman, and the young urbane Etonian accountant. Hillman died in December 1934 just as the company went public and d'Erlanger took a leading part in bringing his father's banking house to invest in the company. There was already one other financial institution entering the field of air transport—Whitehall Securities, founded by the first Lord Cowdray [q.v.], managed by (Bernard) Clive Pearson, and including on its board Captain Harold Balfour, MP, later to become Lord Balfour of Inchrye. In 1935, thanks largely to d'Erlanger and Balfour, Hillman's Airways merged with United Air Lines owned by Whitehall Securities, and was renamed British Airways Ltd. The result was a powerful independent airline with substantial financial backing which could challenge the state-supported Imperial Airways Ltd.

D'Erlanger became a director of British Airways on its formation and, following the report of the committee chaired by Lord Cadman [q.v.], when Imperial Airways and British Airways were merged to form the state-owned British Overseas Airways Corporation, he joined the board of BOAC from its official beginning on 1 April 1940.

Before this, when war was clearly imminent, d'Erlanger began negotiations in 1938 with the air member for development and production at the Air Ministry, Air Marshal Sir Wilfrid Freeman [q.v.], for an auxiliary force of private pilots, too old or unfit for military service, who might be used to ferry aircraft from manufacturers to squadrons in time of war. At first the Air Ministry was lukewarm but, when war was declared in September 1939, Air Transport Auxiliary rapidly came into being at White Waltham with d'Erlanger as commandant. During the next six years 1,215 men and women from fourteen nations ferried some 308,000 aircraft of 147 different types in all weathers and often in the most difficult conditions, for the loss of 173 lives, sixteen of whom were women. There is a memorial in St. Paul's Cathedral with their motto: 'Aetheris Avidi', 'Eager for the Air'.

Before the war ended, d'Erlanger began discussions with Sir Harold Hartley, chairman of the Railway Air Services, about the formation of a new airline for domestic and European services. The result was the formation on 1 August 1946 of British European Airways, which took over the former services of the independent airlines, including those of Railway Air Services and BOAC's European routes, under the chairmanship of Sir Harold Hartley, with d'Erlanger as managing director.

When Hartley became chairman of BOAC in July 1947, d'Erlanger took the chair of BEA but—following a dispute about the level of subsidy with the minister of civil aviation, Lord Pakenham (who later became Earl of Longford)—he resigned on 14 March 1949 and returned to the City. He was succeeded as chairman of BEA by Lord Douglas of Kirtleside [q.v.]. Early in 1956, after the resignation of Sir Miles Thomas, d'Erlanger was appointed chairman of BOAC at a time of change and reconstruction which caused him much worry and concern. He was knighted in 1958 but retired from BOAC in 1960 to devote himself to City affairs as chairman of City and International Trust Ltd., of the General and Consolidated Investment Trust Ltd., and of the Moorgate Investment Company Ltd.; deputy chairman of the Provident Mutual Life Association, and a director of John Mackintosh & Sons Ltd., and of Philip Hill Investment Trust Ltd., with which Erlangers had merged. He settled down to enjoy a less onerous life at his home at 11 Hyde Park Street in London. Surrounded by a circle of friends, he had wide interests, which included the Royal Yacht Squadron. Two years later he died suddenly, 15 December 1962, at his home in London.

'Pops' d'Erlanger's chief contribution to British aviation was to bring together early commercial airline interests and adequate finance in the years before the war of 1939-45, and to consolidate their scattered remnants to form BEA under state ownership in 1946. His imaginative formation of the Air Transport Auxiliary in 1939 provided a valuable source of flying experience which might otherwise have remained untapped. This was a contribution to the war effort which, because it fitted no Service mould, went largely unrecognized. Always pleasant, often worried, never happy with officialdom, d'Erlanger had an innate reserve which, combined with difficulty in communication, kept him from still greater attainments. In aviation he was a gifted amateur in a tough professional field; in finance he was very much the professional who was often among amateurs.

D'Erlanger married in 1937 Gladys Florence, daughter of H. J. Sammut, by whom he had one son and two daughters.

[*The Times*, 17 December 1962; R. E. G. Davies, *A History of the World's Airlines*, 1964; personal knowledge.]

PETER MASEFIELD

DE SOISSONS, LOUIS EMMANUEL JEAN GUY DE SAVOIE-CARIGNAN, VISCOUNT D'OSTEL, BARON LONGROY (1890-1962), architect and town planner, generally known as Louis de Soissons, was born in Montreal, Canada, 31 July 1890, the younger son of Charles, 37th Count de Soissons and his wife, Anne Marie Julie, Countess Poniatowski Rozanski-Rozwadowski. The house of Soissons is descended in lineage from Charlemagne on one side and his contemporary Wittikind, King of Saxony, on the other. Louis and his brother, Peter, lived in England from childhood and chose to make it their home. He kept the Catholic faith of the family.

His early education was at Bewshers, Colet Court, and private. He knew early that he would be an architect and in his teens he went to the École des Beaux Arts in Paris, at the Atelier Pascal Nenot Recoura et Duquesne, where he took three medals. On returning to England he was articled to J. H. Eastwood, became Tite prizeman (1912), and RIBA Henry Jarvis student (1913) at the British School at Rome.

In 1914 he tried for a line regiment but short sight precluded this. He served with the RASC and later had liaison duties with the Italian Army. He was mentioned in dispatches, appointed OBE (1918) and awarded the croce di guerra, and was made a cavaliere of the Order of the Crown of Italy. He worked with the Claims Commission where his fluent French and Italian were useful.

After the war there were brief partnerships, first with Philip Hepworth and then with George Grey Wornum, when destiny placed a finger upon him. Letchworth Garden City was to have a successor at Welwyn. (Sir) Ebenezer Howard [q.v.] and his fellow directors needed a planner and in April 1920 de Soissons was appointed, with the duty also of company architect. He was a man of action, clear-minded, decisive, and forceful, and presented his first plan in June. Its subsequent development and implementation revealed interests and skills which proved to be in excellent balance for the enterprise and it is a singular tribute to his talent that nearly sixty years later it is evidently working well. On behalf of the Garden City Company he had the final decision about the work of other architects in the town, but it was never exercised without respect for his fellow professionals.

In 1922 he married Elinor Maude Penrose-Thackwell, by whom he had three sons. They set up their first home in the embryo new town and he lived in or near it from then onward, believing that such a responsibility should not be discharged from a distance. He knew that while a plan could provide a strategy, it was the detail that would touch people's feelings. The results are evident in the pleasure of moving around the town and in the active affection that it generates.

What is known of his thinking and values has to be derived mainly from his work and conversation, for he wrote little. He perceived architectural quality without prejudice about style, but had a personal affection for the Italian Renaissance, the eighteenth-century work of England and America, especially Nantucket, and the elegance of Regency Brighton, Cheltenham, and Leamington. He was too independent to be directly influenced by any of this or by Welwyn's immediate predecessors, Letchworth (which he did not much like) and Hampstead Garden Suburb, though, like Hampstead, his town was conceived as a combination of a formal Renaissance civic centre (with industry unexpectedly but successfully adjacent), surrounded by informal residential areas. These were innovatively planned and invested with exceptional natural charm. It was one of his main contributions to the garden city movement that despite their informal and natural character, his streets and housing are distinctively urban in character and are not villages writ large.

His low- and middle-income housing was done with concern and skill, and he was one of a small group with whom Edward VIII as Prince and King discussed housing problems. The part of Welwyn which he touched most personally has been designated a Conservation Area and the town as a whole is a landmark in the history of planning. He did much other housing and served on the Central Housing Advisory Committee and the Burt Committee, appointed after 1945 to promote innovation in construction.

He was greatly pleased by an invitation just before the war to design barracks for the Brigade of Guards and after 1945 to rebuild Carlton House Terrace for the Foreign Office—but sadly both had to be cancelled. He did much-liked work at Cheltenham. As senior partner in the extended post-war firm of Louis de Soissons, Peacock, Hodges and Robertson, he was responsible for the George VI memorial in Carlton Gardens, the Hobbs memorial gates at the Oval, the fine restoration of Nash terraces in Regent's Park, and a great variety of other work. He was architect to the Duchy of Cornwall estate and the Imperial War Graves Commission for Greece and Italy (later the Commonwealth War Graves Commission). He believed in personal commitment in design and was the final arbiter in the office. He conveyed his ideas with decisive comments and quick sketches, and expected them to be carried out exactly. He was more open minded about modern work in the office than his personal tastes might suggest.

In 1923 he was made FRIBA, MTPI, and SADG, but he was not an 'institute' man and preferred to put effort into the Architectural Association School (1929-33) where he was a vice-principal of the Upper School and a tough, incisive critic; later into the Royal Academy, to which he was elected in 1953 (having become an ARA in 1942) and where he served as treasurer from 1959, and into the Royal Fine Arts Commission (1949-61). He was also involved with F. R. Yerbury [q.v.] in founding the Building Centre. He was awarded the RIBA distinction in town planning in 1945 and was made CVO in 1956, the honour which he most greatly valued.

He loved good food and wine, sculpture, and paintings (James Woodford and Charles Cundall were among his close friends), but he did not particularly enjoy theatre or music. He read quickly and enjoyed the best current architectural journals, especially French, Italian, and Scandinavian. He was a devotee of whodunits and of classics (Dickens, Dumas) and Zane Grey. He was gregarious and his friends were anyone who gained his respect, whatever they were and wherever he found them. He made every day an event for those with him at the time, for he had great vitality and a strong sense of fun. Religious or political compatibility was irrelevant. When he walked into a pub he would look quickly around and give a greeting, and he resented any lack of response. He was not a sporting man himself but enjoyed the thought of field sports. Walking holidays gave him pleasure at one stage. He was a member of the Athenaeum and the Arts Club, but not a club devotee. Among his contemporaries he admired Sir Edwin Lutyens, with whom he once worked briefly, Sir Giles Gilbert Scott, H. S. Goodhart-Rendel [qq.v.], (John) Charles James, and Frank Lloyd Wright. His own closest collaborator in his firm was Kenneth Peacock, with whom he designed the war cemeteries.

He was a pioneer but did not see himself in this light. He was first, last, and always an architect; not a theorist but a maker of theory, and though he wanted the challenge of major set-piece architecture, Welwyn Garden City is likely to be viewed in history as his great achievement, especially its plan and its residential areas. He died at the London Clinic 23 September 1962. There is a posthumous bronze bust at Welwyn Garden City by James Woodford, which was exhibited at the Royal Academy Summer Exhibition 1968.

[Private information, personal knowledge.]

WILLIAM ALLEN

DE STEIN, SIR EDWARD SINAUER (1887–1965), merchant banker, was born 16 June 1887 at 9 Palace Gate, London, SW7, the eldest of the three children of Baroness Clara de Stein, sole heir of Baron de Stein of Antwerp, and of her husband, Sigmund Sinauer, who took her name. The elder of de Stein's two sisters married Herwald Ramsbotham (later Viscount Soulbury). The younger sister, like de Stein himself, did not marry and kept house for him with elegance all their adult lives. De Stein was educated at Eton, where, although small in stature, he distinguished himself at games and was a quite outstanding player of speed and agility in the Field Game. For many years afterwards he took down famous scratch sides to play against the school.

He went on to Magdalen College, Oxford, where he was immensely popular and already noted for his wit and skill as a raconteur and for his many artistic gifts. He obtained a second in history in 1910. He was sufficiently talented as a pianist to think seriously of becoming a professional, but decided to read for the bar and was called by the Inner Temple in 1912. When war broke out in 1914 he volunteered immediately and served throughout in the King's Royal Rifle Corps, emerging unscathed as a major, one of the few survivors of that talented generation of friends.

After the war de Stein entered the City where, after a short time with Carter & Co., merchants of Lothbury, he started in partnership with the Hon. Michael Herbert and later formed his own merchant bank, under his own name, in 1926 in partnership with the Hon. John Mulholland. Edward de Stein & Co. engaged in the financing and development of industrial and commercial enterprises and in the management of investments for private clients and institutions. He formed a number of investment trusts and, although a comparative newcomer to the City, his reputation for shrewdness and his transparent honesty enabled him to enrol as directors some of the best-known names in investment and banking circles. This integrity led him to pick and choose his clients, his associates, and his partners with exacting care.

His major financial operations were comparatively few: Columbia Graphophone, later to be merged with His Master's Voice to form Electric and Musical Industries; Gallaher, the tobacco manufacturers; and Mercantile Credit, the pioneer hire-purchase company. All these became large and successful undertakings. In 1960 Edward de Stein & Co. merged with Lazard Brothers.

De Stein was mercurial and impatient, and most reluctant to read memoranda on economics or market research; he distrusted the judgement of all theoreticians. His success lay in his ability to size up, mostly intuitively, the prospects of a company and of the industry in which it operated, and then to find the right men to carry through his ideas. Strangely, for one of his financial ability, he was bad at figures and relied on others to do this work for him. He excelled in his judgement of people and, having picked them, he trusted them. He was seldom deceived.

During the war de Stein was from 1941 director of finance (raw materials) at the Ministry of Supply, a position of great complexity which he filled with distinction and for which in 1946 he was knighted.

His interest in philanthropic work played a great part in his life. He worked first in connection with Toc H and was always particularly interested in boys' clubs in the poorest parts of London. He founded and fully endowed a club of his own near Shepherd's Bush. There he frequently entertained the boys on the piano. He played football, cricket, and tennis with them when visiting their camps, and at the age of fifty-five challenged the best of them to a 100-yard sprint and was beaten only by a short head. In 1949 he became chairman of the British Red Cross finance committee and on his retirement in 1963 received the certificate of honour, class 1.

His wit and quick mind showed themselves in the writing of light verse and essays. In 1919 he published a collection of parodies entitled *Poets in Picardy*, and he continued to contribute to *Punch*. In the early twenties he produced a short collection of verses for circulation among his City friends, entitled 'Poems from an E.C. Chair'. Throughout his life he entertained his family and friends with his amusing poems, skits, and clerihews. To his early musical and literary gifts he added later a skill in the painting of water-colours, and he exhibited at the Royal Society of Painters in Water Colours. For other relaxation in a busy life, he did extremely skilled tapestry work. He was a keen sportsman, a fine fisherman, and an excellent shot. He developed an interest in landscape gardening and created a remarkable water-garden at his fishing cottage at Fulling Mills near Easton on the Itchen. His love of beauty and history led him to buy Lindisfarne Castle on Holy Island, where he acted as a philanthropist to the islanders and became an enthusiastic but somewhat inaccurate bird watcher. He gave the castle to the National Trust. He was a discriminating collector of pictures and china, and his London house in Montpelier Square was filled with things of beauty.

De Stein had innumerable friends in every walk of life. He died at Fulling Mills 3 November 1965, and it was found that, unknown even to his family, he had continually made loans and gifts to young people to enable them to make a start in life and to buy their own homes. In his will he left a large sum to form the Easton Trust to found hostels where boys from schools for the maladjusted could be helped to enter normal life.

A portrait by John Napper is in the boardroom of Gallaher Ltd. and another by Edward I. Halliday is owned by Mercantile Credit Co. Ltd.

[Private information; personal knowledge.]

M. R. NORMAN

DE SYLLAS, STELIOS MESSINESOS (LEO) (1917–1964), architect, was born at Holmwood, Surrey, 24 July 1917, the younger son of Stelios de Syllas, painter, and his wife, Veronica Rose Palatiano. He was educated at Haberdashers' Aske's and Christ's College, Finchley, and in 1933 entered the Bartlett School of Architecture, University College London, which under (Sir) Albert E. Richardson [q.v.] had the strong academic flavour of the École des Beaux Arts, Paris. But his sympathies lay in another direction and in 1936 he transferred for his final two years of training to the progressive and turbulent Architectural Association School, which harboured amongst its staff and students lively protagonists of the modern movement in architecture. In this atmosphere he at once became an energetic activist, always relating his left-wing social and political beliefs to his approach to architecture, and in 1938 was one of the student editors who launched the polemical architectural quarterly, *Focus*, which combined student contributions with those from distinguished allies of an older generation. In 1939 he took his diploma with honours and was one of eleven contemporaries at the AA school whose strong architectural convictions and positive attitude to the social function of building brought them together to start the firm of Architects' Co-Operative Partnership (later Architects' Co-Partnership, or ACP).

The war interrupted the development of this partnership and de Syllas joined the Research and Experiments Department of the Ministry of Home Security. In 1943 he went to the British West Indies as assistant architect to Robert J.

Gardner-Medwin in the Colonial Development and Welfare Organization to work on a programme of buildings for education, housing, and health — his first opportunity to combine his practical and imaginative approach to architectural problems with his social idealism. In 1945 he was appointed architect and planning officer to the Government of Barbados, where he was responsible for the master-plan of Bridgetown. He returned to England and the partnership in 1947 and designed several innovatory school buildings, notably the secondary modern school at Chaddesden in Derbyshire. But his experience in the West Indies had given him a strong desire to continue to work in the less developed countries, on the challenging task of building in the tropics, and in 1954 he established a branch office for his partnership in Nigeria. There his principal buildings were a number of low-cost schools, some individual houses in differing climatic areas, the Bristol hotel in Lagos, and a large housing development to serve the Volta River project at Akosombo in Ghana. He was always searching for fresh solutions to architectural problems, technically and, when possible, socially: his later buildings in England included the remarkable roof-top extension to Simpsons in Piccadilly, and in 1962 he was responsible for his partnership's winning design in the limited competition for St. Paul's Cathedral Choir School on a controversial site in New Change, a building constructed after his death and his most enduring monument.

A man of enthusiastic energy, he pursued his overseas commitments without any diminution of his interest in architectural affairs at home. He was elected to the council of the Architectural Association in 1956 and was next in line for its presidency when he died. He was active in the association's pioneering Department of Tropical Studies and was largely responsible for the establishment of the link between the association and the University of Science and Technology at Kumasi. In 1963 he was chairman of the RIBA Commonwealth Architects' Conference.

De Syllas was tall and striking in appearance, and with his Greek blood and family background was characteristically animated and fluent in movement, talking and gesticulating continuously. Warm-hearted and gregarious by nature, his readiness to communicate in several languages was not inhibited by an imperfect command of some of them, which was always compensated for by his genuine charm and sincerity. Full of stimulating ideas and with an infectious optimism he got on notably well with young people, whose outlook he found refreshing. He believed in combining practice with teaching and was an invigorating teacher at the AA school. Strongly to the left in his politics, his social attitudes were reflected in his private life when in 1951 he became an active participant in founding St. Julian's, Sevenoaks, a successful communal experiment where his family lived for some years.

In 1942 he married Phoebe, widow of A. W. Nicol and daughter of Ralph Lucas, engineering designer. His family was two stepsons, a son, and a daughter. He died in a road accident near Le Kef in Tunisia 30 January 1964, whilst working on a project for new schools for the Tunisian Government.

[*Architects Journal*, 12 February 1964; private information; personal knowledge.]

ANTHONY COX

DEVINE, GEORGE ALEXANDER CASSADY (1910-1966), actor and theatre director, was born 20 November 1910 in Hendon, the only child of Giorgios Devine, bank clerk, of Hendon, and his wife, Ruth Eleanor Cassady. He was educated at Clayesmore School, of which the founder and headmaster was his uncle Alexander Devine, and at Wadham College, Oxford, where he read modern history. One of his tutors was Lord David Cecil. As president of the Oxford University Dramatic Society in his last year, he established a foothold in the professional theatre by inviting (Sir) John Gielgud to direct the 1932 OUDS production of *Romeo and Juliet* in which Devine played Mercutio in company with (Dame) Peggy Ashcroft's Juliet and (Dame) Edith Evans's Nurse, and Christopher Hassall's [q.v.] Romeo.

Devine left Oxford without taking Schools to embark on a London acting career. At the same time, he attached himself as business manager to the firm of Motley, the stage design partnership of Elizabeth Montgomery, Margaret Harris, and her sister (Audrey) Sophia Harris (died 1966), who later became Devine's wife (1939) and the mother of his only child, Harriet.

It was in the Motley studio that he first met Michel Saint-Denis, director of the Compagnie des Quinze, who for the rest of his life he acknowledged as his master. With Saint-Denis and others he set up the London Theatre Studio (1936-9) which attempted a revolution in British stage training. After the war (which Devine spent mostly in Burma as a captain in the Royal Artillery, and during which he was twice mentioned in dispatches), he resumed his alliance with Saint-Denis at the Old Vic Centre: a tripartite offshoot of the Old Vic Company, comprising a school (directed by Glen Byam Shaw), the Young Vic touring troupe (directed by Devine), and a never-completed experimental theatre (in the charge of Saint-Denis). From its opening in 1947 the Centre produced an astounding crop of young actors, directors, and designers, and when the governors of the Old Vic closed it down in 1952 their action provoked a storm of professional outrage and parliamentary criticism.

Up to this time Devine had spent most of his working life as a teacher-administrator, but with the break-up of the Vic Centre, he turned to freelance directing: partly of opera at Sadler's Wells and Covent Garden (where he directed the première of Sir William Walton's *Troilus and Cressida*, 1954), and partly of the Shakespeare repertory at Stratford-upon-Avon (collaborating with Gielgud and Isamu Noguchi in the 'Japanese' *King Lear*, 1955).

In 1956 he resumed his reformist mission as artistic director of the newly formed English Stage Company at the Royal Court Theatre. The ESC's original policy was to persuade established novelists to write for the stage, a policy abandoned after the production of John Osborne's *Look Back in Anger* (1956) which released a tidal wave of new plays by hitherto unknown young playwrights including John Arden and Arnold Wesker. Until the end of the decade the Court was the spearhead of the so-called 'breakthrough' movement, challenging the reigning conventions of dramatic craftsmanship and reasserting the theatre's role as a platform for radical opinion.

Throughout this spectacular period Devine remained personally inconspicuous. After the first season he directed very few new plays himself (excepting those by his close friend Samuel Beckett); and when he acted on the Court stage it was usually to save money. His purpose was to create a free space where the best talents could collaborate in pushing the theatre from the periphery to the centre of English cultural life: a purpose partly acknowledged in 1958 when he was appointed CBE 'for services to drama'.

Devine's 'writers' theatre' was a place where material of a kind formerly restricted to club performances found a public outlet. He was not the originator of this idea, but he was the first English director to make it work. He succeeded through an unshakeable determination, entirely untouched by narrow obsessiveness. In opening his doors to unknown writers and directors he also kept them open to eminent pre-war colleagues like Ashcroft and Laurence (later Lord) Olivier: and in keeping an open space for the rebel artists under his roof he took great care not to play the rebel with his own management committee. He remained a dedicated teacher, and the creator of an exemplary theatre in which the technician was respected no less than the actor and the writer. His final years were spent with his former London Theatre Studio pupil, the designer Jocelyn, daughter of Sir A. P.

Herbert. In her company he died in London 20 January 1966.

[Irving Wardle, *The Theatres of George Devine*, 1978.]   IRVING WARDLE

DEVONS, ELY (1913-1967), statistician and economist, was born in Bangor, North Wales, 29 July 1913. His father, David Isaac Devons, was a Jewish minister from Vilna who had arrived in Britain in 1902 on a Russian passport at the age of twenty-one. Devons's mother, Edith Edelstein, like his wife, came from Ireland and was ten years younger than her husband. Devons was the second eldest in a family of three boys and three girls. One of his younger brothers, Samuel, was professor of physics at the university of Manchester in the fifties when Devons held the chair of applied economics.

Devons attended a number of different schools as his family moved to Stoke-on-Trent, Portsmouth, and then Manchester, ending up at North Manchester Municipal High School before entering the university of Manchester. In the course of a chance encounter in the street he was persuaded by Harold Laski [q.v.] to study economics and graduated in 1934 with first class honours in the school of economics, politics, and modern history. He was awarded the Drummond Fraser research fellowship and used it to pursue research for the MA degree at Manchester into British production statistics. A by-product of this research was his first published article, 'Output per head in Great Britain, 1924-33', which appeared in the *Economic Journal* just after his twenty-second birthday.

His career as a statistician began in 1935 with a post under Glyn Hughes as economic assistant on the staff of the Joint Committee of Cotton Trades Organizations in Manchester. In March 1940 he joined the Central Economic Information Service—a small group of economists and statisticians from which developed at the end of the year both the economic section of the War Cabinet Secretariat and the Central Statistical Office. Devons quickly made his mark as one of a number of Manchester men, including John Jewkes, (Sir) D. N. Chester, and (Sir) Harry Campion, who played a major part in the early days of these bodies. His special responsibility was to assemble the secret statistics accumulating in various parts of Whitehall and issue them in a form convenient for the central direction of policy. In this he was extremely successful and the work he initiated in 1940-1 had a revolutionary effect on the presentation of official statistics, down to the format and type-face in use. Government statistics never afterwards looked so dull, discontinuous, and inaccessible. It was a job which he repeated in the Ministry of Aircraft Production and again for the OEEC in 1950

when he took a hand in the first issue of their statistical bulletins.

Devons was not the man to steep himself in statistics without considering the lessons they pointed. He had a chance to combine the two when Jewkes, now in charge of aircraft planning, asked him to move from the Central Statistical Office and rejoin him as chief statistician. In the next four years Devons came to exercise an increasingly dominant role in the Ministry of Aircraft Production, taking over from Jewkes as head of the planning department in 1944. His experience in the planning of aircraft and aircraft components formed the background to much of his later thinking and writing about economic and administrative problems and provided him with the material for his *Planning in Practice* (1950), a classic of its kind.

At the end of the war, after some hesitation, Devons returned to Manchester as reader and later professor of applied economics. He remained there for much of the time as dean of the faculty of economic and social studies, until his appointment in 1959 to the chair of commerce at the London School of Economics. Nearly all Devons's published work was composed during his years in Manchester. His *Introduction to British Economic Statistics*, a critical guide displaying an unrivalled knowledge of official statistics, appeared in 1956. A collection of *Essays in Economics* followed in 1961. But his main contribution was the stimulus he provided to his distinguished colleagues. The staff seminar which he conducted with (Sir) Arthur Lewis has been described by Professor Harry Johnson as 'the most devastatingly critical forum in the country into which a careless economist could blunder.'

The move to London was not altogether a success since international trade was not Devons's normal field of interest. But as convener of the economics department he was again the moving spirit, an initiator of structural change, able to think and plan in terms of the institution as a whole. He was largely responsible for the introduction of the new M.Sc. degrees in economics and econometrics and helped to raise money for graduate fellowships in support of them. In 1965 the title of his chair was changed from commerce to economics. While at the LSE he served from 1959 to 1965 as a member of the Local Government Commission and acted as consultant to various government departments and foreign governments.

A victim of insomnia, Devons was an omnivorous reader and had a particular appetite for government publications, especially minutes of evidence. He loved debating and was given to paradox and skittishness. This put many people off who failed to notice how embarrassingly right his forecasts, even the more extravagant ones, generally proved to be. He was always in command of the relevant facts, never willing to bow without question to received opinion, and possessed of an acute and firm judgement rooted in common sense. He hated arrogance, dogmatism, and—most of all—humbug. He had an eye for the weakness of an argument and for the workable solution to a problem. To a rare combination of administrative skill and intellectual power was added an impressive firmness of character which gave to his personal life an integrity and incorruptibility even in small matters.

Devons's published work seems slight and his career disappointing in relation to his intellectual gifts. This partly reflects his disenchantment with technical economic analysis, partly his preference for administrative tasks, but perhaps most of all a detachment which sprang from lack of ambition. He was not a natural writer or man of action. But he had a capacity for leadership which in the post-war years never found full expression.

Devons died in London 28 December 1967 after two years of almost continuous ill health. He had to contend throughout the last twelve years of his life with repeated bouts of illness in the middle of arduous administrative duties. He was survived by his wife, Estelle Wine, a concert pianist from Dublin and a pupil of Solomon, whom he married in 1939. They had two sons and one daughter.

[Memoir and bibliography in a posthumous collection of *Papers on Planning and Economic Management*, ed. Sir Alec Cairncross, 1970; private information; personal knowledge.]

ALEC CAIRNCROSS

DE WIART, SIR ADRIAN CARTON (1880–1963), lieutenant-general. [See CARTON DE WIART.]

DICK, SIR WILLIAM REID (1878–1961), sculptor, was born in Glasgow 13 January 1878, the son of Francis Dick, a journeyman engine-fitter, and his wife, Elizabeth Reid. He served a five-year apprenticeship as a stone-mason's assistant and, in 1906–7, studied at the School of Art in Glasgow when it was perhaps at its strongest as a training centre for quite a few artists who later made considerable reputations. His inborn Scottish thoroughness, combined with this grounding, no doubt accounted for his sound craftsmanship and practical approach to the various commissions for which he was chosen, for he was at his best when working to a brief. Physically he was not a big man but he was robust, tough, dynamic in spirit, and convivial in nature.

In 1907 he came to London, where he remained for the rest of his life, living in St. John's Wood until 1938 and, thereafter, in nearby Maida Vale. He first exhibited at the Royal Academy in 1908 and, except for the years 1916–18, when on army service in France and Palestine, continued to do so every year until his death. Elected an associate in 1921 and a Royal academician in 1928, he was also president of the Royal Society of British Sculptors from 1933 to 1938. He served on the Royal Fine Art Commission from 1928 and the Royal Mint Advisory Committee in 1934–5. He did not, however, neglect his native land, exhibiting at the Royal Scottish Academy and, following his appointment as KCVO in 1935, becoming the King's (later the Queen's) sculptor in ordinary for Scotland from 1938 and being made an honorary Royal Scottish academician in 1939. In 1948 he received the Albert medal of the Royal Society of Arts 'for national memorials in living stone'; this is undoubtedly the aspect of his work for which he gained most distinction.

Reid Dick had several early successes, for example the bronze group 'Femina Victrix' (1914), purchased by the National Gallery of New South Wales, but it was through the memorials required after the war of 1914–18 that he made his impact. The first of real importance was in the Kitchener Memorial Chapel in St. Paul's Cathedral where, working in collaboration with the surveyor, Sir Mervyn Macartney, Reid Dick carved (1922–5) a fine 'Pietà' and altar panel, the recumbent figure of the field-marshal, and two guardian saints. The discipline of these sculptures within their setting, and their clarity, were to become features of all his similar subsequent commissions.

Next he carved the huge 'Lion', eighteen feet in length, above the Menin Gate in Ypres, which was erected in 1927, and modelled the large, gilded-bronze 'Eagle' which surmounts the RAF memorial on the Thames embankment at Westminster. There followed memorials to the second Viscount Leverhulme at Port Sunlight (1930), and at New Delhi in 1932 to Lord Irwin (later first Earl of Halifax, q.v.) and (1935–6) to the Earl (later Marquis) of Willingdon [q.v.] who succeeded Irwin as viceroy of India. He also made memorials to David Livingstone [q.v.] at Victoria Falls, Rhodesia (1931–3), and, among others and much later, to President Roosevelt in Grosvenor Square, London (1948).

Meanwhile, he had chiselled (1938), in *bianco del mare*, a dignified, recumbent effigy of George V for the King's tomb designed by Sir Edwin Lutyens [q.v.] in St. George's Chapel, Windsor. The figure so pleased Queen Mary that Reid Dick was then asked to do one of her also, to be added after her death. Following this commission, and with Sir Giles Gilbert Scott [q.v.] as the architect, Reid Dick was the sculptor of the stone statue of George V (c.1941) alongside the east end of Westminster Abbey.

Even so, over the years, this busy craftsman had found time to produce other important works, for example a bas-relief of 'Children' (1928) around the main doorway of Selfridges in Oxford Street (for which he was awarded the silver medal of the Royal Society of British Sculptors), two colossal groups in Portland stone, entitled 'Controlled Energy' (shire horses held in check), on the river frontage of Unilever House near Blackfriars Bridge (1932), a stone group called 'The Goose Boy' (1937), at the Midland Bank, Poultry, a gilded-bronze figure 'The Herald' (1939) for Reuters' building in Fleet Street, and a bronze statue of Lady Godiva (c.1950) for Coventry, showing the delectable young lady on horseback riding naked through the streets of that city; also a 'Presentation Bell' (1927), 'The *Daily Mirror* Greyhound Trophy' (1928), being a pair of these dogs alert but at ease, and, in association with Sir Edwin Lutyens as architect, two wrought-iron lamp standards (1933) placed outside the west entrance of St. Paul's Cathedral.

There had been in addition many commissions for portrait busts, including, in stone, (Sir) Harry Lauder (1911, q.v.), Lady Diana Duff Cooper (1922), and George V (1934); and, in bronze, Frank O. Salisbury (1927, q.v.), Lord Duveen (1934), George VI (1942), (Sir) Winston Churchill (1943), and Princess Elizabeth (1947). As though all this were insufficient to keep him fully occupied, Reid Dick produced many works of his own volition, among the best being busts and masks of his family and the stone statuette group 'The Child' (1927), his diploma work as a Royal academician.

The immensity of his output is impressive and its standard high, being most telling in association with architecture and in straightforward portraiture.

He died in London 1 October 1961, being survived by his widow, Catherine, daughter of William John Treadwell, of Northampton, whom he had married in 1914; they had a son and two daughters. Fittingly, there is a memorial to him in St. Paul's Cathedral. There are portraits of Reid Dick by Philippe Ledoux (1934, in the National Portrait Gallery), R. G. Eves (1934), and Dick Hart (1951). There are also a head by George Paulin (1935) and a plaster bust by Chintamoni Kar (1953).

[H. Granville Fell, *Sir William Reid Dick*, 1945; *The Times* and *Daily Telegraph*, 2 October 1961; *Guardian*, *Scotsman*, and *Glasgow Herald*, 3 October 1961; Royal Academy records; personal knowledge.]

S. C. HUTCHISON

DIMBLEBY, RICHARD FREDERICK (1913–1965), journalist and broadcaster, was born at Richmond on Thames 25 May 1913, the elder child and only son of Frederick J. G. Dimbleby, and his wife Gwendoline M. Bolwell, the daughter of a Bath surveyor. Educated at Mill Hill School, in 1931 he went to work in the composing room of the family paper, the *Richmond and Twickenham Times*, then edited by his father, who later became a political adviser to Lloyd George. After gaining experience on the *Bournemouth Echo* and the *Advertisers Weekly*, in 1936 Dimbleby thrust his way with typical determination into the Topical Talks Department of the BBC, becoming one of the Corporation's first news reporters 'at a small empty desk in a small and otherwise empty room about to tackle a job which did not yet exist and about which I knew nothing at all'. But his flair, his sense of purpose, and a decided gift for self-assertion made him a pioneer and then a central figure in the development of reporting and public commentary first in radio and then in television. Experience in the Spanish civil war equipped him for service, in 1939, with the British Expeditionary Force in France as the BBC's first war correspondent. In fact his career was a succession of 'firsts'.

Subsequently Dimbleby covered the campaigns in the Middle East, East Africa, Greece, and the Western Desert. Recalled to London in 1942, he was the first BBC correspondent to fly with Bomber Command (to Berlin in 1943) and he had twenty further missions to his credit. In battle his instinct was to go forward, but a suffocating censorship and the BBC's own muddled policies about war news seemed, too often, to flavour his Mediterranean dispatches with the cosy optimism of rear headquarters. Yet though he was in part a conformist, at heart he was a rebel for the truth and his essential integrity was marked by responsible direction of the BBC's war-reporting team from D-Day onwards and by his own coverage of the final advance into Germany. He was the first reporter into Belsen, on which he filed a classic dispatch. He found time to write a number of books during the war and was always a prolific contributor to newspapers and periodicals.

Television's post-war expansion converted a voice familiar on the radio to one intimate by one's fireside. Remorseless in preparation and in the refinement of his techniques, Dimbleby became the irreplaceable 'anchor-man' for elaborate commentaries on televised state occasions and for the burgeoning political programmes like 'Panorama': a figurehead, universally enjoyed, aspersed, respected, and envied. For years his magisterial presence dominated the screen. But he was also an inde-fatigable contributor to radio, as chairman of 'Twenty Questions' and the peregrinating interviewer of 'Down Your Way', and he busily concerned himself with the conduct of the family paper.

Fortunate in his time and opportunities, Dimbleby exploited them seriously, creatively, and ruthlessly. He had no equal. Where he went first and alone, able competitors have since crowded, and after the collapse of the BBC's monopoly no single personality has reigned over the complete territory of the nation's screens like an emperor. The programmes of compli-cated ceremonial at which he was adept have lost their compelling novelty in the course of broadcasting's evolution. But though his art's product was perishable, he made an enduring mark. His subject-matter, whether a coronation or a general election, was rarely trivial, and viewers followed him readily to the height of his theme.

In later years he was a man of substance, and looked it: bulky, formidable, wearing a mantle of success as if by right, although, like all good performers, he was dogged by fears of failure. A natural belligerence was enriched by struggle with his BBC superiors over matters of administrative and editorial policy where, particularly during the war, wise heads at Broadcasting House were often more addled than their representatives in the field. But behind the revealed persona, suave, sometimes pompous and overbearing, there was a true vein of compassion and humanity which per-vaded his dispatches and often, in private, his actions. His career was sweetened by his sense of humour, and he laughed best at himself.

In 1965 he seemed to reach a peak with his handling of the televised commentary on Churchill's funeral, but on 22 December he died of cancer in St. Thomas's Hospital, London. For five years he had successfully concealed his condition, and undertaken the most intensive and exacting treatment, without ceasing to work in the public eye. His fortitude and will-power were exemplary. The memorial service at Westminster Abbey was a national event, and a torrent of public subscriptions funded, in his memory, a fellowship of cancer research at St. Thomas's Hospital, London University. His stoicism and the cause of his death evoked a universal sympathy, and there was an important social consequence. Millions for whom cancer had been unmentionable now found that a taboo had been lifted.

In 1937 he married his father's personal assistant, Dilys, the daughter of Arthur A. Thomas, a barrister and member of the London County Council. They had three sons, Jonathan, David, and Nicholas, and a daughter,

Sally. Jonathan and David both have successful television careers. Dimbleby was appointed OBE in 1945 and CBE in 1959. In 1965 Sheffield University awarded him with an honorary LLD.

[Jonathan Dimbleby, *Richard Dimbleby*, 1975; *Richard Dimbleby, Broadcaster* (ed. Leonard Miall, 1966); Asa Briggs, *The History of Broadcasting in the United King-dom, vol. iii, The War of Words*, 1970, and *vol. iv, Sound and Vision*, 1979; personal knowledge.]   RONALD LEWIN

DIXON, SIR ARTHUR LEWIS (1881-1969), civil servant, was born in Swindon 30 January 1881, the only son of Seth Dixon, a Wesleyan minister, and his wife, Caroline Lewis. He was educated at Kingswood School, Bath, of which for many years he was later a governor, and entered Sidney Sussex College, Cambridge, where he became ninth wrangler (1902). In 1903 he passed fourth in the open competitive ex-amination for class I clerkships in the home Civil Service, and joined the Home Office. From there it was Dixon's achievement to refashion two of the great public services in this country—the police and fire services—from disparate elements which had scarcely changed since Victorian times. In each of these enterprises he was instrumental in enlarging the powers and responsibilities of the Home Office in relation to the service, and he imposed his own strong ideas on its subsequent development.

On the outbreak of war in 1914 Dixon was put in charge of a 'war measures' division, a position from which he was able to assess the handicaps suffered by police forces and fire brigades alike, due to the absence of any effective system for co-ordination and control. Following raids by Zeppelins, he drew up a successful mutual assistance scheme between fire brigades, and this experience was to be of value in preparing for the war of 1939-45. Then, at the end of the war of 1914-18, the troubles of the police, which had led them to strike, demanded attention. In 1919 the Government set up a committee under Lord Desborough [q.v.] to review matters, and Dixon was appointed to be its secretary. The subsequent reports (1919 and 1920) marked a watershed between the old police service and the new: as Dixon himself put it later, the changes proposed by Desborough offered 'what amounted to a new conception of the police as a service, an integrated system, rather than a collection of separate forces each concerned with its merely local requirements and personnel'.

The 'new conception' had to be worked out in practical terms, and Dixon was placed in charge of a newly formed police division in the Home Office to undertake the radical changes pending;

and from there he rapidly gained the confidence, and frequently the affection, of those concerned with police administration—chief constables, members of police authorities, and the new Police Federation. By temperament a brilliant planner and organizer rather than an administrator, his authority was for upwards of twenty years unique, and it went virtually unchallenged; and his reward came with the realization, when war broke out in 1939, that 183 separate police forces, under his guidance, were already acknowledging not only a local loyalty, but also a loyalty to the idea of a single police service, dedicated to the wider national interest.

Meanwhile Dixon's fertile and ingenious mind, always fascinated by scientific discoveries, was casting about for ways of harnessing science to detective work, and the development of early radio links within forces, the systematic training of detectives, and the establishment of forensic science laboratories, were largely due to his enthusiasm and drive during the inter-war years.

Dixon was promoted to be assistant under-secretary of state in 1932, and four years later he took over the fire brigades division of the Home Office. Convinced that in a future war the real menace would be incendiary, rather than high-explosive, bombs, he set about developing and equipping the fire brigades with the same tremendous drive with which he had modernized the police. Hence he made sure that, on the outbreak of war, the fire-fighting equipment was available in quantity; but it soon became clear that the fragmented organization of the service was a source of dangerous weakness, and when the first heavy air raids came in 1940-1 the Government decided that an immediate and radical restructuring of the whole service was essential. The task of creating the wartime National Fire Service fell naturally to Dixon. The basic plan—the unification of all fire-fighting arrangements, with standard conditions of service—was, characteristically, drawn up within weeks. It was, said the home secretary, Herbert Morrison (later Lord Morrison of Lambeth, q.v.), 'one of the quickest administrative revolutions that ever took place'—and it was brilliantly successful.

In thus modernizing both the fire service and the police, Dixon unquestionably made a large personal contribution towards ensuring the stability of the home front during the war—recognition of which came with a knighthood in 1941 and his promotion to a special rank of principal assistant under-secretary of state.in the same year.

Dixon was a shy man, and to many of his colleagues he seemed aloof and gluttonous for work. He had little social life: he lived, recluse-like, in a succession of private hotels. He inherited from his father abstemious attitudes—he did not smoke, and was a strict teetotaller. He was an active Christian, and gave great help to the British and Foreign Bible Society, of which he was vice-president. He was also a generous benefactor of the Methodist Church, of his old school, and of the Police College. Although Dixon was reserved, he was not cold; those who penetrated the reserve were devoted to him. Listening to music, walking, and keeping abreast of scientific discoveries were Dixon's chief delights, but his interests were wide-ranging, encompassing, for example, geology, palaeontology, astronomy, and nuclear fission—about which he published a book, *Atomic Energy for the Layman* (1950). He was welcomed in many of the observatories and atomic stations of Europe and America, and was a visiting lecturer at Berkeley, California.

Dixon retired from the Home Office 30 January 1946, but he continued to keep in touch with the two services which he had refashioned. From official papers he compiled three (unpublished) administrative histories which record his work.

In 1909 Dixon married Marie (died 1949), daughter of Alfred Talbot Price, architect; she was seventeen years older than he and there were no children. He died in Bournemouth 14 September 1969.

[*The Times*, 16 September 1969; T. A. Critchley, *A History of Police in England and Wales 900-1966*, 1967.]   T. A. CRITCHLEY

DIXON, SIR PIERSON JOHN (1904-1965), diplomatist, was born 13 November 1904 at Englefield Green, Surrey, the eldest of the four children and elder son of Pierson John Dixon, estate agent, and his wife, Helen, daughter of James Ownby Beales, a royal caterer. His Christian names had been handed down from father to eldest son through five generations but he was known all his life as Bob. A delicate undersized little boy he had an unhappy childhood. His father, who was frequently absent from home, dissipated the family fortune built up from the estate agency over several generations and the atmosphere at home was one of tension and scolding. Dixon went first to a second-rate private school, then to Bedford School. There he began winning prizes and by his methodical intelligence and hard work set about raising himself from his unpromising beginnings, without financial support and with little encouragement from his family. He gained a scholarship at Pembroke College, Cambridge, where he obtained first class honours in both parts of the classical tripos (1925-7), was awarded the Porson prize and Craven scholarship (1926), and in 1927 was elected to a junior research fellowship. In the same year he won the Craven studentship which enabled him to spend a year in Greece. He became fascinated by Greece, ancient as well as modern, and seemed set for a classical academic career. However, in 1928 he decided after much hesitation to sit for the Foreign Office examination in which he was placed second in 1929. He resigned his Cambridge fellowship; but he never lost his academic leanings. He wrote a history of *The Iberians of Spain* in 1940, and three carefully researched historical novels: *Farewell, Catullus* (1953), *The Glittering Horn* (1958) about the Empress Theodora, and *Pauline* (1964), about Pauline Bonaparte, written while he was living as British ambassador in the house which she had owned. He was engaged in writing a book on modern diplomacy when he died.

Joining the Foreign Office in 1929, Dixon soon abandoned the 'more discursive academic idiom . . .' and acquired 'a talent for concise constructiveness . . .' Adaptability was indeed among the outstanding qualities which, combined with a clear intelligence and serious application, made Dixon such a valued assistant and adviser to his chiefs. He was quiet, unemotional, cautious in his opinions, and meticulous in mastering the subject-matter in any situation in which he found himself. As his children observed, there was something of the courtier about him, and he was at his best when at the right hand of some statesman or diplomat under pressure. These talents he displayed and developed during his years of service in Madrid (1932), Ankara (1936), and Rome (1938).

In 1940 Dixon returned to the Foreign Office and in the following year began his long association with Anthony Eden (later the Earl of Avon), when, as a member of the Southern Department, he accompanied Eden and Sir John Dill [q.v.] on their mission to the Middle East and the Balkans, when the decision was taken to provide military assistance to Greece in the event of a German attack. Two years later, in 1943, Eden appointed him to be his principal private secretary. In this capacity Dixon found himself admitted to the inner circles of political and strategic debate at the height of the war. He was present at innumerable meetings and discussions between the leading figures of the day. His diaries record, for example, the talks in the prime minister's train on 4 June 1944, when the Normandy landings were postponed for twenty-four hours, and the agonizing debates between the British and American leaders on how to handle de Gaulle when the invasion of France was imminent.

In August 1944 Dixon accompanied the prime minister to Italy when Churchill met the new Italian rulers and formed his judgements about the future of Italy. On Eden's instructions Dixon played his part, with the support of Harold Macmillan, the resident minister, in persuading Churchill to make a peace treaty with Italy; and he played an emollient role in the disputes over whether, and from which scene of operations, forces should be sent to Greece to prevent a Communist takeover after the defeat of the Germans. His diary recorded him in the classic role of the foreign secretary's principal private secretary: 'After an amusing dinner with the P.M. (and Tito) I worked late on records and telegrams, including three to Roosevelt, Stalin and the King, each of which required very individual treatment.'

Dixon accompanied Churchill and Eden to Athens on Christmas Day 1944 when the decisions were taken which resulted in saving the country from Communist rule. He was at the Yalta and Potsdam conferences and after a meeting of the Big Three at the latter wrote in his diary 'I redrafted the Communiqué a few minutes before the 10 p.m. meeting—to the irritation of the drafting committee—but the amendments improved the document from the point of view of presentation. It was hot work juggling with papers balanced on my knee sitting on a chair between Bevin and Attlee.' This ability to produce quickly, in uncomfortable conditions, a form of words reconciling divergent views at international discussions was one of Dixon's most valued qualities.

When Ernest Bevin [q.v.] went to the Foreign Office in July 1945 Dixon remained principal private secretary under him and acted as a liaison between him and Eden in the implementation of a bipartisan foreign policy. Bevin came greatly to rely on Dixon who went with him to Moscow in 1945 and to Paris and New York in 1946. He remained Bevin's right-hand man until in 1948 he went as ambassador to Prague.

With an interval in 1950-4 as deputy under-secretary at the Foreign Office, Dixon now had three foreign postings all of which brought unexpected difficulties and challenges as well as sadness and disappointment. He had not been a month in Prague (where Bevin had particularly instructed him to encourage President Benes and to assure him of British support) when the Communist takeover occurred, his friend Jan Masaryk was alleged to have committed suicide, and the first Czech post-war tragedy was completed under his eyes. As permanent United Kingdom representative at the United Nations (1954-60) Dixon was confronted in 1956 with the Suez crisis and found himself sitting at the Security Council between the representatives of the United States and the Soviet Union, both voting against Britain. He had the unenviable duty of recording the first British veto in that body. He sustained his ordeal with great dignity and self-control and his conduct during this crisis helped Britain to regain respect and influence in the United Nations in subsequent years.

Dixon's embassy to France in 1960-5 was complicated and to a large extent frustrated by other factors beyond his control. It coincided with the first bid by Britain, under Macmillan's administration, with Edward Heath as chief negotiator, to enter the Common Market; and consequently with the first British challenge to the Gaullist conception of Europe. By an arrangement which many thought unwise at the time, but which was supposed to be likely to influence de Gaulle in favour of British entry, Dixon was asked to undertake the duties of permanent British representative at the Common Market negotiations in Brussels in addition to his job as British ambassador in Paris. It was an impossible combination of functions and the physical and moral strain undoubtedly affected his health. Nevertheless Dixon earned the esteem of President de Gaulle, who showed special friendliness to the Dixons when they left Paris in February 1965. Dixon for his part recorded that he had 'always liked de Gaulle and enjoyed my dealings with him, however unproductive the political outcome may have been.'

Dixon was a serious and gentle character. He became an 'operator' of very great skill over the whole field of diplomacy and in Eden's view 'one of the ablest diplomats I have ever known'. He was tireless in personal contact, persistent and persuasive in the more intimate and confidential forms of political discussion, and impeccably loyal. As an adviser he preferred to avoid expressing difficult opinions, perhaps because he saw both sides of the question; and he fell short of becoming a major force in the formulation of Foreign Office policy.

In 1928 Dixon married Alexandra Ismene, widow of Michael Melas and daughter of Shirley Clifford Atchley, first secretary at the British Embassy in Greece. He had two daughters and one son, Piers Dixon, who became Conservative member of Parliament for Truro in 1970.

Dixon was appointed CMG in 1945, CB in 1948, KCMG in 1950, and GCMG in 1957. He died in Egham, Surrey, 22 April 1965.

[Piers Dixon, *Double Diploma*, 1968; personal knowledge.]   EVELYN SHUCKBURGH

DOBSON, FRANK OWEN (1886-1963), sculptor, was born in London 18 November 1886, the younger son of Frank Dobson, an illustrator, whose speciality was flowers and birds, and his wife, Alice Mary Owen. He was educated at Harrow Green School and in 1900 gained a scholarship to Leyton Technical School, which had an art department. In 1902 he became apprentice studio boy to (Sir) William Reynolds-Stephens until he was eighteen. He spent the years from 1904 to 1906 painting and sketching in Cornwall, before successfully applying in 1906 for a scholarship to Hospitalfield Art Institute, Arbroath, where he remained until 1910. After a stay in London, where he continued his artistic training at the City and Guilds School, Kennington, he returned to Cornwall to share a studio with (Sir) Cedric L. Morris in Newlyn where he made his first wood carving in 1913. A visit from Augustus John [q.v.] led to his first one-man exhibition of paintings and drawings at the Chenil Gallery in 1914.

In October of that year Dobson enlisted in the Artists' Rifles and was on active service in France until he was invalided out two days before the armistice. After returning to Cornwall in 1919, where he met Cordelia Johnson, who became his first wife the same year, he re-established himself in London at 14 Trafalgar Studios, Manresa Road, Chelsea, and renewed contact with P. Wyndham Lewis [q.v.], whom he had first met in Cornwall, through Captain Guy Baker. In 1920, as the only sculptor, Dobson exhibited in the Group X exhibition at Heal's Mansard Gallery, showing 'Concertina Man' (1920, in the collection of J. Wyatt, USA) and 'Pigeon Boy' (1920, in the collection of John Pringle), among other works, in the company of other artists, including Lewis, William Roberts, Edward A. Wadsworth [q.v.], and I. Charles Ginner [q.v.].

Following the break-up of Group X in 1921, Dobson was commissioned to make a bronze head (Tate Gallery) of H. H. Asquith (later first Earl of Oxford and Asquith) and held his first one-man sculpture show at the Leicester Galleries (1921). Later in that year (Sir) Osbert Sitwell [q.v.] began three months of sittings in the Chelsea Studio (Tate Gallery) and there he met T. E. Lawrence [q.v.], who was another frequent visitor. The head of Sitwell, in polished brass (1923), is in the Tate Gallery.

On 7 February 1922 the first production of *Façade*, by (Dame) Edith Sitwell [q.v.] and (Sir) William Walton, took place in the Sitwell house in Carlyle Square employing a backdrop designed by Dobson, which was used again for the Aeolian Hall performance on 12 June 1923 and for several productions at the Chenil Galleries in 1926.

Having joined in 1922, from 1923 to 1927 Dobson was president of the London Group, which then represented the avant-garde in contemporary British art.

In an article in the *Burlington Magazine* of April 1925, Roger E. Fry [q.v.] gave warm recognition to Dobson's work, with special reference to 'Lopokova' (1924, Arts Council), 'Marble Woman' (1924, Courtauld Institute), 'Susanna' (1923, Tate Gallery), the first sketch for 'Cornucopia' (1926, Mrs F. Dobson), and 'Cambria' (1924, Manchester City Art Gallery). The model for the last had been shown with the London Group in June. In 1926 an exhibition of European art with sculpture by Dobson, Epstein, Maillol, Despiau, Kolle, Haller, and Mestrovic toured the USA and Canada. The XV Venice-Bienniale included 'Susanna' (National Museum of Wales, Cardiff).

Dobson's marriage was under strain at this time and was eventually dissolved; his second wife was Caroline Mary Bussell, whom he married in 1926. They had one daughter.

Dobson's second one-man show at the Leicester Galleries, in 1927, included, among recent sculptures, the bronze portraits of Robin Sinclair (1925), Sir Eugene Goossens [q.v.], L. H. Myers (1927, q.v.), and 'Tallulah'. He also showed with the London Artists' Association (which he had helped to found) at the same galleries in November. In 1925 the Contemporary Art Society made its first purchase of a work by Dobson—a bronze 'Head of a Girl' (1925) and presented it to the Tate Gallery in 1929. The London Group's Retrospective 1914–18 Exhibition at the New Burlington Gallery included 'Concertina Man', 'Cornucopia', 'Torso' (1933, in the collection of Lord Ivor Churchill), and three drawings. Dobson did not thereafter exhibit with the London Group, although he continued to be a member until the end of 1933.

He began to design and print fabrics and, in 1930, he designed faience panels for Hay's Wharf Building, London Bridge.

In 1930 the over-life-size figure of 'Truth' was bought for the nation by the Contemporary Art Society with the aid of a public subscription and installed outside the Tate Gallery. The year 1934 brought the completion of the large carving of 'Pax' in Portland stone.

A bronze of Margaret Rawlings (Lady Barlow) exhibited at the Royal Academy in 1936 was purchased and given to the Tate Gallery by an anonymous donor in 1937.

In 1937 Dobson designed a silver-gilt loving-cup, 'Calix Majestatis', which was presented to King George VI and Queen Elizabeth by Captain W. Llewellyn-Amos for Holyrood House.

Dobson first exhibited at the Royal Academy in 1933 and became an associate in 1942. Dobson was elected an associate of the Royal Society of British Sculptors in 1938. Following his 'Pax' being shown at the New York World's Fair in 1939, Dobson moved to Bristol, staying first with H. W. Maxwell, curator of the Bristol Museum, where the most complete exhibition

of Dobson's career was held in March 1940. He continued his work for the War Artists' Advisory Committee which brought him to Clydeside and Teesside. In 1941 he moved to Kingsley near Borden, Hampshire. His war work included bronze busts of Admiral Sir William James (1941) and Chief Petty Officer H. J. Whitehorne, DSM (1941), commissioned for the Admiralty.

In 1946 Dobson was appointed professor of sculpture at the Royal College of Art and moved back to London. With the shortage of sculptural materials, he began a series of bird and animal drawings largely studied in London Zoo which he showed at the Royal Academy during the following years. He was appointed CBE in 1947.

He was commissioned to do a large plaster group, entitled 'London Pride', for the 1951 Festival of Britain exhibition at the South Bank. In 1953, he was elected a Royal Academician and retired from the Royal College of Art.

As a man, he was slight in stature with a goatee beard, quite unlike a sculptor in appearance; however, he had a dynamic and cheerful personality dedicated to his students. Duncan Grant described him as 'one of England's greatest sculptors'. His recreations, listed in *Who's Who*, were the cinema, walking to the studio, and talking nonsense; his widow remembered him as always gentle and the kindliest of men.

He died at Princess Beatrice Hospital in London 22 July 1963 leaving a widow and a daughter. A portrait of Dobson by Robert Buhler was exhibited at the Royal Academy Summer Exhibition in 1952.

[*The Times*, 23 July 1963; T. W. Earp, *Dobson*, 1945; Arts Council catalogue *Dobson*, 1966; *Frank Dobson* (plates with a preface by Raymond Mortimer), 1926.]

HANS FLETCHER

DOBSON, SIR ROY HARDY (1891–1968), aircraft engineer, was born at Horsforth, Yorkshire, 27 September 1891, the eldest child of Horace Dobson, farmer, and his wife, Mary Ann Hardy. He became an engineering apprentice with T. & R. Lees, a firm then operating in Hollinwood, near Manchester. He joined the company of (Sir) E. A. V. Roe [q.v.], aeroplane manufacturer, in 1914, becoming its works manager in 1919 and general manager in 1934. He was elected to the board of the company in 1936 and became managing director in 1941, retaining that position until he became in 1958 managing director of the Hawker Siddeley Group Ltd., a company of which A. V. Roe had become a subsidiary in 1935, and to which Dobson was appointed a director in 1944.

On his own initiative, in 1945, Dobson set up

on behalf of Hawker Siddeley an aeroplane company known as A. V. Roe Canada Ltd. and an aero-engine company known as Orenda Engines Ltd., in Toronto, Canada. He was the first president of these companies and later, in 1951, became their chairman. He had many associations in Canada, a country for which he had great affection. He was a director of the Canadian Imperial Bank of Commerce (1955–66). In 1963 Dobson became chairman of the Hawker Siddeley Group and remained in that office until he retired in 1967. Dobson—known the world over as 'Dobbie'—was a man of great vigour and imagination, with a drive and determination which enabled him to make a definitive impact on the development of industry and particularly the aeronautical industry. He was warm-hearted and enthusiastic, if sometimes a little hard on others in his outbursts of anger when things went wrong, but always immediately contrite if he had been too harsh. He was apt, from time to time, to address people in somewhat heightened language, but never to an extent greater than he would readily apply to himself if he concluded that the fault was really his own. He was a colourful man with a tremendous capacity for hard work and for overcoming difficulties. As often with such men, he gathered around him others whose devotion to him increased the more he drove them, although not without the occasional casualty.

The increasing possibility of war in the late thirties gave Dobson an opportunity to develop his talents to the full. During the 1930s A. V. Roe had been engaged in the design of a twin-engined bomber aircraft, the Manchester. As this aeroplane suffered from underpowered and unreliable engines it seemed bound to fail. At the time, the Merlin engine, developed by Rolls-Royce, was designed to be used in fighter aircraft. Roy Chadwick (whose notice Dobson contributed to this Dictionary), who was then chief designer at A. V. Roe, felt that he could redesign the twin-engined Manchester using four of the Merlins. He might thus overcome the problems. This was a proposal which the authorities were loath to accept, if only because they felt that the need for fighters would absorb as many Merlins as could be provided. Dobson faced this problem with characteristic vigour. Somehow four Merlins were obtained and the Manchester prototype was speedily fitted with Merlin engines. From this work emerged the Lancaster, which was undoubtedly the most successful bomber developed by either side in the war. Dobson's ability to procure such a new and vital weapon displayed to the full his energy, determination, and imagination.

With similar vigour Dobson initiated and supervised the provision of resources to manu-facture this aeroplane in quantity in Canada—as he was also doing in English factories. In Canada, however, he was starting from the beginning, and he created a factory which produced an excellent product in large numbers. An aero-engine factory was also set up at the same time. At the end of the war Dobson arranged the purchase by Hawker Siddeley of both the aeroplane and engine units. It was at this time that he set up A. V. Roe Canada Ltd., and Orenda Engines Ltd., as design and manufacturing organizations. Their first product was a successful military aircraft, the Avro CF 100, powered by an engine (the Orenda) designed and built by Orenda Engines Ltd. A. V. Roe Canada also built a prototype jet-propelled civil aircraft which was almost certainly the first jet civil machine to fly. It was slightly ahead of the Comet, designed by Sir G. de Havilland [q.v.] in England, although it did not enter passenger service, as did the Comet, which therefore became the first jet-propelled aircraft to carry commercial passengers.

Under Dobson's chairmanship, A. V. Roe Canada proceeded from these successes to design and build, in conjunction with the Canadian Government, prototypes of a very advanced fighting aircraft which became known as the Arrow. In retrospect it can be seen that this very costly venture was probably beyond the financial resources of a country with the small population then possessed by Canada, and the Arrow, although technically successful, was cancelled in a storm of controversy. Dobson, perhaps sensing that there were limits to the investment which Canada could make alone in military development, had already extended the business of A. V. Roe Canada into other areas: particularly railway engineering, in which he made a series of company acquisitions.

Despite his heavy responsibilities in Canada, Dobson continued to develop his interests in England. After the war A. V. Roe designed and built what was then the revolutionary delta-winged Vulcan bomber and entered the civil aviation field with the Avro 748, an aeroplane still (1978) being built and widely used. On becoming a director of the Hawker Siddeley Group, and subsequently its managing director and then its chairman, Dobson did much to widen the company's aeronautical interests, particularly in the early 1960s, when he initiated the acquisition of the de Havilland, Blackburn, and Folland companies, so forming, with the existing Hawker Siddeley aviation interests, a strong aeronautical unit which eventually became Hawker Siddeley Aviation Ltd. Simultaneously he initiated early moves to bring the company into areas of engineering other than aeronautics. He retired from his chairmanship in 1967 at the age of seventy-five. He died at

King Edward VII Hospital, Midhurst, Sussex, 7 July 1968.

Dobson was created CBE in 1942, was knighted in 1945, and was awarded an honorary fellowship of the Royal Aeronautical Society in 1956. In 1916 he married Annie Smith (died 1954). They had two sons, one of whom was lost in a flying accident in 1946, and a daughter. There is a portrait in pastels by Tom Pervis in the Club House of the British Aerospace Corporation in Manchester.

[Hawker Siddeley Group Ltd. records; private information; personal knowledge.]

ARNOLD HALL

DOODSON, ARTHUR THOMAS (1890-1968), mathematician and oceanographer, was born at Boothstown near Worsley in Lancashire 31 March 1890, the second son of Thomas Doodson, the manager of a cotton mill in Boothstown, who later moved to Rochdale and then to Shaw near Oldham, and his wife, Eleanor Pendlebury, of Radcliffe, Lancashire. Doodson went to the village school and evening classes and studied as a pupil teacher before attending Rochdale Secondary School and, in 1908, the university of Liverpool. He gave up the idea of teaching when he became seriously deaf and this may have led him to give up chemistry, though he was also encouraged to specialize in mathematics by Professor F. S. Carey. He gained a first class B.Sc. in chemistry and mathematics in 1911 and a first class honours degree in mathematics in 1912, winning a prize for geometry.

His deafness made it difficult for him to get a job and he accepted a post as meter-tester for Messrs. Ferranti but two years later obtained a more congenial post at the Testing and Standardizing Department of the Corporation of Manchester. In 1916 he was appointed to a post at University College, London, under Karl Pearson [q.v.] to do statistics but this was soon changed to ballistics for the War Office. In 1914 Doodson had been received into one of the churches of the community known as 'The Churches of God in the Fellowship of the Son of God', a breakaway sect from the Plymouth Brethren, and from then on his life was dominated by religion, to the exclusion of much social intercourse. It was therefore sad and paradoxical that he was obliged to work for some years on duties to which he had a conscientious objection. Nevertheless he did some impressive computations, producing tables of Riccati-Bessel functions and of sines and cosines of radians. He was awarded the M.Sc. degree of Liverpool University in 1914 and their D.Sc. in 1919.

By then he had acquired an aptitude and

a liking for computational problems and he started what was to be the most important collaboration of his life, with Professor J. Proudman, who, having been introduced to the problem of ocean tides by (Sir) Horace Lamb [q.v.], had succeeded in getting shipowners to endow a Tidal Institute at Liverpool. Proudman was appointed its honorary director and, recognizing that Doodson had all the qualities necessary to make the Institute a success, arranged for him to be made its secretary. His work with this Tidal Institute constitutes Doodson's greatest achievement.

From small beginnings Doodson built up the Tidal Institute until it was recognized worldwide as an authoritative source of tidal theory, observation, and analysis. He was associate director of the Institute from 1929 to 1945. Doodson's own work was mainly on the computational aspects, his skill at which complemented Proudman's expertise in tidal dynamics. His engineering ability also allowed him to design and install complicated tide-predicting machines in many countries. He was active too in studying meteorological effects on tides and, after the Thames floods of 1928, made intensive studies of coastal flooding, inventing the word 'surge' and many of the techniques which are still (1978) used in forecasting dangerously high highwaters.

Doodson also had administrative charge of a growing Institute and was skilled at the financial aspects. He was reported as saying that he was a mathematician by training, an engineer by preference, and an accountant by force of circumstances. He was certainly gifted, skilled, kind, and had a quiet sense of humour. As soon as hearing-aids became available he made full use of them. His probity and his accounting skills were put to good purpose by the International Union of Geodesy and Geophysics when in 1954 Doodson was made president of the finance committee. He also served as the first director of the permanent service for mean-sea-level of the International Association of Physical Oceanography.

For many years Doodson was an honorary lecturer of the university of Liverpool. In 1930 he was awarded the Thomas Gray memorial prize by the Royal Society of Arts for the benefit of navigation of his prediction of tidal currents. In 1933 he was elected fellow of the Royal Society and in 1953 an honorary fellow of the Royal Society of Edinburgh. He was appointed CBE in 1956.

In 1919 Doodson married, first, Margaret, daughter of J. W. Galloway, a tramways engineer, of Halifax. They had a daughter, who died in 1936, and a son, whose mother died shortly after his birth in 1931. In 1933 Doodson married Elsie May, daughter of W. A. Carey, who survived him. Doodson died at Birkenhead 10 January 1968.

[J. Proudman in *Biographical Memoirs of Fellows of the Royal Society*, vol. xiv, 1968; personal knowledge.]   H. CHARNOCK

DOUGLAS, CLAUDE GORDON (1882-1963), physiologist, was born in Leicester 26 February 1882, the second son of Claude Douglas FRCS, honorary surgeon to Leicester Royal Infirmary, and his wife, Louisa Bolitho Peregrine, of London. His elder brother, J. S. C. Douglas, was professor of pathology at Sheffield University, and his cousin, J. A. Douglas, was professor of geology at Oxford. He was a scholar at Wellington College, but moved to Wyggeston Grammar School, Leicester, in order to study science. He went up to Oxford in 1900 where he was a demy of Magdalen College. In 1904 he obtained first class honours in natural science (animal physiology), after which he stayed on in the physiological laboratory working for the research degree of B.Sc. under the supervision of J. S. Haldane, whose notice he was to contribute to this Dictionary. He was also to contribute the notice of M. S. Pembrey, of Guy's Hospital, where in 1905 Douglas took up a London University scholarship and completed his medical degree (BM, B.Ch.) in December 1907. Six months earlier he had been elected to a fellowship and lectureship in natural science at St. John's College, Oxford, a position he held for forty-two years. He proceeded to the degree of DM in 1913.

Douglas's scientific career falls naturally into three parts, the first, his collaborative work up to 1914 with J. S. Haldane on breathing in man, the second, his work during World War I on physiological aspects of gas warfare, and the third, back in Oxford, after Haldane's departure from the physiological laboratory, on general metabolism in man, successively as university demonstrator (1927), as reader (1937), as titular professor (1942), and, after he had passed the retiring age, as departmental demonstrator up to 1953.

It was Douglas's good fortune to join the physiological laboratory when work on the regulation of body oxygen and carbon dioxide concentrations, and exchange of these gases through the lungs, was still developing. He quickly became the best-known and the most permanent of the younger colleagues of Haldane, who had published since the turn of the century a series of papers which transformed the subject of respiration. Douglas's name appears on some ten of the most important papers over this period which show an insight into the principles of control physiology three or four decades ahead of their time.

Douglas and Haldane provided a quantitative description of the transport of carbon dioxide by the blood between cells and lungs, and the facilitatory effect on it of oxygen transport in the opposite direction. This work complemented the earlier work of Christian Bohr, K. A. Hasselbalch, and S. A. S. Krogh, of Copenhagen, who had showed the facilitatory effects of carbon dioxide on oxygen transport. Work of this kind allowed Douglas and Haldane to develop a practical and bloodless method for measuring the rate of pumping of blood by the human heart under various conditions.

Detailed and meticulous measurement allowed Douglas and J. S. Haldane (with some mathematical assistance from J. B. S. Haldane, q.v.) to elucidate the equilibria between the oxygen-carrying substance haemoglobin and the concentrations of oxygen and carbon monoxide. They went on to show that certain conditions, notably residence at high altitude, altered the equilibria, an observation which has not been refuted, and has been partially confirmed. Ingenious reasoning led them to conclude from this probably correct observation that oxygen could be transported against the concentration gradient across the lung capillary membranes ('oxygen secretion'). The question was open at the time, and the resulting controversy between them and their friends Krogh and (Sir) Joseph Barcroft [q.v.], of Cambridge, was one of the entertainments of early twentieth-century physiology. Subsequent developments decided the controversy against Oxford, but the basic observation remains unexplained (in 1979), although it might be accounted for by changes in the intracellular concentration of a recently discovered reactant (2-3 diphosphoglycerate).

During this period Douglas began to measure the rate of uptake of oxygen and of the output of carbon dioxide by collecting expired air in a large canvas gas-bag. The Douglas bag became well known for its convenience for measuring energy expenditure in coal-miners, bricklayers, housewives, cricketers, and others.

Douglas served in the Royal Army Medical Corps in World War I, reaching the rank of lieutenant-colonel. When gas warfare started in 1915 he was the serving officer in France with the detailed knowledge and deep understanding of respiratory physiology that allowed interpretation of the effects of the alarming new weapon. He held several appointments in the British Expeditionary Force related to gas warfare before being appointed physiological adviser to the Directorate of Gas Services in 1917, where he worked with (Sir) Harold Hartley. He was awarded the MC in 1916, was four times mentioned in dispatches, and was appointed CMG in 1919. He contributed

Douglas, C. G.   D.N.B. 1961-1970

extensively to the official history of the war, and Hartley felt that his chapter dealing with the development of gas warfare was 'by far the best summary of the use of the new weapon'.

After the war Douglas returned to Oxford where he collaborated with J. G. Priestley in setting up and running a novel and thorough' practical course in human physiology. The course was taken by all Oxford medical undergraduates over a period of some thirty years; many will remember Douglas's demonstrations on himself of the effects of asphyxia.

J. S. Haldane having left the physiological laboratory, Douglas's interests moved towards the assessment of metabolic processes in man in the light of the new insights provided by the rapid expansion of biochemistry. With a succession of research students, including F. C. Courtice, he applied the new knowledge to the interpretation of quantitative measurements. His conclusions put him in the vanguard of those who questioned the fashionable, though erroneous, view that carbohydrate was the sole source of energy for muscular contraction.

During World War II Douglas remained in Oxford, teaching and helping with administration in college and the laboratory. After the war and before his final retirement in 1953 he supervised the work of three more research students including (Sir) Roger Bannister.

From 1920 onwards he was increasingly involved in government committee work, some of which he took over from J. S. Haldane. The committees concerned, among other topics, chemical warfare, muscular activity in industry, health and safety in mines, conditions in hot and deep mines, research on pneumoconiosis, breathing apparatus for the National Fire Service, the Gas Research Council, heating and ventilation of buildings in relation to post-war reconstruction, and diet and energy requirements. As a chairman or member, Douglas prepared his papers meticulously, listened carefully, but spoke comparatively seldom. When he did, he usually reintroduced practical common sense when this was lacking.

He was a devoted senior member of St. John's College, which was his home for twenty-eight years. He held the major college offices of vice-president, dean, steward of the Senior Common Room and keeper of the Groves. The fine gardens flourished under his direction.

He was a formidable walker, and a keen and very knowledgeable gardener and photographer. He had a great fund of stories and was an excellent host in college and at home. Douglas was unmarried and lived with his younger sister, Miss Margaret Douglas, for twenty-four years.

In 1911 Douglas won the Radcliffe prize; in 1922 he was elected FRS and was on the council of the Royal Society (1928-30). He was an *ad hominem* professor at a time when Oxford had few such. In 1945 he was awarded the Osler memorial medal, and in 1950 he was elected to an honorary fellowship of St. John's.

Regarding Douglas's personal contribution to his early and best-known joint work in academic physiology, very probably the lion's share came from Haldane's genius. However, Douglas's extraordinarily high standards of accuracy, his energy, his rare 'common sense' and general competence must have contributed greatly to the joint achievement. His capacity as an independent scientist was obvious to his younger colleagues and to readers of his writings on chemical warfare.

Between the wars the departure of Haldane and the scanty material support received by his branch of physiology (Douglas and Priestley ran their excellent practical classes without technical assistance for sixteen years) rendered his achievement in his field of interest difficult; the Oxford laboratory was more concerned with the exciting advances in neurophysiology of the school of Sir C. S. Sherrington [q.v.]. Nevertheless, the younger workers for whom Douglas was responsible received plenty of support, good-humoured encouragement, and advice, and the work in general metabolism deserves to be better known. Douglas died 23 March 1963 after a street accident in Oxford.

There is a portrait in oils by Arthur Pán (1950/1) in St. John's College, Oxford.

[D. J. C. Cunningham in *Biographical Memoirs of Fellows of the Royal Society*, vol. x, 1964, where numerous sources of information about Douglas before 1945 are acknowledged; personal knowledge.]

D. J. C. CUNNINGHAM

DOUGLAS, WILLIAM SHOLTO, BARON DOUGLAS OF KIRTLESIDE (1893-1969), marshal of the Royal Air Force, was born in Oxford 23 December 1893, the second son of the Revd Robert Langton Douglas, secretary of the Church of England Temperance Society, and his first wife, Margaret Jane, daughter of Percival Cannon, printer. Descended from the Red and Black Douglases of ancient Scottish history, his father was a man of great intelligence and diverse interests, who relinquished his orders and later became director of the National Gallery of Ireland. Douglas's domestic background changed with bewildering speed from that of the Anglican Church to the home base of a widely travelling art critic and historian, and finally, when his parents were divorced shortly after his seventh birthday, to a maternal establishment in London where he lived with his mother and two younger brothers in considerably straitened circumstances. His father, fast acquiring a new family, continued to increase his accomplishments and reputation, ending his life as an American citizen, a Roman Catholic, and an acknowledged authority on the history of Italian art.

Despite the commitments of a second and later a third family, his father managed to see that Douglas had a good education, and after due preparation at local schools he went to Tonbridge, then in 1913 to Lincoln College, Oxford, where he won a classical scholarship and sang in the Bach Choir. Before he could take a degree, or show any inclination for a career, all choice was brutally resolved by the outbreak of war. He immediately joined the Royal Field Artillery, and within a few months he was in France. He found land warfare dull, and with the impulsive energy which was to mark him throughout his life he responded to a call for volunteers to join the Royal Flying Corps. By the beginning of 1915 he was training as an observer, and within a few days he was flying reconnaissance patrols. The back seat of an aeroplane still did not satisfy him, and he quickly won a pilot's course. After training he was sent to No. 8 Squadron on the western front, where he rapidly proved himself an aggressive and intelligent airman. He was heavily engaged throughout the fierce fighting of 1915. In 1916 he returned to England, then spent much of the year in Scotland forming and training 43 Squadron; he so proved his quality that in 1917 he led it back to France as commander. He was again involved in continual and bitter air combat, and his squadron suffered heavy losses at the hands of the Richthofen Staffel. His period of command ended when a take-off crash dispatched him to hospital in England.

His naturally assertive nature turned him away from reconnaissance and bombing roles to the fighter or scout type of unit which the air war had then developed, and he was happy to gain command of No. 84 Squadron, flying SE5s, and to lead it into further heavy fighting in France. He finally completed four tours of operations on the western front, and he was credited with six victories in combat. Among those he met in battle was the German fighter pilot Hermann Goering, whose death warrant he was to sign thirty years later. By the end of the war Douglas was a very seasoned and hardened major in the fighter arm of the Royal Flying Corps, awarded the MC (1916) and the DFC (1919), and three times mentioned in dispatches. In circumstances where a pilot's life was measured in days he had lasted nearly four years, and he was still fighting in the last week of the war. Despite the offer of a permanent commission, the tremendous reaction of the war's end separated him from the Service, and caused him to reject the

possibility of returning to Oxford for his degree. Handley-Page Aircraft Company was forming an air transport section, and wanted pilots. Douglas applied for a civil commercial pilot's licence and was issued with No. 4, landing a job with Handley-Page, and became one of the first of the airline captains, working the British and cross-Channel services. But post-war malaise still gripped him. He was discontented with the routine of civil flying. He thought of following in his brilliant if erratic father's footsteps as an art critic, but the pull of aviation was too strong. Finally, after a chance meeting with Sir Hugh (later Viscount) Trenchard [q.v.], he rejoined the air force, in 1920, with a permanent commission in the rank of squadron-leader. He was now launched upon his career. Universally known as 'Sholto', he was a burly man of middle height, giving an impression of great strength and power, occasionally approaching that of a tiger about to pounce. He claimed to be acutely shy with people, but concealed it so well as to instil fear into nervous subordinates, while his manner sometimes came dangerously close to pomposity.

From 1920 until 1936 he served in flying schools, staff appointments, and the Imperial Defence College; with one foreign post, when he was senior RAF officer in the Sudan—and sang in the cathedral choir in Khartoum. He built up a solid reputation as a professional officer who looked and talked like one of the bulldog breed, but who proved on closer inspection to be disconcertingly intelligent without the drawback of over-sensitivity. By 1938 he was an air vice-marshal, once more on the Air Ministry staff. Chance, and particularly timing, play a great part in the military man's career. They served him well; he was the right man at the right place at the right time. He was given the new post of assistant (in 1940 deputy) chief of air staff, responsible for training and for specifying new equipment; in short for the future performance of a Service once more on the brink of war. In this capacity he was compelled to force some very unpalatable truths upon senior officers and politicians, a task from which he did not shrink. At the outbreak of war, which he greeted in a mood of 'sombre anger', he was striving to force the new aircraft types through the factories and into service, pushing the first developments of radar, and attempting to convince the army and navy of the importance of air operations to their own survival. He found some difficulty in keeping his energies solely focused on his own task. At his Air Ministry desk he had to endure the agonizing months of the Norwegian and French campaigns, and watch the RAF's growing power cut down again by its losses in those disasters, followed by the almost unbearable tension of the Battle of Britain. In this struggle he resisted, with indifferent success, an over-powering impulse to urge a change of tactics on Sir Hugh (later Lord) Dowding [q.v.], commander-in-chief of Fighter Command. Dowding elected to meet the enemy as and when he could intercept them; Douglas favoured the assembly of a large defensive force in the air to do the maximum damage to the bombers, so that, even if allowed to drop their bombs first, enemy striking power would be steadily de-pleted. As the only fighter pilot among the senior officers of the air staff his views carried great weight, and when Dowding left Fighter Com-mand in November 1940 he succeeded him, with the rank of air marshal, and a KCB (1941).

His immediate task was to fight the German night air offensive known to history as 'the blitz', with all its problems of radar detection and con-trol. His second, which he tackled with particu-lar relish, was to exploit the daylight victories of the Battle of Britain into an air offensive across the Channel, to engage and destroy the Luft-waffe, and to demonstrate British resistance to the rest of the world. At the same time he built Fighter Command from its dangerously weak condition in 1940 to the formidable strength it achieved two years later. When he was appoin-ted commander-in-chief Middle East, at the end of 1942, by now an air chief marshal, the entry of Russia and the United States had transformed the war. He arrived in Cairo shortly after the battle of El Alamein, and was plunged at once into the wide diversity of operational and diplomatic problems which always distin-guished that area. He took part in the Cairo conference on the future conduct of the war in November 1943. Among his greatest problems was the ill-fated Allied campaign in the Aegean sea, for which he carried a share of the respon-sibility, and which brought him into some conflict with Eisenhower and Sir Arthur (later Lord) Tedder [q.v.] at Supreme Allied Com-mand Mediterranean, but before he left Middle East the Axis forces in Africa had been elimi-nated, Sicily and Italy invaded, and Italy knocked out of the war. None the less it had been a difficult time, and it was with relief that he returned, at the beginning of 1944, to be commander-in-chief of Coastal Command.

His third major command appointment came at a time when the most desperate engagements of the Battle of the Atlantic had been fought, and the naval-air combinations of the Allies had won a large degree of control. The last danger with which he had to contend was the German use of the schnorkel submarine. Nominally under the direction of the Admiralty, Douglas was left in practice to work out his operations with his fellow naval commanders. He was able to extend and strengthen the Allied control of the seas by the application of all the new techniques and aircraft now available, culminating in the supremacy necessary to the Anglo-American invasion of France in June 1944. This provided the last great flurry of activity in the strike and reconnaissance squadrons of his command, and as the enemy was forced back into Germany he was able, for the first time in nearly four years, to feel some lightening of the weight of command responsibility. His great experience with other nations and Services was needed, however, in the difficult situation existing in defeated Germany, and in July 1945 he was appointed commander-in-chief British Air Forces of Occupation, under General Montgomery (later Viscount Montgomery of Alamein). Beginning with problems involving the repatriation of nationals whose countries were now under Russian occupation he became increasingly involved, to his intense dismay, with the dif-ferences which heralded the cold war. He de-tested his job, hated the atmosphere of despair inherent in a ruined and defeated country, and determined to retire from the Service. But while in the process of doing so in January 1946, he was promoted GCB and marshal of the Royal Air Force, becoming one of the only two officers ever to reach that rank without being chief of air staff. At the same time he was nominated to succeed Montgomery as commander-in-chief British Forces in Germany and military governor of the British zone, and under pressure from the Cabinet, he accepted the appointment. The very aspect of command in Germany which he had most disliked was now intensified, for he was the British member of the four-power Allied Con-trol Council, with all its difficulties and tensions. He was doubtful of the propriety of the Nurem-berg trials, and to his distress found that he had to confirm sentences passed on the German leaders following their trials for war crimes. Although he dreaded the responsibility he was forced to resist attempts by the British Cabinet to judge the issue for him in London, and the strain of all these tensions culminated when he signed the document confirming the executions. This was but one of many such judgements, and he welcomed the end of his appointment, when it came in November 1947. He subsequently cited it as the unhappiest period of his life.

After his return to England he retired in 1948 from active duty, and was awarded a peerage. He was then able to declare, without the inhibitions normal to a serving officer, that his political views had always been those of a moderate socialist, and he took his seat in the House of Lords on the Labour benches. This alone made him a somewhat unusual member of the higher military hierarchy. In 1948 his wide experience in aviation brought him a directorship in the British Overseas Airways Corporation, and in 1949, not without some opposition from political anti-militarists, he was appointed chairman of British European Airways. With relish he proceeded to prove that he was no figurehead, by forceful and shrewd management of that company during the emergence of the jet airliner, and he continued to lead BEA, with outstanding success, until 1964. Once more he was doing work which he loved. When he left BEA in 1964 the jet revolution was complete, and it had grown into a large profit-making national airline. He became chairman of Horizon Travel Ltd. in the same year. During the last four years of his life he had to endure increasingly arduous ill health and he died in hospital in Northampton 29 October 1969. His great abilities, persistence, and capacity for sustained hard work had kept him intensively engaged until his seventieth year, and he had filled posts of the highest responsibility for twenty-three consecutive years. He commanded loyalty and affection in those who worked for him, and a guarded respect from his opponents. In 1941 he had been elected an honorary fellow of his college, in 1950 he was made an honorary companion of the Royal Aeronautical Society, and in 1956 he was president of the International Air Transport Association.

In 1919 Douglas married Mary Howard; the marriage was dissolved in 1932 and in 1933 he married Joan Leslie, daughter of Colonel Henry Cuthbert Denny. With the dissolution of this marriage, he married in 1955 Hazel, daughter of George Eric Maas Walker and widow of Captain W. E. R. Walker; they had one daughter.

There is a portrait of Douglas by Eric Kennington and another by Sir James Gunn, both in the Imperial War Museum. A drawing by H. A. Freeth is the property of the Ministry of Defence.

[Lord Douglas of Kirtleside, *Years of Combat*, 1963, and *Years of Command*, 1966; Air Historical Branch (RAF); private information; personal knowledge.]

PETER WYKEHAM

DOVER WILSON, JOHN (1881–1969), Shakespearian scholar. [See WILSON.]

DOWDING, HUGH CASWALL TRE-MENHEERE, first BARON DOWDING (1882–1970), air chief marshal, was born at Moffat, Dumfriesshire, 24 April 1882, the eldest in a family of three boys and one girl of Arthur John Caswall Dowding, a schoolmaster of Wiltshire stock, and his wife, Maud Caroline, daughter of Major-General Charles William Tremenheere, chief engineer in the Public Works Department in Bombay.

During his early schooldays at St. Ninian's,

Moffat, he lived at home enjoying the combination of kindly parents who were also the respected headmaster and his wife. He entered Winchester, his father's old school, in 1895, where he spent four not entirely happy years. His lack of facility with the classics led him to join the army class, thence to choose an army career.

By way of the Royal Military Academy, Woolwich, he became a gunner in the Royal Garrison Artillery, following the advice of his family. His subaltern's life in Gibraltar, Ceylon, and Hong Kong was that of a typical young gunner officer. After transfer to a mountain battery in 1904, he spent six years in India, half the time with a native battery. He relished the strenuous, solitary, and often dangerous life on manœuvres in the Himalayan foothills. Subsequently (1912–13), two years at the Staff College, Camberley, coincided with his developing interest in aviation. In his own time he learned to fly at Brooklands, the flying school run by the firm of Vickers, and obtained his Royal Aero Club pilot's certificate No. 711 early in the morning of the same day as he passed out from Camberley, 20 December 1913. He then took a three-month course at the Central Flying School at Upavon, where his flying instructor was (Sir) John Salmond [q.v.] and his assistant commandant H. M. (later Viscount) Trenchard [q.v.]. Dowding returned to the Garrison Artillery in the Isle of Wight as a Royal Flying Corps Reserve officer.

When war was declared in 1914 he was appointed commandant of the RFC Dover camp whence the squadrons left for France. Thereafter he served at home and in France with Nos. 7 and 6 Squadrons, both as observer and pilot and then as flight commander with No. 9 Squadron. He specialized in early experiments in wireless telegraphy. Appointed to command No. 16 Squadron at Merville in 1915, Dowding in many ways found it a testing time. His nickname from Camberley days of 'Stuffy' appeared to younger aircrew to suit his older, more withdrawn, and austere approach to flying duties. His general reputation was not advanced by a brush with Trenchard over a supply of propellers, although Dowding proved that he himself had the better technical knowledge. Promotion followed regularly until by 1917 he was a brigadier-general; however, another brush with Trenchard in 1916, when Dowding commanded the headquarters wing of HQ Royal Flying Corps, probably denied him field command for the rest of the war.

Becoming, not without difficulty, a permanent officer in the newly created Royal Air Force in 1919, Dowding was group commander at Kenley and then chief of staff at Headquarters, Inland Area. His name became prominent as the organizer of the second and some subsequent Hendon pageants. A posting as chief staff officer to Air Headquarters, Iraq, in 1924 provided further opportunities for active flying. In 1926 he became director of training at the Air Ministry and achieved a much-needed rapport with Trenchard, who was now at the height of power as the chief of air staff. So far did Dowding gain Trenchard's confidence that he was sent in 1929 to Palestine to report on the need for Service reinforcements when an Arab rising seemed imminent. His balanced reports won favour with Trenchard.

After a brief spell in command of the Fighting Area on return from Palestine, Dowding joined the Air Council in 1930 as air member for supply and research. His period of office saw continuous revolutionary changes in the design and construction of aircraft. It saw the development of all-metal monoplanes like the Hurricane and Spitfire, early work on the Stirling and other heavy bombers, and the development of eight-gun armament and especially of radar. Dowding's practical bent, his insistence on experimentation and trials, and his imaginative grasp of aircrew requirements often led him into conflict with colleagues or other holders of received orthodox opinions. Although Dowding was willing to listen to his scientific advisers, it was clear that he formed his own opinions. His title changed to air member for research and development when in 1935 supply became another member's responsibility.

It was fitting that Dowding was appointed AOC-in-C of the new Fighter Command in 1936. The fifty-four-year-old widower moved to Stanmore where his sister Hilda was hostess for him. (Dowding had married in 1918 and his wife died suddenly in 1920.) For the next four years in Fighter Command he dedicated himself to preparing the air defences of the United Kingdom. The introduction of efficient land-line communications, operations rooms, improved VHF R/T, and above all the completion of the chain of radar stations round the east and south coasts were his concern. Together with these went the creation of new squadrons of Spitfires and Hurricanes. The announcement that Sir (later Lord) Cyril Newall [q.v.] was to be appointed chief of air staff in 1937 must have been a blow to any hopes Dowding may have had of achieving that office. He bore this just as stoically as he endured the five separate indications between August 1938 and August 1940 of Air Ministry intention to terminate his active service on grounds of age.

Although a massive Luftwaffe attack did not come, Dowding had to fight a constant paper war to resist diversions of his modern fighters from home defence. Single-mindedly, Dowding sought to retain in readiness the number of squadrons he deemed essential to resist the destruction of his force and the invasion of the country. The loss of fighters in Norway was small compared with the fighter reinforcements demanded by the French premier after the German assault on France. In an appearance at his own request at a Cabinet meeting on 15 May, and in his historic letter to the Air Ministry of 16 May 1940, Dowding set out the stark issues of survival or irremediable defeat. On 20 May the War Cabinet decided that no more fighter squadrons should leave the country. Providing fighter cover at long range during the withdrawal from Dunkirk provided successful combat experience for Dowding's men, but at the cost of further losses of aircraft and pilots. At this time a sympathetic working relationship between Dowding and his AOC No. 11 Group in south-east England, Air Vice-Marshal (later Air Chief Marshal Sir) Keith Park was confirmed and deepened in the summer and autumn of 1940. A similar sympathetic accord was established with his colleague, Lieutenant-General (later General) Sir Frederick Pile, GOC-in-C Anti-Aircraft Command.

The Battle of Britain was fought tactically at Group and Sector Operations Room level. But it is to Dowding that praise must go for his over-all mastery of the air weapon. The deployment of his forces, his rotation of squadrons which had been heavily engaged, his constant regard for reserves of aircraft and personnel, indicated skill of a high order. In addition to commanding the struggle by day for air superiority over south-east England, Dowding spent most nights in monitoring the development of airborne radar and other techniques to meet the threat of the night bomber. His complete personal commitment partly explains his failure to control the clash of tactics and personalities which developed between Park and Air Vice-Marshal Leigh-Mallory [q.v.] (AOC No. 12 Group) over the use of squadrons in big wing formation. Dowding was replaced at Fighter Command on 25 November 1940 by the deputy chief of air staff, Air Marshal Sholto Douglas (later Lord Douglas of Kirtleside, q.v.). Dowding was undoubtedly very tired. He was also a victorious airman and an embarrassingly senior officer.

To many, Dowding's replacement so soon after his victory in Britain's first great air battle appeared ungrateful. Some unusual mark of recognition might have tempered the eventually inevitable decision to appoint a new commander for Fighter Command in its more offensive role. Dowding was persuaded by the prime minister to visit the United States on behalf of the Ministry of Aircraft Production. The trip was not successful. Dowding was inclined to put forward his own views which were not always in accord with those of Britain's permanent representatives there. On his return in June 1941 he was asked to prepare a dispatch on the Battle of Britain. This was ready before October, the date of his retirement as indicated to him by the Air Ministry.

The prime minister expressed 'indignation' when he learned of this intention and virtually commanded Dowding to accept an appointment in the Air Ministry involving the scrutiny of RAF establishments. At the same time he took possession of a book *Twelve Legions of Angels* which Dowding had submitted for clearance. The new appointment was not to Dowding's taste and before long the old arguments with the Air Ministry reappeared. At his own request he eventually retired in July 1942 but his book was suppressed under the wartime regulations until 1946.

In his retirement Dowding devoted himself to a study of spiritualism and theosophy. His nature had always been contemplative and philosophical. He published several books—*Many Mansions* (1943), *Lychgate* (1945), *God's Magic* (1946), and *The Dark Star* (1951). He wrote articles for newspapers and gave lectures on occult subjects. His second marriage in 1951 brought him a wife and companion who shared his beliefs. He gave up shooting and became a vegetarian.

As a young officer Dowding seemed set for an honourable but conventional soldier's life. Aviation opened new possibilities for his devoted spirit and inquiring mind. He became a dedicated airman, rising almost to the top of his profession. His stern sense of duty, added to his well-founded competence in practical flying matters, made him a formidable advocate for views strongly held. No easy compromiser or politician, he often aroused hostility, sometimes unwittingly. His vision was intense but narrow. His high moment was in the Battle of Britain. Few served their country more selflessly and courageously. His life had many bleak and lonely periods but his old age was mellow, surrounded, as he was, by the affection of family and friends. After the war Dowding became a legendary figure to the Battle of Britain pilots and one of his proudest moments was to receive a standing ovation from his so-called 'chicks' at the première of the film *Battle of Britain* in 1969. In his later years as a senior officer Dowding had an erect lean figure. He was dour in aspect with an almost expressionless face. This appearance coupled with his sparing use of speech had a daunting effect on some who met him for the first time. But a twinkle in the eye and a slight pursing of the lips showed his inner kindliness and humour to those of whom he approved. He died at his home in Kent 15 February 1970. His ashes are interred in West-

minster Abbey. Dowding was appointed CMG in 1919, CB in 1928, KCB in 1933, GCVO in 1937, and GCB during the Battle of Britain in 1940. In 1943 a barony was conferred on him and he took the style of his old headquarters, Bentley Priory.

His first marriage was in 1918 to Clarice Maud Vancourt, daughter of Captain John Williams of the Indian Army and the widow of an army officer, who had one daughter by her first marriage; in January 1919 she gave birth to a son. She died suddenly in 1920. Dowding's second marriage was in 1951 to Muriel, widow of Pilot Officer Maxwell Whiting, RAF, and daughter of John Albino. Dowding was succeeded by his only child, Wing Commander Derek Hugh Tremenheere Dowding.

There is a pastel drawing (1939) by Sir W. Rothenstein in the Imperial War Museum, a portrait (1942) by Sir W. Russell at Bentley Priory, and one by F. Kenworthy-Browne in the possession of the family. A bronze by David Wynne was exhibited in 1968 at the National Portrait Gallery.

[*The Times*, 16 February 1970; Basil Collier, *Leader of the Few*, 1957; Robert Wright, *Dowding and the Battle of Britain*, 1969; private information.]   E. B. HASLAM

DRAX, SIR REGINALD AYLMER RANFURLY PLUNKETT-ERNLE-ERLE- (1880-1967), admiral. [See PLUNKETT.]

DRAYTON, HAROLD CHARLES GILBERT (HARLEY) (1901-1966), financier, was born 19 November 1901 at Streatham, the elder of two sons of Bob Drayton (apparently christened Bob not Robert) and his wife, Annie Keep. His father, who came from Lincolnshire, was employed by the London County Council as a gardener. His mother died when the boys were still very young and they thereafter were mostly brought up in the house of a family called Low, who had recently arrived in Croydon from Dinnet in Aberdeenshire. Alexander Low, a sanitary inspector, had several children and Drayton subsequently married one of the daughters.

Soon after leaving school at the age of thirteen Drayton got a job as office boy in the St. Davids' group of companies in Dashwood House, Old Broad Street. He was hired by J. S. Austen, an able solicitor whom Lord St. Davids [q.v.] had enlisted to help run his investment trust companies. Austen spotted the boy's talent, encouraged and befriended him, and indeed subsequently bequeathed to him his estate in Suffolk. Drayton had at that time read little except the Bible (he later always maintained that Ecclesiasticus contained all the principles of finance that any business man needed) and turned his attention to reading what was lying around the office: financial newspapers, journals, and company reports. He turned out to have an uncanny knack of assimilating and remembering figures and the encyclopedic knowledge that he acquired came to make him indispensable. By 1928 he had become manager of Securities Agency and it was not long before the economic blizzard swept across the world and his powers were tested. He revealed the courage and tenacity of purpose for which he became known. Lord St. Davids died in 1938 and Drayton became *de facto* head of the group, but the outbreak of war prevented him for some time from exercising his new responsibilities to the full.

The first assignment on which his reputation began to be built had been the management and liquidation of the Lloyd George Political Fund. This entailed close co-operation with certain companies in which there were large shareholdings. His success led to the adoption of a new policy in the St. Davids' investment trusts of buying into companies in difficulty or in their infancy and helping them with money and advice. Some 20 per cent of the trusts' money was committed in this type of investment, largely unquoted on the Stock Exchange, and the policy was the subject of criticism by those who thought that investment trusts should not interfere in company management. In fact the technique was so successful that in 1945 a larger-scale operation was launched in the Industrial & Commercial Finance Corporation. The financial results were most gratifying; Drayton picked his companies well and without interfering with management was able to inspire it.

During the war Drayton was appointed as one of the commission of three who went to the Argentine to prepare the ground for the sale of the then British-owned Argentine Railways. The sale was consummated a year or two after the war ended and shareholders got their money and had reason to be satisfied.

In the 1945 general election Drayton stood as Liberal candidate for Bury St. Edmunds, where at least he saved his deposit. He took no further active part in politics, but was always ready to give his views in favour of freedom of action and thought. For the next twenty-one years he settled down to heading the group which in 1971, five years after his death, was renamed the Drayton Group. He was chairman of the larger trusts in the group. He also took over the chairmanship of British Electric Traction in 1947 and he was responsible for two big decisions during his term of office. He successfully resisted the nationalization of the buses under the Attlee Government and a good many opponents of nationalization were encouraged by his show of independence. Then he took the decision to back independent television, and it needed great courage to see this through. After two years the losses amounted to six million pounds at which point some of the largest participants wanted to withdraw, but typically he bought them out; his faith was justified and the reward was rich.

Drayton had many other business interests. He was chairman of Mitchell Cotts which led to journeys all over Africa. He was chairman of United Newspapers and was largely responsible for building up the group because of his ability to make acquisitions. He was a director of the Midland Bank and of Eagle Star Insurance. He served his term as chairman of the Association of Investment Trusts and was treasurer of the Institute of Directors on its resuscitation in 1946.

In all these offices Drayton showed his constructive independence and a personal touch. He had originality, conviction, and courage. Smoking his pipe, he would make quick decisions on which he never went back. He was forthright, obstinate, and reliable like the countryman he always remained. A portrait of him by David Jagger hangs in the British Electric Traction office at Stratton House and presents him as broad-shouldered and determined. He never received any official recognition of his achievements—perhaps on account of his unwillingness to compromise and conform. Had he been a better public speaker he might have been more widely known.

His chief interests outside the City were country pursuits which centred around Plumton, the estate near Bishop's Stortford which J. S. Austen had left to him. He became an enthusiastic farmer, pampered his pigs, loved his garden, and enjoyed entertaining his friends at shooting parties. He was high sheriff of Suffolk in 1957. He became a discerning book collector—at first specializing in eighteenth-century pamphlets, then Kiplingiana, and later in fine illustrated books. He learnt to like the best and this applied not least to claret, which he dispensed generously.

In 1926 he married Christine Collie Low. There were no children of the marriage which was a very happy one, but he was exceedingly popular with the children of his friends. Indeed, Drayton gave confidence to all with whom he came into contact and was an active ally and friend. He died 7 April 1966 at his house in Kensington Palace Gardens and an enormous concourse attended his memorial service in St. Paul's Cathedral.

[Private information; personal knowledge.]
ANTONY HORNBY

DRYSDALE, CHARLES VICKERY (1874–1961), electrical engineer, physicist, and social philosopher, was born at Barnstaple, Devon, 8 July 1874, the only son of Dr Charles Robert Drysdale and his wife, Dr Alice Drysdale Vickery. Although eventually becoming senior physician to the Metropolitan Hospital, London, his father was also adept at engineering and took part in the building of the Great Eastern steamship in 1847 and also engaged in railway surveying in Switzerland and Spain. Both C. V. Drysdale's parents were founder-members of the Malthusian League.

Following private schooling, Drysdale obtained his technical education at Finsbury Technical College and at the Central Technical College, South Kensington, where he was awarded the Siemen's medal. After a brief period as confidential scientific assistant with Nalder Bros. & Co. he turned to educational work and became associate head of the Applied Physics and Electrical Engineering Department of the Northampton Institute, London, a position which he held from 1896 to 1910. During this period he was awarded the degree of D.Sc. (London, 1901) and he developed a great interest in the design of electrical measuring instruments. Over the next six years, in association with Messrs H. Tinsley & Co., he supervised the manufacture of many of his inventions. Some of his instruments—for example, the alternating-current potentiometer and the polyphase watt-meter—survive as high-precision instruments, although perhaps his greatest achievement was the phase-shifting transformer which later became the basis of servo-mechanisms throughout the world.

In January 1918 he joined the Admiralty Experimental Station at Parkeston Quay, Harwich. There he became involved in the development of a 'leader' cable system designed to enable a ship to steer along a cable laid on the sea-bed. After the end of the war the Admiralty Experimental Station moved to Shandon in Scotland and Drysdale became the scientific director in 1920. When later in 1920 the Station changed its name once again and became the Admiralty Research Laboratory, Drysdale was appointed the first superintendent and eventually moved with the Laboratory to Teddington in 1921. Whilst superintendent he also found time to continue his researches into leader-cable problems and, on the conclusion of this work, turned his attention to the fire control of naval gunnery in which great precision was required to control the elevation and bearing of large warship guns under severe rolling and pitching conditions. In October 1929 Drysdale left ARL to become director of scientific research at the Admiralty and in 1934 he retired from Admiralty service.

Drysdale lived a very full and energetic life and had a wide range of interests outside his scientific activities. He was a staunch supporter and member of the Malthusian League. On the death of his father in 1907 he and his wife became co-secretaries of the League and he himself assumed the editorship of the League's journal, the *Malthusian*. In February 1921 he replaced his ageing mother as president of the League, a position which he retained until it was finally wound up in September 1952. In 1921 and 1925 he acted as president of Neo-Malthusian International Conferences in London and New York.

Drysdale was a man whose conservative, individualistic philosophy determined his actions and views throughout his life. He gradually changed the Malthusian League from its earlier emphasis on the relationship between over-population and poverty to one of better eugenic selection. His determined and dogged support for Malthusian and neo-Malthusian principles antagonized many of the leading figures of the day and reduced the League's effectiveness in achieving its objectives. Nevertheless it exerted a significant influence upon the family planning movement as a whole and led to Drysdale being made a member of the National Birth Control Council when it was formed in 1930.

A prolific writer, Drysdale published many original scientific papers, as well as many contributions on Malthusian and neo-Malthusian principles. He became a fellow of the Physical Society in 1898, a member of its council in 1936–9, and Duddell medallist in 1936. A founder fellow of the Institute of Physics, he served on the board during 1924–5 and was a vice-president during 1932–6. He was also a member of the former Optical Society and became its president in 1904. He was made a fellow of the Royal Society of Edinburgh in 1921 and a member of the board of managers of the Royal Institution from 1934 to 1936. He was also a fellow of the Royal Statistical Society. He was appointed OBE in 1920 and CB in 1932.

In 1898 he married Bessie Ingman Edwards, a teacher at Stockwell College. They had one daughter, who died at the age of thirteen in 1914, and an adopted son. After the death of his wife in 1950 he spent his last years with his nephew in Sussex and died in Bexhill 7 February 1961.

[Rosanna Ledbetter, *A History of the Malthusian League 1877–1927*, 1977; *Journal of the Institution of Electrical Engineers*, vol. vii, no. 80, August 1961; *Year Book*, Royal Society of Edinburgh, 1960–1; *Nature*, vol. cxc, 15 April 1961; private information.]

A. B. MITCHELL

DUFF, SIR JAMES FITZJAMES (1898-1970), professor of education and vice-chancellor, was born in Cambridge 1 February 1898, the second son, who was followed by two daughters, of the classical scholar, James Duff Duff, fellow of Trinity College, and his wife, Laura Eleanor, daughter of Sir William Lenox-Conyngham of Springhill, county Londonderry, and sister of the geodesist (Sir) Gerald Lenox-Conyngham [q.v.]. From Winchester (1910-16), where he was a scholar and prefect of chapel, Duff enlisted in the Royal Flying Corps. He obtained his pilot's wings, but in 1918 was invalided out after a serious crash and returned to Winchester as a temporary master. In January 1919 he took up at Trinity College, Cambridge, a scholarship won at the age of sixteen. Physically unhandy—he never drove a car and in later life was a notably incompetent golfer—he made his mark by his style of conversation, an inimitable mixture of quotation, banter, and sheer nonsense, with which he delighted his friends to the end of his life. He obtained a first in part i of the classical tripos in 1920 and a second in part ii of the economics tripos in 1921.

After a year as assistant lecturer in classics at Manchester he became in 1922 lecturer in education at Armstrong College, Newcastle upon Tyne, under (Sir) Godfrey Thomson, whom he always revered as his master in this field. In 1925 he was seconded as educational superintendent for Northumberland County Council, and acquired from his travels about the county to rural schools a permanent love of the north-east and its people, especially the miners.

In 1927 he returned to Manchester as senior lecturer in education and in 1932 he became professor. A progressive conservative in education, he was a warm admirer of the grammar school and highly successful in training teachers for it, but his influence was not confined to his department. He was prominent in the affairs of the university at large, and his verbal dexterity found a congenial outlet as public orator; at all periods of his life he had an outstanding gift for felicitous speeches on big occasions.

In 1937 he accepted, under some pressure, the wardenship of the Durham colleges in the university of Durham. It was a difficult moment. A damaging quarrel between Armstrong College and the College of Medicine at Newcastle, the other two members of the federal university, had led to a royal commission, as a result of which the university was recognized in two divisions—King's College, Newcastle, and the Durham colleges. Heads of the two divisions, who were to alternate as vice-chancellor, were appointed by orders in council; Lord Eustace Percy [q.v.] went to Newcastle and Duff to Durham.

The Durham colleges in 1937 were a small academic community of less than 400 students, somewhat inbred and old-fashioned and with a strong ecclesiastical bias. The imposition of a new warden from above was not wholly welcome, and it needed wisdom, vision, and much tact to set the Durham division on the course of expansion necessary for its survival. Duff possessed these qualities abundantly, and with them a style of humour which could often win an argument or help to solve a problem by a sense of the ludicrous. But owing to the war of 1939-45 it was not till the late forties that he could really set about the task of creating a modern university with a full range of departments in science as well as arts, which should yet remain residential and collegiate, able ultimately to stand on its own feet independently of Newcastle. The separation did not take place till 1963, three years after Duff's retirement, but it was his work that had made an independent Durham possible. Many new university buildings bore witness to the extent and variety of his achievement, and one of his latest acts as warden was to lay the foundation stone of a new college.

His advice was widely sought outside Durham. He gladly accepted membership of the Asquith commission on higher education in the colonies (1943-5) and of the commission on higher education in West Africa (1943-4), chaired by W. E. Elliot [q.v.], where he was happy to succour the Durham-linked missionary college of Fourah Bay; of the Indian Government's universities commission (1948-9); and of a two-man inquiry into university government in Canada (1964). He played a leading part in the foundation of the university of Sussex (1961) as chairman of its academic advisory committee. In a different field he was a governor of the BBC (1959-65); for most of this period he was vice-chairman and for a few months temporary chairman, and he bore much of the responsibility for the submissions made to the committee (1960-2) chaired by Sir Harry (later Lord) Pilkington. He was knighted in 1949, and received honorary degrees from Aberdeen (1942), Durham (1950), and Sussex (1964). In 1967 he was a visiting professor at the university of Toronto.

In his last year at Durham Duff was unanimously invited by the city council to become mayor, a signal tribute to one who had never been an elected councillor, and in 1964, to his equal surprise and pleasure, he was appointed lord-lieutenant of Durham, a post unusual for an academic but in his case a most appropriate acknowledgement of his standing in his adopted county.

Duff combined a keen and lucid and well-stored mind with a commanding personality. Always completely master of the business in hand and intolerant of anything bogus or pretentious, he was a formidable chairman and could be a ruthless interviewer; even on informal occasions his ripostes were sometimes devastating. But they left no sting, and the warmth of his personal interest and the breadth of his sympathy won him great affection, especially from the young. In private life he was an unfailingly stimulating and humorous companion, never seeming too busy for an unhurried conversation with a friend and delighting in his garden and the countryside. He never married, but his home at Durham and afterwards at Low Middleton Hall on Tees-side was shared first by his mother and later by his sister Hester, and made a happy centre for an unusually close-knit family. He died suddenly in Dublin after a visit to relatives in Ireland 24 April 1970.

A portrait by Henry Lamb (1958) hangs in the Great Hall of Durham Castle and another by L. A. Wilcox (1966) at Grey College, Durham University.

[*The Times*, 27 April 1970; university of Durham *Gazette*, 30 September 1970; private information; personal knowledge.]

WALTER HAMILTON

DUNCAN, GEORGE SIMPSON (1884-1965), New Testament scholar, was born in Forfar 8 March 1884, the son of Alexander Duncan, tailor's cutter, and his wife, Isabella Brown. From Forfar Academy he went on to Edinburgh University where he obtained first class honours in classics in 1906 and then went as an exhibitioner and sizar to Trinity College, Cambridge, where he obtained a first class in part i of the classical tripos in 1909. He studied also at St. Andrews, Marburg, Jena, and Heidelberg.

In 1915 he was ordained to the ministry of the Church of Scotland and became an army chaplain. On the second Sunday after Sir Douglas (later Earl) Haig [q.v.] took command of the British Armies in France, Duncan was appointed to GHQ. A remarkable bond of affection developed between them, the older man during the dark days of war deeply appreciating the sermons of his chaplain. A photograph in St. Mary's College bears the inscription 'to my Chaplain, 1916 to the end, in all gratitude, D. Haig'. In 1966 Duncan published *Douglas Haig as I Knew Him*. He was twice mentioned in dispatches and was appointed OBE.

In 1919 Duncan succeeded to the chair of biblical criticism in St. Andrews. His work in the New Testament field brought him international reputation. The latest of his three chief works, *Jesus Son of Man* (1948), interprets freshly the message of Jesus in the light of the elusive concept 'son of man', thus anticipating later more detailed interest. In 1934 he contributed *Galatians* to the series of Moffatt Commentaries—at the time probably the best exposition in the English language. His earliest major work, *Saint Paul's Ephesian Ministry* (1929), boldly and independently proposed an Ephesian origin for all the 'imprisonment epistles'. Duncan wrote that 'the Ephesian origin of (the Epistle to the Philippians) ought to remain no longer a matter of dispute'. New Testament scholars are not so easily silenced; but the view has never been better presented. Reviewers said that 'it read like a detective story'; and this remains true even if it is possible to think that in the end the wrong man is charged. In 1948 Duncan became president of the Society for New Testament Studies, of which he was a founder-member.

Appointed principal of St. Mary's College, St. Andrews, in 1940, he ranked second only to the principal of the university and began to exercise an increasing influence in academic affairs. He was deeply involved in the discussions which in 1954 issued in an Act 'making provision for the reorganization of University education in St. Andrews and Dundee'. At the same time he upheld with tenacity the ancient privileges and position of the college of which he was principal. Crossing swords with Principal Sir James Irvine [q.v.] demanded courage. But his fairness and reasonableness were recognized when he was appointed vice-chancellor (1952-3).

Already, in 1949, he had been moderator of the General Assembly of the Church of Scotland, the Duke of Gloucester being lord high commissioner. He visited Germany as guest of the Foreign Office, to 'strengthen the links between the Church of Scotland and the Evangelical Churches, Luther and Reformed'. Thus by an odd turn of fortune's wheel, after a second world war he met on cordial terms church leaders of the people fought by the army he had served in the first.

Among his friends Duncan numbered Bishop Hans Lilje of Berlin, and Bishop Bergrav of the Church of Sweden. His knowledge and admiration of the Reformed Churches in Czechoslovakia and France grew. This appreciation was reciprocated: he became honorary D.Theol. of Paris and honorary professor of the Reformed Church College of Debreçen and of Budapest. Honorary doctorates in divinity came from Edinburgh and Glasgow and in laws from Edinburgh and St. Andrews.

Duncan showed an immediate interest in the New English Bible venture. He was present at the first meeting of the joint committee in 1947 and was member of the New Testament panel and a translator. His contributions were always scholarly and sensible. He broadcast on television when the New Testament appeared and was acclaimed as a natural in this exacting medium.

Duncan possessed an enviable common touch, always breaking through an external appearance of peppery pomposity. Academic eminence never estranged him from ordinary people, whether soldier or ex-serviceman, parish minister or parishioner. But his students claimed his principal attention. Their interests he assiduously promoted: in the classroom, from which they went out knowing better the exacting standards that true scholarship demands; in university court among the crosscurrents of academic politics; in his own home, where the perplexed probationer or ordained man was always welcome and never left without help. With less fire he would not have accomplished what he did; with less humanity he would not have engendered such affection.

Duncan married first, in 1923, Amelia Hay Norden (died 1924); in 1929 he married Eliza Muriel, daughter of the late James Smith, doctor of medicine, of Edinburgh; they had one son. Duncan died in Dundee 8 April 1965. A portrait by Alberto Morrocco is at St. Mary's College.

[Private information; personal knowledge.]
J. K. S. REID

DUNDAS, LAWRENCE JOHN LUMLEY, second MARQUESS OF ZETLAND (1876-1961), public servant and author, was born in London 11 June 1876, the elder surviving son of the third Earl, later the first Marquess, of Zetland, viceroy of Ireland (1889-92), and his wife, Lady Lilian Selina Elizabeth Lumley, third daughter of the ninth Earl of Scarbrough. Educated at Harrow and Trinity College, Cambridge, he joined the staff of Lord Curzon [q.v.], then viceroy of India, as an aide-de-camp in 1900, having previously visited Ceylon, Egypt, and Kashmir. In the autumn of the same year he set out for home via Baluchistan, Persia, and Russia. In the next few years he travelled extensively, spending twelve months in China and Japan.

For some years a prospective Conservative candidate, and unsuccessful at Richmond in Yorkshire in 1906, the Earl of Ronaldshay, as he was from 1892 until he succeeded his father in 1929, entered Parliament at a by-election in 1907 as member for the Hornsey division of Middlesex. He held this seat through successive elections until 1916. He again visited India in 1911-12 and served in 1912-14 as a member of the royal commission on the public services in India. In 1917 he took up the post of governor of Bengal in which he served with marked success until 1922. With dexterity, resolution, and sympathy, he dealt with the stresses of the concluding years of the war; with terrorism; with the rise of non-co-operation; with the anxieties of the Muslim community over the fate of Turkey consequent on the Paris peace con-

ference; with grave disorders in Calcutta in 1921; and with the introduction in that year of the diarchical system of government under the India Act of 1919. On the material side he did much for irrigation, agriculture, and for the rural co-operative movement, and he initiated a major campaign against malaria. His wise and tactful handling secured him throughout the full support of his Indian ministers in dealing with political unrest. He left Bengal with established respect and popularity among both Indians and the important European commercial population and was commemorated by a portrait by Fiddes Watt and a statue by John Tweed.

Appointed GCIE in 1917, he was made GCSI in 1922 and sworn of the Privy Council. He made no attempt to re-enter the House of Commons; declined the high commissionership in Egypt which went to Lord Lloyd [q.v.]; and was disappointed of the viceroyalty of India in succession to Lord Reading [q.v.]. In 1931 he refused an invitation to serve on the commission about to be appointed by the League of Nations to study the causes of dispute between China and Japan. But the report in 1930 of the Simon commission brought immediate recognition of the value he could make to the solution of the Indian problem. An active and constructive member of the Indian Round Table conferences of 1930-2, and of the joint select committee of both Houses of Parliament, from which there emerged the Government of India and the Government of Burma Acts of 1935, he was the obvious successor when Sir Samuel Hoare (later Viscount Templewood, q.v.) moved from the India Office to the Foreign Office in June 1935. Zetland's success in piloting the India and Burma Bills through the House of Lords, in face of the doubts as to their wisdom entertained by important elements in Parliament, was a marked personal achievement.

When Zetland took office, the viceroyalty of Lord Willingdon [q.v.] was soon to be followed, in 1936, by that of Lord Linlithgow [q.v.]. The close and understanding personal terms on which Zetland and Linlithgow were to work together over four testing years contributed greatly to the handling of the major political issues which marked the period. In 1937 came the introduction of provincial autonomy and the decision of the Congress majority in six provinces to take office, consequent on personal explanations given by Linlithgow with Zetland's approval. In the same year came the separation of Burma from India, when Zetland became in addition first secretary of state for Burma and worked in close liaison with the governor, Sir Archibald Cochrane. There were preparations for the federation of India to which the necessary minimum of princely adherences had not been obtained by the time the outbreak of war put an end to further progress. Major issues in a different field were the Waziristan operations of 1936–8; the United Kingdom trade agreement with India; the Chatfield defence commission; and Muslim reactions to the Anglo-Egyptian treaty and the settlement of the Palestine question.

On the outbreak of war in 1939 the viceroy proclaimed a state of war emergency—India not being a dominion came automatically into the war on proclamation. The Princes and the Muslim League ministries gave immediate support to the war effort. The Congress had already committed itself to non-co-operation in the event of war unless India herself was free and now sharply condemned the proclamation of war without India's consent. The Congress ministries resigned. The remaining months of Zetland's period of office were spent in earnest endeavours by himself and the viceroy to remove misunderstandings about British war aims and the constitutional future of India. In March 1940 Zetland was wounded and had a narrow escape from death when Sir Michael O'Dwyer [q.v.] was shot dead in London by one Udhan Singh. When Churchill formed his Government in May, L. S. Amery [q.v.] succeeded Zetland whose approach to the Indian problem differed so fundamentally from Churchill's that his inclusion in the Government was scarcely possible.

Thereafter Zetland devoted himself primarily to his extensive and varied non-official interests. In addition to his duties as a great landowner in Yorkshire and Scotland, he was an active supporter of the Territorial movement. As a steward of the Jockey Club in 1928–31 he had done much for racing, and his family colours were carried by a number of winners from his stud over many years. Provincial grand master of freemasons of the north and east ridings of Yorkshire from 1923 to 1956, he continued to play a prominent part in county business in Yorkshire as lord-lieutenant of the north riding from 1945 to 1951, and in Scotland as governor of the National Bank of Scotland. He was active in the Royal Central Asian, the India, and the Royal Asiatic societies. President of the Royal Geographical Society (1922–5) and a trustee until 1947, he took an active interest in its work and gave full support to the Mount Everest expedition of 1924. He played no small part in building up the National Trust, of which he was chairman from 1931 until 1945.

In the field of authorship, his contribution was important. He published a striking trilogy of books on India and her neighbours: *Lands of the Thunderbolt: Sikhim, Chumbi and Bhutan* (1923); *India, a Bird's-eye View* (1924); and *The Heart of Âryâvarta, A study of the Psychology of Indian Unrest* (1925). All show his deep feeling

for Indian philosophy and thought. It was to the profound impression created by the last, which had the distinction of being translated into Sanskrit, that he owed his election to the British Academy in 1929. In a different field there followed the authorized biography of Curzon (3 vols., 1928) which he was invited to write by the literary executors of his former chief; his edition (2 vols., 1929) of the letters of Disraeli to Lady Bradford and Lady Chesterfield; and in 1932 the authorized biography of the first Earl of Cromer. In 1935, shortly before becoming secretary of state for India, he published *Steps Towards Indian Home Rule*. He received the honorary LLD of Cambridge and of Glasgow and the honorary Litt.D. of Leeds. He was appointed KG in 1942.

Zetland was conciliatory, persuasive, but unbending on any issue of principle, and wholly indifferent to personal considerations. The range of his activities and the success with which he pursued them testify to the skill with which he organized his life and his capacity to combine a mastery of significant detail with a full appreciation of broader issues.

He married in 1907 Cicely Alice (died 1973), daughter of Colonel Mervyn Archdale; they had two sons and three daughters. The younger son was killed while serving with the RAF in 1942. The elder, Lawrence Aldred Mervyn (born 1908), succeeded to the titles when his father died at the family residence of Aske in Yorkshire, 6 February 1961.

A portrait by Sir Oswald Birley of Zetland in the robes of the Garter hangs in the house of the Royal Geographical Society. A portrait by R. Hedley, in hunting costume, is at Aske; another, by T. C. Dugdale, in masonic regalia, is in Freemasons' Hall, Duncombe Place, York.

[The Marquess of Zetland, '*Essayez*', 1956; Sir Gilbert Laithwaite in *Proceedings* of the British Academy, vol. xlvii, 1961; private information; personal knowledge.]

GILBERT LAITHWAITE

DUNNE, SIR LAURENCE RIVERS (1893–1970), metropolitan magistrate, was born in London 4 October 1893, the second son of Arthur Mountjoy Dunne and his wife, Alice Sidney, daughter of Sir John Lambert. His father retired after a highly successful career at the Calcutta bar with a sizeable fortune and Dunne, who became his sole heir after his brother was killed in action during the war of 1914–18, never needed to work. He was educated at Eton and Magdalen College, Oxford, and himself served in the war in the 60th Rifles in Flanders, Macedonia, and in 1919 in the troubled area of Trans-Caucasia. He was thrice mentioned in dispatches and awarded the MC and the croix de guerre with palms.

Dunne was called to the bar by the Inner Temple in 1922 and rising steadily in his profession gained a large practice at the common-law bar. In 1936 he became a metropolitan magistrate and in 1948 chief metropolitan magistrate, a position he held until his retirement in 1960. In the same year (1948) he was elected a bencher of his Inn and was knighted. He was deputy chairman (1948–64) and chairman (1964–6) of the Berkshire quarter-sessions.

As chief magistrate Dunne was renowned for his integrity and fair-mindedness. It was his proud boast, in his later years, that when, each morning, he walked through Covent Garden market to his court at Bow Street, the porters greeted him with a cheerful and friendly 'Good morning, Guv'. He had made his mark earlier with his impartial handling of the vexed problem of alien internees in the Isle of Man; with his masterly report on the Bethnal Green tube shelter disaster in March 1943; and when, despite extra-legal pressure, he sent to prison a group of workers in the gas industry who had in the difficult post-war years undoubtedly broken the criminal law of the land. He showed courage in his handling of a number of extradition and deportation cases which came before him, never letting his undoubtedly conservatively patriotic instincts interfere with his interpretations of the laws of the land. He presided, during a time when English society was in a state of flux and uncertainty, as head of the chief court of first instance in the land, with a total disregard of public opinion, which in his view was usually wrong. His judgements were sometimes reversed on appeal. He was totally unperturbed: he had meted out justice according to his lights. His chief attribute as chief metropolitan magistrate was that he never showed fear or favour to anyone—and those who appeared before him knew it. He won the complete confidence of lawyers, police officers, officials of his Bow Street court, and even of the criminals who appeared before him. He was a man whom everyone trusted, even when his judgement was the reverse of what they expected.

Many of his friends believed that 'Laurie' Dunne could have achieved much higher office in the legal hierarchy. But he had no such ambition. He was a man of very many parts who was bent on enjoying his life within the limits of the call of duty. He was a strikingly handsome man with a fund of good stories at his command. He was an immensely popular member of the Garrick Club on the committee of which he served several terms, and where he played enthusiastically bad bridge.

But his chief love was sport. In his youth at Eton he showed great promise as a cricketer. Later he became a low-handicap golfer at the Berkshire Club. But above all, his chief enthusi-asms were shooting and fishing. He exulted in bringing down the highest-flying pheasant with apparent nonchalance with a shot from a single barrel. It may be added that he looked after his own guns, as he always tied his own flies. Fishing was his real passion. On the Scottish rivers—particularly the Tay and the Spey—he was often the envy of his fellow salmon fishers, and as a dry-fly fisher for trout many considered him outstanding in the country. While his wife was alive he loved his Mill House at the junction of the Kennet and Lambourn rivers, but after her death in 1967 his real home was the Houghton Fishermans Club at Stockbridge on the river Test. There, during the trout fishing season, he spent nearly all his days; there, one June evening, he scored a record bag of trout. The next day, 30 June 1970, he died quietly in his chair, watching Wimbledon on television.

In 1922 Dunne married Armorel, daughter of Colonel Herman Le Roy-Lewis; they had one son, killed at Cassino in the war of 1939–45 on his twenty-first birthday, and one daughter who died in 1965.

[Personal knowledge.]   DAVID FARRER

DUNROSSIL, first VISCOUNT (1893–1961), Speaker of the House of Commons. [See MORRISON, WILLIAM SHEPHERD.]

DYSON, SIR GEORGE (1883–1964), musician, was born at Halifax, Yorkshire, 28 May 1883, the eldest of the three children of John William Dyson, blacksmith, and his wife, Alice Greenwood, a weaver. In spite of poverty his parents had a cottage piano and George began to play at the age of five and to compose music when he was seven. He earned his first fee, as an organist, at the age of thirteen. He left Halifax in 1900 to take up an open scholarship at the Royal College of Music (organ and composition). At the RCM he studied composition with (Sir) C. V. Stanford [q.v.]. He played percussion in the orchestra and after a run-through of a new work by Stanford, Dyson played the piece from memory on the piano—early evidence of his phenomenal musicianship. In 1904 he was awarded the Mendelssohn travelling scholarship to Italy, Austria, and Germany. His first major composition, Siena, was played at Queen's Hall in 1907. In the same year he began his teaching career, first at the Royal Naval College, Osborne (1908–11), later at Marlborough (1911–14), and Rugby (1914).

On the outbreak of war he enlisted in the Royal Fusiliers and in 1915 became brigade grenadier officer, 99th Infantry brigade. His extraordinary versatility was manifest, for his Grenade Warfare (1915) became an army textbook. He was invalided home from France in

1916 suffering from shell-shock. During convalescence he worked for Edmund Speyer in a barrister's office. In 1917 he took the Oxford D.Mus. and in 1919 was commissioned major in the Royal Air Force to organize military bands. With (Sir) H. Walford Davies [q.v.] he composed *The Royal Air Force March*. He was appointed music master at Wellington in 1921, and in 1924 master of music at Winchester. He became director of the Royal College of Music in 1937, the first alumnus to do so, and retired in 1952 to Winchester, where he and his wife settled down among their old friends.

Dyson was a fastidious craftsman. His zest was shown in a stream of literary and musical works. He wrote three books—*The New Music* (1923), *The Progress of Music* (1932), *Fiddling While Rome Burns* (autobiography, 1954)—all of which showed great acuity of mind. His published musical output included twenty-eight instrumental compositions and ninety-two for voices. His best-known work is *The Canterbury Pilgrims*, portraying Chaucer's characters in music of great sympathy, wit, and grace. His three church services are in the repertoire of the cathedrals and college chapels. He wrote much for the 'Three Choirs' Festival. His most important compositions were: *In Honour of the City* (1928), *The Canterbury Pilgrims* (1931), *St. Paul's Voyage to Melita* (1933), *Nebuchadnezzar* (1935), *Quo Vadis* (1939), *Music for Coronation* (1953), and *Sweet Thames Run Softly* (1954). Everything he wrote was well made, but lacked a strong personal idiom which might have brought greater success. Both as a musical thinker and composer Dyson was a liberal conservative.

In *Fiddling While Rome Burns* he wrote, 'I am really what the eighteenth century called a Kapellmeister', and he often said that he could have succeeded in almost any career and it was chance which made it a musical one. Dyson's brilliant all-round qualities were particularly evident in his teaching appointments. At Marlborough, Beverley Nichols said of his first lesson with Dyson, 'This was, I think, one of the few "supreme moments" of my long life' (Beverley Nichols, *Father Figure*, 1972). At Wellington his arrival was described as 'positively elemental' for he had the rare gift of communicating and maintaining enthusiasm and his dry humour would round off a performance of a complex contemporary piece with 'Anyway, it's a lovely piano, isn't it'. At Winchester he exercised benevolent despotism not only in the college but the county round about. He kept the clever boy at full stretch and could coax a choir or orchestra to rehearse a two-hour programme in an hour and a half and give a performance better than was thought possible; even if he did remind

them, 'You are supposed to be a symphony orchestra not an elastic band'.

Dyson changed the friendly and humanistic trend of the Royal College of Music to a small, tough, high-quality school for the training of professional musicians. He had an astringent style and brought the College to high professional and international repute. His administration covered the war period and the early post-war years of reconstruction. His decision in 1939 to keep the College open in London showed courage and foresight. He cut his own salary by half and slept in the College throughout the bombing. His ability for administration and financial acumen were outstanding and his innovations in government grants, buildings, syllabuses, and pensions, proved of lasting benefit. His love and pride for the Royal College of Music included ordinary people as well as talented musicians, as was exhibited in his generous tribute to a deceased College servant (*RCM Magazine*, vol. li, no. 2).

Outside the College his main work and interest was centred in the Carnegie United Kingdom Trust, of which he became a trustee in 1942 and chairman (1955-9). He considered the support of musical and artistic productions, by means of guarantee against loss, to be one of his major contributions to society.

Dyson was knighted in 1941 by King George VI, whom he had taught at Osborne, and was created KCVO in 1953. Many academic honours were conferred upon him, including FRCM (1929), Hon. RAM (1937), FICS (1950), FRSCM (1963), Hon. LLD Aberdeen (1942), and Leeds (1956). He was granted the Freedom of the Worshipful Company of Musicians (1944) and in 1963 the mayor and corporation of Winchester made him a freeman of the city, which symbolized what Dyson himself felt to be true—that Winchester was his spiritual home.

His most striking physical characteristics were his piercing blue eyes and his ready laugh. He had a vivid personality and a great capacity for enjoyment. He loved hill-walking and was an accomplished carpenter. His main driving force was dedication to home-made music, shown so well in his work and interest in the Winchester Music Club and Festival, and, later, when he became the first president of the *National Federation of Music Societies* (1935). He had great respect for first-rate professional musicians but little for the 'artistic temperament', pretentious talk about music, and 'academic' musicians. He had an agreeable and most attractive element of mischief in his nature—playing 'Pop Goes the Weasel' with one hand and 'God Save the Queen' with the other—and an endless fund of stories.

In 1917 Dyson married Mildred Lucy (died

1975), daughter of Frederick Walter Atkey, a London solicitor. Their daughter Alice (born 1920), became a medical social worker. Their son Freeman (born 1923), FRS (1952), became professor of natural sciences at the Institute for Advanced Study, Princeton, New Jersey. Dyson died in Winchester 28 September 1964.

A portrait of Dyson painted by Anthony Devas (1952) is in the possession of the Royal College of Music.

[George Dyson, *Fiddling While Rome Burns*, 1954; *The Wykehamist*, November 1964; *Royal College of Music Magazine*, vol. lxi, no. 1; *Yorkshire Post*, *The Times*, and *Daily Telegraph*, 30 September 1964; *Sunday Telegraph*, 4 October 1964; *Hampshire Chronicle*, 3 October 1964; *Music Trades Review*, June 1954; private information; personal knowledge.]

KEITH FALKNER

E

EADY, SIR (CRAWFURD) WILFRID (GRIFFIN) (1890-1962), public servant, was born 27 September 1890, in Argentina, the eldest of the two sons and one daughter of G. Griffin Eady, railway engineer, and his wife, Lilian, daughter of General John Miller. He was educated at Clifton and at Jesus College, Cambridge, where he graduated with first class classical honours in 1912.

Eady entered the Home Civil Service in 1913. Bad sight precluded military service in the war, and after short apprentice spells in the India Office, the Home Office, and the Department of Foreign Trade, he was transferred in 1917 to the Ministry of Labour, where he was to stay for twenty-one years, the last three as secretary to the Unemployment Assistance Board. By this time he had become a principal assistant secretary, and his reputation for energy, determination, and resourcefulness in administration and for a positively creative skill in negotiation and in dealing with people was securely established.

His next move was to the Home Office, in October 1938, as a deputy under-secretary of state, where he applied himself with great effect to an overhaul of the country's air-raid precautions. That completed, he moved again in April 1940, to take charge, as a deputy chairman of the Board of Customs and Excise, of the arrangements for the new purchase tax introduced in that year's budget. In December 1940 he became chairman of the Board.

In July 1942, after declining an invitation to become the editor of the *Observer*, he was appointed a second secretary in the Treasury; there he remained until his retirement. For the first part of this time he was in charge of overseas finance. In this capacity he was deeply involved, alongside Lord Keynes [q.v.], in the construction of the post-war international monetary arrangements, and in the negotiations for the Anglo-American and Anglo-Canadian loan agreements of 1945-6. He also oversaw, and in the more important instances (notably Argentina) himself undertook, the negotiation of financial and trade agreements to cover the sterling balances accumulated during the war. In August 1947 he led the British delegation to Washington for the talks that preceded the decision to suspend the obligation of sterling convertibility which had been required of the United Kingdom under the Anglo-American loan agreement of 1945. During the latter part of this period he was also much engaged in working out the legislative and practical arrangements consequent upon the decision to nationalize the Bank of England.

The sustained endeavours of the five years from 1942 to 1947 told on his health, and for the last few years in the Treasury he relinquished responsibility for overseas finance and concentrated on home finance. During these years he devised, and persuaded all concerned to adopt, a plan for a voluntary levy—which quickly became known as the 'Eady levy'—to be paid by British cinema exhibitors into a fund for the benefit of British film production.

He retired from the Civil Service in 1952 and became a director of Richard Thomas & Baldwins and of the Steel Company of Wales.

Eady was at his best with something specific to organize and administer, which engaged his energy, his constructive powers, and his skills in negotiation and handling people. The apogee of his career was in the ten years before 1942, when he was given a succession of such assignments. The move to the Treasury in 1942 presented a new challenge in the unfamiliar field of international finance. Eady looked back upon his work with Keynes on the Bretton Woods negotiations and the post-war loan agreements as one of the most exciting experiences of his life, and upon Keynes himself with affection and admiration. For all that it was not an easy collaboration: Eady's mind did not move with the facility of Keynes's in matters of international finance, and, though Keynes came to respect Eady's qualities, he was sometimes impatient at Eady's reluctance to follow his own darting thought. That reluctance, however, was often justifiable: it was that of a man determined not to be diverted by intellectual coruscation from satisfying himself that the arrangements to be made would be workable and in his country's interests. Thus Eady's experience and gifts as an administrator and negotiator complemented Keynes's speed and ingenuity of thought. In 1947 Eady's qualities came into their own again: first in the sterling balance negotiations in Delhi, Cairo, and Baghdad—a difficult and exhausting mission—and later, when it fell to him to convince the American Government not only that the United Kingdom could not continue to sustain the obligation of sterling convertibility but also that she must be allowed to continue to make drawings under the 1945 loan agreement of which that obligation had originally been for them an indispensable condition. His mastery of the detail, his powers of exposition and negotiation, his evident personal integrity, and his capacity to command trust and confidence never served his country better than then.

Eady was appointed CMG in 1932; CB in 1934; KBE in 1939; KCB in 1942; and GCMG in 1948. He became an honorary fellow of Jesus College, Cambridge, in 1945.

Eady had a lifelong interest in the theatre, not only as a spectator and as an amateur performer but also as a playwright. One of his plays was performed with some success in the West End in the 1920s. In later years his interest in the theatre extended to the cinema. He held directorships of the Old Vic Trust, the Glyndebourne Arts Trust and the National Film Institute.

He was for many years the principal of the Working Men's College, retiring in 1955. He gave generously of his enthusiasm and energies to guiding its academic, financial, and social affairs, and made the most of his opportunities for recruiting young civil servants as voluntary evening-class tutors at the college. To this Dictionary Eady contributed the notices of Otto Siepmann and Sir Richard Hopkins.

In appearance, Eady was small, compact, and uncompromising; in manner he was lively, direct, and totally unpompous. His unflagging enthusiasm and zest for life were matched by unfailing kindness and generosity to others, and sustained by the close warmth of his family life. In 1915 Eady married Elisabeth Margaret (died 1969), daughter of Max Laistner. They had two sons, the younger of whom made himself at once the delight and envy of his father by establishing himself as a film director. Eady died in hospital in Lewes 9 January 1962.

A portrait of Eady by Theodore Ramos hangs at the Working Men's College.

[*The Times*, 10 and 16 January 1962; private information; personal knowledge.]

ROBERT ARMSTRONG

EASTON, HUGH RAY (1906-1965), stained-glass artist, was born in London 26 November 1906, the younger son of Frank Easton, a West End medical practitioner, and his wife, Alice Muriel, daughter of William Howland, once mayor of Toronto, and granddaughter of Sir William Howland, lieutenant-governor of Ontario, Canada. He was educated at Wellington College, and later studied languages at the university of Tours in France. The claim that he studied at the Architectural Association is not substantiated. The further broad claim that he 'studied Art in France and Italy' suggests that he was an intelligent sightseer rather than an enrolled student.

In the early period of his life, when his future was uncertain, he found that he had a natural talent for drawing and painting, which was directed towards the decoration of churches by his hobby of brass-rubbing. In the designing of stained glass he was influenced by the work of (Sir) J. Ninian Comper [q.v.] and Christopher

Webb. In craftsmanship he received instruction from the firm of Blacking, of Guildford. He set up his first studio in Cambridge, where he found intellectual stimulus among members of the university.

At the beginning of World War II he volunteered, and, as a commander, RNVR, was a naval adviser in the censorship division of the Ministry of Information. After the war he constructed a studio from a partly bombed house in Hampstead. He then settled in Holbein Place, near Sloane Square, with a workshop in Harpenden.

In the course of his life Easton designed over 250 windows. These included work in the cathedrals of Canterbury, Durham, Ely, Exeter, Winchester, Brechin, Grahamstown, George, Aklavik, and Ypres; in Westminster Abbey and Romsey Abbey; in the Dutch Church of Austin Friars, the parish churches of Chelsea and Warrington, and the City Temple; in Chatham Barracks and Portsmouth Dockyard; St. Bartholomew's and Westminster hospitals, and the Cardiff Royal Infirmary; in the halls of Inner Temple, and of the Fishmongers' and Clothworkers' companies; at Lloyd's of London, and in the town halls of Bishop's Stortford and Hertford; in Clare College, Cambridge (his earliest commission), Wellington College, St. Edward's School (Oxford), Clifton College, Wycliffe College (Glos.), Kingswood School chapel (Bath), and Bedford Modern School. He also designed windows for Rolls Royce. From his maturity until his death he could choose which commissions he would accept.

His success prompted criticism. He was taken to task for eschewing the current vogue for abstract design. Rather, his historical importance may well lie in his rational resistance to that idiom. Apart from the fact that a non-representational treatment would not have met the reasonable demands of his clients, he rightly felt that the traditional function of stained glass had been as a figurative teaching aid. To him personally this gave scope to his love of drawing, and was an outlet for a whimsical inventiveness which is well illustrated in one of his windows at Durham, where he composed the halo of St. Cuthbert from the circling sea-birds of Lindisfarne. A desire for clear expression led him to break away from the lingering clichés of the gothic revival, and to introduce a classical flavour into his drawing.

More controversial was his tendency to vignette his figure-groups on a background of clear glass, instead of infilling with architectural frameworks in the conventional manner. This admitted more light, but his designs were regarded as unstructural. His procedure may be justified in so far as windows are not really structural features, but are rather breaks in the structure, as his open design rightly stressed. In fact it is likely that as a good craftsman he foresaw that when eventually his clear backgrounds were corroded and darkened by dirt in the atmosphere, a silvery effect would be produced which would foil his golden patterning. The beauty of what he envisaged can be appreciated in Winchester Cathedral when the windows to celebrate the reign of George V and the coronation of George VI are seen each day after evensong in the soft light of dusk. His style is more validly criticized because his overworked draughtsmanship did not accord with the crystalline nature of glass and the sense of halation proper to an art which manipulates light.

Happily Easton's greatest artistic achievement was also his most important and most accessible work—the 'Battle of Britain' window at the extreme east end of Westminster Abbey. Its all-over tapestry of interwoven symbols exactly emulates what a Flemish or French glazier of the sixteenth century might have devised for such a site.

As a man, Easton was blessed with an accomplished social manner, and had the gift of making friends. But many of these bear witness to an almost morbid reticence—which may account for a lack of known portraits. He never married. His true fulfilment and solace lay in his art: hence its intensity. He died in King Edward VII's Hospital for Officers in London 15 August 1965.

[*The Times*, 16 August 1965; private information; personal knowledge.]

BRIAN THOMAS

EBBUTT, NORMAN (1894-1968), journalist, was born in London 26 January 1894, the elder son of William Arthur Ebbutt, journalist on the staff of the *Morning Leader* and later on the *Daily News* and *News Chronicle*, and his wife, Blanche Berry. It was in his mother's county, Cheshire, that Ebbutt had his formal education at Willaston School, Nantwich. He left school in 1909 and, in his determination to learn languages, went successively in the next few years to Berlin where he taught English, to Barcelona where he worked in a commercial office, and to St. Petersburg where he was tutor to the sons of a Russian army officer. In 1911, before going to Russia he worked in Paris for a short time with the *Daily News*. In 1914 he joined *The Times* in London, but in November of that year he became a lieutenant in the Royal Naval Volunteer Reserve and served until the end of the war, mainly in the Atlantic Patrol and on the North America station. After the war he took up

work again in the foreign department of the *The Times*. In 1925 he was sent to Berlin to be assistant correspondent under H. G. Daniels. The next year he began his eleven years as chief correspondent in Germany.

In the Berlin office he set himself to learn everything that could be learned about the country first under Stresemann and Brüning (he knew Brüning especially well) and then under Hitler. As Hitler consolidated his power Ebbutt reported events with deep seriousness and with much mental anguish. He uncovered the phase of German rearmament, described the crushing of political opponents and Jews, and in particular reported on every turn in the struggle between Hitler's Government and the Protestant Churches. Within the Protestant ranks Ebbutt had an especially valuable informant who frequently gave him sure information about the religious struggle and also about the tensions among leaders of the state, party, and army.

Under Geoffrey Dawson and his deputy editor, R. M. Barrington-Ward [qq.v.], *The Times* was strong in its support of Neville Chamberlain's policy of appeasement. On 23 May 1937 Dawson wrote privately to H. G. Daniels saying that he did his utmost, night after night, 'to keep out of the paper anything that might hurt their [German] susceptibilities'. Evidence from within *The Times* office later suggests that Dawson meant not that he cut Ebbutt's dispatches but that he did not print readers' letters or special articles which he judged to be alarmist or viewy. There is little to suggest that Ebbutt's dispatches were subject to direct political censorship by Dawson. But Ebbutt sometimes sent in his copy late and at greater length than he had promised earlier in the day; and his care to avoid giving a shallow picture could make his sentences over-involved and his qualifications over-elaborate. For such reasons some of his dispatches were cut in the sub-editorial room, causing Ebbutt more than once to complain. But the purport of his dispatches remained clear beyond doubt.

Constantly he was attacked in the German press for what appeared day by day in the columns of *The Times*. On 9 August 1937 the German authorities asked *The Times* to withdraw him on the grounds that 'his journalistic work does not meet with their approval'. Far from complying, *The Times* supported Ebbutt in a leading article on 17 August. On 19 August he was served with an expulsion order, and left Berlin within two days.

A month later, while in Sussex, he suffered a severe stroke which left him heavily paralysed, with speech impaired, for the next thirty-one years. He died at Midhurst, West Sussex, 17 October 1968.

The impact of Ebbutt's work on German affairs came not from the occasional outstanding article but from the cumulative force of all his dispatches. They were the more effective by being written with an evident care not to overstate, not to over-simplify, not to assume too much when evidence was tentative. Although his messages may not have influenced a British Government set upon appeasement, they helped in educating people in Britain about the true nature of Hitler's regime. American correspondents in Berlin privately acknowledged his influence on their own work. He had few relaxations: he was remarkably good at tennis, but was at his easiest when presiding night after night at a Berlin restaurant table where he and his colleagues from several countries exchanged news and views on the German ferment. At such times he could sit back: a man squarely built, looking out quizzically and expectantly through his thick spectacles, smoking matches as he repeatedly lit his pipe, smiling delightedly when anyone made a telling point in discussion.

Ebbutt was twice married: first, in 1918, to Louise Ingram, daughter of W. I. Crockett, of Henderson, Kentucky, by whom he had a son and a daughter; secondly, in 1942, after the first marriage ended in divorce, to Mrs Gladys Olive Cayford Holms, daughter of Frank William Apps, who nursed him throughout his long illness.

[*The Times*, 19 October 1968; *The Times* archives; personal knowledge; private information; *History of 'The Times'*, vol. iv, part II, 1952; Sir Evelyn Wrench, *Geoffrey Dawson and Our Times*, 1955; Donald Mclachlan, *In the Chair: Barrington Ward of The Times*, 1971.]   IVERACH McDONALD

ECCLES, WILLIAM HENRY (1875-1966), physicist and engineer, was born at Barrow in Furness, 23 August 1875, the son of Charles Eccles, blacksmith and, later, engineer, and his wife, Annabella. In later life Eccles said that it was while working in his father's workshop that he had usefully learnt about the design of metal structures. He was educated at private school and in 1894 went as a national scholar to the Royal College of Science, South Kensington, where, in 1898, he was awarded a B.Sc. with first class honours in physics. In 1898 he became a demonstrator in the physics department. In 1899 he was appointed to be one of Marconi's assistants, helping him with his pioneering work on transatlantic wireless signalling, but in 1901 he left him to become head of the mathematics and physics department of the South Western Polytechnic, Chelsea. In 1901 he also became D.Sc. (London). His boyhood interest in the

design of mechanical structures led to his appointment, in 1910, to a readership in graphic statics (i.e. structural engineering design) at University College, London. Although 'wireless' was always his chief concern, this interest in mechanical design, particularly of masts for wireless transmitters, continued throughout his career. On the death of Silvanus Thompson [q.v.] in 1916, he was appointed professor of applied physics and electrical engineering at the City and Guilds College, Finsbury. In 1926 he retired, at the age of fifty-one, to become a private consulting engineer.

During the active part of Eccles's working life 'wireless' developed from the first transatlantic experiments of Marconi into widely used commercial radio, and public broadcasting. Throughout that time Eccles was in close contact with nearly every aspect of the subject, as research worker, member of advisory committees, president of learned societies, writer of articles and textbooks, patentee, and expert witness. For many years he was the leading (and almost the only) independent physicist working in the field of radio science, first at universities and later as a consultant.

Eccles's early researches were concerned with explaining the behaviour of the 'coherer' which was used in early wireless receivers. It consisted of a loose aggregate of small metal particles contained in an insulating tube; normally it had a fairly high resistance, but if a radio-frequency voltage was momentarily applied to it, the particles 'cohered' together and it became a good conductor. It was difficult to get repeatable results from these devices and there were many suggestions to explain their behaviour. Eccles developed experimental methods which gave reliable results, and suggested a theory to account for them.

Eccles next turned his attention to the thermionic triode which had come into use during the war of 1914-18. He was one of the first to represent its action algebraically in terms of the self- and mutual-conductances of its electrodes. He used the device as a piece of laboratory equipment, in circuits not related to wireless signalling. One of the most ingenious of these produced rectangular wave-forms of relatively low frequency; it was developed in collaboration with F. W. Jordan and, known as the Eccles-Jordan circuit, it was later one of the first to be used for counting pulses.

Eccles is most widely remembered for his theory of the upper atmospheric layer, which had been postulated by Oliver Heaviside [q.v.] in 1902, to explain Marconi's transmission of signals across the Atlantic over the huge 'hump' of intervening ocean. In a paper written in 1912 Eccles showed in detail how this 'Heaviside layer' could result from ionization of the upper atmosphere. Although his theory was incomplete it paved the way for those more detailed explanations which were provided, in the 1920s, by (Sir) Edward Appleton [q.v.] and others. Before he could develop a theory Eccles needed to study how wireless waves travelled over large distances; but commercial wireless transmissions were too scarce, and too irregular, to provide the information; instead, therefore, he made measurements on those naturally occurring 'atmospherics' which are radiated by lightning flashes.

As one of the few independent scientists with a knowledge of wireless, Eccles was called upon to give advice on a wide variety of problems. Before, and during, the war of 1914-18 he was adviser to the War Office, the Army Council, the Air Force Wireless Technical Committee, and the Admiralty. He was the honorary secretary of the Conjoint Board of Scientific Societies whose report led to the formation of the Department of Scientific and Industrial Research in 1916. The rapid development of wireless just after the war led to important problems of organization and politics, amongst which were the part played by amateurs in transmitting and receiving, the relative functions of private industry and government, the best kind of transmission for Imperial communication, and the organization of public broadcasting. Between 1918 and 1926 Eccles was deeply involved in the numerous discussions of these matters.

Those who worked with Eccles in committee and discussion recalled particularly his friendship, his courtesy, and the trouble he took to familiarize himself with technical matters. He was unusually effective as an expert witness in court where, by recalling the scientific background at the time when an invention had been made, he would emphasize the problems which had been overcome before the 'obvious' had been achieved.

In 1926-7 Eccles was president of the Institution of Electrical Engineers; earlier, in 1919, he had been active in arranging for the establishment of a wireless section, of which he was the first chairman, in that Institution. In 1928-30 he was president of the Physical Society, and in 1929 became the first president of the Institute of Physics, which was started to represent the 'professional' activities inappropriate to the Society. A lifelong interest in amateur wireless led, in 1923, to his presidency of the Wireless Society of London, later the Radio Society of Great Britain.

Eccles was elected a fellow of the Royal Society in 1921, an honorary president of Union Radio Scientifique Internationale (URSI) in 1934, and a fellow of Imperial College in the same year.

In 1924 he married his secretary, Nellie Florence, some twenty years his junior, the daughter of Robert Henry Paterson, a railway clerk; they had no children. Eccles died at Oxford 29 April 1966.

[J. A. Ratcliffe in *Biographical Memoirs of Fellows of the Royal Society*, vol. xvii, 1971; private information.]   J. A. RATCLIFFE

EDE, JAMES CHUTER CHUTER-, BARON CHUTER-EDE (1882-1965), parliamentarian. [See CHUTER-EDE.]

EDWARDS, EBENEZER (1884-1961), miners' leader, was born 30 July 1884 at Chevington in mid Northumberland, one of the eleven children of William Edwards, president of a miners' union lodge and a disciple of Charles Bradlaugh [q.v.], and his wife, Esther Fish. 'Ebby' Edwards first went underground in 1896: from 1904 he worked in the collieries at Ashington. In 1908 he went on a miners' scholarship to Ruskin College, Oxford, but left after only ten months, out of sympathy with the socialist criticism which led to the 1909 secession. Back in Northumberland, Edwards joined the Marxist Plebs League, from which sprang the Central Labour League, and encouraged the spread of radical socialist views within the coalfield. In 1912 he became president of the Ashington miners' lodge and thereafter was politically active within the Labour Party, to which the union was affiliated. In May 1918 the local Labour representation committee, disregarding the electoral truce observed by the party's national executive, ran Edwards as its candidate in a by-election in the 'miners' seat' of Wansbeck division, against a Coalition Liberal non-miner. Edwards, a staunch supporter of Robert Smillie [q.v.] expressed the doubts of the socialist wing of the party about the justice and outcome of the war and gained some public attention, but lost the election, although narrowly, and lost again at the general election in December. In 1920 the Northumberland miners made him their financial secretary and in 1926 their representative on the executive of the Miners' Federation, the loosely structured central organization of the district unions.

The events of 1926—a general strike largely precipitated by the miners' grievances, its abrupt calling-off by the Trades Union Congress, the miners' isolated persistence and ultimate surrender—left the Miners' Federation deeply shaken. Edwards, who in 1926 played a useful but minor role, in 1928 served on a committee of inquiry within the union which censured A. J. Cook [q.v.], the controversial general secretary, for an act of irresponsibility during the strike. In 1929 Edwards stood for another mining constituency, Morpeth, and held the seat for Labour; in Parliament his sole concern was with labour aspects of the coal industry; he lost the seat in 1931 and did not stand again. Recognized in the union as a man who combined integrity and socialist principles with common sense and caution, Edwards became in 1930 vice-president and in 1931 president. He took over Cook's duties during the latter's final illness and after his death in 1931, and in 1932 succeeded him as general secretary, a post he retained until the Miners' Federation (renamed Mineworkers' Federation in 1933) was dissolved in 1944. Thus his influence was considerable, perhaps dominant, in the politics of the union during most of the critical period between the disaster of 1926 and the triumph of 1946, when the miners achieved their long-declared prime aim, the nationalization of the coal industry.

He had much to contend with: massive unemployment of miners, unsympathetic governments, constant calls to renewed confrontation from the militant Left, insistence by the coal-owners on district (and not national) agreements—paralleled by a yearning for autonomy on the part of many district unions. In 1937 a breakaway Nottinghamshire union was coerced and cajoled back into the fold; and after wartime circumstances had enabled the union to negotiate national agreements again, the weak Mineworkers' Federation was persuaded to convert itself at the end of 1944 into the more integrated National Union of Mineworkers. In the pre-war years Edwards could gain from owners and governments little for the miners—although he himself served on the 1935 royal commission on safety in mines—but during the war a measure of State intervention helped to produce large wage advances and other benefits. Throughout the period Edwards steered the union away from confrontations, arguing that it was 'better to mark time than to march backwards': he rebuked the militant Left when necessary, although he shared some of their views, worked with Communists in the executive, and generally commanded respect from that direction. By concentrating on rebuilding union strength he gave the union a steady course which contrasted with the ups and downs of earlier decades. It was fortunate for the nation that unemployment had much declined by 1939: the miners were sufficiently mollified to work for the war effort and, under the committed guidance of Edwards, who saw the war as an anti-fascist cause, they gave the governments no more than a moderately rough ride. By 1946 the miners had a stronger union, high wages with negligible unemployment, and nationalization, each in some part the result of Edwards's leadership. In this year he took what seemed to him a logical step, resigning from the secretaryship of the National Union of Mineworkers and becoming chief labour relations officer of the National Coal Board: he retired in 1953.

Edwards thought of himself as an international socialist. Secretary of the Miners' International Federation from 1934 to 1946, he became an opponent of 'fascist' regimes, a strong supporter of the republican cause in the Spanish civil war, and a critic of British appeasement. In 1945, serving for a second year as president of the Trades Union Congress, he campaigned for trade-union representation at the United Nations.

Ebby Edwards was a skilful negotiator and administrator, seldom ruffled, competent in analysis and with statistics, a man of few words but an effective speaker and writer, not flamboyant in manner like his predecessor Cook and hence not as deeply remembered, but more widely trusted. In appearance he was a Northumberland miner of the period: stocky, thin featured and clean shaven, often cloth-capped, with humorous blue eyes, and he spoke broad 'pitmatic'. He lived simply and was reticent about his family life. In 1911 he married Alice Reed, a miner's daughter. One of his children, Dennis, became secretary of the Miners' International Federation in 1966. Ebby Edwards died 6 July 1961, a month after his wife, at their home at Gosforth, leaving an estate valued at £5,600.

[The Times, 8 July 1961; R. Page Arnot, The Miners, a History of the Miners' Federation of Great Britain, 2 vols., 1949-53; A. R. Griffin, The Miners of Nottinghamshire, 1914-1944, 1962; Labour Magazine, April 1932; Dictionary of Labour Biography.]

P. E. H. HAIR

EDWARDS, LIONEL DALHOUSIE ROBERTSON (1878-1966), sporting artist, was born at Clifton, Bristol, 9 November 1878, the youngest of the family of eight children of Dr James Edwards (formerly a Chester physician) of Benarth Hall, Conway, North Wales, and his third wife, Harriet Maine, of Kelso. He received little formal education and country pursuits engrossed him from childhood. He was initially destined for the army, a career for which he showed no aptitude, and his artistic gifts, inherited from his maternal grandmother, who had been a talented favourite pupil of George Romney [q.v.], were encouraged by his mother. In his teens he received brief training, helped financially by scholarships, at W. Frank Calderon's School of

Animal Painting in Baker Street, London, some anatomical instruction there from Dr Armstead, and he also attended night classes at Heatherleys. While still a student he was elected a member of the London Sketch Club.

In 1898 some of his drawings of the famous wild cattle at Chillingham were accepted by *Country Life*, and a further six or seven years working for periodicals in London were made endurable by frequent expeditions by bicycle, or sometimes on a borrowed horse, for a day with hounds in the Home Counties. In 1904, during a holiday on Exmoor, the artist's first exhibition, held in the parish hall at Porlock, of staghunting subjects was a successful sell-out.

After marriage in 1905 to Ethel Ashness-Wells, daughter of a brewer, a union which brought sixty years of great happiness and which produced three sons and a daughter, Edwards and his wife first lived on the border of south Oxfordshire and then in 1909 moved to Worcestershire, both hunting regularly, first on borrowed and then on their own horses, with the artist himself fulfilling many commissions.

In 1912 North Wales became once more his home. In World War I he entered the Army Remount Service, being promoted captain in March 1915, and had, as he said, 'four years of nothing but horse'—an experience which inevitably educated his eyes for equine conformation—and on demobilization he maintained that enforced artistic abstinence had freshened his style.

By disposition Edwards was dedicated to a country way of life; hunting was his great pleasure and he saw sport with ninety-one different packs. In 1921 he moved to West Tytherley near Salisbury and for forty-three years was a member of the Hursley Hunt committee. As early as 1901 he had been made an associate of the Royal Cambrian Academy of Art, in 1926 he became a full academician of that body, and the following year a member of the Royal Institute of Painters in Water Colours. In 1931 he exhibited at the Royal Academy, 'A Hunt in the Snow: The Heythrop'.

All his long life he possessed immense tenacity and diligence as an artist, always carrying a sketch-book in his riding-coat pocket. During the 1920s he began his series of studies of different hunting countries, often in fluent water-colours, his favourite medium. Sensitive landscape backgrounds of packs as diverse in venue as the Quorn, the Beaufort, the Meath, and the Devon and Somerset made these pictures memorable. He understood sport from the inside—the implications of weather con-

ditions, of hound work, of horsemanship, and the esoteric niceties of costume and equipment. This knowledge, allied to his eye for a country, placed him in a unique category as a sporting artist. Whether he was depicting hunting in the shires and provinces, racing scenes at Newmarket, polo at Tidworth, pigsticking in Tangiers, or bullfighting in Spain, he could always evoke the thrill and magic of the moment and also capture with uncanny veracity the likeness of a horse. He painted many of the important equine heroes of his time, such as Mahmoud, Golden Miller, Team Spirit, and Arkle.

As an illustrator he excelled and much of his best work was accomplished for his own articles and books—all written in a clear, vivid style, the most important being *My Hunting Sketch Book*, vols. i and ii (1928 and 1930), *Famous Foxhunters* (1932), *My Irish Sketch Book* (1938), *Scarlet and Corduroy* (1941), *Reminiscences of a Sporting Artist* (1947), and *Thy Servant, the Horse* (1952). Outstanding were his studies for the books of sporting verse by William Henry Ogilvie published between 1922 and 1932.

In later years he held exhibitions at the Tryon Gallery in London, the last one in 1964, and many popular prints were made from his pictures, bringing his work before a wide public. By nature courteous and modest, he was also generous to a degree to aspiring sporting painters. His perceptive insight as a dedicated countryman, combined with his graphic talent as an artist, proved a considerable influence on twentieth-century sporting art, introducing a more subtle approach with appreciation of a landscape being as vital to a composition as an eye for horse and hound. Industrious and prolific to the very end of his long life, he died 13 April 1966 at his home, Buckholt, West Tytherley.

[Lionel Edwards, *Reminiscences of a Sporting Artist*, 1947; *Horse and Hound*, 23 April 1966; *The Times*, 14 April 1966; private information.]   STELLA A. WALKER

ELIOT, THOMAS STEARNS (1888–1963), poet, playwright, critic, editor, and publisher, was born in St. Louis, Missouri, 26 September 1888. He was the youngest son in the family of seven children of Henry Ware Eliot, a successful industrialist, and his wife, Charlotte Chauncy Stearns, a woman of literary interests. His mother wrote two books, one a biography (1904) of her father-in-law, William Greenleaf Eliot, who after completing his course at the Harvard Divinity School had gone in 1834 to settle in St. Louis. He founded the first Unitarian church in the city, and was also the founder of Washington University there. But for a humility which he transmitted to his grandson, it would have been named Eliot University. Mrs Eliot's second book (privately printed in London in 1926 at her son's behest) was a dramatic poem about Savonarola. A respect for family tradition and a predisposition to intense religious experience may have come to Eliot through her.

His family, as Eliot wrote, 'zealously guarded' its New England connections. He himself, after spending seven years (1898-1903) at Smith Academy (another of his grandfather's foundations) in St. Louis, was sent back to Milton Academy in Massachusetts in 1905, and then in 1906 to Harvard University. He completed in three years the four-year course, and received his BA in 1909. He wrote later that in St. Louis he had felt himself to be a New Englander, but that in New England he felt himself to be a Southwesterner. He was later to experience, with ambivalent feelings, further deracination.

He planned at this time to become a professor of philosophy, and to that end entered the Harvard Graduate School. In 1910 he took his MA and then went to the Sorbonne for a year. On his return to Harvard he began to write a doctoral dissertation on the philosophy of F. H. Bradley [q.v.]. The conception of 'immediate experience' as a means of transcending appearance and achieving the 'Absolute' had an effect upon Eliot's own thought, but other influences had also begun to make themselves felt. At Harvard his principal teacher was Irving Babbitt, who in a notable book excoriated *Rousseau and Romanticism*. Eliot's anti-romantic tendencies perhaps derived from him. Another intense interest came in 1908 when he was introduced to the poetry of Jules Laforgue, of whom he would say that 'he was the first to teach me how to speak, to teach me the poetic possibilities of my own idiom of speech'. A little later he studied intensively the languages Sanskrit and Pali, and read a good deal in Indic religion, admiring especially its concern with diligently working out a means of transcending individual selfhood. Gradually these interests were to coalesce.

While still an undergraduate Eliot had contributed a few poems to the *Harvard Advocate*, the later ones exercises in Laforguian irony. In 1910 he composed his first mature poem, 'The Love Song of J. Alfred Prufrock'. In 1914, after having assisted in philosophy courses at Harvard, he was awarded a travelling fellowship by the university. He went to study for the summer in Marburg, but the outbreak of war in August obliged him to make his way, in a less leisurely fashion than he had intended, to Oxford. He continued there, at Merton College, under the supervision of Harold Joachim [q.v.], his study of Bradley's *Appearance and Reality*.

The year 1914-15 proved to be pivotal for Eliot. He came to three interrelated decisions. The first was to give up the appearance of the philosopher for the reality of the poet, though he equivocated a little about this by continuing to write reviews for philosophical journals for some time thereafter. The second was to marry, and the third to settle in England, the war notwithstanding. He was helped to all three decisions by Ezra Pound, whom he met in September 1914. Pound had come to England in 1908 and was convinced (though he changed his mind later) that this was the country most congenial to the literary life. He not only encouraged Eliot to marry and settle, but he succeeded (where Eliot had failed) in having some of Eliot's poems published. The first to appear was 'Prufrock' in *Poetry* (Chicago) for June 1915. This was a bizarre lament for the surrender of deeper impulses to elegant proprieties. The mysterious interstices of this poem, its mixture of colloquialism and elegance, and its memorable ironies were established with great confidence. The portrait of enervation was executed with contradictory energy.

In the same month that 'Prufrock' was published, Eliot married. His wife was Vivien Haigh Haigh-Wood, an Englishwoman with aspirations to be a painter or writer. The marriage proved most unhappy, and unhappiness, fostered by the war, and by what he once described as a lifelong aboulia, became the tenor of much of Eliot's verse. Domestic anxiety may have encouraged him to search out images of ruin and devastation, which joined with the international disasters of the war and the evils of modern industrial society. The witty, humorous side of his nature—well known to his friends—found only sporadic written expression, in the partly satirical cast of his first volumes of verse, in the flamboyant *Sweeney Agonistes* (1932) and, more genially, in *Old Possum's Book of Practical Cats* (1939).

After his marriage Eliot resisted the urgings of his parents that he return with his wife to the safe side of the Atlantic and teach philosophy. They did not cut him off, but, while they wished their son to finish his dissertation, they did not give enough money for full support. To manage at all, Eliot took up school-teaching. His first position was at High Wycombe Grammar School from September to December 1915, after which he changed to Highgate Junior School and taught until December 1916. During this period he had completed and submitted his dissertation, which was found acceptable, and in April 1916 he was set to return to Harvard for his oral examination. But the ship did not sail and he made no further efforts to secure his doctorate. Teaching did not prove a satisfactory way of life, since it left him no leisure time, and in March 1917 he shifted to a position in the colonial and foreign department at Lloyds Bank in London, and kept at it for eight years, until November 1925. When the United States entered the war he was rejected for active service, on medical grounds, and his subsequent efforts to volunteer for military or naval intelligence were also unsuccessful. After the peace treaty was signed, the bank put him in sole charge of dealing with debts and claims of the bank and Germans. He manœuvred dexterously among the complications.

But his principal work during this period had to be conducted at night: this was the conquest of a position as both poet and critic. As poet he had to create a new style, and as critic to validate it. He wrote many reviews and essays, and, with a sparseness already habitual, a few poems. In 1917 he published *Prufrock and Other Observations*, in 1919 *Poems*, in 1920 *Ara Vos Prec* (which included the two previous volumes). An American edition of his verse to date also appeared in 1920 under the title *Poems*. The same year he collected his prose pieces and published them under the title *The Sacred Wood*.

The combination of careers sapped his strength and kept him on the verge of breakdown. Vivien Eliot's health was also bad, and the drugs which she increasingly required to alleviate her migraine and nervous pains were a new source of tension for her husband. In 1921 Eliot felt ill enough to consult a neurologist, who advised him to take three months' convalescent leave. With the consent of Lloyds Bank, Eliot went in October to Margate and in November, for a psychiatric consultation, to Lausanne. While in Switzerland, where he remained into December, he brought to completion *The Waste Land*, the long poem on which he had been working seriously since late in 1919. The publication in 1971 of the original manuscript of this poem (edited by his second wife, Valerie Eliot), after it had been missing for almost half a century, explained and confirmed Eliot's acknowledgement, in the poem's dedication, of his debt to Ezra Pound. It was Pound who helped him sift the final version from many drafts and false starts.

The Waste Land appeared with considerable fanfare on both sides of the Atlantic late in 1922. Although many readers found it outrageous, it gave Eliot his central position in modern verse. The work brought poetry into the same atmosphere of innovation which characterized music and painting of the time, and as with those arts, its effect was not of tentative but of consolidated experiment. In later life Eliot would speak severely of *The Waste Land* as 'just a piece of rhythmical grumbling', but in fact it broke with traditional structure and prosodic conventions, and if it grumbled, did so for a generation as well as for the poet himself. What appeared to be bits of actuality adventitiously juxtaposed with fragmentary allusions from literature, opera, and popular song, were actually parts of a mosaic with definite outlines. Eliot brought together various kinds of despair, for lost youth, lost love, lost friendship, lost value. Sombre and obscure, the poem also offered some possibilities of renewal (though these were not immediately recognized) in its blend of pagan vegetation rites, Christian resurrection, and exhortations from the *Upanishads*. In spite of many shifts of scene, it was anchored firmly in London, and with all its mustering of past ages, it spoke sharply to its own time.

After *The Waste Land* it was incumbent upon Eliot to choose between immobile lamentation, never his mode, and a new journey of the spirit. His next poems, including 'The Hollow Men' (1925), 'Journey of the Magi' (1927), and 'Ash-Wednesday' (1930) testified that he had found his direction not in Indic religion but in Christianity. The process had been taking place, he said, 'perhaps insensibly, over a long period of time'. The year 1927 was almost as momentous as 1915: he was confirmed in the Church of England and he became a British subject. Soon thereafter, in his preface to a book of essays, *For Lancelot Andrewes* (1928), he characterized himself as 'classical in literature, royalist in politics, and anglo-catholic in religion'. (He would later regret the phrasing, though not the stances.) His politics became steadily more conservative. To the astonishment of admirers of his early work, in which the Church had played a less dignified role (as in 'The Hippopotamus'), Eliot became active in many church activities, participating as church warden, committee member, and lay apologist. His most resolute effort in this field was his book, *The Idea of a Christian Society*, published just after the onset of war in 1939. The ideal of an organic society had been implicit in his work almost from the beginning, though represented chiefly by depiction of its opposite; but the explicitly Christian form of the society was a summation of his later views.

The more lasting and effective expression of his spiritual quest came in *Four Quartets* (1944), a group of four poems which were interrelated but first published separately, *Burnt Norton* (1935), *East Coker* (1940), *The Dry Salvages* (1941), and *Little Gidding* (1942). Written in conversational and lyrical modes, the poems confront the problems of history, art, virtue, and mortality; the search for religious truth is subtly, expertly blended with the search for aesthetic expression, and both are shown to be the poet's intimate, lifelong pursuit. The language is triumphantly varied and modern; the imagery blends divebombers and the London underground with almost immemorial symbols of spiritual life. *Little Gidding* concludes with a vision of paradisal completeness for which his early verse, with its satirical portrayal of the infernal aspects of modern life, and his middle verse, instinct with purgatorial pain and hope, seem preparatory.

From 1922 Eliot devoted much of his time to work as editor and publisher. He founded in that year a new quarterly review, the *Criterion*, and became its editor, at first not printing his name so as to avoid complications at Lloyds Bank. The review was primarily literary, but its interests extended to social and political subjects as Eliot expanded the range of his own enquiries. He wished, he said, to create a place for the new attitudes to literature and art, and to make English letters a part of the European cultural community. He published work by the leading writers on the Continent as well as in England and America. A crisis ensued in 1925 when the patron of the *Criterion*, Lady Rothermere, withdrew her support. About the same time Eliot left the bank to become a director in the publishing firm of Faber & Gwyer (later Faber & Faber), and shortly afterwards the firm took over the review. It resumed publication as a monthly until June 1927, and then as a quarterly until January 1939, when the last number appeared. Although its circulation was modest, the *Criterion* had a large following among intellectuals. Besides his work for the review, Eliot took responsibility for his firm's selection of poets, and his taste set a standard; to be published by Eliot's firm was the ultimate guarantee. His own work was translated into many languages, and the latest poet in Arabic, Swahili, or Japanese was more likely to sound like Eliot than like earlier poets in those languages. His eminence became, in fact, a hazard to young poets who felt that their fundamental aesthetic problem was to avoid imitating him.

In the thirties Eliot took up seriously a form which had always attracted him, poetic drama. His first efforts were for a Christian pageant, *The Rock* (Sadler's Wells, 1934), and led the following year to *Murder in the Cathedral*, a play about the martyrdom of Thomas à Becket which was produced in Canterbury Cathedral chapter house. Eliot showed great skill in exploring dramatically the psychology of both martyrdom and political assassination. His later plays dwelt, seemingly, on secular matters, but with various degrees of obliquity explored problems of conscience in profane circumstances. *The Family Reunion* (Westminster Theatre, 1939) deals with sin and expiation; its hero returns to England after an absence of many years and believes himself pursued by the Furies for the putative murder of his wife. This play had a great success in the commercial theatre, as did, ten years later, *The Cocktail Party* produced by Henry Sherek [q.v.] (Edinburgh Festival, 1949), a play about ways of existence and redemption. The last two plays were *The Confidential Clerk* (Edinburgh Festival, 1953), in which the search for parentage by three foundlings—a staple of Greek comedy—becomes an existential search for identity; and *The Elder Statesman* (Edinburgh Festival, 1958), in which the title character has gradually to shed his pretences and come to terms with his real self. All these moral comedies were written in verse, which Eliot increasingly brought as close to prose as possible, on the theory that a more obvious metric would seem unnatural and distracting on the modern stage.

Eliot's dramatic talent was not negligible, but it was limited; his criticism, along with his verse, is more certain to last. In *The Sacred Wood* he enunciated certain cardinal principles. The essay, 'Tradition and the Individual Talent', held that a new work of art alters the arrangement of the 'existing monuments', so that tradition is not to be understood as a fixed entity, but as a changing one. He also made here his famous comparison of the writer to a catalytic agent, who joins the literary tradition to the experience and language of his own time. Against the romantic conception of self-expression, Eliot described the creative process as an escape from personality. The writer, he said in his essay on 'Hamlet', has to find an 'objective correlative' for his emotion. This process had become more difficult since the seventeenth century when, as he argued in 'The Metaphysical Poets' (*Homage to John Dryden*, 1924), there took place 'a dissociation of sensibility', so that poets could no longer feel a thought 'as immediately as the odour of a rose'. A mental disjunctiveness had led to what he sometimes regarded as the 'cultural breakdown' of the twentieth century.

Eliot's essays on these matters, on the Elizabethan dramatists, on Milton and the romantic poets, on Dante and Baudelaire, and on such contemporaries as Joyce, Pound, and Lawrence, became focal points of modern criticism. Many of them, as he said, offered a theoretical basis for his poetic practice. He did not wish this basis to be taken as systematic, and often insisted that particular ideas required expression at particular times, and were polemical rather than dogmatic. As his religious bent became more pronounced, both in his verse and in his life, he strove to see literature as part of a larger spiritual enterprise. His book, *After Strange Gods* (1934), based on lectures he gave at the university of Virginia in 1933, bore the sub-title 'A Primer of Modern Heresy', and tried to pick a path among contemporary writers according to the degree of orthodoxy or heterodoxy he found in them, the former being exalted. The result was a simplification of his position which he regretted and afterwards suppressed. But his other critical volumes, such as *Selected Essays* (1932) (expanded later), *On Poetry and Poets* (1957), and *To Criticize the Critic* (1965), have commanded and kept attention. His later criticism is less confidently assertive than his earlier, which he sometimes repudiates, yet it abounds in untrammelled and precise discriminations.

Eliot's later life became rather stately. In 1932-3 he went back to the United States for the first time to give the Charles Eliot Norton lectures at Harvard. (These were published as *The Use of Poetry and the Use of Criticism*, 1933.) At this time he arranged a permanent separation from his wife, and provided for her support. On his return to London he lived with various friends; his longest stay was with the critic John Hayward [q.v.], who shared Eliot's flat from 1946 to 1957. His wife died in 1947. The following year Eliot received the Nobel prize for literature, and also the Order of Merit. He was to receive eighteen honorary degrees; he was an honorary fellow of Merton College, Oxford, and of Magdalene College, Cambridge; and he was an officer of the Legion of Honour. With his plays on Broadway and in the West End, his best lines on every lip, his opinions cited on all manner of subjects, he was the man of letters *par excellence* of the English-speaking world. He was also a man of generous spirit and firm friendship.

In 1957 Eliot married (Esmé) Valerie, oldest daughter of James Fletcher, of Headingley, Leeds, with whom he lived in great contentment for the rest of his life. He died in London 4 January 1965. His ashes were buried in St. Michael's church in East Coker, the place from which his ancestors had emigrated to the United States and the scene of the second *Quartet*. A memorial service was held in Westminster Abbey where a stone has been placed to his memory.

In appearance Eliot was tall and a little stooped. His beaked nose encouraged him to describe himself in one poem as an 'aged eagle'. Though even in youth he was an impressive and powerful presence, he had a vein of self-mockery, and was known to play practical jokes. In conversation he spoke with great deftness, and often with fine wit. If seized by an idea, he would follow it to its end, oblivious to others' attempts to interrupt, but he could also be silently attentive. His courtesy, self-abnegation, and kindness in difficult situations were celebrated. In later life his affection for his second wife, to whom he wrote the dedicatory poem of *The Elder Statesman*, was proudly manifest.

There is an early portrait of Eliot by Wyndham Lewis in the National Gallery in Durban, South Africa, and a late one by Sir Gerald Kelly, in the possession of the family. The best photographs are by Edward McKnight Kauffer and by Angus McBean, the latter at the London Library of which Eliot was president from 1952 until his death. The National Portrait Gallery has a bust by Sir Jacob Epstein.

[Introductory matter in Valerie Eliot's edition of the manuscript of *The Waste Land*, 1971; Lyndall Gordon, *Eliot's Early Years*, 1979; private information.]

RICHARD ELLMANN

ELLIOTT, THOMAS RENTON (1877-1961), physician and physiologist, was born at Willington, Durham, 11 October 1877, the eldest son of Archibald William Elliott, who had a local retail business, and his wife, Anne, daughter of Thomas Renton, of Otley, Yorkshire. He went to Durham School where he was head boy, played rugby and cricket for the school, and won the fives challenge cup. He obtained a leaving exhibition to Cambridge where his father's two elder brothers, Sir John Eliot [q.v.] and Thomas Armstrong Elliott, in their time had been second and eighth wrangler respectively. Elliott himself entered Trinity College to read natural sciences as a prelude to a career in medicine. He obtained first class honours in both parts of the tripos (1900-1) and would certainly have obtained a fellowship of his college had not a misunderstanding caused him to apply too late, a severe attack of typhoid fever having delayed his graduation. His abilities and maturity had, however, already marked him out and scholarships were forthcoming to allow him to proceed to research. A fellowship of Clare College followed.

His interests focused on the autonomic nervous system and in six short years he produced a sequence of papers which in the words of his near contemporary, Sir Henry Dale [q.v.], 'were of well-nigh incomparable brilliance and authority for a worker so young in years and experience'. He had grasped the significance of the similarity between the action of the sympathetic nerves and that of adrenaline; and, on this basis, he put forward the concept of the chemical transmission of nerve impulses. But Elliott was a quarter of a century in advance of his time. His work was received with scepticism, not least by some to whom he was bound by strong ties of personal loyalty and esteem. This was a severe blow and it was probably for this reason that in 1906 he left Cambridge for London and resumed his medical studies at University College Hospital. He obtained his MD in 1908, and in 1910 was appointed an assistant physician on the staff. A Beit fellowship followed and in 1913 he was elected FRS and in 1915 FRCP.

Before Elliott could do more than pick up the threads of his interrupted research, war broke out. Within a month he was in France and for the next four years he drove himself relentlessly. He was twice mentioned in dispatches and appointed to the DSO (1918) and CBE (1919). Not only had he large responsibilities as a consultant physician but he became, under the cloak of his seniors, the projection on to the battlefield of the committee which later became the Medical Research Council. His aptitude for imaginative administration was by now apparent.

The Haldane commission had severely criticized clinical education in London: it found the academic structure scarcely more than the apprenticeship system under another name and clinical professorships in general simply titles of seniority. The radical solution proposed was the creation of academic departments in clinical subjects with whole-time professors at their head. Elliott was an obvious choice for such a post at his old hospital where he remained professor of medicine until 1939.

His task was formidable. Not only had he to translate an idea into a living and operative organization but he had to overcome the opposition of colleagues whose traditional standards had been so summarily displaced. He succeeded and made his department a prototype. But, after a few abortive attempts, he abandoned personal research. From then on he acted vicariously. His constructive criticisms of research proposals and his perceptive appreciation of scientific intent brought out the best in young workers. It was no accident that Elliott was the only person ever to serve three terms on the Medical Research Council. He was always in demand when major policy was at issue and his ability to identify potential talent was uncanny. Increasingly, as the years passed, he came to be quietly consulted by those who had the responsibility for large decisions, not only in research, but in academic and medical policy at the highest levels. He was a Beit and a Wellcome trustee and served on the Goodenough committee on medical education in 1942-4. Throughout his active life and beyond into his retirement his was the substance behind many constructive achievements with most of which his name was never connected.

By ordinary standards this should have been thought a successful life. But despite the robust appearance and genial laugh with which Elliott moved in the background of power, it seemed that this was no lasting satisfaction to him. In his early career he had glimpsed what to him were the real heights and it was by this measure that he judged the worth of his later life.

In 1918 Elliott married Martha, daughter of A. K. McCosh of Airdrie, and had three sons and two daughters. He died 4 March 1961 at his home, Broughton Place, Peeblesshire. His portrait by Henry Lamb hangs in the library of University College Hospital medical school.

[Sir H. H. Dale in *Biographical Memoirs of Fellows of the Royal Society*, vol. vii, 1961; *British Medical Journal* and *Lancet*, 11 March 1961; *Nature*, 6 May 1961; private information; personal knowledge.]

HAROLD HIMSWORTH

ELLIS, Sir ARTHUR WILLIAM MICKLE (1883-1966), physician and regius professor of medicine in the university of Oxford, was born in Toronto, Canada, 4 May 1883, the eldest son of William Hodgson Ellis, professor of chemistry in the university there, and his wife, Ellen Maude Mickle. Ellis was educated at Upper Canada College and the university of Toronto where he took his BA with honours in natural science (1906), MB with honours (1908), followed by MD by thesis. After a short period of clinical training he was appointed resident in pathology at the Lakeside Hospital, Cleveland, Ohio, and demonstrator in pathology in the Western Reserve University medical school (1909-10). This was followed by appointment as assistant resident physician at the Hospital of the Rockefeller Institute, New York (1911-14). There he made contact with a group of young physicians and pathologists, including Swift, Homer Smith, Tom Rivers, and many others, who had been drawn to the Institute by their interest in medical research. Their friendship and professional contacts provided a valuable link with American medicine and were responsible for the warm hospitality which his pupils later enjoyed in many American medical schools. In New York he first engaged in serious clinical research and published a number of papers with Swift on the intensive treatment of neurosyphilis (the 'Swift-Ellis' treatment).

At the outbreak of war, Ellis came to England with the Canadian Army Medical Corps in which he rose to the rank of major. In 1915-17 he commanded No. 5 Canadian Laboratory with the British Expeditionary Force in France and then served as assistant adviser in pathology with the Fourth Army. He was four times mentioned in dispatches and was appointed OBE in 1917. During this period he was befriended by Sir William Osler [q.v.], a fellow Canadian and then regius professor of medicine in Oxford, and it was undoubtedly Osler's influence which led him to take up clinical medicine in England after demobilization. He worked for a time at Guy's Hospital with a grant from the Medical Research Council and in 1920 was appointed assistant director of the newly formed medical unit at the London Hospital. A chair in medicine was established there in 1924 and after a controversial passage between the Medical College and the university, Ellis was appointed as the first professor of medicine at the London Hospital.

During the twenty years' tenure of his chair, Ellis's outstanding contribution was to foster, by his example and by his shrewd selection of men, the growth and influence of full-time university departments of medicine, particularly in the metropolis. The appointment of university professors in charge of full-time clinical units in the London medical schools had been recommended by the Haldane commission in 1913 in order to improve medical teaching and research which hitherto had been carried out by honorary part-time consultants. Ellis was particularly qualified for such a post by his training in pathology and his research work at the Rockefeller Hospital. He was elected MRCP in 1920 and FRCP in 1929. His clinical experience was at first limited and on appointment his main objective was to train himself and his staff to be no less proficient in clinical diagnosis and treatment than his colleagues, many of whom practised with great distinction in Harley Street. In this aim he was eminently successful, so that students and qualified doctors alike were attracted to his unit where daily attendance and teaching in the wards were supplemented by a live interest in clinical research. Ellis was an indifferent lecturer and had little use for the examination coaching in which the more popular teachers indulged. He excelled in instruction at the bedside and in the personal training he gave to the members of his staff. He repeatedly emphasized that errors of diagnosis more frequently arose from faulty observation than from misinterpretation, and he abhorred intellectual dishonesty and authoritarianism in the teaching and practice of medicine. He was a man of great humanity and humility who believed that the academic physician must be first and foremost a good doctor. His success as a teacher was by example rather than by precept; he had a deep personal regard for his patients who throughout his career held him in great respect and affection.

During the twenties, largely due to wartime discoveries and the growth of more critical attitudes, the discipline of clinical science was beginning to make an impact on the traditional practice of medicine, and post-war travelling fellowships to the United States produced a generation of young physicians who returned to question the dogmas and oracular pronouncements of some of their teachers. Ellis developed a remarkable faculty for selecting and attracting men of promise from his own hospital and elsewhere, and of guiding them into careers of great diversity and distinction. Lord Brain, Lord Evans [qq.v.], Sir Robert Aitken, and a large group of professors and specialists graduated from his unit and were largely responsible for the high reputation which the London Hospital enjoyed as a medical centre. Ellis's research activities, as with most of the clinical professors at this time, were cramped by his administrative and teaching duties and by shortage of trained staff. Over the years, however, he made a number of contributions in the field of metabolism and endocrinology, but notably in the correlation of the clinical and pathological features of renal disease, summarized in his Croonian lectures for 1941 on the natural history of Bright's disease (*Lancet*, 3, 10, and 17 January 1942). He was strongly influenced by the work of the German nephrologists Volhard and Fahr whom he visited after the war, and the work of his associates on experimental renal hypertension greatly clarified the relationship between high blood pressure and kidney disease.

At the outbreak of war in 1939 Ellis became an adviser in medicine to the Ministry of Health and later director of research in industrial medicine under the Medical Research Council. In 1943 he was appointed regius professor of medicine in Oxford and held this post until the age of retirement in 1948. The post-war years brought difficult problems in medical organization, particularly in Oxford where there was a sharp controversy over the formation of an undergraduate clinical school. Ellis had little skill as a committee chairman and his health began to suffer. Nevertheless he carried on his clinical work and teaching with great patience and enthusiasm and enhanced his reputation for professional integrity and for unstinting helpfulness to patients and pupils alike. He was awarded the Moxon medal of the Royal College of Physicians in 1951 for his distinguished contributions to the knowledge of diseases of the kidney, and he was knighted in 1953.

In 1922 Ellis married Winifred Hadley, daughter of (Sir) William Foot Mitchell, member of Parliament for Saffron Walden and lord of the manor of Quendon, Essex. His marriage brought him a rich family life—he had one son and two stepdaughters—and friendships within a wide social circle far outside the field of medicine. Two activities he particularly enjoyed were duck shooting in Essex and salmon fishing in Iceland. This social background, together with his own not inconsiderable wealth and Canadian forthrightness, made him an excellent host to his friends, pupils, and colleagues, and the annual Boat Race parties at Bedford House, Chiswick Mall, were a major social event. On retirement from Oxford he returned to his house in Chiswick Mall, which had been the scene of so many happy occasions in the past, but his last years were clouded by his wife's prolonged and serious illness until her death in 1965. He died in London 20 May 1966.

[*Lancet* and *British Medical Journal*, 4 June 1966; personal knowledge.]

CLIFFORD WILSON

ELSIE, LILY (1886-1962), musical-comedy actress, was born at Wortley, near Leeds, 8 April 1886. Her parents were supposedly William Thomas Cotton, a theatre proprietor, and his wife, Elsie, who helped in the wardrobe. But it was widely rumoured that 'little Elsie' was in fact the illegitimate daughter of the gay and delightful Elsie Cotton and the Lord Buchan of the day. Lord Buchan was known as the 'PA' (pocket Adonis) and may have given his high-spirited mistress, Elsie Cotton, the lodging-house which she successfully ran in Salford, near Manchester, where 'little Elsie's' early childhood was spent.

Whatever the facts of her origins, it is said that the extremely respectable grandparents of 'little Elsie' were outraged at their daughter's behaviour, and behaved cruelly to her child who was of a shy and delicate nature. There was never any question of the child going on the stage but 'little Elsie' soon showed a faculty for mimicking the vaudeville celebrities. By the time she was eight 'little Elsie's' imitations of (Sir) Harry Lauder, Vesta Tilley [qq.v.], and others were well known in Salford and Manchester, and in 1896 she was engaged to play the title-role in *Little Red Riding Hood* at the Queen's Theatre in Manchester. The pantomime ran for twelve months. At the age of twelve 'little Elsie' was appearing at many music-halls in Hull and Bristol. At the age of fourteen she acted for a year in a farce, *McKenna's Flirtation*. Now named 'Lily Elsie', she went to London, which she found a frightening city, and appeared in suburban pantomimes, but returned to Manchester where she was spotted by (Sir) George Dance and brought back to London to play Princess Soo-Soo in *A Chinese Honeymoon* in 1903. The song 'Egypt my Cleopatra, why do you haunt me?' brought her first notable success and its fame spread throughout the world. Years later old sailors long since returned from sea were haunted by its refrain.

George Edwardes subsequently gave Lily Elsie many small parts in London and in the provinces. These included *Lady Madcap*, *The Cingalee*, *The Little Michus*, *The Little Cherub*, and *The New Aladdin*. It was while playing for him in *See-See*, in which she was the one member of the cast with the taste to wear oriental make-up, that Edwardes took her to Vienna to see Franz Lehar's *The Merry Widow*, and to offer her the leading role. In spite of her doubts about her voice being adequate, or her physique strong enough to act and dance such an exacting part, she was prevailed upon to accept the part of the Marsovian heiress, Sonia, at a salary of £10 a week. The success of *The Merry Widow* at Daly's Theatre (1907) made theatrical history.

Cecily Webster, the last surviving member of the original company, remembered Lily Elsie on the first night waiting for her final entrance in the third act. The house had cheered itself hoarse and was in a state of ecstatic hysteria. Lily Elsie, with the typical modesty which was to remain with her all her life, turned and whispered: 'I think they like us!'

Overnight Lily Elsie had the town at her feet. On the stage she seemed mysteriously beautiful with her perfect Grecian profile, enormous blue eyes, and hauntingly sad smile. She appeared as a completely new type of leading lady, lacking the fashionable pertness or arch coyness. She emanated a quality which made all men want to protect her, and all women to emulate her. Tall, cool, and lily-like, she moved with lyrical gestures in a slow-motion grace, and people praised her lilting walk.

Lily Elsie's voice was strong, youthful, and pure. She could dance with an abandon which a critic said 'was as surprising as it was enchanting', and if she possessed only a limited vitality and her acting ability was no greater than was needed for such forms of entertainment, her early years on the stage had given her the experience to be in all respects and *par excellence*, a 'star'.

Lily Elsie wore exquisite Empire-style dresses made by the fashionable Lucile (Lady Duff Gordon) and her large black hat of the last act was copied by the thousand. Photographs of Lily Elsie were everywhere to be seen, with special supplements in the magazines. Her face adorned chocolate boxes, biscuit tins, and advertisements for face creams; she was the favourite on the popular picture-cards.

King Edward VII saw *The Merry Widow* four times from a box. Lily Elsie's regular devotees in the stalls included many intellectuals of stage and literature including (Dame) Rebecca West and Lillah McCarthy [q.v.] and such varied personalities as (Sir) Winston Churchill, Lord Salisbury [q.v.], and the Duchess of Rutland who insisted upon Lady Diana Manners and her other daughters studying every move she made as she considered that here lay the acme of elegant distinction. From the cheaper seats in the house the young (Sir) Noël Coward and Ivor Novello [q.v.] watched and listened with awed admiration.

After a record-breaking run of 778 performances, *The Merry Widow* was succeeded by Leo Fall's *The Dollar Princess* (1909) in which Lily Elsie achieved the almost impossible by maintaining her former success.

King Manoel of Portugal, staying at Buckingham Palace, visited Daly's Theatre twice in one week and gossips talked of his infatuation. Lloyd George, a friend of Edwardes, formed a habit of watching Lily Elsie from the wings. One ardent lady enthusiast saw the production two hundred times.

Subsequently Edwardes decided to revive Oscar Straus's *A Waltz Dream* (1911) and to give Lily Elsie the role earlier played by the effervescent Gertie Millar [q.v.]. The music and the leading lady's sweet sadness were praised, but the Ruritanian plot was considered too trite. Lehar's *The Count of Luxembourg* (1911) gave Lily Elsie her next opportunity: for the role of Angèle Didier, Edwardes paid her £100 a week. The new King and Queen were present at the first performance in which Lily Elsie and her partner waltzed up a staircase. Before the end of the run she left the cast to marry the extremely handsome and dashing twenty-six-year-old Ian Bullough.

Thus, in 1911, after only four years as Queen of Daly's, Lily Elsie retired to become the châtelaine of Meggernie Castle in Perthshire. Her husband was a son of a textile manufacturer of Accrington, and the brother of Sir George Bullough who built himself a castle with a ballroom big enough to accommodate two thousand guests on the island of Rhum. Lily Elsie had always been of a shy and retiring disposition and many aspects of her fame had frightened and exhausted her. Country life suited her temperament and she led a very happy life in the Highlands surrounded by dogs, riding to hounds, fishing, and playing golf.

'Gone but not forgotten' read the captions to the galaxy of photographs which resulted from Lily Elsie's spasmodic visits to London and to her photographer friends, Messrs Foulsham and Banfield and Miss Rita Martin. Dressed in Empress Josephine gowns, swathed in chinchilla with diamonds at her neck, Lily Elsie appeared more beautiful than ever. Fashions changed, but somehow she was able to assimilate them successfully; later she even made the shingle and the fashionable low 'headache' bands of the twenties appear becoming when she was presented at Court.

During the war of 1914-18 Lily Elsie returned to the stage for several charity performances, including a star-cast production of *The Admirable Crichton* by (Sir) James Barrie [q.v.] in which she played Lady Catherine Lazenby. (Sir) J. J. Shannon painted her in the desert-island costume, the only reputable portrait of her to exist.

Even at an early age Elsie had found her stage work extremely tiring. During the run of *The Merry Widow* she was frequently absent from matinées and one newspaper called her the 'occasional actress'; but it was eventually discovered that she had long been suffering from a form of anaemia. This was no doubt the reason for an unusually early menopause and for a certain frigidity. Elsie became depressed that her marriage could not be considered entirely successful. Her always delicate health deteriorated. Thinking that theatrical work would be of benefit, her husband encouraged her to return to the stage, in a musical-love-drama named *Pamela* (1917) at the Palace Theatre. Although Lily Elsie was said to be as remarkable and beautiful as ever, the play and music were below standard and the success of this venture was in no way comparable to that of her former appearances. Undaunted, ten years later Lily Elsie again appeared in London and her gallant husband sat proudly in a box on the first night of *The Blue Train* (1927), a Viennese adaptation, in which his wife gave her accustomed elegance and distinction to a musical comedy in which she was able to do little more than wear the short sacklike dresses and cloche hats of the time. Critics and public alike acclaimed her youthfulness, and the *Daily Mail* wrote that she still possessed 'a kind of magic'.

When Ivor Novello offered Lily Elsie a 'straight' part in his comedy *The Truth Game* (1928) she accepted in the knowledge that such activity would take her mind off the fact that her marriage had now inevitably broken down; she obtained a divorce in 1930; Ian Bullough died in 1936. By degrees it became obvious that Lily Elsie had become somewhat of a hypochondriac. Much time was spent in sanatoria in Switzerland; but on returning to England— 'cured like a ham', as she said—she became fractious, and quarrelled not only with relations and devoted friends, but with servants. Thenceforth she frequented one nursing-home after another. It was difficult for her remaining friends to track down her whereabouts, but she seemed contented to remain by herself, unknown and forgotten.

She suffered from severe headaches, and her bouts of inertia and deep melancholia increased. Leucotomy—an operation to destroy certain tissues of the brain—was successful: the headaches disappeared and Lily Elsie became of a much calmer, happier disposition. Still considered too neurotic to live on her own, it was fortunate that she was sufficiently well-off to be taken care of in expensive nursing-homes where she was surprisingly popular with all the staff. 'The bones hold my face up', she said when a friend told her that she was as beautiful as ever. Although she had always disliked being 'recognized' in public and was extremely happy in her anonymity, she was not displeased when one morning her Australian nurse ran in and said: 'You never told me you were a movie star! The man in the next room has a collection of picture postcards and all of them are of you.'

Lily Elsie died in a London nursing-home 16 December 1962.

The National Portrait Gallery has her portrait by Sir J. J. Shannon.

[D. Forbes-Winslow, *Daly's*, 1944; W. Macqueen-Pope and D. L. Murray, *Fortune's Favourite, The Life and Times of Franz Lehar*, 1953; A. E. Wilson, *Edwardian Theatre*, 1951; W. Macqueen-Pope, *Carriages at Eleven*, 1947, and *Shirtfronts and Sables*, 1953; Raymond Mander and Joe Mitchenson, *Musical Comedy*, 1969; personal knowledge.]   CECIL BEATON

EVANS, SIR CHARLES ARTHUR LOVATT (1884–1968), physiologist, was born 8 July 1884 in Birmingham, the son of Charles Evans, who taught music—violin and piano—and his wife, Alice Harriett Hipkins. His interest in science appeared to be uninfluenced by his family background. He was educated at Birmingham Upper High Street Elementary School and the Council Secondary School, which he entered on the science side at the age of thirteen. Chemistry was taught by a travelling master, who went round a number of schools and obviously made an impression on at least one pupil, as the young Lovatt Evans left school at the age of fourteen in order to become an assistant to his itinerant teacher. He assisted his further education by correspondence courses and by studying at the Birmingham Municipal Technical School. At the age of sixteen he

started work in the department of physiology in Mason Science College, Edmund Street, Birmingham. He then embarked on the enterprise of obtaining a university degree, matriculated as an external candidate of the university of London in 1907, and graduated as B.Sc. in 1910. During that period he earned his living as steward in the physiology department, and by a series of teaching posts—lecturer in physiology at Handsworth Technical School (1902–8), demonstrator in physiology at the Birmingham Midland Institute (1904–7), and interim lecturer in physiology, university of Birmingham. While there was no doubt that he came up the hard way, he retained great affection and interest in the university of Birmingham. He proposed the toast of the university at the annual dinner on Founder's Day in 1930, and he was awarded an honorary LLD in 1934.

When he graduated in 1910 he intended to make a career in chemistry. But at the conclusion of the examination he was offered the Sharpey scholarship by Professor E. H. Starling [q.v.] in the department of physiology in University College, London. This was the beginning of an association and friendship with Starling, which lasted till Starling's death in 1927. He worked with Starling for five years, mainly on the metabolisms of the heart, and during this period he also studied medicine at University College Hospital, qualified MRCS, LCRP in 1916, and in addition obtained the degree of D.Sc.

He then joined the RAMC and continued his association with Starling at the Royal Army Medical College at Millbank, where Starling was in charge of the anti-gas department. For two years he was occupied with a number of problems related to gas warfare—effects of arsine, phosgene, hydrocyanic acid, and mustard gas; general anti-gas training at Aldershot, efficiency of respirators and field trials held on Porton Down.

After demobilization in 1918 Lovatt Evans was appointed to the chair of experimental physiology in Leeds. He must have made a considerable impact on physiology in a short time, for this was only eight years after his first degree and part of that time had been spent in qualifying in medicine and in performing war work. However, he remained in Leeds for only one year, leaving to accept an invitation by (Sir) H. H. Dale [q.v.] to join the staff of the National Institute for Medical Research at Hampstead, from which he went in 1922 to the chair of physiology in St. Bartholomew's Hospital. In 1926 he went to the Jodrell chair of physiology in University College, London. His two predecessors in that chair were still working in the department as Foulerton professors of the Royal Society. Starling died in

1927, but A. V. Hill and Lovatt Evans worked together for twenty-three years. They had a common interest—the application of the methods of the exact sciences to biological problems. Lovatt Evans worked on the chemical side and Hill on the physical, and they must have had a great influence on the younger people who went through the department.

During the war of 1939-45 Lovatt Evans left London to work at the Chemical Defence Experimental Establishment at Porton Down. He later resumed his chair at University College until his retirement in 1949, when he returned once more to Porton and continued to work there until shortly before his death.

Lovatt Evans was only given a relatively short time to use his scientific talents in a purely academic background. His early struggles meant that he was twenty-six when he graduated in 1910, and his first period at University College was partly occupied in obtaining a medical qualification. It was thus only after the war that he was free to pursue academic research. His first interest with Starling was the metabolism of the heart and lungs studied by Starling's heart-lung preparation, and it was here that he became interested in the role of lactic acid in muscle metabolism. He published a number of papers on cardiac, voluntary, and smooth muscle in relation to lactic acid and heat production. During this work he developed the heart oxygenator preparation which enabled the metabolism of the heart to be studied without the complication of the lungs. This early work of Starling and Lovatt Evans laid the foundations for open-chest surgery. He later published a series of papers with (Sir) F. G. Young and others on the conditions affecting the storage of glycogen.

His early interest in problems related to chemical warfare was renewed again in 1939 and yet again in 1949 when he retired from the Jodrell chair. He became interested in anti-cholinesterones and analysed the three ways in which they affected respiration by broncho-constriction, by neuromuscular block, and by central respiratory failure. He later turned to an investigation of sweating in the horse, and produced interesting results on the mechanism of sweat control, which in the horse appeared to be controlled by adrenaline in the blood rather than by nervous control. His last published work was on the toxicity of hydrogen sulphide, and at the age of eighty-three he cannulated the six different blood vessels required and carried out the titrations to estimate the sulphide concentrations.

Lovatt Evans made a great contribution to teaching by his herculean effort to produce fourteen editions of Starling's *Principles of Human Physiology* between 1930 and 1958. He also wrote *Recent Advances in Physiology* which ran to four editions and included Spanish translations. His administrative capacity was not only freely felt at University College, but he also made a great contribution to the Royal Veterinary College, where he acted as chairman of the council 1949-63. His work was recognized by the conferment of the first honorary fellowship of the college. He also served on the Medical Research Council in 1947-50, and was chairman of the Military Personnel Research Committee from 1948 to 1953.

Lovatt Evans was amongst the first physiologists to recognize the importance of the new and growing subject of biochemistry. It may seem strange to the present generation that the place of biochemistry had to be contended, and it was the physiologists rather than the chemists who led the way. Lovatt Evans was a founder-member of the Biochemical Society, but always hoped that the two disciplines would keep close together, and for a considerable time the annual general meetings of the Biochemical and Physiological Societies took place on successive days at University College.

Lovatt Evans was elected FRS in 1925. He was Sharpey-Schafer lecturer (university of Edinburgh, 1939), Louis Abrahams lecturer (Royal College of Physicians of London, 1946), Stephen Paget lecturer (Research Defence Society, 1949), first Bayliss-Starling lecturer (Physiological Society, 1963), and William Dick memorial lecturer (Edinburgh, 1965). He was an honorary member of the Physiological Society, the Biochemical Society, the Italian Society of Experimental Biology, the Ergonomics Society of which he was a founder-member, and a foreign member of the Royal Physiographical Society, Lund. He was a fellow of University College, London, and of the Royal Veterinary College, London. In 1934 he received the LLD from the university of Birmingham, and in 1957 the LLD from the university of London. He was knighted in 1951.

In 1911 Lovatt Evans married Laura Stevenson from Hanley, Stoke-on-Trent, the daughter of an operatic singer. She herself had a good mezzo-soprano voice. They had two daughters, one of whom lived in Copenhagen at the beginning of World War II and worked for a time as assistant to Professor S. A. S. Krogh. Lovatt Evans's happy home life was reflected in a friendly personality, which was able to elicit an immediate response in a wide range of people. His early struggles made him appreciate independence in others, and he believed in letting people show what they could do on their own without too much assistance. He was widely read and enjoyed discussions on a great variety of topics. He had also some skill painting in water-colours. His knowledge of the early physiologists was profound and he was an excellent raconteur who could conjure up for his listeners the characters he knew so well.

Perhaps his greatest characteristic was a capacity to inspire confidence both in his friend-. ship and in his judgement—probably because he was basically a simple man. He saw things in a straightforward way; his own motives were not complex and he did not look for complex motives in others. This simplicity of living was obvious when he went to live in Winterslow near Porton and tended his garden with enthusiasm and care. He looked after his wife during a trying illness, and after her death lived alone in his cottage. A man with such a capacity for friendship could not be lonely, and visits to and by his daughters and his colleagues in Porton meant much to him. He died 29 August 1968 at Winterslow, near Salisbury, within a year of giving up active work.

A portrait of Lovatt Evans hangs in Porton Mess.

[I. De Burgh Daly and R. A. Gregory in *Biographical Memoirs of Fellows of the Royal Society*, vol. xvi, 1970; personal knowledge.]

D. H. SMYTH

EVANS, SIR GUILDHAUME MYRDDIN- (1894-1964), civil servant. [See MYRDDIN-EVANS.]

EVANS, HORACE, BARON EVANS (1903-1963), physician, was born 1 January 1903 at Dowlais near Merthyr Tydfil, elder son of Harry Evans, musician, and his wife, Edith Gwendolen Rees. His grandfather was a pharmacist in Dowlais and his father, who conducted the famous Dowlais Choir, subsequently became a prominent musician in Liverpool and conductor of the Liverpool Philharmonic Orchestra. Horace Evans was educated at Liverpool College, and, following his father's death, at the City of London School. He gained admission to the London Hospital Medical College on a science scholarship. His student career was unremarkable save for some considerable difficulty in passing his examinations and it was his selection by (Sir) Arthur Ellis [q.v.] as house physician to the medical unit which marked him as a man of promise. Following this post he held a series of appointments, surgical, obstetric, and in anaesthetics and pathology, which provided a broad basis for his future career as general physician. He qualified in 1925, obtained his MB, BS in 1928, took his MD and MRCP in 1930, and was made FRCP in 1938. He became assistant director of the medical unit in 1933 and this was shortly followed by appointment as assistant physician to the London Hospital in 1936 and as full physician in 1947. He subsequently became consulting physician to the Royal Navy and to the Royal Masonic Hospital, the Royal Buckinghamshire Hospital, Poplar Hospital, King Edward VII Hospital for Officers (where he died), and King Edward VII Sanatorium at Midhurst.

Evans's great achievement and reputation as a physician was based on his long service to the royal family, which had for many years past had close ties with the London Hospital. In 1946 Evans succeeded Lord Dawson of Penn [q.v.] as physician to Queen Mary, became physician to King George VI in 1949, and from 1952 until his death was physician to the Queen. This distinguished service brought him many honours. He was appointed KCVO in 1949 and GCVO in 1955, and was created a baron in 1957, taking as his territorial title Merthyr Tydfil which made him an honorary freeman in 1962. The university of Wales conferred on him an honorary D.Sc. and the Royal College of Surgeons their honorary fellowship.

Horace Evans was a general physician of a high order and he grew in stature as his work expanded in breadth and importance. Yet it is doubtful if he would have achieved such high distinction had he not been singled out by Ellis to join a group of young physicians who were to become leaders in their profession in this country and abroad. Ellis had the great gift of recognizing special promise in his students and he selected Evans at a time when he showed no particular academic ability or evidence of the great personal qualities which emerged in later years. It was from Ellis that Evans learned the fundamental clinical discipline of careful, unhurried, and informed history-taking and physical examination which has distinguished the British clinical method since the time of Thomas Sydenham [q.v.]. This, combined with profound suspicion of dogma and theory, and a proper humility when faced with a difficult clinical problem, were Ellis's special qualities and Horace Evans learned and applied them with great diligence. It has been said that he was the last of the great general physicians of his time. This is a reflection of the changing character of medical practice and of medical responsibility during the post-war years. The explosive growth of the biological sciences—physiology, biochemistry, medical physics, and pharmacology—had placed a high premium on medical specialization and scientific medicine. In both diagnosis and treatment, the traditional physician had become increasingly dependent on the laboratory worker for technical information about his patients. Evans realized, and impressed on all those he taught, that these developments and the accumulating scientific data they provided, increased rather than diminished the need for the personal physician with a critical judgement based on broad general experience, and with an individual approach to the patient, which was too often prejudiced by the scientific team-work of a large hospital. This basic discipline alone could not, however, have produced in Evans more than a competent general practitioner had it not been grounded in a personality of resilience, compassion, and understanding. This was combined with a remarkable physical presence, in the sick-room and the hospital ward, of which all who came in contact with him—patients, nurses, and colleagues—became instantly aware. Much of his sympathy and understanding stemmed unfortunately from his personal family misfortunes. His younger daughter died in tragic circumstances and his wife suffered prolonged ill health; but even during his own final illness from which he died, 26 October 1963, at the age of sixty, he showed immense fortitude, imperturbable humour, and continuing interest in students, patients, and the colleagues who sought his advice and help.

As his consultant career became more demanding Evans had less and less time to devote to research and his published work was negligible. With Ellis and Clifford Wilson, however, he made an intensive study of Bright's disease and the substance of this work was embodied in Ellis's Croonian lectures for 1941 to the Royal College of Physicians on the natural history of Bright's disease (*Lancet*, 3, 10, and 17 January 1942). This was the speciality in which Evans excelled and he contributed an authoritative chapter on this subject to Price's *Textbook of the Practice of Medicine*. At the London Hospital he gave freely of his time to the nursing staff as their consultant physician. His clinical teaching was simple, practical, and reflected the immense experience of a wide variety of 'problem' disorders which came his way from all parts of the world. Outside the hospital his interests included the Medical Society of London of which he became president, the British Heart Foundation of which he was a founder-member, and the Royal College of Physicians which he served as examiner, senior censor, and vice-president. His greatest service to the College was, however, the part he played in its translation from Trafalgar Square to its new and modern home in Regent's Park. It was largely through his influence that the College received magnanimous financial support from the Wolfson Foundation, which made the rebuilding possible. His many professional distinctions included the Hunterian professorship of the Royal College of Surgeons and the

Croonian lectureship of the Royal College of Physicians (1955). Whilst his voice, his appearance, his gait, and his attitude at the bedside always appeared to indicate a relaxed and unhurried personality, Horace Evans appeared to have few relaxations. Surprisingly he was not musical and his father's grand piano provided only a repository for the signed photographs of a cosmopolitan array of his many grateful and famous patients—prime ministers, foreign heads of state, film stars and financiers, sportsmen and artists alike. His main diversion was the racecourse, and he was an excellent judge of horses. He was a regular visitor to Monte Carlo but throughout his life took no active part in sporting or outdoor activities.

In 1929 Evans married Helen Aldwyth Davies, daughter of a former high sheriff of Glamorgan; they had two daughters. Portraits of Evans by Sir James Gunn are in the London Hospital and (a copy) in the Royal College of Physicians.

[*Lancet* and *British Medical Journal*, 2 November 1963; personal knowledge.]

CLIFFORD WILSON

EVATT, HERBERT VERE (1894-1965), Australian judge and statesman, was born at East Maitland, New South Wales, 30 April 1894, the third in a family of six surviving sons. His father, John Ashmore Hamilton Evatt, born in India of English descent, kept a public house. He died when Evatt was seven. His mother, Jeanie Sophie, daughter of John Scott Grey, engineer, moved the family to Sydney, where he won scholarships to Fort Street High School and the university of Sydney and graduated brilliantly: BA (1915), MA (1917), LLB (1918), and LLD (1924). He volunteered for service in the war of 1914-18 in which two of his younger brothers were killed, but was rejected because of poor eyesight, the result of excessive study; eyesight also prevented his realizing great promise at cricket and rugby football, but he long remained a sports administrator and contributor to *Wisden*.

The war over, Evatt was admitted to the bar of New South Wales. He had mixed in radical political circles while at the university, joined the Australian Labour Party, and in 1925 he was elected an ALP member of the State legislative assembly. After quarrelling with the ALP premier, J. T. Lang, he held his seat in the 1927 election as an independent. His practice flourished, he appeared in leading constitutional cases in the High Court of Australia, and in 1929 took silk.

In 1930, by majority decision of the federal ALP, Evatt was appointed a justice of the

High Court of Australia, against the wish of the Labour prime minister, J. H. Scullin, and his attorney-general, who wished to economize by leaving the post vacant; there was no question of Evatt's professional competence, but the suggestion of political choice caused him to be received coolly. He soon secured respect because of his energy, knowledge, and extraordinary memory, and came to be regarded as second only to (Sir) Owen Dixon in juristic skill, inferior perhaps in analytical virtuosity and style but superior in feeling for the social relations of law and awareness of contemporary world developments in legal theory. In constitutional cases, Evatt favoured expansive interpretation of positive federal powers, as in *Brislan* (1935) 54 CLR 262 (control of telecommunications) and *Burgess* (1936) 55 CLR 608 (treaty implementation), but he criticized the extreme literalism of some pro-federal interpretation based on *Engineers* (1920) 28 CLR 129 and favoured by Sir John Latham [q.v.]; he sought doctrines which might protect the States against federal coercion, as in *Garnishee* (1932) 46 CLR 155, 246 (enforcement of intergovernmental agreements) and *West* (1937) 56 CLR 657 (fiscal relations). He helped to develop a view of the guarantee of interstate trade freedom (s. 92) which greatly lessened its impact on all governmental action; see especially *Vizzard* (1933) 50 CLR 30; but after apparent endorsement by the Privy Council, this was eventually abandoned. He also penned many important judgements in private law cases. During a world tour in 1938 he cemented pen friendships with famous judicial contemporaries, in particular Lords Atkin and Wright [qq.v.] in Britain, and Felix Frankfurter in the United States. He used his leisure in historical research and writing, often partisan but with brilliant insights, and published *The British Dominions as Mandatories* (1934), *The King and His Dominion Governors* (1936), *Injustice Within the Law* (1937), *Rum Rebellion* (1938), and *Australian Labor Leader* (1940), besides many papers in learned journals.

In 1940 Evatt, feeling that his talents should be employed more actively to aid his country at war, resigned from the High Court and obtained election to the Commonwealth Parliament as an ALP member in the House of Representatives. In October 1941, on the accession to power of Labour under John Curtin [q.v.], Evatt was appointed attorney-general and minister for external affairs, and continued in those posts under Curtin and after his death under J. B. Chifley [q.v.] through the Labour electoral victories of 1943 and 1946, until in 1949 Labour lost the general election to the Liberal-Country Party coalition led by (Sir) Robert Menzies.

As a federal minister, Evatt had a pervasive influence on all aspects of governmental policy and activity, owing to his intellectual ascendancy over most of his colleagues, and to the tangled legal and international problems facing the war and post-war Governments. His greatest impact on Australian and world history was in foreign affairs. During visits to the United States and Britain in 1942-3 he fought with reasonable success for an Australian share in war-policy making, and for the allocation of greater resources to holding and repelling the Japanese. He attended the San Francisco conference 1945 with an elaborate programme of proposals to amend the Dumbarton Oaks and Yalta drafts concerning the structure and powers of the United Nations. He became the main spokesman for the small and middle powers, with whose support he carried many of his amending proposals in whole or partly. His main achievements were the extension of the competence of the General Assembly, inclusion of full employment as a world social objective, closer definition of the duties of trustee and colonial powers towards undeveloped peoples and of enforcement procedures, and modification of the veto power in the Security Council so that procedural matters could in some cases be determined by majority vote. He was president of the United Nations General Assembly for its third session (1948-9) which saw the Declaration of Human Rights and the admission of Israel to the United Nations. He greatly expanded Australia's diplomatic corps, established a distinctive Australian foreign policy, and by procuring in 1942 Commonwealth adoption of the Statute of Westminster 1931, he completed the legal structure of Australia's external sovereignty.

Evatt's early efforts at reforming Australia's federal system (1942-4) failed, but in 1946 he steered through an addition to the Constitution expanding federal social services powers. His drafting of the Chifley Government's bank nationalization Act (1947) and advocacy on its behalf in High Court and Privy Council (1948-9) were less successful, the main provisions being held invalid. In 1948-9 he succeeded in checking the disruptive activities of Communist trade-union leaders, and established the Australian Security Intelligence Organization.

Evatt held his seat when Labour was defeated in 1949, and after an unsuccessful attempt to obtain appointment to the bench in New South Wales, he continued as deputy leader of the federal ALP under Chifley, and as leader after Chifley's death in 1951. When the Menzies Government attempted to proscribe the Communist Party by legislative fiat (1950-1), Evatt appeared as counsel for objectors to the Act at the High Court proceedings in which it was held constitutionally invalid; he then stumped the country for a 'no' vote at the referendum of 1951 by which Menzies attempted to validate his proposals. The narrow defeat of the referendum was largely due to Evatt's campaign, based on civil liberty and rule of law arguments. By 1954 it seemed possible that Evatt would soon lead his party back to power, but the electorate was closely divided, and the adroit disclosure of the Petrov affair by Menzies, shortly before the general election of 1954, tipped the balance in the latter's favour. Petrov, a Russian diplomat in Canberra, defected under persuasion from the Evatt-created security service and gave information about spy rings. A royal commission report showed that the Russians had made only trivial contacts and collected mostly worthless information in Australia. Evatt should have laughed at the affair, but stung by the election loss and by the false references to him and his staff in Petrov documents, he tried unsuccessfully to establish that the disclosures or at least their timing were due to a political conspiracy against him and his party. He appeared before the royal commission until his intemperate behaviour caused withdrawal of his leave to appear, and he earned derision by quoting in Parliament a letter written him by the Russian foreign minister, Molotov, in reply to a letter from Evatt, denying the Petrov allegations. Hitherto Evatt had been a moderating, even at times conservative, influence in the Labour Party, but the Petrov affair brought to a head his growing suspicion that right-wing, anti-Communist colleagues influenced by Roman Catholic social thought were conspiring against him and trying to alter the Labour Party's socialist aims. His move against them resulted in a party split in March 1955 and the formation of the breakaway Democratic Labour Party, dedicated to keeping him out of office. Evatt made gestures towards healing the breach, but without success, and led the ALP to defeat at the general elections of 1955 and 1958.

In 1960 Evatt retired from Parliament and was appointed chief justice of the Supreme Court of New South Wales. Ill health prevented his making any significant mark in this position and compelled his resignation in 1962. He died in Canberra, 2 November 1965; the nation's leaders buried him, and the United Nations General Assembly stood silently in his honour.

Evatt was a great Australian, whose generous purposes were flawed in the execution by faults of character and temperament. He was excessively vain, impatient of criticism, suspicious of colleagues, and insensitive to the feelings of subordinates.

He was sworn of the Privy Council in 1942, was an honorary bencher of the Middle Temple, a fellow of the Royal Australian Historical Society, and president of the trustees of the Public and Mitchell libraries of New South Wales, and received many honorary degrees for his international activities. Two volumes of his speeches on world affairs were published— *Foreign Policy of Australia* (1945) and *Australia in World Affairs* (1946)—and his Holmes lectures at Harvard appeared as *The United Nations* (1948).

In 1920 Evatt married Mary Alice Sheffer, who did much to encourage and guide his patronage of modern art in Australia; they had a son and a daughter. A portrait by Arnold Shore is in the possession of the family and one by W. E. Pidgeon is in the Supreme Court of New South Wales, Sydney.

[K. Tennant, *Evatt, Politics and Justice*, 1970; A. Dalziel, *Evatt the Enigma*, 1967; R. Murray, *The Split*, 1970; P. Hasluck, *The Government and the People 1939–41*, 1952 and *1942–45*, 1971; L. Zines, 'Mr. Justice Evatt and the Constitution' in *Federal Law Review*, vol. iii, 1968–9; personal knowledge.]
GEOFFREY SAWER

EVERSHED, (FRANCIS) RAYMOND, BARON EVERSHED (1899–1966), judge, was born 8 August 1899 at 8 Clay Street, Stapenhill, Burton-upon-Trent, the residence of his father, Frank Evershed, a solicitor, the fourth son of Sydney Evershed, MP, JP, of Albury House, Burton-upon-Trent. His mother, (Frances) Helen, was the daughter of Thomas Barnabas Lowe, of Burton-upon-Trent. He was an only child. He was educated at Clifton College and Balliol College, Oxford, where in 1921 he obtained a second class in *literae humaniores*. He was elected an honorary fellow of Balliol College in 1947 and was president of Clifton College in 1951. During World War I he served in France as a second lieutenant in the Royal Engineers in 1918–19.

He was called to the bar by Lincoln's Inn in January 1923. The Society elected him a bencher in 1938 and he served as treasurer in 1958. He went into Chancery chambers at 11 New Court, Carey Street, and by his outstanding ability and intense application he attained immediate success, becoming a King's counsel in 1933 in the remarkably short space of ten years, at the phenomenally early age of thirty-three. As a silk he constantly appeared in the House of Lords and the Privy Council.

World War II brought him a succession of heavy responsibilities which only his capacity for sustained hard work enabled him to carry out. His ambition to fly in the Royal Air Force was unfulfilled. He exchanged private practice for public duties and served as chairman of the Central Price Regulation Committee from 1939 to 1942 and regional controller of the Nottinghamshire, Derbyshire, and Leicestershire coal-producing region from 1942 to 1944.

When in April 1944 he was appointed a justice of the Chancery division of the High Court and knighted he was at forty-four one of the youngest men ever raised to the bench. His further promotion in April 1947 to be a lord justice of the Court of Appeal was both expected and approved by the profession generally. A fortnight later he was appointed chairman of the committee on practice and procedure in the Supreme Court, which considered the means of reducing the cost and increasing the dispatch of litigation. The committee finally reported in July 1953 and many of its recommendations were adopted.

Meanwhile in 1949 Lord Greene [q.v.], the master of the Rolls, was appointed a lord of appeal in ordinary and Evershed succeeded him. In 1956 Evershed was raised to the peerage. He remained master of the Rolls for thirteen years, longer than any of his predecessors since Lord Esher [q.v.] in the nineteenth century. As master of the Rolls he was statutory keeper of the records; he was also chairman of the Historical Manuscripts Commission from 1949 to 1962. He was active in promoting the work of the Record Office at a time when it was becoming difficult to find room for the rapidly increasing accumulation of documents. When Evershed resigned the mastership of the Rolls in 1962 he was appointed a lord of appeal in ordinary. He retired in 1965.

Lord Evershed's judgements were consistently sound, though they were sometimes criticized for being over lengthy and elaborate. He was critical of the increasing tendency of Parliament to pass statutes in terms of detailed exposition, leaving the judges only the limited function of mere verbal interpretation. He was invariably courteous and considerate to all who appeared before him.

Evershed was of middle height, sturdily built, dark and good looking, and he had a notable capacity for making and retaining friends. He had a pleasantly subtle wit which made him an excellent companion; yet he was modest, and even somewhat shy. Deeply devoted to music, he had a well-trained baritone voice. One of his permanent memorials in the Inns of Court is the Bar Musical Society which arranges regular concerts by accomplished performers in their halls. When Deborah Rowland (later Judge Rowland) founded the society in 1952 Evershed became its first president, remaining so until his death. He was an active working president whose co-operation and influence assured the society's successful establishment.

Evershed's multifarious activities included membership of many public committees including the committee on land compensation and betterment presided over in 1941-2 by Sir A. A. (later Lord) Uthwatt [q.v.]. From 1950 he was British member of the Permanent Court of Arbitration at The Hague. He was chairman of the Pilgrim Trust from 1959 to 1965. Numerous universities awarded him honorary degrees and he was elected FSA in 1950. To this Dictionary Evershed contributed the notice of Lord Somervell of Harrow.

In 1928 Evershed married (Cicely Elizabeth) Joan, daughter of (Sir) Charles Alan Bennett, later a justice of the Chancery division. There were no children of the marriage, and the title became extinct when Evershed died suddenly of a heart attack at his home, Wormegay Grange, Setch, near King's Lynn, 3 October 1966.

In Lincoln's Inn hall hangs the conversation piece, 'A Short Adjournment' by R. Norman Hepple, representing Evershed among a group of members of the Court of Appeal. Another portrait of Evershed by Christopher Sanders was exhibited at the Royal Academy Summer Exhibition of 1956.

[*The Times*, 4 October 1966; personal information.]　　　　　　　　　F. H. COWPER

F

FABER, SIR GEOFFREY CUST (1889–1961), publisher, was born in Malvern 23 August 1889, the second son of the Revd Henry Mitford Faber, a housemaster at Malvern College, by his wife, Florence Ellen, daughter of George Nathaniel Colt, barrister. The Faber family, Yorkshire in origin, had long associations with education and the Church. Faber's paternal grandfather, a fellow of Magdalen College, Oxford, was a brother of Father F. W. Faber [q.v.] and a nephew of G. S. Faber [q.v.]. Having received his public school education at Rugby, where his friends included Philip Guedalla [q.v.], Maurice Collis, and Michael Sadleir [q.v.], Faber proceeded with a scholarship to Christ Church, Oxford, where he obtained a double first in classical moderations (1910) and *literae humaniores* (1912). His publishing career began almost immediately afterwards when in 1913 he joined the Oxford University Press; but it was interrupted by the war. From 1914 to 1919 he was with the London Regiment (Post Office Rifles), saw service in France and Belgium, and in 1916 was promoted captain. During the war he published two volumes of verse, *Interflow* (1915) and *In the Valley of Vision* (1918).

In the first post-war election at All Souls College, Oxford, in November 1919, Faber became a prize fellow, an event which, perhaps more directly than any other, shaped the course of his future life (he remained a fellow until he died). It was some time, however, before the pattern of his career became clearly established. In 1920 he joined the board of Strong & Co. Ltd., the brewers, of Romsey, a firm with which he had family connections; and, although he never practised as a barrister, he was awarded the Eldon law scholarship and was called to the bar by the Inner Temple in 1921. By 1923, having abandoned both brewing and the bar, Faber was in negotiation with his All Souls colleague (Sir) Maurice Gwyer [q.v.], later chief justice of India, whose wife had inherited a prosperous but highly specialized publishing firm, the Scientific Press Ltd. Its fortunes were founded on the *Nursing Mirror*, a successful weekly paper for trained nurses; and round this paper had grown up a small but profitable list of medical books designed for the same public. The Gwyers, ambitious to enter the field of general publishing, invited Faber to join them; and he became chairman of a successor company, Faber & Gwyer Ltd. Over dinner at All Souls, Faber consulted Charles Whibley [q.v.] about the appointment of a literary adviser. Whibley suggested T. S. Eliot [q.v.] and Faber, who

had had in mind only the engagement of a part-time 'talent scout', was so impressed and charmed by Eliot at their first meeting that he shortly afterwards invited him to become a member of his board.

After four years of only moderately successful trading the Gwyers were ready to liquidate the business. Faber, determined to continue although the difficulties seemed almost insuperable, found a way out of the impasse. The *Nursing Mirror* was disposed of very advantageously; the Gwyers withdrew their interest; and Faber, with his own capital, transformed the firm into Faber & Faber Ltd.

During the years which followed, his great driving force, courage, and tenacity were gradually rewarded. Not only did his firm acquire a distinguished reputation—its list was studded with the names of some of the most promising young writers, poets in particular, who made their first appearances in the thirties—but he himself became a prominent figure in the world of publishing. After serving on the joint advisory committee of publishers and booksellers, he joined, in 1934, the council of the Publishers' Association; in 1937 he became treasurer; and in 1939 was made president. In this position he had to face a grave crisis which, after the outbreak of war in 1939, threatened the publishing, bookselling, and printing trades—and to some extent the entire literary profession in this country. Sir Kingsley Wood [q.v.], chancellor of the Exchequer, introduced purchase tax in July 1940 which was intended to include books. Faber was among those who felt that this might virtually stifle the nation's literary output during the war and would do irreparable damage not only at home but also abroad. With speed and efficiency he marshalled a large and influential body of supporters who launched an attack on the imposition of the tax which finally led the Government to exempt books from its operation. Faber remained chairman of the Publishers' Association until 1941; and in 1944 performed his last major service to the book trade by helping to establish the National Book League, of which he became first chairman in the following year.

Faber's other interests were many and varied: the countryside—his houses, first in Cardiganshire and later in Sussex, meant much to him; astronomy—he was chairman of the Radcliffe trustees; farming; shooting; fishing; the chairmanship of a Conservative Party committee which produced an admirable report on secondary education written by himself. At one time he even thought of standing for

Parliament. Two major elements in his life, however, call for special mention: the estates bursarship of All Souls and his own writing.

In 1923, at the age of thirty-three, Faber succeeded Geoffrey Dawson [q.v.] as estates bursar, an office which he held until 1951. His bursarship was marked by large-scale building activity on the college's Middlesex estates, by the expansion and consolidation of its rural estates, and by a sharp rise in income. His only failure was his inability to persuade the college to persist with a project close to his heart—the direct farming of some of its own land.

Faber's prose is more likely to endure than his poetry, yet there is little doubt that the poetry was to him the more important. The title he gave to his collected poems, *The Buried Stream* (1941), is significant. This volume contains all that he wished to preserve of his two earlier collections, together with work written subsequently; and after his death his family published privately *Twelve Years*, a long reflective poem of nearly 400 lines written between 1941 and 1953 and much revised during the remainder of his life. Although his verse seldom attains the force, compression, and inevitability which renders poetry memorable and permanent, it is never meretricious and often very moving particularly when it deals with deeply felt personal emotions. Moreover, the fact that he was himself a poet was a vital factor in the creation and maintenance of the Faber poetry list, particularly during the early years when the chairman of an undergraduate society described him as 'the godfather of modern English poetry'.

Faber's minor prose works were *Elnovia* (1925), a light-hearted and eventually rather dated fantasy; *A Publisher Speaking* (1934), a collection of addresses; and an account of the history of the All Souls bursarships (1950) printed privately. His major works, likely to prove permanent, were *Oxford Apostles* (1933) and *Jowett* (1957). Partly because of his family links with Father Faber, he became fascinated by the great figures of the Oxford Movement; and in particular by J. H. Newman [q.v.]. The book which resulted is authoritative. The struggles between the Movement and its enemies and within the Movement itself are detailed with lucidity and great narrative power; the characters involved are presented with sympathy, intelligence, and insight. *Jowett*, the result of many years of research, particularly in the Balliol archives, is a portrait not only of its subject but of the many academic and religious controversies in which he played a central part.

One further literary achievement deserves recording—his edition of John Gay [q.v.] in the Oxford Poets series, published by the Oxford University Press in 1926. He accepted an invitation to undertake this in 1913, but because of the war and his multifarious activities in the years immediately afterwards it was not completed until 1925. Despite these interruptions and distractions the edition is distinguished and satisfying, marked not only by erudition and industry but also, even when dealing with such matters as punctuation and spelling, by an instinctive sureness which reflects his innate sympathy with Gay's work and temperament.

In 1920 Faber married Enid Eleanor, third daughter of Sir Henry Erle Richards, Chichele professor of international law and diplomacy and a fellow of All Souls. They had two sons and one daughter. The elder son, Richard Stanley Faber, joined the Foreign Service and the younger, Thomas Erle Faber, a physicist, became a fellow of Corpus Christi College, Cambridge. Faber was knighted in 1954. In 1960 he resigned the chairmanship of Faber & Faber Ltd. and was appointed to the newly created post of president which he held until his death at Midhurst 31 March 1961.

In his later years Faber's appearance was that of a successful and cultivated man of the world: rubicund, heavily built, bald, with a slight military moustache; a man at home at the dinner-table or the bridge-table, at a shoot or a concert; happy watching, from his Sussex garden, his Ayrshires returning to be milked. Beneath this exterior lay a shy and introspective personality. Although he was justly proud of his achievements, he remained always a little uncertain of himself and in particular of his ability to communicate successfully with other people. To those to whom he had given his confidence and affection he remained unswervingly loyal and dependable: it is probable that he never fully realized how much affection others in return felt for him.

In 1952 Henry Lamb executed a number of portrait drawings: one is possessed by the Faber family, one by All Souls College, and one by Faber & Faber Ltd.

[T. S. Eliot, *Geoffrey Faber, a memorial address*, privately printed, 1961; *The Times*, 1, 5, and 6 April 1961; *Burke's Landed Gentry*, 1952; private information; personal knowledge.]   CHARLES MONTEITH

FACHIRI, ADILA ADRIENNE ADALBERTINA MARIA (1886–1962), and her sister, D'ARANYI, JELLY (1893–1966), violinists, were born in Budapest 26 February 1886 and 3 May 1895, the first and third of the three daughters of Taksony Aranyi de Hunyadvar, chief of police in Budapest, and his wife, Adrienne Nievarovicz de Ligenza, the fourteenth child of a Pole of good family from the Cracow district. Adrienne was the niece of Josef Joachim, the celebrated violinist and friend of Brahms. The entire family was musical and both girls began their musical training as children at the piano; Béla Bartók, as a student of twenty-two, was among their teachers and became a lifelong friend. It was as violinists, however, that the two entered the Budapest Academy of Music as children; they became pupils of the great violinist Jenő Hubay.

Adila began to play in public when she was fourteen, winning the approval of Budapest critics and the affection of audiences not only for her playing but also for the charm of her personality. In 1906, the year of her début in Vienna, she won the artists' diploma of the Budapest Academy and, although an impresario at once offered her a favourable contract, she went to Berlin to become the only private pupil of her celebrated great-uncle.

Although Joachim died in 1907, Adila's work with him had lasted long enough to imbue her with the principles which made him one of the most admired of musicians, a virtuoso whose gifts and personality were entirely dedicated to music rather than to display. It also brought her into contact with Joachim's circle, musicians as important as Grieg, Humperdinck, Casals, Ysaÿe, and the distinguished English musicologist, (Sir) Donald Tovey [q.v.]. Her work under Joachim included not only the standard concertos and the violin and piano works of the nineteenth-century masters but also the music of eighteenth-century composers, including the accompanied and unaccompanied violin music of Bach. At the same time, she never disdained effective show pieces by composers like Saint-Saëns, Sarasate, and Wieniawski.

At the time of Joachim's death, Adila was already winning a reputation as an unusually gifted violinist much influenced by Joachim but also capable of enjoying well-written display works. Joachim had planned to conduct her début in Berlin, with the Philharmonic Orchestra there, in November 1907, and the concert was given in spite of his death; the impression Adila made opened the doors of many other important concerts for her, and she travelled widely, introducing Jelly as a supporting artist and as her partner in Bach's D minor Concerto for Two Violins. Jelly's formal training thus ended by the time she was fourteen.

Joachim had planned Adila's English début, and she found in 1909 that her great-uncle's English friends and disciples—people of eminence in English music and social life—were eager to demonstrate their enthusiasm for her playing. Apart from their relationship with the much-lionized Joachim, the d'Aranyis were related through the violinist's banker brother, Henry Joachim, to the Russells, so that they began to move among the friends of Bertrand (later Earl) Russell [q.v.] in the intelligentsia. Their liveliness, personality, and quite un-English attractiveness made them welcome in England, and they kept the friends whom they made on their first visit throughout their lives. Fanny Davies, the pianist pupil of Clara Schumann, and Sir Henry Wood [q.v.] became, like Donald Tovey, friends and colleagues.

Thus, when war broke out in 1914 during their second English tour, and kept them in this country, they settled down to become a regular part of English musical life, assisted by such friends as the ex-prime minister Asquith and Balfour over any difficulties arising from their nationality. When, after 1919, their international careers could be resumed, England remained their base. Wartime music-making, much of it at private concerts in great houses, turned Adila's attention to chamber music (slow movements rehearsed, it is said, with tears and an intensity of emotion) rather than to concerto playing. The cellist Guilhermina Suggia was happy to play chamber music with the two sisters: other equally eminent friends gathered round to deal with a remarkably catholic selection of works, many of them unfamiliar, for chamber ensemble.

In November 1915, Adila married Alexander P. Fachiri, an American lawyer of Greek descent, and adopted her husband's name for professional purposes. In 1919 Alexander Fachiri took British citizenship and practised in international law. They had one daughter. Fachiri was, too, an accomplished cellist who had sometimes thought of making music his career, but a retiring disposition had made him unhappy at the thought of public performance. Nevertheless, he became effectively involved in his wife's chamber-music performances. Throughout this period Adila accepted frequent engagements to appear with Jelly in such works as the concertos for two violins by Bach and Gustav Holst [q.v.], the latter work having been written for and dedicated to the two sisters.

The death of Adila's husband, 27 March 1939, restored her to the concert platform. Her broad, powerful style, responsive and high-spirited but essentially classical, remained unimpaired, and her readiness to tackle new music was as great as it had ever been. She was in demand as a teacher, and although after the war of 1939-45 she settled near Florence, in Italy, she returned from time to time to play in London, where she was last heard in 1957, playing in Bach's Double Concerto with her sister. She died in Florence after a short illness 15 December 1962.

It was customary, during the lifetime of the two sisters, to contrast the classical style of Adila Fachiri with the more impulsively romantic playing of Jelly d'Aranyi. The two were, however, such frequently and perfectly matched partners in many works of a variety of styles and periods that to hear them together was to realize that, essentially, they were in complete musical sympathy. Although Joachim died before he could become a direct influence on the younger of his two great-nieces, it seems that Adila passed on his tradition to her sister.

Jelly d'Aranyi's career began at the age of fourteen when she became the pupil of Hubay at the Budapest Academy of Music. During the 1920s and 1930s, when Adila Fachiri was heard less frequently in public as a soloist, Jelly d'Aranyi combined recitals with concerto performances with major European orchestras and established a reputation in the United States of America. As well as Bach's unaccompanied violin works, she played the concertos of Szymanowski, Respighi, and Vaughan Williams, whose *Concerto Accademico* was dedicated to her; she also played his *The Lark Ascending* very frequently. Her recital repertory included Ravel's *Tzigane*, perhaps the most important of all the works dedicated to either of the sisters; she played it both in its original version, with piano accompaniment, and in its later form as a work for violin and orchestra. She played the violin and piano sonatas of Bartok, written for her and her sister, and the sonatas of John Ireland, (Sir) Eugene Goossens [qq.v.], and Richard Strauss.

Jelly was partly responsible for the rediscovery of Schumann's Violin Concerto, and she first played it to the public in 1938. This concerto, dismissed as an inferior work by Clara Schumann, the composer's widow, had been allowed to become forgotten. What Jelly apparently called a 'game' with a wineglass on an improvised ouija board put her on to the track of a work she did not even know existed (the Violin Concerto was not at that time listed in catalogues of Schumann's compositions). It was found in the composer's manuscripts in the Prussian State Library.

Apart from her many appearances with her sister Adila, Jelly formed a close friendship and effective musical partnership with the pianist Myra Hess [q.v.]. The two played violin and piano music both in Britain and the United States. In 1933 Jelly suggested and began to carry out a series of charity recitals in English cathedrals. Her 'Pilgrimage of Compassion', as the series began to be called, happily

extended itself far beyond her original plan. She was appointed CBE in 1946.

When Adila Fachiri retired and settled in Italy, Jelly d'Aranyi followed her after a short time. She died in Florence 30 March 1966.

The d'Aranyi sisters were both fine violinists of technical accomplishment and widely sympathetic musicianship. The teaching of Hubay and the strict artistic discipline of Joachim, which controlled their natural impulsiveness, made their appearance together memorable in music as diverse as that of Bach and their contemporary composers. In spite of their apparent differences of style, they brought the same tradition and same outlook to whatever music they played together.

Between the world wars the musical parties at their studio in Chelsea were much appreciated by their friends, for distinguished artists found in a pleasure to play or sing for such sympathetic and understanding hostesses.

Their popularity among eminent men and women came from a readiness of response to events, personalities, and surroundings, and was the result of charm which, on the platform, was inclined to be spectacular. Virtually self-educated, they read widely and were always ready to speak their minds, sometimes with a startling disregard for conventional notions of tact. Not only through the musical tradition they served, but also through richness of personality, they impressed themselves on the world as women of unusual gifts, both personal and musical.

There is a portrait of Adila Fachiri by the German artist Nelson (*c.* 1907). Portraits of Jelly d'Aranyi have been painted by Neville Lytton (1919), de Laszlo (1928), and Charles-Louis-Geoffrey-Dechaume. (Sir) William Rothenstein sketched her in 1920.

[*The Times*, 1 April and 17 December 1962; Joseph MacLeod, *The Sisters d'Aranyi*, 1969; personal knowledge.]   IVOR NEWTON

FAIRLEY, SIR NEIL HAMILTON (1891–1966), physician, was born in Inglewood, Victoria, Australia, 15 July 1891, the third of the six sons of James Fairley, a bank manager in Inglewood, and his wife, Margaret Louise Jones. Four of the sons qualified in medicine, one becoming senior physician to the Royal Melbourne Hospital. Fairley took pride in being of Scottish extraction, his grandfather having emigrated to Australia from the village of Hamilton in Lanarkshire.

From his school, Scotch College, Melbourne, where he finished as dux, Fairley went on to study medicine in Melbourne University, qualifying with first class honours in 1915. In 1916 he was commissioned in the Australian

Army Medical Service and went to Egypt as pathologist to a military hospital. There he developed an interest in research, particularly into practical problems of current interest, which was to last him throughout his life. He became a meticulously careful worker whose findings were of lasting value. He never spared himself in his efforts to achieve the object he had in view, and expected the same devotion to duty from those who worked under him. His kindly and friendly disposition, however, gained him the devoted loyalty of his colleagues and subordinates, whose interests he never failed to promote. His ability to gain enthusiastic co-operation was a keynote to the success of his ultimate *magnum opus*.

In 1919 Fairley went to London, where he spent some months in the Lister Institute and obtained his MRCP (London) and DPH (Cambridge). He returned to Australia in 1920 as first assistant to the director of the Walter and Eliza Hall Research Institute, Melbourne. In 1922 he was appointed medical research officer of the Bombay Bacteriological Laboratory, where he continued his early work on schistosomiasis and other worm infections of man and domestic animals. He developed a blood test, and, later, a simpler skin test which were of value in early diagnosis, and, in the case of farmyard animals, in the detection of infection, a matter of considerable economic importance. He also studied sprue in India, and devised improved methods of treatment, though he failed to discover the cause of the disease, which he himself contracted. After recuperating in Britain, Fairley returned to the Walter and Eliza Hall Research Institute in Melbourne where he investigated snake venoms and snake-bite, and showed that the wider 'gape' of the viper's jaw enabled it to inject more venom than other snakes, thus adding to the deadly efficacy of its bite.

In 1929 Fairley settled in London, filling an appointment in the Hospital for Tropical Diseases, and lecturing in the London School of Hygiene and Tropical Medicine. He ran to earth the cause of severe, sometimes fatal, cases of hepatitis which cropped up at irregular intervals in sewer workers, showing that it was an infectious and preventable disease, leptospirosis, contracted from sewer rats.

Later, in Cairo in 1941, he showed that sulphaguanidine was a specific cure for acute bacillary dysentery, a discovery which proved of particular value during the battle with the Japanese for Port Moresby, when a severe outbreak of 'Shiga' dysentery ravaged the Japanese but was successfully controlled in the Australian troops.

In the latter part of his life Fairley's predominant interest was in malaria and its prevention. Prior to World War II he paid several visits to a malaria research unit in Salonika to study blackwater fever, a complication of malaria, and while there became well acquainted with the malaria problems of Macedonia. This was to stand him in good stead later. After he became consultant in medicine to the Australian troops in Middle East Force in 1940 it came to his knowledge in 1941 that plans had been made to send British and Australian troops to Macedonia in support of the Greek Army. With a British colleague, also well acquainted with the dangers of Macedonian malaria, he succeeded, after some argument, in persuading General Sir Archibald P. (later Earl Wavell [q.v.], to change these plans and deploy the troops in a less dangerous locality. As it transpired, this achieved nothing, as the Allies were turned out of Greece before the onset of the season of malaria transmission.

When Japan entered the war he left Egypt for the South Pacific theatre, and in due course was promoted brigadier, and director of medicine in the Australian Medical Service, and, later made chairman of the Combined Advisory Committee on Tropical Medicine, South Pacific Area, directly responsible to General MacArthur, appointments which gave him much authority. He was quick to realize that the outstanding medical problem in that area was malaria. Attempting to salvage as much quinine as possible from Java, one of the main sources of supply, he went there and succeeded in purchasing some 120 tons, which was loaded on two ships. Neither got through to Australia, and Fairley himself escaped on the last ship to make the journey successfully, reaching Australia to face a desperate situation. The only potent anti-malarial drug other than quinine known at that time was mepacrine (atebrin), hitherto manufactured chiefly in Germany. Fairley journeyed post-haste to London and Washington to plead at the highest level for the urgent manufacture of adequate supplies. His mission was successful, but, back in Australia, he was sadly disappointed to find that a daily dose of mepacrine, administered under the regulations which existed at the time, failed to prevent infection with malaria in hyperendemic areas.

Determined to discover a drug which would confer complete protection (Fairley had hopes that one of the new sulphonamides, sulphamerazine, would fill this role), he organized and directed a massive research project, involving teams of entomologists, pathologists, and clinicians, and the co-operation of hundreds of volunteer human 'guinea-pigs' from the troops. He succeeded in proving, beyond any possible doubt, that mepacrine, when taken daily *with unfailing regularity*, was effective in suppressing malaria. Quinine and sulpha-merazine were unsuccessful under the severe conditions imposed in these tests. The previous failure of mepacrine was clearly due to irregular administration and consequent failure to maintain the necessary blood level of the drug. Fairley's lucid exposition of his findings convinced the army commander, and, later, all senior officers who were summoned to a conference on the subject. Orders were issued making officers commanding units (and not, as in the past, medical officers, who were too few and far between) responsible for ensuring that the troops received and swallowed the daily dose. Further, these officers were made accountable to higher authority should any of their men develop malaria. The result was dramatic. Malaria ceased to be a problem, not only in the Australian Army, but in the other commands where this procedure was adopted and followed. This proved of vast importance in the latter days of the war.

After World War II Fairley returned to London to resume teaching and to become one of the elder statesmen in the field of tropical medicine. In 1946 he was appointed to the Wellcome chair of tropical medicine in the university of London. The advice he was able to give on the precise timing of the different developmental phases of the malaria parasites, information acquired during the experimental investigations of his teams in Australia, was of the greatest importance in the discovery of the exoerythrocytic phase of the parasites.

Unfortunately his health began to fail at a comparatively early age, slowly bringing his active life to an end. He resigned from his chair in 1949 and died at his home in Sonning 19 April 1966.

Fairley was elected a fellow of the Royal Society in 1942. In 1918 he was appointed OBE, in 1941 CBE, and in 1950 KBE. He was awarded many honorary degrees and medals by universities, colleges, and learned societies. He was honorary secretary of the Royal Society of Tropical Medicine and Hygiene from 1930 to 1951 and its president in 1951-3.

In 1919 Fairley married Violet May Phillips. They had one son, now retired after holding a commission in the Australian Army. This marriage was dissolved in 1924, and in 1925 he married Mary Evelyn, daughter of Herbert R. Greaves, of Bombay. They had two sons, both of whom obtained medical qualifications. The younger, Gordon Hamilton Fairley, was already a leading authority on oncology when he fell a casual victim to a bomb placed under his car by a dissident group. A portrait of Fairley by William Dargie, painted in 1944, is in the possession of the family.

[*Medical Journal of Australia*, vol. ii, 1969, p. 991; private information; personal knowledge.]   JOHN BOYD

FARJEON, ELEANOR (1881-1965), writer, was born in London 13 February 1881, the third of five children (the second boy died in infancy) of Benjamin Leopold Farjeon [q.v.], a prolific Victorian novelist of Jewish descent, and his wife, Margaret, second child of the celebrated American actor Joseph Jefferson. The Farjeons' Hampstead home was a meeting-place for actors, writers, and musicians; the theatre was an essential part of the children's education. The family brimmed with talent. Harry, the eldest, became a distinguished teacher at the Royal Academy of Music; Joe (J. Jefferson Farjeon) and Herbert made their names as writers. Eleanor Farjeon had no formal education, but had the run of her father's 8,000 books; she was absorbed in reading, writing, her family, and her imaginative life. 'I cannot remember being without a headache; I cannot remember one night of restful sleep. . . . I was a dreamy, timid, sickly, lachrymose, painfully shy, sensitive, greedy, ill-regulated little girl.' Immersed far beyond childhood in a world of private fantasy which she shared with her elder brother, she was thirty before she was able to come to terms with reality. *A Nursery in the Nineties* (1935) is her account of the years ending in her father's death.

Ben Farjeon died in 1903, leaving no money. It became important that his daughter, now twenty-two, should emerge from her dreams and write for her living. It was a slow, painful process; but she began to form friendships, and her creative energy found direction. Edward Thomas [q.v.] and his wife Helen became close friends; it was largely through Eleanor Farjeon's participation in Thomas's growth as a poet, and through the shock of his death in France in 1917, that she came to maturity in her own writing. These crucial years in her development are described in *Edward Thomas: The Last Four Years* (1958).

In the autumn of 1917 she rented a cottage near Amberley in Sussex, and for two years lived alone: making her own decisions, standing on her own feet. It was the culminating experience of her emergence from the chrysalis. These Sussex years produced her most memorable single work, the romantic fantasy *Martin Pippin in the Apple-Orchard* (1921). Its reception, and particularly a perceptive notice by (Dame) Rebecca West, established her as a writer. The book was not written for children, but to amuse Victor Haslam, a serving officer in France, to whom it had been sent in instalments; its appeal to the romantic young was considerable, however, and when it was reissued in 1952 it was as a children's book.

In 1920, with new confidence, she returned to Hampstead, where she was to spend the rest of her life; and books began to flow. She had published a first volume of poems, *Pan-Worship*, in 1908; and in 1916 *Nursery Rhymes of London Town* had appeared. Now children's verses, songs, stories, rhymed alphabets, traditional tales retold, and miscellanies poured out. As 'Tom Fool' she wrote a topical verse a day for thirteen years for the *Daily Herald*; as 'Chimæra' she wrote a weekly poem throughout the twenties for *Time and Tide*. Her first fantasy, *The Soul of Kol Nikon* (1923)—heavily influenced by the Celtic Twilight—had earlier appeared in serial form in the *Irish Review*; it led her towards her most considered work between the wars, a number of delicately fanciful novels, inspired by fairytales. Few of them are likely to find readers now. By 1930 she could find a publisher for whatever she cared to write. The following years saw several happy collaborations with her brother Herbert, notably a Victorian operetta *The Two Bouquets* (Ambassadors, 1936, published as a novelette, 1948) and a children's play *The Glass Slipper* (St. James's, 1944, written at the request of Robert Donat, q.v.), later (1955) turned into a full-length book: *The Silver Curlew* was also successful as both play (Arts, 1949) and book (1953). Among the most attractive of her adult books are *Ladybrook* (1931), *Humming Bird* (1936), *Miss Granby's Secret* (1940), and *Ariadne and the Bull* (1945).

The books which will last, however, are the children's books. There Eleanor Farjeon had real mastery. The best of them were reissued—even in a few cases written—in the last fifteen years of her life, when her stature as a children's writer became clear in a remarkable second flowering. *Silver-Sand and Snow* (1951) and *The Children's Bells* (1957) contain the best of her poetry; the finest of her short stories are in *The Little Bookroom* (1955), the collection which won for her the outstanding honours in the field: the Library Association's Carnegie medal and the first award of the international Hans Andersen medal. In 1959 she was awarded the American Regina medal for her work for children.

Eleanor Farjeon—she never married—had a genius for friendship. Among the many to whom she opened her generous heart were a few who took advantage of her, swans who turned out to be geese; but although she never lost a strain of unworldliness, she came to grips with the world, and was a wise and practical adviser to the many who brought their troubles to her. She was a good business woman, astute in managing her affairs; but at the same time much given to impulsive and extravagant gestures. She loved to make everything larger than life, to find drama in daily affairs; always her astonishing energy, her fun, and her intelligence delighted, and sometimes exhausted, her friends. A shrewd critic, she knew the perils of her own facility in writing, and survived them. She inspired warm affection; in later life as a comfortably shaped old lady to whom writing and talking were equal delights. Her place in the company of the best writers for children is assured; she made few concessions to a child's immaturity, but her work marvellously contains a child's sense of wonder and expectancy.

She was received into the Roman Catholic Church in 1951; and died in her mews cottage in Hampstead 5 June 1965.

[Eleanor Farjeon, *A Nursery in the Nineties*, 1935, and *Edward Thomas: The Last Four Years*, 1958; Eileen H. Colwell, *Eleanor Farjeon*, A Bodley Head Monograph, 1961; Denys Blakelock, *Eleanor: Portrait of a Farjeon*, 1966; *The Times*, 7 June 1965; unpublished memoirs and papers; private information; personal knowledge.]

JOHN BELL

FARREN, SIR WILLIAM SCOTT (1892-1970), aeronautical engineer, was born in Cambridge 3 April 1892, the son of William Farren, printseller and taxidermist, by his wife, Harriet Emma Scott. He was educated at the Perse School and gained an entrance scholarship at Trinity College, Cambridge, where he obtained a first class in part i of the mathematical tripos (1912), became a senior scholar in 1913, and graduated with first class honours in the mechanical sciences tripos of 1914.

He then joined British Thomson-Houston at Rugby; within a year, however, Mervyn O'Gorman had persuaded him over to Farnborough to join the band of young graduates—mainly Cambridge men, among them F. A. Lindemann (later Viscount Cherwell) and F. W. Aston [qq.v.], (Sir) Melvill Jones, (Sir) George Thomson, and (Sir) Geoffrey Taylor—whom O'Gorman was collecting to expand the Royal Aircraft Factory (later to become the Royal Aircraft Establishment) into a major national centre of aircraft research, development, and design. Farren became head of the aerodynamics department, learned to fly, and played a significant role in the design of the SE 5a, a highly successful combat aircraft which went into large-scale production. At the height of the submarine menace in 1917 he was made responsible for the immediate production of a flying-boat, the CE 1; under his supervision the machine was designed and built in only seven months. Farren, with limited experience as a test pilot, then successfully took it aloft on its first flight.

In 1918 Farren joined Armstrong Whitworth Aircraft, but although he continued to act as consultant to that firm until 1937, he returned to Cambridge in 1920 as lecturer in aeronautics and engineering under Melvill Jones, who had been appointed to the newly established chair in aeronautical engineering. Jones believed in augmenting theoretical work and wind-tunnel experiments in research by observation in flight on experimental aircraft. Farren provided much of the instrumentation needed for such flight work, as well as designing Jones's first wind tunnel and its balances; he was officially appointed university lecturer in engineering under the new university statutes of 1926, and was elected a fellow of Trinity College in 1933. He also lectured on the strength of aircraft structure at the Royal College of Science in 1922-31.

At the approach of war, he left Cambridge for the Air Ministry in 1937 to become deputy to (Sir) David Pye [q.v.], the director of scientific research. In 1939 Farren became deputy director of research and development of aircraft under (Sir) Roderic Hill [q.v.], and in 1940 moved with him to the newly created Ministry of Aircraft Production, later succeeding Hill as director of technical development; he was one of the original 'boys in the back room' of Lord Beaverbrook [q.v.]. In 1941 he returned to Farnborough as director of the Royal Aircraft Establishment: the four most gruelling years of his life followed, during which rapid advancement in aeronautical techniques was essential for Britain's survival. Farren gave a sense of team spirit to the greatly expanded RAE, skilfully welding the old Farnborough hands with those recruited 'for the duration', and with the assistance of W. G. A. Perring [q.v.] and H. L. Stevens he galvanized the entire Establishment into a dynamo of activity. At the same time he began laying firm foundations for the future, and gave impetus to research which would keep up the momentum of aeronautical development after the war; like Sir Wilfrid Freeman [q.v.] and others, he saw clearly the imminent revolution from the jet engine and supersonics. He also played a leading part in setting up the new RAE airfield and facilities which were subsequently built at Bedford.

Farren was nearly fifty when he returned to the Royal Aircraft Establishment, and, in spite of an interval of twenty years, he brushed up his old flying skills with enthusiasm: in the next four years he flew anything he could lay his hands on—Spitfires, Thunderbolts, Lancasters, Meteors, or captured German fighters and bombers. He regularly flew a Spitfire around in the early morning, to freshen himself up before the working day. Farren took immense pride in his workshops, and was himself a skilled detail designer and a meticulous craftsman; the personal example which he set gave him great strength in dealing with his staff: pilots, craftsmen, scientists, and engineers, all alike felt the inspiration of a man who really knew what he was talking about.

At the beginning of 1946 he joined the Blackburn Aircraft Company as technical director, and in late 1947 moved to a similar position with A. V. Roe at Manchester, where he remained until 1961; in 1956 he had also become technical director of Hawker Siddeley Nuclear Power Company, and he was a director of Hawker Siddeley Aviation from 1959. During his years in industry after the war his two major projects were on the advanced design of the Vulcan 'V Bomber', a tailless aircraft which proceeded to do yeoman service with the Royal Air Force, and the stand-off supersonic 'Blue Steel' missile which went into successful production for the V Bomber Force. He retired in 1961, although he maintained contact with Hawker Siddeley as consultant.

Both before, during, and after the war of 1939-45, Farren's influence, and the services he rendered to the Aeronautical Research Committee (re-named Council in 1945) and its various committees, were considerable. He also played a leading part in the setting up of co-operative wind-tunnel facilities by industry to supplement the official facilities. His contributions to aviation were recognized by many honours: he was appointed MBE in 1918; CB in 1943, was knighted in 1952, and elected FRS in 1945; Manchester University conferred on him an honorary D.Sc. He was made honorary fellow (1953) of the American Institute of the Aerospace Sciences, as it was then called, and also (1959) of the Royal Aeronautical Society, of which he was president in 1953-4; he had been an ordinary fellow of that society for many years, and in 1956 he received its gold medal.

Farren was a deeply sensitive man, at first meeting giving an impression of brusque reserve and even slight coldness, but further acquaintance revealed a passionate devotion to aeronautics and a determination to set himself the highest professional standards, whether as research scientist, designer and engineer, pilot, teacher, or administrator. He possessed a fount of restless and ubiquitous energy, with a profound belief in the virtue of getting things quickly out of the laboratory and into the air as the final test of any aeronautical development, and of understanding the way in which pilots and aircrew handled things when in the air. His pupils from early Cambridge days testified to his gifts as a lecturer, his knack of inspiring those who were keen to learn—whether brilliant or not—and his unfailing help and guidance to younger men. He was a cheerful, loyal, and sympathetic friend, who had a deep love of the English countryside, and enjoyed sketching from a boat in the Cambridgeshire fens.

He married in 1917 Carol Erica, daughter of William Warrington; they had one daughter. His first wife died in 1963, and later in the same year he married Mildred Alice Hooke, OBE (died 1977), formerly headmistress of Bradford Girls' Grammar School. She devotedly tended Farren through the five years of his final illness: he died in Cambridge 3 July 1970. A portrait of him by Frank Eastman (1960) hangs in the headquarters of the Royal Aeronautical Society, London.

[*The Times*, 6, 13, 14, and 15 July 1970; *R.A.E. News*, vol. xxiii, No. 7, July 1970; Sir George Thomson and Sir Arnold Hall in *Biographical Memoirs of Fellows of the Royal Society*, vol. xvii, 1971; private information; personal knowledge.]

MORIEN MORGAN

FARRER, AUSTIN MARSDEN (1904–1968), philosopher, theologian and biblical scholar, was born at Hampstead, London, 1 October 1904, the son of the Revd A. J. D. Farrer, a Baptist minister, and his wife, Evangeline Archer. From St. Paul's he went to Balliol College, Oxford, as a classical scholar in 1923, and read classical honour moderations, *literae humaniores*, and theology, getting first classes in each (1925, 1927, and 1928). He won a Craven scholarship in 1925 and the Liddon studentship in 1927. Despite a Nonconformist upbringing and a period of Spinozistic pantheism in his youth, he became, and consistently remained, a member of the Church of England, 'catholic' in doctrine and 'high church' in style. He was made deacon in 1928 and ordained priest in the following year, serving his title at All Saints', Dewsbury. In 1931 he returned to Oxford, never to leave it, at first as chaplain and tutor of St. Edmund Hall until 1935, then as fellow and chaplain of Trinity until 1960, in which year he became warden of Keble College, remaining so until he died.

Farrer had as penetrating a philosophical mind as anyone of his generation, though the truth of this—which puts him on a par with such practitioners as J. L. Austin [q.v.] and Gilbert Ryle—will not be apparent outside the relatively small circle of those who engaged in philosophical discussion with him. His especial genius lay in his ability to penetrate through the cloud of detail to the essential structure of a problem or the essential features of some doctrine. As a corollary of this he could on occasion give a remarkably illuminating exposition of the thought of some philosopher (Aristotle in particular) with whom he was in sympathy or partial sympathy. Though he assisted in the teaching of philosophy while at Trinity, he did not think of himself as a professional philosopher by vocation. Indeed he sometimes showed some impatience with the laborious and detailed work by which some professionals would pursue the goal of establishing once and for all some limited piece of philosophical truth. Though no Platonist, he perhaps had a somewhat Platonic conception of philosophy—that it is essentially dialogue, that there can be no formulation of the truth so lapidary that it cannot be misunderstood, and that what needs to be said in some context depends upon what is being misunderstood in that context. He did indeed believe that it was the duty of philosophically minded Christians to attack the intellectual roots of infidelity; but he was very far from thinking that there could be a kind of *summa* in which this was once and for all achieved.

He described his own intellectual goal as 'to understand how the first cause works through the secondary causes by using and not overriding the activity proper to their created nature', and as 'to discern what kind of natural philosophy is most congenial to Christian belief'. In his view this involved on the one hand rescuing the concept of substances (or of persistent focuses of activity) from the philosophical limbo in which it was at the time at which he began his work, and, on the other hand, the working out of a tenable account of human freedom. Ancillary to both of these tasks was the giving of a reasoned reply to the logical positivism which seemed, in the forties and early fifties, to have established empiricism on a sure foundation.

These themes are prominent in *Finite and Infinite* (1943) and *The Freedom of the Will* (1958), which are the two of his writings in which he dealt with philosophical themes which pass outside the scope of philosophical theology. Neither book is entirely accessible. Farrer used to say that *The Freedom of the Will* was written in a 'novelettish' manner; and indeed it has a certain sprightliness of style which prevents some readers from taking it as seriously as it deserves. But it contains, for example, an analysis of the concept of predictability, an attack on epiphenomenalism, and an account of the relation between intention and execution, all of which are, characteristically, studded with metaphor, impatient of detail, and in places too fast-moving for the reader to keep up, but which are profoundly illuminating. What Farrer threw out in these passages was in each case subsequently maintained much more carefully and laboriously, but sometimes much less suggestively, in books and learned articles.

The originality of *Finite and Infinite* was on a larger scale. It was rare indeed in the late thirties and early forties to find a defence of metaphysics which really appreciated the force of positivism; but the importance of the book lies in its main thesis, namely that the crucial issue in philosophical theology is the question of what is involved in thinking of ourselves as genuinely unitary centres of activity. But the book is undeniably difficult, partly from the nature of the subject matter, partly from the presentation. Farrer's style was always elegant, sometimes mannered, sometimes racy, sometimes movingly eloquent. But he always wrote, as he thought, in dialogue; and it is sometimes essential to know whom he is arguing with, or what distant allusion is being caught up, if one is to get the significance of what he is saying. In consequence the book, while it influenced many, did so in intangible ways, and did not become the explicit focus of much controversy.

The key to his biblical work is his concern with 'how the first cause works through the secondary causes' together with his belief (expressed, for example, in his 1948 Bampton lectures, *The Glass of Vision*) that religious truth can be communicated to human intelligences only through images. This leads to the conclusion that the divine message will have been conveyed through the shaping of the imagery characteristic of the tradition within which the inspired writer worked. The problem, therefore, for the biblical exegete was to identify this imagery. Farrer's strong poetic streak may have been over-influential here. (He was an extremely adept versifier, not only of Augustan pastiche; but there was a great deal more of the poet in him than just this.) It seems that the consensus of biblical scholars finds much of Farrer's exegesis altogether too imaginative. But even if his conjectures are seldom right, this does not detract from the importance of his question how inspiration is to be conceived of nor from the good sense of the general outlines of his answer to it.

Farrer did not wish to be considered for the Nolloth chair in the philosophy of religion and was inexplicably not appointed to the regius chair of divinity. He continued as tutor and chaplain at Trinity, assiduous and accessible, even if not always communicating entirely successfully with the slower among his pupils. His open-house in his rooms in the evening for beer and conversation with the chaplain surprised those who thought of him as a dedicated intellectual whose relaxation was sophisticated conversation (in fact his relaxations included upholstery and an allotment). Unlike some fellow chaplains he took the pastoral side of his college life extremely seriously. *The Crown of the Year* (1952), a collection of his chapel sermons, shows the eloquence, luminous piety, and remarkable brevity of his pulpit manner. He was in demand as a preacher outside the college, in Oxford, Abingdon, and elsewhere. In the pulpit and at the altar there was a dignity and *auctoritas* about him far removed from the lightness and approachability of his everyday manner.

He responded increasingly as time went on to calls upon him to contribute to Christian apologetics, in popular lectures to undergraduates, in books such as *Saving Belief* (1964) and *Love Almighty and Ills Unlimited* (1962), and in trans-Atlantic lecturings. As an apologist he had the defect of his very quick mind; even when trying to be simple he cannot altogether avoid epigrammatic and allusive writing, and the argument is sometimes so compressed that the more pedestrian reader can fail to notice its existence.

To many pupils, as to many members of his wider audiences, he was sheer inspiration; some were out of their depth with him. He became increasingly aware of the latter, and it was on the whole a relief to him to give up the life of a college tutor on becoming warden of Keble. As head of a college he combined dignity with ready accessibility; and surprised some of his colleagues by his grasp of college affairs and by the rapidity and firmness with which he conducted governing-body business.

Farrer became an honorary fellow of Trinity College in 1963 and a fellow of the British Academy in 1968.

In 1937 Farrer married Katharine Newton. They had one daughter. He and his wife were an excellent partnership, having many common interests (she, too, was a writer, of crime stories, but with aspirations towards more serious work). Their domestic style was cultivated, tasteful, and to appearance leisured, though Farrer was in truth unobtrusively conservative of his time. He died in Oxford 29 December 1968 suddenly and unexpectedly, leaving behind him many writings which were posthumously published and many of which are of very high quality. In the judgement of many there was no abler Christian thinker among his contemporaries.

In Keble College hall there is a portrait in oils painted posthumously by G. Speake in 1970. A pencil sketch by Powys-Evans is in the possession of the family.

[*The Times*, 30 December 1968; E. L. Mascall in *Proceedings* of the British

Academy, vol. liv, 1968; personal knowledge.]   I. M. CROMBIE

FEARNSIDES, WILLIAM GEORGE (1879-1968), geologist, was born 10 November 1879 at Horbury, Yorkshire, the eldest in the family of two sons and one daughter of Joshua Fearnsides, a grocer, and his wife, Maria Green, of Horbury near Dewsbury. Fearnsides was educated at Wheelwright Grammar School, Dewsbury, of which he became head boy, and at Sidney Sussex College, Cambridge. Going to Cambridge with a West Riding county major scholarship in 1897 he later became a scholar of the college. He first intended to become a chemist but was persuaded to study geology by Cambridge geological staff. He gained first class honours in the natural sciences tripos (part i, 1900, and part ii, 1901, winning the Harkness scholarship in geology).

Leaving Cambridge in 1901 Fearnsides went as an indentured apprentice to Westinghouse, Pittsburgh, but left abruptly after a violent altercation with a foreman, working his way home by taking various menial jobs. Back at Cambridge the same year he established himself as a freelance supervisor and coach in geology. Elected a fellow of Sidney Sussex in 1904 he became a Taylor and college lecturer in 1908, and in 1909 was appointed university demonstrator in petrology. Between 1901 and 1913 he taught and researched on the Lower Palaeozoic rocks of Wales and Scandinavia: he became an authority on the Lower Palaeozoic of Wales.

In 1913 he was appointed first Sorby professor of geology at Sheffield University. In this post he developed an interest in economic geology, being convinced that the essential function of a provincial department was to assist local industry; he gradually did more and more consulting work. At the outbreak of World War I he advised on formerly imported supplies for the steel industry and gave a paper to the Surveyors' Institution on the influence of water in macadam road construction. In 1914 in his Sorby lecture to the Sheffield Society of Engineers and Metallurgists he survived the structural analogies between igneous rocks and metals, influenced by some early work at Cambridge on tin/copper alloys in association with chemists. During World War I he published papers on supplies of refractories, iron ores, and other minerals, and on structural and other aspects of the Yorkshire and Derby coalfields. In 1916 he presented a comprehensive address on the mineral requirements of the British iron and steel industry to the Society of Engineers, for which he was awarded their Bessemer premium. He played a decisive part in

the establishment of a Refractories Department. at Sheffield in 1917, and in the development of the semi-silica brick based on the complementary expansion/contraction of silica/clay. He became an authority on moulding sands.

In 1928-32 Fearnsides was vice-president of the Midland Institute of Mining Engineers. At the 1933 British Association meeting at Leicester when president of Section C his presidential address was a comprehensive survey of the geological structure and history of the whole Midland area during the Upper Carboniferous, using evidence from Geological Survey maps and from mine plans and boreholes: he discussed this subject again in 1936 in his presidential address to the Yorkshire Geological Society. In 1930 he had advised the Attock Oil Company on geological matters in India and Burma and in 1938 again assisted that Company on English prospecting in the Carboniferous—work that led to greater geological understanding but no economic success. About this time the Anglo-Iranian Oil Company through its subsidiary, the D'Arcy Exploration Company, started oil exploration in the UK and Fearnsides was retained as a geological adviser to this enterprise. He assisted with geological advice only, firmly stating at the outset that 'he would drink all the oil he found in Britain' (in spite of the seepages he must have known about in coal-mines and on the surface). He assisted in the selection of the company's licence area in the East Midlands where the Eakring oilfield was discovered in 1939 and subsequently a number of other fields. He was also interested in the D'Arcy licence area in East Yorkshire because of its potash prospects in the Permian.

During World War II, coal production, supplies of minerals, refractories, and water supplies to airfields occupied his time. He was president of the Geological Society 1943-5 (his presidential addresses were never published). He retired from Sheffield in 1945. In 1947 he became geological adviser to the West Midlands Division of the National Coal Board for an important borehole programme and other underground work. About this time he assisted the development of the Mountfield gypsum mines in Sussex. Later, at the age of seventy-six, he travelled in Rhodesia on mineral consulting work. At Sheffield he advised on foundations for heavy buildings and on motorway geological problems.

In addition to honours already mentioned he was awarded the gold medal of the Surveyors' Institution in 1914, the Greenwell medal of the North England Institute of Mining Engineers in 1917, and the Murchison medal of the Geological Society in 1932. He was elected FRS in 1932 and served on its council in 1936-7.

From 1931 to 1934 he was dean of the faculty of pure science at Sheffield. Sidney Sussex elected him to an honorary fellowship in 1946.

Fearnsides, known to his contemporaries as 'Bones', was a strong personality who spoke his mind without inhibitions. He was exceptionally energetic both mentally and physically and a tireless walker. He found writing uncongenial and laborious, preferring the spoken word. Indeed, he had an excellent singing voice, which enabled him to join choirs. His many contacts as consultant made him a mine of geological information, some of it regarded as confidential by lesser men, which he delighted to impart in stimulating provocative conversation. His brusque manner covered a basic shyness and a poetic, even mystical, attitude to nature and the vast scale of geological and astronomical time. He was regarded with great respect and some affection by officials of the National Coal Board. He was for years one of the great names in British economic geology. He loved travel, was a shrewd business man, was interested in current affairs, and was generous in an anonymous way.

In 1911 he married Beatrix (died 1973), daughter of William Whitehead Watts, FRS. It was a supremely happy marriage; they had two daughters, the younger of whom was killed by a land-mine in Italy in 1945, and the elder of whom married O. M. B. Bulman, FRS. Fearnsides died in Sheffield 15 May 1968.

[O. M. B. Bulman in *Biographical Memoirs of Fellows of the Royal Society*, vol. xv, 1969; personal knowledge.]   N. L. FALCON

FEETHAM, RICHARD (1874-1965), judge, and last survivor of 'Milner's kindergarten', was born 22 November 1874, the youngest of the five sons of the Revd William Feetham, vicar of Penrhos, Monmouthshire, and his wife, Mary, daughter of the Ven. William Crawley, archdeacon of Monmouth. He was educated at Marlborough (1887-92) and at New College, Oxford, where he took a first class in classical honour moderations in 1895 and a second class in *literae humaniores* in 1897. He then read for the bar, to which he was called by the Inner Temple in 1899, and joined the legal staff of the London County Council. He also engaged in voluntary social work in the East End of London, where he renewed his acquaintance with Lionel G. Curtis [q.v.], who had been his senior at New College. It was Curtis who was responsible for Feetham's being invited to South Africa in 1901, to join the band of young men from Oxford (and especially from New College) recruited by Sir Alfred (later Viscount) Milner [q.v.] to recreate an administrative structure for the Transvaal, after its annexation

in 1900. Feetham was concerned with local government, first on the East Rand and then in Johannesburg, where he was town clerk in succession to Curtis from 1903 until 1905. After Milner's departure from South Africa in 1905, Feetham served both as legal adviser to Lord Selborne [q.v.], Milner's successor as high commissioner, and as a member of the Legislative Council of the Transvaal from 1907 until the establishment of the Union of South Africa in 1910.

Feetham was, indeed, one of the intellectual architects of South African unification. Members of 'Milner's kindergarten' had formed the Fortnightly Club, a discussion group modelled on the New College essay society. On 4 October 1906 Feetham read to this group a seminal paper entitled 'Some Problems of South African Federation and Reasons for Facing Them'; this paper became the basis of an extended statement of the advantages of closer union of the South African colonies, which was endorsed by the high commissioner and published as the Selborne Memorandum. It was this initiative which acted as a catalyst in the movement which culminated in the National Convention which drafted the Act of Union in 1909.

In 1915 Feetham was elected as a member (for Parktown) of the South African Legislative Assembly. As a private member, he successfully promoted a Bill regulating the adoption of children; he also carried a motion amending the budget of 1917. In addition to his parliamentary duties, he served from 1916 to 1919, as a lieutenant in the 1st battalion of the Cape Corps (a unit of Cape Coloured servicemen).

In 1918 he went to India as a member of one of the Southborough committees on Indian reforms, and was chairman of the committee on functions. In 1923 he resigned from Parliament, on his appointment as a judge of the Transvaal division of the South African Supreme Court. In 1924 he undertook what was possibly the most difficult, and certainly the most controversial, task of his career, when he accepted appointment by Ramsay MacDonald as chairman of the Ulster boundary commission, set up under article xii of the Irish Treaty of 1921. His fellow commissioners were Eoin (otherwise John) MacNeill [q.v.], from the Irish Free State, and J. R. Fisher, from Northern Ireland. Feetham attempted to conduct the work of the commission as an exercise in logic rather than politics, taking a strict legalistic and, in the opinion of his critics, a restricted interpretation of the loose and ambiguous language of article xii. Such chance as the commission had of solving the problem of the boundary was destroyed when the *Morning Post*, 7 November

1925, published an unauthorized, but remarkably accurate, forecast of its findings. Thereupon MacNeill resigned, and this action was interpreted as an indication that the commission's findings would be unacceptable to the Irish Free State. The ensuing political crisis, during which it appeared possible that the Irish Free State might repudiate its debt to Britain, left Feetham unmoved in his resolution to continue the commission's work. The matter was eventually taken out of the hands of Feetham and his remaining colleague, after a meeting at the House of Commons, 3 December 1925, between them and Stanley Baldwin, W. T. Cosgrave, and James Craig (prime ministers of the United Kingdom, the Irish Free State, and Northern Ireland), and W. L. S. Churchill (chancellor of the Exchequer) [qq.v.]. Feetham then agreed that the report should be withdrawn; a letter from him to Baldwin, explaining the principles of interpretation which he had adopted, was published in *The Times* of 18 December 1925. Feetham found himself the object of criticism, some of it envenomed, both then and, sporadically, for the next forty years; he made no public reply. The judicial detachment of his work became evident when the report of the commission was published in 1969.

Feetham was called away from the South African bench on two further occasions: to act as chairman of the local government commission in Kenya in 1926, and to be adviser to the Shanghai Municipal Council on the question of the Shanghai boundary in 1930-3. He was also chairman of the Transvaal Asiatic Land Tenure Act commission (1923-5).

In 1931 Feetham was appointed judge-president of the Natal Provincial division of the Supreme Court; in 1939 he was appointed as a judge of the Appellate division. After his retirement from the bench, in 1944, he served from 1946 to 1949, as chairman of the Witwatersrand land titles commission. From 1940 until 1952 he was chairman of the governor-general's National War Fund, which was concerned with the rehabilitation of ex-servicemen and the care of their dependants.

From 1938 until 1965 Feetham served on the council of the university of the Witwatersrand, of which he was vice-chancellor from 1938 to 1948 and was elected chancellor, in 1949, in succession to J. H. Hofmeyr [q.v.]. As chancellor he led the university in its prolonged but unsuccessful opposition to the imposition upon it of racial segregation by Act of Parliament. In 1957 he was joint president, with the chancellor of the univerity of Cape Town, A. van de S. Centlivres [q.v.], of a conference of the two universities, from which emerged *The Open Universities in South Africa*, a reasoned statement of opposition to apartheid in higher education. (It was, perhaps, an indication of the influence of the 'kindergarten' in the public life of South Africa that both chancellors and five other members of the conference were New College men.) He also published a series of closely argued pamphlets, criticizing the constitutional manœuvres by which the South African Government succeeded in circumventing the South Africa Act in order to remove the Cape Coloured population from the common voters' roll. He also served as chairman of a committee of the associated church schools, which considered the future of private education. To this Dictionary Feetham contributed the notice of Sir Patrick Duncan.

Feetham retired as chancellor of the university of the Witwatersrand in 1961, but continued as a member of its council until shortly before his death in Natal 5 November 1965. His work was commemorated by the annual Chancellor's lecture, founded by the university council, and by the Richard Feetham memorial lecture, founded by the students' representative council. Having been appointed CMG (1924), Feetham was further honoured twice—he became honorary LLD of Witwatersrand (1949) and Natal (1958).

Feetham was a man of commanding presence, well over six feet in height, with a bass voice of remarkable power and range. He could appear as austere and aloof; he was impatient of prolixity in speech or writing; and he could be a courteous but devastating critic of shoddy or disingenuous argument. To those whom he admitted to his confidence, however, he displayed warmth and sympathy, enlivened by a subtle and responsive sense of humour.

He married, in 1920, Leila, daughter of L. W. Christopher, of Ladysmith; and he was survived by his widow, a son, and two daughters. There is a portrait of him by Waldo Dingemans in the Senate Room of the university of the Witwatersrand.

[Lionel Curtis, *With Milner in South Africa*, 1951; Leonard Monteith Thompson, *The Unification of South Africa*, 1960; personal knowledge.]　　　　　G. H. L. Le May

FELLOWES, Sir EDWARD ABDY (1895-1970), clerk of the House of Commons, was born in London 23 June 1895, the elder son of William Gordon Fellowes, barrister-at-law, of 17 Onslow Gardens, London SW7, and his wife, Marian Augusta Hamilton. He was educated at Marlborough (1909-14) and was accepted for admission to Merton College, Oxford, in 1914. That year, however, he obtained a commission in the Queen's Royal

West Surrey Regiment, with which he saw much active service on the western front, attaining the rank of captain, being sent to hospital suffering from gas poisoning, and being awarded the MC. He did not take up his place at Oxford after the war; and in 1919 he was appointed to a clerkship in the House of Commons.

During the later part of his earlier years in the House Fellowes proved himself a notable clerk to the Public Accounts Committee. In 1932 he was joint author with J. W. Hills, MP, of the enlarged second edition of the latter's book *The Finance of Government*.

In 1937 Fellowes was appointed second clerk assistant. In this post he set himself to modernize the departmental machinery for administering the elaborate rules which the House had already made for parliamentary questions; his reforms were to prove of lasting value. In 1942-4 he commanded the Palace of Westminster company of the Home Guard. He was appointed CB in 1945.

In 1948 Fellowes became clerk assistant. In this post, as first chairman of the House of Commons Staff Board, he began the modernization of staff relations at the House.

In 1954 Fellowes succeeded Sir Frederic Metcalfe as clerk of the House. He was appointed KCB in 1955. In 1958-9 he submitted a comprehensive memorandum to the select committee on procedure set up that session. His proposals for further devolution to committees of legislative business and for changes in the House's hours of sitting proved too radical for the times; but a number of his detailed suggestions were adopted. In 1960-1, in evidence before the Committee of Privileges in the case of the petition concerning Anthony Neil Wedgwood Benn (who, although he had succeeded to a viscountcy, wished to remain eligible for election to the House of Commons), Fellowes's clear exposition of the impossibility of remedy short of legislation formed part of the process leading to the Peerage Act of 1963.

Fellowes and (Sir) T. G. B. Cocks, the second clerk assistant, were joint editors of the sixteenth edition of T. Erskine May's *Treatise on the Law, Privileges, Proceedings, and Usage of Parliament*, published in 1957. In 1960 HMSO printed Fellowes's *Selection from the Volumes of Decisions from the Chair*, compiled mainly for the use of presiding officers of Commonwealth legislatures.

Fellowes had begun to interest himself in colonial legislatures early in his career, under the inspiration of a senior colleague, (Sir) Bryan Fell. From 1945, under the guidance of the clerk of the House, Sir Gilbert (later Lord) Campion [q.v.], he took a leading part in the

organization of a system (which still continues) of visits by Commonwealth parliamentary officials on attachment to the House of Commons. He himself paid a number of official visits overseas, notably in 1947 to Ceylon (the first such visit ever made by a clerk at the Table from the Commons) and Nigeria, where he sat as president of the House of representatives during several sessions. At the same time he was concerned to promote the changes in the organization of the Clerk's Department which these developments made desirable; and he keenly supported the work of the Commonwealth Parliamentary Association. His services to the Commonwealth were recognized in 1953 by his appointment as CMG, and were recorded in the resolution of thanks passed by the House on his retirement.

In the later years of his service Fellowes extended his interests beyond the Commonwealth, as a member of the Association of Secretaries General of Parliaments, of which he was president in 1956-60.

Fellowes retired at the end of 1961. In thanking him for his services, the leader of the House, Iain Macleod [q.v.], described him as one of the great clerks of the House of Commons. Fellowes indeed possessed a rich combination of the qualities needed for that office. An extensive knowledge of procedure and a deep understanding of its significance (derived in part from researches into the history of the Public Business Standing Orders, on which he left unpublished papers) were balanced by formidable powers of organization. In both fields he had an acute instinct for what was likely to become important and a rare energy in making the necessary preparations to deal with it. His character was well summed up to the House by the leader of the Opposition, Hugh Gaitskell [q.v.], as fair-minded, full of common sense, decisive, and genial. To this Dictionary Fellowes contributed the notice of D. C. Brown, Viscount Ruffside.

After his retirement Fellowes was chairman of the General Advisory Council of the BBC (1962-7) and of the Council of the Hansard Society, and from 1964 till his death first chairman and then president of the Study of Parliament Group. In 1964 he became a member of the Royal Society of Arts. In his younger days he took part enthusiastically, if with no unusual skill, in a number of sporting activities, particularly shooting; and he was always a keen golfer.

In 1921 Fellowes married Ella Mary (died 1976), daughter of Lt.-Col. John Macrae-Gilstrap, of Eilean Donan, Ross-shire. They had three daughters. Fellowes died at his home at Scole, Norfolk, 28 December 1970.

A pen-and-ink drawing by Geoffrey Fletcher

(1961), showing him in the clerk's wig and gown sitting at his desk in his room at the Commons, is in the possession of the family.

[*The Times*, 30 December 1970; *Marlborough College Register; History of the Queen's Royal Regiment*, vol. vii, compiled by Col. H. C. Wylly; *Commons Hansard*, 19 December 1961; private information; personal knowledge.]   DAVID LIDDERDALE

FERGUSON, FREDERIC SUTHERLAND (1878-1967), bibliographer, was born in Stoke Newington, London, 26 December 1878, the elder son of William Sutherland Ferguson, secretary to the Edinburgh Stock Exchange and later a member of the London Stock Exchange, and his wife, Helen Atkin. He had one brother and one sister. Educated at the Grocers' Company School, Hackney Downs, London E9, and at King's College, London, he did not take a degree; but in 1897, at the age of eighteen, he entered the firm of Bernard Quaritch, the well-known antiquarian booksellers. Here he received the training and acquired the experience which made him not merely a successful bookseller but one of the foremost bibliographers of his time, specializing above all in early English printed books.

Much of Ferguson's profound bibliographical knowledge was derived from examining the many private collections that came his way in the course of business, and his skill in recording bibliographical details attained a meticulousness that has rarely been equalled. Indeed, his unrivalled familiarity with types, ornaments, and devices made it possible for him accurately to identify hitherto undated books, and to detect the work of secret presses. Hence his outstanding contribution to *A Short-Title Catalogue of Books Printed in England, Scotland & Ireland, and of English Books Printed Abroad, 1475-1640*, known as the STC, the first edition of which appeared in 1926. In the words of the editors, A. W. Pollard [q.v.] and G. R. Redgrave, Ferguson was 'largely responsible for any bibliographical polish which the catalogue possesses'. He himself took over the joint editorship of the next edition.

After service with the Cameronians (1916-18), Ferguson returned to Quaritch, becoming managing director of the firm in 1928, a position he held until 1943. This proved to be a period of growing prosperity for the book trade, due in part to the great expansion of public and university libraries throughout the English-speaking world.

In his new position, it must be admitted that Ferguson could sometimes try the patience of his colleagues on account of his uneven temper. His outbursts were sudden, though brief, and reconciliations usually followed. Nor can it be said that he was a satisfactory manager of men. He tended to lack humour. His own standards made him impatient and intolerant of those less rigorous and perfectionist in their methods. On the other hand, he was by nature generous and open-handed, wholly without guile, and immensely hard working. He was short of stature and physically robust, and this typified his doggedness of character.

In 1947 Ferguson retired finally from the firm he had served with such devotion, and the last twenty years of his life were spent working in the British Museum on his *magnum opus*. This was a comprehensive catalogue of early British books. His practice was to note down on cards or slips every possible bibliographical feature, especially variants, for which he had an astonishing gift of detection. Dwelling on points that might have escaped less conscientious scholars, his progress was inevitably slow, and the completion of so huge a work would have required the undivided attention of a lifetime even longer than that which he was to enjoy. The assembled material was left to the British Museum, where it was to remain a mine of information for scholars.

While working on his catalogue Ferguson had a room to himself, and he was granted every facility by the museum authorities. To members of the department of printed books, and indeed to any member of the public who approached him with a bona fide problem, he was always ready to be of assistance. On the other hand, he could be a dilatory correspondent; and although he was patient with most enquirers and showed a fundamental humility, he was merciless with colleagues in whose work he detected slovenliness and inaccuracy.

His own publications were few, but of great distinction. The first was *Title-Page Borders used in England and Scotland, 1485-1640* (1932), written in collaboration with R. B. McKerrow [q.v.], with a supplement published in 1936, both issued by the Bibliographical Society. This was followed in the same year by a bibliography of Sir George Mackenzie, the seventeenth-century lawyer, practically the founder of the library of the Faculty of Advocates in Scotland, published for the Edinburgh Bibliographical Society. It was characteristic that to the Advocates' library Ferguson presented at this time 200 volumes from his own private collection, which, having been printed in Scotland in the sixteenth and seventeenth centuries, were works of great rarity.

During these fruitful years, Ferguson commuted from his home in Southgate, and he regularly spent one day each week at the Bodleian Library, Oxford. It was Oxford in fact which recognized his services to scholarship, while repairing his lack of formal academic qualifications, by the grant of an honorary degree of MA on 26 February 1955. This was followed on 8 July of the same year by the award of an honorary LLD by the university of Edinburgh, on which occasion due reference was made to his gift of valuable law books to the library of the Faculty of Advocates.

His eminence in the bibliographical field was such as to make it natural that he should be elected president of the Bibliographical Society (1948-50), honorary president of the Edinburgh Bibliographical Society (he had been its president from 1935 to 1936), and president of the International Antiquarian Booksellers' Association (1934). The Bibliographical Society gave him its gold medal in 1951, a much-coveted award.

Ferguson's private life was happy. In 1905 he married Bessie, a nurse by training, daughter of Henry Holmes Leonard, a surveyor. They had a son and three daughters. Ferguson was an affectionate but strict father, for whom the acquisition of knowledge and the passing of examinations by his children was a particularly serious matter. Nevertheless, his family was united, and when in 1966 his wife died, after a long illness, he was left desolate. His situation was rendered more poignant by the fact that he was obliged to sell his house and his precious collection. He died at Newport, Isle of Wight, 4 May 1967.

In an age renowned for bibliographical studies, especially in Britain, Ferguson was a major figure, worthy to be ranked alongside A. W. Pollard, R. B. McKerrow, his one-time collaborator, and Sir W. W. Greg [q.v.]. In addition to a scholarly *œuvre*, he left a reputation for thoroughness without which bibliography must cease to be an exact science; and it was as such a science that Ferguson cultivated it single-mindedly over nearly six decades.

[Private information.]   E. W. F. TOMLIN

FERGUSSON, SIR (JOHN) DONALD (BALFOUR) (1891-1963), civil servant, was born at Bebington, Cheshire, 26 August 1891, the eldest of the four sons of the Revd J. M. Fergusson, DD, a minister of the Episcopalian Church of Scotland, and his wife, E. C. E. Evans. He was educated at Berkhamsted School and Magdalen College, Oxford, where he took a third class in classical moderations in 1912 and first class honours in modern history in 1914. At the outbreak of World War I he was gazetted to the Royal West Kent Regiment and thence to the 1st Hertfordshire Regiment with whom he saw action at the Somme and Passchen-

daele. Following demobilization in 1919, he entered the Treasury where he served as private secretary to successive chancellors of the Exchequer—Austen Chamberlain, R. S. Horne, Stanley Baldwin, Winston Churchill, Philip Snowden, and Neville Chamberlain [qq.v.]—and he became an assistant secretary in 1934.

The turning-point of Fergusson's distinguished career came in 1936: in that year he was promoted quite exceptionally from assistant secretary direct to the post of permanent secretary to the Ministry of Agriculture and Fisheries in succession to Sir Charles J. Howell Thomas. This proved to be an inspired appointment by Sir (N. F.) Warren Fisher [q.v.] Fergusson was a countryman at heart and very quickly his attributes—high intellectual ability, complete sincerity, considerable political sensitivity (all tempered by a pleasing personality and an almost mischievous sense of humour)—were widely recognized throughout Whitehall and appreciated by those who worked under his command. On his appointment as permanent secretary his major task was to help the minister, W. S. Morrison (later Viscount Dunrossil, q.v.), to lift agriculture from the depths of the great depression of the early thirties and to plan an organization for a food production campaign in the event of a second world war. Legislation was passed to encourage the improvement of grassland and thereby the fertility of the land; 50,000 tractors were purchased as a reserve; the membership of the county war agricultural executive committees was secretly designated; and detailed schemes for departmental reorganization laid down. As a result it was possible to put the Ministry on a war footing both at headquarters and in the country immediately on the outbreak of war in 1939.

The next five years witnessed nothing short of a revolution in British agriculture from what had been pre-war a widely neglected national asset to an effective and highly efficient instrument for food production. And much of the credit for this goes to two men: R. S. (later Viscount) Hudson [q.v.], who was the minister of agriculture and fisheries from 1940, and Fergusson, who was responsible for the efficient operation of the department in giving effect to the minister's policy. The transformation of a relatively small introvert Ministry into an effective food production department involved considerable augmentation of staff both throughout the country and at headquarters and at professional and administrative level. The introduction of experts in their various fields, but with little previous experience of the machinery of central government, was effected with the minimum of friction; and under Fergusson's sensitive and wise guidance both the existing and the new staff were soon operating as an effective and purposeful team.

The immediate task was to increase food production and this was achieved through the medium of the country war agricultural executive committees acting as the minister's agents in their direct contacts with the farmers. A national farm survey was undertaken so that assistance could be channelled in the most worthwhile direction. Farmers were called upon to plough up grassland, to improve farm drainage and buildings, to apply appropriate fertilizers, and in many cases to grow approved crops. Financial assistance was made available under various schemes and direct help given on a repayment basis through the drainage, machinery, and labour services set up by the war agricultural executive committees. Farmers could appeal against any directions they felt to be unreasonable. But much was achieved by discussion and persuasion and only as a last resort was the power of dispossession invoked and the land taken in hand.

Hudson, as minister, maintained close contact with the work of the war agricultural committees through his personal liaison officers —men of standing in the farming scene in their respective areas, covering a number of counties, who kept themselves well informed on any special problems and difficulties confronting the committees. He was an experienced politician with tremendous drive and a great sense of urgency. He could be quite ruthless in overcoming opposition but was prepared to listen to criticism provided it was genuine and not obstructive. Fergusson was fearless in standing up to his minister if he thought he was wrong or unwise or in too great a hurry, and this was never resented. Hudson's forceful drive and Fergusson's wise and calm judgement proved indeed a fortunate combination for wartime agriculture.

Fergusson was already giving thought to the policy for agriculture after the war—to be embodied in the Agriculture Act of 1947—when in 1945, after protestations overcome only by a word from Churchill, he was transferred from the Ministry of Agriculture to become the permanent secretary of the recently created Ministry of Fuel and Power. Here he was faced with the difficulties, administrative and personal, of combining in a new Ministry the separate and sometimes conflicting interests involved in coal, petroleum, gas, and electricity, each anxious to preserve its own identity at all costs.

Additionally, he was called upon within a few weeks (after the 1945 election) to prepare for the nationalization of coal. Thereafter he had to deal with the fuel crisis of 1947, the nationalization of electricity and gas in two successive years, and with the problem of coal and petrol rationing—more difficult in peacetime than in war.

In spite of these burdens, Fergusson left behind, when he retired in 1952, a coherent and efficient organization as well as a reputation for wise leadership, fairness, and human understanding. He was created CB (1935), KCB (1937), and GCB (1946).

After retirement he became a director of the Prudential Assurance Company and of the Agricultural Mortgage Corporation. In 1954 he sat on the committee set up to inquire into the methods and policy of the National Stud. Fergusson died 4 March 1963 at his farm in Ebbesbourne Wake, near Salisbury in Wiltshire.

He married in 1918 Phillis Mary (died 1971), elder daughter of C. F. M. Cleverly, artist, and had three sons and one daughter. One son was killed in action in 1944.

[*The Times*, 7 March 1963; personal knowledge.] C. H. A. DUKE

FETHERSTONHAUGH, SIR HERBERT MEADE- (1875-1964), admiral. [See MEADE-FETHERSTONHAUGH.]

FIELD, (AGNES) MARY (1896-1968), producer of children's films, was born in Wimbledon, London, 24 February 1896, the second daughter of Ernest Field, a solicitor, and his wife, Evelyn Lucy Daniel. She was educated at Surbiton High School and Bedford College, London, where she gained her MA with distinction in Commonwealth history. She had no intention of devoting herself to the cinema. 'If I had any thought of a career,' she said, 'it was of writing.' She began as a schoolmistress, teaching history and English. She returned to university life as a research scholar, specializing in the history of the Newfoundland fishing industry. She was then asked to check the accuracy of some films about the Commonwealth. Her feeling as a teacher, stirred up by the potentialities of the cinema as an educational force, persuaded her to alter course, and in 1926 she joined Bruce Woolfe at British Instructional Films.

After a year spent dealing with the supply of educational cinema to schools she moved to the production side, worked her way up from continuity girl to director, and made one feature film, a comedy called *Strictly Business* (1931). The genre did not suit her and she reverted to documentary and educational films. 'They cost so little', she said, 'that you can experiment.' And indeed she was a partner in experiment, first at British Instructional Films and later at

Gaumont British Instructional Films, to which, together with Bruce Woolfe, she transferred in 1934.

These were fruitful years. She collaborated with one of the undoubted geniuses of the British cinema, the unassuming Percy Smith, a man so shy that, as Anthony Asquith [q.v.] used to say, when he shook hands he turned his head and looked the other way. But with Mary Field a partnership flourished, and together they made a series of films which were to be famous not only in Britain but on the continent of Europe and in the United States: first *The Secrets of Nature* and, after 1934, *The Secrets of Life*. These were nature films, sometimes detailed studies of plants. The dandelion or the bindweed might, with the benefit of slow-motion photography, be shown gradually growing and flowering. A delighted audience was thus enabled to follow in a few minutes the development of a life which in actuality lasted perhaps weeks, perhaps months. 'Slow-motioned and speeded-up adventures in plant life', John Grierson wrote: 'how beautiful they have been, with Bruce Woolfe, Mary Field, and Percy Smith staking a claim for England better than any . . .'

The films won high honours. *The Tortoise-shell Butterfly* was awarded the *diplôme d'honneur* at the 1935 International Cinema Festival in Brussels; *The Tough 'Un* (a study of the dandelion) carried off an Italian gold medal. But Mary Field would probably have wished to be remembered for her contribution to a still more specialized area of cinema: her work with children's films. She approached the problem at a time when there was a good deal of high moral disapproval of children's enjoyment of the cinema and when there were few films designed to give pleasure to a young audience. Mary Field had to make a case for children's cinema. She made it by producing hundreds of films to which children naturally responded and which they could relish without adult reproach.

In 1944 Mary Field married Gerald Thornton Hankin, an inspector in the Ministry of Education, who shared her belief in the value of cinema as an agent in education. In the same year she became executive producer for J. Arthur Rank's Children's Entertainment Films Department; among the pieces produced under her aegis was the charming and popular *Bush Christmas* (1947), made in Australia. When the Rank Organization was forced to retrench she worked for a time in 1950 with the British Board of Film Censors. In 1951 she became executive officer of the Children's Film Foundation, a non-profit-making organization supported by all the main sections of the industry—producers, specialist producers, exhibitors, and renters. There are many who owe her a debt of gratitude for her share in the creation of children's film matinées. From 1959 until her retirement in 1963 she was a consultant on children's films for a major British television company.

She was a fellow of the British Film Academy and of the Royal Photographic Society; she was also chairman of the Brussels International Centre of Films for Children. In 1951 she was appointed OBE in recognition of her work for children's education. Mary Field was a tireless worker. In 1954 she toured in Australia, New Zealand, and India, and she advised and lectured everywhere. Ultimately she was recognized as a world authority on children's films. She used infra-red photography in order to study audience reaction. Her conclusions about the tastes of children and their behaviour in the cinema were published in her book *Good Company* (1952), the theme of which was characteristic of her well-balanced nature.

In appearance she was tall, dark until advancing years changed her colouring; she added to her stature by wearing her hair dressed high on her head. In manner she was friendly and with a pleasant eagerness; she was receptive to ideas, she listened. Friends recall with amusement that this highly professional woman had a taste for hats of an extravagance at variance with the scholarly sobriety of her work.

In addition to *Good Company* she wrote several other books and educational articles about films for children. She was president of the British Federation of Business and Professional Women, and president emeritus of UNESCO's International Centre of Films for Children. She was honorary FRPS, FBKS, and FBFA. She died in Worthing, 23 December 1968. She had no children.

[*The Times*, 24 December 1968.]

DILYS POWELL

FINCH, GEORGE INGLE (1888-1970), physicist, was born at Orange, New South Wales, 4 August 1888, the eldest son of C. E. Finch, chairman of the Land Court of New South Wales. He was educated at Wolaroi College, New South Wales, his university training being in the main at the Federal Technical High School in Zürich (1906-11). Here he graduated with distinction as D.Tech.Chem. He studied as research assistant both there and later at the university of Geneva. It was at Zürich that Finch also laid the foundation of his distinguished career as an Alpine climber. Finch's career as a research chemist at the Royal Arsenal and a demonstrator at Imperial College, London, was interrupted by World War I. He served in France, Egypt, and Macedonia, was mentioned in dispatches, and appointed MBE in 1917.

Finch's association with Imperial College was renewed in 1919 when he returned as a demonstrator; and he was promoted to a lectureship in electrochemistry in 1921, the year of his marriage to Agnes Isobel Johnston. They were to have three daughters. He was appointed to a professorship in applied physical chemistry in 1936, a post he held until 1952. He served a further five years as director of the National Chemical Laboratory in India; he lived in retirement in Upper Heyford, Oxfordshire.

Finch's initial scientific researches were concerned with the effect of catalysts on the combustion of gases. It was his interest in platinum as a catalyst which led Finch to the study of surface effects which destroyed its efficiency. Here he collaborated initially with (Sir) G. P. Thomson in the use of electron diffraction, which demonstrated the existence of a contaminant on the surface. These investigations led Finch to build a new electron diffraction unit (the 'Finch camera') which initiated a very fruitful period of researches into surface structure and the properties of thin films. Finch's appreciation of the technological aspects of his work showed very clearly in his study of 'Beilby layers' (Sir G. T. Beilby, q.v.) —surface properties produced by mechanical polishing. After an intensive study of this 'liquid-like' layer produced on a variety of crystals, he applied his experience to industrial problems associated with wear in internal combustion engines: this led on to studies of the action of lubricants and to the influence of chemical compounds in lubricants on bearing surfaces.

The study of electrodeposition by Finch and his co-workers began in 1936, the main emphasis being on the mode of growth of the deposit and the adhesion of the deposit to the base. The substrates were found to divide into two categories, 'inert' and 'active'. The former included, in the main, polished metals, the latter, crystalline metal surfaces. Two extreme types of growth were found, 'lateral' and 'outward'. This latter form was due to essentially three-dimensional initial aggregates with relatively poor adhesion and was associated with 'inert' bases. In lateral growth, associated with 'active bases', the initial growth started as a two-dimensional form with a well-defined geometrical relationship between the deposit and the base. This form led to good adhesion.

Finch further investigated the effect of other factors, such as both composition and temperature, on the formation of thick electrolytic deposits. He summarized the general results of his studies at a conference of the Electrodepositors Technical Society in 1951.

During the war of 1939-45 Finch acted from 1941 as scientific adviser to the fire division of the Ministry of Home Security. He was partly concerned with the training of personnel, partly with investigations of fires started as the result of bombing. He initiated a series of studies on the growth of fires in furnished rooms using small-scale models, which was the start of investigations on fire prevention in the construction of buildings. Finch also led a group at Imperial College on the development of incendiary bombs and developed a modified flash bomb used in night photography by the RAF.

The contributions of Finch and his co-workers to physics and to engineering were recognized by his election to the Royal Society in 1938, and by the award of the Royal Society Hughes medal in 1944. He was president of the Physical Society from 1947 to 1949 and appointed Guthrie lecturer in 1950. His scientific services in other countries were recognized in Belgium by his appointment as commander of the order of Leopold II in 1938, and in France as a chevalier of the Legion of Honour in 1952.

Finch's interest in mountaineering began in his schooldays, but became a serious activity during his student period at Zürich. It was here that he developed his mountaineering skills and became recognized as an authority as well as an outstanding personality. He dispensed with guides—his excellent physique, judgement, and meticulous preparation making these unnecessary. His first ascent of the north face of the Dent d'Herens in 1923 was regarded as a classic in opening up this route.

Finch also made an outstanding contribution, with George M. Mallory [q.v.] in the 1922 Mount Everest expedition, both in climbing and as a pioneer in the use of oxygen. He took an important part in the development of the (open circuit) type of apparatus which was used in the attempt on the summit, and with Bruce he led the second climbing post to 27,300 feet. His account of his expedition, *Der Kampf um Everest* (1925), as well as the earlier *The Making of a Mountaineer* (1924) and the later *Climbing Mount Everest* (1930) are well worth reading apart from their interest to a mountaineer. Finch founded the Imperial College Mountaineering Club in 1929, and took a very keen interest in its activities. His services to mountaineering were recognized by his election as president of the Alpine Club in 1959.

He died in Upper Heyford 22 November 1970.

[M. Blackman in *Biographical Memoirs of Fellows of the Royal Society*, vol. xviii, 1972; personal knowledge.]   M. BLACKMAN

FISHER, JAMES MAXWELL McCONNELL (1912–1970), ornithologist, writer, and broadcaster, was born in Clifton, Bristol, 3 September 1912, the eldest son of Dr Kenneth Fisher, a master at Clifton College who later became headmaster of Oundle, and his wife, Constance Isabel, daughter of James Boyd, yarn agent, of Altrincham, Cheshire. Fisher was educated at Eton, where he was a King's scholar, and, from 1931, at Magdalen College, Oxford where he obtained second class honours in zoology in 1935. He served as ornithologist on the Oxford University Expedition to Spitsbergen in 1933, and won the OU Challenge Sculls in 1934. After graduation he taught briefly at Bishop's Stortford College and from 1936 to 1939 was assistant curator at the Zoological Society of London.

Fisher's interest in birds was kindled at an early age by his uncle, Arnold W. Boyd, a former editor of *British Birds*. In the late 1930s Fisher played a leading part in the organization of the British Trust for Ornithology, of which he was honorary secretary from 1938 to 1944. In collaboration with (Sir) Julian S. Huxley he set up the Trust's Hatching and Fledgling Enquiry (subsequently the Nest Record Scheme), a task which involved the co-operation of professional and amateur ornithologists.

In 1939, and again in 1949, Fisher and other young naturalists carried out a survey and count of the breeding populations of the North Atlantic Gannet. In 1938–9 he began a study of the Fulmar, which had greatly increased its geographical range during the previous century. This important work was brought to a wide readership in his book *The Fulmar* (1952).

From 1940 to 1946 Fisher worked in Oxford on the food of the Rook. It was at this time that he wrote some of the books which had such a stimulating influence on popular interest in birds. These were *Birds as Animals* (1939, reissued 1954), *The Birds of Britain* (1942), and *Bird Recognition* (3 volumes, 1947, 1951, 1955). Perhaps his most influential publication was *Watching Birds* (1940, revised by Jim Flegg, 1978) which became one of the best-selling Pelican paperbacks. At a time of general stress these books brought to a wide public a combination of scholarship and an enthusiastic appreciation of the charm of birds.

His primary interest was still in sea-birds, and this took him to many of the islands in Britain and northern Europe where these birds nest. On 18 September 1955 Fisher was lowered on to Rockall from the helicopter of HMS *Vidal*. He was the first professional naturalist to land on this rocky islet, which became the subject of his book *Rockall* (1956).

Disappointed at not succeeding to the directorship of the Edward Grey Institute of Field Ornithology, Oxford, Fisher turned to publishing. From 1946 to 1954 he was natural history editor at Collins, the publishers, and one of the founders of their New Naturalist Library, a series of scholarly books on British natural history.

Fisher's interest in birds as part of the environment led him inevitably, and fortunately, to conservation. During some twenty-five years he made over 1,000 broadcasts, of which about 200 were on television, thus publicizing current research in ornithology and other natural history fields and explaining the aims of conservation. He was for many years on the council of the Royal Society for the Protection of Birds, receiving its gold medal in 1961, and also served on the Survival Service Commission of the International Union for the Conservation of Nature. In 1966 he became a member of the National Parks (later Countryside) Commission and in 1968 was appointed deputy chairman, a post he held until his death. His work was recognized by the award of the Bernard Tucker medal of the British Trust for Ornithology (1966), the Arthur Allen award of Cornell University (1968), and the silver medal of the Zoological Society of London (1969). Fisher was a fellow of the Royal Geographical Society, the Linnean Society, the Geological Society, and the Zoological Society.

James Fisher was a tall, broad-shouldered man and a good climber, an attribute that proved particularly useful in his work on cliff-nesting sea-birds; he was also deeply interested in music. With his infectious enthusiasm and sense of humour it is not surprising that he had a wide range of friends and collaborators. One of these was the American artist and ornithologist Roger Tory Peterson, with whom he travelled throughout the United States, a journey which resulted in their book *Wild America* (1956). Fisher admired the realism of John Clare and the lucidity and precision of Gilbert White [q.v.] more than the aestheticism of W. H. Hudson [q.v.]. Yet he was quite at home with poetry and had an excellent 'feeling' for fine books.

In 1936 Fisher married Margery Lilian Edith, daughter of (Sir) Henry S. E. Turner, formerly of the Civil Service, and later controller of meat and livestock at the Ministry of Food (1940–50); they had three sons and three daughters. Together they wrote a life of Sir Ernest H. Shackleton [q.v.], which was published in 1957. Fisher died in a car accident at Hendon, north London, 25 September 1970. There is a bust by Elizabeth Frink in the possession of the family.

[*The Times*, 28 September 1970; K. Williamson in *Bird Study*, vol. xvii, 1970; R. T. Peterson in *British Birds*, vol. lxiv, 1971; private information; personal knowledge.]

GWYNNE VEVERS

FISHER, SIR RONALD AYLMER (1890-1962), mathematical statistician and geneticist, was born 17 February 1890 at East Finchley, the youngest of the four sons and seven children of George Fisher, of Robinson and Fisher, auctioneers, of King Street, St. James, London, and his wife, Katie, daughter of Samuel Heath, solicitor, of London. His twin brother was stillborn. He was educated at Harrow (1904-9), whence he obtained a scholarship to Gonville and Caius College, Cambridge, graduating as wrangler with distinction in 1912. He spent a further year at Cambridge with the Wollaston studentship, studying statistical mechanics, the quantum theory under (Sir) James H. Jeans [q.v.], and the theory of errors.

Although during his education Fisher specialized in mathematics, he had also at an early age developed strong biological interests, and while at Cambridge he became keenly interested in evolutionary and genetical problems. Financial stringency, however, compelled him to take a statistical post in the Mercantile and General Investment Company, after working on a farm in Canada for some months. On the outbreak of war in 1914 he did his best to join the army, but his defective eyesight prevented this. Instead he spent the years 1915 to 1919 teaching mathematics and physics at various public schools. In 1917 he married Ruth Eileen, daughter of H. Grattan Guinness, MD. There were two sons and seven daughters (one of whom died in infancy) of the marriage. The elder son was killed in air operations over Sicily in 1943.

During the war years Fisher actively pursued his scientific researches, and in 1919 he was simultaneously offered a post as chief statistician at the Galton laboratory under Karl Pearson [q.v.], then at the height of his fame, and a newly created post of statistician at Rothamsted Experimental Station, the largest and oldest agricultural research institute in the United Kingdom. He chose Rothamsted, which he thought would give him much greater opportunity for independent research. In this he was undoubtedly right. While at Rothamsted not only did he recast the whole theoretical basis of mathematical statistics, he also developed the modern techniques of the design and analysis of experiments, and was prolific in devising methods to deal with the many and varied problems with which he was confronted by research workers at Rothamsted and elsewhere. *Statistical Methods for Research Workers*, which first appeared in 1925, and was greatly expanded in later editions, was essentially a practical handbook on these new methods. It made them generally available to biologists, who were not slow to take advantage of them.

While at Rothamsted, Fisher pursued his studies on genetics and evolution, and undertook a series of breeding experiments on mice, snails, and poultry; from the last he confirmed his theory of the evolution of dominance. *The Genetical Theory of Natural Selection*, which was published in 1930, completed the reconciliation of Darwinian ideas on natural selection with Mendelian theory.

In this book he also developed his theories on the dysgenic effects on human ability of selection in civilized communities; the major factor responsible he believed to be the parallel advancement in the social scale of able and of relatively infertile individuals, the latter because of their advantages as members of small families, with consequent mating of ability with infertility. He regarded the reversal of these trends as a matter of paramount long-term importance, and for a time played an active part in the affairs of the Eugenics Society. His immediate practical proposal of family allowances proportional to income was, however, so much at variance with the current thought of the time that he found few followers. Indeed his warnings of the dangers of dysgenic effects on human populations have gone unheeded to the present day.

During these years the importance of his work came to be widely recognized both at home and in the United States. He was elected to a fellowship at Caius in 1920, awarded an Sc.D. at Cambridge in 1926, and elected a fellow of the Royal Society in 1929.

In 1933 he succeeded Karl Pearson as Galton professor of eugenics at University College, London. Both here, and later at Cambridge, he made many further important contributions to the theory and practice of statistical inference. He did not, however, inherit the responsibilities for statistical teaching previously attached to the Galton laboratory: these were assigned to Pearson's son, Egon, as head of a newly created department of statistics.

The Galton laboratory offered opportunities for the experimental breeding of animals which had not been available at Rothamsted. Nor was the study of human genetics neglected. An outstanding practical achievement was the development of the study of the genetical aspects of blood groups; this led to the unravelling of the complexities of the rhesus system, knowledge of which has saved many infant lives.

During these years Fisher continued to live in Harpenden and kept close contact with Rothamsted, finding temporary accommodation there when University College was evacuated at the beginning of the war. In 1943 he accepted the Arthur Balfour chair of genetics at Cambridge, which R. C. Punnett had held until 1940. He was re-elected to a fellowship by Caius, later continued for life, and was elected president of the college in 1956. He retired from the chair in 1957 but remained at Cambridge until his successor was appointed in 1959. He then accepted a research fellowship in the Division of Mathematical Statistics of the Commonwealth Scientific and Industrial Research Organization at Adelaide where he remained until his death 29 July 1962.

During his later years Fisher was the recipient of many honours. He was awarded the Royal medal of the Royal Society in 1938, the Darwin medal in 1948, and the Copley medal, the highest award of the society, in 1956. He was knighted in 1952. He was a foreign honorary member of the American Academy of Arts and Sciences, an associate of the National Academy of Sciences of the United States of America, a foreign member of the Royal Swedish Academy of Sciences and of the Royal Danish Academy of Sciences and Letters, and a member of the Pontifical Academy of Sciences. He was an honorary D.Sc. of London University and also received recognition from several foreign universities.

To those who gained his friendship and respect Fisher was a charming man to work with, stimulating and generous in his ideas. In conversation he brought not only a vast store of knowledge, but also an independent mind of great vigour and penetration to bear on almost any subject. His eccentricities, though sometimes embarrassing, were a constant source of entertainment to his friends. In spite of his frail frame he was physically tough and enjoyed excellent health.

The originality of his work inevitably resulted in conflict with accepted authority, and this led to many controversies, particularly with Karl Pearson and his followers. He could be unforgivably hostile to those who in his opinion criticized his work unjustly. Nevertheless he undoubtedly enjoyed the cut and thrust of scientific controversy. His pungent verbal comments were well known; though frequently made without malice, they were nevertheless disconcerting to those of less robust temperament.

A portrait by A. R. Middleton Todd (1957) hangs in the hall of Caius College, Cambridge. There is an earlier portrait by Leontine Camprubi (1952) in Cox Hall, university of North Carolina. A copy of this hangs in the university of Adelaide.

[F. Yates and K. Mather in *Biographical Memoirs of Fellows of the Royal Society*, vol. ix, 1963; P. C. Mahalanobis, *Sankhya*, vol. iv, 1938; Joan Box, *R. A. Fisher. The Life of a Scientist*, 1978; private information; personal knowledge.]   FRANK YATES

FLANAGAN, BUD (1896-1968), comedian, was born Chaim Reeven Weintrop 14 October 1896 in Hanbury Street, London, the fifth son and the youngest of the ten children of Polish immigrants, Wolf Weintrop, the owner of a barber's shop and tobacconist's in Whitechapel, and his wife, Yetta, or Kitty, Price. The 'Weintrop' became Winthrop on the birth certificate, and Bud's Hebrew names, Chaim Reeven, became Robert. He went to school in Petticoat Lane. At the age of ten he was a call boy at the Cambridge Music Hall, and at the age of twelve he made his theatrical début in an amateur talent contest at the London Music Hall in Shoreditch, performing conjuring tricks as Fargo, the Boy Wizard.

In 1910, inspired by the American vaudeville acts he had seen, he walked to Southampton, and passing himself off as an electrician, sailed on the SS *Majestic* for New York. There he jumped ship, and spent the years that followed earning his living variously as a Western Union messenger boy, in a feather-duster factory, and selling newspapers. He had a one-line part in a play called *The Wild Beast*, and in 1911 he joined a vaudeville act called *Campus Days* which toured America. The following year he acquired a partner, and their double act appeared in New Zealand, Australia, and South Africa.

In 1915 he decided to return to England, and in Birmingham he joined the Royal Field Artillery. In an *estaminet* in the village of Poperinghe in France, he met his future partner, an actor named Chesney Allen, but they did not meet again until after the war. On 21 March 1918, at Vandelle Wood, Flanagan was gassed and temporarily blinded. He was sent to 14 General Hospital in Deauville.

Returning home in February 1919, he formed a double-act called Flanagan and Roy (with Roy Henderson). He had decided to call himself Flanagan as an act of revenge against a sergeant-major of that name who had made his life miserable in the artillery. This act, and another called Flanagan and Poy, were both unsuccessful, and by 1922 he was back in London driving a taxi.

In 1923 the urge to perform reasserted itself, and he walked all the way to Glasgow in search of work. In 1925 he met and married his wife Anne, 'Curly', daughter of Johnny Quinn who was well known in Ireland as the 'Singing Clown'. In 1926 their son, Buddy, was born. 1926 was the year when he again encountered Chesney Allen, who was then doing a double-act called Stanford and Allen in Florrie Forde's touring revue. They agreed to team up, and Flanagan and Allen, an act which was to endure for twenty years, came into being. It was not immediately successful; in fact, at one point, so discouraged were they that they decided to exploit a shared passion for horse-racing and became bookmakers.

But the act was improving all the time; Chesney Allen's patient dignity, perfectly wedded to Bud's gleeful roguery, was beginning to delight audiences, and in 1927 they attracted the attention of Valentine Charles Parnell, booking manager to the Variety Theatre Controlling Company and later director of the mighty Moss Empires, whose principal theatre was the London Palladium.

In 1929 Flanagan and Allen made their London début at the Holborn Empire. They were an immediate success, and the following year they appeared in their first royal command performance at the London Palladium, in the presence of King George V and Queen Mary.

Val Parnell had conceived the idea of combining the talents of Flanagan and Allen with those of a group of comedians: Nervo and Knox, Naughton and Gold, Carryl and Mundy, and Eddie Gray, in order to present a new kind of show at the Palladium. The first of these shows was an enormous hit, and soon this riotous assembly of comics was to become known as the 'Crazy Gang', with Bud Flanagan as its undisputed leader.

Between 1931 and 1939 Flanagan and Allen appeared in many shows, some with the Crazy Gang—they included *London Rhapsody* (1931) and *The Little Dog Laughed* (1939)—some without, including *Life Begins at Oxford Circus* (1935), *Many Happy Returns* (1937), and, in 1933, a musical comedy at the London Hippodrome, *Give Me a Ring*.

During the war years they appeared in *Black Vanities* (1941), at the Victoria Palace, and *Hi-De-Hi* (1943), at the Palace Theatre. Between shows, Flanagan and Allen toured the provinces, giving performances for the troops, which included a tour of France immediately after D-Day.

In 1945 ill health forced Chesney Allen to retire from the act, and Flanagan, encouraged by Jack Hylton [q.v.], decided to carry on alone. In 1947 the Crazy Gang reassembled in *Together Again*, and from then until 1959 Flanagan appeared in an extraordinary succession of long-running shows: *Knights of Madness* in 1950, *Ring Out the Bells* in 1952, and *Jokers Wild* in 1954. In 1956 *These Foolish Kings* ran for 882 performances. At last, in 1959, Bud Flanagan, then sixty-three years of age, gave his last performance with the Crazy Gang. In that year's birthday honours list, he was appointed OBE.

Flanagan and Allen appeared in many films. Among them were: *A Fire Has Been Arranged* (1934), *Underneath the Arches* (1937), *Alf's Button Afloat* (1938), *Gasbags* (1940), *We'll Smile Again* (1942), and *Here Comes the Sun* (1945).

He wrote many of his own songs. They include: 'Free', 'Dreaming', and the song with which he is most closely associated, 'Underneath the Arches'.

During three reigns he was a great favourite with the royal family, and between the years 1932 and 1965 he appeared in no fewer than fifteen variety command performances.

He was a tireless worker for charity, both through the Grand Order of Water Rats, and through his own Leukemia Fund, which he initiated as a memorial to his son, Buddy, who died in 1955. Bud Flanagan himself died in a hospital in Sydenham, London, 20 October 1968.

There is a portrait of Bud Flanagan, by Robert O. Lenkiewicz, in the museum of the Grand Order of Water Rats.

[Bud Flanagan, *My Crazy Life*, 1961; Colin MacInnes in the *Spectator*, 25 October 1968; *The Times*, 21 October 1968; *Who's Who in the Theatre*.]   SID COLIN

FLECK, ALEXANDER, BARON FLECK (1889–1968) industrial chemist, was born in Glasgow 11 November 1889, the only son of Robert Fleck, coal merchant, and his wife, Agnes Hendry, daughter of James Duncan, coal clerk. He was educated at Saltcoats Public School and Hillhead High School, but family circumstances compelled him to leave at the age of fourteen. By then, however, his heart was set on a scientific career and, undaunted by the practical difficulties, he set about achieving his ambition in the only way open to him—by entering Glasgow University as a laboratory boy. His keenness to learn brought him to the notice of Frederick Soddy [q.v.]. By attending, first at evening classes and then as a full-time student, he gained an honours degree in chemistry at the age of twenty-two. Later, in 1916, he was awarded a D.Sc. for a thesis entitled 'Some Chapters on the Chemistry of the Radio Elements'. In 1911 Fleck joined the university's teaching staff under Soddy, continuing his work on the chemistry of the radioactive elements, which foreshadowed the later conception of isotopes. Much later, he contributed the notice of Soddy (in addition to that of Sir W. A. Akers) to this Dictionary. In 1913 he joined the staff of the Glasgow Radium Committee with his own laboratory for radiological work on cancer and seemed set for an academic career.

The war of 1914–18 changed his plans and in 1917 he went to Wallsend as chief chemist to the Castner Kellner Alkali Company, which was associated with Brunner Mond & Co., and manufactured a range of chemicals for wartime industry. He soon made his presence felt as both an individual and a chemist, and in 1919 he became works manager. With insatiable curiosity, he believed in seeing and trying for himself. An excellent example was over a dispute about working conditions with the process men on the sodium plant. The work was hot and arduous but Fleck spent a week on shift-work doing a process worker's job and thus rapidly won the respect of the workmen.

The formation of Imperial Chemical Industries in 1926, incorporating Brunner Mond with Nobel Industries, the United Alkali Company, and British Dyestuffs Corporation, had a significant effect on Fleck's career, for it gave his talents wider scope. One result of the merger was to concentrate the activities of the Wallsend works, the Allhusen works at Gateshead, and the Cassel Cyanide works at Maryhill, Glasgow, on one new site at Billingham. This was later called the Cassel works and became one of the principal factories of ICI's General Chemicals Division. Fleck was transferred to Billingham with responsibilities for the planning and operation of the new works. Although there were many technical difficulties, the human problems were greater, for families had to be moved from Glasgow and Tyneside. The fact that most of those who were transferred settled happily, with no wish to return to the Clyde or the Tyne, was clear evidence of Fleck's success in dealing with human problems.

In 1931 Fleck was appointed managing director of the General Chemicals Division with its headquarters in Liverpool. He returned to Teesside as chairman of the Billingham Division in 1937—one of the world's great centres of chemical manufacture. It was an important target during the war of 1939–45 and attracted well over a hundred high-explosive bombs. Fleck's daily meetings with his directors and works managers were an inspiration to all to keep the factory in operation, whatever the difficulties. In 1944 he was appointed to the ICI board but did not relinquish his highly successful chairmanship of the Billingham Division until the war ended. As an ICI director, his main responsibilities were the Billingham Division, Central Agricultural Control—the company's organization for marketing agricultural products—and the development of the new Wilton site on Teesside. He was chairman of Scottish Agricultural Industries from 1947 to 1951. He was appointed a deputy chairman of ICI in 1951 and, two years later, at the age of sixty-three, he was elected chairman, a post which he held until his retirement in 1960.

In this high office Fleck remained unspoilt and unchanged, always courteous and approachable, with a fine sense of humour and an engaging sense of the ridiculous. Wherever he went in the company—and he travelled widely —he was respected for his scientific acumen, his quietly firm leadership, but, above all, for his deep interest in people. He was always a great source of encouragement to the company's younger members, while he himself liked to hear their own views so that his thoughts about the future direction of ICI did not become outdated. Thus, as ICI's chairman, he was no distant figurehead—rather 'he was and was seen to be the wise father of a very large family' (Sir Peter Allen). He was best in this role at the twice-yearly meetings of ICI's Central Council when he presided over a gathering of some 500 representatives of the employees with a firmness moderated by geniality and understanding, which evoked the best from all present. He also enhanced the value of these meetings by initiating the practice of giving a full account of the company's fortunes in his opening addresses.

Despite Fleck's preoccupation with ICI it was astonishing how much else he was able to achieve. From 1953 to 1955 he was chairman of the Coal Board Organization Committee; from 1957 to 1958 of the Prime Minister's Committee on the Windscale Accident; and from 1958 to 1965 of the Scientific Advisory Council. He chaired a government committee on the fishing industry which reported in 1961, and in 1958 he was president of the British Association for the Advancement of Science—most appropriately, the annual meeting was held in Glasgow where Fleck unveiled a plaque commemorating the work of Soddy.

During his chairmanship of ICI his ties with the university world were re-established. Honorary degrees were conferred on him by several universities—LLD (Glasgow), and D.Sc. (Durham) in 1953; D.Sc. (Nottingham) in 1955, D.Sc. (Oxford) in 1956, D.Sc. (London) in 1957, and D.Sc. (Trinity College, Dublin) in 1958. He was elected a fellow of the Royal Society in 1955, becoming treasurer and vice-president of the Society in 1960. He was elected an honorary fellow of the Royal Society of Edinburgh and of the Manchester College of Science and Technology in 1957. One of his most treasured honours was to be made a freeman of Saltcoats, his boyhood home.

Characteristically, Fleck marked his retirement by establishing four Fleck awards to be given to young people in ICI who showed promise. From 1960 to 1962 he was president of the Society of Chemical Industry, and he retained his directorship of the Midland Bank, to which he had been appointed in 1955. From 1960 to 1965 he was chairman of the

Nuclear Safety Advisory Committee. In 1963 he became chairman of the International Research and Development Company and president of the Royal Institution. Fleck was awarded the Castner medal in 1947 and the Messel medal in 1956.

To the recognition he gained in industry and in the academic world were added other high honours. He was appointed KBE in 1955—for services to the Ministry of Fuel and Power—and was created a baron in 1961.

In 1917 Fleck married Isabel Mitchell (died 1955), daughter of Alexander Kelly, a farmer. There were no children of the marriage. Fleck died 6 August 1968 in Westminster Hospital, London.

There are two portraits of Fleck: one, painted by Lawrence Gowing in 1957, is in the National Portrait Gallery, and the other, painted by Edward Halliday (1960), is in Imperial Chemical House.

[*The Times*, 7, 9, 10, and 13 August 1968; private information; personal knowledge.]

C. M. WRIGHT

FLEMING, IAN LANCASTER (1908-1964), writer, was born in London 28 May 1908, the second of the four sons of Valentine Fleming, who became Conservative member of Parliament for South Oxfordshire in 1910 and was killed in France in 1917, when he was posthumously appointed to the DSO. His mother was Evelyn Beatrice St. Croix, daughter of George Alfred St. Croix Rose, JP, of the Red House, Sonning, Berkshire. She was ambitious for her sons and her dominant personality was perhaps in some part responsible for Ian Fleming's early lack of confidence. Peter Fleming, the traveller and writer, was his elder, Richard Fleming, merchant banker, a younger, brother. Ian Fleming was educated at Eton where he was overshadowed by Peter's brilliance but proved an outstanding athlete, becoming victor ludorum two years in succession, a feat only once equalled. By the wish of his mother he entered the Royal Military College, Sandhurst, but he withdrew in the following year and continued his education privately in Austria, Germany, and Switzerland.

Having failed to enter the Foreign Office in 1931, he joined Reuters news agency and in 1933 reported the historic trial in Moscow of some British engineers on charges of espionage and sabotage, an experience he was not to forget. Between 1933 and 1939 he worked successively as a banker and a stockbroker in the City of London. Throughout the war he held a key position in the Naval Intelligence Division in Whitehall as personal assistant to the director of naval intelligence, rising to the rank of commander. His particular interest was the organization of 30 Assault Unit dedicated to the task of seizing material of value to intelligence. Soon after demobilization he became foreign manager of the Kemsley group of newspapers, and continued to hold the post after Roy Thomson (later Lord Thomson of Fleet) acquired the concern, resigning finally at the end of 1959. For the last years of his life he worked only as a writer. In 1952 he had married Anne Geraldine Mary, eldest daughter of the Hon. Guy Lawrence Charteris, son of the eleventh Earl of Wemyss, and divorced wife of the second Viscount Rothermere. The Flemings' only child, a son, was born in that year.

The wedding had taken place in Jamaica, where Fleming had built a house in 1946, and where it was to become his habit to spend the winter months working on the successive adventures of his famous creation, the secret agent James Bond ('007'). Beginning with *Casino Royale* in 1953, one of these books appeared every year until 1966. The success of the series, though immediate, was not overwhelming until the publication in 1958 of *Dr. No*, the first of his books to be filmed. Thereafter his economic position and his world-wide fame were assured.

On the publication of *Casino Royale* it was apparent to many that a remarkable new writer had arrived on the scene, in the tradition of Buchan, Dornford Yates, and Sapper [qq.v.], although at that stage almost certainly more promising than any of these had been. Original in construction, the book contained many of the elements which were to become Fleming's hallmark: evident familiarity with secret-service activities (not least those of his country's enemies), portrayal of the kind of rich life to be found in exclusive clubs, smart restaurants, and fashionable resorts, obsessive interest in machines and gadgets and in gambling, an exotic setting, a formidable and physically repulsive villain, a strong sexual component, a glamorous and complaisant but affectionate heroine, and—of course—James Bond himself. Bond, at any rate on the surface, was a carefully constructed amalgam of what many men would like to be—and of what perhaps rather fewer women would like to meet: handsome, elegant, brave, tough, at ease in expensive surroundings, predatory and yet chivalrous in sexual dealings, with a touch of Byronic melancholy and remoteness thrown in.

Some would say that Fleming never surpassed, perhaps never quite equalled, his achievement in *Casino Royale*. Certainly there is a power and freshness about the book which, in an age less rigidly hierarchical in its attitudes to literature, would have caused it to be hailed as one of the most remarkable first novels to be published in England in the previous thirty years. Yet, as the series continued, the author extended and deepened his range, attaining a new pitch of ingenuity and technological inventiveness while discovering in himself a gift for descriptions of landscape and of wild life, in particular birds and sea-creatures, pushing out in the direction of a more audacious fantasy, as in *Goldfinger* (1959), and also towards a greater realism, as in *The Spy Who Loved Me* (1962). In *You Only Live Twice* (1964) he produced a striking synthesis of these two impulses, though in narrative and other respects the book was unsatisfactory; and the last volume, *The Man with the Golden Gun*, published in 1965 after his death and written when his health had already begun to fail, was sadly the weakest of the series: it never received his final revision. It was during convalescence from a heart attack that he began to write the children's stories *Chitty-Chitty-Bang-Bang* which were later to be filmed.

It is arguable that *Dr. No* is at least as absorbing and memorable as any of the other books, with its unrelaxed tension, its terrifying house of evil, and the savage beauty of its main setting on a Caribbean island, a locale which Fleming made part of himself and which always excited his pen to produce some of his best writing. But one cannot forget *Moonraker* (1955) for the vivid, rounded depiction of its villain, Hugo Drax, and what is probably the most gripping game of cards in the whole of literature, nor *On Her Majesty's Secret Service* (1963) for its idyllic seaside opening and the vigour of its skiing scenes. Indeed, there is hardly a page in all the 3,000 and more of the saga that does not testify to Fleming's ability to realize a unique personal world with its own rules and its own unmistakable atmosphere. His style is plain and flexible, serving equally well for fast action, lucid technical exposition, and sensuous evocation of place and climate; if it falls here and there into cliché or the language of the novelette, it never descends to pretentiousness. The strength of his work lies in its command of pace and its profound latent romanticism.

Fleming travelled widely from an early age and his interest in foreign places is reflected in his journalism, of which two volumes are collected, as well as in his fiction. His pursuits included motoring, golf, bridge, and underwater swimming, but his reading and his cultural interests generally were wider and deeper than might be thought common in writers of his stamp. He acquired an unusual collection of first editions of books which marked 'milestones of human progress'. His friendships were many and enduring. He was humble about his work

and, though totally professional in his approach to his task, did not take himself seriously as a literary figure, perhaps to the detriment of his standing in critical circles.

He died in Canterbury 12 August 1964 less than a month after the death of his mother. A portrait of him by Amherst Villiers was reproduced in the limited, signed edition of *On Her Majesty's Secret Service*.

[Fleming's own writings; John Pearson, *The Life of Ian Fleming*, 1966; *Burke's Landed Gentry*.]   KINGSLEY AMIS

FLETCHER, REGINALD THOMAS HERBERT, BARON WINSTER (1885–1961), politician, was born 27 March 1885, the second son of Nicholas Fletcher and his wife, Dinah Wright. His father, who had been twenty-fourth wrangler in 1873, was for many years professor of mathematics at the Royal Naval College, Greenwich, and Rex, as he was always known, entered the *Britannia* in 1899. He served in the war of 1914–18 in destroyers, seeing action at the Dardanelles, and serving in the Grand Fleet, the Channel Patrol, the Light Cruiser Force, and the Naval College, Dartmouth. After the armistice he served at the Admiralty on the naval general staff as head of the Near-Eastern section, Intelligence Division. He was promoted lieutenant-commander in 1922 and retired from the navy in 1924.

In the meantime he had turned to politics, and although his family background was Conservative he contested Basingstoke unsuccessfully as a Liberal in 1922. He was elected for the same constituency in 1923 with a majority of 348 but lost it at the general election of 1924. Selected as prospective candidate for Tavistock, he nursed it assiduously for three years, and at a by-election in 1928 lost it by only 173 votes to a Conservative VC. But for the intervention of a Labour candidate he would undoubtedly have won, and Fletcher began to wonder whether Labour was not destined to take the place of the Liberal Party. He joined the Labour Party in 1929, but did not stand as a candidate until 1935. Then, at Nuneaton, he turned a Conservative majority of 2,464 into a Labour majority of 5,237.

This notable success led some to think of him as one of the coming men of the Labour Party, but although in it, he was never really of it, and in the House of Commons he spoke almost with the detachment of an independent. He made his name chiefly on naval matters. When war broke out in 1939 he rejoined the navy and was posted to the London docks, where he worked arduously, supervising the fitting of guns to merchant ships. He next became chief staff officer at the Grimsby naval base, where he dealt with east-coast convoys. He now had the rank of commander. On the formation of the coalition Government in 1940 A. V. Alexander (later Earl Alexander of Hillsborough, q.v.) became first lord of the Admiralty and invited Fletcher to be his parliamentary private secretary. Fletcher held the post until the end of 1941, when it was announced that he, with three other Labour members, was to be made a peer to strengthen the Labour Party in the Lords. Fletcher, who could trace his ancestry back to William Fletcher, of Cartmel, at the end of the seventeenth century, in 1942 took the title Baron Winster, of Witherslack, in the county of Westmorland. He soon found himself at ease in the House of Lords, where he spoke his mind, especially on naval matters, with even more independence than in the Commons. He was a joint author of a Penguin Special *The Air Defence of Britain* (1938).

When the Labour Government was formed in 1945 Attlee invited Winster to be minister of civil aviation, which made him a minister of Cabinet rank (but without a seat in the Cabinet), and he was sworn of the Privy Council. The post was in the circumstances important and controversial. Owing to the war, Great Britain had been able to pay little attention to civil air transport, and although Winster's Conservative predecessor, Lord Swinton, had formulated some plans Winster's task was virtually to recreate British civil aviation at a time of American world dominance and rapid technological development. To these inevitable difficulties there was added an unnecessary one—the pin-pricking opposition of the civil aviation group of the Parliamentary Labour Party led ironically by the member who had succeeded Winster at Nuneaton and had unfortunately marked out the Ministry of Civil Aviation for himself. They made it their aim to get Winster removed, and were in the end successful, but in the fourteen crucial months in which he held the post Winster's achievements were substantial and in most respects enduring. He decided to retain Swinton's proposed three airline corporations, but in view of the Labour victory at the polls thought it right to alter the balance of public and private elements in them. In the end the Cabinet, yielding to the civil aviation group, insisted that they should be wholly public; but, while nationalizing all scheduled air transport operations, Winster was able to keep open a wide field for charter operators, and the machinery then devised was sufficiently flexible to permit changes according to the public mood.

Winster inherited a grave dispute with the United States about the right of airlines to pick up passengers freely, a dispute which was not merely hindering the growth of civil aviation but darkening the whole field of Anglo-American relations. The British policy, that of sharing out the traffic in equal proportions, had been called 'order in the air', but Winster agreed to a less doctrinaire and restrictive policy, produced at a conference in Bermuda which has stood the test of time. He personally negotiated the agreements with Canada and Australia.

When Winster took office there were no British aircraft suitable for civil aviation and he skilfully relied on expedients—converted bombers and a limited number of American purchases—while laying with his colleagues sound plans for a new generation of British aircraft. He would have kept some flying-boats in service, but they were abandoned by his successors.

Heathrow had already been selected as the site of London airport but when Winster took office it consisted of only one runway. Within four months the first commercial service had begun from it, and before he left it had already become one of the busiest and best-equipped airports in the world. If his plans had not been subsequently modified, the need for a third London airport which caused so much controversy in the seventies might have been avoided. Heathrow was state-owned, but Winster resisted the nationalization of all aerodromes and encouraged municipalities to build their own.

Winster's policy with regard to the airline corporations and aerodromes was embodied in the Civil Aviation Act, 1946, a major statute whose piloting between Conservative advocates of private enterprise and Labour technocrats and malcontents required considerable skill. When it had received the royal assent, Attlee thought it politic to placate the civil aviation group by removing Winster, and in October 1946 it was announced that he was to be governor and commander-in-chief of Cyprus.

It was not a post Winster would have sought for himself, and he regarded his time in Cyprus as exile. But he did his duty conscientiously, and it was no fault of his that no constitutional progress could be made. Cyprus had been without a constitution since 1931, when the governor's house had been burnt, and it was Winster's task to make some progress towards agreement on a new constitution. But the Greek Cypriots would have nothing short of *enosis*, union with Greece, while the British Government's attitude was that no change in the status of Cyprus could be contemplated. In the hope of reaching some agreement, the political exiles were allowed to return and the Greek Orthodox community was allowed to fill the vacant archiepiscopal see, the choice falling on Archbishop Makarios. A consultative assembly, drawn from representative elements in the island, was set up in 1947 to make recommendations for a form of constitution which would 'secure the participation of the people in the direction of internal affairs'. In reply to Greek Cypriot demands for fully responsible government a dispatch to Winster from the Colonial Office in May 1948 made specific proposals for a legislature consisting of 4 official members, 18 elected by territorial constituencies, and 4 by the Turkish community. The proposals were approved by 11 to 7 in the assembly, but when the seven dissentients refused to take any further part therein, progress became impossible; on 12 August 1948 Winster informed it that it was dissolved, although the British offer would remain open.

Constitutional failure should not conceal the considerable progess which was made economically, socially, and educationally. A ten-year programme of development had been announced in 1946, and Winster particularly interested himself in the improvement of agriculture. But with the breakdown of the constitutional talks he saw no point in remaining in Cyprus and he left in February 1949. He had been appointed KCMG in 1948.

Back in London, Winster took an even more independent line than ever before, and his strictures on left-wing members of his party were biting. He played no further great part in public life, however, and died at his home at Crowborough, Sussex, 7 June 1961.

Fletcher married in 1909 Elspeth, daughter of the Revd Henry Joshua Lomax, of Buxted, Sussex. His wife was delicate and took little part in his public life. There were no children and the title died with Winster.

Short of stature with a ruddy, weather-beaten countenance, Winster enjoyed good wine and food. He was equally at home in the countryside and in the restaurants and clubs of London. He was not an orator, but in private he was excellent company with a rich treasure of anecdotes on which he could draw and a wit which could on occasion be mordant but seldom rankled.

[Personal knowledge.]

IVOR BULMER-THOMAS

FLEURE, HERBERT JOHN (1877-1969), professor of geography and anthropology, was born in Guernsey 6 June 1877, the only son and younger child of John Fleure, a member of an old family of Guernsey, Alderney, and Sark ancestry, and his wife, Marie Le Rougetel, of Jersey. John Fleure, accountant to the States, Guernsey, died at the age of eighty-

seven when his son was only thirteen. Fleure lived to be ninety-two; father and son thus had the combined lifespan of 166 years.

Early childhood and youth in Guernsey were periods of great strain consequent on Fleure's very delicate health and blindness in one eye, such that at the age of fourteen home education was all that could be sustained. He read alone in great depth for his years and, when well enough, explored his native island, thus developing at a very early age an intense love of natural history associated with a deep interest in the comparatively new Darwinian theories of evolution. By 1897 his health had somewhat improved and he gained an open scholarship to Aberystwyth University College of Wales. He read zoology, geology, and botany, graduating with first class honours in zoology in 1901. In the following year he was awarded a college fellowship to study abroad and until 1904 he read physical anthropology and marine biology in the Zoological Institute at Zürich. He obtained his D.Sc. Wales in 1904 and returned to Aberystwyth where until 1907 he was first an assistant lecturer and later lecturer in zoology, geology, and botany. In 1907 he was appointed lecturer with responsibility for all teaching of geology, zoology, and geography; after 1908 he was head of the department of zoology and interim head of the department of geology, until in 1910 he became professor of zoology and lecturer in geography.

In 1917 Fleure realized a long-cherished ambition on his appointment to a newly created chair of anthropology and geography at Aberystwyth. It was within the framework of these two disciplines that he felt able to develop his philosophy, advancing widely based concepts of man's physical and social evolution in diverse world environments and periods of time. From his early study of the biological sciences, zoology, botany, and geology, he came first to have a scientific understanding of the physical environment and its ever-changing forms. From later studies in anthropology and archaeology he gained understanding of man's physical and social evolution and inheritance. In geography, then an academic discipline only in its early formative years in this country, he found a subject wherein he could best express his philosophy, investigating the full environment of nature underlying man's progress towards the mastery of nature itself. Through his teaching, the Aberystwyth school associated with his name attained great fame. In 1930 he accepted an invitation to be the first occupant of a newly created chair of geography at Manchester, where he remained until deferred retirement in 1944. He was subsequently Tallman visiting professor at Bowdoin College, Maine (1944-5), and visiting professor at both Alexandria and Cairo universities (1949-50), and in 1946 an honorary lecturer at University College, London.

Fleure was an inspiring teacher and a fluent and elegant writer. His first major work, *Human Geography in Western Europe*, appeared in 1918; and until well beyond his eightieth year his literary output continued unabated, his publications including the Frazer lecture, Oxford (1947), and the Herbertson memorial lecture (1952). He collaborated with H. J. E. Peake (whose notice he contributed to this Dictionary) in the ten-volume series of *The Corridors of Time* (1927-56) and in 1951 he completed a large and classical text on a *Natural History of Man in Britain*.

Fleure was also a far-sighted administrator and from 1917 until 1947 he held office as honorary secretary and honorary editor of the publications of the Geographical Association of which he was president in 1948. He transformed the status and role of the Association and rendered services of immeasurable value to the teaching of geography at all educational levels in this country. He fought tenaciously for his subject and became known to a vast circle of teachers and scholars the world over. Among the many honours which came to him was the fellowship of the Royal Society (1936), the first to be awarded to a professional geographer. He served as president of three sections of the British Association for the Advancement of Science (anthropology, geography, corresponding societies). In his time he was president of the Cambrian Archaeological Association, the Royal Anthropological Institute (of which he was Huxley medallist and lecturer, 1937), the Manchester Literary and Philosophical Society, and the Folk Lore Society. He received the Daly medal of the American Geographical Society; the research and gold medals of the Royal Scottish Geographical Society; and was an honorary fellow of the Royal Geographical Society whose Victoria medal he received in 1946. He was an honorary member of the Italian Anthropological Society and the Hungarian Geographical Society; received the Order of Leopold of Belgium; and honorary degrees from Edinburgh, Wales, and Bowdoin.

Fleure's somewhat frail stature, his humility, and quiet personality concealed an unending store of energy generously expended in a life crowded with services for the community in which he lived. Leisure time in the accepted sense never existed, but he was very much a home lover and with his family an ardent student of music. His deep understanding of, and sympathy with, people in all walks of life, in small no less than larger issues, brought for him a quality of enduring affection which few have the fortune to engender in such measure.

Although he moved to the mainland, Fleure sustained his interest as a Channel Islander to the end of his days. In 1910 he married Hilda Mary, daughter of the late Revd Charles H. Bishop who in his time had served as a Methodist minister in Guernsey. They had two daughters and one son, John Lawrence, who entered the Directorate of Overseas Surveys. Fleure died at his home in Cheam, Surrey, 1 July 1969. There is a portrait by Leslie Garnett at the national headquarters of the Geographical Association where also the Fleure Library perpetuates his name.

[Alice Garnett in *Biographical Memoirs of Fellows of the Royal Society*, vol. xvi, 1970; private information; personal knowledge.]

ALICE GARNETT

FLINT, SIR WILLIAM RUSSELL (1880-1969), artist, was born in Edinburgh 4 April 1880, the eldest son of Francis Wighton Flint, commercial artist, and his wife, Jane Purves. His younger brother, Robert Purves Flint (1883-1947), also became a painter. Flint was educated at Daniel Stewart's College and at the age of fourteen was apprenticed for six years as a lithographic artist to a firm of printers. In the evenings he studied at the Royal Institution School of Art. In 1900 he moved to London to take up a post as illustrator to medical publications. After eighteen months he moved to a part-time job with Dickinson's, the paper makers, spending half the week studying at Heatherley's. He next spent four years (1903-7) as a staff artist on the *Illustrated London News*.

By the end of this time he was able to become a freelance, graduating from the illustration of magazine stories to books, one of the first of which was an edition of the *Imitation of Christ* in 1908. He illustrated a number of classics for the Medici Society and in 1913 won a silver medal at the Paris Salon for a group of illustrations to the *Morte d'Arthur*.

Flint had exhibited regularly from 1905 in the water-colour section of the Royal Academy. In 1917 he became a full member of the Royal Society of Painters in Water-Colours, over which he was to preside in 1936-56. But he painted also in oils, was elected to the Royal Institute of Oil Painters in 1910 and was elected ARA in 1924 and RA in 1933. He held many successful one-man shows and excellent reproductions of his water-colours made his work widely known. His figure compositions with their gracefully arranged nudes and semi-nudes were attractive but tended to become an over-sweetened formula. In his landscapes, which he painted for preference in Scotland, Spain, or southern France, his ability to render water, sand, and trees with a full control of his transparent medium was especially notable. His drawing was clever and his brush invariably assured. He was a modest and unassuming man, a fine and versatile craftsman, entirely detached from everything that was controversial or experimental in the art of his time. He was knighted in 1947 and in 1962 a retrospective exhibition of his work was held in the diploma gallery of the Royal Academy.

In 1905 Flint married Sibylle (died 1960), sister of (Sir) Murray Sueter [q.v.]. They had one son, Francis Murray Russell Flint, who became a well-known painter. Flint died in London 27 December 1969.

[*The Times*, 30 December 1969; Arnold Palmer, *More than Shadows*, *A biography of W. Russell Flint*, 1943; *Famous Water-Colour Painters: W. Russell Flint*, introduction by G. S. Sandilands, 1928; *Drawings by Sir William Russell Flint*, 1950; private information.]   HERBERT B. GRIMSDITCH

FLOREY, HOWARD WALTER, BARON FLOREY (1898-1968), experimental pathologist and the main creator of penicillin therapy, was born in Adelaide 24 September 1898, the youngest child and only son of Joseph Florey, an Oxfordshire shoemaker who had emigrated in 1885. Joseph's first wife had died in 1886, leaving two daughters, and he married Bertha Mary Wadham, an Australian, in 1889, who bore him two daughters and a son. By 1906 he had built up a shoe manufacturing business with branches throughout Australia. Howard Florey went to Kyre College and St. Peter's Collegiate School, Adelaide. He was clever, hard-working, and determined, winning six scholarships and many prizes. He was also good at games, representing his school (and later his university) at tennis, football, and in athletics. In 1916 he entered Adelaide University medical school, where he was usually first in his class (winning three scholarships). There his critical mind led him to thoughts of research. He qualified as MB, BS, in 1921. In 1918 his father died suddenly, his business was found to be insolvent, and the Florey family was translated from wealth to poverty. Florey's medical studies were secured by his scholarships, but his ambition for research rather than a well-paid post in Adelaide was maintained with some personal misgivings. In 1921 he was awarded a Rhodes scholarship and, having qualified in medicine, he worked his passage to England as a ship's surgeon, arriving 24 January 1922.

In Oxford, Florey enrolled in the Department of Physiology under Sir Charles Sherrington [q.v.], and at Magdalen College. Sherrington recognized his drive and creative independence of mind, and became his most influential guide and friend. In 1923 Florey obtained a first class in the honour school of physiology, then stayed on, at Sherrington's invitation, to study the blood flow in the capillaries of the brain. He made some discoveries and devised a method for inserting transparent windows in living tissues which he later used in various parts of the body to answer questions by direct, simple observation. In October 1924 he moved to Cambridge as John Lucas Walker student in the Pathology Department under Professor H. R. Dean who, with Sherrington, felt that a more experimental approach to pathology could be achieved by an active young physiologist. Florey had spent the summer vacation with the third Oxford University Arctic Expedition as medical officer, and though it provided no major excitements, he never forgot this experience of human comradeship and of the colourful beauty of the Arctic. In Cambridge he continued his study of blood-flow changes in inflammation and thrombosis—problems which remained a major interest for the rest of his career. He submitted this work for an Oxford B.Sc. in 1925, and was congratulated by his examiners. In the same year he was awarded a Rockefeller fellowship to go to the United States to learn micro-surgical techniques. He spent three months with Dr A. N. Richards in Philadelphia and then went to Chicago to work out methods for the study of mucus secretion. Since his Arctic expedition Florey had suffered bouts of indigestion. Investigation had revealed a mucous gastritis and, experimenting on himself, he became interested in mucus, the mechanism of its secretion, and its importance in protecting the mucous membranes. It was a line that led by logical stages to his work on penicillin.

While in America, Florey accepted the offer of a Freedom research fellowship at the London Hospital. He took up this post in June 1926, but it proved not entirely congenial since the laboratories were more concerned with routine than research. But he found a collaborator in (Sir) Paul Fildes, with whom he experimented on a treatment for tetanus, and he often slipped away to work for a few days in Oxford or Cambridge. In 1926 he married Dr Mary Ethel Hayter, daughter of John Hayter Reed, an Adelaide bank manager, whom he had known as a medical student in Adelaide. London life suited neither of them, and when Florey was offered the Huddersfield lectureship in pathology at Cambridge he returned eagerly in October 1927 to the same room which he had occupied before going to America. He now had a new laboratory boy—

the fourteen-year-old Jim Kent, who was to stay as his indispensable and devoted assistant for the next forty-one years, and who contributed so much to the success of his research projects. Florey had become a fellow of Gonville and Caius College and its director of medical studies, but he had (or made) ample time for research. He had embodied work on the flow of blood and lymph, in a thesis for a Cambridge Ph.D. which was conferred in 1927. During the next four years he began several fruitful lines of study and with various collaborators published twenty scientific papers. One of these lines in particular had momentous consequences. In 1922 (Sir) Alexander Fleming [q.v.] had accidentally discovered an agent in mucoid secretions which dissolved certain bacteria. He called it 'lysozyme' and supposed that it might normally prevent infection. It proved, however, to act only on relatively harmless bacteria, and little further work was done on it. Florey took up lysozyme in 1929, because he thought that its presence in mucus might explain an antibacterial action he had observed and also the natural immunity of some animals. He studied lysozyme in animals, publishing two papers in 1930. Though the results did not suggest that lysozyme was necessary to natural immunity, Florey retained a determination to discover its nature and mode of action.

In 1932 Florey was appointed Joseph Hunter professor of pathology at Sheffield University, a choice which surprised orthodox pathologists who still considered him a physiologist. However, there were experienced pathologists in the department who could maintain the routine work while Florey infused vitality into the teaching and research. One of his projects was on the control of the spasms in tetanus by curare combined with mechanical artificial respiration—the basis of the modern treatment. He made important advances in the field of gastro-intestinal function. Lysozyme remained a major interest, although one constantly frustrated by the lack of adequate biochemical collaboration.

In 1934 the chair of pathology in Oxford became vacant on the death of Georges Dreyer [q.v.]. Florey was appointed in 1935, being strongly supported by (Sir) Edward Mellanby [q.v.], secretary of the Medical Research Council. The Sir William Dunn School of Pathology, designed by Dreyer himself on a grand scale, had become something of a mausoleum. Florey came into this partial vacuum with Dr Beatrice Pullinger (from Sheffield) and Jim Kent. Between them they brought the department to life at all levels— teaching, research, and technical assistance. They were hampered by lack of money and Florey had to spend much time in fund-raising.

The Medical Research Council and the Rockefeller Foundation were his main benefactors, but the sums obtained now seem absurdly small. There was little to be had from the university, and Florey was disappointed that pre-clinical departments like his own did not receive any substantial help from the £2 million Nuffield benefaction which was mostly spent on clinical research and teaching at the Radcliffe Infirmary.

Florey brought his department to life largely by attracting young postgraduates who had their own grants. The quality of their research and his own work attracted others and within a few years the Oxford School of Pathology was among the best in the world. Florey expanded his own lines of research to include these new recruits, forming teams in which each contributed some special expertise, and over which he kept a general but not authoritarian control. One such project was the study of the lymphocyte; another was gastro-intestinal function; a third was the study of the micro-circulation by cine-photography. But the most productive of all—perhaps of all time— was the work which led to the practical use of penicillin.

Florey had interested a biochemist, E. A. H. Roberts, in lysozyme, who purified it by 1937. He had also engaged a young refugee biochemist, (Sir) Ernst B. Chain, and asked him to discover how lysozyme dissolves bacteria. Chain found that it is an enzyme which attacks a specific bacterial structure. Reviewing the literature on lysozyme, Chain read the paper by Fleming, published in 1929, describing the chance discovery of a penicillium mould that apparently dissolved bacteria. Since this 'penicillin' (as Fleming called the active agent) attacked a wider range of bacteria than lysozyme, Chain was interested. He found many earlier reports of the antibacterial action of other moulds and organisms, but he also found an actual culture of Fleming's mould in the School of Pathology, with which he began experiments in 1938. Florey had not been particularly interested in penicillin, even though Dr C. G. Paine in his own department in Sheffield had tried it locally, with some success, on eye infections: he had been more concerned with the antibacterial substances produced by the body than by moulds. But he agreed with Chain that a study of such extraneous activities might widen a research which now seemed to be reaching a dead-end in lysozyme, and they decided to work together on three known substances produced by microorganisms, including penicillin. The project was mentioned to the Medical Research Council in January 1939, and again in September, when a request for a special grant yielded £25 and the possibility of £100 later. However, the Rockefeller Foundation granted $5,000 (£1,200) per annum for five years, a considerable sum in those days. Experiments showed that penicillin was the most promising of the substances chosen for study, and might have therapeutic as well as scientific importance. Thereafter the project became a team one. N. G. Heatley undertook the production of the mould filtrate; Chain, later joined by E. P. Abraham, worked on the chemistry, while Florey and Dr Margaret Jennings carried out the animal work and, with Professor A. D. Gardner, the bacteriology.

On Saturday 25 May 1940 there was enough partially purified penicillin to discover if it could protect animals from an otherwise lethal infection—a crucial test. Eight mice were injected with virulent streptococci, and an hour later four of these had injections of penicillin. All four untreated mice were dead in a few hours, all the treated mice were alive and well next day. Florey's remark, 'It looks promising', was a typically laconic assessment of one of the most important experiments in medical history. The results of a large series of such experiments, published in August 1940, completely confirmed the initial promise. Florey tried to persuade British drug firms to produce enough penicillin to treat human cases, but they were already hard-pressed by wartime needs and damage and when he failed he turned his own department into a factory. Descriptions of the physical, chemical, biological, and administrative difficulties fill many papers and books, and all that can be said here is that they were overcome by collaborative perseverance and ingenuity, and by Florey's energy, determination, and personal example. Beginning in January 1941, there was a limited trial under his direction by Dr C. M. Fletcher on patients at the Radcliffe Infirmary, Oxford. The cases chosen were mostly those of otherwise hopeless infection. Though only six could be treated systematically, and even these with restricted doses, the results were practically conclusive. Penicillin had been shown to overcome infections which were beyond any other treatment.

In June 1941, with Mellanby's approval, Florey and Heatley went to the United States to try to enlist commercial help. Florey's old friend, Dr A. N. Richards, promised government support for firms prepared to develop large-scale methods of production, and three accepted. While Heatley remained to assist, Florey returned to Oxford to direct an even greater production effort in his department. This allowed a completely conclusive trial on 187 cases in 1942, largely carried out by Florey's wife. In the summer of 1943 Florey, with (Sir) Hugh Cairns [q.v.], undertook on the battlefields of North Africa a trial of penicillin in the treatment of war wounds, and six months later he went to Russia with information on the new results. Meanwhile commercial production had, at last, begun in Britain, and this revealed that technical methods had been patented in America. Florey was criticized for having 'given away' a valuable commercial asset. But the information which Florey gave in America had been freely offered earlier in Britain, where it was then considered unethical for doctors to patent medical discoveries. Such discoveries continued to be made at the School of Pathology on later antibiotics, and the official attitude to patents had by that time changed. In 1949 a complete account of the Oxford work was published as a two-volume book, *Antibiotics*, by Florey and six of his collaborators. In all, he was also the author or co-author of thirty-two scientific papers and over thirty published lectures and reviews on the subject.

In scientific and medical circles the Oxford achievement had been recognized and applauded. Florey had been elected a fellow of the Royal Society in 1941, before the penicillin work had been established. Thereafter many other honours followed. He was knighted in 1944, and in 1945 he shared the Nobel prize for medicine with Chain and Fleming. The general public, however, tended to regard Fleming as the creator of penicillin therapy. He had, of course, discovered the antibacterial power of a rather rare sort of mould, shown that it was non-toxic to animals, and had used it, without much success, as a local antiseptic in a few cases. He had also suggested that it might be injected locally. But he had not during the next ten years developed his discovery or aroused interest in it, and, in any case, in the 1930s sulphonamides had captured the medical imagination. Fleming had taken no part at all in the Oxford work, although his cultures had prompted it. When the tremendous fact of penicillin therapy became popular news, Florey was unwilling to talk to reporters. Fleming had less reserve, and articles appeared in which he was portrayed as the hero of a long struggle to harness his discovery, producing large amounts of penicillin at St. Mary's Hospital, London, for use there or at Oxford under his direction. Such distortions, continuing uncorrected for many years, created a general impression that only Fleming's name should be associated with penicillin.

After a period of work on the use of antibiotics in tuberculosis, Florey returned in the mid 1950s to his early research interests. He used electron microscopy and marker techniques in new studies of mucus secretion and of vascular changes which can cause thrombosis. As always, he encouraged young workers to participate, and because his interest in the leucocytes was leading into the wider fields of immunology and cytogenetics, his department was ready to move into another new era. Florey, always the best animal surgeon in the department, regularly did long experiments undistracted by his emergence as a public figure. In this latter role he surprised those who had known him as something of a firebrand, since he accepted high official responsibilities with patience and even pleasure. He was concerned with the foundation of the Australian National University, paid many visits to Canberra, and was personally involved with the design, building, and organization of the John Curtin School of Medical Research. Though he refused to become the School's director, he retained his association with the university and was its chancellor in 1965. In 1960 Florey was elected president of the Royal Society, and he brought to it a vitality which rejuvenated what was a rather staid organization and made of its officers and staff a team with a new sense of purpose. A major change was the move from the Society's elegant but cramped quarters in Burlington House to the far more spacious Carlton House Terrace. He also widened the Society's interests to include applied science and demography, and he opened its doors to lively discussion meetings and study groups which extended its already great influence.

In 1962 Florey became provost of the Queen's College, Oxford, and relinquished his chair of pathology. The move puzzled colleagues who thought that, after a life concerned with the clear objectives of science and scientists, he would find the clever meanderings of college politics tiresome. For a time, it seems, he did; but mutual adjustments led to a pleasant working relationship and he was able to contribute practical improvements, as he had done before in every appointment. The college gained its European studentships and the Florey Building, and something of a new outlook. In return, he received the pleasure of a gracious style of living. He had always appreciated the college system in Oxford and Cambridge, and had much enjoyed the fellowship of Lincoln College which he had held since 1935 (he was made honorary fellow in 1962). In 1965 he was created a life peer as Baron Florey and a member of the Order of Merit. He had become a commander of the Legion of Honour, and had received the USA medal of merit, the Royal and the Copley medals of the Royal Society, honorary degrees from ten British and eighteen foreign universities, and other world-wide honours, medals, and prizes.

In 1966 Ethel Florey died after some years of disabling ill health. They had one son and one daughter. In 1967 Florey married Dr Margaret Augusta Fremantle, daughter of the third Baron Cottesloe, and formerly wife of Denys Arthur Jennings. She had worked with him at the School of Pathology since 1936. For some years Florey had suffered from angina, unkown to his colleagues, and it was from a heart attack that he died suddenly in Oxford 21 February 1968.

As a scientist, Florey had an extraordinary flair for choosing expanding lines of research; the ability to reduce a problem to simple questions answerable by experiment; great industry and determination; and an honesty that allowed of no self-deception. Equally important, he could inspire others to work almost as hard and well as himself. He published over 150 scientific papers (excluding reviews and lectures) but the vast amount of experimental work entailed is only revealed by his notebooks. *General Pathology* (1954), the textbook edited by Florey and published in four editions, reflects the progressive teaching at his School. As a person, despite his outward geniality and humour, he was a man of profound reserve. He did not show his deeper feelings and he had few, if any, close friends. Ethel Florey's ill health and, in particular, her progressive deafness, had from the first marred the happy companionship which both had expected from their marriage. Yet she had made a supreme effort to overcome these physical handicaps in her work on penicillin. Outside his own laboratory, Florey's main enjoyment was in travel, which in later years became world-wide. From his first arrival in Oxford in 1922 he took every opportunity to go abroad, working in foreign laboratories, learning languages, and, above all, appreciating the history, art, architecture, and music of the countries he visited. His letters to Ethel before their marriage are full of these experiences, and they reveal him as sensitive, lonely, unsure of himself, and deeply concerned for human troubles—a picture of himself very different from the one he presented to the world. 'I don't think it ever crossed our minds about suffering humanity', he said publicly of his reasons for starting work on penicillin. But in 1923, in a letter to Ethel, he wrote of 'the appalling thing of seeing young people maimed and wiped out while one can do nothing'. He was referring to untreatable infections. He, perhaps more than anyone before him, helped to achieve their defeat.

There is a portrait at the Royal Society, London, by Henry Carr; at the Sir William Dunn School of Pathology, Oxford, by Frederick Deane; at St. Peter's Collegiate School, Adelaide, by William Dargie (1963); and by

Allan Gwynne-Jones (1963) at Adelaide University. There is also a bronze head by John Dowie in Prince Henry Gardens, Adelaide.

[Gwyn Macfarlane, *Howard Florey. The Making of a Great Scientist*, 1979; Lennard Bickel, *Rise up to Life*, 1972; E. P. Abraham in *Biographical Memoirs of Fellows of the Royal Society*, vol. xvii, 1971; personal knowledge.]   R. G. MACFARLANE

FLOWER, SIR CYRIL THOMAS (1879-1961), deputy keeper of the public records, was born 31 March 1879 at Warminster, Wiltshire, the only child of Thomas Flower, who practised medicine there, as his father had done. Thomas Flower, cousin of Henry Fawcett [q.v.], the blind statesman, married Jessie Susan, daughter of William Pope, of Biggleswade, Bedfordshire; he died in 1881.

Cyril Flower won a scholarship at St. Edward's School, Oxford, and entered Worcester College, Oxford, as senior scholar; he obtained a first in classical moderations (1899) and a second in *literae humaniores* (1901) and entered the Public Record Office in 1903.

His first nine years were spent mainly in the legal search room; he joined the Inner Temple and was called to the bar in 1906. He began in 1910 the work on the Curia Regis Rolls which he was to continue for fifty years. In 1912 he moved to the secretary's office to assist R. A. Roberts and later A. E. Stamp. In November 1914 he went to the War Office as a private secretary to the director of contracts; a year later he was commissioned in the Royal Garrison Artillery and went with his battery to France in August 1916. In October he was severely wounded; and, on 'light duty', he returned to army contracts in 1917 and remained there until he was demobilized in June 1919. For his services in contracts he received the croix de guerre.

Returning to his former post at the Public Record Office, Flower also became the legal member and secretary of the inspecting officers' committee which arranged, with the departments concerned, schedules of the records which were to be preserved or destroyed. In 1926 he became secretary of the Office when Stamp succeeded Sir Henry Maxwell Lyte [q.v.] as deputy keeper; on Stamp's death in March 1938 Flower was appointed deputy keeper by the master of the Rolls, the statutory keeper of the records. In October the Office celebrated the centenary of the Public Record Act of 1838. Flower was appointed CB the following January.

His nine years as deputy keeper included the six wartime years. The dominating problem in 1938 was the safety of the records and the

protection of the Office in the event of air attacks. Flower could not bring himself to believe that war was imminent or inevitable, but plans were made for evacuating records to several temporary repositories in the country, and for instructing staff in ARP services. Evacuation of the records began apace in late August 1939 and continued with breaks until 1942; some two thousand tons of records were dispatched from Chancery Lane and the repository for modern records at Canterbury to seven centres in the country ranging from the jail at Shepton Mallet in Somerset to Belvoir Castle in Lincolnshire. Flower kept in touch with the Office custodians there and visited most of them. The records remaining at Chancery Lane were assembled on the lower floors. With this large-scale dispersal of the records, the closing of the literary search room, and the departure of many members of the staff to military service or to other government offices, the staff remaining at Chancery Lane were organized mainly on an ARP footing. Flower took more than his share in this arduous business, patrolling the vast building during 'alerts' and spending at least one night a week on this duty.

Although situated in a heavily bombed area, the Public Record Office escaped serious damage throughout the war; and the records remaining there and those in the country repositories were intact. Flower was unwilling to reassemble them before Japan was out of the war. The work began in earnest in September 1945 and in June 1946 he was able to report to the master of the Rolls that the records had returned safely to the strongrooms at Chancery Lane; the modern records formerly at Canterbury were lodged temporarily in some of the wartime 'deep shelters' in the London area.

As chairman of a depleted inspecting officers' committee Flower co-operated with departments under pressure from the paper shortage committee in preparing new schedules to shorten the periods for retention of documents. On the other hand, as the executive member of the Historical Manuscripts Commission and chairman of the British Records Association's council, he was much involved in their efforts to prevent documents of historical importance in private hands from being swept away in the drive for salvage. Another of his official activities was his membership of the committee for the control of official histories of the war; and he succeeded R. A. Butler (later Lord Butler of Saffron Walden), then president of the Board of Education, as chairman of the editorial board of the official medical history of the second war.

Another institution under Flower's charge

during the war was the Institute of Historical Research of which he was honorary director from 1939 until 1944, arranging for the several compulsory wartime moves of the Institute, its library, and stocks of the Victoria County History.

His connections with learned societies were many: fellow of the Society of Antiquaries from 1921 and vice-president in 1939-43; secretary of the Canterbury and York Society in 1906; treasurer of the Pipe Roll Society from 1938. He served on the council of the Selden Society from 1937 and was president in 1949-52; for the society he edited *Public Works in Mediaeval Law* (vol. xxxii, 1915, vol. xl, 1923) and prepared an *Introduction to the Curia Regis Rolls, 1199-1230* (vol. lxii, 1943).

His major contribution to scholarship was his transcription and editing of the Curia Regis Rolls. *Curia Regis Rolls, Vol. I, Richard I.-2 John*, delayed by the first war, was published in 1922, the fourteenth volume (1230-32) in 1961. There remained in manuscript his transcripts (with assistance latterly from former colleagues) for a further twenty years, already indexed. Medievalists over the decades welcomed this important series and reviewers were particularly appreciative of the elaborate indexes. Flower was a first-rate compiler of indexes, especially of subject indexes.

He was knighted in 1946 and elected FBA in the following year. He retired in 1947 on his sixty-eighth birthday, after forty-four years in the Office, of which the last nine were the most strenuous.

Flower married in 1910 Helen Mary Harding, daughter of David William Thompson, an Irishman, and a retired inspector of schools in the Punjab; they had one daughter. On his marriage Flower moved from his mother's house in Ealing to the house next door. A church-warden and a manager of the local Church of England schools for forty years, Flower was in politics as in outlook unshakeably conservative. He played rugby for school and college, and for Middlesex in 1904-6: a fourteen-stone forward, over six foot two 'and fast for a big man'. Despite his severe wounds and some deafness he continued to live an active life, retained an equable temper and remarkably good health up to the end. He died peacefully in his sleep at his home in Ealing 9 August 1961.

[Sir David L. Evans in *Proceedings* of the British Academy, vol. xlviii, 1962; personal knowledge.]   DAVID L. EVANS

FOLLEY, (SYDNEY) JOHN (1906-1970), biochemist, was born at Swindon, Wiltshire, 14 January 1906, the younger child and only son of Thomas John Folley, who served for more than forty years as an engine fitter in the Great Western Railway Running Shed at Swindon, and his wife, Katie Baggs. Folley's parents were anxious to make it possible for their children to take full advantage of every educational opportunity and they must have felt well rewarded for their sacrifices for Folley's scholastic career was brilliant. For six years he attended the Swindon and North Wilts. Secondary School and Technical Institution, being awarded an exhibition at Hulme Hall, Manchester University, in 1924. In 1927 he obtained a first class honours degree in chemistry at Manchester University, coming out at the head of the list.

Folley's first research was in colloids under D. C. Henry's direction, from which he obtained an M.Sc. He then changed to biochemistry, and joined the biochemical laboratory of H. S. Raper, Brackenbury professor of physiology at Manchester. In 1931 he was awarded the degree of Ph.D. (Manchester) for a thesis on plastein and was then appointed assistant lecturer in biochemistry in the university of Liverpool. In 1932, on Raper's recommendation, he was appointed research assistant in the physiology department at the National Institute for Research in Dairying at Shinfield, Reading. He stayed in this department, becoming its head in 1945, working almost entirely on the physiology of lactation, until his death.

His work on lactation developed along three main lines: the metabolic aspects of milk formation, the endocrinological aspects of mammary growth and milk secretion, and the neurophysiology of milk secretion. The early work of the physiology department was necessarily confined to small laboratory animals, mainly rats and guinea-pigs, and to such cows as could be made available by other departments. About 1937 Folley realized the value of goats as prototype ruminants for lactational research, and during 1938 and 1939 he started to build up a herd of British Saanen goats, which played a major part in the department's work on the mammary gland.

The work on the metabolic aspects of lactation started immediately after his arrival in Shinfield, first, on the relation between blood electrolytes and the lipid constituents of milk; secondly, on the alkaline phosphatase of the mammary gland, and later on endocrinological aspects of lactation in which his interest had been aroused by contact with (Sir) Alan S. Parkes. The outbreak of war in 1939 kept applied research of this kind in the forefront for many years. In the late 1940s, however, Folley studied the respiratory metabolism of slices of mammary gland from ruminants and non-ruminants using [14]C. The results contributed significantly to knowledge of mammary metabolism.

Folley's first work on the endocrinology of lactation arose from the finding in laboratory animals that oestrogen inhibited lactation, but he discovered that in cows the inhibition was only temporary and was accompanied by very prolonged increase in the concentration of milk solids, a phenomenon which he called the 'enrichment' effect. The preparation by (Sir) E. C. Dodds and his colleagues of di-ethylstilboestrol and related artificial oestrogens, soon to be available in large quantities, enabled observations on oestrogenized cows to be carried out on a much larger scale as a wartime project. However, the work did not get beyond the pilot experiment stage.

Another wartime project arose from Folley's work on the effects of thyroxine and iodinated casein in increasing milk production, but, as with the oestrogen work, no worthwhile results in terms of over-all milk supply were obtained. Folley's interest in the hypophysical lactogenic hormone prolactin arose from his meeting with (Sir) F. G. Young, the first fruit of which was the idea that lactogenesis involved a complex of anterior hypophysical hormones, of which prolactin and adrenocorticotrophin were the most important. Much of the work at Shinfield in the 1960s dealt with prolactin secretion and the milk-ejection reflex involving oxytocin, the secretion of which was found to be stimulated by suckling or other stimulation of the udder and, in conditioned animals, by auditory and visual signals associated with milking-time.

In his undergraduate days Folley was something of an athlete, representing Manchester University at cross-country running and being secretary of the Swimming Club. It is a sad irony, therefore, that for much of his life he had to struggle with physical disabilities—attacks of tuberculosis in 1931 and 1938, and in 1946 a severe deterioration in vision. By April 1959, following a disastrous operation, he became almost totally blind at the age of fifty-three. This stunning blow would have incapacitated many people permanently, but his dogged resolution and fortitude enabled him to carry on to a surprising extent.

Folley had wide interests outside science, mainly in the arts. In his own words: 'For many years I have been interested in the arts, particularly music, painting, ballet, cinema, architecture, etc. and I have formed collections of drawings and paintings by contemporary French and English painters and of gramophone records for the reproduction of which I have assembled a fine electrical reproducer.' There can be no doubting Folley's intellectual capacity and the value of his contributions

to science. When he joined the Institute in 1932, the newly established department of physiology at Shinfield was housed in a converted back-bedroom of the old manor house. When he died at Reading Hospital, 29 June 1970, after having been head for twenty-five years, the department occupied a prominent place in world research on the physiology of lactation.

Among his many honours were his fellowship of the Royal Society (1951) and his honorary doctorate of the university of Ghent (1964). He was a member of many learned societies and advisory bodies—for example, the Medical Research Society's committee on human fertility (1945-7) and the World Health Organization's scientific group on lactation (1963). He wrote numerous scientific papers and reviews.

His outstanding quality was his utter devotion to his department and his colleagues in it, a devotion which was wholeheartedly reciprocated. Yet he was in no sense insular or introverted. His wide travels included three visits to the USA and he also welcomed overseas visitors at Shinfield. Although he was unable to handle anything with a light touch, his colleagues outside the department regarded him with respect and admiration, as witness the symposium on lactogenic hormones planned by Ciba Foundation to honour him on his retirement but perforce dedicated to his memory.

He was twice married, first, in 1935, to Madeline, the daughter of Francis James Kerr, of Altrincham, Cheshire, and, then, when in 1947 this marriage was dissolved, to Mary Lee Muntz, the daughter of Canon William Lee Harnett, of Wolverton. There were no children of either marriage.

[Alan S. Parkes in *Biographical Memoirs of Fellows of the Royal Society*, vol. xviii, 1972; personal knowledge.]   ALAN S. PARKES

FORBES, (JOAN) ROSITA (1890-1967), traveller and writer, was born 16 January 1890 at Riseholme Hall, Lincoln, the eldest of the six children of Herbert James Torr, landowner, and his wife, Rosita, daughter of Duncan Graham, of Lydiate, Willaston, county Chester. Her childhood and upbringing were conventional, leaving her with few recollections beyond an early familiarity with horses and an enjoyment of reading. Her marriage in 1911 to Colonel Ronald Foster Forbes which took her to India and Australia ended in divorce in 1917.

Her first book, *Unconducted Wanderers* (1919), describes a journey round the world with a woman friend which terminated in North Africa. There Rosita Forbes made her first contact with the Arab world, in the ferment in which the Middle East had been left by the defeat of Turkey in the war. She met leading personalities in Cairo, Damascus, Beirut, and elsewhere, and laid the foundation of her lifelong interest in Arab affairs. She also planned the adventure on which rests her claim to be taken seriously as an explorer: her journey in the winter of 1920-1 across the Libyan desert to the oasis of Kufra, which lay beyond the frontiers of Italian occupation and within the territory of Sayed Idris el Senussi (later King Idris of Libya). Only one European expedition, that of Gerhard Rohlfs in 1879, had previously visited Kufra.

Rosita Forbes disguised herself as a Muslim, taking the name of Khadija and inventing a Circassian mother to account for imperfections in her Arabic. She had introductions to the Italian authorities, who tried to prevent her moving outside the zone they controlled, and to the sheikhs of the Senussi. She had, too, the good fortune to travel with Ahmed Hassanein Bey, the Egyptian scholar and explorer. Their journey by camel across the desert to the oasis, reached on 15 January 1921, was arduous and at times difficult, the return through Egypt by the Siwa oasis hardly less so, and Hassanein Bey's knowledge of the terrain and personalities concerned was vital to the success of the venture. Rosita Forbes's *The Secret of the Shahara: Kufara* (1921) decidedly under-played her companion's share in the expedition and gave rise to resentments which long persisted.

After her second marriage, to Colonel Arthur Thomas McGrath, in 1921, she continued to use Rosita Forbes as her professional name and to travel as energetically as before. In 1922 she visited the Yemen, again disguised as 'Khadija', and made plans with H. St. J. Philby [q.v.] for a traverse of the Rubʻ al Khali, the then unexplored 'Empty Quarter' of Southern Arabia. The plan was left in abeyance while she undertook a commission to write the life of al-Raisuni, the Moroccan brigand chief notorious for his kidnapping exploits in the early 1900s, whom she visited in his Atlas mountains retreat. *El Raisuni, the Sultan of the Mountains* was published in 1924, by which time Rosita Forbes was on her way to join Philby for the Rubʻ al Khali crossing, with a valuable commission from the *Daily Telegraph* in her pocket. When the British authorities in Aden refused the necessary permits, owing to unrest in the region, she undertook instead an ambitious trek through Ethiopia, accompanied by Harold Jones, a photographer with whom she made a film; *From Red Sea to Blue Nile* (1925) was one of her most successful books. Another visit to the Middle East produced *Conflict: Angora to Afghanistan* (1931); and in 1931 a tour of South America with her husband revealed new horizons. In

1936 she took off from Kabul on a journey through Afghanistan to Samarkand. A judicious combination of social introductions in high places, and spontaneous friendships *en route*, was the typical pattern of this as of other journeys.

Rosita Forbes's travels, recorded in a series of lively books, were interspersed with lecture tours on both sides of the Atlantic, and by rounds of visits in Europe, accompanied by her husband, to the kings, presidents, and other notables. She herself went more than once to India, disturbing the traditional routines of Government Houses and enjoying the anachronistic splendours of the princely states. In London, the McGraths kept house in style, entertaining widely. She was a strikingly handsome woman, affecting the bright colours which suited her dark hair and eyes; as far afield as Aden, British officials had heard of her huge Ascot hats, and librarians of learned societies were amazed by her high heels and sophisticated make-up.

Rosita Forbes played her part in two world wars: she was twice decorated for driving ambulances in France in the first, and in the second she lectured in support of the war effort in Canada, the United States, and Great Britain. In her later years she was attracted to the Caribbean, and in 1939-40 the McGraths built Unicorn Cay on Eleuthera in the Bahamas, which became their permanent home and where her husband died in 1962. Rosita Forbes died at Warwick, Bermuda, 30 June 1967. She left a vivid and highly personal account of her life in numerous travel books, and in two autobiographies, *Gypsy in the Sun* (1944) and *Appointment with Destiny* (1946), which were abridged and reissued as *Appointment in the Sun* (1949).

Although she made no major discoveries, Rosita Forbes was a bold and successful traveller. Her courage and resource were extraordinary, as was her extreme toughness in the exacting conditions of desert travel and her range was world wide. Her achievements were recognized by the award of the gold medals of the Royal Antwerp (1921) and French (1923) Geographical Societies and of the silver medal of the Royal Society of Arts (1924).

A portrait by Stella Bowen is privately owned.

[Her own writings; A. M. Hassanein Bey, *The Lost Oases*, 1925; H. St. J. Philby, *Forty Years in the Wilderness*, 1957; *Burke's Landed Gentry*; private information; personal knowledge.] DOROTHY MIDDLETON

FORBES-SEMPILL, WILLIAM FRANCIS, nineteenth BARON SEMPILL (1893-1965), representative peer for Scotland, engineer, author, and airman, was born 24 September 1893 at Devonport, the eldest in the family of two sons and two daughters of the eighteenth Baron Sempill, soldier and landowner of Craigievar Castle, Aberdeen, and his wife, Gwendolen Emily Mary, elder daughter of Herbert ap Roger of Kington St. Michael, Wiltshire. As the master of Sempill, he was educated at Eton (E. W. Stone's House) and then from 1910 to 1913 served an engineering apprenticeship in the workshops of Rolls-Royce Ltd. at Derby.

When war was declared in August 1914, the master of Sempill—always known as Bill to his friends—joined the Royal Flying Corps as an engineer second-lieutenant at Farnborough, and learnt to fly at the Central Flying School at Upavon. He obtained the Royal Aero Club Aviator certificate No. 922 on 9 September 1914. Combining engineering with flying duties, he transferred from the RFC to the Royal Naval Air Service in January 1916, with the rank of flight commander and on 1 April 1918 to the newly formed Royal Air Force as a lieutenant-colonel. He was then promoted to colonel.

In June 1918 when Sir (William) Sefton Brancker [q.v.] led a two-man 'Royal Aircraft Commission of Great Britain' to the United States with Sir Henry Fowler, chief of munitions production, to advise on aircraft development and production, Sempill went as personal assistant and technical adviser. He learned much about America and even more about how to conduct a mission—which stood him in good stead when, in 1921, he was invited to lead a technical mission to Japan to set up an Imperial Japanese Naval Air Service. As a result the Japanese were equipped with British aircraft, trained by British pilots, and an aircraft factory was built, initially staffed by British design and production teams. Ironically it laid the foundations for Japanese naval air operations twenty years later. Sempill's success in Japan led to his being invited to head similar missions successively to Greece, Sweden, Norway, Chile, Brazil, and Argentina and to be awarded numerous foreign decorations.

Back in England in 1924, Sempill began twelve years of enthusiastic flying as an unofficial ambassador for British aviation at home and overseas. Flying a succession of light aeroplanes he competed—without success—in the King's Cup air races of every year from 1924 to 1930, used light aeroplanes consistently to make weekend visits to friends, in 1925 flew himself to Berlin to lecture, and in 1926 flew in eight hours fourteen minutes from Lands End to John o'Groats in a De Havilland Moth.

Sempill had joined the Royal Aeronautical

Society in 1917; in 1926 he was elected chairman of its council, and, from 1927 until 1930 he was the society's president. His successor, (Sir) Richard Fairey [q.v.], said of him in October 1930: 'Of all the presidents I have served Sempill must stand out as one of the greatest. Thanks to his vigour the society is now immensely stronger than when he first took over.' Out of 137 meetings during his term of office he presided over 135.

Sempill was active in numerous other aeronautical interests—on the Aeronautical Research Council, on the councils of the Air League and the Navy League, as deputy chairman, and then chairman, of the London Chamber of Commerce between 1931 and 1935, as president of the British Gliding Association from 1933 to 1942, and as president of the Institution of Production Engineers from 1935 to 1937. In 1930, 1931, and 1932 he arranged for the German airship *Graf Zeppelin* to fly to England to pick up passengers, first at Cardington and then at Hanworth to take passengers on air cruises. His flights abroad included these: Stag Lane to Dublin and back just before Christmas of 1925, Norway to Aberdeen in 1930, a flight to Australia and back in his Puss Moth G-ABJU in 1934, and in 1936 a non-stop flight from Croydon to Berlin in eleven hours in a British Aircraft Corporation Drone ultra-light aeroplane—and nine hours non-stop back with a tail wind.

Through all of this Sempill lived an active social life centred around the Royal Aeronautical Society and its leading lights of the 1920s and 1930s—Lord Wakefield, Sir (William) Sefton Brancker, (Sir) Richard Fairey, (Sir) Frederick Handley Page [qq.v.], and Peter Ackland.

Colonel the Master of Sempill succeeded his father as Lord Sempill 28 February 1934. He had married in 1919 Eileen Marion, only daughter of Sir John Lavery, RA [q.v.]. By her he had two daughters, Ann, and June, who was killed while driving an ambulance in Kensington during an air raid in 1941. After fighting tuberculosis for many years Lady Sempill died 18 July 1935. In 1941 Sempill married Cecilia Alice, elder daughter of Bertram Edward Dunbar-Kilburn, of Sandford St. Martin, Oxfordshire, and by her he had three daughters. Sempill rejoined the Naval Air Service in 1939 and retired in 1941. He died in Edinburgh 30 December 1965 and was succeeded by his eldest daughter, Ann Moira (born 1920).

A very Scottish, thick-set, figure of medium height—he always wore full Scottish evening dress on all suitable occasions—practical, stubborn, and convivial, Sempill was an enthusiastic propagandist for aviation and 'flying for fun'. He was a sound engineer, an excellent cook who, whenever possible, baked his own bread, and a successful amateur farmer at Dedham in Essex and Craigievar Castle, Aberdeen. Sempill was excellent company and made a host of friends throughout his life.

Among his publications is: *The Air and the Plain Man* (1931). There is a portrait of Sempill, by an unknown artist, in the Royal Aeronautical Society.

[*Journal of the Royal Aeronautical Society*, May 1966; *The Times*, 31 December 1965; personal knowledge.]   PETER MASEFIELD

FORESTER, CECIL SCOTT (1899-1966), novelist, was born Cecil Lewis Troughton Smith in Cairo 27 August 1899, third son and fifth child of George Foster Smith, schoolmaster and author of elementary Arabic textbooks, and his wife, Sarah Medhurst Troughton. Smith took the name Forester for professional purposes in 1923. From an early age he was able to read with ease. With his brothers, he conducted long battles with lead soldiers and naval campaigns with paper ships, drawing up army lists and naval operation orders in Nelsonian style. He frequented the public library, forming the lifetime habit of reading at least one book a day. His omnivorous reading included Gibbon, Suetonius, 'dozens of naval histories', and Harmsworth's Encyclopaedia, besides G. A. Henty and R. M. Ballantyne [qq.v.], Harry Collingwood and Robert Leighton. This, added to rigorous cramming for scholarships at his elementary school in London, revealed the weakness of Forester's eyesight.

A Christ's Hospital scholarship having been withdrawn at the last moment because of the size of his father's income, Forester, aged eleven, joined the fourth form at Alleyn's School. After an unhappy start, he did well enough to be offered some public-school scholarships, settling for an internal offer of two years' free tuition. He moved next to the sixth form (science) at Dulwich College. He was a good cricketer and keen games player.

Between the ages of twelve and sixteen, Forester grew five inches annually. An army medical examination at seventeen revealed a weak heart, precluding his recruitment in 1917. This was an unhappy time for Forester. His vivid imagination enabled him to picture his contemporaries' sufferings 'with terrible realism', sharpening his distaste for civilian complacency. Overshadowed by his eldest brother who had qualified aged twenty, Forester entered Guy's Hospital as a medical student, but he came to the conclusion that he was unfitted for medicine. His thoughts turned increasingly to writing, and the novelist's instinct triumphed over family opposition.

Forester's first attempts at fiction taught him that 'the better part of the work is done before pen is put to paper'. The artistic standard he set himself (he called it 'beauty') was first met by *Payment Deferred* (1926), a compelling narration of a murderer being accused of a crime he did not commit. In 1931 Charles Laughton acted in a successful stage version, and the story was also later filmed. *Brown on Resolution* (1929) collates the themes of the command of the sea, the service of England, and 'the man alone', which dominate Forester's best work. Yet the story has a curious moral; the heroic death of an illegitimate son, after his mother dies of cancer, advances his father's naval career. Forester's best biography was *Nelson* (1929). *Death to the French* (1932) reveals an acute insight into the British army during the Peninsular War. Rifleman Dodd, separated from his regiment, shows the value of Sir John Moore's training. *The African Queen* (1935) convincingly depicts a dedicated woman's love driving a weak man to heroic efforts on England's behalf. This was later filmed and, although the ending was altered, is generally considered to be the best of the various films made of Forester's books.

The General (1936) is a striking study of Lieutenant-General Sir Herbert Curzon, a professional British officer, whose rapid rise to high command in the war of 1914-18 ends during the German offensive of March 1918. The novel stresses Curzon's devotion to duty and unbending sense of honour, without glozing his narrow outlook and sympathies.

During these years Forester was combining the writing of books with journalism; from 1936 to 1937 he was a correspondent in Spain during the civil war, and he was also in Czechoslovakia when the Germans occupied Prague in March 1939.

In 1937, with the publication of *The Happy Return*, Forester created his best-known character, Horatio Hornblower, a sensitive and gifted individual, the flowering of whose talents within the chain of naval command revealed the author's understanding of Nelson's navy, and of seapower. Forester's command of the historical detail of the period was due to his chance purchase, some time previously, of three volumes of the *Naval Chronicle*, a journal published during the Napoleonic wars. Between 1937 and 1962 appeared twelve Hornblower stories, tracing the rise of the hero from midshipman to admiral. The books were written in a terse, effective style, well suited to the portrayal of the self-doubting but self-disciplined Hornblower, whose complex personality was brilliantly evoked. Hornblower's activities were confined, during the thirty years of the stories (1793 to 1823) to the Atlantic, Baltic, Mediterranean, and Caribbean. In *The Hornblower Companion* (1964), which contains a candid account of the creation and writing of the Hornblower books, Forester explained frankly why this was the case: 'These were the only waters with which Hornblower's biographer was familiar while writing about the closing years of the Napoleonic Wars.' One of the Hornblower novels, *A Ship of the Line*, was awarded the James Tait Black memorial prize for 1938.

During the war of 1939-45 Forester, always conscious of the shared British-American heritage, contributed much to British and American propaganda, producing short stories and articles, illustrating the British war effort, for American publication. When America entered the war he was co-opted as an American propagandist and became a familiar figure in the Pentagon. He accompanied a United States warship on one of its missions. In 1943 he was invited by the British Admiralty to sail in the *Penelope*, an experience which resulted in his writing *The Ship* (1943), of which half a million copies were printed and distributed throughout the fleet. The book was a brilliant portrait of trained individuals working as a team. Forester was also a frequent contributor to the *Saturday Evening Post*, in which *The Commodore* (1945) appeared as a serial.

In 1945 the Allied Governments foresaw the possibility of protracted Japanese resistance. Forester, now settled permanently in the United States, was given the freedom of the Navy Department, Washington, with number two priority on air transport. He busied himself with writing 'logistics for the common man', stories about the Pacific war (*The Man in the Yellow Raft*, published posthumously in 1969).

Forester, a shy man, thin-lipped and highbrowed, had a quiet sense of humour. He enjoyed bridge and travel. However, arteriosclerosis curtailed his mobility from 1943 onwards, and a severe stroke in 1964 confined him to a wheelchair. He died in Fullerton, California, 2 April 1966.

In 1926 Forester married Kathleen, daughter of George Belcher, schoolmaster, and had two sons. The marriage was dissolved in 1944. In 1947 he married Dorothy Ellen, daughter of William Foster, ship-broker. A bust by Cynthia Drummond is in the possession of the family.

[C. S. Forester, *The Hornblower Companion*, 1964, and *Long Before Forty*, 1967; *The Times*, 4 and 6 April 1966; private information.]   NEIL HUXTER

FORMBY, GEORGE (1904-1961), comedian, was born in Wigan, Lancashire, 26 May 1904, the youngest in the family of two sons and two daughters of James Booth and his wife, Eliza Hoy. George Hoy Booth was born blind and remained sightless until the age of two when a paroxysm of sneezing during a river trip across the Mersey left him with normal, if weak, vision. His father, a successful music-hall comedian in the Lancashire 'droll' tradition under the name of George Formby, had adopted the name of Formby on seeing the word painted on the side of a railway wagon in Wigan station.

Formby senior had no intention of letting his younger son follow him into the music-halls and, as young George's ambition was to become a jockey, he took the boy away from school at the age of seven and found him employment as a stable-boy in a racing-stable at Bishop's Cannings. He engaged a schoolmaster willing to give the boy an hour's tuition a day for £1 a week, but the teacher became more interested in studying form than in educating the stable-lad, so Formby grew up, and remained all his life, almost totally illiterate.

In 1921, when Formby was sixteen, three events combined to change his life. He grew too big to become a jockey, his father died, and watching a show at the Victoria Palace, London, one evening he saw a comedian made up to look like his father, doing his father's act in its entirety. Taking the not unreasonable view that if anybody was entitled to earn money by copying what his father had created it was himself, he found a management willing to give him a chance and he made his professional début at the Hippodrome, Earlestown. He called himself George Hoy, using his mother's maiden name, saying that he would not use the name Formby until he was top of the bill, as his father had been. In three years he had achieved this and from 1923 he was known as George Formby Junior. The ukelele was a popular parlour instrument in those days and in Barnsley, in 1925, Formby played one on the stage for a bet. For some reason this was wildly successful and from then on Formby stopped impersonating his father and developed his own style.

He soon became an established success in provincial variety theatres. In 1929 he began recording the cheerful, cheeky songs which were a feature of his act, and in the middle 1930s he began making films. He had, in fact, already starred in a film, but it was a silent, five-reel drama of the turf, *By the Shortest of Heads* (1915), made when he was an eleven-year-old stable-lad. In 1934 he made his first comedy talkie, *Boots! Boots!*, in a tiny studio above a garage at Albany Street, London. This was followed in 1935 by a similar low-budget, slapstick comedy, shot between engines revving up in the garage below, *Off the Dole*. The profits earned by these films in northern cinemas so impressed Basil Dean that he signed Formby to a seven-year contract with Ealing Studios.

Then followed the series of well-made and highly successful films which established Formby as an international star: *No Limit* (1935), *Keep Your Seats, Please* (1936), *Feather Your Nest* (1937), *Keep Fit* (1937), *I See Ice* (1938), *It's In The Air* (1938), *Trouble Brewing* (1939), *Come On George* (1939), *Let George Do It* (1940), *Spare a Copper* (1940), and *Turned Out Nice Again* (1941).

At the conclusion of the Ealing Studios contract Formby moved over to Columbia Pictures, perhaps with an eye on the elusive American market, and made *South American George* (1941), *Much Too Shy* (1942), *Get Cracking* (1943), *Bell-Bottom George* (1943), *He Snoops to Conquer* (1944), *I Didn't Do It* (1945), and his last film, *George in Civvy Street* (1946).

Ealing Studios released their films in Russia and Formby became so popular there that in 1943 he was awarded the Order of Lenin. Official recognition came a little later in his own country, and then not for his comic talents but for his strenuous work in entertaining the troops. In 1946 he was made a modest OBE.

In 1947 Formby returned to the stage and made a series of tours abroad. In 1952 he was enjoying a huge personal success in the London production of *Zip Goes a Million* when a severe heart attack forced him into partial retirement, although he continued to make occasional stage appearances and he ventured successfully into television.

In 1924 Formby married a fellow performer, Beryl Ingham, known as The World Champion Clog Dancer, and four years later she hung up her clogs to devote herself, full time, to controlling her husband's career and life; an authoritative role for which she was formidably well equipped. There were no children of the marriage. On Christmas Day 1960 she died. Six weeks later Formby announced his engagement to a schoolteacher, Miss Pat Howson. But on 6 March 1961, three weeks before their wedding, he suffered another heart attack from which he died in hospital in Preston.

The Times obituary said that 'he added nothing to the amateur's range, only perfected his technique'. Certainly Formby's phenomenal success seemed illogical to those seeking a rational reason for it. He was top of the bill at theatres from the age of nineteen, he made over 200 gramophone records, all his twenty-two films made money, for six years running he was named as this country's top box-office attraction, and for ten years he was the highest paid performer. Yet in terms of creative comedy he seemed but lightly gifted. He presented himself as a gormless Lancashire lad, irrepressibly cheerful, surviving and triumphing over circumstances by a mixture of luck and innocent guile. He sang in a squeaky voice, giggled a great deal, grinned vast, toothy grins, scampered through innumerable chases, and played the ukelele-banjo—a dreadful instrument which combined the imprecision of the ukelele with the loudness of the banjo.

But Formby possessed a quality which in his case was more important than depth of originality; he was a born entertainer with an unquenchable urge to beguile. Perhaps helped by the iron control exercised over his private life by his wife, when he made a public appearance his personality and the pleasure he was getting from giving pleasure proved irresistible: it was said that he never once played to a 'bad house'.

And, of course, he was a product of his time. He was essentially a provincial comedian and his public, as his success with Russian audiences would seem to indicate, was the 'proletariat'. In those grim, grey days of depression and imminent war he held out a reassurance that there was a special Providence which took care of simple people, if they were kind-hearted and stayed hopeful. It could be said that during the thirties and early forties the figure of George Formby seemed to ordinary people to ride above the murky waters of existence like a rubber duck; child-like, cheerful, and unsinkable.

[*The Times*, 7 March 1961; John Walley, *George Formby Complete*, 1973; the George Formby Society; personal knowledge.]

FRANK MUIR

FORSTER, EDWARD MORGAN (1879-1970), novelist and man of letters, was born in London 1 January 1879, the only son of Edward Morgan Llewellyn Forster, architect, and his wife, Alice Clara, daughter of Henry Whichelo. His great-grandfather was Henry Thornton [q.v.] of the Clapham Sect, and his great-aunt, Marianne Thornton, left him £8,000 which enabled him to go to Cambridge and be financially independent enough to exist as a writer. He repaid his debt by writing her biography in 1956. His maternal grandfather had been a drawing master and came of a family of artists. When Forster was an infant, his father died, and he was brought up by his mother and a gaggle of maiden aunts in an atmosphere suffused with doting care. His childhood home at 'Rooksnest' at Stevenage was evoked in his novel *Howards End*, but his mother moved in 1893 so that he might go as a day boy to Tonbridge School. He did not admire public schools or their products whom he described as having 'well-developed bodies, fairly developed minds and undeveloped hearts'. His unhappiness there melted and his potentialities appeared only when he went in 1897 as a classical exhibitioner to King's College, Cambridge, where, as he wrote later, 'They taught the perky boy that he was not everything, and the limp boy that he might be something'.

The man who taught him that he might be something was his supervisor, Nathaniel Wedd, who first encouraged him to write. Wedd gave him the confidence to be sceptical of worldly values. (So did Samuel Butler [q.v.] from whom he learnt that although money often distorted men's values, it was nevertheless important and could help them to discover what was really valuable in life.) His other mentor at King's, G. Lowes Dickinson [q.v.], whose biography he wrote in 1934, suggested that the best undergraduate societies were those in which men sought truth rather than victory in discussion. He was an Apostle, and in that society first met the undergraduates, two to three years his junior, who were to form the Bloomsbury set with whom he was to remain always on affectionate terms though preserving a certain detachment. The essence of his undergraduate days is memorably recorded in the first chapter of his second (and his favourite) novel The Longest Journey (1907). He was placed in the second class of part i of the classical tripos (1900) and part ii of the historical tripos (1901).

On leaving King's, Forster travelled in Italy and Greece, countries which meant much to him and symbolized a style of life which he contrasted with the puritanism of northern Europe. He soon began writing short stories which were later gathered together in The Celestial Omnibus (1911) and The Eternal Moment (1928). But in 1905 he found his true medium and published his first novel Where Angels Fear to Tread in which one of the characters, Philip Herriton, was modelled on his friend at King's, the musicologist E. J. Dent [q.v.], just as in his second the undergraduate Ansell was to some extent taken from another friend, Alfred Ainsworth. His third novel, set in Italy, A Room with a View, appeared in 1908 and Howards End followed in 1910. In 1912 he went with Lowes Dickinson for the first time to India. At this time when living with his mother at Weybridge he published little. He began a novel on India and another entitled Arctic Summer but got stuck in both after the first few chapters. Another, Maurice (1971), completed in 1914, came easily; but it was then unpublishable and he chose to allow it to appear only after his death. It is about homosexuality and Forster defiantly gave it a happy ending.

Forster asked his biographer not to dissemble about his private life. He in no way resembled Oscar Wilde [q.v.] or sought the milieu of international homosexuals: he longed only for a loving and stable relationship with someone not of his own class. This was denied him until the 1930s when he achieved such a relationship which endured with great happiness until his death. His homosexuality made the Greek poet, C. P. Cavafy, especially sympathetic to him when they became acquainted during the war, when Forster was serving with the International Red Cross in Alexandria, and he took pride in being the first to promote Cavafy's reputation in England in Pharos and Pharillon (1923).

In 1921 Forster returned to India where he became the private secretary of the Maharaja of Dewas State Senior, a curious experience which he described in The Hill of Devi (1953). This second visit had the effect of releasing what was to be judged his masterpiece, A Passage to India (1924). It was awarded the Femina Vie-Heureuse and James Tait Black memorial prizes; and it led to his being invited to give the Clark lectures at Cambridge entitled Aspects of the Novel (1927), his most substantial piece of literary criticism. He continued to write criticism and biographies, and became a notable broadcaster. These essays and talks were collected in Abinger Harvest (1936) and Two Cheers for Democracy (1951). The latter reflects Forster's growing concern during the thirties and forties with political and social questions. He was twice president of the National Council for Civil Liberties, the liberty of the individual being the political cause nearest his heart. Despite his distaste for politics he thought it his duty to join other artists in the International PEN Club and protest against Nazism; he displayed more judgement than many of them in discerning what issues were at stake. After the war he helped to write the libretto of Benjamin Britten's opera Billy Budd and saw three of his novels dramatized for the stage. He became the sage of humanism.

When his mother died in 1945 Forster had to leave Abinger Hammer where for the past twenty years he had lived. He had been a fellow of King's in 1927-33 and in 1946 was elected an honorary fellow and invited to make his home there; he moved into the set of rooms which Wedd had occupied. Life at King's enabled him to make friends among each new generation of undergraduates. Friendship had always meant much to him. T. E. Lawrence and Siegfried Sassoon [qq.v.] in the period between the two wars were particularly close, and he knew Thomas Hardy, D. H. Lawrence [qq.v.], and W. H. Auden well. On his eightieth birthday at a luncheon, friends from over the world came to honour him, among them George Seferis, the Greek poet and ambassador. Many writers of a younger generation admired him, among them William Plomer, Angus Wilson, and L. P. Hartley. Two of his dearest friends were Jack Sprott, professor at Nottingham University, and Joe Ackerley, the literary editor. He lived at King's until his death at Coventry 7 June 1970. He refused a knighthood, which after the war Attlee somewhat inappropriately offered him, but became a CH in 1953 and was admitted to the Order of Merit on his ninetieth birthday. He received eight honorary degrees.

These honours recognized that, second only to D. H. Lawrence, Forster was the most important British novelist of his generation. His works were translated into twenty-one languages, and his work began to be intensively studied, especially in America where Lionel Trilling's perceptive study in 1944 established his place in the canon. He was particularly venerated in India for his sympathy with the movement for independence and with both Hindu and Muslim culture. Whereas T. S. Eliot [q.v.] was the defender of the Christian and conservative heritage in English culture, Forster spoke for liberal humanism. No one wrote with greater simplicity or originality in defence of such well-worn concepts as liberty, democracy, and tolerance. He was unafraid of the contradictions in life which he believed liberals ought to face: that friendship may mean being hard on friends; that freedom and art depended on money and inequality; that racial prejudice was iniquitous but that it was folly to deny that chasms between cultures and races existed and that the bridges between them were flimsy; that his working-class friends needed houses but that the new housing estates meant the death of rural England and destroyed man's healing contact with nature. But if a choice had to be made he would make it. 'If I had to betray my country or my friend I hope I should have the guts to betray my country.' His works were full of aphorisms: 'panic and emptiness', 'the life of telegrams and anger', 'only connect'.

He distrusted size, pomp, the Establishment, empires, politics, the upper classes, planners, institutions. He put his trust in individuals, small groups and insignificant people, the life of the heart and mind, personal relations. His sense of humour and of the absurd was highly developed. In appearance diffident and his ragged hedgerow of a moustache unimpressive, he could be melancholy and low temperature— he once said 'I warmed both hands before the fire of life, And put it out'; his vitality went into the characters in his novels and his writing. He spent nothing on himself and hardly ever took a taxi. Money was spent on his friends, particularly on the young who came from the working class. He loved music, paradoxically for one who distrusted greatness, Beethoven and the romantics, but also much modern music so long as he could hear passion in it. Sharp though his judgements on people and events could be, and keen though his eye was for pretentiousness or anyone on the make, he had a natural courtesy, great powers of affection, and a gift of gnomic wisdom which appeared not only in his works but in his life.

Forster was drawn as a child by George Richmond. A portrait in oils by Edmund Nelson and a red chalk drawing by Sir William Rothenstein are at King's; a portrait in oils by Roger Fry (1911) is in a private collection in London.

[*The Times*, 8 June 1970; Patrick Wilkinson, *E. M. Forster at King's*, 1970; B. J. Kirkpatrick, *A Bibliography of E. M. Forster*, with a foreword by E. M. F., 1965; Lionel Trilling, *E. M. Forster, a study*, 1944; K. W. Gransden, *E. M. Forster*, 1962; Wilfred M. Stone, *The Cave and the Mountains, a study of E. M. F.*, 1966; *Aspects of E. M. Forster*, ed. Oliver Stallybrass, 1969; P. N. Furbank, *E. M. Forster, a Life*, vol. i, 1977, and vol, ii, *Polycrates Ring, 1914-1970*, 1978 (the authorized biography); Francis King, *E. M. Forster and his World*, 1978; personal knowledge.]   ANNAN

FOSTER, SIR HARRY BRAUSTYN HYLTON HYLTON- (1905-1965), Speaker of the House of Commons. [See HYLTON-FOSTER.]

FOUGASSE (pseudonym), cartoonist. [See BIRD, (CYRIL) KENNETH.]

FOX, SIR CYRIL FRED (1882-1967), archaeologist and museum director, was born at Chippenham, Wiltshire, 16 December 1882, the first son of Charles Frederick Fox, FSA, a bank official, and his wife, Henrietta Maria Paul, of Saffron Walden in Essex. His sister married Bernard Gotch, the water-colour artist. He was of Hampshire stock with roots in the Isle of Wight, and the family returned to that county during his boyhood. From a preparatory school in the Isle of Wight he went on to Christ's Hospital, then (1895-8) still in London, but though he did well his days there were arid, for he was always a countryman at heart. Diphtheria and other illness led to his leaving school at sixteen to take up market gardening at Worthing. He was already gaining an interest in the antiquities of the countryside, and in Sussex he encountered a Cambridge bacteriologist Louis Cobbett, who obtained for him a position as a clerk at the Bovine Tuberculosis Research Station at Stansted in Essex. Removal of this institution to Cambridge in 1912 led Fox into exploring the antiquities of the

Cambridge region. Having already served in the Essex Yeomanry (TA), when war broke out he received a commission. But further illness kept him in England and after the war he returned to the research station as superintendent of its field laboratories. However, post-war reorganization made his future there uncertain, and at thirty-six Fox turned to archaeology as a career.

He gained entry to Magdalene College, Cambridge, in 1919, as a part-time student of archaeology, at first reading for the English tripos, and was much encouraged by Professor H. M. Chadwick [q.v.] who had him transferred to work for a Ph.D. In 1922 he had assembled his material for a thesis, which was published in 1923 as *The Archaeology of the Cambridge Region*. This was a landmark in archaeological thinking, and gave Fox an immediate standing among scholars. He was elected a fellow of the Society of Antiquaries of London in the same year, and was appointed to an assistantship in the Museum of Archaeology and Ethnology at Cambridge.

In 1924 Fox was nominated keeper of the National Museum of Ireland, but the electors' choice of an Englishman was not confirmed at higher level, a German archaeologist Walter Bremer being appointed. (Sir) R. E. M. Wheeler had, however, already persuaded Fox to apply for the keepership of archaeology under him as director at the National Museum of Wales, and though Cambridge would have liked to retain him, he accepted the Cardiff position. Two years later in 1926 he succeeded Wheeler as director, and guided the affairs of the National Museum of Wales until his retirement in 1948. Fox's time as director saw great developments. A monumental new building was in hand, and he brought to fruition the plans for the Welsh Folk Museum at St. Fagan—rural craftsmanship was always dear to Fox's heart. And Fox, though he himself never spoke Welsh, achieved the unifying of the regional and local museums of the principality by affiliation to the National Museum.

Fox served with distinction on public bodies such as the royal commissions on ancient and historical monuments in Wales and in England, and on the Ancient Monuments Board of the Ministry of Works. Yet he never allowed these duties or the administration of a great national museum to slow his own impetus to pursue research. The museum had a long tradition of fieldwork to give life to its collections, and this was congenial to the countryman's outlook; Fox seized every opportunity for such activity, as the stream of publications testifies. Wales provided him with all the expanding variety of terrain and problems he needed for the rest of his long working life.

In 1932 Fox followed his Cambridge regional study with another classic, *The Personality of Britain*. In this work he carried the new trends of thinking then current in human geography into prehistory and protohistory. 'This study of Britain as an environment for Man' was produced as one of four major discourses for the International Congress of Pre- and Protohistoric Sciences in London that year. It shows Fox as an exponent of the distribution map as an archaeological tool, and many of the maps were made in fruitful collaboration with Miss Lily Chitty. Its dual division of Britain into highland and lowland zones (sometimes called Fox's law) is not nowadays so much followed in detail, but the work had a strong influence on the thinking of a whole generation, and the concept of a 'Jurassic Zone' as a determinant through the whole of the human historical geography of Britain still holds its place.

Fox's archaeological studies ranged widely in time, and each is a pioneer model of its class. His many perceptive excavations of burial mounds in Wales led through individual reports to his *Life and Death in the Bronze Age* (1959). Work on the Cambridgeshire dykes led naturally to a full field survey of Offa's Dyke as the great boundary between England and Wales, the successive reports being brought together in a British Academy publication (1955). Finds of the Iron Age in Wales yielded a number of important papers and Museum monographs, culminating in his *Pattern and Purpose: a Study of Early Celtic Art in Britain* (1958).

Fox's study of rural houses in Wales was also most influential. The three volumes he produced (with Lord Raglan) on *Monmouthshire Houses: a study of building techniques and smaller house plans from the 15th to the 17th centuries* (1951-4) did much to give a respectable scholarly status to work on such buildings among social and economic historians, and, most important, in the Royal Commission on Historical Monuments for England. The whole subject of vernacular architecture owes much to Fox.

In 1934 Fox was president of the Museums Association, and in 1935 was knighted for his services to museums. In 1940 he was elected fellow of the British Academy. He served as president of the Society of Antiquaries of London 1944-9, through the crucial post-war years, and was awarded the Society's gold medal in 1952. He was an honorary D.Litt. of Wales (1947) and an honorary fellow of Magdalene (1952). He was held in high esteem by his colleagues, as marked by the volume of twenty essays, *Culture and Environment* (1963), in his honour.

Fox was one of the leading archaeological

thinkers of a fruitful generation. He was a man of energetic enthusiasm, capable of inspiring colleagues and friends. He was a rapid worker, as the flourish of his penmanship reveals; he was not given to laboured reworking of completed tasks. He had a deep love of literature and poetry, paying great attention to the words he wrote. He had a fine visual memory, which he did not, however, allow to impede the flow of his original creative thought. Fox saw the past as a continuum leading into the present. His interests lay above all in the landscape, and in all forms of human craftsmanship. He is remembered for the humanism he brought into archaeological interpretations.

In 1916 Fox married Olive, daughter of the Revd Arthur Congreve-Pridgeon, vicar of Steyning in Sussex. She was drowned off the Gower Peninsula in 1932; by her he had two daughters, Helen Felicity, an art critic, and Dr Penelope Eames, author of a work on medieval furniture (1977). He married secondly in 1933 Aileen Mary, an active archaeologist, daughter of Walter Scott Henderson, of Farnham in Surrey; they worked much together in the field. He retired to Exeter, where she held a position of university lecturer in archaeology. There were three sons of this marriage. Fox died in Exeter 15 January 1967.

There are portraits of Fox at the National Museum of Wales (a drawing by Evan Walters, 1937), the Society of Antiquaries in London, and in possession of the family. There is also an ink drawing by Leonard Monroe (1939) in private hands.

[Stuart Piggott in *Proceedings* of the British Academy, vol. liii, 1967; W. F. Grimes in *Archaeologia Cambrensis*, 1967; Sir Mortimer Wheeler in *Culture and Environment* (ed. I. Ll. Foster and L. Alcock, 1963, with bibliography); private information; personal knowledge.]   E. M. JOPE

FOX, HAROLD MUNRO (1889–1967), zoologist, was born in Clapham 28 September 1889, the eldest of the two children and the only son of Georg Gotthilf Fuchs, once a captain in the Prussian army, and his wife, Margaret Isabella Campbell, daughter of Lt.-Col. Andrew Munro from Sutherland, who held a commission in the 19th (Yorkshire) Regiment. His sister, Alison Settle, OBE, became the editor of *Vogue*. His parents separated when he was very young. At the age of thirteen he became a day-boy at Brighton College, from where he obtained a scholarship to Caius College, Cambridge, in 1908. He graduated in 1911, with a second class in part ii of the natural sciences tripos, having obtained a first class in part i, and then spent a

year working at the Plymouth Laboratory, followed by ten months at Naples. In 1913 he became a lecturer in zoology at the Royal College of Science, London. On the outbreak of war he joined the Army Service Corps and changed his name to Fox. He served in Egypt, Salonika, and the Balkans, and during part of the war, because of his linguistic abilities, he was attached to French and Italian units in Palestine.

After the war he returned to London for six months before becoming a lecturer at the school of medicine in Cairo. During the summer of 1919 he had spent some time at the Plymouth Laboratory, and discovered that the small flagellate *Bodo* could be used to detect respiratory surfaces of aquatic invertebrates. His thesis on this subject, written in Cairo, gained him a fellowship at Caius College, Cambridge (1920). While in Cairo Fox paid frequent visits to the Gulf of Suez. Here he discovered that the regular cycle of spawning in the sea-urchin *Diadema* was restricted to a few days near new moon. This led to a review of available information on lunar periodicity, and to the publication in 1928 of *Selene, or Sex and the Moon*. Returning to Cambridge to take up his fellowship, he quickly organized an expedition to Egypt to study the fauna of the Suez canal (1924). This was a major zoogeographical opportunity, and it was taken fully. Experts were recruited to study the collections, and Fox pressurized them all into publishing at the same time. This study established that the Bitter Lakes acted as a barrier to the majority of animals that might migrate from the Red Sea to the Mediterranean. The true importance of this barrier has only lately been realized. As an indirect consequence of the building of the Aswan high dam the salinity of the Bitter Lakes has been reduced and more animals now enter the Mediterranean.

The most important of Fox's researches began in 1923, when at the Roscoff Laboratory in Brittany he examined the red-green blood of the fan-worm *Spirographis*. The pigment had been called chlorocruorin by (Sir) E. R. Lankester [q.v.] in 1867, and some of its properties had been established, but Fox's critical experiments demonstrated its function and chemical nature. He returned to various aspects of this work over the next thirty years. In 1927 Fox was appointed to the chair of zoology at Birmingham, and after fourteen years transferred to Bedford College, London. The years at Birmingham and Bedford College were filled with active research. He pioneered work on metabolic rates in various environments, and at different latitudes. Also, with H. Ramage, he made the first spectrographic analyses of the rarer elements in a variety of animals. Fox became an international authority on respiratory pigments. He was elected FRS in 1937, président d'honneur of the Zoological Society of France in 1955, and was appointed Fullerian professor of physiology at the Royal Institution for 1953-6. He also received the gold medal of the Linnean Society (1959), an honorary D.Sc. from the university of Bordeaux (1965), and the Darwin medal of the Royal Society (1966).

During all this intense research activity, for forty years he edited *Biological Reviews of the Cambridge Philosophical Society*, making it the finest journal of its type in the world. His own writings were concise and clear, and he would not tolerate lower standards in his authors. As an editor he was severe, but authors generally confessed that their manuscripts were improved by his attentions. His teaching, like his writing, was always meticulously prepared, with an emphasis on elegance and clarity. He retired in 1954, but continued editing, and developed an interest in ostracod crustaceans, on which he published ten papers between 1962 and 1967.

He married, firstly, in 1917, Léonie Thérèse, the daughter of Henri Roger, an official with the Suez Canal Company. They separated while he was professor at Birmingham. He married, secondly, in 1931, Natalia Lvovna, daughter of Lev Yulevich Mertens, of Saratov, Russia. There were no children of either marriage. For the rest of his career 'Natasha' shared with him a dislike of pretence, a love of travel, and considerable linguistic ability.

When he was ten or eleven years old Fox had been run over by a horse-bus which caused him to be a patient for almost a year in St. George's Hospital, London. However, he was left with no permanent disability and became a good shot and an accomplished horseman, ballroom dancer, and swimmer. Strikingly handsome throughout his life, Fox had great vitality which gave him a rapidity of speech and a constantly questioning mind. He was for many years a member of the Savile Club. He remained a keen horseman throughout his retirement, and died in London 29 January 1967 while on his usual weekend ride.

[J. E. Smith in *Biographical Memoirs of Fellows of the Royal Society*, vol. xiv, 1968; personal knowledge.]   J. GREEN

FOX, SIR LIONEL WRAY (1895-1961), chairman of the Prison Commission, was born 21 February 1895 in Halifax, the son of Samuel Fox, boiler makers' draughtsman, and his wife, Minnie Wray. He was educated at Heath Grammar School, Halifax, and Hertford College, Oxford, but joined the army on the outbreak of war in 1914. He served with the Duke of Wellington's Regiment, reached the rank of captain, was mentioned in dispatches, and awarded the MC and the Belgian croix de guerre. Having entered the Civil Service top in his year Fox joined the Home Office as an assistant principal in 1919. From 1925 to 1934 he was secretary to the Prison Commission and there learned to put into effect the combination of exactitude of mind and deep humanity of feeling which characterized his career. In 1934 he was appointed deputy receiver to the Metropolitan Police district and he was acting receiver in 1941-2 before returning to the Prison Commission as chairman.

Rejoining the Commission in the middle of the war, Fox had to lead his service through the most arduous years in which prisons and borstals were damaged by enemy action. After the war he had to grapple with the problems of overcrowding and shortage of staff which indeed remained his preoccupations until in February 1959, in helping to compose the white paper on 'Penal Practice in a Changing Society', he was able to propose and support the biggest prison building programme for a century. He did not live to see its completion or the later increased influx of prison population.

While still secretary to the Prison Commission Fox published *The Modern English Prison* (1934), in the second chapter of which he discusses the problem of deterrence and reformation. He recalls the principle set out in the Gladstone committee report of 1895 that 'prison treatment should have as its primary and concurrent objects deterrence and reformation'. Remarking that experience showed that 'deterrent power lies fundamentally not in *severity* of punishment, but in *certainty* of detection and punishment', he goes on 'it then becomes possible, without impairment of the principle of deterrence, to remove from the prison regime any features introduced to emphasize its deterrent aspect which prove to be incompatible with the concurrent duty "to turn the prisoners out of prison better man and women than when they came in" '. He concludes that 'the most effective method of protection, *if it can be done*, is to reform the offender'. In 1952 Fox published *The English Prison and Borstal Systems* which will remain a standard work, not only because it depicts the system at a particular time but also because of its contribution to scholarship, for in it can be traced the history and principles of criminology. He also wrote for the *Encyclopaedia Britannica* and the *British Journal of Delinquency*.

Fox's name will be associated with the drafting of the new prison and borstal rules under the Criminal Justice Act of 1948. He also helped to institute corrective training, preventive detention, and the detention centres; and developed the open borstal and the open prison system, leaving to his successors a rich variety of both systems. He saw the beginnings of the scheme for the provision of prison welfare officers and he was chairman of the council and of the executive committee of the Central After-Care Association from its inception in 1949 until he retired from the Prison Commission in 1960. He then became visiting fellow of the Institute of Criminology at Cambridge.

Fox left as distinctive a mark on the service as Sir Evelyn Ruggles-Brise [q.v.] who alone served longer than Fox, and his influence on prison affairs was as important as that of Sir Alexander Paterson [q.v.]. At a memorial service for Fox held in Wormwood Scrubs prison chapel the secretary of state spoke of him as a charitable and single-minded man who succeeded to and embellished a great tradition. 'At the latter end of his life he achieved many of the reforms to the perfection of which he had devoted long years.' Fox held firmly to the belief in which he grew up, feeling strongly about the unjustifiable harshness of imprisonment, to which his fiery temperament reacted. He did not volunteer information about his brother, Ralph Fox, who was killed fighting on the Republican side in the Spanish civil war, but he felt very warmly about him, as one who had shared his strength of conviction. Fox was an intimidating adversary in argument about prison matters: he had not only detailed experience but a fine mind. His many friends had to accept an awkward diction and sharpness of manner before they came to the warm-hearted and charming personality which underlay the natural reserve which he seemed to cast aside more easily abroad than at home. He was held in great esteem in the international world. He was a member of the long-established International Penitentiary Commission and when its duties were taken over by the Social Defence section of the United Nations he rapidly became a leader in that sphere. He was president of the United Nations European Consultative Group on the prevention of crime and the treatment of offenders from 1951 until 1960, and was elected honorary president of the second Quinquennial United Nations Congress held in London in August 1960, over which illness prevented him from presiding. He died in London 6 October 1961.

Fox was appointed CB in 1948 and knighted in 1953. In 1921 he married Marjorie Bailey, daughter of Charles Henry Horner, of Halifax; they had one son and two daughters.

In 1964 the International Penal and Penitentiary Foundation published a volume of studies in penology dedicated to Fox which included tributes to his work.

[Private information; personal knowledge.]
BUTLER OF SAFFRON WALDEN

FOX, TERENCE ROBERT CORELLI (1912–1962), chemical engineer, was born in London 2 May 1912, the only son of Corelli Fox, electrical engineer, and his wife, Mabel Ballard; he had two sisters. He was educated at Regent Street Polytechnic Secondary School and began his career as an engineer at Jesus College, Cambridge, which he entered in 1930 to study for the mechanical sciences tripos. In that examination he had unparalleled success, getting a starred first in 1933, with all possible prizes. (Sir) Charles F. Inglis [q.v.] was head of department at the time and is reported to have said: 'There is nothing that young man has written that I would not gladly have put my name to.' Fox's tripos result may have coloured his later views: he retained a perhaps unwarranted faith in the efficacy of examinations.

Fox then spent four years in the Billingham division of ICI as a mechanical engineer. The oil hydrogenation plant was in the early stages of development and the dangerous nature of the work gave Fox a permanent anxiety for safety.

In 1937 Inglis persuaded Fox to return to Cambridge, as a university demonstrator; he became a fellow of King's in 1941, and a university lecturer in 1945. He was an outstanding teacher. His lectures were vividly given, for Fox had histrionic gifts: the laws of mechanics were sometimes illustrated by practical demonstrations involving the dynamics of the lecturer as when he propelled himself across the floor on a chair by the swinging action of his legs which did not touch the ground. The lectures were amply supported by duplicated sheets of notes beautifully written in the unmistakable backhand, the size of which seemed designed for writing tripos answers on index cards; its minute characters invited the use of a magnifying glass.

Fox's great opportunity came in 1945 when Cambridge University accepted the offer from Shell of about £450,000 for a chemical engineering department. His appointment in 1946 as Shell professor caused a stir in the small world of chemical engineers as it was then. The appointment was in many ways remarkable: Fox had published no research papers, nor did he ever; he was not at that time an established member of the chemical engineering profession.

Fox immediately took to his job with enthusiasm, spending the first year in the United States where the subject was well established; he returned to plan the Cambridge course for which the first students were accepted in 1948. He grasped at once the necessity of establishing a tripos course of high intellectual content which would command respect in Cambridge and elsewhere. Hence his course included enough of the existing technological material to be acceptable to industrialists, but the technology was taught in such a way as to illustrate the application of the fundamentals of fluid mechanics, chemical thermodynamics, and other sciences which form the academic basis of chemical engineering. In this rigorous teaching Fox raised the tone of the subject and foreshadowed by at least ten years a similar move in the United States.

Another innovation introduced by Fox and later followed by most chemical engineering, and indeed engineering, departments was in the style of teaching experiments. In their gift, Shell had allowed for the purchase of large equipment, but Fox insisted on keeping the capital, using the interest for research and for small experiments to teach principles rather than practice. His wisdom prevented the Cambridge department from being lumbered with large pieces of equipment which would undoubtedly have become white elephants.

There were several reasons why Fox never published any research: his perfectionist outlook made publication difficult; his inclinations were pedagogical rather than creative; he was an invaluable critic and a scholarly expositor rather than an inventor or discoverer. But he promoted research in his department: he gave shelter and encouragement to Francis T. Bacon with his fuel-cell team at a crucial stage in the development of the cell which eventually went to the moon; he supervised a number of research students, who were devoted to him; he actively encouraged his staff to do research though it was a little bizarre to be told, on having derived some new piece of theory, that 'it would make a good tripos question'. He never published a textbook though his lecture notes were better than many: his notes were usually rewritten every year and most of the books published from the Shell department owed something to Fox.

His desire for rigour, though admirable in academic matters, made life difficult in questions of administration; here he suffered from what was described as pathological conscientiousness which often made him a trying colleague. He found it difficult to delegate fully, and it was said that he would use as much effort in spending ten shillings as £10,000. These traits naturally led to strain and he suffered a succession of nervous breakdowns in the early 1950s which caused his resignation from the Shell chair in 1959. But he had some notable successes as head of department: for example, the building to house the Shell department was largely designed by Fox whose engineering and artistic talents would have made him an admirable architect; his must be one of the very few post-war buildings in Cambridge about which there have been no complaints.

Fox's talents were combined with a striking and attractive personality. Of tall and slender build he had the fine-drawn, dark good looks which indicated his Italian ancestry. He had all the outward marks of a brilliant King's man: widely read, he was an entertaining conversationalist. His fund of anecdotes—as of the distinguished King's economist discovered in his bath by a zealous tourist—lightened the tea-time talk in the Shell department. But he was a reserved man with few close friends. He never married which was a pity for he showed great consideration for those around him and was the kindliest of men: but marriage is not for perfectionists. He died in a London hospital 5 October 1962.

[*The Times*, 6 and 9 October 1962; personal knowledge.]   J. F. DAVIDSON

FOYLE, WILLIAM ALFRED (1885–1963), bookseller, was born 4 March 1885 in Shoreditch, London, the seventh child of a seventh child of a seventh child. It was to this that he attributed his remarkable visionary and intuitive gifts. He was one of the eight children (six sons and two daughters) of William Henry Foyle, a wholesale grocer, and his wife, Deborah Barnett. He was educated at Dame Alice Owen's School, Islington. In 1900 he sat for, and failed, the Civil Service entrance examination. He then attended a short course at King's College, London. His first appointment, in 1902, was with (Sir) Edward Marshall Hall, KC [q.v.], who collected old silver, and frequently sent his young clerk to the sale-rooms. Books were always Foyle's passion, and he took the opportunity of bidding for any interesting lots.

Foyle started trading as a bookseller by selling his own school books. In 1903, at the age of eighteen, he opened, with his brother Gilbert, his first bookshop in Islington. He bought books wherever he could find them—in the sale-rooms, from students, from private people, and from second-hand bookshops. One shop he visited was in New Oxford Street, run by a young lady, Christina Tulloch. She was the daughter of William Tulloch and Helen Gifford, both children of seafaring people from the Shetland Isles. Thinking him a poor student, she let him have the books very cheaply. He persuaded Christina to become his partner and his wife. They married in 1907 and were to have two daughters, and one son, who died. One of the daughters, Christina, was to become a director of the bookselling business which Foyle later expanded. She was to achieve renown by her literary luncheons held for over half a century.

Foyle lived for and dreamed about books. He seldom forgot a title. He went to endless trouble to track down unusual or rare books for people, and his stock and his reputation grew. In 1907 he took larger premises in Charing Cross Road, in order to stock books on every subject—art, theology, music, education, and other subjects. Foyles became a Mecca for booklovers. Foyle was an authority on the lives of booksellers of the past, and he modelled himself on Thomas Guy, founder of Guy's Hospital, and James Lackington, of the 'Temple of the Muses' [qq.v.]. He even had a soft spot for the 'unspeakable' Edmund Curll [q.v.]. He determined to create the greatest bookshop in the world, and he succeeded.

He began to trade in new books in 1912, and the first publishers to give him credit were William Heinemann [q.v.], through John Dettmer. The shop always needed more space, and so Dickensian premises in Manette Street, off Charing Cross Road, were bought from the Revd Basil Bourchier, then vicar of St. Anne's, Soho, and, in 1929, a splendid four-storeyed building was opened by the lord mayor of London, Sir J. E. Kynaston Studd [q.v.].

'Willie' Foyle was a very unusual and deceptive man. An adored if neglectful parent, overflowing with high spirits, mischievous, seldom serious, few people recognized the acute mind that lay behind the fun and the laughter. Extremely sensitive, quite feminine, he was a considerable artist and pianist. He was an individualist, a loner, no lover of committees, and the few clubs he belonged to were of the Bohemian variety, where he met his raffish friends, Townley Searle, Pino Orioli, and A. J. A. Symons, with whom he started the First Edition Club, with elegant premises in Bedford Square. Another partnership followed. A. J. A. had a great admiration for a solitary and eccentric bookseller, Christopher Millard. Millard was devoted to sailing, and owned a dinghy, with which he explored the estuaries of the Blackwater and the Crouch. To Symons, this seemed delightful and very soon he and Willie Foyle became the owners of a seven-ton yacht. The happy days, sailing on the Essex rivers, gave him a love for the country and he made his home in Maldon.

In the twenties he began Foyles literary lectures. These talks were held in the bookshop on Wednesday evenings, and an enraptured audience listened to the Sitwells, Arthur Conan Doyle, T. H. Hall Caine, and Walter de la Mare [qq.v.]. In every new development in bookselling Foyle was first. Foyles began the Book Club in 1937 and it acquired a quarter of a million members. When Foyles opened in 1903, bookselling was a peaceful, leisurely occupation, and customers were few and far between, but William Foyle foresaw the great demand for books that would come with the extension of

further education and the increased wealth of the people, and when this happened, after the war of 1939-45, he was ready for it.

In 1945 he bought the twelfth-century Premonstratensian Abbey of Beeleigh, situated on the River Chelmer, in Maldon, Essex. In this beautiful setting he was able to indulge his passion for collecting rare books, and he formed one of the great libraries. Among his treasures are many incunabula: Caxtons, Wynkyn de Worde, Kolberger, Shakespeare's folios, and a superb collection of fourteenth- and fifteenth-century illuminated manuscripts.

Although money was one of the last things Foyle thought about, he died a millionaire, a state which was perhaps due in some degree to his cautious daughter Christina, who had learned many hard lessons from years of facing creditors, and her extraordinarily able husband, Ronald Batty. Foyle died at his home in Essex 4 July 1963.

His portrait was painted by Thomas Cantrell Dugdale, and is in the library at Beeleigh Abbey.

[*The Times*, 6 June 1963; *Bookseller*, 8 June 1963; personal knowledge.]

CHRISTINA FOYLE

FRAENKEL, EDUARD DAVID MORTIER (1888-1970), classical scholar, was born in Berlin 17 March 1888, the son of a wine merchant, Julius Fraenkel, who was a first cousin of Ludwig Traube and an uncle of Ernst Fraenkel, and his wife, Edith Heimann. He attended the Askanisches Gymnasium, where the classical teaching was of a high order, but on entering the university of Berlin in 1906 enrolled as a student of law. An unbaptized Jew had little chance of obtaining a professorship, and Fraenkel was unwilling to become a schoolmaster. He greatly profited from his training in Roman legal science, in which he never lost his interest. But the famous public lectures given by Wilamowitz, and also a long conversation when he asked the great man to advise him how he might spend his time on his first visit to Italy, impelled him at all costs to become a student of classical philology. In Berlin he learned much from Diels, Eduard Meyer, Norden, Schulze, and above all Wilamowitz; but in 1909 he transferred to Göttingen, where he greatly profited from the teaching of Leo and Wackernagel, and in 1912 took his degree with a thesis about Middle and New Comedy which showed great promise.

After working for two years on the Latin Thesaurus in Munich, Fraenkel habilitated in Berlin in 1917, and was appointed Privatdozent; in 1920 he became Professor Extraordinarius. Two years later appeared the most remarkable of all his books, *Plautinisches im Plautus*. Other scholars, especially since the important papyrus discoveries of Menander, had studied Plautus, chiefly for what he could teach them about his Greek originals; Fraenkel loved him for himself, and did much to make clear the nature of his own specific contribution to his adaptations of Greek plays.

In 1923 Fraenkel became full professor at Kiel, in 1928 he moved to Göttingen, and in 1931 to Freiburg im Breisgau. He became a leading figure in his profession, and helped to found the periodical *Gnomon;* he often visited Italy, and kept in touch with Giorgio Pasquali in Florence. In 1928 he published *Iktus und Akzent im lateinischen Sprechvers;* although he later disowned the main conclusions of this learned book, it contains much valuable matter. In 1931 appeared *Kolon und Satz*, the most substantial product of his lifelong interest in the order of words. In the summer of 1933, the year when the National Socialists came to power, Fraenkel was forbidden to teach, and the next year he moved to Oxford. In August 1934 he was elected to a Bevan fellowship at Trinity College, Cambridge, but in November he applied for the Corpus chair of Latin at Oxford, and largely through the influence of A. E. Housman [q.v.] Fraenkel was elected. He was naturalized in 1939.

He found it difficult to settle down in an environment so different from what he was accustomed to, and at first and for long after alienated many well-wishers by his tactlessness and insensitivity. But although he terrified many of his pupils, his teaching from the first made a profound impression. He lectured effectively on Catullus, Virgil, and Horace; but he exerted special influence through his famous seminars on Aeschylus's *Agamemnon*, in which he went through the play in more time than it took Agamemnon to capture Troy. In 1950 he brought out an edition of the *Agamemnon* in three volumes, containing the most detailed commentary ever devoted to a Greek text. Although some of the author's judgements may be questioned, it makes a massive contribution to Greek scholarship.

As time passed, Fraenkel become accustomed to English life, and radically revised his attitude. He found that although Oxford undergraduates were ignorant of secondary sources, by comparison with German students they often knew their texts thoroughly, and were thus excellent subjects for the instruction he could impart. The affection for Oxford and the English which he had developed was heartily reciprocated by his pupils and his younger colleagues; and when he retired from his chair under the age limit in 1953 he was elected an honorary fellow of Corpus Christi College, given a large

room in which to keep his books, and enabled to continue to hold his famous seminars. After the war of 1939-45 he resumed his connections with the Continent. He was in touch with many German scholars; but the country he loved most was Italy, where he often taught and lectured, and where he received the freedom of the city of Sarsina, birthplace of Plautus.

In 1957 he published a learned and humane book on Horace; in 1962 a short book about another favourite author, Aristophanes; and in 1968 an important study of Latin word-order and prose rhythm; a two-volume selection from his many learned articles appeared in 1964. He remained active in teaching and research until his death.

Fraenkel was one of the most learned classical scholars of his time. In an age when few dared to attempt excellence in Greek and Latin, he was eminent in both, and was also well acquainted with metric, linguistics, Roman legal science, and the monuments of ancient art. Above all he was an interpreter of texts, and brought to the work the entire apparatus of modern learning. He was denied the gift of divination, and he had little sympathy with any literature or art which might be considered decadent; thus his *Horace* suffered from his failure to appreciate Hellenistic poetry together with his inability even to entertain the notion that the regime of Augustus was not in all ways admirable. But with his vast learning he combined a deep love for Mediterranean life and an imaginative sympathy with almost all its manifestations which gave his teaching an exhilarating quality. Like his master Wilamowitz he was first and foremost a teacher and only in second place a writer, hard though this is to credit for those acquainted only with his vast output of learned work. As a teacher he had certain defects. He was not quick in the uptake, and could seldom elicit suggestions from his hearers; he tended to extremes of praise or blame, and many of his pupils found him frightening. But all this was nothing in the face of his boundless enthusiasm for the study of the ancient world, his tireless eagerness to help anyone whom he supposed in any way to share it, and his imaginative sympathy with the writers and the civilizations which were the objects of his study.

He was a fellow of the British Academy (1941-64), and was awarded the Kenyon medal in 1965. He received honorary degrees from the universities of West Berlin, Urbino, St. Andrews, Florence, Fribourg, and Oxford.

In 1918 Fraenkel married Ruth von Velsen, who gave up a promising academic career for his sake, and sustained him with unfailing love and loyalty. They had three sons and two daughters. On learning of the death of his wife,

Fraenkel chose not to survive her and died in Oxford 5 February 1970.

[S. Timpanaro in *Atene e Roma*, NS 15, fasc. 2–3, 1970; H. Lloyd-Jones in *Gnomon*, vol. xliii, 1971; Gordon Williams in *Proceedings of the British Academy*, vol. lvi, 1970; personal knowledge.]

HUGH LLOYD-JONES

FRANCIS-WILLIAMS, BARON (1903–1970), author, journalist, and publicist. [See WILLIAMS, EDWARD FRANCIS.]

FRANKLIN, CHARLES SAMUEL (1879–1964), radio telecommunications engineer, was born in Walthamstow 23 March 1879, the thirteenth child of James Charles Franklin, a carpenter and builder, and his wife, Martha Bulbeck. He received his engineering and scientific training under Silvanus P. Thompson [q.v.] at Finsbury Technical College, after which he worked briefly in Manchester and Norwich. In 1899, at the age of twenty, he joined the Wireless Telegraph and Signal Company (later Marconi's Wireless and Telegraph Company) with which he remained associated until his retirement in 1939.

During the Boer War Franklin helped to introduce wireless communication in South Africa for military use, returning to Britain in 1902 to act as wireless operator for Guglielmo Marconi. They sailed across the Atlantic to demonstrate the reception of wireless messages up to a range of 1,550 miles from the Poldhu transmitting station in Cornwall. From 1904 to early 1906 Franklin demonstrated radio equipment in Russia. He began a long personal association with Marconi to whom he remained devoted throughout his life. They often experimented far into the night. From 1908 to 1916 much of their work was done in isolated wireless stations along the coast, and during this period Franklin was at his happiest. He worked in the short-wave, ultra-short, and micro-wave spectra, and had many important patents.

By 1913 Franklin had patented techniques of using a thermionic valve as a radio frequency generator. He had devised a photographic method of recording radio signals and designed a regenerative receiver of high sensitivity. From 1916 to 1920, working with Marconi, he developed the short-wave beam principle which led to the first beamed short-wave system. He devoted particular attention to the design of efficient reflectors which concentrated radiation into a narrow searchlight-like beam, and he built a special short-wave transmitter employing tubes of his own design. At Inchkeith a rotating parabolic reflector station transmitting on a wavelength of 6 metres demonstrated the possibilities of a radio beacon for navigation.

Franklin designed a special spark transmitter operating in compressed air, and his inductance capacity oscillator (the 'Franklin Drive') formed an essential part of the short-wave beam communication system.

During 1923 and 1924 Franklin installed a short-wave station at Poldhu. He and Marconi conducted tests between it and Marconi's yacht, *Elettra*, chiefly to determine the day and night ranges and reliability of signals transmitted on wavelengths of 97 metres or less, with and without reflectors, and also to investigate the angle and spread of the beam. On 97 metres and 12 kW, daylight signals were received across 1,250 nautical miles and night signals at a range of 2,320 nautical miles. Later, reception was reported in the USA and Australia. The beam transmitter and flat grid aerial system designed by Franklin (the Franklin Beam Aerial) formed the basis of world-wide short-wave communication. A necessary part of the system was Franklin's invention of the concentric feeder for the transmission of the very high frequency currents to and from the aerial arrays, the forerunner of the coaxial cable.

In 1922 Franklin assisted in the design and installation of the transmitter and aerial system of 2LO, London's first broadcasting station, and his team was responsible for running it initially. Later he designed the transmitters and aerial system for the BBC station at Alexandra Palace which transmitted the world's first regular television service in 1936. He retired from the Marconi Company in 1939, but acted as a research consultant to them for some years afterwards.

Among the awards which Franklin received were the Morris Liebmann memorial prize of the Institute of Radio Engineers (NY) in 1922; the James Alfred Ewing medal of the Institution of Civil Engineers in 1936; and in 1949, the Faraday medal of the Institution of Electrical Engineers for 'his distinguished work in radio engineering, and more particularly for his development of the beam aerial and other devices that made long-range high-frequency communication a practical possibility'. Also in 1949 Franklin was appointed CBE.

Franklin was a small, frail, diffident, modest man who seldom spoke unless spoken to, and was happiest working in seclusion. During his Poldhu days, when told of a problem which had baffled his colleagues, he would wander off alone across the headland. Suddenly, he would squat down motionless upon the cliff-top, remain there for perhaps an hour or more, oblivious of wind and weather, then return and state exactly where the fault lay. He would be right.

In 1918 Franklin married Catherine, daughter of John Griffiths, a lime and coal merchant. They had no children. When he retired from the Marconi Company in 1939, he moved back to Mullion Helston near Poldhu where his wife died in 1946. Later he returned to London where he died at Woodford Green 10 December 1964.

[Marconi Company Archives; *Nature*, 13 February 1965; *The Times*, 16 December 1964; W. J. Baker, *A History of the Marconi Company*, 1970; private information.]

E. D. P. SYMONS

FRANKS, ROBERT SLEIGHTHOLME (1871–1964), theologian, was born 1 April 1871 at Redcar, North Yorkshire, the eldest son of the Revd William James Franks, Congregational minister, and his wife, Ann Eliza, daughter of Robert Sleightholme, of Whitby. He was educated at Sir William Turner's Grammar School, Redcar, and St. John's College, Cambridge, where he graduated in mathematics in 1893. Later he studied theology at Mansfield College, Oxford, under A. M. Fairbairn [q.v.]. After a brief period as tutor in the college, Franks was ordained at Prenton Road Congregational church, Birkenhead, in 1900. In 1904 he became lecturer in theology at Woodbrooke, Selly Oak; then in 1910 he went to what was to be his life's work as principal of the Western College, Bristol, where he remained until 1939, devoting his life to training young men for the Christian ministry. He received an honorary LLD from Bristol University in 1928.

It was as a theologian that Franks was chiefly known. His most notable book was *A History of the Doctrine of the Work of Christ*, first published in two volumes in 1918 and subsequently republished in a single volume in 1962. It was for this work that Franks was awarded the D.Litt. by Oxford in 1919. It is a historical study of ecclesiastical doctrine. The subject is presented as a microcosm of Christian doctrine, and four syntheses or total views of doctrine are enumerated: Greek, Mediaeval, Protestant orthodoxy, and modern Protestant. Around these points the historical study turns. The whole massive work was to some extent a development of a small earlier work, *The New Testament Doctrines of Man, Sin and Salvation* (1908).

Some years later Franks presented his own interpretation of this doctrine in *The Atonement* (1934). The method as well as the conclusion were alike remarkable, for Franks argued for the Abelardian view of the Atonement and sought to prove it by the method of Anselm. He aimed to show that love rather than life is the key word in the doctrine; and he hoped that the method adopted would provide theology with a metaphysical basis.

Years later, while in his eighties, Franks published *The Doctrine of the Trinity* (1953), a most lucid historical survey, in which, after an examination of the New Testament 'matrix' of the doctrine, he traced its development in the Patristic period, and with remarkable balance and proportion outlined subsequent thought from Aquinas to Barth.

Although predominantly a theologian, Franks was profoundly interested in the philosophy of religion and especially in its metaphysic. In 1929 he published *The Metaphysical Justification of Religion*, lectures delivered at King's College, London. Reared in the Ritschlian school of theology, he quickly came to see the need for a firmer metaphysic through studying both Troeltsch and Scheiermacher, whose *Christian Faith* supported an experiential theology with a philosophical basis. As the King's College lectures show, Franks carried his quest for a metaphysic of religion through the works of C. H. Weisse, whose fundamental motive was to show the congruence of Christianity with reason largely understood.

Franks published several shorter pieces either in learned journals or symposia. He was a contributor to the *Dictionary of Christ and the Gospels* and other works edited by James Hastings [q.v.]. Although he represented the best of a theological liberalism later out of fashion, he was unusual in that, unlike most Protestant theologians of the period, he valued the work of the medieval scholastics. Not only in his main book but also in an essay contributed to *Amicitiae Corolla* (1933) we see especially in his treatment of Alexander of Hales how deep his learning in this period was. Franks found in Alexander a more sympathetic spirit than in Aquinas, believing that the experientialism of Alexander lived in the mystics, Quakers, Pietists, and Moravians, leading to Schleiermacher, until Barth, like a new Aquinas, challenged the whole method.

Throughout his long life Franks held to his conviction that the subjective element in Christianity is somehow fundamental and that it could be given a sound philosophical basis. This meant that he was at odds with the theology of Karl Barth, which he regarded as altogether unsatisfactory.

Essentially a scholar, Franks was a shy, devout, and kindly man, a sound mathematician and a keen musician. In 1902 he married Katharine, daughter of Joseph Shewell, of Redcar, and had two sons and two daughters. He lived long enough to be in the gallery to see his elder son, Oliver Shewell Franks, take the oath as a life peer in 1962. He died in Bristol 20 January 1964.

[Private information; personal knowledge.]

JOHN HUXTABLE

FRASER, Sir FRANCIS RICHARD (1885-1964), professor of medicine and first director of the British Postgraduate Medical Federation, was born in Edinburgh 14 February 1885, the seventh child of (Sir) Thomas Richard Fraser [q.v.], professor of materia medica in the university, and his wife, Susannah Margaret Duncan. He went from Edinburgh Academy to Christ's College, Cambridge, where he obtained a first class in part i of the natural sciences tripos in 1907; he then gained his MB with honours in Edinburgh in 1910. He proceeded MD in 1922. While a hospital resident in 1911 he was host on behalf of his indisposed father at a private dinner to Abraham Flexner, the American medical educationist. This facilitated his appointment in 1912 as assistant in medicine at the Rockefeller Institute, New York. He was thus among the first young British medical graduates to seek research training in the United States in preference to Central Europe. He worked on poliomyelitis and on the action of digitalis. In 1914 he became an instructor in medicine under W. T. Longcope in Columbia University at the Presbyterian Hospital, New York, where he was also assistant physician. In 1915 he relinquished this post to volunteer for service in the Royal Army Medical Corps in which he worked first as a pathologist and later as physician on active service in France, and in 1919-20, now lieutenant-colonel, he was consulting physician to the Army of the Rhine.

Following the Haldane report recommending the creation of university clinical units, Sir Archibald Garrod [q.v.] had been appointed professor of medicine at St. Bartholomew's Hospital medical school in 1920 and Fraser was appointed assistant director, succeeding his chief as professor and director later that year. These were exciting times with the upsurge of scientific standards in clinical studies, for which Fraser set an example by enlisting the co-operation of the leading respiratory physiologists, J. S. Haldane and (Sir) Joseph Barcroft [qq.v.], in research on the breathlessness of heart disease. In 1925 and in 1928 Fraser travelled widely in the medical schools of North America as well as Australia.

The whole-time university academic units were not always given a full range of control and responsibility in the voluntary hospitals. In 1934, when Fraser was appointed the first professor of medicine in the new British Postgraduate Medical School at Hammersmith, he ensured that all the medical beds were under the control of his academic assistants. He had a unique capacity for the perception of academic promise and the young men on his staff were given full opportunities while still under thirty to deploy their talents as clinical teachers and investigators.

With the help of his colleague, E. H. Kettle [q.v.], in pathology, the new school became a Mecca for the training of medical teachers. Joint staff rounds for the exchange of experience and the final analysis in clinico-pathological conferences became quite famous. Later there was hardly a centre in the English-speaking world which did not owe something to the spirit created by Fraser at Hammersmith. This achievement was entirely due to the exemplary personal attributes of all concerned, for the slump of the thirties had left the projected buildings incomplete and the new centre was created in extremely cramped quarters.

With the outbreak of war in 1939, Fraser was seconded to the Ministry of Health as consultant adviser on the organization of civilian hospitals in wartime. Even facing severe depletion of civilian doctors, Fraser ensured maintenance of standards by building up a skeleton clinical pathological service in all areas of the country. In September 1941 he became director-general of the Emergency Medical Services; he was knighted in 1944. During this disturbed and strenuous period, he never lost touch with the need to think ahead to the end of the war and postgraduate training needs. Many meetings and discussions took place to bring together the school at Hammersmith and the famous London specialist hospitals (beginning with Maudsley, Queen Square, Great Ormond Street, and Moorfields) as the embryo British Postgraduate Medical Federation. He recommended the appointment of postgraduate medical deans in all medical schools of Great Britain to meet the needs of returning Royal Army Medical Corps personnel. His foresight was remarkable and the university postgraduate deans held the first of many (still continuing) conferences in the month the European war ended.

Fraser had realized from the beginning of his career in postgraduate medical education that the Hammersmith school was only the spearhead of a wider movement which must spread to many thousands of general practitioners, and to this end he ensured the use of other general hospitals in London, thus paving the way for the later growth and creation of postgraduate teaching centres in the larger district hospitals in the rest of England. All these functions were written into the charter of the university of London's British Postgraduate Medical Federation, of which he became the first director in 1946, holding this post until 1960.

During his professional life, medicine was in transition. Fraser gave it vigorous and far-sighted leadership. Through his deep involvement in academic medicine and his experience in the emergency medical service, he influenced the creation of a high standard of service to the sick, on a pattern subsequently developed in the National Health Service. Tireless in his work, he would leap from a night train in the early morning with a bundle of journals already digested. His lectures became personal tutorials. He strode from the rostrum up and down the gallery, popping questions to his alerted listeners. His list of headings was ostentatiously torn up at the end of each session, so that he never repeated his presentations in the same way. In ward teaching he exemplified thoroughness by spending at least an hour on the details of one patient. 'Never let a student ever see you do anything second-rate' was his exhortation to his juniors.

He was quite unflappable in a crisis and never revealed exasperation. He thought carefully through every major problem and arrived at meetings with a solution, persuading others to agree with him with a kindly twinkle in his eye. With all this drive he combined sympathy and understanding which helped many individuals through their human dilemmas and difficulties.

His research experience and interests spread into many fields including poliomyelitis, heart failure, thyroid disease, disorders of neuro-humoral transmission, the latter concept revolutionizing physiological thinking in the late thirties. He held many honorific lectureships—Goulstonian, Croonian, Harveian, Flexner among others. His services to the Pharmacopoeia Commission extended over twenty years. From 1947 to 1949 he was deputy vice-chancellor of the university of London. Edinburgh and London conferred the honorary LLD upon him and in 1948 he was appointed commander of the Order of Orange-Nassau for his war services to the Netherlands.

In his youth he was a rugby player. His holidays were usually spent fishing near a family home in Argyllshire at the southern end of Loch Shiel. Interested in ornithology and botany, even his relaxations were directed to continuous occupation of his active mind. His warm-hearted unflagging idealism was blended with an austere belief that idleness is a sin.

In 1919 he married Mary Claudine Stirling, daughter of Colin Donald and widow of his second cousin, Captain J. A. Fraser. They had one son. Fraser died in Hammersmith Hospital 2 October 1964.

[*British Medical Journal*, 10 October 1964; *Lancet*, 17 October 1964; personal knowledge.]   JOHN McMICHAEL

FRASER, HUGH, first BARON FRASER OF ALLANDER (1903–1966), draper, company chairman, and philanthropist, was born in Glasgow 15 January 1903, the only son of Hugh Fraser,

drapery warehouseman, and his wife, Emily Florence McGown. He was educated at Glasgow Academy and Warriston School, Moffat. His mother was influential in allowing him to leave school in 1919. She wanted him to train as an accountant, but after a few months he had his way and entered his father's business, a large emporium in Buchanan Street, Glasgow. He learnt the business from the bottom, partly from his own mistakes, and to such purpose that his father made him managing director in 1924 when he was only twenty-one. Three years later he became chairman on his father's death. The young chairman had ideas for expansion, but he bided his time until 1936 when he defied economic depression and began to extend his business by acquiring other stores in Glasgow. His finances became stretched but credit was forthcoming from banks impressed by his remarkable qualities of vision, imagination, shrewdness, and, above all integrity.

After 1939 the war made expansion difficult, but he did buy an Edinburgh store in 1940. His business prospered to such an extent that in 1948 he was able to float the House of Fraser Ltd. as a public company with a capital of one million pounds. Those who bought ordinary shares then were to have the value of their investment multiplied tenfold in a few years. This success was due to two things: first, Fraser's thorough knowledge of the drapery business; this enabled him to see and grasp opportunities for improving the profits of businesses which he aquired; and secondly his brilliant and original idea, copied later by several entrepreneurs, of selling the freehold properties of the shops and then obtaining leases on them at rents acceptable to the purchasers and not higher than could be met by improved management. This gave him the cash to finance his early acquisitions. He first 'invaded' London by acquiring the John Barker group in 1957. Here he had won the confidence and support of the directors. The 'battle' for Harrods was more serious, since the board was hostile and there was another competitor. Fraser's success in 1959 was regarded as a Pyrrhic victory by those who thought he had paid too much and who did not know their man. By this time the House of Fraser had perhaps larger interests in the length and breadth of England than in Scotland, but Fraser's office in Buchanan Street remained his headquarters to the end, even if he had constantly to go to London and occupy his suite in the Savoy. Twice, his bids for Scottish companies failed. In the first, his wish to help friends who wanted to keep control of SMT in Scotland could not allow him to make a financially unjustifiable offer. In the second he was frustrated by the determined directors of Lyle & Scott and certain circumstances of which they took legal advantage. But when an attempt was made in 1964 to gain control of the *Glasgow Herald*, he did fight successfully to acquire the newspaper and keep its control in Glasgow. He had been a Glasgow town councillor for eight years from 1938, though not in his element, because, while he took his share of committee work, the undue prolongation of business not unreasonably irritated him. He was happier in 1959 when he applied himself with vigour to the expansion of the tourist industry in the Scottish Highlands. The complex of facilities created at Aviemore is a tribute to his vision and enterprise.

In 1960 Fraser created, in memory of his mother, the Hugh Fraser Foundation, with a capital of over two million pounds. This differed from most charitable foundations in two respects: it was not publicized, and its objects were not closely restricted. Fraser had sought suggestions for the objects to which his benefaction might be devoted, but he reflected that trusts had often been created to meet a contemporary need and were later in difficulties because that need had been met and they were unable to devote funds to other causes. Consequently, with unexampled generosity and foresight, he gave power to his trustees to make payments in their sole discretion to any person, fund, institution, or society, whether in Scotland or elsewhere.

Fraser was an honorary LLD of St. Andrews (1962) and was created a baronet in 1961 and a baron in 1964. He spoke once in the Lords, but not very effectively. He was no orator and he disliked public appearances. He was secretly a benefactor to many who were old, infirm, or sick. Unlike other successful millionaires he made and kept friends; he did not want power so much as to succeed; not for him to bury his talent in the ground.

Slim, unostentatiously but well groomed, with a trim moustache and a flower in his buttonhole, an endless smoker of cigarettes, with a Scots voice perhaps rather rough when first heard, he was highly strung, a warm-hearted man who enriched the life of all who knew him. He liked to be at home at week-ends to play snooker with his doctor and then to have a four at bridge where he was as shrewd as he was bold. He enjoyed a flutter at Monte Carlo or some other Continental casino where, as he said, he was very lucky. Some would say that he was lucky in business too, but there his success was based on knowledge, on hard work, on careful and accurate calculations, and above all on his shining integrity.

Fraser was always a family man. He had the great good fortune in 1931 to found a happy home for himself by marrying Kate Hutcheon, daughter of Sir Andrew Jopp Williams Lewis, shipbuilder, former lord provost of Aberdeen. From her he had support, inspiration, and advice for the rest of his life. Fraser's home was his refuge in days of difficulty and disappointment, and his greatest delight in success and triumph was to share it at his own fireside. They had a daughter and a son Hugh (born 1936) who succeeded his father as chairman of the House of Fraser and other companies. Fraser died at his home near Glasgow 6 November 1966; his son succeeded to the baronetcy but disclaimed the barony.

A portrait of Fraser by Sir James Gunn hangs in Harrods; one by Alan Sutherland is in the House of Fraser office in Glasgow; both are owned by the family, as well as another by Frank Eastman.

[G. Bull and A. Vice, *Bid for Power*, 1958; G. Pottinger, *The Winning Counter*, 1971; private information; personal knowledge.]

T. M. KNOX

FRASER, WILLIAM, first BARON STRATHALMOND (1888-1970), industrialist, was born in Glasgow 3 November 1888, the second son among the eight children of William Fraser, who founded and became managing director of the Pumpherston Oil Company, and his wife, Janet Loch. He was educated at the Glasgow Academy and the technical college where he worked in the department endowed by James Young [q.v.], founder of the Scottish shale oil industry. In 1909 Fraser joined his father's firm and visited the United States and Canada on technical investigations. He was appointed a director in 1913 and joint managing director in 1915. During the war of 1914-18 he was instrumental in creating the Scottish Oil Agency by the amalgamation of the six Scottish shale oil marketing organizations; he was appointed CBE in 1918 in recognition of his work in increasing home oil supplies in wartime. Also in that year he was chosen by Sir John (later Lord) Cadman [q.v.] to go to the United States as chairman of the Inter-Allied Petroleum Specifications Commission to co-ordinate supplies for the armed forces. He was thus before the age of thirty beginning to attain a prominent position in the oil industry. In due course he was to become the acknowledged leader in all matters to do with Middle East oil, which ultimately involved most of the countries bordering the Persian Gulf and the major international oil companies of the world. A keen analytical mind and forceful character allied to great foresight and imagination ideally suited him for the task, to which he devoted his time and energies to the exclusion of other professional and business interests.

At the end of the war the Anglo Persian Oil Company considered how best to develop a market in the United Kingdom for its products. The shale oil companies under the direction of Fraser had already been merged into the one company, Scottish Oils Ltd., and Lord Greenway, chairman of the Anglo Persian, knew Fraser and recognized his abilities. Scottish Oils, which could never survive on its own once liquid petroleum became freely and cheaply available, was taken over by Anglo Persian, Fraser joining the board of the main company in 1923 in charge of production. His sphere of activity was thus greatly enlarged and it was not long before he visited Persia and began to play an active part in the development of the oilfields. In 1928 he was appointed deputy chairman, and although he never completely broke his connection with his native Glasgow, he could no longer live away from London and, with his family, moved to Surrey.

At the time of his visit to Persia in 1923 the modest oil production of 3 million tons per annum was being drawn from the only oilfield yet discovered. By then it was clear that there were many times this capacity waiting to be tapped in neighbouring oil-bearing structures once they had been explored and developed. A much stronger organization on site and at London headquarters would be needed and it was Fraser's first task to build this up, which he did with conspicuous success. The vast size of the oil reserves in the Middle East only awaiting the drill must have convinced him that whatever problems the Anglo Persian might have, the supply of raw material was not likely to be one of them. His early association with the production activities showed him that there need be no limit to the volume of crude oil available to the company; its further growth must lie in the expansion of markets and it was to this that he proceeded to devote his attention. At the same time, while there was no need to worry about the physical aspects of production, all must depend on the maintenance of relations with the governments of the producing countries, and on this subject he spent much, if not most, of his time.

Through the thirties Fraser was deputy to Cadman and he succeeded him as chairman of the company in 1941. He was intimately concerned with the development of oil production from Iraq, where oil was found in 1927, and from Kuwait, the first discovery there being in 1938. Companies jointly owned by British, American, French, and Dutch interests were formed to hold the concessions in these countries and these connections brought Fraser into close touch with the leaders of the American oil industry. At this period he was engaged in discussions with the Persian Government, who in 1932 had repudiated their 1901 agreement. After overcoming many difficulties a new agreement was signed with Reza Shah, which remained in force until 1951 when Persia nationalized the oil and seized the company's installation.

By the late thirties, Fraser's complete mastery of his subject and his shrewdness had made him pre-eminent in the industry on Middle East affairs; particularly the heads of the large American companies had confidence in him. Had it not been for this, the British Petroleum Company (the successor of the Anglo Persian) would never have been able to take the lead in the group of British, American, Dutch, and French companies which resumed production in 1954 from Persia, or to have obtained the lion's share of the production rights in the group.

To bring the company's markets into line with their ever-growing availability of crude oil, discussions were held with several large refining and marketing companies; in 1931 Fraser led in the formation of the Shell-Mex & BP to enlarge the market for the company's products in the United Kingdom and of a somewhat similar arrangement in the East and Africa for the joint refining and sale of products in that area. It is significant that in 1951 when 77 per cent of the company's oil supplies were cut off by the Persian nationalization, the reaction might easily have been to surrender part of the company's markets to competitors. Fraser had no doubt that the markets were the most valuable asset and, against considerable opposition, he insisted that they must be retained and supplied at all costs. This courageous action was fully justified in the event, especially when normal production was resumed three years later.

Fraser's most important public appointment came in 1935 as petroleum adviser to the War Office, which continued through and after the war of 1939-45. In 1939 he was knighted. In 1951-2 he was chairman of the oil supply advisory committee. It was not, however, through public appointments that he played his part in the nation's affairs, but rather as the right-hand man for the Government to consult in international oil affairs, particularly where relations with the United States and Middle East governments were concerned. Nor did he hesitate to come forward with advice, or even strictures, on his own initiative when he thought it was needed. His company's success in developing oilfields in the Middle East countries had aroused envy and even apprehension among some of his competitors; this, allied to a feeling that oil reserves in the United States had been unduly depleted in the war years, led to a threat that British properties in the Middle East might be used to redress the balance. It was fortunate that Fraser's determination and courage were there to prevent anything like this happening. It was perhaps not unnatural that certain government circles should favour such a solution to Lend-Lease debt repayment, but Fraser was unwavering in his insistence that such a sacrifice would be disastrous to the country. When he retired in 1956 his company was producing 50 million tons of crude oil per annum.

In 1955 Fraser was created a baron, taking the title of Baron Strathalmond, of Pumpherston, thereby recalling his family connection with the Scottish oil industry. Other appointments which he held were directorships of the Burmah Oil Company, the Great Western Railway, and the National Provincial Bank. He was awarded the Institute of Petroleum Cadman memorial medal in 1945 and in 1951 became an honorary LLD of Birmingham University.

His portrait, painted in 1948 by (Sir) James Gunn, hangs in Britannic House, London, headquarters of the British Petroleum Company. Tall and distinguished in appearance, he may have seemed awe-inspiring and a little remote, an impression not, however, shared by those who knew him well. No one could have been less dour, more full of humanity and humour, or more closely in touch with his staff. As a young man in Glasgow he was a first-class football and tennis player; later in life his sports were golf and shooting.

In 1913 Fraser married Mary Roberton (died 1963), daughter of Thomson McLintock, chartered accountant, and sister of Sir William McLintock [q.v.]; they had one son and one daughter. Strathalmond died in London 1 April 1970 and was succeeded by his son, William (born 1916).

[Private information; personal knowledge.]
J. M. PATTINSON

FRAZER, ALASTAIR CAMPBELL (1909-1969), pharmacologist and food scientist, was born at Orpington, Kent, 26 July 1909, the second son of Wilson Ray Frazer, civil servant in the Local Government Board, and his wife, Grace Haldane Robbs. He was educated at Lancing, of which he was a scholar, and from 1926, at St. Mary's Hospital Medical School, university of London, where he graduated in medicine and surgery in 1932. He taught physiology and pharmacology at the medical school for ten years, and for two periods was acting head of the department of physiology. In 1942 he was appointed independent reader in pharmacology in the university of Birmingham, being promoted professor of pharma-

cology in the following year. From 1937 to 1945 he held a Sir Halley Stewart research fellowship. He received a London D.Sc. in 1945, having achieved a Birmingham MD in 1943 and a London Ph.D. in 1941.

At St. Mary's Hospital Medical School Frazer had developed a special interest in the mechanism of the absorption of fat from the gut and in the physical chemistry of emulsions of fat, and both in London and in Birmingham he gathered around him a group with a lively interest in these subjects. The study of sprue, a tropical disease in which absorption from the gut is defective, led to a growing interest in the chemistry and biochemistry of food, and in nutrition in general, while as a pharmacologist Frazer was naturally concerned with toxic substances, in both food and drugs. In 1953 an honours degree course in medical biochemistry was started by Frazer in the department of pharmacology at Birmingham, and an alteration of name, both of the chair and of the department, from 'pharmacology' to 'medical biochemistry', which was instituted in 1956, illustrated an important development in Frazer's interests.

For many years he was an adviser to the Government on overseas developments, and in this connection he travelled widely in the Caribbean area and in Africa. In 1955 he chaired a committee on medical health policy in Uganda, and in 1961 was chairman of a commission to advise on research in East Africa. His concern with nutrition and toxicology involved him nationally and internationally in bodies set up to advise about the control of food and drugs. When the Ministry of Health set up a committee on the safety of drugs in 1963 Frazer was appointed a member, and shortly before his death he had been made chairman in succession to Sir Derrick Dunlop. He was a member of the Agricultural Research Council for many years.

Frazer was a lucid and compelling speaker and was widely invited to take part in conferences and to give lectures, both at home and abroad. He possessed to a remarkable degree the ability to move from a subject of medical and scientific significance, which had no obvious or direct practical importance, to one of industrial consequence. He was much in demand as a consultant in industry, where he was able to advise on the possible practical application of an observation which at first appeared to be of academic interest only. At the time of his death he was president both of the British Food Manufacturing Industries Research Association and of the British Industrial Biological Research Association.

Frazer's resignation from his university post in 1967 to become the first director-general of the newly established British Nutrition Foundation was surprising to many but not totally unexpected to those who appreciated the width of his interests. The Foundation had been recently set up by a group of academic scientists and industrialists to promote co-operation between industry and non-industrial bodies in all aspects of nutrition, and particularly in research. Frazer's appointment involved a move from Birmingham to London, and the building up of an entirely new institution, a duty which he tackled with zest and effectiveness. But with his early and unexpected death two years later one can only surmise what might have happened under a longer period of his vivid leadership.

Frazer was a large man whose beard added to his striking appearance. He radiated good humour and friendliness and much enjoyed the good things of life and endeavoured to ensure that those around him could do likewise. He delighted to travel to distant parts and had friends in many countries. He was an honorary foreign member of the Société Gastroentérologie de Belge, of the Royal Flemish Academy of Sciences, and of the Société Philomathique de Paris. He was appointed CBE in 1962.

He was the author of many medical and scientific publications; his monograph, *Malabsorption Syndromes*, was published in 1968.

In 1943 Frazer married Hilary, younger daughter of Ralph Eddowes Garrod, a chemist, of London, and three sons and one daughter were born of the marriage. Frazer died suddenly in London 14 June 1969 aged fifty-nine.

[*The Times*, 17, 21, and 24 June 1969; *Lancet*, 28 June 1969; personal knowledge.]

F. G. YOUNG

FREETH, FRANCIS ARTHUR (1884-1970), industrial chemist, was born at 9 Eaton Road, Birkenhead, 2 January 1884, the elder son of Edward Henry Freeth, master mariner, and his wife, Catherine Hinde. F. A. Freeth, who was an intensely patriotic man, was proud of his military connections. His great-grandfather, General Sir James Freeth, was a Peninsular War veteran and later quartermaster-general (1851-4), and his grandfather and two great-uncles were major-generals. His father was commissioned in the Royal Naval Reserve; he himself became a major in the Territorial Army in the Cheshire Regiment and his son served in the Royal Navy.

In Freeth's young days there was no money to spare for much beyond essentials. His schooling was local, first at Yardleys in Birkenhead and later at Audlem Grammar School where in 1897 the Cheshire County Council had installed a small chemical laboratory. This, in his own words, 'fired me off properly; there

was nothing but chemistry for me'. Through the goodwill of an aunt the possibility of a university career became open to Freeth and his brother and after a preliminary failure, due to a lack of the necessary mathematics and the loss of a year through illness, Freeth was admitted to the university of Liverpool in 1902. Here he came under the influence of F. G. Donnan [q.v.] who had become professor of physical chemistry in 1904, and after obtaining a first class in chemistry in 1905 Freeth worked with Donnan for a year and obtained an M.Sc. (1906). Later he contributed the notice of Donnan to this Dictionary, as he did that of Sir James Swinburne.

He worked for a year with Hignetts tobacco factory as an analyst and in September 1907 joined Brunner Mond & Co., the alkali manufacturers at Northwich, a company which later became one of the two leading partners of the amalgamation of 1926 in which ICI was formed.

Chief chemist by 1909, Freeth rapidly made his mark as a physical chemist in the rich scientific soil of Brunner Mond. With friends, made by correspondence with the world-famous Dutch school of physical chemists, he himself became a world figure in a rather recondite but important branch of physical chemistry: the phase rule, which governs the equilibria and behaviour of soluble salts. With his able team of assistants at Winnington, who always remembered him with affection, he produced a large data bank of isotherms of many systems of inorganic salts in water for everyday use which was still in demand fifty years later.

When the war broke out Freeth was mobilized on 4 August 1914. He went to France in February 1915 and was recalled in March. Characteristically he refused at first but was told that if he did not obey he would be put under arrest.

The crisis for which he and other chemists were summoned home was the grave one of high explosives. There was a shortage of ammonium nitrate in particular and the knowledge of how to make it was rare. Freeth and his brother-in-law, H. E. Cocksedge, were among the few who had the knowledge—not only had it but with their phase-rule knowledge could devise no less than three processes for its manufacture. Lord Moulton [q.v.], director-general of explosives supply, gave them a free hand under Brunner Mond's management and the explosives crisis was surmounted. That it was indeed a crisis is illustrated by Moulton's saying to Freeth at one time, 'My dear Freeth, do you realize the safety of England depends on this?', to which Freeth replied 'In that case, Sir, I'll tell you the truth, I'm certain that these processes will all work'—and they did.

For his war work Freeth was rewarded, rather modestly perhaps, with appointment as OBE. Then, as the great increase in chemical research got under way, Freeth was in the van of events in Brunner Mond, collecting men from the universities, making scientific contacts abroad, setting up an industrial laboratory second to none in ability and equipment. His insistence on technique and on quality stamped itself on the company and set the pattern from which ICI in later years was markedly helped on the road to world pre-eminence. In these days academic honours came to Freeth: a doctorate from Leiden (1924), a D.Sc. from Liverpool (1924) and, in 1925, an FRS. Later came many other academic distinctions, and he served as president, vice-president, and member of council of several learned societies.

After the formation of ICI Freeth was separated from his beloved laboratory and set on a different road which ill suited him. He was not at ease in the area of research policy discussions, his health suffered, he began to drink heavily, and in 1937 he broke down. ICI pensioned him and retained him as a consultant. However, with his usual spirit, Freeth, with his brother's help, pulled himself round, stopped drinking, and during World War II was able to engage in some secret experimental work on special weapons and operational devices.

As a suitable end to a distinguished career Freeth, fully recovered in health, was re-engaged by ICI in 1944 and remained with the company for eight happy years. His work concerned research liaison for the company and in this period he devised and introduced the ICI Fellowship Scheme for postdoctoral research at universities.

Freeth's accomplishments in the scientific world, which served his country and his employers so well, were more than balanced by his success in the human sphere. He believed passionately in service to the nation and to science. His faith in science and what it could and did achieve under his leadership was ceaselessly preached and ultimately accepted by the company he worked for and by a host of others in industry. He had a profound effect on the fortunes of Brunner Mond and of ICI, not only by the application of his own doctrines but also by his choice of young men who became the leaders of the chemical industry. A larger proportion of the early ICI executive directors were 'Freeth men' than came from any of the other founding companies—thirteen out of the first fifty-five. Freeth was a good judge of the young, though, like anyone else, he had his failures. He was also wonderfully good with young people; he never talked down to them and always gave the impression that he was really interested in what they had to say. He did not always insist on the highest academic performance in his recruits if they had ideas which seemed potentially first class.

Freeth's style in conversation, an art he loved, was often vehement to the point of extravagance. An excellent example is his comment upon the Brunner Mond directors: 'What are they doing, examining last month's costs with a microscope when they should be surveying the horizon with a telescope?'

In his farewell speech in ICI he said, on receiving a presentation, 'Mr Chairman, ladies and gentlemen, I am told that somebody has accused me of saying that if the Ministry of Fuel and Power were boring for coal and they went through a layer of gold nine feet thick they would throw it away because they wouldn't know what to do with it. Sir, I only said four feet thick.' In talk Freeth was full of ideas; they poured forth, brilliant, sound, unsound, even crackpot. But in reflection more criticism was applied and the seething cauldron would simmer down.

He had great energy and sometimes worked himself excessively hard. He had an immense host of friends and acquaintances, although he was rather a snob; but he was always ready and able to help one by knowing the right man to approach. He was amazingly good company. He was an artist, a wide and deep thinker in spite of his verbal fireworks, an actor manqué perhaps, vain, eager for praise and renown, sensitive, easily hurt, basically humble. Sir Cyril Hinshelwood [q.v.] once spoke of Freeth's fundamental optimism: 'He spake ill of very few and well of many.' Perhaps one might end with his own words: 'I have always observed that it is the cheerful people who get things done and that in dark times one must tell oneself that tomorrow will be a better day.'

In 1910 Freeth married Ethel Elizabeth, daughter of G. N. Warbrick, of Silecroft, Northumberland. They had one son and two daughters. He died in a nursing home at Church Crookham, Hampshire, 15 July 1970.

[Sir Peter Allen in *Biographical Memoirs of Fellows of the Royal Society*, vol. xxii, 1976; private information, personal knowledge.]

PETER ALLEN

FRENCH, SIR HENRY LEON (1883–1966), civil servant, was born in Southsea 30 December 1883, the third son of Frederick Edward French, leather seller, and his wife, Eliza Mingay. He was educated privately at Southsea and later at King's College, London. In 1901 he joined the Civil Service by open competition and was appointed as a second-division clerk to the Board of Agriculture. He was promoted to the first division as an assistant head of branch in 1909. Thereafter he progressed to assistant secretary in the Ministry (1920-9), principal assistant secretary (1929-34), and second secretary in 1934. In 1936 he was seconded to the Board of Trade as director of the food (defence plans) department, and after the outbreak of war in 1939 became permanent secretary of the Ministry of Food where he remained until September 1945. He retired from the Civil Service in the following year.

French's reputation as a strong administrator rests mainly upon the remarkable success of the Ministry of Food during the war of 1939-45. He had little to do with the Ministry of Food during the war of 1914-18 when some of the foundations, such as food rationing, of the later Ministry were well laid. His main concern then had been with agricultural policy and production. In 1917-19 he was general secretary of the food production department of the Board of Agriculture, having been secretary to Lord Milner's departmental committee on home food production and joint secretary to Lord Selborne's committee on agricultural policy. It was not until 1936 that French became concerned with food rather than agriculture.

However, his long career with the Ministry of Agriculture proved to be of considerable value during the second war when the acute shortage of shipping placed increasing importance upon the production of food within the United Kingdom. The relationship between the Ministries of Agriculture and Food became strained in 1940 and 1941 owing to wide differences of opinion about food production policy. French had much to do with the 'concordat' reached between the two ministers (R. S., later Viscount, Hudson and Lord Woolton, qq.v.) which settled policy for the rest of the war.

The success of the Ministry of Food during the war was due to the combination of highly expert knowledge of the food industries throughout the world, a flexible and imaginative approach to new problems and opportunities, strong leadership and public relations, and sound administration. French contributed in varying degrees to these factors.

The food rationing system, fair and efficient and well enforced, reflected the strong administration of the Ministry of Food, which was remarkable for a wartime Ministry whose staff exceeded 55,000 at one time, with a mere handful of permanent civil servants and a very wide mixture of imported talent. French attached high importance to good organization to ensure efficient operation. To some, indeed, his insistence on formal channels of communication was excessive and restrictive, especially when speed of decision was essential. But this was not surprising for a man who was principal establishment officer of a large department during the inter-war years when promotion was desperately slow, who was already fifty-six when war broke out, and who had spent thirty-eight of those years in one department.

At certain key moments, however, French showed surprising flexibility. For example, when Lord Woolton made it clear that he opposed the dual direction of the commodity divisions of the Ministry (i.e. a trade director and a civil servant side by side) French altered the organization immediately so that each division had only one head (usually the trade director). Likewise, he accepted the appointment of a commercial secretary virtually in parallel with himself as permanent secretary. Again, when it became necessary to deal with the very wide range of foodstuffs which were not rationed, French decided that points rationing would be introduced at once alongside the ordinary rationing system, despite strong opposition from most of his trade advisers.

Unhappily, these bursts of flexibility rarely extended to those aspects of administration termed 'establishment matters'. His formal, rigid attitude to such matters, which certainly reflected his own career between the wars, was exemplified most clearly by his failure to come to terms with E. M. H. Lloyd [q.v.], a brilliantly imaginative man, impatient to the point of irresponsibility, as it must have seemed to a civil servant as orthodox as French. Lloyd had made a great contribution to the work of the Ministry of Food in 1917-19. His ideas, often novel and unconventional, found expression in much of the early work of the food (defence plans) department and of the Ministry of Food. The failure of the two men to work together was a matter of concern: when Lloyd persuaded some outstanding men to join the Ministry on the outbreak of war, French refused to endorse the appointments because they had not gone through the proper establishment channels.

On the other hand, French's selection of trade advisers and other staff from the food industries, most of which were settled well before the outbreak of war, contributed greatly to the success of the Ministry. Every section of the food industries—manufacture, distribution, import, storage, transport—agreed to release their senior management to the Ministry and many of the men were party to the pre-war planning. The result was that when war came, the Ministry of Food came into existence almost fully grown and able to execute quickly the plans already in existence. The trade advisers and their staff worked with dedication and determination for as long as war lasted. French's choice of people was amply justified.

The strong leadership and good public relations of the Ministry came, however, mainly from ministers and especially Lord Woolton. Fortunately, the qualities of the two men were mainly complementary. French, never strong in negotiation or in weighing up the views of the other party, left major issues of policy increasingly to the minister and the strong central staff which was built up after 1941. Lend-Lease which virtually ended Treasury control of the Ministry for the duration of the war, at least as far as overseas purchasing was concerned, was left almost entirely to the Food Mission in Washington and the central staff in London. Likewise, French contributed little to the constant struggle for shipping space to meet food import requirements. He showed little interest in the problems of feeding Europe after the war or in the work of UNRRA and the FAO. Once the Ministry was firmly established and its strength both in Whitehall and overseas clear, French seemed to feel that he had made his major contribution and could now leave more and more to others.

To some people French was unapproachable and vain. He made up his mind about people quickly and rarely changed it. Like many civil servants, the war brought him an eminence which he had never expected to attain. He quoted frequently the reported remark of an Indian minister after French's visit to India in August-September 1944: 'French, this is the greatest day in the history of India.' And he seemed to believe it.

Despite these weaknesses, he made a real contribution to the success of the Ministry of Food which owed much to the sound foundations he laid in 1936-9 as director of the food (defence plans) department.

After his retirement, French occupied a number of posts in the film industry into which his close personal relations with the Rank family took him. He brought to the industry his continued interest in good organization and sound administration. But again, he found it more than difficult to come to terms with the creative people. From 1946 to 1957 he was director-general of the British Film Producers Association and he was president from 1957 to 1958. During the same years he was director-general of the Commonwealth Film Corporation and chairman of the Film Casting Association Ltd. He was associated with the Festival of Britain in 1951 and was first chairman of the Festival Gardens Ltd. He was chairman of the UNESCO Co-operating Body on Mass Communications (1946-53) and attended UNESCO conferences in 1947 and 1950.

French was appointed OBE (1918) and CB (1920); KBE (1938), KCB (1942), and GBE (1946).

In 1903 he married Zenobia Clare (died 1954), daughter of Charles Grimes, FRGS, of Southsea; they had one daughter. The marriage was dissolved by divorce in 1929 when French married Violet (died 1975), daughter of G. R. Huntley, of Streatham.

French died in London 3 April 1966.

[Private information; personal knowledge.]
JOHN WALL

FREYBERG, BERNARD CYRIL, first BARON FREYBERG (1889-1963), lieutenant-general, was born 21 March 1889 in Richmond, Surrey, the seventh son of James Freyberg, a surveyor, and the fifth by his second wife, Julia Hamilton. The family emigrated to New Zealand in 1891 and settled in Wellington, where James Freyberg joined the Forestry Department. Bernard Freyberg was educated at Wellington College, New Zealand, where he distinguished himself as a swimmer. After leaving school at the age of nearly sixteen, he took up dentistry, and after qualifying in Otago (1911), practised his profession for a couple of years. He had already formed the ambition of swimming the English Channel, for which he trained assiduously in the Waihou and Waikato rivers, an interest which early began to be rivalled by his soldiering with the local territorials, and by 1912 he had been gazetted in Morrinsville as a second lieutenant. He could not resist the opportunity for change afforded by the dock strike of 1913 and volunteered as a stoker in the *Maunganui* en route to Sydney. On his return he obtained a stoker's certificate and then set off for America.

His adventures from then on are both legendary and obscure but, before the end of August 1914, he had somehow got himself to London where he perhaps contrived to meet (Sir) Winston Churchill. Through Churchill's influence he became a temporary lieutenant in the Royal Naval Volunteer Reserve and was soon given command of A company in the Hood battalion of the Royal Naval Division. He led his company in the Antwerp adventure, Churchill's brain-child, and brought it back via Ostend from the subsequent débacle, the first of Freyberg's four evacuations by sea.

The division was next assigned to Gallipoli. Freyberg sailed with the Hood battalion 28 February 1915. Among the other officers of a brilliant mess were Arthur Asquith (son of the prime minister), (Sir) A. P. Herbert, and Rupert Brooke [q.v.]. When Brooke was buried on Scyros 23 April, Freyberg helped carry his coffin and dig his grave.

The division's role was to cover the landings

of the main force by a mock landing in the Gulf of Xeros. Freyberg managed to persuade his superiors to entrust the task of diversion to him rather than risk many lives for a job which a bold and powerful swimmer could achieve alone. After dark, 25 April, he swam ashore and lit a series of flares along the beaches. He then swam back again and was got safely aboard his ship. For this he was appointed to the DSO, the first of his many decorations.

In the later fighting on Gallipoli he was severely wounded in July but recovered rapidly, and by 19 August he was not only back with his battalion but was its commanding officer. He remained with the battalion for the rest of the campaign, and after the evacuation of the Dardanelles in January 1916 he returned to England. The division had gone directly to France and was now reformed as 63rd division, although without losing its anomalous character. Freyberg was confirmed in command of the Hood battalion with the rank of lieutenant-colonel, and left for France with it in May. His first major battle on the new front was in November on the Somme. Within forty-eight hours he was four times wounded but he refused to be evacuated until the advanced position, captured largely because of his leadership and example, had been consolidated against counter-attack. He was awarded the Victoria Cross.

His wounds were severe, and detained him in hospital and on leave until March 1917. In April, as brigadier-general, he was given command of 173rd brigade of 58th division—thus ending his service with the Royal Naval Division and his men of the Hood battalion—and distinguished himself in the May fighting at Bullecourt. In September, during the third battle of Ypres, he suffered multiple wounds and had to spend three months in hospital in England. On his return to the front he was given command of 88th brigade of 29th division, near Passchendaele, a grim name which he never forgot. He was in much of the major fighting of 1918, including the last battle of Ypres, where he won a bar to his DSO. He ended the war, ardent to the last, with a successful dash to forestall the demolition of a bridge at Lessines just before 11.00 hours on Armistice Day, winning a second bar to his DSO. He had already been mentioned in dispatches five times, wounded six times, and the French Government now awarded him the croix de guerre with palms. His eldest brothers, Oscar and Paul, had not been so lucky: Oscar was killed at Gallipoli in 1915 and Paul in France two years later.

In England, although deprecating heroics himself, Freyberg had become a byword for heroism and a friend of many people in positions of influence. In spite of a hankering to go to Balliol where some of his Hood friends had been educated, he had by now recognized his *métier* and resolved to become a professional soldier; his peacetime army career was interrupted briefly in 1922 by an unsuccessful attempt, under Liberal auspices, to win a seat in the House of Commons. He had passed the staff course at Camberley in 1920, and served for a time with the Grenadier Guards until, in 1929, he was given command of the 1st battalion of the Manchester Regiment. But soldiering had not altogether ousted his earlier ambitions, and he made three attempts to swim the Channel—in 1925, when he failed by only 500 yards, and again twice in 1926. In 1931-3 he was assistant adjutant and quartermaster-general of the Southern Command, and by 1934 was a major-general. In 1937, however, his strikingly successful career received its first real check, under the axe of Leslie (later Lord) Hore-Belisha [q.v.]. He was declared medically unfit, and indignantly challenged his examiners to climb Snowdon: they refused—he went, alone; he was retired with the rank of major-general. For the next two years he interested himself in business and industry as a director of the Birmingham Small Arms Company. He also revived his interest in politics and in 1938 was adopted as prospective Conservative candidate for the Spelthorne division of Middlesex.

On the outbreak of war in 1939 he was recalled to the army, and offered his services to the New Zealand Government. With the warm approval of Sir Edmund (later Lord) Ironside, Lord Gort [qq.v.], and Winston Churchill he was appointed general in command of the 2nd New Zealand Expeditionary Force, 23 November. He flew to New Zealand and met the War Cabinet and thereafter obtained from the New Zealand Government a document—his 'charter'—which gave him wide powers of decision over the organization, administration, and employment of the forces under his command, which were to be trained in Egypt and to fight as a single unit.

5th brigade, one of the three in the newly formed New Zealand division, was diverted to England in 1940, where it was to remain to strengthen the defences against the threatened invasion, and stayed there until the end of the year when the threat had receded. So it was not until March 1941 that Freyberg had his division together as a whole in Egypt, with all three brigades, under the over-all command of Sir Archibald (later Earl) Wavell and Sir Henry Maitland (later Lord) Wilson [qq.v.]. In a matter of days the division embarked for Greece, an enterprise about which Freyberg had considerable but private misgivings: his diary says, 'the situation is a grave one; we shall be fighting against heavy odds on a plan that has been ill-conceived and one that violates every principle of war'.

What had begun as a forlorn hope soon became a fighting withdrawal in the face of an enemy far greater in numbers and vastly superior in all the materials of war. This withdrawal was followed by an evacuation which owed its success to the British Navy as well as to the fighting troops and their commanders. The essential Freyberg was revealed in his refusal to obey Wavell's orders to leave by air, staying with his men to the end.

Two of his brigades had been evacuated to Crete, the third to Egypt. When Freyberg halted in Crete to see his troops he found Wavell who had come to see the situation for himself. Wavell ordered Freyberg to take command of the island and hold it against the expected German invasion by sea and air. With a very few and inefficient tanks, obsolete artillery and little of it, a grave shortage of arms and equipment, virtually no air force, and every kind of supply problem, it was a desperate undertaking. Freyberg performed prodigies in the three weeks before invasion began, 20 May 1941. But the enemy, landing by glider and parachute, gained a foothold on the airfield at Maleme, after fierce fighting. This enabled them to land men and weapons by air. Given this and their total command of the sky, their success was now certain, even though an attempted sea invasion was destroyed by the Royal Navy. The best that Freyberg and his troops could do was to keep an unbroken front, mount counter-attacks whenever possible, avoid encirclement, and withdraw to the southern evacuation beaches. Once again, the Royal Navy brought salvation.

After his return to Egypt an inter-services inquiry fully exonerated Freyberg for the loss of Crete, and indeed praised him warmly for his conduct there and in Greece. He now pressed on with reorganizing the division and training it for desert operations. Both he and the division played a vital part in the battle of November–December ('Crusader') for the relief of Tobruk but, through no fault of its commander, the division suffered heavy losses. Sir Claude Auchinleck had succeeded Wavell as commander-in-chief Middle East, and he and Freyberg differed profoundly in their views about the use of brigade groups and the handling of armoured forces. It was with some relief, therefore, that Freyberg received orders to take the division to Syria.

The reverses suffered by the Eighth Army in the summer of 1942 in its battles with Rommel made it necessary for the division to return to the fray. Freyberg brought his men back from Syria in a lightning march which covered 1,200 miles in under eight days and they arrived in time to prevent the withdrawal of the Eighth

Army from becoming a rout. The division was surrounded by German armour at Minqar Qaim but broke out in a night battle, Freyberg himself being wounded and coming out on a stretcher. The division withdrew safely to the Alamein line where it played an important part in checking Rommel's further advance.

On 10 August 1942, Freyberg returned from hospital, a tonic to the division which had suffered heavily in ill-advised offensives during his absence. Sir Harold Alexander (later Earl Alexander of Tunis, q.v.) now succeeded Auchinleck as commander-in-chief Middle East, and Bernard Montgomery (later Viscount Montgomery of Alamein) took command of the Eighth Army. Montgomery and Freyberg held the same views about the role of armour and the use of brigade groups and the two were in close agreement in the operations which followed: the defensive battle of Alam Halfa, when the division held the main southern flank while Rommel's armour ground itself to a standstill; and the decisive battle of Alamein when the Eighth Army at last went over to a victorious offensive. Freyberg and his division were in the thick of the initial fighting, the breakthrough, and the pursuit which followed.

After a bold assault by one of its infantry battalions had cleared the Halfaya Pass and ensured the way into Libya, the division was given a rest until after the fall of Benghazi. When Montgomery felt ready to undertake dislodging Rommel from the El Agheila positions he sent Freyberg and the division, with armour under command, in a left hook round Agheila which narrowly failed to cut off Rommel's retreat. A further attempt at Nofilia went even closer to success. Rommel continued his withdrawal but could not hold Tripoli which was taken 23 January 1943, the division among the leading British forces. During a halt there, Churchill paid a visit and at a parade of the whole division hailed Freyberg as 'the salamander of the British Empire'.

Rommel now took up a strong position on the Mareth Line. Montgomery decided to try and turn the defence by a left hook through the Tebaga Gap and assigned the job to Freyberg and his division which was so strongly reinforced for the operation that it temporarily became the New Zealand Corps. Contact was made with the enemy 21 March, and the course of the subsequent fighting made Montgomery decide to switch (Sir) Brian Horrocks and his X Corps from the frontal attack to the more promising one on the left flank. The move was a success and Rommel was forced to abandon the Mareth Line. Difficult actions in mountainous country followed but the German and Italian forces were now pinned between First and Eighth Armies and the end was inevitable.

By 13 May 1943 Tunis had fallen and the war was over in North Africa.

Ever since the entry into Libya the New Zealand Government had been considering whether its division, like the 9th Australian division, should be withdrawn to the Pacific. Freyberg was consulted at that time and, after sounding out the feeling of the division, favoured staying in North Africa. The Government, warmly applauded by Churchill, had then decided in favour of staying. Now that the fighting in North Africa was over, the question came up again. There were strong political and administrative arguments for transfer to the Pacific front. And the New Zealand Government was also concerned lest Freyberg's own professional career should suffer if they exploited his loyalty to keep him with the division: by ability and experience he was well qualified to command a corps, or even an army. In the event, it was again decided by the Government to keep the division in the Mediterranean theatre; and Freyberg, a lieutenant-general since 1942 although only commanding a division, made it clear that he wanted to go on leading his New Zealanders. At least one of those who might have succeeded him, Brigadier (Sir) Howard Kippenberger, had no regrets: 'campaigning without the General seemed unthinkable,' he said. Indeed, the men of the division were as devoted to Freyberg as he was to them, and in the minds of many they were as inseparable as the two parts of a centaur.

After a period of rest and reorganization, during which 4th brigade was equipped with tanks and reincorporated, Freyberg took the division to join the Eighth Army on the Sangro front in Italy. There they met their old enemies from Crete, the German paratroops, amid conditions very different from the desert. The days of widely flanking left hooks and deep armoured penetration in terrain the mastery of which had earned for the division the description 'ball of fire' were for the time being over. A fierce battle which had opened in great promise settled into a grim winter campaign and by Christmas there was stalemate.

In January 1944 the division was switched to the command of the Fifth Army and the Cassino front. Freyberg became GOC New Zealand Corps once more, this time with two British divisions under command and a regiment of American armour in support. His task was to try to break through at Cassino where two formidable onslaughts by the Fifth Army had already failed. In spite of the controversial destruction of the monastery and the town of Cassino by aerial bombardment, two powerful attacks by the corps failed to get through, although narrowly. Losses were heavier than the New Zealand Government was prepared to go on accepting, and towards the end of March the division was withdrawn to a quieter sector of the front.

Alexander now turned to the planning and execution of the May offensive which took place in the south-west sector of the front and broke through to link up with the Anzio bridgehead and drive through to Rome. The division conformed on the north of the main advance and took part in the pursuit north of Rome; it went on to play a conspicuous forcing role in the advance towards Florence. According to Sir Oliver Leese, in command of the Eighth Army, if it had not been for Freyberg and his division the whole advance of the Eighth Army would have had to be held up for fresh formations to be brought in. Meanwhile, Freyberg's only son, Paul, an officer of the Grenadier Guards in the British 1st division, had been reported missing in Italy on 24 February. It later transpired that he had been taken prisoner, escaped, and made his way to Vatican property at Castel Gandolfo. He was then smuggled into the Vatican City in the boot of a papal car, and was finally collected by his father after the liberation of Rome in June.

The division was transferred in August to the Adriatic front, where Freyberg was injured in an air accident. But his impatient resilience and powerful constitution soon had him out of hospital again and he commanded the division in the difficult advances to the Senio river. When the spring offensive opened 9 April 1945, the division took the front running and raced ahead so fast that, when the Germans in Italy capitulated 2 May, it was already in Trieste and Freyberg had won a third bar to his DSO. Once more at an ending Freyberg had moved with such speed as to gain a vital position before the guns became silent, the armour halted, and the infantry grounded arms.

So ended Freyberg's last campaign and that of the division with which he had become identified. In 1945 he was appointed governor-general of New Zealand, an appointment so successful that it was extended in 1950 at the request of the New Zealand Government. When the extension ended in 1952 he was appointed lieutenant-governor and deputy constable of Windsor Castle.

Freyberg was a large man physically, six feet and one and a half inches tall and very powerfully built. He was large also in other ways: large-minded, lion-hearted, magnanimous, and great of soul. So closely was he identified, in the war of 1939–45, with his New Zealand Division that it was difficult to recall the one without the other. Freyberg moulded the division into a superb fighting machine, but the New Zealanders provided the material and they in turn had their effect on the mature Freyberg, modifying the stiffness of the British-trained regular soldier. The combination of men and commander produced, behind an appearance of casualness, a disciplined camaraderie within all ranks which stood the test of some of the severest fighting and heaviest casualties of the war. When Montgomery first took command of the Eighth Army he remarked that the New Zealanders did not seem to salute much. 'If you wave to them they'll wave back,' Freyberg replied. The great Churchill parade at Tripoli was another sort of reply. When spit-and-polish were required Freyberg knew that his division could be counted on to produce them with the best. The confidence he inspired in his men was founded not only on the standards of courage and endurance and fire that he himself exemplified, but on his respect for them and his tireless solicitude for their welfare in and out of battle. 'You cannot treat a man like a butler and expect him to fight like a lion', was a favourite saying of his. He was known to all his men by sight and was never far from where the fighting was hottest. His imperturbability under fire was the subject of endless anecdote—he was a man who 'did not know the use of fear'. As 'the General' he was a myth, and as 'Tiny' he was a mascot, and he had the sort of fame in the world at large which normally comes only to the commanders of armies.

He had the gift of finding and keeping senior officers of the same toughness and aggressive competence as himself and he controlled them by a natural authority, a formidable presence, a total integrity, which did not need the support of outward forms. He commanded the division for five long years in and out of battle and, in spite of all the changes in men and fortune, the division which fought in the last campaign was recognizably the same and fought with the same *élan* as the division which fought in Greece and Crete and at Sidi Rezegh. This was Freyberg's doing. He was an example not only to his own men but to his equals and superiors in rank. Many a corps commander felt he had to live up to his redoubtable subordinate; and even Montgomery was known to acknowledge the help which Freyberg gave him.

Nor should Freyberg's contribution to the war on the high political level be overlooked. He was in effect a sort of plenipotentiary of the New Zealand Government, although answerable to it and deeply aware also of the problems of the British War Cabinet. Here he had the advantages of the expatriate, an equal understanding of both his countries, and a sense of their common cause. His modesty and his objectivity about himself, and his discretion in dealing with the perplexities of a loyalty both common and divided, evoked and met with corresponding qualities in the members of the

New Zealand and the British Governments and produced a relationship which was a model of its kind. In this particular role he is important for constitutional history, for the history of the relations between the United Kingdom and the Dominions and the United States, at a time of great stress. It was not by his decision that the New Zealand Division stayed and contributed so much to victory in North Africa and Europe, but the confidence felt in him by both his Government and his troops had been fully earned and was a vital factor in the ultimate success.

Freyberg received an honorary LLD from St. Andrews in 1922 and another from Oxford in 1945. He was appointed CB in 1936 and KCB as well as KBE in 1942, CMG in 1919 and GCMG in 1946, and was raised to the peerage in 1951. In 1922 he married Barbara, daughter of Sir Herbert Jekyll and widow of a brother-officer, the Hon. Francis Walter Stafford McLaren, MP, killed in 1917. She also made a distinguished contribution by organizing welfare for the troops during the second war and was appointed OBE in 1943. She was as popular as her husband in New Zealand when he was governor-general, and was appointed GBE in 1953. She died in 1973. Their only son, Paul Richard (born 1923), succeeded to the title when his father died at Windsor 4 July 1963.

Two portraits painted by Peter McIntyre are in the possession of the family. There is a portrait in the Imperial War Museum painted by Ambrose McEvoy in 1918; another portrait by Peter McIntyre painted during the second war is in the Wellington Art Gallery; and there is a painting by Edward I. Halliday, executed shortly before Freyberg's death, in the Auckland War Memorial Museum. There is a bronze bust by Oscar Nemon in New Zealand House in London and a replica of it in the Defence Ministry in Wellington, as well as a posthumous bronze by Nemon in Freyberg's tablet in the Soldiers' Corner of the crypt of St. Paul's Cathedral.

[*Official History of New Zealand in the Second World War 1939-45*, War History Branch, Department of Internal Affairs, Wellington, New Zealand; Douglas Jerrold, *The Royal Naval Division*, 1927; Peter Singleton-Gates, *General Lord Freyberg*, *V. C.*, 1963; Sir Howard Kippenberger, *Infantry Brigadier*, 1949; private information; personal knowledge.]   D. M. DAVIN

FULLER, JOHN FREDERICK CHARLES (1878-1966), major-general, was born 1 September 1878 at Chichester, son of the Revd Alfred Fuller, rector of the parish of West Itchenor, by his wife, Selma Marie Philippine de la Chevallerie. His father was descended from Roundheads, and his mother from Huguenots, by which Fuller explained his own heretical attitude to accepted dogma, the prime motive of his life. At an early age he developed a dislike of the conventional religious background in which he lived, first at Chichester, then at Lausanne, Switzerland, to which his parents moved when he was eight. Three years later he was sent to a preparatory school in Hampshire, from which he went to Malvern College at the age of fourteen. He stayed there for two years, detesting public-school life, as he said. The wishes of his maternal grandfather directed him towards the army, for which he showed no more enthusiasm than he had for Malvern, for the 'crammer' to which he went at the age of seventeen, or for the Royal Military College, Sandhurst, where he spent a year in 1897-8. He showed little brilliance, was not interested in sport, and took to reading works of history and fiction of his own choice.

Fuller was commissioned in 1898 into the 43rd, the 1st battalion Oxfordshire Light Infantry, and joined them in Ireland where he led the idle life of an infantry subaltern until the battalion was sent just before Christmas 1899 to participate in the South African war; he was promoted lieutenant two months later. Appendicitis removed him from the unit, and after his convalescence and return he spent the final six months of the war as an intelligence officer and for the first time began to take an interest in his profession. This died when he rejoined the battalion in 1902 just before it was sent to India, where he whiled away the boredoms of garrison life in studying Hindu religion and philosophy, including yoga, an interest which was to endure. Illness came to his aid again, this time in the form of a severe attack of enteric fever, and he was sent back to recuperate in England in 1906.

He had obtained his captaincy in 1905, and, in order to avoid a return to India, he applied for and obtained a post as adjutant of a militia battalion, shortly afterwards converted into the 10th Middlesex as a unit of the new Territorial Army. He enjoyed the independence of the job, and the association with keen part-time soldiers. It led to his first attempts at writing, in the form of training pamphlets for his unit. In 1911 the prospect of returning to his regiment loomed, and in order to avoid it he decided to try to enter the Staff College. His first attempt in 1912 failed; 1913 found him successful. By this time, at the age of thirty-five, he was applying himself seriously to his profession and also employing his pen, not only in training pamphlets but also in articles for the *Army Review* and the *Journal* of the Royal United Service Institution. He continued to do this at the Staff College, his principal theme,

from which he was never to waver, being that weapons and their intelligent use were of much greater importance than either numbers of men or adherence to the classic dogma evolved from previous campaigns.

This brought him into conflict with the established teaching of the college, and, in retrospect, he considered it fortunate for him that August 1914 struck, the college broke up half-way through the two-year course, and Fuller went off to organize train movements in and out of Southampton docks. He found this interesting at first (and it brought him the temporary rank of major, made substantive in September 1915), but he wished to get nearer the front. After a spell on the staff at Tunbridge Wells, he joined the headquarters of VIII Corps in France in July 1915 as a GSO 3, from which he was promoted (February 1916) as GSO 2 of 37th division. The division was broken up after the fierce and bloody battles of that summer on the Somme, and Fuller went, as temporary lieutenant-colonel, to a similar post in the Third Army headquarters of Sir Edmund (later Viscount) Allenby [q.v.], involved to a great extent with training and organization. In these appointments he had time to think about the conduct of the war, write a little about it, and achieve a reputation as an efficient, methodical staff officer of sardonic humour, given to trenchant criticism.

Then came the turning point of his life, his posting as GSO 2 (later GSO 1) to the newly formed headquarters of the Tank Corps—or Heavy Branch, Machine-Gun Corps, as it was first called, commanded by (Sir) Hugh Elles [q.v.]—in late 1916. Although up to this point he had little knowledge of tanks, he was quick to see an opportunity to find fulfilment for all the frustrations which had built up in him: from *tabula rasa* to develop an entirely new arm, new methods of fighting the enemy, new ways of training. This novel and exciting task drew out all that was best in him and the plan for the famous battle of Cambrai (November 1917), for which he was largely responsible, was both his achievement and his reward. Its success led to consideration of more ambitious plans and ideas, and the decision to establish a tank branch of the general staff in the War Office under the leadership of Fuller, in July 1918. In preparation for this he and his colleagues at Tank Corps headquarters had developed 'Plan 1919', based on the performance of an experimental tank which had reached the speed of 20 m.p.h. Its concept was revolutionary: the deployment of fast tanks with a range of 200 miles in mass and depth, changing the whole idea of a tank from a slow trench-crossing fortress, working closely with infantry, to a truly mobile arm replacing cavalry in its historic role, a concept which was to be translated into reality in the war of 1939-45.

The end of the war in 1918 put paid to it, and Fuller, to his intense frustration, found all his plans shelved and the army intent on returning to its pre-war pattern, giving high priority to imperial policing. As an outlet he poured his energy into his pen, the first effusion, perhaps the most significant of all his writings, being the essay with which he won the gold medal of the Royal United Service Institution for 1919 (printed May 1920), in which he set out the blueprint for a new model army based on tanks, wholesale mechanization, and exploitation of wartime scientific and technical developments, notably wireless, aircraft, and gas. It was followed by other articles which provoked much controversy, in the midst of which he left the War Office and in 1923 went as a senior instructor to the Staff College. His mind and pen both now became more active, although the publication of many of his lectures and writings was suppressed for a time. It was in fact a disastrous posting. Hitherto the range of his imagination had been kept in check by the practical responsibilities of his job. But from now on his thoughts and writings became more theoretical, complicated, and less likely to be implemented, as he plunged deeper and wider in his search for theoretical bases for his ideas, making him vulnerable to those critics—and they were many—who were only too ready to point out that this forty-five-year-old colonel (he had been promoted in 1920) had hardly ever commanded any body of men and none at all in action.

In 1925 he published *The Foundations of the Science of War*, and the following year he became military assistant to the new CIGS, Sir George (later Lord) Milne [q.v.]. Fuller, with others, had high hopes that he and Milne together would transform the army into a 'new model', but opposition was too great and Milne too cautious. The breaking point came over Fuller's selection in 1927 to take command of what was intended to be an experimental mechanized force, but which was watered down to a standard infantry brigade and garrison on Salisbury Plain with only temporary *ad hoc* control over a few mechanized units. Fuller refused the command, and sent in his papers, but was persuaded to withdraw his resignation and went off to be GSO 1 to the 2nd division at Aldershot, commanded by Sir Edmund (later Lord) Ironside [q.v.]; in 1929 he was given command, at last, of an infantry brigade, first in the occupation army on the Rhine and then in Catterick, until he was promoted major-general (September 1930) at the age of fifty-two, and placed on half-pay. In 1931 he was offered command of Bombay District, with hardly any

soldiers in it; this he refused, and remained on half-pay until retiring at the end of 1933.

Meanwhile he had lectured frequently and his pen had been hard at work. In 1932 he published one of his most authoritative works, *Lectures on F.S.R.*, vol. iii, which showed him both at his best and at his worst. Dealing with general ideas and prognostications, he showed brilliance of imagination, much of it prophetic, on how armoured forces should be organized and employed; but when he began to develop concrete examples of how detailed operations should be executed, he began to disappear into a fairyland of mobile 'anti-tank castles' or 'laagers' from which the tank formations would sally forth like medieval knights to do battle and return, accompanied by 'swarms of motorized guerrillas' and copious clouds of gas, great emphasis being laid on the defensive aspect of a defensive-offensive strategy. The organization of armoured forces and the operations carried out by General Guderian, said to be his pupil, in France and Russia in the war of 1939-45 bore little relation to this pattern, although the development of German armoured forces did owe much to the visionary inspiration of Fuller as well as of (Sir) Basil Liddell Hart [q.v.].

Free of the cares of office, Fuller devoted the rest of his life to writing, probing deeper and deeper into the past and wider afield in his search for the truth. It led him into curious by-ways, the first being towards an idealized form of Fascism with which he was associated in the thirties; he spent some months in 1935-6 with the Italian forces in Abyssinia. Between his retirement and the outbreak of war in 1939 he published ten books, including his *Memoirs of an Unconventional Soldier* (1936).

Since 1923 he had been delving deeply into military history, and this study was to bear fruit in the two-volume *Decisive Battles* (1939-40), followed by *The Decisive Battles of the U.S.A.* (1942). From an apostle of future armoured warfare he had changed into an historian, although he re-edited his *F.S.R.* vol. iii lectures as *Armoured Warfare* in 1943. A short history of the war of 1939-45 (1948) could be regarded as a pot-boiler; but the major work on which his reputation as a historian must rest was *The Decisive Battles of the Western World, and their Influence upon History* (3 vols., 1954-6). Thenceforward he was able to bask in the sunshine of a prophet restored to honour in his own country, the gadfly which had lost its sting, sharing the limelight with Liddell Hart, engagingly modest in his lack of jealousy towards one who had stolen much of his thunder. At the same ceremony at the Royal United Service Institution both received the Institution's Chesney gold medal, October

1963. Fuller was appointed to the DSO in 1917, appointed CBE in 1926, and CB in 1930. Known to his friends as 'Boney', he was described (about 1918) as 'a little man with a bald head, and a sharp face, and a nose of Napoleonic cast . . . a totally unconventional soldier [whose] attacks on the . . . heirarchy were viewed in the spirit of a rat hunt; a spirit he responded to with much vivacity, and no little wit.'

In 1906 Fuller married Sonia, daughter of M. Karnatzki, of Warsaw; it was a happy lifetime partnership although they had no children. He died at Falmouth 10 February 1966.

[Fuller's own writings; *The Times*, 11 and 16 February 1966; B. H. Liddell Hart, *The Tanks*, 2 vols., 1959; private information; personal knowledge.]   MICHAEL CARVER

FYFE, DAVID PATRICK MAXWELL, EARL OF KILMUIR (1900–1967), lord chancellor, was born 29 May 1900 in Edinburgh, the only child by his second marriage of William Thomson Fyfe, an inspector of schools, to Isabella Campbell, a schoolteacher. After George Watson's College, Fyfe went up to Balliol College, Oxford, where he obtained a third class in *literae humaniores* (1921) and failed to become president of the Union, but made friends in the inner circle of English conservatism which it was his life's ambition to enter. Like John Buchan and Brendan Bracken [qq.v.] he was fascinated by the romantic and aristocratic side of English political life, which had not yet been entirely submerged by the egalitarian tide of the twentieth century. There was nothing sordid in this. As Fyfe himself said of those who accused Buchan of snobbery, 'they never understood the living sense of history of the Scot'.

It was one of the paradoxes of politics that the Maxwell Fyfe report on the organization of the Conservative Party in 1949 proposed reforms, particularly in the selection of parliamentary candidates, which were of value to the party in the mid twentieth century, but which also produced, as Maxwell Fyfe was disconcerted to find, unromantic men of obscure interests and views. It was another paradox that his career was to be ended with savage abruptness by another Scot with an equally romantic attachment to English political traditions, Harold Macmillan.

Maxwell Fyfe had highly developed the barrister's power of getting up a complex subject quickly. He was called at Gray's Inn in 1922 and went into chambers at Liverpool with (Sir) George Lynskey [q.v.]. In 1934 he took silk and in 1936 he became recorder of Oldham.

In the meantime he had been returned to Parliament in 1935 as member for the West Derby division of Liverpool. His appearance was unusual for a man seeking advancement on the Tory political ladder. His body was pear-shaped, and beneath a large square bald head there were dark heavy eyebrows and a face of middle-eastern pallor and swarthiness. Like many stocky men he had inexhaustible physical energy which he devoted to his legal and political careers. He recorded that 'during the Assizes I was constantly conferring from 9 a.m. until 10.30, in Court (with a short interval for lunch) until 5.15 p.m., then on the 5.25 from Liverpool or 5.45 from Manchester, reaching London at 9. Then in the House until after the 11 o'clock division, then back on the midnight train to the North . . .' It was also appreciated that 'Under that forbidding shell, He does himself extremely well', and his personal popularity at the bar and at Westminster was great; his simple integrity was manifest.

In 1942 Maxwell Fyfe was appointed solicitor-general and knighted, the attorney-general being Sir Donald (later Lord) Somervell [q.v.]. When Somervell became home secretary in the caretaker Government of 1945 Maxwell Fyfe succeeded him as senior law officer, and was sworn of the Privy Council. Although the general election of July 1945 removed him from office after only a few months, his successor, Sir Hartley (later Lord) Shawcross, allowed him to continue as deputy chief prosecutor at Nuremberg. There he won international recognition for a brilliant forensic success. In particular he brought down a conceited tyrant by his use of a traditional English legal weapon. Goering ('the most formidable witness I have ever cross-examined') lost his dominant position in the court-room.

Maxwell Fyfe not only gave continuous support to his party in its intense struggle against the Labour Government, but also played a prominent part in the movement for European unity centred on Strasbourg. Unusually for a British lawyer, he was a strong advocate of the European Convention on Human Rights, to which the United Kingdom eventually acceded. He was proud of the fact 'that I have done something positive as well as negative in regard to tyranny, which so many of my generation in the twentieth century have accepted without a murmur', and never entirely forgave his seniors in the new Conservative Cabinet for their veto on Britain's entry into Europe. He saw further than many of his contemporaries, and was anxious that Britain should enter Europe on a tide of goodwill—and also on terms more favourable than were to be obtained twenty years later. 'Posterity, rightly, will deal harshly with those who quenched this flame and who did not see, until it was too late, that idealists are often the truest realists in mighty enterprises.'

Maxwell Fyfe had become home secretary in the Conservative Cabinet in October 1951, an office in which he was a firm upholder of the traditional principles of law and order. His was the controversial decision not to grant a reprieve to Bentley who, with Craig, had been convicted of the murder of a police officer. In 1953 Fyfe was appointed GCVO after successfully completing the official duties connected with the coronation, and in October of the following year he became lord chancellor with the title of Viscount Kilmuir. Had he not done so, his chances of succeeding Eden in January 1957 might have been very strong. As it was, Kilmuir took an active part in polling the Cabinet in order to inform the Queen that a clear majority favoured Macmillan. In the Suez episode Kilmuir had been an unrepentant and unwavering supporter of a policy of Thorough. The shock to the party and to the country was therefore all the greater when in July 1962 he was dismissed, together with six other Cabinet ministers, at seven hours' notice. Macmillan claimed that new blood was needed but Kilmuir's successor, Lord Dilhorne, was only five years younger, and patently more to the Right than Kilmuir himself. Kilmuir did not attempt to hide his anger at the way in which he (who had once said that 'loyalty was the Tories' secret weapon') had been treated. He accepted an earldom, but refused to take any further part in legal or political affairs, surrendered his pension, and went into the City. This sudden move, which did not escape criticism in legal circles, should not be ascribed entirely to pique. Kilmuir did not enjoy judicial work, and as this is almost the only activity open to an ex-lord chancellor, he seized the opportunity offered by an invitation from the Plessey Company to be its chairman. Life in the City more than satisfied Kilmuir's desire for constant activity, but it was more of a strain than he had expected. His health was no longer good, and he found it difficult to adjust himself to the interests, values, and conversation of industrialists.

Although he held the Great Seal for over seven years—with the exception of Halsbury, longer than anyone since Eldon—Kilmuir left little permanent mark on English law. He was not a great reformer like Jowitt or Gardiner, nor a great jurist like Simon or Simonds. Indeed, his judgement in *DPP* v. *Smith*, [1961] AC 290 on the mental element required for a conviction of murder, although concurred in by four law lords, attracted an exceptional amount of juristic criticism throughout the Commonwealth. Kilmuir held that it was unnecessary for the Crown to prove that the accused actually

intended to kill or to cause grievous bodily harm if a reasonable man was entitled to conclude from the evidence as a whole that the accused must have had that intention: the test of criminal liability was to be objective and not subjective. The principle so laid down as reversed by the Criminal Justice Act, 1967. But, as always, Kilmuir was patient, courteous, and indefatigable—he personally examined the claims of every candidate proposed for the lay magistracy. His devotion to his work left him with little time for ordinary recreations, but he seldom refused an invitation to a dinner party if the hostess was notable for birth, beauty, or intelligence. He also achieved most of the honours which come to a lord chancellor—the honorary fellowship of his college, and honorary doctorates of ten universities. He was rector of St. Andrews (1955–8) and visitor of St. Antony's College, Oxford, from 1953.

Fyfe married in 1925 Sylvia Margaret, daughter of William Reginald Harrison, civil engineer, of Liverpool, sister of Rex Harrison, the actor. They had three daughters, one of whom predeceased him. Kilmuir died at his house at Withyham in Sussex 27 January 1967. His widow married Earl De La Warr in 1968. Kilmuir's estate was sworn for probate at £22,202.

There are portraits of Kilmuir at Balliol (by Christopher Sanders), at St. Antony's (by A. C. Davidson-Houston), at Gray's Inn (by Simon Elwes), and one by Harold Knight in the possession of the family. A pastel by Dame Laura Knight is in the Imperial War Museum.

[The Earl of Kilmuir, *Political Adventure*, 1964; *The Times*, 28 January 1967; private information; personal knowledge.]

R. F. V. HEUSTON

FYFE, SIR WILLIAM HAMILTON (1878–1965), headmaster and university vice-chancellor, was born in London 9 July 1878, youngest of the three sons of James Hamilton Fyfe, a barrister and journalist, and his wife, Mary Elizabeth Jonas. Henry Hamilton Fyfe [q.v.] was his eldest brother. His father died young, and his mother had little on which to bring up the family. Fyfe won a scholarship to Fettes College, Edinburgh, and then in 1897 went on to Oxford with a postmastership at Merton College, being placed in the first class both in classical honour moderations (1899) and in *literae humaniores* (1901). After taking his degree, he taught at St. Peter's College, Radley, for two years. William Sewell's [q.v.] lavish foundation had by then settled down to quieter ways; but in retrospect Fyfe found his Radley time an idyllic existence.

In 1904 he returned to Merton as a fellow and principal of the postmasters, the senior disciplinary officer of the college. There he remained till 1919, being also tutor in classical honour moderations, and producing translations of Tacitus' *Dialogus, Agricola, and Germania* (1908), and of *The Histories* (1912). During this pre-war period he was one of a number of younger dons clustering on (Archbishop) William Temple [q.v.], who was then a fellow of Queen's. They were active as propagandists for university reform, particularly for a wider opening of the university to members of the working class.

In World War I Fyfe was commissioned in the Territorial Force (unattached list) in February 1915, and after service in training officer-cadets and in intelligence, he ended the war (with the rank of major) in resettlement work, having been posted to the general staff in 1917. He was also made officier d'Académie Française.

In 1919 he left Merton to become headmaster of Christ's Hospital, at Horsham, Sussex. The old (and original) Christ's Hospital (in the City of London) had entered the English tradition with Charles Lamb [q.v.]. That gave it appeal to Fyfe; but even more attractive was the fact that it admitted only those boys whose parents were unable to meet the fees normally paid elsewhere. As he was later to put it: 'Poverty cuts diagonally across classes. So the boys came from very different backgrounds—an educational advantage which other Public Schools are seeking to acquire.' Fyfe soon became known as a new and unexpected type of headmaster, approachable and humorous, ready to experiment and encourage sensible change. Older hands might grouse; but the younger—boys and masters alike—gave him their devotion. To this period belong his Loeb translations of Aristotle's *Poetics* and 'Longinus' *On the Sublime* (1927).

In 1930 a party of British headmasters (including Fyfe) visited Canada. One result was the offer to him of the post of principal and vice-chancellor of Queen's University, Kingston, Ontario, which he accepted, and held till 1936. The Scottish Presbyterian ethos of Queen's was still much as T. R. Glover [q.v.] had experienced it thirty years earlier (Glover and D. D. Calvin, *A Corner of Empire*, 1937). Now also came the depression of the thirties. But Fyfe raised money for his university, and initiated a kind of intra-Canada 'Rhodes scholarship' system that brought it many able students from other provinces.

In 1936 he left Canada for Scotland to be principal of Aberdeen University. He thought the outlook 'a bit dour'. That was true politically; but not otherwise, for, though World War II was soon to freeze expansion plans, he quickly won over and brought the best out of the shyer (and perhaps prouder) Scottish students, who could well have begun thinking (with many of their professors) that so unconventional a principal was not quite *sérieux*.

The years in Scotland (till Fyfe's retirement in 1948) were increasingly devoted to public work. As chairman of the advisory council on education in Scotland, as member of the Scottish advisory council on the treatment and rehabilitation of offenders, and perhaps above all as a member of the inter-university council for higher education in the colonies he found stimulus and interest in subjects which appealed to his liberal temperament. He had a major part in the founding of the institutes which became the universities of Ibadan and of Ghana. He also brought out an edition of Aristotle's *Poetics* (1940), prefacing it with a characteristic note: 'The translation . . . is that of Ingram Bywater which the editor, a Satyr to his Hyperion, has ventured to alter slightly in a few places.'

His years of retirement he spent in Blackheath, and he was developing there a new and very successful career as a broadcaster till failing eyesight compelled him to give it up.

Fyfe was a great educator, and his liberal outlook (grounded on a simple Christian faith) made him an ardent advocate of a type of society in which abilities of all kinds could flourish without privilege unfairly tipping the scales. By some of his colleagues this was misconstrued —'Charming fellow, Fyfe,' said one, 'a pity he has such poisonous politics.' But anyone less poisonous it would have been hard to find, and Fyfe was no clever-silly left-winger. Fyfe was also possessed of a gracious informality of manner; and a very considerable verbal felicity and style that, allied to humour, was at once arresting and could in a flash put a case in a wholly new light. Three lines on a postcard from him said more than many a man could say in a long letter. Few of his calling can in recent times have so unobtrusively and effortlessly had so sane and pervasive an influence on so many over so great an area of the world.

Fyfe was knighted in 1942, held honorary doctorates from Canadian, British, and American universities, was elected a fellow of the Royal Society of Canada in 1932, and became an honorary fellow of Merton College in 1948. He was chairman of the governors of Gordonstoun 1945-8.

Fyfe married in 1908 Dorothea Hope Geddes (died 1977), daughter of John Forbes White, LLD, flour-miller in Aberdeen, and a local patron of the arts. Of this singularly happy marriage there were three children, two sons (the elder of whom, Maurice, became a Canadian QC), and a daughter.

Portraits (oils on canvas) of Fyfe are at Christ's Hospital (M. Ayoub), Queen's University, Kingston, Ontario (Lilias T. Newton), and Aberdeen University (J. Kenneth Green). Another version of the Ayoub portrait, a smaller work by the same artist, is at the Rowett Research Institute, Bucksburn, Aberdeen. A bronze bust by T. B. Huxley Jones (1945) is in Aberdeen Art Gallery; and the family possesses a pencil drawing by J. B. Souter.

[*The Times*, 15 and 18 June 1965; *Postmaster*, vol. iii, no. 4, December 1965; *Oxford*, vol. ix, no. 1, 1945; *The Blue*, vol. xlii, no. 3, September 1965; *Proceedings*, Royal Society of Canada, fourth series, vol. v, 1967; *Aberdeen Chamber of Commerce Journal*, vol. xliv, 1962–3; *Aberdeen University Review*, vol. xli 2, no. 134, 1965; *Press and Journal* (Aberdeen), 16 June 1965; private information; personal knowledge.]

A. H. K. SLATER

G

GADDUM, SIR JOHN HENRY (1900-1965), pharmacologist, was born 31 March 1900 at Hale, Cheshire, the eldest child in the family of four boys and two girls of Henry Edwin Gaddum, a silk importer who was made an honorary MA of Manchester University for his devotion to charitable work, and his wife, Phyllis Mary, daughter of Alfred Barratt, a first cousin of Sir Samuel Hoare (later Lord Templewood, q.v.), and of Richard D. Acland, bishop of Bombay, by whom Gaddum was married in 1929 to Iris Mary Harmer, MB, B.Chir., MRCP, daughter of Sir Sidney Harmer, FRS. Miss Harmer did outstanding clinical research under Sir Thomas Lewis [q.v.]. There were three daughters of the marriage. In the male line Gaddum's ancestry was partly of German origin.

At Rugby, Gaddum won prizes in mathematics, physics, and astronomy. He entered Trinity College, Cambridge, in 1919 on an entrance scholarship, later won a senior scholarship, read medicine and obtained first class honours in part i of the mathematical tripos (1920), and second class honours in part ii of the natural sciences tripos in physiology (1922). In 1922 he entered University College Hospital, London, qualified in 1924, but in his final MB in Cambridge failed twice in medicine. Later Cambridge gave him a Sc.D.

In 1925 Gaddum was initiated into pharmacological research by J. W. Trevan, FRS, at the Wellcome Research Laboratories in Beckenham, and three years later was accepted as assistant to (Sir) Henry Dale [q.v.] at the National Institute for Medical Research in Hampstead, where he spent six extremely fruitful years of research. He became keen to take charge of a department of his own and, when he did not succeed in getting the chair at Birmingham University, in 1934 he accepted the chair of pharmacology at the Egyptian University of Cairo where his friend G. Anrep was professor of physiology. His stay there was short, but made a deep impact lasting long after he had left. He stayed for only one and a half years because once he was out of the country his colleagues in England realized they could not afford to lose him. He was appointed professor of pharmacology at University College, London, in 1935. Three years later, he accepted the chair at the College of the Pharmaceutical Society, London. During the war of 1939-45 he worked at the Chemical Defence Research Station, Porton, and was in part responsible for deciding on the drug to be carried by British agents to be used for rapid self-destruction in case of serious emergency. For a short time he served as a temporary lieutenant-colonel in the army, and if gas warfare had started he would have been physiologist to the 21st Army Group when France was invaded. In 1942 he accepted the chair of materia medica in the university of Edinburgh and might well have remained there until his retirement but for the invitation in 1958 to become director of the Institute of Animal Physiology in Babraham, Cambridge. He accepted and within a few years the Institute became one of the great international centres for research in physiology and pharmacology. His work brought him wide national and international recognition. He became corresponding and honorary member of scientific societies and academies in France, Italy, Germany, and South and North America. He was elected fellow of the Royal Society in 1945; was a fellow of the Royal Society of Edinburgh, and a year before his death was knighted and awarded an honorary LLD at Edinburgh.

The two main lines of research he pursued throughout his life were the mode of action of drugs and the development of specific and sensitive methods for biological assay. The modern development of bioassay owes much to him. He stressed and demonstrated the need for making parallel estimates on different assay preparations in order to identify an unknown pharmacologically active substance in a tissue extract. He formulated the concept of competitive inhibition. An important statistical contribution was his report, in 1933, to the Medical Research Council on methods of biological assay depending on a quantal response, and he was instrumental in getting a mathematical and statistical approach to bioassay accepted in this country.

He developed new methods of bioassay for acetylcholine, adrenaline, 5-hydroxytryptamine (5-HT), substance P, and thyroxin, and introduced a new method for extracting histamine from blood. With this method he showed that the blood histamine rises after extensive cutaneous burns. He constructed new pieces of apparatus, such as a flow recorder, an outflow recorder, a micro-bath, and his famous push-pull cannula, a device to perfuse small regions of tissue in brain and to detect substances liberated from them by appropriate stimuli.

A few fundamental discoveries stand out amongst Gaddum's many contributions: the discovery in 1931, with von Euler, of substance P, a vasodepressor peptide in extracts of brain and intestine. The demonstration in 1933, with W. Feldberg, of the role of acetylcholine as synaptic transmitter in sympathetic ganglia. Three major contributions in the fifties to the pharmacology and physiology of 5-HT—(1) evidence for specific tryptamine receptors, M and D receptors, in smooth muscle; (2) the finding that LSD was a specific potent 5-HT antagonist on smooth muscle; (3) the mapping out, together with A. H. Amin and T. B. B. Crawford, of the distribution of 5-HT in brain and demonstrating a different distribution in brain of the enzymes for its formation and destruction. Gaddum was the first who tried to explain the schizoid changes that LSD produces by interference with the 5-HT metabolism of brain.

In 1939 he wrote a book which appeared in German only (translated by W. Feldberg): *Die gefäßerweiternde Stoffe der Gewebe*. He also wrote a textbook on pharmacology which appeared in 1940, had its emphasis on principles of drug action, was written with a remarkable feeling for essentials, and was unsurpassed in its charm when, as so often, his sense of humour broke through. No wonder the book became so popular that it passed through five editions and was translated into German, Spanish, and Japanese.

Gaddum was tall, rather ungainly, and looked as if he didn't care how he was dressed. He had his coats made with large 'poacher's pockets' in the lining to take quite large books or bundles of papers which had the effect of making a brand new coat look out of shape and shabby after a day's wear. When he was thinking deeply or wondering how to answer a question he would run his right hand up through his hair making it even more untidy than usual, but when he looked at you so trustingly and earnestly, you forgot he had a moustache which looked as if it had been accidentally stuck to his lip. When watching him carry out an experiment, one was struck by the delicate skill of his large, rather clumsy-looking hands. What endeared him to his friends was that he was completely unprejudiced; that he was open to unorthodox ideas put forward by colleagues, giving them the benefit of the doubt until further work should clarify the issue; that he was ready to admit ignorance. He was always friendly to strangers and on journeys easily got into conversation with anyone who happened to be about, thereby acquiring a lot of unusual and odd information, which appealed to him. His formidable intelligence was unsophisticated and carried with it an attractive naïvety. He enjoyed nature in all its manifestations, loved to play with figures, was fond of light and nonsense verse, and had a large stock of quotations derived from sources such as Lewis Carroll and Hilaire Belloc [qq.v.]. Gaddum died at Cambridge 30 June 1965.

In 1966 the British Pharmacological Society created the Gaddum Memorial Trust to commemorate Sir John's services to pharmacology in the form of the Gaddum Memorial Lectures. They are given at intervals at meetings of the British Pharmacological Society and published in its journal. The lecturers are chosen by the members of the society from young scientists who have made important contributions in the field of pharmacology or related subjects.

A drawing of Gaddum by Robert Tollast hangs in the hall at the Agricultural Research Council, Babraham.

[W. Feldberg in *Biographical Memoirs of Fellows of the Royal Society*, vol. xiii, 1967; private information; personal knowledge.]

W. FELDBERG

GAITSKELL, HUGH TODD NAYLOR (1906–1963), politician, was born in Kensington 9 April 1906, the younger son of Arthur Gaitskell, of the Indian Civil Service, and his wife, Adelaide Mary, daughter of George Jamieson, who had been consul-general in Shanghai. He was educated at Winchester and New College, Oxford, where he obtained a first class in philosophy, politics, and economics in 1927. His special subject for his final schools was 'Labour movements' for which G. D. H. Cole [q.v.] was his tutor. Gaitskell's rather simple and individual radicalism as an undergraduate led him naturally into the Labour Party. But he was incapable of dilettantism. He threw himself into support of the general strike of 1926, doing practical and obscure work. When he left Oxford with a number of careers open to him he chose to spend a year as tutor in charge of extra-mural classes in Nottingham; then moved to London in 1928 as a lecturer in political economy at University College where he became head of the department of political economy and university reader in 1938. In the meantime he had stood unsuccessfully as Labour candidate for Chatham in 1935.

Gaitskell early formed the central and unshakeable conviction that socialism was about social justice—an ideal in his own words 'in no way inspired by class hatred'. He favoured a rather radical measure of nationalization, mainly to facilitate economic planning; but he utterly rejected the idea that socialism was synonymous with nationalization. The proper aim of a Labour government in his view ought to be a practical, relevant, and radical course of economic and social reforms which would permanently change and improve society, but would always leave more to be done. In the field of foreign affairs he was prepared to draw conclusions from which many of his colleagues and friends at first flinched. In 1934 he witnessed the crushing of the Austrian Labour movement and sprang into action with vigour and energy to raise funds in Britain and organize relief. He was not content with the conclusion that a socialist must oppose Fascism; he saw that democratic socialism also involved opposition to dictatorship from the Left. But Fascism was the imminent danger and in the thirties Gaitskell became convinced that war with Hitler was inevitable and that everything possible must be done to prepare for the onslaught. He tried but failed to shake the emotional bias of the Parliamentary Labour Party against conscription.

During the war Gaitskell served as a temporary civil servant, first in the Ministry of Economic Warfare, then went with Hugh (later Lord) Dalton [q.v.] to the Board of Trade. His great administrative ability attracted the attention of politicians and officials alike. In 1945 he was returned to Parliament as Labour member for South Leeds, a seat which he retained until his death. In 1946 he was made parliamentary secretary at the Ministry of Fuel and Power, taking over as minister in 1947, when he was sworn of the Privy Council. In February 1950 he joined the Treasury as minister of state for economic affairs.

The year before, Gaitskell had made a major impact, although behind the scenes, on national policy. He was given partial authority at the Treasury during the absence of Sir Stafford Cripps [q.v.] through illness. Concluding that devaluation was necessary he convinced Cripps and other leading ministers and prepared all the necessary measures with high efficiency and absolute secrecy.

In October 1950 on Cripps's resignation, Attlee made Gaitskell chancellor of the Exchequer at the age of forty-four. This opened out the prospect of ultimate leadership of the party. It was then that Gaitskell's combination of qualities led him to take a number of immense risks, each of which put his career at issue and each of which took him a step nearer his goal. Personal ambition of a kind this was: but Gaitskell was not after mere personal power and position—he wanted to stand for something in public life and to represent the modernized Labour Party of his vision. For this goal he fought with tenacious and challenging courage. His ambition was great but it was without stratagem or intrigue.

Aneurin Bevan [q.v.] was the chief obstacle in the way by reason of his high ability and passionate ambitions and his capacity to evoke devoted adherence to a concept of the Labour Party very different from Gaitskell's. This conflict of concepts was the true issue between Gaitskell and Bevan almost immediately after he became chancellor: not health service charges nor even the cost of rearmament. That

was why Gaitskell stubbornly turned down the pleas of colleagues in Cabinet and party who saw the dispute as relatively trivial. At bottom lay the struggle between the idea of a party of government and a party of protest.

While the party was in opposition after 1951, strong controversy arose over German rearmament on which many in the centre of the party shared the views of the Left. Gaitskell saw that the American alliance, which he wholeheartedly welcomed, and steadfastness against the advance of Russian Communism was involved. Again he and Bevan took opposite sides. In 1954 the party narrowly approved German rearmament, and Gaitskell defeated Bevan for the treasurership; he did so again in 1955. On Attlee's resignation in December Gaitskell was elected leader of the Labour Party over Bevan and Herbert Morrison (later Lord Morrison of Lambeth, q.v.) by the largest majority hitherto recorded. Bevan had been prepared to stand down if Gaitskell would do the same in order to allow Morrison to be elected unopposed; but Gaitskell considered that the party should have a choice. He showed his capacity to handle men by effecting a compromise with Bevan whom he made shadow foreign secretary in 1957; two years later they visited Russia together. The older rival had by now accepted the younger's supremacy.

It was not until the general election of 1959 that Gaitskell became a national figure. He fought the campaign with vigour, ease, and enthusiasm, confident of victory. Later he admitted to friends that his promise not to raise income tax was a misjudgement. He won national respect by his unprecedented gesture of appearing on television at 1 a.m. to concede defeat when many returns were yet to come in. Bitterly disappointed at his frustrated hopes of victory, he bore himself with dignified composure, encouraging his supporters to rally from the setback.

On the morrow of defeat he once again put his leadership in issue over clause iv of the party's constitution which amongst other things declared nationalization as an objective of the Labour Party. The lesson he drew from defeat was that the party was hopelessly handicapped so long as socialism seemed to be identified with nationalization. He put forward an alternative which stressed as the objectives of the party social justice, equality, planning. But he underrated the opposition to his proposals. Under great pressure he gave ground: the original clause iv and his new draft were both to be endorsed. The battle was lost but Gaitskell won the war for the concept of a party of power. Hardly was this conflict over than Gaitskell was involved in another—the toughest of his leadership. Against his strong advice to the annual conference at Scarborough in 1960 it carried a resolution in favour of unilateral disarmament. With unconcealed emotion Gaitskell called on his supporters to 'fight, fight, and fight again to save the party we love'.

At the beginning of the following twelve months Gaitskell frankly faced the probability that he would be defeated at the next conference and that this would almost certainly involve his retirement from the leadership, perhaps his withdrawal from public life. But he never for a moment considered compromise on a cardinal issue. In fact the party rallied to him and at Blackpool the previous resolution was overwhelmingly reversed. Gaitskell had at last, with immense courage, created the party he wanted. In 1962 he led it—against the advice of many close friends and with the support of his former critics—to oppose British entry into the EEC on the terms proposed. By then he was generally accepted as Britain's next prime minister. But he died suddenly in London 18 January 1963, and it was left to his successor to lead to victory a party with which it was possible to govern.

Gaitskell was often regarded as rational and unemotional. Bevan's gibe about a desiccated calculating machine seemed to many to have some of the truth in it. Certainly Gaitskell's forte was an appeal to reason: this he regarded as the mark of a good man and, in the end, as the most potent way of winning opinion. He developed an unusual mastery of logical argument in speech: with impeccable logic he would exhaustively set out the arguments for his case. Sometimes his supporters on the benches behind him in the House of Commons were in despair that there would not be a single fresh point for them to make after he had sat down.

But beneath these rational forms Gaitskell was driven by deeper emotions. Faith and conviction compelled him to bring certain issues—often prickly and dangerous ones—before the bar of rational public opinion. But for the emotion—the crusading spirit—that underlay his outward lack of emotion Gaitskell would never have made so deep an impression on public opinion. Of those who thought like himself he wrote: 'while accepting the ultimate emotional basis of moral valuation, they had great faith in the power of reason . . . to persuade men to see the light' (Introduction to Evan Durbin's *Politics of Democratic Socialism*, 1964).

A further source of Gaitskell's political strength was that politics was not the whole of his life: he had other resources on which he could fall back. He enjoyed a lively social life, good food, and good living, and had a solid family relationship. He would never be led, in

great matters, into the kind of compromise which men will make who must at all costs stay in public life. But had he lived to become prime minister his highest qualities would have come into play: his talents were creative and needed power to unfold. He had an intellectual framework into which specific reforms and policies would have fitted; nor would he have flinched from taking unpopular measures. He would have stood out as a man of principle who could look facts in the face and would, if necessary, risk all on an issue on which he felt a righteous cause to be at stake. He was appointed CBE in 1945 and received an honorary DCL from Oxford in 1958.

Gaitskell married in 1937 Anna Dora, divorced wife of David Frost, daughter of Leon Creditor. She was created life peeress within a year of her husband's death. They had two daughters. A portrait of Gaitskell by Judy Cassab is in the National Portrait Gallery where there is also a bronze head by L. C. Bevis. A drawing by Stephen Ward is in the possession of the family.

[*Hugh Gaitskell, 1906-1963*, ed. W. T. Rodgers, 1964; Hugh Gaitskell, 'At Oxford in the Twenties', in *Essays in Labour History*, ed. Asa Briggs and John Saville, 1960; Philip Williams, *Hugh Gaitskell*, 1979; personal knowledge.]

PATRICK GORDON WALKER

GALLACHER, WILLIAM (1881-1965), working-class agitator and politician, was born in Paisley 25 December 1881, the fourth of seven children of an Irish father, John Gallacher, labourer, and his Scottish wife, Mary Sutherland. He was seven when his father died; nine when he refused any longer to attend a Catholic school where he was frequently beaten for not attending Mass on Sunday; ten when he began his first job, an early morning milk-round, while still at a board school. At twelve he left school and started work as a grocer's delivery boy. Soon he had his first struggle—a successful one—with an employer, when he refused to deliver an order after time on his half-holiday. Apprenticed in 1895 as a brass-finisher, he became in due course an engineer. For a short time (1909-10) he worked as a ship's steward.

In 1906 he joined the Social Democratic Federation. In the years preceding the war of 1914-18 he was active in the building of the shop stewards movement in Scotland. During the war, when chairman of the Clyde Workers' Committee, he played an important part not only in industrial disputes but also in support of rent strikes and in the anti-war campaign.

In 1916 he was sentenced to twelve months' imprisonment for sedition; in 1919 to three months for rioting.

Gallacher was amongst those in Britain who enthusiastically welcomed the Russian revolution in 1917, and he became an active supporter of the Soviet Union. His political views took an important turn in 1920. Until then he had been strongly against workers' participation in Parliament, and advocated 'direct action' both for immediate advances and in order to overthrow the capitalist system. One of his earliest writings was a pamphlet, of which he was co-author with J. R. Campbell, entitled *Direct Action*, published in 1919 by the Scottish Workers' Committees. Now, in Moscow for a congress of the Communist International, he read Lenin's newly published *Left Wing Communism, an Infantile Disorder*, in which his own anti-parliamentarianism was strongly criticized. Influenced by this and by personal discussion with Lenin, he discarded his former attitude, and he was later to demonstrate in action how ably a Communist revolutionary could fight in Parliament for his point of view. He helped to found the British Communist Party in 1920-1. In 1921 he served three months for sedition and in 1925 he was one of the members of the party's executive sentenced to twelve months for 'seditious libel' and was thus in prison during the general strike of 1926.

Gallacher unsuccessfully contested Dundee in 1922 and 1923, and West Fife in 1929 and 1931 before he was elected to Parliament for that constituency in 1935; he retained the seat for fifteen years. Historically the most notable event of his very active parliamentary career was his lone opposition to the visit by Neville Chamberlain to Germany for the momentous meeting with Hitler at which the Munich agreement was signed. On 28 September 1938, after Chamberlain had received approval for his journey from all other parts of the House of Commons, Gallacher said: 'No one desires peace more than I and my party, but it must be a peace based upon freedom and democracy and not upon the cutting up and destruction of a small State. . . . I protest against the dismemberment of Czechoslovakia.' When he lost his seat in the general election of 1950 he declared that he had been a working-class agitator before entering Parliament, and also while a member, and he would continue to be one. And so it was; he continued as chairman of the Communist Party, an office which he had held since 1943, became its president in 1956, and after his retirement in 1963 was made an honorary member of its executive committee. He died in Paisley 12 August 1965; at his funeral he was honoured by the presence of tens of thousands of his fellow citizens.

Gallacher wrote four books of memoirs, the last published posthumously. Other publications, in addition to pamphlets and articles, included *The Chosen Few: A Sketch of Men and Events in Parliament* (1940); *The Case for Communism* (1949); *The Tyrants' Might is Passing* (1954). In all his activities he displayed enormous vigour and enthusiasm. As a speaker he had a lively, humorous style, was full of optimism and encouragement for those whom he sought to influence, and was a master hand at exposing all forms of hypocrisy. His writings, especially the memoirs, possess a remarkable literary quality—the quasi-dramatic style brings to life in a vivid way both the writer himself and the other men and women whom he presents. The personal quality which most endeared him, and earned him the admiration of all who knew him, was his entirely selfless devotion to principle, his complete honesty.

A man of medium height, stockily built, he had a brisk and vivacious manner. A quick smile, full of humour and humanity, would accompany his frequent witty remarks, and as a raconteur he would act out the parts with lively movement and gesture. There is a fine bronze bust of Gallacher, by a Russian sculptor, in the Paisley Museum and Art Galleries, and a portrait in oils by E. Eisenmeier remained in the artist's possession.

In 1913 Gallacher married Jean Miller, daughter of John Roy. From that time she was his close and dearly loved companion through all his active and sometimes stormy life, until her death in 1962. They had two sons who died at birth and two adopted sons (his nephews) both of whom died in 1944 while serving with the armed forces.

[W. Gallacher, *Revolt on the Clyde*, 1936 and 1949, *The Rolling of the Thunder*, 1947, *Rise Like Lions*, 1951, and *Last Memoirs*, 1966; *Daily Worker*, 13 and 14 August 1965; *The Times*, 13 August 1965; *Essays in Honour of William Gallacher*, Humboldt University of Berlin, 1966; personal knowledge.]

RALPH MILLNER

GAME, SIR PHILIP WOOLCOTT (1876-1961), air vice-marshal, governor of New South Wales, and commissioner of the metropolitan police, was born 30 March 1876, the second son in the family of eight children (five boys and three girls) of George Game, a member of the Baltic Exchange, of Broadway, Worcestershire, and his wife, Clara Vincent. After Charterhouse and the Royal Military Academy, Woolwich, he joined the Royal Artillery in 1895. He saw action in South Africa (1901-2), was promoted captain, mentioned in dispatches, and awarded the Queen's medal with five clasps. He graduated from the Staff College in 1910, and won the Chesney gold medal of the Royal United Service Institution for that year, with a wide-ranging essay on imperial defence policy. From then on he was caught up in the succession of staff appointments from which he scarcely escaped during his subsequent service. From the general staff at the War Office he went to France in November 1914 as a major on the staff of the 4th Army Corps. He soon made his mark, and was appointed to the DSO in April 1915, moving in July to the staff of 46th division as temporary lieutenant-colonel.

The decisive change in his career came in March 1916 when in order to meet the urgent need to strengthen the staff of the Royal Flying Corps, of which Brigadier-General H. M. (later Viscount) Trenchard [q.v.] was then in command, he was transferred by GHQ as general staff officer I, much against his will. At first he was extremely unhappy. He was less likely to achieve his ambition of active command, and he found the atmosphere of this new and highly technical service entirely uncongenial. He felt that 'General Trenchard would prefer someone of his own type—a hustler'. But in fact Game provided exactly the support that Trenchard needed, turning his 'mysterious thought processes' into clear and persuasive language, and, as mutual confidence grew, able to stand up to his chief when necessary. Trenchard was to refer to him as 'the best staff officer I have ever had or ever seen'.

Promoted temporary brigadier-general in October 1916 Game remained at Trenchard's right hand and gradually became fully committed to the air arm. He learned to fly, and became a member of the Royal Air Force on its establishment in 1918. After a brief period as general officer commanding South-Western Area, he became director of Training and Organization (air commodore) in March 1919 after Trenchard's reappointment as chief of air staff. He was closely concerned with the white paper of December 1919 on the future of the RAF, and with the continuing battle to secure the RAF's independent role. After promotion to air vice-marshal in January 1922 he was in 1923 at last given a chance to command, as air officer commanding RAF India. But he had been in India only a few months when he was called home urgently as indispensable, for what the Air Ministry in a formal letter called his 'unique administrative qualities'. Appointed air member for personnel, he remained one of the senior members of the Air Council until he retired at his own request in 1929.

Game was still only fifty-two, and in 1930 he was appointed governor of New South Wales. He arrived in Sydney in May, and soon found himself in a turmoil of political and constitu-tional controversy. The depression had hit Australia very hard, with the collapse of wheat and wool prices. In October J. T. Lang, the explosive leader of the Labour Party of New South Wales, won a general election on a programme of resistance to orthodox measures for dealing with the slump, and attacked the payment of interest to the 'bondholders'. Game was determined to maintain the neutrality appropriate for the King's representative. As a result he was roundly abused by the anti-Labour forces, especially when he eventually agreed to Lang's demand for the appointment of additional members to the second chamber. To compel Lang to fulfil the state's obligations, the Commonwealth Government, acting under hastily passed legislation which was upheld by the courts, tried to require that taxes should be paid direct to the Commonwealth of Australia and not to the state. Lang directed that state officials should ignore the Commonwealth proclamation. Game held that this was a direct breach of the law, and dismissed Lang. An election followed and Lang was decisively defeated. The governor's action was the subject of bitter controversy. Its critics have maintained that it is for the courts, not for the governor, to resolve disputes between state and Commonwealth. But the circumstances in which prerogative action of this kind can be taken were (and are) not clearly defined. There can be no doubt about the gravity of the situation. Game acted against Lang with the utmost reluctance, but he felt that things could not be allowed to drift. The argument continues. The rest of Game's tenure, until 1935, was uneventful and happy.

On Game's return home he was offered and accepted the succession to Lord Trenchard, whose brief period as commissioner had transformed the metropolitan police. No doubt Trenchard felt that his most trusted staff officer could be relied on to carry his changes through. Ironically they soon fell out over the future of Trenchard's most cherished project, the Metropolitan Police College at Hendon. Game did not accept Trenchard's strongly held view that the higher ranks in the police, as in the Services, should be filled by young men recruited direct as officers and trained for responsibility. Further experience only strengthened Game's early views, and when the post-war national police college was being considered Game asserted strongly that 'we have, and will have, in the ranks, the material to fill all senior posts'. Game was consistent, his own most trusted adviser was not one of the officers brought in by his predecessor but (Sir) George Abbiss, the only one of the assistant commissioners who had risen from the ranks.

Game's calm judgement fitted him admirably

for the impartial maintenance of public order in the East End during the clashes between the Fascists and their opponents. The organization of the force for its manifold wartime duties, and the reshaping required to meet constantly changing wartime conditions, gave full scope for his administrative talents, and he himself gave an outstanding personal example by being out and about in the heaviest air raids. Genuinely unassuming, he did not attempt to make an impact on the general public, who were content to accept that everything was under control, but he gained the respect of all who came in contact with him. Urged on by his sense of duty and of the personal integrity which shines through every account of him, he was a fanatically hard worker, sometimes criticized for doing too much himself. He went to great trouble to improve relationships with the Police Federation, and his deep feeling for the individual came out clearly in his handling of individual cases. He was in fact sometimes misled by his inclination to think that he would get better information and advice from the constable he met on his rounds than from those higher up.

Despite his continuing physical activity he was remarkably prone to accident. He had acquired a limp from a serious skating accident in the twenties. His assumption of office as commissioner was delayed by a broken kneecap, and he suffered three fractures of the leg during his period of office. Despite poor health in the later stages of the war he characteristically deferred his retirement until the selection of his successor could be made with the end of the war in sight. He retired in 1945, and lived in retirement until his death at his home in Sevenoaks 4 February 1961. His wife, Gwendolen Margaret, daughter of Francis Hughes-Gibb, whom he had married in 1908 and with whom he had lived happily for more than fifty years, survived him, and died in 1972. They had two sons, one of whom died on active service in 1943, and one daughter.

Game was slight in build and quiet in speech: a striking contrast to his predecessor as commissioner, 'Boom' Trenchard. He was unpretentious in his habits, for example often taking public transport in preference to his official car. A good horseman, he was an execrable driver.

His many high distinctions reflect his responsibilities: DSO (1915), CB (1919), KCB (1924), GBE (1929), KCMG (1935), GCVO (1937), GCB (1945).

There are two portraits in oils—one by R. G. Eves in Government House, Sydney, and another by M. Mulvey at Scotland Yard.

[Andrew Boyle, *Trenchard*, 1962; B. Foott, *Dismissal of a Premier*, 1968; H. V. Evatt, *The King and his Dominion Governors*, 1936; Metropolitan Police records; the Game correspondence in the Imperial War Museum; private information.]

KENNETH PARKER

GARDINER, SIR ALAN HENDERSON (1879–1963), Egyptologist and linguist, was born at Eltham 29 March 1879, the younger son of Henry John Gardiner, later chairman of Bradbury Greatorex & Co. Ltd., and his wife, Clara Elizabeth Honey. H. B. Gardiner [q.v.], the composer, was his elder brother. He was educated at Charterhouse and having as a schoolboy developed a taste for ancient Egypt, and having become an admirer of Gaston Maspero after reading one of his books, he was sent to Paris for a year to attend Maspero's lectures at the Sorbonne before going to Queen's College, Oxford. He obtained a second in classical moderations (1899) but in the finals in Hebrew and Arabic he got a first (1901). Maspero's lectures had been a disappointment and some private lessons by F. Ll. Griffith [q.v.], a brilliant scholar but poor teacher, were equally of little assistance, so that Gardiner formed himself entirely by his own efforts. In this he was greatly helped by his understanding father who made him financially independent, so that Gardiner never had to earn his living; the only post he ever held was a readership in Egyptology at Manchester University (1912–14). This financial independence Gardiner considered as an obligation, and deserved only if in exchange he gave to his chosen subject of Egyptology all his time and energy.

His father insisted that after Oxford he should spend three months in his office, and this business training proved of considerable use all his life, and inspired his businesslike approach to research and publishing. In 1902 Gardiner moved to Berlin for the next ten years to co-operate in preparations for an Egyptian dictionary sponsored by four German academies (Berlin, Munich, Leipzig, and Göttingen) and directed by Professor Erman. To that dictionary Gardiner devoted most of his time and energy preparing Egyptian texts for excerption. At Erman's suggestion, he specialized in the study of hieratic writing and made prolonged stays at Leiden, Paris, and Turin, copying hieratic manuscripts on papyrus and ostraca (sherds or limestone chips) and translated them later for the dictionary. He was also in these years Laycock student in Egyptology of Worcester College, Oxford.

Some shorter articles Gardiner published as

a schoolboy and before he went to Berlin: but it was in 1904 that his real scientific output started. That year saw his first large-scale article on an inscription describing the installation of a vizier in Pharaonic Egypt; in 1905 appeared 'The Inscription of Mes' dealing with a great civil lawsuit at the time of Ramesses II. From then on hardly a year passed without an article in a periodical or a book throwing new light on some problem of Egyptology. Books he devoted to his favourite line: publication of new texts, their translation, and commentary on them: *The Admonitions of an Egyptian Sage* (1909), *Notes on the Story of Sinuhe* (1916), the satyrical letter of *Papyrus Anastasi I* (1911), *Egyptian Letters to the Dead* (1928), and the mythological story of Horus and Seth and other papyri given to the British Museum by (Sir) Chester Beatty [q.v.] (1931–5), as well as in 1939 (with J. Capart) a large papyrus dealing with a robbery in a royal tomb. The colossal Wilbour papyrus, a taxation ledger, led Gardiner from literary to administrative texts, and in a publication of three volumes (1941–8) he dealt in a masterly way with the obscure subject of Egyptian taxation. At the same time another three volumes of *Ancient Egyptian Onomastica* (1947) made accessible the surviving examples of ancient Egyptian lexicography. In transcription only, that is without translation or commentary, Gardiner published *Late-Egyptian Stories* (1932), *Late-Egyptian Miscellanies* (1937), and *Ramesside Administrative Documents* (1940), making these three classes of texts accessible to scholars in reliable copies at a low price, for Gardiner, though himself a wealthy man, always carefully planned every publication of his to give the most at the cheapest possible price.

In 1927 Gardiner published his *Egyptian Grammar*, the bestseller among Egyptological publications. Its third edition in 1957 was still reprinted after the author's death, for besides the grammar of the language it contains exercises to translate from and into Egyptian, a detailed list of hieroglyphic signs, and an Egyptian–English and English–Egyptian vocabulary. It also adopts the modern method of leading the learner gradually from simple to more complicated rules, keeping his interest by exercises from the earliest stage.

Now and then Gardiner joined another scholar. Thus in 1917 he published the Egyptian inscriptions from Sinai with T. E. Peet [q.v.], and with J. Černý he collaborated on *Hieratic Ostraca* (1957). With A. E. P. Weigall, he compiled *A Topographical Catalogue of the Private Tombs of Thebes* (1913) and did much towards their preservation and recording by Norman and Nina de Garis

Davies. He himself wrote the text to two of Mrs Davies's volumes which appeared in the Theban Tomb Series which he edited with Davies in 1915–33. Between 1916 and 1946 he acted for a total of thirteen years as editor of the *Journal of Egyptian Archaeology*. He edited three volumes on the temple of Abydos (1933–8) and from 1935, in collaboration, seven volumes of the religious texts on Egyptian coffins.

While studying for publication the inscriptions brought from Sinai by (Sir) Flinders Petrie [q.v.], Gardiner noticed a small number of short inscriptions in a hieroglyphic writing which was clearly not Egyptian. Since the number of characters was very limited, the writing was very likely alphabetic and Gardiner concluded that this was the postulated pictographic ancestor of the Phoenician alphabet. He announced his discovery to the British Association in Manchester in 1915, and considered it always and quite rightly as his most important discovery, for it has thrown light on the origin of our own writing. His explanation has been generally accepted.

The writing of the *Egyptian Grammar* led Gardiner to linguistics. He was keenly interested in the subject and gave much thought to its problems. It was, however, only in 1932 that *The Theory of Speech and Language* appeared to the great relief of his Egyptological friends who regretted that linguistic theories kept Gardiner away from Egyptology. The reviewers were far from enthusiastic about the book to Gardiner's discontent, for he sometimes thought that it was the best of all he had written. In 1940 he published *The Theory of Proper Names*.

Gardiner was a man of great self-discipline. He liked, it is true, a good two months' summer holiday spent either in the country or on travel, but for the rest of the year working weeks were of seven days. He was an encouraging example to any scholar who came to know him personally, of whom there were many. Even larger perhaps was the number of those who wrote asking him for information or advice: Gardiner never left a letter unanswered. In his work he was favoured by his powerful physique, which enabled him to make brisk daily walks, and once a week to play tennis with great zest. Evenings, however, were devoted to relaxation, often to music, especially to playing the fiddle (he never said 'violin'). It was just in time, when his strength began to fail, that he finished, in 1961, his last book *Egypt of the Pharaohs*. He called it his 'swan song', feeling that the end was not far. But not quite yet: two articles of his appeared in 1962 exactly one year before his death.

Gardiner supplicated for and obtained the D.Litt. at Oxford in 1910 and in 1929 he was elected FBA. He received honorary degrees

Gardiner, A. H.

from Durham and Cambridge and was an honorary or corresponding member of many foreign learned bodies. He was an honorary fellow of his old Oxford college, the Queen's, from 1935, and in 1948 he was knighted.

In 1901 Gardiner married, in Vienna, Hedwig (died 1964), daughter of Alexander von Rosen, King's Counsellor for Hungary; they had two sons and one daughter. Gardiner died at his home, Court Place, Iffley, Oxford, 19 December 1963.

An oil-painting of Gardiner by Tad. Styka hangs on the staircase in the Griffith Institute (Ashmolean Museum), Oxford. A bibliography of his work down to 1948 can be found in the *Journal of Egyptian Archaeology*, vol. xxxv, 1949.

[Sir Alan Gardiner, *My Working Years*, privately printed, 1962; J. Černý in *Proceedings* of the British Academy, vol. 1, 1964; *Journal of Egyptian Archaeology*, vol. 1, 1964; private information; personal knowledge.]

J. ČERNÝ

GARDINER, SIR THOMAS ROBERT (1883–1964), civil servant, was born at Cork 8 March 1883, the son of Matthew John Gardiner, a Post Office surveyor, who held appointments in Ireland and subsequently in Scotland, and his wife, Elizabeth Granger. He was educated at Lurgan College, in county Armagh, and subsequently at the Royal High School, Edinburgh. He went to Edinburgh University, and graduated MA with first class honours in history and economic science in 1905. The university later was to give him an honorary LLD degree (1949). His Irish and Scottish provenance was always a source of great pride, and he never lost his rich and highly individual brogue. He entered the Post Office in 1906 and after service as an assistant surveyor went to its headquarters in 1913, serving from 1914 to 1917 as private secretary to the secretary of the Post Office, (Sir) Q. E. C. Murray, whose notice Gardiner wrote for this Dictionary, an aristocrat and autocrat of great ability. Gardiner's own autocratic style, though partly inborn, no doubt owed something to his close contact with Murray during his formative years. He then had a short period in the Ministry of Reconstruction, followed by fifteen years in the London Postal Service, the last eight as controller, probably the most exacting managerial post in the Post Office. Following the Bridgeman report, which was critical of what it regarded with some justice as an ivory tower mentality in the headquarters administration, Gardiner was brought back by Sir H. Kingsley Wood [q.v.] to headquarters in 1934 to serve as deputy director-general, under

(Sir) Donald Banks, who also returned to headquarters, in his case from the controllership of the Post Office Savings Bank. As deputy director-general Gardiner undertook the chairmanship of the reorganization committee, which was responsible for the replacement of the old surveyors, in charge of the postal service and the commercial side of the Telephone and Telegraph Services, by regional directors, heading an integrated organization embracing the regional engineering service. In 1936 he succeeded Banks as director-general of the Post Office, a post he held till his retirement in 1945.

The testing of the civil preparations to deal with air attack at the time of the Munich crisis in 1938 showed that they could not all be left to be handled by the small air-raid precautions department set up in 1935. Sir John Anderson (later Viscount Waverley, q.v.) was appointed lord privy seal, with responsibility for civil preparations against air raids: and he asked Gardiner to serve as head of the small office that was to co-ordinate the work of all the departments now enlisted to make adequate preparations. The respect in which Gardiner was already held in Whitehall made him an ideal choice for this difficult task. His outstanding managerial ability, coupled with Irish charm, enabled him to organize and push forward, in the short time available before war broke out, preparations covering not only air-raid precautions services but also the police and fire brigades, emergency hospital arrangements, evacuation plans, and liaison with the fighting services. He became permanent secretary of the Ministry of Home Security, which was created on the outbreak of war in 1939.

In the autumn of 1940 he returned to his post of director-general of the Post Office, where he directed the vital communication services of the nation during the war years. There can have been few holders of the top position in the Post Office who have stamped the impact of their personality on it as Gardiner did. He combined great natural ability with a down-to-earth practicality, reinforced by his experience as an assistant surveyor and as assistant controller of the London Postal Service, and he changed the whole style of management in the Post Office. When he retired there could have been few to dispute the claim of the British postal service to be the best in the world, and the telecommunications services, if not perhaps equally pre-eminent, enjoyed an enviable reputation. After his retirement Gardiner's services were greatly in demand. He confined himself to public work, but within this field the range of his activities was wide. In 1946 he became a member of the royal commission which examined the organization and pay of the senior ranks of the Canadian Civil Service. In 1947–8 he did pioneering work as chairman of the Stevenage New Town Development Corporation; and from 1949 to 1951 he was vice-chairman, and for a time acting chairman, of the National Dock Labour Board. He was also a government director of the Anglo-Iranian Oil Company from 1950 to 1953. The postal service being highly labour-intensive, Gardiner had been necessarily heavily involved in staff matters, and he was a natural choice as chairman of the committee of three appointed in 1948 by the prime minister to deal with cases of civil servants removed from confidential work because of alleged association with subversive organizations. He chaired a committee on the organization and pay of architects, engineers, and surveyors which reported in 1951, and in 1952 he chaired a similar committee dealing with accountants. He was a member of the royal commission on Scottish affairs from 1952 to 1954 and served from 1953 to 1956 on a committee chaired by Lord Waverley on the medical and dental services of the armed forces.

Despite his wide range of experience and achievement, Gardiner always felt himself to be a Post Office man first and foremost. Almost to the end of his life, he was wont to drop in on his successors as director-general of the PO and tell them, more in sorrow than in anger, of what he regarded as instances of failing to meet his own exacting standards for Post Office services. The surveyors of the Post Office, the predecessors of the present directors of the postal regions, have a proud history, counting among their number Anthony Trollope [q.v.], and Gardiner was conspicuous among heads of the Post Office for his recognition of the importance of provincial managerial experience for the men and women who were to hold the highest offices in the Post Office. For the administrative class in the PO at that time he had something less than unqualified admiration, though this did not prevent him from recognizing outstanding ability wherever it was to be found.

Gardiner was appointed KBE in 1936, KCB in 1937, GBE in 1941, and GCB in 1954. In 1919 he married Christina Stenhouse; they had no children. Away from work his main interest was his family, including those who remained in Ireland. For recreation he most enjoyed walking, and was a keen golfer in his younger days; later his delight was to spend summer or autumn holidays in the Scottish Highlands.

Physically Gardiner was an imposing figure, tall and upright; and he had a dominating personality, combined with natural charm but also with a capacity to be ruthless when he judged it necessary.

Until the age of fifty-five his experience had been confined to the Post Office, and in the main

to the postal service, but it came as no surprise to those who knew him that, having moved within five years of normal retiring age into Whitehall, he had quickly become a dominating figure in fields where he was previously unknown, and had earned such wide respect and admiration as to be in great demand in so many different fields on his retirement. He died 1 January 1964 at the Hospital of St. John and St. Elizabeth in St. Marylebone, London.

[*The Times*, 2 January 1964; private information; personal knowledge.]

DONALD SARGENT

GARROD, SIR (ALFRED) GUY (ROLAND) (1891–1965), air chief marshal, was born in London 13 April 1891, the third son of Herbert Baring Garrod, barrister-in-law of Hampstead, London, and his wife, Lucy Florence Colchester. It is worthy of note that Garrod numbered among his immediate forebears no less than three fellows of the Royal Society: his grandfather, Sir Alfred Baring Garrod, and two uncles, Sir Archibald Edward Garrod, KCMG, and Alfred Henry Garrod [qq.v.], all three of whom were physicians of distinction. He was educated at Bradfield College whence he proceeded by way of an open classical scholarship to University College, Oxford. Garrod obtained a second class in classical moderations in 1912 and a third in *literae humaniores* in 1914. His outside interests included the Officers' Training Corps and the OUDS, of which he was a leading member.

At the outbreak of World War I Garrod, with so many of his young fellow countrymen, joined the army where, helped no doubt by his OTC experience and his skill as a rifle shot, which gained him a bronze and a silver medal at Bisley, he was commissioned into the Leicestershire Regiment in August 1914. He was wounded near Ypres in November 1914 and invalided to the United Kingdom. Later, he learned to fly and was seconded to the Royal Flying Corps in 1915. He spent most of his wartime service overseas. He was thrice mentioned in dispatches and awarded the DFC and MC. When war ended, Garrod planned a career in industry but Sir H. M. (later Viscount) Trenchard [q.v.], who was at this time putting together the elements of the peacetime Royal Air Force, persuaded him to return and in August 1919 he accepted a permanent commission in the Royal Air Force.

Between the wars Garrod filled a wide variety of posts. He was a natural selection for Staff College appointments and was a student at the Royal Naval Staff College, Greenwich (1921–2), the Imperial Defence College (1933), and the Royal Air Force Staff College (1923–7) where he was a member of the directing staff. Among other interesting inter-war posts was that of chief instructor to the air squadron at his old university (1928-30). He was promoted to air commodore in 1936.

By the outbreak of World War II Garrod, now an air vice-marshal, was serving in the Air Ministry as director of equipment, the duties of which included ensuring that hundreds of thousands of items of technical and other equipment (from barrack stores to complete engines and airframes) were available in due proportion to Royal Air Force units all over the world. In July 1940 Garrod succeeded to the appointment which was undoubtedly the climax of his Service career—that of air member for training, a new post on the Air Council created to take charge of the vitally important programme of air force training. In 1934 the personnel strength of the Royal Air Force was 30,000. By September 1939 it had grown to 174,000 and by the end of the war, including Dominion and Allied personnel, the total came to well over one million. Most of these men and women were trained to exacting standards and nearly 200,000 of them were aircrew. This was an achievement of massive proportions and it played a significant part in the Allied victories in the air. Of course the programme was too vast to be confined to Britain; it involved, for example, the creation of no less than 300 flying training schools. From the start therefore the training programme was conceived as a Commonwealth effort. As air member for training on the Air Council, Garrod played a leading role in these developments.

In 1943 Garrod was posted overseas where his appointments included those of deputy Allied air commander-in-chief, South East Asia, and (briefly) at the end of the war, as commander-in-chief, Royal Air Force, Mediterranean and Middle East. After the war Garrod served as Royal Air Force military representative on the Military Staff Committee of the United Nations and head of the Royal Air Force delegation, Washington. He retired in 1948 in the rank of air chief marshal.

In the seventeen years which remained to him Garrod followed a wide variety of interests. He held several business posts, wrote extensively on Royal Air Force subjects, and was a member of the advisory panel on official military histories of the war. He became warden of his old school, Bradfield College (1959), an honorary fellow of University College, Oxford (1947), and an honorary steward at Westminster Abbey. The university of Aberdeen awarded him an honorary LLD. He was appointed OBE in 1932, GBE in 1948, CB in 1941, and KCB in 1943.

Garrod was essentially a man of many parts.

Aside from his mainstream activities, he was as a young man an excellent athlete, winning his half blues for cross-country running and rifle shooting in which latter capacity he was of international class representing Britain in competitions in the early twenties. He had an abiding interest in music and was himself an excellent violinist. Thus, Garrod belonged to that select body of men who combine military, artistic, and athletic virtues.

In appearance, Garrod was of average height, softly spoken, and possessed of a distinctly academic air though there was nothing academic about his activities in the military sphere. He was endowed with the important quality of approachability to the young and he was an enthusiast for pressing new ideas to practical conclusions. He made a great success of his career as an airman but he would have been equally at home as an academic or as a professional man. In conversation Garrod was restrained, friendly, and courteous. His contributions never strayed outside the bounds of fact and reason.

In 1918 Garrod married Cicely Evelyn Bray, ARRC, a nursing sister, the daughter of John Bray, estate agent, of St. Leonards-on-Sea, Sussex. After Lady Garrod's death in 1960, in 1961 Garrod married Doris Baker, the widow of Samuel J. Baker. There were two children, a son and a daughter, of the first marriage. Garrod died 3 January 1965 at his home in Malvern, Worcestershire.

A portrait in oils of Garrod by the war artist, Alfred Reginald Thomson (1943) is in the possession of the Imperial War Museum.

[*The Times*, 5, 8, and 12 January 1965; private information.]   M. J. DEAN

GATER, SIR GEORGE HENRY (1886-1963), administrator, was born at Britford, Wiltshire, 26 December 1886, the son of William Henry Gater, solicitor, of Winslowe House, West End, Southampton, and his wife, Ada Mary Welch. He was educated at Winchester, in Morshead's house, and at New College, Oxford, where he gained a fourth class in classical moderations (1907) and a second class in modern history (1909). He remained a devoted Wykehamist all his life. He also obtained a diploma in education at Oxford (1909); and in 1912 he was appointed assistant director of education at Nottingham. Between 1914 and 1918, beginning as a second lieutenant he rose to command the 9th Sherwood Foresters, the 6th Lincolnshire Regiment, and the 62nd Infantry brigade. He saw service in Gallipoli, Egypt, and France, was wounded twice, was four times mentioned in dispatches, was appointed to the DSO (1916, and bar,

1917), made CMG (1918) and a commander of the Legion of Honour, and was awarded the croix de guerre. After the war, he was director of education for Lancashire from 1919 until 1924, when he became education officer of the London County Council.

Both in Lancashire and in London Gater organized most successfully the machinery to work the Education Act of 1918, gaining the respect and affection of administrators, teachers, and scholars. He became clerk to the LCC in 1933 and permanent under-secretary of state for the colonies in July 1939, in succession to (Sir) A. C. Cosmo Parkinson [q.v.]. After short terms in the Ministry of Home Security (jointly with Sir Thomas Gardiner, q.v.) and the Ministry of Supply, he returned to the Colonial Office in 1942 and served there till his retirement in 1947.

War with Japan brought the Colonial Office into the front line, and it was deeply involved in the economic and political aspects of the war effort and in the relations of the United Kingdom with the United States. Both during and after the war, Gater had to steer a succession of secretaries of state on the transition from the old colonial system to social and political arrangements more in keeping with the spirit of the time.

Throughout his career Gater was essentially an administrator. His original sphere was that of education, but it was as an organizer and director of education, not as a teacher, that he made his mark. As a civil servant, he could not attempt to be a master of every subject; his mastery lay in his grasp of the essential issues, and his appreciation both of the indispensability of experts and of the need for providing the experts with a sound administrative organization within which they could work. Ministers and officials alike felt that his was a steady hand at the helm. He had also the good commander's gift of personal interest in, and care for, the welfare of those who served under him.

While with the London County Council, he was responsible, along with E. P. Wheeler, for volume xviii of the council's *Survey of London*, covering the Strand and the parish of St. Martin-in-the-Fields, and with F. R. Hiorns for volume xx, concerning Trafalgar Square and its neighbourhood.

After his retirement he became chairman of the School Broadcasting Council for the United Kingdom, and a member of the BBC General Advisory Council. He was an honorary fellow of New College, and of the Royal College of Music, and a co-opted member of the Oxford-shire Education Committee.

But his main interest in his later years was in the welfare of Winchester College. He had been elected a fellow (i.e. a member of the governing body) by the headmaster, second master, and assistant masters, in 1936, and was warden from 1951 to 1959. He succeeded Lord Simonds, who became lord chancellor, and was a magnificent figure, but not inclined to make or approve changes.

Two main problems confronted the school in 1951, and were solved by 1959, thanks very largely to Gater. The seventeenth-century building called 'School' was too small, and the idea of a new and larger school hall had been in the air since 1919; and the munificent gift by Sir George Alexander Cooper of the seventeenth-century panelling banished from the chapel by William Butterfield [q.v.], the architect, persuaded all doubters that a room worthy of it must be built. Opinions differed about where it should be, but Gater's indefatigable efforts and infallible tact led to complete unanimity, and the building designed by Peter Shepheard is Gater's lasting memorial.

A very different problem was the disrepair and obsolescence of nineteenth-century buildings, including the boarding-houses, and eighteenth-century staff houses, built to be run by a number of servants. Here the expertise was provided by Ruthven Oliphant Hall, a former scholar of the college, who was then an architect in private practice but afterwards became bursar. Much money was needed and Gater persuaded the governing body to issue an appeal, and Anthony W. Tuke, chairman of Barclays Bank, to organize it. Enough money was raised, and the programme was completed.

Meanwhile the governing body had to appoint a new headmaster, and it was mainly Gater who brought about the very successful appointment of (Sir) H. Desmond P. Lee.

Gater was already a parent when he became warden. He had married in 1926 Irene, daughter of (John) Bowyer Buchanan Nichols, of Lawford Hall, Manningtree, a former fellow of Winchester, and their only child, Anthony, had entered Morshead's in 1946, staying there till 1952, when he followed his father to New College. Lady Gater had outstanding gifts both as a hostess and as a decorator. The Gaters delighted the teaching staff, members of the school, and a wide circle of friends and neighbours, with a constant succession of dinner parties, tea parties, and other entertainments, and they left the warden's lodgings much more beautiful and much more comfortable than they found them. Lady Gater ran the National Gallery canteen for midday concerts during World War II and was appointed MBE in 1946, and died in 1977.

Gater was knighted in 1936, appointed KCB in 1941, and promoted to GCMG in 1944. He died 14 January 1963 at St. Joseph's Nursing

Home, Boars Hill, Oxford, and his ashes were deposited in Winchester College cloisters.

[*The Times*, 15 January 1963; *Wykehamist*, 12 February 1963; personal knowledge.]

PATRICK DUFF

GATES, REGINALD RUGGLES (1882–1962), botanist, geneticist, and anthropologist, was born 1 May 1882, near Middleton, Nova Scotia, he and a twin sister being the eldest of the three (the other was a daughter) children of Andreas Bohaker Gates and his wife, Charlotte Elizabeth Ruggles. His father was a large farmer and fruit-grower, holding 600 acres three miles outside Middleton; he was also a manufacturer, in the third generation, of a medicine derived from native roots, herbs, and barks which attained considerable fame. The Gates family, in America and then Canada, was descended from Stephen Gates, who was born at Higham in Essex and settled in Massachusetts in 1638. Earlier ancestors included Sir John Gates [q.v.], who was a gentleman of the bedchamber to Henry VIII and a member of the Privy Council of Edward VI. Ruggles Gates's great-great-grandfather was a half-brother of Major-General Horatio Gates [q.v.], a well-known leader during the American Revolution. His mother was a great-great-granddaughter of Brigadier-General Timothy Ruggles, who played a prominent part on the loyalist side during the American Revolution. During the revolution he was obliged to flee and was rewarded with a grant of 10,000 acres of land in Nova Scotia. These antecedents had a marked effect on Gates and it was typical of him, with his strongly loyalist views, that his greatest admiration should have been for the memory of Brigadier-General Ruggles.

The family was an isolated one, and up to the age of nine Gates was taught by his mother, who had been a schoolteacher. She was also a very keen botanist, and this awakened his interest in the subject. He then attended Middleton High School, where he rapidly qualified for college entrance. In 1899 he went to Mount Allison University, Sackville, Nova Scotia, graduating in 1903 with first class honours in science. He spent a year at McGill University, where he became a demonstrator in botany, and attended the seminars of Rutherford [q.v.]. After teaching for a year at his former secondary school, he supported himself with scholarships until he was offered a senior fellowship at the university of Chicago, where he graduated as Ph.D. in 1908. At both Sackville and Chicago he came under the influence of a number of eminent biologists and greatly profited by his close association with them. It

was at Chicago that he first developed his interest in the genus *Oenothera*, which he used for many long years for a remarkable series of cytological studies. His discoveries were outstanding. To quote a single example, he was the first person to observe the phenomenon of non-disjunction of chromosomes. This was as early as 1908, and by 1914 final clarification was achieved. It is a pity that Gates's name is not attached to the phenomenon of non-disjunction; as frequently happened, he was many years ahead of his time. In 1915 he published a book *The Mutation Factor in Evolution, with particular reference to Oenothera*. He made it clear that mutation could be of two kinds, namely, that of single genes (which was then the specific interest of geneticists), but also of major chromosome rearrangements. This was but the first of many books on genetics which he was to write.

In 1910 Gates paid his first extensive visit to Europe, visiting France, Italy, Switzerland, Germany, Holland, and England, which he immediately recognized as his spiritual home. In 1911 he came to England, continuing his researches at the Imperial College of Science. From 1912 to 1914 he was lecturer in biology at St. Thomas's Hospital. He lectured on heredity and its relation to cytology at Oxford in 1914, and was associate professor of zoology in the university of California in 1915–16. During the latter part of the war of 1914–18 he acted as an instructor in aerial gunnery to the Royal Flying Corps. Early in 1919 he was appointed reader in the botany department of King's College, London, and became professor of the department in 1921. He was elected FRS in 1931, at the early age of forty-eight. His work as a teacher was quite outstanding. He had a phenomenal memory and could at once help students and others in their researches. He was able to extend the facilities for cytological and cytogenetical work and the number of Ph.D. students continually increased. The writer of this notice is indebted to Dr Norah L. Penston, who was a member of his staff at King's College for a number of years, for the following tribute: 'He was most assiduous in the supervision of his many research students, paying a daily visit to the research laboratory and seeing every one of them, and the daily meetings round the tea-table were always lively and stimulating affairs. There were also three or four meetings a term for research students and staff at which in turn we gave papers. Professor Gates was helpfully critical about presentation and content of these papers. Above all he would correct—privately—any errors we had made in reference to the work of earlier authors. He was most particular about this himself, and was helped by a phenomenal memory.' His work at King's

College came to an end at the beginning of World War II. The department was evacuated and greatly reduced in numbers. Gates returned to America, resigning his chair in 1942 at the age of sixty. From then on he spent most of his time at Harvard University, where he was research fellow in botany and anthropology and much enjoyed collaboration with his old friend, Professor E. A. Hooton. He finally came back to live in London in 1957.

In addition to his devotion to research in botany and cytology Gates became especially attracted at an early age to anthropology and human genetics. His contributions in these fields were also outstanding. Two examples may be selected from very many. He realized at a very early stage that many racial differences could not be accounted for by single genes, or indeed by multifactorial inheritance. If some racial differences, for example, skin colour, in regard to which parental types can be recaptured in essentials by segregation in a relatively small F_2 or backcross, and if further crosses show that the segregants breed true, it must follow that the number of gene pairs involved is small. He proposed two to five, acting additively and without dominance and recessiveness. This finding remains true and is generally accepted nowadays. Another contribution (in collaboration with Dr P. N. Bhaduri) was the discovery in Gates's late seventies of a Y-borne gene determining the characteristic of hairy ear-rims in certain populations. This finding remains the only well-proven example of a Y-borne gene in man.

Throughout the whole of Gates's working life he carried out numerous expeditions to a wide variety of countries. These were often lengthy and led to many valuable research contributions, mainly botanical in his earlier years and afterwards very largely anthropological. He collaborated very happily with his hosts and gave numerous courses of lectures. These activities continued until the last year of his life, and, indeed, he published no less than thirteen papers during his last two years and left eight awaiting publication. His final expedition, during the last year of his life, was, appropriately, to India, and lasted for six months. He was received with much honour and friendliness and research assistants were appointed to accompany him. He made numerous anthropological observations and measurements and gave many lectures.

Gates was married three times. His first marriage, in 1911, was to Dr Marie Charlotte Carmichael Stopes [q.v.], the well-known palaeobotanist and advocate of birth control, who was a daughter of Henry Stopes. This marriage very soon broke up and was annulled in 1916. In Marie Stopes's writings and in quotations from her there are personal references to Ruggles Gates which could not help being very hurtful to a sensitive man. Many of these damaging references are not correct or justified. He married, secondly, in America in 1929, Miss J. Williams. This marriage too was dissolved. There were no children. His third marriage, in 1955, was to Laura Greer, daughter of Albert J. Nowotny of New Braunfels, Texas, and widow of Samuel R. Greer, of Tyler, Texas. This marriage proved ideally happy. Mrs Gates, who was a graduate in social science, accompanied him on all his numerous expeditions to many parts of the world. She was able to act as a very valuable assistant, and her skill as a photographer was a great help to him.

Gates had a phenomenal and photographic memory, mastered many languages, and was thoroughly conscientious. Although some of his researches led him to be quite wrongly branded as a racist, he was a fervent critic of Fascism and Nazism. His views are best summarized in his own words: 'To say that all men are equal has not got us very far. It is more accurate to say that all men are different, and then to respect each other's differences.' He was vice-president of the Linnean Society, of which he was a fellow, and a member of its council, and vice-president and fellow of the Royal Anthropological Institute. To these and many other societies he gave much time and attention. Mount Allison awarded him an LLD, and London a D.Sc.; he became a fellow of King's College, London. He published many books and a great number of scientific papers.

There is a portrait in oils by A. Connors (1940) in the Fraser-Ruggles Gates Room at Mount Allison University, Sackville, New Brunswick, Canada.

[Autobiographical notes left by Gates in the possession of Mrs Laura Ruggles Gates; J. A. Fraser Roberts and F. A. E. Crew in *Biographical Memoirs of Fellows of the Royal Society*, vol. x, 1964; personal knowledge.]

J. A. FRASER ROBERTS

GEDYE, (GEORGE) ERIC (ROWE) (1890–1970), journalist, was born at Clevedon, Somerset, 27 May 1890, the eldest son of George Edward Gedye, provisions merchant of Bristol, and his wife, Lillie Rowe. He was educated at Clarence School, Weston-super-Mare, and Queen's College, Taunton, and matriculated at London University. After an unsuccessful start as a would-be journalist and author he was gazetted in August 1914 from London University Officers' Training Corps to the 12th battalion of the Gloucestershire Regiment and served from November 1915 on the western front. He was wounded on the Somme in September 1916. In May 1918 he joined the Intelligence Corps and was mentioned in dispatches. During the advance into Germany he was attached to the cavalry, and served on the British military governor's staff in Cologne and on the Inter-Allied Rhineland High Commission until 1922.

In that year Gedye's real life-work began. As he himself put it, 'Lord Northcliffe came to Cologne, had a nervous breakdown and appointed me local correspondent there of *The Times* and the *Daily Mail*.' He had a flying start. In January 1923 the French occupation of the Ruhr was extended because of a German default in coal deliveries and Gedye was on the spot. Within a few days he was promoted from an obscure local correspondent to the well-paid post of 'our special correspondent' on the staff of *The Times*. During the next two years his dispatches from the Rhineland describing the French plans for the establishment of separatist states 'led' the paper for a longer period than any foreign correspondent had ever achieved, and he came to be regarded by the French as one of the main obstacles in the way of their intrigues to establish what Gedye called 'government by desperadoes'. His most famous scoop was his eyewitness account of the assassination by young German nationalists of Heinz, given by the French the title of 'president of the Autonomous Palatinate', in the Hotel Wittelsbacher Hof in Speyer. Gedye afterwards described this period in *The Revolver Republic* (1930), an exciting piece of contemporary history which perhaps remains his best book. He noted wryly that, while the German press regarded his dispatches at that time as 'objective', when he turned his attention to manifestations of extreme German nationalism in the Rhineland his lack of 'objectivity' was immediately deplored. This provides an important clue to Gedye's character throughout his life. He was always passionately opposed to extremism and violence wherever he found it—and he found it often enough in the Central Europe of the 1920s and 30s, which he continued to interpret vividly for the readers of a variety of newspapers until the outbreak of war in 1939.

In 1925 *The Times* sent him as its Central European correspondent to Vienna, which became his home for the next thirteen years. In 1926 he moved to the *Daily Express* and in 1929 to the *Daily Telegraph*. From 1929 he also represented the *New York Times*. His experience of Central Europe was summed up in his book *Heirs to the Hapsburgs* (1932), a study of political, economic, and social conditions in an area which, as he rightly foresaw, would be a source of increasing trouble in the years to come. In these years he also produced a charming guide-book to his beloved Austria, *A Wayfarer in Austria* (1928). He covered the darkening scene in Vienna, the suppression of the Socialists, and the murder of Dollfuss, but his coverage of the most tragic events of all, the Nazi invasion of Austria and the proclamation of the *Anschluss*, was rudely cut short. In 1938 he was expelled from Austria by the Gestapo at three days' notice. When he left Vienna by rail, seen off on the platform by a mixed crowd of colleagues and Gestapo officials, his dachshund was seen at the window with its paw raised in the Nazi salute. Gedye moved his base to Prague, but only worked for the *Daily Telegraph* for a few months longer. In 1939 he published another book of contemporary history, *Fallen Bastions*, in which he severely criticized Chamberlain's appeasement policy. Rather surprisingly, for the *Daily Telegraph* was anything but enthusiastic about appeasement, the paper considered the book so partisan that he could not credibly carry on as an 'impartial' correspondent. The editor announced that he had resigned by 'mutual consent'. 'That', commented Gedye, 'is correct. It is equally correct that Herr Hitler invaded Czechoslovakia by "mutual arrangement" with President Hácha.'

When the Germans marched into Prague in March 1939 Gedye, with two other British correspondents, took refuge in the British Embassy to avoid arrest under a Gestapo warrant and was allowed to leave the country with a safe conduct a week later. He then became Moscow correspondent of the *New York Times*, for which he had continued to work in Prague after the break with the *Daily Telegraph*, and from 1940–1 correspondent in Turkey. He was employed on special military duties in the Middle East from 1941 until the end of the war, when he returned to Vienna, first of all for the *Daily Herald*, and then for the *Observer* and the *Manchester Guardian*. In 1946 he was appointed MBE. In 1954 he became head of evaluation for Radio Free Europe. He retired and returned to England in 1961 and settled in Bath.

That Gedye was the greatest British foreign correspondent of the inter-war years can hardly be disputed. By his style and personality he contributed a great deal to the aura of romance which surrounded the profession at that period. He was brown-haired, thin, grey-eyed, and electrically energetic. Among other foreign correspondents he was the best of colleagues and companions.

In 1922 Gedye married Elisabeth Bremer of Cologne who died in 1960. His second wife, whom he married in 1948, was Alice Lepper of Vienna, daughter of Bernard Mehler, a factory owner. They had one son. Gedye died on 21

March 1970 in Bath. In retirement he started work on an autobiography. The few chapters which he completed are in the Imperial War Museum.

[Newspaper cuttings and obituaries; private information; personal knowledge.]

HUGH GREENE

GENÉE, DAME ADELINE (1878-1970), ballet dancer, was born 6 January 1878 in the village of Hinnerup, Jutland, the second daughter of Peter Jensen and his wife, Kirsten. The survivor of twins, she was named Anina Margarete Kirstina Petra.

She was encouraged to dance by her parents, who were musical, almost as soon as she could walk. When she was only eight her paternal uncle, Alexander, who had taken the stage name of Genée, and his wife, the Hungarian Antonia Zimmermann, became, in effect, her guardians; they were internationally well known, he as a dancer-choreographer and she as a dancer, and with unremitting thoroughness they set about the self-appointed task of making Adeline a ballerina. Alexander, in particular, was to govern her early career almost completely, until she was well over twenty and already known; only when she was twenty-four did she cease to hand over to him her weekly earnings. On her uncle's advice she was renamed Adeline, after the opera singer Adeline Patti. She first danced in public in Christiania (Oslo) in 1888, at the age of ten.

Her aunt and uncle ran, and were the leading performers in, a small touring company, in which Adeline's career began, in Scandinavia and Germany. At the age of eighteen she made her mark at the Opera House in Berlin and a little later in Munich where, for the first time, she danced Swanilda in *Coppélia*, a role which was to remain her speciality. In 1897, when she was nineteen, she came to London, with a contract for six weeks at the Empire Theatre in Leicester Square. The six weeks turned into an engagement of ten years during which Adeline Genée achieved a reputation unrivalled in Britain by any dancer since Marie Taglioni [q.v.] in the 1830s and 40s, and a popularity for which, among dancers, there was no British precedent.

She undertook six tours of America, in 1908 (twice), and 1909, 1910-11, 1912-13, and 1914; in 1913 she also visited Australia and New Zealand. During her reign at the Empire she revisited Copenhagen in 1902, had the first of several engagements in Paris in 1907, danced at Daly's Theatre (London) in 1905, and, in the same year, danced before Edward VII and Queen Alexandra at Chatsworth. Her American and antipodean tours did not break her link

with London, for she was back at the Empire in 1909 and at the London Coliseum in 1911. In 1914, also at the Coliseum, she had her 'farewell performance'. In 1910 she had married Frank S. N. Isitt (died 1939), an English business man with theatrical and aristocratic connections; they had no children. But for the advent of war, her 'farewell' in 1914 might have been the genuine end of her professional career; in fact she returned to the Coliseum in 1915, 1916, and 1917, danced at the Alhambra in 1916, and did not really end her professional dancing until after a charity performance at the Albert Hall in 1917. Even after that occasionally she could be tempted to appear in other charity programmes until finally, in 1933, she danced once more at the Coliseum, in Sir Oswald Stoll's [q.v.] brief resuscitation of the pre-war music-hall ballet which had passed out of fashion.

By then she had long since begun a second career. Towards the end of the war she joined forces with Edouard Espinosa, the dancer and teacher, and Philip Richardson, editor of the *Dancing Times*, in an attempt to systematize and improve the lamentable and ramshackle standards of ballet teaching in Britain. Out of their combined efforts the Association of Operatic Dancing was founded in 1920, with Genée as its first president. In 1931 the Association instituted the Genée gold medal, an annual award which has remained the highest available to a student dancer in Britain. Thanks to Genée's friendship with Queen Mary, the AOD received a royal charter in 1935. Genée remained president of the Royal Academy of Dancing, as the AOD was renamed, until 1954.

Sir Max Beerbohm [q.v.] wrote: 'Genée! It is a name that our grandchildren will cherish. . . . And Alas! our grandchildren will never believe, will never be able to imagine, what Genée was.' Genée was petite, fair-haired, impudently pretty, and her dancing, trained by her uncle in the predominantly Franco-Danish tradition, was very neat in footwork, light and quick; she was, technically, a virtuoso by the standards of her day and she could jump well. Tamara Karsavina, Serge Diaghilev's leading ballerina, greatly admired her and Diaghilev himself tried to persuade her, when she was forty-three, to join his line of eminent Russian ballerinas in his renowned production of *The Sleeping Princess* at the Alhambra, London, in 1921. She refused this invitation because 'I did not like his entourage'.

Of Genée's many ballets *Coppélia* was the only one of enduring value; the others were lavish, relatively ephemeral, productions which the Empire's trinity of Katti Lannea, C. Wilhelm, and Leopold Wenzel had made the prevailing music-hall fashion. Among these were *Alaska*,

The Belle of the Ball, Cinderella, Old China, Our Crown, High Jinks, and *The Milliner Duchess.* The most popular of all Genée's solos was the 'Hunting Dance' from *High Jinks;* this, along with, for instance, *A Dream of Roses and Butterflies* and *The Dryad,* became part of her permanent touring repertory. Some of her dances were insertions into the general production, arranged by her uncle or herself. *The Love Song,* in which the young Anton Dolin partnered her and in which she appeared in her very last performance at the Coliseum, was one of her inventions, devised for a charity programme in London in 1932. It was part of the repertory of the English Ballet Company which visited Copenhagen in 1932 with Genée as its sponsor and leader. This was the first group of British ballet dancers to go abroad—a snowdrop indication of the growth of ballet in Britain which Genée had done so much to encourage. This visit symbolized, too, her dual loyalties—to Denmark and to Britain. Britain had become her home, but she always maintained her close affection for the country of her birth. In 1950 she was created DBE; three years later she became commander of the Order of Dannebrog—only the second woman to receive this high Danish honour. She was also created an honorary D.Mus. of London University. In 1967 the Genée theatre at East Grinstead was named after her.

Genée's fame was achieved at a time when ballet, in Western Europe generally and particularly in Britain, was low in reputation. Her ballet was part of a music-hall show, with what that implies of unrefined taste; and the large casts of dancers among whom she was the star were, to say the least, of very moderate quality. It was a kind of entertainment which was to be swept aside by the new aesthetically ambitious, revolutionary ballet of the Russian Diaghilev. Yet Genée raised her kind of ballet to an unprecedented quality and popularity. And she made it highly respectable; there was an almost comically ironic contrast between the innocent propriety of the Empire's ballerina and the notoriety of the Empire's promenade as a rendezvous for light ladies. Innocent, indeed prudish, though Genée was, and subservient for an astonishingly long time to the rule of her uncle, she nevertheless had a mind of her own, as she was to show during the formative years of the Royal Academy of Dancing. And by any standards she was a great dancer—one whom the Americans compared with Anna Pavlova, largely to Genée's advantage. She died in Esher, Surrey, 23 April 1970.

Illustrations of an oil painting of Genée by Wilhelm Funk and a statuette by Una Troubridge, together with reproductions of drawings and photographs, are to be found in the biography mentioned below.

[Ivor Guest, *Adeline Genée: A Lifetime of Ballet under Six Reigns,* 1958.]

JAMES MONAHAN

GEORGE, GWILYM LLOYD-, first VISCOUNT TENBY (1894-1967), politician. [See LLOYD-GEORGE.]

GEORGE, LADY MEGAN LLOYD (1902-1966), politician. [See LLOYD GEORGE.]

GIBBS, SIR PHILIP ARMAND HAMILTON (1877-1962), writer, was born in Kensington, London, 1 May 1877, the fifth of the seven children of Henry James Gibbs, a civil servant in the Board of Education, and his wife, Helen Hamilton. His names were registered at birth as Philip Amande Thomas. His father who, apart from being unable to afford the fees, looked upon public schools as the 'most horrible dens of bullying and brutality' guided his children with firm devotion through the processes of self-education, setting an example oddly at variance with the policy of the department which employed him. He had some literary talent and published one or two novels: three of his sons and a daughter (Helen) all published books. One son became a successful dramatist and novelist under the name of Cosmo Hamilton; another was Arthur Hamilton Gibbs who published *Rowlandson's Oxford* (1911) and subsequently established himself as a novelist in the United States where he became an American citizen.

Philip Gibbs had no doubt that his future lay in Fleet Street. He entered the publishing house of Cassell at £2. 10s. a week and while there wrote his first book, *Founders of the Empire* (1899). He moved next to the post of editor of Tillotson's literary syndicate, offshoot of a family printing firm at Bolton, Lancashire, where his task was to buy articles, short stories, and other serial matter from amenable authors and resell the rights at a profit to provincial and overseas newspapers. In 1902 he reached Fleet Street when he was appointed a literary editor on the *Daily Mail* by the future Lord Northcliffe [q.v.]; but this was not altogether successful and after a brief period with the *Daily Express* he went to the *Daily Chronicle.* An interlude with the unsuccessful *Tribune,* a quality newspaper founded in the Liberal interest to challenge the politics and the supremacy of *The Times,* provided Gibbs with the material for *The Street of Adventure* (1909): 'the first Fleet Street novel.' The book went through many editions but Gibbs's royalty earnings were seriously depleted by legal costs incurred by a threatened libel action. His next novel, *Intellectual Mansions, S.W.* (1910), was killed stone dead when suffragette leaders bought up the entire edition and bound it in the colours of their movement.

Although he had not been trained as a reporter, Gibbs proved himself to be exceptionally proficient in that role when he rejoined the *Daily Chronicle* in 1908. His eyewitness accounts annotated many of the headlined events of these years, among them the battle of Sidney Street; and he distinguished himself by his dogged exposure of the claim of Dr Cook, the American explorer, to be the first man to reach the North Pole (1909). His facile pen and fluent style were allied to a staunch concern for accuracy which was rarely compromised by his strong sentimental bias. He was a correspondent for the *Daily Graphic* with the Bulgarian Army in the Balkan war of 1912. In 1913 he went to Germany for the *Daily Chronicle* to counter 'the harm created by newspaper hate-doctors and jingoes'. Based on interviews with representative Germans, his articles mirrored his conviction that there was 'a lot of peace-mindedness in Germany'. But within twelve months he was in Paris, awaiting his credentials as a war correspondent.

In 1915 he was chosen as one of the five newspapermen permitted to wear the official green brassard of a designated correspondent with the British Expeditionary Force. Displaying resources of stamina belied by his unimpressive physique and nervous temperament, he saw the bloodiest aspects of the fighting through the next three years. His impressions were recorded in dispatches which were published jointly in the *Daily Chronicle* and the *Daily Telegraph*, and widely circulated in the United States and the dominions. Their publication in volume form—*The Soul of the War* (1915), *The Battles of the Somme* (1917), *From Bapaume to Passchendaele* (1918), and *Realities of War* (1920)—confirmed him as the best-known British war correspondent. He was appointed KBE in 1920 and made a chevalier of the Legion of Honour.

In 1919 Gibbs undertook the first of several lecture tours in the United States: 'the greatest experience of my life, apart from the war.' Many in his audiences were surprised by the powerful resonance of his voice, which contrasted strongly with his modest presence. He became a persuasive advocate of Anglo-American solidarity. Later that year Gibbs, who was himself a Roman Catholic, achieved a notable *coup* when he became the first journalist ever to obtain an interview for publication with a pope.

In 1920, disgusted at editorial support of Lloyd George's policy of reprisals in Ireland, Gibbs resigned his well-paid post on the *Daily Chronicle*. He edited the *Review of Reviews* in 1921-2, but thereafter worked on a freelance basis, depending primarily on fiction writing for his livelihood. In 1921 he visited Russia to study conditions on behalf of the Imperial Famine Relief Fund. He embodied his experiences in a novel called *The Middle of the Road* (1922) which, like most of the fifty others he wrote, owed its characterization and local colour to his newspaper-conditioned response to the passing show. Consequently, although widely read, his fiction rarely warranted critical attention.

His liberal sympathies were naturally attracted to the League of Nations, and his visits to Geneva in the first post-war decade provided the substance of *Since Then* (1930), his study of Europe in the twenties. It was followed by further non-fiction works in which he expressed contemporary uncertainties and fears: *European Journey* (1934), *England Speaks* (1935), *Ordeal in England* (1937), and *Across the Frontiers* (1938).

In 1935-6 Gibbs was a member of the royal commission on the private manufacture of and trading in arms: 'an interesting experience, though very time-wasting.' In 1938 he went again to Germany and returned, as he had twenty-five years earlier, 'unable to believe that war was inevitable'. Again, within a year he was in France as a war correspondent, representing the *Daily Sketch;* but paper shortages involved his recall. He reverted to the novelist's life with an interval in 1941 when he went to the United States as a lecturer for the Ministry of Information; his experiences were summarized in *America Speaks* (1942).

Failing eyesight was a serious handicap in later years although skilled surgery came to his aid when blindness threatened. His first volume of professional reminiscence, *Adventures in Journalism*, had appeared in 1923. He now wrote three more volumes in the same genre: *The Pageant of the Years* (1946), in which is reproduced a drawing of Gibbs by Sir Muirhead Bone; *Crowded Company* (1949); and *Life's Adventure* (1957), which has a drawing by Sava. A portrait by Alfred Priest is in the possession of the family. Gibbs died in Godalming 10 March 1962.

In 1898 he married Agnes Mary (died 1939), daughter of a Somerset rector, the Revd William John Rowland, brother of (Dame) Henrietta Barnett [q.v.]. They had one son, Anthony, who also became a novelist.

[Sir Philip Gibbs's own writings; private information.]   REGINALD POUND

GIBSON, WILFRID WILSON (1878-1962), poet, was born 2 October 1878 at

Hexham, Northumberland, one of the younger children in the large family of John Pattison Gibson, chemist, of Hexham, an amateur archaeologist and photographer of note, and his wife, Elizabeth Judith Frances Walton. He was educated at private schools and by his half-sister, Elizabeth Cheyne Gibson, who wrote poetry and encouraged him in his wish to be a poet. After publishing some highly romantic volumes, he began to find his authentic voice in The Stonefolds (1907), which dealt with the lives of ordinary people. After this, in some thirty books of verse-plays and long and short poems, he wrote of the poor of town and country in a plain idiom that reflected their plain speech; he spoke for, and aroused sympathy for, the northern people among whom he had grown up. He was admired by some of the best poets of his time—(Philip) Edward Thomas [q.v.] and Robert Frost, as well as Rupert Brooke [q.v.].

The crucial event in Gibson's career was his move to London in 1912, where he lived above Harold Monro's [q.v.] Poetry Bookshop. John Middleton Murry and Katherine Mansfield [qq.v.] introduced him to the patron (Sir) Edward Marsh [q.v.], and he became a contributor to Marsh's five volumes of Georgian Poetry (1912-22), adding a strong individual note that was recognized by his contemporary John Freeman [q.v.]: 'He is without imitators and almost without rivals in his poetic mode. He is one of the most prolific of writers and also one of the most realistic. . . . He takes his subjects from common life. . . . His lyrics are all point, acute, clear, often piercing, unsuperfluous in expression.'

Through Marsh he met the young Rupert Brooke, and with him and others brought out the short-lived quarterly, New Numbers, which printed in December 1914 the 'War Sonnets' that were soon to make Brooke's reputation as a war poet. One result of this collaboration was that Brooke bequeathed to Gibson, Lascelles Abercrombie, and Walter de la Mare [qq.v.] a third share each of his property, including the proceeds of his poems—which sold in unprecedented numbers in the decades following Brooke's death on the Greek island of Skyros in April 1915.

In 1915 Gibson married Geraldine Audrey, daughter of Charles Uniacke Townshend, land agent, of Dublin. This was another debt to Monro, as she had been his valued assistant at the Poetry Bookshop; she had also been at Newnham College, Cambridge. Brooke's legacy enabled Gibson to live as a poet, never following another profession, though sometimes in later days his wife had to take in paying guests.

In the first years of the war Gibson made several attempts to enlist, but was turned down for his poor eyesight. In 1917, after returning from a successful lecture tour of the United States, he was accepted by the Army Service Corps, and served until 1919. His writings of this time include the well-known war poem entitled 'Breakfast':

'We ate our breakfast lying on our backs Because the shells were screeching overhead. . .'

In this and 'The Return' he showed his compassion for the ordinary man and woman, and in 'The Lament' wrote movingly of 'the heartbreak at the heart of things'.

The high point in his career was the publication of his Collected Poems by Macmillan in 1926—Macmillans of New York had paid him the same compliment nine years earlier. The London collection, based on twenty earlier books, is impressive for its variety as well as its length—of nearly 800 pages. After it he published some fourteen more books, including four during the war of 1939-45—with titles, like The Alert (1941), which showed his continued preoccupation with war. An often-anthologized short poem, 'The Shepherd', describes lambs being delivered while bombers fly overhead.

After 1926 his literary standing fell—Robert Frost was concerned about it as early as 1928. He had built up his reputation as the spokesman for the inarticulate poor, and lived on into a time when a self-conscious working class preferred to speak for itself. Also he tended to write too much and revise too little. Too many of his longer passages lack the liveliness of 'Hoops' (1914), about circus people, or the sheer compulsion of 'Drove-Road' (1917), justly reprinted in the Oxford Book of Twentieth Century Verse (1973).

As a person Gibson was attractive. The photograph of him in the Collected Poems shows a boyish-looking face, fair hair, pincenez, and a slight figure. He had a genius for making friends; D. H. Lawrence [q.v.] said in 1913 that he was 'one of the clearest and most lovable personalities I know'. The Gibsons' marriage was a happy one—despite the tragic loss of their daughter Audrey in a landslide in Italy in 1939. They lived in Gloucestershire, in Pembrokeshire, and round about London, never in the Northumberland that remained Gibson's inspiration. Geraldine died in 1950, the year of Gibson's last book, Within Four Walls. Gibson himself died at Weybridge in Surrey 26 May 1962. A second daughter, Jocelyn, survived him, and a son, Michael, who published over thirty books, including some on his special subject, the history of roses.

[Records in Hexham Library; private information.]   R. N. Currey

GIFFARD, SIR GEORGE JAMES (1886–1964), general, was born at Englefield Green, Surrey, 27 September 1886, the eldest son of George Campbell Giffard, clerk of the journals, House of Commons, and his wife, Jane Mary Lawrence. Educated at Rugby and the Royal Military College, Sandhurst, he was commissioned into the Queen's Royal Regiment in 1906. Seconded to the King's African Rifles in 1911, he first saw active service in tribal warfare in East Africa during 1913–14; he remained with that regiment throughout the war of 1914–18 and, from 1916 onwards, distinguished himself in the campaign against Colonel von Lettow Vorbeck in German East Africa. As temporary major in command of the 1/2 KAR, he had to operate in very difficult country of bush, desert, and forest, with his men much exposed to malaria. In October 1917, when the German offensive power broke and they set off in retreat, Giffard's battalion pursued them into Portuguese East Africa. Raised to the temporary rank of colonel while still only thirty-one, he was given command of a three-battalion column in February 1918 and again followed von Lettow Vorbeck through the bush, covering 435 miles in a month. With masterly skill the Germans avoided envelopment and maintained their guerrilla operations until the armistice. Giffard, who had been wounded in the campaign, was appointed to the DSO. Besides four mentions in dispatches, he received the French croix de guerre and the Portuguese Order of St. Benedict of Aviz.

He was selected for the first post-war course at the Staff College, Camberley, in 1919. In July 1920 he was appointed as a staff officer to the inspector-general of the Royal West African Frontier Force, only returning to the Queen's Royal Regiment in England in 1925. From 1928 to 1931 he was a GSO 2 at the Staff College, Camberley, and after attending the Imperial Defence College in 1931–2, he took command of the 2nd battalion of his regiment at Aldershot as lieutenant-colonel. On promotion to full colonel in July 1933 he was posted to the 2nd division as GSO 1 and played a prominent role in designing and carrying out the unconventional tactical exercises introduced by its commander, Archibald (later Earl) Wavell [q.v.]. In 1935–6 he was aide-de-camp to the King. In 1936 Giffard, promoted major-general, became inspector-general of African Colonial Forces, which included, with other units, the Royal West African Frontier Force and the King's African Rifles. He was appointed CB in 1938. Mid 1939 saw him in London as military secretary to the secretary of state for war, Leslie (later Lord) Hore-Belisha [q.v.], but after seven months he was posted as GOC under Wavell once more,

in Palestine and Trans-Jordan. In June 1940, after France had collapsed, he was appointed commander-in-chief West Africa, a new command set up because, with the closing of the Mediterranean, the area had become one of great strategic importance: a key staging-post for British convoys round the Cape and a link in the air route to Egypt, as well as a valuable source of raw materials.

In this post Giffard, who was promoted general and appointed KCB in 1941, successfully tackled a host of complex political and military problems with skill and zeal, carrying through a rapid expansion—indeed, transformation—of the army and organizing the training of some 200,000 Africans, many of them for service in fighting formations: two West African divisions and one from East Africa were later to serve under his command in Burma. When, in June 1942, Lord Swinton arrived as resident Cabinet minister, he and Giffard worked in concord and mutual respect. 'No one but he could have accomplished what was done,' Swinton wrote afterwards. 'With tireless energy and infinite patience he inspired his new officers with something of his own knowledge and genius for handling Africans.'

In the spring of 1943 the Mediterranean was reopened, West Africa's strategic importance declined, and it was possible to release Giffard to command Eastern Army, India, when Wavell asked for him in the post. Morale there was low, training inadequate, malaria rife. Setbacks since the loss of Burma had proved that British and Indian troops needed more self-confidence and new fighting methods before they could deal effectively with the triumphant Japanese. Throughout that summer Giffard supervised intensive training in jungle warfare and instituted strict anti-malaria precautions and other measures against tropical diseases.

When South East Asia Command was set up under Lord Louis (later Earl) Mountbatten, Giffard became commander-in-chief of 11th Army Group, responsible to the supreme commander for all troops in Ceylon and the Indian Ocean bases and for the operations of the 14th Army, which was formed in October 1943 under William (later Viscount) Slim [q.v.]. 11th Army Group should have included the Chinese-American forces in northern Burma, but for largely personal reasons the American General Stilwell ('Vinegar Joe', as he was known) refused to place them under Giffard's command; however, he did consent to serve under Slim's individual control.

Since Giffard's prime task thus became to support 14th Army on the Arakan and central Burma fronts, it was fortunate that he and Slim worked so perfectly together. He reorganized the rear areas of an exceptionally wide and difficult front which was served by most inadequate roads and railways. With calm understanding and rock-like loyalty he backed Slim without interfering and shielded him at times of crisis. Slim paid many tributes to Giffard in *Defeat into Victory* (1956): 'he understood the fundamentals of war—that soldiers must be trained before they can fight, fed before they can march, and relieved before they are worn out. He understood that front-line commanders should be spared responsibilities in the rear, and that soundness of organization and administration is worth more than specious short-cuts to victory.'

Unfortunately Giffard's relationship with Mountbatten was less satisfactory. Although the supreme commander liked him personally, and admired his professional ability and above all his integrity, and although he resisted strong American pressure to have Giffard removed, he came to criticize the general's caution, his slowness of reaction at certain crucial moments, and his failure to inform him in time of military developments and their implications. While the outcome of the desperate fighting at Imphal and Kohima was still uncertain, matters came to a head in May 1944 when Giffard told Mountbatten that he could not provide enough divisions for both monsoon and post-monsoon operations. Nor could he agree to Mount-batten's checking his programme to see if more troops could be extracted. Mountbatten there-upon told Giffard that he had lost confidence in him and must have a younger, more aggressive commander. In any case, he proposed to replace 11th Army Group with a new command to be called Allied Land Forces South East Asia, for which Giffard would be acceptable neither to the Americans nor to Chiang Kai-shek.

Giffard took his dismissal without bitterness and with a clear conscience. Although in the difficult position of being 'under notice' for six months while negotiations for a successor dragged on, he behaved with exemplary courtesy, unselfishness, and loyalty. Once the Japanese invasion forces had been crushingly defeated at Kohima and Imphal, as Giffard had correctly forecast, it was possible, after June, to take greater risks in order to exploit success and, by fighting through the monsoon, to maintain unrelenting pressure on the Japanese retreating in disorder to the Chindwin river and beyond. Giffard, who was appointed GCB that year, eventually left for England in November 1944. Slim wrote: 'we saw him go with grief. I and others built on the foundations he laid.'

Despite his great contribution to victory, Giffard remains probably the least known of all British generals who held high command in the war of 1939–45. Genuinely disliking pub-licity, he was unspectacular in style, not at his best when making speeches or arguing a case at top-level Allied conferences, but good at talking to individuals and small groups. He was a tall, erect, good-looking man with a firm but friendly look and a dignified presence.

He became aide-de-camp general to the King in 1945–6, and on his retirement in August 1946 he settled in Winchester. He served as president of the Army Benevolent Fund and, in 1945–54, as colonel of the Queen's Royal Regiment, colonel commandant of the Royal West African Frontier Force, the King's African Rifles, and the Northern Rhodesia Regiment. With his usual enthusiasm and thoroughness he took up apple-growing and turned a derelict orchard into a thriving, prize-winning concern. He also kept bees, watched birds, and fished on the Hampshire Avon. A man of high principles and deep religious faith, he spent his life trying to conform to what he saw as God's will; the letters he wrote to his wife, whose poor health prevented her from accompanying him on his many postings overseas, contain frequent heart-searchings over actions and decisions. In 1959 a coronary thrombosis obliged Giffard to curtail severely his physical activities, but with characteristic energy he took up tapestry and rug-making. That someone with such large hands could produce such fine work was surprising. Giffard died at Winchester 17 November 1964.

In 1915 he had married Evelyn Norah, second daughter of Richard Margerison, FRCS, of Winchester, who survived him by less than a fortnight; they had one daughter. A pencil portrait was drawn specially for the *Sunday Times* (18 August 1946) by Robin Guthrie.

[*The Times*, 19 November 1964; Sir George Giffard, Dispatches covering operations in Burma and north-east India and in Assam and Burma (Supplements to the *London Gazette*, 13 and 30 March 1951); Earl Mountbatten, *Report to the Combined Chiefs of Staff by the Supreme Allied Commander South-East Asia 1943–1945*, 1951; S. W. Kirby and others (Official History), *The War against Japan*, vols. iii–iv, 1961–5; Lord Slim, op. cit.; Lord Swinton, *I Remember*, 1949; *Chief of Staff: The Diaries of Lt.-Gen. Sir Henry Pownall*, vol. ii, 1940–4, ed. Brian Bond, 1974; P. J. Grigg, *Prejudice and Judgment*, 1948; H. Moyse-Bartlett, *The King's African Rifles*, 1956; private information; personal knowledge.]

ANTONY BRETT-JAMES

GINSBERG, MORRIS (1889–1970), socio-logist and moral philosopher, was born in

Lithuania 14 May 1889, the son of Meyer Ginsberg, tobacco manufacturer. Morris Ginsberg migrated to England where he attracted attention as a talented undergraduate reading philosophy at University College, London, which he entered in 1910. Such a migration was common enough at that time but, as Maurice Freedman (his junior colleague, friend, and admirer as joint editor of the *Jewish Journal of Sociology*) remarked, 'there can have been few Talmudic scholars, entirely Yiddish-speaking until their adolescence, who transformed themselves into members of the austere English middle class'. Part of the interest of Ginsberg's life and an essential key to his character lies in the long bridge he successfully crossed from an obscure Lithuanian Jewish community and a childhood education in classical Hebrew to a prominent position in English social studies at the London School of Economics. Much of his early life will probably remain obscure: for he was determinedly reticent about his youth, refused to record his personal memories, and clearly wished to be remembered mainly, even exclusively, through his writing and teaching.

His unusual quickness of mind and lucidity of expression earned him recognition at UCL before World War I when he was a Martin White and John Stuart Mill scholar. He obtained his BA in philosophy with first class honours in 1913, and his MA in 1915. His philosophical career began there as assistant to Professor G. Dawes Hicks [q.v.] who maintained a position as a realist philosopher at a time when idealism was dominant in other British universities. While the connection with UCL and the grounding of his life's work in philosophy was maintained, it is with sociology and the LSE that Ginsberg is mainly associated from 1914 when he was first invited to be a part-time assistant to L. T. Hobhouse [q.v.]. Permanent tenure did not come to him until 1922, but his service to the School continued thereafter for more than forty further years as reader (1924), successor to Hobhouse in the Martin White chair of sociology (1929), and as an emeritus professor (1954) who undertook part-time teaching well into the 1960s. Prevented from active service by poor eyesight in World War I the legend and indeed truth is that he stood in for four of the regular teaching staff including Major Clement R. Attlee and Sergeant R. H. Tawney [qq.v.].

His association with and devotion to Hobhouse began while he was at UCL where he collaborated in a comparative anthropological study which became a classic—L. T. Hobhouse, G. C. Wheeler, and M. Ginsberg, *The Material Culture and Social Institutions of the Simpler Peoples* (1915). Subsequently and throughout his working life Hobhouse was the dominant influence and he devoted himself to the same essential problems of the liberal tradition, the understanding of the evolution of mankind, materially, socially, culturally, and morally. At the centre of this tradition was a preoccupation with the idea of moral progress and its economic and social correlates: and around that central problem he undertook wide exploration of how variations in social structure were related to moral belief and behaviour, steadily searching on the one hand for the basis of a rational ethic and, on the other, for a definition of the prospects for social institutions expressing reason and justice.

The pursuit of these intellectual concerns required both philosophical sophistication and an immense knowledge of social history. Ginsberg acquired both to a degree surpassing that of any of his contemporaries and demonstrated them in a long series of books, essays, and lectures. His prose style was economical and unpretentious, carrying lightly a vast erudition. The titles convey the theme of these sustained interests—*Moral Progress* (1944), *The Idea of Progress: A Revaluation* (1953), *On the Diversity of Morals* (1953), and *Reason and Unreason in Society* (1947). His last published work, *On Justice in Society*, which appeared in 1965, is a characteristic essay in analysis of the concepts of justice, equality, rights, and duties and their application in criminal law, contract, and international relations.

His contribution to these difficult and enduring problems of ethics in society gives him a permanent place in twentieth-century scholarship. His reputation as a sociologist is, however, less secure. After Hobhouse he was the major British sociologist between the wars. But the rapid development of the subject after World War II passed him by. Attention shifted mainly to American work towards which he was gently but firmly dismissive, regarding most of its leading exponents as verbose and pretentious. It was not that his own erudition was in any way limited. On the contrary, he was familiar with the major and minor European authors, appreciated the importance of Max Weber in Germany and Emile Durkheim in France, and quick to provide a critical introduction of Vilfredo Pareto to the English-speaking world. He was aware of and lectured on German phenomenology a generation before it became fashionable in America and Britain.

Yet the weight of his teaching continued to rest on the interests he inherited from Hobhouse and conceded little or nothing to the eagerness of his post-war students to come to grips with the growing volume of American empirical sociology, the development of quantitative methods, and, later, of Marxist and phenomenological approaches to sociological theory. A rapidly expanding profession of sociology with diverse methods and theories replaced the coherent blend of moral philosophy and social inquiry of which Ginsberg had succeeded Hobhouse as the leading scholar. The question of the relation between moral and social evolution, which they both addressed with painstaking scholarship, remained important but no longer occupied the centre of the subject.

As an academic notable Ginsberg was widely recognized and admitted to fellowship of the British Academy in 1953. He also held honorary degrees from London, Glasgow, and Nottingham, and was an honorary fellow of LSE. He was Frazer lecturer in 1944, Conway memorial lecturer in 1952, and Clarke Hall lecturer in 1953, the year in which he received the Huxley medal and gave the Huxley lecture. In 1958 he gave the Herbert Spencer lecture. In 1942-3 he was president of the Aristotelian Society.

As a man he won and kept strong affection from colleagues and students. He was respected for his integrity, loved for his gentleness, and admired for his informed intellectual power. His two outstanding qualities of humility and academic assurance were often remarked. Both were real in him and appeared to others as an attractively paradoxical character—a kind of self-effacing arrogance. Holding a chair in a subject held suspect by many scholars, his own standards were of the highest demanded by academic tradition. He will be remembered professionally through his writing, personally as 'a small, quiet, serious yet friendly man, curled up in an old armchair, surrounded by walls of books, looking as if he had grown out of them'.

A private and rather lonely man, he was seldom exuberant, often sad, and sometimes despairing. He remained something of an outsider, having travelled far from his East European origins without alienating himself from the religion of his forebears. In 1931 he married Ethel, daughter of Arthur William Street, fellmonger. They had no children. They lived in Highgate where she died in 1962 and he 31 August 1970 at the age of eighty-one.

There is a portrait by Claude Rogers (1960), at the LSE.

[R. Fletcher (ed.), *The Science of Society and the Unity of Mankind: A Memorial Volume for Morris Ginsberg*, 1974; *The Times*, 1 and 14 September 1970; personal knowledge.]

A. H. HALSEY

GLENNY, ALEXANDER THOMAS (1882-1965), immunologist, was born in Camberwell 18 September 1882, the third son among the five children of Thomas Armstrong Glenny, a stockbroker's clerk and Plymouth Brethren minister, and his wife, Elizabeth Foreman. He was educated at Alleyn's School and at Chelsea Polytechnic where he attended evening classes and from where he obtained his London B.Sc. On leaving Alleyn's School in 1899, he joined the Wellcome Physiological Research Laboratories, then at Herne Hill, to work as a technician on the understanding of his headmaster that he would have the opportunity to study for a science degree.

At the Wellcome Laboratories he became closely involved in work associated with the immunization of horses for the production of antitoxins and his meticulous care, orderly approach, and general efficiency in this work led to his appointment in 1906 as head of the Immunology Department. In this capacity he was responsible for the production, control testing, and potency assays of all the antitoxins produced by the Wellcome Laboratories, a heavy responsibility particularly during the 1914-18 war when the demand for antitoxins became immense. Again in 1939 when war broke out Glenny was responsible for meeting even greater demands, particularly for tetanus and gas-gangrene antitoxins. To these were added vast requirements for diphtheria toxoid, because of the diphtheria immunization campaign which was launched on an extensive scale throughout Britain in 1941, as well as for tetanus toxoid required for the active immunization of all members of the British armed forces.

In addition to his routine commercial work in supplying therapeutic and prophylactic immunological products, Glenny was actively engaged in fundamental research particularly in relation to the mechanisms of antibody production. His work on the primary and secondary responses in immunized animals was one of his most outstanding contributions. He and his colleague H. J. Südmersen worked out experimentally in guinea-pigs, rabbits, goats, sheep, horses, and man, using diphtheria toxin/antitoxin mixture as antigen, the pattern of the primary and secondary antibody responses, which were shown to be slow and small for the primary while rapid and large for the secondary, and demonstrated how, by altering the time interval between the primary and secondary antigenic stimuli, the secondary response could be considerably modified. These findings form the basis of modern schedules of immunization of man and animals and apply to virtually all responses to antigenic stimuli. Another outstanding contribution was the discovery that diphtheria toxin which had lost its toxicity by formalin treatment, and was referred to as toxoid, still retained its ability to induce the formation of antitoxin when injected into animals. There was some controversy at the time as to whether Glenny or Gaston Ramon, working in France, could claim priority for this discovery; nevertheless Glenny was the first to demonstrate the efficacy of toxoid in man, a finding which formed the basis for the present-day highly effective products used in the active immunization of man against both diphtheria and tetanus. A third equally outstanding contribution was his discovery that alum-precipitated toxoids were considerably more powerful as regards their antigenic activity than toxoids alone. As a result, aluminium salts are now widely employed as adjuvants in many of the prophylactic antigens used for the protection of man and animals against infectious diseases. All three of these discoveries laid the foundations for the modern immunization procedures, particularly for those in which toxoids are used.

Other researches undertaken by Glenny, although probably of less practical importance but nevertheless fundamental, included the development of the concept of avidity by demonstrating that the firmness of binding of antitoxin to toxin depended on the particular antitoxin used and the discrimination of toxins produced by bacteria, particularly the gas-gangrene organisms, on the basis of the different antibodies they induced in animals.

Glenny had an exceptional intellect, he was full of new ideas, and had an original approach to experimentation. He had a passion for organization in which he was highly competent, an attribute which enabled him to carry out fundamental research in addition to the routine duties demanded of him by the commercial organization in which he worked. He was a great stimulus to the young people who worked under him and who highly respected him, although he was by no means easy to get on with. He was not a very happy man and somewhat disappointed that his work was not receiving the attention he felt it deserved. But this was probably due to his lack of interest in publishing his results and when he did his papers were somewhat complicated and difficult to follow; much of his work remains unpublished. Nevertheless, recognition eventually came, although rather late in life, when he was elected to the Royal Society in 1944 at the age of sixty-two and was awarded the Addingham gold medal and the Jenner medal, both in 1953.

He retired from the Wellcome Laboratories in 1947 after forty-eight years' service during which he had established the Laboratory as one of the leading immunological centres in the country. After his retirement he spent much of his time writing up his unpublished work but in 1960 his memory began to fail and five years later, 5 October 1965, he died in Croydon. He married in 1910 Emma Blanche Lilian Gibbs

and had two sons, one of whom died in a road accident in 1940, and one daughter.

[C. L. Oakley in *Biographical Memoirs of Fellows of the Royal Society*, vol. xii, 1969; personal knowledge.]   DAVID EVANS

GLENVIL HALL, WILLIAM GEORGE (1887-1962), politician. [See HALL.]

GODFREY, WALTER HINDES (1881-1961), architect and antiquary, was born in London 2 August 1881, the eldest son of Walter Scott Godfrey, who at that time was conducting a small wine business, and his wife, Gertrude Annie Rendall, of Bristol. The elder Godfrey later became, under the influence of C. H. Spurgeon [q.v.], a minister of religion. Meeting with ill success in his pastorate, he turned to socialist agnosticism without, however, relaxing a puritanical sense of mission which bore hard on his family. In 1891 W. H. Godfrey was sent to Whitgift Middle School, Croydon, and, four years later, gained a scholarship to the Upper or Grammar School, where he remained until 1898. He also studied at the Central School of Arts and Crafts. He was subsequently articled to James Williams who had succeeded to the practice of the distinguished Victorian country-house architect, George Devey. In 1900 he joined the architectural section of the London County Council. Already keenly interested in the antiquities of London he was elected in 1901 a member of the Committee for the Survey of London which C. R. Ashbee [q.v.] had founded in 1894 with the object of publishing monographs and parish surveys recording ancient buildings in the metropolitan area. Godfrey was at once involved in preparations for the first of the Chelsea volumes and this led to his authorship of all the four volumes which appeared between 1909 and 1927. The Survey was always one of his main interests. He edited several further monographs and parish volumes and was engaged on the monograph on the College of Arms at the time of his death.

In 1903 Godfrey left the LCC and returned to the office where he had served his articles. Williams having retired, the practice was conducted by his partner, Edmund Livingstone Wratten, who took Godfrey as an assistant on a two-year agreement. Before the term was out Wratten had married Godfrey's sister, Gertrude. Wratten and Godfrey then formed a partnership as successors to James Williams, commencing practice in 1905. Commissions were few at first and Godfrey had time to write a study of George Devey, his firm's original founder, which was awarded the RIBA essay silver medal in 1906. He also prepared illustrations for Garner and Stratton's *Domestic Architecture in England during the Tudor Period* (1908), including elevations and a perspective of the oriel window of Crosby Hall, Bishopsgate, then threatened with demolition. Simultaneously he contributed an architectural study of the hall to Philip Norman's monograph in the Survey of London series. This excited the interest of (Sir) Patrick Geddes [q.v.] who was connected with the Town and Gown Association which was building, on a site in Chelsea, a headquarters for the British Federation of University Women. Geddes instigated the removal of the hall to the Chelsea site, Godfrey acting as architect. The hall was successfully transferred in 1909–10.

From 1915 to 1919 Godfrey was employed in the Accounts Division of the Ministry of Munitions. Thereafter, he resumed practice with Wratten and, after the latter's death in 1925, continued on his own. In 1926 he became a FRIBA. The recession of the early thirties induced him to give up his London office and in 1932 he retired to Lewes where, by extraordinary good luck, he was offered the most inspiring and lucrative task of his career—the restoration of Herstmonceaux Castle for Sir (Herbert) Paul Latham. Other restorations and a few houses followed and up to 1939 Godfrey combined the running of a modest domestic practice with the writing of papers, mostly on Sussex antiquities.

In 1940, when London became subject to air attack, a conference was held at the RIBA to consider the need for a central body charged with the recording of historic buildings which might be damaged or destroyed. The outcome of this was the formation of the National Buildings Record, with Lord Greene [q.v.], master of the Rolls, as its chairman and Godfrey as its salaried director. From 1941 until his retirement in 1960 the conduct and development of the Record (now the National Monuments Record) were the main concern of his life. In addition, however, he conducted, with the assistance of his son, Emil, two notable restorations of war-damaged buildings: the Temple Church and the old parish church of Chelsea. The latter had been almost completely demolished by a bomb in 1941 but the records which Godfrey had made as a young man enabled him to achieve a highly satisfactory reconstruction.

Godfrey was the author of many books, including, besides the volumes on Chelsea in the Survey of London, *A History of Architecture in London* (1911, enlarged edition 1962), *The Story of Architecture in England* (2 vols., 1928 and 1931), and *The English Almshouse* (1955). To this Dictionary he contributed the

notices of Sir John James Burnet and Sir Charles Archibald Nicholson. He was a member of the royal commission on historical monuments from 1944 and of the advisory committee on buildings of special architectural or historic interest at the Ministry of Housing and Local Government from 1945. In 1950 he was appointed CBE.

He married in 1907 Gertrude Mary (died 1955), daughter of Alexander Grayston Warren. They had one son and three daughters. Godfrey was a man of slight build, pleasant appearance, and agreeable disposition, though with a somewhat egocentric streak inherited from his father. An excellent profile photograph, by his friend Mary Gillick, accompanies his history of the London Survey Committee in the *London Topographical Record*, vol. xxi (1958), fig. 4.

[Obituary notice by J. Summerson in *London Topographical Record*, vol. xxii, 1965, pp. 127–135.]   JOHN SUMMERSON

GODFREY, WILLIAM (1889–1963), cardinal, seventh archbishop of Westminster, the younger son of George Godfrey, and his wife, Maria Garvey, was born in Liverpool 25 September 1889, his widowed mother's twenty-first birthday. He went to school at St. John's, Kirkdale. His début serving at the altar is remembered for the words: 'I'll never leave it.' In 1903 he entered Ushaw College, Durham, and from then onwards his studies took place within ecclesiastical establishments. From Ushaw he went to the Venerable English College, Rome, gaining with evident credit the customary doctorates in philosophy and theology at the Gregorian University, in 1913 and 1917 respectively. He was ordained priest in 1916.

His only parish appointment was as curate at St. Michael's, Liverpool, in 1917. In January 1919 he returned to Ushaw as classics master, becoming later professor of philosophy and, in 1928, of dogmatic theology. Students felt the weight of his dictated notes but asked for his spiritual conferences in their own time. He published *The Young Apostle* (1924) and *God and Ourselves* (1927). Godfrey's regularity and personal piety were bywords. His afternoon walk was followed by lengthy prayer before the Blessed Sacrament—a lifelong pattern. Between 1921 and 1930 he contributed to the *Ushaw Magazine* mainly on spiritual theology and the history of Douai College. Although his lighter side was not for students, he delighted his colleagues with mimicry on the French horn. As a student himself he had been an impersonator of no mean ability at the English College. Perhaps it was memory of these days which inclined him in his last years to treat sometimes acid and pointed imitations of himself as a permissible form of criticism and to allow students the occasional privileges of 'court jester'.

In 1930 the Holy See appointed him to succeed Archbishop Hinsley [q.v.] as rector of the English College, Rome. Here he entered fully into college life, sang in common-room concerts, and shared students' tours during *villeggiatura*. It was said that his favourite expression, both as rector of a seminary, and later as archbishop, was 'I've got my eye on you', and the accompanying twinkle in his eye did not disguise his determination to maintain strict control over all aspects of pastoral work and initiative. His example was, like his Italian, flawless.

In 1930 he became domestic prelate to Pope Pius XI and a member of the Supreme Council for the Propagation of the Faith, in 1935 a member of the papal mission to Malta and honorary canon of Vittoriosa, in 1937 counsellor in the papal mission for George VI's coronation, and in 1938 apostolic visitor of all seminaries in Great Britain.

A British mission to the Holy See had existed since 1916. The coronation visit gave the Holy See a chance to discuss with Government an apostolic delegation in London, if diplomatic reciprocity were not feasible. The announcement in November 1938 of Monsignor William Godfrey as first apostolic delegate to Great Britain raised few bogies. He was consecrated archbishop of Cius in December. His instructions were *mettere le radici* (put down roots). Typically, he settled on a suburban house, avoiding any semblance of diplomatic status.

He played a part in Pope Pius XII's efforts for peace but protocol hindered his war relief work until the Holy See's unique position for helping prisoners and internees in the Far East was appreciated. He was then heavily committed, and peace only intensified the work of tracing and resettling war victims. More direct diplomatic involvement came through the request of the Polish Government in exile in London for normal diplomatic links with the Holy See. The delegate was appointed chargé d'affaires. He cherished his order of Polonia Restituta, and felt to the end the grief of Poland's betrayal.

In 1953 the delegate was appointed archbishop of Liverpool. He was distressed at no longer being the personal representative of the Pope in Britain but he settled down to pastoral work easily enough. He made no great changes (except in Sir Edwin Lutyens's [q.v.] design for the new cathedral), and edified priests and people by his prudent zeal. The weather-eye was well open but he could relax happily with his priests.

In December 1956 Pius XII appointed him, in succession to Cardinal Griffin [q.v.], seventh archbishop of Westminster and additionally in 1957 apostolic exarch to the Ukrainians of the Byzantine rite in England and Wales. As always his first care was the spiritual life of his priests. He provided systematic instruction for the people with a four-year syllabus of catechesis.

Godfrey's years at Westminster saw diocesan increases of 50,000 in population, 5,000 in the annual baptismal rate, 37 new churches, and 11,000 new school places. These figures of quiet but steady increase best reflect Godfrey's achievements. In a position which inevitably made him a spokesman for the Roman Catholic body in England and Wales, he seemed unable, and perhaps unwilling, to capture national attention as had been done during the war by Cardinal Hinsley, and later by Godfrey's successor, Cardinal Heenan. His pastoral letters neither sought nor obtained headlines, with one deliberate exception: the 'poodle' pastoral which suggested that pets as well as their owners should join in a family fast day! As a public speaker he was not captivating though his unassuming sincerity was patent.

Pope John XXIII created Godfrey cardinal priest of the title of SS. Nereus and Achilles in his first consistory in 1958 and in 1961 appointed him a member of the Central Preparatory Commission, whose task was to examine and recast the *schemata* for discussion in the second Vatican Council.

This proved the climax of Godfrey's service to the Church. His day altered. He began with official papers at 5.15 a.m. and returned to them for a couple of hours later in the day. The Commission met eight times in 1961–2, always for ten days. The cardinal's frequent interventions found favour with many of the Commission members; his theological and ecclesiastical stance can be gauged from a comment of a highly conservative curial official characterizing Godfrey as '*un po' classico*'.

The first session of the Council (October–December 1962) made heavy demands on his failing energies. That a fatal illness had already struck him in the late summer of 1961 remained a closely guarded secret throughout the session from which in fact he returned home to die. His interventions in the debates gave no hint of his physical condition and even when the Council Fathers laid violent hands on the work of the preparatory commissions, whatever he felt inwardly was not passed on.

He died 22 January 1963 at Westminster Hospital in London, and among his last words were: 'The Church gave me everything'—promptly answered by: 'You gave everything to the Church.' That was true but the period for his particular contribution was clearly passing.

Pope John, the beginner of the *aggiornamento*, telegraphed: 'We placed all our trust in him.'

There is a portrait by A. R. Thomson (1960), and a bust by Arthur J. Fleischmann (1959), at Archbishop's House, Westminster. There is also a portrait at Upholland College by Hilda Swift.

[*The Red Hat*, Westminster, 1959; *The Times*, 23 January 1963; *Westminster Cathedral Chronicle*, March 1963; *Wiseman Review*, spring 1963; *The Venerabile*, summer 1963; personal knowledge.]

THOMAS HOLLAND

GOLLANCZ, SIR VICTOR (1893-1967), publisher, was born in London 9 April 1893, the son of orthodox Jews, Alexander Gollancz, a jeweller of Polish descent and brother of Sir Hermann and Sir Israel Gollancz [qq.v.], and his wife, Nellie Michaelson. Gollancz was educated at St. Paul's School and as a scholar of New College, Oxford, where he won the Chancellor's Latin essay prize (1913) and obtained a first in honour moderations (1914). He did not take a degree but joined the university OTC at the outbreak of war and was commissioned in the Northumberland Fusiliers. In 1916-18 he was seconded to Repton School where he found satisfaction and excitement in teaching; he always looked back on that period as one of the happiest in his life. Characteristically it was brought to an end because his civics class was thought to promote anti-war fervour. He was posted to Singapore but was back in England early in 1919.

Gollancz began publishing in 1920 with Benn Brothers where in 1923 he was joined by his friend Douglas Jerrold [q.v.]. When the book department became a separate company Gollancz, as its managing director, launched out on sumptious productions such as the Players' Shakespeare and *The Sleeping Princess* with designs by Bakst, and, at the other end of the scale, Benn's Sixpenny Library. In 1928 he founded his own firm, by no means holding the equity but with articles of association which gave him complete power as governing director. He had Stanley Morison [q.v.], the typographer, create a house style for all his publications and advertising, and the appearance of his first books with typographical jackets, printed in black and magenta on yellow paper, became famous. They showed that an innovator was at work whose new approach to economical, standardized production and lavish, forceful advertisements certainly revolutionized publishing methods.

Almost instant success came with R. C. Sherriff's successful play, *Journey's End*, which had prodigious sales. A fast-growing and distinguished list included the novelists Daphne du Maurier, Elizabeth Bowen, and Dorothy Sayers [q.v.]. The crime novels which he published were among the most respected in the country. He was a knowledgeable amateur of music which he strongly represented. He was quick to see the attractions of a 'bargain' and his books of some thousand pages on music, popular philosophy, politics, and omnibus collections of fiction writers, all selling at low prices, broke new ground.

A new and significant venture, the foundation of the Left Book Club in 1936, in resistance to the rise of Fascism and Nazism, proved to be a rallying point for the Left and the Popular Front and ultimately doubtless a factor in the Labour Party's landslide victory in 1945.

'V. G.', as he was generally known in publishing circles, had, he wrote, a *mana*—a power to influence people—and this, coupled with his driving personality, enabled him to sell his books with *brio* and endow his firm with a more individual character than had yet been seen. That same spirit enabled him at a public meeting to raise a collection 'five times as much, despite obvious handicaps, as the most beautiful woman in the world'.

As a public speaker Gollancz could be spellbinding, and his appearances at public meetings became more and more frequent as his concern for what he felt to be the great evils of the time increased, culminating in the fifties and sixties in his support for nuclear disarmament and the campaign for the abolition of capital punishment. His conception of the Left Book Club provides one of the keys to his complex personality, exemplifying qualities rare in a commercial publisher: scholarship and flair combined with political and social conscience and an always shrewd business sense. His firm always prospered, for he never allowed his highly developed human and political emotions to spoil his profits. But he would never bring out a book which militated against his convictions: he refused, for instance, to publish highly profitable memoirs by Nazi generals, and years after the ending of hostilities would not take part in the Frankfurt International Book Fair. But it was he who started the Save Europe Now movement in 1945 to relieve starving Germany. He could all too closely identify both with sufferers and with their persecutors. His unsparing work on behalf of the Jews in Germany was the main cause of a nervous breakdown during the war; yet in 1961 he published a pamphlet setting out the reasons why Eichmann should not be condemned to death for genocide at his trial in Israel. The mystical or religious side of his character is reflected in his books, *A Year of Grace* (1950) and *From Darkness to Light*

(1959) and his membership of the London Society for the Study of Religion. It may well be that he entered publishing primarily with the object of educating people and this is borne out by a remark he made after the war of 1914-18 to his brother-in-law expressing indecision whether to become headmaster of Winchester or prime minister.

Gollancz was a man of extreme contrasts, polarities of feeling manifest in his behaviour which, in moments of insight, he found irreconcilable to the point of illness. He revelled in self-indulgence and once confessed in a television interview that he had too often compromised with Mammon. He could be from day to day both parsimonious and magnificently generous, kind and hostile, fearless and frightened. He was a Jew who believed in Christian ethics but could not accept the religion as a whole. A friend once said to him that when his joy in living overflowed to embrace his friends, he was a Jew; only when frightened and depressed did he turn to Christianity; he did not deny this.

Gollancz's indelible mark on British publishing made a correspondingly deep impression on American publishers whom he visited annually—always accompanied by his wife, his inseparable companion. Like many men who have led a full life, he knew and fascinated many people, but, as becomes clear in his posthumously published *Reminiscences of Affection* (1968), he had few intimate friends. His only recreations were music and bridge, and with his wife he built up a unique private collection of English pottery.

In 1953, on his sixtieth birthday, he was presented with the grand cross of the German Order of Merit in recognition of his help to the German people after the war; and in 1960 he was awarded the Peace prize of the German Book Trade. In 1965 he was knighted.

In 1919 Gollancz married Ruth (died 1973), an artist daughter of Ernest D. Lowy; her family had been active in the suffragette movement; her sister married R. N. Salaman [q.v.]. They had five daughters, the eldest of whom, Livia, became governing director of the firm and continued to run it in her father's tradition after his death in London 8 February 1967. Four portraits by his wife remained in the possession of the family.

[Victor Gollancz, *My Dear Timothy*, 1952, and *More for Timothy*, 1953; *Bookseller*, 11 February 1967; *The Times*, 9 February, 1967; private information; personal knowledge.]

JAMES MACGIBBON

GOOCH, GEORGE PEABODY (1873-1968), historian, born at Porchester Gate,

London, 21 October 1873, was the third son and youngest child of Charles Cubitt Gooch, merchant, who had been first a clerk and then a partner in the firm of George Peabody [q.v.] which had become J. S. Morgan & Co. The father had married Mary Jane, daughter of the Revd Edmund Blake, rector of Bramerton in Norfolk, and was over sixty when his youngest son was born. His second son, (Sir) Henry Cubitt Gooch (1871-1959), was Conservative MP for Peckham (1908-10) and chairman of the LCC (1923-4).

Gooch quickly became an omnivorous reader in his father's library, but when he went to Eton in 1886 he disliked the life of the place and disapproved of the curriculum. He moved to King's College, London, when he was only fifteen and found there a considerable stimulus, in spite of a certain emphasis which was given to theology. He went on to Trinity College, Cambridge, where his four happy years awakened his interest in social work and his fervour for Liberalism, as well as fortifying his ambition to enter Parliament. He obtained a first class in the historical tripos (1894) and in 1895 the Members' English essay prize and the Lightfoot scholarship. In the autumn of 1895 he studied for three years in Berlin and, similarly, in the following year he went to hear the lectures of famous historians in Paris.

He failed to gain a fellowship at Trinity in 1897, but, being a man of independent means, and not very anxious to become engrossed in a purely academic career, he rejected advice to consider similar posts elsewhere. He taught a little at Mansfield House, at the Working Men's College, and at Toynbee Hall; and he undertook social work at Camberwell as well as with the Church Army, regarding this, in part at least, as a training for public life.

Perhaps the factor which really decided his course of development was the South African war, and he put it on record that the summer of 1899 was 'one of the most harrowing memories of my life'. Henceforward, it was not so much the social question but rather the problems of empire, diplomacy, and war which stood in the forefront of his mind; and, apart from the tragedy of the conflict itself, he was troubled by the bitterness of the resulting controversy and the split in the ranks of the Liberals—a split which affected the discussion of foreign policy down to 1914.

At the time of the great victory for the Liberals in the general election of 1906 Gooch became one of the members of Parliament for Bath, although he twice failed to secure re-election in 1910 and was equally unsuccessful at Reading in 1913. He tried to stand 'midway between socialism and individualism', favoured old-age pensions and the licensing Bill of 1908, and attacked the Liberal imperialism of the foreign secretary, Sir Edward Grey (later Viscount Grey of Fallodon, q.v.), criticizing in particular the connection with Russia and her conduct in Persia. In 1911 he became joint-editor with J. Scott Lidgett [q.v.] of the *Contemporary Review*, of which he had been a director since 1907; it was not until 1960 that he gave up the editorship and not until the year of his death that his last little contribution to the journal appeared. He had set out to make the *Contemporary* 'the leading monthly in the field of foreign affairs'.

All the while he had been developing as a historian, however, and, although not technically a pupil of Lord Acton [q.v.], he was assisted by him in the preparation of his first dissertation on *English Democratic Ideas in the Seventeenth Century* (1898). It won him the Thirlwall prize but not his Trinity fellowship. It was Acton who suggested that he should produce the *Annals of Politics and Culture* (1910), a book which itemized political events on the left-hand pages, and the contemporaneous cultural events on the right. Two important works which came a little later—*History and Historians in the Nineteenth Century* (1913) and *Germany and the French Revolution* (1920)—offered subjects well within the range of Acton's interest, and in fact were imposing extensions of two chapters which Gooch had produced for the *Cambridge Modern History*. Gooch rightly regarded his historiographical volume as his finest production, although this branch of scholarship still remained neglected in England, and it was the revised edition of the book in 1952 which had the bigger sales, the wider effect.

Late in life, Gooch claimed that he had arrived independently at the view of ideas as 'not the effect but the cause of public events'; but he followed that formula more literalistically than Acton—missing therefore some of the paradoxes which the latter loved to discover in the historical process.

The outbreak of war in 1914 was more painful to Gooch than to most people, for he was attached to German historians and German scholarship, and in 1903 he had married Sophie Else Schön, an art student from Zittau, Saxony; they had two sons. To the end of his life he believed that Grey before 1914 had been too much of a *Realpolitiker*, and not only in 1917 but also fifty years later he felt that Grey's pre-war policy was one which tended to make war more probable though it ensured that Britain should not be isolated if a conflict actually took place.

Even in his historical writing he had lately become more profoundly engaged in diplomatic subjects and contemporary affairs. In 1919 he joined Sir Adolphus Ward (whose notice he contributed to the Dictionary) in the editing of the three-volume *Cambridge History of British Foreign Policy* (1922-3). In 1924 Ramsay MacDonald, who was both prime minister and foreign secretary, invited him to edit the *British Documents on the Origins of the War*—overruling his Foreign Office advisers who, however, were glad to be overruled, since Gooch's was a name calculated to satisfy even the most hostile opponents of the policy of Grey. Gooch, for his part, showed the hard core of steel which sometimes lay behind his ostentatious sentimentalities, and insisted on having a fellow editor, having indeed the formidable H. W. V. Temperley (whose notice he contributed to this Dictionary) to help him in possible conflicts with officialdom. The main difficulties, however, proved to be the result of efforts by foreign powers to stop the publication of one document or another. The thirteen volumes were published between 1926 and 1938.

This side of Gooch's work culminated in the two volumes of *Before the War: Studies in Diplomacy*, which appeared in 1936 and 1938. The full study of the documents had transformed his treatment of the Persian problem and persuaded him that Grey had tried to do more good than it would have been prudent for him to make public at the time. Some of the old criticisms of Grey had come to have a more marginal relevance. It was now possible to see that the options open to a statesman were fewer than had been imagined. And Grey, the victim of processes, was sometimes insufficiently aware of the direction in which events were taking him.

After the outbreak of war in 1939 Gooch moved out to London and henceforward he produced for the *Contemporary* essays based on his reading of eighteenth-century history. These he turned into books on *Frederick the Great* (1947), etc.; alternatively he would publish reminiscences, portraits of famous people whom he had known.

His wife had returned to the Catholicism in which she had been brought up and he would walk with her to the church door, not denying for his own part, the possibility of the supernatural, but not convinced that religion could be squared with historical experiences. He was the most generous of men although in respect of himself he was austere, having no car, not caring for taxis, and, at least in his old age, living a most Spartan life. His Liberal friend, F. W. Hirst [q.v.], said that, if he were on the bench, Gooch 'would never send even the most hardened criminal to the gallows'. Yet it was Gooch who, during the controversy over capital punishment, thought that insufficient charity was being shown to the victims of murder, and specified classes of killing which ought still to be punishable by death.

He wrote without anguish, with too easy a mind and too easy a memory, yet he tried hard to make Englishmen understand Germany after the war of 1914-18; and the policies of Sir Edward Grey—the main subject of his self-questioning—drove him to the kind of sincerity and high pressure which can bring touches of originality. He received an honorary doctorate from Durham (1921), was elected FBA (1926), and in 1935 received an honorary fellowship at Trinity College, Cambridge, and an honorary doctorate from Oxford. He was appointed CH in 1939, received the German order Pour le Mérite in 1955, and in 1963 was admitted to the Order of Merit. He had been almost blind for a few years when he died at his home at Chalfont St. Peter, 31 August 1968.

[G. P. Gooch, *Under Six Reigns*, 1958; Sir Herbert Butterfield in *Proceedings* of the British Academy, vol. lv, 1969; private information; personal knowledge.]

H. BUTTERFIELD

GOOSSENS, SIR EUGENE (1893-1962), conductor and composer of music, was born in London 26 May 1893. He came from a musical family of Belgian origin: his grandfather and father, both named Eugene, were both conductors of the Carl Rosa Opera Company, and his mother Annie was the daughter of the operatic bass singer Aynsley Cook. Eugene was the eldest son of the family; his younger brothers were Adolphe, a horn player who was killed in World War I at the age of eighteen, and Leon, the well-known oboist. His sisters Marie and Sidonie are equally well known as harpists.

Goossens was educated at the Muziek-Conservatorium in Bruges and the Liverpool College of Music: from the latter he won a Liverpool scholarship to the Royal College of Music in London in 1907. Here he studied the violin with Achille Rivarde, piano with J. St. Oswald Dykes, harmony with Charles Wood [q.v.], and counterpoint with Sir Frederick Bridge [q.v.]. He was later admitted into Sir Charles Stanford's [q.v.] composition class. He began his professional career in 1912 as a violinist in the Queen's Hall Orchestra under Sir Henry J. Wood [q.v.]. He was rejected for military service in World War I on medical grounds, and began his conducting career with various opera companies, including the Beecham Opera Company in 1916 and the British National Opera Company: he was also a guest conductor with the London Symphony Orchestra, the Philharmonic Orchestra, and various provincial orchestras, the Royal Choral

Society, and the Handel Society. He conducted for the Diaghilev Ballet during their London seasons: this involved performing a number of unusual works, especially modern ones, as Diaghilev had a very forward-looking taste in music and liked to present as many new works as possible.

Goossens was by now becoming known as a composer as well as a conductor: his choral work *Silence* was performed at the Gloucester Three Choirs' Festival of 1922 together with the *Colour Symphony* by Goossens's near contemporary (Sir) Arthur Bliss: both works were put into the programme at the request of Sir Edward W. Elgar [q.v.]. Goossens continued to compose in all forms for the rest of his life, and in the 1920s he was regarded as a member of the avant-garde of British music.

In 1923 Goossens was appointed conductor of the Rochester Philharmonic Orchestra in New York State. This orchestra had been founded by George Eastman, head of the Eastman Kodak Company, who believed in the civilizing influence of music without pretending to have any technical knowledge of it himself. In the eight years which Goossens spent at Rochester he established the orchestra's reputation, and it became one of the leading orchestras in the United States. Goossens conducted at Rochester during the winter season, returning to London in the summers. In 1923 he conducted Delius's incidental music to James Elroy Flecker's [qq.v.] play *Hassan* in Basil Dean's famous production: in 1926 he composed and conducted incidental music for Margaret Kennedy's [q.v.] play *The Constant Nymph*, again directed by Basil Dean. His first opera, *Judith*, with a libretto by E. Arnold Bennett [q.v.] was produced at Covent Garden on 25 June 1929 under the composer's direction.

In 1931 Goossens was appointed conductor of the Cincinnati Symphony Orchestra, a position which he held till 1947: he was the musical director of the Cincinnati May Festival eight times, and made a number of guest appearances as conductor in New York, Boston, Philadelphia, San Francisco, Detroit, and other American cities, as well as conducting opera. On 24 June 1937 he conducted the first performance of his opera *Don Juan de Mañara* at Covent Garden as part of an unusually large repertory of operas performed in honour of the coronation of King George VI. Goossens conducted a number of other operas during this season.

In 1947 Goossens went to Sydney as conductor of the Sydney Symphony Orchestra and director of the New South Wales Conservatorium. He remained there till 1956, when he resigned after a law case, and considerably improved the standards of both institutions. After this he returned to England and made a number of guest appearances with orchestras in many countries. He was knighted in 1955. In 1934 he had been made chevalier of the Legion of Honour.

Apart from his two operas Goossens wrote a choral work, *The Apocalypse*, generally considered one of his finest compositions, two symphonies, a sinfonietta, a concertino for double string orchestra, and an oboe concerto for his brother Leon, as well as chamber music (including a work for his brother and two sisters), songs, and piano music. Though his music was frequently played in the 1920s and 1930s, performances of it have become rarer in recent years. This is probably due to changes in musical fashion, as Goossens always wrote expertly for whatever combination of voices or instruments he was using. Of his two operas *Judith*, in one act, develops and sustains the dramatic action successfully: in *Don Juan* he had to face competition with Mozart, and in addition had to set a libretto by Arnold Bennett, who was more at home writing novels than in dramatic works and was consequently unable to produce striking stage effects. Also the company assembled for the first performance was very much an *ad hoc* one, and not all the singers were really experienced. Goossens's style is chromatic, but does not approach the 'total chromaticism' of Schoenberg: there is always a tonal feeling in it. And Goossens had a very lively and varied feeling for colour. As a person he was charming, witty, and cultured, as may be seen from his autobiography, and he was always willing to help younger musicians. He was very much an all-round musician, of a kind which are not often found nowadays, and his conducting was invariably musical and alive.

Goossens was married three times: first, in 1919, to Dorothy Millar, daughter of Frederick C. Smith Dodsworth, and they had three daughters; secondly, in 1930, to an American, Janet Lewis, who bore him two daughters; thirdly, in 1947, to Marjorie Fetter Faulkrod, who survived him. In 1951 he published an autobiography, *Overture and Beginners*, describing the events of his life up to 1931 and also giving a good deal of information about the lives of his grandfather and father. A projected second volume was never completed. While returning from a visit to Switzerland he was taken ill on the aeroplane and died in Hillingdon Hospital 13 June 1962. There is a bronze bust of Goossens by Frank Dobson (1927).

[Grove's *Dictionary of Music*; Eugene Goossens, *Overture and Beginners*, 1951; private information; personal knowledge.]

HUMPHREY SEARLE

GORE, WILLIAM GEORGE ARTHUR ORMSBY-, fourth BARON HARLECH (1885-1964), statesman and banker. [See ORMSBY-GORE.]

GORE-BROWNE, SIR STEWART (1883-1967), soldier, and settler and politician in Northern Rhodesia (Zambia), was born in London 3 May 1883, the elder son of (Sir) Francis Gore-Browne, who was called to the bar in that year and took silk in 1902, and his wife, Helenor, elder daughter of John Archibald Shaw-Stewart. He was educated at Harrow, and passed into the Royal Military Academy at Woolwich in 1900. He was commissioned to the Royal Field Artillery and sailed for South Africa, but by the time he arrived there the war was over. After eighteen months, Gore-Browne returned home to a very happy period as a young peacetime officer. One of his favourite pastimes was motor racing at Brooklands, which his uncle built. In 1911 he was appointed to the Anglo-Belgian boundary commission, which was to determine the boundary between Northern Rhodesia and the Belgian Congo. After the commission finished its work early in 1914 Gore-Browne, who was much attracted by the country and its peoples, set out from Ndola to march to Mpulungu on Lake Tanganyika. His purpose was to look for land on which to settle. 'One day, after we had been on the march for several weeks', he later recalled, 'we came to a lake in a cradle of hills. I knew I had found what I was looking for.' The lake was called Shiwa Ngandu.

Gore-Browne returned to England just in time to go to France with the Expeditionary Force in August 1914. For his part in the battle of the Somme he was appointed to the DSO (1917) and was mentioned in dispatches. In 1921 he retired from the army with the rank of lieutenant-colonel, for he had decided to go back to Northern Rhodesia to build the home of his dreams. An immense task awaited him, but he knew exactly what he wanted and with single-minded purpose set out to achieve it. In a remote area in the far north of Northern Rhodesia, at Shiwa Ngandu, Gore-Browne constructed a great country mansion and estate, using local materials to the fullest extent, recruiting and training African builders, carpenters, and blacksmiths. By the time the work was completed, Shiwa had its own schools, hospital, chapel, shops, post office, playing fields, club, and aerodrome—and homes of a high standard for the workers and dwellers on the 23,000 acre estate. The force with which Gore-Browne drove himself and his workers comes out in the name given to him by the Bemba—'Chipembere', or rhinoceros.

In 1935 Gore-Browne was elected to the Legislative Council and before long became leader of the unofficial members. In 1938 the governor nominated him to represent African interests. He was knighted for his services in 1945. Gore-Browne's knowledge and personal experience of the Africans were considerable and for years he had his finger more firmly on their political pulse than anyone. He strove for a better understanding of the need to consider the African as a political being. In this he was ahead of his time and when, as a result, he lost the support of the Europeans, he resigned the unofficial leadership at the end of 1946, although remaining a member of the Legislative Council.

Gore-Browne had formed an early association with (Sir) Roy Welensky, whose development from trade-union leader to politician took place under his tutelage. Later the two men spoke out forcibly against the rule of the Colonial Civil Service in Northern Rhodesia and were together involved in early moves towards the establishment of the Federation of Rhodesia and Nyasaland. This alienated much of Gore-Browne's African support, although in later stages he came out strongly against federation. In 1951 he resigned from the Legislative Council and retired to Shiwa Ngandu. Nevertheless, he remained in close touch with his early protégé, Harry Nkumbula, leader of the African National Congress, and later with Kenneth Kaunda, founder of the United National Independence Party. Gore-Browne attempted a come-back in politics as a UNIP candidate for one of the National seats in the 1962 general election, but failed to gain enough European votes to qualify. This was a bitter disappointment to him.

Gore-Browne was a man of strong personality and ability. In politics he was a powerful leader, often at odds with the governor and his officials. On his estate, his style was patriarchal: an old-fashioned country squire; a benevolent autocrat deeply concerned in the life and welfare of his people, whom he regarded and treated as friends; a cultivated man possessed of an extensive library; in bearing military, monocled, courteous, and hospitable. Shiwa Ngandu is his lasting memorial.

Gore-Browne married in 1927 Lorna Grace Bosworth, daughter of the late Professor Edwin Ellen Goldmann; they had two daughters. The marriage was dissolved in 1950. Gore-Browne died at Kasama, in Zambia, 4 August 1967.

A pastel portrait by a member of the Northern Rhodesia provincial administration, Ian Mackinson, is at Shiwa Ngandu.

[*Horizon Magazine* of the RST Group, vol. vi, no. 7, July 1964; Harry Franklin, *Unholy*

Wedlock, 1963; Sir Roy Welensky, *Welensky's 4,000 Days*, 1964; private information.]

EVELYN HONE

GORER, PETER ALFRED ISAAC (1907-1961), biologist and geneticist, was born in London 14 April 1907, the second of the three sons of Edgar Gorer, a noted collector of oriental art, and his wife, Rachel Alice Cohen. In his youth Peter Gorer showed little evidence of future distinction. After leaving Charterhouse, in 1924, he became a dental student at Guy's Hospital, London, but rapidly transferred to medicine, which better suited his temperament and love of natural history. His interest in biology was greatly stimulated by T. J. Evans.

Gorer interrupted his medical studies for a while to undertake research in physiology and wrote a major review and a short original piece about the physiology of hibernation; he received a second class B.Sc. (London) in 1929. At this time he also developed an interest in unsolved problems of genetics and heredity, and more particularly the genetics of immunity of disease, including cancer. His analytical approach was foreshadowed by a satirical note, which he wrote as a student, on the quantitative study of tumours. Much later he delighted an after-dinner audience by a witty, but effective, irreverence for terminology in a discourse entitled 'Transplantese'.

After qualifying MRCS, LRCP in 1932, Gorer was able to study genetics with J. B. S. Haldane [q.v.] at University College, London. Their relationship developed into a lifelong empathy. Also at University College, which was an intellectual lodestone for biologists, Gorer was influenced by D. M. S. Watson and (Sir) E. J. Salisbury and became friendly with George Payling Wright. In 1934 Gorer joined the Lister Institute where he studied the genetic and immunologic basis of the resistance to infection and the synergism between serotherapy and chemotherapy against V. Septique. He was a colleague of D. W. W. Henderson [q.v.]. Dismayed by the tumour immunologists' almost total ignorance of the principles of genetics, Gorer initiated his future life's work on the genetics of individuality by investigating marker substances (antigens) on the surface of red cells and tissues. Gorer decided that the most direct approach to this problem was to define the antigens of normal tissues and then to determine what additional contributions to antigenicity, if any, were peculiar to the tumour itself.

The early experiments were performed by comparing the reactions of serum from a group A donor (himself) against the red cells from two different strains of mice. Later refinements included the immunization of rabbits and mice with red cells or tissues from a predetermined donor strain followed by absorption of irrelevant antibodies. In this way Gorer defined four distinct antigens, I, II, III, and IV. These studies, started at the Lister Institute, were continued when Gorer returned to Guy's in 1940. His genetic knowledge influenced his research as a pathologist and he published detailed analyses of the frequency and form of diseases of the kidney and liver in different mouse strains. His research slowed during the war of 1939–45, when he was required to take on a heavy teaching load. He was also greatly affected in 1945 by the death from tuberculosis of his wife, Gertrude Ernestine Kahler, the former wife of a German refugee. They had been married for only three years and had no children. In 1946 Gorer left London and joined George D. Snell and Sally Lyman Allen in Bar Harbor, Maine, in a collaboration which formed the basis for many future developments in immunogenetics. Snell, who had been following the susceptibility of mouse hybrids to transplanted tumours, had evidence that resistance or susceptibility was often linked to genes controlling the normal development of the tail. In an important series of studies Gorer, Lyman, and Snell demonstrated the close linkage between the presence of Antigen II (thereafter called H–2) tumour susceptibility and the morphological marker, 'fused' tail. Gorer also initiated, with L. W. Law, studies on immunity to the mouse mammary tumour virus and then had the frustration of seeing all but a fragment of the data lost in the fire that consumed the Jackson Laboratory.

While at Bar Harbor Gorer made the acquaintance of, and in 1947 married, Elizabeth Bruce Keucher, the librarian and secretary to the laboratory director, C. C. Little. The marriage was a particularly happy one. They had a son and a daughter.

On his return to England in 1947 Gorer was appointed reader in experimental pathology at Guy's under Payling Wright. He had minimal teaching responsibilities (he taught only pathology to dental students) and complete freedom of research, in which he was assisted by a young Polish refugee and former medical student, Mrs Z. B. Mikulska. He had few students, but of those who were stringently trained by him, E. A. Boyse, J. R. Batchelor, G. Hoecker, O. Pizzaro, and D. B. Amos achieved independent recognition as immunogeneticists.

As Gorer's work progressed and the validity of his conclusions was established, the appreciative proportion of his audience gradually increased. He was responsible for many technical innovations, always striving for greater precision, flexibility, and reliability. He was generous in an unusual way. As an example, he solved the problem of a universally applicable agglutination reaction after several years of intense investigation. The solution involved the addition of fluid from one particular ovarian cyst. He had enough of the fluid for several years' work in his own laboratory. Instead of capitalizing on this he spent further industrious months testing high molecular weight polysaccharides until he found a substitute which gave acceptable results and which anyone could obtain. For much of his working life his only space was a single room of perhaps 250 square feet; no telephone, no secretary, and not even a glassware washer. Even so, Gorer was generous with his ideas. With time, more and more scientists sought his advice and he was much sought after at international meetings. So freely did he give of his time that his total number of publications barely exceeded fifty. Some of his written papers have continued to influence scientific thought and contain ideas which have been as yet incompletely explored. These include 'Interactions between Sessile and Humoral Antibodies in Homograft Reactions', 'Synergic Action between Isoantibody and Immune Cells in Graft Rejection', 'The Antigenic Structure of Tumours', and 'Pathological Changes in F_1 Hybrid Mice Following Transplantation of Spleen Cells from Donors of the Parental Strains'. He also introduced the concept of low-dose enhancement. Gorer has been primarily responsible for the application of genetic principles to immunology and was one of the most important contributors to the study of organ and tissue graft rejection, tumour immunity, and the genetics of immune responsiveness.

There were many sides to Gorer's nature. His manner was unobtrusive, with a slight streak of shyness, sometimes reflected in his relationship with shy people. Often he was content to be a silent member of a group until, with diffidence, he would imperceptibly begin to lead the conversation. He had great patience and gentleness with those with a real desire to learn, and he had no time for the pompous or bombastic. He could also be abrasive and an indefatigable debater who was the despair of his host by developing new concepts until the stars faded and the scotch had long since gone. His humour was delicate and his knowledge of the theatre and the arts extensive. He was a dry-fly expert, a certain winner in casting tournaments, and a prized consultant to a leading tackle maker. Above all, he was a creative thinker with the desire, but sometimes the inability, to communicate with those of lesser intellect and depth of understanding.

Of the honours Gorer received, only one, admission as a fellow to the Royal Society in 1960, pleased him deeply. Gorer died at Haywards Heath, at the early age of fifty-four, 11 May 1961.

[P. B. Medawar in *Biographical Memoirs of Fellows of the Royal Society*, vol. vii, 1961; Guy's Hospital *Gazette*, vol. lxxv, 1961; personal knowledge.]   D. B. AMOS

GOUGH, HERBERT JOHN (1890-1965), engineer and expert on metal fatigue, was born in Bermondsey 26 April 1890, the second son of Henry James Gough, a civil servant in the Post Office, and his wife, Mary Anne Gillis. Gough attended the Regent Street Polytechnic Technical School and won a scholarship to University College School. After a brief interlude as a pupil teacher, he was an apprentice at Messrs Vickers, Sons & Maxim from 1909 to 1913, when he was appointed a designer draughtsman. During this period he obtained a B.Sc. (Hons.) in engineering from London University and later received a D.Sc. and Ph.D.

In 1914 he joined the staff of the National Physical Laboratory in the engineering department, where he stayed until 1938, becoming superintendent of the department in 1930 in succession to Sir Thomas Stanton. During World War I Gough served in the Royal Engineers (Signals) from 1914 until May 1919, rose to the rank of captain, and was twice mentioned in dispatches. He was appointed MBE (military) in 1919.

During his period at the NPL Gough established the science of the behaviour of materials under fatigue conditions. Fatigue failure is failure due to repeated application of a load much lower than that necessary to produce failure in a single application and is one of the most frequent causes of breakage in service. Gough, working initially under the inspiration of Stanton and with many able young scientists and engineers such as D. Hanson, H. L. Cox, A. J. Murphy, C. E. Elam, and W. A. Wood, established that fatigue failure occurs because the metal undergoes plastic deformation. He discovered that this was due to slippage inside the metal crystals and, using X-rays (a new tool at the time), showed how safe ranges of stress could be forecast. He also attacked the problem of fatigue under conditions when differently directed stresses are applied simultaneously, explaining how to predict 'lives' under these conditions. Having developed means of estimating stresses in chains, hooks, and rings, Gough applied the principles to the design of lifting gear. He also demonstrated how the designer of mechanical structures needs to allow for the increased stresses arising at fillets, lubrication holes, keyways, and splines. All of this work was of immense practical significance for it enabled designs to be much more economic, replacing 'rule of thumb' by quantitative procedures. Gough also investigated fretting corrosion where moving metal parts touch, cold pressing of metals, lubrication, and welding. He published *The Fatigue of Metals* in 1924 but much of his later work was not widely known until the publication of his presidential address to the Institution of Mechanical Engineers in 1949.

Gough entered the War Office in 1938 as the first director of scientific research. In 1942 he was appointed CB and became director-general of scientific research and development at the Ministry of Supply, remaining there until 1945 when he joined Lever Brothers and Unilever Ltd. as engineer-in-chief. Gough's responsibilities at the Ministry were very wide, for they concerned physical research, signals, and chemical research, and included the Radar Research Station at Malvern under (Sir) John Cockcroft [q.v.], the Chemical Station at Porton under Davidson Pratt, and the Rocket Station at Aberporth under (Sir) Alwyn Crow. Gough handled the obvious problems of demarcation very well. Although director-general, he took an active personal interest in unexploded bomb disposal.

During the period 1945-50, as a member of the Guy Committee Gough took an active interest in the establishment at East Kilbride of the Mechanical Engineering Research Laboratory (later the National Engineering Laboratory) by the transfer of his old division from the NPL; and assisted in defining its first research programme.

Besides his CB, Gough was decorated with the medal of freedom with silver palm by the United States Government for his work as chief liaison officer on scientific research and development for the United Kingdom and received many medals and prizes from the Institutions of Mechanical Engineers, Civil Engineering, Automobile Engineers, and the Royal Aeronautical Society. He was elected to the fellowship of the Royal Society in 1933, and served on its council in 1939-40.

Gough retired from Unilever in 1955 but retained his interests and in particular helped to organize a number of large international scientific conferences. He died suddenly at Rottingdean 1 June 1965 after a round of golf, a game of which he was very fond. He was survived by his wife Sybil Holmes whom he married in 1918 and who bore him a son and a daughter.

Gough's colleagues speak of the energy, drive, and enthusiasm which he brought to all that he did. He was by all accounts a strong and forceful personality and applied himself with equal energy to the study of the fatigue of metals and to an analysis of his golf score.

[S. F. Dorey in *Biographical Memoirs of Fellows of the Royal Society*, vol. xii, 1966; *The Times*, 4 June 1965.]

ANTHONY KELLY

GOUGH, SIR HUBERT DE LA POER (1870-1963), general, was born at Gurteen, county Waterford, 12 August 1870, the elder son (there were no daughters) of (General Sir) Charles John Stanley Gough, GCB, VC [q.v.], and his wife, Harriette Anastasia, daughter of John W. de la Poer, formerly MP for county Waterford. He was educated at Eton and Sandhurst and commissioned in the 16th Lancers in 1889. Regimental service in India in the 1890s provided ample leisure to display his first-class horsemanship in racing and polo, and he also took part in the Tirah Expedition in 1897. The following year he married (Margaret Louisa) Nora, daughter of Major-General H. C. Lewes. In the South African war he displayed characteristic dash and impulsiveness when relieving Ladysmith against orders, but later the same qualities cost his mounted-infantry regiment heavy casualties in an ambush at Blood River. Nevertheless he ended the war with an enhanced reputation. From 1903 to 1906 he was an instructor at the Staff College and subsequently commanded the 16th Lancers. In 1911 he returned to Ireland as a brigadier-general commanding 3rd Cavalry brigade at the Curragh.

By the end of 1913 there was considerable speculation both inside and outside the army about the position of the armed forces should the Government be obliged to impose the policy of Home Rule for Ireland by force. In December, in an attempt to dispel anxiety, the secretary of state for war, Colonel J. E. B. Seely (later Lord Mottistone, q.v.), discussed the constitutional position with senior officers, making it clear *inter alia* that officers domiciled in Northern Ireland would not be compelled to take part in possible hostilities there. By mid March 1914 trouble appeared imminent and certain precautionary movements of troops in Ireland (and of naval forces) were agreed upon by a Cabinet committee. Seely summoned Sir Arthur Paget, the commander-in-chief in Ireland, to London and instructed him to brief his officers on the lines agreed upon in December: in event of hostilities in Northern Ireland, Ulster-domiciled officers might 'disappear' but other officers who for conscientious reasons were unwilling to carry out their duty were to say so and be dismissed the Service.

Seely was thus initially to blame for obliging officers to make a fateful choice on hypothetical orders, and for presenting Paget with six possible contingencies rather than definite orders. All might still have been well had Paget possessed a cool head and a clear mind, but he lacked either, apprehending fearfully that a number of officers would refuse to go to Ulster if ordered. By his first confused and emotional harangue to senior officers in Dublin on the morning of Friday 20 March 1914 he created the very dilemma which he feared. Contrary to the Government's opinion that precautionary moves might be carried out without resistance, Paget declared that he expected the country to be ablaze by the following day. He was extremely confused about how the troops should react if hostilities occurred. He then stressed the difficulty he had had in obtaining concessions from the War Office and ordered commanders to put the following terms to their officers: officers actually domiciled in Ulster would be exempted from any operations and would be allowed to 'disappear'; any officers unwilling to serve would immediately be dismissed from the Service. In answer to a question from Gough, Paget replied that 'domiciled in Ulster' was to be strictly interpreted, and he added rudely 'You cannot be held to come under that clause. You need expect no mercy from your old friend in the War Office' (i.e. Sir John French, the CIGS, q.v.). Gough left the meeting very angry at his personal treatment and under the impression that the army was to be used to coerce Ulster prior to the passing of the Home Rule Bill. He determined to resign, and although he did not attempt to influence the officers of his brigade, the great majority freely opted for the same course. In reporting this outcome to Paget, Gough stressed in writing that while he and his officers were quite prepared to maintain law and order they were not willing to *initiate* active military operations against Ulster.

Paget addressed all the officers of the Cavalry brigade at the Curragh on the morning of Saturday 21 March. Mixing reassurance with threats he failed to convert Gough and the officers who had decided to resign. He now said that senior officers refusing to do their duty would be court-martialled. He also falsely stated that the terms he had offered derived directly from the King; he would not obey the orders of 'mere politicians' (according to some accounts the phrase he used was 'those dirty swine of politicians'). So the War Office received a signal from Dublin on the evening of 21 March, 'Regret to report brigadier and fifty-seven officers 3rd Cavalry Brigade prefer to accept dismissal if ordered North'.

Gough and his regimental commanding officers were summoned to the War Office to be reprimanded by Seely, but by the time they arrived on the Sunday morning 22 March Asquith had become aware of the muddle which Seely and Paget had between them created and was insisting that order must be promptly restored to avoid a real military mutiny. He made it clear to Seely that there were no grounds for punishing or dismissing Gough and the others who had only taken a choice forced on them by Paget. Meanwhile Lord Roberts [q.v.] had discovered that Seely now repudiated the alternatives presented by Paget and the elderly field-marshal conveyed this information to Gough. The latter therefore reported to the War Office on the Monday morning 23 March fortified in the integrity of his position. He first saw Sir John French who assured him that there had been a misunderstanding and offered his word that the army would not be asked to enforce the current Home Rule Bill upon Ulster. But he felt unable to put his assurance in writing. French then took Gough to see Seely, Paget and the Adjutant-General Sir (John) Spencer Ewart [q.v.] also being present. Seely vainly attempted to browbeat Gough who stubbornly demanded a written assurance. French broke the deadlock by tactfully suggesting that Gough needed documentary proof to convince his own officers. Seely capitulated and left for a Cabinet meeting while Ewart drafted a statement. After lunch Seely received the statement as revised by the Cabinet in Asquith's handwriting, but when Gough called to see it only Seely and Lord Morley [q.v.] were present. Undeterred by the confusion caused by his previous instructions, Seely then took the remarkable step, with Lord Morley's assistance, of adding two paragraphs, the latter affirming that (the Government) had 'no intention whatever of taking advantage of the right to crush political opposition to the policy or principles of the Home Rule Bill'. When the statement had been copied French handed it to Gough who requested a quarter of an hour to study it together with his two colonels, his brother 'Johnnie', who was BGS to Sir Douglas Haig at Aldershot, and Sir Henry Wilson, the DMO [qq.v.]. They were still not entirely satisfied, so Hubert Gough added the rider 'I understand the meaning of the last paragraph to be that the army will not be used under any circumstances to enforce the present Home Rule Bill on Ulster'. Sir John French added 'That is how I read it. J. F.'

The Government speedily repudiated the two 'peccant paragraphs' and Seely, shortly followed by French and Ewart, resigned. Gough had apparently triumphed, although as he explained to a friend at the time, his obdurate stand had been inspired more by resentment at the War Office and Paget's attempt to bully than by the Ulster issue. But his triumph was not unblemished: officers who had agreed to do their duty in Ireland resented the acclaim accorded him; and there was strong feeling among Liberal and Labour politicians that the Government had stooped to bargain with a rebellious group of officers. In fact Gough was innocent of the imputation of political intrigue, but he suffered from his reluctant association with Henry Wilson who was hand-in-glove with the Opposition and crowing over Gough's triumph as his own.

In the short term, however, the brilliant cavalryman's career suffered no ill effects from the Curragh incident. He led his brigade with distinction during the opening weeks of the war in 1914 and was promoted major-general in command of the newly formed 2nd Cavalry division in the first battle of Ypres. Further promotions followed in rapid succession: after the battle of Neuve Chapelle in March 1915 he was given command of 7th division and in July he was promoted lieutenant-general in command of I Corps, which played a prominent part in the battle of Loos, though Gough himself was in no way to blame for the disaster. Jealousy at his rapid rise was offset by his wide reputation for moral as well as physical courage. His chief failings were his hot temper and his tendency to quick, impulsive judgements. A fighting general *par excellence*, Gough discovered that as a Corps commander he was remote from the battle and could not visit the front frequently without arousing the resentment of his divisional commanders. This frustration was intensified before the battle of the Somme in 1916 with his promotion to command of the Reserve (soon to be titled Fifth) Army. 'It was not that he enjoyed pitching men into battle to be killed or wounded,' a biographer remarks, 'simply that he was confident of his ability to lead soldiers successfully in the dreadful tasks to which they were committed.'

In the third Ypres campaign in 1917 Gough's Fifth Army was placed on the left wing and given the major role in the first phase of the offensive. Gough was never sanguine about the prospects of a complete breakthrough into open country, but he differed from GHQ in believing that it was essential to secure all short-range objectives on the first day rather than by a series of short advances. Fifth Army. was initially successful on its left but made little progress on the right. When heavy rain and stubborn resistance held up the second and third attacks in mid August, Gough vainly asked Haig to call off the offensive. Second Army took over the major role in September and Fifth Army's reputation declined. Gough's personal relations with his subordinate commanders remained good but his chief of staff,

Neill Malcolm, had a brusque manner which caused resentment and uncertainty about his general's real feelings. By the end of the campaign Haig had gained the impression that units had become reluctant to serve in Fifth Army.

In March 1918 the Germans were expected to launch an all-out spring offensive with an army strongly reinforced from the eastern front. The British Fifth Army was holding a vulnerable forty-two mile sector between Gouzeaucourt and La Fère with a fully stretched front line and very meagre reserves. Haig was aware of this weakness but gave the Third Army of Sir Julian Byng (later Viscount Byng of Vimy, q.v.), which was on Gough's left, priority because of the vital need to protect the Channel ports, and because he assumed that the French would quickly reinforce Gough's sector in a crisis. When on 21 March Ludendorff launched his main blow against Fifth Army's front he enjoyed a local superiority of about eight to one. Gough decided he could not hope to hold out in the forward battle zone but must fight a delaying action to save his army from complete destruction while preserving an intact line until British and French reinforcements arrived in strength. Unfortunately for Gough, Pétain and Foch both proved reluctant to commit reserves to the British sector for several days, and to make matters worse one of his Corps commanders interpreted Gough's orders as permitting disengagement and withdrawal to the Somme. This precipitate action forced the two adjacent Corps to conform and by 24 March leading German units were already across the river. Nevertheless the German offensive was already losing momentum in the face of Fifth Army's stubborn resistance when Gough was informed, on 27 March, that he was to be replaced by Sir Henry Rawlinson [q.v.] and the staff of Fourth Army on the following day. Haig attempted to keep him employed in France but Lloyd George and Lord Derby, the war minister, insisted (3 April) that he be sent home immediately. Gough's brilliant career thus came to an abrupt end and the official inquiry which he had been promised was never held. 'His treatment', Haig admitted to a brother officer of them both in February 1919, 'was harsh and undeserved: but after considerable thought I decided that public opinion at home, whether right or wrong, demanded a scapegoat, and that the only possible ones were Hubert or me. I was conceited enough to think that the army could not spare me.'

In 1919 Gough accepted the thankless appointment of chief of the Allied military mission to the Baltic but he was speedily recalled by Lloyd George. He was appointed GCMG in 1919. No further employment followed and in October 1922 he was retired with the rank of full general. He had been created KCB in 1916, and KCVO in 1917. In 1922 Gough stood as a Liberal candidate at a by-election at Chertsey but was narrowly defeated. After a few years of farming in Surrey he took up a successful career in business.

However, Gough's chief preoccupation in the long life that remained to him was to vindicate his own and his army's reputation against the slurs cast upon them over the operations in March 1918. In 1924 he was reconciled to Haig and went with Lady Gough to stay with the Haigs at Bemersyde. In 1928 he was a pall bearer at Haig's funeral. In 1931 he published his own dignified and restrained account of the campaign in *Fifth Army*. As the tragic episode began to be viewed more objectively and new evidence appeared Gough's conduct of the retreat tended to be not merely exonerated but praised as a remarkable exercise of generalship in adverse circumstances. This trend in various histories and memoirs culminated in the belated but none the less welcome amends made by Lloyd George in 1936 in the volume of his *War Memoirs* dealing with the episode. No official government action followed, but in awarding Gough the GCB in 1937 King George VI made it clear that Gough's and Fifth Army's honour were fully restored.

In 1939 Gough was still in vigorous health and eager to serve in a military capacity. He formed the Chelsea branch of the Home Guard in 1940 and later commanded a London Zone until he was finally retired in 1942. At the age of eighty he was still an active chairman of numerous companies. Lady Gough, by whom he had a son who died in infancy, and four daughters, died in 1951. Gough then devoted his time to writing his memoirs and published *Soldiering On* in 1954. He survived all other senior commanders of World War I by many years and died at his home at 14 St. Mary Abbots Court, London W14, 18 March 1963.

There is a drawing by Francis Dodd (1917) in private possession. In the National Portrait Gallery are a bust by Patricia Kahn (1961–2) and a chalk drawing by Sir William Rothenstein (1932). A portrait in oils was painted by Frank O. Salisbury.

[A. H. Farrar-Hockley, *Goughie*, 1975; A. P. Ryan, *Mutiny at the Curragh*, 1956; Geoffrey Brooke, *Good Company*, 1954; private information.]   BRIAN BOND

GOWERS, SIR ERNEST ARTHUR (1880–1966), public servant, was born in London 2 June 1880, the younger of the two sons among the four children of (Sir) William Richard Gowers [q.v.], physician, and his wife, Mary, daughter of Frederick Baines, of Leeds. He was educated at Rugby School and at Clare College, Cambridge, of which he was a scholar and, from 1949, an honorary fellow. Having gained a first class in the classical tripos in 1902, he entered the Civil Service and was posted to the Inland Revenue Department, later transferring to the India Office. He was called to the bar (Inner Temple) in 1906. He acted as private secretary to several parliamentary under-secretaries, including Edwin Montagu [q.v.], and in 1911 moved to the Treasury as principal private secretary to David Lloyd George, then chancellor of the Exchequer. In the following year Lloyd George made him chief inspector in the National Health Insurance Commission (England), the establishment of which in that year under the terms of the National Insurance Act of 1911 was the most complex task which had yet faced the Civil Service. He held this post for five years.

In 1917 Gowers became secretary to the Conciliation and Arbitration Board for Government Employees. In 1919 he was made director of production at the Mines Department (Board of Trade), and a year later he was promoted to take charge of the department as permanent under-secretary for mines. In 1927 he became chairman of the Board of Inland Revenue, and in 1930 he retired from the Civil Service although not from public service.

Gowers renewed his association with mining by becoming chairman of the coal mines reorganization commission, established by the Coal Mines Act of 1930. After five years the commission acknowledged failure because of the opposition of colliery owners to the amalgamation of mines. Despite this setback Gowers went on to become chairman of the coal commission set up in 1938, and by 1942 such progress had been made that he was able to announce that all unworked coal in Britain had become the property of the coal commission.

He was also chairman of the manpower subcommittee of the Committee of Imperial Defence, the body which produced the famous schedule of reserved occupations. In 1939 he was appointed regional commissioner for civil defence for the London region, and in 1941 was promoted to senior regional commissioner. From then on he bore the main responsibility for civil defence in London until the end of the war, co-operating successfully with the leader of the London County Council, Charles (later Lord) Latham [q.v.].

After the war Gowers undertook a number of public tasks such as the chairmanship of the Home Office committee of inquiry into the closing hours of shops (1946–7), and the chairmanship of the royal commission on capital punishment (1949–53). From 1948 to 1957 he

was chairman of the National Hospitals for Nervous Diseases, Queen Square, London, an institution which his father and other pioneers of modern neurology had made world-famous towards the end of the nineteenth century.

Gowers may be regarded as one of the greatest public servants of his day. He presided over numerous official bodies and committees of inquiry besides those already mentioned. Among the matters he investigated were the admission of women into the senior branch of the Foreign Service, and the preservation, maintenance, and use of houses of outstanding historical or architectural interest. His courtesy, his fine sense of humour, and his unfailing clarity of expression explain why his services were so frequently sought.

Gowers's literary style was lucid and urbane. His writings include a two-shilling booklet *Plain Words: a Guide to the Use of English*, issued in 1948; its sequel *ABC of Plain Words* (1951); *The Complete Plain Words* (1954), which combined the two earlier works; *A Life for a Life? The Problem of Capital Punishment* (1956); and a revision of *Modern English Usage* (1965) by H. W. Fowler [q.v.]. The first of these, *Plain Words*, was written at the invitation of Sir Edward (later Lord) Bridges [q.v.], then head of the Civil Service, to serve as an introduction to a course of instruction for entrants to the service in the writing of simple and unambiguous English, on which Gowers was known to be insistent. The books on 'Plain Words' show his regard for brevity and precision as the leading virtues in factual writing. Throughout his life he crusaded against the faults which have made 'officialese' a term of opprobrium, and in favour of simple and direct English. His customary mood of amiable scepticism is revealed in many passages, for example in his remark about the fashionable use of the word 'repercussion': 'Many officials must have echoed in their own way the cry of Macbeth, who knew more about repercussions of this sort than most people,

"Bloody instructions which being taught return To plague th'inventor".'

Since *Plain Words* exhibited the profound influence of H. W. Fowler, it was natural that the Oxford University Press should have turned to Gowers to revise *Modern English Usage*, a task which he completed in his eighty-fifth year. One of his principal aims was to leave unimpaired the peculiar flavour that had endeared Fowler to so many people. Here and there he softened some of Fowler's astringency and removed some of his more idiosyncratic remarks. The revised *Modern English Usage*, characterized by the same fastidious care for 'proper words in proper places' that the first author had displayed, nevertheless showed much originality, both in newly written articles (e.g. 'abstractitis', 'sociologese') and within the articles on older topics. In an age of possibly declining standards of written English Gowers provided clear guidance to anyone who turned to him for a ruling on matters of linguistic dispute.

Gowers's work with the royal commission on capital punishment made him a convinced abolitionist: his personal views are set down in his book *A Life for a Life?*

Gowers was made an honorary D.Litt. of Manchester University and was elected an honorary associate of the Royal Institute of British Architects. He was appointed CB in 1917, KBE in 1926, KCB in 1928, GBE in 1945, and GCB in 1953.

He married, in 1905, Constance (MBE 1946, died 1952), daughter of Thomas Macgregor Greer, solicitor and politician, of Ballymoney, county Antrim, by whom he had one son and two daughters.

Gowers spent his later years pig-farming in West Sussex and he died at Midhurst, Sussex, 16 April 1966. There is a portrait in oils by Meredith Frampton (1943) at the Imperial War Museum, and a bronze bust by Loris Rey (1943).

[*The Times*, 18 April 1966; *Listener*, 6 May 1965; Oxford University Press archives.]

R. W. BURCHFIELD

GRAHAM BROWN, THOMAS (1882-1965), neurophysiologist and mountaineer. [See BROWN.]

GRAY, SIR ALEXANDER (1882-1968), economist and poet, was born 6 January 1882 at Lochee, Dundee, the third son of John Young Gray, and his wife, Mary Young. His father was then art teacher at Dundee High School and to this school Gray went before going on to the university of Edinburgh, where in 1902 he took first class honours in mathematics and was awarded a gold medal. In 1905, after study in Edinburgh, Göttingen, and Paris, he took a second degree, again with first class honours, in economic science and was awarded the Gladstone memorial prize. At Edinburgh one of his fellow students was John Anderson (later Viscount Waverley, q.v.) with whom he formed a lifelong friendship. Anderson and he were placed first and second in the Civil Service examination in 1905 and were assigned to the Colonial Office and the Local Government Board respectively. It is said that he went to congratulate Anderson on being placed first in the examination, and when asked how he could possibly know what had not yet been announced,

explained that he had been told officially he was second and only one man could be ahead of him.

Gray spent sixteen years in the Civil Service before his appointment in 1921 to the Jaffrey chair of political economy in Aberdeen. During that time he was mainly occupied with problems of social insurance. After four years with the Local Government Board, and three with the Colonial Office, he was transferred together with Anderson to the National Health Insurance Commission in 1912 and left it in 1919 to go to the insurance department of the newly formed Ministry of Health. These years as an administrator stood him in good stead later both as a teacher of economics and as a member of innumerable public bodies, giving to his handling of classes and committees alike a sense of the realities of government.

Meanwhile his first book, *The Scottish Staple at Veere*, had appeared in 1909. Although based on notes left by Professor John Davidson this involved Gray in extensive research and developed into a full-scale study of the early organization of Scottish foreign trade. It drew also on his powers as a linguist since much of the material was in Dutch. Gray was one of the few British economists able to speak the Dutch language and had an almost complete monopoly in reviewing the works of Dutch economists for the *Economic Journal*.

In 1911, a few years after joining the Civil Service, he submitted the winning essay for a prize of a hundred guineas given by Dr J. Peddie Steele on the occasion of the quincentenary celebrations of the university of St. Andrews, a distinction of which he was specially proud.

Gray's published work as an economist is largely on the development of economic thought. It is marked by simplicity, clarity, and above all humour and readability. His *Development of Economic Doctrine* (1931) took many years in the writing and eventually delighted a generation of undergraduates who found other textbooks dull by comparison. In the same vein but aimed at a wider audience was his *Socialist Tradition, Moses to Lenin* (1946), completed in wartime after an even longer period of gestation. Gray disarmingly confessed his dislikes— singling out Marx, Lassalle, and Rousseau— as well as naming those like Fourier whom he felt to be kindred spirits. Although never doctrinaire or partisan, he expressed his own views with candour and forthrightness in the form of critical comments on the ideas of others.

Apart from these two volumes, Gray published little in economics, putting teaching in front of publication. A lecture on *Some Aspects of National Health Insurance* appeared in 1923 and a later lecture on family allowances was expanded into a book, *Family Endowment* (1927), which took a critical and rather hostile view of the campaign then in progress, arguing that the wage bargaining process would be transformed by payments of allowances out of general taxation, so that strikes, for example, might be much longer and more successful.

Gray's emphasis was on political economy rather than on the more quantitive and scientific aspects of the subject. He warned his audience against unwarranted precision resting on inappropriate assumptions and underlined the limitations of mathematical techniques in the formulation of economic policy. He was very much alive to the complexity of economic problems and their involvement in wider human motives and interests.

Gray had a lively and vigorous prose style, which showed to particular advantage in his prefaces and addresses: for example, the prefaces to his successive volumes of translations of songs and ballads from German, Dutch, and Danish and his entertaining presidential address to the economics section of the British Association in 1949. He was also a poet of distinction whose work is represented in most anthologies of modern Scottish verse. His interest in verse translation originated in the preparation in 1915 of an English version of *J'accuse!*—a work in German in which were scattered passages of verse. His success in handling the translation of these passages encouraged him to tackle German songs and ballads and, later, songs by Heine for his own amusement, and he discovered that much of it went better into Scots than English. Although begun with no thought of Schumann or of the *Dichterliebe* cycle, the translations fit perfectly the Schumann settings and are among his best work. His first translations (*Songs and Ballads chiefly from Heine*, 1920) was followed by a volume of German ballads, *Arrows* (1932); *Sir Halewyn* (1949), translations mainly from Dutch originals; and *Four and Forty* (1954). The last of these, which appeared when he was already over seventy, is an outstanding rendering into Scots verse of forty-four Danish ballads, undertaken to while away overnight railway journeys to London.

In addition to his translations, Gray published several volumes of his own verse, some in English, some in the Scottish dialect. Most of these are included in his *Any Man's Life* (1924) and *Gossip* (1928); a selection from his poems edited by Maurice Lindsay appeared in 1948. These were all short lyrics, predominantly in English, and are more introspective and nostalgic than one might expect. They also give expression to deeper and more personal responses to the human situation than his other writings and many of the best of them show his characteristic deftness and wit.

Gray was very much a Scot and strongly rooted, with a profound understanding of his country. In his last work, *A Timorous Civility* (1966), published only in a very limited edition, he brought together a number of his essays and addresses in which he ranged over Scottish literature, history, and character with authority, insight, humanity, and wit. But he was also a European and had no sympathy for a narrow nationalism or for what he took to be attempts to revive artificially the use of Lallans.

It was above all as a teacher that Gray excelled. It was his deeply felt belief that the first duty of a professor was to lay down a clear conspectus of the subject to his first-year class. Those who took his classes at Aberdeen, where he was particularly happy, or at Edinburgh, to which he moved in 1935, never ceased to look back with pleasure on his lectures on political economy. In the days after the war when a class of 400 first-year students would gather to hear him in the Pollock Hall in Edinburgh, he would sit playing the organ until the appointed hour and then turn and begin his discourse. He spoke with authority, humour, and a ready command of language and addressed himself to the imagination as much as to the intelligence of his students. He was equally concerned for their educational attainments and general welfare.

In the twenties, and even more in the thirties, Gray was kept busy on a series of government committees, at first dealing mainly with National Health Insurance but later with issues relating to pay and employment, labour disputes, unemployment assistance, and so on. He was a member of the royal commission on national health insurance (1924-6) and of the White Fish Commission (1938) and chairman of a number of courts of inquiry under the Industrial Courts Act. He was also chairman, during and after the war of 1939-45, of many of the appeals tribunals set up by the Ministry of Labour, retaining the trust of all parties in this work. Later he served as chairman of the Scottish Schools Broadcasting Council and was a member of the Fulbright commission. He found time also to act as chairman of the executive committee of the Youth Hostels Association in its early years (1931-5); and he was president of the Scottish Economic Society (1960-3), and a vice-president of the Royal Economic Society from 1955 until his death.

Amongst other distinctions Gray was appointed CBE in 1939 and knighted in 1947. He held honorary degrees from four universities, including the two in which he taught for thirty-five years. After his retirement in 1956 he was invited to stand as rector of Edinburgh University, but declined.

Gray's conversation, enriched by a slight burr, was an assured and steady flow of comment on the world's affairs. He was a most witty and entertaining speaker, without contrivance or show, and with a ready fund of quotations and modern instances to draw upon. But there was also a good deal of the preacher in him and it was at the moral rather than the technical level that what he had to say made the deepest impression.

Gray was short, with a ruddy complexion, and an out-of-doors farming appearance. He led a full and happy family life, marrying in 1909 Alice, daughter of William Gunn, solicitor in Edinburgh. They had one son and three daughters. He died in Edinburgh 17 February 1968, shortly after the death of his wife.

A portrait by A. E. Borthwick painted at the time of Gray's retirement hangs in the Secretary's office at the university of Edinburgh.

[Private information; personal knowledge.]
ALEC CAIRNCROSS

GRAY, SIR ARCHIBALD MONTAGUE HENRY (1880–1967), dermatologist, was born 1 February 1880 at Ottery St. Mary, south Devon, where his father, Frederick Archibald Gray, was a general practitioner. His mother was Louisa Frances Waterworth, and he was the only son and the eldest of four children. He was educated at Cheltenham College and University College and Hospital, London. In 1903 he qualified MRCS, LRCP and obtained his London MB with honours; in 1904 he gained his BS with honours in obstetrics. For the next five years he held resident and junior appointments at University College Hospital and the Hospital for Women, Soho Square. He proceeded MD in 1905 in midwifery and diseases of women and was awarded the university medal. He was admitted MRCP (1907) and FRCS in 1908 when he was elected a fellow of University College, London. He decided to specialize in obstetrics and gynaecology and became the first obstetric registrar at University College Hospital, where he performed the first Caesarean Wertheim operation in England.

In 1909, however, the post of physician for diseases of the skin at University College Hospital was offered to Gray who after six months' study under J. Jadassohn at Berne took up this appointment which he was to hold until 1946. His career was interrupted by the war of 1914-18 during which he was attached to the general staff at the War Office with the rank of lieutenant-colonel in the Royal Army Medical Corps. From 1918 to 1919 he was consulting dermatologist with the army in France; and was mentioned in dispatches and appointed CBE. After the war he was for many years honorary consulting dermatologist to the Royal Air Force; in 1931-3 he was a member of the government committee on the medical services of the Navy, Army, and Air Force.

At University College Hospital Gray secured for his department a good allocation of beds and also rooms in the medical school. The latter facilitated the installing of Dr W. Freudenthal from Jadassohn's clinic at Breslau in the early Nazi period, and the eventual establishment of a readership in cutaneous histology. From 1920 to 1934 Gray was also in charge of the skin department of the Hospital for Sick Children, Great Ormond Street. There he made important observations on the rare disease *sclerema neonatorum*, which he reported in 1926 to the American Dermatological Association. His work in paediatric dermatology was extended by his appointment by the London County Council as consulting dermatologist (1935-51) to Goldie Leigh Hospital.

From 1916 to 1929 Gray was editor of the *British Journal of Dermatology*. It was partly for the purpose of financially supporting and controlling this journal that he suggested the formation of the British Association of Dermatology which came into being in 1921. He was president in 1938-9 and its treasurer from 1940 to 1960 during which time he quintupled its funds. From these, on Gray's inspiration, the Association in 1957 contributed towards the new building for the Royal College of Physicians in Regent's Park on condition that a room be named after Robert Willan [q.v.], one of the founders of dermatology.

From 1935 Gray represented London University on the governing body of the Postgraduate Medical School at Hammersmith. With Sir Francis Fraser [q.v.] he planned the expansion of the school into a federation of specialist institutes which materialized in 1947 as the British Postgraduate Medical Federation. Gray was a member of its governing body until 1960. During the same period he was first chairman of the committee of management of the Institute of Dermatology which had taken over the affairs of the London School of Dermatology of which he was also chairman. In the urgent task of finding adequate in-patient accommodation he was helped by his experience in carrying out, with Dr Andrew Topping, the survey of London hospitals for the Ministry of Health, the report of which was published in 1945. It was not, however, until 1959, the year before Gray retired from the chairmanship, that the Institute was officially recognized as a member of the British Postgraduate Medical Federation.

In 1913 Gray was editor and one of the secretaries of the dermatological section of the 17th International Congress of Medicine in London. This may well have been the mainspring of his subsequent enthusiastic encouragement of international contacts. He was vice-president of the 8th International Congress of Dermatology at Copenhagen in 1930; and president of the 10th International Congress in London in 1952. His reputation abroad was shown by his election as honorary member of twelve foreign societies.

Gray contributed to sections on skin diseases for the official medical history of the war of 1914-18 and for *Nomenclature of Diseases*, Royal College of Physicians (1931), and he wrote the skin diseases section for eight editions of Price's *Textbook of the Practice of Medicine*. He was the first dermatologist to give the Harveian oration to the Royal College of Physicians (1951), his subject being the history of dermatology from the time of Harvey.

Gray was honorary secretary of the Royal Society of Medicine (1919-24), treasurer (1926-32), president (1940-2), and was president of its section of dermatology (1931-3). He served on the Goodenough committee on the organization of medical schools (1942-4) and in 1948-62 he was adviser in dermatology to the Ministry of Health. University College Hospital and medical school were naturally primary recipients of his services and influence. From 1926 to 1935 he was both dean of the medical school and chairman of the medical committee of the hospital. In 1948 he became chairman of the medical school council and a member of the board of governors of the hospital, holding the former post for four years and the latter for five. His work for the university of London as a whole was even more important: member of the senate (1929-50); dean of the faculty of medicine (1932-6); chairman of the professoriate committee (1941-50); member of the commission which visited Trinidad to investigate the practicability of starting a medical school there; member of the court (1947-58); member of the General Medical Council, representing the university (1950-2); chairman of the board of management of the London School of Hygiene and Tropical Medicine (1951-61); and vice-chairman of the council of the School of Pharmacy (1949-64). In 1958 the university conferred on him an honorary LLD. He was knighted in 1946 and appointed KCVO in 1959. In the following year he gave up his private practice.

Gray's physical appearance was unimpressive. He was small and drably dressed. His voice, however, was clear and strong, and his speaking and writing were lucid and cogent. Of his dermatological prowess he was unduly modest, but in administrative work he was more sure of his talents and he enjoyed holding the reins of government. He held his opinions so strongly that he was at times impatient with those who disagreed. But he was essentially friendly, of liberal outlook, and kind and helpful to younger men and women, especially those hampered by prejudices against race, sex, or religion. He had few avocations and lived simply, with a touch of disdain for aesthetic pleasures.

In 1917 Gray married Elsie, daughter of F. Bernard Cooper, solicitor, of Newcastle under Lyme. They had one daughter and a son, John Archibald Browne Gray, who became professor of physiology at University College, London, and later secretary of the Medical Research Council. Gray died in London 13 October 1967. There is a portrait by Rodrigo Moynihan in the Willan Room at the Royal College of Physicians, London.

[*The Times*, 14 October 1967; *British Journal of Dermatology*, December 1967, and Special Jubilee issue, 1970 (G. B. Dowling on 'The British Association of Dermatology, 1920-70'); Oscar Gans in *Hautarzt*, vol. xviii, 1967; Brian Russell, *St. John's Hospital for Diseases of the Skin, 1863-1963*, 1963; private information; personal knowledge.]

W. N. GOLDSMITH

GRAY, LOUIS HAROLD (1905-1965), physicist and radiobiologist, was born in London 10 November 1905, the only child of Harry Gray, a minor civil servant, of Barnes, London, and his wife, Amy Bowen. He was educated at Latimer School and then as a scholar at Christ's Hospital, whence in December 1923 he won an exhibition to Trinity College, Cambridge. Cambridge and Trinity profoundly influenced Gray. Thereafter he always wore the Trinity tie. More importantly, he had gone up as an enthusiast well grounded in the basics of physical sciences but unversed in biology or the humanities; Cambridge not only broadened his outlook but consolidated his dedication to science. Cambridge was a most exciting place for physics. The Cavendish Laboratory, headed by Sir Ernest (later Lord) Rutherford [q.v.], was most productive of reports and ideas by future Nobel prizemen. Gray became a disciple of the Cavendish method. He gained good firsts in the natural sciences tripos, parts i and ii (1926 and 1927), achieving a senior scholarship in the process. He was then honoured (1928) by admission to the Cavendish. His postgraduate work there on the interaction of radiation with matter led to his Ph.D. and a prize fellowship at Trinity in 1930.

Meanwhile Gray (known as Hal) had

become engaged to, and in 1932 married, the first blind girl to be admitted to Cambridge University, Frieda Marjorie, daughter of William John Picot, procureur du roi of Alderney in the Channel Islands. She read English and theology at Girton and subsequently Newnham Colleges, studying from braille books and with the help of readers, among them Gray who was thus introduced to English literature as a relaxation and became dedicated to the New Testament way of life. Himself always sincere and never bigoted, he was at times naïve and unworldly. There were two sons of the marriage.

Feeling perhaps that there was more to life than nuclear physics Gray was attracted by an invitation in 1933 to establish a physics laboratory to measure radiation in the treatment of cancer at Mount Vernon Hospital, Middlesex, recently converted from a tuberculosis sanatorium. There he went in 1934 as senior physicist and Prophit scholar of the Royal College of Surgeons. Those were challenging days, for treatment by X-rays and the γ-rays of radium was in transition from an empirical art to scientific measurement. St. Bartholomew's and the Middlesex (teaching) hospitals had professorial departments of medical physics (F. L. Hopwood and Sidney Russ) and the Cancer Hospital, Fulham Road, had W. V. Mayneord developing methods of dosimetry. Gray, fired by the opportunities offered by the director, Sir Cuthbert Wallace [q.v.], and the pathologist, J. C. Mottram, accepted the post, even at a financial loss, provided he was able to spend most of his time on research. In his fellowship thesis Gray had formulated a theory—now known as the Bragg-Gray principle (see also Sir W. H. Bragg, q.v.)—for deducing the energy absorbed by a material exposed to gamma rays from the ionization within a small gas-filled cavity in the material. At Mount Vernon he was to apply his theory to X-rays and, later, in suitably adapted form to the new radiation, neutrons.

So began a new commitment: the improvement of survival of sufferers from cancer. A new science, biology, had to be learnt from the ground-roots and appropriately Mottram introduced Gray to the broad bean, the root growth of which could be measured reliably, cheaply, and statistically to reveal the dynamics of growth and give relations of dose (radiation) versus effect. The biological effects of the new neutron radiation had to be compared with those of the well known α, β, and γ radiations from radium and with X-rays. Gray, now supported by John Read, planned and built, with support from the British Empire Cancer Campaign, a 400 kV neutron generator. This inexpensive but efficient machine yielded the first quantitative results demonstrating the increased biological effectiveness for cellular damage, of neutrons compared with X-rays. In this work Gray and Read expressed their neutron 'dose' values in 'energy units'—foreshadowing the adoption by the International Commission on Radiological Units some fifteen years later (1953) of the unit 'rad' for measuring all types of ionizing radiation. Today, the Commission through the International System of Units has the physical unit of dose redefined as the Gray (= 100 rad)—Resolution 9 of the 15th Conférence Générale Poids et Mesures, 1975.

Gray, a conscientious objector, remained throughout the war of 1939-45 at Mount Vernon. After the war, in 1946, he was recruited by the secretary of the Medical Research Council, Sir Edward Mellanby [q.v.], to head the laboratory side of the radiotherapeutic unit (in the Hammersmith Hospital), which had been expanded to encompass the advances made possible by nuclear fission. Gray collected about him a team which in five years made dramatic discoveries in the basic science of radiobiology; but differences of opinion on the strategy of the research between him and his medical director (and the Medical Research Council) led to his resignation in 1953. To Gray, who was emotionally wholly committed to the relief of cancer by radiotherapy and, now from his own theoretical deductions and limited observations, to fuller investigation of the role of oxygen in radiobiological effect, this was a grievous time. However, within a few months the British Empire Cancer Campaign established for Gray, as director, their own research unit in radiobiology at Mount Vernon Hospital. Time had been lost, but Gray, as able as a theoretician as with his hands, competent administratively and universally respected, reorganized his life and work. In due course he collected around him many of his former colleagues and a succession of new ones to found a school of international repute. Unhappily for science, within ten years he suffered a severe stroke which left him physically handicapped. Gray, undismayed, returned to work, but perhaps did too much, for within two years he had a second stroke and died at Mount Vernon Hospital, 9 July 1965. His ashes were taken to the family vault in Alderney, an island where he was proud to have roots and to which he returned each year. One of his favourite methods of relaxation was to lie on his back in the water and look up at the colours of the cliffs in Telegraph Bay, which he thought the most beautiful place in the world.

Many awards and honours were conferred on Gray. He was elected a fellow of the Royal Society in 1961 and made an honorary D.Sc.

of Leeds University in 1962 and an honorary member of the American Radium Society. He received the Barclay medal of the British Institute of Radiology in 1960, and the Bertner award in 1964. In 1953 he was Silvanus Thompson memorial lecturer at the British Institute of Radiology. He is commemorated by periodic L. H. Gray memorial conferences. Nothing could be more apt, for Gray above all loved people and scientific discussion. His enthusiasm was as infectious as his laughter, and his contacts were world-wide. In the two decades between 1945 and 1965 he was a member of numerous national and international committees, and president of the International Congress of Radiation Research, 1962. Perhaps he was even more at home in learned societies, great and small—the Royal Society, the British Institute of Radiology (of which he was president in 1950), the Hospital Physicists Association (of which he was chairman, 1946-7), and the multidisciplinary Association for Radiation Research, of which he was the founder and first chairman (1959-60).

[J. F. Loutit and O. C. A. Scott in *Biographical Memoirs of Fellows of the Royal Society*, vol. xii, 1966; *British Journal of Radiology*, vol. xxxviii, 1965, 706-7; *International Journal of Radiation Biology*, vol. ix, 1965, 509-11; private information; personal knowledge.]   J. F. LOUTIT

GREEN, GUSTAVUS (1865-1964), aero-engine designer, was born in Hounslow, Middlesex, 11 March 1865. He subsequently took the surname of his stepfather Samuel Green. At the age of about sixteen he moved to Hastings where he was in turn a jeweller and hairdresser; in 1897 he moved to Bexhill-on-Sea where he established a cycle business. He became interested in the internal combustion engine, taking out his first patent in 1900, but it was not until 1904 and 1905 that he patented the method of cylinder construction which was to form the basis of his subsequent designs. The Green Motor Patents Syndicate was formed to exploit his patents, his principal partners being Henry Francis Pelham-Clinton-Hope (later eighth Duke of Newcastle) and Joseph Miller, dental surgeon. The Syndicate became a private limited liability company in 1906. It manufactured small stationary engines and motor cycles until the war of 1914-18, but in 1906 produced two cars, one of which was exhibited in March at Cordingley's automobile exhibition at the Royal Agricultural Hall, London. Colonel J. E. Capper, superintendent of the Balloon Factory at Farnborough, was attracted by the lightweight construction of the engine and invited Green to design an 80-hp

airship engine. This water-cooled V.8 engine was the first of Green's engines to use a single overhead camshaft (patented in 1908) which, with his patented cylinder construction, was to be a characteristic feature of all his subsequent aero- and marine engines. Intended for the *Nulli Secundus*, it was not used until 1910 in the airship *Gamma*.

A 35-hp 4-cylinder engine appeared in 1908 followed by a 60-hp version the following year. The latter engine, in an aeroplane built by Oswald Short [q.v.] and his brothers, enabled J. T. C. Moore-Brabazon (later Lord Brabazon of Tara, q.v.) to win in 1909 the *Daily Mail* £1,000 prize for the first circular flight of one mile by a British pilot in an all-British aeroplane. For the five years prior to World War I Green engines were the most successful British aero-engines, powering seven Michelin Trophy winners. In 1910 Patrick Y. Alexander sponsored a competition to encourage the design and construction of British aero-engines. Although the 35-hp Green engine was the only one to complete the tests, it produced slightly less power than required and so no prize was awarded. The following year the competition was opened to foreign engines and a 60-hp Green engine gained the first prize of £1,000. In 1913 the Sopwith Bat-boat powered by a 100-hp 6-cylinder Green engine won the £500 Mortimer Singer prize for sea-planes and in 1914 a 120-hp 6-cylinder Green engine won the £5,000 prize offered by the War Office in the Naval and Military Aeroplane Engine Competition.

Marine versions of all these engines were produced and in 1912 Fred May, an exponent of racing motor boats, acquired the assets of the Syndicate to form the Green Engine Company Ltd., with Gustavus Green as technical director and a minority shareholder. The company acquired new premises at Edwin Road, Twickenham, in 1914. During the war Green was asked to build engines for Thornycroft Coastal Motor Boats for which Thornycroft were unable to provide sufficient engines. 12-cylinder 300-hp and 18-cylinder 450-hp engines were produced, culminating in a 24-cylinder 1,000-hp engine in 1920 of which only a prototype was produced. After the war the company continued to produce marine versions of its pre-war aero-engines until the company was wound up in 1930.

Green was a gifted mechanic rather than a trained engineer. Although in 1908 his patented features allowed the construction of light and powerful engines for that period, he made little subsequent technical progress. The engines produced in the 1920s were virtually identical to those produced in 1908 and he had been left behind by the scientific and technical advances in engine design which had taken place during the war. Green had little interest in production engineering or sustained development programmes and the company for the most part only built prototype engines. The production of the smaller engines was carried out by the Aster Engineering Company of Wembley and the large wartime marine engines by Peter Brotherhood Ltd., of Peterborough.

In 1893 Green married Beatrice, daughter of James Easton, a carpenter, and they had one son and three daughters. He retired in 1925 and devoted the rest of his life to the hobby of clockmaking. In 1958 it was brought to the attention of the Royal Aeronautical Society that Green was still alive and on 15 January 1959 he was made an honorary companion of the Society in recognition of his contribution to early British aviation. He still retained the alert, distinguished appearance which had characterized him throughout his life. He died at the age of ninety-nine 29 December 1964 at his house in Twickenham.

[*Autocar*, 3 March 1906, pp. 396-7; *Engineering*, 1910-20; *Flight*, 1909-22; (*The Motor Ship and*) *Motor Boat*, 1914-23; *Aeroplane*, 18 April 1917, pp. 971-2; H. F. Cowley, *Gustavus Green*, (privately circulated), 1958; British patent specifications; Public Record Office files BT31/11579/89387; BT31/20790/123108; BT31/14161/130990; private information.]   P. R. MANN

GREGORY, FREDERICK GUGENHEIM (1893-1961), plant physiologist, was born Fritz Gugenheim 22 December 1893 at 236 Tufnell Park Road, London N19, the third son and fourth of the eight children of Carl Gugenheim, a manufacturing jeweller, who was a Jewish expatriate from Germany, and his wife, Laura Maison, the daughter of a haberdasher. They spoke German at home and Fritz first learnt English at a kindergarten. He was educated at Owen's School, Islington, where his record was outstanding and where he was well known for his insatiable curiosity and wide range of interests. The influence of a remarkable science teacher concentrated his mind on science and in 1911 he won the school prize for that subject. In 1912 he went to Imperial College, where he was to spend the rest of his career. His intention was to read chemistry, but he became so excited by (Sir) J. B. Farmer's [q.v.] lectures on botany that he changed his mind and graduated ARCS in 1914 and B.Sc. (London) in 1915, both with first class honours in botany, and was awarded the Forbes memorial medal and prize. He was awarded the DIC in 1917, the M.Sc. in 1920, and the D.Sc. in 1921.

Having been exempted on medical grounds from military service in the war of 1914-18, following his graduation and with a Board of Agriculture scholarship, Gregory joined the Research Institute of Plant Physiology set up by V. H. Blackman [q.v.] in 1913 with its headquarters at Imperial College. He began work at the Cheshunt Experimental Station on the physiology of greenhouse crops. While there he was the victim of the antipathy, not uncommon at this time, for people with German names, and suffered some personal abuse and the loss of important experimental records. This experience led him to change his name by deed poll in 1916. Gregory spent three years at Cheshunt and then returned to Imperial College on appointment to a graded post in the Research Institute.

In his experiments on the growth of cucumbers at Cheshunt he was struck by the profound differences in growth pattern between plants grown at constant temperatures at different times of year. Aware of Blackman's ideas about expressing growth history in mathematical terms, Gregory suggested that photosynthetic efficiency could be expressed by a quantity he termed the 'net assimilation rate', calculated by dividing the plant's dry weight by its leaf area and the number of hours of light. Some of his assumptions were challenged by G. E. Briggs, the Cambridge physiologist, and a lively controversy ensued. In the event this led to the primary concepts of this quantitative type of growth analysis being defined and much productive work followed in many parts of the world. His contribution to this topic brought Gregory into prominence as quite a young man.

After his return to London he spent a short while measuring effects of small electric currents on plant growth as part of Blackman's investigations. However, Gregory's real interest remained in the analysis of plant growth and he soon returned to this field of enquiry. In 1919 he began a long series of studies on the growth of the barley crop. He set himself the task of defining equations to fit growth data, using correlation and regression methods, and with great ingenuity drew clear inferences about the effects of some climatic factors on growth. There were youthful errors in this work which he later freely admitted. Nevertheless the investigations were of a pioneering type and remained the only serious work of its kind for many years. It was undoubtedly the most influential work of Gregory's career, and determined the development of this aspect of physiology.

Facilities for the necessary fieldwork were supplied by Rothamsted Experimental Station where Gregory came into contact with (Sir) R. A. Fisher [q.v.]. For his next experiments (aided by research students), which dealt with the effects of the major plant nutrients in controlling growth, he enthusiastically adopted Fisher's recently introduced factorial techniques. When summing up ten years of work in a paper (published in 1937) on the effects of these nutrients, he characteristically attempted broad generalizations. He linked together the several aspects of metabolism into a scheme of chemical reactions which attracted great attention. This paper was the forerunner of others based on greatly increased factual knowledge.

In 1926 F. J. Richards [q.v.] joined the staff of the Research Institute and there began a collaboration which lasted for thirty-two years. Starting with a study of the effects of the major nutrients on assimilation and respiration in barley, the scope of the investigations gradually extended to become mainly the responsibility of Richards.

In 1928, at the invitation of the director of agriculture, Gregory visited the Sudan to advise on cotton-growing by irrigation. He quickly set up factorial experiments which were so successful that his report became the basis for guiding the further development of crop agronomy in the Sudan and contributed directly to its prosperity. He became a member of the advisory committee of the Empire Cotton Growing Corporation and of the London committee on agricultural work in the Sudan.

In 1929, when Blackman became head of the biological laboratories at Imperial College, Gregory was given the title of assistant professor of plant physiology and assistant director of the Research Institute. He now gave lectures on plant physiology for the first time. In the succeeding decade he diversified his interests in keeping with his new responsibilities. The laboratories became known for publications concerned with vernalization and photoperiodism—in which Gregory played a major role—and on transpiration, stomatal behaviour, and carbohydrate metabolism, which benefited from his stimulating support and encouragement. He was always in demand for advice both at the college and at the several research stations where staff of the Research Institute were located. On Blackman's retirement in 1937 Gregory became professor of plant physiology and in 1947 director of the Research Institute.

The war of 1939-45 disrupted the work at Imperial College and the staff were dispersed to stations outside London. Gregory remained at his Hampstead home and travelled as necessary to see his staff. After the war his energies were directed to re-equipping the London laboratories, where he again initiated teaching and research. Gregory was elected a fellow of the Royal Society in 1940 and served on the council from 1949 to 1951. He was awarded the Royal medal in 1957. He served on the governing body of the Glasshouse Crops Research Station. He was elected a foreign associate member of the United States National Academy of Science in 1956—only the second botanist to be so honoured. Many Commonwealth students came to benefit from his teaching and the Indian Society of Plant Physiologists elected him to membership.

Gregory was a cultured and sensitive man of many moods. He was excitable, talkative, argumentative, and something of a rebel. At the same time he was a philosopher with a compassionate nature and well known for many kindnesses. His mind always seethed with ideas derived from a fertile imagination and great erudition acquired by avid reading since childhood. He entered passionately into all his activities and his strongly expressed opinions and speculations evoked in others responses ranging from awe and respect to outright hostility. His vivid personality provided inspiration to all with whom he came in contact and attracted to his laboratory numerous overseas visitors. His astonishing catalytic power may perhaps prove to have been his greatest contribution to the progress of plant physiology.

Gregory had a deep appreciation of the arts and music was an essential part of his life. He turned for relaxation and solace to playing the piano and to musical composition. He remained a bachelor and the focus of his life for more than forty years was Imperial College. He acknowledged his debt for the opportunities he had had by the gift to the college of his Royal medal and his collection of books and by a legacy which created the Frederick Gregory Fund for the benefit of the Botany Department.

Gregory's health began to deteriorate some years before he retired and he found it increasingly difficult to fulfil his duties. He therefore retired as soon as he reached his sixty-fifth birthday. His retirement was marred by increasing ill health and by loneliness due to the loss of his youngest sister and of his housekeeper who had been his nanny in early childhood, to both of whom he was devoted. He died in Hampstead Hospital 27 November 1961. There is a posthumous portrait of Gregory in oils, by Edgar Kohler, at the Imperial College of Science and Technology, South Kensington, London.

[Archives of Imperial College; Helen K. Porter and F. J. Richards in *Biographical Memoirs of the Fellows of the Royal Society*, vol. ix, 1963; private information; personal knowledge.] H. K. PORTER

GRIFFITH, ALAN ARNOLD (1893-1963), aero-engineer, was born 13 June 1893 in London, the eldest of the three children of

George Chetwynd Griffith, a widely travelled explorer, journalist, and author, who lived for a time in South Africa as a special correspondent of the *Daily Mail*, and in the 1890s took his family to live in Douglas, Isle of Man, where he died in 1900. A. A. Griffith's mother was Elizabeth Brierly.

Griffith's early education was somewhat unsettled, but in 1906 he went to the Douglas Secondary School whence in 1911, with a Sir W. H. Tate science scholarship, he entered the Mechanical Engineering School at the university of Liverpool. In 1914 he graduated B.Eng. with first class honours in mechanical engineering and won the Rathbone medal and the University scholarship in engineering, which enabled him to do research for a year on the surface resistance to heat flow between metal and gases. He gained his M.Eng. in 1917 and D.Eng. in 1921, both at Liverpool, for work done after he joined the Royal Aircraft Factory (later the Royal Aircraft Establishment), Farnborough, in July 1915.

Griffith was a gifted applied mathematician with an intuitive grasp of the laws of nature which made him equally at home in the theories of materials, structures, aerodynamics, and heat engines, to all of which he made notable contributions. Probably the best known of these is the work, in which (Sir) G. I. Taylor collaborated, described in the paper read in December 1917 before the Institution of Mechanical Engineers, called 'The use of soap film in solving torsion problems'. It can be shown that if a soap film is stretched across a hole cut to the shape of the cross-section of a uniform bar, and if the film is distended by inducing a pressure difference between the two sides of the film, then the contours of the bubble are related to the stress distribution in the bar when it is twisted. This and subsequent work in the same field, which had valuable practical applications, earned him the nickname of 'Soap-bubble Griffith'.

In 1920 Griffith published his outstanding paper, 'Theory of Rupture' (*Phil. Trans. A.*, 1920), on the behaviour of materials, resolving the discrepancies between ideal and observed strength by postulating that materials contained cracks or other flaws which induced local concentrations of stress. This was a new conception on which all subsequent theories of fracture strength rely. It led Griffith to show experimentally that very high strengths can be obtained from fine-drawn filaments.

Contemporaneously with this fundamental work, Griffith was investigating propeller problems and this led him to the study of turbine blading. He realized that the blades of existing turbines, designed as the walls of passages, were working inefficiently and that big improvements in efficiency could be obtained by treating the blades as aerofoils. His classic Royal Aircraft Establishment report on the subject is called 'An aerodynamic theory of turbine design' (July 1926). In it he demonstrated that the gas turbine was a feasible aircraft engine. He conceived it as the combination of an axial flow compressor, an axial flow turbine, and a propeller. He did not, however, associate the gas turbine with jet propulsion, as did (Sir) Frank Whittle's momentous invention of 1929. What Griffith did, after a lapse of time, which is difficult to explain, was to develop in the 1930s by a series of experiments the high efficiency axial compressor. A. A. Rubbra has therefore described him as 'the true originator of the multi-stage axial engine'.

Griffith was away from Farnborough from 1928 to 1931, as principal scientific officer in charge of the Air Ministry Laboratory at South Kensington. He moved back to become head of the Engine Department where, *inter alia*, he conducted the axial compressor experiments with his talented assistant Hayne Constant [q.v.]. The pioneering work he did came to the notice of E. W. (later Lord) Hives [q.v.], then general manager of Rolls-Royce, and as a result, in 1939 Griffith became research engineer at Derby, directly responsible to Hives for aero-engine research. He remained with Rolls-Royce for the rest of his working life.

In the early 1940s he brought to fruition a design he had been working on for some years, the 'contra-flow' engine in which each wheel of the multi-stage design had turbine and compressor blading. This design, delightful in conception, had serious practical defects and represents one of Griffith's rare failures. After it was dropped he concentrated on more conventional axial flow designs and played a valuable part in the basic designs of the successful Avon jet engine, and the Conway by-pass jet engine.

More and more Griffith became interested in the vertical take-off and landing of aircraft and produced highly imaginative military and civil designs in which his comprehensive knowledge of aerodynamics and of thermodynamics were effectively combined. His ideas found their first practical expression in a test-rig which became famous as the 'flying bedstead'. This was essentially a framework carrying two Rolls-Royce Nene engines which not only gave direct lift for hovering but provided air from their compressors to the jets used for control.

The first free flight of this device took place on 3 August 1954, when it rose about 10 feet and was controlled successfully. It 'flew' for $8\frac{1}{2}$ minutes, and many other trouble-free flights followed. These led to the design by Short & Harland of the SC.I aircraft in which four

Rolls-Royce RB 108 engines, designed specifically for jet lift, provided vertical take-off and one RB 108 was used for propulsion. This aircraft first flew in March 1957 and achieved complete transition from jet-borne to wing-borne flight in April 1960.

It was in June of that year that Griffith retired, though so far as his developing ill-health allowed, he continued as a consultant to Rolls-Royce.

Griffith was a tall, slim man of somewhat serious demeanour, but, on closer acquaintance, engaging and amusing. He had little taste for publicity, as evidenced by the fact that he seems, though the author of numerous papers, to have published nothing after 1928. The brilliance of his work was nevertheless widely appreciated, and he became a fellow of the Royal Society in 1941, CBE in 1948, and silver medallist of the Royal Aeronautical Society in 1955.

In November 1925 he married Constance Vera, the daughter of R. T. Falkner, of the Army Catering Corps. They had one son and two daughters.

He died in hospital at Farnborough 13 October 1963.

[A. A. Rubbra in *Biographical Memoirs of Fellows of the Royal Society*, vol. x, 1964; F. W. Armstrong, 'The Aero Engine and its Progress—fifty years after Griffith', commemorative lecture at the Royal Aeronautical Society, 18 November 1976, published in the *Aeronautical Journal*, December 1976; personal knowledge.]   KINGS NORTON

GRIFFITHS, EZER (1888-1962), physicist, was born 28 November 1888, at Aberdare in Glamorgan, the eldest of the six sons of Abraham Lincoln Griffiths, a colliery mechanic, and his wife, Ann Howells. In addition to their six sons, the Griffiths also had three daughters. The high academic ability in the family is evidenced by the fact that two of Ezer's brothers attained good academic positions and published books.

Ezer Griffiths was educated at the Aberdare Intermediate School and University College, Cardiff, where he studied physics; he obtained first class honours and was awarded the Isaac Roberts research scholarship and a fellowship of the university of Wales. He later proceeded to the degree of D.Sc. in that university. At the age of twenty-three he presented a paper on magnetism to the Institution of Electrical Engineers. After researching at Cardiff until 1915, he joined the heat section of the National Physical Laboratory (NPL), Teddington, where he remained until his retirement in 1953.

Griffiths's life interest was the theory of heat and he worked at Cardiff with the principal E. H. Griffiths (who was no relation of his and whose notice he wrote for this Dictionary) on the specific heats of a number of metals at low temperature to test the theories put forward by Einstein, F. A. Lindemann (later Viscount Cherwell, q.v.), and others. This work formed the substance of papers in the *Transactions of the Royal Society* in 1913 and 1914.

At the National Physical Laboratory, Griffiths became one of the leading world authorities on the subject of heat insulation, heat transfer, evaporation, and related matters. Many of his hundred or so published papers give accounts of work done in collaboration with other members of staff, but he was generally the senior author. He published three books, *Methods of Measuring Temperature* (1918), *Pyrometers* (1926), and *Refrigeration, Principles and Practice* (1951). He was also responsible for articles in Sir R. T. Glazebrook's [q.v.] *Dictionary of Applied Physics* and in Sir T. E. Thorpe's [q.v.] *Dictionary of Applied Chemistry*.

Griffiths's most important work was associated with refrigeration and he became one of the world's leading authorities on the subject. In 1923 he was one of a team sent to Australia to examine the problems of the transportation of apples to England. In 1930 he went to New Zealand to study matters related to the refrigerated transport of lambs.

At the other end of the temperature scale, Griffiths measured the specific heats and heat conductivities of iron and its alloys, the subject of many of his published papers. In 1935 he and R. W. Powell were jointly awarded the Moulton medal of the Institution of Chemical Engineers for their studies on the evaporation of water from surfaces.

Immediately before and during the war of 1939-45, Griffiths worked on such problems as the vapour trails made by modern aircraft and on the cooling of armoured fighting vehicles for crew comfort.

Shortly before his retirement, Griffiths was invited by the Medical Research Council and the Admiralty to help in the study of the influence of extremes of conditions of temperature on human beings. The experiments he conducted provided much useful information on the effects of radiation on man.

Griffiths was secretary and later vice-president of the Physical Society; recorder of Section A of the British Association; president of the Institute of Refrigeration (then known as the British Association of Refrigeration) from 1936 to 1938 and later chairman of the Institute's Research Committee; president of the Institute of Engineers-in-Charge; president of the Institut International du Froid from 1951 to 1959 and subsequently honorary president;

and chairman of the governing body of Twick-enham Technical College. He also served on many of the committees of the Department of Scientific and Industrial Research and the British Standards Institution.

When Griffiths was elected a fellow of the Royal Society in 1926 he was the youngest ever to have been so honoured; in 1950 he was appointed OBE.

Griffiths was a kindly and popular man with a somewhat high-pitched voice in which he was wont to regale the company with his apparently unending fund of humorous anecdotes. He was a regular attender at overseas meetings of the Institut International du Froid and he was a most interesting travelling companion. Griffiths never married, but lived with one of his sisters at Teddington until his death 14 February 1962.

[C. G. Darwin in *Biographical Memoirs of Fellows of the Royal Society*, vol. viii, 1962; personal knowledge.]   D. T. LEE

GRIGG, SIR (PERCY) JAMES (1890-1964), public servant, was born in Exmouth 16 December 1890, the eldest of the three sons of Frank Alfred Grigg, a carpenter. His mother's maiden name was Crocker; she was the daughter of a tailor and had been a children's nurse. Shortly after their son was born, the Griggs moved to Bournemouth, and 'P. J.', as he subsequently became widely known in Whitehall, was educated at an elementary school from which he gained a scholarship to Bournemouth (Secondary) School, and, in 1909, entered St. John's College, Cambridge, as a senior scholar. He graduated with first class honours in both parts i (1910) and ii (1912) of the mathematical tripos, and, in 1913, was placed first in the examination for entrance to the administrative class of the Civil Service, and appointed to the Treasury.

In June 1915 Grigg was permitted to apply for a commission in the army, but was rejected on account of short sight; a few months later he tried again, and this time was accepted. He joined the RGA as a second lieutenant, and served in Eastern Europe until 1918 when he was transferred to the Office of External Ballistics where he worked until the war ended. One of his colleagues there was Gertrude Charlotte, daughter of the Revd George Frederick Hough, and a niece of the bishop suffragan of Woolwich. They married in July 1919 after Grigg had returned to the Treasury. The marriage was childless.

Sir N. F. Fisher [q.v.], permanent secretary to the Treasury, speedily recognized Grigg's ability, and in 1921, when Sir Robert Horne (later Viscount Horne of Slamannan, q.v.) became chancellor of the Exchequer,

Fisher persuaded him to appoint Grigg as his principal private secretary. 'P. J.' remained in this post for almost ten years, in which time he served five chancellors including Stanley Baldwin (later Earl Baldwin of Bewdley), A. Neville Chamberlain, Philip (later Viscount) Snowden, and (Sir) Winston Churchill [qq.v.] with whom Grigg worked for nearly five years from 1924 to 1929.

The decade between 1921 and 1930 was a period of momentous developments in the economic and financial policies of the Governments led by Lloyd George, Bonar Law, Stanley Baldwin, and Ramsay MacDonald, and Grigg saw many changes of direction and gained invaluable experience as an administrator. He accompanied Baldwin and Montagu (later Lord) Norman [q.v.], governor of the Bank of England, to Washington for the negotiations leading in 1923 to the settlement of British war debts to the United States; he was working with Churchill when in 1925 it was decided that the pound sterling should return to the gold standard at its pre-war parity. He saw the development of the crisis in the coal industry and the general strike of 1926, and supported the chancellor of the Exchequer in dealing with some of the financial problems that faced the Labour Government in 1930 and 1931 leading to Snowden's decision to abandon the gold standard and to the formation of the 'national' Government.

Snowden was still chancellor when Grigg ceased to be his principal private secretary, and became chairman of the Board of Customs and Excise. After a month he was transferred as chairman of the Board of Inland Revenue. Grigg himself wrote that 'it was known that the Inland Revenue would have to produce a scheme for taxing Land Values against the Budget of 1931, and the Chancellor wanted to have somebody at the head of it whom he knew and who knew him and how his mind worked'.

His uneventful tenure of this post did not last long. At the end of 1933 Sir Samuel Hoare (later Viscount Templewood, q.v.) asked him to go to India to succeed Sir George Schuster as finance member of the viceroy's executive council. For the next five years Grigg applied his mind, with its respect for order and efficiency, to the intractable problems of the subcontinent in which the Government of India Act of 1935 extended quasi-self-government to the provinces and the Congress Party grew steadily in power. He sought to improve communications and create better conditions in the rural areas, but his efforts were unpopular with Congress, and all his five budgets were rejected in the Assembly and had to be enacted by the viceroy's certificate.

When he returned to London in 1939 Grigg

expected to succeed Sir Warren Fisher as permanent secretary to the Treasury, but he was disappointed and was offered instead the Colonial Office or the War Office. He chose the War Office. Grigg wrote that, at the outbreak of war in 1939, the impression of the War Office left on his mind was 'one of considerable confusion'. He set out at once to improve this situation. In 1940 he became chairman of the standing committee on army administration set up to increase efficiency in organization and to simplify procedure, and when, in November 1941, Sir Alan Brooke (later Viscount Alanbrooke, q.v.) became chief of the imperial general staff, the two worked closely together in the necessary reorganization of the army. Their co-operation became even more effective when, in February 1942, Churchill took the unusual step of appointing Grigg to be secretary of state for war when he dismissed H. D. R. (later Viscount) Margesson [q.v.], following the fall of Singapore. Brooke confided to his diary, 'Thus started a long association with P. J. Grigg for which I thank heaven. I received nothing but assistance and support during the whole of our time together and could not have asked for anyone better to work with. One of the quickest and ablest brains I have ever met. A slightly suspicious nature at times until one had gained his confidence. A heart of gold!'

For three years, from the military and naval disasters of 1942 to the victories of 1945, Brooke and Grigg collaborated in the arduous task of creating the British military organization and the efficient, well-trained armies that fought successfully in North Africa and Europe until Hitler was defeated. Throughout this time Grigg was Nationalist MP for East Cardiff, and when the 1945 election brought about the downfall of Churchill's Government, Grigg lost his seat and ceased to be secretary of state for war.

It was fortunate for the British war effort that Grigg and Brooke, two men who were never afraid to speak their minds with brutal frankness, should have had complete confidence in each other's ability and absolute trust in each other's integrity. From his early years as a principal private secretary Grigg with his passion for efficiency had often been regarded as intolerant and arrogant. John C. C. (later Viscount) Davidson [q.v.], parliamentary private secretary to Baldwin when he was president of the Board of Trade, was critical of Grigg as a colleague. 'P. J. wasn't a really attractive person', he said, 'because he lacked human sympathy and was intolerant.' Years later, Herbert Morrison (Lord Morrison of Lambeth, q.v.) described Grigg in unflattering terms: 'Grigg had a considerable flair for frank speech,

aggravated by a hot temper. I recall a day at No. 10 when we were all waiting to enter the Cabinet Room. I was chatting to Sir James and we began mildly to disagree. In a matter of a moment or two he was denouncing me and being extremely rude. I mildly enquired who was having a row with whom.' Sir John Anderson (later Viscount Waverley, q.v.), another civil servant turned minister, who was present on this occasion, said 'It's all right, Herbert. You need not be upset. It's just James's way of talking. He can't help it.'

Grigg undoubtedly prized competence and precision above tact and diplomacy, but he was able to win the confidence of statesmen as widely different in outlook as Philip Snowden and Winston Churchill. The former described him as a civil servant of 'exceptional merit', and the latter, while he was chancellor of the Exchequer, expressed the greatest admiration for his gifts and character. R. M. Barrington-Ward [q.v.], editor of *The Times*, referred in his diary to a dinner with the permanent secretary at the War Office in which they talked together about Churchill. 'Much talk of Winston', he wrote, 'whom he knows better than most people both in his strong and his weak points', and added, 'He has a fine intelligence and courage. I have a great regard for him and respect for his common sense' (Donald MacLachlan, *In the Chair, Barrington-Ward of The Times*, 1971).

The fact that Churchill selected Grigg to be secretary of state for war in a time of grave crisis shows clearly enough that the prime minister had no doubts about his capacity as an administrator.

After his defeat in the general election of 1945 Grigg found himself at the age of fifty-four without employment. In 1946, however, he became the first British executive director of the International Bank for Reconstruction and Development, and, in 1947, he was appointed financial adviser and then director of the Imperial Tobacco Company. He also held directorships of the Prudential Assurance Company and the National Provincial Bank.

In 1948 he published his autobiography, *Prejudice and Judgment*. He was appointed chairman of the Bass, Ratcliff & Gretton Company in 1959, and on its merger with Mitchells & Butlers, Birmingham, in 1961, became chairman of the new group.

In 1954, in consequence of the recommendations of a committee on departmental records of which Grigg was chairman, responsibility for the Public Record Office was transferred from the master of the Rolls to the lord chancellor. Grigg was chairman of an advisory committee on recruitment to the forces which, in 1958, recommended improved pensions and allowances for the armed forces.

Grigg was appointed KCB in 1932 and KCSI in 1936; he was sworn of the Privy Council in 1942, became an honorary fellow of St. John's College, Cambridge, in 1943, honorary LLD of Bristol University in 1946, and honorary bencher of the Middle Temple in 1954. He died in a London hospital 5 May 1964.

[*The Times*, 7 May 1964; P. J. Grigg, *Prejudice and Judgment*, 1948; Arthur Bryant, *The Turn of the Tide, 1939–43*, 1957; Herbert Morrison, *An Autobiography*, 1960; Philip, Viscount Snowden, *An Autobiography*, 2 vols., 1934; H. Montgomery Hyde, *Baldwin. The Unexpected Prime Minister*, 1973.]   H. F. OXBURY

GUGGENHEIM, EDWARD ARMAND (1901–1970), authority on thermodynamics, was born in Manchester 11 August 1901, the elder son of the family of three children of Armand Guggenheim, a senior partner in E. Spinner & Co., importers of cotton and exporters of cotton cloth, and his wife, Marguerite Bertha Simon. Originally of Swiss nationality, his father became a naturalized British subject in 1906 and was the Swiss consul in Manchester from 1917 to 1923. Edward was educated at Terra Nova School, Birkdale, Southport, and, from the age of fourteen, and with a junior scholarship, at Charterhouse. In 1917 he gained a senior scholarship and was head of house in his last year, when he won another scholarship, to Gonville and Caius College, Cambridge. After obtaining a first class both in the mathematical tripos, part i (1921), and in chemistry in the natural sciences tripos, part ii (1923), he spent the next two years doing research under the supervision of (Professor Sir) Ralph H. Fowler [q.v.], who inspired Guggenheim's lifelong interest in statistical mechanics. Despite his excellent academic record, however, he failed in his application for a fellowship at Gonville and Caius; so great was his disappointment that it was only the persuasion of that eminent lawyer, A. D. (later Lord) McNair, which prevented him from giving up science and reading for the bar. Instead, he continued his scientific studies in Denmark, first with Professor J. N. Brønsted and then with Professor N. Bjerrum at the Royal Agricultural College in Copenhagen. He was greatly gratified by his election in 1951 as a foreign member of the Danish Academy of Sciences and the invitation to deliver the Bjerrum memorial lecture nine years later.

He returned to England in 1931 to accept the hospitality of Professor F. G. Donnan [q.v.] (himself a renowned thermodynamicist) at University College, London, and wrote his first book, *Modern Thermodynamics by the Methods of W. Gibbs* (1933). Its outstanding display of scholarship, elegant presentation, and maturity of thought established his reputation and revolutionized the teaching of the subject. Nevertheless, his search for a senior university post over the next few years was surprisingly unsuccessful. After a year as visiting professor of chemistry at Stanford University, California (1932–3), he was a temporary lecturer at Reading University (1933–5), an assistant lecturer at University College, London, and, following promotion to a full lectureship, a reader in the chemical engineering department at Imperial College. During this period he produced a series of important scientific papers which gained for him a Cambridge Sc.D.

At the outbreak of war in 1939, his services were quickly enlisted by the navy and later by the Montreal Laboratory of Atomic Energy (1944–6). His greatest satisfaction was associated with the neutralization of German magnetic mines which initially wrought such devastation of our supply ships. One mode of defence, the setting up of an applied magnetic field to simulate the magnetism of ships and thereby to actuate the trigger mechanism and destroy the mine, was in danger of being abandoned on the recommendation of Professor F. A. Lindemann (later Viscount Cherwell, q.v.), adviser to the first lord of the Admiralty, but calculations by Guggenheim clearly showed that the method would be successful, a conclusion unambiguously confirmed by experimental trials on the Canoe Lake, Portsmouth. The defeat of the magnetic mine was then ensured.

In 1946 Guggenheim returned to his prewar post at Imperial College and was elected a fellow of the Royal Society. In the same year there quickly followed an appointment at Reading University, as professor of chemistry and head of department, a post which he held until his retirement in 1966. During this period, he was chairman of the publications committee of the Faraday Society and in 1967 was elected an honorary life member, a distinction limited to ten persons, for his outstanding contributions to physical chemistry and to the Society. As a member of the commission on symbols and units of both the International Union of Pure and Applied Physics and the International Union of Pure and Applied Chemistry and of the symbols committee of the Royal Society, his personal contribution was widely praised. Nevertheless, of more than 100 scientific papers and 11 books, over half appeared during his professorship.

In 1934 he married Simone, the daughter of August Ganzin, of Toulon; this happy marriage ended twenty years later, in 1954, by her death in tragic circumstances. His second marriage, to Ruth Helen (known as Peggy) Clarke, widow of Major Charles Fleming Aitken, took place in 1955. There were no children of either marriage. Guggenheim was a man of great culture, being keenly interested in music, literature, and the theatre, and was a master of five languages, besides being an accomplished chess player. One of his greatest pleasures was his beautifully maintained garden of four acres in Caversham, containing a swimming pool and tennis court for his relaxation. Sadly, a severe illness during 1963–4, from which he only partially recovered, greatly restricted his activities until his death in Reading 9 August 1970.

[F. C. Tompkins and C. F. Goodeve in *Biographical Memoirs of Fellows of the Royal Society*, vol. xvii, 1971; *The Times*, 11 August 1970.]   F. C. TOMPKINS

GUINNESS, RUPERT EDWARD CECIL LEE, second EARL OF IVEAGH (1874–1967), philanthropist, was born in London 29 March 1874, the eldest of the three sons of Edward Cecil Guinness [q.v.], who was created Earl of Iveagh in 1919, and his wife, Adelaide Maria, daughter of Richard Samuel Guinness, MP, of Deepwell, county Dublin, a distant cousin of her husband. Rupert Guinness was born heir to great family wealth and also to the heavy responsibilities carried by his father who in 1868 became the sole proprietor of the St. James's Gate Guinness brewery in Dublin and in 1886, when Guinness became a public company, its first chairman. Rupert Guinness took on the chairmanship of the Guinness Company in 1927 when his father died, and held it for thirty-five years, during which the company developed under his guidance and grew into a multinational group with worldwide interests and activities. In 1962 he relinquished the chairmanship to his grandson (Arthur Francis) Benjamin Guinness.

Rupert Guinness was educated at a preparatory school, St. George's in Ascot, and then at Eton (1888–93). He was a slow reader and achieved no success at all in academic subjects, except in science where his passionate curiosity in practical scientific questions became evident, a quality which marked many of the activities of his long and full life. He was very powerfully built and was said to be 'one of the strongest boys who ever went to Eton'. Besides rowing in the Eton eight which won the Ladies plate at Henley (1893), he won the diamond sculls in 1895, and in 1896 by winning both the diamond sculls and the Wingfield sculls he became undisputed amateur champion. The two later successes were achieved

during a year he spent at Trinity College, Cambridge.

Water, however, continued to exercise its attraction. In 1903 he built a 90 ft. racing yawl, the *Leander*, with which he won the King's Cup at Cowes and the Vasco Da Gama Challenge Cup in Portugal. He was later asked by the Admiralty to raise the naval force that became the London division of the Royal Naval Volunteer Reserve, a task which he undertook during the nine years preceding the outbreak of World War I, at which time he took over command of the division.

In 1899 he became a director of Arthur Guinness, Son & Co. Ltd., but had little opportunity to become much involved with the company's affairs because of the outbreak of the Boer War, and in 1900 he was in South Africa working with the Irish hospital, donated to the war effort by his father, as aide to its commander, Sir William Thomson [q.v.]. He was appointed CMG in 1901 for his services in South Africa.

Returning to England, Rupert Guinness began to interest himself seriously in politics and, after becoming a member of the London County Council, was adopted in 1903 as Conservative candidate for the Haggerston division of Shoreditch, but there were five years of hard political work to come before he reached Westminster. In 1903 he married GWENDOLEN FLORENCE MARY ONSLOW (1881–1966), who was born 22 July 1881, the elder daughter of William Hillier Onslow, the fourth Earl of Onslow [q.v.] and his wife, Florence Coulston, daughter of the third Baron Gardner. Gwendolen Onslow had lived a rather sheltered life at Clandon Park in Surrey and for a large part of each year in France. She was a good linguist, with strong intellectual interests, and held pronounced political views, derived from her family background. She had a distinguished career herself in politics and her first experience of them, shared with her husband, was the seven years of political work in their East End constituency. In the general election of 1908 Rupert Guinness was elected to Westminster and served as the member for Haggerston, Shoreditch, until 1910, when he failed to hold the seat in a general election. After this setback Rupert and Gwendolen Guinness, both enthusiastic supporters of imperialist ideals, visited Canada and were immensely struck by the opportunities in this new country for enterprising emigrants from home. Guinness determined to establish an organization in which emigrants could be effectively taught and trained for the very different conditions of life in Canada. He bought Woking Park Farm with 550 acres, close to his own estate at Pyrford, and set up the training establishment he had in mind. By 1914 it had trained over 200 future emigrants. Gwendolen Guinness sought to establish a similar training organization for women in Canada, but war prevented its development.

Guinness was appointed CB in 1911. In 1912 he was elected member for the south-eastern division of Essex, a constituency which later became the borough of Southend. He continued his un-interrupted representation of the borough until he succeeded in 1927, on his father's death, to the earldom of Iveagh. His wife stood at the by-election caused by this event and was elected. She in her turn continued to represent the borough with great success and an increas-ing majority at each election until she retired from politics in 1935 after eight years in the House of Commons.

Rupert Guinness's interest in science and the practical applications of scientific research was stronger at this time of his life than his interest in politics, and he was particularly fascinated by the techniques and potentialities of preventive medicine. He was fortunate in being able to combine his interest with the material means to support research and ensure that results were carried through. He involved himself deeply in the running of the Lister Institute of Preventive Medicine, endowed by his father, of which he was a governor for many years. He took a close interest in the work of (Sir) Almwroth Wright and (Sir) Alexander Fleming [qq.v.], both of whom became his lifelong friends, and this interest resulted in the setting up of the Wright-Fleming Institute of Microbiology, of which he was chairman for the greater part of the Institute's life, and which made many contributions to medical knowledge in the fields of allergy control, antibiotics, and preventive medicine techniques.

Rupert Guinness's scientific interest was also strongly directed towards agricultural questions and particularly the problems of dairy farming. He was convinced of the possibility of reducing the incidence of bovine TB in children by producing clean milk. Before 1914 he had designed and made bottling and sterilizing equipment for use with his dairy herd at Pyrford. He stimulated and financed practical and successful research at the Rothamsted Institute, with (Sir) E. John Russell [q.v.], the director, and Dr Hanneford Richards, into the best ways of making and storing farmyard manure. His intense and practical interest in farming questions was strongly developed on a much larger scale, after the war, when he was involved in very large-scale farming at Elveden in Suffolk.

The outbreak of World War I found Rupert Guinness commanding the London division of the RNVR and anxious to find the right employment in the war effort for the thousand trained men, collected and trained largely by his own efforts in the preceding years. To his and their dismay they found themselves limited to military activities on land only. It was hard to accept after so many years of patient prepara-tion. Rupert Guinness's efforts were then directed to the carrying out of recruiting drives throughout the country, which were vigorous and successful. In 1916 he was promoted to acting captain and made ADC to the King, the first RNVR officer to be so honoured.

His large London house, 11 St. James's Square, had been turned by his wife into an office for the organization of relief measures for prisoners of war. Gwendolen Guinness was appointed a member of the National Prisoners of War Fund and in 1920 was appointed CBE for the extensive work which she did in this field.

In 1916 they both went again to Canada, his mission this time being to find volunteers to serve in the Royal Navy. This was a difficult and frustrating assignment and was only par-tially successful. Finally he was demobilized to do what he was perhaps above all qualified to do for the war effort, namely, grow and produce more food at home.

Work undertaken with the Rothamsted Institute on clean milk and on the use of farmyard manure was carried out at Rupert Guinness's Pyrford farm, with his dairy herds there. One discovery from this work led to the establishment of the Agricultural Develop-ments Company to work and put on the market ADCO, a material made basically from straw which, when mixed with refuse, made usable manure.

Tuberculin-tested milk was now being pro-duced from the Pyrford herd and the battle had been joined to make it available to people everywhere. In 1920 Rupert Guinness—or Viscount Elveden as he had now become since the elevation to an earldom of his father in 1919—became one of the founders and the first chairman of the Tuberculin Tested Milk Producers Association, with offices in St. James's Square. This active pioneer work for clean milk eventually led to universal accep-tance of the principles involved and a big reduction in the incidence of bovine TB in children.

Rupert Guinness had been working closely also with the Research Institute in Dairying of University College, Reading, with its first director, Professor Stenhouse-Williams, and later with his successor, Professor H. D. Kay, and by contributing substantial material help to the Institute enabled it to set up its own experimental farm, Shinfield Manor, near Reading. The major part he played in the development of the Institute was publicly recognized in the conferment of the degree of honorary D.Sc. by the university of Reading, of which he later became chancellor. Lady Elveden was closely involved in this pioneer agricultural work at Pyrford. Her interest was recognized when she was asked to open the new National Institute for Research in Dairying in 1924. Another of the agricultural organizations to which they both gave help and lifelong affection was the very successful Chadacre Agricultural Institute, founded by his father, near Bury St. Edmunds. He was chairman of the Institute for a great many years.

In 1926 the Elvedens paid a six-month visit to India, at the time when Lady Elveden's brother-in-law, Lord Irwin (afterwards the first Earl of Halifax, q.v.), was viceroy. On 7 October in the following year the first Earl of Iveagh died and Lord Elveden inherited the great Elveden estate. The house was vast and magnificent and the estate probably provided the finest shooting in the land. The upkeep of both on the Edwardian scale would have been a colossal and probably impossible task, physically and financially. Lord Iveagh had very many other responsibilities, his chairmanship of the Guinness Company, his many charitable, scientific, and agricultural commitments, his other houses and estates in England, Ireland, and Italy. Lady Iveagh was an active member of Parliament and had many activities in public life. The idea of running and managing Elveden in the old style was daunting. For one year, however, it was maintained in full to cover the visit to Elveden in 1928, with a shooting house-party, of King George V and Queen Mary. From then on, however, the emphasis in Elveden management changed and Lord Iveagh started the task, which he had set himself, of converting Elveden into an efficient and economic farming unit. He intended to establish a tuberculin-free dairy herd on the huge scale that Elveden farming required. He intended to show that the light 'breckland' of the Elveden estate could be used efficiently for food production, and that the wasteland could be reclaimed for effective farming as well as for supporting game. The enterprise was an immense one and the planning, labour, and investment required was on a large scale. It began with an extensive programme of destruction of pests and fencing and draining of reclaimed land. The work of farming it was largely experimental and novel methods were needed. He improved the fertility of much of the light land by a policy of heavy cropping of lucerne. By the end of his life Elveden had the largest dairy farm in England: producing over half a million gallons of milk a year. The experiment succeeded largely because of Lord Iveagh's driving persistence and determination

to carry it through and because he had the means to experiment on so large a scale, and the resources to be able to accept losses on the farm in the early years before the enterprise could become fully efficient and eventually profitable.

The entire Elveden establishment could not be maintained, but during the 1930s Lady Iveagh maintained and used the new wing of the house. She was deeply engaged in politics and entertained political friends there. She became chairman of the National Union of Conservative and Unionist Associations. She was active in the House of Commons and was a most competent broadcaster and speaker. Lord Iveagh also took on many duties in public life. He was a lieutenant of the City of London, deputy lieutenant of Surrey and Essex. He received honorary degrees from universities in Britain and Ireland in recognition of his agricultural work. In both countries he supported a great many causes covering scientific, medical, agricultural, and direct charitable endeavours and took an active part in the direction of as many of them as possible. He took a particularly active part as chairman in directing and expanding the Guinness Trust in England and the Iveagh Trust in Dublin, housing charities established originally by the first Lord Iveagh.

In the 1930s also the Guinness Company had taken the important step of building a major new plant, the Park Royal brewery, to brew Guinness stout in London. The decision to build was made during the 'economic war' with Ireland and followed very direct talks between the Government and Lord Iveagh. One important consequence of this decision was that during the war of 1939–45 the Company was able to keep production going reasonably well in both countries and maintain a supply of Guinness throughout Great Britain.

Shortly before the outbreak of war Lord Iveagh presented his splendid Dublin town-house in Stephens Green, which he had inherited from his father, to the Republic of Ireland and, named Iveagh House, it became the Department for Foreign Affairs of the Irish Government.

Throughout World War II the concentration at Elveden was on increasing production of food and the successes achieved resulted in wide acclaim in this country, but just as the war was ending Lord and Lady Iveagh suffered the shattering blow of the death on active service in Holland of their only son Arthur, a major in the 55th Suffolk and Norfolk Yeomanry. In 1936 he had married Lady Elizabeth Hare, younger daughter of the fourth Earl of Listowel, and left three children, the eldest of whom, (Arthur Francis) Benjamin, was to succeed Lord Iveagh as head of the family and chairman of the Guinness Company.

Recognition of Lord Iveagh's achievements in so many fields came in full measure in later life. In 1955 he was appointed to the Order of the Garter. When he was presented with the first Landowners gold medal at the Royal Agricultural Society in 1958, nonagenarian Charles Bathurst, Viscount Bledisloe [q.v.], handed it over to the eighty-five-year-old Lord Iveagh with the words 'it is so nice to give it to an up and coming young man'. In 1964 Iveagh was made a fellow of the Royal Society, an honour which moved him deeply.

The Guinness Company moved after the war into a new phase of growth and diversification, industrially and geographically, and Lord Iveagh was pleased to encourage and preside over these developments. He presided also over the massive celebrations of the bicentenary of the Guinness Company in 1959. Now he began to consider the time had come to give up some of the many offices he still held. He resigned from the chairmanship of the Wright-Fleming Institute in 1957. In 1962 he resigned from the chairmanship of the Guinness Company and he and Lady Iveagh gave up their regular prize-giving visits to Chadacre. In 1963 he resigned from the chancellorship of Trinity College, Dublin. He was sad not to be able to attend the ceremony at Trinity when John F. Kennedy was presented with an honorary degree. As chancellor he had conferred honorary degrees on Sean T. O'Kelly [q.v.] and Eamon De Valera. Both Lord and Lady Iveagh felt that in his last years they had successfully tidied up and disengaged from the innumerable enterprises in which they had together spent their lives. She died at Pyrford 16 February 1966 and he died soon after, also at Pyrford, 14 September 1967. They were survived by their three daughters. They are buried at Elveden.

There are portraits of both Lord and Lady Iveagh at the Park Royal offices of Arthur Guinness, Son & Co. Ltd.; a portrait of Rupert and his brother Ernest by J. Sant (1891); a portrait of Lord Iveagh by H. Oliver; a portrait of Lady Iveagh by John Gilroy and a portrait of Lord and Lady Iveagh, standing in coronation robes, also by John Gilroy; and a portrait of Lord Iveagh by the same artist (1955) at Iveagh House, St. James's Square, London.

[H. D. Kay in *Biographical Memoirs of Fellows of the Royal Society*, vol. xiv, 1968; G. Martelli, *The Elveden Enterprise*, 1952; private information; personal knowledge.]

R. A. McNeile

GUNN, Sir JAMES (1893-1964), painter, was born in Glasgow 30 June 1893, the son of Richard Gunn, a Glasgow tailor, and his wife, Thomasina Munro. When he was five years old he was taken every Saturday to the studio of A. B. Docherty, for he was already drawing from what was in front of him, a course of study which speaks of a precocity frowned upon today for no good reason. He was educated at Glasgow High School. He went on to the Glasgow School of Art when he was fourteen, but fell out with Maurice Griffenhagen, the director, whose paintings were perhaps too romantic for the young Gunn. He spent a year or two in commercial work. Then Clouston Young the engraver advised his parents to send him to the Edinburgh College of Art, where he stayed for three years before going to the Académie Julien, Paris. In Paris he worked under Jean-Paul Laurens.

It was from this time and a holiday in Spain that his painting took its shape. The French virtues of paint applied bluntly and freshly, a broad tonal design, and colours close together, stood Gunn in good stead for the rest of his life not only in his portraits but also in the hundreds of landscape sketches, of which he used to speak in his later years but never showed. But it must have been the visit to Spain which was of most value. Though his life as a painter was interrupted by the war of 1914-18, in which he enlisted with the Artists' Rifles and was commissioned with the 10th Scottish Rifles, the lessons of Velazquez came to fruition in the thirties with the portrait of Father Vincent McNab, and the three portraits of James Ferrier Pryde. It is not only the shadows cast by the figures that make them so substantial but also the pattern of tone which gives the men the look of being cut out by the action of the light. The conversation piece of Belloc, Chesterton and Baring (1932), and the portrait of Lord Crawford (1939), both of which are in the National Portrait Gallery, were also painted in colours sombre but never muddy; now the paint was more thinly applied—a technique which foreshadowed his later pictures, such as the famous portrait 'Pauline in the Yellow Dress' and the portrait of Delius in Bradford (1933), in which the blind composer sits listening, with his attenuated and useless hands laid on a rug.

Portraits of prime ministers, field-marshals, judges, dons, and bankers were among the many which he executed with close attention to design and to the texture of clothes, though his best sitters, perhaps, were writers, such as Belloc, or artists, such as Sir W. O. Hutchison, the president of the Royal Scottish Academy.

A later success was his painting of George VI and his family in a room at Windsor, with what, at the time, seemed 'a degree of needless scrupulosity'. In the state portrait of Queen Elizabeth II painted in 1956 Gunn paid his respects to a tradition which came from

Van Dyck by way of Sir Joshua Reynolds, Thomas Gainsborough, Sir Thomas Lawrence [qq.v.], and Sir Gerald Kelly (all of whom, except Gainsborough, were presidents of the Royal Academy). It was, however, a disappointment. A further disappointment were the many copies of it made by young artists who, unsupported by a good design or rich paint, added one more evidence of imperial decline to our embassies.

In boardrooms and college halls the visitor is often stopped by one of Gunn's portraits, severe and even bitter in expression, painted with scrupulous distinction, with nothing evaded, neither the wrinkled hands nor the pinstripe suit. The sitter neither flaunts his ruffs, nor makes any effort to charm or daunt the spectator. The gravity of the man is met by the honesty of the painter, but it is an honesty which does not boast of exposure or disrespect. Neither sitter nor artist doubts the place that each has in society. For that reason, as well as for the precision of the workmanship, and the pleasure in catching a likeness (perhaps his greatest pleasure at the end of his life), Gunn's portraits will sustain their power after more gifted and peremptory painters have ceased to please.

As for those less gifted but more in keeping with fashion, Gunn suffered from their indifference even when in 1953 he was made president of the Royal Society of Portrait Painters in succession to Augustus John [q.v.]. It is true that after a long wait he was made an associate member of the Royal Academy (1953), and then treasurer. He became RA in 1961. He was knighted in 1963. He received honorary degrees from Manchester (1945) and Glasgow (1963). His sombre and elegant figure, his kindly handsome face, seemed to carry with them a weight not only of dignity but of a sense of neglect which would have been erased if he could have heard the enthusiasm of young artists who saw for the first time four of his best portraits in his memorial display at the summer exhibition at the Royal Academy in 1965.

In 1919 Gunn married Mary Gwendoline Charlotte, daughter of Captain H. E. Hillman, RN, by whom he had three daughters. In 1929 he married, secondly, (Marie) Pauline (died 1950), daughter of A. P. Miller; they had one son and one daughter. Pauline was the model of some of the best known of Gunn's paintings. Gunn died in a London hospital 30 December 1964. There is a portrait of him by Sir W. O. Hutchison in the Royal Scottish Academy in Edinburgh, and two drawings by William Dring (1954) in the artist's possession. There are two bronze busts: by Christine Sabatini (1955) and G. H. Paulin (1958), of which casts are in the possession of the family.

[*The Times*, 1 January 1965.]

PETER GREENHAM

GWYNNE-VAUGHAN, DAME HELEN CHARLOTTE ISABELLA (1879-1967), botanist and leader of women's Services in both world wars, was born 21 January 1879 in Chapel Street, Westminster, the elder daughter of Captain the Hon. Arthur H. Fraser (died 1884), of the Scots Guards, and his wife, Lucy Jane, daughter of Robert Duncan Fergusson, a major in the Royal Ayrshire and Militia Rifles. Lucy Fraser married in 1887 Francis Hay-Newton, her step-brother, the son of her father's second wife. Since he was a member of the consular service, Helen was brought up mainly abroad. Educated by governesses except for a final year at Cheltenham Ladies' College, she endured several years of the social round common to girls of the Victorian upper classes, before entering King's College, London, in 1899. There she won the Carter gold medal for botany in 1902 and graduated B.Sc. in botany, with second class honours, in 1904. In 1907 her thesis on fungi was accepted for the degree of D.Sc. in the university of London.

Helen Fraser began her teaching career in 1904 as a demonstrator at University College, London, for V. H. Blackman [q.v.]. In 1905 she became assistant lecturer at Royal Holloway College, moving to a lectureship at the University College of Nottingham in 1907. Two years later she became head of the department of botany at Birkbeck College, London, where except for her periods of war service she was to spend the rest of her career. In 1911 she married her predecessor in that post, Professor David T. Gwynne-Vaughan.

Early in her career Helen Gwynne-Vaughan distinguished herself both in botany and in public affairs. She read papers on fungi to the British Association in 1906 (jointly with V. H. Blackman) and in 1909; she became a fellow of the Linnean Society, a member of the university of London board of studies in botany, and a university examiner. As a girl she had worked with her mother in girls' clubs in St. Marylebone and she remained for some years secretary of a Paddington girls' club. With Dr Louisa Garrett Anderson she founded in 1907 a university of London Suffrage Society. Her interest in feminist politics stopped short of militancy, however, and she disapproved of the suffragettes' extremism.

David Gwynne-Vaughan died following the rapid onset of tuberculosis in 1915. His widow's first task was to order his papers and prepare for publication his last work on palaeobotany. But she soon needed some more challenging work than that offered by university teaching in wartime. Through the agency of Louisa Garrett Anderson she was appointed in February 1917 joint chief controller of the newly formed Women's Army Auxiliary Corps. Mrs. Chalmers Watson, who had founded the corps, directed operations at home while Helen Gwynne-Vaughan took up her duties in France. She proved an energetic and able organizer, with a flair for creating an *esprit de corps* amongst the nearly 10,000 women under her command. The new corps was designed to free men for combat from the numerous essential jobs associated with maintaining an army in the field. This unprecedented organization had to face much prejudice and obstruction. Not only did many army officers dislike working with women, but persistent rumours of immoral behaviour in the corps reached the British press. These resulted in an inquiry which vindicated the corps completely. In January 1918 Helen Gwynne-Vaughan was appointed CBE and three months later the Queen assumed the position of commander-in-chief of the renamed Queen Mary's Auxiliary Army Corps, in recognition of their work during the battle of Ypres.

Helen Gwynne-Vaughan's success with the QMAAC made her an obvious candidate to take over the Women's Royal Air Force after the dismissal of the Hon. Miss Violet Douglas-Pennant as commandant. Having neither sought nor wanted the job, she found herself transferred in September 1918 to head a force designed to replace 30,000 men with women immediately and with an eventual recruitment target of 90,000. In her fifteen months' command she cleared away most of the administrative encumbrances that had helped to bring down her predecessor, and established an efficient force. She left when the WRAF was beginning to be run down, in December 1919, having been appointed DBE shortly before her resignation.

She returned in 1920 to head the Birkbeck botany department, being appointed professor in 1921. In 1920 Glasgow University gave her an honorary LLD. Turning to politics to absorb her extra energies, she stood for North Camberwell without success in the London County Council elections of 1922 on behalf of the London Municipal Society, and fought the three subsequent parliamentary general elections as a Conservative candidate for the same constituency. Following her third failure she withdrew from national party politics, but strong conservative sympathies and a certain sense of *noblesse oblige* kept her active on a large number of committees. In 1924 she was a member of the royal commission on food prices.

The 1920s saw her most important botanical work, including the award of the Linnean Society's Trail medal for research on protoplasm in 1920 and the publication of two textbooks on fungi. In 1928 she was president both of the Mycological Society and of Section K of the British Association. In 1929 she was appointed GBE 'for public and scientific services'.

Dame Helen was among those who saw an early need for rearmament. In 1934–5 she helped form 'Emergency Service', an organization to prepare women for service in wartime. This in turn provided recruits for the Auxiliary Territorial Service in 1938–9, and in July 1939 she became the ATS's first director. With her accustomed and undimmed energy Dame Helen laid a firm organizational foundation for the service, but other failings led to her enforced resignation in 1941. She was, as some officials had feared, not in step with the spirit of the times. The ATS under her direction was top-heavy with officers, too apt to be chosen for their social class rather than ability. At the same time the conditions in which all ranks were forced to serve were needlessly austere, a reflection of the director's own ascetic approach to life. She insisted that women must be treated no differently from men and indeed, that their comforts must come second to those of the fighting forces. The image of the ATS did not encourage recruitment and this, combined with Dame Helen's disagreements with senior officers over the rank and status of the service, brought about her removal. She returned to Birkbeck, whence she retired in 1944. A long and active retirement followed and for many years she worked full time but unpaid as honorary secretary to the London branch of the Soldiers, Sailors and Air Force Association. She died 26 August 1967, at the RAF convalescent home at Sussex-down, West Sussex.

Dame Helen Gwynne-Vaughan was formidably intelligent, self-denying, and possessed by a strong sense of duty. In personal appearance she was striking, in her youth a statuesque, fair beauty. Her tastes were all for learning, research, and organization; she had little feeling for any of the arts and in her scientific work may have been held back from even greater achievements by a deficiency of flexibility and imagination. In middle age she became a vegetarian, lived very frugally, and began to dress more severely than in her stylish youth. Few people found her lovable, and yet she could be warm-hearted and very generous. She inspired devotion and hero-worship amongst some of her younger staff, but her dealings with other officials, especially men, were often overbearing and inept. She appeared to lack humility and scorned to use her charm. In retrospect, however, her human failings were insignificant beside the very considerable achievements of her life.

She published some twenty-five scientific studies, most of them on the reproductive system of fungi. Two textbooks, *Fungi. Ascomycetes, Ustilaginales, Uredinales*, and (with B. Barnes) *The Structure and Development of the Fungi* were published in 1922 and 1927 respectively. In 1942 her autobiographical *Service with the Army* appeared.

A portrait of Dame Helen at the age of thirty was painted by Philip de László in 1909 and hangs in Birkbeck College. The Imperial War Museum has a portrait by Sir William Orpen (1918), and a bronze by Julian Allan was exhibited by the Society of Portrait Sculptors in 1953.

[Molly Izzard, *A Heroine in her Time*, 1969; J. M. Cowper, *The Auxiliary Territorial Service*, 1949, and *A Short History of Queen Mary's Auxiliary Army Corps*, 1966; *Transactions of the British Mycological Society*, vol. li (2), 1968; unpublished papers of the War Office and the Ministry of Aviation, Air Historical Branch, at the Public Record Office.]   ALICE PROCHASKA

H

HACKING, SIR JOHN (1888-1969), chartered electrical engineer, was born 16 December 1888, at Crawshaw Booth, Lancashire, the only son and the eldest of three children of William Edward Hacking, engineer, of Burnley, Lancashire, and his wife, Martha, only daughter of Albert Birtwistle, of Crawshaw Booth. He was educated at Burnley Grammar School and Leeds Technical Institute.

After five years of engineering experience with the Newcastle upon Tyne Electric Supply Company—NESCO, the pioneer in Great Britain of integrated electricity supply—in 1913 Hacking joined Merz & McLellan, a firm of electrical consultants. On their behalf, he was engaged from 1915 to 1923 on the electrification of the Central Argentine Railway and, from 1923 to 1933, on projects in South Africa, at the London office, and in India, where he dealt with the electrification of the Bombay-Baroda Railway and the Great India Peninsula Railway.

On returning to England, Hacking, as engineer of Merz & McLellan, supervised the construction of the Central Electricity Board's mid east England 132 kV transmission grid. He was appointed as the Board's deputy chief engineer in 1933 and became chief engineer in 1944. After the outbreak of war in 1939, the CEB had to cope with a change in the pattern of transmission, due to reduced demand in cities and residential areas and a rapid increase in electricity usage in remote war factories. Consequently, lines intended initially for the interconnection of generating stations within each region became, in effect, elements of a national transmission system, with emergency reinforcements to permit supplies in bulk from areas of surplus to those with expanded demands. Such conditions brought many problems, but, by the co-ordinated efforts of Hacking's department and the regional staffs, supplies were well maintained, in spite of enemy action and drifting barrage balloons. A contribution to this engineering success was the CEB's well-founded tradition, encouraged by Hacking, of technical integrity.

When the electricity supply industry was nationalized in 1947, the CEB and company and local authority undertakings were abolished. The British Electricity Authority was established to own and operate generating stations and main transmission systems and to sell electricity in bulk to the new area (distribution) boards. Hacking's appointment in 1947 as deputy chairman (operations) of the Authority was welcomed throughout the industry, for he was a well-liked and respected engineer. The Authority's difficulties were many; the integration of 650 separate undertakings of various sizes and characteristics raised problems of engineering, finance, administration, and human relations. Above all, there was a severe shortage of generating capacity. Load shedding and black-outs were frequent and, with demand rising more rapidly than the increase in generating plant, Hacking inherited a problem of the utmost gravity, for the nation's recovery from war shortages depended on a trustworthy supply of electricity. Hacking, though not himself a specialist in generating matters, gave good leadership to his team of engineers by applying first-aid measures to mitigate the shortage of generating plant capacity, although it was more than a decade before the deficiencies were overcome. Under Hacking's engineering management, a start was made on the design of more advanced generating stations and the first four of the Authority's nuclear stations. The building of a new—and much needed—transmission system of 275 kV was also begun.

Hacking retired from his deputy chairmanship of the British Electricity Authority in 1953 and returned to Merz & McLellan as a consultant until his final retirement in 1966. He made several overseas tours on his firm's behalf, principally in South Africa, Nigeria, and Australia.

In his youth Hacking was a keen cricketer, captaining his local team for several years, but, when injury ended his bowling, he became instead a week-end golfer, though never to the neglect of his wife, children, and, later, his grandchildren, for Hacking was a good family man. To those outside his family, Hacking, though by nature quiet and reserved, was friendly and sincere; a considerate and honourable man, on whom his friends knew they could rely.

Hacking was knighted in 1949. He served as president of the Electrical Research Association, of the British Electrical Power Convention, and of the Institution of Electrical Engineers in 1951-2, being appointed an honorary member of that Institution in 1962.

In 1917 in Buenos Aires Hacking married Janet Stewart, only child of Alexander Stewart Scott, of Newcastle upon Tyne, and his wife, Elizabeth, second daughter of William Davison, of Ovington, Northumberland. They had one son and one daughter. Hacking died at Orpington Hospital 29 September 1969.

[Private information; personal knowledge.]

CECIL T. MELLING

HAILEY, (WILLIAM) MALCOLM, BARON HAILEY (1872-1969), public servant, was born in Newport Pagnell 15 February 1872, the third son of Hammett Hailey, medical practitioner, and his wife, Maria Coelia, daughter of John Clode. He was educated at the Merchant Taylors' School and at Corpus Christi College, Oxford, where he was a scholar and subsequently (1925) an honorary fellow. He obtained first class honours in classical moderations (1892) and *literae humaniores* (1894). In that year he passed third into the Indian Civil Service and was posted to the Punjab in the following year. In 1901 he became colonization officer for the Jhelum Canal Colony. The great canal systems of the Punjab had brought water to millions of acres which had once been desert and it was the task of the colonization officer to apportion this new land to peasant families from more crowded areas and to build up a prosperous community. In his later life Hailey looked back to this as a time of intense and creative satisfaction and when raised to the peerage it was from Shahpur that he took his territorial designation.

In 1907 came the inevitable call to the secretariat, first to the Punjab but a few months later, in 1908, to the Finance Department of the Government of India. There he displayed that ability to digest quickly a mass of complicated facts, to summarize, to seize on the essential, and to reach a clear and sound decision which was the hallmark of a good secretariat officer and at which he excelled throughout his life. In 1912 he was appointed first chief commissioner of the new province of Delhi, where he pressed on energetically with the building of the new capital. He was in this post until 1918 although for part of the time he was on deputation to the reforms committee whose advice to the secretary of state culminated in the Montagu–Chelmsford reforms, and in 1919 he became finance member of the viceroy's Executive Council. This was probably the appointment of his whole life in which he felt least satisfaction.

In 1922 Hailey was transferred to the more congenial post of home member and leader of the government bloc in the Legislative Assembly. The Assembly consisted of 40 nominated members and 103 elected; a government majority was thus far from certain. But although the viceroy might pass legislation over the head of the Assembly, it was an obvious matter of policy that this should occur only exceptionally. The constitution was designed for the education in public life of Indian politicians; it provided, incidentally, a political education for officials, for whom it became necessary to persuade where previously they had simply decided. Hailey set himself to learn the neglected art of oratory. He acquired a style which was formidable, more rotund and magisterial than the pithy phrases in which he had recorded decisions on files, but for that reason not unwelcome to Indian hearers whose English had been modelled on Burke and Macaulay. But later the House of Lords was to find him more informative than persuasive; he did not always catch the mood of that House.

Hailey attached great importance to the principle of dyarchy, by which subjects such as education and local self-government were transferred to Indian ministers wholesale, instead of step by step upwards from below. He was wholly committed to gradual constitutional progress towards responsible democratic government, but there was a second aim, to ensure that communal strife was prevented. In the Punjab, of which province Hailey became governor in 1924, this meant keeping the balance between Hindu, Sikh, and Muslim. Hailey inherited a dangerous agitation about the management of Sikh gurudwaras (temples) which, by a combination of firmness and conciliation, he successfully brought to a conclusion within a year. But the overriding danger was that party divisions should coincide with religious ones; this Hailey, and his successors until partition, succeeded in avoiding by a coalition of Muslim, Sikh, and Hindu landed interests, usually opposed by urban commercial and financial interests. The two aims of keeping the peace and educating the people in democracy were hard to reconcile, but increased prosperity for the peasant might prove the solution. For this Hailey looked to canals and irrigation, better seed, the use of fertilizers, and co-operative banks rather than to the reform of social life in the village by exhortation and education.

In 1928 Hailey was transferred to the governorship of the United Provinces, where the political problem took a different form: Muslims were a majority in the cities but in the countryside the peasantry were overwhelmingly Hindu and except in the west it was hard to believe in prosperity for land so desperately overcrowded. Muslim landlords and Hindu business men could be found as ministers but even with a limited franchise popular support for them was not markedly spontaneous; at the first election on a wider franchise, the province voted overwhelmingly for the Indian National Congress. During Hailey's time in office this party had much popular backing but was only intermittently prepared to co-operate with the Government; the task of educating the people in democracy was therefore hard to keep in view. Hailey, however, did not, like many officials, lose sight of the main object and was deeply involved in the next stage of constitutional progress. He was called to London for the Round Table Conference of 1930–1 and played an important part in the discussions which led to the Government of India Act of 1935.

Hailey left the United Provinces in 1934 when he was sixty-two. Until then he had never taken his leaves in England but always in India itself. He was raised to the peerage in 1936 and continued to act as an adviser to successive secretaries of state for India. But already he had begun his second career. In his Rhodes lecture of 1929 J. C. Smuts [q.v.] had proposed a comprehensive survey of Africa; Hailey, on his retirement from India, became the director of this survey, which was conducted from Chatham House. The result, *An African Survey*, was published in 1938. It had been a formidable task. Expert contributions covered politics, administration, and education as well as soil erosion, irrigation, and the improvement of crops. But none of this material was incorporated without digestion. Hailey completed a journey of 22,000 miles, in the course of which he discussed questions on the spot with everyone he could, from governors to village headmen. With this experience behind him, he recast every contribution in his own stately style, summarizing the discussion and recording a carefully guarded verdict.

There are a million weighty words in the survey. More important than mere size was its influence. In the Colonial Office, extracts were made of every passage suggesting action or policy and a discussion was started on how it could be implemented. For the next fifteen years the influence of these measured pronouncements was felt, perhaps most strongly in the immediate post-war years. Hailey believed that Africans should, and before long would, take over political power in their own continent; he expressed this belief more freely in conversation than in print, where he was monumentally discreet; it was a time when current thinking on colonial questions would have postponed any such advance for half a century. The settlement that Lord Lugard [q.v.] had made with the Emirs of Northern Nigeria had provided not merely a model but a doctrine; the 'native authority', which meant first the Emir, later the Emir in Council, was regarded by many as a means of constitutional development in accordance with African tradition and preferable to Western parliamentary institutions. Hailey more than anyone put this concept in its proper place; 'indirect rule' was a temporary stage, one that had proved useful but had become out of date except as a form of local government.

At the outbreak of war in 1939 Hailey was asked by the colonial secretary to visit the African colonies and to make recommendations on what should be done to secure their full contribution. One of his recommendations was the appointment of Africans to the Colonial Administrative Service, a proposition to which there was still influential opposition. His far-sighted advice was accepted for the West Coast but failed to win acceptance for the East and Central African territories. On his return from this tour in the summer of 1940, Hailey was asked to go at once to the Belgian Congo as head of an economic mission, of which it was the purpose to secure as much as possible of French and Belgian Africa against German penetration. Metropolitan France and Belgium were of course in German hands. For the rest of this year he was active in assistance to the governor-general of the Belgian Congo and the Gaullist authorities in French Africa. The Congo's economic contribution to the war effort, particularly in respect of uranium, was of the first importance and Hailey was instrumental in securing financial support for the local authorities and making possible a series of trade agreements.

One of the proposals in *An African Survey* had been that the Government should provide funds for African studies and in 1940 this bore fruit in the Colonial Research Fund. On his return from the Congo, Hailey became chairman of the committee which allocated the resources of this Fund; he was also chairman of the International African Institute and thus in a key position with regard to African research. It was a field in which he himself continued to be an active practitioner; he published several books on colonial dependencies, based on lectures, and followed these by a survey in four volumes of Native Administration in the British African Territories, with a fifth volume on the High Commission Territories then attached to South Africa (1950–3). These were books for the specialist in administration by the leading authority on the subject. In 1952, when he was eighty, he undertook a second edition of *An African Survey*. This was no matter of a few amendments; too much had happened. Again he travelled throughout Africa and again each chapter was entirely rewritten. During much of the five years of unremitting toil on this vast task, Hailey was afflicted by cataract and at one stage every document had to be read to him. The second *Survey* was published in 1957 in his eighty-sixth year; it was no less authoritative than the first and the power to select essentials from a mass of detail was still unerring. But it was less influential, because by this time the initiative had passed from the Colonial Office to the colonial peoples. Hailey's last book, *The Republic of South Africa and the High Commission Territories*, was published in 1963 when he was ninety-one.

Hailey was essentially a public servant rather than a politician. He described himself as 'no party man but a lifelong cross-bencher'. His early training in the Indian Civil Service had accustomed him to hear both sides of a case with an open mind and then form an opinion; this remained his habit until the end. As an administrator, he believed in choosing the man for the job and leaving him to do it with a minimum of interference. After his retirement from India, the possibility that he might return as viceroy was widely discussed in India, although Lady Hailey's uncertain health would have proved an obstacle. If he was disappointed, he neither showed nor referred to it but threw himself into his new work on Africa and into the active chairmanship of many voluntary bodies. Few men contributed so much to the transition from bureaucratic rule to democracy in India; few so much to the peaceful transfer of power in Africa. But he outlived his own achievement by ten years and the men he had influenced were already out of office when he died.

Hailey was a man devoted to work, as his record of achievement shows; but he loved to get away from it for a day's fishing or a week in the jungle. One of his minor achievements was the creation of what was originally called the Hailey National Park, a wild-life sanctuary in the foothills of the Himalayas. He could tell a story against himself but the humour which sparkled in his conversation was usually ironic; he was respected by all and loved by those who knew him best, but he was not a man who revealed easily the inmost springs of his being nor did he act or speak on impulse. He was perhaps regarded more often with awe than with affection.

He was appointed KCSI (1922), GCSI (1932), GCIE (1928), GCMG (1939), sworn of the Privy Council (1949) and admitted to the Order of Merit (1956). The list of his academic honours is formidable. His appearance was always striking; the look of the eagle which marked him as a governor was much softened by a gentler and sweeter expression in old age. There is a portrait by Sir James Gunn at Chatham House and a copy by Robin Bell in Rhodes House, Oxford, where thirteen volumes of personal press-cuttings and other papers have been deposited. He was a Rhodes trustee in 1946-66.

Hailey married in 1896 Andreina Alessandra, daughter of Count Hannibale Balzani of Italy. His only son was killed in the war of 1939-45. His only daughter died in 1922; after her death Lady Hailey's health deteriorated seriously and she died in 1939. Hailey died in Putney 1 June 1969 at the age of ninety-seven.

[Sir Frederick Pedler in *Journal of the Royal Society of Arts*, March 1970, and in *African Affairs*, the Journal of the Royal African Society, February 1970; private information; personal knowledge.]   PHILIP MASON

HALDANE, JOHN BURDON SANDERSON (1892-1964), geneticist, was born 5 November 1892 in Oxford, the only son of John Scott Haldane [q.v.], and his wife, Louisa Kathleen, daughter of Coutts Trotter, of Dreghorn. J. S. Haldane came from an old Scottish family, and achieved distinction as a physiologist. He was a younger brother of Richard Burdon Haldane (afterwards Viscount Haldane) and an elder brother of Elizabeth Sanderson Haldane [qq.v.]. J. S. Haldane was an important educational influence on his son, who from an early age was allowed to help him in his experiments. The father also had a continuing interest in the philosophical and religious implications of science, an interest which was shared by the son, although the former's views were idealist and in general sympathetic to religion whereas the latter became an increasingly outspoken materialist. Mrs J. S. Haldane, who wrote her autobiography (*Friends and Kindred*, 1961), also came from a Scottish family. She held strong views on political matters, being a passionate feminist and a passionate imperialist. J. B. S. Haldane's younger and only sister was to become well known as the writer, Naomi Mitchison.

Haldane was educated at the Dragon School, Oxford, then known as Lynam's, and at Eton College, which he disliked intensely. At both schools he had at first to put up with more than the usual amount of bullying, perhaps because of a combination of short temper and intellectual arrogance, but his large size and aggressiveness in time made him relatively immune. He won a mathematics scholarship to New College, Oxford, where he obtained first class honours, both in mathematical moderations (1912) and in *literae humaniores* (1914). The war broke out two months after he graduated. He served in the Black Watch, and was wounded in France in 1915. After running the Nigg Bombing School from August 1915 until March 1916, he was sent to Mesopotamia, where he was again wounded, and then to India, where he lectured at a bombing school. He returned and in October 1919 became a fellow of New College, where he did research in physiology, and published a number of papers in genetics. In 1922 he was appointed reader in biochemistry at Cambridge under (Sir) F. Gowland Hopkins [q.v.]. In 1925 he was dismissed from his readership at the instigation of the 'Sex Viri' because he had been quoted as co-respondent in a divorce case. Haldane appealed, and was reinstated in 1926. Following this appeal, the 'Sex Viri' changed their name, perhaps to avoid

Haldane's proposed translation, 'sex weary', and there has been no subsequent harassment of university officers on account of their private lives. Another consequence of these events was that in 1926 Haldane married his first wife, Charlotte Burghes, née Franken (died 1969), a journalist who later wrote several books, including two volumes of autobiography; this marriage ended in divorce in 1945. Charlotte had one son by her previous marriage to Mr Burghes. Haldane had no children by either of his marriages.

While still holding his readership at Cambridge, Haldane also became 'officer in charge of genetical investigations' at the John Innes Horticultural Research Station in 1927, a post he held until 1936. He was elected a fellow of the Royal Society in 1932. He also held the Fullerian professorship of physiology at the Royal Institution from 1930 to 1932. In 1933 he resigned from Cambridge to occupy the chair of genetics, and then of biometry, at University College, London. In 1945 he married a former student, Helen Spurway, who later became a lecturer in his department. Helen Spurway survived him, and died in India in 1978. In 1957, before retirement age, Haldane retired from UC to become a member of the Biometry Research Unit at the Indian Statistical Institute, Calcutta. In 1961 he and his wife became Indian citizens and in 1962 he was appointed head of the Laboratory of Genetics and Biometry established by the Government of Orissa at Bhubaneswar. He died of rectal cancer in Bhubaneswar, India, 1 December 1964.

Haldane's major contribution to science was in uniting Darwinian evolution theory with Mendelian genetics. A series of papers starting in 1924 worked out the consequences of natural selection acting on populations with a Mendelian system of heredity. Haldane's work, together with that of (Sir) R. A. Fisher [q.v.] and Sewall Wright, re-established Darwinian natural selection as the accepted mechanism of evolutionary change. He continued working in this field all his life, but made significant contributions in many other areas. His early work in biochemistry helped to establish a mathematical theory of enzyme action. He did much to encourage the development of human genetics, both by his own contributions and through discussion with others, particularly at University College. Other fields to which he contributed ranged from cosmology to animal behaviour and from the origin of life to the physiology of diving. His great strengths as a scientist were an ability to reduce complex systems to simple mathematical equations, an extraordinarily wide range of interests which enabled him to see connections missed by others, and a gift for lucid and vivid exposition. He was less successful as an experimenter; it is significant that his main experimental contributions were to the physiology of diving, when the two main techniques, the handling of gases and experiments on human subjects, including himself, were ones he had learnt from his father when a child. This work, carried out during the war of 1939-45, started when he was invited to investigate the disaster in the submarine *Thetis* by the Amalgamated Engineering Union and the Electrical Trades Union, many of whose members had died in the accident. He subsequently worked on behalf of the Royal Navy on the physiological effects of gases at high pressures. He also undertook physiological work for the Royal Air Force and the Ministry of Aircraft Production. Because of the bombing of London, Haldane and most of his staff moved to Rothamsted Experimental Station from 1941 to 1944.

Haldane was one of the most effective popularizers of science, as indicated by his books, *Daedalus* (1924), *Possible Worlds* (1927), *The Inequality of Man* (1932), and by his weekly articles in the *Daily Worker*. These essays contain a unique combination of original scientific insight, verbal wit, appeal to everyday experience, and radical political and philosophical criticism. In *My Friend Mr Leakey* (1937) he combined the same elements in a collection of children's stories.

Haldane's political activity was overwhelmingly influenced by the rise and fall of Hitler. He became a socialist when a student, but a socialist of a liberal and lukewarm kind. In his early essays he is more interested in taking a swipe at God than at the ruling class. He played little part in organized political activity until the 1930s. During this period he became increasingly associated with the Communist movement, for which he was an indefatigable and effective speaker, although he did not join the Communist Party until 1942. He visited Spain three times during the civil war, and advised the Spanish Government about defence against gas attacks and air raids. This experience led him to publish in 1938 his book *A.R.P.*, which attempted a quantitative estimate of the likely effects of air raids in the coming war. In 1940 he became chairman of the editorial board of the *Daily Worker*, a post he held until 1950 when the board was disbanded. In the years immediately after the war, his political position became increasingly untenable because of the debate over the Russian geneticist Lysenko. Until the end of his life Haldane continued to assert that there was some positive content to Lysenko's science, but he was also aware that many of the things said by Lysenko, and in support of Lysenko, were wrong, and that unjustifiable interference with scientific research was taking place in Russia. Although he was reluctant openly to condemn or criticize the Soviet Union or the Communist Party, his lack of sympathy with their policies ultimately led him to resign his membership of the party. No public announcement of his resignation, which took place *c.* 1950, was made; he later said that he had resigned 'because of Stalin's interference with science'. His final years in India were devoted to teaching and to encouraging research in biometry and genetics.

Haldane was honorary D.Sc. (Oxford, 1961), an honorary fellow of New College, Oxford (1961), and he had a doctorate of the university of Paris. He was awarded the Italian Feltrinelli prize and the Kimber award of the United States Academy of Sciences in 1961. His other honours and awards are too numerous to mention.

There is a portrait of Haldane by Claude Rogers at University College, London.

[Ronald Clark, *J. B. S.*, 1968; N. W. Pirie in *Biographical Memoirs of Fellows of the Royal Society*, vol. xii, 1966.]

J. MAYNARD SMITH

HALL, WILLIAM GEORGE GLENVIL (1887–1962), politician, was born at Almeley, Herefordshire, 4 April 1887, the eldest of the five children of William George Hall and his wife, Elizabeth Holl, of New Radnor, Radnorshire. His forebears had been settled as yeoman farmers in Herefordshire and Radnorshire for many generations. Glenvil Hall's parents were devout Quakers and his father devoted his life to pastoral work for the Home Mission of the Society of Friends.

Hall was educated at the Friends' School, Saffron Walden, and then worked in London as a clerk in various branches of Barclay's Bank. His leisure hours quickly revealed what was to be his lifelong devotion to the needs of the poor, the weak, and the unfortunate. He gave himself unstintingly to social work among the men and boys of the East End of London, at Hoxton and at Toynbee Hall, and lived for some years in Whitechapel the better to identify himself with those he wished to serve. He was one of the first to encourage the Boy Scout movement in Hoxton and Whitechapel and lectured at Toynbee Hall on economic and social history.

The poverty Hall encountered had a profound effect on his sensitive and idealistic nature. He became a socialist and in 1905 joined the Independent Labour Party for which he worked and spoke until 1914. Although a Quaker, on the outbreak of war Hall had no doubt that it was his duty to enlist. After two years as a private in the Queen's Westminster Rifles, he was commissioned in 1916 in the East Kent Regiment (the Buffs) and later served with the Tank Corps until the end of the war, during which he was wounded and mentioned in dispatches.

On his demobilization in 1919 Hall determined to devote himself entirely to the Labour cause. He joined the Labour Party and became its full-time financial officer, a post he held for twenty years. He was the unsuccessful Labour candidate for the Isle of Ely at the general election of 1922, for Bromley in 1923, and for Portsmouth Central in 1924. During this last campaign the Marquess of Tavistock created a minor sensation by taking the chair at one of Hall's meetings, saying that he had been impressed by Hall's personality and thought that he was the sort of man the country needed in Parliament. In 1929 Hall won Portsmouth Central but lost it in 1931. Thereafter he remained out of Parliament until 1939 when he was returned at a by-election for Colne Valley, Yorkshire, a seat he held until his death.

In 1933 Hall fulfilled a long-standing ambition and was called to the bar by Gray's Inn. He did not have the opportunity to practise, however, until he re-entered the House of Commons in 1939, when he joined the chambers of (Sir) Valentine Holmes [q.v.].

Hall was by now deeply committed to a political career and his resolve had become the more determined during the thirties as each year seemed to bring war nearer. During the war years he was faithful in his attendance at Westminster where he was also a very popular officer of the Palace of Westminster Home Guard. When Attlee formed his administration in 1945 Hall was appointed to the exceedingly onerous post of financial secretary to the Treasury, where he served with the utmost devotion and steadfastness, particularly during the difficult times of the austere budgets of Hugh Dalton and Sir Stafford Cripps [qq.v.]. The task of defending their unavoidable severity fell in large measure on Hall's shoulders and during the long nights of debate on the committee and report stages of the finance Bills the sustained attack by the Opposition was faced with unfailing good humour and moderation by Hall. It was an exhausting task and his colleagues remembered with gratitude how time and again as the dawn broke through the windows of the House of Lords chamber (which the Commons were then using) the first rays lighted on Hall who had battled through the night in charge, sometimes almost alone, of the government front bench. In addition Hall, with all his other ministerial work, was called upon to take part in international gatherings: the final Assembly of the League of Nations and the Paris peace con-

Hall, W. G. G. D.N.B. 1961-1970

ference in 1946, and as a British representative at the United Nations Assembly in 1945, 1946, and 1948. In 1947 he was sworn of the Privy Council.

In 1950 Hall was succeeded by Douglas Jay as financial secretary, but was soon elected chairman of the Parliamentary Labour Party. During the two years in which he held this post Hall's tact and good judgement and the goodwill and support of his colleagues were of inestimable value to the parliamentary party, which had undergone the stress of office in the most critical post-war years during which constant austerity and restraint had been the order of the day.

In the 1951 general election, as a result of which the Labour Government fell, Hall faced a formidable challenge from the Liberal candidate, Lady Violet Bonham Carter (later Baroness Asquith of Yarnbury, q.v.) who had Conservative support; but he held his seat with a majority of over 2,000, which in 1955 he increased to over 3,000, and in 1959 to over 6,000.

Tall and romantically good-looking in his youth, Hall retained to the end of his life his ascetic good looks and the spare figure and light step of a young man. A portrait of him by T. Binney Gibbs, painted in 1932, is in the possession of the family. Hall was one of those people of deep sincerity and feeling who contribute so greatly to the real strength and abiding vitality of a democratic parliamentary system.

After 1951, Hall, a widower, although happy in his children and their families and in his very many friendships in all parties and the respect he everywhere enjoyed as a senior parliamentarian, still found plenty to do, besides his work in the House and his unflagging attention to his duties in his constituency. In 1950, 1951, and 1952 he attended the Consultative Assembly at Strasbourg. He was also active in the Commonwealth Parliamentary Association and made several journeys under its auspices. He was a participant in the work of the NSPCC; in 1952 he became a member of the BBC advisory council and in 1959 he became president of the United Kingdom Alliance.

In 1921 Hall married Rachel Ida (died 1950), daughter of the Revd Robert Bury Sanderson, a Church of England clergyman; they had a son and a daughter. Hall died in London 13 October 1962.

[Private information; personal knowledge.]
STOW HILL

HALL, (WILLIAM) STEPHEN (RICHARD) KING-, BARON KING-HALL (1893-1966), writer, and broadcaster on politics and international affairs. [See KING-HALL.]

HAMBRO, SIR CHARLES JOCELYN (1897-1963), merchant banker, was born in London 3 October 1897, into a banking family of Danish origin, which settled in Dorset and the City in the first half of the nineteenth century. He was the elder son of (Sir) C. Eric Hambro (1872-1947), who was Conservative MP for the Wimbledon division of Surrey in 1900-7 and a partner in C. J. Hambro & Son, the family firm; his grandfather (Sir) Everard Alexander Hambro was a director of the Bank of England. His mother, Sybil Emily (died 1942), was the daughter of Martin Ridley Smith of Warren House, Hayes, Kent, and his wife, Cecilia, daughter of Henry Stuart (1808-80), of Montfort, Isle of Bute, a descendant of George III's prime minister, John Stuart, third Earl of Bute. In 1929 Hambro's parents were divorced and his father at once remarried. He had a younger brother and two sisters.

Hambro was at Eton from 1910 to 1915—in the cricket XI in 1914, and its captain in 1915, when he took seven wickets for six runs against Winchester. He went straight from school to Sandhurst, and by the end of the year was an ensign in the Coldstream Guards. He survived two years of the western front, receiving the military cross for conspicuous bravery in action. On demobilization in 1919 he went for a brief spell of training to the Guaranty Trust Company in New York, and then into the family firm, of which he soon became secretary. He played an important part in its merger with the British Bank of Northern Commerce, which led to the establishment of Hambros Bank in 1921. In 1928, when only thirty, he was elected a director of the Bank of England, and for a spell in 1932-3 he put all other work aside in order to establish, under the direction of Montagu C. (later Lord) Norman [q.v.], the bank's exchange control division to deal with some of the consequences of the ending of the gold standard.

His commanding presence—he stood six feet three inches tall—and driving personality were backed by equal strength of character, loyalty, and charm. He made a notable impact in several spheres of work, particularly on the Great Western Railway, the most successful of the four great British railway companies. He became a director of it in 1928, and deputy chairman in 1934. From 1940 to 1945 he was nominally chairman, but war work took up much of his time.

On the outbreak of war with Germany in 1939, at the invitation of (Sir) Ronald Cross, the minister, Hambro joined the Ministry of Economic Warfare. In August 1940 Cross's successor Hugh (later Lord) Dalton [q.v.] brought Hambro into the new secret service he was forming under the Ministry's cover, the

Special Operations Executive (SOE). SOE's purpose was to stimulate resistance in enemy-occupied territory, and Hambro's vigour, energy, and originality were valuable to it. He began in charge of Scandinavia, and visited Sweden in November 1940. There he arranged for some highly successful smuggling of ball-bearings, and for some sabotage in Swedish harbours, which provoked difficulties with the Swedes. He also, through the anti-Nazi journalist Ebbe Munck, initiated contacts with resistance-minded Danes, which bore useful fruit in the summer of 1944. Dalton thought highly of his Scandinavian work, and Hambro was created KBE in 1941.

From December 1940 to November 1941 he added to his responsibilities oversight of SOE's nascent French, Belgian, Dutch, and German sections, and from November 1941 for five months he was deputy head of the whole organization, in the rank of squadron leader, Royal Air Force. (Rank in SOE meant little.) He initiated an important development in January 1942, when he persuaded the Norwegians to help form an Anglo-Norwegian planning committee, from which several highly successful small operations derived, particularly the destruction on 27/8 February 1943 of the heavy-water plant at Vemork near Rjukan. When a further stock of heavy water was destroyed, in a separate operation, on its way to Germany, the Germans' search for an atomic bomb was utterly dislocated. By that time Hambro had become the executive chief of SOE (called CD) and been promoted to air commodore. Dalton's successor, the third Earl of Selborne, had appointed him in April 1942 to succeed (Sir) Frank Nelson [q.v.] when Nelson's health gave way—on the ground that a man who could run the Great Western Railway could run anything. An early and important task for Hambro was to arrange with Colonel William Donovan, his American opposite number, who visited London in June 1942, for co-operation between SOE and the American Office of Strategic Services. Occasional rivalries should not obscure a great deal of close and rewarding interchange.

Hambro's multifarious acquaintances in the business world were often useful to SOE. During his seventeen months of leadership, this small but lively service was transformed from a body still struggling to establish its worth into a recognized, and often highly efficient, military tool. Hambro cannot claim undue credit for this development, much of which arose from the general political and military course of the war, and some of it from the excellent work of his predecessor, Nelson, and from technicalities too abstruse even for him. A well-placed observer described him in retrospect as 'always the gentleman, among the professionals'; he was certainly not a professional in the secret-service world.

Hambro and Selborne could not agree over a protracted dispute about control over SOE by the commander-in-chief, Middle East; and early in September 1943 Hambro had to resign. Another weighty post was soon found for him. He spent the last eighteen months of the war in Washington as head of the British raw materials mission: this was cover for supervising the exchange of information between the United Kingdom and the USA which led to the first man-made nuclear explosions in July and August 1945.

He then returned to the City, and became prominent; not only in Hambros Bank, of which he was made chairman when his uncle Olaf died in 1961. He also diversified, through the Union Corporation, into mining, among other interests; supported several charitable trusts; worked himself harder than he worked his subordinates; and escaped whenever he could to Dixton Manor near Cheltenham to shoot. He married in 1919 Pamela (died 1932), daughter of John Dupuis Cobbold, DL, of Ipswich, and his wife, Lady Evelyn, daughter of Charles Adolphus Murray, seventh Earl of Dunmore; she bore him a son and three daughters. By his second wife, Dorothy (daughter of Alexander Mackay, of Oban), whom he married in 1936, he had another daughter; he had twenty-four grandchildren living when he died, in his Marylebone home, at the height of his powers and reputation, 28 August 1963.

[M. R. D. Foot, *SOE in France*, 1966, and *Resistance*, 1976; Bickham Sweet-Escott, *Baker Street Irregular*, 1965; *The Times*, 16 July 1915, 29 and 31 August, 2 and 3 September 1963; private information.]

M. R. D. FOOT

HAMILTON, CHARLES HAROLD ST. JOHN (1876-1961), writer, better known as FRANK RICHARDS, was born 8 August 1876 at 15 Oak Street, Ealing, the sixth in a family of five brothers and three sisters. His birth certificates states that his father, John Hamilton, who married Marian Hannah Trinder, was a carpenter. In fact, John Hamilton was a journalist, and sometime bookseller and stationer, of unstable temperament who enjoyed confusing officialdom. He died when Charles was seven, after which the family moved house frequently. Of Charles Hamilton's early years little is known and he was reticent on the subject. He attended various church schools in the west London area and possibly private schools as well—never, he once said, a state school—and acquired a good knowledge of

Latin and French, along with an enduring passion for the classics.

By his own account he received his first cheque for a short story at the age of seventeen from a 'Mr M' who cut later payments from five guineas to four pounds on finding that his contributor was a stripling. Hamilton concentrated his efforts on boys' papers, notably those of Trapps, Holmes & Co. and Pearsons, and never had difficulty in getting his work accepted. In 1907 the Amalgamated Press started a boys' paper, the *Gem*, following it in 1908 with the *Magnet*, and Hamilton turned out 'long, complete' stories for these weeklies for more than thirty years. He still found time to write elsewhere, under many pseudonyms, and maintained an annual output of one and a half million words. Once, when pressed, he wrote 18,000 words in a day. In the *Gem*, as Martin Clifford, he wrote about a school called St. Jim's, which had originally appeared in *Pluck*, and to which Tom Merry and his friends moved from Clavering College to become the 'Terrible Three' of the Shell. Hamilton's favourite came to be the *Magnet* in which, as Frank Richards, he wrote about Greyfriars School and its 'Famous Five' of the Remove, who included Harry Wharton, Frank Nugent (a self-portrait), and the 'dusky nabob' Hurree Jamset Ram Singh. Greyfriars' most famous character, however, was Billy Bunter, the Fat Owl, the prevaricating tuck-hunter for ever waiting for a postal order which never came. Bunter became a legend in the lifetime of his creator who liked to recall that an editor to whom he had outlined the character many years earlier had failed to 'see much' in him.

The outbreak of war put an end to the *Gem* in 1939 and the *Magnet* in 1940. Their circulation had been ailing under strong competition from the D. C. Thomson boys' papers. For Hamilton this was a hard blow. Although he had earned upwards of £2,500 a year, a substantial income for those days, he had spent freely and helped to sustain the casinos of Europe. As a literary prodigy he was then almost unknown; but in the post-war mood of nostalgia his talents were again in demand and Billy Bunter began to appear between hard covers. More than thirty Bunter titles were published, first by Charles Skilton (for whom Hamilton offered to write at his old rate of 30s. per thousand words) and later by Cassell. From 1952 Hamilton wrote Bunter scripts for television, the chief role being played by Gerald Campion. Bunter Christmas shows were also staged in London.

Hamilton's autobiography, published in 1952, greatly disappointed his followers, chiefly because it ignored his origins. It was written in the third person, as by Frank Richards. By now he was Frank Richards and it was under this name that his evasive entry appeared in *Who's Who*. His eyesight had deteriorated but he kept going with the aid of a heavily inked typewriter ribbon. Visitors to his bungalow at Kingsgate-on-Sea, near Broadstairs, found an old-fashioned, reserved figure in black skull-cap, dressing-gown, and trousers cycle-clipped against the cold. Belated fame did not affect him.

George Orwell [q.v.] and others criticized Hamilton's school stories on the grounds that they were wholly escapist, nurtured snobbishness, and represented foreigners as funny. The mentality, Orwell complained, was that of 'a rather exceptionally stupid member of the Navy League in the year 1910' (*Horizon*, March 1940). Replying, Hamilton maintained (*Horizon*, May 1940) that the aristocratic virtues were worth preserving and that foreigners *were* funny. He made no apology for excluding sex from his stories. At all times he was alert to defend his work from condescension and misrepresentation: he threatened legal action on hearing that his tales were to be discussed in a book provisionally titled *The Penny Blood*. He was aware that many parents would have preferred their children to read the *Boy's Own Paper*, but he was unashamed of giving harmless pleasure to the masses. His never-ageing characters were compounds of cheek and manliness; even the bounders had redeeming streaks. If there were 'barrings-out' at Greyfriars, the example did not infect his readers. Hamilton was little influenced by earlier writers on school life. He simply cultivated the already flourishing market for school tales, avoiding the ferocities of the Jack Harkaway stories and the *Angst* of *Eric, or Little by Little*. A suggestion by Orwell which rankled was that, since not all the stories under his pen-names could have been written by one man, they had been couched in a style easily copied, with standardized ejaculations like 'Yarooh'. Hamilton always resented the use of 'his' pseudonyms by stand-in writers. His admirers, endlessly analysing his work in specialist magazines, claimed that they could always detect the work of other hands. Hamilton's style was curiously repetitive and strewn with classical allusions, but he rarely failed to bring his characters to vigorous life. He appears to have created at least thirty schools. As Owen Conquest he founded Rookwood with Jimmy Silver & Co. in the *Boys' Friend*; as Hilda Richards he launched Bessie Bunter of Cliff House School in the *School Friend*; and as Ralph Redway he wrote many Wild West tales. Under his *Gem* name of Martin Clifford he penned a fanciful account of Frank Richards's schooldays at a backwoods school in Canada. His editors joined in the game of laying false trails. Many of his contemporaries who wrote for the juvenile market were astonishingly prolific, but it is unlikely that anyone exceeded Hamilton's lifetime output, which had been put at the equivalent of nearly a thousand ordinary novels.

Hamilton, who never married, died at his home on Christmas Eve 1961.

[*The Autobiography of Frank Richards*, 1952; E. S. Turner, *Boys Will be Boys*, 1948, revised edn. 1957; Brian Doyle, *Who's Who of Boys' Writers*, 1964; files of *Collector's Miscellany*, *Collector's Digest*, and *Story Paper Collector* (Manitoba); private information.]   E. S. TURNER

HAMILTON FAIRLEY, SIR NEIL (1891–1966), physician. [See FAIRLEY.]

HAMILTON FYFE, SIR WILLIAM (1878–1965), headmaster and university vice-chancellor. [See FYFE.]

HAMMOND, SIR JOHN (1889–1964), animal scientist, was born 23 February 1889, at Briston, Norfolk, on the farm of his father, Burrell Hammond, a tenant of Lord Hastings. He was the eldest of four children and was christened John after his grandfather who, besides being a farmer and a veterinarian, was one of the founders of the Red Poll breed of cattle. His mother was Janette Louise Aldis, the daughter of a Norfolk schoolmaster with his own school at East Dereham.

Hammond received his schooling at Gresham's School, Holt, and at Edward VI Middle School, Norwich. In 1907, on the advice of T. B. Wood, he was sent to Downing College, Cambridge, to study agriculture, his Latin having failed to gain him admission to the Royal Veterinary College. As his tutor recommended, he took the natural sciences tripos in which he gained a second class in part i (1909). In 1910 he obtained the diploma in agriculture, with distinction in all biological subjects. Added to his farming background, his university training in pure and applied biology and the influence of one of his teachers, F. H. A. Marshall, were to enable him in his life's work to change the traditional study of animal husbandry into an empirical science of animal production of which he was the creator. Marshall gave direction to his research, particularly in the physiology of reproduction.

At the outbreak of war in 1914 Hammond joined the 7th battalion of the Royal Norfolk Regiment and served as captain and company commander with the BEF in France until invalided home in 1916. Later he was staff captain, 201st Infantry brigade.

Hammond's career in animal science began in earnest after the war with his appointment in 1920 as physiologist in the Animal Nutrition Institute at the school of agriculture in Cambridge. In 1931 he became superintendent of the Animal Research Station, where he remained until retiring in 1954. Since the budget for research was meagre, never to exceed £10,000 a year, he experimented on strains of rabbits inbred for characteristics he wished to study in farm animals. Even for the latter—for example, horses and cattle—he chose diminutive breeds, such as Shetland pony mares and Dexter cattle, to increase the numbers he could afford to keep. With these and collections of pigs and sheep, his researches encompassed the animal life cycle from fertility and conception through pregnancy to birth, growth and development, lactation, and the inheritance of the next generation. His ideas and methods are well illustrated in his books—among which are *The Physiology of Reproduction in the Cow* (1927) and *Growth and the Development of Mutton Qualities in the Sheep* (1932). He was also on the editorial boards of the *Journal of Agricultural Science*, the *Empire Journal of Experimental Agriculture*, and the *Journal of Dairy Research*.

Faithful to his dictum that 'science isn't science until it is applied', Hammond promoted the results of his research in many ways. From those on growth in live animals he worked with producer organizations at home and abroad in developing standards for carcass assessment which are now in international use. His early interest in artificial insemination, officially discouraged for a time, led to the formation of the country's first Cattle Breeding AI Centre at Cambridge in 1942, which became the model for a new breeding system, now developed nationally, for the genetic improvement of cattle for milk and beef. During the war of 1939–45 he supervised with great success the Downing College Estate farms on the heavy clay of Cambridgeshire.

Hammond, although very tenacious of his ideas for livestock improvement, was by nature extremely gentle and kind, and incapable of making an enemy. With his very tall, spare build and his healthy complexion of a countryman, he was an outstanding figure among gatherings of farmers and scientists among whom he was equally at home. He was an inveterate world traveller and invitations from many governments and national organizations of producers to survey their animal industries provided him with opportunities which he relished. Whenever possible he went by train and in daylight, breaking his journey each evening, to enable him to make diary entries of the farming along his route. Hammond had rowed for his Cambridge college and kept an interest in its Boat Club throughout his life. He remained active and fit by cycling daily to and from his work and by gardening intensively to produce abundant fruits and vegetables from which his family and the families of his research students benefited. His interest in genetics overspilled from the laboratory to the garden, where he bred numerous strains of polyanthus.

In 1916 Hammond married Frances Mercy, daughter of John Goulder, a farmer, and they had three sons. He became the first president of the British Society of Animal Production. He was appointed CBE (1949) and received a knighthood in 1960. He was elected a fellow of the Royal Society in 1933 and was made a fellow of Downing College in 1936. Honorary doctorates were conferred on him by the universities of Iowa (1932), Louvain (1953), Durham (1956), Copenhagen (1958), Leeds (1961), Crakow (1963), and by the Hochschule für Bodenkultur, Vienna (1952). He was made a commander of the Order of Orange-Nassau (1946) and Commenda al Merito della Republica Italiana (1954), and was elected foreign member of many academies of agriculture and veterinary science. He died in Cambridge 25 August 1964.

[W. K. Slater and J. Edwards in *Biographical Memoirs of Fellows of the Royal Society*, vol. xi, 1965; E. O. Whetham in *Journal of Animal Production*, vol. iv, part i, 1962; personal knowledge.]   J. EDWARDS

HAMMOND, WALTER REGINALD (1903–1965), cricketer, was born at Dover 19 June 1903, son of William Walter Hammond, a corporal in the Royal Garrison Artillery who later became a major, and his wife, Charlotte Marion Crisp. His early days were spent in oversea stations in China and Malta, but he later scored so prolifically at Cirencester Grammar School that he made his first championship appearance for Gloucestershire only a few weeks after his seventeenth birthday. He did little at first, and in 1922 he was suspended after five matches because his residential qualification was not completed. But he had been quietly developing under the guidance of his county colleague George Dennett, and in 1923 he became a regular member of the side after scoring 110 and 92 against Surrey in the opening match.

In 1925, with 1,818 runs, 68 wickets, and 65 catches, Hammond established himself as an all-round cricketer of unusual promise, and a thunderous 250 not out at Old Trafford took him to the West Indies with MCC. At Bridgetown he made 238 not out in his first representative match, but he then became dangerously ill with blood-poisoning following a mosquito bite. His strong constitution carried him through twelve operations, but in 1926 he played no cricket at all. A coaching engagement in South Africa helped to restore his health, and in 1927 he announced his return to the English scene by becoming the first player since W. G. Grace [q.v.] in 1895 to score 1,000 runs in May. This achievement actually took only twenty-two days, and it included a century in each innings against Surrey, 187 in another onslaught on Macdonald at Old Trafford, and in the final match 192 out of 227 in 2½ hours against Hampshire. In a wet season he scored nearly 3,000 runs, with 12 centuries, and he played in all five tests in South Africa in the winter. The following summer saw his most spectacular all-round achievement when at Cheltenham he made 139 and 143 against Surrey, took Hobbs's wicket, and set up a world record of 10 catches; and then against Worcestershire made 80 in his only innings and bowled throughout the match to take 9–23 (catching the tenth) and 6–105: all this in one week's cricket.

In his prime Hammond was an exciting cricketer. As a bowler, with his upright side-on action and late swerve from leg, he could have played for any county even if he never made a run; he stood in the slips with an air of disengagement, but his eye and anticipation were so keen that he accepted the sharpest chance without appearing to move; and his batting had the stamp of the classic era, because it was never idiosyncratic or empirical. It was founded on an instinctive but rigorous technique: on a ruined wicket at Melbourne in 1937 there would be an innings of 32, when England declared at 76–9, which at that time no other batsman could have played. Above medium height, thickset, and broad-shouldered, Hammond was nevertheless very quick on his feet, and even when he was hammering the ball to the boundary, straight past the bowler, on the off through a ring of extra-covers or with his favourite stroke off the back foot past cover's left hand, his batting never lost its distinguishing grace and dignity. But he gradually turned his back on mere adventure. It began with the abandonment of the hook which had pulverized the county bowlers of the twenties. With (Sir) Jack Hobbs [q.v.] retiring, it fell on him to meet the oppressive challenge of the Australian (Sir) Donald Bradman. Bowlers, too, became increasingly negative, and although the controlled ferocity was never more than dormant, the time would come when O'Reilly could contain and frustrate him by bowling on his legs.

In his first encounter with the Australians in 1928–9, Hammond disciplined himself to the requirements of the timeless test. In a victorious series he made 905 runs at 113·12, with 251 at Sydney, 200 at Melbourne, 119 not out and 177 at Adelaide. They were all solid, responsible innings, devoid of quixotry or self-indulgence, and Hammond had reached his commanding maturity.

Looking back on the abundance of the thirties, Hammond said deprecatingly that 'It was all too easy'. In this great decade he helped B. H. Lyon to take Gloucestershire to second place in the championship. In 1933 with 3,323 runs (his largest aggregate) he headed the English averages, which he continued to do, in every season but one, for the rest of his career. He was an automatic choice for England whenever he was fit, although he had a dismal series against Australia in 1934, making only 162 in eight innings, and out there two years later half his test aggregate came in a single innings of 231 not out at Sydney. But at Lord's in 1938 he played his finest test match innings, 240 in 6 hours after 3 wickets had fallen for 31. In this season he began to play as an amateur, and thereafter he captained both Gloucestershire and England.

In the war Hammond joined the Royal Air Force, serving in the Middle East and South Africa, but he was seen in an occasional match at Lord's and in 1945 he scored 121 and 102 in one of the victory tests against the Dominions. But he was already troubled by the fibrositis which helped to bring his career to its sadly anti-climactic end. After captaining a home series against India he was asked to take a side to Australia in 1946-7 before English cricket had recovered from the war. The tour was a disaster in every way. The three completed tests were all lost, the traditional rivalry was soured by personal antipathies, and Hammond, fighting a private battle against illness, could not provide the expected leadership. He totalled only 168 runs in four tests and had to drop out of the fifth. The Palladian style had always been characterized by an impassive detachment, a grandeur which was beyond self-identification, so that the player had seemed to be aloof from his own achievement. Now the run of failure and misfortune produced an almost total withdrawal, and detachment began to look like apathy or indifference. Hammond batted mechanically, avoided his own team and his hosts alike, and neglected the captain's social duties. At the end of the tour he announced his retirement and he played only two more first-class games.

In his career he made 50,493 runs at 56·10, with 167 centuries, took 732 wickets at 30·58, and made 819 catches. His highest score was 336 not out against New Zealand, and he made three other scores over 300 and thirty-two over 200; seven times he made two centuries in a match. In 140 test innings he scored 7,249 runs at 58·45, with 22 centuries, took 83 wickets at 37·83, and made 110 catches. He twice scored double centuries in consecutive test innings, and for Gloucestershire in 1938 he hit seven centuries in eight innings.

In 1929 Hammond married Dorothy, daughter of Joseph Barker Lister, wool merchant, of Bingley. The marriage was dissolved and in 1947 he married Sybil Ness-Harvey, of Durban. He settled in South Africa where, after losing his capital by unwise investment in the motor trade, he was appointed coach and groundsman to Natal University. He died in Durban 1 July 1965. A memorial service was held in Bristol Cathedral and the county club opened an appeal fund for his widow and their son and two daughters.

[Ronald Mason, *Walter Hammond*, 1962; W. R. Hammond, *Cricket My Destiny*, 1946; *Wisden's Cricketers' Almanack*, 1966.]

M. M. REESE

HAMSHAW THOMAS, HUGH (1885-1962), palaeobotanist. [See THOMAS.]

HANBURY-WILLIAMS, SIR JOHN COLDBROOK (1892-1965), industrialist, was born at Henley-on-Thames 28 May 1892, the only surviving son of (Sir) John Hanbury-Williams who was military secretary to Lord Milner in South Africa and Earl Grey [qq.v.] in Canada before serving from 1914 to 1917 as chief of the British military mission with the Russian Army headquarters in the field. From 1920 to 1934 he was marshal of the Diplomatic Corps. The family had originated in Worcestershire but acquired an estate at Pontypool and developed the ironworks there; they were influential with the Duke of Marlborough in bringing William of Orange to this country and attained particular national prominence in the person of Sir Charles Hanbury Williams (1708-59, q.v.).

Hanbury-Williams's mother was Annie Emily, eldest daughter of Emil Reiss, a family which had business interests in the Far East. After education, like his father, at Wellington College, Hanbury-Williams joined the firm in London and Manchester. He served in France during the war of 1914-18 with the 10th Royal Hussars and at GHQ, British Army, was mentioned in dispatches, and was invalided out of the Service after the cessation of hostilities. On returning to the family business, he travelled extensively in China and Japan.

In 1926 Hanbury-Williams accepted an invitation to join Courtaulds Ltd., a company which by this time had already established itself as world leader in the rayon or artificial silk industry, and of which Samuel Courtauld [q.v.] had been chairman since 1921. The growth of the firm had been greatly accelerated since the war and there was a need for initiative and leadership which Hanbury-Williams amply provided. Within a couple of years he was carrying much responsibility in the commercial field—particularly overseas—participating in top-level negotiations with rayon producers in other European countries, and fulfilling the administrative task of establishing the manufacturing companies which were set up on the Continent. In 1928 he was appointed a director of Snia Viscosa, an Italian associate company, a position which he held until his death. To Hanbury-Williams was due the initiative and foresight which finally led to the manufacture of 'Cellophane' in this country, and several years later he was responsible for Courtaulds participating with Imperial Chemical Industries Ltd. in the development of nylon.

In 1930 Hanbury-Williams was appointed to the board; he became a managing director in 1935, deputy chairman in 1943, and in 1946 succeeded Courtauld as chairman. When he retired in 1962 after the unsuccessful takeover bid by Imperial Chemical Industries, the assets of Courtaulds had multiplied nearly four times, and under his leadership the company had taken its place amongst the largest industrial concerns in Great Britain. One of his board colleagues once remarked that he was 'determined and stern in his business dealings, yet courteous and kind in his treatment of individuals'. During his chairmanship of the company, schemes were introduced for recognition of long service by employees, as well as for employee participation in the company's fortunes by means of co-partnership. Although he remained true to the diplomatic tradition of his family, he combined this with an unfailing spirit of democracy in all his personal relations.

In 1928 Hanbury-Williams paid his first visit to the vast interests of Courtaulds in the United States, with which he later became much involved. Some twelve years afterwards it was his unhappy lot to represent the company in the negotiations which took place between the British and American Governments prior to the passing of the Lend-Lease Act in 1941, and which culminated in the loss by the company—and, indeed, by Britain—of an asset of very great value.

A member of the royal household for many years, Hanbury-Williams filled the office of gentleman usher from 1931 to 1946, thereafter serving as extra gentleman usher to King George VI and then to Queen Elizabeth. In 1950 he was knighted and in 1956 appointed CVO.

In 1936 Hanbury-Williams was appointed a director of the Bank of England. He served for many years as a member of the committee of Treasury, and from 1940 to 1941 was in charge of foreign-exchange control. In 1949 upon the retirement of Lord Catto [q.v.] he was invited to succeed him as governor; although singularly fitted for this high distinction, with characteristic integrity of purpose he declined because of his commitment to Courtaulds, but continued as a director until 1963 and was active in many ways throughout his long period of office.

Hanbury-Williams served under Lord Selborne at the Ministry of Economic Warfare in 1942; led a goodwill trade mission to Egypt in 1945; was appointed a lay member of a committee which sat from 1947 to 1953 to consider and make recommendations on the practice and procedure in the Supreme Court with a view to reducing the costs of litigation; in 1948 he chaired a committee appointed by the prime minister to investigate the ordering procedure for civil aircraft; in 1943 and again in 1958 he was high sheriff of the county of London.

Hanbury-Williams was actively associated with the raising of funds for various charitable, educational, and philanthropic causes, amongst which were the King George VI National Memorial Fund and King George's Jubilee Trust. Invited in 1954 by the Duke of Edinburgh to serve on the council of the study conferences which he inaugurated, Hanbury-Williams undertook the task of honorary treasurer and subsequently acted also until his death as a trustee of the Fund which was established. The first of these conferences was held in Oxford in 1956 and a second in Canada in 1962.

In 1928 Hanbury-Williams married Zenaida, daughter of Prince Michael and Princess Julia Cantacuzene. Her family had left Russia in 1917 and settled in the United States, her mother being granddaughter of General Grant. There were two daughters and one son of the marriage.

Hanbury-Williams died in London 10 August 1965. A portrait by David Jagger is in the possession of Courtaulds Ltd. and a copy is with the family.

[Private information; personal knowledge.]

NORMAN H. HUDSON

HANCOCK, ANTHONY JOHN (TONY) (1924-1968), comedian, was born at Small Heath, Birmingham, 12 May 1924, the second of three sons of John Hancock, hotelier, and his wife, (Lucy) Lilian Thomas. He was educated at Durlston Court, Swanage, and Bradfield College, Reading. Much of his youth was spent in Bournemouth where his father, himself a part-time professional entertainer, ran a hotel.

Here he met many people from the lighter side of the entertainment world. Attempts to find employment in ordinary life were less than successful. He was, briefly, in the Civil Service and his subsequent job, at a Birmingham tailor's, lasted just under three hours.

Enlisting in the RAF in 1942, Hancock toured with ENSA (Entertainments National Service Association) and the Ralph Reader 'Gang Shows'. Demobilized in 1946, in 1948 he appeared at the Windmill Theatre, a variety house whose girl-predominated turns had much pleased the mainly male wartime audiences and whose proud motto was 'We Never Closed'.

But it was to be with the BBC, both in radio and on television, rather than on the stage that Hancock's name was to be made. Graduating from such wireless attractions as 'Workers' Playtime', 'Variety Bandbox', and 'Educating Archie', where his catchphrase of 'flippin' kids!' became well known and widely copied, he was given on 2 November 1954 his own programme, 'Hancock's Half-Hour', which was an immediate success.

To add incongruity to his fictional and somewhat squalid East Cheam background, his name was elaborated into Anthony Aloysius St. John Hancock. The programme owed much to the presence in the cast with him of Bill Kerr, Kenneth Williams, and, particularly, Sid James. It owed perhaps most of all, for Hancock was incapable of producing his own material, to Alan Simpson and Ray Galton, his scriptwriters. The strength of the Half-Hour lay in the fact that it relied on comedy of character and situation rather than on set jokes and it had none of the musical interludes with which such programmes were normally interrupted. Hancock played an unsuccessful actor, full of pretentiousness and snobbery and deeply prejudiced. In one of the John Freeman 'Face to Face' interviews on BBC television, he said: 'The character I play isn't a character I put on and off like a coat. It's a part of me and a part of everybody I see.'

Throughout the 1950s television was becoming increasingly efficient and popular and vastly expanding (ITV appeared in 1954) and in due course in 1956 the Hancock programme was transferred to this medium and to the huge audience which it by then commanded. Here the success was even greater and for a few years there was no comedian of comparable popularity. His face fitted to perfection the character which had up to then been purely a wireless voice. There were the heavy jowls, the creases, the sunken and pouchy eyes, the turned-down corners of the mouth. There was a fresh catchphrase ('Stone me!'). Sid James, his partner in the constant disasters—financial, social, and professional—which beset them,

had a face along similar lines. The programme frequently found them, bored to tears, after lunch on a Sunday afternoon and with rain falling. One of the episodes began with the following series of groans, treasured by the whole viewing public, from Hancock: 'Ahh. Oh dear. Mm. Oh dear, oh dear. Ahh, dear me. Ahhh. Stone me, what a life.'

Bored indeed with his by now familiar comedy routines, his attempts to branch out into other comic realms brought real disaster with them. Seldom has such a dazzling career disintegrated so swiftly. He abandoned Sid James and Galton and Simpson. He made three poor films. There was an unsuccessful ITV series. He began drinking heavily and could not remember his lines. His first marriage (to Cicely Romanis in 1950) broke up in 1965 and his second marriage to 'Freddie' Ross, his public relations agent, in the same year ended in divorce a week before his death.

Tony Hancock was the last of a cherished line of English comedians whose stock-in-trade it has been to have about them a seedy air of vanished sartorial grandeur and of better times, Burlington Berties every one of them. There was George Robey's bowler hat and frock-coat, with the red nose and heavy, arched eyebrows to go with them. There was Billy Bennett ('Almost a Gentleman') with his defiant bow-tie and dickey and boots. And with Hancock it was the Homburg hat, the shabby fur-collared overcoat, and the grand manner, all so splendidly out of place either in a fish and chip parlour or at home at 23 Railway Cuttings, East Cheam. And to accompany the run-down clothing there was the look of total gloom and despondency and a deep resentment against life.

J. B. Priestley, writing enthusiastically on the special characteristics of purely English humour, a brand so incomprehensible to other nations, says that Hancock, in the television sketches written for him by Alan Simpson and Ray Galton and which suited him so perfectly, 'seemed to combine an unconscious despair and hatred of show-business with more than a touch of genius for it, finally giving him deep at heart a deathwish'. Priestley was sadly right and in the end Hancock died by his own hand in Sydney, Australia, 25 June 1968.

[Roger Wilmot, *Tony Hancock—'Artiste'*, 1978; Eric Midwinter, *Make 'em Laugh*, 1979; *The Times*, 26 June 1968.]

ARTHUR MARSHALL

HANCOCK, SIR HENRY DRUMMOND (1895-1965), civil servant, was born in Sheffield 17 September 1895, the only child of Percy Griffen Hancock, manufacturer of electroplate, and his wife, Margaret Drummond. His father died three years later, the business passed out of the family, and his mother moved to Portsmouth. After periods at school in France and Germany, Hancock was educated at Haileybury and as a scholar of Exeter College, Oxford. In the war of 1914-18 he served in the Sherwood Foresters and the Intelligence Corps, and was mentioned in dispatches.

In 1920 he entered the administrative class of the Civil Service, and was appointed to the Ministry of Labour. He early became secretary of a committee of inquiry into the working of the Trade Board Acts. Then followed a period, which included the general strike, when he was private secretary to Sir Horace Wilson, the permanent secretary.

During the ten years from 1928 Hancock was deeply involved in the problems created by unemployment. He first helped to administer various schemes for the transfer of unemployed workers to places where industry was expanding. In 1929 Labour took office, and J. H. Thomas [q.v.] was made lord privy seal to head a team to stimulate and co-ordinate schemes for the relief of unemployment. Hancock was appointed to be his private secretary, a post in which he showed his quality, although the financial orthodoxy of Philip (later Viscount) Snowden [q.v.] as chancellor of the Exchequer left Thomas without the resources to make any impact on the problem. When Labour went out of office in 1931, Hancock returned to the Ministry of Labour to deal with the problem of assisting those who had exhausted their right to unemployment benefit. He helped to frame the legislation which set up the National Assistance Board, and in its early years was a member of its staff, helping to build the first nationwide organization to take over responsibilities hitherto left to the Poor Law.

In 1938 Hancock was transferred to the Home Office to take charge of a division concerned with the expenditure of local authorities, who had been called on to administer a system of air-raid precautions. There he put the arrangements for financing Civil Defence on a sound footing.

In 1941 he was sent to the United States as secretary-general of the British Purchasing Commission and the British Raw Material Commission. His work there earned him a CMG (1942). He returned to England in 1942 to be deputy secretary of the Ministry of Supply, where he had three strenuous years at the hub of war production.

With the return of peace in 1945 and a Labour Government in power, the centre of gravity moved back to the social services, and Hancock moved with it, becoming deputy secretary,

under Sir Thomas Phillips, of the new Ministry of National Insurance, established to frame and administer the comprehensive scheme, based on the Beveridge plan, which replaced and extended the former separate and partial schemes of health and unemployment insurance, old-age and widows' pensions, and workmen's compensation. Hancock was appointed KBE in 1947 and this, and his appointment to succeed Phillips as permanent secretary in 1949, showed how his work was regarded. He was appointed KCB in 1950.

By 1951 the National Insurance scheme was established and Hancock was moved to a new field of activity, as permanent secretary to the Ministry of Food. The end of rationing could now be foreseen, and it became Hancock's business to dismantle the system of wartime controls and state purchase, so that the remaining functions of the Ministry of Food could be absorbed into what thus became the Ministry of Agriculture, Fisheries and Food. In 1955 this work was done, and Hancock was appointed chairman of the Board of Inland Revenue, a post which he filled with distinction until he retired in 1958.

All through his career in the Civil Service, Hancock had shown remarkable versatility, and was moved from one criticial point to another as the need arose, particularly when some new organization was to be created or some major development of policy had to be steered. In the last ten years he had been permanent head of three major departments, and the principal adviser of three Labour and five Conservative ministers. For him retirement simply meant a change of occupation, and he continued to work as hard as ever. Of his new activities, the most onerous were the chairmanship of the Local Government Commission for England, appointed under the Act of 1958 to review the boundaries of county and county borough areas, and membership of the boards of two large companies, Booker Bros. McConnell & Co., and the Yorkshire Insurance Company. To all these he was deeply committed and never spared himself, winning affection by his kindness as well as respect for his thoroughness, clear thinking, and wisdom. No business problem was too much trouble; and, even more important, he was always ready to listen sympathetically and helpfully to the working and personal problems of his colleagues, young and old. In 1962 he was promoted GCB. But he had taken on too much. On 24 July 1965 he died suddenly while abroad on business.

His dedication to work left him little time for outside activities, but he read widely, was fluent in French and German, and had a considerable knowledge of antiques and architecture. In his younger days he was a great walker, and knew many country churches and country houses. But London was his home throughout his working life except in the war; he never owned either a house or a car.

In 1926 he married Elizabeth, elder daughter of Engineer-Captain Henry Toop, RN, of Portsmouth; they had one son and one daughter. The son, Peter Henry Drummond Hancock, was elected in 1971 to membership of the council of the Institution of Civil Engineers.

[*The Times*, 26 July 1965; private information; personal knowledge.]   EDWARD HALE

HANDLEY PAGE, SIR FREDERICK (1885–1962), aircraft designer. [See PAGE.]

HANKEY, MAURICE PASCAL ALERS, first BARON HANKEY (1877–1963), secretary to the Cabinet, was born at Biarritz 1 April 1877, the fifth child and third son of Robert Alers Hankey and his wife, Helen, daughter of William Bakewell, lawyer, of Adelaide, South Australia. His father, whose health was delicate, had spent some years as a sheep farmer in Australia. Hankey, like his father, was educated at Rugby School. He was gazetted a probationary second lieutenant in the Royal Marine Artillery in 1895; passed out first with the sword of honour from the Royal Naval College; and took first place in all his examinations at Eastney Barracks, Portsmouth. He served in the *Ramillies*, flagship on the Mediterranean station, in 1899–1902 and was then transferred to the Naval Intelligence Department in the Admiralty. There he served on committees on the defences of the principal naval bases at home and overseas (1905–6) and on naval war plans (1906–7). In 1907 he returned to the Mediterranean as intelligence officer. In 1908 he was appointed an assistant secretary in the Committee of Imperial Defence and in 1912 was promoted secretary at the early age of thirty-five.

The outbreak of war in 1914 brought him additional responsibilities in the secretaryship of the War Council, the Dardanelles Committee, and the War Committee. When the War Cabinet Secretariat was established in December 1916 he became its chief, and after the war combined the secretaryship of the Cabinet with that of the Committee of Imperial Defence, to which in 1923 was added the clerkship of the Privy Council. He retained these three positions until he retired from official life in 1938.

To these exacting activities at home he added a number of important tasks in the international sphere. Amongst the most important were the secretaryship of the British Empire delegation at the Paris peace conference in 1919 and later at the same conference the secretaryship of the innermost Council of Four (Lloyd George, Clemenceau, Orlando, and Woodrow Wilson). He was British secretary at the Washington conference (1921) and the Genoa conference (1922); secretary of the Imperial conferences of 1921, 1923, 1926, 1930, and 1937; secretary-general to the conferences on German reparations in London (1924) and Lausanne (1932), the Hague conferences of 1929 and 1930, and the London naval conference in 1930.

Hankey's mind was capacious, his memory large and exact, his persistence relentless, and his tenacity invincible: characteristics of many public servants. But Hankey had supplementary qualities which brought him into the ranks of the really great administrators. He had more than the usual allotment of tact with those volatile politicians who were his daily masters. He served with equal success men as widely dissimilar in temperament as Asquith, Lloyd George, Bonar Law, Baldwin, Ramsay MacDonald, and Neville Chamberlain. If he did not like all of them to an equal degree, they all trusted his integrity and used him to sort out some of the rough animosities which constantly arise between ambitious men. They relied also upon his prodigious memory and his extraordinary application to the problems which confronted them. On questions of defence in particular his opinion and advice were constantly sought, and he had no hesitation about responding. In the first war it was difficult for ministers to get an objective inter-Service point of view from the official Service advisers: each upheld in confident terms the professional views of his own Service. There was no machinery by which comprehensive strategic advice could be obtained. Hankey filled the gap, and his memoranda on broad strategic questions, always deeply considered, resembled the thorough reports submitted by the Joint Planning Staff to the Chiefs of Staff Committee and the prime minister in the second war. Obviously Hankey's memoranda did not carry the same authority, and inevitably from time to time they roused the suspicion and hostility of the Admiralty and the War Office. But they were always well informed, often imaginative and prescient, and invariably cogently expressed.

Hankey's greatest achievement was the creation of the Cabinet Secretariat which first came into existence in 1916. From the time of the Liberal electoral victory of 1906, the scope and complexity of government responsibilities had increased; but the only official record of Cabinet proceedings—a very subjective one—was the prime minister's letter to the sovereign.

Responsibility for executing decisions lay with individual ministers in the Cabinet: the danger of confusion and negligence was considerable. With the onset of war in 1914 the consequences of misunderstandings could well have been disastrous. Hankey saw clearly the need for some effective articulating machinery and to him must go the chief credit for the formation of the Cabinet Secretariat. He laid down the principles which have continued to guide its performance. From time to time it has been viewed with suspicion, by the Treasury in particular, and not much less by the Foreign Office and the Service departments: it has remained right at the centre of power and inevitably the secretary of the Cabinet has more direct contact with the prime minister than any other official could hope to have.

When the war was over and Lloyd George, in whose eyes Hankey was indispensable, had fallen from power in 1922, the system came under heavy attack. Bonar Law, the new prime minister, professed to think the Cabinet Secretariat an extravagance. This stimulated the Treasury into an all-out attempt to obliterate the Cabinet Office once and for all. The Foreign Office gladly joined in the hunt and some prominent newspapers were anxious to be in at the kill. Hankey defended his creation with skill and vigour and by making judicious concessions here and there kept it in existence. In this process it became more and more obvious to him that, if a Cabinet Secretariat were to make its appropriate and invaluable contribution to the conduct of government, its ambitions must be restricted by modesty.

After this somewhat bitter defensive action Hankey was even more careful not to abuse his position and his successors have followed his example. If the Cabinet Secretariat were to attempt to override the great departments of State and to make pretensions to superior knowledge, it would fail in its co-ordinating and articulating duty. Hankey came to understand this very clearly, and it was for this reason that he was so often acceptable as secretary-general of various international conferences. He was by no means without ambition and he held strong opinions on many subjects, but he knew that for the successful conduct of the business of the Cabinet and of any other committees and conferences the secretary must be self-effacing. The system remains the envy of many other nations.

After his retirement in 1938 Hankey was created a baron (1939) and in that year joined Neville Chamberlain's War Cabinet as minister without portfolio. When Churchill became prime minister in May 1940 he made Hankey chancellor of the Duchy of Lancaster, without a seat in the War Cabinet, and subsequently in 1941 paymaster-general, from which office he was dismissed in March 1942. Churchill was a notable example of the fact that prime ministers rarely have much time for the political figures favoured by their predecessors. Moreover, he was never much in sympathy with men of strict habits and moralizing tendencies. Whereas, as a secretary, Hankey had been excellent and silent in Cabinet, as a minister he talked too much. Churchill was irritated especially by Hankey's insistence in 1941–2 that the battle of the Atlantic ought to have priority over strategic bombing, largely valueless at that time.

Nevertheless, in spite of Churchill's waning confidence, Hankey did some useful work as ministerial chairman of Cabinet committees, where his capacious mind and knowledge of government business were most valuable. His chairmanship of the Cabinet's Scientific Advisory Committee brought him into a new world, and the many scientists, whose work he facilitated by his high administrative skill, honoured him with a fellowship of the Royal Society (1942). After his dismissal from office he continued, at the request of Ernest Bevin [q.v.], to be chairman of two ministerial committees, and he accepted the unpaid chairmanship of several official committees right up to 1952.

In his retirement Hankey busied himself with his memoirs of the first war. The publication of these was banned by three successive prime ministers (Churchill, Attlee, and Macmillan) on security grounds, and after the deletion of certain passages they finally appeared in two innocuous volumes in 1961 under the title of *The Supreme Command 1914–1918*. In 1945 Hankey published his Lees Knowles lectures on *Government Control in War*; in 1946 *Diplomacy by Conference*; and in 1951 his Romanes lecture on *The Science and Art of Government*—all subjects of which his practical experience was unrivalled.

Success and promotion in Whitehall are more often derived from the skilful mobilization and use of the written and the spoken word than from qualities of personal leadership. Hankey in office was certainly too busy on matters of extreme national significance to give very much consideration to the personal problems of his own staff, and his natural gifts did not lead him in that direction. The harsh trial of official business was seldom mitigated by the exercise of charm and humour. His subordinates admired his extraordinary qualities and they were proud to share in the splendid organization he had created and to be praised when they did well. But their admiration for their chief was greater than their affection.

In person Hankey was not impressive. He was no more than 5 feet 5 inches in height, his figure was inelegant, and it seemed to many observers that he was always in a hurry, running from one crucial position to another. He had a large head and massive brow, and the tones of his voice were light and pleasant. He was busy always, and his moods of relaxation were known only to his family. Part of his scanty leisure was occupied with music to which he was devoted throughout his life. His private life was founded upon the principles of Christianity and a strict observance of the rites of the Church of England. His religion was of the type known as 'muscular Christianity'. He took a cold bath every morning, he was an advocate of alfresco meals in unwelcoming weather, he was persistent in physical exercise, and his favourite method of locomotion was on his feet. He was a man of temperate habits. He preferred a diet of whole-meal bread, raw vegetables, fresh fruit, eggs, and nuts, and this sustained him in full vigour until he was nearly eighty-six.

In 1903 Hankey married Adeline Hermine Gertrude Ernestine (died 1979), daughter of Abraham de Smidt, who had been surveyor-general in Cape Colony but had settled in England in 1890. A woman of strong character and outstanding practical ability, she took over the burden of family affairs and created a happy background in which her over-stretched husband was able to enjoy himself with their three sons and one daughter. There was no self-indulgence about his enjoyment, and he took pains to devise games and activities for them and to stimulate their imagination and their interest in history and current affairs. The secret of the family happiness was the mutual and constant devotion of Hankey and his wife.

Hankey received a grant of £25,000 for his services in the first war. To his private secretary he gave a box of small cigars. He was appointed CB (1912), KCB (1916), GCB (1919), GCMG (1929), and GCVO (1934). He was sworn of the Privy Council in 1939. He held honorary degrees from Oxford, Cambridge, Edinburgh, and Birmingham. He died in hospital in Limpsfield 26 January 1963 and was succeeded as second baron by his eldest son, Robert Maurice Alers (born 1905), a member of the Diplomatic Service.

The National Portrait Gallery owns a portrait of Hankey by Sir William Orpen. There is also a sketch of Hankey intended for inclusion in a picture of the Versailles peace conference by Orpen in the British Embassy in Paris. A portrait of Hankey in his room in the Cabinet office by Robert Olivier is reproduced in *Diplomacy by Conference*.

[*The Times*, 28 January 1963; Stephen Roskill, *Hankey, Man of Secrets*, 3 vols., 1970-4; contemporary biographies and memoirs; private information.]

GEORGE MALLABY

HARARI, MANYA (1905-1969), publisher and translator, was born at Baku 8 April 1905, the fourth child and youngest daughter of Grigori Benenson, a Jewish financier, by his wife, Sophie Goldberg. While Benenson amassed an enormous fortune Manya's childhood was spent amid the opulence of a rented top floor of Volkonsky's Petersburg house, and at Redkino, a splendid country estate. In 1914 the family migrated to London from Germany where they had been visiting. Manya was educated at Malvern Girls College and Bedford College, London, graduating with second class honours in history in 1924. Her father refused to establish new domicile roots and, while he was building up another financial empire which crumbled in the Wall Street crash, the family home was usually a luxury hotel.

In 1925 Manya's awakened interest in the Jewish question, both from a religious and political point of view, led to a Palestine visit where she met Ralph Andrew Harari, a notice of whom appears below. They were married in that year. Bored by the social round in Cairo she began to study, and was shocked by, social conditions in Egypt. Visits to Palestine, where she worked in a kibbutz in 1926, and welfare work in Cairo failed to quell a growing restlessness of spirit. In 1932 she reached a long pondered decision and became a Roman Catholic; she remained emphatic that this in no way detracted from her Jewish identification. Later, frequently visiting London, she was associated with the inauguration of the Sword of the Spirit movement by Cardinal Hinsley [q.v.] in 1940; she worked on the *Dublin Review* and then edited her own periodical, the *Changing World*; when publication ceased in 1942 she anticipated her husband in joining the Political Warfare Department as a translator.

In 1946, with Marjorie Villiers as her partner, Manya Harari founded the Harvill Press, a small publishing house specializing in books on religion, metaphysics, the arts, and psychology. In 1954 Harvill became a subsidiary of Collins, with Manya and her partner continuing to direct the enterprise. It was as the publisher, and joint translator with Max Hayward, of Boris Pasternak's *Dr. Zhivago* (1958) that Manya Harari's name became widely known. She also helped to introduce to British and American readers Konstantin Paustkovsky, Alexander Solzhenitsyn, Andrei Sinyavsky, Ilya Ehrenburg, and Yevgeni Yevtushenko, thus providing expression for what might be regarded as the free voice of Russia. Her discernment as a publisher was matched by her outstanding gifts as a translator.

Working from an attic room in her London

home in Catherine Place, poised between typewriter and telephone, with manuscripts, authors, intermediaries, their friends, and friends of their friends all jostling for priority, clutching a huge box of cigarettes and for ever smoking, Manya Harari never lost her softness of voice and gentleness of manner; physically she was so slender that her whole presence seemed contained in the intensity and pallor of exquisitely drawn features. Totally without vanity and oblivious of her material surroundings she pursued her diverse causes with passionate resolution. However busy, she never could bear to be tied to one environment.

In 1948 she went to Palestine as a reporter. In 1955 she made her first return journey to Russia, visiting Moscow, Leningrad, and Redkino. She was to return in the spring of 1956 and again in the winter of 1961.

When her husband became seriously ill in 1968 Manya Harari already knew that she herself had only months to live. Characteristically she kept the knowledge to herself until he died in May 1969 and continued to work on an autobiography until a few days before her own death in London 24 September 1969, having found an almost total serenity in her all-embracing religious faith.   P. J. V. ROLO

HARARI, RALPH ANDREW (1892–1969), merchant banker, art scholar and collector, was born 28 October 1892 in Cairo, the third child and elder son of (Sir) Victor Harari Pasha, civil servant, financier, and leading member of Egypt's Anglo-Jewish community, by his wife, Emma Aghion. The hospitality of their Cairo home, spanning the years from Cromer to Killearn [qq.v.], provided a valued meeting point between British administrators, resident diplomats, visiting notabilities, and the Turco-Egyptian establishment. Harari was educated at Lausanne and Pembroke College, Cambridge, where he obtained first classes in both parts of the economics tripos (1912–13) and a boxing blue. Back in Egypt in 1914 he participated, as a junior officer, in the Palestine campaign of Sir Edmund (later Viscount) Allenby [q.v.], later serving as finance officer to his father's old friend (Sir) Ronald Storrs [q.v.], then military governor of Jerusalem. In 1920 he was appointed director of trade and commerce in the new mandate under Sir Herbert (later Viscount) Samuel [q.v.], also an old family friend. In 1925 he returned to Egypt to help his father's business enterprises.

In 1939 Harari was imaginatively appointed economic adviser to GHQ Middle East, with the rank of full colonel, but no visible signs of any supporting establishment. His duties were unspecified, his services ubiquitous. His advice, modestly conveyed in oracular pronouncements, was widely sought; he became, in effect, a one-man 'think-tank'. Recalled to London for consultation with Lord Keynes [q.v.] after the end of the desert campaign, he was recruited, on the basis of his Cairo reputation, by Peter (later Lord) Ritchie-Calder, then director of plans in the Department of Political Warfare; colleagues were impressed by his shrewdness and practical humanity; for his services Harari was appointed OBE.

After the war he remained in London as managing director of the merchant banking firm of S. Japhet & Co., later taken over by the Charterhouse group of companies whose board he then joined.

Alongside a career moulded by family tradition Harari made his own way as an art scholar and collector. Becoming interested in Islamic metal work in the twenties he emerged as its leading expert and collector, contributing the authoritative chapter 'Metalwork after the early Islamic period' in the *Survey of Persian Art* (6 vols., 1938–9); he donated his own collection to the Cairo Museum. In the early thirties he began to collect Beardsley drawings, then out of fashion. Adding to these after the war, he eventually formed the largest private collection which notably enriched exhibitions in London (1966) and New York and Los Angeles (1967), and has now been acquired by the Victoria and Albert Museum. His Beardsleys were complemented by paintings and drawings of Rouault, Lautrec, Segonzac, Sickert, John, Gavarni, and Keene. It was said of Harari that 'he was essentially sensitive to style taken to the point of mannerism'; perhaps inevitably his attention turned to Japan. Before 1958 he had collected one important album of Hokusai (1760–1849) sketches; from then onwards he became increasingly fascinated; while concentrating on Hokusai, he acquired a representative range of Japanese paintings and drawings. An exhibition, organized after his death by the Arts Council at the Victoria and Albert Museum, was the first public glimpse of this unique collection which, amassed without the aid of any vast financial resources, had already inspired and delighted Japanese art scholars.

Harari was also a collector of people; he believed in good food, good wine, and civilizing communication. He and his wife made an art of hospitality at their London home. Both believed passionately in the healing power of reason and persuasion; their influence, so diverse in its impact, was probably more pervasive than they knew; they were both good listeners and very undemanding in their friendship. They had one son, Michael Harari, who became a psychiatrist. Ralph Harari died in London 26 May 1969.

[Manya Harari, *Memoirs*, 1972; *The Harari Collection of Japanese Paintings and Drawings*, compiled by J. Hillier, 3 vols., 1970-3; private information; personal knowledge.]

P. J. V. ROLO

HARDWICKE, SIR CEDRIC WEBSTER (1893-1964), actor, was born 19 February 1893 at Lye in Worcestershire, the eldest of three children and only son of Edwin Webster Hardwicke, medical practitioner, and his wife, Jessie Masterston. He was educated at King Edward VI Grammar School, Stourbridge, and at Bridgnorth School. At first intended to follow his father's profession, he failed in a preliminary examination and was then allowed to follow his own desire. He joined the (Royal) Academy of Dramatic Art and in 1912 had some small part and understudying experience at the Lyceum, His Majesty's, and the Garrick theatres.

In 1913 he joined the Shakespeare Company of (Sir) Frank Benson [q.v.] which gave him experience in the provinces, South Africa, and Rhodesia; and in 1914 he was in the Old Vic Company, still struggling for recognition. Up to this point he had not shown any remarkable acting talent, nor did it seem that he was taking his stage career very seriously; for when he joined the army at the end of 1914 he remained a soldier for no less than seven years, becoming in 1921 the last British officer officially to leave the war zone. Even so, he felt himself a misfit in civil life in post-war England. According to his own account in his autobiography *A Victorian in Orbit* (1961) it was a chance visit to the Birmingham Repertory Theatre directed by (Sir) Barry Jackson [q.v.] which gave him 'for the first time' the desire to do something worth while as an actor.

Starting his career again virtually from scratch, Hardwicke joined Jackson's company in January 1922, and for two years remained in Birmingham playing a wide variety of increasingly important parts. In February 1924 Jackson took over the Court Theatre in London and gave Hardwicke the chance of repeating there the three parts in *Back to Methuselah* which he had already created. This production was followed in March by *The Farmer's Wife* in which Hardwicke's share was a quite extraordinary performance in a 'character' part as Churdles Ash, a bent and sharp-tongued old farm labourer. The piece did not at once find popular favour in London, but Jackson's faith in it held steady and he nursed it to success. In the end, largely owing to the growing fame of Hardwicke's performance, it had a run of 1,324 performances, one of the longest in theatrical history. After this triumph,

Hardwicke found himself in constant demand for important parts over a wide range of contrasted styles. In 1926 a crusty old misogynist in *Yellow Sands;* in 1928 Captain Andy in *Show Boat*; in 1929 the highly sophisticated King Magnus in *The Apple Cart*; in 1930-1 the sinister Edward Moulton-Barrett in *The Barretts of Wimpole Street*. In 1932 at the Malvern Festival he played Abel Drugger in *The Alchemist* and gave contemporary audiences a chance to understand why David Garrick in his day had been inspired to make this comparatively minor part into a *tour de force* of comic acting. In 1933 as the doctor in *The Alchemist* and gave contemporary audiences a chance to understand why David cess and was rewarded with a knighthood in 1934. Nor did his run of good fortune end there, for his next two plays, *Tovarich* (1935) and *The Amazing Doctor Clitterhouse* (1937), both lasted over a year. In 1936 he gave at Cambridge the Rede lecture on 'The Drama Tomorrow'.

The year 1938 brought Hardwicke to an altogether new phase in his career. He went to America, and made his first appearance on the New York stage as Canon Skerritt in *Shadow and Substance*. After a good run in this play, followed by a tour, he went on to Hollywood, where he was destined to spend almost the whole period of the war of 1939-45 making films designed in general to keep up the morale of an embattled Britain. His acting on film was effective enough but not of the same high quality as his stage work and like other leading stage actors he had a dislike of the scrappy way in which film acting has to be done. But he was one of a group of fine British players above military age whose contribution to the war effort lay in this field.

Hardwicke returned to London in 1944 and for four rather unsettled years he shuttled back and forth between London and New York, sometimes to act, sometimes to direct, but without finding anything very rewarding. In 1948 he joined the Old Vic Company at the New Theatre to play Sir Toby Belch, Doctor Faustus, and Gaev in *The Cherry Orchard;* but it was about this time that he confessed to a friend that he was finding the competition in London too hot for him. He returned to New York and spent the rest of his career there making himself invaluable either to play the lead in, or to direct, the more important plays brought over from London. He died in New York 6 August 1964.

He was twice married: first (1927) to an English actress Helena Pickard (died 1959); secondly (1950) to an American actress, Mary Scott. Both wives divorced him; he had a son by each.

[Sir Cedric Hardwicke, *Let's Pretend*, 1932, and *A Victorian in Orbit*, 1961; *The Times* and *Daily Telegraph*, 7 August 1964; private information; personal knowledge.]

W. A. DARLINGTON

HARDY, SAM (1882-1966), footballer, was born at Ashton-under-Lyne 17 April 1882, the son of James Hardy, a labourer at an ironworks, and his wife, Sarah Wadsworth. After attending the Newbold Church School, Chesterfield, he was employed by a Chesterfield draper, absenting himself on Saturday afternoons to play football. Although destined to rank among the great goalkeepers in the game's history, he was originally a centre-forward and only went into goal when one day the selected incumbent did not appear. He caught the attention of the Chesterfield club, then in the second division, and joined them in April 1903 at a wage of 5s. a week. When Liverpool won the second-division title in 1904-5 they scored six goals against Chesterfield but were so well impressed by Hardy's potential that they paid £500 for his transfer. They went on to win the League championship in the following season, and Hardy, taking over from E. Doig, made thirty appearances in the side.

Hardy's international career began in 1907, and although it was interrupted by the war, he was capped twenty-one times for England between 1907 and 1920 and he also played in three 'Victory' internationals in 1919-20. With R. Crompton (Blackburn Rovers) and J. Pennington (West Bromwich Albion) he formed a celebrated defence that played together for several pre-war seasons, and in 1908-9 England defeated Wales, Ireland, and Scotland without conceding a goal (Hardy incidentally saving a Scottish penalty). This feat had not been accomplished by any of the four countries since the international championship was instituted in 1883, and it had not been repeated by any English side seventy years later, although Scotland achieved it in 1925-6.

In May 1912 Hardy moved to Aston Villa, together with J. Harrop, a centre-half, for a combined fee of £1,250. He replaced W. George, a former English international, in the Villa goal, and in his first season with the new club they finished second to Sunderland in the League. Sunderland were therefore favourites to win the 'double' honours when the two teams met in the Cup final, which was played on the old Crystal Palace ground and was watched by 121,919 spectators. After an hour Hardy was injured in a collision with an opposing forward and eventually had to leave the field for repairs, Harrop taking his place in goal. He returned with a bandaged leg but kept his goal intact, Villa winning by the only goal. Next season they were again runners-up in the League, this time to Blackburn Rovers, and in the first season after the war Hardy gained another Cup-winner's medal when they beat Huddersfield Town, of the second division, 1-0, after extra time. In August 1921 Hardy moved to Nottingham Forest, who headed the second division during his first season with them. He finally retired in 1925, aged forty-two, after a career of 552 League appearances.

He was known in the game as 'Silent Sam', a name which epitomized his unobtrusive style. Goalkeepers in his time did not come out and seek to dominate the penalty area in the modern fashion. At 5ft. 10 in. and weighing 12 stones, Hardy was able to look after himself, but the laws did not give goalkeepers the physical protection they now enjoy and mostly they stayed on their line and relied on accurate handling and instinctive positioning and anticipation. Hardy's anticipation was such that he seemed to magnetize the ball into his arms, and only an unforeseeable deflection would oblige him to go at full length to save it. In 1908 'the famous warden', as the newspaper called him, wrote an article for the *Liverpool Echo* entitled 'Aspects of a Difficult Art'. Goalkeepers, he said, were born and not made, and he placed anticipation as the highest of their natural gifts. Himself he made a habit of watching the striker's foot as a clue to the likely power and direction of the shot.

Goalkeepers, he added, must be phlegmatic, and in his own demeanour on and off the field Hardy was a model professional in days when the game itself, and especially those who played it for a living, were lowly regarded. His insistence throughout his playing career on living and training at his Derbyshire home showed an unusual independence in a professional footballer. Having assisted Nottingham Forest on the administrative side, he later kept an interest in the game by acting as a scout for Aston Villa. For many years he was licensee of the 'Gardener's Arms' in Chesterfield, and he was proprietor of a number of billiard halls. He died at his home at Newbold 24 October 1966, leaving a widow and three sons. He had married c.1908.

[The *Liverpool Echo*; the *Derbyshire Times*.]

M. M. REESE

HARLECH, fourth BARON (1885-1964), statesman and banker. [See ORMSBY-GORE, WILLIAM GEORGE ARTHUR.]

HARMAN, SIR CHARLES EUSTACE (1894-1970), judge, was born in London 22

November 1894, the second son of John Eustace Harman, an eminent junior of the Chancery bar and a popular bencher of Lincoln's Inn. His mother was Ethel Frances, daughter of Henry Birch, a housemaster at Eton who had been tutor to Edward VII. Throughout his life Harman retained a strong filial attachment to his father's memory and admiration for his professional skill and wisdom.

Harman won the third scholarship in the 1908 election at Eton where he played the wall game both for College and the school, and for some years after 1918 he used to return regularly as a vociferous and savage player for the bar. He gained a classical scholarship at King's College, Cambridge, and went up in the autumn of 1913, but the outbreak of war interrupted his career. He was commissioned in the Middlesex Regiment and after the battle of Loos in 1915 he was a prisoner until 1918, a time in which he acquired fluent French, good Italian, and some Russian. He returned in 1919 to Cambridge where by his own account he spent much time in re-creating the undergraduate life and institutions he had known before the war. For the Marlowe Society he gave a memorable performance as Falstaff in Shakespeare's *Henry IV Part I*. He won the university's Winchester reading prize and the Charles Oldham Shakespeare scholarship and, reading for a war degree, secured first classes in both parts of the classical tripos, graduating in 1920.

Harman was called to the bar by Lincoln's Inn in 1921 and quickly attracted business at the Chancery bar. He took silk in 1935. In 1947 he was appointed a judge of the Chancery division with the customary knighthood and in 1959 was promoted to the Court of Appeal and sworn of the Privy Council. As an advocate Harman's style had sometimes an abrasive quality which was not endearing, but he was a careful and conscientious counsel of whom solicitors were rightly confident that a client's case would be thoroughly and firmly presented. As a judge he proved much more patient and urbane than many of his friends had expected. He was ever ready to listen attentively to a well-presented argument. His judgements were robust and clear, showing a deep respect for legal scholarship combined with common sense. His style was lucid and his vocabulary flexible, as befitted a classical scholar and wide reader. Although his interlocutory remarks were sometimes characterized by a disconcerting judicial waywardness, he was not inclined to wit or epigrams in his judgements, but the language in which he clothed them, particularly his extempore judgements, endowed them with a peculiar vigour. He brought to his cases a combination of a powerful mind and a wide knowledge of and profound respect for orthodox law.

At the end of every sittings Harman would be on the first available boat-train to Holyhead. All his vacations were spent at Tully, his home on the west coast of county Mayo, and the setting of holidays from early boyhood. There he devoted himself mainly to outdoor pursuits. As a naturalist he had studied and knew his country intimately. He was a good shot and a first-class fisherman, whose happiest hours were spent on the river which flowed past, and occasionally under, his front door.

Harman developed a gruff and sometimes intimidating manner to cover a shy disposition, but his asperities were matched by great kindliness to others. Although in some respects a solitary man, he nevertheless delighted in good talk, good company, and good living. He gave devoted service to Lincoln's Inn, of which he became a bencher in 1939 and treasurer in 1959. It would have been strange if he had passed a bystander unnoticed as he strolled back to the courts after lunching at the bench in Lincoln's Inn. Six feet four inches tall, broad and upstanding, wearing a tall silk hat and an overcoat of elegantly Edwardian cut, with a military moustache and a monocle appropriately slung on a length of fishing line, he was a striking figure; and the manner matched the man.

In 1924 Harman married Helen Sarah, daughter of Colonel Herman Le Roy-Lewis; they had two sons, one of whom, Jeremiah, followed his father to the Chancery bar and became a Queen's counsel in 1968. The other, Nicholas, became a well-known writer and broadcaster on economic and political subjects.

In June 1970 failing sight and hearing compelled Harman to retire and he died in London 14 November. He was buried by his own wish in the churchyard of his Irish parish church.

Portraits by David Rolt and Juliet Pannett are in the possession of the family.

[Private information; personal knowledge.]
DENYS B. BUCKLEY

HARRIS, JOHN WYNDHAM PARKES LUCAS BEYNON (1903-1969), writer, best known under the name of JOHN WYNDHAM, was born at Knowle in Warwickshire 10 July 1903, the elder son of George Beynon Harris, a barrister-at-law of Welsh descent, and his wife, Gertrude Parkes, the daughter of a Birmingham ironmaster. The younger son, Vivian Beynon-Harris, became the author of four light novels published between 1948 and 1951. Because his parents separated when he was eight, John gained a wide experience of English

Harris, J. W. P. L. B.   D.N.B. 1961-1970

preparatory schools before being sent to Bedales from 1918 to 1921.

He then tried his hand at several careers, including his father's profession of law, farming, commercial art, and advertising, but a small private income—coupled with something in his temperament—made it difficult for him to settle to anything. He began to write short stories. An early affection for the novels of H. G. Wells [q.v.] prompted him towards science fiction. He sold a slogan to an American science fiction magazine in 1930 and, encouraged by this minor success, wrote fiction published in American magazines like *Wonder Stories* and *Amazing Stories*, under the name of John Beynon Harris.

Honour demanded an attempt at the English market. The *Passing Show*, in its third midsummer double number for 20 July 1935, launched a new serial in nine parts, 'The Secret People', by John Beynon. Harris had gone; Beynon sounded more literary. His was an unlikely tale of a man and woman captured by pygmies under a Sahara which was being flooded to create the New Sea; it was published as a book in 1936. It was successful enough to encourage both Wyndham and the magazine to try again for, in May 1936, the *Passing Show* began serialization of 'Stowaway to Mars', published as a book (*Planet Plane*) in the same year. Both these novels were reprinted in the 1970s.

The war brought a halt to this stop-go career. Wyndham became a civil servant and worked as a censor; later, in 1943, he joined the Royal Corps of Signals, working in a cipher office with the rank of corporal, and playing his part in the Normandy landings.

After the war, Wyndham had to start again. He was a familiar figure at the Penn Club in Bedford Place, just off Russell Square in London, and knew the publisher (Sir) Robert Lusty, then a director of Michael Joseph Ltd. One day he brought Lusty a manuscript, saying: 'This is a novel I've managed to write. I don't quite know what to do with it and I thought you might advise me.' Michael Joseph published the novel in 1951, as *The Day of the Triffids*. In the same year it was serialized in five parts in *Collier's* magazine and from then on Wyndham's was a famous name—for he had shuffled through his generous supply of forenames and arrived at 'John Wyndham'. His story of the perambulating vegetable menace which takes over a Britain stricken with blindness was an immediate success. The inferior MGM film version (1963) starred Howard Keel. The novel sold as well and steadily as a Penguin book as did any by Agatha Christie.

The Kraken Wakes was published in 1953. The story is one of interstellar invaders who settle on the sea-bed and flood the land. It provides a chance for the type of mild surrealism—motor boats chugging up Oxford Street—which Wyndham enjoyed, and it brought more success. Wyndham's most powerful novel, *The Chrysalids*, was published in 1955; a puritanical post-nuclear war community in Labrador oppresses its children, who eventually discover telepathic powers and break free. A similar theme, this time with the children unsympathetically cast, emerged in *The Midwich Cuckoos* (1957), the story of a sleepy English village where all the women are astrally impregnated at the same time. The novel was filmed with notable success as *Village of the Damned* (1960), starring George Sanders. A sequel followed, *Children of the Dammed* (1963), which owed less to Wyndham and more to commerce. *The Outward Urge* appeared in 1959; this time Wyndham had found a collaborator, 'Lucas Parkes'. Thus, Harris economically used up his two remaining forenames. This story depicted an English family, the Troons, venturing into space, but Wyndham was less successful on Arthur C. Clarke territory. Although *Trouble with Lichen* (1960) has its supporters, it is an indecisive attempt to tackle the debating point of 'Immortality: Is it Democratic?' *Chocky*, published in 1968—and ominously serialized in the magazine *Good Housekeeping*—was a too cosy account of a boy taken over by an interstellar something. *Web* was published posthumously in 1979.

Among Wyndham's many short stories, collected in such volumes as *Jizzle* (1954) and *The Seeds of Time* (1956), special mention must be made of the collection *Consider her Ways* (1961), a strikingly nasty glimpse of a future world where men are extinct and gigantic breed mothers perpetuate the species.

In 1963 Wyndham married Grace Isabel Wilson, a teacher and long-term member of the Penn Club. They had no children. Wyndham died 11 March 1969, in Petersfield, Hampshire.

Although the vogue for Wyndham's type of 'cosy catastrophe' as one critic termed it, may have passed, Wyndham's importance in the rebirth of British science fiction after the war of 1939-45 was second to none. His very English style ('the Trollope of science fiction', according to one reviewer), coupled with the Wellsian gift for exploring emotive ideas, brought him international success and encouraged others to strike out in the same way. Writers as diverse as John Christopher, Charles Eric Maine, J. G. Ballard, and Christopher Priest owe him much. Indeed, it can be claimed that, however hesitatingly, Wyndham established a flourishing school of writers.

[Donald H. Tuck, *The Encyclopaedia of Science Fiction and Fantasy*, vol. i, Chicago,

1974; Sir Robert Lusty, *Bound to be Read*, 1975; private information; personal knowledge.]   Brian W. Aldiss

HARRIS, TOMÁS (1908-1964), artist, art dealer, and intelligence officer, was born 10 April 1908 in Hampstead, London, the youngest son and sixth of the seven children of Lionel Harris and his Spanish wife, Enriqueta Rodriguez. His father had founded the Spanish Art Gallery in Bruton Street and was responsible for importing almost all the important works of art which came from Spain into England in the years before and after the war of 1914-18. Tomás was educated at University College School and at the age of fifteen won the Trevelyan-Goodall scholarship to the Slade where he studied from 1923 to 1926, concentrating mainly on sculpture. He continued his studies in the arts by spending a year at the British Academy in Rome, but in 1928 he decided to become an art dealer. He set up a small gallery of his own first in Sackville Street and then in Bruton Street, but after a short time moved it to join his father at the Spanish Art Gallery. He continued to run the latter after his father's death in 1943. He was also a talented amateur musician, and played the piano, the saxophone, and other wind instruments.

As a dealer Harris continued the policy of his father and brought to England not only Spanish paintings, including works by El Greco, whose importance was only just beginning to be recognized, but also medieval tapestries, oriental carpets, Renaissance jewellery, and other *objets d'art* in which the palaces and religious houses of Spain were rich. He had an astonishing instinct for discovering works of art in unexpected places, and on one occasion bought a group of panels from a fifteenth-century German altarpiece which were among the contents of an outhouse at a country sale in England. He had a reputation for absolute probity which sometimes aroused the jealousy of his less successful competitors.

At the beginning of World War II Harris joined a branch of intelligence which was later dissolved and in 1940 was transferred to the Security Service where his intimate knowledge of Spain was of great value. His greatest achievement in this field was as one of the principal organizers of 'Operation Garbo' which was the most successful double-cross operation of the war and which seriously misled the Germans about Allied plans for the invasion of France in 1944. The success of the operation, which was described by a senior commander as worth an armoured division, was mainly due to the extraordinary imaginative power with

which Harris directed it. In 1945 he was appointed OBE.

Even during the war Harris did not completely relinquish his activities as an artist and in 1943 he held a one-man show at the galleries of Reid and Lefèvre in King Street. After the war he gradually freed himself from his commitments as a dealer and spent more and more time in Spain, first at Malaga and then in Majorca where he designed and built a house at Camp de Mar. Here he was able to paint as much as he wanted, and he also experimented with making ceramics and stained glass and designing tapestries, three of which were woven at the Royal Tapestry Factory at Madrid. His great versatility enabled him to master all the technical problems involved in these activities with astonishing ease.

At the same time he devoted much time to collecting, concentrating first on drawings by the two Tiepolos (which were shown by the Arts Council in 1955) and later on the engravings of Dürer and the etchings of Rembrandt. His greatest achievement was, however, to form a magnificent collection of etchings and lithographs by Goya which in 1979 was accepted on part payment of death duties and is now in the British Museum. Finding that the standard works on Goya were seriously misleading he decided to write a book about the etchings himself and the result was the two volumes published in 1964 which became the standard work. In writing this he was helped by Juliet Wilson.

In 1931 Harris married Hilda, daughter of Ernest Campbell Webb, of London; there were no children of the marriage.

Harris died in a motor accident in Majorca 27 January 1964. In 1975 an exhibition of his work was held at the galleries of the Courtauld Institute, to which his widow and sisters had presented a fine collection of textiles formed by his father and himself. Harris was notable for his warmth, his generosity, and the enthusiasm with which he threw himself into any undertaking.

There is a self portrait, painted in 1954, in the Courtauld Institute galleries.

[Private information; personal knowledge.]   Anthony Blunt

HART, Sir BASIL HENRY LIDDELL (1895-1970), military historian and strategist, was born in Paris 31 October 1895, the younger son of the Revd Henry Bramley Hart, Wesleyan minister in Paris, and his wife, Clara, daughter of Henry Liddell. He was educated at St. Paul's School. In 1913 he went up to Corpus Christi College, Cambridge, to read history, but on the outbreak of war in 1914 he obtained a temporary commission in the King's Own Yorkshire Light Infantry. Posted to France in September 1915, he was invalided home after a shell-burst at Ypres; he returned to the front in the spring of 1916, only to be rendered *hors de combat* by gas on the Somme. Deep thought about his intense experiences on the western front permeated his subsequent military ideas. As adjutant (temporary captain) of training units of the Volunteer Force in 1917-21, he evolved new methods of instruction and an original battle drill. These attracted the attention in 1919 of two generals, Sir Ivor Maxse [q.v.] and Winston (later Lord) Dugan, who were responsible for compiling a post-war *Infantry Training* manual, much of which, although junior in rank, Liddell Hart was to revise or compose. His concepts did not always survive the War Office sieve, but he promulgated them with characteristic assurance in articles and lectures. He transferred to the Army Education Corps in 1921 with a regular commission, but his health wrecked his professional career; he was placed on lieutenant's half-pay in 1924, and retired as captain in 1927 'on account of ill health caused by wounds'. Nevertheless, he was already launched as a military thinker.

Oppressed by the slaughter on the western front, which he ascribed to inflexible generalship and bull-at-a-gate offensives, he sought by intellectual analysis to prevent or ameliorate any recurrence, taking as his slogan 'if one wishes peace one should understand war'. His key concepts were the 'expanding torrent' and the 'indirect approach'. The former, drawing on techniques employed in the German offensive of March 1918, emphasized fluidity, continuous forward motion, and the vital need to reinforce spearheads by immediately available reserves. The latter stressed tactical and strategic outflanking, the paramount virtue of surprise, and the importance of striking not at an opponent's main body but at nerve centres such as headquarters and lines of communication. Between the wars he expounded these principles volubly, and his *Strategy—The Indirect Approach* appeared in different forms in six editions between 1929 and 1967. Some felt that as he elaborated his theories they became more a philosophy of life than a *vade mecum* for the commander, but it is unquestionable that their forceful and lucid reiteration had a seminal and liberating effect on educated soldiers at home and abroad.

With the inter-war pioneers of British armoured development—J. F. C. ('Boney') Fuller, (Sir) Percy Hobart [qq.v.], (Sir) Charles Broad, and (Sir) Giffard Martel (a notice of whom Liddell Hart contributed to this Dictionary)—his affinity was two-way. They discussed with him their practical experiments and forward thinking; he stimulated in argument and provided a public forum for the unorthodox group, struggling as it was against conservatism and the 'cavalry spirit'. As military correspondent of the *Daily Telegraph* in 1925-35, and as correspondent and defence adviser of *The Times* in 1935-9, he assiduously charted the efforts of the pioneers of mechanization, while also turning a critical eye on broader aspects of the British military machine, and registering the progress of German rearmament. His intimate contacts with the Service hierarchy, both at unit levels and in Whitehall, gave him an unequalled insight into dead wood and growth points. He was cultivated by the alert, and rejected by closed minds.

Wide reading in military history gave his theories backbone. Over thirty books he wrote included studies of Scipio Africanus (1926), Sherman (1930), Foch (1931), and (1934) of T. E. Lawrence [q.v.], with whom he had a warm *rapport*. A man of sturdy loyalty, he devoted much time to defending Lawrence against his denigrators, as he did in the case of David Lloyd George, whose war memoirs owed much to his assistance. His Lees Knowles lectures for 1932-3, on 'The Movement of Military Thought from the Eighteenth to the Twentieth Century', were published as *The Ghost of Napoleon* (1933). In 1930 *The Real War* (enlarged and reissued as *A History of the World War*, 1934) made a controversial indictment of the command of Earl Haig [q.v.]. Widely read by military students—indeed, often 'required reading' in military colleges—Liddell Hart's writings advanced his authority.

This seemed at a peak in 1937-8, when the war minister, Leslie (later Lord) Hore-Belisha (whose notice he wrote for this Dictionary), enlisted him as unofficial adviser. He gave a creative impulsion to Hore-Belisha's reforms, but when the connection waned in mid 1938 it had damaged him: the reforms (although mainly salutary) were resented and the minister himself was distrusted by the military establishment, where Liddell Hart was felt to have enjoyed an excessive influence—particularly over senior appointments. In November 1939 *The Times* accepted his resignation, tendered in August after mounting frustration over his inability to publish the truth as he saw it. He thus lost both power-bases, and the issue in July of *The Defence of Britain* had even raised doubts about the stability of his judgement. Its stress on the current need for defence rather than offence seemed inconsistent with his ardent advocacy of the 'expanding torrent'.

Throughout the war of 1939-45 he was excluded from positions of influence. This was not surprising, since he advocated a compromise peace and consistently opposed 'total war'. (Sir) Winston Churchill, who had sought his advice in the thirties, made no further overtures. Journalism and private consultation were his lot, and pain as he watched the Germans in 1940, and other belligerents later, apply the ideas he had preached. The latter were not his alone, but he had been an especially perceptive prophet: he had fertilized the British Army—particularly the Royal Tank Corps—and in Germany men like Field-Marshal Reichenau and General Guderian acknowledged his stimulus, although it was perhaps not so directly influential as their post-war confidences suggested.

After 1945 he recovered from his eclipse. *Persona grata* with captive German generals, he recorded his interrogations in *The Other Side of the Hill* (first issued 1948, and enlarged in 1951), for long a source-book on their attitudes, and his edition of *The Rommel Papers* (1953) became an enduring text. *The Tanks* (2 vols., 1959) lifted regimental history on to the highest plane, and years of preparation resulted in his posthumous *History of the Second World War* (1970). Here his strength as a military analyst was qualified by limitations, for in describing a total war he overlooked its totality in terms of sociological, economic, and political consequences.

During the post-Hiroshima years he denounced 'massive retaliation' and denied, in speech and writing, that the existence of nuclear weapons would proscribe warfare at lower levels, in which he was as prescient as in his warning that antidotes must be prepared for the coming plague of guerrilla insurgency. But in his Indian summer it was as a sage that he most happily contributed to military affairs, and wrote, among much else, several notices for this Dictionary. States House, Medmenham, became a place of multi-national pilgrimage; the gamut ran through chiefs of staff to graduate researchers. His study was lined with photographs of statesmen and soldiers with whom he had shared a dialogue—his 'rogues' gallery'—and a later collection, the 'young rogues', who represented the cream of a new generation of military historians, beneficiaries of his passionate tutorial dissection of their writing and the incessant dialectic of his conversation. His ideas, moreover, were still a weapon: in 1967 the Israelis affirmed that their war that year had been won by 'the true strategy of indirect approach', and Yigal Allon inscribed a photograph to 'the captain who teaches generals'.

Unusually tall, light of frame, with a busy inquisitive air, he struck one as like a secretary-bird. But his eyes were Robin Goodfellow's, puckish and smiling; his laughter effervesced,

and an ill-concealed streak of vanity endeared more than it offended. Brocade waistcoats and an indefinably dandiacal pose reflected his eccentric but deeply informed studies of feminine fashion, about which the experts approached him on their own level. As a young officer he had reported for leading newspapers on lawn tennis and rugby, and his lifelong addiction to war games, chess, and croquet (in which he was described as a fiendish opponent) refreshed rather than reduced his competitive spirit.

In 1918 he married Jessie Douglas, daughter of J. J. Stone; they had one son. The marriage was dissolved, and in 1942 he married Kathleen, daughter of Alan Sullivan, of Toronto, and widow of Henry Philbrick Nelson, FRCS. In 1963 he was awarded the Chesney gold medal of the Royal United Service Institution, in 1964 Oxford made him an honorary D.Litt., and in 1965 he was elected an honorary fellow of Corpus Christi College, Cambridge. He was a founder-member of the Institute of Strategic Studies, president of the Military Commentators' Circle in 1953-70, and an honorary member of the United States Marine Corps. In 1965-6 he was visiting distinguished professor at the university of California, and also in 1965 he was presented with a Festschrift, *The Theory and Practice of War*, edited by Michael Howard. He was knighted in 1966. A unique archive, the hundreds of files containing his correspondence and voluminous papers, is lodged in King's College, London.

He died 29 January 1970 at his home at Medmenham. A drawing by Sava Botzaris (1938) and two portraits by Eric Kennington (1943) are in the possession of the family.

[Basil Liddell Hart, *Memoirs*, 2 vols., 1965; *The Times*, 30 January 1970; R. J. Minney, The Private Papers of Hore-Belisha, 1960; Kenneth Macksey, *Armoured Crusader: Major-General Sir Percy Hobart*, 1967; Sir Giffard Martel, *An Outspoken Soldier*, 1949; private information; personal knowledge.]

RONALD LEWIN

HARVEY, HILDEBRAND WOLFE (1887-1970), marine biologist, was born 31 December 1887 at Streatham, London. He came of a family which had been professional for three centuries and was the elder son of Henry Allington Harvey, paint manufacturer in the firm of Foster, Mason & Harvey of Mitcham, Surrey, and his wife, Laetitia, daughter of Peter Kingsley Wolfe, a descendant of General James Wolfe [q.v.], of the battle of Quebec in 1759. After attending Gresham's School, Holt, Norfolk, from 1902 to 1906, he entered Downing College, Cambridge, in 1906, to read natural sciences. He gained a second class in both parts of the tripos (part i in 1909 and part ii—specializing in chemistry—in 1910).

Early he developed a love of small boats. Possession of a certificate as master mariner (yacht) led to his service in minesweepers and patrol vessels in the RNVR during the war of 1914-18. His skill at navigating these in stormy waters in all seasons, including northern winter nights, became legendary.

In 1921 he joined the staff of the Marine Biological Association of the United Kingdom as administrative and hydrographical assistant. He was to spend the rest of his working life (he retired in 1958) in Plymouth and was destined to become one of the founders of systematic research on the biological productivity of the sea. He was to develop a combination of qualities rarely found in one man. He was a gifted synthesizer of existing knowledge able to see the relevance of and to co-ordinate pieces of knowledge drawn from widely different disciplines. From these he constructed powerful hypotheses. At that early stage he rarely discussed them with colleagues except in pursuit of further factual knowledge. This ability to take the constructive broad view was combined with the patience to undertake meticulously designed experimental work needed to test his hypotheses. He had a gift for minimizing the time spent on experiment by his intuitive flair for rejecting work likely to be unproductive. He was a master of the experimental method and of presentation of results in elegant, precise, and concise language.

Consequent on the terms of his appointment his early work was on the physical oceanography of the western English Channel. At that time useful measurements were largely confined to salinity and temperature and the theory for interpreting these in shallow seas was much behind that available for the waters of the deep ocean. Though Harvey quickly saw that an understanding of biological productivity which his colleagues sought needed a more biochemical approach, a decade was needed for him to find out how best to do it. He had to devise his own quantitative methodology. His first success was a method for analysing one of the forms of combined nitrogen—nitrate—which he considered that marine plants were likely to need. Though no more than semi-quantitative and using a highly corrosive medium it was immediately and widely used by expedition ships. The broad picture obtained with it of world oceans distribution has been confirmed by the far better methods since available.

The publication in 1928 of his monograph on the biological chemistry and physics of sea-water illustrated the ordered and economic way in which he carried through all his researches. It epitomized an exhaustive study to ensure that he himself wasted no time in vain repetition of unnecessary experiments. Other researchers greatly valued it. Harvey had been at Plymouth for twelve years before publishing his classical paper on the rate of diatom growth. He then succeeded in enlisting the help of three specialist colleagues to produce a paper on plankton production and its control, in which the methods of physics, chemistry, plant physiology, and zooplanktology were applied to the waters of the English Channel for a year.

To convey the seminal value of Harvey's continuing work and publications upon marine productivity, one could hardly improve the words in which the Murray committee of the US National Academy of Sciences recommended the award of the Agassiz medal in 1952: 'H. W. Harvey . . . has been the leading student for many years of the changes in the chemical constituents of sea water brought about through the agencies of plants and animals and also of how the availability of nutrient chemicals determines the fertility of the sea. While his field observations have been concentrated mainly in the English Channel and its approaches, many of the conclusions which can be drawn from his work apply to the whole biologically active zone of the marine environment.' Indeed, Harvey's genius lay in recognizing untilled fields ready for strategic research and in his gift for cultivating those fields with maximum production of pertinent knowledge. No effort was wasted in nurturing trivial weeds. He wrote two further books.

In 1945 he was elected to fellowship of the Royal Society, and in 1958 he was appointed CBE.

In 1923 he married Elsie Marguerite, daughter of H. Sanders. The marriage was dissolved and in 1933 he married, secondly, Marjorie Joan, daughter of J. Sarjeant. There was a son of the second marriage.

He was a kindly man who taught quietly by precept. Always considerate, he once offered a colleague a lift in his car, to receive the reply 'No thank you, Dr Harvey, I am in a hurry'. And so he drove through life. He died in Freedom Fields Hospital, Plymouth, 26 November 1970.

[*Journal of the Marine Biological Association of the UK*, 1972, vol. lii, pp. 773-5; L. H. N. Cooper in *Biographical Memoirs of Fellows of the Royal Society*, vol. xviii, 1972; private information; personal knowledge.]

L. H. N. COOPER

HARVEY, OLIVER CHARLES, fourth baronet, and first BARON HARVEY OF TASBURGH (1893-1968), diplomatist, was born at Rain-thorpe Hall, near Norwich, the only son of Sir Charles Harvey, second baronet, and landowner, by his second wife, Mary Anne Edith, daughter of G. F. Cooke, of Holmwood, Norwich. He was educated at Malvern College and at Trinity College, Cambridge, where he obtained a first in part i of the historical tripos in 1914. He served throughout the war in France, Egypt, and Palestine, and was mentioned in dispatches.

In 1919 Harvey entered the Diplomatic Service and after postings at home and to Rome and Athens became in 1931 head of Chancery at the embassy in Paris. From then on his career was an alternation between Paris and London where his service at the Foreign Office was closely related to that of Anthony Eden (later the Earl of Avon). In January 1936 Harvey was promoted counsellor and became private secretary to Eden whom he served with a dedication to which his *Diplomatic Diaries* bear eloquent witness. He was a convinced believer in Eden's policy of resistance to Fascist aggression and consequently, as his very outspoken diaries show, strongly hostile to Neville Chamberlain's appeasement policies. As private secretary to the foreign secretary Harvey interpreted his duties widely, often proffering advice on matters of internal policy in terms critical of the prime minister's policies and of his interferences in foreign affairs. After Eden's resignation in February 1938 Harvey continued to offer unofficial advice to his former chief. His personal relations with Lord Halifax [q.v.] were good, but he could not feel the same enthusiasm for his policies and he noted that the new foreign secretary was less inclined than his predecessor had been to rely on his private secretary for political counsel, and more in the habit of resorting to the conventional channel, via the permanent under-secretary, for the diplomatic advice he needed. Nevertheless, Harvey stayed on at his post, albeit with diminished influence, until he became minister in Paris in December 1939.

There his time was brief but eventful. France fell within a few months and he was involved in the embassy's odyssey from Paris, via a château in Touraine, to Bordeaux, and evacuation in a British warship. He worked briefly at the Ministry of Information in charge of propaganda to the occupied countries of Europe, but it was no surprise that Eden, who had returned to the Foreign Office in December 1940, took the first opportunity of reappointing Harvey as his private secretary, in June 1941, although he was by now well above the rank normal for the post. Thenceforward Harvey was closely involved in all the complicated issues which beset the Foreign Office during the war. He accompanied Eden on three trips to Moscow, the first at the dramatic moment when the Germans had just been stopped thirty kilometres away in December 1941, and once to the United States. He was closely involved too in the controversies over the employment of Darlan and Giraud, the struggle over the recognition of the National Committee of de Gaulle, the difficulties with the exiled Polish government, and the like. In all these questions his advice was forward-looking, realistic, and on the side of the new forces which he believed would emerge in the open at the end of the war. His *War Diaries* show him as very critical of Churchill and Roosevelt for their inability to recognize these new forces, and his admiration for Eden in this period was not unqualified, though he continued to hope for his succession as prime minister and discouraged him from accepting the vice-royalty of India. He continued as private secretary until 1943 when he became assistant under-secretary, and in 1946 he succeeded Sir Orme Sargent [q.v.] as deputy under-secretary (political), the second highest professional post in the Foreign Office, and one in which he worked closely with Ernest Bevin [q.v.] whom he much admired.

In 1948 Harvey was appointed ambassador in Paris in succession to Duff Cooper (later Viscount Norwich, q.v.). He had served there twice before and he had accompanied King George VI and Queen Elizabeth on their state visit in July 1938 (when he received the grand cross of the Legion of Honour), and his intimate acquaintance with European and in particular French problems made his appointment natural, almost inevitable. His embassy was a very different one from the dazzling performance of the Coopers which he did not seek to emulate. He was strict in excluding from the embassy any Frenchman in any way tainted by collaboration with the Germans but filled the beautiful house in the Faubourg St. Honoré with small and well-selected parties of leading Frenchmen, mainly drawn from the political parties then ruling France. The food was delicious, the Harveys' distinguished collection of modern paintings ornamented the salon vert, and the discriminating style of their entertaining was exactly suited to the ethos of the Fourth Republic, whose leading statesmen were mostly men of intelligence and taste but without the pretentiousness which came later. Harvey's tenure of the British Embassy coincided with one of the least acrimonious periods of Anglo-French relations, and to this his personal contribution was far from negligible. His own style was entirely devoid of pretentiousness. His appearance was deceptively mild and owlish; in fact, as his diaries show, he was a man of strong convictions, even passions.

On his retirement from Paris in 1954 Harvey was created a baron and later in the same year he succeeded his half-brother as fourth baronet. He took little part in the debates in the House of Lords although he attended with some regularity, sitting on the cross-benches and normally voting on the Labour or Liberal side. His retirement, spent in London with winters in the south of France, was peaceful and uneventful. He enjoyed his trusteeship of the Wallace Collection, and was active in the Franco-British Society, of which he became chairman.

Harvey was appointed CMG (1937), CB (1944), KCMG (1946), GCMG (1948), and GCVO (1950). In 1920 he married Maud Anners (died 1970), daughter of Arthur Watkin Williams-Wynn, a landowner of Coed-y-Maen, Montgomeryshire. Lady Harvey was a woman of unusual charm and distinction of appearance who was a great help to Harvey in his career. They had two sons, the elder of whom, Peter Charles Oliver (born 1921), succeeded to the baronetcy and the barony when his father died at his London home 29 November 1968.

[*The Diplomatic Diaries of Oliver Harvey, 1937-1940*, ed. John Harvey, 1970; *The War Diaries of Oliver Harvey, 1941-1945*, ed. John Harvey, 1978; private information; personal knowledge.]   W. E. HAYTER

HASSALL, CHRISTOPHER VERNON (1912-1963), poet, biographer, playwright, and librettist, was born in London 24 March 1912, the son of John Hassall [q.v.], the painter and illustrator, and his second wife, Constance Maud, the daughter of the Revd Albert Brooke Webb, rector of Dallinghoe, Wickham Market, Suffolk. He was the younger brother of Joan, the wood-engraver, who decorated many of the title-pages and jackets of his books. He was educated at Brighton College and Wadham College, Oxford, which, because of a family financial crisis, he left without taking finals. After leaving Oxford, where he played Romeo with (Dame) Peggy Ashcroft, (Dame) Edith Evans, and George Devine [q.v.] in the OUDS *Romeo and Juliet*, a notable production directed by (Sir) John Gielgud, he spent some years as an actor.

Such was the range of Hassall's gifts, that only a few of his achievements can be listed. In poetry, *Penthesperon* (1938) won him the Hawthornden prize; and *Crisis* (1939), a sonnet sequence, the A. C. Benson medal. *S.O.S. . . . 'Ludlow'* (1940) was published soon after he had joined the Royal Artillery as a gunner. In 1941 he was commissioned, and in 1942 he joined the Army Education Corps in which he attained the rank of major. *The Slow Night*, containing

some of his most moving poetry, was published in 1949, and *The Red Leaf* in 1957. He did not live to see the publication of *Bell Harry, and Other Poems* (1963) which contained a sequence of forty sonnets in memory of his friend, the poet Frances Crofts Cornford [q.v.]. In poetic drama, *Christ's Comet*, an Easter play for which he also composed the music, was written for the 1938 Canterbury Cathedral Festival, and *The Player King* was the Edinburgh Festival play of 1952. *Out of the Whirlwind* (1953) was the first secular play to be staged in Westminster Abbey since the Reformation.

In another field, not unrelated, Hassall's original libretti for cantatas and operas by, amongst others, Antony Hopkins, (Sir) Arthur Bliss, (Sir) William Walton, and Malcolm Arnold, and his English versions of foreign works, notably *Bluebeard's Castle* of Bela Bartok, placed him foremost among contemporary librettists. His libretto for Walton's *Troilus and Cressida* (1954) was described by Ernest Newman [q.v.] as 'the best poetic opera text since Hofmannsthal'. In the field of biography, *The Timeless Quest* (1948) was a life of the actor, Stephen Haggard. His major biography, *Edward Marsh: Patron of the Arts* (1959, awarded the James Tait Black memorial prize) is a lasting contribution to the cultural and social history of the first half of this century, and was the result of his long friendship with 'Eddie' (as he was always known). Hassall also contributed the notice of Marsh to this Dictionary. *Ambrosia and Small Beer*, a record of their voluminous correspondence, appeared posthumously in 1964 as did also his life of *Rupert Brooke* (1964) though he was able to complete and revise the text before his sudden death.

Hassall also had a flair for lighter verse and in 1935, with the lyrics he composed for *Glamorous Night*, he started his collaboration with Ivor Novello [q.v.], an association which, over many years, was to enable him financially to devote time to his more serious work. His public and recorded recitals of drama and poetry, in which he frequently included the work of his favourite metaphysical poets, were well known; his deep appreciation of the poetry was matched by the fine quality of his voice.

Hassall's lifetime covered a period of accelerating and often hectic change in the arts. Temperamentally, he was not always in sympathy with the new developments. Though his interest in the younger poets never flagged, his own work showed a concern to further and expand the traditional, rather than a desire to break with it. His poetry, sometimes lyrical and sometimes ruminative, almost conversational, was always direct in theme and statement. At its best, it was distinguished by depth and clarity of feeling, with a startling felicity of expression. Hassall knew or had met an extraordinarily wide range of people, most of them connected with the arts, and he was an exceptionally good raconteur; his sense of humour was highly infectious, and he loved the argumentative evaluation of a poem, a painting, a piece of music, so that his company was a constant source of pleasure and enrichment. He was a councillor and fellow of the Royal Society of Literature and a governor of the London Academy of Music and Dramatic Art.

During the last six years of his short life he lived at Tonford Manor, near Canterbury, a fortified house dating from the twelfth century which he carefully restored. Here, with the towers of the cathedral visible across the watermeadows to the east, he worked in surroundings which he loved. Half a mile from the house stands the small church of St. Nicholas in which he regularly worshipped, and it was here that he was buried on 2 May, after his sudden collapse and death in a train 25 April 1963. The funeral service was in the crypt of Canterbury Cathedral, a measure of the love in which he was held, and an honour of a kind that would have greatly pleased him.

In 1938 Hassall married Evelyn Lynett, daughter of Eustace Chapman. They had a son and a daughter.

A pen-and-wash drawing by Joan Hassall, 1936, which is reproduced in *Ambrosia and Small Beer*, is in the possession of Sir Geoffrey Keynes. An early portrait in oils (*c*. 1931), by Joan Hassall, is in the possession of the artist, as is the block of a portrait (wood engraving) by Joan Hassall, reproduced on the title-page of *Penthesperon* (1938). There is also a miniature portrait by Enid Mountfort.

[Christopher Hassall, *Ambrosia and Small Beer*, 1964; *The Times*, 27 April 1963; personal knowledge.]   JOHN GUEST

HATRY, CLARENCE CHARLES (1888-1965), company promoter and financier, was born in Belsize Park, Hampstead, 16 December 1888, the eldest son of Julius Hatry, silk merchant, by his wife, Henriette Ellen Katzenstein. He developed as a contemplative child, ingrown, inventive, and self-sufficient. He was educated at St. Paul's School and at eighteen, following the death of his father, assumed responsibility for a failing family business which collapsed with liabilities of £8,000. By the time he was twenty-three, however, Hatry was established as an insurance broker and soon earning £20,000 a year. The close of the war of 1914-18 provided opportunities for his undoubted talents and among his outstanding operations was the purchase of Leyland Motors for a reputed £350,000 and its

sale in less than twenty-four hours for nearly double that figure.

Much of his flair was that of a shrewd gambler. His small Commercial Bank of London, registered in 1920, was used as a springboard to further activities in the purchase and reorganizing of stores, glass manufacturers, and jute companies, and by that year his successful operations had netted him a private fortune of £2¼ million. He acquired an estate in Sussex and a house in Upper Brook Street. His yacht *Westward* was the world's second largest and his horse Furious won the Lincolnshire Handicap in 1920. Following the economic slump which began in 1921 Hatry eventually sold his homes and horses, laid up his yacht, and pumped £¾ million into his companies. By 1924, when the economic climate changed, he was making a fresh start. A year later he had organized the nucleus of the Austin Friars Trust group which was registered in 1927. Industrial concerns, including department stores and steel firms, were taken over and reorganized to emerge as the Drapery Trust and Allied Ironfounders, starting a style in industrial mergers which was to become an economic fashion nearly forty years later.

Aided by an assistant named Edmund Daniels from the former Commercial Bank, Hatry exploited the money market which provided funds for local corporations and another of his companies was Corporation and General Securities Ltd. Introduced by Daniels, an Italian named John Gialdini became associated with Hatry's enterprises. The trio planned a bid for the shares in a group of companies named United Steel, which was accepted by more than 90 per cent of the shareholders in April 1929. The election of a Labour Government in May resulted in a nervous stock exchange, falling prices for shares, and Hatry trying unsuccessfully to raise the money for the United Steel stock. Gialdini suggested issuing unauthorized bonds for Gloucester, Wakefield, and Swindon as a stopgap. When the inevitable crash occurred Hatry voluntarily appeared before the director of public prosecutions and confessed to forgeries which involved the three corporations in substantial losses. Losses by private investors were claimed to be about £15 million. He and Daniels and two other directors appeared at the Old Bailey in January 1930 before Mr Justice Avory [q.v.] after Gialdini had absconded to Italy and on the fifth day, after the prosecution had completed its case, changed their plea to guilty. Sentenced to the maximum term of fourteen years' penal servitude, Hatry began this sentence only after his appeal had been dismissed. Daniels was sentenced to seven years, the other directors to five and three years.

Hatry was released in 1939 by the home

secretary. In the same year he published *Light Out of Darkness* in which he sought an economic and social alternative to the financial burden of modern armaments. Between 1940 and 1950 he established himself for the third time as a successful financier, but again failed to maintain his position. In 1962 he set up a group of companies for industrial cleaning and at the time of his death was actively engaged in negotiations with Scottish knitting companies. He died in a London hospital 10 June 1965, a man who had been almost furtively generous to friends and down-and-outs but whose financial brilliance was offset by an over-confidence and over-optimism which seemed unfortunately to blind him to the sharp outlines of reality.

In 1909 Hatry married Violet, daughter of Charles Ferguson, of independent means.

[Michael Pearson, *The Millionaire Mentality*, 1961; private information.]

LEONARD GRIBBLE

HATTON, SIR RONALD GEORGE (1886–1965), horticultural scientist, was born in Hampstead, London, 6 July 1886, the youngest child of Ernest Hatton, a barrister of the Inner Temple, and his wife, Amy, daughter of William Pearson, KC, the brother of Professor Karl Pearson, FRS [q.v.], the distinguished biometrician. Hatton was educated at Brighton College and Exeter School and as an exhibitioner at Balliol College, Oxford, 1906–10. He obtained a fourth class in modern history in 1910. He then worked as a labourer on a farm near Bristol and wrote a book, *Folk of the Furrow*, published in 1913 under the pen-name of Christopher Holdenby. In 1912 he went to study agriculture at Wye College in Kent. It was the Wye College Fruit Experimental Station which became the East Malling Research Station in 1914 with Hatton as its acting director after its first director had left on military duties; Hatton was appointed director in 1918.

Hatton devoted the next thirty years of his life to the development of the Research Station into the leading fruit research institute in the world, enlarging its area from 22 to 360 acres and its staff to more than 80. His enthusiasm and financial acumen were invaluable assets because, in economically difficult times, he was able to raise funds for this expansion from fruit growers, the Empire Marketing Board, and the Treasury. His best-known contribution to research was the study of the effect of rootstock on scion growth and fruiting of apples, pears, and plums. In the course of this work he classified and standardized fruit tree rootstocks, including those which became known as the Malling series and are widely used wherever apples are grown commercially. His influence on horticulture, and fruit growing especially, extended far beyond his own investigations; with his research team he transformed the subject from folklore to a science. He emphasized field experimentation, always with a practical objective, exact measurement, and keen observation. He recognized the limitations of the horticulturalist when his crops are attacked by pests and diseases, and encouraged work on control measures.

Hatton stimulated his staff to collaborate with others and a particularly effective liaison was with the John Innes Horticultural Institute; this resulted in the production of the Malling-Merton apple rootstocks bred specially for southern-hemisphere countries but one of which proved to be the most successful stock for Cox's Orange Pippin in England. The basis of fruit-tree physiology was laid by collaboration with the Institute of Plant Physiology of the Imperial College of Science, London.

Many graduate students came to East Malling to study for higher degrees after 1932 when the university of London recognized the Station as suitable for this purpose. Consequently Hatton's influence was spread to the many countries from which these students came, and he was invited to visit and advise on fruit growing in Australia, Canada, Ceylon, Java, New Zealand, South Africa, and the United States of America. He retired in 1949.

Hatton published many papers on diverse aspects of fruit culture in scientific and other journals. He was instrumental in starting in 1919 the *Journal of Pomology* which became the *Journal of Horticultural Science* in 1948; he was joint editor from 1924 until 1947. He was the first director of the Imperial (now Commonwealth) Bureau of Horticulture and Plantation Crops when it was established at East Malling in 1929. Its journal, *Horticultural Abstracts*, begun in 1931, reviews the world literature on fruit and other tree crops and became the standard source on those subjects. Hatton also played a leading role in the Royal Horticultural Society, which awarded him the Victoria medal of honour in 1930 and elected him vice-president in 1952.

Among his many distinctions were his appointment as CBE in 1934, his knighthood in 1949, and his elections to fellowship of the Royal Society in 1944 and of Wye College in 1949.

In 1914 Hatton married Hannah Rachel, daughter of Henry Rigden, of Ashford, Kent; they had one son. In his retirement Hatton continued his enthusiasm for horticulture in his garden as a successful grower of fruit and flowers. He died at his home in Benenden 11

November 1965 and, by his request, was buried in the East Malling churchyard adjoining the land of his Research Station. His portrait painted by Reginald Lewis hangs in the committee room at Bradbourne House, which, with its estate of nearly 200 acres, Hatton had added to the Research Station lands in 1938.

[T. N. Hoblyn, 'R. G. Hatton' in East Malling *Report*, 1948; W. S. Rogers, 'Sir Ronald Hatton' in East Malling *Report*, 1965; E. J. Salisbury in *Biographical Memoirs of Fellows of the Royal Society*, vol. xii, 1966.]   A. F. Posnette

HAVELOCK, Sir THOMAS HENRY (1877–1968), naval mathematician, was born in Newcastle upon Tyne 24 June 1877, the son of Michael Havelock, marine engineer, of Newcastle upon Tyne, and his wife, Elizabeth Burn Bell. Four of their six children (two boys and two girls) survived to maturity, but only the eldest girl married. For most of his life Thomas Havelock lived with his younger sister and his brother, who became a director of the Moor Line. Love of ships ran strongly in the Havelock family. At first Thomas hoped to become a draughtsman in the Neptune Works of Swan, Hunter & Wigham Richardson on Tyneside, but while waiting for an apprenticeship to fall vacant he entered Durham College of Physical Science in Newcastle upon Tyne, and his nascent gifts for mathematics and physics burst forth. Completing a B.Sc. course in 1895 at the age of eighteen, he stayed for a further two years of postgraduate studies in the college before entering St. John's College, Cambridge, in 1897, first as a pensioner and the following year as a scholar. Nevertheless, all his life he was faithful to his love of ships.

In 1898 Havelock suffered serious injury, which impaired his health for the rest of his life, when some railings, which he had climbed in order to get a better view of Lord Kitchener [q.v.], who had come to receive an honorary degree, gave way outside the Senate House at Cambridge.

Despite the consequent interruption of his studies, Havelock was placed in the second division of class 1 in part ii of the mathematics tripos in 1901, with J. E. Wright alone above him in the first division. In 1902 he shared the Smith's prize with Wright, and was awarded an Isaac Newton studentship. He was elected to a six-year Gregson fellowship in his college in 1903, but in 1906 returned to Armstrong College (as the Durham College of Science had become in 1904) as a special lecturer in applied mathematics. He received a D.Sc. there (by examination) in 1907. He was elected to a

fellowship of the Royal Society in 1914, and the following year Armstrong College created a second chair of (applied) mathematics especially for him. His damaged health ruled out active service in the war of 1914–18.

Havelock's scientific work lay in two main areas: the passage of light through materials and naval hydrodynamics. Although he wrote some twenty papers on the first of these, they did not attract lasting attention, and Havelock himself appears to have lost interest in optics by 1930. He did, however, do pioneering work on the wave resistance of ships and related problems, topics which interested him into his eighties. His most significant contributions started in 1923 after he had discovered a much neglected, but fundamental, paper by J. H. Michell (1898). In following years he applied and generalized its methods with conspicuous success. He discovered much about the way a ship's resistance to motion depends on the form of its hull. Later in his life he answered sophisticated questions about the trim and the heaving and pitching of a ship. But he never allowed mathematical abstraction to lead him too far from the real world. He constantly compared his theory with experiment, and sought to improve the extent of the agreement between the two.

His impact on this branch of naval architecture was strong and fully recognized in his lifetime. He was made an honorary member of the Royal Institution of Naval Architects in 1943, and awarded their first William Froude gold medal in 1956. Durham University conferred an honorary DCL in 1958, and Hamburg an honorary D.Sc. in 1960; he became an honorary fellow of St. John's in 1945. The French Academy of Sciences made him a corresponding member in 1947. He was the featured guest of the United States Society of Naval Architecture and Marine Engineers in 1950, and in 1963 the United States Office of Naval Research paid him the unusual compliment of collecting together and publishing sixty of his papers on hydrodynamics. He was knighted in 1951.

In 1928 Havelock became the head of both the pure and applied mathematics departments in Armstrong College. He maintained strong links with the Department of Naval Architecture, of which he became honorary acting head for three years from 1941, when Sir Westcott Abell [q.v.] retired. He was vice-principal of Armstrong College from 1933 to 1937, and took a leading part in the negotiations which brought it and the College of Medicine together to form King's College of the federal university of Durham at Newcastle upon Tyne. He was sub-rector of King's College from 1937 to 1942, and retired from his chair in 1945. His benevolent influence as a university statesman was permanently recognized by the university when in 1968 it opened Havelock Hall for student residence.

Havelock owed much of his success, and perhaps also his longevity to the devoted care of his sister, Alice, who survived his death at home in Gosforth 1 August 1968 by only a few weeks.

[*Cambridge Express*, 26 November 1898; *Cambridge Weekly News*, 25 November 1898; J. H. Michell, *Philosophical Magazine* (series 5), vol. xlv, 1898; P. H. Roberts, *Bulletin of the London Mathematical Society*, vol. ii, 1970; A. M. Binnie and P. H. Roberts in *Biographical Memoirs of Fellows of the Royal Society*, vol. xvii, 1971; W. C. S. Wigley (ed.), *The Collected Papers of Sir Thomas Havelock on Hydrodynamics*, US Office of Naval Research ACR-103, 1963.]

P. H. ROBERTS

HAVILLAND, SIR GEOFFREY DE (1882–1965), aircraft designer and manufacturer. [See DE HAVILLAND.]

HAWKE, SIR (EDWARD) ANTHONY (1895–1964), judge, was born 26 July 1895, the son of (Sir) (John) Anthony Hawke [q.v.], judge, and his wife, Winifred Edith Laura, daughter of Nicholas Henry Stevens, surgeon, of London. He had one sister. He was educated at Charterhouse and in 1914 went to Magdalen College, Oxford. His undergraduate career was interrupted by the outbreak of World War I, after which he did not return to Oxford. Instead he studied law and was called to the bar by the Middle Temple in 1920.

Hawke joined the Western circuit and the Devon sessions. As the years passed his practice became more confined to the Central Criminal Court where he was junior prosecuting counsel in 1932, third senior prosecuting counsel in 1937, second senior prosecuting counsel in 1942, and senior prosecuting counsel from 1945 to 1950. Among the trials in which he prosecuted were those of the murderers Neville Heath and Daniel Raven and of the two men found guilty of the chalk-pit murder, one of whom was a former minister of justice in the government of New South Wales.

Hawke began to occupy official positions, holding the recordership of Bath from 1939 to 1950 and the deputy chairmanship of Hertfordshire quarter-sessions from 1940 to 1950. He became a bencher of his Inn in 1942 and in 1950 was appointed chairman of the county of London quarter-sessions. In 1954 he was knighted and made common sergeant of the City of London. Held in high esteem, he could look forward to prospects of further promotion and indeed succeeded Sir Gerald Dodson as recorder of London in 1959, in which year also he became a member of the standing committee on criminal law revisions.

With such a background and experience of the criminal law he was a successful and highly respected recorder whose gaiety, handsome and debonair appearance, and keen sense of humour made him a popular friend throughout and beyond the legal profession. One of the last cases to come before him at the Old Bailey was that in which Christine Keeler was convicted of perjury, when he showed himself, especially in the sentence which he imposed, possessed of a superb judicial temperament which enabled him to conduct the trial free from any consideration of events (concerning the accused) which caused considerable public and political concern for the security of the State—events which had occurred before the perjury and had led up to it.

In 1962 Hawke became treasurer of his Inn. When in this capacity he exercised his right to nominate honorary benchers, he showed his interest in cricket by nominating Sir Learie (later Lord) Constantine, who thus became a valued and popular colleague of the other benchers of that Inn. Hawke was also a keen golfer. As a master of the bench his qualities of kindness, wisdom, and humour endeared him to his fellows. He also added the weight of his authority, as editor, to the fifteenth edition of Roscoe's *Criminal Evidence*.

In 1931 he married Evelyn Audrey Lee Davies (died 1977); they had one daughter. Hawke died in Italy 25 September 1964 while on holiday at Menaggio, Lake Como.

[*The Times*, 26 September 1964; personal knowledge.] FRED E. PRITCHARD

HAWKINS, HERBERT LEADER (1887–1968), geologist and palaeontologist, was born in Reading 1 June 1887, the only son of John Luther Hawkins and his wife, Mary Elizabeth Leader. His father was a master baker and the family were Quakers. Hawkins was educated at Reading School and afterwards at the Grammar School at Kendal, Westmorland. He entered Manchester University with a classical scholarship in 1905 and transferred from classics to geology. He gained a first class honours degree in that subject and the first Mark Stirrup palaeontological scholarship in 1908. A further two years of postgraduate work resulted in his M.Sc. in 1910. During this time he settled upon what was to be his principal palaeontological research—the study of fossil echinoids. In 1909 he was appointed part-time lecturer at the University College of Reading and, even before completion of his studies at Manchester, was given a full-time post which enabled him to initiate and develop the department of geology in that institution which became the university of Reading in 1926. Hawkins was appointed professor of geology in 1920, the year in which Manchester University awarded him the degree of D.Sc. He was elected a fellow of the Royal Society in 1937, by which time he was recognized as the foremost specialist on fossil Echinoidea in the United Kingdom.

Between 1909 and 1965 Hawkins published 102 scientific communications, almost one-half of which report his fossil echinoid research mainly on the morphology of the Holectypoida. Meticulous observation, new techniques, and laborious, patient dissection revealed new morphological features which Hawkins interpreted in terms of phylogeny. Particularly admirable papers were his 'Morphological Studies on the Echinoidea Holectypoida and their Allies' in twelve parts between 1917 and 1922; 'The Morphology and Evolution of the Ambulacrum in the Echinoidea Holectypoida' (1920); 'The Occurrence, Structure, and Affinities of Echinocystis and Palaeodiscus' (with S. M. Hampton, 1927); 'The Lantern and Girdle of some Recent and Fossil Echinoidea' (1934); and the description of the remarkable Cravenechinus (1946). The papers are illustrated with fine drawings made by himself.

Another aspect of his writing concerned certain philosophical aspects of palaeontology, its contribution to evolution extrapolated into the future, and its implications for mankind. This phase culminated in *Humanity in Geological Perspective*, the Alexander Pedler lecture in 1938 which achieved international acclaim when it was republished the following year by the Smithsonian Institution. The lecture reveals Hawkins as an accomplished writer, an imaginative thinker, and a man with a deep concern for humanity.

As a teacher Hawkins was unusual. He lectured without notes. He was concerned to fire the imagination and engender a devotion to the subject. His students found his lectures entertaining, enjoyable, and often inspired performances. Lucid simplicity often disguised deep profundity but he left the documentation of his assertions to the students' own reading. Whatever the success of this approach, of six students who had gone on to higher degrees, four eventually occupied chairs in British universities and two attained high office in the National Geological Surveys.

Hawkins made significant contributions to British Tertiary stratigraphy, periglacial phenomena, and some aspects of economic geology. He was much in demand as lecturer and president of minor natural history societies and served as president of the geological section of the British Association for the Advancement of Science (1936).

He was awarded the Lyell medal of the Geological Society (1940) and served as its president (1941–2). He took great interest in the Geologists' Association, serving as president (1938–40); he was elected honorary member in 1949. The *Proceedings of the Geologists' Association*, vol. 78, part i, 1967, comprising papers by his students and associates, was issued as a Festschrift for his eightieth birthday. He was president of the Palaeontographical Society from 1943 to 1966.

Tall and spare, moustached, with brilliant blue eyes, he was gentle and friendly, benign and entertaining, ever ready to talk about his subject at any level. He partly had and partly assumed a bewildered helplessness in face of administrators, technologists, and rich benefactors, as a consequence of which a new building, cash endowments, superb collections, and fine books fell into his hands to form the nucleus of a department which on his retirement in 1952 he was able to bequeath to his successor and as professor emeritus to watch its continuing expansion and success. In 1961 he was appointed consulting geologist to the Thames Valley Water Board.

In 1912 Hawkins married Amy, daughter of Alexander Morrison Mitchell, a photographer. They had two sons and a daughter. His wife died in 1953 and in 1955 Hawkins married Sibyl Marion Hampton, his former research student, who survived his death which occurred in Reading 29 December 1968.

[P. Allen in *Biographical Memoirs of Fellows of the Royal Society*, vol. xvi, 1970; personal knowledge.]   F. HODSON

HAYWARD, JOHN DAVY (1905–1965), anthologist and bibliophile, was born in London 2 February 1905, the younger son and second child of John Arthur Hayward, surgeon, of Wimbledon, London, and his wife, Rosamond Grace, daughter of George Rolleston, physician [q.v.]. Educated at Gresham's Holt School, Norfolk, he spent a period in France before going up to King's College, Cambridge, in 1923 where he graduated with second classes in English in 1925 and in modern and medieval languages, part ii, in 1927.

How far the course of Hayward's life was influenced by the disabling illness which first became manifest about the age of ten is difficult to determine. He was afflicted with incipient facio-scapulo-numeral muscular dystrophy, which gradually affected the muscles of the face and both limb girdles. Although he was not seriously handicapped until his early twenties, the progressive wasting of the affected muscles rendered him increasingly helpless. The greater part of his adult working life was spent in an invalid chair, and his activities were inevitably circumscribed to a degree which might have broken the spirit of a less resolute man.· In fact, he not only successfully followed the career of author, editor, critic, and book-collector, but he also fulfilled until his last months a remarkably busy social programme.

He was fortunate in having substantial private means, or the difficulty of earning a living might have proved insuperable. Even so, he gained a certain amount by his books, his articles, and editorial work, and he left a sizeable fortune. The tendency to cantankerousness in his character may have been due as much to heredity (his mother had a quick temper) as to the humiliating consciousness of physical defect. If he could be difficult and curmudgeonly in his dealings, and sometimes scabrous in his conversation, he had a gentler side to his nature. He was able to win the affection of children; he admired many accomplished women; and he proved a loyal friend. He might have married, but he felt that this would have imposed an excessive burden on the partner. The result was an existence of cruel restrictions; but, in spite of this, he managed on the whole to enjoy life.

In the 1930s Hayward ran a minor *salon* in his flat in Bina Gardens, Gloucester Road, where T. S. Eliot, (Sir) Geoffrey Faber [qq.v.], and F. V. Morley would meet to compose and exchange light verse in several languages. This resulted in the privately printed *Noctes Binanianae* (1939), twenty-five copies of which were issued; one of them is in the Eliot Collection in the Houghton Library at Harvard. Hayward's literary career was notable for the production of works of erudition, and for the study and collection of books, for which he had a passion. As he remarked in a broadcast talk in 1949: 'Pleasure may be as good a justification for collecting as any other. The pleasure of pursuit, the pleasure of discovery, the pleasure of possession—they all combine to gratify the mind and the senses.'

He edited the *Collected Works* of Rochester (1926), published while he was still an undergraduate, the *Complete Poetry and Selected Prose* of Donne (1929), *The Letters of Saint-Évremond* (1930), Swift's *Gulliver's Travels* (1934), and Swift's *Selected Prose Works* (1949). He also compiled the following anthologies: *Nineteenth Century Poetry* (1932), *Silver Tongues* (1937), *Love's Helicon* (1940), *T. S. Eliot: Points of View* (1941), *Seventeenth Century Poetry* (1948), *Dr. Johnson* (1948), *Donne* (Penguin Poets, 1950), *T. S. Eliot: Selected Prose* (1953), The

Penguin Book of English Verse (1956), *The Faber Book of English Verse* (1958), *Herrick* (Penguin Poets, 1961), and *The Oxford Book of Nineteenth-Century English Verse* (1964).

Hayward was appointed CBE in 1953. Among the offices which he held were those of editorial adviser to the Cresset Press; editorial director of the *Book Collector*; and vice-president of the Bibliographical Society. He was also honorary foreign corresponding member of the Grolier Club, New York, and honorary member of the Association Internationale de Bibliophilie, Paris.

During the period of the war, Hayward, who found himself isolated at first, had been the guest of Lord Rothschild. In 1946 Hayward and Eliot set up house together at 19 Carlyle Mansions, Cheyne Walk, Chelsea, employing a French housekeeper; and this association was to last until Eliot's second marriage in January 1957. Hayward was said to have felt the break keenly. Thereafter, instead of the French housekeeper, he employed a manservant, who also cooked for him, and during his last months he engaged a trained nurse. On 17 September 1965 Hayward died at home, in extreme helplessness and some depression of spirits. He left his valuable books and his letters from authors—above all T. S. Eliot—to King's College, Cambridge, where there is now a Hayward Room in the library.

Hayward will be remembered for his steadfast pursuit of literary excellence, his fidelity to the profession of letters, and his cultivation of numerous literary friendships.

There is an ink-and-wash portrait of him in the National Portrait Gallery by Anthony Devas (c.1950), and a head and shoulders by Robert Lutyens in the possession of the family.

[Private information; personal knowledge.]
E. W. F. TOMLIN

HENDERSON, DAVID WILLIS WILSON (1903–1968), microbiologist, was born 23 July 1903 at Partick, Lanark (now part of Glasgow), the only child of John Henderson, accountant, and his wife, Mary Wilson. He attended Hamilton Academy where he became interested in science. On leaving school he insisted on going to work on a farm but left, somewhat dramatically, because the farmer's methods were unscientific. He enrolled as a student of agricultural bacteriology at the West of Scotland Agricultural College and Glasgow University in 1921 and graduated (B.Sc. in agriculture) in 1926. In 1927 he became adviser in dairy bacteriology under the Ministry of Agriculture and Fisheries and a member of the staff of Armstrong College, then part of the federal university of Durham. There he submitted the thesis,

'A study of certain anaerobes isolated from sheep and their significance in certain sheep diseases', for which he was awarded an M.Sc. in 1930.

Henderson joined the Lister Institute of Preventive Medicine (London) as a Carnegie research fellow in 1931, continued with a Beit memorial research fellowship (1932–5), and was a member of the bacteriological staff of the Lister's serum department until 1946, where he dealt mainly with the immunology of the Salmonella and Clostridium species. He was awarded a Ph.D. degree by London University in 1934 for a thesis, 'Studies on the spore-bearing anaerobes with experiments on active and passive immunity', and a D.Sc. in 1941.

In 1940 the Cabinet decided to form a biology group under the auspices of the Medical Research Council to assess the threat posed by microbiological agents used against man and to devise methods for protection. (Sir) Paul Fildes was appointed to be its director and Henderson was seconded to it, becoming a prominent and active member. The group was housed in the Chemical Defence Experimental Establishment at Porton, Wiltshire. CDEE was internationally well known for its work on aerosols, meteorology, physiology, and toxicology, and possessed a multidiscipline staff augmented during the war years by several eminent scientists and supported by a wide diversity of skilled artisans. The new unit exploited these resources to the full. Henderson, who had previously liaised with CDEE in demonstrating that inhaled clostridial toxins could be lethal to mice, now extended his interest to infection by the aerosol route. The whole experience profoundly influenced Henderson's thinking and in later days he insisted that staff of various disciplines in his establishment must be free to collaborate on projects 'at bench level' without the straitjacket imposed by a rigid divisional structure. Henderson played a key role in Anglo-American wartime liaison on microbiological defence, for which he was awarded the US medal of freedom, bronze palm, in 1946.

At the end of the war most of the biology team returned to their civilian work. Their *ad hoc* experiments had shown that microbiological weapons posed a threat which needed systematic evaluation and required a multidiscipline staff working in properly equipped and purpose-built laboratories on the basic biological, biochemical, and physical factors involved. Henderson, who had been asked to form such a group, was determined not to accept less. Eventually the Cabinet instructed the Ministry of Supply to implement the programme and Henderson was appointed chief superintendent (later changed to 'director') of the Microbiological Research Department in 1946. An advisory board was formed with Lord Hankey [q.v.] as chairman and many eminent scientists as members. The building of the new laboratories, which began in June 1948, was completed in 1951. Their design was considerably in advance of other microbiological laboratories, and MRE soon became recognized as a place where experiments could be, and were, done properly.

As director of MRD (later MRE) Henderson showed many pronounced but often contradictory character traits, nevertheless his ethos permeated the staff. He became a patriarchal figure who could brook no effective deputy. Often overbearing towards his staff, he fiercely protected them from outside interference and was determined to prevent the local and headquarters' administration from intermeddling so that the scientists could concentrate on research. He displayed charm and patience in listening to staff describing their problems; he knew them all by name and remembered what they said. This produced an almost family atmosphere. Visits to individual laboratories were frequent and unannounced; if he found the occupants 'run off their feet' he would help with any job, however menial. In public he could be relied upon to back his staff, even if he was determined to speak his mind in private afterwards and he expected the same behaviour from them. He could be very patient in helping those who, due to their inexperience, had fallen into difficulties while trying to do the right thing. He assessed exactly what he wanted scientifically from each member of staff and just how many of their peculiarities and vagaries he would endure to get it. In contrast he credulously trusted as friends and loyal supporters those who told him what he wanted to hear and was distressed at their rapid abandonment of his principles after he retired. By nature a prima donna he could be forthright, sometimes rude, and occasionally plainly offensive. Anything he regarded as bureaucratic obstruction received rough and peremptory treatment. He enjoyed creating crises for his line management who found him exasperating, temperamental, and difficult, and were outraged at his habit of passing problems over their heads to the highest levels. Nevertheless his technical judgement was greatly valued by all. In his outbursts of temper, which were sometimes real, but more often employed for dramatic effect, his English slowly degenerated into an incomprehensible Glasgow dialect. In contrast he could charm staff into working on some applied problem he wanted solved by making it appear as pure research probably leading to a Nobel prize.

Perhaps Henderson's greatest achievement was in creating an environment in which each could give of his best, and then helping and encouraging everyone to do even better. Many of his staff had reason to be grateful for the guidance and interest which he displayed in the early stages of their careers. Since Henderson's duties as director left him little time for personal research, he concentrated on setting objectives for research groups and then injecting his ideas from time to time as the work progressed, and in this way his personality permeated all fields of research. He reviewed the scientific achievements of the new establishment in a paper given to the Royal Society in 1955. Retaining a special interest in infection by the aerosol route, he later studied 'mixed infections' (the effect that one infection can have on the course of another) during a sabbatical year. He was a martinet on safe procedures and the high standards set in MRE had a considerable influence in the microbiological field.

Henderson's extramural activities included being an original member of the Society for General Microbiology, serving on its committee from 1947 to 1951, and being president from 1963 to 1965. The prestige gained by Henderson and MRE was recognized by his appointment as CB in 1957 and as a fellow of the Royal Society in 1959.

In 1930 Henderson married Beatrice Mary Davenport, daughter of Sir Westcott Abell [q.v.], professor of naval architecture at Armstrong College. She died in 1952 and in 1953 he married Emily Helen, daughter of D. Theodore Kelly, of New York, a prominent lawyer and vice-president of Manhattan Life. Pat, as she was generally known, held a Ph.D. in bacteriology from Yale University and had researched at Camp Detrick on the pathogenesis of infectious diseases and the acquisition of drug tolerance by bacteria. She combined a charming personality with considerable scientific ability and had a superior talent as an editor of scientific material. They bought a fifteenth-century cottage at Great Durnford, Wiltshire, whose large curtilage bordering on the River Avon afforded them the relaxation of gardening and fishing, and here they entertained friends and visiting scientists from all over the world. Although Henderson was fond of children and they liked him, there was no issue from either marriage.

In 1959, when the Ministry of Supply was dissolved, Henderson and others fought vainly to have MRE transferred to civilian control. It passed to the War Office and then to the Ministry of Defence. The change from the flexible and enlightened methods of the Ministry of Supply to the doctrinaire Civil Service attitudes of the Ministry of Defence, with its complex administration, worried and depressed Henderson, who developed hypertension. Always a heavy smoker, he became increasingly subject to respiratory infections. He retired as director in 1964 but continued as a research worker studying viral aerosols until 1967. He died at home in Great Durnford 16 August 1968.

A portrait by Kohler, taken from the photograph in the *Biographical Memoirs* listed below, hangs in the Centre for Applied Microbiology and Research at Porton Down.

[L. H. Kent and W. T. J. Morgan in *Biographical Memoirs of Fellows of the Royal Society*, vol. xvi, 1970; obituary notice in *Journal of General Microbiology*, vol. lx, 1970; *Proceedings of the Royal Society, London*, B, vol. cxliii, 1955; personal knowledge.]

HAROLD DRUETT

HENRIQUES, SIR BASIL LUCAS QUIXANO (1890–1961), club leader and magistrate, was born in London 17 October 1890, the youngest of the five children of David Quixano Henriques, who had an import and export company in Manchester and London, and his wife, Agnes, who was a greatniece of Sir Moses H. Montefiore [q.v.]. The family of Quixano Henriques, originally Sephardic Jews from Portugal, settled in Jamaica, as did many of their countrymen, following the persecutions of the sixteenth and seventeenth centuries. There they achieved some prominence, holding minor office in the legal and military establishment of the island. In the nineteenth century one branch of the family transferred its considerable import/export business to England, where the riches of the Victorian empire provided well-established merchants with a profitable base. There was, therefore, ample wealth to sustain the family of David Henriques in a life-style of comfort and elegance and to provide for Basil and his wife a modest investment income throughout their lives.

Like his elder brothers, Basil was sent to Harrow (1904–7), but he was not a great scholar and he left before obtaining a place at Oxford. Careful tuition at home and abroad did, however, produce the desired result and he entered University College, Oxford, in 1909. Once again he found difficulty in facing the world of books and barely managed to get a degree, obtaining a third class in history in 1913. The other side of Oxford, however—its wealth of personalities, of ideas, and of social theories—was the formative influence in his life. Two people in particular contributed to his development and to the shape of his future; one was (Sir) Alexander H. Paterson [q.v.] and the other Claude J. G. Montefiore [q.v.]. Paterson and his social theories were fairly new to Henriques but the writings of Montefiore and his work for the liberalization of Jewish ritual and practice in England was part of his family background.

His mother was related to the Montefiores and was herself immersed in the liberal tradition. But British Jews, in the early part of the twentieth century, were deeply divided in the matter of their religious practices. The strict orthodoxy of some, particularly those more recently arrived from Europe, was seen by liberal intellectuals as a barrier to the anglicization which they wished to achieve for all Jews who found a home in England. Moreover, many members of old-established Jewish families had come to admire the Anglican tradition and to appreciate the social cohesion brought about by the use of a rich living language in the everyday liturgy of the English Church. Claude Montefiore was the chief spokesman for those who held these views. One of his books, *The Bible for Home Reading* (2 parts, 1896 and 1899) came into the hands of Henriques while he was still at Harrow; it impressed him deeply. At Oxford he threw himself into the liberal Jewish movement, organizing English–Hebrew services and rousing sluggish and disinterested undergraduates to co-operate with him. He showed his capacity for persuasion by joining with Claude Montefiore and the chief rabbi to promote the establishment of an academic post in rabbinical studies. The first holder of this post was Herbert M. J. Loewe, who became Henriques's brother-in-law.

This lifelong interest in the religious life of British Jews was the Mount Sion of Henriques's intellectual and emotional perspective. His Parnassus was the study and practice of club work among underprivileged boys and young men. The source of this enthusiasm was the work of Alec Paterson, who, although he was living in the East End of London, maintained his links with Oxford and came up frequently to talk to undergraduates about his club and its members. Henriques, convinced that such social intervention was necessary and indeed admirable, went to stay at the Oxford and Bermondsey Mission, and decided, as a result of this experience, that social work, and particularly club work, was to be his profession. His family at first opposed him. He persuaded them, however, that he had no other ambition and they agreed to support him, suggesting at the same time that he should concentrate his energies on work among East End Jews whom he might help to 'anglicize' by the provision of the kind of social service he had in mind. Thus, his two interests became one and he spent the rest of his life among the Jewish people of Commercial Road and Berner Street (later renamed Henriques Street) as club leader and magistrate.

He had no easy task; the boys to whom he first offered club membership were mostly the sons of first-generation immigrant Jews from Russia, Latvia, Poland, and parts of Eastern Europe. Some of them were resolutely Jewish, speaking no English and refusing to give up their strict orthodoxy. Others, particularly the Russian Jews, already possessed, or were easily converted to, the revolutionary views that had been preached in the political and industrial organizations which flourished at the turn of the century in the Jewish East End. To both these groups the religious component of Henriques's social programme must have seemed unwelcome. He himself was aware of the conflict between the religious orthodoxy of the immigrant and the liberal practices he taught in his club. He does not seem to have appreciated the irony that the very street where his settlement was founded and which was later to bear his name had been the centre of the activities of the Russian Jewish anarchists. His first club, the Oxford and St. George's in the East Jewish Boys Club, was opened in March 1914—an inauspicious time for innovations. Henriques joined the army (the 3rd battalion East Kent Regiment) in 1915 but exercised a kind of remote control over his club through his wife, Rose Louise, daughter of James H. Loewe, a linguist and at one time secretary of the Jewish Colonial Trust, and granddaughter of Louis Loewe, linguist [q.v.]. They were married in 1916. Since she had founded the girls' club, at whose centre she remained for more than thirty years, she was already part of the organization. There were no children of the marriage.

Henriques's war service was of historic interest since he was in command of the first tank to be used in the war and to fire on the enemy. Although his first commission was held in the Buffs, he was seconded, in 1916, to the newly formed Tank Corps (the heavy branch of the Machine-Gun Corps). He was wounded in the first tank attack on the Somme in 1916, and returned to England. Later, as reconnaissance officer, he showed great skill and bravery, was twice mentioned in dispatches, and gained the Italian silver medal.

When the war was over he returned to the Oxford and St. George's Club but the original buildings were too small to house the new activities he had in mind. With courage and determination he set out to find money for premises in which there could be a meeting-place for older club members, a luncheon club for social workers and teachers, a room for religious services, and the various club rooms for the boys and girls for whom this whole enterprise had been undertaken. The Jewish community, particularly the liberals of the older British families, supported him generously.

Having founded his settlement he remained there for more than thirty years, stimulating its development and directing its gradual moves from the original cramped premises to the spacious Bernhard Baron Settlement in Berner Street. Henriques retired as warden in 1947.

Although he had always fostered self-government in his boys' and girls' clubs, Henriques was by nature something of an autocrat, with firm opinions which he expressed with great force. These were, of course, derived only partly from his experience of life among East End Jews; his beliefs were, in the main, those of a successful and powerful group of people whose secular model was the British nation state. It is not, therefore, suprising that he should see the magistracy as central to the work of care and control that he wished to do. With his usual skill he had himself made a magistrate in 1924 and served faithfully on the bench until he retired in 1955. Since his club work was primarily with young people, he had some share in the discussions that preceded the setting up of the new 'welfare' juvenile courts in 1933 and must have observed the sharp rise in the number of children appearing before the new courts once their welfare function had been made explicit. It is arguable that Henriques found his greatest enjoyment in sitting as chairman of the East London Juvenile Court, to which he was elected in 1936. There was, of course, a difference between those who came to the settlement (well-intentioned and aspiring Jewish families) and those who appeared in the juvenile court. Henriques himself was fond of saying that the strength of Jewish family life, its habits of prayer and sobriety, helped to prevent delinquency. Those who knew him as a magistrate, therefore, while admiring his firm kindliness, noted that his understanding of some of the problems of young offenders and their families, and, in particular, of young girls and women, was limited by his experience and his imagination. Nevertheless, as magistrate, settlement warden, and social worker, he remained an important figure in the world of the London East End poor.

The final human judgement upon him must be made in the two areas of his endeavour. As social worker, club leader, and magistrate he gave himself entirely to those whom he sought to serve, striving at the same time to impose his own standards of self-control and moral rectitude upon people who had no share in the kind of upbringing which produced them. In the first half of the twentieth century this did not appear to be incongruous or patronizing. Alexander Paterson had shown how privileged young men could give service to those less fortunate; from the community of British Jews, Basil Henriques emerged to follow this example in his social work among the East End Jewish community. To all his practical work, however,

there was another dimension, his liberal Judaism. He was tireless in his efforts to modernize and simplify the Jewish rituals. If this were done, he believed, not only would the Jewish faith survive among later generations of British Jews, but the anglicizing of immigrant Jews would be easier to achieve. Since his own identification with the British state was complete, he was doubtful about the establishment of a Jewish state, fearing that 'nationality' would take the place of religion in the heart of the Jew'. Thus the foundation of the state of Israel was not, for him, an undiluted blessing, nor did he think it should be for any British Jew who was already a citizen of a proud empire. With these simple but strong beliefs in righteousness, religious practice, civic duty, and national pride, Henriques attempted the kind of social work which was characteristic of the first part of the twentieth century. Such ideas and style of social work did not survive into the second part.

In appearance Henriques was majestic—six feet three in height and broad-shouldered. In his early years he had a shock of fair hair, which thinned and silvered fairly rapidly, but he was an upright, strong figure until just before his death.

His written work was considerable, although much of it is merely of historic interest. Among his books are *Club Leadership* (1933, reprinted thrice), *The Indiscretions of a Warden* (1937), *The Religion of the Jew* (with A. Marmorstein, 1946), *The Indiscretions of a Magistrate* (1950), *Fratres, Club Boys in Uniform* (1951), *Club Leadership Today* (1951), *The Home-menders, the Prevention of Unhappiness in Children* (1955), and pamphlets on Judaism, juvenile delinquency, boys' clubs, and printed sermons and prayers.

Henriques was appointed CBE in 1948 and knighted on his retirement from the East London Juvenile Court in 1955. He died in a London hospital 2 December 1961. There is a portrait by June Mendoza (1955) at the East London Juvenile Court, Bow Rd., London.

[Lionel Loewe, *Basil Henriques*, 1976; *The Times*, 4 December 1961, and the *Magistrate*, vol. xviii, I, 1962; W. J. Fishman, *East End Jewish Radicals 1875–1914*, 1975; private information; personal knowledge.]

SARAH McCABE

HESS, DAME (JULIA) MYRA (1890–1965), pianist, was born in London 25 February 1890, the daughter of Frederick Solomon Hess, a textile merchant, and his wife, Lizzie, daughter of John Jacobs, shopkeeper and moneylender of London. She was the youngest of four children of whom the eldest was her only sister.

She grew up in a typical Jewish home in north London.

Myra Hess's general education, to her lasting regret, was of the superficial kind then deemed adequate for a young girl. But thanks to her obvious musical talent she was given piano and cello lessons from the age of five. The cello was abandoned when she began more serious study at the Guildhall School of Music, where her teachers were Orlando Morgan (piano) and Julian Pascal (theory). By far the most formative musical influence in her life, however, was that of Professor Tobias Matthay, with whom she studied piano for five years after winning the Ada Lewis scholarship at the Royal Academy of Music in 1903. She always maintained that he was her 'only teacher', and he regarded her as his 'prophetess'.

Myra's official début took place on 14 November 1907, when she gave an orchestral concert at the Queen's Hall in London, conducted by young (Sir) Thomas Beecham [q.v.]. She played concertos by Saint-Saëns and Beethoven (the G major, with which she was later so often associated), together with an obligatory group of solos. Newspaper reports of the concert, and of her first solo recital given at the Aeolian Hall two months later, were mainly enthusiastic. Yet engagements came in slowly and were rarely well paid, so for some years her livelihood depended to a large extent on teaching.

Her first great success came in Holland in 1912, when she took the place of an indisposed colleague to play the Schumann Concerto in A minor with the Concertgebouw Orchestra under Willem Mengelberg. This had a welcome effect on her career in England, where engagements with music clubs and orchestras steadily increased. Visits abroad became impracticable during the war of 1914-18; but on 17 January 1922 Myra made a highly successful American début with a recital at the Aeolian Hall, New York. Thereafter, up to 1939, she divided each year between a North American tour in the winter, concerts in England and Holland in the spring and autumn, and a working holiday, often in the country, during two summer months.

In the early part of her career Myra played a considerable amount of contemporary music, although even then she tended to favour the classical and romantic repertoire. This, and her abiding lack of interest in virtuosity, might suggest a rather forbidding character. But her strength of character was tempered by graciousness and an enchanting sense of humour, which bubbled out irresistibly not only in everyday life, but also whenever she played a lighthearted Scarlatti sonata or Mozart finale. Moreover, in spite of agonies of nerves before every concert, as soon as she stepped on a platform (a shortish but comfortable-looking woman, invariably dressed in black) her deceptive air of serenity made audiences feel that they were her friends, and that the only thing which mattered was the music they were about to enjoy together.

Myra delighted in taking part in chamber music. In the 1920s she regularly joined the London String Quartet for a week's music-making at the Bradford Chamber Music Festival; in the 1930s she had a sonata partnership with the Hungarian violinist Jelly d'Aranyi [q.v.]; and she appeared at the Casals summer festivals in Perpignon and Prades in 1951 and 1952. More important, and wholly characteristic, was her decision on the outbreak of war in 1939 to cancel an American tour in order to remain in England and organize, and take part in, the remarkable series of daily chamber-music concerts which she instituted at the National Gallery in London, with the assistance of Sir Kenneth (later Lord) Clark, the director. They ran uninterruptedly for six and a half years (apart from a short break at the end of the war), were attended by over three-quarters of a million people, and only ceased (to her bitter disappointment) when repairs to the war-damaged Gallery became inevitable.

The finish of the concerts allowed Myra to resume her regular tours in Holland and the United States where she was greeted as a beloved, long-absent friend, and as one who had served music and her country so selflessly. Audiences sensed, too, that her powers of interpretation had acquired a new simplicity, directness, and depth. Whereas formerly her quest for sheer beauty of sound had sometimes interfered with her sense of musical line, she had now achieved such complete technical control that she could concentrate entirely on the shape and meaning of a work, knowing that her fingers would reproduce exactly what her inner ear dictated. Furthermore, her instinctive understanding of whatever music awakened her love and interest had become unerring.

From the late 1950s Myra became increasingly troubled by arthritis of the hands and severe circulatory problems. Her last concert appearance was on 31 October 1961 at the Royal Festival Hall, London, when she played the Mozart Concerto in A major, K. 488, under Sir Adrian Boult. Although she still managed to give occasional lessons to a few gifted pupils, she lacked the physical and mental strength to reorientate her life in a way which might have made retirement tolerable. It was a sad end to a great career. She died at her home in St. John's Wood, London, 25 November 1965. She had never married.

The gramophone recordings made between

1928 and 1959 (a list is in both the books about Myra Hess cited below, but that in Marian McKenna's book is more complete) give little idea of the quality of her playing. She hated recording and, as Professor Arthur Mendel wrote, 'performance for her was *essentially* communication to an audience'. The recording which comes closest to capturing her beauty of tone, human warmth, and deep musical understanding, is probably the Beethoven Sonata in E major, Op. 109, issued in 1954. Of her few publications, immense popularity was achieved by her piano transcription (1926) of the chorale-setting from Bach's Cantata No. 147, familiarly known as 'Jesu, Joy of Man's Desiring'. Few artists have been so closely associated with one piece of music.

For her services to music Myra Hess was appointed CBE (1936), DBE (1941), and commander of the Order of Orange-Nassau (1943). She received the gold medal of the Royal Philharmonic Society (1942) and honorary degrees from the universities of Manchester (1945), Durham, London, St. Andrews (all 1946), Reading (1947), Cambridge (1949), and Leeds (1951).

A charcoal drawing of her (1920) by John Singer Sargent is on loan to the Museum of Fine Arts, Boston, and a bronze bust (1945) by (Sir) Jacob Epstein belongs to the Royal Academy of Music, London.

[The Myra Hess papers and the National Gallery Concerts papers in the British Library; *Grove's Dictionary of Music and Musicians*; Denise Lassimonne and Howard Ferguson (eds.), *Myra Hess by her Friends*, 1966; Marian C. McKenna, *Myra Hess, a Portrait*, 1976; personal knowledge.]

HOWARD FERGUSON

HETHERINGTON, SIR HECTOR JAMES WRIGHT (1888-1965), university vice-chancellor, was born at Cowdenbeath 21 July 1888, the elder son of Thomas Hetherington who in 1889 moved to Tillicoultry where he ran a business as a pharmaceutical chemist and became a JP, and his wife, Helen Mundell, a farmer's daughter. Hetherington was educated at Dollar Academy and the university of Glasgow (1905-10), where, having a career in the Church in mind, he took honours degrees, at first in classics and then in philosophy and in economics (1910). In 1911 he won a Ferguson scholarship in philosophy, open to graduates of all Scottish universities. His social conscience was sharply aroused by the poverty and squalor he saw in Glasgow and this concern for his fellow men was strongly reinforced by the influence of his professor of moral philosophy, Sir Henry Jones [q.v.], of whom he

wrote a biography. In 1910 Jones appointed him as lecturer in his department, a post he occupied until 1914, apart from a short time in 1912 when he resided at Merton College, Oxford, to study with H. H. Joachim [q.v.]. During these years he also acted as secretary and then as warden of the Glasgow University Settlement. In 1914 he became a lecturer in philosophy at the university of Sheffield and from 1915 to 1920 was professor of logic and philosophy at University College, Cardiff.

The turning point in his career was his appointment in 1920 at the early age of thirty-two as principal and professor of philosophy at the small and struggling University College in Exeter where his noteworthy achievement was to secure from the University Grants Committee academic recognition and financial support for the College. The delicate and persistent negotiations involved in this episode he later recalled in his racy and illuminating brochure, *The University College at Exeter* (1963). His evident flair and liking for academic administration did not prevent him, however, from accepting the chair of moral philosophy in Glasgow in 1924 and he found great satisfaction in being (after A. D. Lindsay, later Lord Lindsay of Birker, q.v.) a successor to his former chief. But in 1927 his interest in administration prevailed and he took up the post of vice-chancellor of the university of Liverpool where, by his conciliatory skill and his social adroitness, he smoothed away longstanding but petty antagonisms between the senate and the lay council of the university and strengthened the links between the university and the city. In co-operation with Frederick Marquis (later Lord Woolton, q.v.), the treasurer of the university, he placed the finances on a much firmer footing and secured benefactions for an extension to the students' union and a handsome new building for the university library. He also played a prominent part in the amalgamation of the four voluntary hospitals in the city and brought them into closer relationship with the faculty of medicine.

His success at Liverpool made him a clear choice in 1936 for the post of principal of the university of Glasgow which is a regius appointment. He had now come home to his own university over which he presided with conspicuous wisdom, tact, and firmness until his retirement in 1961. During his long tenure which spanned the war years of 1939-45 and an era of unprecedented university expansion, he transformed the university by his vision of what its function should be in a modern setting. By 1961 it was a vastly different place from that to which he had come as principal twenty-five years earlier: it was three times the size in staff and student members, enriched with many new buildings, much wider in the range of its activities, and of greater standing in every respect. With a realistic sense of priorities he actively encouraged the modernization of many existing departments, and initiated or fostered the establishment of a goodly number of new ones in every faculty. In furtherance of his policies he devoted unremitting personal attention to the making of sound academic appointments at all levels and during his reign he was involved in the selection of over 100 new incumbents of professorial chairs. He concerned himself also with the siting and planning of the new buildings, an interest which led to his election as an honorary ARIBA. He was skilful too, as he had been in Liverpool, in attracting generous financial support from private and corporate benefactors. Yet the task he envisaged for himself was not a wholly easy one. Hetherington, astute academic politician though he was, had need of a resolute determination on many occasions when quasi-autonomous heads of departments were in his view obtuse or unreasonably obstructive. But it says much for his qualities that his senate soon came to take pride in his leadership and increasingly admired and respected him. He won its affection too by his human sympathies and his pastoral interest in his staff and their families. With the student body he had especially friendly relations; and the interest of graduates in their university was kept alive by his annual Christmas letter written to them in an engagingly chatty manner and having a world-wide circulation. The one problem he was not able to solve completely was the relationship between the university and the partially affiliated Royal Technical College which later became the university of Strathclyde. On the other hand he was brilliantly successful in effecting a renaissance in the medical school which he had 'found in a perilous state' and bedevilled by rivalries between the university, two other independent medical schools, and two teaching hospitals.

In wider arenas of academic affairs outside Glasgow Hetherington came to play a progressively influential role, not least when questions of academic freedom and the independence of universities were concerned. He was chairman of the Committee of Vice-Chancellors and Principals from 1943 to 1947 and again from 1949 to 1952, and his close personal friendship with four successive chairmen of the University Grants Committee was invaluable in ensuring a mutual understanding between the two bodies. He also had easy high-level contacts with a number of government departments which frequently proved useful to universities. University interests also benefited from his association with various trusts and foundations, including the managing trustees of the Nuffield Foundation (vice-chairman, 1947-65), the Research Awards Committee of the Leverhulme Trust (chairman 1933-58), and the Carnegie UK Trust (life trustee). At the same time these trusts themselves gained much from the fertility of his ideas for expanding the fields of their beneficence. He visited the universities of Canada and the USA on many occasions and formed particularly enduring links with those in the USA. Very appropriately he was chairman from 1951 to 1956 of the Committee on Awards to Commonwealth (Harkness) Fellowships, tenable in the USA. In 1955 he visited India to advise the Indian Government about universities and in 1957 was chairman of a commission on the constitution of the university of Malta. He took a prominent part in organizing the quinquennial congresses of Commonwealth universities, every one of which he attended from 1921 to the first overseas gathering in 1958 in Montreal, where he gave the keynote address on 'Expanding Education'; indeed it was very largely due to him that the congresses were revived after the war, in 1948. He interested himself also in the founding of new universities in developing countries and was chairman of the Colonial Universities Grants Committee, 1942-8. As the years went by his exceptionally wide experience, his balanced judgement on all aspects of universities' aims and problems, and his personal popularity gave him a unique position so that he came to be recognized as the unchallenged doyen of vice-chancellors throughout the Commonwealth.

In the domain of more general public service he practised the good citizenship that he preached and was frequently called upon for help. He was a member of the royal commission on unemployment insurance, 1930-2; member and chairman of various trade boards, 1930-40; chairman of an inquiry into wages in the cotton industry in 1935 and 1937; chairman of a royal commission on workmen's compensation, 1939; member of the National Arbitration Tribunal, 1940-8; vice-chairman of the Council on Adult Education in HM Forces, 1942-8; and member of the Industrial Disputes Tribunal, 1948-59. He was also chairman of the Committee on Hospital Policy in Scotland, 1942; president of the National Institute of Social and Economic Research, 1942-5; president of the Scottish Council of Social Service, 1945-9; and president of Section L (Education) of the British Association at its Edinburgh meeting in 1951. He was chairman too of a Royal Fine Art Commission for Scotland (1957-64) and of the School Broadcasting Council for Scotland. In all, he held office as chairman, president, or deputy, of over fifty educational and charitable bodies and was a member of the committees of many more.

His career was such that the philosophical studies in which it was expected he would become eminent came to claim less and less of his attention and in any case his major interest had always been in the practical applications of moral philosophy and its relation to the general welfare, and relatively less in logic and metaphysics. In 1918 he published *Social Purpose* (with J. H. Muirhead, q.v.); in 1920 *International Labour Legislation*, based on his participation in the League of Nations Labour Conference (1919) in Washington; and in 1924 *The Life and Letters of Sir Henry Jones*. Apart from these three books many of his more important addresses on education and on economic and social topics were published in the transactions of the societies concerned or as pamphlets. In writing, as in public speaking, he had a distinctive and felicitous style which combined precision with elegance and a marked warmth of feeling. His many memoranda, reports, and addresses on a wide variety of occasions were models of their kind.

Tall and well-built and always physically in good trim, he had a commanding presence, a frank and open countenance, a generally relaxed demeanour, a ready smile, a genial sense of humour, and an easy friendliness which made him welcome everywhere. Much that he did seemed to be effortless or almost casual but it was invariably based on mastery of the facts and careful preparation. When advocating any policy or cause which he supported he relied on quiet reason and eschewed emotional appeals. Although often enough he did battle with hard-hitting opponents, he had few, if any, personal enemies. It was his knowledge, shrewdness, fair-mindedness, and wide sympathies, which gave him the standing he was accorded. He was from early years frugal in his personal life and his chief relaxation and only addiction was golf, a game in which he was more than usually proficient. He died suddenly, in the Westminster Hospital, 15 January 1965, while on a visit to London.

In 1914 he married (Mary Ethel) Alison (died 1966), of Alva near Tillicoultry, daughter of William Reid, the rector of Alva Academy and later headmaster of Shettleston Academy, Glasgow. She herself was a Glasgow graduate and a friend of his student days; possessing all the qualities desirable in a principal's wife, she was as popular everywhere as he was and afforded him great support and happiness throughout his life. They had two sons, the younger of whom, (Hector) Alastair, was editor of the *Guardian* 1956-75. Created a knight in 1936, Hetherington became KBE in 1948 and GBE in 1962. He was an honorary graduate of eighteen universities in Britain, Canada, and the USA, and an honorary fellow of a number of professional bodies. In 1958 he received the Howland memorial prize from Yale 'in recognition of marked distinction in the art of government'; and in 1961 he was made an honorary freeman of Glasgow. A strikingly lifelike portrait by (Sir) W. O. Hutchison (1938) is in the possession of the university of Liverpool and is reproduced in the biography listed below; another by Stanley Cursiter painted in the 1950s hangs in the hall of the Royal College of Physicians and Surgeons, Glasgow; a third, which controversially depicts him as a man of stern and masterful character and now hangs near the Senate-room in Glasgow, was commissioned by his Glasgow colleagues in 1961 and painted by David Donaldson.

[Sir Charles Illingworth, *University Statesman: Sir Hector Hetherington*, 1971; *The Times*, 16 January 1965; private information; personal knowledge.]

JAMES MOUNTFORD

HILBERY, SIR (GEORGE) MALCOLM (1883-1965), judge, was born 14 July 1883 at 30 Hilldrop Crescent, Islington, London, the fourth child in the family of five sons and one daughter of Henry Hilbery and his wife, Julia Moncaster Mitcheson. One of the sons died in infancy. His father was a City of London solicitor who soon afterwards opened offices at 4 South Square, Gray's Inn, and was the founder of the firm of Henry Hilbery & Son.

Hilbery was educated at University College School and, without passing through a university, he became a member of Gray's Inn, around which his life was principally centred thereafter. In his bar examinations he obtained a certificate of honour and he was also granted an Arden scholarship by his Inn. After his call to the bar in 1907 his first chambers were at 6 Crown Office Row in the Temple. He devilled for (Sir) Patrick Rose-Innes, afterwards a county court judge, and acquired a good miscellaneous practice. He was a keen yachtsman and kept a boat at Poole Harbour. During the war of 1914-18 he served as an RNVR lieutenant in minesweepers.

After resuming his practice at the bar he was elected a bencher of Gray's Inn in 1927 and was appointed recorder of Margate in the same year. He took silk in 1928. With chambers now at 2 King's Bench Walk he had a large civil practice and enjoyed a high reputation in running-down cases. As a student at Gray's Inn he had been an assiduous member of the Debating Society and he was a good and elegant speaker. As an advocate he had tact and discrimination in adapting himself to his tribunals, combining authority with restraint. He achieved clarity of exposition based on thorough preparation so that his points were perfectly thought out and lucidly marshalled.

When in January 1935 he was nominated commissioner of assize on the South-Eastern circuit it was evident that he was approaching the end of his career at the bar and in pursuance of an Act of Parliament of that year authorizing the appointment of two additional judges to the King's Bench division, he was one of those. On receiving the customary honour of a knighthood he took as the motto going with his coat of arms the words 'Nosce teipsum'.

He proved a reliable judge trying cases with ability and good sense, so that he was rarely reversed on appeal. He was a firm upholder of the common law. Although his practice had been chiefly in civil litigation and he had never appeared in a murder case at the bar, he became one of the ablest criminal judges. In 1948 he tried James Camb, the liner steward who was convicted of murdering a passenger by pushing her through a porthole into the sea.

Hilbery served as treasurer of Gray's Inn in the fatal year 1941 when the Inn was devastated by bombardment and the hall, chapel, and library burnt. After the fires he saw to it that the walls of the hall should be 'capped' to prevent deterioration so they could form the basis of the post-war rebuilding of the hall in replica.

In the affairs of the Society he exercised great authority and influence as chairman of the house committee, while his detailed knowledge of gardening had enabled him to render valuable service as master of the walks and chairman of the garden committee. His knowledge of painting was employed in the interests of the Society in guiding the acquisition of portraits. He himself was a discriminating collector of Dutch masters. After the rebuilding of the Inn he made his home at 5 Gray's Inn Square. His book, Duty and Art in Advocacy (1946), was presented to every student of the Inn on his call to the bar. In 1954, when the Duke of Gloucester was treasurer of Gray's Inn, Hilbery acted as his deputy. He was chairman of the Berkshire quarter-sessions from 1946 to 1963 and in 1959, when he was senior puisne judge of the Queen's Bench division, he was nominated a privy councillor. He retired from the bench in 1962.

Hilbery was perhaps the last of the high court judges in the grand manner. Tall and slender with a long, grave, impressive face, he consciously upheld the image of judicial dignity and impassivity whether in or out of the court. His height lent itself to the loftiness of manner which he cultivated in speech and demeanour. He prided himself on speaking little on the bench and as a reminder he wrote down and carried about with him the words of the psalmist: 'I held my tongue and kept silence, yea, even from good words, but it was pain and grief to me.' Though he gave the external impression of reserve and solemnity, in private and in congenial company he was an interesting conversationalist on a wide range of topics, well versed in English literature and with a dry ironic wit.

He was for many years chairman of the board of governors of the Royal Masonic Hospital. He was a prominent member of the Royal Thames Yacht Club, and until late in life he continued to sail.

In 1915 he married Dorothy Violet Agnes, daughter of Lieutenant-Colonel St. John Christophers, who survived him. They had one adopted son, Michael Seymour, who was in the Royal Navy and died when he went below in an attempt to rescue his shipmates after his 'Q' ship was torpedoed. Hilbery died at Bourton-on-the-Water 18 September 1965.

There is a portrait of Hilbery by William Dring (c. 1960) in the possession of the family. A copy of the portrait hangs in the Pension Chamber at Gray's Inn and another copy in the boardroom of the Royal Masonic Hospital.

[The Times, 20 and 24 September 1965; Graya (the magazine of Gray's Inn), Michaelmas term 1960 and Michaelmas term 1965; private information; personal knowledge.]   F. H. COWPER

HILDITCH, THOMAS PERCY (1886-1965), chemist, was born at Tollington Park, North Islington, London, 22 April 1886, the eldest of the three children and the only son of Thomas Hilditch, a boot manufacturer's agent, and his wife, Priscilla, daughter of Frederick Hall, London agent of a Welsh tile-manufacturing company. From 1900 to 1904 he was educated at Owen's School, North Islington, and in 1904 went to University College, London. As an undergraduate he studied under Professors Sir William Ramsay and J. Norman Collie [qq.v.], was awarded the Tufnell scholarship in 1906, and graduated with a first class B.Sc. degree in 1907. He became an associate of the Institute of Chemistry by examination in 1908. Between 1907 and 1911 he undertook research under Dr Samuel Smiles in London, Professor L. Knorr at the university of Jena, and Professor P. A. Guy at the university of Geneva, being the holder of an 1851 Exhibition science research fellowship for part of this time. In 1911 he was awarded the degree of D.Sc. by the university of London and was elected a fellow of the Institute of Chemistry.

Hilditch's postgraduate career fell into two parts: from 1911 to 1926 he worked for Joseph Crosfield & Sons, soap manufacturers, of Warrington (still in existence as part of Unilever Ltd.), as a technical research chemist, and from 1926 until his retirement in 1951 he was the first holder of the Campbell Brown chair of industrial chemistry at the university of Liverpool.

At Crosfields Hilditch worked under the technical directorship of Dr E. F. Armstrong and was engaged, during the war years, in the successful development of catalytic methods for preparing acetic acid and acetone from ethanol. After the war, attention was directed to the study of the catalytic hydrogenation of fats and oils and other substances resulting in the publication by Armstrong and Hilditch of a series of thirteen significant papers. These appeared from 1919 to 1925 in the *Proceedings of the Royal Society*, series A, under the general title 'A Study of Catalytic Actions at Solid Surfaces'. Through their investigations both Armstrong and Hilditch realized how little was known about the chemical nature of animal and vegetable fats and Armstrong's presidential address to the Society of Chemical Industry in 1925 was entitled 'A Neglected Chapter of Chemistry — Fats'. Half a century later that description no longer applied, thanks, mainly during the first half of the intervening period, to the labours of Hilditch and his research colleagues. Despite the inadequacy of the techniques then available for the study of fats and the fact that almost all his research students began as inexperienced workers who had to be trained, the flow of results steadily mounted to become an impressive contribution to our knowledge of natural fats.

Continuing his Crosfield interest, Hilditch studied the hydrogenation of unsaturated fats and their constituent acids. He also investigated their autoxidation and uncovered a fundamental link between these two processes. In addition fatty acids of unknown or uncertain structure were isolated and identified. His major contribution, however, was a study of the composition of the natural fats. This involved the development of satisfactory analytical procedures both in respect of their constituent acids and — a more difficult problem — their constituent glycerides, the application of these procedures to a wide range of fats, and the compilation, critical assessment, and correlation of data available both from the Liverpool laboratories and from other sources. The first two of these tasks were undertaken by Hilditch and his research students, the last was Hilditch's responsibility

alone and was masterfully achieved in his book *The Chemical Constitution of Natural Fats*, which appeared in four editions (1940, 1947, 1956, 1964), the final edition being jointly written with P. N. Williams. This work remains a monument to Hilditch's industry and insight and a valuable compilation to which reference is still frequently made.

Hilditch was elected a fellow of the Royal Society in 1942 and appointed CBE in 1952. He received many other awards including the Lampitt medal from the Society of Chemical Industry, and the Chevreul medal from the French Groupement Technique des Corps Gras. The American Oil Chemists Society organized a symposium in his honour at Houston in 1965. Although his chair was a research appointment and his undergraduate teaching was confined to one course of honours lectures he contributed in many ways to the administrative life of the university and served on the committees of various professional societies concerned with chemistry.

His research students came from Britain and from overseas. Hilditch was not an easy man to know and in the early months of their research career his students regarded him with respect and awe and sought so to conduct their research as to avoid his caustic comments on inadequate work or shoddy thinking. Slowly those first impressions gave way to respect and affection for one who was always fair and frequently generous. Long after they graduated most kept in touch with their teacher and friend. Many of them continued to work with fatty acids in an industrial or academic environment and added further to our knowledge of fatty-acid chemistry. Hilditch was pleased to chart progress and they were glad to build on the foundation which he had so carefully laid. His contribution to fat chemistry will long be remembered and his name will always be associated with the pioneering labour of the quarter century during which he occupied the chair in Liverpool and which immediately preceded the development of those chromatographic and enzymic techniques which extended even further our knowledge of fatty-acid chemistry and biochemistry.

Hilditch was married three times: in 1912 to Elizabeth Monica Lawrence (died 1929), by whom he had three daughters; in 1929 to Eva (died 1949), widow of John Stephen Parsons, and daughter of John Richardson, coal merchant; and in 1952 to Margery, daughter of George Davies, haulage contractor, who survived him. Always a prodigious worker he found his recreation in gardening, walking, and watching cricket. A regular worshipper, he served his church (All Saints, Oxton) in many capacities and was regarded by his friends there as a shy and reserved man of great humility. He died at his home in Birkenhead 9 August 1965.

[R. A. Morton in *Biographical Memoirs of Fellows of the Royal Society*, vol. xii, 1966; private information; personal knowledge.]

F. D. GUNSTONE

HINDLEY, JOHN SCOTT, VISCOUNT HYNDLEY (1883–1963), business man and administrator, was born 24 October 1883 in Margate, the son of the Revd William Talbot Hindley, vicar of Holy Trinity, and his wife, Caroline, daughter of John Scott. He was educated at Weymouth College and as a teenager had some ideas of going up to Oxford but was warned by a friend of his father that he would find it a games-playing place and a poor preparation for business. As he had already decided to enter industry, he went down the pit, as an apprentice on the engineering side of a Durham colliery. He soon changed over to the commercial side of the business. It was in the large-scale distribution of coal at home and abroad that he first made his name as a capable and energetic man of affairs. Between the wars he became chairman in 1938 of the large and in those days well-known coal merchanting and coal exporting concern, Stephenson, Clarke Ltd. He was also associated with the direction of one of the most conspicuous colliery groups in South Wales, the Powell Duffryn Steam Coal Company Ltd. He was on the board of a considerable number of other companies and as early as 1931 he had become a director of the Bank of England. He was a man who by diligence and capacity made himself a position in business life and a personal fortune, starting with few social advantages. He possessed a genial manner and a sense of humour, a capacity for working with many sorts of people, high executive ability in the day-to-day conduct of business, and an extremely shrewd judgement. He was knighted in 1921, created a baronet in 1927, and Baron Hyndley in 1931.

Hyndley became associated with coal business at a time when the coalmining industry reached and passed the peak of its nineteenth-century development. Coal had enjoyed something like a monopoly of the market for energy during the first great phase of European industrial expansion. It lost that position in Britain after 1913. The coal industry had to find its way through a period of painful contraction, through disturbed, often bitter, industrial relations, and two world wars. These were the conditions in which Hyndley, as a prominent man of business, became associated with national politics and administration.

He first entered government service during the war as a member of the coal controller's export advisory committee in 1917. Between the wars, he was commercial adviser to what was then the Mines Department, a small department with inferior personnel and limited powers, which was the only existing medium of communication between government and the coal industry at that time. When the second war began, the coal industry ran into grave difficulties, arising partly out of the decline of the industry in the previous twenty years, partly out of the demand for men for the army when France fell in 1940. This latter emergency stripped the mines of workers just when the munitions drive, with its need for coal, was getting into its stride. The Mines Department did not survive the 1941–2 fuel crisis; it was replaced in 1942 by the much larger, wider, and better-staffed Ministry of Fuel and Power. Hyndley became the Ministry's controller-general and carried the main responsibility for coal output and distribution under the first minister of fuel and power, Major Gwilym Lloyd-George (later Viscount Tenby, q.v.). Hyndley was thus associated with the fuel effort during the most critical years of the war. But his position was awkward, for the Ministry also possessed a secretary directly responsible to the minister. The personal resolve of the two men concerned was needed to avoid trouble, on the whole successfully. It should be said, however, that Hyndley's undoubted capacity for business was better suited to day-to-day administration and creating the confidence needed for the running-in of a new large organization than to weighing distant alternatives and laying down long-term policy. He resigned at the end of 1943 to be succeeded by Sir Hubert Houldsworth [q.v.].

For the next three years Hyndley devoted himself largely to his business interests. But the coal industry was towards the centre of the political stage after the war and Hyndley with his intimate knowledge of its problems seemed too valuable a man to lose. When the mines were nationalized in 1946 it was Hyndley who was asked by the Attlee Government to take on the heavy and thankless post of first chairman of the National Coal Board. This he held until 1951, when he was again succeeded by Houldsworth. Hyndley brought loyalty, hard work, and fortitude to his five years at the Board. He established excellent personal relations with, and earned the liking of, a deeply divided industry. How far the organization he helped to set up was wholly effective for the long-term requirements of fuel and power policy is another question. It could not be answered out of an examination of his efforts alone, for the establishment of the Board was much influenced by contemporary political and economic conditions. Hyndley was shrewd rather than adventurous. But he certainly assisted to close one chapter in the history of British coal mining and to open another. To that extent he left his personal mark on the economic development of Britain at the time. He was appointed GBE in 1939 and advanced to a viscountcy in 1948.

In 1909 Hindley married Vera, daughter of James Westoll, of Coniscliffe Hall, Darlington; they had two daughters. The titles therefore became extinct when he died in London 5 January 1963.

[*The Times* and *Colliery Guardian, passim;* private information; personal knowledge.]

W. H. B. COURT

HINSHELWOOD, SIR CYRIL NORMAN (1897-1967), physical chemist and biochemist, was born in London 19 June 1897, the only child of Norman Macmillan Hinshelwood, chartered accountant and friend of Charles Dickens, by his wife, Ethel Frances Smith. After his father's death in Canada in 1904, his mother brought him back to London and took a little flat in Chelsea which was their London home for sixty-four years and in which he died. Hinshelwood often spoke of his debt to his mother. It was due partly to their affection and devotion to one another that he never married. His mother died in 1959.

Hinshelwood went to the Westminster City School and won a Brackenbury scholarship at Balliol College, Oxford, in 1916. Instead of going up at once he went as a chemist to the Explosives Supply Factory at Queensferry, where he came under the dynamic leadership of K. B. Quinan. In his Nobel oration Hinshelwood described how the testing of the stability of explosives impressed on him the mysteries of chemical change and its dependence on the energy and environment of the molecules. At Queensferry he soon found opportunities for his innate gift for research and was known as the boy wonder, having been promoted assistant chief laboratory chemist.

In January 1919 he went up to Balliol and while he was still an undergraduate three papers he had written at Queensferry on the decomposition of solids were published by the Chemical Society. Having won distinction in the shortened war degree course in 1920 he was elected to a research fellowship at Balliol. A year later he became a tutorial fellow of Trinity where he taught until 1937. For twenty years his researches were done in the cellars of Balliol and the outhouses of Trinity, which had been adapted to the teaching of physical chemistry in the university. Before the war the researches of Lord Rayleigh [q.v.] and Irving

Langmuir had directed attention to the elucidation of the kinetics of gaseous reactions by means of the molecular kinetic theory. Hinshelwood was quick to see the possibilities of this method of attack. In 1921 Nernst prophesied that he and his colleagues in Berlin would 'settle this whole business of gas reactions within a year'. But the problem of gas reactions was settled in Oxford by Hinshelwood in 1926 in his first book, *Kinetics of Chemical Change in Gaseous Systems,* so far as concerned the first of the three stages of a scientific theory which he specified in his presidential address to the Royal Society in 1957. 'The first is that of gross over-simplification, reflecting partly the need for practical working rules, and even more a too enthusiastic aspiration after elegance of form.' The second stage was reached in the third edition of his book in 1933: 'when the symmetry of the hypothetical systems is distorted and the neatness marred as recalcitrant facts increasingly rebel against uniformity.' There remained to be attained the third stage 'when a new order emerges, more intricately contrived, less obvious, and with its parts more subtly interwoven, since it is of nature's and not of man's contriving'.

Hinshelwood's first book was a milestone in chemical literature. The young Oxford chemist outdistanced his more famous competitors: first by his imaginative approach in which, with the help of his pupils, he quickly investigated a wide range of gaseous reactions of various types while others were making a more minute investigation of single reactions. Hinshelwood worked quickly and he had a flair for spotting the significant features of each reaction so that his thoughts advanced on a broad front. His experimental techniques were simple and elegant and he wasted no time, sometimes running risks, as when he evaporated an explosive liquid by the warmth of his hand.

Then he had acquired a mastery of the calculus which, backed by his intensive study of the papers of Clerk Maxwell [q.v.] and the *Kinetic Theory of Gases* of (Sir) James Jeans [q.v.], became a most powerful instrument in his mathematical analyses of his results. There were five exciting years when the materials for the first edition of his book were being collected; the book itself was a model of clarity of exposition, covering the whole field with fresh insight. For reaction involving two or more molecules the kinetic theory in many cases gave a reasonable picture of the mechanism as dependent on the energy of activation, the energy needed by a molecule to enable it to react. There was, however, the intriguing problem of the unimolecular reaction in which the proportion of the molecules that reacted in unit time was independent of the pressure and apparently therefore of collisions with other molecules or with the surface of the vessel. Only one such reaction was known in 1926, the decomposition of nitrogen pentoxide, and there were rival theories due to Perrin and to F. A. Lindemann (later Viscount Cherwell, q.v.). Perrin supposed that the rate was dependent on the absorption of energy from outside the system. Lindemann suggested that the molecules were dependent on gaining energy by collision, a quick process, but that, having gained energy, time was needed before it was distributed between the constituents of the molecule to produce an unstable state. Lindemann predicted therefore that unimolecular reactions would be found in which the rate would be independent of the pressure, except at very low pressures, when the time needed for the active state to occur would be the governing factor. By 1933 Hinshelwood had discovered many unimolecular reactions in his studies of the decomposition of organic vapours and shown that at very low pressure their rate of reaction was diminished as Lindemann had predicted.

Among the complications which came to light under closer examination was the chain reaction in which molecules when they react energize other molecules, the mechanism first invoked by Nernst to explain the high quantum yield of some photochemical reactions. The work of Christiansen and Semenov had emphasized its importance and Hinshelwood discovered frequent instances of its occurrence. Another field which he investigated, by adding various gases and vapours to the systems he was studying, was homogeneous catalysis.

The exploration of the complexities of the apparently simple reaction between oxygen and hydrogen occupied Hinshelwood and his pupils for several years before he reached the conclusions given in his Bakerian lecture which threw fresh light on the causes of the explosive limits of mixtures of the two gases under various conditions.

As a college tutor Hinshelwood was unsurpassed. All his pupils became his friends. He understood so well the difficulties facing young men in learning and he guided them with an unfailing touch, fitting them for the great responsibilities which many of them were to assume. Tolerant of their follies, he commanded universal devotion and respect. Both in tutorials and in lectures the clarity and vision with which he could present a subject appealed both to the clever and to the dull. He was an ideal supervisor of research. By his daily presence in the laboratory and his close attention to any detail of their research his students were imbued with his own critical attitude towards techniques, evaluation of results, and style of presentation.

In 1937, following the retirement of Frederick Soddy [q.v.], Hinshelwood was elected as Dr Lee's professor with responsibility for the teaching of both physical and inorganic chemistry. This meant great changes in his life. He moved from Trinity to Exeter, and as the old chemical department of the Museum provided no facilities for physical chemistry he continued to work in Balliol and Trinity until the generosity of Lord Nuffield [q.v.] provided him in 1941 with a fine Physical Chemistry Laboratory, when the cellars and outhouses of Balliol and Trinity returned to their former uses after honourable service to science for nearly a century. Hinshelwood took his responsibility for the two large departments very seriously, but administration irked him. Luckily one or two of his younger colleagues took much of the detailed work off his shoulders. Under his inspiring leadership his laboratory soon became an important centre of research. At one time, nine of his colleagues were fellows of the Royal Society.

In 1936 Hinshelwood found a new interest in the study of the chemical kinetics of living cells, on which life and growth depend. Each cell, he said, resembled a chemical factory in miniature, dependent on a complex of interlocking reactions, each with its own specific enzyme. He chose for his point of attack in this new field the adaptation which certain bacteria showed in accommodating themselves to their environment when their supplies of foodstuff were changed and their gradual adaptation even to substances initially poisonous to them: a matter of critical importance in the adaptability of hostile organisms to substances aimed at their destruction. Having investigated several instances of this adaptability of bacteria, Hinshelwood and his pupils became involved in controversy over what was said to be their fallacy, of assuming the inheritance of acquired characteristics, and neglecting the possibility that the occurrence of mutants and natural selection are the real factors at work. Hinshelwood had never ruled out the possibility of mutation which would by analogy be a fairly rare occurrence, and he described systems in which the changes originated in the selection of mutants. In other examples he proved his point by plating a number of bacteria after short exposure to a new environment, and showing that all of them continued to show normal growth under the new conditions. Other techniques provided confirmation. The convincing evidence he produced has gradually converted many of the sceptics and adaptation in the Hinshelwood sense became an accepted theory, with its grave implication for immunology. His active investigation of the kinetics of the growth of micro-organisms continued to the end of his life. When he moved to London in 1964, a senior research fellowship at Imperial College provided facilities and he gathered round him young and enthusiastic helpers.

In 1946 Hinshelwood collected the results of ten years of investigation in a book of great originality, *The Chemical Kinetics of the Bacterial Cell*, in which he traversed the whole problem of cell organization. In 1966 came his last book, *Growth, Function and Regulation in Bacterial Cells*, with A. C. R. Dean as his co-author. For thirty years he had been striving to see 'how the main characteristics of life, in its physical manifestations', as exhibited by uni-cellular organisms 'emerge from the interplay of the laws of nature', and his last book was a brilliant summary of the progress made in this quest.

The breadth of Hinshelwood's outlook and his severely critical attitude towards what each generation regards as fundamental was shown in a remarkable manner in his monograph *The Structure of Physical Chemistry* in 1951. It represents his individual point of view of the structure and continuity of the whole subject and in it he insists on the limitations of the current working notions, so that young chemists should not invest them with more ultimate significance than they contain. In this con-nection he quoted *Alice in Wonderland*, 'Some-how it seems to fill my head with ideas, but I don't know exactly what they are'.

One of the great merits of Hinshelwood's lectures was defining the merits of the known and unknown with a clarity which was rein-forced by his dry, pithy humour. There is a philosophical vein running through the pages of *The Structure of Physical Chemistry* as they progress from the world as a molecular chaos to the growth and structure of the living cell.

During the years at Oxford honours came to Hinshelwood from many quarters: the Faraday and Longstaff medals of the Chemical Society, the Davy, Royal, Leverhulme, and Copley medals of the Royal Society into which he had been elected in 1929. He received many honor-ary degrees and was the natural choice as presi-dent of the Chemical Society (1946-8) for its centenary in 1947 and as president of the Royal Society (1955-60) for its tercentenary in 1960, having been its foreign secretary from 1950. He was knighted in 1948 and in 1956 he shared a Nobel prize with his friend Semenov for their contributions to chemical kinetics. In 1960 he was admitted to the Order of Merit. In 1964-5 he was president of the British Association. He was an honorary fellow of Trinity, Balliol, Exeter, and St. Catherine's Colleges, Oxford. From 1934 onwards he was a delegate of the Oxford University Press and the steady growth of their scientific publications owed much to his initiative and advice, while with his literary interests his influence was felt in other fields.

Hinshelwood's aesthetic tastes dated back to his boyhood. He loved beauty in all its forms and his taste was catholic, in literature, music, the arts; and the aesthetic value of a scientific law. His paintings reveal his sensitive eye for form and colour and much of his leisure in later years was spent listening to his set of Beethoven records. He was a discerning col-lector of Chinese porcelain and Eastern carpets which adorned his professorial rooms. His great pleasure in his visit to China was to find men alive to the secrets of the glazes of the Ming period, with whom he discussed the aesthetics of Chinese porcelain. It was his catholicity which gave him such a full life and made his influence felt in so many fields.

Hinshelwood had a genius for languages and an aesthetic sense of their form and beauty. He wrote exquisite English prose of perfect clarity. He was proficient in French, German, Italian, and Spanish, and he knew also Russian and Chinese. He was equally versed in the classics and his presidential address to the Classical Association was an example of his range of learning and the elegance with which he used it to exemplify his philosophy of language and his passionate belief in the essential unity of the intellectual disciplines. He illustrated the individuality and illogicality of languages by the idiosyncracies of German genders, the code of Arabic plurals, and the difficulties attending the transition from classi-cal Chinese to modern usage. One of Hinshel-wood's finest occasional papers was his centen-ary essay on Dante's imagery. The acute visual perception with which Dante described the many episodes in the *Divina Commedia*, which Hinshelwood quoted, appealed to him as a painter. From his boyhood he had been inter-ested in painting. The little palette he used he had bought when he was nine. The exhibition of more than a hundred of his oil-paintings at Goldsmiths' Hall after his death showed his mastery of the medium to express the wide range of visual images he was trying to portray, whether it was the portrait of a friend or pupil, the college cat, the interiors of the Oxford rooms he loved so dearly, or the colour and life of the streets of London. One ambitious picture showed the stride of a racing eight rowing up the barges at Oxford, a historic record of a bygone scene. Hinshelwood's fine draughts-manship and sense of composition brought them all to life.

In 1964 Hinshelwood left Oxford at the termination of his professorship and returned to his Chelsea flat. His help and advice were quickly in demand, as a consultant to several great industrial organizations; he was also a valued member of the Arts Council and a trustee of the British Museum, the chairman of council of Queen Elizabeth College, London, chairman of the scientific advisory committee of the National Gallery, and chairman of the education committee of the Goldsmiths' Company, to whose court he had been elected in 1960. His connection with the company was one of the great pleasures of his closing years and he left the company the largest legacy they had received for many years because, he said, 'he admired so much what they did for individuals and for the relief of suffering'. His last years were specially happy. He was free of administrative duties; his mind was as fresh and fertile as ever: he had time to paint the streets and parks of London, and to revel in his Beethoven and Wagner records. When he died at home 9 October 1967, at the peak of his powers, the last things on which his eyes must have rested were his beloved Chinese porcelain and Eastern rugs.

There are portraits by Sir Gerald Kelly at the Royal Society and at the Chemical Society; by Edward I. Halliday at Exeter College, Oxford; by Douglas Anderson (presented by his pupils) at the Physical Chemistry Laboratory at Oxford; by Charles Pickard; and a self-portrait at Goldsmiths' Hall.

[*The Times*, 12 October 1967; *Chemistry in Britain*, vol. iii, 1967; personal knowledge.]

HAROLD HARTLEY

HIVES, ERNEST WALTER, first BARON HIVES (1886-1965), chairman of Rolls-Royce engineering firm, was born 21 April 1886 in Reading, the twelfth child of John William Hives, a schoolmaster, of Reading, and his wife, Mary Washbourne. He was educated at Redlands School, Reading. After working in a Reading garage, in 1903 Hives got a job in the garage of C. S. Rolls's car sales company. After a brief period with another sales firm, he joined the Napier company where he spent three years. In 1908 he joined Rolls-Royce, the company he was to serve for nearly fifty years. He was originally engaged at Derby to supervise experimental work. A great deal of this was road testing and he became one of the firm's outstanding drivers in the major automobile trials which were a feature of the European scene before the 1914-18 war. He was one of the first men to achieve 100 m.p.h. on the racing track.

The outstanding reputation of the Rolls-Royce company rests of course on the work of many gifted people. Among them, however, four stand out above the rest. One of them, C. S. Rolls, died in 1910 before his work for the motor car company he helped to create was complete, but the other two founders, (Sir) (Frederick) Henry Royce [q.v.] and Claude Johnson, built an organization based on talented and meticulous engineering which gained and kept world-wide admiration. The fourth of the great Rolls-Royce characters, whose reign began in 1936 and lasted for twenty years, was Hives.

The war of 1914-18 naturally brought great changes. Royce designed his first aero-engine, the 12-cylinder Eagle, in 1915 and in that year Hives began its development. In 1919 it powered the twin-engined Vickers-Vimy bomber on the first direct flight across the Atlantic. Other notable engines followed, all of which were developed under Hives's direction. Of these the Kestrel marked perhaps the greatest single advance and from it sprang the R engine which powered the winning Schneider Trophy racers of 1929 and 1931. This engine was the precursor of the Merlin which powered the Hurricanes and Spitfires which won the Battle of Britain. Hives, who had been responsible for the Merlin's development, became responsible also for its production, for in 1936 he succeeded to the general works management of the factory and a year later was elected to the board. He became managing director in 1946 and chairman of the Rolls-Royce company in 1950. In 1957 he retired.

It was in May 1941 that the first British jet-propelled aeroplane, powered by the Whittle W1 gas turbine engine, flew. (Sir) Frank Whittle's company, Power Jets Ltd., was collaborating with other companies and, by 1942, particularly with the Rover company. In that year Hives decided 'to go all out for the gas turbine' and arranged with the Ministry of Aircraft Production to take over the Rover gas turbine establishment while Rover took over from Rolls-Royce the production of the Meteor tank in which a variant of the Merlin engine was installed. This was perhaps the most important policy decision in Rolls-Royce history and, under Hives's direction, the company rapidly moved into a commanding world lead in the design development and manufacture of gas turbine aircraft engines.

Hives was a leader of men, especially engineers. He seemed rarely, if ever, to seek advice but he never resented criticism from subordinates. He carried responsibility with supreme self-confidence, was delighted by success, and undismayed by delay in achieving it: there was never in his philosophy room for failure.

He was a sturdy man of medium height. Outside his domestic life, he lived for Rolls-Royce. In the run up to World War II and in the war itself he developed intimate contacts with the Royal Air Force and the government departments which supplied it, and official confidence in the company was such that it operated government contracts with an unusual degree of autonomy, justified indeed by its basic understanding of what the service wanted and of its own technological and production abilities. Moreover, Hives, through his relationships with ministers, Service chiefs, and senior civil servants, had an undoubted influence on government policy.

Recreations played only a small part in Hives's life, but he did play golf occasionally and he sometimes fished, and all those who on their visits to Derby stayed overnight at the Rolls-Royce guest house on the banks of the Trent remember the post-prandial games of snooker—a game for which he had a predilection comparable only with his liking for the songs of Ethel Merman, which provided the background music.

Hives became an MBE in 1920, a Companion of Honour in 1943, and a baron in 1950. He was an honorary D.Sc. of Nottingham (1949), an honorary LLD of Cambridge (1951), and an honorary D.Sc.(Eng.) of London (1958). He was awarded the gold medal of the Royal Aeronautical Society (1935).

He married, in 1913, Gertrude Ethel (died 1961), daughter of John Alfred Warwick, a merchant sea captain, and Caroline Drusilla Pumphrey. They had four sons and three daughters. Hives died 24 April 1965 in the National Hospital for Nervous Diseases, London. He was succeeded in the barony by his eldest son, John Warwick Hives (born 1913).

His portrait by (Sir) James Gunn (1954) is at The Bendalls, Milton, Derby, the house of his eldest son. A copy of this portrait is in the head office of Rolls-Royce, 65 Buckingham Gate, London SW1.

[Harold Nockolds, *The Magic of a Name*, 1938; W. A. Robotham, *Silver Ghosts and Silver Dawn*, 1970; Frank Whittle, *Jet, the Story of a Pioneer*, 1953; Ian Lloyd, *Rolls-Royce. The Years of Endeavour*, 1978, *Rolls-Royce. The Growth of a Firm*, 1978, and *Rolls-Royce. The Merlin at War*, 1978; private information; personal knowledge.]

KINGS NORTON

HOBBS, SIR JOHN BERRY (JACK) (1882-1963), cricketer, was born at Cambridge 16 December 1882, the eldest of the twelve children of John Cooper Hobbs, a slater's labourer, and his wife, Flora Matilda Berry. As his father became a professional at Fenner's and later groundsman at Jesus College, cricket was immediately a central function of Jack Hobbs's life, and although he never had any formal coaching, he would get up at six to practise on Parker's Piece. He was educated at the local Church of England boys' school and the first cricket team for which he played was that of the church choir in which he sang. His promise in local cricket earned him a trial with Surrey in 1903 (after Essex had ignored his application), and he was paid 30s. a week, £1 in winter, while he qualified by residence.

Surrey were rebuilding after the triumphs of the 1890s and as in the previous season he had made 696 runs in 13 innings for Cambridgeshire, in 1905 Hobbs was given as immediate opportunity as soon as he was qualified. In his first match, against the Gentlemen of England, he made 18 and 88, and was awarded his county cap when he followed this with 28 and 155 against Essex in his first championship game, reaching the century in 2 hours. After three summers of consolidation under the guidance and example of Tom Hayward, his first great opening partner, he went to Australia in 1907-8. Left out of the first test, he made 83 at Melbourne and until his test career ended in 1930 he was never again omitted by England when he was available.

In 1909 he came within 81 runs of reaching a thousand in May, which he would probably have done had he not been rested against Oxford. In this prolific month he made 205 out of 371 in 165 minutes against Hampshire, 159 out of 352 against Warwickshire, and a century in each innings in the return match at Birmingham. Hobbs had established his authority in all English conditions, and he completed his apprenticeship when in 1909-10 he faced South Africa's battery of spin bowlers on their native matting. The googly was a new weapon in the bowler's armoury and many of the leading batsmen of the era had been routed by it. Hobbs admitted that he could not yet spot it from the hand, but on this tour he subdued it by going down the pitch and attacking it off the front foot. Although the series was lost, his average in the tests was 67, the next highest being 33, and on the tour he made 1,194 runs. His mastery of spin, coupled with the bowling of S. F. Barnes [q.v.], largely won the rubber in Australia in 1911-12, because after H. V. Hordern had taken 12 wickets in the first test, which was lost, Hobbs put him to the sword with centuries in the next three. At Melbourne he and W. Rhodes set up a record of 323 for the first wicket, made in 4½ hours.

In South Africa in 1913-14 he made 1,489 runs, 700 more than anyone else, and in the following summer, when Surrey were champions for the only time in his career, he made 11 centuries, 3 of them over 200. At Bradford he hit 5 sixes and 11 fours in making 100 out of 151 in 75 minutes, and against Yorkshire at Lord's he and Hayward had the last of their forty century partnerships. This was his high noon, when he was unchallenged as the leading batsman in the world, the supreme technician on any sort of wicket. Although audacity was sometimes tempered by his increasing responsibility to the side, the characteristic style was a fluent aggression which dictated to the bowlers. The worse the conditions, the more he set himself to dominate through attack.

But the ripeness is all. By 1914 Hobbs had scored 25,587 runs, made 65 centuries, played in 28 tests. The war years should have been his prime, and at thirty-six he could not be certain of recovering his old ascendancy. But in the event all these figures were to be more than doubled, and he was to garner the richest harvest the game has known. When he retired in 1934 he had made 61,237 runs, at an average of 50.65, and 197 centuries, 98 of them after his fortieth birthday.

At first Hobbs showed much of the old aggression: 205 not out against the Australian Imperial Forces when the next score was 38; with J. N. Crawford 96 in 32 minutes, scored in bad light and drizzle, to defeat Kent in his postponed benefit match; with Sandham in 1920 190 in 90 minutes against Northamptonshire; a century in 65 minutes on a fiery pitch at Leicester. But in 1921 a muscle injury was followed by an ulcerated appendix which nearly cost his life. He played only 6 innings in that year of plenty and thereafter he tired more easily and his batting was less adventurous. Adapting his style to the physical possibilities, he now dominated the bowlers off the back foot. The runs rolled in, but their gathering was never mechanical. A Hobbs innings was scrawled with his personal signatures as, all technical problems now instinctively resolved, he deployed the fullness of his art.

At Bath in 1923 he made his hundredth century, and at Taunton two years later he both equalled and overtook the record of 126 centuries set up by W. G. Grace [q.v.]. In this season of 1925 he scored 10 of his 16 hundreds in the first 12 games, and he led the English averages with 3,024 runs at 70.32. Next year his 316 not out for Surrey was the highest innings ever played at Lord's and in the final test at the Oval, with Sutcliffe, a masterly century on a turning wicket helped to recover the Ashes from Australia. In 1928 he had an average of 82, and when he went to Australia in the winter a team-mate said that for him the tour was like a royal procession as he visited for the last time the grounds where he had given so much pleasure. At Melbourne his 49, made when the pitch was most lethal, enabled England to get 332 to win the match in conditions so bad that they were not expected to reach a hundred. Gradually, however, the years took their toll and he had to rest while minor strains and injuries took longer to clear up. His final century in first-class cricket was scored in Duckworth's benefit at Old Trafford in 1934, and the crowd sang 'Auld Lang Syne'.

All but 2 of Hobbs's 61 tests were played against Australia and South Africa: in 102 innings he made 5,410 runs at 56.94, with 15 centuries. In his career he shared in 166 opening century partnerships, an average of 1 every 8 innings, the highest being 428. Sixty-six were with Sandham, 40 with Hayward, 26 with Sutcliffe (15 in tests). Hobbs 6 times made 2 centuries in a match; he reached 1,000 runs in a season 26 times; he scored centuries both home and away against every county. In the Gentlemen v. Players fixture he had his own little cluster of records: an aggregate of 4,050, the highest individual score of 266 not out, and centuries at Lord's, the Oval, and Scarborough. In all grades of cricket he made 244 centuries, the last in 1941.

At medium pace with a late swerve he was also a useful bowler. He opened the bowling in three tests in South Africa in 1909–10, and in 1920 he even headed the English averages with 17 wickets at 11.82. In the field he was brilliant, lurking at cover with deceptive casualness to trap the unwary. In Australia in 1911–12 he ran out 15 opponents.

Surrey made Hobbs a life member in 1935, the MCC in 1949; his knighthood in 1953 was the first conferred on a professional cricketer; the Hobbs Gates at the Oval and a pavilion on Parker's Piece stand as tangible memorials of his career. But in a wider sense Hobbs was remembered as a potent symbol of the game, the small boy's idol, known to thousands who never saw him play. No other great player has inspired so much personal affection, nor permitted such a high degree of personal identification. His obvious integrity had something to do with this, his modest and disciplined way of life, his deep but unobtrusive religious beliefs, and his unassuming pleasure in his own achievement. But he was loved because he was so evidently an ordinary man, exceptional only in the endowment of a particular genius which he was humble enough to see in its proper perspective. He never expected to inherit the earth because of it, nor even to be hired as a radio pundit on matters outside his experience.

With the proceeds of his benefit in 1919 Hobbs opened a sports shop in Fleet Street in which he continued to take an active interest after he left the game. In 1906 he married Ada Ellen, daughter of Edward G. Gates, of Cambridge; they had three sons and a daughter. He died at Hove 21 December 1963, only a few months after his wife.

[J. B. Hobbs, *My Cricket Memories*, 1924, *My Life Story*, 1935; Louis Palgrave, *The Story of the Oval*, 1949; Ronald Mason, *Jack Hobbs*, 1960; *Wisden's Cricketers' Almanack*, 1936, 1963, 1964.]   M. M. REESE

HOBHOUSE, SIR JOHN RICHARD (1893–1961), shipowner, was born 27 February 1893 at Hadspen House, Castle Cary, the third son of Henry Hobhouse [q.v.], Liberal member of Parliament for East Somerset, and his first wife, Margaret Heyworth Potter, sister of Beatrice Webb [q.v.]. He was educated at Eton where he was a King's scholar and at New College, Oxford, where he studied botany and zoology; he later became an ardent and knowledgeable gardener. In the war of 1914–18 he served as a captain in the Royal Garrison Artillery and was awarded the MC in 1917. From 1920 he was a director of the Ocean Steam Ship Company of Liverpool, with his cousins, Richard and Lawrence Holt, Leonard Cripps, and Roland Thornton, and was chairman from 1953 until he retired in 1957. He was also a director of the Royal Insurance Company from 1933 to 1961 and chairman in 1954–7.

Throughout his working life Hobhouse was an outstanding and dedicated professional shipowner. He made important contributions to the progress of British liner trade between Europe and the Far East, where his companies were the principal operators. For in an era when shipowners were regarded, and with some justice, as remote and unapproachable, he travelled extensively in Asia and established easy formal relations with a wide range of Eastern traders. His early scientific training gave him a ready understanding of the commercial aspects of marine technology. He rationalized many traditional methods of carrying tropical produce and in particular he pioneered the bulk movement of vegetable oils and also of liquid latex, which brought immense wealth to Malaysia and revolutionized modern upholstery. And he was for a long time one of the Government's principal advisers on the shipment of explosives and other dangerous goods in peace and war. He was well trusted by the trade unions and he displayed notable determination, patience, and foresight in the affairs of the National Maritime Board, the National Dock Labour Board, and the ports industry, all of which he served effectively for long periods. He did as much as any man to determine the conditions which kept the large and essential element of Chinese ratings in service on British merchant ships throughout the war of 1939–45.

In that war Hobhouse was initially deputy regional commissioner and later the Government's chief shipping representative in the north-west. As chairman of the Liverpool Steam Ship Owners' Association in 1941–2 he played a leading and constructive part in establishing the General Council of British Shipping, which thereafter represented the interests of all British shipowners; he was chairman in 1942–3. He was knighted in 1946 for his war services and later received the Order of Orange Nassau for his help to Dutch shipping based on Britain. In 1948–50 he was chairman of the National Association of Port Employers.

A member of the council of the university of Liverpool for many years until 1957, he was treasurer in 1942–8, and president of the council in 1948–54. He was a pro-chancellor in 1948–57. He gave much time to the university's business and carried a large responsibility for planning its post-war development. He received the honorary degree of LLD in 1958. He was a member of the council of the Liverpool School of Tropical Medicine from 1932 to 1961 and its chairman from 1949 to 1955 and took an intense and beneficial interest in the School's affairs.

Hobhouse was a magistrate from 1929 to 1957. He became an imaginative member of the juvenile panel and was for several years a highly successful chairman of the chancellor of the Duchy of Lancaster's advisory committee in Liverpool. He was deeply concerned with many Liverpool charities and specially its Personal Service Society which, under his guidance, did much valuable and original work.

Hobhouse inherited from his Somerset forebears a compelling sense of obligation and a profound belief in the worth of individuals. A man of courage and decision, he was equipped with a penetrating and practical intellect coupled with exceptional vigour which gave a forceful and even aggressive slant to an essentially kindly and unselfish character. These attributes flourished in Liverpool, which in his time retained much of its Victorian pride and independence. Thus he was widely respected for his clear and direct approach, his exacting standards, and his power of logical analysis, but he was generally regarded as a formidable and somewhat uncompromising personality. Yet his substantial achievements owed much more to quite other characteristics. For men trusted him and turned to him in their private and public difficulties because they relied on his absolute integrity and his broad wisdom, drawn from deliberate observation and reflection; above all they knew that while unfailingly anxious to help he would seek no personal credit for anything he did or suggested. In every enterprise which he touched his direct contribution was significant and his example drove others to greater efforts and higher standards.

In 1926 Hobhouse married Catherine,

daughter of Henry Stewart Brown, produce broker; they had three sons and two daughters. He died at his home in West Monkton, Somerset, 9 May 1961.

[Private information; personal knowledge.]

JOHN NICHOLSON

HOBSON, SIR JOHN GARDINER SUMNER (1912–1967), attorney-general, was born 18 April 1912 at Long Clawson Hall, Melton Mowbray, the son of Major Gerald Walton Hobson of the 12th Lancers and his wife, Winifred Hilda, daughter of John Gardiner Muir, JP, DL, of Farmingwoods Hall, Northamptonshire. He was educated at Harrow and at Brasenose College, Oxford, where he was a scholar and obtained second class honours in history in 1934. He was called to the bar by the Inner Temple in 1938. Hobson's background, like his bearing and his inclination, tended towards the military. He was a keen territorial. In the war of 1939–45 he served in the Northamptonshire Yeomanry, rising to the rank of lieutenant-colonel, as his father had done in the first war, and serving with the British Expeditionary Force in France in 1940 and with the First Army in North Africa. From 1944 to 1945 he was at the headquarters of the 21st Army Group, with special responsibilities for tracked and armoured vehicles. He was mentioned in dispatches, and appointed OBE in 1945.

Hobson's virtues and abilities, particularly in the field of organization, were those of a soldier, although he used to say that he learnt more as head boy of Harrow than at any subsequent period of his life. His capacity for leadership was enhanced by a deep love and knowledge of country matters. He was a skilled horseman, an enthusiastic rider to hounds, and a first-class shot. Every year he made his holiday in Scotland in order to stalk. His practice at the bar reflected this provenance. Questions under the Agricultural Holdings Acts or local Water Acts were his speciality on the Midland circuit. He was at his most characteristic when prosecuting a poacher. As chairman of Rutland and of Bedfordshire quarter-sessions, and as recorder of Northampton (1958–62), he played a full part in the public life of the shires. He took silk in 1957.

It was the chance of Eden's resignation in 1957 which brought Hobson into the House of Commons as Conservative member for Warwick and Leamington. Although his arrival was accidental, his capacity for hard work and clear expression became immediately apparent. He was soon elected to the powerful backbench 'One Nation' group. In February 1962 he became solicitor-general and in July attorney-general. He was knighted in 1962 and sworn of the Privy Council in 1963.

Some disagreeable duties fell to Hobson during the last few years of the long and stale Conservative administration. Inevitably the disgrace in 1963 of his old school and regimental friend, John Profumo, involved him in painful labour. He prosecuted the spy Vassall in 1962 and played the leading role before the Radcliffe tribunal which followed the revelations in Vassall's trial. In the course of the inquiry, Hobson felt obliged to press two journalists to disclose the sources of their information. When they refused to answer, Hobson procured their committal to prison for contempt of court, a course of duty which he fully realized would bring down upon himself, his Government, and his profession the full weight of a displeased press, as indeed it did.

Hobson had a leading part to play in the crop of extradition and deportation cases which plagued the home secretary at this period. The most famous of these, the Enahoro case (1963), led to Hobson being 'reported' to the benchers of his Inn by a fellow bencher, Reginald Paget, an old hunting companion, for unprofessional conduct on two counts. The masters of the bench held that the charges were unfounded.

When the Conservatives went into opposition in 1964, Hobson became even more valuable to them. The front bench relied increasingly on his advice and particularly on his uncanny power of drafting. He could produce perfect clauses, and amendments to clauses, absolutely on the spot. From his short period in office he had acquired an unrivalled knowledge of the art of the parliamentary draftsman. He was not exciting; but many of his colleagues thought he was the best law officer the Conservative Party had produced since the first Viscount Hailsham [q.v.].

Hobson's return to private practice at the bar was less successful. He was never a showy advocate and never one to court publicity and his previous connections had been provincial rather than metropolitan. Financially the years after 1964 were lean. In the autumn of 1967 it was strongly rumoured that his circumstances had compelled him to seek a judicial appointment, for which he was excellently suited: he was clear, firm, compassionate, hard-working, and the soul of honour. But he complained one evening of a crippling pain in the leg and the next evening (4 December) he was dead, killed by an entirely unsuspected tumour of the brain.

In 1939 Hobson married Beryl Marjorie, daughter of A. Stuart Johnson, of Henshall Hall, Congleton, Cheshire; they had three daughters.

[Private information; personal knowledge.]

CHARLES FLETCHER-COOKE

HODGSON, RALPH EDWIN (1871-1962), poet, was born in Darlington, county Durham, 9 September 1871, the sixth son in the family of seven boys and three girls of Ralph Hodgson, coal merchant, and his wife, Mary Graham. He was proud that William Bewick [q.v.], the painter, was his grandfather's cousin. Hodgson never wished to talk of his life and often employed his gift of imagination when irked by an insensitive questioner; myths and fantasies about him have resulted. His father died when he was still a small boy, and the family broke up. Hodgson lived with friends at Gatton in Surrey where his love for the countryside, birds, and dogs was nurtured. In his teens he travelled to America where he was employed in the Thalia Theatre, New York, apparently as an assistant scene-painter.

In the early nineties he was working in London as a black-and-white artist upon newspapers and magazines, signing some of his work 'Yorick'. For a short period from 1912 he edited *Fry's Magazine of Outdoor Life* for C. B. Fry [q.v.]. In 1913 he founded 'The Sign of the Flying Fame', publishers, with Claud Lovat Fraser [q.v.] and Holbrook Jackson, which made an important contribution to printing design.

During these years he was writing poetry, but as it did not satisfy him he destroyed it. His first published poem, 'The Storm Thrush', appeared in November 1904, in the *Saturday Review*, to which he thereafter contributed regularly. In 1907 he published his first collection of poems: *The Last Blackbird and Other Lines*. His second, *Poems*, followed in 1917, and it is upon this slim volume that his reputation is founded. It contains 'The Song of Honour', for which he had been awarded the Polignac prize in 1914; and in 1933 A. E. Housman [q.v.] said of this poem that it 'is one of the best of the twentieth [century]'; it is sufficient on its own to assure Hodgson's position in English literature.

Hodgson gave up writing when he joined the forces at the start of the war of 1914-18; he resumed writing after the war, but spasmodically. A third collection came out in 1958, *The Skylark and Other Poems*, and his *Collected Poems* in 1961.

Hodgson felt passionately for animals, and for the sanctity of nature; he also possessed a unique vision of man and humanity, set in a commanding sweep of historical imagination. These matters, close to his heart, are reflected in his poems, humorous sometimes, and lyrical, but always powerful and individual. He was careful to remain aloof from poetic trends and schools; he believed that poets are the mouthpiece only for lines inspired beyond them and he did not write unless an inner compulsion demanded it. He avoided prose as he did not wish to dull his 'muse'; the poems he had left us bear the quality of being distillation of matured emotions which have achieved a form perfect of their expression. He was the sternest of self-critics and his total production was small, but at its best is of a high lyric order.

Hodgson enjoyed friendship with many other writers of his day, such as Masefield, de la Mare, Sassoon, Drinkwater, and Eliot [qq.v.]. Besides being a poet, Hodgson was a singular character with varied gifts and interests. He was an artist, and in particular a fine characterist both with pencil and brush, and as a mimic. He was a spirited conversationalist, an enthusiastic book collector, and in youth he had been an ardent boxer. He bred bull-terriers, was a judge at Crufts, and was also a keen billiards player. He was particular about his clothes, but in appearance was likened to a gamekeeper, in tweed.

In 1920 he inspired the campaign to end the trafficking in birds' feathers for women's apparel, which ended successfully with the passage of the Plumage Act of 1921. He was lecturer in English at Sendai University, Japan, from 1924 to 1938, when he retired to live in America. He died in his farmhouse in the remote countryside of Ohio 3 November 1962.

In 1896 he married Janet Chatteris who died in 1920; in 1921 he married Muriel Fraser; this marriage was dissolved in 1932, and in 1933 he married Aurelia Bolliger. He had no children.

Hodgson was awarded the insignia of the Rising Sun in 1938; received an award for distinguished achievement from the American Academy and National Institute of Arts and Letters in 1946; and gained the Queen's gold medal for poetry in 1954.

The following portraits exist of him: a watercolour by Katherine Mayes *c.*1916, 'Lieutenant Hodgson in uniform'; two by Sir William Rothenstein have been published, one in *Men and Memories* (vol. ii, 1932), the other in *Twenty-Four Portraits* (2nd series, 1923); a circular bronze medallion, Hodgson's head in low relief, by T. Spicer-Simson (1922), of which the mould and a cast are in the National Portrait Gallery; and an oil painting by Kikuo (1934). The whereabouts of the original Rothenstein portraits are not known; the remainder are in the possession of the family.

[Private information; personal knowledge.]

COLIN FENTON

HOLDEN, HENRY SMITH (1887-1963), academic botanist and forensic scientist, was born at Castleton, near Rochdale in Lancashire,

30 November 1887, the elder of the two children (both sons) of Henry Carlton Holden, locally employed as a clerk, and his wife, Betsy Cockcroft. He was educated at the local grammar school and, on a scholarship, at Victoria University, Manchester, where he graduated with second class honours in botany in 1909. His father, who seems to have been a less than ideal husband and parent, had died whilst he was still at school, and his mother had to go to work to support him and his brother Ernest during their education. He himself helped to support Ernest through university as soon as he was able to do so.

Immediately after graduating, Holden joined the staff of University College, Nottingham (as it then was), as an assistant lecturer, and in 1911 gained his Manchester M.Sc. He remained at Nottingham for twenty-seven years, rising through the academic hierarchy to the chair of botany (1932) and the headship of the department of biology. This period was interrupted only by a wartime post (1916-19) as a bacteriologist in the Royal Naval Hospital, Plymouth.

Holden published in all, mainly in the *Annals of Botany* and the *Journal of the Linnean Society*, twenty-five papers on botanical subjects. At first these dealt largely with plant anatomy, but later he specialized in palaeobotany, especially that of the coal measures. His earlier published work gained him a D.Sc. from Manchester in 1921. He was elected a fellow of the Linnean Society in 1910, and of the Royal Society of Edinburgh in 1927. He proved to be a most effective academic teacher, able, according to report, to enliven his lectures with an impressive display of ambidexterity on the blackboard.

Holden had two careers, and his reputation rests mainly on his second. During the latter part of his academic period he began to be consulted by the local police on scientific problems which they encountered and on the uses of science in crime detection, and this work grew rapidly into his main interest. (According to one source, the association started by his being consulted by the local CID superintendent, who was a keen cricketer, about the care of the grass on his cricket pitches.) Thus when the locally inspired forensic science laboratory, one of the first in the country, came under the Home Office in 1936, Holden was appointed its first director, with a scientific staff of two graduates and two technicians. His surviving staff remember him for his enthusiasm, his forceful personality, and the drily witty encouragement which he gave them. As he said to one of them: 'Forensic science is a practical job, and all you have to do is to get in ten years' experience as quickly as you can.'

He soon became a, if not the, leading forensic scientist in Britain, and was both tireless and effective in educating the police about the ways in which science could help them. His advice was frequently sought by the Home Office during the late 1930s, when the present forensic science service was taking shape. In 1946 he was appointed director of the larger and more prestigious Metropolitan Police Laboratory, where he provided the scientific evidence in several of the most notorious crime cases of the post-war years (for example, the Haigh, Heath, Hume, and Raven murder trials).

His health, however, began to deteriorate, and he suffered a stroke in 1951. On recovering from this, he moved to the less arduous post of forensic science adviser to the Home Office, from which he retired in 1958 to resume working in the British Museum (Natural History) on his palaeobotanical research 'before I go completely ga-ga'. On his retirement he was appointed CBE (1958).

Professionally Holden was a considerable 'character', with a blunt, down-to-earth manner of expression which made him popular with the police officers who consulted him, but which, with its sardonic side, could also make him a little intimidating. Privately he was a man of simple conventional tastes—his home and garden, cricket, fell-walking, and the countryside. He paraded no particular religious beliefs and was inactively conservative in politics. He undoubtedly appreciated very much the status and deference which his position in the world of forensic science and his CBE brought him.

In 1917 he married Annie Janet, the daughter of Richard Hamer, a civil engineer, of Oswestry. They had a son and a daughter. Holden died 16 May 1963 in Dene Hospital, Caterham, near his Surrey home. In 1974 the university of Nottingham established the H. S. Holden botanical lectures, to be given annually to a public audience.

An excellent photograph of Holden is reproduced with his obituary in the *Journal of the Society for the Bibliography of Natural History*.

[*The Times*, 18 May 1963; *Journal of the Linnean Society*, vols. clxxv and clxxvi; *Royal Society of Edinburgh Year Book*, *1964*; *Journal of the Society for the Bibliography of Natural History*, vol. iv, pt. 4; private information; personal knowledge.]

H. J. WALLS

HOLLAND, Sir EARDLEY LANCELOT (1879-1967), obstetrician, was born 29 October 1879 at Puttenham, Surrey, the eldest son of the rector, the Revd Walter Lancelot Holland, and his wife, Edith, daughter of Canon Edward Revell Eardley-Wilmot. He was educated at

Merchiston Castle, Edinburgh, and gained a Warneford entrance scholarship to King's College Hospital, London. He qualified in medicine in 1903 and in 1905 obtained his MB, BS London, and FRCS England. He held a number of resident house appointments at King's College Hospital, Paddington Green Children's Hospital, Soho Hospital for Women, and Queen Charlotte's Maternity Hospital; and spent a year in Berlin where he worked with the distinguished gynaecologists, Olhausen, Bumm, and Orth. In 1907 Holland was appointed obstetric registrar and tutor at King's College Hospital and in the same year obtained his London MD. In the following year he took the membership of the Royal College of Physicians.

Holland was appointed to the honorary staff of King's College Hospital in 1914; but in 1916 moved to the London Hospital as obstetric and gynaecological surgeon: a more important appointment which offered greater facilities for research as well as a greater volume of clinical experience. He was unable to take up his appointment until 1919, serving in the meantime as a surgical specialist in France with the Royal Army Medical Corps.

Soon after his appointment to the London Hospital, Holland embarked upon his research into the causes of stillbirth, encouraged therein by the Ministry of Health. In 1922 an official ministry report was published which contained the results of what was a classical piece of original research. Of particular importance was the establishment of the fact that in breech deliveries it was cerebral injury which was the major cause of the high stillbirth rate in those cases.

Holland also had an appointment to the staff at the City of London Maternity Hospital which he served for a number of years and in which he retained great interest. He held a number of public appointments of importance: member of the royal commission on population; of the Central Midwives Board; and of the council of King Edward's Hospital Fund. Between 1937 and 1940 he was adviser in obstetrics and gynaecology to the Ministry of Health and when war broke out in 1939 he became responsible for organizing the evacuation of pregnant women from London to the country. He took charge of the emergency service in Hertfordshire and East Anglia; an experience which gave him many ideas about the development of a national maternity service. Many of these ideas were incorporated in a report made by the Royal College of Obstetricians and Gynaecologists which was consulted by the Ministry of Health on various aspects of the maternity services in relation to the National Health Service which was to come into

being in 1948. Holland was president of the College in 1943–6 and so had a very major say in the pattern of development of the maternity services at that time. Prior to his election as president Holland had served the College in many capacities: he had been active in its foundation in 1929; and as its honorary treasurer in 1930–9 had played no small part in establishing its financial stability.

Professionally Holland's main interest and greatest contributions were in the field of obstetrics rather than gynaecology. He was not an outstanding abdominal surgeon but his skill in vaginal surgery was very considerable. This undoubtedly stemmed from his early training in Germany where this type of surgery was more frequently undertaken than in England. He always retained the closest links professionally with colleagues in Germany and established many firm friendships with leading gynaecologists there. Holland's teaching abilities were considerable as one might expect from a man who had such a very strong personality. He was extremely forthright and direct; found it difficult to suffer fools gladly; and was at times almost irascible and unreasonable. This did not always make him at one · with his contemporaries and his colleagues. Nevertheless, his sincerity and the force of his personality made everyone realize the great contributions he had made to his speciality. With a professional life as crowded as was his, he yet found time to have a flourishing and successful private practice, which, however, he never allowed to divert him from his teaching, research, and public duties. He always maintained that private practice was secondary to his other professional commitments, which he took most seriously.

Holland's contributions to obstetric and gynaecological literature were considerable. He was a master of the written word. For several editions he shared authorship with T. W. Eden of a *Manual of Obstetrics* and later became its sole author. For many years this textbook, which ran into twelve editions, was the one most widely read by undergraduates in all the British medical schools. He collaborated with Aleck Bourne in editing two volumes of a *British Obstetric and Gynaecological Practice* (1955) which also, at the time, had a very wide circulation. He served the *Journal of Obstetrics and Gynaecology of the British Empire* as editor for a number of years and played no small part in establishing it as one of the leading journals in the speciality's literature in the world.

Holland made a special study of the obstetric details which surrounded the pregnancy and labour of Princess Charlotte of Wales [q.v.] who died in childbirth in 1817. The tragic circumstances which surrounded her death, which was followed by the suicide of Sir Richard Croft [q.v.] the obstetrician in charge of the Princess during her pregnancy, always fascinated him, and his knowledge of the intimate details which could be gleaned from all that had been written about this event was very extensive. His lecture, 'Princess Charlotte of Wales: a triple obstetric tragedy', was published in 1952.

Retirement at West Dean near Chichester was serene and pleasant for Holland. He enjoyed his family, his beautiful house, and even more beautiful garden. He continued in his literary activities long after his period of active medical practice had ended. His professional achievements received fitting recognition: honorary degrees from Dublin, Birmingham, and Leeds, an honorary MMSA and honorary FRCS of Edinburgh, and a knighthood in 1947, the year after he retired from the London Hospital.

In 1913 Holland married Dorothy Marion (died 1951), daughter of Dr Henry Colgate, of Eastbourne; they had three daughters. In 1952 he married Olivia (died 1975), daughter of Leslie L. Constable, JP, of Fittleworth, Sussex. Holland died at West Dean 21 July 1967. A memorial service was held in Chichester Cathedral. The Royal College of Obstetricians and Gynaecologists has a portrait of him by Sir James Gunn.

[Personal knowledge.]   JOHN PEEL

HOLLAND, SIR (EDWARD) MILNER (1902-1969), lawyer, was born 8 September 1902 at Sutton and was the second son in the family of two sons and two daughters of (Sir) Edward John Holland DL, JP, a publisher, and his wife, Selina Hobson. Sir Edward had a long career as a member of the Surrey County Council, of which he was chairman, and he was knighted in 1929. His first son was killed in the war of 1939-45.

Milner Holland was educated at Charterhouse and at Hertford College, Oxford. At Charterhouse he was awarded a classical leaving exhibition and at Hertford, where he obtained a classical scholarship in 1921, he was junior and senior scholar and won the Gordon Whitbread prize and the Talbot gold medal (both in classics). He achieved second class honours in classical moderations (1923) and a third class in *literae humaniores* (1925). He also received a second class in both jurisprudence (1926) and in his BCL degree in 1927. In the bar final examination of the Council of Legal Education he was awarded a certificate of honour. In addition, he received from the Inner Temple as a law student a Profumo prize.

In 1927 Milner Holland was called to the bar by the Inner Temple. He became a pupil of Wilfrid M. Hunt, who had an exceptionally busy and varied practice as a Chancery junior. On finishing his pupillage he obtained a room in chambers in 7 New Square, Lincoln's Inn, and he remained a member of those chambers until his death. In the twelve years following his call to the bar he built up a substantial practice, mainly in the Chancery division, and he supplemented his income by lecturing for the Council of Legal Education. In 1931 he became assistant reader in equity to the Council and in 1935 he was appointed reader. During this period he lectured on company law for the Council. Following the outbreak of war he joined the RASC as a 2nd lieutenant and he served in the army until 1945. In 1943 he became deputy director of personal services at the War Office with the rank of brigadier and in that capacity he was heavily engaged in the negotiations with the Treasury concerning army pay, allowances, and pensions. In recognition of his services in this field he was appointed CBE in 1945.

At the end of the war he returned to his practice at the bar. He was fortunate in finding his old chambers still available, together with a sufficient nucleus of pre-war barristers to constitute a viable set of Chancery chambers. He quickly re-established himself as an outstanding Chancery practitioner and in 1948 he took silk. He had in the meantime been called by Lincoln's Inn 'ad eundem' and in 1953 he became a bencher of that Inn. In 1951 he was appointed attorney-general of the Duchy of Lancaster and attorney and sergeant within the County Palatine. In 1957-8, and again in 1962-3, he was chairman of the General Council of the bar and in 1957 he was elected a member of the Pilgrims. During this period he was a member of the 'Bank Rate' and 'Vassall' tribunals. From 1958 to 1962 he was a member of the Council on Tribunals and in 1962 he became vice-chairman of the Inns of Court Executive Council. In 1963 he was appointed chairman of the London Rented Housing Survey which produced a valuable and exhaustive report (published in 1965) about the result of investigations into the housing shortage and the hardships suffered by tenants in the Greater London area. He was knighted in 1959 and made a KCVO in 1965.

In the post-war period Milner Holland established his reputation as a great persuasive advocate not only at the Chancery bar but also in the field of local government and in the parliamentary corridors. The cases in which he was engaged as counsel, in the main successfully, were numerous and varied and included cases dealing with the Burmah Oil Company, the Fitzwilliam peerage, the will of George Bernard Shaw [q.v.], and the litigation relating to 'Spanish champagne'.

His success as an advocate was due partly to his extensive knowledge of the law but still more to his understanding of human nature which enabled him to select and deploy the arguments which were most likely to appeal to whatever tribunal he was addressing at the time.

The mental strain of Milner Holland's practice would have been intolerable but for the recreations and hobbies in which he indulged. He was a keen golfer and had numerous other interests including the construction of wireless sets and the study and photography of wild flowers. He was also a very popular and skilful after-dinner speaker. In all these pursuits Milner Holland was a perfectionist and his concentration on any hobby in which he was for the time being absorbed no doubt helped him to bear the strain of his professional life.

It may seem surprising that in spite of his outstanding achievements in his profession as an advocate and the judicial qualities that he had shown in the inquiries in which he had taken part Milner Holland did not accept appointment as a high court judge. This was probably due to some extent to his feeling that he had done his duty, so far as public work was concerned, by taking part in numerous inquiries and other activities which involved great expenditure of time and energy without any remuneration. Another reason was that he wanted to spend more time in the various non-legal pursuits which appealed to him and he preferred the independence which is in theory (but not always in practice) available to an advocate more often than to a judge. There can be no doubt that, had he been willing to accept a judgeship, he would have been a most valuable addition to the bench.

In 1929 he married Elinor Doreen, of Malvern, daughter of Frederick Archibald Leslie-Jones, a schoolmaster. They had two sons. Milner Holland died in a nursing home in Brighton 2 November 1969.

[Personal knowledge.]

RONALD COZENS-HARDY HORNE

HOLLAND, SIR HENRY TRISTRAM (1875–1965), eye surgeon, missionary, and philanthropist, was born 12 February 1875 at the Cathedral Close in Durham, the second son in the family of three sons and one daughter of Canon William Lyall Holland, then a Cathedral canon, as was his own father. Henry Holland's mother was Mary Gertrude, daughter of Canon Henry Baker Tristram, a naturalist [q.v.]. Holland spent most of his youth in his father's parsonage at Cornhill-on-Tweed in Northumberland, leading a rumbustious life, which included hunting with five packs of hounds and bird-watching. He was educated at Loretto School from 1889 to 1894, and later, with distinction, at Edinburgh University Medical School, where he became MB and CHB (1899). He was a medallist in anatomy and a prizeman in surgery. Having decided while still an undergraduate that he should be a medical missionary, he joined the Punjab Mission of the Church Missionary Society in 1900, remaining with it for forty-eight years. Though he spent some time in Kashmir, his main life's work was in the CMS Hospital at Quetta, 5,500 feet up in the mountains of Baluchistan, where he soon established a reputation for cataract surgery. Holland became FRCSE in 1907.

In 1911 a Hindu philanthropist built a special hospital in Shikapur, Sind, on condition that Holland worked there with a team especially to perform eye operations for six weeks every year. This work continued through the years, and Holland himself performed more than 60,000 operations for cataract alone. Visitors came from all over the world, and despite repeated offers of important posts elsewhere he always preferred to remain in the Punjab. Even so, he found time for travel throughout India and into Kashmir and Afghanistan on missionary and medical duties, and in the remoter parts of Baluchistan his name became a legend.

In 1935 Quetta Hospital was completely destroyed by an earthquake and he was buried in the ruins, but was rescued by his elder son. It was chiefly through Holland's subsequent efforts that money was raised to erect, for the CMS and Church of England Zenana Missionary hospitals at Quetta, much finer buildings than before. Holland's name will also be remembered in connection with temporary eye camps that he used to establish in areas where blindness was rife. Over a period of some months he and a team of surgeons would then operate on hundreds of cases. In addition he was a founder-member of the Royal Commonwealth Society for the Blind.

Holland was secretary of the CMS Punjab Medical Executive Committee for thirty-two years, and also the Society's medical adviser for that area. He had a very considerable share in the planning of medical policy, not only of the Church but also of the Government. He received the Kaiser-i-Hind silver medal in 1910, the gold medal in 1925, and a bar to it in 1931. He was appointed CIE in 1929 and knighted in 1936.

He was always a fearless and outspoken

evangelist, both among the Pakistanis and among his own people, and his life deeply influenced generations of British soldiers and officials. After his official retirement from CMS missionary service in 1948 he and Lady Holland returned to the North-West Frontier a number of times at the invitation of local chieftains. On each occasion he performed cataract operations at Quetta or Shikapur. In 1960 came the announcement that Holland and his son, Ronald W. B. Holland, had been honoured with the Ramon Magsaysay award, presented annually to outstanding persons who have served their fellow-men with distinction. Both Sir Henry and Ronald Holland travelled to Manila to receive it. The citation stated that father and son had saved the sight of about 150,000 people. In his speech in reply Sir Henry concluded with the words, 'All that has been accomplished is only due to the Lord Jesus Christ, whose ambassadors we have tried to be'. Among his other distinctions, Holland was an honorary member of the Section of Ophthalmology of the Royal Society of Medicine, and of the Oxford Ophthalmology Congress. He was vice-president of the Pakistan Society.

To this Dictionary Holland contributed the notice of Sir (A.) Henry McMahon, the military political officer who designated the frontier between Baluchistan and Afghanistan.

In 1910 Holland married Florence Ethel (died 1975), daughter of the Revd J. Tunbridge. They had two sons and a daughter. Both the sons became eye specialists.

Holland died in hospital in Farnham, Surrey, 19 September 1965.

[Sir Henry Holland, *Frontier Doctor*, 1958; *The Times*, 20 and 25 September 1965.]

P. D. TREVOR-ROPER

HOLLAND, SIR SIDNEY GEORGE (1893–1961), prime minister of New Zealand, was born at Greendale, Canterbury, New Zealand, 18 October 1893, the fourth son of Henry Holland, who was to be mayor of Christchurch and a member of Parliament, and his wife, Jane Eastwood. Educated at West Christchurch District High School, Sidney Holland was employed at 5s. a week in a hardware firm at the age of fifteen; then joined his father's haulage firm. He enlisted in the ranks in 1915; was later commissioned, but was invalided out in 1917. After lengthy convalescence he formed with his eldest brother the Midland Engineering Company; there followed vigorous participation in Christchurch business and in Conservative political activities. He succeeded his father as member for Christchurch North in 1935. As a new member of Parliament, he spoke as an experienced business

man with a long record in local public affairs. His attitude was independent and unabashed; and he immediately became an effective spokesman for uncomplicated ideas, dear to the 'average man', to which he was to show lifelong loyalty. He believed in free enterprise, operated by enlightened employers. He loved the Empire, and the British way of life, and he thought that the best hope of world peace lay in co-operation between the Empire and the United States which he was willing to promote even by tariff reductions for America's benefit. He believed in healthy sport, in family life, in freedom within the limits of decency and law, in laws set out so clearly that those affected could read and readily understand. Above all, he plunged into national politics with buoyant energy, infectious optimism, quickness of apprehension, and skill in boyish repartee. He revelled in the rough and tumble, the challenge and comradeship, of parliamentary life.

The Opposition in 1935 had just suffered shattering defeat. Its leaders had held office during depression-time distresses and were blamed for what they had done and had left undone; and its two main elements, farming and commercial, were allied only uneasily. Holland's robust, earthy common sense appealed to both camps, and under the conditions of war after 1939, he found a new role. The ruling Labour Party refused to have a coalition, but a War Cabinet was set up alongside the domestic Labour Cabinet. It comprised the senior members of both parties: the younger members of the Opposition were left free to argue that loyalty to the Empire and the war effort was consistent with eternal and vocal vigilance in domestic politics. Holland was the most effective member of this group, and in November 1940 he became leader of the National Party and of the parliamentary Opposition. Thereafter party politics took on new life, though from June to September 1942 Holland and his leading supporters joined the short-lived two-party War Administration. Over the next few years Holland welded together farmers and business men—he bought a farm and took a characteristically active personal interest in farming without losing touch with industry. He also helped to frame a Nationalist policy which was rather more than the mere negation of Labour's ideas. Both operations were achieved on a common-sense, practical level, with little regard for long-term theoretical problems. The National Party simply promised to preserve the material benefits of Labour's social security, while restoring, under free enterprise, the spiritual values of liberty, individual initiative, and loyalty to the traditions of the Empire.

This broad programme, which corresponded

closely to the aspirations of the middle rank-
ing man-in-the-street, had been sketched
while Holland was a back-bencher. It was now
preached with exuberant confidence and gained
increasing support as the Labour Party seemed
to have exhausted its mandate and as the
electorate increasingly wearied of wartime
controls. In November 1949 the National Party
won an overwhelming victory, and Holland
became prime minister and until 1954 minister
of finance. In office he remained consistently
his practical, non-doctrinaire, cheerful self. He
learned from men, not from books or documents, and his policies were derived less from
principle than from shrewd reactions to problems as they arose.

In domestic matters, Holland proclaimed the
virtues of free enterprise and accelerated the
dismantling of wartime controls; but there was
no revolution. Indeed, when in power he
realized that some pre-election policies must be
modified and he frankly acknowledged—and
benefited from—the lessons of experience.
Coal-mining, broadcasting, and civil aviation,
for example, remained under public ownership.
Some longstanding promises were of course
honoured, and certain fixed ideas expressed
with characteristic extravagance. In 1950, for
example, the upper house of Parliament, the
nominated Legislative Council, was abolished
with éclat, and in the following year an industrial dispute was handled as a section of the
current international 'cold war', with New
Zealand's Communists seen as a traitorous
fifth column. In 1942 Holland had destroyed
the War Administration in protest against the
Government's handling of a coal-mining stoppage; in 1951 the battle against the waterside workers seemed part of a crusade against
militant labour, preached with the vehemence
of contemporary American witch-hunting, and
fought with the traditional techniques of strike-
breaking. Holland's Government insisted on
fighting this particular battle to total victory,
sealed its triumph with a successful snap
election which helped to secure a further six
years of power, and proposed to follow overseas
precedents with a drastic restriction of civil liberties. It appreciated the force of resulting protests, however, and characteristically retreated
to provisions that were 'middle-of-the-road'
conservative. The language of Holland and his
colleagues could be virulently anti-'socialist',
but the Welfare State was not dismantled, or
even greatly modified.

A similar pattern appeared in New Zealand's
foreign policies. She continued to hope that her
safety could still be based primarily on her
Commonwealth associations and on a world-
wide system of collective security; but as the
cold war intensified and a Japanese peace

treaty appeared imminent she felt an increasing
need for an American guarantee. Holland's
Government responded promptly to the United
Nations' call for help for American forces in the
Korean war, and in 1951 New Zealand joined
Australia and the United States in the ANZUS
treaty of mutual guarantee. In 1954 she
accepted the wider-based Manila Pact, which
also aimed at strengthening regional security.
This was followed in 1955 by the little-noticed
decision, reached as a result of Commonwealth
discussions, to transfer New Zealand's military
commitment from the traditional Mediterranean area to South-East Asia. Holland's
Government, however, saw these developments
as entirely compatible with New Zealand's
traditional relationships with Britain, America,
and the United Nations. He himself used
superlative—even embarrassing—language to
describe New Zealand's devotion to the Empire
and to the United States.

Holland retained a firm grip over his Cabinet
and over New Zealand until his retirement
through ill health in September 1957. His
strength and buoyancy of personality, his
friendliness and loyalty, his skill in parlour
tricks and interest in sport, his success in parliamentary combat, fighting with 'the cutlass
rather than the rapier', his directness, sincerity,
and lack of subtlety, all helped to build a powerful public image. His life was in the world of
action, not of the mind, and he faithfully
reflected the views—and prejudices—of a
broad sector of New Zealand opinion. He was
sworn of the Privy Council (1950) and
appointed CH (1951) and GCB (1957).

In 1920 Holland married Florence Beatrice,
daughter of Arthur Fostyn Drayton, of Christchurch; they had two sons and two daughters.
He died at Wellington 5 August 1961.

[*The Times* and *Evening Post* (Wellington),
5 August 1961; M. Bassett, *Confrontation
1951*, 1972; F. L. W. Wood (Official
History), *The New Zealand People at War—
Political and External Affairs*, 1958; *Round
Table, passim;* R. S. Milne, *Political Parties
in New Zealand*, 1966; *New Zealand Listener*,
18 August 1961; K. Jackson, *The New
Zealand Legislative Council*, 1972; New
Zealand Ministry of Foreign Affairs: *State-
ments and Documents 1943–1957*, 1972; A. H.
McLintock (ed.), *An Encyclopaedia of New
Zealand*, 1966.]   F. L. W. WOOD

HOLLINGWORTH, SYDNEY EWART
(1899–1966), geologist, was born 7 November
1899 in Floore, Northamptonshire, a county to
which he later contributed much as a geologist,
the son of Charles Hollingworth, a foreman in
the Army Ordnance Department, and his wife,

Alice Masters. He was educated at Northampton School and saw active service, during which he was wounded, for a short period before the end of World War I. Entering Clare College, Cambridge, he took a first in part i of the natural sciences tripos in 1920, and a first in part ii (geology) in 1921, being awarded the Harkness scholarship in that year. At Cambridge he came under the strong influence of J. E. Marr, the Woodwardian professor, and Alfred Harker, reader in petrology [qq.v.].

In 1921 Hollingworth joined the staff of the Geological Survey of Great Britain; soon the director, (Sir) J. S. Flett [q.v.], assigned him to the new unit then being formed in Cumberland, based on Whitehaven, which was designed primarily to resurvey the West Cumberland coal and iron-ore fields. Here he had among his colleagues Bernard Smith as district geologist, Tom Eastwood, F. M. Trotter, and W. C. C. Rose. Living and working in this district where extractive industry was important brought him many friends, among them Charles Edmonds, trade-union leader and able amateur palaeontologist. His official work took him to the Brampton, Whitehaven, Gosforth, and Cockermouth districts of Cumberland, and he was a contributor to the revised 1-inch maps and the published memoirs covering each of these districts. At Brampton, with Trotter, he worked in the north-eastern part of the northern Pennines. The collaboration not only produced a controversial correlation of Upper Carboniferous strata, but also the concept of the Alston Block that has influenced profoundly the interpretation of the structure of these mountains (1932). At Cockermouth he was concerned with the Skiddaw slates and Borrowdale lavas, and particularly with the Carrock Fell gabbro, where his detailed mapping brought out conclusions at variance with those of his former teacher, Harker. The description in the Cockermouth memoir, published posthumously in 1968, is a memorial to Hollingworth's work in the best tradition of the Cambridge school. Meanwhile in his spare time he had become interested in the glaciation of the Eden country, a subject he was to use to gain his London D.Sc. in 1931. Before the Cumberland unit moved to South Kensington, in 1935, Hollingworth was transferred to the West Midlands, and commenced field-work in the Cambridge district, completing meanwhile his Cumbrian studies. His last link with that area was his synthesis of the information on the gypsum-anhydrite deposits of the Eden Valley and his comparison of these with the salt deposits of south Durham and north Yorkshire. He was among the first to recognize the rhythmic character of the chemical sedimentation, just as in his time he was also an able advocate of rhythmic clastic sedimentation in the Carboniferous.

With the onset of World War II, Hollingworth became a member with J. H. Taylor [q.v.] of a team whose task it was to bring up to date and amplify geological knowledge of the Jurassic ironstones of the region including his native county. These were the chief domestic source of iron-ore, playing an important part in the expansion of steel production necessary for the war effort. His contribution to the problems of superficial structure was particularly significant.

When war ended Hollingworth accepted an invitation to succeed W. B. R. King [q.v.] as Yates-Goldsmid professor of geology at University College, London. There it quickly became apparent that his overflowing enthusiasm for his subject, especially as a field discipline, made him an inspiring teacher. Not only did he increase the department's space, equipment, and standing, but he also embarked with his colleagues upon new areas of research, firstly in the Caledonian mountains of Norway, and later, after a prospecting trip to the Andes in search of sulphur in 1951, to Chile. Here he began to relate his long-standing interest in geomorphology to the stages of enrichment of the 'porphyry'-type copper deposits; one of his able young assistants has since become a leading expert on this type of deposits, nowadays the chief source of the world's copper. Hollingworth's affection for the high Andes grew with the years, and it was very fitting that his wish that his ashes should be scattered among them was realized. He died 23 June 1966 after attending his last London University senate meeting before retiring. He is remembered for his quick-witted contributions to discussion at the Geological Society of London, of which he became a fellow in 1922. He served on its council for a total of seventeen years, was secretary from 1949 to 1956, vice-president in 1956-8 and 1962-4, and president in 1960-2. His work was recognized with the award from the Lyell fund in 1938, and the Murchison medal in 1959. He was active in promoting the engineering geology group of the society, and was himself a consultant to the Metropolitan Water Board. In 1964 the Geologists' Association, for which he had led a number of field meetings, took the unusual step of electing him an honorary member.

In 1927 he married Anne Mary Lamb of Egremont, who bore him two sons and survived him after a happy married life.

[M. K. W., 'Sydney Ewart Hollingworth' in *Proceedings of the Geological Society, London*, 1636, 1967; Sir Edward Bailey, *Geological Survey of Great Britain*, 1952, p. 257; personal knowledge.]   KINGSLEY DUNHAM

HOLLIS, Sir LESLIE CHASEMORE (1897-1963), general, was born at Walcot, Bath, 9 February 1897, the son of the Revd Charles Joseph Hollis, curate of Bath Abbey church, by his wife, Marion Chasemore. He was educated at St. Lawrence College, Ramsgate, and was commissioned as probationary second lieutenant in the Royal Marine Light Infantry in April 1915. In November of the same year he was posted to the *Duke of Edinburgh* as acting lieutenant. The ship was one of four coal-burning cruisers forming the first cruiser squadron, commanded by Sir Robert Arbuthnot [q.v.], a part of the Grand Fleet based on Scapa Flow. Hollis's action station was in the foretop, and from there he had a clear view of events at the battle of Jutland 31 May 1916. The day was disastrous for the first cruiser squadron, three of the four ships being sunk. The *Duke of Edinburgh* was the sole survivor, and fortunately suffered no casualties. Later in the war Hollis took over his first command, as lieutenant in charge of the Royal Marine detachment in the *Coventry*, in the Harwich Force.

After the war Hollis served in various ships—becoming captain, Royal Marines, in 1921—until in 1927 he was selected for the naval staff course at Greenwich; he passed out in December 1928, and was then appointed as intelligence officer on the staff of the commander-in-chief Africa station, with headquarters at Simonstown; the first of a succession of staff appointments, Hollis always regarded those three years as the happiest of his life. In 1932 he was brought home to the plans division of the admiralty as a captain in the local defence section which dealt with the sea defences of ports at home and abroad, including Singapore, work which brought him into contact with his opposite numbers in the War Office and Air Ministry. After serving four years in plans division, and having been promoted major in 1935, Hollis expected to go to sea again and was to join the *Hood*. However, Sir Maurice (later Lord) Hankey [q.v.], secretary to the Cabinet and to the Committee of Imperial Defence, and himself a Royal Marine officer, asked for him, and thus in the spring of 1936 Hollis found himself secretary of the Joint Planning Subcommittee, and one of the military assistant secretaries of the Committee of Imperial Defence.

The Committee of Imperial Defence had a small, specially selected, staff from the three Services, which formed part of the Cabinet Office. Hankey was the secretary and head of the whole office, but when he retired in 1938 the responsibilities were divided, Edward (later Lord) Bridges [q.v.] becoming secretary of the Cabinet, and Hastings (later Lord) Ismay [q.v.] becoming secretary of the Committee of Imperial Defence. Ismay had been Hankey's deputy, and so Hollis served under him (from 1936) for the important years of preparation for war (becoming his deputy in 1938), and then through the war itself, to succeed him when he retired at the end of 1946—nearly eleven unbroken years in all.

The tempo of work steadily quickened with the inevitable approach of war, and as the size of the office was rigidly controlled, the load on each of the assistant secretaries became heavier. When war came in 1939 Hollis had already proved his capacity for the tasks which lay ahead, and had enough experience to take his place as a key member of the machinery for the conduct of world-wide operations. When (Sir) Winston Churchill became prime minister in 1940 he also assumed the title of minister of defence, and appointed Ismay as his chief staff officer, military deputy secretary to the War Cabinet, and an additional member of the Chiefs of Staff Committee. Hollis took over as secretary of this committee, and as Ismay's deputy, he became responsible for the organization and efficiency of the military side of the War Cabinet secretariat, which became known as the office of the minister of defence. He remained in this position for six years, being promoted lieutenant-colonel, colonel, and brigadier, until in November 1943 he became an acting major-general.

Ismay found in Hollis just the man whom he could rely on to keep the office going at maximum efficiency, leaving Ismay himself free to serve the prime minister and the chiefs of staff in ways which fell outside the daily routine. Increasingly, as the scope of the war widened, Hollis found himself acting as Ismay's alternate, and the two played Box and Cox on the many journeys abroad taken by the prime minister and chiefs of staff. Perhaps one would be in London 'minding the shop', while the other would be in Washington, or further afield. The system had to be such that, wherever the prime minister, the members of the War Cabinet, and the chiefs of staff might happen to be, they were served with the same efficiency and dispatch as they had become accustomed to in London. That this result was achieved was largely due to Hollis.

At the end of 1946 he succeeded Ismay in the post of deputy military secretary to the Cabinet and as chief staff officer to A. V. Alexander (later Earl Alexander of Hillsborough, q.v.), who had been appointed to the newly established Ministry of Defence. Finally, in 1949, he achieved the ambition of all Royal Marine officers by becoming commandant general of the Corps. His appointment was a surprise to some, as he had been for so many years on the staff, but his knowledge of all the people in high position enabled him to play a decisive role in saving the Corps from the abolition proposed after the war. He was appointed successively CBE, CB, and, in 1946, KBE. He was promoted full general in 1951, and in the same year was appointed KCB. He retired in 1952, and spent some time writing two books of reminiscences and a biography of Prince Philip, Duke of Edinburgh, *The Captain General* (1961). He also served the English-Speaking Union as director of current affairs, and became director of a few commercial enterprises. But he suffered increasingly from ill health, and gradually gave up his occupations.

Hollis was full of common sense, completely loyal, and straight as a die. No matter what the load of work or the stress of war might be, he held his course calmly: he estimated afterwards that he had attended more than 6,000 meetings of chiefs of staff during those years, without counting innumerable other meetings and conferences. He was no intellectual, but he had the ability to deal with even the most stubborn or truculent of men, from the prime minister downwards, without losing his balance and with unfailing tact; indeed, Churchill described him as 'a tower of strength'. His mind was practical, he had a dry and lively sense of humour, excelled as a raconteur, and he was Ismay's constant ally in creating a relaxed and confident atmosphere, even in the darkest hours; there was no bickering or self-seeking under their aegis, and no such odious division between 'frocks' and 'brass hats' as had occurred in the previous war. He suffered from asthma, but never allowed this to affect his work: he was rarely away for even one day throughout the war—days which normally began at 7.30 and only ended in the small hours of the next morning. In appearance, Hollis was stocky—about five feet eight inches tall—and of upright carriage; his brown hair was brushed back and parted in the middle, and he wore a short moustache. Brisk in his movements, he was impassive when working.

He married in 1923 Rose May (died 1978), daughter of Alfred Fraser of Folkestone: they had no children. His wife had been previously married to Juan de la Torre Bueno, by whom she had two daughters, and from whom she had obtained a divorce. Hollis died at Cuckfield, Sussex, 9 August 1963.

[Sir Leslie Hollis, *One Marine's Tale*, 1956, and *War at the Top*, 1959; Admiralty records; private information; personal knowledge.]

IAN JACOB

HOLMES, ARTHUR (1890-1965), geologist, was born at Hebburn, near Newcastle upon Tyne, 14 January 1890, the son of David Holmes, a cabinet-maker, and his wife, Emily Dickinson, a schoolteacher. On both sides he was descended from Northumberland farmers. Educated at Gateshead High School, he gained a scholarship to Imperial College, London, in 1907. In 1909 he took the London B.Sc. in physics, and then, under the influence of W. W. Watts, he changed over to geology for his ARCS in 1910. Research under R. J. Strutt (later Lord Rayleigh, q.v.) on radioactivity in rocks led to the DIC and eventually placed him in a premier position in this subject. After an expedition to Portuguese East Africa to study Pre-Cambrian granites, Tertiary lavas, and *inselberg* geomorphology, during which he contracted malaria and blackwater fever (making him unfit for military service when war came), in 1912 he became demonstrator in geology at Imperial College. There he continued his researches into radioactivity, petrogenesis, and physical geology until 1920. In 1914 he married Margaret Howe of Gateshead and settled in Chelsea; they had one son. His wife died in 1938 and the following year he married the distinguished petrologist Dr Doris Livesay Reynolds.

The period up to 1920 was a happy and productive one, with much writing, including the first edition of his book *The Age of the Earth* (1913), and his influential *The Nomenclature of Petrology* (1920) and *Petrographic Methods and Calculations* (1921). From 1921 until it failed in 1924 he was chief geologist of an oil prospecting company in Burma, returning in the latter year to take the readership offered by the university of Durham to restart the teaching of geology in the Durham division, where it had lapsed after the death of J. F. W. Johnston [q.v.] in 1855. This was quickly upgraded to professorial rank, and Holmes remained in Durham until his translation to the regius chair of geology at Edinburgh in 1943, having provided the Durham school with a splendid beginning. In 1956 he became professor emeritus.

These are the bare facts of a distinguished career which made a deep impact on Earth science in at least three major areas. Holmes's pioneer work with Rayleigh and the fact that he became the focus for research on radiometric dating of rocks based upon the constant rate of decay of uranium, thorium, and potassium led not only to the establishment of the age of the Earth, but to the development of a time-scale independent of the fossil record. In the fifty years following his first papers in 1911, Holmes contributed altogether sixty-nine books and articles to the discussion of the geological implications of radioactivity. He very well realized that, as the techniques for determining small amounts of the radioactive elements and their decay products in rocks improved, adjustments of the numbers in the time-scale would be necessary. This was particularly the case after the introduction of mass-spectrometry made possible the separate estimation of the isotopes of these elements. Thus, while his earliest figure for the age of the Earth was of the order of 1,600 million years, by the end of his life it had become clear that our planet originated more than 4,000 million years ago. Both estimates are, however, of a different order of magnitude from the 20–40 million years arrived at by Lord Kelvin [q.v.] on the assumption of an Earth cooling with no spontaneous source of heat. Holmes also considered the wider implications of the new approach to the Earth's thermal history, arriving at important conclusions regarding convection in the substratum and resulting migration of continents, which anticipated by many years conceptions which were to become basic to the breakthrough in global tectonics of the 1960s.

Holmes's second major field was in the origin of alkali-rich igneous rocks. Here his interest had been stimulated by the material he had collected in Mozambique, but collaboration with the Geological Survey of Uganda during his years at Durham enabled him to extend this. As he did so he gradually moved towards hypotheses demanding reactions between emanations and crustal material. Interest in Africa also led Holmes to study the unique rocks of the diamond pipes, giving insights into the composition of the substratum or mantle, to use the current term. He also became deeply involved in the controversy which raged during the 1940s and 1950s over the origin of granite. He started with orthodox views involving differentiation of deep-seated melts, but moved, in concert with his wife, Dr Reynolds, towards the advocacy of solid-state reactions in crustal materials stimulated by diffusing mineralizers. Experimental study of hydrothermal systems at high temperatures and pressures since the 1950s have shown that change of substance as contemplated by the Holmeses can indeed take place, but it cannot yet be said that this enables magmatic melts to be excluded from consideration in the granite problem.

Arthur Holmes's lectures at Durham were models of clarity, and, though his students only came to realize the fact later, they were no mere statements of orthodox views, but were full of original ideas over the whole range of physical geology. Towards the end of his Durham years he published them as *Principles of Physical Geology* (1944). This book set forth his philosophy of the subject, which won wide international acclaim. Through his read-able style, Holmes probably achieved a wider audience than any other geologist of his time.

Many honours came his way. He was elected FRS in 1942; his honorary foreign memberships included those of the Academy of Sciences of the Institute of France, the Royal Swedish Academy, the Royal Academy of Sciences of Amsterdam, and the geological societies of America, Belgium, Stockholm, and Cornwall. The Geological Society of London awarded him its Murchison medal in 1940, and its highest honour, the Wollaston medal, in 1956. In the same year he received the Penrose medal of the Geological Society of America. The university of Edinburgh recognized him with an honorary LLD in 1960, and the Royal Society of Edinburgh with its Macdougall-Brisbane prize in 1965. He was awarded the Vetlesen prize, which has a standing similar to a Nobel prize, in 1964.

He was a quiet, unassuming man without ambition to be a public figure, loving music from Grieg to Stravinsky, impressionist paintings, and poetry, and helpful to all genuine seekers after the truth about the Earth. He died at home in Putney, London, 20 September 1965.

[F. H. Stewart and L. R. Wager in *The Phanerozoic Time-scale* (1964); K. C. Dunham in *Biographical Memoirs of the Fellows of the Royal Society*, vol. xii, 1966; Kingsley Dunham in *Dictionary of Scientific Biography*, vol. vi, 1972; personal knowledge.]   KINGSLEY DUNHAM

HOLMES, SIR GORDON MORGAN (1876–1965), neurologist, was born in Dublin 22 February 1876, the son of Gordon Holmes and his wife, Kathleen, daughter of John Morgan, from whom she inherited Dellin House, Castlebellingham, county Louth, which his father farmed. He had three brothers and one sister. From Dundalk Educational Institute he went on to Trinity College, Dublin—a tall broad-shouldered boy with black hair, athletic, and brilliant. Having won a scholarship he graduated BA in 1897 as senior moderator in natural science and gold medallist. He qualified in medicine in 1898 and at the age of twenty-three left Dublin on the Stewart scholarship in nervous and mental diseases for two years of graduate work abroad.

At Frankfurt he found an excellent opportunity to study the histology of the nervous system under Karl Weigert and neuroanatomy under the famous Ludwig Edinger who soon made Holmes an instructor in his university course of neuroanatomy and eventually urged him warmly to remain as his assistant. But Holmes decided to return to Ireland. On his way through London he heard of a vacancy as house-physician in the National Hospital for Nervous Diseases, Queen Square, for which he successfully applied in 1901. At this time there were two world centres for neurological study: Paris, at the Salpêtrière, and London with its National Hospital. Holmes, who proceeded MD in 1903 and was elected FRCP in 1914, moved up from house-physician to resident medical officer, then in 1904 to the new post of pathologist and director of research. In 1909 he became honorary physician to the hospital and in 1912 he turned over the pathology laboratory to S. A. Kinnier Wilson [q.v.], who was in turn followed in 1914 by a permanent pathologist, J. G. Greenfield. Holmes was also associated for a long period with the Charing Cross and Seamen's hospital and also Moorfields.

Holmes had become a restless, indefatigable investigator and this was the time for the pathological and physiological analysis which was to pave the way for more adequate therapy. The physicians of the National Hospital brought their independent skills and differing genius to this neurological centre, long called the National Hospital for the Paralysed and Epileptic. Advancing up the ladder of seniority on the staff, they served patients without remuneration and conducted graduate teaching, like the early Greeks, without university organization.

When Holmes entered the clinical field, with his knowledge of anatomy and neuropathology, he proceeded to make of neurological examination a relatively exact science. At the same time, like Sir William Gowers and J. Hughlings Jackson [qq.v.] he collected and recorded his observations of patients with neurological lesions.

From 1901 to 1911 his publications dealt in general with neuropathology, and neuro-anatomy. By 1911 he had turned to clinical neurophysiology, working with (Sir) Henry Head [q.v.] of the London Hospital, a neurologist of great vision and originality. They studied the role of the human cerebral cortex in sensory perception, using the critical, sometimes quantitative, methods devised by Head. Holmes applied these tests with scrupulous exactitude. The formidable study which followed (*Brain*, 1911) showed that the optic thalamus was 'the seat of physiological processes which underlie crude sensations of contact, heat and cold', while the cortex had to do with the more discriminative aspects of sensation.

With the outbreak of war in 1914 Holmes became consulting neurologist to the British Army. His Goulstonian lecture on 'The Spinal Injuries of Warfare' (1915) showed how quickly he had changed the focus of his attention. A brilliant series of publications followed, which dealt with the function of man's cerebellum and the effect of cortical lesions on vision and on somatic sensation. In conjunction with the surgeon, (Sir) Percy Sargent, Holmes made various studies of battle casualties which involved the nervous system. He was appointed CMG in 1917 and CBE in 1919.

In 1920 he wrote a chapter for *Nelson Loose-Leaf Medicine* including (Sir) F. M. R. Walshe in the authorship. It was entitled 'An Introduction to the Study of Diseases of the Nervous System'. From 1922 to 1937 Holmes was editor of *Brain*, following Head in this highly influential editorial post. He was elected a fellow of the Royal Society in 1933, gave the Ferrier lecture in 1944 and was a member of council in 1945-6. In 1935 he was president of the 2nd International Congress of Neurology when it met in London.

Holmes rarely referred to his own philosophy of life. But in 1934 when he was principal speaker at the Opening Exercises when the Montreal Neurological Institute was founded, he said: 'The student of neurology must equip himself with that intellectual honesty and independence which refuse to submit to authority or to be controlled by preconception . . . But on the other hand, he must have the courage to formulate, when ready to do so, observations into hypotheses or rational generalisations, for, as Francis Bacon had told us, "truth can emerge sooner from error that from confusion".'

His contributions to the physiology of the cerebral cortex, thalamus, and cerebellum of man were important, and the role he played as critic and editor was of great value; but his contribution as a teacher of teachers was outstanding, and he attracted many postgraduate students from abroad. He was a formidable man, of driving energy, with little use for diplomacy or compromise, still less for committees or after-dinner speeches. But his logical thinking and lucid exposition made him unsurpassed, especially as a teacher of small groups.

In 1918 Holmes married Rosalie (died 1963), daughter of the late Brigade Surgeon William Jobson, a charming woman with an unfailing sense of humour. She had studied at Oxford and had later qualified in medicine. They found a house, 9 Wimpole Street, large enough for their home and consulting rooms. There, three daughters were born to them. The house was damaged by bombs during the war of 1939-45 and Holmes moved to Farnham, Surrey, where he enjoyed cultivating a large garden. He retired from the National Hospital in 1941 and gradually gave up his London commitments, but he continued to serve throughout the war as a consultant for the Emergency Medical Service. He was knighted in 1951; received several honorary degrees, and honorary membership of many foreign neurological societies; was awarded the Conway Evans prize in 1952; and was an honorary fellow, gold medallist, and Hughlings Jackson medallist of the Royal Society of Medicine.

In 1946 Holmes published the *Introduction to Clinical Neurology* and in 1954 he wrote a short history of the National Hospital (which has a portrait of him by Harold Knight). In 1956 his *Selected Papers* were edited by Sir F. M. R. Walshe in a volume dedicated to Holmes on the occasion of his eightieth birthday by the guarantors of *Brain*. Holmes died at his home in Farnham 29 December 1965.

[Sir F. M. R. Walshe in *Biographical Memoirs of Fellows of the Royal Society*, vol. xii, 1966; *British Medical Journal*, 8 January 1966; Wilder Penfield in *Journal of the Neurological Sciences*, vol. v, 1967; *Munk's Roll*, vol. v, 1968; personal knowledge.]

WILDER PENFIELD

HOOKE, SAMUEL HENRY (1874-1968), biblical scholar and oriental linguist, was born in Cirencester 21 January 1874, the elder son of Henry Mann Hooke, evangelist for the Plymouth Brethren, and his wife, Elizabeth Loudoun. Educated at Wirksworth and St. Mark's School, Windsor, he left school early, on his father's death, to provide for his mother and brother by teaching in a preparatory school in Clifton and by setting courses and examining for Wolsey Hall. He was thirty-three when he went as exhibitioner to Jesus College, Oxford, where he took a first in theology (1910) and a second in oriental languages (1912) and won five university prizes. There he joined the Church of England and began the radical critique of his faith which, with his undiminished passion for the Bible, was to make him an exciting and beloved teacher for nearly sixty years.

In 1913 he became Flavelle associate professor of oriental languages and literature at Victoria College, Toronto, where during the war he also taught English literature and history. Through the unfettered enquiry which characterized his teaching, his leadership in the Student Christian Movement, then a centre of religious ferment, and his genius for friendship with people of all ages, he exercised a powerful influence over his pupils which eventually excited the suspicions of conservative parents, and he was encouraged to resign. A year later, in 1926, he returned to London with a Rockefeller fellowship in anthropology, to study those Babylonian, Assyrian, Hittite, and Egyptian texts from which he derived his distinctive ideas about myth, ritual, and kingship. In 1930

he was appointed to the Samuel Davidson chair of Old Testament studies at London. Retirement in 1942 brought only a change of activity. He became a master at Blundell's School (where he played the violin in the school orchestra), and was then appointed examining chaplain to the bishop of Coventry. In 1958 he went to Ghana as a visiting professor, and four years later he was lecturing in Rhodesia.

He was Schweich lecturer in 1935, president of the Folk Lore Society in 1936-7, a fellow of the Society of Antiquaries from 1937, president of the Society for Old Testament Study in 1951, and Speaker's lecturer at Oxford in 1956-61. He was awarded the British Academy Burkitt bronze medal for biblical studies (1948), the honorary DD of Glasgow (1950), and the honorary D.Th. of Uppsala (1957); and he was elected honorary fellow of Jesus College in 1964.

Hooke was an indefatigable writer, constantly contributing articles and reviews to dictionaries and periodicals, editing for twenty-three years the *Palestine Exploration Quarterly*, producing 100,000 chain references for new editions of the Bible, translating the Bible into Basic English, all in addition to writing his fourteen books on the Christian faith and on the Old Testament and its background. But he will be remembered chiefly as the innovator and pioneer of what others have called the Myth and Ritual School. He edited two symposia, *Myth and Ritual* (1933) and *The Labyrinth* (1935), in which the contributors set forth the evidence for the existence of recurring patterns in the religions of the ancient Near East and for the influence of these patterns on the Old Testament. His aim was 'to build a bridge between the three disciplines of Anthropology, Archaeology, and Biblical Studies'; and this he continued to do in his Schweich lectures and later writings.

He had a sturdy, athletic frame: at Oxford he played cricket, rugby, hockey, and tennis for his college and golf for the university; in Canada he became a strong swimmer and skater, and built his own summer cottage on an island in Lake Muskoka. He had immense mental, as well as physical, energy and mastered languages as readily as games, in spite of deafness which caused a monotonous booming in his public diction. He was a competent man, except in the way he drove a car. He had a boisterous, schoolboy sense of humour and a warm-hearted friendliness. He wrote poetry and was a connoisseur of wine. He loved teaching and was beloved by those he taught. Above all he was a deeply religious man, with the kind of faith to which doubt serves only as a growing point.

Hooke married young, and his wife Alice, a young Yorkshire teacher, soon became a permanent invalid, more and more dependent on him until her death in 1945. In 1946 he married Beatrice Emily Wyatt, daughter of a London banker, Louis Holland Kiek, and gained through the children of her first marriage a family life such as he had not known since childhood. From 1958 they lived in Buckland, where he took enthusiastically to gardening and village life. And there he died 17 January 1968, four days before his ninety-fourth birthday.

[E. C Graham, *Nothing is here for Tears: a memoir of S. H. Hooke*, 1969; private information.]   G. B. CAIRD

HOOPER, SIR FREDERIC COLLINS, first baronet (1892-1963), industrialist, was born at Bruton, Somerset, 19 July 1892, the only son of Frederic Stephen Hooper, wine merchant, by his wife, Annie Collins. He was educated at Sexey's School, Bruton, and at University College, London, where he read botany and became a fellow in 1957. On the outbreak of war in 1914 he was commissioned into the Dorset Regiment and served on the western front.

Demobilized in 1919, he spent the next two years in Athens with the Ionian Bank. In 1922 he was recruited to Lewis's, the Liverpool department store, by F. J. Marquis (later the Earl of Woolton, q.v.), its managing director and a pioneer in the training of university graduates for industry. Marquis later wrote of Hooper: 'he was successful in everything except his personal relationship with his seniors. I promoted him to the board so that he had nobody to quarrel with except me—and I felt I could take it.' In 1942, after two years as joint managing director of Lewis's, Hooper resigned in quest of a political career. At the invitation of Sir Kingsley Wood [q.v.], chancellor of the Exchequer, he set up the Political Research Centre. Designed to keep Conservative doctrine alive during the wartime party truce, it produced several papers on post-war policy: and in conjunction with Lord Hinchingbrooke's Tory Reform Committee it published a series of pamphlets, *Forward—by the Right!*, which sold 250,000 copies. Some of the more senior Conservatives, however, found its doctrines disobligingly radical. The death of Wood in 1943 removed Hooper's most powerful patron, and in the following year the Political Research Centre was extinguished from above. Nor could Hooper find a Conservative constituency association willing to adopt him. But it was during those wartime years that he made his reputation as a broadcaster, succeeding Sir Norman (later Lord) Birkett [q.v.] in the pseudonym 'Onlooker'.

From 1945 to 1946, as director of business training at the Ministry of Labour, he speeded the resettlement of returning ex-service men. That task completed, he formed his own business consultancy firm. His first client happened to be Schweppes, the mineral-water company; and when he recommended that they find a new managing director, he was promptly invited to accept the appointment himself. He did so (in 1948) on the understanding that a modest salary should be supplemented by a commission on the company's annual profits. Fifteen years later, on the eve of his intended retirement in 1963, the prosperity to which he had raised Schweppes was reflected in personal emoluments approaching £100,000 a year.

He was far-sighted in labour relations. 'The time', he wrote, 'is no longer opportune—even if it were desirable—for management to insist on mechanical obedience or the sack.' He laid down that his employees should be told at the earliest possible moment of changes in company policy or fluctuations in its fortunes; and that all businesses should establish profit-sharing schemes and a promotion structure flexible enough to satisfy both ambition and enthusiasm. Strikes and other disturbances, he maintained, were nearly always the fault of bad managers. Such doctrines, which have since become the platitudes of harmonious industrial relations, were not widely accepted in Hooper's day. Many of them he embodied in his dynamic *Management Survey*, published in 1948 and since reprinted several times. A contented labour force was his first concern, advertising his plaything and delight. With that master of puns Stephen Potter [q.v.] and the artist George Him, he added an entirely new county, Schweppeshire, to the map of England. It was under his leadership, too, that the company built up an international reputation for its soft drinks.

Hooper gave an increasing amount of his time to public service, particularly to problems of national defence. Between 1954 and 1956 he sat on committees of inquiry into the organization of the Royal Air Force and into the employment of national service men. In 1957 he became chairman of the advisory board set up by the Ministry of Labour to ensure the smooth transition to civilian life of officers and other ranks, many of whom had been obliged to retire prematurely as a result of cuts in defence expenditure. He was successful in persuading retired officers not to despise industry, and industrialists not to regard officers as Colonel Blimps. In 1960 he became adviser on recruiting to the minister of defence. Again he dispelled the myth that service in the regular forces was the last refuge of the boneheaded or the destitute; and the imaginative use of television advertising which he recommended sent recruiting figures soaring. Ashridge Trust, the Royal Academy of Dancing, the Royal College of Nursing, and the Institute of Directors were other bodies whose fortunes he helped to guide. He was knighted in 1956 and received a baronetcy in 1962.

'Eric' Hooper held, indeed he flourished, opinions not always found in a boardroom. He had a particular regard for trade-unionists, journalism, the regular army, the wines of St. Émilion, the brisk wit of the United States, and the therapeutic qualities of egg farming. He detested tax fiddlers, pop singers, ostentation, and the fizzy drinks upon which the prosperity of his firm depended. He collected modern pictures, designed a beautiful garden at his house in Kent, and loved the ballet. He also supported the contemporary theatre both as a patron and as an increasingly disenchanted playgoer. A tall, heavily built man with several chins, he was nevertheless a nimble ballroom dancer, and a cunning but sometimes bad-tempered tennis player.

His first marriage, in 1918, was to Eglantine Irene, daughter of Thomas Augustine Bland, of Yelverton, Devon. They had one son, Anthony Robin Maurice (born 1918), who succeeded him to the title, and a daughter. The marriage was dissolved in 1945, when he married Prudence Avery, daughter of Basil Elliott Wenham, of Barnt Green, Worcestershire, by whom he had a daughter. He died in London 4 October 1963.

[*The Times*, 5 October 1963; private information; personal knowledge.]   KENNETH ROSE

HORNER, ARTHUR LEWIS (1894-1968), miners' leader, was born 5 April 1894 in Merthyr Tydfil, the son of James Horner and his wife, Emily Lewis. His father, when only sixteen, had tramped from Northumberland to South Wales looking for work which he found as a railway porter, and subsequently as foreman at the goods yard. Emily Lewis, born in Penybont, near Llandrindod Wells, moved with her parents into the coalfield where her father was killed in a pit explosion. The first Merthyr Co-operative Stores was established in the Horner front room, with Emily responsible for running it.

Arthur Horner was the eldest son among seventeen children, eleven of whom died at birth or in early childhood. After passing the labour examination at eleven and a half years old, he was allowed to leave school to become a junior clerk in the railway office. He was active in sport as a boxer, footballer, and runner. His parents and home life were deeply religious and he developed as a remarkable boy preacher. At seventeen he was persuaded to enter a Baptist college for a two-year course of theological training, but abandoned it after some six months, having become more interested in politics.

Horner joined the Independent Labour Party, then a strong movement in the Merthyr borough with James Keir Hardie [q.v.] as leader. Horner soon became known as an agitator and could only obtain work in the mines under an assumed name. Consequently in the war of 1914-18 he was not exempt, as a miner, from military service, and as a conscientious objector was on the run from the authorities. He dodged across to Ireland where he served for a time in James Connolly's Citizen Army, under the name of Jack O'Brien. Returning to Britain, he was arrested upon landing and imprisoned. He was officially discharged from the army in January 1919 'in consequence of incorrigible misconduct' for refusing to wear uniform. His autobiography, written after retirement, takes its title *Incorrigible Rebel* (1960) from the terms of his discharge. Sentenced to a further term of imprisonment, he was elected checkweighman for the Mardy Colliery and obtained his release from prison after a period of hunger strike.

Horner rose to prominence as a leading member of the British Communist Party which he joined when the party was founded in 1920. He stood unsuccessfully as a Communist candidate for the Rhondda East parliamentary constituency in 1929, 1931, and 1933, and after his first visit in 1923 he went frequently to the Soviet Union. He led delegations of miners to several of the Communist states, including China, and visited the British battalion in Spain on two occasions during the civil war to meet Welsh miners serving there. But Horner was an independent thinker and this sometimes brought him into conflict with the Communist Party as it did in 1931 when he was in strong disagreement over tactics during a South Wales miners strike.

The lock-outs of miners during 1921 (when Horner went to prison for unlawful assembly) and 1926, and the general strike, had provided the environment for Horner's rise to leadership of the South Wales miners. Short, plump, and genial, a brilliant and forceful speaker and debater, a close friend and collaborator of A. J. Cook [q.v.], the national secretary of the Miners' Federation, Horner was able to influence policy both in South Wales and nationally during this difficult period. His progress in the union, however, was abruptly interrupted by his expulsion from the South Wales Miners' Federation in 1930 when the Mardy miners lodge, with its leaders, was expelled for supporting Horner as a Communist candidate against the official miners candidate in the 1929 parliamentary election. In 1932 Horner was sentenced to fifteen months' imprisonment for his part in the resistance of Mardy people to an attempt by the Rhondda council to distrain furniture from a family said to be in arrears of rates.

In January 1934 Horner re-entered the union as miners' agent for the anthracite part of the coalfield where non-members were eligible to stand for union full-time posts. In 1936 he was elected president of the South Wales Miners' Federation and in 1937 after a long campaign reached agreement with the colliery companies to end the 'company unions' in the pits where they operated. In the same year he negotiated a coalfield wages structure which became the forerunner of a similar national structure in 1955.

Although acknowledged to be a most able and outstanding trade-union personality, Horner's political views were used to prevent his serving on the General Council of the Trades Union Congress. But in 1944 he represented the TUC at the Congress of the American Federation of Labor in New Orleans and at the Latin-American Union Conference in Colombia.

Horner played a leading part in the formation of the National Union of Mineworkers in January 1945; he then became national production officer; and in 1946 national secretary; he was consequently closely involved in the discussions with the TUC and the Labour Government which brought about the nationalization of the mines. Thereafter Horner was able to secure many important reforms, including new legislation for safety measures, holidays with pay, a retirement pension scheme, and the raising of miners' wages from among the lowest to among the highest. With not many years' practical experience as a mineworker, he was quick to assimilate facts and their significance; his political convictions made him less influential than he might have been in the trade-union movement as a whole, but in his own union he was highly respected and his abilities fully recognized by friend and adversary. He retired in 1959, when he received the freedom of Merthyr Tydfil, and died in Wembley, Middlesex, 4 September 1968.

In 1916 he married Ethel Mary Meyrick; they had three daughters. A portrait by Kazatkin is in the possession of the family.

[Private information; personal knowledge.]

WILL PAYNTER

HORRABIN, JAMES FRANCIS (1884-1962), artist, lecturer, cartoonist, and left-wing socialist, was born in Peterborough 1 November 1884, the eldest son of James Woodhouse Horrabin, a cutler with a small business, and his wife, Mary Pinney, of Sheffield. Although born in Peterborough, which he subsequently represented in Parliament, and although his mother came from Stamford in Lincolnshire, where he himself attended Stamford Grammar School, 'Frank' Horrabin had throughout his life marked Yorkshire sympathies and even a trace of a Yorkshire accent. This, though presumably derived from his father, was much strengthened when he went to study at the Sheffield School of Art. There he began as a designer in metal and found employment in Sheffield as a metal-work designer. He very soon abandoned that interest in favour of line drawing. In 1906 he secured a post as staff artist on the *Sheffield Telegraph*, whence he proceeded in 1909 to become art editor for the *Yorkshire Telegraph and Star*. After two years he decided to move to London, to work on the *Daily News*—which later became the *News Chronicle*—and the London *Star*, where his humorous serial drawings endeared him to the readers. For the *News Chronicle* he created the characters of Japhet (son of Noah and brother of Ham and Shem) and Happy. Various books arose from these and other characters whom Horrabin invented: for example *Japhet and Fido* (1922), *Mr. Noah* (1922), *More About the Noahs—and Tim Tosset* (1922), and *The Japhet Book* (1925). *The Japhet and Happy Annual* appeared in 1926. The *Star* saw the adventures of the two office-girls, Dot and Carrie—which also were reprinted in book form (1922). Horrabin's connection with the two newspapers lasted until 1960, with a brief interlude from 1917 to 1918, when he was a rifleman in the Queen's Westminster Rifles. His Dot and Carrie strip was still appearing at the time of his death in the *Evening News*, to which it was transferred after the *Star* ceased publication in 1960.

Neither Japhet nor Dot and Carrie had any definite political character, except in so far as the journals in which they had their being indicated a generally radical attitude in their creator, and Horrabin, although he did draw other cartoons, and some caricatures, was never a cartoonist of the calibre of Sir David Low or William Henry (Will) Dyson [qq.v.] or other of his contemporaries. His gift emerged, rather, as a talent for drawing maps and diagrams (which he later showed could be used for propagandist purposes); and he became prominent in this field when in 1919 he was chosen to illustrate H. G. Wells's [q.v.] *Outline of History*, which appeared in 1920. His 200 and more contributions, which included, in addition to maps and charts, imaginative reconstructions of animals and life in prehistoric times, were immensely successful and continued to appear in the many revisions of the book. As Wells himself said in his original preface, 'In Mr. J. F. Horrabin he [Wells] has had the good fortune to find not only an illustrator but a collaborator'. The result was that Horrabin undertook more work of the same kind, illustrating Lancelot Hogben's *Mathematics for the Million* (1936) and *Science for the Citizen* (1938), and the 1939 edition of *Glimpses of World History* by Jawaharlal Nehru [q.v.]. Meanwhile, he produced by himself a number of atlases of different kinds for students and in 1923 a textbook of geography.

These were low-priced books, intended for adult students with small resources, for Horrabin very early had become a left-wing socialist. Before the war of 1914-18 he had been converted to the guild socialism advocated by A. R. Orage [q.v.] and Samuel George Hobson in the *New Age*, and by G. D. H. Cole [q.v.] and William Mellor in the *Daily Herald*; and when the National Guilds League was formed in 1915 he was a member of its first executive committee. Even before that he had enlisted in the cause of 'independent working-class education', and when (James) Dennis Hird, the principal of Ruskin College, which was founded in 1899, broke away from Oxford connections to start, with trade-union support, the Central Labour College in Earl's Court, he became one of its most ardent supporters, writing, lecturing, and even acting for it (playing the name part in a performance of G. B. Shaw's [q.v.] *Blanco Posnet*)—although without any of the rancour and malice shown by some Marxist educationists to their competitors, the Workers' Educational Association, founded in 1903. He was the first editor of *The Plebs*, the organ of the National Council of Labour Colleges. For a short while he was a member of the Communist Party.

As a socialist, after the general strike of 1926 he turned his attention to Parliament and was Labour member for the Peterborough division from 1929 to 1931, though he soon became disillusioned with the second Labour Government and joined eagerly in the attempts, by G. D. H. Cole and others, to bring its policy back on course: and when the New Fabian Research Bureau had reformed and revitalized the Fabian Society, he collaborated with Rita Hinden and Arthur Creech Jones [q.v.] in creating the Fabian Colonial (now Commonwealth) Bureau and providing it with a monthly anti-imperialist journal. When Creech Jones in 1945 became Colonial Secretary, Horrabin succeeded him as chairman of the Bureau until 1950; but he also continued to take an active part in it, and wrote a regular column for the monthly *Socialist Commentary*, edited by Dr Rita Hinden.

Horrabin was twice married—first, in 1911, to Winifred Batho, a fellow worker in the Labour College movement: after this marriage was dissolved he married in 1948 Margaret V. McWilliams, whose previous husband was a business traveller. He had no children. He died at his Hendon home 2 March 1962.

[*The Times*, 3 and 6 March 1962; personal knowledge.]   MARGARET COLE

HORSBRUGH, FLORENCE GERTRUDE, BARONESS HORSBRUGH (1889-1969), politician, was born at Edinburgh 13 October 1889, the youngest of the three daughters of Henry Moncrieff Horsbrugh, chartered accountant, of Edinburgh, and his wife, Mary Harriet Stark Christie. She was educated at Lansdowne House, Edinburgh, and St. Hilda's, Folkestone.

She entered Parliament in 1931 as the senior of the two members for Dundee. She held this seat continuously until she was defeated in the general election of 1945. She successfully introduced two private members' Bills, one aimed at preventing the drinking of methylated spirits in Scotland, and the other concerning children. The latter resulted from her appointment as chairman of the departmental committee on adoption societies, which prompted her to introduce the private member's Bill which passed into law as the Adoption of Children (Regulation) Act of 1939. In that year she was appointed CBE, having been created MBE in 1920. Her interest in the welfare of children continued and, after she became parliamentary secretary to the Ministry of Health shortly before the outbreak of war in 1939, she was able to play an active role in the arrangements which had to be made in order to evacuate children and other priority classes from London and other large cities. She retained this position until 1945, working devotedly at the unusual tasks caused by the war. In 1944 she was injured by a bomb blast during a raid on London. Towards the end of the war the Ministry of Health drafted the National Health scheme, upon which Florence Horsbrugh did much preparatory work. She was to see this come to fruition in the National Health scheme passed by the post-war Labour Government.

In the caretaker Government of 1945 she was parliamentary secretary to the Ministry of Food at a time when the minister was John (later Lord) Llewellin [q.v.]. This was a particularly difficult time for food supply and distribution, and Florence Horsbrugh's participation ceased when she was defeated at Dundee in 1945. Thereafter she became Conservative candidate for Midlothian and Peebles, but in the general election of 1950 she was defeated by the Labour candidate. However, pure chance allowed her to enter Parliament in that election, for the Conservative candidate for the Moss Side division of Manchester had died before polling day, causing the election to be postponed. Florence Horsbrugh was rapidly nominated as Conservative candidate and was elected a fortnight later with a handsome majority in an 'extended general election'. When the Conservatives formed a Government in 1951 (Sir) Winston Churchill appointed Florence Horsbrugh as minister of education. This was not at first a Cabinet post, but when it became so in 1953, Miss Horsbrugh became the first woman to hold a Cabinet post in a Conservative government.

Throughout her life Florence Horsbrugh had also been interested in international affairs. In 1933, 1934, and 1935 she was a delegate to the League of Nations Assembly, and in 1945 she was a delegate to San Francisco, where the United Nations charter was drawn up. She also led the United Kingdom delegation to the seventh session of the general conference of UNESCO in Paris.

Miss Horsbrugh resigned office in 1954 and left the Government, whereupon she was created GBE. Her public life continued, for she was a delegate to the Council of Europe and the Western European union from 1955 to 1961. In 1959 she was made a life peer.

Academic circles, too, were glad to honour her. In 1946 the university of Edinburgh granted her an honorary LLD, and in the same year the Royal College of Surgeons of Edinburgh conferred honorary fellowship of their college upon her, the first time in their 440 years of existence that they so singled out a woman. Indeed, by her quiet example, Florence Horsbrugh did much for the cause of women. She was the first woman to be member of Parliament for Dundee, to move the address in reply to the King's speech (1936), to be both a privy councillor (1945) and a GBE, and to be a Conservative Cabinet minister.

On her death at her home in Edinburgh at the age of eighty, 6 December 1969, it was said of her that she was one of the best-equipped party politicians of all the women in Parliament. She was a brilliant and attractive speaker. She was spirited in controversy and never shrank from the rough and tumble of the party fight. She had a wonderful sense of humour and despite her somewhat rather severe appearance she was a warm-hearted and generous friend.

[*The Times*, 8 December 1969; private information; personal knowledge.]

KATHARINE ELLIOT

HORTON, PERCY FREDERICK (1897-1970), artist, was born at 38 Jersey Street in Brighton 8 March 1897, the eldest of three sons of Percy Horton, a Brighton bus conductor, and his wife, Ellen Batchelor. Despite the family's financial hardship, all three boys prevailed: Harry, the middle son, became a schoolteacher; Ronald, the youngest, became, like Percy, an artist and art teacher; as for Percy, after attending the Brighton Municipal School, he was first propelled towards recognition by a scholarship to the Brighton College of Art, where he was awarded prizes for drawing and pictorial composition and from which he graduated with distinction in 1914.

After a wartime prison ordeal as a conscientious objector (he was condemned to solitary confinement in Edinburgh's Calton Gaol), and, following the long recovery which this necessitated, he studied in 1918-20 at the Central School of Arts and Crafts in London, taught for two years at Rugby School (1920-2), and then won a Royal exhibition (at that time only one was awarded each year) to the Royal College of Art in South Kensington. There he became ARCA, graduating with distinction in 1924, whilst also winning the coveted college drawing prize for that year—against such talented classmates as Edward Bawden, Eric Ravilious [q.v.], (Dame) Barbara Hepworth, and Henry Moore.

There followed six quiet and productive years, teaching at Bishop's Stortford College, where Horton served as art master. In 1929 (Sir) William Rothenstein [q.v.] was looking for a draughtsman of distinction to add to the staff of the Royal College of Art. Horton was appointed to the post where he remained for the next nineteen years, thereby setting the standards for a generation of the nation's brightest young talents.

Percy Horton was an accomplished portraitist. During the war of 1939-45 (which Horton's passionate opposition to Fascism led him to support), the RCA was evacuated to Ambleside, and Horton produced a series of fine paintings of the Lake District and of its people. For the National War Records, he drew portraits and painted scenes in war factories: these pictures are now in the War Museum in London.

As a logical award for so many years so well spent in dedication to art and to young artists, Percy Horton was called in 1949 to Oxford, where he took over the mastership of the Ruskin School of Drawing and Fine Art from Albert Rutherston. The contrast between the hardships of his youth and the opulence of Oxford—he was given membership of New College in 1949—must have caused poignant reflections in the intelligent, sensitive mind of the Brighton bus conductor's son.

During his new appointment Horton drew and painted many of the heads of houses and senior tutors at the universities of Oxford and Cambridge. When (Sir) Roger Bannister astonished the world by running his historic four-minute mile in 1954, it was Percy Horton whom Exeter College commissioned to do his portrait.

And, always, Horton painted landscapes—above all, the landscape of his native Sussex. For many years he was to use the gamekeeper's tower in Firle Park as his painting headquarters. He would be seen in fine weather in a panama hat and pale alpaca jacket, crossing the countryside to his subject: he was strong and would be carrying a large panel of hardboard, a substantial easel, and a very big knapsack containing campstool and a complete oil-painting outfit. These landscapes were carefully composed and closely observed, with, always, a strong sense of form and pictorial structure.

Instead of singing a graceful swan song at Oxford whilst covered in that honour he so richly deserved Horton found himself plunged instead into a struggle for the very survival of the fine arts in the university: for the next fifteen years he fought courageously, often against powerful opposition, to keep the Ruskin School of Drawing alive. He succeeded, sometimes calling on old friends like Henry Moore or Sir Jacob Epstein [q.v.] to lend their support; but when he retired from Oxford in 1964, the struggle had exhausted him, and his friends noticed that something had gone out of him.

Percy Horton's aim as an artist might be summed up in these words of Gustave Courbet: 'I have studied the art of the masters and the art of the moderns, avoiding any preconceived system and without prejudice. I have no more wanted to imitate the former than to copy the latter; nor have I thought of achieving the idle aim of "art for art's sake". No! I have simply wanted to draw from a thorough knowledge of tradition [informed by] the reasoned and free sense of my own individuality.'

Horton's pictures can be seen today in the Tate, the National Portrait Gallery, the Ashmolean, the Fitzwilliam, the Imperial War Museum, the Leeds City Art Gallery, and in municipal galleries throughout Britain. His life was one of service, of lasting friendships, and of accomplishment against adversity.

Friends of Percy Horton, in remembering him, are likely to recall his marvellous powers of mime, saying, 'Why, he could have been an actor!' His students (two generations of British draughtsmen are in his debt) are more likely to remember the concentration with which he

entered upon his demonstration drawings, remembering, too, his erudition in the study of the Old Masters: it is unlikely that anyone knew more than Percy Horton about the golden section—the divine proportion. It is astonishing that such a man should ever have been sent to prison. But from this indelible experience of his young manhood to his final triumph—and time of trial—as Ruskin master of drawing at the university of Oxford, Horton's life was a remarkable study in contrasts. He was a very good violinist and participated all his life in string trios and quartets.

In 1921 he married Lydia Sargent, the daughter of George Smith, a prosperous corn merchant of Derbyshire. She was a remarkable woman of Quaker background eleven years Horton's senior. By the time of her marriage she had already been a suffragette, a policewoman (one of the earliest), and, with Joan Beauchamp, co-editor of the anti-conscription journal, *Tribunal*, during the war of 1914-18. After that war she became a journalist on the *Daily Herald*; but it was during the war years that she and Horton had discovered a common cause and a common courage. Horton died in St. George's Hospital, Tooting, London, 4 November 1970. John Ward, RA, a former pupil of his, spoke movingly at the funeral; Henry Moore was there; and, in lieu of a formal ceremony, a movement was played from a Mozart violin concerto in commemoration of Horton's lifelong interest in music. Horton was survived by his wife, and his daughter. There is a self-portrait (1936) in oils in the Arts Council Collection and another self-portrait in oils in the Ashmolean Museum, Oxford.

[Private information.]   PHILIP MORSBERGER

HOSIER, ARTHUR JULIUS (1877-1963), pioneer farmer, engineer, and inventor, was born at Shawford, Somerset, 16 October 1877, the twelfth and youngest child of Joshua Hosier, tenant dairy farmer, by his second wife, Sarah Fricker, a farmer's daughter from Frome. His was the fourth generation of farmers beginning with his great-grandfather, Joshua Hosier, who operated the stage-coach between Frome and London. One day this forebear befriended an apparently penniless young stranger by lending him money and a horse. Years later Joshua was summoned to the court of George III and it was revealed that the stranger was the Prince of Wales, later George IV. His reward was the free tenancy of a royal farm, Laverton Manor, for three generations. From such humble beginnings Arthur Hosier was to build up in his lifetime a farming complex which by 1954 extended to 22,000 acres, much of which he and his family owned.

Hosier's apprenticeship was the hard life of under-capitalized tenant farming. As a boy he had to help with milking cows before a four-mile walk to Bradford on Avon Grammar School and to return for evening milking. Although his terms were shortened by harvesting and other farm work, every year he took a prize at school. At nine years of age he learned to operate a steam threshing engine and when he left school, aged thirteen, he and his brother took the threshing tackle away for long periods on contract work. At the age of nineteen he and a brother took the tenancy of another farm and prospered selling milk at 5*d.* per gallon. By dint of hard work they increased their farming enterprise so that by the age of twenty-four Arthur Hosier was married and had his own farm tenancy. Then began a long career of inventing, first, a side-rake which was years ahead of its time. He also designed a mechanical milk filter which gained a medal at the London Dairy Show in 1904 but which failed to prosper for lack of engineering support. In the same year his brother-in-law, Uriah Whatley, died, leaving his engineering business in a precarious condition. Hosier gave up his farm and stepped into the breach. This proved to be an important step in his education; for six years he steadily gained knowledge of farming and engineering, being particularly successful in water supply, greatly assisted by the discovery that he was a natural water-diviner.

In 1910 Hosier returned to farming with his brother Joshua to grow corn on a large scale. They steadily increased their capital so that in 1920 they were able to purchase the 1,700-acre Wexcombe estate, a poor downland area in Wiltshire worth about £5 per acre. This became Hosier's home for the rest of his life. He developed the concern which firmly established his name in agricultural circles. He had foreseen that after the 1918 armistice cheap imported cereals would again become available and the way ahead must lie with low-cost milk production, a formidable challenge on this derelict Wiltshire downland with few buildings and no roads, which produced little other than rabbits.

Although the milking machine had been invented some twenty years earlier, installations were few in number, probably fewer than 1,000 in the whole United Kingdom. Moreover, they still constituted a hazard for the health of the cow and the hygiene of the milk, though potentially mechanical milking could reduce costs by saving labour. Probably deriving some inspiration from developments in the antipodes (his brother, Sidney, had emigrated to Australia in 1919), Hosier met the challenge with a novel idea which, in a paper given some years later to the Farmers' Club, he called 'Open-Air Dairying',

but which was generally known as 'the Hosier system'. The central feature of the system was a portable milking installation which Hosier, using an Australian term for a cowstall, called a 'bail'. The original design provided six stalls abreast forming part of a four-wheeled structure with a roof. This was moved daily, about its own length, by a tractor or a winch. It was fitted with a releaser-type milking machine, much of which was of Hosier's own design and manufacture. Initially the engine and vacuum pump were installed on the roof but for the second prototype a converted shepherd's hut was used to house the machinery, which was soon increased by the addition of a boiler to produce hot water for cleaning and sterilizing, a dynamo for electric lighting, and later a refrigeration unit for cooling the milk.

Following the first experiments in 1922, Hosier found that the cows and the operators could survive the hardest winters and were healthier, even at altitudes above 800 feet. Together with his meticulous attention to hygiene these open-air conditions resulted in high-quality milk. His labour costs were less than half, and his capital costs in buildings and equipment a mere fraction of the conventional cowshed system. A potential set-back at a very early stage was a slump in the price of milk— from nearly 3*s.* to 6*d.* per gallon. Hosier countered this by taking milk daily by road some eighty miles to London where he retailed it (at cut price) for cash until the business was sold on advantageous terms to United Dairies.

While low-cost milk production continued to be the keystone and gave rise to many more original developments, share milking for example, Hosier did not neglect his farming in the broader sense. He developed a system which he called 'alternate husbandry' — ploughing up pasture and grassing down arable as opportunity offered. This gave him scope for more new ideas such as ploughing, pressing, seeding, and harrowing in one operation, and the invention of many devices for bush clearance, hay and silage making, and cereal harvesting. He designed a portable poultry unit enabling some 5,000 laying hens to accompany each dairy herd, using the same land.

Hosier was an outstanding pioneer. His love of hard work and his flair for original thought lasted until his death. He was reserved, even dour, at first acquaintance and had a deep-rooted aversion to officialdom and committees. Nevertheless he gave freely of his knowledge and was generous in support of charities and young farmers. He was a Methodist lay preacher throughout his life. In 1949 he was appointed OBE and in 1951 Cambridge University conferred on him the honorary degree of LLD. He married in 1901 Ruth (died 1950), daughter of George William Smith, a tenant farmer, of Broad Blunsdon. They had two sons and three daughters. In 1953 Hosier married Florence Joyce Orchard, of Collingbourne, by whom he had one daughter. He died at Wexcombe 3 April 1963.

[*The Times*, 6 April 1963; A. J. and F. H. Hosier, *Hosier's Farming System*, 1951; C. S. Orwin, *A Pioneer of Progress in Farm Management*, University of Oxford Agricultural Economics Research Institute, 1931; private information; personal knowledge.]

H. S. HALL

HOTINE, MARTIN (1898–1968), geodesist and photogrammetrist, was born in Putney 17 June 1898, the tenth child and fourth son of Frederick Martin Hotine, a retired army officer and journalist, and his wife, Mary Louisa Golder. After an education at Southend High School and the Royal Military Academy, Woolwich, he was commissioned into the Royal Engineers on 6 June 1917, the head of his entry. He saw active service in Persia, Iraq, and India, and then went up to Magdalene College, Cambridge.

In 1925 Hotine was appointed research officer to the Air Survey Committee. Although the subject was new to him he devoted his considerable mathematical ability, experimental aptitude, and tremendous energy to devising practical methods of using air photographs for topographic mapping. In 1927–31 he was attached to the geographical section of the general staff at the War Office, but retained his interest in photogrammetry and in 1931 published his book *Surveying from Air Photographs* which was to be the standard textbook in English for many years to come. Most of the next three years was spent in Central Africa on observation for the measurement of the 30th Arc of Meridian and this practical work aroused his interest in geodesy and developed his appreciation of the basic survey needs of undeveloped countries. From 1934 until 1939 he served in the Ordnance Survey where he initiated the retriangulation of Great Britain, completed nearly thirty years later. In spite of severe financial restrictions, he insisted on the highest technical standards and introduced several innovations; he also insisted that however good the work it must become useless if the stations could not be recovered. The pillars on hill tops all over the United Kingdom are visible monuments to his ability to combine a practical viewpoint and scientific work of the highest order.

When war broke out in 1939 Hotine was appointed deputy director of survey in the British Expeditionary Force and, later, director of survey in East Africa, whence he returned to England in 1941 to become director of military survey, uniquely responsible for the army's maps and the aeronautical charts needed by the Royal Air Force throughout the world. He retained this post, with the rank of brigadier, until 1946. One of his major achievements was the development of the closest co-operation with the United States Army Map Service, ensuring that in the mapping field the utmost was extracted from the skill and resources of both nations.

In 1946 Hotine became director of what was to become the Directorate of Overseas Surveys. It was designed to provide a central agency to undertake major surveys overseas beyond the capacity of local organizations. The concept of the organization was his own and to his steady leadership during the next seventeen years is due much of its success. While at the Directorate, Hotine was president of the Commonwealth Survey Officers' Conference in 1955, 1959, and 1963. That this conference, attended by delegates from up to thirty nations, became accepted as a model of its kind was due to his insistence on most careful planning followed by informal and friendly meetings, coupled with his firm but tactful presidency.

Despite his involvement in overseas surveys and mapping, Hotine found time to devote his mind to developments in the science of geodesy and became a recognized world authority, especially in three-dimensional geodesy and in the mathematics of projection systems. He retired from the Directorate in October 1963 and within a month became a member of the research staff of the United States Coast and Geodetic Survey, working mainly at Boulder, Colorado, on geodetic problems. He completed five years in America, during which he wrote his major scientific work *Mathematical Geodesy*, published in 1969 by the United States Environmental Science Services Administration.

Hotine was appointed CBE in 1945 and CMG in 1949, the year in which he retired from the army. In 1947 he was awarded the Founder's medal of the Royal Geographical Society and in the same year became an officer of the United States Legion of Merit. In 1955 he was the first recipient of the President's medal of the Photogrammetric Society of London. The gold medal of the Institution of Royal Engineers was awarded to him in 1964, and in 1968, just before he died, he was awarded the gold medal of the United States Department of Commerce. He died in Woking 12 November 1968.

In 1924 Hotine married Kate Amelia, daughter of George Pearson, of Rochford,

Essex; they had three daughters. There is a portrait by L. M. Carmichael at the head-quarters of the Directorate of Overseas Surveys, at Tolworth, Surrey.

[*Nature*, 28 September 1963; *Royal Engineers Journal*, March 1969; private information; personal knowledge.]　　　R. A. GARDINER

HOWITT, SIR HAROLD GIBSON (1886-1969), chartered accountant, was born at Nottingham, 5 October 1886, the second son of Arthur Gibson Howitt, printer and litho-grapher, and his wife, Elizabeth Archer. He was educated at Uppingham and retained an active interest in the school throughout his life, becoming chairman of the trustees (1949-67). In 1904 he was articled to W. R. Hamilton, chartered accountant, of Nottingham, qualify-ing in 1909 and joining W. B. Peat & Co. (later Peat, Marwick, Mitchell & Co.) in London in the same year. In 1911 he accepted a partner-ship in their Middlesbrough office and re-mained a partner until his retirement in 1961.

Howitt was always a believer in hard work and physical fitness. The amount of pro-fessional and public work he got through was remarkable. As a young man he played rugby for Midland Counties and Harlequins, and throughout his life he treated holidays as an opportunity for vigorous physical exercise. His energy, and a taste for adventure, were early called into play when in 1910, in the first of two professional visits to the Donetz coal basin, he reached the Vagliano anthracite collieries, after stowing away on a goods train, to find the miners on strike and the place in chaos. He stayed for three months, paid the wages with money brought in under Cossack guard, and got the place working again. The sternest test of his resilience and enterprise came soon after-wards, in the war of 1914-18. On 4 August 1914 he left his office in Middlesbrough and joined the 4th battalion, the Green Howards; he served throughout the war, mainly in France but for a short period in Egypt and Palestine, and was appointed to the DSO and awarded the MC, being mentioned in dispatches four times. In a renowned exploit in March 1918, borrowed by John Buchan [q.v.] for his novel *Mr. Standfast*, he was captured during the German advance at St. Quentin; observed and was impressed by his captors' preparations for the next move; broke free from his guards; and after running back, part of the way in the glare of a burning dump, regained the British lines, having dis-covered where he was by hearing in the dark-ness a familiar British oath.

In 1919 Howitt returned to Peat's, in their London office, where he remained for the rest of his working life. Within a few months he had embarked on the long series of public com-missions and inquiries which were the out-standing feature of his career. Beginning with the commission on Southern Rhodesia (1919-20, chaired by Viscount Cave, q.v.), he dealt with major valuation problems, several of them in colonial territories, up to the com-mittee on the financial structure of the Colonial Development Corporation (1959). From 1932, when he was appointed to the reorganization commission on pigs and pig products, he was prominent in agricultural inquiries and even found time to run a small farm of his own. He was involved in fixing the compensation due to several nationalized industries at home and abroad: coal (1946), Argentine Railways (1947), Anglo-Iranian Oil (1951), and Cable and Wire-less (1956). He was also concerned with cost control questions from Lord Bridgeman's com-mittee on the British Legion (1930) to the British Transport Commission (1957), and he rendered distinguished service on the Air Council throughout the war of 1939-45. This main wartime duty he managed to combine with being chairman and deputy chairman of BOAC (1943-8), a member of the council of the NAAFI (1940-6), chairman of the Building Materials Board, and financial adviser to the Ministry of Works (1943-5). He was an effective and lucid speaker, a patient and courteous negotiator, always charming and friendly.

In the long list of Howitt's services the best known was his membership, with Lord Cohen and Sir Dennis Robertson [q.v.], of the original Council on Prices, Productivity, and Incomes (1957-9), popularly known as 'The Three Wise Men', the forerunner in the search for a national incomes policy. With some reluctance, Howitt himself came to the conclusion that attempts to regulate the industrial economy were the price of full employment and the existence of powerful associations of labour and employers.

He was a member of the council of the Institute of Chartered Accountants in England and Wales (1932-61), its president in 1945-6, and president of the International Congress of Accountants in London in 1952. After his retirement from practice he wrote the *History of the Institute of Chartered Accountants in England and Wales 1880-1965* (1966).

His charitable activities, often concerned with financial matters, were many, and were often directed to the needs of young people. He was a member of the council of Toynbee Hall (1922-51) and of the United Services Trustees (1946-66), and was master of the Merchant Taylors' Company in coronation year 1953. Howitt was knighted in 1937 and appointed GBE in 1946; he became a magistrate in Hampstead in 1942 and was chairman of its bench in 1950-8; and was an honorary DCL of Oxford (1953) and honorary LLD of Nottingham (1958).

Howitt married in 1917 Dorothy Wentworth (died 1968), daughter of William Henry Radford, of Sherwood, Nottingham; they had one son and three daughters, the son A. W. Howitt being senior executive partner in Peat, Marwick, Mitchell & Co., management consultants. Howitt died at Barnes 30 November 1969.

A portrait in oils by Frank O. Salisbury is owned by the Institute of Chartered Accountants in England and Wales.

[Private information.]   WALTER TAPLIN

HUDSON, ROBERT GEORGE SPENCER (1895-1965), geologist, stratigrapher, and palaeontologist, was born at Rugby 17 November 1895, the eldest of the four sons and the six children of Robert Spenser Hudson, carpenter and joiner, and later mayor and first freeman of Rugby, and his wife, Annie Wilhelmina Goble, of Bicester, Oxfordshire. Hudson was educated at the Lower School of Lawrence Sheriffe, Rugby, which he left in 1913. At the age of eighteen he became a student teacher at Elborow Boys' School, and, in September 1914, he entered St. Paul's Training College for teachers at Cheltenham. In 1916 he joined the Artists' Rifles and in March 1917 was gazetted to the 2nd battalion, Royal Warwickshire Regiment, in which he served as a machine-gunner. He was wounded in France, invalided back to England, and discharged with the rank of second lieutenant.

In autumn 1918 he entered University College, London, to read geology. He won the London University geology scholarship in 1919 and the college's Morris prize; he was secretary and later president of the college's geological club, the Greenough Club. In 1920 he graduated B.Sc. with first class honours. After graduation he was appointed to a part-time demonstratorship in geology at University College, London, a post which he held for two years and which he combined with postgraduate research. Through the influence of his professor, E. J. Garwood, Hudson's attention was directed to north-west Yorkshire, where a study of the Yoredale rocks formed the basis of his thesis for the M.Sc. degree, which was awarded by London University in 1922. This work was to mark the beginning of his association with the geology of the Carboniferous rocks of Yorkshire, an association which was to last for a quarter of a century. In 1922 Hudson was appointed assistant lecturer at Leeds University. From this time he identified himself with Yorkshire rather than

with his birthplace, a regional identity which was to persist throughout his adult life. In Leeds his ability as a teacher was quickly recognized and he established a remarkable rapport with his students who cheerfully assisted him in many of his projects, collecting suites of fossils from particular areas and breaking many hundreds of feet of drill hole core.

In 1927 he became lecturer at the university of Leeds and in 1939 he was appointed to the chair of geology, a post which he resigned in 1940 to become a research fellow. At this time Hudson published palaeontological papers in the *Transactions of the Leeds Geological Association*, of which he was editor from 1927 to 1940, and in the *Transactions of the Leeds Philosophical and Literary Society*. He became involved in caving and potholing, serving on the organizing committee and later on the council of the British Speleological Association. Later, when in Iraq, he explored some of the more spectacular potholes in the Zagros mountains. Although involved in many activities outside his teaching and research commitments he still found time to deliver evening lectures to the Workers' Educational Association in Leeds and, after the outbreak of war, he assisted the commissioner for Civil Defence in the North-Western Region from 1940 to 1942.

In 1942 Hudson left Leeds University to become a consultant geologist, retained by a number of companies engaged in carrying out oil exploration programmes on the Carboniferous rocks in Yorkshire and contiguous counties. It was perhaps inevitable that he should become involved in petroleum geology, for much of his work on the palaeogeography and palaeoenvironment of the Carboniferous rocks, although of academic importance, was also of significant relevance in the interpretation of oil sources, traps, and reservoirs. Interest in Britain's onshore oil prospects developed during the inter-war years and shortly after the outbreak of hostilities in 1939 the Eakring field came into production, an event of considerable strategic importance.

In February 1946 Hudson was appointed to the staff of the Iraq Petroleum Company as geologist and macro-palaeontologist and for the next six years was to take an active part in field-work, mapping, collecting fossils, and interpreting structures in the Middle East, from north Iraq to south-west Arabia. He entered into these new duties with tremendous enthusiasm and although initially agreeing to spend eight months in the area, he extended this to a year, returning to London in February 1947. Although engaged in applied economic geology he had not yet abandoned academic commitments and from 1947 to 1958 he was an honorary lecturer in geology in University College, London, serving on the geology board of studies of the university of London in the years following. In 1958 he became an honorary research associate at University College, London, and from then to 1961 continued to publish papers on corals, brachiopods, and stromatoporoids from the Mesozoic of the Middle East.

In 1959 Hudson was appointed to a lectureship in palaeontology at Trinity College, Dublin, where his former student, W. D. Gill, held the chair of geology. In 1961 Hudson himself was appointed to the chair of geology and mineralogy, a position which he held until his death.

From 1923 to 1950 Hudson published some eighty-seven papers dealing with Carboniferous stratigraphy and palaeontology of the midlands and north of England. From 1953 to 1961 twenty-four papers dealt with the Permian and Mesozoic palaeontology and stratigraphy of the Middle East, covering a vast area from Iraq, through Lebanon, Israel, and Oman to Saudi Arabia. From 1964 to his death he returned once again to his first interest, the Dinantian, and, in collaboration with postgraduates and colleagues, wrote five papers dealing with the stratigraphy and palaeontology of the Lower Carboniferous of Ireland.

Hudson made important contributions to the palaeontology, stratigraphy, and palaeogeography of the Carboniferous of the north of England and the Mesozoic of the Middle East. His palaeontological work embraced the Lower Carboniferous rugose corals, erecting the genera *Rhopalolasma*, *Cravenia*, *Hettonia*, and *Rylstonia* (the last three names deriving from Yorkshire place-names). He described the ontological development of many rugose genera, introducing the term *rhopaloid septum* and, in the siliceous sponges, erected the genus *Erythrospongia*. In interpreting phasal faunas he introduced the term *homeofaunas* and, in defining the position of fossil-type material within a hierarchical framework, coined the term *lectosyntype*. In his work on Mesozoic stromatoporoids from the Middle East he erected the genus *Actostroma* from the Jurassic of Israel and the genus *Steinerina* for a Jurassic hydroid. The Namurian goniatite genus *Hudsonoceras* was named in Hudson's honour by E. W. J. Moore in 1946.

Hudson, known affectionately to his students, colleagues, and friends as 'Hud', was a burly man with a ruggedly handsome face, clipped moustache, and candid grey eyes which gazed at the world with a direct frankness. Although of more than average height, this was masked by his stocky build. His left jaw was marked by a bullet wound dating from World War I, an asymmetric chin-dimple crimped by scar tissue. His irrepressible enthusiasm and often unorthodox views made him excellent company and he was a great talker. He recounted with animated and unfeigned gusto his field experiences in the Middle East. His sense of values was both inflexible and simple; geology occupied the pre-eminent position and clothes, motor cars, and other material things, and his own personal comfort, came very low on the scale. He was a superb teacher, teaching by example rather than by precept. A tireless and dedicated worker, even in his last years he was usually to be found in his department up to midnight on most evenings, both during term and vacation. He could be indiscreet, inevitable in the light of his spontaneity, and in academic politics he was patently guileless, not to say naïve.

In 1921 he was elected a fellow of the Geological Society of London. He was elected to the council of the Yorkshire Geological Society in 1923, edited the Society's *Proceedings* from 1934 to 1947, and served as its president from 1940 to 1942. In 1931 he was awarded the Wollaston Fund by the Geological Society of London. From 1939 to 1944 he was secretary of Section C of the British Association. He became a member of the council of the Geological Society of London in 1952, being elected a vice-president for two years in 1955 and being awarded the Society's Murchison medal in 1958. When the Palaeontological Association was formed in 1957 he was invited to become its first president. In 1961 he was elected a fellow of the Royal Society and in 1962 a member of the Royal Irish Academy and a fellow of University College, London. In 1964 he became president of the Irish Geological Association and at the time of his death was serving his second term in that office. In 1964 he was also elected chairman of the committee for science and its industrial application of the Royal Dublin Society, and during his chairmanship saw many geological papers published in the *Proceedings* of the Society. In his honour the Royal Dublin Society published the Hudson Memorial Numbers in 1966, which consisted of four papers of which Hudson and his colleagues at Trinity College, Dublin, were co-authors, together with an appreciation and a bibliography.

In 1923 he married Dorothy Wayman, daughter of Edward James Pocock Francis, gentleman of London. The three children of this marriage, one son and two daughters, all entered the teaching profession. This marriage was dissolved and in 1947, in London, he married Jane Naden, daughter of Cecil Philip Airey, schoolmaster, of Keighley, Yorkshire; they had three sons and a daughter. Hudson died at Trinity College, Dublin, 29 December 1965.

[C. J. Stubblefield in *Biographical Memoirs of Fellows of the Royal Society*, vol. xii, 1966; J. S. Jackson in *Scientific Proceedings of the Royal Dublin Society*, vol. ii(A), 1966; W. H. C. Ramsbottom in *Proceedings of the Yorkshire Geological Society*, vol. xxxv, 1966; W. D. Gill in *Proceedings of the Geological Society of London*, no. 1636, 1967; private information; personal knowledge.]

JOHN S. JACKSON

HUGHES, EDWARD DAVID (1906-1963), organic chemist, was born in Criccieth 18 June 1906, the youngest of nine children of Hugh Hughes, farmer, and his wife, Anne Roberts. Both his parents were of North Welsh stock. He attended Portmadoc Grammar School and was greatly encouraged in his studies by the head science master, W. J. Hughes, who influenced young Edward to enter university. In 1924 he entered University College, Bangor, and was awarded the B.Sc. degree with first class honours in chemistry in 1927. In 1927 he commenced part-time and in 1928 full-time research under Dr H. B. Watson, on prototropy, a subject of great interest to the head of the department, Professor K. J. P. Orton, who stimulated Hughes's interest in mechanistic organic chemistry, a field he was to espouse for the rest of his life. He was awarded the Ph.D. degree of the university of Wales in 1930.

In 1930 Hughes gained a postdoctoral fellowship to work with Professor (Sir) C. K. Ingold [q.v.], which led to a very fruitful collaboration over the next thirty-three years. Ingold had just been appointed to a chair of chemistry at University College, London, and master and pupil arrived at the same time. During the early thirties Hughes held a series of postdoctoral fellowships including a Ramsay memorial fellowship and temporary positions on the staff of UCL, leading to his appointment as lecturer in 1937. His early years at UCL, in conjunction with Ingold, culminated in the recognition, in 1933, of two distinct mechanisms of nucleophilic substitution, the unimolecular and the bimolecular (S_N1 and S_N2) and a bimolecular mechanism of elimination (E2). A unimolecular mechanism of elimination (E1) was also tentatively advanced. This nomenclature came to be widely acknowledged as the basis of the classification of organic mechanisms. In 1932 Hughes obtained the M.Sc. and in 1936 the D.Sc. of the university of London. He was awarded the Meldola medal of the Royal Institute of Chemistry in 1936.

On the outbreak of war in 1939 the chemistry department of UCL was evacuated to Aberystwyth and Bangor, Hughes and Ingold going to the former. When in 1943 the chair of chemistry at Bangor became vacant, Hughes was appointed and at the conclusion of the war organized the rapid rebuilding of his department. During his five years at Bangor he extended his work on substitution and elimination reactions and also initiated work on isotope separation, with a view to using isotopes as indicators of mechanisms. He paid frequent visits to UCL where collaborative research was continuing with Ingold and his students.

His stay at Bangor was short—he was appointed professor of chemistry at UCL (1948), deputy head (1957), and head of department (1961). In 1949 he was elected a fellow of the Royal Society and in 1954 a fellow of University College, London. He bore more than his share of extra-departmental activities and was much in demand as a chairman because of his expeditious handling of business. He was on many committees of the Chemical Society, and was honorary secretary in 1950-6 and vice-president in 1956-9. He also served the college as chairman of the Ramsay advisory council.

His publications, over two hundred papers, cover most of the then known aspects of organic reaction mechanisms, many of which were discovered by Hughes and his co-workers. In assessing Hughes's scientific work, Ingold wrote: 'It can certainly be said that this work has changed the aspect of organic chemistry, by progressively replacing empiricism by rationality and understanding, to a degree which is now manifest in the terminology and teaching of the subject, and in the research activity all along its advancing frontier.'

Hughes was essentially a humane man. It was a great tragedy both for him and his department that his headship, from which he derived so very much satisfaction, was so brief. A little-known aspect of his life was his breeding and racing of greyhounds; he was known on the course as 'the Prof.'. He was an indefatigably hard worker; the fact that he accomplished so much in so many fields was due to the orderliness of his approach.

In 1934 he married Ray Fortune Christina, daughter of the Revd Ll. Davies, of Brecon, and their only child, Carol Anthea, was born five years later. He died in University College Hospital 30 June 1963.

[C. K. Ingold in *Biographical Memoirs of Fellows of the Royal Society*, vol. x, 1964; personal knowledge.]   ALLAN MACCOLL

HUME-ROTHERY, WILLIAM (1899-1968), first Isaac Wolfson professor of metallurgy in the university of Oxford, was born at Worcester Park, Surrey, 15 May 1899, the only son of Joseph Hume Hume-Rothery, a barrister and patents lawyer, and his wife, Ellen Maria Carter. His great-grandfather was Joseph Hume (1771-1855), the radical politician [q.v.]. The family soon moved to Cheltenham, where William, with his two young sisters, spent most of his childhood. After preparatory school he joined Cheltenham College as an entrance scholar (1912). Following the outbreak of World War I, a military career seemed almost inevitable. In 1916 Hume-Rothery took the army entrance examination, achieved fifth place and a prize cadetship, and passed into the Royal Military Academy, Woolwich, as a gentleman cadet. A distinguished military career might very well have lain ahead of him, but for a circumstance which altered his whole life. In 1917 he contracted cerebrospinal meningitis. He recovered but the nerves of hearing were destroyed, leaving him completely deaf, and the army was closed to him.

The study of science attracted him and in 1918 he went up to Magdalen College, Oxford, to read chemistry in the honour school of natural science. His college elected him to a demyship and he took a first in 1922. In his fourth year, a research year, he was introduced to optical microscopy, which he exploited later in his career. Possibly at this time Hume-Rothery developed an interest in intermetallic compounds, especially those the compositions of which did not conform to the formal valency rules of contemporary inorganic chemistry.

Hume-Rothery joined the Royal School of Mines after graduation, and worked under (Sir) H. C. Carpenter [q.v.] on various intermetallic compounds, obtaining his London Ph.D. in 1925. This was a period of great importance in his career. Publications arising from his London work contained the first mention of the influence of the electronic characteristics of metals on the nature of the alloys formed between them. In 1925 Hume-Rothery returned to Oxford and worked on the constitution of alloys, successively as a senior demy of Magdalen, an Armourers' and Braziers' Company research fellow (1929-32), and a Warren research fellow of the Royal Society (1932-55). Personally and professionally, this was an exciting period. In 1931 he married Elizabeth Alice, the third daughter of Herbert Reginald Fea. She was a former editor of the *Geographical Magazine*. His work flourished and he developed his ideas, based on high-quality experiment, on the influence of atomic sizes, valency electron concentration, and electrochemical differences between metals on the nature of alloys. His tenure of the Warren research fellowship was particularly productive and he did not lack for research students, to whom he was invariably kind and generous in his supervision. His daughter Jennifer was

born in 1934. His Oxford D.Sc. was awarded in 1935, and the fellowship of the Royal Society followed in 1937.

Hume-Rothery became a fellow of Magdalen College in 1938, the year in which he received his first official university appointment as lecturer in metallurgical chemistry. He strove continuously for recognition of his subject in Oxford teaching. The establishment of a Metallurgy Department in Oxford was a long process, not helped by World War II; developments included Hume-Rothery's election to a readership in 1955 and culminated in his election as the first Isaac Wolfson professor of metallurgy in 1958, and the opening of a new building for an independent department in 1960. These events were assisted by industrial and commercial interest, particularly that of (Sir) Isaac Wolfson, and were a tribute to Hume-Rothery's brilliance and steadfastness of purpose. He made a subject which had hitherto been largely empirical into something more precise and scientific, demonstrating that metallurgy could be treated as a scientific discipline in its own right.

Many honours came his way, including the Sir George Beilby memorial award (1934), the platinum medal of the Institute of Metals, the Francis J. Clamer medal of the Franklin Institute (1949), the Royal Netherlands Academy Roozeboom gold medal (1950), and the Luigi Losana prize medal (1955). Honorary degrees were conferred by the universities of Manchester and Sheffield (1966); he was appointed OBE in 1951. Retirement came in 1966; and the news of his sudden death in Oxford 27 September 1968 shocked the metallurgical world. The success of his work, summarized in 178 papers and seven books, assures his place in metallurgical history.

Those who were privileged to enjoy the Hume-Rotherys' hospitality saw how happy was his family life at Headington and later at Iffley, where he regularly attended the old church. He overcame his deafness magnificently and it never interfered with his enjoyment of life. He was a water-colourist of note, and a keen fisherman.

[G. V. Raynor in *Biographical Memoirs of Fellows of the Royal Society*, vol. xv, 1969; private information; personal knowledge.]

G. V. RAYNOR

HUNTER, SIR ELLIS (1892-1961), industrialist, was born in Great Ayton, Yorkshire, 18 February 1892, the younger son of William Hunter, the headmaster of the local village school and his wife, Alice Davison. He attended Middlesbrough High School and subsequently was articled to a firm of local accountants, qualifying in 1914. During the war of 1914-18 he worked in the steel department of the Ministry of Munitions. After the war he became a local partner in W. B. Peat & Co., and then in 1928 a general partner in the enlarged firm of Peat, Marwick, Mitchell & Co., after acquiring his fellowship of the Institute of Chartered Accountants the previous year.

In the early thirties Hunter as an accountant was intimately concerned with the fortunes of the steel industry in Middlesbrough. But he found accounting limiting and, following the traumatic experiences of the steel firms, in the early thirties especially, he left the profession and in 1938 accepted the offer of becoming deputy chairman and then soon afterwards also managing director of Dorman Long. He retained the managing directorship of the company for the rest of his life and in addition became chairman in 1948. He was primarily responsible for re-establishing the company on a firm financial basis and for carrying through major developments, which, though delayed by the war of 1939-45, involved new iron-ore unloading and handling, new blast-furnaces and mills, and open-hearth tilting furnaces at a new steel plant at Lackenby. The developments fully maintained the position of Dorman Long as a leading steel-maker using molten iron as distinct from the users of predominantly scrap and cold pig-iron. It might be claimed that the major developments at Dorman Long proceeded with an undue, but understandable financial caution and did not always make use of the new techniques — for example, the basic oxygen converter which was then being installed in some competing countries.

Hunter, as an accountant coming into the steel industry, was at first received somewhat coolly by the more traditional steel-makers but with his firmness of character and his intellectual ability he soon made his mark in the higher counsels of the industry. In 1945 he became president of the British Iron and Steel Federation and was to remain president until 1953, an exceptional tenure in an office normally held for two years only. Prior to the war the major guidance of the industry's affairs had been in the hands of the independent chairman of the federation, Sir Andrew Duncan [q.v.], with the president playing a minor role. Duncan remained chairman till his death in 1952, but the significance of the roles became progressively reversed during Hunter's presidency.

Hunter's early impact on the policies of the industry was seen in his influence in securing a sharing, through the Industry Fund, among all steel-makers, whether they used scrap or pig-iron, of the benefits from the artificially maintained low price of scrap. Then, as a result of a recommendation from a committee under Hunter, the Federation established the British Iron and Steel Corporation (Ore) in 1948 to provide for the central purchasing of all imported iron ore on behalf of all the firms in the industry. Hunter himself regarded as one of his special contributions the leading part he played in the drawing up of the first post-war development plan for the industry. This involved reconciling the development aims of the companies with the often broader objectives of the Federation's technical advisers. The plan was publicized as a government white paper in 1946. On a more personal note, during the early post-war discussions with Sir Oliver (later Lord) Franks, then permanent secretary at the Ministry of Supply, on the industry's future, Hunter showed remarkable clarity in stating the then unpopular case for the industry's pre-war arrangements with the European cartel under a regime of supervision by the Import Duties Advisory Committee.

Hunter's main achievement, however, was in successfully leading the industry, in conjunction with Sir Andrew Duncan, in the opposition to nationalization which successfully delayed it till 1951 and then, on the change of Government, soon led to denationalization. The key feature of his leadership of the industry during this period was his attempt to dissociate the issue from politics. He consistently advocated a solution which would have left the firms bearing their separate financial responsibilities but subject to an over-all supervision that would effectively reflect the public interest. The key discussions on this issue took place in 1947 with Herbert Morrison (later Lord Morrison of Lambeth, q.v.) who was delegated by Attlee, the prime minister, to see if a compromise solution to the nationalization issue could be achieved. At a number of meetings, notably in October 1947, at which Hunter, with Andrew Duncan and (Sir) Robert Shone met Morrison and John Wilmot (later Lord Wilmot of Selmeston, q.v.), it appeared that a solution had been reached under which companies would have remained under their present ownership but subject to public supervision over prices, development, and any collective activities undertaken by the industry. There would also be a further right for the Government to acquire companies for reasons either of 'defence or default'. The solution, though recommended by Morrison, was subsequently turned down by the Cabinet and nationalization became effective during the life of the short-lived 1950-1 Labour Government with its slender majority.

Hunter remained president of the Federation until the new Conservative Government, elected in October 1951, promptly set in motion the denationalization of the companies and established a supervisory Iron and Steel Board with powers over the industry in relation to prices and development, much on the lines of the earlier discussions with Morrison, though without the provisions for nationalization in cases of 'defence or default', but instead with provisions for state investment if this proved to be necessary. In 1953 Hunter ceased to be president of the Federation, but until 1959 still had a major influence on the policies of the industry.

Hunter had an austere manner which at first was somewhat intimidating. This austerity, however, was relieved by two crucial characteristics. He had a strong sense of principle and, though accommodating and clear minded in assessing points of detail, retained firmly the ideals which he held of aiming to combine public accountability with a decentralization of risk-bearing and of managerial responsibility. His other important characteristic was a kindness and simplicity which endeared him greatly to all those who had an opportunity of knowing him more intimately than was possible in normal business dealings. His apparent sternness was coupled with a shyness and reserve which sometimes failed to reveal his true kindness, his pleasure in the Yorkshire countryside, and his wide general reading.

In 1918 he married Winifred Grace, daughter of J. W. Steed, of Essex; they had two daughters. He derived great pleasure from returning to his wife and family at Howden Gate, Northallerton, for week-ends after the problems and controversies which were an inevitable part of his life as a leading figure in the steel industry in the post-war years when it was the centre of so much debate. In all his dealings, whether at Dorman Long in Middlesbrough, or in representing the industry in London, he maintained a calmness of manner, a thoughtfulness, and a clearness of understanding which made it a delight to be associated closely with him.

Hunter's reputation spread far outside the industry and he was twice asked if he would accept nomination as president of the Federation of British Industries. But he declined this invitation, no doubt feeling that, with the problems of Dorman Long and the steel industry as a whole, he had difficult enough issues to tackle. He was knighted in 1948 and appointed GBE in 1961. He died at his Yorkshire home 21 September 1961.

[*The Times*, 22 September 1961; B. S. Keeling and A. E. G. Wright, *The Development of the Modern British Steel Industry*, 1964; personal knowledge.]

ROBERT SHONE

HURST, SIR CECIL JAMES BARRINGTON (1870–1963), international lawyer, was born at Horsham Park, Sussex, 28 October 1870, the youngest son of Robert Henry Hurst, barrister, recorder of Hastings and Rye (1862–1905), and member of parliament for Horsham between 1865 and 1876, and his wife, Matilda Jane, daughter of James Scott, of the Nunnery, Rusper, Sussex. From Westminster School he went on to Trinity College, Cambridge, where he obtained a second in part i and a first in part ii (1891–2) of the law tripos.

Called to the bar by the Middle Temple in 1893, his masters in chambers were the future Lord Justice Scrutton and Mr Justice Bray [qq.v.]. After a year as junior counsel to the Post Office on the South-Eastern circuit (1901), he was appointed, in 1902, as assistant legal adviser to the Foreign Office. In this capacity he became active in international affairs, first, in 1907, as legal secretary to the British plenipotentiaries at the second Hague peace conference, then, in 1908, as a British delegate at the London naval conference. In 1910 he was appointed a member of the commission to report on the *Alsop* claim which had been referred to His Majesty's arbitrament by the United States and Chilean Governments. After 1912 he was much involved as British agent in the work of the British–American Claims Arbitration Tribunal. He took silk in 1913.

Hurst was promoted legal adviser to the Foreign Office in 1918. He had served in 1917–18 on the Phillimore committee which prepared an early draft for the Covenant of the League of Nations. But the work which had the most direct reflection in the Covenant as eventually adopted was his co-operation with David Hunter Miller, the American delegate, the outcome of which was presented, early in 1919, to the League of Nations Commission of the peace conference in the form of the so-called 'Hurst–Miller' draft. Among Hurst's own proposals was one for a Permanent Court of International Justice. As a member of the Paris peace conference he played an important part also in the drafting of the peace treaties. Writing to the Foreign Office in May 1919 (Sir) James Headlam-Morley [q.v.] remarked 'Hurst really carried the thing through entirely on his own shoulders, and it is owing to him more than to anyone else that there is a treaty of any kind to present to the Germans.'

In 1919–20 Hurst visited Egypt as a member of the mission headed by Lord Milner [q.v.]. When a commission of jurists was set up under the Washington conference on naval disarmament of 1921–2 to examine and report on the laws of war, Hurst was nominated a British member. He attended the Assembly of the League of Nations as a substitute delegate in

1922, 1924, and 1925, and as a delegate in 1926, and always played a leading creative role. He was prominent in the negotiation of the Treaty of Locarno of 1925.

A man of immense energy and dedication, endowed with a strong sense of moral principle and a devotion to public service, Hurst enjoyed the constant respect of his colleagues. Kindness, courtesy, and absolute integrity characterized his work, in which he set himself an exacting standard of scholarly perfection. He became assistant legal adviser at the Foreign Office at a time when legal institutions were powerful in policy-making, and it was largely he who invested the post of legal adviser with the prestige and eminence it subsequently carried. For Hurst regarded his function as that of a jurist involved in international affairs; not merely a writer of opinions, but a representative of his Government and a creator of policy at international conferences. One of his successors, Sir Gerald Fitzmaurice, had observed that by the time Hurst left the Foreign Office he had established an influence comparable to that of the permanent under-secretary. Foreign lawyers particularly were impressed by Hurst's lack of insularity and his receptiveness to foreign ideas. Indeed, his friendship with Henri Fromageot, his French counterpart, did much, in the words of Lord McNair, 'to ensure the co-operation, or minimize the divergence, of the British and French governments in implementing the Treaty of Versailles'.

Anxious to foster the development of an integrated and authoritative literature of international law, Hurst was convinced that there existed a vital need for the participation in the development of the subject by Foreign Office lawyers who were so closely involved with its practical application. He actively encouraged his colleagues to shed light on the purely legal aspects of their work, without ever jeopardizing the essential secrecy of political transactions. Within the limitations which the nature of his work imposed, Hurst himself published a number of important articles on a wide range of international legal questions. These have been republished as his *Collected Papers* (1950). It was largely because of his 'happy blend of scholarship with practical experience', that Hurst was able to exert such a marked influence on the growth both of policy and of legal thought.

In 1919 Hurst provided the initiative in founding the *British Year Book of International Law*, the first English periodical specifically devoted to this field of study. He himself served until 1928 as its chief editor. He also took an active part in the establishment of the Grotius Society, of which he became president in 1940.

In his last four years at the Foreign Office, Hurst appeared as counsel in several cases heard before the Permanent Court of International Justice. In 1929 he was elected a judge of the Court, of which he was president in 1934-6. Appropriately, it was the first Viscount Finlay [q.v.], who had been his former leader at the ·bar, whom Hurst succeeded in 1929 as the second British judge elected to the Court. There his gifts of diplomacy and scholarship were to be combined to even greater effect than hitherto. Hurst's aim as a judge was to strengthen the prestige and authority of the Court's pronouncements, striving always to achieve unity and minimize disagreement by means of exhaustive deliberation. It was the example he set by his far-sighted judicial philosophy which earned him the presidency after so short a time. He played a decisive part in formulating the many majority judgements with which he associated himself. While recognizing that the right to dissent was essential to the viability of any international tribunal, he was convinced that the ultimate effect of the indiscriminate production of dissenting opinions would be to undermine the standing of the Court's decisions. Yet, being conscientious in his adherence to principle, Hurst himself occasionally found it necessary to have recourse to this liberty. His preference for the textual method of treaty interpretation, which involved him in meticulous analysis of several important international conventions, bears out Lord McNair's view of him as a traditionalist. Hurst remained a judge until the dissolution of the Court in 1946, upon its replacement by the International Court of Justice. In the meantime, during the war of 1939-45 he spent three years as chairman of a Home Office panel for appeals against orders of detention under Regulation 18B; then became the first president of the War Crimes Commission, in 1943-5.

Hurst was appointed CB (1907), KCB (1920), KCMG (1924), and GCMG (1926); he was elected a bencher in 1922 and was treasurer of the Middle Temple in 1940. He was president of the Institute of International Law and an honorary LLD of Cambridge and Edinburgh. Throughout his career he enjoyed the full support of his wife, Sibyl Gabriel, daughter of (Sir) Lumley Smith, a judge of the City of London court, whom he married in 1901. She died in 1947, leaving two sons and a daughter. Hurst himself lived to be ninety-two, and died at his home, Rusper Nunnery, 27 March 1963. A portrait by W. Dring presented to Hurst in 1948 by the Grotius Society is reproduced in the *British Year Book of International Law*, vol. xxvi, 1949.

[*British Year Book of International Law*, vol. xxvi, 1949 (Sir Eric Beckett) and vol. xxxviii,

1962 (Lord McNair); *Annuaire de l'Institut de Droit International*, vol. l (ii), 1963 (Sir Gerald Fitzmaurice); *International and Comparative Law Quarterly*, vol. xiii, 1964; David Hunter Miller, *The Drafting of the Covenant*, vol. i, 1928; Sir James Headlam-Morley, *A Memoir of the Paris Peace Conference 1919*, ed. Agnes Headlam-Morley and others, 1972.]

E. LAUTERPACHT

HUSSEY, CHRISTOPHER EDWARD CLIVE (1899-1970), architectural historian and architectural contributor to *Country Life* for fifty years, was born in London 21 October 1899, the only son and elder of the two children of Major William Clive Hussey, of the Royal Engineers, and his wife, Mary Anne, eldest daughter of the Very Revd George Herbert, dean of Hereford. His father was the second son of Edward Hussey, of Scotney Castle, Kent. His parents encouraged his interest in buildings, writing, drawing, and the theatre, all of which had developed before he went to Eton; and it was through his activity as a journalist there that he sent his first, non-architectural, contribution to *Country Life* in 1917. In 1918 he served as second lieutenant in the Royal Field Artillery. At the instigation of H. Avray Tipping, who was the principal architectural writer on *Country Life* and a family friend and who wanted him to join the editorial staff, Hussey then went up to Oxford, where he spent the years 1919-21 at Christ Church. He read modern history (in which he gained second class honours in 1921) and devoted time to dramatics and journalism; and while an undergraduate he wrote his first country house articles for *Country Life*. In 1920 he became a member of the editorial staff. In the course of the next fifty years he contributed nearly 1,400 signed articles, as well as being editor from 1933 to 1940, and only his exceptional powers of concentration and industry enabled him to write on planning, landscape, historic towns, and the modern movement as well as country houses, with a regular flow of notes on topical subjects for the leader page, and occasional letters signed 'Curious Crow, Tunbridge Wells'. Rightly it is the list of his articles which dominated the bibliographical tribute to him in *Architectural History*, 1970. Not only did he sustain the standard already set out by Avray Tipping and Sir Lawrence Weaver whose notice Hussey later wrote for this Dictionary, but he made the weekly country house article into a tradition which was strengthened as architectural history became established as a subject and documentary research became accepted as an integral part of it. It is particularly remarkable

that he was able to sustain the theme throughout the war of 1939-45.

His regular articles were the basis of a number of his books, *Eton College* (1922), *Petworth House* (1926), and *English Country Houses: Early Georgian* (1955), *Mid Georgian* (1956), and *Late Georgian* (1958). That trilogy was the distillation of over thirty years' work and the last volume helped prepare the way for the reassessment of the Victorian country house. His most important book was *The Picturesque* (1927). It was also the most revealing in showing how much he owed to his paternal and maternal background and the links which they forged with eighteenth-century attitudes to literature and landscape. From the early 1920s his grandfather's house and garden at Scotney, to which he was the heir, played an increasingly important role in his life, inspiring and influencing much of his writing, particularly on landscape, which culminated in his *English Gardens and Landscapes 1700-1750* (1967), the counterpart of his trilogy on Georgian country houses. Scotney also lay behind his concern for the practical issues of property management and preservation.

Although moved by the past, Hussey was never a remote aesthete: he believed in the continuity of tradition and its practical application. That is apparent in his lifelong admiration for and enjoyment of the architecture of Sir Edwin Lutyens [q.v.], whose *Life* he wrote in 1950 in connection with the three memorial volumes on his architecture by A. S. G. Butler; his articles on Lutyens span a period of forty-nine years. Similarly he wrote about Sir Robert Lorimer in 1931, and later contributed the notices of both Lutyens and Lorimer to this Dictionary. By 1931 Hussey had also become interested in modern architecture and in 1933 he was chairman of an exhibition of industrial art at Dorland Hall. He took an active part in public work, particularly for the National Trust and the Historic Buildings Council for England, where his soundness of judgement was highly valued. His presidency of the Society of Architectural Historians from 1964-6 recognized not only his special contribution to the establishment of a subject which did not exist in England when he began work but also his influence on growing public awareness of the point of preservation. Hussey was honorary ARIBA (1935) and an associate of the Institute of Landscape Artists. He was also FSA (1947) and was appointed CBE in 1956.

In fact he was a remarkably rounded figure, who enjoyed all he did and did all he enjoyed, whether it was writing and research, painting in water-colour, which was a strong family tradition, gardening and planting trees, shooting writing verse and lyrics, or choosing cattle for his prize Sussex herd at Scotney. In 1936 he married Elizabeth Maud, daughter of Major P. Kerr Smiley. They had no children. Hussey inherited his uncle's property in 1952, and thereafter he and his wife devoted much effort to the maintenance and improvement of the untouched early Victorian house and its picturesque setting, which he left to the National Trust. He died at Scotney 20 March 1970. A bronze bust by Tait McKenzie and a portrait by John Ward are at Scotney Castle.

[*The Times*, 21 and 25 March, 23 April 1970; *Country Life*, vol. cxlvii, p. 767; *Newsletter* of the Society of Architectural Historians, May 1970; *Victorian Society Annual*, 1969-70; *Architectural History*, 1970, for an almost complete bibliography; 'The Husseys and The Picturesque', *Country Life*, vol. clxv, pp. 1438 and 1522; private information; personal knowledge.]

JOHN CORNFORTH

HUTCHISON, SIR WILLIAM OLIPHANT (1889-1970), landscape and portrait painter, was born at Kirkcaldy 2 July 1889, the fifth child in the family of four sons and two daughters of Henry William Hutchison, of Kinloch, a Kirkcaldy business man, and his wife, Sarah Hannah Key. He was educated at Kirkcaldy High School, Cargilfield, and later at Rugby School. As a boy he showed considerable promise as an artist and wished to become a painter but his family were set on him entering business. In 1911 he spent a period in Paris, primarily to perfect his French but he also took this opportunity to study at the Atelier Delacluse. It was during this year that he struck up a lifelong friendship with another Scots artist, (Sir) James H. Gunn [q.v.]. After his return from Paris he dutifully entered the timber business but after a short time he rebelled and obtained his father's permission to enter the Edinburgh College of Art. He used to say that his father agreed to this because he had had a picture accepted by the Royal Scottish Academy. This was a portrait of his younger sister Nancy, exhibited in 1911.

It was while he was studying in Edinburgh that Hutchison came under the influence of the water-colourist E. A. Walton, an influence evident in much of his early work, especially his landscapes. He became very friendly with Walton and his family and eventually, in 1918, married Margery (died 1977), the Walton's youngest daughter. The marriage was a particularly happy one. They had two sons, Henry Peter, born 1919, and Robert Edward, born 1922, and one daughter, born 1935.

Hutchison served in the Royal Garrison Artillery during the war of 1914-18, in Malta and in France, where he was severely wounded. Shortly after his demobilization, late in 1918, he and his wife took a studio flat in York Place in Edinburgh. They remained there only until 1921, when they moved to London. At first they lived at Mulberry Walk in Chelsea but two years later moved to Ladbroke Road, Holland Park, and became near neighbours of James F. Pryde [q.v.], another Scottish artist who had long been settled in London. Hutchison practised as a portrait painter and had some measure of success. He exhibited regularly at the Royal Academy. He joined the Savage Club and had a wide circle of friends, mainly connected with the arts. In particular, he became a close friend of James Pryde.

In 1929 Hutchison bought an old vicarage in Suffolk near to Wickham Market and he spent his time either in London or Suffolk. In 1932 he was persuaded to apply for the post of director of the Glasgow School of Art, was successful in the competition, and took up his post in the following year. He remained director until 1943, when he retired to devote more time to painting. Although he had had no teaching experience, he made an excellent director. He painted very much in the academic tradition but was always ready to help and encourage students and young artists who aspired to the avant-garde. Sir Basil Spence, who for a time served on Hutchison's staff, said of him: '. . . his liberal understanding and enthusiasm for everything young brought the activities of the school into close harmony with the building itself [designed by Charles Rennie Mackintosh, q.v., a close friend of Hutchison]. It was during Bill Hutchison's term that many distinguished artists were produced as confidence was high and enthusiasm was a characteristic of those years' (letter to *The Times*, 14 February 1970).

After he relinquished the directorship in Glasgow, Hutchison moved to Edinburgh and took the upper part of a house in Eglinton Crescent in the west end of the city. He converted the principal floor into a handsome studio and elegant living-room. He again devoted his energies to portrait painting and became deeply involved in the affairs of the Royal Scottish Academy, of which he had been elected an associate in 1937 and a full academician in 1943. He served on the council of the Academy and in 1950 succeeded Sir Francis Mears as president, a post he held until 1959. He was knighted in 1953. Shortly after he relinquished the presidency he returned to London, where he had maintained a studio at Cheniston Gardens Studios in Kensington since shortly after World War II. He held an exhibition in London in 1964. He continued to be very active as a portrait painter and from

1965 served as president of the Royal Society of Portrait Painters, of which he was elected a member in 1948.

Hutchison is best known for his portraiture but throughout his career he painted landscapes of great charm and sensitivity. He painted many distinguished people, including the Queen, Prince Philip, and the Queen Mother. His full-length portrait of the Queen in Thistle robes, painted for the Edinburgh Merchant Company in 1956, is probably one of his finest works. Amongst his other portraits can be mentioned J. Ramsay MacDonald (now in the House of Commons), Dorothy L. Sayers (in the National Portrait Gallery, London), Sir James Gunn (his diploma picture in the Royal Scottish Academy, which is perhaps his finest male portrait), and Sir Sydney A. Smith, for which he received a gold medal in the Paris Salon of 1961.

Hutchison was a retiring and modest man but he had a good speaking voice and was in demand as a public speaker. He was also a great raconteur and his reminiscences of his early days in London were a never failing source of pleasure and amusement to his family and friends. In appearance he was a tall, fair, distinguished-looking man with strong features, his face scarred by a war wound.

Hutchison continued working right up until his death at home in London 5 February 1970. He died very suddenly while writing a letter to The Times, leaving two uncompleted commissions in his studio.

A number of portraits of Hutchison exist: the Royal Scottish Academy possesses an oil painting by his friend (Sir) James Gunn (1952) and a bronze bust by George H. Paulin (1953). A small portrait by Gunn, painted in 1911, is in the Scottish National Portrait Gallery, and there are self-portraits in Kelvingrove Art Gallery, Glasgow, and in Kirkcaldy Art Gallery. A number of self-portraits are also in possession of the family. Kirkcaldy Art Gallery has a group of paintings, both portraits and landscapes, given by the artist: these include a portrait of the artist's mother, which he himself considered to be one of his most successful works.

[Papers and correspondence of Sir W. O. Hutchison, National Library of Scotland; Scotsman and Glasgow Herald, 10 February 1970; The Times, 9, 12, and 14 February 1970; Annual Report of the Royal Scottish Academy, 1970, pp. 9–10; private information; personal knowledge.]

R. E. HUTCHISON

HUXLEY, ALDOUS LEONARD (1894–1963), man of letters, was born at Laleham,

a house near Godalming, 26 July 1894, the third son of Leonard Huxley [q.v.], an assistant master at Charterhouse and subsequently editor of the Cornhill Magazine, by his first wife, Julia Frances Arnold, a granddaughter of Thomas Arnold of Rugby and niece of Matthew Arnold [qq.v.]. As a grandson of T. H. Huxley [q.v.] and great-grandson of Dr Arnold, Aldous Huxley inherited both a passionate interest in science and the pursuit of truth, and his high sense of moral purpose. Mrs Humphry Ward, the novelist [q.v.], was his aunt; (Sir) Julian Huxley his eldest brother.

Huxley was educated first at Prior's Field, a successful avant-garde school founded by his mother, then at Hillside, a near-by preparatory school, from which he won a scholarship to Eton in 1908. Shortly after arriving there he suffered the first of three traumatic experiences: the premature death of his mother at the age of forty-five. Huxley was wholly devoted to her, and this sudden loss when he was only fourteen came as an appalling shock and deprivation. Then, scarcely more than two years later, he contracted an infection of the eyes (keratitis punctata) which sent him virtually blind and obliged him to leave Eton before the end of his eighth term. He faced this calamity with extraordinary determination and courage; taught himself to read braille, to type, and to play the piano; he continued his education doggedly with a series of tutors. In the spring of 1912 his sight had improved sufficiently for him to walk alone, to read large print with the aid of a magnifying glass, and to have hopes of going to Oxford. In October 1913 he went up to Balliol. There, despite his irreparably damaged sight, he read assiduously for a degree in English literature (in which he obtained a first, in 1916, as well as winning the Stanhope prize), developed a taste for Proust and the French symbolists, but also found time to play jazz and take part in amateur theatricals. By then Huxley was immensely tall (6 feet 4½ inches), and so thin that he was accurately described as having to 'fold himself and his legs, like some gigantic grasshopper, into a chair'. But what people noticed most particularly was his unaffected charm, his extraordinarily mellifluous voice, his sense of humour, and, above all, his gentleness. In later life, many people who disagreed profoundly with some of his views and deplored his propensity for entertaining the most improbable hypotheses (a by-product of his immense intellectual curiosity) nevertheless found it impossible to quarrel with this most lovable of men. For in addition to gentleness, there was an innate modesty and a sweet reasonableness about him that disarmed contention. His first year at university was intoxicating and he took everything that Oxford had to offer. The spell was broken by the outbreak of war in August 1914, and almost simultaneously by the third of the personal tragedies which afflicted him before he came of age: the suicide of his gifted elder brother Trevenen.

It was while he was still an undergraduate that Huxley started writing poetry chiefly but also short stories, and first discovered that he had 'some kind of natural gift for it'—a gift that supported him and his family for the rest of his life. It was also while he was at Oxford that, towards the end of 1915, he was taken to Garsington, home of the pacifist member of Parliament Philip Morrell and his wife, Lady Ottoline [q.v.], where he met most of the younger and more advanced writers and painters of the day. Huxley was both alarmed and fascinated by this immensely talented and varied *galère*, but after he left Oxford he spent part of the war years working on the land there (he was totally unfit for military service), and came to regard Garsington as one of the seminal factors in his education. More important, it was there that he met and became engaged to Maria Nys, the eldest daughter of a well-to-do Flemish family from Courtrai which had sought refuge in England; it was nearly three years, during which Huxley taught at Repton and Eton, before they could get married in July 1919. They set up house in Hampstead, and lived for some time in great financial stringency on Huxley's earnings as a journalist; their only child, Matthew, was born in April 1920.

The next ten years saw the emergence of Huxley as a novelist and short-story writer of marked originality, whose pungent wit, uninhibited dialogue, and frank discussion of subjects hitherto considered taboo in fiction, quickly won him a public, and a place as 'cultural hero' among the young. His first novel, *Crome Yellow* (1921), was shortly followed by *Antic Hay* (1923) and *Those Barren Leaves* (1925), all of which satirized contemporary society, through characters who challenged or flouted accepted conventions and were not always without resemblance to living people. The novels were interspersed by collections of brilliant short stories, including *Mortal Coils* (1922), *Little Mexican* (1924), and *Two or Three Graces* (1926). In addition, volumes of essays and books of travel made a regular appearance, among them *On the Margin* (1923) and *Jesting Pilate* (1926): in all a dozen books in eight years—a remarkable achievement for a man almost bereft of sight. Moreover, they made him money, and amply justified the faith his publishers had shown by offering him a three-year contract, at £500 a year, as early as 1923—an arrangement which

was renewed at intervals, in varying terms, up to his death. But it was 1928, the year in which his most ambitious novel to date, *Point Counter Point*, was published, which saw him become a best-seller both in Britain and America. The years 1925 to 1937 were among the happiest in Huxley's life. With the gradual easing of his financial position, he and his wife were able to spend more time abroad, especially in Italy, where they became close friends of D. H. Lawrence [q.v.], whose *Letters* Huxley edited (1932); they also visited India and the Far East, as well as Germany, Spain, the West Indies, and Mexico; in 1928 they bought a house near Paris, and later a villa at Sanary, near Toulon, which they occupied on and off from 1930 to 1937. There Huxley painted a good deal as well as wrote, entertained, and visited friends. In the intervals, regular visits were paid to London for the publication of a book or the production of a play (Huxley remained mistakenly convinced that he could become a successful dramatist), or to Italy for refreshment of his delight in Italian painting and architecture.

Early in 1937 the Huxleys began a prolonged visit to America, and by 1938 they had finally decided to remain there. It has been suggested that this was a result of the threat of war already developing in Europe, that Huxley was turning his back on the ugly prospects ahead (he was an ardent supporter of the Peace Pledge Union, for which he lectured and wrote pamphlets). Huxley himself, however, believed that the clear sunlight of California would enable him to see and read better, and he heard encouraging reports of a new American method, invented by Dr W. H. Bates, of improving the vision of partially sighted people. In this, according to his own and his wife's reports, he was not disappointed. By the middle of 1939 he was able to read and write without spectacles, and in 1942 he published his conclusions in *The Art of Seeing*. By then his writing had taken an entirely fresh turn. The 'philosophy of meaninglessness', as Huxley himself described it in *Ends and Means* (1937), which had informed all his early work and proved so potent a liberating force for his readers, no longer satisfied him. Something positive, something transcendental, something which would set mankind on the road to a fuller realization of its potential, was what he sought. He found it, he believed, in a form of mysticism derived in part from oriental philosophy, but largely from his own intuitive aspirations. 'Men and women', he wrote, 'are capable of being devils and lunatics. They are no less capable of being fully human', and for the rest of his life he devoted himself to trying to persuade them to be so. The books which followed, *The Perennial Philosophy* (1945), *Science, Liberty and Peace* (1946), *Themes and Variations* (1950), and *Brave New World Revisited* (1958), and in a sense also *Grey Eminence* (1941), spelt out the temptations which life presents in the modern world with its materialist values and dangerous technological advances, and suggested ways of overcoming them. The ways were unorthodox, and of such originality that they inevitably exposed him to accusations of abandoning reason for mumbo-jumbo. Huxley was unmoved, and later his views found powerful support among some of the best minds of the day. Similarly, the novels of that period, *After Many a Summer* (1939) which won the James Tait Black memorial prize, *Time Must Have a Stop* (1944), *Ape and Essence* (1948), and *The Genius and the Goddess* (1955), were distinguished by a combination of irony and compassion with a profound regard for humanity which lifted them on to a different plane from his earlier novels. In that context, Huxley wrote two fictional Utopias: one, *Brave New World* (1932), was a nightmarish prognostication of a future in which humanity has been destroyed by science; and the other, *Island*, published exactly thirty years later, was a picture of the good life possible for humans if only they would behave rationally. It was ironic that the former, despite its pessimism, should prove easily his most popular (and many good judges continued to think his best) novel, while the latter was clearly unsatisfactory as fiction but comprised his most sustained, imaginative, and moving account of *la condition humaine*, which for Huxley was ever 'the beast in view'.

In 1953 Huxley's interest in the therapeutic value of hypnosis was extended to other methods of releasing the human body from the domination of its ego: notably the use of mescalin and other psychedelic drugs such as LSD. His own experiments with these, and the practical use which he believed could be made of them, he described in *The Doors of Perception* (1954) and *Heaven and Hell* (1956). He was subsequently much criticized for the part he was thought to have played in encouraging young people to take these drugs, although he had warned that they must be used with caution. The year before his first experiment, his wife, Maria—his 'dragoman', as he called her for her practical good sense and tact—was seriously ill; she died from cancer early in 1955. A year later Huxley married Laura Archera, an Italian concert violinist and psychotherapist from Turin, whom he had first met some years earlier. But it was not long before Huxley himself contracted cancer of the tongue, in 1960. The disease at first yielded to radium treatment (he refused surgery

because it would have impaired his speech), and the next three years were spent indefatigably writing, lecturing, and attending conferences in America and all over Europe. This was interrupted, in May 1961, by the catastrophic fire which totally destroyed his home in Los Angeles, leaving him 'a man without possessions and without a past'. Huxley accepted the disaster philosophically, describing it as 'a sign that the grim reaper was having a good look at me'. A year later the cancer returned, this time incurably. By the autumn of 1963 his condition was hopeless, although he remained stoically detached and serene to the end. He died in Los Angeles 22 November 1963. In 1971 his ashes were returned to England and buried in his parents' grave at Compton cemetery, Surrey.

An oil portrait by his uncle, John Collier (1926), is privately owned; there is an ink and wash drawing by A. Wolmark (1928) in the National Portrait Gallery, and a drawing of Huxley and the Revd H. R. L. ('Dick') Sheppard by (Sir) David Low (1938) in the Tate Gallery. (Sir) William Rothenstein drew Huxley several times and one of these (1922) is reproduced in *Twenty-Four Portraits* (2nd series, 1923).

[*Listener*, 16 October 1947; *Aldous Huxley: a Memorial Volume*, ed. Sir Julian Huxley, 1956; *Letters of Aldous Huxley*, ed. Grover Smith, 1969; Laura Archera Huxley, *This Timeless Moment*, 1969; Sybille Bedford, *Aldous Huxley: a Biography*, 2 vols., 1973–4; personal knowledge.]   IAN PARSONS

HYDE, SIR ROBERT ROBERTSON (1878–1967), founder of the Industrial Welfare Society, was born in London 7 September 1878, the second son among the five children of Robert Mettam Hyde, of Paisley, and his wife, Marjorie Stoddart Robertson, of Inverary. His father was a constructional civil engineer who had been responsible for laying the first submarine cables in South America but he fell upon hard times and died in 1888. Hyde grew up in circumstances of considerable poverty: his formal education ended at Westbourne Park School in 1893 when he went on to work in commerce. In 1901 he was able with the help of friends to enter the theological faculty of King's College, London. He was ordained deacon in 1903 and priest in 1904 and began his ministry in the East End as curate at St. Saviour's, Hoxton.

From the beginning Hyde was concerned with boys' clubs and in 1907 he became warden of the hostel settlement in Hoxton founded in memory of F. D. Maurice [q.v.]. There he came into contact with many movements, interests, and people normally beyond parish bounds. From 1912 to 1916 he combined his work at the Maurice Hostel with the living of the parish church of St. Mary.

In 1916 there came a dramatic change in Hyde's career when he was asked by Seebohm Rowntree [q.v.], who was helping Lloyd George, to take charge of the boys' welfare department in the Ministry of Munitions. Hyde knew the essential nature of boys and how well they could respond if given the opportunity to develop. He was a born leader, whose humanity, kindliness, and humour shone out of him, and he soon had a band of friends and admirers, among them the reputedly cold industrialists and employers with whom he came in contact. These men rallied round him when in 1918, irked by the constrictions of civil-service procedures, he broke away from the Munitions Ministry and set up an organization of his own: the Boys' Welfare Association. Sir William Beardmore (later Lord Invernairn, q.v.) was his first chairman: and, with a characteristic flash of imagination and audacity, Hyde obtained the consent of King George V to his son, Prince Albert, becoming the first president.

Entirely self-financing, supported by industry itself, and dedicated to the advancement of humanitarianism in industry, the Association was soon firmly established as a repository of valuable and practical knowledge which prompted and led the way to new legislation and as a reliable instrument for the selection and training of welfare practitioners. This was due largely to Hyde's practical idealism, enormous energy, and powers of persuasion. On royal suggestion the name was changed in 1919 to that of the Industrial Welfare Society to conform with the wider responsibilities it had been urged to undertake; and it was with the IWS as it became familiarly known that Hyde's name was principally associated.

Hyde made a considerable impact on British industry and commerce in the provision of basic welfare such as lavatories, canteens, changing-rooms, and other amenities. He campaigned for pension funds for workers, for apprentice schemes for young people, for the introduction of medical officers in factories, for recreational facilities where the community did not provide them, for works magazines, and for suggestion schemes. His whole method of working was by widespread visiting, walking factory floors, talking to all and sundry, and by providing the very practical expertise necessary to introduce these schemes. He had the ability of not boring people or putting over his ideas in highfalutin' terms. He argued that it was just common sense to treat human beings decently if you wanted them to work and co-operate decently.

Meanwhile, between the Duke of York, as Prince Albert had now become, and Hyde a genuine friendship had developed, to their mutual benefit. Hyde was able to give the Duke an intimate understanding of the industrial and commercial life of Britain such as no previous member of the royal family had possessed. Together they conceived and carried through the venture known as the Duke of York's camps, where boys from industry and the public schools met and mixed, to their great mutual benefit, at summer camps in an unselfconsciously egalitarian atmosphere. The last of these camps was held at Balmoral in 1939 by invitation of the Duke, by then King George VI.

In 1932 King George V conferred the MVO upon Hyde in personal recognition of his services to his son who in 1949 himself bestowed a KBE upon his old friend. To Hyde's deep sorrow, his acceptance of the knighthood led to his being required by the Archbishop of Canterbury to relinquish holy orders.

In 1950 Hyde retired as director of the Industrial Welfare Society and was given the official title of founder. The society, subsequently renamed the Industrial Society, became the largest joint management–union body specializing in man management, industrial relations, communication, and the development of young people.

Hyde was an unpretentious and lovable man of medium stature and buoyant step. He loved people, and his impelling charm and sincerity when talking to anyone made that person feel that no one mattered more. He published a comprehensive book on *The Boy in Industry and Leisure* in 1921 and an autobiography in 1968.

In 1917 Hyde married Eileen Ruth (died 1970), second daughter of Dr George Parker, of Cuckfield. They had one daughter and a son who was reported missing in Italy in 1943. Hyde died at Haslemere 31 August 1967. A portrait of him by Sir James Gunn is the property of the Industrial Society.

[Sir Robert Hyde, *Industry was my Parish*, 1968; private information; personal knowledge.]   JOHN GARNETT

HYLTON, JACK (1892–1965), dance-band leader, pianist, composer, and impresario, was born in Bolton, Lancashire, 2 July 1892, son of George Hilton, a Bolton millhand, and his wife, Mary Greenhalgh. He was educated at the Higher Grade School in Bolton. He learned to play the piano as a child, becoming an accompanist at the age of ten. He later changed the spelling of his name to Hylton. His first professional engagement was at Rhyl, in summer

1905, as assistant pianist and singer with a pierrot troupe. Afterwards he conducted for touring revues, musical comedies, pantomimes, and ballet.

Hylton went to London in 1913 and worked in a music-publisher's office. He made his London début in October 1913 when he was engaged as cinema organist at the Alexandra, Stoke Newington. In 1920 he worked as a double-act with Tommy Handley [q.v.] at Bedford Music Hall. He was assistant pianist in cabaret at Queen's Hall roof, joined the resident band, and became its leader. On 28 May 1921 he made his first records with the 'Queen's' Dance Orchestra for 'His Master's Voice' and, as Jack Hylton's Jazz Band, for Zonophone. When he heard the first American records by Paul Whiteman's Orchestra, he set out to emulate the style of orchestration. In this he was very successful. He left Queen's Hall roof briefly in 1922, but returned to install a new band, with his name on the labels of *all* his subsequent records.

It was then that he opened a London office, employing many first-class dance-band musicians and placing bands in the Piccadilly Hotel and the Kit-Cat Club (1925), while at the same time touring with his principal band, which was generally recognized as the finest show-band in the British Isles. On 4 September 1927 he took his band in an Imperial Airways biplane from Croydon to Blackpool, circling the tower and playing another new song ('Me and Jane in a 'Plane') so that holiday-makers could hear it. He appeared with his band in *Shake Your Feet* (London Hippodrome, 20 July 1927); *Life Begins at Oxford Circus* (Palladium, March 1935); *Swing is in the Air* (Palladium, 29 March 1937); and *The Band Wagon* (Prince's, 26 December 1938).

Hylton toured Europe many times, with great success, particularly in Germany (1928, 1928-30, 1931, 1932), France (1928-31), and Italy (1931). However, he was unable to take his band to the USA owing to restrictions imposed by the American Federation of Musicians. He went there alone in December 1935 and appeared conducting a specially formed American band for six months.

Hylton created a sensation in the popular-music world in October 1931 by signing a contract with the fairly newly formed Decca Record Company after ten years with 'His Master's Voice'. However, he returned to the latter early in 1935 and remained with this label until war conditions prompted him to disband in April 1940.

In 1935 he had appeared in the film *She Shall Have Music* and the theatre also made a strong appeal to him. He began a new career as a theatrical impresario immediately after dis-

banding, touring with the London Philharmonic Orchestra. He became associated with the Daniel Mayer Company and revived *Peter Pan* (1940), continuing the annual presentation of this popular show until December 1948. He entered the West End field of theatre management by presenting *Lady Behave* (His Majesty's, 24 July 1941), following the success of this with such outstanding productions (mostly musical) as *Jack and Jill* (Palace, 26 December 1941); *The Merry Widow* (revived, His Majesty's, 4 March 1943); *Hi-de-Hi* (Palace, 3 June 1943); *The Love Racket* (Victoria Palace, 26 October 1943); *Duet for Two Hands* (Lyric, 27 June 1945); *For Crying Out Loud* (Stoll, 6 August 1945); *Follow the Girls* (His Majesty's, 25 October 1945); and *No Room at the Inn* (Winter Garden, 3 May 1946).

Hylton also composed many popular songs, especially at the outset of his career as a band-leader—'Mooning' (1921); 'Singing' (1922); 'Little Miss Springtime' (1922); 'Joyce' (1923); amongst them. He featured as a vocalist on a number of early recordings, with label-credit, which was very unusual at that time.

Hylton provided opportunities and encouragement to others. Over the years he featured many prominent musicians and popular vocalists (Sam Browne, Dolly Elsie (his own sister), Arthur Askey, Stanley Holloway, George Formby Jr., Tommy Handley, and Leslie Sarony); launched the bandleading careers of several famous personalities by giving them employment (for example, the trumpeter Jack Jackson, the trombonist Ted Heath, the saxophonists Noel 'Chappie' d'Amato and Billy Ternent, and the violinist Hugo Rignold). He often employed European musicians (the trumpeter Philippe Brun, the trombonist and arranger Leo Vauchant, and the saxophonist André Ekyan). In 1921-2 he included the American negro clarinetist 'Ed' Jenkins in his band, thus affording the first example of a mixed-race dance or jazz band in England.

Hylton made musical history on 10 February 1927 by taking down the music of *Shepherd of the Hills*, which was dictated to him over the newly opened transatlantic cable by the British composer Horatio Nicholls, who was then in New York. While motoring to Hayes, Middlesex, to record the new song the following morning Hylton was involved in a near-fatal car accident in fog. Hylton survived, dying nearly four decades later, 29 January 1965, in London.

For most of the two decades of his band-leading, Hylton set the standard for most of the others to follow, offering a variety act in the band itself, playing not only dance music, for which it is said Sir Edward Elgar [q.v.] and (Sir) William Walton wrote some arrangements, but modern concert music, 'hot' jazz, comedy routines, and even ballet music. He appeared in six royal command variety performances, and received the decorations of the Légion d'Honneur and Officier de l'Instruction Publique from the French Government.

Hylton was thrice married: first, in 1922, to Florence Parkinson (Ennis Parkes), the revue artist and composer, who died in 1957. This marriage was dissolved, as was Hylton's second marriage, to Friederike Kogler (died 1973). He married, thirdly, in 1963, Beverley Prowse, who, in 1973, married Sir Alex McKay. There were two daughters of the second marriage. He also had a son.

[*The Times*, 30 January 1965; private information.]   BRIAN RUST

HYLTON-FOSTER, SIR HARRY BRAUS-TYN HYLTON (1905-1965), Speaker of the House of Commons, was born in Ewell, Surrey, 10 April 1905, the only son of Harry Braustyn Hylton Hylton-Foster, barrister, and his wife, Margaret Isobel Hammond-Smith. He had one sister. He was educated at Eton and Magdalen College, Oxford, where he obtained a first class in jurisprudence in 1926. He was called to the bar by the Inner Temple in 1928 and in the same year was legal secretary to the first Viscount Finlay [q.v.] at the Permanent Court of International Justice. In the war of 1939-45 he served in the intelligence branch of the Royal Air Force Volunteer Reserve and was deputy judge advocate in North Africa, then in Italy. He was successively recorder of Richmond (1940-4), Huddersfield (1944-50), and Kingston upon Hull (1950-4). He was also chancellor of the dioceses of Ripon (1947-54) and Durham (1948-54). He took silk in 1947.

In 1945 Hylton-Foster failed to win a seat at Shipley; but in 1950 he was returned as Conservative member for York and held this seat again in 1951 and 1955. In 1959 he was returned for the safe Conservative seat of the Cities of London and Westminster.

In 1954 Hylton-Foster was knighted on becoming solicitor-general, and he appeared for the Crown in several important trials, one notable case being the Brighton conspiracy trial of 1958. In the courts, as in the House, he was lucid and quietly persuasive. In 1957 he was sworn of the Privy Council.

In the Parliament of 1959 Hylton-Foster's life was dramatically changed when he was elected Speaker of the House of Commons and sacrificed a legal career in which he seemed destined for the highest office. There was some controversy over this election: during preliminary conversations the prime minister had indicated that his party might support a Labour member as Speaker if the man were Sir Frank Soskice (later Lord Stow Hill), who indicated, however, that he did not wish to serve. The Labour Party felt that some other Labour men were worthy of consideration and on the day of the election made a protest. However, Hylton-Foster was unanimously elected and at once both sides rallied to him, for the protest had been about procedure and not about the man. In his speech of acceptance Hylton-Foster disclaimed the compliments which had been paid to him but claimed to love and revere the House: 'an institution so much greater than the sum of all of us of whom at any one time it is composed.'

The characteristics which had marked his work as solicitor-general—clarity, modesty, wit, and gentleness—Hylton-Foster now showed as Speaker. The days had gone when a prime minister could say of a Speaker 'We trembled at the rustle of his gown'. Discipline now had to be evoked rather than imposed. Hylton-Foster could be strict in his rulings, but he often gave them with a light touch and a happy turn of phrase which disarmed his critics. He ruled the House with urbanity and charm, always calm and unruffled, master of the understatement. He appeared to carry the burden of his office lightly, with the saving grace of not taking himself too seriously. Only those who knew him intimately realized how sensitive he was and how deeply he was hurt when a member charged him with being unfair.

In 1964 Hylton-Foster was unanimously re-elected Speaker by the new Parliament in which the Labour Party formed the Government. In the following year Parliament celebrated the 700th anniversary of Simon de Montfort's Parliament: Hylton-Foster was host to all the Speakers of the Commonwealth and in Westminster Hall presented the Queen with a congratulatory address on behalf of the Commons. He had returned to his duties before he was physically fit following an emergency hernia operation in the autumn of 1964. On 2 September 1965 he died suddenly after collapsing in a London street.

In 1931 he married Audrey Pellew Clifton Brown, daughter of Douglas Clifton Brown (later Viscount Ruffside, q.v.), who was Speaker in 1943-51. There were no children. She was created a life peeress in 1965. There is a portrait of Hylton-Foster in the Speaker's state rooms by Edward I. Halliday and at the Inner Temple by Sir William Coldstream.

[Private information; personal knowledge.]
                    MAYBRAY-KING

HYNDLEY, VISCOUNT (1883-1963), business man and administrator. [See HINDLEY, JOHN SCOTT.]

I

ILLING, VINCENT CHARLES (1890–1969), petroleum geologist, was born at Jullundur, Punjab, 24 September 1890, the younger son of Thomas Illing, a non-commissioned officer in the Indian Army Rifle Brigade, and his wife, Annie Payton. After an early education at army and other schools in India and Malta, he was thirteen when his father retired to Hartshill, near Nuneaton, Warwickshire. His mother, who came from a family long established in the area, was ambitious for him and sent him to King Edward VI Grammar School, Nuneaton. From there he won an open scholarship to Sidney Sussex College, Cambridge (1909). Under the inspiration of W. G. Fearnsides [q.v.], a fellow of the college, an early ambition to join the Indian Civil Service was overtaken by a fascination for geology. He was a keen athlete and soccer player, but an ankle injury ruled him out from university selection. He graduated with first class honours in parts i (1911) and ii (1912) of the natural sciences tripos, winning the Harkness scholarship in 1914, which allowed him to continue researches on the trilobite fauna of the Cambrian rocks at Hartshill, begun while mapping the area as an undergraduate. The results were published in the *Quarterly Journal of the Geological Society* in 1915, in a classic paper entitled 'The Paradoxidian Fauna of part of Stockingford Shales'.

In 1913 he was appointed demonstrator in applied geology at the Imperial College of Science and Technology, South Kensington, and was asked to develop a course in petroleum geology. Starting from scratch, he saw clearly that geology was an integral part of the problem of oil exploration and production, which was most important now that war was threatening. He built up the course gradually, reading and thinking much about oil occurrences and oilfields, particularly in America. He became lecturer in 1915, assistant professor in 1921, and professor of oil technology in 1935. He was an inspiring lecturer and teacher of geology with a flair for capturing the imagination of students. He seemed to have almost inexhaustible energy in the field. A good judge of character and ability, he took a great interest in his students and their subsequent careers.

After a short note in *Nature* (1917) on British oil shale prospects, his first paper on oil, 'The Search for Subterranean "oil-pools" in the British Isles' (*Geological Magazine*, 1919), was a reaction to the exaggerated ideas held by some politicians. It was a lucid scientific review, which was somewhat pessimistic about the prospect of the discovery of oilfields below the British land area.

In 1915 he made the first of his many visits to Trinidad. In 1920 he returned on a two-year leave of absence to Trinidad to map the Naparima region for a local oil company. The fieldwork was exceptionally arduous: he examined over 9,000 pits and 100 trenches using, it is believed for the first time, heavy minerals to correlate sediments.

After returning to Imperial College, during vacations he carried out geological studies in the Polish and Romanian oilfields and in the Pechelbronn oil-mine in France. These engendered an interest in maximum oil recovery and led to experiments on the processes of oil, gas, and water movements in porous media. This was his greatest contribution to petroleum geology. His main conclusions were published in 1933 in the *Journal of the Institution of Petroleum Technologists* with the title 'The Migration of Oil and Natural Gas'. In this article he introduced the concepts of primary and secondary migration, the former from the source rock into the reservoir rock, the latter concerning the movement and concentration of hydrocarbons within the reservoir rock. Other papers followed and in 1945 the American Association of Petroleum Geologists published his much quoted account of 'The Role of Stratigraphy in Oil Discovery' in its *Bulletin*.

In 1942 he gave an important address to the Geologists' Association entitled 'Geology Applied to Petroleum', a valuable synopsis and statement of his philosophy of geological education. He had early decided to combine academic and consulting work to ensure that his teaching had the authority of practical experience. At this he was remarkably successful, being closely associated with industry throughout his career. The financial stringency of his early days no doubt provided some of the motivation, but he had a lifelong conviction that knowledge and scientific discoveries should not be an end in themselves but should be co-ordinated between one discipline and another and applied to the welfare of mankind.

In the early 1920s he became a consultant to the Cowdray Group, and thereafter practised widely as a petroleum consultant, as well as being adviser to some mining ventures. He travelled extensively. For part of every summer from 1928 to 1939 he carried out geological surveys in Venezuela. This led to a long association with the Ultramar oil company and the discovery of their Mercedes oilfields at the start of the war of 1939–45. In 1946 he formed Petroleum Scientific Services Ltd. as a vehicle for his advisory services to companies in the Caribbean. As work expanded this was changed in 1950 to V. C. Illing & Partners. He also assisted in the formation of Seismograph Services Ltd. which flourished exceedingly. In 1947, at the request of the Government, he successfully arbitrated with the Mexican Government over compensation due to Mexican Eagle (owned by Shell) for their nationalized properties. For several years he advised the Nigerian Government on the future development of their oil resources, established by Shell and BP in partnership.

In 1958 he was appointed adviser to the Gas Council on gas exploration of land areas in Britain. With the American industry developing marine rigs to explore the Gulf of Mexico, the discovery of gas at Groningen in Holland rekindled his interest in the gas and oil potential of the North Sea basin. But he advised the Gas Council to leave exploration to the industry, purchasing any gas found. His last assignment was a search for underground reservoirs suitable for gas storage to meet peak demands. This required the drilling of many shallow boreholes, which revealed much new data on Cotswold geology.

Illing joined the Geological Society in 1913. He was awarded its Lyell Fund in 1918 and its Murchison medal in 1944. He served on its council in 1927-8. He was on the Institute of Petroleum's council from 1930-41 and 1947-8, was one of its vice-presidents in 1942-5 and in 1948. He was the first English geologist to be elected an honorary member of the American Association of Petroleum Geologists. He was elected FRS in 1945, honorary associate of the Royal School of Mines in 1951, and a fellow of Imperial College in 1958. On retirement in 1955 he was made emeritus professor of oil technology in the university of London.

Short in build and of quiet disposition, Illing was a man of great determination with an abundance of physical and mental energy and enthusiasm. A sincerely religious man, his scrupulous integrity and honesty won the confidence of all he advised and worked with. His career was characterized by enduring personal relationships. Brought up in austerity, he lived unostentatiously, mindful of the needs of others. He contributed generously in later years to charities and other organizations. He was fond of classical music and gardening, and enjoyed a happy family life. In 1919 he had married Frances Jean (died 1975), eldest daughter of Hugh Leslie, headmaster of a school in Perth. At the time she was teaching in London. They had one son and four daughters. In spite of a cancerous condition he never mentioned, he worked until a few weeks before his death at his home at Cheam, Surrey, 16 May 1969. V. C. Illing & Partners continues under the direction of his son. A posthumous portrait, which is in the possession of the family, was painted by Elva Blacker, and is reproduced in the Royal Society memoir.

[N. L. Falcon in *Biographical Memoirs of Fellows of the Royal Society*, vol. xvi, November 1970; private information; personal knowledge.]   N. L. FALCON

INGHAM, ALBERT EDWARD (1900-1967), mathematician, was born at Northampton 3 April 1900, the son of Albert Edward Ingham and his wife, Annie Gertrude Whitworth. He had an elder brother and three younger sisters. The father was a craftsman employed by a firm of boot and shoe manufacturers and was awarded a modest honorarium by his firm for the original idea of making shoes waterproof—the 'veldtschoen'. Ingham was educated in Northampton and at King Edward VI's Grammar School, Stafford, where he won the prizes open to a clever boy. In December 1917 he gained an entrance scholarship at Trinity College, Cambridge, going into residence in January 1919 after a few months in the army. In part ii of the mathematical tripos (1921) he was a wrangler with distinction and in 1923 won a Smith's prize and an 1851 senior exhibition.

In 1922, his first year of candidature, he was elected a prize fellow of Trinity, Cambridge. The electors saw in his dissertation a depth and maturity already marking him out as a leading scholar of his generation. He enjoyed four years of research (1922-6) without commitments to teach, spending some months in Göttingen. In 1926 he was appointed reader in the university of Leeds. In 1930, on the sudden and untimely death of F. P. Ramsey, he returned to Cambridge as fellow and director of studies at King's College, with a university lectureship. He was elected a fellow of the Royal Society in 1945. In 1953 (after two years as Cayley lecturer) he was appointed reader in mathematical analysis. He retired from regular college teaching in 1957.

Ingham was an outstanding member of the G. H. Hardy [q.v.] and J. E. Littlewood school of mathematical analysis, which from its beginnings in the first decade of the twentieth century attained world-wide fame in the third. The deep-lying and beautiful theorems which are Ingham's memorial have meaning only for the expert. They yield, however, information about elementary properties of the numbers 1, 2, 3, . . .; one illustration may interest the reader. In 1742 Christian Goldbach asserted that every even number is the sum of two prime numbers. Trials point overwhelmingly to the truth of the assertion. Nevertheless, to this day, no one has been able to *prove* it.

Searches for a rigorous proof lead to complex analysis of the Hardy-Littlewood pattern. In these endeavours mathematicians may be likened to mountaineers who establish camps at increasing heights striving to reach a summit.

Ingham was the embodiment of meticulous accuracy; nothing slipshod came from his hand, his tongue, or his pen. As a lecturer he won higher praise than did any other teacher in the faculty. Kingsmen whom he taught individually were grateful for the gentle patience and the standards of perfection towards which, to their lasting gain, he encouraged them. By nature shy, modest, and reserved, he was friendly and hospitable, and instinctively kind to anyone lonely or troubled. Like many shy people, he was quick to win the affection of children. His life was simple. He had no car and never possessed a radio, let alone a television set. He was an expert photographer. He enjoyed cricket, as a spectator when there was no opportunity for a game.

Ingham's thirty-two research papers, models of incisive reasoning, solved difficult problems. Moreover, they opened up avenues for other workers which are still being explored. Ingham's method and Ingham's theorem are quoted repeatedly in mathematical works. His one book, *The Distribution of Prime Numbers* (1932), is a classic. A major service to the community of mathematicians is his perspicacious and meticulous editing of the papers in number-theory in volume II of G. H. Hardy's *Collected Papers* (1967).

From 1932 Ingham had the devoted support of his wife Rose Marie ('Jane'), daughter of Canon Albert Darell Tupper-Carey. They were ideally complementary, Jane as quick in thought and action as 'A. E.' was deliberate. They had two sons, Michael and Stephen. Characteristically one of the best rooms in the house was turned into the 'workshop' for handicraft, indoor games, and other recreations of the family, friends, and pupils. Michael, an astronomer, followed his father in 1961 as a fellow of King's; later he moved to the Observatory at Oxford, and became a fellow of New College in 1968.

Every summer 'A. E.' and Jane packed their rucksacks and walked among mountains. It was on such a holiday that he died. On 6 September 1967, on a high path near Le Buet in Switzerland, his heart failed and he lived for only a few hours.

[J. C. Burkill in *Biographical Memoirs of Fellows of the Royal Society*, vol. xiv, 1968; King's College, Cambridge, *Annual Report*, 1967; personal knowledge.]

J. C. BURKILL

INGOLD, SIR CHRISTOPHER KELK (1893–1970), organic chemist, was born at Forest Gate, a London suburb, 28 October 1893, the son of William Kelk Ingold and his wife, Harriet Walker Newcomb. On account of his father's health, the family moved to Shanklin, Isle of Wight, whilst he was still an infant; his father died when Christopher was only five years old, and his sister Doris only two.

Ingold attended Sandown Grammar School and Hartley University College, now the university of Southampton; he obtained his B.Sc. honours degree as an external student of the university of London in October 1913. He then proceeded to Imperial College, London, to undertake research with Professor J. F. Thorpe, FRS; he left in 1918 to spend two years as a research chemist with the Cassel Cyanide Co., Glasgow, but returned to Imperial College as a lecturer in organic chemistry in 1920. From that year commenced the series of papers on organic chemical reactions, which secured for him the D.Sc. degree of the university of London in 1921, election to the Royal Society in 1924 at the early age of thirty, and the chair of organic chemistry at the university of Leeds, where he succeeded Professor J. B. Cohen, FRS, in 1924. In 1930 Ingold returned to London as professor of chemistry at University College, in the department then headed by Professor F. G. Donnan, FRS [q.v.], and in succession to Professor (Sir) Robert Robinson, FRS. When Donnan retired in 1937, Ingold became director of the laboratories, retaining this position until his retirement in 1961; thereafter he took an active part in the life of the department as professor emeritus and special lecturer. As a mark of affection and esteem, the new chemistry department at University College, London, was named the Ingold Laboratories on 25 September 1970.

Ingold was a chemical genius, an excellent physicist, and a talented mathematician; he published 744 papers, and he invented the domain of physical organic chemistry. The concepts, classifications, and terminology of theoretical organic chemistry, which he introduced and supported experimentally, provided a framework of principles that has opened a prospect and a programme for the unlimited unfolding of the theme 'how organic chemistry works', and has influenced profoundly the development of the whole of chemistry. A conspectus of the results achieved is given in his monumental book *Structure and Mechanism in Organic Chemistry* (1st edn. 1953, 2nd edn. 1969). Ingold's ideas, his system, and his nomenclature are now accepted and universally employed.

At Imperial College (1913–24), Ingold's

early work with Thorpe dealt with spiro-compounds, unsaturated and cyclic compounds derived from halogenated acyclic molecules, and polycyclic structures in relation to their homocyclic unsaturated isomers. Independent work was carried out on the synthesis of methanetriacetic acid, the reversibility of the Michael reaction and its relationship to proto-tropy, the mutarotation of sugars, the structure of benzene, and the additive formation of four-membered rings.

At Leeds (1924–30), investigations embraced electrophilic and nucleophilic addition reactions, elimination reactions, kinetics of ester hydrolyses, electrometric titration curves of dibasic acids, hydrolytic stability maxima, mobility, equilibrium, and mechanisms in proto-tropic and anionotropic systems, free radicals, molecular rearrangements, and electrophilic aromatic substitution. The latter work led to a prolonged and bitter controversy with Professor (Sir) Robert Robinson of the university of Manchester. The theoretical frame of induction and conjugation, as modes of polarization and polarizability, was set up (1927), and led to an electronic theory of organic reactions. The physical mechanism of mesomerism ($\equiv$ resonance) was recognized (1929) as a consequence of quantum theory and as a factor of molecular stability.

At University College, London, this work was extended and supplemented by kinetically controlled studies on the mechanisms (E1, E2) of elimination, the mechanisms (S_N1, S_N2, S_Ni) of nucleophilic (aliphatic) substitution at a saturated carbon atom and their stereochemical consequences, which led to solution of the forty-year-old mystery of the Walden inversion, the establishment of relative configuration (1937, 1950), of absolute configuration (1951), for the specification of which the Sequence Rule was devised (in association with Dr R. S. Cahn and later with Professor V. Prelog), the concepts of steric retardation and steric acceleration, and the mechanism of the Wagner rearrangement. Electrophilic additions to simple olefins, and electrophilic and nucleophilic additions to conjugated systems were further investigated. The Leeds work on ester hydrolysis was expanded to include esterification and led to the concepts of acyl-oxygen and alkyl-oxygen fission, and the kinetic recognition of six of the eight predicted mechanisms. Studies of the kinetics of aromatic C-nitrations showed these reactions to be electrophilic bimolecular substitutions (S_E2) involving the nitronium ion NO_2^+, which was identified cryoscopically and spectroscopically and isolated as the crystalline perchlorate; these studies led to work on N-nitration and O-nitration. Kinetic work was undertaken on

the mechanisms (S_E1, S_E2, S_Ei) of electrophilic (aliphatic) substitution at a saturated carbon atom and their stereo-chemical consequences, and on homolytic substitution at a saturated carbon atom. The mechanism of the benzidine and semidine rearrangements was kinetically elucidated. Three brilliant incursions were made into molecular spectroscopy on the ground state and first excited state of benzene and the first excited state of acetylene. Latterly (1953–65), a study was made in association with Professor Ronald Nyholm, FRS, of the mechanism and stereo-chemistry of the substitution reactions of octahedral cobalt(III) complexes.

At Imperial College, Ingold was friendly, helpful, purposeful, but remote. At Leeds, he became less remote, took up cricket, became an expert bird-watcher, and started rock-climbing. At University College, London, he became much less other-worldly; he took up motoring, kept up his bird-watching, became a keen mountaineer making climbs in North Wales, the Lake District, Skye, and the French Alps. After 1945 he spent much time on the rehabilitation of chemistry in France and Spain, and commenced to travel extensively. He motored alone (although over sixty years old) through Greece and Turkey, and once drove as deep as possible into the Sahara desert. Later, he took up fishing and (at the age of seventy-one) water-skiing. Ingold combined extraordinary imagination, insight, initiative, and ingenuity in his work, and determination with a dash of dare-devilry in his character. The rigorous and forceful way with which he dealt, in print, with opposition and criticism were in complete contrast to his personal kindness, patience, and courtesy.

The contributions of Ingold to chemistry were recognized by many honours and awards: the Meldola medal by the Royal Institute of Chemistry (1922); the Bakerian lecture (1938), the Davy medal (1946), and a Royal medal (1952) by the Royal Society; the Pedler lecture (1957), the Longstaff medal (1957), and the Faraday lecture and medal (1962) by the Chemical Society; the Paracelsus gold medal (1964) by the Swiss Chemical Society; and the Norris award (1965) by the American Chemical Society. He received the degree of D.Sc. *honoris causa* from the universities of Leeds, Sheffield, Southampton, Oxford, Dublin, Bologna, Paris, and Montpellier, from McMaster University and the National University of Ireland, and the degree of Ph.D. *honoris causa* from the university of Oslo. He held visiting lectureships at Stanford, Cornell, Notre Dame, Illinois, Kansas, Connecticut, Minnesota, and McMaster Universities, and a National Science Foundation fellowship at Vanderbilt University. He was a corresponding member of the Royal Academy of Sciences of Spain, an honorary counsellor for Higher Scientific Investigations in Spain, an honorary foreign member of the Weizmann Institute, Israel, of the New York Academy of Science, of the American Academy of Arts and Sciences, a fellow of the Royal Society, of the Royal Institute of Chemistry, of Imperial College, visiting professor at the university of Ibadan, Nigeria, and a foreign academician of the Bologna Academy of Science. He was president of the Chemical Society (1952-4), a member of the academic planning board of the university of East Anglia, and was knighted in 1958.

In 1923 Ingold married Edith Hilda Usherwood, Ph.D., D.Sc. (London), daughter of Thomas Scriven Usherwood, schoolmaster at St. Dunstan's College, Catford, and later at Christ's Hospital, Horsham, Sussex, of Church End, Finchley. He died at his home 12 Handel Close, Edgware, 8 December 1970, and was survived by his wife, his elder daughter Sylvia (a graduate in medicine), his son Keith, FRS associate director of the division of chemistry of the National Research Council of Canada, his younger daughter Dilys (a graduate in geography), and seven grandchildren.

[Charles W. Shoppee in *Biographical Memoirs of Fellows of the Royal Society*, vol. xviii, 1972.]   C. W. SHOPPEE

INGRAM, SIR BRUCE STIRLING (1877-1963), editor of the *Illustrated London News*, was born in London 5 May 1877, the second son of (Sir) William James Ingram, and grandson of Herbert Ingram [q.v.], who founded the publication, the world's first illustrated weekly newspaper, in 1842. Bruce Ingram was educated at Winchester and Trinity College, Oxford, where he took a third class honours degree in jurisprudence (1897). After leaving Oxford he was given some technical training with a lithographic printing firm but was soon serving his journalistic apprenticeship by editing, with the help of a secretary and an office boy, the *English Illustrated Magazine*, and by producing, for the *Illustrated London News*, a special supplement on the war in the Transvaal. He clearly impressed the directors with his journalistic potential, for when the editorship of the paper became vacant in 1900 he was offered the post, at first on a probationary basis.

As grandson of the founder Ingram may have been fortunately placed to have won so distinguished a position at the age of twenty-two, but he was quick to justify the family's confidence and to demonstrate his remarkable ability to adapt an essentially Victorian publication to respond to the rapid and at times almost revolutionary changes of the twentieth century without sensationalism and without discarding its tradition and authority. He took over at a difficult time. There were strong competitors in the field, and the recent development of the photographic half-tone gave daily newspapers the opportunity of carrying regular up-to-date illustrations. For the first time the daily press could challenge the illustrated weeklies, and daily picture papers such as the *Graphic* and *Daily Mail*, which had been launched in the last decade of the nineteenth century, became a real threat to their continued existence. Ingram responded to the challenge by concentrating on the quality of printing, reproduction, and paper, exposing the weaknesses of the high-speed newsprint processes which the dailies had to use. He adapted the slow and expensive Rembrandt intaglio for rapid printing and after much patient experiment was able to introduce the photogravure process. He had a fine chance of emphasizing his point about the value of quality on the death of Queen Victoria. The memorial issues produced to mark the end of the reign, and of an era, were strikingly successful, and have since become valuable as collector's items. They also provided sufficient reassurance for the company that the young member of the family was capable of upholding the traditions of his grandfather. His appointment was confirmed, and within a few years he was also made editor of the *Sketch*.

When war broke out in 1914 Ingram was a lieutenant in the East Kent Yeomanry. From 1916 until the end of the war he served in the Royal Garrison Artillery on the French front, being promoted to the rank of captain and awarded the Military Cross (1917), the OBE (military, 1918), and three times mentioned in dispatches. He was able throughout the war to keep in reasonably close contact with his office in London, and thus to supervise the paper's coverage of the war, which extended to an additional weekly supplement history of the war, published on Wednesdays, as well as the normal weekly edition, published on Fridays. Because of its fairness and the high quality of its coverage of these events the *Illustrated London News* was used by the Government to help make known abroad the extent of Britain's, and the Commonwealth's, war effort. The same compliment was paid to the publication in the war of 1939-45 when Ingram, still its editor but now too old for active service, was more directly involved in the day-to-day production. During this war he never missed a day at the office, even at the height of the blitz (when a bomb destroyed most of the paper's archives).

He was always an active editor, and those who worked with him recall that even in his eighties he would crawl around the floor of his editorial office laying out the photographs for each weekly issue. He was astute in his judgement of writers—he chose G. K. Chesterton [q.v.] in 1905 to write the weekly Notebook feature, and on his death in 1936 picked the young (Sir) Arthur Bryant to succeed him. Inevitably some parts of the paper reflected some of his prejudices: he was suspicious of modern art, so Picasso was ignored; and he was tone deaf, so music tended to be neglected. But such eccentricities did not tarnish his reputation as an editor, which rested securely on his achievements in communicating, over a period of sixty-three years, the actuality and atmosphere of Britain, its character, temper, and achievements, in a style that has not been equalled.

Two of Ingram's particular interests throughout his life were archaeology and the collecting of pictures. He had, as a youth, twice visited Egypt, and these tours stimulated a lifelong curiosity in archaeology that was reflected in the regular reports on the subject which have always been a feature of the *Illustrated London News*. When he was twenty Ingram began to collect illuminated manuscripts, but after selling his collection in 1936 he concentrated his attention on collecting paintings and drawings, particularly on marine subjects. He published, in 1936, *Three Sea Journals of Stuart Times*, based on a study of naval manuscripts and journals, and from this developed his main preoccupation as a collector. Pre-eminent among his large collection were the works of the Dutch marine artists Willem van de Velde the Elder and the Younger (he contributed a note on their drawings to the catalogue of an exhibition held in 1937), 700 of which were presented to the National Maritime Museum to mark his eightieth birthday; but if the Dutch and Flemish schools remained his favourites Ingram also collected many representative works by artists less well known, and the largest part of the collection, which at one time consisted of more than 5,000 works, was devoted to the English schools. Among other museums that benefited from his collection were the Fitzwilliam at Cambridge, the Birmingham Art Gallery, and the Royal Scottish Museum. During the war Ingram commissioned, and subsequently presented to the nation, the Battle of Britain roll of honour in the Royal Air Force chapel in Westminster Abbey.

As a collector Ingram was exceptionally generous in his attitude to lending, and many tributes were paid both to his readiness to deprive himself of large parts of his collection so that others could see and enjoy them in public exhibitions, and to the hospitality he showed towards other collectors and students at his home, in Great Pednor, Buckinghamshire. He was honorary keeper of drawings at the Fitzwilliam Museum, vice-president of the Society for Nautical Research, vice-president of the Navy Records Society, and honorary adviser on pictures and drawings to the National Maritime Museum.

As well as editor of the *Illustrated London News* from 1900 to 1963, and of the *Sketch* from 1905 to 1946, Ingram was chairman of the Illustrated London News and Sketch Ltd., director of Illustrated Sporting and Dramatic News Ltd., and president of Illustrated Newspapers Ltd. He was knighted in 1950 and awarded the Legion of Honour by the French Government in the same year, and given the honorary degree of D.Litt. by Oxford University in 1960. He married, in 1904, Amy, daughter of John Foy, who died in 1947, and secondly Lily, daughter of Sydney Grundy, who died in 1962. There was one daughter of the first marriage. Ingram died at Great Pednor Manor, Buckinghamshire, 8 January 1963.

[*The Times*, 9 January 1963; Sir Arthur Bryant, 'Our Notebook', *Illustrated London News*, 2 January 1960; Luke Herrmann and Michael Robinson, 'Sir Bruce Ingram as a Collector of Drawings', *Burlington Magazine*, May, 1963; private information; personal knowledge.]   JAMES BISHOP

IRELAND, JOHN NICHOLSON (1879–1962), composer, organist, and pianist, youngest child of Alexander and Annie Ireland [qq.v.], was born at Inglewood, Dunham Massey in the sub-district of Altrincham, Cheshire, 13 August 1879. Both parents were well known in literary circles, his father being editor and part-owner of the *Manchester Examiner* and his mother the biographer of Jane Welsh Carlyle. Owing to his mother's delicate health he was sent as a boarder to a dameschool in Bowdon and later to Leeds Grammar School. At fourteen he entered the Royal College of Music, London, studying piano with Frederic Cliffe and organ with Sir Walter Parratt [q.v.]. A year later both his parents died, but he was able to continue his musical studies through a small allowance. At sixteen he was the youngest student to be awarded a fellowship of the Royal College of Organists, and a year later he was appointed assistant organist and choirmaster of Holy Trinity church, Sloane Street. In 1897 he received a composition scholarship and studied with (Sir) Charles Stanford [q.v.] until 1901. In 1908 he was made a Mus.B. of Durham University which in 1932 conferred on him an honorary doctorate.

In 1904 Ireland was appointed organist and choirmaster of St. Luke's, Chelsea, a post he held for twenty-two years, during which time he composed the greater part of his church music. In 1909 his Phantasy Trio in A minor won the second prize in W. W. Cobbett's chamber music competition and the following year his Violin Sonata in D minor was given first prize out of 134 works submitted from all over the world. It was, however, with his second Violin Sonata (1917) that he achieved full recognition, and he 'awoke one morning to find himself famous'. Meanwhile he had become acquainted with the writings of Arthur Machen, whose work was characterized by mystery, romanticism, and the macabre. Ireland had always been attracted by the prehistoric atmosphere and relics of the remoter parts of the Sussex Downs and Channel Islands, and the influence of Machen can be heard in the individual musical style of the piano suite *Decorations* (1913) and the orchestral *The Forgotten Rite* (1913).

In 1923 Ireland was appointed professor of composition by the Royal College of Music and examiner for the Associated Board of the Royal Schools of Music, and in the following year the academic distinctions FRCM and honorary RAM were given him. The next fifteen years were his most prolific as a composer. During this period he wrote his Cello Sonata and Piano Sonatina, performed at festivals of the International Society for Contemporary Music in 1924 and 1929, Piano Concerto in E flat (1930), *Legend*, for piano and orchestra (1933), *A London Overture* (1936), and the choral work *These Things Shall Be*, commissioned by the BBC for the coronation of King George VI in 1937, together with the greater part of his large and important contribution to song and piano music.

Retiring from his professorial duties at the Royal College in 1939—his composition pupils included E. J. Moeran [q.v.], Alan Bush, Humphrey Searle, Benjamin Britten, and Geoffrey Bush—he planned to spend the rest of his life in Guernsey, but the German occupation of the Channel Islands in 1940 forced him to return to England. However, his stay in Guernsey had given him the inspiration for one of his finest piano works, the Island Sequence, *Sarnia* (1941). During the war years he lived outside London and, still active as a composer, wrote the Epic March (1942) and after the war the Overture *Satyricon* (1946) and music for the film *The Overlanders* (1947). In his final decade he left the studio in Gunter Grove, Chelsea, which had been his home for almost the whole of his creative life, and retired to Rock Mill, a converted windmill looking out over the South Downs and Chanctonbury Ring. His failing eyesight did not permit much creative work, but his friend Mrs Norah Kirby

was at hand to relieve him of business worries and cope with the many friends and young music students who were eager to visit him. Shortly after his eightieth birthday a John Ireland Society was formed which has done much to propagate his music both in public concerts and on gramophone records, and which has sponsored the publication of some of his early chamber music.

Ireland described himself as 'England's slowest and most laborious composer' and certainly his output of major works was comparatively small. He never wrote a symphony, but neither did Debussy or Ravel, two elder contemporaries whose music he greatly admired, and who influenced his individual pianistic style. Even in his songs and piano music he wrote with great deliberation and self-criticism, and never let a work be published until he was satisfied with it in every detail. As a song-writer the literary background he inherited from his parents found full and prolific expression in his setting of English poets from Shakespeare and Blake to Masefield, Housman, Thomas Hardy, and many other poets of the present century. Many years ago the music critic Edwin Evans summed up the quality inherent in his music as 'a scrupulous artistic sincerity'.

Friendship was an essential ingredient of his life, and he valued the company of his intimate friends, whom he preferred to meet individually. In 1927 he married Dorothy Phillips, a piano student at the Royal College of Music, but the marriage was never consummated and was soon annulled.

Ireland died 12 June 1962 at Rock Mill and was buried at Shipley, Sussex, the headstone on his grave being of prehistoric sarsen stone. There is a memorial window to him in the musicians' chapel of the Church of the Holy Sepulchre, Holborn, and a plaque at his birthplace. A portrait by Arnold Mason is privately owned; the National Portrait Gallery has one by G. Roddon. A portrait bust by Konstam is privately owned.

[John Longmire, *John Ireland: Portrait of a Friend*, 1969; Appreciation and Biographical Sketch in *Catalogue of Works* compiled by Norah Kirby, 1968; *Cobbett's Cyclopedic Survey of Chamber Music*, 2nd edn., 1963; private information; personal knowledge.]

JULIAN HERBAGE

IRONSIDE, ROBIN CUNLIFFE (1912–1965), painter and writer, was born 10 July 1912 in London, the elder son of Reginald William Ironside, medical doctor, and his wife, Phyllis Laetitia, daughter of Sir (Robert) Ellis Cunliffe, solicitor to the Board of Trade, who later married A. R. Williamson, stockbroker. He was educated at Bradfield and the Courtauld Institute. In 1937 he was appointed assistant keeper at the Tate Gallery. In 1946 he resigned in order to devote himself to painting, writing about painters, and occasional stage design. While at the Tate he served as assistant secretary (1938–45) to the Contemporary Art Society. Of his introductions to books, *Wilson Steer* was published in 1943, while he was still at the Tate. Other works were written in his years of independence: *Pre-Raphaelite Painters*, *British Painting since 1939*, and *David Jones* (all 1948). He translated from the French E. and J. de Goncourts' *French XVIII Century Painters* (1948). His last writings were *Andrea del Sarto* (1965) and 'Van Eyck' (both for the *Old Master Drawings* series). The latter was unfinished at the time of his death.

His contributions to *Horizon* in the 1940s included articles on 'Burne-Jones and Gustave Moreau' (June 1940), 'The Art Criticism of Ruskin' (July 1943), and 'Comments on an Exhibition of English Drawings'—a circulating exhibition (September 1944). As an art historian and critic he combined a complete independence of accepted opinions with a rare suavity and precision of style. In particular he rejected the respect and admiration accorded to the New English Art Club, the focus of the most serious British painting, disliking its infiltration by the innovations of the Impressionists and other major Continental artists. He believed that what he termed the Club's 'crude corporate vigour', combined with the scandal of the Oscar Wilde trials and the early death of Aubrey Beardsley [qq.v.], had killed the imaginative tradition which had derived from William Blake and Samuel Palmer and been carried on by Rosetti and Burne-Jones [qq.v.], a tradition which 'has been kept flickering in England ever since the end of the eighteenth century, sometimes with a wild, always with an uneasy light, by a succession of gifted eccentrics' ('Comments on an Exhibition of English Drawings'). Ironside, unable to type, wrote with a stylish hand.

Original, highly informed, and elegantly presented as are his writings, it is rather for his paintings that he will eventually be accorded the recognition he deserves. At present, remote from all prevailing 'movements', they have suffered almost total neglect outside a small circle of ardent admirers. Ironside's paintings, whether in oils or gouache, are mainly of esoteric subjects—for example, 'Rose being offered in a Coniferous Wood', and 'Musical Performance by Patients in a Condition of Hypomania'. They are highly complex in colour and composition, and are skilfully executed. Ironside's rejection of generally accepted attitudes extended far beyond those of the relatively traditional New English school. His convictions were the precise opposite of those held by most of his own and the immediately preceding generation. There was, in fact, scarcely one of the ideas, accepted almost without question by those who regarded themselves as representative of what was most progressive, which he did not disregard in his practice as a painter, question searchingly in his writings, and often ridicule in his talk. He rejected, for instance, the belief that ' "formal relationships", "pattern", "structure", etc., have any absolute value in a picture as though it had practical functions requiring firmness or commodity', or that colour was 'an abstract element to be praised or criticized for its own sake as one would the colour variations of a wallpaper or a carpet' (*Horizon*, June 1940). He dismissed 'appeals to artists to cultivate a sense of paint, a sympathy with the material in which they are working' as 'appeals for the cultivation of affinities with nothing. Since paint, or stone, yields unquestioningly to the most diverse treatment, there can be no nicety of relation requiring establishment between them and the artist' ('Comments on an Exhibition of English Drawings'). A conception of the nature of the arts as appealing to faculties that could be isolated from the hopes and frustrations of living he stigmatized as an imposture ('The Art Criticism of Ruskin', *Horizon*, July 1943). Ironside took nothing for granted and at an early age had evolved his highly personal style of painting and his attitude towards the arts.

His achievements as a painter are the more remarkable in view of his total lack of formal training. They are remarkable too, for the conditions under which a number of his paintings were created. At the end of a long working day at the Tate he would dine out, conduct himself with a leisurely calm, and then sit down to paint (or write) as though midnight were the dawn of a working day, until his strength failed him. Moreover, his constitution was frail and he neglected his health.

He first exhibited in 1944 at the Redfern Gallery, London, with his brother Christopher and others; later at the Hanover Gallery, at the Arthur Jeffries Gallery, London, and at Durlacher's, New York. He is represented at the Tate Gallery, the Boston Museum, and the Leicester Art Gallery. In spite of his accomplishments as painter and writer he would have been unable to maintain himself after leaving the Tate without working for the theatre. He made designs for *Der Rosenkavalier* (Covent Garden, 1948), *Silvia* (Covent Garden, 1952), *A Midsummer Night's Dream* (Edinburgh Festival, 1954), and *La Sylphide* (Sadler's Wells, 1960), the last three in collaboration with his brother Christopher, with whom he also designed medals and coins, and a huge royal coat of arms as a centrepiece of Whitehall's coronation decorations—a rococo explosion of gilded aluminium, which is preserved in Australia.

Ironside was unmarried. He died in London 2 November 1965, and a retrospective exhibition was held the following year at the New Art Centre.

[Sir John Rothenstein, 'Robin Ironside', *London Magazine*, October, 1966; personal knowledge.]   JOHN ROTHENSTEIN

ISAACS, ALICK (1921-1967), medical scientist, was born in Glasgow 17 July 1921, the eldest in the family of three sons and one daughter of Louis Isaacs, shopkeeper, of Glasgow, and his wife, Rosine, daughter of Jacob Lion, leather merchant, of London. The surname 'Isaacs' was bestowed on his grandfather, Barnet Galinsky, when he arrived in England in the 1880s, having emigrated from Lithuania. Alick's mother, who trained as a schoolteacher, came from a more substantial Jewish family which had produced two lord mayors of London. His childhood was a happy one; among his early hobbies were music and chess, which became lifelong interests. At Pollokshields Secondary School, where he was a popular pupil, he studied physics and chemistry but not biology. In 1939 he entered the faculty of medicine at Glasgow University. Here he proved an unusually bright student and won a number of prizes and medals. In 1944 he obtained his MB and Ch.B.

After a year of house appointments Isaacs decided that clinical medicine was not his *métier* and moved with a scholarship to the department of bacteriology under Professor Carl Browning. Here his early work was on streptococci, and this was impressive enough for him to be awarded in 1947 a Medical Research Council studentship under Professor C. H. Stuart-Harris in the university of Sheffield. Here began his work on influenza which became his main preoccupation for the rest of his life. In 1948 he received a Rockefeller travelling fellowship and went to work under (Sir) F. Macfarlane Burnet in Melbourne; there he remained for two years.

He soon struck out on lines of his own, being fascinated by the 'interference phenomenon'. It had been known for some time that one virus, live or inactivated, had some ability to suppress the growth in a cell of another virus, even though it was unrelated to the first. Working with Margaret Edney, he produced a series of papers analysing the interference between active and inactive influenza viruses in the allantoic cavities of developing

hens' eggs. It was shown that the interference did not concern the uptake of virus by the cell but was effective in the cell's interior.

Isaacs returned to England in 1951 to work at the National Institute for Medical Research at Mill Hill; here the work on interference continued. With a visiting worker, Dr J. Lindenmann from Zurich, he carried out experiments which had far-reaching results. It appeared that when an interfering experiment had been carried out *in vitro*, there was considerable interfering activity in the fluids surrounding the treated tissues; it seemed that these had been stimulated to produce fresh interfering activity. Isaacs and Lindenmann named the active agent 'interferon'. An entirely novel defence mechanism against viruses had been discovered, valuable because it was directed against viruses of many kinds and not only against that which had elicited it. Interferon was soon being studied by workers in Britain and abroad and its mechanism was coming to light. A number of international symposia have been devoted to its study.

There were high hopes that there was here a natural chemotherapeutic agent, active against viruses and with great potentialities in medicine. These have not yet materialized, but success may come when the substance can be made in larger quantity. Be that as it may, Isaacs discovered something of fundamental importance in biology, not necessarily related only to defence against viruses.

During this productive period of work on interferon Isaacs was also busy with the work of the World Influenza Centre under the World Health Organization. This had the duty of comparing influenza strains from all over the world and monitoring the changes which are continually taking place in the antigenic composition of the virus. In 1955 Isaacs's work on influenza gained him an MD with honours at Glasgow University. In 1962 he received an honorary MD from the Catholic University of Louvain in Belgium and he was elected FRS in 1966.

All Isaacs's work showed originality; he was a pioneer, not a follower of current trends. On a personal level he had a great capacity for friendship and was commonly full of *joie de vivre*. However, during his later years he suffered from a number of episodes of intense depression. He was nevertheless appointed as head of the virus division at Mill Hill in 1961; but the episodes recurred and on 26 January 1967 he died in University College Hospital, London, of a recurrence of intracranial haemorrhage.

He was married in Melbourne in 1949 to Susanna Gordon, a paediatrician and child psychiatrist, daughter of Herbert James Foss, pianist and composer: they had become engaged during his time in Sheffield. They had twin sons and one daughter.

[Sir Christopher Andrewes in *Biographical Memoirs of Fellows of the Royal Society*, vol. xiii, 1967; private information; personal knowledge.]   C. H. ANDREWES

ISITT, DAME ADELINE GENÉE- (1878-1970), ballet dancer. [See GENÉE.]

ISMAY, HASTINGS LIONEL, BARON ISMAY (1887-1965), general, was born at Naini Tal, India, 21 June 1887, younger son of (Sir) Stanley Ismay, a member of the viceroy's legislative council and later chief judge of the Mysore Court, by his wife, Beatrice Ellen, daughter of Colonel Hastings Read. He was educated at Charterhouse and the Royal Military College, Sandhurst. Entering the Indian Army in 1905, he was posted in 1907 to the 21st Prince Albert Victor's Own Cavalry, acquiring the Frontier medal and clasp and becoming adjutant of his regiment. But he felt the need to gain wider military experience, and was thus by a quirk of fate forestalled from serving on any of the main fronts during the war of 1914-18, for he was seconded to the King's African Rifles as captain, and landed at Berbera 9 August 1914; in 1917-19 he was with the Somaliland Indian Contingent, and with the newly formed Camel Corps in 1919-20. All efforts to return to his regiment failed, and he remained in Somaliland until 1920, distinguishing himself in operations against 'the mad Mullah'; he was appointed to the DSO and promoted major, having been temporary lieutenant-colonel in 1919.

Granted a year's leave on medical grounds, he met and married in 1921 Laura Kathleen (died 1978), only daughter of Henry Gordon Clegg, of Wormington Grange, Gloucestershire; they had three daughters. His qualities, already recognized, then took him to the Staff College, Quetta, and they were confirmed in the passing-out report of his commandant, who declared: 'I consider this officer one of the two best, if not the best, of the students who have passed through my hands.' Thereafter Ismay was lost to regimental soldiering; in 1923 he spent a brief period on the staff at Army HQ India, and in 1924 was nominated to the vacancy reserved for an Indian Army officer at the new RAF Staff College, Andover. At the end of 1925 he was appointed assistant secretary to the Committee of Imperial Defence under Sir Maurice (later Lord) Hankey [q.v.].

Five years at the Committee of Imperial Defence, spent particularly in preparing the substratum of what became the War Book,

gave Ismay an exceptional insight into the ways of Whitehall. When his appointment ended in December 1930 his ability had already marked him as potential successor to Hankey, and the recognition of it in the New Year's honours list of 1931 created a problem of protocol: by some failure of communications he was gazetted as both CB in the civil list and CIE in the India Office list: Ismay opted for the former.

The India Office wished to create a Committee of Imperial Defence in Delhi, and Ismay was now pressed to accompany the new viceroy, Lord Willingdon [q.v.], as military secretary with the organization of an Indian Committee of Imperial Defence—a scheme which eventually proved abortive—among his duties. He was promoted colonel, and although he hoped for command of a cavalry regiment, in 1931 he obediently went east, where he enjoyed a privileged view of the Raj in action. Nevertheless, those two years were a parenthesis and hardly equipped him for the responsibilities, which he took up on his return to the War Office in 1933, of GSO 1 Intelligence Eastern Europe.

Shortly before he left India, Ismay's polo pony slipped while he was playing in the Prince of Wales's tournament; concussion deafened his left ear, but he never allowed this disability to impede a long life of talk and conference. After his return to London there occurred a distressing sequence of deaths in his wife's family, which, however, brought her the inheritance of Wormington and substantial resources. Since Ismay was independent of mind, although a man of devoted loyalties, this independence of means merely increased his value as an objective adviser freed from the restrictions of an officer *de carrière*.

In 1936 Ismay moved into his predestined place as deputy secretary to Hankey at the Committee of Imperial Defence. The succession was not inevitable, for the Treasury and the Foreign Office were eager to take over the Cabinet Office, and it was not without a struggle that the secretaryship of the CID (although not the rest of Hankey's empire) was handed over to Ismay after Hankey's retirement in 1938. Inadequacies of government policy made the months before and immediately after the outbreak of war in 1939 the most frustrating of his life. But in April 1940 Neville Chamberlain appointed (Sir) Winston Churchill as chairman of the Ministerial Co-ordinating Committee, responsible for guiding and directing the chiefs of staff, assisted by 'a suitable central staff under a senior staff officer, who would be an additional member of the chiefs of staff committee'. The man he chose was Ismay, who had been promoted major-general in 1939.

Churchill planned to make a 'garden suburb' by assembling a central staff of his own henchmen. Ismay's first personal contribution to the war effort was to stonewall over this dubious proposal. In consequence, when Churchill became prime minister and minister of defence in May 1940, retaining Ismay as his chief staff officer, the military secretariat which Ismay evolved developed into a machine of unsurpassed quality because those whom he chose to man it—(Sir) Leslie Hollis [q.v.], (Sir) Ian Jacob, and others who serviced the war administration—were apt for the task and not a prime minister's idiosyncratic miscellany. Moreover, drawn as they were from the staff of the Committee of Imperial Defence or elsewhere in Whitehall, they provided continuity as well as competence.

For the remainder of the war, Ismay's position was unique: none of the other belligerents, neither President Roosevelt's Harry Hopkins, nor Hitler's adjutants, provided an equivalent. Hundreds of Churchill's famous minutes and the replies to them were personally handled by Ismay, who commanded the prime minister's absolute trust. He was the essential link with the chiefs of staff, on whose committee he sat without executive powers of embarrassment. Difficult Allies respected him as much as did difficult colleagues. On delicate missions abroad, amid growing responsibilities for the most secret matters, from 1940 to 1945 Ismay endured strains more continuous than any battle-commander, and sometimes equally intense. Not even Sir Alan Brooke (later Viscount Alanbrooke, q.v.) was so exposed to the exigencies and exhaustion of intimate work with Churchill by day and by night. Shrewd, resilient, accessible, emollient in diplomacy but of an unbreachable integrity, Ismay created a role as entrepreneur which, in its range and value, surpassed that of his master Hankey in the previous war. As Ismay himself put it, 'I spent the whole war in the middle of the web.' He became lieutenant-general in 1942 and full general in 1944, and Churchill's 'resignation honours' gave his services the rather curious recognition of his appointment as CH. The next prime minister was not satisfied, and Clement (later Earl) Attlee's final victory list in June 1946 appointed Ismay GCB, and in the following New Year's honours he was created a baron.

Peace did not allow Ismay to 'put up his bright sword'. He retired from the army in December 1946, after largely reorganizing the defence system and setting up the Ministry of Defence. By the following spring he was back in India, as chief of the viceroy's staff and Lord Mountbatten's right-hand man in the days of the 'great divide'. He went there at his own suggestion, although he was anguished by the fear that the coming abandonment of India would be a betrayal of the guardianship to which he and his father had been dedicated, and as his country had also once seemed to be. He was by then a tired man, driven by a sense of duty; but again his performance as a catalyst, a tranquillizer, and a constructive negotiator was exemplary. Trusted by all parties, by his calmness and accumulated wisdom he balanced the mercurial energy of Mountbatten, who more than once dispatched him to London to conduct critical negotiations. Ismay took no pride in the clinical act of partition, although he accepted its draconian necessity, and he declined the grand cross of the Star of India, content merely with the order of release from what he described as the most distasteful assignment of his career.

In the event there was no release. He had hardly been back in England a few weeks when—early in 1948—Attlee appointed him as chairman of the council for the Festival of Britain—a job which, as Ismay himself said, called for strategic planning no less difficult than a military campaign. Shortly after its successful conclusion in September 1951 Churchill returned to power and, by a decision only less idiosyncratic than his subsequent summons of Lord Alexander of Tunis [q.v.] to the Ministry of Defence, made Ismay secretary of state for Commonwealth Relations. In practice the arrangement proved profitable, since Churchill drew heavily on Ismay's own experience of defence matters. It was a natural consequence when, only six months later, Ismay was chosen to be the first secretary-general of NATO and transferred to Paris.

Once more 'the man with the oil-can' went unwillingly; his achievement was brilliant and historic, for all his gifts—clarity of mind, winning charm, intellectual and social dexterity, combined with an unequalled *tact des choses possibles* and a keen appreciation of good press and public relations—were required and applied in the fusion of fourteen nations for a common, self-defensive end. When he retired in April 1957, in his seventieth year, international acclaim recognized his unsparing efforts in providing NATO with an ordered structure and harmony of purpose which could hardly have been anticipated when he took office. He was immediately appointed KG. Other honours had already been bestowed: he was sworn of the Privy Council in 1951, and received honorary degrees from Queen's University, Belfast, Bristol, and Cambridge. He was chairman of the National Institute for the Blind in 1946-52, and president from 1952, as well as being director of various companies and schools, and a deputy-lieutenant for Gloucestershire from 1950.

His retirement was marred by ill health, but in 1960 he was able to publish his self-effacing *Memoirs*. He had already assisted Churchill with *The Second World War* (1948-53). 'Pug' to all the world, he was the personification of honesty, loyalty, and human warmth, with an irresistible smile and that inner core of steel which made his presence at the heart of affairs so effective. An unashamed *bon viveur*, who also enjoyed racing and polo, tennis, and bridge, he nevertheless believed that the best thing in life is to seek to do the State some service. He died 17 December 1965 at Wormington Grange.

Portraits by Anthony Devas, and Allan Gwynne-Jones (1959), and a drawing by Augustus John, are in the possession of the family. A head-and-shoulders study for the full portrait of Ismay in Garter robes, also by Gwynne-Jones (1958), is in the National Portrait Gallery. Cheltenham town hall has a portrait (*c*.1918) by Mark Birley.

[Sir Ronald Wingate, *Lord Ismay*, 1970; Stephen Roskill, *Hankey, Man of Secrets*, 3 vols. 1970-4; Sir Winston Churchill, *The Second World War*, 6 vols. 1948-53; *The Memoirs of Lord Ismay*, 1960; *The Times*, 20 December 1965; private information.]

RONALD LEWIN

IVEAGH, COUNTESS OF (1881-1966), philanthropist. [See under GUINNESS, RUPERT EDWARD CECIL LEE.]

IVEAGH, second EARL OF (1874-1967), philanthropist. [See GUINNESS, RUPERT EDWARD CECIL LEE.]

J

JACKSON, Sir BARRY VINCENT (1879-1961), theatre director, was born at Northfield, a Birmingham suburb then in the county of Worcester, 6 September 1879, the second son and the youngest child by ten years of George Jackson, provision merchant, and his wife, Jane Spreadborough. His father, founder of the Maypole Dairies, was a wealthy man who loved the arts; he named his younger boy after the actor Barry Sullivan [q.v.]. Unusually for that time, Barry Jackson was encouraged to go to the play; he never forgot his earliest experiences in Birmingham, particularly Shakespeare by the company of (Sir) Frank Benson [q.v.] and by such artists as Wilson Barrett [q.v.], Ada Rehan, and Hermann Vezin [q.v.]. Even before going to a preparatory school, he was taken abroad; later, except for eighteen months in Geneva, studying French and the theatre when he was sixteen, he was educated entirely by a tutor. In adolescence he began to paint; but his father wished him to be an architect. For five years he worked in a Birmingham office until he decided at twenty-three that this was not his vocation.

Thenceforward his life was in the theatre. In 1907 he and several of his friends, notably two young insurance officials, H. S. Milligan and a tall, black-haired youth, John Drinkwater [q.v.], then beginning to write poetry, founded the Pilgrim Players. From the work of this amateur company which within five years presented twenty-eight plays of literary and aesthetic worth, there rose in February 1913 the Birmingham Repertory Theatre, later among the most honoured institutions of its kind in Britain; one intended, in Jackson's words, 'to serve an art instead of making that art serve a commercial purpose'.

After more than three years in planning, the Repertory took only four months to build. Once the site behind New Street Station had been secured in June 1912 and the plans had been completed that October, Jackson's life and the story of his theatre would be inextricably linked. In February 1913 the Repertory Company opened, with *Twelfth Night*, in the house—holding 464 people and called in a Drinkwater poem 'the captive image of a dream'—that would be used for over fifty years; a building ahead of its time, its auditorium descending to the stage in sharply raked steps. The money was Jackson's; he sent off the première by reading, 'rather bashfully', the rhymed iambics of Drinkwater's prologue and its often-quoted phrase, 'We have the challenge of the mighty line; / God grant us grace to give the countersign.'

A grey-eyed, urbane man, six feet tall and a conspicuous figure at any gathering, Jackson seemed, outwardly, to change little during his life. Although only a moderate actor (and he gave this up after the first Repertory years), he was always naturally authoritative. In those early days he would sometimes direct the play or design the sets. The programme he chose had an uncommon range; he saw his theatre not as a West End annexe but as 'a revolving mirror of the stage'. Birmingham, where some people spoke slightingly of 'a rich man's toy', responded sluggishly. Jackson, to begin with, was uncompromising; although it was the period of the theatre theatrical, he had no orchestra at the Repertory and even banned curtain-calls. Slowly the theatre did collect a following; when, mid way through the war, Jackson was commissioned in the navy, Drinkwater carried on the work, and his own *Abraham Lincoln* (Birmingham, 1918) was the first of many Repertory plays to reach London (1919). On Jackson's return his life again became inseparable from the changes and chances in Station Street. He saw such a triumph as the opera *The Immortal Hour* (1921) by Rutland Boughton [q.v.], which he presented later in London (1922); and in 1923 there arrived the famous production of the pentateuch *Back to Methuselah* by G. B. Shaw [q.v.], directed by H. K. Ayliff, which established a lasting friendship between dramatist and manager. Earlier, Jackson had experimented with the then radical idea of Shakespeare in modern dress by presenting *Cymbeline* (1923).

Birmingham remained oddly aloof. At length, among startled protests, Jackson—who for all his urbanity could be resolute—closed the theatre until an audience was guaranteed. Meanwhile, he devoted himself to London and to the presentation of *The Farmer's Wife* (1924), the Dartmoor comedy by Eden Phillpotts [q.v.], done long before in Birmingham and now a steady success at the Royal Court. The Repertory was reprieved; but Jackson continued a London career which was progressively complex. In 1925 he leased the Kingsway as well as the Royal Court; during that year, when he was knighted for services to the stage, he put on the modern-dress *Hamlet*, known popularly as '*Hamlet* in plus-fours', and in the next year *The Marvellous History of Saint Bernard*, his own version of a French mystery play by Henri Ghéon.

The period from the mid twenties to the early thirties was Jackson's most strenuous time. At Birmingham his theatre prospered artistically. He believed in the inspiration of youth; no friend of the star system, he yet made his own stars. The Repertory had produced such players as Gwen Ffrangcon-Davies, (Sir) Cedric Hardwicke [q.v.], (Sir) Ralph Richardson, and Laurence (later Lord) Olivier; people were speaking of it as the university of the English stage. In 1929, besides his active London management, Jackson increased his responsibilities by planning the Malvern summer festival with the lessee of the local theatre. Living now on the Malvern Hills, he thought the town would be unexampled for a festival, which he dedicated at first to Shaw. When Jackson left the London stage in 1935 he had still two or three Malvern seasons before he concentrated on Station Street. Birmingham had had another scare; in the spring of 1934, after spending not less than £100,000 on the Repertory within twenty-one years, Jackson insisted that the city must finally prove itself. After a year he was able in 1935 to transfer his interest to a local trust, giving the theatre, in effect, to the city, although he remained its governing director. In 1938, tired of apathy among the townsfolk of Malvern, he withdrew from the festival after nine years of ardent and costly toil.

Generous and sensitive, Barry Jackson could not forgive ingratitude; several times he was sharply hurt. The last occasion came in 1948 when, after he had restored the fortunes of the Shakespeare Memorial Theatre at Stratford-upon-Avon during three celebrated post-war seasons of reorganization (which also established Paul Scofield as an actor and Peter Brook as a director), his contract was not renewed. Thereafter he gave himself entirely to the Birmingham Repertory, putting on, among other successes, the three parts of the rarely staged *Henry VI* (1953) and in 1956 a *Caesar and Cleopatra* which went to Paris. He relied more and more on a trusted staff. After severe illness he was in his theatre for the last time during the first two acts of *Antony and Cleopatra* at a matinée on 15 March 1961; on Easter Monday, 3 April, he died in Birmingham. He was unmarried.

Barry Jackson, practical visionary, connoisseur, and philanthropist, asked, above all, for style and for living speech. He wrote, translated, or adapted, several plays himself, among them *The Christmas Party* for children (1914), *The Marvellous History of Saint Bernard* (1925), and *Doctor's Delight* (from Molière, 1945). He was an honorary freeman of Birmingham (1953); he held the honorary degrees of MA and D.Litt. from the university of Birmingham, the LLD from St. Andrews, and D.Litt. from Manchester. A lover of opera, in 1949-55 he was a director of the Royal Opera House, Covent Garden. A portrait of him by Harold Knight is in the London offices of the Actors' Benevolent Fund; and the new Birmingham Repertory Theatre (opened in 1971) has portraits by Harold Knight and Sir A. J. Munnings.

[John Drinkwater, *Discovery*, being the second book of an autobiography, 1897-1913, 1932; George W. Bishop, *Barry Jackson and the London Theatre*, 1933; J. C. Trewin, *The Birmingham Repertory Theatre: 1913-1963*, 1963; private information; personal knowledge.]   J. C. TREWIN

JACKSON, WILLIS, BARON JACKSON OF BURNLEY (1904-1970), electrical engineer and educationist, was born in Burnley 29 October 1904, the only son of Herbert Jackson, parks superintendent, and his wife, Annie Hiley. He was educated at Burnley Grammar School. His association with electrical engineering began as an undergraduate in the university of Manchester where he held the Burnley Educational Committee scholarship (1922-5). The award in 1925 of a B.Sc. with first class honours and a graduate research scholarship led to research and an M.Sc. in 1926. From 1926-9 he was lecturer in electrical engineering at Bradford Technical College. A straightforward academic career lay ahead but in 1929 the award of an industrial bursary by the 1851 Exhibition Committee enabled Jackson to join the Metropolitan-Vickers Company and to come under the influence of (Sir) A. P. M. Fleming, whose notice he subsequently wrote for this Dictionary. This set Jackson on a life's work embracing both industry and education and inspired him with the wish to bring the two more closely together.

Jackson's first contact with Metropolitan-Vickers was a brief one and was followed by further academic experience—at Manchester College of Technology (1930-3), and research at Oxford (1933-6) under E. B. Moullin [q.v.]. The Oxford period defined his main technical interest—the behaviour of electrical insulating materials—and provided a major research contribution, the demonstration of dipole rotation in solids and its influence on dielectric loss, for which he was awarded the D.Phil. of Oxford and the D.Sc. of Manchester in 1936.

Jackson's return to Metropolitan-Vickers as Fleming's personal assistant brought him directly into contact with policy on industrial research and on the training of graduates for industrial careers. This rounded off his extended apprenticeship in industry and academic life. Thirteen years after graduating from the Electrotechnics Department of Manchester University he returned as its professor. He rapidly established a reputation by the enthusiasm he communicated to students, both in lectures and in tackling projects of an advanced kind. His research group on dielectrics was sufficiently developed by the outbreak of war to be charged, in collaboration with the Signals Research and Development Establishment, with the study of dielectrics needed for radar. Such a study required the development of precise measurements of dielectric properties at centimetre wavelengths and Jackson's group pioneered the use of resonator techniques for this purpose. Theoretical work on the behaviour of waveguide junctions laid the foundations for others to develop. Jackson's wartime group gained an international reputation, largely as a consequence of his shrewd selection of the problems to be tackled, and his drive which infected all his team.

Unwilling to allow the demands of wartime research to diminish his interest in education, Jackson was a major contributor to a remarkably far-sighted document, published in 1942 by the Institution of Electrical Engineers' Education and Training Committee. His anticipation of many of the post-war educational developments was converted to reality during the period 1946-53 when he filled the chair of electrical engineering at the Imperial College of Science and Technology. This period, possibly the most fruitful of his career, effected a transformation in all aspects of his department—undergraduate courses, postgraduate courses, and research—creating the most forward-looking electrical engineering university department in the country. His philosophy was essentially simple and is summarized in the quotation from his presidential address to the British Association for the Advancement of Science at Leeds (1967)—'the ultimate purpose of technology and engineering is to apply established scientific principles and other relevant knowledge to productive ends'. All the changes he initiated were directed towards ensuring that his students appreciated this. The majority of the innovations he made—final-year student projects, student colloquia, emphasis on the properties of materials as a major factor in engineering, courses in economics, industrial sociology, and other 'relevant' subjects—are now universally accepted, but at the time were regarded as revolutionary. His success lay in the skilful selection of staff sympathetic with his views and in giving them his complete support. Research was revitalized and he created lively groups in the fields of control, solid-state electronics, information theory, microwaves, and ultrasonics—subjects all novel at that time.

Election as a fellow of the Royal Society in 1953 in recognition of his research in insulating materials and microwaves completed this phase of Jackson's career. A new challenge was offered by his appointment in 1954 as director of research and education at Metropolitan-Vickers in succession to Sir Arthur Fleming. This was a key post, carrying as it did responsibility for the apprentice school—recognized universally as the best of its kind in Britain and the nursery for several generations of distinguished British electrical engineers—and for the research department. Jackson's reorganization of the research department into groups, each directly linked to a product division of the company, bore fruit in the form of designs for advanced products such as mass-spectrometers and linear accelerators. Despite such forward-looking innovations, Metropolitan-Vickers could not survive as an independent unit and the formation of a partnership with the British-Thompson-Houston Company as Associated Electrical Industries was the first of a series of changes leading to the eventual emergence of GEC as the major British electrical company. By 1961 such changes led to a merger of Metropolitan-Vickers and BTH laboratories. Jackson left industry to return as head of the Electrical Engineering Department at Imperial College, and as pro-rector from 1967.

In 1953 Jackson was appointed as a member of the royal commission on the Civil Service and thereafter he was continually in demand for public services, especially in the fields of technical education and relations between university and industry. Amongst many such duties were membership of the University Grants Committee (1955-65), presidency of the British Association for Commercial and Industrial Education (1961-70), and the chairmanship of the Industrial Research Committee of the Federation of British Industry (1958-60). His experience of industry led him to stress repeatedly the need for a comprehensive pattern of technical education, which would supply not only graduate engineers but also craftsmen and technicians to provide essential support. He was therefore opposed to the recommendations of the Committee on Higher Education (chaired by Lord Robbins, 1961-3) for massive expansion of the universities, fearing that employment opportunities would not increase sufficiently rapidly to meet the aspirations of a greater number of graduates and that concentration on the university sector would lead to a shortage of properly trained technical support staff. The change from colleges of advanced technology to technological universities was one which he especially regretted. Despite his failure to prevent these decisions, he did succeed, by his chairmanship (1956-7) of a special committee of the Ministry of Education on 'The supply and training of teachers for technical colleges' in re-emphasizing the important role of the technical colleges.

The recommendations in his report, published in 1957, led through a new Technical Teacher Training College in Wolverhampton and a residential Further Education Staff College in Blagdon, to a marked improvement in the morale of technical college staff.

Jackson's technical and committee abilities came together through his involvement with the Engineering Advisory Committee of the BBC (1948-53) and as chairman of the postmaster general's Television Advisory Committee at the period when colour television was being introduced. The technical choice lay between the American NTSC system, the French SECAM, and the German PAL but was complicated by the desire to reach a common European standard. Jackson guided difficult discussion and gained Britain's complete support for PAL at the 1967 meeting of the International Radio Consultative Committee. The rapid introduction of colour television in Britain followed. Despite these exacting tasks, Jackson published many books, articles, and reports.

During the 1960s, technical education was of major concern to the developing countries and Jackson was involved in several new ventures in Africa and India. He played a major part in a collaborative operation, funded in large part by the Commonwealth Office and the Federation of British Industry, which resulted in the creation of a new high-level technological institute in India: the Indian Institute of Technology, Delhi.

As chairman of the Scientific Manpower Committee (1963-4) and of the Committee on Manpower Resources for Science and Technology, Jackson initiated a series of studies on the factors influencing the supply of trained personnel for industry. He had no illusions regarding the uncertainties inherent in predicting future requirements but succeeded in impressing upon his educational colleagues the importance of meeting such requirements with the resulting creation of several new types of course, particularly at postgraduate level, aimed at bridging the gap between universities and industry.

Jackson deservedly received many recognitions for his work—a knighthood in 1958, a life peerage in 1967, and honorary degrees and fellowships from many British and overseas universities. He was president of the Institution of Electrical Engineers in 1959-60 and of the British Association for the Advancement of Science in 1967.

Jackson brought a vitality and freshness of approach which was readily communicated to the very wide range of people in industry and education with whom he worked. An unfailing good humour, often extending to a schoolboy-like sense of fun, ensured harmonious personal relations but did not deflect him from pursuing his chosen aims with determination. His load was always a heavy one and although an indication in 1966 that his life would not be long led to some reduction in his commitments, he continued to discharge his duties with his customary high sense of responsibility. On 16 February 1970 he collapsed at his desk in Imperial College and died the following day.

In 1938 Jackson married Mary Elizabeth, daughter of Robert Oliphant Boswall, D.Sc., senior lecturer in mechanical engineering at Manchester University. There were two daughters.

[D. Gabor and J. Brown in *Biographical Memoirs of Fellows of the Royal Society*, vol. xvii, 1971; *The Times*, 18, 20, and 23 February 1970; *New Scientist*, 26 February 1970; *IEE News*, April 1970; private information; personal knowledge.] JOHN BROWN

JAMES, REGINALD WILLIAM (1891-1964), physicist, was born in London 9 January 1891, elder son of William George Joseph James and his wife, Isabel Sarah, daughter of George Ward, a commercial clerk. Both his father, by trade an umbrella-maker and shopkeeper in Praed Street, Paddington, and his mother were keenly interested in natural history and science; so, not surprisingly, the boy specialized in science at the Polytechnic Day School, Regent Street, and the City of London School. He was awarded a London County Council scholarship (1907), an entrance scholarship for natural sciences at St. John's College, Cambridge (1908), and the Beaufoy mathematical scholarship in 1909: he entered St. John's College as a foundation scholar in October of that year.

First classes in both part i (1911) and part ii (physics, 1912) of the natural sciences tripos were followed by two disappointingly unproductive years in the Cavendish Laboratory, which was at that time ill-equipped for research and lacked adequate provision for supervision of the beginner. During this five-year period, however, he formed an enduring friendship with another student, (Sir) W. L. Bragg [q.v.], which strongly influenced James's career as a professional physicist in later years.

In July 1914 James was on the point of departure from Cambridge to take up a junior lectureship in Liverpool when by pure chance, and in the most casual way, he was invited to join Shackleton's [q.v.] Antarctic Expedition as physicist. His acceptance, without hesitation, represented a clean break from the anticipated regular and orderly academic life in favour of adventure which might well—and in the event did—involve severe hardship and danger. The crushing of *Endurance* in the ice in October 1915, and the grim and hazardous existence on Elephant Island which followed until the rescue ship arrived in August 1916, were a severe test for one not accustomed to such harsh conditions, from which nevertheless he emerged with honour, having earned the affectionate respect of his companions.

There now followed two years on the western front in World War I, where in January 1917, having been commissioned into the Royal Engineers, he joined the sound-ranging section set up in 1915 by W. L. Bragg. James played a large part in the development of an efficient technique and towards the end of the war was appointed officer in charge of the Sound-Ranging School, with the rank of captain.

James's entry on a normal academic career was thus delayed for five strenuous years, but his appointment in 1919 as lecturer in physics in Manchester University, where Bragg was the newly appointed professor, was followed by nearly twenty years of successful original research and brilliant teaching in the department, recognized by promotion to senior lecturer (1921) and reader in experimental physics (1934). It would be difficult to exaggerate the importance for X-ray crystallography of his beautiful quantitative experimental measurements of X-ray reflexion (with W. L. Bragg and C. H. Bosanquet). When combined with the theoretical studies of (Sir) C. G. Darwin, D. R. Hartree [qq.v.], and I. Waller they threw a flood of light on the fundamental physics of the process of reflexion, and at the same time furnished much more powerful methods than were previously available for the analysis of complex crystal structures. First applied by James and Wood to barium sulphate, and afterwards to various other fairly complex structures, their use finally made possible the triumphantly successful attack on the formidable problem of the silicates, the most important constituents of the Earth's crust.

In December 1936, when nearly forty-six, James switched his domestic life and professional career as suddenly as in July 1914 when, at twenty-three, he left academic life for Shackleton's Antarctic. Long regarded as a confirmed bachelor he married; apparently settled in his readership in Manchester, he accepted the chair of physics at Cape Town.

Hints of the impending marriage had been picked up during the autumn of 1936 when it was noticed that James was regularly accompanied at the Hallé concerts by Annie Watson (generally known as Anne), second mistress and senior classics mistress at the Manchester High School for Girls, the only daughter of John Watson, a commercial traveller, of Rochdale. In 1937 they left Manchester for Cape Town, where their three children were born—John Stephen in 1938, David William in 1940, and Margaret Helen in 1943. The marriage was exceedingly happy; deeply devoted to their young family, they had many other interests in common, including James's strong feeling for the classics, derived from his schoolboy 'required reading'.

When James took up his professorship, the teaching of physics in the department was very good; his major effort was therefore directed to establishing research in crystallography; the papers which began to appear in the international journals were evidence of his success, and members of his team were welcomed as visiting workers in established laboratories overseas. Later, the demands of the higher administration of the university necessarily encroached upon his departmental effort; his period of office as acting principal and vice-chancellor coincided with the Government's attack on academic freedom, and James led the fight in its defence. To the thoroughness and total integrity which characterized all his work he now added a degree of political acumen and a high order of statesmanship in meeting conditions not previously encountered in the universities. His wife's support in these troubled times was invaluable, as it was in 1949 during a period of enforced rest following serious heart trouble.

It remains to speak of his splendid book, *The Optical Principles of the Diffraction of X-rays*, first published in 1948 and reprinted several times. Masterly in both content and presentation, essential reading for all serious workers in the field, it is a fitting monument to his profound understanding of the fundamental physics on which X-ray crystallography is based.

James's diverse and distinguished career attracted various honours and awards—the Polar medal (1918), a Rockefeller research fellowship in Debye's laboratory at Leipzig (1931-2); fellowship of the Royal Society came rather late but 'at last in 1955 his many services to science were appropriately recognized by his election to the Society' (W. L. Bragg in the memoir listed below), an honour which brought him and his many friends great satisfaction. Meanwhile he had been appointed to fellowship of Cape Town University (1949-56) and had served a term as president of the Royal Society of South Africa (1950-3); in 1957 the University of the Witwatersrand conferred on him its honorary D.Sc.

He retired from the chair of physics in December 1956, from university office as acting principal and vice-chancellor in December 1957, and died at his home in Cape Town

7 July 1964. A new physics building was completed shortly afterwards, and was named the R. W. James Building: a portrait, painted by Bertram Dumbleton, commissioned by the University Council early in 1964, and intended for the Administration Building alongside other similar official portraits, was brought to the R. W. James Building at the express request of the physics staff of the day, and hangs there now. No more suitable tributes could have been paid to the high esteem in which James was held by the university as a whole and by his departmental staff in particular.

[W. L. Bragg in *Biographical Memoirs of Fellows of the Royal Society*, vol. xi, 1965; private information; personal knowledge.]

W. H. TAYLOR

JAMESON, SIR (WILLIAM) WILSON (1885-1962), professor of public health, medical officer, and medical adviser, was born at Craigie, Perth, 12 May 1885, the second of the three children and elder son of John Wilson Jameson and his second wife, Isabella Milne. His father, who was joint manager of a bank in Perth, died when Jameson was six and his mother, who had been a schoolteacher and came from Aberdeen, returned there for the sake of its educational opportunities. After ten years at the Grammar School Jameson entered King's College in Aberdeen University where he graduated in arts (1905) before transferring to Marischal College to qualify MB, Ch.B., with distinction, in 1909. He had been a notable athlete at school, but beyond playing rugby football for the university he gave little attention to games thereafter, except for golf to which he remained addicted. He was active in student affairs and president of the students representative council in 1907; the human understanding and diplomatic ability which were to be the characteristics of his later life were already evident.

After qualifying, Jameson went to London, where he spent a year in resident posts at the Prince of Wales General Hospital and then for two years worked on tuberculosis at the City of London Hospital for Diseases of the Chest, Victoria Park. He obtained the MD, Aberdeen, with commendation in 1912, his thesis dealing with the treatment of pulmonary tuberculosis. After a year at Eastbourne in general practice he went as an assistant medical officer to the Hackney Hospital (1913) and then worked for a time at St. George's Home in Chelsea (1914). He became a member of the Royal College of Physicians of London in 1913 and obtained the DPH in 1914 after attending a part-time course at University College. Professor H. R. Kenwood chose Jameson from that course as an assistant lecturer in the department and Jameson thus entered the first of the three phases of his main medical work.

From 1915 to 1919 Jameson was in the Royal Army Medical Corps, working mainly on hygiene and laboratory services, and serving in France and Italy. After demobilization he returned to the teaching of public health at University College and in 1920 became medical officer of health for Finchley and deputy medical officer of health for Marylebone. The first edition of his *Synopsis of Hygiene*, with F. T. Marchant, was published in 1920. In 1922 he was called to the bar by the Middle Temple; in 1925 he became medical officer of health for Hornsey, and in 1926 a lecturer at Guy's Hospital. He continued to teach at University College and in 1929 took up the post of first professor of public health at the London School of Hygiene and Tropical Medicine in Keppel Street.

This was the first and in some ways the most important of Jameson's major appointments, rather for its consequences than for its immediate effects. The London School was the first independent postgraduate school in London University and it gave a fresh impetus to the teaching of preventive medicine and medical administration, not only in Britain but throughout the world. Jameson became dean in 1931 and in the years which followed he, more than any man, contributed to the success of the School. He travelled widely in North America, Burma, Malaya, West and East Africa, and Europe. The reputation of his brilliant group of colleagues, including such men as W. W. C. Topley, P. A. Buxton, R. T. Leiper [qq.v.], (Sir) Graham Wilson, Major Greenwood, and (Sir) A. B. Hill, as well as that of Jameson himself, brought students from all over the world to Jameson's own course for the diploma in public health as well as for the courses on bacteriology and tropical medicine and hygiene. Jameson's own personal quality as a teacher matched that of the best of his colleagues and the course he organized was perhaps more broadly based than any other in that field at the time. In other fields of medicine in London he became a most important influence amongst his contemporaries in informal discussion which prepared the way for the changes in the organization of British medicine which clearly had to be made.

The outbreak of war in 1939 temporarily brought the diploma course to an end, and Jameson had to deal with the evacuation of the departments of the School which amongst other things contributed so much to the Emergency Public Health Laboratory Service. He was invited in 1940 to act as part-time medical adviser to the Colonial Office and this brought him in contact with Malcolm MacDonald who became minister of health in May and who invited Jameson to become chief medical officer on the retirement of Sir Arthur MacNalty [q.v.] in November.

Jameson remained chief medical officer of the Ministry of Health and the Board (later Ministry) of Education until 1950. He had to deal with the problems of maintaining the nation's health and developing the emergency services required to deal with casualties and other civilian needs arising from the large movements of population, particularly of children, and from wartime conditions. His report on the nation's health in six years of war was published in 1946. It was difficult enough to keep services going in such conditions, but there were two great contributions which were largely inspired by Jameson. One was the special attention given to the nutrition of children and expectant mothers, for which Jameson chaired an advisory committee to the Ministry of Food. The other was the introduction of a nation-wide scheme for immunization against diphtheria which not only prevented the epidemic increase which might have been expected in wartime but actually brought about the near-elimination of the disease.

Jameson was a member of the Goodenough committee which in 1942–4 reviewed medical education in Britain, and made a major contribution to the planned reorganization which took place after the war. During the war, too, his personal influence was directed towards better public information on health, not only on immunization, but on such subjects as tuberculosis and venereal disease, on which he was one of the first people to broadcast, and on the more mundane but extremely important problem of controlling the prevalence of the head louse and the itch mite.

In addition to its wartime responsibilities the Ministry of Health, consequent upon the Beveridge report, was called upon to produce a plan for a national health service, which it did in a white paper in February 1944. From then until the introduction of the National Health Service in 1948 there was constant negotiation and preparation, changed only in method by the advent of a Labour Government in 1945. Jameson was one of the most important influences in these developments and he remained chief medical officer through the difficult transition period until the Service was nearly two years old. At no time was Jameson's capacity for attracting the support of leading figures in the profession and obtaining their confidence more manifest or more important. That the Health Service was achieved without a final breach between the Government and the medical profession was perhaps as much due to Jameson as to anyone.

After he retired in 1950 Jameson became medical adviser to the King Edward's Hospital Fund for London, and in the next ten years most of the important educational work of the Fund in hospital administration, nursing administration, and catering was established, largely due to his influence and with his direct participation in the teaching. He gained universal esteem in an organization in which the medical influence had previously been almost entirely that of the leading consultants in London teaching hospitals. He did more than anyone to broaden the interests of the Fund and to lead it into supporting some of the less glamorous and yet extremely important areas of hospital work. Despite periods of ill health he continued working even after the death of his first wife in 1958 and finally retired in 1960.

Jameson was elected FRCP in 1930, knighted in 1939 while still at the School of Hygiene, and appointed KCB (1943) and GBE (1949) while at the Ministry of Health. He received a number of honorary degrees, was Harveian orator and Bisset Hawkins medallist of the Royal College of Physicians, and received the Lasker award of the American Public Health Association. He was master of the Society of Apothecaries and he received the United States medal of freedom.

Wilson Jameson was of middle height and modest presence, with a high forehead and an air of unfailing benignity. He was cool, persuasive, and always lucid; his friendly voice never lost its Aberdonian intonation. He made many friends in the medical and other circles in which he moved, but his intimates were few. His students and colleagues held him in an admiration and affection, the justification for which he was never able to understand. He did not want the honours that were heaped upon him. His remark that 'It's a terrible thing to have a sense of your own dignity' could never have been made of him. But in his generation no member of his own profession earned that dignity more.

In 1916 Jameson married Pauline Frances, daughter of James Paul Helm, sheep farmer, whom he had met while still a medical student; they had two daughters. In 1959 he married Constance, daughter of Dr Herbert Dobie. Jameson died in London 18 October 1962.

[Neville M. Goodman, *Wilson Jameson, Architect of National Health*, 1970; private information; personal knowledge.]

GEORGE GODBER

JARVIS, SIR JOHN LAYTON (JACK) (1887–1968), racehorse trainer, was born in Newmarket 28 December 1887, the third and youngest son of William Arthur Jarvis, racehorse trainer, and his wife, Norah, daughter of

James Godding, also a racehorse trainer. Jarvis was educated at Cranleigh School, Surrey. On leaving school he served his apprenticeship as a jockey with his father, and rode the winner of the Cambridgeshire Handicap (Hackler's Pride) at the age of sixteen. His increasing weight put an end to his career as a jockey. He then assisted his father, accompanying the horses to meetings until he set up as a trainer himself in 1914.

Within a few years Jarvis provided a steady stream of winners. His first major success was in 1921, with the colt Ellangowan, in the Two Thousand Guineas. Jarvis provided winners for the same race in both 1928 (Flamingo) and 1939 (Blue Peter). The One Thousand Guineas also fell to his horses thrice: in 1924 (Plack), 1934 (Campanula), and 1953 (Happy Laughter). Jarvis won the St. Leger once, in 1931 (Sandwich). His horses also won the Derby twice, in 1939 and 1944 (Blue Peter and Ocean Swell).

Jarvis knew best how to train middle-distance horses and stayers, but he was also a skilled handler of faster horses. He trained to great advantage the outstanding sprinters Honeyway and Royal Charger. Jarvis set himself the highest standards, working his horses as hard as himself. It was often said that his horses consequently looked on the light-framed side, but it was a tribute to his profound equine understanding that they were capable of winning in spring, mid season, and autumn, thus confounding the paddock critics, who decried them by saying they were 'over the top'.

Jarvis trained from 1922 until his death for the fifth Earl of Rosebery [q.v.], and his son, the sixth earl.

Jarvis was a forthright person and left no doubt about his views. He was somewhat quick-tempered, although his bark was worse than his bite, and altercations would be over as quickly as they started. He could be kind, always keen to help those, especially the young, who wished to make their way.

Jarvis went annually to South Africa, where he appreciated the warmer climate. There he made many close friends and came to hear of a young jockey, John Gorton, who was employed by Lord Rosebery on Jarvis's suggestion and rode a Rosebery horse (Sleeping Partner) to victory in 1969, in the Epsom Oaks.

Jarvis was always meticulous, in his stables and in his other activities. He served on committees in the town, and, for several years, until advised against it for medical reasons, was on the town council in Newmarket. Among his relaxations were shooting and hare-coursing. He won the Waterloo Cup, the most cherished coursing prize, with Jovial Judge, and the Barbican Cup with Junior Journalist. Also a pigeon fancier, his bird was winner one year, and runner-up the next, in the Lerwick race.

Jarvis regularly attended functions at the Subscription Rooms, Newmarket's racing club. He was knighted for his services to racing in 1967.

In 1914 Jarvis married Ethel Edina, daughter of Thomas Leader, a racehorse trainer of Newmarket. They had one daughter. Jarvis died 19 December 1968 at his home in Newmarket, on the eve of a visit to South Africa.

[Jack Jarvis, *They're Off*, 1969 (autobiography); private information; personal knowledge.] K. M. NORMAN

JEFFERSON, SIR GEOFFREY (1886-1961), neurosurgeon, was born in Stockton, county Durham, 10 April 1886, the son of Arthur John Jefferson, a general practitioner surgeon, and his wife, who had been a nurse, Cecilia James. He was educated at Manchester Grammar School and Manchester University. It was not until he came to take his higher surgical qualifications that he showed signs of emerging from the average run of the better of his contemporaries. After qualifying in 1909 and the customary house appointments, he took a step which was decisive for his future: probably to fill in time between posts he became in 1911 a demonstrator in anatomy under (Sir) Grafton Elliot Smith [q.v.], then the leading authority in the country on the structure of the brain, and thus acquired his lifelong interest in the problems of the nervous system.

Jefferson obtained his FRCS in 1911 and his MS London with gold medal in 1913. In 1914 he married Dr Gertrude Flumerfelt, a Canadian, and settled in Victoria in British Columbia. As soon as war broke out he returned to England and in 1915, with his wife, joined the Anglo-Russian Hospital in Petrograd where they remained until the collapse of the Russian armies in 1917. He subsequently went to France in a special unit dealing with gunshot wounds of the head.

By this time he was attracting attention and after the war he was given facilities by the Royal College of Surgeons to work up his experience. But neurosurgery was still regarded as a sideline of general surgery and Jefferson was unsuccessful in his application for the post of assistant surgeon at his own teaching hospital. Three years previously, however, he had been appointed to the staff at Salford and as visiting surgeon to the Ministry of Pensions hospital for head injuries. On this basis he continued his work on the significance of structure in the nervous system, the effect of injury on this, the localization of cerebral tumours, and the problem of consciousness. In 1926 he was largely responsible for the foundation of the Society of British Neurological Surgeons, of which he remained secretary until 1952.

His reputation in his subject was now becoming international. In 1926 Manchester provided a small neurological department for him and in 1933 he was appointed as a part-time visiting surgeon to the staff of the National Hospital for Nervous Diseases in London. But Jefferson did not sever his connection with Manchester where in 1939 a special chair of neurosurgery was created for him. Again war came to interrupt his plans: he became consultant adviser in neurosurgery to the ministries of Health and Pensions and it was through his efforts that neurosurgical centres were established throughout the country. These it was his delight to goad, inspire, and enliven by a series of benevolent pastoral visits.

Jefferson had now emerged as one of the personalities of British medicine. His inimitable style, as well as his searching mind, made him much in demand as a lecturer both in this country and abroad. He was recognized as a man who had expanded beyond the bounds of his speciality and increasingly he was drawn into wider issues. In 1947 he was elected to the Royal Society and the Royal College of Physicians. He was appointed CBE in 1943 and knighted in 1950. In the following year he retired from his chair. From 1948 to 1952 he was a member of the Medical Research Council and from 1953 to 1959 chairman of the newly created Clinical Research Board. Throughout he retained close personal contacts with the Ministry of Health and he was the trusted adviser on medical matters in many universities. It was in this, his second career, that his personality came fully into its own.

Throughout his life Jefferson enjoyed being a law unto himself. He never said anything that was not worth hearing and never said it in a way that was expected. He was provokingly unaware of time and he had his own ideas about what constituted importance either in men or things. Wherever he was, an aura of unbuttoned ease and percipient humour reigned and, in this, difficulties shrank to their due proportions and pretensions were abashed. Yet, despite his sleepy look, he missed nothing and, when it came to assessing a situation, he could make the most apt, original, and sometimes devastating comments, colloquially and with disconcerting simplicity. But the basis of Jefferson's unique authority was the mind behind the wit. Although benign, his insight into human affairs was never clouded by sentiment and he was impervious to wishful thinking, especially by others. His perspicacity became legendary in his lifetime and his salty aphorisms were treasured with delight by his contemporaries.

Jefferson died in Manchester 29 January 1961. His health had been precarious for several years but he disregarded this with his customary mild nonchalance. It was typical that his last remark to his physician should have been 'That was life, that was'. His widow died less than a fortnight later. She had been founder and medical director of the Family Welfare Service in Manchester. They had two sons, both of whom entered the medical profession, and one daughter. His portrait, by Sir Gerald Kelly, hangs on the staircase of the Royal College of Surgeons of England, Lincoln's Inn Fields, London. A further portrait by Frederick Deane is hung in the Jefferson Memorial Library at the Royal Infirmary, Manchester.

[Sir Francis Walshe in *Biographical Memoirs of Fellows of the Royal Society*, vol. vii, 1961; *British Medical Journal*, 4, 11, and 18 February 1961; *Lancet*, 4 February 1961; private information; personal knowledge.]

HAROLD HIMSWORTH

JENKINS, DAVID LLEWELYN, BARON JENKINS (1899-1969), judge, was born at Exmouth, Devon, 8 April 1899, the third son and fifth of the seven children of (Sir) John Lewis Jenkins, KCSI, an Indian civil servant whose father was a farmer of Glansawdde, Carmarthenshire. David's mother, Florence Mildred, was the daughter of Sir Arthur Trevor, KCSI, niece of W. S. Trevor [q.v.], and a granddaughter of Captain R. S. Trevor of the 3rd Bengal Cavalry who was murdered with Sir William Macnaghten [q.v.] in Kabul in 1841. Captain Trevor's widow with her seven surviving children was eventually able to return by way of India to England. An eighth, born in captivity, died in India shortly after release.

Although his ancestry on both sides was Welsh and his family was predominantly associated with the Indian Service, Jenkins never had a home in either Wales or India. His father had bought a house in Exmouth as a home for his family where the children seem to have spent an exceedingly happy childhood in the care of their mother, when she was not in India, and at other times of an aunt. Their father joined them during his periods of home leave once in every three years. In 1912, following Sir John's death, the family moved to Kew.

In the same year Jenkins won a scholarship at Charterhouse, where he became a really good schoolboy classical scholar, won all the prizes open to him, and became head of the school. He gained a Domus exhibition in classics at Balliol, but shortly afterwards was called up for military service. Commissioned in July 1918, he was in France with the 12th (Service) battalion of the Rifle Brigade for a few weeks before the armistice was signed. Demobilized early in 1919 he went up to Balliol where he obtained a first class in classical honour moderations (1920) and a second in *literae humaniores* (1922). He was a Craven scholar and proxime accessit for the Ireland in 1919 and proxime accessit for the Hertford in 1920.

In spite of the long family connections with India, it did not attract Jenkins, although his brothers Sir Evan and Sir Owain Jenkins both had distinguished careers there. While still at Charterhouse Jenkins had decided that he wished to go to the bar. He became a student member of Lincoln's Inn while he was an undergraduate and secured a Tancred studentship. He was called to the bar in 1923 and became a pupil of J. E. Harman (father of the future Lord Justice Harman, q.v.), thus gaining the advantage of seeing one of the largest and most varied junior Chancery practices of the day. Harman died suddenly at about the end of the pupillage and Charles Harman and Jenkins together dealt with winding up his practice. After a period in the chambers of Edward Beaumont, Jenkins was invited to move to J. H. Stamp's chambers at 11 New Court, of which Raymond (later Lord) Evershed [q.v.], a Balliol friend and later master of the Rolls, was already a member. Jenkins devilled extensively for Stamp, who was standing junior counsel to the Inland Revenue, built up a sound junior practice of his own at the Chancery bar, and took silk in 1938.

His career as a leader was soon interrupted by the war of 1939-45 in which he held a temporary commission in the Royal Army Service Corps, serving for a time as adjutant of a training unit with the temporary rank of major. In 1943 he transferred to the Political Warfare Executive branch of the Foreign Office under Sir Robert Bruce Lockhart [q.v.] who, when Jenkins returned to the bar in 1945, wrote that in the 'mercurial atmosphere' of the branch Jenkins's 'even temperament and dispassionate judgement' had been of great value.

Jenkins returned to the bar rather apprehensively, but his experience of revenue work with Stamp led to his being frequently selected to lead for the Inland Revenue and this was a type of work in which he excelled. In 1946 he was appointed attorney-general of the Duchy of Lancaster. In 1947 he was promoted to the Chancery bench and two years later to the Court of Appeal. During his ten years there his judicial excellence was demonstrated by the remarkable regularity with which any dissenting judgement of his was upheld in the House of Lords. In 1959 he was appointed a lord of appeal in ordinary.

Jenkins was a shy man and his manner was somewhat withdrawn, but among friends he was the best of company. His figure was slight and he retained the spareness of his youth. His appearance was suggestive of some slim and cautiously intent bespectacled bird. Behind his glasses were a pair of markedly humorous and observant eyes. His wit was incisive, good humoured, and inclined to an irreverent approach to conventional judgements. When on becoming a judge he applied for a grant of arms he is reported to have proposed as his motto the injunction 'Up Jenkins'. At the Foreign Office, when his colleagues were seeking to capsulate in a single sentence the cause for which the Allies were fighting, after a moment's reflection Jenkins exclaimed: 'I have it: To make the world SHAEF for democracy.'

Jenkins's quality as a judge, like his wit, closely resembled that of Lord Bowen [q.v.], his Victorian predecessor. Among his contemporaries he excelled in penetrating analysis and lucid exposition. He had probably the best judicial brain of his day.

Jenkins served for some time as chairman of the lord chancellor's Law Reform Committee and presided over a number of other important committees concerned with law reform including the Leasehold Committee which reported in 1950, and notably the Company Law Committee whose report in 1962 was Jenkins's last and probably his most notable contribution to law reform. In the following year ill health compelled him to retire. He died after a long sad illness in London 21 July 1969.

Jenkins never married. He was a bencher of Lincoln's Inn (1945), an honorary fellow of Balliol (1950), a governor (1953-65) of Sutton's Hospital in Charterhouse, and chairman for some years of the Tancred studentship trustees. He was knighted in 1947, sworn of the Privy Council in 1949, and became a life peer in 1959. There is an excellent likeness of Jenkins in a conversation piece 'The Short Adjournment' hanging in the hall of Lincoln's Inn by Norman Hepple.

[Private information; personal knowledge.]

DENYS B. BUCKLEY

JENKINSON, SIR (CHARLES) HILARY (1882-1961), deputy keeper of the public records, was born at Streatham 1 November 1882, the youngest of the six children of William Wilberforce Jenkinson, land agent, by his wife, Alice Leigh Bedale. He was a nephew of F. J. H. Jenkinson [q.v.]. He was educated at Dulwich College and Pembroke College, Cambridge, where he was a scholar and graduated with first class honours in classics (1904). He entered the Public Record Office at the beginning of 1906 and after a formative period of training under C. G. Crump [q.v.] he worked chiefly on the arrangement and classification of records of the medieval exchequer. In 1912 he was put in charge of the literary search room with a general instruction to reorganize its services in the light of the criticisms made in the first report of the royal commission on public records. His work there and in the reorganization after 1922 of the repairing department and of the repository to which he moved from the search room in 1929 probably constitutes his most valuable contribution to the Office and its users. He was appointed secretary and principal assistant keeper in 1938 and was deputy keeper from 1947 until his retirement in 1954. During these years plans were made for the wartime dispersal of a great part of the records to temporary accommodation in the country and for their safe return afterwards, for the acquisition of buildings at Ashridge in Hertfordshire to supplement the storage at headquarters, and for the establishment of the intermediate repository at Hayes in Middlesex to meet the needs of departments in housing non-current records and preparing them for transfer to the Public Record Office. A photographic service was brought into being and new forms of publication were planned with the co-operation of a consultative committee of historians, but Jenkinson was unable to play the part he would have chosen in the reorganization of the Office which followed the publication, shortly after his retirement, of the report of the committee on departmental records.

In 1915 Jenkinson was commissioned in the Royal Garrison Artillery and he served in France and Belgium from 1916 to 1918. He was then employed as GSO 3 at the War Office until he was demobilized in 1920. During part of the war of 1939–45 he was lent to the War Office to advise on the protection of archives in occupied enemy territory and served in Italy and Germany.

His extra-official interests were directly related to his official work. Within a few years of the start of his official career he had become honorary secretary of the Surrey Archaeological Society and had taken a leading part in founding the Surrey Record Society, whose volumes, edited on principles laid down by him as general editor and designed to provide reliable texts of documents of local history, with introductions setting out their administrative context, have earned a high place among record publications. He also became associated with his colleague Charles Johnson [q.v.] in the work on medieval handwritings which was published in 1915 under the title *English Court Hand*. This was followed by various papers on post-medieval scripts culminating in his *Later Court Hands in England from the Fifteenth to the*

Seventeenth Century (1927). From 1911 to 1935 he was the Maitland memorial lecturer at Cambridge, his subject being English palaeography and diplomatic from the Conquest to 1485, and from 1920 he was lecturer and from 1925 until 1947 reader in diplomatic and archives at King's College, London. Between 1920 and 1925 he also lectured on palaeography and archives for the new school of librarianship at University College, London. His *Manual of Archive Administration*, undertaken for the Carnegie Foundation, was published in 1922 and reissued with some revision in 1937. This pioneer work had a unique influence on the development and practice of record-keeping in England and through it and his many lectures and other writings on the topic he merited the description 'doyen of archivists' given him by a French colleague.

For some years before 1932 the need for an influential national organization committed to promote the preservation and accessibility to students of documents in local or private custody and at risk of dispersal or destruction had exercised the minds of many interested people. After prolonged negotiations and discussions in which Jenkinson took a prominent part the British Records Association was formed. As joint secretary until 1947 and afterwards vice-president he directed its policy and was its chief propagandist. Among the achievements for which he and the Association could fairly claim a share of the credit were the establishment of local record offices throughout the country and the inauguration of university diploma courses in archives for the training of staff. Jenkinson was himself instrumental in persuading the university of London to enlarge the school of librarianship at University College into a school of librarianship and archives with separate diploma courses for each branch. He himself gave the inaugural lecture of the archives course with the title 'The English Archivist: a New Profession'. In 1943 he formulated through the British Records Association proposals for legislation to control local and private archives. For the most part they proved to be too controversial and had to be abandoned, but out of them came the establishment of the National Register of Archives which later took permanent form as a branch of the Historical Manuscripts Commission. On being appointed deputy keeper of the public records he became executive historical manuscripts commissioner and chairman of the directorate of the National Register, and after his retirement as deputy keeper, the Commission, Register, and Association retained his active interest.

Over the years he formed friendships with archivists in many countries and had a high reputation among them. He was the British representative on the committee set up in 1948 under the auspices of Unesco to draft proposals for an International Council on Archives and when the new council was formed he was elected one of its vice-presidents.

In the course of his lifetime Jenkinson played a leading part in establishing in England principles which should govern the care of records, in rousing public interest in their preservation, and in providing for the professional training of their custodians, who should be, as he preferred to call them, archivists rather than amateurs with antiquarian tastes. His gift for personal relationships undoubtedly went far to promote the cause he had at heart, although his pursuit of perfection betrayed him into a doctrinaire advocacy of ideas and practices which created difficulties and brought frustration. He was generous in the help given to students and old pupils and his official contacts often developed into personal friendships. He was a delightful host, a connoisseur of good food and wine, an ardent gardener, and an amateur of eighteenth-century domestic architecture and furnishing, cultivating at home the feeling for good craftsmanship and interest in its methods which displayed itself in his official publications on seals and the binding of Domesday Book.

Jenkinson was for many years a prominent fellow of the Society of Antiquaries, and he was also a fellow of the Royal Historical Society, and president of the Jewish Historical Society and the Society of Archivists. He was appointed CBE in 1943 and was knighted in 1949, and was an honorary fellow of University College, London, and an honorary LLD of Aberdeen (1949).

He married in 1910 Alice Violet (died 1960), daughter of Andrew Knox Rickards, who made many contributions to the Victoria History of her own county, Bedfordshire; there were no children.

A sketch of Jenkinson made by Michael Ross in 1945 is in the Public Record Office. There was also an oil-painting by the same artist. Jenkinson died in London 5 March 1961.

[Biographical memoir in *Studies Presented to Sir Hilary Jenkinson*, ed. J. Conway Davies, 1957; *Essays in Memory of Sir Hilary Jenkinson*, ed. A. E. J. Hollaender, 1962; *The Times*, 7, 9, and 11 March 1961; *Archives*, vol. v, No. 25, 1961; private information; personal knowledge.]   H. C. JOHNSON

JENNINGS, SIR (WILLIAM) IVOR (1903–1965), constitutional lawyer, was born in Bristol 16 May 1903, the son of William Jennings, carpenter and joiner, and his wife, Eleanor Jane Thomas. He was educated at Queen Elizabeth's

Hospital, Bristol Grammar School, and St. Catharine's College, Cambridge. He obtained first classes in part i of the mathematical tripos (1923) and both parts of the law tripos (1924–5), was Whewell scholar in 1925, and was clearly destined for a university career. He was appointed Holt scholar of Gray's Inn in 1925 and Barstow scholar in 1926 and was called to the bar in 1928.

Jennings's first appointment was as lecturer in law in Leeds University in 1925–9. From there he went to the London School of Economics and Political Science, first as lecturer, then in 1930 as reader in English law. He remained there as a teacher of public law until 1940, and this period saw the production of his most original and creative work. The mutual stimulus of colleagues such as Harold Laski, (Sir) Hersch Lauterpacht [qq.v.], and William Robson, with whom he was in close contact, undoubtedly acted as a ferment on them all.

In these eleven years he produced eleven substantial books. Some of these were legal treatises intended for the practitioner, the official, or the student. They included treatises on the poor law code, the law of housing, the law of public health, the law of town and country planning, and a vast tome on the law relating to local authorities, published soon after the great consolidating Local Government Act, 1933. These works were produced at extraordinary speed but they were scholarly and accurate. Although mainly of vocational interest, they displayed the author's remarkable gift of lucid and succinct exposition.

The books which represent his greatest intellectual achievement were also written during these vital years. The most distinguished of them is *Cabinet Government*, first published in 1936. This was instantly recognized as a masterly analysis of the principal characteristics of the Cabinet system. It is immeasurably superior to anything which had preceded it. To obtain the information on which it was based, Jennings had read widely and deeply in the memoirs and biographies of statesmen past and present; and he presented the material in a clear and systematic manner which has never been surpassed. The book still holds its place as a standard work on the subject, and will continue to be read even though it is now challenged in certain aspects of the subject by a more recent study. Other literary incursions into the sphere of politics during this period consisted of a large work on *Parliament* (1939) which again displayed the author's extraordinary power of exposition; a provocative and highly original book entitled *The Law and the Constitution* (1933); a short study on *Parliamentary Reform* (1934); and a work entitled *A Federation for Western Europe* which appeared in 1940.

In that year Jennings was appointed principal of University College, Ceylon. Two years later the college became a university and Jennings its first vice-chancellor. His energy, skill, and foresight resulted in a vast expansion on a new site; and the standards he laid down were high.

His services as constitutional adviser were in considerable demand after the war, not only in Ceylon, where he was a member of the commission on the Ceylon constitution, but in other countries which were becoming independent states—for example, he was the constitutional adviser and chief draughtsman to Pakistan in 1954-5 and a member of the Malayan constitutional commission in 1956-7.

The concluding phase of Jennings's career began when he returned to England in 1954 as master of Trinity Hall, Cambridge. In 1961-3 he was vice-chancellor of the university and while holding that office, in 1962 he was appointed to the Downing professorship in the laws of England in succession to E. C. S. Wade. From 1955 to 1958 he was chairman of the royal commission on common land.

His interest in the Commonwealth was shown in 1938 when he produced in collaboration with C. M. Young a casebook on the *Constitutional Laws of the British Empire*. In 1949 he delivered the Waynflete lectures at Magdalen College, Oxford, on 'The Commonwealth in Asia', and in 1956 he published *The Approach to Self-Government*. He delivered a course of lectures on 'Problems of the New Commonwealth' in 1958 at the Commonwealth Studies Center at Duke University. His final literary contribution in this field was on democracy in Africa. Jennings believed in the new Commonwealth; he saw the problems confronting its political leaders without illusions; but he did not foresee the forces which have caused repeated wars between India and Pakistan, the exclusion of South Africa, and the disappearance of parliamentary government on the Westminster model throughout Africa.

Towards the end of his life Jennings resumed the study of British government and politics; but his long absence led to a loss of the freshness and originality which had marked his earlier work. It was a mistake to complete and publish (1960-2) a long study of *Party Politics* in three volumes which he had begun before leaving England in 1940.

Jennings was knighted in 1948, and appointed QC in 1949 and KBE in 1955. He was elected FBA in 1955, became a bencher of Gray's Inn in 1958, and received honorary degrees in law from the universities of Bristol, Southampton, Ceylon, Leeds, Belfast, Hong Kong, Manchester, and Paris.

His outstanding characteristic was his extraordinary capacity for both intellectual and practical work. Every task which he undertook he accomplished rapidly, efficiently, and in an apparently effortless manner. In politics he was left of centre; but his work was not politically tendentious though sometimes controversial and was generally marked by good judgement and common sense. He had no known recreations apart from an occasional walk with his dog and an insatiable interest in books. He never gave offence, but it was difficult for even close colleagues to penetrate a certain aloofness which seemed to inhibit a more intimate knowledge of the man.

In 1928 Jennings married Helena Emily, daughter of Albert Konsalik, of London; they had two daughters. He died in Cambridge 19 December 1965. Trinity Hall has a drawing by Michael Noakes.

[*The Times* and *Guardian*, 20 December 1965; personal knowledge.]   W. A. ROBSON

JERROLD, DOUGLAS FRANCIS (1893-1964), author and publisher, was born at Scarborough 3 August 1893, the only son of Sidney Dominic Jerrold, district auditor, and his wife, Maud Frances Goodrich. He came of a famous literary family which had originated with Douglas William Jerrold [q.v.], one of the earliest contributors to *Punch*. Jerrold was a scholar of Westminster where he was captain of the school, and of New College, Oxford, where he read history but never took his degree owing to the outbreak of war. He joined the Royal Naval Division with which he served in Gallipoli and France and of which he published a history in 1923. He was severely wounded on the Somme and he suffered from the effects of this for the rest of his life.

In 1918 he became a civil servant in the Ministry of Food, transferring in 1920 to the Treasury where he remained for three years. He then became a publisher, first with Benn Brothers (1923-8) where he collaborated with (Sir) Victor Gollancz [q.v.], then as director (1929-45) and chairman (1945-59) of Eyre and Spottiswoode. He was also editor of the *English Review* (1930-6) and the *New English Review* (1945-50). As a publisher he tended to publish books by authors who reflected his own views, and among them were Winston Churchill, Francis Yeats-Brown, J. B. Morton, Major-General J. F. C. Fuller, Mrs Parkinson Keyes, Hector Bolitho, and Professor David Douglas.

Jerrold was very much a mixture of opposites. He was not an easy man with whom to work, for he was liable to change his opinions, not on fundamental principles but on their practical application, at very short notice. By nature there can be no doubt that he was kindly disposed towards his fellow-men, but he had a tongue like an asp, and he could be extremely rude. Much, however, must be forgiven him on the score of temper, for he was rarely out of pain owing to his wound. His approach to a problem was rather French than English, which was probably due to the fact that his grandfather, Blanchard Jerrold [q.v.], had lived much in Paris. One of his outstanding characteristics was his affection for France, where he was a confirmed Bonapartist.

In British politics Jerrold was very definitely a man of the Right. He would undoubtedly have liked to become a member of Parliament, but on the only occasion on which he endeavoured to be adopted as a candidate—for South Kensington—he was rejected by the selection committee. At Oxford he had been a Liberal, and was secretary of the Oxford Union. When the Spanish civil war broke out Jerrold emerged as a strong supporter of General Franco, and for a time he was unquestionably drawn to Hitler. He sympathized with Churchill and Lord Lloyd [q.v.] in their opposition to Baldwin in the thirties, and he made no secret of his views in his writings, which did nothing to recommend him in official Conservative circles.

In the years immediately preceding the war of 1939-45 his views carried a good deal of weight in right-wing circles, although he was never very popular personally, and his flirtations with Hitler and Sir Oswald Mosley caused him to be regarded with some suspicion by more conventional Conservatives: yet some of his policies, such as the importance of a property-owning democracy, were later adopted by the Conservative Party. As editor of the *English Review* his object, to quote his own words, was 'to restate the Conservative case in terms which would appeal to the man in the street and the man on the land; to offer them not a deferred path to the Socialist gaol but a new path to another goal'.

It is significant that he was never recommended for an honour by any Conservative prime minister, and he resented the fact. In religious matters Jerrold's attitude was much the same, for although he was a staunch Catholic he was often very critical of the policy of Rome in temporal affairs.

Somewhat surprisingly Jerrold was a good deal of a clubman, and at one time or another he belonged to the Athenaeum, Carlton, Garrick, Authors', Pratt's, and Hurlingham, where he used to play croquet which, with bridge, was perhaps his only real relaxation. The Authors' Club was for many years his preoccupation outside his publishing and literary work, and in the difficult period after the second war when he was its chairman he did a good deal to keep it going. This particular activity was rendered the easier for him since the club

at that time was housed in Whitehall Court where he had a flat.

Jerrold was a prolific writer, but most of his more serious literary work was ephemeral and of a political nature. His novel, *Storm over Europe* (1930), was dramatized in London in 1936 with Mary Newcomb in the female lead. His autobiography, *Georgian Adventure*, was published in 1937. At the time of his death he was writing *An Introduction to the History of England*, but he had only concluded the first volume (1949) which took it down to the loss of Normandy. His style was not always easy, but the attraction of what he wrote lay in the fact that he definitely had something to say, however unconventional.

In 1919 Jerrold married Eleanor, daughter of Henry Arnold; they had no children. He died in London 21 July 1964.

[*The Times*, 23 July 1964; Douglas Jerrold, *Georgian Adventure*, 1937; private information; personal knowledge.] CHARLES PETRIE

JOHN, AUGUSTUS EDWIN (1878-1961), artist, was born 4 January 1878 at Tenby, Pembrokeshire, the third child in the family of two sons and two daughters of Edwin William John, solicitor, of Haverfordwest, and his wife, Augusta, third child of Thomas Smith, plumber, of Brighton. Augusta died when Augustus John was six years old. His childhood was loveless and unhappy. After attending Greenhill School, Tenby, a boarding school at Clifton, near Bristol (not the College), and St. Catharine's School, Tenby (1891-3), which had less than ten pupils, he went to an art school in Tenby. There he determined to become an artist, and in 1894 departed for the Slade School of Art in London. At the Slade he appeared as a neat, timid, unremarkable personality, but he impressed by his intense application to his work and his study of the Old Masters at the National Gallery. In the summer holiday of 1897 in Pembrokeshire he injured his skull by striking a hidden rock when diving into the sea. The precise physical effect of the accident is impossible to ascertain, but he returned to the Slade that autumn a man transformed. Henry Tonks [q.v.] had described his previous work as 'methodical'; it was now of a startling brilliance, and the John legend came quickly into being. At the Slade he learnt much from Tonks as a draughtsman but little as a painter. 'I was never apprenticed', he wrote, 'to a master whom I might follow.'

In the autumn of 1898 he visited Amsterdam for a great Rembrandt exhibition, and other cities in the Netherlands. This he was able to afford by winning the summer composition prize with 'Moses and the Brazen Serpent' (now at University College, London), an extraordinary achievement for a student. It was a brilliantly executed 'anthology' of features from the works of those whom he most revered—Rubens, Rembrandt, and Michelangelo and other Renaissance painters. Its composition was at certain points confused, but mastery of complex composition, even though it eventually became his predominant preoccupation, John rarely achieved. Understandably the work made a profound impression and John left the Slade that summer a heroic figure. The following spring he held at the Carfax Gallery the first of his many one-man exhibitions, which was a success and earned him £30. This enabled him to make another of his numerous visits abroad—mostly to France—to Vattetôt-sur-mer with Charles Conder, (Sir) William Orpen [q.v.], and Ida Nettleship (his future wife), Albert Rothenstein (Rutherston), and his brother (Sir) William Rothenstein [q.v.], who began his 'The Doll's House' portraying his own wife, Alice, and Augustus John. Some of them left later for Paris, where John studied Daumier, who reinforced the lesson he was learning from Rembrandt—that of seeing broadly and simply. In company with Conder, he spent many nights in Montmartre *boîtes*; his days he passed in the Louvre in intense study of the Masters.

In 1901 John married Ida, the eldest of the three daughters of John Trivett Nettleship [q.v.], animal painter and brother of Henry, Edward, and Richard [qq.v.]. Ida, who had been a fellow student at the Slade, bore John five sons (the second of whom, Sir Caspar John, was first sea lord, 1960-3) before she died in Paris in 1907. In 1903 he had met Dorothy (known as Dorelia, died 1969), daughter of William George McNeill, a mercantile clerk, of Camberwell. Dorelia also had a son by John by the time of Ida's death, and subsequently two daughters. John also had two other illegitimate daughters (1915 and 1922) and a son (1935). But it was Dorelia who was the dominant figure from 1903 until the end of John's life. Their relationship was extremely complex. She appeared to tolerate his innumerable infidelities. One day about 1939 Richard Hughes and she were walking together with a little boy, one of Augustus's illegitimate sons, when she exclaimed, 'There's one thing about John I've never got used to . . . Time after time *he's late for lunch*'.

From 1901 until 1902 John was an art instructor in the university of Liverpool, where he became an accomplished etcher and formed a lifelong attachment to gipsies. In 1903 he and Ida moved to Matching Green, Essex, where the following year they were joined by Dorelia. John's restlessness impelled him to be constantly on the move: he travelled about, often in a caravan with members of his family, often alone on foot, mainly in Provence, and also in Italy, Ireland, Scotland, and Wales. Later in his life John observed: 'I am just a legend; not a real person at all.' To a friend he wrote 'I am in a curious state . . . wondering who I am. I watch myself closely without being able to classify myself. I evade definition—that must mean I have no *character*.' He hated solitude, in which he was miserable and lost confidence, yet he wrote of Wyndham Lewis [q.v.]: 'What a mistake it is to have a friend—or, having one, ever to see him.' Towards his friends he could display—arbitrarily, as the mood took him—affectionate loyalty and hospitality and unmitigated venom. Many of those who knew him were aware that he often believed himself to be a 'hollow man', lacking a basic self and—in spite of his formidable industry—a basic purpose. Such a belief by a weak man, a failure, would be natural enough, but John was far otherwise; all his life he did almost exactly as he wished, and no painter of his generation was more illustrious from his Slade days, when fellow students would paste together drawings he had thought worthless, torn up, and thrown away. He became a legend long before he had reached middle age: the great artist, the great lover, the great Bohemian. It is scarcely an exaggeration to say that—outside academic circles—he was worshipped: he was splendidly romantic in appearance, a draughtsman of rare mastery, and a notable painter.

The disparity between his own lack of a sense of personal identity, his awareness of his shortcomings, as both man and artist, and his legendary public reputation was anomalous. John early attained mastery as a draughtsman (to cite two among many examples of this: 'Studies of a male nude with a staff' and 'Ida Nettleship, Ursula Tyrwhitt and Gwen John', both *c*.1897), but his progress as a painter was slower. By the turn of the century it too had matured, as is apparent in 'Merikli' (his wife Ida) of 1901-2 and, far more impressively, in 'Estella Cerutti' of 1902 (both in Manchester City Art Gallery). From then onwards until the late 1920s, when his painting began to deteriorate, he produced a succession of masterly works, his powers enhanced by his knowledge of modern Continental masters: among others Puvis de Chavannes, Manet, Sisley, Pissarro, Monet, Degas, Bonnard, and Rouault.

The war of 1914-18 (in which he was physically unfit to serve) did not immediately affect the quality of his painting, as is shown by his portraits, for example those of George Bernard Shaw and Arthur Symons, but in spite of, or possibly because of, his immense social and professional success at the Versailles peace conference—'he held court in Paris', Francis

Stevenson recorded—he began to paint and draw less well. To take a single instance of each: his 'In Memoriam Amedeo Modigliani' (c.1920) compared unfavourably with most of his earlier paintings, while 'Ronald Firbank' (c.1917-19) hardly compares with the least of his Slade drawings. After the late 1920s from time to time the deterioration was splendidly arrested. For instance, 'Joseph Hone' of 1932 and 'Matthew Smith' of 1944 (both at the Tate Gallery) combined nobility of form and resonant colour with a profound insight into character.

Decline is no more precisely explicable than its reverse, but there were circumstances in John's life and his attitude towards his art which contributed to it. His conduct of life, especially his restlessness and his addiction to alcohol, combined to undermine his immensely powerful constitution. As early as 1932 T. E. Lawrence wrote: 'John is in ruins.' Moreover, his growing preoccupation with large-scale imaginative painting was unsuited to the fulfilment of his greatest talents, which were for portraiture and landscape, and the combination of both. Another likely cause of his decline was his increasing preoccupation with imagination. When his work, of whatever kind, was firmly based on what he saw, he often showed himself a master. But he became ever more preoccupied with a form of painting which he described as being 'without any direct reference to "visual nature"' but dependent on the power of invention, which he lacked, namely the big composition. Opening an exhibition at the Tate in 1939, he said: 'When one thinks of painting on great expanses of wall, painting of other kinds seems hardly worth doing.' And where did this preoccupation eventually lead him? Referring to an attempt lasting for years to create a gigantic triptych, 'Les Saintes-Maries de la Mer with Sainte Sara l'Egyptienne', he had, in 1961, to make the agonizing confession: 'The triptych is no good and never will be.' His earlier and most famous large-scale 'imaginative' painting, 'Lyric Fantasy' (1911-15, at the Tate Gallery), was in fact an assembly of portraits, including one of Dorelia, two of children, probably his sons Caspar and Romilly, and the setting resembled Wareham Heath, Dorset. John's genius was for penetrating observation of 'visual nature' and its interpretation in terms audacious yet lyrical. Without the presence of 'visual nature' he was lost.

Besides contributions to the *Journal of the Gypsy Lore Society* and articles on painting, he was persuaded to write *Chiaroscuro, Fragments of Autobiography*, published in 1952, a book marked by a medley of passages of beauty and wit and, in contrast, ponderousness of phrase and entire absence of order. A second volume, *Finishing Touches* (not published until 1964),

like its predecessor, contained fine passages but was even more fragmented. Of the many exhibitions of John's work the principal were the retrospective at the Royal Academy in 1954 (of which he had been a member since 1928), and those at the National Portrait Gallery in 1975, one covering his art and the other his life. Among the honours conferred on him the highest was the Order of Merit, in 1942. He had become RA in 1928.

He died 31 October 1961 at his home, Fryern Court, in Fordingbridge, Hampshire. To cite defects in his character and his work is not difficult, but—to quote Lawrence again— he was 'a giant of a man' and although, on account of changing fashion and indiscriminate praise, his reputation declined, he is likely to be recognized as one of the masters of his age.

There is a memorial statue (1967) by Ivor Roberts-Jones at Fordingbridge. Among John's self-portraits, one (an etching) is in the Bradford City Art Gallery; one in the National Museum of Wales; and one in chalk (c.1901) at the National Portrait Gallery. Also at the National Portrait Gallery are a chalk portrait by (Sir) William Rothenstein (1924); a whole-length canvas by (Sir) William Orpen (1900); and a bronze cast of the head by (Sir) Jacob Epstein (1916). A portrait as a young man by (Sir) William Rothenstein is in the Walker Art Gallery, Liverpool, and a pastel by the same artist is in the Bradford City Art Gallery. Three oils were done by Matthew Smith, one of which (1944) is in the Museum of Fine Art, Montreal, and a portrait sketch and a pencil drawing were made by Ambrose McEvoy. In the Manchester City Art Gallery is a portrait by S. MacColl (oil on panel), and in the National Museum of Wales is one by T. C. Dugdale (1943).

[Michael Holroyd, *Augustus John*, 2 vols., 1974 and 1975; Augustus John, *Chiaroscuro*, 1952, and *Finishing Touches*, 1964 (autobiographies); Malcolm Easton and Michael Holroyd, *The Art of Augustus John*, 1974; Malcolm Easton and Romilly John, *Augustus John* (National Portrait Gallery, 1975); *Augustus John* (Beaverbrook Newspapers, 1962), with an introduction by Sir John Rothenstein; personal knowledge.]

JOHN ROTHENSTEIN

JOHNS, WILLIAM EARL (1893-1968), writer, journalist, and creator of the children's popular fiction character 'Biggles', was born 5 February 1893 at Hertford, the eldest son of Richard William Eastman Johns, a tailor, and his wife, Elizabeth Earl. He was educated at Bengeo School and Hertford Grammar School, also attending evening classes at the local art school.

After leaving school he completed indentures with a firm of surveyors. Taking a job in Norfolk, he fulfilled an ambition to become a soldier by enlisting as a part-time private with the Norfolk Yeomanry. He was called up for active service on the outbreak of World War I. In the autumn of 1914 he married Maud Penelope Hunt, daughter of a Norfolk clergyman, and their only son was born in March 1916.

Johns served with the Yeomanry at Gallipoli and then with the Machine-Gun Corps in the Salonika campaign, transferring to the Royal Flying Corps in 1917. He was commissioned as second lieutenant on 26 September, training as a pilot. After several postings as a flying instructor, he joined No. 55 Squadron at Azelot, France, in August 1918, flying DH4 bombers on long-range raids into the Rhineland.

On 16 September the squadron raided Mannheim. Johns's aircraft was damaged by anti-aircraft fire and, as he returned to base, he found himself fighting a battle with Fokker DVII's of Ernst Udet's famous Jadgstaffel. Johns's observer was killed and Johns, wounded, crashed and was captured. At Strasburg he was tried and condemned to death for 'war crimes', accused of indiscriminate bombing of civilian targets, but saved by the possibility of an armistice. He spent the rest of the war in prisoner-of-war camps, attempting two escapes.

He remained in the Royal Air Force until 1927, being promoted to flying officer in 1920. He flew in RAF displays and was on the organizing committee of the Hendon air display.

In 1923 it was Johns who, as recruiting officer, admitted T. E. Lawrence [q.v.] into the RAF as 'Ross'; he wanted to reject him for giving a name that was obviously false, but accepted him under orders. Later, Johns exploded the myth that Lawrence's identity in the RAF was ever a secret; from the first day, one officer warned another that 'aircraftman second class Ross' dined with Cabinet ministers.

By 1923 Johns had left his first wife and met Doris May Leigh. In 1924 they had set up home in Newcastle. On leaving the RAF Johns became an aviation illustrator (sharing a studio with the illustrator Howard Leigh, Doris's brother) and then tried his hand at journalism. In 1932 he became founder-editor of the monthly *Popular Flying*. It was in this magazine that he first introduced 'Biggles', the archetypal RFC pilot. The first collection of these stories appeared as *The Camels are Coming* (1932). By the time of his death, Johns had written ninety-six 'Biggles' books and his airman had been consecutively a World War

I 'ace', a freelance adventurer, a World War II squadron-leader, and, finally, an 'air-detective' at Scotland Yard.

Johns's output was prodigious. In the 1930s he wrote regularly for the *Modern Boy*, *Pearson's Magazine*, and *My Garden*, as well as editing *Popular Flying*. In April 1938 he also edited a weekly, *Flying*. In 1939, owing to his criticism of government air defence policy, he was dismissed from his editorships. At the outbreak of war he lectured to the Air Training Corps (in whose foundation he had been involved) and wrote for the *ATC Gazette*. He also wrote specialized aviation books for the Air Ministry and Ministry of Information. Johns's 'Biggles' stories had an immense impact on recruitment to the RAF.

'Worrals of the WAAF', the female counterpart of 'Biggles', was created by Johns at the request of the Air Ministry to promote the Women's Auxiliary Air Force, and a similar demand from the War Office for a soldier hero was met by the creation of 'Gimlet'—a commando.

After ten years in Scotland, where Johns indulged in his favourite pastimes of shooting and fishing, he and Doris Johns moved to Park House, Hampton Court, in the mid 1950s. When he died at Park House 21 June 1968, he had published 169 titles: 104 under 'Biggles'; 11 under 'Worrals', 10 under 'Gimlet', 10 science-fiction adventures, 5 'Steeley' novels, 8 miscellaneous juvenile titles, 11 adult thrillers, and 6 non-fiction titles. His works were translated into fourteen languages, issued in braille, serialized in newspapers and magazines in Britain, Australia, and Europe, broadcast on radio in Britain, Australia, and South Africa, televised by Granada TV, turned into strip cartoons, and issued as cassette recordings. After Enid Blyton [q.v.], Johns was the most prolific and popular children's writer of the time.

In his later years, and after his death, Johns came under attack from children's librarians and others who accused him of racialism, outmoded concepts, and stereotype characters. Although some of his books reflect the prejudices of his times, a reading of his works reveals his tremendous, almost puckish, sense of humour, and his habit of making fun of his own supposed prejudices. The critic Stanley Reynolds summed up the secret of Johns's success: 'The appeal is that "Biggles" is a flier and Captain Johns writes wonderously about flying . . . The writing is so vivid that it sticks in your mind and years after you remember it.'

Popular in Service circles and the book world, Johns, with his short bulky figure and his well-groomed grey hair and ready smile, was greeted enthusiastically by his wide range of friends.

A craftsman, he always delivered his work on time and to the exact length required.

[RAF officers' records, Ministry of Defence; W. E. Johns, articles in *Popular Flying*, June 1933, June 1935, and June 1936; Kriegsarchiv, Bayerisches Haupstaatarchiv, Munich; Alan Morris, *First of Many—The Story of the Independent Force, RAF*, 1968; *The Times*, 22 June 1968; *Guardian*, 6 January 1979.]   PETER BERRESFORD ELLIS
PIERS WILLIAMS

JOHNSON, CHARLES (1870-1961), assistant keeper of the public records and historian, was born at Newcastle upon Tyne 2 May 1870, the only child of Edmund White Johnson, timber merchant, by his wife, Elizabeth Hannah, daughter of his senior partner, John Herring. He was educated at Giggleswick School and Trinity College, Oxford, which he entered as a classical scholar in 1888. After obtaining a first class in *literae humaniores* (1892) he entered the Public Record Office in 1893 and, except for a brief period on loan to the army contracts directorate of the War Office in 1918, he remained there until his retirement in 1930. After the outbreak of war in 1939 he was recalled to take charge of the records stored for safe-keeping in Culham College and finally retired in 1946.

For much of his official career Johnson was engaged in the arrangement and reclassification of the ancient miscellanea and files of the Chancery brought together from the Tower and Rolls Chapel. He also contributed substantially to various texts and calendars published by the Office. He was secretary of the advisory committee on publications appointed by the master of the Rolls in 1912, and a member of the Inspecting Officers and Manorial Records Committees.

Extra-officially he collaborated with two of his colleagues, C. G. Crump (whose notice he contributed to this Dictionary) and Arthur Hughes, in producing the standard edition of *Dialogus de Scaccario* (1902), and he was largely responsible for the Domesday section of the *Victoria History of the County of Norfolk* (1906). With his colleague (Sir) C. H. Jenkinson [q.v.] he produced *English Court Hand* (1915) which became a standard work for the student of the handwritings of medieval records. He was a general editor of the series of Helps for Students of History published by the Society for the Promotion of Christian Knowledge between 1918 and 1924 and himself contributed three handbooks to the series: *The Public Record Office* (1918), *The Care of Documents and Management of Archives* (1919), and *The Mechanical Processes of the Historian* (1922).

In 1913 he became interested in proposals for a dictionary of medieval Latin and when, in 1924, the British Academy, in furtherance of a plan for an international dictionary of medieval Latin sponsored by the International Academic Union, set up two committees to collect materials from British and Irish sources he was appointed secretary of the committee concerned with the post-Conquest period. The committees united in 1931 and in 1934 the *Medieval Latin Word-List from British and Irish Sources*, edited by the joint secretaries, was published by the Oxford University Press. The next stage of the project, the revision and amplification of the materials leading to the publication of the *Revised Word-List* (1965), was carried through and plans prepared for the final stage of the full-scale dictionary with Johnson as principal initiator and guide.

After his retirement in 1930 much of his time was devoted to the editing of some of the basic texts of English medieval history. He accepted the invitation of the Oxford University Press to continue the *Regesta Regum Anglo-Normannorum* begun by H. W. C. Davis [q.v.] and with the assistance of H. A. Cronne completed the second volume, covering the reign of Henry I, which was published in 1956. His translations of *Dialogus de Scaccario*, Nicholas Oresme's *De Moneta* with a selection of *English Mint Documents*, and Hugh the Chantor's *History of the Church of York, 1066–1127*, were published in Nelson's series of Medieval Classics in 1950, 1956, and 1961 respectively, and his edition of the *Register of Hamo de Hethe, bishop of Rochester, 1316–52* was issued by the Canterbury and York Society over the years 1914 to 1948. He made frequent contributions of articles and reviews on historical topics to learned journals and served on the councils of several learned societies. He was a fellow of the Royal Historical Society and of the Society of Antiquaries and a vice-president of both, a founder-member of the Canterbury and York Society, its joint secretary for many years and later a vice-president, a member of the council of the Pipe Roll Society, and a member of the committee of the Institute of Historical Research from 1933 to 1945 and of the management committee of the Victoria County History from its formation in 1933 until 1955. His services to scholarship were recognized by his election as a fellow of the British Academy in 1934 and his appointment as CBE in 1951.

Johnson's career spanned a period of transformation in historical studies in England resulting in part from the development of new expertise in the use and interpretation of records, to which he himself greatly contributed. His influence was particularly felt in medieval history, where he helped to promote a new understanding of the interrelation between records and administration and to encourage a scientific rather than an antiquarian approach to the interpretation of documents. His meticulous scholarship and exhaustive knowledge of the records supported by a grasp of the intricacies of administration and finance earned for him a unique authority among his colleagues and the many scholars throughout the world who sought his advice.

He was of shy and modest disposition, laconic in speech, and disposed to overestimate his hearer's knowledge, but most rewarding when drawn out in question and answer. He had great serenity of spirit and generosity of heart, never bitter in controversy and never wounding in criticism. His loyalty to his friends was absolute. As a young man he took pleasure in walking, cycling, and rowing and, though never of a robust appearance, he had a toughness of physique which carried him through some serious illnesses in later life. A few years after his fiftieth birthday he began to wear a beard, largely in consequence of a serious and disfiguring accident. He died suddenly at his home in Hampstead 5 November 1961.

He married twice: first, in 1907, his cousin Mabel Catherine Rudd, who died in 1947; secondly, in 1950, Violet Margaret, eldest daughter of Arthur Mutrie Shepherd, of Boars Hill, Oxford. There were no children of either marriage.

A pencil sketch of Johnson made by his friend Laurence Binyon [q.v.] about 1892 is in the possession of the Athenaeum. A copy signed by Johnson is in the Public Record Office library.

[H. C. Johnson in *Proceedings* of the British Academy, vol. li, 1965; *The Times*, 7 November 1961; private information; personal knowledge.]   H. C. JOHNSON

JOHNSON, HEWLETT (1874-1966), dean successively of Manchester and Canterbury, was born in Manchester 25 January 1874, the third son of Charles Johnson, wire manufacturer, and his wife, Rosa, daughter of the Revd Alfred Hewlett, who for more than half a century worked in the parish of Astley where he was known as the 'Spurgeon of the North'. Johnson was educated at Macclesfield Grammar School and the Owens College, Manchester, where he took a B.Sc. in 1894 and won the geological prize. In 1898 he became an associate member of the Institute of Civil Engineers. Although he was trained for a business career, his knowledge of the slums of Manchester combined with his religious upbringing led him to offer his services to the Church Missionary Society.

He entered Wadham College, Oxford, and gained second class honours in theology in 1904. By then his liberal churchmanship made him unacceptable to the Church Missionary Society. He was ordained to a curacy in the parish of St. Margaret, Altrincham, as deacon (1905) and priest (1906). Although his outspoken and radical views were not appreciated by some of the wealthy industrialists in the neighbourhood, his ability so impressed the parish that within three years there was a successful petition to the bishop that he should be made vicar. His work was quickly recognized beyond the boundaries of the parish and in 1919 he became an honorary canon of Chester and in 1922 rural dean of Bowden. In the same year he was elected by his fellow clergy a proctor in Convocation.

An interesting venture during the Altrincham period was his editorship of a theological magazine *The Interpreter*. During the years of its history (1905-24) many leading theological scholars of the day contributed to it. Meanwhile Johnson continued his studies and in 1917 obtained the degree of BD at Oxford and in 1924, for his work on the Acts of the Apostles, the DD.

In 1924 when Ramsay MacDonald was prime minister, Johnson was appointed to the deanery of Manchester. He quickly proved that he possessed many of the qualities looked for in a dean. He preached well; he looked every inch a dignitary of the Church; he was keenly interested in civic affairs; and he had considerable charm. He was helped by his first wife, Mary, daughter of Frederick Taylor, merchant, of Broughton Park, Manchester, whom he had married in 1903. She was much loved in Manchester. In 1931 she died and in that year Johnson was transferred to Canterbury. It has sometimes been supposed that the appointment was motivated by political considerations. But MacDonald had moved far to the right and had he thought that Johnson would prove susceptible to Communist influence it is unlikely he would have considered his nomination. Rather, would it seem that it was on the recommendation of Archbishops Lang and Temple [qq.v.], both of whom had been impressed by Johnson's work in Manchester.

At the time of his appointment to Canterbury, Johnson's political affiliations were indeed uncertain. He was interested in industrial conditions; he deplored the massive unemployment; he felt the Government should do more to ease economic inequalities. But in so far as he favoured one solution rather than another, it was the theory of Social Credit as propounded by Major C. H. Douglas [q.v.]. In 1931 he was still looking to Alberta rather than to Moscow. Johnson, who had a passion for foreign travel—he claimed to have visited every cathedral in Europe—did not find his way to Russia until 1937. The rise of Fascism in Germany and Italy and his outspoken support of the Republican Government in Spain had already predisposed him in favour of the Soviet experiment. He went, he saw, and was conquered. Thereafter he became an indefatigable speaker for the Left Book Club in association with (Sir) Victor Gollancz and John Strachey [qq.v.]. Nor, later, did he modify his views. No matter what adverse reports reached him—of secret trials, terrorism, concentration camps, the atrocities of Stalin, the invasion of Hungary—he was unmoved. His loyalty to the official line of the Russian Communist Party was unflinching. He held fast to what he wanted to believe and dismissed from his mind anything which might shatter his illusions. His writings on Soviet achievement, particularly *The Socialist Sixth of the World* (1939) which had an enormous sale in many languages, help to explain the man. The significance of the book lies in what is ignored. Having decided that Soviet Communism was helping the cause of human betterment, he refused to criticize.

After the war Johnson travelled even more extensively. He paid a number of visits to Eastern Europe and went also to the United States and Canada, Australia, Cuba, and of course on several occasions to Russia where in 1951 he received the Stalin peace prize. He was especially fascinated by China which he had first visited in 1932 in the cause of famine relief. He returned there in 1952 and went again in 1956, 1959, and finally in 1964 at the age of ninety. He was as enthusiastic for the Peking, as he had been for the Moscow, regime, although it was said that the criticism and counter-criticism of the two expressions of Communist rule were a cause of embarrassment to him, had he been capable by then of embarrassment.

The political interests and journeyings, and more especially the pronouncements of the 'Red Dean', were themselves no small source of embarrassment to other people. Foreigners did not always understand his position in the hierarchy. In 1947 the archbishop of Canterbury issued a statement ending with: 'The Dean's office and jurisdiction in this country does not extend beyond the confines of the Cathedral body of which he is head. Outside those limits he speaks and acts only for himself. The Archbishop of Canterbury has neither responsibility for what the Dean may say or do, nor the power to control it.' The factors which made Johnson a controversial figure nationally and internationally caused difficulties also in the diocese and in the city and at times relationships were almost intolerable. In 1940 the canons of

the cathedral publicly dissociated themselves from their dean's political utterances. Johnson was careful, however, to give no grounds for his removal; but eventually 'events came to a head', as he put it. '. . . the Canons wanted me to go—and said so, vehemently.' His resignation took effect in 1963.

Nevertheless there were in Johnson's makeup conservative and aesthetic strains which were fulfilled in his work at Canterbury where he cherished the dignity of the ceremonial and the music in the beautiful setting of the cathedral. His critics had to respect his many gifts: he was a man of wide culture with an informed appreciation of the arts. As a preacher he continued to be eloquent and forceful. He endeared himself to many by his acts of personal kindness. He was invariably gracious. If it was never easy to know when he was speaking as chairman of the editorial board of the *Daily Worker* or as dean of Canterbury Cathedral, it must in fairness be said that he had so adjusted himself that he was unconscious of any inconsistency.

Towards the end of his life Johnson returned to psychical research which had aroused his interest when he was a young man. It had overcome his spiritual doubts and led him to the priesthood; it was his conviction that it would ultimately lead Marxists to a belief in personal survival. But in the final pages of his autobiography, *Searching for Light* (1968), he made it clear that his own belief was based on his faith in the resurrection of Christ.

Some years after the death of his first wife Johnson married, in 1938, Nowell Mary, daughter of his cousin, the late Revd George Edwards; they had two daughters. Johnson died in Canterbury 22 October 1966.

A portrait painted by his second wife is in the Deanery, Canterbury. A portrait by the Russian painter Gerassimov and a bust by the Russian sculptor Tomsk are in the possession of the family. The National Portrait Gallery has a bust by Vera Mukhina. A bust by Sir Jacob Epstein is privately owned.

[Hewlett Johnson, *Searching for Light*, 1968; private information; personal knowledge.]
                                        A. M. STOCKWOOD

JOHNSTON, THOMAS (1881–1965), politician and newspaper editor, was born 2 November 1881 at Kirkintilloch in Dunbartonshire—a small town which grew up around the site of a fort on Antonine's Wall. Johnston was proud of his association with so ancient a settlement and this undoubtedly contributed to the intense feeling for Scotland and its history which shaped and dominated his career. He was the eldest child in the family of one son and two daughters of David Johnston, a provision merchant, and his wife, Mary Blackwood. Johnston was educated at the local Board school and later at Lenzie Academy. At that time it appears that he had not considered going to university. But he had a natural talent for writing narrative and, after some unsuccessful employment as a clerical assistant in law and insurance, his opportunity came when a distant relative handed over to him a small printing establishment and the editorship of two weekly papers. Johnston had by this time become an enthusiastic member of the early socialist movement and with the assistance of some of his idealist friends the socialist weekly, *Forward*, was launched in 1906 on a capital of £60. After some years of difficulty Johnston succeeded in making *Forward* viable. Johnston's *The History of the Working Classes in Scotland*, published in 1920, sold well and was of great benefit to *Forward*. During the twenty-seven years of his editorship the newspaper was a vigorous and often violent exponent of national and municipal socialism. Johnston's early introduction to political life had been in the town council of Kirkintilloch, where he successfully founded the first Scottish municipal bank.

His real entrance into politics came in 1908 when, having entered Glasgow University as a non-graduating student in moral philosophy and political economy, he took the lead, as chairman of the recently formed university Socialist Society, in running James Keir Hardie [q.v.] for the rectorship, in which contest Hardie, although he did not win the election, polled 123 votes, a respectable total. The competent conduct of this campaign earned Johnston a high place in the political and social life of the university, and the ease and friendliness with which he mixed therein was remembered for many years.

During the war of 1914–18 Johnston conducted *Forward* from a strongly anti-war basis —so much so that in January 1916 his newspaper was suspended for printing a frank but inaccurate report which it had published of a meeting between Lloyd George and trades unionists, which was constantly interrupted. After several weeks of agitation—and an interview of Johnston by Lloyd George—publication was allowed to be resumed, to the great benefit of *Forward*'s circulation and, presumably, its profits.

In the election of 1918 Johnston stood for West Stirlingshire (near Kirkintilloch) but, not unexpectedly, he was defeated. However, rather to his surprise (and clearly not much to his enthusiasm) he gained the seat in 1922 and held it till the Labour defeat of 1924. But for good or ill he was returned in 1925 at a by-election for Dundee, then a two-member constituency. He left Dundee for his homeland of West Stirlingshire in 1929, and that remained his parliamentary base as long as he continued to sit in the House of Commons—that is, until 1945.

Johnston made his mark in the House, first as a rather unorthodox supporter of an all-party approach to the various problems created by unemployment, secondly by his vigorous attacks on companies with overseas interests which paid what he considered excessive dividends. In the Labour minority Ministry of 1929–31 he was at first under-secretary of state for Scotland and later lord privy seal (with a seat in the Cabinet). He did well in both posts but the MacDonald Government fell in the financial crisis of 1931. Johnston's views, which he later expressed in a pamphlet (1934), of this crisis, in which he saw the sinister hand of international finance, cost him his seat, which he regained in 1935.

The years 1935–9, which he describes in his memoirs as 'The Years the Locust Ate', saw Johnston in regular attendance on the back benches of the House of Commons but despairing of arousing public opinion to the reality of the menace of Hitlerism which, having travelled widely and read much, he completely understood.

But though he did not appreciate it, it was this very situation which led the way to the most constructive part of his career. The Government, in preparation for the possibility of war, set up a system of regional commissioners for Civil Defence to take over some of the immediate functions of government in the event of emergency. Johnston was selected as regional commissioner for Scotland in 1939, with Lords Airlie and Rosebery as his deputies. It was the turning point of his career. Henceforth, while not abandoning his political beliefs, he devoted himself to the social and economic interests of Scotland and the revitalization of its life. In his work to this end he was greatly stimulated by the discovery that in the crisis of 1939 and afterwards men like Rosebery and Airlie, as well as others of lesser degree, were happy to work with him in spite of his controversial past. It was the renewed confidence he gained from the way in which Scotland accepted him in his new position that enabled him to make such success as could be achieved of the very difficult problem of evacuating children in September 1939.

Again much to his surprise, Johnston was in February 1941 summoned to Downing Street and made secretary of state for Scotland, an office he held with great distinction till 1945. He made it a condition of his appointment that he should be assisted on a non-party basis by a Council of State consisting of all the living ex-secretaries of state for Scotland. This highly unorthodox experiment, which only two such unusual people as Johnston and Churchill could have allowed, worked well until the return to party politics in 1945. It enabled Johnston to push through such important legislation as the Act creating the North of Scotland Hydro-Electric Board, a measure which has done more for the economic health of Scotland than any legislation in modern times. Successful as it turned out to be, when it was launched the hydro-electric scheme aroused great controversy among landed, sporting, and amenity interests. The first scheme undertaken, Loch Sloy (Loch Lomond side), went successfully through. The crisis came over the proposal to harness the Tummel at Pitlochry, involving a pleasant stretch of the glen. Argument over the Pitlochry scheme (many of the villagers feeling it would ruin the area as a summer resort) became so fierce that in 1945 Johnston, who had ceased to be secretary of state on the formation of the Labour Government, felt compelled himself to assume the chairmanship of the North of Scotland Hydro-Electric Board. His skill in public relations, together with his drive and energy, forced through the scheme. It was a great success, contributing greatly to the prosperity of Pitlochry.

Thereafter the harnessing of Highland water power went ahead with only minor difficulties and today, with its constructive work almost complete, it functions smoothly. The Hydro-Electric Board, from which he resigned in 1959, was Johnston's great post-war achievement—although he did useful work for a period after 1945 as chairman of the Scottish Tourist Board, as a forestry commissioner, and as chairman of the Broadcasting Council for Scotland.

Few were better at handling the press than Johnston. Himself a born journalist, he took conferences with ease and his confidential meetings with editors were notable for the ideas he put forward to test the movement of Scottish opinion. To this Dictionary Johnston contributed the notices of John Wheatley, James Maxton, and the first Baron Kirkwood.

Although Johnston was so prominent in public life he had few intimate friends. There was an inner core of reserve and modesty which he allowed only a few to penetrate. Thus, when in 1951 the university of Aberdeen offered him its chancellorship, he only accepted the appointment after consulting these intimates as to his fitness in the public eye for such an academic post. Johnston was president of the Scottish History Society from 1950 to 1952. Among the honours conferred on him were CH (1953); the position of freeman of Edinburgh (1944), of Campbeltown in Argyllshire (1945), and of Kirkintilloch; and LLD

(Glasgow, 1945). Typically, he refused a peerage offered to him in 1945.

In 1914 Johnston married Margaret F. Cochrane, who died in 1977 at the age of eighty-seven. They had two daughters. He spent his last few years in retirement at his home in Milngavie, not far from his birthplace. He died there 5 September 1965.

There is an official portrait (1956) by (Sir) James Gunn in the Scottish National Portrait Gallery. There is also a bronze head (1953) by Gladys Barron in the headquarters of the Hydro-Electric Board in Edinburgh.

[Thomas Johnston, *Memories*, 1952; personal knowledge.]   WILLIAM ROBIESON

JONES, ARNOLD HUGH MARTIN (1904-1970), historian of Greece and Rome, was born at Birkenhead 9 March 1904, the son of John Arthur Jones, then on the staff of the *Liverpool Post* and later (1908-24) editor of the *Statesman* of Calcutta, and his wife, Elsie Martin, daughter of a clergyman. A. H. M. Jones's grandfather was a Wesleyan Methodist minister. Jones himself, however, became an agnostic. He was educated at Cheltenham College and, from 1922, at New College, Oxford, where he took a first class in both classical honour moderations (1924) and *literae humaniores* (1926), and won the Craven scholarship (1923). His fluency in the classical languages was such that in later years he would read the Church Fathers in hospital with the zest and rapidity with which others might have devoured novels.

In 1926 he was elected to a fellowship at All Souls, whither he returned after being reader in ancient history at the Egyptian university of Cairo from 1929 to 1934; he always greatly valued his connection with the college. From 1939 to 1946 he was lecturer in ancient history at Wadham College, Oxford. During the war of 1939-45 he served first in the Ministry of Labour, then in intelligence at the War Office. His experience of wartime direction of labour helped to suggest to him that a shortage of manpower explained the regulations that tied all sorts of men to their occupations in the late Roman empire. He had already gained a high reputation as a historian, and became professor of ancient history, first at University College, London (1946), and then at Cambridge (1951), where he was a fellow of Jesus College.

Jones's interests lay not so much in political, diplomatic, and military history, which has mostly absorbed the attention of students of Greece and Rome, or in the history of ideas, as in social and economic conditions and still more in institutions and administration. To the analysis of these subjects he brought the most comprehensive knowledge of written texts, literary, juristic, epigraphic, and papyrological, over a period extending from classical Greece to the reign of Heraclius. In his younger days he took part in excavations at Constantinople and Jerash, and he had a keen interest in architecture, which led to his writing accounts of the buildings of New College and All Souls and Worcester colleges for the *Victoria History of the County of Oxford*, vol. iii (1954). It is rather curious that he made little use of archaeological evidence for the ancient world, even for the social and economic history on which it can chiefly throw light. Before and during his tenure of the post at Cairo, he travelled widely in the Near East, and at all times he liked to see for himself the lands in which Graeco-Roman civilization had flourished, but topographical knowledge too is not conspicuous in his works.

In the earlier part of his career he read extensively in modern scholarly literature, but as time went on, he cared less to know what others had written. He did not indulge in polemic, and he was confident that in setting out what he saw as certain or probable, on the basis of his mastery of original evidence, he would have much to say that was true, which others had not discerned. This confidence was generally justified. He was indeed fairly criticized for relying too often on easily accessible collections of inscriptions rather than on the most reliable publications. In no other respect might his scholarly accuracy be impugned. Ignoring most modern works, he would invariably cite and often quote the full evidence on every problem, so that every reader could form his own judgement; as he expressly says, this often showed how little basis there is for any solution. He could indeed hardly have written so much and over so wide a range from personal scrutiny of the evidence, if he had not restricted himself as he did. His practice resembled that of Fustel de Coulanges, whom he rivalled in the range of his knowledge, which no contemporary historian of antiquity equalled.

The candour with which Jones presented his material was matched by the soberness and good sense of his judgement. To all this he added, again like Fustel, a marvellous clarity in exposition. Every sentence was crystal clear; every paragraph marshalled the facts and arguments with lucidity and force. This came so naturally to him that, once he had thought out a subject, he hardly ever needed to blot a word in the first draft. For that matter, he would not readily amend the manuscript in deference to objections, and with one exception, in republishing his works, he altered them very little. Rationally and carefully formed, his convictions were hard to shake.

His first book was *A History of Abyssinia*

(1935), written in conjunction with Elizabeth Monroe, and reprinted in 1955 as *A History of Ethiopia*. In 1938 he published *The Herods of Judaea*, his principal essay in narrative history, a readable survey for the general public. Meantime, in 1937 his *Cities of the Eastern Roman Provinces* had come out, a large work that was corrected and brought up to date with the help of collaborators just before he died. It traces the diffusion of the Greek city from Alexander to Justinian, and though useful, too much resembles an arid gazetteer. But it was the groundwork for *The Greek City from Alexander to Justinian* (1940), in which he not only analysed the process of diffusion, but also the relations between the cities and the Hellenistic monarchies and central government at Rome, the developments in their internal institutions, their economic basis, and their cultural functions. Replete with information, this is also a grand synoptic work, reprinted as a paperback without change in 1979. Jones developed M. I. Rostovtzev's insight, in stressing the gulf between the cities and the peasantry they exploited. The cities themselves came wholly under the control of local magnates, who he thought were chiefly landowners. In later works, too, Jones argued, against what had been received doctrine, that trade and industry were of relatively little importance in the Roman economy and were insignificant as a source for the wealth of the ruling class. He also gave a powerful exposition of the view, familiar enough, that the decay of civic patriotism, due to excessive central control and the burden of taxation, helps to explain the fall of the Roman empire; later he was to give more weight to barbarian invasions than to internal decay.

As this book shows, Jones's own mildly socialist leanings made it easier for him than for most classical scholars to discard the aristocratic prejudices of Greek and Roman writers. Hence his *Athenian Democracy* (1957) gives a sympathetic account of that system, but it was characteristic of him also to enquire how Athenian democracy actually worked. His *Studies in Roman Government and Law* (1960), another collection of seminal articles which relate to the Roman principate, betray the same concern with institutions and their operation. They first illustrate his mastery of Roman public and criminal law; a posthumously published book, *The Criminal Courts of the Roman Republic and Principate* (1972), unfortunately takes too little account of a new and revolutionary theory. It shows some falling off of his powers, like his last excursions into the history of the classical periods, *Sparta* (1967) and *Augustus* (1970), which were designed for general readers or students. For their benefit he also compiled select volumes of evidence and a summary of his *magnum opus* on the late Roman empire. For scholars he planned *The Prosopography of the Roman Empire*, edited the first volume (1971) and made substantial contributions to it: this was in itself an immense work. His pen was indeed never inactive.

Meantime in 1964 he had issued *The Later Roman Empire AD 284-602*, two volumes of text and one of notes, which he added when the text was in page proof. Parts of it were founded on memorable articles which were collected, with important pieces on unconnected subjects, in *The Roman Economy* (1974). It is sub-titled 'A Social, Economic and Administrative Survey'; even the narrative sketch of some three hundred pages with which it begins contains numerous excursuses on these matters. A. Momigliano remarked that 'the unusual form of this book cannot be explained without the English tradition of Royal Commissions, social surveys, Fabian Society pamphlets. A. H. M. Jones is clearly in the direct line of the Webbs and Hammonds, indeed of Booth and Beveridge.' This does not imply that the work is ahistorical. The process of evolution is everywhere on show. What is omitted is the record of sentiments and beliefs. Jones cared more about ecclesiastical organization than about saints or theologians. That did not make him underrate the importance of ideas. *Constantine and the Conversion of Europe* (1948), the best of his books of *vulgarisation*, had totally rejected the notion that Constantine was no more than a rational political schemer; Jones later found new evidence to prove the authenticity of the documents that illustrate Constantine's religiosity. Still he now made little of spiritual developments. Nor will every one think that his new interpretation of the break-up of the empire is an improvement on that given in his *Greek City*. But the book remains the greatest contribution in English to Roman imperial history since Gibbon, astounding not only for the abundance of information but for its acumen, sweep, coherence, and elegance in presentation.

Jones was elected a fellow of the British Academy in 1947, and was president of the Society for the Promotion of Roman Studies from 1952 to 1955. He was a fellow of All Souls from 1926 to 1946. His contributions to Roman law and Church history earned him respectively doctorates in law from Cambridge (1965) and in divinity from Oxford (1966). New College made him an honorary fellow.

Jones was a little man, somewhat bowed, with sparse, sandy hair and keen eyes; he spoke swiftly, softly, and jerkily (and lectured, not very attractively, in the same style); he used few words and had no small talk. Always known as 'Hugo', he was friendly and easily accessible, treated all as his equals, and was generous in praise where he thought it due; the development of social and economic study of the ancient world at Cambridge owed much to his example and encouragement. In private affairs one could turn to him for kind and judicious advice.

Shortly before his retirement was due, he died suddenly on a sea-crossing from Brindisi to Patras 9 April 1970. He had previously been subject to various illnesses, but they hardly disturbed the copious flow of his publications. In 1927 he married Freda Katharine Mackrell, a medievalist, who survived him with two sons and a daughter.

[John Crook in *Proceedings* of the British Academy, vol. lvii, 1971; private information; personal knowledge.]   P. A. BRUNT

JONES, ARTHUR CREECH (1891-1964), politician, was born in Bristol 15 May 1891, the second of the three sons of Joseph Jones, journeyman lithographic printer, and his wife, Rosina Sweet. Until 1905 he attended Whitehall Boys' School, winning a scholarship which enabled him to study French, mathematics, and commercial subjects for an extra year. He then worked in a solicitor's office in Bristol and prepared at evening classes for the Civil Service junior clerks' examination. In 1907 he entered the service of the War Office. For almost ten years he served in several departments of the Civil Service, including the Crown Agents' Office. At this time he was called plain Arthur Jones, but later he made greater use of his more distinctive second name and was known to all but his closest friends as Creech.

When he began to question the dogma of the Methodist Church, of which he was a member until 1912, he joined, in 1910, the Liberal Christian League. Through lectures which he organized for its study group, on the relationship between religion and politics, he met some of the leading radical churchmen and politicians. Creech Jones fulfilled his membership pledge to personal social service by becoming, in 1913, a founder-member and honorary secretary of the borough of Camberwell trades and labour council. By now unable to subscribe to certain tenets of the Nonconformist faith he became a humanist and an international socialist. While serving as honorary secretary to the Dulwich branch of the Independent Labour Party in 1913 he arranged meetings for the party's anti-conscription campaign; he joined the South London Federal Council against Conscription and, in 1915, the No-Conscription Fellowship. For his ideals he was imprisoned from September 1916 to April 1919. Imprisonment was particularly hard for him to bear as rambling and sketching had been his chief relaxation. However, he read history, politics, and economics as determinedly and widely as possible in the circumstances and emerged with greater understanding of his own character, abilities, and vocation.

On release Creech Jones resumed work for the local trade-union movement and was also appointed secretary of the National Union of Docks, Wharves, and Shipping Staffs and editor of its journal, *Quayside and Office*. When his union amalgamated with the Transport and General Workers' Union in 1922 he was promoted national secretary of the administrative, clerical, and supervisory group. As such he travelled to the Ruhr with Ben Tillett [q.v.] and Samuel Warren in 1923 to report on the effect of French occupation on the workers.

Although he had long been interested in the theory of colonial rule, Creech Jones's first practical contact with African problems was in 1926 when he began to instruct Clements Kadalie, general secretary of the South African Industrial and Commercial Workers' Union, on trade-union organization. In 1928 the Workers' Educational Association published his handbook *Trade Unionism To-day* which was much used in the colonies.

After unsuccessfully contesting the Heywood and Radcliffe constituency in Lancashire in 1929 Creech Jones left the union to become organizing secretary of the Workers' Travel Association, on the management committee of which he had served since its inception in 1921. Always an ardent traveller, by 1939 he had visited Palestine and most countries in Europe and written of his experiences in the Association's journal, *The Travel Log*.

Events in Germany convinced Creech Jones that he should again stand for Parliament and in 1935, as a member of the Labour Party, he was elected for the Shipley division of Yorkshire. Immediately his interest in colonial affairs became apparent and he was invited to join the Labour Party's advisory committee on imperial questions, of which he became chairman in 1943; this enabled him to make an important, continuous contribution to the formation of the party's colonial policy. In 1937 he was chosen one of the first members of the Trades Union Congress colonial affairs committee. Multifarious problems from every part of the Empire were submitted to him to bring before the notice of Parliament, the British public, the trade-union movement, and the Labour Party. His energy, enthusiasm, and persistence made him an acknowledged expert in colonial affairs; his warm friendliness, approachability, and 'colour-blindness' brought him the trust and affection of colonial peoples.

Meticulous attention to detail enabled him, where others had failed, to pilot through Parliament, as a private member's Bill, the Access to Mountains Act in 1939: a cause very dear to his heart.

From May 1940 to June 1944 Creech Jones served in the Ministry of Labour as parliamentary private secretary to Ernest Bevin [q.v.]; there he worked for the interests of conscientious objectors and immigrant labourers, for the rehabilitation of the disabled, and the education and vocational training of the armed forces. As an executive committee member of the Fabian Society he founded in 1940, with Dr Rita Hinden, the Fabian Colonial Bureau. Through the Bureau he extended his work for colonial peoples and collected the information upon which, in 1943, the Labour Party based its policy statements for post-war action. He paid his first visit to colonial territories in 1943–4 as vice-chairman under Walter Elliot [q.v.] of the commission on higher education for West Africa.

In August 1945 Creech Jones entered the Colonial Office as parliamentary undersecretary of state; from October 1946 he held office as secretary of state until his narrow defeat in the general election of 1950. He did a great deal to reorganize the Colonial Office and to reshape the Colonial Service in order to meet the changed and increasing needs of the colonies, founding the Colonial Development Corporation and fostering colonial research projects. He paid several visits to the colonies and represented Britain at the United Nations during the debates on the cession of the Palestine mandate in 1946 and 1947–8. In preparing British dependencies for political independence Creech Jones was deeply involved in reforming their constitutions and promoting their economic and social development. In 1948 Ceylon achieved independence, the first colony with a non-European population to do so. Creech Jones presided over the Montego Bay conference on West Indian federation in 1947 and over the first African Conference at Lancaster House in 1948.

Creech Jones emphasized adult education as a necessary preliminary to self-government. Adult education in Britain had always interested him. He was a governor of Ruskin College (1923–56) and, from 1954, of Queen Elizabeth House, Oxford; he was also a vice-president of the Workers' Educational Association and a vice-chairman of the British Institute of Adult Education.

While out of Parliament, Creech Jones continued to work for the Commonwealth by writing, lecturing, chairing conferences for the Fabian Colonial Bureau, acting as chairman and delegate for the British Council of Pacific Relations, and leading deputations to ministers from the Anti-Slavery Society and the Africa Bureau. He opposed the federation of British

Central Africa and supported the cause of Tshekedi Khama [q.v.]. In the general election of 1951 he fought an unsuccessful campaign in Romford. Essex, but he won a by-election at Wakefield, Yorkshire, in 1954 and represented that constituency until his resignation due to ill health in August 1964. His interest in these ten years returned to international responsibility for developing countries and the promotion of international understanding in colonial affairs and he travelled to many Commonwealth countries as a Commonwealth Parliamentary Association delegate.

Creech Jones was not a brilliant speaker in the House of Commons but he was respected for his knowledge and integrity by members of all political parties. He was sworn of the Privy Council in 1946. He died in London 23 October 1964. In 1920 he married Violet May (died 1975), younger daughter of Joseph Tidman, with whose family in Goose Green, Camberwell, he had lodged when he first moved to London.

[The papers of Arthur Creech Jones, Oxford University Colonial Records Project, Rhodes House Library, Oxford; the papers of the Fabian Colonial Bureau, ibid.; the papers of the Anti-Slavery Society for the Protection of Human Rights, ibid.; British Labour Party records, Transport House; private information.]   PATRICIA M. PUGH

JONES, SIR (GEORGE) RODERICK (1877–1962), newsagency head, was born at Dukinfield, Cheshire, 21 October 1877, the son of Roderick Patrick Jones, hat salesman, of Manchester, and Christina, second daughter of William Gibb, of Kilmarnock. Gibb, a cousin of Archbishop A. C. Tait [q.v.] took control of the boy's education. When Jones's father died, he was sent to live with Gibb's married daughter in Pretoria, South Africa.

The move decided his career. Quick-minded, eager, ambitious, Jones became a Pretoria journalist in his teens. Speaking Afrikaans like a Boer, he gained the confidence of Paul Kruger, president of the Transvaal Republic. To him he translated the telegram sent by Joseph Chamberlain [q.v.] after the Jameson Raid. Immediately the raiders had been captured and brought to Pretoria Jones interviewed (Sir) L. S. Jameson [q.v.], who later became a friend, exclusively for Reuters. Jones was eighteen. His long career of notable service to the British newsagency had begun.

Always a keen horseman—he was later master of the Cape hounds—Jones was arrested by the British as a spy and then covered the early part of the Boer War as a correspondent with the British cavalry. He was soon a man of note. Louis Botha and Jan Christian Smuts [qq.v.] later became his friends. (All his life Jones had the gift of turning eminent acquaintances into friends. They stayed with him after his fall.) When in 1902 Reuters needed an editor for its South African desk in London, Jones, then both Reuters' senior cable correspondent in Cape Town and chief sub-editor on the *Cape Times*, was chosen. He was twenty-four, self-confident, soon on personal terms with Baron Herbert de Reuter, son of the agency's founder and then its head. Having pressed his claim to swift promotion, he returned to Cape Town in 1905 in full charge of Reuters' South African operations. When the Baron committed suicide in 1915, Jones was called to London and given control of the company, thus fulfilling the hope he had expressed six years earlier of succeeding de Reuter.

Reuters' finances were in a mess. With the aid of Mark Napier, the company's chairman, Jones beat off all opposition and raised loans enabling the two of them to buy Reuters in 1916. In 1919, when Mark Napier died, Jones became chairman and managing director, posts which he held until his resignation in 1941. He built up the agency's services and restored its fortunes. He had the vision to see that Reuters' future would be safe only if the whole of the British press owned it. The refusal of the London newspapers to share fifty-fifty with the provincial papers made this impossible. The provincial press, through the Press Association, became the major shareholders with Jones. Ironically, it was only after Jones had gone that his original plan could be realized.

Jones's absolute power—the provincial representatives who formed his board knew little of international news handling—enabled him to personify Reuters in himself. Small, dapper, decisive, he became a public figure. He travelled widely. He received honours from France, Italy, Greece, and China, as well as being made a KBE in 1918. Naturally autocratic, he became imperial. Reuters' prime purpose lost his attention.

By the outbreak of war in 1939 he no longer commanded the confidence of his senior colleagues, but the board was loath to accept their representations. When France fell it seemed no action would be possible in wartime. However, within a year the issue had been forced. With war imminent Jones had agreed to accept government help to maintain Reuters' news services to South America. To Jones, who had been chief executive and director of propaganda in the 1918 Ministry of Information, such wartime co-operation was natural. One or two directors were uneasy, but the board approved. Jones did not disclose to them that his agreement with the Government also covered far more questionable matters. The Ministry deliberately betrayed him. When Jones's good faith was challenged by one of his directors at a board meeting on 4 February 1941, he resigned.

Jones took the blow with dignity and stoicism. He gave his version of events in his memoirs, *A Life in Reuters*, published in 1951. Until 1955 he remained a member of the council of the Royal Institute of International Affairs which he had joined in 1927. He was a delegate to the Congress of Europe at The Hague in 1948. He never lost his interest in South Africa. He was chairman of the governors of Roedean School from 1950 until his death at Rottingdean 23 January 1962.

In 1920 Jones married Enid, only daughter of Colonel Arthur Henry Bagnold—Enid Bagnold, the well-known novelist and playwright. They had three sons and a daughter.

[Sir Roderick Jones, *A Life in Reuters*, 1951; *The Times*, 24 January 1962; personal knowledge.]   WILLIAM HALEY

JONES, OWEN THOMAS (1878–1967), geologist, was born in Beulah near Newcastle Emlyn, Dyfed, 16 April 1878, the only son of David Jones, a farmer, and his wife, Margaret Thomas, whose other child, a daughter, died at the age of six. Until he attended Pencader Grammar School in 1893, he spoke only Welsh, and he continued to speak his mother tongue for the rest of his life. In 1896 he won the Keeling natural sciences scholarship in the University College of Wales, Aberystwyth; and four years later graduated with first class honours in physics. In the same year he became an exhibitioner at Trinity College, Cambridge, and was successively Wiltshire prizeman and Harkness scholar. He obtained a first class in both part i (1902) and part ii (1903) of the natural sciences tripos.

In 1903 Jones joined the Geological Survey of Great Britain. Having already developed an interest in Lower Palaeozoic sediments, the traditional speciality of Cambridge geologists, and the predominant rock type of Wales, he was fortunate enough to join a team of distinguished field geologists, led by (Sir) Aubrey Strahan (later to become director), who was then engaged in mapping the western part of the south-Welsh coalfield. This period was an important phase in Jones's career. The maps, in the preparation of which Jones played a major role, especially with his contribution to the Haverfordwest and Milford Haven sheets, are masterly. Concurrently Jones spent his free time investigating the Plynlimon mountains. In 1909, by using a variety of field and labora-

tory techniques including correlation by graptolitic assemblages, he showed that the geological core of the mountains is an anticline of Ordovician slates and grits.

In the wake of this burst of intellectual and physical energy his appointment as the first incumbent of the chair of geology at Aberystwyth in 1910 and, at the same time, the award of a doctorate of science (Wales) and the Sedgwick essay prize (Cambridge) for his researches, came as no surprise to his colleagues.

At Aberystwyth Jones was long remembered as a tall, fair, unconventional young man who taught all aspects of geology with equal authority, and who disappeared into the hills, the moment term ended, to chase stratigraphic boundaries so that by 1912 he had mapped 1,800 square miles of west mid-Wales and, in so doing, had discovered the central Wales syncline. This discovery was to be the key to a new and deeper insight into the evolution of geosynclines to which he gave memorable expression in his outstanding presidential address to the Geological Society in 1938.

In 1919 Jones succeeded to the chair of geology at Manchester University; although he enlarged our understanding of the economic geology and geomorphology of north-west England, his main commitment continued to be the study of Welsh rocks. Consequently, when he was appointed to a chair in Cambridge in 1930, his research interests were in accord with what had always been expected of the Woodwardian professor of geology. Indeed, by that time he had made two further major contributions: firstly by establishing the Llandovery series as an internationally acceptable standard measurement of geological time; secondly, by showing that fossil brachiopods, when properly understood and more precisely classified than hitherto, could be used for correlating Lower Palaeozoic strata. He retired in 1943.

Jones's enthusiasm for geology never abated and, although it was a constant source of encouragement for all those who wished to seek the benefit of his unique knowledge, acute observation, and awesome memory, it also discomforted those who espoused inadequate interpretations, especially of field data. An example of this is Jones's demonstration that contorted sediments exposed in Denbighshire do not represent small-scale folding of rocks, as P. G. H. Boswell [q.v.] had so obdurately believed, but are, rather, beds which had slumped while still in an unconsolidated state. This discovery stimulated an entirely new approach to the dynamics of past sedimentary basins. Jones began his climactic field studies of the 1940s, which were undertaken jointly with (Sir) William J. Pugh and which resulted in the identification of an early Ordovician shore-line and a laccolithic intrusion in the Builth–Llandrindod Wells area, partly to prepare for a Geological Congress meeting in Britain but mainly to refute the ill-founded model then in vogue.

O. T. Jones died at Cambridge 5 May 1967. His last paper, published within a year of his death, was written in Welsh and had, as its theme, the distribution of the blue stones of Carn Meini of Pembrokeshire which, of course, occur as far afield as Stonehenge. In his old age, 'O. T.' may have felt an affinity for those outposts of the land he loved so deeply.

In the course of his life he received many academic honours. He was twice president of the Geological Society (1936–8 and 1950–1), which awarded him its Lyell medal in 1926 and its Wollaston medal in 1945. He was elected a fellow of the Royal Society in 1926 and, in addition to serving as a vice-president in 1940–1, received its Royal medal in 1956. He was an honorary LLD of the university of Wales and an honorary fellow of geological societies of other countries, including the United States of America.

In 1910 Jones married Ethel May, daughter of William Henry Reynolds, of Haverfordwest, and had a daughter and two sons, one of whom was awarded the DFC and was killed in a flying accident in 1945.

[*The Times*, 6 May 1967; *Nature*, vol. ccxiv, 17 June 1967; W. J. Pugh in *Biographical Memoirs of Fellows of the Royal Society*, vol. xiii, 1967; private information; personal knowledge.]   ALWYN WILLIAMS

JOUBERT DE LA FERTÉ, SIR PHILIP BENNET (1887–1965), air chief marshal, was born at Darjeeling in India 21 May 1887, the fourth child of a family of four daughters (two of whom died young) and two sons of Colonel Charles Henry Joubert de la Ferté, of the Indian Medical Service, and his wife, Eliza Jane, eldest daughter of Philip Sandys Melville, of the Indian Civil Service. He was of part French descent, for his grandfather had come to England in 1840 and, after being naturalized in 1885, distinguished himself by designing and engraving a fourpenny Inland Revenue stamp which was to be used for over forty years.

The Joubert children had a sound upbringing, but had a reputation for recklessness. At the age of nine, Philip was sent to school in England, a severe test for a youngster brought up in the East. However, he found solace by reading novels about flying and submarine adventures, books which undoubtedly coloured his future outlook. Since it was impossible to return to India for school holidays, he went to family friends in the country and to an aunt in the south of France. These visits developed in him those self-reliant qualities which were to become evident later, since by the age of eleven he was travelling alone between England and France and was thrown entirely upon his own resources.

It was intended that he should join the army, whereas he himself had a strong desire to join the navy. Parental influence prevailed and he was dispatched to Harrow. He qualified for the Royal Military Academy, Woolwich, at his second attempt and passed out at the lower end of his term, gaining a commission in the Field Gunners in 1907. After five years as a second lieutenant, Joubert regained his desire to fly or to operate a submarine. Quite by chance, his parents had taken a house at Weybridge, adjacent to Brooklands race track. Brooklands soon afterwards became an aerodrome. In 1912 Joubert set out to learn to fly and was given official permission to do so at his own expense. He was soon granted Royal Aero Club certificate No. 280. After a course at the Central Flying School at Upavon, he was attached to the Royal Flying Corps (Military Wing) in March 1913 as a flying officer. He was at last financially independent, and had joined the RFC at a time which favoured his future prospects. He was a fully qualified young army officer, fit and keen to believe in the importance of powered flight, and with the added advantage of being able to speak French.

Joubert was promoted to the rank of temporary captain when war began in 1914, and proceeded to France with No. 3 Squadron. Within a week, flying a Blériot and armed with a pistol, he made aviation history by being one of the two pilots to make the first reconnaissance of enemy lines. He was mentioned in dispatches for the first time two months later— in all he was to be mentioned seven times. He was then recalled to England in 1915 to raise a new squadron. That task completed, he was promoted to the rank of temporary major and given command of No. 15 Squadron in France.

Events moved swiftly as the war developed and he was fortunate to be given command of No. 1 Squadron, in succession to (Sir) (William) Geoffrey Salmond [q.v.], at a significant time because it covered the battle of Loos. His younger brother, John Claude, also of No. 1 Squadron and also a pilot, had had the misfortune to be shot down in March 1915 over Holland and remained a prisoner of war for the rest of the war.

Early in 1916 Joubert was invalided out of France with 'trench feet'. When he had recovered he was ordered to form a new squadron, No. 33. Very shortly afterwards he was promoted to the rank of temporary lieutenant-colonel and given command of No. 5 Wing in Egypt. There Joubert's experience and flair for improvization were put to good use since No. 5 Wing's resources were not large and its aircraft were out of date. Joubert left Egypt early in 1917 with many important lessons learned from the fighting in Sinai, particularly in the handling of both air and ground operations. He was appointed to the DSO for his efforts. After only a few months in England in command of No. 21 Wing, he was transferred to No. 14 Wing which he took to Italy after a short stay in France. The move to Italy was an important step in his career since he had now established himself as a leader, a practical airman, a sound administrator, and a good commander in the field—all essential qualities for higher command. These qualities were recognized in 1918 by his appointment to command the RFC in Italy. At this time he was awarded the Order of Saints Maurice and Lazarus, the Cavaliere, and the croce di guerra. Later he was appointed CMG in 1919, CB in 1936, and KCB in 1938.

At the conclusion of the war, he was given command of No. 2 Group at Oxford and received a permanent commission in the Royal Air Force (as the RFC became in April 1918) as a wing commander. No. 2 Group was moved to the Recruits Depot at Uxbridge where Joubert's administrative and leadership qualities were tested to the full because he had both to deal with 1,500 restless and undisciplined Dominion cadets anxious to return home, and to participate in the country's milk distribution during the nationwide railway strike. He emerged from both tests with an enhanced reputation. The following year, 1920, he attended the Army Staff College at Camberley; his happy days there were a welcome respite.

In 1922 he was promoted to group captain and appointed an instructor to the recently formed RAF College at Andover. This period was vital for his subsequent career, for it provided a forum for the formulation of future air policy. On leaving Andover he served as deputy director of personnel and in the directorate of manning at the Air Ministry. In 1926 he became the first RAF instructor at the Imperial Defence College, another milestone. He remained there for three years, being promoted to air commodore when he left. After some nine months in flying training, in which he took every opportunity of modernizing his airmanship, he was posted as commandant of the RAF Staff College, where he remained for three years. This was an admirable post because it enabled him to witness the implementation of the plans made by the Air Council in 1922, and the development of an air policy, broadly

conceived and flexible in its application. Above all, Joubert sought to bring the other two Services into closer co-operation. His quick brain infused both a spirit of enthusiasm and a sense of urgency into staff and pupils alike.

In 1933 he was promoted to air vice-marshal and a year later appointed as air officer commanding the Fighting Area of Great Britain—the forerunner of Fighter Command. In this post he devoted much time to studying the air tactics which were gradually evolving from the techniques employed by fighters during the war of 1914-18 to those of the more modern fighters then in service. It was during this period that he took charge of British air defence during the annual air exercises. Promoted to air marshal in 1936, he was appointed for the first time as AOC in C Coastal Command, a post in which he hoped to stay for some time in view of his earlier affection for the sea; but this was not to be, for in 1937 he was sent to India as AOC: the least satisfying of his appointments because the authorities in London were inevitably preoccupied with the dangerous course of events in Europe. Although Joubert made his needs known, he was frustrated by his superiors' inability to face the military facts of life in the Far East where even the nucleus of a modern air force was sadly lacking. Fortunately for Joubert himself, his stay in India was cut short when he was recalled to England at the outbreak of war and appointed air adviser on combined operations. There were, however, more pressing needs for his services elsewhere, and he became assistant chief of air staff with special responsibility for the practical application of radar in the RAF. Much of the ultimate success of the radar war was due to Joubert's realization at this early stage of its great possibilities, both in defence and offence. It was also during this period that he gave his regular broadcasts on the air war; his large audience was evidence of his decided talent in this medium.

In June 1941 he was promoted to air chief marshal and became, for the second time, AOC in C Coastal Command, his own favourite (if not his most successful) command. During the seventeen months he was there, much needed to be done to reduce the very heavy U-boat attacks upon Allied shipping in the Atlantic. The command became better equipped, with more aircraft and superior weapons which enabled tactics to improve. Because Joubert was so well informed about radar, air-to-surface vessel radar became the most effective aid in the anti-submarine war. Joubert also made good use of the civilian scientists available to him to analyse results and to promote greater efficiency with the limited facilities available. These innovations were to have a profound effect upon the

Command in the days ahead. It was not a period in his life which was free from criticism and his own outspokenness on the use of air power led to a clash with the Admiralty, which caused him to be moved and appointed inspector general of the RAF, a post he held until his retirement in 1943.

Fortunately for Joubert he was recalled after only a month of retirement to join the staff of Admiral Mountbatten (later Earl Mountbatten of Burma) in the South East Asia Command as the deputy chief of staff (information and civil affairs). Perhaps his most successful venture in this posting was to create a South East Asia Command newspaper which was delivered almost daily to the troops throughout the Command. After the fall of Rangoon, Joubert returned to England for hospital treatment. He finally retired in October 1945.

After some nine months of rest and recuperation he returned as a civilian to the Air Ministry for another year as director of public relations. Joubert permitted himself the luxury of only a short rest before he embarked upon a most successful but exhausting 'coast to coast' lecture tour of the United States talking on his favourite subject, air power. Joubert frequently also gave expression to his thoughts in print and one book, *The Third Service* (1955), provoked considerable controversy amongst the various Services and Ministries. He was by no means universally popular. In appearance Joubert was just under six feet tall, broad in proportion, with a fine complexion, sparkling eyes, and a very healthy look. He had a strong character combined with great charm and an engaging personality.

Joubert first married in 1915 Marjorie Denison, the youngest daughter of Frederick Joseph Hall, of Sheffield; this marriage, of which there were two daughters, was dissolved in 1948, the year in which he married Joan Catherine Cripps, the daughter of Frederick Bucknell. To this Dictionary he contributed the notices of Sir (Ernest) Leslie Gossage and Sir Oliver Swann. He died at the RAF Hospital, Uxbridge, 21 January 1965.

A portrait by Sir Oswald Birley was destroyed by fire at Joubert's old favourite mess of Headquarters Coastal Command; another portrait, by (Sir) James Gunn (1941), is now in the Imperial War Museum.

[*The Times*, 22 January 1965; *Daily Telegraph*, 22 January 1965; Sir Philip Joubert de la Ferte, *The Fated Sky*, 1952; private information.]   EDWARD CHILTON

K

KARLOFF, BORIS (1887–1969), actor, was born William Henry Pratt in Camberwell 23 November 1887, the son of Edward John Pratt, of the Indian Salt Revenue Service, and his wife, Eliza Sara Millard. He was the youngest of nine children, eight of them boys; one brother became a judge in the high court of Bombay and another was Sir John Thomas Pratt, an expert on China for the Foreign Office. Young William gained his first interest in the stage from a third brother, who acted under the name of George Marlowe.

In 1894 the family moved to Enfield, and William was educated at Merchant Taylors' School and Uppingham; in 1906 he moved to King's College, London, and studied for the Consular Service. In fact he elected instead for a stage career, but in deference to family feeling sailed to Montreal before beginning it. Despite his striking looks and inimitable voice, his young manhood was not a period of great success. He acted with repertory companies all over Canada, and when jobs were hard to find he worked on farms and fairgrounds. In 1911 he adopted Karloff, an old family name, adding Boris because it seemed to fit. The new name got him a steady job at Kamloops, where he worked until 1912, subsequently joining a company in Prince Albert, Saskatchewan. In 1917 he joined a touring company of the play *The Virginian* starting in Chicago and ending in Hollywood, where he stayed.

Gradually extra work came his way, and by 1919 he was playing villains in Douglas Fairbanks films. During the twenties he worked fairly steadily without being at all well known. His best role in silent films was as the mesmerist in *The Bells* (1926), but the first years of sound found him again reduced to playing bandits and minor gangsters. In 1930 he was fortunate to find a good stage role in Los Angeles in *The Criminal Code*. When this was filmed he was offered the same part, of a convict who, with gait and gestures which were to become very familiar, kills a stool-pigeon. This led to several roles in 1931, including the unexpected one of the hypocritical effeminate reporter in *Five Star Final*.

When James Whale was casting *Frankenstein*, he saw something unusual about the shape of Karloff's head which might make him effective as the monster. Weighed down under much uncomfortable make-up, Karloff was sensationally effective in the role, extracting pity as well as revulsion for the monster. His name did not appear on the credits, the intention being to surround the role with mystery, but immediately the film was released he was a star, and in his next films, *The Old Dark House* (in which he played the deaf mute butler) and *The Mummy*, his name appeared on the bills in larger letters than the titles. In 1932 he was the Chinese villain in *The Mask of Fu Manchu*, and in 1933 he returned to England for *The Ghoul*. This period, though exciting, had typecast him, and in his occasional non-horror roles (*The Lost Patrol*, *The House of Rothschild*) he showed that he had become an over-emphatic actor.

Returing to horror films, he was successful in *The Black Room* and *The Bride of Frankenstein*, although he himself felt that the monster should not have been allowed to talk. Lean years followed, horror films being unfashionable, and he was reduced to playing Mr Wong in a low-budget series of detective films. In 1939 *Son of Frankenstein* revived his stature somewhat, though he played the monster, for the last time, rather disappointingly as a soulless killer. The popularity of horror films revived during the war, and Karloff starred in a series of 'mad doctor' films, in which his intentions at least were always honourable. It was clear that he was never to find another role like the monster, and that Hollywood regarded him as no more than a useful addition to low-budget offerings; yet ironically his name was known throughout the world.

Karloff determinedly made a name for himself in other fields, notably the Broadway stage. He successfully caricatured his own image in *Arsenic and Old Lace* (1941), was a kindly professor in J. B. Priestley's *The Linden Tree* (1948), and Captain Hook in *Peter Pan* (1950). He also issued several recordings, in which he recited fairy tales and ghost stories, and edited volumes of similar material; and he was a noted Hollywood cricketer.

At the end of World War II Hollywood began to offer him more distinguished roles, such as the leading part in his first colour film, *The Climax* (1944), smooth comedy villainy in *The Secret Life of Walter Mitty* (1947) and, curiously, an Indian chief in *Unconquered* (1947). He had also some success with Val Lewton, a producer of 'intellectual horror' films: *The Body Snatcher* (after Robert Louis Stevenson, q.v.) (1945), *The Isle of the Dead* (1945), and *Bedlam* (1946). Thereafter he was unsuccessful in Hollywood, except in television.

In Britain he played patch-eyed Colonel March of Scotland Yard in a 1955 TV series, and in 1958 secured two thrillers better than Hollywood was likely to offer: *Corridors of Blood* and *Grip of the Strangler*. In 1959 he retired to a Sussex village to enjoy cricket. He died at Midhurst, Sussex, 2 February 1969, shortly after completing a moving performance in a TV series, *The Name of the Game*, as a Czech writer caught in the cold war.

Karloff's deep and cultured voice was widely imitated. He deserved better roles, although his acting range was limited.

He was married three times, in 1923 to Helene Vivian Soule, in 1929 to Dorothy Stine, and in 1946 to Evelyn Helmore (*née* Hope), who survived him. There was one daughter of the second marriage.

[Richard Bojarski and Kenneth Beals, *The Films of Boris Karloff*, 1974; Peter Underwood, *Horror Man*, 1972; Denis Gifford, *Karloff, the Man, the Monster, the Movies*, 1973.]   LESLIE HALLIWELL

KEBLE MARTIN, WILLIAM (1877–1969), botanist. [See MARTIN.]

KEILIN, DAVID (1887–1963), biologist, was the third child and second son in the family of seven children of Hirsh Davidoff Keilin, a business man, and his wife, Rachel Strelsin. He was born in Moscow 21 March 1887, but in the 1891 pogrom the family was exiled to the west. They settled in Warsaw where the father opened men's wear shops and where Keilin was educated at the Górski Gymnasium. In 1905 he completed pre-medical courses at the university of Liège; but, being asthmatic, he was persuaded to abandon thoughts of a medical career. Moving to Paris, he began to study the arts and philosophy. Obliged one day to shelter from a storm, he found himself attending a lecture on entomology by Maurice Caullery (later foreign member of the Royal Society). So impressed was Caullery by this new pupil that, at the end of the course, he invited Keilin to join him in research. Keilin had found his *métier*. In 1915 Keilin accepted an invitation to Cambridge to become research assistant to George H. F. Nuttall [q.v.], the first Quick professor. Keilin held Beit fellowships from 1920 to 1925, became lecturer in parasitology in the latter year, and in 1931 succeeded Nuttall as Quick professor of biology and director of the Molteno Institute. He remained active in research until he died.

In Paris Keilin began studies of life-cycles of parasitic insects, and also of protists (microorganisms) that parasitize insect larvae. From 1909 onwards his original work brought him wide recognition. His experiences focused his attention on two themes which dominated his later work. These were the often extraordinary evolutionary adaptations of fly larvae to the parasitic mode of life, and the overriding importance of respiratory requirements in the control of insect life-cycles. When Keilin reached Cambridge he joined Nuttall in work, often tedious and sometimes hazardous, on the reproduction of lice. These were a major scourge in the war of 1914–18. Keilin also continued the work he had undertaken in Paris. It is remarkable that in the thirty-nine papers which he published between 1914 and 1923 there are descriptions of eight new genera and twelve new species of parasitic protists. His work on the life-cycle of the horse bot-fly was a turning point in Keilin's career. Although it revealed new vistas in biochemistry for Keilin, he continued parasitological work, though on a diminishing scale. In 1944 he published his final paper in this field: a 66-page monograph on respiratory adaptations in fly larvae. This work was to produce a typical example of Keilin's commitment to scientific enquiry: he translated the manuscript of his monograph from the original French, and extensively revised and up-dated it, as a relief from tedium during illness.

The red larvae of the bot-fly contain haemoglobin—better known as the red pigment of blood. While trying to determine the fate of this haemoglobin during metamorphosis, Keilin examined tissues of the adult fly with a spectroscope. He could find no haemoglobin, but he found a reddish pigment with a quite different absorption spectrum. He detected this pigment, which he named cytochrome, in a wide range of organisms: from bacteria and plants to mammals. He showed that cytochrome is an iron-protein compound (as also is haemoglobin) and that it plays an essential role in cell respiration. Cytochrome becomes oxidized by oxygen and reduced, through co-operation with appropriate enzymes, by cell metabolites (breakdown products of foodstuffs). Through rapid interchange between its oxidized and reduced states, cytochrome is an essential link between the oxygen which is absorbed by a living cell and the oxygen-requiring processes within the cell. When these findings were published in 1925 biochemists' opinions about the nature of intracellular respiration were in disarray. Keilin's discovery was to a great extent responsible for the development of biochemistry into an exact science: a development in which he was to play a dominant role. Between 1925 and 1931, when Keilin, single-handed, was establishing the basic facts about cytochrome, he held a full-time appointment as lecturer, demonstrator, and researcher in parasitology. Cytochrome was a spare-time occupation. In later years Keilin's biochemical activities included work on haemoglobin and its analogues, on oxidizing enzymes, and on spectroscopic techniques. He also studied anabiosis (the ability of small organisms to suspend life processes for long periods) and the history of cell biology. His lectures on cytochrome and related topics endeared him to student audiences, as much for his enthusiasm as for his carefully rehearsed and striking lecture demonstrations. He retired from his chair in 1952.

Keilin received in 1915 the D.Sc. degree (Sorbonne) and the Prix Passet of the Société Entomologique de France. He became a fellow of the Royal Society in 1928, delivered the Society's Croonian lecture (1934) and Leeuwenhoek lecture (1958), and was awarded the Society's Royal medal (1939) and Copley medal (1952). He greatly valued his election to the Académie des Sciences de l'Institut de France, as *membre correspondant* (1947) and *membre associé étranger* (1955), and his honorary fellowship of Magdalene College (1957). He received honorary degrees from the universities of Brussels (D.Sc., 1946), Bordeaux (D.Sc., 1947), Liège (MD, 1951), and Utrecht (MD, 1957). A fund set up by friends and colleagues after his death endowed a biennial Keilin lecture and medal under the auspices of the Biochemical Society.

In 1913, in Paris, Keilin married Anna, daughter of David Hershlik, a town councillor of Wielun (Russian Poland). To their only child, Joan, fell the task of completing the manuscript of a book which Keilin had been writing for many years. This personal account of the history of cytochrome reveals much of his character and philosophy. His approach to research was strictly pragmatic: he allowed no preconceived hypotheses to influence his thinking. He always carried a list of deceptively simple ideas for experiments. These, he confidently expected, contained the key to a current problem: and this often proved to be the case. Despite his absorption in work at the bench he was very tolerant of interruptions. He would give a cheerful welcome to anyone in need of guidance or advice. Coupled with a disarming modesty was a remarkable intuition, an ability to pass the right judgement, and an encyclopedic knowledge of biology. Fluent in Russian, Polish, French, and English, he enjoyed the works of nineteenth-century authors—from Tolstoy to Dickens and Thackeray. That, with quiet strolls near his home and the pleasures of entertaining friends, was the extent of his relaxation. Francis M. C. Turner, another Magdalene man, wrote: 'David Keilin wore the mantle of his world-wide distinction as an invisible garment . . . He was a most remarkable and lovable person, patient and wise, with so great a spirit in so small a frame.' He died in Cambridge 27 February 1963.

There is an ink and wash portrait by H. A. Freeth (1952) in the National Portrait Gallery.

[D. Keilin, *The History of Cell Respiration and Cytochrome*, 1966 (ed. J. Keilin); *Magdalene College Magazine and Record*, vol. vii, 1963; T. Mann in *Biographical Memoirs of Fellows of the Royal Society*, vol x, 1964; obituary notices in *Parasitology*, vol. lv, 1965 and in *Journal of General Microbiology*, vol. xlv, 1966; E. F. Hartree in *Biochemical Journal*, vol. lxxxix, 1, 1963; private information; personal knowledge.] E. F. HARTREE

KEITH, JAMES, BARON KEITH OF AVONHOLM (1886-1964), judge, was born 20 May 1886 at Hamilton, the eldest child of (Sir) Henry Shanks Keith, merchant and authority on local government, and his wife, Elizabeth, daughter of John Hamilton. Educated at Hamilton Academy and Glasgow University, where he graduated MA with first class honours in history (1906) and thereafter LLB (1908), Keith was admitted to the Faculty of Advocates in 1911 and rapidly acquired a large practice before its interruption by war service. Commissioned in the Seaforth Highlanders in 1914, he served in France where a wound put an end to his active service; later, having been attached to the Egyptian Army, he held official appointments under the Sudan Government. So attracted was he by the Sudan he seriously considered making his career in that country's service, but eventually decided to return to practice at the Scottish bar. He recovered at once his extensive junior practice in all types of work, and especially work concerned with local government, licensing, and property law. He took silk in 1926. His advocacy was notable for its masterly presentation of law and fact and marked by integrity, perception, and contempt for the verbose. He was elected dean of the Faculty of Advocates, the chosen leader of the Scottish bar, in 1936.

In 1937 Keith was appointed lord commissioner of justiciary and senator of the College of Justice, and took his seat upon the bench with the judicial title of Lord Keith. This appointment was warmly welcomed by the profession as a whole. A strong, conscientious, and hard-working judge of independent mind, both in the Outer House and subsequently in the Inner House, Lord Keith manifested in his opinions the same forthright and lucid presentation reinforced by cogent powers of reasoning as had distinguished his advocacy. When in due course Keith came to sit in the First Division, that court was presided over by Lord Cooper (whose notice Keith contributed to this Dictionary), a profound scholar and an innovator impatient of the obsolete or pettifogging. While Lord Keith was his colleague, the lord president presided, but did not necessarily dominate. Keith was noted for his independence of approach, and his not infrequent dissenting opinions still illuminate the law no less than do the opinions he delivered when concurring with the majority.

Keith was a very effective member of the royal commission on marriage and divorce (the Morton commission) to which he was appointed in 1951, and his incisive and independent views are reflected in the Report. His preference for a clean break on divorce so far as property rights are concerned, although not a popular view, has practical social advantages. On another major social issue he had the courage to change his mind. Before the royal commission on capital punishment reported, Keith supported the retention of the death penalty for deliberate murder; after the Homicide Act, 1957, he advocated the abolition of this punishment.

In 1953 when Lord Normand [q.v.] retired as lord of appeal in ordinary, Keith had to make another crucial decision affecting his career. Although judicial office in the House of Lords is perhaps the highest aspiration of an English lawyer, this is not necessarily true of Scottish judges who have spent their professional lives in Edinburgh, and who have over the years developed strong social, cultural, and personal ties in Scotland. Keith was essentially a Scotsman in speech, outlook, and life-style, and, of course, a member of the close-knit community—geographically and professionally—of the Scottish bench and bar. It was no easy matter to decide to move to London from the Georgian New Town of Edinburgh with easy access to Muirfield, where he could find relaxation in golf. However, since a strong Scottish judge was required in London to replace Normand, Keith consented to be 'drafted', and found perhaps more fulfilment as lord of appeal in ordinary from 1953 to 1961 than he had anticipated. On being created a life peer in 1953 he took the title of Keith of Avonholm. In the same year he was sworn of the Privy Council, and, when he sat in the Judicial Committee of the Privy Council, earlier interests in the law and administration of other countries overseas were revived. Even after he retired as lord of appeal in ordinary he continued to sit from time to time on the Judicial Committee of the Privy Council. In the highest courts in London he was both liked and respected by his English colleagues, and in 1953 he was elected an honorary bencher of the Inner Temple. His contributions in the highest appellate courts were fresh, original, and not infrequently dissenting. Several of his dissenting speeches, such as in *White & Carter (Councils) Ltd.* v.

McGregor, 1962 SC (HL) 1 (a case on anticipatory breach of contract), point to the solutions which may well eventually prevail. It was said that there was a kind of perennial youth about Keith. He changed little over the years and despite his interest in outdoor sports he seemed to walk alone. His mind was independent, always alert to consider an argument, and his speech direct. There was nothing superficial in his legal thinking.

A man of exceptional physical and mental energy, with a special interest in scholarship and the young, throughout his professional life in Scotland Keith gave freely of his time and counsel to various aspects of public service. He was a trustee of the National Library of Scotland from its foundation in 1925 to 1937, and succeeded Normand as convener of the standing committee of trustees. From 1942 to 1946 he was chairman of the Scottish Youth Advisory Committee appointed by the secretary of state for Scotland, and in 1943-9 was chairman of the Scottish Probation Council. Other bodies on which he served included the Scottish advisory committee on physical training and recreation, the Scottish Council for National Parks, the Red Cross Society, and the Scottish Youth Hostels Association.

For about two years before he died Keith lost completely the use of his legs, an affliction which was particularly grievous to one of his interests and temperament. He accepted his condition with his accustomed courage and without self-pity.

In 1915 Keith married Jean Maitland, daughter of Andrew Bennet, solicitor, of Arbroath; they had one son and two daughters. The son, Henry Shanks Keith, in 1971 took his seat as a senator of the College of Justice and lord commissioner of justiciary with the judicial title of Lord Keith. His father died in Edinburgh 30 June 1964.

[*The Times*, 1 July 1964; *Scots Law Times*, 1936 (News) 45, 1937 (News) 117, 1953 (News) 205; *Glasgow Herald*, 1 July 1964; private information; personal knowledge.]

T. B. SMITH

KEMSLEY, first VISCOUNT (1883-1968), newspaper proprietor. [See BERRY, (JAMES) GOMER.]

KENNEDY, (AUBREY) LEO (1885-1965), journalist, was born at Brighton 6 February 1885, the second of the four sons of (Sir) John Gordon Kennedy, minister plenipotentiary in Bucharest from 1897 to 1905, and his wife, Evelyn, daughter of Colonel Edward Wilbraham. He was educated at Harrow (1899-1903) and Magdalen College, Oxford, receiving his BA in 1906. He joined *The Times* under G. E. Buckle [q.v.] in 1910 and was put in the foreign sub-editors' room to learn something of the working practice in Printing House Square. He was sent to Paris in 1911. When the Balkan wars broke out in 1912 he went to report them from Serbia, Romania, and Albania. During the war of 1914-18 he served successively in the King's Own Yorkshire Light Infantry, the Intelligence Corps, and the Scots Guards; he was mentioned in dispatches and gained the MC. All his three brothers were killed in action; the memory of their deaths strengthened his own determination to do all he could in his writings to avert another war.

In 1919, after Kennedy returned to *The Times*, Henry Wickham Steed [q.v.], then editor, sent him round Europe to gather all the information he could about the changes brought about by the Versailles treaties. Power politics became Kennedy's main concern, which was never to leave him throughout his working life. The title of his first book, published in 1922, *Old Diplomacy and New 1876-1922*, could as fitly be applied to scores of the leading articles which he was to write for *The Times*. His interest led him to be a founding member of the Royal Institute of International Affairs in 1920.

Kennedy's main work began in 1923 when G. Geoffrey Dawson [q.v.] returned for his second period as editor of *The Times*. Dawson appointed Kennedy a foreign leader writer and sent him from time to time as a special correspondent in European capitals. Broadcasting was still only beginning; television news and comment were unknown; *The Times* under Dawson was regarded as the voice of Britain's ruling class. Kennedy, quiet, earnest, dark-haired, courteous, soldierly, with a military officer's sweeping moustache, was an excellent ambassador for the newspaper and he talked confidentially with many of the European ministers over the years. Whenever he wrote a leader, he used to say, he felt the chanceries of Europe looking over his shoulder. He took his responsibilities seriously, weighing every word, seeking a way out of every problem. He had more than one period of absence through strain.

His inner torment increased when Hitler began his aggressive moves. On the one hand he saw the German dictatorship for the evil it was and he maintained that Hitler meant all that he had written in *Mein Kampf* about Germany's need to expand. In 1937 he wrote a forthright book, *Britain Faces Germany*. Here he differed from Dawson and R. M. Barrington-Ward [q.v.], the deputy editor. He wished them to give clearer warning to the country about the dangers which would arise if Neville Chamber-

lain's appeasement policy failed. On the other hand, Kennedy, abhorring the thought of another great war, believed that much of the Versailles treaty had to be rectified. Here he was at one with Dawson and Barrington-Ward, and it was Kennedy who wrote the first draft of the renowned leading article in *The Times* of 7 September 1938.

The leader suggested, as the international tension was coming near to snapping point, that Prague might consider ceding the Sudeten lands and other border areas for the sake of peace. Dawson persuaded Kennedy to rewrite part of the leader and then hastily tinkered with it himself. It emerged ill-considered and ill-timed. In Britain and abroad it was immediately regarded as an appalling forecast of British official policy, yet the immediate storm of protest did not deter Chamberlain and Daladier from forcing Prague to make the concessions at Munich. In his private diary Kennedy wrote (17 October 1938) that in penning the leader he had been moved by three influences: by the general line of thought in Printing House Square, by Neville Chamberlain's confidential hint the previous May that he would not refuse the cession of the Sudeten lands, and by Lord Halifax's [q.v.] no less confidential remark in a letter to Dawson a little later that he would not rule out a solution by means of a plebiscite.

Little more than a month after Munich Kennedy returned to the other strand in his thinking. In a personal letter published by *The Times* he gave warning of the dangers of further German expansion. Dawson occasionally allowed him such outlets. Kennedy got on well with Dawson but he and Barrington-Ward found it harder to agree on policy. Barrington-Ward had been editor for less than a month when in October 1941 he suggested that Kennedy should do less work inside the office and be more free to take on outside work. Kennedy, then fifty-six, preferred to leave altogether and went to the European service of the BBC until the end of the war. He lived afterwards for some years in north Yorkshire. He published a life of Lord Salisbury (1953), and edited (1956) for Lady Derby the letters which the fourth Earl of Clarendon [q.v.], foreign secretary from 1865 to 1866 and 1868 to 1870, wrote to Lady Derby's mother, the Duchess of Manchester.

In 1921 Kennedy married Sylvia Meysey-Thompson, who died in 1968; they had three daughters. He died in Westminster Hospital, London, 8 December 1965. He was the archetype of the conscientious, liberal-minded, and deeply troubled intellectual who tried in vain to cope with the evil of Hitlerism without incurring the evil of another great war.

A portrait of Kennedy by Frank Eastman is with his family.

[*The Times* archives; *The History of The Times*, vol. iv, 1952; Kennedy's private papers; personal knowledge.]

IVERACH MCDONALD

KENNEDY, MARGARET MOORE (1896-1967), writer, was born in London 23 April 1896, the oldest of the four children of Charles Moore Kennedy, a barrister, originally from Loughlash, county Derry, and his wife, Elinor Marwood. She was educated at Cheltenham Ladies' College and Somerville College, Oxford, where she was the younger contemporary of Dorothy Sayers and Vera Brittain [qq.v.] and obtained second class honours in history in 1919. She had started to write as a schoolgirl, but she did not publish anything until 1922 when her first book, *A Century of Revolution*, a textbook about the French revolution and nineteenth-century France, appeared.

Her first novel, *The Ladies of Lyndon* (1923), followed a year later, and her second, *The Constant Nymph*, which made her name, in 1924. The 'Sanger's Circus' of this novel was inspired by a painting which Margaret Kennedy had seen of Augustus John [q.v.] and his wives; the book also revealed a serious approach to the fight for the freedom of the arts from the customs and beliefs of the day. Many people found it shocking. The book was a best-seller, and was translated and read in many parts of the world by a whole generation of high-, middle-, and lowbrow readers. It was praised by older writers as disparate as Arnold Bennett, Thomas Hardy, A. E. Housman, H. G. Wells [qq.v.], and Jean Giraudoux. Margaret Kennedy was lionized as the author of *The Constant Nymph*, but she did not allow this success to impress her too forcibly. She was professional enough not to be daunted by having her name linked strongly with one book so early in a writing career which was to last another forty years. *The Constant Nymph* was rewritten as a play (New Theatre, 1926) by herself and Basil Dean, and several film versions have been made. *Escape Me Never* was staged at the Apollo in 1933, when Elisabeth Bergner made her first appearance in London. Another successful play was *Autumn* (1937), written with Gregory Ratoff.

In 1925 Margaret Kennedy married (Sir) David Davies, then a barrister, who was a county court judge from 1937 to 1947 and thereafter a National Insurance commissioner. He was knighted in 1952. They had a son and two daughters. Her elder daughter, Mrs Julia Birley, also became a novelist. Although a wife

and mother, Margaret Kennedy continued to write, always at home, in her bedroom, or on a drawing-room table. She wrote sixteen novels in all. The most successful, after *The Constant Nymph*, were *The Feast* (1950) and *Lucy Carmichael* (1951), both Book Society choices, and *Troy Chimneys*, which won the James Tait Black memorial prize for 1935. *The Feast* was also a Literary Guild choice in the United States; many consider it to be her best work.

Throughout her working life she was interested in craftsmanship and in the best way of expressing an imaginative theme. Her choice of subject was varied and she set out to entertain the reader with a good story, handling her narrative with assurance. She believed social comedy to be her forte. A woman of intellectual austerity, wide reading, and a highly developed critical sense, she first made readers aware of her critical acuity in her short biography of *Jane Austen* (1950). She demonstrated it even more clearly in *The Outlaws on Parnassus* (1958), a serious study of the art of fiction, and its decline in public esteem in the twentieth century. She was a fellow of the Royal Society of Literature.

Margaret Kennedy was a reserved woman, who was happiest in the circle of the family and a few close friends. Her strong moral sense did not dampen her sense of gaiety. She was tall and slender; was an accomplished pianist with a fine singing voice; and she also had a passion for mountain walking. She was emotionally crushed by the death of her husband in 1964, and was just recovering from the shock when she died in her sleep at the house of a friend at Adderbury, Oxfordshire, 31 July 1967.

In the possession of the family are a bronze bust of Margaret Kennedy by Frank Dobson and a water-colour portrait painted by the American artist Eliot O'Hara in 1948.

[*The Times*, 1 August 1967; private information.]

RICHARD BENNETT

KENSWOOD, first BARON (1887-1963), professional violinist and economist. [See WHITFIELD, ERNEST ALBERT.].

KENT, DUCHESS OF (1906-1968). [See MARINA.]

KENYON, JOSEPH (1885-1961), organic chemist, was born 8 April 1885 at Blackburn, Lancashire, the eldest child in the family of four sons and three daughters of Lawrence Kenyon, a gardener, of Blackburn, and his wife, Mary Anne Southwarth. Kenyon's was no easy education: indeed it was by his own considerable efforts that he ascended the educational ladder. However, a young man of his great scientific intellect and strength of character was not to be denied the benefits of higher learning. After leaving the Blackburn Secondary Higher Grade School in 1899 he became, at the age of fourteen, a laboratory assistant at the Municipal Technical School, Blackburn. He continued his education on a part-time basis, with two years' full-time study while he held the John Mercer FRS scholarship, until he graduated, with honours, as a B.Sc. (London) in 1907. He was awarded the degree of D.Sc. of the university of London in 1914.

His first research was done while he was still an undergraduate, when he published three papers with (Sir) R. H. Pickard [q.v.], whose research assistant he was in Blackburn, and whose notice Kenyon later wrote for this Dictionary. One of these papers, on the resolution of secondary octyl alcohol into its optically active forms, was to be the beginning of a lifelong interest in stereochemistry. At the time of this early work, no general method was available for the resolution of compounds like alcohols, which contain no groups by which they can form salts with acids or bases. The formation of such salts with optically active forms of acids or bases is the basis of Pasteur's classic method of resolution. Pickard and Kenyon surmounted this difficulty by converting the alcohol into its half-ester with phthalic acid, which, being a dibasic acid, left one acidic group free in the half-ester, so that salt formation with the optically active bases brucine and cinchonidine was made possible. The two different (diastereoisomeric) salts could then be separated, and the (+)− and (−)− forms of the *sec*-octyl alcohol obtained from them by hydrolysis.

In his subsequent scientific work, Kenyon, using these methods, accomplished many experimentally difficult and laborious resolutions, and devoted himself assiduously to attempting to elucidate the extremely puzzling relationship (or apparent lack of it) between chemical constitution and optical activity.

Although these papers are classics, it is probably for his work on the steric course of nucleophilic substitution reactions that Kenyon will be best remembered. Some of these reactions, but not all, are accompanied by inversion of configuration (the celebrated 'Walden Inversion'). The problem, which arose from the absence of any simple relationship between configuration and optical rotation, was to determine the one stage out of several in a series of reactions in which an optically active starting material was finally regenerated in its enantiomeric (inverted) form, in which the inversion had occurred. With his colleagues, notably H. Phillips, and using the techniques

which he had previously developed, Kenyon solved this problem by designing reaction cycles such that only one of the whole series involved cleavage of a bond at the centre of the asymmetry in the molecule, so that only in this one reaction was inversion possible. This breakthrough, taken with the classic work and theories of Hughes and (Sir) C. K. Ingold [q.v.] at University College, London, was crucial to our understanding that inversion always occurs in bimolecular processes at an asymmetric carbon atom, but that in unimolecular processes various stereochemical consequences are possible, racemization being the typical result. This conclusion was most important, since it is fundamental to our understanding of the mechanism of what it possibly the most general process in the whole of organic chemistry.

Many other contributions to organic chemistry were made by Kenyon during the course of his professional life. With various colleagues, including Phillips, M. P. Balfe, C. L. Arcus, and A. G. Davies, he published over 160 papers, mainly on stereochemistry and its relationship to reaction mechanisms.

In 1906 Kenyon obtained his first academic post—that of assistant lecturer at Blackburn Technical College. He was promoted to lecturer in 1907. During the war of 1914-18 he was engaged with H. D. Dakin [q.v.] and J. B. Cohen in war research at Leeds University on the synthesis of Chloramine-T as a possible antidote to 'gas gangrene'. From 1916 to 1920 he was at Oxford with W. H. Perkin [q.v.], working on dyestuffs chemistry in collaboration with the British Dyestuffs Corporation.

In 1920 Kenyon was appointed head of the department of chemistry at Battersea Polytechnic, where he remained until his retirement in 1950. His was the inspiration that created at Battersea one of the best chemistry schools in the country. Such was Kenyon's character, however, that while achieving this as well as making his distinguished research contributions, he became one of the best-loved and respected figures not only in his own department but in the chemical community in general. Particularly was this true in London, where he gave freely of his wisdom and expertise as a member of the university board of studies in chemistry and of the university of London senate, as vice-president and council member of the Chemical Society, and in various capacities for the Royal Institute of Chemistry of which he was a fellow for fifty years. His distinction was recognized by the Royal Society by his election to the fellowship in 1936, and by the university of Surrey by the naming of a laboratory after him.

After his retirement from Battersea, Kenyon

spent two periods as visiting professor at the university of Alexandria, and one at the university of Kansas. He also continued his research and was for some years still a member of the London University board of studies.

In 1917 Kenyon married Winifrede Agnes, daughter of Cornelius Foley, of Cork. They had one daughter. Kenyon died at his home in Petersham 12 November 1961.

[E. E. Turner in *Biographical Memoirs of Fellows of the Royal Society*, vol. viii, 1962; *Journal of the Royal Institute of Chemistry*, vol. viii, 1962, p. 117; *The Times*, 17 November 1961; personal knowledge.]

G. H. WILLIAMS

KERMACK, WILLIAM OGILVY (1898-1970), biochemist and mathematician, was born 26 April 1898 at Kirriemuir, Angus, the only son of William Kermack, postman, and his wife, Helen Ogilvy. His mother died in 1904 and his upbringing fell largely upon his father's sister. The local school, Webster's Seminary, provided him with a stimulating education which was typical of rural Scotland at that time. Kirriemuir has been vividly described under the name of 'Thrums' in the novels of another of its natives, Sir James M. Barrie [q.v.].

Kermack was awarded a bursary and entered the university of Aberdeen in 1914. In 1918 he graduated MA with first class honours in mathematics and natural philosophy and B.Sc. with special distinction in mathematics, natural philosophy, and chemistry. He then served six months with the Royal Air Force. From 1919 until 1921 he worked, under the influence of W. H. Perkin [q.v.] and (Sir) Robert Robinson, at the Dyson Perrins Laboratory, Oxford, which had recently been constructed from a generous donation by C. W. D. Perrins [q.v.]. It was then that Kermack developed a lifelong interest in the chemistry of heterocyclic compounds. A promising research career in charge of the chemical department of the Royal College of Physicians Laboratory in Edinburgh seemed to be over at the age of twenty-six when an accident in the laboratory resulted in his total and permanent blindness. A lesser man might have succumbed, but Kermack's subsequent achievements in chemistry, mathematics, and in other areas of endeavour were to be accomplished under this cruel hardship. In his later years he modestly attributed this triumph over adversity to the help and support of his many friends, scientific collaborators, and, above all, to a devoted wife.

Kermack began to apply his highly original mind and remarkable memory to collaborative research with his colleagues at the Royal College of Physicians Laboratory. He also supervised a series of research students in chemistry, working for postgraduate degrees at the university of Edinburgh. Over a period of years he developed methods for the synthesis of heterocyclic compounds with antimalarial activity in order to determine the basic principles. These studies greatly facilitated the production in Britain of mepacrine, a drug which was used extensively as a prophylactic and therapeutic agent in areas where malaria was endemic during the war of 1939-45. Kermack also returned to mathematics as a part-time intellectual exercise. One result of this was his collaboration with A. G. McKendrick on the mathematical theory of epidemic disease and on the conditions under which transmissible disease could attain a steady endemic state. Their conclusions published over the period 1927-40 were a major advance in epidemiology. Later in Aberdeen Kermack was to collaborate on a wide variety of problems of biochemical and biomedical importance, notably on the mode of action of antimalarial drugs and on the development and use of antibodies labelled with fluorescent dyes in scientific and clinical research.

In April 1949 Kermack moved to Aberdeen as the first MacLeod-Smith professor of biological chemistry. He was fifty, blind, a distinguished synthetic organic chemist and mathematician, but he had no previous experience of teaching at the undergraduate level or of administrative problems in a university. It needed all his sterling qualities of character and undoubted intellectual ability to overcome these handicaps. He took his full share of teaching undergraduates science and medicine, but was always his best with small groups where he could stimulate discussion. It was a measure of his ability that within a few years he was able to foster and expand a department which came to enjoy a high reputation for both teaching and research. He took an active part in the general life and work of the university and of the associated research institutes in the Aberdeen area. His influence became considerable on faculty and other committees because he was consistently a man of science in all matters. His phenomenal memory served him in good stead when he served as dean of the Science Faculty (1961-4)—an office which he filled with distinction.

Kermack naturally depended entirely on others to read to him and he could be very demanding. At the same time he had an outstanding ability to identify, summarize, and recall the crux of any scientific or administrative argument after a paper had been read to him once. Kermack loved an argument and delighted in being able to discuss new ideas. The duty of reading to him usually became a stimulating affair.

Well-built and muscular, he enjoyed long walks, always accompanied by his wife or a friend. He sought relaxation in chess and books which had been recorded on records or tapes—curiously he never really mastered braille. He frequently used a small portable radio to keep abreast of current affairs. His political views were to the left but were somewhat modified after a visit to Moscow in 1961 to attend the International Congress of Biochemistry.

Kermack's life revolved around his work, from which he derived an inner sense of contentment. He could be formal and remote but usually he was a cheerful and gentle man with a puckish sense of humour and an insatiable interest in people and scientific matters. After his retirement in 1968 he continued his collaborative work with various colleagues and was actively preparing the manuscript of a book when he died suddenly in Aberdeen 20 July 1970.

Kermack received the D.Sc. degree from the university of Aberdeen (1925), an honorary LLD from the university of St. Andrews (1937), and was elected a fellow of the Royal Society (1944). A fellow of the Royal Society of Edinburgh from 1924, he served on its council from 1946 to 1949. In 1925 he married Elsábeletta Raimunda, daughter of Raimundo Blásquez, of Anguilas, Spain. They were a devoted couple and had one son. A good photographic likeness was presented by his friends to the university of Aberdeen.

[J. N. Davidson, F. Yates, and W. H. McCrea in *Biographical Memoirs of Fellows of the Royal Society*, vol. xvii, 1971; personal knowledge.]   P. T. GRANT

KETTON-CREMER, ROBERT WYNDHAM (1906-1969), biographer and historian, was the elder son of a Norfolk squire, Wyndham Cremer Cremer of Beeston, and his wife, Emily, daughter of Robert Bayly, timber merchant. Born 2 May 1906, at his mother's family home in Plymouth, he lived always near Cromer where his father's land adjoined that of an eccentric bachelor great-uncle, Robert Ketton of Felbrigg. At Harrow and at Balliol College, Oxford, where he was an exhibitioner, bouts of rheumatic fever permanently impaired his health. For that reason, after obtaining a second in English in 1928, he decided to live at home, write books, and help his father to nurse the Felbrigg estate back to life. Robert Ketton had made that property over to the boy's father early in 1924 before flitting suddenly to Kent, on condition that the family should change its name to Ketton-Cremer.

The family moved with deep misgiving into Felbrigg. The lovely seventeenth-century house had been left, like everything else, in a state of such appalling neglect that restoration could only be an arduous work of many years. It was promptly transformed, nevertheless, into a scene of happiness and hospitality, and when young Ketton-Cremer inherited it on his father's death in 1933 his first book had been well received. It was entitled *The Early Life and Diaries of William Windham* (1930), a remote collateral predecessor, who had been Pitt's secretary at war and a friend of Burke and Johnson. His literary output branched thereafter into the two channels of full-scale biography and local history.

Ketton-Cremer published major biographies of *Horace Walpole* (1940) and *Thomas Gray* (1955). The latter book won the James Tait Black memorial prize and the Heinemann Foundation award. He felt an affinity with both subjects because, like himself, they never married and came to terms with the fact that they were natural celibates. He did not live to write a projected biography of Matthew Prior, but his contribution to the history of Norfolk is unlikely ever to be surpassed. It consists partly of five volumes of collected essays (1944-61), descriptive of personalities and events, and composed in an urbane style of polished but pungent lucidity. It consists also of a long work entitled *Norfolk in the Civil War* (1969) and *Felbrigg: The Story of a House* (1962) which he alone could have written, and which is much the most personal and revealing of his books.

Ketton-Cremer's sense of duty matched his sense of history. His public role as a prominent landowner and man of letters was conducted against a background of many unrecorded kindly offices. His more conspicuous activity included service as a major in the Home Guard (1941-5), as chairman of his magistrates' bench (1948-66), and as high sheriff (1951). He was a trustee of the National Portrait Gallery, and he combined chairmanship of the Norwich Diocesan Council for the Care of Churches with membership of the regional committee of the National Trust. A fellow of the British Academy (1968), and a governor of Gresham's School, Holt, he helped to promote the university of East Anglia which conferred on him an honorary degree (1969). He derived much pleasure from his election as a fellow-commoner of Christ's College, Cambridge (1966), and gave the Rede lecture at Cambridge (1957) on Matthew Prior, the Warton lecture for the British Academy (1959) on lapidary verse, and the Lamont memorial lecture at Yale (1960) on Gray as a letter-writer.

Ketton-Cremer's gentleness and modesty earned a rare measure of affection and respect. He was a practising Christian and devout churchman, sustained by an unshakeable Anglican religious faith which he did not ask his friends to share. He kept a wide range of friendships in repair on both sides of the Atlantic, and took a warm personal interest in the individual welfare of everyone who worked or lived on his estate. Loving the fine arts, and fascinated by antiquarian studies, his knowledge and instant command of illuminating detail were extraordinary. But his most absorbing passion was forestry and he planted on a substantial scale. His appearance, personality, and library, all strongly suggested the eighteenth century, in which he would have been thoroughly at home.

The most bitter sorrow of Ketton-Cremer's life was the death on active service in Crete in 1941 of his younger brother, Dick, while serving in the Royal Air Force. Despite differences in tastes and temperaments they exhibited the same serenity and charm and were completely in accord. When their mother died in 1952 Ketton-Cremer became the last survivor of a family circle which had always been exiguous. Although faithfully served, he experienced increasing frustration as his health, which worried his friends more than it did him, visibly deteriorated. On 12 December 1969 he died peacefully in hospital in Norwich, bequeathing Felbrigg with all its contents and land to the National Trust.

There is an unfinished portrait of Ketton-Cremer by Allan Gwynne-Jones at Felbrigg.

[Personal knowledge.]   PHILIP MAGNUS

KILLEARN, first BARON (1880-1964), diplomatist. [See LAMPSON, MILES WEDDERBURN.]

KILMUIR, EARL OF (1900-1967), lord chancellor. [See FYFE, DAVID PATRICK MAXWELL.]

KING, EARL JUDSON (1901-1962), clinical biochemist, was born 19 May 1901 in Toronto, Canada, the elder son of the Revd Charles W. King, Baptist minister, and his wife, Charlotte Stark. He was educated at Brandon College and McMaster University, Ontario, graduating in 1921 in chemistry and biology and then continuing to a master's degree in chemistry and, at Toronto University, to a doctorate of philosophy in 1926.

King was offered a research post in the newly founded Banting Institute in Toronto where he engaged in the study of the biochemistry of silicosis, an occupational lung disease caused by the inhalation of siliceous dust by miners and others employed in various dusty trades. In 1928 he went to London to work in the Lister Institute where he became interested in organic phosphate compounds and the phos-phatase enzymes which were his second life-long research subject. He then worked for a short period in the Kaiser Wilhelm Institute at Munich before returning to the Banting Institute in 1929, where he was promoted to associate professor and in 1931 became head of the biochemical section.

In 1934 he returned to London on being invited to take charge of the chemical pathology department of the new British Postgraduate Medical School at Hammersmith Hospital, a post he retained for the rest of his life. He was appointed reader in chemical pathology in the university of London in 1935 and made professor in 1945.

At Hammersmith, E. H. Kettle [q.v.], the first professor of pathology, was building up an outstanding academic department with research and teaching based on the best modern hospital practice. The influence of the Hammersmith school was to be felt in all English-speaking countries and King played a full part in this development. He realized the growing importance of accurate biochemical data for the diagnosis and treatment of disease and he pioneered the quantitative analysis of blood constituents which came to replace the somewhat empirical tests of the previous generation. In particular he was dissatisfied with the relatively large volumes of blood required for the methods then current and he displayed much ingenuity in refining the analyses so that they could be performed on the amount of blood readily available from a finger prick. The successive editions of his book, *Microanalysis in Medical Biochemistry* (1946), were used world-wide in clinical laboratories. This was but one of his many books and articles.

In the meantime King continued his main research interests in the biochemistry of silicosis and the properties of the phosphatase enzymes. His reputation was such that a constant stream of research students and others came to work with him for varying periods before returning to their own laboratories; many were from overseas and King's methods and ideas became internationally well known. An indication of his influence is given by the almost universal use, until very recently, of the eponymous King-Armstrong unit for alkaline phosphatase measurements, making his name a household word in every clinical laboratory in the world.

The lung damage of silicosis was widely believed to be caused biochemically by the sharp-edged crystals of silica inhaled into the pulmonary tissue. Silica was believed to be almost completely insoluble in body fluids. King rapidly disproved both of these assumptions. He demonstrated that silica slowly and continuously dissolved to produce a toxic action on near-by cells and that the damage was mysteriously linked to the fineness and number of dust particles. This solubility theory of silicosis opened a large programme of research, into the normal physiology of silica in animals, the effect of other compounds in enhancing or reducing the silica effect, and the complications which resulted from the frequent coexisting tuberculous infection in human cases. In 1937 public interest was aroused into the closely related coal-miners' pneumoconiosis and King commenced experimental work to throw light on the great differences in morbidity from lung disease between different coalfields in the United Kingdom. He became a self-taught and accomplished experimental pathologist and extended his interest to the effects of inhaled asbestos fibres—a very early indication of the widespread concern about the use of asbestos which was to follow twenty-five or thirty years later.

At the outbreak of World War II, King accepted responsibility for pathology laboratories in a number of hospitals in the Middlesex sector, a task which involved much travelling under difficult wartime conditions. It was not very long before his talents were required on a wider scale and he developed methods for the estimation in blood of some new anti-malarial drugs and chemicals which undoubtedly helped in their introduction, with important consequences for the troops in tropical climates. King also headed an investigation into methods for determining haemoglobin—his findings were rapidly adopted and formed the basis of the methods nowadays in everyday use. He spent some time in India as an adviser to the armed forces on laboratory methods and was made consultant in medical biochemistry, with the rank of brigadier, to the Royal and Indian Army Medical Corps. From 1950 he was consultant in biochemistry to the Royal Army Medical Corps.

After the war King became progressively involved in scientific administration. His great ability was widely recognized and he occupied positions of importance in the British Postgraduate Medical School, the university of London, and various scientific societies. He was, for example, chairman of the Biochemical Society (1957-9) and editor of the *Biochemical Journal*. Shortly after the war he founded the Association of Clinical Biochemists, the first scientific society devoted entirely to the relatively new speciality of clinical biochemistry which King had done so much to establish. He then turned his attention to international scientific matters and, as a result of his efforts, the International Federation of Clinical Chemists was founded; he became its first chairman (1952-60). He became an honorary MD of Oslo and Iceland, and was an honorary

member of many societies. He was Chadwick lecturer in 1955.

By 1955, because the Postgraduate School had grown to such an extent, a decision was taken to launch a public appeal for funds to extend the buildings. King took a prominent part in this work and, in particular, spent much time and energy in seeking funds in North America. It was on an exhausting trip to the United States that he was taken ill; he recovered but remained in ill health for the next two years. One night he died suddenly, 31 October 1962, at his home in Wembley, Middlesex, after a characteristically busy day spent at London University Senate House.

In appearance King was stocky and compactly built. He moved briskly and spoke abruptly. As his record shows, he had a prodigious appetite for work and a fine talent for spotting scientific discoveries ripe for development or individual scientists who would repay encouragement. His interests outside his work were few, but he derived a never-ending pleasure from meeting people and from social intercourse with different people of every nationality. His main recreation during the summer was touring and camping on the Continent, often combined with attendance at a scientific congress and he was never happier than when exploring a foreign country he had not visited previously, accompanied by his wife (herself a biochemist) and his two daughters. In 1927 he had married Hazel Marion Keith, of Lethbridge, Alberta, who had been a fellow student at Brandon College.

He is remembered with affection in laboratories all over the world by workers who enjoyed the generous hospitality of his laboratory and home. Clinical biochemistry was one of the fastest developing new medical sciences during the second and third quarters of the twentieth century. King's contribution was second to none.

There is a bust of King by Anthony Gray in the possession of the family.

[*Biochemical Journal*, vol. lxxxix, 1963; *Enzymologia*, vol. xxv, 1963; *Annals of Occupational Hygiene*, vol. vi, 1963; private information; personal knowledge.]

I. D. P. WOOTTON

KING, WILLIAM BERNARD ROBINSON (1889-1963), geologist, was born 12 November 1889, at West Burton near Aysgarth in Yorkshire, the younger son of William Robinson King and his wife, Florence Muriel Theed. He was very much a son of the Yorkshire dales and records of the Kings as yeoman farmers in Wensleydale reach back to 1640. King's elder brother died at the age of twenty-one. King was educated at Uppingham School and Jesus College, Cambridge. He attained first class honours in part ii of the natural sciences tripos in 1912, being awarded the Harkness scholarship.

King was appointed to the Geological Survey of Great Britain in October 1912. At the outbreak of the war of 1914-18, King became a 2nd lieutenant in the 7th battalion of the Royal Welch Fusiliers, and from 1915 until the end of the war was in France with the Royal Engineers. There he advised on water supply and well production, the driving of mine galleries and construction of dugouts so that they remained dry, and numerous other matters which earned him appointment to the OBE (military division) and two mentions in dispatches. In 1920 he became demonstrator and assistant to the Woodwardian professor of geology at Cambridge; in 1931 he became Yates-Goldsmid professor of geology at University College, London; and from 1943 to 1955 was Woodwardian professor of geology at Cambridge. He became a fellow of Jesus College, Cambridge, in 1920 and of Magdalene College, Cambridge, in 1922.

King's scientific work, embodied in more than fifty publications, was concerned mainly with the stratigraphy of the Lower Palaeozoic and of the Quaternary, the Cambrian palaeontology of the Dead Sea and the Persian Gulf, pioneer work on the geology of the floor of the English Channel, hydrogeology, and military geology. The last three topics were closely connected with his outstanding service with the Royal Engineers during both world wars. He ended the first as a captain, and the second as a lieutenant-colonel. In the second war he was awarded the military cross for bravery in the Dunkirk evacuation. From 1941 to 1943 he was attached to GHQ, Home Forces, from which was to develop the invading 21st Army Group. It was because of King's advice on the geological conditions which would permit the rapid construction of strike airfields that the original choice of Cotentin and Cherbourg for the invasion of France was changed to Normandy. He was also concerned with the early investigations into the outcrop of Quaternary peats and clays on the invasion beaches of Normandy, the understanding of which proved to be crucial to the success of the operation.

King occupied many important offices in learned societies, serving as secretary of the Geological Society of London, 1937-40 and again 1944-6, and as president from 1953 to 1955. He was president of the Yorkshire Geological Society in 1949 and 1950 and of Section C of the British Association in 1951. In 1949 he was elected a fellow of the Royal Society.

King was extensively honoured for his work, in this country and abroad. He was a foreign correspondent of the Palaeontological Society of India, the Geological Society of America, and the Geological Society of France. In 1947 the university of Lille conferred on him an honorary doctorate for the work he had done in two world wars, and Rennes did the same in 1952, mainly for his researches in the English Channel. The Société Géologique de Nord awarded him the Gosselet medal in 1923 and the Geological Society of France presented him with its Prestwich medal in 1945. The Geological Society of London, which had recognized King's early promise with the Wollaston Fund in 1920, presented to him the prestigious Murchison medal in 1951.

In 1916 King married Margaret Amy Passingham, daughter of Charles Alvin Gillig and his wife who, upon their divorce, assumed her maiden name of Passingham. The Kings had two daughters, one of whom, Cuchlaine, became professor of geography at Nottingham. King died at Northallerton Hospital 23 January 1963. Throughout his academic career, the quiet friendship, hospitality, and help which King and his wife offered to his students will be an abiding memory to all who came under his influence.

There is a portrait in pencil by John Hookham (1953) in Magdalene College, Cambridge.

[F. W. Shotton in *Biographical Memoirs of Fellows of the Royal Society*, vol. ix, 1963; *The Times*, 26 January 1963.]

F. W. SHOTTON

KING-HALL, (WILLIAM) STEPHEN (RICHARD), BARON KING-HALL (1893-1966), writer, and broadcaster on politics and international affairs, was born at Blackheath 21 January 1893, the eldest of the three children and the only son of (Admiral Sir) George F. King-Hall, and his wife, Olga, daughter of Richard Ker, of the diplomatic service and MP for Downpatrick. She came of an Ulster family with not only diplomatic but also literary associations. His grandfather (Sir William King Hall distinguished himself during the second Chinese war) and uncle were also admirals. His father, a liberally minded man, held religious convictions of an evangelical cast. He was also a lifelong teetotaller, as was his son. After early schooling at Lausanne, King-Hall was educated for the Royal Navy, at Osborne and Dartmouth. He was in action at Jutland in the *Southampton*, the 'little ship' of his naval affections. After the war he wrote the first Admiralty manual on cruiser tactics.

Having been awarded the gold medal of the Royal United Service Institution in 1919, he went on to serve in the Training and Staff

Duties Department of the Admiralty. In 1920-1 he passed through the Royal Naval Staff College, afterwards proceeding as a torpedo lieutenant to the China Squadron, until the end of 1923. From 1925 to 1926 King-Hall was intelligence officer to Sir Roger (later Lord) Keyes [q.v.] in the Mediterranean Fleet. In 1928 he was promoted commander, and called to work on the naval staff.

Though King-Hall's feeling for the navy was deep, he had early confided to his family his impatience with some of its traditional practices. He shared his generation's revulsion from war. Though never a pacifist, he pinned hopes on disarmament. He had, moreover, long cultivated the talents that would make him a publicist. He wrote much for the press under a pseudonym. On the China station he had produced his first book under his own name, *Western Civilization and the Far East* (1924). *Imperial Defence* (1926) attracted a preface by Viscount Haldane [q.v.]. Meanwhile his verve had overflowed in the improvization of ships' entertainments with results that would prove fruitful in the theatre.

In 1929 King-Hall resigned from the Service to take a research post in the Royal Institute of International Affairs. His slender finances, now supporting a family, were transformed by the success of a naval comedy, *The Middle Watch* (1930), produced in collaboration with Ian Hay (John Hay Beith, q.v.), which ran for two years, and was to be five times filmed. He was now poised to become one of the most popular interpreters of current events of his generation.

As organizer of discussions at the Institute King-Hall met authorities in many fields, including J. M. (later Lord) Keynes [q.v.], whose respect he gained, and whose influence became apparent in his work. He made no claims as an original thinker, but saw himself as a mediator, whose information would be 'respected by the expert, and acceptable to the general reader'. His strongly held opinions, sometimes simplistic, at other times lit by genuine insight, were those of a liberal internationalist, who was early alert to the rising menace of Fascism. His independence was patent. The press had forfeited much public confidence, and an audience lay ready. From 1930 till 1937 he broadcast a talk on current affairs every Friday in the BBC 'Children's Hour'. His directness and warmth, (not without an occasional breeze from the quarter-deck), combined with his rare gift for reducing complexities to simple language, enthralled, not only the children, but many adults, including such diverse personalities as Lloyd George, the Duke of Westminster, and Lord Perry, chairman of Ford Motor Company Ltd.

By 1935, when King-Hall left the staff of Chatham House, he was not only a radio celebrity, but a widely published journalist, in demand as a lecturer at home and abroad, a name in the theatre, and a prolific author. (His books would eventually total forty.) In 1934-5 he published *Our Own Times*, a voluminous contemporary history, which went through four editions. An invitation to the board of the United Kingdom Provident Association gave him practical insight into insurance and investment. In 1936 came his most characteristic venture. Single-handed, save for family and a few friends, and with no capital, he undertook to post a weekly letter to subscribers to the *King-Hall News Letter*. At first there were 600. In three years there were 60,000. The *King-Hall News Letter* became, without advertisement revenue, a self-financing institution. His touch remained personal, but always with an eye to world horizons. Again and again he returned to the need for preparedness to meet the threat of Hitler. On the eve of war he contrived to infiltrate a German version to individuals in the Reich, provoking a vehement reaction from Goebbels and Hitler himself.

In October 1939 King-Hall entered the House of Commons as National Labour member for Ormskirk, unopposed under the wartime truce. This climax to long-cherished parliamentary ambitions proved hollow. He could endure the yoke of no party, even the loosely associated National Labour remnant soon becoming too constrictive. He resigned from it in February 1942. As an Independent, he was appointed chairman of the Fuel Economy Publicity Committee. But his speaking did not catch the House's ear. He vented his wartime energies in administrative and propaganda work. His foundation of the Hansard Society in 1944 attested his devotion to Parliament as an institution. He lost his seat to (Sir) Harold Wilson in 1945, and failed as Independent candidate at Bridgwater in 1950.

Meanwhile King-Hall's appeal as a publicist had declined somewhat from its pre-war peak. He appeared on television, but it was too late for him to match there his earlier success on radio. Fashions in journalism had changed. Yet his personal following remained considerable. When, in 1959, rising costs threatened the *News Letter*, pressure from subscribers persuaded him to continue it, though at less frequent intervals. His flow of books was unabated. In them he argued strenuously for European union. Quick to seize the implications of the atom bomb, he put a reasoned case for unilateral nuclear disarmament by Britain, though he never countenanced agitation by unconstitutional means.

Though many good things lie scattered in his

writings, King-Hall left no memorial commensurate with his dispersed talents. He saw himself as primarily an educator and former of opinion. As such he remains a distinctive figure, unlikely to be overlooked by students of his time. He was a companion of infectious vitality. In appearance he realized the traditional idea of the sailor, short and sturdy, with a merry eye and a pugnacious chin.

King-Hall's last years were overshadowed by the death of his wife. In 1919 he had married (Amelia) Kathleen (died 1963), daughter of Francis Spencer, an associate of Cecil Rhodes [q.v.]. He had met his wife in Cape Town as a midshipman. They had three daughters. He had been knighted in 1954, and in January 1966 he received a life peerage. He died in London 2 June 1966.

There is a drawing by David Low in the National Portrait Gallery.

[*The Times*, 3 June 1966; private information.]   E. R. THOMPSON

KIRKPATRICK, SIR IVONE AUGUSTINE (1897–1964), diplomatist, was born in Wellington, India, 3 February 1897, the elder son of Colonel Ivone Kirkpatrick of the South Staffordshire Regiment, a descendant of a branch of a Scottish family which had settled in Ireland in the eighteenth century. But his talents for public service may have come more from his mother, the daughter of (General Sir) Arthur Edward Hardinge [q.v.], later commander-in-chief, Bombay Army, and governor of Gibraltar. She was a former maid of honour to Queen Victoria. Her grandfather, Viscount Henry Hardinge [q.v.] served in the Cabinets of Wellington and Peel, and was later governor-general of India, 1844–8. Her first cousin, Charles Hardinge, Baron Hardinge of Penshurst [q.v.], was permanent under-secretary of the Foreign Office, 1906–10 and 1916–20, and viceroy of India, 1910–16. Ivone Kirkpatrick spent much time with his mother between the ages of seven and ten in Switzerland, Belgium, and Germany, learning French and German.

Kirkpatrick, a Roman Catholic through his mother, went to Downside in 1907. He was commissioned in the Royal Inniskilling Fusiliers in November 1914, when he was still only seventeen years old. He was severely wounded in action against the Turks in August 1915. Fit for duty six months later, he spent the rest of the war on intelligence and propaganda work, the last year of it in neutral Holland in charge of a network of British agents operating in German-occupied territory. In February 1919 he passed the Foreign Office examination.

After a year in Brazil Kirkpatrick spent the unprecedentedly long period of ten years in the Western Department of the Foreign Office. In these years he made his reputation as a rapid, reliable, and incisive worker, eager for responsibility. He gained experience of international negotiations, and became well known to senior officials and ministers.

After three years in Rome (1930–3), Kirkpatrick went in August 1933 as head of Chancery (first secretary) to Berlin. There he remained for over five years, as chief of staff to two very different ambassadors, Sir Eric Phipps and (from April 1937) Sir Nevile Henderson [qq.v.]. By his personality, his energy, his wide range of German acquaintance, he acquired in Berlin a position of real authority and influence. His long service there culminated in the Czechoslovakian crisis and the Munich settlement. In his memoirs (*The Inner Circle*, 1959), Kirkpatrick made clear his detestation of the Nazis and his conviction that they must be resisted, while leaving open the question whether they should have been opposed at the time of Munich. However, his views seem to have made little impression on those of Sir Nevile Henderson. Kirkpatrick was loyal to his service and political chiefs, and accepted his duty to authority. He wrote of Henderson: 'He was a human chief for whom it was a pleasure to work . . . except for a few angry outbursts when I tried to prove that war was inevitable.'

Kirkpatrick returned to London in December 1938. After a variety of posts he found what suited him when in February 1941 he became foreign adviser to the BBC, and six months later controller of its European services. He was back in the sphere of wartime propaganda, where he had operated with such zest twenty-five years before, and here for three years he made a major contribution. One interlude, in May 1941, found Kirkpatrick employed to identify and interview Hitler's deputy, Hess, after his flight to Scotland.

From August 1944 until the end of the war Kirkpatrick was in charge of organizing the British element of the German Control Commission. He then went for a few months as British political adviser to General Eisenhower at Supreme Allied Headquarters, until its disbandment. After two years as assistant under-secretary in charge of Foreign Office information work, he served from 1947 to 1949 as deputy under-secretary for Western Europe, and then for a year as permanent under-secretary of the German Section of the Foreign Office—the former 'Control Office for Germany and Austria'. In these last two posts he worked closely with Ernest Bevin [q.v.], for whom he came to feel deep respect and affection. In 1950 he went as high commissioner to Germany. His three years of office included, most notably, the negotiation and signature (May 1952) of the immensely important and complex series of Bonn Conventions, which eventually restored sovereignty to the Federal Republic; and, in parallel, the first steps towards German rearmament. As high commissioner—one of the three joint sovereigns of Western Germany—Kirkpatrick carried immense responsibility; and in his brisk, authoritative, relaxed way he shouldered it easily enough. He established good relations with Chancellor Adenauer, but not so close and cordial as those of his predecessor, General Sir Brian Robertson (later Lord Robertson of Oakridge).

In November 1953 Kirkpatrick succeeded Sir William (later Lord) Strang as permanent under-secretary in the Foreign Office. His three years in office—under three foreign secretaries, Eden, Macmillan, and Selwyn Lloyd—presented the usual infinite variety of problems; but they culminated, only three months before his retirement, in the Suez crisis. His part in this has certainly, whether deservedly or not, scarred Kirkpatrick's reputation. He has been severely criticized in several books, but they are not based on full information. In his own memoirs he is reticent, writing that these events were so recent and controversial that he did not propose to comment on them. Yet he wrote enough to show how strongly he had felt, and to suggest that he may have been over-influenced by the lessons he drew from his German experience of the thirties—the need to stand up at all costs against outrageous conduct. Many members of the Foreign Service were indignant at the intensely secretive handling of the crisis, and blamed Kirkpatrick for it. But the secrecy may have been imposed on him. Kirkpatrick may have been guilty of no more than fulfilling a civil servant's duty of loyalty to his political chiefs.

Yet it may be doubted whether Kirkpatrick was well fitted, by temperament, training, and experience, to fill this post at what was—as it is easy, in retrospect, to see—a period of rapid decline in British power. In appearance and manner, Kirkpatrick was small, slight, brisk, dapper, decisive, self-confident; and his mind matched. Superficially outgoing, he was not an easy man to know well. He took pride in thinking, working, and deciding fast—perhaps too fast. He had little use for research or analysis or for prolonged discussion. It may be significant that he was probably the only man in the senior branch of his service with no university education, or indeed any formal education after the age of seventeen, although he had been accepted by Balliol in October 1915. He was combative, even aggressive. He had no great respect for foreigners. He had great courage, and great

appetite for responsibility. He had carried great responsibilities through a period of great apparent British power. By 1956, he may have over-estimated what remained of it. Few people did not. But if anyone should not, it is the head of the Foreign Office.

Kirkpatrick was appointed CMG (1939), KCMG (1948), GCMG (1953), KCB (1951), and GCB (1956).

Kirkpatrick served as chairman of the Independent Television Authority from 1957 to 1962. In addition to his memoirs he wrote *Mussolini, Study of a Demagogue* (published posthumously in 1964). In 1929 he had married Violet Caulfield, daughter of Colonel Reginald C. Cottell. They had a son, who went up to Balliol in place of his father in 1950, and a daughter. Kirkpatrick died at Celbridge, county Kildare, 25 May 1964.

[Ivone Kirkpatrick, *The Inner Circle*, 1959; personal knowledge.]   CON O'NEILL

KNIGHT, HAROLD (1874-1961), painter, was born in Nottingham 27 January 1874, the eldest son of William Knight, a local architect, and his wife, Elizabeth Lindsay Symington, whose rigid puritan temperament did not make for a happy home life for the family of three brothers and two sisters. It is probable that Harold's reserve, which was to grow on him, had its roots in those early years, when natural instincts were sternly repressed. He was educated at Nottingham High School, and went on to the Nottingham School of Art, where he soon made his mark as an outstanding student. Wilson Foster was a strong influence, and Harold learnt how to imitate nature faithfully.

It was here that he met Laura Johnson (Laura Knight, q.v.), whom he was to marry much later, but he was in no way emotionally involved with her; the atmosphere at home made him concentrate on his painting, which he determined should be his career. He entered the competitions for provincial students held yearly at the South Kensington College of Art in London, and won gold, silver, and bronze medals. In 1895 he won a British Institute travelling scholarship worth £50 a year for two years. He elected to remain for a year in Nottingham in order to sell his paintings and add to the scholarship. The following year he went to Paris, studying with Jean Paul Laurens and Benjamin Constant, but did not find the French ateliers congenial and returned to Nottingham before the year was up. It is surprising to note that he did not appear to be at all influenced by the new wave in Paris, the artistic centre of Europe, where those painters who succeeded the early Impressionists were pushing out the boundaries of art further than they had been before.

He had kept up his friendship with Laura Johnson, and when she and her sister were taken by an aunt for a painting holiday at Staithes, a fishing village near Whitby on the Yorkshire coast, Harold was invited to join the party. There was a small artists' colony at Staithes, and Harold decided to remain for a time. He made a modest livelihood selling his work to dealers in Nottingham. Laura, too, remained with her sister, and painted scores of studies of the fisherfolk, selling them when she could, and living on a small allowance from an uncle.

Harold sent pictures to the Royal Academy in London, and had a few small canvases taken. In 1902 his painting of a fishing boat, 'The Last Coble', was bought by the trustees of the Holbrook Bequest and presented to the Nottingham Museum and Art Gallery. Laura had a picture, 'Mother and Child', accepted by the RA, which was sold. Both were at last making a little money.

On 3 June 1903 Harold Knight, then nearly thirty and Laura Johnson, then twenty-six, were married. Their long, individual careers from this point onwards were closely connected, and Harold's development is considered alongside that of Laura.

KNIGHT, DAME LAURA (1877–1970), painter, was born 4 August 1877 at Long Eaton, in Nottinghamshire, the youngest of the three daughters of Charles Johnson, of no settled occupation, and his wife, Charlotte Bates. Johnson left his wife and family when he discovered that the Bates lace manufactury was on the downgrade, leaving Charlotte to bring up her daughters by teaching art in Nottingham schools. She was determined that Laura, who early showed a talent for drawing, should be properly trained. Laura was educated at Brincliffe School and at St. Quentin in northern France, where an aunt who lived there promised to get her a place in a Paris atelier. This did not materialize, to Laura's bitter disappointment, and she returned home, entering the Nottingham School of Art when she was fourteen. Here she met the prize student, Harold Knight [q.v.]. Like him, she was much influenced by the naturalistic methods taught at the School, and when she went to live in Staithes her studies and painting were all on firmly traditional lines. Also, like him, she entered regularly for the South Kensington College of Art competitions, and won gold, silver, and bronze medals, as well as a Princess of Wales scholarship.

After their marriage, the Knights remained in Yorkshire for a time, but decided if they were going to advance with their work they ought to move. In 1905 they took a number of their canvases to London, and were much encouraged when Ernest Brown, a partner in Brown & Phillips (Oliver Brown, q.v.), of the Leicester Galleries gave an exhibition of their work. Some pictures were sold, and a substantial cheque from Brown enabled them to sail on a cargo boat to Holland, which they had always wanted to visit. They remained for some weeks in Amsterdam, where Harold was able to study the paintings of the artist he admired most, Vermeer, and Laura was entranced by the picturesque nature of everything. On their return they sold a sufficient number of pictures between them to go to Holland again the following year, staying at Laren, well known to Dutch artists. In 1906 Harold had a picture, 'A Cup of Tea', accepted by the RA, and Laura had a Dutch interior taken. Harold's picture was hung on the line and bought for the Brisbane Gallery. They were able to go to Holland for a year, and brought back a large number of canvases, some of which they sold, but many had to be burnt or painted over. They decided to leave Staithes and move to Newlyn, in Cornwall.

The colony of artists at Newlyn, led by Stanhope A. Forbes [q.v.] and his wife, Elizabeth Armstrong, rejected the idealized subjects that had made so much Victorian painting dull and lifeless. They insisted on 'the simple truth of nature' in art, with an emphasis on painting out of doors. Laura had always preferred working in the open, and the marvellous quality of the Cornish light was a constant inspiration. Harold also painted out of doors, but he had a feeling for interiors and reflected light. Each had developed a strongly individual style, and both were selling their pictures at the Leicester Galleries, and getting known in London.

(Sir) Alfred James Munnings [q.v.], already being talked about as a talented artist, came to Newlyn. Harold did not care for the uninhibited young man in the check suit and yellow neckerchief, but Laura began a friendship with him which was to last. She was attracted by his overwhelming vitality, which matched her own exuberant temperament. She was in her element at Newlyn, painting the effects of sun and light on the naked bodies of bathers. She loved large canvases, and was tireless in making scores of studies. Her painting, 'Daughters of the Sun', exhibited at the RA in 1909 was praised as a stunningly effective painting, but she priced it too highly (at £600) and it did not sell. (This fixation about the monetary value of her work was to grow.)

The temperamental differences in the Knights' work and their divergence of outlook was apparent. In spite of the aims of the Newlyn group, Harold kept to his own vision, what Norman Garstin in *The Studio*, December 1912, called 'the authoritative formulae of the art establishment of former centuries'. It was generally agreed that he was not interested in experiment and analysis; lucidity of statement was the dominating factor of his work. He lacked emotional force; his goal, as always, was mastery of his medium, and this he achieved. Laura's paintings showed an opulence of style and a flamboyance which was part of her nature. She painted a huge canvas, 'The Green Feather', in a day, and sent it to the Carnegie Institute of Pittsburgh, Pennsylvania, which had an International Exhibition every year. It got an honourable mention and was sold to the National Gallery of Canada for £400—the best price, Laura said, she had ever been paid for a day's work.

In 1912 Harold became seriously ill with infected teeth, and neither he nor Laura began painting again for six months. Harold had begun to get commissions for portraits, and they could now save money. They also made friends with new arrivals at Newlyn, Augustus John [q.v.] and his wife, and (Sir) Barry Jackson [q.v.], a wealthy theatre impresario from Birmingham.

After the outbreak of war in 1914, Harold, who was a conscientious objector, was directed to work as a farmer's labourer. Their savings diminished. In 1916 Laura received an unexpected Canadian Government commission, through a critic who was an admirer of her admirable technique, to paint soldiers bathing at Witley Camp. This turned out to be a non-event; instead, she worked there on studies of boxing, though she had never attempted anything like it before. The finished canvas was one of the most realistic paintings she had ever achieved, and the resulting publicity added to her growing fame.

Soon after the end of the war, the Knights moved to London. Harold was now established as a portrait painter. Laura, always ready to try something new, got permission to work behind the scenes of Diaghilev's Ballet Company. Through Barry Jackson she was allowed to work backstage in the theatre. In 1922 she was invited to go to America as one of the European representatives on the jury for that year's International Exhibition at Pittsburgh. On her return, she and Harold took a long lease of 9 (the number was later changed to 16) Langford Place, St. John's Wood, which was to be their permanent home and where each had a studio.

Harold's now established reputation as a meticulous, skilful portrait painter continued to bring him many commissions. In 1926 he was invited to go to Baltimore to paint Dr John Finney of the Johns Hopkins Memorial Hospital; the generous fee enabled him to bring Laura to America and she made many studies in the negro wards of the famous hospital.

An honour which filled her with pride came in 1927, when she was elected associate of the Royal Academy, after A. J. Munnings had put her name forward several times without success. She was the second woman ARA, the first being Annie Swynnerton, then eighty years old.

Laura had always been interested in the technical problems of drawing movement, and she now began to work in a field that had fascinated her since childhood, the circus. Munnings introduced her to Bertram Mills [q.v.], the owner of Mills's Circus, who gave her permission to go where she liked during rehearsals, and soon she was producing studies of trapeze artists, acrobats, tumblers, jugglers, contortionists, as well as dwarfs, clowns, and the circus animals. She painted a huge canvas, 'Charivari', which brought in nearly everyone in circus life; it was exhibited at the Royal Academy summer exhibition in 1929 and was caricatured in *Punch*, with politicians portrayed as the various circus performers.

Harold was elected ARA in 1928. In 1929 Laura was appointed a Dame Commander of the British Empire, an honour which she accepted with pride, but which did not prevent her from travelling round with a circus, her friends there puzzled why she should now be officially a Dame when she had obviously always been one. From circus life she went on to paint gipsies at Epsom and Ascot, working in an old Rolls-Royce fitted up as a miniature studio. Her long-standing friendship with Barry Jackson led to her going to the Malvern festival, which he had founded. Harold went with her every year, and they met many celebrities of the time, including G. Bernard Shaw [q.v.], whom Laura painted. But the portrait was not considered to be successful, either as a likeness or a painting.

Harold's reputation continued to grow in this genre. A portrait of the pianist Ethel Bartlett playing on a grand piano was exhibited at the RA summer exhibition in 1929 and was highly praised for its charm and beautiful sense of colour. In 1933, a fine portrait of the lord bishop of Truro was exhibited at the RA summer exhibition and enhanced his reputation as a first-class painter of pictorial realism; it was described as a restrained and dignified piece of work. In fact, Harold could achieve a great deal more than pictorial realism, as is shown in his portrait of W. H. Davies [q.v.], which conveyed the character of the poet through the expression in the eyes. The portrait is in the Merthyr Tydfil Art Gallery.

In 1936 Laura was elected RA, the first woman to become a full member of the Royal Academy. She served on the selection and hanging committee, and was later involved in a row over a portrait of T. S. Eliot by

P. Wyndham Lewis [qq.v.], which the Academy had rejected. Augustus John resigned from the Academy in protest, and Laura tried to act as mediator. It was now well known, however, that she was not sympathetic to new ideas in art, and she took the side of the Academy in the dispute.

Harold was elected RA in 1937. The Knights were living in Colwall, near Malvern, when war came in 1939. They were hit financially, as several portrait commissions which Harold had accepted were cancelled. Laura was soon working, as the War Artists' Advisory Committee had come into being, and she did a number of paintings for them. Her most notable canvas was for the Ministry of Munitions, of a woman munitions worker called Ruby Loftus screwing the breech ring in a Bofors gun, a delicate operation thought impossible for a woman to do. Laura's photographic eye for detail and command of technique brought an extraordinary reality to the painting, one of the best she had ever achieved. It is in the Imperial War Museum, London.

Then came a unique assignment. In 1946, at the age of sixty-eight, Laura went to Nuremberg to paint what was to be a pictorial record of the war criminals' trial; she was rated officially as a war correspondent. Harold had left their home in London and was living in the Park Hotel in Colwall. Laura wrote to him frequently, describing the scenes in court. She made scores of sketches, and her final large picture of the prisoners in the dock was unusual for her, in that it was surrounded by vivid impressions of their crimes. It is now in the Imperial War Museum, London.

Back in England, she and Harold returned to Langford Place. Harold's health had long been failing, and he found it difficult to paint because of arthritis. Laura took him to Colwall, which he liked better than any other place in England, and he died there 3 October 1961, at the age of eighty-seven. His work was summed up variously, with the emphasis on its pictorial quality, but there was no question about his great achievements as a superb master of his craft. If he was not the English Vermeer, he brought many of the fine qualities of the Dutch Old Master into his work. Some critics wondered why he had not attained a higher eminence. Perhaps there is something in the remark which Laura made more than once: 'I stood in his way.' She never tried to explain how.

In addition to RA, Harold was an honorary member of the Royal Institute of Oil Painters, the Royal Society of Portrait Painters, and the Royal West of England Academy. He is represented in many public collections, including the Welsh National Gallery, Cardiff; Merthyr Tydfil Art Gallery; the Tate Gallery, London; the Diploma Gallery, Burlington House, London; and in the art galleries of Leeds, Rochdale, Preston, Newcastle upon Tyne, Nottingham, and Manchester; abroad in the Municipal Gallery, Perth, Australia; and in Brisbane, Cape Town, and New Zealand.

Laura put on an exhibition of Harold's pictures, and spent her remaining years arranging for exhibitions of her own work. These showed her astounding range in oils, watercolour, etchings, and pencil drawings, with subjects which included landscape, seascape, the Cornish sunlight on nudes, circus scenes, gipsies, ballet dancers and actors, bomber crews and balloon sites in wartime, and the Nuremberg trial, all executed with incredible facility. A retrospective exhibition in the Diploma Gallery at the Royal Academy in the summer of 1965 was the accolade of her long career. She went to an exhibition of her work, '75 years of Painting', at the Upper Grosvenor Galleries in 1969. This was her swan-song. She was unable to go to an exhibition of her work put on at Nottingham Castle during the Nottingham Festival, 1970, though she made a gallant attempt to do so. She died at her home in London 7 July 1970, in her ninety-third year. There were no children of the marriage.

Laura, in addition to RA, was an honorary member of the Royal Society of Painters in Water-colours, the Royal Society of Painter-Etchers and Engravers, the Royal West of England Academy, the Society of Women Artists, and the Royal Portrait Society. Her honours include the gold medal, San Francisco, 1915, and an honorary mention, Paris Salon, 1928. She is represented in many public collections, including the National Portrait Gallery, the Diploma Gallery, Royal Academy, the Victoria and Albert Museum, the Tate Gallery, the British Museum, and the Imperial War Museum; as well as in collections abroad. She wrote *Oil Paint and Grease Paint* (1936), *A Proper Circus Omie* (1962), and *The Magic of a Line* (1965). She was awarded an honorary LLD by St. Andrews (1931) and an honorary D.Litt. by Nottingham (1951).

In the National Portrait Gallery are a self-portrait by Laura Knight (1913) and a self-portrait by Harold Knight (1923).

[Janet Dunbar, *Laura Knight*, 1975; Norman Garstin, 'The Art of Harold and Laura Knight', *The Studio*, vols. lvii, 1913, and lix, 1916; *The Studio*, vols. xcvi (1928), cii (1931), cvi (1933), cx (1935); private information; personal knowledge.]　　　JANET DUNBAR

KNOLLYS, EDWARD GEORGE WILLIAM TYRWHITT, second VISCOUNT KNOLLYS (1895-1966), business man and public servant, was born at St. James's Palace, London, 16 January 1895, the only son (he had one sister) of Francis Knollys [q.v.], first Viscount, private secretary from 1870 to 1910 to the Prince of Wales who became King Edward VII, and from 1910 to 1913 to King George V, and his wife, Ardyn Mary, daughter of Sir Henry Thomas Tyrwhitt, baronet.

Knollys was educated at Harrow (1903-12) and New College, Oxford. He served in World War I, first in the 16th London Regiment (Territorial Army) and then in the Royal Flying Corps, where he flew in balloons as an observer. He was awarded the DFC, the Order of the Crown of Belgium, and the croix de guerre, and was appointed MBE. In 1924 he succeeded his father.

Despite encouragement, then and later, notably from the Prince of Wales (later King Edward VIII), to follow his father's footsteps in royal service, Knollys decided to break away and make a business career for himself. After studying accountancy, he joined Barclays Bank and spent three years in Cape Town (1929-32) as local director of Barclays (Dominion, Colonial & Overseas). Thence he moved to the insurance business, being appointed in 1932 a director in London of the Employers Liability Assurance Corporation, of which he became managing director the following year. Most of the Employers' business lay in North America, and it was in the handling of these American clients and managers that Knollys's remarkable talent for personal relationships, patient negotiation, and hard work first came to light. Overcoming initial difficulties, Knollys soon won wide respect as a leader in his field which after the war of 1939-45 was widened by the merger, in 1960, of the Employers' with the larger Northern Assurance. Knollys was the first chairman of the joint company.

In the early years of the 1939-45 war, Knollys became deputy commissioner for Civil Defence, South-Eastern Region, before being appointed, in 1941, governor and commander-in-chief of Bermuda and made KCMG. This post, traditionally filled by a senior serving general, had become a sensitive one. Under Anglo-American wartime agreements, a naval and air base had been leased to the United States. Considerable problems were created by the arrival on the little British island of large numbers of American servicemen and construction staff. Knollys's sure touch with Americans, his tact and intelligence with all, enabled him to excel in the task he had been sent to perform.

In 1943 he was appointed first full-time chairman of the British Overseas Airways Corporation. During the four years of his chairmanship, the Corporation was trans-formed from what was virtually RAF Transport Command, with its rough and ready passenger amenities, to an airways system such as the United States had kept going, with suitable aircraft, throughout the war. BOAC was operating with converted war planes, and Knollys saw that the one special element it could offer was courtesy, kindness, and understanding. These qualities, filtering down from the chairman's office, where a firm polite charm and elegantly good manners prevailed, permeated the staff.

In 1947 Knollys—known to all his friends as 'Edgey' (an abbreviation for Edward and George, the names of his two godfathers Edward VII and George V)—returned to his business career, but four years later was again lent to the Government. The outbreak of the Korean war in June 1950 had resulted in scarcity and high prices for many raw materials, thus threatening the economic stability of Western Europe, particularly Britain. Knollys's task (with the rank of minister) was to represent Britain at the International Materials Conference in Washington. Once again, his gifts of getting on with people, especially Americans, equipped him to perform a formidable feat in protecting British interests. For this, he was promoted to GCMG in 1952.

In 1956 Knollys became chairman of Vickers Ltd., the large shipbuilding, engineering, steel, and aircraft concern, on to whose board he had been brought four years earlier. In some respects it was a curious appointment. For all his financial acumen and ability to handle people, Knollys had no knowledge of industry and no technical qualifications. Nevertheless, he brought to Vickers his customary sense of style, epitomized by the decision, taken under his chairmanship, to give Vickers a new and fitting London headquarters. The result was the Vickers tower at Millbank, which by general consent made a welcome contrast to the giant concrete matchboxes obscuring the London skyline.

Knollys's influence on Vickers's financial fortunes was less spectacular. He was only partially successful in steering the company away from its traditional armament-producing role into other, more varied activities. Some of the men chosen, under his chairmanship, for top management posts did not prove to possess the special flair and skill needed for the exceptionally difficult task facing the company. Knollys retired from his post in 1962, but continued as chairman of the English Steel Corporation (which he had become in 1959) until 1965.

Knollys was elected FRSA in 1962. A good shot and golfer, a respectable fly fisherman, a keen gardener, and, in his later years, a *peintre de dimanche*, Knollys found the best relaxation from hard work in a country setting. Tall, well-dressed, and good-looking, he combined a sense of well-bred self-assurance with a certain diffidence of manner, accentuated by a nervous habit of adding the unnecessary phrase 'in that way' to many of his sentences. Much of his small stock of spare time was given to charitable interests, particularly the RAF Benevolent Fund, of whose council he was chairman for many years. He was a trustee of Churchill College, Cambridge.

In 1928 Knollys married Margaret Mary Josephine, daughter of Sir Stuart Auchincloss Coats, baronet. There were a son and daughter of the marriage, the former, David Francis Dudley Knollys (born 1931), succeeding to the viscountcy on Knollys's death, which occurred in London 3 December 1966.

A portrait of Knollys, with his wife, son, and daughter, by R. Norman Hepple, was exhibited at the Royal Society of Portrait Painters in 1955.

[Private information; personal knowledge.]
F. T. R. GILES

KRONBERGER, HANS (1920–1970), leader in the physics and engineering of nuclear reactors, was born in Linz, Austria, 28 July 1920, the younger child and only son of Norbert and Olga Kronberger. His parents were Jewish and his father had inherited a family business of leather merchants. The Anschluss caused Hans to go into hiding but he managed to leave Austria and come to England where King's College, Newcastle, accepted him in the 1938 entry as a student in mechanical engineering. In May 1940 he was interned as a 'friendly enemy alien', first in the Isle of Man and then in Australia, but he was able to continue his studies to some extent and learn from more experienced people who were similarly interned. When released in 1942, he returned to King's College and in 1944 took a wartime honours degree in physics. He began a Ph.D. for Birmingham University, which he completed in 1948. In 1946 he joined (Sir) F. E. Simon's [q.v.] team in the 'Tube Alloys' project. In 1946 he heard that his mother and sister had died in a Nazi concentration camp.

Simon was an exceptionally fine director and Kronberger learnt quickly. Heinz London [q.v.] was also a member of the team and he and Kronberger became close friends and collaborators. London had deep scientific insight and Kronberger showed rare ability in extending a scientific idea into practical hardware. Soon they were both transferred to the new atomic energy establishment at Harwell. Kronberger first worked with London on the separation of carbon-13 and oxygen-18 by means of columns and low-temperature distillation. Next, he made some of the early important contributions to the separation of the isotopes of uranium by means of a bank of centrifuges. Here, and in some of his later work, he found scope for his considerable mathematical talents.

The government decision to build a uranium diffusion plant at Capenhurst had put a great strain on the atomic energy organization. American information and knowledge were not available and qualified staff were scarce. Kronberger in 1951 was the obvious choice as research manager of the components development laboratory. Many novel components and control devices had to be invented; new instruments had to be developed and older types of instruments had to be modified. Kronberger's performance was scintillating. In the language of the scientific laboratory, he had wonderful hands. Those same hands would sometimes make deeply felt music.

Two years later, he was promoted to be head of the Capenhurst development laboratories and in 1956 he became chief physicist, under Leonard Rotherham, of the research and development branch of the Industrial Group of the Atomic Energy Authority. As part of these wider duties he continued a personal association with the Capenhurst laboratories where various methods of isotope separation were being applied to hydrogen, lithium, and boron, and where the centrifuge method of separating the isotopes of uranium continued to receive attention. Kronberger succeeded Rotherham as director in 1958.

By the early sixties the Authority was committed to operating an experimental fast reactor at Dounreay; to developing the prototypes of two thermal reactor systems at Windscale and Winfrith respectively; and, because of the encouragement of Sir J. D. Cockcroft [q.v.], to having a large share in the Organization for European Economic Co-operation and Development Dragon reactor at Winfrith. By then Kronberger was scientist-in-chief of the Reactor Group, one of the groups arising from the split of the Industrial Group. He was faced with streams of problems, some familiar and some new. Many of them arose from the need for special materials that could survive reactor conditions. Some were solved by skilful technology (e.g. impregnated graphite) and some were avoided by cancelling the project (e.g. abandoning beryllium as a reactor material). As work proceeded, the reactors all seemed to be successful but when they were being extended to the stage of large nuclear power stations, additional engineering problems arose and these could only be solved by an integrated national effort, including the most powerful nuclear engineering companies. This was the position when Kronberger died, a year after he had been appointed a member of the Atomic Energy Authority.

Much of Kronberger's work is still secret or is not attributable to him but he did become well known from his lectures on hydrostatic extrusion and on the desalination of sea water. He served as a member of the United Nations scientific advisory committee and of the advisory committee of the International Atomic Energy Agency. He was appointed OBE in 1957 and CBE in 1966; he was elected FRS in 1965 and was awarded the Royal Society's Leverhulme tercentenary medal in 1969.

Life brought to Kronberger some happy times when his sunny disposition blossomed but he had much more than a normal share of grief and his life ended tragically with his suicide. He married, in 1951, Joan Hanson (née Iliffe) widow of Dr Neil Hanson, who was killed in a climbing accident. She died in 1962, after suffering from an inoperable brain tumour for nine years. Kronberger died at his home in Cheshire 29 September 1970 and was survived by two daughters and a stepson.

[L. Rotherham in *Biographical Memoirs of Fellows of the Royal Society*, vol. xviii, 1972; personal knowledge.]

PENNEY

L

LACHMANN, GUSTAV VICTOR (1896–1966), aeronautical engineer, was born 3 February 1896 at Dresden, Saxony, the younger son of Gustav Anton Lachmann, industrialist, and his wife, Leopoldine Wilvonseder; both were Austrian and their elder son Edward became professor of literature and German philology at Innsbrück University. In 1902 the family moved to Darmstadt, where Gustav entered the Realgymnasium and in 1908 joined fellow students in building a glider in emulation of Otto Lilienthal and the Wright brothers. In 1914 he volunteered for the 24th Hessian Life Dragoons and was assigned to the eastern front, being commissioned in 1917, wounded in action, and awarded both the Eisenkreuz and the Hessische Tapferkeits Medaillon. Transferring from the cavalry to the Fliegerkorps as a fighter pilot, he crashed, sustaining a broken jaw and leg injuries; in hospital he contemplated the cause of the stall that had interrupted his flying career, deducing that sudden loss of lift at high incidence and low airspeed could be due to airflow stagnation. With a ladies' hairdrier and a simple wooden model wing having spanwise slots discharging air from the under surface tangentially on to the upper surface, so as to re-energize the boundary layer, he used tobacco smoke to visualize the airflow, which behaved exactly as expected. In February 1918 he drafted a patent specification to protect his invention, which he believed would prevent stalling. Rejoining his unit on the western front, he was wounded in aerial combat and awarded a second Eisenkreuz.

On being invalided out in 1918, Lachmann found that the German patent examiners refused to accept the principle of his invention; he then enrolled at Darmstadt Technical University for a three years' course in mechanical engineering and aerodynamics, graduating in June 1921 as Diplom-Ingenieur. By chance, he saw an account in *Flugsport* of the previous year's demonstration at Cricklewood of a slotted wing patented by (Sir) Frederick Handley Page [q.v.] and immediately challenged its priority. The German patent examiners insisted on experimental proof, so Lachmann asked Professor Ludwig Prandtl to conduct the requisite wind-tunnel tests, for an agreed fee of 1,000 marks (£50), which Lachmann borrowed from his mother; the result (65 per cent increase in lift) convinced the Patent Office, which granted the original application backdated to February 1918, some eighteen months earlier than Handley Page's master patent, which, however, Lachmann could not afford to contest in court. In August 1921 the two inventors met amicably

in Berlin and agreed to collaborate, retaining their separate rights in their own countries, but pooling them elsewhere; Handley Page retained Lachmann as his consultant during his forthcoming three years' research in Prandtl's Aerodynamic Institute at Göttingen, thus providing useful income for Lachmann at trivial cost to himself, because of the prevailing low value of marks in relation to sterling.

In 1923 Lachmann's thesis, 'The Slotted Wing and its Importance for Aviation', was accepted by Aachen Technical University for the degree of doctor of engineering, the oral examination being passed 'with distinction', coupled with the award of the Borchers plaque. Having gained workshop experience in the Opel motor car factory at Russelheim, Lachmann spent one year as a designer at the Schneider aircraft works in Berlin, then in 1925 became chief designer at the Albatros aircraft works at Johannisthal, where he designed two biplanes: the single-engined L 72 for express delivery of Verlag Ullstein's *Berliner Zeitung am Mittag* and the twin-engined L 73 eight-passenger transport; both had slotted ailerons and flaps for low-speed control, but only the L 72 had leading-edge slots. In 1926, before the L 73 had flown, Lachmann resigned from Albatros to join the Ishikawajima aircraft works in Tokyo as technical adviser on the design of a biplane, which he also flight-tested, as no test pilot had been engaged.

The following year Lachmann married Evelyn Wyatt Haigh, widow of the late British vice-consul at Tokyo; their only daughter, Evelyn Leopoldine, was born in 1929, when they moved to England, where Lachmann became engineer in charge of aerodynamics, stressing, and slot development at Handley Page Limited.

In 1932 Lachmann became chief designer at Cricklewood, to exploit Herbert Wagner's 'tension-field' system of stressed-skin metal construction for cantilever monoplanes, being responsible for the HP 47, Harrow and Hampden bombers, while George Volkert dealt with production problems arising from the new technology. In 1936 Volkert resumed as chief designer, while Lachmann initiated a research department at Edgware to develop an advanced tailless monoplane. In 1939 war broke out before this had flown and Lachmann, still technically an 'enemy alien', was interned in Canada, whence Lord Brabazon or Tara [q.v.] secured his transfer to the Isle of Man, where he undertook non-military design studies till 1947. He became a naturalized British subject in 1949. However, internment had affected his marriage, which was dissolved in 1950. He married, secondly, Catherine Elizabeth Beggs in 1951; there were no children.

In 1953 Lachmann became head of the Handley Page Research Department at Radlett, to develop laminar airflow control by suction, a difficult technique promising enhanced performance and economy for long-range aircraft, but this project ended in 1965, when Lachmann retired to continue his researches privately at his home at Chorleywood, where he died suddenly on Whit Monday, 30 May 1966.

'Gus', as he was known to his colleagues, combined generous chivalry with an excellent command of English and a lively wit, matching that of Sir Frederick Handley Page, whom he was prepared to defy on any important point of principle. His honours included fellowship in 1938 of the Royal Aeronautical Society (which awarded him both the Taylor and the Wakefield gold medals), the honorary degree of D.Eng. of the Technical University of Aachen in 1959, and honorary fellowship of the Wissenschaftliche Gesellschaft für Luft und Raumfahrt in 1962.

Lachmann's publications on aerodynamics (particularly boundary layer control) were numerous; he was the author of *Leichtflugzeugbau* (Munich, 1925) and also edited *Boundary Layer and Flow Control*, 1961.

[Private information.]   C. H. BARNES

LAMBERT, MAURICE (1901-1964), sculptor, was born in Paris 25 June 1901, the elder son of George Washington Lambert, ARA, the painter who towards the end of his life also turned his attention towards sculpture, and his wife, Amelia Beatrice Absell, an Australian. He was the brother of the musician, Constant Lambert [q.v.]. His father was born in Leningrad of an American father and an English mother. When Maurice Lambert later applied for a passport, he found he had no official nationality, and had to apply for nationalization as a British subject. He was educated at Manor House School, Clapham. From the age of seventeen he was apprenticed to F. Derwent Wood [q.v.] and worked as his assistant for five years.

Lambert's work first appeared in public in 1925, at a mixed exhibition in the Goupil Gallery, Regent St. He exhibited fourteen pieces, in various styles. But it was at a subsequent exhibition at the same gallery that he demonstrated his true talent with a head 'Ceres', carved from hard red African gritstone. Its simplicity yet realism indicated the direction in which Lambert might be moving and this impression was confirmed at an exhibition of the Seven and Five Society at the Beaux Arts Gallery in 1928. The fourteen works which had appeared in the first exhibition had, by contrast, shown a great diversity of styles, derived from (Sir) Jacob Epstein, Frank Dobson [qq.v.], Brancusi, and others. Lambert's first one-man exhibition was at Messrs Tooths' Gallery in 1929. It was there that his talent as a carver became particularly apparent. He had used a variety of materials—for example, marble, alabaster, African hardwood, Portland stone, metal—and, in some cases, combined more than one of these. One work, for example, entitled 'Hooked Fish', was made of aluminium, plate glass, three-ply wood, selenite, and concrete.

In 1932 the Tate Gallery accepted a gift of an alabaster carving, 'The Swan', which had been exhibited in his next one-man show at the Lefevre Galleries. This was a just reward, since an offer of his 'Man with Bird' had been rejected by their trustees three years earlier, though it was later accepted by the Victoria and Albert Museum.

He first exhibited at the Royal Academy in 1938. His exhibit, entitled 'Head of Woman', in bronze, was purchased for the nation, under the terms of the Chantrey Bequest, and became the second example of his work to be housed in the Tate. Although elected as an associate of the Royal Academy in 1941, he did not exhibit there again until 1945 because of his war service, at first in the ranks of the London Welsh Regiment and subsequently as a captain in the Royal Welch Fusiliers. After the war he exhibited regularly in the summer exhibition. He was a fellow of the Royal Society of British Sculptors from 1938 to 1948, when he resigned; he was re-elected in 1951. In 1949 he was awarded that society's silver medal for 'Pegasus and Bellerophon', which had been exhibited at the Academy during the previous year. From 1950 to 1958 Lambert was master of the Royal Academy Sculpture School, and was elected Royal academician in 1952.

His best-known work, a life-size bronze statue of the ballerina Dame Margot Fonteyn, was another purchase for the nation under the terms of the Chantrey Bequest. It was bought in 1956 and remains at the Royal Ballet School, White Lodge, Richmond Park. Another well-known work, 'The Lark Ascending', made from a 250-year-old church oak gate-post, was acquired for the Rutherston collection, Manchester City Art Gallery.

His other works include an equestrian statue of King George V for Adelaide, South Australia; a statue of Viscount Nuffield for Guy's Hospital; carvings in Portland stone for the Associated Electrical Industries building, Grosvenor Place, London; the Duke of Edinburgh's trophy for shooting and running (a drinking cup in silver and gold); a fountain for Basildon, Essex, and another for the presidential palace, Baghdad, on which he was at work during his last illness. He also did a great number of portrait busts of, among others, Dame Edith Sitwell, Kingsley Martin, J. B. Priestley, the Maharani Sahiba of Cooch Behar, Frank Herbert, Sir Gerald Kelly, Sir Henry Rushbury, and Lord Devlin. Among them, there are bronzes of rare distinction, in which a sense of repose and unity does not detract from the character portrayal.

Lambert's undoubted early promise as a sculptor was never really fulfilled since, in later years, he became dogged with the illness which finally caused his death. However, the breadth of his imagination, especially in the use of such varied media, is evident throughout his work, and this contribution to the advancement of sculptural interpretation was the signpost to the future. He took a particular delight in feats of virtuosity such as a flight of fish going through the arms of a sea-god. It was this skill and experience as well as his driving conscience which made him such a fine teacher in the Academy Schools. He was a physically strong man: he had been a boxer in his early days, and was once employed as an inspector of advertisement posters whose duty was to ride many miles round and about London on a bicycle. He spent much of his time at London Zoo studying the animals and birds and also took daily early morning runs round Regent's Park.

In 1926 Lambert married Olga Marie Stuart, daughter of Stuart Gordon Morrison; they had no children. He died in a London hospital 17 August 1964.

[*The Times* and *Daily Telegraph*, 20 August 1964; private information.]

HANS FLETCHER

LAMBURN, RICHMAL CROMPTON (1890-1969), author, known as Richmal Crompton, was born 15 November 1890 in Bury, Lancashire. She was the second of the three children of the Revd Edward John Sewell Lamburn, schoolmaster and curate, by his wife, Clara Crompton. She had an elder sister and younger brother. She was named Richmal after her mother's sister. This unusual Christian name has been in her mother's family since the early 1700s. Her father taught at Bury Grammar School and the family lived in Bury for many years.

Richmal Crompton attended St. Elphin's Clergy Daughters' School in Warrington, Lancashire, and later in Darley Dale, Derbyshire. She gained a founder's scholarship to the Royal Holloway College, London, in 1911. She was awarded a university scholarship in 1912, and the college's Driver scholarship in classics in 1914. Whilst a student she supported the campaign for women's suffrage, was a member of the hockey, tennis, and boating clubs, and took a leading part in college theatricals.

After gaining second class honours in classics (1914) at London University, Richmal Crompton taught from 1915 to 1917 at her old school. She then became classics mistress at Bromley High School for Girls in Kent from 1917 to 1924. During this period Richmal Crompton began to write short stories, including one featuring the robust, anarchic schoolboy, William Brown. This was published in the *Home Magazine* in February 1919. Further stories about William appeared in this monthly publication. The stories were transferred to the *Happy Mag.*, and in 1922 George Newnes Ltd. published a selection in two books entitled *Just-William* and *More William*. Other William books followed, becoming so popular that between 1922 and Richmal Crompton's death in 1969 the series ran to thirty-eight titles. By 1977 some nine million William books had been sold, and translations have been made in Gaelic, Finnish, Swedish, Norwegian, Danish, Dutch, French, Spanish, Portuguese, Italian, German, Icelandic, and Czech. By 1977 there had also been four William films, a radio series, and two television series. Yet Richmal Crompton by her own account at first considered William a 'pot-boiler', and her ambition was to write adult novels. She produced thirty-nine, but they never achieved a fraction of the success of her William books.

After an attack of poliomyelitis in 1923 Richmal Crompton lost the use of her right leg. Although able to walk with a stick she was advised by her doctor to give up teaching because of the difficulty in travelling. This was the turning-point in her life as she was then able to give her energies wholeheartedly to writing. Some years later, when her niece made a sympathetic reference to her disability, Richmal Crompton declared that she had led 'a much more interesting life because of it'.

During the war of 1939-45 she was a voluntary worker in Bromley's fire service. (Her irritation with some of the officialdom she encountered is reflected in one or two comical William episodes.) Most of her adult life was spent in Kent—some thirty-six years at Bromley Common, and over fifteen years at Chislehurst. She did not marry. As her stories suggest, Richmal Crompton was quick-witted and amusing. Despite sometimes appearing vague, she was extremely well ordered and methodical. She became interested in mystical interpretations of Christianity while remaining a staunch member of the Church of England. Politically she was a Conservative, although her early William books are an interesting critique of Conservative values.

Richmal Crompton supported several charitable organizations, including the Muscular Dystrophy Group and the British Polio Fellowship. Always drawn to young people, she kept a drawerful of toys at her home for child visitors, and happily accepted arduous roles in children's games. She loved teaching, and many of her ex-pupils were grateful for the help and extra coaching which she gave them. The character of William Brown was partly inspired by episodes in the lives of members of her family: when first writing about William she drew upon her memories of the childhood of her brother, John, and that of her nephew.

Richmal Crompton created other attractive fictional characters including Jimmy, a younger boy, in 1949; but William Brown eclipsed them all. Tough and resilient, he became typical of the outdoor, non-bookish child. His author's insight, acute observation, and engaging irony have ensured his appeal. William's name, like that of the heroes of classical legend, acquired meaning even for people who had never read the stories in which he featured. Richmal Crompton continued to write about him until shortly before she died, 11 January 1969, at Farnborough Hospital, Kent.

[Patricia Craig and Mary Cadogan, 'That Boy Again', in the *Sunday Times* magazine, 6 February 1977; Brian Doyle, *Who's Who of Children's Literature*; private information.]   MARY CADOGAN

LAMPSON, MILES WEDDERBURN, first BARON KILLEARN (1880–1964), diplomatist, was born at Killearn, Stirlingshire, 24 August 1880, the second son of Norman George Lampson and his wife, Helen Agnes, daughter of Peter Blackburn, of Killearn, who had been member of Parliament for Stirlingshire, and niece of Lord Blackburn [q.v.]. He was the grandson of Sir Curtis Miranda Lampson, first baronet [q.v.]. Educated at Eton, Lampson passed in 1903 into the Foreign Office. He was selected as secretary to the missions of Prince Arthur of Connaught [q.v.] to Japan in 1906 and 1912. With interludes in the Foreign Office and at Sofia, he served in Tokyo and Peking and acquired knowledge of both Japanese and Chinese. In 1919–20 he was temporarily in Siberia as acting high commissioner, and in 1921–2 he was in the British delegation at the Washington conference.

Lampson next became head of the Central European Department with responsibility for the application of the peace treaties with Germany and her European allies, including the complications of German reparations and the Franco-Belgian occupation of the Ruhr. After the Dawes conference, the question of international security took first place and it fell to him to co-ordinate, under Sir Austen Chamberlain [q.v.], the negotiations leading to the Locarno Treaty of 1925.

Late in 1926 Lampson was sent as minister to Peking, a task of exceptional difficulty. There was no effective government of China. The Southern Nationalist (Kuomintang) forces, in their drive against the Northern warlords, had occupied Hankow. Anti-foreign feeling was rising. The British Government were advocates, consistently with non-intervention, of a conciliatory policy towards the Nationalist movement. Lampson began with a visit to Hankow by warship for friendly and informal contact with Eugene Chen, foreign minister in the as yet unrecognized Kuomintang leadership. The immediate effect was good, but in January 1927, a fortnight after Lampson's departure for Peking, the storming of the foreign Concessions at Hankow and Kiukiang by mobs touched off a crisis. London ordered out naval reinforcements and a Shanghai Defence Force and, almost simultaneously, announced to both sides in the civil war some practical steps which Britain might be prepared to take towards meeting Chinese aspirations. In 1928 a settlement of the recent incidents cleared the way for the recognition in December of the new National Government of China, of which Chiang Kai-shek had emerged as president. Lampson went to Nanking for this purpose, and concluded a treaty recognizing China's tariff autonomy, subject to non-discrimination.

In December 1933 Lampson was appointed high commissioner for Egypt and the Sudan where he was again faced with unfulfilled national aspirations, but in the special context, with the advent of Hitler and Mussolini, of British strategic requirements. Two main questions, the Sudan and the presence of British troops in Egypt, had defied previous efforts at agreement. But the danger to both Egypt and the Sudan, portended by Mussolini's ambitions and his invasion of Ethiopia, produced the miracle of an all-party Egyptian delegation with whom the Anglo-Egyptian Treaty of Alliance of 1936 was signed in London. Egypt became fully sovereign and Lampson the first British ambassador. He had been appointed CB in 1926, KCMG in 1927, and was promoted GCMG in 1937.

The treaty stood the stress of the critical war years from 1939 until the turn of the tide at Alamein in 1942. It was Lampson's steadfastness, wisdom, and determination which ensured a stable military base in Egypt for the Eighth Army and the Mediterranean Fleet. In 1940 a British Cabinet minister took up residence in Cairo to co-ordinate Middle Eastern problems, leaving unchanged Lampson's responsibilities as ambassador in Egypt. The 1936 treaty made his a key position in the peculiar situation where Egypt, while granting all facilities for a wartime Allied base, remained non-belligerent almost throughout the war, even when Axis forces overran her borders. The hesitant, or pro-Axis, influences which gathered round the court, the wayward character of the young king, and the chronic antipathy between the latter and the Wafd Party were, however, factors of material concern. The moment came in February 1942 when, supported by armed force, Lampson drove to Abdin Palace and delivered an ultimatum to King Farouk to recall the pro-Allied Wafd to power. Controversy still lingers round this action and Lampson's relations with the king. But whatever the criticisms, the Wafd when in office showed unwavering steadiness in the all-important period preceding Alamein.

Lampson was sworn of the Privy Council in 1941 and raised to the peerage in 1943. As the war drew to its close, Egypt's desire for the revision of the treaty grew, but that issue had not come to a head when, in March 1946, Killearn was appointed, although well beyond retiring age, special commissioner in South-East Asia. This was an emergency post, based on Singapore, created to cope with the political aftermath of the Japanese surrender. On arrival, Killearn concluded that the task of averting the famine then threatening Malaya, Indonesia, Indo-China, Siam, and Burma must precede all else. With no executive authority and in the face of ill-informed but in some cases bitter local hostility, he nevertheless by reason, persuasion, and the force of his personality induced agreement amongst the differing national authorities, stimulated the local production of vital foodstuffs, rationalized their transportation and distribution, and steered starvation away from the peoples of South-East Asia. In politics he was called upon to assist in the negotiations between the Dutch and the Indonesians; and the Linggadjati Agreement of 25 March 1947, bringing the first glimmerings of peace to Indonesia, was the result of his patience and diplomatic skill. He then turned to the furtherance of regional collaboration between the governments of the territories of South-East Asia, who before the war had thought only in parochial terms, and here too achieved a considerable measure of success.

In some ways a figure out of another century, but with feet firmly on the political ground of his day, Killearn tempered vigour with caution

and impact with the perceptiveness and skills of an outstanding negotiator: a loyal friend and a tough adversary. Over six feet five inches in height and eighteen stone to match, he combined the massive figure and the fearlessness of one of Dumas's musketeers with rare political sagacity, inner modesty, and common sense. To the Chinese he was the man-mountain unmoved by a hundred cups of rice wine. Forthright towards Whitehall, he was undaunted in handling critics and adversaries and in facing menacing situations. An unsparing worker until all hours, he yet found time for racing, shooting, learning to fly when over fifty, and collecting Chinese porcelain. After his retirement in 1948 business interests took him often abroad; and he was assiduous in the House of Lords.

In 1912 Lampson married Rachel Mary Hele, younger daughter of William Wilton Phipps, whose death in 1930 marred Lampson's years in China. They had two daughters and one son, Graham Curtis (born 1919), who succeeded his father as second baron and as heir presumptive to the baronetcy, succeeding to the latter in 1971. In 1934 Lampson married Jacqueline Aldine Leslie, daughter of Professor Marchese Sir Aldo Castellani. She did not spare herself in providing a background full of life and interest at the residency in Egypt; and in the war years in caring for the welfare of servicemen. Of this marriage there were also one son and two daughters.

Killearn died in Hastings 18 September 1964.

[Trefor E. Evans, *Mission to Egypt, 1934–1946*, 1971; *The Killearn Diaries, 1934–46*, ed. Trefor E. Evans, 1972; *The Times*, 19 September 1964; private information; personal knowledge.]   MICHAEL WRIGHT

LANCHESTER, GEORGE HERBERT (1874-1970), automobile engineer and inventor, was born 11 December 1874 at Hove, Sussex, the youngest of the five sons and of the eight children of Henry Jones Lanchester, architect, of Hove, and his wife, Octavia, daughter of Thomas Ward, coachbuilder of London. He was educated at Clapham High School, London, which he left at the age of fourteen to be apprenticed to his brother, Frederick William Lanchester [q.v.], who was works manager and designer of the Forward Gas Engine Company in Saltley, Birmingham.

After three years' apprenticeship and attendance at evening classes at the Midland Institute, without passing any examinations, he spent a year in the drawing office and became works manager in his turn in 1893, a position he held for four years. During those years he helped his brother Frederick to make the first British four-wheeled petrol car, the Lanchester experimental car of 1895, and to rebuild it. In 1897 he resigned to join his brother as his chief assistant and was responsible for all work in progress while four more experimental models were made, including the Phaeton two-seater to which the Automobile Club awarded a gold medal.

When the Lanchester Engine Company was formed in 1899 he was in the same position, a 'Pooh Bah' as he described it, in charge of jigs, gauges, and works supervision. He continued as such during the production of five new models for the market until the company became bankrupt and was reconstructed as the Lanchester Motor Company in 1905. He came into his own only in 1909 when, after his brother had gone to the Daimler Company, he became designer and subsequently chief engineer and technical director of the Lanchester Company and redesigned the six-cylinder and four-cylinder cars which appeared as 38-hp and 25-hp models in 1910 and 1911 respectively. During the war of 1914–18 the Lanchester armoured cars, which were used on the Russian front, were based on the 38-hp chassis.

He designed the Lanchester 40 of 1919, the 21-hp car of 1923, and a succession of other models, all renowned in motoring circles, until he left the company in 1936. From his designs came also an armoured car with which the XIth Hussars and later the XIIth Lancers were equipped and a scout armoured vehicle which anticipated by ten years the cars of the war of 1939–45. When the Lanchester Company was absorbed by Daimler he joined the Alvis Company in 1936 and designed their Silver Crest car.

In 1939, as consultant to the Sterling Armament Company, he was responsible for the production of sound-ranging vehicles for the Dutch Government, and showed his versatility by redesigning the Schmeissen 9-mm gun into the Lanchester sub-machine-gun which was used by the British and Australian navies. In 1945 he became consultant to the Russell Newbery Diesel Engine Company, full time until 1952 and part time to 1961.

He was admitted member of the Institution of Mechanical Engineers in 1927 and subsequently fellow. To that body and the Institution of Automobile Engineers, of which he was president in 1943–4, he contributed three technical papers (two of them jointly with F. W. Lanchester). He was consultant editor of the *Automobile Engineers' Reference Book* and was active in the Veteran Car Club, frequently making the London to Brighton run.

An engineer to his finger tips, he was widely admired as a great engineer and designer but his distinct achievement is not easily identified. So much of it in the earlier years was inseparable from that of his well-known brother, F. W. Lanchester, in whose shadow he devotedly stayed. Even so his contribution was vital to the many basic innovations made under the name of Lanchester, to which numerous aspects of modern car design and production may be traced. Thereafter he developed independently, for as long as possible, their characteristics of high quality, mechanical efficiency, comfort, and security. Vitruvius was his ideal engineer. An undue modesty, kindness, and zest for life governed his personality.

He married in 1907 Rose Winifred, daughter of William Thomas, building contractor, by whom he had a son and a daughter. After her death in 1955 he married in 1961 Mary, daughter of William Stevenson, cutler and silversmith. He died 13 February 1970 at Chulmleigh, Devon.

[Anthony Bird and Francis Hutton-Stott, *Lanchester Motor Cars*, 1965; P. W. Kingsford, *F. W. Lanchester*, 1960; private information.]   P. W. KINGSFORD

LANE, SIR ALLEN (LANE WILLIAMS) (1902–1970), publisher, was born Allen Lane Williams in Bristol 21 September 1902, eldest of the four children of Samuel Allen Gardiner Williams, a municipal architect, and his wife, Camilla Matilda Lane. He went to Bristol Grammar School, and although he did not particularly distinguish himself there, he was to remember the school with pride and affection.

In 1919, when not yet seventeen, he went to work in the Bodley Head, the publishing house of John Lane [q.v.]. Its founder was a kinsman of Allen Lane's mother, and he was childless but anxious that the family name should survive and remain associated with the firm he had led to fame. He therefore stipulated that on joining him Allen change his name by deed-poll. Henceforth he was known simply as Allen Lane. Simultaneously his parents, two brothers, and sister also adopted the surname Lane.

Allen Lane learned the book trade from the bottom up. He ran errands, looked out and packed books in the warehouse, made deliveries, and after some time became London traveller for the Bodley Head. For several years he lived with John Lane and his socially active American wife, and thus began to take part in London's literary life.

By the time 'uncle' John died in 1925, the Bodley Head, which had been in decline for some years, was in serious trouble. Although only twenty-three, Allen Lane became a director, but the next ten years were not accompanied by much success, nor did his becoming chairman in 1930 lead to any marked improvement in the firm's fortunes. There were disagreements with other members of the board, and this lack of mutual confidence came to a head when Allen Lane failed to convince his colleagues that cheap paperback reprints might be the company's salvation. He therefore decided to strike out on his own, with his brothers Richard, and John (who was killed in action in the navy in 1942): in July 1935 the first ten Penguins were published at sixpence each. Experienced publishers predicted that the venture would fail as similar attempts had in the past. One of them, Jonathan Cape [q.v.], from whose list six of the first ten titles and three of the next had come, was sympathetic but had insisted that Allen Lane should pay him an advance of £40 each (instead of the £25 offered); he later told him: 'I thought you were bound to go bust, and I thought I'd take four hundred quid off you before you did.' Booksellers, too, gave the Penguins a lukewarm reception, but the situation was saved by Woolworth's, whose chief buyer was persuaded by his wife to place a substantial opening order. The public soon took the bright and well-printed little books to their hearts; presently the trade was won over, and a few months after its shaky start it was clear that the new venture was a success, although nobody could have predicted that here indeed was the beginning of a world-wide revolution. Early in 1936 Penguin Books were formally established in their own right, and a few months later Allen Lane resigned from the Bodley Head, which was about to go into liquidation.

Within two years some important new series were launched: in April 1937 the first of the Penguin Shakespeares came out, and in May the first group of Pelicans, whose co-editor, (Sir) William Emrys Williams, who has contributed to this Supplement, was to play a conspicuous part in the development of the entire range of Penguin Books. In November that year Edgar Ansel Mowrer's *Germany Puts the Clock Back* was the first of a rapidly expanding series of Penguin Specials. With these Allen Lane achieved a phenomenal success which entitled him to much more paper than would otherwise have been the case when the war brought rationing. More important, they played a notable part in swinging British public opinion towards the need to fight Hitler.

As Pelicans and Penguin Specials developed, more and more of them were specially commissioned, and Allen Lane ceased to be a publisher merely of paperback reprints. In his choice of advisory editors and authors he proved that he had a remarkable instinct for the kind of books people *needed*; he also had the ability to persuade them that these were the books they *wanted*. The missionary and the merchandiser went hand in hand. He combined this flair with a zestful enthusiasm which inspired a wide circle of editors and members of his staff, notable among whom were Eunice Frost and Kaye Webb. Many business associates testified that they would agree to requests from him which they would never have granted anybody else. Early fears by some writers—for instance, George Orwell [q.v.] in 1936—that paperbacks were going to harm their earnings were soon found to be groundless. On the contrary, Penguin's standing quickly became such that many distinguished authors, whether novelists or men of learning, were proud to be on Allen Lane's list.

The Penguin's rapid rise to popularity was, Allen Lane thought, because it combined dignity with an engaging flippancy. Perhaps without realizing it, with this epithet he had also described himself. He was always neat and spruce to the point of elegance, yet completely unselfconscious; an attentive listener, although not for too long at a stretch; and he had a boyish, sometimes mischievous, smile which showed his sense of fun and adventure. He was neither a literary critic in any serious sense, nor a scholar of anything; but he was a publisher to his fingertips. He attracted able specialists with whom he liked to exchange ideas and whom he entrusted with putting them into practice. Some of his most far-reaching and distinguished publishing ventures came out of casual encounters: so it was with the Penguin Classics, for many years under the editorship of Dr E. V. Rieu, himself the translator of the first and most successful volume, *The Odyssey* (1946); so also with The Pelican History of Art, edited by (Sir) Nikolaus Pevsner, who also had Allen Lane's patient support in producing the forty-odd volumes of *The Buildings of England* (1951–74).

When his own interest was engaged and he had confidence in a person, Allen Lane could be staunchly loyal. But when he was beset by doubts, he tended to become distrustful and irresolute. If drastic action became inevitable, it sometimes took forms that could only be called wayward. Such was the notorious dismissal of Tony Godwin, the editorial director who had eagerly accepted the challenge of leading Penguins into their second generation, had at first been given great encouragement, but failed in the end to retain Allen Lane's support.

In 1936 the Bodley Head had published the first British edition of James Joyce's *Ulysses*. Although Allen Lane had broken away by then, he could claim the credit for this courageous decision, taken in a somewhat adverse climate.

Years later he took a similar risk in publishing the unexpurgated text of D. H. Lawrence's *Lady Chatterley's Lover*. The successful defence in a *cause célèbre* at the Old Bailey in the autumn of 1960, brilliantly conducted by Gerald (later Lord) Gardiner, brought Allen Lane his greatest moment of triumph.

In the wake of the trial Allen Lane made Penguin Books into a public company but retained financial control through various trusts, among them the Penguin pension fund, which he generously endowed to secure the back-service rights of existing employees; and the Allen Lane Foundation, which his later benefactions turned into a major charitable trust. But even here his tendency to procrastinate had unfortunate results: vast sums of estate duty had to be paid because he died less than a year after taking the action his advisers had urged upon him again and again. He retired as joint managing director in 1967.

In his younger days travel had been one of his main relaxations, and he visited most parts of the world. To be his companion on a journey and share the gusto with which he savoured new experiences was a delight. In later years he spent more and more time on his farms: he took farming seriously and became thoroughly professional at it. He loved to plan new buildings or extensions, employed outstanding architects, and paid particular attention to landscaping at the Penguin headquarters at Harmondsworth. Good design came high on his list of priorities in all things.

When he was found to be suffering from cancer, with only two years to live, he bore his illness with fortitude. In April 1969 he celebrated fifty years in publishing with the first British paperback publication of *Ulysses*—a piece of symmetry that appealed to his sense of occasion. In the same month, at the last of the many glittering parties for which he was famous, authors, publishers, and booksellers paid tribute to him. For most of them it was also a poignant leavetaking. He died in hospital near London 7 July 1970.

Even Allen Lane's critics would not deny that his achievement was enormous. At his death the company he had founded thirty-five years earlier had published between six and seven thousand books, distributed in about four hundred million copies, and catering for readers of every age and interest. There were of course indifferent and bad books among them. There were projects which had been conceived with high hopes but failed. But no publisher can have brought so much pleasure and enlightenment to so many people: Allen Lane made social history.

In 1941 he married Lettice Lucy, elder daughter of Sir Charles William James Orr,

KCMG, former governor and commander-in-chief of the Bahamas. They had three daughters. Lane was knighted in 1952, and appointed CH in 1969. The universities of Birmingham, Bristol, Manchester, Oxford, and Reading gave him honorary degrees; he was an honorary fellow of the Royal College of Art and a foreign honorary member of the American Academy of Arts and Sciences. In 1969 he was the first publisher to be awarded the Albert medal of the Royal Society of Arts. A portrait by Bryan Kneale (1960) is privately owned. A life-size group portrait by Rodrigo Moynihan (1955), 'After the Conference: The Penguin Editors', hangs in the entrance hall at Penguin Books.

[Sir W. E. Williams, *Allen Lane: A Personal Portrait*, 1973; J. E. Morpurgo, *Allen Lane King Penguin*, 1979; *The Times*, 8 July 1970; private information; personal knowledge.]

HANS SCHMOLLER

LATHAM, CHARLES, first BARON LATHAM (1888–1970), public servant, was born 26 December 1888 at Norwich, the eighth of ten children of George Lathan, tanner, and his wife, Sarah Ann Mason. Charles changed his name to Latham to avoid confusion, he said, with his elder brother George, who was Labour member of Parliament for the Park division of Sheffield from 1929 to 1931 and from 1935 until his death in 1942.

Latham left the local elementary school in Norwich at the age of fourteen and was employed as a clerk, first in Norwich and later in London. After commissioned service in the war of 1914–18 in the Royal Sussex Regiment, he qualified as a member of the London Association of Accountants and played a leading role in its development into the Association of Certified and Corporate Accountants, of which he became, and for three years remained, president. In the meantime, Latham had made his mark as the sole Labour member of Hendon Urban District Council (1926–31), and on the London Labour Party, but three attempts to enter Parliament as a Labour candidate in 1922 and 1923 (Hendon) and in 1924 (Central Wandsworth) were unsuccessful. In 1928 Herbert Morrison (later Lord Morrison of Lambeth, q.v.), who liked using aldermanic vacancies to strengthen his party in departments in which it was weak, secured Latham's election as an alderman of the London County Council (1928–34) to augment the Labour group's financial skill. In 1934–46 he represented South Hackney on the LCC, and was again an alderman in 1946–7.

On Labour gaining control of the LCC for the first time in 1934, Latham was given the key office of chairman of the finance committee. He stood out from the other members of the group largely because of his driving energy, and became very much Morrison's right-hand man. When Morrison relinquished the leadership of the LCC in 1940 to become minister of supply (and later home secretary and minister of home security), it seemed natural and inevitable that Latham should take his place, but although he was his party's choice, he got off to a slow start. He lacked Morrison's geniality and ability to put a case with humour: he gave the impression of aloofness, but this veiled a warmth and generosity which brought him deep and lasting friendships. His characteristics of hard work and thoroughness soon established him as the acknowledged leader of the Council, in what was probably the most difficult period of its history. During this period, in 1942, he was raised to the peerage to strengthen the Labour Party in the House of Lords.

The mobilization and operation of the Civil Defence services during the long lull with which the war began and the heavy air attack in London which followed, owed a great deal to Latham's own energy and to his successful co-operation with Sir Ernest Gowers [q.v.], the regional commissioner of the London Civil Defence Region. The senior officers at County Hall, who worked for him, considered him a model of clarity and firmness, and his decisiveness and effectiveness won their respect and admiration. He said good-bye to them with a characteristic phrase: 'Give members the advice you think they should have, not the advice you think will please them: they can give themselves that.'

Great though were the problems posed to the administration of London by the war, Latham had found time and energy to prepare for the days of peace and, at meetings frequently held in the basement of County Hall during air raids, the County of London Plan and the Council's post-war housing programme were the fruits of his enterprise. Financial support for the London Philharmonic Orchestra was also due to Latham's initiative.

Latham left County Hall in 1947 to become chairman of the London Transport Executive. He had been a member of the London Passenger Transport Board since 1935 and of the London and Home Counties traffic advisory committee since 1933. On completion of his term as chairman in 1953, he returned, not with any great sense of satisfaction, to his accountancy practice. From his early days, when he was a member of the government-appointed economy committee (1931) under Sir George (later Lord) May [q.v.], until his more mature years, everything he tackled was marked by

a rugged independence of mind and, at a stage where many men would have been prepared to sit back in retirement, he was not too proud to accept and fill with distinction minor roles as a co-opted member of the LCC's housing committee (1957) and as a member of the Metropolitan Water Board. From 1945 until 1956 he held the appointment of lord lieutenant of Middlesex with dignity and with obvious enjoyment. He was a founder member of the Administrative Staff College, Henley (1946-59), of the standing advisory committee on the pay of the higher Civil Service (1956-67), and of the Council of Europe (1960-2). As a member of the House of Lords, he continued his interest in local government and was always helpful to the LCC in its legislation; he bitterly opposed the creation of the Greater London Council.

In 1913 he married Maya Helen, daughter of Louis George Allman, of Hendon. The marriage was dissolved in 1957. They had one son (who died in 1959) and three daughters. In 1957 he married Sylvia May, widow of Alexander Kennard. He was succeeded in the barony by his grandson, Dominic Charles (born 1954). He died 31 March 1970 in the Middlesex Hospital.

[*The Times*, 2 April 1970; private information; personal knowledge.]   A. E. SAMUELS

LAWRENCE,   SIR   (FREDERICK) GEOFFREY (1902-1967), judge, was born in London 5 April 1902, the eldest of three sons of Frederick James Lawrence, master butcher, and his wife, Lilian Kate Burden. From the City of London School he went with an open scholarship in classics to New College, Oxford, where he obtained a first class in honour moderations (1923) and a second in *literae humaniores* (1925) and in jurisprudence (1926).

Music was in the family, for his mother was a teacher of singing, and by the time Lawrence had arrived at Oxford he was already an accomplished violinist and a capable pianist. He joined the Oxford University Musical Club of which he became president. Together with his brother, a classical exhibitioner at Merton and a cellist, he formed the Magi String Quartet. The viola player was Mrs Joseph, the daughter of Robert Bridges [q.v.], the poet laureate, and the wife of H. W. B. Joseph [q.v.]. The quartet became well known in university musical circles and Lawrence played the first violin in the orchestra of the Oxford Bach Choir under Sir Hugh Allen [q.v.]; he also gave violin recitals, when he was generally accompanied by Jean Hamilton, the pianist who was to marry the future Lord Redcliffe-Maud. When Lawrence left Oxford he became tutor to the two sons of Jan Masaryk, the Czechoslovakian diplomat, who were both anxious to enter the university but needed extra coaching. Lawrence travelled with them to America and Prague and became close friends with the ill-fated family.

Lawrence next joined the Middle Temple where he was awarded a Harmsworth law scholarship and was called to the bar in 1930. Work at the bar was then very hard to get and Lawrence had no private means. But he was able to stay with a relation in Brighton while he was a pupil of Eric Neve who in 1929 had one of the best junior practices in Sussex. Neve had probably more work than he could cope with himself and was able to pass on some of it to Lawrence. Being exceptionally mature and having an unusual command of English, Lawrence made an immediate impression locally and on the South-Eastern circuit and before long was able to make a reasonable living. Neve was then in the chambers of Norman (later Lord) Birkett [q.v.] in Temple Gardens, which had a number of Sussex solicitors as clients, and Lawrence entered those chambers although in reality—until his marriage in 1941—he carried on his practice from the house in Brighton where his mother continued her profession as a teacher of singing.

By the beginning of the war of 1939-45 Lawrence himself had the best junior practice in south-east England and this took him to London where he frequently appeared in the High Court. After the war, feeling perhaps that he was not receiving the attention he was entitled to in the chambers he had first joined, Lawrence moved elsewhere. By 1950 he had one of the largest junior practices in London and in that year, with some reluctance, he took silk, and before long became greatly in demand in a remarkably varied range of cases. He was briefed in fashionable divorce suits, both civil and some criminal cases, complicated local government inquiries, and 'led' the future Lord Wilberforce in the litigation in the Chancery division on the subject of 'Spanish' champagne.

While recognized by the legal profession as a most gifted advocate Lawrence was not yet well known to the public. But in 1957, an Eastbourne doctor, John Bodkin Adams, was charged with murdering in 1950 one of his patients, Mrs Morrell, a wealthy old lady who, as the evidence showed, was unlikely to have lived for more than a few weeks. It was the case for the prosecution that the doctor had given his patient overdoses of morphine and heroin in order to shorten her life. At the time the doctor was in attendance he was aware that he was to receive a legacy of a case of silver and a conditional gift of a pre-war Rolls-Royce motor car subject to the consent

of the old lady's son. Lawrence was briefed to lead Edward Clarke (later a judge) for the defence. In the hope that the doctor would have an impartial trial outside Sussex the case was transferred to the Old Bailey where it was heard before Mr Justice (later Lord) Devlin and lasted seventeen days. The attorney-general as the leading counsel for the prosecution built up a powerful body of specialized medical evidence which included the testimony of the nurses who attended the old lady during her last illness. Well instructed on medical matters and helped by an experienced junior counsel, as well as the unexpected production of the notebooks kept by the nurses at the time, Lawrence cross-examined the medical witnesses, often at great length, with the greatest skill, thereby laying the foundation for the defence that the so-called overdoses were in fact the only treatment the doctor could give to alleviate pain and distress. Refusing to call the doctor as a witness—because as Lawrence told the jury the accused could not be reasonably expected to remember the details of what had happened so long before—Lawrence secured an acquittal. In the climate of opinion which then prevailed this was generally hailed as a somewhat unexpected triumph. In the following year he secured the acquittal of the chief constable of Brighton on a charge of conspiracy to obstruct the course of justice. Lawrence was by now at the top of his profession and could generally obtain whatever fees he wanted.

Lawrence was successively recorder of Tenterden (1948-51) and Canterbury (1952-62) and was chairman of the West Sussex quarter-sessions. He was chairman of the General Council of the Bar (1960-2) and in that capacity visited America to address the American Bar Association in New York where his speeches much impressed American lawyers. He was chairman of the National Incomes Commission in 1962-4, was knighted in 1963, and in 1965 was made a High Court judge. He remained on the bench for an unusually short time for years of unremitting work in court and late nights occupied in reading briefs affected his constitution, never too robust, and ended in serious illness.

In appearance Lawrence was short, slight in build, with good features and his voice was attractive and well modulated. He had in the most unusual measure the power to attract the attention of his listeners—whether in or out of court—to what he was saying. It was said that he could make even the pattern on the carpet sound interesting. But he was not himself much interested in the needs of others. Courteous, sophisticated, and urbane, he was probably at his best in cross-examination when he could lead a suspecting—or unsuspecting—witness very politely along a path from the end of which there was no return. But underneath his good temper was a sense of great determination and persistence. He was considered the equal of most of the notable barristers of the early part of the twentieth century, although lacking the stature of some of them. As a lawyer he was neither exceptionally learned nor profound (he was perhaps too busy and had too many other interests to wish for either of these qualities) but he was clever enough to be able to argue complicated matters of law without much apparent effort. If he had a weakness it was that he was too much of a perfectionist which led him somewhat irrationally to suppose he was unsuited for appointments outside the law as being too much of an adventure for an essentially cautious person; but which, had he accepted or looked for them, might have imposed less strain on his health.

While he had not the physique of an athlete Lawrence was interested in agriculture, enjoyed yachting, swimming, and games in general—particularly cricket, of which he was a shrewd and knowledgeable observer.

In 1941 Lawrence married Marjorie Avice, daughter of Charles Angelo Jones; they had no children. His wife shared very fully his love of music and country life. Lawrence died at Midhurst, Sussex, 3 February 1967.

[Private information; personal knowledge.]
D. M. GOODBODY

LAWRENCE, FREDERICK WILLIAM PETHICK-, BARON (1871-1961), social worker and politician. [See PETHICK-LAWRENCE.]

LAWSON, EDWARD FREDERICK, fourth BARON BURNHAM (1890-1963), newspaper proprietor and soldier, was born in London 16 June 1890, the elder son of William Arnold Webster Levy Lawson, of the Scots Guards and Royal Bucks Hussars, who succeeded his brother H. L. W. Levy-Lawson [q.v.] as third baron in 1933, and his wife, Sybil Mary, daughter of Lieutenant-General Sir Frederick Marshall. Their younger son, William, was killed in action in 1914. Lawson was educated at Eton and Balliol College, Oxford, where he obtained third class honours in modern history in 1913 and played polo for the university. He then started his press career with the Daily Telegraph, first as a reporter in Paris and later in the New York office, where he found himself at the outbreak of war in 1914. He returned to England and was immediately mobilized with his father's old regiment, the Royal Bucks Hussars, into which he had already been commissioned. In 1915 he went with his regiment to the Middle East and acted as landing officer at Gallipoli, subsequently taking part in the Palestine campaigns and the entry of Lord Allenby [q.v.] into Jerusalem. At the early age of twenty-six he was transferred to command the Middlesex Yeomanry. For his services he was appointed to the DSO (for the cavalry charge at El Mugghar), awarded the MC, and thrice mentioned in dispatches.

After the war, Lawson returned to his press career with the Daily Telegraph under his uncle, Lord Burnham. At the same time he maintained his interest in the Royal Bucks Hussars and was one of the prime enthusiasts in ensuring the success of their transformation from cavalry to artillery and their merger with the Berkshire Yeomanry into the 99th (Bucks and Berks) Field Brigade Royal Artillery, which he commanded in 1929-33 and of which he then became honorary colonel.

In 1938 he received the compliment, rare for a non-regular officer in peacetime, of appointment as commander Royal Artillery 48th (South Midland) division, with the rank of brigadier. In that capacity he went to France soon after the outbreak of war and took part with distinction in the Dunkirk campaign. When the evacuation began, he and his staff were detached from their division to assist in the organization of the final defence perimeter round Dunkirk, a task which he carried out with calm and skill and for which he was appointed CB (1940).

Returning to England, he continued in his CRA appointment until in 1941 he was promoted major-general as general officer commanding the Yorkshire division. To his regret, because he preferred service in the field to an office, he held this command only a few months before being appointed senior military representative at the Ministry of Information, and at the same time, director of public relations at the War Office. For those appointments, which he held until the end of the war, he was admirably qualified by his army and press careers and he gained the complete confidence both of the Army Council and of Fleet Street.

He succeeded to the title on his father's death in 1943 and in 1945 retired from the army but continued until his death to take a lively interest, especially in Territorial matters. His press career ran coincident, except for the two wars, with his army life. When his uncle disposed of the Daily Telegraph in 1927 to Sir William Berry (later Viscount Camrose, q.v.), Lawson remained as general manager, an appointment which he held until the outbreak of war in 1939 and which he resumed as managing director in 1945 until his retirement in 1961. Apart from his responsibility for the administration of the Daily Telegraph he took a keen interest in Fleet Street affairs generally, and in 1934 he was elected vice-chairman of the Newspaper Proprietors (later Publishers) Association and held that appointment, except for the war years, until 1961. In 1946-61 he was chairman of the labour executive of the NPA and gained a reputation for common sense and fair dealing, which commended itself to both management and unions. In 1955 he published *Peterborough Court, the Story of the Daily Telegraph*. He was for many years an active supporter, member of the council, and from 1946 vice-chairman of the Commonwealth Press Union. With his wife he took part in the major conferences and tours in Canada (1950) and India and Pakistan (1961).

Burnham had many outside interests. Freemasonry was one, and he became provincial grand master of Buckinghamshire masons in 1946. Another was racing, and he was a successful owner under both Pony Club and Jockey Club rules. He hunted with the Whaddon Chase and shot over his Buckinghamshire estates with enthusiasm almost until his death. He was essentially a countryman, and he treated animals, especially horses and dogs, as people. He knew no fear. He was a man of some shyness and reserve, but his warmth of character and kindness soon came through with closer acquaintance and friendship. He had a quiet but incisive sense of humour, great common sense, fairness and honesty. His advice to a staff officer was: 'Never be rude on paper. Never have a *small* row. Learn how to make a short speech.' He was himself one of the best after-dinner speakers of his generation. He loved good wine and good food and his staff mess in France was a by-word for both.

Burnham enjoyed a perfect family life. In 1920 he married Marie Enid (died 1979), daughter of Hugh Scott Robson, of London and Buenos Aires; they had two sons and one daughter. His wife was president of the Girl Guides Association of England in 1961-70 and of the Bucks Red Cross in 1936-64. Their elder son, William Edward Harry (born 1920), succeeded his father when he died in London 4 July 1963, having commanded the 1st battalion Scots Guards in 1959-62. Their younger son, Hugh, maintained the family tradition with the *Daily Telegraph*.

There are portraits of Burnham in the possession of the family by T. C. Dugdale and Edward I. Halliday.

[Private information; personal knowledge.]
         L. D. CROSS

LAYCOCK, SIR ROBERT EDWARD (1907-1968), soldier, was born in London 18 April 1907, the eldest surviving son of (Sir) Joseph Frederick Laycock and his wife, Katherine Mary, daughter of Hugh Henry Hare and formerly Marchioness of Downshire. His father, who had been appointed to the DSO in 1900, was in 1918 commander of a brigade of the Royal Artillery, and was one of the very few Territorial officers to be appointed KCMG (1919) for services in the field. Laycock was devoted to his father, and probably inherited a soldierly disposition from him.

'Bob' Laycock was educated at Eton and the Royal Military College, Sandhurst, where he became senior under-officer. He was commissioned as an officer of the Royal Horse Guards in 1927. His wide interests included scientific ones, and he took every professional opportunity to enlarge his knowledge of these; as a result, on the outbreak of war in 1939, he found himself GSO 2 Chemical Warfare at BEF headquarters in France. From this unrewarding post he was transferred to England to attend the first wartime course at Camberley. He thus took no part in the first battle of France.

In the period succeeding the fall of France, Sir Roger (later Lord) Keyes [q.v.] was founding the Commandos, and requested Laycock's services which he had in fact already volunteered. This double event saved him from the threat of another CW appointment. An ideal officer for Special Service employment, Laycock was promoted to lieutenant-colonel, and early in 1941 he sailed for the Middle East in command of 'Layforce', an enlarged battalion of five Commandos.

The little force carried out several minor but hazardous tasks with varying success until it was allotted the daunting mission of rearguard action in the British defence of Crete. Throughout this action (May-June 1941), Laycock's personal assistant was Captain Evelyn Waugh [q.v.]. The experience of the British disaster in Crete is reflected in Waugh's novel *Officers and Gentlemen* (1955). Laycock and Waugh were in the last British ship to leave the island.

Later in 1941 Laycock took part in the unsuccessful raid led by Lieutenant-Colonel Keyes (the admiral's son) on Rommel's supposed headquarters, and after the action he escaped into the Libyan desert and lived for nearly two months behind the enemy lines. He afterwards declared that he owed his survival to his knowledge of the habits of foxes, and in gratitude he never went hunting again.

Early in 1942 Laycock was ordered back to England from Egypt to command the Special Service brigade, his main duties being its training, organization, and planning, in concert with the Combined Operations Command of Lord Louis (later Earl) Mountbatten. Various raids on the Continent resulted; it was rightly said that 'Laycock made the Commandos what they were'.

In 1943 Laycock was again in the front line when he led an assault in the Sicily landings, and faced a harder military task at Salerno where, against a more numerous and heavily armed enemy, and for the loss of half his small force, he successfully held bridgehead positions for eleven crucial days. For his action in Sicily he was appointed to the DSO, and for his action at Salerno he was awarded the medal of the United States Legion of Merit.

In October 1943 he was promoted major-general, as the inevitable successor to Mount-batten when the latter was transferred to the South-East Asia Command. As chief of com-bined operations, Laycock's later war service was less spectacular, but remained as valuable and highly valued. He was appointed CB in 1945. In the same year he stood for Parliament in the general election, as Conservative candi-date for Bassetlaw, where his chance of victory was slender since the sitting member was Frederick John Bellenger who had made a name in Parliament as 'the soldier's friend'.

After his defeat he was reappointed chief of combined operations and remained in the post until 1947. He then retired to the family house at Wiseton, near Doncaster, and the manage-ment of his property. In 1954, on the advice of the secretary of state for war, his friend and contemporary Antony (later Viscount) Head, Laycock was appointed governor and commander-in-chief of Malta.

He entered on his new duties at a critical time. Dominic Mintoff was rising to political mastery, and represented the popular desire for independence and for the abolition of the British position on the island. To add to Lay-cock's difficulties some in authority deliberately gave him misleading advice for interested reasons. Negotiations with the Independence Party broke down at the end of 1958, and the British Government suspended the constitu-tion. During that time of conflict Laycock remained none the less a much esteemed and effective governor. His term of office was twice extended, and when he retired in 1959 he had successfully initiated a five-year development plan.

In 1935 he married Angela Clare Louise, daughter of William Dudley Ward, a privy councillor, and Liberal member of Parliament for Southampton, 1906-22; they had two sons and three daughters. Laycock was appointed KCMG in 1954; he held the posts of high sheriff (1954-5) and lord-lieutenant (from 1962) of Nottinghamshire, and in 1960 he was appointed colonel commandant of the Special Air Service and the Sherwood Rangers Yeo-manry. An enthusiastic horseman and yachts-man, he also maintained many intellectual and other interests; he was an inveterate reader and collector of books, and his versatility included such minor accomplishments as Bond Street barbering. His acquaintance and friendships were among a very wide variety of people, and his gaiety and modesty placed him among those rare beings who seem to have no enemies.

In the last years of his life he was troubled by an arterial disorder which gave him continual pain in one leg. An operation failed to cure it, and he was threatened by the need for amputa-tion. Typical of his impetuous spirit, he once called at a hospital to make an immediate appointment for this purpose, and was some-what indignant on being told that preliminary discussion must involve delay. On 10 March 1968 he collapsed from a heart attack while walking from church at Wiseton and died instantly.

[*The Times*, 11 March 1968; personal know-ledge.]   CHRISTOPHER SYKES

LAYTON, WALTER THOMAS, first BARON LAYTON (1884-1966), economist, editor, and newspaper proprietor, was born in London 15 March 1884, the son of Alfred John Layton, of the Chalet, Fulham Park Rd., London SW, and his wife, Mary, FRCO, daughter of Walter Johnson, schoolmaster. He had two brothers and one sister. Both his parents were musical and he himself showed musical and mathe-matical talent; his mother was a gifted organist, as was one of his brothers, and he himself sang as a chorister of St. George's before Queen Victoria during her Diamond Jubilee celebra-tions at Windsor. He was educated at King's College School, London, and Westminster City School. He went up to University College, London, early, graduating in 1903 with third class honours in history. The following year he was placed in the second division of inter-mediate science (economics) at the age of twenty. Thence he went to Trinity College, Cambridge, achieving first classes in both parts i (1906) and ii (1907) of the economics tripos. In 1908 he was, with J. M. (later Lord) Keynes [q.v.], appointed lecturer in economics, becoming a fellow at Gonville and Caius (1909-14) and Newmarch lecturer at University College, London (1909-12).

Layton married in 1910 (Eleanor) Dorothea, daughter of Francis Beresford Plumptre Osmaston, of Stoneshill, Limpsfield, Surrey. She was also a Cambridge graduate, also musical, also blonde and handsome: she de-scribed him then as 'the next best-looking man in Cambridge to Rupert Brooke'. Layton re-tained into late middle age his tall, lean, athletic figure, fair hair, and blue eyes. Their seven children (three boys and four girls) were brought up with open-air and musical backgrounds and, despite Layton's many and prolonged missions abroad and travels for political and academic purposes in Britain, family life was a serious matter for both parents; often, some thought, too soberly and seriously taken. Lady Layton (died 1959) zealously joined in her husband's activities, especially in Liberal Party politics, and in 1961 Layton published *Dorothy* (as she was always known), a touching biographical picture of her.

Layton's career, like that of Keynes, fell into three distinct sectors: academic, political and public service, and business. First, his mathematical bent showed itself early in his admiration for what Alfred Marshall—and before him J. Horne Tooke and William Newmarch and W. S. Jevons [qq.v.]—had emphasized as the dependence of 'economic science' on the 'measurable in money terms'; thus Layton derived, through their works, his lifelong respect for, and addiction to, statistics; thence also his only substantial and scholarly work *An Introduction to the Study of Prices* (1920). He made careful studies of separate industries for his lectures, which stood him in good stead for his 1914-18 work for the Ministry of Munitions and led to his key appointments in that war: to the famous Milner [q.v.] Mission to Russia (1917)—on which he narrowly escaped Lord Kitchener's [q.v.] fate in the *Hampshire* by having to change ships at the last moment—and the Balfour Mission to the USA that same year, for all of which he was appointed CBE. He was made CH in 1919. His readiness with facts and figures, often when no one else could offer more than wild guesses, became legendary in many national and international conferences during and immediately after the war of 1914-18; so it was natural that he should become a member of the Consultative Economic Committee of the League of Nations, and in due course director of the Economic and Financial Section of the League, in which position he developed that Section's service of statistics which was to prove so valuable as the 1920s and 1930s unfolded. Like many of his Cambridge and other fellow economists— Keynes, Dudley Ward, E. Hilton Young (later Lord Kennet, q.v.), R. J. Stopford, Sir Basil P. Blackett [q.v.], Sir Cecil Kisch—Layton had gradually and naturally turned from the academic sector to that of public affairs; and also to Liberal Party politics. In the early 1920s, the League, the domestic British political wrangling over the Peace of Versailles, and the breaking-up of the Coalition and the Lloyd George-Bonar Law balance gave Layton from then onwards his deep concern with world (especially European and Anglo-American)

affairs, the safeguarding of peace through the League, and the need for economic growth and monetary stability for the world as a whole.

His work was, however, to take a third and unexpected direction: into Fleet Street in the shape of the editorship of that prestigious weekly *The Economist* which he was to refashion and direct from 1922 to 1938. Here, too, wheels came full circle, for its founder (James Wilson, q.v.) and his more famous son-in-law (Walter Bagehot, q.v.) between 1843 and the latter's death (1877) had turned to Sir Robert Giffen [q.v.], Tooke, Newmarch, and other statisticians in order to build the paper up as the world's premier source of economic and financial statistics. The paper had been in the hands of trustees for the Bagehot daughters, the last of whom (Mrs Russell Barrington) had by the 1920s come to the opinion that— with safeguards for the paper's editorial integrity and for its proprietors—it should be sold. The story of the way in which Layton, aided by the Cadburys and others with funds, not only organized the purchase of *The Economist* but also made sure of his own editorship is told in its centenary volume *The Economist 1843–1943* (1943); but the sale was not to occur till 1928. Between the advent of Layton merely as editor on behalf of 'the dear old ladies'' trustees in 1922 until the sale in 1928, he was to refashion the paper, its policies, and its writers to serve the ravaged world economy. In that task his experience in the war, and at various international monetary and other conferences after it, proved invaluable. New or refurbished sections of the paper gave much more substance and space to international affairs each week, and the 'facts and figures' multiplied apace.

It was during these years that Layton became closely identified once more with his fellows who were Liberals and of Cambridge origin: especially with Keynes and (Sir) H. D. Henderson [q.v.]. Both of these had become publicists: Keynes through the (then) *Manchester Guardian*, Henderson through the *Nation* and both through the feature and correspondence columns of the daily press (still numerous in those days). The Liberal Party had begun its long fission and decline; the British economy as well, with unemployment leading to the 1926 general strike and to that split between economists which has widened to this day and over which the spirit and works of Keynes still brood. Between Keynes, Henderson, Layton, and others active in the Liberal Party the 1928 *Liberal Yellow Book* was planned and brought to publication, with help from funds from the Cadbury family. Layton, learning of the possible sale of his paper, formed a syndicate of buyers, among whom were counted Cadburys, City firms, and (as to 50 per cent) the group organized by Brendan (later Viscount) Bracken [q.v.]. It was a period of amalgamations among papers, even of disappearance for many like the *Nation*, *Morning Post*, and *Daily News*. Liberals were saddened by the absorption of the latter into the *News-Chronicle*, but heartened by Keynes's becoming chairman of the *New Statesman and Nation* and the unexpected appointment of Layton as editorial director to the *News-Chronicle* while remaining editor of *The Economist*.

Thus the 1930s opened the third sector of Layton's career: that of editor and chief business director of a famous weekly for intellectuals and of two 'dailies', a morning and an evening (the *Star*). He was at the full stretch of his remarkable powers, approaching the age of fifty. Still expanding and modernizing *The Economist*, Layton had to associate other, younger men with him as aides in more and more specialized writing and fact-gathering. Of these the best known was Geoffrey (later Lord) Crowther, who not only spent a third of his time on *The Economist* but two-thirds helping Layton run two daily papers on the opposite side of Bouverie Street, eventually (in 1938, after 'Munich') taking Layton's editorial mantle at *The Economist* and allowing Layton to concentrate on the daily papers. From 1945 to 1953 Layton was also a director of Reuters.

Layton and Crowther had not altogether 'gone along with' the 'appeasers' over Hitler's depredations and over the impotence of the leading powers in the League of Nations. Accordingly when tasks were assigned for the conduct of the British war effort from 1939 to 1945 neither of the two found himself in as controlling a position as his talents would have justified. Layton was director-general of programmes in the Ministry of Supply from 1940-2, chairman of the Executive Committee, Ministry of Supply, 1941-2, chief adviser on programmes on planning in the Ministry of Production, 1941-3, and head of Joint War Production Staff, 1942-3. Both men returned to direct their papers as war ended; but while *The Economist* under Crowther went from strength to strength, the *News-Chronicle* and *Star* under Layton (with Crowther as a fellow director) went into decline in the intensifying struggle for survival in Fleet Street in the face of the unfavouring public attitude to the Liberal Party, and with the growing popularity of television. The two dailies eventually had to be closed down, though not until the mid sixties, by which time Layton and Crowther had resigned their positions on them. Some public criticism and some employees' natural resentment much upset both men at the time; but Layton had already lost his wife in 1959 and

was ageing, while Crowther had resigned his editorship of *The Economist* and entered the business field.

In the post-1945 world Layton, with his wife's unfailing help until her death, worked hard for the causes of Anglo-American understanding, European unity, the United Nations, and the Liberal Party. But despite many speeches at many meetings, or perhaps because of them, Layton's seemed a lonely voice, and his life lonely, in his last decade or so. His many grandchildren were a recompense, but he was more and more of a stranger in the Britain and the world of the 1950s and 1960s. The monuments to his life's work are his influence over so many younger men (especially the very many who served *The Economist*) and his organizing the security and editorial integrity of that famous weekly paper, now a world-wide more than a British institution. As a young Cambridge (and London) don, Layton never belonged to the Bloomsbury (or any other) 'set'. He was no aesthetic authority or even amateur, save in music. He did not value 'the good things of life' but rather led an austere life and impressed it on his home and family. He had little sense of humour or of 'occasion'. He was impatient of cant, and could devastate a purveyor of falsities or mere guesses. He was no great public speaker. Of somewhat diffident manner, he was often taken to be weak; but he had a fierce fighting spirit on his many principles. An essentially shy man with a slight stammer, he never lost the look of the bright young man of Cambridge in the first decade of this century. He survived most of his fellows in that time and place, but he contrived to pass on to two younger generations something of the values they were to see overthrown or discarded.

Layton was knighted in 1930, was created first Baron Layton in 1947, and was a member of the Legion of Honour and of many other foreign orders. Gonville and Caius made him an honorary fellow in 1931 and he had honorary degrees from Columbia and Melbourne.

He died in Putney Hospital 14 February 1966. He was succeeded as baron by his eldest son, Michael John Layton, who was born in 1912.

[*The Times*, 15, 16, 18, and 23 February 1966; private information; personal knowledge.]
GRAHAM HUTTON

LEARMONTH, SIR JAMES RÖGNVALD (1895-1967), surgeon, was born in Gatehouse of Fleet, Kirkcudbright, 23 March 1895, the elder son of William Learmonth, headmaster of Girthon School, Gatehouse of Fleet, and his wife, Katherine Craig. William Learmonth was an Orcadian, his wife an Ulster woman.

Young Learmonth received his primary education at Girthon School under the eye of his father, a strict disciplinarian and a scholarly man who wrote a book on Kirkcudbrightshire and Wigtownshire. He went on to Kilmarnock Academy, then in 1913 to Glasgow University as a medical student. On the outbreak of war he was commissioned in the King's Own Scottish Borderers with whom he served in France and Scotland until 1918 when he returned to university. He won many prizes and medals and in 1921 qualified MB, Ch.B. with honours and the Brunton memorial prize for the most distinguished graduate in medicine of his year.

After periods as house-surgeon and house-physician in the Western Infirmary, Glasgow, Learmonth served as assistant to Professor Archibald Young from 1922 to 1924. He had a keen interest in original work and obtained a Rockefeller research fellowship which took him to the Mayo Clinic in 1924. There he met his wife, Charlotte Newell, daughter of F. G. Bundy, of St. Johnsbury, Vermont. She was at that time director of the department of social work at the clinic and they were married in 1925. After what he described as the happiest year of his life Learmonth returned to Glasgow in 1925, first as assistant to the regius professor of surgery and later as dispensary surgeon to the Western Infirmary, the main teaching hospital of Glasgow University. There he wrote several pioneer papers on the inheritance of blood groups which were well received. His interest in the subject stemmed from his student days when he worked with J. M. Graham in Edinburgh on blood transfusion. He proceeded Ch.M. in 1927 and FRCSE in 1928. In that year he was invited to return as a member of the staff of the department of neurosurgery at the Mayo Clinic where he spent the next four years in the rigorous and exacting field of brain surgery. He was not a man who could shed the problems of his patients at the hospital door and these years, although professionally valuable, took a great toll of his reserves.

When the regius chair of surgery in Aberdeen became vacant in 1932 Learmonth was elected and for the next seven years worked happily there in the company of such distinguished colleagues as (Sir) Stanley Davidson in the chair of medicine and (Sir) Dugald Baird in obstetrics. It was in Aberdeen that he turned his energy to the study of disease of the arteries which became his life's work and for which he became internationally famous.

In 1939 Learmonth succeeded Sir David Wilkie [q.v.] in the chair of surgery at Edinburgh University. The onset of war with its problems of providing emergency medical services away from the large cities which were vulnerable to air attacks left little time for building up a university department. But he directed his considerable organizing ability towards helping the war effort and at Gogarburn hospital near Edinburgh he set up an outstanding unit for the treatment of injuries of the peripheral nerves. In 1946 he took over the regius chair of clinical surgery in addition to his own. This resulted in a single division of surgery and he used this opportunity to establish special departments of plastic, thoracic, paediatric, and urological surgery, all of which achieved international renown. He was also keen to promote surgical research and appointed the first senior lecturer in experimental surgery as deputy director of the Wilkie surgical research laboratory.

Learmonth's experience in the Mayo Clinic had persuaded him of the value of interchange of ideas and experience between the various departments in surgery. In Edinburgh, as in most centres in Great Britain, there was very little of this. Each chief with his group of acolytes tended to regard himself as wholly independent and self-sufficient. Inevitably this created an aura of infallibility and rigidity, in which new ideas found difficulty in becoming established. Learmonth was determined to break down these barriers and instituted Saturday morning staff meetings in his own units and in others whose chiefs were sympathetic to his efforts. They were not without their intimidating moments since a feature was the discussion of complications occurring in the unit. For a young surgeon to appear before so many distinguished seniors to explain the errors of his ways could be a chastening experience, but a sympathetic hearing was the rule. Gradually more and more units joined these staff meetings and eventually hospitals outside Edinburgh took part.

Learmonth's intelligence made him delight in the exchange of ideas especially with young men whose enthusiasm had not been blunted by the day-to-day cares of professional life. In many ways he was at his best at research meetings in his own department where his natural generosity of heart went out to young men striving without much success to seek solutions to the many problems which beset surgery. His integrity made care of patients something of an ordeal to him since he became inevitably involved with their personal problems. In particular the responsibility of operating on children gave him many sleepless nights. No doubt a more detached outlook would have made things easier for his staff, nurses, and his family and friends, but it was accepted that conscientiousness was the very stuff of his being.

His reserve was not easy to break down and

it became crustier in the face of pretentiousness or arrogance, when he was capable of quite frightening tight-lipped antagonism of which many people retained unhappy memories. Like all highly intelligent and energetic men, he tended to see the best solution to a difficult problem quickly and expressed his views articulately. When they were not accepted immediately, he could be forceful and not always politic in committee. In fact committee work was not congenial to his character and the lobbying and prolonged negotiation inseparable from it gave him little pleasure. Nevertheless his concept of the proper role of a university in society made him serve on many cognate committees including the University Grants Committee and the Medical Research Council.

Professionally Learmonth was one of the surgical giants of his time. His influence was world wide and during his term of office in Edinburgh famous men from all over the world came to his department to see his work in peripheral vascular disease. Much of his surgical philosophy and experience was distilled in his lectures. His Listerian oration (1952) reiterated his profound conviction that today's research is tomorrow's practice and that the university hospital is the proper medium in which to nourish it. His Macewen lecture delivered in the university of Glasgow before the Association of Surgeons was an account of his great experience of vascular disease in children. The Horsley memorial lecture of the British Medical Association (1952) recounted his pioneer work in association with Dr John Gillies, his anaesthetist and close friend, on hypotensive anaesthesia, a technique by which it is possible to reduce bleeding at operation by artificially lowering the patient's blood pressure; a method which had passed into standard use, particularly in neurosurgery.

In 1934 Learmonth was appointed surgeon to the royal household in Scotland and in February 1949 surgeon to the King upon whom he was to operate in the following month. He was appointed CBE in 1945, KCVO in 1949, and was made a chevalier of the Legion of Honour in 1950. He received a number of honorary degrees and his honorary fellowships included that of the American College of Surgeons and of the Royal Medical Society. In 1954 he visited Canada and Australia as the Sir Arthur Sims travelling Commonwealth professor. In 1956 he retired from his chair and bought a house in the attractive Border village of Broughton where he spent eleven very happy years, during which he served on the court of Glasgow University. The frequent visits of his two children, James and Jean, with their children brought him great joy. An unexpected side to his character, known only

to his intimates, was a puckish sense of humour, a gift for mimicry, and a habit of playing the tunes of his student days on the mandolin: 'at the end of the day, he was a delightful companion'. He died at Broughton 27 September 1967. Typically he would not have a portrait painted or a memorial service after his death.

[Private information; personal knowledge.]

D. M. DOUGLAS

LEATHERS, FREDERICK JAMES, first VISCOUNT LEATHERS (1883-1965), shipping expert and government minister, was born 21 November 1883, at Ratcliff, Stepney, Middlesex, the son of Robert Leathers, carpenter, and his wife, Emily Seamen. His father died in Frederick's infancy, leaving the family in somewhat difficult circumstances. Young Frederick entered commercial life at the age of fifteen, joining a company called Steamship Owners Coal Association which was subsequently merged with William Cory & Sons Ltd. At that time Corys was closely associated with P&O Company, then led by Sir James L. Mackay (later the Earl of Inchcape, q.v.), who was quick to appreciate the energy and ability of his young subordinate. Soon, while little more than a boy, Leathers was working closely with Mackay and performing many confidential services for him. Leathers was promoted fast and by 1916 became the managing director of William Cory; he quickly became a director or chairman of many other companies mainly concerned with coal or shipping auxiliary services, such as lighterage. During the war of 1914-18 he was called upon to advise the Ministry of Shipping on port problems.

During the inter-war years his main task at Corys, which for long had had a powerful position in the coal-bunkering trade, was to build an equally strong position in the rapidly growing business of oil-bunkers. Indirectly more significant for his future was his introduction to (Sir) Winston Churchill by Brendan (later Viscount) Bracken [qq.v.]. Churchill was at that time in the political wilderness because of his opposition to the Government of India Bill and Lord Inchcape sympathized with his stand. Before long Churchill became a director of two of Cory's subsidiaries and, in this way, came to form a high opinion of Leathers's commercial knowledge and capacities. In May 1940 Churchill pressed the minister of shipping to appoint Leathers adviser to the Ministry on all coal problems. Almost at once, when France fell, Leathers was faced with the very difficult problem of dealing with the vast quantity of coal destined for France, much of it already on the water. (Shipments of coal to France had been 1,800,000 tons in May and an even larger tonnage had been planned for June.) Leathers's intimate knowledge of the trade and the persons concerned with it enabled him to dispose of this great quantity by 'persuasion, cajolery and sometimes even stronger methods'. No one else could have performed this task so quickly, thus freeing the ships for further service.

A year later, in May 1941, the prime minister amalgamated the Ministries of Shipping and Transport and appointed Leathers minister of war transport. At the same time he was created a baron. In spite of his ignorance of political procedure, he proved an admirable choice—not only did he have a comprehensive knowledge of the shipping, port, and inland-transport industries, but he also knew most of the leaders in these spheres and already had an inside knowledge of the working of the Ministry of Shipping. Moreover, he enjoyed the very great advantage over his predecessor in that he had, and was known to have, the steady support of the prime minister; thus there was an end to the steady sniping from the Ministries of Supply (which had not yet been able to work out the precise imports needed for the multifarious materials it controlled) and of Food (which consistently understated its stocks). As the official historian (Miss C. B. A. Behrens) says: 'The intricate system of controls and committees began to take a shape that permitted all the various demands on ships in the United Kingdom to be considered together, and adjusted to each other and to the supply.'

The shipping position was acute at the time Leathers took office; at the same time the first optimistic hopes of the United States shipping aid, derived from the president's directive of 1 May, began to fade under the influence of obstruction from the US Services and administrative difficulties in American government agencies. Nevertheless, Lend-Lease and other forms of US aid were soon giving effective help. The North Atlantic was the shortest supply route available for many of the most needed commodities but, prior to Lend-Lease, the shortage of hard currency prevented full advantage being taken of this short haul. In 1942 the shipping shortage grew even more acute and reached its climax in March 1943. The vast US shipbuilding programme was by then increasing the pool of tonnage at the Allies' disposal but the US Services pre-empted a wholly disproportionate share of the pool because of their wasteful and inexperienced use of ships. It thus fell on Leathers and the British Merchant Shipping Mission in Washington to exert every power of persuasion and logic on their opposite numbers in favour of an over-all allocation of Allied shipping resources in proportion to the needs of the various military theatres, the maintenance of areas of Allied responsibility such as Africa, the Middle East, the Indian Ocean, and Australasia, and the British import programme. It would be idle to pretend that this was ever completely achieved, the demands of the US chiefs of staff and theatre commanders being almost invulnerable, but by the end of 1943 the ideal had been accepted in theory and great progress had been made towards implementing it in practice.

During 1943 Leathers attended the Casablanca, Washington, Quebec, and Cairo conferences which were convened to fix and co-ordinate Allied strategy. Strategy had to be correlated to shipping availability. At Casablanca Leathers was not formally consulted and it soon became clear that the plans there agreed were beyond the carrying resources of Allied shipping. At Washington and subsequent conferences Leathers and his staff were fully consulted and operational plans brought gradually within the shipping possibilities. One of his particular aims at Washington was to secure 200 standard US war-built ships on bare-boat charter; previous aid had been largely on a voyage-by-voyage basis, the uncertainty of which prevented any precise programming. There was the further consideration that the US had more ships than seamen whereas the British had a pool of seamen provided by the survivors of sunk ships. These 200 ships became a leitmotiv, and one of the great moments of Leathers's life came as he was quietly sipping a drink (which he did sparingly and seldom) in a New York hotel on his way back from Washington; the street was suddenly filled with hubbub as an escorted motor-cycle dispatch rider arrived to deliver a message from the president that the 200 ships would be provided.

Leathers, who was appointed CH in 1943, also accompanied the prime minister to Yalta and Potsdam, but proceedings there were more political than practical and he was not able to achieve any of his aims in the sphere of transport.

When Churchill returned to power in 1951, he recalled Leathers to become secretary of state for the co-ordination of transport, fuel, and power, as an 'overlord' of the three departments. The experiment was not a happy one. The statutory powers, the executive, and planning staffs remained with the individual departments, leaving the co-ordinators helpless, a situation far from Leathers's taste. He retired in 1953 and resumed his business interests, becoming first Viscount Leathers, of Purfleet, in the New Year honours of 1954. He was an honorary LLD of the universities of Leeds (1946) and Birmingham (1951), and an honorary member of the Institution of Naval Architects. He was also an underwriting member of Lloyd's, warden of the court of the

Worshipful Company of Shipwrights, and president of the Institute of Chartered Shipbrokers. He died in London 19 March 1965.

In 1907 he married Emily Ethel, daughter of Henry Baxter, of Southend, Essex. They had two sons and a daughter, who all survived him. The title passed to his elder son, Frederick Alan (born 1908).

There are portraits by (Sir) James Gunn (1943) and Maurice Codner (1952); both are in oils and in the possession of the family.

[C. B. A. Behrens, *Merchant Shipping and the Demands of War* (official history), 1955; private information; personal knowledge.]

FRANCIS KEENLYSIDE

LE BAS, EDWARD (1904-1966), painter and collector, was born 27 October 1904 in Hampstead, London, the youngest of the three children and only son of Edward Le Bas and his wife, Anna Le Grand. The Le Bas family was of Anglo-French descent, originally from Jersey and had become wealthy through the exertions of Edward Le Bas senior in building construction and the manufacture of industrial steel products. Le Bas was educated at St. Peter's Preparatory School, Eastbourne, and at Harrow (1918-22); he went up to Pembroke College, Cambridge, and graduated with a BA from the University Architectural School in 1925. He had briefly studied painting in France in 1922 and on leaving Cambridge he attended the Royal College of Art, South Kensington, under (Sir) William Rothenstein [q.v.]. His decision to become a painter displeased his father; his allowance was cut to £150 a year and he lived in modest circumstances in Golden Square.

In 1933 Le Bas first exhibited at the Royal Academy ('Lady with a Siamese Cat') and was included in group exhibitions at the Lefevre Galleries, sharing his first one-man show there with (Dame) Ethel Walker [q.v.] in 1936. Still life, landscape, and figures in interiors were (and continued to be) his principal subjects. There were landscapes of the Hertfordshire countryside near Standon and later of the coast at Rye Harbour where he had a cottage. As a boy, Le Bas had spent some summers at Le Touquet and thereafter was frequently in France, on painting expeditions to Brittany, Collioure, Nice, and Roquebrune. His preference was for tranquil landscapes and busily peopled views of harbours and seafronts (Rye, Brighton, Dieppe). More representative, however, and among his best works are genre pieces of friends in interiors, of London pubs and restaurants, very much in the tradition of the Camden Town Group. The influence of W. R. Sickert [q.v.] and Vuillard are especially evident in such paintings with their combination of robust portraiture and a spatial complexity brought about by his predilection for patterned surfaces, mirrors, artificial lighting, and the juxtaposing of figures and still life. Friends remember the Vuillardesque atmosphere and furnishing of the sitting-room in his flat in Bedford Square where he lived in London until taking a studio-flat shortly after the war of 1939-45 in Glebe Place, Chelsea, where he lived until his death.

After the death of his father, Le Bas became financially independent, indeed wealthy, and from the later 1930s dates his extraordinary generosity in buying young painters' work as well as his discerning purchase of pictures by the masters of the modern French school—Pissarro, Cézanne, Vuillard, Bonnard (whose 'Bol de Lait', c.1934, Le Bas left to the Tate Gallery), Derain, Braque, and Picasso. But when his collection came to be shown at the Royal Academy ('A Painter's Collection', 1963) it was seen that he had a remarkable eye for the best in modern British painting and there were groups of pictures of the highest quality by Sickert, I. C. Ginner, Sir Matthew A. B. Smith, Dame Ethel Walker [qq.v.], Duncan Grant, and Harold Gilman.

Le Bas did not neglect the young and unknown particularly among painters of the Euston Road School (with some of whom Le Bas shared aesthetic affinities) and those artists who emerged in the 1940s such as Robert Colquhoun and Robert MacBryde, F. John Minton [qq.v.], and John Craxton. Many painters were among his friends. Charles Ginner's professionalism was a continual example to Le Bas; Ginner was to be grateful for the younger painter's support at a time when his reputation had plummeted; they frequently worked together and during the war often dined together in Leicester Square almost every night. Later painter friends included Vanessa Bell [q.v.] and Duncan Grant; Le Bas painted with them and Eardley Knollys in Asolo in 1956, at Roquebrune in 1959, and with Grant and Knollys in Spain in the early 1960s.

In 1939 Le Bas held his last one-man exhibition in England (at the Lefevre Galleries with Mark Gertler, q.v.) and thereafter exhibited annually at the Royal Academy, of which he was elected an associate in 1943 and an RA in 1954. He was elected to the London Group in 1942 (with Lawrence B. Gowing, Frances M. Hodgkins [q.v.], and others). In 1957 he was appointed CBE. Overcoming his distinct aversion to one-man shows, he held two successful exhibitions at the Hammer Galleries, New York, in 1956 and 1961.

Le Bas was a tall, well-built man who wore a neatly trimmed beard for most of his life. He lived comfortably, spending most of his money on travel and pictures; expensive cars were the only sign of his wealth. Although not a social man, he was extremely convivial, giving memorable if somewhat haphazard parties and suppers for his friends in Glebe Place where pictures covered the walls and were stacked against the skirting boards. Intemperate habits considerably reduced the quantity and quality of his painting during his last years though his 1964 'Lady with a Parasol' (private collection, London) is notable for its assured composition and lyrical colour. Above all Le Bas was a colourist owing much to Bonnard and it is as a discriminating, though never slavish, descendant of the modern French school that he is best remembered. He also had something of the witty observation of Degas, Lautrec, and Sickert's London genre scenes—an amusing hat, a striking profile, or a perfectly placed little dog. And such a painting as 'Interior at Long Crichel' (exhibited at the RA, 1952) shows that he could design a contemporary conversation piece on a large scale and retain his personal sense of colour—something rare in modern British painting. Le Bas posed for the figure of Christ in Duncan Grant's 'Crucifixion' at Berwick Church, Sussex (1943), and there is a small portrait by Grant (c.1947, estate of the artist). Good examples of work by Le Bas can be found in the Tate Gallery, London, various provincial galleries, New South Wales, America, and many private collections.

Le Bas was unmarried. He died at Sway in the New Forest 18 November 1966.

[*Catalogue of Modern British Paintings, Drawings and Sculpture* (Tate Gallery, 1964); private information.]   RICHARD SHONE

LEE, SIR (ALBERT) GEORGE (1879-1967), engineer-in-chief of the General Post Office, was born at Conway, North Wales, 24 May 1879, the son of George Henry Payne Lee, a Post Office engineer, and his wife, Maria Agnes Bosmell. He grew up in Conway, leaving there to attend the Collegiate School, Llandudno. Little is known about his activities in the years after he left school.

Lee's lifelong career in telecommunications began when he joined the Post Office Engineering Department as an engineering assistant in London in November 1901, at a time when his father was engineer-in-charge of the Bangor section of the North Wales District of the Post Office. This was a period when the Post Office was integrating the diverse local services, which operated under the general oversight of the National Telephone Company, into a co-ordinated national whole. It was also a time when the application of scientific principles was beginning to produce important improvements and opportunities.

Lee's innate drive and potential began to show itself in this fertile environment, for he made small but significant contributions to the redesign of experimental air-core loading coils on the 'new' London-Birmingham telephone cable. Within five years he had graduated as B.Sc. (London) after part-time study at Northampton Institute, Finsbury Technical College, and King's College, London.

By 1908 Lee had begun to contribute articles of increasing authority to technical journals and to establish his reputation as an expert on telephone transmission theory and practice. During the four years between 1908 and 1912 he experienced both 'field' management and command, and achieved his father's rank of sectional engineer, at Bolton. Returning to the London headquarters in 1912, Lee was responsible for leading teams in the final stages of engineering integration of the national telecommunications systems into the over-all Post Office network. On the outbreak of war in 1914 he was given a commission in the Royal Engineers Signal Service, becoming officer in charge of GHQ Signals Area. Lee received the MC and continued his military service throughout the subsequent years of peace as lieutenant-colonel, Royal Corps of Signals (Supplementary Reserve).

When Lee returned to the Post Office his imagination was captured by the rapidly developing use of radio communications. Throughout the 1920s radio-telephony and -telegraphy for international communication was his interest. In 1921 he acted as British delegate to the Inter-Allied Radio Conference in Paris. In 1921-2 he visited Egypt and India to develop 'wireless services' with Britain. In 1923 he began work on transatlantic telephony in conjunction with the Atlantic Telephony and Telegraphy Company. This was at first experimental and included the building of Rugby Radio Station and, in 1926, the opening of a successful commercial service. From such beginnings developed, in the late 1920s and early 1930s, an Empire-wide communications system of immense strategic and commercial significance.

In December 1931 George Lee was appointed engineer-in-chief, a post he held until his retirement from the Post Office in 1939. These were difficult years, with the aftermath of the depression, the rapidly changing international scene, and the threat of war.

When World War II broke out Lee became director of communications, research, and development, Air Ministry, and in 1944 was appointed senior telecommunications officer in the Ministry of Supply. After the war he was a member of the scientific advisory council of the Ministry of Supply and served as a member of the royal commission on awards to inventors from 1946 to 1955.

In 1929 Lee was vice-president of the Institute of Radio Engineers of America—the first Englishman to hold that honour. He was elected president of the Institution of Electrical Engineers for the year 1937-8. He was appointed OBE in 1927 and a knighthood was conferred upon him in January 1937.

Although he was an internationally recognized electrical engineer, a careful and meticulous administrator, and a man who cared about his fellow engineers, George Lee yet remained unknown as a person to his colleagues and staff. He was accepted and sought-after within the bounds of his official and professional activities but, to those who were even close colleagues, little was ever disclosed of the man, his deeper interests, his family, or his innermost thoughts. Memory and photographs evoke a short, neat, precise man looking out through small circular spectacles, the very confines of which seemed to exclude reference to any matter other than that in hand. Yet it is upon Lee's imaginative, specific judgements that the superstructure of much of today's global communications soundly rests.

In 1903 Lee married Susie Lydia (died 1944), daughter of William Tanner; they had one daughter. In 1950 he married (Ivy) Laura Powell. Lee died at home in Chalfont St. Giles 26 August 1967.

[Post Office records; Journals of the Institution of Electrical Engineers and the Institution of Post Office Electrical Engineers; private information; personal knowledge.]

JAMES H. H. MERRIMAN

LE FANU, SIR MICHAEL (1913-1970), admiral of the fleet, was born in Lindfield, Sussex, 2 August 1913, the son of Commander Hugh Barrington Le Fanu, Royal Navy, and his wife, Georgiana Harriott Kingscote. He came of an Irish Huguenot family and was educated at Bedford School and the Royal Naval College, Dartmouth. After the usual junior officer's training at sea and ashore, he spent three years in destroyers before specializing in gunnery in 1938. After qualifying he was appointed to the staff of the commander-in-chief, Mediterranean, until in October 1939 he left to become gunnery officer of the cruiser *Aurora*. There his character and personality developed to a remarkable degree and he was mentioned in dispatches for his competence and bravery during the Norwegian campaign; and was awarded the DSC for his services in a very successful night action against a heavily escorted Italian convoy in November 1941.

In June 1942 Le Fanu joined the staff of the commander-in-chief, Home Fleet, as gunnery assistant and was most successful in training numerous new and refitted ships. From March 1944 until the end of the year when he was promoted commander he served as gunnery officer of the new battleship *Howe* which joined the Far Eastern Fleet and operated with distinction in the Indian Ocean and the Pacific. As a commander he was appointed liaison officer to the American 3rd and 5th Fleets, a post which he held until the end of the war with Japan. He distinguished himself by his clear thinking, his ability to mix well, and by his humour. With a United States captain he was responsible for the arrangements for the surrender of Japan abroad the battleship *Missouri* on 2 September 1945. Le Fanu was awarded the Legion of Merit in recognition of his services to the US Navy.

It had become clear that Le Fanu was an officer of altogether exceptional ability. He had been granted two years' seniority during the war which enabled him to be promoted commander at the early age of thirty-one; and after the war his appointments were planned to give him the necessary experience for the highest rank.

A spell ashore as experimental commander at the Portsmouth gunnery school was followed by sea service as executive officer of the cruiser *Superb*, where he again showed his gifts of leadership and his ability to get the most out of officers and men. Promoted captain in 1949, he went as naval assistant to the controller: useful experience of Whitehall. Then followed, in 1951, his first command: of the 3rd Training Squadron at Londonderry, where the main activities were anti-submarine, a task which was new to him. In 1952-3 he was employed on special duties in the Admiralty under the chief scientist in order to investigate the many problems of atomic warfare. There followed a year at the Imperial Defence College before taking command in 1954 of HMS *Ganges*, the boys' training establishment at Harwich. He moved next to the aircraft carrier *Eagle* (1957-8), an important command in which he was a great success and quickly gained the respect and confidence of naval aviators. On promotion to rear-admiral in 1958 Le Fanu was a well-qualified officer with experience in almost every sphere of naval activity.

His first appointment as admiral was in the newly created post of director-general, weapons (1958-60), where he found many difficult problems connected with the development of new equipment. His next post was as second-in-command of the Far East station (1960-1), where he gained golden opinions by the flexibility of his thinking and by his mental and physical endurance. In the important appointment of controller of the navy (1961-5), with a seat on the Board of Admiralty, he followed through a radical reorganization of the material departments. He was promoted vice-admiral in 1961 and full admiral in 1965.

In that year Le Fanu was appointed to the command of the three Services in the Middle East with his headquarters at Aden where conditions were most difficult both in the city and in the hinterland. He was able to develop a very high morale at a time of withdrawal and disillusion and the evacuation was conducted with skill and precision.

It had long been clear that Le Fanu would become first sea lord, a post to which he was duly appointed in 1968. It was a time of reductions in the fleet when the decision to phase out the aircraft carriers had already been taken. But by great personal efforts at home and abroad, and by skilled advocacy and intelligent administration in Whitehall, he retained the confidence of the Service and maintained its morale. In October 1970 he should have taken over the post of chief of the defence staff—the highest position in any Service—but illness intervened. He retired at the age of fifty-six with the rank of admiral of the fleet and died in London 28 November 1970. He was appointed CB (1960), KCB (1963), and GCB (1968).

Le Fanu was perhaps the most unusual officer of his generation in the navy. He was an exceptional leader and administrator and he had the knack of getting his point of view across to politicians. Moreover, he was well read and well informed on many subjects, not exclusively naval; besides being witty he had a useful talent for pithy verse. While he could be very firm when necessary he gained most of his aims by sympathy and kindness. Nothing was ever too much trouble and he displayed a deep sense of gratitude to friends. When he had the opportunity he gave much of his time to boys' clubs; for he had the common touch and knew no barriers of rank, or age, or class.

In 1943 Le Fanu married Prudence Grace, daughter of Admiral Sir Vaughan Morgan; they had two sons and one daughter. It was a very happy marriage and his wife took a full share in all social activities—wheeled by Le Fanu or carried up gangways, for she had been crippled by polio when she was a girl. She died in 1980.

[Navy records; personal knowledge.]
PETER GRETTON

LEIGH, VIVIEN (1913-1967), actress, was born Vivian Mary Hartley in Darjeeling, India, 5 November 1913, the only surviving child of Ernest Richard Hartley and his wife, Gertrude Robinson Yackje. She spent the first six years of her childhood in India, where her father was a junior partner in a firm of exchange brokers in Calcutta. Her mother, who was of French-Irish descent, carefully superintended her small daughter's upbringing, and the books and music which early appeared in the nursery had a warm welcome. In 1920 the Hartleys returned to England and placed their daughter in the Convent of the Sacred Heart in Roehampton, where Maureen O'Sullivan was a fellow boarder. Even as a child, Vivian Hartley was a leader in style, and her beautifully chosen clothes not a little coveted. Although bored by conventional school lessons, Vivian Hartley lost no opportunity in absorbing what interested her, and her letters home urged many extra lessons in ballet, piano, and violin. Visits to the theatre fed the child's dramatic instinct, and she took part each term in school productions, making her début as Mustardseed in *A Midsummer Night's Dream*.

When Vivian Hartley was thirteen, her parents extended her education by taking her on a European tour. This decision, which included study in schools and convents in France, Italy, and Bavaria, gave her fluency in three languages, and a liberal experience of great value. She made the utmost use of her five years abroad, visiting the great art galleries, attending opera, concerts, and the theatre, while her natural taste for beauty and quality was nourished by the international fashion designers. When she returned to England at eighteen, she was abundantly prepared to conquer the theatre world. Her clear green-blue eyes, chestnut hair, and delicate features were enhanced by a flawless complexion, and she walked with an assured grace.

Scarcely had she enrolled as a student at the Royal Academy of Dramatic Art, when she announced her engagement to a young barrister, Herbert Leigh Holman. The fashionable wedding which followed in December 1932 at St. James's, Spanish Place, and the establishment of a new pattern of living engrossed her until after the birth of her daughter in October 1933. Characteristically, this was recorded in her diary—'Had a baby—a girl'. Gradually, however, her ambition to become an actress again grew restless, and in August 1934 she interrupted a family yachting cruise to return home, just in case she should be called for a small part in a film. Her reward came in one line in the film *Things are Looking Up*, with (Dame) Cicely Courtneidge. More small parts now began to come her way, and she decided upon the stage name Vivien Leigh.

Less than a year after her entry into films, Vivien Leigh was given the stage opportunity she needed, when casting had been held up for a young actress to play a leading part in *The Mask of Virtue* by Carl Sternheim. Since the first requirement was exceptional beauty,

Vivien Leigh conquered everyone concerned at the first interview. The play, produced at the Ambassadors Theatre in 1935, was not a success, but the young actress was acclaimed 'a star of unusual promise'. It was very much to her credit that the adulation she received did not turn her head, but like the good professional that she wished to be she took the exposure of her inexperience intelligently and began to learn her craft.

Within twenty-four hours of her successful press reviews, Vivien Leigh had signed a five-year contract with (Sir) Alexander Korda [q.v.], but she had to wait another year before Korda was ready to cast her: in *Fire Over England* (1937). The occasion, when it came, was fateful, bringing her into professional relationship with Laurence (later Lord) Olivier. They were soon very much in love. She was already an admirer of his acting, and the four months working daily together on the film was deeply influential in her subsequent development. Aware of her limitations, and working constantly to overcome them, Vivien Leigh eagerly accepted the challenge to play Ophelia to Olivier's Hamlet, when the Old Vic production was invited to appear in Elsinore, Denmark, in June 1937. Under expert tuition, her voice—which had been light and small—gained in strength, and her willingness to learn so won her director's admiration that she was cast for Titania in the Old Vic production of *A Midsummer Night's Dream* at Christmas 1937.

With the offer to play Scarlett O'Hara in the film *Gone with the Wind* (1939), Vivien Leigh saw her first chance to break the image of a Dresden china shepherdess—a comparison she despised. Although she had no sympathy for Scarlett, the actress could recognize 'a marvellous part' when she saw one, and she seized and exploited every facet of her heroine, who gave her both an Oscar award and international status as a film star.

Following the dissolution of their previous marriages, Vivien Leigh and Laurence Olivier were married in California in August 1940. They made the film *Lady Hamilton* (1941), then returned to England—Olivier to service in the navy, and Vivien Leigh to establish a wartime home for them both. She was eager to return to the theatre, making her appearance in *The Doctor's Dilemma* by G. Bernard Shaw [q.v.] at the Haymarket in 1942. This was followed a year later by a three-month tour of North Africa, in which she appeared in a concert party with Beatrice Lillie for the armed services. In a letter home she confesses to 'one of the most exciting and often the most moving experiences I have ever had'.

Vivien Leigh had been an actress for almost ten years before her capacity to carry the action of a play was tested. In Thornton Wilder's *The Skin of Our Teeth* (Phoenix, 1945), as Sabina, she showed a new authority in her work, and evidence that she could now stand unsupported. In 1947 her husband was knighted. In a demanding ten-month tour of Australia and New Zealand with Olivier and the Old Vic Company, in 1948, she had abundant classical opportunities to prepare her for the tragic role of Antigone, in which she made a great impression when they returned to London in 1949. Critics, who had been cautious over her early successes, observed that 'this is a new Miss Leigh altogether', and complimented her on her extended vocal range and 'fanatical force of character'.

The actress was now seen in full maturity; and when she appeared as Blanche in *A Streetcar Named Desire* at the Aldwych in October of the same year she received a storming ovation for a performance of uncommon subtlety, and filled the theatre for eight months. Another Oscar award was given her for her film performance in the same role.

While she appreciated her film successes, it was more important to her to succeed as her husband's equal in the theatre. Her great joy was to act with Olivier, and in spite of her fears that she was not yet ready for the demanding variety of Cleopatra, she accepted the challenge to appear under their joint management in the two plays on alternate nights: *Caesar and Cleopatra* by Shaw and *Antony and Cleopatra* by Shakespeare, at the St. James's, 1951. Under her husband's direction, she gave a performance which satisfied both scholars and the general public.

The Oliviers' first season together at Stratford-upon-Avon in 1955 culminated in a powerfully effective production of *Titus Andronicus* by Peter Brook. In May 1957 this production was selected to represent the Memorial Theatre Company on a prestige tour of European capitals for the British Council. On such occasions, Vivien Leigh appeared in her natural element—a distinguished guest, a gracious hostess, and totally professional. Colleagues paid warm tribute to the unvarying quality of her performances, which remained constant throughout a gruelling social programme. Her tact and consideration for the press were tireless and individual. However, she repeatedly began to suffer from manic phases in which she lost physical control of herself and abused her husband verbally in public. Olivier finally decided that he could no longer tolerate the situation.

In 1957 Vivien Leigh and Laurence Olivier appeared together for the last time, at the Stoll Theatre in *Titus Andronicus*. It was during this run that Vivien Leigh interrupted a debate in the House of Lords to protest—without avail—against the projected demolition of the St. James's Theatre.

The last decade of her life, although marked by the same high level of performance, in plays by Jean Giraudoux and (Sir) Noël Coward, among others, had lost its radiance. Her marriage to Olivier was dissolved in 1960; they had no children. She continued to act, making a new reputation for herself in the musical *Tovarich* in New York, 1963, but her delicate constitution could not sustain a career single-handed; the fire of a shared grand passion for the theatre had gone out. Her career had been interrupted from time to time by nervous collapse when she drove herself too hard and by the tuberculosis which caused her death 8 July 1967, in London, during preparations for her appearance in Edward Albee's *A Delicate Balance*. That night the exterior lights of London's West End theatres were darkened for an hour.

Portraits of Vivien Leigh include an oil-painting (unfinished) by Augustus John, held in a private collection in America; an oil-painting, as Blanche DuBois in *A Streetcar Named Desire*, 1950, by A. K. Lawrence, given to the British Theatre Museum at Leighton House, London; and an oil-painting as Henriette in *The Mask of Virtue* by Diet Edzard, 1935, privately owned.

Vivien Leigh received the knight's cross of the Legion of Honour in 1957.

[Anne Edwards, *Vivien Leigh, A Biography*, 1977; *Who's Who in the Theatre*; Felix Barker, *The Oliviers*, 1953; Alan Dent, *Vivien Leigh—a Bouquet*, 1969; Gwen Robyns, *Light of a Star*, 1968; *Observer*, 16 February and 16 October 1949; private information.] FREDA GAYE

LEIPER, ROBERT THOMSON (1881–1969), professor of helminthology, was born 17 April 1881 in Kilmarnock, Scotland, the eldest of three children of John Leiper, a tailor, and his wife, Jessie Aird. His father's family came of farming stock, their connection with agriculture going back several centuries. John Leiper moved to England after Robert's birth, but succumbed to tuberculosis in 1895. Leiper went to Warwick School where the science taught was minimal, but he was able to work in the Technical College and to attend university extension lectures in Leamington. His initial interest in science was stimulated by visits to Millport Marine Station with his cousin, J. F. Gemmill, FRS, but, on leaving school at the age of sixteen, he had shown no marked ability in any specific scientific discipline. He went for a year to Mason College, Birmingham, where he matriculated in physics, mathematics, English, and Latin.

Leiper then began to study medicine at Glasgow University where his talents soon blossomed. He won a number of medals and prizes and while still in the university was appointed honorary librarian at the Millport Marine Station, experience which anticipated his later unique work in scientific literature. He graduated in medicine in 1904 but dismissed this career in favour of helminthology in which he was to be recognized as the world authority. Within a year of his graduation he was appointed by Sir Patrick Manson [q.v.] as helminthologist at the newly founded London School of Tropical Medicine. With Manson's encouragement he became involved in a long series of expeditions, chiefly in tropical regions, which was to extend over the years to all the continents except Australia, a curious omission being any visit to India. His travels in the tropics enabled him to make a vast collection of helminths from various animals and birds which he brought back to London, for his interest in helminthology was catholic and to him man and other forms of life ranked equally in scientific interest.

In 1905 Leiper went to Accra to study the infection known as 'Guinea worm'. This was caused by a helminth *Dracunculus medinensis* which caused an ulcerated skin condition. The causative vector was supposed to be the water flea, *Cyclops*, which became infected with the helminth from its water habitat when the latter was contaminated from sores on the legs of infected persons; but it was not known how it could infect man. Leiper solved this problem by a convincing experiment. He fed a monkey on bananas to which he had added infected cyclops. After the lapse of several months the monkey became infected, proving that infection is acquired by ingesting cyclops in drinking water.

In 1912 Leiper visited West Africa, to try and find the vector of the disease called Calabar swelling which causes lesions under the skin and also affects the eyes, even leading to blindness. The cause is a filarial worm called *Loa loa* but the method of infection was not known. After extensive experiments he finally incriminated a fly of the genus *Chrysops*.

A major medical problem in Egypt, affecting a third of the population, was the disease schistosomiasis caused by certain helminthic parasites. To study this problem Leiper decided to go to the East, where the condition existed in animals. At this time, 1913, Japanese researchers had shown that one species, *Schistosoma japonicum*, developed certain stages (cercariae) in water snails and that mice exposed to the water of rice fields where the disease was rife became infected. Leiper was able to verify this work by 1914, but, with war imminent, had to return to London, bringing with him mice which had been exposed to water containing cercariae from infected snails. In one of those mice which survived the journey to London male and female schistosome parasites were found. During this sojourn in the East Leiper studied a wide variety of other helminths which added considerably to knowledge of these species.

All this work proved of major assistance as preliminary to what was to prove one of the most important and fruitful of Leiper's achievements. On the outbreak of war in 1914 many British troops were dispatched to Egypt and it was evident that a major hazard would be schistosomiasis. A Bilharzia mission was appointed with Leiper in charge with the temporary rank of lieutenant-colonel. Leiper at once set out to discover molluscs infected with cercariae. The mission established a field station in the village of El Marg in which the children showed nearly 100 per cent of infections with a schistosome, *S. haematobium*. By 1915 an extensive survey of Egyptian snails containing cercariae had been made and there, and subsequently in London, Leiper's studies had elucidated the main details of the life histories of the Egyptian species of parasites causing human schistosomiasis, *S. haematobium* and *S. mansoni*. The vector snails of these two infections were shown to be *Bulinus contortus*, *B. dybowski*, and *B. innesi* causing infections of *S. haematobium*, and *Planorbis boissyi* those of *S. mansoni*. Many animal experiments with mice, guinea pigs, and monkeys proved conclusively the method of infection in humans through contact with water contaminated with cercariae. This work of course indicated the methods of prevention of the disease which could be applied for the protection of troops and Leiper was able to make the appropriate recommendations. There was some controversy over whether there were actually the two species of schistosoma mentioned, the criteria being differences in the egg of the parasite. That there are in fact two species Leiper proved conclusively as the result of experiments.

Leiper's interests in his work were divided between the practical study of the life cycles of helminths and the taxonomy of the group. In 1919-21 he was director of the prosectorium of the Zoological Society of London. This formed a close link with his place of work at the London School of Hygiene and tropical Medicine where he became director of parasitology (1924-45) and gave him unrivalled opportunities for his studies in comparative zoology. In the university of London he became

professor of helminthology in 1919. In 1923 he founded the *Journal of Helminthology*.

In 1925 Leiper acquired Winches Farm near St. Albans which became the Institute of Agricultural Parasitology. Small as this unit was its importance may be judged from the fact that no fewer than four of those who worked there were elected FRS. After Leiper's retirement from the London School in 1945 it became the field station of the School, a status it already had in fact if not in name. In 1929 Leiper founded the Commonwealth Bureau of Helminthology which he administered at Winches Farm and, after 1945, at the White House in St. Albans. On retirement as director in 1958 he remained as consultant helminthologist.

Leiper was a soft-spoken man, whose quiet manner gave no indication of the determination of his character. When engaged in controversy with colleagues, a not infrequent occurrence, if opposition was apparently complete, he was often able to get his way almost without his opponent being aware of it, for he had a subtle and devious mind. He was intensely loyal to those he considered worthy and performed kindly actions to individuals who remained quite oblivious of the source of their good fortune. In his scientific work, as well as in administration of his department and of the affairs of the London School of Hygiene and Tropical Medicine, he was far-seeing and his advice at times prevented what might otherwise have been difficult situations.

Leiper proceeded D.Sc. of Glasgow in 1911 and MD in 1917 with the Bellahouston gold medal. He was elected FRS in 1923 and FRCP in 1936, and appointed CMG in 1941. Among the distinctions he received were the Mary Kingsley medal of the Liverpool School of Tropical Medicine and the Bernhard Nocht medal from the Tropeninstitut of Hamburg. A long list of zoological names honours his work.

In 1908 Leiper married a Welsh girl, Ceinwen Saron Jones (died 1966), a dentist; they had one son and two daughters. Leiper died in St. Albans 21 May 1969.

[P. C. C. Garnham in *Biographical Memoirs of Fellows of the Royal Society*, vol. xvi, 1970; private information; personal knowledge.]   H. E. SHORTT

LEITH-ROSS, SIR FREDERICK WILLIAM (1887-1968), civil servant and authority-on finance, was born in Mauritius 4 February 1887, the younger son of Frederick William Arbuthnot Leith-Ross, of the Oriental Bank in Mauritius, and his wife, Sina Van Houten. On his father's side he was the descendant of two old Aberdeenshire families. His mother was Dutch, her father, Sam van Houten, having been prominent in the political life of Holland and for a long time the leader of the Liberal Party there. Before he was three Leith-Ross and his brother were brought home to Scotland to live with their paternal grandfather, John Leith-Ross, at Arnage Castle in north-east Aberdeenshire.

In 1898 he won a scholarship to Merchant Taylors' School and in December 1904 he won the Warner exhibition and an honorary scholarship at Balliol. He got first classes both in honour moderations and *literae humaniores* (1907 and 1909) and had hoped to stay up for a fifth year, read law, and enter the bar. The extension of his exhibition for a fifth year depended upon college approval and, as Leith-Ross had had some minor troubles with authority, it was indicated that this might not be given. He accordingly sat the Civil Service examination and passed top. His first choice was the Indian Civil Service but, owing to defective eyesight, the medical examiners disqualified him for India. He was then offered a vacancy in the Treasury. He was assigned to the finance division, the head of which was John (later Lord) Bradbury [q.v.]. Fate, as much as choice, thus played an important part in Leith-Ross's future career.

After two years' departmental employment Leith-Ross was appointed a private secretary to the prime minister, H. H. Asquith (later first Earl of Oxford and Asquith). This appointment gave him an invaluable insight into public affairs at the very centre. It also started a personal friendship with both Asquith and his wife which, in the case of the latter, lasted for over thirty years. For Asquith himself Leith-Ross had the greatest admiration.

In November 1913 Leith-Ross returned to the Treasury on promotion to first-class clerk (now principal). This, in pre-1914 days, was rapid promotion even in the Treasury. He was assigned to the third division which, amongst other matters, dealt with Civil Service pay. As the war developed this increased in importance and Leith-Ross showed his skill as a negotiator. He also found time to edit *Frederick Goodyear: Letters and Remains, 1887-1917* (1920).

After a short time with the Cabinet Secretariat Leith-Ross, in March 1920, was invited by Bradbury to join him in Paris as British member of the Finance Board of the Reparation Commission. This was his introduction to international finance and he spent five frustrating but otherwise happy years in Paris. He liked France and he was educated in an appreciation of good food and wine. In the main the work comprised conference after conference attempting to resolve the insoluble problems of reparations. The Commission was disbanded in February 1925 and Leith-Ross returned to the Treasury to act under Sir Otto Niemeyer as deputy controller of finance with special responsibility for foreign debts and credits, including reparations and exchange questions.

In 1928 Leith-Ross suffered a severe internal haemorrhage, from which he took several months to recover. About the same time Niemeyer left the Treasury for the Bank of England. The top posts at the Treasury were reorganized and, at times, Leith-Ross found the new arrangements frustrating.

Early in 1929 Leith-Ross spent some months in Egypt negotiating a settlement of various post-war claims against that country. Later that year he accompanied the chancellor of the Exchequer, Philip (later Viscount) Snowden [q.v.], for whom he had a high regard, to the Hague Conference which was considering the Young plan. He played a major role in the discussions behind the scenes. He was also much involved in the 1931 financial crisis.

In March 1932 Leith-Ross was appointed chief economic adviser, a post which was misnamed, but which carried permanent-secretary status. His existing functions continued but he added to them the duty of acting as British representative on a number of international bodies. For the next two years the preparatory committee for the World Economic Conference, discussions with the United States on war debts, and with the Germans on German payments, bulked largely in his activities.

Then came a task which brought him considerable publicity. Early in 1935 China approached the British Government for a loan of £20 million to support her financial and economic position which had been undermined by the American silver policy. The other 'consortium' powers, the United States, France, and Japan, were unwilling to be associated with an investigation of the position on the spot and in August 1935 Leith-Ross left for China, via Japan. Except in a few financial circles his activities were not welcomed by the Japanese. Nevertheless he worked out with the Chinese authorities a plan for changing their currency from the silver dollar to paper. In the short term the currency reform was a success. To what extent, if any, this success affected Japan's attitude to and action against China is difficult to say.

In 1938 Leith-Ross negotiated a revised German payments agreement to ensure the service of the Austrian guaranteed loans and in 1939 he had economic and financial discussions with the Romanians and the Greeks. He was not a critic of Chamberlain over Munich, but he regarded the Polish guarantee as unwise because it could not be implemented in practice.

With the outbreak of war in 1939 Leith-Ross became director-general of the Ministry of Economic Warfare. He was no longer a negotiator with a small team of advisers. He became head of a heterogeneous department, staffed from many sources and with a wide variety of functions. Initially there were arrangements to be negotiated with Allied and neutral Governments. This Leith-Ross liked doing but, as time passed, his duties became more those of dealing with complaints and fobbing off grievances. Moreover, with the destructive side of economic warfare he was temperamentally unsympathetic. He was, therefore, not sorry in 1942 when Hugh (later Lord) Dalton [q.v.], the minister, asked him to take over general charge of post-war economic policy questions, constructive work which he liked. He took a large part in the preparatory work for the United Nations Relief and Rehabilitation Administration and he became a deputy director-general in its European regional office and later chairman of the European committee of its Council (1945-6). In 1946 was published his *UNRRA in Europe*.

In March 1946 Leith-Ross accepted a five-year appointment as governor of the National Bank of Egypt. Politically these were difficult years, but Leith-Ross's relations with Egyptian ministers and officials were, in general, friendly. His principal problem was Egypt's sterling balance. His other main concern was with the Bank's 'nationalization'. This came about in a compromise form just as Leith-Ross's term of office was expiring.

On his return to England in 1951, Leith-Ross was invited to become a director, first of the National Discount Company and then of the National Provincial Bank. Within a year he became deputy chairman of the latter (1952). Shortly afterwards he joined the board of the Standard Bank, eventually becoming director.

In many ways the next fifteen years were the years of his working life which he most enjoyed. Directorship of the Standard Bank involved much travelling which he had always liked. He felt that his work was constructive and forward looking. He was associated with colleagues whom he respected and who liked and respected him. His financial activities as a civil servant had given him a valuable background on which to draw and, possessing a first-class memory, he was able to do this. At board level he was a cogent speaker whose opinions, because of their inherent wisdom, carried great weight. His pleasant sense of humour was a valuable asset, both as a chairman and as a negotiator. In appearance he was a tall, erect,

somewhat heavily built man, with a pleasant twinkle in his eye which could be discerned even through his glasses. He dressed neatly and well and remained faithful to a pocket-watch and chain.

He received many honours: CB (1925), KCB (1933), KCMG (1930), and GCMG (1937). In the last few years of his life he wrote an autobiography, *Money Talks* (1968). In this he gave his personal views on monetary policy over the period from 1920, which clearly sometimes differed from the official and accepted opinions.

Leith-Ross married in 1912 Prudence, daughter of R. J. Staples; they had one son and three daughters. Leith-Ross died in the Isle of Man 22 August 1968.

[Sir Frederick Leith-Ross, *Money Talks* (autobiography), 1968; private information; personal knowledge.]   HAROLD PARKER

LETT, SIR HUGH, baronet (1876-1964), surgeon, was born at Waddingham, Lincolnshire, 17 April 1876, the son of Richard Alfred Lett, MD, who had graduated in Dublin in 1869 and subsequently went into practice in Lincolnshire, and his wife, Bithiah, daughter of William Appleford. He was the eldest of eight children, one of whom, Phyllis, became known as a contralto, and another, Eva, principal of Ripon Diocesan Training College. Lett was educated at Marlborough College; in later years he became a governor and president of the Marlburian Club. He started as a preclinical student at Leeds, then entered the London Hospital in 1896. He was a dedicated student: qualified MB, B.Ch. (Victoria) at Leeds in 1899, took the diplomas of the Royal Colleges in 1901, and was elected FRCS in 1902. In his earlier years he was active in the students' union as president of the cricket and fencing clubs. After qualification he held most of the resident appointments; in 1902 he became surgical registrar; in 1905 assistant surgeon to the hospital; in 1909-12 surgical tutor; and in 1915 full surgeon.

Lett served as lecturer in anatomy and clinical and operative surgery. His writings covered many subjects: in 1905 he published a study of ninety-nine cases of advanced breast cancer treated by removal of the ovaries, a portent of things to come. Although a general surgeon, his main interest was in urology and for many years he was in charge of the hospital's urological department. He was an excellent teacher and always showed great courtesy to his patients and the nurses; but in the operating theatre he had a tendency to irritability which seemed out of character.

During the war of 1914-18 Lett was attached to the Anglo-American Hospital at Wimereux

(1914–15) and to the Belgian Field Hospital at Furnes (1915), and was a major in the Royal Army Medical Corps. For his services he was appointed CBE in 1920.

He retired from active surgical practice in December 1934, becoming consulting surgeon to the London Hospital. He was now free to exercise his great abilities as a medical statesman. On the council (1927–43), he was president of the Royal College of Surgeons for three years from 1938, a period spoiled by the anxieties of the war. He took a personal interest to safeguard the valuable possessions of the College and was later associated with the rebuilding of the Hunterian Museum which had been destroyed in an air raid. He was a Hunterian trustee in 1942–62 and chairman in 1955–9. In 1936 he delivered the Bradshaw lecture on 'Early Diagnosis of Renal Tuberculosis' and in 1942 the Thomas Vicary lecture on 'Anatomy at the Barbers Surgeons' Hall'.

Lett was created a baronet in 1941, and in 1947 appointed KCVO in recognition of his work for the King Edward's Hospital Fund of which he had been an honorary secretary since 1941. He was the first chairman of the Staff College for Ward Sisters established by the Fund.

During the war he was chairman of the Committee for the Allocation of Medical Manpower. In 1946–8 he was president of the British Medical Association at a time when the National Health Service was coming into being and he gave the presidential address on 'Medicine in the Post-War World'. He was also president of the sections of surgery and urology of the Royal Society of Medicine (1932–3) and of the Hunterian Society (1917), and an honorary fellow of both. In 1911 he became a liveryman of the Worshipful Society of Apothecaries, and a freeman of the City of London, and played an active part in its activities. He joined the court in 1931 and was master in 1937–8. He was also a Masonic grand officer. He received an honorary DCL from Durham and an honorary Sc.D. from Cambridge.

He was a tall, thin man of serious demeanour, kindly and affable, and without any affectation. He was meticulous in all his professional dealings, and was an admirable committee chairman with a wealth of experience and common sense. He was interested in music and himself became an accomplished cellist. In his latter years his eyesight failed; he died at his home at Walmer in Kent 19 July 1964.

In 1906 he married Helen (died 1963), daughter of the famous surgeon (Sir) Buckstone Browne; they had three daughters.

Portraits by Sir James Gunn are in the possession of the Society of Apothecaries and the Royal College of Surgeons.

[*The Times*, 20 July 1964; *Lives of the Fellows, Royal College of Surgeons*, 1970; *British Medical Journal*, 21 April 1956; *Lancet*, 25 July 1964; *London Hospital Gazette*, vol. lxvii, no. 4, October 1964; private information; personal knowledge.]

A. M. A. MOORE

LEWIS, CLIVE STAPLES (1898–1963), writer and scholar, was born in Belfast 29 November 1898, the younger son of Albert James Lewis, a local solicitor, and his wife, Florence (Flora) Augusta, daughter of the Revd Thomas Hamilton. She had been a graduate of Queen's College in mathematics and logic. Lewis's mother died when he was nine, whereupon he was sent first to Wynyard House, a moribund preparatory school in Watford, and later (briefly) to Campbell College, Belfast, where he came under the influence of one excellent master, J. A. McNeill, who introduced him to Arnold's poetry. For reasons of health he was moved early in 1911 to a preparatory school at Malvern, whence he entered Malvern College with a scholarship. His years at these schools were not happy but at the College he discovered the riches of Celtic and Norse literature and made a friend, Arthur Greeves, with whom he was to correspond for nearly fifty years. In September 1914 he was sent for private tuition to W. T. Kirkpatrick, a former headmaster of Lurgan College, then living at Great Bookham, Surrey; 'Kirk's' fixed regimen and acutely logical mind exerted a lasting influence. With him Lewis read Latin and Greek authors, but otherwise followed his own inclinations, relishing particularly works of William Morris and George Macdonald [qq.v.], with results that can be traced in his own poems and romances. In December 1916 he won a classical scholarship to University College, Oxford, but when he went up in April 1917 despite having failed responsions, it was to train in the university Officers' Training Corps. He was gazetted to the Somerset Light Infantry, crossing to France in November 1917, and was wounded in the battle of Arras in April 1918; his convalescence lasted until the end of hostilities. In January 1919 he returned to Oxford to read for classical honour moderations. During his convalescence had begun his intimate and somewhat perplexing friendship with Mrs J. K. Moore, the mother of an Officers' Training Corps friend who had been killed in the war; with her and her daughter he set up house in Oxford, later moving to The Kilns, Headington Quarry, on the outskirts of Oxford. There he attended to Mrs Moore's wants until her death in 1951, and he continued to occupy the house until his own death.

In Oxford a small college club, the Martlets, encouraged his literary and dialectical bent; he twice met W. B. Yeats [q.v.], and formed lasting links with Owen Barfield, who was to become his solicitor and philosopher-critic. He began a long narrative poem eventually published as *Dymer* (1926) under the pseudonym Clive Hamilton. In 1920 he obtained a first class in classical honour moderations, in 1921 the Chancellor's English essay prize with an essay on Optimism, in 1922 a first in *literae humaniores*, and in 1923 achieved the same class in English language and literature. His attempts at fellowships being at first unsuccessful, he took a temporary post as lecturer in philosophy in his own college, but in 1925 Magdalen elected him as a fellow and tutor in English language and literature, a post he held for nearly thirty years. Throughout this period he had rooms in New Buildings, where initially he taught Anglo-Saxon, philosophy, and political theory as well as English literature. To live on the same staircase as J. A. Smith [q.v.] was, he said, a liberal education; and at Magdalen also he benefited from acquaintance with C. C. J. Webb and C. T. Onions [qq.v.]. But the main influences on his thinking at this time were the writings of Samuel Alexander and G. K. Chesterton [qq.v.]. From agnosticism he moved, almost reluctantly, to theism and finally committed himself to the Christian position—a movement reflected in his first allegorical work, *The Pilgrim's Regress* (1933), written during a fortnight's holiday in Northern Ireland in 1932. It was in his Magdalen rooms that a few friends, known as the Inklings, met weekly over a long period; amongst them were J. R. R. Tolkien, H. V. D. Dyson, Nevill Coghill, and R. E. Havard, who became Lewis's doctor. They were joined in 1939 by Charles Williams [q.v.] with whom Lewis had strong affinities.

Several years of wide reading in medieval literature bore fruit in *The Allegory of Love* (1936), which combined a study of medieval allegory with a new account of 'courtly love'; the chapters on Chaucer, Gower, and Spenser marked the emergence of a powerful and attractive critic; the work gained Lewis the Hawthornden prize and he was soon in demand as a speaker and lecturer. *A Preface to 'Paradise Lost'* (1942) was based on lectures given at the University College of North Wales in 1941, and *The Abolition of Man* on the Riddell lectures given at Durham University in 1943; the former retains its value as an introduction to epic in general; the latter presented an indictment of certain methods of teaching English then gaining ground. *The Screwtape Letters* (1942), an imaginary correspondence between an experienced devil and a subordi-nate, appealed to a different and far wider public, as did a series of broadcast talks on Christian topics which began in August 1941 and were later published. Lewis became internationally well known, but he continued to teach at Oxford, where in 1942 he founded the Socratic club, a Christian discussion group of which he was president until 1954. By the end of the war he had completed a trilogy of allegorical science fiction books involving planetary journeys but with some scenes (such as the college meeting in the opening chapters of *That Hideous Strength*, 1945) set in the contemporary world. A fourth, unfinished, interplanetary story, *The Dark Tower*, was published posthumously in 1977. A retelling of the myth of Cupid and Psyche under the title *Till We Have Faces* (1956) was more subtle but less popular. The Narnia series of seven children's tales Lewis began in 1948; they revealed a new facet of his imaginative gifts, recognized by the award of the Carnegie medal for *The Last Battle* (1956).

Despite his popularity as a lecturer to Oxford undergraduates his claim to the Merton chair of English literature was passed over in 1946, when his evangelical commitments were thought by some of his colleagues to be too pronounced; and similar considerations weighed against him when he stood for the chair of poetry in 1950, though the list of his supporters then was almost embarrassingly impressive. In 1944 he had given the Clark lectures in Cambridge and these provided materials for his most substantial book, *English Literature in the Sixteenth Century* (1954). It is a brilliant and genial work of criticism on the grand scale, providing, amongst many other things, a salutary reappraisal of humanism, and glowing pages on Hooker and Spenser. It made him the choice for the chair in English medieval and Renaissance literature established at Cambridge in that year, but he had to be persuaded to accept it, and even when he migrated to Magdalene College, which had immediately offered him a fellowship, he regularly returned (by train) to Oxford for week-ends and vacations; Magdalen (in 1956) and University College (in 1959) elected him to honorary fellowships and he kept his Oxford friendships in good repair. But an attempt to entice him back when the Merton chair again fell vacant came to nothing and it was for Cambridge audiences that he reshaped one of his standard Oxford courses on medieval thought and belief into *The Discarded Image* (1964) which, like two collections of studies, was published posthumously. Freedom from tutorial tasks gave him leisure to complete two other critical works, and a stream of papers and manuals on Christian topics flowed from his pen (he never typed) until shortly before his death. He had resigned his chair a few months earlier, when Magdalene made him an honorary fellow. He was elected Gollancz prizeman in 1937 and FBA in 1955; among his honorary degrees were DD (St. Andrews, 1946) and D.Litt. (Laval, Quebec, 1952). He declined appointment as CBE.

In 1956 Lewis married Helen Joy Davidman of New York in the Oxford register office, an expedient to avoid extradition for her and her two sons by her former marriage to William Lindsay Gresham. An illness of hers that seemed to be mortal led to the repetition of the ceremony in Anglican form in the Churchill Hospital in 1957. A year later she unexpectedly recovered and there was a halcyon interval before she died in 1960. Under the pseudonym N. W. Clerk, Lewis poignantly set down his sense of loss in *A Grief Observed* (1961).

The clarity and forthrightness of his critical and theological writings, his Johnsonian command of forceful apopthegm, apt quotation, and homely comparisons, his ready wit (which sometimes appeared in contributions to *Punch*), a general humanity which showed itself in a relish for talk in a country pub—all these qualities made for his wide appeal. All his critical work was compelling, based as it was on wide reading and enthusiasm, but it also invited criticism from other scholars. His powers as a disputant, which first showed themselves in *The Personal Heresy* (with E. M. W. Tillyard, 1939), made him a formidable defender of Christian values at a time when perplexities and ambiguities flourished. He had not only an imaginative understanding of morality but also, as a former pupil wrote, 'a poet's gift for visual and even tactile splendours and a wickedly accurate and entertaining eye for human frailty' (*Tablet*, 30 November 1963). The strain of 'fine masculine cheerfulness' which he found in Scott and Dunbar is evident in most of his work. *The Problem of Pain* (1940) reveals another side of his nature; and at least two of the later books, *The Four Loves* (1960) and *An Experiment in Criticism* (1961), show a perceptiveness and delicacy which some earlier readers had not expected to find. He lived more in the world of literature and the imagination than in the technological age; for diversion he preferred to read Kipling or Rider Haggard rather than modern poets or novelists. He showed little interest in college, university, or public affairs, and if he looked at *The Times* it was only to do the crossword. Impatient of political nostrums, he had a firm belief in ceremony and order, but he was no ritualist. The Ulster elements in his make-up showed in certain Protestant and individualist attitudes which distinguished him from

Chesterton, to whose role as lay apostle he may be said to have succeeded. For the 'cult of culture' he had a profound distaste. He was sometimes taken for a farmer, or a butcher. Fond of walking but not of travel, after 1918 he only once crossed the Channel, and that was when he took a brief holiday with his wife in Greece and the Aegean in 1960. Lewis died at The Kilns after a series of painful and wearing illnesses, 22 November 1963. He was buried at Holy Trinity church, Headington, Oxford.

Assessments of his character and achievements were attempted by a varied group of friends and pupils in *Light on C. S. Lewis* (1966). In the United States admiration for his Christian writings attained the dimensions of a cult, and it is from America that anthologies and similar works (including several dissertations) have largely come. The most serious study is by G. Kranz (Bonn, 1974, with a full bibliography).

[C. S. Lewis, *Surprised by Joy: the Shape of my Early Life*, 1955; W. H. Lewis (ed.), *Letters of C. S. Lewis*, 1966; C. S. Kilby and D. Gilbert, *Images of C. S. Lewis*, 1973; Helen Gardner in *Proceedings* of the British Academy, vol. li, 1965; Roger Lancelyn Green and Walter Hooper, *C. S. Lewis, a Biography*, 1974; Humphrey Carpenter, *The Inklings*, 1978; Walter Hooper, ed., *They Stand Together: the Letters of C. S. Lewis to Arthur Greeves (1914–1963)*, 1979; personal knowledge.]   J. A. W. BENNETT

LEWIS, JOHN SPEDAN (1885–1963), shopkeeper and industrial reformer, was born in London 22 September 1885, the elder son of John Lewis, a Somersetshire draper who from 1864 built up a successful retail business in Oxford Street, and his wife, Eliza, daughter of Thomas Baker, draper, of Bridgwater. She had been one of the earliest students at the college in Hitchin opened by Emily Davies [q.v.], which became Girton College, and was a teacher at Bedford High School before her marriage.

Spedan Lewis won a Queen's entrance scholarship to Westminster School, where he studied classics as a day boy. On his nineteenth birthday he joined his father in the Oxford Street shop. Declining an invitation to stand for Parliament as a Liberal in 1910, he devoted the rest of his life to shopkeeping and to a farsighted practical experiment in the reform of industrial organization. He believed that the rewards of capital should be limited and that the true profits of industry should go to the workers. Dividends on capital should be fixed and limited and working owners or senior employees should be content with professional earnings. But he was worried at the effect of distributing the profits to the workers on the capital needs of an expanding business. Apparently unaware of earlier experiments in profit-sharing and co-ownership, Lewis first conceived a solution to his problem in the autumn of 1910 when he was recovering from a serious riding accident which left his health permanently impaired. His concept was that residual profits should be distributed annually to the employees in proportion to their pay in the form of non-voting shares carrying a fixed dividend which they would be free to sell without affecting the control of the business.

Lewis began putting these ideas into effect in 1914, when he took charge of the unsuccessful drapery business of Peter Jones Ltd. in Chelsea which his father had acquired some years earlier. After disagreements with his father, he exchanged his profitable partnership in the Oxford Street shop for sole control of Peter Jones in 1916. To his father's trading principles of honesty, good value, and wide assortment, he added close control of merchandizing and expenses together with energetic experiment. In 1920 he secured formal reconstruction of the company, whereby the few outside holders of ordinary capital accepted a fixed dividend, and he distributed some preference shares to the employees.

Owing to Lewis's ill health and difficult trading conditions, profit-sharing then lapsed until 1924 when Lewis was reconciled with his father and resumed his partnership at Oxford Street. He became the sole partner in this firm on his father's death in 1928, having by agreement acquired the share of his younger brother Oswald (1887–1966), Conservative member of Parliament for the Colchester division of Essex (1929–45). He amalgamated the two shops to form a single business organized as an open partnership for the benefit of the employees. Lewis formed the public company, John Lewis Partnership Ltd., in 1929 when the two shops had fewer than 2,000 employees—or partners, as they were called— and annual sales under £2 million. He transferred all the equity capital of this company to trustees on behalf of the employees, by means of an interest-free loan to the business of nearly a million pounds, to be repaid gradually out of profits.

Under Lewis's dynamic management the business expanded rapidly, while sharing its profits as he had planned. He achieved considerable improvements in efficiency: he established central buying and detailed budgetary control long before these techniques were generally used in retail distribution. In 1950 he completed a second and irrevocable trust settlement under which all the equity of the business is permanently held by trustees on behalf of the employees. When Lewis retired as chairman in 1955 the Partnership had over 12,000 members and annual sales of more than £25 million.

Lewis aimed to share with his partners not only the profits but also the knowledge and power which go with ownership. He took pains to ensure good communications between workers at all levels; and published weekly from 1918 a house journal which gave full information about the business and also provided an unusual additional means of communication by printing, with official comments, anonymous letters from readers. He did not aim to share the decision-making functions of management; he provided for democracy in industry by making management accountable to the managed, on the basis of a formal constitution specifying the rights and responsibilities of all members of the Partnership. Largely by the force of his personality, he attracted to his Partnership a wide variety of recruits from other occupations. One of five women graduates he engaged for senior positions became his wife in 1923. She was Sarah Beatrice Mary (died 1953), daughter of Percy Hunter, of Teddington, Middlesex, a graduate of Somerville College, Oxford, later for many years deputy chairman of the company. They had two sons and a daughter.

Lewis was an emotional, combative, and outspoken man, often appearing arbitrary and domineering. He had tremendous nervous energy and drove his colleagues hard, yet retained the admiration and affection of most of them by his idealism, infectious enthusiasm, and sheer charm of manner. He had a deep sympathy with the underdog. His single-minded dedication to the development of a real sense of common interest among the ever-increasing number of workers of all kinds in his Partnership carried it through the stresses of the early years when so many, inside and outside, were both sceptical and distrustful.

He was basically a philosopher, looking for the underlying 'nature of things' in everything he did and particularly in all his dealings with people. He had wide-ranging interests and a versatile, sensitive, and unconventional mind. He had an abiding love of the classics and was president of the Classical Association in 1956–7. He was devoted to natural history, particularly entomology and botany, and served on the council of the Zoological Society. At his country estate, at Longstock in Hampshire (which subsequently became the property of the John Lewis Partnership) he created beautiful water-gardens and an arboretum. He played chess and golf, enjoyed music and the arts, read voraciously, and, above all, loved to talk. He had a fine sense of the dramatic and was strikingly impressive as a public speaker, although he seldom spoke at gatherings of any importance outside the business. He published *Partnership for All* in 1948 and *Fairer Shares* in 1954.

He died at Longstock 21 February 1963. A portrait by Anthony Devas and a bronze head by Benno Elkan are in the possession of the John Lewis Partnership.

[Private information; personal knowledge.]
BERNARD MILLER

LEY, HENRY GEORGE (1887-1962), organist, pianist, and composer, was born 30 December 1887, the eldest child of the Revd Gerald Lewis Henry Ley, rector of Chagford, Newton Abbot, Devonshire, and his wife, Beatrice Hayter-Hames, who came from a family long settled in that area. Through both his parents, Henry Ley had connections with many Devon dynasties—a background which deeply influenced him.

Musical talent, displayed at an early age, came to the notice of Sir Walter Parratt [q.v.], who admitted Ley in 1896 to the choir of St. George's, Windsor, where he was soon recognized as something of a prodigy. From Windsor and its admirable disciplines Ley went as their first music scholar in January 1903 to Uppingham. He left in December 1904 with an exhibition to the Royal College of Music and in 1906 he won the much-coveted organ scholarship at Keble College, Oxford, of which he later became an honorary fellow.

In 1909, to everybody's astonishment, Ley was chosen, whilst still an undergraduate, to be organist of Christ Church, Oxford. The appointment and the dean, Dr T. B. Strong [q.v.], who made it, were severely criticized; but the decision proved to be justified, and Ley's early years at the House firmly established his reputation as a great organist. He proceeded to the degrees of MA (1913) and D.Mus. (1919). From 1923 to 1926 he was choragus of the university.

His fiery rhythms and passionate feeling were exciting innovations in English organ-style. Ley was judged even finer as a solo-pianist, and when (Sir) W. G. Alcock, himself a master of the instrument, called him the Paderewski of the organ, he was referring partly to the pianistic element in Ley's playing. This executive skill was achieved despite a malformation of Ley's left foot. In addition to his Christ Church appointment, from 1916 to 1918 Ley was precentor of St. Peter's College, Radley, and from 1919 to 1941 was on the teaching staff (organ) of the Royal College of Music.

In 1917 Ley married Evelyn Mary (died 1946), daughter of the Revd Charles Abel Heurtley, vicar of Binsey: she was a poet whose lyrics inspired her husband in many imaginative settings. But Oxford after 1919 had seen great changes, and Ley began to feel that he had completed his work there. In 1926, after refusing several important invitations, he went as precentor to Eton College and curtailed his recital activities. From that time, apart from the valuable effect of his work in Eton, his influence was chiefly felt in the Royal College of Music, where he became a venerated figure.

In 1941, during an air raid, Ley's beautiful home in Eton was destroyed with all its contents—a disaster from which he and his wife never fully recovered. They stayed at Eton only three more years before moving to Devon in 1945 for what might have been a happy retirement. But Evelyn Ley, already ill, did not survive the change, and Ley's own health began to deteriorate in the comparative isolation of country life. In 1949 a happier time began when he married Mary Elizabeth, daughter of the Revd Charles Walford of Ascot-under-Wychwood, whose loving care sustained him until his death. There were no children of either marriage. After his retirement in 1945 Ley continued to examine for the Royal College of Organists and to give recitals. He was president of that College in 1933 and 1934 and of the Incorporated Association of Organists in 1952 and 1953. He became FRCM (1928), honorary FRCO (1920), and honorary RAM (1942).

Throughout his career Ley was an active composer of church and organ music, short choral pieces, and songs: some of his anthems enjoyed wide popularity and were sung in many countries of the English-speaking world. His style, not highly individual, was based on the English cathedral tradition and the work of his teachers, Sir C. V. Stanford and Charles Wood [qq.v.]. His music was always well composed, expressive, and eminently effective, reaching its best level in the early songs, which are imaginative and beautifully laid out. It was of them that Sir C. Hubert H. Parry [q.v.] wrote 'your songs . . . go right to the fore-front of any English songs . . . in modern times'. To this Dictionary Ley contributed the notices of Basil Harwood and Sir (Henry) Walford Davies.

Ley was a modest, generous, and much-loved man—with a character whose substance was enriched by wide interests outside his own art. He had an exuberant joy in life and a keen appreciation of the quirks of personality which he observed among his fellow-men. He loved England and knew intimately her byways and village churches, as well as her cathedrals and mountains. Devoted as he was to steam railways and the men who ran them, the proud moments of his life were not only his playing at coronations, but also, and perhaps even more, his journey in the driver's cab of a west-country express train. His musical achievements touched two generations and are still important: his human and personal influence was even more unforgettable and far-reaching.

Ley died at his home in Metcombe, Ottery St. Mary, 24 August 1962.

[*The Times*, 27 August and 6 September 1962; private information; personal knowledge.]   THOMAS ARMSTRONG

LIDDELL HART, SIR BASIL HENRY (1895-1970), military historian and strategist. [See HART.]

LILLICRAP, SIR CHARLES SWIFT (1887-1966), naval constructor, was born at Ford, Devonport, 12 November 1887, the eldest of the five sons of Charles Lillicrap, of Hastings, naval constructor in the Royal Dockyard, Devonport, and his wife, Selina Jane Chapman. He received his early education at Stoke School, Devonport, and entered HM Dockyard School, Devonport, as a shipwright apprentice at the age of fourteen. After four years he was awarded a cadetship in naval construction in 1906. After one year at the Royal Naval Engineering College, Keyham, he completed the three year course in naval architecture and ship construction at the Royal Naval College, Greenwich, passing out in 1910 with a first class professional certificate.

His first appointment in the Royal Corps of Naval Constructors in 1910 was to Devonport dockyard and in February 1913 to the *Superb* for a year's sea service. In 1911 he married (Harriet) Minnie (died 1961), a schoolteacher, the daughter of Richard Shears, of Plymouth. They had two sons and one daughter.

In March 1914 Lillicrap was appointed to the Naval Construction Department of the Admiralty, where he was engaged on the design of the Royal Sovereign class of battleships and subsequently on a group of large monitors, minesweepers, and other craft. It was during this period that he served as secretary to the landship committee under the chairmanship of the director of naval construction (Sir) Eustace Tennyson-d'Eyncourt [q.v.]; it was from the work of this committee that the first tanks were produced for the army. For this Lillicrap was appointed MBE in 1918.

In 1917 he had assumed responsibility for cruiser design on promotion to constructor and in 1921 was responsible for the design of the cruiser-minelayer *Adventure*. In the same year he was appointed lecturer in naval architecture at the Royal Naval College, Greenwich. This was the time of the Washington Treaty (1922),

which imposed rigorous limitations of tonnage and gun calibre, and Lillicrap was responsible for the design of the 10,000 ton 8-inch gun cruisers of the Kent class. He received the Board of Admiralty's commendation for his work on this design. He was responsible for subsequent designs of variants of the County class, including the *Surrey* and *Northumberland*, the construction of which was cancelled in 1928 when the London Naval Treaty was implemented.

Although naval construction activity was low at this time, design work and research and development continued and among this the development of electric welding occupied an important place. Lillicrap made a special survey of welding in 1930 and cultivated an interest that was the subject of several papers in journals and before learned societies and which was to colour his entire career and lead to the presidency of the Institute of Welding (1956-8). Lillicrap's next design, the Arethusa class, featured an extensively welded forward end.

In 1936 he was promoted to assistant director of naval construction and took responsibility also for the design of submarines. The rearmament programme and the outbreak of World War II vastly increased naval design and construction and by 1941 Lillicrap was the senior officer in the Naval Construction Department, Bath, where he played the major part in adapting the organization to the wartime pattern of work. In 1944 he was promoted director of naval construction, the year in which he was appointed CB; he held this post until his retirement in 1951. In January 1944 he also became head of the Royal Corps of Naval Constructors. In 1947 he was appointed KCB. He was also made an officer of the Legion of Honour by the French Government and a grand officer of the Order of Orange Nassau by the Dutch.

He was always active in the work of the learned societies connected with his profession. He was a member of the council of the Royal Institution of Naval Architects from 1937 until his death, becoming vice-president in 1945, and an honorary vice-president in 1955. He was a member of the council of the Institute of Welding and of the British Welding Research Association and was president of each body. He presented papers on 'The uses of electric arc welding in warship construction' to the Naval Architects in 1933, and 'Welding as applied to Shipbuilding' to the Institute of Welding in 1935, and the literature of these institutions is rich with other contributions from his pen.

Lillicrap was a liveryman of the Worshipful Company of Shipwrights and was its prime warden in 1958. He took an active interest in the education and welfare of shipyard apprentices and was for many years chairman of the Worshipful Company's committee for awards to apprentices. He was a member of the board of governors of the Imperial College of Science and Technology for nearly twenty years and in 1964 was elected to a fellowship in recognition of his valuable service. He was awarded the honorary degree of D.Sc. (Eng.) by Bristol University in 1951.

His retirement from Admiralty service marked a change in emphasis rather than a cessation of work. In addition to his work for the institutions, he became a director of J. Samuel White & Co., the Island Transport Co., Henry Bannister Ltd., and Marinite Ltd.

In earlier years his recreations included walking. His major diversion was, however, books, and he became a collector of first editions which reflected his scholarship and erudition. A notable admirer of Dr Samuel Johnson, he was president of the Johnson Society in 1955-6. He was by nature and inclination a student with broad sympathies and wide interests. He was a man of great energy, directness of purpose, and charm, who enjoyed being with people and made friends readily. He died at Lincoln 17 June 1966.

[*The Times*, 20 June 1966; personal knowledge.]   R. J. DANIEL

LINDSAY, JOHN SEYMOUR (1882-1966), designer and metalworker, was born in London 16 May 1882, the fourth son and youngest surviving child of William Henry Lindsay, iron merchant and proprietor of Lindsay's Paddington Ironworks, and his wife, Alice Charlotte Garman. His mother died in 1892, leaving Seymour and a brother to be brought up by a maiden Garman aunt in their father's house.

Lindsay was educated at home, and early showed talent for drawing and painting, a characteristic he shared with many of his family. At the age of seventeen he was apprenticed to Leonard Ashford, designer and draughtsman, of 5 John Street, Adelphi, and later joined the firm of Higgins and Griffiths, electrical engineers, of 21 Orchard Street, London W.1, as a designer of electrical fittings, lamps, etc.

On the outbreak of war in 1914 Lindsay joined the London Rifle Brigade as a private and served in France. He was awarded the DCM and promoted to officer rank in the field. He was wounded in September 1916, and invalided home.

After the war Lindsay rejoined Higgins and Griffiths, and extended his range of designs to gates, balustrades, and other ironwork. In the early 1930s he started his own business, employing a blacksmith in Suffolk. He did much work for Sir Herbert Baker, Sir Edwin Lutyens, and (Sir) Albert Richardson [qq.v.]. This included, for Baker, ironwork in the Bank of England (1921-37), wrought-iron altar rails, vestry stairs balustrade and lectern at the Church House chapel, Westminster (1937-40), and ironwork in branches of Barclays Bank throughout London; for Baker and Lutyens the designing of light-fittings and ironwork in the Government Buildings in New Delhi; for Lutyens the gates for Roehampton Hospital, and the ironwork in the Midland Bank, Poultry (1929-37); for Richardson the iron staircase and weather-vane of Trinity House, Tower Hill, and the restoration of ironwork at St. James's, Piccadilly, and St. Alfege, Greenwich.

On his own account Lindsay made, for the chapel of St. George and the English Martyrs in Westminster Cathedral, the bronze screen (designed by L. H. Shattock in 1930) which was only erected after World War II. In 1946 he designed the silver altar rails, and plate for the altar (a pair of candlesticks, a pair of candelabra, and a cross) of the Battle of Britain memorial chapel (dedicated in 1947) in Westminster Abbey, which were made by Garrards, and the wrought-iron lectern for the roll of honour.

During World War II Lindsay was appointed to the Ancient Monuments Department (Ministry of Works) to advise on what ironwork should be preserved, and what melted for munitions. During this time and until his retirement in 1952, he made a comprehensive record of ironwork in and on public buildings, palaces, and of especial interest.

On retirement he joined Messrs Grundy, Arnatt Ltd., metalworkers, who carried out his designs for numerous architects.

In 1914 he published in the *Architect* a series of articles, illustrated by himself, on domestic ironwork, which were a prelude to his later works, *Iron and Brass Implements of the English House* (1927, revised 1964), and *An Anatomy of English Wrought Iron* (1964), both illustrated by himself. His skill as a draughtsman, able to suggest the substance and surface texture of metal, vied with a very considerable technical and historical knowledge of ancient and obsolete domestic implements and ironwork. Such knowledge led him to favour the historicist in his designs.

Lindsay joined the Art-Workers' Guild in 1930, was made a fellow of the Society of Antiquaries in 1942, and a fellow of the Royal Society of Arts in 1949.

He was a perfectionist, sometimes irascibly so, a man of charm and modesty, of whom it might be said that collaboration was the thief of fame. He was scarcely ever seen without his huge-brimmed black felt artist's hat, and his recreations were appropriately sketching, and painting in water-colour and oil. He was a member of the Langham Sketching Club. He was also a skilful maker of toys and models, and a collector of ancient domestic ironwork, some of which he gave to the Victoria and Albert Museum. Lindsay died at the Stud Farm, Sulhampstead Abbots, Berkshire, 8 January 1966, and was survived by his widow Iris, daughter of Alfred Bennett, whom he married in 1959. His first wife, Mildred Ethel Williams, whom he married in 1915, died in 1948; they had one daughter.

[Sir Herbert Baker, *Architecture and Personalities*, 1944; Sir Nikolaus Pevsner, *The Buildings of England: London*, vols. 1 and 2, 1952 and 1957; private information; personal knowledge.]   MARIAN CAMPBELL

LINSTEAD, SIR (REGINALD) PATRICK (1902–1966), experimental organic chemist and university administrator, was born in London 28 August 1902, the second son of Edward Flatman Linstead, pharmaceutical chemist, of London, and later manager of Burroughs Wellcome and Company (later the Wellcome Foundation), and his wife, Florence Evelyn Hester. His brother, (Sir) Hugh Linstead, became MP for Putney (1942–64) and secretary and registrar of the Pharmaceutical Society. Linstead attended the City of London School from the age of eleven to seventeen. Initially, due to his mother's influence, he was most interested in the arts, especially English literature. These interests, although not destined to lead to a career, were retained in later life and supplemented by a comprehensive knowledge of English and American nineteenth-century history. In October 1920 Linstead entered Imperial College, South Kensington, and commenced his study of chemistry. At that early stage Professor (Sir) Jocelyn Thorpe, the head of the department, commented: 'A young man came to me to-day who will make his mark in the world.' On graduating with first class honours in 1923, Linstead commenced research with Thorpe and G. A. R. Kon and obtained the Ph.D. degree in 1926. After continued studies as one of Thorpe's research assistants, he worked for a year with the Anglo-Persian Oil Company. In 1929 Linstead returned to Imperial College as a demonstrator and subsequently as a lecturer in organic chemistry. Until 1938 research was supervised by a triumvirate of Kon, E. H. Farmer, and Linstead. In 1938 Linstead was appointed Firth professor of chemistry at the university of Sheffield. A year later, after the death of his wife in childbirth, he accepted a chair of organic chemistry at Harvard University.

At the outbreak of war in 1939 Linstead was drawn into the British and American Government rdx (cyclonite, a research department explosive) programme. In 1942, on extended leave from Harvard, he returned to the United Kingdom as deputy director of scientific research at the Ministry of Supply. Resigning the Harvard chair in 1945, Linstead was appointed director of the government Chemical Research Laboratory at Teddington. After four years he returned to Imperial College as professor of organic chemistry and member of the board of studies; subsequently he became head of the department when Professor H. V. A. Briscoe retired in 1954. In 1953 he was appointed dean of the Royal College of Science. In October 1954 the rector Sir Roderic Hill [q.v.] suddenly died and Linstead was appointed as his successor. As Linstead was from the academic staff this promotion was a break with tradition. During his term of office, which began in 1955, Imperial College was expanded greatly in numbers of students and academic staff. Facilities for teaching, research, and student welfare were improved by the addition of new buildings and equipment. A new student hall of residence, provided by anonymous donation, was named in Linstead's honour after his death.

Linstead was awarded the Harrison memorial prize (1929), the Meldola medal (1930), and the Hofmann medal of the German Chemical Society (1939). He became D.Sc. (London, 1930), honorary MA (Harvard, 1942), and honorary D.Sc. (Exeter, 1965). He was appointed CBE in 1946 and knighted in 1959. He was elected to the fellowship of the Royal Society in 1940 and became vice-president (1959–65) and foreign secretary (1960–5) of that body. In addition, both the Chemical Society (1946–9, 1950–3, and 1954–7) and the Royal Institute of Chemistry (1949–51) elected him as vice-president. Linstead's diverse accomplishments were recognized by his appointment as a governor of Charterhouse, the London School of Economics and Political Science, and the London Graduate School of Business Studies, and as a trustee of the National Gallery (from 1962). He was twice president of the Science Masters' Association, and a member of the council of the Royal Albert Hall. Linstead was frequently consulted by the Government. His wise counsel was accepted by many, including the National Resources (Technical) Committee, the Ministry of Works Advisory Committee on Building Research and Development, the Committee on the Technique of Control of Government Scientific

Research and Development, and the Advisory Council on Scientific Policy. In the formulation of educational forward planning Linstead's influence was significant: he was a member of both the Central Advisory Council for Education, chaired by Sir Geoffrey (later Lord) Crowther (1956-60) and the Committee on Higher Education, chaired by Lord Robbins (1961-4).

Linstead investigated the synthesis, tautomerism, and cyclization of unsaturated mono- and dicarboxylic acids. During these studies, he extended the Kolbe's electrochemical reaction to the synthesis of natural products. Linstead's study of hydrogen transfer from donor to acceptor molecules using quinones, olefins, or dihydroaromatic compounds is classic. His greatest contributions were in the chemistry of the phthalocyanin, porphyrin, and chlorin pigments and their metal derivatives. These studies led naturally to an investigation of photosynthesis and the verification of the structures of chlorophyll and bacteriochlorophyll. During the war of 1939-45 Linstead completed significant studies relating to the chromatographic characterization of metals including uranium. He revised Cain and Thorpe's *The Synthetic Dyestuffs* (with Thorpe, 1933), and wrote *A Course in Modern Techniques of Organic Chemistry* (with J. A. Elvidge and M. Whalley, 1955), and *A Guide to Qualitative Organic Chemical Analysis* (with B. C. L. Weedon, 1956), all notable treatises.

Linstead possessed insight and sound judgement and was masterly in both discussion and organization. His enthusiasm for chemistry was infective and he was popular with research collaborators and students alike. Linstead's diplomacy and administrative skills always ensured he was enthusiastically followed. Using his knowledge as a conciliatory gift, he encouraged students to diverse interests and sponsored the establishment of an Arts and Music Library at Imperial College. His great chemical reputation and popularity ensured no shortage of excellent research collaborators. As a teacher Linstead was an innovator. He established an undergraduate tutorial system at Imperial College and introduced specialization and research projects for third-year chemistry undergraduates.

In 1930 Linstead married Aileen Edith Ellis Rowland, daughter of J. Abbott, a fellow research worker at Imperial College. His wife tragically died in 1938 giving birth to his only child, a daughter. In 1942 Linstead married Marjorie, daughter of W. D. Walters, of Aberdare. She had an Oxford doctorate and subsequently became principal of Lady Spencer Churchill College of Education at Wheatley, Oxford. On 22 September 1966 Linstead

suddenly died at St. George's Hospital, London, having suffered a heart attack. His portrait, by Edward Halliday, hangs in the rector's house at Imperial College.

[D. H. R. Barton, with H. N. Rydon and J. A. Elvidge, in *Biographical Memoirs of Fellows of the Royal Society*, vol. xiv, 1968.]

A. G. M. Barrett and D. H. R. Barton

LITTLEWOOD, SIR SYDNEY CHARLES THOMAS (1895-1967), solicitor and principal architect of England's legal aid system in civil proceedings, was born in Bournemouth 15 December 1895, the elder son of Charles Sydney Littlewood, of Southampton, and his wife, Sarah Ann Harris. His father from 1892 devoted his life to the service of the Hampshire police force, retiring in 1920 as a much-respected superintendent to live in Bromley, Kent.

On leaving school Littlewood first worked as an office boy with a firm of country solicitors and after that for a year as a constable in the same police force as his father. Then the war of 1914-18 changed the course of his life. Serving with the Loyal North Lancashire Regiment he won his subaltern's commission on 21 September 1915. Soon he transferred to the Royal Flying Corps and joined 35 Squadron, BEF, as a flying officer. On 1 June 1916 he was shot down behind the enemy lines near Armentières and captured. Till the end of 1918 he was held a prisoner at various camps, where his extensive range of reading included the classics, law, politics, and Egyptology. On demobilization in 1919 he chose the legal profession as his career and after two years in articles was, in May 1922, admitted as a solicitor. With a characteristic sense of duty, he joined the Territorial Army in 1926 when so many resiled from such service and became a captain in the 6th East Surrey Regiment.

By 1932 (when he resigned his commission) Littlewood was making his mark in his profession, having commenced in 1928 a partnership with Messrs Wilkinson Howlett & Co. which was to last for thirty years. His talent for advocacy was being exercised mainly in magistrates courts: later, to an increasing extent, it served him well in the specialized field of town planning enquiries. In 1940, aged forty-five, he was elected to the Council of the Law Society which in 1944 nominated him for appointment by Lord Simon to the Committee on Legal Aid chaired by Lord Rushcliffe [qq.v.] 'an all party and no party Committee containing judges, barristers, solicitors, social workers and politicians of great eminence and experience' (Sir David Maxwell-Fyfe, later Earl of Kilmuir, q.v.). Its unanimous and historic report (1945) was against control of any scheme by the

Government or by local authorities: it was in favour of control 'by the lawyers themselves'.

The Government adopted the basic scheme recommended in that report and decided to place its control in the hands of the Law Society with its large secretariat. To draft in detail the scheme itself and the statutory instruments needed to implement the provisions of the proposed Bill a Legal Aid Committee was constituted consisting of twelve members of the Council of the Law Society, all of whom later became presidents, three members of the Bar Council, each of whom became a High Court judge (the senior was the writer of this notice), and one of the lord chancellor's staff. Littlewood was aptly selected to be its chairman, and presided with whole-hearted enthusiasm and conspicuous success over its meetings, many of which called for his admirable compound of fairness, common sense, and legal acumen.

Within the Law Society there were originally many doubts as to the wisdom of the scheme and 'no other single person contributed more to winning the support of a traditionally conservative body to an idea which was entirely novel and at the same time far reaching in its effects' (Sir Denys Hicks, member of the Committee). Moreover, the Committee sat over a period when relations between Littlewood's Council and the Bar Council were strained as never before or since. In addition to the voluminous intricacies of the scheme and its regulations and the hesitations of colleagues, he had to face the fact that a small but forceful section of his Council and its secretariat, having realized how high a proportion of barristers' civil practices would come under the scheme, sought so to frame it as to give, by its disciplinary procedures, the Law Society a hold on the bar. No praise could be too high for the way Littlewood dealt with all difficulties.

As a result, under Littlewood's guidance there was produced a scheme which, when put to the test, worked with singular smoothness for matters which might or did become the subject of proceedings in courts of civil jurisdiction. The grant and control of legal aid in criminal cases has always remained a matter for the courts under quite a different system. Control by the Government was avoided; the independence of each branch of the legal profession was maintained; and both branches co-operated in administering the scheme in an economic manner. Expense to the taxpayer was rigorously controlled and two decades later remained only a fraction of 1 per cent of the cost of the National Health Service. The scheme soon became the envy of other civilized countries.

For his successful work Littlewood was knighted in June 1951. He continued with unabated zest to take a leading part in the administration of the scheme for the rest of his life. In 1959, he became, in addition, president of the Law Society and was generally regarded as being an outstanding holder of that office.

His notable activities were, however, not confined to his work for that Society. His impressive stature, his keen and commonsense approach to new problems, and his patent integrity resulted in his being in demand in several spheres. Within that of the law, he had been president of the Justices' Clerks' Society in 1944-5. A little later his specialized experience in town and country planning matters often led to his being briefed at enquiries as a leading advocate instead of a QC: and in 1956 he became legal member of the Town Planning Institute, an appointment in which he took pride.

Because of Littlewood's interest in medical matters he became a member of the South-West Metropolitan Regional Hospital Board in 1952, chairman of the Council of Professions Supplementary to Medicine in 1961, and chairman of the departmental committee on experiments on animals whose deliberations in 1963-4 resulted in much-needed control of laboratories and protection for the animals used there. His flair for finance led to his becoming a member of the commission that de-cartelized the Krupp organization in Germany and to his chairmanship of the Westminster Fire Office.

It was, however, Littlewood's presidency of the London Rent Assessment Panel from 1965 to 1967 (an appointment by Richard Crossman on the recommendation of Dame Evelyn (later Baroness) Sharp) that brought him most into the public eye. He thus became, as was intended, the leading authority on those provisions of the Rent Act of 1965 which set up tribunals to determine 'fair rents'. Left-wing Labour MPs having found fault with him for not invariably reducing the current rents, Littlewood forcefully criticized them for failing to understand what the word 'fair' meant in the Act they had just passed. Their much-headlined threats to call for his resignation subsided in due course.

Littlewood's classically impressive presence—Olympian, to quote a close colleague—and his strong personality tended on initial acquaintance to obscure the warmth and humanity of his character. Fond of the company of his fellow men, he took pleasure in his membership of the Garrick Club, the Company of Basketmakers, and his dining clubs. His leisure interests included extensive reading, shooting, and gardening. His death at King Edward VII Hospital, Midhurst, 9 September 1967 closed the career of a man of all-round knowledge and great ability who would have made an admirable High Court judge had that office then been open to solicitors.

Littlewood's first marriage, in 1919 to Evelyn Myrtle Prior, a farmer's daughter, was childless and ended in divorce: the second, patently happy, was in 1934 to Barbara ('Bill'), daughter of Dr Langdon-Down, herself a solicitor who practised in Guildford and was a magistrate. In due course she became president of the Surrey Law Society and president of the International Federation of Business and Professional Women: her combination of charm and calm ability provided her husband with notable support and wise counsel in testing times. Their son Paul, born in 1936, also became a solicitor.

[Ministry of Defence records; private information; personal knowledge.]

ERIC SACHS

LIVENS, WILLIAM HOWARD (1889-1964), soldier and inventor, was born at Lincoln 28 March 1889, the only son of Frederick Howard Livens, chief engineer of the firm which became Ruston & Hornsby, by his wife, Priscilla Mary Abbott. He was educated at Oundle and Christ's College, Cambridge, where he took the natural sciences tripos and graduated in 1911. He played lacrosse and water-polo for Cambridge and captained the rifle-shooting eight, making a record score against Oxford. He was in the English shooting eight in 1910. Writing was another of his interests and on going down from Cambridge he worked for *Country Life*.

In September 1914 he was commissioned in the Royal Engineers and served as a brigade signal officer. He was one of the remarkable group of officers drawn from the most varied professions which Colonel (later Major-General) C. H. Foulkes [q.v.] recruited for the Special Companies RE which in 1916 was re-formed as the Special Brigade RE, with twenty-one companies. It was organized to retaliate in kind for the German gas attacks at Ypres in April 1915. Foulkes quickly realized Livens's forceful character and inventive talent and when the first British cloud gas attack at Loos on 25 September 1915 revealed certain deficiencies in appliances, he sent Livens back to England to secure improved components before the next attack which was timed for 13 October. Livens obtained what seemed necessary, commandeered a Pullman compartment on a leave train, ordered lorries from GHQ to meet him at Boulogne, and arrived in time to remedy the deficiencies.

In July 1915 the Germans had used portable liquid fire projectors at Hooge. Livens suggested the design of much more powerful flame projectors and while these were being made was sent home to train a company to operate them. Two projectors were discharged successfully by his company on the 18th divisional front just before the infantry attack of 1 July 1916 which marked the opening of the battle of the Somme. This was the sector on which a notable advance was made on that day. Since the large flame projector was unsuitable for the more open warfare which followed, Livens invented a new method of throwing burning oil into the German trenches. This developed into the Livens projector: by means of a charge of black powder he fired an oil drum, fitted with a bursting charge and percussion fuse, from a slightly larger oil drum, dug into the ground. It was easy to fire a number simultaneously with a range of several hundred yards and they were used successfully just before several infantry attacks in the fighting on the Somme. To substitute gas for oil was not difficult and thus produce a heavy gas concentration near to the burst of the drum. During the winter of 1916-17, with the help of his father, Livens perfected the design of a bomb containing thirty pounds of liquid phosgene, the most lethal gas, which could be fired in large numbers simultaneously by electric fuses from drawn steel tubes closed at one end. The range could be varied by the size of the black-powder charge. Several thousand phosgene bombs were fired into the German trench system in preparation for the battle of Arras in April 1917. This was the first of many similar discharges which inflicted heavy casualties on the Germans whose respirators were penetrated by the high concentration of phosgene near the burst of the bomb. The Livens projector was the gas weapon most feared by the Germans; but when they copied it they made it more accurate and, by the addition of pumice, more persistent and thereby lost the advantage both of its simplicity for mass production and of its lethal character.

Livens combined great enterprise and initiative with a flair for seeing simple solutions of problems. He was quite imperturbable and the failure of one idea never prevented him from producing another. He gave up the command of his company to act as liaison officer between the Special Brigade and the Ministry of Munitions and towards the end of the war was employed entirely in the Ministry. He was awarded the MC, appointed to the DSO, and mentioned in dispatches.

Lacking the stimulus of war, and having independent means, Livens toyed thereafter with various inventions but found himself forestalled by earlier patent applications. In later life he became interested in spiritualism. In the war of 1939-45 he worked in the Ministry of Supply on gas projects, but this form of warfare was not employed.

In 1916 Livens married Elizabeth Price (died 1934); they had three daughters. He died in London 1 February 1964. There are portraits by A. G. Walker and Hilda Kidman in the possession of his family.

[*The Times*, 5, 6, and 11 February 1964; C. H. Foulkes, '*Gas*', *the Story of the Special Brigade*, 1934; personal knowledge.]

HAROLD HARTLEY

LLOYD, EDWARD MAYOW HASTINGS (1889-1968), British and international civil servant and world food expert, was born 30 November 1889 at Hartley Wintney, Hampshire, the fourth son of Edward Wynell Mayow Lloyd, headmaster, and his wife, Eleanor Elizabeth Hastings, of Hartford House, Hartley Wintney. Lloyd was educated at Rugby School and Corpus Christi College, Oxford, where he obtained second classes in classical honour moderations (1910) and *literae humaniores* (1912).

After leaving Oxford, in 1913 Lloyd decided to join the Home Civil Service and was posted to the Department of Inland Revenue. With the outbreak of war, he was moved to the War Office Contracts Department, where he spent three years. In May 1917 the Ministry of Food was formed and Lloyd was to spend three years in that remarkable Ministry working with E. Frank Wise. He was especially concerned with the development of a successful food rationing system which was to become the foundation of the system introduced during World War II.

From 1919 to 1921 Lloyd had his first experience as an international civil servant when he was seconded to the Economic and Financial Section of the League of Nations Secretariat. In 1921 he returned to Whitehall and was posted to the Ministry of Agriculture. In 1926 he was seconded to the newly created Empire Marketing Board as assistant secretary and in 1933 he became secretary of the Market Supply Committee. These were to be the decisive years for his future career. Through the Empire Marketing Board and the Market Supply Committee he was brought immediately into touch with that tragic paradox which was to perplex so many governments for so long (and indeed continues)—the development of large surpluses and low prices of basic foodstuffs at a time when much of the world's population is undernourished and, far too often, actually starving.

Lloyd was soon brought into contact with a number of outstanding men who were determined to find some solution to this immense problem—notably, Henry Wallace, John (later Lord) Boyd Orr, S. M. Bruce (later Viscount Bruce of Melbourne, q.v.), and Frank Macdougall. Although their success in tackling these problems before the war was very limited (apart from one or two International Commodity Agreements) these men were all influential in persuading President Roosevelt to make the remarkable decision to call an international conference on food and agriculture in the middle of the war. From the International Conference on Food and Agriculture in Hot Springs, Virginia, in May 1943 was to come one of the early United Nations specialized agencies—the Food and Agriculture Organization.

In 1936 the Government established the Food (Defence Plans) Department to make preparations for feeding the population of the United Kingdom in time of war and Lloyd was seconded to it as assistant director. His important contributions to the successful planning activities of the Department have not received the credit they deserve. His knowledge of the food rationing system introduced towards the end of the war was invaluable. Equally valuable was his personal knowledge of many people in the food trades who were to join the Department at the outbreak of war and to be so largely responsible for the success of the Ministry of Food. In addition, he was instrumental in persuading men from other walks of life to join the Ministry. Outstanding examples were—(Sir) Herbert Broadley, (Sir) Maurice I. Hutton, John (later Lord) Redcliffe-Maud, and K. A. H. Murray (later Lord Murray of Newhaven).

With the outbreak of war, the Ministry of Food was established and Lloyd became principal assistant secretary in charge of what later was to become the General Department of the Ministry. From the early days of the Ministry, Lloyd's personal problems were to become more and more serious. They finally came to a head in 1942, when he was posted to the Middle East as economic adviser to the minister of state.

Lloyd's personal problems were reflected in his increasingly unhappy relationships with (Sir) Henry L. French who was the director of the Food (Defence Plans) Department, and later the permanent secretary of the Ministry of Food. This was caused largely by the widely differing characters of the two men. French was a determined and ambitious man who understood organization and management disciplines and was more concerned with running a successful and well-organized Ministry than with the vast problems which were arising, mainly from the sinking of so many food ships.

Lloyd was gentle, self-effacing, intellectual, and more interested in the problems themselves than in organization and management. He did not find it easy to explain problems and solutions to ministers and business men. From the time when F. J. M. (later Lord) Woolton [q.v.] became minister of food in 1940 and the Ministry was reorganized, Lloyd's standing within the Ministry diminished steadily.

The culmination of these disappointing days came with the transfer in 1941 of (Sir) Edward Twentyman from the Treasury to the Ministry of Food. Twentyman became second secretary and head of the General Department, which was increasingly responsible for matters of policy, including claims for shipping space, relations with the American Government and its departments after Lend-Lease was established (through the British Food Mission in Washington), relations with the Combined Food Board and with the governments of liberated countries as well as for providing the Ministry's main contact with all other government departments in Whitehall. When Twentyman was transferred to Washington in 1943 Lloyd remained in the Middle East whilst Maud and Broadley were each in turn to become deputy secretary and second secretary of the Ministry and to lead the General Department.

Possibly the most disappointing event in that period was the decision that Lloyd should not be a member of the United Kingdom delegation to the Hot Springs conference in May 1943. More than any member of that powerful delegation Lloyd was familiar with the major problems of food and agriculture. He was also personally acquainted with many of the leading delegates who attended the conference. His extensive experience since 1926 was thus not to be available.

However, after a brief spell as economic and financial adviser to UNRRA for the Balkan countries, Lloyd spent 1946 and 1947 with the Food and Agriculture Organization. He returned to the Ministry of Food as an undersecretary in 1947 and retired in 1953. In 1956 he became president of the Agricultural Economics Society and was a consultant to Political and Economic Planning from 1958 to 1964.

Lloyd's publications included *Stabilisation* (1923), *Experiments in State Control* (1924), and *Food and Inflation in the Middle East 1940–1945* (1956).

In 1918 Lloyd married Margaret Frances, daughter of Rollo Russell, and granddaughter of Lord John Russell [q.v.]. They had two sons and one daughter. He was appointed CMG in 1945 and CB in 1952. He died in a London hospital 27 January 1968.

[*The Times*, 29 January 1968; personal knowledge.] JOHN WALL

LLOYD, SIR THOMAS INGRAM KYNASTON (1896-1968), civil servant, was born at Shifnal, Shropshire, 19 June 1896, the eldest of three sons of John Charles Lloyd, corn merchant, and his wife, Henrietta Elizabeth Brown. He went to Rossall School and left in 1915 with an open scholarship in mathematics to Gonville and Caius College, Cambridge. Owing to the war, however, he entered the Royal Military Academy, Woolwich, was commissioned second lieutenant in the Royal Engineers in 1916 and promoted lieutenant in 1917. He served in Egypt and Palestine and was mentioned in dispatches. In 1919 he went for a year to Caius where he read history but took no examination.

Lloyd entered the Civil Service in 1920 and was posted to the Ministry of Health. In 1921 he was lent to the Colonial Office, to which he was permanently transferred the following year. His first posting was to the Nigeria Department, but in 1926 he moved to the Middle East Department where he served until in 1929 he was appointed private secretary to the permanent under-secretary of state, Sir Samuel Wilson [q.v.]. In 1929 he was promoted principal and later in the year was selected to be secretary of the Palestine commission, an assignment for which his service in the Middle East Department specially fitted him and which he discharged with great ability. Thereafter, from 1930 to 1938 he worked in the Colonial Service Department, where he was especially concerned with the personal records and careers of members of the Colonial Civil Service. He made a particular point of meeting as many of them as he could, and thus acquired an unrivalled knowledge of their qualities for promotion.

In 1938 Lloyd was appointed secretary of the royal commission on the West Indies under the chairmanship of Lord Moyne [q.v.], who later paid tribute to his 'really remarkable efficiency and devotion to duty'. The commission's report led to the enactment in 1940 of the first Colonial Development and Welfare Act. In 1939 Lloyd was promoted assistant secretary and in 1940, following the collapse of France, took charge of a new department dealing specially with relations with the French colonies. In 1942 he was made head of the Defence Department. In 1943 he became assistant under-secretary of state, supervising the West African and Eastern departments. In this year he was appointed CMG. Four years later, in 1947, he succeeded Sir George Gater [q.v.] as permanent under-secretary of state and was appointed KCMG, followed by KCB in 1949 and GCMG in 1951. He retired in 1956.

In nine years as permanent under-secretary,

Lloyd, T. I. K.

Lloyd served four secretaries of state. This was a period of economic and social expansion, notably the development of university colleges, made possible by Colonial Development and Welfare funds. The territorial responsibilities and the strength of the Office and Colonial Service were at their maximum and many improvements in organization and training were introduced. Lloyd devoted great care to planning coherent sequences of promotions and transfers. Despite an endless series of political problems, such as the Malayan emergency, Mau Mau in Kenya, terrorism in Cyprus, and the deposition of the Kabaka in Uganda, significant constitutional changes were introduced, including ministerial self-government in the Gold Coast, the West Indies Federation, the Federation of the Rhodesias and Nyasaland, and the Federation of Nigeria. The foundations were laid for the independence of Ghana and Malaya in 1957.

This would have been an indigestible menu for any permanent under-secretary. Lloyd's orderly mind enabled him to delegate without losing control of essentials, concentrating his effort where it was most needed from time to time. His advice was always shrewd and well informed, and expressed with masterly precision and economy of words. His qualities were well summed up in *The Memoirs of Lord Chandos* (1962): 'Tom Lloyd was an example of the best in the Civil Service, wise and salty in his judgements, never in a panic or a hurry, enlightened and broad-minded on colonial policy, a good judge of men, insistent that humour must be among their qualifications. It is certainly amongst his. Some said that he did not allow his imagination to walk abroad, but only took it out on a lead for a short time. If this were true I should be far from saying that it was a fault in the permanent head of a department. A little deflation from time to time is as good a thing for Ministers as it is for monetary policy. With all this, he had perhaps too much loyalty for some of his particular swans who had turned, in the stress of colonial affairs or under the erosive influence of Government Houses, into geese.'

Lloyd did not seek further government employment after retirement. He accepted a directorship with Harrisons & Crosfield Ltd., and he was a governor and member of Rossall School council from 1956 until his death. He very rarely missed a meeting and his wisdom and experience were of very great value. But for the most part he devoted himself to his family and his grandchildren, and to his personal hobbies, particularly gardening and philately, to both of which he applied himself with expert knowledge and enthusiasm. His garden at Faggots End, Radlett, was described in *Country Life* as probably the most beautiful in Hertfordshire.

Lloyd married in 1922 Bessie Nora, daughter of G. J. Mason, of Penn, Staffordshire, who owned a chain of grocery shops. Lloyd died at his home 9 December 1968. The elder of his two sons, G. P. Lloyd, entered the Colonial Service in 1951.

[Private information; personal knowledge.]

HILTON POYNTON

LLOYD-GEORGE, GWILYM, first VISCOUNT TENBY (1894–1967), politician, was born at Criccieth 4 December 1894, the younger son and the fourth of the five children of David Lloyd George (later Earl Lloyd-George of Dwyfor, q.v.) and his wife, Margaret, daughter of Richard Owen, a substantial farmer of Mynydd Ednyfed, Criccieth. He was educated at Eastbourne College and Jesus College, Cambridge. After the outbreak of war in 1914, he served at first in the 38th (Welsh) division on the western front in France. Later he commanded a battery of artillery on the Somme and at Passchendaele, rose to the rank of major, and was mentioned in dispatches. His letters written in Welsh to his father in 1917–18, with their references to 'the Hun', show that he shared to the full the 'patriotic' emotions of the time.

After the armistice he became almost inevitably involved in the career of his father, then prime minister and apparently at the zenith of his popularity and authority. Gwilym Lloyd George attended the Paris peace conference with the British delegation in 1919 and took an active interest in foreign policy questions over the next three years. Inexorably, he became involved in Liberal politics in Wales and in the 1922 general election was elected to Parliament as National Liberal member for Pembrokeshire (the native county of his grandfather) with a majority of 11,866 over Labour. He retained his seat in 1923 against Conservative and Labour opposition, and was made a junior Liberal whip but was narrowly defeated by a Conservative in the 1924 election. However, this rebuff did not deflect him from continuing to take an active part in Liberal politics, especially in his father's campaigns for land reform and for combating unemployment with a public-works programme.

In 1925 his father made him managing director of United Newspapers, including the *Daily Chronicle*. He also became a junior trustee in May 1925 of the National Liberal Political Fund, as the 'Lloyd George Fund' had now been rechristened. In 1945 the remnants of the fund were to be transferred to his sole possession. His father privately attacked him for 'indolence' and he resigned his directorship in 1926. But he still maintained a warm relationship with his father, and largely escaped the family bitterness kindled by the growing estrangement of his parents as a result of his father's relationship with his private secretary, Frances Stevenson.

In the 1929 general election Gwilym Lloyd George returned to Parliament, regaining the Pembrokeshire seat in a three-cornered contest: he was to retain it for the next twenty-one years. He was a loyal supporter of his father in the turmoil that afflicted the parliamentary Liberal Party during the period of the second Labour Government in 1929–31. However, when the 'national' Government was formed under J. Ramsay MacDonald, Gwilym Lloyd George served briefly (September–October) as parliamentary secretary to the Board of Trade. But, like his father and his sister Megan [q.v.] (then member for Anglesey), he turned against the Government after the decision to call a 'doctor's mandate' election. He particularly objected to any proposal to introduce tariffs and resigned from the Government on 8 October. After the general election, which saw the 'national' Government victorious by a huge majority, he joined his father, sister, and his family relative, Goronwy Owen, in a four-member 'party' of Welsh Independent Liberals opposed to the Government.

Throughout the thirties he was a loyal supporter of his father's domestic and foreign policies. He accompanied him on his notorious visit to Hitler at Berchtesgaden in the summer of 1936. However, when war broke out again in September 1939, it was confirmed, as in 1931, that Gwilym Lloyd George was far less hostile to Conservatism than were either his father or his sister, Megan. He again became parliamentary secretary at the Board of Trade and served there, under first Chamberlain, then Churchill, until February 1941, when he became parliamentary secretary to the Ministry of Food. He was now carving out a new career of his own, and this was confirmed in June 1942 when he was appointed to the vital new post of minister of fuel and power, an office he held until the 1945 general election.

Here he proved to be an able and tactful minister. He devised an effective system of fuel rationing and persuaded domestic consumers to exercise economy. He helped stimulate the miners into vastly increased coal production. He worked closely with Ernest Bevin [q.v.], the minister of labour, in starting the 'Bevin boys' scheme to increase the labour force and in instituting a national minimum wage for miners, fixed at a higher rate than in other industries. Most important of all, in October 1943 he implemented some wide-ranging changes in the management of the coal industry. Lloyd George recognized that the private-enterprise system was inefficient and totally inadequate for raising coal production. In a memorandum to the Cabinet on 7 October 1943 (WP446) he proposed that the Government secure operational control over the mines and become the direct employer of the various managements for the duration of the war. Although Churchill's personal veto prevented outright nationalization, sweeping changes were instituted which saw the setting up of a National Coal Board with wide powers over production targets and industrial relations. Lloyd George's major achievement was to secure a dramatic increase in the nation's fuel supplies during the wartime period. He was, however, unsuccessful in an attempt to turn the electricity supply industry into a public corporation, a scheme advocated by himself and Herbert Morrison (later Lord Morrison of Lambeth, q.v.).

After Lloyd George's father died in March 1945, he himself went on to confirm both his steady drift towards the Conservatives and his new stature as a politician in his own right. He narrowly (by 168 votes) held Pembrokeshire in the 1945 general election, then standing as a 'National Liberal and Conservative'. He insisted in public speeches that no major issues now divided the Liberals and the Conservatives, and that the fight against the 'socialist menace to liberty' was paramount. It was noticeable that he adopted the hyphenated form 'Lloyd-George' and also that he declined the chairmanship of the parliamentary Liberal Party after the defeat of Sir Archibald Sinclair (later Viscount Thurso, q.v.). In the February 1950 general election he was defeated in Pembrokeshire by a Labour candidate, Desmond Donnelly, but in October 1951 was comfortably returned for Newcastle upon Tyne (North) instead. He thus preserved the Lloyd George tradition in the Commons as his sister Megan had been narrowly defeated at Anglesey at the same time. Churchill had spoken for him at Newcastle and had a high regard for his administrative abilities and conciliatory approach. He appointed Lloyd-George to the sensitive post of minister of food in October 1951 and he remained there for three years. Here he presided successfully over a difficult transitional period which saw the ending of food rationing in 1954, and savings in the bill for food imports. The previous year had seen him elected an honorary fellow of his former college, Jesus, Cambridge.

His success saw him promoted in October 1954 as home secretary, an office which he combined, appropriately, with the new Ministry of Welsh Affairs. He retained these portfolios when Eden succeeded Churchill as prime minister in 1955. His most important achievement at the Home Office was to pilot what became the 1957 Homicide Act through the Commons. This modified the severity of the law in murder cases, although Lloyd-George was now firmly opposed to the abolition of capital punishment (after having been an abolitionist as recently as 1948). When Harold Macmillan became prime minister in January 1957, Lloyd-George was one of those removed from office ostensibly to make way for younger men, though his successor at the Home Office was the scarcely youthful R. A. Butler (later Lord Butler of Saffron Walden).

Lloyd-George then went to the House of Lords as Viscount Tenby. He continued to play a part in public life. He served as chairman of the council on tribunals in 1961, a body created to scrutinize administrative tribunals and ministerial inquiries. This council helped add to the safeguards for individual citizens against omissions and errors by departmental officials. He also remained active in his native Wales, serving as president of the University College of Swansea, president of the London Welsh Rugby Football Club, and president of the Football Association of Wales. In 1961 he succeeded Lord Birkett as president of the Fleming Memorial Fund for Medical Research.

Gwilym Lloyd-George was notable for forging a career for himself, independently of his distinguished father. He had a far happier and more fulfilling career than do the sons of many great men. He also avoided the storms that beset his father's political and personal life. Although increasingly a somewhat conservative, almost squirearchical, figure himself, he remained on the best of terms with his father, mother, and sisters. A warm-hearted, humorous man, who was an excellent mimic, he was especially well liked in the House of Commons, where his knowledge of parliamentary procedure led some to speculate that he might have been nominated as Speaker. He was an able, if not outstanding, minister, in a variety of departments. His work at the Ministry of Fuel and Power during the war was a significant contribution to victory through the building up of the nation's energy supplies. A popular, placid figure, he made his own distinctive contribution to the Lloyd George political tradition.

He married in 1921 Edna Gwenfron (died 1971), daughter of David Jones, of Gwynfa, Denbigh; they had two sons. He died at St. Thomas's Hospital, London, 14 February 1967. He was succeeded in the title of Viscount Tenby by his elder son, David (born 1922).

There is a pen-and-ink sketch of Lloyd-George in the University College of Swansea. In 1955 Maurice Codner exhibited a portrait in the Royal Society of Portrait Painters.

[Lloyd George letters (20,467C) in the National Library of Wales, Aberystwyth; papers in the private possession of the Hon. William Lloyd-George; *The Times*, 15 February 1967; *Guardian*, 15 February 1967; *Western Mail*, 15 February 1967.]

KENNETH O. MORGAN

LLOYD GEORGE, LADY MEGAN (1902-1966), politician, was born in Criccieth, Caernarvonshire, 22 April 1902, the third daughter and youngest of the five children of David Lloyd George (later Earl Lloyd-George of Dwyfor, q.v.) and his wife, Margaret Owen. Her early years were overshadowed by her father, who entered the Liberal Government in 1905 and finally became prime minister in December 1916. Megan was brought up in a strongly political atmosphere, first at No. 11, then at No. 10, Downing Street. Since the death of the eldest daughter, Mair, in 1907, Megan had succeeded her as foremost in her father's affections. She was at first tutored privately; later she was educated at Garratt's Hall, Banstead, and in Paris. She stayed with her father during the Paris peace conference in 1919 and accompanied him to several subsequent international conferences, often acting as his hostess. After his fall from office, she accompanied him to the United States in 1923; afterwards, she spent a year in India as the guest of Lord Reading [q.v.].

By her mid twenties she was widely regarded as her father's likely political heir. In 1928 she secured the Liberal nomination for Anglesey and was returned to Parliament in the 1929 general election. She showed considerable gifts as a parliamentarian, and soon built up a reputation in her own right. She made a sparkling maiden speech in 1930 on rural housing. In later sessions she made some notable interventions on agriculture, unemployment, and Welsh affairs. She also delivered powerful public speeches on foreign affairs and disarmament, as befitted an executive member of the League of Nations Union. Throughout the thirties she faithfully followed her father's radical line. She opposed Ramsay MacDonald's 'national' Government and was one of the family group of four Welsh Independent Liberal members led by Lloyd George after the 1931 general election. She often urged co-operation between the Liberals and Labour; even at this early period, there were rumours of her joining the Labour Party. But her father kept her faithful to Liberalism. She was a forceful supporter of his 'new deal' programme in

1935 for combating unemployment. She also followed her father in foreign policy, and accompanied him on his visit to Germany in 1936, during which they met Hitler. However, Megan was an uncompromising critic of appeasement from the Abyssinia crisis onwards. She remained a fierce opponent of Chamberlain's Government after the outbreak of war, and played a major part in persuading her father to speak, with devastating effect, in the debate of 7-8 May 1940, which led to Chamberlain's resignation.

During the war Megan emerged more distinctly as an independent public figure. Her father was now ageing rapidly, and died in March 1945. Shortly before, his earldom had led to her becoming Lady Megan. She served on wartime consultative committees for the ministries of Health and Labour, and on the salvage board for the Ministry of Supply. She was a member of the Speaker's conference on electoral reform in 1944. But she was most prominent as a leading figure on the unofficial, non-party Woman Power Committee, concerned with the wartime employment of women, and with women's rights. She was also apprehensive of the post-war policies to be adopted by the Liberal Party. With such colleagues as (Sir) Dingle Foot, she urged that the Liberals align themselves unambiguously on the left. She rejected any possible alliance with the Simonite 'National Liberals'. In the event, she hung on to her seat at Anglesey with a much-reduced majority over her Labour opponent at the 1945 general election.

Lady Megan was now foremost among those striving to prevent the Liberals drifting to the right. She feared that the emergence of Clement Davies [q.v.] as the party's leader in 1945 meant a further erosion of its radicalism. When made deputy leader of the Liberal Parliamentary Party in January 1949 she demanded that the party shed its right-wing elements. In the parliament of 1950-1, with two other Liberal members, she was criticized for often voting with the Labour Government in defiance of the official party policy. The Conservatives put up a candidate against her in Anglesey in the general elections of 1950 and 1951: in the latter year she was defeated by her Labour opponent, after over twenty-two years in the House.

After 1951 Lady Megan was much involved with Welsh affairs. She was president of the Parliament for Wales campaign, which attracted over a quarter of a million signatures. In 1952 she declined invitations both to continue as Liberal candidate for Anglesey, and to seek re-election as vice-president of the Liberal Party. She did so in terms which suggested that the parting of the ways was not far off. In April 1955 she announced that she was joining the Labour Party as it now appeared to be the essential voice of British radicalism: it was a decision she had taken privately two years earlier. She played an active part in the following general election; Labour regarded her as a major force in winning over former Liberal voters. Her opportunity to return to the House came in a by-election at Carmarthen in February 1957. In a fiercely fought contest, she defeated her Liberal opponent by over 3,000 votes. In three subsequent general elections she built up her majority to over 9,000. She now took part in debate mainly on Welsh questions and on agriculture, but was never asked to speak from the Opposition front bench. She did not receive office when Labour returned to power in 1964. The general election of March 1966 was fought in her absence through ill health. Soon afterwards, 14 May 1966, at her Criccieth home, Bryn Awelon, she died of cancer. Just before her death she had been appointed CH.

Lady Megan never married. Her relationship with her father was close; but she opposed his second marriage, to Frances Stevenson, in 1943. She also differed from her brother, Gwilym (a notice of whom appears above), who moved over to the Conservatives as she herself moved left. In almost thirty years in the Commons she never attained office; she was a backbencher when she died, although she might have become a minister of state had she recovered. But she brought rare gifts to British political life. She was a superb speaker, in Welsh or English. Her speeches in the House, while somewhat infrequent, powerfully focused attention on such issues as rural housing and regional unemployment. She was a regular and effective broadcaster: her many outside interests included membership of the BBC advisory council. She was a devoted Welsh patriot. She became a bard of the National Eisteddfod in 1935 and the first woman member of the Welsh Church Commissioners in 1942. She was a woman of vivacity and charm, with a wide range of friends inside and outside politics. Her particular loves were the theatre and ballet; she was also a keen tennis player. With her quick gestures and eager wit, she symbolized much of the Lloyd George magic. She was in many ways ideally equipped to serve as the heir to her father's brand of independent radicalism, but her talents went largely unused.

A portrait by Henry Lamb was exhibited at the Royal Academy in 1953.

[Lloyd George papers in the National Library of Wales, Aberystwyth; A. J. P. Taylor (ed.), *Lloyd George: a Diary by Frances Stevenson*, 1971; Kenneth O.

Morgan (ed.), *Lloyd George: Family Letters, 1885-1936*, 1973; 'profile' in the *Observer*, 4 June 1950; *The Times*, *Guardian*, and *Western Mail*, 16 May 1966; *Carmarthen Journal*, 20 May 1966; *Baner ac Amserau Cymru*, 2 June 1966; private information.]

KENNETH O. MORGAN

LOCKHART, SIR ROBERT HAMILTON BRUCE (1887-1970), diplomatist and writer, was born 2 September 1887 in Anstruther, Fife, the eldest of the five sons of Robert Bruce Lockhart, headmaster of the Waid Academy, and his wife, Florence Stuart, daughter of John McGregor. A younger brother was J. H. Bruce Lockhart, headmaster of Sedbergh School (1937-54), and another, Sir Rob Lockhart, became a general in the Indian Army. His only sister, Freda, made a reputation as film critic and journalist.

Bruce Lockhart took pride in having 'no drop of English blood' in his veins, his mother being Highland, the Lockharts Lowlanders. He won a foundation scholarship to Fettes College at the age of twelve but failed to fulfil his scholastic promise and, as he recorded in *My Scottish Youth* (1937), spent five years 'in the worship of athleticism'. To rid him of this fetish, his father sent him to work under an austere professor in Berlin, then to Paris. This paternal move was an important influence on his subsequent career for it opened up the horizon of foreign countries; and learning fluent German and French developed his talent for mastering languages which later stood him in good stead. His wide reading in the literatures of the languages he learned shaped his own style.

For three years (1908-10) Lockhart was a rubber planter in Malaya where his mother's family had interests. Acute malaria brought him home and he then entered the consular service, passing first in his examinations. In January 1912 he went to Moscow as vice-consul. Owing to the illness of his chief, he was acting consul-general during the war years and very much in the centre of the efforts to keep Russia in the war. But in 1917, some six weeks before the Bolsheviks took over, he was quietly recalled to London 'on sick leave', in reality because of an affair with a Russian Jewess which was 'being talked about'. Early in 1918, when the British Government wished to establish unofficial relations with the Soviets, Lockhart returned to Russia as head of a special mission, bearing a letter of introduction to Trotsky from Litvinov then still in England. When Anglo-Soviet relations deteriorated, Lockhart was arrested in September for 'espionage' and imprisoned in the Kremlin for a month before he and Litvinov were exchanged. For what is known in the Soviet Encyclopaedia as 'the Lockhart conspiracy' he was condemned to death *in absentia*. It was clear, however, that he had never believed in the wisdom of anti-Bolshevik intervention and had only unwillingly acquiesced in Allied policy. Later he wrote of coping with 'an impossible situation' and how the interventionists would 'never forgive' him for his advocacy of understanding with the Bolsheviks.

Lockhart's health had suffered, probably as much from hard living as the strain of his work, and it was not until November 1919 that he was appointed commercial secretary at the British legation in Prague. In a politically insignificant career there he formed a deep affection for the Czechoslovak people, and Dr Benes and Jan Masaryk became his close friends for the rest of their lives. He had a weakness for living beyond his means and to reinstate his finances he left the Foreign Service for international banking in October 1922 and continued to spend most of his time in Central Europe which had become his natural habitat. Although banking was certainly not his *métier*, his conviviality smoothed negotiations. In 1924 he was received into the Roman Catholic Church.

Lockhart had already been summoned to see Lord Beaverbrook [q.v.] after the Moscow débâcle and in 1928 he joined the *Evening Standard* as editor of the Londoner's Diary, a job which he performed until 1937 with superb urbanity. An early scoop was the first English interview, in 1929, with the exiled Kaiser Wilhelm II. It was during this period that he wrote his first book, *Memoirs of a British Agent* (1932), in which his Russian years are brilliantly recorded. It had an immediate success and was reprinted eighteen times between 1932 and 1946. It was followed by *Retreat from Glory* (1934) and *Return to Malaya* (1936). After 1937 authorship became his career, for his books were successful in America as well as in the United Kingdom. But he continued to write occasional journalism and undertook some lecturing in Europe and the United States.

After the outbreak of war in 1939 Lockhart rejoined the Foreign Office. In 1940 he was appointed British representative with the provisional Czechoslovak Government in exile; in 1941 he became a deputy under-secretary of state and took over the direction of the Political Warfare Executive which co-ordinated propaganda in enemy and enemy-occupied countries. He was appointed KCMG in 1943, continued in his post until the end of the war, and described his experiences in his first post-war book *Comes the Reckoning* (1947). There followed a number of other books, based mainly upon his memories of people and events.

Lockhart's books are likely to be remembered, for his easy, natural style, his knowledge of Russia and Central Europe during four stormy decades, and his many friends in high places make his writings useful subsidiary historical records as well as enjoyable reading. He had a flair for making friends wherever he went, was much loved, restless, and kind. His personality shone through his books and his enthusiasm for his friends, Scotland, and fishing is always infectious. One of his most attractive books was *My Rod, My Comfort* (1949). He was handsome in a rugged way, with an endearing smile, and, no matter how pressed for time, was always ready to exchange reminiscences, particularly if they were about Scotland and his school, Fettes, which was a big influence in his life. This had something to do with a boyish quality in his character which he never lost and which was his attraction, yet a weakness. The posthumous publication in 1973 of the first volume of his Diaries, for 1915 to 1938, provided an illuminating addition to his writings but showed him to have been self-indulgent and extravagant to an extent which somewhat undermined his reputation.

In 1913 Lockhart married Jean Haslewood, daughter of Leonard Turner, an Australian; they had one daughter who died at birth and one son. They became estranged at an early stage and the marriage was dissolved in 1938. In 1948 he married Frances Mary, daughter of Major-General Edward Archibald Beck. Lockhart's last years were spent in sickness and he died in Hove 27 February 1970.

[Lockhart's own writings; *The Times*, 28 February 1970; private information; personal knowledge.]   JAMES MACGIBBON

LOCKWOOD, SIR JOHN FRANCIS (1903-1965), university administrator, was born 6 July 1903 at Preston, Lancashire, the only son and elder child of John Lockwood, stockbroker, of Preston, and his wife, Elizabeth Speight. Lockwood was educated at Preston Grammar School, where he was active in sport and mountain walking. In 1922 he was awarded a classical scholarship at Corpus Christi College, Oxford, where he obtained a first class in classical honour moderations, and a second in *literae humaniores* (1926).

After a short period as assistant lecturer in Latin at the university of Manchester in 1927, in the same year he was appointed by University College, London, as senior assistant lecturer in classics. He was lecturer in Greek there from 1930 to 1940. When war began in 1939, the college's classics department moved to Aberystwyth. In 1940 Lockwood was appointed University College's tutor to arts students and a London University reader in classics. In 1945, when University College returned to London, he became professor of Latin. In this post Lockwood showed himself an excellent teacher and departmental administrator.

In 1950-1 Lockwood was dean of the faculty of arts of London University; in 1951 also he was elected chairman (until 1958) of the governing delegacy of Goldsmiths' College, where a building was later named after him. As dean of a faculty he joined the university senate committee which was administering a scheme of special relationship with colleges in Africa and the West Indies.

By now it was widely believed that Lockwood might be a successful college head. The governors of Birkbeck College, the main function of which is to provide facilities for the taking of degrees by mature students, elected him to the vacant mastership on 1 October 1951. He consequently resigned his professorship and stopped teaching, but became a member of the senate. Some people needlessly wondered whether Lockwood would understand the college fully, despite his experience of cramped working space and damage done by German air raids at University College in Gower Street, and which Birkbeck College had also suffered in Fetter Lane. But he at once grasped that Birkbeck students were maturer than those at day colleges, and that the college lacked sufficient space. Even before his mastership began he successfully insisted that the college should move at once into its internally unfinished new building alongside the Senate House in Malet Street.

From 1952 to 1955 Lockwood was London University's public orator. A lover of English and never prolix, he showed, in short speeches whereby he presented candidates for honorary degrees, a ready wit and a sense of epigram as much 'Lockwoodian' as 'classical'. From 1953 to 1955 he was also chairman of the Collegiate Council, in 1954-5 deputy vice-chancellor, and in 1955 became a member of the Court—the controlling financial body. He was vice-chancellor from 1955 to 1958, assuming his appointment a fortnight before the installation of Queen Elizabeth, the Queen Mother, as chancellor of the university. At the invitation of the Inter-University Council for Higher Education Overseas, in 1954 he went with a mission led by Sir Eric (later Lord) Ashby to Kampala, to investigate the possibilities of making Makerere College a university centre for Kenya, Uganda, and Tanganyika. From 1956 to 1961 he was a member of the United States-United Kingdom Educational Commission. Lockwood's knowledge, wisdom, and gaiety endeared him to American scholars and administrators alike: he had a 'modesty, cordiality and humour that made working with him a delight'. He went to the United States several times.

In 1956, when the Ford Foundation had granted £357,000 to help students and artists who had left Hungary after the revolt, Lockwood was the British representative at the discussions in Vienna between the Foundation and representatives of other countries willing to accept Hungarian students. When his vice-chancellorship ended in 1958 he became chairman of the Secondary School Examinations Council and joined the Inter-University Council for Higher Education Overseas, on whose policy he had a decisive influence. He also did good work for the Association of the Universities of the Commonwealth committee on universities overseas. In 1958 he became chairman of a Colonial Office working party on higher education in East Africa. With the help of his hard-worked team his report (1958-9) led to the development of a single university of East Africa, federal in structure, of which Kenya, Uganda, and Tanganyika each had a constituent college. Lockwood became a member of the East African University's Provisional Council and of the Council of the University College at Nairobi, Kenya. His attention was then drawn to West Africa. In 1957 he led a delegation to the University College at Ibadan, and in 1958 he went to Sierra Leone and Ghana as leader of the grants committee on higher education in Ghana. He also visited Basutoland. The following year he was a member of an Anglo-American Commission (chaired by Sir Eric Ashby) surveying higher education in Nigeria, whose independence celebrations he attended in 1960, the year in which the new university of Nigeria opened at Nsukka. From 1960 to 1964 Lockwood was chairman of the West African Examinations Council. In 1961 Lockwood advised against the creation of a university in Mauritius because of the difficulties of staff recruitment and finance.

Meanwhile, as chairman of the Secondary School Examinations Council (1958-64) Lockwood produced a report, which was accepted, recommending that a Schools Council for Curriculum and Examinations should be established before the academic year 1964-5. Lockwood's name is also associated with influential reports on sixth-form studies and the English language examination, which influenced the GCE system.

In 1961 Lockwood became senior consultant in a UNESCO and International Association of Universities study of the role which institutions of higher education in South-East Asia were playing and should play. After the requisite travels he was just able to write the preface to its summary report before his death.

In 1962, when he was knighted, Lockwood attended a conference on higher education in Madagascar and was elected chairman of the new Voluntary Societies' Committee for Service Overseas, which sent trained young volunteers to developing countries. When the British share in this scheme was publicly criticized, Lockwood explained and defended the policy in some detail. He became a member of a new Council of Volunteers in 1964.

Two years before his death Lockwood chaired two final projects, in Central Africa and Northern Ireland. After a visit to Northern Rhodesia, he recommended the establishment of a university at Lusaka (this later became the university of Zambia). In Northern Ireland he participated in the decision to site a university at Coleraine (the New University of Ulster, founded in 1965).

Meanwhile, at London University, Lockwood chaired committees and served on councils (such as those of the Medical College of St. Bartholomew's Hospital, the Postgraduate Medical Federation, Westfield College, and the Royal College of Art). From 1960 to 1963 he was a member of the university of Wales commission on its own structure.

Lockwood wrote articles of merit and originality, and, in the second revision of Smith's smaller Latin-English dictionary (corrected, improved, and enlarged), he produced almost a new work.

Despite his administrative and advisory commitments overseas, Lockwood spent most of each academic session in administration at Birkbeck College. His conduct as master was far from overbearing, since headstrong actions and controversial policies were distasteful to him. His anger was mild and short-lived, his forgiveness quick and permanent. At meetings his lively sense of humour was restrained under the pressure of serious business except when he was not himself presiding, but when he was host at a party he was gay and seemingly carefree. His speech was restrained and his English careful and artistic, giving rein to word-play only in the concocting of Anglo-Latin and Anglo-Greek menus for certain 'classical' lunches or dinners at college. An 'arts' man, he made no fetish of the classics; in politics a moderate, he held to the principle of merit alone in appointments. He was readily accessible to all—staff, students, and strangers. A Christian, he was renowned for certain qualities displayed everywhere at home or abroad, and, some thought, shown at their best in the team-work of committees: stamina, courage, persistence; gentleness, sympathy, bonhomie; objectivity, thoroughness, conciseness;

skill, diplomacy, and leadership of a new kind.

To face growing problems at Birkbeck in 1963-5 he summoned all his powers. After 1962 the two main issues were the extent to which the college could and should admit school leavers, and the justification of its bold proposals for physical expansion. Deep and divergent were opinions among the teachers, but by hard work Lockwood held the college together. There was some opposition to his own views, but he was vindicated as time passed, although the problems remained unsolved.

He could have retired in 1965 but Birkbeck's governors extended his mastership until the age of sixty-seven. However, he died at his home at Winchmore Hill 11 July 1965. The Inter-University Council recorded especially his tireless energy, vision, persuasiveness, and new approach to meeting the education needs of countries in Africa, and the trust inspired among leading academics and politicians there; and stressed his generosity and hospitality at Birkbeck College. Sir Christopher Cox wrote: 'The present [1950-65] packed chapter in the story of British and American co-operation in assisting African education virtually coincides with the Lockwood period; in it no Englishman except Sir Charles Morris and Sir Eric Ashby has played so influential a part.' Sir Eric Ashby himself wrote: 'Changes in British policy about overseas universities during the ten years 1955-1965 were mostly caused by Lockwood's thinking and imagination.'

Lockwood had a happy marriage; in 1929 he had married Marjorie, daughter of William Basil Clitheroe, a primary-school headmaster, and his wife, Katherine. They had a son and a daughter. He was a man of middle height and build and moved with a nimble and almost bounding walk. Clean shaven always, he kept short his light-brown hair which with age did not cover all the sinciput above his forehead. A portrait in oils, of him and Lady Lockwood together, by Norman Hepple, is at Birkbeck College.

[Lockwood Reports; minutes of the governors of Birkbeck College and the senate of the University of London; the Inter-University Council; *The Lodestone* (magazine of Birkbeck College); press notices; private information; personal knowledge.]   E. H. WARMINGTON

LOMBARD, ADRIAN ALBERT (1915-1967), aero-engineer, was born in Coventry 9 January 1915, the second son and third child of Arthur Henry Lombard, toolmaker, and his wife, Louisa Bartlett. Lombard was educated in Coventry at the John Gulson Central Advanced School and afterwards in night classes at the Technical College. In 1930 he joined the Rover Company, beginning his training in the drawing office. He left in 1935 to join Morris Motors where, still only twenty years old, he was in charge of engine stress calculations.

In 1936 he returned to the Rover Company and later became part of the design team under Maurice Wilks which in 1940 was given the task of making the Whittle W2B jet engine suitable for production. In the same year the team moved from Coventry to Clitheroe and at nearby Barnoldswick a factory was equipped to manufacture the engine. Thereafter, Lombard's main professional preoccupation was to be with the jet engine—more correctly, the aircraft gas turbine.

Lombard's production design, known as B 26, employed a different combustion system from (Sir) Frank Whittle's W2B and was in fact the precursor of the highly successful Nene and Derwent engines which Lombard designed in 1944 and 1945.

Early in 1943 E. W. (later Lord) Hives [q.v.], of Rolls-Royce, and Spencer Wilks, the chairman of Rover, completed a historic deal by which the Rover Co. exchanged their interest in the Whittle engine and the Clitheroe and Barnoldswick factories for the Rolls-Royce Tank Engine Factory at Nottingham. The Rover engineers concerned were given the choice of staying with Rover and transferring to tank engine production or staying with the jet engine work and joining Rolls-Royce. Few chose the latter, but one who did was Lombard.

Lombard had to create a fresh design organization and, with first-class recruits from Rolls-Royce, Derby, he quickly developed an efficient team. At Barnoldswick, he produced the W2B Whittle engine, of which 100 (at 1,700 lb. thrust) were built and used in the early Gloster Meteor twin-engined fighter aircraft. At the same time he supervised the design of the more powerful Derwent I engine (at 2,000 lb. thrust) which was interchangeable with the W2B in the Meteor. The Derwent I Meteors were in 1944 the first jet-fighters to be used by the RAF.

Meanwhile Lombard had supervised the design of the Rolls-Royce Nene engine which first ran in 1944, achieving a world record thrust of 5,000 lb. After the war the engine's design was sold to Pratt & Whitney in the USA and Hispano-Suiza in France. Twenty-five of the engines were sold to Russia, and a Russian version subsequently engined large numbers of MiG fighters.

In January 1945 Lombard began the design of the Derwent V engine, which was tested seven months later—an achievement which remains a testimony to Lombard's talent as a mechanical designer. Furthermore, in October 1945 a Meteor with Derwent V engines broke the world speed record at 603 mph.

In 1945 Lombard's team designed the Avon engine, rated at 6,500 lb. thrust. During the design of this engine Hives decided to transfer the technical and design centre to Derby, where Lombard became chief designer (projects). The Avon proved to be a major success and provided the power plants of the Vickers Valiant, Hawker Hunter, English Electric Canberra, and English Electric Lightning. The Avon also powered the Fairey Delta experimental aircraft (the first to exceed 1,000 mph), and was the first Rolls-Royce civil aircraft jet-propulsion engine, being used in the de Havilland Comet and the Sud Aviation Caravelle.

In 1952 Lombard became chief designer (aero), and in 1954 chief engineer, of Rolls-Royce. In this period he was engaged on the Conway engine which became noted internationally in both military and civil roles. The Vickers VC10, with four Conway engines, was one of the finest civil jet aircraft of its time.

Under Lombard's leadership, the Conway was succeeded by the Spey, the engine of the Buccaneer strike aircraft and the RAF Phantom, and the RB211, which engined the Lockheed Tri-Star, was developed.

Lombard served on the council of the Royal Aeronautical Society, on the Air Registration Board, and on the Aeronautical Research Council. Jointly with (Sir) Stanley Hooker, he was awarded the James Clayton prize of the Institution of Mechanical Engineers. He was appointed CBE a month before his death.

Lombard lacked formal training in aerodynamics and thermodynamics but was one of those good engineers who have an intuitive grasp of the laws of nature. He was also an able leader of a team. Hooker, who knew Lombard well, aptly described him: 'He was dynamic in action, energetic in application, and determined in argument, but withal he had a strong sense of humour and a ready wit.'

Lombard was a short, square person with an attractive smile, liked and respected by all who knew him. When he died, suddenly in Derby 13 July 1967, he was at the apex of his career, having been appointed director of engineering (aero) in 1958 and a director of Rolls-Royce.

In 1940 Lombard married Joan, daughter of George Chaffard Taylor, engineer. They had three sons, the second of whom died in infancy.

[S. G. Hooker, 'Adrian Albert Lombard, CBE', *Journal of the Royal Aeronautical Society*, December 1967; personal knowledge.]   KINGS NORTON

LONDON, HEINZ (1907-1970), physicist, was born 7 November 1907 at Bonn, the younger of the two sons of Franz London, mathematics professor at Bonn University, and his wife, Luise Hamburger. His father died when he was only nine and he was guided towards science by his brother Fritz, seven years his senior, who became a leading figure in quantum chemistry. Following school in Bonn, Heinz studied at several universities (Bonn 1926, Berlin Technische Hochschule 1927, and Munich 1929 to 1931), where he was inspired by the lectures of Planck, von Laue, and Sommerfeld. He then started research in low-temperature physics at Breslau University under (Sir) F. E. Simon [q.v.], from whom he received a thorough grounding in thermodynamics, a discipline which London regarded with almost religious reverence. With the advent of Hitler in 1933, Simon decided to leave Germany and London joined his group soon afterwards in Oxford.

In Breslau he looked for the appearance of resistance in a superconductor as the frequency of an alternating current was raised. Although he failed to find an effect because his frequency could not be raised sufficiently, his Ph.D. thesis (Breslau, 1933) contained important new ideas about the nature of the superconducting state, which he then developed at Oxford in collaboration with his brother Fritz. Their 'phenomenonological' theory of superconductivity (1935) was an important step in the eventual development of the fundamental theory by John Bardeen, Leon N. Cooper, and John R. Schrieffer (1956). In 1936 London moved to Bristol, where he again took up the high-frequency resistance problem and at last found the effect in 1940. The effect was later more thoroughly studied by (Sir) A. B. Pippard, and provided further vital clues to the fundamental theory. In parallel with his work on superconductivity, London also contributed to the understanding of superfluidity in liquid helium, most importantly by his thermodynamic interpretation of the fountain effect.

Early in the war, London was among the many German refugees who were interned, but he was soon released to work on problems of isotope separation for the atom bomb project (at Bristol and Birmingham universities, Imperial College, ICI Witton and Winnington, and Ministry of Supply, Mold, Flintshire). In 1944 he was effectively leader of the Birmingham team. The anomaly of having a foreigner engaged on top-secret work was eliminated by the simple expedient of naturalization (1942). After the war he joined the new AERE at Harwell as principal scientific officer and was later senior principal scientific officer (1950) and deputy chief scientist (1958). There he continued for a while his isotope separation work, collaborated in various technical cryogenic projects, and worked on various ingenious ideas for the technical exploitation of superconductivity. His main contribution, however, was his invention of a new method of cooling to extremely low temperatures—the 'dilution refrigerator'. His first proposal of the basic idea in 1951 was very bold since it depended essentially on the use of the rare isotope helium 3, which was not then available in anything like sufficient quantities. However, helium 3 did soon become commercially available and after years of difficult development work (in collaboration with E. Mendoza and H. E. Hall) the dilution refrigerator eventually worked at Manchester in 1965. It has since been manufactured commercially and in making readily accessible the millidegree range of temperatures it has revolutionized low-temperature physics in recent years. London's fundamental contributions were recognized by the award of the first Simon memorial prize in 1959 and by his election as a fellow of the Royal Society in 1961.

Although London regarded himself as an experimentalist and most of his scientific life was spent in laboratories, he will be remembered more for his original ideas and inventions than for the experimental work he carried out himself. Indeed, he was rather 'ham-handed' and things rarely went right until the actual manipulation was left to his assistants. He was much valued as an informal consultant and ideas man and could be relied on to get down to the fundamentals of a problem, especially if it involved classical disciplines such as electrodynamics or thermodynamics. In the familiar circle at the Harwell lunch table he would lose his customary shyness and hold forth in a lively way on a multiplicity of topics. In spite of a somewhat withdrawn manner and a stooping stance, which made him look sad, he was very happy in his family life after his second marriage and much enjoyed simple recreations such as walking, climbing, and cycling. These recreations had to be much restricted after a mild coronary thrombosis in 1966, but he continued to be scientifically productive until the end of his life. Always a heavy smoker, he died of lung cancer at home in Oxford 3 August 1970.

His first marriage (1939) to Gertrude Rosenthal ended in divorce and he subsequently (1945) married Lucie Meissner by whom he had two sons and two daughters.

[D. Shoenberg in *Biographical Memoirs of Fellows of the Royal Society*, vol. xvii, 1971; private information; personal knowledge.]   D. SHOENBERG

LONGMORE, SIR ARTHUR MURRAY (1885-1970), air chief marshal, was born 8 October 1885 at St. Leonards, New South Wales, Australia, the youngest son of Charles Croker Longmore, station master at Yarrara. He was brought to England by his mother when seven years old and educated at Benges School, Hertford, and Foster's Academy, Stubbington. As a boy the sea held a great attraction for him and, after showing considerable aptitude at school, he entered *Britannia* as a naval cadet in May 1900. After receiving his commission into the Royal Navy in 1904, his early career followed the normal pattern of a junior officer. During this period young Arthur Longmore took a great interest in, and followed the exploits of, the early pioneers in aviation.

It was a coincidence that, in 1910, when commanding a torpedo boat based at Sheerness, one of the early flying schools was being established at Eastchurch on the near-by Isle of Sheppey. Such was Longmore's enthusiasm for aviation that he was one of the first four naval officers selected to attend a course of flying instruction there. In less then two months he was awarded Royal Aero Club certificate No. 72 which put him high among the ranks of the pioneers of naval aviation.

There followed a brief period as a flying instructor at the newly opened Central Flying School, where (Sir) John Salmond [q.v.] was also an instructor. After this he took command of Cromarty Air Station and subsequently of the experimental seaplane station at Calshot where he was able to pursue his great interest in the development of floatplanes. Prior to the introduction of aircraft carriers, these were regarded as the most suitable aircraft to provide support for the Royal Navy. When war broke out in 1914, Longmore was sent to Dunkirk to carry out some of the first bombing missions during which the small bombs were literally thrown over the sides of the cockpit. After a few weeks of these haphazard and largely ineffectual operations, Longmore was given the task of forming and commanding No. 1 Squadron, Royal Naval Air Service, which had considerable success in the Dunkirk area against Zeppelins, then beginning to attack England with increasing frequency.

It came as a disappointment to Longmore to be transferred back to naval duties in January 1916, when he was appointed to *Tiger* of the first battle-cruiser squadron as a lieutenant-commander, relinquishing the rank of wing commander, RNAS. This was to be his last sea-going appointment and it gave him a unique opportunity to be present at the Battle of Jutland during which the experience he had acquired as an airman made him an admirable adviser on air matters to the commander of the battle-cruiser force. In this capacity he was highly critical of the failure to make adequate use of aircraft during the battle and considered that they could have made an invaluable contribution in the reconnaissance role.

After a brief spell in London on the Air Board where he was responsible for aircraft and equipment development, Longmore, now a wing captain, RNAS, went to Malta where he joined the staff of the commander-in-chief, Mediterranean, and was responsible for air operations. On 1 April 1918 the Royal Air Force was formed and he became a lieutenant-colonel RAF and was given his first RAF command, the Adriatic Group at Taranto, a post he held until after the armistice in November 1918. He waged a vigorous and successful campaign against U-boat bases in the Mediterranean, for which he was appointed to the DSO in 1919.

The post-war years were unstable and frustrating for the new Service and Longmore filled several posts for short periods before being posted to Iraq in 1923 as a group captain on the staff of Air Headquarters. This was a period of great interest for him since Iraq had been placed under 'air control' by the Cairo Conference of 1921; this gave the RAF its first opportunity to demonstrate its capability for controlling large sparsely populated areas of difficult terrain. Longmore should be given much of the credit for the success of the experiment which was later extended to Aden and other theatres. He was appointed CB on his return home in 1925 for a tour of duty in the Air Ministry as director of equipment.

He then became commandant of the RAF College at Cranwell and shortly afterwards was promoted to air vice-marshal at the early age of forty-five. His great experience and somewhat gregarious nature qualified him admirably for this appointment. He passed two of the happiest years of his career in the Lincolnshire countryside where he was able to indulge his enthusiasm for hunting and shooting. Under his guidance the permanent college building was completed at Cranwell and opened in 1933.

After leaving Cranwell he commanded in succession Inland Area and Coastal Area which later became Fighter Command and Coastal Command respectively. These years involved him in constant struggles to preserve his forces against the wholesale reductions and economies which were prevalent, and it was not until 1933, when he was promoted to air marshal and in the following year when he became commandant of the Imperial Defence College, that the RAF began to expand to meet the growing threat from Germany. At the Imperial Defence College he devoted much time and effort, with little response, to fostering closer relations between the three Services.

For a brief period in 1939-40 he was commander-in-chief, Training Command, and, as such, played a notable part in initiating the highly successful Empire air training scheme under which thousands of wartime aircrew were to be trained in Canada, Rhodesia, and elsewhere in the British Empire. Shortly after the outbreak of war, however, he was transferred to the important post of AOC-in-C, Middle East, which turned out to be his most challenging appointment. When he assumed command in May 1940, the pressing demands of the European theatre had resulted in a serious dearth of modern aircraft and equipment in the Middle East. In the following month, Italy declared war and Longmore's small force was soon heavily involved with the Italian Air Force in North Africa, Greece, and Abyssinia. As he slowly built up and modernized his squadrons, their commitments, notably in Greece, became increasingly heavy.

On 9 December 1940 the offensive in the Western Desert opened with all the air support that Longmore could assemble. It turned out to be the first British success of the war on land and the Italian Air Force in North Africa was virtually immobilized. Unhappily the triumph was short-lived when Germany came to the assistance of her Italian ally both in Africa and in Greece. Within four months the Germans had recaptured all the Army's earlier gains and had overrun Greece. Longmore was compelled to withdraw the RAF from the Western Desert into Egypt and to evacuate the Greek airfields. Nevertheless his losses were not unduly heavy and he could now count upon a much larger and more modern force than had been available when he assumed command. Severe losses on the enemy had been inflicted.

In May 1941 he was recalled to London for consultation and was made inspector-general of the RAF, a post which he held until the following year when he retired officially from the Service, having been appointed GCB.

After his retirement he returned to his home in Lincolnshire and contested the March 1942 by-election in Grantham as a Conservative candidate. He was, however, narrowly defeated. His RAF career was not finished as, in August 1943, he was recalled to serve on the Post-Hostilities Planning Committee, which considered problems concerned with the reshaping of combatant countries in peacetime. This valuable work took him to his final retirement in May 1944, but he continued to help the war effort by joining a voluntary organization, the 'Yachtsmen's Emergency Service'. As a lifelong sailing enthusiast he was of immense value to this organization which provided waterborne transport for the invasion fleet forming up in the Channel ports. From the end of the war until his death he led an active life and gave a great deal of his time to the War Graves Commission, of which he was vice-chairman. He also continued to indulge his love of sailing as a member of the Royal Yacht Squadron. He died 10 December 1970 at Little Trees, Broomfield Park, Sunningdale.

Longmore was twice married: firstly in 1913 to Marjorie, only child of William James Maitland, of Witley Manor, Godalming. They had three sons, two of whom joined the RAF, one being killed in action in 1943, and one of whom joined the Royal Artillery, and one daughter. Marjorie died in 1959 and Longmore married, secondly, Enid, the widow of Lt.-Col. Geoffrey Bolster, in 1960. During his long and distinguished career he received many foreign decorations—from Belgium, France, Italy, and Greece—and he wrote his autobiography, *From Sea to Sky*, which was published in 1946. He also wrote a chapter on air forces in *The Era of Violence, 1898-1945*, New Cambridge Modern History, vol. xii (1964). His portrait was painted in 1939 by Sir William Rothenstein and is in the possession of the Royal Air Force College.

[*The Times*, 12 December 1970; Sir Arthur Longmore, *From Sea to Sky*, 1946.]

DAVID LEE

LONGSTAFF, TOM GEORGE (1875-1964), mountain explorer, was born 15 January 1875 at Summergangs Hall, Hull, the eldest son of Llewellyn Wood Longstaff and his wife, Mary Lydia, daughter of Thomas William Sawyer, of Southampton. It was his father who made possible the first Antarctic expedition under Captain Scott [q.v.] by an early contribution of £25,000. Longstaff was educated at Eton and Christ Church, Oxford, where he obtained a third class in physiology in 1897. He proceeded BM, B.Ch. in 1903 and DM in 1906 (Oxford and St. Thomas's), but he never took up regular practice thereafter.

Although he often visited the Alps during his childhood and adolescence, it was not until he was twenty-two that Longstaff began serious mountaineering; then, during several Alpine seasons, he learnt the art under the tuition of some of the leading Alpine guides of the period. In 1903 he undertook a climbing expedition in the Caucasus where, with his single companion, L. W. Rolleston, he made the first ascent of five peaks.

In 1905 Longstaff went to the Himalaya with two Italian guides, Alexis and Henri Brocherel, with the intention of exploring the vicinity of Nanda Devi. His plans were curtailed when he accepted an invitation to join C. A. Sherring, deputy commissioner of Almora, on a journey to Tibet. Before setting off, however, Longstaff and his guides spent a month exploring the eastern approaches to Nanda Devi, and reached a 19,000 ft. col on the rim of the basin which gave them the first view of its interior. The Tibetan journey took them through little-known country to Lake Manasarowar, the source of the river Sutlej. On the way, Longstaff and the Brocherels made a bold attempt to climb Gurla Mandhata (25,350 ft.). Swept away by a snow avalanche which carried them 3,000 feet down the mountainside, they renewed their ascent next day but abandoned the attempt 1,000 feet below the summit after they had spent the night in the open at an altitude of 23,000 feet.

Two years later Longstaff returned to the Himalaya with the same guides, this time accompanied by Charles Bruce [q.v.] and Arnold Mumm. They approached Nanda Devi from the west and, by discovering and crossing the Bagini pass (20,000 ft.), they reached the middle gorge of the Rishi Ganga, the only outlet from the basin. From there, Longstaff and the guides made the ascent of Trisul (23,360 ft.), climbing the final 6,000 feet in a single day. This was to remain for twenty-three years the highest summit reached. They then attempted to penetrate the upper gorge of the Rishi Ganga into the Nanda Devi basin. Although they failed, the first party to accomplish this project twenty-seven years later owed its success largely to this reconnaissance. They spent the rest of the summer exploring the glaciers of the Kamet group.

In 1909 Longstaff turned his attention to the Karakoram. It was there that he made his most notable contribution to geography when, accompanied by A. Morris Slingsby, he crossed the legendary Saltoro pass to discover the upper portion of the Siachen glacier, one of the greatest ice-streams outside polar regions, and the lofty massif of Terim Kangri beyond. Then, with D. G. Oliver he followed the Nubra river to its source in the glacier; and continuing up the glacier was able to confirm his identification. These discoveries established the position of an important section of the continental watershed between the Indus and the Tarim basin of Chinese Turkestan.

All these expeditions he conducted with Spartan simplicity, unencumbered by elaborate equipment and living largely upon local produce. This was from choice, not necessity; for he was a keen exponent of light travel which not only gave him freedom of movement but enabled him more easily to establish contact with the local people and to achieve close harmony with his chosen environment. Following the tradition of the nineteenth-century travellers he recorded detailed observations of the natural history of the regions he visited; but his special interest was ornithology. His affection for mountain people and his understanding of their way of life are revealed in his autobiography, *This My Voyage* (1950).

In 1910 and 1911 Longstaff climbed in the Canadian Rockies. During the war of 1914-18 he served in India and, as assistant commandant of the Gilgit Scouts (1916-17), in the course of his duties travelled widely in the Hindu Kush. In 1922 he joined the second expedition to Mount Everest where his experience of high-altitude climbing and his medical knowledge were of great value to the party. Apart from this, his pioneer travels during this period were in the Arctic. He took part in two expeditions to Spitsbergen (1921 and 1923) and three to West Greenland (1928, 1931, and 1934).

Longstaff's short, spare frame belied his exceptional powers of endurance; but his dynamic character was revealed by a high-bridged, patrician nose and lively eyes, and emphasized by a jutting red beard. For more than half a century he was a leading figure in geographical and mountaineering circles. He served for many years on the council of the Royal Geographical Society, as vice-president in 1934-7, and as honorary secretary in 1930-4. In 1908 he was awarded the Gill memorial and in 1928 the Founder's medal. He was elected president of the Alpine Club in 1947 and made an honorary member in 1956. It was, however, through his personal contacts that his influence was most widely felt. His great experience was at the disposal of all who sought it and successive generations of young mountaineers and explorers owed much to his encouragement and sage advice. He would discuss their plans with as much enthusiasm as though he himself were taking part in their projects, and he was equally generous in his praise of their success. He never hesitated to say what he thought and he was fiercely critical of humbug and ostentation. Typical was his remark to a member of one of the many abortive attempts to climb Everest which in his opinion received excessive publicity: 'For Heaven's sake climb the wretched thing and let's get back to real mountaineering.'

In 1911 Longstaff married Dora Mary Hamilton, daughter of Bernard Scott, MRCS, of Bournemouth; they had seven daughters. The marriage was dissolved in 1937 and in 1938 he married Charmian Dorothy Isabel, daughter of Duncan James Reid, MB, CM, of Ealing, London, with whom he settled in Wester Ross. In this wild setting, so well suited to his tastes, he spent the main part of his last twenty-five years, keeping open house to his wide circle of friends, including many of the foremost naturalists of the day, and visited, as always, by young men seeking his advice. He died there 26 June 1964.

[Private information; personal knowledge.]

ERIC SHIPTON

LORAINE, SIR PERCY LYHAM, twelfth baronet (1880-1961), diplomatist, was born in London 5 November 1880, the second son and second child in the family of two sons and two daughters of Rear-Admiral Sir Lambton Loraine and his wife, Frederica Mary Horatia, daughter of Captain Charles Acton Broke, of the Royal Engineers, who brought him the Suffolk property of Bramford Hall, Ipswich. Loraine was educated at Eton (1893-9) and New College, Oxford (1899), but left to serve in the South African war (Queen's medal with five clasps). He passed into the Foreign Office in 1904. In his first two posts—Constantinople (1904) and Tehran (1907)—he learnt Turkish and Persian. In 1909 he was posted to Rome, and in 1911 temporarily to Peking. He next served in Paris (1912) and Madrid (1916).

In 1918-19 he was appointed to the peace conference delegation in Paris, but found that working for tired and overburdened men was disheartening; more congenial was battling with the Bolsheviks in Eastern Europe. In October 1919 he was appointed a member of the mission which thwarted Bela Kun in Hungary, and from there went immediately to Poland where he witnessed the Polish success in repelling the Bolshevik armies from Warsaw; he helped to abate extravagant Polish frontier demands.

The foreign secretary, Lord Curzon (later Marquess Curzon of Kedleston, q.v.), had spotted Loraine's zeal, and in 1920 offered him the counsellorship in Tehran to help win ratification for 'his' treaty; but Loraine, who had just inherited Northumbrian estates, pleaded home business, and joined Curzon's personal staff. The two north-country landowners, with their shared feudal outlook, found that they had much in common; nevertheless Loraine was astounded when in July 1921 Curzon begged him to become minister to Persia and salvage what he could from a treaty which the Persians had rejected. Loraine early recognized Reza Khan (later Reza Shah Pahlevi) as the likely winner of the local struggle for power; he appreciated Reza's directness. But his assignment was dogged by conflicting British obligations—to the sheikh of Mohammerah in the oil province of Arabistan, and to Reza, who was bent on controlling all Persia. In bad faith, Reza seized the sheikh and removed him to Tehran, where he later died. Loraine spent much effort trying to correct this injustice.

After three years as minister in Greece (1926–9), he was in 1929 appointed high commissioner for Egypt and the Sudan, succeeding the imperious Lord Lloyd [q.v.]. But here his technique of establishing personal relations with a leader failed him. Leaving King Fuad to sort out differences with his ministers yielded neither a treaty with Britain nor mitigation of the tussle between king, parties, and Residency. To Loraine's mortification he was replaced and in 1933 transferred to Ankara. However, even appointment to the Privy Council (1933) did not reconcile him to that 'godforsaken hole'.

But he was mistaken. His Turkish service was a triumph. He established with Mustafa Kemal relations even closer than those with Reza Shah. They played bridge and poker together, talked far into the night, and agreed on Anglo-Turkish friendship. All through Loraine's life he had felt a personal attachment to his own king; he relished Edward VIII's visit in 1936, and was saddened by his abdication. He left Turkey when he was appointed ambassador to Italy at the beginning of 1939, shortly after Kemal's death. He was then confident that Anglo-Turkish friendship was firm.

Loraine had approved of the Munich agreement and was distressed when Hitler occupied Prague and Mussolini Albania. He saw Mussolini only twice and was snubbed over British policy. He stood his ground, but fought a losing battle. For a while Loraine's good relations with Count Galeazzo Ciano kept Italy neutral, but Hitler's success in France encouraged Mussolini to declare war upon the Allies on 11 June 1940.

On his return to England Loraine much resented official failure to use his talent; Churchill would not see him; he thought his Middle East experience wasted; and he spent the war in frustration. After the war, he took with zest to horse-racing, a hobby which dated from Egypt. He bred some classic winners, was elected to the Jockey Club, and helped to innovate the photo-finish. To this Dictionary Loraine contributed the notice of James Rennell Rodd, first Baron Rennell.

Since Loraine's elder brother had been killed in a flying accident in 1912 he succeeded to the baronetcy when his father died in 1917. Tall, discreet, immaculately dressed, he nevertheless looked forbidding; he would have liked to unbend, but found this difficult, being essentially shy. He never discussed ideas, and preferred cards or backgammon to chat. His memory was excellent and his judgement good, but he delegated too little, and was wordy on paper.

In 1924 he married Louise Violet Beatrice (D.G.St.J.), elder daughter of Major-General Edward James Montagu-Stuart-Wortley, CB, CMG. Their happy marriage was marred by failure to produce an heir. A friend described Loraine as disclosing 'more and more an essential humanity' as he mellowed with age; a photograph of 1954 leading in the winner of the 2000 Guineas bears this out. He was appointed CMG in 1921, KCMG in 1925, and GCMG in 1937. He died at his London home 23 May 1961. A portrait was painted by T. Geraldy in Paris in 1913. The National Portrait Gallery has a photograph of him in his Turkish period.

[Gordon Waterfield, *Professional Diplomat*, 1973; Piers Dixon, *Double Diploma*, 1968; *The Times*, 24, 26, and 30 May 1961; personal knowledge.]   ELIZABETH MONROE

LOVATT EVANS, SIR CHARLES ARTHUR (1884–1968), physiologist. [See EVANS.]

LOW, SIR DAVID ALEXANDER CECIL (1891–1963), cartoonist and caricaturist, was born in Dunedin, New Zealand, 7 April 1891, the third and youngest son of David Brown Low and his wife, Jane Caroline Flanagan. His father, a business man of wide interests, was of Scottish and his mother of Irish descent. Their families had emigrated to New Zealand in the mid nineteenth century; neither had previously produced an artist.

Low's days at Christchurch Boys' High School ended when he was eleven, and thenceforth his youth was happily spent in the family house on the outskirts of Christchurch. There he read excursively in his father's library but devoted most of his time to drawing, rigging for himself a makeshift studio, and working from models, animate and inanimate, which he found available in the immediate surroundings. A determination to earn his living as an artist met with the usual parental opposition which was, however, tempered when one of his drawings was reproduced in the Christchurch *Spectator* before his twelfth birthday.

Although for a short period he attended a local school of art, he found it more profitable to learn by the hard process of trial and error, and to discover (in his words) that 'one could draw a thing if one understood it, but usually got lost if one did not'. A pile of old copies of *Punch* had introduced him to the work of Charles Keene and Phil May [qq.v.]. 'Once having discovered Phil May', he later wrote, 'I never let him go.' Already encouraged by having many of his sketches accepted by local papers, he obtained his first regular appointment as political cartoonist on the *Spectator*, his second on the *Canterbury Times*. Success turned his thoughts and ambitions towards Australia and, eventually, England.

The Sydney *Bulletin* in Australia had a reputation for the fostering of talent, and no doubt this influenced Low in 1911 to accept an offer of six months as its Melbourne political cartoonist. There followed some years of general work for the *Bulletin* until in 1914 he became the paper's resident cartoonist at Melbourne. The *Bulletin's* basic policy was to oppose established authority, particularly when power was wielded by politicians alleged to be taking themselves too seriously. By temperament and upbringing the young artist had radical leanings; and William M. Hughes [q.v.], known in Australia as 'our Billy', who in 1915 became prime minister and was generally believed to be getting above himself, afforded just the target Low needed for the exercise of his pictorial wit. The artist did not spare Hughes, ridiculing both the man and his policy, and his cartoons were later collected in *The Billy Book* (Sydney, 1918) which had a wide sale. His portrait drawings of local worthies were more restrained; and when a selection was published in book form (Sydney, 1915) the artist confessed in a foreword that his caution derived from the fear of arousing resentment, a self-imposed curb on freedom of expression which his later career proved to be merely a temporary expedient.

Low's future as cartoonist was assured during these years in Australia. His technique matured from a highly finished, rather academic manner to the more confident economy of line which became so characteristic a feature of his later work.

His cartoons were now becoming known in England and the Cadbury Press offered him a place on the staff of one of its newspapers. In November 1919 he arrived in London, and for the next eight years he was political cartoonist to the *Star*, an evening paper with a strictly Liberal policy, vehemently opposed to the coalition Government of Lloyd George. Lloyd George, indeed, succeeded Hughes as the principal butt of Low's satire, and was often depicted astride the 'coalition ass', a grotesque and obstreperous double-headed animal, which the cartoonist had concocted to symbolize the alleged ineptitude of the coalition. Already, however, Low's cartoons relating to foreign affairs were of more serious import, and not infrequently prophetic, as, for example, the drawing (1922) of the intransigent Poincaré driving the democratic German Weimar Government at the point of the bayonet into the outstretched arms of totalitarianism.

In 1926 Lord Beaverbrook [q.v.] persuaded Low to join the *Evening Standard* as political cartoonist. Both proprietor and artist well knew that the policies in which Low believed would be frequently in conflict with those advanced in other parts of the paper. The agreement (by letter dated 6 December 1926) contained a clause that the artist was 'to have complete freedom in the selection and treatment of subject matter . . . and in the expression therein of the policies in which you believe; and that this fact will be given prominence in all our announcements . . . when you join the staff of the *Evening Standard*' (copy of letter in the Beaverbrook Library, London). Low's cartoons were often the subject of bitter criticism from readers, and occasionally of friendly remonstrance on Beaverbrook's part, but they were always printed except on the rare occasions when the paper's legal advisers raised the alarm.

In the years leading up to the war, although Low in his cartoons continued to record in the *Standard* the features and foibles of politicians at home, and to survey the national scene from his own highly critical and individual angle, affairs abroad, particularly those of countries under the heel of dictatorship, became his main theme. Hitler was depicted, often two or three times a week, as a militant pigmy strutting across the page; and Mussolini was also a constant subject of Low's derision, portrayed with dark half-shaven jowl and threatening mien, truculently defying the League and the irresolute democracies. In consequence, from 1933 the *Evening Standard* was banned from Germany, and later from Italy. The Nazis continued to be sensitive to criticism in the British press, and particularly resented Low's cartoons, as Lord Halifax [q.v.] was made well aware during his visit to Germany late in 1937. Goebbels, invited to meet Halifax at the British embassy, took the opportunity of contrasting the restrained behaviour of the German press at the time of the abdication in 1936 with 'the shameless fashion in which our Press was for ever attacking the Führer' (Lord Halifax, *Fulness of Days*, 1957). These reactions were later privately conveyed by Halifax to Low who so far relented as to introduce a composite character named 'Muzzler', fusing the features of Hitler and Mussolini without being identifiable as either; but after the invasion of Austria the cartoonist absolved himself from all such restraint.

In the immediate pre-war years Low's cartoons were reproduced by radio transmission throughout free Europe, the Americas, and the Commonwealth; and he thus became a figure of world-wide prestige, resented and feared in the totalitarian countries as Raemaekers and Will Dyson [q.v.] had been in the Germany of an earlier generation. In 1940 Low was reliably informed that he had been included in the Gestapo list for elimination.

In 1949 Low resigned from the *Evening*

Standard. 'Black Friday' was how Beaverbrook described the day he received Low's letter of resignation. There was no quarrel: Beaverbrook's great admiration for Low's work and the close friendship between them remained constant until the end. Low needed a change, a need engendered by a characteristic fear of 'becoming a British institution', as he had already been described by a foreign newspaper; and the exigencies of post-war paper control no longer allowed him space for a full-sized cartoon, a technical point which decided the issue. In 1950 he joined the *Daily Herald*, then the mouthpiece of political and industrial Labour, and during the next three years either amused or bewildered readers by depicting the Trades Union Congress as an endearingly massive and clumsy draught-horse, the last and not the least famous of his pictorial symbols. From 1953, in semi-retirement, he contributed three cartoons a week to the *Manchester Guardian*.

Churchill described Low as 'the greatest of our modern cartoonists. The greatest because of the vividness of his political conceptions, and because he possesses what few cartoonists have—a grand technique of draughtsmanship' (*Thoughts and Adventures*, 1932). Certainly his technique of heavy black lines and masses, applied with brush and crayon, was peculiarly well adapted to modern methods of reproduction and, irrespective of content, aesthetically satisfying to the eye. Carried out under the stress of journalistic requirements—during the currency of the *Evening Standard* agreement he was contributing five cartoons a week—his drawing was bold in conception and execution, restoring to English caricature a vitality and irreverence which had been lacking since the early nineteenth century. Adopting a method begun by James Gillray [q.v.], he portrayed living characters as butts, represented in varying shapes and images of fantasy, made familiar to the reader by constant use of accessories chosen as expressing the quiddity of the subject caricatured. Baldwin's pipe, for example, J. H. Thomas's dress-shirt (token of his alleged pleasure in dining out in full splendour), Goering's bemedalled girth, Neville Chamberlain's umbrella, all received regular attention. He also invented imaginary characters to symbolize policies and attitudes of mind, the most famous of whom was 'Colonel Blimp', a name added to the dictionaries to connote a muddle-headed type of complacent reactionary. The colonel was depicted by Low as an elderly gentleman, usually in a Turkish bath, bald and rotund, with a long white two-pronged moustache, delivering himself of self-contradictory aphorisms.

Although Low in his cartoons hit hard at folly and hypocrisy, and could state his theme with grim earnestness—the memorable drawings he contributed to the *Evening Standard* in the spring of 1940 perfectly reflected the mood of the nation—in the usual run his natural kindliness showed itself and 'cheerfulness was always breaking in'. His cartoons were sometimes bitter, occasionally perhaps brutal, but (except abroad) were seldom resented by those depicted, who were indeed often eager to obtain the original drawing. Low used to say he was incapable of disliking people whom he met, and he was frequently on friendly terms with those whose ideas he attacked in his cartoons. (Even the imaginary Colonel Blimp, for all his obtuse absurdity, became for many readers a not unlikeable figure of fun.) The pictorial commentary Low contributed to light-hearted articles on aspects of contemporary life in England was a popular feature of the papers for which he worked. The mocking self-portrait he introduced into these articles, as into many cartoons, of a squat gesticulating figure belied his real appearance which, with his heavy eyebrows, fine alert eyes, and dark pointed beard, was one of distinction.

Low throughout his career considered his work as a caricaturist to be at least as important as the political content of his cartoons. 'It lies within the bones of the caricaturist himself', he wrote, 'to decide whether he will be a mere drawer of funny pictures or a worthy satirist; . . . whether beneath the surface of his cartoons lies nonsense or the visible operation of human intellect in the presentation of truth' (from the foreword by Low to H. R. Westwood, *Modern Caricaturists*, 1932). Perhaps the finest examples of his work as a caricaturist, as distinct from that of a cartoonist, appeared in the *New Statesman*. Many selections from Low's cartoons were published in book form. They include *Lloyd George & Co.* (1921); *Low's Political Parade* (1936); *Europe Since Versailles* (1940); *Low's War Cartoons* (1941); *Years of Wrath: A Cartoon History, 1932–45* (1949); and *Low Visibility: A Cartoon History, 1945–53* (1953). To the 'Britain in Pictures' series Low contributed *British Cartoonists, Caricaturists and Comic Artists* (1942). Mention too should be made of his ten double-page illustrations for H. G. Wells's *The Autocracy of Mr. Parham* (1930); and of his twelve double-page illustrations in water-colour for *The Modern 'Rake's Progress'* (1934) for which (Dame) Rebecca West wrote the words and in which he satirized the current scene in the Hogarthian manner. In 1956 his autobiography was published.

In 1920 Low married Madeline Grieve Kenning, of New Zealand; they had two daughters. He was knighted in 1962. He had been made an honorary LLD of the university of New Brunswick in 1958. He died in London 19 September 1963.

A self-portrait in oils is at the National Portrait Gallery which also possesses some 400 of his studies for caricature of a wide range of personalities. Letters and other papers in connection with Low's career are at the Beaverbrook Library, London, besides over 2,000 of his original drawings, mainly cartoons for the *Evening Standard*. In the library at New Zealand House, London, there are, besides seventy original cartoon drawings, a set of copies of books written or illustrated by the artist.

[*The Times*, 21 September 1963; *Low's Autobiography*, 1956; private information.]

D. PEPYS-WHITELEY

LUBBOCK, PERCY (1879–1965), author, fourth son of Frederic Lubbock, merchant banker, and his wife, Catherine, daughter of John Gurney, of Earlham Hall, Norfolk, was born in London 4 June 1879. He was the grandson of Sir J. W. Lubbock [q.v.] and nephew of Sir John Lubbock (later first Baron Avebury, q.v.). He was educated at Eton, in the house of A. C. Benson [q.v.], and as a scholar at King's College, Cambridge. In 1901 he was placed in the first class of the classical tripos. As an undergraduate he eschewed games but the love of birds and flowers and rural landscape, which remained with him throughout life, prompted long expeditions into the East Anglian countryside.

In 1906 he resigned from an uncongenial post in the Board of Education after his election as Pepys librarian at Magdalene College, Cambridge, on the recommendation of A. C. Benson, then a fellow. For two years he enjoyed a semi-academic life with rooms in college, but in 1908 he resigned in order to devote himself entirely to literature and writing. (He had already published, in 1906, *Elizabeth Barrett Browning in her Letters*.) One fruit of his term as librarian was the publication, in 1909, of *Samuel Pepys*, which, although to some extent superseded by later more elaborate studies, deserves to hold its place in Pepysian biography as a concise and clearly written introduction to the *Diary*.

Between 1908 and 1914 Lubbock contributed regularly to *The Times Literary Supplement*, writing several main articles which he was urged in vain to republish as a volume. It was during this period that he first met Henry James [q.v.], the author who was to have so strong an influence on Lubbock's concept of literature and indeed on his literary style. James died in 1916, and in the following year Lubbock saw through the press and wrote a short general preface for three of James's unfinished works—*The Ivory Tower*, *The Sense of the Past*, and *The Middle Years*. In 1920 he edited, in two volumes, a selection of James's *Letters;* and he contributed the notice of James to this Dictionary.

The Craft of Fiction, Lubbock's main critical work, was first published in 1921 and has been many times reprinted, both in this country and abroad. (A new edition appeared a few years before his death.) The author confined his theme to a consideration of the technical aspect of the novel: 'how it is made is the only question I shall ask'. He fulfilled his object by a series of analyses, or rather dissections, of certain novels (including those by Tolstoy, Flaubert, Henry James, and Thackeray), setting forth his views and theories in straightforward terms, free from jargon. This critical study of the form and design of the novel has proved of enduring value not only for its insight and freshness of outlook but, incidentally, as pointing the way to an appreciation of the art of reading.

Earlham, Lubbock's best-known work, was first published in October 1922. It describes in detail the background of a late Victorian childhood spent during the holidays in an old Norfolk house which for generations had been the home of the Gurneys. Each room of the house, the garden and beyond, members of the family, past and present, all are affectionately described in tranquil and measured prose. The book appeared at a time when readers could at least put behind them, or at least temporarily forget, the horrors of war, and so lose themselves in these memories of a serene vanished world. It at once became something of a bestseller.

In 1923 Lubbock showed another facet of his craft as writer. *Roman Pictures* is a social comedy, seen through the mind of a young English tourist in Rome at the turn of the century. Naïve the narrator may appear to be, but he observes his characters—natives, visitors, and exiles—with an ironical yet good-humoured detachment which impliedly points the contrast between them and the splendour of the architectural background to which they are largely indifferent.

Lubbock's only novel, *The Region Cloud*, appeared in 1925. It attracted little attention, perhaps justifiably, for the underlying theme, the affectation of genius, is too concentrated, and there is throughout a certain diffuseness of thought and expression. The central character, Channon, was inspired by a chance encounter Lubbock had in Toledo, in 1906, with (Sir) Hubert von Herkomer [q.v.], the Victorian painter.

In *Shades of Eton* (1929) Lubbock limited his survey to the time he was there during the

1890s, a studious imaginative boy who did not quite fit into the conventional pattern of the period. It gave scope to his skill in portraying character, particularly of those masters who, weathered by Eton, had taken the rank of monuments by the Gothic richness of their mouldings. Of these may be instanced Frank Tarver, the handsome and patriarchal French master, whose teaching, with a splendid disregard of the phrases one may require at Boulogne, recalled 'the spacious days of the Grand Tour, of the English gentleman rolling across the Continent in his travelling chaise'.

Lubbock on several occasions published 'sketches from memory' of his friends: of *George Calderon*, for example, in 1921, and also for this Dictionary; and of *Mary Cholmondeley* (1928), whose 'outspoken' novels, exposing the frailties of clergy and county, were once on the shelves of many country-house libraries. Mention, too, should be made of his selection (1926) from a vast quarry of notebooks, of the *Diary* kept between 1897 and 1925 by A. C. Benson, with an introduction and connecting narrative of Benson's life. Finally, in 1947 was published what proved to be his last work, *Portrait of Edith Wharton*, American writer and discerning admirer of Henry James.

In 1926 Lubbock married Lady Sybil Marjorie Scott (died 1943), younger daughter of the fifth Earl of Desart, widow of W. C. Cutting of New York, and mother of the author, Iris Origo. They lived in Italy, first in the Villa Medici in Fiesole, then in a house, Gli Scafari, designed for them at Lerici on the Gulf of Spezia.

In appearance Lubbock was tall and in later years bulky. His sight had been failing for some time and at the end he was almost totally blind. He was not unhappy, living amid beautiful surroundings, solaced by the music that most delighted him, that of Wagner, Brahms, Schubert, enjoying and contributing to good conversation, and read to by young friends. He died at Lerici 2 August 1965.

(Sir) Edmund Gosse [q.v.], writing in 1923, regarded Lubbock as one of the best prose writers of his time. His works, although relatively few, were diverse, and each was a careful and sincere piece of prose, attuned to its purpose, quiet, efficient, and well-mannered. His literary style could be complex, even involved, but it was never affected or obscure. Before the end of his life he had the satisfaction of knowing that there was a revival of his reputation, especially as a critic, a recognition reflected in his appointment, in 1952, to CBE.

[*The Times*, 3 August 1965; private information.]   D. PEPYS-WHITELEY

LUCAS, FRANK LAURENCE (1894-1967), author and scholar, was born 28 December 1894 at Hipperholme in Yorkshire, the elder son of Frank William Lucas, headmaster of the Grammar School, and his wife, Ada Ruth Blackmur. Educated at Colfe's Grammar School, Lewisham, where his father was then headmaster, and at Rugby, he went up to Trinity College, Cambridge, in 1913 with a classical scholarship and in 1914 won the Pitt university scholarship and the Porson prize for Greek iambics. In November 1914 'Peter', as he was always called, was commissioned in the Royal West Kent Regiment, serving throughout the war on the western front. The *Official History* mentions 'a daring and resourceful reconnaissance by Lieutenant F. L. Lucas, 7/R. West Kent, conducted whilst British shrapnel was bursting behind him', which brought the first indication of the German retreat to the Hindenburg line. After being dangerously wounded in 1916 and gassed in 1917, he was transferred to the Intelligence Corps.

Back in Cambridge in 1920, he won the Chancellor's medal for classics and a Browne medal for Latin ode, was placed in the first class in part i of the classical tripos, and was elected to a fellowship in classics at King's. His first two published works were in this field, *Seneca and Elizabethan Tragedy* (1922) and *Euripides and his Influence* (1924), but he was then attracted to the newly established English faculty. Meanwhile in 1920 he had married the novelist Emily Beatrix Coursolles ('Topsy') Jones, and had become associated with the Bloomsbury group of writers and artists.

His career as a writer now entered its most productive and versatile period. His edition in four volumes of the plays of John Webster (completed 1927) was hailed as a supreme work of scholarship. A first book of poems, *Time and Memory* (1929), was admired ('he has written some V. G. Poems' wrote T. E. Lawrence [q.v.] in a letter) and was followed by *Marionettes* (1930) and *Poems 1935* (1935). His early semi-autobiographical novel, *The River Flows* (1926), was followed by two historical novels, *Cécile* (1930) and *Dr. Dido* (1938). Also in the thirties two of his plays reached the London stage. In criticism, where many will think his special talents lay, *Authors Dead and Living* (1926), *Tragedy in Relation to Aristotle's Poetics* (1927), still a standard work after fifty years, and *Eight Victorian Poets* (1930) were followed by *Studies French and English* (1934), the fruit of a lifelong love of French literature and civilization, and *The Decline and Fall of the Romantic Ideal* (1936), perhaps his best work of historical criticism.

In 1932 he married his second wife, Prudence

Dalzell Wilkinson: their passion for wild scenery and arduous walking is vividly displayed in their companion-guide to Greece, *From Olympus to the Styx* (1934).

He had now an international reputation as a writer. In the later thirties he earned a second reputation, as an outspoken opponent of totalitarianism. His *Delights of Dictatorship* (1938) and *Journal under the Terror 1938* (1939) reflect those times. During the war of 1939-45 he was employed at the Government Code and Cypher School at Bletchley Park in Buckinghamshire where he worked on the intelligence side of decodes of German Army and Luftwaffe high-grade ciphers. The value of his work there was recognized in 1946 by his appointment as OBE. In 1940 he married his third wife, the Swedish psychologist Elna Julie Dagmar Constance Kallenberg, by whom he had a daughter and a son. Of his first two marriages, both of which were. dissolved, he had no issue.

In Cambridge after the war he resumed lecturing and writing with all his old energy and in 1947-62 was reader. Dr Leavis and his school were then in the ascendant in the English faculty, however, and to him their attitude to literature was an aberration. His own settled outlook had been shown in the brilliant chapter on English Literature which he contributed to Harold Wright's *Cambridge University Studies* (1933). It was that of an uncompromising traditionalist in the line deriving from Sainte-Beuve and exemplified by his own friend and mentor Sir Desmond MacCarthy [q.v.], who remained for him always 'wisest of readers of to-day'.

His two large volumes of verse translation, *Greek Poetry for Everyman* (1951) and *Greek Drama for Everyman* (1954), met a popular need. *Style* (1955) was illuminated by a wealth of examples drawn from a lifetime of voracious reading in half a dozen literatures. In *The Search for Good Sense* (1958) and *The Art of Living* (1959) he returned to his old love of the eighteenth century; and another earlier interest was revived in *The Drama of Ibsen and Strindberg* (1962) and *The Drama of Chekhov, Synge, Yeats and Pirandello* (1963).

Lucas was an immensely clever man, 'The man is magnificent, a mental athlete', to quote Lawrence again. Yet in some moods he himself valued most highly the life of action, and thought the most useful years of his life had been those of the two wars. The dominant impression he made was of an exhilarating and masterful vitality. Gay and charming in congenial company, he could also be formidable and, once he had decided on a course of action, was apt to pursue it with a single-mindedness which, despite a native considerateness towards others, could sometimes be disconcerting. In appearance, he retained in later life 'the sensitive face of a poet' which after half a century Henry Williamson remembered in him as a schoolboy.

He died in Cambridge 1 June 1967.

[Cyril Falls, *Official History of the Great War. Military Operations, France and Belgium, 1917*, vol. i, 1940; Clive Bell, *Old Friends*, 1956; *The Letters of T. E. Lawrence*, ed. David Garnett, 1938; private information; personal knowledge.] R. H. L. COHEN

LUKE, SIR HARRY CHARLES (1884-1969), colonial administrator, was born in London 4 December 1884, the eldest child and only son of Joseph Harry Lukàch, an international man of business of Hungarian descent, and his wife, Eugénie Caroline Zamarska, of Vienna. The family name was changed to Luke in 1919. Joseph Lukàch was born in Detroit in 1856; his parents had gone to the United States with Kossuth after the abortive Hungarian uprising of 1848, in which the father had been one of Kossuth's captains.

From a preparatory school at Farnborough Luke went to Eton in 1898; from both schools he retained vivid memories of Queen Victoria. Leaving Eton at the end of 1902, Luke spent some time in the United States before going up in 1903 to Trinity College, Oxford, of which in 1952 he became an honorary fellow. None of his many honours gave him greater satisfaction. He obtained a second class in modern history in 1906 and after visiting Jamaica and Haiti went back to Oxford in 1907 to prepare himself for a prolonged journey in the Levant with his friend Harry Pirie-Gordon. With his parents he had already visited most countries in Europe, and had met many of the leading figures in the world of letters and the arts. His Levant tour took him to Greece, Turkey, Cyprus, Palestine, Syria, and northern Mesopotamia.

Luke's first official appointment was as private secretary (1908) and aide-de-camp (1909) to the governor of Sierra Leone. In 1911 he served in the same capacity in Barbados and in May-July was attached to the Colonial Office. From 1909 to 1911 he was a second lieutenant in the London Yeomanry. In October 1911 he was transferred to Cyprus, where he was successively private secretary to the high commissioner, assistant secretary to government (1912), and commissioner of Famagusta (1918). During the war he had served in 1915-16 as a political officer on the staff of Admiral Sir Rosslyn Wemyss (later Lord Wester Wemyss, q.v.) in the eastern Mediterranean. In 1919 he was back in the Levant, on the staff of Admiral Sir John De

Robeck [q.v.] in Constantinople and the Black Sea. In 1920 he was British chief commissioner in Georgia, Armenia, and Azerbaijan. In the same year he began to make a reputation on a wider stage, having been appointed assistant governor of Jerusalem. With the governor, Sir Ronald Storrs (whose notice he contributed to this Dictionary), Luke did much to preserve and renew the beauty of the Holy City. After a spell as colonial secretary of Sierra Leone (1924-8), Luke returned to Palestine as chief secretary in 1928. He was acting as high commissioner when on 23 August 1929 violent riots broke out between Arabs and Jews. By his promptness and resolution in summoning British troops from Egypt, Luke prevented a major catastrophe.

In 1930 Luke went to Malta as lieutenant-governor, a post which he held for eight years during which, as the secretary of state for the colonies was later to recall, he made a 'distinguished contribution . . . towards the preparation of the Island for the ordeal which lay before it'. It was largely due to Luke's unflinching and unremitting efforts that Maltese society at all levels was integrated with that of its British ally. Moreover, Luke was the first to recover and maintain so many of the monuments of the unique history of the Maltese Islands, the pride of the Maltese people and an attraction of international fame. While in Malta he refused the offer of two governorships, having reason to believe that he would be appointed to Cyprus; but in 1938 he was given his last official post, as governor of Fiji and high commissioner for the Western Pacific. In this capacity it fell to him to negotiate with his French colleagues in the New Hebrides; and by his tact and flair he was largely responsible for the adhesion of French territories in the Western Pacific, notably New Caledonia, to the Allied cause.

On his retirement from the service in 1943, Luke was for three years chief representative of the British Council in the Caribbean. Apart from travel—he visited Easter Island in 1952 and Nepal and Sikkim in 1965, besides renewing links with Palestine and Mexico—Luke had two other main interests. He was a member of the Order of St. John of Jerusalem, of which he was bailiff of Egle, bailiff grand cross, and registrar for the last two decades of his life. He was the chief promoter of the fraternal relations which now link the English order both with the Protestant European branches of the order and with the Sovereign Military Order based in Rome, of which he was made a grand officer of merit in 1966.

Luke's literary output was prolific. He published a bibliography of Sierra Leone in 1910 and *The Fringe of the East* in 1913. He wrote other books on the Levant, on Malta (1949), and on Cyprus (1957). He wrote also on the Caribbean and the South Seas, and, in collaboration, a witty cookery book, *The Tenth Muse* (1954). His autobiography *Cities and Men* (3 vols., 1953-6) was one of the best to appear in his generation. It showed him as one of that great line of British proconsuls who regarded themselves as entrusted with a mission which sprang less from Whitehall than from conscience and culture. In his rational and ardent patriotism, combined with a prismatic cosmopolitanism, Luke had few equals. He did indeed live, as his friend Ronald Storrs said, 'the most unwasted life of any man I have known'.

Luke was appointed CMG in 1926, knighted in 1933, and promoted KCMG in 1939. He was a D.Litt. of Oxford (1938) and an honorary LLD of Malta.

In 1918 Luke married Joyce Evelyn, daughter of Henry James Leigh Fremlin, of the Indian Cavalry. The marriage was dissolved in 1949. There were two sons, the elder of whom, Peter, gained renown for his play *Hadrian the Seventh* founded on the novel of that name by F. W. Rolfe whom his father had once known.

Luke died in Cyprus 11 May 1969; his ashes rest in the crypt of the conventual church of the Order of St. John of Jerusalem at Clerkenwell. He was painted in 1933 by E. Caruana-Dingli; the portrait is in the possession of the family.

[Sir Harry Luke, *Cities and Men*, 3 vols., 1953-6; private information; personal knowledge.]   STEWART PEROWNE

LUMLEY, LAWRENCE ROGER, eleventh EARL OF SCARBROUGH (1896-1969), public servant, was born at York 27 July 1896, the second son of Brigadier-General Osbert Victor George Atheling Lumley and his wife, Constance Ellinor, daughter of Captain Eustace John Wilson Patten, and a grandson of the ninth earl. He was educated at Eton, the Royal Military College, Sandhurst, and Magdalen College, Oxford. His elder brother was killed in action in 1914 with the 11th Hussars. Lumley himself served from 1916 on the western front and was wounded with the 11th Hussars, whose history he wrote in 1936. He graduated in 1921 and in 1922 entered the House of Commons as Conservative member for Hull East, held the seat until 1929, and re-entered the House two years later as member for York, which he represented until his appointment as governor of Bombay in 1937.

Lumley's appointment to Bombay coincided with the coming into operation of provincial autonomy, and his long parliamentary experience in the House of Commons, his tact, skill, and interest contributed materially to its smooth introduction once the Congress majority had decided in 1937 to accept office, and thereafter to its easy working until the Congress ministries resigned on the outbreak of war and responsibility for the government of the presidency devolved on the governor.

In August 1942 the Congress demand for the withdrawal of British political control, coupled with the threat of mass civil disobedience if this were not conceded, was followed by the arrest of the Congress leaders throughout India. The All-India Congress Committee was in the Bombay presidency, and it fell to Lumley to order the arrest and internment of M. K. Gandhi [q.v.] and the other leaders. When in February 1943 Gandhi began a three weeks' fast and the Government of India refused to intervene unless he and the Congress were prepared to give the appropriate guarantees for co-operation, the difficult resulting local reactions were handled by Lumley with great address. These major political strains notwithstanding, Lumley's excellent relations with local political leaders, and the high esteem in which he was held, were reflected in a major contribution to the war effort by the Bombay presidency over recruitment, war charities, and the provision of comforts for the troops—British and Indian.

Lumley returned from the governorship of Bombay in 1943 and in 1945 succeeded his uncle as eleventh Earl of Scarbrough. From 1921 to 1937 he served with the Yorkshire Dragoons, of which he was honorary colonel in 1956–62. In 1946 he became an honorary major-general (acting major-general 1943–4). For many years thereafter he gave invaluable help as president to the West Riding Territorial and Auxiliary Forces Associations. For a brief period in 1945 parliamentary under-secretary of state for India and Burma in Churchill's caretaker Government, he served in 1945–6 as chairman of a commission of great importance on Oriental, Slavonic, East European, and African studies, the recommendations of which were not only accepted, but acted on. His interest in Asia was at all times close. President of the Royal Asiatic Society in 1946–9; the East India Association in 1946–51; the Royal Central Asian Society in 1954–60; he was chairman of the School of Oriental and African Studies in 1951–9 and of the Commonwealth Scholarship Committee in 1960–3. In 1956 he was special ambassador to the coronation of the King of Nepal.

Always actively interested in county business, he was lord-lieutenant of the West Riding of Yorkshire and of the city of York from 1948 and chancellor of the university of Durham

from 1958. His services in these fields were recognized by the honorary DCL of Durham and by the LLD of Sheffield, Leeds, and London. As high steward of York Minster from 1967 he achieved an outstanding success in his leadership and active support of the appeal for the York Minster Fund. Throughout his life an active freemason, he was grand master of the United Grand Lodge of England from 1951 to 1967 and thereafter pro-grand master.

Scarbrough, who had been made GCIE on appointment to Bombay in 1937 and GCSI on the conclusion of his term in 1943, was appointed KG in 1948, lord chamberlain of HM Household in 1952–63, and a permanent lord in waiting from 1963. He was sworn of the Privy Council in 1952, appointed GCVO in 1953, and received the Royal Victorian Chain in 1963.

Scarbrough's career was one of great distinction and variety. Dignified and impressive in his public appearances as lord chamberlain, a most successful governor in very difficult circumstances, inspired throughout by a strong sense of public service, as an individual he was easy, friendly, relaxed, with a quick sense of humour and great personal charm.

He married in 1922 Katherine Isobel (died 1979), daughter of Robert Finnie McEwen of Marchmont, who throughout his career gave him invaluable help, more particularly during the war years in Bombay over the provision of comforts for the troops, curative work in hospitals, and convalescent depots, and the welfare of nurses and women workers. She was appointed DCVO in 1962 and received the Kaisar-i-Hind gold medal in 1941. They had four daughters and a son, Richard Aldred (born 1932), who succeeded his father as twelfth Earl of Scarbrough when he died at Sandbeck 29 June 1969.

A full length portrait of Scarbrough in Garter robes by Sir James Gunn hangs in Freemasons Hall in London; and there is a portrait by Derek Hill at Sandbeck. There is also a portrait in India, the property of the Bombay freemasons, by W. Langhammer.

[Private information; personal knowledge.]
GILBERT LAITHWAITE

LUTHULI, ALBERT JOHN (1898 ?–1967), president-general of the African National Congress, was born, according to his own calculations, in 1898 in Southern Rhodesia, the second surviving son of John Bunyan Luthuli, an evangelist and interpreter at a Seventh Day Adventist Mission at Solusi near Bulawayo. His family came from the strongly Congregationalist Zulu community, mainly of small farmers, of Groutville near the coast in Northern Natal.

Luthuli's mother, Mtonya, had come with her mother from the royal kraal of Cetewayo to Groutville where she became a Christian and learnt to read, although not to write.

After his father's death in Rhodesia, his mother eventually returned to Groutville where his uncle Martin Luthuli had now been elected chief. She grew vegetables, and laundered for white people in the nearest town of Stanger to keep Luthuli at school. Teaching was almost the only career open to an educated African, so Luthuli went from the local school to the Ohlange Institute, then to the Methodist Institution at Edenvale to qualify as a teacher. In 1918 he was appointed to a one-teacher country school. There, living with a deeply Christian family, he took stock of his own upbringing, was confirmed in the local Methodist church, and became a lay preacher.

A bursary in 1920 took Luthuli to Adams College, a Congregational foundation near Durban, where he stayed on to train teachers in his turn. He founded the Zulu Language and Cultural Society; and became a lifelong soccer fan. His interest in the organization of African and inter-racial sport continued throughout his life. The subjects he taught were Zulu, school organization, and music. Singing was a particular strength in his life: he sang well and his voice was part of his charisma. He could inspire hope in situations which might have been marked only by bitterness and frustration. He himself drew courage from hearing 'Nkosi sikelel' iAfrika' (God Save Africa), the anthem of African determination, hope, and endurance. Profoundly influenced by the Christian outlook he found at Adams, Luthuli saw that Christianity was relevant to the problems of society; a recognition he expressed through political action.

In 1927 Luthuli married Nokukhanya Bhengu, granddaughter of a hereditary Zulu chief; they had seven children. Their home was at Groutville but Luthuli continued to work at Adams. After insistent requests from the Groutville tribal elders Luthuli agreed to stand for election as chief of the Umvoti Mission Reserve. Unwilling to leave the life of teaching, he yet felt an obligation to serve his own community. When he became chief in 1936, in contrast to the orderly life at Adams College, he found himself confronted daily with the besetting problems of poverty and land hunger, and with the destruction of families resulting from migratory labour and the pass system.

He founded with some success the Natal and Zululand Bantu Cane Growers Association to assist the small-scale growers, and when an advisory board to the South African Sugar Association was set up Luthuli served on it until 1953. As the city of Durban expanded

there came the problem of land rights. With the future Bishop Zulu, Luthuli revived the Mission Reserve Association and assisted the Umlazi Mission Reserve in negotiations with the Durban Corporation and the Native Affairs Department.

Such work brought Luthuli into public affairs and some associations brought him into touch with white people, notably the Natal Missionary Conference affiliated to the Christian Council of South Africa. He served as a Natal delegate and later as an executive member. In 1938 he was a delegate to the International Missionary Conference in Madras. This, and a lecture tour in the United States on missions in 1948, gave him opportunities of seeing South Africa in a wider perspective.

In 1945 Luthuli was elected to the executive of the African National Congress in Natal and became steadily more involved in national questions. This hitherto moderate body was taking new shape, partly because of disillusionment with the ineffectual Native Representative Council, called a 'toy telephone', which had been established by J. B. M. Hertzog [q.v.] in 1936 and to which Luthuli was elected in 1946. The end of the war and the four freedoms of the Atlantic Charter brought a more militant attitude; young militants set up a Youth League of the ANC. With the return of the white Nationalist Party to power in 1948 came a succession of measures to implement the blueprint of apartheid, to control all forms of organized protest, and to silence individual dissenters. Natal leadership of the ANC was not rising to the occasion and in 1951 Luthuli, supported by the young militants, became president of Congress in Natal. Defiance of unjust segregation laws by non-violent, passive resistance had already been centrally planned and in 1952 Luthuli brought Natal into the Defiance Campaign and into close co-operation with the Indian Congress. This marked a momentous personal decision for Luthuli whose past approach had been that of 'knocking in vain, patiently, moderately and modestly at a closed and barred door'. He himself did not defy, but organized and inspired. Summoned to Pretoria he was told that he must choose between the ANC and his chieftainship. His decision was to resign from neither. The Government deposed him, but both the title and the standing of chief continued to be accorded him by his people. In a statement after his deposition he concluded 'the road to freedom is via the Cross'.

At the end of the year he was elected president-general of ANC. In 1953 he was banned, in terms of the Riotous Assemblies Act and the Criminal Law Amendment Act, from the major cities and from attending public gatherings. A second banning order was imposed in 1954 when this had expired and he was about to lead a massed protest against the enforced removal of Africans from Sophiatown and elsewhere. It ran for two years and confined him to the magisterial district of Stanger in which Groutville lay. In early 1955, after a stroke, permission had to be obtained to allow him to be moved to a hospital in Durban.

Luthuli was debarred from attending the Congress of the People held at Kliptown near Johannesburg in June 1955. The Freedom Charter which it adopted brought ANC policy into question and put Luthuli into a defensive position over the extent of control exercised in ANC affairs by Communist members of the Indian Congress and the White Congress of Democrats. Luthuli's vision of a democratic multi-racial South Africa and his immediate aim of mustering non-violent opposition to apartheid made him place great importance on the inter-racial Congress Alliance. ANC itself did not have a clear policy so much as a bundle of aspirations. Luthuli was no theorist, was little concerned with the political colour of his allies, and tended to shelve some problems. Moreover he led a loosely knit movement in which spirit outshone organization. He realized the difficulties of organizing a national campaign to oppose the Bantu Education Act of 1953 which transferred control of African education to the Native Affairs Department. Many would choose a bad education rather than none at all. Nevertheless he supported the principle of mass opposition to this new threat and although the campaign of 1955 was not successful it left its mark by giving centrality to the issue, showing publicly the strength of African rejection.

Luthuli's second ban ended in 1956 and he was able to deliver his presidential address to Congress in person, his theme: the struggle must go on. But on 5 December he was one of 156 people arrested on a charge of high treason. Another was Z. K. Matthews [q.v.], a former colleague of Adams College, and author of the Freedom Charter. Luthuli was eventually released on bail and at the end of 1957 with some sixty others discharged. The trial continued until March 1961 when the remaining accused were acquitted of conspiring to overthrow the state by violence.

In this period Luthuli's dignified bearing, authority, and gravity, as well as his sense of humour, became well known. He was a guest at the houses of prominent white people in Johannesburg and he warmed to the concern of Bishop Ambrose Reeves who took charge of the Treason Trial Defence Fund. Luthuli had often regretted the lack of involvement by white

Christians in the sufferings of black Christians and warned that black people would come to reject the white man's God and the paternalism of white Christians.

In 1958 the Africanist wing of the ANC withdrew from Congress to form the Pan African Congress, a lack of African unity which was a bitter blow to Luthuli. He now toured the larger cities speaking to white and multi-racial audiences as well as from Congress platforms. At a meeting in Pretoria in 1959 he was assaulted by young whites who objected to an African addressing a study-group of white people. His restraint and dignity on this occasion increased his personal renown. The sincerity and urgency of his speeches made a strong impression: his opposition to apartheid and to racialism was in the cause of peace.

In December 1958 Luthuli was again able to attend the annual conference of Congress in Durban at which it was decided to intensify the campaign against the pass system. In May 1959 a third banning order was served on Luthuli, lasting for five years. In 1960 he called for a national day of mourning after the shootings at Sharpeville in the Transvaal and at Langa in the Cape at the start of the anti-pass campaign called by the Pan African Congress. Congress in its turn now called for the burning of passes and Luthuli, in Pretoria for the treason trial, ceremoniously burnt his passbook. The Government declared a state of emergency and outlawed both the ANC and the Pan African Congress. Luthuli was arrested. His health was declining and the next five months were spent mainly in the prison hospital. His prison sentence suspended on health grounds, he returned to Groutville and to banishment. When South Africa's continued membership of the Commonwealth was debated in March 1961 Luthuli cabled *The Times* advocating South Africa's expulsion.

At Groutville in 1961 he learned that he had been awarded the Nobel peace prize for 1960. He was allowed to travel to Oslo to receive it and in his address spoke of the paradox that such an award should be made to a man from a country where 'the brotherhood of man is an illegal doctrine'. From Oslo he returned to banishment.

In 1964 the last and severest ban was imposed, forbidding access even to the neighbouring town of Stanger. Now virtually under house arrest, as far as his health allowed he worked on the land or in his small shop. He had few visitors but in 1965 Senator Robert Kennedy went to see him. On 21 July 1967 Luthuli was struck down by a freight train while crossing a narrow railroad bridge near his home. He was buried in the graveyard of the Groutville Congregational Church. Some 7,000

Africans, some wearing the uniform of the banned ANC, and a few hundred whites, many of them diplomats, gathered to pay tribute to him. His old friend Alan Paton gave the address but was forbidden by law to quote anything that Luthuli had ever said or written. 'The great story of his life', Paton said, 'is the story of his fortitude.'

In 1968 Luthuli was awarded the United Nations Human Rights prize. Luthuli spoke for his people, voicing both anguish and aspiration; he succeeded too in focusing world attention on the destructive effects of the apartheid system which debased personality, destroyed relationships, and threatened peace.

[Albert Luthuli, *Let My People Go*, 1962; Mary Benson, *Chief Albert Lutuli of South Africa*, 1963, and *South Africa: The Struggle for a Birthright*, 1966; Alan Paton, *The Long View*, ed. Edward Callan, 1968; Edward Callan, *Albert John Luthuli and the South African Race Conflict*, 1962; personal knowledge.] ANNE YATES

M

MacARTHUR, Sir WILLIAM PORTER (1884-1964), director-general of the Army Medical Services, was born at Belmont, county Down, 11 March 1884. He was the second child and only son of John Porter MacArthur, partner in a firm of tea-importers in Belfast, and his wife, Margaret Rainey, daughter of William Baird of Donemana and grandniece of Andrew Baird, FRS. His father's forebears had emigrated from Argyll in the latter part of the eighteenth century. MacArthur received his medical education in Queen's University, Belfast, and graduated MB, B.Ch., RUI, in 1908. He proceeded DPH, Oxon. (1910), MD, Belfast (1911), FRCP Ireland (1913), DTM&H, Cantab. (1920), and FRCP London (1937).

In 1909 MacArthur joined the Royal Army Medical Corps as a lieutenant and while serving in Mauritius from 1911 to 1914 acquired a keen interest in tropical medicine which remained with him throughout his life. He treated cases of typhoid fever with a polyvalent vaccine which he himself prepared and claimed considerable success. For the excellence of this work he was officially congratulated by the director-general. In 1915 he was posted to the British Expeditionary Force in France where he served until he was wounded and invalided home in 1916, and appointed to the DSO.

In 1919 MacArthur became commanding officer and chief instructor at the Army School of Hygiene at Blackpool. In 1922 he was transferred to the Royal Army Medical College in London as professor of tropical medicine, an appointment which he held until 1929 and again in 1932-4. Before taking up his duties he studied 'medical' entomology at the London School of Tropical Medicine and acquired a comprehensive collection of those arthropods which are disease vectors. This collection became the basis of a unique and valuable course of entomology which he introduced into the training curriculum at the College. He was greatly esteemed as teacher and lecturer and his enthusiasm and initiative did much to raise the standard of instruction. In subsequent appointments, as consulting physician to the army (1929-34) and as director of studies and commandant of the Royal Army Medical College (1935-8), he maintained his interest in teaching. His bent was towards clinical and preventive medicine rather than to research, but he made one important original discovery. He found that so-called idiopathic epilepsy (believed to result from constitutional or inborn causes) could in certain cases be caused by invasion of the brain by the larval or cysticercus stage of the pork tapeworm, *Taenia solium*, a common parasite of pigs in the East, with which man can become infected. Sixty-three cases of men invalided out of the army with idiopathic epilepsy were traced and in all of them cysticercus infection was found. After vigorous representations by MacArthur their condition was accepted as attributable to service and retrospective disability pensions were granted.

After an earlier period in the War Office as deputy director-general of the Army Medical Services (1934-5), MacArthur was made director-general in 1938, with the rank of lieutenant-general. It was a somewhat unhappy appointment: his experience of the administrative aspects of the Medical Services was limited and he chafed at the restrictions imposed by red tape. Sensing the imminence of war in 1938, for instance, he side-tracked a ruling by a cabinet subcommittee and laid in a much-needed store of equipment for medical field units due to be mobilized when war was declared. This earned him a severe rebuke from the financial authorities but found its justification a year later. Although well able to cope with peacetime problems, he found himself somewhat at sea in the hurly-burly of war when quick decisions had to be given on matters of which he had inadequate past experience. His difficulties were not lessened by the fact that on certain subjects, notably the functions of psychiatrists in the army, he did not see eye to eye with the adjutant-general. He was distressed by a press campaign which adversely, and in his opinion unjustly, criticized the Medical Services. This, however, he was well able to counter: he addressed members of Parliament and representatives of the press with such success that the campaign came to an abrupt end. But an injury to his right arm gave him severe pain for a long time and made sleep difficult, and this, combined with the cumulative worries and frustrations of his appointment, undermined his health and led to his resignation in 1941, a year before the normal termination of his period of office. He had been appointed CB in 1938 and KCB in 1939, and was honorary physician to the king in 1930-41.

In his later years MacArthur found a congenial outlet for his energy as lecturer in tropical medicine and additional member of the faculty of medicine at Oxford, as consultant in tropical diseases at the Royal Masonic Hospital, and as editor of the *Transactions* of the Royal Society of Tropical Medicine and Hygiene. He was colonel commandant of the Royal Army Medical Corps in 1946-51.

Although dedicated to his professional

career, MacArthur had other absorbing interests. Pride in his Highland ancestry and love for all things Gaelic played a great part in his life. He had been one of the founders of the Gaelic Society in Queen's University and to perfect his knowledge of the Gaelic language, which he came to speak fluently, he spent long holidays in the far west of Donegal. Later in life he frequently visited Argyll where he found the Gaelic dialect very similar to that of Donegal, and so he was able to converse freely with the country people and to hear their folklore. He was fascinated by the mysterious Appin murder, on which he wrote a short book (1960), and of which a fictitious account is woven into R. L. Stevenson's *Kidnapped*.

MacArthur was also well versed in Old English and had a working acquaintance with Latin. This repertoire enabled him to read and interpret original documents and records and so to pursue his lifelong hobby, the study of medical history. He was particularly interested in the epidemic diseases and scourges of bygone years. He wrote graphic accounts of the outbreaks of typhus (gaol) fever which recurred in Britain and elsewhere. He was convinced that the Plague of Athens (430 BC) was neither the disease now known as plague, nor, as has been suggested, smallpox or ergotism, but was in fact typhus fever. He made a close study of the medical aspects of the great famine in Ireland (1845-6) and has given a detailed account of the epidemic of typhus fever which added to its horrors. His investigations into the Black Death and other outbreaks of bubonic and pneumonic plague were equally exhaustive. He studied closely the incidence of leprosy in medieval Britain and reached the conclusion, now generally accepted, that it was relatively rare in Britain, the so-called lazar-houses being used as almshouses and very rarely for lepers. He was firmly convinced that Robert the Bruce was not a leper, although this is commonly asserted, and he produced strong circumstantial evidence to support his contention.

His researches were the basis of papers published in various journals and of numerous lectures. He was a lecturer of outstanding ability, capable of holding his audience enthralled, speaking from memory, using no notes, and interlarding his remarks with long word-perfect quotations. Medals awarded in appreciation of his historical researches were: the Arnott (1929), Chadwick (1935), Robert Campbell (1951), and the Scott-Heron (1957). MacArthur was of medium height and build. His Celtic ancestry revealed itself in his robust bearing and forthright manner. He possessed vast stores of energy, and tenaciously pursued to its conclusion any task which he undertook. There is a portrait, signed 'Lewis', in the head-

quarters mess of the Royal Army Medical Corps in Millbank.

In 1914 MacArthur married Marie Eugénie Thérèse, third daughter of Louis Ferdinande Antelme, MD, of Mauritius; they had two sons, the elder of whom became a director of the Rank Organization and the younger, Ian, member of Parliament for Perth and East Perthshire in 1959. MacArthur died in London 30 July 1964.

[Dossier of MacArthur's writings in the muniments room of the Royal Army Medical College; private information; personal knowledge.]   JOHN BOYD

MACASSEY, SIR LYNDEN LIVINGSTON (1876-1963), industrial lawyer, was born 14 June 1876 in Carrickfergus, Larne, the eldest son of Luke Livingston Macassey, a civil engineer of Belfast and later a barrister and parliamentary draftsman in London, and his wife, Agnes White. He was educated at Upper Sullivan School, Holywood, county Down, Bedford School, Trinity College, Dublin, and the university of London. He was trained as an engineer, at one stage serving an apprenticeship on the Clyde where he was later to figure so prominently in labour disputes. Having thus begun his career as an engineer, he shortly turned to law, being called to the bar in 1899 by the Middle Temple. He received a BA and LLB from Dublin in 1900 (proceeding to MA and LLD in 1905). From 1901 to 1909 he lectured on economics and law at the London School of Economics, while building up a practice at the bar sufficient to enable him to take silk in 1912. From 1903 to 1906 he was secretary to the royal commission on London traffic, for which he visited the major cities of the United States.

It was during the war of 1914-18 that Macassey's combination of the professions of engineer and lawyer made his services of peculiar value to the Government. From 1914 to 1916 he was a Board of Trade arbitrator in shipbuilding and engineering disputes. He was particularly involved in the industrial unrest among munitions workers on the Clyde. He was a member of a government commission on Clyde munition workers' grievances and in that capacity produced, together with A. J. Balfour, a report in 1915 recommending some reforms in the Munitions of War Act of 1915 (Cd. 8136). The report is an enlightened document anticipating some developments in labour law which were not to follow for many decades; for instance, the report saw as a corollary to the munition worker's obligation to obtain a clearance certificate before leaving employment, a right on the worker's part not to be dismissed save for reasonable cause.

Macassey was, however, shortly to figure in the Clyde labour troubles in a less libertarian role. One of the principal sources of labour unrest in the munitions industry was the Government's need to dilute the workforce, which had hitherto been largely composed of engineering craftsmen and confined to those who had served their time as apprentices. The dilution consisted of introducing women workers and men who were not time-served ex-apprentices. Resistance to this dilution became a left-wing cause; and in January 1916 Macassey was sent to the Clyde as the head of a body of dilution commissioners whose task was to put the Government's policy into effect. Macassey's skill and experience as a labour arbitrator enabled the commission quickly to secure agreement to dilution in some of the crucial munitions plants on the Clyde, and he seems to have combined effectiveness with moderation in the pursuit of unions' and employers' acceptance of dilution. At another level, however, the dilution commissioners are remembered for their action taken to suppress the Clyde Workers' Committee (CWC) which was leading the agitation against dilution. It seems to have been Macassey himself who was instrumental in convincing the Ministry of Munitions that the CWC was responsible for agitation and that it would be desirable to 'deport' its leaders to other parts of the country. In March 1916, Kirkwood and four others were duly 'deported' at the instance of the commission, an incident whose echoes were long heard among engineering workers. Historians now debate whether there was an official plot to destroy the CWC. Perhaps the more attractive theory is that advanced by Dr José Harris which tends to discount notions of an official plot but attaches great importance to Macassey's direct personal knowledge of conditions on the Clyde from his days as an apprenticed engineer there. Thus he could write in 1915 that many workmen would come to see him personally and unburden their souls about the troubles on the Clyde. At all events, the CWC deportations either contributed to or coincided with the acceptance of dilution on the Clyde, and Macassey could turn his attention to enforcing dilution in Barrow-in-Furness. The year 1917 saw him appointed KBE and the director of shipyard labour for the Admiralty until 1918. From 1917 to 1919 he served on the War Cabinet committees on labour and on women in industry. He then became one of the labour assessors for the British Government on the Permanent Court of International Justice at The Hague, where in 1920 he represented the employers in the court of inquiry at which Ernest Bevin [q.v.] earned himself the title of 'the Dockers' KC' by his advocacy of the workers' case. In 1922 Macassey wrote *Labour Policy—False and True*.

In later years Macassey occupied many honorific positions in public life, being in turn at times a bencher (1922) and treasurer (1935) of the Middle Temple, and honorary fellow and chairman of the governors of Queen Mary College, university of London, master of the Drapers' Company, and president of the Institute of Arbitrators. He also had a long association with the Scottish Amicable Life Assurance Society Ltd., being its president until 1962.

In 1903 he married Jeanne, only child of Robert McFarland of Melbourne and Barooga, New South Wales. They had two sons and one daughter. He died at his London home in Queen's Gate 23 February 1963.

[*The Times*, 25 February 1963; José Harris, *William Beveridge, a Biography*, 1977.]

M. R. FREEDLAND

MacBRYDE, ROBERT (1913-1966), painter of still life and figure subjects. [See COLQUHOUN, ROBERT.]

McCREERY, SIR RICHARD LOUDON (1898-1967), general, was born at Kibworth Harcourt, Leicestershire, 1 February 1898, the eldest son of Walter Adolph McCreery, of Bilton Park, Rugby, and his wife, Emilia McAdam. He was educated at Eton and the Royal Military College, Sandhurst, and was commissioned in the 12th Royal Lancers in 1915. He served with the regiment in France from 1915 to 1917 and again from August to November 1918, winning the MC for a fine reconnoitring action with his troop which enabled the 50th division to advance quickly and effectively. After the war, and despite the leg wound he received in France which the doctors claimed would prevent his riding, McCreery quickly established himself as one of the greatest horsemen of his generation, winning the Grand Military gold cup at Sandown Park twice (once on a favourite mare, Annie Darling), as well as many other steeplechases; winning also sword, lance, revolver, and dummy thrusting competitions at Olympia, hunting regularly, and playing polo for his regiment, eventually leading it to victory in the inter-regimental competition in 1936.

It was not just as a horseman, however, that McCreery established a reputation; he was also an exceptionally promising soldier. He went to the Staff College in 1928; from there he was appointed brigade-major of a cavalry brigade. From 1935 to 1938 (when he was promoted colonel) he commanded the 12th Lancers, and made his regiment work hard and train hard. Only the best would do, no matter what was in hand, so that when in 1940 they found themselves arguing the toss with the German Panzer troops, the 12th Lancers acquitted themselves with unrivalled distinction. By then 'Dick' McCreery himself was commanding 2nd Armoured brigade. At the outbreak of war in 1939, he had been principal staff officer to Harold Alexander (later Earl Alexander of Tunis, q.v.), then commanding 1st division at Aldershot, and they served together in France during the *drôle de guerre* period from September 1939 to May 1940. During the last phase of the battle for France, so gallantly and skilfully did McCreery conduct the withdrawal of his brigade that he was appointed to the DSO. He was promoted major-general, and commanded an armoured division in England for two years, before going to the Mediterranean theatre in 1942, at first as adviser on armoured fighting vehicles at GHQ Cairo. On Alexander's arrival there, McCreery returned to his old master as chief of staff, and wielded decisive influence during the Alamein battle. Long afterwards McCreery broke his silence in an article (1959) in his regimental journal, criticizing Lord Montgomery's tactics in this battle, and his behaviour after it. Alexander described McCreery himself as that rare creature, a brilliant staff officer and an inspiring commander. In 1943 he became lieutenant-general and took command of X Corps, and in the critical Salerno battles his calm courage, personal example, and dynamic influence did much to carry the day. During the subsequent fighting in 1943 and 1944 he was regularly at the front line so that his thrusting subordinate generals would often find McCreery further forward than they were. He was appointed CB and KCB in 1943. In September 1944 he assumed command of the Eighth Army, and after the Gothic Line battles, closed up to the Senio river in preparation for the great spring offensive of 1945. This was a brilliant success, and after a battle lasting twenty-three days the enemy forces surrendered unconditionally on 2 May 1945.

After the war McCreery commanded the British Forces of Occupation in Austria, and was the British representative on the Allied Commission for Austria in 1945-6. During this time he had considerable success in negotiating with Marshal Koniev and earned the respect of the Russians with whom he had dealings. He was appointed KBE in 1945, and advanced to full general in 1946. When Sir Archibald Nye [q.v.] became governor of Madras in 1946, Lord Alanbrooke [q.v.] wanted McCreery to succeed him as VCIGS, but Montgomery disagreed and a compromise was found in (General) Sir Frank Simpson. McCreery commanded the British Army of the Rhine in 1946-8, during the difficult period of its run-down and retraining in peacetime, and finally he was the British Army representative on the United Nations Military Staff Committee in 1948-9. He was appointed GCB and retired in 1949, although he continued until 1956 in the post of colonel commandant of the Royal Armoured Corps, which he had held from 1947.

McCreery was deeply religious, and very much a family man. After his retirement he devoted his time to the many demands which were made on it, especially to his regiment: he was colonel of the 12th lancers in 1951-60, and of the amalgamated 9th/12th Lancers in 1960-1. He was also colonel of the 14th/20th Hussars, and the 3rd/4th County of London Yeomanry. He gave much of his time to racing and was steward at both Wincanton and Sandown; also to boys' clubs; and he took pride in his horses, his home at Stowell Hill, Templecombe, his farm, his garden, and his flowers. He was a man for whom nothing was too much trouble. Everybody—family, friends, and regiment, soldiers, gardeners, servants, or nannies—received his consideration and kindness.

McCreery seemed to be composed of gentler, simpler elements than most men and with a rare clarity of heart and mind: a man of fierce loyalties and without humbug. A legendary horseman, he came to be at once the doyen and the conscience of the British cavalry of his day. He died in London 18 October 1967, and at the memorial service the Bishop of Sherborne, who had been chaplain-general to the forces, in reminding the congregation of McCreery's goodness and courage remarked his unusual gift of being both master and servant. In 1928 he married Lettice, second daughter of Lord Percy St. Maur; they had four sons and a daughter. A portrait by Denys Fildes is in the possession of the family, and a full-length copy of it hangs in the 9th/12th Royal Lancers officers' mess.

[Private information; personal knowledge.]

JOHN STRAWSON

MACFADYEN, SIR ERIC (1879-1966), rubber industry pioneer, was born in Whalley Range, Manchester, 9 February 1879, the fifth and youngest son among the seven children of the Revd John Allison Macfadyen, minister of Chorlton Road Congregational church, Manchester, and his wife, Elizabeth Anderson, of Greenock. From Lynams (the Dragon) School, Oxford, he won a scholarship to Clifton College. He was happy there, worked hard, and was head of his house. Below average height, he was tough and self-reliant. Group games did not catch his interest, but he revelled in swimming and running.

A classical scholarship took him to Wadham College, Oxford, for two years before he joined the Imperial Yeomanry and served in South Africa as a trooper in 1901–2. He had the normal soldier's life, which he took in his stride, but came to an abrupt stop when he was knocked down by a mule in the lines and run over by a wagon, which broke his shoulder, split his jaw, and damaged an eye. He was succoured by an English family owning a neighbouring farm, who showed him such devotion that the only final souvenir of the disaster was a monocle needed to hold up the ruptured eyelid.

Invalided out with the Queen's medal and three clasps, he returned to Wadham, involved himself also in university politics, and became president of the Union in 1902. He became a lifelong friend of a former president, J. A. (later Viscount) Simon [q.v.]. Macfadyen had inherited his father's gifts as a speaker and developed into a skilled debater, master of his brief, with an engaging wit and the rare faculty of making his hearers believe he was really presenting their own thoughts. Based on his classical training his English was impeccable and throughout his life he prepared all his own writing by hand. Later still he was a regular writer to *The Times* on matters of public interest written with amazing acumen and foresight. On every occasion his letter headed the correspondence columns.

In 1902 he obtained a second class in *literae humaniores* and headed the list of entrants by examination to the Malayan Civil Service; he served in several departments until 1905. The reason for his departure was amusing and characteristic. Observant as always, he formed the opinion that his department was being consistently overcharged, so he resigned the service, went into partnership with a Chinese friend, and proceeded to quote against public tenders published by his old department. On the very first occasion an ex-colleague warned him that he was so much below all other prices that acceptance would mean ruin and he must withdraw to save his skin. The kindly advice was refused, the contract awarded, executed at a profit, and Macfadyen was launched as a contractor.

From this it was a short step into planting. He joined as a 'creeper' Jebong Estate on which a small area had been planted with rubber. He learned fast. A little later, with financial help from a Manchester lawyer friend of his father, he began planting rubber. Enough letters to his sponsor survive to show the self-sacrifice, devotion to duty, and skill with which sites were chosen, lines built for labour, their

supplies of food and pay assured, jungle cleared, and drains laid before planting even started. This precision and attention to detail not only satisfied his sponsor but, more important, won the unbounded confidence of his labour force of Chinese and Malays, who were intelligent, if illiterate.

He became master of every branch of the plantation industry and a little later joined as senior partner to form Macfadyen Wilde & Co., the leading firm of visiting agents. Progress was swift and distinctions were heaped on him. He helped to form the Planters' Association and was its chairman, hence his sobriquet 'The Planters' Friend'. At different times he was chairman or president of most of the rubber associations; and he was awarded the gold medal of the Rubber Growers' Association in 1952. He was also a member of the Federal Council of the Federated Malay States in 1911–16 and in 1919–20.

His planting career reached its peak when he joined the board of Harrisons & Crosfield Ltd., the East India merchants, in January 1919 at the end of a spell as a commissioned officer in the Artillery, which had included service in France. In his thirty-six years as director with them he extended, guided, and consolidated their planting interests in Malaya. In 1955 on retirement from the board he became life-president of two of their largest plantation groups, Golden Hope and London Asiatic, household names for rubber and oil palms.

In 1923 Macfadyen made an incursion into politics when in December he won Devizes for the Liberals. But his heart was not in it and in the election of 1924 he lost the seat without regret. His outside interests ranged widely. He helped his friend, Sir Malcolm Watson [q.v.], in his work for the Ross Institute, which effectively stamped out malaria from Malaya, and was its chairman from 1946 until 1958.

He was years ahead of his time in stressing in *The Times* and elsewhere the need to look forward, planning for growth while preserving amenities. He gave practical evidence of his creed by his chairmanship of Letchworth Garden City.

In 1943 he was knighted for services to tropical agriculture when he completed service as a member of the Imperial College of Agriculture, Trinidad, and became life-president. West now joined East in salute to the industry's greatest living figure.

In 1920 Macfadyen married Violet Lucy Stanley, daughter of E. H. S. Champneys, of Otterpool Manor, Sellindge, Kent. The wedding was in Klang; Malayan royalty attended; the crowd was enormous, such was his popularity. They had three sons and three daughters. At home at Meopham Bank near

Tonbridge he and his wife farmed on a considerable scale, he on hops and barley and she in high-yielding Guernseys. At well over sixty he was a captain in the Home Guard based on Meopham and used to visit his outposts at night with the same care as on the veld. At seventy-five he made his last trip to the East, calling at the height of the bandit hostilities on estates which had not had a visit since the emergency began and dangling at his knee an old pistol from South African days with which he reckoned to give a good account of himself.

He died at his home 13 July 1966.

[Private information; personal knowledge.]
LEONARD PATON

MacGILLIVRAY, SIR DONALD CHARLES (1906-1966), colonial administrator, was born in Edinburgh 22 September 1906, the second son of Evan James MacGillivray, KC, of Wimbledon and Ringwood, Hampshire, a Scotsman who lived and practised at the bar in England, and his wife, Maude, eldest daughter of Charles J. Turcan, merchant, of Leith. He was educated at Sherborne School (1920-5) and at Trinity College, Oxford (1925-9) where he obtained third class honours in philosophy, politics, and economics in 1928. At school and at Oxford he was well liked by his contemporaries but showed little sign of his innate talents. He entered the Colonial Administrative Service in 1928 and underwent the normal year's training at Oxford before going out to Tanganyika in 1929.

In his first year spent in the Dar-es-Salaam secretariat his superiors noted the ability to grasp the essentials of intricate problems which showed so often later and he was soon recognized as a potential 'high-flyer'. However, in accordance with the practice of the service, he was posted (1930-4) to districts in the Lake Province to obtain a thorough grounding in district administration. Although still junior he had temporary charge of districts more than once and showed interest in native affairs and customs. When he revisited this area in 1956 after an interval of twenty years he was remembered and warmly welcomed by a large assembly of African chiefs. His work was recognized by his appointment as MBE in 1936. From 1935 to 1938 he returned to Dar-es-Salaam to serve as private secretary to the governor, Sir Harold A. MacMichael [q.v.], whom he followed to Palestine in 1938.

In Palestine he returned for a time to district work first in Galilee (1942-4) and then as district commissioner Samaria. He next became under-secretary to the Palestine Government which made use of his ability as a diplomat by posting him to duty as liaison officer first with the Anglo-American committee and then with the United Nations Special Committee on Palestine. He then served as colonial secretary in Jamaica (1947-52) showing great tact and political skill in his dealings with local political leaders.

Instead of the governorship which would normally have followed his time in Jamaica, where he had on occasion acted as governor, he was next selected for service in Malaya as deputy high commissioner to General (later Field Marshal) Sir Gerald Templer. The two men arrived together on 6 February 1952. They had never met before being posted to Malaya and they presented a total contrast in temperament and professional background. It was, however, a very successful partnership. Templer was concerned mainly with the co-ordination and direction of civil and military resources in the campaign against Communist insurgents in Malaya. While Templer was out and about in his cyclonic tours of the Malay States MacGillivray took over the direction and control of the complex federal government system of Malaya. There were intricate negotiations to conduct with the Malay rulers and political leaders over constitutional questions and communal disputes on such matters as common citizenship and recruitment to the public service. MacGillivray also instituted—though with limited success—developments in local government.

When Templer left Malaya in June 1954 MacGillivray succeeded him as civil high commissioner but not as military director of operations. Malaya was now moving towards independence. The transition was a difficult and uncertain period. Apart from communal questions there were two main political organizations, Party Negara under Datuk Onn, and the Alliance led by Tunku Abdul Rahman, as yet untested by national elections. As the parties jockeyed for position MacGillivray had to preserve an impartial balance without losing the confidence and goodwill of either. The situation became the more difficult as the Alliance began to press for a more rapid move to self-government than some observers judged wise. It was a problem which fully extended MacGillivray's gifts as a diplomat and conciliator. However, his quiet, cool, courteous but sometimes rather aloof manner were well-adapted to the situation—which might easily have gone off the rails but to his credit did not. In the first national elections held in July 1955 the Alliance established its claim to be the future Government of an independent Malaya by a landslide victory at the polls. The outstanding problems of constitution-building were resolved by negotiations based on the recommendations of the Reid

Commission. Malaya became independent in 1957.

MacGillivray then retired from the Colonial Service and settled in Kenya where he bought a farm in the Highlands at Gilgil. But the same restless absorption in work which marked his career throughout drew him away from farming to public life in East Africa. He became chairman (1958–61) of the council of Makerere College in Uganda and then of the council of the university of East Africa (1961–4). When the British Government appointed a commission to report on the constitutional problems of the Federation of Rhodesia and Nyasaland in 1960 MacGillivray became its vice-chairman. Apart from holding company directorships, notably in banking, he became the director (in 1964) of the United Nations Special Fund for the East African Livestock Development Survey. He thus continued to travel widely and to drive himself hard until cancer brought his working life to its end. He died in hospital in Nairobi 24 December 1966 at the age of sixty.

In 1936 he married Louisa Mai, daughter of Marvyn Knox-Browne, of Aughentaire Castle, county Tyrone. They had one son. His MBE in 1936 was followed by appointment as CMG (1949), KCMG (1953), and GCMG (1957).

Slight of build, quiet in manner, and to those who did not know him well at times rather reserved, MacGillivray had a lively mind, a sense of humour, and a capacity—indeed a personal need— to absorb himself in the work in hand. In his successful career as a colonial administrator he was a man of his time. In the era of decolonization it was patient skill rather than drastic action, above all sympathetic and intelligent diplomacy which was needed to resolve the problems of dependent territories as they moved towards independence. In this context and in this way MacGillivray made a notable contribution.

[Private information; personal knowledge.]

J. M. GULLICK

McGOWAN, HARRY DUNCAN, first BARON McGOWAN (1874–1961), business man, was born in Glasgow 3 June 1874, the only son and second of three children of Harry McGowan, brass fitter, and his wife, Agnes, daughter of Richard Wilson. He went to Hutchesontown school and then, on a bursary, to Allan Glen's School, both in Glasgow, and at fifteen joined Nobel's Explosives Company, Glasgow and Ardeer, as an office boy. Without capital, influential connections, or technical training of any kind, McGowan made his way as a professional manager in the firm which was the largest subsidiary of the Anglo-German Nobel-Dynamite Trust Company. It dominated the explosives trade of the British Empire, secured to it by agreements between the Trust and other makers in Europe and America in return for undertakings not to compete in their 'exclusive territories'. As assistant to Thomas Johnston, Nobel's powerful, ingenious, and not over-scrupulous general manager, McGowan was early introduced to elaborate industrial diplomacy on a world-wide scale.

In Canada, between 1909 and 1911, McGowan played a large part in constructing Canadian Explosives Limited (1910), later Canadian Industries Limited, a merger of explosives firms jointly owned by Nobels, who had control, and Du Pont, the largest American explosives business. CIL became much the largest chemical business in Canada. The Du Pont alliance, greatly enlarged and elaborated, became at length the centrepiece of ICI's foreign policy until, in the late forties, the American authorities broke it up with the anti-trust suit *US* v. *ICI*. McGowan himself was deeply impressed by the Du Pont business and by Pierre S. du Pont and others of the family. Where they led, in later years, he would often follow.

The Nobel-Dynamite Trust was destroyed by the outbreak of war in 1914, leaving Nobel's Explosives much greater freedom of action. McGowan used it to carry through a merger of almost the entire British explosives industry, and at much the same time he was closely concerned with moves, backed by the Government, to bring about a similarly comprehensive merger of British dyestuffs businesses. In 1918 he became chairman and managing director of Explosives Trades Limited, renamed in 1920 Nobel Industries Limited. In 1919 he joined the board, on its formation, of British Dyestuffs Corporation. No one had ever held so great a position in the British chemical industry.

McGowan's aim in forming Nobel Industries was to move resources out of explosives, for which—rightly—he foresaw no very bright peacetime future, into other activities, especially the motor industry and its associated trades. Influenced by Du Pont, he directed £3 million in 1920 into General Motors, alongside Du Pont's much larger investment, and considerable sums went also into Dunlop, Lucas, and other British firms servicing the motor trade. Until the crash of 1929 the General Motors investment was very successful and judicious sales provided capital for ICI's expansion in the late twenties.

Nobel Industries Limited provided the model for McGowan's largest conception: Imperial Chemical Industries Limited. The formation in

Germany, in the autumn of 1925, of IG Farbenindustrie threatened to overwhelm the British chemical industry by sheer weight of concentrated industrial power, and McGowan, prodded by Reginald McKenna [q.v.], proposed a defensive merger between the four largest British chemical businesses: Nobel Industries; Brunner, Mond; United Alkali Company; and British Dyestuffs Corporation. Sir Alfred Mond (later Lord Melchett, q.v.) originally had plans for a different merger for his firm, including the IG and an American firm, Allied Chemical & Dye, but his scheme broke down on the refusal of the latter to come in, and in New York in September 1926 Mond and McGowan agreed upon the merger which brought ICI into existence.

On 31 December 1930, after the death of Melchett, McGowan became chairman and sole managing director of ICI. It was a daunting moment. ICI was staggering under the impact of the slump on over-optimistic expansion, and by 1935 about 10 per cent of the capital of the business had been lost. McGowan's strategy for recovery depended heavily on a world-wide network of trading agreements with almost every producer of any importance at home or abroad, including Du Pont, IG, and producers of alkali in Western Europe, the United States, and Russia. Elaborate cartels regulated output, prices, selling areas, and exchange of technical knowledge in fertilizers, dyestuffs, alkali, the products of hydrogenation, and indeed nearly every article of any importance in any branch of the chemical industry.

McGowan was a dictator and his dictatorship antagonized his board. In 1937 they rebelled, taking the opportunity offered by the failure of McGowan's personal speculations, carried out on credit from brokers which at one time reached £1.9 m. In the winter of 1937 McGowan's career was apparently in ruin. He had been rescued from bankruptcy, but Sir William McLintock [q.v.] had advised the board that they could no longer have confidence in him, and they had chosen his successor, the second Lord Melchett. On Christmas day Melchett had a heart attack, putting him out of action for a year. The board's nerve broke, and they recoiled from dismissing McGowan. He remained chairman until 31 December 1950. He had outfaced adversity and won.

As a business man, McGowan was not of the stature of Sir Charles Tennant [q.v.] who had been one of the founders of Nobel Explosives, of Lord Leverhulme [q.v.], or even, perhaps, of his colleague, Alfred Mond. He lacked their creative flair. What he had was force, vitality, and courage, and his great appetite for power was balanced by his ability to use it and a total acceptance of responsibility.

He told the second Lord Melchett that he did not accept 'the theory . . . that competition is essential to efficiency'. Instead, he relied on the cartel system which was characteristic of the chemical industry for many years, and he defended it in the House of Lords as 'a medium for the orderly expansion of world trade'. For success, ICI had to be strong enough to enforce the respect of foreign competitors, and McGowan and Mond repeatedly said that the object of founding ICI—'Imperial in aspect and Imperial in name'—was to make the British chemical industry strong enough in its 'natural markets'—Great Britain and the British Empire—to develop the export trade and to build healthy and varied manufacturing enterprises in the United Kingdom, Canada, South Africa, Australasia, and other countries as they become capable of supporting them.

In the circumstances of the thirties, with productive capacity throughout the world running far ahead of effective demand, no such policy would have been possible without the protection of cartels, behind which the main centres of ICI's strength, in the United Kingdom, could be reorganized and modernized. McGowan's most important service to the nation was to see what needed doing in the chemical industry and to do it, which above all required will-power: his essential quality.

Florid of countenance, sanguine in expression, fond of good living, he could be brutal; he was often coarse; his relations with his family were stormy; his judgement, especially in his own affairs, was sometimes faulty; but when everything has been said against him, and plenty can be said, one fact remains: he rescued the British chemical industry from the threat of extinction in the twenties, and in the thirties set it on the way to the technological revolution of the fifties and sixties. In a period chiefly remarkable for the failure of British will and nerve, McGowan's nerve never broke and his will prevailed.

McGowan was appointed KBE in 1918 and created a baron in 1937. In 1903 he married Jean Boyle, daughter of William Young, of Paisley, who died in 1952. They had two sons and two daughters. McGowan died in London 13 July 1961 and was succeeded by his elder son, Harry Wilson (1906-66).

There is a portrait of McGowan by Sir William Orpen at Imperial Chemical House, London, and another, by Harold Knight, is in the possession of the family.

[W. J. Reader, *Imperial Chemical Industries, a History*, vol. i, 1970; private information.]
W. J. READER

McKIE, DOUGLAS (1896-1967), historian of science, was born 15 July 1896 at Ebbw Vale in Monmouthshire, the elder son of James McKie, a Scottish soldier and farmer, and his wife, Janet Moseley. He was educated at Tredegar Grammar School and he chose the army for his career. In 1915 he entered Sandhurst for a shortened wartime course and was later commissioned in the South Wales Borderers with whom he served for eighteen months in France until he was severely wounded at Passchendaele in 1917. After many months in hospital he rejoined his regiment at home and was with them in the army of occupation in Germany when he was selected for a Staff College course. However, in view of his physical handicap due to his wound he decided to leave the army in 1920. He then entered University College, London, where he read chemistry under the stimulating influence of F. G. Donnan [q.v.]. After taking his B.Sc. with first class honours in 1923 he spent several years in research which gained for him a Ramsay memorial medal (1925) and a Ph.D. (1928). In addition it gave him the experience of the pangs and excitements of experimental research, the quest of new techniques and the critical appraisal of results, which later made his studies of the work of the old masters of chemistry so realistic and sympathetic after he had found his *métier* and turned to the history of science. In 1925 he became a part-time assistant to Professor Abraham Wolf in the department of the history and philosophy of science in which he was to spend the next forty years. Later under McKie's stimulating leadership it became the leading centre of that subject in Britain. McKie became lecturer in 1934, reader in 1946, and succeeded to the chair in 1957, retiring as an emeritus professor in 1964.

With his wide interests and sympathy McKie was never a narrow specialist. He read widely and with his retentive memory and human interest in individuals he got a broad perspective of the history of science from the seventeenth century to recent times, and he left an impressive record of books and papers. In spite of their wide coverage they are never superficial as McKie had a quick eye for the significant and for those episodes which have played a crucial part in progress. The strength of the school he developed owed much to the example he set in his lectures and in the quality of everything he wrote.

In 1935 he published with N. H. de V. Heathcote *The Discovery of Specific and Latent Heats*, which led to his lifelong study of Joseph Black [q.v.]. Also in 1935 there appeared his important book embodying his intimate studies of the scientific work of Lavoisier. This led twenty years later to his membership of the committee of the French Académie des Sciences responsible for the editing and publishing of Lavoisier's correspondence and laboratory records. McKie devoted much time to the planning of this work, for which he was made a chevalier of the Legion of Honour in recognition of his services to France. His second book on Lavoisier in 1952 dealt with his public work as an administrator and economist and with his contribution to education as well as with his scientific work. In his last years he was still at work on Lavoisier, collecting material for a definitive life and preparing for publication Lavoisier's laboratory note-books; both these projects he left unfinished.

He ran in parallel with his early work on Lavoisier's chemistry a historical study of the phlogiston theory with J. R. Partington [q.v.], which was published as a series of papers in *Annals of Science* between 1937 and 1939. At this period too, he became involved in a study of a remarkable precursor of Lavoisier and eventually published in 1951 a facsimile reprint, with critical introduction, of *The Essays of Jean Rey*.

Shortly before his death McKie published his edition of Thomas Cochrane's *Notes from Doctor Black's Lectures on Chemistry 1767/8* (1966). The various manuscript versions of Black's lectures had been the subject of a series of papers, part of the material which McKie had been collecting for years for the first full-length portrait of the Scottish chemist who published so little but exercised so great an influence on his contemporaries. McKie had traced Black's missing correspondence and all the background work had been done when illness overtook him.

McKie's rich store of knowledge and his critical judgement were always most generously available to his friends. The planning of the tercentenary volume: *The Royal Society, its Origins and Founders* (1960) owed much to his advice. He contributed to it the opening article, 'The Origins and Foundation of the Royal Society of London', a definitive account of the events leading up to the birth of the Royal Society and of the intellectual climate in which it was formed. Written in McKie's clear narrative style and with its admirable balance, like all McKie's writing, it is the standard account of a great episode. He also contributed the chapter on science and technology to the *New Cambridge Modern History*.

McKie's services to the history of science were manifold. Many of the later generation of historians were trained under his watchful eye. In 1936 he founded the *Annals of Science*, which he edited with scholarly care until his death. He was proud of his Scottish ancestry and his election into the Royal Society of Edinburgh in 1958 gave him special pleasure. He was also a fellow of University College, London, of the

Royal Institute of Chemistry, of the Royal Society of Arts, and of the Society of Antiquaries. In 1963 the division of the history of chemistry of the American Chemical Society gave McKie the Dexter award in recognition of his international eminence as a scholar.

McKie had a serious operation in 1964 and died in London 28 August 1967. In 1922 he married Mary, daughter of Thomas Smith, of Kirkby-la-Thorpe, who had been his wartime nurse. Their only child, Dr Duncan McKie, a mineralogist, became a fellow of Jesus College, Cambridge.

[*Annals of Science*, March 1968; *The Times*, 31 August 1967; private information; personal knowledge.]   HAROLD HARTLEY

MACKINTOSH, HAROLD VINCENT, first VISCOUNT MACKINTOSH OF HALIFAX (1891–1964), man of business and public servant, was born in Halifax, Yorkshire, 8 June 1891, the eldest of three sons all destined to enter the confectionery business founded by their father, John Mackintosh, and his wife, Violet, daughter of James Taylor, of Clover Hill, Halifax. Mackintosh was educated at Halifax New School, a private grammar school where he became head boy and captain of the hockey and cricket teams. On leaving school in 1909 he went to Germany, working at the family's factory there for two years to learn both the manufacturing and selling side of the business. On the death of his father in 1920 he became chairman of the family firm, having meanwhile served during the war of 1914–18 in the Royal Naval Volunteer Reserve. The growth of the business was in no small part due to Mackintosh's belief not only in quality but also in large-scale publicity schemes. His enthusiasm for advertising led to his presidency of the Advertising Association (1942–6), of the National Advertising Benevolent Association (1946–8), and from 1949 to a great deal of organization for the International Advertising Convention over which he presided in 1951.

Business interests apart, Mackintosh recorded that he worked throughout his life for three causes—thrift, Sunday schools, and medical research. He was involved in the negotiations which brought about the amalgamation in 1928 of the two building societies in Halifax into 'The Halifax', and it was through his work for the building society movement that he had come to join the board of Martins Bank. His connection with the savings movement began when he became a trustee of York County Savings Bank and vice-president of the Trustee Savings Banks Association. In 1941 he was elected Yorkshire member of the National Savings Committee and in the same year he

was appointed vice-chairman. In 1943 he succeeded Lord Mottistone [q.v.] as chairman of the Committee and in 1946 he became head of the Savings Movement on the retirement of Lord Kindersley [q.v.] from the presidency. Mackintosh was responsible for the publicity for wartime saving, based on War Savings Weeks which changed their theme as the war progressed: War Weapons Week, Warships Week, Wings for Victory, Salute the Soldier, and Thanksgiving. After 1945 the movement again became National Savings based on the same organization which had been so successfully expanded during the war: local savings groups wherever they could be formed, in schools or factories, streets or villages, with a well-built structure of local, district, and regional committees, the last with their representatives on the National Committee. Mackintosh travelled more than 20,000 miles a year in the cause of savings and was very popular with the movement's voluntary workers. The general public knew him well through his broadcasts and public appearances. Newspaper men liked his frankness, his unfailing good humour, and his accessibility. The National Savings Committee benefited greatly by his wide experience of advertising and modern publicity methods.

Mackintosh's second interest sprang from his early upbringing in the Methodist Church of which he was a staunch supporter. He was chairman of the central board of finance, a director of the Methodist central buying association, and joint treasurer of the Home Missionary Committee and of Ashville College, Harrogate. He was president of the National Sunday School Union (1924–5) and of the World Council of Christian Education and Sunday School Association (1928–58), continuing as chairman until his death, and as honorary treasurer of the British committee. He was also a vice-president of the national council of the YMCA.

In 1926 Mackintosh became secretary of a campaign started in Yorkshire for cancer research and in 1936 its chairman. Again his flair for publicity was put to good use in raising money and Yorkshire Cancer Research Centres were established at the universities of Leeds and Sheffield.

Before the second war, Mackintosh's acquired the chocolate business of A. J. Caley in Norwich and in 1947 Mackintosh decided to make his home in Norfolk, mainly to be within easier reach of London and his work for National Savings. He became interested in the proposals for the new university of East Anglia, was chairman of the promotion committee in 1959, but died before he could be officially installed as first chancellor.

Beneath a brusque exterior Mackintosh had a warm, friendly, and generous nature. He was one of the most popular after-dinner speakers in the country with a fund of stories told in his rich Yorkshire brogue. One of his recreations was farming and his herd of Jersey cows won him trophies in all big agricultural shows. He was president of the Yorkshire Agricultural Society (1928-9) and in 1960 president of the Royal Norfolk Agricultural Society. Another interest was the collection of early Staffordshire pottery and in 1938 he published a book on *Early English Figure Pottery*. He had also a fine collection of paintings, particularly works of the Norwich school. In 1959-64 he was a member of the Arts Council.

Mackintosh was appointed a JP in 1925, deputy lieutenant for the West Riding of Yorkshire in 1945, an honorary freeman of the county borough of Halifax in 1954, and an honorary LLD of Leeds in 1948. He was knighted in 1922, created a baronet in 1935, baron in 1948, and viscount in 1957. He sat in the House of Lords as an independent member.

In 1916 Mackintosh married Constance Emily (died 1975), daughter of Edgar Cooper Stoneham, OBE, an accountant in the Civil Service, and born on the same day as himself. It was an intensely happy marriage. They had a daughter and one son, John (born 1921), who succeeded as second viscount on the death of his father in Norwich 27 December 1964. Portraits of Mackintosh by Cowan Dobson are in the possession of the family and at the offices of the company at Norwich and Halifax.

[Lord Mackintosh of Halifax, *By Faith and Work*, ed. A. A. Thomson, 1966; *The Times*, 29 December 1964; private information; personal knowledge.]   INMAN

MACKINTOSH, JAMES MACALISTER (1891-1966), public health teacher and administrator, was born in Kilmarnock, Scotland, 17 February 1891, the younger son of James Dunbar Mackintosh, solicitor, and his wife, Janet Macalister. He was educated in Glasgow at the High School and university, graduating MA in 1912 before commencing medical studies which were interrupted by the outbreak of war in 1914 in which he served in France with a commission in the 6th Cameron Highlanders. After being wounded at the battle of Loos he returned to Britain and graduated MB, Ch.B. in 1916. He went back to France as a captain in the Royal Army Medical Corps in 1918.

After the war Mackintosh decided on a career in public health. He took his DPH in 1920, obtained his MD in 1923 with high commenda-

tion, and in 1930 was called to the bar by Gray's Inn. In 1920 he began the movement from post to post which was the career pattern of the public health officer of those days. Four years in Dorset were followed by two in Burton-on-Trent and three in Leicestershire. In 1930 he became county medical officer of Northampton, where he spent perhaps the happiest years of his professional life. He soon established himself as an expert on rural housing and his reports are a permanent contribution to social history on that subject. His interest was not limited to the siting, construction, and sanitary amenities of rural cottages, but included the lives, habits, and financial resources of their inhabitants. The influence of housing on health was one of his abiding interests and in 1952 he published a book on *Housing and Family Life*.

In 1937 Mackintosh was appointed chief medical officer in the Department of Health for Scotland, and he was there for four years. Arriving shortly after the publication of the Cathcart committee's report on the Scottish health services, Mackintosh looked forward to presiding over the developments which would give effect to its recommendations; but the war clouds were gathering and he devoted himself to the task of organizing the emergency medical services in Scotland. The improvised but effective emergency medical service hospitals which sprang up all over the country were not only a major contribution to the war effort but later proved a godsend to the regional hospital boards which took them over in 1948. He served on the Feversham committee which in 1939 recommended the amalgamation of the voluntary mental health services and led to the eventual formation of the National Association for Mental Health.

Mackintosh found central government a disappointing experience, and welcomed the opportunity in 1941 of becoming professor of public health in his old university of Glasgow. Three years later he moved south to become professor of public health in the university of London and dean of the London School of Hygiene and Tropical Medicine. Wartime tenants occupied a large part of the School building, a sixth of which, including the department of public health, was a derelict ruin through bomb damage. All teaching, except some courses in tropical medicine, had been in abeyance for five years, and most of the pre-war staff had disappeared. He gave up the deanship after five years to devote himself to the department, but in those five years he had directed the rebuilding of the bomb-damaged part of the building, completely reorganized and restarted the course for the DPH, and set the School on its feet again.

Mackintosh was as well known internationally amongst public health workers as in his own country. His interest in international public health started in 1941 with a prolonged visit which he paid to the United States. He was appointed a general adviser on civil defence, and he toured practically every state of America. This was the first of his many visits to the United States. His greatest activities in the international field were carried out under the World Health Organization. He was invited to take part in meetings of experts on public health administration and to act as a consultant on rural housing. His advice was also sought on such matters as public health teaching, and, with Professor Fred Grundy, he carried out an important study on the *Teaching of Hygiene and Public Health in Europe* (1957). His introductory general survey to the first report on the World Health Situation, published in 1959, was a notable contribution on the theory and practice of international public health. After retiring from his chair in 1956 Mackintosh acted as director of the World Health Organization division of education and training from 1958 to 1960. He then returned to the United States for two years as an adviser to the Avalon and Milbank Foundations. After he finally retired he continued to write despite his failing health, and his essays on *Topics in Public Health* were published in 1965, the year before his death.

In 1943 he was elected FRCP of London and Edinburgh. He received the honorary LLD of Glasgow in 1950 and of Birmingham in 1961.

A legend grew up that Mackintosh did not take kindly to administration—but he was in fact an able, practical, and flexible administrator. Nevertheless, his greatest contribution was as teacher and interpreter of public health. He had a flair for interesting exposition in both formal and informal speaking and his gift for clear, attractive, and persuasive writing was outstanding. He had a keen interest in the historical origins and trends of social policy and institutions, and gave to his students a firm sense of the necessity to look back in order to go forward. His interest in social attitudes and his feel for their importance in determining trends in health through changing individual behaviour was unique in his day. He was a social philosopher and diagnostician whose sensitive awareness of the importance of public opinion and individual behaviour in public health was conveyed most clearly in his Heath Clark lectures (1951). As administrator and teacher he had the gift of imagination with which to add an extra dimension to the facts of health and social policy. He has been described as the poet of public health and

indeed published privately a slim volume of verse under the title *Airs, Waters and Places*. On first acquaintance he gave a deceptive impression almost of frailness and diffidence which belied his resilience, charm, and immense capacity for friendship. He was reflective, original, gay, and warm of heart. It was typical that in middle age he wrote an admonitory letter to himself to be opened on retirement.

In 1919 he married Marjorie, daughter of David Strathie, chartered accountant, of Glasgow; they had one son and two daughters. Mackintosh died in Bristol 20 April 1966.

[*Lancet* and *British Medical Journal*, 30 April 1966; private information; personal knowledge.]   J. H. F. BROTHERSTON

MACKWORTH-YOUNG, GERARD (1884-1965), Indian civil servant and archaeologist, was born in London 7 April 1884, the eldest of the four sons of (Sir) William Mackworth Young [q.v.], lieutenant-governor of the Punjab in 1897-1902, and his second wife, Frances Mary, eldest daughter of Sir Robert Eyles Egerton, lieutenant-governor of the Punjab in 1877-82. His great-uncle was the poet Winthrop Mackworth Praed [q.v.]. He was King's scholar at Eton, in the Newcastle select, and as an Eton scholar went up to King's College, Cambridge, where he took a first in part i of the classical tripos (1906). In 1907 he followed family tradition by passing into the Indian Civil Service.

His career in the Service was devoted and distinguished: under-secretary to the Government of the Punjab (1913), under-secretary to the home department of the Government of India (1916-19), deputy commissioner for Delhi (1921), deputy secretary of the army department of the Government of India (1924) and secretary (1926); in 1929 he was appointed CIE. Possessor of a fine tall wiry physique, capable of walking fifty miles a day, he was a natural choice for government excursions into the wilds, and in 1912 he was dispatched on a three month's journey to Toling and Tsaparang in western Tibet, places scarcely visited by Europeans since the seventeenth century when, it is credibly reported, a Jesuit mission reached Tsaparang and converted the king to Christianity.

The journey was in fact an excursion into Cathay, and Gerard Young was to write eloquently of temples and treasures, of a valley with temperatures rising to well above 100°, and of the spectacle of Toling monastery, crimson and white and roofed with the gold for which ever since Herodotus the region had been famed. In 1916 he married Natalie Leila Margaret (died 1981), daughter of the late Sir Walter

Francis Hely-Hutchinson, who had been Cape Colony's last governor. After the Tibetan expedition it was not surprising that the honeymoon should be spent in travel, and the pair set out from Simla on a two months' trek to Kulu and back—a journey which a wedding guest prophesied would kill the bride but which in fact, for she too was a strong walker, she triumphantly enjoyed.

Good fortune as well as natural endowment was on the side of Gerard Young. In 1932 a legacy enabled him to retire at forty-eight and pursue the diverse intellectual and artistic interests which have often inspired the public servant of his period and background. He had for some time been working on a verse translation of *The Epigrams of Callimachus*: graceful, lucidly annotated, the result was published in 1934. Free now to indulge his feeling for the ancient world, in 1932 he enrolled as a student of the British School of Archaeology in Athens, and modestly accepted among the young postgraduates of the institution the position of a beginner. He had, however, taken advice on finding a niche in classical archaeology. Astutely he mastered the technique of the still camera; and in collaboration with the then director of the School, Humfry Payne [q.v.], who wrote the text, he produced in 1936 a standard photographic catalogue, *Archaic Marble Sculpture from the Acropolis*. Meanwhile with a young archaeologist, James Brock, as partner he undertook between 1935 and 1938 excavations in the island of Siphnos, and to the publication in the British School *Annual* contributed a carefully documented section on Roman graves of the first century AD.

In 1936 the death both of Humfry Payne and of his successor left the School without a director. Gerard Young was a comparative newcomer to archaeology, but he had the qualifications which the times demanded—sufficient scholarship, knowledge of the job, great administrative experience. And he was both well-to-do and generous; the School was to be deeply indebted for his benefactions. He remained as director until the outbreak of war in 1939, when he joined the staff of the British legation in Athens. On the German occupation of Greece he returned to India, first as joint-secretary of the War Department, and in 1944 as an honorary officer of the Archaeological Survey.

After the war he went back to Athens to take charge of the reopening of the School; he finally retired in 1946. He did not, however, retire from something which all his life had been his major pleasure—music, and especially singing. With a handsome bass-baritone voice and near-professional standards which at one time encouraged two years' study in Munich, he had sung in opera in Simla and given *Lieder* recitals in Athens; indeed he was practising almost to the day of his death. The value of his book *What Happens in Singing* (1953), a study of vocal mechanics and in particular resonation, was recognized by both teacher and practitioner.

The formal and the engagingly adventurous were mingled in his character as in his life. His friendship, always kind, always generous, was enlivened by ready fun; and in his manner, suddenly and charmingly illuminated by a blazing smile, the habit of authority rarely betrayed itself. Nevertheless he had no lack of self-respect, and it was in an effort to avoid, as he put it, confusion with all the other Youngs that he first had his four children, two boys and two girls, christened Mackworth and then himself in 1947 took by deed poll the hyphenated surname of Mackworth-Young. He died at Windsor 28 November 1965. Robert Christopher, his elder son, in 1958 became librarian at Windsor Castle; a portrait of his father by Sonia Mervyn is in his possession.

[*Annual Report* of the council of King's College, Cambridge, 1966; private information; personal knowledge.] DILYS POWELL

MACLEOD, IAIN NORMAN (1913-1970), politician, was born at Skipton, Yorkshire, 11 November 1913, the second child and eldest of three sons of Norman Macleod and his wife and second cousin Annabel, daughter of Rhoderick Ross, a doctor on the isle of Lewis. His father, the son of a crofter on the island, was a popular and respected doctor in Skipton for nearly thirty years. Of wholly Scottish ancestry Macleod was brought up in Yorkshire, although in 1920 his father bought for a small sum a property, Scaliscro, on Lewis, where the family often spent the holidays and where Macleod was taught to shoot and to play bridge. His roots were at least as much in the Highlands as in Yorkshire.

As a child Macleod conceived an enduring love of poetry, for which he had a Macaulayan memory, and which he himself wrote. Neither at Fettes College, however, nor at Gonville and Caius College, Cambridge, where he got a second in history in 1935, were his intellectual gifts revealed. He was fond of rugby and cricket, although only a moderate player, and he always remained a keen follower and spectator of most sports. Apart from poetry and a little acting, Macleod's chief interests at Cambridge were bridge and gambling. He spoke only once at the Union and joined none of the political clubs, but he formed the Cambridge Bridge Club and made himself president. He was a top-class player.

After Cambridge Macleod was given a place in Thomas de la Rue, whose chairman he had met at the bridge table, but he had no interest in his job, which he was in any case often too tired to do, having spent most of the night playing bridge. De la Rue's forbearance lasted two years, whereupon Macleod claimed to be reading for the bar, perhaps to please his father. His manner of life at Cambridge and in London, although not in accord with the Protestant ethic, had its reasons. His earnings from bridge were on average more than ten times the £3 a week he gained from de la Rue, and his intellect was well trained.

In September 1939 Macleod joined the Royal Fusiliers as a private, and after being commissioned in the Duke of Wellington's Regiment in April 1940 he was sent to the BEF which was already in retreat. Near Neufchâtel he was badly wounded in the thigh and returned to hospital in England. In 1941 Macleod married Evelyn Hester, daughter of the Revd Gervase Vanneck Blois, rector of Hanbury, Worcestershire, whose first husband, Mervyn Charles Mason, had been killed at sea in 1940. A boy and a girl were born in 1942 and 1944. Macleod's early soldiering extended him no more than had university or commerce. It was only at Staff College in autumn 1943 under the stimulus of high-class competition that he realized the extent of his abilities and determined to use them. He landed on D-Day as DAQMG of the 50th Northumbrian division, and served in France until his division returned to Yorkshire in November 1944.

He was on leave at Scaliscro when the general election of 1945 was announced. There being no Conservative organization in the Outer Hebrides, Macleod supplied it. His father, who supported Churchill although a Liberal, was elected chairman and Macleod the candidate. Since there was no one else present, this was not a difficult meeting. Defeat in the election was, however, certain, and Macleod's creditable 2,756 votes out of nearly 13,000 cast left him at the bottom of the poll.

Macleod was demobilized as a major in January 1946 and shortly afterwards joined the Conservative Parliamentary Secretariat. On the amalgamation of the new Secretariat with the Research Department in 1948 Macleod, now one of the party's few experts on the social services, was put in charge of home affairs. In 1946 he had been adopted as Conservative candidate for Enfield, then a safe Labour seat; only after it divided into two in 1948 did he seem likely to be successful. At no time in his life was Macleod well off. Until 1952, when he virtually gave it up, bridge remained necessary for paying the mortgage on his home in Enfield and other expenses. He wrote a weekly bridge

column for the *Sunday Times* and in 1952 published the lively and authoritative *Bridge is an Easy Game*.

Elected in 1950 for Enfield West with a majority over 9,000, Macleod wisely concentrated on the subjects he knew best: health and social services. An original member of the One Nation Group he edited with Angus Maude the group's pamphlet *One Nation* (1950). He was not given office when the Conservatives regained power in 1951 but became chairman of the Conservative parliamentary health and social services committee. As such, on the second reading debate on the National Health Service Bill on 27 March 1952 he was likely to be the third speaker after the minister and Dr (later Baroness) Summerskill, the shadow minister, a good position when the House would be well filled. However, a maiden speaker was given precedence. Bitterly disappointed, Macleod decided not to speak and threw away his notes. But when Aneurin Bevan [q.v.] followed the maiden speaker, Macleod changed his mind again and also his speech. Bevan was a much better target than Dr Summerskill, and by now Churchill was in the House. Macleod's opening sentence, 'I want to deal closely and with relish with the vulgar, crude and intemperate speech to which the House of Commons has just listened', followed shortly afterwards by the remark that to have a debate on the National Health Service without Aneurin Bevan 'would be like putting on Hamlet with no one in the part of the First Gravedigger', established his hold over the House. Complete master of his subject in all its details, Macleod dealt effectively with several interruptions from Bevan, and his victory over the most formidable debater in the Opposition was not in doubt. Six weeks later Churchill appointed him minister of health. At that time the Ministry, which had lost its responsibilities for housing and for planning, was a declining department, and its minister was not in the Cabinet. Nevertheless, to achieve the post in one jump from the back benches and to become a privy councillor at the age of thirty-eight was remarkable.

Two months later Eve Macleod was struck by meningitis and polio; eventually she was able to walk again with the aid of sticks. Despite her disability she continued to work tirelessly in the constituency and to help Macleod in every way she could. Macleod's own health was already bad. He suffered from ankylosing spondylitis, a form of rheumatoid arthritis which attacks the spine and which made it progressively more difficult for Macleod to move his back, neck, or head. Its effect was no doubt aggravated by his wartime injury which made walking difficult and led to a slanting of the pelvis. Social occasions when he had to stand or look up were an increasing trial. The pain was virtually permanent for the last twenty years of his life. It was unflinchingly borne.

Macleod's ill health and that of his wife naturally sharpened his sympathy for the suffering of others, which was demonstrated during his visits to hospitals and by his successful efforts to humanize their administration and to encourage help from voluntary organizations. Although the last man to parade his concern, he was both in private and in public life notably and genuinely compassionate. Otherwise, as minister of health Macleod was sound but not spectacular: money was scarce, and housing had much higher priority; consolidation was the only possible course. Macleod showed himself a quick and competent administrator, and as always was good in the House. His reputation steadily grew, but promotion did not come until Eden's reshuffle in December 1955 when Macleod entered the Cabinet as minister of labour.

Macleod's predecessor, Sir Walter Monckton (later Viscount Monckton of Brenchley, q.v.), had been given by Churchill the task of maintaining good relations with the trade-union leaders. But conciliation had bred inflation, and by 1955 greater heed had to be paid to the economic effects of conceding wage claims. If Macleod could not be as open-handed with the unions as Monckton had been, his employment policies followed the ideal of 'One Nation'. He tried to improve relations in industry by persuading employers to treat their employees as responsible individuals, and he favoured the introduction of a code of practice setting out the rights of workers, contracts of service, and redundancy payments: all later achieved. In 1957 he was glad to be able to announce the beginning of the end of national service. But it was his defeat of Frank Cousins in the bus strike in 1958 which first made Macleod a national figure. He himself was unhappy about some aspects of the lengthy struggle, in particular the forced departure from his department's traditional role of mediator; but in public his handling was firm and sure, and he accompanied it with a biting attack on Hugh Gaitskell [q.v.], one of several notable parliamentary performances at this period. Sometimes speaking without notes, Macleod always presented a clear argument heavily buttressed by detailed facts, which his photographic memory had no difficulty in retaining. His phraseology was colourful and often witty: 'I cannot help it if every time the Opposition are asked to name their weapons they pick boomerangs.'

Macleod had his misgivings over Suez but he was not sufficiently involved to consider resig-

nation. Although he got on well enough with Eden, his relations with Macmillan were far closer. With the planning for the 1959 election Macleod was closely concerned. Immediately afterwards he was made secretary of state for the colonies, the social and political demands of the appointment necessitating a move from Enfield to a flat in London. With Macmillan's support Macleod deliberately speeded up the movement towards independence in Africa. Conferences on Kenya, Tanganyika, Nyasaland, and Uganda quickly succeeded each other; Hastings Banda and Kenyatta were released from jail. Within a few years Macleod's policy had the appearance of inevitable rightness, but at the time it was strongly opposed by the Conservative right wing. In the Lords, Salisbury delivered a strong personal attack on the colonial secretary (7 March 1961) for adopting, especially 'to the white communities of Africa, a most unhappy and an entirely wrong approach. He had been too clever by half.' Salisbury went on to accuse Macleod of bringing into the sphere of politics the bridge technique of seeking to outwit his opponents—the white settlers. Highly sensitive, Macleod seemed unduly put out by this onslaught, but his assessment turned out to be correct. 'Too clever by half' stuck, and almost to the end it distorted many people's picture of Macleod.

It was not true of his African policy, let alone of the man. A calculating man would never have set about dismantling the British Empire so openly and with something approaching enthusiasm; he would have feigned reluctance. Macleod was fully aware that he was going against the grain of his party and damaging his own prospects. In early 1961 he thought he might well be forced out of office by the end of the year. Yet he stuck to his policy, convinced that speedy de-colonization in Africa was vital. Elsewhere he was less successful: both the South Arabian and the West Indian federations were short-lived. But Britain's withdrawal from Africa in peace instead of with ill grace and in bloodshed was Macleod's greatest political achievement and put him perhaps second only to Joseph Chamberlain [q.v.] among reforming colonial secretaries.

In October 1961 Macleod was moved. Over Northern Rhodesia he had become overexposed both in the Cabinet and in the party. Sure of the correctness of his policy and aware of the dangers of going too slowly, he had sometimes been inflexible over details. He became chancellor of the Duchy of Lancaster, leader of the House of Commons, and chairman of the Conservative Party organization. The first job was a sinecure; the other two doubtfully compatible; nor did Macleod's occasional abruptness of manner and impatience with the slower-witted make him an ideal choice. Yet, he was well fitted to be party chairman. If his African policies had done him harm in the party, they had done the party itself a lot of good and had given Macleod a broad cross-party appeal. His attitude at home was similarly attractive, especially to the young. He always called himself a Tory, regarding 'Conservative' as stodgy and uninspiring. (Not surprisingly, Macleod's book on *Neville Chamberlain* (1961), amongst the dullest of Conservatives, was disappointing; he wrote it because he admired Chamberlain's work for social reform.)

It was the element of romanticism or poetry in Macleod which, as much as the liberalism of his political views, helped to attract the young and uncommitted. Macleod's faith in democracy was unusually strong for a democratic politician. He knew that a party's policy had to be much more than an invocation of past dogmas; it had to learn from the voters as well as try to lead them: width of appeal was vital. For Macleod winning elections by being a national party was only part of the Tory task. If the country was one nation, this was not inevitable: the one nation had to be preserved and constantly re-created.

Unfortunately Macleod had become chairman of the party when the Government's fortunes were beginning to decline. Its economic policy was unpopular, and a series of by-election disasters followed. Macleod never shirked the battle, and in private was full of suggestions and expedients for lessening the party's unpopularity. He was, too, always resourceful in the Government's defence in the House of Commons. But a modern party chairman, like a modern football manager, is judged by results. For that reason, as well as his unpopularity with the Right over Africa, Macleod in the leadership crisis in 1963 was not seriously in the running to succeed Macmillan.

Whether or not he occasionally nursed hopes that in a deadlock the party might turn to him, Macleod's usually sure-footed political judgement failed him during the leadership controversy. His subsequent refusal to join Douglas-Home's Government was due in part to his belief that Macmillan's successor should have been chosen from the House of Commons and that Douglas-Home, too exclusively associated with foreign affairs, could not win an election; and in part to the view that having said, in his support for R. A. Butler (later Lord Butler of Saffron Walden), that he would not serve under Douglas-Home, it would be dishonourable to change his mind. Others might retract or waver but not he. 'One does not expect', he said,

'to have many people with one in the last ditch.'

Having imprudently jeopardized his political career, Macleod shortly afterwards became editor of the *Spectator*, a post which he held until the end of 1965, and a director of Lombards Bank. As an editor he was unstuffy and approachable, and always gave full freedom to his writers, even though a good deal of the political writing in the paper was to say the least inconvenient to him. While not devoid of the politician's egotism, he was far more egotistical in print than in life. This made his journalism unrepresentative of the man, but it made his weekly column enormously readable. Macleod considerably added to his unpopularity in his party by publishing an article in the *Spectator* (17 January 1964) on the leadership row. Although under some pressure in his constituency to explain himself, the prudent course was unquestionably silence.

After the 1964 election, Douglas-Home invited Macleod to join the shadow Cabinet, which he did, with steel as his subject; an unfortunate choice since, with a tiny majority, the Labour Government was not anxious to hurry on its plans for nationalization. Nevertheless Macleod made many effective speeches in the country in order to rehabilitate himself. He felt his abilities fitted him to be party leader and prime minister, but knew he had too much to live down and too much distrust to dispel. Well before Douglas-Home resigned in 1965, Macleod had decided not to stand for the succession. Appointed shadow chancellor of the Exchequer by Edward Heath, for whom he had voted, his eyes were henceforth firmly fixed on No. 11.

Macleod was not an economist and had no inclination to become one. Experience had engendered doubts about the possibilities of detailed management of the economy by the Treasury, and he always believed that an Opposition should not over-burden itself with policy. For these reasons Macleod avoided large theoretical pronouncements as shadow chancellor, but at a time of almost continuous economic trouble for the Government his natural ability and his eye for essentials as well as his loathing of unemployment made him an outstandingly effective Opposition spokesman. Before the 1970 election Macleod was aware that he had been pushed too far in the non-interventionist direction and that this would have to be redressed in office.

A belief in opportunity, although with proper safeguards for the less fortunate, was a consistent theme throughout Macleod's career. Accordingly he embraced the idea of a radical reform of the system of taxation with enthusiasm and intense industry. The package of tax reform enacted in the early years of the Heath Government had been closely prepared by Macleod and his team in opposition.

Macleod was a superb orator in Parliament and on the platform. He was probably the best conference speaker in any party since the war. Small in height, and bald on the top of his head since his Cambridge days, his large forehead seemed to have difficulty in encasing his brains. Added to this arresting appearance, his unusually resonant voice had a dramatic intensity which excited his audience, and easily moved it to laughter or enthusiasm. Macleod was a brilliant communicator not only in the sense that he spoke and wrote exceptionally well, and was a master of television, but in the more important sense that he had something to say. Never trendy—he had a profound contempt for the BBC and for a period near the end refused to appear on its programmes—he was totally unpompous, and his opinions reflected both freshness of mind and stability of attitude.

He regarded the Commonwealth Immigrants Bill of 1968 as a betrayal of the Kenyan Asians, and although the shadow Cabinet supported the Government, Macleod together with fourteen other Conservatives voted against it. When his friend, Nigel Fisher, was in trouble with the far Right in his constituency, Surbiton, in 1969, Macleod made it clear that if Fisher was pushed out he would leave too. He had strikingly shown his loyalty to other friends in trouble before. Although his ill health seemed to get even worse in the last two years of his life, he remained good and amusing company.

When his mother died during the 1970 election, Macleod suspended his electioneering for a week. He returned to make two extremely telling television appearances. On 20 June he was made chancellor of the Exchequer, but had no chance to make his mark before being taken ill on 7 July. He was operated upon for appendicitis and returned to 11 Downing Street. But the years of ill health and pain had taken their toll, and he died there after a heart attack 20 July 1970. He was buried at Gargrave, Yorkshire, near his parents and his sister.

A posthumous portrait by Alfred Janes hangs in the Constitutional Club.

[Nigel Fisher, *Iain Macleod*, 1973; private information; personal knowledge.]

IAN GILMOUR

MacMICHAEL, SIR HAROLD ALFRED (1882–1969), colonial civil servant, was born at Rowtor, Birchover, Derbyshire, 15 October 1882, the eldest son of the Revd Charles Mac-Michael, later rector of Walpole St. Peter,

Wisbech, near Kings Lynn, and his wife, Sophia Caroline, eldest daughter of the Revd Alfred Nathaniel Holden Curzon, fourth Baron Scarsdale, and sister of G. N. Curzon (later Marquess Curzon of Kedleston, q.v.). He began his schooling at Kings Lynn, but on the preferment of his father to a living near Bedford, went to Bedford Grammar School. Here he distinguished himself not only in learning but also at games; he won the public schools fencing championship in 1901. In that year he also won an open scholarship to Magdalene College, Cambridge, where he obtained first class honours in the first part of the classical tripos (1904), and, in 1905, a first class in the Arabic examination for the Sudan Political Service. He began work in the Sudan in October 1905; from then on his nickname, given in affection by all his British friends, was 'MacMic'.

After a short training period in Khartoum, he was posted to Kordofan province, then eight days travel by Nile steamer and camel from Khartoum. He at once showed himself a hard worker, keen on research and on devoting spare time to the study of local ways; his maps, done from camel-back, were so accurate as to be still in use in the Sudan for many years after his death. In 1912 he produced a scientifically arranged book on the pedigrees and customs of the tribes of northern and central Kordofan, and in 1913 a monograph on the camel brands of Kordofan. He next served in the Blue Nile province, and in 1915 was transferred to Khartoum province as a senior inspector. He was renowned for his preference for the written minute over the spoken word; even on safari, he was known to shout from tent to tent for a written answer to some note.

When war broke out in 1914 he longed to enlist, but his wish was not fulfilled until 1916, when he was appointed political officer to the expedition against Ali Dinar in Darfur—service which earned him three mentions in dispatches and an appointment to the DSO. Conquest of Darfur gave the Sudan Government 150,000 square miles of new territory to administer, and in this task MacMichael's knowledge of the Darfur tribes was recognized by all to be a great asset.

While on leave in England at the end of 1918, he shepherded a delegation of Sudanese notables who came to London to congratulate the King on his victory. He then tarried, awaiting appointment to an Anglo-French Commission delegated to fix the western boundary of the Sudan. When this did not materialize, he was considered for a post first at Aden, and then, under (Sir) Gilbert Clayton [q.v.], in Cairo. Neither post was firmly offered, and in November 1919 he returned to Khartoum as assistant civil secretary, turning down the firm offer of the Egyptian post which had arrived in January 1920; as civil secretary from 1926, he several times served as acting governor-general. His love of research was constant. When *Sudan Notes and Records* first came out in 1918, he wrote in it on the Nubian elements in Darfur; in 1922 he produced the two-volume *A History of the Arabs in the Sudan* that entitles him to rank as a historian. In it, he came to the conclusion, both from observation and from consultation of the *nisbas* or genealogical papers kept by some Sudanese families, that Arabs had first reached the area through Abyssinia, coming in search of gold, ivory, and slaves, before the time of Christ; these first-comers had been reinforced, again from Arabia, in about the eighth century AD; later, in the thirteenth and fourteenth centuries, others had travelled south from Egypt in search of conditions more like those in Arabia, possibly at the time of the overthrow of the Christian kingdom of Dongola (1351).

In 1928, in London, he gave the Sir Richard Burton memorial lecture of the Royal Asiatic Society, and was awarded its Burton medal.

Never for a moment did he think that Egypt's claim to the Sudan had any historical warrant. The Sudanese were by his standards a nation in their own right, whose strength had been assisted by British management, and who would not stand for rule from Cairo. He was an advocate of the use of local languages, and believed firmly in the devolution of authority to local dignitaries, notably in the southern Sudan, where he dismissed Arab teachers, technicians, and even merchants, and instituted Sunday instead of Friday as the day of rest. He was sure that there was a happy medium between the blind accordance of support which would encourage them to flout public opinion, and the refusal of it which would deprive them of prestige and authority. He generated loyalty, and respect tinged with awe, among British subordinates, to whom he preached the doctrine that 'duty has no possible significance, and the idea of duty no justification, unless it be in terms of religion, whether you define religion in terms of dogma or not'.

They learnt with dismay, therefore, in 1933, that the governor of the mandated territory of Tanganyika was to be their new governor-general, and that MacMichael was to take up the succession in Tanganyika. It was after he had arrived there that *The Anglo-Egyptian Sudan* (1934) appeared. In Tanganyika he saw the native farmer as progressive, requiring less capital, and running fewer risks than the European, who ought nowhere to encroach on native farmland. Tanganyika lay too far south to be immediately affected by Italy's conquest of Abyssinia, but MacMichael's years there were

those when Hitler revived his claim to Germany's lost colonies. This claim affected investment in the territory, but it seemed to MacMichael, as it did to London, strategically out of the question.

At the end of 1937, on the expiry of Sir Arthur Wauchope's [q.v.] term as high commissioner and commander-in-chief in Palestine, MacMichael was appointed to succeed him; he was responsible for Trans-Jordan also. He arrived in Jerusalem in March 1938 and at the height of an Arab rebellion which was costing the British dearly in lives and money. Not only were the Arabs fighting the British and the Jews, but Arab extremists were murdering moderate Arabs. In August, the secretary of state (Malcolm MacDonald) visited MacMichael to see the scene for himself, and in October MacMichael returned the visit, asking in London for heavy reinforcement of the British military, which settled matters for the time being. The British force thus mustered was the biggest assembled since the war of 1914-18, and by the autumn of 1938 the revolt had burnt itself out.

In 1937 it was still possible to make policy from the high commissioner's office. By 1938 the impact of events in Europe had removed the seat of all power to London. MacMichael, who had always thought the Balfour declaration too lightly given, at first believed in a bi-national state under British tutelage. He was in charge when the British Government, despairing of getting Jews and Arabs to agree to any plan, imposed its own solution in the Palestine white paper of 17 May 1939.

This white paper, forced on Britain by the need to prepare for war with Germany, was the despair of the Jews, who saw it was robbery of their last hope at the darkest hour of their history. MacMichael had come to Palestine as a man blessed with good Arabic, but no Hebrew; they therefore saw him as biased and hostile. Only when, in the course of time, his papers were opened in the British Public Record Office, did the Jews realize how justly he had judged their case. By 1943 the pressure for Jewish immigration from both Europe and America had caused him to revise his view; to meet it, he began to argue that partition, with unlimited immigration into the Jewish sector, was the only desirable solution because it was decisive. Most Arabs did not care for him either. When war broke out and he was instructed to deport their leaders, the men deported found him unbending in manner and less friendly than his predecessors.

In February 1940 he had to announce land transfer regulations which rendered him still more unpopular with the Jewish community. Both Jew and Arab found him stern but resolute in many unpleasant duties, including mobilization of all manpower and property, dictation of the crops to be grown, and—for the Jews—deduction from their quota of immigration certificates of the number of immigrants who had arrived illegally.

Among the most exacting of his wartime tasks was the negotiation of relations with Free France over Syria and Lebanon. General de Gaulle resented Britain's contribution to the liberation of the Levant States, and suspected the British of designs on them. Sometimes these complications took on a lighter note and tickled MacMichael's sense of humour. For instance, when the Amir Abdullah of Trans-Jordan, who was a good judge of a horse and had won some thousands at Cairo races, spent it on a flutter amongst the tribes in Syria, the French complained to London and London to MacMichael. Shortly afterwards General Catroux, who was de Gaulle's representative in the Levant, visited Jerusalem and repeated the complaint: 'I had the pleasure', said Mac-Michael, 'of taking the key from my watch-chain, unlocking my file, and handing him my note to the Colonial Office explaining that I could not control the Amir's racing earnings. "You will not hear of this again", said Catroux.'

With the liberation of Africa and the removal of the German threat to Palestine, Jewish terrorism increased and on 8 August 1944 the Stern Gang made a determined attempt to murder both the MacMichaels. MacMichael was unhurt, but Lady MacMichael slightly wounded; the ADC and driver were severely wounded. But MacMichael's term of office was up; he left Palestine in September 1944.

From October 1945 until January 1946 he worked for the British Government on a con-stitution for Malaya, getting the agreement of the sultans and rulers of the Federated and Unfederated Malay States to arrangements for independence which would unite them while permitting the powers to retain certain strategic strongpoints. Early in 1946 he was sent to Malta to negotiate a form of constitutional government which would reconcile its impor-tant strategic position with its poverty. There-after, from his home in Teynham in Kent, he took part in the work of the advisory council of the Joint East African Board. Towards the end of his life, he and his wife moved to Folkestone. It was at Folkestone that he died 19 September 1969.

He wrote another book, *The Sudan* (1954), and he was also a confirmed collector—of first editions, of Sassanian seals, of stamps. His Blue-John (Derbyshire spar) china was one of the largest collections in private hands. To this Dictionary he contributed the notice of Sir Hubert Huddleston.

He married in 1919 Agnes de Sivrac Edith (Nesta) (died 1974), daughter of Canon J. Otter Stephens, vicar of All Saints, Tooting Graveney; there were two daughters of the marriage. He was appointed to the DSO (1917), and awarded the Order of the Nile by the ruler of Egypt (1930) for his work in the Sudan. He was appointed CMG in 1927, KCMG in 1932, and GCMG in 1941. He also held the Star of Ethiopia, awarded by Ras Tafari on his corona-tion as emperor in 1930. To his delight, he was made an honorary fellow of his Cambridge college in 1939. A good photograph of him is kept in the record of distinguished persons at the National Portrait Gallery.

[Sudan archive, Durham University; private papers at St. Antony's College, Oxford; private information; personal knowledge.]

ELIZABETH MONROE

MacNALTY, SIR ARTHUR SALUSBURY (1880–1969), expert in public health, was born 20 October 1880 at Glenridding, Westmorland, the son of Francis Charles MacNalty, physician, and his wife, Hester Emma Frances, daughter of the Revd Arthur D. Gardner, fellow of Jesus College, Oxford. He spent his early boy-hood in the Lake District. He was educated privately in the south while his father was in general medical practice in Winchester. He was first at Hartley College, Southampton, and later in St. Catherine's Society, Oxford, before enter-ing Corpus Christi College, Oxford. He was therefore rather late in taking a degree in natural science (physiology), in which he obtained a second class in 1904, and the BM at the age of twenty-seven. His Oxford DM followed four years later in 1911. He became MRCP in 1925 and was elected a fellow in 1930 having taken the diploma in public health in 1927. Those are the bare academic bones of a slightly un-orthodox career in preventive medicine, for one who chose to work in the central rather than a local health department. Most of the leading figures in what was then called public health rose through the services of local authorities in the manner of Sir Arthur Newsholme and Sir George Newman [qq.v.].

MacNalty began a career as a clinical physician following a special interest in chest diseases, which led him to the Brompton. Chest disease at that time meant mainly pul-monary tuberculosis and the central health department—then the Local Government Board—was engaged in the establishment of county and county borough services for the tuberculous. MacNalty was recruited in 1913 as a member of the small team of specialists required to promote a 'sanatorium' and 'dispen-sary' service throughout the country. Most of his subsequent career was centred upon this service and he did not move around the special sections as most of the more generally trained medical staff were expected to do. Even medical practitioners active today are seldom conscious of the dominant position of tuberculosis control in local authority health responsibilities from 1910 to 1948. MacNalty played a large part in the central guidance of the development of those services. A succession of departmental reports written by MacNalty culminating in the 1932 report on tuberculosis testify to his special interest in the epidemiology and treatment of tuberculous infections. He had, however, contributed substantially to the Ministry of Health's work on other infections—especially virus infections of the central nervous system. He was a close friend of Sydney A. Monckton Copeman, the last member of the departmental staff to become a fellow of the Royal Society, and they worked together on virus diseases. It has been said of him that he was 'a medical reporter before all else'.

His official career as a member of the staff transferred to the new Ministry of Health in 1919 advanced when he became one of the six senior medical officers in 1932. Later he was the first to become deputy chief medical officer. That post became established under Sir George Newman [q.v.] whom he succeeded in 1935 as only the ninth chief medical officer since (Sir) John Simon's [q.v.] first appointment in 1855. At that time MacNalty was not well known amongst public health medical staff in the country, but his standing in his own field of medicine was high.

MacNalty was chief medical officer from 1935 for a little over five years. In that time there were not only the preparations for civilian services in time of war but important changes in legislation including the first major revision of public health law since 1875, a new Midwives Act (1936), a Cancer Act, and a Medicines and Pharmacy Act. The Ministry of Health was rapidly becoming involved in the hospital building programmes of local authorities and in the development of specialist services. The public health laboratory service developed from an emergency service planned for wartime on the basis of a survey initiated by MacNalty. Others were involved in these changes and MacNalty has been given little of the credit for them, but they did occur at the right time and, if not an innovator he was at least ready to support innovation. In a departmental reorganization in 1940 he retired at the age of sixty, although sixty-five was the usual age, and made way for the more dynamic leadership of his successor. MacNalty then turned to the work for which he will be mainly remembered, as editor-in-chief of the official medical history of the war. He continued that task for a quarter of a century and completed it shortly before his death in 1969. He gave this work the same devoted attention he had always applied to writing and at the same time indulged his real passion for history especially, but not exclusively, related to medicine. His knowledge of history and literature was exceptional and his writing extensive. There have been few such contributions to the history of medicine. To this Dictionary he contributed the notices of Sir Arthur Newsholme, Sir Andrew Balfour, and Sir George S. Buchanan.

In 1913 he married Dorothea (died 1968), the daughter of the Revd C. H. Simpkinson de Wesselow. They had two daughters.

At the end of his long life (he died at home in Epsom, Surrey 17 April 1969), perhaps none remained who had known MacNalty's whole range of activity and therefore could make a fair assessment. He was an unassertive and reserved man, few of whose staff knew him well, despite his occasional social gestures. Yet he was well liked by those few who came to know him in his later life. He was unfortunate in being thrust into the most responsible medical administrative post in the country at the moment when it was exposed to unprecedented strains. One felt he stepped aside with relief; there are few who are prepared to cede leadership gracefully in that way and turn to another career as he did. With his death went the last of the team of medical inspectors of the Local Government Board who succeeded the original medical officers of the Privy Council, John Simon's first team. MacNalty had been a student at Oxford when Sir William Osler [q.v.] was regius professor. He was an honorary fellow or freeman of many societies, including the Royal Society of Edinburgh, and was also a freeman of the City of London.

[*The Times*, 18 and 21 September 1969; personal knowledge.]　　　　G. E. GODBER

McNAUGHTON, ANDREW GEORGE LATTA (1887-1966), Canadian soldier, scientist, and public servant, was born at Moosomin, Saskatchewan, 25 February 1887, the elder son of Robert Duncan McNaughton, a prosperous storekeeper of Highland blood, and his wife, Christina Mary Ann, daughter of William Armour, also of Scottish descent. McNaughton grew up in the free, outreaching pioneer life of the prairies, was educated at Bishop's College School, Lennoxville, Quebec, and at McGill University where he graduated with honours in electrical engineering (1910) and went on to research work in high-voltage electricity; he obtained his M.Sc. in 1912 and remained as lecturer.

He had qualified for a commission in the British Army, but served in the Canadian militia, and was placed on active service in August 1914. He served in France and Belgium as battery commander and heavy artillery brigade commander, but he made his mark as corps counter-battery officer (1917–18). In this novel role he developed techniques of flash spotting, sound-ranging, aerial reconnaissance, intelligence recording, and artillery tactics, which succeeded and which deeply affected military thinking and procedures in these fields. He was appointed to the DSO (1917), CMG (1919), and in 1920 McGill University conferred an honorary LLD on him in recognition of 'his remarkable ability as an officer of artillery'.

McNaughton continued in the Canadian Army after the war as director of military training with the rank of acting brigadier-general. In 1921 he attended the Staff College senior division at Camberley where his report called him: 'An officer of exceptional attainments, with immense powers of concentration, and great strength of character.' In 1923 he was appointed deputy chief of the Canadian general staff. In 1927 he attended the Imperial Defence College in London. In 1929 he was promoted major-general and made chief of the Canadian general staff, a post he held until 1935.

In this period McNaughton was a responsible and significant figure not only in the maintenance of some military force in Canada in the face of public disinterest and parsimony, but in the invention of the cathode ray direction finder, a direct ancestor of radar, in the development of communications and mapping in the Canadian north, in the development of Canada's international and commonwealth position, in the inception of finite proposals and an unratified treaty for the St. Lawrence Seaway, in transatlantic air and postal service, and in a Trans Canada Airway. In the problems presented by the depression of 1930 and the years following, he ardently advocated unemployment relief camps and projects. The widespread unemployment and the concentration of the single unemployed in work camps led to problems of public order with which he grappled.

Before the Conservative prime minister, R. B. (later Viscount) Bennett [q.v.], was defeated in the elections of 1935, he prevailed upon McNaughton to become president of the National Research Council which co-ordinated and promoted scientific and industrial research in Canada in the public interest. Here his character, experience, and talents overcame the suspicions and animosity of the new Liberal Government and made it possible for the National Research Council to play its proper part later in the war effort of Canada.

From December 1939 to December 1943 McNaughton commanded the Canadian troops in the United Kingdom as general officer commanding successively of 1st Canadian division, VII British Corps, I Canadian Corps, and First Canadian Army. He brought to the tasks which these commands imposed, as to everything he did, his ardour, his knowledge, his integrity, his drive, and his devotion to Canada. The Canadian troops in Britain were made ready for battle. The employment of Canadians in Trondheim (April 1940), Calais or Dunkirk (May 1940), in Brittany (June 1940), Spitsbergen (August 1941), Northern Norway (July 1942), at Dieppe (August 1942), in the Canary Island (October–December 1942), Sicily and Italy (1943) was considered by McNaughton, and they were used in Brittany, in Spitsbergen, at Dieppe, and in Sicily and Italy.

In these years and in this work, the conflicts arose which led to McNaughton's removal from the command of First Canadian Army. They raised in personal terms what was, in essence, an issue of principle. McNaughton believed that Canada could field and furnish a whole army of volunteer Canadians, under Canadian control but taking its place in the whole scheme of things. He recognized that parts of it could and would be detached from time to time, but proceeded on the basis that it would go into battle as a whole Canadian Army under his command. The British looked on Canadian formations as part of their own forces, under Canadian command when purely Canadian, but subject always to higher British control in battle, and to the policies which were determined in inner councils to which Canada was a stranger.

J. L. Ralston [q.v.], Canadian minister of defence, Lieutenant-General Ken Stuart, the Canadian chief of general staff, and Major-General Harry Crerar, among others, thought that Canadians should fight detached, if necessary, rather than remain poised and unused in the United Kingdom. Thus first a division and an army tank brigade, then an armoured division and a corps headquarters went to Italy, and the rest of First Canadian Army became in its tactical use a headquarters and Canadian troops at British disposal, dependent on non-Canadians for its plenitude. Such a disposition of Canadian troops could only work if its Canadian commanders had the confidence of the British generals under whose command they would have to serve. In 1943 General Sir Alan Brooke (later Viscount Alanbrooke, q.v.), chief of the imperial general staff, and General Sir Bernard Paget [q.v.], under whose command First Canadian Army then came, both expressed the view that McNaughton was not suited to command an army in the field. McNaughton, who saw in it machinations by Ralston and Stuart, had to accept the situation, and resigned.

He returned to Canada and in 1944 retired from the army with the rank of full general. He refused to join the political opposition and accepted the invitation of Mackenzie King [q.v.] to become Canada's first Canadian governor-general. Within three weeks and before his appointment was announced, a conscription crisis arose in Canada. There were not enough trained infantrymen ready to volunteer for overseas service in the field. Ralston threatened to resign and did so on the issue of conscription to provide infantry reinforcements. King had already appealed to McNaughton to take his place and carry on, without conscription, to save the country from the disunity which had rent it in 1917 on the same issue. In this spirit, to meet a national emergency and for unity as well as from conviction and personal requital, McNaughton accepted and was sworn in on 2 November 1944. Within twenty days the effort to meet the crisis without conscription had failed; King introduced conscription. The Government survived. The crisis passed. McNaughton ran for Parliament in 1945 at Grey North in February and in Qu'Appele, his native riding, in the general election of June. In both he was defeated. On 21 August 1945 his resignation was accepted.

Subsequently he served as chairman of the Canadian section of the Canada-United States Permanent Joint Board on Defence (1945–59); president of the Atomic Energy Control Board of Canada (1946–8); Canadian representative to the United Nations Atomic Energy Commission (1946–50); permanent delegate of Canada to the United Nations (1948–9); chairman, Canadian section of the International Joint Commission (1950–62). In this last work he became a powerful antagonist of the Columbia River Treaty providing Canadian water power for American purposes. In and out of office he opposed it and proffered his own plan. He then joined and led a fight to deny Canadian water resources to the United States on a continental basis.

In the midst of this fight, he died at Montebello 11 July 1966 and was buried in Beechwood Cemetery, Ottawa. He married in 1914 Mabel Clara Stuart, daughter of Godfrey Weir, of Montreal; they had one daughter and three sons, the eldest of whom adopted the surname of Leslie.

Professor F. H. Underhill, an acid and fearless critic, called McNaughton 'the greatest Canadian citizen of his day'. Few who served with McNaughton in any of his activities would disagree with this assessment. He was a leader of men and attracted to himself, in his daily life, devotion and admiration. He had the gift of convincing whoever he was talking to that they and their opinions mattered to him. But it was by his own devotion to the principles which moved him in his public life, and by the shining talents with which he advanced them, that he made his mark and reputation. He fought fiercely and fairly in every endeavour and to the end. At Crerar's funeral when he was asked how he was McNaughton said, 'I'm seventy-eight and I'm still in every fight'. He lost his major battles because the primary ideals of Canadian nationalism, to which he was dedicated, were in the wide practical scheme of things where he sought to apply them secondary roots of action and decision, moving no one but Canadians. He suffered from a fullness of confidence, a consciousness of the rightness of his views, and continuing bitterness against those who thwarted them, Brooke, Ralston, Stuart, and Montgomery, an ingenuous ignorance of political factors in Mackenzie King's Canada, and an inability to dissemble—failings which each in their way were virtues.

McNaughton was appointed PC (Canada) in 1944, CB in 1935, and CH in 1946. He was a strikingly photogenic person and eloquent likenesses appear in the biography by Swettenham. There is an oil painting of him by Mrs K. S. Brydone-Jack on loan to the Public Archives of Canada. The Imperial War Museum has a pencil drawing by William P. Roberts.

[John Swettenham, *McNaughton*, 3 vols., Toronto, 1968–9; James Eayrs, *In Defence of Canada*, 2 vols., Toronto, 1964–5; J. W. Pickersgill and D. F. Forster, *The Mackenzie King Record*, 4 vols., Toronto, 1960–70; C. P. Stacey, *Six Years of War*, Ottawa, 1955, and *Arms, Men and Governments*, Ottawa, 1970; personal knowledge.]

PETER WRIGHT

MacNEICE, (FREDERICK) LOUIS (1907–1963), writer, was born in Belfast 12 September 1907, the youngest of three children of the Revd John Frederick MacNeice, then rector of Holy Trinity, Belfast, by his wife, Elizabeth Margaret, daughter of Martin Clesham, of Galway. Originally a Galway man, Louis MacNeice's father was from 1908 to 1931 rector of Carrickfergus; in those early years his mother was often ill, his father preoccupied and remote: 'My mother was comfort and my father was somewhat alarm.' His only brother, William, was a mongol and MacNeice was much dependent for company on his sister, Caroline Elizabeth, who was later to marry (Sir) John Nicholson, third baronet. The death of their mother in 1914 was a severe blow, which threw a sombre shadow over MacNeice's adult recollections of childhood, imparting to much of his poetry a poignant sense of the impermanence of men and things. The children were looked after by a cook and a governess until 1917, when their father brought home a new wife, Georgina Beatrice, second daughter of Thomas Greer, of Sea Park, county Antrim, and Carrickfergus; she brought 'much comfort and benevolence' into their lives. MacNeice's father became bishop of Cashel and Waterford in 1931, bishop of Down and Connor and Dromore in 1935, and died in 1942. In later life MacNeice came to appreciate him, as well as the family background of Galway, Dublin, and Connemara which acted as a counterpoise to that element of stern Ulster reticence which he did not always find it easy to accept in his own character.

When MacNeice was ten, he was sent to Sherborne preparatory school—at that time a happy place, and he was happy in it. In the autumn of 1921 he went with an entrance scholarship to Marlborough, where he enjoyed rugby and running on the Downs, and specialized in the classics. (Sir) John Betjeman, Bernard Spencer, John Hilton, Graham Shepard, and Anthony Blunt were among his contemporaries; they remained lifelong friends. MacNeice matured rapidly and even precociously in an aesthetic and intellectual ambience, wrote a great deal of verse, and developed a persona which took pride in an opposition to science as well as religion, a contempt for politics, and a scepticism of all values except the aesthetic.

In 1926 he won a postmastership to Merton College, but Oxford was at first disappointing; he found much of the work arid, and his Marlborough friends were in other colleges. But he continued to write—chiefly poems and stories of satire and fantasy—and in time became friendly with other poets, notably W. H. Auden, Stephen Spender, and Clere Parsons. He took a first in classical honour moderations in 1928, and eagerly devoured the philosophy prescribed for 'Greats', ranging beyond it in quest of a system to replace a world founded on the religion he had lost, with one founded on reason. But his obsession with the logic of poetry ran counter to any other logic, and his quest did not find a solution either then or later, although it was to be a continuing drive which underlay all his poetry. His Oxford studies did, however, give him a firm intellectual foundation, and in spite of emotional strains, his last year there—1930—was a year of successes. He got a first in *literae humaniores*, edited *Oxford Poetry* with Stephen Spender, published his first book of poems, *Blind Fireworks*, and, on the

security of a lecturership in classics at the university of Birmingham, he married Giovanna Marie Thérèse Babette ('Mariette') Ezra, stepdaughter of (Sir) John Beazley [q.v.].

Industrial Birmingham and its university were a rude shock after the youthful snobberies and 'preciousness' of the Oxford aesthetes; MacNeice had to revise his ideas of how and what to teach, and he confronted the problems inevitable to a man who honestly wants to fulfil his obligations, whether to his employers or to his wife, yet who at a deep level regards his creative writing as more important than anything else. According to his posthumous autobiography, *The Strings Are False* (1965), he and his wife at first withdrew from these problems into a 'hothouse' of their private world, in which he wrote a novel, *Roundabout Way* (1932), under the pseudonym Louis Malone. The book he soon came to see as a fake, and it was not a success. But he was unable to shut off the outside world, and at Christmas 1933 he wrote *Eclogue for Christmas* with 'a kind of cold-blooded passion' which surprised him. His son Daniel was born in 1934, and about this time MacNeice also began to take more interest in the life of Birmingham and the university, where there was then a remarkably able group of people; he became a lasting friend of the head of his department, Professor E. R. Dodds, his lifelong mentor who became professor of Greek at Oxford; of Ernest Stahl, a lecturer in German and later Taylor professor at Oxford; and of John Waterhouse, a lecturer in English. And among the students he came to know R. D. Smith, with whom he was later to be associated at the BBC, and Walter Allen. MacNeice was also becoming known as a poet through his contributions to *New Verse* and other periodicals and his second volume of *Poems* (1935), and he was at work, with Dodds's encouragement, on his translation of Aeschylus' *Agamemnon* (1936), which is of permanent value.

Looking grimly at the outside world in 1933 he had wanted to 'smash the aquarium'; instead, in 1935 his own golden bowl was broken when his wife abruptly left him. He had to turn his mind to domestic problems, and reconcile himself to the fact of rejection. His autobiography dissimulated the grief and concentrated on the gain of freedom: 'I suddenly realized I was under no more obligation to be respectable.' But freedom and loneliness made him restless, and at Easter 1936 he and Anthony Blunt visited Spain. His Birmingham years may have made him more conscious of social and political injustice, but he does seem to have seen only the pictures of Spain and not the whole picture, with its intimations of turmoil to come. On his return, he felt he could not endure the reminders of his broken marriage, and in the summer of 1936 he accepted a post as lecturer in Greek at Bedford College, London. He then went to Iceland with W. H. Auden, a journey about which they subsequently wrote *Letters from Iceland* (1937).

MacNeice discharged his university duties in London punctiliously, although living the literary life and moving gradually away from 'the old gang who were just literary' towards 'the new gang who were all Left'. The Group Theatre produced his *Agamemnon* in 1936, which was well received, and, less successfully, his *Out of the Picture* in 1937. His life at this period was 'a whirl of narcotic engagements'—parties, private views, and political meetings and arguments. But, although he was left-wing in his sympathies, he was never himself formally committed to the revolutionary Left, and he found the Communist Party unacceptable; nor can the whirl have been too narcotic, for in the single year 1938 he published another book of poems, *The Earth Compels*; two prose works written to commission, *I Crossed the Minch*, and *Zoo*; and a critical book, *Modern Poetry*, which exhibited a close study of metrics and a keen eye and ear, drew upon a wide range in the classics and English, and showed a great balance of judgement. And in August he began a long poem, *Autumn Journal* (1939), which it took him the rest of the year to finish. This poem is a long lyric meditation on the preceding years, with revocations of childhood, sharp glimpses of the contemporary scene, sombre autumnal premonitions of national catastrophe, and a rejection at times overt of contemporary political nostrums.

He paid a second visit to Spain early in 1939 and found it much changed; Barcelona was on the eve of collapse and Franco's cause triumphing. This, and the outbreak of war with Germany, brought his dilemmas to a head: he had also been in the United States that spring, and now, loitering in Ireland, he decided to take leave of absence from Bedford College, and go back to America to try to find a woman he had met earlier, and see if events might make up his mind for him. His visit was a success, and he enjoyed lecturing at Cornell, but by July 1940 it had become clear to him that if he stayed there he would be 'missing history'. In the event he was forced to stay on, due to peritonitis, and he did not get back to England until December. He was rejected for active service because of bad eyesight, and joined the BBC Features Department in May 1941. There, under Laurence Gilliam, MacNeice applied his mind to the principles and techniques of his new medium and to exploiting it to creative ends. His mastery was apparent in such programmes as the series 'The Stones Cry Out', 'Alexander Nevsky', and 'Christopher Columbus'. He adapted his old love of the stage to radio drama, and produced at least two memorable contributions: *He Had a Date* (1944), an elegy for his friend Graham' Shepard who had been killed on convoy duty; and *The Dark Tower* (1946), a synthesis of two favourite themes, the morality quest and the parable.

During the war years he also produced three more books of poetry, *The Last Ditch* (1940), *Plant and Phantom* (1941), and *Springboard* (1944), and another critical work, *The Poetry of W. B. Yeats* (1941). In 1942 he made a fresh start in family life by marrying Hedli Anderson, the actress and singer; his son Daniel rejoined him from Ireland, and in 1943 his daughter Corinna was born.

The Features Department provided him with security and employment which he found useful, satisfying, and compatible with his vocation as poet. It was natural to continue in this work after the war, more especially as Gilliam had recruited other stimulating colleagues, many of them also poets—W. R. Rodgers, Rayner Heppenstall, Terence Tiller, and, on occasion, Dylan Thomas [q.v.]. Rodgers and Thomas in particular became his close friends, as did Francis (Jack) Dillon, the producer. MacNeice was proud of his skill in this medium and took pleasure in the company and technique of the teams with which he worked. The BBC of those years, and Gilliam particularly, knew how to get loyalty and dedicated work out of the intractable race of poets, and drove them with relaxed reins. MacNeice was given leave to visit Ireland in 1945—an Antaean and necessary return to his origins; his curiosity about the wider world was also given scope and he had many assignments abroad—to Rome, to India and Pakistan (in 1947 and again in 1955), to the United States (1953), to the Gold Coast, and to South Africa.

In 1949, to mark the Goethe bicentenary, the BBC produced his version of *Faust*—a major undertaking on which he worked in collaboration with his old friend Ernest Stahl. He had published another collection of poems, *Holes in the Sky* (1948), and the following year *Collected Poems 1925-1948*. From January to September 1950 he was on leave from the BBC as director of the British Institute in Athens, and he stayed on until the following March as assistant representative. Again, he led the double life: conscientious in discharging his duties, while writing—in spite of the rueful 'This middle stretch of life is bad for poets'—the poems published in 1952 as *Ten Burnt Offerings*. Back in London, MacNeice was beginning to be strongly conscious of time slipping away, and in elegiac mood he began *Autumn Sequel* (1954), a complement and reprise of *Autumn Journal*; he was in the midst of writing this when Dylan Thomas died, in November 1953, and grief for that death strongly marked the mood of the poem. He published no more until *Visitations* in 1957— the year in which he received an honorary doctorate from the Queen's University, Belfast. In 1958 he was appointed CBE.

But some desperate discontent was working in him, and a desire for renewal. In 1960 he and his second wife separated, and in 1961 he gave up full-time employment in the BBC to be freer for his own work. He felt himself to be in a fresh creative phase of which *Solstices* (1961) was the first harvest; he delivered the Clark lectures in 1963 (published as *Varieties of Parable* in 1965), and he went to Yorkshire that summer to make a programme, *Persons from Porlock*, which involved recording underground. He insisted on going down with engineers to see that the sound effects were right and caught a severe chill. By the time his sister discovered how ill he was and made him go into hospital it was too late; he died of virus pneumonia in London 3 September 1963.

Before his death MacNeice had been assembling the poems for *The Burning Perch* (1963). Of this he wrote, 'I was taken aback by the high proportion of sombre pieces, ranging from bleak observations to thumbnail nightmares . . . All I can say is that I did not set out to write this kind of poem: they happened.' It was a central tenet of his critical theory that the poet cannot be completely sure of what he has to say until he has said it, and that he works towards his meaning by a 'dialectic of purification'. And in a sense what gives MacNeice's poetry its excitement is the tension between his mastery of words and technique, and the uncertainty for which he was trying to find a resolution. It was fortunate for him as a poet that he did not find it, for perplexity over the irreconcilables in life was the yeast that fermented his best work. Any comprehensive theoretical solution would have been sterilizing.

Even so, his escape from the frigidities of his classical education had been narrow, as he realized in *Modern Poetry*: 'Marriage at least made me recognize the existence of other people in their own right and not as vicars of my godhead.' And it was in Birmingham that he learnt to respect the ordinary man, and came to form his own conception of what a poet should be: '. . . able-bodied, fond of talking, a reader of the newspapers, capable of pity and laughter, informed in economics, appreciative of women, involved in personal relationships, actively interested in politics, susceptible to physical impressions.' But this description omits the qualities which made MacNeice special as a poet: the capacious mind with full memory; the dazzling skill with metaphor and image and symbol; the control of verbal technique—'the sharp contemporary tang of his scholar-poet's idiom', ranging from lyric to acute observation, even slapstick; the basic seriousness, the search for a belief which could explain without destroying the delight of 'the drunkenness of things being various'. The absence of a firm and forming conviction meant that he was open to experience but often passive in his acceptance of it, however creatively he might give back the experience in poetry. He was himself aware of this: 'But the things that happen to one often seem better than the things one chooses. Even in writing poetry . . . the few poems or passages which I find wear well have something of accident about them . . .' And in the same passage of his autobiography he expressed the feeling that what makes life worth living is the surrenders to the feelings and sensation which the given moment may present.

As poet and critic, and as man—humanist and stoic—MacNeice was all of a piece. Once he had found himself and his deepest themes he developed as a tree develops, the years adding rings and ruggedness to the trunk and density of branch and foliage, but the basic shape not changing. As the tree, rooted where it stands, must accept and surrender to the winds and seasons, so MacNeice stoically and passively accepted whatever life brought him next. And in the end it was that passiveness, the stoical confidence in his power to survive, which brought about his death.

A portrait by Nancy Coldstream (Mrs Spender) remained in the possession of the artist. From a death-mask in the possession of Hedli MacNeice, their daughter Corinna has made drawings.

[Louis MacNeice, *The Strings are False*, 1965; private information; personal knowledge.]   D. M. DAVIN

McNEILL, Sir JAMES McFADYEN (1892– 1964), shipbuilder, was born 19 August 1892, at Clydebank, the youngest of three sons of Archibald McNeill, shipyard foreman, and his wife, Isabella McKinnon, daughter of a farmer on the Island of Arran, who died a few days after James was born. The boy was sent to an aunt in Arran, where he spent his early childhood. His father died when he was nine.

His education began at Clydebank High School, from which a scholarship took him to Allan Glen's School in Glasgow, noted for its technical bias. In 1908 he started an apprenticeship at the shipyard of John Brown & Co. Ltd., Clydebank. Winning a Lloyd's scholarship in naval architecture, he undertook a sandwich course at Glasgow University, combining academic work with practical training in the shipyard, and graduated B.Sc. in 1915 with special prizes in mathematics, naval architecture, and engineering.

Having joined the Royal Naval Volunteer Reserve in 1911, McNeill transferred to the Officers' Training Corps at university, and on graduating was commissioned as a second lieutenant in the Royal Field Artillery Lowland brigade, proceeding to France in 1916. Promoted captain in 1917, he served with the 21st divisional artillery and was awarded the MC at Amiens (1918); then promoted major, he was mentioned in dispatches.

Returning to Clydebank in 1919, McNeill was assistant naval architect from 1922 till 1928, when he became principal naval architect and technical manager. During the inter-war years McNeill was responsible for the design of a wide variety of ships for different owners and trades, but the work which brought him his greatest acclaim was in the sphere of large passenger liners.

As an apprentice he had seen the construction of the *Aquitania* and, in the period after World War I, he shared in the planning of liners for Canadian Pacific Steamships, New Zealand Shipping Co., Union Castle Line, and other leading companies. He is best remembered for his collaboration with the Cunard Company in the production for their North Atlantic service of the *Queen Mary* and the *Queen Elizabeth*, which went into service in 1936 and 1940 respectively. The considerable advance in size and speed of the *Queen Mary* presented problems in design and construction which were successfully resolved under McNeill's assiduous and skilful guidance. Not least of these was the launching of such a large ship in the restricted waters of the river Clyde, and its accomplishment in 1934 was the subject of a classic paper delivered by McNeill to the Institution of Naval Architects in 1935.

The respect in which McNeill was held by owners and subcontractors alike was matched by his relations with senior Admiralty officials who greatly valued his opinions and cooperation, especially during World War II, when the Clydebank yard made a singular contribution to naval building.

In 1948 he assumed the office of managing director and in 1953, when the Clydebank works became a separate company in the John Brown Group, McNeill was appointed managing director and deputy chairman. The completion of the Royal Yacht *Britannia* in 1954 brought him his appointment as KCVO. He had already been created CBE in 1950. He retired from executive duties in 1959 and relinquished the deputy chairmanship in 1962.

In addition to his Clydebank posts, McNeill held at various times directorships in the Firth of Clyde Dry Dock Co. Ltd., the Rivet, Bolt and Nut Co., the North West Rivet, Bolt and Nut Co. Ltd., and the British Linen Bank.

His attainments were recognized by his university in 1939 when it conferred on him the honorary degree of LLD. He also greatly prized the fellowship of the Royal Society (1948). In 1950 the Royal Society of Arts named him Royal Designer for Industry. His native town made him a burgess of the burgh of Clydebank.

His concern for the technical institutions of his profession led McNeill to serve as a vice-president of the Institution of Naval Architects and as president of the Institution of Engineers and Shipbuilders in Scotland (1947-9). In 1956-7 he was chairman of the standing committee of the Association of West European Shipbuilders. In addition, he was president of the Shipbuilding Conference (1956-8). He was a member of the general and technical committees of Lloyd's Register of Shipping, and of the court of assistants of the Worshipful Company of Shipwrights.

McNeill had an integrity of purpose and the determination and drive to attain his objectives, coupled with a modesty of manner which disguised his underlying ability. A staunch member of the Church of Scotland (for a time he was preses of Wellington church in Glasgow), he did not flaunt his beliefs but lived according to them. His busy life did not permit much time for recreation which for him took the form of an occasional game of golf.

In 1924 McNeill married Jean Ross, daughter of Alexander McLaughlan, a Glasgow glass merchant. They had one son. McNeill died in Glasgow 24 July 1964.

[Andrew McCance in *Biographical Memoirs of Fellows of the Royal Society*, vol. xi, 1965; private information; personal knowledge.]

J. BROWN

MAFFEY, JOHN LOADER, first BARON RUGBY (1877-1969), public servant, was born in Rugby 1 July 1877, the younger son of Thomas Maffey, commercial traveller, and his wife, Mary Penelope, daughter of John Loader, of Thame. He was educated at Rugby and was a scholar of Christ Church, Oxford, of which he was later an honorary student. He entered the Indian Civil Service in 1899 and transferred to the political department in 1905. He served with the Mohmand field force in 1908 and had a distinguished career in the North-West Frontier Province of India where the Pathans described him as 'a sort of honorary Pathan'. He was political agent, Khyber (1909-12), deputy commissioner, Peshawar (1914-15), and chief political officer with the forces in Afghanistan in 1919. In 1915-16 he was deputy secretary in the foreign and political department of the Government of India; and from 1916 to 1920 private secretary to the viceroy, Lord Chelmsford [q.v.], during a difficult period when, apart from the strains of war, the Government of India, the prestige of which had suffered from the handling of the Mesopotamia campaign, was faced with a growing pressure in political circles for constitutional advance. During the visit of E. S. Montagu [q.v.] as secretary of state for India, which resulted in 1918 in the Montagu-Chelmsford proposals for constitutional reforms, Maffey's tact, experience, and knowledge played an important part in smoothing relations between the viceroy and the secretary of state. Maffey was chief secretary to the Duke of Connaught [q.v.] during his visit in 1920-1.

As chief commissioner, North-West Frontier Province (1921-4), it fell to Maffey to deal with the rescue of Miss Mollie Ellis, a girl of seventeen who had been carried off by tribesmen, who had killed her mother, into the Tirah, and was held for a ransom which he refused to give. Realizing that a military pursuit might be fatal to the girl, he asked Lilian Agnes Starr of the Peshawar Medical Mission, to go into the tribal area and intercede, which she did successfully, for Miss Ellis's release.

Maffey was an outstanding expert on the North-West Indian frontier. Frontier policy was a matter of sharp controversy in the immediate post-war period. The alternatives were the so-called close border policy of non-interference, for long successfully applied, save in Waziristan, or a fixed long-term policy of roads, regular troops well forward, and scouts widely placed in Mahsud country. Maffey, as chief commissioner, with the full support of the finance member, Sir W. Malcolm (later Lord) Hailey [q.v.], was strongly in favour of the close border policy and the curtailment of expenditure on Waziristan, already very high at a time of great financial stringency. The governor-general's Council, including the commander-in-chief, Lord Rawlinson [q.v.], unanimously agreed, and so recommended to the secretary of state. But, after discussion with Rawlinson and the Committee of Imperial Defence, which favoured developing lateral communications, even at greater cost, the home government decided in favour of road construction, and the permanent control of Waziristan by military occupation, if no better means could thereafter be suggested. The viceroy (Lord Reading, q.v.) and the commander-in-chief changed their view and accepted this conclusion. Maffey, however, was not prepared to compromise. Although the responsible authority for the North-West Frontier, he had not been consulted, and on the day his pension was due in 1924 he resigned from the Service.

In 1926 he was selected to be governor-general of the Sudan, a vast area with complex racial and political problems, which was still recovering from the troubles following the death of Sir Lee Stack [q.v.] in 1924. He governed with great distinction, helped by the deep affection and respect felt for him by all alike over seven years of steady development including the development of Gezira, and a marked rise in general prosperity. Always keenly interested in natural history, he took the opportunity to visit Eritrea, Ethiopia, and the source of the Nile. An observant traveller, his report to the Government on Italian aspirations in Abyssinia showed how well he understood whither Mussolini was tending in the creation of an Italian empire.

In 1933 Maffey was appointed permanent under-secretary of state for the colonies, a post in which he served until 1937. His overseas tours, his contacts with administrative staffs and with non-officials, were of the greatest value to him at the Colonial Office. After retirement he held directorships in the City (Rio Tinto Company and Imperial Airways) until 1939 when, on the outbreak of war, he was chosen to be the first United Kingdom representative in Eire at a time of great difficulty and importance. He held this post with the greatest success until 1949. Irish neutrality; the position of Ulster; the presence in Dublin of representatives of Germany, Japan, and Italy; the possibility of difficulties over the use of Eire ports by the Allies, were all among the major issues which he had to face. His success was complete; his integrity was accepted and respected by Eire; his kindness and understanding, his discretion, tact, skill, and diplomacy in dealing with individuals, whether in or out of office, in the political field were outstanding. He maintained throughout cordial relations with Mr de Valera personally, while retaining at all times the confidence and esteem of Ulster. When the time came for him to retire he was very greatly missed and the warmest tributes were paid to him in the Irish press and by Irish political and other spokesmen.

Tall, of craggily distinguished appearance, authoritative, firm, Maffey had a sense of humour, capacity to take decisions, skill in quickly assessing a situation and reaching a logical and correct conclusion, cool and steady judgement, loyalty to his officers, sense of duty and service, kindness and understanding, all of which instilled confidence and universal respect through his career.

Maffey was appointed CIE (1916), CSI (1920), KCVO (1921), KCMG (1931), KCB (1934), and GCMG (1935). He was raised to the peerage in 1947. In 1907 he married Dorothy (died 1973), daughter of Charles Long Huggins, of Hadlow Grange, Sussex, and had two sons and one daughter. Rugby died at Bungay,

Suffolk, 20 April 1969 and was succeeded by his elder son, Alan Loader (born 1913). A portrait of Rugby by P. A. de László was hung in Government House, Peshawar. Another, by the same artist, is in Christ Church, Oxford.

[Private information; personal knowledge.]

GILBERT LAITHWAITE

MAJOR, HENRY DEWSBURY ALVES (1871-1961), theologian, was born in Plymouth 28 July 1871, the eldest child of Henry Daniel Major, an Admiralty clerk, and his wife, Mary Ursula, daughter of W. Alves, Admiralty commissioner at Haulbowline, Ireland. In 1878 the family emigrated in the *Lady Jocelyn* to Kati Kati Settlement, founded by G. V. Stewart, in the Bay of Plenty, New Zealand, where the climate was congenial for the father's asthma. By then Major had two brothers and a sister. His mother, an admirer of John Keble [q.v.], exercised a strong religious influence. After tuition from his father, he was influenced by the Revd William Katterns, the local vicar, well known for his ostrich farm, a traditional high churchman, who encouraged Major in 1890 to enter St. John's College, Auckland, where his outlook was broadened by the warden, William Beatty, an admirer of S. T. Coleridge and F. D. Maurice [qq.v.].

As his father opposed his ordination, Major had to support himself in the vacations. In 1895 he gained a pass BA in the university of New Zealand. Bishop W. G. Cowie [q.v.] of Auckland ordained him deacon in 1895, and priest in 1896. He served a curacy at St. Mark's, Remuera, from 1895 to 1899, where Beatty was then vicar, and also gained his MA (1896), with first class honours in natural sciences, having specialized in geology. In 1899 he married Mary Eliza, daughter of Charles Cookman McMillan, JP, of Remuera and Waingaro, New Zealand, the brother of (Sir) William McMillan of New South Wales. There were two sons, one of whom was killed in action in 1941, and one daughter of the marriage. Shortly before he was married Major moved into the diocese of Wellington as acting vicar of Waitotara, where he began to have the ear trouble which gradually rendered him deaf. He was later also to have great trouble with his eyesight. In 1900 he became vicar of St. Peter's, Hamilton, but left in 1902 because the vicarage was unsatisfactory and he wished to study Biblical criticism in England. He returned to New Zealand once only, in 1929, a visit which inspired his *Thirty Years After. A New Zealander's Religion* (1929).

Having entered Exeter College, Oxford, in 1903, he was taught by William Sanday and S. R. Driver [qq.v.] and W. C. Allen. His family lodged at 26 Polstead Road and he served as curate to C. A. Whittuck, vicar of St. Mary the Virgin. He was a founder of the Origen Society; and one summer acted as *locum tenens* at Longworth for J. R. Illingworth. In 1905 he took first class honours in theology. W. C. Allen suggested his name for the vacant chaplaincy at Ripon Clergy College to its principal, John Battersby Harford, an evangelical. The college had been founded in 1897 by William Boyd Carpenter [q.v.], bishop of Ripon, an eloquent evangelical who had developed broad church leanings. Major later wrote *The Life and Letters of W. B. Carpenter* (1925), and he also contributed Carpenter's notice to this Dictionary. He went to Ripon in January 1906, proved an immense success, and was appointed vice-principal in the same year. Later in the year he brought his family to live at Beech Grove, South Crescent. Both the bishop and the dean, W. H. Fremantle, an Erastian broad churchman and a disciple of Benjamin Jowett and A. C. Tait [qq.v.] influenced him, but even greater was the impression made by Hastings Rashdall [q.v.], one of the governors.

Major's first overt link with theological liberalism came with his contribution 'St. Paul's presentation of Christ' in *Lux Hominum*, edited by F. W. Orde Ward (1907). That year the Majors visited the Holy Land, and, during a severe illness immediately upon his return, Major decided to throw in his lot completely with Anglican liberal churchmen. He joined the Churchmen's Union (later the Modern Churchmen's Union) and from 1910 became a fanatical advocate of modernism. He started the *Modern Churchman* in 1911, as a successor to the *Liberal Churchman*, to which he had contributed articles, some of which he republished in *The Gospel of Freedom* (1912). His editing of the *Modern Churchman*, from which he did not retire until 1956, was brilliant and often vitriolic, despite the fact that he was gentle when met in person. He also commenced the series of Conferences of Modern Churchmen, the first of which was held at the Spa Hotel, Ripon, in 1914. He was, in addition, responsible for the Modern Churchman's Creed and the Modern Churchman's Library.

In 1911 Boyd Carpenter retired from Ripon, having just appointed Battersby Harford a canon there. The changes created problems for Major, who had worked happily with Harford and had grown to admire the bishop, whom he had served as Holden librarian. The new bishop, T. W. Drury, a pronounced evangelical, appointed as the principal C. H. K. Boughton, a sincere but unimaginative member of his own school, who, though a good administrator, was unpopular with the students. Boughton sought to remove Major but in 1915 he himself was moved by the offer of the living of Calverley.

Major did not become principal; instead Battersby Harford reassumed the post as war work, in addition to his canonry.

Major, who had acted as curate of North Stainley from 1908 to 1911, then became rector of Copgrove, where he remained until the end of the war, helping neighbouring parishes and writing *Memorials of Copgrove* (1922). Like Rashdall, he was determined that the college should reopen, with himself as principal, in a university setting. This was achieved in 1919 when Ripon Hall opened in Parks Road, Oxford. Many liberal churchmen emerged from the college, for example Norman Sykes, James W. Parkes, Oliver Fielding Clarke, Robert D. Richardson, and Charles Jenkinson. In 1921, after Major had taken part in the renowned Modern Churchmen's Girton Conference, at which Rashdall and J. F. Bethune-Baker [q.v.] had expounded their degree Christology, there was an attempt to arraign him for heresy by the Revd C. E. Douglas, an expert in Convocation law and founder of the Faith Press. This caused Major to write *A Resurrection of Relics* (1922), and to be named 'Anti-Christ of Oxford'. In 1925 Major went to the United States to deliver the William Belden Noble lectures at Harvard. These were published in 1927 as *English Modernism; its Origin, Methods, Aims*. In term-time he lived closely with his pupils at Ripon Hall, while his family occupied Copgrove Cottage, Bagley Wood, and later a house at Eastleach Turville. In 1929 Major moved near Bicester when he was appointed vicar of Merton by Exeter College, Oxford.

The years 1930–48 saw Major, though getting older, deafer, and white-haired, running Ripon Hall, editing the *Modern Churchman*, and organizing the conferences. He remained the leading apostle of modernism, much abused by the *Church Times*. In 1933, at the suggestion of R. W. Macan, he moved the college to Foxcombe Rise, which had recently been the home and laboratory of the Earl of Berkeley [q.v.]. The site was beautiful but Boars Hill was three miles from Oxford. In 1937 Major wrote, with T. W. Manson and C. J. Wright, *The Mission and Message of Jesus*, showing he retained the belief that Mark's Gospel was the eyewitness testimony of Peter. He had first expounded this idea in *Reminiscences of Jesus by an Eye-witness* (1925) which had gained him his Oxford DD (1924). In 1938 he rejoiced at the publication of the report *Doctrine in the Church of England*, which he regarded as giving modernists the right to worship and serve in the Church of England.

In World War II the main buildings of the college became a hospital, and Major moved into Tutor's Lodge, keeping the college going with a handful of students. When the college expanded again in 1946 it faced the problem of finding a successor to Major. The appointment of R. D. Richardson aroused controversy and bitterness, but the situation was redeemed by the appointment in 1952 of Bishop G. F. Allen, who had departed considerably from Major's theology. When Major died in 1961 the college seemed to be flourishing under W. G. Fallows, later bishop of Sheffield, but in 1975 it amalgamated with Cuddesdon College. In 1964 the college chapel was refurnished in memory of Major and a Latin inscription described him as 'Praeceptor impiger, et eruditus, veri sine metu studiosus, pastor diligens, hospes liberalis'. By then Major's modernism had been rendered old-fashioned by the new theology of John A. T. Robinson and Paul Van Buren.

Major was a firm believer in the Godhead, but uncertain of traditional Trinitarianism. He was devoted to the person of Jesus Christ, but sceptical of the Virgin Birth, the physical Resurrection, and other miracles. His faith in after-life was firm. He favoured reunion with nonconformists, considering episcopacy as a non-essential advantage of the church. Although he had affection for the Book of Common Prayer, he advocated its revision and himself attempted it in an article entitled 'Towards Prayer Book Revision' in G. L. H. Harvey (ed.), *The Church and the Twentieth Century* (1936). His attitude to the Church of Rome is seen in *The Roman Church and the Modern Man* (1934). His special delight was the study of the New Testament in Greek. When at Oxford he had won the Canon Hall Greek Testament prize. Apart from his notice of Carpenter, Major also contributed to this Dictionary, jointly with J. M. C. Toynbee, the notices of the classical scholars Percy and Ernest Arthur Gardner. His most distinguished pupil was Ian T. Ramsey, bishop of Durham; others were F. L. Cross, Alan Richardson, H. F. D. Sparks, G. F. Woods, and A. Tindal Hart. In 1941 E. W. Barnes [q.v.] appointed Major an examining chaplain and an honorary canon of Birmingham. Much vilified in his lifetime, he was greatly loved and revered by those who knew him well. He died at Merton Vicarage, Bicester, 26 January 1961, and was buried in Merton churchyard. There is a portrait by Alphaea Garstin (1926) and a bust by Marguerite Milward (1950) at Ripon College, Cuddesdon.

[*Modern Churchman*, 1911–78; private information; personal knowledge.]

A. M. G. STEPHENSON

MALLESON, (WILLIAM) MILES (1888–1969), actor, dramatist, and stage director, was born in Croydon 25 May 1888, the son of

Edmund Taylor Malleson, manufacturer, and his wife, Myrrha Bithynia Borrell. He was educated at Brighton College, where he was head of the school, captain of cricket, and a good footballer; at Emmanuel College, Cambridge, where he graduated in history in 1911 and passed part i of the Mus.Bac. examination; and at the (Royal) Academy of Dramatic Art.

A young man variously gifted and of a serious turn of mind, with an interest in sociology and a natural bent for the arts, Miles Malleson was nevertheless best known to fame as one of the subtlest and most resourceful stage clowns of his generation. He very soon found that as an actor his face was his fortune. It was an eccentric collection of strongly contrasted features, in which prominent cheek-bones were offset by an almost complete absence of chin. By exaggerating these contrasts with make-up and allowing the intelligence to drain out of his eyes, he could turn himself to a veritable grotesque which set critics hunting in their descriptive vocabularies for apt comparisons, the happiest of which was perhaps A. V. Cookman's 'an enraged sheep'. In a gentler mood he could tinge his satire with pathos, as he did in his incomparable presentation of Sir Andrew Aguecheek. But it was inconceivable that he could ever have persuaded audiences to accept him in any completely serious part. Nature had decreed otherwise and he was wise enough to accept her ruling. At the Court, under J. B. Fagan [q.v.] and at the Lyric, Hammersmith, for (Sir) Nigel Playfair [q.v.] he was able to perfect his particular talent.

Malleson's serious side had, however, its outlets in the theatre. He was an ambitious dramatist and a stage-director of skill. He was a quite prolific writer of 'plays with a purpose' which reflected what one of his friends described as the Shelleyan idealism of his private character. His aim in these plays was always to help on the cause of some social or political reform; but he was apt to allow the urgency of his purpose to show through the pattern of his play, and so lose the attention of playgoers who wished to be entertained rather than instructed. Only once, with The Fanatics (1927), in which he was pleading for greater freedom for the younger generation and its ideas, did he achieve a long run. Otherwise, as in Six Men of Dorset (1938), the play about the Tolpuddle Martyrs, which he wrote in collaboration, he had to be content with critical respect.

During the thirties Malleson made a start in a new direction by writing for the films and occasionally acting in them also. In 1937 he became the first chairman of the Screen Writers' Association, and when war broke out in 1939 he continued to collaborate in film work.

However, it was always the living stage upon which his heart was set; and in 1943, when London was no longer under intensive air attack and the theatres could once again be run with confidence, he returned to the classic stage as old Foresight in (Sir) John Gielgud's production of Love for Love, which ran for a year, after which he stayed on with Gielgud for a repertory season. After that he joined the Old Vic Company, which was making theatrical history at the New Theatre under the leadership of Laurence (later Lord) Olivier and (Sir) Ralph Richardson, and for another year (1945–6) played a round of important parts for them, and went with them to New York.

Malleson rejoined the Old Vic Company for the 1949–50 season and played the name part in The Miser (his own adaptation from Molière). This version was acclaimed a success; and during the last years of his career Malleson devoted his writing talents chiefly to the work of finding an equivalent in English for a whole series of Molière plays. In these, perhaps, consists his chief claim to be remembered as a dramatist.

Malleson was thrice married: his first marriage (1915) to Lady Constance Mary Annesley (who was on the stage as Colette O'Niel and who died in 1975) was dissolved in 1923; he then married a medical student, Joan Graeme Billson, who as Dr Joan Malleson became a pioneer of family planning. She died in 1956. The marriage had been dissolved and in 1946 Malleson married an actress Tatiana Lieven. Malleson died in London 15 March 1969.

[The Times, 17 March 1969; Daily Telegraph, 16 March 1969; personal knowledge.]

W. A. DARLINGTON

MALLON, JAMES JOSEPH (1875–1961), warden of Toynbee Hall, was born 9 May 1875 in Manchester of Irish parents, Felix Mallon of county Tyrone and his wife, Mary O'Hare, of county Down. He had two sisters. Educated at Owens College, Manchester, he was drawn at once into what was to prove the main pursuit of his life, social work with the 'under-privileged', at first in the Ancoats Settlement, devoted to the poor of Manchester. Mallon was to become known in time as 'the Father O'Flynn of the Labour movement', lively, fluent, charming and always in demand, a man who, above all else, enjoyed life. His obituary in The Times described him as 'the most popular man east of Aldgate Pump'.

In 1906, when he was appointed secretary of the National League to Establish a Minimum Wage, Mallon moved from Manchester to Toynbee Hall, which he was to serve as warden from 1919 to 1954. There were some misgivings at first since he was not an 'Oxford man', but 'Jimmy' soon became known as a born committee man, conscientious but with a welcome touch of informality, even of irreverence. He was a member of thirteen of the first Trade Boards to be set up after the Trade Boards Act of 1909, and honorary secretary of the Trade Boards Advisory Council. During the war of 1914-18 he served on several of the committees set up under the Profiteering Act and as part of the reconstruction machinery, and he was almost equally active during the war of 1939-45, when he advised Lord Woolton [q.v.] on the provision of food and refreshment in London's air-raid shelters. By then, it was said of him that he knew the East End as an actor knew Charing Cross Road. His friends, who were many, included actors, and he was largely responsible for the foundation of the Toynbee Hall Theatre and later (in 1944) of the Children's Theatre.

It seemed natural that in 1937 Mallon should become a governor of the British Broadcasting Corporation: his tenure, interrupted in 1939, when the number of governors was reduced, continued from 1941 to 1946. One of his broadcasts, a postscript of 1943 following a visit to the United States, was very widely acclaimed. So, too, was his interest in the People's Palace, the Whitechapel Art Gallery, and the London Museum. He also served as a member of the executive committee of the British Empire Exhibition (1924) and the Departmental Committee on the Cinematographic Films Act.

At Toynbee Hall he was the life and soul of an established institution, the place of which in local and in national life was changing considerably during Mallon's long and popular wardenship. Above all, he strengthened its community links and emphasized its educational activities, so that it was sometimes known in his time as 'the poor man's university'. He had been an early member of the executive committee of the Workers' Educational Association, of which he later became honorary treasurer and was prominent in its counsels. He was a strong advocate of the raising of the school-leaving age and of the expansion of further and higher education, including part-time education. He was closely associated, too, with the Workers' Travel Association. In bodies like this he found his ideals.

Educational and cultural interests mattered more to Mallon than 'straight economics' which he approached in much the same way as R. H. Tawney [q.v.]; and while he served on Ramsay MacDonald's Economic Advisory Council and wrote booklets on the minimum wage and women's work (he contributed the notice of Mary Reid Anderson to this Dictionary) and articles from time to time on social and economic subjects for the *Observer*, the *Daily News*, and the *Manchester Guardian*, he

made no professions to scholarship. The only book he published was *Poverty Yesterday and Today* (1930), with E. C. T. Lascelles. He was happy, however, to receive an honorary doctorate from Liverpool University in 1944: he gave a characteristically stimulating talk in Liverpool in that year on 'the place of the pub in the community'. He was also awarded an honorary MA by Manchester in 1921. He had served in 1929-31 on the royal commission on licensing.

Mallon hoped at various times to become a Labour member of Parliament, once for Burslem in the Potteries, where the WEA was very strong, but his effervescence—and complete lack of *gravitas*—did not help him either with selection committees or with the electorate. 'In this and many other constituencies,' he twinklingly told a Burslem audience in 1944, 'I have been rejected by large and enthusiastic majorities.' Although he may have regretted this failure, it was his persistent cheerfulness in dismal times of depression and war which always impressed his contemporaries. He was an energetic chairman of the 'London Council for Voluntary Occupation during Unemployment' during the worst years of the 1930s. It was as natural that he should be made a Companion of Honour in 1939 as that he should have been made a BBC governor. In 1955 he was awarded the Margaret McMillan medal.

In 1921 he married Stella Katherine, eldest daughter of the editor A. G. Gardiner [q.v.]. They had no children. In retirement, he hoped to write his autobiography to replace an earlier manuscript destroyed during the bombing of London. This was an unrealized ambition, but his work at Toynbee Hall is commemorated in a garden facing Commercial Street known as the Mallon Garden. There is also a bronze bust of Mallon by Sir Jacob Epstein (1955) in the dining hall. Mallon died in London 12 April 1961.

[*The Times*, 13, 14, 15, and 20 April 1961.]
ASA BRIGGS

MANLEY, NORMAN WASHINGTON (1893-1969), Jamaican statesman and lawyer, was born at Roxburgh, Manchester, Jamaica, 4 July 1893, the eldest son of Thomas Albert Samuel Manley, planter and produce dealer, and his wife, Margaret Ann, daughter of Alexander Shearer, penkeeper. His father was part Negro and part English and his mother of part Irish descent. He was educated at elementary schools and at Jamaica College where he excelled both as scholar and as athlete, setting many inter-scholastic records (his 100 yards record lasted for forty years although equalled by his elder son Douglas in 1942). In 1914 he became a

Rhodes scholar and entered Jesus College, Oxford, to read law.

In 1915 Manley enlisted as a private in the Royal Field Artillery, became a first-class gunner sergeant, and won the MM. He declined a commission.

Returning to Oxford in 1919, he graduated BA in 1921, obtained his BCL with second class honours, and was called to the bar (certificate of honour) by Gray's Inn. Admitted to practise in Jamaica in 1922, after spending a year as a pupil in chambers in London, he showed brilliance immediately and soon became the foremost lawyer of the day. Appointed KC in 1932, by the time he had given up active practice in 1955 he had appeared in every important or sensational case both civil and criminal in Jamaica. He was not only the leader of the Jamaica bar but that of the British West Indies as well. He added to his reputation by appearances in England, successfully defending a Jamaican charged with murder, and became the first Jamaican counsel to appear before the Judicial Committee of the Privy Council in the Karsote trade-mark case which he won (*De Cordova and others* v. *Vick Chemical Co.*, [1951] WN 195 (PC)).

Yet all this success at the bar was not enough for Manley. By 1936 he was brooding that 'the law was emotionally and intellectually too bankrupting' and that he would have to 'find a way into a wider life'. In 1938 the wider life opened. In May of that year labour disturbances plagued Jamaica as well as others of Britain's colonies in the Caribbean. There was deadlock between employers and labour; Manley offered his services as mediator and succeeded in restoring industrial peace. Later that year he founded Jamaica's first political party, the People's National Party, with the chief aims of universal adult suffrage and self-government for Jamaica. In the first elections, in 1944, having won adult suffrage, both he and his party were defeated. In 1949 the PNP again suffered defeat, but Manley won a seat. It was not until his third try (1955) that the party succeeded and Manley became chief minister of Jamaica.

In the elections of 1959, under the new constitution which gave Jamaica internal self-government, Manley's party won 29 seats against the 16 which went to the Jamaica Labour Party of Sir Alexander Bustamante. But in 1961 Manley called a referendum to decide whether or not Jamaica should remain in the Federation of the West Indies which had been established in 1958. The electorate voted 'No' and Manley, who was a pro-Federationist, had to call new elections in 1962 to decide which party should lead the country into full independence. His party lost, and in 1967 lost again. Finally broken in health Manley gave up the leadership of his party and left Parliament in 1969, only a few months before his death in Kingston, Jamaica, 2 September 1969.

It was ironic that Manley who had done more than anybody else to win self-government for Jamaica was denied the honour of leading the country into independence and it was given to his cousin and arch political rival, Bustamante, to become Jamaica's first prime minister, although for most of his political life Bustamante had opposed self-government.

Manley received an honorary LLD from Howard University in 1946 and from the university of the West Indies (posthumously) in 1970. In 1969, also posthumously, he was made a National Hero of Jamaica and in 1971 a public statue was erected to his memory by the Government.

Norman Manley was in every sense a big man. Whether in things of the intellect, in the skills of the law, in the arts of life, in public dedication, his was the genius of total and unselfish commitment. He gave to Jamaica a logic and a method which benefited all who formed its modern public life. The foundations of Parliament and the law owe a great deal of their strength to his legal and constitutional skill, and as in the troubles of 1938 when he first assumed a public role he continued at all times to stand athwart the dangers of national turbulence and divisiveness.

Manley married in 1921 in England his cousin Edna Swithenbank, who subsequently won considerable renown as a sculptress. She was the daughter of the Revd Harvey Swithenbank, an English Methodist missionary who had married Ellie Shearer, sister of Manley's mother. There were two sons of Manley's marriage, the younger of whom, Michael, succeeded his father as leader of the PNP and in 1972 became prime minister of Jamaica; the elder, Douglas, won a seat and became minister of youth and community development.

[*Daily Gleaner*, 3 September 1969; *Norman Washington Manley and the New Jamaica. Selected Speeches and Writings 1938–68*, ed. Rex Nettleford, 1971; personal knowledge.]

T. E. SEALY

MANN, SIR JAMES GOW (1897–1962), master of the Armouries of the Tower of London and director of the Wallace Collection, was born in Norwood, London, 23 September 1897, the only son of Alexander Mann, Scottish landscape painter, and his wife, Catherine Macfarlane Gow.

Leaving Winchester in 1916 in the middle of World War I, Mann joined the Oxfordshire Yeomanry (Royal Artillery, Territorial Army) in which he served in Flanders and Italy, rising to the rank of major. At the end of the war he entered New College, Oxford, in 1919, remaining there after he had taken his BA degree in modern history in 1920 to take a B.Litt. in 1922, with a thesis on armour. After obtaining his degree he was appointed assistant keeper of fine arts at the Ashmolean Museum, Oxford, under C. F. Bell, the keeper, where, although he had little contact with arms and armour, the great love of his life, he laid the foundation of his wide knowledge of other art fields. In 1924 he was appointed assistant to the keeper of the Wallace Collection but, although he now worked in a museum containing an important armoury, he was not in charge of it, since it was the principal interest of the keeper, S. J. Camp. At that time Mann wrote the introduction to the English edition of a book by Oswald Graf Trapp, *The Armoury of the Castle of Churburg* (1929), in the compilation of which he had already contributed. At the same time he was working on the *Wallace Collection Catalogue of Sculpture* (1931) which, since the objects cover a wide range both of place and period, demonstrated the quite exceptional breadth of his knowledge. In 1932 Mann left the Wallace Collection to become deputy director of the newly formed Courtauld Institute of the university of London, a post which included a readership in history of art in the university, but he returned to the Wallace Collection at the request of the trustees in 1936 as keeper, a position he retained until his death, although from 1946 in the rank of director.

Both his proven organizing ability and his wide knowledge of arms and armour made him an ideal choice for the post of master of the Armouries at the Tower of London, which fell vacant in 1939 on the death of Major J. Charles ffoulkes, whose notice Mann wrote for this Dictionary. The outbreak of World War II meant that both collections had to be packed away immediately, but on the return of peace Mann had the opportunity of rearranging both. The Armouries of the Tower had hitherto been old-fashioned in the methods of display and had been without trained museum staff of any kind. Mann began to reorganize the Armouries both as a modern exhibition, and as a properly constituted national museum with efficiently trained curatorial and conservation staff. His wide influence in the artistic world made it possible for him to attract very substantial grants from the National Art-Collections Fund and Pilgrim Trust for the purchase for the Armouries in 1942 and 1952 of pieces of the greatest historical and artistic importance from the Norton Hall collection, originally formed by Beriah Botfield [q.v.], and the William Randolph Hearst collection.

After a generation in which a great part of the nation's heritage of fine English armours

had been exported, Mann induced the authorities to reinstate the Armouries purchase grant. He began a series of important exhibitions at the Tower including in 1957 the first to cover the armours made in the Royal Workshop at Greenwich founded by Henry VIII.

His most productive period scholastically was from 1929 to 1945, when he produced, among a stream of papers on armour and cognate subjects, a very important series in *Archaeologia* on European medieval and Renaissance armour which formed a firm foundation stone on which his successors have built.

Mann's two papers on the Sanctuary of the Madonna della Grazie, near Mantua, resulted from his discovery that the armours decorating this church were not of *carta pesta*, as had been thought, but contained parts of a number of exceptionally important and rare fifteenth-century armours. He also published the surviving inventories of the Gonzaga armouries in two papers in the *Royal Archaeological Journal* (1939 and 1945). His paper, 'The Etched Decoration of Armour' (British Academy, 1940), opened up new ground by linking the history of arms with the early history of etching plates for printed illustrations.

An excellent committee man, who was constantly in demand, throughout his life Mann played an influential part in organizations concerned with art history. He was a member of the committees of the Exhibition of British Art (1934), of Portuguese Art (1955-6), and of British Portraits (1956-7), all of which were held at the Royal Academy. In 1937 he visited Spain at the request of its Government to inspect the measures taken to protect works of art during the civil war. From 1943 to 1946 he was a member and honorary secretary of the British committee for the restitution of works of art in enemy hands. In 1944 he became director of the Society of Antiquaries of London, and from 1949 to 1954 was president, and thereafter honorary vice-president. In 1946 he was appointed surveyor of the Royal Works of Art, a post he held until his death. At different times he was also trustee of the British Museum and of the College of Arms, governor of the National Army Museum, chairman of the National Buildings Record, vice-chairman of the Archbishop's Historic Churches Preservation Trust, a member of the advisory committee of the Royal Mint, of the Royal Commission on Historical Monuments, and of the Historic Buildings Council. He was knighted in 1948 and appointed KCVO in 1957. He was a fellow of the British Academy (1952).

The fact that his last major work, the *Catalogue of the European Arms and Armour* of the Wallace Collection, published only weeks before his death, was in some ways unsatisfactory was no doubt due to the distractions of these many calls on Mann's time and energy. However, it was his very wide interests in many artistic fields which made it possible for Mann to reinstate arms and armour in the main stream of art-historical studies. His own interest in the subject had begun when he was five, if not earlier, and, throughout the greater part of his life, he was the unchallenged authority on most aspects of it.

Mann's apparently reserved and even austere manner concealed a charming and warm personality. He was always ready to make time to encourage and help younger enthusiasts in his field.

In 1926 Mann married Mary (died 1956), daughter of the Revd Dr George Albert Cooke; they had one daughter. In 1958 he married Evelyn Aimée, daughter of Charles Richard Hughes. Mann died at his London home, 23 Chapel Street, Westminster, 5 December 1962.

A chalk drawing by A. K. Lawrence was exhibited in the Royal Academy summer exhibition of 1955.

[Francis J. B. Watson in *Proceedings* of the British Academy, vol. xlix, 1963; *Armi Antiche*, 1962; *Waffen- und Kostümkunde*, 1963; private information; personal knowledge.]   A. V. B. NORMAN

MAPSON, LESLIE WILLIAM (1907–1970), biochemist, was born 17 November 1907 in Cambridge, England. He was the only child of William John Mapson and his wife, Elizabeth Chapman. His father was a steward for the Pitt Club in Cambridge and his mother had a position as a housekeeper. He was only eleven years old when his father died. His mother was then left with the entire care and support for the boy's education. Some help was forthcoming, for Leslie had a long association with the Very Revd Geoffrey Hare Clayton, afterwards archbishop of Cape Town, and with the Revd C. P. Hankey, dean of Ely. His personal acknowledgement of these friendly contacts gave an indication of his living Christian faith supporting his fine intelligence and his affectionate nature. This continued through a life devoted to his work and to helping others, whether in his home or in his professional activities.

At the age of ten Mapson went to the Cambridge and County High School. After leaving school in 1926 he began in the following year to study for a pharmaceutical career. However, having been recognized as a talented pupil he was encouraged by his former chemistry teacher to read natural science. He entered Fitzwilliam House (later Fitzwilliam College)

at Cambridge in 1928. This led to his taking both parts of the natural sciences tripos— part i in which he gained a second class (1929) and part ii, in 1930, in which he also gained a second, with biochemistry as the principal subject. In 1932 he joined the enthusiastic band of research workers which surrounded their professor, (Sir) F. G. Hopkins [q.v.], in his school of biochemistry in Cambridge. This was an exciting time for the study of nutrition and of enzyme catalysis. Marjory Stephenson [q.v.] had developed her superb microbiological technique for studying the catalytic activities of a bacterium. J. B. S. Haldane [q.v.] was then the reader in biochemistry in Cambridge. The ideas arising from the study of nutrition and the properties of enzymes provided the basis for Mapson's decision to embrace a career in scientific research. In later years he referred to his early contacts with Hopkins, Haldane, and M. Dixon as being instrumental in developing his interest in biochemistry.

Mapson's next research was on a nutritional problem with B. C. Guha, a well-known authority on the subject. But there was another aspect of these activities for the student just starting to find his place in the scientific hierarchy. The future was highly uncertain in those days of the recession of the 1930s and the support to be derived from teaching in college or in a university department was apt to be meagre. Mapson then obtained a position with a commercial venture connected with the whaling industry. This work which he carried out in the Biochemical Department allowed him to be registered as a student for the degree of Ph.D. under the supervision of Haldane and Hopkins. The work involved the most intense activity at repeated intervals. Working in the basement of the department Mapson provided a picture of keenness and modesty with his great effort almost concealed by a quietness of manner. He was able to show how a concentrated preparation containing a supplementary factor for nutrition could be prepared from the liver of the whale during the normal disposal of the catch. His experiments and critical conclusions from this work formed the basis for his doctoral dissertation. It happened that after taking his Ph.D. degree in 1934 there was apparently no satisfactory research appointment available for him.

Mapson left the laboratory and accepted the post of lecturer in biochemistry at Portsmouth College of Technology. Here his powers as a teacher for the students in pharmacology were greatly appreciated. However, in 1938 he was appointed as a scientific officer to the Food Investigation Board of the Department of Scientific and Industrial Research. After the outbreak of the war in 1939 he was seconded to the Dunn Nutritional Laboratory of the Medical Research Council in Cambridge. Mapson also became a member of the vitamin C subcommittee of the Accessory Food Factors Committee of the Medical Research Council. (The report of this was published in 1953 as 'Vitamin C Requirement of Human Adults, Special Report No. 280'.) These activities were followed by an enthusiastic approach to the problem of the biological significance of this vitamin. Mapson as a true biochemist was essentially concerned with the relation of the two aspects of a process: the study in a living organism and the analysis of the process *in vitro*. He never lacked enthusiasm and was never depressed for long by an unsuccessful experiment. He quickly made a decision for a new approach. Throughout his scientific career there was a collaboration with many different workers and a mutual appreciation was always apparent. In 1950 he became principal scientific officer of the DSIR and in 1956 senior principal scientific officer, a post from which he retired in 1967. He published many research papers.

He was twice married, first to Muriel Dodds in 1932 (there was one son who did not survive); secondly to Dorothy Lillian Waldock in 1949 whose father John George Montague Pell was in charge of the classical literature in the bookshop of W. Heffer & Sons in Cambridge. There was one daughter, Elizabeth, of his second marriage. He and his wife lived in the village of Hauxton, Cambridgeshire, where they were active members of the church community where he was much respected. Mapson was a governor of the Melbourne Village College from its foundation.

Mapson was appointed to a fellowship of the Royal Society in 1969, a year before he died at his home, Lolworth, Cambridgeshire, 3 December 1970. He was also an honorary professor at the university of East Anglia.

[Robert Hill in *Biographical Memoirs of Fellows of the Royal Society*, vol. xviii, 1972.]

ROBERT HILL

MARGESSON, (HENRY) DAVID (REGINALD), first VISCOUNT MARGESSON (1890-1965), politician, was born in London 26 July 1890, the third of the five children and the elder son of (Sir) Mortimer Reginald Margesson, for many years private secretary to the Earl of Plymouth. A happy childhood in Worcestershire, and descent on his father's side from generations of 'squarsons', imbued him with a love of life, a sense of duty, and middle-of-the-road Conservative beliefs, while from his mother, Lady Isabel Augusta Hobart-Hampden, daughter of the sixth Earl of Buckinghamshire, he inherited formidable energy and organizing capacity, but not her advanced Liberal ideas.

His abilities were entirely non-academic. At Harrow (1904-7) and Magdalene College, Cambridge, rather than study, he devoted his time to sport and friendship. He went down early without a degree to seek his fortune, unsuccessfully, in the USA. The war overtook his indecision about a career and developed the talents and experience which later distinguished him as chief whip.

Knowing nothing whatever about soldiering except how to ride, he volunteered as a trooper in the Worcestershire Yeomanry. In November 1914 he was commissioned and served with the XIth Hussars throughout the war in Europe, adapting rapidly to the horror of trench warfare, becoming regimental adjutant within two years, and remaining so until 1919, retiring with the rank of captain. He was gassed and won the MC—characteristically, for 'helping to pull the line together'.

With peace, he resumed country life, having in 1916 married France, only child and heiress of Francis H. Leggett, the New York wholesale provision merchant, whose wife was a close friend of Lady Isabel. Predictably the calendar of sport and village good works were not enough to satisfy Margesson's post-war urge for further patriotic service. Instead of becoming a master of foxhounds he was recruited by Lord Lee of Fareham [q.v.] as a Conservative candidate in the general election of 1922.

Unusually for a young Tory in east London, Margesson won the Upton division of West Ham. He was chosen to second the address in his maiden and only speech as a back-bencher. Before losing his seat the following year, he had become both attached to government, as parliamentary private secretary to the minister of labour, and compulsively addicted to the House of Commons and the politico-social life which lay behind it.

His magnetic, busy personality had caught the eye of Stanley Baldwin (later Earl Baldwin of Bewdley) and the chief whip (Sir) B. M. Eyres-Monsell, who wanted Margesson back in a safe seat. In October 1924 he regained Rugby for the Conservatives and started his sixteen-year period in the whips' office, forgoing any further experience as an ordinary back-bencher. In 1926 he was appointed a junior lord of the Treasury. By 1931 he had become Baldwin's preferred choice, over senior colleagues, to succeed Eyres-Monsell as parliamentary secretary to the Treasury on the formation of the first 'national' Government. He was sworn of the Privy Council in 1933.

Margesson threw himself into the work of

serving a Labour prime minister leading an overwhelmingly Conservative coalition, the more determined because he was saddened by the recent breakdown of his marriage due to a basic incompatibility of temperament, his wife having cultural aspirations which he did not share. They separated but were not divorced until 1940. They had one son and two daughters.

He remained in the key position of government chief whip for the next nine years with growing knowledge, authority, and influence, managing the House of Commons for the prime minister of the day, for such very different characters as MacDonald, Baldwin, Chamberlain, and Churchill, each of whom chose to retain Margesson for his pronounced efficiency and complete loyalty.

In manœuvring a huge unwieldy majority, 'national' in name but disparate in party loyalty and doctrine, Margesson developed a strict political discipline to muster in the government lobby every vote he could. His sanctions were few, apart from his considerable influence upon ministerial appointments and some remaining power of patronage, which he refused to use for the undeserving. His best day-to-day disciplinary weapon was his own redoubtable presence. He was a striking figure, tall, very good-looking, always immaculate, often in morning dress superbly cut.

The prestige of his position and his charm, combined with his driving force, worldly-wise common sense and terse, often profane, humour, made it difficult for straying party members, summoned to the chief whip's room as to a headmaster's study, to resist his arguments and stand by their convictions when they differed and was bent on changing them. Even so, those with a will and strongly held views of their own practised their nonconformity, usually with mutual understanding and respect.

Among the opponents of government policies, Margesson had to contend with four future prime ministers. He was scrupulously fair in dealing with the small Labour Opposition, whose difficult task he recognized. His courtesy and consideration won him Clement (later Earl) Attlee's lasting esteem. Likewise Harold Macmillan, searching for remedies for the chronic unemployment that afflicted his Stockton constituents during the depression, accurately described himself as for many years a difficult and awkward member, who never at any time received anything from Margesson except the most complete courtesy and sympathy. In February 1938 the resignation of Anthony Eden (later the Earl of Avon) provided a focus for those malcontented with Chamberlain's foreign policy and presented a running challenge, especially after Munich, to the formal unity of the Conservative parliamentary party,

which it took all Margesson's tact and skill in the management of men to preserve.

Yet his most persistent opponent was (Sir) Winston Churchill, splitting the Conservatives in the House on the India Bill, isolating himself over the abdication, and warning of the perils of German rearmament and any policy of appeasement. Despite their conflicts of view and Margesson's considerable success in depriving Churchill of a greater following, each respected the other's position and they shared a personal friendship which never broke down.

There were distinct sides to Margesson's personality. The martinet in the Commons was all that some critics may have seen. Those who had business with No. 12 Downing Street soon recognized the value of the procedural expertise and parliamentary guidance that Margesson, accompanied by (Sir) Charles Harris, private secretary for over forty years to successive parliamentary secretaries to the Treasury, consistently provided for the prime minister at No. 10.

Almost all MPs became personally fond of Margesson, including most of those who complained that he was hard in his methods; for off parade he was a different man, basically kind especially to the young and to his subordinates, indulging his gift for friendship, full of fun, a most sought-after guest delighting in social and sporting activities as a relaxation from the nagging demands of a chief whip's work.

When war came Margesson remained totally loyal to Chamberlain, but as the months passed he began to recognize, with the Commons, that Britain could not fight a war on a division of political opinion, and that a national coalition was essential, but impossible under Chamberlain because the Labour Party would never accept his leadership. The sudden drop, despite all Margesson's efforts, in the Government's majority after the Norway debate on 8 May 1940 revealed the inevitable.

When two days later Churchill became prime minister, Margesson, with Chamberlain's complete assent, transferred his loyalty to the new prime minister who, through years of disagreement, 'had formed the opinion that he was a man of high ability, serving his chief, whoever he was, with unfaltering loyalty, and treating his opponents with strict good faith'. Until Churchill, in October 1940, also succeeded Chamberlain as leader of the Conservative Party, it needed all Margesson's power of persuasion to procure a similar transfer of loyalty to the new prime minister among the Conservatives in Parliament, many of whom remained true to Chamberlain and distrustful initially of Churchill's judgement. In December, with his political power-base assured, Churchill determined to try out Margesson's organizing ability further by promoting him secretary of state for war, much against his will. To take over the War Office, with no previous departmental experience, and indeed while serving as a private in the Palace of Westminster Home Guard, was a searching test. Again he succeeded, with credit in the Commons and much respected by the general staff, but conscious that endless reading and high policy-making were not his sphere.

In February 1942, after defeats in North Africa and Singapore, Churchill felt compelled to yield to public clamour for ministerial changes. Margesson was abruptly sacrificed, though personally without blame. The manner of his enforced resignation was unfortunate in that he first learned that he was to be replaced by his own permanent under-secretary, from Sir (P.) James Grigg [q.v.] himself. Though hurt, Margesson never allowed himself any trace of grievance, outdoing even Churchill in magnanimity. He accepted a viscountcy but disliked leaving the House of Commons. He attended but did not speak in the Lords though he remained a powerful influence in the Conservative Party and with Churchill. He was still only fifty-two. Thenceforward his energies and zest for English life were deployed, no less conscientiously, in City directorships, as a trustee, and, adjutant-like again, in managing affairs no longer for prime ministers but for his friends.

Margesson was neither a commander nor a creator but cast by nature for the exacting role of chief whip. His efficiency exposed him to the criticism that he sometimes enabled ministers and policies to survive in the Commons longer than their merits warranted; but not much longer. His decade of office was one of great uncertainty and division of opinion, within as well as between the political parties in Parliament as in the nation itself. Opposition was never coherent, continuous, or widespread enough to present a valid alternative. In discouraging the Government's enormous majorities from fragmenting into separate rival groups and in duly and punctiliously respecting the rights of the official Opposition, Margesson strove to maintain the essential working of the British parliamentary system at a time when other democratic assemblies were lurching into dictatorship or subdividing into impotence.

Margesson died 24 December 1965 at Nassau, Bahamas, on an annual visit with friends, leaving three surviving children of whom his younger daughter married M. M. C. (later Lord) Charteris, private secretary to Queen Elizabeth II. He was succeeded by his only son, Francis Vere Hampden (born 1922), then information officer at the British Consulate-General, New York. Such was Margesson's activity and modesty that he seems never to have sat for his portrait.

[*The Times*, 28 and 30 December 1965 and 5 January 1966; W. S. Churchill, *The Second World War*, vol. ii, 1949; Sir John Colville, *Footprints in Time*, 1976; private information.]
J. E. B. HILL

MARINA, DUCHESS OF KENT (1906–1968) was the youngest of the three daughters of Prince and Princess Nicholas of Greece. Her father was the third son of King George I of Greece and her mother was the Grand Duchess Helen, daughter of the Grand Duke Vladimir, uncle of Tsar Nicholas II. Born in Athens 13 December 1906, she enjoyed a particularly happy early childhood, spent mostly in the Greek capital and at the enchanting palace at Tatoi at the foot of Mount Parnes. Her parents, although for their position not wealthy, provided a comfortable home life, which combined discipline with affection and understanding. A childhood visit to her maternal grandmother gave her glimpses of the splendours of the Russian court, but her own upbringing was simple, the home atmosphere in many ways English; the children's governess, Miss Kate Fox, although firm and at times severe, was held in affection throughout her life by the Princess and her two sisters.

The Princess early acquired fluency in her native language, in English which was habitually spoken within the family, and also in French. She was brought up in the Greek Orthodox Church and her affection for the country of her birth survived all its disturbed history, even though this brought two periods of exile. The first was in 1917, when political upheavals forced Prince Nicholas and his family to seek refuge in Switzerland. Some four years later they returned to Greece, but in 1922 were again driven into exile. The family settled in Paris, where Princess Marina went for a time to a finishing school run by Princess Mestchersky, an old friend of the family.

Their financial position and social life were now greatly altered. Nevertheless their Paris days were happy. Prince Nicholas was able to make profitable use of his artistic talents and Princess Nicholas devoted her time and some of her slender wealth to helping less fortunate Russian refugees. Princess Marina aided her mother, and also developed her good taste in clothes, many of which she made for herself. So began her lifelong reputation as one of the best-dressed women of her time. After her marriage her elegance greatly influenced the style and appearance not only of other members of the British royal family but also of the British public, while her choice of British fabrics, especially cotton, did much to revive home industries.

In 1923 her eldest sister Olga married Prince Paul of Yugoslavia and in 1934 the next sister, Elizabeth, married Count Toerring-Yettenbach of Bavaria. In August of that year Princess Marina became engaged to Prince George [q.v.], fourth son of King George V and Queen Mary, whom she had met from time to time when she visited London. Princess Marina rapidly won the hearts of the British people. Her attractive beauty and obvious happiness made her wedding in Westminster Abbey on 29 November 1934 a notable event. Prince George had been created Duke of Kent shortly before his marriage and the duchess quickly adapted herself to her new role as a member of the British royal family, fulfilling her varied engagements with graceful conscientiousness. Her home life, as in Greece, was unobtrusive and simple. The duke and duchess particularly enjoyed converting into a pleasant home Coppins, near Iver, Buckinghamshire, the Victorian house which was left to the duke by his aunt, Princess Victoria [q.v.]. At their London home in Belgrave Square they extended their hospitality to a widely ranging circle of people: artists, authors, actors, besides those associated with the charitable organizations in which the duke and duchess were especially interested.

The death of the duke in a flying accident in Scotland while serving with the Royal Air Force, 25 August 1942, was a cruel blow. The eldest son, Prince Edward, who succeeded as second duke, had been born 9 October 1935; their daughter, Princess Alexandra, on Christmas day the following year; and Prince Michael on 4 July 1942. The duchess did not for long allow her loss to interrupt her war work. She had trained as a VAD, but her principal energies were devoted to the WRNS, of which she had become commandant (later chief commandant) in 1940. She took a detailed and continuing interest in this Service and it was generally accepted that her taste in dress influenced the attractive uniform designed for it. Her other concern was the bringing up of her family in an atmosphere which was well ordered and relaxed.

Her public duties increased with widowhood. She replaced the duke in many of the organizations of which he had been president or patron, and in his work as an unofficial factory inspector. As president of the Royal National Lifeboat Institution she was active in visiting many small harbours; her constant attendance at Wimbledon as president of the All England Lawn Tennis Club was indicative of her genuine interest in the game; and towards the end of her life she took seriously her duties as

chancellor of the newly formed university of Kent. Another deep and constant concern was for those suffering from mental illness: manifested in her patronage of the National Association for Mental Health. Nor did she abandon the interest in painting and music which she had so closely shared with her husband.

A number of her duties took her abroad. In 1952 she made an extensive tour of the Far East, beginning and ending at Singapore and including Hong Kong and Sarawak. As colonel-in-chief of the Queen's Own Royal West Kent Regiment she saw some of its troops in operation against the rebels in the Malayan jungle. She represented the Queen in 1957 at the independence celebrations of Ghana and in 1966 at those of Botswana and Lesotho. On these and other tours in Australia, Canada, Mexico, and South America her charm and natural friendliness increased the prestige of British royalty overseas. Although basically shy and diffident she never allowed this to stand in the way of her duties and showed great courage in the adverse events of her life. Her warm-heartedness and generosity made for her strong friendships and she retained from childhood a sense of humour and interest in people which made her an enchanting companion. During her last years she was happy in the marriages of her eldest son and of her daughter, and found much enjoyment in her grandchildren's progress. After her son's marriage she was known as Princess Marina, Duchess of Kent, and moved to Kensington Palace so that her son might have his independent establishment at Coppins. She had been appointed CI and GBE in 1937 and GCVO in 1948.

Financially the post-war years were far from easy. There was no provision for her in the Civil List and the situation was only partially eased through the sale of many of the art treasures which she and the duke had acquired before the war. She died at Kensington Palace after a short illness 27 August 1968. At the time of his death her husband's body had been placed in the vaults of St. George's Chapel, Windsor, but at her wish they were now buried side by side in the private burial ground at Frogmore.

Two of her three portraits by P. A. de László, portraits by Judy Cassab, and a pair by the Russian artist Sorine of the duke and herself are in family possession. There is also a full-length portrait of her by (Sir) William Dargie, the Australian artist, in the hall of the Clothworkers' Company, of which she was a freewoman, and there are two portraits by Simon Elwes in the possession of the Queen's Regiment, and one by Norman Hepple in the possession of the Corps of Royal Electrical and

Mechanical Engineers, of which she was the colonel-in-chief.

[*The Times*, 28 August and 6 September 1968; Arthur S. Gould Lee, *The Royal House of Greece*, 1948; Jennifer Ellis, *The Duchess of Kent*, 1952; J. Wentworth Day, *H.R.H. Princess Marina, Duchess of Kent*, 2nd edn. 1969; Stella King, *Princess Marina*, 1969; private information.]

G. K. S. HAMILTON-EDWARDS

MARKS, SIMON, first BARON MARKS OF BROUGHTON (1888-1964), retailer and business innovator, was born in Leeds 9 July 1888, the only son of Michael Marks and his wife, Hannah Cohen. His father, who only a few years earlier had come to England as a poor Jewish immigrant from Poland, set up in 1884 a stall in the open Kirkgate market with a slogan 'Don't ask the price—it's a penny'. In 1894 he went into partnership with Thomas Spencer; in 1903 the firm became a private limited company; and when Michael Marks died in 1907 Marks and Spencer Ltd. was a chain of sixty penny bazaars.

Simon Marks was educated at Manchester Grammar School and spent two years on the Continent studying languages and business methods. He joined his father shortly before his death and became chief merchandiser. He was appointed director in 1911, and in 1916 assumed control as chairman, the position he occupied for forty-eight years during which he transformed the company into one of the most progressive retail organizations in the world and a national institution.

He was greatly influenced by his father and was fond of saying that he learned his social philosophy 'from Michael Marks and not Karl Marx': to put people always first. He maintained that there were three factors of success for a retail business: the customers, the suppliers, and the staff, all of whom must derive benefits and contentment from their association.

At school Marks met Israel (later Lord) Sieff who married in 1910 his eldest sister, Rebecca. Marks married Sieff's sister, Miriam (died 1971), in 1915 and asked him to join the board of Marks and Spencer. The two men, who were to be friends, partners, and associates for over sixty years, shared the same outlook on life and business; 'that David and Jonathan relationship had permeated throughout our lives', wrote Marks.

During the war of 1914-18 he joined the Royal Artillery as a signaller, but following the issuing by the British Government of the Balfour Declaration he was seconded to Chaim Weizmann [q.v.] to establish and direct the Zionist headquarters in London. He had met Weizmann in 1913 who was then teaching biochemistry at the university of Manchester and this friendship converted Marks to a fervent belief in technology and gave him his first experience of statesmanship.

By 1916 Marks was in full command of his father's business, following a Chancery court's ruling against the executors of the Spencer estate who wanted to have its control. In 1926 Marks and Spencer was incorporated as a public company and in that year Sieff left his family textile firm to become its full-time vice-chairman and joint managing director.

Marks called the twenties the formative years when, following an intensive study and a fruitful visit to America in 1924, he laid down the principles which not only revolutionized his own business but were to have an effect on the whole of British retailing and beyond it. 'We believe', said Marks at the first annual general meeting in 1927, 'that we are filling a long-felt want in providing sound quality goods at inexpensive prices, which the public cannot get elsewhere . . . .It is our aim and object to get as much produced in this country as possible.'

The war put an end to the penny price point. During his American visit Marks had been impressed by the goods offered there within the dollar limit. On his return, the new pricing policy, with a five-shilling ceiling, enabled Marks and Spencer to use economies of co-ordinated large-scale production and distribution to create a range of clothing for the family. To ensure better and more consistent quality, the company established its own technological organization to research and test materials and garments, to set specification standards, and to enforce quality control. This was a revolutionary step for a retailer to take.

'St. Michael', the brand name of Marks and Spencer, was registered in 1928 and gradually all the goods sold in the stores were to be produced under this name to the company's own specifications. Since the company would not own factories, a massive educational programme was required for suppliers and soon Marks was able to say that 99 per cent of the goods were British made.

The capital available from the public issue of shares made it possible to implement the policy of progressive enlargement, rebuilding, and modernization of the stores, and of the continuous improvement of standards, both for the customers and the staff. Very little was spent on advertising. Marks always laid great stress on the importance of direct communications through good human relations and personal contact; he introduced efficient stock control to speed up the flow of goods directly from factories to stores. 'The stores were for him a kind of fairyland', wrote the company's historian; 'it gave him deep pleasure to see the transformation.' He took particular pride in the affectionate nickname of 'Marks and Sparks' by which his organization had become known to the public.

Over the years he built up a wonderful relationship with the customers, the suppliers, and the staff. He was the most human of employers and the social amenities for his staff were outstanding. From the beginning, the company initiated an enlightened welfare policy, starting with the provision of a good hot midday meal and extending to medical, dental, catering, and social services, generous pensions, and comfortable quarters. All this created a family-like atmosphere. Marks, though a perfectionist himself, was very protective towards people who worked for him.

During the war of 1939-45, while the company helped with its welfare services, for instance feeding evacuees, Marks served as deputy chairman of the London and South Eastern Regional Production Board and as adviser to the Petroleum Warfare Department. A co-founder of the Air Defence Cadet Corps before the war, he served as one of the first directors of British Overseas Airways.

Marks, with his genius for merchandising, will be remembered especially as the initiator of high-quality clothing at reasonable prices. His retailing revolution was based on the principle that the main function of distribution was to tell the manufacturer what the public needed, and assist with expert advice on technology, production engineering, and so on. His dynamic and imaginative reform reached its climax after the Second World War, when he helped to bring about a social revolution by attracting customers in every class and making it possible for every woman to be well dressed. The expansion into foodstuffs followed a similar path, with emphasis on quality and freshness as he himself had an almost fanatical interest in hygiene and cleanliness.

His sensitivity almost amounted to intuition and with it went the faculty of criticism and self-criticism. He was always ready to examine and re-examine both merchandise and systems, to reconsider any approach that had taken root, even though he had brought these ideas into being, or had approved them. He often said to those he led and guided: 'I am the greatest rebel of you all.' Very impatient with rising costs, he started in 1956 the 'good housekeeping campaign' to simplify his business and eliminate unproductive paperwork. This led to higher efficiency, lower prices, and a greater sense of involvement among the staff.

This 'operation simplification' was widely reported and caught the popular imagination, bringing civil servants, administrators, and business men to study it. Marks had a strong sense of social responsibility and was ready to give generous help to those who wanted to learn from his success. Also, personally, he was warmly and lavishly generous. His interests included the Royal College of Surgeons, University College, London, Manchester Grammar School, the British Heart Foundation, and always Israel. 'Rich men must learn to give,' he once said, 'for some it is the hardest lesson of all and some of them never learn it.'

Marks was knighted in 1944 and raised to the peerage in 1961; the speeches he made in the House of Lords showed pride in British achievement and a desire to enhance it. Parallel with his love for England was a passionate commitment to Zionism which could always claim his high-pressure energy and resourcefulness and the services of his family. He was president of the Joint Palestine Appeal and honorary vice-president of the Zionist Federation.

Honours conferred on him included the honorary D.Sc. (Economics) of London, LLD of Manchester and Leeds, Ph.D. of the Hebrew University of Jerusalem; the honorary fellowship of the Royal College of Surgeons, of the Weizmann Institute of Science, and of University College, London. In 1962 he was the first recipient outside the United States of the Tobé award for the most distinguished retailers.

Marks conveyed an impression of youthful enthusiasm and spontaneous warmth, with his sensitive and mobile features, a small agile body, and quick expressive gestures. His soft and appraising eyes, under heavy eyebrows and a full head of hair, would light up with intense curiosity or emotion. His spirit was vibrant but his manner and humour were understated. He had a mercurial personality: soft in sympathy but passionately relentless in determination, with an earthy sense of fun, particularly at the expense of pomposity.

He had great personal charm and was a good companion, with an extraordinary zest for life and a capacity to surprise. He liked to be surrounded by his family in his Grosvenor Square flat or the Berkshire farm; he had one son and one daughter. Once an ardent tennis player, he enjoyed the theatre and concerts, collecting French Impressionists or antique furniture, and reading. Most of all, he liked people: he was very modest and simple in his approach, able to talk with all kinds of people and quick to understand their problems and points of view. He died in London 8 December 1964 at the head office of Marks and Spencer, where his portrait by Frank O. Salisbury hangs in the boardroom. He was succeeded in his title by his son, Michael (born 1920).

[Goronwy Rees, *St. Michael, A History of Marks and Spencer*, 1969, and *The Multi-Millionaires*, 1961; S. J. Goldsmith, *Twenty 20th Century Jews*, New York, 1962; Woodrow Wyatt, *Distinguished for Talent*, 1958; Marshall E. Dimock, *Administrative Vitality*, 1959; *The Times*, 9 December 1964; *Observer*, 30 June 1968; Israel Sieff, *Memoirs*, 1970; private information; personal knowledge.]   .SIEFF

MARQUIS, FREDERICK JAMES, first EARL OF WOOLTON (1883–1964), politician and business man, was born in Salford 23 August 1883, the only child of Thomas Robert Marquis, saddler, and his wife, Margaret Ormerod. From Ardwick higher-grade school he went to Manchester Grammar School and thence to the university where he read mathematics, chemistry, physics, and psychology and obtained his B.Sc. in 1906. He could not afford to accept the offer from London of a research fellowship in sociology but became senior mathematical master at Burnley Grammar School and part-time mathematics and science lecturer in the evening technical school. Increasingly concerned as a young man with problems of poverty, he deliberately acquired first-hand experience of them, first from the Manchester University settlement at Ancoats Hall (where he first met J. J. Mallon [q.v.], later one of his close friends, who was then starting his campaign against sweated labour), and later from bachelor life in Burnley. He was a research fellow in economics at Manchester in 1910 and obtained his MA in 1912.

Led away from schoolmastering by his social concern, Marquis became assistant to an enthusiastic Congregational minister, T. Arthur Leonard, founder of a co-operative association in near-by Colne for organizing family holidays with the help of undergraduates during their long vacations. This was the one decision of all those mentioned in his memoirs which he says that he was wrong to take. Six months later the misdirection was corrected. Fred Marquis took a step which led decisively to all the subsequent stages of his life. He became the warden of a unique social settlement, oddly named the David Lewis Hotel and Club Association, in the Liverpool dockland. Amply provided with funds, it consisted of a 'sleep-shop' (where for sixpence a night a man could get a clean bed), a 'people's palace' (club, meeting-rooms, library, temperance bar), and a theatre seating 800. The warden was under obligation, besides organizing social activities, to undertake research into the social problems of the neighbourhood, and not to allow in the club any party politics or religious teaching.

Soon Marquis was asked by the vice-chancellor of the university of Liverpool to become warden of the university settlement as well: this widened the scope of the club work and enabled the warden to get new premises built which could serve as a centre in dockland both of research and of collegiate life for the residents. There Marquis himself lived and in 1912 brought with him as his bride an old Lancashire friend, Maud Smith, by temperament and training the ideal wife for any warden, who was to prove no less invaluable a partner in each of her husband's later posts. Their joint efforts had many kinds of success. A school dental clinic was established, about which such good propaganda was made at the next municipal elections that Liverpool was induced to start dental clinics throughout the city. Similar results followed the establishment of a pioneer maternity clinic, and the warden's name was rightly linked with the movement to decasualize dock labour. On occasion his timely appearance would save the situation when Protestants and Catholics were nearly at each other's throats.

Rejected on health grounds for military service when war broke out in 1914, Marquis was already well enough known in Whitehall to be given some urgent work by one of the shrewdest officers in the Local Government Board. But as this did not satisfy him, he got himself appointed by the War Office as an economist and was told to find, first, blankets for the armies of France, Belgium, and Italy, and then equipment for Romania and Russia. He became secretary of the Leather Control Board and then civilian boot controller, securing the goodwill of manufacturers and distributors with such success that the whole scheme could soon be left to the boot industry's own federation, with only a small headquarters staff of temporary civil servants, (Sir) Adrian Boult among them. This proved to be the prototype for control of standard articles during the war of 1939–45.

Success in large-scale public administration had significant effects on Marquis. It confirmed his conviction that normally the public could best be served by business men competing for the public's favour without control by Government: only in times of scarcity, such as a war, should use be made of regulations or the Civil Service. As soon, therefore, as he thought that leather supplies were adequate he sent in his resignation as controller and at the same time resigned from the Fabian Society. While his war work had impressed Marquis with the competence and patriotism of the great majority of business men, many of them had been equally impressed by Marquis. For the rest of his life he was to be subject to frequent offers of highly profitable employment.

From several possibilities he now chose to accept the secretaryship of a new post-war federation of the boot industry. This body was to have 'high public purpose': to maintain the reputation made by British boot manufacturers in war, extend their trade, and work in such harmony with the trade union that there should never be a strike—in short, to prove the Marquis theory that welfare and profits are inseparable partners in a well-organized industry. He proved a highly successful secretary, while substantially increasing his income by freelance journalism and learning to put his theory into words. Soon there came the opportunity to put his theory into practice.

Boot business took Marquis to the United States and with him went Rex Cohen, one of a family which had established in Liverpool, Manchester, and Birmingham the highly successful department store of Lewis's and, as a philanthropic by-product, the David Lewis Club. Marquis drafted for Cohen the report to Lewis's on the American stores they visited and on their return he received a surprising invitation. Although since its foundation more than sixty years before Lewis's had been an exclusively Jewish family firm they now asked Marquis (who had no Jewish blood) to join their board. After a characteristic pause he accepted the invitation, on his own terms: a salary not much higher than his present one, and at the end of two years either side to be free to cancel the arrangement without ill feeling. Before the two years were up he did offer his resignation, but neither then nor at any time was there danger of its acceptance. He became joint managing director in 1928 and chairman in 1936. The firm went from strength to strength, the gentile quickly and happily became its moving spirit and remained, except during war, its tutelary genius until 1951, in due course arranging a marriage of convenience between Lewis's and the London firm of Selfridges; with the London John Lewis partnership there was no connection.

Although Marquis wanted to make money, he wanted still more to prove by his own practice that that was compatible with public service. So, literally, he walked the shop, studied the customer, questioned the firm's buyers, exploited American experience, took major risks—and constantly increased the turnover and profits of the business. But he was soon finding time for much besides the firm: not for local or national party politics but for meetings of a private luncheon club in Liverpool and dinner parties where leading business men and city fathers met. Among the results were the municipal airport at Speke and a major public

relations effort to attract industry to Merseyside.

Whitehall meanwhile had not forgotten him. It was Sir Horace Wilson who from his personal knowledge of Marquis was chiefly responsible for first bringing him into national affairs and later for securing his appointment by Neville Chamberlain in 1940 as minister of food. During the pre-war period Marquis was one of three commissioners for areas of special distress through unemployment—in his case Lancashire and the north-east coast; and he was a member of advisory councils to the Overseas Development Committee (1928–31), the Board of Trade (1930–4), and the Post Office (1933–47). A committee under Frank Pick [q.v.], studying relations between art and industry, appointed a special group, under Marquis's chairmanship, on women's fashion trade. Years later the value of this work was recognized when a rejuvenated Royal College of Art made him one of its honorary fellows. Other recognition came more swiftly. Besides his public service Marquis had turned the Retail Distributors Association of which he was president (1930–3) and chairman (1934) into a national body of some influence. In 1935 he was knighted and in 1939 created a baron as Lord Woolton.

Meanwhile he had deliberately widened his experience by joining the boards of the Royal Insurance Company and Martins Bank and becoming a council member of Liverpool and Manchester universities. But from 1936 onwards Marquis was more involved, behind the scenes, in war preparation than in any private business. In 1937 he was one of a four-man government committee, nominally concerned with fire brigades but secretly charged with the general problem of defending civilians under conditions of heavy bombing. Later that year he was one of a small high-powered group under Lord Cadman [q.v.] on the aircraft industry which greatly influenced the future of British aviation and the course of the coming war. Before long Marquis was absorbed in another crucial inquiry, under Lord Hailey [q.v.], which decided that deep shelters should not be built for civilian protection. Within hours of completing this work, in April 1939, he was called to undertake the clothing of the army.

Before agreeing to serve he made a characteristic reconnaissance. Although the country was within four months of war he found chaos in Whitehall: politicians without organization or sense of urgency, administrators overworked and leaderless. He decided how much authority he needed; went personally and got it, from the head of the Treasury, Sir Warren Fisher [q.v.], and (through Horace Wilson) from the prime minister; and only then accepted the job. On 30 August he reported its completion—and for the rest of his life regarded this as the most difficult and anxious work he ever did. He had contrived to cover this wide field of public and private activity because he never stopped working, had no inclination to spend time on games or cultural enjoyment, and knew how to delegate.

When war broke out Woolton was asked to become director-general of the Ministry of Supply. This he accepted with uncharacteristic speed, because he thought non-political war service preferable to ministerial office and was well aware that in sending him to the House of Lords Chamberlain had him in mind for a Cabinet post.

Woolton did not have his way for long. Parliamentary and press critics of the Government had quickly found a 'sitting rabbit' in the Ministry of Food; a new minister was needed; the choice of Woolton in April 1940 was obvious enough to those who knew his work and in the eyes of the press and public it was a positive gain that he was politically unknown. Feeding an island population of fifty million, previously accustomed to import two-thirds of its food supplies from cheap world markets, throughout an indefinite period of air and sea attack was a tougher problem than clothing the British Army in four months. Woolton was responsible for solving it. On taking office he found none of the chaos of unpreparedness with which he had had to cope when called on to clothe the army. Much had been done before war broke out to accumulate supplies, print ration books, and arrange for leading members of the food industry to join the staff. By 1940 a large department had been working for some months. The chief civil servant, Sir Henry French [q.v.], who had himself been in charge of preparations from the start, differed greatly from Woolton in temperament as well as training, and at first it seemed unlikely that they could work happily together: the eventual closeness of their collaboration was the real secret of the Ministry's success. Woolton's most obvious contribution was in his dealings with the public. Through broadcasts lengthily rehearsed under the expert guidance of Howard Marshall, public meetings, weekly press conferences and private meals with newspaper proprietors, and by personally dealing with a great volume of daily correspondence, he became the popular 'uncle Fred' who gave people, especially housewives, the impression of personal concern for them—taking them into his confidence, warning them in advance of shortages, admitting and correcting occasional errors of judgement. Many a child who was wayward with his food was threatened with the displeasure of Lord Woolton.

But he was much more than a superb presenter of his case. Inside the Ministry he gradually built up morale, from the depths in which he found it to an increasingly high level, despite the appalling loss of essential foods throughout the summer of 1940 as one source after another was cut off, air raids destroyed stocks and essential food services in Britain, and submarine attacks on shipping were intensified. In particular, he brought the squabbling business men and civil servants into partnership, paying them personal visits in their offices, goading them with occasional rude memoranda (channelled correctly through French), and putting new ideas at a premium. Nor did he hesitate to cut bureaucratic corners or exploit personal friendships in the Treasury and elsewhere in Whitehall.

As minister of reconstruction from November 1943 to May 1945 and a member of the War Cabinet, Woolton had no relations with the public, no power base in a major Whitehall department, no political party behind him; and the eighteen months of this appointment did not enhance his reputation. His work had chiefly to be done through the reconstruction committee of the Cabinet, and as chairman of this committee he was not in his element. All other members were long-term party politicians. In determination to avoid mass unemployment after the war they were united, and Woolton easily obtained unanimous approval for the famous white paper pledging all parties to maintain 'a high and stable level of employment'. Agreement was also reached on housing policy, and commissioners were appointed to review local government boundaries. But as the end of the war came into sight, with the prospect of a general election, the party leaders looked to their business, compromise became impossible, and no reconstruction minister could expect his colleagues to agree on future policy for land, national health, social insurance, or electricity.

In the caretaker Government Woolton was lord president of the Council. The Labour election victory which followed faced Tories with as grave a party prospect as that of a hundred years before. That the election five years later reduced the Labour majority to single figures, and that of 1951 brought Churchill back as prime minister, with a Tory majority which was to increase its size in 1955 and again in 1959, was an astonishing achievement. Much of the credit was due to R. A. Butler (later Lord Butler of Saffron Walden), the moving spirit in the process of rethinking Tory policy to match post-war British circumstances. But for electoral victory the party had to be galvanized into new energy, reorganized from top to bottom, refinanced, its social base extended, and a new army of constituency workers mobilized. Of this complete restructuring Woolton was, quite unexpectedly, the architect. He had joined the Conservative Party as the

1945 election results were coming in and next year, after a brief show of reluctance, he accepted Churchill's invitation to become party chairman. By 1955, when he gave way to Oliver (later Lord) Poole, the work was done. Woolton himself served as lord president of the Council (1951-2), chancellor of the Duchy of Lancaster (1952-5), and as minister of materials, to wind up the Ministry (1953-4).

Tall, fastidiously dressed, and consciously squaring his shoulders, Woolton was a formidable figure both in private and on the platform. He never enjoyed good health but his courage and ruthless determination to succeed proved irresistible—even in 1952 when he was thought to be dying. His first wife (who died in 1961) was a major element in his success, invariably telling him what she thought, in a downright north-country idiom which he loved even when his vanity or tendency to be pompous was under fire. Despite his wide business experience he was no economist or intellectual, and he became a successful speaker only because he took great pains to learn the art. His critics, particularly in the Labour Party, consistently underrated his powers, questioning the sincerity behind his bland manner and envying the undoubted reach of his popular appeal. He was frankly scared of Churchill and never became intimate either with him or, through lack of social self-confidence, with other leading Tory politicians. But he won their affectionate respect, nor did he lose as party politician the trust which he had won from housewives as minister of food. For he was an endearing man of strong principle who thought hard, cared fiercely both for individuals (especially the young) and for his country, and was humble enough never to stop learning.

He was chairman of the executive committee of the British Red Cross Society (1943-63), a governor of Manchester Grammar School, chancellor of Manchester University from 1944, and received honorary degrees from Manchester, Liverpool, Cambridge, McGill, and Hamilton College. He was sworn of the Privy Council in 1940, made a CH in 1942, and created a viscount in 1953 and an earl in 1956. In 1962 he married Dr Margaret Eluned Thomas. By his first marriage he had a daughter and a son, Roger David (1922-69), who succeeded him when he died at his home at Walberton 14 December 1964.

A bronze portrait bust by Lady Kennet remained the property of her family. A portrait by Sir James Gunn hangs in the Whitworth Hall of Manchester University.

[*The Memoirs of the Rt. Hon. the Earl of Woolton*, 1959; personal knowledge.]
REDCLIFFE-MAUD

MARSDEN, SIR ERNEST (1889-1970), atomic physicist and science administrator, was born at Rishton, near Blackburn, 19 February 1889, the second of the four sons (there was also one daughter) of Thomas Marsden, originally a weaver and later a draper and hardware dealer, and his wife, Phoebe Holden. Ability at school led Marsden to scholarships at Queen Elizabeth's Grammar School, Blackburn, and then to the university of Manchester in 1906, where he took the honours course in physics, at first under (Sir) Arthur Schuster [q.v.]. He had to supplement his scholarship by teaching at Manchester Grammar School.

From 1907, the influence of Ernest Rutherford (later Lord Rutherford of Nelson, q.v.), who had succeeded to Schuster's chair, made him interested in radioactivity. Assisting Hans Geiger by counting *a*-particles fired down a glass tube, Marsden found they were diffusely reflected from the tube walls. On Rutherford's suggestion, he found that *a*-particles are scattered through large angles from a metal surface, the scattering varying with the atomic weight of the metal. These startling results, published in 1909, led Rutherford to conceive the nuclear theory of atomic structure (1911). After a brief period teaching physics at East London College, Marsden returned to Manchester in 1911 as John Harling fellow, continuing experiments with Geiger which tested Rutherford's predictions and left no doubt about the truth of his conception. Marsden was twenty-four when he took part in these experiments, since recognized as one of the most beautiful series of experiments ever performed. Marsden succeeded Geiger as lecturer and research assistant (1912), publishing research papers (with collaborators) on radioactivity until he was appointed professor of physics at Victoria University College, Wellington, New Zealand (1914).

Soon after taking up his new post, Marsden, who had been active in the Manchester OTC, was granted a commission in the New Zealand Territorial Force and volunteered for overseas service with the Expeditionary Force (Divisional Signals), but was seconded to the Royal Engineers Sound Ranging Section in France. He perfected techniques for the artillery to engage enemy batteries successfully, was mentioned in dispatches, and awarded the MC (1919); he resumed Territorial service in New Zealand (1920), retiring with the rank of major (1928).

After the war Marsden played an active part as university teacher and administrator at Victoria College, and showed his gift of getting what he wanted by obtaining a new physics department. He took a wide interest in science beyond the university, lecturing provocatively, planning to continue research on a wide range of topics appropriate to New Zealand—efficiency of coal and electricity, properties of timbers, and earthquakes. He persuaded the New Zealand Government to support the Apia Observatory (formerly German) after the war. Often his enthusiasms did not last, for he believed 'the exhilaration and excitement are always in the chase—the conclusion is invariably an anticlimax' but frequently others were inspired to take up the torch.

Marsden claimed that the secret of keeping interested was to change jobs every ten years. In 1922 he became assistant director of education. For the next four years he contributed a gust of fresh scientific air to a system that was facing up to the liberal aspirations of the post-war world; he maintained his scientific interests in his spare time. In 1926 when the New Zealand Government invited Sir (Henry) Frank Heath [q.v.] to advise on the application of science to industry, Marsden accompanied him on his investigations.

The Heath report led the Government to establish a Department of Scientific and Industrial Research with Marsden as permanent secretary. Scientific units formerly administered by other state agencies formed the nucleus of the new department. Marsden threw himself into the new job with infectious enthusiasm, disarming informality, a real feeling for people, and an impatience with red tape. The units assembled in DSIR all dealt with physical sciences, but the needs of New Zealand, where farming was the only worthwhile industry, were mainly biological. Though a physicist, Marsden showed remarkable ability to deal with other sciences and with applied rather than basic research. His policy was to demonstrate to particular industries that research is worthwhile and co-operation in research is practical; the establishment, with industry support, of research associations to serve the wheat, dairy, wool, tobacco, and hops industries of New Zealand ranks high in Marsden's achievements. A Plant Research Bureau was established (despite Agriculture Department opposition) with sections responsible for plant diseases (especially mycology) and fruit research. Additional units conducted research on soils, entomology, fats, and plant chemistry, or undertook geophysical exploration and physical testing. Marsden played a very personal role in the promotion of these agencies.

The economic depression of the early 1930s set back government science. Marsden became depressed and threatened to return to academic work, but stayed on, despite salary cuts, at the request of the prime minister, and experienced the challenge offered by New Zealand's first Labour Government (1935) when science received increased funding, counterbalanced by closer ministerial direction. He was appointed CBE in 1935.

The New Zealand DSIR played a vital part in World War II, seeking import substitutes, servicing munitions production, developing dehydrated foods, and improving submarine detection. Marsden played a special part in radar and nuclear science. The New Zealand Cabinet directed him to proceed to England in April 1939 for training in radar production, at the request of the secretary of state for air. At Bawdsey Manor he learned how New Zealand could enter the new field and obtained prototype equipment whereby radar sets were produced for HMNZS *Achilles*, for aerial use, and for tank landings in the Solomon Islands. As scientific adviser to the New Zealand fighting services, Marsden held the rank of lieutenant-colonel and was promoted honorary colonel on proceeding to the Empire Scientific Congress in 1946.

In December 1943, Marsden, in military uniform, encountered (Sir) James Chadwick and (Sir) Mark Oliphant in a Washington hotel lobby. Guessing (to their consternation) why two nuclear physicists were there, he put in a word for New Zealand participation in the 'Manhattan project'. Several leading New Zealand scientists of succeeding years gained invaluable experience by taking part in atomic energy development in Canada, USA, and Britain. He was elected FRS and appointed CMG in 1946.

Marsden had been the right man to establish government science in New Zealand on a broad liberal basis embracing basic and applied research related to the economy; for the post-war period he believed he was not the right man. After he had renewed contacts with British scientists during the war, London beckoned him. He retired from DSIR to become New Zealand scientific liaison officer in London (1947–54). He represented New Zealand at scientific conferences and councils, reporting on such matters as renewing oil prospecting and developing an iron industry from magnetite iron sand ore. A project to write Rutherford's life was unfulfilled but he delivered the Rutherford memorial lecture in South Africa on his way back to New Zealand where he retired in June 1954. He threw himself into work for advisory bodies and societies, promoted New Zealand's participation in the IGY and Transantarctic Expedition (1957–8), the use of geothermal energy, and oil prospecting that led to the discovery of gas-condensate fields, and was greatly in demand as a lecturer. He was knighted in 1958.

Marsden's contributions to science and to the Allied war effort were recognized by the USA (medal of freedom, bronze palms), Sweden

(Royal Swedish Order of the North Star), and by honorary degrees from Oxford (1946), Manchester (1961), and the Victoria University of Wellington (1965). He presented several commemorative lectures and published about eighty papers and articles.

Ernest Marsden, less than average height, remained a neat, brisk figure all his life. His voice retained an attractive Lancashire intonation. He was genial, puckish, never boring, full of fun and the excitement of science, with a zest for life, expressive eyes, and a brain like a needle. His contagious enthusiasm and dynamic energy excited the enthusiasm of others, stimulating them to do their best. He had a gift of communicating with the layman, was therefore a favourite with the press, and could fascinate children.

In his retirement Marsden's main (but not sole) interest was in the effects on human health of variations in radiation from soils, rocks, seafood, tobacco, and petrol additives. He travelled widely for his research and conferences, with Lady Marsden his constant companion and assistant. He advised the Republic of China (Taiwan) on scientific development. He suffered a stroke in 1966 but retained an active interest in science, although confined to a wheelchair. He died at Lowry Bay 15 December 1970.

In 1913 Marsden married Margaret (died 1957), daughter of Hartley Sutcliffe, of Colne. They had a daughter and a son. In 1958 he married Joyce Winifred, daughter of W. A. Chote, of Wellington. There is a portrait by Olive Laurenson (1968) in the Royal Society of New Zealand, Wellington, and another, by Joan Fanning (1969), in the possession of the family.

[C. A. Fleming in *Biographical Memoirs of Fellows of the Royal Society*, vol. xvii, 1971, including a section by J. Chadwick; personal knowledge.]   C. A. FLEMING

MARTIN,(BASIL) KINGSLEY (1897-1969), editor, was born at Hereford 28 July 1897, the second of the four children of the Revd David Basil Martin, then a Congregational minister, by his wife, Charlotte Alice Turberville. His second name was a tribute by his parents to the memory of Charles Kingsley [q.v.]. Kingsley Martin was devoted to his parents. His father was a man of unqualified integrity, a pacifist, a socialist, something of a rebel in religious matters, and to some extent persecuted. Memories of him and his fight, never embittered, against the odds deeply coloured Kingsley Martin's own complex personality.

His formal education began as a day boy at the Hereford Cathedral School; the prominent dissenter's son was not happy there. In 1913,

however, better days came to the whole family when they moved to London on Basil Martin becoming a Unitarian minister at Finchley. Kingsley Martin completed his school education as a day boy at Mill Hill. Whilst still there he appeared before a conscientious objectors' tribunal and in 1917-18 he served eighteen months in France as a member of the Friends' Ambulance Unit. He went up to Magdalene College, Cambridge, in 1919; got a first in both parts of the historical tripos in 1920-1; spent a year as a visiting scholar at Princeton; returned to Magdalene with a bye-fellowship into which he was first elected in 1920; and started his first job as an assistant lecturer in politics at the London School of Economics in 1924. He was a close friend of his immediate superior, Harold Laski (whose notice he contributed to this Dictionary) but got on bad terms with the director, W. H. (later Lord) Beveridge [q.v.]; and in 1927 gladly accepted an appointment as a leader writer on the *Manchester Guardian*. Again, he was not really happy with the job or with the editor, C. P. Scott [q.v.]; his three-year contract was not renewed.

Martin returned to London and on 1 January 1931 was appointed editor of the *New Statesman*. In this appointment J. M. (later Lord) Keynes [q.v.] played a principal part. Two months later the *Nation* was amalgamated with the *New Statesman*; in 1934 the *New Statesman and Nation* took over the *Week-End Review*. Martin remained editor until December 1960. He had thought of journalism as a career before he became a university teacher; as editor he had a recurring and powerful longing to return to academic life. By the time he became editor he had to his credit his two most important and lasting books, *The Triumph of Lord Palmerston* (1924) and *French Liberal Thought in the Eighteenth Century* (1929). He had also been, with W. A. Robson, a co-founder and joint editor of the *Political Quarterly*, and indeed continued in that position until the summer of 1931. His editorship of the *New Statesman and Nation*, however, was his real life's work.

When Martin took over, the journal had become a somewhat parochial production of a Fabian character, running at a loss. The circulation of the combined *New Statesman and Nation* was about 14,000. When Martin gave up the circulation was over 80,000 and the advertising revenue over £100,000. The thirties were, of course, the golden age for weeklies; and many of the new readers were primarily attracted by the literary part of the paper, with which Martin had the wisdom not to interfere. But it was the political part, which he controlled closely, which changed its position from sectarian insignificance to world-wide influence. Initially, he caught a tide of opinion in Britain, one of a passionate desire, however muddle-headed, for 'progress' (conceived mainly as a matter of socialism at home and peace abroad). Martin's *New Statesman* became a kind of Bible for many intellectually minded people. He articulated their thoughts. Later, his somewhat naive anti-imperialism gained him many converts in Africa and Asia. His religion and his pacifism were discarded, the latter very slowly. In the late fifties he was, with J. B. Priestley, a founder of the Campaign for Nuclear Disarmament, although his enthusiasm for it came to slacken. He abandoned his sympathy for Communism less reluctantly but as slowly. Only in the fifties did he finally see Stalinism for what it was. His socialism, on the other hand, always remained, whilst never taking so simple a form as even half-hearted support of the Labour Party. The fact, however, that the paper never followed a narrow party line was an important cause of its success.

In politics, Martin was always a mixed-up Peter Pan. He was clever but confused; bright on top, gloomy below; saw problems as polygons to which he had usually at least two, and frequently changing, solutions; kept *au courant* with the *fait accompli* (a favourite joke), but was a very bad prophet; lacked the strength of mind to form firm and consistent judgements; assembled, and to a great extent trained, a team of brilliant writers, but picked some distinctly odd advisers; was often sloppy rather than scholarly; had little interest in 'practical politics'; was valiant for truth, but not above an occasional suppression of it for the sake of a cause; struck more often than not a querulous rather than a positive note

On the other hand, his very success as editor largely derived from his being a weather-vane, highly sensitive to every puff of gossip and opinion; his deliberate discontinuity, week by week, made for liveliness; he could write nothing that was unreadable, and his obvious desire for truth, with an equally obvious uncertainty as to where it lay, touched a chord in many minds as racked as his own by the difficulties of choosing the right line to follow in such difficult times. In his time, and especially in the thirties, Martin was the archetypal Englishman of the intellectual Left.

His personal life was in keeping with his public one. Academically educated, he gave more time to talk than to reading or reflection; usually mean, he could be dramatically generous; deeply kind-hearted, he could be capricious and rude; masculine in intellect, his feminine quarrels were numerous. Fascinated by women, his sex life was unstable. In 1926 he married Olga Walters, but she left him eight years later, eventually became an eccentric recluse, and died in 1964. The marriage was

legally ended in 1940. In the thirties Martin began a companionship with Dorothy Woodman which lasted for the rest of his life but bound neither of them to exclude sexual relationships with others.

After his reluctant retirement from his editorship in 1960 Martin travelled even more frequently and widely than previously. He published two volumes of autobiography, *Father Figures* (1966) and *Editor* (1968). He died at Cairo 16 February 1969. His portrait in oils by an Indian artist, Albert Whishan, hangs in the boardroom of the *New Satesman*, and a drawing by Edmund Kapp in the editor's office. He was frequently caricatured by Low and by Vicky, who made the most of a forelock which stuck up straight from his forehead. There are also excellent drawings by Michael Ayrton.

[C. H. Rolph, *Kingsley*, 1973; Edward Hyams, *The New Statesman*, 1963; *Kingsley Martin*, ed. Mervyn Jones, 1969; private information; personal knowledge.]

FRANK HARDIE

MARTIN, HUGH (1890-1964), ecumenical student leader and publisher, was born 7 April 1890 at Glasgow, the son of the Revd Thomas Henry Martin, minister of the Adelaide Place Baptist church, Glasgow, for thirty years (1888-1918), and his wife, Clara Thorpe. His early initiation into the spirit of the ecumenical movement came in 1910 as a 'student observer' at the World Missionary Conference at Edinburgh, an experience which was to be a permanent inspiration to him. He was educated at the Glasgow Academy, the Royal Technical College, Glasgow, and at the university of Glasgow where he won the university's Henderson Biblical prize in 1913 and graduated MA with honours in the same year. He was also awarded the Baptist Union scholarship for the student with the highest percentage of marks in the Baptist Theological College of Scotland, where he studied theology (as well as at Trinity College, Glasgow) from 1909 to 1914. Placed on the Baptist ministry's probationers' list in 1914, he was transferred to the main ministerial list in 1920.

This progression would normally have led to a career in the regular Baptist ministry but Martin had become fascinated with the possibilities of work among students and in 1914 accepted a proposal to serve as assistant secretary of the Student Christian Movement, which was then rapidly developing, under the leadership of Tissington Tatlow, whose notice Martin wrote for this Dictionary, into a powerful force in the universities and colleges of Britain. This position meant that Martin was in charge of the Movement's publications, and their distribution in Britain and abroad, an experience that led him to an insight into the intricacies of publishing and helped to turn an amateur publisher into a very skilled practitioner. It also introduced him to the World's Student Christian Federation and the friendship in their student days of many of the future Church leaders of Europe and North America. He was treasurer of the World Federation from 1928 to 1935.

Martin's skill as a committee man and as a chairman, capable of reconciling vastly opposing points of view, was seen in the preparation for the 1924 Conference on Politics, Economics, and Citizenship (COPEC), of which Martin chaired the preparatory committee and William Temple [q.v.], later archbishop of Canterbury, chaired the conference itself.

The aftermath of COPEC created a new attitude to social affairs and politics in British Church life, and Hugh Martin was alert to see in it a new reading public. Taking a shrewd publishing risk, he persuaded the Student Christian Movement to establish in 1929 its publications department as a separate limited company to be known as 'SCM Press'. Martin and his immediate colleagues—Alex Walker, F. R. Reader, and Kathleen Downham—forged links with authors and publishing houses in Europe and North America and built up a varied list of significant theological and sociological titles. In 1937 they brought off their chief publishing *coup* by establishing the Religious Book Club which soon attained a membership of 18,000. Each member received six books a year of a standard length at two shillings a copy. All the books were specially commissioned and dealt with many of the urgent public and theological issues of the day, especially during the Munich period and beyond. Martin himself wrote or edited several of the books which illustrate his capacity for bringing groups together to discuss the content of manuscripts. One of the best of many such larger books was the *Teachers' Commentary* (1932), which went into many editions.

On the outbreak of war Martin became director of the Religious Division (1939-43) in the Ministry of Information, a post for which he was ideally suited because of his wide knowledge not only of the British Churches and their leaders but of the religious situation in the countries that were now Britain's enemies. He was careful to elucidate what were the spiritual issues at stake in the war, and to avoid propaganda that appeared to support war aims which were un-Christian. He returned to the SCM Press as managing director in 1943, and succeeded William Paton [q.v.], who died that year, as Free Church leader of the newly formed British Council of Churches.

As the war ended discussion began on the attitude of the British Churches to their Christian counterparts in Europe. From such deliberations arose Christian Reconstruction in Europe, and eventually Christian Aid. Martin was on the committee of CRE and also served the Friends of Reunion (1933-43). In the early days of the British Council of Churches (1942) he housed the Council in the SCM Press offices in Bloomsbury Street. This nursing of infant organizations was typical of Martin's practical approach to Christian co-operation and Church unity. He saw the SCM Press as an instrument of debate and concern for unity and was happy to have authors of all Christian traditions on his list. On his retirement in 1950 he served as vice-president of the British Council of Churches and in 1952-3 as moderator of the Free Church Federal Council.

Perhaps his most lasting memorial is the *Baptist Hymn Book Companion* (1962) which he edited while also presiding over the revision of the Baptist *Hymn Book* (1962). He regarded this work as a tribute to the Baptists of Scotland, whose faith he had never forsaken. He was an honorary DD of Glasgow University (1943) and in 1955 was made a Companion of Honour.

In 1918 he married Dorothy Priestley Greenwood; they had two adopted sons. Martin died 1 July 1964 at East Grinstead.

[*Baptist Quarterly*, October 1964; *Baptist Handbook*, 1965; private information; personal knowledge.] CECIL NORTHCOTT

MARTIN, WILLIAM KEBLE (1877-1969), botanist, was born 9 July 1877 at Radley, near Oxford, the sixth child in the family of five sons and four daughters of the Revd Charles Martin, warden of St. Peter's College, Radley, and his wife, Dora, younger daughter of George Moberly [q.v.], and sister of R. C. Moberly [q.v.]. George Moberly was an intimate friend of John Keble [q.v.]. In 1891 the family moved to Dartington and Keble Martin was sent to Marlborough College, where he remained until 1895. In 1896 he went up to Christ Church, Oxford. Among his tutors were S. H. Vines [q.v.] and A. W. Church. Keble Martin became especially interested in mosses, and made the acquaintance of G. C. Druce [q.v.]. He obtained a pass degree in Greek philosophy, botany, and church history in 1899. Keble Martin then attended Cuddesdon Theological College, and was ordained in 1902. From 1902 to 1909 he was a curate, successively, at Beeston, Ashbourne, and Lancaster.

Throughout these years Keble Martin devoted his spare time to the study of flowers. He became adept at drawing the plants which he observed, while simultaneously cataloguing them precisely. He preferred the wild flower to the cultivated, assembling related plants together on plates in order to portray an example of each species. He was interested in colour-contrast, delighting in the depiction of pale flowers against their dark foliage. Together with Gordon T. Fraser, he edited the *Flora of Devon* (1939) for the Botanical Section of the Devonshire Association, of which he had become a member in 1930.

In 1909 Keble Martin became vicar of Wath-upon-Dearne, near Rotherham, Yorkshire, being married the same year to Violet, daughter of Henry Chaworth-Musters, of Colwick Hall, Nottingham. They had two sons, one of whom died at the age of two, and three daughters. In the winter of 1917 Keble Martin volunteered to go overseas as a temporary chaplain to the armed forces, and was assigned to the 34th Northumberland Fusiliers in France. In 1920 he published *A History of the Ancient Parish of Wath-upon-Dearne*. In 1921 he became rector of Haccombe and Coffinswell, near Torquay. He now found more time for his flower studies and drawings, but was also an assiduous parish priest. He designed a new church at Milber, which was later built according to his plan, with three diverging naves before the altar.

When Keble Martin's flower plates were exhibited at the International Botanical Congress held in Cambridge in 1930, he gained recognition as a botanist of note. He had already, in 1928, been elected a fellow of the Linnean Society. A move to Great Torrington, North Devon, in 1934 left him with little time for botany, although he sometimes managed to attend meetings of the Linnean Society in London, where his drawings were exhibited. His attitude was then, as it had been formerly, that 'If some of our members fancy that modern science is not compatible with the Christian faith, it may be of some help to them to be assured that this is not at all the case. These two aspects of truth complete one another. We speak of natural law, let us call it the trustworthiness of nature, mercifully provided for us.'

During the war of 1939–45 Keble Martin continued his parochial work at Torrington and, in 1943, moved to the benefice of Combe-in-Teignhead with Milber. He was anxious to have a parish which would be less exacting than Torrington, and also to see that his plans for a church at Milber were implemented. He achieved both these objects with the move. However, Keble Martin was ageing and Milber was hilly and so, in 1949, he resigned his benefice and retired to Gidleigh, near Chagford. He continued to work part-time for neighbouring churches, replacing clergy who were absent or ill.

Keble Martin's wife had a stroke in 1957 and

a heart attack in 1960; she died in 1963. In 1960 his eldest daughter died of leukaemia. He was encouraged during this difficult time by the possibility that his coloured drawings of flowers might be published. An appeal was launched with the support of several well-known botanists and the encouragement of the Duke of Edinburgh, who wrote an introduction to the book. It was published as *The Concise British Flora in Colour* in 1965 and became a best-seller. Exeter University awarded Keble Martin an honorary D.Sc. in 1966 and in December of that year the Post Office asked him to submit designs for postage stamps. Four stamps with his designs were issued in 1967.

Keble Martin married, secondly, in 1965, Florence (Flora) Lewis, a widow. He then busied himself with writing his autobiography, *Over the Hills* (1968). He died at his home at Woodbury, near Exeter, 26 November 1969.

[W. Keble Martin, *Over the Hills*, 1968; *The Times*, 28 November 1969.] C. S. NICHOLLS

MARTINDALE, CYRIL CHARLIE (1879–1963), priest and scholar, was the only child of (Sir) Arthur Henry Temple Martindale and his first wife, Isabel Marion, daughter of Captain C. F. Mackenzie. Although the family originated in Martindale in the Lake District, Martindale himself was born in Kensington 25 May 1879 in the home of his grandfather Ben Hay Martindale, general manager of the London and St. Katharine Docks Company. His mother having died within some months of his birth and his father being in the Indian Civil Service, he was brought up by his aunts in the family home. Precocious and lonely, he early developed scholarly and somewhat exotic tastes. At the age of ten he asked for and got an ancient Egyptian grammar as a Christmas present. As a schoolboy at Harrow he seems to have been influenced by the *Yellow Book* culture. After leaving Harrow, he became a Roman Catholic in 1897 and later in the same year entered the Jesuit novitiate. He was to become the most famous English Jesuit of the twentieth century.

In the course of his Jesuit training Martindale went to Campion Hall, Oxford, where his classical scholarship reached its full flower. In addition to firsts in honour moderations (1903) and *literae humaniores* (1905), he won the Hertford and Craven scholarships (1903), the Chancellor's Latin verse and the Gaisford Greek verse prizes (1904), was twice placed second for the Ireland scholarship, and was later awarded the Derby scholarship (1906) and the Ellerton theological essay prize (1907). He was ordained in 1911; taught at Stonyhurst from 1913; then in 1916 returned to Oxford to lecture in classics. The war of 1914–18 altered the whole nature of his apostolate. The university had been turned into a vast hospital and Martindale began to minister to the spiritual needs of the wounded soldiers. Suddenly, this shy, donnish priest discovered in himself a totally unexpected ability to communicate with these tough Australians, perky cockneys, and taciturn Scots.

Although he stayed on at Oxford for some years after the war, his interest in pure scholarship was declining and in 1927 Martindale joined the staff of Farm Street church in Mayfair, where his spiritual clientele was drawn from every level of society—from dukes to dustmen. He was, for example, involved in the declaration of the nullity of the (ninth) Duke of Marlborough's marriage to Consuelo Vanderbilt. Equally he involved himself in such enterprises as a settlement for working-class boys in the East End of London. He became known for his sermons, which were not the rhetorical exercises of a Bernard Vaughan [q.v.], but the direct, reasoned, taut productions of a man who never used three words where one would do. His reputation as a broadcaster grew rapidly, so able was he to present the abiding truths in language which could be grasped by the average man and yet appealed to the mind of the sophisticated intellectual.

Whereas his earliest written works—such collected pieces as *Waters of Twilight* (1914) and *The Goddess of Ghosts* (1915)—reflected his classical preoccupations even whilst these were related to his Christian convictions, Martindale soon turned to more directly religious themes. One of his greatest achievements was to rescue the trade of hagiography from its cliché-ridden conventionality. He produced, over the years, in addition to biographies of such contemporaries as R. H. Benson and C. D. Plater (whose notices he also contributed to this Dictionary), a score of saints' lives which presented their subjects in the round and in the context of their age. He published over eighty books, some sixty pamphlets, and hundreds of articles, all aimed at the presentation of Christian truth in a way which would show it to be intellectually respectable and genuinely humane. Like his friend Teilhard de Chardin, although in a less spectacular way, he was regarded with some suspicion by ecclesiastical authorities who found his fresh, almost pioneering approach to theological ideas too novel for their taste.

Meanwhile Martindale was becoming internationally known. Two concerns in particular were responsible for this development. His university background involved him in a Roman Catholic international university movement. He was also to become a member of the central committee which planned the Eucharistic Congresses which occur periodically in different parts of the world. He visited Switzerland, Yugoslavia, and Hungary in 1923, Poland, Hungary, and Germany in 1924, and in 1928 New Zealand and Australia. Later he travelled to South Africa and South America. Wherever he went, he was in demand for sermons, lectures, discussions, speeches, retreats, broadcast talks. His sea voyages opened his eyes to another problem—the spiritual needs and anxieties of sailors. They too were added to his already excessively large 'parish', just as he concerned himself with the activities of a home for mentally defective boys.

In April 1940, having been invited to give a course of lectures in Denmark, Martindale arrived in Copenhagen on the very eve of the German invasion. This meant that he was marooned there until the end of the war. He chafed at his exile at a time when he felt he was not sharing the dangers of his fellow countrymen; his health, always precarious, was seriously affected. However, he lived and worked on for almost eighteen years after his return to England in September 1945. He retired from Farm Street in 1953 and died at Petworth, Surrey, 18 March 1963.

A portrait by Simon Elwes is at Campion Hall, Oxford, and a bronze relief by Rosamund Fletcher at the Farm Street residence.

[Philip Caraman, *C. C. Martindale*, 1967; personal knowledge.]   THOMAS CORBISHLEY

MASEFIELD, JOHN EDWARD (1878-1967), poet laureate, was born at The Knapp, Ledbury, Herefordshire, 1 June 1878, the son of George Edward Masefield, solicitor, and his wife, Caroline Louisa Parker. He was left an orphan at a very early age, and was brought up by relatives. His childhood on a late Victorian farm was followed by education at the King's School, Warwick, and in the *Conway* where he began to learn, from the age of thirteen, the seamanship which informs much of his most authentic writing. He crossed the Atlantic and for several years worked in a carpet mill in Yonkers, New York, and travelled around in America doing menial jobs. Yet Masefield found time to read widely in the English poets, and Chaucer, Shelley, and Keats, in a foreign land at the impressionable age of seventeen, served to stimulate his love and reverence for England and its countryside. He also developed a passionate sympathy with the unfortunate, the persecuted, and the weak, which enabled him in the fullness of time to write his narrative masterpiece *Reynard the Fox*.

By 1897 he had made his way back to England, where he first attracted attention with *Salt Water Ballads* (1902); in his next volumes, *Ballads* (1903, revised and enlarged 1910), and

Ballads and Poems (1910), there was a surer touch, and the 'Dirty British coaster with a salt-caked smoke stack . . .' betokened a new and rousing voice in English poetry which owed as much to Rudyard Kipling [q.v.] as to Masefield's own sea-going experience: he was never ashamed to admit the influence of other writers. He had by then settled in London and he began to contribute, with the help and encouragement of friends, to the *Outlook*, the *Academy*, and the *Speaker*, and in 1907 he began to work on the *Manchester Guardian*.

The Everlasting Mercy (1911), Masefield's first major poem, was a shock to the literary world. Significantly it is a narrative, redolent of life as he knew it, a mixture of beauty and ugliness and couched, in places, in the language of the tap-room. This form was especially his, and in *Dauber* (1913) he tells, again as a poetic story, of the conflict facing the artist set amongst philistines and frustrated in his artistic ambition. Here was a man who had sailed before the mast writing a narrative poem about a life at sea he knew and understood.

The zenith of Masefield's achievement as a poet came in 1919 with the publication of *Reynard the Fox*. No English poet since Chaucer had called up the vision of the English countryside so effectively as he did there, with his powers of honest and accurate observation and his mastery of metrical pattern and pace. In this, as in many other poems, he drew upon his childhood at Ledbury for that real experience of rural life and the natural world which was a mainspring of vitality in much of his best work.

However, Masefield was not simply a poet. Over the years he wrote naval histories, and edited selections of the works of various poets and dramatists, some in collaboration with his wife. Many critics judged his *William Shakespeare* (1911) to be a work of scholarship, or at least of such imaginative power as to make it appear that he had entered into Shakespeare's very thought processes: his warm humanity and capacity for feeling for other people made his judgements appeal to all but the most desiccated of scholars.

As a novelist Masefield showed that he could tell a tale in prose as compellingly as in poetry, and with the same lucid clarity which effaced any sense of the author intervening between reader and events or characters. In *Lost Endeavour* (1910) there is hardly a false note: the force of his imagination makes it more than just a racy story for boys, although it is certainly that too. It is a variation on a theme close to the heart of all his work: that hope and idealism and energy can never be completely frustrated or overcome by mundane human considerations. In *The Bird of Dawning* (1933) the elements are the same: on one level it is a parable about

sustained bravery and tenacity on the old China clippers, on another, a gripping tale told by a man with a blazing imagination.

As a playwright, Masefield was less convincing. He came nearest to success in the rather uneven *The Tragedy of Nan* (Royalty, with Lillah McCarthy, q.v., 1908); the theme was another favourite of his—that human problems come nearest to solution in a state of nature. Next he embarked on a historical play, *The Tragedy of Pompey the Great* (Stage Society, Aldwych, 1910), in which an uncharacteristic torrent of words often fogs the main issues. Although Masefield was devoted to the theatre, and did much to promote poetry reading and amateur dramatics (stimulated by his friends W. B. Yeats and Gilbert Murray, qq.v.), both in the little theatre in his garden at Boars Hill, Oxford, and elsewhere, nevertheless his plays lack the sense of reality which imbues his poetry and much of his prose. One thing which he did well, however, was religious drama with such plays as *Good Friday* (1916), *The Trial of Jesus* (1925), and *The Coming of Christ* (1928).

He was also a great entertainer of children, and his perennially youthful heart never lost the sense of surprise and wonder which could be seen in his eyes. There are few more enchanting children's books than *The Box of Delights* (1935), or *The Midnight Folk* (1927), written for children of all ages, for anyone willing to fly on the wings of imagination to magic lands where witches and strange animals abound.

As poet laureate, a post to which he was appointed in 1930 when Ramsay MacDonald was prime minister, Masefield felt bound to do what he thought was expected of him, and dutifully produced occasional pieces for thirty-seven years. He took his responsibilities in this capacity very seriously, and the Order of Merit which he received in 1935 was warmly acclaimed. For many years he was a popular visitor to the United States and in Europe, where he gave numerous lectures and lecture-tours as laureate. It was significant that in 1940 he should have been stirred so deeply by the miracle of Dunkirk that he wrote one of his finest short prose works on this subject—*The Nine Days Wonder* (1941). All that had gone before, including his own distinguished service in the Red Cross in France and the Dardanelles during the war of 1914-18, prepared him for this work: it was the proud and loving Englishman who spoke, the man who believed that the spirit of goodness would, in the end, prevail. His life had always been modestly dedicated to helping the weak against the strong, the fox against the hounds; his innate courtesy was appreciated by all who knew him, and his sensitivity and integrity were never questioned by contemporary poets. More, perhaps, of his work appeared in print than a more self-conscious writer or a less courageous man would have permitted, but the reward for chancing his arm so often was, on occasion, to produce a work which no other man of his age could match. Masefield was awarded honorary degrees by the universities of Oxford, Liverpool, and St. Andrews; he was appointed C.Lit. in 1961. He was president of the Society of Authors from 1937, and of the National Book League in 1944-9. He died at his home near Abingdon 12 May 1967.

He married in 1903 Constance (died 1960), daughter of Nicholas de la Cherois Crommelin, of Cushendun, county Antrim; they had a son who died in action in 1942 and a daughter, Judith, who illustrated some of his books. Portraits of Masefield by William Strang and Henry Lamb hang in the National Portrait Gallery; Sir William Rothenstein drew him twice: one drawing is reproduced in *Twenty-Four Portraits* (1st series, 1920), and the other is in the Fitzwilliam Museum, Cambridge. There are also portraits of him by Sir John Lavery, John Mansbridge, and Norma Bull.

[John Masefield, *So Long to Learn*, 1952, his poems, and other works; *The Times*, 13 May 1967; W. J. Entwhistle and E. Gillett, *The Literature of England, A.D. 500-1960*, 4th edn., 1962; Constance Babington Smith, *John Masefield: A Life*, 1978; personal knowledge.]   D. R. W. SILK

MASSEY, (CHARLES) VINCENT (1887-1967), diplomatist, patron of education and arts, and first Canadian-born governor-general of Canada (1952-9) was born in Toronto 20 February 1887, the elder son of Chester Daniel Massey, industrialist and philanthropist, and his wife, Anna Dobbins Vincent. His brother, Raymond, became a well-known actor. The house in Toronto in which he grew up was the home of his grandfather, Hart Almerrin Massey, who had built up the family business for the manufacture of farm implements (Massey-Harris, later Massey-Ferguson), renowned wherever farm machinery is used. The Masseys were descendants from an immigrant ancestor who had come to Salem, Massachusetts, from Cheshire, probably in 1630. Vincent's mother came from Pennsylvania, of Huguenot ancestry. Massey was educated at St. Andrews College, Toronto, the university of Toronto (BA 1910), and at Balliol College, Oxford, where he obtained a second class in modern history (1913). He was later made an honorary fellow of Balliol, where he endowed the Vincent Massey fellowship.

Despite these deep roots set in North American soil, or perhaps as a reaction to his Puritan background, Vincent Massey, from his first visit to England when an adolescent, nourished a deep attachment to England and English life. Thus, in his autobiography, he writes: 'I have never felt away from home in England. This cannot be explained by heredity.' Perhaps it was his sojourn at Oxford, where he spent 'two of the happiest years I can remember' (*What's Past is Prologue*, 1963) which started a deep attachment which was to last a lifetime.

Early in his career, Massey gave evidence of his distinctive, imaginative, and creative qualities as a patron of education, arts, and letters. While still an undergraduate at Toronto, he recognized the need for equipping the extra-curricular life of his fellow students. Having been made an executor of the substantial estate left by Hart Massey, he set about the planning of Hart House, completed in 1919, which, in its neo-Gothic setting, provided the university of Toronto students with their main centre for a wide variety of extra-curricular activities—debating, art, books, theatre, photography, and sport.

On his return to Toronto from Oxford in 1913, Massey became lecturer in modern history at the university of Toronto, and dean of residence at Victoria College (1913-15). It was while he was dean that he married, in 1915, Alice (died 1950), eldest daughter of (Sir) George Parkin [q.v.], principal of Upper Canada College, Toronto, and organizing secretary and first administrator of the Rhodes scholarships. They had met while Massey was at Oxford, when Alice's father dispensed hospitality to Rhodes scholars and other Oxford undergraduates at his home in Goring-on-Thames. The Masseys had two sons.

Massey served on the staff in the Canadian Army in the war of 1914-18 and attained the rank of lieutenant-colonel. His administrative abilities became evident first as associate secretary of the War Committee of the Cabinet, and, later, after the end of hostilities, as secretary of the Repatriation and Employment Committee, working on the re-establishment of ex-servicemen. This 'intensive course on the machinery of government in Ottawa' gave him his first experience of the working of the federal structure, which was to stand him in good stead.

This was followed by a period as president of the family business, Massey-Harris (1921-5), which was coupled with the development of his activities as a patron of the arts, education, and letters, nourished by the philanthropy of the Massey Foundation which he set up from the assets of the Massey estate. The Massey Foundation was the first trust of its kind in Canada and, apart from building Hart House, helped to finance music, scholarships, a convalescent home for Canadian officers in England in the war of 1939–45, and the construction of Massey College for graduate students in the university of Toronto, influenced by Massey's Oxford experience. Moreover, Massey built up one of the great collections of Canadian art as well as making a contribution to English art, both as a patron and as a trustee of the National Gallery in London (1941–6) and chairman (1943–6). He was also a trustee of the Tate Gallery (1942–6) and was chairman of the board of trustees of the National Gallery of Canada (1948–52). He chaired the royal commission on national development in the arts, letters, and sciences (popularly known as the Massey Commission, 1949–51), whose report has rightly been called 'one of the great Canadian nationalist documents of our time'. Massey Hall, the main concert hall in Toronto, had been built by Hart Massey.

Massey also made contributions to the development of Canadian diplomacy. In 1925 W. L. Mackenzie King [q.v.] wished him to enter the Cabinet as minister without portfolio, but Massey failed to be elected to a parliamentary seat. Instead he attended the Imperial Conference in London, 1926, the year in which he was appointed first Canadian diplomatic representative to the United States of ministerial rank. Massey was named high commissioner in London in 1930, but the defeat of Mackenzie King resulted in the appointment of Howard Ferguson by Sir (later Viscount) R. B. Bennett [q.v.], the Conservative leader, instead.

Between 1932 and 1935 Massey was himself more successful as a political organizer than he had been as an aspiring politician. From 1932 to 1935 he was president of the National Liberal Federation, and proved not only an effective fund-raiser but also, through his organizing skills, one of the architects of the Liberal victory over the Conservatives in 1935. The newly re-elected Mackenzie King again named Massey to represent Canada in London, where he was to remain as high commissioner for the next eleven years (1935–46).

Although at times relations between the high commissioner and Ottawa may have been rather strained by the impression that he might be succumbing to 'sinister British influences' (*What's Past is Prologue*), there is no doubt about the zest and skill with which both Vincent and Alice Massey tackled their work in London in peace and in war. Their long term in London brought out for all their many friends and admirers to see and enjoy the partnership which had been firmly established in their married life. Alice Massey was a remarkable woman in her own right: intelligent, enthusiastic, imaginative, compassionate, and forceful.

This partnership, which radiated mutual affection and happiness, attracted a wide circle of friends, which included the summit of English society as well as the most influential Canadians. During the war years the Masseys organized two centres for Canadian soldiers, both officers and other ranks, to meet some of their needs for recreation and meals when on leave. In addition, they set up and financed, through the Massey Foundation, a convalescent home for Canadian officers in a large country house near Hereford, known as 'Garnons'. The Masseys were tireless in their wartime activities—Alice personally writing to the bereaved families of all Canadians killed in the war. Both their sons, Lionel and Hart, were on active service, and both suffered wounds.

In everything he did Massey was always concerned with excellence, quality, beauty, and form. This was the case before he became a national figure as Canada's representative in London and Washington. As time went on, he became more concerned with tradition, and looked especially to England for examples worthy to be followed. Thus, the Crown and the traditions of English society and all it stood for seemed to him a sure course for Canadians to follow, presumably because it had stood the test of time for the British in peace as in war. *The Sword of Lionheart and Other Wartime Speeches* (1943) reveal the depth of Massey's conviction in this respect, and the care and excellence with which he expressed it. For those who worked for him in preparing these texts, it seemed that he polished his speeches so that they shone like his shoes, and that he could stroke even a cliché until it purred like an epigram.

The height of Massey's career came when he was named Canada's first native governor-general, 25 January 1952. For seven years he toured the country serving the Crown. That he took on this job and discharged it with distinction bespoke a strong constitution, as well as his acknowledged commitment to the traditions associated with the Crown. He understood all it stands for in both Canadian and British history. To the normal strains of living up to his exceptionally high standards was added the burden that he had lost the devoted support of Alice, who died in July 1950 at Batterwood House, the Massey home near Port Hope, before he took office.

'If I had done anything to make its [the Crown's] reality vivid to the people of Canada, as something that was important to them and that belonged to them', he wrote in his autobiography, 'I was content. Nothing touched me quite so much as this comment in a Canadian newspaper: "He made the Crown Canadian", that was what I had tried to do.' Whether he entirely succeeded is for historians to judge, rather than those who happen to share his attachment to tradition, including that pertaining to the Crown. The obituary notice in *The Times*, 1 January 1968, noted that Massey 'was always conscious of the vice-regal traditions and felt that the outward trappings were important. . . . He did much to encourage ceremonial during his stay at Rideau Hall,' but added, 'in spite of all the ceremonial, Government House during his time was not an isolated unapproachable fortress governed by pomp and privilege. To it came actors, writers, union leaders and educationists. The place hummed with activity, social and intellectual.' Massey was short of stature, thin and wiry, dark, with finely chiselled features, and elegant in bearing. For every occasion he was always impeccably dressed.

With his heredity grounded in Puritan New England, Massey tried to interpret England for Canadians and Canada for the English. His heart, however, was captured early in his life by the sophistication of upper-class aspects of English life, and he could not escape from its toils. He became a member of the Privy Council (1941) and a Companion of Honour (1946). He received an honorary DCL from Oxford, and honorary degrees from many other universities. He was Romanes lecturer at Oxford (1961) and was an honorary fellow of the Royal Society of Canada. He died in London 30 December 1967.

Three official portraits of Massey were painted by Lillias Torrance Newton, the well-known Canadian portrait painter. One, depicting him as governor-general, hangs in Government House in Ottawa, another is in Hart House, university of Toronto, and the third is in the possession of the family.

[Vincent Massey, *Good Neighbourhood and Other Addresses*, 1931; *The Sword of Lionheart and Other Wartime Speeches*, 1943; *On Being Canadian*, 1948; *Speaking of Canada, Addresses*, 1959; *What's Past is Prologue, Memoirs*, 1963; *The Times*, 1 January 1968; personal knowledge.]   GEORGE IGNATIEFF

MATHEW, SIR THEOBALD (1898–1964), director of public prosecutions, was born in London 4 November 1898, the elder son of Charles James Mathew, barrister, and his wife, Anna, daughter of James Archbold Cassidy, of Monasterevan, county Kildare. Educated at the Oratory School, he served with the Irish Guards during the war of 1914–18 and was awarded an MC in 1918 when a lieutenant. The following year he was appointed aide-de-camp to Sir Alexander Godley [q.v.].

In 1921 Mathew was called to the bar by Lincoln's Inn, but practised for only four years in that branch of the profession before taking steps to have himself disbarred and becoming articled to the well-known firm of London solicitors, Charles Russell & Co., whose senior partner, Sir Charles Russell, Bt. [q.v.], was an uncle of his wife. In 1928 he was admitted a solicitor and became a partner in the firm. In April 1941 he left private practice and joined the Home Office as a wartime civil servant. A year later he became head of the criminal division of that department where he remained until his appointment as director of public prosecutions in 1944.

As head of criminal division, his work brought him to the personal notice of Herbert Morrison (later Lord Morrison of Lambeth, q.v.), then home secretary, who quickly formed a high opinion of his talents. It was Morrison who recommended his appointment as director of public prosecutions to the prime minister on the retirement of Sir Edward Tindal Atkinson [q.v.]. At the time, the appointment caused a certain amount of surprise and comment in legal circles as he was the first solicitor to hold that office, which had hitherto been regarded as one reserved for the bar. It proved, however, to be a completely successful appointment, and one which amply justified Morrison's confidence.

In 1946 Mathew was appointed KBE and this year found him presiding over a rapidly expanding department. The problems of the immediate post-war years were manifold and, on the part of the director of public prosecutions, called for administrative as much as legal skills. Mathew's talents in both spheres were quickly apparent and his ability to win the loyalty and affection of a greatly increased staff (most of them straight from the forces) was a mark of his success.

He was a good lawyer, but perhaps what is more important in someone concerned with the administration of the criminal law, he had an abundance of common sense and great humanity. Allied to these qualities was a keen sense of humour. He was one of the most approachable holders of high office, which was symbolized by his insistence that the door of his room be kept open, save when he was in conference. He was incisive and could reach decisions quickly with the authority of a clear mind. He was also a master of the written word and managed to stamp all his letters and minutes with his own brand of urbane literacy.

He sat on numerous official committees concerned with aspects of the administration of criminal justice and his advice was frequently sought and generously given. He had a strong feeling for his office and its constitutional role and was always ready to lecture on the subject. He was fond of opening his lectures with the words, 'I direct no one and there's no such thing as a public prosecution', to underline the principle that criminal justice in this country rests basically on the rights and duties of the private individual.

Of medium height and lithe figure, Mathew had a pair of eyebrows of memorable bushiness. Away from the calls of office he was very much a family man and had a keen interest in horse racing.

He died in London 29 February 1964, a few months short of retirement. During the twenty years he held office, he had served under eight attorneys-general, and had become something of a father figure to the many on his staff who had grown up under his benign and efficient reign. Although brought up in the law—his father a silk, his grandfather was Lord Justice Mathew [q.v.], and an uncle was the inimitable Theo Mathew [q.v.] of 'Forensic Fables' fame —he was refreshingly free of those foibles often associated with lawyers in the lay mind.

Mathew married in 1923 Phyllis Helen, daughter of Cyril Russell, stockbroker, and granddaughter of Lord Russell of Killowen [q.v.], a nineteenth-century lord chief justice. They had one son, John Charles, who became a senior Treasury counsel at the Central Criminal Court, and two daughters.

[Private information; personal knowledge.]
MICHAEL EVELYN

MAUGHAM, WILLIAM SOMERSET (1874–1965), writer, was born in Paris, at the British Embassy, 25 January 1874, youngest of the four sons of Robert Ormond Maugham, solicitor and legal adviser to the embassy, by his wife, Edith Mary, daughter of Major Charles Snell, of the Indian Army. His grandfather, Robert Maugham [q.v.], and his brother, Frederic (later Viscount) Maugham [q.v.], were both eminent lawyers.

Maugham lived in France until he was ten, when his father died (his beloved mother having died two years earlier), and he was transported to the guardianship of his uncle, the Revd Henry Macdonald Maugham, vicar of Whitstable, Kent; he was educated at the King's School, Canterbury, and then at Heidelberg University, where he attended lectures for a year but did not take a degree. French was his first language, and during his later childhood he was a foreigner in his own country; he stammered, and he was unhappy both at school and in the vicarage. His escape was travel, which was to become a lifelong habit. At sixteen, on the suspicion that he had tuberculosis, he was sent for a time to Hyères on the Riviera. He read de Maupassant and became familiar with French authors. His uncle wanted him to go into the Church, but he had £150 from his father's estate, and in 1892 he enrolled as a medical student at St. Thomas's Hospital, London. He completed the course, but at the same time he continued to read omnivorously and to keep

a writer's notebook. When he began to work in the wards he was 'exhilarated' by his contact with 'life in the raw', and in 1895 he was for three weeks an obstetric clerk in the slums of Lambeth, which he found 'absorbing'.

His first novel, Liza of Lambeth, was published in 1897; its vivid portrayal of low life gave it a mild succès de scandale, and Maugham, who later that year qualified MRCS, LRCP, was encouraged to abandon medicine for literature. He went to Spain, which was to become, after France, the country of his heart, and lodged in Seville. He read; he travelled; he wrote. After his return to England, he published further books without making any mark, although he attained a certain entrée into literary and social circles, where a lack of money humiliated him. In 1903 his first play, A Man of Honour, was performed by the Stage Society, but not until 1907, at the age of thirty-three, did he wake one morning to find himself, at last, famous. Lady Frederick had been mounted as a stopgap at the Court theatre, but its success was so sweeping that within a short time Maugham had four plays running simultaneously in the West End, and a sketch by (Sir) Bernard Partridge [q.v.] in Punch (24 June 1908) showed the shade of Shakespeare turning enviously from the playbills. From then onwards Maugham never looked back. His wit was sharp but rarely distressing; his plots abounded in amusing situations, his characters were usually drawn from the same class as his audiences and managed at once to satirize and delight their originals.

The theatre was never entirely to satisfy him. Although he attempted to use it as a platform for less amiable subjects, he was constrained by the exigencies of the managers and by his audiences' expectations. Yet by the mid twenties he was an acknowledged master of light, sometimes mordant comedy. He attempted serious themes with courage and assurance, but the public wanted to be amused. In 1933 he ceased writing plays altogether, but already as early as 1911 he had retired temporarily from the theatre to work on his long novel, Of Human Bondage. He was to correct the proofs under the admiring eyes of (Sir) Desmond MacCarthy [q.v.] in a small hotel at Malo, near Dunkirk; the two men were drivers in an ambulance unit for which they had volunteered at the outbreak of war in 1914. MacCarthy became one of the most vociferous of Maugham's literary advocates, but his voice was never wholly to prevail against those who regarded public success as evidence of vulgarity.

In 1915 Maugham was recruited into the Intelligence Department; his facility with languages made him a 'natural' for the work, and he was sent to Geneva where he posed with no great difficulty as a literary man. Willie

Ashenden, his *alter ego* in many spy stories and novels, was born of this experience. In 1917 he was selected by Sir William Wiseman to go to Russia, where the overthrow of the Tsar threatened to lead to a Russian withdrawal from the war. He was to say later that he believed that, had he gone six months earlier, he might have averted the Bolshevik revolution and held Kerensky to the Allied cause. By the time Lenin came to power, Maugham's health had temporarily failed, and after spending three months in a sanatorium he remained an invalid for the next two years.

The war years were also eventful in his literary and private life. In 1916 he married Gwendoline Maude Syrie Wellcome, daughter of the philanthropist Thomas John Barnardo [q.v.], after being cited co-respondent in her divorce from (Sir) Henry Wellcome [q.v.]. Their liaison had existed for some years, but the marriage was not happy. By the time Maugham and his wife were again together for long enough to set up house, he had discovered a new interest: the East, which he first visited in the year of his marriage. Travelling in the company of a young American, Gerald Haxton, who became the companion of his middle years, he 'stepped off his pedestal', as he put it. So far as the British were concerned, Haxton was an undesirable alien; Maugham could not both live in England and retain his friendship. He went frequently on his travels, and in 1928 decided to live permanently in the south of France. His marriage had been dissolved the previous year; he and Syrie, who became a fashionable interior decorator, had one daughter, Elizabeth Mary ('Liza'), whose second husband was Lord John Hope (later Lord Glendevon).

Of Human Bondage was published in 1915. It was less noticed in wartime London than in New York, where Theodore Dreiser reviewed it with enthusiasm. It remains Maugham's most impressive literary work, and by the time of his death was said to have sold ten million copies. *The Moon and Sixpence* (1919), *The Painted Veil* (1925), and *Cakes and Ale* (an elegant piece of literary malice, 1930), followed and found a prompt public. Having quit the theatre, he discovered a fertile new field in the short story and was widely regarded as the supreme English exponent of both the magazine squib and the more elaborate *conte*.

At his home, the Villa Mauresque at St. Jean, Cap Ferrat, he entertained smart company with stylish generosity, although he himself ate sparsely of the lotus he offered others: he worked steadily. His prose style changed little; he prided himself on his plain speaking and lack of literary frills. He was never a modern: he neither favoured experiment nor disdained public success. His books sold hugely; one short story, *Rain* (1921), was filmed several times. No one denied his intelligence, but the more severe critics never conceded his importance. He affected indifference.

In 1940 he had to leave France in a coal boat: he was on the Nazi's wanted list. He went to America, where he lived quite modestly: although rich, he refused to be too much at his ease while England was in sore straits. In 1944 he published his last substantial novel, *The Razor's Edge*, in which he paid tribute to the ascetic mysticism he had encountered in India and of which he was more an admirer than a practitioner. He returned to France after the liberation and resumed life at the Villa Mauresque. Gerald Haxton had died in America in 1944 and Alan Searle, a man of more reliable stamp, took his place as Maugham's private secretary.

During the twenty years which remained to him, Maugham established himself in many eyes as a cosmopolitan oracle. He had a talent for worldly moralizing, already displayed with concise elegance in *The Summing Up* (1938), and he now turned to the essay, although he continued to write short stories and historical novels. Some of the stories were filmed, with his usual success, and he himself appeared on the screen to provide introductions. He had become perhaps the most famous living English author, and claimed casually that sales of his books exceeded 64,000,000 copies; yet he was not a happy man. He was rather short, about five feet seven, and prognathous in appearance, with olive complexion and penetrating eyes. He was tortured by his stammer, and by the conviction that he was unloved. He was drawn to religion, although he affected sturdy agnosticism. He was very widely read, but claimed to be uneducated. His tongue was sharp and he could make enemies easily, yet he was capable of great courtesy, and his uncensorious scepticism brought comfort as well as diversion both to millions of readers and to private acquaintances. His conversation was urbane and he was a good listener no less than an amusing commentator. His old age was soured by public wrangles with his daughter and, in the regrettable memoir *Looking Back* (1962), with the ghost of his wife, who had died in 1955. However, he could be kind as well as caustic. He was a thoughtful correspondent and a generous private critic of unsolicited manuscripts. In 1947 he founded the Somerset Maugham Award, which gives young writers an opportunity to travel. He died in hospital in Nice 15 December 1965, and left a substantial legacy, including his books, to the King's School, Canterbury, where his ashes were interred, next to the library he had endowed.

He was appointed CH in 1954, and C.Lit.

in 1961. He was a fellow of the Royal Society of Literature, a commander of the Legion of Honour, and an honorary D.Litt. of the universities of Oxford and Toulouse. On his eightieth birthday the Garrick Club gave a dinner in his honour; only Dickens, Thackeray, and Trollope had been similarly honoured.

There are many portraits of Maugham: Sir Gerald Kelly painted him about thirty times—for example, 1911, in the National Portrait Gallery; 1935, privately owned; and 1948, at the King's School, Canterbury); a bronze by (Sir) Jacob Epstein (1951, lent by the Tate Gallery) is in the National Portrait Gallery, where there is also a portrait by P. Steegman (1931). A drawing by Sir William Rothenstein is reproduced in *Contemporaries* (1937), while the best-known portrait, by Graham Sutherland (1949), is in the Tate Gallery. Others, by Marie Laurencin (1936), H. A. Freeth (1946), and Vasco Lazzolo (1953), are in private hands.

[W. Somerset Maugham, *The Summing Up*, 1938; *The Times*, 17 December 1965; Robin Maugham, *Somerset and All the Maughams*, 1966; Frederic Raphael, *Somerset Maugham and his World*, 1976; Richard B. Fisher, *Syrie Maugham*, 1979; personal knowledge.]

FREDERIC RAPHAEL

[Ted Morgan, *Maugham, a Biography*, 1980.]

MAXWELL, SIR ALEXANDER (1880–1963), civil servant, was born in Northern Etchells, Cheshire, 9 March 1880, the eldest son of the Revd Joseph Matthew Townsend Maxwell, a Congregational minister, and his wife, Louisa Maria Brely Snell. Educated at Plymouth College he went up to Christ Church, Oxford, where he obtained first classes in honour moderations (1901) and *literae humaniores* (1903) and gained the Matthew Arnold (1904) and the Chancellor's English essay (1905) prizes.

In 1904 he entered the Home Office where he was private secretary to successive secretaries of state. He was made an assistant secretary in 1924. In 1917 Maxwell had been acting chief inspector of reformatory and industrial schools. Brief though his tenure was, it was probably then that he became interested in delinquency, an introduction which served him in good stead in 1928 when he became chairman of the Prison Commission. There he and (Sir) Alexander Paterson (whose notice he contributed to this Dictionary) worked in close partnership. The first open borstal was started in 1930 at Lowdham Grange in Nottinghamshire: the idea was Paterson's but the administrative form and substance were Maxwell's.

In 1932 Maxwell became deputy under-secretary of state at the Home Office and in 1938, when Sir Samuel Hoare (later Viscount Templewood, q.v.) was home secretary, Maxwell was promoted permanent under-secretary, a post he held for the next ten years, becoming, by common consent, the doyen of his fellows. In this significant office, in war and in peace, Maxwell's qualities were seen at their best. Upon the Home Office rests the duty not only of maintaining law and order but also of safeguarding the liberty of the subject. That the man and the duty were in Maxwell fitly joined his political chiefs have testified. Templewood recorded that 'Alexander Maxwell in particular helped me with wise and stimulating advice. How lucky I was to have him! . . . Unruffled amidst all the alarms and excursions that periodically shake a Ministry of public order, he possessed the imperturbable assurance essential to a department of historic traditions.' After Maxwell had retired, J. (later Lord) Chuter-Ede [q.v.], taking the chair for Maxwell's Clarke Hall lecture in 1949, said that 'Whether he was dealing at the Home Office with broad questions of policy or with particular cases he never forgot that the decisions reached would affect, not some undifferentiated mass of humanity, but individual lives, every one of which had its peculiar problems and potentialities'.

The imprisonment of enemy aliens, the treatment of those detained under the 18B regulations, and the particular case of the Mosleys illustrate both the explosive questions of policy and particular cases with which Maxwell was called upon to deal. Many aliens had been deported to Canada. It was clearly on his advice that the Government in 1940 sent out Paterson to sift from the rest those whose sympathies were genuinely with this country. In offering advice Maxwell always knew when to press his point and when not. He had the appearance and in some ways the temperament of a don, but he was at the same time a great administrator, firm and just in disciplinary matters and generous in praise.

Maxwell's supreme administrative gift was founded on his sheer intellectual power and capacity for work—he was usually first in the office and last out. He was able to illuminate problems, and propound solutions which were seen to be the obvious course, but which had not been apparent to his subordinates, though they were far from stupid, until he showed them the way. He was able, moreover, to set forth the principles of a subject in felicitous prose, perhaps best demonstrated in a note on the home secretary's duty to advise the sovereign on the exercise of the prerogative of mercy, a judge having expressed a contrary view: the judge subsequently acknowledged his error.

Withal, Maxwell had a nice sense of humour and was amongst the most humble and gentle of men. When speaking once of deterrence he said, 'most of us, when we travel by train, intend to buy a ticket; it is just the presence of the ticket collector at the barrier which clinches the matter'. If one rang him at home, where his doctor wife practised, he would always answer, 'Dr Maxwell's telephone', perhaps a typical blend of modesty and wisdom.

In 1919 he had married at the Friends Meeting House at Jordans Dr Jessie McNaughten Campbell, daughter of the Revd John Campbell, of Kirkcaldy; they had two sons. It was so like Maxwell that he and his wife, with their two sons as waiters, should give annual parties at Toynbee Hall for the Home Office charladies, all of whom, it was said, he knew by their first names. Maxwell was appointed CB in 1924, KBE in 1936, KCB in 1939, and GCB in 1945. A valuable committee man, he presided in 1936 over the inquiry into the work of metropolitan police courts and in 1949 he was a member of the royal commission on capital punishment. From 1948 to 1950 he was a governor of Bedford College. He died 1 July 1963 at his home at Coldharbour, near Dorking.

[*The Times*, 2 July 1963; Viscount Templewood, *Nine Troubled Years*, 1954; private information; personal knowledge.]

DUNCAN FAIRN

MAXWELL, GAVIN (1914–1969), writer and conservationist, was born 15 July 1914 at Elrig in the county of Wigtown, the youngest of three sons and four children of Lieutenant-Colonel Aymer Edward Maxwell and his wife, Lady Mary Percy, fifth daughter of the seventh Duke of Northumberland and sister of Lord Eustace Percy (later Lord Percy of Newcastle, q.v.). His grandfather was Sir Herbert Eustace Maxwell, seventh baronet [q.v.]. His father died in October 1914 of wounds received at Antwerp.

He was educated at Stowe and at Hertford College, Oxford, where he studied estate management and graduated in 1937. He later described his degree as 'a useless achievement'. From his boyhood he had a strong interest in all aspects of natural history and began to build up at this time a major collection of wild geese at his family home of Monreith. After a few half-hearted attempts to establish himself in conventional employment he followed an instinct to travel and set out alone for east Finmark to study the habits of the eider duck. After the outbreak of war in 1939 he took a commission in the Scots Guards and in 1941 was seconded to Special Operations Executive, in which he instructed, with the rank of major. In due course his service brought him to the west coast of Scotland. After a medical discharge from the army in 1944 he returned there and bought the island of Soay, off Skye, where he started a shark fishery venture. This was a commercial failure but it gave him rich material for his first book, *Harpoon at a Venture* (1952).

He went into freelance journalism and pursued it without much interest: he found the research tedious and the style cramping. More to his liking was portrait painting, at which he had considerable ability. Between 1949 and 1952 he tried to earn his living in London as a portrait painter. He took up sporadic residence in a remote cottage by the sea at Sandaig in west Inverness-shire. He also began to travel and to write about the people and places which he visited. In 1953 he went to Sicily to discover the story of Salvatore Giuliano, a young Sicilian separatist who was killed in 1950. His researches resulted in *God Protect me from my Friends* (1956) and a study of Sicilian life, *The Ten Pains of Death* (1959). Early in 1956 he travelled to southern Iraq with Wilfred Thesiger, after which he wrote a study of the marsh Arabs, *A Reed Shaken by the Wind* (1957). He returned from Iraq with an otter, and later acquired another. The personality and habits of these two animals prompted Maxwell to write the enchanting *Ring of Bright Water* (1960), a delicate sketch of the natural beauty of the wild sea coast coupled with a poignant account of a man's relationship with his animals. This was later made into a film. Two other books on the same theme followed—*The Otter's Tale* (1962) and *The Rocks Remain* (1963)—but the visionary gleam was gone. He was now writing for money and his rustic retreat had become a modernized holiday camp. His literary innocence was restored in *The House of Elrig* (1965), a candid autobiography of a sensitive boy mentally and physically adapting to the rigours of an aristocratic upbringing. This was followed by a history of the Moroccan house of Glaoua, *Lords of the Atlas* (1966). His two final books were *Seals of the World* (1967) and *Raven Seek thy Brother* (1968).

In 1962 he married Lavinia Jean, eldest daughter of Sir Alan Frederick Lascelles, but the marriage was not a success and was dissolved two years later. Maxwell was in fact a bisexual, but in his leaning to adolescents of his own gender he was gentle in his affection, and many gained sophistication and wisdom from his patronage. In character he was impetuous and improvident, distrustful of affection and not free from fits of sudden malice. In conversation he was determined and concise and given the subject of his choice he would illuminate it with the light from a very penetrating mind. He was hypersensitive to beauty in many forms and had a rare gift of expressing in words what he saw and felt. His wit was subtle, devastating, or cruel, as the occasion suited. He had much courtliness and charm, but his temper was mercurial and he might insult even his friends with some conviction, although the insult would be just as speedily repaired. Those who knew him loved him: but acquaintances were often treated to the other side of his complex personality.

In business matters he was over-sanguine, yet in other respects he was a reasoning pessimist, anticipating misfortune and looking upon good luck as a bonus earned against the odds.

As a natural historian his name was respected though his views were often controversial, but as a humanitarian he was perhaps less well known. His lasting shock at the condition of the Sicilian peasants led to his involvement with the Dolci Trust. He was a member of, among other groups, the Wildfowl Trust and the Fauna Preservation Society, and was president of the British Junior Exploration Society. He was also a fellow of the Royal Society of Literature, the Royal Geographical Society, and the Royal Zoological Society (Scotland).

In 1968 the house at 'Camusfearna'—by which name he immortalized his west-highland retreat—was burnt down and he moved to Eilean Ban, a small island off Kyle of Lochalsh. Here he conceived a scheme for a wildlife park but this idea was only in its infancy when he fell ill with an inoperable cancer. During the short illness which followed his strength of character was impressively displayed. He died at Inverness 7 September 1969 with dignity and a minimum of fuss.

There is a pencil drawing of Maxwell by (Sir) Peter Scott, dated 1946.

[Gavin Maxwell, *The House of Elrig*, 1965; Richard Frere, *Maxwell's Ghost*, 1976; personal knowledge.]   RICHARD FRERE

MAXWELL FYFE, DAVID PATRICK, EARL OF KILMUIR (1900–1967), lord chancellor. [See FYFE.]

MEADE-FETHERSTONHAUGH,   SIR HERBERT (1875–1964), admiral, born in London 3 November 1875, was the third of four sons of Richard James Meade [q.v.], Lord Gillford, later fourth Earl of Clanwilliam and admiral of the fleet, and his wife, Elizabeth Henrietta, daughter of Sir, Arthur Edward Kennedy [q.v.], governor of Queensland.

Entering the *Britannia* in 1889, Meade served as midshipman in the *Canada*, a fully rigged steel corvette on the North America station. He was promoted lieutenant in 1897, while serving in the *Iphigenia* in China. In 1901 he joined the *Ophir*, a liner commissioned for a state visit to India by the Duke and Duchess of York, later King George V and Queen Mary. After enjoying command of two early destroyers, he joined

the *Venerable*, second flagship in the Mediterranean, in 1902. In 1904 a cable accident on her forecastle was nearly fatal. Indomitable spirit restored him to duty two years later, with a permanently shortened leg and a wound pension. Seldom free from pain, he refused to be handicapped and resumed tennis and riding. As first lieutenant of the Admiralty yacht *Enchantress* from 1906 he earned promotion to commander in 1908.

After two years in the Mobilization Department of the Admiralty Meade returned to destroyers in 1912 as a divisional leader in the *Goshawk*, and to the general advantage held sea commands for most of the war. Under (Sir) Reginald Tyrwhitt [q.v.], a leader after his own heart, his vigorous part in the Heligoland Bight action on 28 August 1914, including sinking the destroyer V.187, brought appointment to the DSO and promotion to captain in December. In the *Meteor* he was in the forefront of the action with German battle cruisers near the Dogger Bank on 24 January 1915. After torpedoing the *Blücher* his ship was disabled and was towed back to Immingham. In the light cruiser *Royalist* he joined the Grand Fleet, and at Jutland, late on 31 May 1916, with the *Caroline* carried out a torpedo attack on German battleships which only they identified as hostile. After commanding the cruiser *Ceres* Meade returned to the Admiralty in 1918 and became chief of staff to the commander-in-chief Rosyth the next year.

In 1921 Meade was selected to command the battle cruiser *Renown* for the Prince of Wales's visit to India, China, and Japan, and was appointed CVO in 1922. He then became captain of the Royal Naval College, Dartmouth (1923), until promoted to flag rank in 1925. He was appointed CB during this year.

As rear-admiral commanding Mediterranean destroyer flotillas 1926–8, Meade was in his element. Rejecting the official historian's dictum that the disappointing results achieved by destroyers during the night after Jutland were solely due to the limitations of the torpedo, he cultivated methods which, although no comparable opportunity arose, were fruitful in the war of 1939–45. He was promoted KCVO in 1929 and to vice-admiral the following year. In 1931 he was given command of the royal yachts and appointed honorary naval aide-de-camp. After inheriting the property of Up Park in 1930 from Miss Fetherstonhaugh (to whom H. G. Wells's mother had been housekeeper) Meade assumed the additional name of Fetherstonhaugh by royal licence, but remained 'Jimmy' Meade to his friends. He was promoted to admiral in July 1934, became an extra equerry to the King on relinquishing command later in the year, and was promoted GCVO. Two years later he retired at his own request. He was reappointed extra equerry in each succeeding reign.

The House of Lords saw little of him when he was sergeant at arms in 1939-46, for on the declaration of war he turned convoy commodore, transferring to the Home Guard when invasion seemed imminent, in the hope of getting to closer grips with the enemy. Later he happily became a lieutenant RNVR in the Small Vessels Pool, which provided runner crews and miscellaneous services. Not every ship returning to Spithead for replenishment when supporting the Normandy landings recognized him in this role, but those who did saw in him a heartening example of service. He died 27 October 1964 at Up Park, near Petersfield.

In 1911 Meade married Margaret Ishbel Frances (died 1977), eldest daughter of Edward Carr Glyn, bishop of Peterborough; they had two sons and two daughters.

A portrait by Sir Oswald Birley hangs in Up Park which was made over to the National Trust in 1954.

[Private information; personal knowledge.]
P. W. BROCK

MEEK, CHARLES KINGSLEY (1885-1965), anthropologist and colonial administrator, was born 24 June 1885 in Larne, Northern Ireland, the son of James Brady Meek, a Presbyterian minister, and his wife, Mary Elizabeth McCarter. Educated at Rothesay Academy and Bedford School, he went up to Brasenose College, Oxford, as a Colquitt exhibitioner at the relatively mature age of twenty-one. His undergraduate days were remarkable only for a decision to change his career: having graduated BA in theology in 1910, he entered the Colonial Administrative Service. In 1912 he was posted to Nigeria. This was the time when F. J. D. (later Lord) Lugard [q.v.] decided to use his new post of governor-general to extend his policy of indirect rule from the successful north to a suspicious south. Fundamental to this was an exact knowledge of traditional institutions. From this point of view, much of Nigeria was still something of a blank map. As commissioner of the decennial census of 1921, Meek was able to exploit the interest he had pioneered in the social anthropology of the peoples he administered. With the publication of *The Northern Tribes of Nigeria* (1925), an ethnological account which became far more important than the census survey it was intended to be, he introduced to the outside world a large number of tribal groups of whose existence it had hitherto been unaware.

By then, however, Meek's talents had been recognized by his appointment in 1924 to one of the two posts of government anthropologist established by Nigeria. An early fruit of this happy selection was the appearance of his *A Sudanese Kingdom* (1931), a study of 'divine kingship' among the Jukun-speaking peoples. This was followed in the same year by *Tribal Studies in Northern Nigeria*, still a work of reference for many of the lesser-studied peoples of the region. Meek, who had been promoted to the rank of resident and transferred to Southern Nigeria in 1929, resigned from the Colonial Service because of ill health in 1933. He now devoted the second half of his life to the scholarly study of the field in which he had gained such a rich experience in his first career.

Largely self-taught in ethnological science, with some help from R. R. Marett and C. G. Seligman [qq.v.], for Meek to have written *A Sudanese Kingdom* was a noteworthy achievement. In recognition of this and his record of anthropological research, in 1934 he was granted leave by Oxford University to supplicate for the degree of D.Sc. Two years later the Royal Anthropological Society (he was a fellow of both the Royal Anthropological Institute and the Royal Geographical Society) awarded him its Wellcome gold medal. Following the appearance of his greatest single undertaking in the Nigerian Service, his *Law and Authority in a Nigerian Tribe: a Study in Indirect Rule* (1937), a meticulous analysis of legal and political institutions of the highly individualistic Ibo people of south-eastern Nigeria in which he sympathetically disproved the apparently anarchic nature of their acephalic society, he was appointed to the Heath Clark lectureship in the university of London for 1938-9. These lectures, delivered at the London School of Hygiene and Tropical Medicine by Meek, W. M. Macmillan, and E. R. J. Hussey, published as *Europe and West Africa* (1940). To this Dictionary Meek contributed the notice of E. P. C. Girouard.

In 1943 Meek was elected to a senior research fellowship at his old college. His experience and advice were valuable to the Colonial Office as it set about designing a fresh style of training course for its putative post-war administrative cadets, and when these 'Devonshire' courses started in 1947 he was appointed to the university lectureship in anthropology earmarked for this programme. A long association with the International Institute of African Languages and Cultures meant that Meek was also closely involved in plans for its Ethnographic Survey. In 1946 he published *Land Law and Custom in the Colonies*, a work he subsequently revised in the Colonial Research Studies series as *Land Tenure and Land Administration in Nigeria and the Cameroons* (1957). He also produced

Colonial Law (1948), a bibliography of African land law and tenure.

On Meek's retirement in 1950, his college paid him the unexampled tribute of electing him tutor and supernumerary fellow, with continuing membership of the governing body. Modest to a degree—he used to deprecate his own contributions as an anthropologist when set beside those of his younger, professionally trained colleagues—and a general favourite among dons and pupils alike, he found life in the common room as congenial as his colleagues found his presence there. He took an interest in all members of the college and their families (a trait particularly manifest at Christmas), and was always ready for a round of golf. If his kind of applied anthropology has grown up over the years so that it has become fashionable to denigrate it as illustrating the subservience of the science to colonial administration, his reputation as a distinguished pioneer of anthropological studies in Nigeria remains secure. Along with the work of P. A. Talbot and R. S. Rattray, his was the first detailed scholarly account of the diverse peoples of West Africa.

On leaving Oxford in 1957, Meek moved to Tunbridge Wells. He did not lose his interest in Africa, and it was a tribute to his standing among the new phenomenon of academic Africanists that he was invited to contribute the first article to the first issue of the *Journal of African History* (1960). He chose as his theme 'The Niger and the Classics: the history of a name'. His last years were somewhat marred by ill health. He died at Eastbourne 27 March 1965.

Meek married in 1919 Helen Marjorie (died 1960), daughter of Lieutenant-Colonel C. H. Innes Hopkins. They had two sons, the elder of whom also joined the Colonial Administrative Service and became head of the civil service in Tanganyika.

[*The Times*, 14 April 1965; *West Africa*, 24 April 1965; *The Brazen Nose* (Brasenose College magazine), 1965; *Colonial Office List*, 1932; private information; personal knowledge.]   A. H. M. KIRK-GREENE

MENON, VAPAL PANGUNNI (1894-1966), Indian public servant and author, son of C. Sankunni Menon and his wife, Vapal Kunhikutty Amma, was born 30 September 1894 in Ottopalam, a town in the Malabar district of the Madras presidency, now part of Kerala State. The circumstances of his family were modest, but this was no handicap to his intellectual development or his enterprise. He decided, after matriculating from Ottopalam High School, that he had completed his formal education, and ran away from home in order to avoid being sent to college.

Menon's first employment was with the Imperial Tobacco Company in Bangalore; then, independently, as a contractor in the Kolar gold-fields. His first venture in this unfamiliar business succeeded, but his second was disastrous. Penniless, but too proud to return to his family, he travelled northwards, far from the scene of his failure. After a short experience as schoolmaster in Bhopal, he decided to seek employment with the Government of India. On his journey he was helped by an old Sikh, who gave him twenty rupees with his blessing, saying that he would consider himself repaid if Menon would one day, in turn, help another in need. In Simla, Menon found another benefactor in a fellow Malayali, Anantan, then a superintendent in the Home Department of the Government of India. Anantan took him into his home and also found him a clerk's post in his department.

Menon was now in his twentieth year; and the year, 1914, was a political and constitutional watershed. The war of 1914-18 and India's share in it strengthened her claim for an advance towards self-government. The recommendations of the Montagu-Chelmsford report took shape in the Government of India Act, 1919, and thereafter constitutional progress marched by stages of commission and conference to the Government of India Act, 1935. The subject of constitutional reform was handled in the Home Department, and Menon made good use of his opportunity to become expert in this field. His ability was noticed, and rewarded with the title of Rao Bahadur. He joined the new Reforms Office in 1930, and went to London in 1931 as a member of the secretarial staff of the second Indian Round Table conference. In 1933 he was assistant secretary in the Reforms Office, in 1934 under-secretary, and in 1936 deputy secretary under (Sir) Hawthorne Lewis, the reforms commissioner.

The outbreak of war in 1939 frustrated the hope of achieving the federal scheme of the Act of 1935, and the political parties in India seized the opportunity to press their respective, irreconcilable claims as conditions for co-operation with the war effort. The Reforms Office was brought directly into the sphere of the governor-general's responsibilities, becoming part of his secretariat. Menon was appointed CIE in 1941, and in the next year succeeded H. V. Hodson as reforms commissioner, in which capacity he occupied a key position of trust and influence as constitutional adviser to the last three viceroys of India.

The progress towards independence unrolled, against a background of varying fortunes of war and increasing communal bitterness, in a series of three-cornered entanglements between the ruling power, the Congress Party, and the

Muslim League. In the Simla Conference of 1945, in discussion of the Cabinet mission's proposals, the formation of the so-called interim Government, and the final evolution and acceptance of the plan for the transfer of power, and in all the manœuvring between these stages, Menon played an indispensable role. In May 1947 Menon saved from shipwreck Lord Mountbatten's negotiations with the party leaders, by successfully advocating his own plan for an early transfer of power to two central Governments with dominion status, in substitution at the last moment for the unacceptable formula favoured by the British Cabinet. Mountbatten had the highest regard for Menon's judgement and character.

Menon had been appointed CSI in 1946. On 3 January 1948 he received at the governor-general's hands the unique distinction of a certificate conferring on him the dignity of a knight commander in that Order, without the title and insignia which, as a servant of the independent Government of India, he could not accept.

Shortly before independence Sardar Vallabhbhai Patel [q.v.], the deputy prime minister of India, had chosen Menon to be, as secretary of the States Department, the instrument of integrating the Indian states with the new dominion. In less than two and a half years Menon had completed the task. More than 550 states, great and small, half a million square miles, and 87 million people were added to India. The solution was summary, but realistic; and except in disputed Kashmir and in Hyderabad, it was accomplished peacefully.

When Patel died in December 1950 Menon had lost, in the space of three years, two powerful patrons. The British-Indian Government had recognized and rewarded his exceptional talents; and, had Patel lived, these would have been employed for longer in his country's service. But Menon's spectacular record, and his close association with Patel, had attracted envy and ill will in high places. After a short appointment as governor of Orissa in 1951, then as member of the Finance Commission, he was retired from service prematurely in March 1952.

But his retirement in Bangalore was productive. He fulfilled a promise to Patel by writing two books, *The Story of the Integration of the Indian States* (1956) and *The Transfer of Power in India* (1957), two masterly first-hand historical documents. A much shorter work, *An Outline of Indian Constitutional History*, was published in 1965.

Modest, for all his success, frank and tenacious of purpose, Menon had many friends and few enemies. He was a staunch Indian patriot, and at the same time a friend and admirer of the British and their institutions. In this there was no conflict of loyalties. Menon contributed much to the reconciliation of differences between Britain and India, and he was one of the main architects of the bridge which ultimately spanned them.

In 1925 Menon had married Anantan's niece, who bore him two sons. This marriage was dissolved, and in 1941 he married Anantan's widow, Srimati Kanakamma, who had brought up his sons with her own daughter as one family, and who survived him when he died in Jubbulpore, Madhya Pradesh, 1 January 1966.

[*The Times*, 4 January 1966; Alan Campbell-Johnson, *Mission with Mountbatten*, 1951; H. V. Hodson, *The Great Divide*, 1969; private information; personal knowledge.]

W. H. J. CHRISTIE

MENZIES, SIR STEWART GRAHAM (1890–1968), head of the Secret Intelligence Service, was born in London 30 January 1890, the second son of John Graham Menzies, of independent means, and his wife, Susannah West, daughter of Arthur Wilson [q.v.], of Tranby Croft. After the death of John Menzies his widow married in 1912 Lieutenant-Colonel Sir George Holford, an officer in the Life Guards and equerry-in-waiting to Queen Alexandra and extra equerry to King George V.

Stewart Menzies was educated at Eton where he won no academic distinctions but was a popular boy and a fine athlete who was master of the beagles, and president of the Eton Society ('Pop') in 1908 and 1909. Immediately on leaving school he joined the Grenadier Guards in 1909 but was transferred to the Life Guards in the following year. While in the army he acquired a love of horses and of hunting which remained with him for the rest of his life and to which he returned with special zest after his retirement. His country home was in Wiltshire and he hunted mainly with the Duke of Beaufort's hounds. He was well into his seventies when a fall in the hunting field started a decline in his health. While resident in London, Menzies enjoyed an active social life. He was a great frequenter of White's Club and also belonged to St. James's and the Turf.

Menzies first came into contact with the intelligence world during the war of 1914–18. He was sent to France in 1914 with the British Expeditionary Force and in 1915, after recovering from a gas attack, was assigned an intelligence appointment at GHQ. The work appealed to him and he showed a flair for it, which was aided by his knowledge of European languages. He ended the war with the DSO and MC and the rank of brevet major and in 1919 was again selected for an intelligence appointment: military liaison officer with the Secret Intelligence Service, also known as MI6. He thus began a career in professional intelligence which was to continue for thirty-two years. He was promoted colonel in 1932 and retired from the Life Guards in 1939.

Menzies became 'C' in full command of the Secret Intelligence Service only three months after the outbreak of war in 1939. It was a crucial moment in the history of his service. Between the wars it had been starved of funds by successive Governments and consequently entered the war ill-prepared for the tasks demanded by total warfare. Expansion and reconstruction had to take place simultaneously, and these tasks were further complicated by set-backs such as that at Venlo, when Gestapo men crossed the German-Dutch border to capture two SIS officers who had gone there to contact agents of the underground opposition in Germany. The whole character of the service gradually changed. Hitherto the staff had been recruited mainly from retired Service officers; now that it could attract men and women of talent from all walks of life the management problems were new and intricate. Added to these Menzies had to steer his service through a complicated maze of inter-Service relations, created by the existence of a new British secret service—SOE—and a new American service—OSS—operating in parallel with his own in neutral and enemy territories. In these circumstances it was to take some time before SIS could develop a momentum of its own and forge those links with Allied intelligence and resistance organizations which were to prove valuable in the later stages of the war.

Besides commanding SIS, Menzies was responsible for the over-all supervision of the Government Code and Cipher School (GC & CS), whose greatest achievement in the war of 1939-45 was the breaking of the German 'Enigma'. This was an electro-magnet enciphering machine, which generated a wide range of separate ciphers in use by the German army, navy, and air force. German experts had rendered their machine so sophisticated that by the outbreak of the war they considered it safe even if captured. It was therefore used to communicate vital German war secrets. These began to be made available by GC & CS by the end of 1940 and by the end of 1943 they were decrypting as many as 40,000 naval and 50,000 army and air force messages a month. It is therefore not difficult to imagine the crucial importance of this source of intelligence to the Allied war effort. But it was also a highly vulnerable source for the security of which Menzies was finally responsible. This could mean refusing some forceful operational commander the right to act on one of its intelligence leads if by so doing he might endanger the source. In retrospect this responsibility was

admirably discharged and the secret of the GC & CS's remarkable cryptographic successes was preserved until the end of the war. Not surprisingly, with such excellent information at his disposal, Menzies's influence with the prime minister, War Cabinet, and chiefs of staff was considerable.

The stamina and toughness Menzies displayed during the war years came as something of a surprise to those acquainted with his easy and affluent way of life between the wars. Running his service and supervising GC & CS meant exceptionally long hours of office work, besides which he became in time a member of Churchill's intimate circle of war advisers. This meant being on call to brief the prime minister at any hour of the day or night. On such occasions he had to answer for more than his own responsibilities for he was the only intelligence director to enjoy this privileged position. As an intelligence man his strength lay in a quick grasp and understanding of operational issues and in his shrewd management of a network of powerful contacts. Organization and long-term planning were not his strong points. He preferred the getting of intelligence to the mosaic work of the assessors and in this respect he resembled one of his American opposite numbers, Allen Dulles, another man to enter intelligence from a patrician background.

To many foreigners Menzies came to seem the personal embodiment of an intelligence mystique they believed characteristically and historically British. Whatever the truth of this, it contributed to his international influence and was a potent factor in establishing the Anglo-American and other Allied intelligence alliances. During the war years his service had a greater role to play than ever before. By the time he retired in 1951 the pressures of the cold war had caused the intelligence world to develop in major ways, and to acquire potent technological resources: a very different world from the one he had entered in 1919.

Menzies was appointed CB in 1942, KCMG in 1943, KCB in 1951, and received a number of foreign decorations.

In 1918 he married Lady Avice Ela Muriel Sackville, daughter of the eighth Earl De La Warr. He obtained a divorce from her in 1931 and in 1932 married Pamela Thetis (died 1951), daughter of Rupert Evelyn Beckett, nephew of the first Baron Grimthorpe [q.v.], and divorced wife of James Roy Notter Garton. He married thirdly in 1952 as her fourth husband, Audrey Clara Lilian, daughter of Sir Thomas Paul Latham, first baronet. Menzies had one daughter by his second wife. He died in London 29 May 1968.

[*The Times*, 31 May and 6 June 1968; private information; personal knowledge.]

MERRIMAN, FRANK BOYD, BARON MERRIMAN (1880-1962), judge, was born at Knutsford 28 April 1880, the eldest son of Frank Merriman, JP, of Knutsford, and his wife, Mariquita, fourth daughter of John Pringle Boyd. N. J. Merriman [q.v.] was his great-uncle. Boyd, as he was called by most who knew him well, was educated at Winchester where he won the English speech prize and played an active part in the debating society. Circumstances did not permit him to enter a university and he became articled to a firm of Manchester solicitors. Later he decided to go to the bar and he was called by the Inner Temple in 1904. He became a pupil in the chambers of the future lord chief justice, Gordon (later Viscount) Hewart [q.v.].

In the war of 1914-18 Merriman served with distinction in the Manchester Regiment and on the staff. He was thrice mentioned in dispatches and in 1918 appointed OBE. On his return to civilian life he made such rapid progress that in 1919 he was able to take silk. In 1920 he was appointed recorder of Wigan. In the meantime he took a keen interest in politics and was adopted as Conservative candidate for the Rusholme division of Manchester. In 1924 he won this seat after a contest with the Liberal candidate C. F. G. Masterman [q.v.] and retained it until his elevation to the bench in 1933, when he joined other Wykehamists of his generation who also became High Court judges. He gave up the recordership of Wigan when in March 1928 he succeeded Sir Thomas Inskip (later Viscount Caldecote, q.v.) as solicitor-general. This period of office ended in June 1929; in January 1932 he was reappointed, until in September 1933 he became president of the Probate, Divorce, and Admiralty division and was subsequently sworn of the Privy Council.

The Admiralty work of the division was much shrunken by a world-wide decline in shipping. Probate work continued much as it had been before his appointment, but the flood of divorce cases increased and continued to do so during the whole of his presidency. His work in that office was carried out with great energy and efficiency, none the less because he had little experience in the class of work he had to perform. He had previously had a substantial practice as a junior and as a silk at the common law bar on the Northern circuit and in London. One memorable case in which he appeared was an action brought by Captain Peter Wright against Lord Gladstone [q.v.] arising out of defamatory statements made by Wright concerning W. E. Gladstone. The thankless task of appearing for Wright he performed with ability, tact, and good taste which won general admiration.

In September 1929 Merriman appeared before the commission appointed to report on the Palestine disturbances of August 1929. He led the team of barristers who appeared for the Palestine Zionist Executive and the Zionist Organization. The complaints made by his clients against the Mufti of Jerusalem and the Palestine Arab Executive were that they were influenced by the general political motive of determined opposition to the policy of the Jewish National Home based on the Balfour Declaration.

At the bar Merriman was vigorous and fair in controversy and the same qualities were recognized by his fellow members of the House of Commons. On the bench he was above all conscientious and anxious to give of his best, never sparing himself in the attempt to arrive at a just conclusion in every case. Some indication of the amount of work which devolved on him and the other judges of the division is shown by comparison of the numbers of divorce petitions presented in 1933, when he was appointed, then under 5,000 in the year, with the figure of over 50,000 reached in 1947. The judicial strength of the division increased from three to eleven before the end of his presidency.

The Act of 1937 which enlarged the grounds for divorce was no doubt in part responsible for this vast increase in the work, but Merriman never questioned the propriety of the Act. As a judge he did all he could to surmount the difficulties in his way and, in spite of a temperament which led him at times to explosions of anger, always directed at what appeared to him to be unjust or otherwise objectionable, he earned the respect and affection of those who practised before him. He was a just and upright judge who remained in office until he died at the age of eighty-one without losing the capacity to deal judicially and thoroughly with each case which he had to try. At the last he was engaged in a matrimonial appeal in the House of Lords upon which he was due to deliver his opinion on the day of his death. The greater part of it was included in the opinion of one of the colleagues who had been sitting with him.

During a happy childhood at Knutsford as a member of a large family with many relations in the neighbourhood, Merriman developed a love of music, the theatre, and sport, particularly fishing and golf. These interests were with him to the end. He did not abandon his attachment to Knutsford which he visited regularly when opportunity offered in order to take part in various church and civil occasions and where he retained many friendships. In London he was a popular member of the Savile Club and at the Inner Temple he became a bencher in 1927 and in 1949 deputized for King George VI as treasurer. In 1941-6 he was chairman of the bishop of London's commission on City churches. He was an honorary member of the American and Canadian bar associations and received an honorary LLD from McGill University. He was knighted in 1928, created a baron in 1941, and appointed GCVO in 1950.

In 1907 Merriman married Eva Mary (died 1919), second daughter of the late Revd Henry Leftwich Freer, by whom he had two daughters. In 1920 he married, secondly, Olive McLaren (died 1952), third daughter of Frederick William Carver, of Knutsford. In 1953 he married, thirdly, Jame Lamb, younger daughter of James Stormonth, of Belfast. Merriman died in London 18 January 1962. A portrait by John Merton is in the possession of the family.

[Private information; personal knowledge.]

HODSON

MERTON, SIR THOMAS RALPH (1888–1969), physicist, was born at Wimbledon 12 January 1888, the only son of Emile Ralph Merton and his wife, Helen, daughter of Thomas Meates. His father was for a time a partner in the family business of Henry Merton & Co. founded by his eldest brother in London in 1860; another brother, William, had founded the Metallgesellschaft in Frankfurt-am-Main in 1881. Merton was educated at Farnborough School and at Eton where he had the good fortune to come under Dr T. C. Porter, the physics master, who encouraged him to start research. In the interval between leaving Eton in 1905 and going up to Balliol in 1906, Merton worked at King's College, London, where he made a lifelong friend of (Sir) Herbert Jackson [q.v.] and met J. W. Nicholson. He went to Balliol with a distinguished group of Etonians, including Julian Grenfell and Ronald Knox [qq.v.] and (Sir) Julian Huxley. In view of his delicate health and his promise as an investigator, the university allowed Merton to go straight to a research thesis without taking final schools, a unique privilege well justified by subsequent events. His investigation of the physical properties of solutions of caesium nitrate was awarded a B.Sc. in 1910.

Meanwhile Merton had been reading widely and his active brain was busy with ideas for improving the techniques of spectroscopy which was to be the main field of his researches. While still a schoolboy he had equipped a room in his home as a laboratory and after his marriage in 1912 his spectroscopic laboratory was moved to his London house in Gilbert Street. Two years later war broke out and Merton, having been rejected for active service on grounds of health, was commissioned in 1916 as a lieutenant in the Royal Naval Volunteer Reserve in the secret service; his distinguished services, in identifying the secret ink carried by German spies in their clothing and inventing a new means of secret writing, won a mention in dispatches.

After 1913 a steady stream of papers came from Merton's private laboratory which had the latest spectroscopic equipment. His early work was on the absorption spectra of solutions, but he soon changed to the spectra of gases and to astrophysics, which were to be the main fields of his investigations. All his early papers dealt with some significant problem and they were distinguished by the beauty and accuracy of his experimental techniques. In 1916 he obtained his D.Sc. (Oxford) and was appointed lecturer in spectroscopy at King's College, London. In the same year his first joint paper with J. W. Nicholson appeared. It was a fortunate chance which brought together Nicholson's brilliant mathematical analysis and Merton's experimental skill. The paper dealt with the broadening of spectrum lines in a condensed discharge and by an ingenious technique Merton measured the discontinuities in the lines due to their partial breaking up into components under the influence of the magnetic field between adjacent atoms. Two other joint papers appeared applying the same technique to the measurement of the spectra of hydrogen and helium. In these papers the distribution of intensity of some stellar lines was reproduced in the laboratory for the first time.

In 1911 Balliol elected Merton to a research fellowship and the university made him reader (from 1920 professor) in spectroscopy. He worked on a series of problems, usually with a young student as his assistant. He had been elected into the Royal Society in 1920 and in 1922 gave the Bakerian lecture to the Royal Society with (Sir) Sydney Barratt on the spectrum of hydrogen. They cleared up a number of discrepancies in the secondary spectrum of hydrogen which were shown to be due to the hydrogen molecule, and they also showed the profound influence that traces of impurities can exert on gas spectra.

In 1923 Merton left Oxford to live at Winforton House in Herefordshire, the estate he had acquired with three miles of salmon fishing in the Wye. Merton was a good shot and a most skilful fisherman. He caught the second largest salmon taken in the Wye, weighing 63 pounds. He transferred his laboratory to Winforton, so that he was able to combine a sporting life with his scientific research to the great benefit of his health.

One of the notable services Merton rendered to science was as treasurer of the Royal Society. His knowledge and experience of affairs benefited the society in many ways. He formed a finance committee of experts to control its finances, and it was on his initiative that charitable bodies were given power to invest in equities, where they had previously been limited to gilt-edged. The income of all the society's funds showed a large increase during the treasurership which he held from 1939 to 1956, an unusually long period.

In his early days at home Merton had exposed a number of phosphorescent salts to cathode rays and was surprised at the short period of the afterglow. To investigate this further he had exposed a mixture of salts with appropriate excitation and emission bands to the rays and had found that under these conditions the afterglow was much increased. He did nothing about it at the time but in 1938 he received a letter from Sir Henry Tizard [q.v.] asking for just this, without saying why. Shortly afterwards Merton was asked to join the Air Defence Committee and he was told of the application of his invention in the two-layer long-persistence radar screens which contributed so much to victory in the Battle of Britain.

Merton's other war inventions included the black paint which reduced the proportion of light reflected from bombers in a searchlight to less than one per cent; the use of nitrous oxide to accelerate fighter aircraft in battle; and a diffraction range-finder for fighters which was used against doodlebugs.

There is a gap of nearly twenty years between Merton's scientific papers of 1928 and 1947. But in these years he was busy in the laboratory and was taking out patents for his inventions. In 1947 Merton published two papers in a new field for him—microscopy. The first described an ingenious form of interference microscopy. But he soon returned to his lifelong interest in diffraction gratings, where his inventive genius is seen at its best. The rarity and expense of good diffraction gratings led Merton to devise in 1935 a method of copying them without loss of optical quality by applying a thin layer of a cellulose ester solution to an original plane grating. This pellicle he detached after evaporation of the solvent and applied its grooved surface to the moist gelatine film on a glass plate. After evaporation of the water the gelatine was found to bear a faithful record of the original rulings.

In 1948 Merton made an important basic advance in the science of ruling diffraction gratings. Since 1880 these had been ruled groove by groove by the method used by Rowlands. In place of this Merton ruled a very fine helix continuously on a steel cylinder which he then opened out upon a plane gelatine-coated surface by his copying method. No lathe could, however, rule a helix free from periodic errors of pitch and these Merton eliminated by means of a very simple and ingenious device. It consisted of a 'chasing lathe' by which a secondary helix was cut on the same cylinder with a tool mounted on a 'nut' lined with strips of cork pressed upon the primary lathe-cut helix. This device eliminated entirely the periodic errors as they were averaged by the elasticity of the cork.

Merton then handed over these processes to the National Physical Laboratory for further development and they have formed the basis of a considerable research programme. The 'blazed' gratings made by the Merton–NPL method became of great value in making available cheap infra-red spectrometers of high resolving power which have many applications in research and industry. The ruling of long gratings by this method has made possible their use for engineering measurements and machine tool control.

In 1930 Merton's eldest son, John, brought home the drawing prize from Eton: a turning-point in both their lives. It awoke in Merton some latent interest and he spent months in Italy with his son seeing all the great collections of Renaissance paintings. His study of the techniques of the Florentine painters was reflected in his son's pictures. Then he began to make his remarkable collection of pictures of the period 1450–1520. Merton had a photographic memory, great knowledge of pigments, and good aesthetic judgement which was shown by the fine quality of his collection. His outstanding acquisition was a delightful portrait of a young man by Botticelli. From 1944 until his death Merton was a member of the scientific advisory board of the National Gallery and its chairman from 1957 to 1965. He was also a trustee of the National Gallery and of the National Portrait Gallery from 1955 to 1962, in recognition of his high standing as a connoisseur.

In 1947 Merton bought Stubbings House, near Maidenhead, a small mansion in lovely grounds. Its spacious rooms made an admirable setting for his collection of pictures. His laboratory was probably the last private physical laboratory in Britain. He continued his research and papers and patents continued to appear. In 1957 he had several serious operations and thereafter he rarely left his home. He died there 10 October 1969. He was knighted in 1944 for his services during the war and in 1956 he was appointed KBE. He was awarded the Holweck prize in 1951 and the Rumford medal of the Royal Society in 1958.

In 1912 Merton married Violet Marjory (died 1976), daughter of Lieutenant-Colonel William Harcourt Sawyer; they had five sons, the eldest of whom painted a portrait of his father which is in the possession of the family.

[*The Times*, 13 October 1969; Sir Harold Hartley and D. Gabor in *Biographical Memoirs of Fellows of the Royal Society*, vol. xvi, 1970; personal knowledge.]

HAROLD HARTLEY

MIDDLETON, JAMES SMITH (1878–1962), secretary of the Labour Party, was born 12 March 1878 at Primrose Terrace, Clarborough, near Retford, the son of Alfred Edward Middleton, book-keeper, and his wife, Martha Odam, who had been a straw-plaiter. Later his father moved to Blackburn to work on a Lancashire newspaper, and still later to Cumberland, where he settled in Workington and became proprietor of the *Workington Star*. There was a second son of the marriage, and a daughter who died young.

Middleton was educated at a variety of elementary schools; in his farewell address to the Labour Party conference of 1944 he spoke of spending a period as a 'half-timer' in Rochdale. On finishing his schooling he went into his father's printing establishment as a 'boy-of-all-work'; but his interest lay less in his work than in politics. Both his father and his mother were socialists, and he became very early an unpaid officer in the local working-class movement. He was secretary of the Workington trades council, of the local branch of the Independent Labour Party, and after the foundation of the Labour Representation Committee which became the Labour Party he was local secretary of that also. It was in connection with his political work that he met his first wife, Mary Muir, who was also an ardent socialist and acted for some time as his assistant; they were married in 1900. But Middleton was getting restive in Cumberland, and in particular he was in some disagreement with his father over conditions in the printing works which he thought incompatible with socialist principles. He therefore decided to move to London.

He made the move in 1902, and for a while worked on a North London paper. But Joseph Bowerbeck, a railwayman who was chairman of the Workington trades council, had written a letter of recommendation to Ramsay MacDonald, who had not long been secretary of the Labour Representation Committee. Middleton was invited to lunch, and shortly afterwards was taken on as assistant secretary, part-time at first and after 1904 full-time; he had vivid memories of doing his work for the party in MacDonald's bedroom in the early days, and after the 1906 election of attending and taking notes at the first meeting of the new Parliamentary Labour Party.

Middleton was well placed, at the centre, for making contacts with his heroes in the party such as James Keir Hardie [q.v.]; and with the MacDonalds he and his wife had a very close friendship. He thought Margaret MacDonald one of the finest women in the world, and she for her part had a great admiration for Mary Middleton, with whom she collaborated particularly in schemes to assist working-class mothers and children. After Mary's untimely death in 1911 Mrs MacDonald started the first baby clinic in Britain as a memorial to her friend; but it had hardly come into existence before she herself died, and thereafter Middleton's relations with his chief became less close.

During the years before war broke out in 1914 Middleton continued to work hard and faithfully as assistant secretary to the Labour Party, meantime collecting a personal library, attending performances of plays by G. B. Shaw [q.v.], and eagerly making acquaintance with as many foreign socialists as possible, such as Jean Jaurès and Camille Huysmans. In the days of 'social unrest' just before the war, he had left-wing sympathies, as was shown by his signing the manifesto of the rebel Guild Socialists, led by G. D. H. Cole [q.v.] and William Mellor, when they came so near to capturing the Fabian Society. But his position as a subordinate official gave him little scope; and it was not until war broke out that he came into the public eye. This was as secretary to the War Emergency Workers' National Committee, a clumsily titled body which began its existence as the result of a conference held on 6 August 1914, when for the first time representatives of all sections of the working-class movement came together and decided to form an organization to protect standards of living and the democratic way of life under war conditions. This organization was housed in the Labour Party offices; and as running it looked like involving a great deal of work and travelling to provincial centres, too much to be carried by Arthur Henderson [q.v.] who in 1911 had succeeded MacDonald as party secretary, Middleton was given the post of secretary to the committee and made responsible for organizing all its multifarious activities during the war years. This he did to excellent effect, under the guidance of Sidney Webb [q.v.], for whose abilities Middleton developed a deep respect; he managed to keep on good terms with all its sometimes awkward personalities, and received the warm congratulations of that none too easy character H. M. Hyndman [q.v.].

When the war was over, the committee was allowed to lapse; Middleton returned to his earlier status, and though when Henderson took over the Home Office during the 1924 Labour Government he was given the title of acting secretary he did not find the arrangement a happy one, and when in 1929 he was offered a similar role refused to consider it unless he were entrusted with proper responsibility. (Henderson's well-known difficulty in delegation was an unfortunate trait of his.) Middleton's demands were met; and after Henderson's retirement in 1934 he served as party secretary until 1944, when he left public life with an eloquent speech to his last annual conference in which he passionately urged his comrades to 'remember the International'. He had been offered an honour in the spring of 1931, but declined it.

In 1913 Middleton married Alice Todd (died 1935), by whom he had a daughter. In 1936 he married Lucy Annie, second daughter of Sidney Cox, brass wire-drawer. She was a strong socialist, member of the ILP, who had stood for Parliament, with Middleton as her agent, in 1931, and in 1945 and 1950 was elected for the Sutton division of Plymouth. Middleton, after a long and peaceful retirement, during which he wrote a number of entries for this Dictionary, died at his London home 18 November 1962.

[Labour Party annual reports and conference reports; reports and minutes of the War Emergency Workers' National Committee; J. S. Middleton in *The Webbs and Their Work*, ed. M. Cole, 1949; personal knowledge; private information.]

MARGARET COLE

MILLS, PERCY HERBERT, first VISCOUNT MILLS (1890–1968), politician and industrialist, was born 4 January 1890 at Thornaby-on-Tees, the fourth child of Daniel Mills, wholesale confectioner of Stockton-on-Tees, and his wife, Emma Brown. His career was that of a self-made man who rose by his qualities of intelligence and character from a comparatively humble origin to become one of the most respected Cabinet ministers in the Governments in which he served. He was educated at the North Eastern County School, Barnard Castle, county Durham, but in 1905, aged fifteen, he left the North for London where he served his articles with W. B. Peat & Co., chartered accountants.

After completing his training he married in 1915 Winifred Mary, daughter of George Conaty, engineer and manager of Birmingham Tramways, by whom he had a daughter and a son. In 1919 Mills entered the firm of W. & T. Avery Ltd. (later also Averys Ltd.), weighing machine manufacturers of Birmingham, in whose employment he remained for thirty-eight years thereafter until his retirement in 1957. His original position was that of financial assistant to (Sir) Gilbert Vyle, managing director, under whom he became general manager in

1924. In 1927 he was appointed to the board and, following Vyle's untimely death in 1933, became managing director of the firm which was to be his industrial base in years to come.

On the outbreak of war in 1939 he was appointed, first, deputy director of ordnance factories in the Ministry of Supply and later in the dual capacity of controller general of machine tools (1940–4) and head of the production division in the Ministry of Production (1943–4). His services were acknowledged by a knighthood in 1942.

It was during this period that he made friends with and gained the confidence of many senior civil servants who were to be his collaborators in years to come: and, more, importantly, of Harold Macmillan, parliamentary secretary to the Ministry of Supply, 1940–2. They were close friends thereafter and, to the end of his life, he and Winifred used to dine *en famille* with Macmillan once a week.

In his memoirs Macmillan recorded of the machine tool control: 'Here one man emerged as the supreme figure trusted by all—even, after considerable struggles, by the Ministry of Aircraft Production.' This was Percy Mills. The war being concluded, Mills became head of the economic subcommission of the British element of the control commission for defeated Germany. During this time he obtained a reputation for toughness with Russian and French chauvinism which not only earned him the respect of the representatives of those countries, but the admiration of his British colleagues. While determined to reduced Germany's war potential he insisted that its civilian industries must be maintained and assisted towards recovery.

To this period belongs an incident with a touch of the Nelsonian blind-eye to it. The submarine yards of Bloehm & Voss were to be blown up according to instructions, but as their implementation approached Whitehall started to waver. On the arrival of a telegram which Mills suspected might contain orders countermanding the operation, he left it unopened and departed to ensure that existing orders were carried out. On returning with the mission accomplished, he opened the telegram, the contents of which were as he had supposed. After dictating his regrets that it had arrived too late to be implemented, he commented: 'They've nearly brought us to our knees in two wars running. We can well do without them.'

Following completion of his work on the control commission and his appointment as KBE in 1946, he became president of the Birmingham Chamber of Commerce in 1947, and in 1949 accepted the chairmanship of the newly established National Research Development Corporation, a post which he held until

1955. In 1951 he became honorary adviser on housing to Harold Macmillan, by this time minister of housing and very senior in the Cabinet, who had been asked to take over the relevant Ministry, to which it was widely suspected that the recently elected Conservative Party had made promises which they might be unable to keep. The problem was to mobilize production, for example brickmaking facilities. Mills set up Regional Housing Boards to do this; thus the Government implemented its promises and Macmillan's trust in and admiration of his colleague grew correspondingly. His memoirs give a picture of how he saw his friend, '. . . what we should do without him, I shudder to think. He approaches every problem with realism and precision; his suggestions are at once bold and ingenious; and he has a quiet persistence which enables him to get his way. . . . With his quiet but inflexible will [he] has really moulded the whole Ministry to our purpose. I could have done nothing without him.'

In 1953 Mills was honoured with a baronetcy and in 1955 reached the retiring age for executives at Averys, becoming non-executive chairman of the board and accepting appointments to other industrial boards coterminously. Two years later Macmillan became prime minister, and Mills was created Baron Mills in order to take his seat in the House of Lords as minister of power, a position which he held for two years until 1959, when he became paymaster general until 1961. There followed a further period in the Cabinet as minister without portfolio and deputy leader of the House of Lords in 1961-2 until Macmillan's reconstruction of the Cabinet, whereupon Mills, created a viscount in 1962, stepped out of political life to rejoin the board of Electric and Musical Industries and became chairman of, and later special adviser to, their electronic subsidiary, a post which he held until his sudden and unexpected death, 10 September 1968. He had left his Kensington home to post the morning mail and fell dead beside the post-box in Hornton Street. his widow survived him until 1974. He was succeeded in the peerage by his son, Roger Clinton (born 1919).

Mills's character was a blend of toughness and friendliness, bluntness and courtesy, seriousness of purpose and gaiety, combined with a formidable intelligence, power of decision, and intuitive insight. To his prime minister he was 'wise old Percy'. To an industrial colleague he was 'a tough driving chief executive'. To Civil Service colleagues he was remembered as a fount of gaiety and much recalled laughter. No one more enjoyed a bachelor dinner party, good food, and good wine, than Percy Mills. Notwithstanding his toughness and drive, it was recorded at Averys that 'his instinctive sense of management and the handling of men were always ahead of their time'. As president of the Birmingham, Wolverhampton, and Stafford district of the Engineering and Allied Employers' Federation, he once allowed a union representative to overreach himself. Suddenly and quietly Mills cut in: 'That is an impertinence.' After a painful interval the culprit, unable to improvise an escape-route, apologized. 'Thank you,' said Mills, smiling instantly and passing to the next business. The urbanity of his later years was learnt. 'When I was young,' he once remarked, 'I had a pretty fiendish temper. But I have learnt to control it. It isn't the right way to treat people and it achieves nothing.' That in the achievement of power he learnt humility could be a fitting epitaph for one of the most politically influential industrialists of his time.

[Harold Macmillan, *Tides of Fortune*, 1945–1955, 1969; private information; personal knowledge.]   HALSBURY

MILNER, JAMES, first BARON MILNER OF LEEDS (1889-1967), politician and lawyer, was born 12 August 1889 at Scholes near Leeds, the eldest son of James Henry Milner, solicitor, and for some years city coroner, and his wife, Elizabeth, daughter of Robert Tate, of Leeds. He was educated at Easingwold Grammar School, Leeds Modern School, and the university, where he obtained his LLB in 1911. He joined the family firm, J. H. Milner & Son, of Leeds and London, and eventually succeeded his father as senior partner.

At university Milner was an active member of the Officers' Training Corps; he became an officer in the Territorial Army and went as adjutant with his regiment to France after the outbreak of war in 1914. He served with great distinction, ending the war with the rank of major, the MC with bar, and a mention in dispatches. Wounded and taken prisoner, he twice attempted to escape but was recaptured. His wounds left him with a permanent limp and long afterwards, at the age of seventy-one, he had to have a leg amputated.

Milner's reflections during the war had brought him to the decision that he must support the Labour Party. Returning to Leeds to resume his lawyer's life, he became an active member of the local Labour Party and served on the city council in 1923-9. At different times he was either chairman or deputy chairman of the Improvements Committee when there was considerable replanning of the centre of the city. The Headrow of Leeds became one of the best-known streets in the country: Milner was responsible for the choice of the name and active in the negotiations which brought Lewis's to the city and to the Headrow. In 1928–9 Milner was both deputy lord mayor of Leeds and president of the Leeds Labour Party.

A man of courage, ability, and driving force, Milner was prominent in the general life of Leeds: a founder of the Leeds Civic Trust, president of the Leeds Law Society, vice-president of the Leeds Thoresby Society and of the Leeds National Savings Committee; an honorary member of the Leeds chamber of commerce and a patron of the Leeds Trustee Savings Bank. His valued help and advice were in constant demand and never refused; for he was abundantly blessed with the gifts of compassion and kindness.

In 1929 Milner became member of Parliament for South East Leeds and held the seat until 1951. He was quickly a noticeable figure in the House and had a fine record of active and responsible work. He became parliamentary private secretary to Christopher (later Viscount) Addison [q.v.], served on the Select Committee on Capital Punishment (1931), and went to India in 1932 as a member of the Indian Franchise Committee. From 1935 he was on the chairmen's panel of the House of Commons, and in 1943–5 he was chairman of the Fire Committee in charge of Civil Defence of the Houses of Parliament. In 1943 he became chairman of the Committee of Ways and Means, and thus deputy Speaker; he was sworn of the Privy Council in 1945. As chairman of the British Group of the Inter-Parliamentary Union he went frequently abroad—he was especially fond of travel—and in 1949 he was leader of the parliamentary delegation to Ceylon to present a Speaker's chair and mace to its new Parliament. He led parliamentary delegations to Austria in 1948 and Turkey in 1953.

The great disappointment of Milner's parliamentary life came with the return of the Conservatives to power in 1951 when the Labour Party nominated him to be the new Speaker, but Churchill had already decided to appoint W. S. Morrison (later Viscount Dunrossil, q.v.). For the first time since 1895 the House divided on the choice of a Speaker, due to the great resentment on the Labour benches that Milner, who had so frequently occupied the Speaker's chair since 1943, should have been passed over. It was also felt that their party leaders had not been sufficiently forceful in their negotiations with Churchill in pressing Milner's claim. Created a baron in 1951, Milner served for a time as a deputy Speaker of the House of Lords.

Milner, always affectionately known as 'Jim', was a tall, handsome, and distinguished looking man, who would stand out in any company. He took his public and political work with remarkable seriousness: never spared himself and was always approachable. He was made a freeman of the city of Leeds and was the Crown representative on the court and council of Leeds University of which he was an honorary LLD. He was a deputy lieutenant of the West Riding of Yorkshire; a vice-president of the Association of Municipal Corporations and of the Building Societies Association, and a past president of the Society of Yorkshiremen in London.

In 1917 Milner married Lois Tinsdale, daughter of Thomas Brown, of Leeds. They had two daughters and a son, Arthur James Michael (born 1923), who succeeded to the title when Milner died at his home in Leeds 16 July 1967.

[Private information; personal knowledge.]
S. Pearce

MILNER HOLLAND, Sir EDWARD (1902–1969), lawyer. [See Holland.]

MITCHELL, Sir PHILIP EUEN (1890–1964), colonial administrator, was born in Wimbledon 1 May 1890, the fifth son of Hugh Mitchell, barrister, late captain in the Royal Engineers, and his wife, Mary Catherine Edwards Creswell. His father practised in Gibraltar and Mitchell was educated in Spain until the age of thirteen when he went to St. Paul's School, where he was a prefect and in the eleven and fifteen. In 1909 he won an open scholarship to Trinity College, Oxford, where he obtained a second class in honour moderations in 1911.

Mitchell joined the Colonial Service in 1912 as an assistant resident in Nyasaland, fought throughout the war in the King's African Rifles, being awarded the MC and mentioned in dispatches, and after return to civil duty was transferred in 1919 to Tanganyika, where he spent the next eight years as a district officer. It was an important, formative period in his career for he lived in close contact with Africans, especially during the war when his 'battalion was almost continuously on the march living off the land'. He recorded that there was 'little comfort or relaxation, hardly any reading matter, but much time to get to know the African intimately'. He became fluent in three African languages and being an alert and intelligent observer acquired a profound knowledge of Africa and its peoples. He became convinced that education was 'the key to the future in which lay the destiny of Africa'.

In 1926 Mitchell was selected by the governor, Sir Donald Cameron [q.v.], who regarded him as the best district officer he had met, as assistant secretary (secretary from 1928) of native affairs, to put into operation his new system of native administration, somewhat misleadingly termed indirect rule. This was to base local authorities upon traditional institutions adapted to modern conditions. Mitchell proved an ideal agent and also the perfect foil, for Cameron, who lacked Mitchell's understanding of the Africans, might have been tempted to enforce his system with religious fervour; Mitchell was a realist who recognized that 'any system was but a means to an end (the progress and welfare of the people concerned) and had no intrinsic value in itself'. Under his supervision the system proved highly successful and came to be accepted as the model for colonial administration at that time.

In 1934 Mitchell was promoted chief secretary but he had barely assumed duty before, in 1935, he was appointed governor of Uganda. By contrast with Tanganyika, where he had been building a new administration upon the ruins of war, in Uganda Mitchell found a 'comparatively old-established government pursuing its tranquil way'. He subjected it to a rigorous appraisal, revitalized it, and gave it a new direction. He was particularly concerned with the quality of African leadership, seeing the need for an 'élite equal to the European in education, culture, and sophistication'. He sought to create this by developing higher education: through his efforts Makerere became the University College and Mulago the Teaching Hospital for East Africa.

In 1937 Mitchell was offered the governorship of Tanganyika but although there was no post he desired more he felt it his duty to remain to complete the tasks he had begun in Uganda. The war, however, soon brought new assignments of increasing responsibility elsewhere. In 1940 he became deputy chairman of the Governors' Conference to co-ordinate the East African war effort. In 1941 he was appointed to the staff of Sir A. P. (later Earl) Wavell [q.v.] with the rank of major-general to organize the administration of territories conquered or won back from the Italians. In 1942 when he was appointed governor of Fiji, it lay as the next step in the Japanese onrush, morale was low, and relations with the Americans left much to be desired. He organized and inspired its defence. With New Zealand help he raised the Fiji Military Forces, who soon earned a reputation as amongst the best of colonial troops. He established a relationship with the Americans of such mutual friendship and respect that, in spite of strong anti-imperialist sentiment, when British territory was recaptured it was taken for granted that he should assume the administration.

But his heart remained in Africa and there he returned in 1944 as governor of Kenya. His first concern was to improve co-operation between the East African Governments. After protracted consultations the East Africa High Commission was established with responsibility for the administration of common services and he guided it through its formative stages. In Kenya itself he believed strongly that 'all communities should have a share and a vital interest in the government according to their needs and capacities', and political advances were made to enable them to do so. The establishment of the Royal Technical College and the Muslim Institute provided facilities for higher education, and a major inquiry was set in train with the object of improving use of the land.

Unfortunately the outbreak of Mau Mau soon after his retirement in 1952 overshadowed his achievements. He was criticized for failing to foresee the danger and to take steps to avert it. But much of this was based on wisdom after the event. Mitchell was one of the main architects of East Africa, especially in laying the foundations for higher education. Few governors brought equal qualities of heart and mind to their task. With his brilliant intellect and outstanding experience Mitchell understandably at times became impatient with conventional attitudes which he considered out of date or unimaginative; this earned him a reputation for arrogance. But he was always accessible, ready to hear the other side, and gave credit where due. He was a well-built man and a keen sportsman: sailing, riding, shooting, fishing, and golf, at all of which he was highly proficient. He had a wide circle of friends, was a generous host and amusing raconteur.

Mitchell was appointed CMG in 1935, KCMG in 1937, and GCMG in 1947. He held the Brilliant star of Zanzibar, was a knight of St. John, and had the American Legion of Merit. In 1925 he married Margery, daughter of John D'Urban Tyrwhitt-Drake, of Port Alfred, Cape Province; they had no children. Mitchell died in Gibraltar 11 October 1964.

[Sir Philip Mitchell, *African Afterthoughts*, 1954; manuscript diaries, 1927-42, 15 vols., deposited at Rhodes House, Oxford; *The Times*, 13 October 1964; private information; personal knowledge.]

JOHN RANKINE

MONCKTON, WALTER TURNER, first VISCOUNT MONCKTON OF BRENCHLEY (1891-1965), lawyer and politician, was born 17 January 1891 in the village of Plaxtol, Kent, the eldest of the three children and elder son of Frank William Monckton, paper manufacturer, and his wife, Dora, daughter of William Golding. He was educated at Harrow, where he developed an early love of cricket, and, despite the fact that he could hardly see out of one eye, became a good wicket-keeper and was given his flannels; he played in the redoubtable Fowler's match of 1910 against Eton, as did his friend Harold Alexander (later Earl Alexander of Tunis, q.v.). Although he won an exhibition to Hertford College in 1910, Monckton went as a commoner to Balliol to join an immensely brilliant set of undergraduates. He obtained a third in classical honour moderations (1912) and a second in history (1914). In 1913 he was elected president of the Union, and in that capacity met Edward, Prince of Wales, who was then at Magdalen.

On the outbreak of war in 1914, despite the fact that his vision had not prevented him playing cricket or hunting, Monckton found it well-nigh impossible to join any of the armed forces, and in a state of frustration he decided to take the preliminary examinations for the bar. Eventually, with the help of his younger brother who was serving in the Queen's Own West Kent Regiment, he was commissioned into that regiment and served in France; he was awarded the MC in 1919. He was called to the bar the same year by the Inner Temple, and soon built up a flourishing and varied practice at the common law bar. In 1930 he took silk; he was recorder of Hythe (1930-7), chancellor of the diocese of Southwell (1930-6), and attorney-general to the Prince of Wales (1932-6).

In 1933 Monckton became constitutional adviser to the Nizam of Hyderabad and also the Nawab of Bhopal [qq.v.] at a time when the Round Table conference had produced a scheme for a federal India to which it was hoped the princes would accede. It fell to Monckton to advise and negotiate for the Nizam and other princes, and endeavour to obtain some reasonable concessions for them. After the Government of India Act had been passed in 1935 the princes had to decide whether or not to join the proposed federation and in the summers of 1935 and 1936 Monckton visited Hyderabad to advise the Nizam. The latter, a Muslim ruling a largely Hindu State, was anxious to retain his independence and his treaty rights with the British Crown. Monckton felt that the future of Hyderabad was best assured by accession to federal India under favourable terms.

From his second visit Monckton was recalled by the King to England where a crisis was developing. After the accession of the Prince of Wales to the throne, Monckton had been appointed attorney-general to the Duchy of Cornwall, a post he was to hold with a break of one year until he became a member of the Government in 1951. In that capacity he was deeply involved in events which culminated in the abdication in December 1936. He was the King's closest confidant and attended innumerable meetings on his behalf with the prime minister and other members of the Cabinet in an effort to find an acceptable solution to the constitutional crisis arising from the King's determination to marry Mrs Simpson. From 3 to 11 December Monckton was the King's sole companion at Fort Belvedere, from where he travelled frequently to London trying desperately to avoid what now seemed the inevitable. On the night of 11 December after the King had renounced the throne and broadcast to the nation he and Monckton drove together to Portsmouth where the *Fury* was waiting to take him into exile. On 1 January 1937 Monckton's name appeared in the honours list as a KCVO and as a mark of esteem, on the same day, King George VI dubbed him first knight of his reign. Until after the outbreak of war Monckton continued to act as go-between for the new King and the Duke of Windsor on financial and other matters.

After the outbreak of war in 1939 Monckton was appointed chairman of the Aliens Advisory Committee which heard appeals by those detained without trial under regulation 18B as being persons suspected of bearing allegiance to the enemy. Anxious to play a more positive part in the war, he applied to join the RAFVR, but instead the prime minister appointed him director-general of the Press and Censorship Bureau. In April 1940 he was appointed deputy director and in December director-general of the Ministry of Information, with his old friend, Cyril (later Viscount) Radcliffe, as his deputy.

In October 1941 Monckton was sent on a government mission to Russia, from where he went to Cairo as director-general of propaganda and information services; as such he was a member of the Middle East War Council. In February-May 1942 he acted as minister of state pending the arrival of R. G. (later Lord) Casey after the departure of Oliver Lyttelton (later Viscount Chandos). Later that year he paid a visit to the United States and Canada at the invitation of their respective Bar Associations and in January 1943 went on an official visit to Sweden. A difference of opinion with Churchill in April 1942 had put him out of favour but until the end of the war he was engaged in various government tasks. Although he had taken little active part in politics since his Oxford days and he was not a member of Parliament, he was restored to favour and appointed solicitor-general in the caretaker Government in May 1945. Ten years earlier he had refused this office. His most important task was to lead the United Kingdom delegation on the Reparations Commission in Moscow and Potsdam.

After Labour came into office in July, Monckton returned to the bar and immediately acquired an immense practice largely in appellate work and before parliamentary committees and at public inquiries. In January 1946 he paid the first of many post-war visits to Hyderabad, arriving some months ahead of the Labour Government's Cabinet mission which was led by the secretary of state, Lord Pethick-Lawrence, who was accompanied by A. V. Alexander (later Earl Alexander of Hillsborough) and Monckton's old friend, Sir Stafford Cripps [qq.v.]. Events had moved fast in the ten years since his last visit and Monckton had to try to convince the Nizam, who was a man of stubborn determination, that the chances of Hyderabad retaining independence were fast becoming remote.

Returning to India in April he joined the Hyderabad delegation to the Cabinet mission, whose plan left the future relations of the princely States and independent India open to negotiation, since British paramountcy would not be transferred. In November Monckton returned again to consult the viceroy in the hope of securing 'a reasonably sure prospect of survival' for the Faithful Ally of the British Government, the title granted to the Nizam by King George V. Monckton's efforts were of no avail. Early in 1947 Lord Mountbatten was appointed the last viceroy of India and charged with the duty of presiding over the grant of independence. Monckton now had the unenviable task of trying to persuade the intractable Nizam that the future of Hyderabad, the largest of the princely States, would be best safeguarded by an alliance of some nature with India. This was quite unacceptable to him and his more extreme followers. Monckton refused to give up the struggle and fought relentlessly after the transfer of power in 1947 to achieve a reasonable settlement, knowing full well that an independent Hyderabad was well-nigh unattainable. At last, to everyone's astonishment, the Indian Government agreed in June 1948 to accept the proposals which Monckton had worked out to the great advantage of the Nizam. Tragically the extremists in Hyderabad completely rejected them, and in September 1948 the State was occupied by the Indian Army. Throughout his long association with the Nizam, Monckton demonstrated his outstanding qualities of wisdom and firmness, and an immense loyalty for those whom he was advising.

In February 1951, at Churchill's wish, Monckton succeeded to the seat of Bristol West in the by-election following the death of Oliver Stanley [q.v.]. Two days after the general election in October he was summoned by the prime minister, expecting to be appointed a law officer again. To his surprise he was offered the post of minister of labour and national service. When he hesitated on the grounds of inexperience, the prime minister replied that his qualification was that he had no political past. Monckton replied 'I take it you do not expect me to have any political future'. Despite his diffidence he was a most successful and popular minister at a time of industrial strife and strikes. Monckton was quick to appreciate that, nevertheless, the unions numbered amongst their leaders men of good sense and moderation, and there grew up between them a warm relationship based on trust and mutual respect for the other's point of view, which was a unique achievement for a Conservative minister of labour. Inevitably he had critics to say he was weak and too conciliatory. He had an infinite capacity for seeing round and beyond the immediate problem, and with great insight and wisdom he was able to propose a just solution. Thereafter he never wavered, but inevitably there were occasions when his advice was not accepted. It was the policy of the Government to avoid friction with the unions at almost all cost and it is in this light that Monckton's political record must be judged.

After an exceptionally long and ardous spell of four years at the Ministry of Labour he moved in 1955 to defence. Although it was thought that this would give him a respite, he found himself at the heart of an international crisis. In July 1956 Colonel Nasser expropriated the Suez Canal Company, and although Monckton supported the strong stand taken by the Government, he was opposed to military intervention. Passionately loyal to his colleagues, and reluctant to resign lest he bring down the Government, he became paymaster-general in October 1956 and retired from the Government in January 1957. He was created a viscount and in the same year was made president of MCC in succession to Lord Alexander of Tunis. Having been president of Surrey County Cricket Club between 1950 and 1952, he was again elected in 1959, and remained in office until his death. In 1957-64 he was chairman of the Midland Bank and in 1958-65 chairman of the Iraq Petroleum Company.

In 1959 Monckton found himself burdened with another task fraught with difficulties. He was asked by the prime minister to preside over an advisory commission in preparation for the review in 1960 of the constitution of the Federation of the Rhodesias and Nyasaland. The report recommended changes in the constitution which would benefit Africans, changes in the racial policy of Southern Rhodesia, and envisaged the possibility of secession from the Federation. Monckton had spent many months travelling to all parts of the territory, returning regularly to England to attend to the affairs of the bank. The strain involved had a serious effect on his health. Several times in his career his health broke down under the prolonged pressure of dealing with problems with which he perhaps identified too closely.

Monckton was a governor of Harrow and standing counsel for Oxford University (1938–51). He received honorary degrees from Oxford, Bristol, and Sussex. In 1957 he was made an honorary fellow and visitor of Balliol and in 1963 he became the first chancellor of Sussex University. He was appointed KCMG in 1945, sworn of the Privy Council in 1951, and promoted GCVO in 1964.

Monckton was completely unpretentious and a man of immense charm. He was warm and sympathetic, and was frequently called upon for his advice and help, which he was never known to refuse. He was chairman of St. George's Hospital (1945–51) and of the Barristers Benevolent Association. In 1914 he married Mary Adelaide Somes (died 1964), daughter of Sir Thomas Colyer Colyer-Fergusson, third baronet; they had a son and a daughter. The marriage was dissolved in 1947 and in that year he married Bridget Helen, daughter of the ninth Lord Ruthven (a title to which she succeeded) and formerly wife of the eleventh Earl of Carlisle. Monckton died at his home at Folkington 9 January 1965, and was buried at Brenchley, where his ancestor, the Revd John Monckton, had been vicar in 1651. He was succeeded by his son, Gilbert Walter Riversdale (born 1915). There is a portrait by Sir James Gunn at the Midland Bank.

[Lord Birkenhead, *Walter Monckton*, 1969; private information; personal knowledge.]

DAVID KARMEL

MOORE-BRABAZON, JOHN THEODORE CUTHBERT, first BARON BRABAZON OF TARA (1884–1964), aviator and politician. [See BRABAZON.]

MORANT, GEOFFREY MILES (1899–1964), anthropologist and statistician, was born in Battersea, London, 15 July 1899, the third child of Henry Morant, headmaster of an elementary school in Lambeth, and his wife, Maria Elizabeth Miles. He was educated at Battersea Secondary School and, after service with the Machine-Gun Corps in World War I, at University College, London. He obtained a B.Sc. in applied statistics (second class honours, 1920), an M.Sc. in 1922, and a D.Sc. in 1926. He held Board for Scientific and Industrial Research and Crewdson Berington studentships and an 1851 exhibition from 1920 to 1926. In 1932 he won the Weldon memorial prize.

Morant was on the staff of the Department of Applied Statistics and was a pupil of Professor Karl Pearson [q.v.]. By the late 1920s Morant was the acknowledged leader of the biometric school of physical anthropologists. Much of his early work appeared in *Biometrika* (of which he was assistant editor). His first paper, 'On Random Occurrence in Space and Time when followed by a Closed Interval' (1921), was soon followed by a number of important contributions to physical anthropology setting new and critical standards. These included 'Tibetan Skulls' (1923) and 'Racial History of Egypt' (1925). In 1926 he showed that the so-called Iberian inhabitants of Neolithic Britain were of Nordic not Mediterranean origin. Subsequent work confirmed Morant's views, which were unconventional at that time. Four important studies on 'Palaeolithic Man' appeared in the *Annals of Eugenics* (1926–30). In 1935, in collaboration with Pearson, he produced a lavishly illustrated study of the 'Wilkinson' head of Oliver Cromwell. This showed the relic to be the Protector's head and shed new light on his death and the disposal of the remains. This work led to advances in forensic medicine first used in the trial of Dr Ruxton.

When Hitler came to power Morant was disturbed by the manner in which his discipline was being perverted for political ends. In an article 'An attempt to Estimate the Variability of Various Populations' (1939) in *Zeitschrift für Rassenkunde* he destroyed the foundation of Nazi theories of 'pure race'. This was followed in 1939 by *The Races of Central Europe* (with a preface by J. B. S. Haldane [q.v.], in which, by using blood groups and anthropometry he showed that the Germans were racially the most heterogeneous group in Europe. In 1939 the *Biometrika* Trust published a bibliography of Karl Pearson's work prepared by Morant from material given him by Pearson.

At the outbreak of World War II Morant joined the Ministry of Information. But by 1942 he was applying his anthropometric methods to help the Medical Research Council's Army Personnel Research Committee. The first report (1943), written jointly with (Sir) Austin Bradford Hill, analysed the heights and weights of 1,600 men in the Royal Armoured Corps; later (1945) a more detailed study of 2,000 tank personnel gave the information needed to design tanks with the optimal space for the crew. From 1944 Morant worked at the Physiological laboratory (the RAF Institute of Aviation Medicine) at the Royal Aircraft Establishment, Farnborough. He prepared many reports for the Flying Personnel Research Committee. These covered three main topics: surveys of heights and weights of men and women recruits to the RAF with comparisons with earlier similar surveys; body measurements of aircrew to provide the information needed for improving the fit of Services clothing, and for the detailed design of aircraft cockpits, seats, and their controls: statistical analyses of research projects at the School, such as the effects of fluoride on dental caries; and experimental studies of decompression and air sickness. Morant worked closely with those making the decisions—the cockpit design teams and the cutters preparing the patterns for the clothing. In this way his work had an important and immediate application.

At the end of the war Morant returned briefly to academic work at University College. This was a period of great disappointment for him. He had expected that the understandings he had had with those in authority before the war would ensure his getting a senior appointment in the department of anthropology or anatomy. But the senior staff had died, others had moved away, and the appointment he had expected had been filled. He therefore returned to the Institute of Aviation Medicine, retiring in 1959.

Morant had an old-world courtesy, a rather diffident manner, and a charming smile which was immediately attractive to the many much younger laboratory members with whom he worked so successfully. He was tall and handsome, with striking dark eyebrows. His modesty prevented many of his colleagues in the Services realizing his eminence as an anthropologist. It also perhaps prevented him pushing earlier and harder to ensure his return to academic work at the end of the war. His kindness to many by helping to prepare publications often went unrecorded at his request. He was an eminent anthropologist who made a unique contribution to the needs of the Services in the later part of his career. He was appointed OBE in 1952.

He married first, in 1922, Geraldine Wynne, who died in childbirth in 1923. The child also died. In 1928 he married Mary Evelyn, daughter of Ernest Hitchcock, caterer, and had one son and one daughter. He died at his home at Bishop's Waltham, Hampshire, 3 July 1964.

[*The Times*, 9 and 13 July 1964; Joan Box, *R. A. Fisher. The Life of a Scientist*, 1978; private information; personal knowledge.]

JOHN C. GILSON

MORGAN, SIR FREDERICK EDGWORTH (1894–1967), lieutenant-general, was born in Paddock Wood 5 February 1894, the eldest son in a family of nine children of Frederick Beverley Morgan, timber merchant, and his wife, Clara Elizabeth, daughter of Edgworth Horrocks, of Paddock Wood, Kent. He was educated at Clifton College and the Royal Military Academy, Woolwich, from which he was commissioned into the Royal Artillery in 1913. He returned from India with the Lahore Divisional Artillery in 1914 and served continuously in France and Belgium throughout the war, taking part in most of the major battles and being twice mentioned in dispatches. Early in the war he was blown up and suffered severe shell-shock, but he returned later to serve on the staff of the Canadian Corps. From 1919 to early 1935 he served with his regiment in India. He passed through the Staff College, Quetta (1927–8), and subsequently held staff appointments first in India and later at the War Office.

In 1938 Morgan was for a short period GSO 1 to the 3rd division, but was then given command of the support group of the 1st Armoured division, with which he went to France in 1940 during the retreat of the British Expeditionary Force, took part in the fighting south of the Somme, and escaped from Brest. Between 1940 and 1943 he held a succession of appointments at home culminating in the command of I Corps. This he relinquished in March 1943 when appointed as COSSAC (chief of staff to the supreme allied commander (designate)). He was faced with the gigantic task of preparing a plan for the invasion of north-west Europe and a follow-up attack on the heart of Germany with an eventual force of 100 divisions. Morgan set up his headquarters at Norfolk House in St. James's Square where he assembled an Anglo-American staff representing all three Services. Although a number of studies for a landing on the coast of Normandy had already been made, Morgan and his team faced enormous difficulties. The chief of the imperial general staff, Sir Alan Brooke (later Viscount Alanbrooke, q.v.), after outlining the problem is alleged to have remarked 'Well, there it is. It won't work, but you must bloody well make it.' If in the end Morgan failed to provide a plan which satisfied the eventual executants, they could not have managed without it. He devoted himself tirelessly to the task, working seven days a week and sleeping beside his desk. The happy relations he fostered in his inter-Allied staff was a remarkable achievement in view of the misunderstandings and differences of opinion sometimes prevalent between the Allies on a higher level.

The inadequacies of COSSAC's planning in 1943 and early 1944 were principally due to two factors: the absence of a supreme commander and the shortage of means then available. Despite the representations made by Churchill and the British chiefs of staff at the Quebec conference in August 1943, it was not until after the appointment of General Eisenhower and his deputy commanders at the end of 1943 that the Americans fully grasped the size of the problem and began to make provision for it. The planners' most acute difficulty was undoubtedly the lack of a sufficient number of landing-craft (the Pacific theatre and to some extent the Mediterranean then enjoyed a higher priority), but there were many other serious deficiencies, including ships and aircraft for lifting airborne troops. When the prime minister showed General Montgomery (later Viscount Montgomery of Alamein) a draft of COSSAC's plan at Marrakesh at the end of December 1943, the latter at once submitted a trenchant memorandum arguing that in its present form it was impracticable. In particular Montgomery pointed out that the allocation of only three infantry divisions for the initial landing would entail far too narrow a front: 'By D + 12 a total of 16 divisions have been landed on the same beaches as were used for the initial landings. This would lead to the most appalling confusion on the beaches, and the smooth development of the land battle would be made extremely difficult—if not impossible.' Montgomery significantly extended the scope of the landings and also strengthened the command structure; his plan called for an attack by two armies side by side, Second British Army on the left with three divisions in line, and First US Army on the right with two divisions. Montgomery himself held the executive command of 21st Army Group, under Eisenhower's supreme direction, until after the break-out was achieved.

Nevertheless the great expansion of the forces available for Overlord and the consequent modifications of the plan in the first five months of 1944 should not obscure the fact that COSSAC and his staff had laid the essential foundations for the greatest amphibious operation ever undertaken. Among the many novel features of Morgan's plan perhaps the most remarkable and successful was the provision for large-scale maintenance from artificial harbours (or Mulberries) a method not previously attempted in war. In 1950 Morgan published a valuable and interesting account of the work of the COSSAC team entitled *Overture to Overlord*.

When, early in 1944, he was relieved on the arrival of the British and American commanders with their own chiefs of staff, Morgan was appointed deputy chief of staff at Eisenhower's headquarters. His advice to the supreme commander frequently conflicted with the views of Montgomery, who later recorded of Morgan in his *Memoirs* (1958) that 'He considered Eisenhower was a god; since I had discarded many of his plans, he placed me at the other end of the celestial ladder'. In September 1945 Morgan took on probably the most difficult and ultimately most unhappy assignment of his career as chief of operations in Germany to the United Nations Relief and Rehabilitation Administration (UNRRA). During the next year he applied his qualities of drive, intelligence, and sympathy to the desperate problems presented by at least a million displaced persons. Although remarkably successful in some aspects of his work, he speedily became disillusioned with UNRRA, which he believed was being exploited by more sinister organizations. In January 1946 he created a furore by asserting at a press conference that a secret organization existed to further a mass movement of Jews out of Europe. Although his suspicion was possibly well founded, critics held that he should not have made a public statement while officially concerned with provision for numerous Jewish refugees. Six months later he was dismissed after alleging that UNRRA organizations were being used as a cover for Soviet agents who were fomenting trouble among displaced persons. This episode is related in full and strikes an uncharacteristically bitter note in Morgan's autobiography *Peace and War, a Soldier's Life* (1961).

'Freddie' Morgan was a tall, cheerful soldier with a fresh complexion and blue eyes. Behind a somewhat untidy appearance and a droll sense of humour he concealed one of the sharpest minds of his generation in the army. His charm and courtesy were invaluable assets in a senior staff officer, yet these qualities were compatible with a strong personality and great courage in voicing unpopular views. Throughout his career he displayed ability and competence well above the average.

In 1946 he retired from the army with the honorary rank of lieutenant-general. In 1951 he succeeded Lord Portal of Hungerford as controller of atomic energy, and witnessed Britain's first atomic tests at the Monte Bello islands in October 1952; and in 1954–6 he was controller of atomic weapons under the Atomic Energy Authority.

He was appointed CB in 1943 and promoted KCB in 1944. He was a commander of the US Legion of Merit and of the French Legion of Honour, and held the American DSM and the croix de guerre. He was a colonel commandant of the Royal Artillery from 1948 to 1958. In 1917 he married Marjorie, daughter of Colonel Thomas du Bédat Whaite, of the Army Medical Service; they had a son and two daughters. Morgan died at Northwood, Middlesex, 19 March 1967.

A charcoal drawing by S. Morse-Brown (1947) is in the possession of the family and is reproduced in *Peace and War*.

[*The Times*, 21 March 1967; private information.]   BRIAN BOND

MORISON, STANLEY ARTHUR (1889-1967), typographer, was born at Wanstead, Essex, 6 May 1889, the only son and second of three children of Arthur Andrew Morison and his wife, Alice Louisa, daughter of Charles Cole, clerk, of Hackney. His father, an unsuccessful and intemperate commercial traveller, deserted the family when Morison was fourteen, a sufficient reason for Morison's leaving Owen's School, Islington, in 1903 and finding paid work. After a phase of sharing his mother's agnosticism, he was received into the Roman Catholic Church in December 1908. Unhappy as a clerk with the London City Mission (1905-12), he spent his spare time in museums and public libraries. *The Times* printing supplement of 10 September 1912 concentrated his mind on the study of letters, printed and written, and early the following year he was fortunate in securing a post as assistant in the office of the *Imprint*, a new monthly periodical devoted to design in printing. When the *Imprint* seemed likely to fail in the following year, the editor recommended Morison to Wilfrid Meynell, husband of Alice Meynell [q.v.] and managing director of Burns & Oates, Roman Catholic publishers, who took him on his staff. Morison afterwards felt deeply grateful to the Meynell family for help and encouragement.

In 1916 he made known his conscientious objection to war service. His appeal against conscription on religious and moral grounds was dismissed, and on 7 May 1916 he was taken to prison. Eventually he accepted alternative employment and by the time the war ended he was engaged in farm work. Meanwhile, on 18 March 1916 he had married Mabel Williamson (died 1961), a schoolteacher. Not until many years later did Morison learn that she was not seven but seventeen years older than himself. Morison never spoke of his marriage: late in 1926 he made a settlement on his wife and they separated. He had formed a close relationship, undoubtedly amorous but as certainly chaste, with the American typographer, Mrs Beatrice Lamberton Warde, who was by his bedside when he died.

After the war Wilfrid and his son, (Sir) Francis Meynell, found him temporary employment until, in June 1921, he went as typographer to the Cloister Press near Manchester. The press was liquidated in July 1922, and Morison was never again full-time employed. He acted as freelance consultant to several publishers; but his position as Britain's greatest authority on letter-design was won by the success of a programme for the production of a series of typefaces proposed to the Monotype Corporation in 1922 leading to a part-time appointment as typographical adviser lasting until 1954. A dozen typefaces made to his specifications, some rendering old designs, others drawn by living artists, became those most commonly used for book-printing in Great Britain and to a large extent abroad.

Morison's writings, some two hundred books, articles, collections of specimens, reviews, and prefaces, strongly affected the taste and enlarged the knowledge of experts and amateurs concerned with book-production. A succession of learned essays in the annual the *Fleuron* (1923-30), founded in conjunction with Oliver Simon [q.v.], discovered much that was of value in the history of type and its relation to the work of scribes and writing masters. The final one, 'First Principles of Typography', was reprinted as a book (1936) in thirteen editions and seven languages during Morison's lifetime. On weekly visits to Cambridge, where he was part-time typographical adviser to the University Press, he was the perfect collaborator for the printer, Walter Lewis, from 1923 until 1945 and his successor, Brooke Crutchley, until 1959.

Morison's great services to *The Times* over thirty years made him known to a wider public and as more than a technician. His appointment as typographical adviser was the result of his caustic comments on the paper's drab and old-fashioned look made in 1929 to a representative. His views, reported to the manager, were taken seriously at the highest levels and led eventually to his being asked to submit proposals. That he did throughout 1930 and 1931, advocating typographical changes including the abandonment of the ornamented gothic for the title. As a consequence a new typeface was cut and when the paper first appeared in *The Times* New Roman on 3 October 1932 almost all correspondents found it a relief to their eyes. Morison's position at *The Times* developed into something much more than adviser on printing. He edited and largely wrote the four-volume *The History of The Times* (1935-52) and was for two years, 1945-7, editor of *The Times Literary Supplement*. He was consulted about organization and appointments of personnel, and even for a time about editorial policy; but this last anomaly ended in 1952. He retired from *The Times* in 1960. His researches in newspaper history brought him in touch with Lord Beaverbrook [q.v.], who entertained him in the years 1948-63 to winter holidays in the Bahamas and on the Riviera. To this Dictionary Morison contributed the notices of Barrington-Ward and St. John Hornby.

Morison's involvement with the *Encyclopaedia Britannica* began in 1949, when he met the publisher, William Benton, and in 1961 he was added to the editorial board. He made periodic visits to Chicago (the city that came nearest to rivalling London in his affections) and enjoyed Mediterranean cruises in Senator Benton's yacht.

During the war of 1939–45 he seldom spent a night out of London. The preface to *Blackletter Text* (1942) describes his experiences in a catastrophic air raid when his rooms, most of his books, and his work in progress were destroyed.

Morison far excelled other typographers of his day in point of erudition; and his choice of type-designs, prompted by a fastidious mind and a sensitive eye, was enduring. His capacity for gaining the confidence of managements and commanding the skill of technicians made him a leader in his profession of consultant. Consequently, his influence on book-printing was powerful, and he exerted it in favour of an austere and traditional style, with an improved repertory of type. His reform of *The Times* unfortunately failed to survive a need for stringent economy. As a scholar he was quick to grasp essentials but inaccurate in details, and in the lectures of 1957, delivered when he was James P. R. Lyell reader in bibliography at Oxford in 1956–7, he undertook a task for which he had insufficient knowledge.

Cambridge University, where he had been Sandars reader in 1931, honoured him with the degree of Litt.D. in 1950, and so did Birmingham and Marquette (Wisconsin, USA). He was elected FBA in 1954 and appointed Royal Designer for Industry in 1960; but he declined three offers of knighthood. His lesser honours would make a long catalogue.

He was vigorous and did not spare himself. In middle life he worked very hard and travelled a great deal in search of information. His talk was pugnacious in a humorous way. Victorian in morals, on other subjects he would differ without bitterness, though he had no doubts. In politics he was radical: spoke contemptuously of the Roman Curia, resented monarchy, and thought capitalism was wrong but invincible. Communist friends dissuaded him in 1921 from applying for membership of their party. Apart from the breviary, which he always carried, he read only for information, increasingly about liturgy and ecclesiology: in music he cared only for plain chant. His fine collection of books (presented by Sir Allen Lane, q.v.) is kept in a 'Morison Room' at Cambridge University Library.

He was of spare build; wore spectacles (steel-rimmed) from his youth up, the lenses thickening as he aged. Dressed invariably in a black suit with a white shirt and black tie, outdoors with a rather small black hat, he struck strangers as looking like a Jesuit.

Given handsome parting presents from *The Times* and the Monotype Corporation and a generous subsidy from Senator Benton, he lived his declining years in great comfort in a double suite of rooms in Whitehall Court, Westminster, and indulged a discriminating taste in food and wines. He was still visiting Chicago in 1966; but by May 1967 he had taken to a wheelchair because of spinal weakness and he could hardly see. He died at home, 11 October 1967. He had taken a close interest in the form of the requiem Mass offered in Westminster Cathedral on 18 October.

There is a charcoal drawing (1924) by (Sir) William Rothenstein at Cambridge University Press. A sketch for this drawing, dated 1923, is in the possession of the Monotype Corporation.

[Nicolas Barker, *Stanley Morison*, 1972; S. H. Steinberg in *Proceedings* of the British Academy, vol. liii, 1967; personal knowledge.]
H. G. CARTER

MORRIS, SIR HAROLD SPENCER (1876–1967), president of the Industrial Court, was born at 21 Compton Terrace, Highbury, London, 21 December 1876, the second son of (Sir) Malcolm Alexander Morris, FRCS (Edin.), and his wife, Fanny Cox, of Dorchester on Thames. Malcolm Morris, who with his family moved in September 1887 to 8 Harley Street, London (from their then address of 63 Montagu Square), from which address he thereafter practised, had a distinguished career as a consulting surgeon and as a specialist in skin diseases.

Harold Morris was educated at Westminster School, Clifton College, and from 1894, at Magdalen College, Oxford, where he read law, graduating in 1897 with a fourth class degree. Having joined the Inner Temple he was called to the bar on 26 January 1899. Amongst those called the same night there were three others who, as in his case, later became benchers: in 1949 on the fiftieth anniversary of their call to the bar (as indeed on some later anniversaries) the four dined together in Hall in company with and to the delight of their fellow benchers. The other three were John (later Viscount) Simon [q.v.] who to his other high offices had added that of having been lord chancellor from 1940 to 1945, Rayner (later Lord) Goddard who became lord chief justice of England in 1946, and the Hon. Victor Alexander Russell, a popular and respected practitioner in the Probate, Divorce, and Admiralty division.

Morris practised at the common law bar and was a member of the South-Eastern circuit. For anyone who had been building up a practice in the years after 1899 the outbreak of war in 1914 must have come at a time which could cause grievous professional upset. Particularly might this be so in the case of someone with a young family. In 1904 Morris had married Olga, the daughter of Emil Teichman, of Chislehurst. It was a happy marriage. They had four daughters and one son. The son, Malcolm John Morris, followed his father into the legal profession: he was called to the bar by the Inner Temple in 1937, became QC in 1959 and a bencher (in his father's lifetime) in 1965. He held various recorderships and then became a judge at the Central Criminal Court where he sat in the period before his untimely death in the year 1972.

Being anxious to serve in the war Morris was commissioned in the Coldstream Guards on 2 June 1916: in June 1918 he was transferred to the Flying Corps as deputy assistant adjutant-general: he became a court-martial officer with the rank of major: he was mentioned in dispatches and in 1919 he was appointed MBE.

Being demobilized in February 1919 and returning to the bar he successfully re-established himself and took silk in 1921. As an advocate he was competent: as a speaker either in court or on social occasions he was pleasing, lively, and interesting. He possessed a natural buoyancy and gaiety and courtesy: he had good looks. The combination of all these qualities seemed to augur for him a legal career of promise which, whether or not likely to take him to the highest flights of the bar or to participation in the heaviest and most lucrative type of cases, could lead to a thriving practice with prospects of elevation to the High Court bench. He became recorder of Folkestone in 1921, holding the post until 1926. In November 1922 he entered Parliament as National Liberal member for East Bristol but in the general election of the following year he lost the seat.

In 1925 he was asked to be chairman of a court of investigation to consider a dispute in the woollen industry. His success in that capacity doubtless led to his being invited (as he was in 1925) to succeed Sir William Warrender MacKenzie (later Lord Amulree, q.v.) as chairman of the Railways National Wages Board and to his being appointed in the following year (1926) to succeed Sir William as president of the Industrial Court—a position which he continued to hold until 1945. He was knighted in 1927.

In the period before Morris accepted these positions his health was for a time not good. If as a consequence of ill health there are interruptions in the work of a busy barrister a disruption of practice with consequent anxiety and loss is likely to result. The advantage of a secure position freed from the stresses and strains of life at the bar becomes inevitably an attraction. Morris was probably so in-

fluenced. Though his appointment as president of the Industrial Court was to a position of great national importance and prestige it meant in Morris's case that after only four or five years in silk he would have to abandon any prospects of building up a large practice and of any possible future appointment to the High Court bench.

He had the qualities which fitted him to be an admirable president of the Industrial Court: he was wise as well as being impartial. Assuredly his tenure of the presidency during years of economic difficulties and anxieties gave satisfaction and inspired confidence. For a short time (from 1930 to 1935), he added to his work by being chairman of the Coal Wages Board after the passing of the Coal Mines Act of 1930. Even after his retirement in 1945 he continued to render public service in that, very acceptably, he sat judicially from time to time at Middlesex quarter-sessions, at the Central Criminal Court, and in other courts.

His happy appreciation of and understanding of life at the bar inspired him to write in 1930 an entertaining book, *The Barrister*: years later, in 1960, came an autobiographical volume of much interest which he called *Back View*. He died at his home in Kew 11 November 1967. There is a portrait by Walter Russell in the possession of the family.

[Sir Harold Morris, *Back View*, 1960; *The Times*, 13 November 1967; personal knowledge.]   MORRIS OF BORTH-Y-GEST

MORRIS, WILLIAM RICHARD, VISCOUNT NUFFIELD (1877-1963), industrialist and philanthropist, was born in Worcester 10 October 1877, the son of Frederick Morris, who was then working for a draper in Worcester, and his wife, Emily Ann, daughter of Richard Pether, of Wood Farm, Headington. He was the eldest of a family of seven of whom only a sister survived beyond an early age. His father was an Oxford man and to Oxford he returned to farm when Morris was three. The boy grew up in Cowley and went to the village school. After a short period with a local bicycle firm he started on his own at the age of sixteen with a capital of £4. By 1901 he could advertise himself as 'Sole maker of the celebrated Morris cycles'. In 1902 he showed a model of a motor cycle of his own design, and about this time he started on motor-car repairs. In 1903 he went into partnership but this soon got into financial difficulties, and he salvaged only his personal kit of tools. He resumed business under his own name and by 1910 he was described as motor-car engineer and agent and garage proprietor. He was by then well advanced on his project for a car of his own; the Morris-Oxford was announced at the 1912 Motor Show when he received an order for 400 cars. The first was produced in April 1913: the original bull-nosed 8.9 hp two-seater which did 35–50 miles to the gallon, had speeds ranging up to 50 miles per hour in top gear, and was priced at £165.

Morris was a hard-working, conscientious, enthusiastic, and attractive young man, with plenty of self-confidence. He had no formal training as an engineer, but was good with his hands and had a shrewd eye for the potentialities of the newly developing internal combustion engine. In a rapidly expanding industry he had a large number of competitors, but in some ways being in Oxford was an advantage. The richer undergraduates, and even senior members of the university, were interested in the motor car and Morris was quick to learn from the variety of cars which passed through his hands. Not having the wide-ranging engineering facilities of some industrial towns he had to concentrate largely on assembling components made by others. This gave him greater flexibility and involved much less capital. He was also free to concentrate on design and improvement. He was a shrewd bargainer with, but also a reliable customer for, his suppliers. He had the courage, flair, farsightedness, and singlemindedness of the successful business man, who knew how to choose men and attract their loyalty.

Since his premises in Longwall, next to New College, were unsuitable for large-scale production Morris acquired property at Temple Cowley, including the buildings of what had formerly been Hurst's Grammar School, where his father had gone to school. Early in 1914 he visited the United States to secure components for his second model—the 11.9 hp Morris-Cowley. During the war of 1914–18 the Cowley factory made a small number of cars but was engaged mainly on munitions. For his services Morris was appointed OBE in 1917.

He was quickly ready to produce cars to meet the post-war boom: the firm of Morris Motors Ltd. was incorporated in July 1919 and by September 1920 was selling around 280 cars a month. Then came the slump. By February 1921 the company had a large bank overdraft, owed even more to suppliers, and production was obstructed by the accumulation of supplies and unsold cars. Morris then took the dramatic decision which proved the turning-point in his career: to cut the price of the 4-seater Morris-Cowley by £100 to £425 and other models by smaller sums. Within three weeks all the completed cars had been sold and the factory was running short of supplies—400 cars were sold in March 1921. Other manufacturers reduced their prices but at the Motor Show in the autumn Morris made further reductions. By 1923 Morris Motors were producing some 20,000 cars a year and by 1926 some 50,000, or about a third of the national output. Morris had established himself as one of the major producers of the popular car.

In that year Morris joined with other companies to finance the Pressed Steel Company, located at Cowley, to supply car bodies to the industry. And in the same year the new public company of Morris Motors (1926) Ltd. was established to take over Morris Motors Ltd. and three other firms already owned by Morris, supplying bodies, engines, and radiators. The City advised that an issue only of preference shares would not attract the investor and that either Morris should market some ordinary shares or allow the preference shares some part of the profits. He declined the advice; the issue of £3 million cumulative preference shares was oversubscribed and he retained the ownership of the whole of the ordinary shares with a nominal value of £2 million. He combined this policy with ploughing back the surplus trading profit. Thus in 1924–5 Morris Motors Ltd. had paid £2,030 on its preference shares, nothing on its ordinary shares, and retained net profits of £822,000 in the business which was thereby provided with cheap capital for its expansion.

The company weathered the depression of the early thirties by shifting the emphasis to smaller models: the Morris Minor of 1931 sold at £100 and claimed to do 100 miles per hour and per gallon. In the meantime in 1930 Morris had registered the MG Car Company which produced the famous MG sports car; and acquired the Wolseley Company in 1927, as well as the SU Carburettor Company which in 1927 became Morris Industries Ltd., the holding company for all Morris's interests. In 1935 Morris Motors acquired the Wolseley and MG companies from him and in 1939 Morris Commercial Cars, Morris Industries Export, and the SU Company. By now the ordinary share capital of Morris Motors consisted of £2,650,000 in 5s. shares, all owned by Lord Nuffield as he had now become. In 1936 one-quarter of these was issued to the public at 37s. 6d. and at the end of the first day their price closed some 4s. higher. This put Nuffield's financial interest in the company at some £16 million, and with Morris Garages and another company he wholly owned, and the proceeds of the sales, he had a fortune of over £20 million.

Although Morris had started to give money away as early as 1926, when he endowed the King Alfonso XIII chair of Spanish studies at Oxford, his major benefactions started from around the period of the public issue; indeed, in order to fulfil his desire to become a public benefactor on a large scale he had to have large sums more readily available. During his lifetime

Nuffield gave away some £30 million, with the main general aim of reducing human suffering. His £2 million endowment in 1936 for the medical school at Oxford made the university one of the main centres for medical research and teaching. He claimed he had always wanted to be a surgeon and in 1948 he gave a quarter of a million to the Royal College of Surgeons for the establishment and maintenance of a residential college. He was a generous benefactor of the Oxford hospitals and also of Guy's, St. Thomas's, Great Ormond Street, and hospitals in Birmingham, Coventry, Worcester, and elsewhere. His especial sympathy for the crippled was shown in his provision for what became the Nuffield Orthopaedic Centre at Oxford, in the Nuffield Fund for Cripples (1935-7), and the Fund (1935-45) for orthopaedic services in Australia, New Zealand, and South Africa. In 1939 he gave over a million pounds to form the Nuffield Provincial Hospitals Trust; and in the same year over a million and a half for a Forces Trust.

The very imaginative Trust for the Special Areas, created in 1936 by a grant of £2 million, with the important contribution it made to bringing new industries to depressed areas, was part of the general pattern. The primary purpose of Nuffield College, founded in 1937 with the grant of a site in Oxford and some £900,000 in cash, was the study of social, economic, and political problems. And the first three objects of the Nuffield Foundation, founded in 1943 by the gift of 4.8 million ordinary shares (then worth about £10 million), were the advancement of health and the prevention and relief of sickness; the advancement of social well-being; and the care and comfort of the aged poor. Most of the good Nuffield did lived after him, for the bulk of his money went on endowments and buildings. The Nuffield Foundation continued to distribute its large annual income among a wide-ranging variety of research projects and pioneering activities.

Although Nuffield declined to participate in the shadow factory scheme devised before the war because he disagreed with the basis upon which it was organized, he set up organizations for the manufacture of tanks in 1937 and of aircraft in 1938. During the war of 1939-45 Cowley became the headquarters of the Civilian Repair Organization. After the war Morris Motors went on to produce its two-millionth car in October 1951. In the following year the company merged with the Austin Motor Company in the formation of the British Motor Corporation, of which Nuffield became first chairman. Six months later he retired and became honorary president. He continued

regularly to attend his office in the headmaster's study in the former Hurst's Grammar School, but he was no longer the dominant figure. Since the late thirties he had spent an increasing amount of his time on his numerous benefactions and on his annual long sea trips, on which he excelled at deck games. Unlike many rich men he did not develop new pursuits or figure in the gilded world. His pleasures were simple—the Huntercombe Golf Club and the company of convivial friends and kindred spirits. He was an uncomplicated man with a strong belief in the old-fashioned virtues of hard work and honesty. He was an individualist who disliked committees and took very little part in organized public affairs. When he did, his views were of the same homespun variety combined with a firm belief in the freedom and opportunities afforded by private enterprise. He knew his own mind, and could make large and imaginative decisions of which there is plenty of evidence in his careers as industrialist and benefactor. He was essentially a kindly man, concerned at the sufferings of others. He read very little and notwithstanding all the money he gave for academic activities and research was not greatly interested in the results—only medical problems and progress excited his direct interest.

In 1929 Morris was created a baronet, in 1934 a baron as Lord Nuffield, and in 1938 a viscount. He was appointed GBE in 1941 and CH in 1958. He was an honorary DCL of Oxford (1931) and in 1937 received an MA which made him a voting member of the university and 'one of us'. He was a doctor of six other universities, three of them Australian. He was elected FRS in 1939 and honorary FRCS in 1948. He was an honorary fellow of St. Peter's, Pembroke, Worcester, and Nuffield colleges in Oxford and an honorary freeman of seven towns, including the cities of Oxford, Worcester, Cardiff, and Coventry.

In 1904 Morris married an Oxford girl, Elizabeth Maud (died 1959), daughter of William Jones Anstey; they had no children. His heirs were the numerous benefactions which he liked to bear his name. He died at Nuffield Place 22 August 1963 and was cremated at a simple private service and his ashes buried in the parish church at Nuffield. He showed his confidence in the college carrying his name by making it his residuary legatee and assigned to it his coat of arms. Nuffield Place, his home for thirty years, became the responsibility of the college.

Nuffield College has a bronze bust by Madame Lejeune and a portrait of Morris by Sir Arthur Cope which was presented to him by the staff and workpeople of Morris Motors in 1929. It shows him as a youngish man standing on Shotover, with Oxford spires in the background.

[P. W. S. Andrews and Elizabeth Brunner, *The Life of Lord Nuffield*, 1955; Robert Jackson, *The Nuffield Story*, 1964; personal knowledge.]   D. N. CHESTER

MORRISON, HERBERT STANLEY, BARON MORRISON OF LAMBETH (1888-1965), Labour politician, was born in Brixton, London, 3 January 1888, the youngest in a family of four girls and three boys of Henry Morrison, police constable with a weakness for the bottle, and his wife, Priscilla Caroline Lyon, daughter of a carpet fitter in the East End of London. His mother had been in domestic service and, with six surviving children, the early years were hard but not marked by lack of the basic necessities. An eye infection shortly after birth deprived Morrison of the sight of his right eye, although this was a handicap which he generally overcame. He was educated at one of the Board schools set up under the 1870 Education Act, and, from the age of eleven, at St. Andrew's Church of England School, Lingham St., which he left at the age of fourteen to become an errand boy. After a spell as a shop assistant and as a switchboard operator (which gave him more time for reading), minor journalistic efforts helped to provide a living, and from 1912 to 1915 Morrison worked as circulation manager for the first official Labour paper, the *Daily Citizen*. From April 1915 he became part-time secretary of the London Labour Party and thereafter politics, either as an organizer or as a member of Parliament, was his sole occupation: and politics to Herbert Morrison meant the Labour movement. In his early years he took part in the local forums, heard such famous figures as George Bernard Shaw and Keir Hardie [qq.v.], and in 1906 he joined the Brixton branch of the Independent Labour Party. Following a common trend among left-wingers in London, he found this a rather pro-Liberal, north of England or Nonconformist type of organization, and himself preferred the more direct socialism of the Social Democratic Federation to which he transferred in 1907. To the London Left, free trade, anti-landlordism, and Home Rule for Ireland were all meaningless; Morrison was preoccupied — it was his lifelong preoccupation — with transport, health, education, and housing as provided by the local authorities for the citizens of the larger towns, and, above all, for London. Later he left the SDF and rejoined the ILP because he saw that it was more likely to win elections and achieve actual changes. As part of this interest he attended the Lambeth Metropolitan Borough Council — he was often the sole visitor — and unsuccessfully contested the Vauxhall ward for the ILP in 1912. In 1910 he had become secretary of the South-West London Federation of ILP branches and his work led steadily to the decision of the London Trades Council to call a conference and form the London Labour Party. After he became secretary to this new organization, in 1915, Morrison talked less and less about political theory, though he was opposed to the war of 1914-18 and to conscription. His concern was entirely with winning elections and carrying out pragmatic reforms, the common feature of which was to remedy social grievances in a manner which showed no prejudice against either governmental action or state ownership. If he resisted Poplarism, he also rigorously opposed any Communist move 'to pour sand' into the Labour Party machine.

In many respects Morrison's greatest achievements in politics were in London between 1920 and 1940. He began by bringing his organization intact through the war of 1914-18, going on to win fifteen out of 124 seats in the 1919 London County Council elections. He realized that more was gained by steady work and preparation, by mastery of the immediate subject and its possibilities, than by all the street-corner oratory which so delighted the older generation of socialists. This work required the finding and training of candidates not only for the LCC but for the elections in twenty-eight boroughs. Once elected, these men had to be taught how to make speeches, conduct committees, and actually run the machinery of local government. In late 1919 the London Labour Party won a majority or became the largest party in sixteen boroughs. In 1919 Morrison became mayor of Hackney and in 1922 a member of the London County Council. He was soon the dominating figure.

Elected to Parliament for Hackney South in 1923 and 1929, Morrison was a strong supporter of Ramsay MacDonald and in the second Labour Government became minister of transport (1929). He proved to be a first-class minister, and was responsible for the 1930 Road Traffic Act and for the London Passenger Transport Bill of 1931. In the latter case, Morrison had been leading the Labour group on the LCC in opposition to a proposal to form a privately owned monopoly of London Transport. He became minister of transport just in time to prevent the Bill from passing and introduced his own measure, the creation of the London Passenger Transport Board. As a progenitor of the Board, Morrison was a firm believer in the autonomous public corporation as the best instrument for controlling a nationalized industry. He argued the case in his book *Socialization and Transport* (1933), which was in part a defence of his views against criticism from within the Labour Party. Other possibilities, such as workers' or joint control of an industry or management by a government department, had a strong traditional appeal to some socialists. By winning acceptance for his own view, Morrison in effect determined the form which was later given to the post-war nationalization Acts. He also insisted on fair compensation for stockholders and on the obligation to demonstrate the advantages of nationalization industry by industry. Because, as he thought, the case had not been made out for nationalization of the steel industry, he was opposed to that commitment in Labour's programme.

It was in the 1930s that Morrison achieved his greatest hold on the Labour Party. In part this was due simply to his personality and ability. A short, stocky figure with a quiff of hair combed back from his forehead, he was a first-rate debater and public speaker. He could put his party's view in the most reasonable, lucid, and engaging manner while never suggesting weakness and he was always ready to counter every attack. Also his achievements in London were a tonic to the Labour Party just when it most needed one. The annual conference found him in his element.

After Labour's exhilarating rise to power in the early 1920s, there had been the disappointing experiences of the two minority Governments, the defection of Ramsay MacDonald, and the débâcle of the 1931 general election. Morrison had begun in 1931 by wishing to remain in office with MacDonald, but after much hesitation he eventually stayed with the rest of the party when the 'national' Government was formed. In the face of these setbacks, the capture of the LCC in 1934 and the steady achievements thereafter were a most welcome sign that Labour could win and govern, achievements which in London were due to Herbert Morrison. Under him the LCC reformed public assistance, kept Poor Law officers out of the hospitals, built a new Waterloo Bridge despite government opposition, introduced the green belt, and pushed ahead with slum clearance and school building. Morrison was, in fact, a rather unusual type of Labour leader. He had not come up through the trade-union movement, nor was he one of the middle-class intellectuals who formed the other major group in the senior ranks. A working-class boy who was largely self-educated, he had risen by virtue of his organizational, tactical, and argumentative skills and he had no signs of a social inferiority complex. Indeed his bearing was a mixture of cockney brashness and the self-confidence which arose from knowledge, competence, and a solidly based political position. His clothes

and his furniture were always bought at the Co-op. A further facet of Herbert Morrison's character which emerged strongly after his re-election in 1935 was his love of the House of Commons. As might have been expected, despite a shaky start, he took pleasure in mastering its rules of procedure. He was never overawed by the Palace of Westminster, but he valued its historical traditions and became an expert at using the House of Commons as part of the machinery of government.

His absence from the Commons from his defeat in 1931 until the general election of 1935, when he was re-elected for Hackney South with a majority of 5,000 was, however, to have a crucial effect on his subsequent career. Clement Attlee, hitherto junior to Morrison, who had been a Cabinet minister already, found himself deputy leader of the small group of Labour MPs in 1931 and when the leadership fell vacant in 1935 on George Lansbury's retirement, Attlee's claims were preferred to those of Morrison or Arthur Greenwood [qq.v.]. When a 'national' Government was formed in 1940, Morrison became minister of supply and then, from October, home secretary and minister of home security. In large part this appointment arose from his close knowledge of London and Londoners because the chief task was to reassure the citizens that all possible measures were being taken to preserve them from air attack.

Herbert Morrison visited all the areas and units involved in Civil Defence, and, after some reluctance to remove fire-fighting from its local government base, he created the National Fire Service to secure better co-operation and more rapid action, and provided a proper Civil Defence uniform. This did much for morale, as did the Morrison indoor table shelter; and he went on to institute a Fire Guard with regular fire-watching duties. In all these activities Morrison typified the irrepressible London civilian who made a joke out of nights at the office or the factory, who rallied round after the raids, and would not let any German actions depress him.

In many ways, the climax of Morrison's career was the Labour landslide of 1945. He had prepared the ground for it in several respects. In the actual chain of events leading to the election, Morrison had played a considerable part. In 1940 he had insisted that the Labour Party divide the House at the end of the debate on the Norwegian fiasco and had thus given the impetus which led to the resignation of Neville Chamberlain. As one of the small group of Labour leaders who successfully occupied high office through the war, he had shown that such men could rule most effectively. And, when Churchill asked the Labour Party to continue with the Coalition until Japan was defeated, Morrison was instrumental in insisting that this was unsatisfactory and that the country wanted a general election.

It has often been said that Morrison constructed and managed the machine which channelled the enthusiasms of 1945 into decisive action at the ballot box. Of this there is less evidence. The Conservative Party had almost totally abandoned its organization while Transport House had kept in operation. But there was no expert electioneering on either side. As with the LCC campaigns, all that was done was to provide candidates, explain the legal position, and produce a manifesto and some centrally directed propaganda. But because Morrison had done this before in London and played a large part in the similar process at a national level in 1945, he, not unfairly, received a large measure of the credit for the victory.

Although he had many subsequent achievements and his highest offices and honours were bestowed after 1945, some aspects of his career raised doubts and Morrison himself had disappointments, which made this period perhaps less happy than the previous years had been. As the results of the election of 1945, when Morrison was elected for Lewisham East, became known, he suggested that Attlee should not accept the royal commission to form a Government until the parliamentary party had met to elect a leader. Ernest Bevin and Attlee himself resisted this argument; Sir Stafford Cripps and Harold Laski [qq.v.] agreed with Morrison; Attlee ended the matter by going to the palace. Morrison in his *Autobiography* (1960) denied that, in supporting delay, he was seeking the post of prime minister for himself. Yet Laski, Ellen Wilkinson, and the others who were active on this occasion were quite clear that their candidate was Morrison and that he had given them his complete support. In fact, Morrison pressed his case in meetings of various Labour groups for several days after Attlee had been designated prime minister.

Again, in 1947, when Cripps was alarmed about the lack of leadership on economic affairs, Morrison became involved in the situation. But, in spite of these frictions, not uncommon in all Governments, few would deny Morrison the credit for many of the successes of the post-war Labour Government. When he was minister of supply in 1940, Morrison had had some difficulty with economic problems, a field which he never mastered as thoroughly as he had general administration and the social services. This difficulty cropped up again between 1945 and 1947, when he was responsible, as lord president of the Council, for economic planning and co-ordination. In 1947 this task was given to

Cripps at a new Ministry of Economic Affairs and Morrison was left to lead the House of Commons and to plan and carry through the legislative programme of the Government. In this task he excelled. His experience over the London Passenger Transport Act made him the authority on all the earlier nationalization measures, particularly of transport and electricity. Experienced members of the press lobby said it was a joy to watch him introduce these Bills, picking his way through the complexities and skirting the dangers like a cat walking across a mound of cans and broken bottles.

When it came to the question of steel, he was never adamant about public ownership and had wanted this item omitted from the 1945 election programme. Then, when the Cabinet took up the measure, Morrison was responsible for negotiations with (Sir) Ellis Hunter and (Sir) Andrew Duncan [qq.v.], the steel-masters' leaders. They produced a plan for increasing the powers of the Iron and Steel Board and allowing it to take over any firm which was not amenable to control. Aneurin Bevan, Bevin, and Cripps resisted this scheme throughout the summer of 1947 (when part of the time Morrison was seriously ill). In August the Parliamentary Labour Party discovered the situation, insisted on full nationalization, and the Bill was put in hand in October of that year. Although Morrison was much criticized for his 'hybrid measure', it was the most that could be achieved if the co-operation of the steel-masters was to be retained; and it would have given the Government a substantial measure of control.

In September 1947 Cripps openly admitted that he felt Bevin should take over from Attlee as prime minister, Hugh (later Lord) Dalton [q.v.] should become foreign secretary, and Attlee could remain as chancellor of the Exchequer. Cripps was almost equally critical of Morrison but still tried to win him over. Morrison said that he felt he should be prime minister and he went no further with the conspirators when it was clear that their objective was to elevate his chief enemy, Bevin. He left Cripps to put the proposal to Attlee who stopped the whole business by appointing Cripps to the Exchequer. Morrison's account of this in his *Autobiography* is not entirely frank. Eventually he agreed to be lord president of the Council, in which office he would have to co-ordinate Labour's policies. When Bevin fell ill in 1950, Morrison dithered over whether he wanted to become foreign secretary. The following year Attlee noted that: 'He seemed to want it badly and turned down every other suggestion I made to him, so in the end I appointed him. Rather bad luck for him, as it turned out.' This was because Morrison lacked all feeling for foreign affairs and was unhappy and uncomfortable in it so that his reputation suffered as a result. It is generally agreed that much of Morrison's touch, his sure-footedness in all matters of domestic policy and administration, deserted him when he moved to the Foreign Office in 1951. It has been suggested that for the first time his eyesight troubled him, when so much had to be read. More seriously, his judgement faltered. Even friendly critics pointed out that he knew Londoners perfectly, other English fairly well, the Scots and Welsh were strangers to him, and foreigners incomprehensible. This may not have been fair, but his tenure of the Foreign Office was neither successful nor fortunate. A Morrison Plan for Palestine was quickly disregarded but the chief problem confronting him was the decision of Mr Mossadeq's Government to take over the British-owned oil-wells at Abadan. Morrison was in favour of recovering them and admonishing the Persian Government by direct military action. It was left to Attlee to veto any such idea, pointing out that world and particularly Asian opinion would react violently, that the Persians could not be denied the right to nationalize such assets, and that strong-arm action in defence of commercial interests could no longer be tolerated. Unable to act as he had wanted, Morrison's performance lacked clarity or decisiveness and his short spell at the Foreign Office did considerable harm to his political standing.

In opposition after 1951, Morrison played a prominent part but many felt that he was getting older and was not as effective as he had been in the 1940s. In 1955 Attlee retired and Morrison entered the leadership contest. In his *Autobiography* he says that his weakness was his 'inability to intrigue'. Yet there is small evidence of intrigue on the side of the victor, Hugh Gaitskell [q.v.]. There is little doubt that Attlee held on to the leadership until 1955 in order to prevent Morrison's succeeding. He resigned only when Morrison was sixty-seven and then after declaring that the Labour Party needed a leader who was born in the twentieth rather than in the nineteenth century. As deputy prime minister from 1945 to 1951 and as deputy leader of the party since then, as a man who had contested the leadership with Attlee as far back as 1935, Morrison had undeniable claims to the topmost position. There was also a definite campaign to prevent his succeeding, all of which may justify his meeting such efforts with all the resources open to a politician.

'In politics', it is said, 'there is no friendship at the top', and this appears to have been the case among some of the Labour leaders. Attlee was always on reasonable terms with Morrison but he complained that 'Herbert cannot distinguish between big things and little things' and this was probably one motive behind his desire to prevent Morrison from obtaining the leadership. It was while Attlee was ill in hospital in early 1951 and Morrison was presiding over the Cabinet that divisions arose and Aneurin Bevan and (Sir) Harold Wilson resigned. Attlee blamed Morrison for this and complained that the issue was not kept open for long enough— 'he lost me two of my ministers'.

Herbert Morrison had not got on well with Bevan, but the most publicized disharmony was between Morrison and Ernest Bevin. For some reason, very possibly over trade-union representation on public bodies, the massive leader of the Transport and General Workers Union had decided as early as 1924 that Morrison was anti-union and to this he added a distaste for disloyalty of which he accused Morrison in 1945 when the attempt was made to replace Attlee. While Cripps's move to oust Attlee in 1947 apparently never riled Bevin, he continued to suspect Morrison. A major reason why Attlee had placed Bevin at the Foreign Office in 1945 was the feeling that his relations with Morrison were not easy enough to permit the close co-operation which would have been required had both men occupied posts on the home front.

After the Labour Party lost power in 1951, Morrison remained as a leading and very effective opposition spokesman. He had been elected a visiting fellow of Nuffield College, Oxford, in 1947 and was much aided there by (Sir) Norman Chester, especially when he turned to writing and in 1954 published *Government and Parliament, a Survey from the Inside*. The book was at once acclaimed as a notable account of British government and Morrison himself hoped it would become another Erskine May, the authoritative description which would be renewed every few years and continue long after he had died. While the book had considerable merits, especially in the lucid accounts of parliamentary procedure, the legislative programme, and the nationalized industries, it never attained the stature Morrison hoped for. One reason was that he lacked the academic turn of mind and, while the exposition was excellent, there was little analysis. Deeper criticisms are that the book is a first-rate description of how the system worked in theory, but that Morrison put in too few of the by-ways and circumventions of practice. A brilliant intuitive politician, he did not explain how he played by ear, but set out the actual score as it was on the official hymn sheet.

After his defeat for the party leadership, he rejected all attempts to persuade him to remain as deputy leader, although until the end of that Parliament he was still a frequent contributor to debates, as jaunty and pugnacious as ever. In the dissolution honours of 1959 he was made a life peer and the following year extended his activities by accepting the presidency of the British Board of Film Censors. He was also the signatory of the notice of Eveline Mary Lowe, the first woman chairman of the LCC, in this Dictionary.

Morrison's *Autobiography* appeared in 1960. It provided little new information or insights into the period, but did give some interesting sidelights on the author and his relations with his colleagues. In it Morrison says of Attlee that 'he was one of the best mayors that Stepney ever had'. It would be true to say that Morrison himself was almost certainly the best leader whom the London Labour Party and the LCC have ever had, but it would not be enough. He was a great parliamentarian, effective in debate, a master of legislative and administrative detail, the father of an important account of British government and a man whose sincere desire to create better conditions for all was recognized by everyone engaged in British politics.

He died in Queen Mary Hospital at Sidcup 6 March 1965, and his ashes were scattered in London, on the river.

Morrison married in 1919 Margaret (died 1953), the daughter of Howard Kent, of Letchworth, a clerk at Euston station; they had one daughter. It was not a particularly happy marriage. He married, secondly, in 1955, Edith, daughter of John Meadowcroft, of Rochdale. She wrote an enjoyable account of his second marriage (1977).

There are two portraits in chalk of Morrison, both in the National Portrait Gallery, one by Juliet Pannett (1961), the other by Sir David Low.

[Lord Morrison of Lambeth, *An Autobiography*, 1960; Bernard Donoughue and G. W. Jones, *Herbert Morrison, Portrait of a Politician*, 1973.]   JOHN P. MACKINTOSH

MORRISON, WILLIAM SHEPHERD, first VISCOUNT DUNROSSIL (1893–1961), Speaker of the House of Commons, was born at Torinturk, Argyll, 10 August 1893, the sixth of the eight sons of John Morrison and his wife, Marion, daughter of Ronald McVicar, of North Uist. His father had worked in the South African diamond fields in partnership with William Shepherd, eventually selling out to De Beers, when he settled as a farmer at Torinturk. Morrison was educated at George Watson's College and Edinburgh University where he obtained his MA in 1920, having meantime served in the Royal Field Artillery, reached the rank of captain, been wounded and awarded the MC and three mentions in dispatches.

A Highlander in tongue and soul, Morrison returned from the war determined upon a better world and for this purpose chose to follow a career in law and politics. He was called to the bar by the Inner Temple in 1923 on the advice primarily of the Duke of Atholl and also that of Sir Robert Horne [q.v.], a Glaswegian raconteur whose migration south had already led him to the chancellorship of the Exchequer. But Morrison had to pass through six years and two electoral defeats (in the Western Isles in 1923 and 1924) before finding an English constituency to return him. Sir Thomas Inskip (later Viscount Caldecote, q.v.), in whose chambers Morrison was working as a part-time secretary, was his real sponsor for his adoption by the Cirencester and Tewkesbury division. He was returned at the election of 1929 and held the seat until 1959.

Morrison proved intensely impressive both in mind and body. His nickname 'Shakes' was not derived only from his initials, but also from his love of Shakespeare, and indeed he had something of Shakespeare's sense of music in words and of that psychological penetration which, in a Highlander, is sometimes called 'fey'. The capacity to see deeply into things from afar was enhanced by his appearance. A shock of early white hair overhung the blackest of black eyebrows and the deepest of deep-set eyes. He was vibrant. Certainly Morrison had brains; but also his character was one of the most fascinating in the politics of his generation. It was never safe to predict anything about his views except that they would be unusual or unusually well expressed. He had so much character that he probably influenced the House of Commons when chairman of the 1922 Committee (1932–6) more than he ever did as a minister. He took nearly six years to obtain more than a private parliamentary secretaryship, preferring for financial reasons to continue his legal career. He took silk in 1934 and was recorder of Walsall in 1935. In the same year he became financial secretary to the Treasury and in 1936 minister of agriculture and fisheries in succession to his close friend Walter Elliot [q.v.] whose policy of rescuing British farmers from despair he attempted to continue. He was sworn of the Privy Council in 1936. In 1939–40 he was chancellor of the Duchy of Lancaster and minister of food; in 1940–2 postmaster-general; and from 1943 to 1945 he was minister of town and country planning.

At the time of Munich, Morrison expressed black anger in private but publicly argued that legally the national honour had not been smirched. He did not resign, believing, mistakenly, that more influence could be exerted from within rather than from without. Although the wartime offices which he held were not unimportant, his name was never again one at which the whips grew pale, and he was not given office when the Conservatives returned to power in 1951.

But he lost no whit of his charm and lovability, and a wide circle of friends were delighted when his exclusion from office was followed by selection and election as Speaker. He had in fact been offered this post years before but had generously refused because he knew that Douglas Clifton Brown (later Viscount Ruffside, q.v.) wanted it, and he himself did not. But Morrison was a natural for the job of Speaker who must possess unshakeable dignity, enforce a discipline seasoned with humour, know the rules with all a lawyer's infallibility, and protect the rights of minorities without undermining those of majorities. All these things were well within the compass of Morrison's talents. And if, as he said himself at the time, he had become a little hard of hearing, that defect can at least from time to time be an asset in a Speaker.

The eight years from 1951 to 1959 were certainly the highlight of his career even if they were not all sweetness and light. There was the tempestuous affair of Suez, when feelings rose so high as seriously to threaten the preservation of parliamentary order and the cohesion of the Conservative Party. But the standing of Parliament as an institution unlike some individual reputations remained undamaged and on such occasions the main credit for weathering the storm belongs to the Speaker.

When Morrison announced his retirement in 1959 he said that it was for reasons of health and there was therefore some surprise when shortly afterwards he accepted the governorgeneralship of Australia. Morrison himself had contemplated no such thing and was surprised when his old friend (Sir) Robert Menzies approached him, but he was anxious to continue to serve in some capacity. The viscountcy conferred upon him in 1959 in addition to the GCMG was no more than the traditional *envoi* to a Speaker. An effort by socialist backbenchers to combat his receipt of half the Speaker's pension in addition to the ·governor-general's salary collapsed. In less than a year he died in Canberra 3 February 1961, but not before he had given Australians reason to be saddened by his loss.

In 1924 Morrison married Katharine Allison, daughter of the Revd William Swan, minister of South Leith parish. She was herself an Edinburgh graduate and at the time was reading for the bar. They had four sons, the eldest of whom, John William (born 1926), succeeded to the viscountcy. A portrait of Dunrossil by Sir Oswald Birley is in the possession of the family, another, by E. O. Fearnley-Whittingstall, is in the state dining room of the Palace of Westminster.

[Private information; personal knowledge.]

COLIN R. COOTE

MOULLIN, ERIC BALLIOL (1893-1960), professor of electrical engineering, was born at Sandbanks, near Parkstone, 10 August 1893, the only child of Arthur Daniel Moullin, a civil engineer from an old Guernsey family, and his wife, Charlotte Annie Longman. He was delicate in childhood and was educated privately. He won a scholarship to Downing College, Cambridge, and took a second class in part i of the mathematical tripos in 1913. He then embarked on the mechanical sciences tripos. In 1914 ill health forced him to abandon his studies but the following year he returned and in 1916 obtained a first class in the tripos and gained the John Winbolt prize in 1918. From 1917 to 1919 he was a lecturer at the Royal Naval College, Dartmouth. He then returned to the Cambridge Engineering Laboratory where he was a very active teacher and research worker for the next ten years. During this time he was attached to King's College as an assistant director of studies. In 1929 he was offered the chair of engineering at Oxford but withdrew with characteristic generosity in favour of (Sir) R. V. Southwell [q.v.]. He then accepted the newly founded Donald Pollock readership (under Southwell) and two years later became a fellow of Magdalen College. On the outbreak of war in 1939 he joined the Admiralty Signals Establishment at Portsmouth and in 1942 transferred to the Metropolitan Vickers Electrical Co. Ltd., of Manchester. At the end of the war he was appointed to the chair of electrical engineering at Cambridge, which had just been founded through the sponsorship of the Institution of Electrical Engineers and the British Electrical and Allied Manufacturers Association. He was elected to a professorial fellowship at King's in 1946. He retired in 1960. He was awarded the Cambridge Sc.D. in 1939 and was made an honorary LLD of Glasgow University in 1958.

Throughout his career Moullin was an active member of the Institution of Electrical Engineers. He was chairman of the radio section at the outbreak of war, served on council from 1940-9, latterly as vice-president and then president for the session 1949-50. In 1963 he was made an honorary member of the Institution. He was also a governor of the College of Aeronautics until 1949 and a member of the Radio Research Board of the Department of Scientific and Industrial Research, 1934–42.

He was a prolific writer. Besides a large number of scientific papers, most of which appeared in the *Journal of the Institution of Electrical Engineers*, he published five important books. The first of these, *The Theory and Practice of Radio Frequency Measurements* (1926), had a considerable influence on the development of radio systems. It shows his character-istic combination of experimental and mathe-matical skill. As a boy he had been a radio amateur helped by his father in a workshop at their home in Swanage and almost to the end of his life he delighted in working in the attic laboratory at his home in Cambridge. His great contribution to measurement was the Moullin valve voltmeter and various other instruments and components. His second book, *The Principles of Electromagnetism* (1932), was a widely used teaching book and formed the basis of his own lectures. In 1938 appeared *Spontaneous Fluctuations of Voltage*, a lucid research monograph on a most difficult subject. The fourth book, *Radio Aerials* (1949), was written at Metropolitan-Vickers as a result of Moullin's wartime researches. His last book was the *Electromagnetic Principles of the Dynamo* (1955). Its preface states that most of it was written before the end of 1933, when it was meant to appear as a companion volume to *The Principles of Electromagnetism*, but the pressure of other researches hindered its completion. It is a tribute to the quality of Moullin's work that twenty-two years later the work had not dated appreciably. His central contribution to the study of electromagnetism was his insistence that the sources of fields are their most impor-tant feature and that these sources can be con-trolled by the engineer to achieve desired effects.

The range of subject-matter of these books demonstrated their author's grasp of the whole field of electrical engineering. Moullin disliked all narrow specialization, although on the other hand he was no generalist but had rather a distrust of general statements. He loved detail and delighted in particular cases, on which he focused his powerful mind and which he studied so carefully that they became windows through which one could see a whole landscape. He was an outstanding teacher of engineers, reinforcing his lectures with beautifully designed experi-ments. He was daily in the laboratory, where he showed a personal interest in individual students and in members of his staff, both academics and technicians. From his research students he called out the best. He did not praise often, but his praise was worth having.

Moullin saw no conflict between academic and industrial engineering, being as much at home in the factory as in the college. He treated colleagues in industry as full partners in a pro-fessional enterprise and was an energetic supporter of industrial training schemes. In the university he was a fighter for academic free-dom, which he felt was endangered both by central government and by academics who were not content to be scholars but sought after power and influence.

He had a keen sense of history and was delighted when he inherited, in 1947, the Fief des Eperons in Guernsey. On Queen Eliza-beth's visit to the island in 1957, he carried out, as seigneur, his feudal duty of presenting the gilt spurs to the reigning monarch. His scarlet doctor's gown added a splash of colour to the ceremony. He did much work on Guernsey parish registers and wrote several antiquarian papers for La Société Guern-sesiaise. In his will he endowed a prize at Downing College for the best student in en-gineering or history, two subjects he had made his own.

He married in 1919 Christobel, daughter of Professor Edward Schroder Prior, Slade pro-fessor of fine art at Cambridge, by whom he had two daughters, and secondly, in 1934, Joan Evelyn, daughter of Louis Francis Salzman, who was a medievalist and sometime editor of the Victoria County Histories. Moullin died in Cambridge 18 September 1963.

[Obituary notice in the *Annual Report of Council*, 1963, of King's College, Cambridge; private information; personal knowledge.]

P. HAMMOND

MURRAY, JOHN (1879–1964), educationist and politician, was born 28 February 1879 at Fraserburgh, Aberdeenshire, the eldest son of Francis Robert Murray, fish curer, and his wife, Isabella Watt. He was educated at Robert Gor-don's College, Aberdeen. In 1896 he entered the university of Aberdeen as first bursar, graduat-ing in 1900 with honours in Greek and Latin, having won the Simpson Greek prize and the Seafield Latin medal. In 1901 he went up as an exhibitioner to Christ Church, Oxford, on a Fullerton scholarship. He took first class honours in classical moderations in 1903 and in *literae humaniores* in 1905. In the same year he was elected prize fellow of Merton College, and in 1908 student and tutor of his old college, Christ Church, where in 1910 he became censor. Murray published nothing except the occasional political piece in the *Oxford Magazine* (which he edited from 1911 to 1914) during his years as a don, but the Oxford system of education had made a lasting im-pression.

In 1915 Murray left Oxford to join the

Labour Department of the newly created Ministry of Munitions. By the end of the war he had reached the fairly senior rank of assistant commissioner in the Labour Adviser's Department. In the general election of December 1918 he stood as a Coalition Liberal in Leeds West, and was elected with a large majority. He was soon given minor administrative work to do as officer in charge of a section of the Board of Education concerned with university awards to ex-servicemen. In 1920-1 he was chairman of the Central Committee on Trusts, a body set up under the Profiteering Acts, 1919-20. The committee had powers to investigate and report on price increases, and during Murray's chairmanship published a large number of brief reports, on which little or no action was taken. In 1921 Murray married Ellen, widow of George Harwood (1845-1912, Liberal MP for Bolton) and daughter of Sir Alfred Hopkinson [q.v.]. In 1922 he stood as a National Liberal in Leeds West and retained his seat by a narrow majority in a straight fight against Labour, but in 1923, when the Conservatives fielded a candidate, Murray came third, at the bottom of the poll. In 1924 he retreated to Kirkcaldy, but succeeded only in reducing the Labour majority. He fought a by-election in the safe Conservative seat of Ripon in 1925, his last attempt to re-enter Parliament. Murray was never a leading member of the Liberal Party, but during his brief parliamentary career he spoke lucidly and with originality; in happier days for Liberals he would undoubtedly have achieved office. His speeches in the House showed a certain radicalism: he favoured sympathetic treatment of the unemployed and was an early (and lifelong) advocate of family allowances. In later years he described himself as an individualist and associated with Sir Ernest Benn [q.v.] in the Society of Individualists. Already in the by-election at Ripon in 1925 he had openly disagreed with Lloyd George's plans for nationalization of land and the coal industry, and privately expressed his dislike of what he called 'promise-politics'.

In 1926, after nearly three years in the political wilderness, Murray was appointed principal of the University College of the South West, Exeter, in succession to (Sir) W. H. Moberly. Although Murray at first hoped to return to politics one day, he spent the rest of his working life in the service of the University College, declining in 1929 the vice-chancellorship of the university of Sheffield. He inherited a college with cramped buildings and few endowments, partly engaged in training teachers for elementary schools, but mostly preparing students for external degrees of the university of London. The college had two assets: recognition by the University Grants Committee as a grant-receiving institution; and a magnificent and almost empty site of 150 acres on the northwestern outskirts of Exeter. It was Murray's object to develop these assets until the college became a full university. The first need was money. Murray plunged happily into the business of fund-raising, which he likened to 'a perpetual by-election'. While he was principal the substantial sum of £250,000 was raised for buildings, scholarships, and chairs. He was not the man to suffer a fool gladly—unless a prospective benefactor: the largest benefaction ever received by the college was owing to Murray's tact, firmness, and inexhaustible patience exercised over a period of fourteen years in the face of considerable provocation. Murray sought to combine in Exeter the merits of Oxford and Aberdeen: he promoted the Oxford system of residence and of tutorial teaching and he envisaged Exeter as providing for poor English boys and girls the educational ladder that Aberdeen offered to aspiring Scotsmen like himself. In addition he strove to provide an international dimension to the college by attracting students from Europe, the United States, Africa, and the Middle East. In all this he had considerable success, but the final prize—a university charter—eluded him. He retired in 1951. Murray received three honorary doctorates: LLD from Aberdeen (1930), Litt.D. from Columbia, NY (1939), and, fittingly, D.Litt. from Exeter (1956), conferred at the first degree congregation held by the new university that he had done much to foster.

Murray was eloquent, formidable, autocratic, and in his later years careless of administrative forms. He gave time and money generously to help students and staff. He wrote occasionally for the *Hibbert Journal* and the *Contemporary Review* and circulated privately a humorous fantasy *Shinid* (1938) in celebration of English hospitality in an Irish setting. He was a staunch Christian and as a member of the de la Warr committee on higher education in East Africa in 1936-7 wrote a minority report opposing secular education there; in his view the mission schools should have continued to monopolize popular education even in territories three-quarters pagan—'an educated pagan is a pagan still'. Murray died in London 28 December 1964.

A portrait of Murray by R. G. Eves (1939) hangs in Murray House, a hall of residence of the university of Exeter named in his honour but built on a larger scale than he would have considered desirable.

[University of Exeter MSS; *The Times*, 30 December 1964 and 2 January 1965; private information.]   B. W. CLAPP

MURRAY, MARGARET ALICE (1863-1963), Egyptologist, was born in Calcutta 13 July 1863, younger daughter of James Charles Murray, by his wife, Margaret Carr. James Murray, whose family had been in India for several generations, was managing partner of a firm of Manchester merchants, and was three times president of the Calcutta Chamber of Commerce; his wife was from a Northumbrian family, and had gone to India as a missionary and social worker. Margaret Murray was educated privately in England and Germany, and from the age of sixteen she divided her time between India and England. She resolved to pursue a nursing career, and entered Calcutta general hospital in 1883 as their first 'lady probationer', where she acted briefly as sister-in-charge during an epidemic. She returned to England for good in 1886 (her parents retiring there the following year), but had to give up her intention of becoming a professional nurse because she was too small to qualify for admission. She shared her mother's concern for the social status of women, and was to remain an ardent feminist all her life, participating in the suffragette movement and challenging male dominance in the academic world.

In 1894 she entered University College, London, as a student of Egyptology under (Sir) Flinders Petrie [q.v.], fired by her sister's enthusiasm for his work; Margaret Murray quickly learnt to decipher Egyptian hieroglyphs, and Petrie, realizing her abilities, started her on further research: she thus became the first woman to devote herself fully to Egyptology, and remained Petrie's helpmate and disciple until the end of his life. Despite the fact that she had, as she said, never been to school or passed an examination in her life, in 1899 she became a junior lecturer at University College; she took over the teaching of elementary hieroglyphs, and also developed an interest in anthropology and ethnology (then not considered 'suitable' subjects for women) under the influence of C. G. Seligman [q.v.]. She gave extension lectures at Oxford (1910) and London (1911), and catalogued Egyptian antiquities in the National Museum of Ireland, the Royal Scottish Museum, Manchester University Museum, and the Ashmolean Museum, Oxford. During much of this time she was also nursing her invalid mother (her father died in 1891), and when these responsibilities ceased she went to live near University College; she became successively assistant (1909), lecturer (1921), and senior lecturer and fellow of the college (1922); in 1924-35 she was assistant professor, obtaining her D.Lit. in 1931. She took an active interest in the welfare of the girl students, and was especially remembered for her kindness to the young women doctors who

came from Serbia and later Yugoslavia on postgraduate scholarships. She was a lady associate of the Society of Antiquaries of Scotland from 1900.

Margaret Murray first assisted Petrie in his excavations at Abydos in 1902, but her teaching duties in London increased as she organized the training of students in Egyptology and archaeology, and more of the departmental work fell upon her while Petrie was abroad, so that she could spend little time on fieldwork. She excavated in Malta (1920-3), Minorca (1930-1), and at Petra (1937). In 1938, when Petrie's powers were beginning to fail, she joined his expedition to Tell El Ajjul, ancient Gaza, and concerned herself particularly with the Hyksos cities, where she concentrated on the description of a hoard of gold jewellery and discussed the evidence for Hyksos horse sacrifice. Her work in Palestine was recorded in *The City of Shepherd Kings, Ancient Gaza V* (1952), her name appearing alongside those of Petrie and E. J. A. Mackay.

She was highly industrious, a conscientious cataloguer, and everything she produced was—and remained—valuable to students as a primary record; she published over eighty books and articles on ancient Egypt, including the following: *Guide to the Collection of Egyptian Antiquities in the Edinburgh Museum of Science and Art* (1903); *Ancient Egyptian Legends* (1904); *The Osireion at Abydos* (1904); *Saqqara Mastabas* (vols. i and ii, 1905-37: perhaps her best work); *Elementary Egyptian Grammar* (1905); the useful and much quoted *Index of Names and Titles in the Old Kingdom* (1908); *The Tomb of Two Brothers* (1910); *Egyptian Sculpture* (1930); *Egyptian Temples* (1931); *The Splendour that was Egypt* (1949); *Egyptian Religious Poetry* (1949); *Seven Memphite Tomb Chapels* (with Hilda Flinders Petrie, 1952); and *The Genesis of Religion* (1963). But for so forceful a character, much of what she wrote was unexpectedly pedestrian in style, lacking a sense of historical excitement, and *The Splendour that was Egypt*, one of her best-known works, is vitiated by a chronology slavishly adopted from Petrie, who had erroneously set the archaic dynasties of Egypt a Sothic cycle—well over a thousand years—too early. *Egyptian Sculpture* contains much acute and penetrating observation of detail and is a useful factual account, although the remarkable sculpture of the Saite period receives only a casual reference, and the composition of much Amarna painting is denigrated.

Margaret Murray's scholarship showed breadth of interest rather than profundity; she was not a philologist, and was occasionally guilty of making unsubstantiated statements. Perhaps the main criticism which might be levelled is that she tended to take a myopic view of Egyptian civilization; lack of a proper perspective is particularly evident in her failure to appreciate the important outside influences and contact with Mesopotamia which were manifest in the Proto-Dynastic period. Never again were the Euphrates and Nile valley in such close touch. It was an altogether remarkable phenomenon when imported cylinder seals began to appear, and her account of the Gebel Araq knife, whereon we see a standing figure in the Sumero-Babylonian style between two rampant lions, is defective. Nevertheless, in the assessment of the changing scope of Egypt, Margaret Murray was well versed and sensitive to the internal changes in the long course of Egyptian history. She had great enthusiasm for her subject, and her surprising versatility was displayed, for example, by *Elementary Coptic Grammar* (1911), a useful introduction for students, and the *Coptic Reading Book* (with Dorothy Pilcher, 1933). Her knowledge of hieroglyphs and the language was of the greatest help to Petrie. At heart she was a true archaeologist who enjoyed concentrating on the material remains, and a conscientious cataloguer and recorder, although her works are dull in style and she had no close affinity with those who kept the linguistic record. A woman of courage, a happy explorer, her amusing and strong personality made a marked impact on all who studied with her.

Margaret Murray was also deeply interested in witchcraft and folklore; she was a fellow of the Royal Anthropological Institute from 1926, and was president of the Folklore Society in 1953-5. She became a recognized authority on the subject through *The Witch-Cult in Western Europe* (1921), wherein she rightly drew a sharp distinction between witchcraft and magic. Her theory of the witch-cult was criticized in detail, and her interpretations questioned, but her breadth of learning was always respected. She possessed firm common sense and was quite unsuperstitious, although if she had lived in an earlier age she might have been thought of as a lady fit for burning: when she comminated her enemies her bright blue eyes flashed in dangerous indignation, and she was ready if only in jest to practise magic in order to remove from office a colleague of whose appointment she disapproved. Indeed, on one occasion she cast a spell on an intended victim in a saucepan at the Institute of Archaeology, in the presence of two reputable witnesses, and achieved her aim with conspicuous success. The subject immediately fell ill, and was promoted to some higher and more suitable office. In this instance a rational explanation is the more acceptable, but those who were conscious of Margaret Murray's powers preferred to recall her magic.

She died in London 13 November 1963. A bronze head of her by S. L. Rickard was exhibited in the Royal Academy in 1961.

[*The Times*, 15 November 1963; Margaret Murray, *My First Hundred Years*, 1963; personal knowledge.]   MAX MALLOWAN

MYRDDIN-EVANS, SIR GUILDHAUME (1894-1964), civil servant, was born at Aberystruth, Monmouthshire, 17 December 1894, the second son of the Revd Thomas Towy Evans, of Blaenau, Gwent, Abertillery, Monmouthshire, and his wife, Mary James. He was educated at Llandovery and Christ Church, Oxford, where he obtained first class honours in mathematical moderations in 1914, and subsequently became MA. On the outbreak of World War I he was commissioned in the South Wales Borderers, and served in France and Flanders. In 1917 he was invalided out of the army, and he then joined the prime minister's secretariat. Two years later he became assistant secretary to the Cabinet, and, for the next ten years he was an assistant principal in the Treasury.

In 1929 Myrddin-Evans moved to the Ministry of Labour, becoming in 1935 deputy chief insurance officer under the new Unemployment Acts. Then, in 1938, he was appointed head of the International Labour Division of the Ministry of Labour. From this time until his retirement in 1959 he led nearly all the British delegations to international labour conferences, and it was at once the most congenial as well as the most successful period of his career.

During the war of 1939-45 Myrddin-Evans served as head of the Production Executive secretariat, and he also acted as adviser on manpower problems to both the American and Canadian governments. He was a member of the British delegation to the San Francisco conference in 1945 which established the United Nations, and he served in the British delegation to the General Assembly of the UN between 1946 and 1953. But his outstanding achievement was his work for the International Labour Organization. He had become the representative of the British Government on the governing body of the ILO in 1945, and he was soon elected chairman. In the early months of 1946 negotiations began between the ILO and the UN; and the conclusions of these often difficult discussions, formally embodied in a detailed agreement, owed much to the tact, skill, and competence of the two respective chairmen: Myrddin-Evans for the ILO and Sir A. Ramaswami Mudaliar, of India, for the UN. Myrddin-Evans was chairman of the ILO for three periods of office—a rare occurrence—and he was the first civil servant ever to be elected president of the International Labour Conference. This was in 1949.

He enjoyed great esteem within the ILO and was known all over the world for his remarkable knowledge of international labour conditions and problems. His contribution to the growth and development of the ILO was widely appreciated, and the warmth of his reception on his many visits to different parts of the world was a matter of deep personal satisfaction. On the eve of his retirement from the Ministry of Labour he was appointed chairman of the Local Government Commission for Wales. He greatly appreciated the compliment; and he showed himself once more as an admirable chairman: thorough, positive, always helpful, and he won the respect and the affection of his committee. The Commission's report was published in 1963, a year before his death.

Myrddin-Evans was an active churchman all his life. For many years he was a member of the council of the Baptist Union, and for a time he served as secretary of the Bloomsbury Central Baptist Church in London.

In 1934 he published, with (Sir) Thomas Chegwidden as co-author, *The Employment Exchange Service of Great Britain*. He was appointed CB in 1945, and KCMG in 1947. In 1919 he married Elizabeth (died 1981), daughter of Owen Watkins, of Sarn, Caernarvonshire, and there were two sons of the marriage. Myrddin-Evans died at his London home 15 February 1964.

[*The Times*, and the *Western Mail*, 17 February 1964; private information.]

JOHN SAVILLE

N

NASH, SIR WALTER (1882-1968), prime minister of New Zealand, was born in Kidderminster 12 February 1882, the fifth of the six children of Arthur Alfred Nash, a wool weaver, dyer, and later a clerk, and his wife, Amelia Randle. He was educated at a church school beginning at the age of three. He soon revealed an exceptional memory and won a scholarship to King Charles I Grammar School, but the family could not afford the required uniform, so he left school at eleven. Thereafter he had a variety of jobs, from messenger boy to an analysis clerk in the Ariel bicycle works in Birmingham, where the family moved by stages. Then he opened two sweet and tobacco shops in Selly Oak, where he married Lotty May (died 1961), daughter of Thomas Eaton, plumber, in 1906. They had three sons, the eldest born in Selly Oak.

Apart from helping his father, a Conservative Party agent, on election days, and showing a keen interest in land taxation, Nash revealed little concern for politics in England. He began, however, the very extensive reading which assisted his later political career.

His wife wanted to travel and in 1909 Nash sold his business and sailed for New Zealand with about £800. He settled in Wellington and entered a partnership in a firm of tailors. One of his partners misled him about the firm's debts and Nash lost what money remained after furnishing a house. Then he became a commercial traveller in cloths for suits. He proved a very successful salesman.

In Wellington Nash had become very active as a fund-raiser for the Church of England Men's Society, until the bishop discovered that he thought usury a sin and had refused to deposit the funds at interest. Through a radical parson, he met the leaders of the political Labour movement, Harry Holland and Peter Fraser [q.v.]. He was angry at the brutal actions of special police (mounted farmers) during the 1913 strike, and joined the New Zealand Labour Party formed in 1916. His socialism was not Marxist. He was a Christian socialist, whose thought was chiefly influenced by reading Ruskin, Morris, F. D. Maurice [qq.v.], and Tolstoy. In that year he became a partner (and accountant) in a firm of tailors in New Plymouth, where he started the first Labour Party branch, and stood with other Labour candidates unsuccessfully in the New Plymouth municipal elections in 1919. His introduction of profit-sharing in his firm led to trouble with the chief partner (and suggested that he was not perhaps born to make profits).

Nash set off for England, where he acquired the New Zealand agencies for several publishers. He represented the New Zealand Labour Party at the Second Socialist International in Geneva in 1920. There he met Sidney Webb [q.v.], F. W. Jowett, and other famous socialists. He spoke once only, criticizing Webb's report on socialization as disguised capitalism.

Returning to New Zealand, Nash opened a bookshop and publisher's agency in Wellington—work more to his taste than selling cloths or suits. But in 1922 he was elected secretary of the party and by the mid twenties this took up all his time. Nash was a near perfect secretary. He (and Fraser) made the Labour Party into a national organization. Nash introduced efficient office methods, raised funds, opened branches. He remembered every detail—indeed his memory for facts, figures, and names of people was extraordinary. Most of the other Labour leaders had trade-union, and some of them revolutionary, socialist, backgrounds. Nash brought an element of middle-class and Christian respectability.

As well as working for the party, he helped start the Institute of International Affairs and the Institute of Pacific Affairs. He represented New Zealand at conferences of the latter in Hawaii and in Canada, where he met many leading men and gained in confidence. His knowledge of world affairs was exceeded by only a handful of people in New Zealand.

After two unsuccessful attempts, in a by-election in 1929 he was elected to Parliament, continuing as secretary until 1932. Although not the leaders (Holland and then M. J. Savage were officially those), Fraser and Nash played the biggest part in formulating the policies which, in time of depression, led to the election of the first Labour Government in 1935. Nash wrote the election manifesto.

He became minister of finance, customs, and later marketing, in Savage's ministry (1935-40) and minister of finance and deputy prime minister under Peter Fraser (1940-9). He and Fraser (whose intelligence and political shrewdness Nash greatly admired) made an outstanding team. Nash's contribution to the extensive reforms of 1935-8 was very great. He introduced the system of 'guaranteed prices' for dairy produce which still, much modified, exists. Although caucus rejected his own income-related contributory scheme of pensions, he played a major role in formulating and (as minister of social security) piloting through Parliament in 1938 the great system of pensions, child allowances, and 'free' medicine which was the most extensive system of social security in the world at that time.

In 1936-7 Nash spent months in England unsuccessfully trying to negotiate a new trade agreement whereby Britain would buy virtually all New Zealand's exports at agreed prices and New Zealand would import an equivalent value of British goods. In 1939 he again visited London trying to raise funds to redeem a maturing loan. New Zealand was suffering from over-importing due to local inflation and Nash reacted rather belatedly by introducing import licensing. To this British leaders objected. Nash was given a rough time and only succeeded in raising funds on most arduous terms. Ironically, within a few months New Zealand was at war on Britain's side and Britain was taking New Zealand exports under a bulk purchase agreement.

By 1940 it was clear that the British could not defend New Zealand against attack. In November 1941, just before Pearl Harbor, Nash was appointed minister to Washington—New Zealand's first diplomatic representative in a foreign country. In the United States he was an outstanding success at his chief task, getting New Zealand known. He was a member of the Pacific War Council and, for a time, of the War Cabinet in London. He retained his Cabinet rank in New Zealand and returned temporarily to present his 1943 budget.

Much of Nash's time was taken up with post-war planning. In 1944 he chaired a meeting of the International Labour Organization; he attended the international meetings at Bretton Woods, Geneva, and Havana at which GATT (the General Agreement on Tariffs and Trade) and the International Monetary Fund were created. At these meetings he took an active part. Their aim was to improve post-war economic conditions; to decrease the risk of depression and war. The Labour caucus refused to agree to New Zealand joining the IMF—and Opposition leaders, like (Sir) Sidney Holland [q.v.], agreed with the Labour majority. The IMF was criticized, among other reasons, for involving restrictions on New Zealand's independence.

In 1949 the Fraser Government lost office. Peter Fraser died in 1950 and Nash became leader of the Opposition, almost immediately to be confronted with one of the greatest crises in his career. The Labour leaders, while dealing decisively with the very left-wing Auckland Carpenters' Union, had been unable to dispose of the aggressive, but only partly Communist-led, Waterside Workers' Union in Auckland. The Holland Government acted ruthlessly and wrecked the union with its arrogant leaders. Nash fought hard for freedom of speech, but was much criticized by an anti-union (and cold war) public for saying that his party was 'neither for nor against' the strikers. Labour was defeated

in a snap election in 1951 and again in 1954, when many voters 'protested' by voting Social Credit, not Labour.

At last, in 1957, at the age of seventy-five, Nash became prime minister, elected on a policy which included increased family benefits and pensions, easier access to housing loans, and up to £100 tax rebate when PAYE was introduced. On the day he took office he was informed that overseas funds had dropped disastrously due to over-importing. It seemed like 1939 all over again. This time the Government probably over-reacted with its severe 'black budget' and import controls. In the circumstances of economic severity, and with a parliamentary majority of only one, the Government's scope was restricted. It did abolish compulsory military training, introduce 'equal pay' in the Civil Service, and carry out the reforms mentioned above. It promoted industrial development. But the public recalled the contrast between Labour's promises and the financial stringency which followed. The party was defeated in the 1960 election.

Nash was less impressive as prime minister than as minister of finance. Although quite extraordinarily energetic, he was almost equally dilatory in making decisions. He attended endless petty functions from which a prime minister could have been excused for more exacting duties. He seemed too absorbed in details rather than in broad policy decisions. He was, as always, in some respects, inconsiderate of his assistants. He himself needed only four or so hours' sleep (plus 'cat-naps') and he expected others to be available as required at almost all times. Increasing fame was paralleled by vanity. He amassed the largest private collection of papers in New Zealand which filled his garage and, after culling, weighed ten tons. Every scrap referring to his career—even air tickets—was filed away.

While prime minister he travelled abroad constantly, talking to Krushchev, de Gaulle, Macmillan, Eisenhower. The British high commissioner in New Zealand, Sir George Mallaby, wrote that he was the only New Zealand politician with 'some pretensions to being a world figure' and that 'other world statesmen were ready to listen' (*From my Level*, 1965). Nash led New Zealand delegations to every conceivable conference. He continued as leader of the Opposition until 1963 and MP until his death. His active sympathy for the underdog remained undiminished to the end, as did his hatred of militarism. In 1965 he spoke vehemently at the first two 'teach-ins' against the Vietnam war.

Nash was sworn of the Privy Council in 1946, appointed CH in 1959 and GCMG in 1965. He received honorary doctorates from Cambridge,

Victoria University of Wellington, Tufts College, and Temple University. He died in Wellington after a short illness 4 June 1968. Portraits painted by Evelyn Page and L. Mitchell are in the National Art Gallery, Wellington.

[The Nash papers, New Zealand Archives, Wellington.]   KEITH SINCLAIR

NATHAN, HARRY LOUIS, first BARON NATHAN (1889-1963), lawyer and public servant, was born at 36 Bassett Road, North Kensington, 2 February 1889, the elder son of Michael Henry Nathan and his wife, Constance, daughter of Louis Beaver, jeweller and silversmith, of Manchester. For reasons of health his father retired from his business as a fine art publisher when he was about fifty but continued his activities as a justice of the peace and as a keen Liberal in politics.

Nathan was educated at St. Paul's School where he was a cadet lieutenant in the Corps, of which the future Field-Marshal Viscount Montgomery of Alamein was a member, and vice-president and treasurer of the Union Debating Society. It was perhaps due to his numerous extra-curricular activities that he failed to obtain a scholarship at Balliol and he decided not to go up to Oxford as a commoner, a decision he often regretted in later years. Instead, he became an articled clerk, was admitted a solicitor in 1913, and became junior partner to Herbert Oppenheimer, a brilliant lawyer with a good commercial practice.

As an original territorial officer Nathan reported for duty with the Royal Fusiliers when war broke out in August 1914. He served in Malta and then in Gallipoli and was promoted captain, then major, and as lieutenant-colonel commanded his battalion, a unit of the 29th division, during the evacuations at both Suvla Bay and Helles. Subsequently the battalion was sent to France in time for the first battle of the Somme in July 1916. Shot through the back of the head by a sniper, Nathan was in hospital for eighteen months but made a remarkable recovery although the after-effects lasted for many years.

Returning to his firm, Nathan was introduced to Sir Alfred Mond (later Lord Melchett, q.v.) who became a client. This opened up a new field of interest as Mond was an enthusiastic supporter of the Zionist movement. Nathan became legal adviser to the Zionist Organization, to the Economic Board of Palestine, and later to Pinhas Rutenberg who founded the Palestine Electric Company and to Moses Novomeyski who formed the Palestine Potash Company in 1930 to extract potash from the Dead Sea.

During the war of 1939-45 it supplied half the potash needed by Great Britain.

As a power in the Liberal Party, Mond was also helpful to Nathan in his political career. Unsuccessful as the Liberal candidate for Whitechapel and St. George's in 1924, Nathan won North East Bethnal Green in 1929. In his maiden speech he attacked the government proposal to authorize the Treasury to guarantee loans of £25 million without stating the precise nature of the public utility schemes to be aided. He was soon recognized by the House as an expert on economic and financial matters.

When Ramsay MacDonald formed his 'national' Government in the summer of 1931 Nathan followed Sir Herbert (later Viscount) Samuel [q.v.], the leader of what was left of the Liberal Party, in supporting the new Government on the ground that its immediate function was to put the national finances on a proper basis. After the general election in October in which the Conservatives gained an overwhelming majority, Nathan was disappointed by the course taken by the new Government, stating that it was a fraud under a false alias. He crossed the floor of the House in February 1933 and sat as an independent Liberal for eighteen months before joining the Labour Party. He was bitterly attacked for betraying the Liberal Party but his action was a courageous one, both from the political standpoint and from that of his private interest, because a Labour solicitor might not be popular with the business men who were his clients.

At the general election of 1935 Nathan fought South Cardiff in the Labour interest but did no more than reduce his opponent's majority; a failure due in part to a libel published by the *Western Mail* on the morning of the election for which the newspaper subsequently made a public apology to Nathan in court and paid a substantial sum by way of agreed damages. In April 1937 at a by-election Nathan was returned to the House as Labour member for Central Wandsworth. He became chairman of a committee known first as the Territorial Army Public Interest Committee and later as the National Defence Public Interest Committee, formed to encourage recruiting first for the Territorials, then also for the Auxiliary Air Force, and finally also for Civil Defence. Before war broke out Nathan had realized that soldiers would need help with their home problems and with the agreement of the authorities the Army Welfare Service was built up in the early days of the war. Nathan became command welfare officer of Eastern Command and London District, relinquishing the former in 1941. When in 1943 the Army Council put welfare in London under an assistant adjutant-general it thanked him for his 'outstanding part in welfare work', of which he was the pioneer.

While Neville Chamberlain was still prime minister Attlee asked him to recommend Nathan for a peerage so as to strengthen Labour representation in the Lords. Before this could be done Churchill had succeeded Chamberlain. Nathan was created a baron in June 1940 and Ernest Bevin [q.v.] was elected member of Parliament for Central Wandsworth. The suggestion that Nathan's peerage was used to make a place for Bevin was not correct. Nathan chose as his motto in his heraldic arms the words 'Labor nobilitat'.

When Attlee became prime minister in 1945 Nathan went to the War Office as under-secretary of state and therefore vice-president of the Army Council. In October 1946 he was promoted to be minister of civil aviation and sworn of the Privy Council. This was an entirely new field: he had many problems to tackle, notably the development of the state corporations set up under the Civil Aviation Act of 1946.

In May 1948 he was obliged to resign from the Government owing to the advanced age of his senior partner. He continued active in public affairs and in 1950 became chairman of the Charitable Trusts Committee whose report in 1952 on necessary changes in the law became the foundation of the Charities Act of 1960. In 1957, in collaboration with A. R. Barrowclough, he published a work on *Medical Negligence*. He had served as crown representative on the British Medical Council, was for many years chairman of the governors of the Westminster Hospital Group, and chairman of the executive of the British Empire Cancer Campaign. He was also chairman of the Wolfson Foundation, president of the Royal Geographical Society, and chairman of the Royal Society of Arts.

As a young man Nathan had been one of the managers of the Brady Street Club in Whitechapel, the oldest of the London Jewish boys' clubs. Throughout his life he continued his interest in training for the young, such as the Maccabian Associations which stressed the importance of rendering Jewish youth capable of self-defence. In 1950 he was president of the European organizing committee when the third Maccabiah Games were held at Tel Aviv. It was then that he inspected the Israeli defence forces, noting that they were 'the most formidable, the best trained and the most resolute in the Middle East'.

Nathan's especial qualities have been summed up as loyalty, warm-hearted humanity, and creative imagination. To these might be added enthusiasm and capacity for hard work in regard to anything he undertook to do.

Nathan married in 1919 Eleanor Joan Clara (died 1972), daughter of the late Carl Stettauer, leather merchant. She was of notable assistance to her husband in his political life. A Cambridge graduate and a governor of Girton, she was for many years a member of the London County Council and in 1947-8 its second woman chairman. They had one daughter who married (Sir) Bernard Waley-Cohen and one son, Roger Carol Michael (born 1922), who also became a solicitor and who succeeded to the title when his father died in London 23 October 1963.

A portrait by Henry Carr is in the possession of the family.

[*The Times*, 25 October 1963; H. Montgomery Hyde, *Strong for Service: the Life of Lord Nathan of Churt*, 1968; personal knowledge.]   A. L. GOODHART

NEHRU, JAWAHARLAL (1889-1964), national leader and first prime minister of India, was born in Allahabad 14 November 1889, the eldest child of Pandit Motilal Nehru [q.v.] and his wife, Swarup Rani. Motilal was to become a leading advocate at the Allahabad high court, and he adopted a life-style which matched his professional eminence. He accepted the Anglo-Indian culture of the time and mixed easily with the British rulers of India. Swarup Rani, in contrast, remained uneducated and traditional in her beliefs. Although Jawaharlal had two younger sisters (one of whom was to become Mrs Vijayalakshmi Pandit), his parents were deeply possessive and ambitious for their son. Motilal wanted him to have the best English education money could buy and then to enter the Indian Civil Service and in 1905 took him to England to enter Harrow. After two unsatisfying years Jawaharlal decided to go on to Cambridge where he entered Trinity College. Although Motilal's support enabled him to live in great comfort and to travel widely, he was restless and drifting. He obtained a second class in part i of the natural sciences tripos (1910), which was rather better than he had expected. Meanwhile Motilal had changed his plans for his son and decided he should study law. In October 1910 Jawaharlal moved to London and the Inner Temple to read for the bar. Law too failed to win his interest but he passed the final examinations two years later, leaving in 1912 to return to India.

While Jawaharlal was in Britain Motilal had become active in the Indian National Congress: father and son began their long political dialogue. Jawaharlal was more sympathetic than his father with those Indians who challenged the moderate leadership of Congress. The extremist glorification of the Hindu past, however, had no attraction, and temperamentally he could never accept terrorist violence. His first meeting of Congress, in 1912, did not inspire him and for four years he led an aimless life, living at home and working for his father.

His marriage, on 8 February 1916, seemed only to increase his burdens. Motilal chose the bride. Kamala, daughter of Jawaharmal Kaul, a Delhi business man, was like Jawaharlal a Kashmiri Brahmin. Married at sixteen she was ten years younger than Jawaharlal. Kamala lacked Western education, had little in common with her husband, and in the Nehru household she was bitterly conscious of her inadequacies and felt helpless and jealous of her sisters-in-law. In November 1917 a daughter was born and named Indira, but Kamala's health was poor and by 1920 she was already suffering from tuberculosis.

Jawaharlal was drawn into active politics by Mrs Annie Besant's [q.v.] Home Rule League and showed a relish for agitation which suggested he was at last finding a cause. Then, in 1919, M. K. Gandhi [q.v.] launched his campaign against the Rowlatt Act. To Jawaharlal he seemed to offer brave and effective leadership in striking contrast with the spineless Congress politicians. Only Motilal's profound scepticism stopped Jawaharlal joining Gandhi's movement at once. Events during 1919, however, shook Motilal's faith in British intentions and the shooting of hundreds of Indian demonstrators at Amritsar on 13 April cast doubt on the proposed reforms.

In November 1919 Motilal was elected president of Congress. He urged acceptance of the constitutional reforms, but within twelve months Congress had turned away from electoral politics and embarked on a non-co-operation campaign under Gandhi's leadership. Jawaharlal joined with enthusiasm although he shared neither Gandhi's spiritual and moral preoccupations, nor his commitment to non-violence. In many ways they were worlds apart but the bond between them remained unbroken until Gandhi's death. Motilal, whose name and fortune had given Jawaharlal his start, was left with no option if he were to retain influence, both political and with his cherished son, but to join him in Gandhi's campaign. During these months Jawaharlal first travelled in the countryside and gained some inkling of the conditions in which the overwhelming mass of his fellow countrymen were living. The Westernized intellectual, who generally thought in English, forged links with men who barely if at all understood what he told them. In a way which he found inexplicable they extended to him their trust and confidence. Jawaharlal for the first time tasted the exhilaration of power.

On 6 December 1921 Motilal and Jawaharlal were both arrested and sentenced to six months in prison. After three months it was discovered that Jawaharlal had been improperly convicted

and he was released. Following outbreaks of violence Gandhi had already called off the campaign and this had angered and bewildered Jawaharlal. His doubts disappeared when he attended Gandhi's trial and he returned to Allahabad to organize a boycott of foreign clothes. On 11 May 1922 he was back in prison, this time for eight months. Between December 1921 and June 1945 Jawaharlal was to spend almost nine years in prison. It served perhaps as an escape from the demands of mundane political activity, providing periods of study and reflection which led him later to describe prison as 'the best of universities'.

Meanwhile Congress had split, with Motilal a leader of the group wishing to return to electoral politics. Gandhi was strongly opposed. Jawaharlal was torn by the conflict of loyalty; temperament rather than conviction led him to look for some kind of compromise. He became secretary of the All-India Congress but the movement was in decline and disarray. Drawn into municipal politics, he won widespread respect as chairman of the Allahabad Municipal Board. The actor in him, however, aspired to a larger stage. But national politics were at a low ebb and Jawaharlal was depressed by the divisions in Congress. Kamala lost an infant son in 1924 and her health grew worse. Jawaharlal felt little regret when on 1 March 1926 he left India with his wife and daughter to seek medical treatment for Kamala in Europe. They settled in Geneva, Kamala's health showed little improvement, and European politics increasingly won Jawaharlal's attention.

During his stay in Europe Jawaharlal came in touch with socialist and anti-imperialist groups and laid the foundation of his knowledge of European and world affairs and his interest in both the Soviet Union, which he visited briefly, and China. He also became convinced that India's greatest obstacle in achieving national unity was religion, and that the country could advance socially and economically only through industrialization and socialist planning.

The Indian political scene was transformed by the appointment in 1927 of the statutory commission, chaired by Sir John (later Viscount) Simon [q.v.], and the widespread hostility which this provoked. Early in December Jawaharlal sailed for home to play a leading role in a revived Congress culminating in his election as president, in succession to his father, at the end of 1929. He argued passionately for complete independence. Motilal in contrast accepted the goal of Dominion status. Congress was deeply split and faced a radical revolt. At the end of 1929 the conciliatory initiative of the viceroy, E. F. L. Wood, Lord Irwin (later the Earl of Halifax, q.v.), trapped Jawaharlal in a personal crisis. Gandhi and Motilal at first responded favourably to Irwin's move. Against his judgement Jawaharlal felt unable to disagree. Gandhi saw personified in Jawaharlal the tensions which threatened to tear Congress apart and decided that not negotiations but another Gandhian campaign was the only way to preserve Congress unity. In March 1930 he set out on his 'salt satyagraha' and the next month civil disobedience began. It continued, with a number of breaks, into 1934 but faced increasingly determined and effective government action.

For much of the campaign Jawaharlal was in jail. From 1930 to the end of 1935 he was imprisoned four times and served a total of 1,460 days. Again he used the time to read, to think, and to write prolifically. *Glimpses of World History* (1934-5), written in the form of letters to his daughter, Indira, was followed by his *Autobiography* (1936). Although uneven, the book was written with passion and an engaging yet forthright style. Motilal was also in prison and his health began to deteriorate gravely. Jawaharlal was released at the beginning of 1931 in time to be with his father when he died on 6 February. The political scene did nothing to alleviate his grief. He could not support Gandhi's willingness to negotiate: the clash between nationalism and imperialism, he was convinced, could not be ended through compromise. So he ignored the Gandhi-Irwin Pact, involved himself in the peasant movement in the United Provinces, and was back in prison by the end of the year, irritated equally with Gandhi and with Congress, but unable to see any effective alternative course of action. In May 1935 Kamala's condition worsened and she sailed for Europe for further treatment. In September Jawaharlal's sentence was suspended on compassionate grounds and he flew to join her. She died 28 February 1936. Jawaharlal in his absence had been again elected Congress president and he left at once to return to India.

He arrived to find Congress deep in discussion on whether to accept the 1935 Government of India Act and seek elected office. Nehru was opposed to this but was in the minority and, in spite of his doubts, he campaigned vigorously, travelling over 50,000 miles in five months. To his surprise Congress won a remarkable victory in eight of the eleven provinces. Nehru saw it as a victory for secularism and socialism. He was mistaken: it heralded an intensification of communal feeling and marked a major step on the way to partition.

Congress government in the provinces had less interest for Nehru than the deepening world crisis. In 1937-9 he travelled widely outside India and was not surprised by the outbreak of war. His sympathies were with the Allies but his profound distrust of British intentions left him in anguished frustration. Deeply critical of Gandhi's individual civil disobedience campaign he nevertheless took part, was arrested on 31 October 1940, and, apart from nine months, he was in prison for the rest of the war. The viceroy, the Marquess of Linlithgow [q.v.], had little sympathy with Congress while Britain was fighting for survival. Government viewed Nehru as the most dangerous leader in the country and was happy to see him behind bars. Japan's entry into the war led to the only attempt to break the political deadlock. Sir Stafford Cripps [q.v.] was sent out in March 1942 and Nehru attended the discussions with Maulana Azad [q.v.], the leading Congress spokesman. Nehru hoped for a settlement which would enable Congress to co-operate in the war effort but the mission was a failure. Nehru, disillusioned and bitter, turned to Gandhi and his 'Quit India' movement as the only alternative to the break up of the national movement in a sea of communalism and disintegration. The Congress leaders were arrested and Nehru was in prison for almost three years. There he wrote his *The Discovery of India* (1946), which was part rambling cultural history, part autobiography, part exploration of the freedom movement and its links with the country's past.

When he was released on 15 June 1945 Nehru found M. A. Jinnah's [q.v.] movement for Pakistan a powerful force, and the general elections at the end of the year revealed the extent to which the political world had been polarized between Congress and the Muslim League. Nehru's gifts seemed ill-suited to the protracted negotiations that preceded independence. Deeply suspicious of British policy, even after the Labour Party came to office, unable to recognize the proponents of Pakistan as more than reactionary and self-seeking opportunists, increasingly shocked by the irrational and bloody outbursts of violence, Nehru found it difficult to give decisive leadership and his frustration led, on occasion, to intemperate outbursts. Yet events swept him into power. When Lord Wavell [q.v.] formed a provisional government in September 1946 Nehru became vice-president of the viceroy's council and held the external affairs portfolio. In spite of friction with Muslim League members of the Government Nehru, prime minister in all but name, began laying down policies for independent India.

Meanwhile a virtual war of succession was breaking out with savage rioting in many parts of the country. Nehru was appalled at this 'competition in murder and brutality'. The British Government on its part concluded that only a rapid transfer of power could avert a complete disintegration of civil order. Lord Mountbatten of Burma was appointed to carry this through and he recognized at once that such a transfer could take place only on the basis of partition. Nehru and Mountbatten had much in common and the sympathy and trust between them enabled Nehru at a critical moment in the negotiations to persuade Mountbatten to revise his plans and avoid the danger of India being fragmented. At last Nehru resigned himself to the inevitability of partition and when, at midnight on 14 August 1947, the Constituent Assembly met to usher in Indian freedom, Nehru rose superbly to the occasion with a moving speech, eloquent and magnanimous. The rejoicing was brief, for free India under Nehru's leadership faced critical problems of great magnitude.

As prime minister Nehru dominated the first seventeen years of India's independence. It was in many ways a premiership of character rather than accomplishment, of continuity rather than change, yet what was achieved owed more to him than to any other leader. In building and preserving national unity, in strengthening parliamentary democracy, in seeking development through state planning, and in pursuing a foreign policy of non-alignment, he made a mark unmistakably his own.

Partition and the transfer of power brought massacre and panic; millions were uprooted, hundreds of thousands killed. Order was restored but communal feelings were dangerously inflamed. Gandhi returned to Delhi to try to stop the violence and was assassinated there in January 1948 by a Hindu extremist. Deeply shocked, Nehru told India 'the light has gone out'. For some months his passionate opposition to communalism appeared to be shared by his fellow countrymen, but this reaction was short-lived; within Congress itself Hindu communalists were strongly represented. Their strength was one element behind the election (against Nehru's wishes) of P. N. Tandon as Congress president in 1950. The election was also an attempt by Vallabhbhai Patel [q.v.], long a rival to Nehru and now deputy prime minister, to limit Nehru's power and the influence of his office. The Patel-Tandon domination of Congress was short-lived. Patel died in December 1950, Nehru gathered support in Tandon's working committee and consolidated his power over the party by taking the presidency himself from 1951 to 1954. He accepted the necessity of working with the rightists both in Congress and in Cabinet but his victory established both his undisputed personal supremacy and also the dominance of Government over the Congress organization.

Independence made it necessary to integrate the former princely states whose relationship with the Crown was unceremoniously ended by the British. By 15 August 1947 almost all of them had acceded either to India or to Pakistan. Kashmir, with a predominantly Muslim population but a Hindu ruler, still had not. In October 1947, in an attempt to force the issue, Pathan tribesmen from Pakistan invaded Kashmir. The Maharaja opted for India, troops were sent in to support him, and a brief war between India and Pakistan followed. A Government under Sheikh Abdullah, an old friend of Nehru's, was installed and when the United Nations brought about a cease-fire in the fighting India agreed that a plebiscite should follow. It never did: Nehru's growing reluctance stemmed partly from a rift with the Sheikh who began to speak of an independent Kashmir and was eventually removed and imprisoned without trial, but perhaps more to his conviction that to hold a plebiscite would rekindle the communal violence of partition, place in peril the large Muslim population remaining in India, and strengthen those forces opposing Nehru's stand for a secular state. There is little doubt either that as a Kashmiri Brahmin long attracted by the mountainous beauty of his ancestral home Nehru's emotions were deeply involved in the fate of the state. The cease-fire line hardened into a *de facto* border and Kashmir remained divided. Although a pact between Nehru and Liaquat Ali Khan [q.v.] in April 1950 settled some of the outstanding issues between India and Pakistan, Kashmir remained a matter of bitter dispute.

Nehru used his enormous influence to nurture parliamentary democracy. Impatient as he could be with others, he was endlessly patient in establishing the traditions and conventions of the parliamentary system. The new constitution was inaugurated in January 1950 and India became a republic with a president as its constitutional head, but recognizing the British sovereign as head of the Commonwealth. The Indian union was established as a secular state with a federal structure but a strong centre. In these broad features, as in many of its details, Nehru's wishes were closely reflected. The achievements of the first years were consolidated in the first general election of 1951-2 when both communalist and Communist parties fared badly and Congress scored an overwhelming victory.

In one area Nehru achieved less than he hoped; that of social reform. The opposition to a reform and codification of personal and family law was too strong and it took all of Nehru's personal prestige to carry a number of separate acts providing, among other things, for divorce, monogamy, and equal rights of inheritance for women. The constitution itself formally abolished untouchability. The new constitutional and legal basis for individual rights and liberties had relatively little impact except among urban, Westernized classes, and many other reforms had a similar limited effect. Education was greatly expanded but with a striking imbalance between the urban and rural areas where a large majority of the population remained illiterate.

The other major area where change was sought was the economy. Nehru's belief in industrialization and in state planning, long a source of difference with Gandhi, went back many years. In 1950 the Planning Commission was created, with the prime minister as chairman, and this was followed by three Five Year Plans. The first (1951–6), which concentrated on agricultural production, appeared a great success. When it ended India was self-sufficient in food. But this achievement was not sustained; monsoon failures and the seemingly inexorable increase of population again created the need for imports. The second plan was more ambitious. After the Communist victory in China a sense of competition and national pride was involved in Indian development and Nehru was determined to show that democratic freedom need not be sacrificed to economic progress. The record was mixed. The plan cost nearly twice as much as the first, depended on substantial foreign aid, and eventually had to be cut back. The achievements, nevertheless, were striking: the steel, aluminium, and cement industries were greatly expanded, a number of new industries were started, and industrial production expanded 50 per cent in eight years (1951–9). But for all their success the plans did little to benefit the inhabitants of India's innumerable villages. Landlordism was abolished in the early years of independence, but agrarian conditions proved intractable. Nehru saw a powerful Congress as the key to national unity and he ruefully recognized that at the heart of this power in the states were deeply conservative small landholders hostile to any far-reaching changes. In 1952 the Community Development Programme was begun but change was slow; the economic disparity between rich and poor grew no smaller.

In foreign policy during the late 1940s and the 1950s Nehru's authority was almost unchallenged. He offered support and leadership to fellow Asian nationalists and welcomed the Communist rise to power in China. This concern with Asia brought him into conflict with the United States to whom Nehru's idea of non-alignment in the deepening East–West division seemed at best incomprehensible. One attraction of Commonwealth membership for Nehru was that, in a modest way, it offered a grouping other than the American or Soviet blocs, and enabled India to avoid complete reliance on the United States for foreign aid. In October 1950 the Chinese invaded Tibet and Nehru's enthusiasm for China waned, though he rebuffed Patel and others who urged a policy of confrontation. Thereafter Nehru was always apprehensive of China while still believing Sino-Indian friendship to be the only basis of stability in Asia. This seemed assured by the agreement between them of June 1954 and by the Bandung conference of Afro-Asian states the following year. At Bandung Nehru was unquestionably the elder statesman but it was Chou En-lai who took the centre of the stage. By this time Nehru's sustained advocacy of non-alignment had become more acceptable, or at least accepted, by the great powers. In 1955 Nehru visited the Soviet Union and Bulganin and Krushchev returned the visit later that year. When Nehru condemned the Anglo-French invasion of Suez he was in agreement with the United States, and his visit there in 1956 brought new understanding on both sides. He was less forthright on the Soviet invasion of Hungary and this cost him support both at home and abroad.

If during the fifties Nehru's authority seemed undisputed there were times nevertheless when he bowed to pressure. One was in his response to the movement for redrawing the state boundaries along linguistic divisions. He saw the movement as a threat to national unity and the States Reorganization Act of 1956 was a tactical concession in an attempt to defuse separatism which was only partly successful. Cautious accommodation was also called for in the bitter disputes over the continued use of English as an official language.

In his last years, from 1959 until his death in 1964, Nehru faced increasing pressure internally and externally, and for the first time he experienced public criticism. Congress faced serious challenges from both conservatives and radicals and when in 1959 the Chinese reopened the whole boundary question and established direct control in Tibet right-wing opinion grew markedly. Nehru's room for manœuvre or negotiation narrowed. Heavy internal pressure forced him to approve the invasion of Portuguese Goa in December 1961 which sadly tarnished his reputation as a peace-maker and although the general election shortly afterwards renewed the Congress majority the pressure on Nehru did not diminish. Pressed by an army and by public opinion he agreed to a policy of asserting Indian presence in the border region with China. The discovery of a Chinese road across the desolate Aksai Chin plateau in northeast Kashmir provoked a strong anti-Chinese reaction in India. Nehru was shocked, felt he had been betrayed, and publicly expressed his bitterness. In October 1962 Chinese forces advanced into India but later withdrew to their earlier positions. Nehru believed the Chinese wished to destroy India's non-aligned status and the war certainly finished any idea of an Afro-Asian bloc headed by India and China.

Brief and local as it was, the war was a disaster for India's development plans, and during 1963 Nehru courageously sought to direct the surge of national feeling created by the war into saving as much as possible of the third Five Year Plan. He probably found greater satisfaction in the signing of the Nuclear Test Ban Treaty in August. The East–West antagonism which he had always opposed seemed at last to be diminishing.

On 8 January 1964 Nehru, then seventy-four years old, suffered a serious stroke. For five months he fought to regain his physical powers and was able to resume some of his official duties. The recovery was only partial and was brief, and he died in Delhi 27 May 1964. His only child Indira was prime minister of India from 1966 to 1977, and from 1980.

That Nehru was a good man is profoundly true and lay at the heart of his almost magical appeal. He was also an unusually complicated man, a leader harbouring powerful contradictory impulses: agitator and mediator, a politician often bored with politics and wanting power not for himself but for a cause, a Brahmin not without vanity who loathed caste, an aloof intellectual preferring his own company who had a unique relationship with the Indian masses. The young revolutionary came to face the dilemmas of power, and the impulsive intransigence of the pre-independence years gave way in great measure to a tough practicality. What persisted was the urge to persuade rather than coerce. His public speeches, often rambling and discursive, were in essence a remarkable course of public education, the fruit of a singularly well-furnished mind. Blessed with extraordinary gifts of intellect, of energy and physical resilience, and of a captivating presence, Nehru added to these qualities loyalty, courage, self-discipline, and a dedication to a free and democratic India in which dignity and well-being for the Indian people would be achieved and preserved.

There is a portrait by Edward I. Halliday (1954), and a bronze by Sir Jacob Epstein. A bronze statue of Nehru, holding a dove of peace (1966), is in Aurangabad, western India.

[Jawaharlal Nehru, *An Autobiography*, 1936; *Selected Works of Jawaharlal Nehru*, 1972; Michael Brecher, *Nehru: A Political Biography*, 1959; Sarvepalli Gopal, *Jawaharlal Nehru: A Biography*, vol. i, 1975, vol. ii, 1980; B. N. Pandey, *Nehru*, 1976.]

T. H. BEAGLEHOLE

NELSON, SIR FRANK (1883–1966), organizer of Special Operations Executive, was born at Bentham, Gloucestershire, 5 August 1883, the son of Henry Ellis Hay Nelson, general manager of the Army and Navy Auxiliary Co-operative Supply, and his wife, Catherine Haviland. After education at Bedford Grammar School and Heidelberg, he went to India to work in a mercantile firm in Bombay in which he rose to become senior partner. In the war of 1914–18 he served in the Bombay Light Horse. Subsequently he was chairman of the Bombay Chamber of Commerce and its representative on the Bombay Legislative Council (1922–4) and president of the Associated Indian Chamber of Commerce (1923). In 1924 he was knighted and returned to England. He was Conservative member of Parliament for Stroud from 1924 to 1931 when the depression forced him to resign to go into business.

On the outbreak of war in 1939 Nelson was employed on intelligence work in Basle, but this came to an end with the fall of France when he returned to England. Even before 1939 it had been recognized that the Government would have to weaken any potential enemy by political subversion, sabotage, and other clandestine operations. When war broke out the work suffered from lack of co-ordination, for it was split up between several bodies, responsible to different authorities. By 1940, when the British were left to fight the Axis powers alone, co-ordination was more than ever essential. The War Cabinet consequently decided on 16 July 1940 that all these functions were to be put in the charge of a new body, the Special Operations Executive (SOE), with Hugh (later Lord) Dalton [q.v.], who continued to be minister of economic warfare, at its head. Dalton records that the prime minister then said to him, 'And now set Europe ablaze'. He at once divided SOE into three bodies—SO1 for underground propaganda, SO2 for unacknowledgeable action, sabotage, and the support of resistance in enemy-occupied territory, and SO3 for planning. In August 1940 Dalton appointed Nelson to be head of SO2. The functions of SO3 were assumed by SO2 in January 1941, and in the following August those of SO1 by a separate body called the Political Warfare Executive. From that point Nelson was responsible for all the remaining activities of SOE.

Nelson had a formidable task. Not only was there not a single agent in enemy-occupied France, but SOE was a new body for which no precedent existed. As such it incurred the suspicion and jealousy of the established secret organizations, the Foreign Office, and the Service ministries, all of which were professional bodies which had existed for many years and which were concerned by the inevitable amateurishness at first displayed by SOE. Another difficulty was recruitment, for by the autumn of 1940 most men of ability were employed elsewhere. Above all Nelson found he had to obtain for SOE facilities, such as secret wireless sets, aircraft for parachute training and getting agents into Europe, and special devices for sabotage. But it was no easy task to get these scarce resources unless SOE could show results, and without the resources there could be no results. Finally, Nelson had somehow to get the confidence of Whitehall and the Services.

He set to work at once with tireless energy, and surrounded himself with a group of able people, notably (Sir) Colin Gubbins, who at first took charge of the important job of training and operations and was to finish the war as head of SOE. Gradually Nelson overcame the difficulties by his unshakeable integrity of purpose. It was a disappointment to him when in early 1941 the chiefs of staff ruled against supplying secret armies in Europe by air in favour of the bombing offensive. But he persisted, and by the winter of 1941 SOE was in touch with agents and supporters in most of the countries of occupied Europe. Above all, Nelson made people believe that, given facilities, results could be achieved. In less than two years SOE had become an established force with the confidence of the chiefs of staff, and was recognized in every theatre of war. It is no disparagement of his successors to say that he created the groundwork without which SOE's later successes in Europe and the Far East would have been impossible.

But Nelson was never physically strong, and in 1942 his health began to fail. He resigned in May, was appointed KCMG, and subsequently held appointments as an air commodore in Washington and Germany. He married in 1911 Jean, daughter of Colonel Patrick Montgomerie; they had one son. She died in 1952 and he then married Dorothy Moira Carling. He died in Oxford 11 August 1966.

[Hugh Dalton, *The Fateful Years*, 1957; M. R. D. Foot, *SOE in France*, 2nd impression, with amendments, 1968, and *Resistance*, 1976; Bickham Sweet-Escott, *Baker Street Irregular*, 1965; personal knowledge.]

B. SWEET-ESCOTT

NELSON, GEORGE HORATIO, first BARON NELSON OF STAFFORD (1887–1962), chairman of the English Electric Company Ltd., was born in London 26 October 1887, the eldest child in the family of two sons and one daughter of George Nelson, textile merchant, of Muswell Hill, and his wife, Emily Walsh Lewis. He was educated at City and Guilds Technical College, where he worked under Silvanus Thompson [q.v.]. After gaining a diploma and the Mitchell exhibition, he moved on, with a Brush studentship, to the Brush Engineering Company at Loughborough. He then joined the British Westinghouse Company in Manchester, becoming chief outside engineer at Trafford Park in 1911 and chief electrical superintendent in 1914. In these posts he was responsible for the manufacture and installation of steam and hydro-electric power equipment and electric traction equipment in various parts of the world. He developed many contacts in the steel and railway industries.

Nelson remained with the same company when it joined the Metropolitan Vickers Group, becoming manager of the Sheffield works of Metropolitan Vickers Electrical Company in 1920. He stayed at the works, which specialized in electric traction, for ten years. Sir Holberry Mensforth, who had been works manager at Trafford Park and had subsequently joined the English Electric Company, then persuaded Nelson to become English Electric's managing director. When Mensforth retired in 1933 Nelson was appointed chairman and managing director.

Nelson set the English Electric Company on its feet, expanding the work force, handling men and contracts with great skill, and fully understanding the engineering aspect of his company. In 'clearing the decks' he made some bold, far-ranging, and usually correct decisions which were to alter and broaden the whole concept of the business. When the rearmament programme began he spent many months trying to persuade Service chiefs of the contribution his organization could make, and finally won a contract for seventy-five Hampden bombers. These were followed by 2,470 Halifax bombers and 2,730 tanks. By the end of the war English Electric was undertaking the production of the Canberra bomber to its own design, which was one of the most successful of its time.

In 1942 Nelson went to the United States and Canada as chairman of the United Kingdom tank mission to discuss a joint policy for tank production. He served on the heavy bomber group committee of the Air Ministry from 1939 to 1945, on the reconstruction joint advisory council in 1943–4, on the higher technological education committee in 1944–5, and was chairman of the census of production committee in 1945. He was president of the Federation of British Industries in 1943–4, a most difficult period.

After the war English Electric acquired Marconi's Wireless Telegraph Company, which increased Nelson's responsibilities. He also found time to develop his interest in technical education. His own companies provided much technical training and he served on the governing body of the Imperial College of Science and Technology, on the court of governors of Manchester College of Science and Technology, and on the governing body of Queen Mary College, London. He was president of the Institution of Electrical Engineers in 1955 and of the Institution of Mechanical Engineers in 1957-8. He served as prime warden of the Goldsmiths' Company in 1960. In 1955 Imperial College made him an honorary fellow and granted him an honorary diploma. In 1957 he received an honorary LLD from Manchester. The previous year he received the freedom of Stafford.

Nelson received a knighthood in 1943, a baronetcy in 1955, and was raised to the peerage as first Baron Nelson of Stafford in 1960. In 1913 he married Florence Mabel ('Jane') (died 1962), only daughter of Henry Howe, JP, of Leicestershire. They had one son and one daughter. Nelson died in Stafford 16 July 1962 and was succeeded by his son, Henry George (born 1917), who became chairman of General Electric Company Ltd. from 1968, chancellor of Aston University, and a member of the court of the Bank of England.

There are portraits in oils by Harold Knight (c. 1948), by Maurice Codner (1955) in the English Electric Company London Office, with his daughter by Maurice Codner (1955), with his son by (Sir) James Gunn (1958), and by C. Dil-Capinop (1960) in the English Electric Company Stafford Office. There is a black-and-white sketch by an unknown artist (1955) in the possession of the Institution of Electrical Engineers.

[*The Times*, 17 July 1962; private information.]
                                    C. S. NICHOLLS

NEWALL, CYRIL LOUIS NORTON, first BARON NEWALL (1886-1963), marshal of the Royal Air Force, was born 15 February 1886 at Mussoorie, United Provinces, India, the only son and the second child of Captain (later Lieutenant-Colonel) William Potter Newall, Indian Army, and his wife, Edith Gwendoline Caroline Norton. He was educated at Bedford School and proceeded by way of the Royal Military College, Sandhurst, to a commission in the Royal Warwickshire Regiment at the age of nineteen. After moving with his regiment to India he followed his father's footsteps into the Indian Army, being received into the 2nd battalion King Edward's Own Gurkha Rifles in 1909. Like many young army officers of that day he met his first experience of active service amid the mountains of the North-West Frontier. Inspired by a flying demonstration in India, he learned to fly while on leave in Britain in 1911,

and was awarded Royal Aero Club certificate No. 144.

He received further training at the Central Flying School in 1913 on a special posting from India and returned to Britain in 1914 to join the Royal Flying Corps. Newall served with that corps throughout the war of 1914-18 and in 1919 became a wing commander in the newly formed Royal Air Force during the reorganization that year. In the great and dangerous days of the RFC Newall saw service as a pilot and as a squadron and formation commander. His last posting was to command the elements of the RFC designated to attack German targets from bases in the Nancy area, a development largely occasioned by German air raids on London in 1917. In this last appointment he came under the immediate control of Brigadier-General (later Viscount) Trenchard [q.v.], who was posted in May 1918 to the command of what was to become the Independent Force. In the course of his Royal Flying Corps service, Newall was awarded that rather rare and much prized distinction, the Albert medal, for an act of conspicuous gallantry in dealing with a fire in a bomb store.

The first fifteen years of the Royal Air Force in peacetime, although significant in shaping its future development, were also years of struggle and frustration; its future survival was repeatedly a matter of serious doubt and the new Service was retarded and distorted by financial restrictions. Newall was lucky in that during this period he held three key appointments. From 1922 to 1925 he commanded the School of Technical Training at Halton, a star feature of the peacetime pattern of the Royal Air Force producing airmen apprentices of the highest technical skills. Between 1926 and 1931 he was in charge of the operations and intelligence elements of the Air Staff and, for the last year of the appointment, ranked as a member of the Air Council. Between 1931 and 1934 he commanded the Royal Air Force in the Middle East with his headquarters in Cairo and with a vast range of responsibilities throughout Africa. Early in 1935 Newall rejoined the Air Council as the newly created air member for supply and organization, a post he held for some two and a half years and which embodied responsibility for the organization of the expanding Royal Air Force, for meeting its needs for airfields and quarters, and for supplying it with warlike and non-warlike stores of all kinds. The problems which confronted Newall were of a kind unusual or even unprecedented in time of peace. Between 1935 and the outbreak of war in 1939 expenditure on the Royal Air Force was increased by a factor of more than ten but the problems which arose were not those of scale only. They were complicated by the change from slow biplanes to fast monoplanes with enclosed cockpits, retractable undercarriages, and variable-pitch propellers. It was also necessary to construct and equip new aircraft factories and to deal with the problems of the light-alloy industry and with other specialized needs.

In September 1937 Newall was appointed to succeed Sir Edward Ellington as chief of air staff, a position which with that of secretary of state constituted the two appointments most vital to the future of the Service. His qualifications for the appointment were impressive. He had seen active service, he had held an important overseas command, he had served as deputy chief of air staff, and he had presided for three years over the physical development of the Royal Air Force. No one could have been endowed with a better understanding of the problems. Above all, he had the personal qualities required. He was chief of air staff for three years and few men can have faced a time of greater stress. When Austria was overwhelmed in March 1938 Newall put forward his views on the implications to British security with clarity and force. The Munich crisis, involving as it did partial mobilization, brought the Royal Air Force close to the brink of war. After the crisis was over Newall called his staff together and with great prescience told them exactly what would be the responsibilities facing the Service in 1939. Tensions mounted and in September 1939 Britain was at war again. For the Royal Air Force all the work of the last four years was soon to be put to the test. The problems of the first year of the war were many and arduous: there was the issue of whether fighters should be sent to France; and, when France was overrun, Britain's air defence problems multiplied; there was the threat of invasion; and, finally, the crucial and desperately close issue of the Battle of Britain. It was a heavy burden for Newall to carry.

By September 1940 the Luftwaffe's daylight assaults on Britain had given way to the nightly blitz on London and other big cities. This, too, brought many, although less extreme, problems. In the development of the air war something like a natural break had been reached. It was therefore a suitable moment for Newall to hand over as chief of air staff to Sir Charles Portal (later Viscount Portal of Hungerford). Earlier in the month in which he retired Newall had been promoted to the rank of marshal of the Royal Air Force.

Newall had occupied a position of crucial responsibility, but he, the Air Ministry, and the various secretaries of state, faced some criticism. Alternative views about air policy covering matters of detail as well as of policy came from both Churchill and Attlee, and behind the scenes there were some individual critics as well. Some, but by no means all, of the criticism was apposite. This detracts nothing from the fact that over a period of three years and in most difficult circumstances Newall had proved himself a distinguished leader of the Royal Air Force. Newall was appointed governor-general of New Zealand in 1941 and remained in that office for five years, which included the period when New Zealand was exposed to the threat of Japanese attack. He and his wife worked devotedly to sustain the New Zealand war effort at every level and at the end of their mission they were given a warm and gracious tribute from the prime minister of New Zealand, Peter Fraser [q.v.].

In appearance Newall was slim and slightly over average height. Although an airman, he looked every inch a soldier. He was always immaculately dressed. In times of stress, and in those days this was the normal state, his composure and cheerfulness were beyond praise. His courtesy and kindness to everyone who came into contact with him were a model.

For his services during the war of 1914-18 Newall was appointed CMG and CBE and received decorations from France, Italy, and Belgium. He was appointed GCB in 1938 and GCMG in 1940 and in that year he was also admitted to the Order of Merit. He was created a baron in 1946.

In 1922 Newall married May Dulcie Weddell (died 1924). In 1925 he married Olive Tennyson Foster, the only daughter of Mrs Francis Storer Eaton of Boston, Massachusetts. There were three children of Newall's second marriage, one son and two daughters. Newall died 30 November 1963 at his home in London and was succeeded by his son, Francis (born 1930).

Portraits of Newall by W. G. de Glehn (1931) and by (Sir) Oswald Birley (1941) are in the possession of the family. There are also two portraits by R. G. Eves (1940), one in the Imperial War Museum and the other in the National Portrait Gallery.

[Denis Richards, *Royal Air Force 1939-1945*, vol. i, 1953; *The Times*, 2 December 1963; private information.]   M. J. DEAN

NEWSAM, SIR FRANK AUBREY (1893-1964), civil servant, the third son of William Elias Newsam and his wife, Alice Mary Chambers, was born 13 November 1893 in Barbados where his father was a civil servant. He showed early promise at Harrison College from which in 1911 he went up to Oxford with an open classical scholarship at St. John's College. There could never have been any doubt of his intellectual capacity; that he only obtained second classes in honour moderations (1913) and *literae humaniores* (1915) may be ascribed to the fact that he enjoyed to the utmost the full and varied life the university then afforded.

In the war of 1914-18 Newsam was commissioned in the Royal Irish Regiment. He was in Southern Ireland with his regiment at the time of the Irish rebellion and was wounded by a sniper. Later he was posted to a battalion of his regiment in North India where he served with the 1/30 Punjabis. During the war he was awarded the MC and mentioned in dispatches. After the close of hostilities he again served in Ireland before being demobilized in 1919. He then taught for a period at Harrow while waiting the result of the Class I competition for the Home Civil Service in which he had decided to make his career. His elder brother had entered the Indian Civil Service.

In July 1920 Newsam was assigned to the Home Office where he quickly made his mark among the young assistant principals who, like himself, had served in the army during the war. His intellectual powers were obvious to his seniors. Moreover, as a young man, and indeed to the end of his life, Newsam had much physical distinction. Well-built and good-looking in a rather Latin way, he carried himself as one to whom the good things of life were not only agreeable but came naturally. It was consequently no surprise that in 1924 Sir John Anderson (later Viscount Waverley, q.v.), the permanent under-secretary of state, appointed Newsam his private secretary and kept him in that post for three years after his promotion to principal in 1925. Anderson gave much scope to men whom he trusted and Newsam, who did not fail to master the lessons he learned from Anderson, began to be recognizable as a power behind the throne.

In 1928 Newsam entered a new field when he was appointed principal private secretary to the home secretary, Sir William Joynson-Hicks (later Viscount Brentford, q.v.), a post which almost invariably led to later preferment. It was usually held for a couple of years but Newsam held it until 1933, also serving J. R. Clynes, Sir Herbert (later Viscount) Samuel, and Sir John Gilmour [qq.v.]. It is the measure of his ability, adaptability, and command of the duties of the post, that he served successfully, and to their entire satisfaction, four politicians of widely differing qualities drawn from three political parties. It was this long experience which gave Newsam his intimate knowledge of the working of the political mind. In his later years it was sometimes thought that he tended to approach departmental problems from a parliamentary, rather than an administrative, point of view. If this were a fault it at least smoothed the path of many home secretaries in the House of Commons.

The year in which he was appointed CVO (1933) saw his promotion to the rank of assistant secretary, and his appointment to the charge of a new division. The greater part of his time in the Home Office had been spent at the centre, 'on the staff', and he had much less experience of actual work in a division than his contemporaries. His new division was concerned, *inter alia*, with betting and lotteries, a highly contentious subject on which legislation had long been contemplated. Newsam's competent handling of the first major Bill for which he was administratively responsible, the Betting and Lotteries Bill, owed as much to his exceptional knowledge of what the House of Commons would not accept as to his rapid grasp of the details of a problem which was new to him. The Betting and Lotteries Act of 1934 was almost entirely his handiwork. But his main preoccupation for the next few years was with the grave disorders brought about by the activities of the British Fascists. The point was eventually reached where drastic legislative support for the police became essential. Newsam devised, and got carried through Parliament, the Bill for the Public Order Act of 1936 which put a speedy end to the troubles which had plagued the public and the police alike.

In 1938 Newsam was selected to be principal officer of the South Eastern Region under a plan by which the country would be administered locally through regional commissioners in the event of the breakdown of communications under enemy attack. He took up that post at the outbreak of war in 1939; but in 1940 he was recalled to the Home Office and appointed assistant under-secretary of state in charge of matters of security. His greatest problems arose from the internment of enemy aliens under the prerogative and, under Defence Regulation 18B, of British subjects whose loyalty could not be relied upon. It would have been beyond the power of any man to control measures of this nature without raising criticism. Indeed, throughout the war the Home Office was subjected to criticism from both sides of the political field; but neither Sir Alexander Maxwell [q.v.], the head of the Home Office from 1938 to 1948, nor Newsam, although poles apart in habit of mind, would allow himself to be rushed into hasty decisions or to be governed by caprice in taking them.

In 1941 Newsam became deputy under-secretary of state and in that capacity found additional outlets for his energy and abilities, including the planning of the restoration of the economy of the Channel Islands against their release from German occupation. The plans which, in due course, were successfully put into operation, led to an association with the Channel Islands which gave Newsam great pleasure. He played an important part in the action taken to reform the constitutions of the islands and to develop their legal and administrative systems.

Newsam's final promotion to the top post in the Home Office was delayed until 1948 when he was fifty-five. A man of his ability and achievement might have expected to get to the top at an earlier age; and there were indeed some who wondered whether the long delay might have blunted the keen edge of his efficiency and whether he would now be able to handle a range of business in which, as one home secretary observed, 'a pit yawns for you every morning'. In fact he succeeded above expectation. He threw himself with energy into a variety of matters which had been held up by the war, notably in the field of criminal law and the administration of prisons and borstals; and he carried to a conclusion the plans for co-ordinating the work of the police and for improving the training of police officers which had been formulated much earlier by an older member of the Office, Sir Arthur Dixon [q.v.], and put into storage by the needs of civil defence. And, in accordance with long practice, he bore the final responsibility for advising the home secretary of the day on capital cases.

Newsam retired in 1957. He had been appointed KBE in 1943 as deputy under-secretary, KCB in 1950, and advanced to GCB in 1957. For his services during the war he had been appointed by King Haakon of Norway a commander of the Order of St. Olaf.

The Home Office in the first half of the twentieth century had many outstanding heads —Sir Edward Troup, Anderson, and Maxwell were, in their very different ways, men of extreme talent and character. Even if Newsam, so markedly dissimilar from any of them in natural temperament, cannot quite be placed on their level, he takes a high position among civil servants of his own and previous generations. He was enough of an idealist to be a reformer, and he combined with great professional capacity in administration marked gifts as a negotiator. He was courageous in the formulation of policy and ruthless in its execution; never brow-beaten; as loyal to his subordinates as to his seniors. He had, it is true, some of the defects of these qualities—a measure of impatience and intolerance of views which differed from his own. But no one who watched him at work could fail to admire his efficiency and the force of his personality. Many of those who worked for him came to feel for him affection as well as respect. And the few who knew him well realized that under the hard surface which he showed to the world there was a sensitive spirit and a deep capacity for human compassion.

He died in London 25 April 1964, and was survived by his widow, Jean, daughter of James McAuslin, whom he had married in 1927. They had no children.

[Private information; personal knowledge.]
AUSTIN STRUTT

NICHOL SMITH, DAVID (1875-1962), scholar. [See SMITH.]

NICOLSON, SIR HAROLD GEORGE (1886-1968), diplomatist and author, was born in Tehran 21 November 1886, the third son of (Sir) Arthur Nicolson (who became eleventh baronet and later first Lord Carnock, q.v.), by his wife, Katharine Rowan Hamilton; her sister was the wife of Lord Dufferin [q.v.], viceroy of India. His father was at that time chargé d'affaires of the British Legation in Tehran. His childhood was spent either in constant pursuit of his parents wherever Sir Arthur was *en poste*—the Balkans, the Middle East, Tangier (with which his main childhood memories were associated), Madrid, and St. Petersburg, or in the holidays from school at his mother's Irish home, Shanganagh in county Dublin, and his uncle Dufferin's houses, Killyleagh Castle in county Down and Clandeboye, near Belfast. Years later he was to write that he came to look upon these great Irish houses 'as anchors in a drifting life, as the only places where I ceased to be a pot-plant for ever being bedded out in alien soil'.

After a conventional education at preparatory school and Wellington College, which he disliked, Balliol College, Oxford, supplied the intellectual stimulus and companionship which his natural curiosity and geniality demanded. He obtained a third class in classical honour moderations in 1906, and the following year left Oxford with a pass degree. He received both his BA and MA in 1930. After Oxford he prepared himself for the diplomatic service. To the surprise of his father, who had paid little attention to his studies, he passed with flying colours into the diplomatic service in 1909.

Early in 1911, shortly after his father had become permanent under-secretary of state for foreign affairs in the previous year, Harold Nicolson was sent from London to Madrid, and in January 1912 as third secretary to Constantinople, both capitals which he had known during his father's ambassadorship. While on leave from Constantinople he married on 1 October 1913 in the chapel at Knole, Kent, Victoria Mary (Vita) Sackville-West (a notice of whom appears in this Supplement), only child of Lionel, third Lord Sackville, and his wife (also his first cousin) Victoria, an eccentric and erratic woman who was to cause the Nicolsons considerable disquiet in the years to come. His marriage was the most important event in Harold Nicolson's life. In *Portrait of a Marriage* (1973) their younger son Nigel, born in 1917 (the elder, Lionel Benedict, was born in 1914), has recounted the story of a union, unorthodox in some respects, which was cemented by a mutual understanding and deep affection probably unsurpassed by any literary partnership. In 1914 Nicolson was recalled to London where, as a result of his diplomatic duties which exempted him from military service, he remained throughout the war of 1914-18. In *Lord Carnock* (1930) Nicolson tells the story how, as the junior official sent to the German Embassy on the night of 4 August to retrieve an erroneous declaration of war, he surreptitiously substituted the correct for the incorrect note dispatched by the Foreign Office one hour previously.

In 1915 the young couple bought Long Barn, a medieval cottage near Sevenoaks, where Vita Sackville-West launched upon gardening and poetry, for which she was to become renowned, and where in the intervals between her occupations and his Foreign Office work and writing, they entertained an exclusive group of mutual friends. At the same time Nicolson led a social life in London during the week.

In 1919 Nicolson served with notable success on the British delegation to the Paris peace conference which culminated in the Treaty of Versailles. For weeks he was closeted with the world statesmen, Lloyd George, Clemenceau, and President Wilson, to whom A. J. Balfour caustically referred as 'those three, all-powerful, all-ignorant, men sitting there and partitioning continents with only a child to take notes for them'. For his contribution Nicolson in 1920 was appointed CMG and promoted to first secretary. After the treaty was signed he became assistant to Sir Eric Drummond (later the Earl of Perth, q.v.), the first secretary-general of the League of Nations. It was during his time in Paris that his wife seemed likely to leave him at the height of her emotional involvement with Violet Trefusis. His patience and tolerance of a problem not unfamiliar to himself enabled them to resume their marriage on a basis of mutual understanding.

In June 1920 he was recalled to London where he was mainly concerned with Middle East affairs. Very industrious, he found time to write his first book, *Paul Verlaine* (1921), which was the first of six literary biographies—*Tennyson* (1923), *Byron, the Last Journey* (1924), *Swinburne* (1926), *Benjamin Constant* (1949), and *Sainte-Beuve* (1957). In 1922-3 he attended

the Lausanne conference as secretary to Lord Curzon [q.v.].

In 1925 Nicolson was sent by Sir William (later Lord) Tyrrell [q.v.], then permanent under-secretary, to Tehran. In those days the journey to Persia by sea and overland took longer than a fortnight. At first the British minister, Sir Percy Loraine [q.v.], welcomed Nicolson to the legation in which he had been born nearly forty years previously. But their relations were uneasy. Loraine, a stickler for etiquette and without much humour, resented his new counsellor's disregard for ceremonial, his sloppy dress, his penetrating intelligence, and irreverent tendency to tease. Similar symptoms of alarm were evinced by other pundits in the Foreign Office, like Tyrrell and Sir Ronald Graham [q.v.]. They did not relish being laughed at, however good-naturedly, by a subordinate. When *Some People*, a brilliant selection of essays on 'real people in imaginary situations and imaginary people in real situations', was published in 1927, 'Ponderous Percy', as the minister was known to his staff, called it 'a cad's book'. Between Loraine's departure and the arrival of his successor, (Sir) Robert Clive [q.v.], Nicolson acted as chargé d'affaires. He wrote a dispatch sharply criticizing the Foreign Office's policy in the Middle East, which caused a minor sensation. (Sir) Lancelot Oliphant, who regarded himself as arbiter of Middle East matters, was incensed, and recommended to the Foreign Secretary, Sir Austen Chamberlain [q.v.], that the chargé d'affaires should be transferred to another post.

Nicolson had loved Persia, in spite of the absence of his wife who twice visited him but would not join him permanently. Innumerable daily letters between the two illustrate the wretchedness of their separation. On his recall to London in the summer of 1927 Nicolson, demoted from counsellor to first secretary, was depressed by the sense that his superiors mistrusted his judgement. He seriously considered leaving the service. This, however, he postponed. Instead, he agreed with reluctance to be sent to Berlin. Here too he became chargé d'affaires between two ambassadors during the Weimar Republic. Through his dispatches he quickly achieved a high reputation with the promise of a splendid future in the service. Although repromoted to the post of counsellor under an ambassador, Sir Ronald Lindsay [q.v.], for whom he had a warm regard, Nicolson did not have enough scope for his extraordinary abilities. 'I am a stepney wheel of a car that is seldom taken out of the garage', he complained to his friend, (Sir) Robert Bruce Lockhart [q.v.]. Nor did he care for Berlin in spite of its diversions. His time there was made tolerable by several visits from his wife although she loathed the place, and numerous close friends, including Lord Berners, Edward Sackville-West (later Baron Sackville), Virginia Woolf [qq.v.], Cyril Connolly, and Raymond Mortimer.

During leave in September 1929 Nicolson sent in his resignation from the diplomatic service. In an abbreviated diary which he kept from 1921 until the end of that year he jotted down under 20 December: 'Leave Berlin . . .', adding with characteristic understatement, 'I am presented with a cactus. It symbolizes the end of my diplomatic career.'

To his colleagues, this was an inexplicable step. His prime reason for taking it was the unbearable absences from his wife. The second was the need for money. Upon her marriage his wife had been given an allowance by her mother, and the Nicolsons were therefore somewhat dependent financially upon her. Lady Sackville chose this moment to quarrel with them, and they were anxious to be completely independent of her whims. Nicolson had no capital and his salary was, even for those days, meagre. He was invited through Bruce Lockhart to become a contributor to the 'Londoner's Diary' of the *Evening Standard*. He accepted on the condition that he was not expected to voice Tory opinions or renegue his radical opinions. He embarked upon his career of journalist with the New Year of 1930. But his association with the *Evening Standard* lasted precisely eighteen months. The uncongenial occupation was only relieved by long week-ends spent with his wife. In 1930 the Nicolsons moved from Long Barn to Sissinghurst Castle near Cranbrook in Kent, and jointly created out of practically nothing what became one of the most beautiful and celebrated gardens in Great Britain. Whereas she was the planter, he was the designer. The year 1930 also marked the beginning of the diaries which Nicolson kept until 1962. They were skilfully edited and published by Nigel Nicolson in three volumes (1966–8).

The *Diaries* give a faithful and fascinating day-to-day record of the second half of Nicolson's life. They open on perhaps its least satisfactory period. Impelled by an urge for public service and a laudable desire to excel, Nicolson decided to enter politics. Somewhat rashly he allowed his introduction to be through Sir Oswald Mosley's New Party. In 1931 he unsuccessfully contested the Combined Universities seat as a candidate, and edited the party's weekly journal, *Action*. But when in 1932 Mosley's party turned into the British Union of Fascists, Nicolson, to whom all forms of dictatorship were repugnant, instantly broke with it. He was without a job. As a stop-gap he wrote his second novel (the first, *Sweet Waters*, came out in 1921). *Public Faces* (1932) is an amusing and kindly satire on how in a crisis affairs are conducted in the recesses of the Foreign Office, with a typical Nicolson emphasis on the lesson that honesty is the best policy. He followed this with an intimate and penetrating account of the Paris negotiations of 1919: *Peacemaking 1919* (1933). In 1933 he went with his wife on a well-paid lecture tour of America. It was followed by the biographies, *Curzon, the Last Phase* (1934), *Dwight Morrow* (1935), and *Helen's Tower* (1937). Nicolson also gave numerous broadcast talks, introducing an intimate fireside technique which was both beguiling and extremely popular. His versatility is evident from the fact that he was at the same time writing *Diplomacy*, published in 1939.

From 1935 to 1945 Nicolson was National Labour member of Parliament for West Leicester. His passionate love for the House of Commons, and his unqualified support of (Sir) Winston Churchill were not fully reciprocated. The only office he achieved was that of parliamentary secretary to the Ministry of Information under Alfred Duff Cooper (later Viscount Norwich, q.v.), from 1940 to 1941. (Nicolson contributed the notice of Duff Cooper to this Dictionary.) When superseded in this office he was appointed a governor of the British Broadcasting Corporation (1941–6). Probably his most effective contributions during the war were his weekly 'Marginal Comment' articles in the *Spectator* (1939–52), book reviews in the *Daily Telegraph*, and a Penguin Special *Why Britain is at War* (1939), which sold 100,000 copies within a few months. Nevertheless Nicolson fulfilled a far more valuable role in Parliament than was recognized. He was bitterly opposed to Munich. His knowledge of foreign affairs, his understanding of the French, his championship of de Gaulle with Churchill, and his independence, coupled with his patriotism and strikingly civilized demeanour, always commanded a hearing in the House and the respect of parliamentary committees. His drawbacks were a softness in political combat, an inability to understand or sympathize with the outlook of his middle- and working-class constituents, and a congenital impatience with the humdrum and second-rate.

In 1947 Nicolson threw in his lot unconditionally with the Labour Party, moved thereto, as he put it, by 'cerebral socialism'. He had unsuccessfully contested the general election of 1945 as a National candidate. The National Labour Party had been wound up before the election. He contested North Croydon in a by-election in 1948. It was a half-hearted endeavour. He was defeated. The scintillating after-dinner speaker was no spell-binder on the hustings. Thereafter he abandoned politics, apart from broadcasting, but never received the peerage which would have enabled him to play a useful role without the constituency responsibilities for which he was ill-fitted. Shortly beforehand he had written two very different books, *The Congress of Vienna* (1946) and *The English Sense of Humour* (1947), and now he was to devote the remainder of his life to his true vocation, writing. He was invited to write the official biography of King George V in 1948. *King George V: His Life and Reign* (1952) was the book over which he took most time and trouble, and which ,enhanced his reputation as a brilliant historian as well as biographer. He was appointed KCVO (1953) and was made an honorary fellow of Balliol. He gave the Chichele lecture at Oxford in 1953, and in 1956 stood for the chair of poetry at Oxford, losing to W. H. Auden by only twenty-four votes. In addition to the literary biographies already mentioned, he wrote *Good Behaviour* (1955), *Journey to Java* (1957), *The Age of Reason* (1960), and *Monarchy* (1962). From 1949 to 1963 he contributed weekly book reviews to the *Observer*.

Nicolson found time for supernumerary interests and duties. He was vice-chairman of the National Trust executive committee (1947-68), chairman of the committee of the London Library (1952-7), a trustee of the National Portrait Gallery (1948-64), and president of the Classical Association (1950-1). He was a fellow of the Royal Society of Literature and a commander of the Legion of Honour.

Until his seventieth year Nicolson enjoyed robust health. The death of his wife in 1962 was a shattering blow from which he did not recover. His last years were spent at Sissinghurst in a sad decline, relieved by the affectionate care of his sons and their families to whom he was devoted. He died at Sissinghurst 1 May 1968.

Nicolson was a tiger for work. His mind was rapid and perspicacious; his literary style distinguished for ease, fluency, and wit; he probably never wrote a boring line. He delighted in describing the foibles of human beings, including himself, and yet he was totally devoid of malice or rancour. Although fastidious to a degree verging on exclusiveness, he had a host of friends among the intellectual, artistic, and political élite. He disliked formality and pomposity. The young were devoted to him for the fun as well as wisdom with which he enriched their lives, for he was the most stimulating and entertaining of conversationalists. Indeed his life was rich in diversity of interests. On reaching fifty he admitted to having dispersed his energies too freely in doing too many things, adding in his inimitable way, 'I am still very promising and shall continue to be so until the day of my death'.

Harold Nicolson was stocky in build and cheerful in countenance; jaunty in movement; mischievous and benignant in manner. A drawing in red chalk was done of him by (Sir) William Rothenstein in 1925 and is at Sissinghurst. A life mask, taken by Hamann in Berlin, gives a prosaic likeness of him in middle age.

[Sir Harold Nicolson, *Diaries and Letters, 1930-1962*, 3 vols., ed. Nigel Nicolson, 1966-8; Anne Scott-James, *Sissinghurst, the Making of a Garden*, 1974; Nigel Nicolson, *Portrait of a Marriage*, 1973; Sir Robert Bruce Lockhart, *Diaries*, ed. K. Young, 1973; Sir Oswald Mosley, *My Life*, 1968; Lord Gladwyn, *Memoirs*, 1972; private information; personal knowledge.]

JAMES LEES-MILNE

NICOLSON, VICTORIA MARY, LADY (1892-1962), writer and gardener. [See SACKVILLE-WEST.]

NORMANBROOK, BARON (1902-1967), secretary of the Cabinet. [See BROOK, NORMAN CRAVEN.]

NORMAND, WILFRID GUILD, BARON NORMAND (1884-1962), judge, was born at Aberdour 16 May 1884, the youngest son of Patrick Hill Normand, linen merchant, and his wife, Ellen Prentice. He followed four brothers to Fettes College, went on to Oriel College, Oxford, where he obtained a first in *literae humaniores* in 1906; went next to Paris, and finally to Edinburgh University where he graduated LLB in 1910. So reserved and scholarly was Normand at this stage that few would have predicted for him exceptional success in high office. In 1910 he was admitted to the Faculty of Advocates, and quickly established a busy junior practice until it was interrupted by service as an officer in the Royal Engineers from 1915 to 1918.

On his return to the Scottish bar after the war, Normand developed a substantial practice particularly in the shipping and commercial field, and took silk in 1925. As editor of the *Juridical Review* in the early twenties he contributed also to legal scholarship. In 1929 he held the office of solicitor-general for Scotland for a few weeks and resumed that office after the general election of 1931, when he was elected Unionist member of Parliament for West Edinburgh. His was the responsibility as solicitor-general to pilot through Parliament the important Administration of Justice (Scotland) Act, 1933, which still basically regulates procedure in the Court of Session. Normand was appointed lord advocate and sworn of the Privy Council in 1933, and in 1935 he succeeded Lord Clyde [q.v.] as lord justice general and lord president of the Court of Session. He presided in the highest courts in Scotland until 1947 when he was appointed a lord of appeal in ordinary, an office from which he retired in 1953—although he continued to sit from time to time thereafter both in House of Lords appeals and in the Judicial Committee of the Privy Council. In 1947 Normand was created a life peer. In 1934 he had been elected an honorary bencher of the Middle Temple.

Normand's high reputation as an appellate judge in London and Edinburgh is assured, and it was as such that he was happiest in his professional career. The administrative duties of lord president he did not find very congenial. Moreover, he preferred dealing with legal principles rather than with the weaknesses and shortcomings of men and women. Thus as lord advocate he did not relish his responsibilities for criminal prosecutions, nor did he enjoy the earthier aspect of practice at the bar. His was a specialist rather than a 'general purposes' practice. On the other hand he was keenly interested in the art of pleading, himself favouring clear unemotional and concise exposition. He often quoted the advice of a well-known dean of the Faculty of Advocates, Condie Sandeman—'If you have thought of anything good to say the night before your speech, don't say it.' A typical example of Normand's style was *Cantiere San Rocco, S.A. v. Clyde Shipbuilding and Engineering Co. Ltd.*, 1923 SC (HL) 105 (a case of unjustified enrichment) where Normand was led by Sandeman. English authorities might have been fatal to this case, and Normand therefore argued the appeal in the House of Lords on Scottish and Roman law authorities—translating the Digest with successful effect.

It was painful to Normand, but characteristic, that as lord advocate he refused to recommend his friend Sandeman for elevation to the bench after the latter had allowed his name to be used by a company, the administration of which had been criticized judicially in England.

As a judge in the House of Lords, Normand's grasp of principles and his powers of reasoning enabled him to expound Scots law and English law with authority so as to influence substantially the course of foreseeable legal development. Since the House of Lords since 1966 has reclaimed its earlier freedom to depart from its own precedents, the quality of individual decisions rather than the fact that the House of Lords has spoken has greater importance. Normand fulfilled admirably the special responsibility of a Scottish lord of appeal in recognizing the areas in which Scottish and English solutions may or must be harmonized and areas in which divergences must be stressed. No legal nationalist, he was vigilant for the best interests of Scots law in a United Kingdom setting. Thus he accepted reluctantly (and with sympathy for the Court of ·Session whom he overruled) the statutory anomaly that for fiscal purposes Scottish charities must conform to the requirements of a statute of the Tudor Elizabeth. On the other hand in *A.G.* v. *Prince Ernest Augustus of Hanover*, [1957] AC 436 judicially (but more vehemently extra judicially) he deplored the attitude of the attorney-general who was apparently prepared to accept that pre-Union English statutes could confer British nationality while pre-Union Scottish Acts could not; the anomalous outcome was apparently that the Prince became British in England only.

Normand was distinguished in appearance and bearing, and had a fine head of white hair to the end. Throughout his life he was recognizably a Scot in speech and outlook. Although he might on first impression seem reserved and austere, he could be most courteous and charming in public and in private, and warmed in scholarly circles. During his six years' sojourn in London he was always happy to return home to Scotland, and it was in Scotland that he spent nearly a decade in retirement. These years enabled him to pursue those many scholarly interests which he had always maintained. He was an active trustee of the National Library of Scotland from its foundation in 1925 until his death, and in 1950–3 was a trustee of the British Museum. He was active as chairman of the trustees of the Scottish Museum of Antiquities and of the Carnegie Trust for the Scottish Universities. He served in the capacity of president of the Classical Association of Scotland, of the International Law Association, of the Stair Society, and of the Scottish Universities Law Institute—which he conceived to revive contemporary Scottish legal literature. His scholarship did not lack official recognition: he was an honorary LLD of Edinburgh, an honorary fellow of Oriel and of University College, London, which he served as chairman of its college committee during the era of post-war reconstruction. Somewhat fastidious in extrovert society he enjoyed the company of scholars, old and young. At his death he was working with Dr. J. C. Corson of Edinburgh University on notes to the legal references in the works of Sir Walter Scott. These notes are deposited in the National Library of Scotland.

In 1913 Normand married Gertrude, daughter of William Lawson, banker, of New York; they had a son and a daughter. After his first wife's death in 1923, he married in 1927 Marion Bell Gilchrist (died 1972), daughter of David Cunningham, farmer, of Aberdour. Normand died in Edinburgh 5 October 1962.

[*The Times*, 8 October 1962; *Scots Law Times*, 1935 (News) 113, 1947 (News) 1, 1962 (News) 148; *Glasgow Herald*, 6 October 1962; private information; personal knowledge.]   T. B. SMITH

NORTH, SIR DUDLEY BURTON NAPIER (1881–1961), admiral, was born at Great Yarmouth 25 November 1881, the fourth of the five sons of Captain (later Colonel) Roger North, Royal Artillery and adjutant in the 1st Norfolk Artillery Volunteers, and Fanny Ellen, the daughter of Stephen Beeching, of Tunbridge Wells. He entered the *Britannia* as a naval cadet in 1896 and then served in cruisers, destroyers, and battleships as a midshipman. He became sub-lieutenant in 1902 and lieutenant in 1903. In the battle-cruiser *New Zealand* he took part in the battle of Heligoland (1914). As commander, and in the same vessel, from 31 December 1914 he took part in the battles of the Dogger Bank (1915) and Jutland (1916). After a short period of shore service in the Admiralty, where he was naval assistant to Captain (later Admiral Sir) Lionel Halsey [q.v.], he returned to sea in the battle-cruiser *Australia*. Promoted captain and appointed CMG in 1919, he embarked on a series of world tours by various members of the Royal family as naval equerry. In 1919 he was also appointed MVO, in 1920 CVO, and in 1922 CSI. In 1922–4 he commanded 'C' class cruisers before taking another Royal tour with the Prince of Wales in 1925.

North was then successful in various important posts as captain, being flag captain in the flagship of the Atlantic Fleet in 1926–7, and subsequently flag captain and chief of staff in the Reserve Fleet. In 1930 he became director of operations at the Admiralty, being promoted to rear-admiral in 1932. He then became chief of staff to Admiral Sir John Kelly [q.v.], the commander-in-chief, Home Fleet. There his tact and courtesy combined well with the unconventional attitude of Kelly, who was determined to make the fleet forget the Invergordon mutiny of 1931. In 1934 North was appointed to the command of the Royal Yachts at Portsmouth, a post for which he was well qualified after his experiences as equerry and his friendship with the Royal family, whom he accompanied to Canada in 1939. When war came in September 1939, North, CB since 1935, a vice-admiral since 1936, and KCVO since 1937, had been too long out of touch with the fleet to be appointed to a sea-going command. Instead, he was made flag officer commanding the North Atlantic station and admiral superintendent at Gibraltar, taking up his post in November 1939. He was promoted to admiral in May 1940. The bombardment of Oran by the British fleet under Admiral Sir James Somerville [q.v.], on 3 July 1940, distressed him considerably. He wrote an official letter to the Admiralty in which he criticized the operation and explained how repugnant it had been to all who took part. The letter was ill received and the first lord, A. V. Alexander (later Lord Alexander of Hillsborough, q.v.), proposed that he should be relieved, but Sir Dudley Pound [q.v.], the first sea lord, did not agree that the case was strong enough, whereupon a sharp reprimand was sent instead. This was the start of a lack of confidence in North by the Admiralty which was to have serious consequences.

In September 1940 occurred the incident of the French squadron passing the straits of Gibraltar and steaming on to Dakar where it played a part in repelling the attack of the Franco-British force, an operation of which North was aware unofficially. North had received previous intelligence reports of the French movements, but expected instructions from the Admiralty which were not sent, due to mistakes in the handling of signals. In the event, he took no action to stop the French and this was regarded by the Admiralty as an unforgivable lack of initiative. The first sea lord proposed, and the first lord agreed, that he should be relieved, and this was done on 31 December 1940, despite North's violent protests and demands for an inquiry. On arrival in London in mid January, North saw Pound, the first sea lord, but the interview, and subsequent letters, achieved no inquiry. North joined the Home Guard and in 1942 was appointed flag officer, Yarmouth, as a retired rear-admiral.

After the war he was still convinced that he had been treated unjustly, and so apparently did King George VI who appointed him admiral commanding Royal Yachts, a post which lasted a year only because economies were made. North became GCVO in 1947. The post-war years saw a succession of efforts, some by North personally, some by others, to secure an inquiry. The Admiralty was criticized in several books and articles and North again wrote to Whitehall. In 1953 five admirals of the fleet took up the case with the first lord, J. P. L. Thomas (later Viscount Cilcennin, q.v.), but without result. In 1954 the publication of the official history appeared to clear North, and a bitter debate took place in the House of Commons, in which the first lord emphasized the loss of confidence in North by the Admiralty Board and refused to act. A fiery debate also took place in the House of Lords. Whereas it cannot be disputed that the Admiralty could relieve any officer in whom confidence had been lost, the method used was clumsy and the subsequent handling bungled.

When Lord Mountbatten of Burma, who had been a friend of North's for many years, became first sea lord in 1955, he at once investigated the affair and came to the conclusion that an inquiry would serve no purpose. However, in 1957 the publication of a book by Noel Monks, strongly criticizing the Admiralty, revived the matter yet again, and another debate took place in the Commons. Mountbatten, Lord Selkirk, the new first lord, and Harold Macmillan, the prime minister, spent many hours considering the documents and also met the five admirals of the fleet. The prime minister then produced a carefully balanced statement in which he stressed that North's honour and professional integrity had not been impugned but refused an inquiry into such a well-documented incident. The public generally were satisfied that the statement ended the affair with a vindication of North's honour. North himself was not so content. He died 15 May 1961 at Bridport, Dorset, a sad and bitter man.

In appearance North was of medium height and stocky, with a cheerful round face which usually had a twinkle. He married in 1909 Eglantine, daughter of William R. Campbell of Sydney, New South Wales. She died in 1917 and he married, secondly, in 1923, Eilean Flora, daughter of Edward Graham, JP, of Charminster, Dorset. There were a son and three daughters of the second marriage.

[*The Times*, 16 May 1961; S. W. Roskill, *The War at Sea*, 1954; Noel Monks, *That day at Gibraltar*, 1957; Arthur Marder, *Operation Menace*, 1976; Charlotte and Denis Plimmer, *A Matter of Expediency*, 1978.]
                      PETER GRETTON

NORTH, JOHN DUDLEY (1893-1968), aircraft designer, was born in London 2 January 1893, the only child of Dudley North, solicitor, and his wife, Marian Felgate. He was educated at Bedford School where he learned the elements of the mathematics which he applied so skilfully until the end of his days. After leaving school he became an apprentice in marine engineering. Whilst still an apprentice he won two competitions in the *Aeroplane*, edited at that time by Charles Grey Grey [q.v.]. It was through Grey's advice that his apprenticeship was transferred to the Aeronautical Syndicate and when that venture ended he joined the Grahame-White company. He was still only nineteen when he became its chief engineer. Between 1912 and 1915 he designed and supervised the construction of a number of aeroplanes, one of which was the first British aeroplane to loop the loop. The best-remembered product of this period of extraordinary precocity was the Grahame-White Charabanc which in 1913, piloted by Louis Noël, took nine passengers, including the youthful designer, into the air.

In 1915, when only twenty-two, North joined the Austin motor company as superintendent of its aeroplane division. In this post he was responsible not for design but for constructing the large numbers of RE.7 and RE.8 aircraft which the company produced for the Royal Flying Corps.

At the end of 1917 he joined Boulton & Paul Ltd., of Norwich, a company which, through the aircraft production work it had taken up during the war, had decided to start a design department, of which North was put in charge. The first machine he designed was the Bobolink, a fighter. It was followed by the Bourges, a bomber-reconnaissance aircraft of attractive design and remarkable performance. This aeroplane, of which there were several marks, was the first of a series of high-performance bombers. It was followed by the Bolton and the Bugle and, in 1927, by probably the most famous of North's aeroplanes, the Sidestrand. Towards the end of the 1920s there followed two single-seater fighters, the Partridge, which was a single-engine biplane, and the Bittern, a twin-engine monoplane with a number of original features. The Air Ministry appeared to decide, however, that the forte of Boulton & Paul, and its successor (1934) in the aircraft field, Boulton Paul Aircraft Ltd., was the bomber, and the next selected for service was the Overstrand. Towards the end of the series came that remarkable turret-fighter, the Defiant, which was used in the early days of the war of 1939-45 and aided the Dunkirk evacuation. The last aircraft production run, which came after the war ended, was on the Balliol, an advanced trainer for the Royal Air Force and Fleet Air Arm. Thereafter the only aircraft of note were the delta research aircraft P.111 and P.120, the first to use Boulton Paul power controls. Few designers have to their credit a more remarkable series of aircraft, and a study of them reveals North's outstanding fertility in invention and skill in engineering.

North was one of the first to move away from the wood and fabric of the war of 1914-18 to the tubular and monocoque constructions of the later years. He was always close to the latest development in metal and plastic materials. His particular genius for design in metal was given an excellent opportunity in 1924 when Boulton & Paul became intimately associated with the design and construction of the airship R.101. Its sad fate should not be allowed to obscure the ingenuity of its structure. The over-all design of the skeleton was the work of the Royal Airship Works, but the design of the individual girders, in some parts of the ship a matter of most complicated three-dimensional geometry, was the work of North and his team.

An outstanding characteristic of North's last bombers was their gun turrets. As Boulton Paul became famous for making powered turrets for a variety of aircraft, its work moved progressively away from complete aircraft to the increasingly complex parts thereof. In his last phase as a designer North concentrated more on powered controls—including those of Concorde—and on other powered devices within and without the aeronautical field.

It was North's ideas on control which led to his deep interest in control mathematics and cybernetics, and he developed a wide-ranging knowledge of operational research, ergonomics, and statistics. His profound and imaginative scientific papers include 'The Rational Behaviour of Mechanically Extended Man' (Conference on the Human Operator in Control Systems, Royal Military Academy of Science, 1954), 'Application of Communication Theory to the Human Operator' (third London Symposium on Information Theory, 1955), and 'Manual Control as a Stochastic Process' (published in *Ergonomics*, 1963).

North was a member of the council of the Society of British Aircraft Constructors from 1931 to 1962. It was as the society's nominee that he joined the council of the Air Registration Board and the governing body of the College of Aeronautics at Cranfield, on both of which he worked with characteristic dedication.

As engineer, as designer, as applied mathematician, J. D. North was a great professional. As horticulturalist, gastronome, and cook, he was a great amateur—an amateur in the cricketing sense in that he could keep his end up with the professionals. He was an honorary fellow of the Royal Aeronautical Society and in 1967 he became an honorary D.Sc. of the university of Birmingham. In 1962 he was appointed CBE. Although he seemed indifferent to fame and his course was determined only by logic, he did not scorn recognition and when he was honoured he was greatly pleased. When his years of service to the Air Registration Board were appreciated by a modest presentation he was deeply touched. Perhaps, in his great modesty, he never felt neglected, but in the memories of those who knew him best he will always stand out as a person of distinction whose merit in his lifetime was comprehended by too few. This may have been because his integrity was complete and in things which mattered he could not compromise. North was a tall, heavily built man, bespectacled from youth. His voice was deep, his manner deliberate. On first meeting he could be a little frightening, but it was usually not long before his humour and kindliness came through.

North married in 1922 Phyllis Margaret, daughter of Edward Huggins, clerk to the Norwich Board of Guardians. They had two daughters. He died at his home in Bridgnorth, Shropshire, 11 January 1968.

[H. F. King in *Flight International*, 7 October 1965; obituary notice by Kings Norton, *Journal of the Royal Aeronautical Society*, December 1968; private information; personal knowledge.] KINGS NORTON

NOYCE, (CUTHBERT) WILFRID (FRANCIS) (1917–1962), mountaineer and writer, was born at Simla 31 December 1917, the elder son in a family of two sons and a daughter of (Sir) Frank Noyce, Indian civil servant, and his wife, Enid Isabel, daughter of W. M. Kirkus, of Liverpool. He was educated at Charterhouse, becoming head of the school, and in 1936 he went up to King's College, Cambridge, as a major scholar. He obtained first class honours in the classical tripos (part i, 1939) and in the preliminary examination for part ii of the modern languages tripos (1940), becoming BA in 1940 and MA in 1945. In 1939 he joined the Friends' Ambulance Unit, but in 1940 joined the Welsh Guards as a private. Commissioned in the King's Royal Rifle Corps in 1941, he spent the years 1942–6 in India, first as a captain in intelligence and then as chief instructor at the Aircrew Mountain Centre in Kashmir. From 1946 until 1950 he was an assistant master teaching modern languages at Malvern College and subsequently he taught for ten years at Charterhouse. In the latter period he served for some years on the Godalming Borough Council. He retired from teaching in 1961 in order to give more time to writing.

Already, at eighteen, Noyce was a fine rock climber, partly through the influence of a brilliant older companion, J. Menlove Edwards, with whom he climbed regularly between 1935 and 1937. He survived a serious accident on Scafell in 1937, when he fell 180 ft. and was magnificently held by Edwards on a rope of which two of the three strands had parted. He was badly injured, especially about the face, and the completeness of his recovery was astonishing. In two early Alpine seasons, 1937 (shortly before this accident) and 1938, climbing with either Armand Charlet or Hans Brantschen, both great guides, he made a series of major climbs in very fast times. During the war, when he was stationed in India, his exceptional stamina and capacity to acclimatize were demonstrated when he and Sherpa Angtharkay reached the top of Pauhunri in Sikkim (23,385 ft.) fifteen days after leaving Darjeeling.

In 1946, climbing in a gale in the Lake District, Noyce was blown from his holds and broke a leg, and for some years he climbed to more ordinary standards. He was nevertheless an obvious choice for the 1953 Everest expedition, and at a critical stage it was Noyce and Sherpa Annullu who opened the route to the South Col. Ten days later, Noyce reached the col again, without oxygen, in support of the successful summit climb. Subsequently he had several impressive seasons in the Alps and one (1961) in the High Atlas, but his major ventures were further afield. In 1957 he was turned back by bad weather just below the top of Machapuchare (22,997 ft.), a difficult peak in western Nepal, and in 1960 he led an expedition to Trivor (25,370 ft.) in the Karakoram, Noyce himself being one of the pair which reached the summit. His main reason for joining the Pamirs expedition on which he died was his wish to promote friendship between British and Russian mountaineers.

Noyce was a cultivated, unassuming man with an almost diffident manner. Despite his outstanding achievements, his appreciation of mountains was largely aesthetic and his instincts scholarly and literary. In 1947 he wrote an unusual autobiography, *Mountains and Men*, the first of more than a dozen books. These included two volumes of poetry, *Michael Angelo, a Poem* (1953) and *Poems* (1960); some of the poems were written at 21,000 ft. on Everest. His main reputation was as a mountaineering author. He had a gift for conveying, vividly but with restraint and complete honesty, what mountain experiences were really like. This was skilfully demonstrated in *South Col* (1954), his personal story of Everest and easily his most successful book; but the same approach characterized his two later expedition books, *Climbing the Fish's Tail* (1958) and *To the Unknown Mountain* (1962). An earlier work, *Scholar Mountaineers* (1950), was a study of various historic figures who in different ways were both lovers of mountains and men of thought. He wrote one mountain novel, *The Gods are Angry* (1957). Latterly, he was moving away from purely mountain subjects; in *The Springs of Adventure* (1958) he explored the motives for engaging in any sort of hazardous activity, and in *They Survived* (1962) he made a case study of man's will to survive in desperate situations.

In 1950 he married Rosemary, daughter of Henry Campbell Davies, and there were two sons. He died in the USSR 24 July 1962,

when he and a companion fell, descending from the summit of Garmo Peak (*c.* 21,500 ft.) in the Pamirs. His death cut short a literary career of notable achievement in a particular field, but one whose wider promise was not yet fulfilled.

[*Alpine Journal*, vol. lxvii, pp. 384-91; King's College, Cambridge, *Annual Report*, 1963, pp. 56-9; private information; personal knowledge.]   A. D. M. Cox

NUFFIELD, VISCOUNT (1877-1963), industrialist and philanthropist. [See MORRIS, WILLIAM RICHARD.]

NYE, SIR ARCHIBALD EDWARD (1895-1967), lieutenant-general, was born in Ship St. Barracks, Dublin, 23 April 1895, the youngest but one in the family of three sons and three daughters of Charles Edward Nye and his wife, Mary Sexton. His father was a regimental sergeant-major in the Oxfordshire and Buckinghamshire Light Infantry. His mother was Irish. An outstanding scholar at the Duke of York's Royal Military School, Dover (where he was sent at the age of ten upon his father's death), he was preparing to become an army schoolmaster when war began in August 1914, as the result of which he volunteered for combatant duty. Serving as a non-commissioned officer in France, he was selected for a commission in the Leinster Regiment in 1915. Twice wounded in action and awarded the MC for gallantry thereafter, he was granted a regular commission in 1922 in the Royal Warwickshire Regiment with the demise of the Leinsters, a southern Irish regiment. Lacking any private means, Nye never drank, and helped to pay his mess bills by winning games of billiards. In the military doldrums of the 1920s, Nye's quick, keen mind drew him to the staff. In 1924-5 he attended the Staff College, Camberley. He soon acquired a high reputation, brevet, and accelerated promotion through exchange of regiments. It is a mark of his capabilities that while holding demanding appointments, he managed simultaneously to qualify as a barrister at the Inner Temple in 1932.

Recognized as a potential general officer, Nye was returned to regimental duty to command the 2nd battalion, Royal Warwickshire Regiment in 1937, earned at once a recommendation for higher command, and was appointed to raise the Nowshera brigade in India in 1939. War once again changed his plans, however. Within a few months he was recalled to London and, shortly, promoted major-general as director of staff duties in the War Office, the branch concerned with organization and co-ordination. During the crises of British arms in 1940, his enterprise, moral courage, and mastery of complex politico-military policy impressed the prime minister, (Sir) Winston Churchill, so that when he removed Sir John G. Dill [q.v.] as chief of the imperial general staff in 1941, Nye was one of three possible successors in his mind. But seniority and experience in high command weighed in this selection. Sir Alan Brooke (later Viscount Alanbrooke, q.v.) was chosen; Nye was promoted to lieutenant-general and vice-chief. Fortunately, the two men complemented and had absolute confidence in one another. They carried a formidable work-load for four years until victory in 1945. Nye accompanied Brooke on many of his important journeys during the war. At its end Brooke wished to make Nye adjutant-general but another option was offered, governor of Madras. Retiring with the honours of KBE (1944) and KCB (1946, having been appointed CB in 1942), Nye returned to India in 1946.

His active support for independence there inspired Jawaharlal Nehru [q.v.] to ask him to stay in post when imperial government ended. Further, his firmness and wisdom in the ensuing political, racial, and caste turbulence prompted the Indian Government to suggest his appointment as United Kingdom high commissioner at Delhi when he completed his extension in Madras in 1948. In this second post he developed successfully the new and friendly relationship between the British and Indian governments, enhancing it by skilful diplomacy during the opening and greater part of the Korean war.

Departing from India in 1952 with the honours GCIE (1946) and GCSI (1947), he was appointed high commissioner to Canada. In his four years in Ottawa his most notable success was the extension of British-Canadian trade; perhaps his most difficult political task the representation of his country's policy concerning the Suez Canal. Retiring in 1956, he left many official and personal friends in Canada. He had received the freedom of the capital city, academic honours from Bishop's, McGill, Toronto, and McMaster universities, and was to be appointed GCMG by his own government in 1951. For some years, he held a number of directorships in commercial companies but, in 1962, he returned temporarily to government service as chairman of a committee to consider the reorganization of the War Office. The work of this body—the Nye Committee—influenced profoundly the reshaping of the army's headquarters for the remaining years of the twentieth century. Its influence persists.

Nye made an important contribution to the high political and military policies of his country and often played a crucial part in their execution over more than twenty years. His reputation is, happily, unsullied by any manifestation of jealousy, bitterness, or disregard towards those with whom he served. It is remarkable that he caught the attention of three prime ministers—Churchill, Attlee, and Nehru—each of whom wanted to place him in a significant position.

In 1939 Nye married (Una Sheila) Colleen, daughter of General Sir Harry Hugh Sidney Knox; they had one daughter. Colleen also had two children by her previous marriage to Colonel N. D. Stevenson. Nye died in London 13 November 1967.

There is a pastel portrait by William Dring (1942) and a portrait in oils by Henry Lamb (1942), both of which are in the Imperial War Museum.

[*The Times*, 15 November 1967; official and regimental records; private information.]

ANTHONY FARRAR-HOCKLEY

O

O'CASEY, SEAN (1880-1964), Irish dramatist and author, was born in Dublin of Protestant parents 30 March 1880, the youngest of the five surviving children of Michael and Susanna Casey. His real name was John Casey, but he subsequently Gaelicized his name to Sean O'Cathasaigh and still later changed the surname to O'Casey. His father, who worked as a clerk for the Irish Church Mission, died when John was six; two brothers and a sister who were already approaching adulthood went their several ways. O'Casey with his mother and the remaining brother, who was able to provide but little financial support, lived in the poverty and squalor of tenement life.

O'Casey himself suffered from a painful eye disease which prevented any formal education; but by the age of fourteen he had taught himself to read. From then onwards he read voraciously. His inborn feeling for the splendour of language had been nourished from an early age by reading from the Bible. His bent for the theatre quickly showed itself: two authors in whose work he took special delight were, at their different levels, masters of stagecraft—Shakespeare and Dion Boucicault [qq.v.].

But self-education, though it may be intense and profound, is almost of necessity narrow—especially when it starts late and from illiteracy. Not for many years was O'Casey able to make use of his hard-earned culture to improve his way of life. Until he was thirty he worked as a casual labourer, often unemployed and further handicapped by poor health. Even when he did escape from drudgery, it was into the fervid atmosphere of Irish politics rather than the comparatively calm world of Irish literature. He was in turn a member of the Gaelic League, the Irish Republican Brotherhood, Jim Larkin's union, the Irish Citizen Army, and the Irish Socialist Party. But he was too independent to remain long in any movement. After 1916 he turned seriously to writing plays. Although the first three which he submitted to the Abbey Theatre were rejected, he received encouragement from Lady Gregory and W. B. Yeats [qq.v.]. Not until he was forty-three was his first play staged; but it was quickly followed by others which made it clear that he was a writer of genius.

Genius was a word which came easily to commentators on O'Casey's command of language, once his career was fully launched. His prose had about it an amplitude and a poetic colour which set it apart from and above the drab realism which was the aim of most of his contemporaries; and while many faults of craftsmanship were laid to his charge as his career continued the special magic of his style was never, or very seldom, questioned.

This special quality was seen at its finest in his early plays about the Irish troubles produced at the Abbey Theatre, all written from his own personal experience, and in the six volumes of his magnificent autobiography (1939-54). But even in his least successful plays he showed this quality. He was still unmistakably a genius, but one who had somehow lost his way to the heights.

O'Casey's three Dublin plays established him as a great writer but destroyed him as a dramatist. While the first of them, *The Shadow of a Gunman* (1923), was packing the Abbey Theatre he was still working as a day labourer, mixing cement. After the success of his masterpiece, *Juno and the Paycock* (1924), he turned professional. But his next play *The Plough and the Stars* (1926), of which the setting was Dublin during the Easter rising of 1916 and the main characters non-combatants, gave great offence. When he was awarded the Hawthornden prize in 1926 for *Juno* he was invited to London and he determined to retreat to an exile in England which was to endure for the rest of his life.

An exile indeed it was, and continued to be. O'Casey never understood England, nor she O'Casey. Even the welcome which his Dublin plays received in London was based on a misapprehension. English audiences of the time had little patience with any dramatic dialogue which was not realistic, and they took O'Casey's lyric prose to be the authentic speech of Irish slum dwellers. Consequently when he turned later to more obvious fantasy the English public, expecting more realism, lost interest in his work.

O'Casey in his turn contributed strongly to this misunderstanding. After a perfunctory glance at the London theatre he decided that its aims were too trivial to be worth his attention. A man more worldly wise or less self-assured might have realized that London had much to teach him, both in the way of broader culture and a greater experience of stagecraft; but O'Casey, who had a theory that an artist should develop naturally along his own lines, saw no need for this. As a result, his lack of education remained always in his way.

For example, he had the idea, in itself brilliantly original and destined to be valuable in the hands of later generations, of using different styles of writing in the same play. But because he was not skilled in the various techniques he employed, such a play was foredoomed to failure. His anti-war play, *The Silver Tassie*, with its symbolic second act, was a case in point. Its rejection by the Abbey Theatre in 1928 gave rise to a public dispute between the author and Yeats. Produced in London at the Apollo (1929) it was praised by the critics for its originality, but it did not draw the public. *Within the Gates* (Royalty, 1934), written with a similar disregard of realism, was found incomprehensible by critics and public alike. It gave ample evidence of O'Casey's inability to adapt himself to his new surroundings. It was set in Hyde Park and the characters included a kind of chorus of down-and-outs. Yet there was not a hint of a London atmosphere in the whole composition. It was not surprising that this was the last of his plays to command an important production as a matter of course.

After that he had to fight a losing battle to obtain production of any kind at all, although *Red Roses for Me* was favourably received by the critics when it was produced at the Embassy in 1946. In 1938 O'Casey settled in Devon where he continued to write busily but it was as an increasingly frustrated, disappointed, and embittered man with his mind's eye always on the Ireland which had rejected, and continued to reject, him. For the Dublin International theatre festival of 1958 he was invited to provide a new play. But difficulties were made about its production and O'Casey withdrew the play (*The Drums of Father Ned*) and went on to withdraw all his plays from production in Dublin.

In 1927 O'Casey married Eileen Reynolds, an actress (as Eileen Carey) of Irish Roman Catholic parentage. They had two sons, the younger of whom died in 1957, and one daughter. O'Casey died in Torquay 18 September 1964.

The National Portrait Gallery has a drawing by Powys Evans.

[*The Times*, 21 September 1964; O'Casey's autobiography; David Krause, *Sean O'Casey, The Man and his Work*, 1960; Eileen O'Casey, *Sean*, 1971; private information; personal knowledge.]

W. A. DARLINGTON

O'KELLY, SEAN THOMAS (1882–1966), president of Ireland, was born at Lower Wellington Street, Dublin, 25 August 1882, the eldest son of Samuel O'Kelly, a master boot-maker, and his wife, Catherine O'Dea.

Educated at the Christian Brothers' School in St. Mary's Place and later at O'Connell Schools, North Richmond Street, Dublin, he went to work at the age of sixteen as a boy-messenger at the National Library. During his four years in the library, he quickly made up for the deficiencies in his early education and by the age of twenty had acquired a journalistic skill which was to be his mainstay for many years. In 1903 he became a full-time journalist in periodicals devoted to cultural and political nationalism. Arthur Griffith [q.v.] had returned from South Africa in 1899 to start the Sinn Fein movement, which, originally aiming at an Anglo-Irish dual monarchy, was within little more than a decade to supersede the Irish parliamentary party as the main vehicle of Irish nationalism. In 1903 O'Kelly wrote for Griffith's first newspaper, the *United Irishman* (founded 1899), and in the same year became the manager of the weekly, *An Claidheamh Solais* (the sword of light), the organ through which the Gaelic League carried on the campaign for reviving the Irish language.

O'Kelly was elected in the Sinn Fein interest to Dublin City Council in 1906, thus preceding Eamon de Valera and his future colleagues in Fianna Fail as an active politician. He was an assiduous member of the council, on which he remained until 1932, being especially concerned about the appalling housing conditions in much of Dublin.

O'Kelly was a founder-member of the Sinn Fein volunteers in 1913 and participated in the Easter rebellion of 1916 as a staff-captain to Patrick Pearse, the commander-in-chief of the insurgent forces. Incarcerated, after the surrender, in Richmond prison, Dublin, with his future leader, Eamon de Valera, O'Kelly was deported to Wales, released at Christmas 1916, re-arrested, then escaped to Ireland and participated in the by-election of Longford in May 1917, the second won by a Sinn Fein candidate in opposition to a nominee of the Irish parliamentary party.

In October 1917 Griffith joined forces with de Valera who became president of Sinn Fein, now unequivocally committed to attaining an Irish republic. O'Kelly entered with enthusiasm into the arrangements for the general election of 1918 as Sinn Fein director of organization. He was a candidate for the College Green constituency of Dublin which he won by a handsome majority. (He was to be returned as a deputy for various Dublin constituencies at every general election between 1918 and 1944 inclusive.) When the Sinn Fein deputies met in Dublin on 21 January 1919 to set up the republican assembly known to history as the first Dáil, O'Kelly was present, and at the second meeting in April was elected Speaker. Later in the year he was sent with another emissary to the peace conference at Paris, but the mission was fruitless. Clemenceau refused to receive them and Ireland's claim to self-determination went unheard at Versailles.

He was in Paris and Rome until after the truce of July 1921 which led to the Anglo-Irish treaty of 6 December 1921. When the treaty came up for ratification by the Dáil, O'Kelly followed de Valera in opposition to his old leader Griffith, who on the treaty's ratification became president of the Dáil, a position which he held for a mere six months, dying in August 1922. During the civil war which followed the treaty split, O'Kelly was arrested, but released at Christmas 1923. He then went to the United States to raise funds for those opposed to the treaty.

In 1926 when de Valera decided to found a political party, Fianna Fail, committed to attaining a republic by constitutional means, O'Kelly was a founder member, and edited the first party newspaper. He was not de Valera's initial choice for deputy leader, but when the politician first selected declined, O'Kelly was appointed, and for the next nineteen years remained the *fidus Achates* to the great leader, always at his side except for the occasional visit abroad. The breach with the lineal successors of Griffith, President W. T. Cosgrave [q.v.] and his *Cumann na nGaedhael* party, who were now dedicated to the Commonwealth connection, was complete.

In August 1927 O'Kelly was one of the forty-five new Fianna Fail deputies to take their seats in the Dáil and was for the next five years an active front-bencher while not neglecting his municipal duties. In the general election of 1932 Cosgrave was decisively defeated; de Valera became president of the Executive Council (prime minister) while O'Kelly became vice-president and minister for local government and public health, a post which he held until 1939. As a minister his greatest achievement was the energetic building of 'labourers' cottages', the most conspicuous social service associated with the first Fianna Fail Government. He also headed the Irish delegation to the Imperial Conference in Ottawa in 1932 (the last such appearance by the Irish Free State) and in 1939 deputized for de Valera at the opening of the World Fair in New York.

In a Cabinet reshuffle after the outbreak of war in 1939, O'Kelly was transferred to the Ministry of Finance where he remained for six years, but the post did not suit his talents and he made little impact. At the end of the war in which de Valera's neutrality policy had had all-party support the office of president of Eire fell vacant. At the first election following the adoption of the constitution of 1937 (which gave the name of Eire to the Irish Free State), the major parties agreed on a non-political candidate, the scholar-poet, Douglas Hyde, first president of the Gaelic League, but he was too infirm to seek a second term in 1945, so a contested election occurred. O'Kelly was nominated as the Fianna Fail candidate and the continuing ascendancy of that party was demonstrated by his winning

easily, even without the formality of a speaking tour, securing just under 50 per cent of the votes against two other candidates.

As devised in the constitution of 1937 the office of president was an ambiguous one—something between a head of state and a dominion governor-general; he had no role in foreign affairs, since de Valera wished to continue the tenuous link with the Commonwealth, provided by having heads of diplomatic missions accredited to the King. (This had led to anomalies, as when during the war new diplomatic personnel could obviously not be accredited from Germany and Japan.) In the first post-war general election in February 1948 which brought an end to de Valera's longest term in office, only one party, the new republican party, Clann na Poblachta, led by Sean MacBride, proposed a complete separation from the Commonwealth; but it was paradoxically the new coalition government led by John A. Costello of Fine Gael (traditionally the strongest pro-Commonwealth party) which introduced the legislation establishing the Republic of Ireland outside the Commonwealth (April 1949). Henceforth the official name of the state was 'Ireland', not 'Eire'.

This dramatically altered the status of the president, who was now a full head of state, and O'Kelly quickly realized the potentialities of his new role. He made state visits abroad, to Rome in 1950 and later to Paris, and the Prince of the Netherlands became the first state visitor to be entertained at Arus an Uachtarain (the presidential residence in Phoenix Park, formerly the viceregal lodge). O'Kelly also performed with great dignity the public functions associated with a head of state. In spite of his long association with disputatious politics, as president he 'showed very clearly that he had as fully transcended the political sphere as his natural dignity overcame his diminutive stature' (*Irish Times*, 24 November 1966). At the end of his first seven-year term of office in June 1952 his popularity was rewarded by an unopposed second term, during which he publicly appealed for an end to the post-civil war animosities, which for nearly forty years had inhibited ordinary social intercourse between the leaders of the two major parties that had developed after the Sinn Fein split. In 1953 he made a state visit—the first of many by Irish presidents—to the United States and addressed a joint session of Congress. He also helped to defuse a potential Church–State crisis by mediating between the second de Valera Government and the Catholic hierarchy over some controversial provisions in the Health Act of 1953.

After his retirement in 1959, when he was succeeded as president by de Valera, O'Kelly lived quietly at his country residence in Roundwood, county Wicklow, with his wife Phyllis, who throughout the years in the highest office had proved a benign and affable first lady. He broadcasted his political reminiscences in 1959; they were afterwards published by the *Irish Press* under the title 'Memoirs of Sean T. O'Kelly'. Chatty and anecdotal, they do not add greatly to our knowledge of the period, but display the author's journalistic facility as well as a puckish sense of humour and occasionally a flash of temper, but all suffused with a personal charm which even political enemies found irresistible.

O'Kelly was the recipient of many honorary degrees, among them doctorates from the National University of Ireland, Dublin University, Ottawa, Fordham, and De Paul universities, and Boston College. During his years as president he was awarded the freedom of the cities of Dublin, Cork, Limerick, Waterford, and Galway. In 1958 the Pope conferred on him the gold collar of the Pian Order; he had earlier been awarded the grand cross of the Order of St. Gregory the Great (1933). He also received the grand cordon of the Legion of Honour (France), the grand cross of the Order of Charles III (Spain), the grand cross of the Order of Merit (German Federal Republic), and the grand cordon of the Order of Merit (Italy).

He was twice married, first in 1918 to Mary Kate, second daughter of John Ryan, farmer, of Tomcoole, Wexford, and sister of Dr. James Ryan, a colleague of O'Kelly's in the Fianna Fail government. She died in 1934. In 1936 he married her youngest sister, Phyllis Ryan (an analytical chemist) who survived him. There were no children of either marriage.

O'Kelly died in a Dublin hospital 23 November 1966 and is buried at Glasnevin. A portrait by Leo Whelan is at Arus an Uachtarain.

[*Irish Times*, 24 November 1966; *Irish Press*, 3 July–9 August 1961; the Earl of Longford and Thomas P. O'Neill, *Eamon de Valera*, 1970; J. H. Whyte, *Church and State in Modern Ireland* 1923–70, 1971; private information.]   CORNELIUS O'LEARY

OLDHAM, JOSEPH HOULDSWORTH (1874–1969), missionary, was born in Bombay, India, 20 October 1874, the eldest son of Colonel George Wingate Oldham and his wife, Lillah Houldsworth. George Oldham retired early from his successful career to bring his delicate wife home. Oldham attended the Edinburgh Academy and, passing out *dux* in 1892, entered Trinity College, Oxford, where he obtained a second class in both honour moderations (1894) and *literae humaniores*

(1896), with a career in the Indian Civil Service in mind. His objective changed as the result of a religious conversion and he proceeded to India in 1897 under the auspices of the Scottish YMCA to work among students and government employees in Lahore.

He spent three years in India almost entirely in the company of Indians, an experience which made him sensitive to Indian aspirations. Oldham was then invalided home. In 1901 he entered New College, Edinburgh, completed his theological studies with distinction, and then went to the university of Halle, Germany, to study missionary theory and practice. Although he was never ordained, he became a ministerial assistant at Free St. George's, Edinburgh, and worked to promote the study of missions among students and in Scottish congregations. In 1908 he was summoned to act as full-time organizing secretary for the Edinburgh World Missionary Conference of 1910, which might be regarded as the starting-point of the modern ecumenical movement. The conference acknowledged his remarkable success by unanimously appointing him secretary to a proposed 'Edinburgh Continuation Committee', a job which he described as 'setting out on an uncharted sea and trying to steer a course.'

There was just time before the outbreak of war for Oldham to meet the main mission boards on the Continent, in Great Britain, and in America. The committee promoted a few cooperative ventures of which the most significant was the *International Review of Missions*, established in 1912 with Oldham as editor. He created a distinguished quarterly by his editorials and comprehensive reviews of the year, and by enlisting as contributors not only outstanding missionaries but scientists and administrators. He gained Roman Catholic cooperation and continued as editor until 1927.

The Continuation Committee foundered but Oldham tried to keep the spirit of internationalism alive. His writings included *The World and the Gospel* (1916) which sold over 20,000 copies and helped to lift the sights of war-engrossed Christians to the world beyond Europe, including Africa of which he wrote: 'One of the great issues of history is whether the African races shall create a characteristic life of their own or be made the tool of others.' As the servant of all missions and especially of those hardest hit by the war Oldham approached heads of government departments on such delicate matters as the internment of German missionaries in India and their expulsion from their African spheres. He was successful in preventing the confiscation of German mission properties; he negotiated the terms for the ultimate return of German missionaries and, with

Archbishop Randall Davidson [q.v.], secured the inclusion in the peace treaty of a clause guaranteeing freedom for missions in former German colonies. Government recognition of Oldham's unique position as spokesman for so many missions, his mastery of facts, and his recognition that 'governments must govern', established him as a trusted adviser.

But he was no uncritical ally. After the war he was soon in action over the matter of forced labour in Kenya. Unable to obtain satisfaction from the secretary of state for the colonies, Oldham organized a massive and highly successful protest by politicians of all parties, religious leaders, academics, and editors of the national press.

In 1920 Oldham prepared proposals for a new start in international missionary co-operation, based on an International Missionary Council whose members were to be councils of churches and missions. Oldham became secretary of this newly formed Council in 1921. To further his plans Oldham visited China and India (1922 and 1923) and played a crucial role in securing strong Indian representation in the National Council there. His knowledge of both the Kenyan and Indian scenes thrust him unexpectedly into the role of mediator between European settlers and Indians in Kenya. Oldham worked to get recognition by Government that, whatever the claims of settlers or Indians, African native interests must be paramount. In July 1923 Oldham's principle was embodied in a government statement of policy.

Oldham's lifelong interest in education centred at first in India but his main achievement was in relation to Africa. He aimed to persuade the Colonial Office (in spite of official reluctance) to play a more positive role. Getting the support of several colonial governors and of missionary societies, he formulated a proposal which led to the establishment of the Advisory Committee on Native Education in Tropical Africa in 1923. Oldham was an active member from its inception and, with Sir Frederick (later Lord) Lugard [q.v.], drafted what became an important statement of policy: *Education Policy in British Tropical Africa* (Cmd. 2374, 1925). After visiting institutions for negro education in the southern states of the USA, Oldham arranged for the Phelps Stokes Fund to visit East Africa and make recommendations to Government.

In 1926 Oldham organized the first conference of missionary educators and colonial administrators. He seized on a suggestion made there for an International Institute of African Languages and Cultures. His links with the colonial offices of European Governments and his access to Rockefeller funds enabled him to bring the idea into effect, and Lugard became chairman. From 1931 to 1938 he was administrative director and did the work which made possible Professor B. Malinowski's seminars for young anthropologists and Lord Hailey's [q.v.] impressive *An African Survey* (1938).

In 1924 Oldham had published his most influential book, *Christianity and the Race Problem*. As its author he was invited to visit South and East Africa in 1926. In South Africa he felt that, with the Colour Bar Act, a dangerous boundary had been crossed. 'Racialism', he wrote while there, 'is the deadliest enemy of a humane civilization.' But in Kenya he saw more hope and seriously considered becoming research director to the governor, Sir E. W. M. Grigg (later Lord Altrincham, q.v.). Instead he accepted membership of the Commission on Closer Union between the East African Territories, chaired by Sir E. Hilton Young (later Lord Kennet, q.v.). Oldham and Sir George Schuster wrote its intricate and carefully argued report. Vociferous opposition from the Kenya settlers, coupled with the chairman's refusal to sign, seemed to incline the Government towards handing over control to the settlers. Once more Oldham (this time in partnership with Lord Lugard) organized successful pressure and persuaded the Government to refer the matter to a joint select committee of both Houses of Parliament (1931).

Meanwhile Oldham's thought had turned from politics to the future tasks of Christian mission. *The New Christian Adventure* (1929) summarized the many speeches on both sides of the Atlantic which he made on this theme. A world-wide secular culture needed a new missionary approach—the 'field' and the 'base' of such a mission were everywhere: its chief agents were the Christian laity. To supplement the mastery of nature and control of the future which science was progressively achieving there must be an attitude to life based on relationship—man with nature, man with man, and man with God. He introduced the thought of Eberhard Grisebach and Martin Buber to English-speaking audiences. This 'relational' philosophy found expression in his later books, *Real Life is Meeting* (1941) and *Life is Commitment* (1953).

In 1934 Oldham became chairman of the research committee for the Universal Christian Council for Life and Work and began preparations for the world conference on 'Church, Community, and State'. Repeated efforts by the German Government to get recognition for its church policies brought into sharp focus issues which might have been merely academic in another context. The circulation of the preparatory documents, Oldham's own challenging account of the purpose of the conference as a confrontation between the totalitarian State and the Church and its gospel, together with the many groups which he initiated or addressed—all these constituted an awakening of many Christians, and indeed others, to the issues at stake. As an educative process it was Oldham's greatest achievement and influenced Christian thinking for a generation. Before and after the conference, which was held at Oxford in 1937, essential steps were taken to bring existing ecumenical movements into a single world council whose members would be individual churches. Archbishop William Temple [q.v.] provided the leadership; Oldham the agenda. The latter had first mooted the need for 'something like a world league of churches' in 1921.

Oldham's chief interest was not in ecclesiastical organization however, but in the laity, trying to live their faith in the world. How could they be supported? The *Christian News Letter*, founded in 1939, was one answer; Oldham edited this fortnightly from 1939 till 1945. Another answer was the Christian Frontier Council, Oldham's conception, founded in 1942 as a lay movement which brought together lay expertise and Christian insight.

Oldham's success with groups owed something to the deafness which afflicted him in middle life. The cross-talk of large gatherings became impossible for him to cope with, but the smaller group was ideal. He took infinite care choosing and preparing such groups and planning the venue and subject. He controlled the meetings with well-regulated tolerance, circulating from member to member on his stool, with his vast hearing aid on his knee. Some groups produced corporate findings (for example, *The Era of Atomic Power*, 1947). Others, like 'the Moot', had their outcome in the thought and writings of the members. 'These things changed our lives', Michael Polanyi wrote of the Moot.

In retirement at Dunford, Midhurst, Oldham, stimulated by the faith and enthusiasm of the young leaders of the Capricorn Africa Society, turned again to Africa. He enabled them to meet an older generation of Africa specialists and wrote for them his last book, *New Hope in Africa* (1955).

In 1898 Oldham married Mary (died 1965), only daughter of Sir Andrew H. L. Fraser, later governor of Bengal [q.v.]. They had no children. The universities of Edinburgh (1931) and Oxford (1937) honoured Oldham with the degree of doctor of divinity. He was appointed CBE in 1951. He died 16 May 1969 at St. Leonards.

[Archives in London, Edinburgh, Birmingham, Oxford, Basle, Geneva, and New York; personal knowledge.]   KATHLEEN BLISS

OLIVER, SIR HENRY FRANCIS (1865–1965), admiral of the fleet, born in Lochside near Kelso, 22 January 1865, was the fifth child of Robert Oliver, JP, and his wife, Margaret Strickland, who had seven sons and three daughters. To his father, who came from sound yeoman stock and farmed 2,000 acres of good Border land, and to his talented mother, he owed a strong constitution and a vigorous approach to life.

Entering the *Britannia* in 1878 he joined a navy in which sail, still dying hard, developed fine seamen. More than once his quick reactions averted disaster. On promotion to lieutenant in 1888 he volunteered for surveying. This service offered better pay and unusual activities abroad, but slender prospects, and in 1894 he returned to general service and qualified as a navigator.

After varied service in cruisers he was promoted to commander in 1899. As navigating commander of the *Majestic*, wearing the flag of Vice-Admiral (Sir) A. K. Wilson [q.v.], he became widely known when they took the squadron at high speed from Northern Ireland to the Scillies in thick fog—a severe test of skill and nerve with the navigational aids then available. He was promoted to captain in June 1903, unusually early for a navigator.

Selected by Sir John (later Lord) Fisher, second sea lord [q.v.], to improve the training and status of navigation specialists, Oliver established a school first in the *Mercury*, an old cruiser, and then in the old Royal Naval College in Portsmouth dockyard, with the torpedo gunboat *Dryad* as name ship and floating tender. In 1905 he was appointed MVO, and in 1907, in the new armoured cruiser *Achilles*, led the navy in gunnery skill. Fisher, as first sea lord, summoned him to become his naval assistant, a strenuous post which he retained when Wilson succeeded Fisher in 1910. Returning to sea, Oliver again made gunnery history in the new battleship *Thunderer* in 1912.

Appointed director of naval intelligence and soon promoted to rear-admiral in 1913, he faced increasing responsibilities as war approached. On the outbreak of war, he established wireless interception stations, staffed to decipher enemy messages. In September he preceded (Sir) Winston Churchill to Antwerp to prevent the advancing enemy from making use of German ships moored there. Working long hours with a small Belgian staff he personally disabled the engines of thirty-eight ships with explosive charges.

He was Churchill's naval secretary for a short while, but on Fisher's return as first sea lord in November Oliver became chief of Admiralty war staff with the acting rank of vice-admiral. In this capacity he favoured the Dardanelles operations, introduced taut-wire measuring gear which greatly improved minelaying accuracy, and was a general source of sound advice. In June 1916 he was promoted KCB, having been appointed CB in 1913. In January 1917 Sir J. R. (later Earl) Jellicoe [q.v.] assumed the dual role of first sea lord and chief of naval staff and Oliver became deputy chief of naval staff, with Board status.

Like many of his senior contemporaries Oliver was temperamentally unable to delegate responsibility, even in detail—a major difficulty in creating an effective naval staff—and his 'extraordinary power of continuous mental toil', remarked on by Churchill, was now becoming strained. He was relieved in January 1918, whereupon he was appointed KCMG. In March he became rear-admiral commanding the 1st Battle Cruiser Squadron, Grand Fleet, in the *Repulse*, and saw the German fleet surrender off the Firth of Forth in November. When the Grand Fleet dispersed in 1919 he became C.-in-C. Home Fleet as a vice-admiral in the *King George V*. The Reserve Fleet was later merged with his force.

In 1920 he received an honorary LLD (Edinburgh) and became second sea lord and chief of naval personnel, which gave him the painful task of reducing the Navy List to peacetime needs. The drastic measures taken in 1922 were generally considered as fair and liberal as might be. Promoted to admiral in 1923, in 1924 he declined the Portsmouth Command in favour of the Atlantic Fleet, which he commanded with customary efficiency until 1927. He was promoted to admiral of the fleet and to the GCB in 1928 and retired in 1933. He was restored to the active list in 1940 but was denied wartime employment.

He had married in June 1914 Beryl Carnegy White (later Dame Beryl Oliver, GBE, who died in 1972), the only daughter of Francis Edward Joseph Carnegy, of Lour in county Angus. In the war of 1939-45 Dame Beryl's Red Cross work kept the Olivers much in London, but the admiral regularly visited Scotland for shooting and fishing, his main recreations, together with carpentry. Amongst his other interests the foremost was the Royal National Lifeboat Association, of which he became deputy chairman. The verbal economy which gave him the nickname 'Dummy' (derived presumably from 'Dumby') Oliver did not conceal his solid worth from those who served him. His integrity, justice, foresight, judgement, and seamanship were evident throughout his career. He died at home in London 15 October 1965.

A portrait painted by J. Blair Leighton, presented by the officers of the Navigation School to mark his seventieth birthday, is hung in the present *Dryad*, School of Maritime Operations, the modern successor to Oliver's school. In the Imperial War Museum there is a lithograph by W. G. Burn-Murdoch (presented in 1933) and a drawing by Francis Dodd (1917).

[*The Times*, 18 October 1965; Sir William James, *A Great Seaman, Admiral of the Fleet Sir H. F. Oliver*, 1956; *Portrait of an Admiral, the Life and Papers of Sir H. Richmond*, ed. Professor A. J. Marder, 1952; private information; personal knowledge.]

P. W. Brock

ONIONS, CHARLES TALBUT (1873-1965), lexicographer and grammarian, was born at Edgbaston, Birmingham, 10 September 1873, the eldest son of Ralph John Onions, and his wife, Harriet, daughter of John Talbut, locksmith. Although the traditional occupation of the family had been bellows making, his father was a designer and embosser in metal; the name is of Welsh origin, being based on the form Einion. He was grounded in grammar, first at a Board-school and later at the Camp Hill branch of King Edward VI's foundation at Birmingham, where he came under the influence of the Revd A. J. Smith, a headmaster of sterling character and scholarly outlook, to whom he owed the very means of entering academic life as well as his first contact with lexicography: Smith kept Littré's French dictionary in his class-room, together with fascicules of the *New English Dictionary* as they appeared. At school, too, Onions was much influenced by a Tractarian organist and choirmaster, John Heywood; and his religious sympathies and affiliations were thus permanently established.

With a leaving exhibition he entered Mason College, Birmingham, where he studied for the London BA which he gained in 1892 with third class honours in French, followed in 1895 by his MA. Under E. A. Sonnenschein [q.v.] he learnt *inter alia* to scan Plautus and to write Greek prose; he contributed *An Advanced English Syntax* (1904; frequently reprinted) to a Parallel Grammar Series published by Sonnenschein. The professor of English at Birmingham at this time was Edward Arber [q.v.] who introduced him to (Sir) J. A. H. Murray (whose notice he subsequently contributed to this Dictionary) when the latter was examining at Birmingham in the Oxford Local Examinations. Shortly after (September 1895), Murray invited him to join the small staff of the English Dictionary at Oxford; and at Oxford he lived, except for one short interval, for the rest of his life. There he was soon joined by Henry Bradley [q.v.]; in later years he spoke of passing from Murray to Bradley as a remarkable experience: 'It was to pass from the practical, professional teacher to the philosophical exponent.'

From 1906 to 1913 Onions was entrusted with the special preparation of various portions of the work under the supervision of Bradley and (Sir) W. A. Craigie [q.v.] and then began independent editorial work on the section Su–Sz; he was also responsible for Wh–Worling and the volumes containing X, Y, Z, and so contributed the very last entry to the whole work in the form of a cross-reference (Zyxt, obs. (Kentish) 2nd sing. ind. pres. of SEE v.) which he liked to mention as it was taken, because of its position, as a brand name for a soap. But it was by no means Onions's last word. In 1922, after the death of William Little, the Clarendon Press had commissioned him to revise and complete Little's work on a *Shorter Oxford English Dictionary*. This appeared in 1933, and was continually revised and augmented by him until 1959: in the twenty pages of addenda in the 1944 edition he dealt with 1500 words, mostly the product of war. He shared with Craigie the preparation of the Supplement to the main work (1933) which includes a list of books cited therein that constituted the fullest bibliography of English literature yet made. An equally valuable by-product was his *Shakespeare Glossary* (1911 etc.), the Introduction to which provides a notable survey of Shakespearian usage; throughout the work he was able to draw on his knowledge of the Warwickshire dialect. On the death of Sir Sidney Lee [q.v.] he completed the editing of *Shakespeare's England* (1916), contributing to the articles on Alchemy and the article on Animals as well as providing a glossary of musical terms. Henceforth the Clarendon Press constantly called on him for advice and help, and many Oxford books owe improvements to him. For many years he was the only visitor allowed into the Walton Street office at 'the sacred hour of 9.30' when the day's work was being planned. The files of the Press are rich in his scholarly jottings.

In 1918 he donned uniform and went to the naval intelligence division of the admiralty (where his knowledge of German was put to good use) with the rank of honorary captain, Royal Marines. On his return to Oxford he became university lecturer in English (1920) and later reader in English philology (1927–49). In 1922 he revised for the Clarendon Press the *Anglo-Saxon Reader* originally compiled by Henry Sweet [q.v.], though 'reverence for the opinion of a great master' restrained the correcting hand. On Bradley's death in 1923 Magdalen elected Onions to fill the vacant fellowship; when the statutes were revised shortly afterwards he chose to remain under the old regulations and so remained a stipendiary fellow until the day of his death. In 1940–55 he was librarian of the college and undergraduates and others profited from his constant presence in the dictionary bay of the library; he was equally at home in the senior common room, where his astringent rejoinders to questions on etymology and English usage were much relished. He had been president of the Philological Society from 1929 to 1933, and was elected FBA in 1938. Oxford, Leeds, and Birmingham conferred honorary degrees upon him on the completion of the Dictionary, and he was appointed CBE in 1934. In 1945 he succeeded R. W. Chambers [q.v.] as honorary director of the Early English Text Society, and, partly by enlisting the help of several ex-pupils at Oxford, he did much in the following twelve years to extend its publishing programme. He was editor of *Medium Ævum*, the journal of the Society for the Study of Medieval Languages Literature, from its inception in 1932 to 1956. But the preoccupation of his last twenty years was the *Oxford Dictionary of English Etymology* (1966) which went to press before he died. It treats over 38,000 words and is likely to be his enduring monument.

Onions had an almost personal pride in his mother tongue, which he once described as 'a rum go—but jolly good'. His lifelong study of it bore fruit in the masterly chapter on the English language which he contributed to *The Character of England* (1947), edited by Sir Ernest Barker [q.v.]. His training in the scriptorium of the Dictionary taught him the art of conciseness, as is demonstrated in his tracts for the Society for Pure English and in his article 'Grammar' in *Chambers's Encyclopaedia*. As a lexicographer his strength lay in etymology: he delighted in teasing out the history of such words as syllabus or acne or Shakespeare's 'dildos and fadings'. His grasp of idiom, and his analytical power are well evidenced in the articles in *OED* on *set*, *shall*, *will*, and the interrogative pronouns. To dialectal usages, medieval and modern, he was particularly sensitive. His approach to linguistic and lexical problems was essentially pragmatic. There was something Johnsonian in his attitudes and character (as well as his early struggles). For much of his life he was handicapped by a stammer, and he always had a fellow-feeling for other stammerers; but he was undemonstrative in his likings as in his religion. He married in 1907 Angela, youngest daughter of the Revd Arthur Blythman, rector of Shenington, by whom he had seven sons and three daughters. She died in 1941. He died in hospital at Oxford 8 January 1965. A portrait by William Dring hangs in Magdalen senior common room.

[*A List of the Published Writings of Charles Talbut Onions*, with portrait and preface, 1948; *The Times*, 12 January 1965; personal knowledge.]   J. A. W. BENNETT

ORD, BERNHARD (BORIS) (1897–1961), musician, was born 9 July 1897 at Bristol, the youngest of the five children of Clement Ord, a Quaker and head of the German department at Bristol University, and his wife, Johanna, daughter of Hofprediger G. Anthes, who came of a musical German family. Bernhard was educated from 1907 to 1914 at Clifton College, of which he was a scholar and, later, a governor. He took his ARCO while still at school and won a scholarship to the Royal College of Music, where he studied the organ under Sir Walter Parratt [q.v.] and also excelled at the pianoforte. He was already a devotee of opera, and his nickname 'Boris', by which he became universally known, arose from his enthusiasm for *Boris Godunov*, introduced to London in 1913 by (Sir) Thomas Beecham [q.v.]. After war service from 1916 to 1918, first with the Artists' Rifles and then as a pilot in the Royal Flying Corps, during which he was twice wounded, he returned to the Royal College, where he took up choir training.

It was as organ scholar of Corpus Christi College that he went to Cambridge, in 1919. The next year he founded the Cambridge University Madrigal Society, later to be known for its May Week concerts in massed punts on the river. He became Mus.B. in 1922, and the following year was elected to a fellowship at King's, his father's college, within which as a bachelor he spent the rest of his life. As a freelance musician he was much in demand. Sometimes it was as a continuo player on piano or harpsichord, as for the staging of works by Purcell [q.v.] and Handel produced by Camille Prior and Cyril Rootham, the organist of St. John's College; sometimes as a conductor, as for the Greek play committee's revival in 1921 of Aristophanes' *The Birds* with the music of Sir (Charles) Hubert Parry [q.v.] and of Aeschylus' *Oresteia* with C. Armstrong Gibbs's music (1924). He also conducted a remarkable performance (1928) of Stravinsky's *The Soldier's Tale* in which Lydia Lopokova, the wife of J. M. (later Lord) Keynes [q.v.], was the princess, (Sir) Michael Redgrave the soldier, and Dennis Arundell the narrator. In 1927 he gained valuable experience by working at Cologne opera house.

On the death of A. H. Mann [q.v.] in 1929 Ord was appointed organist of King's College and also of the university. At King's he joined forces with the dean, the Revd Eric Milner-White, in his policy of broadening the repertoire of the chapel music, especially by strengthening the sixteenth-century element. In 1936 he became a university lecturer in music and in 1938 he succeeded Rootham as conductor of the Cambridge University Musical Society. His work for the society greatly broadened his scope and also revealed the range of his musical sympathies. Continuing Rootham's tradition, he conducted a highly successful stage performance of Handel's *Saul* in the Guildhall, with David Franklin in the title role.

The outbreak of war inevitably reduced the number of chapel services at King's. In 1941 Ord handed them over to Dr Harold Darke for the duration and rejoined the air force as a flight-lieutenant, eventually participating in the Normandy landings and the ensuing campaign. Back at Cambridge, he resumed his duties in 1946. His Cambridge University Musical Society concerts included Beethoven's Ninth Symphony and Stravinsky's *Symphony of Psalms*. On the Guildhall stage there were performances of Handel's *Solomon* and of *Pilgrim's Progress* by Vaughan Williams [q.v.], and at the Arts Theatre of Purcell's *Dioclesian* and *King Arthur*. But early in the 1950s Ord's health weakened, and eventually disseminated sclerosis was diagnosed. He retired from the Cambridge University Musical Society in 1954, but for some time continued to conduct concerts at the Festival Hall, including works for varying numbers of harpsichords. It was a great comfort to him that his former organ scholar and assistant (Sir) David Willcocks returned from Worcester Cathedral to take over from him in 1957–8. He then resigned his university lectureship also. He was created CBE in 1958. His last public appearance, in a wheelchair, was in the Senate House in June 1960, to receive the honorary doctorate of music. He died at Cambridge 30 December 1961.

As a musician Ord had exacting professional standards. His score-reading classes were a bracing test. As a choir trainer he inspired a mixture of affection and wholesome fear. Under him the King's choir established, by broadcasting and foreign tours, its international reputation. Durham University made him an honorary Mus.D. in 1955. His abundant geniality was shown in many less serious musical productions, in his generous hospitality, and in his quick sense of humour.

An oil portrait of him at the age of twenty-nine by Hugh Bass and a drawing by Percy Horton (1957) are in the possession of King's College, Cambridge.

[P. F. Radcliffe, *Bernhard (Boris) Ord, 1897–1961*, privately printed for King's Colledge, Cambridge, 1962; private information; personal knowledge.]   L. P. WILKINSON

ORDE, CUTHBERT JULIAN (1888–1968), painter, was born in Great Yarmouth 18 December 1888, the second son in the family of three sons and two daughters of (Sir) Julian Walter Orde, founder and first secretary of the Royal Automobile Club, and his wife, Alice Georgiana, daughter of Frederic Archdale, of Baldock, Hertfordshire. Orde was educated at Framlingham College, and subsequently exhibited regularly at the Royal Academy, the Royal Society of Portrait Painters, and the Royal Institute of Oil Painters, as well as in many other galleries in Britain and in Paris.

Orde joined up at the outbreak of World War I, going to France on 21 August 1914. He was awarded the 1914 Mons star. He was granted a commission in the Royal Flying Corps as a temporary lieutenant flying officer observer on 21 October 1915. On 1 August 1917 he was promoted temporary captain flight commander, being reclassified temporary captain aeroplane and seaplane, Royal Air Force, on 1 April 1918. As a war substantive engagement, he was subsequently promoted major on 16 August 1918. He served throughout the war in France and Egypt, relinquishing his commission on 15 January 1919 on the grounds of ill health.

In the war of 1939–45 Orde undertook war paintings, and in many an RAF mess hung his portraits of pilots, whose expressions he had an outstanding ability to capture. Older than his subjects, he was known to the pilots affectionately as 'Turps' or 'Uncle Orde' or 'The Captain'. Being a handsome, friendly man of great charm, he was most popular in the messes.

Among Orde's more important paintings are those of Viscount Astor, Sir Winston Churchill, Lieutenant-Colonel J. T. C. Moore-Brabazon, and Air Chief Marshal Sir John Salmond [qq.v.].

In 1940 Orde's work was hung in the War Artists Exhibition at the National Gallery and the Art Advisory Committee purchased a number of his portrait studies. In 1942 Harraps published a book of his drawings of pilots of Fighter Command—sixty-four drawings of the pilots he so much liked and admired.

The Imperial War Museum has eight portraits in its collection, in addition to many letters from Orde between December 1939 and August 1945, addressed to the Ministry of Information (Artists Committee), London University. Besides these and his other RAF portraits, Orde carried out portraits for the Royal Aeronautical Society, the Senior United Service Club, the Staff College at Camberley, and the RAF Club in Piccadilly. The RAF Museum, Hendon, owns a number of his portrait sketches and one portrait in oil.

In 1916 Orde married Eileen Wellesley (died 1952), daughter of Arthur Charles Wellesley, fourth Duke of Wellington; they had two daughters. In 1953 he married Alexandra, former wife of Sir Alexander Davenport Kinloch, twelfth baronet, and daughter of Frederick Dalziel, of New York; she had two daughters by her former marriage.

Orde died peacefully 18 December 1968, a few hours after celebrating his eightieth birthday with a lunchtime party of family and friends.

A portrait of Orde by R. Norman Hepple was exhibited by the Royal Society of Portrait Painters in 1958, and another, by Henry Carr, was shown at the Royal Academy in 1959.

[*The Times*, 27 and 28 December 1968; records of the Ministry of Information; private information; personal knowledge.]

MAURICE BRADSHAW

ORMSBY-GORE, WILLIAM GEORGE ARTHUR, fourth BARON HARLECH (1885–1964), politician and banker, was born in Eaton Square, London, 11 April 1885, the only child of George Ralph Charles Ormsby-Gore who became in 1904 the third Baron Harlech, and his wife, Lady Margaret Ethel Gordon, daughter of the tenth Marquess of Huntly. He was educated at Eton and New College, Oxford, where he obtained a second class in modern history in 1907.

Ormsby-Gore was elected, in January 1910, by a majority of eight, Unionist MP for Denbigh, moving in 1918 to Stafford, a seat he retained until he succeeded to the peerage on his father's death in 1938.

Commissioned in the Shropshire Yeomanry in 1908, he joined up when war broke out in 1914 and was on active service in Egypt when in 1916 he joined the Arab Bureau as an intelligence officer attached to the high commissioner, Sir A. Henry McMahon [q.v.]. He was recalled, in March 1917, at the instance of Lord Milner [q.v.], to be his parliamentary private secretary and also, a little later, an assistant secretary to the Cabinet assisting Sir Mark Sykes [q.v.]. Impressed by Zionism while in Egypt, he established cordial relations with its leader in London, Chaim Weizmann [q.v.] who took refuge in his office while the Cabinet approved, on 31 October 1917, the Balfour Declaration, and with whose support he was appointed British liaison officer with the Zionist Mission sent to Palestine in March 1918. He returned to London in August and was a member of the British delegation to the Paris peace conference in 1919. He attended the meetings of the Permanent Mandates Commission, of which he was the first British member, in October 1921 and August 1922. In the winter of 1921–2 he accompanied the under-secretary for the colonies, E. F. L. Wood (later the Earl of Halifax, q.v.) on a mission to the West Indies.

An unusually appropriate apprenticeship thus preceded his appointment, in October 1922, as parliamentary under-secretary at the Colonial Office where he remained until 1929 except for the brief interval of the first Labour Government in 1924 during which, however, he was appointed by its colonial secretary, J. H. Thomas [q.v.], as chairman of an all-party commission which visited East and Central Africa in the autumn, advised against any immediate federation of these territories, and recommended a loan of £10 million, guaranteed by the Treasury, mainly for the improvement of transport, anticipating much of the thinking behind the Colonial Development Act of 1929. In 1926 he visited West Africa and in 1928 Ceylon, Malaya, and Java. He was made a privy councillor in February 1927 and was in charge of the Colonial Office from July of that year until the following January during the Empire tour of the colonial secretary, Leopold Amery [q.v.].

Ormsby-Gore's knowledgeable enthusiasm for the arts, well exemplified in his book *Florentine Sculptors of the Fifteenth Century* (1930), resulted in a long and active association with the work of the major British galleries and museums. He was a trustee of the National Gallery from 1927 to 1934 and again from 1936 to 1941, of the Tate Gallery from 1934 to 1937 and again from 1945 to 1953, a life trustee of the British Museum from 1937, president of the National Museum of Wales from 1937, and was chairman of the Standing Commission on Museums and Galleries in 1949. He inherited a fine family library and although obliged to reduce its size when he ceased to live at Brogyntyn in Shropshire in 1955, he later added many rare books. He was president of the National Library of Wales from 1950 to 1958.

In the 'national' Government of 1931 he was postmaster-general, without a Cabinet seat, and, in November of that year, he became first commissioner of works with a seat in the Cabinet, an office he retained until his appointment as colonial secretary in May 1936. Under his auspices a determined effort was made to improve the architectural standards of new post offices and labour exchanges. He also wrote four volumes in the series *Guide to the Ancient Monuments of England* (1935, 1936, and 1948).

During the two years he was colonial secretary, he had little opportunity for the constructive work for which he was so well equipped by temperament and experience. (Perhaps no other colonial secretary had as much first-hand knowledge of the Colonial Empire.) In the month in which he took office, the Arabs demanded that Jewish immigration into Palestine and purchase of land there should be ended and attacked Jewish lives and property. A royal commission, headed by Lord Peel [q.v.] reported in July 1937 that the mandate was unworkable and recommended partition and the creation of a much truncated but independent Jewish state. This Government, on Ormsby-Gore's recommendation, accepted these proposals. He did not, however, succeed in persuading Parliament to endorse them but only to agree that the scheme might be put before the League of Nations while making clear that Parliament was not committed even to the principle of partition, much less the commission's actual proposals. As the international situation worsened, the British Government became increasingly concerned to appease the hostility of the Arab states to any continuing Jewish immigration. Ormsby-Gore considered himself committed to partition. He was also an outspoken critic of Nazi Germany so that it was hardly surprising that when on his succession to the peerage in May 1938 he felt constrained to offer his resignation, the prime minister, Neville Chamberlain, should have accepted it.

Harlech served as commissioner for Civil Defence in the North-East Region from 1939 to 1940 but his keen and active disposition chafed at the restraints still imposed by Whitehall. In 1941 he became British high commissioner in South Africa. He greatly admired the intellectual range of its prime minister, J. C. Smuts [q.v.], but found little else to admire in the politics and society of that country. The long association between Smuts and Churchill and many other leading British personalities sharply limited the intermediary role of the high commissioner, although his informative reports were appreciated by C. R. (later Earl) Attlee, then secretary of state for the Dominions.

After Harlech's return to London in 1944, he became a director of the Midland Bank, of which he was chairman from 1952 to 1957. It incorporated the London Joint Stock Bank which his great-grandfather had helped to establish in 1836. He was also chairman of the Bank of British West Africa from 1951 to 1961. Under his auspices, staff conditions and training were improved and substantial expansion of commercial business in Africa promoted.

Appointed GCMG in 1938, he was created KG in 1948. He was constable of Harlech Castle from 1938, of Caernarvon Castle from 1946 to 1963, and lord lieutenant of Merionethshire from 1938 to 1957. He received three honorary degrees, and was made an honorary fellow of his former college, New College, Oxford, in 1936. He devoted much time to the university of Wales, of which he was pro-chancellor from 1945 to 1957.

A convinced Conservative, Harlech was prominent in the Tory revolt that ended the coalition in 1922 and remained a firm supporter of Baldwin in the party divisions on Indian reform. He opposed the Hoare-Laval plan to accommodate Italian aggression in Ethiopia (thereby earning from Neville Chamberlain, with Walter E. Elliot and Oliver F. G. Stanley, qq.v., the contemptuous sobriquet of the 'Boys Brigade') and was bitterly hostile to Nazi Germany. Unusually receptive of ideas, he was always outspoken and sometimes impetuous. At the Colonial Office in the twenties he sought to promote scientific research and its application to the medical and agricultural problems of tropical dependencies and took a leading part in the attempt to develop educational policies more consonant with African environments but constructive development was largely frustrated by financial constraints. His hope in 1918 that Zionist objectives might be attained without political domination soon appeared visionary but his acceptance of partition, if inopportune in the international situation in 1938, was a courageous assessment of realities in Palestine. Perhaps his deepest interests were in the arts, especially architecture, of which his knowledge was extensive.

He married in 1913 Lady Beatrice Edith Mildred Gascoyne-Cecil (died 1980), daughter of the fourth Marquess of Salisbury [q.v.]. A lady of the Bedchamber from 1941, she was created DCVO in 1947 and was made an extra lady of the Bedchamber to Queen Elizabeth the Queen Mother in 1953. They had three sons, the eldest of whom was killed in a motor accident in 1935, and three daughters.

Harlech died in Bayswater, London, 14 February 1964 and was succeeded by his elder surviving son, Sir (William) David Ormsby-Gore, KCMG, who had been minister of state for foreign affairs from 1957 to 1961 when he became ambassador in Washington.

There are portraits by David Bell in the National Museum of Wales, Cardiff (1950), by R. Broadley in the Midland Bank (1952), by Ivor Williams in the National Library of Wales, and one by (Sir) Oswald Birley, painted in the mid thirties, is in the possession of the Dowager Lady Harlech.

[*The Times*, 15 February 1964; M. W. S. Weisgal (ed.), *The Letters and Papers of Chaim Weizmann*, Series A, vols. viii and ix, 1977; Martin Gilbert, *Exile and Return*, 1978; *MidBank Chronicle*, March 1964; R. H. Fry, *Bankers in West Africa*, 1976; Permanent Mandates Commission, *Minutes* 1921-7 and 1937; private information.]

K. E. ROBINSON

ORTON, JOHN KINGSLEY (JOE) (1933-1967), playwright, was born in Leicester 1 January 1933, the eldest child in the family of two sons and two daughters of William Orton, gardener, and his wife, Elsie, machinist and charwoman. He was educated at Marriots Road Primary School; and after failing his eleven-plus examination took a secretarial course at Clark's College, Leicester. Bored by a series of office jobs, Orton became interested in amateur dramatics and in 1951 won a scholarship to RADA. Puckish and handsome, Orton did well enough at RADA to earn his diploma in 1953. But he did not enjoy it: 'I completely lost my confidence and my virginity. I was lost. I didn't have a very good time because I found that in the very first term that I wasn't learning anything.'

After a four-month stint at the Ipswich Repertory Company, Orton became disenchanted with acting. Too young and inadequate a performer to get major roles, he was also too ambitious and full of fun for the arid grind he discovered was the regimen of the repertory actor. Returning to London, he set his sights on a literary career. He was ill equipped for this task. The idea of writing was suggested by Kenneth Leith Halliwell (1926-67) whom Orton met at RADA and with whom he lived until his death. Halliwell was seven years Orton's senior and much better educated. He set about to transform Orton into his intellectual equal and constant companion. Orton was especially influenced by the writings of Ronald Firbank whom Halliwell also imitated. Together, between 1953 and 1962, they wrote a series of novels, none of which deserved to be published. The books included *The Silver Bucket* (1953), *The Mechanical Womb* (1955), *The Last Days of Sodom* (1955), and *The Boy Hairdresser* (1956). They lived a hermetic existence first at 161 West End Lane in West Hampstead, moving in 1959 to another bed-sitter in Islington at 25 Noel Road. For a time they existed on Halliwell's small inheritance; but when that ran out they worked at odd jobs six months at a time to subsidize their writing.

By 1957 Orton had begun to write novels and plays on his own. He had no luck; but he had begun to identify in himself a great appetite for anarchy. 'Cleanse my heart, give the ability to rage correctly', prays Gombold, Orton's spokesman in *The Vision of Gombold Proval* (1961)—posthumously published as *Head to Toe* (1971). In the novel, Orton dreamed of a cauterizing verbal power which would create a 'seismic disturbance'. In his writing Orton had not found the right tone or target for his rage. But in public pranks he found another way of satisfying his hunger for vindictive triumph, and one in which the verbal and visual power of his plays were first planted. Under the pseudonym of Edna Welthorpe, he assumed a suburban attitude and wrote letters to a variety of institutions which goaded them into idiotic correspondence. (In later years, Edna Welthorpe would damn and praise Orton's plays in the letters columns of newspapers to stir up controversy.) In 1959 Orton also began to deface public library books by writing false blurbs in the jacket sleeves and pasting outrageous images on book jackets. The cut-up images were well done: concise, irreverent, and very funny. Orton admitted later that he was 'enraged that there were so many rubbishy novels and rubbishy books' in libraries. His prank was intended to shock. He and Halliwell would return the tampered books to the shelves and wait to see if they got a response. In 1962, they did. They were arrested and sent to prison for six months. Prison brought a saving detachment to Orton's writing and clarified his view of life. 'Before prison, I had been vaguely conscious of something rotten somewhere: prison crystallized this', Orton said.

In 1963, after a decade of total literary failure, Orton completed a radio play, *The Ruffian on the Stair*, which was accepted by the BBC and broadcast on 31 August 1964. Between 1964 and 1967 when he died, Joe Orton became a playwright of international reputation. His output was small but his impact was large. By 1967 the term 'Ortonesque' had worked its way into the English vocabulary, a shorthand adjective for scenes of macabre outrageousness. Orton wrote three first-class full-length plays: *Entertaining Mr. Sloane* (1963, produced in 1964), which (Sir) Terence Rattigan called the best first play he had ever seen; *Loot* (presented in 1965); and the posthumously produced *What the Butler Saw* (1967, produced in 1969). Orton wrote four one-act plays: *The Ruffian on the Stair* (1965, produced in 1966), *The Good and Faithful Servant* (1964, produced in 1967), *The Erpingham Camp* (1965, produced in 1966), and *Funeral Games* (1966, presented in 1968). Films were made of *Sloane* (1969) and *Loot* (1970), which also won the *Evening Standard* award for the best play of the year (1966). Orton wrote one original, but unproduced, film script, *Up Against It* (1967).

Orton's plays often scandalized audiences, but his wit made the outrage scintillating. He found people 'profoundly bad and irresistibly funny'. He was the first contemporary English playwright to transfer into art the clown's rambunctious sexual rapacity from the stage to the page. He aspired to corrupt an audience with pleasure. Orton's laughter bore out Nietzche's dictum that 'he who writes in blood and aphorisms does not want to be read, he wants to be learned by heart'. Orton brought the epigram back to modern theatre to illuminate a violent world. 'It's life that defeats the Christian Church, she's always been well-equipped to deal with death' (*The Erpingham Camp*). 'All classes are criminal today. We live in an age of equality' (*Funeral Games*).

Orton searched for a way to marry terror and elation and found it in farce. In his hands, farce became a paradigm of the tumult of consciousness as well as society. Orton fed his characters into farce's fun machine and made them bleed. He found a way of making laughter at once astonishing and serious. A voluptuary of fiasco, Orton's career ended as sensationally as it began. On 9 August 1967 he and Halliwell were found dead in their Islington flat. Halliwell, disturbed by the contrast between Orton's success and his own failure and by Orton's homosexual promiscuity, had battered in his friend's head with a hammer and taken his own life with an overdose of sleeping pills. Orton's death—laced as it was with the irony of his own fascination with the grotesque—had special public interest. No playwright in living memory had met a more gruesome end. It was a great loss to world drama. *The Times* obituary called Orton 'one of the sharpest stylists of the British new wave . . . a consummate dialogue artist and a natural anarch'.

[John Lahr, *Prick Up Your Ears: The Biography of Joe Orton*, 1978; Orton's private diaries; *The Times*, 10 August 1967; private information.]   JOHN LAHR

OWEN, SIR (ARTHUR) DAVID (KEMP) (1904-1970), international civil servant, was born at Pontypool, Monmouthshire, 26 November, 1904, the eldest son of the Revd Edward Owen, of Pontypool, and his wife, Gertrude Louisa Kemp. He was educated at Leeds Grammar School and the university of Leeds, from which he received a degree with economic honours (1926) and the Master of Commerce degree (1929). Between his first and second degrees Owen was assistant lecturer in economics at Huddersfield Technical College.

He was director of the social survey committee of Sheffield from 1929 to 1933, secretary of the Civic Research Division of Political and Economic Planning (PEP) from 1933 to 1936, co-director of the Pilgrim Trust Unemployment Enquiry from 1936 to 1937, and Stevenson lecturer in citizenship at the university of Glasgow from 1937 to 1940.

In 1941 Owen relinquished the post of general secretary of political and economic planning, to which he had been appointed in the previous year, to become personal assistant to Sir R. Stafford Cripps [q.v.] on his mission to India. He remained with Cripps during the latter's terms of office as lord privy seal and minister of aircraft production.

From 1944 to 1945 Owen served as officer in charge of League of Nations affairs in the Foreign Office and was a member of the United Kingdom delegation to the United Nations conference on international organization at San Francisco in 1945. When the preparatory commission of the United Nations was being organized in London in the summer of 1945, he joined the United Nations staff as its first recruit, in the capacity of deputy executive secretary of the preparatory commission.

When the preparatory commission gave way to the United Nations itself and the Organization moved to New York in early 1946, Owen was appointed assistant secretary-general in charge of economic affairs, one of the eight top officials of the Organization. In the late 1940s, the Organization became increasingly concerned with economic development, and in August 1951 Owen became the first executive chairman of the Technical Assistance Board, a position which he retained until in January 1966 the Expanded Programme of Technical Assistance Board merged with the United Nations Development Fund to form the United Nations Development Programme. At that time he became co-administrator of the Programme with Paul G. Hoffman, a post which he retained until his retirement from the United Nations service in 1969.

On his retirement, David Owen was appointed secretary-general of the International Planned Parenthood Federation, a new career which was cut short by his sudden and unexpected death.

Throughout his career David Owen was essentially a pioneer in new areas of public service, first on the national and later on the international level. He relished new challenges, and his enquiring mind and his skill as a pragmatic and informal administrator admirably equipped him to meet them. He was a non-doctrinaire socialist of the old school with a quiet faith in the capacity of humanity to improve its condition and an ardent desire to help it to do so.

His work in social and economic planning in the post-depression years and his service with Sir Stafford Cripps during the war led naturally to strong convictions about the necessity of international co-operation, convictions which he was able to put to the test in the most challenging circumstances in helping to build and operate the institutional structure of the United Nations. He was one of the younger architects of the new world Organization from San Francisco and thenceforth, and had an almost unique record of being associated with the creation of successive new branches on the economic side—first the

Economic Department itself and its Regional Economic Commissions, then the Technical Assistance Board, and finally the fully-fledged United Nations Development Programme, which is by far the largest and most far-flung operation of the United Nations.

Owen was an idealist and enthusiast of a practical and realistic kind. In the emergent international civil service he found a perfect setting for his convictions. 'It is, after all, a fine thing', he wrote, 'to belong to a service which, whatever its failings and frustrations, is engaged in the practical business of trying to establish more effective forms of international co-operation in the pursuit of peace and human well-being.' His concept of the United Nations was that of an activist, although he was very much aware of the shortcomings and difficulties of the world Organization. 'It remains to be seen', he wrote in 1966, 'whether we can rise to the historic occasion or whether we will find ourselves stagnating with modest usefulness in the margin of great events.'

Owen was modest, unpretentious, quick-witted, and of an enquiring turn of mind. Small in stature, with the humour and a touch of the accent of his native Wales, he was a dominant influence in the formative years of the United Nations. His kindness, consideration, and interest in the careers of his colleagues, especially the young and intelligent, had a great effect in the early stages of organization. Later, when he was responsible for setting up the world-wide network of resident representatives of the Technical Assistance Programme, which became the basis of the Development Programme, his ability to find new and promising recruits had a major effect on the development of the United Nations.

Owen loved to travel and to visit his widely dispersed Organization. His method of leadership was a very personal one. He was a voracious reader which prevented him from becoming stale or bureaucratic. He never lost the simplicity and natural friendliness of his youth and was a much beloved colleague. He died at St. Thomas's Hospital, London, 29 June 1970, very shortly after being appointed KCMG. He had also received honorary doctorates from the universities of Leeds (1954) and Wales (1969).

Owen was twice married, first in 1933 to Elizabeth Joyce, daughter of a Methodist minister, the Revd E. H. Morgan, and secondly, in 1950, to Elizabeth Elsa Miller, daughter of Frieda S. Miller, special assistant to the United States ambassador to Britain, 1943, and director of the Women's Bureau of the United States Department of Labour, 1944-53. He had one son and one daughter by his first marriage and two sons by his second.

[Personal knowledge.]   BRIAN URQUHART

P

PAGE, Sir FREDERICK HANDLEY (1885–1962), aircraft designer and manufacturer, was born 15 November 1885 at Cheltenham, the second child in a family of four sons and one daughter of Frederick Joseph Page, master upholsterer, and his wife, Eliza Ann Handley. Educated at Cheltenham Grammar School and at Finsbury Technical College (under Professor Silvanus Thompson, q.v.), in 1906 he was appointed chief electrical designer at Johnson and Phillips Ltd. at Charlton. Joining the (later Royal) Aeronautical Society in 1907, he helped José Weiss to construct an automatically stable aeroplane. Declining an offer from Westinghouse at Pittsburgh, he adopted an aeronautical career after Wilbur Wright's demonstrations in France in 1908. He constructed several aeroplanes for clients and a glider for himself at Woolwich, and in 1909 he moved to Barking, where he registered Handley Page Ltd. specifically to manufacture aeroplanes, and flew his first monoplane on 26 May 1910. After joining the Northampton Polytechnic Institute (later Northampton Engineering College and then the City University) at Clerkenwell as lecturer in aeronautics under Dr Mullineux Walmsley, he installed there a wind tunnel, thereby combining practical course work with investigation of design problems at Barking. His first passenger-carrying monoplane flew across London in July 1911, and the following year another two-seater competed in military trials on Salisbury Plain. He moved to Cricklewood and his first biplane was demonstrated at Hendon before war began in 1914. When (Sir) Murray Sueter [q.v.] at the Admiralty demanded a 'bloody paralyser' to halt the German advance into Belgium, Handley Page produced a large twin-engined bomber for the Royal Naval Air Service, followed in 1918 by a still larger four-engined machine to bomb Berlin, one of each type being the first aeroplanes to fly from England to India. Handley Page was appointed CBE in 1918.

In 1919 Handley Page promoted airlines in Europe, India, South Africa, and Brazil; of these the first survived to become a constituent of Imperial Airways in 1924. Bombers converted to carry passengers and freight were replaced in 1922 by twin-engined airliners and these in 1932 by a fleet of four-engined biplanes, which carried thousands of passengers millions of miles in exceptional comfort over Imperial Airways's routes to Africa and India until 1939. Concurrently the Cricklewood factory produced twin-engined bombers for the Royal Air Force, and also experimental prototypes, one of which was runner-up in the Guggenheim Safe Aircraft competition in 1929. Both this and the American winner achieved full control at low speeds using slotted wings invented in 1918 independently by Handley Page and Gustav Lachmann [q.v.], who later joined the firm. In 1928 the Royal Air Force adopted automatic wing-tip slots, thereby eliminating 'stall-and-spin' accidents, a major cause of fatalities. After 1935 Handley Page manufactured increasing numbers of twin- and four-engined monoplane bombers for the expanding Royal Air Force. He was knighted in 1942 for his contribution to the war effort. Transport aircraft, which were derived from the bombers, assisted in the Berlin air-lift in 1948–9 and equipped the African routes of the British Overseas Airways Corporation.

A pioneer of technological education, Handley Page initiated sandwich courses for his apprentices in 1923, in conjunction with Northampton Engineering College. Elected a fellow of the City and Guilds of London Institute in 1939, he became chairman of its council and executive committee ten years later. In 1946 he was instrumental, with Sir Roy Fedden, in setting up the College of Aeronautics at Cranfield at the behest of Sir Stafford Cripps [q.v.], and remained chairman of its governing body until his death. An autocrat intolerant of governmental interference, he refused to merge with other groups under the plan proposed by the minister of defence, Duncan Sandys (later Lord Duncan-Sandys), because he insisted on protecting his dedicated team of employees, whose loyalty he had earned and esteemed highly. A founding member of the Society of British Aircraft Constructors in 1916, he was twice its chairman and, in 1938–9, its first president. He was also vice-chairman of the Air Registration Board, president of the Institute of Transport 1945–6 and of the Royal Aeronautical Society 1945–7, master of the Worshipful Company of Coachmakers and Coach Harness Makers 1943–4, deputy lieutenant 1954–6 and lieutenant 1956–60 of Middlesex. In debate a master of repartee, well spiced with quotations from the Bible and Gibbon, he was always abreast of current technology and objective in criticism.

The Royal Aeronautical Society awarded him its gold medal in 1960; in the same year he received the Royal Society of Arts Albert gold medal and the German Scientific Society for Aviation's Ludwig Prandtl ring. He was an officer of the Legion of Honour, and of the Ordre de la Couronne (Belgium). This latter honour he received personally from King Albert for saving two bathers at Blankenberge from drowning. The annual Handley Page memorial lecture, first given in May 1963 by Prince Philip, Duke of Edinburgh, is sponsored jointly by the Cranfield Society and the Royal Aeronautical Society.

In May 1918 Handley Page married Una Helen (died 1957), daughter of John Robert Thynne, and they had three daughters. He died in London 21 April 1962. There are two copies of a bronze bust by Charles Pibworth, one in the Royal Aeronautical Society and the other in the possession of the family. A posthumous portrait in oils, also in the Royal Aeronautical Society, was painted by an unknown artist using a set of photographic studies made by Douglas Glass for Handley Page's seventieth birthday.

[C. H. Barnes, *Handley Page Aircraft since 1907*, 1976; *Aeronautical Journal*; *Aeroplane*; *Flight*, 1909 et seq.; private information; personal knowledge.]   C. H. BARNES

PAGET, SIR BERNARD CHARLES TOLVER (1887–1961), general, was born 15 September 1887 at Oxford, the third son and fourth of the six children of Francis Paget [q.v.], regius professor of pastoral theology and canon of Christ Church, of which he became dean in 1892, and was appointed bishop of Oxford in 1901, and his wife, Helen Beatrice, daughter of Richard William Church, dean of St. Paul's. He was educated at Shrewsbury and the Royal Military College, Sandhurst, and was commissioned into the Oxfordshire and Buckinghamshire Light Infantry 13 November 1907.

After a winter with the 2nd battalion (52nd) at Tidworth, he joined the 1st battalion (43rd) in India in February 1908, and was promoted lieutenant in 1910. He returned to England on leave in 1914, and on the outbreak of war was appointed adjutant of the newly formed 5th (service) battalion of his regiment, which he helped to form, and with which he went to France in May 1915. He remained with the battalion until November of that year when he became brigade-major of the 42nd Infantry brigade of the 14th Light division. He was awarded the MC in the same month.

In October 1917 he was employed as a GSO 2, first with the 62nd division, and then on the GHQ staff of Sir Douglas (later Earl) Haig [q.v.].

During the German advance in March 1918 he was wounded for the third time, this time severely in the elbow, which rendered his left arm virtually useless for the rest of his life. He had been appointed to the DSO in January 1918 and was four times mentioned in dispatches.

There followed a series of staff appointments, graduation at the Staff College, Camberley, in 1920, and promotion to major in 1924. In April 1925 he rejoined the 1st battalion of his regiment as a company commander in Cologne, leaving in January 1926 to become an instructor at the Staff College, and in January 1929 a student at the Imperial Defence College.

He was never destined to command a battalion, and his last appointment with his regiment was as commander of the regimental depot at Cowley Barracks, Oxford, in 1930, where he instituted many improvements and left a lasting impression of his personality. One of the achievements of his time there, which he always recalled with pride, was the dedication of the regimental chapel in the cathedral.

The normal three-year tenure of his command was reduced to two, with his return to India as chief instructor at the Quetta Staff College, during which he won distinction for the part he played in connection with the disastrous earthquake in June 1935. For two years (1936–7) he commanded the 4th Quetta Infantry brigade, was promoted major-general in December 1937, and returned to England to become commandant of the Staff College at Camberley (1938–9).

In November 1939 he took over command of the 18th division, then in East Anglia, from which he was summoned 'literally at a moment's notice' in April 1940 to take part in the ill-fated Norwegian campaign. German superiority, both on the ground and in the air, was overwhelming, the ship carrying the artillery and transport of the British troops had been sunk, and the prospects were hopeless. When the Cabinet, unwilling to face further losses of ships, and unable to provide the reinforcements for which the general asked, decided on evacuation, Paget fought a series of skilful rearguard actions, worthy of his distinguished predecessor, Sir John Moore [q.v.], and succeeded, not only in extricating his troops, but also in inflicting heavy losses on the enemy. His achievement brought not only the public praise of the prime minister, but also promotion, though he was never to enjoy a fighting command again.

After Dunkirk he was for a short time chief of staff, Home Forces, and when a German invasion seemed imminent, would never permit the airing of pessimistic views or contemplate the possibility of defeat.

When South Eastern Command was formed in 1941 he was appointed GOC-in-C and promoted lieutenant-general. At the end of the year he succeeded Sir Alan Brooke (later Viscount Alanbrooke, q.v.) as commander-in-chief, Home Forces, a command he held until July 1943, when, having been promoted to general, he was given the responsibility of forming 21st Army Group of fifteen divisions, which was set up in preparation for the forthcoming invasion of Normandy. He was, however, never to achieve the opportunity of commanding in the field the men he had trained for this purpose; the appointment went to General Sir B. L. Montgomery (later Viscount Montgomery of Alamein), fresh from his campaigns in North Africa and Italy.

It was a great disappointment, for he had trained the troops who were to storm the Normandy beaches, the most difficult feat of arms ever attempted by a British army, but he will go down in history as the greatest trainer of British soldiers since Sir John Moore [q.v.], teaching them how to overcome the difficulties of attacking in the face of modern automatic power — 'to bridge', as he described it, 'the gap between the barrage and the bayonet'.

To further this he established a School of Infantry, with divisional battle schools, in which he aimed at creating 'a true offensive spirit, combined with the will-power which will not recognize defeat', as well as battle inoculation in which live ammunition was used during exercises.

Shortly after his death, papers which he had refused to allow to be published disclosed details of Operation 'Skyscraper', prepared by him in the spring of 1943 as a detailed study of the proposed invasion of north-western Europe. It was described as 'a blueprint for the D-Day operations of 1944; there were the same beaches, and the same objectives, while the problems of an opposed landing had all been fully assessed . . . the first key plan of the invasion'.

In January 1944 Paget became GOC-in-C Middle East Forces in succession to Sir H. M. (later Lord) Wilson [q.v.], where he remained until October 1946, when he retired from the army at his own request. During this tenure of command, while no active service was involved, there were many difficulties to be tackled, in dealing with which he added greatly to his reputation. Again he was an outstanding success in carrying out a tough assignment, and few men could have handled, as adroitly as he, such varied problems as the adminis-tration of the Polish base and the mutiny of the Greek brigade in Egypt. He was 'the only man who really understood the problem', observed a prominent Greek official afterwards.

His years of retirement were to be far from idle. Already colonel commandant of the Reconnaissance Corps and the Intelligence Corps, he was appointed to succeed Major-General Sir John Hanbury-Williams [q.v.] as colonel of his regiment, an office which gave him both pride and pleasure. He also became principal of Ashridge College, then devoted to adult education in citizenship, a post which he retained for three years until he became, again to his delight, governor of the Royal Hospital, Chelsea.

There were other activities as well, all of which reflected his care for the soldier, to whom, despite crippling arthritis, the legacy of his wounds, he devoted his last years. Among these were his work for the Forces Help Society, of which he was national chairman, the Lord Roberts Workshops, and not least the Royal Commonwealth Society for the Blind, his efforts for which raised nearly £400,000. He was also governor of the Corps of Com-missionaires.

Shortly before going into complete retire-ment, in 1956, he took his last parade, the passing out of an intake of national servicemen at Cowley Barracks, to whom he paid a moving tribute, in which he told the young soldiers that one of his World War I wounds had cost him his funny-bone, 'which means', he added, 'that I have lost half my sense of humour; it was a good thing I didn't lose my other elbow as well'. Afterwards, to the officers in the mess, he said retirement would mean that, for the first time in his life, he would be living in his own house and have to clean his own shoes; nevertheless, he was looking forward to it.

To those who served with him in the regi-ment, he was its greatest soldier of the century. To many, especially the junior officers, he was rather a frightening person to meet; 'his eyes seemed to bore holes in you' and he made no secret of his dislike of things which he con-sidered to be 'sloppy'. He had an innate shy-ness, as a result of which he appeared not to be entirely at his ease when talking to men, but he was a great champion of private soldiers, and, if their conditions were not as good as he thought they should be, 'the fur flew'. He was without fear, either physical or moral, deeply religious, completely selfless, and devoted to his country.

He was appointed CB in 1940, KCB in 1942, and GCB in 1946. In World War II he was awarded honours from Greece, Belgium, the United States of America, Czechoslovakia, and Norway — the last the grand cross of the Order of St. Olaf.

He married, in 1918, Winifred Nora, his cousin, daughter of Sir John Rahere Paget, second baronet, and they had two sons, both of whom served with distinction in the war of 1939-45. His younger son, Lt. Anthony Francis Macleod Paget, of the Oxfordshire and Buckinghamshire Light Infantry, died of wounds received in a gallant action in the Reichswald in March 1945, for which he was awarded a posthumous DSO and recommended for the VC.

Paget died suddenly at his home, The Old Orchard, Petersfield, Hampshire, 16 February 1961.

There is a portrait by William Dring (1960),

another in the regimental museum at Cowley Barracks, Oxford, and a third by Eric Kennington in the possession of the family.

[*Chronicle* of the 1st Green Jackets 43rd and 52nd and the Oxfordshire and Buckinghamshire Light Infantry, 1960; *The Times*, 18 February 1961; *Guardian*, 22 February 1961; *Oxford Times*, 24 February 1961; private information.]   R. J. OWEN

PANTIN, CARL FREDERICK ABEL (1899-1967), zoologist, was born at Blackheath 30 March 1899, the second child and elder son of Herbert Pantin, head of a family manufacturing company, and his wife, Emilie Juanita, a descendant of the distinguished Abel family which included Pantin's great uncle, Sir Frederick A. Abel [q.v.] who invented cordite, and seven generations before, Karl Friedrich Abel (q.v., 1725-87), after whom he was named, believed the greatest violone player of all time. His brother, W. A. Pantin, FBA, became keeper of the university archives at Oxford.

From childhood Pantin was fascinated by natural history, and at Tonbridge School (1913-17) was recognized as having outstanding scientific ability, and in the words of his headmaster a 'nobility of character' which is the abiding impression of all who subsequently knew him in whatever capacity. After brief service with the Royal Engineers, he went up to Christ's College, Cambridge, as a scholar, in 1919, where, particularly under the influence of (Sir) James Gray and J. T. Saunders he graduated with distinction, obtaining first classes in parts i (1921) and ii (1922, zoology and comparative anatomy) of the natural sciences tripos. He was awarded the Frank Smart prize in 1922. Zoology, long dominated by traditional morphological and systematic studies, was just beginning the experimental and ecological approach, to which Pantin contributed much of the foundation, both directly and indirectly. In 1922 Pantin joined the staff of the Marine Biological Laboratory at Plymouth, embarking on a series of elegant and fundamental investigations into the functioning of the lower animals. His work on amoeboid movement can be seen to contain the elements of the later biophysical approach to the structure of cytoplasm; he investigated the effect of ions on and in tissues and made similarly fundamental discoveries about osmoregulation in flatworms. It was, however, characteristic of his approach, and it is embedded in the philosophy of those many distinguished zoologists whom he taught at Plymouth and later at Cambridge, that physiological mechanism is only meaningful when understood in the context of the biology of the animal in nature, and to this end he would call upon an encyclopedic knowledge of the animal kingdom, backed by what he would call an amateur's grasp of palaeontology and geology, which was in fact of professional stature.

In 1929 Pantin became a fellow of Trinity College, Cambridge, directing studies and lecturing in the department of zoology of the university, but returning regularly to Plymouth to research and run the renowned 'Easter' courses, where his colleagues and pupils included A. V. Hill, (Sir) Frederick S. Russell, (James) Eric Smith, and many other distinguished zoologists. Pantin took his Cambridge Sc.D. in 1933.

Following a period at the Naples Zoological Station in 1933, Pantin published a series of papers on the functioning of the nervous system of the sea anemone: his most influential work. He demonstrated how the organization of the nerve net, and its very low-frequency impulses, could produce the response of different muscles each to its appropriate range of impulse rate, and also create integrated movement and behaviour of a comparatively complex kind in seemingly the simplest of nervous organizations. His work formed a foundation from which much of later neurophysiology and the interpretation of behaviour in neural terms originated. Despite Pantin's contracting tuberculosis, and a consequent loss of robust health for the rest of his life, his work led to fellowship of the Royal Society in 1937, the year in which he organized the now classical *Discussion* of that body on the transmission of excitation in living material.

Pantin worked on the lower animals for the rest of his life, especially the coelenterates and nemertine worms, though with his increasing involvement with the national bodies of his science, to which he gave great service, his research was done more and more through associates and assistants. Yet for thirty-five years his lectures to undergraduates communicated an enthusiasm and excitement of a remarkable kind. He became reader in invertebrate zoology in 1937 and succeeded Sir James Gray as professor in 1959. Thus in the seven years of headship before his retirement, he engaged with great courage and failing strength on two final tasks: the stability of the staff of his department, and the obtaining of new buildings for the Museum of Zoology, and a modern research wing which today bears his name. But in 1964 he was diagnosed as having leukaemia and he died in a Cambridge nursing home 14 January 1967, only a few months after he retired.

Pantin was president of the Linnean Society of London from 1958 to 1960, president of the Marine Biological Association of the United Kingdom (1960-6), during which time he negotiated the transfer of its main support to the

Natural Environment Research Council, and from 1963 till his death, chairman of the board of trustees of the British Museum, Natural History. He received the Royal medal of the Royal Society in 1950, and the gold medal of the Linnean Society in 1964. He became an honorary member of the Royal Society of New Zealand in 1955 and was given honorary doctorates of the universities of São Paulo and Durham. He became an honorary fellow of his old Cambridge college, Christ's. Despite this, those closest to him felt that he did not receive the public recognition he deserved, for he lacked any vestige of ruthlessness or selfishness; he was a man of transparent sincerity and personal charm, who communicated a radiant enjoyment of life and its study.

In 1923 Pantin married Amy, second daughter of Dr James Cruickshank Smith, CBE, Litt.D., LLD, a senior chief inspector of schools in Scotland. She also was a zoologist who qualified in medicine and collaborated in some of his research. They had two sons.

The portrait by Claude Rogers (1959) in Trinity College, Cambridge, is an admirable likeness; that by H. A. Freeth in the Balfour Library of the Zoological Department, Cambridge, was, unhappily, done when his final illness was advanced.

[F. A. Russell in *Biographical Memoirs of Fellows of the Royal Society*, vol. xiv, 1968; *Journal of the Marine Biological Association*, UK, vol. xlvii, 1967; personal knowledge.]

JAMES BEAMENT

PARKINSON, SIR (ARTHUR CHARLES) COSMO (1884-1967), civil servant, was born 18 November 1884 at Wimborne Minster, the only son and younger child of Sidney George Parkinson, a surgeon, and his wife, Elizabeth Trench. He went to Epsom College which he left as head prefect, having won a number of prizes; then went up to Magdalen College, Oxford, as a demy and obtained first class honours in classical moderations (1905) and *literae humaniores* (1907).

In 1908 Parkinson entered the Civil Service and was posted to the Admiralty. The next year he transferred to the Colonial Office where his first assignment was as secretary to the tropical African entomological research committee, and later to a committee investigating the relationship between wild animals and trypanosomiasis. This experience gave him an interest in tropical medicine which lasted all his life.

In 1914 he was appointed assistant private secretary to the secretary of state; but in May 1915 he was released for military service and commissioned as a second lieutenant in the Inns of Court Officers' Training Corps. He served with the King's African Rifles in East Africa from 1917, becoming deputy assistant adjutant-general and temporary major. He was appointed OBE in 1919.

On reverting to the Colonial Office in 1920 Parkinson was promoted principal in the East African department: but later that year he was appointed private secretary to the secretary of state. In 1924 he was moved to the Dominions division of the Colonial Office; and when the two departments were separated in 1925 he was promoted assistant secretary in the Dominions Office. In 1928 he returned to the Colonial Office as head of the East African department, and in 1929 was awarded the Brilliant Star of Zanzibar, third class. His promotion to assistant under-secretary of state, supervising the Middle East, Cyprus, and Aden departments, and his CMG came in 1931. He was advanced to KCMG in 1935; and in 1937 was appointed permanent under-secretary of state, with a KCB in 1938.

Parkinson was cast in a scholar's mould, with a keen sense of history and pride in tradition. Himself a perfectionist he expected perfection in others. He was a bachelor and lived for the Office. But a consequent concern, perhaps over-fastidious, with the niceties of procedure and style was combined with a wide-ranging ability and insistence on upholding Britain's obligations to the colonial peoples. This, together with his invariable personal kindness and humanity, held the admiration and affection of his colleagues. Nevertheless, with war approaching, ministers evidently felt that a more dynamic leadership was needed. A change had been planned for the autumn of 1939 but was deferred because of the outbreak of war until February 1940. Parkinson was then appointed permanent under-secretary of state for the Dominions Office and Sir George Gater [q.v.] took his place at the Colonial Office. The staff were frankly sceptical about the substitution of an officer from outside who, whatever his personal abilities, had little experience of central government and none of colonial affairs.

In May 1940 Gater was released on loan to the Ministry of Supply and Parkinson resumed, on an acting basis, the post to which he had been substantively appointed in 1937. It was therefore Parkinson who piloted the Colonial Office through the dark days of 1940-2, covering the spread of the war to Africa and the loss of British Somaliland; and the loss of Hong Kong, Malaya, Singapore, and the Borneo Territories—military defeats which, however, the contemporary press widely attributed to deficiencies in colonial administration. Parkinson's calmness and comradeship did much to sustain morale during this difficult period of blitz at home and losses abroad.

In 1942 Gater returned to the Colonial Office and Parkinson was seconded for special duties, being 'made available to visit colonies from time to time as opportunity offers, to discuss local problems with Governors as the Secretary of State's personal representative'. There was admittedly a case for such an appointment, since personal contacts had perforce been disrupted by the war. But many people felt that others could have filled it equally well, and questioned the wisdom and equity of again displacing such a wise and experienced administrator.

Parkinson himself accepted his new duties with dignity and threw himself into them wholeheartedly. He visited the Caribbean and Bermuda in 1942–3; Gambia, Nigeria, Kenya, Northern Rhodesia, Nyasaland, Mauritius, Seychelles, Aden, and British Somaliland in 1943; and Ceylon and Gibraltar in 1944. He retired at the end of 1944; but was re-employed during 1945 as adviser on the post-war reorganization of the Colonial Service. In that capacity he visited Fiji and the other Pacific colonies. He had been promoted GCMG in 1942.

Parkinson remained active after his retirement, publishing *The Colonial Office from Within* in 1947. He served on the Epsom College council from 1932 to 1965, being chairman of the executive committee from 1947 to 1961. He was a member of the governing body of University College Hospital, Birkbeck College, and the Old Vic; and as a crown trustee of the City Parochial Foundation from 1951 never missed a meeting until failing eyesight compelled him to resign in 1966. From 1948 to 1966 he served on the delegacy of King's College, London, being a member of the finance committee from 1950 to 1963. From 1956 to 1964 he was chairman of the court of governors of the London School of Hygiene and Tropical Medicine. He received an honorary LLD from St. Andrews.

After his retirement Parkinson moved to Bournemouth to be near his sister. Although he became totally blind in one eye his mind and memory remained fresh to the last. He died suddenly and peacefully in Bournemouth 16 August 1967.

[Private information; personal knowledge.]

HILTON POYNTON

PARTINGTON, JAMES RIDDICK (1886–1965), chemist and historian of science, was born 20 June 1886 in Bolton, Lancashire, the only son and first of the three children of Alfred Partington, bookkeeper, of Bolton, and his wife, Mary Agnes, daughter of Adam Riddick, tailor, of Dumfries. He was educated at Southport Science and Art School and became articled to the Bolton public analyst after his parents returned there in 1901. By private study he qualified for entrance to Manchester University in 1906. After obtaining first class honours in chemistry in 1909 he did research in physical organic chemistry under Arthur Lapworth, held a Beyer fellowship (1910–11), and was awarded the M.Sc. in 1911; his D.Sc. followed in 1918.

An 1851 Exhibition scholarship enabled Partington to work on the specific heats of gases under H. Walther Nernst in Berlin from 1911 to 1913. He was assistant lecturer and demonstrator in chemistry at Manchester University from 1913 until 1919, when London University appointed him professor of chemistry at East London College (renamed Queen Mary College in 1934). His reputation had grown during the war of 1914–18. Soon after it started he joined the army and saw active service as an infantry and engineer officer, becoming a captain. For some time he purified water for the troops on the Somme, working on a barge with (Sir) Eric K. Rideal. In 1916 they were transferred to the munitions inventions department of the Ministry of Munitions and, in the chemistry department of University College, London, headed by F. G. Donnan [q.v.], joined a team developing a method of manufacturing nitric acid, needed for explosives, from atmospheric nitrogen. Partington was appointed MBE (military) in 1918.

Until retiring in 1951 he remained at Queen Mary College, which elected him a fellow in 1959. He continued research on specific heats of gases and other topics, mainly in physical chemistry, and spent much time writing and revising textbooks on inorganic and physical chemistry for students at different levels. These books rather than his experimental work made his name familiar to all chemists, and in their day were influential. His *An Advanced Treatise on Physical Chemistry* (5 vols., 1949–54) contains a wealth of data and is of lasting value.

Partington's historical writings constitute his most enduring work. A meticulous scholar, he taught himself ancient and modern languages, used primary sources whenever possible, and produced a steady stream of books and articles on the history of chemistry, only a few of which can be mentioned. His *Origins and Development of Applied Chemistry* (1935) is a massive study of the production and uses of materials in the Near and Middle East to the end of the Bronze Age, when previous historians of science had started. His military experience added weight to his criticism of earlier writings on the subject in *A History of Greek Fire and Gunpowder* (1960). It is unlikely that a single scholar will again attempt a work on the scale of *A History of Chemistry* (4 vols., 1961–70), which contains in volumes ii–iv a richly documented account of the period since 1500; Partington did not complete volume i, part of which appeared posthumously, so his final views on alchemy remain unpublished.

During the war of 1939–45 Partington's college was evacuated to Cambridge. He lived there until 1964, then moved to Northwich, Cheshire, to be near his sister. His house was full of books, and in his study he could smoke his favourite strong tobacco, but he was often seen in London or Cambridge libraries, reading with intense concentration, constantly writing on slips of paper which he subsequently edited and pasted together to form the manuscript for a tolerant printer. A blunt and outspoken critic of contemporaries whose achievements seemed to him inadequate, he nevertheless gave praise where it was due. Those who knew him in his later years remember a reserved man with a dry sense of humour which reveals itself in the prefaces of some of his books.

Partington was the first chairman (1937–8) of the Society for the Study of Alchemy and Early Chemistry; now the Society for the History of Alchemy and Chemistry, it awards the triennial Partington prize to a young historian. From 1949 to 1951 he was president of the British Society for the History of Science. He received the American Chemical Society's Dexter award for history of chemistry in 1961 and the Sarton medal of the American History of Science Society shortly before he died.

In 1919 Partington married Marian (died 1940), daughter of Thomas Jones, brickworks manager, of Buckley, Chester. They had one son and two daughters. Partington died 9 October 1965 in the Grange Hospital, Weaverham, Cheshire.

A photograph by Ruth Partington hangs in the Chemistry Department, Queen Mary College.

[*The Times*, 11 and 15 October 1965; F. H. C. Butler in *British Journal for the History of Science*, vol. iii, 1966; F. W. Gibbs in *Chemistry and Industry*, 1966; private information; personal knowledge.]

W. A. SMEATON

PAYNE, JOHN WESLEY VIVIAN (JACK) (1899–1969), bandleader, was born in Leamington 22 August 1899, the only son of John Edwin Payne, music warehouse manager, and his wife, Sarah Vivian Clare Gunn, of 10 Church Street, Leamington. Jack Payne first became interested in dance music during his service with the Royal Flying Corps in 1918, playing the piano in various amateur bands in the Service. After demobilization he took up dance music as a profession and formed a small band which secured a position in the Hotel Cecil in London in the summer of 1925. With this he made his first records (Zonophone, Aco). When the BBC began relaying dance music from the hotel, four extra musicians were added, increasing the number to ten. In February 1928 Jack Payne was appointed director of dance music to the BBC, a position he held from 2 March 1928 until 14 March 1932. In that period, he and the BBC Dance Orchestra recorded exclusively for Columbia, and made daily broadcasts of about an hour from Station 2LO, later known as the National Programme. He was the first bandleader to introduce and close each broadcast with a signature tune, in this case Irving Berlin's 'Say It With Music', and was one of the first to announce his music and sing the vocal refrains himself. In April 1930 Jack Payne and the BBC Dance Orchestra appeared at the London Palladium, returning there in August 1931. The full strength of the band was then sixteen, and it remained so for many years.

On leaving the BBC, Jack Payne took his band on nationwide tours, recording for Imperial Records; the labels showed his portrait in place of the gold crown trade-mark, and a gold facsimile of his signature. He is the only dance bandleader in this country to have been accorded this honour. Late in 1932 he and the band appeared as the central figures in a film called *Say It With Music*, for which his arranger, Ray Noble, wrote the score. Towards the end of 1933 the band was reorganized, and continued to record on Rex Records, which had replaced Imperial as the principal product of the Crystalate Gramophone Record Manufacturing Company. At the end of 1935 Jack Payne and his band made another film, *Sunshine Ahead*, on completion of which they visited South Africa very successfully during the summer of 1936.

In May 1937 Jack Payne gave the members of his band two weeks' notice, and retired to his Buckinghamshire farm to concentrate on stock-breeding; but he returned to the popular-music business in January 1938, resumed recording (for Decca), and touring. During the war of 1939–45 he and the band entertained the Services extensively, but within a year of the end of the war Jack Payne again withdrew from the scene and became a very popular 'disc-jockey', host on his own television show, artists' manager, and, finally, manager of a hotel in Tonbridge. The last venture was not a success, and failing health and financial difficulties contributed to his death at the age of seventy.

Jack Payne was also a composer. In 1930 he had published two waltz ballads which were very successful—'Blue Pacific Moonlight' and 'Underneath The Spanish Stars'—and, in 1931, another waltz 'Pagan Serenade', among other numbers. His band was very versatile, and in the course of a single show would play all kinds of popular tunes of the day, mostly romantic but freely intermixed with rousing chorus songs in 6/8 time, *paso-dobles*, Afro-American rhythms, comedy songs involving cameo-sketches in which Jack Payne himself would play cockney, north country, American, and 'Oxford-English' character-parts, and sometimes concert arrangements of standard classics, one of the most popular being Ravel's 'Bolero'. One of his most spectacular pieces of showmanship was to simulate a huge engine, appearing to be running out of the stage backdrop into the stalls of the London Palladium, with the members of the band seated on various parts of the engine, as they played a popular instrumental number of the time (1931) called 'Choo Choo'. As a man, Jack Payne was a perfectionist, a disciplinarian, an obvious leader, frank and sincere to a fault. These characteristics did not always find favour with his associates, but he has left an indelible mark on the pages of the history of British dance music.

Payne was twice married: firstly, in 1923, to Doris Aileen (died 1939), the daughter of Colonel H. H. Pengree, Royal Field Artillery, and secondly, in 1942, to Peggy, daughter of Thomas Andrew Cochrane, LLB (Edinburgh). A daughter was adopted in the second marriage. Payne died at his home in Tonbridge, Kent, 4 December 1969.

There is a cartoon sketch of Payne by Kapp reproduced as the frontispiece to Payne's autobiography, *Signature Tune* (1947), and another by Bond in the *Radio Times*, 17 March 1933, p. 656. A cartoon was also used by the Crystalate Gramophone Record Company for their publicity material in 1932 and for a year or so thereafter.

[Jack Payne, *This is Jack Payne*, 1932, and *Signature Tune*, 1947; Peggy Cochrane, *We Said it with Music*, 1979.]   BRIAN RUST

PEACOCK, SIR EDWARD ROBERT (1871–1962), merchant banker, was born in the manse at Glengarry, Ontario, 2 August 1871, the eldest son of the Revd William MacAllister Peacock, Presbyterian minister, and his wife, Jane McDougall. His father died in 1883, leaving a family of young children; their mother, a woman of great character, struggled to see that they received a good education. Edward Peacock attended Almonte High School, Ontario, then Queen's University, Kingston; he graduated in 1894 'magna cum laude', with the gold medal in philosophy and the silver medal in political economy. He was particularly influenced by a young professor of political science, Adam Shortt, with whom he established a close and lasting friendship. Peacock was by no means afraid of hard physical labour, and in his younger days tackled a variety of jobs—shovelling grain, driving street-cars—to gain cash and experience. Shortly after graduation he accepted a teaching post at Upper Canada College which in 1895 came under the headmastership of (Sir) George Parkin [q.v.]. Peacock proved a successful and popular teacher of English and senior housemaster (1897); at the college he became a close friend of Stephen Leacock [q.v.], and taught him economics in exchange for lessons in French and chess.

In 1902 Peacock made the bold decision to abandon schoolmastering and embark on a financial career: he joined Dominion Securities Corporation, a Toronto financial house, acting first as personal assistant to the founder, E. R. Wood, later becoming a bond salesman. In 1907 Dominion Securities decided to set up a European office in London and sent Peacock over as their first representative. The corporation had been interested, among other ventures, in a group of electric power and traction companies in Spain, Mexico, and Brazil, headed by Dr F. S. Pearson, and when Pearson was drowned in the sinking of the *Lusitania* in 1915, Peacock was one of those given the task of bringing order out of confusion. He became vice-president of Brazilian Traction Light and Power, and president of the Mexican Light and Power Company and of the Barcelona Traction Light and Power Company, administering them until 1924.

His financial abilities, which had early become apparent, were soon well known on both sides of the Atlantic. One of the first to recognize his qualities was Montagu (later Lord) Norman [q.v.], then governor of the Bank of England. In 1921 Peacock was appointed a director of the Bank, the first Canadian to serve on the Court, and immediately he became one of its most active members. His colleagues on the Court included Lord Revelstoke, at that time senior partner in Baring Brothers, who was much impressed by Peacock whom he invited to join Barings. As it was a rule that two directors of the same firm should not serve on the Court simultaneously, on joining Barings Peacock had to resign from the Bank of England; he did so with reluctance, hesitating some time before he acceded to Revelstoke's request in 1924. In 1929, however, when Revelstoke died, Peacock was immediately invited to resume his place on the Court and remained a director continuously until 1946. After his re-election, his responsibilities became heavy once again, especially in the difficult months during the autumn of 1931, when Norman was ill and his duties had to be redistributed; in particular, Peacock was called on to support the deputy governor, Sir Ernest Harvey, in the difficult discussions involving the British Government and bankers in America.

In 1926 he had been appointed European director of the Canadian Pacific Railway Company, the first of various appointments in the field of Anglo-Canadian relations which had a special appeal for him. Another was to the board of the Hudson's Bay Company in 1931, on which he served until 1950. He handled many special negotiations and missions, both financial and otherwise, between Canada and the United Kingdom, and his services were often called on in matters relating to the United States; for example, he went to Washington in 1941 on behalf of the Treasury, travelling at the age of seventy most uncomfortably across the Atlantic in a bomber aircraft, to handle the delicate question of Britain's direct investments in the States and the extent to which they should be used in financing wartime dollar expenditure. Also during the war of 1939–45 he was chairman of the overseas committee of the Canadian National War Services Funds Advisory Board, in which he supervised the financing of welfare agencies for the Canadian forces overseas.

Peacock's qualities were recognized in many other spheres. Shortly after his move to Baring Brothers in 1924 he became a member of the council of the Duchy of Cornwall; in 1929 he became receiver-general of the Duchy. In recognition of his services to the Crown he was appointed GCVO in 1934. The trust and respect which he inspired in members of the Royal Family were evidenced by the invaluable counsel he was able to give to the departing monarch and to his successor, during the delicate situation before the abdication of Edward VIII. 'E. R. P. was a very great help', the new King noted in his chronicle, 10 December 1936.

Peacock was treasurer of King Edward's Hospital Fund for London, and chairman of its finance committee, from 1929 to 1954. During that time he saw many changes and crises in the hospital world and in the role of the Fund: the appearance on the scene of a new hospital authority in London, the London County Council; the threat posed to the voluntary hospitals by the financial crises of the thirties, when grants from the Fund became a life-line to many of even the most historic hospitals; the disruption caused by the war of 1939–45 and the creation of an integrated emergency hospital service; and the establishment of a state system of hospitals by Aneurin Bevan [q.v.] in 1948. Peacock was deeply and continuously concerned to secure that the necessary changes were achieved with a minimum of damage and personal friction.

In 1925 Lord Milner [q.v.] brought Peacock on to the Rhodes Trust, of which Parkin, his early mentor, had been the organizing secretary, 1902–19. Although Peacock himself was born too early to be a Rhodes scholar, it was said at the time of his death that he exemplified all that one might hope a Rhodes scholar to be. Financially too, the Trust benefited considerably from his wise advice, and he has been described as its 'second founder'. He was also chairman of trustees, Imperial War Graves Commission, chairman of the board of management of the royal commission for the Exhibition of 1851, a trustee of King George's Jubilee trust, and a lieutenant of the City of London. He received honorary degrees from Oxford (1932), Edinburgh (1938), and his Alma Mater (1949).

Peacock's services were in constant request at Threadneedle Street, and although he was a non-executive director of the Bank of England, for many years he contributed much to the financial developments and policies of his time. He was, for example, already in his eighty-second year when he played an active part, despite his deafness, in the formation of the Bank-sponsored Commonwealth Development Finance Corporation, an organization designed to provide finance by the City of London and British industry for worthwhile projects in developing countries in the Commonwealth. When he finally retired from Barings at the end of 1954, after helping to guide their affairs soundly through years of great difficulty both at home and abroad, he had achieved a unique position in the financial community as 'the conscience of the City'.

Peacock was endowed with an impressive physical presence; the 'tall, tow-headed and rangy' youth who had gone up to Queen's, Kingston, in 1891 matured into a tall, handsome, impeccably dressed and dignified man, with clear eyes and firm features. As a Freemason and a Presbyterian, Edward Peacock possessed in full measure the quality of 'gravitas', which was, however, coupled with a never-failing enthusiasm, an appreciative sense of humour, and a natural feeling of kindliness towards his fellow men. He never lost his understanding of the young. Endowed by nature with a first-class brain, he developed the wisdom of long experience. He was a man of complete integrity, and once he had made up his mind, which he never did hastily, he would make his decision clearly and definitely, and firmly abide by it. He never lost a night's sleep. He possessed many of the best qualities of a great judge, and was recognized by many as a first-class arbitrator in important matters. Although he was both serious and conscientious in the discharge of his manifold responsibilities, he never appeared to be weighed down by them: he was well read, enjoyed playing not very serious bridge, and was a witty after-dinner speaker; he continued to play golf enthusiastically and competently until almost the end of his days, going round the Swinley Forest course which marched alongside the garden of his delightful house, Boden's Rise, Ascot, it was said in the same number of strokes as his years. After some international conference in Canada he had agreed to play a round of golf. The view from the first tee was shrouded in mist, and his partner was for abandoning the game; Sir Edward drove his ball straight as a die, as was his nature, right through the fog and advanced upon it with steady resolution: there lay his ball in the middle of the fairway in the brilliant sunshine which illuminated the rest of the match.

Peacock's favourite quotation (attributed to Stephen Grellet, 1773-1855) was 'I expect to pass through this world but once; any good thing therefore that I can do, or any kindness that I can show to any fellow-creature, let me do it now; let me not defer or neglect it, for I shall not pass this way again.' When, very late in life, he agreed to the preparation of a coat of arms to fill his rightful place in the Savoy Chapel, the warden of All Souls (Mr John Sparrow) remembered the old sundial, which when asked the hour replied 'Time to be doing good'. So the following motto was most appropriately incorporated in Edward Peacock's coat of arms: *Semper adest hora bene faciendi*.

In 1912 Peacock married Katherine, daughter of John Coates, of Ottawa. It was a long and happy marriage, and having no children of their own, they adopted two daughters. Lady Peacock died in 1948. Peacock died in London 19 November 1962. A portrait painted by (Sir) James Gunn (1941) hangs in Rhodes House, Oxford; another is in the ownership of Baring Brothers.

[*The Times*, 20 November 1962; *Canadian Banker*, vol. lxvii, no. 2, Summer 1960; R. Bassett, *Nineteen Thirty-One*, 1958; J. W. Wheeler-Bennett, *King George VI*, 1958; Frances Donaldson, *Edward VIII*, 1974; private information; personal knowledge.]

ANDREW CARNWATH

PEAKE, FREDERICK GERARD (1886-1970), pasha, founder of the Arab Legion, was born at Ashtead, Surrey, 12 June 1886, the only son of Lieutenant-Colonel Walter Ancell Peake, DSO, of Burrough-on-the-Hill, Leicestershire, by his wife, Grace Elizabeth Ann Fenwicke. He was intended for the navy, and was educated at Stubbington House, Fareham, where he showed little aptitude; he eventually gained entrance to the Royal Military College, Sandhurst, and was commissioned in the Duke of Wellington's Regiment in 1906. Later that year he was posted to India, and, while disliking

the social duties then a prominent feature of Indian army life, he hunted, studied the local languages with enthusiasm, and developed a certain ingenuity, acumen, and resolution of his own.

Early in 1914 he was seconded to the Egyptian Army at his own request, and was sent to join the 4th Infantry battalion in the Sudan; although his applications for front-line duty on the outbreak of war were ignored, in 1916 when the Darfur rebellion broke out he transferred to the Camel Corps under (Sir) Hubert Huddleston [q.v.], and took command of No. 5 company, having been promoted captain in 1915. Due for home leave that year, Peake asked to go instead to Salonika for action against the Bulgarians, and was temporarily posted to No. 17 Squadron, Royal Flying Corps, as observer and later adjutant. Although he outstayed his leave, he was saved from court martial by the sense of humour of General (later Field-Marshal Lord) Milne [q.v.], who merely sent him back to Darfur with a reprimand. However, on the last lap of the journey south he was thrown from his camel and severely dislocated his neck: he spent several months in hospital before a specialist told him that his case was incurable. Later, walking in the hospital gardens and unable to raise his head from his chest, Peake crashed blindly into a tree: the jolt restored his neck to normal with no subsequent ill effect. He had no sooner returned to his unit after convalescence, however, than he developed a liver abscess and was sent home on sick leave. On the return voyage his ship was torpedoed near Alexandria: Peake jumped overboard with a bottle of beer and a packet of sandwiches and was picked up none the worse.

Early in 1918 he was sent to Sinai and took command of a company of the Egyptian Camel Corps, in the British section of the Northern Arab Army; in April they joined T. E. Lawrence [q.v.] with Sharif Faisal's army at Aqaba. Lawrence's task in the final phase of the Egyptian Expeditionary Force's campaign under Sir Edmund (later Viscount) Allenby [q.v.]—especially after many of Allenby's troops were withdrawn to meet the German offensive in Europe of March 1918—was to cut off and contain the large numbers of Turks defending the Hejaz railway and garrisoning the towns from Medina to Damascus. The Egyptian Camel Corps gave invaluable assistance to Lawrence's guerrilla campaign northwards, even if Peake had cause to complain that his men were reluctant to get themselves killed; they had a vital role to play against those Turkish positions inaccessible to armoured cars, and 'The Peake Demolition Co. Ltd.' became adept as sappers, developing the 'tulip' technique for blowing up stretches of railway; their last job before the decisive battle at Megiddo was to cut the Dera'a-Damascus railway in order to disrupt Turkish communications and hinder their retreat. Demobilization soon followed, and Peake returned to HQ in Cairo.

When hostilities ended in 1918, the Trans-Jordanians set up quaint pockets of autonomous government in every town. To each of these a British officer of one kind or another was posted, as representative of the British high commissioner in Palestine. Most of the area was under Occupied Enemy Territory Administration and also formed part of Faisal's Kingdom of Damascus, while the far south still belonged to his father, Husain, Grand Sharif of Mecca; boundaries were undefined, and funds and a tax system non-existent, and civil administration was chaotic. The desert nomads, whom the Turks had made little attempt to control, regarded it as a heaven-sent opportunity to raid the sown, according to age-old custom, and the cultivators of the sown retaliated; the first task was to establish law and security. Peake was sent to administer Aqaba and its environs, and within a year his impartiality had gained the respect and affection of both tribesmen and villagers.

But in 1919 British troops were withdrawn from Trans-Jordan as well as from Syria, following the treaty of Versailles, and Peake returned to his old command of the Egyptian Camel Corps in Palestine with responsibility for policing the eastern frontier south of the Dead Sea. On the establishment of the British mandate in Palestine in 1920, the Camel Corps was disbanded; Peake accepted a position in the Palestine Police, and was posted to supervise internal security in Amman; he found morale and efficiency at a low ebb, and the gendarmerie unpaid, having evidently inherited all the vices and few of the virtues of the Turkish regime. The high commissioner for Palestine, Sir Herbert (later Viscount) Samuel [q.v.], authorized Peake to raise a force of 105 men and officers: the Arab Legion thus came into being, October 1920. At first there was much opposition from the tribesmen, who saw a threat to their traditional way of life, the villagers were afraid of reprisal and reluctant to join, and Peake was obliged to scrape together a few Egyptian and Sudanese ex-servicemen. However, recruitment slowly increased, although uniforms were 'war surplus' (Peake was later to design the uniforms himself), and the soldiers of the new 'Arab Army' were, to their shame, the only men in the area without weapons until Peake managed to find some old German rifles.

Peake attended the Cairo conference of 1921,

at which (Sir) Winston Churchill, Lawrence, and Samuel were also present among many others; while it was in progress, news came that Sharif Abdullah, Husain's second son, had reached Amman to raise a force against the French who had ejected Faisal from Syria. At Lawrence's instigation, Churchill went to meet Abdullah, and persuaded him to accept the emirate of Trans-Jordan under British protection, on condition that he would try to prevent his subjects from troubling the French. The Arab Legion was to be increased to a thousand men, and funds were promised; enlistment gradually became more competitive as the Legion's prestige grew, although arms remained a difficulty; for example, there were ex-Turkish cavalrymen who insisted on swords, and Peake finally obtained from the Cairo Ordnance Depot a 'job lot' which turned out to be part of the Napoleonic army's equipment abandoned in 1801.

Later in 1921 Lawrence toured the country with Peake in an old 'Tin Lizzie' Ford; their esteem and liking was mutual, and Lawrence—a frequent visitor—gave Peake much advice on general policies, and methods of controlling tribal raiding and the threat of incursions from Arabia. Both men foresaw the end of direct British rule, and realized the potency of the Arab awakening.

Peake's early problems arose from the strong anti-French feeling stirred up by Arab officials exiled from Damascus: the French did not hesitate to accuse him of aiding these refugees, many of whom had secured posts in Abdullah's Government and who in turn accused Britain of having handed over Syria to the French. The Balfour Declaration of 1917 was a further cause of friction, and aroused general distrust and fear of Zionism among even the local sheikhs; Peake narrowly escaped death at the hands of a mob enraged by the arrest of an Arab agent, whom Peake had handed over to the Palestinian authorities without being aware of the man's identity. However, Abdullah himself showed unfailing good humour, common sense, and much respect and affection for Peake who consulted him almost daily. A spell of home leave in 1923 was interrupted by a fierce but brief uprising against unfair taxation by corrupt ministers, but another crisis was already on the horizon in 1922: raids by the fanatical Ikhwan from central Arabia, massacring all Muslims who did not belong to their own Wahhabi sect, and slowly increasing in range and ferocity until by 1924 they came within ten miles of Amman. Harry St. John Philby [q.v.], at that time chief British representative, was the first to tell Peake of the imminent danger, and a desert outpost of the Arab Legion was set up to give early warning, although its purpose was defeated owing to the lack of wireless equipment. However, in 1924, with the help of the RAF, a decisive victory was gained over a large force of Ikhwan, who thereafter left Trans-Jordan in peace.

In 1926 the British Government asked Abdullah to take over the south from Ma'an to Aqaba, as a result of Ibn Saud's invasion of the Hejaz; Peake successfully persuaded—by ingenious if unorthodox methods—the inhabitants of those wild and inaccessible mountains to accept the presence of law and order, and the following year an additional three hundred men were recruited to police the area. However, in 1927 Ibn Saud's Wahhabis were again menacing the south, and a detachment of the Trans-Jordan Frontier Force was sent from Palestine to guard the frontier; the Arab Legion was reduced accordingly, but in 1930 (Sir) John Glubb—Glubb Pasha, who was to succeed Peake as the Legion's commander—came as peacemaker and lawgiver to the border tribes, with a small unit of Bedouins. The decade from 1927 brought peace and prosperity to the Middle East, and within a few years of Trans-Jordan's having been one of the most lawless and dangerous countries, tourists began to visit places such as Petra and Jerash in safety. Peake and the Arab Legion, which he had raised and trained from scratch, established law and order, a peaceful community was able to extend the area of cultivation, and the Government could conduct a regular administration. But the years 1936-9 were more difficult, when the Palestinian rebellion put the Legion's loyalty to a severe test; many Trans-Jordanians were sympathetic to the cause of the Palestine Arabs, and had Palestinian family connections. Six hundred extra men were drafted in to protect the oil pipeline against sabotage and to forestall the movement of rebels through the north of the country.

Peake Pasha built the Arab Legion on a firm foundation, establishing a tradition of loyalty and efficient discipline which withstood many shocks from both within and without the kingdom; a stern disciplinarian whose military style was almost Victorian, he believed that it was good policy to appear angry. His character was always unexpected, and his courage legendary; he learned to fly at the age of forty-four, and when on tour the warning code-word 'thundercloud' would precede him from one police post to another. Nevertheless, his men of the Arab Legion were utterly devoted to him for his honesty and kindness, his almost motherly fondness and consideration for their well-being. In height he was above average, upright, with a rubicund complexion set off, in later life, by white hair and moustache, while his piercing blue eyes seemed to read the very soul of a miscreant; for years after he left Trans-Jordan, men would say, 'May Allah remember him for good! His heart was true and simple.'

Peake retired in 1939, having held the British local rank of lieutenant-colonel since 1921; in the Arab Legion he held successively the ranks of brigadier (1920-2), major-general (1922-6), and general or pasha from 1926. He was awarded the Sudan medal with two clasps (1916), and was appointed OBE (1923), CBE (1926), and commander of the Order of St. John of Jerusalem (1934); he was also appointed CMG (1939) in recognition of his services to Trans-Jordan, and held several Middle Eastern decorations and medals. In 1937 Peake married Elspeth Maclean, younger daughter of Norman Ritchie, of St. Boswell's, Roxburghshire; she bore him a daughter, and died in 1967. They retired to his wife's Scottish home, where he served in Civil Defence from 1939, and was acting inspector of constabulary with the local rank of lieutenant-colonel (1942-51); he wrote *A History of Jordan and its Tribes* (1958) and *Change at St. Boswell's* (1961), a history of the village. He died at Kelso 30 March 1970. A portrait of him by the American artist Mollie Guyon (1953) is privately owned.

[C. S. Jarvis, *Arab Command*, 1942; J. B. Glubb, *The Story of the Arab Legion*, 1948; T. E. Lawrence, *Seven Pillars of Wisdom*, 1926; *The Times*, 1 and 6 April 1970; personal knowledge.]   JOHN BAGOT GLUBB

PEAKE, MERVYN LAURENCE (1911-1968), artist and author, was born at Kuling, China, 9 July 1911, the younger son of Ernest Cromwell Peake, MD, Congregational missionary doctor, of Tientsin, by his wife, Amanda Elizabeth Powell. Peake was educated at Tientsin Grammar School, Eltham College, Kent, and the Royal Academy Schools where he won the Hacker prize (1931). After finishing at the Academy Schools he spent two years in an 'artists' colony' of friends on the island of Sark; on the strength of his work he was offered a position at the Westminster School of Art in 1935, where he taught life drawing until 1939. There, too, he met Maeve, youngest of the six children of Owen Eugene Gilmore, MD, FRCS; they married in 1937, and had two sons and a daughter. During the war Peake served in England in the Royal Artillery, being later transferred to the Royal Engineers, but was invalided out in 1943 after a nervous breakdown. For the next two years he was attached to the Ministry of Information, and it was not until just after the end of the war that he was appointed war artist with the rank of captain. In 1946 he returned to Sark with his family, where they spent three serenely happy years; but a retainer from his publisher and a few commissions could not continue to meet the needs of a growing family, and in 1949 they came back to England where Peake secured a part-time teaching post at the Central School of Art, Holborn; this, together with commissioned paintings and illustrations for books, and to a lesser extent his writing, formed the often uneven ground on which he supported his family. From 1957, after the failure of his first and only West End play, *The Wit to Woo*, which was to have solved all their financial problems, he became increasingly incapacitated by what was eventually diagnosed as a form of Parkinson's disease, and by 1960 he was obliged to give up teaching.

After his death in 1968 Peake became best known for his three 'Titus' novels, *Titus Groan* (1946), *Gormenghast* (1950), and *Titus Alone* (1959), which describe the growth of Titus, the seventy-seventh Earl of Groan, in his ancestral home Gormenghast castle, his rebellion against Gormenghast and his restrictive duties, and his attempt to find a new identity for himself in another land. Although showing the influence of Dickens, Lewis Carroll, and Kafka, these books defy ready classification. The term 'fantasy' is perhaps the least inadequate, although Peake's work has nothing of the lightweight or evasive commonly implied by the word: but it is fantasy in being the creation of a fully realized 'other' world, ontologically separate from our own. The strength of *Titus Groan* is the thoroughness with which it is imagined, and the dialectical play throughout of the static, unchanging nature of the castle against the dynamic of the enemies within it. In Gormenghast Peake found the perfect literary expression for his interests as an artist: the slow, heavily descriptive method of the style and the delight in the individualities of people and objects are paralleled in the unmoving character of the castle, the obsessive preoccupation with minutiae which epitomizes the ritual laws which govern it, and the eccentric personalities it produces. Gormenghast castle is the natural home of Peake's imagination, a home to which he was irresistibly drawn, even while as a man and an artist he wished to escape it and explore new worlds. The undertow of Gormenghast drains the life from the portrayal of Titus's rebellion, and the imaginative unity and power of *Titus Groan* is increasingly lost in the succeeding volumes. Yet, considered as a whole, the 'Titus' books remain a massive achievement.

During his lifetime, Peake was known more as an artist, particularly as an illustrator of books. The finest examples are his work for the editions of Lewis Carroll's *The Hunting of the Snark* (1941) and the *Alice* books (1946 and 1954); Coleridge's *The Rime of the Ancient Mariner* (1943); the Grimm brothers' *Household Tales* (1946); and R. L. Stevenson's *Dr. Jekyll and Mr. Hyde* (1948) and *Treasure Island* (1949). Peake also illustrated much of his own work; and his children's books, *Captain Slaughterboard Drops Anchor* (1939) and *Letters from a Lost Uncle from Polar Regions* (1948) are composed round his brilliant drawings. In collections of his individual sketches, *The Craft of the Lead Pencil* (1946) and *The Drawings of Mervyn Peake* (1949), Peake also outlined his views on art as at once intensively subjective and objective. The primary concern of Peake's drawings is with the human figure, rather than with landscape: of Gormenghast he has left us scarcely a pictorial trace. One of the most frequent and powerful of his effects is the portrayal of the frail verticality of his figures struggling against a dense and crushing atmosphere, or else bent or deformed by it: this is also his vision of the lives of the personages of Gormenghast, and of those who rebel against the castle. Later publications, such as his *Writings and Drawings* (1974) and his *Drawings* (1974), showed a return of interest in Peake the artist.

Peake was also recognized in his own day as a poet. Poetry was for him the most moving form of human expression. Much of his poetry for adults appeared in his *Shapes and Sounds* (1941), *The Glassblowers* (1950), *The Rhyme of the Flying Bomb* (1962), and *A Reverie of Bone* (1967). For *The Glassblowers* (and *Gormenghast*) he was awarded the W. H. Heinemann Foundation prize of £100 and an honorary fellowship of the Royal Society of Literature (1951). He is at his best when an experience and its significance for him are fused, as for instance in 'The Glassblowers' or the frightening 'Heads Float About Me', rather than when he reflects on or self-consciously tries to proportion his feelings to his experience. A recurrent motif in his poetry is the idea of a face or body as a building or city, and vice versa: this transference is also seen in the interrelations of Gormenghast and its inhabitants. Peake also wrote children's and nonsense poetry (the latter often in the vein of Lewis Carroll). His poetic impulse is as divided between the serious and the comic as is his *Gormenghast*: Peake would have written more good poetry, as he did the prose of *Titus Groan*, had he fused both sides of his nature in the making of it.

Tall, thin, dark, and haggard, Peake was a romantic figure, whose passionate and intense nature exhausted him: he lived always on 'this desperate edge of now', and wrote to pour himself forth, to empty himself of all his 'golden gall'. In some ways shy and reserved, he was innocently open and generous to all who asked his help. He was enormously sensitive to human suffering, and a visit to Belsen in 1945 (commissioned by the *Leader* to sketch what he saw) left him emotionally scarred. In character he was gentle, gracious, unworldly, and unpractical. He lived in many ways outside convention, wearing strange clothes and behaving in a gently whimsical fashion which puzzled the ordinary. He did not care for 'arrangements' in life: he would gather materials for drawings simply by walking the streets of central London and stopping interesting subjects for on-the-spot sketches; and he would write in the midst of his family circle. It was in part Peake's very proximity to and delight in life which produced his fantasy, and his sense of the individual his art of exaggeration: 'Anything,' he once said, 'seen without prejudice, is enormous.'

Peake died at Burcot, Berkshire, 17 November 1968. Several portraits done by his widow, Maeve Gilmore, remained in her possession. A Mervyn Peake Society was formed in 1975.

[Maeve Gilmore, *A World Away: A Memoir of Mervyn Peake*, 1970, and *Peake's Progress*, 1979; John Watney, *Mervyn Peake*, 1976; private information; personal knowledge.]

C. N. MANLOVE

PEARSALL, WILLIAM HAROLD (1891–1964), ecologist and professor of botany, was born at Stourbridge, Worcestershire, 23 July 1891, the only son and second of the three children of William Harrison Pearsall, schoolmaster, Methodist lay-preacher and distinguished naturalist, and his wife, Mary Elizabeth Green, of Earl Shilton, Leicester. His father moved to Dalton-in-Furness when the son was quite young and became headmaster of Broughton Road School. Pearsall attended his father's school until 1905 and then went to Ulverston Grammar School. In 1909 he was admitted to the Victoria University of Manchester, initially to read chemistry but after his first year he changed to botany, graduating with first class honours in 1913 and gaining a university graduate scholarship. From his earliest days he had accompanied his father on frequent week-end and holiday excursions into the Lake District, where they walked and climbed and also searched for water plants, in which he developed a great interest. The graduate scholarship enabled him to devote himself to a systematic study of the distribution of aquatic plants in the English Lakes. He was awarded his M.Sc. in 1915 and in the following year he joined the Royal Garrison Artillery and saw active service in France, returning to civilian life in 1919 with the permanent and troublesome handicap of quite serious deafness necessitating a hearing-aid.

Now married, Pearsall applied successfully in 1919 for an assistant lectureship under Professor J. H. Priestley at Leeds University, and was promoted to a full lectureship in 1920, when he was also made D.Sc. of Manchester University for his researches on the English Lakes. In 1922 he was made reader in botany at Leeds and held the post until, in 1938, he was appointed professor of botany at Sheffield University. He was elected FRS in 1940 (as was his ancestor W. Pearsall in 1663) and in 1944 succeeded (Sir) E. J. Salisbury in the Quain chair of botany at University College, London, retaining it until his retirement in 1957. He was remembered at University College as a 'near ideal head of department' and an outstandingly good teacher, especially in seminars and informal discussions, and many of his students acquired from his field excursions an intense and lasting interest in the countryside.

Pearsall's earliest scientific publications (1917–21) report those studies of lakes and their vegetation which he began immediately after graduation. Consideration of the mode of erosion of wave-exposed shores, and of the redeposition of the removed material, enabled him to explain the distribution of plant communities in and round Esthwaite Water. The shore vegetation at the north end of the lake was of special interest because it changed with distance from the mouth of the inflow stream which carried most of the incoming silt. Pearsall carefully mapped the plant communities, showing their relation to the water-margin and to the fineness and chemical content of the accumulating sediments. When he remapped the area in 1929 all the zones had advanced into or towards the open water. The general interest aroused by this direct demonstration of 'plant succession' led to the declaration of the North Fen as a national nature reserve in 1954 and to a further mapping in 1967–9 by a group from Lancaster University.

Pearsall next looked at the lakes as a whole in an attempt to account for differences between them. He found a close relationship between physical and chemical features of their shores and water on the one hand and their flora and fauna on the other. Since all occupy ice-deepened rock basins which became ice-free at much the same time, he argued that their present differences must have arisen from differing rates of subsequent change. The *rocky* lakes like Wastwater and Ennerdale must be relatively primitive, the much *silted* lakes like Windermere and Esthwaite were further removed from their initial state and must therefore be more advanced. The rocky lakes have very clear water poor in dissolved substances, scanty vegetation, and trout as the most abundant fish. The silted lakes have water less clear but richer in plant nutrients, much more vegetation, and perch, pike, and eels as the typical fish. The publication of 1921 reporting these findings is characteristic in the adventurous boldness of its inferences from a large body of careful field-work and in the satisfying simplicity of the resulting synthesis. Pearsall's conclusions were found acceptable and stimulated much further research, but doubts arose later when the analysis of deep lake sediments provided a dated record of changes in their chemistry and in the plankton and pollen incorporated in them. There had in fact been great variations in rates of change and some reversals of direction, but these proved explicable in the light of ideas largely suggested by Pearsall himself. His original story had lost in simplicity while gaining in breadth of ecological interest, but the framework remains and continues to illuminate and challenge.

Pearsall's research interests were by no means restricted to lakes. In 1937 and subsequent years he described measurements of those electric potentials of natural soils that he interpreted as oxidation–reduction potentials and whose ecological significance he discussed with customary perceptiveness, and there were further valuable contributions on soils and bogs. In his presidential address to Section K of the British Association in 1954 he drew attention to the increasingly urgent problems of world food production. There followed a series of papers by himself and former pupils on 'production ecology' which undoubtedly influenced the choice of biological productivity as one of two major topics for the International Biological Programme.

Mention must be made of Pearsall's splendid book *Mountains and Moorlands* (1950) in which he drew on all his vast and intimate knowledge of Britain's highland zone and on his capacity for creative imagination and lucid writing. It was written primarily for the amateur naturalist, but it nevertheless provides the university student with an unrivalled introduction to the scientific analysis of familiar ecological phenomena. His *Report on an Ecological Survey of Serengeti National Park, Tanganyika* (1956) is a classic of ecological literature.

Pearsall was one of three biologists principally involved in seeking to establish a British centre for lake research, their efforts resulting in the foundation in 1929 of the Freshwater Biological Association and the leasing of research accommodation for it in Wray Castle by Windermere. Pearsall was closely involved from the start in the development of the FBA's research, playing a very active role in guiding, encouraging, and inspiring the research workers until the end of his life.

Pearsall joined the British Ecological Society soon after its foundation and began his term as president in 1936. From 1937 to 1947 he edited the society's *Journal of Ecology*. At the time of his death he was editor of *Annals of Botany*. He became a member of the Nature Conservancy when it was set up in 1949 and was chairman of its scientific policy committee from 1953 to 1963. This enabled him to exert a powerful influence for the application of critical scientific thought to problems of nature conservation.

A number of academic and other honours came to Pearsall. He was honorary D.Sc. of both Durham (1958) and Birmingham (1963) universities and received the Linnean Society's gold medal for botany in 1963. He was made an honorary member of the British Ecological Society and the Society for Experimental Biology, and a foreign member of the Swedish Phytogeographical Society. He was a fellow of the Institute of Biology and its president in 1957–8.

Pearsall was of tall and slender but athletic build and, with his erect carriage and small close-clipped moustache, had something of the military in his aspect. He was blue-eyed, with fair hair and a pale skin that never tanned deeply despite the amount of time he spent in the open. He was never idle and always appeared vigorous and purposeful, most so, perhaps, when he was striding with obvious enjoyment across a moor or up a mountain, his companions trailing behind him. Those who met him for the first time were at once impressed by his wide knowledge and capacity for penetrating analysis, but they soon discovered his modesty and humanity and an endearing gaiety of spirit. He shared with his father a deep love of fly-fishing and a gift for sketching in pen-and-ink or water-colour. He became a scratch golfer at the age of seventeen.

In 1917 Pearsall married Marjory Stewart, second child of Robert Peter George Williamson, director of education, of Stoke-on-Trent. She was herself a first class honours graduate in botany of Manchester, where she was a fellow student of Pearsall's, and later lecturer in botany at Birmingham and then at Leeds. There were two sons, Alan William Harrison, now historian at the National Maritime Museum, Greenwich; and Ian Stewart, now head of the Fluid Mechanics Division at the National Engineering Laboratory, East Kilbride. In 1970 Dr Ian Pearsall won the Wolfe award for his outstanding contribution to the research of the Department of Trade and Industry on the development of the super-cavitation pump.

Pearsall died at his home in Morecambe 14 October 1964 of a brain tumour. His wife and sons survived him. There is a drawing by Delmar Banner (1961) reproduced in the Royal Society memoir listed below.

[*The Times*, 15 October 1964; A. R. Clapham in *Biographical Memoirs of Fellows of the Royal Society*, vol. xvii, 1971; private information; personal knowledge.]

A. R. CLAPHAM

PEAT, STANLEY (1902-1969), professor of chemistry in the University College of North Wales, Bangor, was born at South Shields, county Durham, 23 August 1902, the eldest in the family of two sons and one daughter of John Peat, mining engineer of East Boldon, and his wife, Ada Bradford. A serious illness in early childhood left him with a permanent curvature of the spine and delayed his formal schooling. An active and fertile brain, however, compensated for this physical handicap and enabled him, in 1915, to win a scholarship to Rutherford College, Newcastle. There he was taught by several dedicated science teachers, including the chemistry master, William Carr, whose love of chemistry fired Peat's imagination. In 1921 he won a State exhibition, an entrance exhibition, and an Earl Grey memorial scholarship to study at Armstrong College, Newcastle (now the university), where he chose to read chemistry, and thus came under the influence of Professor (Sir) W. N. Haworth [q.v.]. Peat graduated in 1924 with first class honours in chemistry, being awarded the Freire-Marreco medal and prize, and was invited to join Haworth's research school. At that time Haworth was carrying out fundamental studies on the structures of simple sugars, and Peat was soon involved in studies on the ring forms of glucose and the structure of maltose. When Haworth moved to the Mason chair of chemistry at Birmingham in 1925, he took with him an enthusiastic group of workers, including Peat as his personal assistant.

Awarded the Ph.D. in 1928, Peat was appointed lecturer in biochemistry in the medical school at Birmingham but he returned to the chemistry department six years later. This brief excursion into biochemistry awakened his interest in biochemical problems and was to influence much of his later research. During the next fourteen years, and in spite of the advent of the war, Peat collaborated with Haworth in a series of investigations on the chemistry of sugars and important polysaccharides such as starch, cellulose, and agar, which resulted in the publication of over forty original papers in, mainly, the *Journal of the Chemical Society*. He was awarded the D.Sc. and promoted to a readership in 1944.

The war, however, brought many changes. Peat carried out work for the Admiralty and, for a time, worked on uranium compounds as part of the project leading ultimately to the atom bomb, but he was never happy in this work. He also served on the cellulose and cordite panel of the Ministry of Supply, and on a committee which was seeking alternatives to Japanese agar for microbiological work. During 1940 he became interested in a series of papers by C. S. Haines, which described the synthesis of starch using a plant enzyme. Haworth and Peat secured a sample of this starch from Haines for examination, and from this initial study stemmed an interest in the biological synthesis and breakdown of starch which continued for the rest of Peat's life. In a series of papers, spanning seventeen years, he described the results of his investigations on starch which gained him world-wide recognition.

Elected a fellow of the Royal Society in 1948, he was appointed in the same year to the chair of chemistry at Bangor, where he quickly established a research school. With W. J. Whelan as his able collaborator, he began to publish widely on starch and a variety of other plant polysaccharides. In recognition of his work, the Chemical Society invited him to give the Hugo Müller lecture in 1959, but a serious illness prevented him from doing so.

In addition to his activities in research, Peat was a dedicated teacher, who took enormous pains over the teaching of organic chemistry to first-year students; he considered this the most important of the undergraduate courses. His clear and concise introduction to modern theories of chemical reactions was a revelation to generations of students. He also served in a wider sphere as dean of the faculty of science at Bangor, on the council and committees of the Chemical Society, and as a consultant to several research associations. From 1959 repeated illnesses prevented him from taking an active part in research, but he was always ready to give advice and encouragement to his colleagues until his death at Bangor 22 February 1969.

In 1939 he married Elsie Florence, younger daughter of Henry H. V. Barnes, dental surgeon of Edgbaston, Birmingham, and they had two daughters. The last years of his life were enriched by the arrival of grandchildren, from whose company he derived tremendous pleasure.

[E. L. Hirst and J. R. Turvey in *Biographical Memoirs of Fellows of the Royal Society*, vol. xvi, 1970; private information; personal knowledge.]

J. R. TURVEY

PENSON, DAME LILLIAN MARGERY (1896-1963), historian, was born in Islington

18 July 1896, the eldest daughter, but not the eldest child, of Arthur Austin Penson, wholesale dairy manager, and his wife, Lillian Alice Martha Brown. After private education she went to the university of London, first at Birkbeck, then at University College. In 1917 she graduated BA with a first in history and in 1921 she became one of the earliest Ph.D.s. She served as a junior administrative officer (1917-18) in the Ministry of National Service; then in 1918-19 worked in the War Trade Intelligence Department. She taught as a lecturer at Birkbeck College in 1921-30; and also part time (1923-5) at East London (later Queen Mary) College.

In 1930 she was appointed to the chair of modern history held at Bedford College for Women. There she had as colleagues, besides some distinguished men, some remarkable women, who helped to give the college a distinctive quality, marked by a high degree of civilization. Among these were Susan Stebbing [q.v.] and Edna Purdie, who became her trusted friends. She opposed the introduction of male undergraduates to Bedford College; a proposal agitated during her later years, but not fulfilled until 1965.

Under her leadership the department of history flourished. Her lectures were immensely enjoyed. They were as carefully prepared as if they had been ceremonial performances for distinguished occasions: polished, lucid, not overloaded with detail, imaginative, at times witty or humorous, beautifully balanced, and economically worded, reflecting deep insight into issues and personalities. For many years her seminar at the Institute of Historical Research was a Mecca for diplomatic historians. In classes and seminars she had little patience with the shiftless; but for the serious she had generosity, patience, and helpfulness. A common epithet of disapproval, uttered in a certain tone of voice, was 'glib'. Eccentric but intelligent undergraduates, who seemed unusually incapable of a reasonable degree of conformity, she was inclined to defend, calling them 'my funnies'.

Her first researches were in colonial history, and bore fruit in The Colonial Agents of the British West Indies (1924) and other publications. Her commitment to diplomatic history seems to have begun with her appointment in 1918 as an editor of the peace handbooks prepared for the Paris peace conference. From this she went on to assist G. P. Gooch and H. W. V. Temperley [qq.v.] on British Documents on the Origins of the War 1898-1914 (11 vols., 1926-38).

Temperley's influence on her was profound. He was for her what a historian should be. She stressed, as he did, the need for adequate linguistic equipment; the usefulness of knowing the folklores, literatures, and geography of the European countries; the need for careful study of private as well as public papers; and the value to the historian of some experience of affairs. With Temperley she produced Foundations of British Foreign Policy (1938) and A Century of Diplomatic Blue Books (1938). The planning of these projects and the business affairs connected with them provided excellent training for the administrator of later years. Had time allowed, she would have produced a magisterial work on Lord Salisbury's diplomacy. Papers in the Cambridge Historical Journal (1935) and in the Transactions of the Royal Historical Society (1943), and the Creighton lecture for 1960 (which by illness she could not deliver) give some idea of the directions the magnum opus would have taken.

Before war came in 1939 Lillian Penson was a person of importance in the university, not without hostile critics and anti-feminist opposition. Dean of the faculty of arts (1938-44), a member of the senate from 1940, in 1945 elected chairman of the academic council (a strategic position), and in 1946 a member of the court, she reached the peak of her career when in 1948 she became vice-chancellor, the first woman known to hold such an office. She had a unique knowledge of the university machine; she was clear-headed, generally tactful, and adept at conciliation, although some persons found her too trenchant for their liking. She was succeeded in 1951 by an old friend, H. Hale Bellot.

In two areas she took a special interest: the Fulbright scheme and colonial higher education. She was a founder-member of the United States Educational Commission in the United Kingdom (1948) and acting chairman in 1953 and 1954. She did more than any other British academic to secure the co-operation of British scholars in this excellent scheme, so rewarding to British and Americans alike. Three successive secretaries in London found her an effective helper and a warm-hearted friend.

The policy for higher education in the colonies, as worked out by the commission under Sir Cyril Asquith (later Lord Asquith of Bishopstone, q.v.) in 1943-5, of which she was a member, involved the establishment of colonial university colleges, brought into 'special relationship' with the university of London, whereby curricula and examinations were conducted jointly by university and colleges. This was intended as a means whereby good standards would be established, preparatory to the colleges becoming independent universities. While ready to adjust London rules to meet colonial circumstances, she resisted in this, as in other connections, 'liberal' pressures for relaxation of standards. She made numerous laborious journeys to the colleges. She had a particular devotion to Khartoum. She became in 1955 a member of the council of the college at Salisbury, Rhodesia. Her view of these developments she set forth, in historical perspective, in a Montague Burton lecture at Glasgow in 1954, *Educational Partnership in Africa and the West Indies*.

In 1951 she was appointed DBE. Cambridge in 1949, the year following the admission of women to degrees there, made her an honorary LLD, one of the first two women, after Queen Elizabeth, to be so honoured; the other was Dame Myra Hess [q.v.]. Oxford made her an honorary DCL in 1956, when the other recipient was ex-President Truman. Among the other seven honorary degrees which she received was the LLD of Southampton (1953) which had also enjoyed a 'special relationship' with London. In 1959 in recognition of what she had done for medical studies, the Royal College of Surgeons made her an honorary fellow. She served three terms as a member of the council of the Royal Historical Society and as a vice-president, and was honorary vice-president from 1959 until her death.

Of middle height, as a younger woman she was slim, of a light and brisk step, and with black hair of rich texture, carefully groomed. In later years, she was of heavier build, of heavier gait, and her hair touched with grey; her face fuller, of complexion somewhat more florid. Generally of kindly expression, she could, as she put it, 'look repressive'. Her eyes were singularly eloquent. She was not loquacious, but when she spoke, she spoke with authority. Early in her career she adopted, and maintained to the end, a professional costume of a two-piece dark suit, with white blouse, its front flounced, and over some thirty years of the same pattern. For social occasions, her dresses were of unobtrusive elegance. She held it important for herself and others to dress suitably to the occasion.

Marks of a puritanical upbringing were never effaced: a belief in work and duty, uneasiness with flippant talk about serious subjects, and integrity of a certain type. Moderately conservative in most ways, she hated the appeasement of the thirties, and admired Churchill. While many saw the public figure—*très autoritaire*, said a Frenchman—only a few saw the other Penson, who believed that the last thing to do with your dignity was to stand on it; the compassionate person given to doing good by stealth; an excellent cook, judge of wines, and raconteur; a connoisseur of detective fiction; fond of country walks and fishing; excellent as hostess or guest; and a good listener. After

two years in which she was gravely incapacitated, she died at Brighton 17 April 1963.

[Private information; personal knowledge.]

ROBERT GREAVES

PEPPIATT, SIR LESLIE ERNEST (1891–1968), solicitor, was born 7 November 1891 at West Hackney, the elder son of William Robert Peppiatt, a mercantile clerk, and his wife, Emily Elizabeth Giles. Until he was sixteen he was educated at Bancroft's School, Woodford, Essex, which he left to be articled to a solicitor. He studied for a time as an external student at London University but did not graduate. He was admitted a solicitor in July 1913 and therefore hardly had started in practice before war broke out in August 1914. He served throughout the war in the London Regiment, reached the rank of major, was twice mentioned in dispatches, and was awarded the Military Cross and bar in 1918. From 1921 to 1935 he was a full-time legal adviser to the British–American Tobacco Company in London. In 1935 he became a partner in the leading City firm of Freshfields, Leese & Munns, one of whose partners had for the past two hundred years in unbroken succession held the appointment of solicitor to the Bank of England. Sir William H. Leese who at the time held the appointment died in 1937. The Bank did not formally appoint a successor but Freshfields (as the firm again became known in 1945) continued to act as solicitors to the Bank. Peppiatt himself was the Bank's principal legal adviser from that time until he retired from practice in 1962. His brother, (Sir) Kenneth Oswald Peppiatt, had become chief cashier to the Bank in 1934. In 1940 Leslie Peppiatt was elected a member of the council of the Law Society, where he was a quiet success. In 1954 he was appointed a member of the disciplinary committee set up under the Solicitors Acts, and in 1958 he was elected president of the Law Society. His year of office was uneventful and at its end in 1959 he was knighted.

Dignified and handsome in appearance and always impeccably dressed, Peppiatt had considerable personal charm and a genuine interest in other people. He deliberately cultivated the character of a simple man not readily capable of understanding or indeed very interested in the technical and tortuous aspects of the issues with which he had to deal. When he spoke he did so in simple terms with a good deal of disarming wit, for he was a master of the 'throwaway line'. In fact he was a very shrewd solicitor who knew that his many important clients wanted him to identify for them what was achievable and not to impress them with a display of legalistic expertise. He was always for the 'broad view'. His presidential address to the Law Society in 1958 therefore did not pretend to any statements of high professional policy; he dealt mainly with the day-to-day problems of remuneration and competition which he rightly considered were of the most interest and importance to his audience of practising solicitors.

Being a kindly man he became intimately connected with the management of a number of important charities. Among them were the King George VI Memorial Fund, the 1930 Fund for the Benefit of Trained District Nurses, and the Solicitors Benevolent Association. He also believed strongly that solicitors did not play as important a role in public life as they should and deplored the criticism that those who did public work did it to attract professional business. He himself set a good example. Although in very busy practice he was from 1949 to 1955 chairman of the discipline committee of the Architects Registration Council; in 1960 he was chairman of the Departmental Committee of Betting on Horseracing; and he also served on the Departmental (Spens) Committee on the Remuneration of Medical Specialists and of Dental Practitioners (1947).

In 1927 Peppiatt married Cicely Mallyn, daughter of George Edward Howse, a company director. They had two sons, one of whom became a solicitor and a partner in Freshfields. Peppiatt died 15 November 1968 at Cleve Cottage, Wisborough Green, Sussex.

[*Law Society Gazette*, 1957-9; private information; personal knowledge.]   H. KIRK

PETHICK-LAWRENCE, FREDERICK WILLIAM, BARON PETHICK-LAWRENCE (1871-1961), social worker and politician, was born 28 December 1871 in London, the youngest of the family of two boys and three girls of Alfred Lawrence, carpenter, who had moved from Cornwall to London and founded a prosperous building firm, and his wife, Mary Elizabeth, daughter of Henry Ridge of Upper Clapton, Middlesex, and granddaughter of Robert Brook Aspland [q.v.], a well-known preacher. His father died when he was three and his mother brought him up as a Unitarian. He was educated at Eton (1885-91) and Trinity College, Cambridge, where he gained first classes in mathematics (part i, 1894) and natural sciences (part i, 1895). He became Smith's prizeman for mathematics (1896), Adam Smith prizeman for economics (1897), and president of the Union (Michaelmas, 1896). Trinity College elected him to a fellowship (1897-1903) but he decided against an academic career and left Cambridge on a world tour, visiting India, the Far East, and the United States.

At Cambridge, Lawrence had met Percy Alden, warden of Mansfield House university settlement in Canning Town, and a friend of William (later Lord) Beveridge [q.v.], and, on his return to London, he went there to work. He also studied law and was called to the bar by the Inner Temple in 1899, but, as he wrote in his autobiography, his social conscience was aroused, and his main interests were the social problems of working people in the East End. He became increasingly sympathetic to the cause of trade unionism. He was Dunkin lecturer at Manchester College, a private hall at Oxford, 1900-1. By the death of his elder brother in 1900 he became a man of property, and could follow almost any career he chose. His inclination was to enter Parliament and he was selected as Liberal-Unionist candidate for North Lambeth in 1901.

However, his attitude changed when he fell in love with a fellow social worker, Emmeline, daughter of Henry Pethick, of Weston-super-Mare. He knew her to be a rebel at heart, and unlikely to accept the attentions of a potential member of Parliament with traditional sympathies. This, together with his strong opposition to the Boer War, made him abandon his prospects at North Lambeth, and he and Emmeline were married in 1901. Lawrence then prefixed his wife's name to his own. Husband and wife now combined their efforts to ameliorate the conditions of those who lived in the East End. To further the cause of the nascent Labour Party Pethick-Lawrence purchased the *Echo*, an evening halfpenny newspaper, and in 1902 became its editor when Percy Alden resigned. J. Ramsay MacDonald was one of his contributors. In spite of increasing the circulation of the paper Pethick-Lawrence could not make it pay and in 1905 he decided to cease publication.

The same year saw the landslide victory of Campbell-Bannerman and the election to Parliament of several representatives of the Labour Party. Pethick-Lawrence thought the millennium was at hand. But within a few months he had become a determined opponent of the Liberal Government. He was asked to defend three suffragettes accused of disorderly conduct, and his sympathy for them led him to take up the cause of women's suffrage with all the ardour he had previously devoted to the working people of the East End. In 1907 he and his wife became joint editors of *Votes for Women*, and proceeded to wage unceasing battle on behalf of the Women's Social and Political Union, founded a few years earlier by Emmeline Pankhurst and her daughter, (Dame) Christabel [qq.v.], who now became close allies of the Pethick-Lawrences.

For the next six years Pethick-Lawrence was absorbed in the struggle to overcome the opposition of the Liberal Government to the grant to women of the right to vote in parliamentary elections. In October 1906 his wife, with others, had caused a disturbance in the House of Commons. She was arrested, and after refusing to be bound over to keep the peace, was sentenced to two months' imprisonment. This first taste of gaol was a claustrophobic experience which her husband feared would cause her a nervous breakdown. With the aid of her father, he persuaded her to comply with the magistrates' order and secured her release.

In 1909 Emmeline was again sent to prison. She was now inured to imprisonment. Her husband wrote that, to his relief, she served this two months' sentence 'with serenity'. In 1912, Pethick-Lawrence himself, together with his wife and Emmeline Pankhurst, was convicted of conspiracy to incite members of the WSPU to cause damage in the West End of London. They were convicted, and despite the jury's recommendation of clemency, they were sentenced to nine months' imprisonment. Pethick-Lawrence and Mrs Pankhurst were ordered to pay the costs of the trial. All three went on hunger strike. The Pethick-Lawrences were forcibly fed, but, after five weeks, were released. As Pethick-Lawrence refused to pay the costs, he was declared bankrupt. This declaration was rescinded a year later.

The Pethick-Lawrences now decided that a more moderate policy should be pursued in the crusade for women's suffrage. Mrs Pankhurst did not agree, and uncompromisingly expelled them from the WSPU. The outbreak of the war of 1914–18 put a new complexion on the struggle. In making munitions and other essential work, for which manpower was depleted by the demands of the armed forces, women took over a variety of jobs previously reserved for men. In 1915 Lloyd George recognized the political advantage to himself of women when he used a WSPU demonstration to overcome trade-union resistance to the use of unskilled women workers. When the war ended, the right to vote, for which the suffragettes had borne so many indignities, was granted without further argument because it was no longer a political danger, and indeed might be a positive benefit, to those in power since 1916, the Coalition Government under Lloyd George.

Ironically the crusade, to which Pethick-Lawrence had devoted some of the best years of his life, was successful, at last, because of events which occurred in a war with which he totally disagreed. He had been a convinced pacifist from the time of the Boer War. When he was called up for military service, he declared himself a conscientious objector, and was drafted to work on the land. In 1917 he decided to seek the opportunity of pressing his views in Parliament. In a by-election he stood for South Aberdeen as a 'peace by negotiation' candidate and was inevitably defeated. He failed again in 1922 at South Islington, but in 1923 he achieved his ambition, and became a Labour member of Parliament, after defeating (Sir) Winston Churchill in a bitterly contested election at West Leicester.

His maiden speech advocated pensions for widowed mothers. He also spoke in favour of a capital levy. But his speeches in the House were not impressive. He was re-elected for West Leicester in 1924. When, in 1925, Churchill, as chancellor of the Exchequer, announced the return to the gold standard, Pethick-Lawrence opposed this measure, although some of his Labour colleagues were in favour of the move. In 1929 the Labour Party won a narrow victory over the Conservatives, and Ramsay MacDonald became prime minister. He appointed Philip (later Viscount) Snowden [q.v.] as chancellor of the Exchequer and Pethick-Lawrence as financial secretary to the Treasury. The latter was not entirely successful in that post. Some members of the House considered him too ready to evade responsibility by referring problems to the chancellor. When Ramsay MacDonald decided to form a 'national' Government in 1931, Pethick-Lawrence and the other junior ministers were dismissed. Sounded about his willingness to serve in the new administration, Pethick-Lawrence had replied that he could not agree with the financial policy being pursued. In the 1931 general election he was defeated.

The following year he visited Russia. Although he saw much to admire in the Soviet system, he decided that he had no wish to see Russian institutions transplanted to Britain.

Pethick-Lawrence was re-elected to Parliament in 1935, for the East Edinburgh division. In the years leading up to the war of 1939–45 he viewed with dismay the growing power of Nazi Germany, but followed the normal party line regarding rearmament and preparation for war. In 1937 he became a privy councillor.

Throughout the war he sat on the Labour front bench, an experienced and much respected member of the party. His youthful enthusiasm had mellowed, and, on occasions in his later years in the House, he clashed with Aneurin Bevan [q.v.], who once referred to him there as 'a crusted old Tory'. In 1942 his autobiography, *Fate Has Been Kind*, was published.

When C. R. (later Earl) Attlee came to power in 1945 he appointed Pethick-Lawrence, who had gained experience in the 1931 India Round Table Conference, secretary of state for India and Burma, and a barony was conferred on him. In 1926 he and his wife had celebrated their silver wedding by a visit to India. They had many Indian friends and were keenly interested in the aspirations of the Indian political leaders. He wholeheartedly agreed with the policy of granting independence to India and Burma.

In 1946 the Government decided to send a Cabinet mission to Delhi, and Pethick-Lawrence led this mission, accompanied by (Sir) (Richard) Stafford Cripps, president of the Board of Trade, and A. V. Alexander (later Earl Alexander of Hillsborough, first lord of the Admiralty [qq.v.]. Its purpose was to convince the Indian leaders that the British people were sincere in offering independence to India and to attempt to obtain the agreement of Congress and the Muslim League to some compromise that could preserve the unity of the country. Throughout the hot weather in Delhi the mission, together with the viceroy, Lord Wavell, conferred interminably with Nehru, Jinnah [qq.v.], and other Indian politicians in the hope of securing agreement to a form of unitary constitution. While Cripps prepared draft after draft of constitutional schemes, Pethick-Lawrence listened patiently to the views of any Indian politician who sought his company. He wrote to his wife: 'People start coming to interview me at 7 a.m. and the last doesn't leave much before midnight. And nothing whatever comes of it! And the heat is stifling.' He was nearly seventy-five.

On returning to London, Pethick-Lawrence admitted in the House of Lords that agreement could not be reached. The chasm between the aims of Congress and those of the Muslim League could not be bridged. He claimed that the mission had been entirely successful in convincing the Indian leaders, for the first time, that Britain was in earnest in offering India independence. The turbulent political situation in India, exacerbated by the intransigence of the two great Indian parties, continued to deteriorate, and on 20 February 1947 Pethick-Lawrence announced Britain's intention, in response to the advice of the viceroy, to effect the transference of power to Indian hands by a date not later than June 1948. The decision was also taken to replace Lord Wavell by Lord Mountbatten of Burma. In April 1947 Pethick-Lawrence, exhausted by the strenuous months of frustrated effort, resigned his office as secretary of state, and retired to his home at Peaslake in Surrey. He still attended the House of Lords and, in the discussions of the legislation granting independence to India and Burma, he continued to support the Government.

His wife, who was the author of *My Part in a Changing World* (1938), died in 1954.

The marriage was childless. Three years later, in 1957, Pethick-Lawrence married Helen Millar, widow of Duncan McCombie and daughter of Sir John George Craggs, chartered accountant. They had been friends for over forty years since the time when Helen herself had been a militant suffragette.

Pethick-Lawrence died in London, 10 September 1961, whereupon the barony became extinct.

Besides his autobiography, he wrote books and pamphlets on mathematics, economics, and women's suffrage. In the National Portrait Gallery are a portrait by Henry Coller (1933) and a carved wooden head by Albin Moroder (1949). There is also a portrait by John Baker in the Pethick-Lawrence House (a local community centre) at Dorking.

[*The Times*, 12 September 1961; *Annual Register*; F. W. Pethick-Lawrence, *Fate Has Been Kind*, 1942 (autobiography); Vera Brittain, *Pethick-Lawrence; a Portrait*, 1963; Roger Fulford, *Votes for Women*, 1957; Hugh Tinker, *Experiment with Freedom*, 1967; *Wavell: The Viceroy's Journal*, ed. Penderel Moon, 1973; India Office records.]

HAROLD OXBURY

PETRIE, SIR DAVID (1879–1961), public servant, was born at Inveravon 9 September 1879, the second son of Thomas Petrie, master millwright, of Inveravon, Banffshire, and his wife, Jane Allan.

After graduating MA at Aberdeen University (1900), Petrie entered the Indian Police in December 1900 and was posted to the Punjab. His early service included a five-year secondment to the Samana Rifles in the North-West Frontier Province. In 1909 he became assistant to the deputy inspector-general, Punjab CID and, in 1911, assistant director with the Central Criminal Intelligence Department of the Government of India. In the same year he won the gold medal of the United Service Institution of India for an essay on 'The maintenance of law and order in India considered in relation to the mutual co-operation of the civil and military power in the country'.

In December 1912 a bomb was thrown at the viceroy and Petrie played a leading part in the ensuing investigation. He remained on special duty investigating subversion and terrorism throughout the war of 1914–18. In January 1915 this took him to the Far East where he met his wife.

During 1921–2 Petrie was on the staff first of the Duke of Connaught, and later of the Prince of Wales, during their Indian tours. As a member of the Public Services Commission, India, 1931–2, and its chairman, 1932–6, he helped to secure concessions which persuaded some subsequently distinguished police officers to pursue careers which they might otherwise have terminated prematurely.

In 1924 Petrie became director of the Intelligence Bureau of the Home Department of the Government of India (as the Central Criminal Intelligence Department came to be called), the first Indian police officer to hold this post. He filled it with great distinction in very troubled times, when law and order were threatened not only by extreme nationalist terrorism but also by Communist subversion. On leaving the Bureau in 1931 he was appointed first a member, and then, in 1932, chairman, of the Indian Public Services Commission. He also became chairman of the Indian Red Cross Society and St. John Ambulance Association and was appointed a Knight of Grace of the Order of St. John of Jerusalem in 1933. Honours had accumulated steadily—the King's Police medal (1914), CIE (1915), OBE (1918), CBE (1919), CVO (1922), and a knighthood (1929).

Petrie retired in 1936. In 1937-8 he visited Palestine with another distinguished retired police officer, Sir Charles Tegart, whose notice he later wrote for this Dictionary, to advise on police organization and counter-terrorism. In 1939, with war threatening, he hoped to find employment with one of the professional intelligence services, but it was not until May 1940 that he was commissioned in the Intelligence Corps and posted to Cairo. He was recalled at the end of November to report to the lord president of the Council, Sir John Anderson (later Viscount Waverley, q.v.), on the organization of MI5 (the Security Service, concerned with the defence of the realm against espionage, sabotage, and subversion), then at the nadir of its fortunes. Precisely how the fortunate choice of Petrie for this task came to be made is uncertain. It is believed that he was first suggested by a former Indian Police officer. He would have been known at least by reputation to Sir John Anderson, who had been governor of Bengal from 1932 to 1937, and he was personally known to Sir S. Findlater Stewart [q.v.], formerly permanent under-secretary at the India Office, who held a key position on the Home Front. In March 1941 Petrie was appointed head of MI5 to carry out his own recommendations and held the newly created post of director-general for the next five years.

The main problems confronting him on taking office were organization and morale. He introduced major changes designed to create a machine capable of bearing the manifold strains of war. These changes were immediately successful. Morale was at a low ebb. Now the atmosphere changed dramatically, and it rose rapidly to the very high level which it maintained for the rest of the war. There was a wealth of talent in MI5 (much, but by no means all of it, recruited during the war), and with sound organization and strong leadership MI5 played a distinguished part in the defeat of Germany's intelligence services which was as complete as that suffered by her armed forces.

Petrie brought to MI5 what it most needed—leadership and administrative ability. But he also had a thorough grasp of the techniques of the work. He was very industrious and did nearly all his own drafting. He always made himself perfectly clear, but was occasionally pompous and inclined to overlook the virtues of brevity and tact in his external correspondence. Thanks to his Indian experience, he understood bureaucracy. He briefed himself with great care for meetings, where he generally spoke little but to the point. Aided by his impressive bearing and distinguished record, he left his comparatively few Whitehall contacts in no doubt that he was vastly experienced and totally reliable, and could safely be trusted with the conduct of a highly secret organization which was still very much on the periphery of government. His relations with Lord Swinton and Alfred Duff Cooper (later Viscount Norwich, q.v.), who were successively *in loco parentis* to MI5, were good, but he made no attempt to cultivate influential people and described himself as a bad publicity merchant for the service.

Petrie was always authoritative and occasionally irascible, but he was also sensitive to the feelings of others. The loyal support which he invariably gave his subordinates won him much respect. With very few exceptions his relations with them were rather formal; as was the custom of his generation, he called even those closest to him by their surnames. Nevertheless, he enjoyed convivial occasions at which he more than held his own. He was a man of perfect integrity and somewhat puritanical morality, a proud Scotsman, a lover of the countryside, and a skilful fisherman.

Petrie finally retired in 1946. He had been appointed KCMG in 1945 and after the war became a commander of the US Legion of Merit and of the Order of Orange Nassau with swords, and was awarded class iii of the Czechoslovak Order of the White Lion.

He married in 1920 Edris Naida (died 1945), daughter of W. Henry Elliston Warrall, a captain in mercantile marine; they had no children. Petrie died at Sidmouth 7 August 1961.

[*The Times*, 8 August 1961; private information; personal knowledge.]

ANTHONY SIMKINS

PETTER, (WILLIAM) EDWARD (WILLOUGHBY) (1908–1968), aircraft designer, was born at Highgate, London, 8 August 1908, the eldest in the family of three sons and one daughter of (Sir) Ernest Willoughby Petter, co-founder and chairman of Petters Ltd., oil engine and aircraft manufacturers of Yeovil, and his wife, Angela Emma, daughter of Henry Petter of Calcutta. His father and mother were related through a mutual great-grandfather.

Admitted to Marlborough College in 1921, 'Teddy' Petter proved an outstanding scholar and preferred literary pursuits and countryside excursions to games. Proceeding to Gonville and Caius College, Cambridge, he gained the Solomons scholarship for 1928–9, and achieved a first class in the mechanical sciences tripos in 1929, tying for the John Bernard Seely prize in aeronautics. By then he had abandoned an earlier intention of joining the Petter oil engine organization at Yeovil, and on leaving Cambridge became a postgraduate apprentice of the Petter subsidiary, Westland Aircraft Works, diligently labouring at the bench in every department. He was a sensitive young man, tall and aesthetic in appearance, and proved of receptive and analytical mind. After two years in the shops he spent six months in the drawing office, but proved a poor draughtsman although sound on technology and a questioner of established ideas. In the spring of 1932 he became personal assistant to the managing director, Robert Bruce, a man of unique technical and business ability. In that year Petter married Claude Marguerite Juliette, daughter of Louis Munier of Geneva, League of Nations official.

In 1935 Bruce retired. Westland was reconstituted as a limited company, with Sir Ernest Petter as chairman, and 'Teddy' Petter was appointed technical director. The staff were apprehensive of his youth and inexperience, and neither the Air Ministry nor the Royal Air Force showed confidence in his talent. Nevertheless, (Sir) Roy Fedden, the well-known designer of Bristol aero-engines, backed by the Air Ministry technical officer at Westland, eventually ensured an invitation to submit a project for a radial-engined fighter, although no contract followed. However, the engineering of this monoplane was sufficiently impressive for Petter to be included among those tendering for an army co-operation two-seater to replace the Hawker Hectors which Westland were currently building. This resulted in the Lysander, an ingenious high-wing monoplane which was designed, built, and flown in the record time of a year, and of which 1,368 were ultimately produced.

Meanwhile Petter had designed a twin-engined light transport which did not proceed beyond the mock-up stage, and had also linked with a French autogiro designer, Lepère, with whom he devised the CL20, a small two-seater rotary-wing machine which Westland built. They commenced six more but abandoned production because of manufacturing demand for Lysanders.

The Whirlwind twin-engined single-seat fighter monoplane with four nose cannons was Petter's next accepted design. The first of these flew in October 1938, three months after the shipbuilding firm of John Brown Ltd. obtained controlling interest in Westland, and subsequently Associated Electrical Industries acquired the Petter holding. Although initial problems with the Whirlwind had to be overcome, orders for 177 followed, the first of which were received by the Royal Air Force in July 1940. That month Petter submitted designs for the twin-engined Welkin—the biggest single-seat fighter till then built—for which he devised an armoured and pressurized cabin for stratospheric operations. Its first flight was in November 1942, but, although 100 were built, changed tactics made the Welkins unnecessary. However, their pressurization system led to the post-war establishment of Westland's Normalair business.

In 1944 a medium bomber with twin turbojets unconventionally located within the fuselage and a propeller-turbine torpedo-plane fighter next engaged Petter's attention. But increasingly he had been attempting to obtain over-all responsibility for manufacture as well as directing the technical department, and this led to conflict with the company board, which resulted in his abrupt resignation. He was aware, through Air Ministry contacts, that the English Electrical Company, which had re-entered the aircraft industry with big bomber contracts just before the war, was initiating a design department and required a chief engineer. He successfully applied, and, because Westland had obtained a contract for the naval fighter, that company permitted him to retain the bomber design. This became the starting point for the English Electrical Company's Canberra, a world success, which first flew in May 1949. 1,329 were built in Britain, Australia, and the United States in post-war years.

Meanwhile Petter was designing a remarkable supersonic fighter, of which a low-speed version was built by Short Brothers Ltd., with which to explore the optimum extent of its acute sweepback. This led to the final design of the Lightning, which had to be completed by F. W. Page because Petter had again become involved in increasingly difficult relations with the manufacturing side and resigned in 1950 to join Folland Aircraft Ltd., a relatively small sub-contractor company, as managing director and chief engineer. These were the positions to which he had aspired at Westland and the English Electrical Company.

Of the several projects which he envisaged in 1951, Petter now concentrated on a private venture low-cost miniature single-seat fighter, the Gnat, but development of its intended Bristol turbo-jet engine was abandoned by the Ministry of Supply. Petter therefore revised his design as the Midge with a smaller engine. This proved an outstanding success when flown in August 1954, with resulting Ministry of Aviation interest and construction of the almost identical Gnat fitted with a more powerful Orpheus engine and flown in July 1955. 300 of these aeroplanes were produced for the Royal Air Force and overseas governments. In August 1959 a two-seater trainer version was flown and 115 were ordered, but at that juncture Folland Aircraft Ltd. was taken over by the Hawker Siddeley Group. Since Petter did not relish again working with a large organization he resigned, although nominally remaining consultant. This brilliant designer then retired to Switzerland 'in search of a life of contemplation' with his wife and three daughters. To his distress, at the age of forty his wife had fallen victim to Parkinson's disease and, after trying many specialists, he now turned to faith-healing. With their youngest daughter, Jenni, they joined a small Swiss religious community of this nature which accepted men, women, and children, later transferring to the same order in France. There he died in Beruges 1 May 1968, his wife surviving him until 26 September 1975.

Petter became a student of the Royal Aeronautical Society in February 1931, an associate fellow in September 1935, and was elected fellow in March 1944. In January of that year, in conjunction with (Sir) Eric Mensforth, he presented a paper entitled 'Aspects of the design and production of airframes with particular reference to their co-ordination and to the reduction of the development period'. He was awarded the society's silver medal in 1950, and served on the council and medals and awards committee from 1951 to 1954. He was made a CBE in 1951 for services to aviation. In later years his hobby was gardening.

[Private information; personal knowledge.]

H. J. PENROSE

PEULEVÉ, HENRI LEONARD THOMAS (HARRY) (1916-1963), British agent in enemy-occupied France, the only son of Leonard Otho Peulevé and his wife, Eva Juliet Dallison, both of British nationality, was born 29 January 1916 at Worthing, where his mother and sister were temporarily in refuge from the

German invasion of France. The family home was in Paris where Leonard Peulevé represented a firm of British seedsmen until the outbreak of war in 1914 when he joined the British Army. At the time of his son's birth he was a staff sergeant-major in the Army Service Corps. When the fighting in France became stabilized as trench warfare, his wife returned with the two children, moving from one place to another as her husband's unit was posted from this sector to that.

The Peulevé agency in France was not revived after the war and the family's wanderings continued while Peulevé sought to make a living, shuttling back and forth between France and England, with a period in Algiers where for a time he was British vice-consul. Thus Harry Peulevé's upbringing was as unsettled as his education was varied. His many schools included a nuns' kindergarten in Algiers, the Shakespeare School at Stratford-upon-Avon, Rye Grammar School, private schools and tutors in England and France, and finally a technical college in London where he took courses in telegraphy and wireless which led him to his first job; technical assistant in the Baird Television Company. From this he went on to the British Broadcasting Corporation in the early days of television, became a cameraman, and was so employed at the outbreak of war in 1939 when he joined the army.

Peulevé was commissioned in the Royal Army Ordnance Corps, worked on the first radar equipment, and later transferred with the rank of captain to the Royal Electrical and Mechanical Engineers, whence in 1942, as one of the earliest volunteers, he was seconded to Special Operations Executive, the paramilitary body created by the British joint chiefs of staff to organize and conduct clandestine warfare in enemy-occupied territories. Peulevé could not have been better fitted for such a task: he was bilingual and could pass as a Frenchman in France; his loyalties to that country and to Britain were equal, indivisible, and dedicated; he had an ingrained ability to make the best, even to take advantage, of the unpredictable; and he was already a specialist in wireless communication as both technician and operator. As though these qualifications were insufficient, nature had provided him with a well-built body, broad-shouldered and suggestive of considerable physical strength. Large grey-green eyes which could on occasion compel without frightening were allied with a persuasiveness remarkable in that it was always muted and made acceptable by his charm of personality. These attributes came together in developing his powers of leadership in circumstances where difference and independence in the men he commanded in the field were uncontained by the disciplines of military training. A final gift stood him in great stead in outwitting and escaping his enemies: he was able to 'withdraw' mentally, to make his mind still in the presence of those he did not want to notice him—a surer disguise than any false beard or dark glasses.

After training in a secret agent's special skills by SOE Peulevé parachuted into the Pyrenees area on the night of 30 July 1942, but, by the pilot's error, he was too low for safe landing and broke a leg. He escaped across the mountains on crutches into Spain where he was imprisoned; he got away and reached England in very poor physical condition. After recuperating he volunteered to try again. In September 1943 he was landed safely by light aircraft and established himself in the Corrèze area and extended his influence to the northern Dordogne, training and arming a large group of resistance fighters which in the course of the months reached some 3,000 men whom he led in extensive sabotage operations, on occasions joining battle in running fights with German occupation troops and inflicting considerable casualties. He acted throughout as his own radio operator in maintaining contact with SOE in London, organizing regular air-drops of supplies of arms and equipment for his increasing forces, as well as agents to assist him.

Despite the Gestapo's determined efforts to find and capture him, Peulevé evaded them until by a stroke of bad luck he was erroneously denounced as a black marketeer and arrested while operating his radio set, on 21 March 1944. Interrogated under torture he refused to talk, and the enemy never discovered who he was and the important part he had played in the clandestine war. Imprisoned in solitary confinement at Fresne for almost a year, he attempted escape, was shot and wounded in the thigh, and, since he was refused medical treatment, himself removed the bullet with the aid of a spoon. Eventually he was taken to Buchenwald where, on the eve of his execution, he was chosen by F. F. E. Yeo-Thomas [q.v.] as one of the two agents who with himself changed identities with Frenchmen dying of typhus. As one of the prison's forced labour group Peulevé was more easily able to escape (11 April 1945); but he was recaptured almost within sight of an advancing American unit by two Belgian SS. He persuaded the two men of the danger of being captured in uniform, suggested they undress, and while they were doing so seized one of their pistols and made them his prisoners, delivering them to the Americans. He was appointed to the DSO, made a chevalier of the Legion of Honour, and received the MC and croix de guerre.

After the war Peulevé worked for the Shell Oil Company in several European countries, Egypt, and Tunis. In 1952 he married Marie-Louise John, a Danish woman, by whom he had a son and a daughter. He died in Seville of a heart attack 18 March 1963.

[*The Times*, 25 March 1963; M. R. D. Foot (Official History), *S.O.E. in France*, 2nd impression, with amendments, 1968; M. R. D. Foot, *Six Faces of Courage*, 1978; private information; personal knowledge.]

SELWYN JEPSON

PHILLIPS, MORGAN WALTER (1902-1963), Labour Party organizer, was born 18 June 1902 at Aberdare, Glamorgan, the eldest son in the family of six children of William Phillips, a coal-miner, and his wife, Sophia Alberta Jones. The young Phillips attended Bargoed elementary school until he was twelve, and then began working in the local pits. He became an active trade-unionist and was chairman of the Bargoed Steam Coal Lodge from 1924 to 1926. He was also politically involved and between 1923 and 1925 was secretary of the Bargoed Labour Party.

Morgan Phillips grew up in a South Wales mining community in a period when industrial and political militancy were at their most lively. He was much influenced by the tradition which in 1912 produced *The Miners' Next Step*, and in the year of the general strike he won a South Wales Miners' Federation scholarship to the 'marxisant' Central Labour College in London. When his two-year course ended, Phillips chose to remain in London rather than return to almost certain unemployment in Aberdare. He became secretary and agent to the West Fulham Labour Party from 1928 to 1930 and he was to remain associated with the borough of Fulham throughout the 1930s. In the early years of the decade he was for a short time on the staff of the National Council of Labour Colleges, and then in 1934 he became Labour Party agent for Whitechapel. Between 1934 and 1937 he was also a member of the Fulham Borough Council and became chairman of its finance committee.

Until this time Phillips's career had been typical of the general run of Labour Party local organizers. His efficiency and competence were, however, beginning to be recognized beyond the boundaries of the London Labour Party, and in 1937 he joined the headquarters staff of the Labour Party at Transport House as propaganda officer. When war broke out in September 1939 he served for a short time in the Ministry of Information; then he became party organizer for the Eastern Counties 1940-1, and in the latter year he returned to head office in charge of the research department: a position which was to become increasingly important as post-war plans came under urgent discussion. In 1944 he was selected by the national executive committee of the Labour Party to succeed J. S. Middleton [q.v.] as national secretary. He faced serious competition for the job, most notably from George R. (later Lord) Shepherd [q.v.], the national agent, Reg Wallis, Lancashire regional organizer, and Maurice Webb, the youth officer. E. Hugh (later Lord) Dalton [q.v.], who was on the selection committee, noted in his memoirs that Phillips's record at Transport House as secretary to the policy committee had been impressive, and that his ability to guide a discussion and state a case in lucid and persuasive terms was well proven. In the selection committee, Phillips had a majority of two votes over Maurice Webb.

Phillips remained national secretary for seventeen years. By the time he was elected, his own political views had moderated considerably from those of his youth, and in the 1950s he was to oppose vigorously the Left groupings within the party, especially the Bevanites. He backed Hugh Gaitskell [q.v.] for leadership during the bitter controversies of these years although he and Gaitskell never seem to have been close personally. Immediately after his appointment in 1944 his central concern was the working efficiency of the Labour organization in the country for the post-war election. Phillips's ability to infuse new energies into political organizations was never better illustrated, and the part which he played in the 1945 victory was widely appreciated. He was a member of the 1945 campaign committee, with H. S. Morrison (later Lord Morrison of Lambeth), C. R. (later Earl) Attlee, Dalton, and Arthur Greenwood [qq.v.], but as regards policy he was much less important at this time than Morrison, who was chairman. In the general elections of 1950 and 1951 his political influence was greater; indeed Herbert Morrison always believed that Phillips, resentful of Morrison's acknowledged part in the 1945 election, contrived to limit and curtail Morrison's place and role in the future. Certainly by the time of the 1955 general election Phillips was in a strong position, and the election campaign was largely run by him from Transport House. The political leadership apparently never or rarely met to discuss strategy; but the poor showing of Labour at the polls led to criticism of Phillips himself.

During this decade Phillips was involved in three main areas of political work. The first, and most important, was the unity of the party which Phillips was convinced should develop around the moderate platform favoured by Gaitskell. Phillips was against a commitment to large-scale nationalization; he favoured the acceptance of German rearmament; and he was strongly opposed to the campaign for nuclear disarmament at the end of the decade. The second concern was the rebuilding of the Labour Party's Youth Section, a matter to which he had referred in his first address as general secretary to the 1944 annual conference. To the 1950 annual conference he explained the new constitution and organization of the Youth League, and he urged the whole party to involve themselves in their youth movement. It remained a minor but troublesome issue for the leadership.

His third notable interest was with the international movement, and he played a leading part in the re-creation of the Socialist International. He presided over several conferences which preceded the establishment of the International in 1948, and was its chairman from that date until 1957. On behalf of both the International and the British Labour Party Phillips travelled widely, including a visit to Moscow and China with an official Labour Party delegation which included Attlee and Edith (later Baroness) Summerskill (August 1954). His last series of visits before he became ill in 1960 were to Central and South America on behalf of the International.

The general election of 1959 took place at a time when Phillips's reputation within the Labour Party was reviving, and although he had no central part in policy-making during the election campaign, his daily press conferences were widely appreciated. He had always been an excellent conductor of meetings with the press, where his qualities of conciseness and well-ordered answers found much favour. Early in 1960 his status within the party was raised from secretary to general secretary, and in the same year he published *Labour in the Sixties*, an influential pamphlet which achieved a wide circulation and evoked intense discussion.

He had begun to think seriously again about a parliamentary career (he had been parliamentary candidate for Central Nottingham in 1931 but withdrew before the general election), and he made several efforts to obtain a nomination. What finally settled the matter was a serious heart attack in August 1960, from which he never fully recovered. He resigned from the general secretaryship in December 1961, and died in a London hospital 15 January 1963, being survived by his wife and their son and daughter. He was buried at Fulham cemetery, and on 12 February a memorial service was held in the Kingsway Hall, at which the Revd Donald (later Lord) Soper officiated and the address was given by James Griffiths, MP. His wife, Norah Mary, whom he had married in 1930, was created a life peer in 1964. She was the daughter of William Charles Lusher, a postman. Phillips's daughter, Gwyneth P. Dunwoody, was Labour MP for Exeter from 1966 to 1970 and for Crewe from 1974 to 1979.

[Michael Foot, *Aneurin Bevan, 1945–1960*, 1973; Bernard Donoughue and G. W. Jones, *Herbert Morrison*, 1973; private information.]   JOHN SAVILLE

PICKLES, WILLIAM NORMAN (1885–1969), general practitioner and epidemiologist, was born 6 March 1885 in Camp Road, Leeds, where his father was in general practice. He was the second of the six sons, of whom five qualified as doctors, of John Jagger Pickles and his wife, Lucy Dobson. Pickles went to Leeds Grammar School and afterwards studied medicine at the medical school of the then Yorkshire College and at the Leeds General Infirmary, where he qualified as a licentiate of the Society of Apothecaries in 1909. After serving as resident obstetric officer at the Infirmary, he began a series of temporary jobs in general practice. In 1910 he graduated MB, BS London, after two failures in the final examination. He proceeded MD in 1918. His first visit to Wensleydale was as a *locum tenens* for Dr Hime of Aysgarth in 1912. After serving as a ship's doctor on a voyage to Calcutta, he returned to Aysgarth later that year as second assistant to Dr Hime. In 1913 he and the other assistant, Dean Dunbar, an old friend from his student days, were able to purchase the practice. Dunbar died in 1934, but Pickles remained in practice in Wensleydale until he retired in 1964, interrupted only by the war of 1914–18 during which he served in the Royal Naval Volunteer Reserve as a surgeon-lieutenant.

'Will Pickles of Wensleydale' achieved fame during his lifetime as the embodiment of the ideal general practitioner or country doctor. He achieved this not by his outstanding intellect, but because of his warm humanity and deep interest in his patients, most of whom were visited in their own homes; surgeries were of little importance. In introducing one of his lectures Pickles said: 'And as I watched the evening train creeping up the valley with its pauses at our three stations, a quaint thought came into my head and it was that there was hardly a man, woman or child in all those villages of whom I did not know the Christian name and with whom I was not on terms of intimate friendship. My wife and I say that we know most of the dogs and, indeed, some of the cats.'

When he was forty-one, Pickles read *The Principles of Diagnosis and Treatment in Heart Affections* by Sir James Mackenzie [q.v.] who had made many important contributions to medical knowledge from his general practice

in Burnley. His example fired Pickles. In 1929 an epidemic of catarrhal jaundice broke out in Wensleydale, affecting 250 people out of the total population of 5,700. Pickles was able to trace the whole epidemic to a girl whom he had seen in bed on the morning of a village fête and who he never dreamed would be able to get up that day. In this enclosed community Pickles was able to trace time and again 'the short and only possible contact', and to establish the incubation period as 26 to 35 days. This was a notable contribution, for it not only established the infective nature of the disease, but also its surprisingly long incubation period. An account of the epidemic in the *British Medical Journal* (24 May 1930) received scant notice at first. Two years later he published in the *Lancet* (2 July 1932) the records of an outbreak of Sonne dysentery; and in the next year he recorded (*British Medical Journal*, 4 November 1933) for the first time in Great Britain an epidemic of myalgia, or Bornholm disease, later known to be an infection with the Cox-Sacchie virus.

In 1935 Pickles described some of his work to the Royal Society of Medicine. After this meeting, a leading article in the *British Medical Journal* stated, 'It may mark the beginning of a new era in epidemiology'. Major Greenwood, the outstanding epidemiologist of the time, suggested that he should write a book on his observations, which was published in 1939 as *Epidemiology in Country Practice*. This became a medical classic, and established Pickles's reputation. It also showed how a country practice could be a field laboratory with unique opportunities for epidemiologists.

Pickles had now become famous. He was Milroy lecturer at the Royal College of Physicians, London (1942), and Cutter lecturer at Harvard (1948). In 1939 he was elected a member of the Royal College of Physicians and in 1963 a fellow, having in the meantime been awarded the Bisset Hawkins medal (1953). In 1946 he shared the Stewart prize of the British Medical Association with Major Greenwood and in 1955 he was elected an honorary fellow of the Royal College of Physicians of Edinburgh and was awarded the first James Mackenzie medal. He received an honorary D.Sc. from Leeds in 1950. In 1953 he was elected the first president of the College of General Practitioners, holding office for three years, during which period the college was given its royal charter. In 1957 he was appointed CBE. In 1965 he became an honorary fellow of the Royal Society of Medicine and an honorary vice-president of the British Medical Association.

In 1917 Pickles married Gertrude Adelaide, daughter of Harry Tunstill, a wealthy mill owner from Burnley who had a holiday house in Wensleydale. They had one daughter. Pickles died in hospital in North Allerton 2 March 1969 and was buried in Aysgarth. His wife died later in the same year. There is a portrait of Pickles by Christopher Sanders at the Royal College of General Practitioners. His epidemiological charts (1931-63) have been deposited at the London School of Hygiene and Tropical Medicine.

[John Pemberton, *Will Pickles of Wensleydale*, 1970; *British Medical Journal* and *Lancet*, 15 March 1969.]

GEORGE PICKERING

PIERCY, WILLIAM, first BARON PIERCY (1886-1966), economist and banker, was born 7 February 1886, the only son and eldest of four children of Augustus Edward Piercy and his second wife, Mary Ann Margaret Heaford. The family lived at Hoxton, Middlesex, and in 1893 William Piercy's father, who was an engineer employed by Vickers Ltd., was killed in a works accident. In 1898, when he was twelve, William Piercy left his local school and entered the City office of Pharaoh Gane, timber brokers. He studied hard in the evenings, and, aided by two small scholarships, he became in 1910 at the age of twenty-four a full-time undergraduate student at the London School of Economics and Political Science. He was secretary and then chairman of the Students' Union, and in the autumn of 1913 he graduated B.Sc. (Econ.), with first class honours, specializing in economic history. Piercy secured a Mitchell research studentship and was appointed lecturer in history and public administration at the school in 1914.

In the war of 1914-18 Piercy was one of the architects of the munitions levy. He was then lent to the Inland Revenue and in 1917 he spent some time in the United States as a member of the Allied Provisions Export Commission, and as a director of the British Ministry of Food. For this work he was appointed CBE in 1919.

The war over, Piercy joined Harrisons & Crosfield Ltd. as trading general manager, and then became joint managing director of Pharaoh Gane.

In the early 1930s Piercy became interested in evolving a system by which the small savings of the general public could be safely channelled into groups of quoted Stock Exchange securities. He played a leading part in organizing the first unit trusts. He was a member of the London Stock Exchange from 1934 to 1942, being a partner of Capel-Cure and Terry when most of his work which brought unit trusts into being was accomplished.

In 1939 Piercy was fifty-three, a successful and mature business man whose fertile inventiveness had already made its mark in the City and whose counsel and ready help were greatly valued in discerning academic and research institutions. His important public services during the war of 1939-45 were rendered with the reticence of a distinguished career civil servant. He headed the British Petroleum Mission in Washington and was probably more responsible than anyone else for the successful introduction of 'pooled' distribution of petrol in place of competing brands. He was successively a principal assistant secretary in the Ministry of Supply and the Ministry of Aircraft Production, and then served as personal assistant to the deputy prime minister, C. R. (later Earl) Attlee. He was created a baron on 14 November 1945.

In the summer of 1945 Lord Catto [q.v.], then governor of the Bank of England, invited Piercy to become the first chairman of Industrial and Commercial Finance Corporation Ltd. (ICFC). The decision to create this Corporation was announced by Sir John Anderson (later Viscount Waverley, q.v.), then chancellor of the Exchequer, to the House of Commons on 23 January 1945. When the Corporation was incorporated on 20 July 1945 with the Bank of England, the English clearing banks, and the Scottish banks as its shareholders, its declared purpose was to provide finance by means of loan or share capital for industrial and commercial businesses in Great Britain particularly in cases where the existing facilities were not readily or easily available.

Catto's choice of Piercy was inspired, for all Piercy's unusually varied experience was germane to the development of this new style of financial institution. Starting from scratch, an effective staff had to be created while all the time the business was growing apace. The first few years were difficult but thereafter the Corporation's profits steadily rose and Piercy showed that it was possible to provide a genuine service for the smaller industrial concerns, and at the same time make a fair profit. When he retired from the chairmanship in 1964 the Corporation had lent some £120 million in nineteen years.

Piercy was primarily responsible for the creation in 1952 of Estate Duties Investment Trust—EDITH as it soon became known—and he remained its chairman until his death. It too met a real need and proved an outstanding financial success. In 1946 Piercy was appointed to the Court of the Bank of England, and in 1950 and again in 1954 was reappointed. He retired from the Court in 1956 on reaching the age limit of seventy. He was a member of the Committee of Treasury for nine of these ten years.

He served until his death as a governor of the London School of Economics and as a member of the senate and of the court of the university of

London. He was a fellow of the Royal Statistical Society from 1922 until his death, and served as its president in 1954-5. From 1946 to 1963 he was president of the National Institute of Industrial Psychology, and chairman of the Wellcome Trust from 1960 to 1965. He was chairman of the Committee of Inquiry on the Rehabilitation, Training and Resettlement of Disabled Persons appointed by the Conservative Government in March 1953 which produced a notable report published by HMSO in November 1956 (Cmnd. 9883).

As chairman of ICFC Piercy succeeded in establishing a new type of financial institution which, having overcome its teething troubles, became an important part of the permanent financial machinery in the City, and this will remain his principal memorial.

Piercy was a fine-looking man with keen perceptive eyes. He had a ready wit and a prodigious memory. His principal interest was in economics and statistics, but he was an avid book collector, and a very wide reader. He enjoyed his walking holidays, especially in the Scottish Highlands.

In 1915 Piercy married Mary Louisa, daughter of Thomas Henry William Pelham, third son of the third Earl of Chichester. She had been secretary of the Students' Union while he was chairman. They had a son, Nicholas Pelham Piercy, born in 1918, who succeeded his father in the barony, and three daughters. Lady Piercy died in 1953 and in 1964 Lord Piercy married as his second wife, Veronica, younger daughter of Mrs Ann Warham. Piercy died in Stockholm 7 July 1966 while attending a meeting of the Kuwait international advisory committee, of which he was a member.

[*The Times*, 9 and 13 July 1966; *Journal of the Royal Statistical Society*, vol. cxxx, part 2, 1967; private information; personal knowledge.]   JOHN B. KINROSS

PIPPARD, (ALFRED JOHN) SUTTON (1891-1969), engineer, was born at Yeovil 6 April 1891, the eldest child in the family of three sons and two daughters of Alfred Pippard, a building contractor, and his wife, Alice, the daughter of John Sutton, a glover. He attended Yeovil School and Merchant Venturers' College at Bristol where, in 1911, he graduated with first class honours in civil engineering. (In 1909 the College had become the faculty of engineering of the university.) He then worked as an articled pupil with the consulting engineer A. P. I. Cotterell, and subsequently as assistant engineer with the Pontypridd and Rhondda Valley Joint Water Board. While there he wrote in his spare time an M.Sc. dissertation on 'The masonry dam' which was accepted by Bristol University in 1914.

Soon after the outbreak of war, having learnt that his sight would bar him from a commission in the Royal Engineers, he joined the newly formed technical section of the Air Department of the Admiralty, to work on aircraft structures and stressing. In association with men such as Alec Ogilvie, (Sir) Henry Tizard [q.v.], and J. L. Pritchard, Pippard made contributions of significance for the improvement and safety of aircraft, for which in 1918 he was appointed MBE. During the next year he and Pritchard published their well-known book *Aeroplane Structures*, and in 1920 Pippard gained the D.Sc. degree of Bristol University. From 1919 to 1922 he was in partnership with Ogilvie in the latter's firm of consulting aeronautical engineers and also gave lectures at Imperial College under (Sir) Leonard Bairstow [q.v.].

This experience convinced Pippard that his proper sphere lay in the academic world. In 1922 he successfully applied for the chair of engineering at University College, Cardiff. Understaffed, with restricted laboratory facilities, the engineering department at Cardiff differed little from those of other British provincial universities at that time, and it is Pippard's achievement that he was chiefly responsible for transforming this situation, turning the teaching of the theory of structures into a scientific discipline, actively promoting and participating in research, and generally raising the intellectual level of civil engineering courses in the country. These activities he continued while holding the chair of civil engineering at Bristol from 1928 to 1933, where, it may be noted, he was succeeded by his former research assistant, John F. (later Lord) Baker.

Though much of Pippard's research, at least up to 1926, had been on aircraft structures, he was not devoted to aircraft as such, but rather to the structural problems they presented. He was by early training and inclination a civil engineer. So when opportunity arose to go to Imperial College, to a department larger than that at Bristol, and with prospects of much closer connections with the Institution of Civil Engineers and the profession, he accepted without hesitation. He remained as professor of civil engineering and head of department at Imperial College from 1933 until his retirement in 1956.

During this period chairs were established under his guidance in hydraulics and concrete technology, four readerships were created, flourishing postgraduate courses were set up in the principal disciplines, and research was undertaken on a scale unprecedented in a British university civil engineering school. Pippard himself continued lecturing and directing research in theoretical and experimental structural analysis, notably on arch dams. His work in 1952-4 for Binnie & Partners on the design of the 116 m high Dokan dam in Iraq was of special importance and opened a new era in a field to which his research assistant, Miss Letitia Chitty, later Telford gold medallist and fellow of Imperial College, went on to make notable contributions. He also gave a good deal of attention to public health engineering, so that a readership in this subject was founded in 1950 and he was chairman (1951-61) of the influential government investigating committee on pollution of the tidal Thames.

Pippard's publications include eighty papers and five books. Of these, *The Analysis of Engineering Structures* (with J. F. Baker) (1936, 4th ed. 1968), became a classic in engineering literature. To this Dictionary he contributed the notices of Sir Alexander Gibb and Sir R. E. Stradling.

Pippard was elected FRS in 1954. He served on the council of the Institution of Civil Engineers from 1944 and was president in 1958-9. In 1964 he received the Ewing gold medal for exceptionally distinguished engineering research. He held honorary degrees from Bristol, Birmingham, and Brunel, was pro-rector of Imperial College (1955-6), and visiting professor at Northwestern University, USA (1956-7). He died at Putney 2 November 1969.

He married in 1918 (Frances Louisa) Olive Field (died 1964) and they had two sons: Dr John Pippard and Sir A. Brian Pippard, professor of physics at Cambridge.

There are two portraits: one at Imperial College painted in 1955 by R. Norman Hepple and another at the Institution of Civil Engineers painted by William Dring in 1958.

[A. W. Skempton in *Biographical Memoirs of Fellows of the Royal Society*, vol. xvi, 1970; personal knowledge.]   A. W. SKEMPTON

PLUCKNETT, THEODORE FRANK THOMAS (1897-1965), legal historian, was born 2 January 1897 in Bristol, the only son of Frank Plucknett, boot stock keeper, who became a shoe-making technologist and taught and wrote books on that subject, and of his wife, Caroline Thomas. Plucknett went from Alderman Newton's School, Leicester, to the Bacup and Rawtenstall School at Newchurch, Lancashire, working there for an external degree of London University and graduating with second class honours in history in 1915. His father then apparently moved to London to make it financially possible for him to become an internal student at University College; and before he was twenty-one he had gained not only his MA but also the Alexander prize

of the Royal Historical Society, both for work on the fifteenth-century Council. In 1918 he went to Emmanuel College, Cambridge, with a research exhibition, and under the supervision of H. D. Hazeltine wrote a thesis published as *Statutes and their Interpretation in the first half of the Fourteenth Century* (1922). This began the conversion of Plucknett from a constitutional historian to a historian of private law; and the LLB degree which it gained in 1920, under regulations later superseded by those for the Ph.D., lent colour to the impression that he was a lawyer. In this conversion the decisive event was his nomination in 1921 to the Choate memorial fellowship, which took him to the Harvard Law School where he was first a student, though doing only research and taking no courses, then from 1923 to 1926 instructor, and from 1926 to 1931 assistant professor. Plucknett's appointment to the faculty was the doing of Roscoe Pound, with whom he edited a volume of readings on legal history; and his leaving Harvard for the London School of Economics seems. to have been the doing of Harold Laski [q.v.]. The reputation which Plucknett had made by his Harvard courses, and partly also by his *Concise History of the Common Law* which was written by dictation in a matter of weeks and published in the United States in 1929, was that of a historian with a creed and a sense of style, both caught in his own later words: 'It is only in text-books that constitutional, economic and legal history are set apart from one another. In real life they are simultaneous, and one man lives all his histories concurrently.'

This was the reputation which brought Plucknett home in 1931 as first holder of what is still the only chair of legal history in England. He held it for the rest of his working life; but from his colleagues in the law faculty Plucknett became increasingly remote. He steadfastly denied that his subject was any use to lawyers: 'It is still too often said that English law can only be understood historically. Now English law may be bad, but is it really as bad as that?' His courses for law students were attended by the interested few, which to him was as it should be; and the remainder of his teaching and all of his professional discourse was directed to historians. His presidency of the Society of Public Teachers of Law in 1953-4 seemed a pleasant incongruity, very different from his term as president of the Royal Historical Society from 1948 to 1952. Plucknett was elected FBA in 1946, fellow of University College, London, in 1950, honorary fellow of Emmanuel College, Cambridge, in 1952, and was awarded the honorary LLD of Glasgow (1958) and Birmingham (1963), and in 1959 an honorary Litt.D. of Cambridge (a perceptive recognition of the pure historian). His last years were clouded by illness and he resigned prematurely in 1963. He died in Wimbledon 14 February 1965.

In the Massachusetts Cambridge, Plucknett met Marie, daughter of Ferdinand Guibert; and in 1923 they were married at her home in Clermont-Ferrand. This became a second home where, unless prevented by war or illness, they spent part of every year; and there he was buried. Apart from these visits he was never long away from their Wimbledon house, next door to which their only son settled after his marriage. Outside his family Plucknett was solitary by habit, having few intimates, all historians; and even with them he kept in touch mainly on professional matters and by correspondence. Formal in speech and dress, amiable and absent in manner, he became elusive to casual inquirers. But to those with a claim on his time he was encouraging and helpful; and his professional life was conducted with a firmness and method unsuspected by most of his colleagues.

Apart from articles and contributions to books by others, Plucknett advanced his subject in two main ways. He was joint literary director of the Selden Society from 1937 and alone from 1946; and though he played a named part in few volumes, a substantial proportion of the society's publications and the continuation of the enterprise itself owed much to his faith in the value of such intractable materials. And then there are his own books. The *Concise History* went into five editions and several languages; and though increasingly daunting to students it remains an essential part of the literature. The other works grew out of special lectures. The Ford's lectures in Oxford in 1947 became *Legislation of Edward I* (1949); the Maitland memorial lectures in Cambridge, commissioned for the centenary in 1950 of the birth of F. W. Maitland [q.v.], became *Early English Legal Literature* (1958); his Creighton lecture of 1953 was published as *The Mediaeval Bailiff* (1954); and the Wiles lectures in Belfast in 1958 became *Edward I and Criminal Law* (1960). The last was written when Plucknett was failing; and though full of ideas, it lacks the realism and immediacy of his best work. If he underestimated the strength of legal logic, he never fell into the converse and more common error of connecting one abstraction only with another. The book on literature is about lawyers; the book on legislation is about social problems, themselves seen as real people in concrete situations. His lack of legal training probably helped, and perhaps his lack of historical training helped too; apart from the supervision of his graduate work, and some early help with documents from

Hubert Hall [q.v.], Plucknett had no instruction after his school days. It may turn out that sometimes he saw wrong, but he always saw for himself; and at least in that, and in the vividness and humour which that alone can generate, he was a true follower of Maitland.

[S. F. C. Milsom in *Proceedings* of the British Academy, vol. li, 1965; private information; personal knowledge.]   S. F. C. MILSOM

PLUNKETT-ERNLE-ERLE-DRAX, SIR REGINALD AYLMER RANFURLY (1880–1967), admiral, was born in London 28 August 1880, the second son of John William Plunkett, later seventeenth Baron of Dunsany, and his wife, Ernle Elizabeth Louisa Maria Grosvenor Burton. He was the younger brother of the future eighteenth Baron of Dunsany [q.v.] and in 1916 on inheriting estates from his mother he assumed by royal licence the additional names of Ernle-Erle-Drax. Thenceforth he was usually known by the surname of Drax.

From Cheam School he joined the *Britannia* and went to sea in 1896. He was promoted lieutenant in 1901 and went on to specialize in torpedo. At his own request he attended the Millitary Staff College, Camberley, and in 1912 he was one of the first officers chosen to undergo the new course of training for staff officers. In the same year he received early promotion to commander and when in 1913 Admiral (later Earl) Beatty [q.v.] was given command of the battle-cruiser squadron, he chose Plunkett as his war staff officer. In this capacity he served in the *Lion* at the actions of Heligoland Bight, Dogger Bank, and Jutland. He was promoted captain in 1916 and ended the war in the cruiser *Blanche* which was employed in laying minefields in the Heligoland Bight close to the enemy's main ports. For his services in the *Lion* he was mentioned in dispatches and he was appointed to the DSO when commanding the *Blanche*.

In 1919 Drax became first director of the new Naval Staff College at Greenwich where he served until 1922. Having proved himself as a brilliant staff officer and thinker and also as a fine captain of a cruiser, he was the ideal person for this appointment. He did much to make staff work respectable in a navy where thinkers were apt to be regarded with suspicion and only the proved seamen admired and promoted. Drax showed that it was possible to be both. He went next as president of the allied naval control commission in Berlin until 1924. In 1926-7 he commanded the *Marlborough* in the third battle squadron.

In 1928 Drax was promoted rear-admiral and in 1929 appointed to command the first battle squadron in the Mediterranean. As director of manning at the Admiralty (1930-2) he was involved in the recovery of the navy's morale after the Invergordon mutiny, an episode for which he had had no responsibility. In 1932-4 he was commander-in-chief America and West Indies, where he cruised widely in his flagship and did much to promote friendly relations with the United States navy. He was promoted vice-admiral in 1932 and admiral in 1936. In 1935-8 he served as commander-in-chief, Plymouth. In 1939 he headed the British section of the Anglo-French military mission to Russia to concert plans against German aggression, a mission which was doomed from the start through no fault of his, for whilst Drax was engaged in vague staff talks at Leningrad, the Russo-German treaty of non-aggression was being negotiated.

In 1939-41 Drax was commander-in-chief at the Nore where he was responsible for the main defences against German attack. After Dunkirk, when Drax worked in close co-operation with his old friend (Sir) Bertram Ramsay [q.v.] at Dover, his inventive mind did much to prepare for the expected invasion. After serving his full time at the Nore, Drax retired and returned to his estates in Dorset where he served as a private in the Home Guard. In the spring of 1943 he volunteered for duty as a commodore of convoy and served until 1945 with the distinction of never losing a ship.

A critic of much of British strategy, Drax privately printed in 1943 a book on the *Art of War* which attacked many aspects of defence policy. Events have vindicated many of his views. Perhaps his greatest contribution to the navy was his promotion of the study of war, a topic which at the beginning of the century was somewhat discouraged due to the flood of technological change. Drax was a founder-member of the Naval Society which from 1913 has issued the quarterly *Naval Review* to encourage new ideas on naval matters and persuade young officers to put their thoughts on paper. Throughout his career Drax studied the art of war and constantly produced new ideas and new policies, based mainly on a thorough study of history. It was little known that he had a particular sympathy for the men of the lower deck and their pay and conditions of service. He was a friend of 'Lionel Yexley' (James Woods), the naval reformer, and invited him to lecture to the staff course—a move looked upon as most radical. Drax was firm but kindly and he inspired great affection from those with whom he served. He encouraged junior officers constructively and was never too busy to advise or if necessary to criticize. In retirement at Charborough he remained busy with the management of his estates and the writing of articles on many subjects. The swimming bath, warmed by rays of the sun, was one invention of which he was very proud.

Drax was appointed CB in 1928 and KCB in 1934. In 1916 he married Kathleen (died 1980), daughter of Quintin Chalmers, MD, and sister of the future Rear-Admiral W. S. Chalmers, the naval biographer and a contributor to this Dictionary. Of an unusually happy marriage there were four daughters and one son. Drax died in Poole 16 October 1967.

[Private information; personal knowledge.]

PETER GRETTON

PODE, SIR (EDWARD) JULIAN (1902-1968), steel executive, was born in Sheffield 26 June 1902, the only son of Edward Pode, a master at the Royal Grammar School, and his second wife, Lilla Telfer. His father died in April 1902 shortly before the boy was born. His uncle, John Pode, took him to the family house at Slade in Devonshire at the age of six; the boy began as a weekly boarder and later became a full boarder at the Mount House Preparatory School at Plymouth. In April 1916 he joined the training ship *Conway*, to leave in April 1918 in a senior position with a report noting his very good executive ability. He first went to sea at fifteen and his life in the navy was very adventurous, since his ships were lost from torpedoes and mines, and finally he had to jump on to the deck of a destroyer from the armed merchant cruiser, *Otranto*, in October 1918 when she was sinking after a collision in a full gale off the west coast of Ireland. He was discharged in March 1919, his eyesight having deteriorated badly under the strain of war. In April 1919 he joined Arthur Leslie Wing (Wm. Wing & Son), chartered accountants in Sheffield, to qualify in 1924.

In 1926 Pode entered the steel industry by joining the staff of Guest, Keen & Nettlefolds Ltd. at the Dowlais Works, as district accountant. In the 1930 slump, when the heavy-steel interests of that company were amalgamated with those of Baldwins Ltd. to form Guest Keen Baldwins Iron & Steel Co. Ltd., he was appointed secretary of the new company. In 1938 he became secretary and joint commercial manager. In 1943 he was appointed assistant managing director, and in 1945 joint managing director.

When, in 1947, the Steel Company of Wales Ltd. was formed for the purpose of modernizing the sheet steel and tinplate industries of South Wales, he was appointed managing director of the new company. For fifteen years, in this role, Pode guided the company through one of the biggest development projects ever carried out in the steel industry, not only raising ingot steel output from half a million to three million tons a year but also converting the old tinplate industry of Wales to the new cold-reduced tinplate by the construction of two works at Trostre near Llanelli and Velindre near Swansea and constructing a large-output sheet complex at Port Talbot, alongside the new strip mill. In addition, the Steel Company of Wales and Richard Thomas & Baldwins jointly introduced the manufacture of the highly sophisticated electric sheet known as grain oriented. The Steel Company of Wales works for this product were at Orb, Newport. Pode's period in charge of the company involved the expenditure of enormous sums of money at these four works, culminating in the decision to build the new port for large ore carriers at Port Talbot, which was not completed until after his death. In May 1961 he was appointed deputy chairman in addition to his position as managing director. In February 1962 he was appointed chairman of the company, and in February 1967 he retired from the board.

Whether in his own company, the Steel Company of Wales, in the iron and steel industry in general, or within the numerous companies with which he was connected as a director, Pode was notable for his quality of leadership combined with a certain humility. He was at all times a good listener, yet in handling people he was fearless and ever ready to set an example if a difficult human decision had to be taken. He took a leading part in the energy advisory council of the Ministry of Power, the Industrial Coal Consumers' Council, and the shipping policy and ore investment committee of the British Iron & Steel Federation. His directorships and interests were many: in particular his long-term membership of the main board of Guest Keen & Nettlefolds and the Steetley Company, chairmanship of France, Fenwick & Co., and his service on the main board of Lloyds Bank, as well as the chairmanship of their South Wales district committee. He was deputy chairman of the Hodge Group until his death.

Pode was high sheriff of Glamorgan in 1948 and a justice of the peace from 1951 to 1966; in 1957 he became an honorary freeman of the borough of Port Talbot, one of the honours he prized most. He was knighted in 1959. From 1962 to 1964 he was president of the Iron & Steel Federation, during which time he exerted great influence on the steel trade and was a particularly outspoken opponent of nationalization; as a past president his influence continued to be considerable. He was, too, a man of wide interests in other fields, with a vivid sense of enjoyment in everything he did, accompanied by considerable skill. As a golfer, for instance, at one time his handicap was 4; he remained a good golfer throughout his life, and with his love of competition he was a difficult man to beat. While an enthusiastic bridge player, he was never an expert, perhaps because of his innate sense of optimism. But his favourite hobby was undoubtedly racing: he was said to have visited every racecourse in the country, and although he owned racehorses he was not remarkably successful until later years when he started breeding bloodstock. He was also a keen farmer and owned a fine pedigree herd of Guernsey cows. Towards the end of his life, he also started to collect pictures, Stubbs and Richard Wilson for example. Never a great reader of books, he could absorb a brief with remarkable rapidity and recall the salient points accurately. There was much humour in him, and his business colleagues always hoped that he would be in to lunch for 'one knew it would be very entertaining'.

In 1930 Pode married Jean, daughter of Frederick Finlayson, colliery owner, and went to live at Great House, Bonvilston, Glamorgan, where he lived until he died, 11 June 1968. They had a son and a daughter. His son, John, as a Frazer scholar from Winchester, took a first in chemistry at Balliol, wrote two chemistry books much used in schools, and became a housemaster at Eton. A portrait of Pode painted by Edward I. Halliday in 1968 hangs in Great House, Bonvilston.

[Private information; personal knowledge.]

W. F. Cartwright

POLLITT, GEORGE PATON (1878-1964), chemical industrialist and farmer, was born 23 August 1878 at Mellor near Blackburn, Lancashire, the younger son and middle child of Joseph Seddon Pollitt, bank manager, and his wife, Charlotte Paton. He was at school in Bruges, where he learnt to speak fluent French and German, took a B.Sc. degree with honours in chemistry (1899) and an M.Sc. (1903) at Owens College, Manchester, and a Ph.D. degree (1902) in the university of Basle after three years' study at Zürich Polytechnic.

On completion of his education he entered the field of industrial chemistry and in 1907 joined the staff of Brunner Mond & Co., manufacturers of heavy chemicals.

On the outbreak of war with Germany in 1914 Pollitt enlisted as motor-cycle dispatch rider and was sent on active service with the BEF immediately. He soon obtained a commission and served with the Intelligence Corps, the Special Brigade RE, and the infantry. His promotion was rapid: in early 1918 he was appointed to command the 11th battalion Lancashire Fusiliers. He had only commanded the battalion for a fortnight when he was wounded and taken prisoner. He remained a prisoner for the rest of the war. His record as a non-professional soldier was remarkable. He was wounded four times, mentioned in dispatches four times, and was appointed DSO with two bars. On demobilization he was granted the rank of lieutenant-colonel.

On leaving the army Pollitt rejoined Brunner Mond and was elected a director. At this time the company was considering taking over from the Government a wartime project to manufacture synthetic ammonia. The Government was interested in the project as a basis for the manufacture of explosives, but the company was more interested in it as a basis for the manufacture of nitrogenous fertilizers. Not all the Brunner Mond directors were in favour of the takeover, but Pollitt was and his view prevailed. A new company was formed, with a capital of £5,000,000, of which Pollitt was appointed managing director. The new company, Synthetic Ammonia & Nitrates Ltd., took over the site of 266 acres, which the Government had bought at Billingham in Durham, near the mouth of the river Tees and, under Pollitt's energetic direction, design and construction work was started. The factory at Billingham later became one of the largest chemical manufacturing complexes in the world.

In 1926 a new company, Imperial Chemical Industries Ltd., was formed by a merger of all the major chemical manufacturing companies in the United Kingdom, including Brunner Mond and Synthetic Ammonia & Nitrates. Pollitt took part in the negotiations leading to the merger and became a director on the first board of the new company. He was one of the very few technically trained directors in the early days of the company. Probably his most important contribution to its success was his insistence on the importance of adequate scientific research. In 1927 he was awarded the gold medal of the Society of Chemical Industry for 'conspicuous services to applied chemistry by research, discovery, and invention'.

Pollitt resigned as an executive director in 1934 but remained on the board until his retirement in 1945.

In 1932 he became interested in farming and acquired some 900 acres in Shropshire. He raised cattle by feeding them on fresh cut grass in the summer and on dried cut grass in the winter. In 1937 he was awarded the silver medal of the Royal Society of Arts 'for the encouragement of arts, manufacture, and commerce' for a paper on 'Recent Developments in Grass Drying'. In 1942 he published a booklet entitled *Britain Can Feed Herself*, in which he claimed that if all the ploughable land in Britain were farmed up to the best standards there would be no need to import food and that the total cost of the food produced would be no greater than the cost of most of the food imported. Although he was convinced that there was no agricultural reason why the plan should not succeed he realized that, for various reasons, political and social, it was unlikely to be adopted.

During the war of 1939-45 he was appointed zone commander of the Home Guard and was given the rank of colonel. He was high sheriff of Shropshire in 1945-6.

In 1947 Pollitt emigrated to Southern Rhodesia where he had bought a farm. He was no longer a young man, and his health began to suffer. He contracted cancer of the larynx and returned to England in 1952 to have it removed. The operation was successful but as a result he found it difficult to speak and make himself understood. He went to live at St. Mawes in Cornwall and became a recluse. He died there 9 March 1964.

Pollitt never married. He was not averse to the company of women and always treated them with courtesy and consideration. He had two nephews, the sons of his brother, whom he treated as his own sons after his brother's death. Both boys took diplomas in agriculture and worked with their uncle on his farms in Shropshire and Rhodesia.

Pollitt was a tall man with a good physique, fair complexion, blue eyes, and close-cut sandy hair and small moustache. He was fond of outdoor exercise and always kept himself in good physical condition. There is a photograph of him in the Intelligence Corps Museum, Ashford. His manner has been described as 'bluff, tactless, and masterful'.

[Major-General C. H. Foulkes, *'Gas!' The Story of the Special Brigade*, 1934; W. J. Reader, *A History of Imperial Chemical Industries 1926–1952*, vol. i, 1970; private information.]   F. T. WOOLNER

POLLOCK, SIR (JOHN) DONALD, baronet, of Edinburgh (1868-1962), physician, industrialist, and philanthropist, was born at Galashiels 23 November 1868, the elder surviving son of the Revd John Barr Pollock, minister of the United Presbyterian Church, and his wife, Margaret, daughter of John Donald, JP, of Edinburgh. He was educated by his father, studied science at Glasgow University, and medicine at Edinburgh where he gained his MB, CM in 1892 and MD in 1895. After qualifying he spent a year or two as a ship's doctor before setting up in practice in the Earl's Court Road, London (1895-1908). He then became private medical adviser and companion to the Duke of Leinster, an epileptic, with whom he travelled extensively until the outbreak of war in 1914 when they settled in Edinburgh. Pollock gave his services to the naval hospital at Granton; he was appointed OBE in 1919 and in 1922 received the honorary rank of surgeon-commander RNVR.

After the war and the Duke's death in 1922, Pollock joined with S. J. L. Hardie and R. W. McCrone in the formation in 1922 of a ship-breaking company, Metal Industries Ltd., of which he remained chairman until 1951. In 1925 the company was asked by the Admiralty if it was interested in salvaging the sunken German ships at Scapa Flow. It was beyond their resources and another company raised all the small ships, some of which, as well as five battleships, were purchased by Metal Industries. In 1933 Pollock's company took over the salvaging and raised another six battleships before work was stopped in 1939. In 1936 they were able to obtain from the Admiralty a lease of part of Rosyth dockyard which enabled them to deal with much larger ships.

At the outset it was realized that it was essential for the company to make its own oxygen at the works and Pollock and McCrone went to Germany to study methods of production before a plant was set up at Charlestown on the Forth. Later they purchased the patent rights for a new method which delivered the oxygen in liquid form and converted it into gas at the purchaser's works. Pollock, who was a very good negotiator, overcame the initial reluctance of the large steel works to change to the new method and factories were opened in Sheffield and Birmingham. Alarmed at this progress the British Oxygen Company raised an action against them for revocation of their patent rights. But before the case was finished the British Oxygen Company asked Pollock and his colleagues to amalgamate with them, which they accordingly did in 1932. Pollock was chairman of British Oxygen from 1932 until 1937 when he became honorary president.

Although his business interests took him frequently to London, Pollock was always active in the public life of Scotland. He was, for instance, a member of the Scottish Milk Marketing Board, the Carnegie Trust for the Scottish Universities, and the economic committee of the Scottish National Development Council. In 1936 he gave £250,000 to form a trust for educational and religious purposes in Scotland and a few years later he founded the £70,000 Pollock Memorial Missionary Trust to provide homes for missionaries of all denominations. He was a generous benefactor of Edinburgh University of which he was lord rector in 1939–45 and where there are Pollock halls of residence. He received an honorary LLD from Edinburgh (1935) and an honorary D.Sc. in 1937 from Oxford where he had established a readership in engineering science and also enabled the Clarendon Laboratory to carry out its research into low temperatures. As a great friend of A. L. Smith [q.v.] he became a member of the senior common room at Balliol. He was a fellow of the Royal Society of Edinburgh and in 1951 a vice-president of the British Association.

Pollock was a man of simple tastes, almost a teetotaller and certainly a non-smoker. He spent little on himself except on etchings of which he had one of the finest collections in the country. He only had two cars in forty years, never had a chauffeur or even a full-time gardener. He took no interest in sports except rugby and sailing and listed as one of his recreations the 'nautical training of young lads'; the others were gardening and engineering. He took a lot of exercise, never put on weight, and was always very fit. He died in Edinburgh 4 June 1962. He was unmarried and the baronetcy which was created in 1939 became extinct.

Edinburgh University has a portrait of him by Stanley Cursiter.

[Private information; personal knowledge.]
R. W. McCrone

POOLEY, Sir ERNEST HENRY, baronet (1876–1966), public servant, was born in London 20 November 1876, the eldest son of Henry Fletcher Pooley, who became an assistant secretary to the Board of Education, and his wife, Susan, daughter of Edward Bond. He was educated at Winchester and Pembroke College, Cambridge, where he obtained second classes in the classical tripos (part i, 1898) and the law tripos (part ii, 1899). He was called to the bar by Lincoln's Inn in 1901 and joined the Board of Education as a legal assistant in 1903. In 1905 he was appointed assistant clerk to the Drapers' Company and in 1908 became clerk. On retirement from office in 1944 he was elected master (1944–5), an unusual honour; and in 1952–3 and 1962–3 he was warden. In 1945 he published an admirable book in the 'Britain in Pictures' series on *The Guilds of the City of London*.

In the war of 1914–18 Pooley served in the Royal Naval Volunteer Reserve and the Royal Garrison Artillery and fought in France and Gallipoli. From 1928 until his death he was deeply involved with King Edward's Hospital Fund for London and from 1929 to 1948 he was a member of the senate and court of the university of London which in 1948 conferred an honorary LLD upon him. He was an honorary fellow of Pembroke College, Cambridge, and also of Queen Mary College, London. He was a member of several important committees, among them the Goodenough committee on medical education and the Fleming committee on public schools, both appointed in 1942.

Pooley was a man of many parts. He was a figure of distinction among the City companies and in several wider fields, especially educational and charitable. He had great administrative abilities and was an unusually good chairman of the many committees on which he served. In that capacity he combined clarity of mind, unusual tactical skill, firmness of will, and good humour. He never allowed an issue to wander into an impasse, and he rarely had to resort to a show of hands. Burly as he was he never had to throw his weight about, for his powers of persuasion were considerable. One of the most difficult, and successful, tasks he undertook was to succeed Lord Keynes [q.v.] when he died in 1946 very soon after becoming first chairman of the Arts Council. It was a challenging assignment for, despite the success of the wartime Council for the Encouragement of Music and the Arts, public patronage of the arts was a relatively new venture in this country. The Arts Council was an innovation, a body liable to pressures from conflicting interests and likely, also, to attract the spotlight of public discussion. There were some, at the time, who criticized Pooley's appointment on the ground that he had no particular knowledge or experience of any of the arts. But he was a decided success in seeing the Arts Council through its first seven vital years. What was chiefly called for in the chairman was common sense and courage, and with these qualities Pooley was abundantly endowed. The members of the Council, appointed by the chancellor of the Exchequer, were all people of considerable standing in the cultural life of the country and their discussions were often of a high voltage. Pooley led them with skill and wisdom. There were, in those early days of trial and error, occasions when differences of opinion were acute. Pooley handled them with quiet but emphatic authority, and if the tension became excessive he always managed to clear the air by some apt—and often humorous—parable. He was a shrewd but very human leader.

Pooley worked hard at his many public commitments, but the care he gave to them was never obtrusive and he never made heavy weather of a task. He was, moreover, a very companionable man. One was glad to be with him on almost any occasion, and especially on the convivial one. He was immensely popular at his favourite London club, the Savile, to whose affairs he gave a generous share of his experience of people and problems. He enjoyed life in a great variety of ways, especially good

hospitality, a good game of bridge, a good night at a play, a ballet, an opera—and even a romp at the Folies Bergère.

Pooley was knighted in 1932, appointed KCVO (1944) and GCVO (1957), and created a baronet in 1953. In that year he married Winifred Christabel (died 1976), the widow of his old friend H. C. Marillier [q.v.] and daughter of Arthur Hopkins, artist. Pooley died in hospital in Chichester 13 February 1966 and the baronetcy became extinct.

[Personal knowledge.]   W. E. WILLIAMS

POPHAM, ARTHUR EWART (1889-1970), keeper of prints and drawings at the British Museum, 1945-54, was born at Plymouth 22 March 1889, the only son of Arthur Frederick Popham and his wife, Florence, daughter of George David Radford, of Mannamead, Plymouth. His parents were cousins, the families being connected in a long-established draper's business, Popham and Radford, in Plymouth. His mother's brother, Sir George Heynes Radford, was a Liberal MP for East Islington and a senator of London University, and her sister Ada Radford married the sociologist Graham Wallas [q.v.]. His father studied architecture, and worked for a time for the Doves Press in the book-binding department. Popham, known to his friends as 'Hugh', was educated at Dulwich College and University College, London; but Sir George Radford, who had taken charge of his education after his parents' death, sent him from there to King's College, Cambridge, where he took a second class degree in classics in 1911. In July 1912 he was appointed assistant in the Department of Prints and Drawings at the British Museum, and he remained in that department (except for war service) until he retired as keeper in 1954. During the war of 1914-18 he served in the Artists' Rifles, and then in the Royal Naval Air Service, as a pilot. He later became a captain in the newly formed Royal Flying Corps. He was awarded the croix de guerre.

The official museum publications for which Popham was wholly or chiefly responsible between his return to duty after the war and his retirement in 1954 were: *Netherlandish Drawings of the Fifteenth and Sixteenth Centuries* (1932, completing the catalogue of Dutch and Flemish drawings, of which four volumes by A. M. Hind, whose notice Popham wrote for this Dictionary, had already appeared); *A Handbook of the Drawings and Watercolours* in the department (1939), a very valuable general guide; *Italian Drawings of the Fourteenth and Fifteenth Centuries* (1950, with Philip Pouncey); and *Drawings of the School of Parma*, which appeared in print only after Popham's retirement, in 1967. Independently of the museum, he was honorary secretary of the Vasari Society (for the reproduction of drawings) from 1925 to 1935, and in 1926 he collaborated with his colleague, (Sir) K. T. Parker, in launching the periodical *Old Master Drawings*, something of a landmark in the history of the study of draughtsmanship, which lasted through fourteen volumes, with Parker as editor, and many contributions by Popham, until the outbreak of the war of 1939–45. His own independent publications during this period were: a small book, *Drawings of the Early Flemish School* (1926); a revised and enlarged catalogue of the drawings exhibited at the Italian Exhibition of 1930 at the Royal Academy (1931); and the catalogue of the Phillipps Fenwick collection of drawings (1935), much of which afterwards found its way, through the generosity of an anonymous donor, into the British Museum.

During the war of 1939–45 he was at Aberystwyth, in charge of the collections which had been removed there for safety; this gave him an exceptional opportunity to study at his leisure not only the drawings from his own museum but also the treasures from the Royal Library at Windsor and from Chatsworth; and as a result he was able to produce, after his return to London as keeper of the department, a general book on *The Drawings of Leonardo da Vinci* (1946), and in 1949 (with Johannes Wilde, q.v.) the catalogue of *Italian Drawings of the XV and XVI centuries at Windsor Castle* in the series published by the Phaidon Press. After his retirement he acted as adviser to the National Gallery of Canada, Ottawa, for the acquisition of drawings, and his catalogue of all the European drawings (other than British) in that collection, on which Kathleen Fenwick collaborated, appeared in 1965. Two other important independent books must be mentioned: his *Corregio's Drawings* (1957) sponsored by the British Academy, and the great three-volume corpus of the *Drawings of Parmigianino* (1971) for the Pierpont Morgan Library, New York—a subject on which he had already produced a small book for the Faber series in 1953. He died 8 December 1970, very shortly before the appearance of this last exemplary piece of scholarship.

In 1949 Popham was elected FBA. He was appointed CB (1954) on his retirement and was elected an honorary fellow of King's College, Cambridge (1955). He would not have called himself an art historian in the modern academic sense; like most museum men of the days before the history of art was taught in British universities, he was self-trained by his daily work, and it was his unrivalled knowledge of the great British Museum collection, as well as of those at Windsor, Chatsworth, Holkham, and elsewhere, that gave special authority to his judgements. As an expert cataloguer, he was interested above all things in establishing the authorship of the works he had to consider. His style of writing was fluent and clear, and strictly disciplined: only very seldom did he allow the natural humour that was evident in his conversation to appear in his published work, which was almost entirely confined to the study of drawings and prints and the history of collecting. But he had many other interests: calligraphy and carpentry, for instance, and many sorts of sport. He was tall and dignified in appearance, with a somewhat melancholy expression which belied his character. In 1912 he married Brynhild (died 1935), daughter of Sydney (later Lord) Olivier [q.v.], governor of Jamaica. There were three children, one of whom, Anne Olivier Bell, has contributed the notice of Vanessa Bell to this Supplement. In 1926 he married, secondly, Rosalind (died 1973), daughter of Sir (William) Hamo Thornycroft [q.v.], sculptor. There were no children of the second marriage. His wives were first cousins. There is a good portrait-drawing of him by David Bell in the British Museum, which is reproduced as the frontispiece to the obituary notice in *Proceedings* of the British Academy, vol. lvii.

[*The Times*, 9 December 1970; *Burlington Magazine*, vol. cxiii, 1971, p. 97; James Byam Shaw in *Proceedings* of the British Academy, vol. lvii, 1971; private information; personal knowledge.]   JAMES BYAM SHAW

POTTER, STEPHEN MEREDITH (1900–1969), writer and radio producer, was born 1 February 1900 in south London, the only son of Frank Collard Potter, chartered accountant, and his wife, Elizabeth (Lilla) Reynolds. He was educated at Westminster School, where he won the pancake and rowed in the eight. He left just in time to be trained and gazetted as a second lieutenant in the Coldstream Guards before demobilization returned him to civilian life in 1919. After a few uneasy months in his father's office he went up to Merton College, Oxford, where he took a second in English language and literature in 1922. For a time he acted as secretary to the playwright Henry Arthur Jones [q.v.], until in 1926 he was appointed a lecturer in English at Birkbeck College, London.

His first book, *The Young Man* (1929), was the inevitable autobiographical novel and caused little stir. In 1930 he published a good short study of D. H. Lawrence, then turned his attention to Coleridge, editing the Nonesuch Press *Coleridge* (1933) and Mrs Coleridge's letters to Thomas Poole in *Minnow Among Tritons* (1934). His main work on the subject, and his most important critical book, *Coleridge and S.T.C.* (1935), was an acute discussion of the duality in the poet's nature. In 1937 he published *The Muse in 'Chains: a Study in Education*, a critical and extremely amusing history of the teaching of English in our universities. G. M. Young [q.v.] wrote of it: 'If I were suddenly commissioned by some Golden Dustman to organize a new university, I think I should send for Mr. Potter and offer him the chair of English literature forthwith.'

All seemed set for a distinguished career as teacher and critic, but marriage and children made financial demands which these pursuits could not resolve, and in 1938 Potter joined the British Broadcasting Corporation as a writer-producer in the Features Department (later he became editor of Features and Poetry). His broadcasting career was long and increasingly successful. Literary features and war documentaries occupied him initially, then in 1943 appeared the first of twenty-nine 'How' programmes, written with Joyce Grenfell. They dealt satirically with everyday subjects, such as 'How to talk to children', 'How to woo', 'How to give a party'; and in 1946 'How to listen to radio' was the first broadcast heard in the newly created Third Programme.

Potter's light touch did a great deal to move radio features on from a rather static form of presentation to an impressionism with natural dialogue and minimal use of sound-effects which was lively, immediate, imaginative, and vivid. Particularly successful were his series of 'Professional Portraits', and 'New Judgments', as well as the broadcast of Nevill Coghill's version of *The Canterbury Tales*. As a radio producer Stephen Potter was clear and unfussy, inspiring confidence and enthusiasm.

In 1945 he did a stint as theatre critic for the *New Statesman and Nation*, and in 1946 a year as book critic on the *News Chronicle*. He was also an occasional and useful member of the BBC 'Critics'. When he had enjoyed the subject under discussion he said so, in refreshing contrast to the superior and grudging assessments of some of his colleagues.

A ten-day power-cut at the beginning of 1947 cancelled all broadcasting and gave Potter the opportunity to dash off, on odd scraps of paper, the book which gave a new word to the language and a new concept to the whole world of sport. This was *The Theory and Practice of Gamesmanship; or the Art of Winning games Without Actually Cheating*, published in November 1947. In it he described how the idea crystallized when he and his friend C. E. M. Joad [q.v.] managed to defeat at tennis two younger and more agile opponents, by subtle and

entirely legal 'ploys' which put them off their game. From this the idea spread to almost all other games, and from them to many other aspects of life. *Some Notes on Lifemanship* (1950) was followed by *One-Upmanship* (1952) and *Supermanship* (1958). By this time the concept and the suffix '-manship' had travelled the world, and the foreign policy of the American secretary of state John Foster Dulles was universally known as 'Brinkmanship'.

For Potter the joke was played out, but for the rest of his life he found it difficult to speak or write naturally, so accustomed had he grown to the jocose gambits and ploys of his own invention. He did, however, manage to forget them long enough to write what many considered his best book, *Steps to Immaturity* (1959), an attractive evocation of his Edwardian boyhood and Georgian schooldays. His choice of title showed a disarming self-awareness, for in many ways he never grew up, and always seemed an immensely likeable overgrown boy. He was such an obsessive games player (squash, tennis, golf, croquet, and always snooker at the Savile Club) that his friends wondered how he managed to do any work at all. He was a reluctant starter when it came to putting pen to paper, a last-minute man, but somehow he met his deadlines. Later, and minor, publications included an anthology, *Sense of Humour* (1954), *Potter on America* (1956), and *The Complete Golf Gamesmanship* (1968). From 1949 until its death in 1951 he was editor of the weekly *Leader*.

Besides English literature he was interested in natural history, birds, and especially music. He once said that he got more from music than from the written word. Beethoven was his favourite composer. Potter was tall and rangy, with rough fair hair which stood on end in spite of absent-minded attempts to dampen and flatten it. In a memorial broadcast Roy Plomley said: 'There was something very special about his trousers. Some men have the kind of hips which keep a waist-band neatly in place: Stephen hadn't.' He smoked in a perilous manner, disregarding ashtrays. He was good company and popular everywhere. It was in a radio interview with Plomley that he deftly demonstrated a tiny but telling gamesmanship ploy. 'Mr Potter,' began Plomley, 'as I've known you for so many years, do you think that on this programme I might call you Stephen?' 'Well,' he replied, 'Why not—Plomley?'

In 1927 Potter married Marian Anderson, daughter of John Arthur Attenborough (Mary Potter, the distinguished painter); they had two sons. This marriage was dissolved in 1955, and in the same year he married Mrs Heather Jenner, daughter of Brigadier C. A. Lyon,

DSO; they had one son who died at the age of sixteen. Potter died in London 2 December 1969.

[Potter's own writings; *The Times*, 3 December 1969; G. M. Young, *Daylight and Champaign*, 1937; private information; personal knowledge.]   JOYCE GRENFELL

POWELL, CECIL FRANK (1903–1969), physicist, was born in Tonbridge 5 December 1903, the elder child and only son of Frank Powell, gunsmith, of 99 High Street, Tonbridge, Kent, and his wife, Elizabeth Caroline Bisacre. His father, from a family long established as gunsmiths in Tonbridge, had been rendered bankrupt by a lawsuit arising from a shooting accident, so that the family circumstances were severely straitened in Powell's childhood. Nevertheless, encouraged by his grandfather George Bisacre, a schoolmaster, who gave him second-hand (and rather ancient) scientific texts, and inspired by the engineering talents of two paternal uncles, one of whom had constructed the first successful motor car in the Tonbridge district, he contrived to have a garden-shed chemical laboratory while a schoolboy. At eleven he won a scholarship to Sir A. Judd's Commercial School (later the Judd School), Tonbridge, whence state and college open scholarships took him to Sidney Sussex College, Cambridge, where he obtained first class honours in parts i (1924) and ii (1925) of the natural sciences tripos, and was placed second in his year for physics. He followed this with research in Rutherford's [q.v.] Cavendish Laboratory, under the direction of C. T. R. Wilson [q.v.], and then moved, as research assistant to Professor A. M. Tyndall [q.v.], to the newly opened H. H. Wills Physics Laboratory of the university of Bristol in 1928. There he spent the rest of his career, becoming lecturer (1931), reader (1946), Melville Wills professor of physics (1948–63), Henry Overton Wills professor of physics and director of the H. H. Wills Physics Laboratory (1964–9), and a pro-vice-chancellor of the university (1964–7). He had been elected to the Royal Society in 1949 and received the Nobel prize for physics in 1950. He was elected president of the Association of Scientific Workers in 1954 and of the World Federation of Scientific Workers in 1957.

Powell's earliest research work, with C. T. R. Wilson, which aimed at improving the performance of cloud chambers, had an engineering 'spin-off' in application to the discharge of steam through nozzles. With Tyndall, during Powell's first four years in Bristol, the nature of gaseous ions was greatly clarified. His research interests then diverged in two very different directions—to nuclear physics and seismology. He undertook the construction of a Cockcroft generator [see Sir J. D. Cockcroft, q.v.] to produce a 700 keV proton beam, and the associated cloud chamber; and he went as seismologist on the joint Colonial Office and Royal Society expedition to Montserrat, West Indies (1935). Another such expedition to Dominica was being planned in 1939, but was frustrated by the war, and at that point Powell's career as a seismologist ended. His high-voltage set came into service in 1939, to be dismantled in 1940 because the space was needed for other war-displaced occupants of the laboratory: but it was in use for long enough to launch him into what was to be his principal line of research. The cloud chamber not being ready, he recorded his proton beam in the emulsion of a photographic plate, tangentially exposed. Then he used the same technique to determine the energy spectrum of a neutron source by registering the tracks of 'knock-on' protons in the emulsion, and at the same time he participated in experiments registering events produced by the cosmic rays in photographic plates stored on high mountains. It was generally thought at the time that the registration of fast particle tracks in emulsion was only suitable for qualitative demonstrations, and could give no results of worthwhile precision; but Powell persisted in following his belief that, with better microscopes, better used, with improved processing techniques, and with the development of new thicker and more silver-rich emulsions, the accuracy and sensitivity of the method could be greatly improved. He was correct, and was rewarded with an important harvest of new phenomena observed in the cosmic rays in the years following the war. The method had an intrinsic advantage over all others for the observation of particle transformations occurring after very short time intervals (because of the high magnification under which the tracks were seen). The resolution of the meson paradox in 1947, revealing that there was a strongly interacting π-meson which transformed spontaneously into a weakly interacting and relatively long-lived μ-meson won him his Nobel prize in 1950. These observations were made in balloon-borne stacks of photographic emulsion, a method which was to reveal a new world of transient 'fundamental' particles during the next decade. Powell organized this research internationally, physicists from twenty or more universities of Europe and elsewhere collaborating in the balloon flights and in the subsequent analysis. From his position thus established as a leader in European collaborative research Powell then played a leading role in the establishment of CERN (the European Centre for Nuclear Research at

Geneva) as fundamental particle research entered the era of giant accelerator machines too expensive for any one nation in Europe. He was chairman of the scientific policy committee of CERN from 1961 to 1963. To the end of his life he continued to play an active part both in the science and in the forward planning of research on fundamental particles.

His politics had been on the left; but in a speech in 1955 on 'The hydrogen bomb and the future of mankind' he said: 'We are in a situation of great difficulty and danger in which it is very important to create a serious and informed body of opinion, all over the world ... [which] must, if it is to be effective, embrace people with conflicting opinions on almost all other issues but who can be united on this', and this represented his political position from then onwards. He was importantly involved in the discussions leading up to the Russell–Einstein declaration of 9 July 1955, of which he was one of the eleven original signatories, and in the setting up of the Pugwash series of conferences on science and world affairs, commencing 7 July 1957. He was elected chairman in 1967, having in fact been the working chairman from the beginning, as deputy to the chairman, Bertrand Russell (third Earl Russell, q.v.), who usually guided the conferences from a distance, prevented by age from attendance. All such duties he performed with great charm, tact, and literary style.

Of medium height, and cheerfully serious disposition, he had among his hobbies landscape drawing with a skilful pencil and the making of his own furniture, preferably from a difficult wood like yew. He had a well-developed sense of humour and was a skilled raconteur: at parties he enjoyed being asked to recite 'The Barge' or to tell some story about his inventive Uncle Horace. As chairman of an awkward confrontation he knew how to lower the temperature with a well-timed joke. As an ex-pro-vice-chancellor at Bristol he was one of his university's leading statesmen at the time of student unrest in 1968, helping to allay suspicions of professors and students alike. He had a love for good English, and particularly liked to find an apposite quotation from the essays of Bacon. One of his greatest joys was an unplanned audience reaction when he gave a lecture on the cosmic rays at Oxford. After he had entered the Sheldonian theatre with the vice-chancellor and bedells in robed procession, his innocent opening words, 'Coming from outer space', brought the house down.

The Royal Society awarded him the Hughes medal in 1949 (the year of his election as fellow) and the Royal medal in 1961; he gave the Bakerian lecture in 1957, and a tercentenary lecture in 1960. The Physical Society of London awarded him the Charles Vernon Boys prize in 1947, and (as the Institute of Physics and the Physical Society) the Guthrie medal and prize in 1969. He received the Nobel prize for physics in 1950 and the Lomonosov gold medal of the Academy of Sciences of the USSR in 1967. He was elected a foreign member of the Academy of Sciences of the USSR in 1958, and of the Yugoslav Academy of Sciences and Arts in 1966. He was an honorary member of the Royal Irish Academy (1959); an ordinary member of the Leopoldina Academy, Halle (1964); an honorary Doctor of Science of the universities of Dublin (1950), Bordeaux (1952), Warsaw (1959), Berlin (1960), Padua (1965), and Moscow (1966); and an honorary fellow of Sidney Sussex College, Cambridge (1966), and of the Institute of Physics and the Physical Society (1962). He was chairman of the Nuclear Physics Board of the British Science Research Council from 1965 to 1968.

In addition to many scientific papers and published lectures, he published, in 1947, with G. P. S. Occhialini, *Nuclear Physics in Photographs*, and, in 1959, with P. H. Fowler and D. H. Perkins, *The Study of Elementary Particles by the Photographic Method*.

He married, in 1932, Isobel Therese, daughter of Johann Artner, an Austrian business executive with I. G. Farbenindustrie. They had two daughters. On 9 August 1969, eight days after he retired from the Bristol chair, he died of a heart attack on an Italian mountain side, at Alpe Giumello, Commune di Casargo, Lago di Como, Italy.

There is a portrait plaque by Desmond Hale Fountain in the H. H. Wills Physics Laboratory, university of Bristol, a drawing by Mervyn Levy and a sculpture by Charlotte Hewer in private hands, and a portrait painting by Bernard Hailstone in the possession of his old school in Tonbridge, Kent. A commemorative plaque donated by the Clifton and Hotwells Improvement Society marks his place of residence from 1946 to 1954 at 1 Downside Road, Clifton, Bristol 8.

[F. C. Frank and D. H. Perkins, with an appendix by A. M. Tyndall, in *Biographical Memoirs of Fellows of the Royal Society*, vol. xvii, 1971; *The Times*, 11 and 16 August 1969; *Scientific World*, vol. xiii, 1969; *Science Today*, December 1969; personal knowledge.]   CHARLES FRANK

POWICKE, SIR (FREDERICK) MAURICE (1879–1963), historian, was born 16 June 1879 at Alnwick, Northumberland, the eldest child of the Revd Frederick James Powicke, a Congregational minister and historian of seventeenth-century Puritanism, and his wife,

Martha, youngest daughter of William Collyer of Brigstock, Northamptonshire. He was named Maurice after F. D. Maurice [q.v.]. In 1886 the family moved to Hatherlow, near Stockport, and Powicke was educated at Stockport Grammar School until, in 1896, he went to the Owens College, Manchester. There he came under the influence of T. F. Tout [q.v.] who turned him into a historian. It was in these years also that Powicke first experienced the pleasure of working in a scholar's library among the books of E. A. Freeman [q.v.] whose library formed one of the earliest departmental libraries in an English university.

In 1899 Powicke went to Balliol College, Oxford, Tout's old college. He became a Brackenbury scholar of the college and read classics with only moderate success, obtaining a second class in *literae humaniores* in 1902. He then returned to history and achieved a first class in that subject in 1903. Meanwhile, he had become a Langton research fellow at Manchester University, a fellowship which he held from 1902 to 1905. This allowed him to do his first serious piece of historical research on Furness Abbey for the Victoria County History of Lancashire; 'I could not', he wrote of this work to Tout in March 1904, 'imagine a better training in the various technical branches of medieval history, the insight into the literature of all centuries, the familiarity with ecclesiastical and manorial and local terminology, the forgotten interests of ordinary political history which it brings.' These casual words in a private letter, written when he was twenty-four, accurately describe the range of Powicke's historical interests and his manner of working on historical subjects during the greater part of his career. Despite his later excursions into European intellectual history, his main work lay in enlarging the 'forgotten interests of ordinary political history'.

With the exception of Tout, who supported him throughout, Powicke at this time was undervalued by those who had the disposal of academic jobs. From 1905 to 1906 he was assistant lecturer at the university of Liverpool, but he failed to get his position renewed, and Tout brought him back to Manchester as assistant lecturer from 1906 to 1908. His election to a prize fellowship at Merton College, Oxford, in 1908 was the turning point in his career and Powicke never ceased to feel a warm attachment to the college which had rescued him from obscurity. A series of important articles in the *English Historical Review* from 1906 to 1909 laid the foundations of his academic reputation and from this date his troubles in getting employment were over. From 1909 to 1919 he was professor of modern history at Queen's University, Belfast;

from 1919 to 1928 professor of medieval history at Manchester; and from 1928 until his retirement in 1947 regius professor of modern history at Oxford. After his retirement he received *Studies in Medieval History presented to Frederick Maurice Powicke*, ed. R. W. Hunt, W. A. Pantin, and R. W. Southern (1948), which contains a full bibliography of his publications to this date. He was given a room in Balliol where he continued to work until shortly before his death. He left his books to Balliol College.

In academic affairs Powicke was a strong supporter of what may broadly be called the Manchester undergraduate course, which laid much more emphasis on training students in historical research than was customary at Oxford. Curiously enough, his early letters show that as a young man he had more doubts about the Manchester system than were apparent later in his career. Certainly, in his last and most influential phase as regius professor, he was committed to attempting to reform the Oxford history course along lines analogous to those which Tout had developed at Manchester. Indeed he believed (wrongly as it turned out) that he had been chosen in order to do this, and it was a bitter disappointment to him when he discovered, as Sir Charles Firth [q.v.] had done before him, that he had insufficient support for carrying out this programme. He never gave up the attempt to reshape the history syllabus, but his main efforts, and nearly all his influence, lay in the congenial work of inspiring and guiding young medieval historians. For this he had an exceptional gift which arose mainly from his power of conveying a tremulous sense of the significance and manifold ramifications of often quite obscure events. Vision and imagination characterized all his historical work. His foremost quality was insight: he illuminated rather than explained; suggested rather than resolved. Consequently few teachers have produced pupils more different from themselves; Powicke encouraged pupils on to their own course in their own way, while remaining himself the most important single influence in their work.

Powicke was the first influential British historian to make his pupils aware of the range of Continental scholarship as it had developed in the last half of the nineteenth century. He was especially sensitive to the scholastic revival instigated by Pope Leo XIII which had been hitherto largely overlooked by British scholars. This awareness extended his imaginative range, but his own work remained firmly rooted in the tradition of English constitutional and institutional history. His first book, *The Loss of Normandy* (1913), showed the pervasive influence of the earlier English antiquaries for whom Powicke always had a special regard; but he approached the subject in his own way with his own characteristic emphasis on details of personalities and places, and a keen awareness that things are never as simple as historians like to think. His next book, *Stephen Langton* (1928), delivered when he was Ford's lecturer for 1926–7, brought English political history into close contact with the development of scholastic theology. It is the most personal of his books and the one in which the influence of sentiment and the imaginative appreciation of the English countryside are most apparent. It was also the book in which, more than anywhere else, he opened up lines of later research. It was followed in 1936 by another work of lasting importance in the same field, produced in collaboration with A. B. Emden. This was a new edition, in three volumes, of *Universities of Europe in the Middle Ages* (1895) by Hastings Rashdall [q.v.]. Although not the most congenial to Powicke's individual genius, this gave him a unique opportunity for showing the great range of his bibliographical knowledge and judgement. In his last two substantial works, *King Henry III and the Lord Edward* (1947), and *The Thirteenth Century, 1216–1307*, the fourth volume in the Oxford History of England, the elaboration of the personal and political aspects of medieval English history was carried to its furthest extremity. These works were the main product of Powicke's years of teaching and research, although his influence was also sustained by a large number of reviews and essays, which showed his extraordinary powers of perception and charm of manner. Among his larger pieces of work, his study and edition of Walter Daniel's *The Life of Ailred of Rievaulx* (1922 and 1950) and of *The Medieval Books of Merton College* (1931) have a high place for their originality of conception and their long-term influence.

Powicke did more than most other British scholars in his generation to rescue medieval studies in this country from the insularity in which, despite all the efforts of the great pioneer William Stubbs [q.v.] they had become embedded. His combination of a strong local and traditional attachment with a widely ranging scholarship and poetic vision made him a decisive force in moulding a new generation of British medievalists.

Apart from his work as a teacher and writer, Powicke was very active in promoting co-operative enterprises in historical scholarship. He saw the Royal Historical Society, of which he was president from 1935 to 1937, as a main instrument in this work. He inaugurated his presidency by putting forward a plan which had an important effect on the society's activities. The series of guides and handbooks and annual bibliographies came into existence as a result of his initiative. Probably the most important of the enterprises he planned was the new edition of the *Concilia* (1737) of David Wilkins [q.v.], of which the first two volumes appeared in 1964, the year after Powicke's death. He also contributed to this Dictionary the notices of his fellow historians, Kate Norgate (with P. Millican), A. G. Little, A. J. Carlyle, and C. C. J. Webb.

In personal appearance Powicke was noticeably small and deceptively fragile; his voice was soft and fluty; he read well, especially such favourite authors as Dickens, and he had a relish for the ridiculous which went with a somewhat macabre and elfish sense of humour. He liked walking and was deeply attached to the Lake District, where for many years he and his family spent most of the summer at their cottage in Eskdale. In 1909 he married Susan Irvine Martin Lindsay (died 1965), daughter of the Revd Thomas M. Lindsay, principal of the United Free College of Glasgow, and the sister of his friend A. D. Lindsay (later first Lord Lindsay of Birker, q.v.). For many years the Powickes' house at 97 Holywell was a place of resort for large numbers of pupils and visiting historians. They had one son, who to Powicke's lasting grief was killed in a road accident in 1936, and two daughters, one of whom, Janet, married Richard Pares, the historian.

He was elected FBA in 1927, and knighted in 1946. He was an honorary fellow of his three Oxford colleges, Merton (1932), Balliol (1939), and Oriel (1947), an honorary doctor of many universities, and a corresponding member of foreign academies in France, Germany, and America. He died in the Radcliffe Infirmary, Oxford, 19 May 1963, after a brief illness.

There are two drawings by J. Oppenheimer, one at the History Faculty Library, Oxford (1955), and one at Balliol (1955). There is also a drawing by R. Schwabe (1944) at Oriel, but the best likeness is a drawing by Walter Stoye (1947) in the possession of the family.

[R. W. Southern in *Proceedings* of the British Academy, vol. l, 1964, with a bibliography of Powicke's published work after 1948; private information; personal knowledge.]

R. W. SOUTHERN

POWNALL, Sir HENRY ROYDS (1887–1961), lieutenant-general, was born in London 19 November 1887, the second son of Charles Assheton Whately Pownall and his wife, Dora Bourne Royds. His father was consulting engineer to the Railway Bureau of Japan, and between the ages of three and eight he was brought up in that country. Later he went to Rugby and from there to the Royal Military

Academy, Woolwich, whence he was commissioned into the Royal Field Artillery in 1906. From 1914 to 1919 he served continuously in France and Belgium, acting as brigade major to the Royal Artillery, 17th division, in 1917–18. He was twice mentioned in dispatches, and was awarded the MC and appointed to the DSO. From 1926 to 1929 he was on the directing staff of the Staff College, Camberley. In 1931 he won a bar to his DSO in action on the North-West Frontier of India. From 1933 to 1936 he served on the secretariat of the Committee of Imperial Defence under Sir Maurice (later Lord) Hankey [q.v.], who was prepared to recommend Pownall as his successor had he not preferred to return to service with troops. From mid 1936 he was commandant of the School of Artillery, Larkhill, with the rank of brigadier.

Thus far there had been nothing exceptional about his career, but his three years at the CID had established his reputation as an exceptionally able staff officer. In the five years preceding the outbreak of war he was promoted no fewer than five times, and his appointment as director of military operations and intelligence at the War Office in January 1938 represented a jump of more than a hundred places in seniority. Long convinced that war with Germany was inevitable, he strove first to secure a definite Continental commitment for the army, then, in the few months remaining (April–August 1939), worked all-out to prepare the British Expeditionary Force to go to France. At the War Office he had enjoyed excellent relations with the chief of the imperial general staff, Lord Gort [q.v.], whom he much admired, so it was not altogether surprising that the latter should select him as his chief of staff when appointed to command the BEF on the outbreak of war; although this entailed—as in 1914—that the two men who knew most about military organization and planning were suddenly removed from the War Office. Pownall sympathized wholeheartedly with Gort in the latter's differences with the secretary of state for war, Leslie (later Lord) Hore-Belisha [q.v.], and after the 'Pill Box affair' Pownall played a considerable part behind the scenes in securing Hore-Belisha's resignation. During the retreat to Dunkirk, Pownall set an admirable example of calmness and foresight, working closely with Gort in the final phase to extricate the BEF from encirclement. He was mentioned in dispatches and appointed KBE.

Unlike Gort, Pownall had clearly retained the prime minister's confidence, for he was given a succession of important commands in potential trouble-spots. After a few months as the first inspector-general of the Local Defence Volunteer Force (later the Home Guard) he was nominated commander-in-chief British Forces in Northern Ireland (1940–1) when German invasion was still a real possibility. When the threat waned he returned to the War Office in May 1941 as vice-chief of the imperial general staff. In November 1941 the replacement of Sir John Dill [q.v.] by Sir Alan Brooke (later Viscount Alanbrooke, q.v.) as chief of the imperial general staff led to a reshuffle among the senior officers at the War Office and Pownall was appointed commander-in-chief Far East. However, Japan entered the war against Britain and the United States before he could effectively take up his command, and in January 1942 he became chief of staff to Sir A. P. (later Earl) Wavell [q.v.] in the short-lived South-West Pacific Command. He was promoted lieutenant-general and for exactly a year from April 1942 took over the Ceylon Command. Once again the enemy robbed him of the opportunity to demonstrate his capacity as a commander, and when the Japanese advance had clearly been arrested he was appointed commander-in-chief Persia-Iraq, succeeding Sir Henry Maitland (later Lord) Wilson [q.v.]. Pownall's ambition was to escape from what he regarded as a backwater into the Mediterranean theatre, but in fact what proved to be his final appointment lay in the other direction. In the summer of 1943 Admiral Mountbatten (later Earl Mountbatten of Burma) had been appointed to the newly created South-East Asia Command, and Brooke—with Churchill's approval—selected Pownall as a highly experienced staff officer to supply a steadying influence as chief of staff. This proved an excellent choice so far as personal relations with Mountbatten and the creation of the large and complex SEAC inter-Allied staff headquarters were concerned; but in strategic terms Pownall's term of office was largely characterized by frustrating changes of plan due to the theatre's low priority in the Allies' grand strategy. In November 1944 Pownall's health broke down, and he retired from the army early in 1945, receiving a KCB. From 1942 to 1952 he was colonel commandant, Royal Artillery.

Pownall was aptly described by his friend and successor as deputy secretary to the Committee of Imperial Defence, Lord Ismay [q.v.], as 'one of the best brains of my vintage in the Army, courageous, competent and cool as a cucumber'. Lieutenant-General Sir Wilfrid Lindsell, who served with 'Henry', as he was universally known, as quartermaster-general of the BEF in 1939–40, wrote of him: 'He certainly possessed all the qualities for success in any branch of Staff work or in Command. He had the essential basis of sturdy common-sense, a well-balanced knowledge of his profession, no fear of taking responsibility and plenty of initiative and energy . . . of a serious turn of mind and always imperturbable in a crisis . . . Quick and precise in manner, he was an energetic worker, bringing to the solution of all his problems a clear well-ordered mind. To all who served under him he was a quiet, courteous and sympathetic chief. He had a remarkable memory and was a masterly writer of minutes and reports.' Lord Wavell found him 'a model of what a senior staff officer should be'.

After retiring from the army Pownall was appointed chief commissioner of the St. John Ambulance Brigade in 1947, becoming vice-chancellor of the Order of St. John in 1950 and chancellor a year later. He was chairman of Friary Meux Ltd. and a member of the committee of Lloyds Bank. For six years he assisted Churchill as military consultant on the latter's *History of the Second World War*. Pownall's chief relaxations were skiing, fly-fishing, and golf. He was an accomplished linguist and a delightful conversationalist with a dry sense of humour.

In 1918 Pownall married Lucy Louttit Gray (died 1950), daughter of William Henderson of Aberdeen and the widow of Captain John Gray, 36th Sikhs, Indian Army, killed at Kut-el-Amara in 1916, by whom she had one son. Pownall died in London 9 June 1961.

There is a life-size oil portrait, three-quarter length, by Simon Elwes, painted when Elwes was official war artist to SEAC; and a miniature (tempera), painted in 1950 by J. W. Pownall-Gray. Both are in the possession of the family.

[*The Times*, 10 June 1961; *Royal Artillery Regimental News*, August 1961; *The Diaries of Lt.-Gen. Sir Henry Pownall, 1933–1944*, ed. Brian Bond, 2 vols., 1972–4; private information.]   BRIAN BOND

POWYS, JOHN COWPER (1872–1963), novelist and miscellaneous writer, was born 8 October 1872 at Shirley, Derbyshire, eldest of the eleven children of the vicar, the Revd Charles Francis Powys, and his wife, Mary Cowper, daughter of the Revd William Cowper Johnson, rector of Yaxham, Norfolk, through whom Powys inherited the blood of the poets Cowper and Donne. Through both parents he came of a long line of country parsons; the Powys family was anciently of Welsh origin, connected in England with the barony of Lilford. When John was seven his father took a curacy at Dorchester, Dorset, and in 1885 became vicar of Montacute, Somerset, so that the conditioning environment on John and his two brothers, Theodore Francis and Llewelyn, was the West Country with which their names

as writers are identified. John was educated at Sherborne School and Corpus Christi College, Cambridge, where he obtained a second in the historical tripos of 1894. He drifted first into lecturing at girls' schools in the Brighton area; then from 1898 to 1909 lectured for the Oxford University Extension Delegacy. Initially he had no wide ambition to be a writer, but in 1896 and 1899 he issued small collections of poems. In 1896 he married Margaret Alice Lyon (died 1947), sister of his Cambridge friend T. H. Lyon; they had one son, Littleton Alfred, who entered first the Anglican, and afterwards the Roman Catholic, priesthood and died in 1954.

In 1905 John Cowper Powys made his first lecture tour in the United States where after 1909 until 1934 he spent the greater part of each year. He drew large audiences by his remarkable eloquence and became a potent force in popular American culture; his standing may be measured by the fact that he was called as an expert defence witness at the court cases arising from publication of *The 'Genius'* by Theodore Dreiser (1915) and *Ulysses* by James Joyce [q.v.] (1922).

In 1915 he published his first novel, *Wood and Stone*, in New York, and thereafter while continuing his profession as lecturer he wrote regularly; and after retiring and returning permanently to Britain he wrote and published steadily until the end of his life, gaining rather than diminishing in power and imagination as time passed. Recognition came slowly, and what may be termed 'official recognition' hardly at all; in 1958 he received the plaque of the Hamburg Free Academy of Arts for outstanding services to literature and philosophy, and in 1962 an honorary D.Litt. from the university of Wales; otherwise he was ignored by those responsible for conferring honours and making awards.

The early novels, *Wood and Stone, Rodmoor* (New York, 1916), and *Ducdame* (1925), received little notice, but *Wolf Solent* (1929) was at once recognized by discerning critics as an important work and the reputation thus established was consolidated by *A Glastonbury Romance* (New York, 1932, London, 1933) although it remained narrow compared with the celebrity of Joyce and Lawrence. *Weymouth Sands* (New York, 1934, published in England as *Jobber Skald*, 1935) and *Maiden Castle* (New York, 1936, London, 1937) had contemporary settings, but with *Owen Glendower* (New York, 1940, London, 1942) Powys began a series of historical novels which included *Porius* (1951), *Atlantis* (1954), *The Brazen Head* (1956), and the related prose retelling of the *Iliad*, *Homer and the Aether* (1959).

Parallel with his novels Powys wrote a series of philosophical essays for the guidance of the 'common man' exposed to the stresses and frustrations of modern urban life: *The Meaning of Culture* (New York, 1929, London, 1930), *A Philosophy of Solitude* (1933), *The Art of Happiness* (1935), *The Art of Growing Old* (1944), and others. His lifelong study of the world's great writers was reflected in *The Pleasures of Literature* (1938), *Dostoievsky* (1947, dated 1946), *Rabelais* (1948), and several collections of essays; but he also appreciated contemporary developments and his *Letters to Louis Wilkinson* (1958) are scattered with perceptive judgements on such writers as Henry Miller, (Sir) Angus Wilson, and Arthur Koestler.

It is by half a dozen novels and an astonishing masterpiece, his *Autobiography* (1934), that Powys will be longest remembered. Introducing a new edition (1967), J. B. Priestley called it 'one of the greatest autobiographies in the English language', seeing its greatness in its subjectivity. Here is no chronicle of events, no parade of famous names, almost nothing of how the author's books came to be written. Instead, we see a man as he saw himself, without reticences, without shame, without regrets, without excuses: a self-portrait unique in English and hardly paralleled elsewhere: the warts certainly displayed, but taken for granted, not underlined; and the humanity, the humility, and the genius unconsciously revealed.

The earlier novels present a minutely observed panorama of the West Country, remembered from the author's boyhood: for most of them were written in America and the terrain was deliberately and lovingly evoked—Dorchester, Montacute, Sherborne, Weymouth. The major historical novels are set in Wales, Powys's home for his last twenty-eight years, and the evocation here is imaginative for he creates a landscape studded with fortresses and peoples it with warriors, magicians, priests, and serfs. Essentially, all his novels—indeed, most of his writings—are concerned with human relationships, often devious, tortured, and hopeless, but enduring. Wolf Solent, John Crow, Dud No-Man, his principal heroes, seem figures arising from himself; but his extraordinary insight into the feelings of women is displayed in a notable group of characters, and a further group of eccentrics and madmen is conceived with the compassion of a Dostoevsky. His faculty of endowing the inanimate with personality produced splendid passages, particularly in *Atlantis* and certain poems like 'The Old Pier Post'. At times his prose is uneven but it reaches and sustains heights of majesty and eloquence denied to more consistent lesser writers.

All members of this remarkable family were striking in appearance and personality, and John Cowper's magnificent head is powerfully seen in Augustus John's frontispiece drawing in *Letters to Louis Wilkinson*, and in Ivan Opfer's frontispiece to the 1934 English edition of the *Autobiography*. The portrait by his sister Gertrude Powys is in the National Museum of Wales.

After retiring, Powys lived at Corwen, and later at Blaenau Ffestiniog, Merioneth, where he died 17 June 1963; his ashes were scattered on the Chesil beach, near Abbotsbury.

[J. C. Powys, *Autobiography*, 1967, *Letters to Louis Wilkinson*, 1958; Louis Marlow, *Welsh Ambassadors: Powys Lives & Letters*, 1936; Derek Langridge, *John Cowper Powys: a Record of Achievement*, 1966; Kenneth Hopkins, *The Powys Brothers*, 1967; personal knowledge.]   KENNETH HOPKINS

PUMPHREY, RICHARD JULIUS (1906-1967), professor of zoology in the university of Liverpool, was born in London 3 September 1906, the only child of Julius Pumphrey, of 7 Marlborough Hill, London, NW, a manufacturer of umbrellas, who traced his descent from James Pomphrey, born about 1490, of Newnham-on-Severn, Worcestershire. Julius Pumphrey's wife, Alice Lilian, was the daughter of Edward Towgood of Hawkes Bay, New Zealand; she had come to England as a child. Pumphrey was educated at Marlborough College (1920-5), where he was greatly influenced by two of his schoolmasters: H. L. O. Flecker, who prompted Pumphrey's lifelong interest in English expression, and the biologist, A. G. Lowndes. It was under Lowndes that Pumphrey learned to know the birds and insects of the countryside. From Marlborough he won an entrance scholarship to Trinity Hall, Cambridge, and gained second class honours in part i of the natural sciences tripos (1927) and first class honours in part ii (1929, zoology and comparative anatomy). He won the Frank Smart prize in 1929 for the best zoologist of the year. He was a fine athlete, rowing in the college boat (whose members called him 'Jerry', a nickname which remained with him) and representing the college at hockey, a game he kept up for many years as a member of the MAs' team. Awarded the Amy Mary Preston Read scholarship in 1929, Pumphrey gained his Ph.D. in 1932 and was then successively Rockefeller fellow at the university of Pennsylvania and Beit fellow at Cambridge (1936-9). From 1930 he was demonstrator in experimental biology and developed the links between this subject and colloid science. He was one of the first to realize the importance of electrical measurement in biology and made some of the early measurements of the electric potential across biological membranes.

As a scientist, Pumphrey is best remembered for his penetrating analysis of the physiology of the senses of hearing and vision in insects and birds. Much of the apparatus used in the initial experiments was constructed with great skill by Pumphrey himself, but he soon started to collaborate with A. F. Rawdon-Smith in the design of equipment which later became standard in electrophysiology. Together they laid the foundations for the understanding of insect hearing. In this work and in Pumphrey's later papers on the sense of hearing in birds and in man, the experimental observations are interpreted using basic physical principles. Pumphrey was always at pains to avoid the tendency, then common among biologists, of 'explaining' animal behaviour in terms of poorly defined concepts. Throughout his career his writings, research, and teaching maintained a degree of rigour and precision which challenged and inspired his pupils and collaborators. He was awarded the Sc.D. degree by Cambridge in 1949 and was elected a fellow of the Royal Society in 1950.

At the outbreak of war in 1939, Pumphrey left Cambridge to research for the Admiralty, first at Portsdown and then in the Signal Establishment at Witley. There he developed a ranging apparatus which was recognized by the Awards Council; he became deputy head of the division responsible fot the development of radar for surveillance and fighter direction.

After returning for a short while to Cambridge as assistant director of research, Pumphrey was appointed Derby professor of zoology at Liverpool University in 1949. His inaugural lecture there, on the origin of language, related his knowledge of animal sounds to his widening interest in the evolution of man and human behaviour. He was noted in Liverpool for the lucidity of his lectures on complex subjects and for his stimulating and astringent comments in faculty and senate meetings. Biology at the university of Liverpool owes much to his work on the academic planning board. He continued for a time his research on insect hearing and vision and wrote a number of valuable review articles on the comparative physiology of these important channels through which animals receive information from the external world.

Pumphrey was married in Cambridge in 1933 to Sylvia Margaret, daughter of W. H. Mills [q.v.], chemist and field botanist. A daughter, Alison Margaret, who became a biochemist, was born in 1936; a son, Nicholas William James (later a research chemist), in 1938, and a son, Richard Stephen Hugh (later a consultant immunologist), in 1944. After 1949 the Pumphreys lived in Hoylake and West Kirby. Pumphrey died in Clatterbridge Hospital, Bebington, 25 August 1967.

[J. W. S. Pringle in *Biographical Memoirs of Fellows of the Royal Society*, vol. xiv, 1968; personal knowledge.]   J. W. S. PRINGLE

R

RACKHAM, BERNARD (1876-1964), museum curator and authority on ceramics, was born in London 26 July 1876, the third son of Alfred Thomas Rackham, Admiralty marshal of the High Court of Justice, and his wife, Anne, daughter of William Stevenson, draper, of Leicester and Nottingham. His eldest brother was Arthur Rackham [q.v.], the illustrator. Rackham was educated at the City of London School and went with an exhibition to Pembroke College, Cambridge, where he took a first in the classical tripos in 1898. He then entered a competition for an assistant keepership at the South Kensington Museum (later the Victoria and Albert Museum) under a scheme whereby the Government aimed to attract Oxford and Cambridge graduates to the museum service. Successful, he was posted to the department of ceramics, where he was destined to remain for forty years, during the last twenty-four of which he was its head.

To Rackham belongs the credit of putting ceramic studies in England on a firm footing, a service which in many fields was also of international significance. Before his time the study of English ceramics was based on facts, assumptions masquerading as facts, and vague traditions. Rackham, by his intellectual vigour and grasp of essentials, reduced this formless mass to order, eliminating baseless assumptions and calling in aid only verifiable and relevant information. The same strict method was applied in other fields. With this disciplined approach he combined a real enthusiasm for art in all its manifestations, ancient and modern, Oriental and Western. For him the aesthetic quality of an object was its ultimate justification.

Shortly after appointment to the museum, Rackham was detailed to register the vast mixed ceramic collection (some 5,000 objects) acquired from the Museum of Practical Geology on its dissolution. This experience underlay his subsequent great and diverse knowledge of ceramics.

Rackham's first publications lay in the field of English ceramics, partly because the main emphasis of the Practical Geology collection lay there, partly because he was charged with reworking the *Catalogue* of the Lady Charlotte Schreiber Collection of English pottery, porcelain, and enamels, the greatest of its kind. The three volumes appeared in 1924-30, only the first volume of the revision having been published previously, in 1915. In 1917 there appeared a complementary *Catalogue* of the English porcelain in the Herbert Allen Collection. These works established the basic categories of English porcelain.

After the war of 1914-18 it fell to Rackham to rearrange the enormous collections of his department. As a fitting complement to this work he undertook the translation from Danish of Emil Hannover's encyclopedic *Keramisk Haandbog* (appearing in three volumes in 1925 as *Pottery and Porcelain*). The previous year he had returned to English studies in *English Pottery*, written with (Sir) Herbert Read [q.v.]. This work represented the first modern classification of all branches of English pottery, and was succeeded by his *Catalogue* (2 vols., 1935) of the vast Glaisher Collection at the Fitzwilliam Museum, Cambridge, still one of the most useful reference works on English pottery.

In 1918 Rackham had turned to an entirely fresh theme in the *Catalogue of the Le Blond Collection of Corean Pottery*, and although he never explored Oriental subjects in great depth, he was perennially interested and stimulated by them, and became a founder-member of the Oriental Ceramic Society. By then he was devoting himself increasingly to the European Middle Ages and Renaissance, particularly tin-glazed earthenware and stained glass. About 1900 he had been invited to help catalogue the works of art inherited by Francis Wyndham Cook, and in 1903 he published his *Catalogue of Italian Maiolica and other Pottery, 8 Cadogan Square*. This experience was the beginning of his special interest and mastery in this field. In 1926 he published a pioneer work on the tin-glazed pottery made in the Low Countries (*Early Netherlands Maiolica*). He contributed important articles on Italian *maiolica* to learned periodicals, and in 1933 brought out a *Guide to Italian Maiolica* in the museum, a masterly work of compression and lucid exposition. The true fruit of his work in this field, however, was seen in his monumental *Catalogue of Italian Maiolica* (1940) in the museum, a two-volume *catalogue raisonné* of the more than 1,400 items in that great collection, and the essential tool in all *maiolica* studies. Rackham's vast erudition in this branch of ceramics was later distilled into the more popular *Italian Maiolica* (1952).

In 1936 a series of articles on stained glass culminated in a *Guide to the Collections of Stained Glass* in the museum, one of the best short summaries of the whole subject in any language. The summit of his work in this field, however, was reached with his *Ancient Glass of Canterbury Cathedral* (1949). This was more than ten years after his retirement, and he continued to publish on various ceramic themes — *A Key to Pottery and Glass* in 1940, *Medieval English Pottery* in 1948, and *Early*

Staffordshire Pottery in 1951. He also published important articles on English and continental glassware, on Limoges enamels, and on continental porcelain.

Rackham, who was a fellow of the Society of Antiquaries, was appointed CB in 1937. He was honorary remembrancer of Guildford, and president of the English Ceramic Circle and of the Guildford Art Society. In 1909 he married Ruth (died 1963), daughter of Francis Adams, of Clapham, a colonial merchant; they had one son and one daughter.

Apart from his scholarly work, Rackham was also a civil servant, charged with the administration of a department. These duties he conscientiously fulfilled, requiring of his subordinates the same high standards which he imposed upon himself. Personally, he was highly strung and eager, overflowing with enthusiasm, and endowed with a keen sense of humour. He was tall and lean, with a bright eye and a strikingly erect carriage even in old age. He died at Liss 13 February 1964.

[*The Times*, 15 February 1964; *Burlington Magazine*, September 1964; private information; personal knowledge.]

R. J. CHARLESTON

RAMAN, SIR (CHANDRASEKHARA) VENKATA (1888–1970), physicist, was born at Trichinopoly, then in the province of Madras, now the Tamil Nadu, 7 November 1888, the son of Chandrasekhara Iyer, and his wife, Parvati Ammal. The family were engaged in agriculture, but his father took an unusual step in becoming a teacher at the local high school. Soon after, when C. V. R. was four years old, his father was appointed a lecturer in mathematics and physics at a college in Vizagapatam.

For eight years Raman studied at the local high school in Vizagapatam, and for two more at the college. His intellectual ability was clear, and he obviously received much encouragement from his parents. He soon qualified to enter a university course and in 1903 went to the Presidency College at Madras. In 1904 he took the BA degree with high honours and was awarded the gold medal for physics, and in 1908 the MA with distinction. At this early age his interest in scientific research became evident, and especially in the diffraction of light. It appeared in two short but interesting articles accepted in the *Philosophical Magazine* (1906) and *Nature* (1907, p. 1908), when he was not yet twenty.

This was an important moment in Raman's career. Science was not much encouraged in India, conditions and facilities for work were poor, and reasonably paid jobs were few. Raman

therefore applied for an administrative post under the Indian Government, won it in examination, and in 1907 joined the Finance Department in Calcutta. He held this post for ten years. Yet his interest in science was not to be dispelled, and he found in Calcutta a place where he could pursue it, namely the Indian Association for the Cultivation of Science, which had been established in 1876. Here he was able in his spare time to do some experimental work, and he published many papers, mostly in English and American journals. A much respected member of the Association was Sir Asutosh Mookerjee, a high court judge and vice-chancellor of the Calcutta University, who recognized Raman's potential and in 1917 invited him to become the Palit professor of physics at the university. At some financial sacrifice, he accepted and a little later also became the honorary secretary of the Indian Association for the Cultivation of Science.

The next fifteen years were very productive. Raman sought and gathered more funds for his work, although through his whole life he maintained that simple experimentation with inexpensive equipment was desirable. Many young Indian scientists went to work with him. His main researches were in acoustics and physical optics, but covered many aspects including vibrations and sound, the properties of musical instruments, diffraction, colour and interference, colloids, the molecular scattering of light, X-rays, magnetism, and magneto-optics. He was always much interested in the optical and magnetic anisotropy of molecules.

The Raman effect, to which his name was given and which ensured his lasting recognition in modern science, was announced in 1928. His book, *Molecular Diffraction of Light*, published in 1922, seemed, in retrospect, to point towards the discovery. For many years he had studied the scattering of light by matter in different states of aggregation, and noticed that colours different from that of the incident beam were produced. White light shone into a flask of clear benzene produced a blue colour. The effect was not the same as had been established much earlier by the third Baron Rayleigh [q.v.] and others, when the different colours in white light are scattered with an intensity related in a continuous way with their wavelength. Using filters and a somewhat crude experimental technique, Raman was able to show that new wavelengths different from that of the individual light appear with a wavelength gap, a 'dark space', between themselves and that of the incident source. The effect was more easily observed by the use of mercury arcs with filters to produce monochromatic incident radiation, and a simple spectroscope to analyse the scattered radiation.

Announcing his discovery in *Nature* (vol. 121, p. 501 and p. 619), Raman recognized that this scattering must in some way be related to new ideas of the quantum theory and the existence of light quanta. In 1905 Albert Einstein had interpreted quantitatively the photoelectric effect, the emission of electrons from metals when irradiated by light of high frequency, in terms of light quanta from which kinetic energy of the electrons had been derived. The Compton effect (1923), the impact of X-rays upon electrons with discrete changes of the wavelength of the X-rays, had also been interpreted in terms of light quanta. The loss of energy from the incident light source in the Raman effect is now attributed to the absorption of molecular vibrational or rotational quanta, but at that time little was known about such vibrations or rotations because molecular spectra had not been interpreted satisfactorily.

Smekal had predicted some time earlier (*Naturwiss*, 1923, vol. xi, p. 873) that the interaction of light energy with molecules might be accompanied by a loss of energy quanta, and Herzfeld (*Zeit. Phys.*, 1924, vol. xxiii, p. 341) had suggested an interpretation in terms of 'intermediate states'. Before Raman, however, no one had shown the effect by experiment, and it is to him that the credit has rightly been given. In his Nobel lecture (1930) Raman mentions the significance of vibrational and rotational energy quanta of molecules. The Raman effect became one of the main methods for the determination of molecular vibrational frequencies and for the specific identification of features of molecular structure. Improvements in technique, with new monochromatic light sources and better handling of samples, and in the recording of spectra have made it easier to measure Raman spectra, and the molecular data thus obtained are now of fundamental value in many branches of physics and chemistry.

Among his other work at Calcutta, Raman studied the sounds of musical instruments, and especially the violin. He examined the vibrations of stretched strings as affected by the mechanical structure of the instrument. He made similar measurements on Indian drums. He was mainly concerned with tonal quality and the occurrence of harmonics. He wrote a series of papers about this for the Indian Association for the Cultivation of Science and a lengthy article on the physics of musical instruments in the *Handbuch der Physik* (vol. viii, 1927).

In 1933 Raman left Calcutta to become the director of the Indian Institute of Science, Bangalore. He had recently received the Nobel prize, and his whole attitude to science differed from that of many of the current Indian administrators. Some difficulties might have been anticipated. At any rate, problems arose over the management and policies of the Institute, so that he soon gave up the directorship. Previously, there had been no department of physics. Raman became professor of physics and established a school in which much distinguished research was carried out during his tenure of fifteen years. Many new data were accumulated from the Raman effect. Also, he explored some new phenomena which had been noticed when light is diffracted by a liquid through which supersonic waves are being passed. With Nagendra Nath he was able to formulate a theory to explain the effects. He found, too, that when X-rays are directed at diamond, unexpected reflexions occur of a different kind from the well-known Laue patterns. He also studied luminescence and other optical properties of minerals.

In 1934 Raman was able to get the Indian Academy of Sciences established, became its first president, and remained so until his death in 1970. Along similar lines to the Royal Society of London, he arranged for the monthly publication of the *Proceedings* of the Indian Academy, in two parts dealing respectively with the physical and biological sciences, and by much hard work and organization this was continued throughout his life.

Before retiring from the Indian Institute in 1948, he managed to obtain grants from private individuals, industry, and the Government of Mysore to build the Raman Research Institute at Bangalore, of which he was the director from its opening in 1949 until his death. As well as the research laboratory, it contains a collection of exhibits of natural historical and scientific interest made by Raman himself. He began new measurements in gem stones. With diamonds, he studied the ultraviolet transparency, fluorescence, luminescence, birefringence, X-ray scattering, specific heat, magnetic susceptibility, photoconductivity, the Faraday effect, and other properties. He was able to separate diamonds into tetrahedral and octahedral types. Some had a blue fluorescence in ultraviolet radiation. He made a sort of taxonomic classification within a large collection of diamonds. As a result of this work, research on diamond still continues in many laboratories today, and although the physics of the solid state and our understanding of lattice defects have advanced considerably, some curious properties of diamonds remain unexplained. Raman gave much thought to the mechanism of human perception of colour, and published a treatise, *The Physiology of Vision*, in 1968. He was honoured by election as the first national professor appointed by the Indian Government.

In the second half of his life he travelled much to Europe and North America. He first visited England in 1921 as Indian delegate to the Universities Congress at Oxford. In his keenness to observe everything possible on his journey he carried in his pockets small equipment such as a Nicol prism, small spectroscope, and diffraction grating, and it is said that he was intrigued by the blue colour of the Mediterranean, which increased his interest in the scattering of light. In 1924 he joined the British Association for the Advancement of Science in a tour of Canada, accepted an invitation of Professor R. Millikan to spend four months at the California Institute of Technology at Pasadena, and attended the centenary of the Franklin Institute of Technology. Later he was a guest of the Soviet Academy of Sciences in Leningrad and Moscow. He took part in the Faraday Society discussions on molecular spectra at Bristol (1929), international congresses of physics in Paris and Bologna (1937), and the twentieth anniversary celebration of the Raman effect at Bordeaux (1948).

Raman became a legendary figure of Indian science. He had a sense of awe and wonder at nature and of the unknown, and an intensely enquiring mind. He was fascinated particularly by the colours of minerals, birds, and butterflies and wrote much about the colours of morning glory, hibiscus, jacaranda, bougainvillea, and other flowers. Late in his life, he sought to understand zonal winds and the properties of the Earth's atmosphere. He was dedicated to science, and worked hard at it, and for it, all his life. His papers, though often short, were marked by great clarity. He published more than 500 papers and four books. Although his access to the foreign literature must have been limited, his publications showed considerable knowledge of the work of leading foreign scientists. He always acknowledged the help of his co-workers. In later years he was disappointed with trends in Indian science. He deplored the emigration of Indian scientists abroad, forced upon them by lack of appropriate funds and facilities. Yet he was also against unnecessarily large expenditure, and regretted, for example, the use of human resources on space science. His rigid defence of an ivory-tower attitude perhaps lost him some friends.

Raman was elected a fellow of the Royal Society of London in 1924, knighted by the British Government in India in 1929, and received the Nobel prize for physics in 1930. He was an honorary doctor of science of the universities of Calcutta, Bombay, Madras, Benares, Dacca, Allahabad, Patna, Lucknow, Osmania, Mysore, Delhi, Kanpur, and Paris; and was appointed honorary LLD of Glasgow University and honorary Ph.D. of Freiburg. He was an honorary member of the Royal Irish Academy, the Royal Philosophical Society of Glasgow, the Academy of Sciences in Hungary, Poland, Romania, and Czechoslovakia, the Munich Academy, the Zurich Physical Society, the Catgut Acoustical Association, and the Indian Science Congress Association; foreign associate of the Paris Academy of Sciences, and a foreign member of the Academy of Sciences of the USSR; and honorary fellow of the American Optical Society, and of the American Mineralogical Society. He received the Matteuci medal of the Italian Academy (1928), the Hughes medal of the Royal Society (1930), the medal of the Franklin Institute of Philadelphia (1940), and the Lenin prize of the Soviet Union (1957), and was president of the Indian Science Congress in 1929. In 1954 the Indian Government gave him the unique title of Bharat Ratna.

In 1907 Raman married Loka Sundari Ammal, who was his constant support in his scientific activities. They had two sons. Raman died in Bangalore 21 November 1970.

There is a portrait in the Raman Research Institute at Bangalore.

[S. Bhagavantam in *Biographical Memoirs of Fellows of the Royal Society*, vol. xvii, 1971; *The Scattering of Light*, Indian Academy of Sciences, Bangalore, 1978.]

H. W. THOMPSON

RANSOME, ARTHUR MICHELL (1884–1967), journalist and author, was born in Leeds, 18 January 1884, the eldest in the family of two sons and two daughters of Cyril Ransome, professor of history, who died when Arthur was thirteen, and his wife, Edith, daughter of Edward Baker Boulton, who had been a sheep farmer in Australia. He was educated at the Old College, Windermere, and Rugby, but he was a reluctant pupil. Doggedly determined from early adolescence that he was going to be a writer, he spent two unprofitable terms at Yorkshire College, Leeds (later to become Leeds University), reading science before he threw in his hand and left for London where he found a job for eight shillings a week at Grant Richards, the publishers. He was then seventeen.

His bohemian life in London, with a brief period in Paris, lasted for some twelve years. He scratched a living by writing stories and articles, some of which appeared in book form; he reviewed and ghosted. His literary friends included Edward Thomas, Lascelles Abercrombie, Gordon Bottomley, Robert Lynd [qq.v.] and his wife Sylvia, and Cecil Chesterton, brother of G. K. Chesterton [q.v.]. There were also actors and artists with whom he would celebrate the sale of an article or a picture by a flagon of Australian burgundy and a meal of macaroni cheese. Many of these met at the studio 'evenings' of Pamela Colman Smith—'Pixie'; he later said that it was from her telling of Negro folk-stories that he learnt so much of the art of narration. He was very poor but nevertheless avidly buying books, and he later attributed his chronic stomach troubles to the meagre and erratic meals of that period.

If there was time for a brief holiday and he could scrape together the fare, he found himself hurrying 'through the big grey archway at Euston that was the gate to the enchanted North' on his way to the Lake District where, before his father had died, his family had spent summer months so happy that the rest of his life seemed an anticlimax. Here he passed much of his time with the family of W. G. Collingwood, adopted as an honorary nephew by the parents, and camping and boating with the children, one of whom was Robin Collingwood [q.v.]. Later, the four children of Dora, the oldest daughter (later Altounyan), were to identify themselves as the Walker children in his books. He hoped to marry Barbara, the second daughter, but this never came about, and it was to escape the unhappy marriage that he did make, to Ivy Constance, daughter of George Graves Walker, in 1909, that he went to Russia in 1913.

The winter of 1912–13 had been one of continual nightmare. A book commissioned by Martin Secker on Oscar Wilde [q.v.] had landed Ransome in a suit for libel issued by Lord Alfred Douglas [q.v.], and though judgment was against Douglas in April 1913 it was a scarring experience. Meanwhile, seeing Russian folklore as the material for a new book of folk-stories retold in a simple vernacular style, he decided to visit Russia itself. Arriving there in 1913, he taught himself Russian, collected folklore, and busied himself with writing a guide to St. Petersburg commissioned by an English firm. After the outbreak of war (which prevented the guide from being published), he supported himself as a newspaper correspondent for the *Daily News*. In 1916 was published *Old Peter's Russian Tales*, the result of Ransome's investigations into Russian folklore. It had considerable success and was reprinted several times. Paying regular brief visits to England, he stayed in Russia until 1919, becoming friendly with Lenin and other Bolshevik leaders, especially Karl Radek, and making himself unpopular with the British Foreign Office by his opposition to foreign intervention in Russian affairs. For a time in 1918 a British mission in Moscow was headed by (Sir) Robert Bruce Lockhart [q.v.], of whom Ransome said '. . . [he] was soon on better terms with Trotsky than I was'. In *Six*

Weeks in Russia in 1919 (1919) he gave a picture of Moscow in those days of starvation and high hopes, and in *The Crisis in Russia* (1921) he defended the Russian revolution and pleaded for a more balanced view of its aims.

By that time he was living in Estonia with Evgenia, daughter of Peter Shelepin (she had been Trotsky's secretary), whom he was to marry in 1924 when his first marriage had been dissolved. His long association with C. P. Scott [q.v.] and the *Manchester Guardian* started in 1919, and such time as he could spare from his newspaper reports he spent in the fishing and sailing that all his life were an absorbing passion. In the *Racundra*, a thirty-ton ketch, built to his specifications at Riga, he cruised round the Baltic in 1922. The log of this holiday was published in '*Racundra's' First Cruise* (1923).

At the end of 1924 Scott sent him as correspondent to Egypt and then in 1925–6 to China, but he was growing increasingly weary of political journalism and longing to settle to his own writing. In March 1929 he began to write *Swallows and Amazons*, an account of four children and their holiday camping and sailing in the Lakes, an evocation of the supreme happiness of his own boyhood holidays. Published in 1930, it was slow to sell. Jonathan Cape [q.v.], the publisher, had received it politely but was more interested in his fishing essays, *Rod and Line* (1929). Nevertheless he persisted, following it up with a further account of the Walker children and their allies the Blacketts sailing Lake Windermere and exploring the fells—*Swallowdale* (1931). But only with his third story, *Peter Duck* (1932), did he soar into the popularity that made his nine other books for children best-sellers. (It was in *Peter Duck* that he first attempted his own illustrations, a practice he was to continue.) *Winter Holiday* (1933) recalled a winter he had spent on the Lakes when he was at preparatory school. There were books such as *Coot Club* (1934) about bird-watching and sailing on the Norfolk Broads, near which he lived for a time from 1935 on the river Orwell, in Suffolk. For *Pigeon Post* (1936) he received the Library Association's first Carnegie medal for the best children's book of the year. He became an honorary D.Litt. of Leeds University in 1952 and was appointed CBE in 1953. He published his last book, *Mainly about Fishing*, in 1959.

Bald, vastly moustached as he became in later life, habitually dressed in a fisherman's sagging tweeds and a thimble of a tweed hat, he still contrived to retain much of the appearance of the round, rosy, bright-eyed schoolboy that can be seen in the early photographs. With it went a boyish charm of manner with its mingling of enthusiasm and fierce indignation;

a deftness of fingers—especially where tying flies was concerned—and a stimulating ability to say something new and unexpected about almost any subject.

He died 3 June 1967 at Cheadle Royal Hospital, Manchester. His second wife died in 1975. He had one daughter by his first marriage. There is a portrait by John Gilroy, 1958, in the Garrick Club.

[*The Times*, 6 June 1967; Hugh Shelley, *Arthur Ransome*, 1960; *The Autobiography of Arthur Ransome*, ed. Sir Rupert Hart-Davis, 1967.]   GILLIAN AVERY

RAVEN, CHARLES EARLE (1885–1964), professor of divinity, was born 4 July 1885 in Paddington, eldest of the three children of John Earle Raven, barrister, and his wife, Alice, daughter of Edward Comber, a Liverpool merchant. His younger brother was Edward Earle Raven who was chaplain of St. John's College, Cambridge (1921–6), and dean from 1927 until his death in 1951. Charles Raven was educated at Uppingham School, in Fircroft House which was then under his uncle, the Revd Tancred Earle Raven. He won a classical scholarship to Gonville and Caius College, Cambridge, and obtained a first class in part i of the classical tripos in 1907, and a first with distinction in part ii of the theological tripos in 1908, specializing in early Christian doctrine. In July 1906, while still an undergraduate, he became engaged to the master's niece, Margaret Ermyntrude Buchanan ('Bee') Wollaston, whom he married in 1910. Raven started his career as assistant secretary for secondary education under the Liverpool City Council (1908–9), where he was miserable; for the first time, however, he saw beyond his middle-class upbringing, to understand the meaning of fellowship and dedication, when he engaged in the work of a boys' club. In 1909 he was offered the position of lecturer in divinity, fellow, and dean of Emmanuel College, Cambridge, provided he would be ordained that December. The idea fitted his newly found sense of vocation, and he took up the post at the beginning of 1910. There he was instantly thrown into a tense college and university controversy as the master, William Chawner, had issued a pamphlet declaring that Christian orthodoxy was indefensible: Raven, *ex officio* at the centre of the ensuing storm, went through a time of intense anxiety.

After the outbreak of war, he was assistant master at Tonbridge School in 1915–17, and a front-line army chaplain in France during 1917–18, where he suffered slightly from being gassed. He returned to Emmanuel and, needing a home for his wife and four children,

accepted the college living of Blechingley (or Bletchingley), Surrey, where he was rector for four years, until he became residentiary canon of the new Liverpool Cathedral from 1924 to 1932. Raven was already well known for his oratory, and as early as 1920 he was appointed a chaplain to the King. Within the life of the travelling preacher he managed to write two important books. *Christian Socialism 1848–1854* (1920) was the first to treat this important Victorian movement historically; he felt strong links with the ideals of Christian socialism, and was one of the chief organizers of the influential Conference on Christian Politics, Economics and Citizenship ('Copec') in 1924: he was its joint secretary from 1920 to 1928, under the chairmanship of William Temple [q.v.], who remained a lifelong friend. In 1923 he published *Apollinarianism*, a sober and fundamental study of a then neglected aspect of primitive Christian thought, which made his name in a different world, that of academic divinity, and gained him the Cambridge DD. In 1932 he was appointed regius professor of divinity at Cambridge. With the chair he held a canonry at Ely cathedral (1932–40), a fellowship at Christ's College, and from 1939 to 1950 the mastership of Christ's.

As professor he had a full audience; he would lecture *extempore*, pacing with restless energy about the room. The lectures were not geared to undergraduates' needs to pass examinations, nor easy to summarize in the form of notes. The austere Cambridge tradition of linguistic knowledge and historical texts he regarded as excellent but far too narrow. He long argued for a wider syllabus, especially to include the place of theology in the modern world, and like many reformers he did not see the reform for which he had worked until after he had retired. But his own lectures took the great Christian themes one by one—God, Christ, Holy Spirit, creation, creed, future life, idea of the Church—and tried to expound them in the context of a scientific world and contemporary social need. The thinkers to whom he loved to point were those who tried to marry faith with the reason and science of their own day: the Alexandrian Fathers in the third century, or the Cambridge Platonists in the seventeenth. The difficulty, as in all his writing, lay in showing how the drastic reinterpretation which he called for would differ from the watering down of Christianity (as he thought it) in the work of scientific modernists such as Ernest William Barnes or James Bethune-Baker [qq.v.]. He had a deeper sense of immediacy—even ecstasy—in religious experience, and a quicker perception of the numinous in nature, which he could more easily make men feel than himself analyse. A brilliant scholar, he had too large a heart to attain the detachment of the pure academic.

From boyhood he loved birds and insects and wild flowers, and as an adult he made himself expert in the history of the life-sciences. He wrote a happy little book, *In Praise of Birds* (1925), painted wild flowers and birds with exquisite precision, and was a pioneer of the photography of birds in flight. His desire to heal the breach between faith and reason turned slowly towards reconciling science and religion: he believed that the evolutionary process could be accounted for only in terms of the movement of spirit. He wrote and lectured more on the theme of science and religion than on any other subject: to him, science meant biology and evolution, and religion a humane and liberal interpretation of Christianity. The most ambitious of these efforts were the Gifford lectures at Edinburgh for 1951-2, published as *Natural Religion and Christian Theology* (1953). But his best books in the field were more modest endeavours to explain early English science; *John Ray, Naturalist* (1942) and *English Naturalists from Neckam to Ray* (1947—which won a James Tait Black prize) were notable contributions to the history of biology. As war approached in the late thirties, liberal divinity was assailed as too facile for the ills of the age. Raven vehemently denounced the swing against reason and the leaders of European intellectual reaction headed by Karl Barth. In his later years as professor he felt grief that young men seemed to be neglecting his type of liberal thought, and it came as a relief when the French Jesuit Teilhard de Chardin won posthumous celebrity for a proposal to reconcile evolution with faith along lines which were in substance those proposed by Raven himself three decades before. In 1962 Raven published the first English biography of de Chardin.

Meanwhile he met the course of the world head on over the question of pacifism. During the twenties he slowly came to adopt the position as faithful to the New Testament, and in 1932 he became chairman of the Fellowship of Reconciliation and two years later one of the sponsors of the Peace Pledge Union with the Revd H. R. L. ('Dick') Sheppard [q.v.]; he delivered an impressive apologia in his Halley Stewart lectures of 1934, *Is War Obsolete?* (1935). This movement lost influence unsteadily from 1937 as the Nazi threat grew, but Raven was a man who committed his heart to a cause and did not waver, in spite of frustration and depression of spirit. At the outbreak of war in 1939 he therefore faced unpopularity and contempt, although he gave unfailing help to refugees in England, and at times even he could not quite be constant, as when he gave thanks in the college chapel for the victory at El Alamein. He would have liked high office in the Church of England, but so much controversy surrounded his name during the years when he was the right age that he was passed over. In 1947, however, Cambridge University unexpectedly summoned him to be vice-chancellor. His two years of office were difficult, with so many returned soldiers crowding two into a room; but Raven confounded prophets who predicted that so charismatic a man could not administer a great institution. As one who had long contended for the advancement of women (including their ordination) he had the special happiness of presiding over the belated but at last unopposed admission of women to full membership of the university, and of bringing the Queen to an honorary degree as the first women graduate in 1948. In the same year he helped to choose J. C. Smuts [q.v.] as the university's new chancellor; they had been friends for many years.

On his retirement from both chair and mastership in 1950, he accepted the position of warden of Madingley Hall, which the university had just bought as a hostel. The Hall needed a good secretary, not one of the principal orators of Europe who felt that it was 'a backwater' offering little scope for his talents; the result was not altogether happy, and he gave up the wardenship in 1954. However, Raven travelled, lectured, and preached more widely than ever after his retirement, visiting the United States several times, Australia and New Zealand (1950), Canada (1952), Russia (1954), and India in 1955-6. He spent much time in visiting schools, too, where he would both preach and talk informally to the boys, and it was said that his ministry to sixth-formers may have been the most influential of his career; he was also a popular figure on radio and television (once the wartime ban on his voice as a pacifist had been lifted), giving a new dimension to religious broadcasting. All his adult life he had been a great preacher and a natural leader of men: tall and spare, with chiselled features, brilliant eyes, a youthful appearance, dynamic energy, and a magical voice, he never spoke without riveting attention; yet he never outgrew a certain nervousness before preaching, and would privately rehearse like an actor in order to speak without notes. On religious subjects he felt passionately, and at his best he could communicate the fervour and agony which were a part of his being. With an evangelical gospel, he was simultaneously an intellectual and a classicist trying to integrate his own faith and that of his hearers into the honest apprehension of a scientific world—a quality which made him wanted as a lecturer and in pulpits everywhere. He retained the magnetic power of his oratory until the end of his life.

Raven was a trustee of the British Museum from 1950, a fellow of the British Academy from 1948, president of the Botanical Society of the British Isles in 1951-5, and fellow of the Linnean Society; and he received honorary degrees from many universities: the one he valued most was a doctorate of science from Manchester. He wrote many books besides those mentioned: the most important were his Hulsean and Noble lectures of 1926-7, combined as *The Creator Spirit* in 1927; *Jesus and the Gospel of Love* (1931); *Evolution and the Christian Concept of God* (1936); *Science, Religion and the Future* (1943, the published version of his Cambridge Open lectures); and *Good News of God* (1943).

Raven's first wife, by whom he had a son and three daughters, died in 1944—a shattering blow, only a year after his own serious illness. After her death his eldest daughter, Mary, presided at the Lodge, until in 1954 he married Ethel, widow of John Moors, of Boston, Massachusetts, with whom he had worked closely in the pacifist cause. She was already eighty, and died on honeymoon within a fortnight of the marriage. In 1956 he married Hélène Jeanty ('Ninette'), a former worker in the Belgian resistance whose first husband had been shot by the Nazis; living partly in Cambridge and partly in Brussels, they dedicated themselves to a mission of reconciliation between students of different races. His only son, John Earle Raven (died 1980), became a fellow and dean of King's College, Cambridge, and an authority upon both ancient Greek philosophy and mountain plants.

Raven died in Cambridge 8 July 1964. A portrait painted in 1949 by Edmund Nelson hangs in Christ's College, Cambridge, and another, by Baron Antoine Allard (1962), is in the possession of the family.

[C. E. Raven, *A Wanderer's Way*, 1928, and *Musings and Memories*, 1931; F. W. Dillistone, *Charles Raven*, 1975; I. T. Ramsey in *Proceedings* of the British Academy, vol. li, 1965; *The Times*, 10 July 1964; Hélène Jeanty Raven, *Without Frontiers*, 1960; personal knowledge.]   OWEN CHADWICK

READ, SIR HERBERT EDWARD (1893-1968), writer on art, critic, and poet, was born 4 December 1893, the eldest of the three sons of Herbert Read, of Muscoates Grange, Kirbymoorside, in the North Riding of Yorkshire, and his wife, Eliza Strickland. Of farming stock, he was always proud of his peasant origins, and gave a memorable account of them in *The Innocent Eye*, a fragment of autobiography (1933). They were also the inspiration of *Moon's Farm*, a poem written for the radio in 1951. When he left his birthplace to go to the Crossley

and Porter Endowed School for orphans in Halifax, he wrote that 'no wild animal from the pampas imprisoned in a cage could have felt so hopelessly thwarted'. After employment as a clerk in the Leeds Savings Bank at the age of sixteen, he entered Leeds University, and felt the literary influence of Blake and Tennyson. At the same time he came under the spell of Nietzsche. On the outbreak of war in 1914 he was commissioned into the Green Howards, and rose to the rank of captain, winning both the MC and the DSO—the type of 'resolute soldier' who organized his men for battle as he would afterwards try to organize the world for peace. His distinguished military record, which included a mention in dispatches, lent an added authority to his pacifism.

He had also, like Guillaume Apollinaire, fought 'on the frontiers of culture'. There was a certain discrepancy between a man so traditional in his way of life, so concerned to create a 'cell of good living' for himself and his family, and the tireless apostle of the avant-garde in literature and art. He was an early pioneer of the modern movement, where his friendship with T. S. Eliot [q.v.] and T. E. Hulme, Ben Nicholson, (Dame) Barbara Hepworth, and Henry Moore, counted for much. Read's imagination was essentially visual. This set him apart from a poet like W. B. Yeats [q.v.] for whom poetry was always, in some degree, incantation, and ranked him with the Imagists who held that only free verse could guarantee to the picture its sharp outline, and to the emotion its unblurred significance. Read's output of verse was not large, but at its best—that is to say, at its most direct and concrete, and at its least explanatory —it had a moving honesty, precision, and power.

Herbert Read was aware of the two forces which shaped his life and gave it a creative tension. As he wrote in *Moon's Farm*: 'the instinctive voice that flows like water from a spring or blood from a wound | and the intellectual voice that blares like a fanfare from some centre in the brain.' It was this second voice which, as time went on, was more generally heard. His public appointments registered an increasing interest in the visual arts. After a short period at the Treasury (1919-22), he became an assistant keeper at the Victoria and Albert Museum (1922-31), and Watson Gordon professor of fine art in the university of Edinburgh (1931-3). From 1933 to 1939 he edited the *Burlington Magazine*. In these years he published *Art Now* (1933), *Art and Industry* (1934), and *Art and Society* (1937), all of which were many times reprinted. Only the outbreak of war prevented the establishment of a Museum of Modern Art in London of which he would have been the first director—for his championship of the Surrealist Exhibition (1936) had marked him out as the principal theorist of non-figurative painting and sculpture, where the intention—as Paul Klee had put it—was 'not to reflect the visible, but to make visible'. In 1947 he founded, with Roland Penrose, the Institute of Contemporary Arts—not as yet another place for study or exhibition, but as 'an adult play-centre . . . a source of vitality and daring experiment'.

Through all these activities, and the numerous publications which accompanied them, Read became an international authority and indeed something of a sage. It was not a role to which he ever pretended, for he was a man of conspicuous modesty, and quite capable himself of resting in uncertainty about the essential matters of life and death. His somewhat uncritical welcoming of the new experiment often reflected his dissatisfaction with the old one. But he believed, profoundly, in the dialectic of tradition and innovation, of anarchy and order, which alone could preserve society from sclerosis. This was the meaning of his single novel, *The Green Child* (1935). His anarchism was philosophical, not political, although he was generally found subscribing to any protest on behalf of personal freedom, and he sat down with the others in Trafalgar Square while Bertrand (Earl) Russell [q.v.] was warning the world against the imminent threat of self-destruction. This nonconformity did not prevent the offer and acceptance of a knighthood in 1953. His anarchist friends were dismayed, but it was observed that the Queen had never dubbed a knight to whom the epithet of 'gentle' was more perfectly applicable.

Read's poetry was the classical expression of a romantic temperament, and his literary criticism emphasized his sympathy with romanticism. His Clark lectures on Wordsworth (1930) showed how a passionate love affair and a passionate political *parti-pris* had simultaneously inspired so much of Wordsworth's greatest poetry, and how its incandescence grew faint when the first had cooled and the second had been betrayed. *In Defence of Shelley* (1936) rescued the poet from the denigrations of T. S. Eliot, with whom Read remained on terms of the closest friendship, although Eliot had quoted Read's opposition of 'character' and 'personality' as an example of 'modern heresy'. Read's philosophy might not unfairly be described as 'aesthetic materialism', but the purpose of his preaching in one book after another was to link the good life with the good artefact. *Education Through Art* (1943) indicated how this might be done.

In 1950 Read returned to his Yorkshire roots at Stonegrave, only a few miles from his birthplace. A beautiful stone house was filled with pictures illustrating the achievement of the school whose prophet he had become. For some years he was a director of Routledge & Kegan Paul, and this, among other things, brought him to London for a few days every alternate week. And these years saw the publication of his Concise Histories of *Modern Painting* (1959) and of *Modern Sculpture* (1964). Much of his time, however, was spent abroad, as a speaker at international congresses. He was not at all a voluble person, but it was remarked that 'when Read does at last open his mouth, you know there's nothing more to be said'. In the last years of his life the poet and the peasant, the philosopher and the paterfamilias, seemed to have realized their separate vocations in a serene and unified way of living. He was twice married: first, in 1919, to Evelyn May Roff, by whom he had one son; and, after the dissolution of the marriage in 1936, to Margaret Ludwig, by whom he had three sons and a daughter. He died at Stonegrave 12 June 1968.

The National Portrait Gallery has a portrait by P. Heron given by Dame Barbara Hepworth and Henry Moore.

[Private information; personal knowledge.]
ROBERT SPEAIGHT

READ, HERBERT HAROLD (1889-1970), geologist, was born at Whitstable, Kent, 17 December 1889, the third of the four children of Herbert Read, dairy farmer, and his wife, Caroline Mary Kearn. On his father's side he was descended from many generations of small farmers in east Kent, from whom he inherited a love of the country. He was educated, with a scholarship, at Simon Langton School, Canterbury, where he became head of the school, and, from 1908, at the Royal College of Science, London, where he graduated with first class honours in 1911, with geology as his main subject. After three years as a junior member of staff, and his acquisition of an M.Sc., he left in 1914 to join the Geological Survey of Great Britain. By then he had already begun the first of his eight successive revisions of a well-established geological classic, Rutley's *Elements of Mineralogy*, which had then reached its eighteenth edition. Fifty-five years later he was at work on his latest revision two days before his death. This simple, straightforward, book well illustrates his ability to muster material clearly and concisely. Throughout his life he wrote and lectured fluently and readily.

His career with the Geological Survey was almost immediately interrupted by the war of 1914-18. After service in the Mediterranean and France with the Royal Fusiliers he was invalided out in 1917 with the rank of corporal. While still a patient in hospital in Sheffield, on 21 June 1917 he married Edith, youngest daughter of Frederick Thomas Browning and his wife, Elizabeth Anne. Their daughter, Marguerite, was the only child.

Between 1917 and 1931, when Read left the Geological Survey, he was concerned predominantly with geological mapping in Northern Scotland. The wide knowledge of crystalline rocks he obtained led to a series of highly influential papers. His work in Banffshire and in Shetland enabled him to recognize that the nature of metamorphic changes varies from region to region as a result of variations in the flow of heat in the Earth's interior. He was among the first to appreciate that many crystalline rocks have been repeatedly metamorphosed; he paid particular attention to the question of the relationship between granites and metamorphic rocks—plutonic rocks, as Read preferred to call them—and the part they played in the Earth's history. One of his lasting achievements was to show how geological history may be recorded in the crystalline rocks formed deep in the Earth's crust and how such information could supplement the classical geological record established through the study of fossiliferous sedimentary rocks. Read's views were influential for they were widely read and were delivered at a time when radiometric methods made it possible, for the first time, to determine the ages of non-fossiliferous rocks. While Read himself did not carry out such investigations he encouraged others to do so; he was always ready to see the virtues of new methods of investigation. He himself was a field geologist of unusual ability, perfectly at home in the countryside where, with his tweed cap and alert figure, he might have been taken for a keeper or farmer.

He influenced the development of geology both through his students and through his publications, particularly through the series of addresses he prepared while presiding successively over the British Association, Section C (1939), the Geologists' Association (1942-4), and the Geological Society of London (1947-8). These and other addresses reprinted in book form as *The Granite Controversy* (1957) established his international reputation and led to his election to the Norwegian, French, and Belgian Academies. In 1939 he had been elected a fellow of the Royal Society from which he also received a Royal medal (1963). He was also awarded the Wollaston, Penrose, and Steinmann medals, the principal awards of the geological societies of London, America, and Germany. He was made honorary D.Sc. at Columbia University (1954), honorary Sc.D. at Dublin (1956), and honorary MRIA (1958).

He was also an honorary member of many foreign societies.

In 1931 he was appointed to the George Herdman chair of geology in the university of Liverpool, whence, in 1939, he moved to Imperial College where he held the chair of geology until his retirement in 1955. There Read became dean of the Royal School of Mines (1943-5), pro-rector of Imperial College (1952-5), and acting head of Imperial College from 1954 to 1955 until (Sir) R. Patrick Linstead [q.v.] became rector. He was an able administrator, and maintained a happy and informal atmosphere in the university departments and scientific societies whose work he led. In 1948 he presided over the 18th Session of the International Geological Congress held in London, a meeting which did much to bring together the geological community after the wartime disruption, and which paved the way for the success of major international geological investigations in the following decades.

Throughout his time at Imperial College he travelled daily from his birthplace at Whitstable, where other members of his family continued to farm. A simple and modest man, Read was profoundly religious and took an active part in the work of his parish, where he served as people's warden for a number of years. It was at Whitstable that he died on Easter Sunday, 29 March 1970.

[J. Sutton in *Biographical Memoirs of Fellows of the Royal Society*, vol. xvi, 1970; personal knowledge.]   J. SUTTON

READ, JOHN (1884-1963), organic chemist, was born in Maiden Newton, Dorset, 17 February 1884, in his father's seventieth year, the younger of two children of John Read, yeoman farmer, and his wife, Bessie Gatcombe. Apart from his sister, Read also had five older half-brothers and six older half-sisters. He was the first member of the family not to become a farmer. Both of his parents descended from a long line of farmers.

He was identified early as a clever boy at the village school at Sparkford, and proceeded after only three years to Sexey's School, Bruton, at the top of the county junior scholarship list, leaving it in due course (1901) as head boy with a senior Somerset county scholarship of £60 per annum. This was followed by four years at Finsbury Technical College, London, where he attended courses in both science and engineering before obtaining the college's diploma and chemistry prize in 1904, and becoming for a short time a college demonstrator in the department of chemistry then headed by Professor Raphael Meldola, FRS. Then followed the award of a London County Council senior scholarship which enabled him to leave

London, which he disliked, for the university of Zürich where he was accepted as a Doktorand by Professor Alfred Werner, then in the prime of his scientific life.

It is clear from his writings that Read enjoyed Zürich University. Not only did he find the scientific scene stimulating and rewarding, but he was able to develop his interest and proficiency in foreign language, an interest which he maintained throughout his life. Although not directly involved in Werner's renowned research on the stereochemistry of inorganic complexes— that is, a study of the consequences of the three-dimensional structure of molecules containing metallic ions—he was greatly influenced by stereochemical concepts being widely discussed in the laboratories there. It was not surprising, therefore, that after a successful defence of his Ph.D. thesis in 1907, two years after his arrival in Zürich, Read decided to spend the remaining year of his scholarship working with (Sir) W. J. Pope [q.v.] at the Municipal School of Technology in Manchester. Pope had earned an international reputation for his studies of the stereochemistry of organic compounds (those based on carbon), and Read's decision was important in determining his career, because in 1908 Pope was appointed to the chair of chemistry at Cambridge, taking Read with him as his assistant. Read became a member of Emmanuel College with the status of advanced student. In 1912 he was granted an honorary MA.

For the next eight years Read was committed to his chemistry and made significant discoveries in the field of organic stereochemistry. That he was not to be deterred is evident from his story of his synthesis of methyl ethyl selenide, which not only has one of the most offensive smells known but can be detected at remarkably low concentrations. In view of this Read felt it wise to synthesize the substance in the open air, namely on the roof of his laboratory. Unfortunately his efforts coincided with a number of garden parties held to celebrate the Darwin centenary, and the subsequent furore forced Read into the fens to complete his work. There he noted that both insects and cows were attracted by the smell: 'Their whole behaviour indicated that they felt they were missing something really good.'

A major change occurred in 1916 when Read, at the age of thirty-two, was appointed to the chair of organic chemistry in Sydney, Australia. After a long and anxious voyage he arrived to find that he was required to give his first lecture that very day. The problems facing him were now very different. Large classes, the design and supervision of the construction of a new chemistry building, and the administration of the department all combined to reduce the time available for research. Nevertheless, Read initiated and pursued what came to be recognized as a significant investigation of the structure (and stereochemistry) of a series of organic materials which he isolated from Australian flora. These studies in the chemistry of natural products were all the more commendable because Read had very little research assistance.

While in Australia, in 1916 Read married Ida, daughter of Arthur Suddards, of Bradford, Yorkshire; they had two sons. Read was very happy in Sydney and his decision, in 1923, to accept an invitation to succeed (Sir) Robert Robinson in the Purdie chair of chemistry at St. Andrews, was not an easy one. The department there, first under Thomas Purdie, with his foresight in recognizing the importance of research in the context of university chemistry (he personally met the cost of erection of the research laboratory and subsequently endowed it), and then under his outstanding pupil, (Sir) J. C. Irvine [q.v.], had a reputation which had been enhanced by Robinson, despite his short stay (1921–2). Read soon settled down in the St. Andrews atmosphere of scholarship and went on to produce a steady stream of original papers as well as a very successful series of textbooks; his *A Direct Entry to Organic Chemistry* (1948) ran to many editions both in Britain and aboard and Read was to receive, in 1949, the 'Premio Europeo-Cortina', a prize of one million lire for the best popular work in the field of physical science published in Europe in the preceding five years.

Read had always been interested in history— indeed, he said that, given a choice, free from the pressures of a science-orientated school, he would have specialized in history, or languages, rather than science, on leaving school. Once at St. Andrews he devoted more time to these interests, building up, and writing about, an extraordinarily important collection of manuscripts, books, and engravings relating to the history of science, and to alchemy. Notable here is his *Humour and Humanism in Chemistry* (1947). His interest in the dialects of Somerset and Dorset also found expression in print. His wide distinction is summarized by the citation of Read as 'one of the most versatile of Scientists as well known for his literary accomplishments as for his researches in organic chemistry' on his receiving the Dexter award (1959) of the American Chemical Society.

Read remained in St. Andrews for almost forty years. He was widely acclaimed during his lifetime and was elected FRS in 1935. In the same year he was awarded the Sc.D. by Cambridge University. He was most proud, however, of the esteem in which he was held by his pupils. He was an excellent teacher and kindly man, who appeared untouched by the hurly-burly of modern chemical life.

Read died in St. Andrews 21 January 1963, just one month short of his seventy-ninth birthday, the last professor of chemistry to hold a life appointment in a British university.

[E. L. Hirst in *Biographical Memoirs of Fellows of the Royal Society*, vol. ix, 1963; J. Read, *Humour and Humanism in Chemistry*, 1947; private information.]

J. I. G. CADOGAN

REDPATH, ANNE (1895-1965), painter, was born in Galashiels 29 March 1895, the second of four children of Thomas Brown Redpath, tweed designer, and his wife, Agnes Milne. She attended Hawick High School and in 1913 proceeded to Edinburgh College of Art and Moray House College of Education. In 1917 she qualified as an art teacher and the following year was awarded her art diploma. After a year's postgraduate work she won a travelling scholarship which took her to Brussels, Bruges, Paris, Florence, and Siena. Her lifelong admiration for Sienese primitives began then.

In 1920 she married James Beattie Michie (died 1958), an architect with the War Graves Commission in France, where they lived, first in the north and then for ten years on the Riviera. Looking after her husband and three sons left little time for painting. 'I could never have sacrificed my family to painting,' she said, 'I put everything I had into house and furniture and dresses and good food and people. All that's the same sort of thing as painting, really, and the experience went back into art when I started painting again.'

In 1934 she returned to Hawick with her sons; her husband worked in London and a gradual estrangement ended in separation. From this year she exhibited regularly at the Royal Scottish Academy and held other exhibitions; from 1951, except for a break in 1954-5, she had at least one one-person show each year in Edinburgh, London, or elsewhere.

In 1949 she moved to Edinburgh, where she lived until her death. Up to that year she had painted still lives and domestic interiors, with a much smaller number of landscapes in the Borders and Skye. Now began the visits to places in France, Spain, Corsica, Italy, Holland, the Canary Islands, and Portugal which continued for the rest of her life. These visits, she found, made her respond to new ranges of colour and kept her approach to painting fresh. The resulting landscapes formed an increasingly important part of her work, but each new colour-range she discovered was also explored in the still lives painted after her return.

Her still lives and domestic interiors were infectiously happy paintings, expressing an intensification of her delight in the harmonious and visually stimulating ambience found in her own home. There, scores of enchanting objects, many of which appeared in her still lives, were juxtaposed with unobvious precision. In the paintings this highly developed decorative instinct blended with her painterly gifts and her fine sense of pictorial construction. The landscapes she painted were always places where people lived: the relation of human dwellings to landscape gave the scene meaning for her.

Her approach to painting (and to life) remained enviably fresh: to the end of her life she made new discoveries. In her last few years her work became more strongly emotive. It was a time not without difficulties. She had a serious illness in 1955 and again in 1959, when for a time she lost the use of her right arm; before it returned she had learnt to paint with her left hand.

There remained five fruitful years during which she visited the Canary Islands, Portugal, Amsterdam, and Venice. The highly enjoyable visual wit and lyrical felicity of much of her previous work was now less evident. Her gifts as a colourist and manipulator of paint were now used with a new vigour and urgency for purely expressive ends. From 'intimism' she had turned towards expressionism, and in doing so produced many of her finest works. These included townscapes, landscapes with buildings, and—a new theme—church interiors in Portugal and Venice. Some of the most satisfying of all her works were painted in her last year.

Like her painting, Anne Redpath's character had a style which delighted those who know her. She had great and very feminine charm, and an integrity which enabled her to enjoy the material success of her last years without being in any way altered by it. To her many friends, her company was one of the more civilizing amenities of Edinburgh.

She was appointed OBE (1955) and received an honorary LLD from Edinburgh (1955). She was elected an associate of the Royal Scottish Academy (1947) and academician (1952); ARA (1960); ARWS (1962). She was president of the Scottish Society of Women Artists (1944-7), and a member of other exhibiting societies. She died in Edinburgh 7 January 1965.

Two self-portraits (drawings) are in the Scottish National Portrait Gallery and the Glasgow Art Gallery and Museum. An oil 'Self Portrait in a Venetian Mirror' (*c*.1956) was formerly in a private collection. Of her three sons, David Michie, RSA, became a painter, and Alistair Michie a painter, sculptor, and fashion artist.

[Terence Mullaly, Arts Council *Memorial Exhibition Catalogue*, 1965; George Bruce *Anne Redpath*, 1974; private information; personal knowledge.]   DAVID BAXANDALL

REED, SIR (HERBERT) STANLEY (1872-1969), newspaper editor and politician, was born in the Ashley district of Bristol 28 January 1872, the son of William Reed, a grocer of Fremantle Villa, Bristol, and his wife, Amelia Whitney. He was educated privately, became a journalist, and in 1897 joined the staff of the *Times of India* in Bombay, then under the editorship of Thomas Bennett. As a young bachelor, Reed entered fully into the lively social life of Bombay at the turn of the century, enjoying sailing, riding, and hunting over the dry rice fields of the surrounding countryside; he was eventually to become an enthusiastic member of the Bombay Light Horse and to command that volunteer body with the rank of lieutenant-colonel.

He married Lilian (died 1947), daughter of John Humphrey, in 1901. They had no children. She fully shared his interest in India where they spent so much of their married life and made so many friends.

From the time of his arrival in India, Reed was keen to travel and see as much of the country as possible, and in 1900 he broke new ground for his newspaper with an extensive tour of famine-affected areas. He sent reports of what he had seen in the countryside not only to his own newspaper but also as its special correspondent to the *Daily Chronicle*. In his book *The India I Knew*, published in 1952, Reed described how he invaded the placid leader-writing sanctum of Bennett with this revolutionary suggestion: 'I am doing little or nothing here. Yet the city is ravaged by plague. Poona is deserted. . . . The Black Death has swept over Sholapur, Surat and Ahmedabad. . . . The embers of the famine are slowly dying and we have nothing about these great happenings.' That was the start of travels which ranged over the length and breadth of India. Reed accompanied King George V and Queen Mary when as Prince and Princess of Wales they toured India in 1905. His dispatches were republished in book form in 1906, with a preface by Sir Walter Lawrence (whose notice Reed wrote for this Dictionary), who abandoned his intention of writing an official record of the royal visit when he found that Reed had virtually done the job for him. During these travels Reed acquired the profound knowledge and sympathetic understanding of the Indian people which were later to stamp his writing as an editor and his speeches as a British parliamentarian.

Reed was appointed editor of the *Times of India* in 1907 and under his control the newspaper became not only one of the two most influential journals in India (the other was the *Statesman*, based in Calcutta on the other side of the subcontinent), but in its general conduct and appearance able to challenge comparison with any English daily. Under the editorship of his predecessor, Lovat Fraser, the status of the *Times of India* had been raised from that of a respectable provincial newspaper into an Indian organ of opinion which Lord (later Marquess) Curzon of Kedleston [q.v.] described as the leading paper of Asia. Reed saw that it lacked two things: a sensible selling price and a comprehensive foreign news service. He persuaded its proprietors to drop its selling price from fourpence a copy to one penny. This led to a fourfold rise in circulation in three days and Reed went on to play a influential role in the Imperial Press Conference in 1909, where the case for cheap telegraphic rates between the countries of the Empire was pressed.

In the war of 1914-18 Reed was director of publicity to the Government of India, and towards its end he was called upon to counsel on the functions and organization of the Central Publicity Board, of which he became vice-president (1918). This was a belated attempt to improve the understanding of the people of India about a war to which they had been committed four years earlier by Lord Hardinge of Penshurst [q.v.], then the viceroy. Reed had, in the columns of his newspaper, written very critically about the military disaster in Mesopotamia and was in consequence not universally popular at Government headquarters in Simla, but he pressed through a number of reforms aimed at helping the press and some sections of the public to understand how and why the war was being fought. The isolation of the Government of India from public opinion at that time, Reed wrote many years later, was almost inconceivable. In 1919 he was created KBE, having been knighted in 1916.

Reed retired from India in 1923 but continued to write for his paper from London for many years. He quickly became involved in British politics and in 1929 unsuccessfully contested the Stourbridge constituency in Worcestershire as a Conservative. But in 1938 he fought and won a by-election in the Aylesbury division of Buckinghamshire. The first suggestion that he should stand for Parliament had come from the socialist statesman, Arthur Henderson [q.v.], when they were both members of the British delegation to the League of Nations in 1924. Reed had certain natural affiliations with the Labour Party but he professed himself unable to swallow nationalization and the capital levy and it was finally his old Indian guru, Sir Walter Lawrence, who persuaded him to enter the lists on the Tory side. He contributed many useful speeches to the House on Indian questions and on a variety of other topics, and, if his independence of mind did not always endear him to the whips, his well-studied briefs ensured him an attentive audience. He and (Sir) Alan Herbert jointly presented a private member's Bill to amend the law of defamation; this ended in the appointment of a committee presided over by Lord Porter [q.v.], which for a variety of reasons could not report until 1948. It was, however, on Indian subjects that Reed spoke most frequently and his support for Indian independence after the war was tempered with regret that Britain had taken so long to complete a process which, he reminded the House, had begun in 1917.

Reed retired from politics in 1950 and, in the House, Philip (later Lord) Noel-Baker said of him that he had rendered great service to the cause of friendship between the peoples of the United Kingdom and those of India and Pakistan, and that with the passing of the Bill which marked the final devolution of the authority of Parliament over India he must have felt that his work had borne fruit.

Reed also wrote, together with (Sir) Patrick Cadell, *India: The New Phase* (1928), which presented a lucid summary of the reforms introduced into India by the Act of 1919. He was also founder of the *Indian Year Book* in 1922.

Reed lived on in London until he died in Westminster Hospital 17 January 1969 at the age of ninety-six.

[*The Times*, 18 and 23 January 1969; H. S. Reed, *The India I Knew, 1897-1947*, 1952.]

EVAN CHARLTON

REID DICK, SIR WILLIAM (1878-1961), sculptor. [See DICK.]

RELF, ERNEST FREDERICK (1888-1970), scientist and authority on aerodynamics, was born in Beckenham, Kent, 2 October 1888, the younger child and only son of Thomas Joseph Relf, business man, and his wife, Marion Weeks. Relf's early education was frequently interrupted by family removals; however, his father, a linguist and very versatile musician, himself took a hand in his son's education. Relf could read music before he could read print, and schooling in the three Rs was matched by musical instruction, both amateur and professional. In 1903 his family home was in Portsmouth; Relf sat the Dockyard entrance examination, won first place, and in January 1904 entered the Dockyard as an apprentice shipwright: this involved part-time attendance at the Royal Dockyard School. Soon afterwards, at sixteen, he was appointed organist at one of Portsmouth's largest churches, and two years later was nearly persuaded to make music his career. But his record at the Royal Dockyard School was outstanding, and in 1909 he won a Royal scholarship to the Royal College of Science. Here he read mathematics and physics as principal subjects, won the Tyndall prize, and in 1912 duly obtained his ARCS with first class honours. In August 1912 he was appointed a junior assistant in the aeronautics section of the Engineering Department of the National Physical Laboratory (NPL) at Teddington; he thus came under the influence of (Sir) Leonard Bairstow [q.v.], then head of the section. When Bairstow left in 1917, the section became an independent Aerodynamics Department; from 1917 to 1920 it was under the direction of (Sir) T. E. Stanton and from 1920 to 1925 of (Sir) R. V. Southwell [q.v.]. Relf succeeded Southwell as superintendent in 1925.

Relf's first thirteen years at the NPL showed his brilliance and versatility as a scientist and engineer. Among his hobbies were electrical engineering and photography; he put both to good use in his aerodynamical and related research. In this period he published some forty scientific papers on a wide variety of topics: from the visualization of flow in liquids to the use of an electrical analogue to determine streamlines; from aeroplane stability to the design and manufacture of a special electrical motor, the problems of which had defeated the electrical industry and which now became standard equipment; from the determination of the virtual inertia in yaw of an airship to the 'singing' of bracing wires; these and many more. His work was regarded as of such importance that he was not called up in 1914, although he was 'attested' and served one day in the Services. In 1919 the Massachusetts Institute of Technology offered Relf its newly founded chair of aerodynamics; he declined the appointment. Later, he took part in two Oxford expeditions, in 1923 to Spitsbergen and in 1924 to Nordaustlandet, under the leadership of (Sir) George Binney. Relf was physicist, surveyor, radio officer, and handyman.

From 1925 to 1945 Relf, as head of his department, had to become an administrator. But he never lost his zest for scientific research, even though now it had to be done by others under his direction. A most human man, he ran his team on the lightest of reins, encouraging original thought by his keen and evident interest and his helpful advice, but still keeping everyone on the appropriate road; in this way he brought out the best in his staff, seven of whom were in due course to be elected FRS. Relf himself was elected FRS in 1936 and appointed CBE in 1944: he also became F.R.Ae.S. (1926) and FIAS (United States) in 1933. He won the George Taylor gold medal of the Royal Aeronautical Society in 1935, and its highest honour, the Society's gold medal, in 1953.

At the end of 1945 Relf left the NPL to take up for five years the post of principal of the newly founded College of Aeronautics at Cranfield. He recruited a first-class staff, and set the college on the right lines, so that in his lifetime it became the Cranfield Institute of Technology, Britain's first postgraduate university.

In 1951 Relf left Cranfield, to devote the remaining years of his life to consultancy and music. He had already become an independent member of the Aeronautical Research Council, a body to which he gave unbroken service, in various capacities, for fifty years (1918-68). For four years he acted as a consultant to his former department at the NPL; he also worked with (Sir) Barnes Wallis and with various research associations. As to music: from his student days, when the proximity of the Royal Colleges of Science and of Music enabled him to expand his talents and to make many friends in the musical world, music permeated and supplemented his scientific life. In addition to playing on piano and organ, he composed much chamber music and some 200 songs. Some of his music, with professional performers, has been broadcast by the BBC.

Relf was of medium height, plump and jolly; a man who engendered a real affection in his wide circle of friends. In 1917, at Plymouth, he married Elfreda Grace, daughter of Frank and Emily Day, of the Royal Naval Ordnance Service; they had no children. He died at his home in Addlestone 25 February 1970. A portrait by Montague Fielden hangs in the Library at Cranfield.

[A. R. Collar in *Biographical Memoirs of Fellows of the Royal Society*, vol. xvii, 1971; personal knowledge.]   A. R. COLLAR

RICHARDS, FRANCIS JOHN (1901-1965), agriculturalist, was born 1 October 1901 at Newton Road, Burton-on-Trent, the third child and second son in the family of four children of Robert Richards, a retail butcher, and his wife, Mary Ann Mayger. Frank Richards was educated at Burton Grammar School where he was an outstanding pupil and where an early interest in biology, fostered at home, was developed by an enthusiastic schoolmaster; in addition he showed an early talent for mathematics. As an outcome of higher certificate examinations, which included a distinction in biology, he was awarded a major borough scholarship. He showed his versatility by taking an active part in debates and theatricals and by becoming a junior member of the local archaeological society. Archaeology remained a hobby throughout his life. Richards also achieved distinction in sport as captain of the school rugby team and as a winner of a victor ludorum trophy. In 1921 he proceeded to the university of Birmingham, where he devoted all his time to his studies, graduating B.Sc. in 1924, with first class honours in botany, followed by an M.Sc. after eighteen months as a demonstrator. He was later awarded the D.Sc. for published work.

In 1926 Richards joined the Research Institute of Plant Physiology at Imperial College, London, under the general direction of Professor V. H. Blackman [q.v.], to assist F. G. Gregory [q.v.], later director of the Institute, in investigations of the mineral nutrition of barley as an important crop plant. After six months in London he moved to Harpenden, where field facilities were provided at Rothamsted Experimental Station. He was soon given an established post as a plant physiologist and remained in Harpenden for thirty-five years. When responsibility for the Institute passed from the Ministry of Agriculture to the Agricultural Research Council he became, by normal promotion steps, a principal scientific officer, and then, by two special merit promotions, senior principal scientific officer and, in 1963, deputy chief scientific officer.

At Harpenden Richards, by degrees, took over from Gregory responsibility for the nutritional aspects of the Institute's research and for training research students in the subject, in which he himself continued to work throughout his career and to which he made a unique contribution which assures him a place in the history of plant nutrition. On Gregory's retirement in December 1958 the Institute was disbanded and to provide for the continuation of Richards's work a research unit was set up, with Richards himself as director. The unit was to be at Wye College, Kent (university of London) and in 1961 Richards moved to Wye, accompanied by his senior colleague, W. W. Schwabe. Here he spent the last few years of his life.

In 1929 Richards published (with Gregory) in the *Annals of Botany* the first of a series of papers on the mineral nutrition of barley which indirectly contributed much to modern fertilizer practice. Making delicate and meticulous measurements and exploiting (Sir) R. A. Fisher's [q.v.] new techniques for statistical interpretation, he firmly established the effects of nitrogen, phosphorus, and potassium deficiencies on assimilation and respiration rates of barley leaves. Subsequent studies probed deeply into the roles of phosphorus and especially potassium in protein synthesis and in the general nitrogen metabolism of plants. The experiments culminated in a demonstration that the amine putrescine, itself toxic, was produced as the ionic substitute for a lack of potassium. Richards's data were subjected to often complex and detailed statistical analysis which provided firm support for the results.

Richards took an interest, which possibly arose from his mathematical hobbies, in the problem of the patterns of leaf arrangements in plants—phyllotaxis. His studies led to a completely new understanding of the relations between the growth of the shoot tip and organ formation. He devised a means of defining the patterns—the 'Phyllotaxis Index' for plane projection and the 'Equivalent Phyllotaxis Index' for a conical surface. For the first time an unequivocal description became possible of phyllotactic systems in terms of radial distances from the centre of the growing point and the angular divergence between primordia which was free from implied hypotheses about the origin of the system. While Richards did not proceed to prove formally the necessity of the Fibonacci angle being the limiting divergence, his contributions published in several papers advanced this subject to an entirely new level and have since stimulated renewed interest in this, perhaps the oldest, problem of plant morphogenesis. Richards was elected a fellow of the Royal Society in 1954.

While still a student Richards had joined a volunteer party to assist Professor R. H. Yapp in a study of the salt marshes of the Dovey estuary of which an important aspect was the vertical accretion of the sward association. In the years following Yapp's death, Richards completed the project and published the results in 1934. He used statistical methods in the analysis of the data, and was the first to employ these techniques in ecological studies.

Richards was a gentle and modest man with a diffident manner which concealed remarkable talents and an astonishing range of general as well as biological knowledge. His reluctance to express his views restricted his influence but his colleagues had the deepest respect for his shrewd analytical mind and clarity of thought as well as for his knowledge. Richards was well known for his hobbies, all scientific, to which he brought both specialist wisdom and technical skill. As examples, he assembled and mounted a superb collection of Lepidoptera and made a collection of palaeolithic artifacts from the classical fields of Rothamsted; he also made a reflecting telescope, grinding the parabolic mirror himself.

Richards married in 1928 Lilian Kingsley Mason, daughter of a Burton timber merchant. They had two daughters and led a quiet domestic life in Harpenden. During the war of 1939-45, Richards served in the Harpenden Home Guard. Soon after the move to Wye his health began to deteriorate and he died at Orchard Bank, Oxenturn Road, Wye, Kent, 2 January 1965.

[H. K. Porter in *Biographical Memoirs of Fellows of the Royal Society*, vol. xii, 1966; private information; personal knowledge.]

H. K. PORTER

RICHARDS, FRANK (pseudonym), writer. [See HAMILTON, CHARLES HAROLD ST. JOHN.]

RICHARDSON, SIR ALBERT EDWARD (1880-1964), architect, was born 19 May 1880 at 33D Middleton Road, Hackney, the eldest of the three children of Albert Edmund Richardson, printer, and his wife, Mary Ann, daughter of Thomas Richardson (not related), of Highgate. He was educated at the Boys British School, Highgate, where he already showed pleasure in buildings and a talent for drawing. In 1895 he was articled to an architect named Page, in Gray's Inn Road, and served subsequently in the offices of Evelyn Helicar (1898-1902), Leonard Stokes (1902-3), and Frank T. Verity (1903-6). As Verity's leading assistant he designed 'mansion flats' in Cleveland Row, St. James's, and Bayswater Road (both 1906), the middle section of 169-201 Regent Street (1908-9), and the façade of the Regent Street Polytechnic, the latter being executed after he had severed his connection with Verity and set up in practice with another of Verity's assistants, Charles Lovett Gill. The contemporary French influence seen in the work for Verity is reflected again in the early works of the partnership, notably flats in Berkeley Street (nos. 19 and 10) executed between 1910 and 1916. A developing taste for an earlier and more distinguished type of neo-classicism is shown in the New Theatre (now the Opera House), Manchester, built in association with Horace Farquharson, 1911-13. The most substantial commission, however, obtained by the partnership before World War I was Moorgate Hall, Finsbury Pavement, EC2 (1913-17), a thoughtful solution to the problem of combining office fenestration with shop windows. This led to a series of similar commissions forming the backbone of the practice for twenty-five years.

With the exigencies of practice Richardson combined an enthusiastic devotion to the architecture of the past, especially the later and at that time unregarded episodes of the classical tradition. With the encouragement of Harry

Batsford [q.v.] he wrote, in collaboration with C. Lovett Gill, his first book, *London Houses from 1660 to 1820* (1911), a pioneering appreciation of the simple elegance of Georgian streets and squares. This was followed by *Monumental Classic Architecture in Great Britain and Ireland in the Eighteenth and Nineteenth Centuries* (1914), a superbly illustrated folio work demonstrating the progress of the classical tradition from the Palladian movement to the mid-Victorian period. This offered a new perspective of stylistic continuity and remains a landmark in British architectural historiography.

Between 1916 and 1918, Richardson served as a lieutenant in the Royal Flying Corps, working at the School of Military Aeronautics at Reading. In 1919 his combination of practical experience and historical learning made him conspicuously eligible for the chair of architecture at the Bartlett School of Architecture, University College, London, where he succeeded F. M. Simpson. This chair he held for twenty-seven years, retiring as professor emeritus in 1946. At University College he effectively exploited his personal qualities as a teacher. Not by temperament an academic, nor indeed a scholar of the more disciplined kind, his history lectures were rhetorical improvisations made wonderfully vivid by a rare talent for impromptu graphic demonstration. In the studios, the same ready pencil, accompanied by an enthusiastic flow of talk and the random play of ideas, endeared him to a whole generation of students.

The practice of Richardson and Gill developed remuneratively through the twenties and thirties with offices in the City, flats in the West End, and a few churches and country houses. In the City, nos. 47-57 Gresham Street (1924) show a departure from classical compromise towards direct statement and this became more manifest in the premises built for Sir Arthur Sanderson and Sons in Wells Street, W1 (1930-2), which was awarded the RIBA London architecture medal in 1932. But although Richardson was sympathetic to the 'modern' tendency towards simplification, the intellectual pretensions of the Continental Modern Movement as expounded in the teaching of Gropius and the propagandist books of Le Corbusier he rejected with contempt. If *The Art of Architecture* (1938), which he wrote in collaboration with his colleague, H. O. Corfiato, was an attempt to fortify the academic position against such provocations, its influence was negligible and in the late thirties Richardson found himself increasingly alienated from the younger generation of architects.

During the war of 1939-45 the Bartlett School was transferred to Cambridge where Richardson spent happy years in a privileged environment which appealed to his sense of tradition. In the post-war world he emerged as a stalwart reactionary, a lively castigator of bureaucracy, and a champion of the preservationist movements then gathering strength. Elected ARA in 1936, he became a full academician in 1944 and president of the Royal Academy ten years later. In this high office he was at once recognized as an agreeably controversial public figure who could be relied upon to say something original, paradoxical, and quite possibly irresponsible, on any subject to which his attention was directed. As a member of the Royal Fine Art Commission from 1939 to 1956 his insights were often valuable and his criticism unsparing. In 1947 he was awarded the RIBA gold medal for architecture and was appointed KCVO in 1956. He was also FSA, honorary MA (Cantab.), honorary Litt.D. (Dublin), honorary RWS, and an honorary fellow of St. Catharine's College, Cambridge.

The partnership with Gill having terminated in 1939, Richardson found, in 1945, a new partner in his son-in-law, Eric Alfred Scholefield Houfe. The works of Richardson and Houfe include the Chancery Lane Safe Deposit (1945-9), the *Financial Times* building, Cannon Street (1955-8), the AEI building, Grosvenor Place (1958), and the chapel and library, St. Mary's College, Twickenham (1961). Restorations of war-damaged buildings include Merchant Taylors' Hall (1953), Trinity House, Tower Hill (with an important extension, 1956), St. Alphege, Greenwich (1959), and St. James's, Piccadilly (1947-54). Written work of this period includes his notice of Sir (Thomas) Edwin Cooper for this Dictionary.

Richardson married, in 1903, Elizabeth (died 1958), daughter of John Byers, farmer, of Newry, county Down; they had one daughter. He died 3 February 1964 at Avenue House, Ampthill, a beautiful late eighteenth-century house which he had acquired in 1919 and where he brought together a remarkable collection of furniture and works of art, including architectural drawings. He is buried in the churchyard at Millbrook, Bedfordshire.

In person Richardson was of middle height, inclining to stoutness in middle age; his countenance was somewhat fleshy with dark hair brushed back, an aquiline nose, and fine grey eyes, heavy-lidded. In deportment and gesture he had something of the air of an old-fashioned actor.

There is a portrait by Sir James Gunn at Clarendon School, Haynes Park, Bedfordshire, and a bust in bronze by Kate Parbury (1953) is in the possession of the family. There are also portraits by Edna S. Rose and Maurice

Codner. The memorial tablet in the crypt of St. Paul's Cathedral has a bronze profile portrait by David McFall.

[Private information; personal knowledge.]

JOHN SUMMERSON

RICHEY, JAMES ERNEST (1886–1968), geologist, was born 24 April 1886 at Ballymully, county Tyrone, the son of the Revd John Richey, priest in the Church of Ireland and rector of Desertcreat, and his wife, Susana Best. Educated at St. Columba's College and at Trinity College, Dublin, he gained the BA degree in natural sciences in 1908 with the award of a senior moderatorship and a gold medal, and continued to take the BAI in engineering in 1909. His published work gained him the Sc.D. of Trinity in 1934.

After a period as demonstrator at Oxford (1910–11) under W. J. Sollas [q.v.] he joined HM Geological Survey in 1911 as a geologist and was assigned to the Scotland office in Edinburgh. It had been recognized from the early days of the science that the remains of a line of great volcanoes ran from Arran northwards through Mull to Skye, and that the volcanic centre in the Mourne Mountains and the lava field of Antrim might be connected with this line. In the early years of this century, Alfred Harker [q.v.] of Cambridge had begun the detailed study on the six-inch-to-one-mile scale in Skye, and when Richey first went into the field a team under C. T. Clough and later (Sir) E. B. Bailey [q.v.] was at work in Mull. It fell to Richey to complete the mapping begun by W. B. Wright of a broad dyke crossing Loch Ba; his meticulous work showed its annular, outward-dipping shape and provided the key to the principal structural element in the complex, a ring-fracture which had permitted the subsidence of a plug of rock more than 1 km wide into the magma-chamber below. It now began to emerge that a series of such ring-subsidences had taken place during the eruptive episode, and that a considerable variety of different rock-types had been emplaced in the fractures. The ring-dyke concept thus enabled successive foci to be defined, and the stages in the evolution of the magmas to be determined. Bailey had previously recognized what he called cauldron subsidence in the much older intrusive complex at Glencoe on the mainland. Now the way was open for the elucidation of the history of the Tertiary volcanoes, the interiors of which had been exposed by the removal of as much as 2 km of the superstructure by erosion during the past 55 million years. A large share of this work fell to Richey, and he became the leading figure in a subject that influenced work on volcanoes, ancient and modern, all over the world.

In World War I he was commissioned in the Royal Engineers in 1914 and served with the Guards Division in France with distinction, gaining the MC. He was demobilized in the rank of captain in 1919. Richey then began the investigation of the Ardnamurchan peninsula, where the ring form of the intrusions is beautifully reflected in the topography, and by 1924 had completed a six-inch survey which for its clear wealth of detail has seldom been equalled. The publication of his map and descriptive memoir in 1930 was a landmark in the subject. Meanwhile, not entirely as part of his official duties, he had begun to look at other centres in the line, to reinterpret Harker's mapping in Skye and that of the Geological Survey of Ireland in Slieve Gullion and the Mourne Mountains, and in an outstanding presidential address to the Geological Society of Glasgow in 1932 he was able to give a new conspectus of Tertiary volcanicity in the British Isles. He was later able to show that quiet upwelling of magnesian magmas alternated with violent periods of explosion when the magma became silica-rich.

Richey's interests were nevertheless far wider than has so far been indicated. From 1925, when he became district geologist, he was actively engaged in the metamorphic areas of Morar, Moidart, and Morvern, and the granitic complex of Strontian. W. Q. Kennedy, J. B. Simpson, and A. G. MacGregor were among his collaborators in this study. He also contributed substantially to geological knowledge of Renfrew and Ayrshire, and later to the eastern Midland Valley of coalfield surveys in Scotland. After his retirement from the Geological Survey at the age of sixty, he set up as a consulting geologist and also gave lectures at Queen's College, Dundee, his wide experience now being brought to bear on many aspects of engineering geology; it is enshrined in a textbook of this subject and in the foreword to the first issue of the *Quarterly Journal of Engineering Geology* (1967).

His work achieved wide recognition. He received the Lyell medal of the Geological Society of London in 1933 and was elected FRS in 1938. The Geological Society of Edinburgh gave him their Clough medal in 1964, and the Royal Society of Edinburgh, of which he was a fellow (1927), general secretary (1946–56), and a vice-president (1956–9), its Neill prize in 1965. He became an honorary member of the Royal Irish Academy in 1967, and was an honorary fellow of the Geological Society of America (1948). The Society of Engineers awarded him its first Baker medal in 1954. His influential work on ancient volcanoes led to his election to the vice-presidency of the International Association of Volcanologists, a constituent body of the International Union of Geodesy and Geophysics, a position he held from 1936 to 1948; from 1950 to 1959 he was chairman of the Royal Society's committee on volcanology. His presidencies included the Geological Societies of Glasgow and Edinburgh, and Section C of the British Association for the Advancement of Science.

In 1924 James Richey married Henrietta Lily McNally from his own home county, and with his charm and Irish wit, sometimes mordant, they made an ideal couple. There were three daughters and several grandchildren. The Richeys were visited at their homes in Edinburgh and Monifieth by geologists from all over the world. Richey was generous with his time and liked to encourage younger men to criticize and re-examine his work. Among his leisure interests, gardening was one of the chief and it is recorded that he had the charming custom of attaching names of friends he wished to remember to his rhododendron bushes. Richey died at Coleshill, Warwickshire, 19 June 1968.

[W. Q. Kennedy and A. G. MacGregor in *Biographical Memoirs of Fellows of the Royal Society*, vol. xv, 1969; A. G. MacGregor in *Year Book*, Royal Society of Edinburgh, 1969; A. G. MacGregor in *Proceedings* of the Geological Society of London, 1969: personal knowledge.]   KINGSLEY DUNHAM

RICHMOND, SIR BRUCE LYTTELTON (1871–1964), editor, was born in Kensington 12 January 1871, the only child of Douglas Close Richmond, who became secretary of the Charity Commission and comptroller in the Exchequer and Audit office, and his first wife, Margaret Cecilia, daughter of Henry Austin Bruce, first Baron Aberdare [q.v.]. At the age of thirteen he headed the scholarship roll at Winchester, where he rose to become prefect of Hall, a member of Lord's eleven, and winner of the prize for Greek prose. A scholar of New College, Oxford, he gained a first class in classical moderations in 1892. His second in 'Greats' (1894) perhaps owed something to his having spent less effort on *literae humaniores* than on organizing chamber concerts and playing cricket for the university, though without achieving a blue. Called to the bar by the Inner Temple in 1897, Richmond made a mark by devilling for the editor of a legal textbook which attracted the notice of G. E. Buckle [q.v.], editor of *The Times*, and led to his being engaged, in 1899, as an assistant editor. In the autumn of 1902 he took over from (Sir) James Thursfield [q.v.] the editorship of *The Times Literary Supplement*, then only a few months old. Under his aegis in the next thirty-five years the '*Lit. Sup.*'—he never became reconciled to its later sobriquet, the '*TLS*'— achieved, in the words of George Gordon [q.v.], a 'position of undisputed and ungrudged authority'. His task was not made easier by the threat, under which he worked daily and loyally for some years, of the sudden, arbitrary extinction of the *Supplement* by Lord Northcliffe [q.v.].

The Times's tradition of anonymity perfectly suited the confident but unassuming character of a man whose entry in *Who's Who*, to the day of his death, did not so much as mention his editorship of the *Literary Supplement*. Apart from an occasional 'letter to the editor', signed 'Templar', on some point of scholarship, he never himself wrote in the *Supplement*, and he enjoined strict secrecy, as much in their interest as in its own, upon his reviewers. These included many men and women already distinguished as divines or dons, in the Services, in politics, and in literature. But his particular flair was for discovering, and encouraging, new talent. He gave their first opportunities for serious critical work to the young novelist Virginia Woolf and the young poet T. S. Eliot [qq.v.]. If both of these individualists confessed to having fretted in the strait-jacket of '*The Times*'s style', Eliot was later to pay an impressive tribute to the mentor who had taught him 'the discipline of anonymity'. The anonymous writer, Eliot recognized, 'must subdue himself to his editor—but the editor must be a man to whom the writer can subdue himself and preserve his self-respect. . . . Good literary criticism requires good editors as well as good critics. And Bruce Richmond was a great editor.' In a period before the proliferation of academic literary journals the *Supplement* under Richmond also enjoyed pre-eminence as a forum for the discussion, in signed articles and letters, of problems of literary history and textual criticism. He was not averse from allowing unsolicited contributors to expose their weaknesses. John Dover Wilson [q.v.] wrote to another regular writer on Shakespearian topics: 'What I admire about the *Lit. Sup.* is its intense impartiality. People growl to me, Why does the *Lit. Sup.* print letters from that ass— ? But I think it is splendid of Richmond to do so, and *so* wise.'

Richmond contributed to this Dictionary the notices of his editor, Buckle, and his friend the music critic, John Fuller-Maitland. His only separate publications were the briefest of brief anonymous guides to Bodiam Castle, in Sussex, and *The Pattern of Freedom* (1940), a prose and verse anthology inspired by the faith that a liberal spirit would outlast the war. Characteristically the anthology, which ranged from Homer, Ecclesiasticus, and Petronius to Henry James, Robert Bridges, and others of

Richmond's *Literary Supplement* contributor-friends, contained no editorial introduction or other overt justification of purpose.

In private life, besides men of letters, Richmond numbered among his friends many musicians, both professional and amateur. After literature, classical and modern, in both of which he was widely read, music was his chief abiding passion: he was a member of the executive committee of the Royal College of Music, as well as a vice-president of the Royal Literary Fund. He lived, in simple elegance, in South Kensington, in a house hung with early and later English water-colours and with drawings—more than one of his wife—by J. S. Sargent. He also leased a small house outside Robertsbridge, in Sussex, where his male guests were inducted in all weathers, with a Henry Jamesian gesture of welcome, into the mystery of the earth-closet some distance down the garden. Childless, Richmond had a strong sense of family, and of kinship with the young, whom he regaled with anecdotes, often embellished if never wholly apocryphal, of the theatre and opera of more than half a century. He had a predilection, conservative almost to the point of prejudice, for Shakespearian acting as exemplified in Sir Henry Irving and Sir P. B. Ben Greet [qq.v.]. Until after his ninetieth birthday he was still a familiar figure, τετράπους (as he would say) with two sticks, and not always approving, at the theatre at Stratford-upon-Avon, where he seldom missed a new production of Shakespeare. He travelled little abroad until late in life, when his distaste for hotels was mitigated by the hospitality of friends, literary or diplomatic, in Italy, Greece, and Egypt.

Richmond received honorary doctorates of letters from the university of Leeds (1922) and from his own university (1930). He was knighted in 1935, and on the last day of 1937 retired from *The Times* to live first in Netherhampton, in Wiltshire, and later at the Old Rectory, Islip, near Oxford, where he died 1 October 1964. He was survived for only six days by his wife, Elena Elizabeth, daughter of William Gair Rathbone, of Liverpool, half-brother of Eleanor Rathbone [q.v.], whom he had married, a stately Edwardian beauty of great charm and intelligence, in 1913.

A pencil drawing of Bruce Richmond in profile (1937) by Frances A. de B. Footner is in the possession of the family. An excellent likeness, full face, by a staff photographer of *The Times* appeared on the front page of the *Literary Supplement* on 13 January 1961.

[*The Times Literary Supplement*, 18 January 1952 and 13 January 1961; *The Times*, 2 October 1964; private information; personal knowledge.]   SIMON NOWELL-SMITH

RICHMOND, SIR IAN ARCHIBALD (1902–1965), archaeologist, was born 10 May 1902 in Rochdale, Lancashire, the elder twin son of Daniel Richmond, a medical practitioner in that town, and his wife, Helen Harper. He was educated at Ruthin School and Corpus Christi College, Oxford; his first publications were written while he was still an undergraduate, so that it was no surprise that, despite a third class in honour moderations (1922) and a second in *literae humaniores* (1924), he was awarded the Gilchrist scholarship to the British School in Rome and the Craven fellowship and Goldsmiths' senior studentship. The two years, 1924–6, which he spent at the British School under the benevolent eye of Thomas Ashby (whose notice he contributed to this Dictionary) developed the interest in Roman military architecture and the methods of the Roman army which were to be his major research interest, although the range of his active work in archaeology was wider than that of most of his contemporaries. As an excavator he served his apprenticeship, first under (Sir) Mortimer Wheeler at Segontium and then under F. G. Simpson at Cawthorn; in later years he was to train and inspire very many archaeologists who have since attained distinction.

Richmond's first major work was the monograph on *The City Wall of Imperial Rome* (1930), illustrated by his own splendid plans and isometric drawings. Thereafter he wrote two books on *Roman Britain* (Britain in Pictures, 1947, and Pelican History of England, 1955—reissued as a hardback, with additions, in 1963), and edited three successive editions of John Collingwood Bruce's *Handbook to the Roman Wall* (1947, 1957, and 1966); at his death he had completed the preparation of a thoroughly revised second edition of *Archaeology of Roman Britain* by R. G. Collingwood [q.v.]; it was seen through the press by his former research assistant, D. R. Wilson, and published in 1969. But the great bulk of his writings appeared in the publications of archaeological societies, particularly in *Archaeologia Aeliana* (Society of Antiquaries of Newcastle upon Tyne) and the *Transactions* of the Cumberland and Westmorland Antiquarian and Archaeological Society, in the *Archaeological Journal*, the *Journal of Roman Studies*, or the *Proceedings* of the Society of Antiquaries of Scotland, to mention only those in which important records of his excavations or of his reassessment of previous discoveries of Roman material were printed. As an excavator he had the precious gift of visualizing how the Roman army would lay out its structures on a given site, so that he was able to effect his excavations with an economy of effort which nobody else has been able to match; and his knowledge of Roman architecture and of the reliefs on the columns of Trajan and Marcus Aurelius, added to his familiarity with the literary sources, often caused his hearers to wonder whether he had not personally witnessed the Roman army at work. He was a dignified and eloquent public speaker, his addresses being notable for the elevation of their style, spoken deliberately as though he was always seeking for the exact word to match his meaning—even when the text of his speech had already been written out, as it more often had. In private he could relax, full of fun and with a twinkle in his eye; there could be no greater contrast than that between his public and his private images. His writings, too, were as notable as those of F. J. Haverfield [q.v.], his predecessor in the mastery of Romano-British archaeology, for the care with which they were composed.

From 1926 to 1930 he was lecturer in classical archaeology and ancient history at The Queen's University, Belfast, his terms of appointment allowing him to spend half of each year on the Continent or in Britain, much of the summer being devoted to excavation, first at Cawthorn and then on Hadrian's Wall. In 1930 he was the obvious choice to return to Rome as director of the British School, but two years later ill health caused him to resign, and for nearly three years he was without a post; but he put the period of his convalescence to good use, completing and seeing through the press the great work on *The Aqueducts of Ancient Rome* (1935) which Ashby's death had left unfinished, and contributing a series of important papers to the Cumberland and Westmorland Society's *Transactions*. In January 1935 he was appointed lecturer in Roman-British history and archaeology at Armstrong College (later King's College, Newcastle) in the university of Durham, where he remained—with a brief break for national service during the war—until 1956; he was given a personal readership in 1943, and a personal professorship in 1950; served a biennium as dean of the faculty of arts, and for several years was public orator. During those twenty-one years he directed a notable series of excavations, both on Hadrian's Wall and at Corbridge, and also in Scotland, at Fendoch and Newstead and Inchtuthil. In 1956 he was translated to Oxford, as the first holder of the chair of the archaeology of the Roman Empire and a fellow of All Souls; he continued his annual excavations at Inchtuthil, in partnership with Dr J. K. St. Joseph, but otherwise he found himself increasingly engaged in advising other excavators, up and down the country, and it was only at Hod Hill in Dorset that he managed more than occasional small-scale digging.

Richmond would doubtless have written more, and more substantial books, but for his readiness to accept the many calls upon his time and energy. His public lectures included the Rhind in Edinburgh (1933), the Riddell memorial in Newcastle (1948), the Ford's in Oxford (1951), and the Gray in Cambridge (1952), but he only published the Riddell lectures, in the stimulating monograph entitled *Archaeology and the After-life in Pagan and Christian Imagery* (1950). From 1944 he served on the Royal Commission on Historical Monuments for England and on the parallel Scottish Commission, contributing substantially to their reports on Roman remains, notably in the English Commission's volumes on Roman Essex and Roman York, and the Scottish Commission's two volumes on the county of Roxburgh. He had been elected FSA in 1931 and served as director of the Society of Antiquaries in 1959-64 and president from April 1964 until his death; no fellow could have had the interests of the society closer to his heart. He was also a pillar of the Roman Society, which he served as its president in 1958-61.

He was appointed CBE in 1958 and knighted in 1964. He was elected FBA in 1947 and received honorary doctorates from Edinburgh, Belfast, Leeds, Manchester, Newcastle, and Cambridge, and was a member of the German Archaeological Institute; he had also served as president of the Society of Antiquaries of Newcastle and of the Bristol and Gloucestershire Archaeological Society.

In 1939 Richmond married Isabel, daughter of John Arthur Little, woollen merchant in Newcastle upon Tyne; they had one son and one daughter. He died in Oxford 4 October 1965.

[Eric Birley in *Proceedings* of the British Academy, vol. lii, 1966; *Journal of Roman Studies*, vol. lv, 1965; *The Times*, 6 October 1965; personal knowledge.]   ERIC BIRLEY

ROBERTSON, ALEXANDER (1896-1970), organic chemist and farmer, was born 12 February 1896 on a farm at Charlesfield, Auchterless (on the Hatton estate), Aberdeenshire, the son of Andrew Robertson, farmer, and his wife, Jane Cantlay. Robertson was the eldest of three children; his twin sisters predeceased him. He was educated at the Auchterless School, where he was accorded the distinction of dux, and then at the Turriff Higher Grade School, which he left in 1914, also as dux. He entered the university of Aberdeen in the same year and, like most Scottish students of that time, took the MA course. He presented botany, chemistry, geology, Latin, mathematics, physics, political economy, and zoology at the preliminary level and in 1915-16 was placed first in the chemistry class. He enlisted in the

Special Brigade, Royal Engineers, in March 1916, and in March 1917 was commissioned in the 2nd Seaforth Highlanders. During service in France he was badly gassed and was discharged from the Service in 1918 with the rank of lieutenant.

After resumption of his studies at Aberdeen Robertson obtained his MA in 1919. With the award of a scholarship from the Lord Kitchener National Memorial Fund he proceeded to study for a degree in science at the university of Glasgow, where Professor G. G. Henderson [q.v.] was head of the chemistry department. In the final examination (B.Sc., 1922) he received special distinction in advanced inorganic, physical, organic, and general technical chemistry. Robertson then obtained a Carnegie research fellowship for two years (1922-4) for research at Glasgow, under Henderson's supervision. In 1924 he obtained his Ph.D. for a thesis entitled 'Studies on the Sabinene Series of Terpenes'. In the same year Robertson was awarded a Ramsay memorial fellowship. However, he resigned this almost immediately in order to accept a Rockefeller international science fellowship to work for two years (1924-6) with Professor (Sir) Robert Robinson at the university of Manchester. During this period he spent six months at the university of Graz, Austria, studying the new and revolutionary technique of microanalysis with Professor Fritz Pregl. At the termination of his fellowship in 1926, he was appointed assistant lecturer in chemistry in the university of Manchester, and resumed his work with Robinson during a period when organic chemistry at Manchester probably reached its greatest days. Robinson and Arthur Lapworth were the two professors; F. Challenger and H. Stephen were senior lecturers, and a group of young men, from all over the world, most of whom were to achieve eminence, assisted the research into the chemistry of the anthocyanins, the alkaloids of the morphine and strychnine groups, and the development of the electronic theory of organic reaction mechanisms.

In 1928 Robertson became reader in chemistry at the East London (later Queen Mary) College in the university of London, and moved in 1930 to the London School of Hygiene and Tropical Medicine as reader in biochemistry. The influence of Harold Raistrick, who was the head of the department, undoubtedly stimulated Robertson's own later researches on fungal metabolites. From London Robertson moved to Liverpool in 1933, to succeed (Sir) Ian M. Heilbron [q.v.] as holder of the Heath Harrison chair of organic chemistry. He occupied this chair with outstanding distinction until he retired in 1957 to devote himself to his second profession—

farming. In Liverpool Robertson designed for organic chemistry a new building, which was completed in 1939, and which fortunately escaped serious damage during the war. In addition to being head of a large and flourishing department, he was pro-vice-chancellor from 1949-54, during which period he had two spells as acting vice-chancellor because of the illness of the vice-chancellor, (Sir) James Mountford. He also served, for varying periods, as chairman of the Departmental Grants Committee, and of the ICI Fellowships Committee, and was president of the University Club from 1951-4. He was elected to the fellowship of the Royal Society in 1941, in recognition of his outstanding contributions to the chemistry of natural products, and was awarded the Society's Davy medal in 1952. He received an honorary LLD of the university of Aberdeen in 1958, was for a time a member of the Advisory Council for Scientific and Industrial Research, and of the University Grants Committee from 1955-9. After his retirement, Robertson acted as adviser in chemistry to the Carnegie Trust for the universities of Scotland (1960-9), and was in great demand as a consultant to various agricultural research institutes and organizations. He was a member of the Agricultural Research Council from 1960 to 1965.

Robertson's scientific excellence is exemplified by his contributions to the chemistry of natural oxygen heterocycles such as anthocyanins (with R. Robinson), to the rotenoids, and to the lichen substances—especially usnic acid—to fungal metabolites such as citrinin, citromycetin, and the sclerotiorin pigments, and to natural pigments such as dracorubin and rottlerin. He also made major contributions to the chemistry of naturally occurring bitter principles, and to nitrogen heterocycles, especially the bacterial metabolite, violascein, and, with H. G. Khorana (later a Nobel prize winner), to indoles and their hydroperoxides.

Robertson's chemistry, like his personal life, was characterized by complete integrity and a total rejection of the second best. During his academic life he always maintained close links with active farming and upon retirement commenced a second career in full-time farming, first in Aberdeenshire and later on a 2,000 acre estate at Roxholme Grange, Lincolnshire, in partnership with his only child and son, Euan.

Robertson was a man of imposing stature, possessed of a natural shyness and dislike for publicity which caused him to refuse many social engagements. This shyness was disguised by a brusque exterior which was frequently misunderstood, but to those favoured few who knew him sufficiently well, he was a different person. It was typical of his character not to leave a record or a photograph with the Royal Society, and to refuse all invitations to sit for a portrait.

In 1926 Robertson married Margaret Mitchell (died 1960), daughter of Alexander Chapman, a farmer and wood merchant, of Forglen, Banffshire; she graduated MB, Ch.B. at Aberdeen in 1919. It was a most happy marriage. Robertson died in Grantham Hospital 9 February 1970.

[R. D. Haworth and W. B. Whalley in *Biographical Memoirs of Fellows of the Royal Society*, vol. xvii, 1971; personal knowledge.]

W. B. WHALLEY

ROBERTSON, SIR DENNIS HOLME (1890–1963), economist, was born at Lowestoft, Suffolk, 23 May 1890, the sixth and youngest child of the Revd James Robertson and his wife, Constance Elizabeth Wilson. His father, who had been a master at Rugby and Harrow, and headmaster at Haileybury from 1884, resigned from Haileybury in the year of his son's birth and took up the country living of Whittlesford, Cambridgeshire, where he died in 1903. During Dennis Robertson's early years his father was his only teacher, but the parental tuition was such that at Eton, where the son became a King's scholar in 1902, he won prizes or scholarships each year and rose to be captain of the School.

His classical education continued at Trinity College, Cambridge, where he was an entrance scholar and gained a first in part i of the classical tripos (1910); he won the Chancellor's medal for English verse three times, and was president of the Amateur Dramatic Club, retaining a lifelong interest and excellence in theatrical activities. In 1910 he moved over to economics; the following year he won a Craven scholarship, and became president both of the Union and of the Liberal Society. In 1912 he took a first in part ii of the economics tripos, J. M. (later Lord) Keynes [q.v.] having been his supervisor. Robertson remained in Cambridge, and in 1913 he won the Cobden prize; in 1914 he was elected into a Trinity fellowship, having written, as the dissertation for the fellowship, *A Study of Industrial Fluctuation*, an important work which set the course for much that was to follow; it was published in 1915, when he was already in the army, and firmly established him as an economist.

He spent the war years in the Balkans, Egypt, and Palestine with the 11th battalion, London Regiment, winning the MC, and returned to Cambridge at the end of 1919. During the next nineteen years his fellowship at Trinity was augmented first by his appointment as university lecturer in economics (1924–8), then

as Girdlers' lecturer (1928–30), finally as reader in economics—a post which he held until he went to London in 1938.

Robertson was pre-eminently a literary economist, both in the negative sense that he was opposed to the reduction of economics to mathematics, and in the positive sense that his contributions were outstandingly well written, in a style peculiarly his own which won the affection of many of his readers. The charm of his textbook *Money* (1922) with its quotations from *Alice in Wonderland* at the heads of the chapters, won for him a reputation as a monetary specialist; but he was much more than that, and even in his writings on money he was continually looking for the causes of monetary disturbances in directions which lay outside the narrowly monetary field. Already apparent in his first book, *Industrial Fluctuations*, the process continued, leading him at one stage to think upon lines which converged with Keynes's, but at another to diverge.

Money, in its original form, was in the 'orthodox' Cambridge tradition of Alfred Marshall [q.v.], just as Keynes's early writings on money were orthodox; soon after finishing it, however, Robertson began to break away. *Banking Policy and the Price Level* (1926) was the most difficult of his books, a voyage of exploration into territory which had not then been charted, and its characteristically picturesque terminology was not very usable. It did, however, mark a turning-point: the turning away from quantity of money towards saving and investment, towards the route which was eventually to lead to Keynes's 'effective demand'. At that stage Robertson and Keynes were clearly working together and influencing one another, and as late as 1928 (to judge by the preface to that edition of *Money*) Robertson believed that they were working on the same lines. But Keynes does not appear to have consulted him in the actual preparation of his own *Treatise on Money*; it is evident from Robertson's review in the *Economic Journal* (1931) that already they were beginning to lose touch. When it came to Keynes's *General Theory of Employment, Interest and Money* (1936), Robertson reacted strongly.

In 1938 he decided to move to London University, accepting the Sir Ernest Cassel chair of economics ('with special reference to banking and currency') at the London School of Economics. Although he nominally held the appointment until 1944, he taught there one year only, for soon after the outbreak of war in 1939 he found himself in the Treasury, as economic adviser or 'temporary administrative officer' to Sir Frederick Phillips, the third secretary in charge of overseas finance. Robertson's brief was to watch and control the balance of payments with particular countries; later he was involved in the preparations on both sides of the Atlantic for Bretton Woods, and took part, with Keynes (here more nearly upon common ground), in the negotiations themselves.

In 1944 he was elected to the chair of political economy at Cambridge, in succession to A. C. Pigou [q.v.] and returned to his rooms in Trinity, the only home he ever had. In those rooms, with the cat-hole in the door and the collection of weird animals on the mantlepiece, he continued to live for the rest of his life. He was a man of courteous charm and sensitive modesty, a warm appreciation of the work of others, and enjoyment of the company of the young. Nevertheless, these years were hardly happy. They were spent in a struggle against what had become Keynesianism, against the new orthodoxy which he felt to be 'no less rigid than that against which it was, or conceived itself to be, a revolt'. It was very uncomfortable to take that line in Cambridge; although in the outside world (in the world of finance as well as in other universities) he had many sympathizers, in Cambridge he felt himself to be isolated, and he suffered from it. This appears in his later writings, even in his *Lectures on Economic Principles* (1957-9), published after his retirement in 1957.

He was a member of the royal commission on equal pay (1944-6) and of the council on prices, productivity, and incomes (1957-8). He received honorary degrees from the universities of London, Manchester, Durham, and Sheffield, as well as Harvard, Columbia, Amsterdam, and Louvain. He was appointed CMG in 1944 and knighted in 1953. He was a fellow of the British Academy from 1932, and of Eton in 1948-57—the distinction which he valued most highly; he was president of the Royal Economic Society in 1948-50, and was a member of various foreign learned societies. He never married. He died in Cambridge 21 April 1963.

It is not easy to sum up the issue between Keynes and Robertson in a few lines, in a manner fair to each. Certainly it was not a matter of logic, nor of knowledge of the world; it was more probably a difference in point of view, in the things which one or the other judged to be important, and the things which he was willing to leave out of account. Keynes (at least in the thirties, although much less in his final Bretton Woods phase, when Robertson and he again came closer together) had fixed his eye on the economic situation as seen at the moment, and had asked, 'What do we do about it? In what direction should its present course of development be changed?' Whereas Robertson, from 1912-14 onwards, had been

looking at fluctuations; he was concerned with the 'cycle' as a whole. His objective was stability; the dampening of fluctuations, not indeed their elimination, for some fluctuation, he held, was 'appropriate'. That must imply judicious use of encouragement, at the right time, and of restraint, at the right time. In certain later versions of Keynesianism that balance came back, and one of them might, in the end, prove to have been Keynes's own. But what Robertson feared was that Keynes's teaching would lead, in practice, to the over-use of encouragement, and, in order to make that possible, at the same time to the over-use of restraint—an outcome which many people have felt that he was right to fear.

A chalk drawing of Robertson by Francis Dodd (1939) is in the Marshall Library, Cambridge.

[*The Times*, 22 April 1963; Sir John Hicks in *Proceedings* of the British Academy, vol. i, 1964; private information; personal knowledge.]   JOHN HICKS

ROBERTSON, DONALD STRUAN (1885-1961), classical scholar, born in London 28 June 1885, was the fourth child and only son of Henry Robert Robertson, etcher and painter, and his wife, Agnes Lucy Turner. His eldest sister was Agnes Arber [q.v.], the botanist. He went as a day-boy to Westminster School whence he won a major entrance scholarship at Trinity College, Cambridge. He was placed in the first class in part i of the classical tripos in 1906 and in part ii in 1908, specializing in classical archaeology. His distinctions included the Members' Latin essay prize in 1906, the first Chancellor's medal in 1908, and the Stewart of Rannoch (1905), Pitt (1907), and Charles Oldham (1908) scholarships. He competed for a Trinity fellowship with a dissertation on the story of Lucius as told by Apuleius and by pseudo-Lucian; and successful at the first attempt was elected in 1909.

In the same year he married Petica Coursolles, daughter of Major Charles Jones of the Royal Artillery, to whom he had become engaged after an acquaintanceship as brief as the marriage was successful. She was one of six sisters, all distinguished, nieces of Robert Ross, the friend of Oscar Wilde [q.v.]; one of them, E. B. C. Jones, the novelist, married F. L. Lucas [q.v.], writer and critic. Their first child, Charles Martin, later professor of classical archaeology at Oxford, was born in 1911; he was followed in 1913 by Giles, who became professor of fine art at Edinburgh. In 1911 Robertson was appointed assistant lecturer on the classical staff at Trinity, joining Ernest Harrison and Francis Cornford [q.v.]. On the outbreak of war in spite of a slight congenital lameness he was commissioned in the Army Service Corps, in which he rose to the rank of major. He returned in 1919 to lecturing and supervising at Trinity, and in 1928 he succeeded A. C. Pearson (whose notice he contributed to this Dictionary) as regius professor of Greek.

Between the wars Robertson lived a full and happy life in his Bateman Street house, where many of the most interesting and distinguished figures of the university young and old, as well as visiting scholars, were to be encountered. His wife was an enthusiastic, although unpretentious, hostess, whose gentleness gave reassurance to those who sensed a certain intellectual austerity in their host.

From the beginning archaeology and literature were the fields of classical scholarship which engaged Robertson's interest. He was sensitive to the visual arts and had a keen enjoyment of poetry in many languages, although largely indifferent to what in his day was called 'modern'. It was on archaeology that he first lectured, but soon after his return in 1919 he turned to Greek literature; he took particular pleasure in his course on poetry from Homer to Aeschylus, which attracted large audiences. His delivery was rapid and his matter highly compressed, but he spoke with patent sincerity touched at times with eloquence, especially when Homer or Pindar was his subject. He gave also specialist courses both on literature and on textual criticism.

His first book was *A Handbook of Greek and Roman Architecture* (1929) which covered some of the same ground as the sections on architecture which he contributed to volumes iv-vi of the *Cambridge Ancient History*. It was a masterly survey by one who clearly had it in him to write far more than a textbook. He revised it for a second edition in 1943 and it has been several times reprinted. In 1969 the word *Handbook* was dropped from the title.

The work for which he will be best remembered is his text of the Metamorphoses of Apuleius published in the Budé series (Paris, 3 vols., 1940-5). Robertson spent many years over the collation of the manuscripts, whose relationship he established, and produced a greatly improved text accompanied by an apparatus criticus remarkable for its economy. The work on Pindar to which he looked forward in his inaugural lecture was never achieved.

Robertson would no doubt have published more had he been less in demand as a member of boards and committees, where his sagacity and incisiveness were highly valued, and had he been less prodigal of time in helping and advising others. In particular the publication from the notes of Sir William Ridgeway [q.v.] of the second volume of *The Early Age of Greece*

(1931), in which he assisted his friend and colleague Andrew Gow, required much time and labour. In addition he contributed numerous articles to learned journals, and his duties as examiner were heavy. And perhaps he was aware that the law of diminishing returns applies even to scholarship, and hence he diverted some of his energies to the study of Icelandic sagas and, especially in his later years, to Persian poetry.

In 1941 he suffered a stunning blow in the loss of his wife, killed by a bomb while on duty as an air-raid warden. Before the end of the war he moved from his house to rooms in college. He had always taken part in the administration of its affairs and from 1947 to 1951 he served as vice-master; his wit and wide range as a conversationalist made him an admirable college host. At the end of his term of office, which was shortly after he reached retiring age as professor, he suffered a breakdown in health, and although at length he made a good recovery he was compelled to give up his long bicycle rides through the Cambridgeshire countryside of which he was a strong admirer.

Robertson received honorary degrees from the universities of Durham, Glasgow, and Athens, and was elected FBA in 1940. He was a man of more than ordinary integrity and uprightness. His nerves were somewhat tense and he may at times have concealed less completely than he supposed the irritation provoked by stupidity, but he rarely displayed impatience, and never with the young. In a Cambridge which had its share of critical and irascible characters he was never spoken of but with affection and respect.

A young colleague of great promise at Trinity, George Cary (son of Joyce Cary, q.v.), died in 1953, and Robertson became occupied in helping his widow, Margaret, daughter of Sir Eric Phipps [q.v.], formerly ambassador in Paris, to prepare for publication her husband's work on the Alexander Romance. They were married in 1956 and Robertson spent his last years in their house in the Madingley Road. He died after a series of strokes in Cambridge 5 October 1961.

Trinity College has a chalk drawing of Robertson by Neville Lewis.

[F. H. Sandbach in *Proceedings* of the British Academy, vol. xlviii, 1962; *The Times*, 6 October 1961; personal knowledge.]

D. W. LUCAS

ROBERTSON, SIR HOWARD MORLEY (1888-1963), architect, was born in Salt Lake City, Utah, 16 August 1888, the second child and younger son in the family of three children of Casper Ludovic van Uytrecht Robertson of

Liverpool and his wife, Ellen Duncan, of Ohio. He came to England to be educated at Malvern College, and in 1905–7 he attended the Architectural Association School of Architecture, then located in Tufton Street, Westminster. This was followed by a course at the École Supérieure des Beaux Arts in Paris (1908–12), where he qualified with the French Architectural Diploma in 1913. He gained practical experience as an assistant in architects' offices in London, Boston, New York, and on a project in Le Touquet which brought him into contact with his future partner.

During World War I, Howard Robertson served in the army with distinction in France, 1915–19, being promoted to the rank of colonel and awarded the Military Cross, Legion of Honour, and USA Certificate of Merit: he was also appointed Officier de l'Étoile Noire. On his return to England he joined with John Murray Easton in private practice as 'Easton and Robertson'. In 1920 he joined the teaching staff of the Architectural Association School of Architecture, which had by then moved to Bedford Square, to aid in the integration of student instruction with experience from office and site. He became a friend and travelling companion of the school's secretary, F. R. Yerbury [q.v.]. He was appointed principal of the AA School in 1926 and later director of education from 1929 to 1935, and it was during this period that the school achieved the distinction of being the first to receive final recognition of its diploma for full qualification. Robertson never allowed administrative matters to interfere unduly with lectures and personal contact through studio tuition. His aim was to teach broad principles, as reflected in his writings on theory and composition, urging students thereafter to find things out for themselves.

He had thus a considerable influence during what was a period of aesthetic reassessment. His teaching proved more progressive than his own designs, so often hampered by restrictions: although at one time he was a member of the Congrès International d'Architecture Moderne international avant-garde group, he withdrew because it was too partisan. By trips abroad, however, he kept in close touch with current movements both in Europe—particularly France, Sweden, Holland, and Italy—and in the United States where in 1927 he renewed his acquaintance with and married a former architectural pupil, Doris Adeney, daughter of John Reynolds Lewis of Melbourne, Australia, and his wife, Sara Day. They had no children.

In due course it became necessary to devote all his time to a thriving and varied practice which merged in 1931 with that of Stanley Hall under the three names, until it was again reconstituted after World War II. He had become FRIBA in 1925 and later honorary AIA. In 1933 he was awarded the RIBA Godwin and Wimperis bursary for his report on Continental schools. In this period he spent a short while in the then tense atmosphere of the Bauhaus.

His most notable commission, which was designed with his partner, Easton, was the permanent exhibition hall for the Royal Horticultural Society, which was awarded the RIBA architecture bronze medal in 1928, one of many similar awards to the firm in later years: he received RIBA architecture bronze medals in 1936 and 1937. Amongst the buildings in which Robertson was personally most closely involved were the British Pavilion at the 1925 Paris Exhibition of Decorative Arts, and further national exhibition pavilions at Brussels in 1935, Johannesburg in 1937, and New York World's Fair in 1939 when he received the distinction of being made 'honorary citizen of the city of New York'; interior designs in hotels such as the Berkeley, Savoy, and Claridge's, and in several large liners for the New Zealand Shipping Company; a hotel, bathing-pool, and pavilion at Prestatyn, North Wales; the printing works for the Bank of England; the post-war reconstruction of libraries at the universities of Keele and Newcastle; the Faculty of Letters at Reading University, where he was honoured with a D.Litt. in 1957; Hatfield Technical College; and various office buildings, blocks of flats, and schools. Although Robertson's architecture tended towards the traditional rather than the modern, his teaching was most progressive and his school produced many architects of the modern movement.

During World War II Howard Robertson devoted much thought to designing the original standard industrial-type hostels used by the Ministry of Works, at the same time preparing typical schemes of interior decoration, the warm friendliness of which contributed to the hostels' success. In 1947 he served the Architectural Association as president during the centenary year, and thereafter remained on the advisory council. On the RIBA council he was vice-president 1938–40 and president 1952–4, also serving on the Building Industries National Council. In 1949 he was awarded the Royal gold medal for architecture, and in the same year was elected ARA, becoming full RA in 1958. He was knighted in 1954.

In the international field Howard Robertson was technical adviser to the secretary-general in connection with the League of Nations building in Geneva and also a member of the jury which assessed the international competition for Parliament buildings in Ankara. Later, in 1947 he achieved the distinction of being selected to be British representative on the international board of design for the United Nations headquarters in New York, in which he showed courageous firmness for ethical as well as aesthetic rectitude. His last major work was the vast and immensely complicated Shell Centre on the south bank of the river Thames, which was fated to receive from the critics less understanding tolerance than Robertson himself was wont to show to others. He was a man of parts, liveryman of the Goldsmiths' Company, with a keen appreciation of modern paintings and sculpture and of music—reflecting a worldly wisdom lightened by humour, which he was always ready to share. His career and personal credo are summed up in a series of autobiographical articles entitled 'Obbligato to Architecture' in the *Builder*, April to June 1962. Among his other writings are *The Principles of Architectural Composition* (1924) and *Modern Architectural Design* (1932).

Eric Kennington's portrait of him, which is in the possession of the Architectural Association, records him with bushy eyebrows, furrowed forehead, and clear gaze, ably expressing the penetrating mind behind a deliberate manner of speaking, which to the end retained inflection from the country of his birth. There is also a presidential portrait by Rodrigo Moynihan (1954) which hangs in the Royal Institute of British Architects.

After a long drawn out illness Howard Robertson died in London 5 May 1963.

[Sir Howard Robertson, 'Obbligato to Architecture', *Builder*, April-June 1962; personal knowledge.]　　　　　R. E. ENTHOVEN

ROBERTSON SCOTT, JOHN WILLIAM (1866-1962), journalist, author, and founder-editor of *The Countryman*, was born 20 April 1866 at Wigton in Cumberland, the second of eight children (the first died in infancy) of David Young Crozier Scott, commercial traveller and temperance orator, and his wife, Janet, daughter of John Robertson. His Border origins were wholly rural. He was educated at Quaker and grammar schools. His parents, who held broad and Liberal views, welcomed many like-minded visitors of several nationalities to a home that was 'serious but not austere, of great affection and care'. Robertson Scott wrote of his father, as one who had much to do in setting the course of his life, that he was 'not only a teetotaller and a non-smoker, but a believer in cold baths and a disbeliever in bottles of medicine'. His parents were members of the Evangelical Union, but the family went to Quaker, Wesleyan, and Congregational services 'impartially'.

They moved to Carlisle about 1876 and,

three or four years later, to Birmingham where his father was summoned to take charge of the organization to which he had devoted already a disproportionate share of his time and energies, the Independent Order of Good Templars. One of Robertson Scott's first jobs was as secretary to Joseph Malins, head of the grand lodge of the Good Templars in England; but he had already decided on a career in journalism. His father died at the age of forty-three, when he was still in his teens. As the eldest surviving son he accepted the challenge and supported his mother, brother, and three sisters on meagre journalistic earnings. In retrospect he was grateful for 'a realizing sense of what poverty is'. The first payment had come from C. P. Scott [q.v.] of the *Manchester Guardian*, and he was contributing to several national journals when H. J. Palmer offered him a staff appointment on the *Birmingham Gazette*; but he had to leave when he stipulated that, as a Liberal, he should write nothing in support of the Conservative cause. He was working again as a freelance when, in 1887, he was invited by W. T. Stead [q.v.] to join him on the *Pall Mall Gazette*. He worked for six years on that paper under Stead and then (Sir) Edward T. Cook [q.v.]. When Cook left to found the *Westminster Gazette* in 1893, Robertson Scott accompanied him and wrote a daily feature, 'Round the World'. In 1899 he transferred to the *Daily Chronicle* under H. W. Massingham [q.v.] but resigned with him in November of that year on the issue of the Boer War, with which the proprietors were in sympathy.

It was then that Robertson Scott decided to live and write in the country. He acquired a cottage at Great Canfield in Essex and 'invented that pioneer in rural journalism and authorship, "Home Counties "'. In 1902 he was invited by J. St. Loe Strachey [q.v.] to contribute farming articles to the *Country Gentleman*. In the next few years, using the same pseudonym, he was closely associated with the *World's Work* and the *Field*; he also wrote hundreds of articles and several books in a style peculiarly his own. They were for townspeople, about farmers and smallholders, farm workers and landowners, how they lived and made a living, omitting the technicalities. He travelled the country and made frequent visits abroad, notably to Holland and Denmark. His energy was prodigious; his journalistic output remarkable. In 1906 he married the talented Elspet (died 1956), daughter of George Keith, of HM Customs. They had no children. Together they contributed to the life of rural Essex, forming at Dunmow the Progressive Club for 'men and women of markedly different upbringings and associations, politics, denominations and incomes', and producing in Lady Warwick's big barn plays by Synge, Barrie, and Bensusan.

When war broke out in 1914 Robertson Scott was above military age. He paid two visits to Holland, then sold his Essex property and went to Japan. Looking ahead to the period of post-war reconstruction, he had in mind two studies: one of the small-farming system and rural life in Japan, the other (never accomplished) of large-scale farming in the American Middle West. While in Japan, gathering material with characteristic penetration and vigour, he started and edited with official backing a monthly, the *New East;* he refused to adopt a propagandist approach and tried to explain Japan and the Japanese to the West and Western ideas to the East. In 1916 appeared, in both English and Japanese, his book *Japan, Great Britain and the World;* but it was not until 1922, a year after his return home by way of the United States, that his copious notes were published as *The Foundations of Japan,* long the standard work in English on the rural life and people of that country.

On his return Robertson Scott resumed his journalistic writing, became an enthusiastic adviser to the National Federation of Women's Institutes (he published, in 1925, *The Story of the Women's Institute Movement*), and was a hard-working member of the Liberal Land Committee which produced *The Land and the Nation* (1923-5). At this time he contributed to the *Nation* a series of four articles which grew to twenty-four and was published anonymously as *England's Green and Pleasant Land* (1925), his best-selling book. It described frankly and penetratingly, through the people and their talk about neighbours and themselves, the life of a contemporary village. *The Dying Peasant and the Future of His Sons* followed a year later, and both books will be of permanent value to historians.

In 1923 Robertson Scott had moved to the Cotswold hamlet of Idbury in Oxfordshire. Four years later, at the age of sixty-one, he founded the quarterly review, *The Countryman.* He and his wife were business and advertisement manager, editor, sub-editor, and principal contributors. Ignoring the advice of friends, and with never more than £500 capital, they made it the most successful venture in periodical publishing between the two world wars. Non-party, though firm enough in opinion, it was to be packed with rural life and character, to place before town, city, and country dwellers vividly and convincingly the facts, and to strengthen the forces of rural progress; but it must entertain, if it were to achieve its more serious purpose. Robertson Scott sold the magazine in 1943 and continued to edit it with full independence for a further four years.

Despite the demands of *The Countryman,* Robertson Scott was active in local government. Housing had been one of his most compelling interests since he contributed to the *Country Gentleman* a series of articles entitled 'In Search of a £150 Cottage', which led to an exhibition at Letchworth opened by the Duke of Devonshire. He was for ten years chairman of his district council housing committee and served under four ministers of health on the Central Housing Advisory Committee. He became a JP and founded the Quorum Club, an educational society with a good library for magistrates. He set great store by the gatherings of 'Village Neighbours' in Idbury School to hear an invited speaker each Sunday afternoon. In 1947, on his retirement, Robertson Scott was made a Companion of Honour. Two years later he was awarded an honorary MA degree by Oxford University.

Self-styled agnostic, Robertson Scott had an infectious faith in mankind and the future based on a belief in the individual worth of ordinary men and women, who would grow in stature as the opportunities open to them increased. All his strivings, tremendous energy, knowledge, and journalistic skill were directed to extending these opportunities. He was always welcoming to people and causes. He was greatly helped by a devoted wife, herself a gifted writer, who provided him with the satisfying home background necessary for the success of single-minded endeavours. He lived until his middle nineties with faculties undiminished and died at home in Idbury 21 December 1962.

There is a portrait in oils by Anton van Anrooy, probably painted in the 1930s, in the offices of *The Countryman* in Burford.

[J. W. Robertson Scott, *The Day Before Yesterday,* 1951; John Cripps, 'J. W. Robertson Scott, C. H.', *The Countryman,* vol. lx, no. 1, 1963; personal knowledge.]

JOHN CRIPPS

ROBINS, THOMAS ELLIS, BARON ROBINS (1884-1962), business man, was born 31 October 1884 in Philadelphia, USA, the son of Major Robert P. Robins of the United States Army, and his wife, Mary, daughter of Thomas de la Roche Ellis. He was educated privately and at the university of Pennsylvania. At the age of nineteen he became the first Rhodes scholar from Pennsylvania to go to Oxford where he was at Christ Church from 1904 to 1907. He read history, but failed to get a degree. He was a member of the Bullingdon Club. He then spent two years in New York in journalism and became assistant editor of *Everybody's Magazine.* He returned to England in 1909 to be private secretary to one of his Oxford friends, the sixth Earl Winterton [q.v.]. In 1912 he became a naturalized British subject and joined the City of London Yeomanry, with which he was mobilized on the outbreak of war in August 1914. He served overseas in the Middle East, being twice mentioned in dispatches and appointed to the DSO. For two years after the armistice he was provost marshal in Egypt and Palestine. After demobilization, he became secretary of the Conservative Club in London (1921–8). From 1925 to 1928 he commanded the City of London Yeomanry Battery of the Royal Horse Artillery, which in 1928 won the coveted King's cup.

Robins was invited in 1928 to join the British South Africa Company (Chartered) as its general manager in Salisbury, Southern Rhodesia. He quickly made his mark with this powerful commercial company, the principal assets of which were the mineral rights in Southern and Northern Rhodesia, and ownership of the railways. On the death of Sir F. Drummond Chaplin he became resident director of Chartered in 1934.

Robins formed a close friendship with Sir Ernest Oppenheimer [q.v.], chairman of the Anglo-American Corporation of South Africa, and of De Beers Consolidated Mines. He served on the board of directors of both of these companies. Amongst many other companies of which he was a director mention should be made of Barclays Bank DCO, Union Corporation, African Explosives and Chemical Industries, Wankie Colliery, Rhokana Corporation, and Nchanga Consolidated Copper Mines. He was an original director, and later chairman, of Rhodesia and Nyasaland Airways; and chairman of its successor, Central African Airways.

His characteristics were a devotion to duty, untiring energy, a readiness to accept the burdens of responsibility, and a willingness to serve the public interest in any field. His interests were much wider than the success of the company which he directed. A keen freemason, he was for twenty years district grand master of Rhodesia. He was commissioner for Boy Scouts in that country and held the Silver Wolf decoration. For his long and devoted leadership in ambulance work he was made knight of the Order of St. John of Jerusalem. For two decades he was chairman of the Southern Rhodesia Agricultural Society.

Soon after the outbreak of war in 1939 Robins joined East Africa Command in Kenya, commanding from 1940 to 1943 the 1st battalion of the Rhodesia Regiment. At the request of (Earl) Wavell [q.v.] he served on the general staff in India in 1943. He returned to Southern Rhodesia to be AA and quartermaster-general of the Southern Rhodesia forces until the end of the war. For his war services he was knighted in 1946.

It was inevitable that Robins should be made chairman and principal organizer of the Central Africa Rhodes Centenary Exhibition held in Bulawayo in 1953, which was opened by Queen Elizabeth, the Queen Mother. He was an original trustee of the Rhodes–Livingstone Institute and of the Rhodes National Gallery. Later he became president of the Royal African Society in London.

Besides his merits as an administrator he was a genial host. His home, June Hill, Avondale, Salisbury, was for thirty years as much a centre of attraction as Government House, to which all Rhodesians flocked, as did all visitors to the country from overseas. He commanded respect, admiration, and the affection of a host of friends of all ages, as of those who served under him.

In 1957 he returned to London and succeeded Christopher Hely-Hutchinson as president of the Chartered Company. He was raised to the peerage as Baron Robins, of Rhodesia and Chelsea, in 1958.

As Cecil Rhodes [q.v.] wished, here was one of his scholars from overseas imbued with the spirit of Oxford who exemplified Christian virtues of truth, courage, and kindliness; and, to a marked degree, of leadership: a man 'sans peur et sans reproche'.

He married in 1912, Mary St. Quintin (died 1974), youngest daughter of Philip Wroughton, DL, MP, of Woolley Park, Berkshire. They had two daughters, and the title lapsed upon Robins's death in Chelsea 21 July 1962.

There is a portrait in oils by (Sir) James Gunn (c.1953) in the possession of the family. A smaller version of the same portrait hangs in the board room at Charter House, Anglo-American Corporation of Rhodesia, in Salisbury, Rhodesia.

[Personal knowledge.] H. St. L. GRENFELL

ROGERS, SIR LEONARD (1868–1962), pioneer of tropical medicine, was born at Hartley House near Plymouth 18 January 1868. He was the seventh son of Captain Henry Rogers, RN, and grandson of John Rogers (1778–1856, q.v.) his father had ten children by his first wife, Jane Mary, daughter of John Samuel Enys, of Enys, and granddaughter of Davies Gilbert [q.v.], and six by his second wife. Rogers was educated at Tavistock Grammar School, Devon County School, and Plymouth College. Rejecting advice to become a mathematician, he entered St. Mary's Hospital medical school in 1886, obtained the English conjoint diplomas in 1891, passed the final examination for the FRCS in 1892—too young to receive the diploma—and later in the same year passed as MB, BS London with distinction in every subject.

In 1893 he passed into the Indian Medical Service and as a regimental medical officer he soon showed such aptitude in conducting research that the director-general marked him down for early transfer to civil employment. On sick leave in the United Kingdom he obtained the MD London (1897) and the MRCP (1898) despite a reproof from the president for poor writing and spelling. On his return to India, Rogers was lent to the veterinary department for research at Múktesar, where he made important discoveries on the control of rinderpest in cattle by inoculation and on the transmission of equine trypanosomiasis (surra) in horses and camels by mechanical contamination of the mouth parts of the biting flies concerned.

His posting to the Bengal civil medical department at Calcutta in 1900 heralded a new era in tropical medicine. He acted for the professor of pathology in the medical college and was the virtual holder of the post after 1904 although not confirmed in it until 1906. He extended the range of his work beyond the confines of his laboratory and paid daily visits to the wards to observe the patients of his clinical colleagues. His discovery of the flagellate stage of the parasite of kala-azar, a most deadly disease of man in Assam (now known to exist throughout the tropics) enabled him to suggest, on grounds of analogy with sleeping sickness of Africa, that antimony administered intravenously as tartar emetic might be curative. It was. He put forward the theory that the disease would certainly prove to be transmitted by a biting insect; it took forty years to prove this to be so.

Observations on the deadly effects of seasnake venom, made, typically, while on vacation at Puri on the Indian coast, led to a study of appropriate physiological research methods in London with Professor A. D. Waller and enabled Rogers clearly to differentiate the effects of colubrine from viperine bites on the vascular and nervous systems.

His work in differentiating amoebic dysentery from the bacterial dysenteries, his discovery of the specific action of emetine in amoebic infections, his cure of early amoebic invasion of the liver by emetine, and his introduction of aseptic aspiration of amoebic abscess of the liver in place of the often fatal open drainage marked a turning-point in the treatment of bowel infection in the tropics.

Rogers recognized that the very high mortality in cholera was due to the sudden loss of most of the body fluid. His treatment by the intravenous infusion of large quantities of sterile salt solution saved innumerable lives;

his work on the need for maintaining a proper balance between sodium, potassium, and calcium ions in the blood plasma led to the introduction of Rogers fluid which remained the standard treatment for cholera for half a century. His advocacy of preventive inoculation of those attending pilgrim fairs in the Ganges valley had a salutary effect on the incidence of the disease. His rescue of leprosy from the doldrums of neglect will probably rank as his major contribution to tropical medicine, for leprosy became curable. The subject appealed to him on both social and scientific grounds. His investigation of the efficacy of the ages-old chaulmoogra oil, of its components and analogues, and his drive to stimulate others to recognize the early stages of leprosy paid handsome dividends and encouraged workers in many lands to take up leprosy research.

Rogers was mainly instrumental in devising plans, and in raising funds, for the construction of the Calcutta School of Tropical Medicine. That school and the British Empire Leprosy Relief Association which he founded in 1923 will remain his most enduring monuments.

After leaving India in 1920 on grounds of health and retiring from the Indian Medical Service in 1921, Rogers was appointed a lecturer at the London School of Tropical Medicine. He was a voluble rapid lecturer, difficult to follow. His appointment as a member of the India Office medical board in 1922 was followed by his promotion as president in 1928, with collateral duty as medical adviser to the secretary of state, a position for which he was not entirely suited; but it gave him access to the vast stores of statistical and meteorological records in the India Office which provided him with material for a long series of papers on the forecasting of epidemics. For some years he was secretary of the Research Defence Society.

In 1911 Rogers was appointed CIE and in 1914 he was knighted. He was appointed KCSI in 1932, and on his retirement in 1933 given the honorary rank of major-general. In 1916 he was elected FRS and was president of the Asiatic Society of Bengal; in 1919 he was president of the Indian Science Congress; and in 1933-5 he was president of the Royal Society of Tropical Medicine and Hygiene, whose Manson medal was among the numerous distinctions he received.

A slim and wiry figure, until his marriage careless of his appearance, capable of extraordinary feats of endurance on his bicycle on remote jungle tracks, a rigid teetotaller and non-smoker who attributed his success in life to the strict religious upbringing which he owed to his father, Rogers had little time for sport or social intercourse. With an uncanny flair for sound investment he amassed a considerable fortune which he gave away during his lifetime to scientific bodies and charitable trusts. His autobiography, *Happy Toil* (1950), showed that he was not unaware of the important part which he had played.

In 1914 Rogers married Una Elsie (died 1951), daughter of Charles Niven McIntyre North, architect, of Forest Hill. They had three sons of whom Professor C. Ambrose Rogers, mathematician, was elected FRS in 1959 during his father's lifetime. Rogers died in Truro after a fall, 16 September 1962. There is a marble bust by a Mr Martre of Bombay in the School of Tropical Medicine in Calcutta.

[Sir John Boyd in *Biographical Memoirs of Fellows of the Royal Society*, vol. ix, 1963; *Burke's Landed Gentry;* personal knowledge.]　　　　　　　　GEORGE McROBERT

ROOTES, WILLIAM EDWARD, first BARON ROOTES (1894–1964), motor-car manufacturer, was born in Hawksworth, Kent, 17 August 1894, the son of William Rootes, a cycle and motor engineer, and his wife, Jane Catt. He was educated at Cranbrook School, and then joined the family workshop until 1913, when he became an apprentice at Singer Cars in Coventry. From the beginning he worked hard, but nevertheless found time for motor-cycle track racing at which he was frequently successful. In 1915 he volunteered as a pupil engineer in the Royal Naval Volunteer Reserve and in 1917 was moved to the flying section of the Royal Naval Air Service, which became part of the Royal Air Force in 1918. On demobilization he became a motor trader and persuaded his younger brother, Reginald (Claud), to leave his Civil Service post at the Admiralty and join him. The brothers started a motor business in Maidstone with a loan of £1,500 from their father who instructed them in the trade of a distributing agency. The business was soon extended to Long Acre, London, and then to the new Devonshire House in Piccadilly when it was built in 1926.

'Billy' Rootes, however, not content with dealing in cars, determined to manufacture them to ensure a steady flow of vehicles for his market. Financial assistance organized by Sir George E. (later Lord) May [q.v.] of the Prudential Assurance Company in 1929 enabled the Hillman and Humber factories in Coventry to be acquired. The business prospered and it became evident that the Rootes brothers had entered the manufacturing business at a favourable time, for a car was rapidly becoming a status symbol and the proud acquisition of an increasing number of families. The Rootes brothers planned new models with an export appeal, such as the Humber Snipe, designed in part to challenge the American market, and the Hillman Wizard, launched in 1931 as 'the car for the roads of the world'. Billy Rootes's determination vigorously to attack the export markets was an important stage in the development of the British car manufacturing business. Reginald founded a branch in Argentina in 1931 at the time of the British Exhibition in Buenos Aires, and in 1932 the Rootes brothers launched the Hillman Minx, which was tested by Billy Rootes himself on roads abroad. It set a new fashion for small cars and became an immediate and lasting success.

Throughout the 1930s further acquisitions took place: Karrier Motors in 1934, Singer Cars, Clement Talbot Ltd., and Sunbeam Motor Car Co. Ltd., in 1935 (these becoming Sunbeam Talbot Ltd. in 1938), and in 1937 Light Steel Pressings Ltd. of Acton, makers of car and vehicle bodies. The policy was to manufacture well-tried and well-known models, preserving their names and distinctive characteristics, but to increase the efficiency of the concerns which they acquired and hence reduce the costs of production and service. Many manufacturing processes were centralized, components standardized and made more interchangeable, and more efficient assembly systems devised.

In the 1930s Rootes served on many national and official bodies, such as the Board of Trade Advisory Council, the Overseas Trade Development Council, the Committee on the Education and Training of Students, the council and executive committee of the British Council, and the Joint Aero Engine Committee (shadow industry), a committee which was formed when war threatened and of which Rootes became chairman in 1940–1. In 1936 the Rootes Group was among the first to join the Government Aircraft Scheme, set up to organize the volume manufacturing of air-frames and aero-engines. Shortly after the outbreak of war Rootes was appointed chairman of the aircraft shadow industry which was later to become linked with the Aircraft Production Ministry of Lord Beaverbrook [q.v.]. He became chairman of the Motor Vehicle Maintenance Advisory Committee in 1941 and chairman of the supply council of the Ministry of Supply in 1941–2. In 1942 he was appointed KBE.

The Rootes factories suffered in the air raids on Coventry in 1940 and on the morning after the blitz of November 1940 Rootes was to be found outside the plant on an upturned box addressing his work-force, encouraging them to return to clear up the mess, and promising that there should be work for all. The former apprentice was demonstrating, as he was to demonstrate time and time again, both his thorough relationship with the motor industry and his abiding loyalty to the Coventry community. Directly after the raid the Coventry Industrial Reconstruction and Co-ordinating Committee was set up on Lord Beaverbrook's initiative and it was inevitable that the chairman should be William Rootes. His drive and assertiveness and his qualities of leadership in rehabilitating industry had consequences both national and local. Many recommendations were usefully applied in other bombed cities and William Rootes's impact through the committee contributed greatly to Coventry's economic recovery. (In a typical report on New Year's Eve, 1941, submitted jointly on behalf of the committee to the regional commissioners, William Rootes and Alderman Halliwell, a dedicated trade-unionist, commented on the refusal of bus drivers to work after 6.30 p.m. Although the unions advised the bus drivers to work late, some failed to turn up and, in consequence, many men lost work and there was a general loss of confidence in the bus service. The report declared: 'In our view, government support must be given to transport undertakings to overcome the . . . lack of a sense of duty among certain of their employees and an absence of the discipline which is the only substitute for such a sense of duty'.)

After the war the Rootes Group embarked on an expansion plan involving the deployment of several million pounds. Wartime plant was converted for the manufacture of cars and the production capacity of the group more than doubled. Exporting was now a vital national necessity. Rootes established departments for service and the supply of parts at Long Island, Chicago, and Los Angeles, and, in Paris in 1950; he was the inspirer and organizer of the first British Car Exhibition to be held in New York, at the Grand Central Palace. In June 1951 he became chairman of the new Dollar Export Board through which he induced British manufacturers to think on a scale commensurate with transatlantic standards. He travelled widely, becoming the foremost salesman for British industry, while continuing as chairman of the Board (by then known as the Western Hemisphere Export Council) until his retirement in March 1964.

In 1963 the Group opened a new £23 million plant at Linwood in Scotland to produce the new small car, the Hillman Imp. This move was in conformity with a national plan to take industry to distressed areas but one may reflect whether such a policy assisted our exporting ability when the car industry needed to compete with large international firms producing cars within a ring fence.

Rootes's personal leadership of the Rootes organization was typified by his determined but costly stand during the Acton strike of 1961. However, in the world of international car manufacturing Rootes was a small group and in June 1964 the American car firm Chrysler took a £12 million interest. The management control remained with the Rootes family but the company benefited from the Chrysler sales network and the injection of American capital for investment.

Rootes was advanced to GBE in 1955 and created a baron in 1959. His brother Reginald had been knighted in 1946. In 1961 Lord Rootes became chairman of the promotion committee of the new university of Warwick which was founded in 1964 on a site on the south side of Coventry provided by the Coventry City Council and the Warwickshire County Council. He instituted an appeal, the Foundation Fund of the university of Warwick, which became the most successful appeal of any of the new universities and by his urbane importuning of his industrial friends rapidly raised more than £1 million. The appeal ultimately raised nearly £4 million. But Rootes himself died shortly after its inauguration, and before he could be installed as the university's first chancellor.

Physically a small, active, restless man, friendly yet with the uncanny ability to read people at a glance, a formidable character with more than a touch of ruthlessness, Rootes was nevertheless an approachable man, with the gift of 'persuading anyone he met that that was the person he had been waiting to see all day'. 'Billy' Rootes was a supersalesman *par excellence* at a suitable time in Britain.

Rootes was a great lover of the country, well known as a breeder of pedigree stock, and devoted to shooting and farming, both in England and in Scotland. In 1916 he married Nora (died 1964), daughter of the late Horace Press. There were two sons of the marriage, both of whom became involved in the Rootes business. The marriage was dissolved in 1951 and in the same year Rootes married (Ruby Joy) Ann, formerly the wife of Sir Francis Henry Grenville Peek, fourth baronet. Rootes died at his London home 12 December 1964 and was succeeded by his elder son, William Geoffrey (born 1926).

[*The Times*, 14 December 1964.]

J. B. BUTTERWORTH

ROSCOE, KENNETH HARRY (1914-1970), professor of engineering, was born at Worsley 13 December 1914, the eldest in the family of three sons and one daughter of Colonel Harry Roscoe, consulting mining engineer, of Primrose Hill, Hanforth, Stoke-on-Trent, and his wife, Elizabeth Ann Schofield. Educated at the High

School, Newcastle under Lyme, He became head of the school, and captain of rugby football, of cricket, and of the rifle team. He went up to Emmanuel College, Cambridge, in 1934. In competition with public school contemporaries he won election as captain of his college XV and college athletic colours for the low hurdles. In 1937 in the rugby match between the university and the Harlequins his arm was broken and was never fully right again. Six months later, being unable to take the mechanical science tripos because of his injury, he was awarded an aegrotat degree. As this result did not satisfy him he stayed up for a fourth year and in 1938 was awarded first class honours. Roscoe had been made a senior scholar on the strength of his second year's work, and on graduation Emmanuel offered him their internal research studentship. He went instead as a technician trainee to Metropolitan Cammell Co. Ltd. of Birmingham where after a year he was offered the post of assistant works manager.

Following his father's example, Roscoe was active in the Territorial Army. He had obtained a commission in the sapper (Royal Engineers) wing of the Officers Training Corps at Cambridge, so at the outbreak of war he was automatically embodied as a lieutenant. Despite his injury he persuaded a doctor to pass him as fit for overseas service and he was drafted to France with the British Expeditionary Force in October 1939, serving as works adjutant to the commander, Royal Engineers, forward sub-area. In the confused situation leading to the fall of France he eventually reached Boulogne, where he distinguished himself with the Welsh Guards defending the pier, for which he was subsequently (27 November 1945) gazetted MC. He was captured and spent the remainder of the war in a German prison camp. An active member of various escape groups, he escaped and was recaptured on three occasions. He finally escaped in April 1945 by breaking away from the column when his camp was being marched east before the advancing Americans.

He spent a large part of his captivity studying. At first without books, he wrote notes from memory, and reconstructed what he could from first principles. Through the Red Cross he passed the London Intermediate Examination in French and German. He enquired of Emmanuel College whether there was any chance of being rewarded the internal research studentship he had refused in 1938. Roscoe's single-minded determination to pursue an academic career in very adverse circumstances, his diligent study, and his help to student engineers, much impressed the camp education officer (Professor) C. J. Hamson, a fellow of Trinity College, Cambridge.

On Roscoe's return to Cambridge he was accepted as a research student by Professor J. F. (later Lord) Baker, who sent him in the summer of 1945 to visit the Building Research Station. There A. W. Skempton drew his attention to M. J. Hvorslev's 'Über die Festigkeitseigenschaften gestörter bindiger Böden' in *Ing. Vidensk. Skr.* A. No. 45, 1937, which Roscoe translated and in which he found the hoped-for germ of his research. The aim was to work with soils in their simplest states (for example, dry, well-graded Leighton Buzzard sand, and saturated reconstituted kaolin clay) and to devise new equipment which would enable the fundamental parameters to be measured (Roscoe's simple shear apparatus SSA Mk. I). Baker set him to work developing a small soil mechanics laboratory for Cambridge University Engineering Department and in December 1946 had Roscoe appointed to a university demonstratorship.

The first decade of Roscoe's subsequent twenty-five years at Cambridge involved activity on many fronts as well as research. He thoroughly reorganized the Emmanuel system of engineering cribs for tripos and May examinations, spending much time himself and with students solving problems, and achieving good results. He became a university lecturer and a fellow of Emmanuel in 1948, and actively presided over the college rugby and athletics clubs. At first from 1946 to 1952 he took command of the Cambridgeshire County Battalion of the Army Cadet Force, then in 1952 he became second-in-command of the university OTC, receiving his Territorial decoration in 1954 and continuing to serve until 1960 with the rank of lieutenant-colonel. From 1952 to 1965 he was tutor and director of studies in engineering at Emmanuel and from 1955 as domestic bursar accepted responsibility for building the new Barnwell hostel, installing new central heating and carrying out extensive renovations of the college.

Busy with these other activities Roscoe made slow progress with his research, and in this first ten years back in Cambridge he published little. Not until 1953 did he describe his SSA in a paper to the Zurich conference, and then with no exposition of tests of a variety of soils. Baker looked for more results from Cambridge soil mechanics, and in 1951 got Roscoe to design and test portal frame foundations that could resist fully plastic bending moments during collapse of a steel frame. Roscoe by then had taught many undergraduates and in 1954 when two of them returned as research students, he at last had the nucleus of his research team. He started them on two research topics which he continued to rework in subsequent years—the study of lateral earth pressure against a rotating short pier foundation and the study of soil in the SSA.

In 1958 the paper on the yielding of soils was published in *Géotechnique*. It won a prize and brought new students to Cambridge. They reworked Roscoe's research topics, helped by advice on soil radiography from Addenbrooke's Hospital, collaboration from Professor (Sir) Charles Oatley's group in scanning electron microscopy, and comments on applied mechanics from Baker's structural plasticity group. The second ten years produced thirty-two papers with Roscoe as author.

Roscoe became a reader in 1965 and for his last five years was fully absorbed in the work of his group, which he described in the Rankine lecture of 1970, published in the same issue of *Géotechnique* that carries his obituary. The Engineering workshops had made him seven marks of his SSA and built many different rigs in which his students could deform blocks of soil between glass plates by moving boundary walls faced with load cells. The work of Roscoe's team received international attention with the widespread development of new computational facilities, because his soil mechanics group was the first successfully to explain the experimentally observed behaviour of soil as that of an elasto-plastic structural material. Roscoe was elected to a chair of engineering at Cambridge in 1968.

In 1945 Roscoe married Janet, daughter of Basil Gimson, a schoolmaster at Bedales. She became a consultant paediatrician at Addenbrooke's Hospital; they had one daughter and an adopted son. The family lived at 4 Millington Road, Cambridge, and were very hospitable. Roscoe died in a car accident near Reading 10 April 1970. He is commemorated in Cambridge University by a prize for the best student in soil mechanics in the tripos.

[A. N. Schofield and C. P. Wroth in *Géotechnique*, vol. xx, 1970; obituary by D. B. Welbourne in Emmanuel College magazine; personal knowledge.]   A. N. SCHOFIELD

ROSS, SIR FREDERICK WILLIAM LEITH- (1887-1968), civil servant and authority on finance. [See LEITH-ROSS.]

ROTHERY, WILLIAM HUME- (1899-1968), first Isaac Wolfson professor of metallurgy in the university of Oxford. [See HUME-ROTHERY.]

ROTTER, GODFREY (1879-1969), government scientist and explosives and munitions specialist, was born in Hampstead, London, 3 September 1879, the youngest of the six children of Charles Godfrey Rotter, export agent, and his wife, Clara Marie Louise Ehrhardt. He was educated at the City of London School. He was admitted to the University College of North Wales, Bangor, in 1898 before he had matriculated, but was permitted to pursue the first year B.Sc. courses and passed the matriculation examinations in June 1899. He completed the honours course in chemistry in 1902 and, after graduation, became the sole research student.

In 1903 Rotter joined the recently formed War Office Explosives Committee experimental establishment in Woolwich Arsenal. This consisted of six chemists and supporting staff, under a senior scientist, O. J. Silberrad, whose notice Rotter wrote for this Dictionary, and had been set up by the reconstituted Explosives Committee, with Lord Rayleigh [q.v.] as president, following an inquiry into defects in the ammunition used in the Boer War. Rotter quickly displayed practical skills. He helped to standardize the tests used to assess the performance of explosives, and their relative sensitiveness to impact and friction.

In 1907, following a major reorganization, the establishment was renamed the Research Department, Woolwich. Dr Silberrad resigned and (Sir) Robert Robertson [q.v.], from the Royal Gunpowder Factory, Waltham Abbey, was appointed superintendent of explosives research. Prior to World War I, Rotter played a notable part in developing a process for the manufacture of the explosive Tetryl and, early in the war, for TNT which was so urgently needed. Later, in order to eke out the TNT, he was concerned with the introduction of 'Amatol', a mixture of TNT and ammonium nitrate, for shell fillings. But he will be best remembered for his invention of the Rotter Impact Testing Machine, still widely used, and for his design of Fuse No. 106 of which 88 million were made and for which he received an award. In 1919 the degree of D.Sc. was conferred on him by the university of Wales for a thesis describing his more important investigations.

During 1917 Robertson's post was restyled 'director of explosives research', and when he moved in 1921 to the post of government chemist, Rotter was his natural successor.

In the years preceding World War II, Rotter's staff became involved in many important developments including the introduction of lead azide as an initiator, the use of wood cellulose (to save cotton) for the manufacture of nitrocellulose, and the introduction of the solventless technique for the production of cordite for guns, assisted take-off devices, and small rocket motors. There were, however, two other developments of great significance. First, a range of flashless propellants, based on nitro-guanidine, was introduced into Service use. Lengthy trials had proved that reproducible ballistics could only be obtained when the crystal size of the nitroguanidine was very finely controlled, and the code name Picrite was given to the material used. Secondly, a search had been made in the 1920s for a high explosive more powerful than TNT, and cyclo-trimethylene trinitramine, which could be made from indigenous materials, was selected for trials. A safe, continuous process for its manufacture was evolved in the early 1930s and, for security reasons, the explosive was named RDX. The production of Picrite pro-pellants and RDX was greatly expanded during the war. Early in 1941 Rotter was much involved in furnishing details of the methods of their manufacture to an American mission, led by Dr J. B. Conant, chairman of the National Research Defense Committee, and this greatly expedited production in the United States.

Rotter retired in 1942 and took up farming with two of his sons near Cardigan, Wales, but he continued to act as a consultant to the Ministry of Supply and to serve on various committees. In February 1942 the roof of a large underground bomb store at Llanberis collapsed and Rotter took charge of the hazardous salvage operations. In November 1944 an explosion of great violence occurred in a similar RAF depot at Fauld, Staffordshire, and Rotter, often at great personal risk, was again responsible for evacuating the explosive stores.

Rotter was a man of sound judgement, who took many important decisions, and was widely respected for his work on military explosives and munitions. He was a first-class public servant, always kind and considerate, and highly regarded by his staff for whose welfare he showed much concern. He was appointed OBE in 1918, CBE in 1925, CB in 1936, and was awarded the George Medal in 1945 for his work in bomb clearance at Fauld. He was a fellow of the Royal Institute of Chemistry and the Institute of Physics. During a long retirement he derived much pleasure from farming activities, and from his hobbies of carpentry, gardening, and writing. He died at the farm-house at Tyhen, Llwyndafydd, Llandyssul, Cardiganshire, 16 February 1969. He married in 1905 Gertrude Elizabeth, daughter of George Plank, accountant, of Upper Clapton, and they had four sons and one daughter.

[*The Times*, 18 February 1969; *London Gazette*, 28 September 1945; private infor-mation; personal knowledge.]

W. B. LITTLER

ROUND, HENRY JOSEPH (1881–1966), wireless pioneer, was born 2 June 1881 at Kingswinford, Staffordshire, the eldest child in the family of two sons and two daughters of Joseph Alfred Round, registrar of births and deaths, Cheltenham, and his wife, Gertrude Rider. His early education was at Cheltenham Grammar School and he later studied at the Royal College of Science, London, where he was awarded the diploma of associateship (ARCS) in mechanics (division first class) in 1901.

Round joined the Marconi Company in 1902 and was sent to the United States where he worked at Babylon, Long Island. Here he experimented with dust-core tuning induc-tances and devised the elements of direction finding. In his spare time at this station he constructed one of the first arc radio telephones. He was recalled to England and became one of the *corps d'élite* working personally with Guglielmo Marconi. Having greatly improved the performance of the Clifden (Ireland) high power transatlantic transmitter, he was sent to South America in 1912 where he performed an outstanding feat of engineering at two wireless stations on the upper reaches of the Amazon. Because of heavy signal attenuation across the jungle the stations were not achieving the contract guarantee, and Round virtually re-designed the stations *in situ* to operate on 4,000 m by day and 2,000 m by night. This was the first time that deliberate use had been made of different wavelengths for day and night working.

On his return to England Round immersed himself in the problems of valve amplification and in 1913–14 patented important valve im-provements, including the indirectly heated cathode. In the same year he patented an auto-heterodyne circuit and a comprehensive transmission system which included the first use of automatic grid bias.

Round was seconded to military intelligence at the outbreak of war in 1914 and was entrusted with the setting up of a network of valved direction-finding stations covering the entire western front. These stations were so successful that Round was recalled to England to super-vise a second network there. On 30 May 1916 the DF stations reported a $1\frac{1}{2}$ degree change in bearing and incessant wireless telegraphy chatter from the German ships lying at Wilhelmshaven. The Admiralty reasoned that they were about to put to sea and ordered the Grand Fleet to the German Bight to intercept them and the following day the Battle of Jutland was fought. In 1920 Admiral Sir Henry Jackson [q.v.] disclosed that the man, the mysterious 'Captain X', primarily responsible for the naval battle, was a certain Captain Henry Round.

Round's other wartime activity was the design of the first telephony transmitters and receivers for airborne use. For services to his country Round was awarded the MC in 1918. (The medal arrived by post because Round felt strongly that this particular honour should be reserved for acts of gallantry and refused to go to the Palace.)

It was with his newly designed transmitting valves, the MT1 and MT2, that in March 1919 a telephony transmitter which he had installed at Ballybunion, Ireland, became the first European station to span the Atlantic with telephony. A series of range tests from an experimental station at Chelmsford with a 6 kW transmitter resulted in enthusiastic reports from wireless amateurs and gave the impetus for the establishment of an entertainment broadcasting service. On 23 February 1920 on a wavelength of 2,500 m, the world's first wireless telephony news service was inaugurated, closely followed on 15 June by the first public broadcast of entertainment, a recital by the Australian *prima donna*, Dame Nellie Melba [q.v.]. Two years later the concerts from 'Two Emma Tock' (2MT) at Writtle led to the establishment of station 2LO at Marconi House in the Strand. Again the transmitter was designed by Round. This was the first station to be taken over by the BBC on its formation in November 1922. The artificial echo system and the Sykes-Round microphone are two of Round's many contributions to the early stages of the art of broadcasting. In parallel with this work Round was redesigning the Marconi high-power station at Caernarvon from spark to valve transmission using fifty-six MT2 valves. On 19 November 1921, using the new equipment, signals from this station were received in Australia.

Appointed chief of the Marconi Research Group in 1921, Round's output was prolific. He designed valve receivers for ships and constructed the first batch of maritime valved transmitters. He designed the 'Straight Eight' broadcast receiver; a gramophone recording system (licensed to the Vocalion Company); and a large-audience public address system which was used to relay King George V's speech at the Wembley exhibitions. He devised a talking picture system which was licensed to Stoll (Visatone) for recording sound on film during the 1930 cinema boom.

In 1931 Round set up in private practice as a research consultant. He worked on ASDIC for the Admiralty between 1941 and 1950, and on echo sounding for the Marconi Company from 1950 onwards, inventing new magneto-strictive devices for use in the production of echo-sounders; the first permanently magnetized nickel transducers and the first belt recording system for echo sounders. In all, his patent applications numbered 117, the last recorded in 1962 when Round was eighty-one.

Round was an individualist as well as an innovator. Physically short in stature he was a nonconformist; he was a robust, bluff extrovert, rather Churchillian even to the cigar. He teemed with ideas and had tremendous energy, carrying out private research after a long working day. He had no regard for protocol and had an aversion to technical mystique. His papers to learned societies were straightforward and lucid. As the most prolific inventor it has had so far, the electronics industry owes him a large debt, and yet he received no British civil honour; the Radio Club of America awarded him the prized Armstrong gold medal in 1952.

In 1911 Round married Olive Wright, daughter of John Evans, saddler; they had two sons and five daughters. The elder son, John, a Spitfire pilot killed in World War II, was awarded the DFC. In 1960 Round married Evelyn Baise, his first wife having died in 1958. He died in the Innisfallen Nursing Home, Bognor Regis, 17 August 1966, after a short illness.

A bust of Round, sculptured by his daughter Jeanne Cordrey, is on display in the technical library of the Marconi Research Laboratories, Chelmsford. Round's book *The Shielded Four-Electrode Valve* was published in 1927.

[Marconi archival collection; private information.]
                                    PETER BAKER
                                    BETTY HANCE

ROWLEY, HAROLD HENRY (1890-1969), Old Testament scholar, was born in Leicester 24 March 1890, the fifth of six children of Richard Rowley, a foreman finisher in a shoe factory, and his wife, Emma Saunt. He was educated at the Wyggeston School, Leicester, and then at Bristol Baptist College and Bristol University, studying also as an external student of London University, where he gained the pass degree of BD in 1912. A year later he graduated BA (theology) at Bristol. Thereafter at Oxford he belonged to St. Catherine's Society and to Mansfield College, and obtained a B.Litt. in 1929. In 1916 he served briefly in Egypt with the YMCA, but ill health forced him to return to England. After a time as minister of a united Baptist-Congregational church at Wells, Somerset, he went to China as a missionary of the Baptist Missionary Society and taught Old Testament in Shantung Christian College until 1929. His interest in things Chinese remained with him in later years and was expressed in his *Submission in Suffering and Other Essays in Eastern Thought* (1951) and his *Prophecy and Religion in Ancient China and Israel* (1956).

His first major published study was *The

Aramaic of the Old Testament (1929): it defended the critical dating of Daniel in the Hellenistic period. In 1930 Rowley became assistant lecturer in Semitic languages in Cardiff, then in 1935 professor of the same subject at Bangor. In 1945 he moved to Manchester as professor of Semitic languages and literatures, a title changed in 1949 to Hebrew language and literature. This fitted Rowley's style, for, though fully competent in Biblical Hebrew and in Aramaic, he did not aspire to mastery of the wider fields of the Semitic languages. The Manchester years were Rowley's great period, and the fine libraries of the city served ideally the genius of one who was meticulous in annotation and bibliography.

He had quickly become one of the leading figures in Old Testament studies in Britain and his counsels were evident in the development of the subject; he was influential in the wider world of scholarship also. As secretary responsible for foreign contacts in the Society for Old Testament Study he entered into correspondence with scholars all over war-torn Europe and did much to restore the community of scholarship which war had disrupted; for this he was uniquely remembered by many.

Rowley's publications were multifarious. *Darius the Mede and the Four World Empires* (1935) and *The Relevance of Apocalyptic* (1944) continued his early research interests. The Schweich lectures for 1948, published as *From Joseph to Joshua* (1950) concerned the dating of the Exodus. *The Faith of Israel* (1956) was a contribution to Old Testament theology; his last major work was *Worship in Ancient Israel* (1967). Volumes like *The Servant of the Lord* (1952), *From Moses to Qumran* (1963), and *Men of God* (1963) collected valuable articles previously published, many of them first given as lectures in the John Rylands Library series. Rowley was active in discussion of the new-found Dead Sea scrolls: his chief study was *The Zadokite Fragments and the Dead Sea Scrolls* (1952). Numerous other biblical and theological themes occupied his pen. To this Dictionary he contributed the notice of T. W. Manson.

Much of his contribution, however, lay not in his own writing but in editing and planning publication. For eleven years he edited the *Book List* of the Society for Old Testament Study and made it into an internationally recognized source. The joint volume *The Old Testament and Modern Study* (1951) was extremely successful. He initiated (1956) the distinguished *Journal of Semitic Studies* and was its joint editor till 1960. Many other works of biblical and theological study were initiated, supervised, or re-edited by him, and in his retirement he undertook even wider respon-

sibilities in advising publishers. He reviewed a vast range of theological literature, often well outside his own field; and he was a member of the Old Testament panel for the New English Bible. In all this he was assisted by his immense library with its notable collection of offprints, bound and indexed. In his later years Rowley sold this library to Union Theological Seminary, Richmond, Virginia, in such a way that he retained it for his lifetime and it passed to that institution at his death.

He received honorary degrees from many universities, became a fellow of the British Academy in 1947, and was awarded the Burkitt medal in 1951. The Norwegian Academy of Science and Letters, the Royal Flemish Academy, the Royal Society of Letters of Lund, and the Society of Biblical Literature (USA) all elected him to honorary or foreign membership. He was president of the Society for Old Testament Study in 1950, and in 1955 a volume in his honour, *Wisdom in Israel and in the Ancient Near East* (Vetus Testamentum Supplements, iii) was published; it contained a select bibliography of his writings up to 1954. He remained active in Baptist affairs and was president of the Baptist Union in 1957–8, as well as serving the Baptist Missionary Society as chairman of its committee.

Rowley was a scholar of great competence and thoroughness rather than an original thinker. He covered all the ground and sifted the literature with extreme care, but did not initiate specific new lines of thought. He worked exceptionally hard and it was said that he thoroughly enjoyed proof-reading. His one hobby was philately. He took no sort of exercise and professed not to know that there were mountains in Wales. His health had never been robust. After retirement from Manchester in 1959 he moved to Stroud. In his retirement he had several illnesses, in the midst of which he was often to be found reading the proofs of some abstruse work. He died at Cheltenham 4 October 1969.

In 1916 he married Gladys Barbara, daughter of Richard Arthur Shaw, commercial traveller, of Bristol. There were four children: one son and three daughters, of whom the second married another Old Testament scholar, Professor Aubrey R. Johnson, FBA.

[G. W. Anderson in *Proceedings* of the British Academy, vol. lvi, 1970; private information; personal knowledge.]   JAMES BARR

RUGBY, first BARON (1877–1969), public servant. [See MAFFEY, JOHN LOADER.]

RUGGLES GATES, REGINALD (1882–1962), botanist, geneticist, and anthropologist. [See GATES.]

RUSHBURY, SIR HENRY GEORGE (1889–1968), painter, draughtsman, and engraver, was born 28 October 1889 at Harborne, then still a country village on the outskirts of Birmingham, the younger son of G. Norbury Rushbury, a clerk, and his wife, Naomi Fennell. The father, when unsuccessfully job-hunting, used to take his son with him on visits to churches and other old buildings, thereby developing the boy's powers of observation and kindling what was to be a lifelong and essential interest in immediate surroundings.

At the age of thirteen Rushbury gained a scholarship to Birmingham School of Art where, from 1903 to 1909, studying at first gold and silversmith's work and later stained-glass design and mural decoration, he became under the stimulating influence of the headmaster, R. M. Catterson Smith, who encouraged the students to make quick drawings of figures in movement, rather than highly finished studies of posed models, but also subjected them to the strict discipline of painting in tempera. Thus, while still very young, and despite the poverty at home, Rushbury was well equipped to perceive and record accurately his environment, particularly townscapes with people going about their daily business, which gave liveliness and scale to his works.

On leaving Birmingham he worked in the Cotswolds for a time, as assistant to Henry Payne at St. Loe's near Stroud in Gloucestershire, making designs for stained glass and helping with a series of tempera paintings for William Lygon, Earl Beauchamp [q.v.], at Madresfield Court, Worcestershire. In 1912 he settled in London, sharing lodgings in Chelsea with his friend Gerald Brockhurst, who had been a fellow student under Catterson Smith. There he met Francis Dodd [q.v.] who taught him the techniques of etching and dry-point.

In 1914 Rushbury married Florence, daughter of Herbert W. Lazell, a lay preacher. After war broke out he joined the army in 1915. He was subsequently transferred to the Royal Flying Corps. His draughtsmanship was soon put to good use and he became an official war artist, producing various documentary drawings which are now in the Imperial War Museum.

After the war Rushbury spent a few months studying under Henry Tonks [q.v.] at the Slade School but soon continued a busy life of drawing and engraving which involved extensive travelling on the Continent each year, particularly in France and Italy. He had first exhibited at the Royal Academy in 1913 and, with scarcely a break in the sequence, continued to do so throughout his career, amassing a total of over 200 works. Their titles alone are evidence of the broad coverage of his interests—for example, 'The Brewery, Sandwich' (1915), 'Walls of Siena' (1923), 'Quai des Belges, Marseille' (1929), 'A Street in Gerona' (1936), 'Stirling Castle' (1946), 'Market, Concarneau' (1955), 'Tenby Harbour' (1962), and 'Orvieto' (1968). Rushbury was a master of the mood of the moment—early morning, a busy forenoon, a drowsy afternoon in the sunlight, or a sultry evening. He was far more than an accomplished topographical draughtsman, for he always seemed to be able to portray the spirit of his subject.

Some of his best work was used to illustrate Sidney Dark's *Paris* (1926), *Rome of the Renaissance and Today* (1932) by Sir James Rennell Rodd (later Lord Rennell, q.v.), and *Fenland Rivers* (1936) by Iris Wedgwood. All three books, excellent as they are in their texts, are greatly enhanced by the clarity and warmth of the drawings, which bring the places visually to life, always maintaining the monumental qualities of the dominant subjects but setting them in the local climatic and social conditions. This was achieved not only by the artist's unerring choice of viewpoints and his skilful use of light and shade but also frequently by including human figures and their transport—as for example (in the *Rome* book) 'The Pantheon' with groups of people chatting, carriages and tramway cars, and 'Palazzo Farnese' with its horses and carts and the fountain playing.

Rushbury was fortunate to be able to depict such scenes before they were despoiled by excessive motor traffic. His output was considerable, as is evident in mixed and one-man exhibitions over a long period of years, and his works, with their blend of scholarly interest and sympathetic rendering, were extremely attractive and, in scale, very suitable for rooms of reasonable size. He also did a series of mural decorations for Chelmsford Town Hall in 1937.

Rushbury was again an official artist during the war of 1939–45, recording the production side of the war effort. At sixty years of age, in 1949, he was elected keeper of the Royal Academy and, as head of its Schools until his retirement in 1964, did much to encourage the students through his experiences and to help them to tread their own paths.

He exhibited regularly with several societies and became a member of the New English Art Club in 1917, of the Royal Society of Painter-Etchers in 1921, and of the Royal Society of Painters in Water-Colours in 1922. He was elected an associate of the Royal Academy in 1927 and a Royal academician in 1936. He was made an honorary associate of the Royal Institute of British Architects in 1948. He was appointed CVO in 1955, CBE in 1960, and KCVO in 1964.

In personality Rushbury was most friendly and club-loving, being a staunch supporter of both the Arts Club and the Chelsea Arts Club. Sir Alfred Munnings [q.v.] said 'Henry could charm a bird off a tree'. In appearance he was somewhat Pickwickian—short and sturdy in stature but with sharp features and alert blue eyes; there was usually a smile on his lips and, as an older man, his face was topped with white hair. He was rubicund, kindly, and an enlivening companion. He died in Lewes, Sussex, 5 July 1968, and was survived by his widow and their two daughters.

There are a number of portraits of Rushbury, of which the family possess a painting by his son-in-law, Theodore Ramos (1962), drawings by Francis Dodd, and a bronze bust by Roland Bevan (1930). The Royal Academy has a terracotta bust by Maurice Lambert (1959). Other paintings include those by Gerald Brockhurst (1929), Neville Lewis (1934), and James Proudfoot (1939).

[Articles in *Draughtsmen*, 1924, and The Studio *Masters of Etching*, no. 18, 1928; *The Times* and *Daily Telegraph*, 6 July 1968; Royal Academy records; private information; personal knowledge.]

S. C. HUTCHISON

RUSSELL, BERTRAND ARTHUR WILLIAM, third EARL RUSSELL (1872–1970), philosopher and social reformer, was born at Trelleck in Monmouthshire 18 May 1872, the younger son of Viscount Amberley (the eldest son of the first Earl Russell, previously Lord John Russell, q.v.) and his wife, Kate, daughter of the second Baron Stanley of Alderley [q.v.]. Russell's mother died of diphtheria in 1874 and his father died in 1876, before Russell was four. The Amberleys were a highly progressive couple, holding unconventional beliefs in morals, politics, and religion. They chose John Stuart Mill [q.v.] to be a kind of secular godfather to Russell. The atheist guardians they appointed to look after their orphaned children were set aside by the courts and replaced by their paternal grandmother, the second wife, and, after 1878, widow of the first Earl Russell, and daughter of the second Earl of Minto [q.v.].

Russell remained in the firm and unremitting care of his grandmother until he went up to Cambridge in the autumn of 1890 at the age of eighteen. The other adults in the household were some unmarried aunts and there were visits from uncles of varying degrees of eccentricity. Russell's education until he left home was in the hands of governesses and tutors. Russell and his elder brother lived in this curious state of sequestration in Pembroke Lodge, a grace-and-favour house in Richmond Park, allocated to Russell's grandfather as a former prime minister. Russell's grandmother, the chief influence on his early development, was a woman of strong, high-minded opinions, morally puritanical, and the adherent of a radical form of liberalism in politics.

Later Russell recalled various impingements of the outside world on Pembroke Lodge in his autobiographical writings, notably being alone with Gladstone at dessert as the great man wondered why he had been served such good port in a claret glass. Russell seems to have had reasonably unobstructed access to his grandfather's large and comprehensive library and valuably exploited the tedium of his childhood years to lay up massive stores of attentive reading for future use. Significant developments of later years announced themselves in a modest way. In 1883 his elder brother, trying to teach him geometry, disappointed him by insisting that the axioms had to be accepted without question. That, Russell subsequently claimed, set him off on his passionate quest for ultimate mathematical truth. A year later his grandmother gave him a Bible for his twelfth birthday, inscribed with the text: 'thou shalt not follow a multitude to do evil'. For all their differences he was to remain as faithful to that text as she did.

In his teens Russell began to have religious doubts, ascribing some influence in this to John Stuart Mill's *Autobiography*. Also important was an atheistic tutor he had when he was sixteen. Soon after that he went to an army crammer's in north London to bring his mathematics up to the state of technical polish required for entrance to Cambridge. Contact with future army officers was deeply shocking to the protected and priggish adolescent Russell. In December 1889 he sat for the scholarship examinations at Trinity College, Cambridge, and with the support of A. N. Whitehead [q.v.], who recognized his still unpolished brilliance, was elected to a minor scholarship.

The Cambridge to which Russell went up in October 1890 was a marvellous place for any intelligent young man fortunate enough to find his way there. To Russell, arriving from the narrow rectitude and bleak avoidance of pleasure practised at Pembroke Lodge, it seemed like paradise. His remarkable qualities of mind were soon detected by his contemporaries and he was made one of the Apostles. He became friendly with many gifted and interesting people: the philosopher J. E. M'Taggart, G. Lowes Dickinson, the Trevelyan brothers—Charles, G. M. [qq.v.], and Robert—and, perhaps most important of all, G. E. Moore [q.v.], at first a classicist, but eventually a philosopher, the strongest early influence on Russell's strictly philosophical thinking.

Russell was placed as seventh wrangler in part i of the mathematical tripos of 1893 and decided to stay up for a further year to read 'moral sciences' (in other words, philosophy). In September of that year he read *The Principles of Logic* of the Oxford idealist F. H. Bradley [q.v.] and formed an admiration of him from which nothing short of the persistent, hard-headed commonsensicality of Moore could rescue him and then only by a process of conversion lasting several years. Closest to Bradley among Russell's philosophical teachers was James Ward [q.v.]; he learnt less from Henry Sidgwick and G. F. Stout [qq.v.]. After a year he secured a first class with distinction in the moral sciences tripos. For a few months he served at the British Embassy in Paris. On 13 December 1894 he married Alys Whitall (died 1951), daughter of Robert and sister of Logan Pearsall Smith, at the Quaker meeting-house in St. Martin's Lane. Robert Pearsall Smith came from a family of rich Philadelphia Quakers and had settled near Hindhead on an evangelical mission. Russell's family opposed the match, in part because of Alys's age (she was five years older than he), in part because of a strain of madness in his own background which seemed to count against his becoming a father. As it turned out he and Alys had no children together.

In 1895 Russell and Alys paid a visit to Bernard Berenson and his wife (who was a sister of Alys's) in Italy. In the same year Russell was elected to a fellowship at Trinity on the strength of a dissertation which was published in 1897 as *An Essay on the Foundations of Geometry*, his first philosophical book. It was closer in subject than in doctrine to his main contributions to philosophy, being concerned to adjust a fundamentally Kantian conception of geometry as the *a priori* science of space to the emergence of non-Euclidean geometries. But even in the pursuit of this somewhat untypical goal Russell was already showing the superbly crystalline style that served him and his readers so well from the 1890s to the splendid memorandum on his association with Ralph Schoenman that he wrote shortly before his death.

After his election at Trinity he and Alys travelled to Berlin. There he studied the theory and practice of Marxism, accumulating the material which formed the basis of lectures at the London School of Economics in 1896 and, later that year, of his first book: *German Social Democracy*. An initial chapter neatly expounds the main theses of Marx and Engels, and crisply

affirms their invalidity; the main bulk of the text is more straightforwardly historical. During the year 1896 Russell paid the first of his numerous, frequently eventful, and often profitable visits to the United States. He and Alys visited Johns Hopkins and Bryn Mawr, at both of which he lectured, and they stayed with William James at Harvard. The conclusion to the first, more or less dependent, phase of his life ended with the death of his grandmother in 1898. Later he was to blame himself for his lack of feeling about this at the time.

It was in the following year that Russell established himself as a seriously professional philosopher, with his first work of genius his *A Critical Exposition of the Philosophy of Leibniz*. M'Taggart, intending to spend the Lent term in New Zealand, persuaded Russell to give his lectures for him. The result was more than anyone had bargained for. Instead of journeyman lectures by a substitute there was a brilliantly imaginative reinterpretation of a major philosopher effected by one of the few qualified to do it. In the course of the task Russell rebelled against the idealism which he and M'Taggart had previously shared.

The main work of the closing years of the nineteenth century for Russell was his great *The Principles of Mathematics*. This was not published until 1930 but the first draft was completed by 31 December 1900. Two important influences were first brought to bear on Russell in the last year of the old century. The first was that of Guiseppe Peano, whom Russell met and talked with illuminatingly at the International Congress of Philosophy in Paris. The other was Gottlob Frege, whose *Grundgesetze der Arithmetik* Russell acquired, to discover that they had been working along similar lines. The central idea of their two philosophies of mathematics was the reducibility of mathematics to logic, first by the definition of the basic mathematical concept of number in terms of the logical concept of class and, secondly, by the derivation of the principles about number from which Peano had shown all pure mathematics to be deducible from more fundamental principles of a logical kind.

Frege had carried out this logicist programme with greater thoroughness and rigour than Russell was ever to do, even in the full formal development of *Principia Mathematica*. Furthermore, Frege based his work on a much more sophisticated theory of meaning than Russell was ever to develop. But he used an obscure diagrammatic notation and he failed to notice the paradoxical consequences which Russell saw resulted from an unrestricted use of the concept of class. Russell first perceived the paradox about the class of classes that are not members of themselves (viz. that if it is a member of itself it is not and if it is not then it is) in June 1902. It preoccupied him to a point of exasperation that could be called agonizing for the next four years until the discovery, or perhaps invention, of the theory of types.

The strain of these years of unrelenting thought of the most powerful originality at the outer limits of abstraction revealed itself in various ways. In February 1902 Russell realized he no longer loved his wife, bluntly told her so, and yet continued to live with her in considerable tension for the next nine years. He seems to have fallen in love with Evelyn Whitehead, the wife of his teacher and collaborator, a love it was impossible for him to declare in public in any way. For many of these years he and Alys lived in grim proximity in a small house in Bagley Wood near Oxford. In 1903 he published his well-known, stylistically rather over-ripe, declaration of cosmic defiance 'The Free Man's Worship' in the *Independent Review*. In 1905 his article 'On Denoting' appeared in *Mind*, perhaps the most influential philosophical article of the twentieth century, for all the uncharacteristic muddle of its expression. In 1907 the public Russell stood for Parliament in Wimbledon as women's suffrage candidate. In 1908 he was elected a fellow of the Royal Society.

By 1909 another large change was about to occur in Russell's life. His work on *Principia Mathematica*, for which he wrote most of the crucial first volume and most of the explanatory philosophical material in the introduction, was nearing completion. In the autumn Logan Pearsall Smith, Alys's brother, brought Lady Ottoline Morrell [q.v.] to visit the Russells in Bagley Wood, setting in motion the first of Russell's major love affairs. Appointed a lecturer at Trinity College, Cambridge, for five years in 1910 he spent a good deal of time there, away from Alys. He canvassed for Ottoline's husband Philip in the election of that year. The first volume of *Principia Mathematica* came out, as also did a volume of collected *Philosophical Essays* of the preceding years. The two later volumes of *Principia* came out in 1912 and 1913.

In 1911, still under forty, Russell was elected president of the Aristotelian Society. He and Alys finally separated and in the spring Ottoline Morrell became his mistress. In October he first met Ludwig Wittgenstein [q.v.], who was to be the stimulus of a bout of original thinking in general philosophy almost as profound as the mathematical philosophizing of his previous decade. Before long he was Wittgenstein's academic supervisor, but was learning as much as he was teaching. One lesson he absorbed

with a reluctance he never wholly overcame was that logic and mathematics are essentially tautological in nature, that they do not describe the relations between independently existing abstract entities, but merely register the consequences of our linguistic and notational conventions.

During the years just before World War I, the period of his closest contact with Wittgenstein, Russell was laying out the main lines of that combination of the major assumptions of traditional empiricism with the techniques of the revolutionized formal logic he had himself so much developed that was to remain his basic philosophical position until his last words on the subject in the late 1940s, as well as coming to be the position of the main group of analytic philosophers of the twentieth century. (Sir) J. Alfred Ayer, in many ways the most Russellian of Russell's interpreters, has rightly observed that Russell's conception of philosophy is somewhat old-fashioned: 'He makes the now unfashionable assumption that all our beliefs are in need of philosophical justification.' From 1911 onwards in a series of powerful and lucid⁊ essays (later brought together, for the most part, in *Mysticism and Logic* in 1918), in the remarkable and remarkably durable *The Problems of Philosophy* (1912) that Russell wrote for the Home University Library and in his Lowell lectures of 1914— *Our Knowledge of the External World*—his ideas about perception, causation, knowledge, truth, and the nature of philosophy itself were elaborated.

Other interests were not extinguished by this outpouring of philosophical creativity. He wrote more sympathetically than at any other time about religion in the *Hibbert Journal*, perhaps revealing the influence of Ottoline Morrell, and tried his hand at fiction in a long story, 'The Perplexities of John Forstice'. In 1913 the Morrells bought Garsington Manor, and thus provided the scenery for a good deal of English intellectual life in the ensuing years. Russell met Joseph Conrad [q.v.] and greatly admired him, giving Conrad's name to both of his sons. A long manuscript he wrote at this time on the theory of knowledge (in his papers but still not published) was devastatingly criticized by Wittgenstein with a damaging effect on Russell's philosophical self-confidence.

In March 1914 he left for the United States to give the Lowell lectures at Harvard. There he met T. S. Eliot [q.v.] who was to report Russell's appearance in cultivated circles in Boston in his poem 'Mr Apollinax'. He also met John Dewey on this visit for the first time, the philosopher who was to be in a way his closest counterpart in the United States, combining as he did large and influential philosophical productivity with a conspicuous public position as social and educational reformer. He also met Helen Dudley who was to follow him fruitlessly to England in the war, one of the more pathetic victims of his amorous energies.

By 1915 Russell was becoming increasingly and turbulently involved in resistance to the war. Around the time that Trinity College was renewing his lectureship he joined the rather militantly pacifist No-Conscription Fellowship. A leaflet whose authorship he acknowledged brought him a fine of £100 in 1916 and, more seriously, removal from his lectureship at Trinity. A brief friendship with D. H. Lawrence [q.v.] flared up around this time and soon died away in mutual recrimination: on Lawrence's side in the portrait of 'Sir Joshua Malleson' in *Women in Love* (1921), on Russell's with an uncharacteristically bitter recollection in *Portraits from Memory* (1956). He was seeing a good deal of T. S. Eliot and his attractive, unbalanced wife Vivienne, supplying money to the husband and a not precisely discoverable degree of amorous affection to the wife. In June of 1916 he met Dora Black, who was to be his second wife, for the first time, and in July Colette O'Niel (Lady Constance Malleson), perhaps his greatest love.

His most coherent and well-organized political book *Principles of Social Reconstruction* was a product of the war years, delivered as lectures at Caxton Hall and then published in 1916. Invited to the United States he was refused a passport by the Foreign Office. In 1917 he gave an initial welcome to the Russian Revolution and, increasingly at odds with the leadership of the No-Conscription Fellowship, resigned from it. Early in 1918 he returned to philosophy with a series of eight lectures, 'The Philosophy of Logical Atomism' (*Monist*, 1918 and 1919), in which the influence of Wittgenstein is much more evident than in anything he had written before, epistemological considerations being altogether outweighed by purely logical ones.

An article he wrote in May 1918, suggesting that American troops would be useful in this country in the strike-breaking role to which they were accustomed in their own, led to his being sentenced to six months in prison (for sedition rather than silliness). Secured the comforts of the 'first division' by the exercise of elevated interest on his behalf, he settled down to write his sparklingly lucid *Introduction to Mathematical Philosophy* (1919), which perhaps owes its smoothness of development and coherence of organization to the monotonous circumstances in which it was composed. Comparing it with some of his later books,

often spasmodic and casual, one might wish he had been imprisoned more often.

The end of the war allowed for a measure of tidying-up in his life. He was in poor financial circumstances with no job and with a deserted wife to support. An admirably succinct and informative pot-boiler, *Roads to Freedom*, gave only temporary relief. A fund raised by G. Gilbert Murray [q.v.] enabled him to deliver at the London School of Economics the lectures that were to be published in 1921 as *The Analysis of Mind*, in which a strong leaning towards behaviourism is evident, but not total acceptance of it. Helen Dudley conveniently returned to the United States. He managed to disentangle himself from his involvements with Ottoline Morrell, for some time an increasingly unwilling object of his desires, and Mrs Eliot. Something like normality seemed to have been regained when in November 1919 Trinity College agreed to reinstate him, the vengeful emotions of wartime having cooled down sufficiently and the surviving younger fellows having come back from the war to outvote their more bellicose seniors.

With the help of J. M. (later Lord) Keynes [q.v.], Wittgenstein's manuscript of the *Tractatus Logico-Philosophicus* had been got out of its author's prison camp. A return to academic life might have seemed, therefore, both practicable and intellectually exciting. What ruled out the possibility was Russell's desire for a family. Believing that Colette O'Niel was unwilling to have children he took up with Dora Black who was not. Early in 1920 he and Dora travelled to Russia where he formed the unalterable conviction of the coarseness and cruelty of the Bolsheviks expressed in *The Practice and Theory of Bolshevism* (1920), a work he was rightly content to see republished without change in 1949, nearly thirty years later.

Their next trip together was to China, which Russell admired as much as he had disliked Russia. That too inspired a book: *The Problem of China* (1922). A bad attack of pneumonia led to reports that Russell was dead. Dewey, also travelling in China, came to his aid. Returning to England in July 1921 Russell resigned the lectureship at Trinity in which he had been reinstated. For in September he got his divorce from Alys and at once married Dora Winifred Black who presented him with a son in November. She was the daughter of Sir Frederick Black, formerly director-general of munitions supply.

In the early twenties Russell established the style of life he was to follow until the war of 1939, which, after a troublesome start for him, left him financially secure and in a condition of unprecedented respectability. He was able to undertake a certain amount of original and seriously reflective philosophical writing. The main instance of that between *The Analysis of Mind* in 1921 and *An Inquiry into Meaning and Truth* in 1940 is *The Analysis of Matter* of 1927, originally given as Tarner lectures in Cambridge in 1925. He put a good deal of work into a new edition of *Principia Mathematica* in 1925, getting a grumpy reaction from Whitehead for his efforts. But most of his writing was popularization or journalism, always lively and amusing, often shallow and somewhat mechanical. *The Prospects of Industrial Civilisation* (1923), which he wrote with Dora, was serious enough, as was *On Education* (1926). Other writings were of lighter weight, the excellent *ABC*s of *Atoms* (1923) and *Relativity* (1925) as good as any popular accounts of the new developments in physics, *Marriage and Morals* (1929) arguing for what most would now see as reasonable permissiveness, *The Conquest of Happiness* (1930), a book that Wittgenstein found quite unbearable, *The Scientific Outlook* (1931), *Education and The Social Order* (1932), *Religion and Science* (1935), and *Power* (1938). Of the same quality are the highly readable essay collections—*Sceptical Essays* (1928) and *In Praise of Idleness* (1935). It was with these, and other, yet more fugitive, writings, that Russell earned his living, met the obligations arising from his and his elder brother's earlier marriages, and sustained such enterprises as his standing as the Labour candidate for Chelsea in the general elections of 1922 and 1923 and the money-engorging progressive school, Beacon Hill, which he and Dora founded in 1927.

Lecturing in the United States was a reliable resource in these financially anxious years. Russell clearly enjoyed the work and threw himself into it with energy and appetite. He was an excellent debater, able to disagree wholly with an opponent without being in any way personally offensive to him. He carried out lecture tours in 1924, 1927, 1929, and 1931. After leaving Dora and the school in 1932 his need for money was a little less pressing, fortunately, perhaps, in view of the state of the American economy.

Beacon Hill School was started in 1927 at Telegraph House, in the country near Petersfield, which Russell had rented from his elder brother. It was not of the utmost progressiveness; although Russell would not have children forced to do academic work, he required them to show a measure of consideration for others. But his reputation ensured that there would be many problem children in the school and a number of rather singular teachers. Carried on by Dora after she and Russell parted, it managed to survive until war began in 1939.

They had agreed to tolerate moderate deviations from strict marital fidelity in one another but that proved hard in practice. In 1930 Dora, who had also had a daughter of Russell's, had a daughter by a young American and two years later a son by the same father. It is not surprising that Russell should have fallen in love with Marjorie Helen Spence, who changed her name to Patricia ('Peter'), and who was originally in the household as a holiday governess for the Russells' own children. Russell and Dora were divorced finally in 1935 and he married Peter Spence the following year. She was the daughter of Harry Evelyn Spence.

Towards the end of the 1930s Russell, now in his sixties, was beginning to favour the idea of a return to the calm and regularity of academic life. He had inherited the title from his brother Frank on the death of the latter in 1931. In 1937 he had been obliged to sell Telegraph House, to which he was devoted, and in the same year he and Peter had a son. He made some tentative gestures towards Cambridge but G. E. Moore was not helpful. He and Moore had examined Wittgenstein for the Ph.D. in 1929, his last academic act for a long time. Unsuccessful at home he turned next to the United States, to the Institute for Advanced Study at Princeton, but nothing came of it. A series of lectures, 'Words and Facts', delivered in Oxford in 1938 (published two years afterwards as *An Inquiry into Meaning and Truth*) showed that he could still take part in the most advanced and up-to-date type of philosophical discussion. He wrote in the book's preface that it was the result of 'an attempt to combine a general outlook akin to Hume's with the methods that have grown out of modern logic'.

In these difficult circumstances George Santayana, unexpectedly enriched by writing a best-selling novel *The Last Puritan* (in which a character based on Russell's brother took a notable part), generously agreed to subsidize Russell with a sum of £1,000 a year. As it turned out he was not called on for very long, since the university of Chicago offered a visiting professorship for the next year starting in the autumn of 1938. Russell and his family left England soon after the death of Ottoline Morrell broke another link with the past. In the autumn of 1939, with the outbreak of war in Europe, Russell moved to another visiting professorship, at the university of California in Los Angeles. Conflict with an unsympathetic right-wing president induced him to leave California before his time was up for what proved to be a bird in a very prickly bush, a chair at the City College of New York.

As a municipal institution City College was

exposed to citizen litigiousness and a lady was induced to sue the New York Board of Higher Education for offering employment to an alien atheist and exponent of free love. A ludicrous judge upheld her plea, Mayor La Guardia was happy to placate conventional opinion which carried a lot of votes, and the outraged protests of a great number of liberal-minded and intelligent Americans went for nothing. Harvard counteracted the insult by inviting him to give the William James lectures there later in 1940 but the practical problem of economic survival remained.

Dr Albert Barnes, inventor of argyrol, came to the rescue, appointing Russell lecturer at his 'Foundation' in Philadelphia at a fairly generous stipend. Russell's duty was to lend a certain broad intellectual respectability to Barnes and his remarkable collection of pictures by lecturing on the history of philosophy. At first things went well enough but eventually Barnes, enraged, it seems, by Peter Russell's knitting during the lectures, found a pretext for ending Russell's contract, which he understood to rule out outside lectures by Russell. At the end of 1942 Russell was given three days' notice to leave. But better times were at hand.

Later in 1943 Russell won an action against Barnes for wrongful dismissal, receiving $20,000 in place of withheld salary. He was invited to lecture at Bryn Mawr. He pushed ahead with the work he had undertaken for Barnes and which was soon delivered to the publisher as *A History of Western Philosophy*, an immediate success from the moment of its publication in 1945 on both sides of the Atlantic and a complete guarantee of financial security to Russell for the rest of his life. By no means a scholarly work it combines lively passages on philosophical themes of the past where they happen to have caught Russell's interest, entertaining biographical material rather in the manner of G. H. Lewes [q.v.], and amusingly processed historical matter of only the most marginal relevance to his main exposition derived from readily accessible sources. To close a splendid year Trinity College once again invited him to rejoin it.

With the war coming to its end he was able to take up this suggestion in the October of 1944. The seal of approval from the philosophical profession of which he had been such a fitful and wayward member was given by the appearance of a volume on his philosophy by a largely distinguished cast of contributors in the 'Library of Living Philosophers'. Once in England again he was quickly recruited by the BBC, and his voice became available for widespread imitation on the popular Brains Trust programme for which his brand of mental

agility and definiteness of opinion was ideal. Now seventy-two he was still avid for romantic episodes, falling in love with the writer Gamel Brenan in 1944 and enjoying an affair with the young wife of a lecturer at Cambridge the year after.

The dropping of atomic bombs on Japan instantly commanded his attention and preoccupied his energies, along with connected political interests, for the rest of his life. At an early stage of his thought on the subject he conceived the idea of coercing Russia, if necessary by the threat of war, to agree to international control of atomic energy, expressing it publicly in 1947. His subsequent denials of this and very limited and reluctant admissions in the face of plain evidence of the fact pose a problem which his biographer Ronald Clark reasonably solves with the conjecture that it was not that Russell had forgotten but that he saw himself as lying in the best of all possible causes, that of getting the human race, as he put it, 'to acquiesce in its own survival'. But his anti-nuclear preoccupation was not to reach its full intensity until 1954.

In the late 1940s and early 1950s Russell was in the happiest circumstances, universally revered, loaded with honours, provided with unlimited opportunities for speaking his mind. He made lecture tours in a great variety of places, among them Switzerland, Scandinavia (during which his flying-boat capsized in Trondheim fjord), Australasia, and, of course, the United States. In his homeland he gave the first Reith lectures on the radio in 1949, published as *Authority and the Individual*. He was admitted to the Order of Merit in 1949, and awarded the Nobel prize for literature in 1950. His private life continued its undulating course. His marriage to Peter Spence collapsed in 1949 and she left with their young son. In the same year he met Alys again. More significant for the future was a new meeting with Edith (died 1978), daughter of Edward Bronson Finch, of New York. He had first met her at Bryn Mawr in the war years, and she was to become his wife in 1952 after his third divorce and to bring him, at last, complete marital contentment. In 1955 they went to live at Plas Penrhyn, Merionethshire, Wales.

A personal cloud over this generally agreeable scene was cast by what he, not unreasonably, took to be the low opinion shared by most philosophers of the new generation of his last major philosophical book: *Human Knowledge* (1948). The book itself was not one of his best. Apart from its last section on inductive reasoning (where he fell back on a method of postulation which he had once criticized as 'having all the advantages of theft over honest toil'), there was little in it that had not appeared in his earlier books. It so happened that the academically ascendant philosophy of that moment was radically opposed both to Russell's idea that the ultimate task of philosophy is justification and to his methodological reliance on formal logic. He and his old pupil Wittgenstein were now totally estranged, particularly after a risible scene at the Cambridge Moral Sciences Club, where Wittgenstein swept out in a hysterical tantrum.

From then on Russell's literary work was largely confined to his own past, as in *Portraits from Memory* (1956), *My Philosophical Development* (1959), and the three volumes of his fascinating but rather fragmentary *Autobiography* (1967, 1968, 1969), and to the political present as in his *Common Sense and Nuclear Warfare* (1959), *Has Man a Future?* (1961), and *Unarmed Victory* (1963).

His most active period as a campaigner against nuclear weapons can be dated from a broadcast of 1954, 'Man's Peril', inspired by the Bikini H-bomb tests. In 1955 he organized a manifesto, signed by Einstein and other scientists. He took part in the first Pugwash conference in 1957 and in 1958 became the first president of the Campaign for Nuclear Disarmament. Two years afterwards, in 1960, he split the CND to form the more militant Committee of 100, dedicated to civil disobedience in pursuit of its aims. It was in that year that Ralph Schoenman first came into Russell's life, which he was to stage-manage, to Russell's increasing discredit, during his tenth decade.

That is not to say that Russell did not take part with full consent in the mass sit-down in Whitehall in February 1961 and in a demonstration the following August, as a result of which he and his wife were sentenced to two months in prison, but detained only for a week because of age and ill health. It was Russell too who said that J. F. Kennedy and Harold Macmillan were more wicked than Hitler. In 1962 in the Cuba crisis Russell wrote powerful letters appealing to various heads of state and retained enough sense of proportion to doubt whether they had any effect whatever. But as he moved into his nineties he became more and more the instrument of Schoenman's one-sided campaign to blame the United States for all the world's misfortunes. Letters written in villainously sub-literate American English appeared over Russell's signature in *The Times*. He became the figurehead of the long-drawn-out buffoonery of a 'war crimes trial' whose bench consisted exclusively of apologists for Russian imperialism, most notably the egregious Sartre. Finally, in 1969, Russell took the step that had driven many of his allies and friends to abandon him politically; he disowned

Schoenman and wrote a funny, lucid, rather insufficiently apologetic account of the relations between them. Shortly afterwards, on 2 February 1970, within three months of his ninety-eighth birthday, he died at his home, Plas Penrhyn.

If Russell's political reputation was low at the time of his death, his philosophical reputation had taken an upward turn from the trough of the late 1940s and the 1950s. The heroes of 'linguistic philosophy', Wittgenstein and J. L. Austin [q.v.], died in 1951 and in 1960, and although Wittgenstein at least remained an object of close and interested study, and even of more or less convincing impersonation in some circles, up to and beyond the date of Russell's death, the influence of Austin effectively died with him. The philosophers of greatest standing in the Anglo-Saxon analytic tradition in the 1960s and 1970s—W. V. O. Quine, Davidson, Putnam, Kripke—have all been more Russellian than anything else.

Although Frege was a more profound philosopher of mathematics than Russell he was not as influential. No one had had a more fundamental and persistent effect on the course of academic, technical philosophy in the English-speaking world than Russell did. Less original than Wittgenstein, and even in some respects than his original mentor, G. E. Moore, he served as a listening-post for his age in which a vast range of movements of thought were perceptively picked up, helpfully simplified, and then sent forth to the world in a lucid and readily digestible form. At times his style, for the most part a magnificent expository instrument, is a little remorseless and mechanical in its determined brightness but he managed to be entertaining about topics that had never been seen before as joking matters.

Russell was an attractive and sociable man, generous with time, money, and attention, no respecter of persons, but the same to all men, even if somewhat ruthless in, and after, his pursuit of women. He was short in stature, but quite sturdy from middle life. In his early manhood he wore a somewhat fleecy moustache. This was removed in deference to the wishes of Ottoline Morrell in 1911 and was not seen again. In his long life he had various quite severe illnesses, among them, not surprisingly, a collapse through nervous exhaustion. But only a very reliable constitution could have kept him going for nearly a hundred years with little diminution of mental vigour and, to the end, with a fair degree of physical capacity. A great pipe smoker, he had a sharp, slightly raucous voice and a highly recognizable whinnying laugh. His articulation was amusingly precise and pedantic.

There is a pencil drawing of him by Sir

William Rothenstein (reproduced in *British Philosophers* by Kenneth Matthews, 1943) and a bust (1953), which he commissioned himself, by (Sir) Jacob Epstein. Another bust (also 1953) was fashioned by Eric L. Edwards. Two portraits in oils, by David Griffiths and Lewin Bassingthwaighte, were painted in the last two years of Russell's life. In the National Portrait Gallery is a portrait by Roger Fry (*c.* 1923). There are many excellent photographs of him in comparatively old age: the best, perhaps, being that by Philippe Halsman in 1958 (reproduced in Ronald Clark's biography).

[Ronald W. Clark, *The Life of Bertrand Russell*, 1975; Alan Wood, *Bertrand Russell—The Passionate Sceptic*, 1957; Bertrand Russell, *Portraits from Memory*, 1956, *Autobiography*, 3 vols., 1967, 1968, 1969; Rupert Crawshay-Williams, *Russell Remembered*, 1970.]   ANTHONY QUINTON

RUSSELL, SIR (EDWARD) JOHN (1872–1965), agriculturalist, was born 31 October 1872 in Frampton on Severn, the eldest of the nine children of Edward Thomas Russell and his wife, Clara Angel, daughter of Captain Samuel Hallet. His maternal grandfather owned barges and had a wharf in Lambeth; his paternal grandfather was in the coal business. His father was initially a schoolmaster with an independence of judgement that led to frequent conflict with his employers and to consequent changes of employment. Disagreement with the managers of his school, and with the conservatism of Gloucestershire farmers, caused a move to Nether Hallam, near Sheffield. Because the school authorities there refused him leave to attend a course by T. H. Huxley [q.v.] in South Kensington, he went to Lee Common, near Tring, but soon disagreed with authority over the enclosure of common land and left for a lay appointment at a Unitarian church in Leicester. By this time Russell was six; he was sent to stay with an aunt in London for a time to escape an epidemic of scarlet fever in Leicester. In 1882 his father moved to another lay appointment at a Domestic Mission in Birmingham. The deaths of two of his children, and the wish for a larger salary, were the cause of that move.

Perhaps because of the varied educational experience that resulted from these moves from town to town, and from several changes of school within a town where his father became dissatisfied with the teaching, Russell made excellent academic progress. Furthermore, his parents prized all aspects of knowledge and had an extensive collection of scientific books. At the age of thirteen he went to the recently opened Technical School in Birmingham and decided there that chemistry would be his vocation. He did very well at that school, but his parents moved to London when he was fourteen, and he was obliged to find work. He was apprenticed to a homeopathic chemist in London, which he found unrewarding, but he made good use of night classes and private reading. Having matriculated, and now nearly nineteen, in 1891 he entered the Presbyterian College in Carmarthen. After a year he went with a scholarship to University College, Aberystwyth, and thence, in 1894, to Owens College, Manchester, where, having graduated B.Sc. with first class honours in chemistry in 1896, he started research on rates of reaction in thoroughly dried gases. For his researches at Manchester he was awarded a D.Sc. by London University in 1901.

Intense exposure to Nonconformist religion, close connection with various missions and charities, and his father's republican sympathies, made Russell dissatisfied with the condition of the urban poor. Pure chemistry was beginning to seem too limited a subject. He therefore went to Copenhagen in 1900 to learn about agricultural co-operatives and the biochemistry of yeast. In 1901 he was appointed lecturer at Wye Agricultural College and found his vocation. Russell was always a great walker: at Wye he learnt that walking around fields was not the same thing as farming them, and that agriculture was not a large-scale solution to town unemployment. In 1903 he married Elnor (died 1965), whom he had met two years earlier at the Manchester Mission, the daughter of Walter Oldham of Manchester, and formerly a merchant of Penang and Singapore. They had five sons and two daughters. One of the sons died in 1926 at the age of sixteen, after a road accident, and another was killed in action in 1945, at the age of twenty-seven. One of the surviving sons, Edward Walter, became professor of soil science at Reading University.

In 1902 Rothamsted Experimental Station was moribund. Then (Sir) A. D. Hall [q.v.] was made director and matters improved. In 1907 Russell moved there and became director in 1912. Rothamsted was no longer moribund, but agricultural research still was. The President of the Board of Agriculture 'could not conceive of circumstances in which the Board would concern itself with research' and the point of view of the Board was stated succinctly that British agriculture was 'dead and it was the Board's business to bury it'. Russell changed such attitudes, and Rothamsted has grown steadily in size and influence. In 1910 a £1 million Development Fund was set up for agriculture, part of which went to Rothamsted. When war began in 1914 Russell became a member of various committees concerned with government-financed research; this brought more grants to Rothamsted. Government finance continued after the war and enabled new departments to be established. But it was an uphill task for there were those in influential positions who thought that Rothamsted should become an institute for routine soil analysis. Russell records the strong opposition he met when setting up a statistics department. He showed skill, amounting to genius, in getting money from private sources. This skill was shown most dramatically when he managed in seven weeks to raise enough money to buy the Rothamsted Estate which the public trustee was proposing to sell for 'development' in 1934. His detestation of money lying idle led to useful, but disconcerting, flexibility in Rothamsted finances.

An accidental observation while at Wye started Russell and several collaborators on a detailed examination of the beneficial effects of partially sterilizing soil with heat or antiseptics. The method would not be practical on a field scale but is extensively used in glasshouses. After his appointment as director he had little time for research, and furthermore he undertook an impressive programme of travel to give advice and to gain experience of agriculture in other climates. He remained an enthusiastic traveller until nearly the end of his life and visited at least twenty countries—some several times. During a visit to Sudan in 1934 he was disturbed by the lack of information exchange between that country and Britain. As a result he initiated the Imperial (now Commonwealth) Agricultural Bureaux.

Russell retired in 1943, but went on working in his new home near Woodstock. He wrote about fifty papers dealing with research, and published many lectures, addresses, and reports on his travels. Among his many books are *Soil Conditions and Plant Growth* (1st edn. 1912, 7th edn. 1937), *World Population and World Food Supplies* (1954), *A History of Agricultural Science in Great Britain, 1620-1954* (1966), and *The Land Called Me* (1956), an autobiography. He was elected FRS in 1917, was appointed OBE in 1918, and was knighted in 1922. He was awarded gold medals from five bodies, and honorary degrees from eleven. Russell was rather short and, in his prime, lean. He moved quickly and walked leaning slightly forward and a little jerkily. When discussing a point of administration or finance he sat with his head tilted slightly to the right and, however complex the proposed arrangement, his bright blue eyes never lost their expression of innocent candour. He died in a nursing home at Goring-on-Thames 12 July 1965, surviving his wife by only a few weeks.

There is a portrait by Edward Hall (1959).

[Edward John Russell, *The Land Called Me*, 1956; H. G. Thornton in *Biographical Memoirs of Fellows of the Royal Society*, vol. xii, 1966; personal knowledge.]

N. W. PIRIE

RUSSELL FLINT, SIR WILLIAM (1880-1969), artist. [See FLINT.]

RUTTLEDGE, HUGH (1884-1961), mountaineer, was born 24 October 1884, the son of Lieutenant-Colonel Edward Butler Ruttledge, of the Indian Medical Service, and his wife, Alice Dennison. He went to schools in Dresden and Lausanne and then to Cheltenham College. In 1902 he went as an exhibitioner to Pembroke College, Cambridge, and in 1906 he obtained a second class in part i of the classical tripos.

His working life was spent in the Indian Civil Service, which he joined in 1908, being appointed to the United Provinces. He was promoted city magistrate at Lucknow in 1917, and its officiating deputy commissioner in 1921. He developed a deep affection for the Himalayan district of Almora, among the foothills and within sight of the big peaks. He became deputy commissioner of Almora in 1925, and settlement officer in 1928. He brought a strict sense of duty and impartiality to his work, but he also found time for both field sports, such as big-game shooting and pig-sticking, and travel in the mountainous parts of his district, where he was a familiar and trusted visitor. A pig-sticking accident gave him a limp, which did nothing to impair his zest for mountain travel, although it prevented him from undertaking difficult climbs.

With his wife and friends, in the 1920s, Ruttledge explored the Milam glacier, tried to reach Nanda Devi, and did a reconnaissance of Mount Kailas. He retired early from the ICS in January 1932, because he wanted to see more of his young family, and also perhaps because of the frustrations of his job. His friend—the Everest mountaineer T. H. Somervell, who shared some of his journeys in the hills, commented: 'I cannot help feeling that one of the reasons for his retirement was that he was so tired of making plans that he knew to be right, to find that the Government always thought they knew better than the man on the spot.'

A useful but not especially distinguished career was followed by an invitation from the committee jointly representing the Royal Geographical Society and the Alpine Club to lead the next Mount Everest expedition. The choice of Ruttledge as leader surprised many mountaineers. However, since Lieutenant-Colonel E. F. Norton, the leader of the 1924

Everest expedition, on which G. L. Mallory [qq.v.] and A. C. Irvine disappeared, was not available in 1933, and his colleagues of a decade beforehand had also aged, the Everest committee was left with no obvious choice of a man to lead a major expedition.

Ruttledge himself confessed that he had had potential greatness thrust upon him, and indeed his abiding modesty was one of his most endearing characteristics. He was genuinely proud to lead the young climbers he had chosen after seeking careful advice. Many of them were more experienced in hard climbing, as opposed to mountain travel, than he himself was. His companions found that to travel with Ruttledge across the high uplands of Tibet was a delight, for he had a keen interest in the strange topography, in the unusual customs of hospitality and bargaining, and in the animals and birds whose lack of timidity he revelled in. He had a sure and friendly touch when dealing with the Dzongpens (governors), the muleteers, and the sherpa and other porters, as well as a natural authority, tempered by a real liking for those who lived in wild places.

Yet it was perhaps unwise to ask Ruttledge to lead the 1933 expedition to Everest. In the years after the war of 1914-18, when he was out of touch with the British climbing scene, a new generation of young, mostly university-trained, mountaineers appeared. Confident and outspoken, they often puzzled and confused their older leader. Ruttledge found it difficult to make up his mind, and when he did, he might reach a decision based on insufficient evidence. At a crucial moment—the selection of climbers to set up Camp V, at 25,700 feet— he chose a mixture of university climbers and soldiers, with their very different disciplines and traditions. In a rarely encountered period of good weather, dissensions aborted the establishment of Camp V. Although the expedition reached a height previously unclimbed (28,100 feet, the missed chance possibly cost the party final success, twenty years before John (later Lord) Hunt's expedition reached Everest's summit. None the less, the expedition returned to England almost united in affection for their leader.

Between the 1933 and the 1936 Everest expedition, which Ruttledge was also to lead, doubt about his leadership began to emerge, and he resigned the offered post several times, uncertain whether he would command the support of the climbers most likely to reach the summit. Finally Ruttledge accepted the leadership of the 1936 expedition. Unfortunately that expedition was defeated by the weather.

In his later years Ruttledge was laird of the tiny island of Gometra, off the coast of Mull.

He enjoyed sailing his boat round the Devonshire coast, and was visited by many of the young climbers whom he had taken to Everest. He wrote two books: *Everest* (1933), and *Everest: the Unfinished Adventure* (1937).

In 1915 Ruttledge married Dorothy Jessie Hair Elder; they had one son and two daughters. Ruttledge died in Stoke, Plymouth, 7 November 1961.

[Hugh Ruttledge, *Everest*, 1933; private information; personal knowledge.]

JACK LONGLAND

RYDE, JOHN WALTER (1898-1961), physicist, was born at Brighton 15 April 1898, the only child of Walter William Ryde, artists' colourman, of Brighton, and his wife, Hannah Louise Buckland, who was related distantly to William Buckland, FRS (1784-1856, q.v.), geologist and sometime dean of Westminster. He was educated at St. Paul's School, which he left in 1913 to continue his education abroad. After a year in France, the outbreak of war forced a return to England where he joined the City and Guilds Technical College, Finsbury, to study under Professor Silvanus P. Thompson [q.v.]. In 1916 Ryde volunteered for service in the Royal Engineers, being posted in due course to France, and receiving a commission just before the 1918 armistice.

After demobilization, Ryde was successful in obtaining an appointment to the scientific staff of the Research Laboratories of the General Electric Company Ltd., then in process of formation under (Sir) Clifford C. Paterson. He was soon awarded a quite senior position in this organization in just recognition of his outstanding abilities. His scientific interests covered a range so extensive as to be quite unusual in this age of specialization. He possessed the gift of being able to familiarize himself with a fresh field of study very rapidly, following this up quite often by a significant contribution to the advancement of the subject. Much of his work was theoretical but he was also a skilled experimenter, a talent he retained throughout his career. Ryde's work at the GEC Wembley Laboratories was thus not confined by departmental boundaries, his final appointment, in 1953, being to the new post of chief scientist.

His earlier work was concerned with electrical discharges in gases, thermionic emission, spectrophotometry, spectroscopic analysis, optical projection systems, and the optical properties of diffusing media. The work on discharges in gases took a sudden turn into a very practical and commercially significant direction in the early 1930s when Ryde and his team developed the first successful high-pressure mercury vapour lamp, later widely adopted for the lighting of streets and industrial installations. This work occupied a major part of his effort for several years, but by the time war came in 1939 the scientific problems were largely solved and Ryde was free to turn his attention to other, more pressing, problems of that time.

It was now that his various leisure-time interests—astronomy, geology, microscopy, mathematical studies—proved of such value; not only was he heavily engaged in various aspects of the war work at the Wembley Laboratories, but he was able to make a number of significant personal contribution to defence matters. A particularly important theoretical investigation, undertaken jointly with his wife—also a skilled mathematician—was concerned with the effect on centimetric radio waves (for example in radar) of meteorological conditions such as rain, hail, cloud, and dust storms. The calculation of the attenuation and echo intensities involved a prodigious amount of computational work and it was gratifying to the Rydes to find that their theoretical predictions were, some years later, confirmed to a most satisfactory degree by direct measurements. Ryde's interest in astronomy also enabled him to make another significant personal contribution during the war. There

was a need for information regarding the illumination from natural sources during hours of darkness and Ryde devised a means for calculating and presenting this information in a form readily usable by those responsible for military operations. The issue of these Ryde Night Illumination Diagrams by the Hydrographic Department of the Admiralty continued until 1947.

After the war he continued to exercise his general influence over the whole of the scientific work at the GEC laboratories, in which organization he was still active at the time of his death.

In 1948 Ryde was elected to fellowship of the Royal Society. He was also a fellow of the Royal Astronomical Society, a fellow of the Institute of Physics, and, for a number of years, played an important part in the affairs of the Royal Institution as chairman of its Davy Faraday Committee.

In 1930 Ryde married Dorothy, daughter of Thomas Edward Ritchie, electrical engineer. They had one son. Ryde died at Marlborough 15 May 1961.

[*The Times*, 19 May 1961; R. Whiddington in *Biographical Memoirs of Fellows of the Royal Society*, vol. viii, 1962; personal knowledge.]   B. S. COOPER

S

SACKVILLE-WEST, EDWARD CHARLES, fifth BARON SACKVILLE (1901-1965), man of letters, was born in London 13 November 1901, the only son of Charles John Sackville-West, later fourth Baron Sackville, and his first wife, Maude Cecilia, daughter of Captain Matthew John Bell, of Bourne Park, Kent. His father was then a major in the King's Royal Rifle Corps who had served in the South African war as aide-de-camp to Sir Redvers Buller [q.v.]. After active service in France during the war of 1914-18 he became in 1918 British military representative on the Supreme War Council and remained in Paris as military attaché from 1920 to 1924. He succeeded his brother as third baron in 1928. Edward Sackville-West was brought up at Knole, the historic family seat near Sevenoaks. He had one sister, to whom he was devoted, but in general he described his boyhood as 'lonely, invalidish, and apprehensive'. Later, he never wanted for friends and social life was a pleasure to him, but his health was always weak and he showed a steady courage in face of it. He was educated at Eton, where his precocious gifts as a pianist were quick to reveal themselves, and there is little doubt that, had he chosen, he could have made for himself a distinguished musical career. His bent, however, was also literary, and after four years at Christ Church, Oxford, reading modern history and modern languages, he travelled in France and Germany, acquiring an easy mastery of both French and German, and a wide knowledge of European art and literature. By the time he came to write his first novel, *Piano Quintet* (1925)—the story of a group of musicians who set out on a European tour—his critical and creative faculties were on their way to full development.

His tastes, like his temperament, were romantic—although the romanticism was generally kept under rational control. Both to himself and to others he could apply the cold douche of common sense. *The Ruin* (1926), with its reminiscences of Knole, was described as a 'Gothic novel', and the theme invited those flights of fantasy and rich tonality of style to which the author's talent lent itself. But it was with *Simpson* (1931) that it seemed as if Edward Sackville-West would make a really significant contribution to the English novel. This was the story of a nurse—a nanny—and the lifelong response to her vocation. Through the circumstances of birth and background the novelist was well placed to understand his subject, but the story of Simpson is no tale of progress from one stately nursery to another. The suburban home at Wimbledon, the officers'

quarters at Aldershot, the boarding-house at Folkestone, and the house in East Prussia on which the war of 1914-18 hardly impinges, are as truly described as the patrician setting in which Simpson serves her brief novitiate. Nor is her career a chronicle of unqualified success; she has one notable failure, and another mission she never lives to complete. The book showed that the sympathies of Sackville-West were as wide as his judgements—when occasion called for them—could be penetrating and astringent. He revised the novel for subsequent publication in 1951, fearing perhaps that it was overloaded with simile, and, here and there, a vocabulary too *recherché*; and that for such a theme and setting the poetic dimension, which his sensibility craved in any work pretending to what De Quincey called the 'Literature of Power', should be less apparent.

For some time his friend (Sir) Desmond MacCarthy [q.v.] had urged him to write a critical biography of De Quincey. No such work had been undertaken since the biography by Alexander Japp [q.v.] in 1877, revised and republished in 1890. Edward Sackville-West had a natural sympathy with his subject, carefully separating De Quincey from the Decadents and the Surrealists with whom he was too often linked. He possessed the scholarship to place De Quincey in the world of the Romantic Movement, to which he essentially belonged, without associating him too closely with men like Wordsworth, who was never able to return his friendship as warmly as it was given, or like Coleridge whose addiction to the laudanum bottle was more incurable than his own. De Quincey, for all his weakness and eccentricity, was shown not only as learned and lovable, but also as a man of character, using his drug as an opiate against pain, not as a key to open the gates of a *paradis artificiel*. Edward Sackville-West achieved exactly the right balance between biography and criticism, reserving his more detailed literary assessments for separate chapters; illustrating the absurdities, the *longueurs*, and the prolixities, into which De Quincey's lack of method too often led him; correcting the exaggerations of his political views; revealing the stubborn intensity of his Christian faith; doing justice to his scholarship, and at the same time exposing the factual errors of one who was compelled by financial necessity to write about too many subjects; but concluding that 'in his finest achievements he rose to those heights of impassioned beauty and truth which proclaim the great writer—the poet and the seer'.

Edward Sackville-West's work on De

Quincey, *A Flame in Sunlight* (1936), which was awarded the James Tait Black memorial prize, is likely to remain a standard work, and the book by which he will be best remembered. He wrote only one further novel after *Simpson—Sun in Capricorn* (1934)—for he had reached a point where the exercise of his critical faculty was beginning to outrun the creative impulse. When war broke out in 1939 he left his apartments at Knole and moved to London, lodging with his relatives, Earl and Countess De La Warr. He joined the Features and Drama department of the British Broadcasting Corporation, where his taste, erudition, and easy mastery of an unfamiliar medium reminded listeners of a world beyond the clash of armies, and were thus a paradoxical, but very real, contribution to the war effort. The walls of his office were adorned with the pictures of the contemporary painters he admired—Max Ernst, John Piper, Graham Sutherland—and his advice on musical questions was always at hand for those who asked for it. He translated Paul Claudel's *L'Otage*, and wrote an original play of his own, *The Rescue*, based on a classical theme, with music by Benjamin Britten, which was successfully broadcast. It showed no flagging of his imaginative powers.

He had never shared the attachment of his cousin, Victoria Sackville-West [q.v.] to Knole, which she would so desperately have liked to inherit—although they had collaborated, happily enough, on a translation of Rilke. In 1946 his father transferred Knole to the National Trust, retaining for his family a lease of part of the house. In 1945 Edward Sackville-West had acquired a charming Queen Anne house at Long Crichel, in Dorset, which he shared with three friends whose tastes were congenial to his own. Four years later he published a volume of literary essays—*Inclinations* (1949)—and here his critical gifts were shown to their best advantage. Malraux and Mauriac, Meredith's 'muscular agnosticism', Dickens and Fromentin, Stendhal and Zola, Delacroix and Henry James—these were among the writers, most of them novelists, whose character and genius he had captured. Particularly challenging was his rehabilitation of *The Sacred Fount* as a masterpiece of Henry James's final period. Apart from the invaluable *Record Guide* (1951), compiled with Desmond Shawe-Taylor, this was his last publication.

In 1949 he was received into the Roman Catholic Church, and among his papers was found the 'Fragment of an Autobiography', in which he tells how this decision—which he never regretted—was inspired, not by a careful balancing of pros and cons, but by a quasi-mystical experience which had come to him many years earlier. At about the same time he bought a house in Ireland at Clogheen in southern Tipperary, where he usually spent nine months of the year, enjoying the social life of the neighbourhood and welcoming his friends from England. When he was in London he took an active interest in the development of Covent Garden opera under Sir David Webster. He inherited his father's title in 1962, but this made no difference to a way of life which gave satisfaction to himself and immense pleasure to others. He died at Clogheen 4 July 1965. He was unmarried and was succeeded in the title by his cousin, Lionel Bertrand (born 1913). There is a portrait in oils by Graham Sutherland (1957).

[Personal knowledge.]   ROBERT SPEAIGHT

SACKVILLE-WEST, VICTORIA MARY (1892-1962), writer and gardener, was born at Knole near Sevenoaks 9 March 1892. Generally known as Vita, she was the only child of Lionel Sackville-West and his wife, Victoria Sackville-West, who were first cousins; her father later (1908) became third Baron Sackville. Knole, the background of her life from infancy until marriage, was one of the largest houses in England, a Tudor palace built round seven courtyards within a 1,000-acre park, and her romantic love of her aristocratic home, combined with her disappointment that as a female she could not inherit it, did much to form both her personal character and her professional career.

Though Vita Sackville-West loved her father, she was always critical of her charming but eccentric half-Spanish mother, and was essentially a lonely child. Educated at Knole by governesses until she was thirteen, she spent long days of solitude immersed in the private pleasures of literature and the country; she later went to a day-school in London. She was a prodigious reader and compulsive writer, having written eight novels (one in French) and five plays by the age of eighteen, all on historical themes, and many poems. Developing alongside a joy in books was a deep love of country pursuits and the fertile farmland of Kent. In her teens, she also discovered the pleasures of travel, visiting France and Italy on numerous occasions (she spoke both languages fluently), and once touring Russia, Poland, and Austria with her mother and her mother's lifelong friend, the immensely rich Sir John Murray Scott. In 1913 she also travelled in Spain.

Her security of background was threatened by two sensational lawsuits: when she was eighteen her father's right to the inheritance of Knole was challenged in the courts in 1910, unsuccessfully; in 1913 Sir John Murray Scott died, leaving her mother a large bequest, and his relatives contested the will. Vita Sackville-West, at twenty-one, tall, handsome, and strong-featured, was called as a witness, and her clear evidence and truthful manner were largely decisive; the jury decided for the Sackvilles.

In 1913 she married (Sir) Harold Nicolson, a notice of whom appears in this Supplement, son of Sir Arthur Nicolson (later Lord Carnock, q.v.), permanent under-secretary at the Foreign Office, in the chapel at Knole, having chosen him from several suitors. Not rich, he was, however, already third secretary at the British embassy at Constantinople, where they lived for a short time after their marriage. In 1914 he was recalled, and they returned to Knole where their first son, Lionel Benedict (a contributor to this Supplement), was born in August. Two months later they moved to London and in 1915 bought a country house, Long Barn, a few miles from Knole, which they kept until 1930 as a main home for herself and a base for her husband whose work was in London or *en poste* abroad.

During these years she developed as a writer from a childish amateur to a prolific professional, successful in the widely different fields of poetry, the novel, and biography. Most important of her books in this period were *Knole and the Sackvilles* (1922), a history of her home and ancestors; *The Land* (1926), a long poem in the manner of the *Georgics* which won her the Hawthornden prize in 1927; and *The Edwardians* (1930), a novel based on Knole, the Sackvilles, and Edwardian society at its extravagant peak. It was an instant best-seller, and though perhaps over-intense, it will hold its place as a period piece, a record of the sumptuous standard of living in a great house where the servants were numbered in hundreds, before the war of 1914–18. She also published some admirable essays and short travel books, of which *Twelve Days* (1928), a book about an expedition in the mountains of Persia, shows a perceptive eye for landscape and wild flowers.

Vita Sackville-West's personal life between 1914 and 1930 was always emotional and sometimes stormy, for she never attempted to rein in her powerful instincts for romance. In 1915 a son was born dead. In 1917 a third son, Nigel, was born in London. For three years, from 1918 to 1921, she had a passionate love affair with a woman, Violet Trefusis, with whom she went off on several occasions, but she returned eventually to Long Barn and resumed her marriage with a husband who was both understanding and forgiving. There were many bonds as well as affection which held them together: one was a shared love of literature; another was the beautiful garden which they were making at Long Barn. Yet another was their social life at week-ends, when they entertained many visitors from London, particularly the literary élite of Bloomsbury, and, though neither took naturally to parenthood, they enjoyed seeing their children at convenient times.

In 1925 Nicolson was posted to Persia, and his wife decided not to accompany him, for she hated diplomatic life, preferring her writing and her garden. However, they wrote to each other every day, a habit they continued all their lives, and she travelled to Persia twice to visit him. Although their marriage was unconventional in every way, for each was basically homosexual, it had become extremely happy; physical relationship had lapsed, but each needed the other to advise, amuse, sustain, and understand. Her most significant relationship during this period, apart from her marriage, was with Virginia Woolf [q.v.], whose extravagant fantasy, *Orlando* (1928), was an open love-letter to her.

In 1929 her husband resigned from the Foreign Office and returned to England to become a journalist, and in 1930 the Nicolsons moved house, giving up Long Barn and buying a ruined Elizabethan mansion, Sissinghurst Castle, also in the weald of Kent, which they planned to restore and where they dreamed of making a great garden from the existing wilderness. The ruined buildings, with the adjacent farm and 500 acres of land, cost £12,000. Vita Sackville-West was thirty-eight, Nicolson forty-three. Their youth was behind them, his career was at a crossroads, and their finances were precarious, but they looked forward eagerly to the new adventure.

From 1930 until the outbreak of war, she worked continuously at her writing and her new garden. In 1930 she wrote a lyric poem of high quality called *Sissinghurst* which appeared the following year; in 1931 she also published a novel, *All Passion Spent*, and another, *Family History*, in 1932; in 1936 a biography, *Saint Joan of Arc*, and in 1937 a life of her Spanish grandmother, *Pepita*. At the same time she and her husband were planning and planting what many consider her finest memorial, the garden at Sissinghurst, a seven-acre garden consisting of linked enclosures formal in shape, but planted with romantic profusion, with an abundance of scented flowers and old roses.

She became more solitary at Sissinghurst than at Long Barn and rarely went to London, where Nicolson spent his week. However, they travelled frequently to France, Italy, and other countries and in 1933 they went on a lecture tour of the United States. Virginia Woolf remained her closest friend and she was deeply distressed by her suicide in 1941.

During the war Vita Sackville-West kept Sissinghurst going and joined the Kent committee of the Women's Land Army, and she wrote prolifically; her most important books were *The Eagle and the Dove: St. Teresa of Avila, St. Thérèse of Lisieux* (1943) and *The Garden*, begun in 1942 and published in 1946, a long poem in the manner of *The Land*. Both these poems, whether successful or not in their entirety, contain lyric passages of unquestionable beauty. In 1948 she was appointed CH for her services to literature. In 1959 she published *Daughter of France*, a biography of La Grande Mademoiselle, Duchesse de Montpensier, and in 1961 *No Signposts in the Sea*, her last novel. By now acknowledged as one of the finest gardeners in England, she wrote a gardening column for the *Observer* from 1946 to 1961, selections from which have been reprinted many times in book form. The intelligence and lucidity which characterized all her writing were as notable in a short gardening article as in a full-scale biography.

By 1950 the garden at Sissinghurst had reached its zenith, and in 1955 she was awarded a gold Veitch memorial medal by the Royal Horticultural Society. The garden was opened to the public every day in summer and in 1961 it was visited by more than 13,000 people, a figure which multiplied after her death when Sissinghurst passed to the National Trust.

In 1961 Vita Sackville-West became gravely ill with cancer, and she died at Sissinghurst 2 June 1962. A portrait of her at the age of twenty-seven by William Strang is in the Glasgow Art Gallery; a painting by P. A. de László (1910) and drawings by (Sir) William Rothenstein (1925) are at Sissinghurst.

[Her own writings; Sir Harold Nicolson's *Diaries and Letters*, ed. Nigel Nicolson, 3 vols., 1966-8; Nigel Nicolson, *Portrait of a Marriage*, 1973; Michael Stevens, *V. Sackville-West*, 1973; Anne Scott-James, *Sissinghurst: The Making of a Garden*, 1975; private information.]   ANNE SCOTT-JAMES

SALISBURY, FRANCIS OWEN (FRANK) (1874-1962), painter, was born 18 December 1874 at Harpenden, one of the family of five sons and six daughters of Henry Salisbury, plumber and glazier, and his wife, Susan Hawes. A very delicate child, he was educated mostly at home by his sister, Emmie. When he was fifteen he was apprenticed to his eldest brother (H.) James Salisbury in his stained-glass works at St. Albans. When the young apprentice displayed a talent for painting, his brother took him to Heatherley's of Newman Street, a drawing academy in London, which he attended three days a week. At eighteen he won a scholarship at the Royal Academy Schools for five years. There he won several medals and awards, including the Landseer

scholarship, which enabled him to go to Italy in 1896.

Salisbury quickly acquired a considerable reputation first exhibiting at the Royal Academy in 1899, after which he was a constant exhibitor, but was never offered membership. This disappointed him very much but he was never embittered. His first Royal Academy exhibit was a portrait of Alice Maude, daughter of C. Colmer Greenwood. Salisbury married Alice (died 1951) in 1901 and they had twin daughters. These were to provide the inspiration for a number of pictures of children which Salisbury painted during the subsequent years.

Heraldry and pageantry were also among Salisbury's interests. A very large composition, 'The Passing of Queen Eleanor', was painted in 1907 and shown at the Royal Academy the following year. This picture led to a commission for the mural 'The Trial of Katherine of Aragon' for the House of Lords. There followed other murals: 'Great Artists of Chelsea' for the Chelsea Town Hall, and works for the Royal Exchange, Liverpool Town Hall, and elsewhere. He also did many paintings for the Corporation of London.

Salisbury recorded many historical events in oils, including 'The National Thanksgiving Service on the Steps of St. Paul's, 1919', 'The Burial of the Unknown Warrior' (11 November 1920), 'The Heart of the Empire' (recording the thanksgiving service for the jubilee of King George V), and the coronation of King George VI. He was commissioned by the Government to paint 'The Signing of the Anglo-Soviet Treaty' (1942), and for the Government of the USSR he painted 'The Battle of Britain'.

Salisbury's gift lay not only in the able depiction of large crowds, and the decorative disposition of figures such as in 'The Sen Sisters', but also in the portraiture of sitters, many of whom were distinguished. He painted five presidents of the United States, five British prime ministers, three archbishops of Canterbury, and a number of leaders of the Church and Salvation Army. These were but a few of his celebrated sitters.

At the same time, Salisbury was interested in religious subjects. As a child he had been brought up in a strictly religious household, a fact which may have had a bearing on his canvases of, for example, Jeremiah, Jonah, Daniel, Moses, Elijah, Isaiah, Ezekiel, and Habakkuk, which he painted in collaboration with Dr. Parkes Cadman of New York. His work is a clear interpretation of the simple truths he found in the Bible, and seven pictures he painted illustrating the Lord's Prayer became well known.

Salisbury worked not only in oils but also in stained glass, and was master of the Worshipful Company of Glaziers in 1933–4.

In 1953 an important exhibition, entitled 'Portrait and Pageant', was held at the Royal Institute Galleries in Piccadilly when nearly 200 of Salisbury's most important works were displayed. One of the most popular works exhibited was 'The Boy Cornwall in the Battle of Jutland, 1916' (the lad who was posthumously awarded the VC for remaining at his gun post during the battle). This portrait had been painted at Scapa Flow in appalling weather where the artist was only partially protected by canvas screens.

Salisbury was appointed CVO in 1938 and was awarded an LL.D by St. Andrews University in 1935. In 1936 he became cavaliere of the Order of the Crown of Italy. He was RP (1917) and RI (1936).

In 1944 Salisbury published his memoirs under the title *Portrait and Pageant*, which was revised with additional material and published as *Sarum Chase* in 1953. He was a man of great charm, an enthusiastic gardener, and the garden at his home, Sarum Chase, in Westheath Road, Hampstead, was a great joy. He always claimed that the Armada signal was sent from that spot as it was the highest point in Hampstead. Besides playing tennis, he was a keen motorist and took considerable pleasure in driving his Rolls-Royce. He was always immaculately dressed and favoured a very high collar with a dark coloured cravat, which emphasized his consciously Victorian appearance.

Salisbury painted a self-portrait in the dress of master of the Worshipful Company of Glaziers. His bust was sculpted in bronze by G. H. Paulin (1945). Salisbury died in London 31 August 1962.

[Frank O. Salisbury, *Portrait and Pageant*, 1944, and *Sarum Chase*, 1953; B. Aquila Barber, *The Art of Frank O. Salisbury*, 1936; *The Times*, 1 September 1962; personal knowledge.]   MAURICE BRADSHAW

SALMOND, SIR JOHN MAITLAND (1881–1968), marshal of the Royal Air Force, was born in London 17 July 1881, the younger of the two sons among the five children of Lieutenant (later Major-General Sir) William Salmond of the Royal Engineers, and his wife, Emma Mary, youngest daughter of William Fretwell Hoyle, of Hooton Levet Hall, Maltby, Yorkshire. John Salmond was thus brought up in a military family at a time when the British Empire offered much in the way of action and adventure to the young man who had such inclination. It was almost a foregone conclusion

that he would go to Wellington College and follow his father into the army. He disliked school and his performance was no better than average. He failed at the first attempt to pass into either the Royal Military Academy, Woolwich, or the Royal Military College, Sandhurst, but was accepted for the latter at his second attempt. This was the first important step towards a career which he craved, and he departed for Sandhurst in 1900 anxious to join the cavalry but doubtful whether his father could afford it. His doubts were justified and, after a modestly successful year at the Royal Military College, he was gazetted to the King's Own Royal Lancaster Regiment.

A brief and somewhat inactive interlude with his regiment in South Africa during the closing stages of the Boer War gave him a taste for the wide open spaces and a great desire for active service. This led him to volunteer for secondment to the West African Frontier Force. He was accepted and departed for Nigeria in 1903, to spend a rough and adventurous three years, mostly up country with considerable responsibilities, an experience which matured him, gave him self-confidence, and also inspired him to indulge in more unusual activities. It was this latter characteristic which led him to take a deep interest in aviation and the endeavours of the early pioneers.

On returning to his regiment from Nigeria, the routine experienced by an infantry officer at home soon began to pall and Salmond seized an opportunity which arose for selected army officers to obtain their flying certificates. He learned to fly at the Aviation Company at Hendon set up by Claude Grahame-White [q.v.] and, on 12 August 1912, was awarded his Royal Aero Club certificate No. 272, subsequently being posted to the first course of the newly established Central Flying School at Upavon. He developed into a competent and reliable pilot and was retained at Upavon as an instructor. This new career not only brought him great satisfaction but, as the war clouds gathered over Europe, revealed to him more clearly than to most of his colleagues, the immense potential of military aviation. When war broke out in 1914 he was sent to France and given command of No. 3 Squadron at Amiens.

In this, his first flying command, Salmond began to show many fine qualities of leadership, humanity, and tolerance which characterized his later success in high office. In 1914 the Royal Flying Corps, led by Sir David Henderson [q.v.], was hardly recognized as a serious component of the military forces, but Salmond did much to develop reconnaissance, artillery spotting, and aerial photography to a point at which army commanders began to find these services indispensable in planning and conducting their operations. Salmond's humanity was well illustrated during a tragic incident when one of his aircraft was blown to pieces while being loaded with bombs. The pilot and several airmen and civilians were killed. Salmond sent everybody except one sergeant away from the scene and insisted on clearing up himself, allowing nobody to return until all traces had been removed.

In April 1915, having been awarded the DSO, he was promoted to lieutenant-colonel and returned home to command the Royal Flying Corps Wing at Farnborough, but such was his operational experience and ability that, within six months, he was back in France in command of one of the three wings of the RFC in the field. The advent of fixed machine-gun firing through the propeller, initially introduced with devastating effect by the Germans in the Fokker Scout, greatly accelerated the development of air fighting and, as the numbers of aircraft on both sides increased, Salmond found himself immersed in the problems of air fighting tactics. Promotion came rapidly and he became a brigadier-general early in 1916, being given command of one of the RFC brigades. But his days in France were numbered and he was sent home to reorganize flying training at a time when there was intense criticism of the RFC due to the serious shortages of aircrew and the inexperience of those being sent out to the squadrons in France. This proved to be a difficult and most responsible job but, with the assistance of Lieutenant-Colonel Smith-Barry, who was a pioneer in what became acknowledged world wide as the Central Flying School method of instruction, Salmond revolutionized flying training and evolved a pattern which has existed with few changes to this day. In particular, pilots were taught manœuvres which had hitherto been considered unsafe, if not impossible, and they began to reach the squadrons with far greater knowledge of the capabilities and limitations of the aircraft.

In August 1917 Salmond was appointed director-general of military aeronautics at the War Office, with a seat on the Army Council of which, at the age of thirty-six, he was the youngest member. He had made a name for himself and his appointment was hailed as a triumph for youth and ability. It was at this time that the amalgamation of the Royal Flying Corps and the Royal Naval Air Service into what eventually became an independent Royal Air Force began to take shape on the initial recommendation of J. C. Smuts [q.v.]. Salmond worked hard to increase the efficiency of the RFC, to improve supplies and aircraft production, and to bring in United States airmen to be trained alongside those of the RFC during

the closing stages of the war. He had not, however, finished with France and in January 1918 he took over from H. M. (later Viscount) Trenchard [q.v.] the command of the RFC in France in time to organize the force to counter Germany's last desperate offensive which started on 21 March. The final battles were hard and bitterly fought and Salmond threw in the whole of the RFC in close support of the sorely pressed armies. Casualties were severe but he directed his squadrons with cool judgement and they played a notable part in the final victory. He had already been made CMG during the previous year and, on his return home for the armistice parade, he was received by the King and appointed CVO.

During Salmond's last months in France, the Royal Air Force had been established as a separate Service, but the demand for rapid demobilization as soon as the war ended made it extremely difficult to preserve the fledgling Service. Salmond was given command of Inland Area, responsible for the air defence of Britain, and there followed several years of immense difficulty and frustration for him in maintaining defences which many thought to be unnecessary in the aftermath of war. He was appointed KCB during this period (1919) and, with Trenchard and (Sir) Winston Churchill, pulled the RAF through the difficult post-war years.

In 1922 he was appointed air officer commanding in Iraq shortly after it had been decided at the Cairo conference of 1921 to introduce 'air control' into Iraq. Salmond thus commanded all the forces in Iraq and his resolute decisions in handling a serious threat to Kurdistan from Turkey greatly enhanced not only his reputation but also that of the RAF, which he used skilfully in a country the desolation of which would have created great difficulties for land forces. He introduced methods of warning tribes by leaflet before an attack and developed various forms of policing from the air which became accepted practice in many other parts of the world.

At the end of this most successful tour in Iraq, Salmond returned home to take over the air defence of Great Britain—the forerunner of Fighter Command—a post which he held until appointed to the Air Council as air member for personnel in 1929. This lasted for only a brief period as Trenchard relinquished the appointment of chief of air staff in 1930, and Salmond succeeded him at the early age of forty-eight. It was said of him that 'if Trenchard laid the foundations of the RAF, Salmond started erecting its superstructure upon them'. Many long distance flights and the winning of the Schneider Trophy marked his tenure of office, but he waged a continual, and ultimately successful, battle to preserve the RAF from being reduced to a purely short-range air defence role. He was created GCB in 1931 and promoted to marshal of the Royal Air Force before resigning in 1933. His brother, Sir Geoffrey Salmond [q.v.], was chosen to succeed him but he unfortunately died a month after the appointment, and John Salmond was recalled for a few weeks before handing over to Sir Edward Ellington.

On his retirement he became a director of Imperial Airways, but he retained such a lively interest in the progress of his old Service that he returned to become chairman of the Air Defence Cadet Corps in 1938 as the clouds of war once again gathered. As soon as war broke out he accepted an invitation to become director of armament production at the Ministry of Aircraft Production, a task to which he applied all his drive and vast experience under the minister, Lord Beaverbrook [q.v.], with whom he did not always agree. His dissatisfaction with Beaverbrook's control of the Ministry caused him to resign in March 1941. Afterwards, at the request of the chief of air staff, he co-ordinated the Air/Sea Rescue and Flying Control organizations at a time when Britain was losing far too many aircrew and aircraft because of in-adequate rescue arrangements. In this post Salmond was highly successful and earned the gratitude of the nation for saving so many valuable lives. In 1943 ill health compelled him to retire from active service, although he never lost interest in the fortunes of the RAF. He lived a further twenty-five years and many honours came his way, including being admitted as a freeman of the City of London in October 1957. He was president of the Royal Air Force Club from 1946.

Salmond was twice married: first, in 1913, to Helen Amy Joy, of Rubislaw, Aberdeen (died 1916), fourth daughter of James Forbes Lumsden of Johnstone House, Aberdeen; and, secondly, in 1924, to Monica Margaret Grenfell (died 1973), elder daughter of Lord Desborough, whose notice she contributed to this Dictionary, and the sister of Julian Grenfell [q.v.]. Salmond himself contributed the notice of Sir C. S. Burnett to this Dictionary. There was one daughter by the first marriage and a son and a daughter by the second. Salmond died at Eastbourne 16 April 1968.

A portrait by C. J. Orde, which hangs in the Royal Air Force Club, shows Salmond as handsome and youthful-looking for his rank and age, with dark hair and a clipped military moustache. Another portrait, by Matthew Smith, remains in the possession of the family; a drawing by Francis Dodd (1917), together with a bronze by L. F. Roslyn (1921), are in the Imperial War Museum. A sculptured head, also by L. F. Roslyn, was exhibited in the Royal Academy in 1940.

[John Laffin, *Swifter than Eagles*, 1964—a biography of John Salmond; *The Times*, 20 April 1968.]   D. J. P. LEE

SAMUEL, HERBERT LOUIS, first VISCOUNT SAMUEL (1870-1963), Liberal poli-tician, administrator, and philosopher, was born 6 November 1870, in Liverpool, the fifth child and youngest of the four sons of Edwin Louis Samuel and his wife, Clara, the daughter of Ellis Samuel Yates, a Liverpool business man. Edwin Samuel moved to London shortly after his son's birth, and, with his brother, Montagu (later Lord Swaythling, q.v.), founded the banking firm of Samuel Montagu & Co. He died in 1877, and Herbert was brought up by his mother. His father's grandfather had been born in Poland of Jewish parents and his mother also came of Jewish stock.

Herbert learnt Hebrew as a child and was raised in strict conformity with Jewish beliefs and customs. He was educated at University College School and, from 1889, at Balliol College, Oxford, where he gained a first class in history (1893). At Oxford Samuel was president of the Russell, the University Liberal Club. While he was at university he informed his mother that he had ceased to believe in Jewish orthodox theology, but he was proud to be a Jew, and continued to conform outwardly with Jewish observances.

The legacy he had received on his father's death was sufficient to enable him to follow whatever career he chose. He was still a school-boy when he assisted his elder brother in his political work in Whitechapel, and later, he recorded in his memoirs (published in 1945): 'From that early date the House of Commons became my objective, and to take part in social legislation my aim.' The scenes of degradation and poverty in the East End of London made a lasting impression on him, and while he was at Oxford, he saw that it was not only in cities that squalor and privation were rife; he found conditions of extreme poverty in the villages of Oxfordshire.

During this time he formed close friendships with Graham Wallas, G. Bernard Shaw, and Sidney Webb (later Lord Passfield) [qq.v.], but although he found himself to be in full agreement with the socialist aim of a funda-mental change in economic conditions, he could not accept that nationalization and the other panaceas offered by the socialist movement were the right means of achieving that aim. In 1895 he was Liberal candidate for South Oxfordshire and was only narrowly beaten; he also fought in the same constituency in the 'khaki' election of 1900, to be defeated by an even narrower margin.

Meanwhile, Samuel had been associated with a political club known as 'The Rainbow Circle', a forum for Liberals and socialists, in which the Webbs, Bernard Shaw, and H. G. Wells [qq.v.] were prominent. The journal of the club, the *Progressive Review*, for a time employed Ramsay MacDonald as its secretary. This periodical did not, however, last long. MacDonald and the editor, William Clarke, could not agree, and Samuel, as one of the directors, decided to terminate MacDonald's engagement. The *Review* was issued for the last time in September 1897. Samuel himself was busily engaged in setting out his views on Liberal policy in which, he argued, social reform must be in the forefront. The outcome of his reflections, *Liberalism: its Principles and Proposals*, was published in 1902 with an introduction by H. H. Asquith.

In 1897 Samuel married his first cousin, Beatrice Miriam, daughter of Ellis Abraham Franklin, a partner in Keyser & Co., another family banking business. Her dowry added to his private means.

In 1902 Samuel was elected to Parliament in a by-election for the Cleveland division of Yorkshire. He was thirty-two. During the ten years of his political apprenticeship he had visited East Africa and studied the problems of the African continent. His maiden speech in the House was made in opposition to the Conservative Education Bill, but, for his first two or three years as an MP, he concentrated mainly on African matters. In particular, he spoke out against the import of Chinese labour into the Transvaal goldfields. When Balfour resigned in 1905 and the Liberals came into office under Campbell-Bannerman Samuel was offered, and accepted, the post of under-secretary of state at the Home Office.

After the overwhelming victory of the Liberals in the 1906 election Samuel continued to serve in the Home Office under Herbert (later Viscount) Gladstone [q.v.]. In the next three years he rapidly made a name for himself in the field of social legislation dealing with measures for the prevention of industrial diseases and juvenile delinquency. He was largely responsible for 'The Children's Charter' (the Children's Act of 1908) introducing juvenile courts, the probation system, and amending the laws relating to reformatory schools, which he called 'Borstals'. In 1908, when Asquith succeeded Campbell-Bannerman, he offered to transfer Samuel to the Admiralty, but Samuel preferred to stay at the Home Office to carry out the programme of social legislation on which his heart was set. While his colleagues, Winston

Churchill and Lloyd George, were setting up labour exchanges and introducing insurance against sickness and unemployment, Samuel was supporting Herbert Gladstone in piloting through Parliament Bills to provide for police superannuation, workmen's compensation for accidents, and the Mines Eight Hours Bill. In 1908 he was sworn of the Privy Council, and in 1909 he joined Asquith's Cabinet as chancellor of the Duchy of Lancaster.

This was the Cabinet that Asquith's daughter, Violet (later Baroness Asquith of Yarnbury, q.v.), described as 'an orchestra of first violins who sometimes played in different keys'. Asquith, however, depicted Samuel as very sensible and loyal. Conscientious, honest, and industrious, he could be relied upon to play in tune with his leader. He supported the prime minister and Lloyd George throughout the long period of discord between the Government and the House of Lords culminating in the defeat of the peers and the Parliament Act of 1911.

Two general elections in 1910 had confirmed the support for Asquith's administration, and, in both, Samuel succeeded in his Yorkshire constituency. Early in the year he had been appointed postmaster-general. His cousin, Edwin Montagu [q.v.], became under-secretary of state at the India Office. While Samuel was postmaster-general he became inadvertently involved in the 'Marconi scandal'. In March 1910 he began negotiations with the English Marconi Company for the erection of a chain of wireless stations covering areas of strategic importance to imperial defence. He decided that the company was the only organization with the necessary expertise to carry out this work, and agreed upon a contract to be submitted to the Cabinet and to Parliament. Before this action could be taken, rumours were widely circulating that Godfrey Isaacs, the managing director of the company, had sold shares in the Marconi Company of America to his brother, Sir Rufus (later first Marquess of Reading, q.v.), the attorney-general, and to Lloyd George, chancellor of the Exchequer. In February 1913 a French newspaper, *Le Matin*, accused Samuel of being implicated in what it described as a Jewish intrigue. Samuel, without hesitation, sued the paper and forced it to retract its story and make an apology. There was never any evidence to support the allegation that Samuel was in any way involved in the imprudent transactions of his two colleagues. The contract with the Marconi Company was eventually ratified.

Throughout this period of controversy Samuel continued to play his part in presenting to Parliament the far-reaching measures put forward by Asquith's Government. He helped to frame the Irish Home Rule Bill and bore his share of the animosity of the suffragettes. Although sympathetic in principle to women's suffrage, he was appalled by the violence of the militants. In February 1914 he became president of the Local Government Board, and continued his task of ameliorating social conditions by extending maternity and child welfare centres and providing for improvements in housing and town planning.

Then came the war. Samuel had been opposed to supporting France or Russia against Germany, but when the Germans invaded Belgium, he was firmly convinced that Britain had no alternative but to fight, and he gave his full support to Asquith when war was declared.

In May 1915 Asquith, encouraged by Lloyd George, entered into a coalition with Bonar Law and the Conservatives. Samuel moved back to his former office of postmaster-general and ceased to be a member of the Cabinet. Asquith promised to restore him to Cabinet rank as soon as a Liberal vacancy arose, and in November, when Churchill resigned from the Government, Samuel became chancellor of the Duchy of Lancaster, as well as PMG, and resumed his seat in the Cabinet. In January 1916 he became home secretary. While he was in that office he assumed responsibility for Irish affairs for a period of three months during which the Easter rebellion broke out in Dublin and Sir Roger Casement [q.v.] was arrested after landing in Ireland from a German submarine.

Throughout 1916 there arose a growing feeling in the House of Commons that Asquith was lacking in the energy and decisiveness required to cope with the problems of war. In December Lloyd George resigned on the same day as Asquith. A new coalition was formed with Lloyd George at its head. Lloyd George invited Samuel to remain home secretary, but Samuel, partly out of loyalty to Asquith, and partly because he was convinced that Lloyd George would fail, refused his offer, and spent the remainder of the war on the backbenches of the House.

As soon as the war ended, Lloyd George, with the agreement of Bonar Law, called an election in which candidates from both Liberal and Conservative parties who supported the continuance of his Government were endorsed as 'coupon' candidates, pledged to sustain the coalition. Samuel, faced with a coupon candidate in his Cleveland constituency, was defeated for the first time in sixteen years. The result of this 1918 election, which confirmed Lloyd George in office, spelt the end of the Liberal Party as a viable alternative to a Conservative Government. While the party was split into rival factions, Samuel's career as a rising politician suffered a set-back from which it never effectively recovered, although he continued to play a prominent part from time to time, particularly when crises arose in British politics. There can be little doubt that his loyalty to Asquith and his inflexible adherence to principles which he believed to be inseparable from Liberal policy inhibited further progress up the political ladder. As his son wrote: 'He lacked the ambition and the ruthlessness that might have given him higher office.'

Samuel in 1919 was approaching fifty years of age; his health was good and he was in the prime of life. It was unlikely that he would remain inactive for long. A new phase in his career began. At the end of the war Palestine was under British military control, and in 1920, when Britain was granted a mandate to administer the country, Lloyd George asked Samuel to become the first high commissioner. With his usual scrupulous regard for proprieties, Samuel, before accepting the post, sought assurance that his Jewish sympathies would not be thought to impair his impartiality as an administrator. On appointment, he was appointed GBE.

In his memoirs (p. 156) Samuel wrote: 'No one with any historical sense could approach without emotion the task which had now so unexpectedly devolved upon me.' As early as 1914 he had talked to Sir Edward Grey (later Viscount Grey of Fallodon, q.v.), the foreign secretary, about the possibility of settling some Jewish refugees in Palestine, and from time to time during the war Samuel had placed memoranda before the Cabinet advocating Jewish claims. In 1917 the Balfour Declaration had stated that the British Government viewed with favour the establishment in Palestine of a national home for the Jews, but without prejudice to the civil and religious rights of existing non-Jewish communities in Palestine.

When Samuel arrived in Palestine he found the country 'almost derelict, politically and materially'. Gradually, over the next five years, he and his staff were able to achieve steady progress in carrying out the purpose of the mandate: prosperous and peaceful development. Some assistance was given to the settlement of Jewish immigrants, but Samuel faithfully pursued the policy set out in a 1922 white paper aiming at a multi-national commonwealth. As he himself wrote: 'Some thought that a national home for the Jews must mean subordination, possibly spoliation, for the Arabs. I did not share that view.' At this time, Samuel maintained a formal connection with his Jewish religion, and occasionally attended religious services, but the dogma and the ritual did not appeal to him. Nevertheless, as Asquith wrote, after a visit to him in Palestine, although he had been brought up under every typically English influence, he remained 'a Jew of the Jews'. To the initial dismay of the French, Samuel received Foreign Office backing for an active policy in Trans-Jordania, thus apparently securing the eastern border of Palestine.

When Samuel's tenure of office ended in 1925, he and his wife planned to settle as private citizens in Palestine, but this was unacceptable to the Government and the Samuels decided to live instead in Italy. Once again, as in 1920, Samuel was not left in retirement for long. During Samuel's period of office in Palestine, Lloyd George had been succeeded by Bonar Law. Bonar Law had retired in favour of Stanley Baldwin who sought Samuel's help with the difficulties of the coal-mining industry. Samuel accepted appointment as chairman of a royal commission to examine the problems of that industry.

The commission reported on 11 March 1926 after what Samuel described as 'the most strenuous six months I have ever done'. Its recommendations included the cessation of the mining subsidy, reduction of the miners' wages to their 1921 level, reorganization of the industry by the amalgamation of smaller pits, improved working conditions, and the state ownership of the royalties. These proposals pleased neither the mine owners nor the miners' leaders. The former rejected the proposals for reorganization; the latter were adamant in their opposition to a reduction in wages or an increase in hours of work. At the end of April the subsidy came to an end and the coal owners declared a lock-out. The General Council of the Trades Union Congress agreed to support the miners in a general strike. Negotiations between the Government and the TUC broke down and the strike began on 3 May.

Samuel had returned to Italy, but on 6 May he hurried to London, and immediately made contact with J. H. Thomas [q.v.], a Labour leader with whom he had co-operated when he was high commissioner in Palestine and Thomas was colonial secretary in Ramsay MacDonald's administration. For the next three days Samuel and the TUC sought for some formula that would be acceptable to the miners' leaders. Samuel felt strongly that a decrease in wages was inevitable but argued that this should be considered in the context of a reorganized industry with improved conditions. He prepared a memorandum for the TUC which he hoped the miners would accept. The TUC knew that he had no backing from the Government for this initiative, but they were conscious that the strike might not succeed. They were concerned about the drain on the unions' funds and ready to seize on some justifiable pretext for ending the strike. Although the miners' leaders would not give in, the TUC considered that the Samuel memorandum promised a reasonable settlement, and, on 12 May, they called off the general strike. Ramsay MacDonald confided to his diary: 'The Samuel document may not be worth the paper it is written upon, but it has enabled the General Council to face the inevitable.'

Baldwin was prepared to put the Samuel report into effect, but the miners refused his offer. They paid bitterly for their obduracy. Samuel commented in his memoirs: 'The General Strike was over to the relief of the whole nation, but the coal stoppage went on. It lasted for six months. The union's funds were gradually exhausted; the worker's savings as well. . . . they were obliged to go back in the end, and on terms far, far worse than they could have had in the beginning.'

Later in 1926 Samuel was appointed GCB. He and his wife abandoned their plan to live in Italy and returned to London. In October Asquith resigned the leadership of the Liberals, and early in the new year Samuel agreed to become chairman of the party and to try, with the co-operation of Lloyd George, to restore the party's fortunes. He was adopted as Liberal candidate for Darwen in Lancashire.

The results of the 1929 general election were a bitter disappointment to the Liberals. Samuel won a narrow victory at Darwen, but the party won only 59 seats, whilst Labour won 288 and the Conservatives 260. Labour under MacDonald was once more in office, but provided the Liberals stayed united, they held the balance and were in a position to oust the Government when they chose to do so. In fact, they did not remain united. The Government introduced a Bill to reorganize the coal industry, covering a reduction in miners' hours of work, limitation of production, and subsidization of exports. Samuel, inevitably, opposed this Bill. He could not accept the principle of subsidies and held firmly to the view that the industry's problems could only be solved by amalgamation of pits and rationalization. Other Liberals, however, supported the Bill, and the Government passed it into law.

The Labour Government was brought down not by the Liberals, but by its own dissensions, arising from the inability of the Cabinet to agree on the measures required to deal with the economic situation in Britain caused by a disastrous recession in world trade. In August 1931 MacDonald and Philip (later Viscount) Snowden [q.v.], chancellor of the Exchequer, in their efforts to save the pound, had to obtain credits from the Federal Reserve Bank. Such credits were dependent upon immediate drastic cuts in government expenditure, including a reduction in unemployment pay. To these measures most of the Cabinet were inexorably opposed. MacDonald offered his resignation to the King.

By chance, at this moment of crisis on 23 August 1931, Lloyd George was seriously ill and Baldwin was not immediately available when George V sent for him. Samuel, as acting leader of the Liberals, was called to Buckingham Palace, and advocated the formation of a 'national' Government with MacDonald at its head. The latter, after some hesitation, agreed to carry on. Samuel once more became home secretary. His satisfaction with this arrangement was very short-lived. The Conservatives, anxious to introduce a protective tariff as one means of combating the trade depression and unemployment, called for a general election. Samuel and his colleagues who opposed this proposal were overruled. The 'national' Government went to the polls, each party advocating its own policy; the Labour dissidents were overwhelmingly defeated and the Government was returned with a large Conservative majority. Samuel, who was now both home secretary and Liberal leader, and those who supported him soon found that they were fighting a losing battle against protection, and, when the Ottawa agreements were signed, introducing imperial preferences, they left the Government at the end of 1932 and went into opposition. In the 1935 election Samuel was defeated at Darwen and his membership of the Commons came to an end. He was sixty-five.

In 1937 he accepted a peerage and went to the Lords as Viscount Samuel, of Mount Carmel and Toxteth, Liverpool. In his final speech in the Commons he had supported Neville Chamberlain's proposals for increasing the Service estimates, and as leader of the Liberals in the Upper House, he expressed approval of the Munich agreement in 1938. When the Conservative prime minister wished to appoint him lord privy seal he refused, and thus turned down his last chance of returning to office. Although he made speeches in the Lords up to the time of his retirement in 1955, his career as a politician really ended with his defeat at Darwen in 1935.

Throughout his life in Parliament he was a much respected figure, but never succeeded in arousing the enthusiasm of his contemporaries. Harold Macmillan wrote that his speeches were always admirably and even persuasively argued, but they had no fire. Aneurin Bevan [q.v.] said that he was one of the very best debaters he ever heard. But Samuel had none of the fervid oratory of Lloyd George or Churchill or the cutting edge of F. E. Smith (Lord Birkenhead, q.v.) in his prime.

In his later years Samuel concentrated on his philosophical studies and produced a number of books and articles setting out his views. He believed that the future could be moulded by man's efforts, and conscious evolution could be accepted as the underlying principle of action. He called himself a 'meliorist', and believed that free will was the essential basis of ethical behaviour. During this period of his life he travelled widely and also became known to a wide public when he took part in the BBC Brains Trust programmes. He became honorary DCL (Oxford), honorary LLD (Cambridge and Liverpool), honorary Litt.D. (Leeds), and honorary Ph.D. (Jerusalem). He was president of many learned societies and delivered the Romanes lecture at Oxford in 1947. In 1949 he achieved high academic honour when he was elected visitor of Balliol. In 1958 he was admitted to the Order of Merit.

Lady Samuel died in 1959. They had been singularly devoted for over sixty years, though she was a hypochondriac and he detested medicines. They had three sons and one daughter.

Samuel's appearance was as unsensational as his oratory or his whole way of life. He was of middling height, with grey eyes, and black hair which turned pure white. Perhaps the central feature was his trim moustache; his whole figure had a trim compact look, which somehow seemed to emanate from and reflect the essence of his personality. Portraits in oils, by Frank O. Salisbury, are in Balliol College hall and in the National Liberal Club. A bust (1944) by Benno Elkan is in the library of the Hebrew University at Jerusalem. Samuel's papers about philosophy and British politics are kept at the House of Lords; those of specially Jewish interest in the Israeli State Archives at Jerusalem.

Samuel died in London 5 February 1963. His son, Edwin (died 1978), who succeeded him as second Viscount, has recounted that he went in great awe of his father, feeling himself to be a sapling under the shadow of a massive oak.

[*The Times*, 6 February 1963; Edwin Samuel, *A Lifetime in Jerusalem*, 1970; John Bowle, *Viscount Samuel*, 1957; Viscount Samuel, *Memoirs*, 1945.]   H. F. OXBURY

SANSOM, SIR GEORGE BAILEY (1883–1965), diplomatist and scholar, was born in Limehouse, London, 28 November 1883, the only son of George William Morgan Sansom, naval architect, by his wife, Mary Ann Bailey, from Yorkshire. He was at school at a *lycée* at Caen, where he acquired a love of France and French culture which lasted throughout his life. After studying in Germany he passed a competitive examination for the British Consular Service in 1903, was appointed to the Japan branch of the Service, and attached to the British legation in Tokyo to study the Japanese language. His subsequent appointments included service in consulates throughout Japan, but he spent the greater part of his official career in Tokyo, where from 1923 onwards he was in charge of the commercial department of the embassy.

From his arrival in Japan Sansom was increasingly charmed and intrigued by Japanese civilization and culture. In Nagasaki, his first post outside Tokyo, he was singing in the chorus of a *nō* play; as well as acquiring in a miraculously short time a thorough knowledge of spoken and written Japanese, he studied Japanese painting and calligraphy, and started a collection of pottery, of which he became one of the foremost non-Japanese connoisseurs. He served as private secretary to two ambassadors, Sir Claude Macdonald and Sir Charles Eliot [qq.v.], and as a young man formed friendships with many future Japanese leaders, and with scholars, who came to see in him a brilliant and meticulous student of all aspects of Japanese history and civilization.

Taking advantage of the leisured pace of official life, Sansom read exhaustively and acquired a profound knowledge of Japanese history and culture. In 1928 he published his first work, *An Historical Grammar of Japanese*, followed in 1931 by *Japan: a Short Cultural History*, which secured him immediate recognition in Japan and abroad as the first foreign writer able to avail himself fully of primary sources in Japanese. His position as indispensable adviser to successive ambassadors, together with commercial and economic work in the embassy, then left him little time for independent study, and his next book, *The Western World and Japan*, was not published until 1950. In 1935 he had delivered a course of lectures at Columbia University, New York, and before the outbreak of war in 1939 he had decided to retire and devote himself to writing and lecturing. His official retirement on pension took place in 1940, but his effective retirement was delayed for seven years by the war; he led a special mission to Japan (1940), served as adviser to a wartime economic mission in Singapore (1941), escaped through Java to Australia, and was appointed minister in Washington (1942-7), where he made a valuable contribution to the determination of Allied post-war policy towards Japan. He finally retired with a GBE in 1947. He had been appointed CMG in 1926 and KCMG in 1935.

As professor of Japanese studies from 1947, and director of the East Asian Institute from 1949 until 1953, at Columbia University,

Sansom was a major influence in the great advance of Japanese studies in the United States. In 1955 he accepted an honorary professorship at Stanford University, California, where, freed from routine work, he spent the last ten years of his life working on his *magnum opus*, the three-volume *History of Japan* (1958-61-64). He was visited by scholars from all over the world, by whom he was regarded as an almost legendary source of knowledge. He was made an honorary fellow of the Japanese Academy in 1934, and received honorary degrees from Columbia, Mills College (California), and Leeds.

In his youth Sansom's official chiefs, while unanimous in acclaiming his outstanding intellectual gifts, had regretted that his appearance was 'small and not impressive', and in his later years strangers might be momentarily deceived by the diffidence with which he was wont to express his views. Ill-informed enquirers about Japanese matters were never rebuffed; perhaps with a twinkle in his eye Sansom would provide the correct answer, but never so as to prick the balloon too rudely. In Japan in the late thirties, when relations with Britain were very bad, he was once involved in a dispute with an officious policeman. He later explained that as soon as he was able to engage the official in discussion about a point in Japanese history the hostility disappeared. What he did not realize was that it was as much his courtesy, charm, and humility which had caused the change.

Although his official career was distinguished, Sansom will be remembered mainly as an interpreter of Japan to the West. Apart from the *Historical Grammar of Japanese*, itself an exploration of uncharted territory, his published works were all elaborations of one theme: the history of Japan from earliest times down to the first decades of the Meiji era. In all of them he made use of material not previously examined by a foreigner, and of contacts available to him only through his unique position in academic circles in Japan. In the *Cultural History of Japan* emphasis is placed on the economic factors affecting the country's political development, and on the introduction and assimilation of Buddhism, and *The Western World and Japan* traces the influence of Western thought as it reached Japan down the centuries. In the *History of Japan* Sansom covers more fully the whole field of Japanese history, providing Western readers for the first time with a balanced assessment of the nation's evolution. All are the work of a mature scholar, master of his complex material, and are typical, in their conciseness, accuracy, and flashes of quiet humour, of the personality of the author.

In 1916 Sansom married Caroline, daughter of Godfrey Weston, from whom he obtained a divorce in 1927. In the following year he married Katharine, formerly wife of Stephen Gordon, and daughter of William Cecil Slingsby, a Yorkshire landowner and naturalist; the marriage was a supremely happy one. Sansom had no children. He died 8 March 1965 on a visit to Tucson, Arizona.

[Lady Sansom, *Sir George Sansom and Japan. A Memoir*, 1972; personal knowledge.]

OSCAR MORLAND

SARGENT, SIR (HAROLD) ORME (GARTON) (1884-1962), diplomatist, was born in London 31 October 1884, the only child of Harry Garton Sargent, of independent means, and his wife, Henrietta Sarah Finnis Stud Mackinnon, whose sister married the fifteenth Duke of Somerset. He was educated at Radley but his childhood was unhappy, his elderly parents being rather possessive and exacting. He was not sent to a university but spent much time in Switzerland preparing for the Diplomatic Service, into which he passed in 1906. He went to Berne in 1917 and in 1919 transferred to Paris, where for seven years he was attached to the 'Ambassadors' Conference'. There Sargent made his name. His excellent French, his sharp intelligence, and his enormous industry were much appreciated by the various ambassadors under whom he served. He was appointed CMG in 1925 and transferred to the Foreign Office, where he was promoted counsellor in 1926 when he was made head of the Central Department, with responsibility for relations with Italy, Austria, Hungary, and the Balkans.

Although a member of the Diplomatic Service, Sargent never left the Foreign Office again. He was believed to suffer from some complaint — perhaps claustrophobia — which made travelling difficult, if not impossible. He certainly resisted all attempts to place him abroad. Nor had he the qualities of a good ambassador, or, indeed, a wife to help him entertain.

At the Foreign Office Sargent became an assistant under-secretary of state in 1933, with additional responsibility for relations with Germany, France, and Poland; deputy under-secretary in 1939; and permanent under-secretary in 1946 for a short spell before his retirement in 1949. He was appointed CB (1936), KCMG (1937), KCB (1947), and GCMG (1948). He never wrote anything for publication before or after his retirement and his influence on events, which was considerable, can only be appreciated by a study of the minutes and memoranda which he poured out as head of the Central Department and as under-secretary and which have become, for the most part, available to the public. He was an advocate of a 'classical' policy for the United Kingdom as laid down in the celebrated memorandum of Sir Eyre Crowe [q.v.] in 1907. Britain could not allow any one power to dominate Europe and the only power capable of such domination was still, during the twenty years which followed Versailles, Germany. Therefore Germany must be 'contained' by alliances, and notably by a Franco-British alliance or the equivalent of an alliance, linked up with French alliances with the small democracies of Central Europe, and, if necessary, but only if absolutely necessary, with the Soviet Union. Failure to resist the occupation of the Rhineland was therefore, to Sargent, the beginning of the end; the Anschluss a disaster; Munich the final and disgraceful capitulation. 'Anybody would think', he was heard to say, 'that we were celebrating a major victory instead of the betrayal of a minor ally.' Attempts to placate or 'appease' the Nazis were naturally not only useless but positively dangerous. Disarmament was suspect. The navy above all must be strengthened; the Empire by hook or by crook preserved. In spite of much superficial cynicism and pessimism it was really a rather simple philosophy, but, given the premises, logical. And it was maintained with a burning intensity which did not, however, penetrate much beyond the room at the end of the first-floor corridor in the Office and the Travellers' Club.

Sargent's view did not, indeed, differ greatly from those of Lord Vansittart [q.v.] who, however, favoured some kind of 'appeasement' of Mussolini with the object of breaking the Axis, which Sargent never believed to be possible. But 'Van' was a crusader, even if an unsuccessful one, whereas 'Moley' Sargent limited his efforts to reasoned papers addressed to the foreign secretary and to nobody else, tending to shrug his shoulders if they failed to convince and to make cynical wisecracks about the follies of politicians to his intimates at his club. As Vansittart observes in *The Mist Procession*, 'Orme Sargent was a philosopher strayed into Whitehall. He knew all the answers; when politicians did not want them he went out to lunch.'

Sargent's immediate predecessor, Sir Alexander Cadogan [q.v.] was, on the contrary, the sensible official with whom the politicians felt they could get on and who carried far more weight with them, more especially since he never regarded problems from a theoretical point of view. Cadogan's *Diaries* bear witness to the extent to which he was irritated by Sargent's Cassandra-like wails.

No portrait of this tall, distinguished man with his thin and sensitive nose has been traced, but Sargent's photograph naturally adorns the permanent under-secretary's room in the Foreign Office which he helped to reorganize under Anthony Eden (later the Earl of Avon) after the war and where he was much loved by his subordinates and indeed by all the staff. A devout Christian, he lived for his work and had few outside interests. He did not collect anything, although he had a real taste in furniture. He cherished his friendships and was happy in retirement in Bath until he fell ill. Violently pro-Suez in 1956 he became before his death an enthusiastic 'European'. He died in Bath 23 October 1962.

[Lord Vansittart, *The Mist Procession*, 1958; Sir Llewellyn Woodward, *British Foreign Policy in the Second World War*, 3 vols., 1970-1; The Earl of Avon, *The Eden Memoirs*, *The Reckoning*, 1965; *The Diplomatic Diaries of Oliver Harvey, 1937-1940*, ed. John Harvey, 1970; *The Diaries of Sir Alexander Cadogan*, ed. David Dilks, 1971; private information; personal knowledge.]
GLADWYN

SARGENT, SIR (HENRY) MALCOLM (WATTS) (1895-1967), conductor, composer, pianist, and organist, was born in Ashford, Kent, 29 April 1895, the only son of Henry Edward Sargent of Stamford, Lincolnshire, and his wife, Agnes Marion Hall, daughter of a Hertfordshire landscape gardener. Henry Sargent, employed in a coal-merchant's business, was a keen amateur musician, an organist, and choirmaster, who carefully fostered his son's talent from the beginning: but the most important early influence was that of Frances Tinkler, an inspiring local teacher who greatly helped Sargent and, some years later, (Sir) Michael Tippett. At Stamford School Sargent was soon noted for irrepressible high spirits and quick intelligence. But his interests were never academic, and other possibilities were elbowed aside in the determined drive towards a career in music.

On leaving school in 1912 Sargent was articled to Haydn Keeton, organist of Peterborough Cathedral, and was one of the last to be trained in that traditional system, so soon to disappear. The discipline involved daily contact between master and pupil in a severe but balanced curriculum: and Keeton was an exacting tutor, old-fashioned perhaps, but highly professional. He taught the counterpoint of Fux, organ-playing in the style of Samuel Sebastian Wesley [q.v.], and piano-playing in that of Mendelssohn and Sir W. Sterndale Bennett [q.v.]. Score-reading and continuo-realization were learnt not as academic subjects but in the daily practice of cathedral music, performed

from the scores of William Boyce and Samuel Arnold [qq.v.]. It was hard work, and Sargent loved it all. 'We had no money', he said in later years, 'and our future was quite uncertain: but it was music, music, music all the way.'

By the end of his articles Sargent was already recognized as a fine player, a composer of marked talent, and a well-equipped professional whose charm, vitality, and technical accomplishment were outstanding. But his ambitions, though ample, were not yet defined. Sometimes he thought of being a solo-pianist and, like a Rachmaninov, playing his own compositions all over the world. He could probably have done this. After a performance of *The Dream of Gerontius* in 1912, however, he told a group of friends about his intention to be 'a second Elgar'. For that destiny he was less well suited.

In 1914 Sargent was appointed organist of Melton Mowbray, and found himself among people able to appreciate his talent and to give him substantial help. It was made possible for him to have piano-lessons from Benno Moiseiwitch; a good orchestra was created for him to conduct in Leicester; opportunities were offered generously. In his Leicester concerts he appeared as pianist, composer, and conductor, and won the approval of Sir Henry J. Wood [q.v.], who invited him to conduct, in the 1921 Promenade Concert season, his tone-poem 'Impressions of a windy day'. The performance was a triumph: but it was as conductor rather than composer that the young man was acclaimed, and on that evening the pattern of his career was settled. For a time he continued to work from his base in the Midlands, but in 1923, invited to join the staff at the Royal College of Music, he moved to London, where in the following year he married Eileen Laura Harding Horne, by whom he had two children, a son, Peter, and a daughter, Pamela. The marriage was terminated by divorce in 1946.

The ten years after 1923 were decisive in Sargent's career, and were a time of unremitting hard work and social activity. He was a restless man, for whom dancing till dawn after a concert seemed to be a necessary relaxation. With no private income and increasing responsibilities, as well as a natural inclination to spend freely, he was obliged to undertake whatever work was offered; and his schedule involved much travel, with varied programmes on limited rehearsal time. Only a musician of great talent and resilience could have done what he did. But he might have been wise to be more selective, even if the experience made him a general-purpose conductor of extreme efficiency, sometimes criticized for not being fastidious but also admired for being totally reliable.

Sargent's responsibilities at this time included the Robert Mayer concerts (1924), the Diaghilev Ballet (1927), the Royal Choral Society (1928) including the spectacular productions of *Hiawatha*, the Courtauld-Sargent concerts (1929–40), and the D'Oyly Carte Opera Company (1930). He conducted many performances of the British National Opera Company and numberless concerts in cities outside London. Among the works entrusted to him for first performance were *Hugh the Drover* by Ralph Vaughan Williams [q.v.], (Sir) William Walton's *Belshazzar's Feast*, and Walton's opera *Troilus and Cressida*.

Success so brilliant and an enjoyment of its glamour so uninhibited were bound to provoke hostility and to 'excite the common artifice by which envy degrades excellence'. There began to be troubles with orchestras which Sargent tried to discipline. Methods that delighted his devoted choralists were less acceptable to experienced orchestral players: harsh things were said on both sides. Some critics described his performances as brash and superficial, and purists objected to adjustments that Sargent made in the scoring of well-known works, even though these were always effective, and generally less drastic than those made by other conductors. Sargent seemed to disregard these attacks: in fact he was deeply hurt, and they added to the strain under which he worked, a strain that was beginning by 1930 to affect the quality of his performances and his health.

In 1932 he suffered a complete breakdown, and there was doubt whether he would recover from the tubercular infection that involved serious abdominal operations. For two years he was out of action, but when he did reappear his performances had all the old zest and a new depth.

In 1944 a fresh blow fell when his much-loved daughter Pamela was smitten with polio and died. For months Sargent was almost a broken man, but music saved him, and he seemed in time to draw inspiration from the experience. There were, however, works that he never conducted again except as a kind of memorial to Pamela, and not a few of his many generous but strictly private benefactions to other sufferers were really an offering to her.

In 1950 Sargent was chosen to follow Sir Adrian Boult as conductor of the BBC Symphony Orchestra and entered the final, most influential, stage of his career. With that orchestra, the BBC Chorus, the Royal Choral Society, the Huddersfield Choir, the Promenade Concerts, and many appearances as guest conductor with other ensembles, he enjoyed unrivalled opportunities for music-making on a great scale. Old prejudices had largely evaporated, and his interpretations were now seen to be equal to those of any conductor in the world; as an accompanist, he was regarded by many exacting soloists as pre-eminent.

His influence in these years was extended by appearances on the Brains Trust, where he effectively represented the common sense and decency of the ordinary citizen, and proved himself more than a match for the plausible intellectuals who often appeared with him. In this as in other activities he used his gifts of personality and showmanship to spread the love of music and to insist upon its place in a good life.

Sargent was now accepted as a valuable ambassador for music, and especially British music, in many parts of the world; and it was on one of his numerous foreign tours that he was taken ill. There was a temporary recovery, and he returned to conducting, but again collapsed in Chicago in July 1967. On his return he was seen to be dying. During the months that remained he continued to present himself with courage and something of the old panache, and made an unforgettable farewell visit to his devoted audience on the last night of the Proms. He died a day or two later at his home in London 3 October 1967.

Sargent's death provoked a remarkable demonstration of public sorrow and admiration. During a career in which social success had played no small part he had won the affection and loyalty of countless ordinary music-lovers who recognized his sincerity and came to share his buoyant love of life and music. He once said in jest that his career had been based on the two Ms, Messiah and Mikado, and there was an element of truth in the comment, which was a characteristic example of his unguarded spontaneity. But he could have added that it also rested on a long record of fine performances, an unfailing devotion to music, and natural endowments of exceptional brilliance.

Sargent's character was a strange blend of simplicity and sophistication, of apparent self-confidence and a deep sense of insecurity. He was an extremely generous man, but could sometimes appear vain and arrogant, displaying a frank enjoyment of fame and success which more cautious persons would have concealed, not from modesty but from fear of ridicule.

The circumstances of his early life had permanently influenced him. If he had enjoyed the privilege of attachment to a great professional orchestra and its conductors he might have become a different musician but not necessarily a better one. As it was, in the tough campaign to make his own way, he won the equipment necessary for the work he had to do, a work that greatly forwarded the interests of British music. After Sir Henry Wood's death in 1944 there was nobody except Sargent who could carry on his particular task; and when Sargent himself passed from the scene his place was not filled.

Sargent was appointed honorary D.Mus. (Oxford) in 1942 and honorary LLD (Liverpool) in 1947, the year in which he was knighted. Among his many other honours were honorary RAM, honorary FRCO, FRCM, honorary FTCL, and FRSA.

There is a bronze bust by William Timyn in the Royal Albert Hall and a portrait in oils by Sir Gerald Kelly. Another portrait in oils by John Gilroy (1967) is in the Garrick Club.

[Charles Reid, *Malcolm Sargent*, 1968; private information; personal knowledge.]

THOMAS ARMSTRONG

SASSOON, SIEGFRIED LORAINE (1886-1967), poet and prose-writer, was born 8 September 1886 at Weirleigh, near Paddock Wood in Kent, the second of the three sons of Alfred Ezra Sassoon and his wife, Georgina Theresa, daughter of Thomas and Mary Thornycroft [qq.v.], sculptors, and sister of Sir J. I. and Sir W. H. Thornycroft [qq.v.]. He was educated at Marlborough College and Clare College, Cambridge, of which he was later an honorary fellow. His father left home when Siegfried was seven and died in 1895, so that the boys were entirely brought up by their mother and her talented family.

He left Cambridge without taking a degree and lived as a country gentleman, hunting, playing cricket, collecting books, and writing poems, of which he privately printed nine pamphlets between 1906 and 1912. These early verses, on the strength of which he was encouraged by (Sir) Edmund Gosse, (Sir) Edward Marsh [qq.v.], and Robert Ross, are graceful, often imitative, full of poetical intent, but without body. He was always 'waiting for the spark from heaven to fall', and when it fell it was shrapnel, for the war of 1914-18 turned him from a versifier into a poet.

He enlisted as a trooper in the Sussex Yeomanry, and in 1915 was commissioned in the Royal Welch Fusiliers and posted to France. He soon became well known for his bravery and was nicknamed 'Mad Jack'. He was awarded the MC for bringing back a wounded lance-corporal under heavy fire, and later unsuccessfully recommended for the VC for capturing a German trench single-handed.

He was wounded in April 1917 and convalescing in England he felt impelled to write a violent attack on the conduct of the war ('I am making this statement as an act of wilful defiance of military authority, because I believe that the war is being deliberately prolonged by those who have the power to end it .ʼ. .'). This he contrived to have read out in the House of Commons, but instead of the expected court-martial, the under-secretary for war declared him to be suffering from shell shock, and he was sent to the Craiglockhart War Hospital, near Edinburgh. During his three months there he made two important friendships: with the young poet Wilfred Owen, whom he encouraged and helped, and with the psychologist and anthropologist W. H. R. Rivers, who became a loved and revered father-figure to him. Eventually he decided to fight again and early in 1918 was posted to Palestine. In May he rejoined his old battalion in France, and in July was wounded again, this time in the head. So finished his military service.

Meanwhile in *The Old Huntsman* (1917) and *Counter-Attack* (1918) his savagely realistic and compassionate war-poems had established his stature as a fully fledged poet, and despite all his later prose and verse, and his growing aversion to the label, it was mainly as a war-poet that he was regarded for the rest of his life.

In 1919 he was briefly involved in Labour politics and was the first literary editor of the reborn *Daily Herald*. This uncongenial task brought him into contact with the younger poet Edmund Blunden, who became a lifelong friend. In 1920 he read his poems on a lecture tour in the United States. Thereafter he lived in London, hunted for a few seasons in Gloucestershire, and brought out volumes of poetry—*Selected Poems* (1925), *Satirical Poems* (1926), and *The Heart's Journey* (1927)—which greatly increased his reputation and represent his full flowering as a poet.

Then he turned to prose, and in 1928 published *Memoirs of a Fox-Hunting Man*, anonymously, though his name appeared in the second impression. This lightly fictionalized autobiography of his early years in Kent, in which he figures as the narrator George Sherston, was an immediate success, was awarded the Hawthornden and James Tait Black memorial prizes, and was quickly accepted as a classic of its kind—an elegy for a way of life which had gone for ever. He continued the story in *Memoirs of an Infantry Officer* (1930) and *Sherston's Progress* (1936), and the three books appeared in one volume as *The Complete Memoirs of George Sherston* (1937).

In 1933 Sassoon married Hester, daughter of the late Sir Stephen Herbert Gatty, chief justice of Gibraltar (1895-1905), and they settled at Heytesbury House, near Warminster in Wiltshire, where Sassoon spent the rest of his life. Their son was born in 1936, and, although the marriage ended in sadness and separation, at

Heytesbury Sassoon continued to find the beauty and the solitude that his writing needed, and he became steadily less inclined to leave home for any reason.

Once established there he began to write his factual autobiography, beginning with *The Old Century and Seven More Years* (1938), his favourite among his books, dedicated to his loved and admired friend (Sir) Max Beerbohm [q.v.], and continuing with *The Weald of Youth* (1942) and *Siegfried's Journey* (1945), which carried his story up to 1920. In 1948 he published a critical biography of George Meredith, and all the time he was writing poetry, published in private or public editions, which culminated in the *Collected Poems* of 1947 (enlarged edition 1961).

In 1957 he was received into the Roman Catholic Church, and the comfort and joy with which his religion filled his last years was celebrated in a spiritual anthology of his poetry, *The Path to Peace* (1960), printed and published by his dear friends, the nuns of Stanbrook Abbey.

Sassoon was strikingly distinguished in appearance, his large bold features expressed the courage and sensitivity of his nature, and he retained his slimness and agility into old age, playing cricket well into his seventies. A dedicated artist, he hated publicity but craved the right sort of recognition. He was appointed CBE in 1951, and was pleased by the award of the Queen's medal for poetry in 1957 and by his honorary D.Litt. at Oxford in 1965, but pretended that such honours were merely a nuisance. A natural recluse, he yet much enjoyed the company of chosen friends, many of them greatly his juniors, and was a witty and lively talker. He loved books and pictures and music, was a brilliant letter-writer, and kept copious diaries.

Sassoon died at Heytesbury 1 September 1967, and was buried in Mells churchyard near his friend Monsignor Ronald Knox [q.v.]. A portrait by Glyn Philpot is in the Fitzwilliam Museum, Cambridge.

[Sassoon's own writings; private information; personal knowledge.]

RUPERT HART-DAVIS

SAUNDERS, SIR ALEXANDER MORRIS CARR- (1886-1966), biologist, sociologist, and academic administrator. [See CARR-SAUNDERS.]

SCARBROUGH, eleventh EARL OF (1896-1969), public servant. [See LUMLEY, LAWRENCE ROGER.]

SCOTT, CYRIL MEIR (1879-1970), composer and writer, was born at Oxton, near Liverpool, 27 September 1879, the third child of Henry Scott and his wife, Mary Griffiths. He had an elder sister; his elder brother had died in infancy. Henry Scott (1843-1918), of Staffordshire descent, was a businessman and a scholar of biblical Greek. His wife Mary, of Welsh ancestry and delicate in health, was musical, and of conventional church-going habits. Cyril Scott's sensitive childhood was spent in middle-class domestic surroundings. The music of the church and of the commonly heard barrel-organ influenced his early improvising at the piano and he began to compose at the age of seven.

After a brief spell at day-school he was enrolled in 1891 at the Hoch Conservatorium in Frankfurt am Main to study piano with Lazarro Uzielli and theory with Engelbert Humperdinck. Eighteen months later he returned to Liverpool to continue his education with a tutor, and piano with Steudner-Welsing. There he met a Swiss merchant Hans Lüthy, a liberal thinker, who greatly influenced Scott's reading, especially in esoteric literature. Filled with what he called 'dogmatic agnosticism' he returned to Frankfurt to study with the renowned Iwan Knorr (1853-1916). Amongst his fellow pupils were Roger Quilter, H. Balfour Gardiner [qq.v.], Norman O'Neill, and Percy Grainger, with whom he was later associated in the Frankfurt Group. The training these musicians received at Frankfurt, so different from the English academies, was to prove a liberalizing force in British music.

Also at Frankfurt Scott met the poet Stefan George who encouraged in him not only his poetic instinct, but a preoccupation with his artistic personality. Through George he met also the stained-glass artist Melchior Lechter, whose almost medieval life-style impressed Scott, and in 1898 he returned to Liverpool with a quite un-English panache, affecting long hair and a stock, but with a seriousness of mind that refuted any charge of affectation.

At Liverpool he met Charles Bonnier, professor of French literature at the university college, who encouraged Scott's interest in poetry. In 1909 and 1910 Scott published translations of Baudelaire and Stefan George. Three volumes of his own very individual poetry were also published. George was instrumental in having Scott's early symphony produced at Darmstadt and in 1900 Hans Richter played the 'Heroic Suite' in Manchester and Liverpool. Both were later discarded, but the Piano Quartet, in which in 1901 Fritz Kreisler played was published by Boosey as opus 16. In 1903 a further symphony was given at the Promenade Concerts, but was also withdrawn to be reworked later as *Three Orchestral Dances*.

The publication of several exotic, but quickly popular, piano pieces (and some settings of the poet Ernest Dowson) earned Scott a reputation which was to overshadow his larger-scale works in Britain. Despite the publication by Stainer & Bell (1924) of the Piano Quintet (for which he won a Carnegie award), Scott's growing reputation was established mainly on the Continent, following the publication (by Schott) in 1909 of his Violin Sonata, and the advocacy of Debussy.

Composition (*A Christmas Overture*, 1906; 'Nativity Hymn', 1913; 'Tallahassee Suite', 1911; and the unconventional Piano Sonata, as op. 66 but later revised, 1909) was complemented by his deepening interest in esoteric philosophies which embraced not only the spiritual but the physical, leading him to naturopathy and homeopathy (and the publication of widely circulated booklets on *Black Molasses*, *Sleeplessness*, and *Cider Vinegar*). He developed his interest in astrological influences, to which he attributed his recovery from pneumonia in childhood. Such preoccupations encouraged his exploratory vision in music, and these ideas being more readily acceptable abroad, he returned to Vienna in 1913 at the invitation of Frau Alma Mahler, the composer's widow, who had been much impressed by the Violin Sonata. There the overture *Princess Maleine* was performed. Later, as *A Festival Overture*, it won anonymously the *Daily Telegraph* prize in 1934.

Interest in England was not entirely lacking, and with performances abroad curtailed by the war, Scott played the solo part in his new Piano Concerto under the baton of (Sir) Thomas Beecham [q.v.] in 1915. Publication of his books *The Philosophy of Modernism* (1917) and *The Initiate* trilogy (1920) was followed by *Music—its Secret Influence throughout the Ages* (1933), developing those theosophical ideas which stemmed largely from his encounter with the supernatural 'Masters' in 1921, to whose spiritual guidance he attributed his direction in music and his marriage that same year to Rose Laure Allatini (Eunice Buckley). His opera *The Alchemist* (for which he had written both words and music) was finally given at Essen in 1925.

In 1939 his life was again disrupted by war and by 1943 it was amicably agreed that his wife and two children (a son and a daughter) should move to London whilst he, with his companion Marjorie Hartston (to whose life Scott's occult philosophies had brought much comfort), should have the use of Percy Grainger's cottage at Pevensey.

Scott had decided to abandon music—but under these influences began work on another opera *Maureen O'Mara*. Compositions at this time were written, like the vast *Hymn of Unity*, in a mood of idealism—but the last years were ones of contentment. Moving to Eastbourne he lived quietly, earning recognition as far afield as Chicago and Australia. A Cyril Scott Society was formed in 1962, and he was elected honorary RAM in 1969. Scott's last appearance in London was in 1969 at a performance by Moura Lympany of his first concerto. He died at his home in Eastbourne 31 December 1970. His ashes were buried in the churchyard of St. Nicolas, Pevensey.

Scott's work, though often in a delicate and mystical tonal world, is far from nebulous. His pioneering in the realms of sound, then largely unexplored, showed a striking independence of mind—and a freedom of tonal resource that was stimulated by the range of his thought and philosophy. That this freedom was expressed, not by sensational means, is the justification of his need for a wholly individual and new style which, in his *The Philosophy of Modernism*, he attributed to a 'certain divine discontent'.

A portrait of Scott by George Hall Neale (1932) was shown at the Royal Festival Hall, London, in the Four-in-One Exhibition (1979), which commemorated the lives of Scott, John Ireland, Sir Thomas Beecham, and Frank Bridge [qq.v.].

[Cyril Scott, *Bone of Contention*, 1969; *Musical Times*, September 1959; A. Eaglefield Hull, *Cyril Scott*, 1918; *Journal of the British Institute of Recorded Sound*, no. 61, January 1976; *Composer*, no. 50, winter 1973/4; private information.]

COLIN SCOTT-SUTHERLAND

SCOTT, JOHN WILLIAM ROBERTSON (1866-1962), journalist, author and foundereditor of *The Countryman*. [See ROBERTSON SCOTT.]

SEMPILL, nineteenth BARON (1893-1965), airman. [See FORBES-SEMPILL, WILLIAM FRANCIS.]

SEWELL, ROBERT BERESFORD SEYMOUR (1880-1964), zoologist, was born at Leamington 5 March 1880, the second son of the Revd Arthur Sewell of Weymouth, who, a schoolmaster and chaplain to the Order of St. John of Jerusalem, lived to the age of 106. His mother, Mary Lee, was the daughter of Henry Franks Waring, a solicitor in Lyme Regis. Both sides of the family were of Wessex stock. He was related to Elizabeth Missing Sewell and her brothers, Henry, James Edwards, Richard Clarke, and William, all five of whom are in this Dictionary.

At Weymouth College the young Sewell tried classics and then mathematics with little success. He then took to biological science and never looked back. After a short period studying zoology at University College, London, he went in 1899 as an exhibitioner to Christ's College, Cambridge, where he was helped and encouraged by (Sir) A. E. Shipley [q.v.]. In 1902 he obtained a first class in part i of the natural sciences tripos, and in 1903 also a first in part ii (physiology, and human anatomy with physiology). For two subsequent years he stayed in Cambridge teaching anatomy and physiology. However, in 1905 medicine called and he entered St. Bartholomew's Hospital, qualifying two years later after many humanizing experiences in the wards.

Then began Sewell's time in India which dominated the rest of his life. In 1908 he joined the Indian Medical Service and was posted as medical officer to the 67th and 84th Punjabi Regiments; but his love of zoology continued to blossom and in 1910 he joined the Marine Survey and the museum in Calcutta as surgeon-naturalist. This involved spending five or six months each year on the *Investigator* and the remainder based on the museum in Calcutta. His primary job was to look after the health of the ship's company, but since hardly anyone was ever ill, biology and oceanography occupied nearly all his time. Initially his publications covered a wide range, including freshwater and terrestrial fauna, but he came to focus on that large group of microscopic Crustacea, the *Copepoda*, on which he soon became an authority. In 1911–13 he was seconded as professor of biology at Calcutta Medical College. Then, on 5 August 1914, the day after the declaration of war, while on leave in England he married Dorothy (died 1931), daughter of William and Matilda Dean, of Chichester. He went at once on military duty, first to Aden as port health officer and later to Sinai and Palestine, where he was mentioned in dispatches.

After the war Sewell returned to India as superintendent and, in 1925, director of the Zoological Survey, living mainly in Calcutta, but establishing wide-ranging connections with Indian scientists. At intervals he continued his former work at sea and evidently found the clubbish male life aboard ship much to his liking. In 1931 he retired from the Indian Medical Service and was appointed CIE.

Then began the third stage of Sewell's life, based mainly in Cambridge, where his old friend John Stanley Gardiner was shortly to retire from the professorship of zoology. Plans were maturing for the John Murray Expedition to the Indian Ocean with the *Mabahiss*, a ship loaned by the Egyptian Government, and Sewell was appointed its leader. This expedition, begun in 1933, lasted more than a year and was a great success: it applied to tropical waters for the first time principles on the role

of light and of chemistry in the seas' productivity; it discovered orographical features of the ocean bed and an azoic region of deep water. Sewell's personal interest continued in the small Crustacea of the plankton and the expedition's collections kept him busy for the rest of his life. He was set in the mould of the great nineteenth-century zoologists, concerned with taxonomy, evolution, and the interaction between organism and environment. Geographical distribution fascinated him and in later years he contributed much biological evidence to Wegner's theory of continental drift which was first embraced by the geophysicists, then discarded, and later confirmed.

During his working retirement at Cambridge, in addition to producing notable scientific papers, Sewell edited more than a score of the volumes of the *Fauna of British India* which stand as a major contribution of zoological science to that subcontinent. In 1946 the independent Government persuaded him to tour India to advise on the expansion of zoological studies and of fisheries. Sewell also had much contact with Indian students in England. Honours came his way: FRS in 1934, presidency of the Linnean Society (1952–5), and of the Ray Society (1950–3). From India came many recognitions including the presidency of the Royal Asiatic Society of Bengal (1931–3); the Barclay memorial medal (1931); the Annandale memorial medal (1947); and the honorary fellowship of the Indian Academy of Sciences, Bangalore (1949), and of the Zoological Society of India (1949).

Sewell was not a man of large stature, nor was he particularly prominent in social qualities, and in his latter days he became somewhat crippled with arthritis. But during his last thirty years he was a well-loved figure in Cambridge and he contributed in no small way to the foundations of modern oceanography. There were two daughters of his marriage and both attained distinction, one in the nursing profession and the other as an English scholar. Sewell died in a nursing-home in Cambridge 11 February 1964.

[C. F. A. Pantin in *Biographical Memoirs of Fellows of the Royal Society*, vol. xi, 1965; *Proceedings of the Linnean Society*, 1963–4, p. 101; personal knowledge.]

E. BARTON WORTHINGTON

SHEEPSHANKS, SIR THOMAS HERBERT (1895–1964), civil servant, was born in the Bishop's Palace, Norwich, 10 January 1895; he was the youngest of the twelve surviving children of the Right Revd John Sheepshanks, bishop of Norwich 1893–1910, and his wife, Margaret, daughter of Dr William Hall Ryott, of Thirsk. Both his father and mother were of strong character and distinguished ancestry—his father's side could boast Anne, John, and Richard Sheepshanks, and his mother's, both Guy Fawkes and Oliver Cromwell [qq.v.]—and Tom Sheepshanks inherited valuable qualities from each. His father as a young man served as a missionary in British Columbia amongst lumbermen, miners, and agricultural workers, and before returning home had crossed China, Mongolia, and Siberia in a little mule-cart in which he slept. The bishop died in 1912, and his wife, who survived him by more than thirty years, refused, despite the threat of air raids during the war of 1939–45, to leave her home in the Close at Norwich, and when her distinguished son visited her she insisted that he went to bed early and ate a proper breakfast.

Like three of his five brothers, Sheepshanks was a scholar at Winchester. He went up to Trinity College, Oxford, as a scholar in 1913, and like so many of his generation volunteered on the outbreak of war; he joined the Norfolk Regiment, and later served in France attached to the Suffolk Regiment, reaching the rank of captain. He did not return to Oxford after the war but entered the Ministry of Health, where he was one of a team of outstanding young civil servants, many of whom rose to high rank in various government departments; promotion was slow in most departments, and Sheepshanks had to wait for seventeen years, acquiring a wide experience of the various branches of the Ministry, until he was promoted assistant secretary in 1936.

In 1935 a step had been taken which was to determine his career: the increasing tension in Europe forced the Government to take measures to protect the civil population against air raids. A small branch had been set up in the Home Office called the Air Raid Precautions Department, the first move in the process which eventually led to Civil Defence and the establishment, on the outbreak of war, of the Ministry of Home Security. Staff was recruited for the new branch from retired Indian and colonial civil servants and from other departments. The most important decision taken was that the ARP services should be organized through the local authorities, which insisted that these services should be grant-aided. Home Office experience of grants was in essence limited to the police grant: it was essential that the Office should be reinforced and strengthened by the appointment of a senior official from the Ministry of Health with wide experience of the local government machine and of the grant system. The choice fell on Sheepshanks who was seconded to the ARP Department in 1937.

There he quickly made his mark. He was supremely competent, ready to take responsibility for what was to be done, to support and encourage those who were engaged in doing it, and always ready to remain on the job and see it through. He quickly established such a position that he became the general counsellor of his colleagues, a development aided by the fortuitous circumstances that, in the first place, he was accustomed to dealing with local authorities and their associations, and had won their respect and confidence; secondly, his immediate superiors were inhibited, either by peculiarities of temperament or by lack of parliamentary experience, from dealing with the political aspects, often acutely controversial, of the work in hand. So to him fell the responsibility for parliamentary business, a responsibility greater than would ordinarily attach to his rank of assistant under-secretary of state. He was the right-hand man of Sir John Anderson (later Viscount Waverley, q.v.) when as lord privy seal Anderson was in charge of the Bill for the Civil Defence Act of 1939. (Sir) Austin Strutt was associated with him in that work, and Sheepshanks shared with him and a couple of clerks working under great pressure in the routine of assembling briefs to get them off to the minister in time. No wonder those who worked for him in quite humble grades felt affection for him: he would give a hand, was tireless himself, and never forgot to say 'thank you'.

On the outbreak of war in 1939 Sheepshanks was made principal assistant secretary at the Ministry of Home Security, becoming deputy secretary in 1942. He played a major role in putting the new Ministry on its feet and keeping it there. The Ministry needed a person of his strong character to cope with some of the personalities who had become regional commissioners in 1939; before he left it he had earned their respect and confidence as a man from whom they would receive sound advice, wise counsel, and help in solving their problems.

In 1943 he was given a special assignment: he was seconded with Sir Thomas Phillips to the minister of reconstruction, Lord Woolton [q.v.], to work out the practical application of the report of Sir William (later Lord) Beveridge [q.v.] on social insurance and allied services: it was common knowledge in Whitehall that Sheepshanks was the draftsman of the white paper on social security. So it was no surprise when he was appointed deputy secretary of the newly established Ministry of National Insurance in 1944. But he did not stay there long, spending 1945–6 in the Treasury as an under-secretary; from there he moved to the Ministry of Town and Country Planning, of which he was soon appointed permanent secretary. In this capacity he was heavily involved in the Bills for the New Towns Act of 1946, and the Town and Country Planning Act of 1947. He was transferred in 1951 to be permanent secretary of the Ministry of Local Government and Planning (later renamed Housing and Local Government), where he remained until his retirement in 1955. He was appointed CB in 1941, KBE in 1944, and KCB in 1948.

Sheepshanks was a man of strong character, high intellectual qualities, and great administrative ability; he had an ingenious mind, and his wide and varied experience was seen in his capacity for careful, wise, and resolute guidance. He was a skilful negotiator who could be blunt and forthright, but those who dealt with him knew that he was always open to argument. Indeed, one of his peculiar traits was that a man with such a calm and collected mind could be so explosive in his speech: the contrast between the extreme caution with which he handled any matter of a political aspect and the austerity with which he expressed himself on paper, and his occasional verbal outbursts, surprised those who did not know him well. He had that extra gift which sensed what would and would not be acceptable to the House of Commons, and ministers of different parties and in different departments were indebted to this gift. He was a skilful draftsman with a persuasive pen which ministers found of real value. He was respected both by those above and below him; those who worked with him were proud to be members of his team, knowing that they might be driven hard, but that he would drive himself hardest of all, and that in times of difficulty he would be as firm and steady as a rock.

He married in 1921 Elizabeth Creemer (died 1977), younger daughter of James Calvert, JP, by whom he had two sons and a daughter. The death of the elder son, a young man of great promise, in Tunisia in 1943, and of the daughter in 1958, were heavy blows to their parents who took a special pride in their family. Apart from his work, Sheepshanks's main interests were his family, reading, and a little golf. On retirement he took on no further governmental work, but concerned himself part time in an undertaking with which his family had an interest. He died in Woking 1 February 1964. He was slightly above average height and sturdily built, with an appearance of solidity and latent strength. Neat and tidy in habits and dress, he avoided every kind of affectation or eccentricity. His spectacles, however, gave him a decidedly owlish look: his quick penetrating glance and the accompanying sharp, upward movement of his head sometimes gave the impression of an angry owl about to pounce, but in repose the effect was of the matured

wisdom with which the owl is traditionally associated.

[*The Times*, 4 February 1964; D. E. Muir (Sheepshanks's daughter), *Lift the Curtain*, 1955; private information; personal knowledge.]   AUSTIN STRUTT

SHEREK, (JULES) HENRY (1900-1967), theatre impresario, was born at 2 Guilford Street, London, 23 April 1900, the younger son of Bernard Scherek, merchant, and his wife, Margarette Jacoby. His schooling was scrappy and unconventional because his father who, after retiring from business in middle life, had become an international theatrical agent, had only one strongly held principle about education: the need for fluency in foreign languages. The boys were therefore sent, when Henry was nine, to the Waren Gymnasium in Germany. He detested this: the discipline was stern and his schoolfellows were young fire-eaters preparing themselves to be officers in the Kaiser's army; but it taught him fluent German. A few years later a less tough school in Switzerland taught him French.

Without a drop of British blood in him, Henry Sherek grew up a passionate patriot for the country of his birth and when war broke out in 1914 he took advantage of the fact that he was a big mature-looking boy to enlist in the army at fifteen. He saw service in the Near East and was severely wounded. After the war and a few more desultory attempts at education, he went at the end of 1923 to the United States, where he spent some eighteen months working first for David Belasco, then for a theatrical agency.

Returning to London he joined his father's agency and carried it on when his father died. He found the work pleasant and satisfying. The qualities which were later to carry him to a high place among play producers were such as to make very easy the less responsible enterprises of an agent. He was a very big man and this, combined with an extraordinary energy and zest for whatever he happened to be doing, made him a noticeable figure in any company.

Born as he had been into the world of entertainment, he enjoyed it at all its levels; but this catholicity of judgement did not blunt his natural good taste. He was ready to like almost any kind of thing, but it had to be good of its kind. He was in fact in all his dealings with life a rare mixture of gourmand and gourmet.

This was true of him literally as well as figuratively. As a boy he had had an enormous appetite and he grew up to be a trencherman of fame. Indeed, in his later years he became a compulsive eater and put on a great deal of weight. This increase of bulk did not seem to affect his energy, although it may well have shortened his life. Yet he never let quantity impair quality. Both in food and wine his choice was excellent.

Likeable, humorous, and kindly, he was a popular figure in all parts of the world to which his talent-spotting journeys took him. He found the life amusing, and its rewards, though uncertain, were enough to keep a pleasure-loving bachelor in comfort—even in luxury, since in 1936 he was engaged by the Dorchester Hotel to supply them with cabaret revues and was given quarters in the hotel. In the same year, however, he realized that a bachelor existence was no longer what he wanted. A friendship of some years with a rising actress Pamela Carme (in private life Kathleen Pamela Mary Corona Boscawen, daughter of the seventh Viscount Falmouth) deepened into love, and in 1937 they were married. His wife ceased to act but became his business partner in management.

From the very first, Sherek showed that as a manager he intended to set his standard of quality high. His opening venture, made before his marriage in the hope of providing him with some working capital, was a light comedy which failed; but his chance for a real start came very soon afterwards, when he was offered the British rights in Robert Sherwood's anti-war play *Idiot's Delight*. It took courage to produce such a piece for a public sick of war talk; but he rose to the occasion and took the risk. The play opened at the Apollo on 22 March 1938 and had an excellent run. Another Sherwood play *The Petrified Forest* came his way a year or two later, but by the time it was staged at the Globe in 1942 Sherek had rejoined the army and had to present it in partnership.

He served from 1941 until he was invalided out in 1944 with the rank of major; among his appointments was that of chief weapon training officer in the Fighting School at Edinburgh. By 1945 he was back in harness as a play producer and adding quickly to his reputation. Over 110 plays were presented or produced by him in London, New York, and Paris. In 1947 and the years following he was sustained by the great success both at home and in America of a fine play, *Edward, My Son*, and this was followed in 1949 by an achievement which must rank as the peak of his career. Reading *The Cocktail Party* by T. S. Eliot [q.v.] he was struck both by its quality and its stage potential and made up his mind, come what might, to produce it.

This decision called once again for his special gift of courage, for the play, obscure as it was and written in a subtle form of verse peculiar to Eliot, might well have been rejected by the ordinary playgoing public; and indeed Sherek did take the precaution of giving it a trial trip at the Edinburgh Festival of 1949. But such was the energy, the understanding, and the care in casting which he brought to his task that the play had a triumphant progress, first in New York and subsequently in London. The oddly assorted team—the ebullient Sherek, the austere Eliot, and his meticulous-minded director, E. Martin Browne—worked so well together that two more of Eliot's plays (*The Confidential Clerk*, 1953, and *The Elder Statesman*, 1958) were similarly launched by them to success in the West End.

Among the many other plays of merit for which Sherek was responsible were *Boys in Brown* (Duchess, 1947); and *Under Milk Wood* (New Theatre, 1956); but perhaps *The Affair* (Strand, 1961) calls for special mention. This stage version by Ronald Millar of a novel by Sir C. P. (later Lord) Snow hung fire among the London managers because it dealt with the internal affairs of a Cambridge college and was thought therefore to have no popular appeal. Characteristically Sherek took that risk and equally characteristically scored a success.

He died 23 September 1967 in Venice after some years of retirement in Geneva.

[Henry Sherek, *Not in front of the Children*, 1959; private information; personal knowledge.]　　　　　　　　　　　W. A. DARLINGTON

SHERIDAN, CLARE CONSUELO (1885–1970), artist and sculptor, was born in London 9 September 1885, the only daughter and second of the three children of Moreton Frewen, landowner and sportsman-adventurer, and his wife, Clara, eldest of the three daughters of Leonard Jerome of New York, the grandfather of Sir Winston Churchill. Clare (who was christened 'Claire' but dropped the 'i') was educated by governesses at her father's Sussex home and at Innishannon, his property in county Cork. She also attended, briefly, a Paris convent and a finishing school in Germany. Holidays were sometimes spent with Churchill and Leslie cousins. At the age of seventeen Clare 'came out' under the aegis of her aunts Jennie (the wife of Lord Randolph Churchill, q.v., who died in 1895) and Leonie (the wife of Sir John Leslie of Glaslough). A restless, artistic girl, she did not take to the round of balls and country-house parties. She spoke fluent French and German but the education bestowed by various unhappy governesses gave her no grounding in English. She tried to educate herself by serious reading, and in this endeavour she was helped by William (known as Wilfred) Frederick Sheridan, a London stockbroker, the son of Algernon Thomas Brinsley

Sheridan, of Frampton Court · in Dorset. Wilfred was amused to learn she had never heard of his great-great-grandfather Richard Brinsley Sheridan [q.v.] and thought he must be the maker of Sheraton furniture.

As well as sketching with her friend Princess Margaret of Connaught, the niece of King Edward VII and later married to Crown Prince Gustaf of Sweden, Clare attempted to write novels. Her parents' friends, Robert Hichens, Rudyard Kipling, and above all Henry James [qq.v.], took pains to advise her but she was discouraged by the opinions of George Moore [q.v.].

In 1910 Clare married Wilfred Sheridan at St. Margaret's, Westminster, and by the outbreak of war she had borne two daughters, Margaret and Elizabeth. She rediscovered her artistic talent when Elizabeth died in February 1914. In her grief Clare sought to model a little angel for the child's grave and as her hands created this monument she knew that her only desire henceforth was to be a sculptor (she refused the term sculptress). Wilfred Sheridan was killed in the battle of Loos in September 1915, a few days after the birth of her son Richard at Frampton Court. Clare remained with her parents-in-law until she settled in a small London studio where she could study under (Sir) William Reid Dick [q.v.]. Her first exhibition under the auspices of the National Portrait Society aroused great interest. Henceforth she was established. Commissions included Asquith the former prime minister and F. E. Smith (later Lord Birkenhead, q.v.). She modelled a head of (Sir) Winston Churchill, her cousin, while he tried to paint her.

The idyll ceased when in 1920 the first Soviet trade delegation reached London. It was headed by Kamenev, who invited Clare to Moscow. Having been refused a visa she boldly set sail with the delegation to Stockholm, where Kamenev procured her an Estonian visa. Civil war was raging in the Crimea and Winston Churchill, the secretary of state for war, was pressing for Allied intervention. With displeasure he learned that his cousin was living in Moscow doing busts of Sinoviev, Dzherzhinsky, Kamenev, Lenin, and Trotsky. When she returned to England Clare found that London society ignored her and Churchill preferred not to see her. Angrily she departed for America.

Clare could have become a successful social portrait sculptor but that was not her desire. After publishing her Russian diaries in 1921 (entitled *Mayfair to Moscow* in America and *Russian Portraits* in England), she travelled in America and Mexico, made friends with (Sir) Charles Chaplin, and was astounded when newspaper columnists announced their engage-

ment. She was introduced to Herbert Swope, editor of the New York *World*, and in the summer of 1922 she returned to Europe as that paper's roving correspondent. Within a short time she had made her name by obtaining scoop after scoop. In the Irish civil war she was the only reporter to interview both Michael Collins and his Republican opponent Rory O'Connor who was besieged in the Four Courts in Dublin. She then accepted a commission to cover the Greek-Turkish war and her vivid accounts of the terrible evacuation of Smyrna brought her to the top rank of professional war correspondents. She interviewed Ataturk, and, in Bulgaria, Stamboulisky, the peasant premier, and King Boris. Then, after interviewing the newly crowned Queen Marie of Romania, she went to Lausanne to cover the international conference. Mussolini invited her to view his nascent organization of young Fascists in Rome, but forbade her to publish his conversations in the New York *World*. Clare, who by now regarded herself as a 'journalist in bronze', returned to America where her children were being schooled and commissions for busts were always available.

A second trip to the Soviet Union, in 1923, proved disillusioning, but she dutifully fulfilled her contract, providing two articles a week for America. However, she had now become *persona non grata* with the Russians. Despite this, on her return to London Clare dared to cajole from Rakovsky, the first Soviet representative in London (who had been governor of the Ukraine), a visa for herself and her brother to tour South Russia on a motor bicycle, which they called 'Satanella'. In 1924, with Clare in the side-car with the luggage, Frewen chugged across Germany and Poland to the Ukrainian border, and continued onwards to Odessa, where they spent a week.

Having arrived safely by ship in Constantinople, Clare decided to take her two children to live on the Bosporus. There she wrote another book, *Across Europe with Satanella* (1925). She then gave up journalism for her true *métier* of sculpture, but this Constantinople sojourn resulted in another book, *A Turkish Kaleidoscope* (1926). In 1925 Clare moved to Algeria where she built a house on the edge of the Sahara (Bab el M'Cid at Biskra). Throughout the remainder of the 1920s and 1930s Clare concentrated on working as a sculptor. However, she had not ceased writing for in 1927 appeared *Nuda Veritas* and in 1936 *Arab Interlude*, among other books which she wrote at the time. In 1937, her son Dick died of appendicitis, aged twenty-one, at Constantine in the Sahara, and as Clare had discovered her true talent through the death of a baby in 1914, now she developed into a new branch of art through another grief. Taking a huge Sussex oak tree from her home Brede Place, she carved it into a memorial for her son. Before, she had done busts of such men as Gandhi, Serge Lifar, and Keyserling; from now on she found artistic fulfilment in carving wood. Seeking solace and to improve her carving technique she spent a summer in an art colony on a Red Indian reservation in the Rocky Mountains, and on returning to London her exhibition of Indian heads whittled from forest trees gave her a new fame. From this experience came *Redskin Interlude* (1938).

During the war, in 1942, she made a bust of Churchill in bronze. After war ended Clare entered the Roman Catholic Church, and moved to The Spanish Arch in Galway. Here she continued to carve and model. Her final memoirs, *To the Four Winds*, were published in 1957.

Clare Sheridan's works are spread over England and Ireland. The collection from Brede Place owned by Jonathan Frewen is often shown at Rye Art Gallery. Her earliest work is in the churchyard at Pepper Harrow, near Guildford. Her bust of Asquith can be seen at the Oxford Union and her second head of Churchill at Chartwell and Harrow School. The most beautiful of her wood carvings, *Rising Christ*, is in the Church of St. Catherine, Hoogstraeten, Belgium; a fine cherrywood *Crucifixion* hangs in Salthill Church, Galway; a dark wood madonna, silver-crowned, stands at Allington Castle, Maidstone, Kent; and several superb wood carvings are often on show at Charlston Manor, Seaford. Many of Clare's works in wood, alabaster, and terracotta were given to friends all over the world. In her last years she sought to work not commercially, but as a medieval artist might, in return for board and stimulating talk.

She died 31 May 1970, and was buried beside Brede church, where stands the great oak madonna memorial to her son, which is probably her best work. A portrait of Clare in her studio by Sir Oswald Birley is in the possession of Lady Birley. In 1919 a bust of her was done by (Sir) Jacob Epstein.

[Clare Sheridan, *To the Four Winds*, 1957 (autobiography); Anita Leslie, *Cousin Clare*, 1976; Mary Motley (daughter), *Morning Glory*, 1961; Shane Leslie, *Studies in Sublime Failure*, 1932; unpublished diaries of Captain Oswald Frewen, RN; private information; personal knowledge.]   ANITA LESLIE

SHERRIFF, GEORGE (1898–1967), explorer and plant collector, was born at Carronvale, Larbert, Stirlingshire, 3 May 1898, the fourth son and youngest of the six children of George Sherriff, a business man and noted amateur photographer, and his wife, Catharine, an ardent horticulturist, daughter of Alexander Nimmo, a business man of Falkirk. Educated at Sedbergh, where he excelled at games, Sherriff, like his brothers, was bent on an army career and went to the Royal Military Academy, Woolwich: he was commissioned in the Royal Garrison Artillery early in 1918. He fought in the Great War in France, where two of his brothers were killed, and he was gassed in June 1918, spending the rest of the war in hospital. In 1919 Sherriff was sent to India and served in a mountain battery at Nowshera, Waziristan, on the North-West Frontier, for which he was mentioned in dispatches. On leave, he delighted in visiting remote districts and the mountains, and when he was invited in 1927 to be British vice-consul in Kashgar, Chinese Turkestan, he readily accepted. He later became acting consul-general until he resigned in 1931, believing, unlike his superiors, that Communist influence in Turkestan would lead, as it has done, to the subjection of that territory.

Whilst at Kashgar, Sherriff took every opportunity to travel widely, reaching Tien Shan in the north and the Khotan in the east. In September 1929 he met Frank Ludlow (1885–1972), who was on his way to the Tien Shan mountains and had been invited to spend the winter at Kashgar by the consul, Frederick Williamson: their interests in ornithology, travel, and plants started a lifelong friendship. Williamson became political officer in Sikkim and was able at the time of Sherriff's resignation to provide passports for both Sherriff and Ludlow to travel to Tibet, thus enabling them to put into operation the plans they had made in 1929. In spring 1933 Ludlow, Sherriff, and Williamson, with his wife, travelled along the central highway in Bhutan from Ha to Bumthang, where they met the maharaja. Sherriff and Ludlow entered Tibet by the Kang La (La = pass), striking the Lhasa road to Nangkartse, and turned west to Gyantse and so back to India: they made 500 gatherings of plants.

This journey initiated a plan to work gradually eastwards through Tibet, collecting plants and birds along the main Himalayan range, until they reached the Tsangpo. In 1934 they worked the Tsona and Mago districts: despite the monsoon and malaria, they procured 600 gatherings of plants. In 1936 they returned, with Dr Kenneth Lumsden, to Tsona, crossing the Nyala La (17,150 feet) into the valley of Chayul Chu, which they followed to Lung. They encountered a semi-barbaric tribe of Daphlas and reached the valleys of the Char Chu and Tsari Chu. Tsari was sacred ground where cultivation and even grazing were forbidden, and the botanical spoils were thus remarkably rich: of the 69 species of *Rhododendron* collected 15 were new to science, as were 14 of the 59 *Primula* species. Whilst Ludlow and Lumsden moved on, Sherriff remained in Tsari, making a circuit of the holy mountain, Takpa Shiri, and discovering the pink *Meconopsis sherriffii*, named, as were six other Himalayan plant species, in his honour. They returned with nearly 2,000 gatherings of pressed plants, two crates of living plants, and innumerable packets of seed. The following year, Sherriff spent the flowering season in Central Bhutan collecting near 'Black Mountain' over 600 gatherings. In 1938 Sherriff and Ludlow were joined by (Sir) George Taylor of the British Museum (Natural History) in their exploration of the drainage of the Tsangpo from near Molo on the Lilung Chu down to Gyala, where they collected herbarium material in vast quantities (almost 5,000 gatherings): 'Taylor collects everything from mosses and fungi upwards to lilies' (Ludlow).

During the war of 1939-45, which temporarily put an end to Ludlow's and Sherriff's plans, Sherriff resumed military service, commanding an anti-aircraft battery in the Digboi oilfields of Assam. Later he entered into political activities in Sikkim, when in charge of the Tibet wool trade in Gangtok and Kalimpong. In April 1943 he was sent as Ludlow's successor to take charge of the British Mission in Lhasa, shortly after marrying Betty, youngest daughter of the Very Revd John Anderson Graham, DD, CIE [q.v.], missionary and founder of the Kalimpong Homes for needy Anglo-Indian children. (There were no children of the marriage.) Continuing to collect within a 60-mile radius of Lhasa, Sherriff made an important series of films of now defunct Tibetan ceremonies. After two years in Lhasa, he settled at Kalimpong in north-east India and, in 1946, with his wife, Ludlow, and Colonel Henry Elliot of the Indian Medical Service, he set out for south-east Tibet and the great gorge of the Tsangpo. The Sherriffs descended the Po Tsangpo to its junction with the Tsangpo at Gompo Ne, but Sherriff began to suffer from an overstrained heart, due to having helped one of his porters over a high pass in 1938, and he and his wife reluctantly left for lower altitudes in India, while Ludlow remained to explore the gorge. In 1949 Ludlow and Sherriff retired from India but both had been planning a final expedition—Sherriff to the Mishmi Hills and Ludlow to the Tsangpo Gorge. Since permits for both were refused, they went to Bhutan with the maharaja's blessing, separating and working the whole of the

alpine and temperate flora from west to east. Ludlow took the west, Sherriff the centre, and Dr J. H. Hicks, the medical officer, with Mrs Sherriff, the east: 5,000 gatherings were made.

The expeditions were carried out almost entirely at the expense of Sherriff, whose thought so matched Ludlow's that they rarely disagreed: but, surprisingly in retrospect, they never came to be on Christian-name terms with one another. Sherriff was able to get the best out of his men, who were well fed, warmly clothed, fairly paid, and very loyal. On the expeditions, Sherriff, highly skilled in the use of both still and ciné cameras, took thousands of photographs, the later ones of which, like the 21,000 plant gatherings (some damaged by wartime bombing), field note-books, and maps are preserved at the British Museum (Natural History). Sherriff was one of the first to use air transport for getting plant material, short-lived seeds as well as mature plants, back to Europe: many crates were sent thus to the Royal Botanic Gardens at Kew and Edinburgh, to the garden of the Royal Horticultural Society at Wisley, and to private gardens. Their best introductions, besides rhododendrons and primulas, included *Paeonia lutea* var. *ludlowii*, which has made possible the breeding of the less heavy-headed cultivars of yellow and yellow-toned tree-paeonies, and, unlike most of their introductions, can be readily grown in gardens throughout almost all of Britain, *Euphorbia griffithii*, *Paraquilegia anemonoides* (*P. grandiflora*), and several superior forms of plants already introduced, like the elusive blue-flowered *Corydalis cashmiriana*. The richness of the areas covered is shown by the fact that of 129 species of primula they gathered, 27 were new, as were 38 out of 140 saxifrages, and 23 out of more than 100 gentians.

Though the Tsangpo Gorge has still to be revisited, the expeditions provided the stimulus for many British Museum expeditions to Nepal when Tibet was closed, so that today the finest collections of Himalayan plants in the world are to be found preserved in the Herbarium at the Museum. Ludlow and Sherriff, both excellent marksmen, presented nearly 7,000 bird skins to the Museum, including specimens of two new species and two new subspecies, one of them named Sherriff's long-tailed wren-babbler, *Spelaeornis soulei sherriffii*. Sherriff's manuscript map of his journeys is now preserved at the Royal Geographical Society, while the negatives and plates of his Kashgar days and seven diaries of the same period are preserved in the Ethnography Department of the British Museum. His ciné films, dating back to 1928 (black-and-white), of Kashgar and the early Bhutan and south-east Tibet expeditions are deposited in the National Film Archive,

London, while the later colour films are in the family's possession and his later diaries are preserved at the Royal Botanic Garden, Edinburgh.

Sherriff ('Geordie') was tall and well built, smart in his appearance, traditional and yeomanlike in his outlook, a countryman with a wide-ranging circle of friends. Yet he had a deep dislike of matters metropolitan and of superficial social life of the cocktail-party type. In 1950 he bought an estate at Ascreavie, near Kirriemuir, Angus, where he created a fine garden from a 'wilderness overrun by rabbits' (Ludlow). Here he grew many Himalayan plants with great success. From 1952 to 1956 he commanded the Angus battalion of the Home Guard and was a member of the Queen's bodyguard for Scotland. From 1952 to 1966 he served on the Angus County Council and District Board and was made a deputy lieutenant of Angus in 1954. He was session clerk of Kingoldrum church from 1955 to 1965. Sherriff was appointed OBE in 1947 and the following year the Royal Horticultural Society bestowed its highest honour, the Victoria medal of honour, on him for his services to horticulture. He died at Kirriemuir 19 September 1967.

A portrait is preserved at the Hunt Botanical Library, Pittsburgh.

[*The Times*, 22 September 1967; H. R. Fletcher, *A Quest of Flowers*, 1975; W. T. Stearn in *Bull. Br. Mus. (Nat. Hist.) Botany*, 5 (5), 1976; R. Desmond, *A Dictionary of British and Irish Botanists and Horticulturists*, 1977; B. Henrey in *Watsonia*, vol. xii, 1978; private information.]

D. J. MABBERLEY

SHIRLEY, FREDERICK JOSEPH JOHN (1890-1967), headmaster of Worksop College and the King's School, Canterbury, was born in Oxford 24 February 1890, the fourth child of William Shirley, carpenter, and his wife, Louisa Ellen Harris. His childhood was poor, but he was greatly influenced by the Anglo-Catholic parish church of St. Barnabas. He was educated at its school, at Oxford High School, and at St. Edmund Hall, where he obtained second class honours in history in 1912. He then taught in private schools, and had the enterprise to read law while commissioned in the Royal Naval Volunteer Reserve in the war of 1914-18. He took second class honours in law in London University (1920) and was called to the bar by Lincoln's Inn.

Shirley found his vocation when, on returning to teaching in 1919, he was given scope for his talents on the staff of Framlingham College in Suffolk and was ordained (deacon 1920, priest 1921). He enjoyed a brief spell as the part-time rector of Sternfield (1923-5). All this prepared him for the challenges he faced on becoming headmaster of St. Cuthbert's College, Worksop, in 1925. This was one of the poorest of the schools founded by Nathaniel Woodard [q.v.], a network of Anglican schools run on more economic lines than most public schools. Shirley set himself to raise its standards and multiply its amenities: new buildings arose, the educational achievements were transformed, and both the grounds and the number of boys were expanded. Everything was stamped with Shirley's personality, which had become powerful and idiosyncratic. If governors of the school were cautious, or pupils non-cooperative, they experienced wrath and a relentless drive; but parents and other visitors were charmed, and increasingly the boys were caught up in the excitement of an ambitious adventure.

This panache was greatly needed at Canterbury, where the King's School, inheriting a tradition of education linked with the cathedral over thirteen centuries, was slow to adapt to modern needs and was burdened by problems of finance and morale. Some boys who moved in 1935 with Shirley from Worksop (to the indignation of his fellow headmasters, whose code was thereby breached) became the nucleus of a renaissance only partly reflected in the school's ever-increasing size and only temporarily halted by the outbreak of war in 1939 and the evacuation to Cornwall.

The success made of Worksop was repeated, but with appropriate variations. Shirley was enthusiastic in acquiring or constructing more spacious premises for his boys around the cathedral and in the city. His building programme was initially made possible by the agreement of the dean and chapter to commute for a cash sum their perpetual obligation to provide King's scholarships; and the programme was crowned by the erection of an assembly hall, now the Shirley Hall. He persuaded two authors, Sir Hugh Walpole and W. Somerset Maugham [qq.v.], who both had unhappy memories of their own schooldays at Canterbury, to vie with each other in generosity among the many benefactors now enlisted. This team of supporters included some members of the royal family as well as many grateful parents.

Shirley's delight in the beautiful surroundings of the King's School inspired him to develop its music and drama to exceptionally high levels. He was also determined that more and more of the boys should proceed to the universities, if possible after winning scholarships, and although he did little teaching in class he attracted an able staff. Victories on the river and the playing-fields were, however, not despised.

The untiring competitiveness which he encouraged arose from his memories of his own underprivileged boyhood and slow start in life, and often amounted to a frank worldliness. But particularly in his later years, the style was so warmly human, and his devotion to the boys under his care was so evident, that he was loved as well as admired. Signing himself John Shirley, he was 'Fred' to the boys. To the end he was lively and affable in his copious conversation. He was a pioneer among headmasters in encouraging a more relaxed, almost domestic, atmosphere in which each individual could discover and develop his own interests. Many hobbies flourished.

Shirley threw himself with an equal zest into his responsibilities as a canon of the cathedral, and in his latter years also as treasurer and librarian, especially since the dean of Canterbury, Hewlett Johnson [q.v.], was handicapped by political unpopularity and old age. He became noted for his eloquence in preaching a simple gospel as well as for his administrative and financial exertions, other aspects of a complex character. He published a number of historical studies, among them *Richard Hooker and Contemporary Political Ideas* (1949). He was DD (Oxford, 1949), Ph.D. (London, 1931), an honorary fellow of St. Edmund Hall, Oxford, and a fellow of the Royal Historical Society and of the Society of Antiquaries.

In 1926 Shirley married Dorothy, daughter of John Howard, a company director. They had two sons and one daughter. Shirley retired from the King's School in 1962 and died in Canterbury 19 July 1967.

Worksop College has a portrait by Blair Leighton and the King's School one by Anthony Devas.

[David L. Edwards, *F. J. Shirley: An Extraordinary Headmaster*, 1969.]

DAVID L. EDWARDS

SHOENBERG, SIR ISAAC (1880-1963), electronic engineer, was born 1 March 1880 at Pinsk, in Russia, the eldest son of Yuli Shoenberg, whose profession was forestry. The family were Jewish. He studied at the Kiev Polytechnical Institute, where he read mathematics, mechanical engineering, and electricity. He always retained a keen interest in mathematics, and later received from Kiev a gold medal for his work in this field.

After graduation, he worked briefly in a sugar beet factory, but in 1905 joined S. M. Aisenstein at St. Petersburg in what in 1907 became the Russian Wireless Telegraph and Telephone Company, and in 1911 the Russian Marconi Company. He was the chief engineer of this pioneer enterprise, responsible for the research, design, and installation of the earliest wireless stations in Russia.

The links between the British and Russian Marconi Companies brought him into touch with England, and he became much attracted to this country, its people, and its liberal system of government. He wanted to develop his mathematics; accordingly, in 1914, he came to London with his wife and four children. He was admitted to work for a higher degree at the Royal College of Science. On the outbreak of war he volunteered for military service, but was turned down on medical grounds. He then joined the Marconi Wireless and Telegraph Company. Since he possessed a remarkable aptitude for the complex business of managing patents, he soon became head of the patents department and then general manager. He became a British subject in 1919.

Shoenberg always had an inborn love of music, and became keenly interested in sound recording, in which, not surprisingly, he had some original ideas. At that time gramophone disc recording in this country was dominated by two firms, the Gramophone Company, otherwise known as His Master's Voice, and the Columbia Graphophone Company, the head of which was (Sir) Louis Sterling. The two men became friends, and Sterling invited Shoenberg to join Columbia and introduce his ideas. So successful was this that in 1928 Sterling appointed Shoenberg general manager.

About this time, the Gramophone Company began to work on television, but when the country was hit by an economic slump, which curtailed the sales of gramophone records, it merged in 1931 with the Columbia Graphophone Company, assuming the new title of Electric and Musical Industries (EMI). Shoenberg became director of research and head of patents under Sterling as managing director. The important question was whether the company should, at a time of severe recession, continue with television, which was showing little promise, and was viewed with scepticism. Mechanical methods had no future, and no electronic solution was in sight.

Shoenberg now showed himself as an inspired visionary. He had supreme faith that the problems eventually could be surmounted by his team. He therefore advised his board to pursue an expensive research programme, and his advice was accepted. Work started, and Shoenberg was everywhere, encouraging and drawing out the members of his teams in exhaustive debates, listening carefully to what they said, and often deliberately taking an opposing view in order to stimulate his juniors into argument. He would then meditate on these discussions and make the strategic decisions.

In 1932 the team succeeded in making an

electronic television picture-generating tube. The pictures were crude, and once again Shoenberg had to decide whether to continue. Courageous as ever, he decided to do so—a decision which was not only fully justified by events, but was also the undoubted origin of the strong position which Great Britain established in the field of television.

In 1935 a government committee under Viscount Ullswater recommended that a public television service should be started by the BBC. Shoenberg had to decide what standard EMI should offer the government, remembering that it would have to remain for a long time, but that the higher it was, the greater both the cost and the technical difficulties. He took a bold scientific risk and recommended 405 lines, a standard far higher than seemed possible with the electronic technology of the time. His decision, which is considered to have been the most difficult that he ever made, was triumphantly vindicated. The 405-line standard was the higher of the two used when the world's first high-definition public television service was opened by the BBC on 2 November 1936.

Shoenberg was outstandingly brilliant. He was not only a trained scientist of most marked ability, but he had a far-reaching imagination controlled, nevertheless, by the rigour of his logic. He was also an excellent linguist, speaking and reading Russian, German, French, and Hebrew, as well as English. Allied to these numerous attributes was a warm and sensitive nature, and great charm of manner. He was a shy man in his private life, and this became metamorphosed in his professional work into a deep suspicion of publicity, which resulted in much of his unique work receiving inadequate recognition until recent times. In 1954 he was awarded the Faraday medal, the highest honour that the Institution of Electrical Engineers can bestow. In 1955 he became a director of EMI, and in June 1962 received a knighthood. In his honour, the Royal Television Society has instituted the Shoenberg memorial lecture, sponsored by EMI, and given by some person of distinction in the science. Shoenberg died at his London home 25 January 1963.

In 1903 he married Esther, daughter of Solomon Aisenstein, hotel owner, and had five children—Mark, a mathematician; Rosalie, a gynaecologist; Alexander, an insurance broker; David, professor of physics at Cambridge University and a fellow of the Royal Society; and Elizabeth, a consultant psychiatrist.

[Private information; personal knowledge.]
D. C. BIRKINSHAW

SHORT, (HUGH) OSWALD (1883-1969), aeronautical engineer, was born 16 January 1883 at Stanton-by-Dale, Derbyshire, the fourth son and fifth child of Samuel Short, engineer, and his second wife, Emma Robinson. His formal education ceased on his father's death but he trained as an engineer by self-help and instruction from his brothers Horace Leonard (1872-1917) and (Albert) Eustace (1875-1932).

Short first worked as an office boy in Derby and founded a showman-aeronaut business with Eustace in 1898. The two brothers built their first passenger-carrying balloon at Hove in April 1901 and moved their factory to Maple Mews, Tottenham Court Road, London, c. 1902. The partnership's first sales were observation balloons for the Government of India (October 1903). In 1905-6 the brothers made contacts in the (Royal) Aero Club and moved their factory to railway arches at Battersea in June 1906. Balloons were sold to, for example, C. S. Rolls, J. T. C. Moore-Brabazon (later Lord Brabazon of Tara) [qq.v.], and T. O. M. Sopwith, and the brothers established a reputation for quality, becoming the club's official aeronauts (1907) and aeronautical engineers (1908).

Eustace and Oswald tried unsuccessfully from 1907 to build aeroplanes designed by club members until Horace left employment with (Sir) Charles A. Parsons in December 1908 to form the tripartite partnership, Short Brothers, Aeronautical Engineers. In March 1909 Wilbur Wright chose Shorts to build six Model A 'Flyers' (the United Kingdom's first batch contract); these were constructed in the UK's first purpose-built aircraft factory, Shellbeach, Isle of Sheppey, and were preceded by Short no. 1 and Short no. 2. In October 1909, in a Short no. 2 powered by an engine designed by Gustavus Green [q.v.], Moore-Brabazon won the *Daily Mail*'s £1,000 prize for the first circular mile by an all-British aircraft. In 1911 Shorts provided the Royal Navy's first two aircraft, becoming principal suppliers to the Naval Wing, Royal Flying Corps (later the Royal Naval Air Service).

Oswald established both Shorts seaplane factory at Rochester (1913-14) and the airship works at Cardington, Bedfordshire (1916); he became wholly responsible for Shorts' designs in 1917 when Horace died. He experimented with light alloy construction from about 1916, pioneering and patenting the smooth-skinned monocoque light alloy construction ('stressed skin') in the UK with 'Silver Streak' (1920). He applied the technology to flying boats in 1924. Oswald persevered with stressed-skin construction in the face of official indifference and sustained Shorts in the 1920s by building omnibus bodies until the Royal Air Force and Imperial Airways accepted stressed-skin aircraft. His technology was licensed in the United States, France, and Japan.

The Short partnership was incorporated as Short Brothers (Rochester and Bedford) Limited in 1919 with Oswald as chairman and joint managing director; he became sole managing director on Eustace's death and retained those posts when Shorts became a public company in 1935. Contracts for Short Empire flying boats for Imperial Airways and Sunderlands and Stirlings for the Royal Air Force in the mid-1930s, and the incorporation of a subsidiary, Short and Harland, in Northern Ireland, marked the peak of his career.

An unassuming, courteous man, whose physical courage was proven as an aeronaut and as an observer on test flights, Short was a lover of music and animal life; his labour relations were paternalistic with a Victorian sense of 'fair play'. His health failed under the stresses of the 1930s and the early war years and, when the Government expropriated the shareholders in 1943, he resigned as chairman and director of Shorts, accepting the honorary title of life president. In these later years he was overshadowed by his protégé Arthur Gouge (1890-1962).

From 1943 Short lived quietly in retirement, latterly at Haslemere, Surrey, increasingly grieved by the loss of his company and haunted by the fear that history would overlook the Short brothers' achievements. He had none of the nation's honours: he declined appointment as MBE in 1919 as inappropriate to the firm's achievements but his peers in the aircraft industry honoured him as honorary FRAeS and president of the Society of Aviation Artists. He was admitted freeman of the City of London (1933), and honorary freeman of the City of Rochester (1949); and he also became FRAS and FZS.

In 1935 Short married Violet Louise Blackburn (née Lister, died 1966); they had no children. He died at his home in Haslemere 4 December 1969.

The Short aircraft company was renamed Short Brothers Limited in 1977 in honour of the brothers but the memorial to Oswald's own genius is the world-wide acceptance of stressed-skin construction.

There is a bronze bust by Dyson Smith at the Royal Aeronautical Society, London; and a portrait by Frank Salisbury at Short Brothers Limited, Belfast.

[*The Times*, 6 December 1969; Harald Penrose, *British Aviation, The Pioneer Years*, 1967.]   GORDON BRUCE

SILLITOE, SIR PERCY JOSEPH (1888-1962), policeman and head of MI5, was born at Tulse Hill, London, 22 May 1888, the second son and second child of Joseph Henry Sillitoe, average adjuster, and his wife, Bertha Leontine Smith. There was also a younger sister. The family suffered from the improvidence of Sillitoe senior. After leaving St. Paul's Choir School in 1902, Percy Sillitoe lived at home for three years during which he received some private tuition. From 1905-7 he worked for the Anglo-American Oil Company and in 1908 became a trooper in the British South Africa Police, a tough, highly disciplined paramilitary force, in what was then Southern Rhodesia. He transferred to the Northern Rhodesia Police in 1911, was commissioned, and in 1913 became engaged to Dorothy Mary, daughter of John Watson, of Elloughton, Yorkshire, surveyor and justice of the peace; he had met her on board ship when returning to Africa from sick-leave. He took part in the campaign in German East Africa, and afterwards served as a political officer in Tanganyika from 1916 to 1920, when he resigned from the Northern Rhodesia Police, came home, and in 1920 married Dorothy, by whom he was to have a daughter and two sons.

A further two years as a Colonial Service district officer in Tanganyika followed, but his wife disliked the life, and after suffering a serious illness himself he resigned in 1922. Prompted by his father-in-law he applied for the post of chief constable in Hull, but this application, and another to Nottingham, were unsuccessful. Sillitoe spent the winter of 1922-3 reading for the bar as a student of Gray's Inn, without finding much satisfaction in his studies and becoming increasingly depressed. However, in the spring of 1923 he applied successfully for appointment as chief constable of Chesterfield and began the career in which he was to achieve distinction.

At Chesterfield, where he stayed two years, Sillitoe made a considerable mark and, after a year as chief constable of the East Riding of Yorkshire, he was appointed chief constable of Sheffield on 1 May 1926. Here he commanded a substantial force badly in need of rejuvenation and strong leadership and faced serious problems of law and order, gangs having at this time virtually complete control of the poorer parts of the city. In the course of five successful years Sillitoe revitalized and modernized the force, broke the power of the gangs by the use of plain-clothes police patrols prepared to use 'reasonable force', and acquired a reputation as administrator, disciplinarian, and resolute upholder of the law.

This led to his appointment in 1931 as chief constable of Glasgow to command a force of 2,500 men, second in size to the Metropolitan Police, and to face problems similar to those which he had mastered in Sheffield. His tenure of the post, which lasted twelve years, further enhanced his reputation. In the words of one of his subordinates, himself a future chief constable of Glasgow, his arrival was 'like a breath of fresh air' from which the whole of the police service in Scotland ultimately benefited. He was appointed CBE in 1936 and knighted in 1942, and the following year was invited to take command of the new Kent joint force in which the county and nine city and borough forces were combined to facilitate planning and co-operation with the fighting Services prior to the invasion of Europe. This was his last police appointment which he held until he became director-general of MI5 on 1 May 1946, in succession to Sir David Petrie [q.v.].

Sillitoe had a commanding presence. To his men he was 'the captain' or 'the big fellow', an autocrat and strict disciplinarian leading in a style which was still acceptable between the wars. In the interests of morale and efficiency he was ruthless in requiring senior officers to retire on qualifying for full pension. He chose his subordinates well, left them to do their work without interference, gave them credit for it with outside contacts, and defended them against criticism. He disapproved of the Hendon Police College experiment, believing that officers should rise through the ranks, but was an advocate of women police. Without himself possessing the policeman's professional skills, or being an original thinker, he was alive to the need to bring technical resources to bear on the prevention and detection of crime. He persuaded the police authorities which he served to loosen the purse strings to provide proper accommodation, transport, communications, and support services for finger-printing, photography, and forensic examination. Resolute, independent, and forthright (as chief constable of Kent he disregarded an instruction to do nothing to prevent the merged forces again becoming independent after the war), his relations with the police authorities were nevertheless generally very good.

Sillitoe wrote in his autobiography that he wished he could persuade himself that his appointment as director-general fulfilled his life's ambition. He had been invited to apply for the post by the Home Office: it was not, he said, one to which the aspirations of a policeman would normally have turned. In fact he was unhappy in it. Times were difficult. His period of office coincided with a high season of Russian espionage and saw the trials of Alan Nunn May and Klaus Fuchs and the defections of Pontecorvo, Guy Burgess, and Donald MacLean. Sillitoe, who had immense concern for his public reputation, had to answer for what with hindsight could sometimes be seen as blameworthy mistakes. The problem of Communists in government service required flexibility and political judgement which were not his strong suits. MI5 needed a different style of leadership from a police force. Moreover, Sillitoe had no liking for people whom he called 'book-learned intellectuals'—a category to which (in his view) many MI5 officers could be consigned. For their part the senior staff of MI5, backed by considerable wartime achievements, had had their own favoured candidate for director-general and resented the choice of an outsider whose career had not tended to develop the particular skills which the post required. A rift developed at a high level which was never closed.

Sillitoe's most valuable contribution was made overseas in extending collaboration with, and promoting organization for security in, the old Commonwealth countries and in assisting colonial Governments to establish machinery to cope with the security problems which accompanied the evolution of colonial rule into self-government. Here the resolution and forthrightness which had helped to make him a successful chief constable again served him well—although his predilection for publicity shocked traditionalists at home.

Sillitoe was made KBE in 1950. Despite setbacks and public criticism he enjoyed Clement Attlee's confidence throughout the latter's premiership.

After retiring from MI5 in 1953 Sillitoe became head of the International Diamond Security Organization established by De Beers to curb the flow of diamonds bypassing the De Beers Central Selling Organization. The main leakage (from Sierra Leone via Liberia) was successfully plugged and the IDSO was wound up in 1957. Sillitoe later became chairman of Security Express Ltd. He died at Eastbourne 5 April 1962. The Strathclyde police have a portrait of Sillitoe painted from a photograph by Malcolm McLellan, who served under him in Glasgow.

[Sir Percy Sillitoe, *Cloak Without Dagger*, 1955; A. E. Cockerill, *Sir Percy Sillitoe*, 1975; private information; personal knowledge.]   ANTHONY SIMKINS

SILVERMAN, (SAMUEL) SYDNEY (1895–1968), lawyer, member of Parliament, and penal reformer, was born in Liverpool 8. October 1895. He was the second of four children, only two of whom survived to maturity, of Myer Silverman, general draper, and his wife, Blanche Stern. Little is known about his mother, except that she came from a long-established Jewish family in Manchester.

The Silvermans were poor, but their poverty

was not that of nineteenth-century industrial labour, for Myer Silverman was a pedlar or, more properly, a chapman, who lived as a small-time entrepreneur among his labouring fellows. He was never materially successful, probably because his sympathy for his impoverished customers did not allow him to enrich himself at their expense. His children therefore had to make their own way. Sydney obtained a scholarship to the Liverpool Institute, a prestigious grammar school, and, from there, two further scholarships, one to the university of Liverpool and the other to Oxford. With characteristic realism he saw that his family could not afford the expense of an Oxford scholarship; he took up the Liverpool offer and began his studies in English literature.

This career was interrupted by the Military Service Act of 1916 which introduced conscription. Silverman, now twenty-one, registered as a conscientious objector. His pacifist beliefs were influenced to some degree by Bertrand (later Earl) Russell [q.v.] but he had his own developing vision of the brotherhood of man, a vision which survived repeated sentences of imprisonment, for his pacifist position was absolute. He rejected completely the arbitrament of war and could not accept any of the alternatives to military service which would rescue him from imprisonment. Serving sentences in gaols as far apart as Preston and Wormwood Scrubs, he learned at first hand of the need for penal reform.

When the war was over Silverman returned to university and completed his degree. In the immediate post-war period, however, jobs in England were hard to come by, especially for one who had refused military service. He applied successfully for a teaching post at the university of Helsinki and went there in 1921. It was the typical academic slavery of early twentieth-century Europe—a six-month semester paid at a pittance, followed by six months unpaid leave. Silverman enjoyed the work sufficiently to stay for four years, learning something, during this time, of the wider world of European politics for which his early training in Liverpool had not prepared him.

Returning to England in 1925, he registered at Liverpool University for a degree in law. This he completed, with distinction, in two years and found himself, in 1927, a qualified lawyer, who could not pay the registration fee (a sizeable amount at that time) that would allow him to practise as a solicitor. He was persuasive enough, however, to obtain a loan of £100 from a hard-headed bank manager. The registration fee was paid and a long and successful career as a solicitor began.

His clients were mostly the poor neighbours of his childhood, whom he defended and supported in landlord-tenant disputes, workmen's compensation claims, and criminal cases. In these early years he learned how much skilled help and support was needed by the labouring poor in their confrontations with the law. His hard work, professional skill, and sympathy for his clients so enlarged his practice that he was joined by other lawyers of the same mind and his firm became one of the best known in Liverpool. In later years, when he entered the House of Commons, he opened an office in London and did much of his own work there.

The imprisoned pacifist and the poor-man's lawyer could not, however, remain content with occasional rectification of individual injustices by legal processes. Political solutions had to be found to the poverty and discrimination which he had suffered and seen others suffer throughout his early manhood. He threw himself into local politics and became a city councillor in 1932. His skill as a speaker and in political manipulation earned him a considerable reputation throughout the industrial North and he was invited to accept the Labour Party nomination for the constituency of Nelson and Colne. He was elected to Parliament in 1935 and retained the seat until his death in 1968.

At the time of his election, the Labour Party was committed to the principle that elected members were there to further the interests of the party in the House of Commons. That meant that every Labour member would have to put general issues concerning the whole country and the whole party before constituency matters. This political stance was particularly suited to Silverman. He became a true House of Commons man, throwing himself into its business and procedures with typical enthusiasm. His constituents, however, were not allowed to suffer. Besides dealing conscientiously with their problems, he wrote constantly for the *Gazette*, the Labour Party weekly of the Nelson area. In this he explained what he was trying to do and described the major issues which were taking up parliamentary time. He was well aware, however, that justice and injustice in Britain and Europe, and matters concerning foreign policy and defence expenditure, could not be dealt with in Nelson but had to be determined in Parliament. His constituents agreed with him and never withdrew their support.

From Silverman's entry into the House of Commons until the slow abandonment of peace in 1938/9 there were no issues which troubled his conscience. The activities of Sir Oswald Mosley and racial attacks on Jews in London and elsewhere were matters for action and protest rather than for a re-examination of his principles. The outbreak of war, however, presented him with a difficult choice. As a pacifist who had served several sentences of imprisonment for his total rejection of force as an instrument of policy, he was bound to oppose any moves that would make war inevitable. However, it was claimed that destruction of the Jews in Europe could be brought to an end only by armed intervention. Silverman accepted this argument and, with many protests about the way in which the war was being fought, involved himself in its furtherance. At the same time he took strong exception to the Churchillian policy of 'unconditional surrender', arguing that carefully drafted peace aims would bring a swifter end to the war. In this, as in many other matters at this time, he was in a minority.

When the Labour Party came into office in 1945 there were many who expected that Silverman's long service and parliamentary skill would be rewarded by a government post. This did not happen either then or in the future. Whatever the reason for his initial rejection by C. R. (later Earl) Attlee, Silverman's later career of opposition to the party establishment ensured that he would remain a backbencher. In the early post-war years, the British Government had serious problems in Palestine. The surviving Jews of Europe were not welcome in the Middle East, since Britain, the mandatory power, feared that there would be difficulties with the Arabs. In this matter Silverman's interests were clearly declared. He approved of open access to Palestine for all refugee and stateless Jews who wished to go there. His parliamentary record does not show him to be a passionate Zionist; his aim was simply to secure for each surviving Jew of Europe the settlement and life-style which he most desired, whether it was in Palestine or Colombia. His advocacy derived its urgency not only from the fact that he himself was an orthodox, though not a practising, Jew, but also because he had been chairman of the British section of the World Jewish Congress and had learned through this organization of the sufferings of his race in Europe. In addition he visited Buchenwald, immediately after it was relieved, as a member of an all-party delegation of members of Parliament who were invited by Eisenhower to go and see what had been happening. Silverman's memory of what he saw never left him.

Opposition to the Government's policy in Palestine and to the treatment of Jewish refugees in general did not endear him to the foreign secretary, Ernest Bevin [q.v.]. Moreover, Silverman was a fierce critic of the foreign secretary's handling of relations with the Soviet Union, for he claimed that Bevin negotiated with Russia as if it were the Communist Party which, in Britain, was both feared and despised; the more appropriate view was that the Soviet

Union was the embodiment of a great people whose rights and dignity should be respected.

His concern with foreign policy and defence arose from his fundamental objection to the use of force. This belief had yielded second place to the need for Jews to survive during the war. When the war was over he campaigned strongly against the use of any kind of nuclear weapons and became a vigorous member of the Campaign for Nuclear Disarmament. The decision of Hugh Gaitskell [q.v.] to oppose the rejection by the Labour Party Conference of a nuclear defence policy made Silverman angry. Later he was expelled from the parliamentary party (along with Michael Foot and three others) for refusing to accept the convention that the Labour Party, in Opposition, did not vote against the defence estimates.

All these concerns: defence, Palestine, and the attitude to the Soviet Union, suggest that Silverman's interests were international. Indeed they were, but the primacy of domestic politics in the concerns of the House of Commons and of the country has ensured that he will be remembered principally for his long campaign for the abolition of the death penalty.

In 1948 the Labour Government introduced a Criminal Justice Bill which found favour with many reformers except that it contained no provision about the death penalty. Silverman introduced a clause which provided for a five-year suspension of the penalty but this was thrown out by the Lords. The Government tried again and suggested that certain types of murder should be excluded from the mandatory death sentence. The House of Lords rejected this amendment too. To obtain the enactment of other parts of the Bill therefore the capital punishment provisions were dropped, but the abolitionists within the House regrouped under Silverman's leadership. Thereafter he was the acknowledged parliamentary protagonist of abolition, although outside the House and in the newly founded Campaign for the Abolition of the Death Penalty he had neither the reputation nor the force of the other determined reformers, Sir Victor Gollancz [q.v.] and Arthur Koestler.

But the battle had to be fought, and won, in the House of Commons. Silverman, at a second attempt, introduced a private member's Bill for abolition in 1956. After obtaining a second reading in the House of Commons, it was defeated in the Lords. Feeling outside the House ran so high that the home secretary, R. A. Butler (later Lord Butler of Saffron Walden), introduced and negotiated through both Houses a compromise Bill which made a distinction between capital and non-capital murder. The provisions of this Act gave rise to many difficulties and anomalies, but there was no opportunity for effecting a change in the law until the

Labour Party took office in 1964. Silverman had been returned to Parliament with an increased majority (in a fierce contest where one of the candidates, although professedly Labour, made his platform the return of capital punishment for all murder). In the light of this resounding success Silverman was given the signal honour of having his proposed private member's Bill for abolition of the death penalty referred to in the Queen's Speech.

In a powerful address, delivered without notes, Silverman moved the second reading of his new Bill. There was now no doubt about the result in the House of Commons and, in due course, the Bill went to the Lords, which had rejected all previous attempts to abolish capital punishment. But the Campaign for the Abolition of the Death Penalty had done its work well and the Bill went through. This was the climax of Silverman's parliamentary career, for he died before the expiry of the five years' suspension period and did not see the completion of one of his great parliamentary endeavours.

As a final assessment of this astute parliamentarian it can be said that he had a passion for justice and equality that kept him well to the left of his party, so that he did not commend himself to the establishment. Besides, he was not good at collective action; most of his battles he fought alone, for he enjoyed twisting the tails of his antagonists and might have been deprived of this enjoyment if he had worked with others. Nevertheless his contribution to the thinking of his party, to the progress of penal reform, and to the welfare of his fellow Jews remains unquestioned. To his constituents and to his agent he was unfailing in his service. They responded with a warm personal devotion to him. He wrote, as he spoke, easily and well, contributing articles to many journals. He produced pamphlets to promote the several campaigns in which he was involved and published one book (with Reginald Paget) which described three cases where the death penalty seemed to have been unjustly imposed (*Hanged, and Innocent?*, 1953).

In 1933 Silverman married Nancy, daughter of L. Rubinstein, whose family had fled to Liverpool from the Russian pogroms in the late nineteenth century. She was an accomplished musician as her father had been before her. They had three sons. Silverman died in hospital in Hampstead 9 February 1968.

A bronze bust by Sam Tonkiss is in Silverman Hall, the Labour Party headquarters in Nelson. A plantation of trees, donated by the World Jewish Congress, grows on a slope outside Jerusalem.

[*The Times*, 10 February 1968; Emrys Hughes, *Sydney Silverman, Parliamentary Rebel*, 1969; E. O. Tuttle, *The Crusade against Capital Punishment in Great Britain*, 1961; House of Commons papers; private information.]   SARAH McCABE

SIMPSON, SIR GEORGE CLARKE (1878-1965), meteorologist, was born in Derby 2 September 1878, the second son and third of the seven children of Arthur Simpson, a small business man who became mayor of Derby, and his wife, Alice Lambton, daughter of Thomas William Clarke, a wharfinger of Sutton Bridge, Lincolnshire. Simpson was educated at the Diocesan School, Derby. He left school at sixteen and entered his father's business, but, as a result of reading popular science in his spare time, joined evening classes to improve his mathematics and persuaded his father to let him sit the entrance examination for Owens College, Manchester, which, to everyone's surprise, he passed at the first attempt.

So, in 1897, Simpson entered Dalton Hall with 'very little education' but, with Professor (Sir) Arthur Schuster's [q.v.] help, was allowed to register for the honours physics degree which he passed with first class honours in 1900. Later Simpson contributed the notice of Schuster to this Dictionary. An appointment as tutor in physics without salary but with free board and lodging, and a university scholarship of £50, gave Simpson financial independence and time for research on the resistance of bismuth to an alternating current in a strong magnetic field on which he published two papers in the *Philosophical Magazine*. Meanwhile he had been accepted by Captain R. F. Scott [q.v.] to join his first Antarctic expedition as a physicist but failed the medical examination for a slight defect which was later corrected by a minor operation.

In 1902 Simpson was awarded an 1851 exhibition to study at the Geophysikalisches Institüt, Göttingen, where he investigated the problem of the Earth's permanent negative charge and showed that this could not be maintained by absorption of negative ions from the atmosphere as suggested by Julius Elster and H. F. Geitel. Believing that this and other problems of atmospheric electricity might best be studied in high latitudes, where the large seasonal variations of solar radiation might have greater effect on the ionization of the atmosphere, he spent a year in Lapland where he obtained continuous records of the atmospheric potential gradient and thrice-daily measurements of air conductivity and ionization. He thus established the diurnal and seasonal variations.

In 1905 Simpson was appointed lecturer in meteorology in Manchester, the first in any British university, but soon afterwards accepted an appointment in the Indian Meteorological Office under (Sir) Gilbert T. Walker [q.v.] and began, in Simla, his lifelong studies of thunderstorm electricity, starting with the electrical charges on raindrops. He found that the charge carried by thunderstorm rain was predominantly positive. He also made the important discovery that large water-drops breaking up in a strong vertical air current became positively charged. This, together with P. Lenard's discovery that freely falling water-drops broke up if they were more than 6 mm in diameter, led Simpson to the view that large raindrops falling from thunderstorms could disintegrate and generate electric charges and fields strong enough to produce lightning. This theory had to be abandoned when it became clear that it was incompatible with the distribution of electric charge within thunderstorms as deduced from measurements of the electric field by C. T. R. Wilson [q.v.], and later by Simpson himself using an ingenious, simple, balloon-borne instrument which produced the first measurements within actual thunderclouds. The Simpson drop-breaking mechanism may, however, be partly responsible for the subsidiary centre of positive charge present in the base of thunderstorms which appears to trigger (rather than generate) lightning flashes.

In 1909 Captain Scott again invited Simpson to join him on an Antarctic expedition. (Sir) C. S. Wright and he made a most valuable series of meteorological and electrical measurements which Simpson published and discussed in three volumes appearing between 1919 and 1923. However, Simpson had to cut short his stay in Antarctica because of Walker's illness in India, whither he returned in 1912 and where he spent the war of 1914–18, part of the time on secondment to the Indian Munitions Board. He married, in 1914, Dorothy Jane (died 1978), daughter of Cecil Stephen, a barrister in New South Wales, who was the son of Sir Alfred Stephen [q.v.] and first cousin of Sir Leslie Stephen [q.v.], the first editor of this Dictionary.

He was elected to fellowship of the Royal Society in 1915 and appointed CBE in 1919.

In 1920 Simpson was invited to succeed Sir (William) Napier Shaw [q.v.] as director of the British Meteorological Office, now under the Air Ministry, and devoted most of his energies during the following eighteen years to building up an efficient unified organization serving the armed forces, civil aviation, and the general public. Heavily engaged in the administration and restructuring of the Office, and in meeting the rapidly increasing demands of aviation, Simpson had little time for research but managed to publish three papers on the

radiation balance of the Earth and atmosphere in 1928–9. Although always interested and active himself, Simpson did not encourage his staff to do research on which the Meteorological Office spent only £393 in 1932 and only £2,830 in 1938 when Simpson retired. His contributions to meteorology and the public service were recognized by his appointment as CB in 1926 and KCB in 1935.

After retirement, and on the outbreak of war, Simpson took charge of Kew Observatory where he continued his research on the electrical structure of thunderstorms and electrification of precipitation until November 1947. His outstanding work in this and related fields was summarized in two very lucid and stimulating presidential addresses in 1940 and 1941 to the Royal Meteorological Society which had awarded him the Symons gold medal in 1930. Among his other honours were D.Sc. (Sydney, 1914, and Manchester, 1906), honorary LLD (Aberdeen, 1925), and honorary FRSE (1947). He served on the council of the British Association from 1927 to 1935 and was a corresponding member of many foreign societies.

Simpson, although physically fit and agile for his years, suffered from deafness which made him appear rather remote and forbidding to his subordinates. He did not suffer fools gladly and could be brusque but, during his latter years at Kew Observatory, he was kind and considerate to all members of his small staff and much concerned to set them a good example in adapting to wartime living. The last years of Simpson's retirement were spent at Westbury-on-Trym. He died in hospital after a short illness 1 January 1965.

His four children have all achieved distinction. Scott is emeritus professor of geology in the university of Exeter; Arthur recently retired as a senior official in the UN Food and Agricultural Organization; Oliver is chief scientist, Home Office; and Jean is a doctor of medicine.

There is a water-colour caricature figure of Simpson by D. G. Lillie (1911) in the Scott Polar Research Institute, Cambridge.

[E. Gold in *Biographical Memoirs of Fellows of the Royal Society*, vol. xi, 1965; private information; personal knowledge.]

B. J. MASON

SIMPSON, PERCY (1865–1962), scholar, was born at Lichfield 1 November 1865, the son of John Simpson, Post Office clerk, and his wife, Emma Gilbert. Through the good offices of Bishop Abraham [q.v.], who found him as a small boy reading in the cathedral library, lent him books, and coached him, he was given a scholarship at Denstone College. From there he went as a scholar to Selwyn College, Cambridge, and after taking a second in the classical tripos of 1887 returned to teach at his old school until 1895. At Cambridge, and as a classics master, he read widely in Elizabethan literature, particularly in the drama; and as early as 1888 he embarked on what was to become his lifework by making a beginning at annotating the plays of Ben Jonson. He moved to Wimbledon in 1896 and in 1899 went to teach at St. Olave's Grammar School, Southwark, no doubt lured by the library of the British Museum and the chance of contact with other scholars. At this period of his life he was carrying very heavy family responsibilities, and it was not until 1913, when he was forty-eight, that relief from these enabled him to give up schoolmastering and devote himself to scholarship. In that year he accepted an invitation to go to Oxford to work for the Clarendon Press. As soon as he arrived Sir Walter Raleigh [q.v.] secured his help as a lecturer in the English faculty and in 1914 appointed him as the first librarian of the new English faculty library. He was elected to a fellowship at Oriel College in 1921; university reader in English textual criticism in 1927 and Goldsmiths' reader in English literature in 1930, a post which he held until his retirement in 1935. He continued to supervise and examine research students for many years, and in 1946, in his eighties, he even returned for a short time to Oriel, of which he had become an honorary fellow in 1943, as a tutor to help with the flood of returned servicemen.

In 1921 Simpson married Evelyn Mary, daughter of James Spearing, of Great Shelford, Cambridge, tutor in English literature at St. Hugh's College, who was already well launched on her work on Donne, with whom her name will always be associated as her husband's will be with Ben Jonson. They had one daughter and one son who died in 1953. The marriage was an ideal partnership in every sense. Like everything else, domestic happiness came late to Percy Simpson, for, except for his epoch-making little book *Shakespearian Punctuation* in 1911, all his important work dates from after 1921, when he was fifty-six, and the edition of Jonson was only completed in 1952, when he was eighty-seven, fifty years from its inception. It was only in his last few years that his mental and physical powers failed and he was moved to his daughter's home at Norwich, where he died 14 November 1962. His widow died in the following year.

The Clarendon Press invited C. H. Herford (whose notice Simpson contributed to this Dictionary) to edit Jonson in 1902. In the following year Herford suggested Simpson should be brought in to assist with the text and commentary. At the initial conference at Oxford the junior editor arrived late, having walked from Reading. (To the end of his life Simpson remained addicted to walking, only in his seventies reducing his daily stint from fifteen to ten miles.) The first two volumes, biographical and critical, mainly the work of Herford, appeared in 1925, followed by the first two volumes of the text in 1927 and 1932. Before the appearance of the last of these Herford died. From this time what he had affectionately described as Simpson's 'impossible standard of perfection', and, no doubt, increasing years made progress almost imperceptible, and in 1937 Evelyn Simpson was brought in as third editor. She laid aside her own work on Donne to help her husband marshal into order the vast amount of material he had amassed over a lifetime, and between them they brought the eleven volumes to a conclusion. Although an editor today would handle the presentation of the text differently, the edition remains one of the great editions of its age. Its commentary is a masterpiece of wide, profound, and exact scholarship.

In two other works Simpson played a notable part in the history of textual scholarship in English. Like all pioneers he lived to see his conclusions questioned; but he was the first to challenge some long-held assumptions. His first, and most original work, *Shakespearian Punctuation*, marks a new era in editorial practice. Before its appearance it had been assumed that an editor could disregard the original punctuation of early printed texts as wholly misleading. Simpson set himself to examine Elizabethan punctuation to discover its principles. His first convert was (Sir) Herbert Grierson [q.v.], who in 1912 produced his edition of Donne's poems, the first edition in old spelling and with old punctuation. The book is now outmoded, since Simpson assumed that what is now seen as largely compositorial pointing was authorial; but progress has been from the position he established. His other major contribution was his study of *Proof-Reading in the Sixteenth, Seventeenth and Eighteenth Centuries* (1935). Here again, although in details he has been proved wrong, he successfully challenged the assumption that authors in those periods never read proofs.

Percy Simpson was a dedicated scholar, prepared to take endless pains to settle a textual point or elucidate a reference. He weighed lightly the risk of never finishing against the compulsion to aim at perfection. Short, rosy-faced, with his blue eyes twinkling behind his spectacles, he loved to give an impression of extreme scholarly ferocity, and recounted with gusto stories of how he had 'floored' some ignoramus. Tales of great scholarly battles, past and present, and of crushing retorts delivered, enlivened the classes he took for research students for many years at Oxford. Although severe to the idle and thoughtless, he was endlessly kind and patient with the serious and delighted in his pupils' later successes. To many young people he communicated, through his strong and simple reverence for great literature and the example of his single-minded pursuit of knowledge, his own belief that the life of service to literature through scholarship is a good and happy life. He received honorary degrees from Cambridge and Glasgow and in 1951 became an honorary fellow of his old college, Selwyn. A drawing by Percy Horton is in the English faculty library at Oxford.

[*The Times*, 16 November 1962; *Oxford Magazine*, 7 February 1963; memoir prefixed to *A List of the Published Writings of Percy Simpson*, 1950; personal knowledge.]

HELEN GARDNER

SINCLAIR, SIR ARCHIBALD HENRY MACDONALD, first baronet, of Ulbster, Caithness, and first VISCOUNT THURSO (1890–1970), politician, was born in London 22 October 1890, the only son of Clarence Granville Sinclair and his wife, Mabel Sands. His father, a lieutenant in the Scots Guards, was the eldest son of Sir (John George) Tollemache Sinclair, third baronet, of Ulbster, Caithness. His mother, a noted beauty of her day, was the daughter of a wealthy New York business man, Mahlon Sands. Sinclair's mother died a few days after his birth, and five years later his father also died, leaving the young Sinclair to experience a rather itinerant childhood as he moved about between the houses of various relations who tried to provide a home for him. Much of his time was spent with his grandfather, Sir Tollemache, or with Archdeacon William Macdonald Sinclair, canon of St. Paul's; and at Temple House, Marlow, Berkshire, the home of his uncle and aunt — Lieutenant-General and Mrs Owen Williams — where he found himself at the heart of fashionable society, for Williams was on excellent terms with King Edward VII.

Educated at Eton and Sandhurst, Sinclair entered the army in 1910 in the 2nd Life Guards, and on the death of his grandfather in 1912 he succeeded to the baronetcy and with it the ownership of some 100,000 acres at the northernmost tip of Scotland. In the days before World War I there were few more glamorous young men in Society than 'Archie'. His good looks, charm, and romantic Highland aura were spiced with a touch of daredevilry which led him to experiment with a primitive

aircraft which he would fly before breakfast. Asquith was captivated, and so was his daughter, Violet; but much the deepest friendship which Sinclair made at this time was with Winston Churchill. At heart Sinclair grew up a somewhat shy and reserved young man with no great liking for the crowded events of the social calendar. Churchill in a different way was also a solitary figure. But he and Sinclair at once discovered that they had a vast amount in common. Both felt that circumstances had deprived them of full parental affection, though both had been sustained by a devoted governess. Both had American mothers and swashbuckling Yankee grandfathers. Both were by training cavalry officers with a shared enthusiasm for polo. It was even the case that both had a slight speech impediment. Sinclair in his early twenties was turning towards politics and ready to trust in an older man as his guiding star; Churchill in his late thirties was already a curiously paternal figure delighted to discover a young disciple. The letters which he and Sinclair exchanged during World War I are remarkable on both sides for their expression of private feeling and read like those of a mutually devoted father and son. Sinclair could write to Churchill in 1916 of 'my keen longing to serve you in politics — more humbly but more energetically than I have been able to in war'.

Sinclair served on the western front throughout the war. Early on he was appointed ADC to the Liberal MP and former secretary for war, J. E. B. Seely (later Lord Mottistone, q.v.), commander of the Canadian Cavalry brigade. In January 1916 Churchill, whose career had been ruined for the time being by Gallipoli, took charge on the western front of the 6th Royal Scots Fusiliers, and for five months Sinclair served as his second-in-command. Sinclair ended the war as a major in the Guards Machine-Gun Regiment. In 1916 while still on service in France Sinclair met and after a whirlwind courtship married Marigold (died 1975), the daughter of Lieutenant-Colonel James Stewart Forbes, and later returned with her to a triumphant civic reception in Thurso.

After the war Sinclair remained for a time in the role of aide to Churchill, serving as his personal military secretary at the War Office (1919–21), and as his private secretary at the Colonial Office (1921–2). But in 1922 he entered Parliament as MP for Caithness and Sutherland, taking his stand as a Liberal supporting the Lloyd George (and thus Churchill) wing of the party. In the House of Commons he built up a reputation as a skilful Opposition speaker, while playing a part in the comprehensive overhaul of Liberal policy which Lloyd

George had initiated. A convinced Scottish Home Ruler, he was chiefly responsible for the Liberal 'Tartan Book', which proposed devolution for Scotland on the lines of the Stormont system in Northern Ireland.

During the second Labour Government of 1929–31 the Liberal Party began to disintegrate, a process accelerated by the formation of Ramsay MacDonald's 'national' Government in August 1931. One section of the party, led by Sir John (later Viscount) Simon [q.v.], wanted outright opposition to the Labour Government in alliance with the Conservatives. In the economic crisis they were prepared to jettison the historic Liberal creed of free trade, and welcome the 'national' Government as the basis of a permanent association with the Tory party. The 'Liberal Nationals', having accepted office in 1931, were gradually to lose their separate identity and to become in effect, Conservatives. Lloyd George, having first welcomed the 'national' Government, swiftly turned against it once it became evident that it would entail the introduction of tariffs, and moved into a position of splendid isolation. Sinclair, who had accepted the thankless task of Liberal chief whip in November 1930, took the same line as Sir Herbert (later Viscount) Samuel [q.v.] and the majority of Liberal MPs. They accepted office in August 1931, Sinclair becoming secretary of state for Scotland (he did not have Cabinet rank until November). In October they agreed to fight a general election in alliance with the Conservatives, and when the Cabinet decided in January 1932 to introduce protection, it was announced that the Samuelite Liberals would remain in the Government under an 'agreement to differ'. No doubt the satisfactions of office were great, and one historian writes that 'the process of extracting the Liberal ministers from the Government has been compared, not wholly unfairly, with that of pulling kittens by their tails from a jug of cream'. But Samuel and Sinclair, who together comprised the Liberal high command, were committed first and foremost to the independence of the party. They believed that free trade must be restored in the long run even if it were sacrificed temporarily for the sake of national unity during the emergency. In the summer of 1932 a series of discussions took place at Sinclair's home in Caithness which led to the resignation of the Samuelite ministers in September, in protest against the conclusion of the Ottawa agreements.

The post of secretary of state for Scotland had offered Sinclair little scope, coming as it did at a moment of financial stringency. A greater opportunity, at first very effectively disguised, presented itself in November 1935.

Samuel, who had led the party since 1931, lost his seat in the general election, and Sinclair was prevailed upon to serve in his place as chairman of the parliamentary party. Sinclair was reluctant to accept the job and the correspondence preserved among his papers helps to explain why. The Liberals were a deeply demoralized party. Their by-election performance since 1931 had been disastrous and in 1935 their strength in the Commons was further reduced to twenty-one MPs. There was no easy solution at hand, but enthusiasts were very ready to blame the quality of the party leadership, and there were many prima donnas at hand with schemes to revive the party's fortunes. With all such prickly individuals Sinclair dealt patiently but firmly, anxious not to discourage the efforts of anyone with something to contribute to the cause. In this he relied heavily on the advice and support of his old friend Harcourt Johnstone, generally known as 'Crinks', who maintained liaison between the Whips' office and the constituencies. Although Sinclair could do little to revive the Liberal vote, he succeeded in turning the parliamentary party into a force more powerful than its numbers indicated. From 1935 onwards the crisis in Europe overshadowed all other political issues. The Baldwin and Chamberlain Governments pursued a pragmatic policy of piecemeal concessions to Mussolini and Hitler. The Labour Party, while adopting a high moral stance of opposition to Fascism and aggression, refused until late in the day to accept the need for rearmament. Under Sinclair the Liberals combined support for collective security through the League of Nations with pressure for a strong air force and secure defences. They were therefore the advocates of a genuine middle way which became increasingly influential, and was indeed adopted by Churchill in his campaign for 'Arms and the Covenant'. In the House of Commons Sinclair and Churchill worked closely together: in condemning the Munich agreement or urging an understanding with Russia they were of one mind. They also combined to seek the establishment of a Ministry of Supply.

At the outbreak of war in September 1939 Chamberlain invited Sinclair to accept office on behalf of the Liberals, an invitation which Sinclair declined. In the critical Commons debate of 7–8 May 1940 which led to Chamberlain's resignation Sinclair joined in the attack, and on 10 May his old friend and ally Churchill became prime minister. Sinclair was appointed secretary of state for air, a post he retained until the dissolution of the coalition in May 1945. Unless or until a biography of Sinclair is written, it will remain difficult to assess precisely his contribution as air minister.

Historians concentrate on strategy, but it may be that Sinclair's most vital contribution was to fight for the allocation of manpower needed to sustain the bomber offensive. The strategic conduct of the war was dominated by Churchill, and the chiefs of staff and Sinclair were well aware that he must rely to a great extent on the professional judgement of the air marshals. In 1941-2, for example, Sinclair was attracted by the idea of the precision bombing of German oil refineries, but had to accept the view of the air staff that with existing equipment this was impracticable. The air marshals probably found Sinclair a considerable asset, for he was always ready to champion them and enjoyed a special relationship with the prime minister. In March 1942 he took a prominent part in the struggle to prevent the Admiralty diverting bombers from strategic bombing to long-range reconnaissance duties in the Battle of the Atlantic, and obtained Churchill's consent for a resumption of the full bombing offensive. Sinclair had developed a strong faith in the value of strategic bombing. When Lord Cherwell [q.v.] circulated his famous memorandum of March 1942 advocating the 'dehousing' of the German population through the bombing of residential areas, Sinclair commented that he found the argument 'simple, clear and convincing'. In recent years the weight of opinion has been strongly critical of the strategic bombing offensive on the grounds that it was ineffectual and wasteful of resources which could have been better employed. This has been accompanied by an ethical revulsion from the use of bombing to terrorize and kill civilians. Sinclair relied on the 'common sense' judgement that a weapon so destructive as bombing must also be important and effective: any secretary for air who thought differently would not have survived the wrath of the air marshals for long. Nor did the moral issue cause him any difficulty, for he believed that the German people must suffer for a war which was their own responsibility, a severe view which most people accepted in the heat of the conflict. None the less Sinclair thought it prudent not to explain the character of the bombing offensive too frankly in public, in case opposition was stirred up on grounds of conscience and the morale of bomber crews affected. In a number of speeches Sinclair asserted that strategic bombing was directed primarily against industrial targets, not against residential areas, and that civilian deaths were the by-product and not the objective of the campaign. The most controversial episode of all, the Anglo-American destruction of Dresden in February 1945, was the outcome of direct instructions from Churchill. Churchill soon began to regret this episode and issued a minute (later withdrawn) describing the attack as 'a serious query against the conduct of Allied bombing'.

Between the wars Sinclair had been able to pay regular attention to his constituency of Caithness and Sutherland, the largest geographically in the United Kingdom. He took care to visit his constituents on annual summer tours, and otherwise kept in touch through his party agent Captain Barrogill Keith, who was also the factor of his estate. The war years cut Sinclair off, and he paid for this in the general election of 1945, coming bottom of the poll in a remarkable result in which only sixty-one votes separated the three candidates. Effectively this was the end of Sinclair's career. After failing to be re-elected in 1950, he accepted a peerage in the first honours list of the post-war Churchill Government, and was created Viscount Thurso, of Ulbster, in 1952. Plans for him to re-enter politics as Liberal leader in the House of Lords were thwarted by illness and he did not take his seat until 1954. For three years he was able to play a prominent part in the debates of the upper house, but it was his fate to spend the remainder of his life as an invalid.

Sinclair enjoyed the world of politics and worked hard at it, but he did not live for his career as Churchill did. He built around himself a secure and happy private life in the company of his wife and children. Except in the war years he guarded his leisure hours. He enjoyed grouse-shooting, won recognition as a very fine salmon fisherman, and played polo and rode regularly until he was about forty. He carefully supervised the accounts of his estate, and kept in touch with his tenant farmers, but was not by inclination an agriculturalist. If his heart was in the Highlands (he was lord lieutenant of Caithness from 1919 to 1964), his home and his vocation for most of the year were in the south-east. To the life of politics he brought both a clear view of his function and certain definite gifts. He maintained that it was not the job of a politician to take on the role of expert in any particular branch of knowledge, but to make use of the knowledge which experts possessed. The task of the politician was to organize, to persuade, and to co-ordinate. In the House of Commons Sinclair was an excellent speaker, alert to the atmosphere of the House, and skilfully casting his arguments in terms which were likely to exercise the maximum appeal. His advisers at the Scottish Office were impressed by his ability to lead a small group of civil servants with great sensitivity and concentration to the point where clear decisions could be taken. Sinclair was in fact an expert in the art of the possible, a consensus politician who naturally developed good relations with congenial figures on the Conservative or Labour benches. A civilizing but never a rugged influence, Sinclair had two great loyalties which account for his two main contributions to public life. He believed in Liberalism and revived it when it was down; and he believed in Churchill and revived *him* when he was down.

Sinclair was appointed CMG in 1922, KT in 1941, and sworn of the Privy Council in 1931. He died at his home in Twickenham 15 June 1970, leaving a wife, two daughters, and two sons. He was succeeded by his elder son, Robin Macdonald Sinclair (born 1922).

There are portraits of Sinclair by (Sir) Oswald Birley and Augustus John, both in the possession of the present viscount, and a portrait of Sinclair as a young man by Sir John Lavery, in the possession of his grandson John. There is also a portrait by William Dring in the Imperial War Museum. A sculpted head by Scott Sutherland (1936), mounted by a stone plaque and seat stands at the end of Sir Archibald Road, Thurso.

[*The Times*, 17 June 1970; Martin Gilbert (ed.), *Winston S. Churchill*: companion volumes iii and iv, 1972, 1977; Violet Bonham-Carter, *Winston Churchill as I Knew Him*, 1965; Sir Percy Harris, *Forty Years in and out of Parliament*, 1947; Sir Charles Webster and Noble Frankland, *The Strategic Air Offensive against Germany 1939-1945*, 1961; Roy Douglas, *The History of the Liberal Party 1895-1970*, 1971; Thurso Papers, Churchill College, Cambridge; private information.]   PAUL ADDISON

SITWELL, DAME EDITH LOUISA (1887-1964), poet and critic, was born at Scarborough 7 September 1887, the eldest of the three children of Sir George Reresby Sitwell, fourth baronet [q.v.], and his wife, Lady Ida Emily Augusta Denison, fourth child and third daughter of the Earl of Londesborough. Through their mother's family Edith and her two brothers, Osbert (a notice of whom follows), and Sacheverell, traced their descent, with a distinct pride of ancestry, to the Plantagenet kings. All three children were destined to make outstanding careers in literature, and in the writings of their youth the backgrounds of the family seat, Renishaw Hall, on the Derbyshire heights not far from Chesterfield, and their grandmother's house, Londesborough Lodge in Scarborough, play an important part, especially in Edith Sitwell's poems.

In her posthumously published autobiography, *Taken Care Of* (1965), she confessed to an unhappy childhood, due, she maintained, partly to her passion for music and literature which ran counter to her parents' interests,

partly to the fact that her looks, although always uniquely striking, and never more so than in later life, were not cast in the mould of conventional Edwardian beauty. It was not until Helen Rootham arrived as governess in 1903 that Edith Sitwell found someone to encourage her natural tastes and liberate her into the world of art. Eventually, in 1914, they took a small flat together in London, where Edith Sitwell lived for the next eighteen years, although she spent most of the summers at Renishaw.

At about the age of seventeen Edith Sitwell discovered Swinburne's *Poems and Ballads* and conceived the ambition to write poetry herself. The gestation was long. It was not until 1913 that her earliest known verses were published in the *Daily Mirror*. In 1915, when her first small volume of poetry, *The Mother*, appeared, she was already twenty-eight.

From that moment her progress was rapid. *Twentieth-Century Harlequinade*, a collaboration between herself and her brother Osbert, appeared with seven of her poems in 1916. In the same year she launched an annual anthology of new poems called *Wheels*, intended as a counterblast to *Georgian Poetry* edited by (Sir) Edward Marsh [q.v.]. It lasted until 1921. All three Sitwells appeared in each number; perhaps its greatest coup was the publication in the issue of 1919 of seven of Wilfrid Owen's war poems.

The key moment, however, when the general public first became aware that a new, highly original poetic personality had arrived on the scene, was the performance of *Façade* at the Aeolian Hall in June 1923 (a private performance had been given fifteen months earlier). *Façade* was a collaboration between Edith Sitwell and a hitherto unknown young composer, (Sir) William Walton, whom the Sitwells had taken under their wing and who lived in Osbert's flat. It created a furore; abuse was showered on it by the majority of the critics; by the end of Edith Sitwell's life it had become an immensely popular concert piece, enthusiastically admired, above all by young people.

Façade dazzled by its verbal wit and fantasy, by its transposed imagery, and by its use of the strong rhythms of dance music, of waltzes, polkas, and foxtrots. Her aim, the author later declared, was to challenge 'the rhythmical flaccidity, the verbal deadness, the dead and expected patterns, of some of the poetry immediately preceding us'. But in the poems she published directly after *Façade*, in *The Sleeping Beauty* (1924) and *Troy Park* (1925), she returned to the elegiac, romantic vein for which she had already shown a unique gift in *Bucolic Comedies* (1923). Although in these poems the technical innovation, which had been so striking in *Façade*, was in abeyance, they were remarkable for their imaginative transmutation of the surroundings and reading of her youth. Perhaps the high point was reached in the concealed autobiography of herself and her two brothers in 'Colonel Fantock', in the opinion of many the supreme poem of her early period. In one of the surprising reversals of mood which were so frequent in her poetic history, in her next long poem, *Gold Coast Customs* (1929), she used the insistent rhythms, the clashing rhymes and assonances with which she had experimented in *Façade*, to create a grimly satiric vision of macabre horror and corruption. *Gold Coast Customs* is a superbly sustained *tour de force* in which the savagery of primitive African tribal life is counterpointed against the heartless luxury of modern plutocratic society.

A poetic silence of some years followed, due in part to the demands made upon her by the prolonged illness of Helen Rootham, with whom she lived in Paris for some years before her death in 1938. During her time in Paris Edith Sitwell developed a platonic passion for the artist Pavel Tchelitchew, a White Russian *émigré*. It was a passion which was to cause her anguish as well as joy. Edith's poetic silence was broken early in the war of 1939-45 by the appearance in 1942 of *Street Songs*, followed two years later by *Green Song*, a sequence of odes in the grand manner which reached its apocalyptic culmination in *The Shadow of Cain*, published in 1947. The long flowing lines, with their apparent ease and simplicity, may be said to be the supreme achievement of a lifetime of devoted apprenticeship to her art: skilfully using an association of ancient and universal symbols she conveyed an extraordinary sense of depth in time and space.

In the poems which followed, her critics have charged her with repeating herself and overexploiting her favourite imagery, although in her last collections, *Gardeners and Astronomers* (1953) and *The Outcasts* (1962), there are several pieces which show that the lyrical impulse of her early days was still alive to make new discoveries of great freshness and tenderness.

In the intervals of writing poetry, which was always her main preoccupation, Edith Sitwell wrote a number of prose works, some potboilers, some of considerable popular appeal, such as *The English Eccentrics* (1933), and two historical works of highly individual and impressive power, *Fanfare for Elizabeth* (1946) and *The Queens and the Hive* (1962). She was also an inveterate anthologist. Among her anthologies, *A Poet's Notebook* (1943) showed the range of her reading and the depths of her

reflections on her art; *The Atlantic Book of British and American Poetry* (1959) in its choice and its commentaries on the work of her favourite poets is as much a final statement of her own poetic ideals and beliefs as a declaration of love for the great tradition of poetry written in English.

Edith Sitwell was awarded honorary doctorates of literature by the universities of Oxford, Leeds, Durham, and Sheffield. She was appointed DBE in 1954 and became a Companion of Literature (awarded by the Royal Society of Literature) in 1963. She became a Roman Catholic in 1955. All her life she was an untiring champion of young poets and other artists whose work had caught her eye. She died in London 9 December 1964.

Her personal appearance was as striking as her personality. She was tall, and the pale oval face with the strong nose and thin lips, the flowing, often bizarre robes she affected, that never owed anything to the vagaries of fashion, the huge aquamarine rings she wore on her long delicate fingers, all contributed to a formidable, even overwhelming impression when she appeared in public. Her capacity for icy, lightning-swift repartee to bores, who were fatally attracted to her, concealed a great sense of fun and also a deep sense of compassion that could immediately be aroused by a genuine tale of misfortune.

The National Portrait Gallery has two drawings of her by Wyndham Lewis whose portrait of her is in the Tate Gallery which has also a portrait by Alvaro Guevara. The Graves Art Gallery, Sheffield, has a portrait by Roger Fry. She sat to her friend Pavel Tchelitchev for six portraits, one of which was lent by the owner, Edward James, to the Tate Gallery. There are reproductions of many photographs and paintings in *Edith Sitwell*, by Elizabeth Salter (1979).

[John Lehmann, *A Nest of Tigers*, 1968; John Pearson, *Façades: Edith, Osbert and Sacheverell Sitwell*, 1978; private information; personal knowledge.] JOHN LEHMANN

SITWELL, SIR (FRANCIS) OSBERT (SACHEVERELL), fifth baronet (1892-1969), writer, was born at 3 Arlington St., London, 6 December 1892, the elder son among the three children of Sir George Reresby Sitwell, fourth baronet [q.v.], and his wife, Lady Ida Emily Augusta Denison, fourth child and third daughter of the first Earl of Londesborough, who was the eldest son of Albert Denison, first Baron Londesborough [q.v.]. Like his elder sister (Dame) Edith [q.v.], and his younger brother (Sir) Sacheverell, Osbert Sitwell was destined to make a unique mark in his generation as a man of letters and a champion of the new movements in the arts of the first quarter of the twentieth century.

Although spending much time at Londesborough Lodge, Wood End, and Hay Brow in Scarborough, houses which belonged to his grandmothers, Osbert Sitwell always considered the ancestral seat, Renishaw Hall near Chesterfield, to which the family regularly moved in summer, as his true and well-loved home. Nevertheless, Scarborough made a deep impression on his boyish imagination, and appears as the background to many of his works of poetry and fiction. Later, the medieval castle of Montegufoni near Florence, which his father acquired in 1909 and subsequently remodelled, became a close rival in his affections, deeply sympathetic as he was to the climate, the arts, and the people of Italy from his first acquaintance with them in his youth.

He began his schooling at a preparatory school for which he appears to have had nothing but loathing, and then went to Eton (1906–9), an experience which in after years he valued chiefly for the opportunity it gave him to read and educate himself in his own way, and to make friends, many of whom were to last him for the rest of his life. Instead of going to university, he was sent to a military crammer, deliberately failed his examination for Sandhurst, but, due to his father's persistence, obtained a commission first in the Sherwood Rangers (1911), and then, some months later, in 1912, transferred to the Grenadier Guards (Special Reserve). As a well-heeled young Guards officer about town, he exploited to the full the opportunities his position gave him to explore not only the brilliant social world of the time, but also, often in the company of his younger brother, the latest manifestations of art, music, and theatre, in particular the Russian ballet. The pages he devotes to these years before the outbreak of war in 1914 in his autobiography are among the most vivid and memorable in that work.

As a serving Guards officer he was mobilized on the outbreak of war. In his writings he was remarkably reticent about his experiences of the fighting, except to record that in spite of the desolation and horrors of trench warfare he found the civilized camaraderie of the Guards a strongly compensating advantage. At the same time he found himself as a poet, and had his first poem published in *The Times* on 11 May 1916, under the title of 'Babel'. In the same year was published *Twentieth-Century Harlequinade, and Other Poems*, which he wrote in collaboration with his sister, Edith.

Having been promoted captain in September 1916, he left the army in 1919, and in November of the same year he moved into what was to remain his London home until almost the end of his life, 2 Carlyle Square in Chelsea, which he shared with his brother until the latter's marriage in 1925, and from which address he directed his unceasing war against everything that smacked to him of the philistine or pompously conventional, in a series of caustic and highly individual pronouncements and polemics.

One of his chief gifts as a writer was for satire, and it is satire that dominates the three novels he wrote between the wars: *Before the Bombardment* (1926), *The Man Who Lost Himself* (1929), and *Miracle on Sinai* (1933). With their passages of bravura description and frequent touches of lively invention, they are highly individual works, although it is difficult not to think that Sitwell lacked some essential gift that goes to make the true novelist. The same limitation may perhaps be found in his short stories. Surprisingly diverse in mood and theme, many of them were delightful and remained fresh to read, although the raconteur rather than the imaginative creator was a little too frequently uppermost. When assembled in *Collected Stories* (1953) they made an impressive volume of over 500 pages.

A more significant contribution to the taste and intellectual temper of his time was made by Sitwell's travel writings. Always on the lookout for new aesthetic experiences and the beautiful or marvellous which had been neglected by a previous generation, he opened the eyes of his contemporaries to many aspects of painting, sculpture, and architecture which were unfashionable at the time. His range was wide, from the Italian essays of *Winters of Content* (1932) to the Far Eastern travels of *Escape With Me!* (1939). To this Dictionary Sitwell contributed the notice of Sir Philip Sassoon.

Throughout Sitwell's adult life he wrote poetry, in which the satiric vein so characteristic of his fiction was strongly in evidence, although tempered, particularly in his poetic portraits from *England Reclaimed* in 1927 to *On the Continent* in 1958, by a warmth of sympathy and a strain of tender nostalgia for a fast-disappearing way of life.

There can be little doubt, however, that his finest achievement was his five-volume autobiography *Left Hand, Right Hand*, which he began writing at the outbreak of the war of 1939–45, and of which the fifth volume, *Noble Essences*, was published in 1950, and a postscript volume, *Tales My Father Taught Me*, in 1962. An exploration of the author's family history and the experiences and encounters of his own life, constructed according to a poetic logic of association rather than chronological sequence, this unique and highly wrought, but always fascinatingly readable, work is remarkable for its combination of shrewd social observation, portraits that are often wittily critical and affectionate at the same time, interspersed with romantic reverie and rhapsodic descriptions of places he had loved. One character dominates: the author's father Sir George, who emerges as a great comic character, living in a world of eccentric fantasy of his own. This is a portrait no doubt with its touches of exaggeration, but with a strong underlying note of exasperated filial affection.

Especially in his middle years Osbert Sitwell was of striking appearance. Tall, with a look of almost princely distinction and soldierly bearing, his formally courteous and aristocratic manners concealed a warmth and generosity of heart which manifested themselves without reservation towards young writers, musicians, and artists, whose gifts he had with immediate sensitive discernment judged to be outstanding. He could be malicious towards those he thought less outstanding and he enjoyed conducting vendettas against hostile critics and writers who had lost his favour.

Sitwell succeeded his father in the baronetcy in 1943, and was appointed CBE in 1956 and CH in 1958. He was made an honorary LLD of St. Andrews in 1946 and an honorary D. Litt. of Sheffield University in 1951. From 1951 to 1958 he was a trustee of the Tate Gallery. In the last phase of his life he was increasingly incapacitated by Parkinson's disease and came to rely heavily on his new assistant and secretary, Frank Magro, who tended him until he died. This caused distress to Sitwell's previous companion of some thirty years, David Horner, who at one time had expected to be left Montegufoni. Instead, the castle and Renishaw were left to Reresby Sitwell, Sacheverell's son, upon Osbert's death at Montegufoni 4 May 1969. Sacheverell (born 1897) succeeded his brother in the baronetcy.

There is a brass bust of Osbert Sitwell by Frank Dobson, which is in the flat at Montegufoni provided to Frank Magro in perpetuity. Another copy is in the Tate Gallery. A water-colour portrait by John Wheatley was exhibited in the Royal Academy in 1946. In 1921 and 1930 (Sir) Max Beerbohm drew cartoons of Sitwell. As a child he appeared in a family group painted by John Singer Sargent (1899). In the National Portrait Gallery is a pencil and water-colour portrait by Rex Whistler (1935).

[Osbert Sitwell, *Left Hand, Right Hand* (5 vols. of autobiography), 1944-50; Max Wykes-Joyce, *Triad of Genius*, part i, 1953; John Lehmann, *A Nest of Tigers*, 1968; John Pearson, *Façades: Edith, Osbert and Sacheverell Sitwell*, 1978; private information; personal knowledge.] JOHN LEHMANN

SKELTON, RALEIGH ASHLIN (1906-1970), cartographical historian, born at Plymouth 21 December 1906, was first registered by the name of Peter, and was known by this name to his friends. He was the second son of John Cecil Skelton, from Long Sutton, Lincolnshire, a marine engineer with the Eastern Telegraph Company, in whose service he moved from port to port. His mother was Agnes Gertrude Gilbert, claiming descent from the family of Sir Humphrey Gilbert [q.v.], for whom Raleigh was a family Christian name. His paternal uncle, who became Engineer Vice-Admiral Sir Reginald Skelton, had been with *Discovery* on the National Antarctic Expedition in 1901-4. Skelton obtained a scholarship at Aldenham School and at Pembroke College, Cambridge, where he took a first in French and German in part i of the modern languages tripos (1927) and a lower second in part ii (1929). He was for two years an assistant master at Berkhamsted School and then entered the British Museum as an assistant keeper in the department of printed books in 1931. Trained to catalogue accessions and to arrange the entries in the museum's general catalogue, he became a highly efficient library technician, who was also turning himself into a scholar by wide and carefully selected reading. His cataloguing brought him into contact with many of the early voyage collections and atlases and he proceeded to master the bibliography and content of those of the early modern period, which provided him with a starting-point for his later studies. He served in the Royal Artillery from 1939 to 1945, first in the Middle East (1941-4), later with the monuments, arts, and archives branch of the Allied High Commission, Austria; he was demobilized with the rank of major.

Returning to the British Museum in 1945, Skelton was seconded to the map room to work with the superintendent, E. W. Lynam, whom he succeeded in 1950, being promoted deputy keeper in 1953. The map room was an autonomous unit in the department of printed books, and Skelton used his considerable powers of organization and command to make it unique. He issued clear, precise instructions on what he wished to have done and drove himself and his helpers hard, but he was always ready to explain his reasons and to listen to suggestions. He was continuously concerned with the housing of the rapidly growing collections in a confined space, the conservation of those collections, the radical improvement of the map-catalogue (which, in a great burst of energy, he and his staff prepared for publication shortly before he retired), good and well-informed service to a growing body of users of the map room for whom he found space, and good relations with other departments in the museum and with cartographical institutions outside it. The result of his labours was the creation of a cartographical laboratory-library which was in the end without equal.

Elected FSA in 1951, Skelton was also involved in the congresses of the International Geographical Union from 1949 onwards, especially that of 1964, for which he mounted and catalogued an exhibition 'The Growth of London' at the Victoria and Albert Museum. He became a member of the IGU commission on early maps in 1952 (and its chairman from 1961), being particularly involved in the organization of *Monumenta Cartographica vetustioris aevi A.D. 1200–1500*, his introduction to volume i (*Mappemondes*) in 1964 giving an account of the project. He became a member of the Royal Society's committee on cartography and served at one time or another on the governing bodies of the Royal Geographical Society (he received the Gill memorial, 1956, and Victoria medal, 1970), the Society for Nautical Research, Royal Historical Society, Institute of Historical Research, British Records Association, and National Central Library. He was awarded the Research medal of the Royal Scottish Geographical Society in 1965.

Skelton's work for the Hakluyt Society, as secretary in 1946–66 and a member of council until his death, was outstanding. He built up its world-wide membership, tightened its editorial standards, got Cambridge University Press to become its publisher (which brought better distribution), and immersed himself in the work of making available early accounts of exploration. He had an exceptional capacity for throwing himself into the problems of each individual editor, acquiring rapidly an expert grasp of his problems and providing assistance, especially contributions on cartographical problems, often unattributed, for successive volumes. His special contribution was in making it possible for J. C. Beaglehole to undertake and complete his classic edition of Captain James Cook's journals, mobilizing subsidies and helpers, selecting a portfolio of charts (1955), and adding sections of his own on each of the three voyages. More than forty volumes were published by the society under his auspices.

Skelton had also much to do with the fluctuating fortunes of *Imago Mundi*, as a corresponding editor from 1950, secretary of its management committee (1959–66), when it was put on a sound footing, and general editor (1966–70). He considerably enhanced its standing as the leading international cartographical journal. Through his association with its founder, Leo Bagrow, he took on the revision and translation of his *History of Cartography* (1964). His friendship with Armando Cortesão led him to take an active part in the preparations for the

500th anniversary of the death of Henry the Navigator. He contributed substantially to Cortesão's edition (with A. Teixeira da Mota) of *Portugaliae monumenta cartographica* (6 vols., Lisbon, 1960), revising and adapting the long English introduction and delivering several papers to the celebratory congress in Lisbon.

In 1962–3 Skelton spent a sabbatical leave at Harvard University, acting as consultant and temporary map curator in order to set the map collections of the Widener Library in order, and lecturing on the history and bibliography of cartography. Later, at the Newberry Library, Chicago, he was a consultant on the cartographical collection and gave the Nebenzahl lectures for 1966 on 'The Study and Collecting of Early Maps: an Historical Survey'.

His work on Cook's early surveys had given Skelton an interest in the early cartography of Newfoundland, which he visited in 1968 to help plan a cartographic bibliography of the island and to receive an honorary D.Litt. from Memorial University whose library has acquired his books and papers.

From 1960 to 1965 Skelton was, with his colleague, G. D. Painter, involved in the study of the newly discovered Vinland map for the then anonymous American owner (Paul Mellon) who was later to present it to Yale University. This research, carried out under conditions of some secrecy, led Skelton to make a masterly survey of the cartography of the northern regions in the later Middle Ages and to add considerably to the authentication of the map (although until his death he was anxious to have it submitted to scientific tests which might establish its authenticity, in which he believed, although he considered it might, conceivably, be a fabrication). The furore which the publication of *The Vinland Map and the Tartar Relation*, by R. A. Skelton, T. E. Marston, and G. D. Painter, created in 1965 plunged him for many months into a whirl of international controversy, from which he emerged with the enhanced respect of both his supporters and those who differed from him.

Throughout this period, Skelton steadily made contributions to the study of English map making and distribution. His 'Tudor Town Plans in John Speed's "Theatre"' (*Archaeological Journal*, vol. cviii for 1951) and his stress on English examples in *Decorative Printed Maps of the 15th to 18th Centuries* (1952) were the first of many detailed studies. His *County Atlases of the British Isles, 1579–1703*, which had appeared over several years in parts, was published within a few weeks of his death. His history of the Ordnance Survey remained unfinished.

Skelton discovered in himself a vein of popular exposition which he exploited in a series of articles in the *Geographical Magazine* from 1953 onwards, using map evidence to bring out precisely what the great explorers had discovered and how the maps that recorded their discoveries often became the fallible guides of the next generation. Collected in *Explorers' Maps* (1958) they had an immediate success. It was, however, to an increasing range of specialists that he became an indispensable guide. He acquired an astonishing familiarity with maps of many periods but on European maps between the fifteenth and eighteenth centuries he became an internationally recognized authority. Always willing to put his knowledge fully at the service of enquirers, he found himself exploring cartographical problems of all sorts and often ended by contributing sections to their books.

In the early sixties Skelton became involved in the selection and presentation of the ambitious series of facsimile atlas publications which Nico Israel, the Amsterdam publisher, began to put out under the imprint Theatrum Orbis Terrarum. For many of them he wrote effective descriptive and bibliographical introductions and after his retirement he acted as a consultant to the firm. He was opposed to reprints which merely re-presented old books without apparatus, but believed in equipping facsimiles with adequate introductions and, where necessary, indexes. He collaborated effectively with D. B. Quinn and Alison Quinn on this basis in the production of Hakluyt's *Principall Navigations* (1589) (Hakluyt Society, 1965).

In 1967 Skelton retired from the British Museum, but worked harder than ever. He completed his fine edition and translation of the Yale Pigafetta MS which was also reproduced in colour-facsimile (Antonio Pigafetta, *Magellan's Voyage*, 1969), and was handling a few hours before he died the final proofs of *A Description of Maps and Architectural Drawings in the Collection made by William Cecil, first Baron Burghley, now at Hatfield House* (1971), which Lord Salisbury presented to the Roxburghe Club and which Skelton had compiled with Sir John Summerson. Three other volumes in which he had a major part were with the printers at the time of his death.

Skelton had a tall, slim figure, and did not in his latter years look his age. He walked with a military stride and never developed more than a slight suspicion of a scholar's stoop. He had considerable physical energy which he employed in walking and gardening. He had also exceptional powers of concentration and endurance, so that he could work long and intensively when writing. He had a clear logical mind which enabled him to seize on essentials in describing or analysing a map or book: he showed the same qualities in argument even if he sometimes

developed a case from too narrow premises. He had strong opinions and his judgements tended to be conservative, but in argument he never defended the claims of established authority when new information was presented to him or when an effective case was made out for a novel interpretation. He made an excellent collaborator, conscientious, sympathetic of approaches other than his own, but always strong-minded in defence of his personal views. His originality lay in his determination to use maps as historical documents in every possible way. He was also determined to mobilize the scattered and largely uncoordinated corpus of information on maps of the early modern period so that the maps should become intelligible and accessible to students and researchers. His development of precise methods and formulae for cataloguing maps, his enthusiasm for the presentation of effective bibliographies of maps and map literature, and his historical understanding combined to make him the leading cartographical historian in his time and an outstanding exponent of what came to be called cartobibliography.

In 1936 Skelton married Katherine, daughter of the late Canon William Arthur Macleod, who had been provost of Wakefield; they had two daughters. After the war they settled at Street Farm, Tilford, near Farnham, which was to be his home for the rest of his life. He was closely concerned in the life of the locality, served three terms on the parish council, was chairman of Tilford Cricket Club (his most cherished distinction), and took an active part in the Surrey Archaeological Society of which he eventually became president in 1968. Skelton died at Farnham 7 December 1970 from injuries received in a road accident.

[*Imago Mundi*, vol. xxv, 1971; private information; personal knowledge.]

DAVID B. QUINN

SLATER, SIR WILLIAM KERSHAW (1893-1970), scientist and agricultural administrator, was born in Oldham 19 October 1893, the only child of James Slater, cotton mill manager, and his wife, Mary Ann Kershaw, who came from a Yorkshire farming family. His early intellectual development was influenced by his uncle, William Kershaw, director of education for Oldham, and by F. Potter, an inspiring science master at Hulme Grammar School, Oldham, where Slater was educated after the age of fourteen.

Slater graduated B.Sc. from the university of Manchester in 1914, with first class honours in chemistry and the Leblanc medal. Rejected for military service because of defective eyesight, he began research, but this was soon curtailed for service with the Explosives Inspectorate.

After the war he became assistant lecturer in chemistry at Manchester University. In 1922, after a year in industry, he got a place in A. V. Hill's laboratory in Manchester, where he turned to biochemistry and obtained for the first time a reliable value for the heat of combustion of glycogen, essential for the interpretation of Hill's experiments on muscle. This success won him a Beit memorial medical research fellowship in 1923, with which he followed Hill to University College, London. Here, under (Sir) J. C. Drummond [q.v.], he continued work on heats of combustion and resolved some obscurities in connection with anaerobic metabolism in lower animals.

Slater's career now took an abrupt turn. Leonard and Dorothy Elmhirst, who had started the Dartington experiment in 1925, wanted the help of a scientist and in 1929, on Hill's recommendation, Slater was invited to join them. He set up a laboratory which was soon useful in nearly every part of the enterprise, and especially in soil surveying and soil improvement. Slater's business abilities early led to his acting as managing director of the two limited companies which were formed to take over the activities of the trading and constructional departments of the estate. When Dartington Hall was registered as a charitable trust, he became one of the trustees, with a still greater administrative load, but he did not abandon science. His unassuming enthusiasm imbued everyone at Dartington with the notion that some understanding of science was both practically useful and intellectually rewarding.

In 1941 the minister of agriculture, Robert S. (later Viscount) Hudson [q.v.], set up the Agricultural Improvement Council as part of his drive to increase the productivity of British agriculture, and in 1942 Slater joined its staff. He there became associated with (Sir) James A. Scott Watson in the creation of the National Agricultural Advisory Service and the establishment of a national chain of experimental husbandry farms and horticultural stations. To Slater must go much of the credit for the sound foundations on which the NAAS was built. He became secretary of the AIC in 1944 when (Sir) John C. F. Fryer moved to the Agricultural Research Council.

Fryer died suddenly in 1949 and Slater succeeded him as secretary of the ARC, a post in which he continued with increasing distinction until his retirement in 1960. Pre-war surveys by the ARC, wartime experience, and a resolve to maintain post-war productivity had led the Cabinet in 1946 to approve a greatly expanded programme of agricultural research. At the outset Slater saw that to realize this programme effectively he would have to work for the abolition of the restrictive administrative procedures with which the ARC was then saddled, and this was achieved with the passing of the Agricultural Research Act in 1956. This Act greatly increased the ARC's responsibilities, and put a much greater burden on the secretary and his staff, but the advantages were shown by more effective research and lower administrative costs. Slater was equally clear that expansion must not be achieved at the expense of quality; he encouraged the appointment of first-class scientists, and his support for the concept of ARC units in universities (originated by W. W. C. Topley, q.v.) secured that essential investment in pure science upon which depended future practical advances.

Slater was appointed KBE in 1951 and elected to the Royal Society in 1957. He was a D.Sc. of Manchester and an honorary D.Sc. of Queen's University, Belfast. He was president of the Royal Institute of Chemistry, 1961-3, a general secretary of the British Association for the Advancement of Science, 1962-5, and chairman of a government committee which proposed the creation of a Natural Resources (later changed to Environment) Research Council. Through Elmhirst, and through his membership of the Colonial Research Council, he had long been interested in the problems of food production in less developed countries, and after 1960 he gave much time to them. He served as British co-ordinator of several UN conferences and was the British representative on the CENTO Council for Scientific Education and Research. He did an immense amount of work for the Freedom from Hunger Campaign, and started the idea of the Food and Agriculture Organization's 1969 *Indicative World Plan for Agricultural Development*. Some of his views are expressed in his book, *Man Must Eat* (1964).

Slater was a big man who was very rarely put out or put off by difficulties, being of an equable temperament and yet extremely tenacious in matters that he considered important. He was a very able negotiator and conciliator, but he would not compromise on essential principles. He was friendly and approachable, and had the loyalty and affection of all who worked with him. He married, in 1921, Hilda, daughter of Augustus Whittenbury, a merchant of Moss Side, Manchester. They had two sons and a daughter. His married life was uniformly happy; his wife died in 1966, and his last years were further clouded by the death of his elder son in 1968. Slater himself died at Midhurst 19 April 1970.

[H. D. Kay in *Biographical Memoirs of Fellows of the Royal Society*, vol. xvii, 1971; *The Times*, 21 April 1970; private information; personal knowledge.]   E. G. Cox

SLIM, WILLIAM JOSEPH, first Viscount Slim (1891-1970), field-marshal, younger son of John Slim, an iron merchant of Bristol, and his wife, Charlotte, daughter of Charles Tucker, of Burnham, Somerset, was born in Bristol 6 August 1891. The family moved to Birmingham at the turn of the century and he began his education at St. Philip's Catholic School and went on to King Edward's School where he showed a flair for literature and the clear thinking which remained a distinctive trait. He was not notable at games but was a keen member of the Officers' Training Corps and his great ambition was to be an army officer. But his parents could not afford to send him to Sandhurst or guarantee the allowance then almost essential for young officers. He took a post with the engineering firm of Stewarts & Lloyds and at the same time succeeded in getting himself accepted by the Birmingham University OTC.

In August 1914 Slim was commissioned in Kitchener's army and posted to the Royal Warwickshire Regiment. With the 9th battalion he first saw active service at Cape Helles and in August 1915 was so seriously wounded at Sari Bair that it seemed unlikely he would ever again be fit for active service. He was posted to the 12th (holding) battalion, but in October 1916, although still officially unfit for active service, went with a draft to his old battalion in Mesopotamia where he was again wounded, gained the MC, and was evacuated to India. He had been granted a regular commission, with seniority from 1 June 1915 in the West India Regiment, but in 1919 he transferred to the Indian Army. From November 1917 until January 1920 he was on the staff at army headquarters, India, becoming a GSO 2 and temporary major in November 1918. In March 1920 he was posted to the 1/6th Gurkha Rifles; as he had not been applied for by the regiment his reception was not cordial, but his ability was soon recognized and he was appointed adjutant. Efficient and strict, he yet became well liked and respected.

In January 1926 Slim entered the Staff College, Quetta, and although he had not the interest in games and horsemanship which counted there for so much, he soon gained the respect and friendship of his contemporaries and was without doubt the outstanding student of his time. On passing out in 1928 he was appointed to army headquarters, India, as a GSO 2 and received a brevet majority in 1930. In 1934 he became Indian Army instructor at the Staff College, Camberley, where colleagues and students testified to the brilliance which earned him the brevet of lieutenant-colonel in 1935. After attending the 1937 course at the Imperial Defence College he went back to India

to command the 2/7th Gurkhas and a little over a year later was sent to command the Senior Officers School at Belgaum, with the rank of brigadier, a few months before the outbreak of war in 1939.

Slim was now given command of the 10th Indian Infantry brigade of 5th Indian division which went to Eritrea in the autumn of 1940. The Italians had occupied Gallabat on the Sudan-Abyssinia border and Slim was sent with a brigade group to retake it and to ensure that the Italians did not advance into the Sudan. Though Gallabat was captured after a hard fight, it was untenable unless the near-by Italian border post, Metemma, could also be taken before the Italians could move up their large reserves. Rather than risk being caught off balance Slim pulled out of Gallabat to positions from which he could prevent the Italians reoccupying it. Subsequent information indicated that the enemy had panicked and would have abandoned Metemma. Of his failure to attack Metemma Slim wrote later 'I could find plenty of excuses for failure, but only one *reason*—myself. When two courses of action were open to me I had not chosen, as a good commander should, the bolder. I had taken counsel of my fears.' Acceptance of blame if things went wrong and praise for his subordinates in victory were characteristic of Slim throughout his career.

Soon after Gallabat he was wounded in a surprise low-flying attack on a vehicle in which he was travelling. On recovering, in May 1941 he was given command, with the rank of major-general, of the 10th Indian division in Iraq and Syria, where he carried out a brief and successful campaign against the Vichy French forces. There followed an advance into Persia where a brisk minor action and much tactful firmness helped to ensure that Persia gave no further trouble during the war.

Much to his disappointment Slim was next recalled to India but his fears of becoming chairborne were dispelled when, on 19 March 1942, Sir A. P. (later Earl) Wavell [q.v.] sent him to Burma to organize a corps headquarters, which carried the rank of lieutenant-general, to take control of the two British-Indian divisions of the army retreating from Rangoon. He brought 'Burcorps' out battered and exhausted but in good heart, and on its disbandment was given command of XV Corps.

Slim's next task was to pull the chestnuts out of the fire in the closing stages of the disastrous Arakan campaign of 1942-3. His handling of this critical situation brought him into conflict with the commander-in-chief Eastern Army, who wished to relieve him of his command; but he had his way, and events vindicated his methods.

By this time Slim had evolved the strategy which was to put an end to the hitherto unbroken success of Japanese infiltration: to cover the approaches to vital areas (at this time Chittagong and Imphal) with well-stocked strongholds which were to stand fast if by-passed, to be supplied by air if necessary, and to cut the supply lines of the infiltrators. The strongholds would thus become backstops against which army or corps reserves would destroy the infiltrators before moving straight into the counter-offensive.

On being given command of the newly formed 14th Army in October 1943 Slim began to build up the administrative organization, including a highly developed air supply system, to underpin his new strategy. At the same time he saw to it that all units in the 14th Army knew what was expected of them. Wherever he went—and he went everywhere—he inspired confidence. In early 1944 the Japanese launched the grand offensive which they hoped would so shatter the Allied forces on the India–Burma border that there would be revolt in India which could be exploited by the so-called Indian National Army. In Arakan the offensive was broken in three weeks and the counter-stroke drove the Japanese from their North Arakan stronghold. At Imphal/Kohima the Japanese 15th Army suffered a disastrous defeat and over 50,000 casualties, of whom more than half were dead, and withdrew in disorder to the Chindwin. These victories earned Slim the CB and KCB and international fame.

During these critical battles Slim was harassed by two unusual command problems. General Stilwell commanding the American–Chinese forces refused to serve under the 11th Army Group, but eventually agreed to take orders from Slim until his own force reached Kamaing within striking distance of his objective of Myitkyina. Fortunately the friendship between Slim and Sir George Giffard [q.v.], who commanded the 11th Army Group, ensured that this awkward situation caused no trouble. The second problem was presented by Major-General Orde Wingate. Though Slim admired Wingate's gift for leadership his confidence in Long Range Penetration was limited, he felt unsure about Wingate himself, and he strongly disapproved of fragmenting tested formations like 70th division to furnish the Chindit columns which seemed to him a private army working for private purposes. Wingate's attempt to exploit his connection with Churchill was a particular embarrassment. But operation Thursday was an Anglo-American commitment, and on 5 March it was Slim who, at the take-off airfield, authorized the fly-in of the Chindit striking force despite last-minute evidence from air-photographs of

Japanese attempts to block the landing-strips.

In the reconquest of Burma, Slim's task was to capture Mandalay and consolidate on the line of the Irrawaddy from there south-westwards to its junction with the Chindwin about 100 miles distant. When on 12 November 1944 11th Army Group was replaced by Allied Land Forces South East Asia (ALFSEA) under Sir Oliver Leese, the 14th Army advance on Mandalay had already begun. Slim had hoped to trap and destroy the reconstituted Japanese 15th Army west of Mandalay on the plain bounded by the Chindwin and Irrawaddy, but by mid December he realized that it had seen its danger and withdrawn across the Irrawaddy. On 17 December he sent ALFSEA a revised plan and the next day gave his corps commanders verbal orders to put it into operation at once. Slim had taken the bit between his teeth and this, added to the fact that earlier he had refused to fly a division into north Burma to contact the American–Chinese forces advancing under General Sultan, was perhaps the beginning of a rift between him and the commander-in-chief ALFSEA which had serious repercussions later, although events had vindicated Slim's handling of the operations.

The new plan put in motion a great two-pronged battle designed to cut the Japanese communications to their main base at Rangoon, envelop and destroy the 15th and 33rd Japanese Armies in north Burma, and isolate the 28th Japanese Army in Arakan for destruction later. The Japanese life-line was to be cut at Meiktila, some 80 miles south of Mandalay, while the two Japanese armies in north Burma were to be held there by what was to be made to seem the advance of the whole 14th Army on Mandalay; a deception which made full use of the romantic appeal of 'the road to Mandalay'. While XXXIII Corps, headed by a division known by the Japanese to have been in IV Corps, drove eastwards on Mandalay, IV Corps, in wireless silence, moved unostentatiously south and established a bridgehead near the confluence of the Chindwin and Irrawaddy. Thence a motorized and armoured column burst through to Meiktila, there to be supplied and reinforced by air.

Great in conception, brilliant in execution, the manœuvre mystified and misled the Japanese who took the thrust south to be the deception and so concentrated on trying to stop the thrust on Mandalay. Thus they were unable to prevent Meiktila being overrun. Their desperate efforts to retake Meiktila collapsed by the end of March and meanwhile the garrison of Mandalay left to fight to the last were destroyed. The failure to retake Meiktila sealed the fate of the Japanese Burma Area Army whose commander-in-chief described it as 'the master stroke'.

On 1 April 1945 Slim began the drive on Rangoon. One corps, with most of the armour, pursued the remnants of the 15th and 33rd Japanese armies down the Mandalay-Rangoon road while another drove down the Irrawaddy valley against the 28th Japanese Army, the remnants of which got penned in the Pegu Yomas and as planned were destroyed later. On 5 May 1945 the 14th Army linked up with the amphibious force which had landed unopposed in Rangoon two days earlier. So ended the brilliant series of victories which went far to substantiate Lord Mountbatten's view that 'Slim was the finest general the Second World War produced'. Throughout the campaign Slim was invariably at hand at vital moments to help if needed.

The day after Rangoon was taken over by 14th Army Slim was told by the commander-in-chief of ALFSEA that he proposed to make a change in the command of 14th Army for the invasion of Malaya, and offered him Burma Command. Slim refused it and said that as it seemed that the high command had lost confidence in him he would apply to the commander-in-chief in India to be allowed to retire. There was dismay in 14th Army and at GHQ India, and it was not long before the direct intervention of the CIGS Lord Alanbrooke [q.v.], resulted in Slim's supercession being cancelled.

He was promoted full general 1 July 1945 and was shortly afterwards himself appointed commander-in-chief ALFSEA, taking up the appointment on 10 August 1945. At the beginning of 1946 he was recalled to England to resuscitate the Imperial Defence College and on completion of his two years as commandant he retired from the army and was appointed deputy chairman of the Railway Executive. This appointment was short-lived for on 1 November 1948 he was recalled to the army to be chief of the imperial general staff and two months later was promoted field-marshal. He visited every British command overseas as well as India, Pakistan, Canada, the United States, Australia, and New Zealand. Before his term had expired he was nominated the next governor-general of Australia. He took office in 1953 and soon established himself in the affections of the Australian people as 'a human being who understands how human beings think'. Lord Casey considered that Australia was very fortunate in having him as governor-general. Slim made it his business to seek out Australia and the Australians and meet them as a man who had something to contribute, and when he relinquished office after an extended term the prime minister of Australia gave it as his opinion that there never had been two people who achieved a greater hold on the affections and regard of the Australian people than had Sir William and Lady Slim.

On leaving Australia in 1960 Slim accepted four active directorships and membership of the board of advice of the National Bank of Australasia. Eleven universities, including Oxford and Cambridge, conferred honorary degrees on him and in 1962 he was master of the Clothworkers' Company. He was a freeman of the City of London and between 1944 and 1960 was colonel of three regiments. In 1963 he was appointed deputy constable and lieutenant-governor of Windsor Castle and became constable and governor the following year, a post which he held until shortly before his death. Before 1939 he published many short stories under the pen-name of Anthony Mills. His book, *Defeat into Victory* (1956), was considered one of the finest published on the war of 1939-45 and sold over a hundred thousand copies. His other two books, *Courage and other Broadcasts* (1957) and *Unofficial History* (1959), a collection of reminiscences many of which had appeared in *Blackwood's*, were also very successful.

His robust appearance and determined jutting chin gave an impression of ruthlessness, but nothing could be further from the truth. Kindly and approachable with a quiet sense of humour so evident in his book, *Unofficial History*, he possessed tremendous fortitude and determination and, in all walks of life, he inspired the confidence given to a great leader. Once a course of action had been decided he carried it through whatever the difficulties: he lived up to his tenet that 'the difficult is what you do today, the impossible takes a little longer'. His humility about his own achievements is exemplified by a remark he made to a friend on learning that he was to be chief of the imperial general staff 'I only hope I can hold it down'.

Slim was appointed CBE (1942), to the DSO (1943), CB and KCB (1944), GBE (1946), GCB (1950), GCMG (1952), GCVO (1954), KG (1959), and was created a viscount in 1960. He married in 1926 Aileen, daughter of the Revd John Anderson Robertson, minister at Corstorphine, Edinburgh. He had one daughter and one son, John Douglas (born 1927), who also entered the army and who succeeded him when he died in London 14 December 1970. After a public funeral with full military honours at St. George's Chapel, Windsor, Slim was cremated privately.

The National Army Museum has a portrait by Leonard Boden. There is also a portrait by T. C. Dugdale.

[Lord Slim's own writings and his record of service; biographical record in the Australian

National Library; S. Woodburn Kirby (Official History), *The War Against Japan*, vols. ii–v, 1958–69; Sir Geoffrey Evans, *Slim as Military Commander*, 1969; Ronald Lewin, *Slim: the Standardbearer*, 1976; private information; personal knowledge.]

M. R. ROBERTS

SMART, WILLIAM GEORGE (BILLY) (1893–1966), circus proprietor, was born. 23 April 1893 at West Ealing, the son of Charles Smart, and his wife, Susan. His was a fairground family, and he began work at the age of fifteen in charge of a hand-operated roundabout on his father's fairground at Slough, Buckinghamshire. After his marriage in 1914 to Nellie, daughter of Harry Digby, he set up his own business as a fairground proprietor, but met with little success. Facing considerable hardship, he bought a pony and cart, collected rags and bones, and again failed. He hired out the pony and cart for 3s. 6d. a week, sold winkles, and dug gardens, while his wife took in laundry. Gradually his fortunes improved, and he again began to build up a fairground business, this time with greater success. By 1939 it had become one of the largest in the country, but was adversely affected by the wartime blackout.

He had always harboured an ambition to extend his business into the world of circus and in 1946, with the backing of his family, he staked all his resources on establishing a travelling circus. The circus grew rapidly to become one of the largest and most successful touring circuses in Britain, and was able to continue when other large circuses were being forced to disband because of steeply rising running costs. Smart's popularity was aided by the advent of television; his show was first screened by the BBC in 1957, and although all but two minutes were blacked out by a technical breakdown, the Smart circus became established as regular and popular television fare at holiday times.

Smart's circus grew to be one of the largest in the world, touring every part of the British Isles, and with permanent quarters and an associated zoo at Winkfield, Berkshire, not far from where Smart began his fairground career. The circus's popularity was greatly aided by the personality of its proprietor; he was a showman on the grand scale, weighed over 20 stone, constantly smoked large cigars, and on one occasion he rode an elephant through the streets of Mayfair and parked it at a meter before inserting a shilling. He performed extensive works for charity, and in recognition was made honorary mayor of Calgary, Canada.

In 1962 Smart made an offer to the town council of Blackpool to lay out and run a 150-acre replica of the Disneyland amusement park in California, but negotiations failed.

Smart and his wife had six daughters and four sons, and boasted an eldest grandson the same age as their youngest son. By maintaining regular television appearances, and combining the circus's winter quarters with a zoo, his family were able to continue the business successfully after his death. At its height the circus owned 150 horses and employed artists of every nationality.

Smart collapsed and died 25 July 1966 while conducting the band at his circus zoo at Ipswich, Suffolk. The funeral was of appropriate magnificence, the procession to his burial at Winkfield including a coffin weighing seven hundredweight, three cars filled with flowers, and a large floral tribute in the shape of an elephant.

[*The Times*, 26 July 1966; private information.]

ALAN HAMILTON

SMITH, DAVID NICHOL (1875–1962), scholar, was born at Buccleugh Place, Edinburgh, 16 September 1875, the younger son of Henry G. C. Smith, a teacher of mathematics and author of several successful mathematical textbooks, and his wife, Camilla Baxter. He was educated at George Watson's College and at the university of Edinburgh, where he took the new honours course in English, graduating in 1895 with a first class. The English professor was David Masson [q.v.], then nearing retirement, but the new course was largely designed and taught by his lecturer, Gregory Smith, later professor of English at Belfast, Nichol Smith's elder brother. When Masson retired in 1895 he was succeeded by George Saintsbury (whose notice Nichol Smith contributed to this Dictionary), who gave the young graduate the task of revising the index to his *History of Nineteenth Century Literature*, an exercise which convinced him, as he was to recall many years later at a dinner of the Saintsbury Club, that 'the only dates in which Saintsbury could be trusted to be minutely accurate were the dates of vintages'.

A fellowship in English now enabled Nichol Smith to pass a year at the Sorbonne, which was mainly spent in studying French literary criticism. One of the first-fruits of those studies was an edition of Boileau's *L'Art Poétique* (1898), a remarkably mature and disciplined piece of scholarship for a young man of twenty-three. For the next few years he supported himself by editing various texts for use in schools, but this Grub Street period ended in 1902 when he became assistant at the university of Glasgow to (Sir) Walter Raleigh (whose notice he also contributed to this Dictionary). In the summer of 1904 Raleigh was appointed to the new chair of English at Oxford, and Nichol Smith obtained the professorship of English at Armstrong College, Newcastle upon Tyne, shortly after his twenty-ninth birthday. The two men were not to be separated for long. Among Raleigh's projects for the Clarendon Press was an old-spelling edition of Shakespeare's plays based on the First Folio, and he invited his old Glasgow assistant to edit it, contriving that he should be appointed to the Goldsmiths' readership at Oxford (1908). Nichol Smith already knew a good deal about the textual problems involved, and was soon to know much more: whereas Raleigh always thought of the project as a simple job—'I had only to remove obvious errors and be in effect a competent printer's reader'. On this question the views of the two men could not be reconciled, and after some years Nichol Smith reluctantly decided to abandon the edition. He continued, however, to give Raleigh valuable assistance in organizing the English school, and later helped his successor, George Gordon [q.v.], in planning the new B.Litt. course.

In 1921 Nichol Smith became a fellow of Merton College and from 1929 to 1946 he was Merton professor of English literature. He was elected FBA in 1932 and received honorary degrees from universities in England, Scotland, France, the United States, and Australia. In later life he travelled a good deal. In 1936-7 he worked at the Huntington Library and in 1946-7 he was at Smith College and at the university of Chicago. In 1950-1 he lectured at the university of Adelaide and he was also Nuffield lecturer in New Zealand. As a lecturer he was judicious, lucid, and endlessly informative rather than brilliant; he was perhaps at his best when supervising the work of the long line of graduate students who came under his care, and who used to revisit him in his book-lined study at 20 Merton Street for the rest of his life.

Meanwhile he was turning his attention increasingly towards the eighteenth century. His edition of *Eighteenth Century Essays on Shakespeare* (1903) had as part of its aim 'to suggest that there are grounds for reconsidering the common opinion that the century did not give him his due'. Much of his later work invited further reconsideration of eighteenth-century literature, notably two series of lectures, *Shakespeare in the Eighteenth Century* (1928) and *Some Observations on Eighteenth Century Poetry* (1937), the latter being the Alexander lectures at the university of Toronto. His Clark lectures on *John Dryden* (1950), a work of his old age, show some decline in his powers. As an editor, and more especially as an annotator, he had few equals. His *Characters from the Histories & Memoirs of the Seventeenth Century* (1918) is

a fine example of the erudition, precision, and editorial good manners which he brought to bear on such work. Among his major editions is one of Swift's *Tale of a Tub* (with A. C. Guthkelch, 1920); *The Letters of Jonathan Swift to Charles Ford* (1935); and (with E. L. McAdam) *The Poems of Samuel Johnson* (1941). An edition of *Gulliver's Travels* on which he had been at work for many years (slowly and meticulously, as was his custom) was unhappily left unfinished at his death. Although he ventured outside his favourite period on a number of occasions, and maintained, fairly enough, that he was not 'cursedly confined to one century', it is for his work in promoting a better understanding of eighteenth-century literature that he will be chiefly remembered. He died at Oxford 18 January 1962.

He married in 1915 Mary, daughter of the Revd George Harford, vicar of Mossley Hill, Liverpool, and honorary canon of Liverpool; they had three daughters and a son, Christopher, killed at Tobruk with the Royal Air Force in 1942. A rather grim drawing of Nichol Smith by Sir Muirhead Bone is in the possession of the family. The greater part of his remarkable collection of books, mainly in eighteenth-century literature, is now in the National Library of Australia at Canberra. A smaller collection of books printed before 1800, and consisting mainly of literary criticism, was presented by him in 1959 to the National Library of Scotland, which also has a considerable file of his correspondence.

[Private information; personal knowledge.]
JAMES SUTHERLAND

SMITH, SIR FRANK EDWARD (1876-1970), industrial scientist, was born 14 October 1876 in Aston Manor, Birmingham, the son of Joseph Smith, an office clerk, and his wife, Fanny Jane Hetherington. Smith was educated at Smethwick Central School, which he left at fourteen to become a laboratory assistant at Smethwick Technical College. He studied part-time at the Birmingham Technical School where he gained honours in inorganic chemistry and magnetism and electricity. He then won a national scholarship to the Royal College of Science, in the face of keen competition from all the schools in the country. This was the first step in his remarkable career. He studied chemistry, mathematics, and physics with some mechanical drawing, geology, and astrophysics. He was awarded the associateship of the RCS in physics (first class) in July 1899. He remained at the Royal College of Science as a part-time teacher and demonstrator, and became much involved in the study of electrical measurements.

When in 1900 the National Physical Laboratory was opened at the Kew Observatory, with (Sir) Richard Glazebrook [q.v.] as its director, F. E. Smith was one of his first assistants. For the next ten years he devoted himself to the establishment of accurate electrical standards and methods of measurement.

The first success was the building of the current balance, which enabled the ampere to be determined with great accuracy. This in turn provided a standard with which to develop a voltmeter better than any then existing. The next problem was to improve the Weston cell as a stable and reproducible electromotive force, which Smith was able to do by a change in the electrolyte. There still remained the problem of the measurement of resistance in absolute units. For this Smith, with financial help from the Company of Drapers and Sir Andrew Noble, FRS [q.v.], developed a method suggested by L. V. Lorenz. The first 'Lorenz machine' was constructed and installed at the NPL where it still is.

These developments led Smith to propose an International Congress on Electrical Units and Standards, and this was held in London at the invitation of the British Government in 1908. The units then decided upon remain substantially those in use today (1981). In 1910 Smith went to Washington to assist the National Bureau of Standards to implement these decisions. Smith had made his mark.

In 1914 the National Physical Laboratory became involved in war work, and Smith made important technical contributions. Ernest Rutherford (later Lord Rutherford of Nelson), Sir J. J. Thomson [qq.v.], and others persuaded the Admiralty to set up a Board of Invention and Research, into which many scientists from the NPL were drawn. It is known that F. E. Smith invented the first magnetic mine which sank a number of German submarines. For this Smith received an award of £2,000 from the Admiralty. He became a fellow of the Royal Society in 1918.

In April 1918 the National Physical Laboratory was transferred to the Department of Scientific and Industrial Research. Glazebrook retired, and the following year Smith left to join the Admiralty. In 1920 he was appointed director of the new Scientific Research and Experimental Department. The Admiralty Research Laboratory was constructed at Teddington, under his control. He was responsible directly to the third sea lord, controller of the navy for the general direction and organization of research work for naval purposes. When research reached a stage where its practical results were to be tested, it was handed over to the departments which were to make use of it. Since these departments were dependent on the director of research for most of their scientific manpower, Smith was able to influence the scientific standards throughout. In 1923, three years after Smith's appointment, (Admiral) Sir Frederick Laurence Field [q.v.], on leaving the post of controller, concluded his report with these words: 'I have no hesitation in stating that the scientific section of the Admiralty, working under the able direction of Mr. Smith, has developed into a most valuable and essential adjunct of the Fleet.'

In 1929 Smith was offered and accepted the post of secretary to the Department of Scientific and Industrial Research. The activities of this Department covered many fields. There were boards concerned with building, chemistry, food preservation, transport, forest products, fuel, metallurgy, radio, water pollution, and the Geological Survey. There were also many other committees for research, and fully operative research laboratories and sub-laboratories in several fields. Smith showed great skill both in organization and consolidation, and in dealing with government departments, politicians, and industrialists. The Industrial Research Associations, which were co-operatives in various fields, were also partly financed by the Department. The Road Research Laboratory was taken over from the Ministry of Transport and later became one of Smith's main interests. He remained secretary of DSIR until 1939.

During these years Smith was active in many other fields. Most scientific organizations set up in the United Kingdom at one time or another had Smith on their governing body, commonly as president. He was on the Royal Society's council from 1922 to 1924, and from 1929 to 1938 was its secretary. He was a member of the Physical Society from 1907, a member of council from 1909, and held many of its offices, including the presidency (1924–6). He was a founder-fellow of the Institute of Physics in 1920 and its president from 1943 to 1946. He was prominent in the British Association for the Advancement of Science for most of his life. He was president of the Junior Institution of Engineers 1935–6 and a governor of the Imperial Institute (1930–8). He became chairman of the technical sub-committee of the Television Advisory Council in 1935.

At the age of sixty-two Frank Smith began a new career in industry. He became adviser on scientific and industrial research to Anglo-Iranian Oil (later British Petroleum), a post he held for seventeen years. He also had a long association with Birmingham Small Arms Co. Ltd.—at first as an unofficial adviser, but in 1944 as chairman of the research committee. In 1947 he became a director, and resigned in 1957 on his eighty-first birthday.

Smith also played an important part during

the war of 1939–45 on advisory scientific committees to various ministries. He was controller of telecommunications equipment, Ministry of Aircraft Production, director of instrument production of the Ministry of Supply, and controller of bearings production at the same Ministry. He was chairman of the Technical Defence Committee MI5 from 1940 to 1946.

The success of Smith's work was recognized by many honours: OBE (1918), CBE (1922), GBE (1939), CB (1926), KCB (1931), and GCB (1942).

Smith was physically attractive, dignified, friendly, and kindly. On the other hand he was very reserved, or even somewhat aloof, and in later years developed an authoritative and somewhat inflexible manner. The brilliance of his mind was generally acknowledged, and he was an indefatigable worker. His academic honours included A.R.C.Sc., D.Sc. (Oxon, 1926, and Sheffield, 1936), LLD (Birmingham, 1930, and Aberdeen, 1931). He also received many distinguished medals. His publications were many, but his original contributions were confined to his time at the National Physical Laboratory. After that time his work was organizational and administrative, and his influence in scientific circles enormous. He was a brilliant lecturer, and much in demand.

In 1902 he married May (died 1961), daughter of Thomas B. King, of Birmingham; they had one daughter. Smith died at Minehead 1 July 1970.

[Charles F. Goodeve in *Biographical Memoirs of Fellows of the Royal Society*, vol. xviii, 1972; private information.]

CHARLES GOODEVE

SMITH, SIR SYDNEY ALFRED (1883–1969), professor of forensic medicine, was born at Roxburgh in the goldfields of Otago in New Zealand 4 August 1883, the youngest child of James Jackson Smith, contractor to the municipality making and repairing roads. His father was a cockney who had emigrated to New Zealand and married another immigrant, Mary Elizabeth Wilkinson, a Yorkshire-woman whose first husband had died young leaving her with six children.

Smith was educated at the village school, became assistant to the local pharmacist, then went to Dunedin as an assistant where he qualified as a pharmacist at the age of twenty-three. He at once began to study medicine and as a part-time student in the faculty of science at Victoria College, Wellington, took his first-year chemistry and physics examinations while holding the post of dispensing chemist in Wellington Hospital.

He went next to Edinburgh University where he won a Vans Dunlop scholarship in botany and zoology which supported him to the extent of £300 spread over three years. He graduated MB, Ch.B. with first class honours and a research scholarship in 1912. After a short period in general practice he rejected this as a career and became an assistant in the department of forensic medicine at the suggestion of Professor Harvey Littlejohn. He obtained his MD in 1914 with a gold medal and the Alison prize. He had already had his first big medico-legal case in the prosecution in 1913 of Patrick Higgins for the murder of his two young sons.

Nevertheless, having already obtained his DPH (1913), he returned to New Zealand where he became medical officer for health for Otago at Dunedin. After the outbreak of war his department would not release him, but on transfer to Wellington he combined civil-health work with duties in various camps with the rank of major in the New Zealand Army Corps.

In 1917 Smith was appointed principal medico-legal expert to the Egyptian Government with a lectureship in forensic medicine at the School of Medicine in Kasr el-Aini, Cairo. The next period of eleven years was probably the most formative in his life for he made original contributions to forensic medicine in ballistics and firearms, and amongst other things he was responsible for the successful investigation of the murder of Sir Lee Stack [q.v.] in 1924.

In 1928 Smith succeeded his old chief in the regius chair of forensic medicine in Edinburgh which he held until 1953, becoming dean of the medical faculty in 1931. In these years his name was associated as an expert witness with many cases, both for the Crown and for the defence — the characteristic of a great and unprejudiced man, for these involved conflict with the established and, until then, unchallenged experts in England, not least of them Sir Bernard Spilsbury [q.v.]. So great was Smith's reputation that his cases on occasion took him as far afield as Ceylon and New Zealand.

During the war of 1939–45 he continued in his old expertise and devoted time to investigating the ballistical properties of various types of official ammunition. He also acted as consultant in medico-legal cases to the army; and he made possible the founding of the Polish medical school attached to Edinburgh University. He was a member of the General Medical Council from 1931 to 1956 and after retiring from his chair became consultant in forensic medicine to the World Health Organization. In 1954–7 he was rector of Edinburgh University which conferred an honorary LLD upon him in 1955; and in the following year he was elected an honorary member of the Royal Society of New Zealand. He was appointed CBE in 1944 and knighted in 1949, and he was appointed also to the Order of the Nile, third class, and to the Polonia Restituta, third class.

A burly, cheerful man, Smith possessed great charm and was a natural academic politician. This, with his alert and logical mind, his wide knowledge and experience, made him an expert witness whose integrity was never challenged. His was the stimulating influence in founding the British Association in Forensic Medicine of which he was first president. But he will perhaps be best remembered for his writing. His text-book, *Forensic Medicine*, was first published in 1925, has gone into many editions, has been translated into Spanish, and was awarded the Swiney prize in 1929. With John Glaister he wrote *Recent Advances in Forensic Medicine* (1931, 2nd edn. 1939); and between 1928 and 1956 he edited four editions of *Principles and Practice of Medical Jurisprudence* by A. S. Taylor [q.v.]. Smith's reminiscences, *Mostly Murder*, were published in 1959.

Smith married in 1912 Catherine Goodsir Gelenick (died 1962), by whom he had one son and a daughter who became a doctor. He died in Edinburgh 8 May 1969. On his retirement from Edinburgh University he was presented with his portrait painted by Sir William Hutchison.

[*Lancet*, 31 May 1969; *British Medical Journal*, 17 May and 7 June 1969; private information; personal knowledge.]

FRANCIS CAMPS

SMITH, THOMAS (1883-1969), superintendent of the Light Division, National Physical Laboratory, was born 6 April 1883 at Leamington Spa. He had an elder brother who died in infancy, a younger brother, and three sisters. He was the son of William Edward Smith, a schoolmaster, and his wife, Dorothy Ann Jameson. Smith was educated at Leamington School where his father was headmaster, and at Warwick School. He entered Queens' College, Cambridge, as a scholar in 1902, was sixteenth wrangler in part i of the mathematical tripos in 1905, and obtained second class honours in the mechanical sciences tripos in 1906. He was a master at Oundle School for one year (1906-7), but, not being happy or successful in this post, he joined the National Physical Laboratory in 1907 where he remained for the rest of his working life. He worked for two years on electricity and on tide prediction, in 1909 he became head of the Optics Division, and when the Light Division was formed in 1940 he became superintendent (1940-8).

Smith was president of the Optical Society (1925-7), and of the Physical Society (1936-8). He was elected a fellow of the Royal Society in 1932. When the International Commission for Optics was formed in 1946, he was chosen, by the general consensus of delegates from many countries, to be its first president (1947-9). He gave the Thomas Young oration in 1949. He was made an honorary member of the Optical Society of America in 1957.

Smith was the author (in a few cases, joint author), of about 170 scientific papers. About 150 concerned the design and testing of optical systems and 10 were on colorimetry. He was interested in the principles underlying the design of optical systems and limited his contribution to practical design problems to some calculations on doublet lenses. He developed algebraic methods of tracing rays without the use of trigonometrical tables. His methods were equally suitable for skew rays and meridional rays and for both spherical and aspherical surfaces. In the presentation of his work he sought the utmost generality and what he considered the most elegant mathematical form. This made his work readily intelligible to only a few and created a resistance additional to that due to the radical novelty of his approach. His algebraic method is very suitable for machine calculation, as are the iterative methods of calculation which he later developed.

In the later part of his work Smith used the mathematical methods of Sir William Rowan Hamilton [q.v.] to calculate image formation from the eikonal rather than from ray tracing. About 1930 he developed very general formulae for image formation in matrix form. He later found that his main results had been anticipated in substance by the astronomer R. A. Sampson [q.v.] in 1898 and made a full acknowledgement. Although he was not the first in this field, it was Smith's work which led to the later use of matrix methods.

Smith came to colorimetry at a time when the logical principles of quantitative colour specification and calculation were being devised. In association with J. Guild he proposed a 'System of Colorimetry' which was adopted by the International Commission of Illumination (CIE).

Smith was a tall, well-built man of considerable 'presence'. In general, he was a man of few words and no small talk, though he would laugh heartily at a clever joke. Many people found him forbidding, and on scientific matters he was indeed a severe and formidable critic, but those who approached him on personal matters found him sincerely kind and sympathetic. He married, in 1913, Elsie Muriel, daughter of E. M. Elligott, a schoolmaster and a relative of the McElligott of Macgillicuddy. They had three daughters and two sons of whom the elder was also a wrangler in the Cambridge mathematical tripos. Smith died 28

November 1969 in his home at Heathfield, Sussex.

[Autiobiographical notes in the archives of the Royal Society; K. J. Habell in *Biographical Memoirs of Fellows of the Royal Society*, vol. xvii, 1971; private information; personal knowledge.]   R. W. DITCHBURN

SNEDDEN, SIR RICHARD (1900-1970), chief executive of the Shipping Federation, was born 18 April 1900 in Edinburgh, the elder son of George Snedden, lawyer, and his wife, Ada Inkpin. He was educated first at George Watson's Boys' College where he became 'dux' of the school. A short period of army service ended with the armistice of 1918 and he proceeded to the university of Edinburgh where he graduated MA in 1921 and LLB in 1922. He was president of the students' representative council, office bearer in many societies, and was acclaimed as an outstanding student. When in 1953 the senate conferred the honorary degree of LLD upon him it was perhaps the honour he valued above all others.

Throughout his life, although small physically and short-sighted, Snedden dominated any gathering, serious or convivial. After taking his degrees he was tempted by the Scots bar but the lure of London prevailed. In 1923 he joined the National Confederation of Employers' Organizations, later to become the British Employers' Confederation, and ultimately the Confederation of British Industry. This, the collective voice of employers' organizations dealing with personnel, was responsible for nominating representatives on the governing body of the International Labour Office at Geneva and its many tripartite conferences. The ILO was designed to reduce world friction by adopting international conventions to standardize conditions of work. Snedden was an ideal apprentice and later a master craftsman in this semi-political world of industrial relations.

He was called to the English bar by the Middle Temple in 1925. He was a member of the British delegations to all ILO conferences from 1923 to 1969, vice-president of the 1955 conference, vice-chairman of the employers' group (1953-60), member of the governing body (1952-60), and leader of the shipowners' group at all maritime meetings in 1942-69. He was vice-president (1955-6) and president (1957-8) of the International Organization of Employers—the international association of employers' organizations.

At Geneva, Snedden attracted the attention of Cuthbert Laws, general manager of the Shipping Federation, the British shipowners' central body for negotiating wages and conditions of seafarers and for the supply of crews.

It was a founder-member of the International Shipping Federation grouping similar bodies in other countries. He became assistant secretary in 1929, secretary in 1933, and chief executive in 1936-62. Hitherto he had had no experience of ship management or the practical handling of ships, but he quickly gained the complete confidence of both sides of the industry. One secret of his success was to make the negotiating board a forum for the discussion of many projects of mutual advantage, not simply a place to argue about wages and hours. In the 26 years of his management, the Shipping Federation became the largest employers' organization in the country, made a major, although necessarily unpublicized, contribution to the war effort, whilst in industrial relations, the industry came to be described by so qualified a judge as Ernest Bevin [q.v.] as a 'model to the rest of the world'.

During the war Snedden's international authority enabled him to co-ordinate in a masterly way the crew arrangements of the Allied merchant fleets in exile. His success was recognized by the CBE in 1942, by the most gratifying honour of honorary captain RNR, and by a number of foreign decorations. He was knighted in 1951, appointed CVO in 1967, and was a member of the Queen's Body Guard for Scotland.

The post-war years, with full employment and virtually no competition, profoundly affected national industrial relations. Sanctity of agreements as the foundation-stone of industrial peace was disregarded—instead came the lightning strike and lightning concession by employers to avoid even a brief stoppage. Snedden never wavered and in his time the shipping industry was almost entirely peaceful. He was frequently in demand for government committees and was a director of several companies, including Monotype and Consolidated Gold Fields. Although highly cultured in the widest sense, he had little time for relaxation, save elementary gardening.

For personal reasons he retired from the Federation in 1962, remaining general manager of the International Federation until 1969.

There was no single clue to Snedden's success. Nature endowed him with intellect, shrewdness, genius for leadership, mastery of lucid English, and geniality except when confronted by empty pomposity. But certain principles were immutable—absolute honesty in collective bargaining, smartness in outwitting the other side being utterly repugnant; meticulous thoroughness which ensured that his case could not be faulted on facts; unlimited patience in understanding opposing views whereby, so often, he produced the acceptable compromise in an apparent deadlock; ruthlessness when bound to oppose but never indulgence in humiliating personalities; a sense of humour and cheerfulness, based on Christian faith, which calmed many a storm and never allowed personal worries to depress others; humanity which made him happiest when working for non-party welfare causes.

In 1926 Snedden married Janet Catherine, only daughter of a schoolmaster, Duncan MacDougall, of Kilchoman, Islay. They had been fellow students and her academic record equally brilliant. It was an ideal partnership which lasted until her death a few weeks before his. There was one son, who was unhappily subject to mental breakdowns, during one of which he brought about the untimely death of his father at Crowborough, 9 March 1970, in the irrational desire to save him from loneliness.

A portrait of Snedden by Mrs Phyllis Bliss is in the possession of the family.

[Private information; personal knowledge.]
H. W. GREANY

SOISSONS, LOUIS EMMANUEL JEAN GUY DE SAVOIE-CARIGNAN DE, VISCOUNT D'OSTEL, BARON LONGROY (1890-1962), architect and town planner. [See DE SOISSONS.]

SOMERVILLE, MARY (1897-1963), educationist and broadcasting executive, was born in New Zealand 1 November 1897, the eldest daughter of the Revd J. A. Somerville, of Gullane, East Lothian, Scotland, who at one time had been chairman of a Scottish school board, and his wife, Agnes Fleming.

Though born in New Zealand, she was brought up in Scotland, very much a daughter of the manse and greatly influenced by the atmosphere of her home where she was always conscious of lack of money but where she was able to establish contact with men of eminence whose interests were literary, educational, and philosophical.

She became a passionate believer in the importance of education, and, having an adventurous mind as well as a great deal of self-confidence, wanted equally passionately to modify the practices of most schools so that these would include the development of children's imagination in addition to the giving of normal scholastic training. She hoped to make a career for herself which would allow her to play a part in achieving this change and, incidentally, earn enough money to ensure her own financial security and that of her family.

This required courage as well as determination, for throughout her energetic life she had to struggle with ill health. Ill health was the main reason why most of her early education took place at home. She also attended the Abbey School, Melrose, and Selkirk High School. She did not go to Oxford, where she attended Somerville College, until she was twenty-four. While she was still an undergraduate she met a fellow Scot, John (later Lord) Reith, then managing director of the British Broadcasting Company but soon (1927) to be the first director-general of the newly created British Broadcasting Corporation.

By the time Mary Somerville met Reith she was already convinced that the new medium of radio broadcasting should be used in schools in order to supplement what she regarded as the over rigid scholasticism of current teaching methods. So, on 24 February 1925, she wrote to Reith suggesting that she should work in radio for nothing or for a nominal sum during her forthcoming long vacation and then be considered for a permanent post at a salary which would meet her needs. Reith was sufficiently impressed by her intelligence and enthusiasm to put her suggestion to J. C. Stobart, his director of education. As a result, and in spite of the fact that she was too ill to sit for her finals in June 1925 and received an aegrotat, not, as expected, first class honours in English, she was appointed in July 1925 to the post of schools assistant to Stobart and embarked upon the work to which she was to dedicate her life.

The timing of her entry into broadcasting was fortunate. In those early days the BBC, under Reith, regarded the function of broadcasting in general terms as educational and was already endeavouring to form an alliance between broadcasters and established educationists so that the BBC could fulfil its educational purposes not only in its routine programmes but in the more specialized areas of school and adult education. Reith's appointment in 1924 of Stobart, previously a Board of Education inspector, as the Company's director of education was an early example of this intention, and Stobart, a classical scholar, proved to be as ready as Mary Somerville to embark upon a new career in broadcasting with an enthusiasm equal to, if different from, hers.

It was significant that Stobart had accepted her unusual suggestion of a trial period of work in broadcasting before agreeing to her appointment because he was uncertain of her willingness to settle down to office routine. This was perceptive, for during the whole of her professional life she was, in a sense, a rebel. She fought unceasingly for the money and the tools she considered necessary to do her job properly, for her own rights and for those of any of her staff she believed to be unfairly treated as a result of the workings of the BBC's administrative machinery.

But what made her so considerable a figure in what Asa (later Lord) Briggs has labelled 'The Golden Age of Wireless' (*The History of*

Broadcasting in the United Kingdom, vol. ii, 1965) was not her battling with the Corporation but her identification with what, under Reith, were its fundamental aims. Her great contribution to broadcasting was, in practice, her insistence upon the duality of the high standards for which the Corporation stood: on the one hand the upholding of what she regarded as Oxford standards of thought, but equally (and after continuous monitoring of the effect of any broadcast at the receiving end) upon the observance of the professional broadcasting standards necessary for any broadcast communication. It is said that she was once rebuked by her seniors for having had the impertinence to ask a distinguished Oxford professor of literature to rewrite a broadcast script. But it was precisely in this duality of approach which her strength lay. She wanted for broadcasting the standard of thinking which, for her, Oxford represented. Yet, in her judgement, even Oxford professors must observe the professional standards of the medium of expression they chose to employ.

It is a tribute both to Mary Somerville and the Corporation that she could be promoted so consistently in spite of their differences about administrative detail. In 1929 she became responsible for all programmes of broadcasting to schools and secretary to the Central Council of School Broadcasting. In 1947 she was made assistant controller to the entire talks division of the BBC and in 1950 controller, talks (home sound), and so became the first woman to rise to the exalted rank of controller within the BBC.

When she retired in December 1955 the Corporation formally stated that 'the BBC's service of broadcasting to schools is Miss Somerville's great monument' and also that 'during her last five years in office' she had brought her mature wisdom to bear upon the difficult and exacting problems which face controller, talks. Outside the Corporation the value of her work was given increasing public recognition. In 1935 she was appointed OBE; in 1943 the university of Manchester awarded her an honorary MA. During 1947 she accepted invitations to visit Australia and the USA to speak and advise upon educational broadcasting; in April 1955 she was presented with a 25th anniversary award from the Institute of Education by Radio-Television in America for her 'outstanding contribution to the development of educational broadcasting during the past quarter of a century'.

Mary Somerville was a very feminine figure, lavishing upon a devoted circle of admirers and friends her continuing intellectual energy and her warmly generous hospitality.

She was twice married: in 1928 to Ralph Penton Brown, by whom she had a son, her only child. She divorced her husband in 1945. Her second marriage, to an old friend, Eric Rowan Davies, took place in 1962, seven years after she had retired from the BBC and only a year before her death at her home in Bath 1 September 1963.

[Asa Briggs, *The History of Broadcasting in the United Kingdom*, vols. i and ii, 1961 and 1965; BBC papers and broadcasts; private information; personal knowledge.]

GRACE WYNDHAM GOLDIE

SOUTHWELL, SIR RICHARD VYNNE (1888-1970), professor of engineering science, was born 2 July 1888 at Norwich, the only son and the second of the three children of Edwin Batterbee Southwell, a director of J. & J. Colman Ltd., Norwich, and his wife, Annie, daughter of Richard Vynne, a farmer and corn merchant of Swaffham. His ancestors were to be found in Norfolk even in Tudor times, when Sir Richard Southwell was a court official and Robert Southwell [qq.v.] a Jesuit poet, who was executed in 1595, but beatified in 1929.

Southwell was educated at King Edward VI School, Norwich, where he received an excellent classical grounding, but turned to mathematics in the last two years. He won an exhibition to Trinity Hall, Cambridge, but eventually entered Trinity College as a commoner in 1907. After winning scholarships and prizes there he graduated with first class honours in both parts of the mechanical sciences tripos (1909 and 1910). He was fortunate to be coached by H. A. Webb, an excellent tutor with a lively interest in the theory of structures. It was thus natural that Southwell's first paper, published in 1912, was on the strength of struts.

Southwell left Trinity College, where he had become a fellow in 1912, in August 1914, to join the army, and was in France by the end of the year. But in May 1915 he was withdrawn to work on the development of non-rigid airships and later moved to the Royal Aircraft Establishment at Farnborough. There, as Major Southwell, he was placed in charge of the Aerodynamics and Structural Departments until demobilized in March 1919. This experience, which brought him in touch with the leading aeronautical engineers of the time, including (Sir) Leonard Bairstow and A. J. S. Pippard [qq.v.], started his lively and enduring interest in the problems of aircraft structures.

He returned to Trinity College but in 1920 became superintendent of the Aeronautics Department of the National Physical Laboratory, where he stayed for five years. During the war his researches had ranged over problems of dynamic and static stability, but now he began his classic work on space frames.

The biplanes and rigid airships of the time had structures which were essentially intricate space frames, and for the next ten years the problems of the great spider-web-like structures of rigid airships stirred Southwell's mind. This period saw the production of six papers on stress determination in space frames; and some related ones on tension coefficients, strain energy, and St. Venant's principle, for which he is particularly remembered. Under him, a department which was primarily aerodynamic produced also a whole series of papers on the critical stability of space frameworks.

When Southwell returned to Trinity College in 1925 his personal research work widened again and papers on vibration and hydrodynamic problems appeared. But from 1924, when the last British airship building programme started, until its cessation in 1931, his heart was in airship structures. He had become a friend of Colonel V. C. Richmond, the designer of the R.101, and acted as his structural consultant at Cardington while A. J. S. Pippard acted in a similar capacity to (Sir) Barnes Wallis, the R.101 designer. All frequently met together with Bairstow on the airship stressing panel of the Aeronautical Research Committee, where the stressing problems of airships were thoroughly discussed and appropriate airworthiness requirements developed.

In 1929 Southwell was invited to succeed C. F. Jenkin, whose notice he contributed to this Dictionary, as professor of engineering science at Oxford. Engineering at Oxford was then scarcely viable and Southwell accepted only after considerable hesitation, but he soon found a way to appoint a reader, E. B. Moullin [q.v.], to strengthen his small department. He showed himself an outstanding teacher with a flair for clarity and precision, and attracted junior staff of notable ability. He also, at Brasenose as at Trinity, engaged the interest of non-engineering colleagues by his lively mind and felicitous humour. He was greatly helped in this by his wife Isabella Wilhelmina, daughter of William Warburton Wingate, a medical practitioner. They were married in Cambridge in 1918 and had four daughters. Their happy marriage created a home which staff and students alike always enjoyed visiting.

It was at Oxford that Southwell's deep understanding and appreciation of the earlier work of Lord Rayleigh and A. E. H. Love [qq.v.] became generally apparent. Rayleigh's Principle in applied mechanics became a feature in his teaching and he never tired of delving into Love's monumental book on elasticity. Although his first book, *Introduction to the Theory of Elasticity for Engineers and Physicists*, did not appear until 1936, he had already written a number of papers in the field.

But the major work of his Oxford period was the development of his relaxation method of analysis. It was known that the simultaneous equations of equilibrium and of compatibility of strains necessary to determine the loads in the members of a highly redundant framework were numerous and often ill-conditioned; and these characteristics became acute in the analysis of the complex space frames of airships. As a result the solution of the simultaneous equations involved became impossible without the adoption of some simplifying physical assumptions. Mathematically this problem invited the use of iterative methods, but the process could be lengthy and the results uncertain. It was Southwell's great contribution in his relaxation method to devise a successive approximation process that at any stage could be physically understood and guided by engineering experience. He started the work in relation to frameworks, but quickly realized the general applicability of the process and, aided by a succession of able research assistants at Oxford and London, developed the method for many fields of engineering science and physics. A whole generation of engineering scientists thus benefited and became adept in using the method. It was only the coming of modern computers that rendered the method largely unnecessary, though still physically enlightening.

Southwell left Oxford in 1942 to become rector of Imperial College, London, in succession to Sir H. T. Tizard [q.v.]. He still carried on the development of the relaxation process in spite of the administrative work of his office, and published his second book on the subject (his first appeared in 1940) in 1946. He retired in 1948 and returned to an earlier home at Trumpington, Cambridge. He continued to be fruitful with papers on engineering science for the next ten years. He died after a long illness in hospital near Nottingham 9 December 1970.

Southwell was honoured by many universities and learned societies. He was elected FRS in 1925 and was knighted in 1948. He was made an honorary fellow of Brasenose College, Oxford (1943), and of Imperial College, London, and Trinity College, Cambridge (both 1950). He won many awards, among them the James Alfred Ewing medal in 1946. For many years he was one of the moving spirits of the International Congress of Applied Mechanics, of which he was president in 1948-52 and treasurer in 1952-6. He was general secretary of the British Association from 1948 to 1956. Throughout his life his colleagues, in whatever capacity, found him a man of great charm and wit; as a Trinity College colleague wrote, 'no one has ever had for me so exquisite a choice of mirth-provoking phrase'.

A portrait by Henry Lamb (1955) is in the possession of Imperial College.

[D. G. Christopherson in *Biographical Memoirs of Fellows of the Royal Society*, vol. xviii, 1972; *The Times*, 12 December 1970.]   A. G. PUGSLEY

SOUTTAR, SIR HENRY SESSIONS (1875–1964), surgeon, was born at Birkenhead 14 December 1875, the only son of Robinson Souttar, member of Parliament for Dumfriesshire (1895–1900), and his wife, Mary Ann, daughter of Philip Dixon Hardy. He was educated at Oxford High School and the Queen's College, Oxford, where he acquired a double first in mathematics (1895–8) and was also interested in engineering. For recreation he rowed and was considered a good oarsman. He went on to the London Hospital where he qualified in 1906 with the MRCS, LRCP and in the same year graduated BM at Oxford. He then held a number of resident hospital appointments and acquired the diploma of FRCS in 1909 continuing his career as a surgical registrar. Three years later he was appointed to the staff of the West London Hospital and in 1915 became assistant surgeon to the London Hospital.

At the outbreak of war in 1914 Souttar was appointed surgeon to the Belgian field hospital at Antwerp and he later described the siege and withdrawal from that city to the coast. He was awarded the Order of the Crown of Belgium and later, when deputy consultant to the Southern Command, was appointed CBE.

Souttar's mathematical background and his engineering skills gave him a broad interest in the world of surgery. He had his own workshop where he designed and made many surgical instruments, which aimed at simplifying or enlarging the scope of existing operative procedures. One invention of his, which has remained in use and known by his name, was a flanged tube made of a soft wire spiral which was introduced down the gullet to overcome obstructions in that organ. He also devised a steam cautery to sterilize and clean breaking-down tumours and ulcers on the surface of the body and he devised and used a most ingenious craniotome (an instrument used to open the skull in brain operations). With the introduction of radium in the treatment of malignant tumours, Souttar was again well in advance of many of his contemporaries. His mathematical skill in assessing dose and the range was very valuable and he chaired many committees in connection with the use of radiation in the treatment of cancer. For implantation he designed a most ingenious 'gun' by which radon seeds could be implanted in or around a tumour with comparative simplicity.

His most dramatic venture in surgery and the one by which he is best known was in connection with the heart. In 1925 surgery of the chest was in its infancy and operations on the valves of the heart unknown. Souttar operated successfully on a young woman with mitral valve disease, devising the approach to the heart which enabled him to make the exploration. He did this by making an opening in the appendage of the left atrium and inserting a finger into this chamber in order to palpate and explore the damaged mitral valve. Actually the condition of the valve did not permit of repair, but this was a pioneer operation on the heart which was not repeated for nearly a quarter of a century. The patient in this case survived for a number of years and this operation is regarded as one of the great landmarks in cardiac surgery. In a lesser way Souttar made medical history by being one of the first people to fly abroad to perform an operation. In 1933 he and his anaesthetists went to India by air, a journey which took nearly a week in each direction.

Outside the practice of surgery Souttar was a man of many parts—he was a good linguist and a competent musician. It is said that he constructed a violin and played on it himself. He was a good artist, as was well demonstrated by the drawings with which he illustrated his well-known textbook *The Art of Surgery* (1929).

Souttar was a member of the council of the Royal College of Surgeons of England from 1933 to 1949 and was vice-president in 1943–4. He was the College's Bradshaw lecturer in 1943 and the Hunterian orator in 1949. He was instrumental in the foundation of the faculty of dental surgery and the faculty of anaesthetists in the College, and was elected an honorary fellow of both these bodies. He was president of the British Medical Association from 1945 to 1946 and was an honorary fellow of the Australasian and the American Colleges of Surgeons. Trinity College, Dublin, gave him an honorary MD in 1933. He was knighted in 1949.

After his retirement in 1947 from the London Hospital Souttar retained his active interest in surgery and was to be seen at surgical meetings where his advice was often sought and always graciously given. In appearance he was a very tall and powerfully built man, dark in his younger days, and impressive looking. He was also noted for his extreme courtesy and kindness, and those who spoke with him could not help but be stimulated by his ingenuity and ideas. He was undoubtedly a great surgeon, but his interests both in surgery and outside were possibly a little too diffuse to allow him to concentrate on any one branch.

In 1904 he married Catharine Edith (died 1959), daughter of Robert Bellamy Clifton, professor of experimental philosophy at Oxford.

They had one son and one daughter. In 1963 Souttar married, secondly, Amy Bessie, widow of Harry Douglas Wigdahl. Souttar died at his London home 12 November 1964; the funeral service was held at St. Marylebone church of which he had been a warden for many years.

[*British Medical Journal* and *Lancet*, 21 November 1964; private information; personal knowledge.]   T. HOLMES SELLORS

SPENCER, SIR HENRY FRANCIS (1892-1964), industrialist, was born at Coseley, Staffordshire, 8 April 1892, the only son of Henry Francis Spencer, boat loader, and his wife, Alice Wassell. He had an older and a younger sister. His early childhood was a period of considerable poverty. His mother when she registered his birth had been unable to sign her name and when Spencer himself left school at thirteen with but a rudimentary education he had a burning resolve to better himself. By the time he was nineteen his father had died and Spencer found himself the family breadwinner for his mother and younger sister. His first employment had been as a sandboy in the Cannon Iron Foundry at Bilston, Staffordshire. But his real ambition was always to go into business on his own account. All his endeavours were directed to this end and in this project he was strongly supported by his wife, Ethel May Southall, whom he married in 1916; they had one daughter.

In 1914 Spencer volunteered but was rejected on health grounds, and together with his future wife and her father, William Southall, started a small iron and steel merchants business at Fullwoods End, Coseley. It was an extremely simple and primitive operation but, by virtue of his tremendous drive, strong personality, a formidable native common sense, and instinctive business acumen, it soon began to prosper. In 1916 he was called up and served with the Royal Engineers and was seconded to the Admiralty. After his discharge in 1918, always conscious of his limited education, he set about improving himself by attending night-school in order to acquire knowledge of accountancy, law, engineering, and metallurgy, which he rightly felt were essential to his career.

With the small company he had created, his dynamic nature began to assert itself and he became recognized in the Wolverhampton and Black Country areas as a formidable personality. He started to take an interest in public affairs and was elected to Coseley Council, subsequently to become chairman of its education committee—education and training were to remain a lifelong and absorbing interest. In the immediate post-war years his business continued to flourish and he acquired a connection with the Ebbw Vale Steel, Iron, and Coal Company which, with its successors, formed a major part of his business life until he died. He was also involved with John Lysaght & Co., who, together with the Ebbw Vale Company, were then the principal manufacturers of flat-rolled steel products. His interest also widened into the tinplate field which was confined to the South Wales area where he was eventually to make such a significant impact. He was an original director of the Steel Company of Wales which he helped to create. The volume of his business was now such that he left Coseley and opened at Wolverhampton a new stockholding centre which at that time was the biggest in Europe for flat-rolled steel products.

His business continued to prosper and he became involved with some other leading industrialists in a most imaginative scheme to create a wide strip mill in the Midlands near Wolverhampton to serve the rapidly expanding motor industry in which flat-rolled steel products were to play such a major and significant part. It seems fair to assume that this project would have been created, but at the time of its conception unemployment, especially in certain areas, had reached such catastrophic proportions that a government directive together with some national finance ordered the strip mill to be built in the severely distressed Ebbw Vale area.

In 1935 H. F. Spencer & Co. became associated with the Richard Thomas organization when the latter took over the assets of the Ebbw Vale Company and Spencer joined Richard Thomas as sheet sales controller, becoming successively commercial manager, assistant managing director, and finally (1952) managing director of Richard Thomas & Baldwins. He was also a member of the council and executive committee of the British Iron and Steel Federation, and was a member of a number of policy-making committees within the larger orbit of the steel industry.

In the mid fifties the Iron and Steel Board decided that the three British strip mills were not adequate to meet requirements and Spencer was the prime mover in the creation of a giant steelworks to be erected on a green-field site at Newport, Monmouthshire. Harold Macmillan, the prime minister, allocated another strip mill to Scotland which of course was in direct competition with the new strip mill at Newport and the three existing strip mills. A difficult situation was created when a world surplus in steel shattered international markets in the early sixties. Spencer was nevertheless determined to see the project through with the maximum efficiency and his determination never wavered. He planned, from the start, to build the Llanwern Works in two-thirds of the time thought sensible for such a project, and he succeeded. He was resolved that the project would be a success and although trading conditions were at a very difficult level he set in motion a trading operation which he felt sure would eventually ensure the complete success of the Llanwern project. The works when opened by the Queen in 1962 were named the Spencer Works.

Spencer displayed a ruthless dynamism in his commercial and business life, yet this was tempered with a broad humanity and complete approachability by no means common amongst men who have clawed their way to the top from humble origins. His relations with the trade-union movement, while firm, were always notable for the degree of co-operation he was able to sustain by reason of the respect accorded to his integrity. He had a keen sense of humour and a wide interest in subjects outside his immediate business life, notably the British Institute of Management of which he became chairman, although his business was always the dominating influence.

He enjoyed family life and the company of his friends and although a ruthless and formidable (although always fair) opponent he would spare no pains to help his friends, colleagues, and subordinates, and sometimes indeed his opponents and enemies. He was knighted in 1963 for services to the steel industry and died in London 31 May 1964.

[Private information; personal knowledge.]
R. A. CROMARTY

SPENS, SIR WILLIAM (WILL) (1882–1962), educational administrator, was born in Glasgow 31 May 1882, the eldest of the four sons of John Alexander Spens, solicitor, and a leading layman in the Episcopal Church of Scotland, and his wife, Sophie Nicol, daughter of Hugh Baird. From Rugby School he became a scholar of King's College, Cambridge, where he obtained a first class in part i of the natural sciences tripos in 1903 and went on to read theology. Immediately after a serious illness, he became in 1907 a fellow of Corpus Christi College, Cambridge: he used to say that his election was due entirely to a knowledge of port which he had studied in Portugal. He became a tutor in 1911 but in 1915 joined the Foreign Office for the duration of the war, becoming secretary of the foreign trade department in 1917. He was appointed CBE in 1918 and made a chevalier of the Legion of Honour and an officer of the Order of the Crown of Italy.

After the war he returned to Cambridge which became his life. For him university management and intrigue were of the essence. He was appointed to the council of the senate in 1920 and a member of the statutory commission for the university in 1923. In 1927 he became master of his college, a position which he held with every ounce of enjoyment until retirement in 1952. In 1931–3 he was a most efficient vice-chancellor of the university and the youngest then within living memory. In 1934 he was appointed a member of the royal commission for the university of Durham and in 1930–9 he was chairman of the Cambridge University Appointments Board. From 1934 he was chairman of the consultative committee on secondary education which reported in 1939 and in that year he was knighted. He received an honorary LLD from Columbia (1933) and St. Andrews (1939).

In the war of 1939–45 Spens held what he regarded as the most important appointment in his (or anyone's) life. As regional commissioner for civil defence in East Anglia he was one of the half-dozen or so in the country to whom the King's power was delegated without responsibility to Parliament in the event of part of the country being cut off by invasion. The qualities which he showed in all his appointments glowed in administration in the King's name and again he was regarded as the acme of efficiency. The borough of Great Yarmouth in gratitude installed him as high steward in 1948.

In 1944 Spens was appointed by Cambridge University as its representative on the governing body of Rugby School, immediately to become chairman on the death of Archbishop William Temple [q.v.]. Spens held the chairmanship until he retired in 1958 in favour of Lord Cilcennin [q.v.]. When he retired from Corpus Christi in 1952 to the Cathedral Close at Ely where he was steward of the chapter, he gave Rugby his fullest and most detailed attention and the benefit of his educational experience. He was instrumental in making the controversial appointment from outside the academic profession of Sir Arthur fforde, solicitor and wartime civil servant, to the head-mastership of Rugby in 1948, maintaining that education and the outside world needed to be closer. Spens was chairman of the Joint Committee of Governors, Headmasters, Headmistresses, and Bursars from 1948 to 1959 and deputy chairman of the Governing Bodies' Association from 1954 to 1959.

When the National Health Service was being organized after 1945, Spens was chairman of the three committees which decided the remuneration of general practitioners, general dental practitioners, and consultants; and from 1947 to 1956 he was chairman of the National Insurance Advisory Committee.

Six feet tall, wearing rimless pince-nez, with a highly domed head, a slow tread, a tight-lipped expression, and little small-talk, Spens was a formidable personality. Napoleonic and

Machiavellian were adjectives applied to him by those with whom he worked. His mastery of detail was supreme. He was punctilious to the last comma in the recording of proceedings. Insistent on having the consideration of all possible relevant data, he would brief himself with the most minute fact. One of the most experienced chairmen in the country, with a rather autocratic manner, he would encourage the same select number in a committee to speak, tending to ignore the presence of persons in whose appointment he had not a hand and disregarding their eminence or distinction in any field other than that which he considered relevant to the committee. Scrutinizing draft minutes, he would sometimes deny that people had been present at a meeting over which he had presided, when in fact they had been there but had been discouraged by him from making any contribution. He would lay his gold watch on the table at the beginning of a meeting and, without appearing to rush the tempo, conclude it, having completed all the agenda, on the exact minute upon which he had decided at the outset. His intellect was so sharp that nothing escaped his notice in any memorandum, although he was short-sighted and not so observant of things off paper, albeit interested in on-the-spot assessments.

As a speaker in a monotone, probably due to tone-deafness, Spens was invariably serious and very much to the point, with only occasionally a rather laboured academic flicker of humour and an infrequent graciousness of expression. In his official appointments he reserved sentiment for Rugby, Cambridge, and the Church of England, of which he was considered to be among the most influential laymen. His only published work was a theological study, *Belief and Practice* (1915), and in 1922-38 he was a member of the Archbishops' Commission on Doctrine. Socially Spens was extremely entertaining with his accounts of people whom he had met and of intriguing incidents in his life. And he was surprisingly susceptible to feminine presence. His wife in this atmosphere helped to humanize him: he enjoyed it when the large bubble of an over-ponderous statement of his was pricked by female comment. His character had its fair share of paradoxes: ruthlessness and kindness, detachment and sentiment, shrewdness and sometimes blind loyalty, keen analysis and unshakeable religious devotion.

In 1912 Spens married Dorothy Theresa (died 1973), daughter of the late John Richardson Selwyn [q.v.], bishop of Melanesia in 1887-90 and thereafter master of Selwyn College, Cambridge. They had three sons, one of whom died in infancy, and one daughter. Spens died in Ely 1 November 1962. A portrait by Sir William Hutchison is at Rugby School and one by Henry Lamb at Corpus Christi College.

[Private information; personal knowledge.]

PHILIP SNOW

SPRING, (ROBERT) HOWARD (1889-1965), journalist and novelist, was born in Cardiff 10 February 1889, the son of William Henry Spring and his wife, Mary Stacey. His father as a boy had run away from his home in county Cork; he was a jobbing gardener who was often out of work. There were nine children, two of whom died in infancy, and Howard was the middle child. The average weekly income was about one pound. When his father died, Howard Spring left school at the age of twelve, worked for a short time as an errand boy, then became an office boy to an accountant in the Cardiff docks. He had to walk through picturesque Tiger Bay to get to work and he received four shillings a week. At the end of his first year, when he asked for a rise, his employer said that he was paying him four shillings a week only because his mother was a widow. Spring therefore found another job as messenger boy in a Cardiff newspaper office. He was happy directly he got there, and stayed in newspaper offices in Cardiff, Bradford, Manchester, and London until 1939 when he retired to Cornwall.

Spring soon saw that the way up was through the reporters' room. He became a very fast and accurate shorthand writer, and at evening classes at the university, for which his editor paid, he studied English, French, Latin, mathematics, and history. From nine in the morning until five or six at night his job was to take over the telephone news reports from district correspondents for the evening paper. Then he switched over to the status of reporter for the morning paper, working all through the evening. From seven to eight he might have a class to attend, then on he would go to pick up a bit of news somewhere. The tail end of another class could be reached when that was done. Back then to the office to write his report; then home to supper and homework. After nine years' service the *South Wales News* was paying Spring thirty shillings a week for reporting for two papers: morning and evening. He applied for a job on the *Yorkshire Observer*, and got it, at fifty shillings a week. His elder brother, a kindred spirit, had died from overwork and malnutrition, and Spring had to help his mother and the younger children. He took a room in Bradford and found the *Yorkshire Observer*, under A. M. Drysdale, a good paper to work for. He worked hard, played golf on the municipal course at Baildon, and talked unceasingly with his new friends. He called these his university years. He was reading regularly and intelligently and did a good deal of book reviewing. Life seemed to him very good.

In the spring of 1915 Spring moved to the *Manchester Guardian* where C. P. Scott [q.v.] was editor, but remained only a few months before joining the Army Service Corps as a shorthand-typist, working eventually at GHQ in France. He had been turned down for active service because of his frail physique. After the war he found his old job on the *Manchester Guardian* waiting for him.

Spring had an almost superstitious belief in the rare moments which signified a cross-roads in his career. In the general election of 1931 he heard that Lord Beaverbrook [q.v.] was to speak in the not too distant Darwen and decided to report the meeting. The approach to the hall lay through the Saturday market swarming with hucksters and pedlars crying their wares. This suggested to him as a title for his *Guardian* article 'The Pedlar of Dreams', a headline which so delighted Beaverbrook that he at once arranged to bring Spring to London to work on the *Evening Standard* where he soon became book reviewer, following Arnold Bennett [q.v.] and J. B. Priestley. The care and judgement which he brought to this task and the institution of a 'Book of the Month' selection made him an influential figure in the book world.

Spring's own first publication was a children's book, *Darkie & Co.*, published by the Oxford University Press in 1932. His first novel, *Shabby Tiger* (1934), and all his subsequent novels were published by Collins and warm and friendly relations always existed between him and the firm. *Shabby Tiger* was followed by a sequel, *Rachel Rosing* (1935). There was nothing about the reception of either to lead Spring to suppose that the next one would be successful all over the world. This was *O Absalom!* (1938), retitled *My Son, My Son!* for publication in America and in subsequent editions in this country. It was a great success in America, was translated into many languages, and filmed. Spring found himself, in middle age, transported from wage-earner to independence. He bought a bungalow on the shores of the Mylor creek in Cornwall and moved there early in the war, giving up his work for the *Evening Standard* in 1939. His next novel, *Fame is the Spur!*, the story of a Labour leader's rise to power, was finished in the early months of 1940. In the next year he began reviewing for *Country Life*. He had written *Heaven Lies About Us, a Fragment of Infancy* in 1939 and now followed it with two autobiographical-philosophical works *In the Meantime* (1942) and *And Another Thing . . .* (1946). In 1972 the three works were published in one volume as *The Autobiography of Howard Spring*. During the war Spring wrote two more novels, *Hard Facts* (1944) and

Dunkerley's (1946). In a curious wartime interlude he went in 1941, with H. V. Morton, in the *Prince of Wales* with Churchill who was meeting President Roosevelt at Placentia Bay, Newfoundland. They went as observers and were not then allowed to write of what they saw.

In 1947 Spring moved to a large Georgian house in Falmouth and settled down to a regular routine of work, publishing *There is no Armour* (1948), *The Houses in Between* (1951), *A Sunset Touch* (1953), *These Lovers Fled Away* (1955), *Time and the Hour* (1957), *All the Day Long* (1959), and *I Met a Lady* (1961). He was a gifted story-teller: his readers found themselves introduced to characters in whom they could immediately become completely absorbed, sharing their problems, trivial or heart-searing, enjoying their lighter moments, and finally parting from them with the greatest reluctance.

After a slight stroke Spring had to give up reviewing for *Country Life*, but he was determined to go on writing and even before he was allowed to walk he was practising with a notebook and pencil. Soon he could write legible words and before long he was at his desk writing his last book, *Winds of the Day*, published in 1964. He had another stroke and died at his home in Falmouth 3 May 1965.

In 1920 Spring married Marion Ursula (died 1976), daughter of George William Pye, a London cotton merchant; they had two sons.

A drawing by Emanuel Levy and a sculpted head by Michael Spring are in the possession of the family.

[Marion Howard Spring, *Howard*, 1967; *Autobiography of Howard Spring*, 1972.]

MARION HOWARD SPRING

STAMP, SIR (LAURENCE) DUDLEY (1898-1966), geographer, was born at Catford, London, 9 March 1898, the seventh and last child of Charles Stamp and his wife, Clara Jane Evans. Charles Stamp was a provision merchant whose children were brought up in the atmosphere of a middle-class family which, in his son's words, 'accepted success through effort as the natural reward of clean living and hard work'. This was Dudley Stamp's attitude to life; it was also embodied in the career of his brother Josiah (later Lord) Stamp [q.v.] whom he held in lifelong affection and admiration.

As a boy, Stamp developed a passion for natural history and geology stimulated by holidays in the Kentish countryside: he established his own 'museum'. He attended University School, Rochester, and despite ill health he was admitted while still only fifteen years of age to King's College, London. He was awarded Tennant prizes in geology and mineralogy and obtained first class honours in the B.Sc. examination in 1917. His first research paper, begun as an undergraduate, on the Silurian rocks of the Clun Forest district, was read to the Geological Society of London when he was nineteen.

Throughout his army service in 1917-19 geology remained a main interest, and service in France and Belgium provided opportunities for geological fieldwork. He returned to King's College, London, as demonstrator in geology. Through his friendship with a student, Elsa Clara Rea, whom he married in 1923, he was led towards geography and they sat for the first honours examination in geography for the BA of the university of London in 1921, Stamp taking a first class. His D.Sc. was awarded in the same year. He then accepted a post as an oil geologist in Burma and in 1923 became professor of geology and geography in the new university of Rangoon.

From this time on Stamp became increasingly concerned with the development of geography as a school and university subject; his early interests in geology and botany undoubtedly guided his approach to geography as the study of relationships between societies and their physical environments and the growth of his special interests in land use and landscape history. Returning to London in 1926 to the Sir Ernest Cassel readership in economic geography at the London School of Economics, he became professor in 1945 and moved to the chair of social geography in 1948, retiring in 1958. Stamp quickly began to apply his belief in the value of geographical methods of survey and analysis to a survey of the land resources of Britain. He formed the Land Utilization Survey of Britain, a project which fired the enthusiasm of colleagues and students. The entire country was surveyed on the scale of six inches to a mile, and one-inch scale maps and county reports were published. Though interrupted by the war of 1939-45 and the loss of material in an air raid, the project was completed in 1948 with the publication of the summary report *The Land of Britain: its use and misuse*. For this work he received the Founder's medal of the Royal Geographical Society in 1949.

The practical value of Stamp's survey became quickly apparent. He was appointed vice-chairman of the Scott committee on land utilization in rural areas (1941-2). As chief adviser on rural land utilization in the Ministry of Agriculture (1942-55) and through his connection with regional surveys, he played an influential part in framing policies for land use and town and country planning for the post-war period. He developed the idea of land classification for planning purposes. His later service from 1958 as a member of the Nature Conservancy, as a member of the royal commission on common land (1955-8), and as chairman of the National Resources Advisory Committee

of the Ministry of Land and Natural Resources in 1965 continued this influence.

The success of his Land Utilization Survey led Stamp to develop a scheme for a World Land Use Survey and maps and memoirs of a number of countries were published under his direction. He wrote widely on problems of population growth, food, resources, and the environment, drawing special attention to variations in the geographical distribution of resources and of man's use of them. That his subject could contribute not only to the understanding of resource problems but to the wise use of land and resources he had no doubt and his principles of land use were widely discussed and adopted. The environment had to be studied as a whole: through an approach that was essentially ecological, understanding could be gained of the great problems of population pressure, the development of hungry lands, the provision of food for starving people. In the Patten Foundation lectures delivered at Indiana University in 1950, and later embodied in the book *Land for Tomorrow, the Under-developed World* (1952), he argued that no world problem was more important than that of matching the world's use of its natural resources with the needs of its people. Effective land-use planning was essential, based on closer understanding of the great diversity of geographical conditions. Stamp was also a pioneer in employing distribution maps to throw light on the causes of geographical variations in disease and mortality and gave the university of London Heath Clark lectures on this subject in 1962.

Sensing that the progress of geography was handicapped by a lack of good school and university textbooks, Stamp began, while still in Burma, to fill the gap. He wrote quickly and a large number of widely used textbooks followed, among them *The World* (1929), first written for Indian schools but later adapted for use in Britain and elsewhere. He forecast, rightly, that a wide market existed for well-written books about land and landscape and became an editor of the successful New Naturalist series to which he also contributed.

Stamp strongly supported the work of many scientific societies: he was president of the Royal Geographical Society (1963-6), of Section E of the British Association for the Advancement of Science (1949), of the Geographical Association (1950), and of the Institute of British Geographers (1956). He took an active part in the work of the Institute of Grocers and was president (1960-3); he was vice-president of the Royal Society of Arts (1954-6). From 1961 until his death he was chairman of the British National Committee for Geography.

Internationally, Stamp was the best known

British geographer of his generation. Through his presidency of the International Geographical Union (1952-6) he encouraged international co-operation in research especially on land use and resources and he greatly enjoyed organizing the 20th International Geographical Union Congress in London in 1964.

Stamp was a modest man, full of life and humour, ever ready to help students and friends. He was a good craftsman, reconstructing with his own hands his home at Ebbingford Manor, Bude Haven, where he lived happily; he gave loyal service to his parish church, the local hospital, and other causes. He was one of the few geographers to develop a serious interest in philately, building a noteworthy collection over the years; he argued successfully for the issue of a special set of stamps to mark the holding of the 20th International Geographical Congress in London. Throughout his life, even to the end, he loved to travel and had an especial fondness for Canada where at one time he intended to make a second home.

Stamp was appointed CBE in 1946 and knighted in 1965. He received the Daniel Pidgeon award of the Geological Society (1920), and the gold medal of the Mining and Geological Institute of India (1922). The American Geographical Society awarded him the Daly medal (1950); he received the Vega medal of Sweden (1954), the Tokyo Geographical Society's medal (1957), and the Scottish geographical medal of the Royal Scottish Geographical Society (1964). The Town Planning Institute elected him to honorary membership in 1944; and he was the recipient of several honorary degrees.

Stamp died 8 August 1966 in Mexico City, while attending a regional Latin-American conference of the International Geographical Union. On his death the geographical societies of Great Britain united to initiate the formation of the Dudley Stamp Memorial Trust to assist young geographers to undertake research involving international co-operation. Stamp's wife had died in 1962; they had one son. A portrait of Stamp by Leslie G. Garnett is in the possession of the Geographical Association.

[*The Times*, 10 August 1966; *Geographical Journal*, December 1966; *Geography*, November 1966; *Agriculture*, December 1966; Institute of British Geographers, *Special Publication*, No. 1 (Dudley Stamp Memorial Volume), November 1968; L. D. Stamp, unpublished autobiography; personal knowledge.]   M. J. WISE

STANIER, SIR WILLIAM ARTHUR (1876-1965), railway engine designer, was born 27 May 1876, in Wellington Street, Swindon, Wiltshire, the son of W. H. Stanier and his wife, Grace, daughter of Robert Ball, of Southport. W. H. Stanier, who spent a lifetime in the service of the Great Western Railway, had moved from Wolverhampton to Swindon in 1871 to become confidential clerk and personal assistant to William Dean, who became locomotive carriage and wagon superintendent in 1877. William was educated at Wycliffe College, Stonehouse, and joined the Great Western Railway in January 1892 as an office boy because he was not yet sixteen.

Stanier's apprenticeship at Swindon Works began on 27 May 1892, and in 1897 on completion of this he went into the drawing office. In 1900 he was appointed inspector of materials, taking charge of an activity of which his own father had been the inaugurator. In 1902 he became technical inspector to the divisional locomotive carriage and wagon superintendent, Swindon; the following year he was appointed acting divisional locomotive carriage and wagon superintendent, London, and in 1904 became assistant to the same superintendent. He was promoted in 1906 to divisional locomotive superintendent, Swindon, and six years later became Swindon's assistant locomotive works manager. In 1920 he was appointed locomotive works manager, Swindon, and in 1922 works assistant to the chief mechanical engineer. Later, as principal assistant to the chief mechanical engineer, as the 'second-in-command' at Swindon was designated, he took the remarkable locomotive *King George V* to the United States to take part in the centenary celebrations of the Baltimore and Ohio Railroad in 1927, and to supervise its running on certain American railroads.

In January 1932 Stanier took office as chief mechanical engineer of the London Midland and Scottish Railway (LMS), the largest of the British railway companies, which had been formed in 1923 by the amalgamation of some of the previously largest and most influential companies. Between them, however, they showed a great diversity of mechanical engineering practice, and Stanier was appointed to establish a standardized code of design and constructional methods; to provide locomotives not only of high thermal efficiency but which also could operate over longer weekly and monthly mileages, and so run the traffic with fewer locomotives. Much of the practice he introduced was based on his lengthy experience on the Great Western Railway, carefully blended with the widely differing requirements on the LMS system. His new standard locomotives—the 'Pacifics'—came to achieve a reputation second to none, both in their overall reliability, and in individual feats of outstanding performance. Stanier also produced a useful 2-8-0 engine, for freight purposes, and a mixed-traffic engine, known familiarly as the 'Black Stanier' or the 'Black Five'. The latter was very versatile and hardly ever broke down. Stanier was also responsible for the 4-6-0 series, known as the 'Jubilees'.

As a chief engineering executive Stanier's charming personality, technical skill, ability to 'get on' with colleagues, and aptitude for team building, quickly brought him a reputation far beyond the railway world. This led him to important consultancies.

In October 1936, with Sir Ralph Wedgwood [q.v.], chief general manager of the London and North Eastern Railway, he was invited by the Government of India 'to examine the position of the Indian state-owned railways'; and in July 1938 he was a member of a committee of inquiry into the causes of a serious accident on the East Indian Railway. At home he was president of the Institution of Locomotive Engineers for the session 1936-7, and again in 1938-9. The outbreak of war in September 1939 led to the postponement of further promising developments on the LMS, but in October 1941 Stanier delivered his presidential address to the Institution of Mechanical Engineers. The war led to a great increase in his responsibilities on the LMS, but in 1942 he was seconded to the Ministry of Production to form one of a team of three full-time scientific advisers. That he could leave the LMS, at such a time, was a great tribute to the team he had built up since his appointment in 1932. In February 1943 he was knighted. In the latter stages of the war, although he was then well beyond normal retirement age his services were still in great demand. He became chairman of Power Jets Limited, a government-owned firm for the development of jet propulsion techniques, and was on the board of several other companies.

Many honours came to him in his later years. In March 1944 he was elected FRS, only the second locomotive engineer to receive such distinction. In 1945 he became an honorary member of the Institution of Mechanical Engineers. In 1957 he was awarded the gold medal of the Institution of Locomotive Engineers and in 1963 the James Watt international medal of the Institution of Mechanical Engineers.

In 1906 Stanier married Ella Elizabeth (died 1957), daughter of L. L. Morse; they had a son and a daughter. He died at his home in Rickmansworth, Hertfordshire, 27 September 1965.

There is a portrait by William Dring (1959).

[Sir Harold Hartley in *Biographical Memoirs of Fellows of the Royal Society*, vol. xii, 1966; O. S. Nock, *Sir William Stanier, an Engineering Biography*, 1964.]   O. S. NOCK

STEIN, SIR EDWARD SINAUER DE (1887-1965), merchant banker. [See DE STEIN.]

STENTON, SIR FRANK MERRY (1880-1967), historian, was born 17 May 1880 at Upper Norwood, Surrey, the third child and second son of Henry Cawdron Stenton, solicitor, of South Hill House, Southwell, Nottinghamshire, and the only child by his second wife, Elizabeth, daughter of Thomas Merry, of Honily, Warwickshire. His parents, who had retired to Upper Norwood in 1879, returned to Southwell in 1886, where his father died a year later. He was a weakly child and was educated partly at the Minster Grammar School, Southwell, partly by private tutors and by his mother. In 1897 he accompanied a family friend to the University Extension College at Reading where at first he gave much of his time to geology and music. However, he came under the influence of W. M. Childs (whose notice he contributed to this Dictionary), then lecturer in history, and in 1899 gained a scholarship in modern history at Keble College, Oxford. There he entered for the first bachelor of music examination, but, on failing, read history and graduated with first class honours in 1902. He spent the next two years at Oxford, working for the *Victoria History of the Counties of England* and coaching. In 1904 he became a history master at Llandovery College, and in 1908 returned to Reading University College as a research fellow in local history. In 1912 he was appointed to the chair of modern history at Reading and continued in that post until 1946. From 1934 he was deputy vice-chancellor of the university and from 1946 vice-chancellor until his retirement in 1950.

Stenton's major works were *The First Century of English Feudalism 1066-1166* (1932) and *Anglo-Saxon England* (1943). The first, which he gave as the Ford's lectures in the university of Oxford, 1928-9, was founded directly on his extraordinary range of knowledge of twelfth-century charters. The second, which brought together all the categories of evidence—chronicles, laws, charters, place-names, coins, and archaeological remains, was the first scientific history of the Anglo-Saxon period. Both these books were remarkable for their continuing importance. Some of his conclusions were later questioned, especially his association of the existence of a free peasantry in the Danelaw with the settlement of large Danish armies in the late ninth century, but his work was so securely grounded in the evidence and his arguments were so meticulous, that it provided the starting point for all later discussion. Some of his shorter essays also were classic studies, especially *The Early History of the Abbey of Abingdon* (1913), *Norman London* (1915, enlarged 1934 and 1960), *The Danes in England* (Raleigh lecture of the British Academy, 1926), and *The Road System of Medieval England* (1937, Creighton lecture of the university of London, 1936).

Stenton's achievement was very much an individual one; he had no support of the kind available in a great university school of history, for the college and university of Reading (university status was granted in 1926) remained small throughout his career. He had unusual innate ability. His first works, the introductions in the *Victoria County History* to the Domesday surveys of Derbyshire (1905), Nottinghamshire (1906), Leicestershire (1907), and Rutland (1908) remain important; his early life of William the Conqueror (1908) was the standard biography until 1964. Furthermore he developed a very wide range of interests. His roots in a small country town set in the old Danelaw, his family's experience as solicitors there, his own training at Oxford where he read the special subject on land tenure, all came together in an early study on *Types of Manorial Structure in the Northern Danelaw* (1910). He retained a lifelong interest in local history, continuing to contribute to the *Victoria County History* (Worcester, 1924, Huntingdon, 1926, Oxfordshire, 1939) and to the volumes of the Lincoln and Northamptonshire Record Societies (1922, 1924, 1930). Following the lead given by J. H. Round (whose notice he contributed to this Dictionary), Stenton was the first scholar systematically to exploit the vast collection of early charters in the British Museum and other repositories. This led to *Documents Illustrative of the Social and Economic History of the Danelaw* (1920). He was one of the founders of the study of place-names. An early work, *The Place-Names of Berkshire* (1911), was followed by a study of the English element in English place-names in the first volume published by the English Place-Name Society (1924), of which he and (Sir) Allen Mawer [q.v.] were joint editors. He also continued a boyhood interest in coins and became both a serious collector of medieval coins and an expert numismatist.

This made him a friend and counsellor to scholars at work in all these fields. His influence was further deepened and extended by his readiness to devote his administrative abilities to the interests which he shared with other scholars. He gave a great deal of time to official bodies and learned societies. He was a member of council of the British Academy (1927-36); chairman of the editorial committee of the *History of Parliament* (1951-65), and of the

committee established by the British Academy for the *Sylloge of Coins of the British Isles* (1956-67); president of the Royal Historical Society (1937-45), the Historical Association (1949-52), the English Place-Name Society (1946-67), the Lincoln Record Society (1942-67), the Berkshire Archaeological Society (1947-60), and the Somerset Archaeological and Natural History Society (1959); and vice-president and chairman of council of the Pipe Roll Society (1945-67). He was also a trustee of the National Portrait Gallery (1948-65). To this work, in addition to his scholarship, he brought an accumulated experience, great practical wisdom, and firm, incisive, but kindly chairmanship.

Throughout his life he remained devoted to the university of Reading, despite many invitations to move elsewhere. He appreciated the friendliness of a small academic community and the easy access which it gave him to the great libraries and repositories of London and Oxford. His appointment as vice-chancellor recognized his pre-eminent reputation, his long service to the university, and his remarkable abilities in committee and as a chairman. He directed the affairs of the university wisely, advocating growth rather than rapid expansion or rash experiment. In 1946-7 the opportunity, created by the university bursar, to purchase Whiteknights Park as a new site, brought out all his administrative flair. Within a few months he was able to reconcile the Ministry of Works, persuade the local authorities, and obtain approval and financial support from the Treasury. Whiteknights is his great contribution to the university.

Stenton was elected FBA in 1926 and an honorary fellow of Keble College in 1947. He received honorary doctorates from the universities of Oxford (1936), Leeds (1939), Manchester (1944), Cambridge (1947), Sheffield (1948), London, Nottingham, and Reading (1951). He was a corresponding member of the Académie des Inscriptions et Belles Lettres in the Institut de France (1947), and of the Monumenta Germaniae Historica (1955), and a corresponding fellow of the Medieval Academy of America (1959). He was knighted in 1948. His pupils and friends presented two volumes in his honour, *Sir Christopher Hatton's Book of Seals* (ed. L. C. Loyd and D. M. Stenton, 1950) for his seventieth birthday and *Anglo-Saxon Coins* (ed. R. H. M. Dolley, 1961) for his eightieth birthday.

Stenton was a small, apparently frail man, whose appearance belied his endurance. He had the fine hands of a pianist and a long face with a great domed forehead. He both looked, and was, wise. In committee he was deliberate and considered. In lectures, for which he used the minimum of notes, the combination of enthusiasm, clarity of thought, and superb scholarship gave an impression of controlled incandescence.

In 1919 Stenton married a former pupil, Doris Mary, only child of Joseph Parsons, carpenter, of Woodley, near Reading. Then a college lecturer, she later became a notable medieval historian and was herself elected FBA (1953). She was not only wife and housewife to Stenton, but also colleague, chauffeuse, and finally nurse. They were an inseparable pair on all his academic excursions. Their home at Whitley Park Farm became a centre of pilgrimage for historians, especially in Stenton's retirement.

He died at Reading 15 September 1967; his wife died in 1971. There were no children. His library, papers, and collection of coins are at the university of Reading except for his index of place-names which is with the English Place-Name Society. There is a bibliography of his works in *Preparatory to Anglo-Saxon England*, edited by D. M. Stenton (1970). There is a portrait at the university by William Dring, painted on the occasion of his knighthood.

[Doris M. Stenton in *Proceedings* of the British Academy, vol. liv, 1968; V. H. Galbraith in *American Historical Review*, vol. lxxvi, 1971; private information; personal knowledge.]   J. C. HOLT

STEPHENSON, (JOHN) CECIL (1889-1965), artist, was born 15 September 1889 at Bishop Auckland, county Durham, the younger son of Robert Stephenson, horse dealer, of Bishop Auckland, and his wife, Elizabeth Jane Newton. He was educated at Bishop Barrington and King James I Grammar Schools, Bishop Auckland, and between 1906 and 1908 at Darlington Technical College, where he decided to become an art student. After enrolling at Leeds School of Art in 1908 he quickly moved to the Royal College of Art and then to the Slade School of Art, where he was taught by Professor Henry Tonks [q.v.]. At the Slade he formed part of an unusually gifted generation, including Paul Nash, (Sir) Stanley Spencer, Edward Wadsworth, David Bomberg [qq.v.], William Roberts, and in particular Ben Nicholson, an artist with whom Stephenson was later to be associated. Before the war, like many other art students of the period, he also travelled to Paris and Italy.

But Stephenson spent the war years making tools, and this interest in mechanics remained with him throughout his life. In 1919 he returned to painting and took 6 Mall Studios, Hampstead, from Walter Sickert [q.v.]. Stephenson lived there until his death, and a similar need for continuity can be found in his employment: in 1922 he was appointed head of art in the architectural department of the Northern Polytechnic, London, a post he held until 1955.

As a painter, though, his career underwent a number of considerable changes. During the 1920s his work pursued a fairly conservative course, concentrating on portraits and landscapes in an able yet unambitious style. Then, in the early 1930s, he found himself in the middle of a group of avant-garde artists—Ben Nicholson, (Dame) Barbara Hepworth, and Henry Moore among them—who settled in the same area of Hampstead. The writer and critic (Sir) Herbert Read [q.v.], another neighbour, called it a 'nest of gentle artists', and there can be no doubt that Stephenson's neighbours stimulated him to pursue a more adventurous direction.

At first, his paintings took as their subject the component parts of the fully operational machinery which filled his studio to bursting point. He enjoyed using his lathes and other machines to repair things for friends, and constructed a wide variety of objects from iron gates and fire-guards to metal furniture and staircases. Stephenson even had a working-scale model railway engine in the garden, where visitors would find themselves invited to take a trip. And in paintings like 'The Pump' (1932), 'The Lathe' (1933), and 'Mechanism' (1933) he made his work directly reflect this ruling passion.

Soon the forms of machinery encouraged him to develop a more angular, minimal language which recalled the work of the vorticists twenty years before. (Stephenson actually titled two of his paintings 'Vortex' in 1939.) The role of brushwork was reduced to a thin blocking-in of the forms, and their vigorous interplay now dominated his compositions. In 1932 he married his first wife Sybil, who later became the wife of the surrealist artist and dealer E. L. T. Mesens. But Stephenson himself was never interested in surrealism and by 1933 his work had become abstract—dependent still on machinery but also drawing on a range of other images that reflected his involvement with architecture and music. Often his paintings of the 1930s relate to the forms of the modernist buildings then beginning to appear in Britain, especially in Hampstead and Highgate. But Stephenson's work can equally well be seen as a series of musical variations on the theme of several favourite shapes: a wedge, a trapezium, and a triangle.

During this decade, when he painted much of his best work and contributed to the second phase of abstraction in twentieth-century British art, he exhibited in many group surveys in Britain, France, and the USA. Notable among them was the '7 & 5 Society' at the Leicester Galleries in 1934, and the 'Constructive Art' show at the London Gallery in 1937. One of his works was reproduced in *Circle*, edited by (Sir) J. Leslie Martin, Naum Gabo, and Ben Nicholson in 1937. A year later Mondrian became a close neighbour and friend, and in 1942 Stephenson married the painter Kathleen Guthrie, the daughter of E. M. Maltby, MRCS, LRCP. She had previously been married to the painter Robin Craig Guthrie and had one son.

By this time the war had dispersed the avant-garde colony which stimulated Stephenson's work. His paintings of the blitz, bought by the Imperial War Museum, returned to a more figurative idiom, and he resumed his interest in drawing from life. But by 1951 he had returned to abstract work, this time on an unprecedentedly large scale, with a 10 × 30 feet mural in fluorescent paint for the Festival of Britain. Stephenson was very excited about the possibilities of painting in collaboration with architects, and in the mid 1950s he was commissioned by Plyglass Ltd. of Harlow to design for their glass laminates. In 1957 his plyglass design on perspex was used on the engineering faculty building of Queen Mary College, London University, and a year later he was awarded a silver medal at the Brussels International Exhibition for a plyglass mural, 185 × 13 feet, made for the British pavilion.

Further recognition came in 1960, when Sir Herbert Read wrote the catalogue introduction for his first one-man exhibition at the Drian Galleries, London, which showed how his very latest paintings had become richer and thicker, worked into impasto textures with the palette knife. In 1963 one of his most memorable works, 'Painting 1937', was purchased by the Tate Gallery. By then, however, this handsome and dignified man had suffered three strokes which left him unable to move or talk, and on 13 November 1965 he died at his Hampstead home. The following year a memorial exhibition was held at the Drian Galleries, and in 1975 a retrospective survey was mounted at the Camden Arts Centre, London. No portraits of Stephenson were executed by other artists, but he did paint his own self-portrait *c.*1919-20 (oil on board), a picture still owned by his widow.

[Michael Collins, 'Introduction' to Camden Arts Centre catalogue, 1975; Jasia Reichardt, 'Musical Abstractions' in catalogue of exhibition at Fischer Fine Art, London, 1976; private information.] RICHARD CORK

STEPHENSON, THOMAS ALAN (1898-1961), marine biologist and artist, was born at Burnham-on-Sea, Somerset, 19 January 1898,

the eldest child in the family of two sons and one daughter of Thomas Stephenson, a Wesleyan minister who shortly afterwards became a tutor at the Wesleyan Trinity College, Richmond, Surrey, and his wife, Ellen, daughter of the Revd George Fletcher, governor (principal) of that college. His early childhood was spent in the large college grounds where, he recalled, 'We were surrounded by flower-gardens, had Richmond Park and the Terrace Gardens and river close at hand'. Here his love of nature began but his surroundings altered after 1904 when his father resumed the normal life of a Wesleyan minister. Schools kept changing, and the longest period from 1909 to 1913 Stephenson spent as a boarder at Kingswood School, Bath.

Stephenson's interest in natural history came from his father, a distinguished authority on British orchids, but his artistic and more intellectual gifts came more probably from his mother's side. Her brother, W. C. Fletcher, was a second wrangler who became chief inspector of Secondary Schools for England. A period spent in Wrexham brought Stephenson into contact with Dr H. Drinkwater, a skilled botanical artist who taught the boy to paint flowers. A move to Aberystwyth in 1914 brought him under the inspiring influence of Professor H. J. Fleure [q.v.], who encouraged his developing interest in sea anemones. In 1915 Stephenson entered the University College of Wales where illness impeded his progress. However, in 1916 Fleure had him appointed student-demonstrator, in which capacity he presented published work for the degrees of M.Sc. and D.Sc. (1920 and 1923). In 1922 he married Anne (died 1977), younger twin daughter of Joseph Dore Wood, of Barry, secretary to the firm which built the South Wales docks. They had no children. She became intimately associated with his scientific work and accompanied him everywhere.

Stephenson did research work at Aberystwyth with a grant from the Department of Scientific and Industrial Research from 1920 to 1923, when he was appointed lecturer in zoology in University College, London. He then proceeded with the preparation of his two-volume Ray Society monograph on *British Sea Anemones* (1928, 1935) which he himself illustrated beautifully. It remains the standard work on these animals, replacing the Victorian book by Philip Henry Gosse [q.v.]. These interests also prepared him for membership in 1928 of the Great Barrier Reef Expedition which spent thirteen months on a small coral formation off the coast of Queensland. In charge of the reef party, he was responsible for the ecological description of what, following subsequent surveys, has become the most intimately known coral area in the world. His work on the development and growth of corals is also of enduring value.

Stephenson there developed a compelling interest in shore ecology, for the study of which he was to find the widest scope following his appointment in 1930 to the chair of zoology in the university of Cape Town. In his ten years there he conducted, with a team of research associates, an impressive survey of the distribution and intertidal zonation of animals and plants along the 1,800 mile extent of South Africa's shores. The long series of reports with their careful determination of species and beautifully designed illustrations are never likely to be equalled. They also formed the basis of all subsequent studies on South African shores.

In 1940 Stephenson returned to England to become professor of zoology at Aberystwyth. There he trained students who made major contributions to the study of intertidal life around Britain, while in 1947 and 1948 he conducted, with his wife, surveys along both the Atlantic and Pacific coasts of North America. He also visited Bermuda in 1952. With unique illustrative skill he described the inhabitants and zonation of typical shores from Nova Scotia and Vancouver to Florida and southern California.

His observations along so many shores revealed a constant pattern of intertidal zonation throughout temperate and tropical regions consisting of a supralittoral fringe inhabited by species of the marine snail *Littorina*, with a midlittoral zone covered with acorn barnacles, and an infralittoral fringe only exposed at low water during spring tides. He made unique contributions to knowledge about the worldwide distribution of intertidal organisms. His work represents the culmination of the descriptive phase in intertidal ecology which was later succeeded by a dynamic phase with concern for energy flow. He was elected FRS in 1951.

Stephenson was a highly skilled miniature artist, the perfect illustrator of the brilliantly coloured and intricately patterned sea anemones. In his little book on *Seashore Life and Pattern* (1944) he revealed his profound interest in pattern which could depend on structure or markings, or on both, with possible changes when the animal moved, all with an underlying mathematical basis.

He died in London 3 April 1961. The book he had planned on *Life between Tidemarks on Rocky Shores* was completed by his wife and published under their joint names in 1972.

[C. M. Yonge in *Biographical Memoirs of Fellows of the Royal Society*, vol. viii, 1962; personal knowledge.]   C. M. YONGE

STERN, SIR ALBERT GERALD (1878–1966), banker and administrator in the production of the first tanks, was the second son of James Julius Stern, senior partner of Stern Brothers, European merchant bankers, by his wife, Lucy Leah Biedermann; he was born at 42 Princes Gate, Knightsbridge, London, 24 September 1878. After an education at Eton and Christ Church, Oxford, he entered the family business and received his professional training at its Frankfurt and New York offices, becoming a partner in 1904. A convinced practitioner of the cult of the strong man, who was committed to take positive independent action in the implementation of administrative cures, he became involved in the launching of a number of important international loans prior to 1914, one of which was an advance of £1,500,000 to the Young Turks. At the outbreak of war his attempt to join the forces by enrolment was refused because of a weak ankle, and an attempt to purchase a place in the war by offering himself and an armoured car with its crew to the first lord of the Admiralty, (Sir) Winston Churchill, also met with a rebuff. Nevertheless, by the end of 1914 he had managed to obtain a commission in the Royal Naval Volunteer Reserve and join the Armoured Car Division of the Royal Naval Air Service. In so doing he became part of the team which was engaged in efforts to find a way out of the deadlock created by trench warfare, attempts aimed, in so far as the RNAS was concerned, at making armoured cross-country vehicles — 'landships' — which would be proof against hostile fire, and would break down barbed wire, cross trenches, and destroy enemy weapons.

From April 1915, as secretary of the Admiralty Landships Committee, of which (Sir) Eustace Tennyson-d'Eyncourt [q.v.] was president, Stern began to exert considerable drive and initiatives in the creation of armoured fighting vehicles. The failure of the spring and summer offensives in France made the need for a solution to the deadlock all the more urgent, and it was he who increasingly took the lead in urging the development of materials and designs compatible with a project which had yet to be fully defined. Suitable armour plate had to be found, guns and engines selected, and above all a decision reached whether the vehicle should be carried on wheels or tracks. While the designers grappled with these problems, Stern took over an office in Pall Mall (at his own expense) in June 1915 and began to run the project, as he said, 'on business lines'. In this he had the support of A. J. Balfour, who had by then become first lord. At about the same time he also came into contact with (Sir) Ernest Swinton [q.v.], who had been among the first to visualize the need for an armoured fighting vehicle carried on tracks and who, as secretary of the Dardanelles Committee of the Cabinet, was engaged in pushing forward his ideas. Thus two imaginative and irreverent intellects were thrown into a mutually agreeable fusion to the benefit of their joint project.

With Swinton formulating the operational requirements and dealing with Whitehall objections, and Stern co-ordinating the essential resources for research, development, and prospective production (and at the same time disentangling the project from Admiralty control), the design of a pilot tracked vehicle—for security reasons presently called the tank—was arrived at in September 1915. While (Sir) William Tritton and Walter Wilson [qq.v.] were solving the immediate technical problems, Stern battled for support among the Ministries and in industry to acquire the necessary resources and priorities. By the end of December the first operational tank had been built, and early in 1916 it was demonstrated to Lord Kitchener [q.v.], Lloyd George, Balfour, and many others, to such good effect that an order for 100 was placed, and Stern was invited to go to the War Office to head a department charged with tank production. But almost simultaneously Lloyd George insisted that tank production should come under him in the Ministry of Munitions, and he made Stern chairman of its Tank Supply Committee. It was the principal feat of this committee that fifty tanks were ready for their first action at Flers, 15 September 1916.

In March 1916 Stern was transferred from the navy to the army (with the rank of major in the Machine-Gun Corps, Heavy Branch—so designated for the purpose of secrecy), and for the remainder of the war he was engaged upon efforts to improve both the quantity and quality of tanks, endeavours which turned him into an advocate of mechanical warfare as a means of reducing casualties among men, and which drove him into heated and often unconventional battles with unbelievers in the Ministry of Munitions and the War Office who knew nothing of tanks and who failed, in his view, to appreciate the immense potentialities of this kind of warfare, and with those among the technicians who seemed to drag their feet. However, his pre-war international contacts made liaison easy for him with the French and the Americans, and he was able to persuade them of the virtues of mechanical-warfare development at a time when some of his own countrymen were lukewarm. In October 1917 he was appointed commissioner for mechanical warfare (Overseas and Allies), was promoted lieutenant-colonel in the newly constituted Tanks Corps, and was instrumental in negotiating a joint Allied programme for the design

and manufacture of tanks—a scheme which never got fully into its stride because the war, hastened to its conclusion by the action of those very tanks, came to its end a year later. The story of his stewardship is told in his book *Tanks 1914–1918: The Log-Book of a Pioneer* (1919). He was appointed CMG in 1917 and KBE in 1918.

Between the wars Stern returned to banking, eventually becoming a director of the Midland Bank, of the Clydesdale Bank, and of the Bank of Roumania, as well as a member of the London committee of the Ottoman Bank, and the head of Stern Brothers on the death of his kinsman, Sir Edward Stern. But the outbreak of fresh hostilities in 1939, while halting an attempt to take over the German oil interests in Romania, brought him swiftly back to the work which had made him famous. In September 1939 he became chairman of the Special Vehicle Development Committee of the Ministry of Supply, charged with the task of building a heavy tank to the specifications of that Ministry. The War Office at first preferred to think in terms of trench warfare on the lines of 1918; Stern brought together his old colleagues from the previous war to assist him, and they designed a model with many characteristics of the 1918 monster tanks. Stern, indeed, was a critic of the priority which before 1939 had been given to smaller tanks, such as were about to revolutionize tank warfare; he complained that there were 'no fighting tanks suitable for trench warfare', and proposed a giant with a twin fourteen-inch gun-turret to tackle the Siegfried Line. But it was soon demonstrated by the Germans in their invasion of France that the days of trench warfare were past. For four years Stern was to continue in the Ministry of Supply, and in 1941 was a so-called independent member of the Tank Board—an interdepartmental organization set up to make decisions about armoured fighting vehicle design, development, and production. But the Board fell short of its aims, due to a certain amount of acrimony between its members, of whom Stern was among the most forthright although not necessarily the most up-to-date in his philosophy of modern warfare. Yet, always foresighted and keen on the gigantic, he had proposed, at the outbreak of war, the construction of 100,000-ton oil-tankers to be built in dry docks in France (the biggest of that class were then only 17,000 tons)—a project which died, of course, with the collapse of French resistance but the feasibility of which was afterwards proven and surpassed.

In the closing years of his life he played a leading part in the court of the Drapers Company, of which he was master in 1946–7; he was high sheriff of Kent in 1945–6, and a deputy lieutenant from 1952. But perhaps his happiest involvement was in connection with the rebuilding of Queen Mary College, London, as chairman of the board of governors, in which he took a dynamic role in acquiring fresh sites and steering the college to a new dignity and prominence—a part he played with characteristic personal contact at all levels of the activity from 1944 to 1963. His interests were widespread, and he took a lively part in everything to which he turned his hand, including peach farming, besides playing most games with vigour and some skill.

Stern married Helen Merryday, elder daughter of Sir Frederick Orr Orr-Lewis, in 1922; they had two sons and two daughters. He died at his home near Maidstone, Kent, 2 January 1966. His widow died in 1974.

[Sir Albert Stern, *Tanks 1914–1918: The Log-Book of a Pioneer*, 1919; B. H. Liddell Hart, *The Tanks*, 2 vols., 1959; Sir Ernest Swinton, *Eyewitness*, 1932; M. M. Postan, D. Hay, and J. D. Scott (Official History), *Design and Development of Weapons*, 1964.]

KENNETH MACKSEY

STERRY, CHARLOTTE (1870–1966), lawn tennis champion, was born in Ealing 22 September 1870, the daughter of Henry Cooper, of Caversham, a miller, and his wife, Teresa Georgiana Miller. Charlotte Cooper was the youngest of six children. Her husband, whom she married in 1901, was Alfred Sterry, a solicitor. They had two children: Gwen, who became a Wimbledon lawn tennis player and represented Britain in the Wightman Cup, and Rex (R. B. Sterry), for many years a committee member of the All England Club. Gwen married Max Simmers who won twenty-eight consecutive rugger caps for Scotland.

Charlote (Chattie) Sterry won the Wimbledon singles championship five times, as Miss Cooper in 1895, 1896, and 1898, and as Mrs Sterry in 1901 and 1908. She was at that time thirty-seven, and the mother of two children. It was a remarkable performance to regain the title for a fifth time after an interval of seven years and in doing so Mrs Sterry inflicted the only defeat sustained by the great Mrs Lambert Chambers [q.v.] at Wimbledon, at the hands of a British player, between 1903 and 1919 (the war years of course intervening).

Charlotte Sterry, slim, active, and always ready to play for her life, was one of the most popular players of her day and no champion has ever enjoyed the game of lawn tennis more than she did. Her game was all attack. She was one of the very few top women players before 1914 who served overhead. Mrs Lambert Chambers served underhand and only changed to over-head after the war. Mrs Sterry came to the net at every opportunity but it was her supreme steadiness, her equable temperament, and her great tactical ability which were the main reasons for her success—rather than any brilliance of stroke. She 'had a go' at everyone and everything and her smiling good temper and great sportsmanship made her as popular in her heyday as did her invincible spirit and irrepressible *joie de vivre* in her old age when she came back to Wimbledon to cheer on the younger generation.

She learnt her tennis at the Ealing Lawn Tennis Club where she was coached, first by H. Lawrence, then by C. H. Martin and H. S. Mahony. In those days there was no winter play and she kept fit in the winter by skipping, running, and walking and playing hockey, at which sport she became a county player for Surrey. She played tennis, of course, in long skirts, an inch or two above the ground, and only kept two rackets, an old one for wet weather and a good one for best. She got her rackets from Slazenger and her husband.always insisted that she should pay for them, the top price for a racket in those days being 30s.

Charlotte Cooper, as she then was, won her first Open singles title at Ilkley in 1893. During the eight years 1894–1901, following the retirement of Miss Lottie Dod, Mrs G. W. Hillyard and Miss Cooper led the field of women's tennis, each of them winning the women's singles title four times during that period; then Mrs Sterry won it once more in 1908. She was also an extremely good doubles player. She won the All England mixed doubles with H. S. Mahony for five successive years from 1894 to 1898 and then with H. L. Doherty in 1900 and with X. E. Casdagli in 1908. As in this latter year she won the All England ladies doubles with Miss Garfit, besides being singles champion, she became a treble Wimbledon champion in one year—a very rare achievement; she also won the triple crown in the Irish championships of 1895 when, in addition to the singles, she won the ladies doubles with Miss E. Cooper and the mixed with H. S. Mahony. She won the Irish mixed again with H. S. Mahony in 1896 and with R. F. Doherty in 1899 and 1900 and the Irish ladies championship another twice, with Mrs Hillyard in 1897 and with Miss E. Cooper in 1900. She won the British covered court mixed doubles in 1898, 1899, and 1900, each time with R. F. Doherty. In the Olympic Games of 1900 she won two gold medals: for the ladies singles and the mixed doubles (with R. F. Doherty).

In addition, she won the Scottish singles championship in 1899 and numerous other championships and challenge cups. These included the singles championships for London

(5 times), Middlesex (7 times), Northern (twice), Northumberland County (thrice).

Perhaps Mrs Sterry's greatest truimph was gained in 1907. This was the year when one of the greatest players of all time, Miss May Sutton of Southern California, aged only twenty, came back to challenge for the Wimbledon title which she had won two years earlier. During her tournaments in Great Britain in that year Miss Sutton only lost one match—to Mrs Sterry at Old Trafford. Mrs Sterry did not defend her Wimbledon singles championship in 1909, but was runner-up to Mrs Larcombe in 1912 and reached the final of the ladies doubles in 1913, eighteen years after gaining her first Wimbledon title.

Mrs Sterry had been deaf since she was twenty-six and in later years lost most of her sight, but her mind and memory remained razor sharp and her morale was excellent. For many years it had been her ambition to be the oldest living Wimbledon champion—both in actual age and in the date of her first championship; and when Lottie Dod, who had won the first of her five championships in 1887 when only fifteen, died at the age of eighty-eight during the Wimbledon championships of 1960, Mrs Sterry was out on her own. She was only three months short of her ninety-first birthday when she flew down unaccompanied from Scotland during the 1961 Wimbledon to attend the champions' luncheon, presided over by the president of the Club, Princess Marina, Duchess of Kent [q.v.], to mark the seventy-fifth year of the championships. She lived happily for another five years before she died at Helensburgh on the Clyde 10 October 1966.

[*Ayres' Lawn Tennis Almanack*, *passim*; Sir John Smyth (with Duncan Macaulay), *Behind the Scenes at Wimbledon*, 1965; Sir John Smyth, 'Memorable Wimbledons' in the Wimbledon Programme, 1966; private information; personal knowledge.]

J. G. SMYTH

STILES, WALTER (1886-1966), plant physiologist, was born at Shepherd's Bush, London, 23 August 1886, the elder child and only son of Walter Stiles, wood carver and architectural modeller, and his wife, Elizabeth Sarah Dury. The family had long been settled in Kent and Stiles's great-uncle, Walter Stiles of Cobham, was the father of Walter Stiles (d. 1967) and grandfather of Walter Stanley Stiles, FRS (born 1901), the physicist.

Stiles was educated at Latymer Upper School, Hammersmith, whither he went with a London County Council scholarship and where he was greatly influenced by the mathematics and senior science master, G. M. Grace, in whose charge at that time were (Sir) Harold Spencer Jones [q.v.], later astronomer royal, G. K. Livers, later professor of mathematics at University College, Cardiff, and D. Orson Wood, who became editor of *Science Progress*. Stiles went up to Emmanuel College, Cambridge, with an exhibition to read natural sciences in 1905, with (Sir) A. C. Seward [q.v.] as tutor. Seward became professor of botany in 1906 and Stiles was transferred to (Sir) F. Gowland Hopkins [q.v.], but his former tutor's influence was such that Stiles concentrated on plant science and worked under F. F. Blackman [q.v.], F. T. Brookes, and (Sir) A. G. Tansley [q.v.]: he won a double first in the tripos, taking part i in 1907 and part ii in 1909.

Stiles's first research papers concerning the anatomy and relationships of certain gymnosperms, notably Podocarpaceae, were written at Cambridge, but in 1910 he was appointed assistant lecturer in the botany department at the university of Leeds with the result that when J. H. Priestley became head of that department, Stiles was won over to plant physiology. Collaborating with Priestley's junior assistant, Ingvar Jørgensen, Stiles took up work on the entry of salts into plant tissues. At the outbreak of war in 1914, Stiles was seconded to the Royal Society sectional chemical committee to work on the preparation of local anaesthetics and, later, on the digestibility of war bread for the society's food (war) committee. In 1918 he transferred to the Food Investigation Board, where he again collaborated with Jørgensen, this time on aspects of food preservation. In 1919, Stiles became professor of botany at University College, Reading, despite tempting offers of advisory work in the food industry abroad. He continued investigations, often through research students, on salt uptake, particularly in connection with aerobic respiration, an area in which he was something of a pioneer, for the next twenty-five years. In 1929 he was elected Mason professor of botany at the university of Birmingham, a post he held until his retirement in 1951.

Stiles was a prolific author: he wrote, often in collaboration with others, over seventy papers and articles, many of them reviews, about plant physiology, particularly for *Annals of Botany*, *New Phytologist*, and *Proceedings of the Royal Society*, and for over forty years contributed pieces on recent advances in the subject to *Science Progress*. Further, he wrote several books and monographs, notably *Carbon Assimilation* (with I. Jørgensen, 1917), *Permeability* (1924), *Photosynthesis* (1925), *Respiration in Plants* (with W. Leach, 1932, 4th edn. 1960), *An Introduction to the Principles of Plant Physiology* (1936, 2nd edn. 1950), and *Trace Elements in Plants and Animals* (1946, 3rd edn. as *Trace*

Elements in Plants, 1961), the first two of which were important monographic reviews in their time, while *Respiration* was a useful student text. His *An Introduction to the Principles of Plant Physiology* was an elementary review of the whole subject: a third edition, which occupied him in his last years, was completed and brought out by Edward C. Cocking in 1969.

Stiles was awarded the Walsingham medal for an original essay on a biological subject in 1911 and obtained a Cambridge Sc.D. in 1922. He was elected to the Royal Society in 1928 and served on its council (1935-7). He was a fellow of the Linnean Society and a founder-member of the British Ecological Society and was associated with the British Association from 1910, serving on its council from 1951 to 1954 and acting as president of Section K at the Cambridge meeting of 1938. He was a corresponding member of the American Society of Plant Physiologists and was later awarded an honorary D.Sc. by the university of Nottingham (1963). After his retirement, in 1952 he was made professor emeritus and, in 1954, a life governor of the university.

Stiles's important research work was carried out at the beginning of his career, his later years being most memorable for his influential textbooks, for he excelled at clear exposition of the labours of others. He was rather detached and awesome to undergraduates, although, on better acquaintance, they found him helpful and understanding. His retiring nature made him a rather inactive participant at scientific meetings, and his lectures, like his written work, were almost painfully careful and perhaps rather dull. Undoubtedly he was more at ease with postgraduates working in his own laboratory on topics of his closest interest. He was one of the few to maintain that nutrient uptake in plants was not merely passive with the transpiration stream, and, although in retrospect his papers may seem prolix and rather naïve, if it is recalled that at the time they were written biochemical knowledge, as a framework in which to put his findings into context, was rudimentary, his approach is at once both understandable and laudably cautious. Of the students from his laboratory who went on to distinguished botanical careers, perhaps the most illustrious was W. O. James (1900–78), who did much to extend and clarify Stiles's original investigations.

In 1920 Stiles married Edith Ethel May, daughter of Charles Harwood, of Earl's Court, London, gentleman and sometime horse-trainer. They had two children, Walter (born 1922), a physicist, and a daughter. Devoted to his wife and family, hardworking and shy, Stiles was of medium height and build with a rather military bearing. He had a lively sense of humour, rooted in his facility with words. He had little time for politics and its practitioners, and, having been brought up in a strict Anglican family, maintained an orthodox religious belief until the end of his life. Stiles was a keen traveller, photographer, and gardener, particularly interested in fruit growing and the collection of varieties in danger of disappearing from cultivation. He enjoyed walking, tennis, and badminton in his younger days, and in old age took up again, rather surreptitiously, his childhood interest in philately, which later proved an excellent investment. He read widely and appreciated recent classical music, notably that of Sibelius. He pursued these interests during retirement at Tilehurst, near Reading, where he continued to write, notably review articles for the *Encyclopaedia of Plant Physiology*, and where he died 19 April 1966.

[*The Times*, 22 April 1966; W. O. James in *Biographical Memoirs of Fellows of the Royal Society*, vol. xiii, 1967; Ray Desmond, *Dictionary of British and Irish Botanists and Horticulturists*, 1977; private information.]

D. J. MABBERLEY

STONER, EDMUND CLIFTON (1899–1968), physicist, was born 2 October 1899 at East Molesey, Surrey, the only child of Arthur David Hallett Stoner, cricket professional, and his wife, Mary Ann, daughter of Thomas Robert Fleet, of Streatham, London. He was educated at Bolton Grammar School and at Emmanuel College, Cambridge, where he was awarded an open exhibition in natural sciences. He obtained a first class in both part i (1920) and part ii (physics, 1921) of the natural sciences tripos. In 1921 he was awarded a Department of Scientific and Industrial Research maintenance grant to carry out research work at the Cavendish Laboratory under the official supervision of Sir E. Rutherford (later Lord Rutherford of Nelson, q.v.). His first paper (1922), jointly with Gilbert Stead, concerned 'Low voltage glows in mercury vapour'; a slightly later paper, with (Sir) L. H. Martin, concerned the absorption of X-rays. The interest engendered by this and related problems of atomic structure led directly to some of Stoner's greatest work in theoretical physics.

In 1924 Stoner was appointed to a lectureship in physics at the university of Leeds. Thereafter he was promoted to a readership in physics in 1927 and to the professorship of theoretical physics in 1939. In 1928 Emmanuel College awarded him a research fellowship, which he retained until 1931. Stoner followed R. Whiddington [q.v.] as Cavendish professor of physics at Leeds in 1951. He took his duties so seriously that his last scientific publication is dated 1954. In 1963 he retired, slightly early, from the chair.

The greatest contributions which Stoner made to theoretical physics came very early and near the end of his scientific career (which was interrupted by war work just when his scientific creativity was at a high point). His early work on X-ray absorption awoke his interest in the distribution of electrons among atomic energy levels. This led to the publication, in 1924, of a paper giving for the first time the distribution, which turned out to be the correct one, that the total number of electrons required to complete a group of quantum number n is $2n^2$. The scheme corresponded to there being a maximum of one electron in each 'possible and equally probable state'. When stated more axiomatically in 1925 by Pauli, who came across Stoner's paper by chance, this very scheme soon became known as the exclusion principle, earning Pauli the Nobel prize. Stoner had pointed out that some evidence regarding this distribution of electrons came from the magnetic moments of the ions of the elements of the first transition series. Thus was laid the basis for Stoner's abiding interest in the magnetism of matter.

A number of other influences were at work in shaping his later scientific researches, namely a love of numerical calculations, a realization of the importance of thermodynamics, and a strong feeling that theoretical and experimental physics must be closely interrelated. Thus he published in 1938 and 1939 two seminal papers on the theory of the magnetic properties of metallic ferromagnets, such as nickel. This theory was called by Stoner the collective electron treatment. Its influence took several decades to spread throughout the mainstream of the physics of solids, but a crescendo of appreciation began about 1960. The concepts called Stoner model, Stoner excitations, Stoner criterion for ferromagnetism, and Stoner parameter became widely used in discussing the ferromagnetism of metals and alloys. A decade after Stoner's death many scientists felt that, had he been alive, he would have been a strong candidate for the Nobel prize. Stoner collaborated in two more pieces of important research. In a joint publication of 1949 a thermodynamic treatment was given of the heat changes during magnetic hysteresis cycles. In 1948 another joint publication laid the basis of the later theory of permanent magnets, magnetic recording tapes, and magnetic thin films.

In 1937 Stoner was elected FRS and in 1938 the university of Cambridge awarded him the degree of Sc.D. He delivered the Kelvin lecture of the Institution of Electrical Engineers in 1944 and the Physical Society Guthrie lecture

in 1955, the respective titles being 'Magnetism in Theory and Practice' and 'Magnetism in Retrospect and Prospect'.

Stoner was essentially modest and kind. Being for most of his life in poor health, partly due to diabetes, which became evident as early as 1919, he nevertheless enjoyed several hobbies, including photography, gardening, and piano playing. His lack of good health gave him an air of frailness which was, however, often deceptive. There was in him some hidden strength allowing him to pursue his chosen aims, notwithstanding the difficulties which frequently beset him. The greatest personal influences in his life were his mother, for whom he cared until her death at the age of eighty-seven, in 1955, and his wife (Jean) Heather, daughter of Herbert Crawford, whom he married in 1951 and who survived him. There were no children. He died in Leeds 27 December 1968.

[L. F. Bates in *Biographical Memoirs of Fellows of the Royal Society*, vol. xv, 1969; personal knowledge.]   E. P. WOHLFARTH

STOPFORD, JOHN SEBASTIAN BACH, BARON STOPFORD OF FALLOWFIELD (1888-1961), anatomist and vice-chancellor, was born at Hindley Green, near Wigan, 25 June 1888, the eldest of the three sons of Thomas Rinch Stopford, colliery engineer from Upholland, and his wife, Mary Tyrer, the daughter of James Johnson of Bolton. He was educated first at Liverpool College, later at the Manchester Grammar School, where he acquired a lifelong devotion to association football. On entering the medical school of the university of Manchester in 1906, he soon gained a position in the university first eleven. He graduated MB, Ch.B., in 1911 with second class honours, having won the Dumville surgical prize and the Bradley memorial surgical scholarship. He became house surgeon at the Rochdale Infirmary, a hospital then staffed entirely by general practitioners. In 1912 he became a demonstrator of anatomy in the university medical school under (Sir) Grafton Elliot Smith [q.v.]. He became lecturer in 1915 and in that year was awarded the MD with gold medal for a thesis on the blood supply of the pons and medulla. In the judgement of successive years of undergraduate students he had become the most popular all-round teacher of anatomy the university had seen for many years. In 1919, when Elliot Smith moved to University College, London, Stopford became professor of anatomy at the early age of thirty.

During the war years of 1914-18 use had been made of Stopford's clinical talents in the study of gunshot wounds of peripheral nerves in the military orthopaedic centre of the Second Western General Hospital. Despite the burden of new duties as professor of anatomy he conducted a peripheral nerve injury follow-up clinic at the Grangethorpe Hospital (Ministry of Pensions) for more than ten years. In 1923 he began his first spell as dean of the medical school, which he relinquished in 1927 only to become pro-vice-chancellor (1928-30), returning to a further spell as dean.

In 1927 he was elected FRS, the first graduate of the Manchester University medical school to achieve this honour. His observations on the pace and quality of motor and sensory recovery following surgical repair of injured nerve trunks led to the publication in 1930 of his book on *Sensation and the Sensory Pathway*. From the peripheral nerve system Stopford turned to a study of the sympathetic system in its practical clinical application to vascular lesions, in collaboration with Professor E. D. Telford.

By 1934 Stopford's administrative qualities had so impressed senate and council that he was invited to succeed Sir Walter Moberly as vice-chancellor. This translation to the world of administration was at first regarded with dismay by many of his colleagues. Indeed Stopford himself was reluctant to abandon anatomical teaching and research, and until 1937 he continued to occupy his anatomical chair. Thereafter, until 1956, he held a personal chair of experimental neurology.

As vice-chancellor, a new career, of outstanding leadership and wide influence, had opened for him. He held office until 1956 and during his time the university doubled its number of students and teaching staff. Stopford's ability as an administrator soon involved him in the affairs of a host of extramural institutions. He was chairman of the Universities Bureau of the British Empire; vice-chairman of the Committee of Principals and Vice-Chancellors; chairman-elect of the General Medical Council (illness prevented him from taking up his duties); and chairman of the council of the Royal Manchester College of Music. He was a member of the Medical Advisory Committee of the University Grants Committee; and vice-chairman of the Interdepartmental Committee on Medical Schools. The impression he made on its chairman, Sir William Goodenough [q.v.], led to his selection in 1943 as vice-chairman of the trustees of the Nuffield Foundation. He had already become involved in the field of the planning of hospital services as chairman of the joint Manchester, Salford, and Stretford Hospitals Board, a forerunner of the regional board pattern of the National Health Service. Added to which there could be cited a whole catalogue of services to his more profes-

sional associations from the Anatomical Society to the General Medical Council. He was also chairman of the John Rylands Library. All this was a heavy burden for a man who had had a severe coronary thrombosis some years before and had weathered a major surgical operation.

Despite the growing compulsion of administrative duties, Stopford's work as a medical scientist was remarkable, particularly in days when collaboration between the scientist and the clinician was rare. The closeness of Stopford's work with clinical colleagues, notably Sir Harry Platt, Sir Geoffrey Jefferson [q.v.], Professor E. D. Telford, and Professor John Morley, remained a leading thread amongst his activities until his retirement, though the nature of the work passed from dissecting room and hospital ward to committee room as the years proceeded. Nevertheless, he prized his reputation as 'the surgeon's anatomist' until his death. In those days clinicians were ill-paid by hospital and university alike and it says much for Stopford that so many of them were ready to put so much unrequited time at his disposal.

By the time his duties as vice-chancellor and his national commitments began to absorb the whole of his time Stopford had published an important monograph (*Sensation and the Sensory Pathways*) and sixty or so other papers. His overriding scientific interests, chiefly neurological in character, lay in work on the supply of blood to the brain, on the loss and recovery of sensation in the peripheral nerves arising from nerve injuries in the war of 1914-18, and on the structure and functioning of the autonomic nervous system.

As a vice-chancellor, Stopford was friendly with all ranks of the university hierarchy who saw him as a man of simple tastes, free from ostentation. Wit was perhaps not the strongest weapon in his armoury. In general his judgements were tolerant, even when confronting the clash of personalities to be found in a university senate. He was known affectionately to his intimates as 'Jock' and was so named in conversation amongst colleagues and undergraduates. The legend was that he and the head university porter would go off most Saturday afternoons to watch their favourite Manchester soccer team together. Stopford was a regular churchgoer next day, as a member of the Presbyterian Church in England, to which he was attracted by his deep friendship with the distinguished theological scholar, T. W. Manson [q.v.]. For a man of such wisdom and powers of judgement, his horizons were sometimes limited. Circumstances had prevented him from acquiring a first-hand knowledge of American universities and teaching hospitals.

However, as a teacher and expositor in speech

and writing, Stopford was direct, simple, and utterly clear, and his reputation as a teacher had remained lively throughout the school. Patient and, with young people, understanding and sympathetic, he aimed at and achieved a clarity superb in its simplicity. Unpretentious in everything he did, he was markedly so in his use of English and often spoke of the campaign he fought (and lost—as have so many others) for the use of the simple word as against the abstruse, for Anglo-Saxon against Latin. Cutaneous sensibility was divided by his predecessors and contemporaries into 'protopathic' and 'epicritic'. For Stopford there was always the 'protective' and 'discriminative' divisions of sensation. With Stopford one was never in doubt, one always knew where one was.

The grave illness of 1943 had left severe consequences which, apart from a highly disciplined personal regime, Stopford had largely ignored. Despite this the then minister of health, Aneurin Bevan [q.v.], applied considerable pressure to secure the appointment of Stopford as first chairman of the Manchester Regional Hospital Board upon which he served until 1953. He brought seemingly unimpaired energy to the task, alongside Dr F. N. Marshall, of reorganizing the hospital services of the region. When in 1948 the new health service came into being he was already sixty years old but the relative, non-controversial, transition from the old system to the new, was a tribute not only to Stopford's character, but to the vigour and industry he had brought to his task.

Stopford naturally attracted a wealth of public honours: honorary doctorates from the universities of Dublin, Leeds, Cambridge, Liverpool, and Manchester. He was appointed MBE in 1920, was knighted in 1941, appointed KBE in 1955; elected FRCP in 1942 and honorary FRCS in 1955, when he was admitted by a Mancunian president and one of his closest friends. Finally, he received the freedom of the city of Manchester in 1956 and in 1958 a life peerage. By then he was a sick man, and was unable to take his seat in the House of Lords. He died at his home at Arnside 6 March 1961.

Stopford married in 1916 Lily Allan, herself an honours graduate in medicine and an accomplished ophthalmologist. She followed her ophthalmic interests until her own and her husband's public duties grew too heavy. Thereafter the health and activities of her husband were her unremitting concern. That, despite considerable ill health, he achieved so much and exerted such continuing influence in so many fields was in large measure due to her complete absorption in his concerns. They had one son.

Stopford's portrait by Sir James Gunn hangs in the Whitworth Hall of the university of Manchester.

[W. Mansfield Cooper in *Biographical Memoirs of Fellows of the Royal Society*, vol. vii, 1961; G. A. G. Mitchell in *Journal of Anatomy*, vol. xcv, pt. 3, July 1961; *Nature*, vol. cxc, no. 4774, p. 391; private information; personal knowledge.]

W. Mansfield Cooper
H. Platt

STRACHEY, (EVELYN) JOHN (ST. LOE) (1901-1963), politician and writer, was born at Newlands Corner, Merrow, near Guildford, 21 October 1901, the younger son and youngest of three children of John St. Loe Strachey [q.v.], for many years editor of the *Spectator*. After the death of Lord Strachie [q.v.] in 1936 Strachey became heir presumptive to the baronetcy created for Sir Henry Strachey [q.v.], secretary to Clive of India. His mother, Henrietta Mary Amy Simpson, was a granddaughter of the Victorian economist Nassau Senior [q.v.]. His sister married the architect (Sir) Clough Williams-Ellis.

Strachey was educated at Eton and Magdalen College, Oxford, which he left after two years, in 1922, without a degree; his parents feared the consequences of further studies on his health following peritonitis. His elder brother had died of pneumonia in his first year at Balliol. But John Strachey had already become known as an undergraduate journalist, as editor, with Robert (later Lord) Boothby, a lifelong friend, of the Conservative journal, the *Oxford Fortnightly Review*; he was also prominent in the Canning Club; wrote poems; and both acted in, and wrote plays for, undergraduate societies. On leaving Oxford he began to work on his father's *Spectator*, writing leading articles and reviews.

In 1923 Strachey joined the Labour Party, under the influence of Sidney and Beatrice Webb [qq.v.], and stood for Parliament unsuccessfully in 1924, for the Aston division of Birmingham, a nomination which he owed to the influence among Birmingham socialists of (Sir) Oswald Mosley, the ex-Conservative member who was candidate for Ladywood. Although Strachey remained a contributor to, and shareholder of, the *Spectator*, he now abandoned his expectation of becoming its editor when his father died, and became an active socialist writer and pamphleteer. With Mosley, he proposed new plans for the resolution of the nation's economic problems in *Revolution by Reason* (1925), and became editor of both the *Socialist Review* and the *Miner*. In 1929 he was returned for Aston and became parliamentary private secretary to Mosley, who had become chancellor of the Duchy of Lancaster in the new Labour Government. He supported Mosley in his campaigns on unemployment in 1930, and followed him into the New Party founded in 1931. For a time he was Mosley's closest collaborator, but broke away after six months, when it seemed that the New Party was turning against Russia, which Strachey had already twice visited.

On leaving Mosley, Strachey asserted himself as an independent member of Parliament, but lost his seat in the general election of 1931. The depression in Britain was by now at its worst, and Strachey found himself drawn towards the Communist Party. He wrote for the Communist cause a succession of influential books: notably *The Coming Struggle for Power* (1932) and *The Nature of Capitalist Crisis* (1935). Strachey was never a member of the Communist Party, although his second wife was, and he would have liked to have been; but the party leaders considered him not altogether dependable and, in any case, so long as he supported the cause, more useful outside than within. Strachey's was, in fact, the most powerful intellectual voice in the Communist movement in this country throughout most of the thirties, and, as such, influenced the Left Book Club, founded by (Sir) Victor Gollancz [q.v.] in 1936 with Strachey's help, which became more of a movement than a book club. Strachey wrote regularly in the club's monthly *Left News*, spoke at its many rallies throughout the country, and provided the club's choice for November 1936 (*The Theory and Practice of Socialism*) and for March 1938, when, in *What Are We to Do?*, he argued for a Popular Front. In the same year his pamphlet *Why You Should Be a Socialist* sold over 300,000 copies.

Although to Strachey socialism still meant Communism, he was by now beginning to move away from Communist orthodoxy. The Nazi–Soviet pact of 1939 in the end disillusioned him about Soviet motives. Other reasons for his break with Communism were: his admiration for J. M. (later Lord) Keynes [q.v.] and for Roosevelt, both of whom, the one in theory, the other in practice, seemed to suggest a middle way in politics; and his interest in and personal experience of psychoanalysis. His book, *A Programme for Progress* (the Book Club choice for January 1940), seemed too Keynesian and angered orthodox Communists even before Strachey finally decided to break with the party after the German invasion of Norway and Denmark in the spring. He did so in a letter published in the *New Statesman* (27 April 1940).

Left without a political base, Strachey joined the Royal Air Force and served some time as adjutant with a fighter squadron, then as public relations officer with a bomber group. He next moved to the Air Ministry, where he eventually joined the directorate of bomber operations and became widely known to the country for his air commentaries after the BBC 9 o'clock news. This fame helped him back into Parliament as a member for Dundee in 1945 and to the post of under-secretary of state for air in Attlee's administration where he dealt skilfully with demobilization and other Service problems. Marked out for promotion, he became minister of food in May 1946.

This appointment was the most critical in Strachey's life. In many ways he was well equipped: he had made himself an able economist; he liked, and understood the meaning of, power; he knew how to use civil servants to their best advantage; he had a gift for political simplification and explanation. All these qualities were necessary, since the Ministry of Food was a politically sensitive department at a time when shortages and rationing continued and, indeed, increased (notably with the introduction of bread rationing) despite the end of the war. Strachey established a temporary mastery over the House of Commons in 1946, but he was bitterly and often unfairly attacked by the Conservative press, particularly the Beaverbrook papers. By 1949 his reputation had been severely damaged by the failure of a plan to increase supplies of natural oil by growing ground-nuts on a large scale in Tanganyika. This scheme originated with the United Africa Company but was thought too large for private exploitation. The Cabinet asked the Ministry of Food to organize the scheme. After several years and over £30 millions had been invested, it was plain that ground-nuts could not be commercially or satisfactorily grown. The affair, exploited to the full by the press, hurt Strachey's political prospects, although he can be blamed only for an initial excess of zeal for the scheme, for failure to start with a 'pilot' plan, and for an excessive reliance on those whom he had named to carry out the scheme on the spot: in particular, his old friend (Sir) Leslie Plummer.

After the general election of 1950, Strachey returned for West Dundee, became secretary of state for war, still without a seat in the Cabinet. The arrest of Dr Fuchs, the atomic spy, had led to doubts about security, and immediately upon Strachey's appointment the *Evening Standard* (2 March 1950) came out with headlines 'Fuchs and Strachey. A great new crisis. War minister has never disavowed Communism.' Strachey was advised not to sue on the grounds that the publicity would do more harm than good, although he wanted to and would certainly have been justified. Although less happy in his new post than at the Ministry of Food, and not in favour of the health service charges which brought the resignation of Aneurin Bevan [q.v.], Strachey greatly admired Attlee's leadership, and remained in the Government until it was defeated in 1951. Thereafter, as shadow minister of war, he set himself to master the complexities of nuclear strategy.

In the years in opposition, Strachey attempted to steer a middle course between Gaitskellites and Bevanites in the Labour movement and accordingly incurred the obloquy of both. He voted for Hugh Gaitskell [q.v.] as successor to Attlee in 1955 and, in the late fifties, drew closer to the official leadership of the party. After Gaitskell died in 1963 Strachey worked for the succession of George Brown (later Lord George-Brown). Nevertheless, (Sir) Harold Wilson named him shadow Commonwealth secretary, and would have included him in his Cabinet in the following year had not Strachey died, in London, following a spinal operation, 15 July 1963.

During the fifties Strachey's main work, in his own view at least, was to attempt a new theoretical statement of his political position in a series of books: *Contemporary Capitalism* (1956), *The End of Empire* (1959), and *On the Prevention of War* (1962). In these the ex-Marxist of the thirties attempted to absorb Keynes, to analyse the real effect of empire on European economies, and to introduce the new theoretical American strategic thinking to a British audience. In 1962 he published a brilliant collection of essays, *The Strangled Cry*, mostly about the intellectual and psychological effect of Communism. In both personal and political life Strachey often seemed indecisive and perhaps evasive. He was, however, a man of great intellectual integrity, charm, and wit to his family and those who knew him well. He remained a man of culture while a politician. Physically, he was tall, somewhat ungainly, with a swarthy countenance relieved by friendly brown eyes. He remained an enthusiastic games player until late in life. As a writer, he was an extremely able expositor of complicated general ideas, whether those of Marx, Keynes, J. K. Galbraith or even Hermann Kahn. He influenced the Labour movement towards Marxism in the thirties; away from it in the forties; and towards a realistic foreign and defence policy in the sixties.

Strachey was twice married: in 1929 to Esther (died 1962), only daughter of Patrick Francis Murphy, a wealthy department store owner of New York, who obtained a divorce in 1933; in that year Strachey married Celia, daughter of an Anglican clergyman, the Revd Arthur Hume Simpson; they had a son and a daughter.

The only known portrait is one by Celia Strachey which remained in her possession.

[Hugh Thomas, *John Strachey*, 1973; private information; personal knowledge.]

HUGH THOMAS

STRATHALMOND, first BARON (1888–1970), industrialist. [See FRASER, WILLIAM.]

STREET, ARTHUR GEORGE (1892–1966), farmer, author, and broadcaster, was born at Wilton near Salisbury 7 April 1892, the younger son of Henry Street, tenant farmer, and his wife, Sarah Anne Butt. At the age of fifteen he left Dauntsey's School, near Devizes, and for the next three years assisted his father at Ditchampton Farm, Wilton. Then he migrated to Canada, where he worked on a farm in North-West Manitoba. Returning home in 1914, he tried to enlist as a soldier, but was rejected because of a congenital malformation of his feet which had prevented him from walking until he was seven. Once again he assisted his father, on whose death in 1917 he took over the farm tenancy.

In 1929, having read what he regarded as an incompetent farming article, he wrote one himself, more or less as a joke. To his astonishment the piece was published by the *Daily Mail*. From that day until his final illness he continued to write. In 1932, encouraged by Edith Olivier, of Wilton Park, he published *Farmer's Glory*, which may be described as a countryman's credo and a farmer's reminiscences. Again to his astonishment, the work was highly successful. During the next three decades he published more than thirty books, either rural novels or cameos of country life. None of the later volumes repeated the success of the first, although *Strawberry Roan* (1932) was filmed. In 1933 he made his first broadcast, which at once established him as a fearless commentator on current affairs in general and on agriculture in particular; he later became a popular member of the 'Any Questions' team. Among his blackest beasts were bureaucrats, egalitarians, anti-foxhunters, and every kind of snob.

In 1937, at the invitation of the Canadian Government, Street toured widely in Canada and America, lecturing on agriculture. Despite his duties as a working farmer and honorary secretary of the local Hunt, he contributed a regular column to the *Farmers Weekly*, which he maintained without interruption for thirty years. This was no easy task, for his brief was technical, unlike that of an essayist who is free to descant on the passing seasons. In more discursive vein he published *Country Calendar* (1935); his family possess a photostat copy of the book's frontispiece, on which Queen Mary had written:

'The King was reading this book at the time of his last illness. Mary R. From the Windsor library.'

Like Dr Johnson, Arthur Street was in every sense bigger than his own books. He was both tall and burly, with ruddy complexion and a head of thick black hair, cut short. In religion an eclectic Anglican, in politics a High Tory, he combined compassion with intolerance, so that generosity sometimes jostled pugnacity. First and last he was an English yeoman. 'Let me', he wrote, 'get my rural status clearly defined; I am merely a humble tenant farmer in the county of Wiltshire.' The soil that bred him was never far from his thoughts. In *Land Everlasting* (1934) he cited a farmer's privilege and obligation: 'It is our duty to serve our land faithfully so that when we die it may receive us in honour and not in shame.' His stature as a writer is immediately self-evident. The maze of human motive interested him, but he did not presume to explore it deeply. Jung he sampled *cum grano;* Freud, with a sceptical chuckle. His novels, therefore, are never more than tales. But as an interpreter of country life, and particularly of farming techniques, he ranked with the best of his contemporaries. Sir Arthur Bryant admired the 'beautiful, direct and Cobbett-like English'. Sometimes he achieved true poetry, as in the passage from *Farmer's Glory* which evokes the skill and satisfactions of ploughmanship. His rural reminiscences have been enriched rather than outdated by the years, because they recall commonplaces which are now rarities. Thus, looking back on the farmfolk of his youth, he wrote: 'Men in search of a new situation wore the badge of their calling in their hats. A carter wore a plait of whipcord, a shepherd a tuft of wool, and cowmen sported some hair from a cow's tail.' Having lived soon enough to see such sights, he survived late enough to become a television celebrity. In 1951 he moved to Mill Farm, on the far side of the Wylye valley, which, like Ditchampton, he rented from the Earl of Pembroke.

In 1918 Street married Vera Florence Foyle, of Wilton; they had one daughter. During his later years he suffered a stroke. After a long illness he died in hospital in Salisbury 21 July 1966.

[Pamela Street, *My Father*, 1969; *Daily Telegraph* and *The Times*, 22 July 1966; private information; personal knowledge.]

J. H. B. PEEL

SWAFFER, HANNEN (1879–1962), journalist, was born at Lindfield, Sussex, 1 November 1879, the eldest of eight children, four boys and four girls, of a Folkestone draper, Henry Joseph Swaffer, and his wife, Kate Eugenie Hannen.

He went to Stroud Green Grammar School, Kent, and later, as he said, continued his education in Fleet Street. First he was appointed a reporter at Folkestone at 5s. a week. An often scornful critic, at the age of eighteen he was banned from the local theatre. A time came when he boasted of having been banned from twelve of forty-one theatres in the West End of London. He joined the *Daily Mail* in 1902 and worked for the future Lord Northcliffe [q.v.] for ten years. His employer, who because of his appearance liked to call Swaffer 'The Poet', made him editor for a while of the *Weekly Dispatch*. Swaffer's best work in his Northcliffe years helped to transform the *Daily Mirror*, after an unhappy start as a women's journal, into a mass-circulation picture paper.

In 1913 Swaffer, seeking fresh employment, invented 'Mr. Gossip' for the *Daily Sketch* as a new and bold kind of gossip feature. Transferring next to the *Daily Graphic* he won even more praise for a gossip page signed 'Mr. London'. After contributing 'Plays and Players' to the *Sunday Times* and being for a few months in 1924 editor of the *People*, he became in 1926 drama critic of the *Daily Express*. In this post he enjoyed full scope for his pungent candour. Campaigning against what he considered the over-Americanization of the stage and the press, he was smacked in the face by an American actress at the Savoy Hotel 'on behalf of America'. Affronts because of his critical trenchancy never perturbed this sharpest of critics. Someone slashed a portrait of him intended for the United States. 'Swaff', as he was now generally known, said, 'I heartily approve. I often feel like slashing my own face when I look in the mirror.'

Another phase of his life opened in 1931 when he joined the *Daily Herald*. In this and other Odhams publications he not only exploited his wide acquaintance with the famous and the notorious but also championed many a cause. One was socialism, to which *Merrie England*, by Robert Blatchford [q.v.], had won him over. He often wrote wisely, sometimes like a wiseacre, and always in a clear, homely style. His habit of pontification on many subjects led him to be termed, to his deep satisfaction, 'The Pope of Fleet Street'. He did not look the part, his appearance suggesting an actor of Sir Henry Irving's day: he wore a wide-brimmed black felt hat, black stock, high collar, dark flowing locks, and a melancholy expression. A kind and witty man, he was known by close friends to be shy under his mask of defiant self-confidence. In middle life he became a Spiritualist, regularly attended seances, and was appointed honorary president of the Spiritualists' National Union, thus becoming titular head of the 500 churches devoted to his faith.

In his prime Swaffer was said to write nearly a million words a year. He was described at a gathering in his honour as the greatest reporter of the era and an immortal of his own time. Speaking in 1959 of his old employers he said, 'I know more about it than any of them. I had to fight the whole lot of them.' Earlier he had denounced a 'new kind of feudalism' among press magnates.

He resigned from the Labour Party in 1957 after a dispute arising out of a campaign to improve mental hospitals. Articles he and others wrote were said to use 'sick and helpless people to attract readers', a charge Swaffer deeply resented.

His publications included *Northcliffe's Return* (1925), *Really Behind the Scenes* (1929), *Hannen Swaffer's Who's Who* (1929), *Adventures with Inspiration* (1929), *When Men Talk Truth* (1934), *My Greatest Story* (1945), and *What Would Nelson Do?* (1946).

He married in 1904 Helen Hannah (died 1956), daughter of John Sitton, a grocer living in Clapham; there were no children. Swaffer lived for many years in a flat overlooking Trafalgar Square in order, he said, to have a front seat when the revolution came. He died in a London hospital 16 January 1962. In the week of his death he wrote, as usual, a commentary on current journalism for the *World's Press News*. The Hannen Swaffer Journalistic Awards announced every year are a memorial to a picturesque personality, who not only enlivened the popular journalism of his time but set an example of often candid gossip which continued to be followed.

A portrait of Swaffer by C. R. W. Nevinson and one by Marcel Poncin and a bust by Macdonald Reid are privately owned. A portrait by Alfred Wolmark and a bust by Douglas Bisset are in the Beaverbrook Art Gallery at Fredericton, New Brunswick, Canada. A portrait by John Myers, an American, hangs in the *Psychic News* office in London, and a bust in bronze by Laurence Bradshaw stands in the hall of Odhams Press.

[*The Times*, 17 January 1962; private information; personal knowledge.]

LINTON ANDREWS

SYLLAS, STELIOS MESSINESOS (LEO) DE (1917–1964), architect. [See DE SYLLAS.]

SYMES, SIR (GEORGE) STEWART (1882–1962), soldier and administrator, was born at Wateringbury, Kent, 29 July 1882, the only son and eldest of three children of Lieutenant-Colonel William Alexander Symes, of the 71st Regiment (Highland Light Infantry), and his wife, Emily Catherine Shore, younger daughter of the second Lord Teignmouth. His father died when he was eight. Educated at Malvern College and the Royal Military College, Sandhurst, he was gazetted to a commission in the Hampshire Regiment shortly after his eighteenth birthday.

In December 1900 he was posted to India to join the 1st battalion of his regiment, and in the next four years he saw service in India, South Africa, Aden, and the Somali Coast. In operations in the Aden hinterland in 1903, to protect an Anglo-Turkish boundary commission from dissident tribesmen, Symes was appointed to the DSO (1904), and mentioned in dispatches. His regiment returned to England and in 1905, dissatisfied with peacetime soldiering, he obtained a transfer to the Egyptian Army. He was posted to the 1st battalion of Egyptian Infantry at Berber in the Sudan in January 1906 and in October of the same year became aide-de-camp to Sir Reginald Wingate [q.v.], the sirdar and governor-general of the Sudan. Symes was promoted captain in 1907 and served in the Blue Nile expedition of 1908. From 1909 to 1912 he was assistant director of intelligence at Khartoum and from 1913 to 1916 private secretary to the governor-general. During these years he travelled much throughout the Sudan and so obtained a knowledge of the country and its people which was to stand him in good stead.

In 1917 Wingate became high commissioner in Egypt and took Symes to Cairo with him. There he became immersed in Egyptian and Arab politics with D. G. Hogarth, (Sir) Gilbert Clayton, (Sir) Ronald Storrs, and (Sir) Kinahan Cornwallis [qq.v.] as colleagues, and, as GSO 1 for the Hedjaz operations, had much to do with the Arab advance on the eastern flank of Sir Edmund (later Viscount) Allenby [q.v.] under the leadership of T. E. Lawrence [q.v.].

After the British victories in Palestine and the establishment of British administration there, Symes, who had been promoted major during the war, retired from the army with the rank of lieutenant-colonel and was appointed governor of the Northern district, a post which he held with such success from 1920 to 1925 that he was chosen to succeed Clayton as chief secretary to the Government. In the difficult situation caused by Arab hatred of the Jewish national home and of Jewish immigration, Symes, supported by Lord Plumer [q.v.], the high commissioner, steered a conciliatory course and was successful in maintaining a high degree of law and order.

In 1928 he was appointed resident and commander-in-chief at Aden. In the three years of his tenure of this office, he promoted reorganization of the services, educational, medical, and economic, and perhaps more important he persuaded the tribal chiefs in the hinterland to co-operate mutually for the defence and better administration of the territory. In 1931 he succeeded Sir Donald Cameron [q.v.] as governor of Tanganyika, a territory severely hit by the world-wide economic crisis. Symes succeeded in combining necessary retrenchment with administrative reform, and strongly supported his predecessor's policy in native administration or, as he preferred to call it, local government.

In 1934 Symes returned to the Sudan as governor-general where he was able to put his ideas into practice. He did much to encourage economic advance, and to develop the role of departmental services in the administration. He deprecated the old-fashioned role of district officers as 'Jacks of all trades', and considered that many of the duties they had previously undertaken should be transferred to specialist departments such as the police, the judiciary, and revenue services. He effected economies by amalgamating provinces and districts.

Symes's experience in Cairo and his acquaintance with many leading Egyptians were valuable during the negotiations for the Anglo-Egyptian Treaty of 1936, and he succeeded in maintaining the Sudan's constitutional position at the expense of relatively minor concessions to the Egyptians. In the two years before the outbreak of war in 1939 considerable preparations were made under his guidance: stores of all kinds and military supplies were accumulated which proved of the greatest value in the 1940-1 campaigns on the Sudan's frontiers.

Until the Italians entered the war in June 1940, Symes was not allowed by the British Government to expand the Sudan Defence Force or to let British civilians of military age leave the Sudan to join the forces. For this he was much criticized locally but his foresight was justified later when the Sudan Defence Force was expanded, and British civilians with Sudan experience were available for service in the new units and in occupied enemy territory administration.

The loyalty of the Sudanese people and their unswerving support for Britain and her allies in the darkest days of the war were a testimony to the policies of Symes and his predecessors in the administration of the country. An Arabic speaker, Symes had many contacts with the Sudanese, both with the educated élite and the country folk. Tall, slim, good looking, he was forthcoming and easy with junior officers and had a friendly open manner in discussion. He was critical of many long-held preconceived ideas and debunked many shibboleths, and in this way effectively shook up the Sudan's administration.

Towards the end of 1940 he left the Sudan and settled in South Africa until the end of the war. During this period he wrote a book of reminiscences, *Tour of Duty* (1946). On his return to England he spent his years of retirement in voluntary work for several charitable causes.

In 1913 Symes married Viola Colston (died 1953), daughter of the late J. Felix Broun of the 71st Regiment; they had one son (killed in the war) and one daughter. Symes was appointed KBE in 1928 and GBE in 1939, CMG in 1917 and KCMG in 1932. He was also the recipient of Turkish, Egyptian, Ethiopian, and Hedjazi decorations. He died at Folkestone 5 December 1962.

[Sir Stewart Symes, *Tour of Duty*, 1946; personal knowledge.]   J. W. ROBERTSON

T

TAFAWA BALEWA, ALHAJI SIR ABU BAKAR (1912–1966), prime minister of the Federation of Nigeria, was born in the village of Tafawa Balewa in Bauchi Province, Northern Nigeria, 12 October 1912. He came of peasant stock; his father, Yakubu, a member of the small Gere tribe, was head of his village, but had originally been a serf of the Emir of Bauchi. His mother, A'ishatu, was of the same tribe. Abu Bakar was their eldest child and was sent first to the village school, then to the Middle School at Bauchi. Thence he went to the Katsina Training College, where he studied with many of the young men from important Fulani and Hausa ruling families who came to political prominence during the latter years of the colonial period. He graduated as a teacher in 1932, and was appointed to a village school in his own province. In 1938 he was a junior master and in 1944 became headmaster of Bauchi Middle School. In 1945 he won an educational scholarship in the United Kingdom to the Institute of Education of London University. On his return to Nigeria he was appointed an education officer and inspector of schools.

While so employed he became a member of the Northern House of Assembly, and soon was prominent as a speaker and political leader. In 1952 he went to Lagos as a Northern member of the Central House of Representatives, and was appointed minister of works. After the establishment of the federal constitution in 1954, Abu Bakar was chosen as one of the three Northern members of the Council of Ministers. As minister of transport he visited the United States in 1955 to study the river transport system on the Mississippi and Missouri with a view to the development of transport on the Niger.

In 1957 when it became possible, under the revised constitution, to appoint a federal prime minister, Abu Bakar was invited by the governor-general to form a Government, a choice which was popularly welcomed. Abu Bakar formed an all-party administration to prepare Nigeria for independence, and successfully led this coalition until after the general election of December 1959 the Action Group Party withdrew. To his disappointment his second administration was formed from only two parties, the Northern People's Congress and the National Council of Nigeria and the Cameroons. During the period from 1957 until Nigeria's independence on 1 October 1960, the British governor-general still presided over the Council of Ministers, and was responsible for the reserved subjects of defence, foreign affairs, and the Civil Service, but Abu Bakar was gradually introduced to the running of these departments so that when independence was achieved he had had considerable experience of their problems, and had on occasions presided over the Council of Ministers in the absence of the governor-general.

Even in these years he had many difficulties to overcome; an upright, conscientious man, he did not easily accept the lower and sometimes corrupt standards of some of his colleagues. He was a Northerner and disliked the humid climate of Lagos, and the noisy brash character of the Southerners. But his greatest handicap was the fact that he was not head of his party, and that general policy had to be referred to the party leader, the premier of the Northern Region, the Sardauna of Sokoto, Sir Ahmadu Bello [q.v.]. Abu Bakar's authority in the House of Representatives depended on the support of party members whose first loyalty was to the party leader and not to him.

After independence in 1960 his difficulties increased. The political parties fell apart, and the unity which had stemmed from the national desire to end colonial rule was gradually eroded. The Southern parties resented the power of the North, and Abu Bakar's task of consolidating the Federation became more and more difficult. In 1962, after disorders in Western Nigeria, his Government suspended the regional constitution and appointed a federal commissioner to administer the Region and restore law and order.

The situation did not improve and after a general election in December 1964, which was boycotted by the NCNC in protest against the NPC, the federal president, Dr Azikiwe, a former leader of the NCNC, hesitated before calling on Abu Bakar to form a Government in January 1965, although the NPC had won a majority of seats. This new Government inherited a critical position: disorders and disturbances continued and an election in the autumn of 1965 reduced the Western Region to a state approaching civil war. The ruling party in the Western Region (the Action Group) split and the other national parties each supported one of its sections. Abu Bakar's coalition was therefore in complete disarray and he himself was much criticized for not intervening to pacify the West. But the attitude of his party and its leader prevented him taking such action.

In January 1966 a number of young army officers determined to put an end to a regime which had failed to stop the disorders. They staged a *coup d'état* in which Abu Bakar was murdered, as were the premiers of the Northern and

Western Regions, the federal minister of finance, and several high-ranking army officers.

During these years of internal unrest and disturbance Abu Bakar's interest and influence in foreign affairs grew and he became a prominent African statesman, influential in the Organization for African Unity, at the United Nations, and in the meetings of Commonwealth prime ministers. His dignified and imposing appearance, his wisdom and common sense gave him a prestige and reputation internationally. His patience and moderation gave his words an authority which the more flamboyant orations of other African leaders lacked; but with all his tolerance and fairness, he left no doubt that he was first and foremost a Northern Nigerian, dedicated to the goal of a Nigeria unified in a federal state. His last achievement a few days before his death was to call and preside over a conference of Commonwealth prime ministers at Lagos to consider the problem of Rhodesia. Due largely to Abu Bakar's dignity, judgement, and authority as chairman, the conference attended by representatives of eighteen countries was a considerable success.

A man of high integrity, he was a strict and practising Muslim, but tolerant of men of other faiths. In 1957 he undertook the pilgrimage to Mecca, and throughout his life showed much interest in theology and the philosophy of religion.

Tall and dignified in his Northern robes, Abu Bakar had a beautiful speaking voice and an excellent command of English. Although modest and unambitious for personal advancement he was determined and strong in carrying out what he considered was right. Shrewd and full of common sense, he was patient and understanding in his attitude to others, and though a patriotic Nigerian he appreciated what the colonial Government had done for his country. Selections of his speeches were published in 1964.

He was appointed OBE in 1952, CBE in 1955, and KBE in 1960. He became a member of the Privy Council in 1961. He had four wives and eighteen children. A portrait by Lady Cumming-Bruce (Lady Thurlow) was presented to the Nigerian Institute of International Affairs in Lagos.

[John Oyinbo, *Nigeria: Crisis and Beyond*, 1971; personal knowledge.]

JAMES W. ROBERTSON

TAWNEY, RICHARD HENRY (1880–1962), historian, was born in Calcutta 30 November 1880, son of Charles Henry Tawney, principal of Presidency College, and his wife, Constance Catherine Fox. The boy was sent to Rugby, and proceeded as a classical scholar to Balliol College, Oxford, in 1899, a year before William Temple [q.v.]. After a first in classical honour moderations and being *proxime* for a Craven scholarship (1901), Tawney only got a second in *literae humaniores* (1903); his father enquired how he proposed to 'wipe out the disgrace', but Edward Caird, the master, told (Sir) Frank Fletcher [qq.v.], 'I grant you his mind was chaotic; but the examiners ought to have seen that it was the chaos of a great mind'. Tawney himself learned more from Rugby and Balliol than he would subsequently acknowledge; typically, he never proceeded to his Oxford MA, although he became a fellow (1918–21), and in 1938 an honorary fellow, of his college.

Tawney himself would trace the major preoccupations of his life to the six years between going down, when he lived for a while at Toynbee Hall, and his marriage in 1909 to Annette Jeanie ('Jeannette'), sister of William (later Lord) Beveridge [q.v.], one of his closest college friends. After Oxford, Tawney 'found the world surprising'; already by 1909, however, he had established himself as a historian and a devoted and inspiring teacher, and had formulated the outlines of a distinctive version of socialism which was later to guide the Labour Party for many years. He had also become a forceful critic of the public schools and Oxford and Cambridge as privileged institutions, and he showed little interest in his comfortable origins or his father's links with India. He was embarking in his own style on a course of his own which eventually inspired Beatrice Webb to dub him a 'saint of socialism' (1935) and Hugh Gaitskell [qq.v.] to describe him as '*the* democratic socialist *par excellence*' 1962).

By 1909 Tawney's historical interests had focused on the late sixteenth to early seventeenth century and its relationships with both the medieval world and the nineteenth and twentieth centuries. His first book, *The Agrarian Problem in the Sixteenth Century* (1912), immediately established him as an authority on economic and social history. It was dedicated to Albert Mansbridge [q.v.] and William Temple, successive pillars of the Workers' Educational Association, which had been formed in 1903; Tawney joined the executive committee in 1905. In 1906–8 he taught political economy at Glasgow University alongside Thomas Jones [q.v.], under Professor William Smart who was busy with the royal commission on Poor Law reform; in 1908 Tawney accepted the pioneer post of teacher for the WEA tutorial classes under Oxford University, which he held until 1914. This proved to be his first source of inspiration, and *The Agrarian Problem* acknowledged a debt to the students of Tawney's tutorial classes, whom he regarded as fellow workers—a class of one tutor and twelve students was, to him, a class of thirteen students. He learned much about English society in those classes, and from them sprang his belief that the only effective way of making necessary changes in society was through education.

His first WEA classes—which quickly became legendary—were held at Rochdale in Lancashire and Longton in the Potteries, and soon after their marriage the Tawneys settled in Manchester at 24 Shakespeare Street, where they lived until just before the outbreak of war in 1914. In Manchester George Unwin, occupant of Britain's first chair of economic history, was one of his early mentors; in 1927 Tawney wrote a memoir of Unwin prefacing his collected papers. Two other Manchester friends, also economic historians, were T. S. Ashton, who became one of his closest colleagues during the last years of his life, and A. P. Wadsworth [qq.v.]. Tawney developed in both himself and his pupils a strong sense of affinity with peasants, and found no difficulty in proving the social relevance of a study of the agrarian history of a remote century, even in the industrial environment of northern England: capitalism had preceded industrialism just as enclosed farms had preceded power-driven factories, and it was in the sixteenth century, he believed, that the erosion of old values and their conflict with the new had become clear. Yet Tawney never showed much enthusiasm for the industrial revolution or the nineteenth century, and was more interested in restraints on economic drive than on commercial or industrial enterprise; he was always suspicious of treating economics as an objective science. He selected themes in economic and social history, therefore, which were concerned with shifts of values in attitudes and relationships, rather than with measurement of economic indicators, like the growth of national income. In 1914 he co-edited with A. E. Bland and P. A. Brown *English Economic History: Select Documents*.

The young WEA prided itself that while it demanded the highest academic standards it was also a thoroughly democratic body at the class level. Tawney, who never thought of himself as an 'educationist', plunged into both the teaching and organizing sides of adult education; he became a champion of extended provision and helped to write, for example, the conference report *Oxford and Working-Class Education* (1908). He remained a member of the WEA executive committee for forty-two years, was vice-president from 1920, and president in 1928-44. He always considered himself not so much a leader as an active member of a 'movement'; the distinction between 'movement' and 'organization' seemed to him crucial,

as did that between 'membership' (whose virtues he stressed) and 'service' which seemed to him to have Rugby-cum-Balliol overtones. It was through WEA experience that Tawney hammered out his ideas about 'equality'; his thought developed from the tradition of Ruskin and Morris, but he extended it through his emphasis on activity rather than on reading.

Tawney's socialism was less intellectual than that of most of his non-working-class contemporaries; at its core was a simple faith in Christian principles, and in this respect also he represented a tradition of Christian socialism which he never fully elucidated. When he talked of the erosion of values, or conflicts between spiritual and materialistic values, he had biblical values in mind: 'Give me neither riches nor poverty, but enough for my sustenance' was both a personal rule and a precept for society. Tawney did not shout either his Christianity or his socialism from the house-tops. He joined the Fabian Society in 1906, and was a member of its executive (1921-33); in 1909 he joined the Independent Labour Party. He had little sympathy with the Marxist-influenced Social Democratic Federation which provided some of the members of his first tutorial classes: he found it sloganizing and sectarian, concerned not with education but with indoctrination. In later years he disagreed with the Webbs about the merits of Communism, and also with Harold Laski [q.v.]. The moral basis of socialism seemed to him beyond argument; in a future socialist society the dominant values would be those which had been appreciated long before Marx or MacDonald.

At the outbreak of the war in 1914, Tawney was director of the Ratan Tata Foundation at the London School of Economics for the study of poverty, and had just produced a monograph (1914) on *Minimum Rates in the Chain-Making Industry*; he was to serve on the Chain-Making Trade Board, 1919-22, but meanwhile the war itself did much to widen and clarify Tawney's beliefs. He enlisted in 1915 as a private in the 22nd Manchesters, and rose to the rank of sergeant, having characteristically refused a commission. During this period he learned to appreciate the French people, especially the peasants, and asserted that in the trenches he discovered more about his fellow countrymen than he had in his tutorial classes. His stress on 'fellowship' acquired a deeper dimension when associated with the fellowship of 'comrades in misery' and sacrifice for the future. Tawney was wounded in courageous action at Fricourt in July 1916 and invalided home to an army hospital in Oxford—a coincidence typical of a life which he once described as 'that terrible thing, an unplanned economy'. He described the other-ranks hospital as a 'workhouse', and, after a surprise visit from Bishop Gore [q.v.], was shocked when the matron asked him 'Why didn't you *tell* us you were a *gentleman*?'—the one word which Tawney never wished to have applied to himself. 'He never suffered stuffed shirts gladly.' The refusal to be fussed over, to be thought a 'gentleman', went even deeper than his refusal to accept high honours in the form of a peerage, which he was to be offered first by MacDonald and again by Attlee.

On his recovery, Tawney served briefly in the Ministry of Reconstruction, and continued to write articles for periodicals; he returned to his old preoccupations in 'A National College for All Souls' which appeared in the *Times Educational Supplement* in February 1917. He was also one of the draughtsmen of an Anglican report on 'Christianity and Industrial Problems' in December 1918. Many phrases from this period of his career have become folk memory. For example: 'It is right that there should be a solemn detestation of the sins of Germany, provided that we are not thereby caused to forget our own.' The remarkably rich prose style was unmistakable: long, sometimes rambling, sentences with upward cadences which were prominent in his lectures; wild, often clashing, imagery referring to the natural world (tadpoles and tigers) as much as to the world of human history; maxims which sounded biblical even when they were not: had English soldiers 'slaved for Rachel' only to come back to have to 'live with Leah'? Avoiding sentimentality, irony was one of his more powerful weapons.

Tawney mistrusted the hasty abolition of economic controls after the war of 1914-18, and wrote an admonitory article on the subject in 1943; he also deplored the unemployment which followed the immediate post-war boom. He stood unsuccessfully as Independent Labour candidate in the general elections of 1918, 1922, and 1924, but between 1918 and 1928 he became a major political influence. He was a powerful member of the Coal Industry Commission under Sir John (later Viscount) Sankey [q.v.] which reported in 1919, and became, as a result, something of a national figure. Working closely with the trade-unionists, Tawney proved a devastating questioner of the coal-owners, and during this commission he developed his views on the disastrous consequences of 'functionless property'. In 1921 the publication of *The Acquisitive Society* persuaded many of Tawney's readers that his was the only correct and constructive way of looking at national problems. He appealed to basic 'principles'—fundamentals which, he claimed, his fellow countrymen usually took for granted. The critique was more powerful than the

somewhat vague remedies suggested, and the lack of attention to both economic and international issues reflected a failure to go far beyond moralizing. There were similar weaknesses in the Labour Party manifesto of 1928, *Labour and the Nation*, which was largely Tawney's work; it too was imprecise, particularly with regard to policies dealing with unemployment and the deteriorating business situation, despite its brave statement that socialism was 'neither a sentimental aspiration for an impossible Utopia, nor a blind revolt against poverty and oppression'.

Tawney's writings on education were more incisive than those on industry; indeed, two Labour Party reports, *Secondary Education for All* (1922) and *Education: the Socialist Policy* (1924), went further than many party members wished, in urging the abolition of all fees in secondary schools and a system of maintenance allowances; similarly, it was he who urged the introduction of a system of comprehensive schools twenty years later. Tawney's belief that politics would be sterile without adult as well as school education was made clear both in party publications and in a large number of newspaper articles. He served as a member (1912-31) of the consultative committee of the Board of Education, and was on its panel of reformers who produced the 'Hadow Report' of 1926, recommending *inter alia* the raising of the school-leaving age to fifteen. For Tawney, education was at the heart of social policy and it was the duty of a democratic state to provide it. He believed that 'to serve educational needs without regard to the vulgar irrelevancies of class and income is part of the teacher's honour'.

In 1919 he served for a time as the WEA's first resident tutor in north Staffordshire, but in 1917 he had become lecturer in economic history at the London School of Economics—an institution to which he returned in 1920 and with which he was to remain associated until 1949, becoming reader in 1923 and professor in 1931. With Eileen Power [q.v.], his colleague there, he produced *Tudor Economic Documents* (1924). He preferred LSE to Oxford or Cambridge for its 'simplicity, . . . its freedom from formality and inhibitions'; yet Tawney eventually became an honorary fellow of Peterhouse, Cambridge, as well as of Balliol, and an honorary doctor of Oxford, Glasgow, Manchester, Birmingham, Sheffield, London, Chicago, Melbourne, and Paris. He was also proud of his membership of the American Philosophical Society, and of his fellowship of the British Academy in 1935; in 1941 he delivered the Academy's Raleigh lecture. He made the first of five tours to the United States in 1920, and one of his last and happiest academic visits was with his wife to Australia in

1955. Nevertheless, he remained an essentially insular figure, although there was one country about which he showed considerable insight and sympathy. During the thirties he paid two visits to China and in 1932 published *Land and Labour in China*, a brilliant survey of agrarian problems, which in the light of later Chinese Communist history contained a prophetic element; interesting affinities have been noted between Tawney's social thought and that of Mao Tse-Tung. They might have surprised Tawney, although he would doubtless have attributed them to peasant influence.

The Economic History Society which Tawney helped to found in 1926 brought him into contact with a new generation of scholars, and he co-edited the *Economic History Review* from 1927 to 1934, with Ephraim Lipson [q.v.]. 'What historians need', he told them, 'is not more documents but stronger boots!' He insisted that the society, like the WEA, should meet in simple surroundings for its conferences, not in expensive hotels; his simplicity could, indeed, sometimes be carried to embarrassing extremes. His house at Mecklenburgh Square was probably the untidiest in London; he smoked heavily, his pipe filled with a cheap mixture bought in bulk, ashes of which were scattered upon carpets rumoured to cover manuscripts of more unpublished masterpieces. His Cotswold cottage at Elcombe was described as 'a charming slum'. But if unaffected humility characterized Tawney's private and public life, his writings during the twenties and thirties certainly did not lack confidence. His reputation as a scholar was consolidated by his best-known historical work, *Religion and the Rise of Capitalism* (1926), based on his Scott Holland lectures of 1922, and dedicated to Bishop Gore. It provoked continuing international controversy about the relationships between religious beliefs and conduct and economic behaviour. A further contribution to what came to be called 'Tawney's century' appeared in 1941: the article on 'The Rise of the Gentry' in the *Economic History Review*, supplemented, after various sharp exchanges, by a postscript in the same journal in 1954. It was a measure of the power of Tawney's historical scholarship that it stimulated counter-attack; while he did not really enjoy academic debate and preferred to withdraw, muttering, into his shell, his private comments remained devastating.

Equality, his Halley Stewart lectures delivered in 1929 and published in 1931, served as a driving-force behind many of the policies of the Labour Government after 1945: although Tawney himself was suspicious of 'trends' and never liked the term 'welfare state', he was one of its principal architects. But, alarmed by the rise of 'the Nazi tyranny' and unsure what ought to be done about it, he was less productive during the later thirties. He mistrusted great concentrations of power as much as the irrationalism of crowds; Hitler was a 'frantic dervish' dealing in 'hoary sophisms', menacing the freedom of the world. When the war began, Tawney was as optimistic as he had been in 1914 that from it a better society could be constructed. Just as he had resumed wearing his old sergeant's tunic during the general strike of 1926, he now joined the Home Guard, wrote an article for the *New York Times* 'Why Britain Fights', and for a year held the post—at times frustrating—of labour attaché at the British Embassy in Washington. He was more at ease as an air-raid warden on patrol in the Gloucestershire hills with the dog which would also accompany him into church.

After the war Tawney continued to follow most of his earlier patterns of activity, and he remained as magnificent a lecturer as ever, tousled, inspiring, and defiant of humbug. He gave the Webb Memorial Trust lecture in 1945, and an inspiring National Book League lecture in 1950. He was a member of the University Grants Committee from 1943 to 1948, stayed on as vice-president of the WEA from 1944 to 1948, and was a main speaker at its jubilee celebrations in 1953; he was also for a time president of the Council for Educational Advance. He had friends and admirers in all sections of the Labour movement, and his eightieth birthday was celebrated by a Festschrift and a dinner at the House of Commons, where people from the world of education, politicians, trade-unionists, and historians, gathered to honour him—notwithstanding his fidgetiness about being treated as a historical figure before he was dead.

His last book, *Business and Politics under James I: Lionel Cranfield as Merchant and Minister* (1958), was as much concerned with shifting values as his first had been. It dealt with 'that seductive border region where politics grease the wheels of business and polite society smiles hopefully on both'. It was a mature and meticulous work, vintage Tawney in style, and dealt with real people, forgotten perhaps, but not abstractions; if the historian 'visits the cellars', he had said, 'it is not for love of the dust but to estimate the stability of the edifice'. Yet the closing years of his life were not, on the whole, very happy. He was disturbed about the state of society and uncertain about the future; the sudden transition from national austerity to affluence made him ponder yet again on what seemed to him false values. He had little sympathy with current fashions in political argument, and felt that even the WEA had lost some of its force. After his wife died in 1958 he was never quite the same, although his marriage had not been without its problems, for his wife had often exasperated him and was wildly extravagant. They had no children. Other deaths, too, affected him, and his dwindling circle of friends were increasingly worried to see his simplicity becoming shabbiness and his humility degenerating into complete lack of care for himself. 'Never be afraid of throwing away what you have,' he had written in his diary in 1912. 'If you *can* throw it away, it is not really yours.'

Tawney died in London 16 January 1962. He was buried at his wife's side at Highgate, and there was a vast congregation at his memorial service at St. Martin-in-the-Fields on 8 February. Psalm XV was appropriate, Hugh Gaitskell gave the address, and the large number of WEA members present must have approved of one additional reading—an unpublished fragment of Tawney's Chicago lecture (1939): 'Democracy a society where ordinary men exercise initiative. Dreadful respect for superiors. Mental enlargement . . . Real foe to be overcome . . . fact that large section of the public *like* plutocratic government, and are easily gullible. How shake them!'

A portrait for Tawney's seventieth birthday by Claude Rogers hangs in the London School of Economics, where there is also a sketch by 'Vicky' of the *New Statesman* (1960); a drawing by John Mansbridge (1953) is in the National Portrait Gallery.

[*The Times* and *Guardian*, 17 January 1962; R. H. Tawney, *The Attack and Other Papers*, 1953, *The Radical Tradition*, ed. Rita Hinden, 1964, and *Commonplace Book*, ed. J. M. Winter and D. M. Joslin, 1972; J. R. Williams, R. M. Titmuss, and F. J. Fisher, *R. H. Tawney, A Portrait by Several Hands*, 1960; T. S. Ashton in *Proceedings* of the British Academy, vol. xlviii, 1962 (which includes an admirable photograph of an unexpectedly tidy Tawney); R. Terrill, *R. H. Tawney and His Times*, 1973; J. M. Winter, 'Tawney the Historian' in *History and Society: Essays by R. H. Tawney*, 1978; Christopher Hill in the *Balliol Record*, 1974; private information; personal knowledge.]

ASA BRIGGS

TAYLOR, EVA GERMAINE RIMINGTON (1879-1966), geographer and historian of science, was born in Highgate 22 June 1879, the third child and second daughter of Charles Richard Taylor, solicitor, by his first wife, Emily Jane Nelson. Her mother ran away when Eva was about three years of age, an event which seems to have marred her young life for the 'sin' of the mother was visited upon her children who were allowed neither toys nor domestic pets.

Eva's sturdy nature turned to hedgerow flowers, birds, and wild animals, and throughout her long life she showed a keen enjoyment of natural history and of gardening. She was educated at home, at the Camden School for Girls, and at the North London Collegiate School for Girls. A scholarship took her to Royal Holloway College and in 1903 she obtained her London B.Sc. with first class honours in chemistry.

Her first appointments were as teacher of chemistry at the Burton-on-Trent School for Girls and at a convent school in Oxford. In 1906 she became a student at Oxford University and subsequently obtained the certificate of regional geography and the diploma of geography, both with a mark of distinction. From 1908 to 1910 she was a private research assistant to A. J. Herbertson, head of the school of geography at Oxford. She spent the next six years in London writing geography textbooks for schools and drafting wall-maps (mainly in collaboration with J. F. Unstead). From 1916 to 1918 she lectured at Clapham Training College for Teachers and at the Froebel Institute. In 1920 she became a part-time lecturer at the East London College, moving a year later to a similar post at Birkbeck College. In 1929 she proceeded to her London D.Sc. in geography; and in 1930 she was appointed (in open competition) to the chair of geography at Birkbeck College, a post which she retained until her retirement in 1944.

Not only was Eva Taylor a brilliant lecturer; she was also a great scholar. Before retirement she published two outstanding works—*Tudor Geography, 1485-1583* (1930) and *Late Tudor and Early Stuart Geography, 1583-1650* (1934). Until a stroke in 1964 damaged an optic nerve, impairing her vision and her mobility, she maintained after her retirement an active interest in geographical and related studies, contributing numerous articles both to learned and to popular journals. Between the ages of seventy-five and eighty-seven she published three remarkable volumes: *The Mathematical Practitioners of Tudor and Stuart England* (1954); *The Haven-Finding Art: a history of navigation from Odysseus to Captain Cook* (1956); and *The Mathematical Practitioners of Hanoverian England* (1966).

In 1938 Eva Taylor chaired the committee appointed by the Royal Geographical Society to prepare a memorandum for the Barlow commission on the distribution of the industrial population. She was also a keen advocate of a National Atlas of Britain as a basis for national and regional planning. During and immediately after the war of 1939-45 she helped the Association for Planning and Regional Reconstruction prepare evidence to the Committee on Land Utilization in Rural Areas and to the Schuster Committee on the

Qualifications of Planners. Birkbeck College remained in London during the war and in the 'phoney war' period she instructed officers of the Eastern Command in map reading and interpretation.

Eva Taylor was twice president of Section E of the British Association for the Advancement of Science. The Royal Geographical Society awarded her the Victoria medal in 1947 and honorary fellowship in 1965. She was a vice-president of the Hakluyt Society, an honorary member of the Institute of Navigation (in 1959 she delivered the first Duke of Edinburgh lecture), and an honorary vice-president of the Society for Nautical Research. In 1949 the university of Aberdeen conferred on her the honorary degree of LLD; and in 1960 she was elected one of the first fellows of Birkbeck College. To mark her eightieth birthday an appeal was launched for funds for an annual lecture to be given in a branch of knowledge to which she had contributed.

Hers was a masterful personality. Beneath her rather formidable manner there was a warm-hearted affection, loyalty, and an unfailing kindness. She was a brilliant talker and raconteur. She was a devoted mother who bore three sons: in 1912, 1915, and 1919; the second died in infancy. She died at Wokingham 5 July 1966.

[Private information; personal knowledge.]

EILA M. J. CAMPBELL

TAYLOR, JAMES HAWARD (1909-1968), geologist, was born at Esher 24 February 1909, the only child of James Taylor of Milngavie, Dunbartonshire, a partner in Balmer, Lawrie & Co., Indian merchants, and his wife, Lilian Dudley Ward Haward, of Spalding, Lincolnshire. His paternal grandfather and great-grandfather were both ministers of the Church of Scotland and his maternal grandfather served with the surveyor-general of India. Taylor spent his early childhood in India. At his preparatory school in Surbiton and at Clifton College, which he entered in 1923, he gained an abiding interest in the classics, but when he went up to King's College, London, in 1926, it was to read a pure science degree, eventually specializing in geology under Professor W. T. Gordon, an old friend of the family. He gained his London B.Sc. with first class honours (1931), became an associate of King's College, was awarded the Tennant and Jelf medals in 1931, and embarked on research in petrology under Dr A. K. Wells. In 1933 he was elected to a Henry fellowship which took him to Harvard to work with R. A. Daly and E. S. Larsen, Jr., and to travel widely in the western states. Research material was collected in the Little

Belt mountains of Montana, and Taylor returned to England with the AM degree in 1934. A difficult year, when he eked out his resources with a demonstratorship at King's College, followed until the autumn of 1935, when he gained one of the four vacancies on the staff of the Geological Survey of Great Britain. His London Ph.D. was awarded in 1936 and he remained on the staff of the Geological Survey until 1948, when he was invited to succeed Gordon the following year as professor of geology at King's College.

James Taylor's early work was directed to the use of the accessory minerals in British granites as an aid to correlation, the material studied being derived from the Oatlands area of the Isle of Man and the Mountsorrel intrusion in Leicestershire. His American studies dealt with the metamorphism of limestone adjacent to intrusive monzonite. However, when he joined the Geological Survey, the director at the time, Dr Bernard Smith, FRS, following the policy of diversifying the interests of his geologists, assigned Taylor to the Midlands unit for work in collaboration with S. E. Hollingworth [q.v.] on the Droitwich 1-inch sheet. Here he was concerned with the sedimentary rocks of the Old Red Sandstone and Trias, with only one small igneous intrusion, the Brockhill dyke. Responding well to the change of scene, he soon demonstrated that he was a first-rate field man. He was elected a fellow of the Geological Society in 1938. With the coming of the war, the regular process of completing the geological coverage of the United Kingdom at the 1:10 560 scale had to be abandoned in favour of intensive work on areas likely to contribute significantly to the war effort. In the Midlands a team was formed to give the maximum possible aid to the ironstone mining industry working in the belt running from Scunthorpe through Corby in Northamptonshire to Banbury. This belt represented Britain's almost sole domestic source of iron ore, and in a short time production was raised to over 20 million tonnes annually. The team, led by T. H. Whitehead as district geologist, consisted of Taylor, Hollingworth, G. A. Kellaway, F. B. A. Welch, and Vernon Wilson. Taylor was particularly concerned with the Northamptonshire area, where, in addition to much detailed surveying, he was assigned the task of investigating the petrography and mineralogy of the ironstones. His memoir on the subject (1949) firmly established him as one of the leaders in this field in Europe. An important result of the team's work was a new understanding of the superficial processes of movement in the ironstone belt, a subject of considerable significance in developing the large open pits necessary to get the required output.

Taylor's return to King's in 1949 as professor of geology by no means ended his work for the Survey, his interest being maintained up to the point of production, with other members of the team, of the important memoir of the stratigraphy, stucture, and reserves of the Northampton Sands ironstone (1951). In 1952 he joined with colleagues from the iron industry to contribute to a symposium on beneficiation at the International Geological Congress in Algiers. Maintaining his interest in the problems of sedimentation, he soon afterwards extended his activities to Northern Rhodesia where he investigated the remarkable lead ore deposits at Broken Hill.

Now his tall, distinguished figure began to be seen in professional circles. He was geological adviser to the Iron and Steel Board from 1954 onwards: he served on the Burden Committee of the British Iron and Steel Research Association from 1950 to 1959, and on the Raw Materials Committee of the British Ceramic Association from 1953 to 1957, being its chairman in 1957. His professional work took him to Portugal, Nigeria, Ghana, Northern Rhodesia, and Newfoundland. The Institution of Mining and Metallurgy benefited from his long membership of its council; he was the chief architect of the new style of publication begun in 1966. He was president of the Mineralogical Society (1963-5), after previous service as treasurer. At one of its most critical periods, when the home and overseas geological surveys were being combined into the Institute of Geological Sciences, he was a member of the parent Natural Environment Research Council.

Taylor's scientific work was recognized by his election to the Royal Society in 1960. He was a member of its council (1963-4), and its representative to the International Union of Geological Sciences meeting at New Delhi in 1964. In the same year he became chairman of the British National Committee for Geology. He was awarded the fellowship of King's College, London, in 1962. He was president of Section C of the British Association for the Advancement of Science at its Aberdeen meeting in 1963, and at the time of his death was president of the International Association of Sedimentologists. An active career of teaching, research, and administration brought him to the front rank of British geologists, but this was prematurely terminated when he was drowned while observing underwater the processes of limestone formation off the Seychelles Islands 25 January 1968. British geology could ill afford to lose his unassuming but wise guidance. He was not married.

[K. C. Dunham in *Biographical Memoirs of Fellows of the Royal Society*, vol. xiv, 1968; Institution of Mining and Metallurgy, *Transactions*, vol. lxxvii, 1968; personal knowledge.]   KINGSLEY DUNHAM

TAYLOR, JOHN HENRY (1871-1963), golfer, was born at Northam, north Devon, 19 March 1871, the second son in the family of four sons and one daughter of Joshua Taylor, a labourer of that village, and his wife, Susannah Heard, midwife, of Barnstaple. Having reached the sixth standard at the local school, Taylor left school at the age of eleven, but took great pains to further his education. He was a frequent reader of Dickens and Boswell, and wrote without any help his own autobiography, *Golf: My Life's Work* (1943). His early life was bound up with Westward Ho!, formed in 1864 and one of the first clubs in England. From school he became a caddie at the club, and after a spell working as a gardener's boy, and a labourer on the construction of Bideford quay, returned to Westward Ho! as a groundsman in 1888, the army and navy having turned him down because of his poor eyesight.

Taylor's sense of justice and powers of oratory might have fitted him for the role of an early trade union leader. If so, his talents were not wasted for as a young man he became the spokesman for a group of club professionals trying to protect the trading interest of their shops. From this movement sprang the Professional Golfers' Association of which in 1901 he became the first president.

Taylor was appointed greenkeeper-cum-professional to the Burnham Club in Somerset in 1891 and from there came his big chance. A match was arranged between him and a renowned Scottish golfer, Andrew Kirkaldy, who was employed at Royal Winchester. Taylor won and Kirkaldy's praise of the young Englishman was such that Taylor succeeded him at Winchester. In 1893 Taylor was emboldened to try his luck in the Open championship at Prestwick, hitherto a purely Scottish preserve. The astonishing accuracy of his long shots to the hole, hit flat-footed with a firm punch and often a little grunt, spread consternation among the Scots.   •

When the championship crossed the border for the first time in 1894, at Sandwich, Taylor became the first English professional to win. He won again at St. Andrews in 1895, coming with a great rush through the rain. In 1896 Harry Vardon beat him in a play-off, depriving him of a hat trick. It was the first of the six times Taylor finished second in the championship, in addition to his five victories. He won handsomely in 1900 at St. Andrews, leading all the way as he liked to do. His fourth victory was in 1909 at Deal and his last in a gale at Hoylake in 1913. Those who watched him there described it as the finest golf they had ever seen.

Among Taylor's other achievements in the game were victory in the French Open and the match-play championship, twice each, in the German Open, and, a feat which is often overlooked, second place in the United States Open in 1900. Even when he was fifty-three he finished fifth in the British Open of 1924, and his score over six rounds, including the two qualifying ones, was lower than that of anyone else.

Highly strung and emotional though he was, Taylor managed to master his feelings and when he had done so, he was, in the estimation of Bernard Darwin [q.v.], perhaps the most clearly inspired player of his age. Resolute to the point of obstinacy, on the golf course he was a true fighter. Together with James Braid [q.v.] and Harry Vardon, Taylor formed the great 'triumvirate' of golf at the turn of the century.

He retired from the Royal Mid-Surrey Club in 1946 after forty-seven years' service there, and the honours began to roll in, for one who had done so much to raise the status of his fellow professionals. In 1950 he was elected an honorary member of the Royal and Ancient Golf Club, a gesture made to two other golfers only up to that time, and later he was given a silver salver signed by all living captains of the club. More than fifty American professionals paid him a similar compliment in 1955, and in 1957 Westward Ho!, now Royal North Devon, paid him the great honour of electing him president of the club where he had started as a caddie.

In 1896 Taylor married Clara Fulford, a teacher. He lost his wife shortly after celebrating their diamond wedding in 1956. He died 10 February 1963 at the village of his birth, being survived by six of his family of three sons and six daughters.

There is a pencil and colour-wash portrait of Taylor by Spy (Sir Leslie Ward).

[*The Shell International Encyclopaedia of Golf*, ed. Donald Steel and Peter Ryde, 1975; Bernard Darwin, *Playing the Like*, 1934; Peter Lawless, *The Golfers Companion*, 1937; J. H. Taylor, *Golf: My Life's Work*, 1943; *The Times*, 11 February 1963; *Country Life*, 19 April 1946.]   PETER RYDE

TAYLOR, SIR THOMAS MURRAY (1897-1962), lawyer and educationist, was born at Keith 27 May 1897, the only son of John Taylor, farmer and head of a firm of cattle dealers, and his wife, Jenny Nichol Murray.

From Keith Grammar School he proceeded to the university of Aberdeen as third bursar in 1915. He was rejected from military service owing to a heart condition. He took a first class in classics in 1919 and won the Ferguson scholarship, open to the four Scottish universities. With a political career in mind, he then studied law in Aberdeen, graduating LLB in 1922 with special distinction in jurisprudence and constitutional law. He read for the bar in Edinburgh, was called in 1924, and took silk in 1945. Passionately concerned for social improvements, he identified himself with the Labour Party and spoke in its interest from 1928. He became prospective Labour candidate for Cathcart in 1930 but resigned in 1931 when he thought it his duty to support the 'national' Government. His resignation from the crown office, where he had been junior advocate depute since 1929 was not accepted, and in 1934 he was appointed home advocate depute. In 1935, however, he left Edinburgh and was delighted to return to Aberdeen and occupy the chair of law in the university. This office, together with the sheriffdom of Argyll (held since 1945) and Renfrew (since 1946) he resigned in 1948 on his appointment as principal of the university.

In background, career, ability, character, and personality he was ideally fitted to be the principal, and, as their leader, he quickly commanded and never lost the confidence and affection of his colleagues. Throughout his tenure of his chair Taylor had been dean of the faculty of law and he was now at last able to be the means of making his faculty, as he had always wished, a school of study and not merely a legal apprenticeship. The last decade of his principalship was a period of university expansion. He was not a man to shirk the challenge presented by a national need, and he did acquire sites and superintend a large building programme, but he resisted, beyond certain limits, an expansion which might conflict with the traditions of his university and jeopardize the excellence of its work. He cemented the good relations between town and gown in Aberdeen, and one project, ever dear to his heart, the restoration and preservation of Old Aberdeen as a mixed community, he saw coming to fulfilment shortly before his death.

He was a highly respected member of the Committee of Vice-Chancellors and Principals, and might have become its chairman had he been prepared to make constant journeys to London. He was the architect and builder of an alliance between the Scottish and the Scandinavian universities, and this work was recognized in 1954 by the conferment of the Swedish Order of the North Star. In the same year he was knighted. He was appointed CBE in

1944. He was an honorary DD of Edinburgh (1952), and an honorary LLD of St. Andrews (1950) and Glasgow (1960). He frequently served as chairman of committees on wages questions and other matters of social concern, but what most excited his imagination was his chairmanship of the Crofting Commission (1951-4), for he had long wanted to do something to preserve the crofting way of life. Always liberal at heart, he came more and more to put the welfare of Scotland above the narrower issues of party politics.

In 1939 Taylor married an Aberdeen graduate in medicine, whom he had known since their student days together: Helen Margaret, daughter of the Revd David Little Jardine, minister of Durisdeer. They adopted a son in 1944 and a daughter in 1945. The happiness of his home was one of the two rocks on which Taylor's life was built. The other was his religion. As he said in one of his sermons (published in *Where One Man Stands*, 1960), he was 'intellectually convinced of the truth of the Christian faith'. He learnt that faith in boyhood, joined the United Free Church in Keith, and there was ordained an elder in the Church of Scotland in 1936. Loyal to his own Church, and a frequent attender and speaker at its General Assembly, he yet had wide sympathies, especially with other Protestant Churches. He was a member of the executive committee of the World Council of Churches (1948-54); from 1955 he chaired its commission on the prevention of war in an atomic age and was one of the two authors of its report (1961). His ecumenical work had taken him to Amsterdam, Geneva, and even to India, but he often enjoyed Continental holidays, especially in north Italy. His faith found expression in sermons delivered, mainly to undergraduates, in King's College chapel, Aberdeen, and elsewhere. No one who heard him preach could fail to be moved by his rigorous argument and the ringing tone of his profound conviction. The same conviction, together with his reflections on law and government, comes out in *The Discipline of Virtue* (1954), his Riddell lectures in the university of Durham.

Tom Taylor (as his friends knew him) had a lovely smile and a beautiful voice; he was a fine singer, whether of hymns in the college choir or of songs at parties in his ever hospitable home; and he loved playing golf. Tall and handsome, he was gay and humorous too when he relaxed with his friends. He could be severe, especially with culprits who tried to shuffle off responsibility for their actions; deceit could not look him in the face. He was free of pomposity, warm-hearted, and loved his fellow men, because, as he would have said, he loved God first. He himself was much loved not only by his intimates but by countless Scots in every walk of life.

Taylor died in Aberdeen 19 July 1962. There are two bronze busts by Gladys Barron, one owned by the family and the other by the university of Aberdeen.

[Memoir in *Speaking to Graduates*, ed. A. M. Hunter and W. Lillie, 1965; private information; personal knowledge.]   T. M. KNOX

TEDDER, ARTHUR WILLIAM, first BARON TEDDER (1890-1967), marshal of the Royal Air Force, was born at Glenguin in the county of Stirling 11 July 1890. He was the younger son of (Sir) Arthur John Tedder, a civil servant in the Inland Revenue who became a commissioner of customs and excise, and his wife, a distant cousin, Emily Charlotte, daughter of William Henry Bryson. The family's ancestry and background were more English than Scottish, and they lived in Scotland only during civil service appointments there. When his father moved back to London, Tedder began his serious education as a day boy at Whitgift Grammar School, Croydon, and went on to Magdalene College, Cambridge. He was placed in the second class of both parts of the historical tripos (1911-12) and was awarded the Prince Consort prize in 1914 for a dissertation on the Navy of the Restoration. He tried for a university tutorship, while his mild interest in his school and college Officers' Training Corps induced him to take a reserve commission in the Dorsetshire Regiment. But as neither civilian nor Service possibilities looked promising he rather half-heartedly applied for the Colonial Service, and finally succeeded in obtaining a cadetship to the administration in Fiji.

He had served only a few months when war broke out. With no great regret Tedder applied immediately for permission to join up, and when the governor showed reluctance to grant him leave he resigned from the Service. His selfless and strenuous efforts to return to his regiment were ironically rewarded, soon after he had put on its uniform, by incapacitation with a minor knee injury, which finally made him unfit for army duty. He thereupon asked for a commission in the Royal Flying Corps and with this third start found his life's work.

After considerable delay he received a wartime course of ground and flying instruction, and in June 1916 he joined No. 25 Squadron in France, where he carried out a tour on bombing and photographic missions. His intelligence and maturity brought him to the notice of Major-General (later Viscount) Trenchard [q.v.] who appointed him, early in 1917, to the command of No. 70 Fighter Squadron. After a year of successful operations he was posted home to a training unit, where he remained until sent to Egypt in 1918. He had become a training expert, and so remained until the end of the war. Between 1916 and 1918 he was three times mentioned in dispatches, and in 1919 he received a permanent commission in the newly formed Royal Air Force, with the rank of squadron-leader. By accepting it he became one of those whose direction in life had been completely changed by the accident of war, and throughout his subsequent career he showed the style of the gifted civilian in uniform, rather than that of the type-cast military man. He had more interest in the theory and organization of air war than in actual flying.

In appearance Tedder had little of the traditional Service officer; with his large dark eyes, prominent ears, kindly and sometimes vague facial expressions, he seemed rather to have strayed from some cloister or quadrangle. In later life he turned this to advantage; in early years it was no help. Resigned to his unexpected career, he continued during the dull post-war years to specialize in training; commanding schools, serving at the Air Ministry, and completing a course at the Imperial Defence College. His interest in the academic side of the military profession grew steadily, and this logically led him to the Royal Air Force Staff College, where he was an instructor and assistant commandant from 1929 to 1931. Leaving with the rank of group captain, for the next two years he commanded the Air Armament School at Eastchurch, and was then posted to the Air Ministry in 1934 as director of training. After two years in this appointment he was nominated as air officer commanding, Far East, and spent the years 1936-8 in Singapore, being promoted to air vice-marshal in 1937.

In 1938 came his first major opportunity to influence future events, when he was summoned back to the Air Ministry to assume the newly created post of director-general of research and development. The British technical preparations for war were at last in full spate, and Tedder threw himself into the complicated work which was fashioning, with desperate urgency, the weapons on which the country's survival would later depend. The new monoplane fighter aircraft, the advanced bomber projects, the development of radar, sophisticated navigation, vastly improved guns, bombs, and rockets, were all under his surveillance, and were pressed forward with all the haste made necessary by the lateness of the political realization of the nation's peril. When war began he continued this work inside the newly established Ministry of Aircraft Production, as deputy member of the air staff for development and production. In 1940 the appointment of the ebullient Lord Beaverbrook [q.v.] to oversee aircraft produc-

tion inevitably involved Tedder in friction with the minister, and through him with the prime minister, whose first view of Tedder was therefore painted in the colours of an obstinate obstructionist. When the Royal Air Force commander in the Middle East asked for him as his deputy the request was refused, and another senior officer was dispatched, but his aircraft was forced down in Sicily, and Tedder was appointed as the second choice.

In late 1940 the outlook in the Middle East, as elsewhere, was grim in the extreme, and it was no better when Tedder was promoted to commander-in-chief in June 1941. Churchill, dismayed by what he thought was a too conservative estimate by Tedder of the RAF strength which would be available for the relief of Tobruk, tried to remove him, but (Viscount) Portal, chief of air staff, threatened to resign if this was done, and Tedder remained in his post. The detailed history of this campaign is a complicated fabric of triumphs and disasters, of which the common factors are continuous operations on a number of different fronts by an air command almost cut off from the home base of Britain, with continuously inadequate resources. Not until the entry of the United States into the war, in December 1941, could any hope be seen for a change in the balance of power, and not until the battle of El Alamein any definite sign of ultimate victory. Throughout this period Tedder's policy had three main prongs: a first-class administrative and technical backing for his squadrons; a continuous attack on the Mediterranean supply lines of the Axis forces in North Africa; and the creation, through his field commander (Sir) Arthur Coningham [q.v.], of a Desert Air Force closely responding to the needs of the army. Like other airmen, Tedder was alive to the danger of the generals and admirals who wanted to split the air arm into small sections each directly under land and sea units. Unlike some of these airmen, he also saw that the only way to ensure the best use of centralized air power was first to prove to the other two Services that only centralization could gain an air situation which would make support possible, and then to produce a better and more responsive support. This is what Tedder's Middle East Air Force did: and it was under its shelter that the Eighth Army retreated to and advanced from Alamein. Tedder was promoted air marshal (1941) and air chief marshal (1942).

His style of command, in these difficult times, was diplomatic and unobtrusive. He was never loud or choleric. He developed an unrivalled power to manage his contemporaries, both military and civil, and kept in close touch with his squadrons by modest, almost furtive, unheralded appearances among them, where his informal dress and manner, his dry wit and lucid explanation, had a greater effect than the most fervent of conventional exhortations. He carried a sketch-book with him, and loved to record things he had seen with simple but vivid drawings. His policies, and his gradually reinforced squadrons, finally produced, with the other two Services and later the forces of the United States, a complete victory in North Africa. In February 1943 Tedder became commander-in-chief of Mediterranean Air Command, under General Eisenhower, with responsibility for all Allied air forces in the area. With the Axis surrender in Tunisia, in May 1943, Tedder's reputation reached a high level and Churchill said to him 'I was told you were just a man of nuts and bolts. It was not true.' Throughout the war, Tedder also retained Portal's confidence and support. Tedder's task required the highest diplomatic ability, yet during the most intensive activity of this period he had to endure the loss of his wife in an air crash, having already lost a son in air operations over Berlin. The first exercises in high-level Anglo-American co-operation were inevitably difficult, arduous, and fraught with complications which could swiftly involve London and Washington, but Tedder acquitted himself with such skill as to keep friction to the minimum, and the successful invasion of Sicily and southern Italy, together with the collapse of the Italian war effort, were all completed by the end of 1943, when Eisenhower was withdrawn to England to plan and command the Allied forces for the invasion of France. With him went Tedder as his deputy supreme commander, with authority over not only the air forces assigned to the invasion (Operation Overlord) but with a call on all Allied air forces which could be brought to bear on the battles, whether assigned or not. This was a unique position, above that of any air commander, and the short time available in which to define it ensured that it contained a large element of ambiguity capable of creating great difficulty, particularly with the Americans. 'Overlord' already enjoyed the personal and detailed attentions of Churchill and Roosevelt. Fortunately Eisenhower's strength and diplomacy were fully developed, and Tedder's wisdom and subtlety, and his complete understanding of the supreme commander, were matched by Eisenhower's support and confidence in him.

The development of 'Overlord' is history. Tedder's great contributions were the top management of the largest force of war aircraft ever directed towards a single objective, his technique for the isolation of the battle area from enemy support by air interdiction, and his use of massive heavy-bomber support of major land force offensive actions (the 'Tedder carpet'). As a fringe activity, he was a continuous and vitally important influence in the not entirely uneventful maintenance of good relations between the major Allied commanders in the field, and with the politicians behind them. He had by now perfected a quite outstanding ability to handle people and resolve differences, and before the final German surrender he was able to exercise it fully. His methods, as in his earlier commands, were first intelligent perception, followed by a gentle, almost apologetic dealing with the protagonists, who were imperceptibly led to adopt the courses he put forward as their own inspired solutions. He seldom allowed the iron in his character to show, but it was there. Throughout the campaign in France and Germany he never lost sight of his foremost precept of the centralized application of air power to the campaign, and nothing would induce him to relax it. By this doctrine he could apply the crushing strength of immense air forces to each part of the theatre as required, as in the intensive attacks on the German forces attempting to break through the Ardennes in January 1945.

As the war ended, Tedder, Marshal Zhukov, and the German Field-Marshal Keitel signed an instrument of surrender in Berlin (8 May 1945) to supplement that signed in Eisenhower's HQ in Rheims. There was nothing left to do but pick up the pieces, and in this he was assisted by his second wife. In memory of Wing Commander H. G. Malcolm, VC, who had been killed in North Africa, she had been establishing and supporting the string of Malcolm Clubs which provided comfort and off-duty relaxation for all ranks of the Service and its civilians, and now he was able to give her his full assistance. During the summer of 1945 the 'Overlord' team broke up, and his future remained uncertain until the Japanese surrender halted the British planning for a Far Eastern campaign. Tedder's reputation stood unrivalled among Allied airmen and he was promoted to marshal of the Royal Air Force in September 1945 and appointed chief of the air staff on 1 January 1946, when he was raised to the peerage.

In the military backwash after a great war even so high an office is seldom onerous, and only the problems of adjusting the Service to peace gave him any difficulty, either as chief of the air staff or when, later in his appointment, he also took his seat as chairman of the combined chiefs of staff committee. In 1948 he published his Lees Knowles lectures as *Air Power in War*. At the end of his four years as chief of the air staff in 1949 he duly retired, but was persuaded to go in 1950 to Washington, during the crucial years of the outset of the cold war, to fill the post of chairman of the British Joint Services Mission and United Kingdom representative on the military committee of the newly formed

North Atlantic Treaty Alliance. At last, in 1951, he was able to step down from high military office. As might be expected, he had been loaded with honours. His college had elected him an honorary fellow during the war; immediately afterwards he received honorary doctorates of five universities, including Cambridge. He had already been appointed CB (1937), KCB and GCB (January and November 1942). He was awarded three decorations by the President of the United States, and fourteen other foreign medals and orders. In 1950 he became chancellor of Cambridge University and vice-chairman of the board of governors of the British Broadcasting Corporation. He was chairman of the royal commission which reported in 1952 on Dundee's claims for a university. From 1954 to 1960 he was chairman of the Standard Motor Company. In 1966 he published his memoirs, appropriately titled *With Prejudice*.

Tedder first married, in 1915, Rosalinde, daughter of William McIntyre Maclardy, of Sydney, Australia; they had two sons and a daughter. After her death in January 1943 Tedder married in October of the same year Marie de Seton (died 1965), younger daughter of Sir Bruce Seton, Bt., and formerly wife of Captain Ian Reddie Hamilton Black, RN. They had one son. Tedder died in Banstead, Surrey, 3 June 1967. His title passed to his son, John Michael (born 1926), who was then Roscoe professor of chemistry, Queen's College, Dundee.

There is a portrait of Tedder by H. A. Freeth and another by Henry Carr, both the property of the Imperial War Museum.

[*The Times*, 5 June 1967; Roderic Owen, *Tedder*, 1952; Lord Tedder, *With Prejudice*, 1966; Air Historical Branch (RAF); private information; personal knowledge.]

PETER WYKEHAM

TENBY, first VISCOUNT (1894–1967). [See LLOYD-GEORGE, GWILYM.]

THIRKELL, ANGELA MARGARET (1890–1961), novelist, was born in Kensington 30 January 1890, the eldest child of John William Mackail [q.v.], classical scholar and later professor of poetry at Oxford, by his wife, Margaret, only daughter of (Sir) Edward Burne-Jones [q.v.]. The three Mackail children—of whom the second, Denis, was also to become a novelist—grew up in Pembroke Gardens, Kensington; in her first book, *Three Houses*, Angela Thirkell describes Sunday visits to her maternal grandparents at The Grange, Fulham, and happy summer and Christmas holidays at their house in Rottingdean. Her early childhood was dominated by nannies with

that mixture of comfort and rigour common to the upper-class young in late Victorian and Edwardian London. When they were brought down from the nursery, the Mackail children found themselves among distinguished people: Sir Edward Poynter [q.v.] was a great-uncle; Stanley Baldwin was her mother's cousin, so was Rudyard Kipling [qq.v.], who gave critical encouragement to Angela's early attempts at poetry.

At the age of fourteen she was sent to the newly established St. Paul's School for Girls, and, as one of its best gymnasts, was chosen to perform at the school's official opening by the Princess of Wales (later Queen Mary) in April 1904. She won prizes for French and German, and in that very musical school was a star performer on the piano; at sixteen she was made a prefect, but left the following year to go to a 'finishing school' in Paris.

In 1911 she married a singer, James Campbell McInnes, by whom she had two sons, Graham, and Colin, the writer; she also had a daughter who died in infancy. But the marriage proved a bitter failure, and in 1917 she obtained a divorce with the custody of her children. The following year she met a young Tasmanian engineer, George Lancelot Allnutt Thirkell, and embarked confidently upon a second marriage; she accompanied her husband to Australia, where they settled down in a small house in the suburbs of Melbourne. Here Angela Thirkell gave birth to a third son, and struggled with domesticity on an inadequate income, in surroundings which were far from idyllic. She began to write: articles, short stories, pieces for Australian radio, and slowly gathered round her a circle of artistic and literary people. But she could never resign herself to living in Australia, and in 1930, taking her youngest son, Lance, she sailed to England, ostensibly on holiday; she never returned.

In bringing up her boys, Angela Thirkell was a martinet: throughout her eleven years' exile, her determination to keep up standards of taste and behaviour drove her to a harshness which alienated her two elder sons. She was not a motherly woman. Her eldest son, Graham McInnes, wrote of her that she could not 'give'. 'Hers was the tragedy of the inarticulate heart'; and he added, 'I have wonderfully amusing, witty and loving letters from her; but to be demonstrative in person, ah! that was different.'

After the break-up of her second marriage she returned to her parents' house and settled down to write books: the charming picture of her childhood, *Three Houses* (1931), was followed by a stream of over thirty highly successful novels, all published by Hamish Hamilton. Her writing did not draw upon the unhappy experiences of her married life: rather she concentrated upon new vistas of tranquillity and laughter, peopled by charming, and, for the most part, well-bred characters. *Ankle Deep* and *High Rising* both appeared in 1933. Her third novel, *Wild Stawberries* (1934), was one of her best, written with complete assurance, and from the first page amusing characters emerge, clear-cut. As well as her dancing wit, she began to portray character with a tenderness and imaginative sympathy which she could never show to those around her, and to create dramatis personae and families who progressed from one book to the next, in settings cleverly adapted from the Barsetshire of Anthony Trollope [q.v.]. *Pomfret Towers* (1938), *The Brandons* (1939), and *Chearfulness Breaks In* (1940) brought her to the outbreak of war and its accompanying effect upon her characters.

She was at times accused of snobbery; but she painted a true and detailed picture of a life which was on the verge of extinction—a truly English way of life, in which many of the characters were wealthy by inheritance, accepting the traditional advantages and responsibilities of the country gentry. The servants who surrounded them were efficient and loyal, seen by their creator as potential comedy parts—in the main lovable, if not quite three-dimensional. In the post-war world she was less happy.

Angela Thirkell was an acknowledged beauty, with a strikingly tall and willowy Pre-Raphaelite grace, and if she had an early fondness for 'clouds of lemon tulle', in later life she preferred to dress in black with a mantilla in the evening, which accentuated an increasingly formidable character. Her speech was rapid, and so when she wrote were her sentences, as if the thoughts informing them were hurrying to be recorded. She became known in society for her 'magnetic if acid personality' and as a brilliant conversationalist, witty, sharp, and erudite. Indeed, her novels showed unusual erudition, based on the culture which she had absorbed from childhood and which, in her Australian exile, she had fought to uphold.

She died 29 January 1961 in Bramley, Surrey, only a day before her seventy-first birthday, and was buried at Rottingdean beside her Burne-Jones grandparents. Her last novel, *Three Score and Ten* (1961), was completed by A. Lejeune. A full-length oil-painting by John Collier is in the National Gallery, Melbourne, Australia; a miniature by the same artist, a portrait of Angela Thirkell as a child by W. Graham Robertson, and a charcoal sketch by J. S. Sargent (1915), are all privately owned.

[*The Times*, 30 January 1961; Angela Thirkell, *Three Houses*, 1931; Graham McInnes, *The Road to Gundagai*, 1965; *Everyman's Encyclopaedia*, 1967; Margot Strickland, *Angela Thirkell: Portrait of a Lady Novelist*; private information.]

THEA HOLME

THODAY, DAVID (1883-1964), botanist, was born 5 May 1883 at Honiton, Devon, the eldest of the six children of David Thoday, an elementary schoolmaster, and his wife, Susan Elizabeth, daughter of Charles Bingham. Both his parents came from villages in the Cambridgeshire fenland where his grandfathers were skilled rural craftsmen, his father from Willingham and his mother from Guyhirne. In 1884 Thoday's father, a man of strong personality, evangelical in religion and radical in politics, moved to London where he continued to teach in elementary schools and later became a headmaster. His son David was educated at Tottenham Grammar School which he left at the age of fifteen to join the Tottenham Pupil Teachers' Centre. The principal, T. E. Margerison, encouraged him to aim at a university career and in 1902 he was awarded a scholarship by Toynbee Hall and was admitted to Trinity College, Cambridge, as a subsizar. At the same time he joined the Cambridge Day Training College, his intention being to become a schoolteacher.

In part i of the natural sciences tripos Thoday read physics, chemistry, and botany. As a freshman his interest seems to have been chiefly in the physical sciences but the stimulating lectures of H. Marshall Ward, (Sir) A. C. Seward, and the plant physiologist F. F. Blackman [qq.v.] attracted him to botany. After being placed in the first class in part i (1905) he was awarded a senior scholarship and in 1906 he obtained a first class in part ii (botany). He was awarded the Walsingham medal in 1908. Later, in 1933, he proceeded to a Sc.D.

Thoday remained at Cambridge for five more years, first as a research student under F. F. Blackman, and from 1909 to 1911 as university demonstrator. During this period he worked on various physiological problems and published several papers of which the best known is on Sachs's 'half leaf' method of measuring photosynthesis. In 1910 he married Mary Gladys Sykes (died 1943), daughter of John Thorley Sykes, cotton broker of Denbighshire: she was a botanist of some distinction, who had collaborated with him in some of his research; she was a graduate of Girton College and was a research fellow of Newnham College from 1909 to 1912.

In 1911 Thoday became lecturer in physiological botany at Manchester University, where he spent seven years, moving in 1918 to the chair of botany at the university of Cape Town. For a botanist with Thoday's breadth of interest South Africa offered wonderful opportunities. He soon embarked on physiological, anatomical, and taxonomic studies on the xerophytic plants in which South Africa's seasonally dry climate is so rich: he became particularly interested in the ericoid (small-leaved) shrubs and the functional significance of their reduced leaf areas.

Although Thoday greatly enjoyed his years at Cape Town, he decided for personal reasons to resign his chair and in 1923 he succeeded Reginald W. Phillips as professor of botany at the University College of North Wales, Bangor, where he remained until he retired in 1949. There Thoday found himself in charge of a small department with extremely limited resources: for some years there were only two members of staff to assist him. In spite of the difficulties, he built up an efficient teaching department and actively continued his research on the water relations and tissue differentiation of plants. In collaboration with Miss A. J. Davey he also studied contractile roots. Among the many papers he wrote at Bangor the most notable were perhaps the series on the succulent *Kleinia articulata* which included work on their peculiar acid metabolism.

After retiring in 1949 Thoday spent two years in Egypt as professor of plant physiology at Alexandria but returned to Bangor in 1952 where he settled down to work on the reactions between host and parasite in Loranthaceae (mistletoes). This he continued until he was nearly eighty and had become crippled with rheumatism.

Thoday had an unusually clear analytical mind and great experimental ingenuity; he had a flair for designing simple but effective apparatus, for instance the widely used Thoday potometer and Thoday respirometer. Though he had comparatively few students, he had great influence on botanical teaching and research, especially through his *Botany: a Text-book for Senior Students* (1915) and his presidential address to Section K of the British Association (1939), in which he put forward ideas on the differentiation of plant tissues which were in some respects ahead of his time. Thoday was elected FRS in 1942 and received an honorary D.Sc. from the university of Wales in 1960.

Thoday was a rather small man, always extremely neat in appearance, and with a modest and unassuming manner. Music, for which he had a critical and discriminating taste, was his chief leisure interest.

Thoday had four sons of whom the third, John Marion Thoday, became professor of genetics at Cambridge in 1959. Thoday died at his home in Llanfairfechan 30 March 1964.

There is a pencil drawing of Thoday by

Margery Alexander in the School of Plant Biology at the University College of North Wales.

[Walter Stiles in *Biographical Memoirs of Fellows of the Royal Society*, vol. xi, 1965; private information; personal knowledge.]
P. W. RICHARDS

THOMAS, FOREST FREDERIC EDWARD YEO- (1902-1964), French resistance organizer. [See YEO-THOMAS.]

THOMAS, HUGH HAMSHAW (1885-1962), palaeobotanist, was born 29 May 1885 in Wrexham, Denbighshire, the second son and third child of William Thomas and his wife, Elizabeth Lloyd, a local farmer's daughter. William Thomas, of Cornish and Leicestershire extraction, was a men's outfitter, a prominent local citizen, JP, Congregationalist, and lifelong Liberal.

After attending the local county school Thomas entered Cambridge in 1904, as an entrance scholar at Downing College. Through the influence of friends and casual reading he had as a boy become interested in natural history, particularly botany and fossils, and he was fired by the idea of biological evolution. In 1906 he obtained first class honours in part i of the natural sciences tripos (botany, chemistry, and physics). Intending to make a career in the Civil Service, he took part ii of the history tripos, obtaining second class honours in 1907. At the same time he continued to research on fossil plants and his first paper (as junior author) was published by the Royal Society in 1908; his first independent paper was published the following year. In 1908 Thomas did well in the Civil Service entrance examination but was offered a post which did not please him.

Instead he chose to live as an independent scholar in Cambridge, earning a precarious keep by coaching students for elementary examinations. For the next few years he followed the usual course of study—the examination of specimens provided in museums or by field geologists. He collaborated with (Sir) A. C. Seward (whose notice he later wrote for this Dictionary) on a study of a collection from Russia. But Thomas, somewhat unusually, chose to study plants preserved as black marks on shale surfaces rather than the three-dimensional petrified specimens, the examination by thin sections of which had been the pride of British palaeobotany.

This work on the Jurassic period led Thomas to begin a fresh study of the Jurassic plants of Yorkshire, which were preserved compressed on shales. This study was inspired by A. G. Nathorst, of Stockholm, who had shown that, after suitable chemical manipulation, such fossils would yield external cuticles or spore membranes. This fact had been known for some time, but it had not been appreciated that cuticles could explain complicated reproductive structures. Consequently, the shale surface fossils were potentially as valuable as petrifactions.

Another Stockholm scholar, Halle, provoked Thomas into collecting his own specimens, studying his results, and returning to collect further material. Thomas repeatedly visited his Yorkshire collecting grounds, selecting his specimens carefully, and concentrating on the study of reproductive parts (which were mostly detached and inconspicuous fossils), in order to advance botanical knowledge. He wrote a valuable paper on *Williamsoniella*, a flower he named himself, relating it to its previously unrecognized stem and to its leaf, which had long been known but was thought to be of a fern. Thomas also wrote a paper, with Nellie Bancroft, on cycad leaf cuticles; his contribution was to show that fossils belonged to two groups—the living cycads, and a very different category. This paper provided a basis for the classification of fossils by leaf cuticles.

Thomas joined the army early in the war of 1914-18 and was an artillery officer in the Royal Field Artillery in France in 1915. Before the battle of the Somme he was transferred to Egypt, on secondment to the Royal Flying Corps, as officer in charge of aerial photography. Sir John Salmond [q.v.] said that the success of the campaign of Sir E. H. H. Allenby (later Viscount Allenby of Megiddo, q.v.) was 'to a great extent attributable to the work that Captain Thomas did'. Thomas was twice mentioned in dispatches, was awarded the Order of the Nile, and appointed MBE. After the armistice he was sent to India to report on the possibilities of aerial survey and on his return to Cambridge assisted in the direction of research in the Aeronautical Department. He played an important part in the foundation of the University Air Squadron.

In 1919 Thomas returned to live in Downing College where Seward was master. The following year he was appointed dean and steward and in 1923 became a university lecturer in botany. In 1923 also he married Edith Gertrude Torrance, from Cape Town, a research student in Cambridge of F. F. Blackman [q.v.]. They had a son and a daughter. The South African connection led to Thomas's work on fossils of that region.

In 1925 he published an outstanding paper on the Caytoniales, an entirely new order of angiospermous plants from the Jurassic era.

Thomas's *Caytonia* was a group of little berry-like 'fruits' each containing seeds, very like a string of currants. Inventing his own technique, which was possible because he could sacrifice many fruits, he worked out the fruit and seed structure from their cuticles and by sectioning them after long swelling in alkali. Success was rare but he showed that the fruit was indeed closed and had a stigma-like part on which he found pollen grains (and he already knew the fossil which produced this kind of pollen). The leaf he discovered by examining with an open mind, all associated fossils of which only one (*Sagenopteris*) had a leaf stalk with a cuticle which matched the *Caytonia* fruit stalk. Thus he launched the Caytoniales as early angiospermous plants, though not claiming them as strictly ancestral.

His paper received a mixed reception, partly because the case he made for identifying the separate parts was not fully convincing. Workers elsewhere confirmed all his main findings, though details were emended. He could have presented a tidier and more convincing case had he been interested in the minute structural points which have no obvious significance but do characterize individual species. Indeed, he was never interested in specific characters. He aroused opposition of another kind deliberately, revealing in this paper that his interest was by no means narrowly concentrated on the fossil but rather on the wider issues that arose from it, such as evolutionary changes and the philosophy of the organization of the plant body. He did deliberate violence to the idea that you can, and in general should, divide a plant into clear categories of organs, root, stem, leaf. In 1933 Thomas wrote a paper on pteridospermous fructifications of South African Triassic plants which was another great contribution to palaeobotany. The plants concerned were a major element of the southern hemisphere Triassic flora. Again he entered the field of debatable plant morphology but there is no doubt of his contribution to knowledge of a major group of plants.

On the outbreak of war in 1939 Thomas joined the Royal Air Force Volunteer Reserve and worked for four years on photographic interpretation. He left in 1943 with the rank of wing commander. In his later years he continued to publish work describing fossils (one two years before he died) but he preferred to publish papers on general botanical ideas and their history. He also wrote the notice of Agnes Arber for this Dictionary.

Thomas never had or wanted a research school in palaeobotany. He did not wish to dominate but to help people to go their own ways independently. He gave unstinting help to many outside palaeobotany, as evidenced by his presidency of the Eastern Counties branch of the Science Masters Association; of the Yorkshire Naturalists; of the botany section of the British Association; of the Linnean Society; and of the British Society of the History of Science. He was active in promoting international co-operation in botany.

Thomas was elected to the Royal Society in 1934 and received the Linnean Society's gold medal in 1960. His most remarkable distinction was to be judged at the Darwin–Wallace centenary in 1958 to be among the twenty biologists who had made the most outstanding contribution to knowledge of evolution, for which he received a commemorative medal. He was a modest and retiring man and the enduring impression is of his thoughtful kindness and the width of his labours. He died in Cambridge 30 June 1962.

[T. M. Harris in *Biographical Memoirs of Fellows of the Royal Society*, vol. ix, 1963; private information; personal knowledge.]

TOM M. HARRIS

THOMAS, SIR (THOMAS) SHENTON (WHITELEGGE) (1879–1962), colonial governor, born in London 10 October 1879, was the eldest of six children, five of them sons, of the Revd Thomas William Thomas, assistant curate at the church of St. Bride, Fleet Street, and his wife, Charlotte Susanna Whitelegge. In 1880 his father moved to a curacy at St. Giles', Norwich, and after 1885 he held vicarships in Cambridgeshire. Thomas was educated at St. John's School, Leatherhead, and Queens' College, Cambridge, where he was awarded a Sedgwick exhibition and was placed in the second class of part i of the classical tripos in 1901. In 1935 he was elected an honorary fellow of his college.

Thomas taught at preparatory schools and was for a time tutor to the son of the Maharaja of Cooch Behar until in 1909 his overseas career began with his appointment as an assistant district commissioner in the East African Protectorate. In 1918 he was transferred to Uganda and in 1921 to Nigeria. In 1927 he went to the Gold Coast as colonial secretary, moving in 1929 to Nyasaland as governor until in 1932 he returned to the Gold Coast as governor. Of average height, clean shaven, well dressed and cheerful in manner, Thomas had a good public presence and was an excellent host. He earned a reputation in Africa as an able administrator; his dispatches and minutes, like his handwriting, were clear and firm. He was a good mixer, played cricket, golf, and tennis, and later in Singapore was a keen racegoer.

In 1934 Thomas was appointed governor and commander-in-chief of the Straits Settlements, high commissioner for the Malay States, and British agent for North Borneo and Sarawak. Although designated commander-in-chief, the governor was not invested with the command of British armed forces in the area. For five years the politically complex States and Settlements maintained their prosperity and racial harmony under the direction of Thomas who was popular with Asian leaders. In 1938 he opened the world's largest naval dock at Singapore.

In September 1939, when Thomas's term of appointment had nearly expired, war broke out in Europe. Although now sixty, he agreed to continue in his post. He used his influence to promote massive financial support from Malaya for Britain's war effort and the maximum output of tin and rubber to earn currency for supplies from the United States. The capitulation of France in June 1940 enabled Japanese forces to move into French Indo-China. Thomas, in London, warned the Colonial Office that, in the event of war with Japan, Malaya could be preserved only by sufficient air or sea forces to prevent an army from landing.

On 8 December 1941 Japanese planes bombed Singapore and two days later sank the *Prince of Wales* and *Repulse* off the east coast of Malaya. Japanese forces landed in north-east Malaya and, with overwhelming air superiority, advanced through the Malay peninsula to Singapore. During the retreat, Thomas's authority was weakened by the appointment at Singapore late in 1941 of a resident minister for Far Eastern affairs, A. Duff Cooper (later Viscount Norwich, q.v.), who did not grasp the implications of a multi-racial society. Thomas and his senior administrators were mindful of Britain's obligations towards the Asian population and treaty relationships with the Malay rulers. To Duff Cooper, the functions of the Far East War Council, of which he was chairman, and the safety of Europeans were paramount. These different conceptions of British responsibilities in the area, which emerged sharply in such matters as evacuation and scorched earth policies, prompted criticism of the civil administration in the European controlled press and caused bitter controversy then and for years afterwards.

On 14 February 1942, after Japanese forces had landed on Singapore Island and invested the city, Thomas informed London that one million people in the city were faced with total deprivation of water within twenty-four hours, that it was impossible to bury the dead lying in the streets, and that pestilence must result. General A. E. Percival [q.v.] surrendered to General Yamashita the next day.

The Japanese interned Thomas and his wife in Changi Gaol, Singapore, in publicly humiliating circumstances. Thomas was transferred in custody in August 1942 to Formosa and in October 1944 to Manchuria, where he was liberated by American forces 25 August 1945. In September he was reunited in Calcutta with his wife who had been interned in Singapore throughout, and they returned to England. Their conduct in internment, in appalling conditions, won the admiration of their fellow sufferers.

After officially retiring in 1946, Thomas was chairman of the Overseas League from 1946 to 1949, and of the British Empire Leprosy Relief Association from 1949 to 1955, a member from 1948 of the governing body of St. John's School, Leatherhead, and a vice-president from 1955 of the Fauna Preservation Society. He endeavoured without success to correct what he felt to be the bias and prejudice in the official history of *The War Against Japan* and to have included in it an adequate appreciation of the war effort of the people of the Straits Settlements and Malay States and their sufferings during the campaign and the Japanese occupation. He wrote a brief record of his unavailing efforts in this respect in 1956.

Thomas was appointed OBE (1919), CMG (1929), KCMG (1931), and GCMG (1937). In 1912 he married Lucy Marguerite (Daisy), who died in 1978, daughter of Lieutenant-Colonel James Alexander Lawrence Montgomery who had retired from the Indian Army and was then commissioner for lands in Kenya. She was a cousin of the future Viscount Montgomery of Alamein. Thomas and his wife were a devoted couple until his death. They had one daughter, who, after the dissolution of her first marriage, in 1965 married the ninth Earl of St. Germans. Thomas died in London 15 January 1962. Although maligned by some of his countrymen, the principles which guided his conduct in 'the greatest disaster in British military history' denied a moral victory to the Japanese conquerors. In Singapore his name is perpetuated in 'Shenton Way', a post-war highway through the business area completed in 1952, in 'Shenton Circus', the busy roundabout near the main Conference Hall, and in 'Shenton House', a skyscraper built nearly thirty years after the war with Japan. There is a portrait of him by a Chinese artist in the Fort Canning archives.

[Papers of Sir Shenton Thomas in the libraries of Rhodes House, Oxford, and the Royal Commonwealth Society; Public Record Office: Colonial Office records; British European Association, Singapore; private information; personal knowledge.]

A. H. P. HUMPHREY

THOMSON, SIR GEORGE PIRIE (1887–1965), chief press censor, Ministry of Information, during the war of 1939–45, was born 30 January 1887 at Jubbulpore in India, the son of Robert Brown Thomson, a civil engineer in the Public Works Department, and his wife, May Forbes, daughter of William R. Pirie [q.v.], moderator of the General Assembly of the Church of Scotland and principal of Aberdeen University. His uncle, the Revd George Pirie, was professor of mathematics at the university of Aberdeen from 1878. Thomson was taken by his parents to Switzerland and until he was six years old was unable to speak anything but French. He began his education in English at George Watson's College, Edinburgh, and joined the Royal Navy at the age of fifteen, claiming that the main reason for this choice was that naval uniform might make him look slimmer. He passed for lieutenant with five firsts and specialized in submarines, which were then (1908) in the very early stages of their development. He spent twenty-five years in the navy, reaching the rank of rear-admiral in 1939. His final appointment before retirement was as second member of the Australian Naval Board (1937–9).

When Hitler invaded Poland Thomson, who had retired from the navy in February 1939, was on holiday in the south of France. Returning to London he presented himself to Churchill, then the first lord of the Admiralty, and received his orders: 'Go at once to the Ministry of Information and give Admiral Usborne a hand with the Press Censorship. He appears to be hard pressed.'

Before war began a machinery for press censorship had been set up, staffed by retired officers from the three Services. On 3 September, a few hours after Britain declared war on Germany, the whole machine collapsed when the British liner *Athenia*, carrying civilians (including many women and children), was torpedoed and sunk without warning by a German submarine, with a loss of 112 lives. Overseas correspondents jammed the censors' office with long cables containing all available details and outward cable traffic came to a halt.

Nine days later another breakdown, of a different kind, occurred. On 4 September, in great secrecy, the British Expeditionary Force had begun its move to France. Silence was broken on 13 September by French radio. Having received permission, the British press issued news items and pictures which had been prepared in advance. Two and a half hours later the War Office cancelled the permission which it had given. By now whole editions had been printed, packaged, and placed in trains and vans for dispatch all over the country and to neutral Ireland. The War Office ordered that all copies of all papers carrying the news should be seized. Police occupied newspaper offices, removed the papers from trains, and stopped private cars, confiscating single copies. Fleet Street reacted with vigour, proprietors intervened forcefully in Whitehall, and three hours later, at 2.30 a.m., the cancellation of the permission was itself cancelled.

This was the situation in which Thomson found himself within ten days of the outbreak of the war, previously having had, as he wrote in his book, *Blue Pencil Admiral* (1947), 'an experience of the Press which was limited to reading my newspaper at the breakfast table'. He showed the frame of mind in which he attacked his new job when he said to a reporter in the very earliest days: 'I should be awfully grateful if you wouldn't address me as "sir".'

The original body of censors, retired officers, had always been used to giving orders or carrying them out, while the journalists were used to challenging authority and arguing with it. Now, however, confidence between press and censorship soon developed; the press learned that Thomson was on their side and would go to the limit to help them. He himself came to trust the press and to know that he could count on it not to let him down.

This relationship was essential to the working of the British censorship system, which was voluntary, with a series of D (for Defence) notices warning of particular topics to be avoided. Items were not submitted for censorship unless there was doubt about whether they conflicted with the D notices. A single set of figures quoted by Thomson in *Blue Pencil Admiral* shows how the system operated and the amount of work involved: '. . . there were over 400,000 separate issues of newspapers during the war . . . [from which] only 650,000 news items were submitted [to censorship]— that is, only one and a half items from each separate newspaper.'

Admiral C. V. Usborne remained at the Ministry of Information until January 1940. After a short interregnum, in December 1940 Thomson became chief press censor, a post he held until the end of the war amidst a swirl of changes in the senior appointments at the Ministry.

It was then decided that the essentials of the system which Thomson had been operating should be continued in peacetime under the title of the Services, Press and Broadcasting Committee, with Thomson as secretary. He was also appointed public relations officer of the Latin American Centre.

Thomson was appointed OBE in 1919, CBE in 1939, and CB in 1946; he was knighted in 1963. He married and had two daughters. He

died at Queen Mary's Hospital, Roehampton, 24 January 1965.

[George P. Thomson, *Blue Pencil Admiral*, 1947; *The Times*, 26 January 1965.]

DAVID WOODWARD

THOMSON, GEORGE REID (1893–1962), lord justice clerk, was born in Glasgow 11 June 1893, the eldest of the four children of the Revd William Rankin Thomson, of the United Presbyterian Church of Scotland, and his wife, Agnes Macfee. The Revd W. R. Thomson spent much of his life as a clergyman in South Africa, and G. R. Thomson received his early education at the South African College, Cape Town. He went up to Corpus Christi College, Oxford, as a Rhodes scholar in October 1911 and obtained a second class in classical honour moderations in 1913. Like many of his contemporaries, he abandoned Oxford at the outbreak of war in 1914. He joined the Royal Fusiliers as a private soldier, was commissioned in the 5th Argyll and Sutherland Highlanders in 1915, and served in Egypt, Palestine, and France. He was wounded in action, promoted captain, and mentioned in dispatches. On demobilization he did not return to Oxford but took his degree in 1920 under the decree which exempted those who had served in the armed forces from further examination. He was elected an honorary fellow of Corpus in 1957.

He entered the law faculty of Edinburgh University in 1919, and graduated bachelor of laws with distinction in March 1922, after having been awarded the Muirhead prize, the Dalgety prize, the Thow scholarship, and the Vans Dunlop scholarship, which he shared with John (Lord) Cameron. He was given the degree of honorary doctor of laws by Edinburgh University in 1957.

He was admitted advocate 1922. He had no legal connections and was an unspectacular pleader and it was some time before solicitors appreciated the virtue of his firm grasp of legal principles, his thorough preparation of even the most trivial case, and his sound common sense. He gradually built up a substantial practice in cases under the Workmen's Compensation Acts and similar fields, but it was not until 1936, when he took silk, that his talent for synthesis and his ability to reduce a complex argument to a few and concisely stated propositions emerged. It was quickly recognized and he acquired a large and broadly based practice. He was an advocate depute from 1940 to 1945.

On the formation of the Labour Government in 1945 he was appointed lord advocate and a member of the Privy Council. The Government had a large legislative programme and the prime minister, Attlee, wished to have his assistance in the Commons. Against his better judgement, Thomson was persuaded to stand for East Edinburgh, where a vacancy was created for him by the elevation of F. W. Pethick-Lawrence [q.v.], the sitting member, to the peerage. Thomson was elected by a substantial majority. His commitment to the Labour Party resulted from his sympathy with the underprivileged, and his approach to political problems was pragmatic and not ideological. This approach, his dislike of rhetoric, and, above all, his contempt for what he called 'the ya-boo' of party strife, and the heated atmosphere of a House of Commons, largely concerned with bitterly fought nationalization legislation, made this an unhappy period in an otherwise happy life.

In March 1947 the office of lord justice clerk fell vacant. Thomson wished for the appointment, but the prime minister felt unable to do without him in the Commons, and Lord Alexander Moncrieff was appointed. This was clearly a stop-gap appointment, and when Lord Moncrieff resigned in October 1947, Thomson was appointed lord justice clerk. He presided over the Second Division of the Court of Session and the Court of Criminal Appeal, and, from time to time, sat as a judge of first instance. He was a patient and attentive judge, courteous to all, rarely interrupting a witness or counsel, and then only in a search for clarification. He desired the truth, but he was very conscious of the limitations of the legal process and, as he put it in an often quoted judgement, 'A litigation is in essence a trial of skill between opposing parties conducted under recognized rules, and the prize is the judge's decision'. His judgements were based on the application of broad legal principles to the ascertained facts, and were couched in simple and sometimes racy language, which reflected his knowledge of human affairs and wide reading. He is said to have quoted Homer in the original Greek in the course of a hearing before him.

His real genius lay in his sincerity, simplicity, and friendliness. In 1925 he married Grace (died 1980), daughter of the Revd Daniel Georgeson, of Bowling. They had no children. They had a most happy marriage and created in their home a centre of hospitality for a wide circle of friends. Every young advocate—and his bride, when acquired—was bidden to and made most welcome at their home, not as a duty imposed by his office, but because they both liked young people and lively minds. He was a discerning collector of modern Scottish paintings, a fisher, and an enthusiastic and skilful golfer, who delighted to select, organize, and captain the Scottish team in the annual match against the English bench and bar.

He was taken ill while on holiday in Spain and died 15 April 1962 at Gibraltar.

[College and university records; private information; personal knowledge.]

DOUGLAS JOHNSTON

THURSO, first VISCOUNT (1890-1970), politician. [See SINCLAIR, SIR ARCHIBALD HENRY MACDONALD.]

TITCHMARSH, EDWARD CHARLES (1899-1963), mathematician, was born at Newbury 1 June 1899, the son of Edward Harper Titchmarsh and his wife, Caroline Farmar. He had an elder sister and a younger sister and brother. His father was minister of the Congregational church at Newbury from shortly before 1899 until 1907, when he was chosen as minister of Nether chapel in Sheffield. There was a strict religious tradition on both sides of his family, and Titchmarsh wrote an account of his family history and restricted childhood with critical but humorous detachment. From 1908 to 1917 he was educated at King Edward VII School, Sheffield; he commented that the pupils were given far too much homework. He first specialized in classics, but failed in Greek in the higher certificate. He then specialized in mathematics and physics, but felt baffled by experiments.

In December 1916 he won the open mathematical scholarship at Balliol College, Oxford, and went up for the Michaelmas term in 1917. He was subsequently on war service for two years, as a second lieutenant, RE (Signals), 1918-19, and was in France and Belgium from August 1918. During this period he lost a great friend, who was also a mathematician. He never talked about his experiences and wrote deprecatingly of his abilities as an officer, but he acquired a useful ability to deal with domestic electrical appliances.

Titchmarsh returned to Oxford in 1919; his tutors were J. W. Russell and, later, J. W. Nicholson. Russell's methods of teaching were grossly over-organized, while Nicholson seldom saw his pupils. G. H. Hardy [q.v.] came to Oxford as Savilian professor of geometry in 1920 and was mainly responsible for Titchmarsh's determination to devote his life to research in pure mathematics. Titchmarsh won the junior mathematical exhibition in 1920 and the junior mathematical scholarship, jointly with H. O. Newboult, in 1921. He was placed in the first class in mathematical honour moderations in 1920 and in the final honours school of mathematics in 1922, taking his BA degree in 1922 and his MA in 1924. In addition, in 1924 he won the senior mathematical scholarship. He spent a year at Oxford working for a D.Phil.

under Hardy's supervision, but never completed the requirements for the degree. He also acted as secretary to Hardy.

In the summer of 1923 Titchmarsh was appointed a senior lecturer at University College, London, and in 1925 reader. In 1923 he obtained by examination a prize fellowship at Magdalen College, Oxford, and remained a fellow from 1924 to 1930, although he only resided occasionally.

In 1925 Titchmarsh married Kathleen, daughter of Alfred Blomfield, JP, who was a farmer and secretary and senior deacon of Titchmarsh's father's church at Halstead, Essex. They had three daughters who all married, and he was always much concerned with family and domestic matters.

In 1929 Titchmarsh became professor of pure mathematics at Liverpool, and in 1931 he was elected Savilian professor of geometry at Oxford to succeed Hardy. This chair carried with it a fellowship at New College, which he held until his death. Hardy had regularly given lectures on geometry as well as subjects connected with his own research, but Titchmarsh said in his application that he could not lecture on geometry and the statute was altered for him. He was a dominant figure in Oxford mathematics for many years and had many research students. As senior mathematical professor he became curator of the Mathematical Institute when it was established, delegating much to his staff. His habits were extremely regular. Both in term and vacations, except for short holidays, he worked in the mornings and after tea, never later than 8 p.m. He had no telephone in his room at the Institute and did not dictate letters. He seldom discussed mathematics, preferring to write everything down, and submitted work for publication in clear manuscripts unless compelled to have it typed. On committees he spoke late and little, but clearly and effectively. He found lecturing difficult and, although he was very clear, he showed little enthusiasm. He was tall and broad-shouldered and a little inclined to stoop. He had dark-brown eyes with strongly marked eyebrows and was rather diffident and shy. As a member of the governing body of New College he served for twenty-two years on the audit and finance committee and for eleven years on the estates committee, as well as being on various *ad hoc* committees. He was a courteous and benevolent sub-warden. Like Hardy he enjoyed watching cricket, and he played in the annual match at New College for the senior common room against the choir school.

His mathematical output was prodigious and remarkably clear. It included important contributions to the theory of Fourier integrals, integral equations, Fourier series, integral functions, the Riemann zeta function, and eigenfunctions of second-order differential equations. A few of his papers were written in collaboration with others, including Hardy, U. S. Haslam-Jones, H. S. A. Potter, and J. B. McCleod. His textbook, *The Theory of Functions* (1932), made easily available much of the theory of functions of a complex and of a real variable which had previously been inaccessible in English. It was written with great clarity, but omitted certain relevant geometrical aspects which he felt were outside his competence. He wrote a short tract, *The Zeta-Function of Riemann* (1930), and later a revised and enlarged edition, giving a connected account of his work on the subject, published in 1952, and also a book (*Introduction to the Theory of the Fourier Integrals*, 1937). The last synthesized his earlier papers on Fourier transforms and was translated into several foreign languages. All the subjects on which he worked were linked in some way, and his work led to results of importance in other fields. He studied a certain type of integral function with a view to applying the methods to the zeta function, and obtained thereby his 'convolution theorem' which is important in functional analysis because it shows that a certain algebra has no zero divisors. In middle life he began to consider the applications of Fourier integrals in quantum mechanics, but only ' as exercises in analysis'. This led to his work on eigenfunction expansions summed up in his two books *Eigenfunction Expansions Associated with Second-order Differential Equations* (part i, 1946, and part ii, 1958). These studies represent an outstanding contribution to functional analysis by completely classical methods. They are concerned with differential operators, both ordinary and partial, and the way in which the continuous spectrum of a perturbed operator degenerates into the discrete spectrum of the unperturbed operator. He also wrote a small book, *Mathematics for the General Reader* (1948), and contributed the notices of G. H. Hardy and G. B. Jeffery to this Dictionary.

Titchmarsh joined the London Mathematical Society in 1922 and was on its council (1925-9, 1932-6, and 1945-8), vice-president (1928-9), and president (1945-7). He received the De Morgan medal in 1953 and the Berwick prize in 1956. He was elected a fellow of the Royal Society in 1931 and received its Sylvester medal in 1955. An honorary D.Sc. was conferred upon him by Sheffield University. He seldom went to mathematical colloquia, but gave an invited address at the International Congress of Mathematicians at Amsterdam in 1954 and attended the congresses at Edinburgh in 1958 and at Stockholm in 1962. He went on a lecture tour in Holland after the Amsterdam Congress, and also later to Liège and Vienna. At the time of his death he was expecting to go to the USSR for a fortnight where his work on eigenfunctions is highly valued. Titchmarsh died at home in Capel Close, Oxford, 18 January 1963.

[Mary L. Cartwright in *Biographical Memoirs of Fellows of the Royal Society*, vol. x, 1964; *Journal of the London Mathematical Society*, vol. xxxix, 1964; *The Times*, 19 and 23 January 1963; private information; personal knowledge.]   M. L. CARTWRIGHT

TRAVERS, MORRIS WILLIAM (1872-1961), chemist, was born at Kensington, London, 24 January 1872, the second son of William Travers, MD, FRCS, and his wife, Anne Pocock, who was descended from the second son (Thomas) of the Revd Thomas Pocock, FRS, chaplain to the navy. At the age of twelve he went to Blundell's School, Tiverton, where he showed an early enthusiasm for science and won the fifth-form prize in chemistry. Since the sixth form was entirely classical he remained in the fifth until he left school to enter University College, London (1889). He obtained his B.Sc. with honours in chemistry in November 1893, but prior to that he had carried out minor research with Dr R. T. Plimpton on the metallic derivations of acetylene, during which he discovered a method of making calcium carbide by heating together calcium chloride, carbon, and sodium. He described the experiment in a paper with the title 'The Preparation of Acetylene from Calcium Carbide' published in the *Proceedings* of the Chemical Society (1893). This work, which has been generally overlooked, anticipated that of Henri Moissan by several months and rapidly developed as an important industry.

On the advice of Professor (Sir) William Ramsay [q.v.], Travers specialized in organic chemistry and went to study with Professor A. Haller at Nancy, but after a year he returned to Ramsay's laboratory at University College as a demonstrator. He returned at a critical time, since in March 1895 Ramsay had reported his discovery of helium and he joined him in working out the properties of this new gas. From then and until the summer of 1900 Travers worked continuously with Ramsay in the search for the missing elements, which the periodic law indicated should exist. It was in the course of this work that he developed many of the techniques for the handling of gases so ably described in his book *The Experimental Study of Gases*, published in 1901.

In May 1898, when examining the residues obtained by evaporating liquid air, Travers and Ramsay discovered the presence of and established by density measurements a further gas which they called 'krypton'. Further examination of liquid-air residues led to the discovery of 'neon' and 'xenon'. In the course of these studies Travers developed an apparatus — now in the Science Museum, South Kensington — for the liquefaction of hydrogen. The full story of these momentous discoveries is vividly told in his books *The Discovery of the Rare Gases* (1928), *William Ramsay and University College, London, 1852-1952* (1952), and *A Life of Sir William Ramsay, K.C.B., F.R.S.* (1956).

In 1898 Travers was appointed assistant professor at University College, London, and in 1904 he became professor of chemistry in University College, Bristol. During the two and a half years he was at Bristol he was very involved in the scheme to promote the college to full university status, and his work and enthusiasm was in no small measure responsible for the movement which culminated in the granting of the university charter in 1909.

In 1906 Travers went to India as director of the proposed Indian Institute of Science at Bangalore. After many difficulties the institute was brought into being in 1911. He retired at the end of his term of appointment and returned to England in 1914. The institute continued to develop along the lines he laid down, and was later to become one of the major scientific research institutes of India.

At the outbreak of war Travers joined the firm of Baird and Tatlock and made many important contributions to the war effort in the building of glass furnaces and in the production of scientific glassware and other glass articles. In 1920 he founded (with F. W. Clark) the firm of Travers and Clark Ltd. which specialized in the construction of glass furnaces and plant for the gasification of coal. The enterprise was abandoned in 1926.

Travers returned to Bristol in 1927 as an honorary professor and research fellow and soon developed a lively research group devoted to the study of the thermal decomposition of organic vapours. This work was discontinued at the outbreak of World War II, when Travers joined the Armament Research Department of the Ministry of Supply as a consultant on explosives. His work involved visiting ordnance factories and advising on technical problems concerning the manufacture of explosives and propellants. Although Travers finally retired in 1949 to Stroud, Gloucestershire, his enthusiasm for science and university affairs remained undiminished. He was a great letter writer, and all his former colleagues and students and friends were always kept well informed of his activities.

Travers was elected a fellow of the Royal Society in 1904. He was president of the

Faraday Society (1936–8) and served for many years on the council of the Institute of Fuel, of which he became a vice-president, and by which he was awarded the Melchett medal. He was president of the Society of Glass Technology (1921–2) and later an honorary fellow of the society.

In 1909 Travers married Dorothy, younger daughter of Robert J. Gray of London and of Melbourne, Australia. They had a son and a daughter. The son, Robert Morris William, is a psychologist who has held chairs at the universities of Ann Arbor and Utah, and who was formerly psychologist to the US Air Force. Travers died at Stroud, Gloucestershire, 25 August 1961.

[C. E. H. Bawn in *Biographical Memoirs of Fellows of the Royal Society*, vol. ix, 1963.]

C. E. H. BAWN

TREVELYAN, GEORGE MACAULAY (1876–1962), historian, third son of (Sir) George Otto Trevelyan [q.v.] and his wife, Caroline, was born 16 February 1876 at Welcombe, the Warwickshire house of his maternal grandfather, Robert Needham Philips, of Manchester. But the country which inspired his boyhood was the moorland of the Northumbrian Border where lay the Wallington property inherited by his father when he succeeded to the baronetcy in 1886. Young George followed his brothers to the house of E. E. Bowen [q.v.] at Harrow and in his last year was allowed to specialize in history, for which he had since childhood felt a vocation, under Townsend Warner. When only seventeen he went up to Trinity College, Cambridge, where he found congenial intellectual companionship. He became an 'Apostle', but his 'greatest friend through life' was Geoffrey Winthrop Young [q.v.], the poet and mountaineer. In his historical studies he benefited from the influence of Acton, Cunningham, and Maitland. Brought up to admire his great-uncle Macaulay as an historian and as a man, he resented Seeley's scorn of Macaulay and Carlyle as 'charlatans' and, later, Bury's description of history as 'a science, no less and no more'. His own essay *Clio, a Muse* (1913), expanded from an article of December 1903 in the *Independent Review* which he had helped to found, was a brilliant plea for history as being also a branch of literature. This essay, with others, was reissued with additions in 1919 as *The Recreations of an Historian* and under the original title in 1930.

After a first class in the historical tripos (1896) Trevelyan won a Trinity fellowship in 1898 with a dissertation, published next year as *England in the Age of Wycliffe* by Longmans,

who thus continued their long association with his family; already at Harrow he had declared himself a Liberal and home-ruler and that period appealed to the young radical as the meeting of medieval and modern thought in England, when the authority of the Church over men's minds was first challenged. The book was addressed to the general public, for he already believed that history was meant to be read. His next book was *England under the Stuarts* (1904) in Methuen's series. Both works showed anti-clerical and anti-authoritarian bias, but their honesty, vivid imagination, and attractive style deserved the success they achieved.

Trevelyan lectured and taught at Cambridge until 1903 when, having the financial means, he left the university for London, impelled partly by his conviction that 'the impalpable restrictions of the Cambridge ethos' discouraged the writing of literary history, partly by his interest in democratic politics and social service, which included lecturing at the Working Men's College in Bloomsbury.

Next year he married Janet Penrose, younger daughter of Humphry and Mary Ward [q.v.]. This marriage, 'the most important and fortunate event' of his life, was overshadowed only by the death in early childhood of their elder son Theodore. Their daughter Mary Caroline, historian of William III and biographer of Wordsworth, married John Moorman, afterwards bishop of Ripon; their younger son, Charles Humphry, fellow of King's, wrote on Goethe and the Greeks. Janet Trevelyan, herself an historian and biographer, was awarded the CH in 1936 for her labours in preserving the Foundling Hospital Site for the children of London and in the movement for play centres. They made their home in Chelsea until in 1919 they left London for Berkhamsted.

Trevelyan had for years known Italy as a walker and his father had introduced him to the Roman scene, already familiar from Macaulay's *Lays*. But it was a present of books on the *Risorgimento* that inspired him to write the trilogy on Garibaldi (1907, 1909, 1911) which made him famous. In the romantic career of this simple, heroic man of action he found a theme which gave scope alike to his enthusiasm for liberty and his narrative genius; besides the necessary research in libraries he traversed the ground on foot or bicycle and conversed with survivors of the campaigns.

Debarred by poor eyesight from combatant war service in 1914, Trevelyan raised and commanded a British Red Cross ambulance unit on the Italian front; he received Italian decorations and was appointed CBE in 1920. In 1913 he had published a *Life of John Bright*, and, after the war, in 1920, he completed a biography of *Lord Grey of the Reform Bill*. Much later, in 1937, he wrote the life of *Grey of Fallodon*, the foreign secretary, whose love of nature and 'grand simplicity' appealed to him profoundly. He wrote Grey's notice for this Dictionary and also one of his father, of whom he published a *Memoir* in 1932. Meanwhile he had written two single-volume books, *British History in the Nineteenth Century* (1922) and *History of England* (1926). Both were popular successes, especially the latter, some of which he had used for his Lowell lectures in 1924 in Boston. At Oxford in 1926 he gave the Romanes lecture on 'The Two-party System in English Political History'. He was now the most widely read and admired of living British historians, unequalled in narrative and descriptive power.

In 1927 Trevelyan was appointed regius professor of modern history at Cambridge. As professor he was unselfish in his help to young researchers and he now embarked on a grand-scale history of *England under Queen Anne*, the three volumes of which appeared in 1930, 1932, 1934. He considered these, along with the Garibaldi trilogy, his best historical work. He had always liked military history and he enjoyed working on a period which saw the stabilizing of conditions at home and England's rise to greatness abroad. The first volume, *Blenheim*, in particular, was a splendid piece of descriptive writing with a fine dramatic fervour.

In 1940 Trevelyan was appointed to the mastership of Trinity College, Cambridge, on the advice of the prime minister, (Sir) Winston Churchill, to whose attack on Macaulay's treatment of Marlborough he had replied in *The Times Literary Supplement* (19 October 1933). Alike in war and peace the master and his wife exploited to the full their opportunities for hospitality; his delight in showing off its beauties led him to publish an admirable historical sketch of the college. His relations with both seniors and juniors were perfect; he was a wise chairman in council, exploding occasionally into devastating comment. Under the new statutes the master's retiring age was seventy with a possible extension to seventy-five; Trevelyan's tenure was unanimously prolonged by the fellows for the full period allowed: he retired in 1951.

During the war he finished the book which has had the largest circulation of all his works, *English Social History* (1944), planned as a companion to his *History of England* but limited by wartime restrictions to a 'survey of the six centuries from Chaucer to Victoria'. This book and the Garibaldi and Queen Anne volumes are likely to be the longest remembered of his writings. Critics will disagree about their order of merit, but it was appropriate that the

Festschrift edited by J. H. Plumb and produced in Trevelyan's honour in 1955 should consist of *Studies in Social History*.

In 1949 Trevelyan published a volume of essays mainly on historical subjects, prefaced by fifty pages of autobiography. He had been, he wrote, 'not an original but a traditional kind of historian', keeping up 'a family tradition as to the relation of history to literature'. From his earliest days he had read poetry with delight amounting to passion and he knew long passages by heart. To him the chief value of history was poetic. Its poetic value depended, however, on its being a true record of actual happenings; in its mysterious power of restoring to us the hopes and fears of real people, most forcibly when we visit the very ground their feet have trodden. With something of a poet's imagination he contrived to re-create the life of long ago. Besides his historical works, all enriched by apt literary allusions, he published several books of literary appreciation: an essay on *The Poetry and Philosophy of George Meredith* (1906), anthologies from Meredith (1955) and Carlyle (1953), and, in 1954, *A Layman's Love of Letters*, his Cambridge Clark lectures, perhaps the most self-revealing of all his works. In 1951 he was president of the English Association.

It has been said that Trevelyan was not a scientific historian. This is untrue if it implies that he was remiss in seeking for and testing evidence or was capable of conscious distortion. He knew that no one can escape personal bias and he freely admitted and tried to correct his own: his volumes on Garibaldi, he said, were 'reeking with bias' and he recognized that his books on English history were similarly slanted. He wrote in the Whig tradition of his great-uncle and father. He admitted too his penchant for 'happy endings', and he reckoned happiness from the standpoint of a patriotic English Liberal. Further, in treating long periods in reasonable compass he was bound to make generalizations which a minute examination of local or personal records or a trained study of statistics in the modern style would have modified. Though he regretted Macaulay's tendency to see his characters all black or all white, his own mind was not analytical and he made no pretence of being a psychologist.

Trevelyan claimed to have no philosophy of history beyond 'a love of things good and a hatred of things evil'. Early in life he rejected the dogmas of Christianity but he respected its moral standards. The essence of religion was to him not a creed but an attitude to life. He found his own inspiration in great poetry and in nature. Wordsworth and Meredith were among his prophets; he believed, like Meredith, in the essential goodness of life and the grandeur of the human spirit. In religion as in politics and in writing history the fiery radical acquired in time greater tolerance and broader sympathies.

In youth he felt a 'physical and spiritual need for long, rapid and usually solitary walks across country'. His *Social History* is replete with nostalgia for the unspoilt beauty of the green island, which eighteenth-century taste had only enhanced, until the industrial revolution largely destroyed it. He had been left by a distant relative a country house in Northumberland, Hallington Hall, near Wallington, the family seat, which after 1928 became a holiday home. He was an active and munificent supporter of the National Trust and similar attempts to preserve what beauty still remained. For many years from its foundation in 1931 he was president of the Youth Hostels Association.

In other matters too he had a strong sense of public duty. He served on the royal commission on Oxford and Cambridge which reported in 1922 and was a trustee of the British Museum and of the National Portrait Gallery. He wisely declined the directorship of the London School of Economics in 1908 and withdrew his name when submitted, with two others, for the governor-generalship of Canada in 1945. He declined the presidency of the British Academy but was proud to be chosen as chancellor of Durham University (1950-8) and as high steward of the city of Cambridge in 1946. In 1930 he was appointed to the Order of Merit. He was elected FBA (1925), FRS (1950), and an honorary fellow of Oriel College, Oxford, and was an honorary doctor of many universities including his own, in which a lectureship was founded in his honour. The Trevelyan scholarship scheme for schoolboys showed how widely his name was respected.

After his retirement from the mastership he continued to live at Cambridge, retreating to Hallington in the summer until the move became too tiring. The decline of European civilization, as he saw it, and especially the degradation of Italy under Fascism had long depressed him. Failing eyesight limited his reading and his wife's death in 1956 after a long illness hit him hard. He died in Cambridge 21 July 1962. In 1965 Side House Farm in Langdale was bought as a memorial to him, thus completing the series of neighbouring farms which he had himself bought and given to the nation.

Physically Trevelyan was tall and energetic, a fabulous walker; later, as a Northumbrian squire, he enjoyed shooting. His austere features and eager glance could be formidable, as could the forthright, though never discourteous, expression of his opinions, following sometimes a long, brooding silence. Normally his conversation, with its selective humour, made him excellent company. He did not conceal his detestation of cruelty, cant, and meanness, but he was incapable of malice and could not easily see defects in a friend. Among his conspicuous virtues were honesty, humanity, humility, and a complete absence of self-consciousness. Old age, as it added dignity to his aspect, taught him patience in adversity, especially when his eyesight was failing, and emphasized the nobility of his character.

A portrait by E. H. Nelson hangs in the hall of Trinity College; there are several drawings: three by Sir William Rothenstein (one, 1913, in Trinity College library, one in the National Portrait Gallery, one in the possession of the family who also have a drawing (1925) by C. Geoffrey), one by Francis Dodd (1933) in the National Portrait Gallery, and one by John Mansbridge; an impressive photograph is reproduced in Plumb's Festschrift.

[*The Times* and *Guardian*, 23 July 1962; G. M. Trevelyan, *An Autobiography and other Essays*, 1949; Sir G. N. Clark in *Proceedings* of the British Academy, vol. xlix, 1963; G. Kitson Clark in *Durham University Journal*, December 1962; J. H. Plumb, British Council pamphlet (1951) reprinted in *Men and Places*, 1963; Owen Chadwick, *Freedom and the Historian*, 1969; Mary Moorman (daughter), *George Macaulay Trevelyan: a Memoir*, 1980; Humphrey Trevelyan, *Public and Private*, 1980; private information personal knowledge.   J. R. M. BUTLER

TUKER, SIR FRANCIS IVAN SIMMS (1894-1967), lieutenant-general, was born in Brighton 14 July 1894, the son of William John Sanger Tucker, a coffee planter in the West Indies who later became a fruit grower in Essex, and his wife, Katharine Louisa Simms. He was educated at Brighton College, whence he went to the Royal Military College, Sandhurst, and seems at about this time to have changed his name to Tuker. In 1914 he was commissioned and attached to the Royal Sussex Regiment, with which he never lost contact, before joining the 2nd King Edward's Own Gurkha Rifles (the Sirmoor Rifles). He served with them throughout the war of 1914-18 in which he was wounded, and saw further active service in the Kuki punitive expedition of 1918 and in 1920 in north-west Persia against the Bolsheviks. In these years were laid the seeds of his exceptional interest, understanding, and affection for the Gurkhas with whom he served, an intense regard which remained undiminished until his death.

In 1925 Tuker entered the Staff College, Camberley. The next ten years were passed in tours of duty with his regiment, alternating with staff appointments. In 1937 he achieved his ambition—command of the 1st battalion of the 2nd King Edward's Own Gurkhas in operations in Waziristan on the North-West Frontier of India. He was appointed OBE and mentioned in dispatches. In the preceding years, as adjutant of the 1st battalion (1920-3) and later in other regimental appointments, he had introduced training methods which discarded the rather stereotyped tactics of the previous twenty years and placed more emphasis on aggressive action to surround the tribesman on his home ground. This training resulted in great successes and under his leadership the 1st battalion attained the highest reputation.

In the years immediately before the outbreak of war in 1939 Tuker published a number of articles on the future pattern of war and the policing of the North-West Frontier. His views on training and his success in command during operations brought him to notice as a keen professional soldier with original and far-seeing views. His criticisms of the tactical methods used in mountain warfare had been justified by the results he obtained in Waziristan. His opinions on the lack of preparedness for war, particularly on the shortage of ordnance factories and arsenals in India, and of tactical training which he considered out of date, raised feelings of uneasiness and suspicion but could not be ignored.

Soon after the outbreak of war Tuker became director of military training at general headquarters, India, with the rank of brigadier. His appointment occasioned much interest and some misgivings, but his views were to be vindicated by the test of war. He was promoted major-general in 1941 and given command of the newly formed 34th Indian division. Shortly afterwards he was appointed to command the 4th Indian division in the Western Desert, and joined then in 1942 at the beginning of the six months' period of disaster culminating in the retreat to El Alamein. Throughout this gruelling period his handling of his division was marked by unusual professional skill, courage and tenacity, and he remained in command of his division throughout the battle of El Alamein and the subsequent advance of Tunisia. The results of his earlier training methods were apparent in the outstanding performance of his division and in particular of the 1st battalion of his old regiment.

Undoubtedly Tuker's greatest military success lay in the bold and daring plan he proposed to break into the left flank of a position of great natural strength which the enemy held on the Tunisian massif after the Mareth Line had been turned by the Eighth Army. A silent attack at Fatnassa meticulously carried out by the 2nd and 9th Gurkhas accomplished an almost im-

possible task during the night of 5/6 April 1943 without artillery support and with casualties so light as to be unbelievable. Such losses reflected the high training and exuberant morale of soldiers trained by a master to perfection. The road from Akarit lay open: the obstacles to the junction of the Eighth and First Armies had been destroyed by Tuker's division in a military operation which with revealing modesty he described as 'so near the borderline of imbecility and impossibility that the outcome could not possibly have lain in my hands'. Tuker was appointed CB and to the DSO and twice mentioned in dispatches.

His division did not see service in the invasion of Sicily and by the time it was employed at Cassino Tuker had fallen sick, the first indications of the disease which was to end his military career prematurely and ultimately to cause his death. On his recovery he was recalled to India (1944). After a period as general officer commanding Ceylon (1945), he was appointed to the command of the IV Indian Corps in Burma. He was in time to direct the last battle which was fought in the monsoon rains to prevent the breakout of the Japanese forces contained by the Fourteenth Army's drive on Rangoon, and to inflict devastating losses on the Japanese.

Returning to India, Tuker commanded the Lucknow District and then in 1946-7 served as commander-in-chief, Eastern Command, a vast area of great sensitivity reaching from Delhi to Assam. His foresight and understanding made a major contribution to the stability of this area, racked by the aftermath of war so recently concluded on its eastern boundaries and perplexed and harassed by birth throes of independence. The only stable factor was the Indian Army which stood firm, secure in the confidence it reposed in the presence of its senior officers. Upon Tuker, within his command, rested the ultimate burden of responsibility. This period of his service is described in his book *While Memory Serves* (1950), and against the background of incalculable confusion which it describes two factors stand forth: the courage and steadfastness of Tuker and the indomitable loyalty and stability of the Indian soldiers under his command.

Tuker was appointed KCIE in 1946 and in the same year became colonel of the 2nd King Edward VII's Own Gurkha Rifles (the Sirmoor Rifles), an appointment which was to him the highest honour of his career. He retired from the army in 1948, having reached the rank of lieutenant-general in 1945.

In 1923 Tuker married Catherine Isabella, daughter of William St. Vincent Bucknall, of Horsham; they had three daughters. His wife died in 1947 and in 1948 he married Cynthia

Helen, daughter of Ronald Gale, of Sevenoaks, and widow of Lieutenant-Colonel Robbie Fawcett of the 9th Gurkhas. They settled at Bosilliac, Mawnan Smith, Cornwall, where they sailed, developed a thriving fruit and flower farm, and Tuker wrote. The majority of his books were concerned with military subjects and were written in the lively style which reflected his zest and interest in anything he undertook. His works included *The Pattern of War* (1948), *Approach to Battle* (1963), and *Gorkha* (1957), a classic on Nepal and the hillmen he so loved and admired, which was awarded the Sykes memorial medal of the Royal Central Asian Society. He also wrote some verse and in 1965 an operetta *May I Call You Julie?*

Never a patient man, Tuker fought against increasing infirmity with his customary courage and determination. He died at his home, Bosilliac, 7 October 1967.

[Regimental records; private information; personal knowledge.]   LEWIS PUGH

TULLOCH, WILLIAM JOHN (1887–1966), professor of bacteriology, was born 12 November 1887 at Dundee, the youngest in the family of two sons and three daughters of Henry Tulloch, hatter, by his wife, Coralie van Wasserhove of Waerschoot in Belgium. He was educated at Dundee High School, became dux of the school and won the Walter Pollock memorial prize. He studied medicine at the university of St. Andrews and graduated MB, Ch.B. with distinction in 1909 at the early age of twenty-one, winning thirteen class medals during his undergraduate course. He became a house doctor at the Royal Infirmary of Hull but within months the university of St. Andrews claimed him to become assistant to Professor L. R. Sutherland in the department of pathology in Dundee. In 1911 he went to Newcastle as assistant in comparative pathology in the Durham College of Medicine and during his time there investigated and diagnosed a fatal case of septicaemic plague, a notable feat for a young bacteriologist.

Tulloch returned to Dundee in October 1914 as lecturer in bacteriology and in the same year was awarded the degree of Doctor of Medicine of St. Andrews with honours for a thesis entitled 'The Influence of Electrolytes on Agglutination'. In the January of the following year he married Florence Sheridan (died 1975); they had one son and two daughters. In March 1916 he entered the Royal Army Medical College at Milbank, where he remained until 1919. He was allotted to bacteriological work and was in contact with Sir David Bruce [q.v.]. He had many stories of Bruce whom he admired greatly. He was engaged on two important problems of great consequence, wound infections, especially the incidence of tetanus, and outbreaks of cerebro-spinal fever in young soldiers in crowded barracks. His work was very much appreciated and he was mentioned in dispatches, promoted major RAMC and appointed OBE (military division) in May 1919. His work in the war years was recorded in Medical Research Council *Special Reports* and also in the *Proceedings* of the Royal Society, Series B, 1918 and 1919.

On his discharge from war service he returned to Dundee to resume his duties as lecturer. He set up the bacteriology department and organized the public health bacteriology in Dundee. He was appointed professor of bacteriology in October 1921, the first occupant of the chair. In addition to his teaching commitments, he was bacteriologist to Dundee Royal Infirmary and responsible for the public health bacteriology not only in Dundee but also in the counties of Angus, Fife, and Perth. His research activities continued and he made important contributions to the subject of gonorrhoea and the serological diagnosis of smallpox. Of all his various duties, the one which he loved best and which was his first priority was the teaching of medical students. He was a dynamic and conscientious teacher—as generations of graduates testified. Indeed many can still recall what Tulloch said and there is no doubt his relations with his students were unique. He called them 'those lovable creatures'. He knew all of them and much about them and he set out to teach them not a dry technical discipline but a living practical subject using his gift for acting, thus making the subject come alive. He educated his students in the widest sense and had no time for lists of facts. His relations with his professorial colleagues and technical staff were friendly and understanding, and his opinion was sought and usually accepted by members of the university and others outside. He was a man of strong religious belief which coloured his life and produced a compassionate relationship with students, colleagues, and others.

Among his many commitments on committees on which he served with distinction he was a member of the General Medical Council from 1949 to 1962 and of the General Dental Council from 1956 to 1959. He was dean of the faculty of medicine from 1945 to 1956 during a time of expansion in the university and carried out the duties and responsibilities of this office with his usual efficiency and tact. One of the last professors appointed *ad vitam et culpam* he retired voluntarily in September 1962 when he was honoured by the university with the degree of D.Sc., the first occasion on which this honorary degree had been awarded. Outside his professional life he was interested in the history of the Dutch Republic on which he was very knowledgeable, and in his time he had been a sprinter, yachtsman, and an expert figure-skater. On retirement he went to live in Hampshire to be near one of his daughters and her family; he doted on his grandchildren. The writer was privileged to spend a week-end with him there and saw him trying to lose a game of chess to a grandson. He still retained his enthusiasm and sharp intellect and questioned the writer closely about recent advances in bacteriology and, as always, pinpointed the weakness in an argument. He remained mentally sharp and kindly in dealing with those with whom he came in contact. He died in Cosham, Hampshire, 26 August 1966.

There is a portrait in oils by A. G. R. Ross (1936) at Ninewells Hospital, Dundee.

[*The College*, vol. xx, 1921-2; J. W. McLeod in *Journal of Pathology and Bacteriology*, vol. xcv, 1968; private information; personal knowledge.]   DAVID M. GREEN

TURNER, EUSTACE EBENEZER (1893-1966), organic chemist, was born in Bromley, London, 22 May 1893, the youngest in the family of one daughter and two sons of John Turner, salesman, and later piano merchant, whose family came from Finchingfield, Essex, and his wife, Annie Elizabeth Coates, from Windermere.

Turner's interest in organic chemistry began at an early age, and while still a schoolboy at the Coopers' Company's School, he practised organic chemistry in a room at his home. He entered East London (now Queen Mary) College, London, with an exhibition in 1910 to study chemistry, and graduated B.Sc. with first class honours in chemistry in 1913. (He obtained a London D.Sc. in 1920.) During the vacation of 1913 a lifelong interest in the chemistry of biaryls bore its first fruit in a piece of research on their preparation by the reaction of Grignard reagents with chromic chloride. This research was conducted with G. M. Bennett [q.v.], who was later professor of organic chemistry at King's College, London, and then the government chemist, and was the basis of Turner's first paper (jointly with Bennett) in the *Journal of the Chemical Society*, vol. cv, 1914.

Turner's interest in biaryls was sustained during 1914 and 1915 when he held a lectureship at Goldsmiths' College, because it was during this period that he expressed doubts, in a published paper, about the validity of the then accepted Kaufler formula for biphenyl, citing as experimental evidence the non-formation of

rings involving the 4- and 4'-position. Such ring formation would have been expected on the basis of the Kaufler formula, in which these positions are represented as being close together. Turner was, of course, correct, as later work by himself and others amply demonstrated.

From 1916 to 1919 Turner was engaged in work on organo-arsenic compounds as chemical warfare agents with (Sir) W. J. Pope [q.v.], whose research assistant he was, at Cambridge, where he was a member of Sidney Sussex College. The interest which he there acquired in the organic chemistry of arsenic was sustained during the next two years during which he held a lectureship in organic chemistry at the university of Sydney, and, in collaboration with G. J. Burrows, he was able to demonstrate optical activity in a quaternary arsonium salt. During his time at Sydney, Turner took part in an anthropological expedition to New Guinea with W. E. Armstrong. Some of the specimens collected on this expedition are in the Sydney Museum.

Perhaps more importantly, and certainly more felicitously, while at Sydney, Turner married in 1921 Beryl Osborne, daughter of Reginald Wyndham, of New South Wales. They had one daughter.

In 1921 Turner returned to England and worked at the Royal Arsenal, Woolwich, until 1923, when he was appointed as senior lecturer at Queen Mary College. In 1928 he became reader at Bedford College in Regent's Park, where he spent the rest of his academic career. The title of professor was conferred upon him in 1944, and in 1946, on the retirement of J. F. Spencer, he became head of the chemistry department. On his retirement in 1960 he was made professor emeritus, and continued to work in the organic chemical field as research director of Biorex Laboratories for several years.

Turner's contributions to modern organic chemistry were inspired largely by his lifelong interests in stereochemistry and biaryls. With R. J. W. Le Fèvre he contributed greatly to the establishment of the correct 'linear' structure of the biaryl system, and explained the occurrence of optical isomerism in biphenyl derivatives substituted in 2-, 2'-, 6- and 6'-positions as being due to restricted rotation about the internuclear bond. Although he made outstanding contributions to other areas of organic chemistry with colleagues at Bedford College, it is for his work in this field that he will be mainly remembered. In the course of this work many fundamental stereochemical concepts (such as that of 'asymmetric transformation') were established. His many distinguished colleagues at Bedford College included Mary S. Lesslie, Margaret M. Harris (with whom he wrote his classic textbook, *Organic Chemistry*, 1952), and D. Muriel Hall.

Turner's distinction was recognized in 1939 by his election to the fellowship of the Royal Society. He was also a fellow of the Royal Institute of Chemistry, and served on the council of the Chemical Society. He was a fellow of Queen Mary College, a freeman of the City of London, and a liveryman of the Coopers' Company. He gave distinguished service on many Bedford College and university of London bodies and was for many years assistant editor of *British Chemical Abstracts*.

Turner was essentially an experimentalist, and the practice of organic chemistry was his abiding interest in life. However, he took an intense personal interest in all his assistants and collaborators, both students and colleagues, both academic and technical. He was a witty and amusing raconteur and mimic with a keen sense of humour and a sometimes disconcerting knack of puncturing the pompous. Turner greatly enjoyed his own pleasant garden, as well as the wider countryside; he was a particularly enthusiastic motorist. He died at his home in Tonbridge 8 September 1966.

[Christopher Ingold in *Biographical Memoirs of Fellows of the Royal Society*, vol. xiv, 1968; *Chemistry in Britain*, 1967; *Chemistry and Industry*, 1966; personal knowledge.]

G. H. WILLIAMS

TURNER, GEORGE CHARLEWOOD (1891–1967), headmaster of Marlborough College and university principal of Makerere College, Uganda, of which he was later made an honorary fellow, was born 27 March 1891, the fourth son in the family of four sons and five daughters of the Revd Charles Henry Turner, later bishop of Islington, and his wife, Edith Emma, daughter of the Revd Alfred Earle MacDougall, who later became a bishop. A large, intelligent, and self-sufficient family, centring on his able and charming mother, set the tone of his character, of the incisive confidence of his judgements and of his instinctive ease and elegance. He was educated at Marlborough and at Magdalen College, Oxford, where from 1910 to 1914 he was a classical demy. At Marlborough he was deeply influenced by the Master, (Sir) Frank Fletcher [q.v.], whose scholarship and force he admired, and at Magdalen he absorbed the traditional values of classical Oxford, though his second class in classical moderations (1912) and second class in *literae humaniores* (1914) hardly represented the outstanding abilities he afterwards displayed.

Commissioned in 1914 in the 23rd London Regiment, from 1914 to 1919 he served on the general staff 47th (London) division, being twice mentioned in dispatches, reaching the rank of major, and in 1918 being awarded the MC. This decoration, according to his own account, he obtained simply by presence of mind; when, armed only with a walking stick, he chanced on some Germans in a dug-out, he at once put up his stick and ordered them in their own language 'follow me!' This they promptly did.

In 1919, matured and hardened by the war, Turner returned as an assistant master to Marlborough, where since 1916 (Sir) Cyril Norwood [q.v.] had been Master. Here, besides working under a great headmaster, Turner found congenial colleagues, particularly C. B. Canning, afterwards headmaster of Canford. Norwood had reorganized Marlborough with outstanding success, and Turner contributed to this phase of all-round achievement; but it was flawed by a rift between the 'aesthetes' or 'intellectuals' and the 'hearties', who, not least on the staff, made a philistine and exclusive cult of games; and when in 1925 Norwood (whose notice Turner contributed to this Dictionary) had left for Harrow and Turner succeeded him as Master, he proved just the person to assuage the conflict without friction.

Turner accomplished this civilizing mission more by example than by precept. He had been a boy at Marlborough, a young master, a housemaster, and he knew what every stratum needed to attain this humane objective, which he summed up in his advice: 'Remember, we are teaching boys, not subjects.' As one boy later put it, 'He didn't do anything; he just was, and that was enough'. In fact he 'did' a good deal, consolidating and rounding off Norwood's reforms, abolishing beating by house captains, and entertaining with elegant hospitality at the Lodge, 'run' for him first by his mother, then by his sister, Ruth. Though he could wield easy authority, he was not aloof, and would often of an evening visit colleagues for a talk. He encouraged the arts and drama, and, himself a good actor, would sing tunefully at school concerts.

Though happy at Marlborough, when in 1939 he was invited to become principal of Makerere University College, Kampala, Uganda, he welcomed the exotic adventure, remarking with typical understatement, 'One can't do the same thing all one's life'. At Makerere he was intrigued by new social conventions; as when one of his students confided that, having got a girl in the family way, he was ready either to marry her or 'pay her family four goats'. 'How much more convenient' wrote Turner, 'are the African conventions than our own!'

Turner's influence at Makerere proved pervasive and important, since many of his students who had studied the humanities and the arts as well as agriculture, science, and technology, took up key positions in East Africa. As at Marlborough, he made his high standards catching by example, and when in 1963 the college became part of the university of East Africa and in 1970 a university in its own right, Turner's influence was further developed. In 1944 he was appointed an honorary fellow of Makerere and in 1945 he was appointed CMG.

In 1947 Turner was appointed headmaster of Charterhouse. Here, after wartime difficulties, his mild but firm regime gave needed time for recovery. Within clearly defined limits, he had always been tolerant; now he remarked, 'at my age I can no longer take too seriously the peccadilloes of the young'. He was particularly helpful and considerate to colleagues, and the big chapel at Charterhouse made a setting for the clarity and wisdom of sermons well adapted to his congregation.

In 1950 Turner was chairman of the Headmasters' Conference; he also made a tour of schools in Australia and helped to establish Kurt Hahn, the founder of Salem in Germany, at Gordonstoun, of which Turner became a governor. He never married, and in 1952 retired to a spacious house in Chichester, which he made a headquarters for his surviving brothers and sisters. He died 11 April 1967 at Chichester.

Turner was small, neat, and handsome, with fine dark eyes and a mellifluous voice. With a successful headmaster's sense of occasion and power of command, he was dignified but never pompous, and, with a singular flair for essentials, made memorable remarks in a polite and sometimes quaintly academic manner. His competence, insight, and kindness made him widely admired and beloved. He was a salutary and civilizing influence in the public school life of his time.

There is an excellent portrait of him at Marlborough by R. G. Eves (1939), and at Charterhouse by Peter Greenham (1952).

[Private information; personal knowledge.]
JOHN BOWLE

TURNER, HAROLD (1909–1962), ballet dancer, was born in Manchester 2 December 1909, the son of Edward Harold Turner, viola player with the Hallé Orchestra and the London Symphony Orchestra, and his wife, Laura Greenwood. He studied dancing with Alfred Haines in Manchester, making his stage début at a pupil show in 1927. Shortly afterwards he went to London and started work first with Léonide Massine and then with (Dame) Marie Rambert, making one of a talented group with such dancers as Pearl Argyle, Diana Gould, and Prudence Hyman, and the choreographers

(Sir) Frederick W. M. Ashton and Andrée Howard. He soon established himself as a strong classical dancer, creating two roles in Ashton ballets, *Les Petits Riens* in 1928 and *Capriol Suite* in 1930. In the same year he partnered Tamara Karsavina in *Les Sylphides* and *Le Spectre de la Rose*. He appeared in Camargo Society performances, as guest artist in 1929–30 at the Vic-Wells Ballet (which later became the Sadler's Wells Ballet and subsequently the Royal Ballet). In 1935 he became a permanent member of the company taking leads in the classical ballets and creating the red knight (*Checkmate*), the blue skater (*Les Patineurs*), and the dancing master (*The Rake's Progress*).

Turner remained with the company except for a brief interval with the International Ballet and the Arts Theatre Ballet and for war service in the Royal Air Force, retiring in 1955 save for an occasional guest appearance. He then taught at the Royal Ballet School and became a director of the Covent Garden Opera Ballet.

Harold Turner's contribution to British ballet was a major one. He was the first outstanding male dancer to win acclaim under his own English name. He was virile, a brilliant technician who shone in such dances as the blue bird in *The Sleeping Beauty* and the peasant's *pas de deux* in *Giselle*. The blue skater in *Les Patineurs* was an astonishing piece of *brio*. He was a considerate partner, a *danseur noble*, who always showed his ballerina to advantage, yet he was versatile enough to dance such character roles as the miller in *The Three Cornered Hat* and the cancan dancer in *La Boutique Fantasque* and to make an impact in a small character role, the chief coachman in *Petrouchka*, which was in fact his last appearance. In addition to the handicap of an English name, he had to overcome the additional handicap, a severe one until recently, of the prejudice against male dancers. His athleticism did much to dispel this prejudice, to make the path of his successors an easier one, and to help in the recruitment of male dancers.

In 1938 Turner married Mary Honer. The marriage was dissolved and in 1944 he married, secondly, Gerd, daughter of Leonard Larsen, civil servant with the Norwegian government, of Oslo. She was herself a dancer and became the senior teacher at the Royal Ballet. There was one daughter of the second marriage.

In 1962 Turner was returning to play the role of the elderly marquis in a revival of the Massine ballet *The Good-humoured Ladies* with a distinguished cast which included Lydia Sokolova. He died after a rehearsal in his dressing-room at Covent Garden 2 July 1962.

Two drawings by T. H. Elliot are in the possession of the family.

[*The Times*, 3 July 1962; *Dancing Times*, August 1971; private information.]

ARNOLD HASKELL

TURNER, WILLIAM ERNEST STEPHEN (1881-1963), chemist and first professor of glass technology in the university of Sheffield, was born in Wednesbury, Staffordshire, 22 September 1881, the eldest son and second of the seven children of William George Turner and his wife, Emma Blanche Gardner, daughter of a London tradesman. His father was self-educated and shared in the precarious employment of those times, being successively railway porter, signalman, ironworks labourer, post-man, and industrial insurance agent; he also served, throughout his working life, as deacon and elder in the Church of the Baptist Brethren in Smethwick.

From the Crocketts Lane Board School in Smethwick Turner went with a county minor scholarship to the King Edward VI Grammar School, Five Ways, Birmingham. After a distinguished school career he entered the Mason (University) College with a school-leaving scholarship and graduated with first class honours in the chemistry B.Sc. (external) of the university of London in 1902. A research scholarship then enabled him to work with Dr Alex Findlay and he proceeded to M.Sc. (Birmingham) in 1904 with the Erhardt research prize. He proceeded to his external London D.Sc. in chemistry in 1911.

An appointment in 1904 as junior demonstrator and lecturer took him to the University College of Sheffield under W. P. Wynne. His interest in the application of science to industrial problems was revealed immediately in a course of lectures in physical chemistry which he prepared for students of metallurgy; in response to requests from metallurgists in industry the lectures were repeated in the evenings. During the spring of 1909 Turner wrote a series of articles for the *Sheffield Daily Telegraph* discussing the employment of scientists in industry. These were serious articles containing much factual information in which the practice of this country was contrasted with that of Germany. When World War I began Turner realized that local industries might welcome help from the scientists in the university and proposed the formation of a technical advisory committee; at the end of September 1914 a university scientific advisory committee was formed with Turner as secretary. As soon as the existence of the committee was advertised questions began to arrive from many of the glass plants near Sheffield. By May 1915 Turner had prepared a report which drew attention to the lack of any scientific method in the glass industry; a department to provide courses in glass manufacture with facilities for research was formed in the following month, and soon afterwards Turner introduced the term 'glass technology', with which his name became associated.

Early in 1916 the committee of the Privy Council for scientific and industrial research provided funds for the new department which were to be administered not by the university council but by a separate body known as the 'Glass Research Delegacy'. The delegacy, composed of industrialists and academic representatives of the senate, in about equal numbers, continued until 1955. Members of the staff regularly visited glass plants, and the research programme was framed with the solution of industrial problems in mind. However, as time passed, the success of the department's activities and the increased employment in industry of people with some education in science changed the nature of the problems. In 1955 the Department of Scientific and Industrial Research made funds available to a newly formed British Glass Industry Research Association. The university department and the Research Association later continued their separate functions in adjacent buildings. Nevertheless, Turner's original concept might still have found favour today; he certainly had an inspired vision of university and industry in co-operation.

The university department had moved to Darnall Road in 1920, when research contracts from a Glass Research Association which existed from 1919 to 1925 made it necessary to find glass-making facilities in an old glasshouse; for many years Turner sought to bring back the department into the university area and in 1936-7 he raised, in a few months, funds from the industry to buy and convert a house ('Elmfield') into a home for the department. It was well equipped with laboratories, a library, lecture rooms, and a museum in which Turner justifiably had great pride.

From the beginning of his work in glass technology Turner's grasp of the importance of communication was evident. In 1916 he founded the Society of Glass Technology of which he was secretary from 1916 to 1922, 1924 to 1937, and 1938 to 1946, and editor of its journal until 1951. The journals of the society are a monument to his hard work and the success of his endeavours. He also played a major role in the formation of the International Commission on Glass. Both institutions flourished. The commission developed a series of triennial meetings attended by nearly 1,000 delegates from more than twenty countries and also became responsible for much international technical co-operation; Turner was the acknowledged and respected leader of these activities.

In 1918 Turner was appointed OBE, in recognition of his services in organizing the application of science to the glass industry. He became FRS (1938), and honorary D.Sc.Tech. (Sheffield, 1954). He was the only person from outside Germany to receive the Otto Schott commemoration medal (1955). In 1943 he received the silver medal of the Royal Society of Arts. He was a founder-fellow of the Institute of Physics, an honorary fellow of the Society of Glass Technology, honorary president of the International Commission on Glass, an honorary fellow of the Institute of Ceramics, an honorary member of the American Ceramic Society, and of the Deutsche Glastechnische Gesellschaft; a foreign member of the Masaryk Academy of Prague; and an honorary freeman of the Worshipful Company of Glass Sellers of the City of London. He was also FSA (1958).

In 1908 he married his first wife, Mary Isobel (died 1939), daughter of John Marshall, a tradesman, of Birmingham. Of their four children (two sons and two daughters), the Revd E. M. Turner, now retired, was for many years rector of Eyam, the Derbyshire Peak District village. The second son, Eric, FBA, was, until his retirement in 1978, professor of papyrology in University College, London, and the director of the Institute of Classical Studies of the university of London. In his early manhood Turner was active in the church and with his first wife he played an important role for many years in the Rutland Hall Settlement in Sheffield. After his first wife's death, in 1943 Turner married Annie Helen Nairn Monro, the well-known glass engraver, who died 21 September 1977. Helen Turner taught in the Edinburgh College of Art and had a studio in Juniper Green, near Edinburgh.

When very young Turner suffered an attack of poliomyelitis which led to atrophy of some muscles of the right arm and general retardation of the development of the right side from the abdomen upwards. This handicap hardly affected him; he was a member of the Swiss Alpine Club and derived tremendous enjoyment from his expeditions which ranged from the mountains of New Zealand and the Alps to the moors near Sheffield. With his first wife, on her fifty-eighth birthday, he walked over the Col d'Herens; leaving soon after daybreak they traversed the Tête Blanche at 12,400 ft. in heavy snow and after fourteen hours reached Ferpécle.

For some time after Turner's retirement from the university in 1945, he worked with Edward Meigh in the joint consulting firm—Glass Technical Services—and maintained his house in Sheffield. His last years were spent in Juniper Green where he died 27 October 1963. A portrait by Edward I. Halliday hangs in the lecture room at Elmfield.

[R. W. Douglas in *Biographical Memoirs of Fellows of the Royal Society*, vol. x, 1964; W. E. S. Turner, 'Memorial Lecture', *Glass Technology*, vol. viii, 1967; private information.]   R. W. Douglas

TURNOUR, EDWARD, sixth Earl Winterton and Baron Turnour (1883-1962), politician, was born in London 4 April 1883, the only child of Edward Turnour, fifth Earl Winterton, by his wife, Lady Georgiana Susan Hamilton, fifth daughter of James Hamilton, first Duke of Abercorn [q.v.]. Educated at Eton and at New College, Oxford, where he studied law, he had hardly begun his third year as an undergraduate when at a by-election in November 1904 he was returned to Westminster as Conservative member of Parliament for the Horsham division of Sussex. Viscount Turnour (the courtesy title he bore) was not yet twenty-two and the youngest member of the House. On his father's death in 1907 he succeeded to the family honours, together with substantial estates in Sussex and Norfolk. As an Irish peer, however, he was not obliged to relinquish his seat in the Commons, which he held continuously until 1951.

Winterton was swiftly installed on the threshold of office as parliamentary private secretary to E. G. Pretyman, financial secretary to the Admiralty. In opposition after the Liberal victory of 1905 he ministered to the ailing Joseph Chamberlain [q.v.]. Freed from these decorous duties in 1908, he made his mark as an astute tactician and pugnacious debater. His talent for insolence and disparagement was much in demand on the Tory benches during resistance to such contentious Liberal measures as the Parliament Bill of 1911 and Home Rule for Ireland. 'There was a little ill-temper,' (Sir) Winston Churchill reported to the King on 19 April 1911, 'and Lord Winterton became conspicuous.' These encounters did not deter the future first lord of the Admiralty from inviting Winterton to become a founder-member of The Other Club or from establishing a lifelong though wary friendship. As much amused by journalism as by journalists, Winterton in 1909 bought an interest in, and briefly edited, a weekly newspaper called the *World*.

In the war of 1914-18 he served with the Sussex Yeomanry in Gallipoli, with the Imperial Camel Corps in the Egyptian Expeditionary Force, and ultimately with T. E. Lawrence [q.v.] in the Hejaz operations that culminated in the fall of Damascus. He was twice mentioned in dispatches. Winterton's intense pride in having worn the King's uniform persisted to the end of his life, cutting across the less romantic loyalties of party politics. He invariably showed more respect for the opponent who had borne arms than for any colleague who had chosen to lie abed on St. Crispian's day.

From 1922 to 1929, except for the brief interlude of the first Labour Government, he held office as parliamentary under-secretary for India and was sworn of the Privy Council in 1924. He received no post in the 'national' Government of 1931 but was a delegate to the Burma Round Table Conference of that year and to the third India Round Table Conference of 1932. In concert with Churchill he pressed repeatedly for a strong defence policy to meet the growing menace of the dictators. His attachment to the Commons prompted him in 1935 to decline a United Kingdom peerage which would have becalmed him in the House of Lords. Baldwin had made the offer as a friendly gesture of regret that no place could be found for Winterton in the new Cabinet. The prime minister was thus stung to anger when in May 1936 he read newspaper reports of a cabal at Shillinglee Park, Winterton's house in Sussex, attended by Churchill and other Conservative dissidents. 'This is the time of year', Baldwin observed, 'when midges come out of dirty ditches.'

Winterton returned to favour on Baldwin's retirement in 1937, when Neville Chamberlain invited him to be chancellor of the Duchy of Lancaster. In March 1938 he was admitted to the Cabinet as deputy to the secretary of state for air, Lord Swinton [q.v.]. Only ten weeks later, however, representing his department in the Commons during an angry debate on rearmament, he failed to convince the House either of the Government's preparedness or of its determination to repair past neglect. A more artful politician might have pleaded that the fault lay less in his advocacy than in the realities of trying to rearm a peace-loving democracy. Winterton preferred to accept the entire blame for his poor performance and asked to be relieved of his duties at the Air Ministry. He remained chancellor of the Duchy with additional duties at the Home Office. In the same year he became chairman of an intergovernmental committee for refugees, an appointment which he held until 1945. Winterton disappointed those of his friends who hoped that he would resign from the Government in protest against the Munich agreement of 1938. On the contrary, his Christmas card for that year bore a photograph of Mr and Mrs Neville Chamberlain, with a comforting quotation from

Horace Walpole: 'Who gives a nation peace, gives tranquillity to all.' In January 1939 he was nevertheless demoted to the sinecure office of paymaster-general without a seat in Cabinet. Churchill offered him no place in the all-party coalition of 1940-5.

Winterton was glad to regain his parliamentary independence. Courteous and good-humoured outside the debating chamber, he scorned the arts of persuasion and compromise demanded of a minister at the dispatch box. He was a dedicated House of Commons man, tireless in preserving its customs and privileges, relishing interjections and points of order more than the plainer fare of legislation and supply. In the absence of an official Opposition, he and a few other oddly assorted members determined that not even a wartime coalition led by Churchill should be spared critical scrutiny. Winterton's closest ally was the Labour member Emanuel (later Lord) Shinwell; the spectacle of patrician Tory harnessed to Clydebank agitator evoked the jibe 'Arsenic and Old Lace', after a popular play of the time. More than once during the war Winterton was offered posts of dignity and importance overseas. He refused them all. But his fidelity to Westminster did bring him two rewarding duties. In 1944 he was appointed chairman of a select committee to consider the reconstruction of the Commons, destroyed by German bombs in 1941. He ensured that the chamber should be rebuilt in its traditional shape and style, whatever loss of modern convenience that might entail. And in 1945 he succeeded David Lloyd George as 'Father' of the House when the former prime minister was created an earl. Later that year after the Labour victory at the general election, he was invited to join Churchill's shadow Cabinet. In 1952 he at last accepted a peerage of the United Kingdom, taking his seat in the House of Lords as Baron Turnour, of Shillinglee.

Eddie Winterton, as he was known by friends and foes alike, epitomized all the virtues and some of the supposed vices of the aristocrat in politics. He was fearless in exposing injustice or in challenging heartless bureaucracy; but he could also be quick-tempered and exceptionally offensive. The intolerance as well as the exuberance of youth persisted beyond middle age, and in the heat of controversy he would make personal allusions better left unsaid. Even while listening to others, he displayed daunting mannerisms: grimly folded arms or knuckles cracking like pistol shots. When he could bear no more he exploded. If his shafts left few wounds, it was because of the affection he inspired as a 'character', almost an institution.

He stood six feet four inches in height, his angular frame surmounted by a long, thin face, sharp nose, pale-blue eyes, and fair hair. In dress he favoured the high-buttoned jacket and narrow trousers of his youth. T. E. Lawrence wrote in *Seven Pillars of Wisdom* that 'Winterton's instinct joined him to the weakest and more sporting side in any choice but fox-hunting'. He was master of the Chiddingfold Hunt and over the years hunted with no fewer than forty packs. At the age of seventy he sometimes spent four days out of five in the saddle. He called his favourite hunter Churchill. At the Beefsteak Club he enjoyed the company of men of letters and himself wrote three discursive volumes of memoirs.

In 1924 he married Cecilia Monica Wilson (died 1974), only daughter of Charles Henry Wellesley Wilson, the second Baron Nunburnholme. There were no children. Winterton died 26 August 1962 at King Edward VII Hospital, Midhurst, and is buried at Kirdford, Sussex. He was succeeded as seventh earl by a distant kinsman, Flight Sergeant Robert Chad Turnour, of the Royal Canadian Air Force. The United Kingdom barony became extinct.

A cartoon by 'Spy' appeared in *Vanity Fair* 16 September 1906 and is reproduced in Winterton's *Pre-War* (1932). There is a drawing by William Roberts in the 1935 edition of T. E. Lawrence's *Seven Pillars of Wisdom*.

[*The Times*, 28 August 1962; Winterton's own writings: *Pre-War* (1932), *Orders of the Day* (1953), *Fifty Tumultuous Years* (1955); Alan Houghton Brodrick, *Near to Greatness: A Life of the Sixth Earl Winterton* (1965); personal knowledge.]   KENNETH ROSE

TURRILL, WILLIAM BERTRAM (1890-1961), botanist, was born at Woodstock, Oxfordshire, 14 June 1890, the eldest of the four sons of William Banbury Turrill, provision merchant and later mayor of Woodstock, and his wife, Mary Homan, who came from a farming family. An early love of natural history was encouraged by his mother who gave him a piece of her garden to cultivate and taught him to prepare biological specimens. He was educated at Oxford High School (1903-6), where he was a contemporary of T. E. Lawrence [q.v.].

On leaving school at sixteen Turrill became a junior assistant in the Fielding herbarium of the department of botany at Oxford, under the curatorship of G. Claridge Druce [q.v.]. In 1909 he became a temporary assistant in the herbarium of the Royal Botanic Gardens, Kew, being appointed permanent assistant (later designated botanist) in 1914, with responsibility for several plant families including *Cyperaceae*, on which he specialized, and *Acanthaceae*. He

continued his education by attending evening classes at Chelsea Polytechnic and graduated B.Sc. (London) with first class honours in botany in 1915. He later obtained his M.Sc. (1922) and D.Sc. (1928) for his work on the flora of the Balkan peninsula. His interest in this region had been aroused during war service (1916-18) in the Royal Army Medical Corps with the British Salonika forces in Macedonia.

After the war Turrill returned to Kew, concentrating, after the reorganization of staff responsibilities in the early 1920s, on the floras of Europe, North Africa, and the Middle East. He continued his association with Chelsea Polytechnic, conducting evening classes on plant taxonomy, plant ecology, and plant genetics (1918-39). He also lectured to the student gardeners at Kew, and to botanical, agricultural, and forestry officers for the Colonial Office, many of whom later repaid his skill and enthusiasm by collecting specimens for Kew. The herbarium collections were considerably enriched also as a result of his own many expeditions, mainly in the Balkans. *Veronica turrilliana*, collected in south-eastern Bulgaria, was named in his honour.

During the war of 1939-45 Turrill returned to Oxford to take charge of the large portion of the Kew herbarium and library which in November and December 1940 was transferred, for safe keeping, to the basement of the New Bodleian Library. During that time he also worked on a series of handbooks for the Admiralty, which described the vegetation of several countries in the war zones. In 1946 he became keeper of the herbarium and library at Kew in succession to A. D. Cotton. He retired from the post 30 September 1957.

Early in his career Turrill advocated a broadly based approach to plant recognition and classification. He sought to include a consideration of anatomy, chemistry, cytology, ecology, and genetics, in addition to the more traditional emphasis on morphology. He was responsible for the innovation at Kew of ecological and genetical herbaria and a seed collection. In 1919 he started an experimental garden attached to the herbarium. Another experimental garden was established at the Wiltshire home of his friend and collaborator, E. M. Marsden-Jones, where Turrill carried out genetical and ecological experiments on species and variants of *Centaurea*, *Silene*, *Ranunculus*, and other genera.

Turrill's reputation as a leading authority on the flora of the Balkan peninsula was established by the publication of *The Plant Life of the Balkan Peninsula* (1929). However, his expertise was by no means confined to this topic. He wrote several books and well over 600 articles on botanical subjects, as well as a botanical history, *The Royal Botanic Gardens, Kew. Past and Present* (1959), and a biography, published posthumously in 1963, of J. D. Hooker [q.v.], to whom he was proud to have been presented during one of Hooker's last visits to the herbarium. Turrill was editor of the *Botanical Magazine* from 1948 until the time of his death; volume clxxiii, part iv (1962) of the magazine was dedicated to him.

Turrill's service to botany and horticulture were recognized by numerous honours and awards. In 1953 he was appointed OBE. The Royal Horticultural Society awarded him a Veitch memorial gold medal (1953) and the Victoria medal of honour (1956). He received the gold medal of the Linnean Society (1958), of which he was vice-president (1949-50). He was president of the Kew Guild (1948-9), of Section K of the British Association (1950), and of the British Ecological Society (1950-1). He was elected a fellow of the Royal Society in 1958. In addition he was a founder member and chairman of the Systematics Association.

A fast writer and an avid reader, Turrill assembled a large private library of books, pamphlets, periodicals, and newspaper clippings. Even after his retirement his capacity for lengthy and painstaking study seemed unlimited but he lacked neither a sense of humour nor generosity towards colleagues.

In 1918 he married Florence Emily Homan. The marriage was particularly happy, for she shared his interests, accompanying him to society meetings and on collecting expeditions; there were no children. Turrill died at his home in Richmond, Surrey, 15 December 1961.

[C. E. Hubbard in *Biographical Memoirs of Fellows of the Royal Society*, vol. xvii, 1971; *The Times*, 16 and 27 December 1961; W. B. Turrill, *The Royal Botanic Gardens, Kew. Past and Present*, 1959.]   P. J. COOTE

TWINING, EDWARD FRANCIS, BARON TWINING (1899-1967), colonial governor, was born in Westminster 29 June 1899, the second son and youngest child of the Revd William Henry Greaves Twining, vicar of St. Stephen's, Rochester Row, and his wife, Agatha Georgina, fourth daughter of Lieutenant-Colonel Robert Bourne, DL, JP. It was generally accepted, but never proved, that Twining's father shared a common ancestor with that branch of the family which had founded R. Twining & Co., the tea and coffee merchants. Twining's maternal grandmother was the sister of the explorer Sir Samuel Baker [q.v.].

'Peter' Twining was a provost's scholar at Lancing where his record in both work and games was nevertheless undistinguished; but he was friendly and likeable and showed signs of enterprise and leadership, becoming house captain, a prefect, and a sergeant in the Officers' Training Corps. At an early age he had decided to be a soldier and in 1917, very low on the list, he entered the Royal Military College, Sandhurst. He passed out bottom of his term in 1918 and was gazetted to the Worcestershire Regiment just before the end of the war, too late for active service.

Between 1919 and the end of 1922 Twining served in Dublin. At the end of 1920 he was appointed battalion, subsequently brigade, intelligence officer. In June 1921 he inadvertently captured President de Valera who was immediately released and signed a truce with Lloyd George two weeks later. Twining was appointed MBE for his services in Ireland.

Seeking, as always, the unusual rather than the usual, Twining was seconded to the King's African Rifles in Uganda in 1923. To normal regimental duties he preferred running a school for the children of African soldiers which sowed the seeds of a lifelong affection for Africans, and acting as battalion intelligence officer, which fulfilled his craving for constant movement untrammelled by authority. His penetrating intelligence reports brought him to the notice of those in high places in London.

After two tours in Uganda, Twining decided at the age of twenty-nine to transfer to the colonial administrative service. After a year's training at Oxford where he did not distinguish himself he was posted back to Uganda in 1929 as an assistant district commissioner. He persistently failed his language examinations; showed no signs of adapting himself to routine office work; and chafed under supervision. He was a self-confident individualist who demanded recognition and worked best on *ad hoc* assignments carrying much personal responsibility. A chance to demonstrate his peculiar talents, which included a flair for showmanship, an ability to organize, and the knack of obtaining the willing co-operation of others of all races, came in 1937 when Twining was charged with organizing the local celebrations for the coronation of King George VI. This task appealed to other elements in his complex nature: an abiding interest in everything regal, stimulated by an unforeseen and informal encounter with the Prince of Wales in up-country Uganda some years earlier, and reflected in his ever-growing interest in crown jewels and regalia. He had, too, an almost boyish delight in and capacity for bringing joy and colour into the lives of other people, especially the poor.

As director of labour (1939-43) in Mauritius Twining was again faced with problems which offered a welcome challenge to his individualistic approach. He was in his element in such tasks as establishing censorship, although as an ex-soldier he had hoped for a more glamorous wartime role. He was appointed CMG in 1943 and a year later was transferred to St. Lucia as administrator, where he revelled in preening his embryo governor's plumes. The affection with which the St. Lucians enfolded him was not merely a response to what he did for them but also to what he did to them. While they admired the skill with which he had bullied London into providing funds for development, they were also aware that it was Twining who had inspired them to make the most of their opportunities. He had realized that development was a matter more of people than of pounds.

Twining was an obvious choice for the governorship (1946-9) of North Borneo, which had been devastatingly impoverished by the Japanese occupation. His task of reconstruction and development was a far larger one, complicated by the traumatic break with the past, whereby the Colonial Office had replaced the Chartered Company as the source of authority.

Before Twining's work was finished he was promoted in 1949 to be governor of Tanganyika, arriving in the Trust territory as a newly appointed KCMG. His policy was to keep Tanganyika racially harmonious and politically stable so as to encourage overseas investment for development. His technique, as elsewhere, was to lead and inspire both the officers of his administration and the multi-racial population as a whole to greater and more relevant efforts. He projected the warmth and friendliness of his ebullient personality by constant safaris during which his imposing presence (he was now over fifteen stone and looked every inch a chief) became known to thousands of Africans and others who had never seen a governor before and who were soon captivated by his Rabelaisian, though otherwise limited, Swahili.

Twining was promoted GCMG in 1953. The visit which Princess Margaret made in 1956 to Tanganyika was a highlight in his term of office, the last two years of which were overshadowed by the rise of Julius Nyerere. Twining had his own ideas about how and when Tanganyika might ultimately become independent, but they were not Nyerere's ideas. Twining underestimated Nyerere's personality and importance just as he underestimated the upsurge of Africanism which was to carry Nyerere to the leadership of the first independent state in East Africa in 1961.

After his retirement in 1958 Twining was created a life peer. He was not an effective public speaker; he did not contribute much to the House of Lords; and he had never cared to be one among many. He spent six months of each year in Nairobi where he had business and other interests. And in 1960 his *History of the Crown Jewels of Europe* was published, followed in 1967 by *European Regalia*.

In 1928 Twining married Helen Mary (May), daughter of Arthur Edmund Du Buisson, JP; they had two sons. In every territory in which Twining served, his wife, a qualified doctor, played a leading role in medical and social welfare activities; she died in 1975.

Twining died 21 July 1967 at his Westminster flat, within a few hundred yards of his birthplace.

[Sir Darrell Bates, *A Gust of Plumes*, a biography of Lord Twining, 1972; private information; personal knowledge.]

JOHN FLETCHER-COOKE

TYNDALL, ARTHUR MANNERING (1881-1961), physicist, was born 18 September 1881, the youngest in the family of three sons and two daughters of Henry Augustus Tyndall, a partner in the firm of Cowley and Tyndall, ironmongers, of Bristol, and his wife, Sarah Hannah Mannering, the daughter of a London linen draper. He was educated at Redland Hill House, a private school in Bristol where no science was taught, except a smattering of chemistry in the last two terms. Nevertheless he entered the University College of Bristol, as it then was, obtaining the only scholarship offered by the city of Bristol for study there, and intending to make his career in chemistry. However, when brought into contact with the professor of physics, Arthur Chattock, who was an outstanding teacher, he decided to switch to physics; he always expressed the warmest gratitude for the inspiration which he had received from him. He graduated as B.Sc. with second class honours in the external London examination in 1903. In that year he was appointed assistant lecturer, was promoted to lecturer in 1907, and became lecturer in the university when the college became a university in 1909. Professor Chattock retired at the age of fifty in 1910 and Tyndall became acting head of the department. Then, with the outbreak of war, he left the university to run an army radiological department in Hampshire, but was eventually persuaded to return to the physics department which seemed in danger of disintegrating without him. In 1919 he became Henry Overton Wills professor of physics at Bristol.

It was in 1916 that he had first met the great benefactor of Bristol physics, Henry Herbert Wills of the tobacco family, pro-chancellor and chairman of a special buildings committee, who was planning with the architect the details of the Great Hall of the university. His first contact with him was a letter to Wills as chairman of the general purposes committee about a site for some accumulators. Out of this arose a friendship, walks to work together across the Clifton Downs, and ultimately Wills's desire to provide a quite exceptional building for physics in the university. Though his intentions were clear earlier, it was in March 1919 that he announced a gift of £100,000 and as much again a year later. In 1922 he died, leaving a further considerable sum to the university. In the same year, together with the architect George Oatley, Tyndall visited the United States to see laboratory buildings and make plans. The H. H. Wills Physical Laboratory, on the highest point of the university's Royal Fort estate, was opened in 1927 by Sir Ernest Rutherford (later Lord Rutherford of Nelson, q.v.).

The creation of this laboratory, and the leadership which Tyndall gave to it before and after the war of 1939-45, was his personal achievement, and the one for which he would wish to be remembered. He would always subordinate his own work and interests to those of the ambitious young men he collected round him, and his greatest pleasure lay in their successes. The Nobel prize awarded in 1950 to Cecil Frank Powell [q.v.] made him quite wild with joy, as did fellowships of the Royal Society and other recognitions of the quality of his colleagues' work. It was from the beginning his ambition to build a research school. When the laboratory was opened, it was much too big for the twelve members of staff and the small honours school, never more than six in the final honours year, and out of scale with anything else in the university. Tyndall's first task was to collect money for endowment and equipment. The Rockefeller foundation provided £50,000 and Melville Wills a further sum of £25,000 for a chair of theoretical physics, named after him and held in succession by (Sir) J. E. Lennard-Jones [q.v.] and by the author of this memoir. That, and in 1933 the influx of very talented refugees from Hitler's Germany, enabled Tyndall to build a really strong school. This allowed Bristol to take part in the explosive development of physics which characterized the inter-war period, a subject which earlier was centred in Cambridge and Manchester. The main achievements during Tyndall's directorship were the work on cosmic rays leading to the discovery of the mu-meson by Cecil Powell, and the strong school of solid-state physics — the term was probably invented there — involving such men as H. W. B. Skinner, Harry Jones, W. Sucksmith, R. W. Gurney, H. Fröhlich, the present writer, and, after the war, F. C. Frank and J. W. Mitchell. Tyndall had the capacity to choose young men who were destined to attain real success in physics.

Tyndall was so wrapped up in their achievements that he seemed too modest about his own personal research, but this was of considerable

distinction. It was mainly in the field of the discharge of electricity in gases. In the early 1920s experiments had been made of the mobility of ions in gases, but the results were very discordant. Tyndall realized that this was because impurities in gases attached themselves to the ions, so that their motion was slowed down. He with a number of young colleagues made use of new techniques, and by the middle 1920s high vacuum methods had progressed to the point where this contamination could be largely avoided. They were able to measure the mobilities of a wide range of ions, and established many of the values accepted today. Details of this work are described in the *Biographical Memoir* published by the Royal Society. In 1938 was published his *Mobility of Positive Ions in Gases*.

From 1940 to 1945 and again in 1946-7 he was pro-vice-chancellor and in 1944-5 acting vice-chancellor. It need hardly be said that throughout his career he took a leading part in the affairs of the university as a whole, particularly in its expansion after the war, though always he shielded his young researchers from involvement unless they wanted to be drawn in. He also took a leading part in the scientific committee work of the country. Elected into the fellowship of the Royal Society in 1933, he served on council from 1941-2 and was vice-president in 1942. He was president of the Institute of Physics in 1946-8, president of the physics section of the British Association in 1952, a manager of the Royal Institution, and president in 1953 of the Science Masters' Association. In Bristol he gave most generously of his time to medical education and the National Health Service. In 1950 he was appointed CBE and in 1958 honorary LLD of his own university. He was also a D.Sc. of both Bristol (1913) and London (1912).

When he retired in 1948 Bristol created him emeritus professor and honorary fellow. From the date of his retirement until his death he was a very active member of the editorial board of the *Philosophical Magazine*, one of the oldest scientific journals in the country since it was founded in 1798. It was he who carried out the day-to-day work of the journal, taking decisions on acceptance or rejection of papers contributed.

Tyndall will be remembered particularly for two things. He presided over part of that phenomenal growth of English physics when it left its traditional home and flourished all over the country. The generosity of the Wills family gave him his opportunity, and he knew how to take it. Whatever Bristol physics achieved owed much to his wisdom, kindness, and uncompromising standards. He also worked during his whole life in what has become one of our great universities. In his department he believed that no effort was too great, and that no time should ever be judged wasted in finding out what everyone thought and in seeing that everyone was heard. Frequently the whole staff accompanied him in a Sunday walk over the Somerset hills, and, if there were any departmental difficulties, it was then that they were resolved. If Bristol's growth from small beginnings has been happy, and relatively free from the strains and frustrations that are sometimes expressed elsewhere, it may be that Tyndall's example in his fifty years there had much to do with it. Many who remember him believe this to be so.

In 1908 he married Lilly Mary, daughter of Frank Smith Gardner, who taught the violin at Clifton College. They had one son and two daughters. The marriage was very happy and the hospitality he and his wife provided for their numerous friends was informal and continuous. Tyndall died suddenly at his home 29 October 1961. His portrait, a gift of colleagues, students, and friends, was painted by (Sir) James Gunn (1948) and hangs in the H. H. Wills Physical Laboratory in Bristol.

[N. F. Mott and C. F. Powell in *Biographical Memoirs of Fellows of the Royal Society*, vol. viii, 1962; private information; personal knowledge.]   NEVILL MOTT

U

UNWIN, SIR STANLEY (1884-1968), publisher, was born 19 December 1884 at Lee in south-east London, the youngest of nine children of Edward Unwin, a London printer and the son of Jacob Unwin, the founder of the printing firm of Unwin Brothers, and his wife, Elisabeth, the daughter of James Spicer, of the paper firm of that name. He was brought up in a devoutly Nonconformist atmosphere and was educated at the School for the Sons of Missionaries at Blackheath and then at Abbotsholme School in Derbyshire from 1897 to 1899. He left after two years due to the burning down of his father's printing works at Chilworth in Surrey, and consequent financial straits. The young Unwin then joined a shipping firm as an office boy but left shortly afterwards to stay in Germany. Here he gained his first experience as a publisher in the German book trade, which proved an important and influential ingredient in his career as a publisher since he was, and remained, the only London publisher of any distinction with a genuine understanding of any book trade outside his own country.

In 1904 Unwin joined his father's younger stepbrother, T. Fisher Unwin, in Paternoster Buildings. The older man was himself a leading and successful publisher and something of a doyen of literary London, and under him Unwin rapidly learnt the craft of publishing, specializing in contracts and the marketing of foreign rights. So successful was he that he embarked on discussions, which proved abortive, about a jointly owned company with his relative. For Unwin, at twenty-eight, knowledgeable, confident, impatient, there was no alternative but to start his own firm. Following a world tour with his future brother-in-law he bought the firm of George Allen & Co. which had recently gone bankrupt. He quickly built a formidable list of authors, established himself as a spokesman on the affairs of the British book trade not only within Britain but all over the world, and became a public personality in his own right. In 1926 he published *The Truth about Publishing* which has become the most authoritative textbook on the subject for generations of people entering the book trade. It has been regularly updated. There are those who feel that in it Unwin set down all the facts but left out all the fun. At first sight this is a real criticism and it is true that Unwin himself rarely played the traditional role of entertainer of budding geniuses sometimes thought to be the only function of literary publishers. He was a hard-headed man who disliked spending his money—even small sums—on what he regarded as trivial matters; and he acquired, and kept, his

authors in a truly professional manner. It was through the advocacy of Professor J. H. Muirhead [q.v.], editor of the Library of Philosophy, that Bertrand (Earl) Russell [q.v.] joined the Allen & Unwin list, though Muirhead disagreed with much of Russell's philosophy. Another helper was A. R. Orage [q.v.], editor of the *New Age*, through whom Unwin acquired the Russian philosopher-mystic George Gurdjieff, as well as Edwin Muir [q.v.], Ramiro de Maetzu, and A. J. Penty. Unwin was also able to pick up authors from other small publishers who failed where he was succeeding. Such authors included Benedetto Croce, August Strindberg, Albert Sorel, James Elroy Flecker [q.v.], Jules Romains, and Sir J. C. Squire [q.v.].

During World War I Unwin published books by conscientious objectors, in the face of much public hostility. During the war period he published *The Framework of a Lasting Peace* (1917), edited by Leonard Woolf [q.v.], and other influential books. Unwin himself was deeply concerned about the nature of the peace to be concluded, but expressed concern most effectively through his publications, which included Woolf's *International Government* (1916), George Lansbury's [q.v.] *Your Part in Poverty* (1917), and *A Century of British Foreign Policy* (1918) by G. P. Gooch [q.v.] and J. H. B. Masterman. Unwin tended to leave fiction publishing to his partner who published some important translations of Russian classics. But, with some honourable exceptions, fiction was not outstanding on Unwin's list and his main interests, reflected in his lists, remained serious works of scholarship, with some topical relevance or at least with the possibility of a wide sale to the literate public. Such a publication was Russell's *The Practice and Theory of Bolshevism* (1920). However, the immediate post-war period saw the acquisition of the translator of Chinese poetry, Arthur Waley [q.v.], to the Allen & Unwin list. This was a productive period for Unwin, for many leading authors, literary and academic, joined the list of the firm—Sydney J. Webb, G. D. H. Cole, R. H. Tawney, G. Lowes Dickinson, G. Gilbert Murray, H. W. Nevinson [qq.v.], and Sigmund Freud. Though Unwin never published George Bernard Shaw [q.v.], he published books about him, which occasioned a heated correspondence with the playwright.

Unwin had strong links with the Fabian Society and in the inter-war years published many left-wing books, including the work of Harold J. Laski [q.v.] and of Leon Trotsky. Another aspect of his character, developed by his parents with their clear religious beliefs, concerned his strong non-sectarian Christian convictions. These led him to publish for C. F. Andrews, and through him the works of several Indian authors, including M. K. Gandhi [q.v.]. In 1936 he published one of the best-sellers of the period—*Mathematics for the Million*, followed by *Science for the Citizen* (1938), both by Lancelot Hogben. In 1937, acting on the recommendation of his ten-year-old son, Rayner, Unwin published J. R. R. Tolkien's *The Hobbit*, followed by *The Lord of the Rings* (1954-5) and other works which were to find a fanatical world-wide readership.

Unwin worked throughout the war of 1939-45, narrowly escaping bombs in the blitz. 'When the raids were at their worst', he wrote, 'it was my practice at home to put on a record of Dvorak's New World Symphony at full blast so that I could hear nothing else.' This was not his only eccentricity, which arose more out of his single-minded wish to get on with his life and work than out of any intention to astonish or amuse. When his cousin Philip was shown the manuscript of his autobiography and ventured to say that the many stories told of Unwin's triumphs could have been tempered with one or two instances where he had not been entirely right or justified, Unwin replied, 'You don't expect me to start writing fiction at my age, do you?' At the office he opened the post himself every day, even on bank holidays. At his Hampstead home tennis was his passion—every Saturday and Sunday afternoon, winter and summer, men's doubles only. When he changed house late in life, the tennis court was completed before the house so that no interruption need be experienced. He had married his wife, (Alice) Mary (died 1971), daughter of Rayner Storr, an auctioneer, in 1914, shortly after he launched his firm, and his family life was exceptionally happy. He had two sons, one of whom, Rayner, succeeded him in his publishing business, and one daughter.

Later successes from Unwin's firm included *The Kon-Tiki Expedition*, by Thor Heyerdahl (1950), acquired in Oslo by his nephew Philip. After the war Unwin travelled widely on business and in 1954 completed fifty years in the book trade. As formerly, in his latter years he continued his interest in the activities of the Publishers' Association and the International Publishers' Association as well as the British Council. He had become president of the Publishers' Association in 1933 and was particularly involved with the vexed question of the net book agreement. Nor with his advancing years was there any diminution in his overriding interest in the firm that he had built from so little and the books that appeared under his imprint.

When Unwin died in London 13 October 1968 he was widely recognized as one of the architects of the British, and indeed the international, book trade; as a publisher of the highest standards of probity in business matters as well as in the quality of the books he published; and as a personality, not without weaknesses, reasonably self-righteous, but one who had contributed importantly to the life and wellbeing of his country over half a century.

Unwin was knighted in 1946 and created KCMG in 1966. Aberdeen University honoured him with an LLD. He also received Belgian, French, and Czechoslovakian decorations. There is a portrait in oils by Oskar Kokoschka in the London offices of George Allen & Unwin Limited.

[Sir Stanley Unwin, *The Truth about a Publisher*, 1960; private information; personal knowledge.]   R. A. DENNISTON

UVAROV, SIR BORIS PETROVITCH (1889-1970), entomologist, was born at Uralsk in south-eastern Russia 5 November 1889, the youngest of three sons of Petr P. Uvarov, a State Bank employee, and his wife, Alexandra. After secondary school education at Uralsk he graduated with a first class degree in biology in the university of St. Petersburg (1910). He was thus able to transform his boyhood enthusiasm for the collection of insects into a profound knowledge of entomology.

After graduation Uvarov held appointments in several provincial departments of agriculture and in 1915 at the age of twenty-seven he was made director of the Tiflis Bureau of Plant Protection. This involved the organization of plant protection stations in Transcaucasia and a thorough entomological exploration of the region. In 1919 he became lecturer in the State University in Tiflis and keeper of entomology and zoology in the State Museum of Georgia. In the face of rampant Georgian nationalism his position was difficult. But among the contingent of British troops in Georgia was Patrick A. Buxton [q.v.] who provided a connecting link with London; and in 1920 Uvarov was given an appointment at the Imperial Bureau (later the Commonwealth Institute) of Entomology under (Sir) Guy A. K. Marshall [q.v.].

Uvarov had made extensive studies of locusts and grasshoppers in south-east Russia; he had not only established his reputation as a taxonomist in this group of insects but he had reached the surprising conclusion that swarming and non-swarming locusts, which are so different in appearance that they had always been regarded as different species, were in fact phases of the same insect. This 'phase theory' provided the basis for much of Uvarov's outstanding contribution to the control of locust plagues.

His official work at the Bureau was the identification of insects sent in from all parts of the Commonwealth, but he also found time to add to his already large output of papers on the taxonomy of grasshoppers; he wrote his classic book *Locusts and Grasshoppers* (1928) which was published in English and in Russian and was the handbook of 'acridologists' (to use Uvarov's own word) for some thirty years. He also prepared a very useful review of the literature on *Insect Nutrition and Metabolism* (1928) commissioned by the Empire Marketing Board; and an even more outstanding review on *Insects and Climate* (1931), the publication costs of which were again met by the Empire Marketing Board.

In the late 1920s there were serious outbreaks of locust plagues in south-west Asia and in Africa. The Committee of Civil Research asked the Commonwealth Institute to undertake investigations into the whole subject of swarming locusts and Uvarov was given the task of organizing and supervising this project. This was the beginning of his real life's work.

His small unit, occupying very restricted quarters in the British Museum (Natural History) soon came to be recognized unofficially as the international centre for locust research. Under the impetus of Uvarov's drive a series of scientific international anti-locust conferences were organized. These served to formulate programmes and to co-ordinate international studies of the locust problem, and they led to the establishment of permanent regional organizations aiming at a continuous study of each locust species in its natural haunts with a view to the prevention of locust plagues. This twin policy of international co-operation and prevention of outbreaks by continuing field studies, was the keynote of Uvarov's teaching. The policy was firmly based in his theory of locust phases.

By 1938 the results were clear enough to form a basis for an international plan for the study and control of locusts. This was to concentrate on the destruction of locusts in their 'outbreak areas', thus preventing the build-up of populations to the crowded state in which the phase change from the 'solitary' to the 'gregarious' form takes place and swarms spread widely over the surrounding countries. The outbreak of war in 1939 prevented the full operation of this plan, but the methods advocated were successfully used against the Red Locust and the Migratory Locust in Africa—species in which the 'outbreak areas' had been discovered and defined. During the war Uvarov's advisory and organizational work grew still further, and in 1945 his unit became the Anti-Locust Research Centre under the Colonial Office. During the

next fourteen years the Centre developed into the foremost laboratory in the world for research in locusts—and, at the same time, it was the co-ordinating centre for much extramural academic research on locusts and for furthering international co-operation in locust control.

Uvarov himself was increasingly under pressure from all parts of the world to advise on locust research and control. He therefore travelled widely. He retired as director of the Centre in 1959 but he remained in office as a consultant and devoted himself largely to the writing of a new book on *Grasshoppers and Locusts*, which would cover the immense advances that had been made in every aspect of the subject since his early classic of 1928 was published. The first volume of the new work appeared in 1966 and he was working on the second volume, which was already far advanced, at the time of his death. The volume was finally produced for publication in 1977 by those of his colleagues most closely acquainted with his ideas.

Uvarov's output of scientific publications was prodigious—in the fields of botany, geography, biogeography, and ecology, as well as locust control. But his major contribution was to taxonomy: in the course of half a century he described 284 genera and over 900 species and subspecies of Orthoptera. His impact on acridoid systematics will long continue to be felt. In his faunistic studies he always stressed the importance of work 'in living nature'. There is no doubt that he was well ahead of his time in showing systematists the value of physiological and ecological studies in relation to museum taxonomy. The theory of locust phases was both a cause and an effect of this broad attitude of mind: he always stressed that the really significant phase differences were not those of external characters, but rather the changes in physiology and behaviour which in turn operated to increase or maintain the high density of populations. The theory of phase transformation continued to dominate the considerations of locust plague dynamics. At one time there was a tendency to discredit the theory because it did not seem to apply to the greatest of all the plague locusts, the Desert Locust. But it was then realized that the Desert Locust underwent the same phase changes but that they took place as the invading swarms, carried by convergent rain-bearing winds, reproduced and multiplied in crowded conditions. Since there were no persisting 'outbreak areas' for this locust, different strategies must be used for control. When a Desert Locust plague broke out in the early years of the war of 1939-45, Uvarov was able to provide a sound biogeographical basis for the large-scale control campaigns. He did not consider that locust and grasshopper problems could ever be solved by chemical methods alone and firmly believed that a radical solution of them must be sought in the ecological field, leading to a gradual replacement of direct control by methods of ecological regulation of populations. (*Entomologicheskoe Obozrenie*, vol. xlviii, 1969).

Uvarov received many honours during his lifetime: CMG (1943), KCMG (1961), FRS (1950), commandeur de l'Ordre Royal de Lion (1948), and honorary D.Sc. in the university of Madrid (1935). He served as president of the Royal Entomological Society of London (1959–61).

Boris Uvarov was a person of small stature but immense toughness and vitality. His own personal interests probably lay in the natural history of insects in the wild, and this led naturally to studies of their classification and taxonomy. But his administrative career brought him into the control of locust pests and in this field he deployed all his gifts of leadership and drive. His objectives were clear: the control of locusts required international co-operation on the one hand and scientific study on the broadest possible base on the other, and he devoted himself to the attainment of these objectives. He succeeded by sheer strength of character combined with scientific integrity. He had a dry sense of humour, an ability to inspire young men coming into locust research, and a capacity to appreciate the importance and to foster the development of relevant fields of science of which he himself had little intimate knowledge or experience. Although he never seemed satisfied and often seemed to bite the hand which fed him, his purpose was honest, his objectives were desirable, and his methods and ideas were sound.

In 1910 he married Anna Federova Prodanjuk (died 1968), daughter of F. and E. Federov. They had one son, who was educated in Britain. Uvarov was naturalized in 1943 and died at his home in Ealing 18 March 1870.

[P. T. Haskell, *In Memoriam* brochure written by colleagues at the Anti-Locust Research Centre (now the Centre for Overseas Pest Research), 1970; V. B. Wigglesworth in *Biographical Memoirs of Fellows of the Royal Society*, vol. xvii, 1971; private information; personal knowledge.]

V. B. WIGGLESWORTH

V

VAUGHAN, DAME HELEN CHARLOTTE ISABELLA GWYNNE- (1879-1967), botanist and leader of women's Services in both world wars. [See GWYNNE-VAUGHAN.]

VERNEY, ERNEST BASIL (1894-1967), physiologist and pharmacologist, was born in Cardiff 22 August 1894, the fourth son and fifth child of Frederick Palmer Verney, who came from Branston, north Devon, and who was both an active farmer and in farming business, and his wife, Mary Ann Burch, who came from Bradford, Somerset. Verney grew up on a farm at Hever, Kent, and in Tonbridge. His education began in Judd School, Tonbridge, and in 1910 he obtained a leaving exhibition to Tonbridge School. He began on the classical but transferred to the scientific side and was encouraged to take up medicine. He was awarded an exhibition in science at Downing College, Cambridge (1913). He gained a first class in part i of the natural sciences tripos (1916) and entered St. Bartholomew's Hospital with the Schuster entrance scholarship in anatomy and physiology. Having qualified MRCS and LRCP in April 1918, he joined the Royal Army Medical Corps as a regimental medical officer.

On demobilization in 1919 he began a year's house physician appointment at St. Bartholomew's and developed an interest in renal function. He then worked as house physician in the East London Hospital for Children (Shadwell). Whilst holding various clinical appointments he obtained the MB, B.Ch. (Cantab., 1921), and the MRCP (London). In 1921 he opted for the academic side of medicine. Professor E. H. Starling [q.v.] appointed him assistant in the department of physiology at University College, London. There Verney began fundamental work on renal physiology. In 1924 he became assistant in the medical unit at University College Hospital under the director, T. R. Elliot. During this period he held junior and fourth-year Beit memorial research fellowships. In 1926 he was appointed to the chair of pharmacology at University College. He became FRCP, London 1928. In 1934 he moved to Cambridge, and in 1946 he became first Sheild professor of pharmacology. In 1961 he retired as emeritus professor of pharmacology. He was then invited to hold a personal chair for three years in Melbourne, Australia, after which he returned to live in Cambridge.

Verney's work was always planned with meticulous care. Much of it was on isolated organs but his aim was to obtain results from animals in conditions which were as near normal as possible; that is, the animals should be healthy, contented, and, when possible, conscious. With colleagues he examined a number of factors responsible for regulating heart rate and blood pressure. Above all, Verney will be remembered for his work on the kidney and on water balance. He showed clearly that water excretion was in part controlled by the hypothalamus and the posterior pituitary, that in conscious animals normal water diuresis followed renal denervation, and that there were central nervous osmoreceptors sensitive to changes in plasma osmotic pressure. He also studied the effects of exercise and emotion on renal function.

Verney had a lively and individual sense of humour. At times his comments were pungent. He was also a man of great kindness. He taught by example how much care must be taken in all details of experimental work. Despite a period of ill health involving two surgical operations, he carried on. He thought nothing of beginning at seven in the morning in order that a demonstration for undergraduates should be perfect and punctual, or of working until ten at night on experimental research. In committees his opinion was highly valued because he did not express a view without careful preliminary study and thought.

When working in Shadwell he met Ruth Eden Conway, who was the resident medical officer. They were married in 1923. She was the eldest daughter of Robert Seymour Conway [q.v.], Hulme professor of Latin in the university of Manchester, and his wife, Margaret Hall. They had two sons and a daughter.

Verney's abilities received wide recognition. In 1936 he was elected a fellow of the Royal Society. He was asked to give a number of public lectures: the Goulstonian of the Royal College of Physicians (1929); the Sharpey-Schafer of the university of Edinburgh (1945); the Croonian of the Royal Society (1947); the Dunham of Harvard (1951); and the John Malet Purser of Trinity College, Dublin (1954). In addition he was elected an honorary fellow of Downing College (1961) and of the Hungarian and Finnish Medical Societies (1938 and 1949). He was awarded medals by the Royal College of Physicians (Baly medal) and by the universities of Liège and Ghent (1946 and 1948). He died in Addenbrooke's Hospital, Cambridge, 19 August 1967, just before presentation of the Schmiedeberg-Plakette of the Deutsche Pharmakologische Gesellschaft.

[I. de Burgh Daly and L. Mary Pickford in *Biographical Memoirs of Fellows of the Royal Society*, vol. xvi, 1970; personal knowledge.]

MARY PICKFORD

VIAN, Sir PHILIP LOUIS (1894-1968), admiral of the fleet, was born in London 15 June 1894, the son of Alsager Vian, secretary to a public company, and his wife, Ada Frances Renault. He was educated at Hillside School and the Royal Naval Colleges at Osborne and Dartmouth. After the outbreak of war Vian was able to arrange a transfer to the new destroyer *Morning Star* which was present at the Battle of Jutland. He was promoted lieutenant in 1916 and served in two other destroyers in turn, thus spending most of the war in small ships. After the war he specialized in gunnery and led the life of the peacetime navy in which, however, he was already showing above-average ability. He was promoted commander in 1929 and in 1932 led a division of one of the Mediterranean destroyer flotillas; then, as a captain (1934), he was put in charge of a flotilla of reserve destroyers which was sent out to defend Malta during the Abyssinian crisis. In July 1936 the Spanish civil war broke out and the ships of the first flotilla, to which Vian had transferred and which was on its way home to pay off, were diverted to Spanish ports. They spent a busy and rewarding period evacuating British subjects, exchanging refugees, and acting as a floating communications centre for the ambassador. Vian's clarity of thought, firm decisions, and astringent signals to Whitehall were outstanding.

Vian then had two years in command of the *Arethusa*, flagship of the third cruiser squadron, where he gained experience of the Mediterranean side of the Spanish civil war. In August 1939 his appointment to command a shore establishment was cancelled and he was sent to be captain of a flotilla of elderly destroyers from reserve which were to be based on Liverpool and used to escort Atlantic convoys. In the new year he was appointed to the fourth destroyer flotilla, consisting of the new and powerful Tribal class destroyers which were working from Rosyth, escorting convoys to and from Scandinavia.

In February 1940 Vian in the *Cossack* led a force of one cruiser and four other destroyers to the Norwegian coast and was then instructed to seize the German ship *Altmark* which was known to be carrying British merchant seamen prisoners. After a long search the *Altmark* was sighted in Norwegian territorial waters but quickly took refuge in Josing Fjord. After some polite but firm discussions with the officers commanding the two Norwegian torpedo boats which had been escorting the *Altmark* down the Leads, and following an interchange of signals with Whitehall, Vian took the *Cossack* into the fjord and sent a boarding party on to the German ship which at the time was going astern out of the ice. After a scuffle with the enemy crew the boarding party rescued the 300

prisoners whom the *Cossack* took home to receive a heroes' welcome. Normally Vian was not an above-average ship handler, but as always in an emergency, his performance was immaculate.

During the Norwegian campaign in the spring of 1940 Vian, in the *Afridi*, was closely involved in many actions and his ship was eventually sunk by dive-bombers after evacuating troops from Namsos. In May he returned to the *Cossack* and the flotilla was based at Scapa during the summer until the peak danger period of invasion when it transferred to Rosyth where Vian spent much time exercising the tactics he would use on German landing-craft in the Channel. In the autumn the flotilla went to Scapa and Vian led a successful night attack on a small German coastal convoy close to the Norwegian coast.

After a long and arduous winter, spent mostly in escorting large ships steaming fast in heavy seas, in May 1941 the flotilla was able to join in the attack on the battleship *Bismarck* whose steering had been crippled by aircraft from the *Ark Royal*. The destroyers, led by Vian, spent an exciting night in very heavy seas, shadowing and attacking the stricken battleship whose fire remained remarkably accurate. Next day, she was sunk by the heavy guns and torpedoes of the big ships.

In July 1941 Vian was specially promoted rear-admiral and left his command. He was sent on a flying visit to Russia to arrange for naval co-operation, but the task was made difficult by obstruction at every level. After reporting to Whitehall, he was appointed to Force K at Scapa, the composition of which varied but which was normally led by the cruiser *Nigeria*. The force was sent to Spitsbergen to report on the situation there and also visited Bear Island where the weather reporting station was destroyed. In August 1941 the force returned to Spitsbergen to destroy the coal-mining facilities, withdraw the Norwegian settlers, and evacuate the Russian colony to their own country. Thus started the first of the Russian convoys. On the return passage to Scapa, Vian took the *Nigeria* and the *Aurora* to attack a German naval force reported at the northern end of the Norwegian Leads. During one of the closest range actions of the war the *Nigeria* rammed and cut in half the German training cruiser *Bremse*.

In October 1941 Vian was flown through the Mediterranean to take command of the fifteenth cruiser squadron at Alexandria. There were few ships available and the enemy forces were greatly superior. The main British tasks were the sustenance of Malta and the prevention of supplies reaching the Axis armies in North Africa. In December Vian successfully bombarded Derna, an enterprise not included in his operation orders. In the same month he took his first convoy to Malta and despite heavy air attacks succeeded in his objective; the Italian fleet which he sighted was luckily engaged in a similar operation to Africa.

In mid February 1942 an operation to supply Malta ended in disaster, not one loaded merchant ship reaching the island; and in the following month Vian's flagship *Naiad* was sunk when he was escorting a cruiser and destroyer from Malta. Towards the end of the month three merchantmen set out for Malta with a strong escort of cruisers and destroyers under Vian's command. It met the Italian battle fleet consisting of a battleship, two 8-inch gun cruisers, a 6-inch gun cruiser, and a number of destroyers. By great bravery and brilliant tactics, the merchant ships remained unscathed from surface attack although enemy aircraft delivered some dangerous hits. In the end, one merchant ship arrived safely, a second was beached at Malta, and the third sunk. The action fully deserved the special message of congratulation from Churchill. During the next Malta convoy, in June, the situation in the desert was worse and even fewer aircraft were available to help. Combined threats by the Italian battle fleet, numerous aircraft, and some U-boats caused the recall of Vian's escorting forces, but two merchantmen reached Malta from the convoy which had approached from the west at the same time, so enabling the island to survive for a further two months when the next convoy arrived.

In September 1942 Vian set out for home by air but his aircraft broke down in West Africa where he contracted malaria. By April 1943 he was adjudged fit for shore service only and appointed to a post on the staff which was planning the invasion of Europe. But before he could take it up he was on his way back to the Mediterranean to take over an amphibious force whose commander had died in an air crash. He had two months to prepare for this new form of warfare and the successful assault on Sicily in July. In August Vian was sent to command a squadron of small aircraft carriers which were to provide fighter cover and tactical support for the invasion of Italy at Salerno in September. Although again he was new to this form of warfare, the squadron's performance was admirable and it was able to remain operating on station for longer than expected.

Immediately after the Salerno operations, Vian was informed that he was to be given the sea command of the Allied navies engaged in the invasion of Normandy. Churchill's personal offer of succeeding Admiral Mountbatten (later Earl Mountbatten of Burma) as chief of combined operations he refused on the grounds that it would be a shore job. He spent two months in training Force J, one of the British amphibious forces. Plans for the naval command were revised and in January 1944 Vian was given command of the Eastern Task Force, the Western Force being commanded by an American. Vian had three British forces under him and flying his flag in the cruiser *Scylla* he spent a testing time during and after the initial invasion. He was next appointed to command the aircraft-carrier squadron which sailed on 19 November to join the British fleet to work with the Americans in the Pacific.

The British were, in comparison with the Americans, inexperienced in this form of warfare against the Japanese, particularly in the techniques of operating for long periods without a return to base for replenishment. Accordingly the task force made four attacks on oil refineries in Sumatra which offered useful practice. After a visit to Sydney, where the logistic arrangements were completed as far as possible, the task force sailed on 23 March 1945 to join the operations already in progress for the capture of Okinawa. Because of the comparative inexperience of the ships they were allotted a separate area in which to work and they attacked with success a chain of islands used by the Japanese to reinforce Okinawa. Despite logistic difficulties due to the small and inadequate Fleet Train the fleet kept the sea for 62 days, broken only by 8 days in harbour in the middle. Confidence was raised by the failure of the suicide bombers to penetrate the armoured decks of the British carriers which were able to operate very soon after a hit. On 25 May the fleet withdrew to Sydney for repairs and maintenance, sailing again on 23 June for further operations. This time Vian's Task Force 37 operated as an integral part of the vast American fleet and despite potential difficulties over command, all went well. The British carriers attacked many targets on the Japanese homeland during this period but on 15 August all operations were cancelled because of the Japanese surrender. After goodwill visits in Australian and New Zealand waters Vian sailed for home and arrived in time to take part in the victory parade in London.

After the war Vian was fifth sea lord at the Admiralty, in charge of naval aviation (1946-8), but his essential qualities were not so suited to peacetime naval life. He was happier as commander-in-chief of the Home Fleet (1950-2) when in his flagship *Vanguard* he was able to go to sea. He retained a superb grasp of the tactical situation and his handling of the fleet was a joy to see. He had been promoted vice-admiral in 1945 and admiral in 1948 and on his retirement in 1952 he was specially promoted admiral of the fleet, a rank normally confined to first sea lords. This was fitting recognition of his remarkable service as a fighting sailor in the war in which no one else continued so long in combatant posts at sea without a break or had such an extensive geographical scope.

Vian's was a complex character who needed knowing well by his juniors if they were to retain his confidence and his inherent shyness seemed to produce an offensive approach. But his loyalty to his seniors was complete however much he disagreed with them and this was not unusual. He had his faults; an apparent intolerance of officers who did not measure up to his high standards of efficiency and initiative and resentment of any differences of opinion in public. He was then abrasive and sometimes abusive. But in private there was no more charming man, and no one with whom matters could more easily be discussed or even argued. His memoirs, *Action This Day* (1960), reveal the man who was so seldom seen in public. They are exceptionally modest, taking blame for failure or mistakes, while giving to others credit for victory or success.

His fighting qualities were superb. He was full of the offensive spirit which he communicated to those under him, but his juniors always knew that he would not take stupid risks. More than once he deferred some action because the odds were too great and he never hazarded his ships when little was to be gained. In battle he seemed to have an inborn instinct for the right decision and he was served by a devoted and competent staff. In harbour he insisted on the highest standards of cleanliness and smartness.

Vian was appointed to the DSO in 1940 with bars in 1940 and 1941. He was appointed KBE in 1942, CB and KCB in 1944, and GCB in 1952.

In 1929 he married Marjorie (died 1973), daughter of Colonel David Price Haig; they had two daughters. He died at his home in Ashford Hill, near Newbury, 27 May 1968. There is a plaque in the crypt of St. Paul's Cathedral near that of the man whom he admired more than any—Viscount Cunningham of Hyndhope [q.v.]. The Royal Naval College, Greenwich, has a portrait by Sir Oswald Birley.

[Sir Philip Vian, *Action This Day*, 1960; personal knowledge.]   PETER GRETTON

VICKY (1913–1966), cartoonist. [See WEISZ, VICTOR.]

VICTORIA ALEXANDRA ALICE MARY (1897–1965), Princess Royal of Great Britain, was born at York Cottage, Sandringham, 25 April 1897, the third child and only daughter of the future King George V and Queen Mary. Among her godparents were Queen Victoria and the Empress Marie of Russia. Known as

Princess Mary until her marriage, her education was private. History and geography were her favourite subjects and in languages, like her mother, she acquired a fluency in French. She was brought up quietly at Sandringham, Marlborough House, and later at Buckingham Palace. As an only daughter among five brothers, her childhood interests tended to the outdoor sports which they enjoyed and for some time she shared their lessons. Her reading was frequently boys' adventure stories, her favourite exercise was riding. She became an expert horsewoman and enjoyed hunting, while her lifelong interest in horse-racing was probably partly inherited from her father and after her marriage encouraged by her husband. She developed a natural interest in botany and an enjoyment of music, possessing a pleasant mezzo-soprano voice. She also took an interest in needlework, making dresses and collecting garments for her mother's Needlework Guild.

During the war of 1914–18 the Princess assisted her mother in many activities, such as those for helping the mothers, wives, and children of men serving with the forces. She took a great interest in VAD work, passing the advanced course in nursing with honours. It was a disappointment to her that she was not allowed to serve in France. Another of her great interests was the Girl Guide movement. She helped also in canteen work, insisting on taking her share of the dull routine tasks. It was her own idea after the war to visit the various women's organizations at a number of places in France. She inherited from her paternal grandfather a good memory for names and faces and, like her mother, possessed untiring energy.

In 1918 Princess Mary came of age and that year went to the Hospital for Sick Children in Great Ormond Street as a VAD probationer. She had early told her mother she thought nursing was her true vocation and her intense care and interest in the children continued long after she left the hospital in 1920.

On 28 February 1922 she married Henry George Charles Lascelles, Viscount Lascelles, elder son of the fifth and himself later sixth Earl of Harewood [q.v.]. It was the first royal pageant since the war and aroused great public excitement and enthusiasm. After her marriage she was known as Princess Mary, Viscountess Lascelles, and after her husband's succession to the earldom in 1929 as Princess Mary, Countess of Harewood, until in 1932 she was created Princess Royal. The many interests she shared with her husband included love of horse-racing and hunting, old furniture, interior decoration, and Yorkshire life. During her father-in-law's lifetime their Yorkshire home was Goldsborough Hall and after his death they moved into Harewood House. Their London home was

Chesterfield House and they occasionally stayed at Portumna Castle, Galway, which her husband had inherited from his great-uncle, the eccentric Marquess of Clanricarde [q.v.].

The Princess in 1918 became colonel-in-chief of the Royal Scots (The Royal Regiment), in 1930 of the Canadian Scottish, and in 1935 of the Royal Signals and later of other signal corps in Australia, Canada, India, and New Zealand, and of the Prince of Wales Own Regiment of Yorkshire in 1958, the Royal Regiment of Canada in 1961, and the Royal Newfoundland Regiment in 1963. In 1926 she was appointed commandant-in-chief of the British Red Cross Detachments.

The war of 1939-45 brought many additional duties. In 1940 she was made chief controller and in 1941 controller commandant of the Auxiliary Territorial Service (later the Women's Royal Army Corps). She was energetic in visiting and inspecting these troops; but she never overcame her dislike of inspecting ranks of men, which she regarded as a man's job. In addition, she paid visits to war canteens and similar welfare organizations.

The war brought its personal anxieties to her and her husband. Their elder son George, Viscount Lascelles, who had been born in 1923, was wounded and taken prisoner in Italy when serving with the Grenadier Guards, and their younger son Gerald, born in 1924, was on active service with the Rifle Brigade. However, the end of the war saw the family once more united. The loss of her husband, who died 24 May 1947, a few months after their silver wedding, increased rather than diminished her activities. She became chancellor of Leeds University in 1951, enjoying her work as such and being particularly gratified that among those upon whom she conferred honorary degrees was her elder son.

During the monarch's absences abroad she was a counsellor of state in 1939, 1943, 1944, 1947, 1953, 1954, 1956, and 1957, as also in 1951 during the King's illness. During the last decade of her life she conscientiously carried out many royal duties. In 1956 she visited France, and the next year Nigeria, while in 1960 she toured for four months in the West Indies, two years later representing the Queen at the celebrations on granting independence to Trinidad. In 1964, as colonel-in-chief of the Royal Newfoundland Regiment, she visited them on the fiftieth anniversary of the re-forming of the regiment in 1914. In October the same year she represented the Queen at Lusaka for the independence celebrations when Northern Rhodesia became Zambia. Only shortly before her death she represented the Queen at the funeral in Stockholm of Queen Louise of Sweden. The Princess died suddenly at Harewood House 28 March 1965.

The Princess was appointed CI in 1919, GBE in 1927, GCVO in 1937. She received the honorary degree of DCL from Oxford and the LLD from Cambridge, Leeds, Sheffield, St. Andrews, Manchester, McGill, Laval, and Lille. She became a Dame Grand Cross of the Venerable Order of St. John of Jerusalem in 1926 and an honorary FRCS in 1927.

A conscientious devotion to her royal duties was perhaps the keynote of the Princess's character. Although she never overcame her shyness, which made many of her official duties a trial to her, she never for that reason avoided them or found them a burden. Once she knew people she could talk with them easily and freely, as many senior girl guides and Red Cross members could testify. She was probably happiest in her home life with her family and in the quiet rural life in Yorkshire, to which county she was particularly attached. Sheffield folk always gave her a warm welcome.

A portrait of the Princess with her husband on horseback by Sir Alfred Munnings is at Harewood House, where there are also portraits by Sir Oswald Birley, Frank O. Salisbury, and J. S. Sargent. That by Birley, relaxed and natural, is regarded by the family as particularly good. She is included in a family group by Sir John Lavery, painted in 1913, now in the National Portrait Gallery. At the Royal Signals Officers Mess, Catterick, there is a portrait of her by Sir Gerald Kelly and the Royal Scots Regimental Museum, Edinburgh Castle, has one painted by Simon Elwes in 1933 and another of her with King George V and Queen Mary, painted by Gerald Hudson for the Regimental tercentenary parade the same year. The WRAC Regimental Museum has a portrait by Edward Seago and the WRAC HQ Mess, Guildford, a portrait by A. C. Davidson-Houston.

[Evelyn Graham (Netley Lucas), *Princess Mary, Viscountess Lascelles*, 1930; M. C. Carey, *Princess Mary*, 1922; James Pope-Hennessy, *Queen Mary*, 1959; *The Times*, 29 March 1965; private information.]

G. K. S. HAMILTON-EDWARDS

VICTORIA EUGÉNIE JULIA ENA (1887-1969), queen consort of King Alfonso XIII of Spain, was born at Balmoral 24 October 1887, the second of the four children and only daughter of Prince and Princess Henry of Battenberg [qq.v.]. Her mother, Princess Beatrice, was the fifth and youngest daughter of Queen Victoria. She was christened Eugénie after her godmother, the Empress Eugénie, but the name Ena, by which she was known before her marriage, was due to the minister misreading her mother's writing of the name Eva.

Her childhood was spent partly at Balmoral and partly in the Isle of Wight, where her father was governor. His death in 1896 deeply affected the Princess, but she concentrated her energies in helping her mother in her philanthropic work and in developing her music in which she showed early and unusual talent.

On 31 May 1906, in Madrid, the Princess married King Alfonso XIII of Spain. In April King Edward VII had conferred on her the style of 'royal highness' and shortly before the announcement of her engagement in March she had been received into the Roman Catholic Church. The change of denomination was not popular in Britain although King Alfonso himself was well liked, partly on account of the courage he had shown at the attempt on his life in Paris in 1905. The wedding was marred by another such attempt: a bomb was thrown at the carriage in which the King and Queen were returning after the ceremony and landed just in front of the carriage, behind the rear pair of horses. Although a number of people were killed and many wounded the King and Queen escaped unharmed and remained composed, albeit greatly shaken. That evening they rode in a carriage unescorted around the streets to assure the people that they were unharmed.

The tragic occurrence had one happier effect in bringing admiration and sympathy to the Queen; there had been suggestions that a British consort might not prove popular with the Spanish people. While respecting the traditions of the country, Queen Victoria Eugénie's ease of manner broke down to a considerable extent the extreme rigidity of the Spanish court. Her friendly manner, her avoidance of involvement in politics, and her help and hard work for the poor, all contributed to the respect and affection in which she came to be held. She particularly encouraged the provision of better hospitals and health facilities, giving much time to the reorganization of the Spanish Red Cross which during the war of 1914-18 became responsible for a scheme of international aid. She also founded a needlework guild, the Ropero de Santa Victoria, and did much to encourage education in a country which had a high rate of illiteracy.

Apart from a still-born son (1910), the King and Queen had four sons and two daughters. The Queen gave much care to the upbringing of her family and faced with fortitude the unfortunate maladies from which three of the sons suffered. The eldest, Alfonso (1907-38), and the youngest, Gonzalo (1914-34), were both afflicted with haemophilia, a disease which ultimately caused their deaths when they were involved in motor-car accidents. The second son, Jaime (1908-75), was born a deaf mute, although with patient and sympathetic training he managed later to learn to speak. The third son, Juan Carlos (born 1913), served as a midshipman in the British navy (1933-5), becoming in 1936 an honorary lieutenant. Both the daughters, the Infantas Beatriz (born 1909) and Maria Christina (born 1911), married and had issue.

In 1931 the municipal elections in Spain showed that republicanism was sweeping the country and to avoid civil war the King, while refusing to renounce his throne, left the country from Cartagena, 15 April, too suddenly to be accompanied by his family. They afterwards joined him in France and lived in exile in Italy. Later the King and Queen decided to separate, but on the King's illness the Queen went to him and was with him when he died in Rome 28 February 1941. She subsequently left Italy for Switzerland. After 1945 she made frequent visits to England, staying often with her only surviving brother, the Marquess of Carisbrooke, until his death in 1960. In 1968 she visited Spain for the first time since her exile to attend the christening of Felipe Juan, first son of Juan Carlos, the elder son of her third son, Don Juan. On this occasion she was received by General Franco and his wife. She died in Lausanne 15 April 1969. In that year her grandson, Juan Carlos, was selected by General Franco as his successor designate as head of state in preference to his father, Don Juan, and on Franco's death Juan Carlos became King of Spain 23 November 1975.

Queen Victoria Eugénie was tall and slender and possessed a gracious ease in her manner and movement. She dressed fashionably and in good taste, many of her clothes being made in Paris. Her favourite colours were grey and blue which set off her English complexion and clear gold hair, features well exemplified in her portrait by P. A. de László which is reproduced in Graham's biography. Another portrait, showing her wearing a mantilla, by the same artist, painted in the King's silver jubilee year, was later placed in the Madrid Modern Art Gallery. She was a Dame Grand Cross of the Sovereign Order of Malta and held the Grand Cross of Maria Louisa and of Public Beneficence of Spain.

[Evelyn Graham (Netley Lucas), *The Queen of Spain*, 1929; David Skene Duff, *The Shy Princess: the life of H. R. H. Princess Beatrice*, 1958; *Daily Telegraph*, 17 April 1969.]

G. K. S. HAMILTON-EDWARDS

W

WADDELL, HELEN JANE (1889-1965), author and translator, was born 31 May 1889 in Tokyo, the youngest child in the family of eight sons and two daughters of the Revd Hugh Waddell and his wife, Jane Martin, of Banbridge, county Down. Her father was a missionary, and both parents inherited a long tradition of service to the Presbyterian confession. Jane Waddell died when Helen was two; Hugh subsequently married his cousin Martha Waddell, brought the family back to Ulster when Helen was ten, and died within a year. Helen was educated at Victoria College and Queen's University, Belfast, where under Professor Gregory Smith she graduated BA with first class honours in 1911, and MA by thesis in 1912. Though she took Latin in the first year of her BA, both degrees were in English; her MA dissertation on Milton was examined by Professor George E. B. Saintsbury [q.v.] of Edinburgh, who remained an inspiring friend and courtly correspondent till his death in 1933. Though she found her stepmother uncongenial, Helen dutifully stayed with her in Ulster till Martha's death in 1919. During these years she published *Lyrics from the Chinese* (1913) and devotional bible-stories later collected in *Stories from Holy Writ* (1949), as well as articles and reviews. She also wrote a play *The Spoiled Buddha* (published 1919), which was performed in 1915 in Belfast with her brother Samuel (who became well known in Dublin as actor and playwright) in the chief role.

Helen went up to Somerville College, Oxford, in late 1920, registering for a research degree; at the invitation of St. Hilda's Hall she gave a successful course of lectures, financed by the Cassel Trust, on medieval mime, but her first acquaintance with the *Carmina Burana* at this time determined the course of her life's work on medieval Latin lyric and medieval humanism. After five terms at Oxford she moved without reluctance to London, where after failing in applications for various university posts she taught at Bedford in 1922-3. The influence of Saintsbury helped her to win the award of a Susette Taylor travelling scholarship from Lady Margaret Hall, and this allowed her two years' study in Paris between 1923 and 1925, where she perfected her French, learnt some German, and above all attained familiarity with the most important Latin poetry of the fourth to the twelfth centuries. After her return she delivered a course of lectures at Lady Margaret Hall in 1926 on 'The Wandering Scholars'.

In the years following her return to London from Paris she published a stream of books which took the academic and literary worlds by storm. *The Wandering Scholars* (1927), for which she was awarded the A. C. Benson silver medal by the Royal Society of Literature and which remains an indispensable introduction for students embarking on medieval Latin studies, provided a historical frame for her creative translations in *Medieval Latin Lyrics* (1929). These books demonstrate the combination of qualities which explain the fascination which she exercised over a wide public—the phenomenal breadth of her original reading, the vivid historical imagination with which she brings an Ausonius or Alcuin or Abelard to life, and the compelling command over language evident in both her poetic translations and in her descriptive prose. She was never an exact Latin scholar, a limitation which she converted into an advantage; for often refusing to reproduce exactly what was said, she created original poems which none the less uncannily mirror the moods of the originals. In an unpublished paper on translation, she emphasises the basic truth that 'the plant must spring again from its seed, or it will bear no flower'; with Fitzgerald, she believed 'better a live sparrow than a stuffed eagle'.

Her greatest achievement was her novel *Peter Abelard* (1933), which has been translated into nine languages, an authentic evocation of the worlds of twelfth-century Paris and Brittany. This was followed by *The Desert Fathers* (1936), a translation of selections of Rosweyd's celebrated edition of *Vitae Patrum* (1615) to which she prefaced a characteristically perceptive and enthusiastic introduction. Earlier she had found time to edit *A Book of Medieval Latin for Schools* (1931, frequently reprinted) and *Cole's Paris Journal* (1931), to translate *Manon Lescaut* (1931) and to write a play about its author *The Abbé Prévost* (1931), and to make a collection of translated stories called *Beasts and Saints* (1934). During the thirties she was overwhelmed with demands to lecture to learned societies. She received honorary degrees from Durham (1932), Belfast (1934), Columbia (1935), and St. Andrews (1936); she was made a member of the Royal Irish Academy (1932) and a corresponding fellow of the Medieval Academy of America (1937). Through her books and subsequently through her engaging personality and affectionate warmth she gained the friendship of such disparate literary figures as AE, (Sir) Max Beerbohm, Charles L. Morgan, George Bernard Shaw, and Siegfried Sassoon [qq.v.]. She breakfasted with Stanley Baldwin, lunched with Queen Mary, and (during World War II) dined with General de

Gaulle. The details of her literary successes and social encounters she recounted in a succession of revealing letters to her sister Meg in Banbridge.

After the appearance of *Peter Abelard* (a sequel to which was planned but never written) her life's ambition was to publish a study of John of Salisbury. But the onset of World War II thwarted this plan. Her activities at Constable's (with which she had long been connected in an advisory capacity, and where she now assumed the assistant editorship of *The Nineteenth Century* under F. A. Voigt, q.v.), her passionate and time-devouring patriotism, and the domestic distractions of a large house in Primrose Hill Road, where her ageing publisher Otto Kyllmann became a permanent resident, left her little leisure for sustained writing. (The occasional translations which she essayed have been gathered by Dame Felicitas Corrigan in *More Latin Lyrics from Virgil to Milton*, 1976.) These pressures, accentuated by a near escape from a German 'doodle-bug' in 1944 and by further bomb damage to her house the following year, took a heavy toll of her nervous energy, and she began to suffer from intermittent amnesia.

An invitation from the university of Glasgow to deliver the W. P. Ker lecture stimulated her to resume her intellectual activities, but this was to be her last sustained contribution. Published as *Poetry in the Dark Ages* (1948), it retraverses the areas of *The Wandering Scholars* which might best have inspired post-war Britain seeking to build the new Troy. By the early 1950s she was increasingly gripped by mental paralysis, and for some years before her death was oblivious to her surroundings. She died in London 5 March 1965. She had never married. Two portraits by Grace Henry (reproduced in *More Latin Lyrics*) are in the possession of relatives in Kilmacrew House, Banbridge.

[Monica Blackett, *The Mark of the Maker, a Portrait of Helen Waddell*, 1973; Dame Felicitas Corrigan, *More Latin Lyrics from Virgil to Milton*, 1976; private information.]

P. G. WALSH

WAGER, LAWRENCE RICKARD (1904–1965), geologist, explorer, and mountaineer, was born at Batley, Yorkshire, 5 February 1904, the son of Morton E. Wager, headmaster of Hebden Bridge Grammar School, and his wife, Adelina Rickard. Wager attended his father's school and Leeds Grammar School. Proceeding with an open scholarship to Pembroke College, Cambridge, he took a first class in the natural sciences tripos (part i, 1925, part ii, geology, 1926), numbering J. E. Marr, Alfred Harker [qq.v.], and C. E. Tilley among his teachers. He engaged in research at Cambridge

until 1929 when he was appointed lecturer in the geology department at Reading University.

During the next ten years Wager carried out extensive explorations in East Greenland, where he over-wintered in 1930-1 and 1935-6, and commenced his classic study of the Skaergaard layered igneous intrusion.

An outstanding mountaineer and rock climber, Wager was chosen to participate in the 1933 Everest expedition, led by Hugh Ruttledge [q.v.]. With (Sir) P. Wyn Harris, he reached a height of some 28,000 feet in the final attempt to reach the summit without the use of extra oxygen.

After distinguished war service as squadron leader in the photographic reconnaissance section of the Royal Air Force, including duty in arctic Russia, in 1944 Wager was appointed to the chair of geology at Durham in succession to Arthur Holmes [q.v.]. He was elected FRS in 1946 and in 1950 moved to the chair at Oxford where, almost from scratch, he created an outstanding department. He was a fellow of University College.

While his work on the Skaergaard intrusion is characterized by a meticulous attention to fine detail that has ensured its permanent place as a keystone in petrological thought, Wager was always keenly aware of the wider implications of his research. For example, in a presidential address to Section C of the British Association in 1958, he built on the early ideas of Lord Kelvin [q.v.] and others to sketch a picture of the evolution of the earth's mantle in terms of convective circulation and crystallization of the kind he had recognized in the Skaergaard intrusion. While more recent opinion might assign a lesser role to convection currents in the formation of layered intrusions than Wager envisaged, convective circulation on the grand scale of the whole earth's mantle became widely accepted as the driving force for Continental drift and the modern plate tectonics, a concept which would have aroused the greatest enthusiasm in Wager had he lived to see its full development.

As a teacher Wager exerted a profound influence through his research students, who became imbued with his enthusiasms and high standards. As a formal lecturer he was less effective, being too honest to oversimplify or gloss over a problem, and rather diffident in his delivery. But few lecturers ever took greater pains in the preparation of their material.

'Bill' Wager was one of the best geological thinkers of his generation and his influence upon his science was deep and lasting. His published work concentrated largely but by no means exclusively on the petrology and genesis of basic igneous rocks, particularly of layered intrusions, stemming from his detailed research on the Skaergaard in the 1930s, which he continued and expanded for the rest of his life. The full breadth of his geological interests and expertise was perhaps only apparent to those who worked closely with him in research or on scientific committees. In research he was single-minded, determined, and an exacting team leader. It was not always easy to work with him but the experience in the end was uniquely rewarding. He set the very highest standards and maintained them himself, this uncompromising honesty and straightforwardness being as characteristic of his personal as of his scientific life.

In appearance, Bill Wager was short, stocky, and tough, with wide-set blue-grey eyes and a very upright bearing. He had a beautiful speaking voice and a precise and elegant use of the English language. In manner, he was modest yet confident; shy and reserved with those whom he knew less than well but displaying a warmth, humanity, and understanding towards the limited number privileged to be counted among his close friends. He generally appeared undemonstrative and was never lavish with praise: when approbation was given, it was really meant. By the same token, if Wager described someone as 'rather a silly chap', it was to be taken as the ultimate in denigration.

Wager's work was recognized by the award of the Lyell Fund (1939), the Bigsby medal (1945), the Lyell medal (1962), all from the Geological Society of London, and the Spendiarov prize from the International Geological Congress (1948). For his achievements in exploration and mountaineering Wager received the Arctic medal (1933) and the Mungo Park medal of the Royal Geographical Society (1936).

In 1934 Wager married Phyllis Margaret, daughter of Edgar Worthington, secretary of the Institution of Mechanical Engineers. She was his constant and unfailing partner, and accompanied him on his 1935-6 Greenland expedition. They had two sons and three daughters, and formed a very closely knit family. Apart from geology, which appeared to occupy his thoughts most of the time, Wager was a keen gardener at his home in Oxford, and a discriminating collector of antique books, particularly those concerned with geology. He died suddenly while visiting London 20 November 1965.

[*The Times*, 22 November 1965; W. A. Deer in *Biographical Memoirs of Fellows of the Royal Society*, vol. xiii, 1967; personal knowledge.]   E. A. VINCENT

WALEY, ARTHUR DAVID (1889–1966), orientalist, was born at Tunbridge Wells 19 August 1889, the second of the three sons of David Frederick Schloss, economist and Fabian socialist, and his wife, Rachel Sophia, daughter of Jacob Waley [q.v.], legal writer and professor of political economy, whose surname the family adopted in 1914. He was the brother of Sir Sigismund David Waley [q.v.].

Arthur Waley was brought up in Wimbledon and sent to school at Rugby (1903-6), where he shone as a classical scholar and won an open scholarship at King's College, Cambridge, while still under seventeen. He spent a year in France before going up to the university in 1907; he obtained a first class in part i of the classical tripos in 1910 but was obliged to abandon Cambridge when he developed diminished sight in one eye due to conical cornea. Rest and Continental travel saved the second eye from being affected and made him fluent in Spanish and German. Although he had got to know (Sir) Sydney Cockerell [q.v.] at Cambridge it was through Oswald Sickert, a brother of the painter, that he was led to consider a career in the British Museum. Sickert was one of a group of friends, mostly either on the museum staff or researchers in the library, who used to meet regularly for lunch in the years before 1914 at the Vienna Café in New Oxford Street, at which Laurence Binyon [q.v.] was one of the 'regulars'. In 1912 Sir Sidney Colvin [q.v.] retired from his keepership of prints and drawings and Waley was a candidate for the vacancy in February 1913, supported by both Sickert and Cockerell. In June he started working in the newly formed sub-department of oriental prints and drawings under its first head, Binyon. Waley's task was to make a rational index of the Chinese and Japanese painters represented in the museum collection; he immediately started to teach himself Chinese and Japanese. He had no formal instruction, for the School of Oriental Studies was not founded till 1916; but by that date Waley was privately printing his first fifty-two translations of Chinese poems, and in 1917-18 he added others in the first numbers of the *Bulletin* of the School and in the *New Statesman* and the *Little Review*. By 1918 he had completed enough translations of poems, mainly by writers of the classic T'ang period, to have a volume entitled *A Hundred and Seventy Chinese Poems* accepted for publication by Constable largely on account of a perceptive review in the *Times Literary Supplement* of the 1917 *Bulletin* poems. In 1919 (Sir) Stanley Unwin [q.v.] became his publisher and remained his constant friend and admirer.

During his sixteen years at the museum Waley's only official publications were the index of Chinese artists (1922), at that time the first in the West; and a catalogue of the paintings recovered from Tun-huang by Sir Aurel Stein [q.v.]

and subsequently divided between the Government of India and the British Museum (1931). His *An Introduction to the Study of Chinese Painting* (1923) was a by-product of his unpublished notes on the national collection and its relation to the great tradition of Chinese painting. He also set in order and described the Japanese books with woodcut illustrations and the large collection of Japanese paintings. He retired from the museum on the last day of 1929 because he had been told that he ought to spend his winters abroad. Waley had started to ski as early as 1911 and he liked to get away into the mountains whenever he could, generally to Austria or Norway and not to the regular runs but as a lone figure on the high snow slopes.

In 1925 began the publication of Waley's largest and probably best-known translation—of the *Genji Monogatari* by Murasaki Shikibu, the late tenth-century classical novelist of Japan, the sixth volume of which did not appear until 1933. This was not the first of Waley's Japanese translations, for it had been preceded by two volumes of classic poetry, selections from the *Uta* (1919) and *Nō* plays (1921); in these he was more concerned with the resonances of the Japanese language, whereas in the *Genji* he aimed rather at an interpretation of the sensibility and wit of the closed society of the Heian court, described in the idiomatic English of his day. Inevitably this already shows signs of dating as the idiom itself becomes remote, but it may be long before it is again possible to enter so sympathetically into the spirit of that refined and élitist world.

The translations of Chinese poetry which he continued to produce for the rest of his life show Waley more as a creative poet, though his lives of Po Chü-i and Li Po show how closely he was aware of their milieux. In his verse translations Waley not only wanted to evoke the mood and intention of the original text but also to convey in the English mode the stresses of Chinese verse form. He denied the influence of G. Manley Hopkins in his use of 'sprung rhythm' but said that he was influenced by him in the phrasing of the Nō plays. In fact the level of his speech rhythm is naturally different from that of Hopkins, with none of its urgent acceleration but rather with the clear phrasing of the flute which he enjoyed playing.

Waley moved with the smooth grace of the skier, his gesture was courtly in salutation, but more characteristic was the attentive, withdrawn pose of his finely profiled head with its sensitive but severe mouth. His voice was high-pitched but low-toned and unchanging, so as to seem conversational in a lecture, academic in conversation. In later life he had a slight stoop which accentuated his ascetic appearance. He enjoyed meeting the sympathetic and their conversation but never spoke himself unless he had something to say; he expected the same restraint in others. His forty years' attachment to Beryl de Zoete, the anthropologist and interpreter of Eastern dance forms, brought out the depth of feeling and tenderness of which he was capable.

As a scholar Waley aimed always to express Chinese and Japanese thought at their most profound levels, with the highest standard of accuracy of meaning, in a way that would not be possible again because of the growth of professional specialization. He was always a lone figure in his work though he was not remote from the mood of his times. Although he never travelled to the Far East and did not seek to confront the contemporary societies of China or Japan, he was scathingly critical of the attitude of the West to their great cultures in the world in which he grew up: hence his scorn for the older generation of sinologists and his hatred of imperialism, as shown in his *The Opium War through Chinese Eyes* (1958).

For over forty years Waley lived in Bloomsbury, mostly in Gordon Square. Although he had many connections with the Bloomsbury group of artists and writers, he was never a member of a clique and his friendships with the Stracheys, the Keyneses, and with Roger Fry [q.v.] dated from his Cambridge days. He was elected an honorary fellow of King's in 1945 but was not often seen there. Other honours also came to him late, election to the British Academy in 1945, the Queen's medal for poetry in 1953, CBE in 1952, and CH in 1956. Aberdeen and Oxford universities awarded him honorary doctorates. After the death of Beryl in 1962 he went to live in Highgate where he was looked after by Alison Grant Robinson, an old friend from New Zealand, who was formerly married to Hugh Ferguson Robinson, and to whom he was married a month before his death at home from cancer of the spine 27 June 1966.

A volume of appreciation and an anthology of his writings was edited by Ivan Morris, under the title *Madly Singing in the Mountains* (1970), a phrase taken from a poem by Po Chü-i which Waley had translated in 1917 and chosen because of its 'joyfulness', as expressed in the lines:

'Each time that I look at a fine landscape:
   Each time that I meet a loved friend,
I raise my voice and recite a stanza of poetry
   And am glad as though a God had crossed
          my path.'

Two notes that Waley wrote on his own work when over seventy, while not factually reliable, contain his own assessment of his translations; that he had made them to the measure of his own tastes and sensibilities, in a 'recherche esthétique'. Forty years earlier he had written: 'If I have failed to make these translations in some sense works of art—if they are mere philology, not literature, then I have indeed fallen short of what I hoped and intended.' It can be asserted that his intention was fully realized.

A bibliography of Waley's work was published by F. A. Johns in 1968. A portrait drawing by Michael Ayrton is in King's College, Cambridge, and a pencil drawing by Rex Whistler is in the National Portrait Gallery.

[Introduction to the second edition of *170 Chinese Poems*, 1962; Ivan Morris (ed.), *Madly Singing in the Mountains*, 1970; *The Times*, 28 June 1966; L. P. Wilkinson in *King's College Annual Report*, 1966; private information; personal knowledge.]

BASIL GRAY

WALEY, SIR (SIGISMUND) DAVID (1887-1962), public servant, was born in London 19 March 1887, the eldest of the three sons of David Frederick Schloss, Board of Trade official and writer on economic and social matters, and his wife, Rachel Sophia Waley, the daughter of Jacob Waley [q.v.]. He assumed the surname of Waley in 1914, as did his brother Arthur David [q.v.]. He was educated at Rugby, where he was head boy, and at Balliol College, Oxford, where he obtained a first class in both classical honour moderations (1908) and *literae humaniores* (1910). He held scholarships at both Rugby and Balliol.

It was the classical preparation for a career in the public service, which he duly joined in 1910, in circumstances which clearly exemplified the man. In order to sit the Civil Service examination, he had to cross the English Channel. The passage was stormy; and, when he arrived in London, he was prostrated by seasickness. But he presented himself at the appropriate place on the following morning; and, when the results were made known, he had achieved first place. The physical hardiness and the single-minded determination which were typified by this incident remained with him for the rest of his career. He was assigned to the Treasury; and it was clear from the outset that the division dealing with external finance was his natural place. But he had been there barely long enough to take his first step on the ladder of promotion—by becoming private secretary to Edwin Montagu [q.v.], the financial secretary to the Treasury, of whom he later wrote a sympathetic biography, published in 1964—when he enlisted in August 1916 and served as a second lieutenant in the 22nd battalion, London Regiment. In the course of his subsequent service in the army he was seriously wounded and was awarded the MC in October 1918. He never spoke of this period of his early adult life; but its effect on his naturally sensitive nature was always clear in the reluctance with which he brought himself to contemplate pain and suffering and the vehement conviction with which he maintained that deliberate cruelty was perhaps the worst of all human sins.

After the war he returned to his old desk in the Treasury, where he was to work for several years in tandem with (Sir) Frederick Leith-Ross [q.v.]. Waley soon became a familiar figure in the world of international finance. He was instantly recognizable—a small, dark man, with alert and flashing eyes; tough and wiry in build; modest and unassuming in manner; often to be seen with head cocked slightly on one side and an impish smile on his face as he pondered the exact phrase which would do devastating justice to the particular brand of higher lunacy which one of his more conventional colleagues happened to be purveying at that moment. He had no great respect for established reputations; and he made short work of pretentious nonsense. But his penetrating intellect was married to a shrewd sense of the feasible; and, although his mind moved quickly, often obliquely, cutting corners and sidestepping obstacles in a way which led some observers to regard him as superficial in his analysis of a problem and over-hasty in reaching a solution, those who worked more closely with him recognized that the darting speed with which he operated was simply the reflection of a restless intellectual vitality which had to explore every avenue and overturn every stone in case the truth might thereby be revealed. Others, who plodded patiently along more conventionally correct paths, were apt to find themselves left behind, puzzled—and sometimes faintly irritated—to understand how it had been done. Neither they nor he himself could wholly account for the way in which his mercurial, intuitive mind had reached an unorthodox conclusion which was nevertheless intellectually defensible but was also eminently practical in its application.

It is the nature of such a man to do business by personal exchange of views rather than by means of the written word; and, by comparison with such contemporaries as John Maynard (later Lord) Keynes [q.v.], Waley left little on personal record. His minutes on official papers were concise—sometimes comments, always penetrating and occasionally sharp, on suggestions and proposals by colleagues; more often, simply directions for action or the draft of a short, pithy, reply to some lengthy telegram from a post abroad which had appealed for help and support from Whitehall at a critical stage in a financial negotiation. There was relatively little to indicate the mental processes which had generated these terse observations; and there was no corpus of philosophy, no continuous commentary on the policies of successive governments, from which one might infer that Waley subscribed to a specific economic theory or that his advice to ministers derived from a particular set of intellectual principles. What mattered to him was to get something done, something which was sensible in the given circumstances, would work in practice, and above all, would do some positive good. An ounce of constructive, pragmatic, compromise, which would do something to liberate the channels of international exchange, to promote a more vigorous flow of trade and a freer movement of people, to alleviate hardship and poverty in the underdeveloped world—this was worth more, in Waley's eyes, than any number of elegant expositions of economic doctrine which would almost certainly be consigned to gather unregarded dust in some other bureaucrat's 'pending' tray.

It was for this reason that the years between the two great wars were probably the finest period of all his career. For some time after 1918 it was permissible to hope that the international community had learned its lesson and that the world might really be rebuilt on more rational and less selfish foundations; and at the Paris peace conference in 1919 and the Lausanne conference in 1922-3 Waley devoted all his formidable intellectual powers to the task of guiding his political leaders, with wisdom and humanity, through the maze of problems generated by reparations, war debts, and the financial reconstruction of Europe under the League of Nations. When the clouds began to gather again, he redirected his attention and his energy to husbanding Britain's resources of gold and foreign exchange for the long haul which he knew lay ahead and reorganizing the administrative structure of the overseas finance division, of which he was by then the head, to take a new and unprecedented strain. He could probably claim greater credit than anyone else for the fact that the structure of exchange control which Britain was compelled to create during the war of 1939-45 was not merely a powerful reinforcement of the nation's military and economic effort but was also administered with common sense and humanity, not least towards those countries whose peoples were Britain's allies but whose territories were occupied by her enemies. He manifested the same combination of qualities when, towards the end of 1944, he was sent to Athens to advise on the economic reconstruction of Greece after the German forces had withdrawn. And, when the war finally came to an end in 1945, he was to be seen at Potsdam and in Moscow, grappling once again with the familiar problems of reparations and inter-Allied debts; and, a little later, in Washington, bending his mind afresh, with undiminished faith, to the enterprise of creating, through the machinery of the United Nations and the related agencies of the International Monetary Fund and the International Bank for Reconstruction and Development, a new financial structure which might match his own enlightened understanding that money should be the servant, not the master, of mankind.

He had not long to serve after the war. But, when he retired in 1948, he embarked on a new life with zest and vigour. He joined the boards of several City companies; took an active part in the work of an international charity for deprived children; was treasurer of the British Epilepsy Association; and became the chairman of the Furniture Development Council (1949-57), the Sadler's Wells Trust, and the Mercury Theatre Trust. The last of these gave him particular pleasure. Although not a maker of music himself, he delighted in music made by others; and the Ballet Rambert, which was controlled by the Mercury Theatre Trust, contributed greatly to the happiness of his later years. In return, he brought to it, as to every enterprise in which he took part, invaluable gifts of common sense, enthusiasm, and simple, unaffected, lightness of heart.

He married in 1918 Ruth Ellen, daughter of Montefiore Simon Waley, stockbroker, and his wife, Florence, daughter of Samuel Montagu (later Lord Swaythling, q.v.) and sister of Edwin Montagu. They had two sons. He was appointed CB in 1933 and KCMG in 1943. He died in London 4 January 1962.

[*The Times*, 5 January 1962; private information; personal knowledge.]   TREND

WALKER, JOHN (1900-1964), numismatist, was born 4 September 1900 at Glasgow, the youngest of the seven children of John Walker, a master carpenter, and his wife, Isabella Watson. His education was at Glasgow, at the John Street and Whitehill schools, until after a brief period of service in the army he entered the university in 1918. He studied a wide variety of subjects including classics, although his principle subject was Semitic languages, and he took first classes in Hebrew and Arabic in 1922. He was a Lanfine bursar and John Clark scholar. To his master's degree he proceeded to add the diploma of the Jordanhill Training College and in 1924 went to teach, as first assistant, at St. Andrew's Boys School in Alexandria in Egypt until 1927. He was next assistant lecturer in Arabic at Glasgow for a year, but went back to Egypt to work for the Ministry of Education from 1928 to 1930. By this time he had already published numerous articles in, for instance, the *Encyclopaedia of Islam* (to which he continued to contribute throughout his life), and had prepared works on *Bible Characters in the Koran* (1931) and *Folk Medicine in Modern Egypt* (1934), based on his close knowledge of Egypt and the Islamic world.

In 1931 Walker was appointed assistant keeper in the department of coins and medals at the British Museum. Thenceforth his scholarship and experience were to be applied mainly to the field of Islamic numismatics, which had been somewhat neglected since the compilation of the museum's *Catalogue of Oriental Coins* by Stanley Lane-Poole [q.v.]. The two volumes which Walker produced at the museum are the monument of his life's work. The first of these, dealing with the Arab–Sassanian coins, was finished in 1939 but published only in 1941; and was at once recognized by the award of the D.Litt. of Glasgow University. At precisely this moment Walker was taken from the museum to serve until 1945 in the Air Staff Intelligence, on account of his special knowledge of Arabic and of the Near East. On his return to the museum he set to work on the next volume of his catalogue, despite the circumstances of post-war disorganization and the assumption of ever more extensive responsibilities. In 1948 he was elected secretary of the Royal Numismatic Society and in 1949 he became deputy keeper of his department at the museum; in 1952 he succeeded as keeper, becoming at the same time an editor of the *Numismatic Chronicle*. He had also from 1937 to 1947 been an additional lecturer at the School of Oriental and African Studies in London University. His own work was maintained, however, and in 1956 there appeared the second volume of his catalogue, devoted to the Arab–Byzantine coins. Only three years later he was responsible, as keeper, for the removal of the department of coins and medals from its temporary housing into rebuilt quarters. His work as secretary of, and from 1956 as chief editor for, the Royal Numismatic Society was assiduous and exemplary, and it was largely his achievement that, by the time of his death, the society's total membership had trebled to about 600 members in all parts of the world.

Walker's scholarly and numismatic publications, over and above the catalogues, include many remarkable and original works. He broke new ground with his fundamental studies of Islamic coinage in Africa with his monograph on the Sultans of Kilwa, and of that in central Asia with his treatise on the second Saffarid dynasty in Sistan; and above all with his discovery of a series of coins issued by Arab governors in Crete in the ninth century,

whose existence had previously been unsuspected. One of his keenest interests was in pre-Islamic Arabia, on which he wrote a number of articles: and another masterly stroke was his identification of a coinage of mixed Arab–Roman type as being of the city of Hatra. The scope of his activity at the museum is further attested by articles on such disparate topics as Italian medals, a Roman coin hoard, and a find of Anglo-Saxon pennies from Tetney in Lincolnshire. His mastery and acumen in all branches of the Semitic languages, ancient and modern, were always of the greatest value in dealing with otherwise intractable problems, and it may be recalled for instance how the history of Cyprus in the fourth century BC was changed, at a blow, by Walker's reading, correct and unhesitating, of a new Phoenician inscription on a coin of the island.

The two-volume *Catalogue of Muhammadan Coins in the British Museum* constituted Walker's chief glory. It dealt with the initial and transitional stages of the Arab coinage, those crucial and almost intolerably intractable sections of the subject which, as Walker sometimes remarked drily, but with a twinkle, 'Lane-Poole had found too difficult'. This was nothing less than the truth, and it was well that these topics had been left over, for a far greater degree of organized knowledge, and especially a mastery of modern numismatic techniques, only developed after Poole's day, were needful to cope effectively with such complexities. In the first volume, the Arab–Sassanian coins comprise all those issues of Sassanian-derived type made for Arab governors in Iran until the general currency reform of Abd-al-Malik; and the wide range of interlocking problems, linguistic, epigraphic, historical, was successfully treated by Walker on the basis of an ordered collection of material from every source, going far beyond the contents of the British Museum's own collection. In particular the interpretation of mint-marks and chronology was such as to throw much new light also on the Sassanians, a topic to which Walker had ever hoped to devote himself one day. The second volume covered the equally complex first period of the coinage of the Arab caliphate, in which extensive use was made of prototypes from the Byzantine empire, together with the Latin-inscribed Arab coins of North Africa and Spain, as well as the Ummayad coins of the post-reform period. The depth and thoroughness with which Walker investigated every ramification of this vast material, and its masterly presentation, form as fundamental a contribution as the first volume to the historical understanding of the vital formative period of the Islamic civilization, in ts relationships to Byzantium and to Iran.

Recognition of Walker's achievement in numismatic scholarship was attested by the award of the Huntington medal of the American Numismatic Society in 1955 and of the medal of the Royal Numismatic Society in 1956. He was elected a corresponding member of the Swedish Royal Academy and a member of the Institut d'Egypte, and in 1958 a fellow of the British Academy; a year before his death he was appointed CBE. A portrait medal of Walker by Paul Vincze was struck for the occasion of his retirement, due in 1965.

Walker's work was his life. He remained a bachelor. But many remember him as a most human personality and the kindest of colleagues, ever generous and helpful with his advice to any who sought it. His very Scottish and sometimes unexpected sense of humour would not only rejoice his friends but on occasion serve to turn a tricky situation. He genuinely delighted in the good things of life, in music and opera, in the civilized enjoyment of food and drink wherein he was a considerable connoisseur, and in the peace of the home where he lived latterly in the Essex countryside. He remained ever a devoted member of the Roman Catholic Church into which he was received as a young man; and endured his last illness with stoic courage. He died in Chelmsford 12 November 1964.

[E. S. G. Robinson in *Proceedings* of the British Academy, vol. lii, 1966; A memoir with bibliography in *Numismatic Chronicle*, vol. v, 1965; personal knowledge.]

G. K. Jenkins

WALKER, THOMAS (1891-1965), professor of horticultural chemistry, was born 5 September 1891 at Newton on the Moor, near Alnwick, the eighth child of the family of three sons and six daughters of Thomas Wallace, a blacksmith and agricultural engineer, and his wife, (Isabella) Mary Thompson. He won a county scholarship to Rutherford College in Newcastle in 1905 and five years later entered Armstrong College of the university of Durham, where he took his B.Sc. degree in 1913, with distinction in chemistry. By this time he had become staff sergeant in the university's Officers' Training Corps, and on the outbreak of war in 1914 he was commissioned and posted to the 3rd Border Regiment. Almost immediately he was sent to France and attached to the Royal West Kent Regiment during the early fighting in France and Flanders. He was one of the 'old contemptibles' who received the 1914 Mons star. Then in 1915 he returned to the Border Regiment, serving with the 29th division in Gallipoli, where he was awarded the Military Cross. In 1916 he was sent back to France and appointed adjutant to the 11th

Sussex Regiment. At Richebourg in July 1917 he received a severe wound which left him with a permanently stiff left knee. He was subsequently seconded to the Royal Engineers for service in the anti-gas department, which continued until his demobilization in 1919. In the 1939-45 war he organized the Long Ashton Local Defence Volunteers, which became a company of the 7th battalion of the Somerset Home Guard, of which Major Wallace was second-in-command.

Wallace joined the staff of the Long Ashton Agricultural and Horticultural Research Station of the university of Bristol in 1919 as assistant to C. T. Gimingham, a former colleague in the anti-gas department. When Gimingham left in 1920 Wallace was appointed agricultural research chemist at Long Ashton and advisory officer in agricultural chemistry for the Bristol Province (the West of England and the West Midlands). This was a daunting assignment for one not familiar with crops, but Wallace quickly demonstrated to the fruit growers of Hereford and the Vale of Evesham that the crippling malady of leaf scorch in plums and apples was a deficiency disease curable by the application of potash. This practical help secured the lasting confidence of the growers and opened up a new field of research.

By intensive and exacting investigations Wallace and his rapidly growing team established the effects of four major plant nutrients and eleven micronutrients on forty-eight crops. These results were embodied in *The Diagnosis of Mineral Deficiencies in Plants by Visual Symptoms*, 1943 and subsequent editions, which remained the standard authority on the subject. During the wartime ploughing-up campaign, Wallace's work was of immense value in correcting soil deficiencies and so bringing into full production thousands of acres previously considered infertile.

In the university of Bristol Wallace was research chemist in agricultural chemistry from 1919 to 1933; deputy director from 1924 to 1943; and director and professor of horticultural chemistry from 1943 to 1957.

However, when in 1924 Wallace was appointed deputy director at Long Ashton, it rapidly became apparent that the director, Professor B. T. P. Barker, was very willing to transfer to his deputy much of the burden of station administration. Consequently, although Wallace's titular directorship covered only the period 1943 to 1957, he exerted a decisive influence on the development of the station for three decades, during which he organized a sevenfold increase in scientific staff with a corresponding growth in buildings and equipment. Outside Long Ashton, Wallace played a major part in the post-war reorganization of the agricultural research and advisory services: he served on numerous committees of the Ministry of Agriculture, the Agricultural Research Council, the National Agricultural Advisory Service, and on the governing bodies of many of the agricultural and horticultural stations, colleges, and institutes. He was a governor of the Royal Agricultural College, Cirencester, in 1944.

As editor from 1943 to 1958 of the *Journal of Horticultural Science* he established its reputation among scientific journals. An Agricultural Research Council Unit was set up within his institute in 1952, so that salaries and expenses arising from this work were carried on a separate grant. Wallace was honorary director of this Unit of Plant Nutrition (micronutrients), and his standing was further recognized by requests for advice which took him to Australia, New Zealand, the United States, France, Spain, and the Caribbean, visits which themselves stimulated a constant flow of workers from these countries to Long Ashton.

Wallace was a man of complete integrity, forthright in his approach both to people and to his scientific work. In his research and in his administrative sphere he would accept nothing improvised or uncertain. He figures in Edmund Blunden's *Undertones of War* (1928) as 'the austere Wallace' and indeed he scorned any form of self-aggrandizement. His director's room was an uncarpeted laboratory with a battered desk and a few wooden chairs. He maintained his soldierly carriage and, to those who did not know him well, he seemed inflexible, but his friends remember him as a brave, kindly man, an inspiring leader, whose great ability, amounting to genius in his own field, was clothed with modesty.

His honours and awards included the D.Sc. of the university of Durham (1931), the Victoria medal of honour of the Royal Horticultural Society (1952), and CBE (1947). He became FRIC (1946) and FRS (1953).

He married in 1917 Gladys Mary, daughter of Robert Johnson Smith, a Merchant Navy captain, and had a daughter, Jean, and a son, Alan, both of whom qualified in medicine. After the death of his wife in 1936, his second marriage, in 1938, was to Elsie Stella, daughter of Colonel John Smyth of the Indian Medical Service. They had one son. Alan and his wife were tragically killed in a plane accident in 1963, leaving two young children to become the responsibility of their grandparents. In 1958 Wallace had a severe illness, but made an excellent recovery. On 1 February 1965 he visited his office at Long Ashton, looking fit and well: on the next day he collapsed and died in Bristol. His portrait, painted in oils in 1957 by John Whitlock, hangs in the committee room of the university of Bristol research station at Long Ashton.

[W. K. Slater and H. G. H. Kearns in *Biographical Memoirs of Fellows of the Royal Society*, vol. xii, 1966; personal knowledge.]

R. W. Marsh

WALTER, JOHN (1873–1968), a proprietor of *The Times*, founded by his great-great-grandfather in 1785, was born in London 8 August 1873, the elder son of Arthur Fraser Walter and his wife, Henrietta Maria, eldest daughter of the Revd Thomas Anchitel Anson, of Longford rectory, Derbyshire. His father was the second son of John Walter the third [q.v.] but succeeded to the control of *The Times* because his elder brother, John, had been drowned while life-saving at Bear Wood in 1870. The subject of the present notice strove throughout his life to be known as John Walter the fifth. Arthur Walter became chief proprietor of *The Times* in 1894 and died in 1910, so John Walter had a long warning of, and schooling in, the responsibilities of Printing House Square.

His heritage was, however, no longer a controlling interest. The complicated financial quarrels in the Walter family which led to loss of control began in 1898, the year John Walter started work on *The Times*. For nearly a decade he had little interest in them. Educated at Eton and Christ Church, Oxford, where he obtained a third class in *literae humaniores* (1897), he served nominally as assistant to C. F Moberly Bell [q.v.], manager of *The Times*. Bell straddled, particularly on the foreign side, both managerial and editorial departments in a way none of his successors did. John Walter's interests were all editorial. He visited the paper's correspondents in Vienna, St. Petersburg, and Berlin, and was often in Paris. He knew de Blowitz, the famous Paris correspondent of *The Times*, well, and wrote his obituary in 1903. Some years later he refused the Paris post. He was present as a representative of his paper at the first Hague Conference in 1899. The same year he attended the retrial of Dreyfus at Rennes. He visited Canada and the United States in 1902. He was based in Madrid as *The Times*'s correspondent for the Iberian peninsula at the time his father died. He had a lifelong affection for Spain. He spent the years 1916–18 as publicity attaché at the British Embassy in Madrid, countering German propaganda; his elder son, John, was to serve in the embassy's press section in the second war.

Nevertheless, in view of his eventual succession, Walter took some part in the abortive negotiations with (Sir) C. Arthur Pearson [q.v.] and when the ensuing ones with Lord Northcliffe [q.v.] succeeded in 1908 it was agreed he should become chairman of *The Times* on his father's death. By 1910 the two years 'honey-moon period' of the new partnership was nearing its end. Walter stepped into twelve agitated and occasionally stormy years, which broke even his patience at the last. Walter's relations with Northcliffe were never simple. The picture of him as an ineffectual man, continually over-ridden, obscures the better lights of his character. He was determined not to be an absentee figurehead like his father who had never had any close working association with *The Times*. John Walter, shortly after he had become chairman, went back to Portugal to report the revolution there.

Walter was convinced that *The Times* needed new blood. But he soon realized that with a man such as Northcliffe, at heart far more a journalist than a newspaper owner, any hope of editorial independence was frail. In 1913, at personal financial sacrifice, he obtained an option to buy back Northcliffe's shares on the latter's death. Meanwhile he soldiered on in his quiet way for the traditions of the paper. Northcliffe at times became impatient with Walter, as he did with everyone else. Yet the two men kept a liking for each other. At last in 1922 Walter's staying power was exhausted. In June he cancelled the 1913 agreement and with it the option. Northcliffe asked him to continue as chairman. Walter, regaining his nerve, agreed, provided the option was maintained. In August Northcliffe died.

In the ensuing battle for *The Times*, involving Lloyd George, the first Lord Rothermere [qq.v.] and others, Walter wisely chose the best ally. When, on 23 October 1922, he and John Astor (later Lord Astor of Hever) became joint chief proprietors of *The Times*, Walter had achieved his aim of ensuring the paper's complete editorial independence. He stayed much the junior partner in a stable relationship, and his chief proprietorship, involving by that time only responsibility for the appointment and dismissal of the editor, lasted until *The Times* and the *Sunday Times* were merged under Lord Thomson of Fleet on 1 January 1967, when his family's long connection with *The Times* came to an end.

Combining great courtesy and an austere manner, Walter was essentially an uncombative man. To hear him describe the arrival at Bear Wood of the issue of *The Times* containing the forged Parnell letter was to realize the generations he spanned. Yet in his ninetieth birthday luncheon speech in Printing House Square he spoke only of the future. He did not feel his position precluded him from letting the editor know his views on public affairs. (He was against *The Times*'s appeasement policy.) He always emphasized that he did so as an ordinary reader, and meant it. His loyalty to his editor's authority was absolute. If he was less forceful than

his predecessors as head of *The Times*, he was more versatile. He painted and drew extremely well. He wrote clear prose. In his nineties he still read *The Times* closely, his dry comments making him an engaging companion. In 1961 he was received into the Roman Catholic Church, as his mother had been. He had known the splendours of Bear Wood, had lived in the Private House at Printing House Square and seen it demolished; he died in a modest flat at Hove 11 August 1968. He never repined.

Walter married in 1903 Charlotte Hilda (Phyllis), youngest daughter of Colonel Charles Edward Foster, of Buckby Hall, Northamptonshire. She died in 1937. They had two sons and two daughters. His second wife, Rosemary, only daughter of James Adair Crawford, ICS, whom he married in 1939, survived him. A portrait of Walter, c.1924, by P. A. de László is the property of *The Times*.

[The Walter papers in the offices of *The Times*; family papers; *The History of 'The Times'*, vol. iii, 1947, vol. iv, 2 parts, 1952; personal knowledge.]   WILLIAM HALEY

WARBURG, EDMUND FREDERIC (1908–1966), botanist, was born in London 22 March 1908, the eldest of the four sons of (Sir) Oscar Emanuel Warburg, a business man and later chairman of the London County Council, and his wife, Catherine Widdrington, daughter of Sir Edmund W. Byrne, judge [q.v.]. The family, of German-Jewish origin, is connected to the botanically illustrious Warburgs resident in Germany, of whom the most noted are Otto Warburg, the systematist, and Otto Warburg, the eminent physiologist, who is most widely remembered as the inventor of the Warburg manometer. For many years Warburg's family home was 'Boidier' at Headley, near Epsom in Surrey, where his father, a keen horticulturist and amateur botanist, assembled a large collection of hardy plants, notably *Cistus*, *Berberis*, and oaks. His father's zeal no doubt channelled Warburg's interest in botany, for, after being educated at Marlborough (1921–7) and going up to Trinity College, Cambridge, as an entrance scholar in mathematics in 1927, he transferred to natural sciences. He was subsequently elected a senior scholar. He obtained a second class in part i of the natural sciences tripos in 1929. Taking botany as his part ii subject in the same tripos, he obtained a first class in 1930.

Whilst an undergraduate, Warburg made a botanical expedition with T. G. Tutin to the Azores, some results of which they published in the *Journal of Botany* in 1932. Warburg was responsible for the introduction to cultivation of *Daboecia azorica*, a species new to science. Before graduating, Warburg wrote an account of the genus *Cistus* with his father as co-author, and shortly afterwards they wrote a useful paper on oaks in cultivation. Meanwhile Warburg prepared a Ph.D. thesis on the cytotaxonomy of the Geraniales, under the supervision of Miss Edith Saunders. On the strength of this, which he obtained in 1937, he was elected a research fellow of Trinity College in 1933. In 1938 he was appointed an assistant lecturer at Bedford College, London, and in 1941 joined the RAF. Attached to the photographic interpretation unit at Medmenham, Buckinghamshire, Warburg found his botanical pursuits restricted. This encouraged him to turn to the humble Bryophyta, a collection of which he had made in the Azores and a group which was to absorb much of his efforts for the rest of his life. After the war, Warburg returned to Bedford College and in 1948 went to the department of botany at Oxford as university demonstrator in botany and curator of the Druce herbarium. His first task was the putting in order of the herbarium, then still at the house of George Claridge Druce [q.v.] in Crick Road, and the supervision of its transfer to the newly built Botany School. At Oxford Warburg's gifts of patient pedagogy, particularly appreciated by the unsure and the amateur, with whom he took immense trouble, his good taxonomic 'eye' and his unexcelled skill as a tireless field botanist endeared him to his pupils and his colleagues. He is remembered for his sound common sense concerning university matters and for his championship of botany in all its branches when it was fashionable for those in authority to promote a rather narrow approach to the subject. In 1964 he was made reader in plant taxonomy and elected a fellow of New College.

Warburg was elected FLS in 1934 and joined the Botanical Society of the British Isles in 1946. For the rest of his life he served on its committees, including the Distribution Maps Committee, whose work resulted in *The Atlas of the British Flora*, and was a member of its council, while from 1949 to 1960 he was editor of its journal, *Watsonia*. Like Druce before him, he was a key figure in the Society, but being a modest man of few words he never dominated it as his predecessor had done. In 1960 he was elected an honorary member and was its president from 1965 until his death. From 1946 Warburg had been a recorder of mosses for the British Bryological Society and was its president from 1962 to 1963. At the time of his death he was engaged in writing a new British moss flora with A. C. Crundwell. This was one of several incomplete projects either begun or contemplated, for it seems that Warburg lacked the drive to carry through major works—an extension of his study of oaks, or of *Sorbus*, on the British species of which he was an auth-

ority, to a monographic treatise or even to a European revision was not his forte, despite the fact that he made several long holidays on the Continent and was acknowledged as an expert on its flora, particularly that of the French Riviera. In consequence most of Warburg's accumulated knowledge and wisdom has been lost, for with so many distracting interests he published relatively little beyond short bryological papers, though in 1963 he edited, in a most scholarly way, the third edition of *A Census Catalogue of British Mosses*.

'Heff', as he was universally known in botanical circles, a nickname ('Heffalump', for he was well over six feet tall, yet a surprisingly good wicketkeeper) bestowed on him by Humphrey Gilbert-Carter at one of his celebrated Sunday tea-parties at the Cambridge Botanic Garden, was the leading field botanist of his day and his knowledge of the British Flora was remarkable in any age. His field classes and excursions were interesting and highly educative without being stuffy, no doubt following in the tradition of Gilbert-Carter. Indeed, Warburg is most widely known as one of the joint authors of the *Flora of the British Isles* (by A. R. Clapham, T. G. Tutin, and E. F. Warburg, 1952, 1962), the first comprehensive scientific Flora to be produced for seventy years, which is dedicated to Gilbert-Carter. Here, particularly in sections on Rosaceae, and on those families with many familiar cultivated plants, on which he was also very knowledgeable, Warburg will be remembered.

In 1948 Warburg married Primrose Churchman, of Melton (the home of her grandfather, Sir William Churchman, Bt., where she was brought up) in Suffolk, daughter of Gilbert Barrett, sometime of the RAF: they first met on a botanical excursion in a Cambridge fen. They had two sons and a daughter and lived at Yarnells Hill, Oxford, where, like his father, Warburg built up a fine collection of hardy plants, notably crocuses on which he was an authority. He was a founder member of the Berkshire, Buckinghamshire and Oxfordshire Naturalists' Trust and later a vice-president, so that it is appropriate that one of their properties, rich in interesting flora, should have been named the Warburg Reserve in 1967 as a memorial to him. He advised the Oxford Preservation Trust and Oxford City on matter aboricultural: the City Council named Warburg Crescent after him in 1969. His name is also commemorated in that of a moss, *Anoectangium warburgii*, a species that he recognized as new in the Outer Hebrides in 1946. Of Warburg's collections, his bryophyte herbarium is preserved in the Fielding-Druce herbarium at Oxford, though type material of his flowering plant species is at the British Museum (Natural History), with duplicates at Oxford, and his collection of *Euphrasia* spp. (eyebrights) is at Cambridge as is the bulk of his living collection of *Sorbus*. He died at Oxford 9 June 1966.

[*The Times*, 11 June 1966; *Nature*, vol. ccxii, 1966, p. 240; *Proc. Bot. Soc. Br. Isles*, vol. vii, 1967, pp. 67–9 (with bibliography); Ray Desmond, *Dictionary of British and Irish Botanists and Horticulturalists*, 1977, p. 639; private information.]   D. J. MABBERLEY

WARNER, SIR PELHAM FRANCIS (1873–1963), cricketer and cricket writer, was born at Port of Spain, Trinidad, 2 October 1873, the son of Charles William Warner, CB, for many years attorney-general of Trinidad, and his second wife, a daughter of a Spaniard, John Joseph Garcia Cadiz, a barrister in Trinidad. Warner was the youngest of his father's eighteen children. He received his early education at Harrison College, Barbados, where he soon showed promise as a cricketer. In his autobiography, *Long Innings* (1951), he wrote: 'I cannot remember when I was not keen on cricket.'

Charles Warner died in February 1887 when Pelham was thirteen. His widow took four of her children to England, and, after an unsuccessful attempt to get in to Winchester, Warner was accepted by Rugby, and went there in September of that year. Always known as 'Plum', he was a delicate boy, but in spite of poor health he was playing cricket for the school within two years, and was captain of the eleven in his last year. He was fortunate to be coached at Rugby by Tom Emmett, who had played for Yorkshire and the Players; his shrewd advice was very helpful to the development of young Warner.

In January 1893 Warner entered Oriel College, Oxford, but, owing to ill health, did not gain his cricket blue until 1895. He was already playing cricket for Middlesex, and when the county met Gloucestershire in the summer of 1894, Warner had the memorable experience of playing against W. G. Grace [q.v.] and being entertained by him and his wife at their home.

Warner's subject at Oxford was jurisprudence, in which he gained a third class in 1896. In the same year he passed his bar final, but was not called until 1900 (Inner Temple).

In 1897 he made the first of his many cricket tours abroad, to the West Indies, as a member of a team led by Lord Hawke [q.v.]. Some controversy was aroused in 1902 when (Sir) F. S. Jackson, whose notice Warner later wrote for this Dictionary, was unavailable, and Warner was selected, in preference to A. C. MacLaren [q.v.], to captain the England test side for the 1903–4 tour to Australia. The sports writers saw little prospect that England would have much chance against the Australians, but the tour proved to

be a great triumph for Warner and the England team, who won the rubber by three matches to two and thus recovered the Ashes.

Eight years later, in 1911–12, when C. B. Fry [q.v.] was unable to accept the invitation to captain England in Australia, Warner was again selected for the task. Unfortunately, he was able to play in only one game and in none of the test matches. After making 151 runs against South Australia at Adelaide in the first match of the tour, Warner had a complete breakdown in health and had to retire to a nursing home for six weeks. In spite of this set-back, England won the rubber by four matches to one.

Warner had joined the Inns of Court Regiment in 1900 and served in the Territorial Army until 1912. During the 1914–18 war he held a commission in the Inns of Court Officers' Training Corps, as the regiment had become. His task was to interview those who wished to transfer from their regiments to the Royal Flying Corps. But he was still dogged by ill health, and after undergoing an operation in 1916, and working for a short time in the Foreign Office, he was invalided from the Service.

He had been captain of Middlesex since 1908, but his greatest success for the county came in 1920, his last year with the side. At the end of July, the county had to win their nine remaining matches if they were to win the championship. Some of those games were very closely contested. They defeated Kent by 5 runs and Yorkshire by 4. In the final game at Lord's, they defeated Surrey, after a very exciting match, by 55 runs with ten minutes to spare. Warner retired from first-class cricket, carried shoulder-high from the field by his Middlesex colleagues. It is Warner's skill as a captain rather than a successful batsman for which he will be remembered.

He played cricket with zestful enthusiasm, and whether he was leading England or Middlesex, he invariably showed a deep understanding of the strategy and tactics of the game and an astute assessment of the strengths and weaknesses of his opponents. The professionals who played with him, among whom were J. W. Hearne and 'Patsy' Hendren, called him 'the General', and supported him with respect and affection.

Throughout his batting career Warner was handicapped by poor health and a frail physique. When he retired he had made nearly 30,000 runs, including 60 centuries. He was not a brilliant batsman of the calibre of Ranjitsinhji or Jack (Sir John Berry) Hobbs [qq.v.], but his technique was sound and he could be relied upon to put up a stubborn defence on a 'sticky' wicket.

His retirement from the field by no means involved retirement from the game. Although he had been called to the bar in 1900, he never practised, and his career as an amateur cricketer was financed mainly by his writing. He began by writing for the *Sportsman* during his tour to the West Indies in 1897. In 1903 J. A. Spender [q.v.] invited him to write a weekly article on cricket for the *Westminster Gazette*. From 1921 to 1933 he was cricket correspondent of the *Morning Post*; in 1921 he also became editor of the *Cricketer*. He was a prolific writer on the game and published many books, including *My Cricketing Life* (1921), *Cricket Between Two Wars* (1942), *Lord's, 1787-1945* (1946), and *Long Innings* (1951).

Warner was chairman of the England Test Match Selection Committee in 1926, 1931-2, and 1935-8, and was appointed joint manager of the side which toured Australia in 1932-3. That tour was marred by the 'body line' controversy. Warner himself regarded this type of attack to be against the spirit of cricket and not in the best interests of the game, but he held aloof from the dispute in Australia, thinking that the tactics employed in the field were the responsibility of D. R. Jardine [q.v.], the captain.

Warner had been elected a member of the Marylebone Cricket Club on 15 March 1892. It was a great pleasure to him to be nominated president of the MCC in May 1950. A unique tribute was paid to him in 1958 when the members' stand at Lord's, built in that year, was named after him. In May 1961 he became the first life vice-president in the history of the MCC.

In 1904 Warner married Agnes (died 1955), daughter of Henry Arthur Blyth, of Stansted, Essex. They had two sons and one daughter.

Warner was appointed MBE in 1919 and knighted in 1937. His portrait, painted by Katherine Lloyd, hangs in the Long Room at Lord's. Another portrait, by A. R. Thomson, was exhibited at the Royal Academy in 1946, and a head, by Myles A. Tyrrell, was shown there in 1955. He died at Midhurst, Sussex, 30 January 1963.

[*The Times*, 31 January 1963; Patrick Morrah, *The Golden Age of Cricket*, 1967; Roy Webber, *The Phoenix History of Cricket*, 1960; Sir Pelham Warner, *Long Innings*, 1951; Laurence Meynell, *'Plum' Warner*, 1951.]   H. F. OXBURY

WARNER ALLEN, (HERBERT) (1881-1968), journalist and author.   [See ALLEN.]

WARR, CHARLES LAING (1892-1969), dean of the Chapel Royal in Scotland, was born 20 May 1892, the younger son of the Revd Alfred Warr, minister of Rosneath, Dunbartonshire, himself a distinguished minister of the Church of Scotland, whose biography he wrote in 1917, and his wife, Christian Grey, fifth daughter of Adam Laing. He grew up in the west of Scotland. He was educated at Glasgow Academy and the universities of Edinburgh and Glasgow. He received his Edinburgh MA in 1914, and was commissioned to the 9th Argyll and Sutherland Highlanders on 5 August of the same year. As he lay dangerously wounded at Ypres in May 1915, he underwent a spiritual experience, the result of which was that he took divinity classes at Glasgow and became assistant minister of the cathedral there 1917-18. He was ordained before the end of the war and became minister of St. Paul's, Greenock, 1918-26.

To the surprise and consternation of a number of more senior churchmen, in 1926 he was appointed minister of St. Giles' Cathedral, Edinburgh. Moreover, to his own astonishment, and initially to the open hostility of the Scottish royal chaplains, he was also appointed both dean of the Chapel Royal and of the Order of the Thistle in the same year. Being only thirty-four years old at the time, King George V called him 'my boy dean'. He held both offices until his death. In the same year, 1926, although there was no vacancy on the list of royal chaplains in Scotland, he was made an extra chaplain to King George V and in 1936 became his chaplain. His friendship with the royal family had begun when Princess Louise, Duchess of Argyll, a daughter of Queen Victoria, had worshipped during the summer months at his father's church in Rosneath and had become interested in the minister's family. He became a close personal friend of George V. He was also chaplain to Kings Edward VIII and George VI and to Queen Elizabeth II. He declined the unanimous nomination for the moderatorship of the Church of Scotland in 1953. Among his many other chaplaincies were those to HM Bodyguard for Scotland (the Royal Company of Archers), the Order of St. John of Jerusalem, the Royal Scottish Academy, the Convention of Royal Burghs of Scotland, the Royal College of Surgeons of Edinburgh, and the Merchant Company of Edinburgh. Among the directorships he held were those of the Royal Edinburgh Hospital for Sick Children and the Princess Margaret Rose Hospital for Crippled Children. As convener of the Church of Scotland committee on huts and canteens for HM Forces throughout the war of 1939-45, he gave most distinguished service in helping the efforts for the troops. For the Church he was convener of the Home Mission Committee and joint convener of the National Church Extension Committee. He was a trustee of the

National Library of Scotland and of Iona Cathedral.

Although his public duties outnumbered those of any other minister, he never allowed them to interfere with his work as a parish minister. 'The best way to run a parish is simply to love your people', he used to say; and he was a great believer in visiting his people, both in their homes and in hospital, and expected the same high standard from his assistants. Although not robust in health, he worked hard himself and expected the same dedication from those around him. Some outsiders knew him more for his participation in the many dignified occasions of Church and State, and it is true that here he did more for the Church of Scotland than any other minister of his time. When performing these duties Warr's punctilious devotion to ceremonial sometimes aroused criticism. As a parish minister he would give quiet and peaceful evening services when the lights were lowered and he spoke from the pulpit in a way which comforted and helped people of all ages for the rest of the week ahead. Those who knew him most intimately will remember him as a man round his own fireside, with a love of people, a sense of fun, a deeply sincere and humble faith, and an almost jealous regard for the vocation of the holy ministry and the dignity and position of the Church. Among his achievements were the lead he gave to the ecumenical movement in Scotland and his part in the restoration of St. Margaret's Chapel, on the rock of Edinburgh Castle, the oldest ecclesiastical building in Scotland still in use as a place of worship.

Warr wrote *The Unseen Host* in February 1916 after being invalided out of the army at the early age of twenty-three. It soon became a best-seller, going into ten editions. Among his other books were *Echoes of Flanders* (1916), *Principal Caird* (1926), *The Call of the Island* (1929), *Scottish Sermons and Addresses* (1930), *The Presbyterian Tradition* (1933), and *The Glimmering Landscape* (autobiography), 1960.

Among his many honours was that of being the only minister of the Church of Scotland to receive the GCVO (1967), having previously been CVO (1937) and KCVO (1950). He was made a deputy lieutenant of the county of the city of Edinburgh (1953), honorary DD of Edinburgh (1931), honorary LLD of St. Andrews (1937) and of Edinburgh (1953), honorary RSA (1927), FRSE from 1936, honorary FRCS of Edinburgh (1955), and honorary FRIBA (1967).

He received a colleague and successor in 1954—an arrangement which turned out neither as happily nor as successfully as he had hoped, and on his retirement from St. Giles' Cathedral in 1962, he joined the Canongate

Kirk. In 1954 the Queen gave him a grace-and-favour house in Moray Place, Edinburgh, where he spent his last years, sometimes rather sadly, remembering Rosneath and the Gareloch, old friends, and the hills of home. He died in Edinburgh 14 June 1969.

He married in 1918 Christian Lawson Aitken (Ruby), the only daughter of Robert Rattray Tatlock; she died in 1961. There were no children.

There is a portrait of Warr (1951) by A. E. Borthwick in St. Giles' Cathedral, Edinburgh, and a bust by Diana Murray is in the Canongate Kirk.

[Charles L. Warr, *The Glimmering Landscape*, 1960 (autobiography); *Year Book of the Royal Society of Edinburgh*, 1968-9; personal knowledge.]   RONALD SELBY WRIGHT

WARRINGTON, PERCY EWART (1889-1961), founder of some public schools, was born at Newhall, Derbyshire, near Burton-on-Trent, 29 December 1889, the elder son of Thomas Warrington, farmer, by his wife, Mary Jane, daughter of William Wright, the registrar of South Derbyshire. Three generations had previously farmed Newhall Park Farm. Warrington attended Stapenhill School, leaving to work on the farm, gaining a knowledge of estate management, and appreciation of antiques and works of art. He had guidance in reading through the help of local clergy. Accepted as an ordinand, he entered Hatfield College, Durham, obtained the licentiate in theology, and was ordained deacon (1914) and priest (1915) at Worcester Cathedral for St. Matthew's Church, Rugby. He moved in 1917 to St. Peter's Congleton in Cheshire where he covered an interregnum. It was said at his departure, 'it was given to few to win the hearts of a congregation so completely'. Warrington accepted in 1918 the benefice of Monkton Combe, a small village with the well-known public school, in the Bath and Wells diocese. He remained there until his death in 1961, an incumbency of forty-three years.

Warrington was an enigma. Small of stature, of immense vitality, serious, sharp-witted, his marked ability was shown in his spare-time work as secretary of the Church Trust Society which aroused the Low Church evangelicals to influence through the field of education. First Wrekin College was acquired in 1921; then followed the founding of Stowe School and Canford in 1923; subsequently, Westonbirt (1928) and Felixstowe (1929) for girls. To further the objective a new trust was developed, incorporating the Church Trust Society, with the rallying title The Martyrs Memorial, extending its influence through advowsons. Other schools came under its aegis, until Warrington's vicarage was the administrative centre of some thirteen public schools. He also had a part in finding resources for a High School in Kenya, for St. Peter's Hall (now College), Oxford, and Clifton Theological College, and committed himself to the restoration of Pentonville Church, London, derelict after the war of 1914-18 and reconsecrated in 1933.

To mark appreciation of Warrington's work, the vice-chairman of governors, Sir Charles King-Harman, acclaimed him in the Mansion House, 25 April 1923, to be the founder of Stowe: 'It was to Warrington's genius . . . and to his financial acumen that the acquisition of Stowe House and the concerting of it into a public school was due. He made this statement lest there should be any mistake in the future, so that generations to come should know who was the real founder of Stowe School.' J. F. Roxburgh [q.v.], the first headmaster, wrote to Warrington on 2 December 1923: 'This is the first anniversary of my appointment to Stowe . . . Without your determination and amazing courage nothing could have been achieved . . . whenever I see the qualities that have enabled you to found Stowe, I know how to value them . . . without you Stowe could never have existed, and I want to tell you how clearly and with what gratitude I realize that fact.'

At the speech-day in 1933, the tenth anniversary of Stowe, the photographs show Warrington in close association with the guest of honour, the Prince of Wales. But disaster was imminent. Warrington had attempted administrative work with the minimum of expense. No one could deflect him, but he could only carry the load by expecting everyone to conform to his speed of action; this made enemies and aroused anxieties. Sometimes involved with the trivial, he also found it difficult to delegate. A large fast car with chauffeur led to whispers of 'feathering his nest'. The less courageous had fears sensitive to insidious conflicting interests alarmed by the power of the movement. All these, with the economic depression, persuaded the Trust that Warrington must go. The way was open through a technical error in the financing of Clifton Theological College. Warrington was deposed, but in the process the latent great financial resources of the schools were lost to the Trust and to the Church. Fifty years later these great schools remained, with a debt to Warrington which could never be repaid. For the Church, Clifton Theological College remained, for Warrington accepted a large measure of responsibility for its financing. With reorganization of theological colleges in the seventies, the union of colleges on this site was called Trinity College, Bristol.

There were unsuccessful attempts to make Warrington bankrupt. A cloud descended upon him; rumour unfairly questioned his dealings; he lived under a kind of judgement. When comments were made upon his isolation in church affairs, few realized the pressures to get him moved from Monkton Combe. When asked why he did not accept attractive offers to leave, his reply was that he had to stay, otherwise it would have been said: 'he had to go in the end.' Disillusioned, especially by what he described as the 'Protestant underworld', he was dangerous in defence; his tongue, always sharp, became vitriolic against hypocrisy, snobbery, place-seeking, and pious sentimentality. Within his parish, the Christian of wealth and opportunity was also his target, but poor people, and the down-and-out, knew they could always rely upon him to be their champion, frequently making a difficult coexistence with the public school in the village, although in later years a happier relationship developed. After the war he concentrated on improving housing conditions and became fully involved in work for the aged. He founded two homes: Claremont House at Corsham in Wiltshire and later Waterhouse at Monkton Combe. These homes stand in his name.

To understand Warrington it must be realized that he was a visionary with an intense sense of his call; as a prophet he was lopsided, but he got things done. In early days he had been influenced by evangelical clergy, especially Richard Weston, vicar of Burntwood in 1886-1923. From such men he sensed the kind of leadership which could meet what was then felt to be Roman Catholic encroachment on the one hand, and the new theological 'modernism' on the other. Warrington's movement was a child of its day, a contemporary reply to the challenge. With it, he saw that opportunities provided by the schools must have an outlet in practical, responsible service.

Warrington never married. He died in Bath 5 November 1961. His portrait by E. Swan, dated 1929, is the property of Trinity College, Bristol.

[*Bath Chronicle and Herald*, 26 April 1923, 29 July 1929, 11 August 1961; *Observer*, 19 November 1961; private information; personal knowledge.] B. J. W. TURNOCK

WATSON, ARTHUR ERNEST (1880-1969), managing editor of the *Daily Telegraph*, was the second son of Aaron Watson, author and journalist, and his wife, Phebe, daughter of John Gibling, of Norwich. Sir Alfred Watson (1874-1967), editor of the Calcutta *Statesman* (1925-33), was his elder brother. He was born 29 February 1880 at Newcastle upon Tyne, where his father was then a leader-writer, and was educated at Rutherford College, Newcastle, at Alleyn's School, Dulwich, and at Armstrong College, Newcastle. Aaron Watson, after two years as London correspondent of the *Newcastle Daily Leader*, had returned to Newcastle as editor, and there from the age of eighteen Arthur Watson received a general grounding in his hereditary craft.

He moved to Fleet Street in 1902 to join the parliamentary staff of the *Daily Telegraph*, but within a few weeks was transferred to the sub-editor's table. Over six feet tall, an unusually low voice and quiet manner which disguised great determination, he showed a rapid and sure judgement of news invaluable in a young journalist. He remained with the paper for the next forty-eight years, interrupted only by service in the war of 1914-18. From the Inns of Court Regiment, he was commissioned as a field gunner, and rose to acting major in command of a battery. A lifelong teetotaller and non-smoker, he returned from France massively imperturbable, with the added experience of handling men. His rise on the *Daily Telegraph* was now swift. In turn night editor and news editor, he was appointed assistant editor in 1923, and on the unexpected death of Fred Miller in the following year succeeded him as managing editor.

Unlike many newspaper editors, Watson deliberately refrained from contributing signed or unsigned articles. Although perfectly capable of writing clearly and forcefully in an emergency, he preferred to leave this to his staff and to apply his energies full-time to overseeing the paper as a whole, and particularly the leader-page. Wholly lacking in personal vanity, he made the minimum of changes in his colleagues' articles, although he would without a rebuke quietly delete a misleading, verbose, or injudicious passage. He was probably unique among Fleet Street editors of his time in frequently visiting the composing-room to make the final adjustments to a leader-column. Apart from lunch at one of his clubs—the Athenaeum, the Union, and the Carlton—he rarely left the office between midday and 9 p.m. or later.

His capacity for sustained work was fully exercised when in 1928 Sir William Berry (later Viscount Camrose, q.v.) acquired control of the paper from Viscount Burnham [q.v.]. The new principal proprietor, who was to mould a respectable but declining newspaper into a successful and powerful organ with more than a million circulation, was in fact as well as name editor-in-chief of the *Daily Telegraph*. Not merely the general policy and character of the paper, but the details of every issue were the constant preoccupation of the new owner. On the managing editor fell the responsibility of carrying out decisions reached in their daily consultations, guiding the staff meanwhile

through a period of constant innovation and expansion.

The two men, temperamentally dissimilar, worked in harmony not only because each admired the other's ability and self-control, but because they shared the aim of producing a fair-minded, responsible, accurate, well-informed newspaper, lively but not sensational. Both men held Conservative views and both were steadfast opponents of the Nazi and Fascist dictatorships. Watson, who had taken the decision to condemn the Munich settlement, would probably not on his own have rallied so quickly to Neville Chamberlain afterwards. By the time the war came, and certainly after Chamberlain fell, there could have been no difference between them over the staunch support Churchill was to receive henceforth from the *Daily Telegraph*.

As the war went on the paper suffered the triple stress of censorship, blackout, and a partly blitzed office. Circulation was pegged and the staff depleted. With peace the *Daily Telegraph*, which had been reduced on most days to four pages, started once more to expand both in size and in scope. Watson had to relinquish to others supervision of the news coverage, but remained in full control not only of the leader-page, but of all special articles and comment until at the age of seventy he retired from the paper in 1950, refusing (it is believed) a knighthood.

He had married in 1904 Lily, daughter of Edward Waugh, of Whitley Bay and Gateshead. They had no children. By 1950 his wife was a permanent invalid in need of the constant care which he devoted to her until her death at the end of 1960. Watson himself, although he suffered a slight stroke in 1967, retained his mental alertness to the end. He died 18 September 1969 in Merton Park, in the bungalow he had built in an enclave cut from the large garden of the house which had been his home for many years and which he had sold after his wife's death.

A good portrait of Watson by Maurice Codner, presented to him by Lord Camrose at a staff dinner on his retirement, was bequeathed by him to the *Daily Telegraph*.

[*Daily Telegraph* and *The Times*, 19 September 1969; private information; personal knowledge.]   H. D. ZIMAN

WATSON, (GEORGE) NEVILLE (1886-1965), mathematician, was born at Westward Ho 31 Hanuary 1886, the elder child and only son of George Wentworth Watson, a schoolmaster and later an army coach, and his wife, Mary Justina, daughter of the Revd George Sandhorn Griffith, rector of Ardley, Oxfordshire. His father was also an eminent genealogist who later took a large part in preparing both editions of Vicary Gibbs's *The Complete Peerage*. Watson was educated at St. Paul's, at that time a distinguished nursery of senior wranglers and Smith's prizemen. Among his contemporaries was J. E. Littlewood, five months his senior, who was to become perhaps the most powerful British mathematician of his time. Watson went up to Trinity College, Cambridge, as an entrance scholar in 1904 and was senior wrangler in 1907. In 1908 he was placed in the second division of the first class of the mathematical tripos. The younger fellows of Trinity at this time included three very distinguished workers in complex variable theory, the field in which Watson was to specialize: (Sir) Edmund T. Whittaker, E. W. Barnes, and G. H. Hardy [qq.v.]. However, Whittaker left in 1906 to become astronomer royal for Ireland and Barnes's interests were turning away from mathematics. Nevertheless his influence was very evident in Watson's early papers, which gained him a Smith's prize in 1909 and a Trinity fellowship in 1910. He left Cambridge in 1914 to become assistant lecturer at University College, London.

The four years which Watson spent in London were very fruitful. It is often the case in problems of mathematical physics that a solution can be obtained in the form of an infinite series or an integral but comparison with observation is frustrated because the solution does not lend itself to numerical computation. Watson's most valuable gift was his ability to bridge this gap. A striking example occurred in 1918. That wireless waves could be propagated over great distances was an undoubted fact, but it was not at all obvious why this should be so. H. M. Macdonald [q.v.], the leading authority on electromagnetic waves, had discussed the question in 1903 and several of the leading theoretical physicists of the day, including Rayleigh [q.v.], Poincaré, and Sommerfeld, had taken the matter further. All took as their model a Hertzian oscillator in an infinite dielectric surrounding a partially conducting sphere. Solutions were obtained, but not in a form which could be compared with observation. Watson was not much interested in problems of physics, but he was generous in helping those who were. Asked to bring his unique expertise to bear on the problem, he was able to show beyond doubt that the model did not explain the facts. It predicted an attenuation of the signal far more rapid than was observed. He was then asked to re-examine the question on the hypothesis that there was a conducting layer in the upper atmosphere as suggested by Oliver Heaviside [q.v.]. He showed that this did, indeed, account for the observations, provided that the layer was at a height of 100 km and of a certain conductivity.

Watson left London in 1918 to become Mason professor of pure mathematics in the university of Birmingham and continued in this post until his retirement in 1951. Though a man of enormous industry, he was a solitary worker and did not found a research school. Much of his time in the early years was devoted to writing an immense treatise on Bessel functions (1922), which will probably never be superseded. He had already, while in London, collaborated with his old teacher, Whittaker, in bringing out a second edition of the latter's *A Course of Modern Analysis* (1915), the first English work on complex variable theory addressed to undergraduates and which remained a steady seller.

The decade 1929–39 was largely devoted to elucidating the work of the remarkable, almost self-taught, mathematician, S. Ramanujan, who had come to England in 1914 and died in his native India in 1920. Ramanujan rarely gave proofs of his statements and some, due to his lack of formal education, were not correct. Watson wrote some twenty-five papers connected with his work, and copied out the whole of his notebooks in beautiful handwriting. They are now in the Mathematical Institute, Oxford.

Watson was an untiring worker on behalf of the London Mathematical Society, above all as editor of its *Proceedings*. He was its president in 1932–3 and was awarded the De Morgan medal in 1947. He was elected FRS in 1919 and received the Sylvester medal in 1946. He was an honorary FRSE and received honorary degrees from Edinburgh and Dublin. Birmingham University chose the name 'Watson Building' for a new building containing, among others, the mathematics departments. In appearance he was dark, and of spare build. Though mathematics was his absorbing interest he was also expert in his private hobbies of railway history and postage stamps. He was a devoted son of Trinity and prints of the college and its members covered his walls.

In 1925 Watson married Elfrida Gwenfil, daughter of Thomas Lane, of Holbeach, Lincolnshire, a farmer. They had one son. Watson died at home in Leamington Spa 2 February 1965.

[J. M. Whittaker in *Biographical Memoirs of Fellows of the Royal Society*, vol. xii, 1966; personal knowledge.]

J. M. WHITTAKER

WATSON, SIR (JAMES) ANGUS (1874–1961), business man and philanthropist, was born 15 January 1874 at Ryton on Tyne, the eldest of the three children and only son of Alexander Watson, a sanitary pipe manufacturer, and his wife, Jane Ann, the daughter of the Revd Thomas Wilkinson, a Baptist minister in Tewkesbury, Gloucestershire. He was educated privately, and in 1903 married Ethel, daughter of James Reid, by whom he had two sons and two daughters. Having started as a junior clerk, his talents and energies enabled him to make rapid progress. After a happy and successful business association with W. H. Lever (later Viscount Leverhulme, q.v.), he became the founder of Angus Watson & Co. Ltd, fish canners, chiefly known for Skipper sardines: the firm became known throughout the world. This business brought him into frequent contact with Norway and its Government. He became founder of Imperial Canneries, Norway, and was made knight of the Order of St. Olaf.

A man of strict puritan principles, Watson was an active Congregationalist, being a leading member of that denomination not only in the Newcastle area but also nationally: he was elected chairman of the Congregational Union of England and Wales, 1935-6. A Liberal in politics and a firm advocate of total abstinence, he was associated with David Lloyd George during World War I in seeking to promote prohibition. In keeping with his puritan principles, Watson gave time and energy to social and educational projects. He was for a while president of the Tyneside Council of Social Service. During World War II he served as northern divisional food officer with the Ministry of Food, 1939-45. For many years he was a JP.

Watson was for some years a member of the staff of the *Spectator*, in which he had at one time a controlling interest, being a partner with (Sir) Evelyn Wrench [q.v.]; and he helped to found the publishing firm Ivor Nicholson & Watson, of which one of his sons was a director. In 1937 he published through this firm a volume of autobiographical reflections, *My Life*. He was a keen golfer, and loved walking and farming. The university of Durham conferred on him the honorary degree DCL and in 1945 he was knighted.

In many ways Watson was typical of the English Nonconformity of his period, much more concerned with practical obedience than theological speculation. While he was concerned to support all forms of the Christian religion and to encourage co-operation between all denominations, he was not deeply concerned about the points of principle on which they differed, though he was much opposed to all forms of Erastianism. To a large extent he had prospered by his own efforts without the advantage of much early education; but this did not lessen his concern that education should be available to all. The wealth derived from his business enabled him to be a generous supporter of many good causes, religious as well as social and educational. His way of life was controlled by strict adherence to his religious principles. To later generations these may have appeared as somewhat narrow and restrictive; but they were the continuing source of his political and social activities as well as of his private life.

He died at home in Newcastle upon Tyne 31 January 1961.

[Angus Watson, *My Life*, 1937; Angus Watson, *The Angus Clan, Years 1588-1950*, 1955.]　　　　　JOHN HUXTABLE

WAUGH, EVELYN ARTHUR ST. JOHN (1903-1966), novelist, was born in Hampstead 28 October 1903, the younger son of Arthur Waugh, publisher and author, and his wife, Catherine Charlotte, daughter of Henry Charles Biddulph Colton Raban, of the Bengal Civil Service. The family originally came from the Scottish Lowlands, and Waugh's mother's family also came from Scotland, for she was directly descended from Henry, Lord Cockburn [q.v.]. Arthur Waugh, in the previous year to Evelyn's birth, had become managing director of Chapman and Hall, once famous as the publishers of Charles Dickens, although by the end of the century the firm had very much contracted, and Arthur Waugh did not have a particularly easy or lucrative life. Himself educated at Sherborne he had sent his elder son there. But the storm created by Alec (Alexander Raban) Waugh's novel based on his school days, *The Loom of Youth* (1917), made it necessary to find another school for Evelyn who was five years younger.

He was sent to the high Anglican public school, Lancing, after some happy years as a day boy at a preparatory school in Hampstead. At first he was unhappy, at a time when the privations of the war years were at their most severe, and when it was the general condition of new boys to be given a bad time at public schools. But he developed his artistic interests, in painting, drawing, and calligraphy, and became editor of the school magazine. He crowned his Lancing career by winning a history scholarship to Hertford College, Oxford, in December 1921. He chose Hertford in preference to his father's old college, New College, out of consideration for his father's strained purse, because the scholarship at Hertford was of greater value. He went up immediately in January 1922, and took happily to Oxford life. At first he was overshadowed by his brother's name, but he soon made many friends in many colleges, and lived a high-spirited life in which social and somewhat rowdy drinking played a larger part than academic study. He developed a lasting antipathy for his history tutor, C. R. M. F. Crutt-well [q.v.], dean, and later head, of the college, who wrote him a severe letter when he obtained a bad third in 1924. Waugh subsequently used the name Cruttwell for derogatory characters in his fiction. Conversely, the origins of many of his characters were to be found in real people.

The next three years, the unhappiest of his life, saw Waugh in a succession of posts as an assistant master, first at a school in Denbigh-shire, caricatured in *Decline and Fall* (1928), then at Aston Clinton in Buckinghamshire, and finally for half a term at a day school in Notting Hill Gate. In his autobiography, *A Little Learning* (1964), he ends what was intended to be only the first volume with an account of a rather half-hearted attempt to drown himself towards the end of his time at the school in Wales. Leaving a Greek inscription on his clothes, he swam out to sea, only to find himself in a shoal of jellyfish which caused him to turn back and decide to live. As a schoolmaster he was easy-going and not unpopular with the boys, but had the candour to recognize that he was very unsatisfactory from the headmaster's point of view. He managed to pursue an active social life; he had made particularly close friends with the Plunket-Greene family and fell deeply in love with the daughter, Olivia, a devout Catholic. She did not reciprocate, but his close friendship with the family had a great influence on him.

While still a schoolmaster Waugh wrote an essay on the *Pre-Raphaelite Brotherhood* which was printed privately in 1926. It came to the notice of the publishing house of Duckworth who suggested that Waugh should write for them a book on Rossetti. By April 1927 Waugh and the teaching profession had had enough of one another. In the autumn of the year he decided to study carpentry seriously with a view to becoming a maker of fine furniture, and he always said that this work gave him greater pleasure than writing ever did. In December Waugh became engaged to Evelyn Florence Margaret Winifred Gardner, daughter of the late Lord Burghclere, whose widow (daughter of the fourth Earl of Carnarvon) was strongly against her daughter engaging herself to a young man with neither income nor occupation. His book on Rossetti was published in 1928 and received some good reviews, but did not solve any problems. It was made very clear to Waugh that if he wanted to marry he must earn some money, and this was the genesis of *Decline and Fall*. When Duckworths jibbed and wanted more alterations than the author would agree to, its publication was undertaken by Chapman and Hall in the absence of his father who might have hesitated to publish his son's work. The

book was an immense success, enthusiastically praised, notably by Arnold Bennett [q.v.] who enjoyed a unique position as a critic of fiction, and Waugh's financial troubles were ended.

In the meantime Waugh had married Evelyn Gardner in June 1928 without the knowledge of her mother. The success of his first novel was soon soured by domestic trouble. While Waugh was writing his next novel, *Vile Bodies* (1930), which proved that he was not a man of one book, but a writer with a rich and developing talent, his young wife was unfaithful to him, and in 1930 he obtained a divorce. When in that year Waugh was received into the Roman Catholic Church by Father Martin D'Arcy at Farm Street, he was quite prepared to face the prospect that he could not, by the law of the Church, contract another marriage while his wife lived. It did not immediately dawn upon him that he had a very good case for arguing that the necessary intention of indissolubility on the part of both parties had not been present. His petition for an annulment made in 1933 was not granted until 1936, and it was not until 1937 that he made a second and enduring marriage to Laura Laetitia Gwendolen Evelyn (died 1973), a first cousin of his first wife, and youngest of the three daughters of the late Aubrey Nigel Henry Molyneux Herbert, half-brother of the fifth Earl of Carnarvon [q.v.].

By that time Waugh had consolidated his position as a writer, and had produced what many critics regard as his finest achievement, in which, as he expressed it, he said all he had to say about a society without religion, a work of masterly construction, full of intensely comical situations which nevertheless illustrate a deeply serious theme. This was *A Handful of Dust* which came out in 1934. It was preceded by *Black Mischief* (1932), a high-spirited story made possible by a visit which the author made to Abyssinia in 1930 for the coronation of the Emperor Haile Selassie which he reported for the *Graphic* and as a special correspondent for *The Times*. He went on from Ethiopia to Aden, Zanzibar, Kenya, the Belgian Congo, and Cape Town, recording his travels in *Remote People* (1931). As a war correspondent for the *Daily Mail* he witnessed Mussolini's invasion of Abyssinia in 1935 and returned there in 1936 to complete his account *Waugh in Abyssinia* (1936). These visits gave him material for a second novel with an Abyssinian setting, *Scoop* (1938). Meantime a visit to South America in 1932–3 resulted in another travel book *Ninety-Two Days* (1934).

When war broke out in 1939 Waugh was thoroughly established in the forefront of the younger novelists, with some entertaining travel books to his credit as well. Moreover he had written a biography of Edmund Campion (1935) which had won him the Hawthornden prize. All his profits from this he made over to Campion Hall, Oxford. He had a country house at Stinchcombe in Gloucestershire near the Severn, and a young wife and the beginning of what was to be a family of three sons and three daughters. But being of military age and aware of the dangers of a civilian job to his inventive talent, he immediately began seeking a commission. It was with great difficulty that he secured one in the Royal Marines; he was seconded for service in the Commandos in November 1940, officially transferring to the Royal Horse Guards in 1942. In 1941 he went to the Middle East and served as personal assistant to (Sir) Robert Laycock [q.v.] throughout the battle for Crete. By the end of the year he was back in England and he did not go overseas again until 1944. He was always a problem to his superiors who found his scepticism disruptive and he was never popular with the men under his command. These defects outweighed his marked physical courage and in March 1943 Laycock told him that he was 'so unpopular as to be unemployable'. It was Laycock, nevertheless, who had proposed him for membership of White's where Waugh had many friends.

In the early months of 1944 he was on leave and writing the novel which was to be very much the most successful of all his books in the United States, *Brideshead Revisited* (1945). Before that major undertaking, he had written, with a fluency and speed quite exceptional with him, *Put Out More Flags* (1942), in which in his best comic vein he developed the character of Basil Seal, whom his readers knew well from *Black Mischief*, who was now shown taking full advantage of all the opportunities which the early stages of the war provided for the advancement of his own fortunes. *Brideshead* was altogether more serious, shot through with a religious theme. It divided the critics, many of whom attributed its exceptional appeal to the American public to its detailed depiction of English aristocratic life.

But Waugh's military career was not yet ended. The prime minister's son, Randolph Churchill, was with Brigadier (Sir) Fitzroy Maclean's mission to Tito's Communist partisans in Yugoslavia, and he asked for Waugh for the sake of his company. In July 1944 Waugh joined the mission. Flying from Bari to Topusko the plane in which Churchill and Waugh were travelling caught fire on landing and as a result of their injuries it was not until September that they finally reached partisan headquarters. At close quarters, and with little to occupy him for most of the time, there was plenty of acrimony, sharpened by Waugh's dislike of the whole idea of co-operating to ensure

that post-war Yugoslavia would be ruled by the Communists, thus placing the Catholic Croats and Slovenes under intolerant atheist masters. He took considerable risks of being court-martialled by reporting to the Vatican, and by the efforts he made to draw attention to what was happening, reporting on the religious situation to the Foreign Office and instigating questions in Parliament.

After the war ended, Waugh's talent lay fallow, although a short visit to Spain in 1946 with Douglas Woodruff resulted in a light-hearted satire, *Scott-King's Modern Europe* (1947), whose humour was applicable to many other government-sponsored commemorations beside that which was the purpose of this Spanish visit, the fourth centenary of the birth of the Dominican Francisco de Vittoria, who, his fellow countrymen maintained, was the real founder of international law and deserved the credit which the Protestant world had generally accorded to Grotius a generation later.

In 1947 Waugh visited Hollywood to discuss the proposed film of *Brideshead Revisited*. No film was ever made because he refused to alter the story as the producers wished, largely that they might satisfy the standards set by the very powerful Catholic Legion of Decency. But the visit was not barren. With time on his hands he became fascinated with Californian burial practices, and the result was *The Loved One* (1948) which, for all its macabre setting, was a highly successful light novel based on Forest Lawn. He made several further visits to America, went to Goa in 1952 for the four-hundredth anniversary of the death of St. Francis Xavier, to Ceylon in 1954, and to Jamaica in 1955.

Meantime in 1950 appeared what was in some ways Waugh's most ambitious work, his only venture into historical fiction, a novel about Saint Helena, the mother of Constantine the Great. He took great pains with this, and the book contains some of his best writing. He used to maintain that it should be read three times because more would be found in it each time.

After a long gestation Waugh's varied war-time experiences came out as a trilogy: in 1952 the first volume, *Men at Arms*, based on his experiences as a Royal Marine, and awarded the James Tait Black memorial prize; in 1955 the second, *Officers and Gentlemen*, drawn from his period with the Commandos and at the Allied reverse in Crete. Then, in 1961 came the final volume, *Unconditional Surrender*, with his experiences in Yugoslavia, the title reflecting the bitter irony that the adventure on which his hero, Guy Crouchback, had set out as on a crusade after kneeling at a crusader's tomb, had ended supporting atheistic Communism. It was only when the trilogy was issued in one volume under the general title of *Sword of*

Honour (1962) that its structural unity and irony stood out in their full strength.

The fifties also saw a slight novel called *Love Among the Ruins* (1953); and in 1957 *The Ordeal of Gilbert Pinfold*, remarkable for the self-portrait of the author with which it begins, and for being based on severe hallucinations which had come upon him as a result of taking remedies for insomnia in too large quantities.

Waugh had found the restrictions of post-war Britain irksome and at one time had seriously contemplated moving to Ireland. It was characteristic of him that at a time when most people, if they moved, chose smaller houses, when he finally made his choice in 1956 it was to a house considerably larger and grander than Piers Court. This was Combe Florey House, six miles from Taunton, on high ground, with an imposing gate-house, and large rooms which he decorated in a flamboyant, Victorian manner. He had acquired a large collection of Victorian narrative paintings which could be bought, in the thirties and forties, for a few pounds, and subsequently greatly increased in value. With the proceeds of two lawsuits he arranged with the manufacturers at Wilton for a replica of one of the more startling prizewinning carpets of the Great Exhibition of 1851. Combe Florey was to be his home for the rest of his life, and was a source of great satisfaction to him. He travelled less abroad, but made one further visit with his daughter Margaret in 1961–2 to South America. When he published all that he wished to preserve of his travel books of the thirties it was under the general title *When the Going was Good* (1946).

Before he was sixty Waugh began to feel that he was growing old, and he rather enjoyed exaggerating the degree of deafness which was afflicting him, using his hearing-aid, generally a large, old-fashioned trumpet, in an aggressive manner, putting it down ostentatiously before an unwelcome speaker.

In 1957 Waugh's friend Monsignor Ronald Knox [q.v.] died after a long illness in which Waugh had shown great solicitude. He was Knox's executor and biographer and he immediately set about filling both offices with great thoroughness, even going out to consult Lady Acton in Rhodesia. The biography of Knox appeared in 1959 and was followed by *A Tourist in Africa* (1960), the result of a second visit to Rhodesia, and finally by the first volume of his autobiography. He never succeeded in completing the second volume. His writing life may be said to have ended before he was sixty, although he lived to be sixty-two. His last years were saddened by the course taken by the Second Vatican Council whose changes in the liturgy he hated. He dreaded the prospect of old age with diminishing faculties in an in-creasingly uncongenial world, but he was spared the ordeal. He died very suddenly on Easter Sunday 10 April 1966, after hearing Mass in the old rite. He was buried in the churchyard adjoining his home at Combe Florey where he had died.

Evelyn Waugh was of less than average height. As a very young man his friend (Sir) Harold Acton described him as faun-like with his reddish hair and light, quick movements; but in middle life he became inclined to portliness, with a reddish face and eyes which seemed to become more protuberant as he glared at the world. His exceptional intelligence brought with it the penalty that he was very easily bored, seeing to the end of situations and conversations before they began, and time hung heavily on his hands. Although he disciplined himself effectively, retiring to Chagford to write his novels, he had few hobbies beyond the collection of Victoriana, did not care for music, and took little interest in public events. But he was continually improvising variants in everyday life, himself writing reports to his children's schools at the end of the holidays as a riposte to the school report, inscribing on his gates 'No admittance on business', and engaging in practical jokes, or behaving quite unpredictably and often very rudely, in an attempt to make everyday life more interesting and amusing. This caused him to be very much discussed by his contemporaries, and gave him some slight relief from his habitual ennui and tendency towards self-hatred. He also did many secret acts of charity and generosity, and when reproached for uncharitableness always replied that without his religion he knew he would be so very much more unpleasant. He told Christopher Sykes that he looked with horror upon Dylan Thomas [q.v.] who in looks, dress, and conversation was in many ways a parody of Waugh: 'He's exactly what I would have been if I had not become a Catholic.' He carried on a large correspondence without employing a secretary, writing everything by hand, and he was as much addicted as Gladstone to the use of postcards which encouraged the economy of language in which he excelled. This was one of the few practical economies in his style of living.

A portrait of Waugh as a young man by Henry Lamb became the possession of Lady Pansy Lamb. A portrait bust by Paràvicini is in the possession of the family. Waugh's manuscripts and letters were acquired by the university of Texas where a room has been set apart for them.

[Evelyn Waugh, *A Little Learning*, 1964, *Diaries*, ed. Michael Davie, 1976, and *Letters*, ed. Mark Amory, 1980; Alec Waugh, *My Brother Evelyn and Other Profiles*, 1967; Frances Donaldson, *Portrait of a Country*

Neighbour, 1967; *Evelyn Waugh and his World*, ed. D. Pryce-Jones, 1973; Christopher Sykes, *Evelyn Waugh*, 1975; personal knowledge.]   DOUGLAS WOODRUFF

WEBB, GEOFFREY FAIRBANK (1898-1970), art historian, was born in Birkenhead 9 May 1898, the only child of John Racker Webb and his wife, Elizabeth Hodgson Fairbank. The father, who had a good position in Booth's Steamship Company, had been married before and there were a number of considerably older half-brothers and sisters. Webb was educated at Birkenhead School, and then served as an able seaman in the RNVR, 1917-19. After the war he went up in 1919 to Magdalene College, Cambridge, where he read English and graduated in 1921 with a third class degree.

After leaving the university he lived for a time in London, where he came to know a number of the members of the Bloomsbury circle, including, in particular, Roger Fry [q.v.] to whom he always maintained he owed a considerable debt. Although he was later to specialize in architecture, Webb, during this period, was not concerned exclusively with this field. Among his first published works were articles on architecture and sculpture in the *Burlington Magazine*, and monographs on Spanish and Georgian art. His chief work during these early years, however, was editing, with Bonamy Dobrée, *The Complete Works of Sir John Vanbrugh* in four volumes (1927, the Nonesuch edition).

In 1929 Webb returned to Cambridge as a lecturer in the extra-mural department. In 1933 he was appointed a university demonstrator and subsequently lecturer (1938), in the faculty of fine arts. He also taught in the department of architecture. It was during this period that he was drawn particularly to the study of the architecture of the late seventeenth and early eighteenth centuries, and to the emergence of what Webb himself termed the Baroque period in English architecture. In 1931 he published some letters and drawings of Nicholas Hawksmoor [q.v.] in vol. xix of the Walpole Society (1931), and in 1937 he wrote a most distinguished short life of Sir Christopher Wren [q.v.]. His interests, however, were by no means confined to this period, and he became deeply concerned with English Gothic architecture in its Perpendicular phase.

For a man of such scholarship and creativity of mind, his published works were comparatively few, and it was perhaps as a lecturer that he left the most indelible impression on that large and privileged number of students, both undergraduate and postgraduate, who were fortunate enough to study under him. His technique was unorthodox and unforgettable. Delivered at high speed, usually whilst pacing restlessly about the platform, and with a wealth of gesture and vivid imagery, often aided by a dashingly free-hand use of the blackboard, his lectures provided a torrent of information and comment which could scarcely fail to fire the imagination and implant the desire for further knowledge in the minds of his listeners. From 1934 to 1937 he was lecturer at the Courtauld Institute of Fine Art, and his work at Cambridge was crowned by his appointment in 1938 as Slade professor of fine art, a post which he held, with the interruption of the war, until 1949. He served on the committee which originally formulated the recommendations which led to the establishment of the tripos in architecture and fine arts.

On the outbreak of war in 1939 he returned to the navy, serving on the intelligence staff of the Admiralty until 1943. He then joined the historical section of the War Cabinet Office, and in 1944 he became adviser on monuments, fine arts, and archives at SHAEF, with the rank of lieutenant-colonel. He ended the war as director, monuments, fine arts, and archives, Control Commission for Germany, British Element, with the rank of colonel. He was mentioned in dispatches and was awarded the croix de guerre in 1945, became an officer of the Legion of Honour in 1946, and achieved the bronze medal of freedom (USA) in 1947.

At the end of the war Webb returned to Cambridge to resume his Slade professorship, but, to his disappointment, no permanent teaching post was available to him in the university. Instead, in 1948 he went to London, where he became secretary to the Royal Commission on Historical Monuments (England), a post which he held until 1962. From 1943 to 1962 he was a member of the Royal Fine Arts Commission. In 1953 he was appointed CBE, and in 1957 he was elected a fellow of British Academy. He was also FSA (1945), and honorary ARIBA (1934).

Inevitably during this time he had less opportunity for his own writing, and there were only two post-war publications of major importance. In 1947 he delivered the Hertz lecture on Baroque art, which appeared in the *Proceedings* of the British Academy, vol. xxxiii, and he wrote the volume on *Architecture in Britain: the Middle Ages* in the Pelican history of art published in 1956. In this book his specialized knowledge of the evolution of the Late Medieval style in England was of particular value. To this Dictionary he contributed the notice of Katharine Ada Esdaile.

Webb was a striking personality. Tall and spare of build, his earlier beard became a war casualty, when he had to don khaki, with only the moustache surviving. An almost permanently raised left eyebrow gave to his face an enquiring, half-humorous expression, which accurately suggested some of the salient characteristics of the man. In his dress he ranged from the almost spectacular untidiness of his earlier years, to a rather tenuous respectability, somewhat erratically achieved, in marriage and later life. He had an infectious sense of humour, and was a great raconteur, his anecdotes being frequently punctuated by loud gusts of laughter. He had a great zest for life. He loved the country and looking at architecture, and the sea and sailing upon it. He enjoyed conversation, good food and wine, and the company of his friends. Above all, he had the rare gift of being able, from the depths of his knowledge and the vivid and enthusiastic way in which he expressed his ideas, of kindling in the minds of his listeners a heightened comprehension and a desire for increased knowledge of the subject he was discussing.

In 1934 he married Marjorie Isabel, the daughter of John Holgate Batten. She was herself an architectural historian, though later she became particularly interested in English sculpture of the eighteenth century, and in 1954 published an important book on John Michael Rysbrack [q.v.]. The similarity of their interests gave scope for much shared enjoyment, both for themselves and their many friends. There were no children of the marriage. In 1948 his wife's long and depressing illness started. He gave her devoted care but the anxiety and calls on his free time were most deleterious to his intellectual life and all that he did before his retirement must be judged against this wearisome background. His wife died in 1962. Shortly after her death Webb's term of office at the Royal Commission came to an end, and he retired to live permanently in the village of Solva on the Pembrokeshire coast in a cottage which he and his wife had acquired some years earlier. It was in Solva that Webb died 17 July 1970.

[M. D. Whinney in *Proceedings* of the British Academy, vol. lvii, 1971; *The Times*, 21 July 1970; private information; personal knowledge.]   JOHN CRITTALL

WEBSTER, SIR CHARLES KINGSLEY (1886-1961), historian, was born at Formby, Lancashire, 25 April 1886, the sixth of the seven children of Daniel Webster, shipping agent, and his wife, Annie Willey. He was educated at Merchant Taylors' School, Crosby, and at King's College, Cambridge, where he was a history scholar. He was placed in the second class in part i (1906) and in the first class of part ii (1907) of the historical tripos, to which he added the university Whewell scholarship in international law (1907). Aiming at an academic career, he combined research with minor teaching appointments in Cambridge and elsewhere. His subject was the history of diplomatic relations in the nineteenth century, the field to which he confined himself until he was well over sixty years old. In 1910 a dissertation, entitled simply 'Foreign Policy' but dealing with the years 1814-18, won him a fellowship at King's. After spending considerable periods in foreign archives, in 1912-13 he was in residence at Cambridge, read two papers to the Royal Historical Society, contributed an article to the *English Historical Review*, and took part in the organizing of the International Historical Congress which met in London in 1913. He accepted the college office of steward, which looked like the beginning of a settled Cambridge career; but in March 1914, at the age of nearly twenty-eight, he was appointed to the chair of modern history in the university of Liverpool.

The outbreak of war in the following summer took him by surprise. The German invasion of Belgium convinced him that Great Britain had a just cause for intervention, but his immediate duty was to his department in Liverpool, and he took this up with characteristic energy. In 1915, however, he volunteered for military service. Defective eyesight debarred him from combatant service, and he took a commission in the Army Service Corps. It was not until the autumn of 1917 that the army made a suitable use of his capacities by transferring him to an intelligence section of the general staff at the War Office of which H. W. V. Temperley [q.v.] was the head. One of Webster's tasks there was concerned with Zionism and the military and political future of Palestine. He became and remained a wholehearted admirer of Chaim Weizmann [q.v.]. Since his research had given him exceptional, indeed unique, knowledge of the last general European peace settlement, in the summer of 1918 he was seconded for two months to the Foreign Office where he wrote the first version of his book *The Congress of Vienna*. This was printed in 1919 as an official handbook. At the peace conference Webster acted as secretary to the military section of the British delegation. This experience confirmed him in the belief that the diplomacy of the twentieth century made a continuous whole with that of the nineteenth, and also in a belief in progress and in Great Britain as a progressive force.

Returning to Liverpool he held his professorship for three more years, also working energetically for the League of Nations Union. One of the leading members of that body was the future first Lord Davies [q.v.], who, with his sisters, had founded the chair of international relations at Aberystwyth. In 1922 that chair became vacant, and Webster was appointed to it, but on conditions which were designed to suit his individual requirements. He was to spend one term in each year at the college; another at any university in the world which might desire his services; and the third in study abroad. Thus for ten years he travelled the world, visiting the Far East twice, and from 1927 the obligation to foreign universities was crystallized as a regular appointment at Harvard. His main historical publication in this period was his book *The Foreign Policy of Castlereagh 1815–22* (1925) which established his position among historians. It provided a full narrative based on the diplomatic sources, and it was the most important contribution to the restoration of Castlereagh to his due place in the history of Europe.

The journeys and exertions based on Aberystwyth had lasted for ten years when Webster was appointed to the new chair of international relations founded at the London School of Economics by Sir Daniel Stevenson [q.v.]. In 1931 he brought out his second Castlereagh volume, covering the years 1812–15. At the School of Economics he became socially very much at home, and he was active in public speaking and journalism. Never much interested in party politics, he was suspicious of well-established institutions and instinctively critical of anything which appeared undemocratic. As the international situation became more menacing, he lost no opportunity of opposing the policy of appeasement.

In the war of 1939–45 the Royal Institute of International Affairs, of which Webster had been an active member since its foundation, set up an organization, later known as the Foreign Research and Press Service, to furnish certain kinds of information and advice to government departments. Webster was head of a section covering the United States, but he lacked opportunities for furthering his personal views. After a successful lecture tour in America in May and June 1941, he was put in charge of the British Library of Information in New York. This involved kinds of business of which he had little or no experience, and he had to relinquish the appointment early in 1942. In the same year the Foreign Office formed a reconstruction department, under Gladwyn Jebb, later Lord Gladwyn. He invited Webster to join it and once again Webster was in the right place. He had a large share in the preparation of plans for post-war security, especially the charter of the United Nations. He was a member of the British delegation to the conference at Dumbarton Oaks and adviser to that at San Francisco. He was appointed KCMG in 1946. His spell of public service continued after the war. In the winter of 1945–6 he became special adviser to his long-standing ally Philip (later Lord) Noel-Baker who was minister of state at the Foreign Office. In this capacity he was an alternate of the pre-

paratory commission of the United Nations, which met in London. He attended the first session of the Assembly. After that his links with the United Nations Organization were through UNESCO and various bodies connected with it.

In 1950 Webster became president of the British Academy, of which he had been a fellow since 1930. He was a steadfast believer in the usefulness of such bodies, especially those of international scope. From 1948 he served for eleven years as a delegate to the Union Académique Internationale. As president of the British Academy he strengthened its links with other learned societies and also with the Treasury. He used his influence to secure the election of fellows at an earlier age than had been usual. Among the many honours which he received were memberships of foreign academies, and doctorates from the universities of Oxford (where he was Ford's lecturer in 1947), Wales, and Rome, and from Williams College; but it is believed that none gratified him more than an honorary fellowship at King's.

During his last years at the School of Economics he finished his two-volume book on the foreign policy of Palmerston from 1830 to 1841, which was published in 1951. Except for an interval of eight years, part of which was covered by Temperley's *Canning*, Webster had thus written the standard history of British foreign policy from 1812 to 1841. He reluctantly gave up his intention of going forward to Palmerston's dismissal in 1851. Neither his general health nor his eyesight seemed likely to stand up to such a strain, even after retiring from his chair in 1953. He deserved all the more praise for accepting, in 1950, a difficult task in a field which was wholly new to him, the official history of the Anglo-American bombing offensive in the recent war. Working in equal collaboration with a younger man, Noble Frankland, who had the necessary Service experience, Webster completed in ten years this major work, than which none in the great series of official histories is better organized, more thorough or more candid. In 1961 he saw the proofs, but he did not live to see the publication of the four volumes. After a short illness he died in London of cancer 21 August 1961.

The qualities which gave its value to his historical work were completeness and strong common sense. His temperament was sanguine; he was optimistic, appreciative, and friendly. In 1915 he married Nora Violet, daughter of Richard Perry Harvey, who had been brought up in Italy. There were no children of this very happy marriage, but Webster was at his best with children and all young people. His physical frame was large and loosely assembled, and his dress untidy. Sometimes impatient or tactless, he was not sensitive to the impression made by his outspoken opinions; but he was so transparently a man of good will that he had no enemies.

[*The Times*, 23 August 1961; King's College, Cambridge, *Annual Report*, 1961; S. T. Bindoff in *Proceedings of the British Academy*, vol. xlviii, 1962; P. A. Reynolds and E. J. Hughes, *The Historian as Diplomat: Charles Kingsley Webster and the United Nations 1939–1946*, 1976; C. Weizmann, *Trial and Error*, 1949; Papers of Sir Charles Webster in the library, London School of Economics; private information; personal knowledge.]   G. N. CLARK

WEBSTER, (GILBERT) TOM (1886–1962), sporting cartoonist and caricaturist, was born 17 July 1886 at Church Street, Bilston, Staffordshire, the son of Daniel Webster, ironmonger, and his wife, Sarah Ann Bostock. He was educated at the Royal Wolverhampton School, where he received his first drawing lessons from Louis Frederick Stiles, the art master.

At the age of fourteen Tom Webster entered the employment of the Great Western Railway as a clerk in the ticket office at Handsworth, Staffordshire. While earning 12s. 6d. a week in that capacity he increased his knowledge of all aspects of sport by daily study of the *Athletic News*. Before he was twenty he had won a five-shilling prize offered by the Birmingham *Weekly Post* for a humorous drawing, and other prizes in competitions run by the Manchester *Evening Chronicle* and the *Athletic News*. Soon afterwards he joined the staff of the Birmingham *Sports Argus*, being paid £2. 10s. for twelve cartoons a week in the third and final year of his contract.

On the outbreak of war in 1914 Webster enlisted in the Royal Fusiliers but was so badly disabled by rheumatic fever in 1916 that he nearly died. Following the end of the war in 1918 he was out of work for a long period and, at one time, so low in funds that he was obliged to sleep on London's Thames embankment.

When told to submit a specimen of his work to the London *Evening News*, he bluffed his way into the National Sporting Club to see the fight between Tommy Noble and Joe Symonds and produced the first running commentary on a sporting event in cartoon form. In 1919 his work in the *Evening News* came to the notice of the paper's proprietor Lord Northcliffe [q.v.] who told the editor of his principal publication, the *Daily Mail*, to give Webster a staff appointment. The editor offered Webster £1,500 a year. Seeing, on the desk between them, a *Daily Mail* headline offering £10,000 for the first flight of the Atlantic, Webster concluded the paper

could afford to pay him more and successfully demanded a starting salary of £2,000 a year.

In 1924 he was the highest-paid cartoonist in the world. Tom Webster was a round-faced man with a broad forehead under a receding hair-line with the parting a little to the left. He had a slightly upturned nose set between large eyes and a wide, generous mouth. As well as in boxing, he found the material for his cartoons in racing, football, cricket, golf, and billiards. He also contributed humorous articles illustrated by himself to the *Daily Mail*.

A highly developed sense of humour gave him a quick eye for the quirks and eccentricities of character and the ridiculous, and enabled him to follow in the best tradition of cartoonists by bringing out personality and recording absurdity. Flamboyant and extravagant in his use of lines, many of them characteristically sharply serrated, he was relatively economic with shading. As well as captions, he made frequent use of 'balloons' to put words into the mouths of his subjects. He depicted horses in human postures, usually with disproportionately bulbous muzzles, and large teeth in contrast to small prick ears. He worked very rapidly, often laughing aloud as he did so, and had a cartoon across three columns on the presses of the *Daily Mail* within a little more than an hour after the fight between Jimmy Wilde [q.v.] and Moore at Olympia.

One of Webster's best-known cartoons was of 'Tishy', a racehorse with its forelegs twisted round each other. This exemplified how exaggeration of the factual, or allegedly factual, inspired his work. The only excuse offered to the public for the failure of 'Tishy' to justify favouritism in the Cesarewitch of 1921 had been that she had crossed her legs in running. As a result of Webster's cartoon the expression 'doing a Tishy' passed into everyday racing parlance.

In 1920, the year after he had joined the *Daily Mail*, Tom Webster visited the United States and sent back a number of cartoons including one of 'Chick' Evans beating Francis Ouimet in the American Amateur Golf Championship. Four years later he played a prominent part in arranging the revue 'Cartoons' at the Criterion Theatre, London, and in 1929 his popularity was recognized by a selection of his cartoons being projected on to a screen in Trafalgar Square for the amusement of Londoners on the night of the general election.

Tom Webster made his first venture into colour when he was one of the artists commissioned to decorate the *Queen Mary* in 1936. He was responsible for the sporting panorama lightly laid on in oils on fourteen panels in the gymnasium.

Having retired from the *Daily Mail* in

1940 Tom Webster resumed work on joining Kemsley Newspapers in 1944. In 1953 he joined the *News Chronicle* before finally retiring in 1956. Each year he had published the best of his work in *Tom Webster's Annual*.

His first marriage was to Mae Flynn in New York in 1929. This was dissolved by divorce in 1933. His second marriage was to Ida, daughter of John Rupert Michael, master mariner, at St. James's Church, Spanish Place, London, 4 December 1935. By his second wife, who was twenty-five years his junior, he had one son and two daughters.

Tom Webster died at his home, 22 Bishopswood Road, Highgate, London, 21 June 1962.

[*Daily Mail* cuttings library; *The Times*, 22 June 1962.]   RICHARD ONSLOW

WEISZ, VICTOR (1913-1966), the cartoonist VICKY, was born in Berlin 25 April 1913, the son of Desider Weisz, and his wife, Isabella. His parents were Hungarian Jewish and he was registered as Hungarian. As a child Vicky showed aptitude as an artist and attended the Berlin Art School before his father died in 1928, ending his schooling and compelling him to become the family breadwinner. He found work on the Berliners' *12 Uhr Blatt*. He published his first anti-Hitler cartoon as a precocious fifteen-year-old. He was a successful caricaturist of theatrical and sporting personalities but his political drawings attracted public attention and the resentment of the Nazis. After the Reichstag fire he lost his job and he was pestered by the Gestapo. Only his Hungarian passport saved him and his family from the concentration camp. Friends arranged an escape to England. In 1938 the *Daily Herald*, the paper of the Labour Party with which his political sympathies lay, was looking for a successor to Will Dyson [q.v.] as staff cartoonist. He was given a brief trial but was unsuccessful. He could barely speak English and his humour was alien. He became a freelance, relying on the indulgence and instruction of professional friends, of whom, with his engaging personality, he had many.

In 1939 he was introduced to (Sir) Gerald Barry [q.v.], editor of the *News Chronicle*, who recognized the verve and peculiar talent of his drawings but also their limitations. The drawings were boisterously funny but they lacked insights into the whimsicality of British humour, the eccentricities of British manners and thought, and the contradictions of British politics. Barry, however, gave him a retainer to do conventional illustrations and pocket sketches. With a patient editor and much friendly advice, he was given a crash course in British humour. He was an earnest student,

setting himself to read the works of Shakespeare to discover the tragi-comic characteristics of the Elizabethan 'clown'. Barry set him his homework—*Alice in Wonderland*, Dickens, Edward Lear, A. A. Milne, back-numbers of *Punch*, and *Wisden* (for the rest of his life Vicky was to ask plaintively 'What's funny about cricket?'). He listened avidly to the BBC, not only to improve his English and to follow the news, but also to dissect the ITMA of Tommy Handley [q.v.]. He frequented the gallery of the House of Commons, and read *Hansard*. He applied himself to the study of political history, the party system, and the uncontinental character of the trade unions. With Richard Winnington, the film critic and fellow cartoonist, he engrossed himself in films, watching the throwaway lines of British understatement and self-ridicule. He discovered pantomime, Gilbert and Sullivan, the football terrace, the dog-track, the public bar and the legal bar, and cockneys with their rhyming slang. After two years, word perfect in English, he could have lectured (as he did later) on the nature of humour itself—wit, wisecrack, satire, music-hall burlesque, pun, Spoonerisms, slapstick, drollery, and situation comedy. All of them he had been rehearsing on the drawing-board.

In 1941 he graduated as staff cartoonist on the *News Chronicle*. Still an enemy alien (he was not granted British nationality until 1946) he was now a British humorist. In wartime circumstances in which sensitive ministers had fairly drastic powers to deal with such people, he was as critical, satirical, funny, or pungent about personalities and policies as his emotional ebullience prompted and his protective editor allowed. He was frequently denounced as an enemy alien, subject to drafting into the Pioneer Corps. He was not easy to handle then or after the war. Gerald Barry was to write a preface to *The Editor Regrets*, a book of his cartoons rejected for good, or sometimes timid, reasons. When Barry left the editorial chair, Vicky became more and more dissatisfied. After fourteen years in which he had established himself as an outstanding cartoonist, he resigned from the *News Chronicle* when it did not publish a bitter cartoon on Kenya.

Vicky, while he deferred to (Sir) David Low [q.v.] as a finer draughtsman, had been vying with him in popularity and, upon Low's semi-retirement, succeeded him as the best cartoonist in Britain. He later joined the *Daily Mirror*, which then had one of the largest daily newspaper sales in the world, and which gave him unlimited scope for his left-wing sympathies. In 1958 he moved to the *Evening Standard*. Lord Beaverbrook [q.v.], whom he had regularly drawn as a diminutive gnome in crusader's armour, had pursued him as he had once pursued Low. As in Low's case, he gave him a contract guaranteeing him complete freedom of expression. Vicky, who was quite incorruptible in terms of money or of flattery, could not resist the opportunity of preaching to the unconverted, the Conservative readers of the *Evening Standard*. The incongruity exaggerated his effects. The Trojan horse stampeded the sacred cows.

From 1954 Vicky drew a regular weekly cartoon for the *New Statesman*. It was a labour of love for which his original fees barely covered his taxi fares. Every Monday morning, he would shyly join the editorial board with an assortment of yard-square drawings, variants of his chosen commentary. He was never conceited about his drawings. He would pass them round one by one and wait for reactions—laughs, rather than comments, which, however, he never resented. He would modestly concede on details but never on his theme, for that was his 'editorial'. If he were challenged on a likeness, he would produce his original, from-the-life, sketch and patiently explain how and why he had exaggerated the characteristics. He once said: 'I don't make fun of a face. I make fun of what is behind that face.'

According to Michael Foot (*Evening Standard*, 21 February 1956), Vicky became the fifth estate of the realm. No public personality, particularly his political friends when they faltered, escaped the ridicule of his pen. His caricatures were impudent rather than malicious: the totem pole Charles de Gaulle, the Micawberish Churchill, the zither-playing Attlee, the White Rabbit Eden, the street urchin Bevan, the Supermac (or, on occasion, Mac the Knife) Macmillan. Indignant supporters protested more often than did the victims, many of whom collected the originals. When he met Truman, Vicky congratulated the President on being more like his own cartoons than he had imagined.

His energy and his output were prodigious. He had no gag men, or caption writers, and he always found his own subjects. He loved good company, good music, and good theatre. He slept badly, relying on the sleeping pills with which he eventually took his life. He rose at 5.45 every morning, breakfasted, listened to the news bulletin, read all the national dailies, and arrived at his newspaper office at 7.30. He would decide upon his topic, do a series of large-scale roughs and, by 3 p.m., deliver the finished drawing. When events were moving fast, he would frequently substitute a fresh cartoon for later editions. He produced six cartoons a week for his newspaper as well as his weekly subject for the *New Statesman*. In addition, he produced painstaking pen-and-ink portraits in the Spy/Beerbohm tradition for the *New Statesman* 'profiles'. These disproved his

modesty about his draughtsmanship. They had the strength of line, incisiveness, and character-penetration of Low at his best.

He was small in height and build, with a large head, bald on top and shaggy on its back and sides. His lively, twinkling eyes were magnified by large, thick glasses. He was exactly like the miniature of himself which frequently figured in his cartoons as the puzzled little man bewildered by events. He was a boon companion, amusing in conversation and abundantly compassionate. Except when he was fighting editors or defending causes, mainly those of the poor and persecuted, he was mild-mannered and endearing.

Even at the height of his career, however, he felt insecure. He was thoroughly worried about the way the world was going and was depressed by the political expediency of his friends in power. He drew a cartoon on the Labour Government's acquiescence in the Vietnam war, took an overdose of sleeping pills, and died in the early morning of 23 February 1966 at the age of fifty-two. His mother, who was eighty-six, died six weeks after the shock of his death. He was four times married, and childless. His fourth wife, Ingelore, whom he married in 1965, committed suicide on the ninth anniversary of his death. He was sketched by his fellow-cartoonists. On that done by Abu, which was reproduced in the *Observer*, cited below, Vicky wrote 'too flattering'.

[*The Times*, 24 February 1966; Sir Gerald Barry and Abu, *Observer*, 27 February 1966; Milton Shulman, *Evening Standard*, 31 October 1958; Cassandra, *Daily Mirror*, 1 February 1954; C. H. Rolph, *Kingsley*, 1973; private information; personal knowledge.]   P. R. RITCHIE-CALDER

WELLINGTON, HUBERT LINDSAY (1879-1967), painter, draughtsman, and art teacher, was born at Gloucester 14 June 1879, the elder of the two sons of Caleb Joseph Wellington, a modestly prosperous printer and paper-bag manufacturer in that city, and his wife, Katherine Potter. Like his father, Hubert Wellington was educated at the Crypt Grammar School, Gloucester, where his artistic talents became evident. In his teens he was drawing with imaginative facility; he was also not only playing the piano with increasing verve but developing his natural ability to sight-read musical scores with fluency.

In spite of some parental foreboding, Wellington moved at the age of eighteen from the Crypt to the Gloucester School of Art and the next year to Birmingham. He entered the more sympathetic and stimulating atmosphere of the Slade School of Fine Art in Gower Street,

London, in 1899. From early sallies to London with his father he had already achieved glimpses of the wider horizons he was seeking, viewing paintings by J. A. McN. Whistler, W. R. Sickert, P. Wilson Steer [qq.v.], Jules Bastien-Lepage, and H. G. E. Degas in dealers' galleries, and having particularly illuminating conversations with the Dutch dealer, van Wisselingh. At Birmingham, preferred by his parents as a more sober environment than London, he had spent more time in the Central Library than in the School of Art, avidly reading and looking at foreign periodicals; it was there that he discovered the *Mercure de France*, the *Revue Blanche*, the lithographs of Steinlen, and, in the *Saturday Review*, the art criticism of D. S. MacColl [q.v.], who later became his staunch champion.

Wellington arrived at the Slade School in 1899 on the same day as P. Wyndham Lewis [q.v.], with whom he managed to remain on surprisingly friendly terms until their last meeting in 1956 at the Tate Gallery at a retrospective exhibition of Lewis's work after he had lost his sight. Wellington made his closest friends in the Post-Impressionist group, which centred around Spencer Gore and Harold J. W. Gilman, and, somewhat later, I. Charles Ginner [q.v.], with Walter Sickert as an enigmatic father figure.

In 1900, at the age of twenty-one, somewhat rashly for a young man without an income, he married Nancy Charlotte Boughtwood (died 1943). He spent the years 1904 to 1916 teaching at the Stafford School of Art to support his wife and two young sons, (Sir) (Reginald Everard) Lindsay and Robert Michael. But he kept in touch with his metropolitan friends; both Gore and Gilman came to stay and to paint with the young family in the country near Stafford. In Wellington's own words: 'for my painting, one of the crucial points was undoubtedly in the summer of 1906, when I joined Gore at Dieppe. Walter Sickert had invited Gore to use his house at Neuville, and I joined them for an immensely stimulating six weeks. Sickert was most generous and encouraging, with endless talk of great practitioners of "la bonne peinture".' The decade between 1906 and 1916 was the most productive period of painting Wellington was to enjoy.

Awaiting call-up in 1916, he introduced Gilman to his beloved Cotswold country; they stayed at the Bell Inn, Sapperton, for the best part of three months, sharing an attic as a studio. Unencumbered by family or other material responsibilities, the artist sank himself joyfully into a concentrated burst of painting, which lasted through that summer. So he developed mainly as a landscape painter, although his many sketch-books were also full of drawings of his family and friends. As a painter, he remained faithfull to the neo-Impressionist style and to 'the divided touch', but as the years went by his sympathies moved further from the world of Camille Pissarro towards the monumental style of Paul Cézanne. In 1926 he wrote: 'Cézanne has changed the face of the world of painting by fundamental constructive and technical perceptions.' Writing about Auguste Renoir at the same time, he said: 'To the painter he stands perhaps more simply and unaffectedly than any man for the primal impulses of delight in what his eyes behold, from which for me the art of painting springs.'

These quotations give a clue to Wellington's increasingly firm orientation towards Paris and current French culture. Beyond the world of painters, he was an early subscriber to the *Nouvelle Revue Française* and so an early admirer of Marcel Proust; in the 1920s scores of Igor Stravinsky's 'Ragtime' and Francis Poulenc's 'Mouvements Perpetuels' joined those of César Franck and Frederic Chopin on top of the piano; and in the late thirties the neo-Thomist writings of Charles Péguy and Jacques Maritain finally led him into the Catholic Church.

The premature deaths of Wellington's two closest friends among painters—Gore in 1914 and Gilman in 1919—and the scattering of the group associated with Camden Town together with the upheavals of the war of 1914–18 (which took him to France with the Survey battalion of the Royal Engineers as a map draughtsman) left him at forty still unestablished as far as a London reputation was concerned. But (Sir) Charles Holmes [q.v.] at the National Gallery, prompted by Charles Aitken and J. B. Manson [q.v.] from the Tate, spotted the potentialities of the articulate and enthusiastic painter-teacher, and proposed in the spring of 1919 that he should launch a new experiment of informal guide lecturing. For two hours each morning six days a week, he talked about the Old Masters as a painter rather than as an art historian. By the time he retired from this field in 1923, his pioneer work, together with that of W. G. Constable, who had inaugurated a similar series at the Wallace Collection, had established a pattern of guide lecturing which has since spread in many directions. He himself, to his own ironic amusement, had acquired a reputation for expertise about Old Masters, and found his advice sought by collectors and dealers. But he had also in occasional art criticism for the *Saturday Review*, the *Nation*, and *Manchester Guardian* established himself as a spokesman for his contemporaries, such as (Sir) Matthew A. B. Smith, Paul Nash [qq.v.] and his brother John, and S. Ivon Hitchens. His monograph on (Sir) Jacob Epstein [q.v.], published in 1924, was regarded by the sculptor as one of the fairest assessments of his aims and work; as was his appreciation of his old acquaintance, (Sir) William Rothenstein [q.v.], published in the same series in 1923. To this Dictionary he contributed the notice of Sir W. M. N. Orpen.

It was the production of the Rothenstein books that brought Wellington back into the world of art schools. Rothenstein, impressed by his tact and sweet reasonableness, invited him in his own words to become his 'chief of staff' at the Royal College of Art, where as registrar and lecturer for ten years (1923-32) he provided a sympathetic link between the establishment world of the Board of Education and the younger generation of Henry Moore, John Piper, and Ceri Richards.

In 1932 he moved from Kensington to become principal of the Edinburgh College of Art, which had recently found itself, thanks to the Andrew Grant bequest, probably the most handsomely endowed art school in Europe. Among the first to take up a Grant scholarship in painting was the subsequent director of the Tate Gallery, (Sir) Norman Reid, who wrote, more than thirty years later: 'Under his direction the college acquired an entirely new vitality . . . particularly, I think because he was genuinely interested in what young people were doing.'

Upon his wife's death in 1943, after more than forty years of exceptionally close partnership, he retired, stunned for the time being, from Edinburgh to Oxfordshire. Unexpectedly in 1946 he was invited by his old colleague, Randolph Schwabe [q.v.], to stand in as professor of the history of fine art at the Slade School. In the event it surprised and touched him that for three years the young should listen to him with such interested concentration. After his fingers had grown too arthritic and his eyesight too uncertain to paint, he prepared for the Phaidon Press an edited version of one of his own favourite books, a translation of the journal of Eugène Delacroix (1951).

The last twenty-three years of Wellington's life were made happier by the companionship and care of one of his former students at Kensington, Irene Bass, whom he married in 1944. A distinguished calligrapher in her own right, a favoured pupil of Edward Johnston [q.v.], Wellington found particular satisfaction in the flowering of her very personal talent.

As a young man, over six feet tall with delicately modelled features, in a halo of reddish golden hair, Wellington was a strikingly romantic figure. In 1921, to protect a delicate skin, he first grew a small vandyck beard, which helped in his later years to enhance his natural distinction of manner. His modesty made him unwilling to advertise his own gifts, but all his life he used his charisma to encourage others. His favourite admonition to the young, taken from François de Sales, was 'live generously', advice which he followed in his own life.

When young Wellington exhibited at the New English Art Club and at the Allied Artists Association, and later at the London Group. Living out of London, he was never a subscribing member of the Camden Town Group, which centred round so many of his friends and contemporaries, although Gore at one time pressed him to leave Stafford to take up a position as their resident secretary. A comprehensive exhibition of his paintings and drawings was held at Messrs. Agnews in 1963, and a memorial exhibition at the City Art Gallery, Gloucester, in 1968. Examples of his work are in the collections, among others, of the Tate Gallery, the Contemporary Art Society, the Arts Council, the Ministry of the Environment, the Ashmolean Museum, and the Gloucester and Southampton art galleries.

Wellington died at Oxford 3 November 1967.

[*The Times*, 7, 9, and 11 November 1967; Leicester Galleries exhibition catalogue, 1926; private information; personal knowledge.]   WILLIAM COLDSTREAM

WEST, EDWARD CHARLES SACKVILLE-, fifth BARON SACKVILLE (1901-1965), man of letters. [See SACKVILLE-WEST.]

WEST, VICTORIA MARY SACKVILLE- (1892-1962), writer and gardener. [See SACKVILLE-WEST.]

WHIDDINGTON, RICHARD (1885-1970), physicist, was born in London 25 November 1885, the eldest of the three children and the only son of Richard Whiddington, schoolteacher, of London, and his wife, Ada Ann, daughter of Richard Fitzgerald of Swords near Dublin. His mother, having left Ireland as a teenager, had been appointed headmistress of a girls' school in north London before she was twenty.

Whiddington attended the William Ellis School at Highgate, and entered St. John's College, Cambridge, as a scholar in 1905. He was placed in the first class in part i of the natural sciences tripos in 1907, as also in part ii (physics) in June 1908. By then he had also completed a London (external) B.Sc. He started research in the Cavendish Laboratory in September, and in the following year was awarded the Hutchinson studentship by his college. In 1910 he gained an Allen scholarship, and in 1911 a fellowship of St. John's, and the degree of D.Sc. of London University. He remained in Cambridge, involved in teaching and research, until the outbreak of war in 1914. In September 1914 he moved to the Royal Flying Corps establishment at Farnborough, where he remained throughout the war as a member of a group which had been given the task of applying the principles of wireless telegraphy to problems of practical communication in the field of battle. Originally gazetted as captain, Royal Flying Corps, Whiddington finished the war as major, Royal Air Force.

Whiddington returned to his college fellowship at the end of hostilities, and was appointed university lecturer in experimental physics in 1919. But he had no sooner been appointed than he resigned. The Cavendish chair of physics in the university of Leeds had remained vacant since 1915, when (Sir) W. H. Bragg [q.v.] had moved to University College, London. Whiddington was appointed to fill the vacancy, and took up his duties in October 1919. He was elected FRS in 1925. By that time he had managed to recruit additional teachers of some seniority to his departmental staff (which consisted of one lecturer and three demonstrators at the time of his appointment), and in 1932 a new building, in the detailed planning of which he had been fully involved, was finally opened.

Whiddington spent the whole of the war of 1939-45 'on loan' to the Government. He was a member of a Royal Air Force officers' selection board for a short time; then with the Admiralty Scientific Research Department dealing with the development of radar for the Royal Navy; finally, he was deputy director of scientific research in the Ministry of Supply. For this service in varied fields he was created CBE in 1946. Shortly before the war ended he had been invited, on behalf of the scientific advisory committee to the Cabinet, to become scientific archivist, but when the war ended he decided he must return to his university post. *Science at War* (1947), with J. G. Crowther as co-author, reflects his activities during his short spell as archivist.

During the sessions 1949-51, at the end of the second of which he retired from his university chair, Whiddington served as pro-vice-chancellor. He had, indeed, for many years taken a wide and effective part in university affairs generally. After retirement Whiddington was president of the Physical Society (1952-4) and scientific adviser to the Central Treaty Organization (1959-63). He lived at Holme next the Sea, on the Norfolk coast, from the summer of 1951 until his death there 7 June 1970.

From Cambridge, during the period 1909-14, Whiddington published sixteen papers describing his researches on the properties of X-rays and electrons, the most important of which established the relation between cathode ray velocity and the capacity of the primary X-rays thereby produced to excite characteristic X-rays in various radiators—as also the relation between the cathode ray velocity and the range of those rays in solid absorbers. For a time, after the war of 1914-18, he continued this general line of research at Leeds, but in 1926, by which time his own department was providing a steady stream of research students, he took up a new field of electron studies in which correlations were sought with optical rather than with X-radiation. Some thirty or more papers, published during the period 1926-39, described the results of this work. It was difficult work, and of high quality, but less likely to be quoted in historical surveys of twentieth-century physics than is Whiddington's earlier work in Cambridge.

Whiddington was married in London on 9 April 1919 to (Laura) Katherine, daughter of Alexander Reoch Grant, a London-based company director. They had one son and one daughter. Miss Grant had served in France with the Women's Auxiliary Army Corps during the last year of the war of 1914-18, and had been mentioned in dispatches. She trained with the Auxiliary Territorial Service before the beginning of the war of 1939-45 and was senior commander at the York HQ at the outbreak of hostilities. When war began she was sent as commandant to Catterick Camp. In 1941 she was appointed MBE. She remained in the Service until late in 1945, holding the rank of controller, and was deputy director, Northern Command, at the time of her return to civilian life. With her two children, she survived her husband. There is a portrait of Whiddington (1951) by A. R. Middleton Todd at the university of Leeds.

[N. Feather in *Biographical Memoirs of Fellows of the Royal Society*, vol. xvii, 1971.]   NORMAN FEATHER

WHITAKER, SIR (FREDERICK) ARTHUR (1893-1968), maritime civil engineer, was born in Ladysmith, South Africa, 17 July 1893, second son of William Henry Whitaker, civil engineer, and his wife, Georgina Primrose Foggo. His father emigrated to South Africa in 1890, but in 1898, after their mother's death, Arthur and his elder brother, Ambler, went to England and were brought up in Liverpool by their uncle, Frederick Whitaker, a schoolmaster. Family life, though happy, was strict and disciplined and Arthur had to work hard at school and university: he never forgot these early lessons, which he applied throughout his life. He went to Liverpool Institute High School and Liverpool University, where he gained first class honours in engineering (1914), a research scholarship, and nomination for an 1851 Exhibition industrial bursary. However, war broke out and, in April 1915, he was sent to Rosyth as a 'temporary draughtsman improver' with the Admiralty—at 4s. per day. Undeterred, he continued his studies and, in 1917, obtained an M.Eng. degree at Liverpool University, which conferred on him the honorary degree of D.Eng. in 1960.

The extent and variety of civil engineering work in the Admiralty provided ideal training for a young engineer. After five years at Rosyth on construction of the naval dockyard and the destroyer base at Port Edgar, Whitaker was sent to Jamaica in 1920 to build an oil fuel installation and found himself acting as naval agent and a member of the Jamaica Marine Board. The 1920s were lean years for the Services and promotion was slow, but Whitaker was broadening his experience and building up his reputation and by 1930 had served at Devonport, the Admiralty, Malta, and Portsmouth, and had been engaged in oil installations, jetties, dredging, and many types of harbour works. Early in 1933 he received accelerated promotion to superintending civil engineer, in charge of the construction of the Singapore naval base, which comprised a dockyard, with a 1,000 ft. dry dock, wharfs, naval, armament, victualling, and fuel depots, barracks, and a small township for expatriate personnel. Work had commenced in 1928 and was in full flight when he arrived. However, in 1934, T. B. Hunter, the civil engineer in chief, Admiralty, retired and Whitaker was summoned home for further accelerated promotion to deputy C.E in C. In January 1940 he succeeded Sir Athol Anderson as C.E. in C.

The country was again at war and Whitaker himself was now responsible for the wide-ranging programmes of naval works at home and overseas. At home, dockyards, naval bases, all types of storage and fuel depots, W/T stations, airfields, and training establishments were expanded and modernized and many new ones built. Much of the storage was underground and many novel requirements had to be met. Overseas, the emphasis was on operational and repair bases, storage, and airfields—scattered all over the world, from Iceland to South Africa and from the West Indies to Australia. For the invasion of Europe special bases and some fifty embarkation yards were built and the department was involved in the design of the Mulberry harbours.

With such a large programme under his control it is difficult to identify any particular project with Whitaker himself, with one exception—the Orkney causeways. The submarine which sank the *Royal Oak* in October 1939 had entered Scapa Flow through one of the four eastern 'sounds'. Having ordered the immediate sinking of additional blockships, (Sir) Winston Churchill asked Whitaker whether all four sounds could be permanently closed by causeways. In that remote area, with depths around 60 ft. and currents up to 12 knots at high tide, this was a daunting task. But Whitaker said the project was possible, directed it personally, got work started in May 1940, and had the sounds effectively blocked by 1942. Completion to road level came in 1945.

Whitaker tackled the biggest construction programme ever undertaken by the Admiralty with energy and determination. By his engineering ability, sense of purpose, and speed of decision, he won the respect and loyalty of all his permanent and wartime temporary staff and welded them into an efficient and close-knit team. Although essentially shy and unostentatious, he was a dominant leader, who drove them to their limits: they responded to his challenge and established a reputation for the department which survived long after his death.

After the war, he chaired the British Organizing Committee for the XIXth Congress of the Permanent International Association of Navigation Congresses in London in 1957 and was a member of the Commission Consultative des Travaux of the Suez Canal Company and, for fourteen years, of the Dover Harbour Board. He was created CB in 1941 and KCB in 1945 and in 1947 was made a commander of the Legion of Honour. He retired from the Admiralty in 1954 and then, for eight years, engaged on harbour and dredging work overseas (mainly in South America) as a partner in Livesey & Henderson, consulting engineers.

Apart from his Admiralty department, his one abiding interest, to which he gave devoted service, was the Institution of Civil Engineers, of which he was a member for forty-nine years and president in 1957-8. He believed that its role was fundamental to the development of the science and practice of civil engineering and he constantly exhorted his own engineers actively to support it. He delivered the 1946-7 Vernon Harcourt lecture on 'Civil Engineering Aspects of Naval Harbours and Bases'. To this Dictionary he contributed the notice of Sir William Halcrow.

He married, in 1923, Florence (died 1978), daughter of John Woods Overend, manager of a marine engineering business in Liverpool. They had one son and two daughters. Whitaker died in Northwood 13 June 1968. A portrait by Maurice and Whitlock Codner hangs in the Institution of Civil Engineers.

[*The Times*, 14 June 1968; private information; personal knowledge.] WILLIAM HARRIS

WHITFIELD, ERNEST ALBERT, first BARON KENSWOOD (1887-1963), professional violinist and economist, was born 15 September 1887 in London, the younger son of John Henry Christopher Whitfield, of London, and his wife, Louisa, daughter of Michael Farren, of Copenhagen. He was educated at Archbishop Tenison's and University College Schools, London, the university of Vienna, and London University. A brilliant pupil at school, Kenswood was forced by economic necessity to accept a commercial appointment in Vienna in 1907 and rose to departmental manager while still in his early twenties. His sight began to deteriorate, however, and after struggling with failing vision for two and a half years he had to consider a new profession.

From an early age he had shown outstanding ability as a violinist and with reluctance he was induced to adopt his musical expertise as a means of earning a livelihood. For some time he pursued his business duties while preparing for a professional musical career, assiduously memorizing as much music as was possible with his remaining sight, and in 1912 he was awarded the Austrian State diploma for teaching music. The following year he made his début as a soloist and his success seemed assured, but with the outbreak of World War I he was obliged to return to London after an absence of eight years, and with barely any vision he endeavoured to establish himself as a concert artist.

Through a chance meeting with Sir (Cyril) Arthur Pearson [q.v.], Whitfield was introduced to the braille system and he joined the St. Dunstan's Blind Musicians Concert Party, but relinquished the position owing to the stress of constant travelling. In 1917, without revealing that his vision was impaired, he succeeded in gaining a post as leader of the orchestra at Wyndham's Theatre in London, and for the first week he memorized all the programme details before admitting his visual handicap, proving that an adequately trained blind musician can fulfil orchestral duties. He remained at Wyndham's for almost two years. He made his first appearance as a soloist in London at the Queen's Hall Promenade Concerts in 1918, and in 1920 he was instrumental in forming the Guild of Singers and Players.

On 13 December 1920 Whitfield married Sophie Madeline, the highly accomplished only child of Ernest Walter Howard, of London and of Hill Head, Hampshire, a descendant of the ducal house of Norfolk. From 1921 to 1923 he won international acclaim for his musical virtuosity and for his introduction of many new British works, but ill health restricted his concert engagements. He embarked on a deeper study of economics, political science, and philo-sophy, and while still perfecting his technique as a violinist, graduated with a B.Sc. degree at London University in 1926. His only daughter was born in 1928 and that year he was made a Ph.D. in London for a thesis on Gabriel Bonnot de Mably, a French pre-Revolutionary philosopher. He reappeared on the concert platform and achieved renown for the mastery of his art.

In 1928 he also was elected to the executive council of the National Institute for the Blind, later becoming honorary joint treasurer, and subsequently he was a British delegate to the World Conference on Work for the Blind in New York in 1931, and other overseas conferences on blind welfare. His son and heir, John Michael Howard, was born on 6 April 1930. Whitfield stood unsuccessfully as a Labour candidate for St. Marylebone, London, in 1931 and for South Buckinghamshire in 1935, and was a co-opted member of the education committee of the London County Council from 1934 to 1939. In 1935 a damaged hand had forced him to abandon his musical career.

He was in France at the outbreak of World War II and in 1941, being unable to return to Britain, he moved to the United States where he undertook musical research for the New York Institute for the Blind. Later he continued this activity in Toronto, in conjunction with rehabilitation programmes for ex-servicemen at the Canadian National Institute for the Blind. On his return to England he became a governor of the British Broadcasting Corporation from 1946 to 1950. He was created a peer on 27 June 1951, during which year he was elected to the presidency of the National Federation of the Blind until 1955. He also became vice-president of the Pembrokeshire Community Council, and in addition he was a member of the Pembrokeshire old people's welfare committee. He served on the committees of several hospitals in the London area and also of schools for the deaf and blind. He contributed to the Columbia Encyclopaedia of Political Science and to various periodicals on blind welfare.

A good-looking man of medium height, Kenswood was a keen walker and enthusiastic swimmer. His puckish sense of humour and persuasive delivery made him a popular and effective after-dinner speaker. His deep passion for music, lifelong interest in political life and current affairs, love of country life, and compassion for less fortunate members of society combined with his personal fortitude to make him a well-liked and fascinating personality.

Kenswood's first wife died on 25 August 1961 at her Pembrokeshire home, Roch Castle, and on 26 July 1962 he married Catherine, widow of Charles Chilver-Stainer and daughter of Frank Luxton. Kenswood died in a London hospital 21 April 1963.

A plaster bust by F. J. Kormis was exhibited by the Society of Portrait Sculptors in 1954.

[*The Times*, 23 April 1963.]

E. T. BOULTER

WHITTARD, WALTER FREDERICK (1902-1966), Chaning Wills professor of geology in the university of Bristol, was born in Battersea, London, 26 October 1902, the youngest of four children of Thomas Walter Whittard, a successful grocer of Clapham, and his wife, Sarah Cotterell.

Whittard attended the County Secondary School at Battersea where his love of natural history influenced him into becoming a founder-member of the school natural history society. While still at school, he was introduced to T. Eastwood of the Geological Survey who inspired in Whittard an interest in geology and advised him, while still a schoolboy, to attend evening classes in geology at Chelsea Polytechnic. There began a lifelong friendship with O. M. B. Bulman (later Woodwardian professor of geology in the university of Cambridge) and C. J. Stubblefield (later director of the Geological Survey of Great Britain). In 1920 he entered Chelsea Polytechnic as a full-time student and his progress was then rapid. In 1922 he became a student in the geology department of Imperial College under Professor W. W. Watts and obtained in 1924 first class honours in geology and zoology in the ARCS examinations and also in geology in his external London B.Sc. Attendance while an undergraduate at D. M. S. Watson's lectures (at University College, London) in vertebrate palaeontology enlarged his interest in palaeontology and this remained with him throughout his life, leading to a succession of papers which ranged from Upper Palaeozoic amphibia to Lower Palaeozoic worms, but those of most importance were his contributions to the study of trilobites.

With the award (in 1924) of a DSIR scholarship, he began his researches on the Valentian rocks of Shropshire under the supervision of Watts, while also pursuing part-time research under D. M. S. Watson on fossil amphibia. Whittard's investigations of the Lower Palaeozoic rocks of Shropshire continued throughout his life; it was his principal research field until his later interest in marine geology developed. In two years he gained his London Ph.D. and in 1926 he entered Sidney Sussex College, Cambridge, with a senior DSIR award. Here he joined in the social life with vigour and rowed for his college with distinction. In two years he completed his work for a Cambridge Ph.D. and published the first of his major papers on the Valentian rocks of Shropshire (in 1928). In 1929 he visited East Greenland as

chief geologist to the 1929 Cambridge expedition under (Sir) J. M. Wordie [q.v.]. This was an experience he greatly valued and he subsequently encouraged his staff and students to join expeditions to Greenland. In 1929 he was awarded an 1851 senior studentship at Imperial College to continue his Shropshire work and in 1930 he received the Daniel Pidgeon award of the Geological Society. In 1931 he was appointed assistant lecturer in geology at Imperial College and then subsequently (1935) to a lectureship. In 1937, at the early age of thirty-four, he accepted the chair of geology at Bristol University, made vacant by the move of (Sir) Arthur E. Trueman [q.v.] to the university of Glasgow. He remained at Bristol for the rest of his life, dying eighteen months before his expected date of retirement.

Until 1960 Whittard returned regularly to Shropshire to continue mapping and collecting and he became the recognized expert, indeed the patriarch, on the geology of the area. His work on the extraordinarily rich harvest of fossils collected over four decades reached its acme with the monograph on the Shelve trilobites, published in eight parts between 1955 and 1966, and effectively complete when he died, although a synthesis of the geology was never finished.

During the war of 1939-45 Whittard was geological adviser to the south-west region of England dealing with problems ranging from the cutting of quartz oscillator plates to water supply.

From the mid 1950s Whittard became increasingly involved in mapping the geology of the English Channel and the results of his work, which partly appeared in published maps in 1962 and 1965, form the basis of the subsequent joint Anglo-French map of the English Channel.

Whittard was a most efficient administrator, rarely overlooking details or failing to appreciate the future implications of apparently innocuous decisions. He built up and ran well a happy department, enlarged threefold during his leadership, served on numerous committees, and executed the move of the department of geology from its old and cramped accommodation into the well-designed Queen's Building in 1958. He simultaneously pursued his research, and was enabled so to do largely because of his natural energy, the long hours he worked, and his remarkable ability to switch his mind back to research from administrative detail almost immediately. His main recreation was gardening and he lovingly supervised the university gardens. He was a shrewd but kindly man.

He was elected a fellow of the Royal Society in 1957 and in 1965 received the Murchison medal of the Geological Society. After visiting Canada in 1965 he was taken ill and died of heart failure at his home at Westbury-on-Trym near Bristol 2 March 1966.

He married in 1930 Caroline Margaret (died 1978), daughter of Albert William Sheppard, an engineer (tool-maker), and they had one son.

[O. M. B. Bulman in *Biographical Memoirs of Fellows of the Royal Society*, vol. xii, 1966; *Proceedings* of the Geological Society, no. 1625 (1965) and 1636 (1967); private information; personal knowledge.]

BERNARD ELGEY LEAKE

WIART, SIR ADRIAN CARTON DE (1880–1963), lieutenant-general. [See CARTON DE WIART.]

WILDE, JOHANNES (JÁNOS) (1891–1970), art historian, was born in Budapest 2 June 1891, the sixth and youngest child of Richard Wilde, a tailor, and his wife, Rosa Somlyaky. Wilde's grandfather had come to Budapest from Bohemia. His parents were devout Roman Catholics who brought him up in an atmosphere of piety and simplicity. He suffered the early bereavement (from tuberculosis) of his father and his elder brother, Paul, who had greatly influenced him. He was educated at the State Gymnasium in Budapest for eight years before entering the university of Budapest in September 1909 to study art, archaeology, and philosophy under Gyula Pasteiner. He remained there until February 1914. The summer term of 1911 was spent at the university of Freiburg-im-Breisgau, and, with a scholarship from the Hungarian Ministry of Education, he continued his studies, under Max Dvořák, at the university of Vienna from October 1915 to July 1917. He was awarded the degree Doctor Philosophiae by Vienna University *summa cum laude* in July 1918 for his thesis 'Die Anfange der italienischen Radierung' which still survives in manuscript.

Wilde's first publication, in 1910, was a translation into his native Hungarian of Adolf Hildebrand's *Das Problem der Form in der bildenden Kunst*, which is an interesting pointer to his own approach to the visual arts. He was also to gain a reputation as a great connoisseur of Hungarian poetry and literature, but his first allegiance was to art and in August 1914 he became a voluntary assistant at the Museum of Fine Arts in Budapest, and after gaining his Ph.D. returned to the Museum's Department of Prints and Drawings as an assistant keeper under Simon Meller, a post he was to hold until December 1922. Here were laid the foundations of Wilde's interest in connoisseurship and the study of Old Master drawings. It seems likely that Meller, who had himself published in 1903

a Hungarian translation of Michelangelo's poems and an article on Michelangelo's role in the Palazzo Farnese (1909), directed Wilde's attention to a master whose work he was later to elucidate so brilliantly. During the short-lived Hungarian Soviet Republic of 1919, Wilde and Frigves (Friedrich) Antal, among others, were directed by György Lukács, the commissar of public education, to sequestrate those privately owned works of art regarded as of national importance. However, in September 1920 Wilde was granted six months' study leave to enable him to accept Dvořák's invitation to lecture at Vienna University. This leave was prolonged several times at the request of the Vienna Academy so that Wilde could prepare, in collaboration with Karl Swoboda, the edition of the collected works of Dvořák, who had died suddenly in February 1921.

Dvořák's death was a cruel personal loss to Wilde and, too young to succeed him as professor, he was invited to join the Kunsthistorisches Museum, Vienna, first as an assistant keeper in June 1923, later becoming keeper. He accepted Austrian citizenship in 1928. Despite his demanding museum duties, Wilde continued to lecture and supervise students until the crisis of the Anschluss and his subsequent resignation from the museum for reasons of conscience in November 1938. He had by then decided to abandon the city and museum for which he so deeply cared, impelled, too, by fear for the safety of his Hungarian-Jewish wife, Dr. Julia Gyárfás (also an art historian), whom he had married in 1930. Assisted by a former pupil, Count Antoine Seilern, they left Austria ostensibly to visit an exhibition in Holland in April 1939, afterwards flying to England where they were the guests of Sir Kenneth (later Lord) Clark and his wife at Port Lympne. A few months of calm and hope followed in which Wilde began to learn to speak English and, at the outbreak of war, he went to Aberystwyth to look after Count Seilern's pictures, stored in the University Library. At the director's request, he began to assist in cataloguing the National Gallery pictures which were in store there, together with the Italian drawings from the British Museum. This happy coincidence led to his friendship with A. E. Popham [q.v.], with whom he was later to collaborate in preparing the published catalogue of Italian fifteenth- and sixteenth-century drawings in the royal collection (1949). Popham was able to persuade the British Museum trustees, in June 1940, to invite Wilde to compile the catalogue of the collection's Michelangelo drawings. But in the same month, during the panic caused by the Nazi offensive in France, Wilde was interned. Despite strong protests from distinguished English friends, he was deported to Canada and only survived the rigours of the concentration camp through the care of a fellow detainee, Otto Demus. In May 1941 Wilde was freed and allowed to live in Buckinghamshire as the guest of Count Seilern who had done much to secure his release. He resumed his Michelangelo studies and began teaching at London University. On 12 March 1947 he had become a British subject, and in 1948 he was appointed reader in the history of art at London University and deputy director of the Courtauld Institute of Art. He officially retired in 1958, although he continued to teach part-time until his seventieth birthday. The title of professor was conferred on him in 1950, he was elected a fellow of the British Academy in 1951, appointed CBE in 1955, and awarded the Serena medal of the British Academy in 1963.

Wilde gained an international reputation for his work on the Italian, especially the Venetian, paintings at the Kunsthistorisches Museum and his many contributions to the problems of dating, style, attribution, and condition appeared in the 1928 Gemäldegalerie catalogue and in the Vienna *Jahrbuch*. His first major work was the reconstruction of the San Cassiano altarpiece of Antonello da Messina from three surviving fragments in Vienna. One of his most important achievements was the systematic use of X-rays as a tool for discovering not only the physical condition of a picture but also as a guide to the individual artist's creative process. His collaboration with the restorer Sebastian Isepp was crucial to this work. By 1928 they were using the facilities of the Röntgeno-logisches Institut of Vienna University, but in 1930 Wilde established at the Kunsthistorisches Museum what was probably the first museum X-ray laboratory for the examination of paintings in Europe. That same year he was one of Austria's two delegates at the Congress of Restorers in Rome. Wilde brought supreme analytical gifts and visual acuity to the interpretation of the X-rays of, for example, Giorgione's 'Three Philosophers' and Titian's 'Gipsy Madonna', the results of which were published in the Vienna *Jahrbuch* in 1932. By 1938, more than a thousand X-rays of works in the collection had been made under his supervision.

The study of Michelangelo's art was, however, the most profound intellectual passion of his life, and his catalogue of the Michelangelo drawings in the British Museum his greatest achievement. Published in 1953, its importance lies far beyond the chance limitations of the collection itself. Rarely has such vast learning and keen sensibility been combined, or found such lucid expression. These same qualities characterize Wilde's six lectures on Michelangelo, which were published posthumously in 1978. His lectures on Venetian painting appeared in 1974. It was one of Wilde's fundamental principles to ask not only why a work of art was conceived in a particular way, but also to try to discover the extent to which its original location determined the artist's formal solution. He exhorted his own students always to be humble before the facts, but, as a pupil of Dvořák, he had also learnt to view art as part of man's spiritual and intellectual expression. These lectures skilfully guide the reader not only through the complexities of neo-Platonism and traditional Christian theology as they shape the subject matter of Michelangelo's major commissions but also through the even more complex processes by which Michelangelo evolved them. In 1952 Wilde also worked on the Michelangelo drawings in the Teylers Museum, Haarlem, and his catalogue of these survives in manuscript.

A tall, sparely built man, Wilde's grave gentle manner masked a rigorous intellect and incorruptible spirit. Those who knew him during his years in England remember his strong jaw and aquiline features, kindly grey eyes behind gold-rimmed spectacles, his silver hair brushed back from a broad forehead. Already frail and slightly stooped, he had a commanding presence. His lectures, always well attended, were delivered with a clear deep voice, in an English enriched by the slow soft drawl of Vienna. Students who may at first have felt in awe of him at tutorials quickly learnt of his willingness to share knowledge and give wise counsel. He would gently guide them with a few lapidary remarks, although he could be crushingly ironic on occasion. Lord Clark has rightly described him as 'the most beloved and influential teacher of art history of his time'. His unsparing generosity may be gauged by one typical gesture. He afterwards presented an inscribed copy of his British Museum Michelangelo catalogue to each of the many contributors to the Festschrift prepared two years earlier in honour of his sixtieth birthday. He died at his Dulwich home 15 September 1970, within three months of his wife's death. They adopted a son, whom they left behind in Vienna in 1939, and who died during the war. He bequeathed a drawing by Rembrandt, his library, and all his manuscripts and notes to the Courtauld Institute. There is a small bronze sculpture, by Ferenczy, showing Wilde as a young man, standing full-length.

[Kenneth Clark, 'Johannes Wilde', *Burlington Magazine*, vol. ciii, June 1961; editorial and obituary (by Michael Hirst) in *Burlington Magazine*, vol. cxiii, March 1971, with bibliography; *The Times*, 15 September 1970; private information; personal knowledge.]   DENNIS FARR

WILDE, WILLIAM JAMES (JIMMY) (1892–1969), professional boxer, was born 12 May 1892 at no. 8 Station Road, Pontygwarth, in the parish of Craig Berthlwyd, near Tylerstown in South Wales, the son of James Wilde, a coal miner, and his wife, Margaret Ann Evans, a miner's daughter. Known as Jimmy from birth, he was the second child, having an elder sister named Mary Anne and several younger than himself.

Educated at a local council school, he was able to leave at the age of thirteen by passing a modest examination that gave him a labour certificate and he went to work in the pits as a boy-helper at the rate of half-a-crown per day. To add to the family budget and to find the money to buy a few luxuries, such as cigarettes, he engaged in boxing bouts at the fairground booths, for which he received five shillings if he won.

As he was rarely defeated in this hazardous profession after an arduous week in the pits, he soon built up a reputation for himself as a glove fighter under the Marquess of Queensberry rules, but also took part in illegal bare-fist contests staged in secret in the Welsh mountains on a Sunday.

Just before his nineteenth birthday, Wilde had become a star performer in Welsh rings and decided to leave the mines and devote his whole time to a boxing career. By now he had married Elizabeth Davies, daughter of Dai Davies, a miner under whom Wilde had served in his apprentice days in the pits. Himself an ardent boxer, Davies had coached Jimmy and taught him the rudiments in the small confines of his bedroom. Wilde's marriage took place at Pontygwarth in 1910 and of the union two sons were born: David, who later took up boxing, and Verdun, who had no inclination for the sport.

Wilde reigned as undisputed flyweight champion of the world from 24 April 1916 until 18 June 1923, and although the weight limit for his class was eight stones (112 pounds), he never went to scale at more than six stones ten pounds (94 pounds), which meant that he was always called upon to meet opponents far bigger and heavier than himself. Among heavyweights the difference of a stone (14 pounds) does not present anything like the handicap that it does among smaller men.

Although he did not weigh much, Wilde possessed long legs and arms, with powerful shoulder muscles. He moved fast and punched with devastating power, his defence being confined to unorthodox bobbing and swaying that made him a difficult target to hit with any accuracy. He owed his amazing muscular development to his early days as a miner when, because of his small size, he could squeeze himself into the narrowest seam to hack away at the coal face with his pickaxe.

Wilde's last paysheet at the Ferndale no. 8 Pit owned by D. Davies & Sons Ltd., dated 1 April 1911, showed him earning the sum of £6. 7s. 9d. for a fortnight's pay, from which was deducted one shilling due to his check-weigher and 1s. 7d. for the services of a doctor, leaving a total of £6. 5s. 2d. from which he had to pay his 'boy' 2s. 6d. a day. It was not much on which to buy a house and bring up a family, hence his decision to become a professional boxer. In the next twelve years he was to earn thousands of pounds with his fistic talent.

By 1911 Wilde could claim, without risk of repudiation, that he had taken part in over 800 contests, but from 1911 until his retirement in 1923, his official record shows 138 well-paid bouts, which included seven British or world-title contests, and the winning outright of a Lord Lonsdale challenge belt. Seventy-eight of his contests during this period, mostly against bantamweights and featherweights, ended within the scheduled number of rounds, his phenomenal punching power earning him such colourful names as 'the Mighty Atom', 'the Tylerstown Terror', and 'the Ghost with a Hammer in his Hands'.

He became a great favourite in the principal boxing arenas throughout the country, especially at the famous National Sporting Club in Covent Garden, London; at the height of his fame his name became a household word. In a triumphant tour of America, from 1919 to 1920, he earned 100,000 dollars. He was beaten only four times: once when he fought against doctor's orders, once by a disputed decision, once by an American far heavier than himself, and in the final defence of his world title against the Filipino, Pancho Villa, in New York, who at twenty-two was Wilde's junior by nine years. For this contest Wilde received his largest purse of £13,000.

On returning to Britain Wilde announced his retirement from active boxing, but he continued to be interested in the sport, both as a manager of boxers and as a promoter of boxing tournaments. He died at Whitchurch Hospital in Cardiff 10 March 1969 just two months before his seventy-seventh birthday, the cause of death being given as acute influenza and severe mental abnormality.

There is a picture of the Prince of Wales shaking hands with Wilde in the ring at the National Sporting Club on 31 March 1919, by Howard Robinson, and there is a caricature of Wilde and his agent, April 1919, by George Belcher.

[*The Times*, 11 March 1969.] GILBERT ODD

WILLIAMS, ALWYN TERRELL PETRE (1888–1968), headmaster and bishop, was born at Barrow-in-Furness 20 July 1888, the eldest son of John Terrell Williams, medical practitioner, by his wife, Adeline Mary, daughter of Richard Peter, solicitor, of Launceston. He was educated at Rossall and went up to Oxford with an open scholarship to Jesus College, where he obtained first classes in classical moderations (1908), *literae humaniores* (1910), and modern history (1911). He won the Gladstone history essay prize in 1909 and in 1911 was elected to a fellowship at All Souls. He was ordained deacon in 1913 and priest in 1914, and in the same year married Margaret Grace, daughter of Colonel Charles Stewart, of Tighnduin, Perthshire; they had no children.

In 1915 the headmaster of Winchester, M. J. Rendall [q.v.], invited him to come and strengthen the history teaching, and a year later Williams was appointed second master, in charge of the scholars in College. In 1924 he succeeded Rendall as headmaster, and the next ten years were, as he wrote later, a time of 'unforgettable happiness'. He was at the height of his powers, mental and physical, and was held in the warmest respect and affection. He was considerate, cheerful, entirely without ostentation, accessible at all times, prompt in business, a man in whom it was natural to put complete trust. He was, into the bargain, a fine historian who took a delight in teaching. Modern history and modern languages were then still held in secondary esteem in the Winchester curriculum, but Williams established them securely alongside classics, mathematics, and science. The special flavour of 'History Bill's' teaching was relished by generations of Wykehamists, some of whom took pains to record the memorable phrases with which he lit up the past. He described the Danes, for example, 'carting off large ecclesiastical candlesticks and shrieking ladies and that sort of thing, pursued by slow, heavy, infuriated Saxons'.

In 1934 he was appointed dean of Christ Church, where his intellectual distinction, warm humanity, and imperturbable common sense well fitted him to combine the duties of head of a college and dean of a cathedral. But his time in Oxford was all too short for in 1939 he was appointed bishop of Durham in succession to H. Hensley Henson [q.v.].

Williams wrote to (Sir) James Duff [q.v.], then warden of the Durham Colleges, that he 'looked forward with great happiness to coming north'. He was already a member of the court of Durham University, he thought the cathedral 'about the most magnificent place there is', and he admired the northern folk. He proved to be a very good bishop, less of a public figure than his redoubtable predecessor, but deeply respected and warmly welcomed everywhere in the diocese, and an excellent judge of men. But as the years went on he became increasingly anxious about his wife's health. Auckland Castle is a splendid edifice, but, even in peace time, offered formidable obstacles to domestic comfort and, indeed, to administrative convenience—there was no telephone in 1939. By the end of the war the bishop, who never complained or spared himself, was suffering severely from an ulcerated stomach, the result of incessant journeying and hastily eaten sandwich lunches. In 1951 he at last agreed to undergo surgical treatment, and a year later left Durham to become bishop of Winchester. He had been deeply attached to Durham, but the move to the softer southern climate and the less isolated situation of Wolvesey Palace was a relief to his wife, and Williams himself rejoiced to return—*quasi domum repetens* in the words of the memorial tablet in the college cloisters—to the place where they had both been so happy.

The move made it easier, too, to carry on his work in connection with the New English Bible, which entailed frequent meetings in London. He had been a member of the joint committee representing the Churches and the Bible Societies since it was set up in 1947, and in 1950 he succeeded J. W. Hunkin, bishop of Truro, as chairman. He was also convener and chairman of the literary panel, whose meetings often took up two days or more. Apart from the members of the joint committee, which had over-all responsibility for policy, more than forty biblical scholars and literary advisers co-operated in the work, and it was Williams's faith in its importance and his firm but unobtrusive authority which kept this large team steady on its course. The New Testament was ready first and was published in 1961, and was an immediate best-seller. Williams retired from Winchester in the same year (his wife had died in 1958) and lived for the remainder of his life in Charmouth, serene and busy to the end. He died there 18 February 1968, when the first instalment of the Old Testament was in the printers' hands. It was published, with the Apocrypha and a revised edition of the New Testament, in 1970.

Williams was a tall, strong man, and he looked out at the world with candid friendly eyes set in a fine, rather narrow face. He had a deep voice, much imitated at Winchester, and a most sincere and frequent laugh. He was fond of hard physical exercise but had no skill at games. At Jesus he had been captain of boats, and nearly forty years on, as dean of Christ Church, would run along the towpath in shirt and shorts encouraging the college boat. He was a great walker, covering the ground with a springy tireless stride. He was a prodigious and very rapid reader with a very retentive and orderly memory. He disliked gadgets and wrote nearly all his letters in his own beautiful firm hand. 'He was', wrote Duff, 'the wisest, kindest and best man that I've ever known'.

As bishop of Winchester Williams was Prelate to the Most Noble Order of the Garter, and his first office was to install Winston Churchill. He was an honorary fellow of Jesus and All Souls Colleges, an honorary student of Christ Church, and DD by decree of Oxford (1925). He received honorary degrees from the universities of Durham (1939), St. Andrews (1939), Glasgow (1951), and Southampton (1962). He was chairman of the commission on training for the ministry whose 'Durham Report' (1944) recommended the setting up of a central body for the selection and training of ordinands. He was a valued contributor to this Dictionary, for which he wrote the notices of Charles Gore, C. R. M. F. Cruttwell, A. C. Headlam, H. Hensley Henson, and C. W. C. Oman. He wrote only one book, *The Anglican Tradition in the Life of England* (1947).

There is a portrait by Sir Gerald Kelly in 'School' at Winchester and one by Rodrigo Moynihan at Christ Church.

[Private information; personal knowledge.]
A. L. P. NORRINGTON

WILLIAMS, EDWARD FRANCIS, BARON FRANCIS-WILLIAMS (1903–1970), author, journalist, and publicist, was born 10 March 1903 at St. Martin's, Shropshire, where his father John Edmund Williams had a farm. His mother was Sally Francis from Montgomery, just across the border in Wales. His schooling was entirely in Lancashire whither his father moved first as a dairyman in Manchester, then back to farming on the moors between Bacup and Todmorden, where Francis and his sister attended school at Rawtenstall. Shortly after the outbreak of war in 1914 the family moved to a better farm at Middleton where Williams completed his formal education at Queen Elizabeth's Grammar School. While there two of his poems were accepted by *Country Life* and the *Weekly Westminster Gazette*, an eccentric enough occurrence for the school to encourage his inclination to be a journalist.

At the age of seventeen, in response to an advertisement, he joined the weekly *Bootle Times* then housed in a two-roomed wooden building adjoining the railway station. There, as an impressionable young reporter, the unemployment in the Merseyside docks and the conditions in the slums impelled him to join the Independent Labour Party. At the same period he forsook religion and became a lifelong

humanist. He secured a post on the Liverpool *Daily Courier* but was impatient to get to Fleet Street and on to a national paper. With a colleague on the *Courier* he decided to buy a horse and caravan and describe a journey through England. The only London newspaper which was interested was the Labour *Daily Herald*, edited by George Lansbury [q.v.], with a small circulation but a prestigious set of contributors. For two articles a week, the travellers were paid four guineas.

There was, however, no staff appointment when he arrived in London at the end of the series in 1922, and Williams earned a fickle living as a freelance until he secured a part-time job on the *Sunday Express*. There he attracted the attention of Lord Beaverbrook [q.v.] when he mastered a couple of Clydesdale horses which had bolted outside the *Express* office in the commotion of the general strike of 1926. Later, following an article which he had written on the controversial sculpture Rima by (Sir) Jacob Epstein [q.v.], Beaverbrook, inconsequentially, appointed Williams as a financial reporter and personally commended him to the moneyed men of the City.

To Beaverbrook's chagrin, when Odhams the publishers in 1929 took over the *Daily Herald*, of which the Trades Union Congress retained a minority interest and Labour Party control, Williams accepted the post of City editor. During the depression and the financial crisis which brought down the Labour Government, he became a significant figure, influential with hostile financiers, with access even to Montagu (later Lord) Norman [q.v.], the redoubtable governor of the Bank of England, and, during his commodity market exposures of the rearming of Germany, a confidant of Winston Churchill.

In 1936 Williams became editor of the *Daily Herald* at a salary of £5,000. The paper soon reached a circulation of two million, a figure which was itself an embarrassment, because, in the paradoxical economics of the newspaper business, it was not drawing the advertising to sustain it. Lord Southwood [q.v.], the chairman of Odhams, wanted a lively paper glowing with an optimism about world events which would encourage trade and therefore advertising. He expected Williams, as Beaverbrook's ex-protégé, to respond. His editor insisted upon treating events, which were goose-stepping to Munich and the war of 1939–45, with the seriousness they deserved. He had the support of the TUC members on the policy board, including Ernest Bevin (whose notice Williams contributed to this Dictionary) and Sir Walter (later Lord) Citrine. But Southwood tried to use financial sanctions to make him dispense with the foreign correspondents who were sending the pessimistic dispatches. Even the outbreak of war did not curb the interference. The break came in 1940 when Williams opened the paper and found that his signed weekly article was missing, removed on Southwood's instructions. He resigned.

He took the opportunity to write a book *War by Revolution* (1940) on the theme of his banned article and *Democracy's Last Battle* (1941). He became a member of the morale committee of the Ministry of Information and when Brendan (later Viscount) Bracken [q.v.] became minister he was appointed in 1941 controller of press and censorship. In that invidious position (the more so because he was the buffer between Churchill and the press, whose criticism Churchill resented) he made censorship tolerable, or at least understandable to the British and foreign correspondents, gaining their co-operation and respect which persisted after the war when he became a world advocate of press freedom. He went with the British delegation in 1945 to the San Francisco conference where his methods of handling the world press, confidentiality in return for frankness, were a new experience for most journalists. In the same year he was appointed CBE and awarded the United States medal of freedom with silver leaves for his war services.

When Labour came into power after the war, the prime minister, Clement Attlee, asked Williams to be his public relations adviser. He relied implicitly on Williams and in his meetings with President Truman and others left the communiqués and press conferences entirely to his discretion. When the secretary-general of the United Nations, Trygve Lie, visited Attlee in London to ask him to release Williams to become assistant secretary-general in charge of public information, Attlee told him that Williams had undertaken to stay with him for at least a year and would not go back on his word.

In the event, Williams stayed two years in Downing Street; went next to Washington as correspondent of the *Observer*; then returned to London as a columnist on the *News Chronicle*. He started a column in the *New Statesman* called 'Fleet Street' which ran for fourteen years and gave the public an insight into the workings of the press which they had never had before. He also tried, unsuccessfully, to make the Socialist *Forward* into a prosperous journal.

In 1951-2 Williams was a governor of the BBC. He had been a frequent broadcaster since the thirties and he went on to become a television personality on a diversity of programmes. He dominated the small screen. The adjective 'leonine' could properly apply to him. His mane, his jowls, his wary look, his crouching shoulders were disconcerting to 'victims' in interrogation programmes but the impression would disappear in his twinkle, his smile, his laugh, and the lighting of the pipe which was his trade mark. Then the warmth of his personality, reflecting years of happy family life and a concern for others, would radiate.

Williams's reputation as an authority on the media was world-wide. He was British representative on the United Nations commission on freedom of information (1949), wrote *Transmitting News* (1953) for UNESCO, and was Regents' professor at the university of California in 1961 and Kemper Knapp professor at the university of Wisconsin in 1967.

He was much sought after as a Labour candidate but his ambitions did not lie in Parliament or in government office. When Hugh Gaitskell [q.v.] prevailed upon him to become a life peer in 1962 he became an assiduous backbencher. But his main activity after the end of the war lay in writing; his publications during this period included *Press, Parliament and People* (1946), *The Triple Challenge: the Future of Socialist Britain* (1948), *Fifty Years' March: the Rise of the Labour Party* (1946), *Ernest Bevin: Portrait of a Great Englishman* (1952), *Magnificent Journey, the Rise of Trade Unions* (1954), *Dangerous Estate: the Anatomy of Newspapers* (1957), *A Prime Minister Remembers* (with Earl Attlee, 1961), *The American Invasion* (1962), and *A Pattern of Rulers* (1965). He was a persistent novelist (*No Man is an Island* (1945); *A Provincial Affair* (1949); and *The Richardson Story* (1951)) whose fiction was better appreciated by the critics than by the customers. His autobiography *Nothing So Strange* was published shortly before he died at his Abinger home 5 June 1970. In it he had remarked 'it would be a fine thing to put on one's tombstone, "The guy had grammar"', an epitaph which he had fully earned both as a writer and as a speaker. He was a literary craftsman whose fluent style survived the paragraphics of the popular press. His wit was caustic and his humour emollient.

In 1926 Williams married Jessie Melville Hopkin whom he had first met when she became an English teacher at his old school. She became a distinguished medical psychologist. They had one son and one daughter.

A portrait by William E. Narraway was included in the 1954 exhibition of the Royal Society of Portrait Painters.

[Personal knowledge.]   RITCHIE-CALDER

WILLIAMS, SIR HAROLD HERBERT (1880-1964), critic and scholar, was born in Tokyo 25 July 1880, the eldest son of James Williams, an Anglican missionary, and his wife, Mary Grindrod. He was educated in Tokyo, at Liverpool College, and finally at Christ's College, Cambridge, where in 1901 he was elected to a scholarship. In 1903 he gained a first in part i of the theological tripos with a mark of distinction for his work on the Old Testament. In the same year he was bracketed for the Carus Greek Testament prize and won the Steel university studentship. In 1904 he was ordained deacon and priest and took up a curacy at Swimbridge, migrating to Ripon Theological College in 1905 as lecturer and chaplain, but returning the following year to Devon as curate of Crediton where he remained until 1909. He then relinquished orders, having seemingly come to want more freedom of judgement than was suitable for a cleric.

His freer thinking was pursued in the university extension lectures which he gave for Cambridge and London. He took his work seriously, even seeking to extend his ministrations into the Oxford province. His lectures were attended by audiences sometimes 350 strong, first in Devon, then in Norfolk, Northumberland, Sussex, Lincoln, Yorkshire, and Derbyshire. As was the custom, he prepared booklets to accompany his courses, which ranged over English literature from Shakespeare upwards, and even took in German—one course was entitled 'Goethe and his times'. The quality of these lectures may be gathered not only from his trenchantly worded syllabuses, but from his book *Two Centuries of the English Novel* (1911) which consists of estimates of a dozen of our greatest novelists, his favourites being Thackeray, Meredith, and Butler—with Conrad to complete the list, on the evidence of a later book. He himself wrote a novel, *Discovery* (1913), preceded by a little book of poems *The Ballad of Two Great Cities* (1912).

His next publications concerned twentieth-century literature, and even more substantially. *Modern English Writers* was published in Britain and America in 1918, reaching a third, revised, edition in 1925. *Outlines of Modern English Literature 1890-1914* appeared in 1920. The amount of reading behind both books is immense.

Meanwhile Williams had married Jean, daughter of Andrew Chalmers, MD, in 1913, and joined the army late the following year, serving with the French forces in the Vosges and later, as captain, with the British in the mechanical transport section of the Royal Army Service Corps. After the war he returned to his old occupations, continuing to lecture and write. Evidently he was a man blessed with the power of working—the weighty *Modern English Writers* of 1918 was presumably written while on active service. And with power of working went the restlessness already discernible in his earlier career. The choices before him were now multiplied, his wife having brought him money. He was called to the bar in 1920 (Inner Temple)

without any apparent intention of practising. In 1921 he again plunged into new paths, breaking all London ties, and settling at Aspenden House, Buntingford, from which he did not return to London until 1950.

The move was no flight into rustication. He now threw himself into public duties of the unpaid kind. He served as a JP, and in 1928 began work as a Hertford county councillor, becoming vice-chairman in 1939 and chairman in 1947, remaining in that office until 1952. He was chairman of the county education committee in 1939-47 and a member of the library subcommittee of which he was chairman for over twenty years until his resignation in 1962. This subcommittee meant a great deal to him: he believed in the work the libraries were doing and did all he could to promote book-borrowing. To these labours he added in 1950-63 those of chairman of the Local History Council, and such church offices as are open to the laity.

The claims of authorship were not, however, neglected. In his first lecture as Sandars reader in bibliography at Cambridge in 1950 Williams told of the occasion when, seemingly by chance, he bought around 1920 two of the 1726 editions of *Gulliver's Travels*, and soon discovered an engaging bibliographical problem. From then on he was caught up into bibliography and editing, but he remained faithful to his earlier interests—he read Swift as a critic, although he expressed his criticism mainly in his reviews of books on Swift in the learned journals, and he continued to write trenchantly, as also gracefully. Whatever the topics he wrote on, and now they were almost wholly Swiftian, he wrote well.

His first book might seem to forbid eloquence—*Dean Swift's Library with a Facsimile of the Original Sale Catalogue and some Account of Two Manuscript Lists of his Books* (1932). A paper in *The Library* in 1935 claimed for Swift the 'History of the Four Last Years of the Queen', and when in 1951 Herbert Davis reached this particular work in his edition of the complete prose, Williams provided him with an introduction as he had in 1941 for *Gulliver's Travels*. His great edition of Swift's poems was published in 1937, a revised edition following in 1958. The edition of the *Journal to Stella* appeared in 1948. On *Gulliver's Travels* Williams was the authority: his first publication on it had been in 1925 when he contributed to *The Library* 'The Motte Editions of *Gulliver's Travels*' almost simultaneous with his edition, complete with long introduction and explanatory notes, of the first of them for the First Edition Club. Later on his discovery, made independently by an American scholar at about the same time, of the superiority of Faulkner's Dublin edition of 1735 provided him with the topic for his Sandars lectures. Fortunately there was much more of Swift left for his continued labours and in 1963 came out the first three volumes of the *Letters* followed in 1965, after his death, by the remaining two. His work on Swift was crowned by his bequest of the old books in his library to the university which had trained him in theology.

Williams was president of the Bibliographical Society in 1938–44 and was elected FBA in 1944 and FSA in 1948. In 1951 he was knighted for his services both to bibliography and to county administration. The university of Durham conferred an honorary D.Litt. on him in 1954. His wife had died in 1948 and the year following he married Pauline Louise (died 1969), daughter of Major C. F. Campbell-Renton, of Mordington and Lamberton, Berwickshire.

As a person Williams was of commanding aspect, aquiline of face and straight of back. There is an excellent portrait of him by John Gilroy (1952) in the County Hall, Hertford. He liked presiding over public meetings and was always completely reliable in the discharge of all offices. At dinner parties—say at the Johnson Club, of which he was a member—he was an affable companion, especially when he could endlessly chat in high-pitched tones about scholarly matters. Some people found him reserved beyond that point of post-prandial bonhomie—he never alluded to his clerical past and it almost seemed that he began a new life in 1909—a life as completely as possible, for so public-spirited a man, devoted to books, especially books of the eighteenth century. When he found his own books praised by one he admired he did not restrain his warm flush of pleasure, having every right to be vain of his achievement in helping the twentieth century to an improved sense of Swift's greatness. Williams died in London 24 October 1964.

[Geoffrey Tillotson in *Proceedings* of the British Academy, vol. li, 1965; *The Times*, 29 October and 3 November 1964; private information; personal knowledge.]

GEOFFREY TILLOTSON

WILLIAMS, IVY (1877–1966), the first woman to be called to the English bar, was born 7 September 1877 at 21 Devon Square, Newton Abbot, daughter of George St. Swithin Williams, solicitor of 12 King Edward St., Oxford, and of his wife, Emma Ewers. She had one brother, Winter (born 17 September 1875), educated at Corpus Christi College, Oxford, barrister at law, killed during World War I, and in his memory Ivy endowed in 1923 two law scholarships at Oxford, one for women only.

Educated privately with her brother, she studied Latin, Greek, Italian, and Russian, travelled in Europe, and spoke French and German fluently. At nineteen she joined the Society of Oxford Home-Students, (later St. Anne's College), under its first principal, Mrs Arthur Johnson, was taught by Edward Jenks and (Professor Sir) William S. Holdsworth [qq.v.], and took a second class in jurisprudence in 1900 and in the BCL examination in 1902. She also took a second class in the London University examination, obtaining an LLD in 1903. Due to the restrictions on women students she was not able to matriculate at Oxford until 7 October 1920, and received her BA, MA, and BCL a week later on 14 October 1920.

In that same year women were first admitted to the Inns of Court and Ivy Williams, who was already forty-two years old, with the sponsorship of Sir John (later Viscount) Simon [q.v.], joined the Inner Temple on 26 January 1920. On 10 May 1922 she was called to the bar by (Sir) Henry Dickens (the son of Charles Dickens, q.v.) on a final bar examination certificate of honour (first class), awarded in Michaelmas term, 1921, which excused her two terms' dinners and thereby gave her priority over some forty women who, though anxious to be called, had either not passed their final examinations or kept the terms required by the ordinances prior to call. Thus, Ivy Williams became the first woman to be called to the English bar, though Ulster-born Frances Kyle had been called six months earlier to the Irish bar.

From 1920 to 1945 Ivy Williams was tutor and lecturer in law to the Society of Oxford Home-Students. She was elected an honorary fellow of St. Anne's College in 1956. She was a dedicated teacher and scholar and devoted endless thought and care to the work and careers of her pupils and to the general advancement of women in the legal profession. In 1923, on the publication of *The Sources of Law in the Swiss Civil Code*, she was awarded the degree of DCL at Oxford, the first woman to be thus honoured. In 1925 she published *The Swiss Civil Code: English Version, with Notes and Vocabulary*. She served in 1930 as delegate to the Hague Conference for the Codification of International Law, under Sir Maurice L. Gwyer [q.v.], and in 1932 as a member of the Aliens Deportation Advisory Committee under Roland Vaughan Williams.

In appearance she was slender, above average height, dark-haired, and possessed of fine blue eyes. Her recreations included tennis, travelling, gardening, the driving. From 1920 she lived at 30 Staverton Road, Oxford, and shared a house near Ludgershall, Buckinghamshire, with Miss Nora MacMunn, tutor in geography and sister of Lieutenant-General Sir George Fletcher MacMunn. Shy and reserved in manner, Ivy Williams was a woman of strong religious belief and the highest principle and to her friends and those who worked with her she was kind, wise, mild, and full of humour. After her mother's death in 1921 she was comfortably off and quietly made a number of generous benefactions to academic, medical, and other causes.

In her later years, realizing that her eyesight was failing, she taught herself to read braille and found so much difficulty that she systematized her learning, first into a booklet and later into a braille primer which was published for the National Institute for the Blind in 1948 and went into more than one edition. She herself had correspondence pupils in many parts of Britain whom she taught to read and write in braille almost to the end of her long life. She died at her Oxford home 18 February 1966. 'Of no one could it more truly be said', wrote Miss Ruth Butler, former vice-principal of the Society of Oxford Home-Students, in her obituary, 'that "she turned her necessity to glorious gain", using in old age for the service of others her powers and enthusiasm which had won her distinction in her youth.'

[*The Times*, 19 February 1966; *Oxford Magazine*; *Solicitor's Journal*; *The Ship*; *St. Anne's College Register*; private information; personal knowledge.]   HAZEL FOX

WILLIAMS, SIR JOHN COLDBROOK HANBURY- (1892-1965), industrialist. [See HANBURY-WILLIAMS.]

WILLIAMS, THOMAS, BARON WILLIAMS OF BARNBURGH (1888-1967), politician, was born 18 March 1888 at Blackwell, Derbyshire, the tenth of the fourteen children (three of whom died in infancy) of James Williams, a miner, and his wife, Mary Ann Parton. When he was two years old the family moved to Swinton in Yorkshire. At the early age of eleven he left school to start work at Thrybergh Hall Colliery where his father and brothers were employed. In his autobiography, *Digging for Britain* (1965), he describes clearly and vividly the harsh and dangerous conditions then prevailing in the coal-mining industry, yet he wanted to follow and share the family tradition of mining. He was to witness personal tragedy. His father, whilst working underground with him, damaged an eye, became totally blind, and died within a few years. Shortly afterwards his elder brother, Richard, received spinal injuries in the pit and spent the next thirty years virtually living in a wheelchair.

After his father's accident Tom Williams went to work at Wath Main Colliery where he began to take an interest in trade union affairs, and at the age of twenty was elected to the branch committee of the union. In September 1910 he was married at the parish church at Wombwell to Elizabeth Ann (died 1977), daughter of Thomas Andrews, of Mexborough. Marriage for a young miner active in the union was an uncertain affair, but fortunately his young bride also came from a mining family. Eighteen months later the young couple experienced a cruel set-back. Williams was unfairly dismissed from work because he dared to suggest to the colliery manager that certain working arrangements were unfair to the men concerned. Given seven days' notice, he was made unemployed. Later he was approached by the members of the Wath Main branch committee to consider applying for the post of steward at the Working Men's Club at Wath upon Dearne. He was successful and the family spent two happy years at the club, though Williams still wanted to return to the coal industry and union matters. He decided to attend evening classes and obtained his deputy's certificate at Barnsley Technical Institute. His path was now open to obtain a higher position in the industry, but he chose instead to start work in 1919 in a new colliery opening up in the district, named Barnburgh Main, where he was later to be elected check-weigher by the men and thus became independent of the colliery management. He was also elected Barnburgh Main's delegate to the delegate meetings of the Yorkshire miners.

His horizons were now widening and he decided to enter local government by becoming the Labour nominee on the Doncaster board of guardians and also a member in 1919 of Bolton upon Dearne Urban District Council. Both these local government positions enhanced his political education and reputation, and Williams seemed set on a parliamentary career. With the backing of the Yorkshire Miners' Association he was officially invited, at the age of thirty-one, to become prospective Labour candidate for Don Valley on 2 October 1920. After a hard-fought general election campaign he was elected to Parliament on 16 November 1922, and was to represent Don Valley continuously until 1959.

He soon made his mark in Parliament and was appointed parliamentary private secretary to N. E. (later Lord) Noel-Buxton [q.v.], the minister of agriculture in the short-lived Labour Government in 1924, and thus began his long and dedicated interest in agricultural matters. It was only one of his preoccupations, for the general strike of 1926 and its aftermath meant for Williams and his fellow miner MPs a traumatic and busy period. They addressed many public meetings throughout the country, explaining the miners' case and collecting funds to alleviate their distress. After the 1929 general election, Williams became parliamentary private secretary to Margaret G. Bondfield [q.v.], the first woman Cabinet minister, who became minister of labour. Then came the fateful 1931 election, and with the majority of his Labour colleagues he went into opposition to the newly formed 'national' Government led by J. Ramsay MacDonald, and was duly put in charge of agricultural matters by the new Labour Parliamentary Committee. On his return to Westminster after the 1935 election, he was again to resume charge of agriculture for the Opposition, and began to build up a formidable reputation in this field. However, it was the outbreak of war in 1939 and the emergence of the coalition Government under (Sir) Winston Churchill which provided him with the opportunity to show his ministerial qualities in agriculture. He became a leading figure during the war years, serving from 1940 as joint parliamentary secretary to the minister of agriculture, R. S. (later Viscount) Hudson [q.v.].

With the election of the Labour Government led by Clement (later Earl) Attlee in 1945, there could only be one choice for minister of agriculture—Tom Williams. Now in the Cabinet (1945–51), he brought to his task all his vast knowledge and experience of the industry. He was responsible for the Agriculture Act of 1947. For the first time the industry was provided with a long-term policy designed to protect the interests of farmers and consumers alike. Indeed, the success of post-war British agriculture was a testimony to Williams's vision and ability.

He suffered from arthritis, which at times tried his temper, but he was a much-loved figure. Sworn of the Privy Council in 1941, he received honorary degrees of LLD from the universities of Cambridge (1951) and Nottingham (1955). In 1961 he was created a life peer, taking the title of Lord Williams of Barnburgh. In the same year he was appointed one of the three members of the Political Honours Scrutiny Committee, and in 1962 he was given the freedom of Doncaster.

He died at his Doncaster home 29 March 1967, and was survived by his wife and their son and daughter.

[Lord Williams of Barnburgh, *Digging for Britain*, 1965; *The Times*, 31 March 1967; personal knowledge.]   PEART

WILMOT, JOHN, BARON WILMOT OF SELMESTON (1895–1964), politician, was born in Woolwich 2 April 1895, the eldest of the four sons of Charles Wilmot, an East Anglian engraver. He attended Hither Green Central School, leaving at the age of fifteen to work as an office boy. He pursued his education at night classes at the Chelsea Polytechnic and King's College, London, where he won the Gilbart prize in banking which enabled him to join the Westminster Bank Piccadilly branch. He rose rapidly, first to the general manager's office and then to the secretaryship of the Anglo-Russian Bank. In the war of 1914–18 he served as an aircraftman in the Royal Naval Air Service, returning to the bank after demobilization.

Wilmot took an early interest in politics, and joined both the Independent Labour Party and the Fabian Society at the age of sixteen. Back from the war, he helped to found East Lewisham Labour Party in 1919. By 1933 this had become one of the ten biggest constituency parties in the country, and for this Wilmot, who stood as candidate in the three elections of 1924, 1929, and 1931, deserves much of the credit. It was through his constituency work that he came to know his wife, Elsa, who was chairman of the women's section and shared her husband's political concerns.

Wilmot came close to taking East Lewisham in the general election of 1929. But in the unfavourable conditions of the 1930s this was not a seat which could be won, and he was glad to become a candidate in an unexpected by-election at East Fulham in October 1933. Fighting a particularly vigorous campaign and benefiting from a mid-term swing against the Government, Wilmot won with a majority of 4,840, overturning the Tory majority (14,521) of the 1931 election. This result gained a significance beyond the improvement in morale and debating strength which it gave to the tiny parliamentary Opposition. In his maiden speech, Wilmot described his victory as a symptom of 'a general feeling, a passionate and consistent desire for peace'. Rightly or wrongly, this interpretation was widely believed, and gave rise to Stanley Baldwin's 'appalling frankness' speech three years later, in which he said that the loss of the Fulham seat 'on no issue but the pacifist' had helped to convince him of the political impossibility of rearmament. In fact, Wilmot was not a pacifist—rather, he was a member of the group which E. H. J. N. (later Lord) Dalton [q.v.] called the 'bloody-minded pacifists' who thought that peace could best be preserved through a strong and effective League of Nations. Wilmot lost his seat in the 1935 election but he remained a national political figure and served for a time on the Party executive, first as a runner-up and replacement, and then in 1940 as an elected member in the constituency parties section. In 1939 he returned to Parliament at a by-election in

Kennington. In 1945 he moved again, this time to Deptford.

Meanwhile Wilmot had seen much of government from the inside, largely through the patronage of Dalton, who chose him in May 1940 as his parliamentary private secretary at the Ministry of Economic Warfare. Because of his close personal friendship with the minister, Wilmot had great influence both at MEW and in Dalton's secret empire, the Special Operations Executive, which dealt with propaganda and subversion. Wilmot's special role was as a personal link with the propaganda staff stationed at Woburn Abbey.

Dalton valued his parliamentary private secretary highly. Wilmot gave the impression (as another friend put it) of 'a shrewd and eminently jolly abbot'. His minister liked both qualities—the irrepressible good humour, and also the canny understanding of the movement, especially the trade union part of it. When Dalton moved to the Board of Trade in 1942, he took Wilmot with him (still as PPS), securing the latter's promotion two years later to joint parliamentary secretary at the Ministry of Supply. This crucial step up the ladder led to a further promotion, after Labour's election victory in 1945, to minister of supply and aircraft production. Wilmot was thus put in charge of an immensely important department with a big staff and a huge labour force, with indirect control over raw material industries. It was an 'executive-administrative' ministry, calling for frequent major decisions from its chief.

Wilmot cut an imposing figure: 'a modern Cockney, a successful child of the pavements', as a 1946 newspaper article put it—tall, well-built, well-dressed, well-brushed, with polish and without accent, big, bustling, a sophisticated man of the world. But while he radiated bonhomie he lacked self-confidence, and he was badly mauled in the major controversy of his tenure of office. In November 1945 Wilmot circulated a memorandum recommending nationalization of iron and steel. This was opposed not only within the industry itself but also by Wilmot's own officials and, crucially, by H. S. Morrison (later Lord Morrison of Lambeth, q.v.). A compromise scheme presented in July 1947 by the two ministers, involving public supervision and partial nationalization, was rejected by the prime minister, and the matter was shelved by the Cabinet. In the course of complex discussions Wilmot lost almost all his allies. 'He was unlucky,' Morrison's biographers have written: 'being outside the Cabinet, he lacked the power to control the destiny of his ministry' (B. Donoughue and G. W. Jones, *Herbert Morrison, Portrait of a Politician*, 1973). Finally, Sir R. Stafford Cripps [q.v.] demanded his sacking, and Attlee was told that he was unpopular even amongst Labour MPs, where his policies found most support. In October 1947 he was dismissed. After first refusing, he accepted a peerage in 1950.

After leaving politics, Wilmot pursued his business interests, building upon his reputation as a Labour politician with a sympathy for the financial world. Wilmot had been seized on early as 'a useful recruit to any company board whose owners or managing-directors saw Labour coming into power' (N. Davenport, *Memoirs of a City Radical*, 1974). By 1949 he was on the board of sixteen companies and served as chairman of six. He also took a keen interest in theatre and opera and was chairman of the governors of the Old Vic and of the trustees of Glyndebourne. Good at public relations and revelling in the limelight, Wilmot was more a communicator and popularizer than a planner or decision-taker. He came from the grass roots, and he had an instinctive appreciation of the feelings of the rank and file. In this sense he was a Party rather than a government man, and his greatest impact was at elections, in the constituencies, and at the Labour Party conference, rather than in the Government in which he held such a crucial but difficult brief.

Wilmot died in London 22 July 1964 and the barony became extinct.

[Public Record Office; Attlee papers; Dalton papers; Gaitskell papers; Morrison papers; M. A. Hamilton, *Remembering My Good Friends*, 1944; E. H. J. N. Dalton, *The Fateful Years*, 1957, and *High Tide and After*, 1962; (ed.) C. P. Cook and J. Ramsden, *By-Elections in British Politics*, 1973 (essay by M. Ceadel); J. Wilmot, *Labour's Way to Control Banking and Finance*, 1935; *Daily Herald*, 14 August, 23 October 1934; 8 July, 21 October 1935; 27 February 1945; 2 May 1946; 25 September 1947; *The Times*, 14 October 1946; 24 July 1964; *Fulham Chronicle*, 29 September 1933; Labour Party Annual Conference Reports; Hansard; private information.]   BEN PIMLOTT

WILSHAW, SIR EDWARD (1879-1968), president of Cable and Wireless (Holding) Ltd. and financier, was born 3 June 1879 at Limehouse, Middlesex, the elder son of William George Wilshaw, a clerk with Fletcher's Dry Dock and later its chairman and managing director, and his wife, Amelia Sewell.

Wilshaw left school at the age of fourteen. In February 1894 he joined the Eastern Telegraph Company Ltd. as a clerk. Although his marriage certificate of 1912 describes him as a 'Director of Public Companies', he did not reach board level at Eastern until later. In

January 1920 he became joint assistant secretary of the Eastern and South African telegraph cable companies. He became secretary of Eastern in September 1922.

During his years with Eastern Wilshaw was closely associated with the Pender family, descended from Sir John Pender [q.v.], who founded British intercontinental submarine telegraph cables on profits from Manchester-based cotton enterprises. From the 1920s, when wireless became a powerful competitor, Wilshaw and the Penders tried to maintain the near-monopoly previously enjoyed by Eastern in the face of the growth of political independence in many countries and of a technology developing beyond Eastern's apparent competence and its management's recognition.

Following an Imperial conference, in 1929 Eastern cable and Marconi wireless telegraph interests were merged, in order to avoid the financial collapse of the telegraph cable companies. The strength of Eastern was demonstrated by its dominance of the merger company in both shareholder control and management allocation. Cutting through several interrelated shareholdings, the new company was first called Imperial and International Communications Ltd. but was renamed Cable and Wireless Ltd. in 1934. Wilshaw, who became general manager and secretary in 1929, was appointed chief general manager in 1933, a director and joint managing director in 1935, and chairman and sole managing director in 1936—a truly spectacular progression.

The new merger company, in common with many others, had a difficult time in the depression years of the 1930s. In 1938, after an Imperial conference, Wilshaw inaugurated the Empire Flat Rate scheme—the first application of a flat rate principle to overseas telegrams. But the continued emphasis of Cable and Wireless on the telegraph and cable field was taking its toll and more economic problems were threatening when World War II broke out. During the war Wilshaw and the telegraph cable operations made an outstanding contribution both to the conduct of the war and, through the use of special rate facilities, to the morale of troops overseas.

Before the end of the war a Commonwealth conference made recommendations aimed at recognizing and accommodating political and technical developments. As had happened previously, Wilshaw bitterly resented the proposed changes which would not only encourage expansion of wireless communication but would also break up Cable and Wireless into several separate locally owned operating corporations in the main Commonwealth countries and leave it with only residual business elsewhere. After a two-year battle with the British Government

Wilshaw lost on the acquisition issue but won good compensation terms for his shareholders.

This was the parting of the ways. Cable and Wireless became a state-owned public company and Wilshaw founded with the compensation moneys an investment trust which developed into the Electra House Group. He was the first governor of the investment trust from 1947 until 1964 when he relinquished the position and became president.

Although he lived at Frinton, Essex, Wilshaw was 'a great and enthusiastic Londoner' (*The Times*, 4 March 1968), whose interests were reflected in the various offices and honorary appointments he held. He was a member of the Court of Assistants (and later prime warden) of the Worshipful Company of Shipwrights, liveryman of the Company of Coopers, master of the Guild of Freemen of the City of London (1920), governor of the City of London College, and member of the City of London Territorial Association. In 1912 he became a member of the Chartered Institute of Secretaries, in which he took a great interest, becoming vice-president and, in 1930-1, president. He commemorated his presidential year of office by giving the Institute a stained-glass window for its Hall in London Wall (the Hall was destroyed in World War II). He was also a lieutenant of the City of London and was very disappointed not to be invited to become lord mayor. London University honoured him with an LLD. In 1939 he was appointed KCMG.

Wilshaw's love of London did not isolate him from Essex where, in 1932, he was elevated to the county bench and his name was added to the Commission of Peace for the county. He also served as a general commissioner of income tax and land tax for the Havering division of Essex.

Later in his life Wilshaw lived almost 'on the job' in a flat in Arundel Street next door to the headquarters at Electra House. He was a stocky man and would pass the time of day with all and sundry. Yet he was by nature an autocrat and it could be said in retrospect that his limited technical appreciation and business outlook caused his company some problems.

In 1912 Wilshaw married Myn (Minnie), the daughter of produce broker William Moar, of Orkney; they had two daughters. Wilshaw died 3 March 1968 at Bryanston Square in the City of Westminster.

There is a portrait by Frank O. Salisbury (1944), which hangs at Electra House.

[Cable & Wireless records; *Zodiac*, 1906-68 (house magazine of Cable & Wireless); *The Times*, 4 and 30 March 1968.]

A. A. WILLETT

WILSON, FRANK PERCY (1889-1963), scholar and bibliographer, was born at Birmingham 11 October 1889, the youngest of the nine children of John Wilson, wholesaler, and his wife, Alice Mary While. He was educated in Birmingham, at Camp Hill and King Edward's Grammar Schools, then at the university of Birmingham, where he took a first class in English (1911) and an MA (1912). He went on to Lincoln College, Oxford, obtaining a B.Litt. in 1913 for a thesis on Thomas Dekker [q.v.] which laid the foundations for much of his later work, and won him the Charles Oldham scholarship. But in September 1914 he volunteered for military service and in 1915 was commissioned in the Royal Warwickshire Regiment. He was badly wounded on the Somme in July 1916, and after much surgery was left with a permanent limp and subject to bouts of infection. After a year in hospital, he served briefly in the Ministry of Food. In 1919 he was invited back to Birmingham by Professor Ernest de Selincourt [q.v.], but returned to Oxford two years later as a university lecturer; he was appointed reader in 1927. Among his pupils was Joanna, daughter of Lancelot Perry-Keene, business manager, whom he married in 1924 and by whom he had three sons and a daughter.

At Oxford he resumed work on Dekker. His edition of Dekker's *Foure Birds of Noahs Arke* was published in 1924, of the *Plague Pamphlets of T. Dekker* in 1925: these were to have been extended to a four-volume edition of Dekker's prose works—a project never abandoned, but never completed (despite a Leverhulme research fellowship in 1938-40 for this work); it should have rivalled the edition (1904-10) of Thomas Nashe [q.v.] by R. B. McKerrow [q.v.]. This edition was Wilson's model, to which he made corrections and additions when reprinted in 1958. An offshoot, *The Plague in Shakespeare's London* (1927), was reprinted in 1963 with a preface, dated five months before his death, drawing attention to new source material and characteristically remarking, 'I have removed from p. 113 a baseless speculation about what Shakespeare was doing in 1603, being now content to say that I do not know'. To him, all work was work in progress.

From 1929 to 1936 Wilson was professor of English at the university of Leeds. It was not only administrative duties, skilfully discharged, but lack of a convenient research library which slowed up his academic work. Fortunately, the Huntington Library, California, offered him a research fellowship in 1933: the first of many transatlantic journeys. He was a visiting fellow at the Huntington again in 1952-3 and 1958; and at the Folger Shakespeare Library, Washington, in 1957. In 1943 he was visiting Carnegie professor at Columbia University, lectured at Smith College, and gave the Alexander lectures at the university of Toronto (published as *Elizabethan and Jacobean* in 1945); in 1952 he was visiting professor at Stanford and Turnbull lecturer at Johns Hopkins; and in 1958 he gave the Ewing lectures in the university of California at Los Angeles (published in *Seventeenth Century Prose* in 1960).

In 1935 he accepted the invitation to be, with Bonamy Dobrée, the general editor of the *Oxford History of English Literature*. This task consumed a great deal of his time, and he himself undertook the volume on English drama from 1485 to 1642. His British Academy lecture on 'Shakespeare and the Diction of Common Life' (1941) and his Clark lectures at Trinity College, Cambridge (1951), published as *Marlowe and the Early Shakespeare* (1953), are a foretaste of this volume; only what he had left more or less complete at his death was published, as *The English Drama 1485-1585*, ed. G. K. Hunter (1969). Determined as he was to enjoy the seeds of promise in this rather lean period, many wished that he had devoted his later years to the flowering of the Elizabethan drama: two fine chapters on 'The English History Play' and 'Shakespeare's Comedies' are salvaged in *Shakespearian and Other Studies*, ed. Dame Helen Gardner (1969). He rescued the plays from the theories of sometimes fashionable critics, who lacked his common sense or scrupulous regard for the texts. The merits of his dramatic criticism are: constant alertness to the exigencies of the stage—he was a promising amateur actor in his early days; keen critical discrimination; unrivalled knowledge of contemporary word usage and phraseology.

The Proverbial Wisdom of Shakespeare (1961) is one of Wilson's many published papers on proverbs. He had long been preparing the third edition of the *Oxford Dictionary of English Proverbs*, with the assistance of his wife; it appeared with her introduction in 1970. Defensively, he would refer to his hobby of collecting proverbs as his tatting, to be done when too tired to write, but he valued proverbs for establishing texts and meanings in Elizabethan authors; he often invoked them for explanatory or illustrative purposes himself.

In 1936 Wilson had been elected Hildred Carlile professor of English literature at Bedford College, London. The congenial combination of college life with reading in the British Museum was interrupted by war and evacuation to Cambridge. Despite his lameness, he joined the Home Guard. In early 1943 he wrote a long essay on 'Shakespeare and the New Bibliography' for the jubilee volume of *The Bibliographical Society, 1892-1942, Studies in Retrospect* (1945), a masterly report on the position at this date; Wilson's personal copy, as revised in 1948, was edited by Dame Helen Gardner in 1970. In it the work of Sir E. K. Chambers, whose notice Wilson contributed to this dictionary, R. B. McKerrow, and A. W. Pollard [qq.v.] is duly appraised. However, the real hero is (Sir) W. W. Greg, whom Wilson regarded as his 'master' and whose notice he also contributed to this Dictionary. Their friendship dates from early collaboration on an edition for the Malone Society of *Every Man out of his Humour* (1920) by Ben Jonson [q.v.]; Greg made Wilson his literary executor. In 1948 he followed Greg as general editor of the Malone Society; the regular flow of volumes, many of them either edited or checked by him, bears witness to the many hours devoted to the society and to helping the volume editors. He did not relinquish this task until 1960, yet found time to edit three pamphlets for the Luttrell Society.

In 1947 Wilson had succeeded David Nichol Smith [q.v.] as Merton professor of English Literature at Oxford. Much of the literary work already referred to was done during the next decade, which proved happy and productive; he enjoyed the proximity of the Bodleian and the society of other Elizabethan scholars. His forceful lectures and his beautiful reading voice were much appreciated, and many research students profited from his advice. On retirement in 1957, he was made a senior research fellow of Merton College for three years. He continued his many services to scholarship. True, especially latterly, there was some fretting over the big books that would never be written, and bouts of ill health were increasingly likely to disrupt plans. By the end of 1962 he was much weakened, and he died at his home on Cumnor Hill 29 May 1963.

He was the most learned Elizabethan scholar of his generation. Yet when he died many referred in the first place, not to his learning, but to the moral stature of the man. In 'Table Talk' reprinted in *Shakespearian and Other Studies*, 1969) he quoted Selden: 'no man is the wiser for his learning; it may administer matter to work in, or objects to work upon, but wit and wisdom are born with a man.' He had an Elizabethan respect for the goddess Ceremony, and always found fitting words for any occasion. He enjoyed good conversation; sometimes he would engineer a repeat if he felt that a 'wit-combat' could be improved upon, but his heart was even more gladdened if he detected some 'grace note' in one of the company. As he wrote of Shakespeare, 'one effect of his comedies is to make us think better of mankind'.

He was made a trustee of Dove Cottage in 1939; elected FBA in 1943; honorary LLD of the university of Birmingham, 1947; honorary fellow of Lincoln College, Oxford, 1948; president of the Bibliographical Society, 1950-2; of the Oxford Bibliographical Society, 1956-7; of the Malone Society, 1960-3; and of the Modern Humanities Research Association, 1961.

A drawing by Gilbert Spencer, in the possession of the family, is reproduced as frontispiece to *Elizabethan and Jacobean Studies Presented to F. P. Wilson in honour of his 70th birthday*, ed. H. J. Davis and H. Gardner (1959), which also contains 'A Select List of the Writings of F. P. Wilson' by H. S. Bennett. Some of the literary manuscripts are in the James Osborn collection in the Beinecke Library, New Haven.

[*The Times*, 30 May and 8 June 1963; Herbert Davis in *Proceedings* of the British Academy, vol. xlix, 1963; private information; personal knowledge.]

JEAN ROBERTSON

WILSON, HENRY MAITLAND, first BARON WILSON (1881-1964), field-marshal, was born 5 September 1881, the eldest of the three sons of Captain Arthur Maitland Wilson, OBE, of Stowlangtoft Hall, Suffolk, and his wife, (Harriet Maude) Isabella, daughter of Colonel Sir Nigel Robert Fitzhardinge Kingscote, GCVO, KCB, of Kingscote, Gloucestershire. Wilson went to Eton and Sandhurst and on 10 March 1900 was commissioned into the Rifle Brigade, with which he had family connections: his uncle, later Lieutenant-General Sir Henry Fuller Maitland, was to become colonel commandant of the 2nd battalion. He joined the 2nd battalion himself in South Africa, after the relief of Ladysmith (28 February 1900), and served with it to the end of the South African war, moving with it to Cairo in 1902.

Intense loyalty as a Rifleman to his regiment and a continuing devotion to Eton were to become two prominent strands in Wilson's life. When he became a general it was rare to find an officer on his personal staff who was not wearing black buttons and he took an abiding interest in all regimental matters, above all during his later years as colonel commandant. He was to be president of the Old Etonian Association in 1948-9 and chairman of the committee for fourteen years, from 1950 to 1964. A strand no less prominent was his enthusiasm for field sports, particularly where horses were concerned, though the physical bulk which caused him to be known from very early on as 'Jumbo', and contributed usefully to an impressive presence, did not make him an easy man to mount.

For his service in South Africa Wilson received the Queen's and King's medals, each with two clasps, and was one of the very few senior officers to be seen wearing Boer War medals in World War II.

In 1907 he went with the 2nd battalion for the first time to India, was promoted captain in 1908, served with the 3rd battalion in Bordon and Tipperary, and was posted in 1911 as adjutant to the Oxford University OTC. As such he had much to do with the generous flow of good young officers into the 'Greenjackets' (that is, the Rifle Brigade and 60th Rifles) when war broke out in 1914.

His own service in World War I, which kept him continuously in France from 1915, was wholly on the staff, almost certainly because he was too good a staff officer to be allowed back to the regimental duty he much preferred. He went out as brigade major in the 16th (Irish) division (General Sir James Steele was in later years to recall him as the best brigade major he ever knew) and was successively GSO 2 of 41st division on the Somme and of XIX Corps in the third battle of Ypres before going, in October 1917, as GSO 1 to the New Zealand division, with which he stayed till the end. He then went to Camberley, in 1919, in the hand-picked group which made up the first post-war Staff Course.

He had been appointed to the DSO in 1917 and was mentioned three times in dispatches. He was promoted major on 1 September 1915 and brevet lieutenant-colonel on 1 January 1919.

After a spell at Sandhurst Wilson returned to the regiment (the first time for twelve years) as second-in-command of the 2nd battalion at Aldershot and then, before taking command of the 1st battalion on the North-West Frontier, spent three years as chief umpire to the 2nd division under Strickland, when the GOC-in-C was a professionally exacting officer in General Sir Philip (later Lord) Chetwode [q.v.]. This played a significant part in Wilson's own professional development and made him fairly widely known.

After three years in India, in which he spent time cultivating tribesmen as well as in shooting, racing, and pig-sticking, and three more as an instructor in the rank of colonel at Camberley, he had to endure nine months on half pay before taking over the 16th Infantry brigade, in January 1934, from Brigadier A. P. (later Earl) Wavell [q.v.]. This was a time of experiment in mechanization and the working out of a role for motorized infantry operating with armour. The concept of the Motor Battalion—a type of unit in which Riflemen were before long to distinguish themselves—was now emerging.

Promoted major-general on 30 April 1935, at a time when commands were hard to come by, Maitland Wilson was again on half pay, this time for nearly two years, until taking over the 2nd division again from his old friend Wavell, in August 1937.

In the summer of 1939, in a threatening international situation, Wilson was appointed GOC-in-C, British Troops in Egypt, in the rank of lieutenant-general, and left England on 15 June (noting that it was Ascot Gold Cup day) to spend the next eight years, covering all of World War II, overseas. He was always, until very near the end of that time, to be found somewhere around the Mediterranean.

Wilson was already high in the confidence of Anthony Eden (later the Earl of Avon), secretary of state for war: they had served together as Greenjackets in World War I. He was soon to win the confidence of Winston Churchill and, unlike some other senior commanders who were less fortunate, was never thereafter to lose it. The operations of the Army of the Nile (as it came to be called) under Wilson's command, with Wavell in the position of C-in-C Middle East, resulted in spectacular successes in the Western Desert of Egypt and Libya against dramatically superior Italian forces—operations in which the action of motorized infantry working with tanks was prominent. After the capture of Tobruk, while Lieutenant-General Sir Richard O'Connor carried on the desert campaign to further successes, Wilson was appointed by Wavell as military governor of Cyrenaica—but not for long. The War Cabinet had decided, with grave misgivings on the part of its military advisers, to send an expeditionary force to help Greece withstand German invasion. The British and Imperial forces available were too weak to be of much help and the opinion was heard in Greece that their arrival would do little more than aggravate a difficult situation. Eden, in Cairo, cabled (21 February 1941) that the expeditionary force required the best commander who could be found and that he, Sir J. G. Dill, CIGS [q.v.] and Wavell all agreed that this was Wilson. His quiet authority was certainly useful in a time of high political sensitivity, while his tactical skill was evident in the conduct of the inevitable withdrawal, which was to end with the evacuation by the British of all mainland Greece and its occupation by the enemy. Wavell met Wilson in Crete and almost at once told him: 'I want you to go to Jerusalem and relieve Baghdad.' Wilson thus found himself GOC British Forces in Palestine and Transjordan. The successful relief of Baghdad, under siege by pro-Axis Iraqis, was followed by the move of British and Imperial forces into Vichy-held Syria and Lebanon, where the use by German aircraft of French airfields had invited a British ultimatum. The inclusion of a Free French contingent in this force was, in spite of the low availability of other troops and political pressure from de Gaulle, almost certainly a mistake. British officers with much experience in the Levant knew that what might be only token resistance from the Vichy side, offered as a matter of professional honour, would almost certainly develop into savage fighting if the Free French came in, which is just what happened. Some tended to blame Wilson (now designated C-in-C Allied Forces in Syria) for an error of judgement but the decision (against which Wavell had argued) was taken in London.

Tension between Winston Churchill and Wavell was growing and in July 1941 the latter was replaced as C-in-C Middle East by General (later Field-Marshal) Sir Claude Auchinleck, with whom the prime minister was going to find it no easier to agree. On 2 July the prime minister urged the new C-in-C to consider Wilson for command in the Western Desert. 'It is much to be regretted', Churchill wrote 'that this advice, subsequently repeated, was not taken.' Auchinleck preferred General Sir Alan G. Cunningham, after his success in Abyssinia, but the appointment did nothing to improve British performance in the field and under Cunningham's successor, General (Sir) N. M. Ritchie, results were even worse and retreat towards the Nile Delta continued. Only when Auchinleck did what the prime minister had latterly been urging and took command himself did the position stabilize, almost in the Delta.

Wilson, who had been made GOC-in-C 9th Army, with his HQ in the Lebanon, had been brought down to Egypt to command troops in the Delta against a possible breakthrough by Rommel. He was then (August 1942) ordered personally by the prime minister, whom he was meeting for the first time, to take over the new command being set up in Persia and Iraq, on the Russians' southern flank and, with its communications and oil, of growing importance. From 23 September 1942 he was to spend eighteen months, based on Baghdad, in complex work more political, administrative, and diplomatic than strictly military: work he was well suited to and did well. The transference of General Alexander (later Lord Alexander of Tunis, q.v.) from the post of C-in-C Middle East to be deputy C-in-C to Eisenhower in January 1943, to assume direction of the last stages of the campaign by Allied land forces in North Africa,

left the position of C-in-C Middle East once more vacant. The prime minister, again in Cairo, had Wilson moved into the post. Since the highest Allied priority in the Mediterranean was the support of Eisenhower's command, Wilson's position was soon to become, in Churchill's hyperbole, that of a general 'with responsibilities but no troops'. On the collapse of Italy later in the year the prime minister saw an opportunity to establish a dominent position in the Eastern Mediterranean before the Germans could prevent it. He cabled Wilson from Washington (9 September 1943): 'This is the time to play high. Improvise and dare.' There was little more that Wilson could do, since virtually all resources were earmarked for the Central Mediterranean, than launch some ill-supported, and in the end unsuccessful and wasteful, small operations in the Dodecanese on Cos, Leros, and Samos. The President consistently refused to allow any forces to be diverted from Eisenhower except for the Far East and would hear of nothing that suggested the slightest possibility of delaying 'Overlord', the operation to open a second front in northwest Europe. On the other hand there was enthusiastic American support for a landing in southern France (Operation 'Anvil', later renamed 'Dragoon'), in which neither Wilson nor the prime minister saw any merit. Wilson would dearly have liked to carry out Churchill's cherished wish to capture Rhodes but the President was adamant. Churchill submitted to his decision but, as he wrote, 'with one of the sharpest pangs I suffered in the war'. The 'bleeding of the Eastern Mediterranean' also brought Churchill into the acutest differences he ever had with Eisenhower, but at the same time it brought him even closer to Wilson, and when Eisenhower was moved from the theatre to take charge of the preparations for 'Overlord', Wilson was from 8 January 1944, on the prime minister's suggestion and with the President's full approval, appointed supreme commander in the Mediterranean in his place. There followed the further operations in Italy, under Alexander's command of the land forces, including the Anzio landing with its disappointingly weak command and slow gains, the steady grind northwards, and the continuing difference of emphasis between the Allies on the relative importance of a landing in the South of France, firmly opposed by Wilson and seen by Churchill only as an extravagant and unnecessary diversion. Churchill, and Wilson with him, would have much preferred strengthening Allied forces in Italy, instead of reducing them, and pressing on up through Austria into Hungary, while exploiting Tito's successes along the Adriatic. Under very strong pressure from the Americans (who harboured hardly justifiable suspicions of British intentions in 'the Balkans') the Riviera landings eventually took place, against almost negligible opposition, and were acclaimed a resounding, if scarcely relevant, success.

Trouble in Greece as the Germans withdrew in the autumn of 1944 required very active Allied intervention but Maitland Wilson was again on the move. Field-Marshal Sir John Dill, head of the Joint Staff Mission in Washington, died there 4 November 1944. The good personal relations he had established and above all Dill's firm friendship with General Marshall had been of the utmost value to the alliance and it was imperative to put in the best available successor. On 21 November the prime minister communicated to Wilson: 'I can find only one officer with the necessary credentials and qualities, namely, yourself.' Wilson, who had been promoted field-marshal, took up the appointment in January 1945 and held it until it lapsed early in 1947. On 23 April 1947 he left for home.

In this, his last post, he had, first of all, having served in one theatre, to find out about four others. He had also to accustom himself to holding a very high-ranking post with no command responsibilities. He was none the less fully occupied acting as trusted intermediary on military matters between the British prime minister and the President, a position which did not change in essence when Roosevelt was succeeded by Truman. Wilson was present at the Yalta and Potsdam conferences and was kept fully informed on all the delicate manœuvring which led up to Hiroshima and Nagasaki.

An active military career which in nearly half a century had moved from the tough but relatively simple warfare of South Africa to involvement in atomic weapons was now at an end. 'Jumbo' Wilson had always been a dedicated professional soldier but as a staff officer early on had given promise of the flair for diplomacy which was possibly to play a more important part in what he achieved than military talent. He was good with people and particularly good with the young and in his retirement he devoted much time and affectionate attention to army cadets.

He was an impressive figure of a man, whose appearance and manner compelled attention and inspired confidence. He usually spoke little but what he had to say was closely, and even sharply, to the point. He had, it was said, 'shrewd little steely eyes', and when he looked at you closely over those half-moon spectacles it could be uncomfortable. He made no pretence to be an intellectual and was rather better in direct confrontation than on paper. His judgement was on the whole sound, though some of his arrangements for operations in the Dodecanese, admittedly at a time of frustration and some confusion, have been criticized. He was much loved by many people and was held in particularly deep affection and respect by young officers who came close to him in personal service. At the same time he could occasionally be guilty of paying perhaps insufficient attention to personal hardship if he thought he saw an overriding need to disregard it. This could have been the result of occasional lapses in imagination.

In addition to his peerage (1946) Wilson's honours included the GCB (1944; KCB, 1940; CB, 1937); GBE (1941); and a wealth of foreign decorations. When elevated to the peerage he chose as supporters to his coat: 'Dexter, a Rifleman, and Sinister, a Bugler, both of the Rifle Brigade in full dress proper.'

In the House of Lords he sat on the crossbenches, as befitted a field-marshal, but took part freely in defence debates. He was active in the affairs of the Royal United Service Institution, the Mounted Infantry Club, and the South African War Veterans' Association, in which he was particularly interested. He was colonel commandant of the Rifle Brigade from 1939 to 1951 and constable of the Tower of London from 1955 to 1960.

His last appearance in public was at Eton on St. Andrew's Day 1964, when the new Regimental Memorial was dedicated in the Cloisters. On the last day of the year he was taken ill and died peacefully at his home, Wheelwrights, Chilton, Aylesbury, 31 December 1964. He was buried with his family at Stowlangtoft and a memorial service was held in Westminster Abbey. For some years he had lived quietly in the Chilterns and close friends say he seemed a lonely man. Wherever he lived his heart remained in Suffolk.

Wilson married in 1914 Hester Mary, daughter of Philip James Digby Wykeham, of Tythrop House, Oxfordshire, and had a son, Patrick Maitland, born 14 September 1915 (by whom he was succeeded on his death) and a daughter.

There are portraits of Wilson by Maurice Codner (Royal Society of Portrait Painters, 1954), and Simon Elwes (exhibited at the Royal Academy Summer Exhibition, 1972).

[*The Times*, 1 January 1965; Field-Marshal Lord Wilson, *Eight Years Overseas*, 1949; *The Rifle Brigade Chronicle for 1965*, ed. Lieutenant-Colonel U. Verney; private information: personal knowledge.]

J. W. HACKETT

WILSON, SIR (JAMES) STEUART (1889–1966), singer, and musical administrator and scholar, was born 21 July 1889 at Bristol, the youngest child of the Revd James Maurice Wilson [q.v.], headmaster of Clifton College and later a canon of Worcester Cathedral, and his wife, Georgina Mary Talbot, daughter of Admiral John Talbot, of Bristol. In addition to his brothers (Sir) Arnold [q.v.] and Hugh and his sister Margaret, he had four half-brothers and sisters of his father's first marriage to Annie Elizabeth Moore (died 1878) of whom the eldest, Mona, was a remarkable woman, greatly loved and respected by him during her long life. Steuart's upbringing was uncomplicated: the family were devoted to one another and cherished by their parents.

Wilson's education, like his background, was conventional. He went to a preparatory school, Grove House, when he was ten. From there he went to Winchester College, where from 1906 to 1909 he was a scholar, and then to King's College, Cambridge, as an honorary exhibitioner reading classics. His gifts as a musician became apparent early and were recognized at Grove House, although there was little in his home life to anticipate them. He took piano lessons and sang regularly in Winchester College and Cathedral; but it was not until the Cambridge period that music—singing—emerged as his central interest. He was fortunate there in having the encouragement of Professor Edward J. Dent and Ralph Vaughan Williams, and in meeting and working with musicians like Gervase Elwes [qq.v.] and Clive Carey, but at no time in his life did he follow any musical course in the orthodox sense. Not surprisingly, he only got a third in the classical tripos at Cambridge (1909).

His first public appearance as a singer was as a soloist and member of the choir in the incidental music written by Vaughan Williams for *The Wasps* of Aristophanes, at the New Theatre, Cambridge, in 1909. The composer was so much impressed by his voice that he wrote a special series of Four Hymns, dedicated to 'J. S. W.', for the Worcester Three Choirs Festival in 1914, an event which was cancelled on the outbreak of war. Wilson had in the meantime succeeded Elwes (killed tragically while on tour in America) as the best-known interpreter of the song cycle, *On Wenlock Edge*, Vaughan Williams's setting of *A Shropshire Lad*, by A. E. Housman [q.v.]. He made his first appearance in opera as Tamino in Mozart's *Magic Flute*, also at the New Theatre, Cambridge, in 1911; but opera was never to be his special field.

When war broke out Wilson joined the 6th battalion of the King's Royal Rifle Corps on 22 September 1914. As a captain, he was twice wounded, the second time seriously; he lost a kidney and a large part of one lung, and ended his military service in Whitehall. Incredibly,

his voice was unaffected by his physical condition (it was a high tenor voice, not in itself of outstanding beauty), and in 1917, while still working at the War Office, he joined Cuthbert Kelly, singing in recitals of madrigals at St. Martin's-in-the-Fields. This led to the founding of The English Singers, as a sextet, in 1920. The group did not become self-supporting until 1921, but from that date they went from strength to strength, with successful tours at home and abroad.

From 1921 to 1923 Wilson taught music at Bedales School. With his own school and family education based on traditional classical values, he found himself out of sympathy with the headmaster's advanced views; but this particular job of music director was not over-exacting and left him free to take professional engagements up and down the country. It also established his connection with what was to become the family centre at Petersfield: Canon Wilson lived at Steep, on the outskirts of the town, in his retirement, and Steuart made it his base off and on for the rest of his life. During the Bedales period, he worked from Steep, cycling backwards and forwards between home, school, and the railway station whence he travelled from one concert fixture to another. He worked hard and under some strain, with the result that he developed a duodenal ulcer which somewhat preoccupied him and for which he had more than one operation in later years. In 1925 he went to live in Notting Hill Gate, London, where he remained until after the war of 1939-45.

Meanwhile, in 1922-3, an offer of material help came from Sir Alexander Butterworth, who had set up a fund in memory of his son George [q.v.], the composer, killed in the war of 1914-18. Wilson was persuaded to accept, and spent two periods in Nice with the Polish operatic tenor Jean de Reszke: six months in 1923-4, and another four in 1924-5. This time of study, with singing lessons from a respected tutor, was the nearest he came to any formal musical training.

English song, English folk-song, German *Lieder* in English (from translations made with his friend Arthur Fox Strangways, q.v.) and oratorios in English are the lasting memorials to this most English of singers. His greatest contribution to the performance of music was the painstaking, scholarly attention he gave to the declamation of the role of the evangelist in the *Passions* of St. Matthew and St. John by Bach. He sang them in the language of the authorized version of the Bible, with impeccable timing, subtle vocal colour, and uncanny clarity of diction. His love of words for singing remained with him long after his voice was, as he said, 'past it'. In addition to his translations of German *Lieder*, he produced new English texts for Haydn's *Creation*, Brahms's *German Requiem*, and the vocal finale of Mahler's *Fourth Symphony*. With Dent, he did much to revive the music of Henry Purcell [q.v.], of whom it was said by his contemporaries that he had 'a peculiar Genius to Express the Energy of English Words', a description which might equally apply to his twentieth-century interpreter.

From 1939 to 1942 Wilson had a short spell in America, at the Curtis Institute of Music in Philadelphia, and elsewhere. He came home partly because of the frustrations he apparently suffered there, but perhaps mainly because he disliked being out of England in wartime. Now fifty-three, he embraced a new career, and he brought to the work of an administrator all the vigour he had previously expended as a performer. In 1943 he was appointed overseas music director to the BBC; and then in 1945 he became music director of the embryo Arts Council of Great Britain. This was at the time when Lord Keynes [q.v.] (a Kingsman like himself) was chairman of the wartime experiment known as CEMA (the Council for the Encouragement of Music and the Arts), and was busy with plans to give it permanent status; the Arts Council was launched as such in June 1945, but did not receive its charter until the following summer, after Keynes's death. Wilson stayed with it until January 1948, then he returned to the BBC as music director, in succession to Victor Hely-Hutchinson. He was knighted in the same year. Thereafter he held several other appointments, including that of deputy to (Sir) David Webster, the general administrator of the Royal Opera House, Covent Garden, from 1950 to 1955 — Wilson had been one of the original trustees of the newly founded Opera House in 1946. Unfortunately, an antipathy developed between Wilson and Webster, and Wilson left Covent Garden. His final, and also unhappy, appointment was as principal of the Birmingham School of Music. He travelled much, at home and abroad, adjudicating and examining, and gradually drifted towards retirement at Petersfield, where he died 18 December 1966.

He married three times: first, in 1917, Ann Mary Grace, younger daughter of Captain Francis Alan Richard Bowles, RN retired, of Sittingbourne, Kent; this marriage was dissolved in 1932; secondly, in 1937, Mary Daisy (died 1960 in India where Wilson was examining for the Trinity College of Music); thirdly, in 1962, Margaret Stewart, widow of Leslie Hunter, of Brockham Green, Surrey, a friend (although younger than he) of Cambridge days. He had four children by his first wife, one of whom, Jonathan, was killed in the war of 1939–45. It was in memory of Jonathan that

he helped to finance the Council for Music in Hospitals: he was one of its vice-presidents, with (Sir) Malcolm Sargent [q.v.] and Frank Howes, the senior music critic of *The Times* with whom he was much in sympathy, and Lord Harewood as president. It should not be forgotten that, highly professional artist as he was, he consistently championed the cause of the amateur music-makers and their sponsors; bodies like the English Folk Dance and Song Society, the International Folk Music Council, and the Rural Music Schools Council owed much to his support.

It may be said that Steuart Wilson was a 'difficult' man. Those who worked for and with him found him stimulating, generous, always exciting; but he was also prickly, and impatient of authority. He hated, in his days as a public servant, hiding behind the anonymity of office. If anything went wrong, he wanted to take the full blame himself; it might almost be said he courted it. His life was a series of confrontations, but in spite of stress, sometimes causing actual illness, he thrived on them.

He overflowed with original ideas, many of them impossible to realize. He was also a good listener to other people's ideas, and if convinced by any of them, was the first to demand immediate action. He cared for the success of all who worked alongside, and there are many who remember his thoughtfulness. He could be a loyal friend, but he was also an implacable enemy. Always revelling in a good fight, he embarked in 1933 on a libel case against the BBC. Much has been written about the 'Case of the Intrusive H', the result of a letter published in the BBC's weekly paper, the *Listener*, in which the writer complained of his pronunciation in a broadcast performance of the *St. Matthew Passion*. Wilson fought and won, and his belligerency was saved from malice by the wit and gaiety of his testimony in court. He used most of the money awarded to him in damages to help his friend Rutland Boughton [q.v.], whose opera *The Lily Maid* he brought to London. Ten years later he was invited to be the BBC's overseas music director.

Wilson was excellent company. His friends remember that the singer of Bach Passion music could also be a wholeheartedly bawdy entertainer in the home, with, among other delights, his inimitable rendering of the apparently innocent folk-song, *The Foggy, Foggy Dew*. He enjoyed entertaining, and was no mean cook, often receiving his guests in the kitchen, clad in his French chef's apron. He was always a good-looking man, and in older age aristocratically impressive. He was not unaware of it and, though far from vain, was sartorially individual. He had, for instance, a collection of embroidered waistcoats and elaborate buttons of porcelain and enamel to go with them. In the later 1940s he could be seen on summer days in a pale-blue-and-white-striped seersucker suit. Six months before his death, in the summer of 1966, he attended the opera at Glyndebourne wearing sponge-bag trousers, a morning coat, a resplendent waistcoat, and a pair of *espadrilles*.

To this Dictionary Wilson contributed the notices of Harry Plunket Greene, Sir George Henschel, Arthur Henry Fox Strangways, and Rutland Boughton. There is a bronze bust of Wilson by David McFall (1966), which is in the possession of the family.

[Margaret Stewart (Lady Wilson), *English Singer: the Life of Sir Steuart Wilson*, 1970; personal knowledge.]   MARY GLASGOW
                                          IAN MACPHAIL

WILSON, JOHN DOVER (1881-1969), Shakespeare scholar, was born at Mortlake, Surrey, 13 July 1881, the eldest of the six children of Edwin Wilson, engraver and scientific illustrator, and his wife, Elizabeth Dover. He won scholarships to Lancing College, where his uncle was headmaster, and to Gonville and Caius College, Cambridge, where he took the historical tripos with a second class in each part (1902-3). In 1904 he carried off the valuable Harness prize for an essay on *John Lyly* (1905). This brought him to the notice of (Sir) A. W. Ward [q.v.], who assigned him two chapters of the *Cambridge History of English Literature* and through whom, after a year's teaching at Whitgift Grammar School, Croydon, he became English Lektor at Helsingfors (Helsinki) in 1906. In that year he married Dorothy Mary, daughter of Canon Edward Curtis Baldwin, vicar of Harston, near Cambridge. Although his temperament responded to the adventure of Finland, he relinquished his post in 1909 and then became lecturer in English literature at Goldsmiths' College, London. His Elizabethan researches, especially on the Marprelate tracts, had brought him into the orbit of the bibliographical triumvirate of A. W. Pollard, (Sir) W. W. Greg, and R. B. McKerrow [qq.v.]. With Pollard there developed an intimate friendship which became 'one of the chief influences' in his life.

Alongside scholarly articles (from 1907) and reprints he brought out his successful anthology *Life in Shakespeare's England* (1911). But in 1912 an invitation to become an inspector for the Board of Education meant that for over twenty years literary scholarship had to accommodate itself to the demands of another career. During his first half-dozen years as an inspector, while he lived in Leeds and did a perpetual round of evening schools throughout the northern counties, his ideal of culture for industrial

workers was strengthened by experience. He wrote a commissioned memorandum on *Humanism in the Continuation School* (1921), on which he was warmly congratulated by Albert Mansbridge [q.v.] among others, and when the scheme for such schools in the 1918 Education Act was ultimately dropped he felt this a betrayal of the nation's youth. He served on the committee on the teaching of English set up in 1919 under Sir Henry Newbolt [q.v.], and wrote part of its report. When he was appointed to the chair of education at King's College, London, in 1924, a wide familiarity with the practicalities of teaching as well as a vision of its high ends underlay his jest that he was not sure what a professor of education was supposed to do. He began the *Journal of Adult Education* in 1926 and, with more enthusiasm, a series of 'Landmarks in the History of Education', for which he did a notable edition (1932) of Arnold's *Culture and Anarchy*.

The professor of education was, however, overshadowed by the Shakespeare scholar he had now become. He has vividly told how he was 'converted' to Shakespeare on a late-night railway journey in 1917 by reading in the *Modern Language Review* an article by Greg which provoked him to a rejoinder. He became 'possessed' with *Hamlet* and, confronted with the problems of its text, was led on to those of Shakespeare's text in general—just when the work of Pollard had suggested that the printed versions might be closer to Shakespeare's manuscripts than it was the custom to suppose. He seized on the clues contained in spellings, misprints, or mislineations; he collected evidence for *Shakespeare's Hand in the Play of Sir Thomas More* (edited by Pollard, 1923). Notes and articles leapt from his pen, and in 1919 the Cambridge Press, looking for a textual expert to join with Sir Arthur Quiller-Couch [q.v.] in editing the New Cambridge Shakespeare, inevitably chose him. This edition (1921-66) henceforth dominated his life.

It was Dover Wilson's analysis and treatment of the text which caused the remarkable impact of the early volumes on the academic world. He also prepared a strongly innovatory text for the beautiful Cranach *Hamlet* (1930), and his long absorption in the problems of this play had its outcome in the appearance of the New Cambridge *Hamlet* (1934), together with *The Manuscript of Shakespeare's 'Hamlet'* (1934) and *What Happens in 'Hamlet'* (1935). With the last of these and his 'biographical adventure', *The Essential Shakespeare* (1932), he captured the imagination of the general public to a degree probably unequalled by any other Shakespeare scholar. Quiller-Couch had withdrawn from the edition on the completion of the comedies, and with the histories Dover Wilson was able to range beyond the text to a vigorous critical reappraisal, which had *The Fortunes of Falstaff* (1943) as an important consequence. He derived satisfaction from becoming at length a professor of English when he was appointed to the regius chair of rhetoric and English literature at Edinburgh in 1935, but in 1945 the claims of his edition, still only half way through, prompted an early retirement. With steady progress and presently the aid of younger collaborators — Alice Walker, his pupil G. I. Duthie, and especially J. C. Maxwell — just after reaching the age of eighty he saw the last play out. Then, after the long-projected *Shakespeare's Happy Comedies* (1962), he was able to add the sonnets before at length becoming blind.

In his determination to fulfil a task undertaken he never lost the spirit of adventure (a favourite word), the optimistic boyish zest, which characterized his attitude to scholarship as to life. Command of detail was accompanied by boldness in hypothesis. Not all his explanations of particular textual phenomena won, or held, assent; the importance of his edition lies rather in its demonstration of new possibilities and methods. He more than anyone established the editorial practice of investigating the nature of the 'copy' through which Shakespeare's plays reached print. As a teacher and lecturer he enjoyed lifelong popularity. His writing has great vivacity in an easy but masterly style; it can only partly reflect the warm and generous personality which inspired widespread affection.

He was elected FBA in 1931 and was appointed CH in 1936. Also in 1936 his Cambridge college made him an honorary fellow. He had taken his Cambridge doctorate in 1926, and subsequently received honorary doctorates from Durham, Edinburgh, Leicester, Lille, London, Natal, and Cambridge. He was a trustee of the Shakespeare Birthplace Trust from 1931, and of the National Library of Scotland from 1946.

He had one son, who died on active service in 1944, and two daughters. His wife died in 1961, and in 1963 he married his widowed cousin, Dr Elizabeth Wintringham, daughter of Sir Joseph Arkwright, bacteriologist [q.v.]. He died at Balerno, near Edinburgh, 15 January 1969.

A portrait by Robert Lyon (1955) is in the university of Edinburgh; there is a bronze bust by the sculptress Julian Allan in the university of Edinburgh, and also at Caius College, Cambridge.

[J. Dover Wilson, *Milestones on the Dover Road*, 1969; H. Jenkins in *Proceedings* of the British Academy, vol. lix, 1973; correspondence and papers in the National Library of Scotland; private information; personal knowledge.]   HAROLD JENKINS

WILSON, JOHN GIDEON (1876-1963), bookseller, was born in Glasgow 9 January 1876, the third of the eight children of James Wilson, a journeyman bookbinder, and his wife, Margaret Miller, who worked as a sheet-folder in the same workshop. He was educated at a Board school in Glasgow till his thirteenth year, when he was apprenticed to the bookselling firm of John Smith & Son, Glasgow, an excellent training ground for young booksellers. Here he began the practice of his immense reading, choosing with independent judgement the best of English prose and poetry.

In 1908, at the age of thirty-two, he married Catherine Smart Provan (by whom he had a son and four daughters) and came south for the rest of his life. For two years he worked with the publishing firm of Constable & Co., London, and then returned to bookselling with the City firm of Jones and Evans. From 1916 to 1919 he served as a soldier in France, winning the medal for meritorious service. He returned to Jones and Evans until 1923, when at the invitation of the proprietors, Messrs. Debenhams, he went to manage the bookshop of J. & E. Bumpus Ltd.

His years at Jones and Evans were perhaps the happiest in Wilson's experience. The modest premises in the City served as a rendezvous for leading figures in the literary world and Wilson followed the tradition of Evans in regarding bookselling not so much as a matter of retail trade as a service in which bookseller and customer met and shared the experience of contact with the precious manifestations of the spirit of man. It was essentially an affair of individuals, and he became the friend and counsellor of many of the finest creative writers of the time.

In the gracious Old Court House at the corner of Marylebone Lane in Oxford Street he was to work on a larger stage with growing fame and growing responsibilities. John Wilson of Bumpus emerged as the most famous English bookseller of his time. Presently a fine room was added to the shop in which he organized notable book exhibitions.

In 1935 the lease of the premises expired and was not renewed, the Court House was demolished, and, Debenhams having lost interest in the bookshop, John Wilson resolved to reestablish Bumpus as his own enterprise. Helped with capital by his friends he acquired the business and as chairman and managing director moved to a site in Oxford Street near Marble Arch. The move did not benefit the business, and Wilson in addition to his practice in bookselling had administrative and financial responsibilities which were uncongenial. He maintained his belief in exact attention to detail and, after the shop was closed, might be found for two hours in a small room writing orders for books, notes, and it was said, addressing labels. This practice obscured his vision of more important aspects of management, and latterly perhaps afforded a refuge from the pressure of financial cares. He found it hard to delegate responsibility, discouraging it in members of his staff; and his generosity in granting credit was abused.

The practice of bookselling was changing: mass production, bulk selling, self-service, and the shadow of the oncoming computer era were warnings that the traditional personal relations of bookseller and customer were 'not for the fashion of these times'. The business dwindled; no provision had been made to meet the renewal of the lease on more arduous terms, there were difficulties which the removal of the shop to Baker Street did not resolve, and in 1959, when approaches were being made for the purchase of the firm, the 'Oracle of the Book Trade' in his eighty-third year retired and went home to his books at Pinner, where, shortly before his death, his sight failed him.

Described as 'massively wise and unassumedly learned' this lovable man was endowed with a rare simplicity. In his shop he might be found conversing with the poet laureate or wrapping up the purchase of a schoolboy. His assessment of authors and their books was quick and sure, and his advice, always valid, was freely given to authors, publishers, and his fellow booksellers.

As chairman of the educational board of the Booksellers Association John Wilson designed the training syllabus for young booksellers, and his manual *The Business of Bookselling* (1930) remains a treasury of good counsel. For some years he edited *The Odd Volume*, an annual miscellany published in support of the Book Trade Provident Society. In 1948 he was appointed CBE.

He died at his home in Pinner 6 September 1963.

[*The Times*, 7 and 11 September 1963; *Bookseller*, 14 September 1963; private information; personal knowledge.]

BASIL BLACKWELL

WILSON, (JOHN) LEONARD (1897-1970), bishop of Singapore and Birmingham, was born at Gateshead Fell, county Durham, 23 November 1897, the second child in the family of one daughter and four sons of the Revd. John Wilson, curate of Gateshead Fell, and his wife, Mary Adelaide, daughter of Thomas Halliday, secretary to the firm of Armstrong Whitworth. He was educated at Newcastle Grammar School and St. John's School, Leatherhead. In 1916 he enlisted in the Durham Light Infantry, and saw service in France. In 1919 he joined the Knutsford Training School, an experiment to equip clergy for the post-war world, and subsequently took a shortened course in theology at the Queen's College, Oxford, where he was influenced by the social and ecumenical thinking of the Student Christian Movement and the theological liberalism of B. H. Streeter [q.v.]. He obtained his BA in 1922. After a brief appointment in 1922-3 to the staff of the Stuart Memorial College, Isfahan, he completed his training in 1923-4 at Wycliffe Hall, Oxford, and was ordained in 1924 to serve the cathedral parish of St. Michael, Coventry. In 1927 he joined the Church Missionary Society, in the expectation that he would become principal of the Old Cairo Boys' School, but his secular manner of life and his christological opinions offended the Society, and he returned from Egypt in 1929 as curate of St. Margaret's, Durham, with charge of St. John's, Neville Cross. As vicar of Eighton Banks, 1930-5, and of Roker, 1935-8, he threw himself into the congenial task of presenting a social gospel in a time of severe deprivation in the north of England.

In 1938 Wilson became archdeacon of Hong Kong, and in 1941 was consecrated bishop of Singapore. He had no time to make an impression on the diocese in normal conditions, since the Japanese conquest involved his internment in the notorious Changi Gaol in 1943. He was repeatedly tortured, on suspicion that the gaol was a centre of espionage, but his endurance, and the courage his ministry inspired in others, convinced him of the reality of the Christian faith, and raised him to an international figure. His tenure of the deanery of Manchester, to which he was appointed in 1949, was unhappy. He saw opportunities for unconventional experiment, while the cathedral authorities wished to re-establish cherished traditions, and it was with general relief that he was nominated bishop of Birmingham in 1953.

Wilson's succession to the controversial Ernest William Barnes [q.v.] was intended to be eirenic, and to concentrate episcopal attention on diocesan and civic, rather than national and theological, issues. He avoided dispute, made few statements on secular affairs, and discouraged his clergy from political action. He faced a diocese seriously understaffed, in which urban replanning, the building of vast housing estates, and the settlement of overspill communities meant the redistribution of churches and the provision of new centres of worship and social life. An appeal launched in 1956 eventually met most needs, and Wilson's liberal and evangelical reputation began to attract more clergy. His cast of mind, and his missionary experience, made him, in his own words, 'almost a fanatic about church unity', and he powerfully supported the Birmingham Council of Churches, founded in 1951, and its local agencies. His episcopate saw a great influx of coloured immigrants into the Midlands, and his example, with the establishment of a special chaplaincy, assured the initial amicable reception which was perhaps the greatest post-war social achievement of the Birmingham churches. He resigned his see in 1969.

Wilson was appointed CMG in 1946 and KCMG in 1968; from 1963 he was Prelate of the Order. He was awarded a Lambeth DD in 1953, and an honorary D.Sc. of the university of Aston in Birmingham in 1969; he was elected an honorary fellow of the Queen's College, Oxford, in 1954. He had an imposing presence and a fine voice. Conscious of his lack of scholarship, he distrusted intellectuals; he was autocratic and impatient of committees; his temper was quick and uncertain; but in personal and pastoral relationships he was generous and gracious. His episcopate in Birmingham cemented a divided diocese, and strengthened the influence of the Church on civic and social life: his understanding of his experience in Singapore stimulated faith in a sceptical and disillusioned age. In 1959 he published *Marriage, Sex, and the Family*.

In 1930 he married Doris Ruby ('Mary') Phillips, the daughter of a merchant trading in Egypt; they had four sons, one of whom died in childhood, and one daughter. Wilson died, in retirement at Bainbridge, Yorkshire, 18 August 1970. His memorial in Birmingham cathedral describes him as 'Confessor for the Faith', in the sense used in the ages of persecution. There is a portrait by Henry Carr (1964) in Church House, Harborne, Birmingham.

[Roy McKay, *John Leonard Wilson, Confessor for the Faith*, 1973; A. Sutcliffe and R. Smith, *Birmingham, 1939–1970*, 1974; personal knowledge.]   J. C. H. TOMPKINS

WILSON, WILLIAM (1875–1965), physicist, was born 1 March 1875 at Goody Hills, near the village of Mawbray on the Solway coast of Cumberland, the eldest in the family of seven sons and four daughters of W. O. Wilson, a farmer, and his wife, Isabella Ewart. His ancestors for some generations had also been farmers. His education began in the village school of Holme St. Cuthbert where he had a master of outstanding ability, John Routledge. Although his reading at that time was mainly in scientific literature, his intention was to take up a career in agriculture. He gained the Longcake scholarship of £40 a year for three years when he was not quite fourteen years of age, and went to the Agricultural College at Aspatria, West Cumberland, as a weekly boarder.

He became a fellow of the Highland and Agricultural Society at the age of seventeen and was awarded a studentship at the Royal College of Science in London when he was eighteen (1893). Here he was exclusively confined to agricultural studies and allied subjects, such as geology, in which he was particularly interested, but he found the mathematical courses dull and, for him, a waste of time. However, he studied mathematics privately in the museum library. The most valuable part of his studies appears to have been the lectures on astronomy by (Sir) J. Norman Lockyer and Alfred Fowler [qq.v.] and the lectures on physics by Arthur Rücker and William Watson. Unfortunately he was unable to attend sufficient lectures to qualify for the associateship and he spent the autumn of 1895 ploughing in the Lowenghyll behind a pair of horses.

The first few posts held by Wilson were not encouraging for a future professor of mathematical physics. He left the Royal College of Science in 1896 without a degree and took a teaching post at a Towcester school. In 1898 he became a mathematics master at Beccles College in Suffolk, and later at Craven College in Highgate.

During this period he determined to study in a German university and, to this end, he taught in the Berlitz School of Languages at Elberfeld, and at branches of the school in Dortmund, Münster, Barmen, and Cologne. This experience enabled him to matriculate and enrol as a student of mathematics in the university of Leipzig in 1902, where he studied under Carl Neumann and Otto Weiner. His earliest research work was an experimental study of the photoelectric effect, for which he was awarded the degree of doctor of philosophy, *summa cum laude* (1906). While at Leipzig he met his future wife, Rose Blanche Lucy, the daughter of Henry Heathfield of Stoke Canon in Devon. They married in 1909 and later had one son, W. F. H. F. Wilson, who subsequently practised as a solicitor in Hereford.

On his return from Germany in 1906 he was appointed an assistant lecturer in the Wheatstone Laboratory at King's College, London, under Professor H. A. Wilson. He continued his work on the emission of electrons from hot bodies until 1917, but his interests began to move towards the new theoretical developments in the theory of relativity and the quantum theory.

His studies of Hamiltonian mechanics under Carl Neumann had prepared him to appreciate the quantum theory of spectra introduced by Niels Bohr and to put forward a considerable generalization of the quantum conditions. Wilson's famous formulae, $\int p_i dq_i = n_i h$ were published in the *Philosophical Magazine* in 1915 and 1916, and, encouraged by J. W. Nicholson (who was then professor of mathematics in King's College), he applied these formulae to the elliptic orbits of the hydrogen atom.

The same results were made shortly afterwards, and independently, by Professor Sommerfeld. In 1922 Wilson generalized his earlier formulae by modifying the mechanical momentum p_i by adding the electromagnetic momentum eA_i, where e is the electronic charge and A_i a component of the electromagnetic vector potential. This result is the foundation of the quantum theory of the emission and absorption of radiation. In 1917 Wilson was awarded the degree of D.Sc. in the university of London.

In 1920 Wilson was appointed to a readership in the physics department of King's College and in 1921 to the Hildred Carlile chair of physics at Bedford College, London. His later writings were on the relation between the general theory of relativity and wave mechanics, but his most important contribution to science in this period was a three-volume work, *Theoretical Physics* (1931-40), which embodies many original and profound insights. Wilson was elected FRS in 1923. He retired in 1944 and died at home in Hereford 14 October 1965.

Wilson was a tall, broad-shouldered man with large brown moustaches. He walked and moved with a striking and unusual manner, almost as if he were one of the original 'Three Musketeers' about to draw and flourish a rapier. His bright and piercing eyes would shine with enthusiasm as he expounded his scientific theories. He ever conveyed an immense vitality and friendliness. He was patient and sympathetic and always ready to find time to elucidate difficulties.

There is a portrait in oils by an unknown artist, in the possession of the family, which depicts Wilson at the age of eighteen.

[G. Temple and H. T. Flint in *Biographical Memoirs of Fellows of the Royal Society*, vol. xiii, 1967; private information; personal knowledge.] G. TEMPLE

WINSTEDT, SIR RICHARD OLOF (1878-1966), Malayan civil servant and Malay scholar, was born in North Parade, Oxford, 2 August 1878, the son of a naturalized Swede, Isaac Olof Winstedt, tailor and outfitter, and his wife, Sarah Mary Castell who belonged to an old-established Oxford family. He seems later to have changed the spelling of his second name to Olaf. His younger brother Eric became a don. Winstedt was educated at Magdalen College School and New College, Oxford. Goitre barred him from athletics. After getting a second in honour moderations (1899) and *literae humaniores* (1901) and taking the Civil Service

examination, he was in 1902 appointed to the Federated Malay States Civil Service (later to be merged into the Malayan Civil Service) and was posted to Perak, a state which had come under British protection only twenty-eight years previously and in which he was to spend ten years. With encouragement from the British resident, Sir Ernest Birch, and his secretary, R. J. Wilkinson, a distinguished Malay scholar, Winstedt made himself familiar with the charming and interesting Malay people and wrote four books in a government-published series called 'Papers on Malay Subjects' covering respectively *Folk Literature* (1907); *The Circumstances of Malay Life* (1909); *Arts and Crafts* (1909); and *Fishing, Hunting and Trapping* (1911). Of these subjects folk literature was the one which was to engage his interest most.

A little later, in collaboration with A. J. Sturrock, Winstedt went on to publish four Malay texts collected from an old traditional story-teller named Pawang Ana; a collection of farcical tales from other Perak story-tellers; and some articles in the *Journal* of the Straits Branch (later Malayan Branch) of the Royal Asiatic Society, a publication to which he was to contribute many times in the course of his life. At this point Winstedt fell ill and was for a long time in a primitive hospital cut off from all books of reference except a few Malay classics which he found it an amusement to parse and analyse. On release from hospital he obtained his first home leave and took his notes to Europe for consultation with the established authorities, most of whom were Dutch. The result was the publication in 1913 of Winstedt's *Malay Grammar* which established his reputation as a scholar. He returned to Malaya and was appointed district officer in Kuala Pilah, an interesting district which contained the court of the Yangdipertuan Besar of the Negri Sembilan and also five little states which followed the local version of Minangkabau matrilineal law. He studied customary law, published more texts and, with Wilkinson, a collection of Malay quatrains (*Pantun Melayu*, 1914); and also carried his language work further in writing *Colloquial Malay: a simple grammar with conversations* (1916) and *An English-Malay Dictionary* (3 vols., 1914-17).

In 1916 Winstedt, one of whose appointments in Perak had been as inspector of schools, returned to the education department, and was stationed in Singapore for fifteen years. His first title was assistant director of education, Straits Settlements and Federated Malay States, and his task was to improve the existing system of education in Malay. He visited Java and the Philippines to study educational systems there and later submitted a report which resulted in 1922 in the closing of two older teacher-training colleges and the founding of the Sultan Idris Training College at Tanjong Malim. Attached to this college was the Malay Translation Bureau, designed not only to prepare textbooks but also to provide literature for the graduates of schools which taught only in Malay. Through the College and the Bureau Winstedt was later able not only to improve school education but also to guide the development of the language to cope with modern needs. The education he introduced was based on the traditional values and virtues of Malay rural life. Since the independence of Malaya he has been attacked for failing to try to direct Malay attitudes towards economic competition with the Chinese and Indians of Malaya, but there are two sides to this question.

Winstedt's sojourn in Singapore led to one of his most productive periods of spare-time writing. In 1920 alone he published two books—*A Dictionary of Colloquial Malay* and a Malay text—and no fewer than twenty-three articles covering history, folklore, ethnology, philosophy, literature, and bibliography. He obtained his D.Litt., Oxford, in that year. In 1921 he started a ten-year period as first president of Raffles College, Singapore, an institution which, with the King Edward VII College of Medicine, was to grow into the University of Malaya. From 1924 to 1931 he was director of education, Straits Settlements and Federated Malay States, and a member of the Legislative Council of the Straits Settlements. In 1925 he published *Shaman, Saiva and Sufi*, a study of the evolution of Malay magic. In 1926 he was appointed CMG. In 1931 he was promoted to be general adviser to the Unfederated State of Johore, an appointment which he held for the last four years of his service in Malaya. This seems to have stimulated his interest in history and, in addition to many shorter writings, he published *A Malay History of Riau and Johore* (Raja Haji Ali's *Tuhfat al-Nafis*—Malay text with English summary, JMBRAS 1932); his own original *History of Johore 1365–1895* (JMBRAS 1932); histories of Selangor and Negri Sembilan (both JMBRAS 1934), and *The History of Malaya* (JMBRAS 1935).

In 1935 Winstedt retired from the Malayan Civil Service and was appointed KBE. He then took up an appointment as lecturer in Malay at the School of Oriental Studies, university of London. In 1937 he was promoted to a readership which he held until he retired in 1946, having been elected FBA the previous year.

London brought Winstedt into contact with original Malay manuscripts, especially those in the Raffles Collection of the Royal Asiatic Society. In 1938 he published in the JMBRAS a romanized and annotated text of the Raffles manuscript of the *Malay Annals* which differed in important respects from versions previously published, and opened up interesting possibilities. The following year he published in the JMBRAS *A History of Malay Literature* which co-ordinated the research of a lifetime in this field. Then came the war and its aftermath. During the Japanese occupation of Malaya Winstedt's Malay language broadcasts helped to keep hope alive in that country; and just after the re-occupation his letter to *The Times* written in conjunction with Sir Cecil Clementi and Sir Frank Swettenham (both of whose notices he contributed to this Dictionary) led to the reversal of the British Government's Malayan Union policy and the institution of a federal government which was to guide Malaya to independence twelve years later.

Between 1947 and his death nineteen years later Winstedt published *The Malays—a Cultural History* (Singapore, 1947), six new dictionaries, several new editions of his more important books, and many articles and reviews. In 1951 he received an honorary LLD from the university of Malaya. During the last years of his life he devoted himself wholeheartedly to the service of the Royal Asiatic Society of which he was either director or president from 1940 to 1964 and a regular voluntary helper even after that. His eighty-fifth birthday was honoured with no fewer than three *Festschriften*. His great contribution to scholarship has been the unearthing and fostering of the cultural heritage of the Malays of Malaya, but he has left later scholars to deal with his subjects in greater detail. The total number of his publications was over 340.

In 1921 Winstedt married Dr Sara Mary Josephine O'Flynn (died 1972), of the Malayan Medical Service, the daughter of a wool-miller of county Carlow. There were no children. Winstedt died in Putney 2 June 1966. The Royal Asiatic Society has a bust by Dora Gordine.

[John Bastin, 'Sir Richard Winstedt and his Writings' in *Malayan and Indonesian Studies, Essays presented to Sir Richard Winstedt on his 85th birthday*, ed. J. Bastin and R. Roolvink, 1964; private information; personal knowledge.]   E. C. G. BARRETT

WINSTER, BARON (1885–1961), politician. [See FLETCHER, REGINALD THOMAS HERBERT.]

WINTERTON, sixth EARL, and BARON TURNOUR (1883–1962), politician. [See TURNOUR, EDWARD.]

WOLFIT, SIR DONALD (1902–1968), actor-manager, was born 20 April 1902 in New Balderton, near Newark, the fourth of the five children of William Pearce Woolfitt, brewer's clerk, and his wife, Emma Tomlinson. He was educated at Magnus School, Newark. From an early age he wanted passionately to be an actor; after a very short, frustrating burst of school-mastering, which he disliked almost as much as being at school, in 1920 he managed to join Charles Doran's touring company. From his eighteenth year he had a complete grounding in the plays of Shakespeare and the touring theatre of the time, from the humblest role as assistant stage manager. It proved invaluable. He played walking-on parts and some of the smallest parts in the great plays. He left Doran to play the small part of Armand St. Just in the autumn tour of *The Scarlet Pimpernel* with Fred Terry [q.v.]. He had cherished an ambition to appear with this management since he first attended a performance at Nottingham in his early teens, and after several unsuccessful interviews with Terry he achieved it in 1923. The Terrys represented the theatre of which he had dreamed; the splendour of the sets and costumes, the assurance and the style of the actors would be remembered and reproduced when Wolfit himself was to appear as Sir Percy.

Matheson Lang [q.v.] gave Wolfit his first chance to appear in London in *The Wandering Jew* in 1924; nearly thirty years later he re-created the leading part under his own manage-ment. After several more years out of London, he was engaged to play good parts at the Old Vic in 1929–30: Touchstone, Cassius, and the King in *Hamlet*. But the season was an unhappy one for him: he never succeeded in disguising his disapproval of actors he did not like personally and in this company he always felt he was on the outside. He was not asked to stay on for another season. In 1930–5 he appeared in plays in the West End and on tour, including for Sir Barry Jackson [q.v.] a tour of Canada in 1931–2, nearly always in good parts in a great variety of plays, among them *She Stoops to Conquer*, *The Barretts of Wimpole Street*, and new plays. His longest run, over fourteen months, was in the highly successful *Richard of Bordeaux* in which he played Thomas Mowbray to (Sir) John Gielgud's Richard; during this he was able to plan his first managerial venture, the Newark drama week, in his home town in 1934.

Wolfit's two seasons at Stratford in 1936 and 1937 brought him much critical acclaim. It was the first time he had been really stretched as an actor, playing good leading parts, and it made him even more determined to save enough money to go into management to tour the plays of Shakespeare. This he managed to do in 1937, and a nine-week tour followed the end of the Stratford season, with many of the actors who had been with him in the company. He added Shylock and Macbeth to Hamlet and Malvolio

which he had already played, and at the end of the tour he was less than £100 out of pocket, which encouraged him enough to plan another for 1938. In January of that year he first appeared as Volpone—one of the parts which suited him best and which he relished playing. For the autumn tour he engaged Rosalinde Fuller as his leading lady, and added *Othello*, *Much Ado about Nothing*, and *Romeo and Juliet*, playing all the plays 'in repertoire' so as to mix in the comedy with the dramatic fare. It was during these early seasons that the younger members of his company grew to recognize the effect the parts he was playing had on his backstage personality; full of laughter for Benedick and Touchstone, jokes were in order during the on-stage dances; but they must be a great deal more careful when *Othello* was played, and *Macbeth* night would see them scuttling out of the way of the wrath to come.

During the summer of 1939 Wolfit took a small permanent company to Dublin, and then asked various 'star' names, who were also friends, to go over for special weeks. After the great success of these plays, several in costume but no Shakespeare, he was again planning his autumn tour when war was declared, and although his leading lady, Rosalinde Fuller, was in America, and only after three separate attempts finally reached England, the tour opened in Brighton. On all sides he was told that Shakespeare in wartime, in the blackout, would spell disaster; he approached every theatre in London, until finally his first West End season opened at the Kingsway in 1940. Although fairly short and not a financial success, it did lead to his season of 'Scenes from Shakespeare' being done at the Strand during the lunch hour. It was during this run that all his scenery and costumes, which were in store, were bombed and completely destroyed. He had also joined the Home Guard at Frensham in early 1940 and managed to combine both activities. By 1941, against all the odds, he had formed a company and was on tour again, and for the first time many people who had never dreamt of going to the theatre, especially Shakespeare, were going and finding it exciting. In this year he added a very good Richard III, and returned to the Strand for the winter and spring. Now came his first attempt at King Lear, not yet exactly as he wanted it, but ever since his first season at Stratford (when he played Kent) he was deter-mined to make it his own, and later in his career he called it 'the brightest jewel in my crown'. His season at the Scala theatre in 1944 brought high praise from the critics, not his habitual supporters, and especially from James Agate [q.v.] for his Lear, but it was forced to close prematurely as the 'doodlebug' attacks on London emptied the theatres. Undaunted, he returned to touring, which included a tour to Cairo and Alexandria, for ENSA, where they celebrated VE day.

Immediately after the war Wolfit embarked on his usual tour of the British Isles, and a season at the Winter Garden in London. His life as actor-manager covered more than twenty-five years. Now his leading lady was always Rosalind Iden. He was disappointed that there was no immediate reward for his war service 'Shakespeare for the masses'. He took a highly successful company to Canada in 1947, and followed it with a visit to New York. His post-war career was largely spent touring until, in 1951, he was invited by (Sir) Tyrone Guthrie to appear at the Old Vic in four spectacular leading parts. He opened the autumn season with Marlowe's *Tamburlaine the Great*, directed by Guthrie. It was a tremendous success, and the critics heaped his performance with praise. Sadly from all points of view this state of affairs did not last. During the four weeks he became impossible to act with, resorting to every tiresome trick on-stage, and even sending notes on their performances to his colleagues. After the Old Vic they paid a visit to Stratford, and here it was found necessary to send for Guthrie, unknown to Wolfit, for him to see what had happened to his production. He was appalled to see the travesty of what had been a magnificent *tour de force*, and spoke forcefully to his leading man. Soon after, Wolfit claimed breach of contract by the governors, and never returned to the Old Vic.

In 1953, coronation year, he presented an excellent series of classical plays at the King's, Hammersmith, with an unusually strong supporting cast; exceptionally well reviewed were his performances as Oedipus. He finished the year with a splendid Captain Hook in *Peter Pan*. For the next year he did little until he found a play, *The Strong are Lonely*, which suited him, and in 1955 was to be his last major production as actor-manager, in London. The last ten years of his life he really enjoyed away from the theatre and allowed himself, at last, to rest a little, without the urge to drive himself and all those round him, ever more on tour. His last appearance on the stage was as Mr Barrett in *Robert and Elizabeth*, with song, when he took over from (Sir) John Clements in 1966-7.

Wolfit never really enjoyed filming, although he gave some excellent performances towards the end of his career, notably in *Room at the Top*, *Becket*, and just before he died as Dr Fagan in *Decline and Fall*.

He was thrice married: first in 1928 to Chris Frances Castor; they had a daughter, Margaret Wolfit, the actress; secondly, in 1934 to Susan Katherine Anthony; they had a son and a daughter; finally in 1948 and for the rest of his life, to his leading lady of long standing, Rosalind Iden, daughter of Ben Iden Payne.

Wolfit was appointed CBE in 1950 and knighted in 1957, the only actor then living to have been twice honoured. He died in London 17 February 1968.

A portrait by Stanhope Forbes is privately owned; Another, by Michael Noakes, hangs in the offices of the Royal General Theatrical Fund.

[Donald Wolfit, *First Interval*, 1954; Ronald Harwood, *Sir Donald Wolfit*, 1971.]

BRIAN MCIRVINE

WOLMARK, ALFRED AARON (1877-1961), painter and decorative artist, was born in Warsaw 28 December 1877, the eldest of the family of four sons and one daughter of Levy and Gitel Wolmark. The Wolmarks, like many other Central European Jewish families, were forced by continuous persecution to leave Poland and they came to London during the 1880s—1883 has frequently been quoted but a date nearer to 1888 seems more likely. The first extant document relating to the artist is his naturalization certificate filled in by his father and sworn by him at the Worship Street police court in the East End of London on 1 January 1894. This document gives the family's residence as 65 Hanbury Street, Spitalfields; Wolmark's forename is given simply as Aaron, and it is probable that he adopted the English name of Alfred at a slightly later date. No record exists of his early education which would have taken place within the Jewish community both in Warsaw and Spitalfields; clearly his aptitude for drawing was brought to the notice of the authorities and he entered the Royal Academy Schools in 1895 where he studied for three years, winning a silver medal for figure drawing in December 1896.

Whilst at the RA Schools he was befriended by Anna Wilmersdoerffer, and it was through her influence that he received several portrait commissions; the financial assistance of the Wilmersdoerffer family also enabled him to return to Poland in 1903, where he executed several important works based on Jewish historical subjects, such as Rabbi Ben Ezra inspired by Browning's poem. These subject paintings are strongly influenced in technique by his studies of Rembrandt, the only artist to whom he had a lifelong devotion, but in his more spontaneous works he was already beginning to lighten his palette. During the next few years his palette continued to lighten, but it was not until he saw the important exhibition, 'Manet and the Post-Impressionists' organized by Roger E. Fry [q.v.] at the Grafton Galleries during the winter of 1910-11, that the full impact of modern French painting was revealed to him.

On 11 July 1911 he married Bessie Leah Tapper, the daughter of Russo-Polish Jewish parents from the East End. They were to have two sons and one daughter. They set off for an extended honeymoon in Concarneau, where Wolmark painted many studies of Breton fisherfolk and harbour life. This series of paintings executed in bright flat areas of heavily applied pigment reduced his subject-matter to its simplest form and led on to the geometric still lives painted immediately after his return to London. The years 1911 to 1915 saw Wolmark at the height of his powers; in addition to painting he turned his hand to the decoration of pots, which he covered in strongly coloured aggressively geometric designs. Interior decoration, the theatre, and stained glass also occupied him at this time. His window for St. Mary's Church, Slough (1915) was probably the most daring piece of modern glass in England. Even the frames he designed for his paintings did not escape his decorative urge, being not only painted, but, at times, covered with geometric collage of patterned wall-papers. His closest associate at this stage was Henri Gaudier-Brzeska (1891-1915), the French artist who had settled in London.

Wolmark despised Bohemianism, and, although he liked to play the part of an artist, especially when frequenting the Café Royal, it was through the elaboration of his dress rather than its disregard that he wished people to be aware of his profession. Passed as medically unfit for military service in 1915, he spent the war years in England. In 1919 he went to New York, where one of his brothers was living, and painted a series of cityscapes; these paintings were shown at the Kevorkian Galleries, New York, in 1920, and mark the last phase of his contribution to *avant-garde* British painting. During the ensuing decades he felt himself increasingly out of touch with the modern movement, and settled down to paint landscapes and figure subjects in a highly personal, expressionistic manner; he also did some teaching, not in art schools but rather in the manner of the old masters taking pupils to work in his studio. In 1928 he held an exhibition at the Lefèvre Galleries of portrait drawings of well-known contemporaries including Israel Zangwill [q.v.], whose complete works he had illustrated for the Globe Publishing Co. three years previously. During his life he held many exhibitions in London, New York, and Paris. An exhibition at the Leicester Galleries in 1948 commemorated his seventieth birthday.

He died in London 6 January 1961. A memorial exhibition of his work was held at the Ben Uri Art Gallery, London, during September and October that year; Wolmark had been one of the prime movers in the setting up of the Ben Uri Art Society in 1915, which did so much to foster artistic awareness among East End Jewry.

There is a massive plaster head of Wolmark by Henri Gaudier-Brzeska which captures his air of self-confidence, tinged with arrogance; the floppy bow-tie and flowing hair hint at the subject's dandified appearance. Bronze casts of this head are in the museums of Southampton, Liverpool, and Birmingham. In the National Portrait Gallery is a self-portrait (1926).

[Personal papers; private information.]

PEYTON SKIPWITH

WOOD, SIR ROBERT STANFORD (1886-1963), educationist, was born in Islington, London, 5 July 1886, the younger son of the Revd John Roskruge Wood, Baptist minister, by his wife, Frances Ann Wren. He was educated at the City of London School and Jesus College, Cambridge, where he was a classical scholar; he obtained first class honours in part i of the classical tripos (1908) and second class honours in part ii of the historical tripos (1909). After two years of teaching, mainly at Nottingham High School for Boys and much activity among Rover Scouts as a commissioner, which led to his being awarded the Scout medal of merit, he entered the Board of Education in 1911 as an inspector of schools. Subsequently he rose to a variety of important posts: principal private secretary to the president of the Board, Lord Eustace Percy (later Lord Percy of Newcastle, q.v.), in 1926-8; director of establishments (1928-36); and principal assistant secretary for technical education (1936-40).

It was in this last capacity that he first came into contact with the small University College of Southampton with which he was afterwards to be associated. The college was experiencing difficulty in raising funds for the new buildings needed for both its university work and the large amount of technical teaching it carried out (there being at that time no Southampton Technical College). Wood attended a conference in 1936 between representatives of the College Council, Board of Education, University Grants Committee, Southampton Borough Council, and Hampshire County Council, and it was largely due to his lucidity of exposition and fertility in suggestions that it was decided that the two local authorities should make increased contributions towards the cost of new buildings.

In 1938 Wood was seconded for special service with Sir John Anderson (later Viscount Waverley, q.v.), then lord privy seal and later home secretary, to whom he was of great assistance in work relating to home security during the war which presently broke out. In 1940 Wood returned to the Board of Education as deputy secretary, an appointment which he held for six years. When the Board's staff moved almost *en bloc* to Bournemouth in October 1940 Wood was left with a few colleagues to advise the president and conduct essential business in London. The advent of R. A. Butler (later Lord Butler of Saffron Walden) to the presidency ushered in a period of great activity in policy making, and it was on Wood that the main responsibility for this fell at a moment when new prospects were opening for technical education, since the Board's staff had previously concentrated on schools and few of its officers were qualified to plan for a world in which science and technology would count for more than the humanities. Wood had already appreciated the need for a new approach when head of the technical branch and had thrown himself into the work involved in planning this, realizing the need for systematic schemes of further education which would provide all areas with facilities ranging from full-time courses of university standing to evening classes and adult work. He was largely responsible for the section on further education in the white paper of 1943, outlining the Government's educational proposals, on which the Education Act of 1944 was based.

After this Act the Board became the Ministry of Education, and it was generally expected that Wood would shortly become its permanent secretary, but the change of government which took place in 1945 prevented this, to his considerable disappointment. Another important sphere of usefulness, however, soon presented itself. On the retirement in 1946 of K. H. Vickers [q.v.], principal of the University College of Southampton, its governors felt that Wood's great experience of dealing with men and affairs and his almost magical ability to find solutions for difficulties made him the ideal man to lead the college to university status, a task which he accepted and accomplished in five years.

Wood threw himself into the work of providing new buildings and equipment, although the building programme had to be carried through not only in the face of the usual post-war difficulties but in a town already fully extended in an effort to replace thousands of houses, port and industrial buildings destroyed during the war. In particular, he continued his predecessor's cherished policy of providing halls of residence for students, having as one of the main objects of his principalship that the university should be a body of scholars leading a communal life. In conjunction with (Dame) Lillian Penson [q.v.], vice-chancellor of Lon-

don University (for whose external degrees Southampton students were then prepared), he conceived the idea of applying the scheme of 'special relationship' with the university of London which was then being developed in connection with the new colonial universities to the University College of Southampton also. This special arrangement became operative in 1950 and worked so well that in response to a petition a university charter was granted to Southampton in 1952. Wood became the first vice-chancellor but retired on grounds of age at the end of the session.

Another major development during Wood's period of office was the establishment of an Institute of Education with a circle of affiliated training colleges, leading to the systemization of teacher training in the area.

In his short stay of six years in Southampton Wood made a deep impression on the life of the university, the town, and the county of Hampshire. His experience as a prominent civil servant enabled him to contribute much to the efficiency of the university, whose numbers almost doubled during this period; he raised very considerable funds for its development and established close contact with the educational authorities of both Southampton and Hampshire. A classic example of the right man in the right place at the right time, he was also a most congenial colleague with a great sense of humour and unfailing courtesy to all alike.

He was appointed CB in 1939 and KBE in 1941, and was made an honorary fellow of Jesus College in 1952, a distinction he greatly prized, and also an honorary member of the Goldsmiths' Company of London. In 1955 he visited Palestine and Iraq to lecture on British universities for the British Council.

In 1922 Wood married Iris Cecilie, daughter of Frederick Arnsby, piano manufacturer; they had one daughter. He died in London 18 May 1963. Southampton University has a portrait by C. Rogers.

[*The Times*, and *Daily Telegraph*, 22 May 1963; private information; personal knowledge.]   A. TEMPLE PATTERSON

WOODS, DONALD DEVEREUX (1912-1964), chemical microbiologist, was born at Ipswich 16 February 1912, the elder son of Walter James Woods, builder and decorator of Ipswich, and his wife, Violet Mabel Cobb. Woods was educated at Northgate School, Ipswich, and became a scholar at Trinity Hall, Cambridge, graduating in 1933 with first class honours in parts i (1932) and ii (1933) of the natural sciences tripos. He remained at Cambridge with a Beit memorial fellowship and took his Ph.D. in 1937. From 1933 to 1939 he worked in association with Dr Marjory Stephenson [q.v.] at Cambridge and under her influence became interested in the metabolic processes of bacteria. In 1939 he joined the Medical Research Council's unit for bacterial chemistry as a Halley-Stewart research fellow, working at the Middlesex Hospital, London. From 1940-6 he was engaged in 'war work' at the Chemical Defence Research Establishment at Porton. At the end of that period he became reader in chemical microbiology in the biochemistry department of the university of Oxford under Professor (Sir) Rudolph A. Peters, and in 1951 he became a fellow of Trinity College, Oxford. He was elected a fellow of the Royal Society in 1952. In 1955 he was appointed to the first chair in chemical microbiology in the United Kingdom, the Iveagh professorship endowed by Arthur Guinness, Son & Company.

Woods's major impact on his science was made in a paper (published during 1940) which was prepared when he was working in the unit directed by (Sir) Paul Fildes. At that time the sulphonamide drugs had become established as the first really effective chemotherapeutic agents for use against bacterial infections. Fildes's group was concerned with the substances essential for the growth of pathogenic bacteria and one of their lines of attack was to analyse animal and vegetable extracts for the essential components. Sulphanilamide was known to inhibit bacterial growth quantitatively and the inhibition was prevented, also quantitatively, by extracts of yeast and other organisms. Woods set out to determine the nature of the anti-sulphanilamide factor in yeast extracts and, within four months, had shown that it was p-aminobenzoic acid. Woods had been trained at Cambridge as a biochemist and, recognizing the similarity of the chemical structures of p-aminobenzoic acid and sulphanilamide molecules, he suggested that the drug could be acting as an inhibitor of an enzyme bringing about some essential metabolism of p-aminobenzoic acid. The idea rapidly received support by extracts of p-aminobenzoic acid in various biological complexes and the demonstration that it formed part of the molecule of folic acid, a substance essential to the functioning of a variety of enzymes important in biosynthetic reactions.

This demonstration by Woods that a chemical analogue of an 'essential metabolite' could become a useful drug appeared to open up a direct approach to the rational development of chemotherapeutic agents by structural modification of other metabolites. Woods was unable to follow this approach himself since he was engaged, for the next six years, in 'war work'. During this period others confirmed the accuracy of his predictions although it was many

years before any 'metabolite analogues' which were effective for the clinical treatment of infections were discovered—mainly because the nature of the selective action of sulphanilamide was not understood at this time and the majority of analogues proved to be non-selective *in vivo*.

When Woods returned to academic life in 1946, p-aminobenzoic acid had been established as the biosynthetic precursor of folic acid and he devoted much of the rest of his research career to elucidating the nature and functions of folic acid in its various forms. During this time, a series of young research workers worked under his guidance and many of these later became leading investigators in other laboratories and universities. Woods was a dedicated teacher and had a gift not only of exposition but also of being able to enlist and maintain the interest of a large number of collaborators, young and old. In 1953 he delivered the first Marjory Stephenson memorial lecture to the Society for General Microbiology and this lecture provides a delightful account both of his work at that time and his approach to the problems of chemical microbiology. He was invited to give the Leeuwenhoek lecture to the Royal Society in 1964 but died at Oxford 6 November 1964 before he could deliver it.

Woods married in 1939 Alison Lillian, daughter of George William Halls, agricultural engineer. There was one daughter of this happy marriage.

[D. D. Woods in *Journal of General Microbiology*, vol. ix, 1953; Ernest F. Gale and Paul Fildes in *Biographical Memoirs of Fellows of the Royal Society*, vol. xi, 1961; private information; personal knowledge.]

E. F. GALE

WOODS, SIR JOHN HAROLD EDMUND (1895-1962), civil servant, was born in Kensington 20 April 1895, the elder son of John Henry Woods and his wife, Annie Alker, both of whom came from Wigan. His father, a gentle, cherubic, scholarly man, had been a wrangler of Peterhouse and spent a few years as mathematical coach at Jimmies before seeking ordination. He was vicar of the dock parish of St. Mark's in South Shields (1909-24) and rector of Glaston, Uppingham (1924-44).

Invariably known as John Henry, Woods was educated at Christ's Hospital where he won classical and other prizes and was captain of rugger, cricket, and fives. In 1912 he became senior Grecian and thus captain of the school, a post to which he was reappointed for a second year. He subsequently became a governor of the school.

In 1913 Woods gained a Williams exhibition to Balliol College, Oxford, but preferred to go straight from school into the army in 1914 when he was gazetted lieutenant in the 22nd battalion, Royal Fusiliers. In 1916 he was very severely wounded in the leg. Invalided out in 1918, he went up to Balliol, and in July 1920 sat for the Civil Service entrance examination before taking his finals. He came out second, and was posted to the Treasury. He was delighted when the MA he had thus missed was given him by the university of Oxford by decree in 1948.

Thus, in his early days, Woods surmounted the severity of his war wounds. Later they were to involve him in forty-five surgical operations, with long periods in hospital; and daily, a major sterilizing job of cleaning and plugging a huge hole in the leg, as regularly as shaving. He could play his beloved cricket, his leg protected by pads, provided he had a runner; and could manage 18 holes of golf. He was a solid figure, but his stick was always in his hand. His conquest of his disability, and the stalwart courage and humour with which he lived his life were essential parts of his lovable and towering personality. The single leisure pursuit with which his injury did not interfere was his listening to good music, of which he was passionately fond. Friendly and indeed gentle, he was a good listener and always had a keen and delightful sense of fun. Perhaps in his early years at the Treasury he yearned for constructive problems rather than the somewhat negative control of expenditure. He went to the Imperial Defence College in 1928, and in 1929 was lent for six months as assistant private secretary to the Prince of Wales. He was appointed MVO in 1930.

Returning to the Treasury, he was given important special assignments. The first of these was to deal with the provision of government credit for employment, giving work such as the building of the new Cunarders. The second was the secretaryship of the Trade Facilities Act advisory committee. In 1931 he was appointed private secretary to Philip (later Viscount) Snowden [q.v.] who was then chancellor of the Exchequer and later lord privy seal. In 1936 Woods became principal private secretary to the chancellor of the Exchequer, Neville Chamberlain, and in 1937-40 to his successor Sir John (later Viscount) Simon [q.v.].

In 1940 Woods, now a principal assistant secretary at the Treasury, was made responsible for the control of expenditure on defence material, and for formulating Treasury policy on the pricing of munitions contracts. This work brought him into close association with the director-general of army requirements (Sir) Robert Sinclair (later Lord Sinclair of Cleeve). In 1943 Sinclair was appointed chief executive at the Ministry of Production, where he was joined by Woods as permanent secretary. This alliance continued through the short life of the caretaker Government of 1945, when Sinclair and Woods moved to the Board of Trade, again under Oliver Lyttelton (later Viscount Chandos).

Within a few months, the post-war election brought to the Board of Trade Sir Stafford Cripps [q.v.], a key man in the new Labour Government. Despite their very different temperaments and habits of work, there quickly grew up between Cripps and Woods the same sort of personal confidence based on deep respect and wise advice that had characterized Woods's relationship with three chancellors. But the work was gruelling, and Woods's problems with his wound had been aggravated by an accident which entailed the loss of an eye. In 1938 the staff of the Board had numbered 2,400, now it was 15,000, with a huge diversity of responsibilities in an era still dominated by controls. Woods inspired the confidence and respect of his senior staff by rigorously delegating responsibility for day-to-day work while remaining firmly in control of important policy developments. Nevertheless the burden of ensuring that the policies of the many different parts of the Board were kept in step was extremely heavy; the risk was, as Woods found, that the Board could hardly advance at all. As he said in a lecture to the Institution of Public Administration, 'Things that ought to happen do not happen while we are making sure that nobody will be upset if they do happen'.

This sort of pressure was not in any way lessened when in 1947 Cripps was replaced by (Sir) Harold Wilson. There can be no doubt that the unremitting overload of work told on Woods's reserves of strength, yet he was called on more and more to undertake special tasks. From 1947 he was a member of the Economic Planning Board. He maintained a close liaison with the Federation of British Industries, whose president and director-general had been colleagues in the Ministry of Production, and, briefly, in the Board of Trade. He spoke pungently and wittily at their export conference in 1946.

Woods gave much thought to the ways of unscrambling the tangle of controls, for he greatly feared that public service would be permanently weakened by the weight and complexity of the bureaucratic machine. The alternative of voluntary methods came in for scrutiny (with the background of their success in the temporary limitation of dividends). At a week-end conference about these problems at New College, Oxford, he observed that voluntaryism sounded to him like the occupational disease of a church organist—an intervention which was very typical of his way of lowering the temperature of a heated debate.

His deep concern with the administrative burden and its probable consequences to departmental efficiency made him an ideal choice as chairman of a Treasury organization committee in 1950, which examined not only the distribution of responsibilities, but also the way the Treasury set about its business.

But this was just one more addition to the incessant overwork, and the effect on his health became well-nigh intolerable. Early in 1951 Woods decided that he must retire from the Civil Service, although only fifty-six; he accepted the invitation of his friend Sir George Nelson (later Lord Nelson of Stafford, q.v.), chairman of the English Electric Company, to join his board as an executive director. Thereafter he played an important part in the expansion of the company's business overseas, and on their behalf he had a close association with the Marconi and other companies.

With the extremes of pressure removed, Woods was able to take on a host of less harassing activities which he wanted to do. First among these, as a devout Christian, he would have put the commitment he felt towards the Church of England. The hard work he put in to helping the archbishops was a great deal more than his obligations as a member of the Central Board of Finance.

Other appointments he felt he should accept as a public duty included membership of the National Institute of Economic and Social Research (president 1952); the committee on the Churchill Falls Power Development, Canada, in 1952; the advisory committee on the Revolving Fund for Industry in 1953; the Waverley Committee on atomic energy in the same year. In 1954 with his friend Sir Harry (later Lord) Pilkington and Sir Maurice Holmes he conducted at high speed the inquiry into the administrative and disciplinary consequences of the Crichel Down affair, and in 1957-9 was a member of the Radcliffe Committee on the monetary system. He was a director of Sadler's Wells Trust Ltd.; a visiting fellow of Nuffield College; a governor of the Administrative Staff College; treasurer of the British School at Rome. He also devoted much time and interest to the William Temple College at Rugby.

In 1930 Woods married Molly, daughter of Noah Henry Baker, of Southgate, who was senior clerk of works, Police Architect and Surveyor's Department, Scotland Yard. They enjoyed a very happy and full married life; they had one son and one daughter.

Woods was appointed CB (1943), KCB (1945), and GCB (1949). In 1962 the ill health which had dogged him since 1916 finally forced him into a wheelchair and the virtual end of his active life, and he died at Haywards Heath 2 December 1962.

[Private information; personal knowledge.]
NORMAN KIPPING

WOOLDRIDGE, SIDNEY WILLIAM (1900-1963), geomorphologist, was born 16 November 1900 at Hornsey, son of Lewis William Wooldridge, bank manager, and his wife, Helen Chadwick. He was educated at Glendale County School, Wood Green. In 1918 he entered King's College, London, to read geology and graduated in 1921 with first class honours. By this time his boyhood interests in exploring the Hertfordshire countryside had flowered into serious study of the Tertiary and Pleistocene deposits of his home area and his first publication appeared in 1921. He joined the staff of the department of geology and geography at King's College: he was awarded the M.Sc. in 1923 and the D.Sc. in 1927. In 1923 he took an active part in the formation of the Weald research committee of the Geologists' Association, thus revealing his interest in a region with which his name was to become very closely associated. In 1928 he received a grant from the Daniel Pidgeon Fund of the Geological Society to assist work on the glaciation of the London Basin, and until about 1930 his research interests were primarily geological, especially into the stratigraphy and structure of the London Basin and the Weald.

From this time onwards he began to acquire his immense reputation as a geomorphologist. He had become lecturer in geography and geology at King's College in 1927 and his teaching and research were directed towards problems of the evolution of land forms. Although laboratory methods continued to play a part in his work, through brilliant observations in the field he contributed greatly both to the study of the development of the land forms of south-eastern England and to the establishment of geomorphology as a scientific field of study in Britain. Wooldridge found a stimulus in the ideas advanced in 1895 by W. M. Davis in explaining the character of the Wealden drainage and in company with a number of fellow workers he prepared a succession of papers throwing new light on both the structure and the erosional history of the Weald. The Weald became a type area for British geomorphology. He established a chronology for south-eastern England based on a series of erosion surfaces at successively lower levels from the summit peneplain at 700 to 900 feet down to the flood plains of the present-day streams, and postulated correlations with upland surfaces elsewhere in Britain. He also elucidated the evidence for the lower Pleistocene (Calabrian) marine transgression in south-east

England. In the now classic *Structure, Surface and Drainage in South-east England* (1939), written with his collaborator D. L. Linton, he reviewed the findings of a phase of work which was of major significance to geomorphology.

To his geomorphological work was added a deep interest in the study of human occupancy of terrain. Especially important was his study of the progress of Saxon settlement upon the loam terrains of south-eastern England. He examined a number of phases in the historical geography of the Weald. At all times he was emphatic that geographical study must be firmly based on the study of the physical environment: in particular, the human geography of south-east England reflected the long course of the preparatory processes whose story he had so brilliantly unravelled.

Wooldridge was also concerned with the practical relevance of his geomorphological work. He criticized the Greater London Plan, 1944, on the grounds of its inadequate relation to the physical geography of the region. He carried out a number of studies of land use problems. As a member of the Waters committee on sand and gravel resources, established in 1946, he contributed his highly detailed knowledge of the superficial deposits especially of south-eastern England. For this work he was appointed CBE in 1954.

In 1942 Wooldridge was promoted to a readership in the university of London. He served during the war years in the Observer Corps. In 1944 he became professor of geography at Birkbeck College where he spent three happy years before returning to King's College as professor of geography in 1947. He had become by this time one of the commanding figures in British geography, a reputation enhanced by his high ability as a teacher, especially in the field. He never tired of leading his students in the search for field evidence, training the 'eye for country' to which he attached so much importance. He had the gift of bringing a landscape to life. It was his passion to bring to young and old the joy which comes from discovering some new fact of landscape history and from fitting it into a developing pattern of scientific knowledge. His classroom lectures were clear and forceful, often provocative. His *Physical Basis of Geography, an Outline of Geomorphology* (with R. S. Morgan), first published in 1937, was a clear exposition of geomorphological principles and became a standard textbook. He loved argument on scientific matters. His students carried his ideas, particularly on field teaching, to other universities and the flowering of British geomorphology in the years after the war of 1939–45 reflected his work.

Wooldridge was married in 1934 to Edith Mary Stephens, herself a teacher of geography, and his colleagues, students, and friends enjoyed visits to their home at Finchley. He lived a most active physical and intellectual life. In addition to his love of walking he played cricket and golf. He was founder president of the Geoids Amateur Operatic Society founded in 1930 with colleagues and students from the geology and geography departments at King's College, London, and the London School of Economics. On stage, he was an impressive Mikado. He gave much of his spare time to the Working Men's College at Camden Town. He was a pioneer in the work of the Council for Field Studies finding, for many years as its chairman, a practical way of expressing his passionate belief in field observation. He also gave his service to Sir John Cass College, to Wye College, and, as chairman of the committee of management, to the Institute of Archaeology of the university of London. He read deeply on theological subjects and, as an active member of the Congregational Church, was in demand as a lay preacher.

He received in 1932 the Foulerton award of the Geologists' Association of which he became an honorary member in 1962; the Geological Society of London gave him the Lyell Fund award in 1936. In 1942 he shared the Murchison grant of the Royal Geographical Society with his fellow worker D. L. Linton. He received the society's Victoria medal in 1957. He was made a fellow of King's College, London, in 1956; was elected FRS in 1959, and in 1960 to the New York Academy of Sciences. He was president of the Institute of British Geographers in 1949–50; of Section E of the British Association for the Advancement of Science in 1950; of the Geographical Association in 1954. In that year he was stricken by illness from which he made a characteristically determined though not a fully complete recovery. He died in London 25 April 1963.

[*The Times*, 27 April, 2 and 8 May 1963; J. H. Taylor in *Biographical Memoirs of Fellows of the Royal Society*, vol. x, 1964; *Geographical Journal*, September 1963; *Geography*, July 1963; *Nature*, 8 June 1963; *Transactions* of the Institute of British Geographers, June 1964; private information; personal knowledge.]   M. J. WISE

WOOLF, LEONARD SIDNEY (1880–1969), author, publisher, and political worker, was born 25 November 1880 in Kensington, the second son of Sidney Woolf, QC, and his wife, Marie de Jongh, both members of the Reformed Synagogue. Sidney Woolf died in 1892, leaving a widow, nine children, and just enough money to enable the sons with the help of scholarships to receive a good education. Woolf was a scholar, first at St. Paul's, then at Trinity College, Cambridge, where he obtained a first class in part i (1902) and a second in part ii (1903) of the classical tripos. He met and was much influenced by G. E. Moore (whose notice he contributed to this Dictionary); Lytton Strachey, Maynard (later Lord) Keynes [qq.v.], and Saxon Sydney-Turner were friends and contemporaries; all of them were Apostles.

Woolf entered the Colonial Service and was posted in 1904 to Ceylon where he very soon showed a capacity for intelligent industry. By 1908 he was assistant government agent in charge of the Hambantota district of the Southern Province and there can be no doubt that he might have risen high in the service. Returning to England on leave in 1911 he found the Cambridge circle of his youth very much extended and already becoming known as 'Bloomsbury'. It included Virginia, a daughter of Sir Leslie Stephen [q.v.]. In 1912 Woolf left the Colonial Service (concerning which he now had political doubts) in order to marry her. At the time of their marriage both Leonard and Virginia Woolf [q.v.] were writing novels. His, *The Village in the Jungle*, was published in 1913; it was followed by *The Wise Virgins* (1914). In 1913 Woolf became a socialist and joined the Fabian Society; he took a special interest in the Co-operative Movement; this led to some political journalism and later to *Co-operation and the Future of Industry* (1919) and *Socialism and Co-operation* (1921). Woolf's political and literary activities were hampered by his wife's precarious mental balance. She had a major breakdown in 1913-14 and again in 1915; in each case recovery was very slow. Until her death her husband did not cease carefully and constantly to act as her monitor and her physician.

Exempted, on medical grounds, from national service, Woolf turned during the war of 1914-18 to the study of international relations and of colonialism. His book *International Government* (1916) formed one of the bases for the British proposals for a League of Nations; in 1920 he published a devastating analysis of imperialist greed: *Empire and Commerce in Africa*. He was editor of the *International Review* in 1919 and of the international section of the *Contemporary Review* in 1920-1. In 1919 he became honorary secretary of the Labour Party's advisory committees on international and imperial affairs; in 1922 he stood unsuccessfully for Parliament as Labour candidate for the Combined Universities.

His wife's health kept Woolf away from London for long periods until 1924. From 1912 he lived at Asham House in Sussex, moving in 1919 to Monks House, Rodmell; but from 1915 until 1924, when they moved to Tavistock Square, they were able to take Hogarth House, Richmond. It was there that the Hogarth Press, beginning in 1917 as a hobby, became one of the most remarkable publishing houses of the time; E. M. Forster, T. S. Eliot, Katherine Mansfield [qq.v.], Freud, Gorki, Maynard Keynes, and the Woolfs themselves were amongst its authors. Woolf spared neither himself nor others in his efforts to make it a success; it became one of the main passions of his life.

Nevertheless he found time to become joint editor of the *Political Quarterly* (1931-59) and literary editor (1959-62). He was also (1923-30) literary editor of the *Nation* and served on the board after it amalgamated with the *New Statesman* in 1931. He wrote *Imperialism and Civilization* (1928), *The Intelligent Man's Way to Prevent War* (1933), *Quack, Quack!* (1935), *Barbarians at the Gate* (1939), and *The War for Peace* (1940). He also attempted a systematic statement of socialism as he understood it in *After the Deluge* (vol. i, 1931, vol. ii, 1939), but these volumes, although they were received with respect, did not excite enthusiasm and, after *Principia Politica* (1953), he made no further attempt to elaborate a complete political philosophy.

The war of 1939-45 was not only the shipwreck of Woolf's hopes for the establishment of international sanity, it also ended his long struggle to preserve his wife from harm; she drowned herself in 1941. He was, however, a man of remarkable physical and moral resilience. He continued to work for the Hogarth Press and for the Labour Party; greatly helped by the sympathy of devoted friends, he rebuilt his life and achieved an extremely happy old age. Living increasingly at Monks House he cultivated his garden and wrote five autobiographical volumes: *Sowing* (1960), *Growing* (1961), *Beginning Again* (1964), *Downhill all the Way* (1967), and *The Journey not the Arrival Matters* (1969). These volumes which, with *The Village in the Jungle*, are likely to prove the most enduring of his works, reveal a very attractive character: highly moral but humorous and tolerant, austerely sceptical but gently humane. Fair, but very forceful in argument he could be convincing when he addressed himself to the intellect rather than to the passions; he exerted considerable influence on others, notably Arthur Henderson, Lord Robert Cecil (Viscount Cecil of Chelwood) [qq.v.] and Philip (later Lord) Noel-Baker. Politically he was prescient and acute in his judgements; but his impatience with stupidity or frivolity, together with a fierce honesty of character, made him an indifferent propagandist. He was a superb organizer and had an organizer's love of detail;

he was happy to serve his party in ward meetings; he was clerk of his parish; he combined high generosity with scrupulous exactitude in money matters. He declined a CH but accepted an honorary doctorate from the university of Sussex in 1964. He died at Monks House 14 August 1969.

A portrait of Woolf by his sister-in-law, Vanessa Bell [q.v.], hangs in the National Portrait Gallery, where there is also a bronze head by Charlotte Hewer. There is another portrait by Trekkie Ritchie (coll. the artist) and a bust by Charlotte Evans is at Monks House.

[Duncan Wilson, *Leonard Woolf: A Political Biography*, 1979; Woolf's own writings; Woolf archive, university of Sussex; private information; personal knowledge.]

QUENTIN BELL

WOOLTON, first EARL OF (1883-1964), politician and businessman. [See MARQUIS, FREDERICK JAMES.]

WORBOYS, SIR WALTER JOHN (1900-1969), industrialist and promoter of good design in industry, was born at Cottesloe, Western Australia, 22 February 1900, the eldest child of Walter Worboys, engineer, by his wife, Amanda Urquhart. He was educated at Scotch College and the university of Western Australia where he graduated in chemistry and geology. He proceeded as a Rhodes scholar to Lincoln College, Oxford, where his supervisor was Nevil Sidgwick [q.v.], and gained his D.Phil. in chemistry in 1925. He then joined Synthetic Ammonia & Nitrates Ltd., a subsidiary of Brunner, Mond & Co., as a research chemist at Billingham and devoted himself to the production of synthetic nitrogen and fertilizers, then in an early stage of development. Brunner, Mond became one of the founder constituents of Imperial Chemical Industries with which company Worboys remained until he retired as commercial director in 1959. During his later years with the chemical industry he carried a full share of its burdens. He was chairman of the Association of British Chemical Manufacturers in 1953-6 and president in 1957-9. He was a member of council of the Society of the Chemical Industry in 1955-8 and gold medallist in 1957, and became a fellow of the Royal Institute of Chemistry in that year.

Worboys's interest in industrial design, always active, was greatly stimulated by his service as chairman of the ICI plastics division from 1942 until 1948 when he became a director of ICI. This was a material lending itself with equal facility to good or bad design. Worboys resolved to exploit the good and to discourage the bad and he employed designers to serve both

aims. Worboys joined the Council of Industrial Design in 1947 and in 1953-60 was its chairman. The Council, started by the Board of Trade in 1944 to encourage good design as a necessary feature of the post-war export drive, had never enjoyed an easy life. There were those who felt that good design could best be determined by market forces, others who saw in any attempt to influence design the hand of government interference. The Council in its early days had perhaps more critics than friends. When Worboys became chairman he decided, probably on the strength of his experience with the Festival of Britain of 1951 in which he took an active part, that if the Council was to make its mark there was an overwhelming need for a permanent exhibition gallery in London. Such a project meant much greater government support. The fact that this support was provided on a pound for pound basis with industry was Worboys's special achievement and his success was due, not only to his enthusiasm and driving force, but also to his ability to convince Whitehall that under his guidance the Council and its Design Centre (as the permanent exhibition was to be called) would develop on sound and productive lines.

In the event, the Design Centre went from strength to strength. Not the least impressive aspect was that it fulfilled the bold and original conception that manufacturers could be persuaded to pay for space on which the goods shown would be selected by another body. The formation of the Design Centre was a turning-point in the fortunes of the Council of Industrial Design. In a world where much that is ugly is created daily, the work of the Council has shone like a good deed in a naughty world. As Sir Gordon Russell, former director of the Council and Worboys's close partner in its work, wrote: 'When the history of the revolt against ugliness comes to be written, it will be seen how important was the work of a very small group of top-ranking businessmen after the last war. Of these Walter Worboys was a natural leader' (*The Times*, 21 March 1969).

Worboys's concern with industry, with design, and with the arts made a clear bond with the Royal Society of Arts. He became a fellow of the Society in 1949, was awarded the bicentenary medal in 1956, and elected a member of its council in 1961. In 1967 he became chairman of council, a post he held until his death.

Some ten years remained to Worboys after he left Imperial Chemical Industries and into this period he compressed a new career. In 1960 he became chairman of BTR Industries and started a much needed programme of modernization and reorganization which contributed a great deal to the subsequent growth and strength of the company. In 1965 the Westminster Bank, of which he was a director, persuaded him to accept the formidable responsibility of chairing the British Printing Corporation whose affairs were then at a low ebb. He held both these posts until his death, and they constituted a heavy burden. During this period Worboys began to undertake new commitments in the educational field. Early in the fifties he had become a governor of Radley College and in 1962 he became chairman of the governing council of Roedean School. Worboys also played a notable part in the great university developments of the sixties by serving as a member of the academic advisory committee for the university of East Anglia and as chairman of the corresponding body for Brunel University. He presided over the government committee on road traffic signs set up in 1961 with results which may be seen in every main road in the land.

In appearance Worboys always seemed active, fit, and alert. He was a man of distinction, endowed with the eye at once of the administrator, the artist, the scholar, and the man of affairs. To all his many activities he brought a sense of style. He set exacting standards, both of behaviour and performance, and with these standards there could be no compromise. His manner could vary from warmth to severity according to need and his tolerance for the imperfect was limited, but at heart he was a most kindly man. He was essentially a man of his times. Justly described in the company's house journal as one of the architects of the modern ICI, he was equally at home in the City, in Whitehall, and in the arts. He accomplished much and the burden it placed on his daily life was cheerfully borne. He found his pleasures in his family, his work, in the arts, and in his country home. His appointment as an honorary fellow of Lincoln College in 1957 gave him especial satisfaction. He was knighted in 1958 and received an honorary doctorate from Brunel University in 1967.

In 1927 Worboys married Ethelwynne Bessie (Betty), daughter of Henry Lavers, an Australian mining engineer; they had one son and one daughter. Worboys died at his London home 17 March 1969. A bronze head of him by Arthur Fleischman is in the possession of the family.

[Sir Gordon Russell, *Designer's Trade*, 1968; ICI; private information; personal knowledge.]   M. J. DEAN

WORDIE, SIR JAMES MANN (1889-1962), polar explorer and scholar, was born 26 April 1889 at Partick, Lanarkshire, the youngest son of John Wordie, carting contractor, and his wife, Jane Catherine Mann. He was a first cousin of Sir James Mann [q.v.]. He was educated at Glasgow Academy and the university where he obtained his B.Sc. with honours and distinction in geology in 1910. He went as an advanced student to St. John's College, Cambridge, reading for part ii of the natural sciences tripos (geology) through which he graduated in 1912. He then began research work in geology. In 1913 the Harkness scholarship in geology was awarded to him, and in 1914 he was appointed university demonstrator in petrology, an office he held until 1917 and again from 1919 to 1923. His work brought him into touch with geologists such as Frank Debenham [q.v.] and (Sir) Raymond Priestley, returned from the second expedition of Captain Scott [q.v.]. These contacts strengthened an interest in Arctic and Antarctic exploration and scientific discovery, already awakened by reading books on travel and mountaineering in his father's library and by working with J. W. Gregory [q.v.].

In 1914 Wordie joined the Antarctic expedition of Sir Ernest Shackleton [q.v.] as geologist and chief of the scientific staff, and so served under a distinguished explorer whom he always acknowledged as his master. The expedition proved arduous and perilous in the extreme. Wordie himself spent a year in *Endurance* drifting 'beset and sinking' in the Weddell Sea; a period of discomfort and danger at Ocean Camp; and a winter marooned on Elephant Island while Shackleton made his epic voyage to South Georgia for help. Wordie ably played his part in maintaining the morale of the expedition; and in spite of its failure to fulfil its exploratory intentions and in spite of the rigours he had undergone, ·brought back important geological specimens and useful observations on oceanography and on the polar ice pack.

Wordie returned in 1917 to a country at war, joined the Royal Artillery, and saw service in France. On his demobilization, the polar regions called him back: in 1919, and again in 1920 he went to Spitsbergen as geologist and second-in-command of the Scottish Spitsbergen expedition under W. S. Bruce [q.v.]. In 1921 he was elected into a fellowship at St. John's College, Cambridge, and henceforward made the college, and Cambridge more generally, the base from which to set out on a long series of Arctic and Antarctic expeditions. He went to Jan Mayen and East Greenland in 1921, 1923, 1926, and 1929 (in the former he made the first ascent of Beerenberg, for he was a dedicated mountaineer); to north-west Greenland, Ellesmere Island, and Baffin Island in 1934 and 1937. The war of 1939-45 put a stop to further polar exploration, but throughout it (indeed from 1923 to 1949) Wordie served on the *Discovery* committee of the Colonial Office which advised on the oceanographical work undertaken by *Discovery I* and *II*, while from 1937 to 1955 he was chairman of the committee of management of the Scott Polar Research Institute in Cambridge of which he was a founder-member.

The young explorer under Shackleton, the leader of expeditions which introduced many young men, notably Gino Watkins [q.v.] and (Sir) Vivian Fuchs, to the polar world, had become the elder statesman of Arctic and Antarctic exploration whose advice was widely sought and always influential. During the war he served for a time as director of the Cambridge sub-centre of the Naval Intelligence Division. His knowledge of local conditions was invaluable to the planning of Operation TABARIN, whose objective was the maintenance of British claims to Graham Land and adjacent territories. This grew into the Falkland Islands Dependencies Survey, whose advisory scientific committee sat under his chairmanship. So it was that, in 1947, Wordie was in polar latitudes for the last time, visiting South Orkney and South Shetland as well as Graham Land. But in his role of elder statesman of polar exploration he continued to be influential, as deputy chairman advising Fuchs when the Trans-Antarctic Expedition was being planned and as chairman of the British national committee for the International Geophysical Year (1954-8). He was also chairman of the British Mountaineering Council (1953-6). He is commemorated by the Wordie Glacier in Graham Land and the Wordie Crag in Spitsbergen.

Closely bound up with Wordie's interests in polar exploration was his service to the Royal Geographical Society. He was a fellow from 1921 and became a member of the council in the following year. He was honorary secretary for no less than fourteen years, from 1934 to 1948, which spanned the difficult war period. After a time as foreign secretary, he was president of the society, from 1951 to 1954, and in that capacity he welcomed back the expedition under Sir John (later Lord) Hunt which made the first ascent of Mount Everest; he became the first chairman of the Mount Everest Foundation.

Wordie's third great absorbing interest was St. John's College, Cambridge, to which he was devoted. He was elected a fellow in 1921 and appointed a tutor in 1923. From 1921 until 1952 (with intermissions) he was director of studies in geography. In 1933 he became senior tutor, an office which he held with that of president from 1950 until (perhaps rather to his surprise) he was elected master in 1952. He held the mastership until 1959, when his health had already begun to fail. As a tutor, Wordie showed himself, though shy, an excellent judge of men, and brought his remarkable memory to bear on

them, their affairs, and their family connections with unfailing accuracy. His filing system seemed, too, to depend on memory, for his large table was littered with papers from which he never failed to extract the document required. As an elder statesman and eventually master, his shrewdness and instinctively accurate judgement of people served the college well; and the college benefited also from the affection he generated in his pupils. As a committee man he was apt to be better at deciding on a line of action (usually the right one) than at justifying it in argument.

Wordie gained the Back grant of the Royal Geographical Society in 1920 and its Founder's gold medal in 1933; the Bruce medal of the Royal Society of Edinburgh (1926); the gold medal of the Royal Scottish Geographical Society (1944); and the Daly medal of the American Geographical Society (1952). He received honorary degrees from the universities of Glasgow and Hull, was an honorary fellow of Trinity College, Dublin, and was a commander of the Order of St. Olaf of Norway. He was appointed CBE in 1947 and knighted in 1957.

In 1923 Wordie married Gertrude (died 1971), daughter of G. T. Henderson; they had three sons and two daughters. He died in Cambridge 16 January 1962. There is a portrait (1954) by Rodrigo Moynihan in St. John's College, Cambridge.

['Exploration's Elder Statesman', in the *New Scientist*, 5 December 1957; *The Times*, 17 January 1962; *Geographical Journal*, March 1962; *The Eagle*, June 1962; personal knowledge.]   B. H. FARMER

WORMALL, ARTHUR (1900-1964), biochemist, was born 17 January 1900 in Leeds, the second child in the family of two sons and two daughters of James William Wormall, a printer and lithographer, and his wife, Anne Phillis. He entered the Boys' Modern School, Leeds, and at seventeen was awarded a senior city scholarship to Leeds University where he read for the honours B.Sc. degree in chemistry under Professor J. B. Cohen. He served in the university Officers' Training Corps and joined the Royal Air Force in 1918. The sudden end to the 1914-18 war in November allowed him to resume his degree course without any serious delay and at the same time become engaged in his first research problem. He was also able to take up a junior appointment as demonstrator in biochemistry in the department of physiology and biochemistry at Leeds. Wormall remained at Leeds University for the next fourteen years and became lecturer (1926) and senior lecturer (1933). He was awarded the degree of D.Sc. in 1930. In June 1928 he was elected to a Rockefeller medical research fellowship and chose to work for about a year with Karl Landsteiner at the Rockefeller Institute in New York and then at the Marine Biological Station, Woods Hole, Massachusetts.

After his return to England Wormall accepted an appointment from the Colonial Office to visit Uganda to investigate some special aspects of sleeping sickness. He returned to Leeds on completing this assignment and became involved in an exacting and heavy teaching load in the physiology department. Nevertheless it was at this time that Wormall made several valuable contributions to the clarification of the nature of serum complement in terms of chemistry of the reactive components and this work stimulated many of the numerous investigations by others on this subject. He enjoyed an increasing reputation as an able investigator in immunochemistry. During this period at Leeds he also became especially interested in the action of mustard gas (di-2-chloroethyl sulphide) and related vesicants on tissue constituents.

In 1936 he was appointed the first professor of biochemistry at St. Bartholomew's Hospital Medical College, London, where he spent much time launching a new department; he remained professor of biochemistry at the Medical School for the rest of his life. As early as 1936 Wormall considered the possibility of using isotopic tracers and he must be recognized as a pioneer worker on this important aspect of immunochemistry. With the outbreak of war in 1939 Wormall moved his department from London to Cambridge where he was accommodated in the Sir William Dunn Institute of Biochemistry. Difficulties resulting from this move, and the heavy academic responsibilities both in London and Cambridge, considerably reduced the amount of his research, but with the cessation of hostilities Wormall and his colleagues returned to London and resumed the task of developing the use of radioactive tracers in immunological investigations.

The development in London University of a B.Sc. (special honours) degree course at the time of his return, together with an extensive reorganization of his own department of biochemistry, occupied much of Wormall's time and he frequently regretted the amount of his energy that had to be given to these and other activities rather than to the research themes of special interest to him. There can be no doubt, however, about the excellent advice he gave to the Board of Governors and College Council — in particular that concerning the purchase of land for future expansion of St. Bartholomew's Hospital. In 1949 Wormall and G. E. Francis organized a course on the use of stable isotopes in biological investigations, the first of its kind

in the United Kingdom, a great success and continued annually for fifteen years. As a result of this special activity, in 1952 Wormall was invited by the university of São Paulo, Brazil, to organize the first Latin-American course in radioisotopes. His efforts, which resulted in a most valuable course, were recognized in 1953 by the conferment on him of a doctorate *honoris causa*.

Although always a busy man, Wormall was never too occupied to give of his time to those who asked for aid. In spite of failing health and long periods in hospital, he remained cheerful and full of hope. In December 1955 he suffered a cerebral thrombosis which kept him away from his work for nearly a year. After a brief return to the department he had a further stroke in April 1962 and from then on he was completely paralysed until he died in St. Bartholomew's Hospital 9 May 1964.

As a Yorkshireman and therefore a cricketer he was probably as pleased by his election to the MCC as he was by his election to the Royal Society, both in 1956. He was immensely proud of his family (in 1925 he had married Eva Jackson) and of his two daughters, whom he missed very deeply when they both married and went to live in the United States. Wormall was a much loved and a highly respected colleague and his large circle of friends was due to his own kindliness and courtesy.

[W. T. J. Morgan and G. E. Francis in *Biographical Memoirs of Fellows of the Royal Society*, vol. xii, 1966.] W. T. J. MORGAN

WORRELL, SIR FRANK MORTIMER MAGLINNE (1924-1967), cricketer, was born at Bridgetown, Barbados, 1 August 1924, the son of Athelston Worrell, mechanical engineer, and was educated at the Combermere School. His first played for the island as a slow left-arm bowler at the age of seventeen, but his batting, in which he was right-handed, developed so rapidly that in 1942-3 he scored his first century, 188 against Trinidad, and in the following season he played the highest innings of his career: 308 not out in an unbroken partnership of 502 with J. D. Goddard. This was a world record for the fourth wicket until he and C. L. Walcott surpassed it two seasons later with an unbroken 574, again against Trinidad, Worrell making 255 not out.

In 1947 Worrell left Barbados for Jamaica and his international career began against the English tourists in 1947-8. He made 294 in three tests, and his 131 not out at Georgetown was the first of his nine test centuries.

In 1948 Worrell began a long and happy association with Radcliffe in the Central Lancashire League, his aggregate of 1,694 in 1951 being a record for the competition. With an eye to the future Worrell took his BA (Admin.) in 1959 at Manchester University.

With many international players taking part, the northern leagues were a stern academy of cricket and Worrell gained valuable experience of English conditions. He learned to play on wickets of varying pace, and he quickened his bowling, relying now on swerve rather· than spin. Thus he was well equipped to take his place in the touring team of 1950 which after losing the first test won the remaining three and became the first West Indies team to win a rubber in England. With his lithe elegance he was perhaps the outstanding batsman in this talented side. He headed the test averages with 539 runs at 89.83, and on the tour he made 1,775 at 68.26, with six centuries, as well as taking 39 wickets. His 261 at Nottingham was then the highest individual score by either country in a test in England, while his stand of 283 for the fourth wicket with E. D. Weekes was the highest test partnership for the West Indies in any part of the world.

In Australia in 1951–2 the West Indies could not repeat their English success. Worrell, with only 337 in ten test innings, was not the only batsman to be unhappy against the Australians' frequent bumpers, although he made 108 at Melbourne, batting almost one-handed after an injury. With the disappointment of their high expectations the side's morale collapsed, there was frequent dissension and they lost four of the five tests. But it was Worrell's most successful series as a bowler, his 17 wickets including 6 for 38 at Adelaide in the only test the West Indies won.

Home series against India, England, and Australia were not years of abundance for Worrell, but he recovered his form when the West Indies came to England in 1957. He easily headed the tour averages with 1,470 runs at 58.80, and his four centuries included a masterly 191 not out in the Nottingham test, when he batted right through the innings. He also took seven wickets in the England innings at Leeds. But the tour was a disappointment for the team, whose confidence characteristically disintegrated after the first test slipped from their grasp when they had seemed certain to win it. They were then beaten three times by an innings.

Because of injuries Worrell captained the side in the last four matches of the tour, and he showed qualities of leadership which led, after various internal struggles, to his appointment as captain in Australia in 1960–1. A remarkable series began with the first tie in the history of test cricket, and although the West Indies eventually lost by two matches to one, the result would have been reversed if two vital decisions had not gone against them. Although personally Worrell had only a moderate tour, his side fulfilled his promise that they would bring back to cricket the spirit of adventure. They were fêted in Australia as victors rather than vanquished, and the Worrell Trophy was instituted to commemorate the Brisbane tie.

Worrell fought his last campaign when he led the West Indies in England in 1963. This was another eventful rubber which the West Indies won 3–1 after a dramatic drawn game at Lord's. Worrell did not do much with the bat, but his 74 not out in 95 minutes at Manchester, with 15 fours, recalled the player he had been in his vintage years.

At the end of the tour he announced his retirement, but he managed the side that defeated the visiting Australians in 1965 and made the West Indies unofficial world champions. In his career he made 15,025 runs at 54.24, with 39 centuries, and took 349 wickets at 29.03. In 51 tests, 25 against England, he made 3,860 at 49.48 and took 69 wickets at 38.73. But although in his prime he was a great batsman, correct but uninhibited, with a free swing whose delicacy concealed its power, statistics do not measure his contribution to the game. It was he who disciplined the West Indies into an organized force in international cricket. The cultural and ethnic differences of the scattered Caribbean islands had made earlier teams unpredictable and at times uncontrollable. Their resolution was easily weakened by disappointment, and insular rivalries had a divisive effect. But under a relaxed and easy manner Worrell inspired his men with his own strength of character and breadth of outlook. His firmness, which at need could be ruthless, prevented the psychological deterioration which had destroyed the tourists of 1951 and 1957, and he welded a team of talented but erratic and temperamental players into the finest in the world. In so doing he raised the status and self-respect of the coloured cricketer.

A lover of England and a true federalist, Worrell was knighted in 1964. He was warden of Irvine Hall (Kingston) (1961–4), then dean of students, Trinidad, of the university of the West Indies. He had a seat in the Jamaican senate (1962–4). He died of leukaemia at Kingston 13 March 1967, and his body was taken to Barbados, where he had bought land for his eventual retirement. A memorial service was held at Westminster Abbey.

In 1948 Worrell married a fellow Barbadian, Velda Elaine, daughter of Mervyn Brewster, photographer; they had one daughter.

[Christopher Nicole, *West Indian Cricket*, 1957; C. L. R. James, *Beyond a Boundary*, 1963; *Wisden's Cricketers' Almanack*, 1968.]

M. M. REESE

WORTHINGTON, SIR HUBERT (1886–1963), architect, was born 4 July 1886 at Broomfield, Alderley Edge, Cheshire, the youngest son of Thomas Worthington, of Manchester, and his second wife, Edith Emma Swanwick. His father was a well-known architect, a friend and adviser of Florence Nightingale [q.v.], and a designer of a number of fine buildings, of which the Albert Memorial and the Minshull Street Courts in Manchester are among the best known. The family firm of Thomas Worthington & Son was carried on after his death by (Sir) Percy S. Worthington [q.v.], a son by his first marriage who was later to receive the Royal gold medal for architecture, and then by Hubert Worthington. In this way the firm had the remarkable record of spanning, in only two generations, and with a consistent standard of excellence, the years 1849 to 1963.

Hubert, who was the youngest of Thomas's eleven children, was educated at Sedbergh School and Manchester University. He achieved an early ambition in life when he met (Sir) Edwin Lutyens [q.v.] in Rome and was allowed to join his office in 1912–13. His career was interrupted by war service and in July 1916 he was seriously wounded when serving with the 16th Manchester Regiment in France. In the extensive period of convalescence which followed, his role as an instructor of infantry cadets gave him an enthusiasm for teaching that was carried on in his post-war lectures at the RIBA and at the universities of Liverpool and Manchester. In 1923 he was appointed professor of architecture at the Royal College of Art. Concurrent with his teaching duties, which he fulfilled with his own personal brand of exuberant scholarship, he practised with the family firm, receiving commissions from his old school at Sedbergh for the war memorial cloister, which he designed in the Lutyens manner, and for the dining-hall at Rossall School.

In 1928 he left the Royal College of Art to return to the family practice and to take up the Slade lectureship in architecture at Oxford in 1929. It was at Oxford, with his design for the new wing of the Radcliffe Science Library, that his work reached the maturity and the certainty of touch which he was to practise for the remainder of his career. Followed by the Garden Buildings at Merton College, the library for New College, the remodelling of the Old Bodleian Library, together with the St. Catherine's Society building, his work demonstrated his own ideal of buildings which were logical, harmonious, and well composed. Apart from work at Oxford, he designed a new series of buildings for Talbot Heath School at Bournemouth, a new boarding house at Eton College, and a number of private houses, the most successful of which is probably Sutton Close, near Dartmouth, designed for Sir Frank Fletcher [q.v.], headmaster of Charterhouse.

With the death in 1939 of his brother, with whom Worthington had worked on numerous projects in Manchester both for the university and the hospital authorities, and with the onset of World War II, a new series of problems had to be faced, but it was the damage caused by the war which led to the work which was to give him his most testing architectural opportunities. There was first the cathedral in his native city of Manchester to resuscitate, a task which he carried on in company with his wife, who had joined the office in 1941. She was Joan, the daughter of Dr S. M. Banham, of Northiam, and they married in 1929, after she had completed her course under Worthington's guidance at the Royal College of Art. They had a son and two daughters. The end-product of their work was a sensitive contribution to the fabric in the Gothic style, carried out with a high quality of workmanship which was the result of their discussions with the craftsmen during their daily visits to the site whenever they were in Manchester.

Equally important was the restoration and rebuilding of the Inner Temple where, alongside work designed by his close friend (Sir) Edward Maufe, Worthington brought back to life the architecture of that fine but sadly damaged part of London. He was also concerned with other war-damaged buildings in London: at Westminster School, the Merchant Taylors' Hall, and the Brewers' Hall. All these buildings demonstrate how Worthington's own particular style of detailing and design enabled him to recapture the spirit of what had gone before, without his having to depart from the grammar he had established for himself early in his career. Equally consistent was his post-war work at Oxford: the new School of Forestry, the School of Botany, the gatehouse at Trinity College, the Besse Building at Pembroke College, and the remodelled Radcliffe Camera. With his appointment as principal architect for North Africa and Egypt for the Commonwealth War Graves Commission, he prepared designs for memorials to the missing at El Alamein, Malta, and Medjes el Bab in Tunisia which, phrased as they were in simple regional variations on his own basic design theme, showed a great sympathy and respect for both spiritual and architectural values. He also worked on designs at Imperial College, London, the Institute of Science and Technology at Manchester University, where the formal staircase is named after him, and the dining-hall at Roedean School where his wife and daughter had been educated.

He had a constant and impish wit which enlivened every meeting he attended. His was a most happy family life and he also enjoyed the regard of a wide circle of friends drawn from all age groups and walks of life, who respected his ideals of sanity, masculinity, and humanity. With Lutyens, Sir Giles Gilbert Scott [qq.v.], and Maufe, he belonged to the end of an era, which was rapidly being overtaken by the modern movement at the time of his death. He said that great architecture should never be forced. It is perhaps the most fundamental quality of his work that he never overreached himself in what he did, but, with a sound grasp of design, a loving eye for detail, and an innate feeling for materials, he ennobled the last days of the neo-classical movement with buildings which were in the best traditions of English architecture. To this Dictionary he contributed the notice of William Curtis Green.

He was appointed OBE in 1929 and knighted in 1949. He was elected ARA in 1945 and RA in 1955. He was a member of the Royal Fine Art Commission from 1945 to 1950 and was the president of the Manchester Society of Architects and a vice-president of the Royal Institute of British Architects. He died in Manchester 26 July 1963.

A memorial window is placed in the regimental chapel at Manchester Cathedral, and a portrait in pastels by William Dring (1956) is in the possession of his family.

[RIBA *Journal*, October 1963; *Builder*, 2 August 1963; *Architectural Review*, January 1977; private information; personal knowledge.]   JOHN SEWARD

WRENCH, SIR (JOHN) EVELYN (LESLIE) (1882–1966), founder of the Royal Over-Seas League and the English-Speaking Union, was born at Brookeborough, county Fermanagh, Ireland, 29 October 1882, the younger son of Frederick Stringer Wrench, of Killacoona, Killiney, county Dublin. His father became one of the Irish land commissioners; his mother, Charlotte Mary, was the third daughter of Sir Alan Edward Bellingham, third baronet, of Castle Bellingham, county Louth.

Wrench was educated at Summer Fields, Oxford, and at Eton, where he was remembered for his kindness towards new boys, and as the best-looking boy in the school. On leaving at sixteen, he travelled on the Continent to learn languages with the idea of entering the diplomatic service. He noticed the lead which the Continent had over Great Britain in the production of picture postcards, and on his return instituted a firm which soon became the largest of its kind in the country. This occupied him from 1900 until 1904 when the firm failed, mainly through too rapid an expansion and lack of capital. This venture, entered into when he was only eighteen, indicated the enterprising spirit which Wrench possessed and its failure in no way lowered his reputation.

The future Lord Northcliffe [q.v.] had observed Wrench's qualities and invited him to join his staff, which he did in 1904. He was editor of the *Overseas Daily Mail* (1904–12) and in addition manager of the export department of the Amalgamated Press from 1907 and sales manager from 1909. Wrench, however, was less interested in success in journalism than in his visions of Commonwealth development awakened by his visits to Canada and the United States. Passionately longing to make a more personal contribution to the unity of Empire, he formed in 1910 the Over-Seas Club. He put his full enthusiasm and energies into this; resigned his newspaper appointments in 1912; and embarked upon a visit to the dominions in 1912–13.

The Club made rapid progress and during the war of 1914–18 its contribution included the Empire Fund to provide tobacco for the forces. It worked in conjunction with the Patriotic League of Britons Overseas, with which it amalgamated in 1918; in 1923 the society was granted a royal charter and became the Over-Seas League.

In 1917 Wrench joined the Royal Flying Corps; he reached the rank of major and served as principal private secretary to Lord Rothermere [q.v.] when air minister, and later as his deputy when controller for the dominions and United States at the Ministry of Information. As a result of his experience in this last appointment Wrench founded in 1918 the English-Speaking Union, which shortly afterwards absorbed the Atlantic Union. A twin organization, the English-Speaking Union of the United States, was formed in 1920.

For many years between the wars Wrench acted as secretary of the Over-Seas League and as editor of the League's journal *Over-Seas* in which his 'Monthly Letter' was enjoyed by many as an informal summary of the previous month's events. He also served two terms as chairman of the English-Speaking Union. In addition he was a contributor, and from 1925 to 1932 editor, of the *Spectator*. He had bought a controlling interest in the *Spectator* from St. Loe Strachey [q.v.] in 1925 and, although he later sold his controlling shareholding to (Sir) Ian Gilmour, he was chairman of the board for the remainder of his life.

Wrench's third major project, the All Peoples Association, founded by him in 1930 was unsuccessful. The wideness of its scope was too idealistic. Its special field in attempting understanding between the English and German peoples was poorly nurtured in the hostile soil of increasing Nazism. The publication of his book *I Loved Germany* (1940) was ill timed and misunderstood.

His marriage in 1937 to Hylda Henrietta, widow of Sir Frederick Henry Arthur Des Voeux, seventh baronet, and a sister of the future Lord Alanbrooke [q.v.] brought him a willing and energetic helper in the many causes in which he was interested. She was Wrench's first cousin, whom he had known all his life. In 1940 they set out on a tour of Canada, the United States, New Zealand, and Australia, but became stranded in India in 1941 on their way back. They quickly found ways of being useful in helping American servicemen. Wrench served from 1942 to 1944 as American relations officer to the Government of India, a post especially created for him by the viceroy.

After the war, working in his home, the Mill House, Marlow, Wrench devoted much of his time to writing. He had already written two personal memoirs, *Uphill, the first stage in a strenuous life* (1934) and *Struggle, 1914–1920* (1935), which portrayed much of the history of his two great organizations. In 1945 *Immortal Years: 1937–1944, as viewed from five continents* had been published. In 1949 his *Transatlantic London: three centuries of association between England and America* emphasized once more his anxiety for close friendship between the English-speaking peoples. By the end of the war he had completed his biography, *Francis Yeats-Brown* (1948). He now added two further biographies, *Geoffrey Dawson and our Times* (1955) and *Alfred Lord Milner: The Man of No Illusions* (1958), in both of which he had been greatly aided by having access to private papers.

In his activities he constantly consulted his wife, whose advice he greatly valued, and her death in 1955 was a great blow to him. Nevertheless his services to the causes he had at heart continued. One result of his later enthusiasms was the foundation in 1958 of the Anglo-Kin Society with the aim of encouraging literary, historical, and topographical research to provide fuller information about places and events in Britain likely to be of interest to the British Commonwealth and the United States. Wrench was a member of the goodwill mission to Virginia in 1957 and from 1959 to 1960 made a tour of Commonwealth countries and southeast Asia. He was president of the Dickens Fellowship in 1961–4 and for many years he was senior trustee of the Cecil Rhodes Memorial Museum Foundation at Bishop's Stortford.

Wrench was a deeply religious person who at one time thought of becoming a missionary. Although he was modest and self-effacing, charming in conversation, some found him somewhat aloof and considered he was not a good mixer. This was probably because he had little time for small talk and social gossip. Where he was concerned with some project close to his ideals he would speak with enthusiasm. Although an idealist, he was at the same time practical. 'Better remove that book', he once said to a porter at Over-Seas League headquarters, indicating an expensive reference book lying on a table, 'or it will get pinched.' With all his idealism he never let go of reality and was prepared to admit that 'perhaps my friends were right when they warned me "not to be too visionary"'. His lively, likeable personality exuded into his literary style, which was pleasantly informal and underlined his sincerity of purpose.

As a young man Wrench had the advantage that his family background, essentially aristocratic, eased his contact with prominent and influential people. Nevertheless this does not detract from the considerable achievements he made through his energy and missionary zeal in founding two major organizations. He was appointed CMG in 1917; knighted in 1932; and in 1960, when the Over-Seas League reached its jubilee and was given the title 'royal', advanced to KCMG. He had earlier received the Order of St. Maurice and St. Lazarus of Italy. Recognition for his work for Anglo-American understanding came through the award by the Royal Society of Arts of the Benjamin Franklin medal for 1964. He received honorary degrees from Bristol and St. Andrews.

In appearance Wrench was ascetic-looking, slim, with an intelligent, earnest expression. This is brought out well in Sir Oswald Birley's portrait in the Royal Over-Seas League London headquarters. Another by Margaret Lindsay Williams is in the London headquarters of the English-Speaking Union.

Wrench died at his home in Marlow, 11 November 1966. A memorial plaque was placed on the wall of his house by the Anglo-Kin Society.

[Wrench's own writings; 'Milestones' in the British Museum Library: a collection of newspaper cuttings and other material relating to Wrench, 1882–1952, 12 vols., including a typescript index; W. V. Griffin, *Sir Evelyn Wrench and his continuing vision of international relations during 40 years*, New York, 1950; Hylda H. Wrench, *Reflections . . . 1879–1955*, privately printed, 1956; *The Times* and *Daily Telegraph*, 12 November 1966; private information; personal knowledge.] G. K. S. HAMILTON-EDWARDS

WRIGHT, SIR NORMAN CHARLES (1900–1970), agricultural and nutritional scientist, was born in Reading 19 February

1900, the second son of the Revd Francis Henry Wright, registrar of the university of Reading, by his second wife, Agnes Mary Dunkley. He was educated at Christ Church Choir School, Oxford, University College, Reading, Christ Church, Oxford (he was a scholar but gained a fourth class in chemistry and physiology in 1922) and (as a Ministry of Agriculture research scholar) at Gonville and Caius College, Cambridge where he proceeded to a Ph.D. (1925). He proceeded to an Oxford D.Sc. in 1937. He had the further distinction of winning a college oar at both universities, oars which graced the walls of his homes thereafter. He spent the years 1924-6 as a research assistant at the National Institute for Research in Dairying at Shinfield, Reading, and the next two years as a Commonwealth Fund fellow in the United States first at Cornell University, NY, and later, in the US Department of Agriculture in Washington, DC, thus beginning his lifelong interest in overseas countries.

On his return to Britain in 1928 he was appointed physiologist to the newly established Hannah Dairy Research Institute, Ayr, and two years later, at the early age of thirty, became its first director. While at the 'Hannah', his interest in overseas countries and foreign travel grew. In 1936-7, as special adviser to the Imperial Council of Agricultural Research in India, he advised the Government of India on the development of its cattle and dairy industries, and in 1945 performed a similar function for the Government of Ceylon. In 1944-5 he was a member of the Anglo-American Scientific Mission to the Middle East Supply Centre and in 1946 was British member of the first FAO mission to Greece.

In 1947 he was invited to succeed Sir Jack C. Drummond [q.v.] as chief scientific adviser to the Ministry of Food; later he became chief scientific adviser (food) of the merged Ministry of Agriculture, Fisheries and Food, a post which he held until he was invited to become deputy director-general of the UN Food and Agriculture Organization in 1959.

Wright was a hard and meticulous worker, and an excellent chairman. He was chairman of the Food Standards Committee from 1947 to 1959 and of the National Food Survey Committee from 1948 to 1959. While combining these roles with that of chief scientific adviser to the parent Ministry he developed his encyclopedic knowledge of agricultural and food sciences, nutrition, and social and economic sciences. He was also chairman of the Agricultural Education Association from 1948 to 1950, member of the Colonial Agricultural Advisory Council from 1947 to 1955, of the Agricultural Research Council from 1950 to 1955, of the Colonial Research Council from

1950 to 1954, and of the National Resources (Technical) Committee from 1950 to 1955, and successively chairman, vice-chairman, and a member of the Committee for Colonial Agricultural Animal Health and Forestry Research from 1946 to 1959. He was chairman of the FAO Programme Committee in Rome from 1953 to 1959.

He stayed with FAO at their headquarters in Rome until 1963 when he returned to London and became for five years secretary of the British Association for the Advancement of Science. He was the first honorary president of the British Dietetic Association (from 1963 to 1969) and addressed the Association on food and the future, a theme to which he devoted much thought during his later years. He became a member of the UN Advisory Committee on the Application of Science and Technology to Development in 1964 and of the Council of the British Nutrition Foundation and of the Nestlé Foundation in 1967, holding all three appointments until his death 16 July 1970 at his home in Kensington, London.

Wright was a wise and kindly man, with a humorous twinkle in the clear eyes beneath bushy eyebrows. He was severely red-green colour blind and therefore could never experience with the normally sighted the joy of returning from desert country to the green fields of England nor of seeing red holly berries against their green leaves. In spite of an apparently strong physique he suffered much from spinal trouble. His chief recreations were travel, which he pursued despite illness, and photography, in which he was skilled and took great pride, particularly over his enrichment of the pictorial archives of the Royal Borough of Kensington. He also enjoyed playing the piano.

In 1928 he married Janet Robison Ledingham, eldest daughter of Dr John Rennie of Aberdeen University. They had one daughter, Mary Elizabeth. The Wrights' homes in Ayr, Kensington, and Rome were centres of warm hospitality, liberally bestowed. That their marriage was a happy one was obvious to all their friends.

Wright was appointed CB in 1955, knighted in 1963, and received the honorary degree of LLD from the university of Leeds in 1967.

[*The Times*, 18 July 1970; *Bulletin of the Ministry of Agriculture, Fisheries and Food*, May 1957; private information; personal knowledge.] DOROTHY F. HOLLINGSWORTH

WRIGHT, ROBERT ALDERSON, BARON WRIGHT (1869-1964), lord of appeal and jurist, was born 15 October 1869 at South Shields, the son of John Wright, marine superintendent, and his wife, Elizabeth Middleton, daughter of John

Carr, of Shields. Wright was not a man to talk much about his early days. All that can be said of his education is that it was good enough to take him to Trinity College, Cambridge, although not until he was twenty-four; and good enough to start him on the way to first classes in both parts of the classical tripos (1895-6) and in part ii of the moral sciences tripos (1897). He decided to go to the bar and was called in 1900 by the Inner Temple. In 1899 he had been awarded a prize fellowship at Trinity; this gave him £200 a year for six years and that income, supplemented by part-time law teaching, kept him going during the long wait for work.

Work at the commercial bar has always been more than half maritime and maybe his father's calling had given Wright an early interest in ships. At any rate he went into the chambers of the future Lord Justice Scrutton [q.v.] who specialized in commercial work. It was heavy work and lucrative, but all beginners had to wait for it, Wright longer than most. After ten years he began to think of full-time law teaching. But then the work came in a sudden rush; from about £300 in one year he jumped to £3,000 in the next.

So Wright had got going before the war of 1914-18 brought with it a great increase in shipping cases, especially in insurance. The Government undertook to bear the risk of war, while underwriters retained the ordinary marine risk; this division was of immense benefit to lawyers who spent much time arguing into which category each casualty fell. In addition to this there was the work of the Prize Court. Wright was given silk in 1917 and at once became one of the leaders of the commercial bar and in constant demand. He was a presenter of material rather than an advocate; clarity and a thoroughness in presentation were what the work needed and these were his great virtues.

Wright was now earning a large income. He lived with his mother, to whom evidently he felt that he owed much, and did not marry until after her death. She enjoyed the delayed prosperity perhaps more than he: 'It's not that we can't afford it, young man,' she was heard to say to an elderly wine waiter, who had unsuccessfully suggested champagne, 'it's no treat to us.' Wright took a long lease of Durley House on the Savernake estate in Wiltshire where he built himself a large law library and laid down an excellent cellar of port.

In 1925 he was appointed to the King's Bench with the customary knighthood. At the bar he had the reputation of being occasionally rough, perhaps because of overwork, but on the bench he was invariably courteous and considerate. He spent much of his time hearing commercial cases and heavy civil litigation. But he did his share of assize work, in general very

successfully, although the extreme monotony of his delivery was a handicap with a jury. In 1931 he presided at the trial at the Old Bailey of Lord Kylsant [q.v.], the shipping magnate, on charges of fraud in a prospectus which involved difficult questions of accountancy.

In 1932 Wright was sixty-three and that is a usual age for promotion to the House of Lords. It is, however, unusual to skip the Court of Appeal. In Wright's case the exception was abundantly justified. He was made a life peer and sworn of the Privy Council. In the House of Lords he found his true vocation. He sat as a lord of appeal in ordinary from 1932 to 1947, except for two years, 1935-7, when he presided in the Court of Appeal as master of the Rolls on the understanding that he would return to the Lords as soon as it was convenient.

Wright was a good judge but as an expounder of the law he was great. He understood the common law intuitively and had a feeling for the way it should develop. He was not content simply to decide an appeal; he wanted to establish general principles. This made him perhaps more completely admired in academic circles than among his colleagues; the expository judgement was then less fashionable in appellate courts than it is today. Wright was the chief creator of the new fashion. His judgements are not short, they do not scintillate neither do they crystallize the law; but the practitioner who searches the speeches of five law lords for 'the sense of the case' will more often find it in Wright's speech than in those of the others.

He did something too to break down the barriers between the practice and the study of the law. In his time the judiciary in general paid little attention to academic developments and not much more to the discussion of common law principles in the courts of the United States and the Commonwealth. Wright wrote articles and gave addresses on legal subjects; by this activity his name became almost as well known in American as in British legal circles. He was elected FBA in 1940. He was chairman of the Law Revision Committee from 1935; many of its reports were enacted into law.

In 1945 Wright became chairman of the United Nations War Crimes Commission which collected the material for the charges at the Nuremberg trial. In pursuit of his duties Wright, now in his mid seventies, made many uncomfortable journeys in converted bombers. He was appointed GCMG in 1948. He believed strongly in the establishment of the Nuremberg tribunal and would not allow that it was set up to administer *ex post facto* law. His article, 'War Crimes under International Law' in the *Law Quarterly Review* (vol. lxii, 1946) is a very important contribution to the jurisprudence on this subject.

In 1947 Wright retired and thereafter led and enjoyed a life of leisure. He sat judicially on a few occasions shortly after his retirement; in his library he 'toyed', as he put it, with legal problems but wrote little. He contributed the notice of Sir Frederick Pollock to this Dictionary. He had no great intellectual interests outside the law. But he liked country life and enjoyed physical exercise. In his youth he was a keen mountaineer. In middle age he learned to ride and in 1928 he married Margery Avis Bullows (died 1980), a champion rider and show-jumper. They had no children. Lady Wright kept a riding school at Durley House. Wright rode frequently in Savernake Forest until the age of ninety when he was seriously injured in a motoring accident. He made a surprisingly good recovery, but it was the end of the exercise and the foreign travel which he and his wife had enjoyed. He died at his home 27 June 1964. He was an honorary fellow of Trinity College, Cambridge, and deputy high steward of the university. There is a portrait by Sir Gerald Kelly in the Inner Temple.

[A. L. Goodhart in *Proceedings* of the British Academy, vol. li, 1965; private information.]
DEVLIN

WYNDHAM, JOHN (1903-1969), writer. [See HARRIS, J. W. P. L. B.]

WYNYARD, DIANA (1906-1964), actress, was born Dorothy Isobel Cox in Forest Hill, London, 16 January 1906, the daughter of Edward Thomas Cox, master printer, and his wife, Margaret Campbell Thomson. She was educated at Woodford School, Croydon. Gifted by nature with a good voice, she went in turn to two notable teachers to have it trained, and at the age of nineteen launched herself on the professional stage. Her blonde beauty served to get her a walk-on part at the Globe in 1925 and in the same year she was taken on tour by Hamilton Deane; in just under a year she played nearly thirty parts, mainly in light comedy. Other touring engagements followed which kept her well employed until, in August 1927, she joined the much admired Liverpool Repertory Company under the direction of William Armstrong [q.v.]. There she remained for two years playing increasingly important parts in plays of increasing weight, gaining steadily in experience and skill until in September 1929 she was ready to make her London début, and to secure a considerable success.

The theatre was the St. Martin's, and the play was *Sorry You've Been Troubled*, and was one of a series of amusing pieces written by the American dramatist Walter Hackett for his wife Marion Lorne, a comedienne of a markedly individual personality. Diana Wynyard's part in this piece was of no great importance, but it needed to be played with assurance, charm, and distinction. So well did the young actress rise to the challenge and so exceedingly beautiful did she look while doing so that a startled London first-night audience took her to its heart upon the spot.

She was soon established as a leading lady in the West End, and was in constant demand. The plays for which she was required were still light in texture, but gradually she showed a certain ambition for more serious work. A visit to America in 1932 widened her horizon and in the following year, returning to London, she played Charlotte Brontë in *Wild Decembers*, taking over the management for part of the run. In 1934 she scored a notable success and a long run in *Sweet Aloes*.

In 1937, having succeeded the American actress Ann Harding as Candida in the play by G. B. Shaw [q.v.], she went with it to Paris, the production having been chosen to represent the British stage in the Paris Exhibition. This was followed, later in the same year, by another Shaw heroine—Eliza Doolittle in *Pygmalion* at the Old Vic; and for the next ten years she maintained her high reputation with appearances in such plays as *Design for Living* (1939), *No Time for Comedy* (1941), *Watch on the Rhine* (1942), and, on tour for ENSA, *Gaslight* (1943) and *Love from a Stranger* (1944).

In 1948 she took a step which was to transform her career and lift her name to a higher plane than any at which she had previously aimed. The governors of the Shakespeare Memorial Theatre who were engaged in a campaign to raise the standard of Stratford acting above the unambitious standard which had satisfied them during the period between the two world wars, invited her to join the company. Up to that point, in a stage career of over twenty-six years, she had shown no ambition to become a classical actress, her sole appearance in a Shakespeare part having been at Liverpool as Titania. She had, however, valuable assets for the task—an excellent voice, a good sense of character, and quick intelligence. She accepted the invitation, and very soon showed that the decision was a right one.

She served the company for the seasons of 1948 and 1949 and in 1949-50 went with them to Australia. During that time she excited admiration in a very wide range of parts; the list included Gertrude in *Hamlet*, Portia in *The Merchant of Venice*, Katherine the shrew, Hermione in *The Winter's Tale*, Desdemona, Lady Macbeth, Beatrice in *Much Ado about Nothing*, Helena in *A Midsummer Night's Dream*, and Queen Katherine in *Henry VIII*. She repeated her performances of Hermione in

London in 1951 and of Beatrice in 1952. She was appointed CBE in 1953: proof of the profound impression she had made.

Among the films in which she appeared may be mentioned *Cavalcade*, *The Prime Minister*, and *An Ideal Husband*.

She was married twice: first in 1943 to (Sir) Carol Reed; secondly, in 1951, to Tibor Csato.

Both marriages were dissolved. She died in London 13 May 1964.

A portrait of Diana Wynyard in *The Silent Knight* by Ethel Gabain was exhibited at the Royal Academy in 1938.

[Private information; personal knowledge.]
W. A. DARLINGTON

Y

YEO-THOMAS, FOREST FREDERIC EDWARD (1902-1964), French resistance organizer, was born in London 17 June 1902, the eldest son of John Yeo-Thomas and his wife, Daisy Ethel Burrows. The Yeo-Thomas family, which had connections with the Welsh coal-mining industry, had established itself in Dieppe in the middle of the nineteenth century. 'Tommy' was sent to the Dieppe Naval College where he early learned to defend his British nationality. Later he went to the Lycée Condorcet in Paris until war broke out in 1914. In spite of all his father's efforts to prevent it, he was determined to take part in the war and was accepted as a dispatch rider when the United States joined in. In 1920 he joined the Poles against the Bolsheviks; was captured and sentenced to death; but managed to escape by strangling his guard the night before his execution was due.

Returning to France, Yeo-Thomas eventually settled down to study accountancy. There followed a variety of employments until in 1932 he became secretary to the fashion house of Molyneux. When war broke out in 1939 he at once tried to enlist, but the two years he had added to his age in the first war now told against him. Eventually he managed to join the Royal Air Force with the rank of sergeant. He completed radar training and was in one of the last boats to leave France when that country fell. In October 1941 he was commissioned and sent as intelligence officer to the 308 Polish Squadron at Baginton. But he was determined to return to occupied France and eventually, in February 1942, with the help of a well-known newspaper and a member of Parliament, he was taken into Special Operations Executive. Here he became responsible for planning in the RF French section which worked in close association with General de Gaulle's Bureau Central de Renseignements et d'Action. It was at this time that he was given the *nom de guerre* 'the White Rabbit'.

After the fall of France small groups of resisters had sprung up all over the country, but they were uncoordinated, ignorant of each other's identities, purposes, or often, whereabouts. It was essential that these efforts should in some way be knit together to work towards the same end. In February 1943 Yeo-Thomas and André Dewavrin, known as Colonel Passy, the head of BCRA, were parachuted into France to join Pierre Brossolette to investigate the potential of resistance groups in the occupied zone. They succeeded in uniting the various groups in allegiance to de Gaulle, pooling their resources to organize a secret army which would spring into action on D-Day. From this mission the three men safely returned in April. But in June the leader and a number of other members of the Conseil National de la Résistance were arrested and its work seriously disrupted. To help restore the situation Yeo-Thomas and Brossolette in September returned to France where movement and meeting together had become much more difficult. In November Yeo-Thomas, concealed inside a hearse, slipped through the controls, and was picked up by Lysander. Brossolette remained behind. In England Yeo-Thomas's urgent demands for supplies for his organization took him finally to the prime minister, Winston Churchill. This interview produced a considerable increase in aircraft for RF section and consequently in weapons and supplies for the resisters in France.

When in February 1944 Yeo-Thomas heard of Brossolette's capture, he arranged to be parachuted into France yet again in order to replace him and also to try to organize his escape. Another visit by one so well known to the Germans as 'Shelley' was courting disaster, which did indeed befall Yeo-Thomas. He was arrested in Paris and his long period of torture and imprisonment began: in Fresnes, Compiègnes, Buchenwald, and Rehmsdorf. Throughout his appalling tortures he said nothing of any value to the enemy. Despite several bold but unsuccessful attempts, he maintained his resolution to escape. At Buchenwald, in September 1944, when Allied agents were being liquidated, he persuaded the head of the typhus experimental station to allow three agents to exchange identity with three Frenchmen who were already dying. Yeo-Thomas, Harry Peulevé [q.v.], and a Frenchman were selected, Yeo-Thomas, in his new identity, was transferred to Rehmsdorf as a hospital orderly. When the camp was evacuated in April 1945 before the advancing Allies he organized an escape from the train when men were engaged in burying those who had died on the journey. Yeo-Thomas was among the ten who succeeded in getting away. Starving, desperately weak from dysentery and other illnesses, he was captured by German troops, posed as an escaping French Air Force prisoner of war, and was sent to the Grunhainigen Stalag. He again organized an escape with ten others who refused to leave him when he collapsed and finally helped him to reach the advancing American forces.

Yeo-Thomas was among the most outstanding workers behind enemy lines whom Britain produced. He was stocky, well built, athletic (he had boxed in his youth), and his blue eyes had a direct and fearless look. His sense of humour revealed itself in a ready smile which, on occasions, broke into open laughter. His character was exactly suited to his task. He was fearless, quick-witted, and resourceful, and his endurance under hardship was supreme. He received the George Cross, the Military Cross and bar, the Polish Cross of Merit, the croix de guerre, and was a commander of the Legion of Honour.

Battered and permanently injured in health, he returned to Britain to be cared for devotedly by Barbara Yeo-Thomas, formerly Barbara Joan Dean. A marriage had ended before war broke out, two children remaining in France with their mother.

After helping to bring to trial several Nazi war criminals Yeo-Thomas returned to Molyneux in 1946 but in 1948 ill health forced him to resign. After a period of recuperation he was appointed in 1950 as representative in Paris of the Federation of British Industries. There, in its different way, he still worked for Anglo-French rapprochement. But his sufferings had taken their toll and he died in Paris 26 February 1964.

[Bruce Marshall, *The White Rabbit*, 1952; M. R. D. Foot, *S.O.E. in France*, 2nd impression, with amendments, 1968; private information; personal knowledge.]

JAMES HUTCHISON

YERBURY, FRANCIS ROWLAND (FRANK) (1885-1970), secretary of the Architectural Association and a founder and first director of the London Building Centre, was born 19 November 1885 at Cricklewood, Middlesex, the youngest son of Francis William Yerbury, clerk, and his wife, Lucy Stinchcomb. His father died early, leaving his widow to bring up the family. An uncle paid for the education of Yerbury's two elder brothers, who went to good schools, but Frank was not so fortunate, a fact which seemed to affect him throughout his life for he was seldom at ease in intellectual circles, while even among his chosen professional friends, such as architects and designers, he always regretted never having become an architect himself. In the hope that he might achieve this, he had accepted at the age of sixteen the post of office boy at the Architectural Association in Tufton Street.

He did not in fact leave the AA until his retirement thirty-six years later, for when the secretary of the Association died suddenly in 1911, Yerbury was appointed to succeed him and thus began his distinguished twin careers as a builder of a great school of architecture and an influential proponent and photographer of modern European building. Indeed Yerbury

became, for his architect friends in London, their prime source of information on and contact with the contemporary architecture and architects in Holland, Germany, Denmark, and Sweden. His excellent photographs of modern European buildings were widely published and his many illustrated books about his travels abroad were avidly read by generations of students to whom contemporary European architecture was still an unknown quantity. Among his books were *Modern European Buildings* (1928), *Modern Dutch Buildings* (1931), and *Small Modern English Houses* (1929). While acting in this way as the leading publicist for new Continental architecture, Yerbury made a great number of friends in architectural circles abroad which were to last throughout his life and even took him on an official wartime mission to Sweden to reassure his Swedish friends about the state of British morale. That he had to travel in the bomb bay of a Mosquito aircraft only reinforced his message. In recognition of his contributions to international understanding and architectural appreciation he had been made a commander of the Swedish Royal Order of Vasa (1929) and became a knight of the Danish Royal Order of the Dannebrog (1951).

As its increasingly respected secretary, he helped successive presidents and principals, especially Robert Atkinson and (Sir) Howard Robertson [q.v.], to build the Architectural Association into a leading centre for architectural education, discussion, thought, and controversy. Under his guidance the AA School even began to challenge the inter-war supremacy of the Liverpool School of Architecture, where his friend (Sir) C. H. Reilly [q.v.] was the professor. While at the AA Yerbury encouraged a colleague, J. K. Winser, to organize a building materials samples room, which was eventually to lead to a third career for Yerbury and one for which he will be long remembered, since out of that modest collection of samples for the benefit of the AA students grew the first Building Centre for the architectural profession as a whole. It was Vincent Vincent, a director of Bovis Ltd., a well-known firm of building contractors, who first saw the possibilities in Yerbury's samples room, for he had recently visited the Architects' Samples Bureau in New York, a commercial information service on building materials. Together Vincent and Yerbury created the Building Centre in 1931 as a non-profit-distributing educational activity to be of help to all concerned with the building industry from materials suppliers to contractors, architects, surveyors, and clients alike. By 1937 the new Centre, having moved from its first home in the Conduit Street headquarters of the Royal Institute of British Architects to its own premises in Store Street, had become almost a full-time preoccupation for Yerbury, and so in that year he resigned from the AA to devote all his energies to directing and developing the London Building Centre, which in due course was to become a model for other cities and indeed for other countries. At the time of Yerbury's death there were nearly one hundred similar centres in operation around the globe.

Yerbury was a convivial, gregarious man, with a flair for international friendships, a great love of travel and a real talent as a photographer. He was also an excellent raconteur and thus a pillar of his favourite Arts Club in Dover Street. As one of the earliest English discoverers of modern Danish design (he had written a short monograph on Kaare Klint's furniture in 1929) he was a staunch supporter of the British Design and Industries Association of which he became a vice-president. He was elected an honorary associate of the Royal Institute of British Architects in 1928 and was made an OBE in 1952. He retired from active work in 1961 and died at Newbury 7 July 1970. He married in 1914 Winifred Constance Bendall, who, with one son and a daughter, survived him. His portrait by Francis Hodge was exhibited at the Royal Academy in 1948 and later hung in the London Building Centre.

[*The Times*, 9 July 1970; private information, personal knowledge.]   PAUL REILLY

YORKE, FRANCIS REGINALD STEVENS (1906-1962), architect, was born in Stratford-upon-Avon 3 December 1906, the only son of Francis Walter Bagnall Yorke and his wife, Mary Ann Stevens, of Langley. He was educated at Chipping Camden School and at what is now the Birmingham University School of Architecture. He was an undistinguished and casual student, though a sensitive draughtsman. His father was an architect, practising in the Midlands with a special interest in vernacular methods of construction with the building crafts. The family house in Redditch was 'redolent of William Morris' and it is probable that it was from this early influence that the son derived the appreciation of natural materials and their associated techniques which he used in later life as a contrast to steel, glass, and concrete.

Yorke's professional life can be divided into two phases. The first was between 1930 and 1939 when he had qualified as an architect and set up in London. The period was the more significant in his development as an architect and as a personality for in his case the two cannot be separated. He was able to attract and often inspire people of talent while the warmth and charm of his nature and his physical presence endeared him to a huge circle of friends. He

looked and dressed like a gentleman farmer, which was what he later also became. Tweed suits (but never hair shirts) went with a powerful, chunky frame, a countryman's clear ruddy skin and mischievous, puckered eyes. His friends called him 'K'.

In this time he achieved a reputation which was unrelated to his actual output as an architect. The few houses which he designed were all built after 1935 (Nast Hyde, near Hatfield, and a terrace in Henley in Arden) were uncompromisingly modern, and express the functionalist forms of the 1930s. These buildings were fewer in number and smaller in size than those of the other architects of the modern movement working in England at the same time. Men like Connel and Ward, Maxwell Fry, and Joseph Emberton were actually less well known. Even when Marcel Breuer of the Bauhaus left Germany and joined Yorke in practice their output did not significantly increase.

During this period he began to travel extensively, meeting architects like Mies van der Rohe and Havlicek, whose work was more formal than that of their English contemporaries. Yorke spoke no foreign language but was immediately understood whether in Moscow or Peking. Typically English in appearance, he was international in outlook. These encounters deepened his convictions while his reputation was also assisted by his career as an architectural journalist and author. *The Modern House*, published in 1934 by the Architectural Press, became an instant and continuing success in the English-speaking world, and had almost as much influence as Le Corbusier's *Vers une Architecture*, published six years earlier. It was followed soon after by *The Modern Flat*, written in 1937 in association with his lifelong friend (Sir) Frederick Gibberd. Yorke also became editor of the annual *Specification* in 1935 and continued with it all his life. Also influential was his association with the Modern Architectural Research Group (MARS), of which he was a founder-member, the British end of the Congrès Internationale des Architectes Modernes, the propaganda arm of the modern movement.

The second phase of his professional life began after the war. The rare building was replaced by the many, the small by the large. In partnership with Eugene Rosenberg and Cyril Mardall, an immense reputation was swiftly achieved with Yorke as the leader. The list of significant buildings subsequently designed by the firm is too long to quote. During the first years he was largely responsible for the Barclay School at Stevenage for which he persuaded the Hertfordshire County Council to commission a work by Henry Moore. The result, 'The Family Group', was the first of Moore's major public works. At Harlow he designed the Ladyshot Estate, with richly textured and intimate housing, recalling his pre-war Henley in Arden work. To this period belongs his own house, a conversion of an old mill at Wootton near Woodstock. The interior, in its organization of space, water, and 'found' materials, is a lyrical concept. Two other buildings in which he took enormous personal pride and care were Gatwick Airport (begun in 1957) and the partnership's own beautiful office building in Greystoke Place, Holborn.

Yorke, the architect, was overtaken by the breathless pace of success and only his unparalleled vitality could keep control of materials and their detailing. He indulged his other interests, in farming, fishing, and the convivial company of the artists he admired and collected. Modern architecture had become accepted and so he wrote little and travelled much. As his life style grew so his architectural impact was diminished. He was always free from conceit, arrogance, or pomposity. His face was perpetually cheerful and his courage indestructible.

Yorke has an assured place in architectural history. He worked within the forms which had been created and his special contribution was a synthesis of the shapes and texture of natural and traditional materials within these confines. He was not one of the theorists of the movement, nor one of its originators; he brought to it a lyrical, spontaneous, even English, approach.

He married Thelma Austin Jones in 1930 and they had twin daughters. He became a fellow of the Royal Institute of British Architects in 1943 and was appointed CBE in 1962 just before his tragically early death 10 June 1962, at St. Thomas' Hospital, London, after a long illness stoically borne.

There is a portrait by Gordon Herickx (1941) in chalk in the possession of his brother-in-law, Cecil Rowland.

[*The Times*, 11 and 12 June 1962; *Guardian*, 16 June 1962; *Architecture and Building News*, 20 June 1962; *Oxford Mail*, 13 June 1962; RIBA *Journal*, July 1962; *Architects Journal*, 20 June 1962; private information; personal knowledge.]   RICHARD SHEPPARD

YOUNG, GERARD MACKWORTH- (1884-1965), Indian civil servant and archaeologist. [See MACKWORTH-YOUNG.]

Z

ZETLAND, second MARQUESS OF (1876-1961), public servant and author. [See DUNDAS, LAWRENCE JOHN LUMLEY.]

CUMULATIVE INDEX

TO THE BIOGRAPHIES CONTAINED IN THE SUPPLEMENTS
OF THE DICTIONARY OF NATIONAL BIOGRAPHY
1901–1970

Abbey, Edwin Austin	1852–1911
Abbey, John Roland	1894–1969
Abbott, Edwin Abbott	1838–1926
Abbott, Evelyn	1843–1901
À Beckett, Arthur William	1844–1909
Abel, Sir Frederick Augustus	1827–1902
Abell, Sir Westcott Stile	1877–1961
Aberconway, Baron. See McLaren, Charles Benjamin Bright	1850–1934
Aberconway, Baron. See McLaren, Henry Duncan	1879–1953
Abercorn, Duke of. See Hamilton, James	1838–1913
Abercrombie, Lascelles	1881–1938
Abercrombie, Sir (Leslie) Patrick	1879–1957
Aberdare, Baron. See Bruce, Clarence Napier	1885–1957
Aberdeen and Temair, Marquess of. See Gordon, John Campbell	1847–1934
Aberdeen and Temair, Marchioness of (1857–1939). See under Gordon, John Campbell	
Aberhart, William	1878–1943
Abney, Sir William de Wiveleslie	1843–1920
Abraham, Charles John	1814–1903
Abraham, William	1842–1922
Abu Bakar Tafawa Balewa, Alhaji Sir. See Tafawa Balewa	1912–1966
Abul Kalam Azad, Maulana. See Azad	1888–1958
Acland, Sir Arthur Herbert Dyke	1847–1926
Acton, Sir Edward	1865–1945
Acton, John Adams-. See Adams-Acton	1830–1910
Acton, Sir John Emerich Edward Dalberg, Baron	1834–1902
Acworth, Sir William Mitchell	1850–1925
Adam, James	1860–1907
Adam Smith, Sir George. See Smith	1856–1942
Adami, John George	1862–1926
Adams, James Williams	1839–1903
Adams, Sir John	1857–1934
Adams, William Bridges-. See Bridges-Adams	1889–1965
Adams, William Davenport	1851–1904
Adams, William George Stewart	1874–1966
Adams-Acton, John	1830–1910
Adamson, Sir John Ernest	1867–1950
Adamson, Robert	1852–1902
Adcock, Sir Frank Ezra	1886–1968
Adderley, Charles Bowyer, Baron Norton	1814–1905
Addison, Christopher, Viscount	1869–1951
Adler, Hermann	1839–1911
Adshead, Stanley Davenport	1868–1946
AE, pseudonym. See Russell, George William	1867–1935
Aga Khan, Aga Sultan Sir Mohammed Shah	1877–1957

Agate, James Evershed	1877–1947
Agnew, Sir James Wilson	1815–1901
Agnew, Sir William	1825–1910
Agnew, Sir William Gladstone	1898–1960
Aidé, Charles Hamilton	1826–1906
Aikman, George	1830–1905
Ainger, Alfred	1837–1904
Ainley, Henry Hinchliffe	1879–1945
Aird, Sir John	1833–1911
Airedale, Baron. See Kitson, James	1835–1911
Aitchison, Craigie Mason, Lord	1882–1941
Aitchison, George	1825–1910
Aitken, Alexander Craig	1895–1967
Aitken, William Maxwell, Baron Beaverbrook	1879–1964
Akers, Sir Wallace Alan	1888–1954
Akers-Douglas, Aretas, Viscount Chilston	1851–1926
Akers-Douglas, Aretas, Viscount Chilston	1876–1947
Alanbrooke, Viscount. See Brooke, Alan Francis	1883–1963
Albani, Dame Marie Louise Cécilie Emma	1852–1930
Alcock, Sir John William	1892–1919
Aldenham, Baron. See Gibbs, Henry Hucks	1819–1907
Alderson, Sir Edwin Alfred Hervey	1859–1927
Alderson, Henry James	1834–1909
Aldington, Edward Godfree ('Richard')	1892–1962
Aldrich-Blake, Dame Louisa Brandreth	1865–1925
Alexander, Mrs, pseudonym. See Hector, Annie French	1825–1902
Alexander, Albert Victor, Earl Alexander of Hillsborough	1885–1965
Alexander, Boyd	1873–1910
Alexander, Sir George	1858–1918
Alexander, Harold Rupert Leofric George, Earl Alexander of Tunis	1891–1969
Alexander, Samuel	1859–1938
Alexander, William	1824–1911
Alexander-Sinclair, Sir Edwyn Sinclair	1865–1945
Alexandra, Queen	1844–1925
Alexandra Victoria Alberta Edwina Louise Duff, Princess Arthur of Connaught, Duchess of Fife	1891–1959
Alger, John Goldworth	1836–1907
Algeranoff, Harcourt	1903–1967
Alington, Baron. See Sturt, Henry Gerard	1825–1904
Alington, Cyril Argentine	1872–1955
Alison, Sir Archibald	1826–1907
Allan, Sir William	1837–1903
Allbutt, Sir Thomas Clifford	1836–1925
Allen, Sir Carleton Kemp	1887–1966
Allen, George	1832–1907
Allen, (Herbert) Warner	1881–1968

Allen, Sir Hugh Percy	1869-1946
Allen, Sir James	1855-1942
Allen, John Romilly	1847-1907
Allen, Percy Stafford	1869-1933
Allen, Reginald Clifford, Baron Allen of Hurtwood	1889-1939
Allen, Robert Calder	1812-1903
Allenby, Edmund Henry Hynman, Viscount Allenby of Megiddo	1861-1936
Allerton, Baron. See Jackson, William Lawies	1840-1917
Allies, Thomas William	1813-1903
Allingham, Margery Louise	1904-1966
Allman, George Johnston	1824-1904
Alma-Tadema, Sir Lawrence	1836-1912
Almond, Hely Hutchinson	1832-1903
Altham, Harry Surtees	1888-1965
Altrincham, Baron. See Grigg, Edward William Macleay	1879-1955
Alverstone, Viscount. See Webster, Richard Everard	1842-1915
Ambedkar, Bhimrao Ramji	1891-1956
Ameer Ali, Syed	1849-1928
Amery, Leopold Charles Maurice Stennett	1873-1955
Amherst, William Amhurst Tyssen-, Baron Amherst of Hackney	1835-1909
Amos, Sir (Percy) Maurice (Maclardie) Sheldon	1872-1940
Ampthill, Baron. See Russell, Arthur Oliver Villiers	1869-1935
Amulree, Baron. See Mackenzie, William Warrender	1860-1942
Anderson, Sir Alan Garrett	1877-1952
Anderson, Alexander	1845-1909
Anderson, Elizabeth Garrett	1836-1917
Anderson, George	1826-1902
Anderson, Sir Hugh Kerr	1865-1928
Anderson, John, Viscount Waverley	1882-1958
Anderson, Sir Kenneth Arthur Noel	1891-1959
Anderson (formerly Macarthur), Mary Reid	1880-1921
Anderson, Stanley Arthur Charles	1884-1966
Anderson (formerly Benson), Stella	1892-1933
Anderson, Sir Thomas McCall	1836-1908
Anderson, Sir Warren Hastings	1872-1930
Andrewes, Sir Frederick William	1859-1932
Andrews, Sir James	1877-1951
Andrews, Thomas	1847-1907
Angell, Sir (Ralph) Norman	1872-1967
Angus, Joseph	1816-1902
Angwin, Sir (Arthur) Stanley	1883-1959
Annandale, Thomas	1838-1907
Anson, Sir William Reynell	1843-1914
Anstey, F., pseudonym. See Guthrie, Thomas Anstey	1856-1934
Anstey, Frank	1865-1940
Antal, Frederick	1887-1954
Appleton, Sir Edward Victor	1892-1965
Arber, Agnes	1879-1960
Arber, Edward	1836-1912
Arberry, Arthur John	1905-1969
Arbuthnot, Sir Alexander John	1822-1907
Arbuthnot, Forster Fitzgerald	1833-1901
Arbuthnot, Sir Robert Keith	1864-1916
Arch, Joseph	1826-1919
Archer, James	1823-1904
Archer, William	1856-1924
Archer-Hind (formerly Hodgson), Richard Dacre	1849-1910

Ardagh, Sir John Charles	1840-1907
Arden-Clarke, Sir Charles Noble	1898-1962
Arden-Close, Sir Charles Frederick	1865-1952
Ardilaun, Baron. See Guinness, Sir Arthur Edward	1840-1915
Arditi, Luigi	1822-1903
Ardwall, Lord. See Jameson, Andrew	1845-1911
Argyll, Duke of. See Campbell, John Douglas Sutherland	1845-1914
Arkell, William Joscelyn	1904-1958
Arkwright, Sir Joseph Arthur	1864-1944
Arlen, Michael	1895-1956
Arliss, George	1868-1946
Armes, Philip	1836-1908
Armour, John Douglas	1830-1903
Armstead, Henry Hugh	1828-1905
Armstrong, Edward	1846-1928
Armstrong, Sir George Carlyon Hughes	1836-1907
Armstrong, Henry Edward	1848-1937
Armstrong, Thomas	1832-1911
Armstrong, William	1882-1952
Armstrong-Jones, Sir Robert	1857-1943
Arnold, Sir Arthur	1833-1902
Arnold, Sir Edwin	1832-1904
Arnold, George Benjamin	1832-1902
Arnold, Sir Thomas Walker	1864-1930
Arnold, William Thomas	1852-1904
Arnold-Forster, Hugh Oakeley	1855-1909
Arrol, Sir William	1839-1913
Arthur of Connaught, Princess. See Alexandra Victoria Alberta Edwina Louise Duff	1891-1959
Arthur Frederick Patrick Albert, prince of Great Britain	1883-1938
Arthur William Patrick Albert, Duke of Connaught and Strathearn	1850-1942
Arthur, William	1819-1901
Asche, (Thomas Stange Heiss) Oscar	1871-1936
Ashbee, Charles Robert	1863-1942
Ashbourne, Baron. See Gibson, Edward	1837-1913
Ashby, Arthur Wilfred	1886-1953
Ashby, Henry	1846-1908
Ashby, Thomas	1874-1931
Asher, Alexander	1835-1905
Ashfield, Baron. See Stanley, Albert Henry	1874-1948
Ashley, Evelyn	1836-1907
Ashley, Wilfrid William, Baron Mount Temple	1867-1938
Ashley, Sir William James	1860-1927
Ashmead Bartlett, Sir Ellis. See Bartlett	1849-1902
Ashton, Thomas Gair, Baron Ashton of Hyde	1855-1933
Ashton, Thomas Southcliffe	1889-1968
Ashton, Winifred, 'Clemence Dane'	1888-1965
Ashwell, Lena Margaret	1872-1957
Askwith, George Ranken, Baron	1861-1942
Aslin, Charles Herbert	1893-1959
Asquith, Anthony	1902-1968
Asquith, Lady Cynthia Mary Evelyn	1887-1960
Asquith, Cyril, Baron Asquith of Bishopstone	1890-1954
Asquith, Emma Alice Margaret (Margot), Countess of Oxford and Asquith	1864-1945
Asquith, Herbert Henry, Earl of Oxford and Asquith	1852-1928
Asquith of Yarnbury, Baroness. See Bonham Carter, (Helen) Violet	1887-1969

Baring-Gould, Sabine	1834–1924
Barker, Sir Ernest	1874–1960
Barker, Harley Granville Granville-. See Granville-Barker	1877–1946
Barker, Sir Herbert Atkinson	1869–1950
Barker, Dame Lilian Charlotte	1874–1955
Barker, Thomas	1838–1907
Barkla, Charles Glover	1877–1944
Barling, Sir (Harry) Gilbert	1855–1940
Barlow, Sir (James) Alan (Noel)	1881–1968
Barlow, Sir Thomas	1845–1945
Barlow, Sir Thomas Dalmahoy	1883–1964
Barlow, William Hagger	1833–1908
Barlow, William Henry	1812–1902
Barnaby, Sir Nathaniel	1829–1915
Barnardo, Thomas John	1845–1905
Barnes, Ernest William	1874–1953
Barnes, George Nicoll	1859–1940
Barnes, Sir George Reginald	1904–1960
Barnes, John Gorell, Baron Gorell	1848–1913
Barnes, Sir Kenneth Ralph	1878–1957
Barnes, Robert	1817–1907
Barnes, Sydney Francis	1873–1967
Barnes, Sir Thomas James	1888–1964
Barnes, William Emery	1859–1939
Barnett, Dame Henrietta Octavia Weston	1851–1936
Barnett, Lionel David	1871–1960
Barnett, Samuel Augustus	1844–1913
Baroda, Sir Sayaji Rao, Maharaja Gaekwar of	1863–1939
Baron, Bernhard	1850–1929
Barr, Archibald	1855–1931
Barrett, Wilson	1846–1904
Barrie, Sir James Matthew	1860–1937
Barrington, Rutland	1853–1922
Barrington-Ward, Sir Lancelot Edward	1884–1953
Barrington-Ward, Robert McGowan	1891–1948
Barry, Alfred	1826–1910
Barry, Ernest James	1882–1968
Barry, Sir Gerald Reid	1898–1968
Barry, Sir John Wolfe Wolfe-. See Wolfe-Barry	1836–1918
Barstow, Sir George Lewis	1874–1966
Bartholomew, John George	1860–1920
Bartlet, James Vernon	1863–1940
Bartlett, Sir Ellis Ashmead	1849–1902
Bartlett, Sir Frederic Charles	1886–1969
Bartley, Sir George Christopher Trout	1842–1910
Barton, Sir Edmund	1849–1920
Barton, John	1836–1908
Barton, Sir Sidney	1876–1946
Bashforth, Francis	1819–1912
Bass, Michael Arthur, Baron Burton	1837–1909
Bassett-Lowke, Wenman Joseph	1877–1953
Bateman, Henry Mayo	1887–1970
Bates, Cadwallader John	1853–1902
Bates, Sir Percy Elly	1879–1946
Bateson, Sir Alexander Dingwall	1866–1935
Bateson, Mary	1865–1906
Bateson, William	1861–1926
Bathurst, Charles, Viscount Bledisloe	1867–1958
Batsford, Harry	1880–1951
Battenberg, Prince Louis Alexander of. See Mountbatten	1854–1921
Bauerman, Hilary	1835–1909
Bax, Sir Arnold Edward Trevor	1883–1953
Baxter, Lucy, 'Leader Scott'	1837–1902
Bayley, Sir Steuart Colvin	1836–1925

Baylis, Lilian Mary	1874–1937
Baylis, Thomas Henry	1817–1908
Bayliss, Sir William Maddock	1860–1924
Bayliss, Sir Wyke	1835–1906
Bayly, Ada Ellen, 'Edna Lyall'	1857–1903
Bayly, Sir Lewis	1857–1938
Baynes, Norman Hepburn	1877–1961
Beach, Sir Michael Edward Hicks, Earl St. Aldwyn. See Hicks Beach	1837–1916
Beale, Dorothea	1831–1906
Beale, Lionel Smith	1828–1906
Beardmore, William, Baron Invernairn	1856–1936
Bearsted, Viscount. See Samuel, Marcus	1853–1927
Beatrice Mary Victoria Feodore, princess of Great Britain	1857–1944
Beattie-Brown, William	1831–1909
Beatty, Sir (Alfred) Chester	1875–1968
Beatty, David, Earl	1871–1936
Beatty, Sir Edward Wentworth	1877–1943
Beauchamp, Earl. See Lygon, William	1872–1938
Beaver, Sir Hugh Eyre Campbell	1890–1967
Beaverbrook, Baron. See Aitken, William Maxwell	1879–1964
Beazley, Sir John Davidson	1885–1970
Beckett, Sir Edmund, Baron Grimthorpe	1816–1905
Beddoe, John	1826–1911
Bedford, Duke of. See Russell, Herbrand Arthur	1858–1940
Bedford, Duchess of (1865–1937). See under Russell, Herbrand Arthur	
Bedford, William Kirkpatrick Riland	1826–1905
Bedson, Sir Samuel Phillips	1886–1969
Beecham, Thomas	1820–1907
Beecham, Sir Thomas	1879–1961
Beeching, Henry Charles	1859–1919
Beerbohm, Sir Henry Maximilian (Max)	1872–1956
Beevor, Charles Edward	1854–1908
Bégin, Louis Nazaire	1840–1925
Beilby, Sir George Thomas	1850–1924
Beit, Alfred	1853–1906
Beit, Sir Otto John	1865–1930
Beith, John Hay, 'Ian Hay'	1876–1952
Belcher, John	1841–1913
Belisha, (Isaac) Leslie Hore-, Baron Hore-Belisha. See Hore-Belisha	1893–1957
Bell, Alexander Graham	1847–1922
Bell, (Arthur) Clive (Heward)	1881–1964
Bell, Sir Charles Alfred	1870–1945
Bell, Charles Frederic Moberly	1847–1911
Bell, Sir Francis Henry Dillon	1851–1936
Bell, George Kennedy Allen	1883–1958
Bell, Gertrude Margaret Lowthian	1868–1926
Bell, Sir (Harold) Idris	1879–1967
Bell, Sir Henry Hesketh Joudou	1864–1952
Bell, Horace	1839–1903
Bell, Sir Isaac Lowthian	1816–1904
Bell, James	1824–1908
Bell, Sir Thomas	1865–1952
Bell, Valentine Graeme	1839–1908
Bell, Vanessa	1879–1961
Bellamy, James	1819–1909
Bellew, Harold Kyrle	1855–1911
Bellman, Sir (Charles) Harold	1886–1963
Bello, Sir Ahmadu, Sardauna of Sokoto	1910–1966
Belloc, Joseph Hilaire Pierre René	1870–1953
Bellows, John	1831–1902
Bemrose, William	1831–1908

Blood, Sir Bindon	1842–1940
Blood, Sir Hilary Rudolph Robert	1893–1967
Bloomfield, Georgiana, Lady	1822–1905
Blouet, Léon Paul, 'Max O'Rell'	1848–1903
Blount, Sir Edward Charles	1809–1905
Blumenfeld, Ralph David	1864–1948
Blumenthal, Jacques (Jacob)	1829–1908
Blunt, Lady Anne Isabella Noel (1837–1917). See under Blunt, Wilfrid Scawen	
Blunt, Wilfrid Scawen	1840–1922
Blythswood, Baron. See Campbell, Archibald Campbell	1835–1908
Blyton, Enid Mary	1897–1968
Bodda Pyne, Louisa Fanny	1832–1904
Bodington, Sir Nathan	1848–1911
Bodkin, Sir Archibald Henry	1862–1957
Bodkin, Thomas Patrick	1887–1961
Bodley, George Frederick	1827–1907
Body, George	1840–1911
Boldero, Sir Harold Esmond Arnison	1889–1960
Bols, Sir Louis Jean	1867–1930
Bomberg, David Garshen	1890–1957
Bompas, Henry Mason (1836–1909). See under Bompas, William Carpenter	
Bompas, William Carpenter	1834–1906
Bonar, James	1852–1941
Bonar Law, Andrew. See Law	1858–1923
Bond, Sir (Charles) Hubert	1870–1945
Bond, Sir Robert	1857–1927
Bond, William Bennett	1815–1906
Bondfield, Margaret Grace	1873–1953
Bone, James	1872–1962
Bone, Sir Muirhead	1876–1953
Bone, Stephen	1904–1958
Bone, William Arthur	1871–1938
Bonham-Carter, Sir Edgar	1870–1956
Bonham Carter, (Helen) Violet, Baroness Asquith of Yarnbury	1887–1969
Bonney, Thomas George	1833–1923
Bonney, (William Francis) Victor	1872–1953
Bonwick, James	1817–1906
Boot, Jesse, Baron Trent	1850–1931
Booth, Charles	1840–1916
Booth, Hubert Cecil	1871–1955
Booth, William ('General' Booth)	1829–1912
Booth, William Bramwell	1856–1929
Boothby, Guy Newell	1867–1905
Boothman, Sir John Nelson	1901–1957
Borden, Sir Robert Laird	1854–1937
Borthwick, Algernon, Baron Glenesk	1830–1908
Bosanquet, Bernard	1848–1923
Bosanquet, Sir Frederick Albert	1837–1923
Bosanquet, Robert Carr	1871–1935
Boswell, John James	1835–1908
Boswell, Percy George Hamnall	1886–1960
Bosworth Smith, Reginald. See Smith	1839–1908
Botha, Louis	1862–1919
Bottomley, Gordon	1874–1948
Bottomley, Horatio William	1860–1933
Boucherett, Emilia Jessie	1825–1905
Boucicault, Dion, the younger	1859–1929
Boughton, George Henry	1833–1905
Boughton, Rutland	1878–1960
Bourchier, Arthur	1863–1927
Bourchier, James David	1850–1920
Bourdillon, Sir Bernard Henry	1883–1948
Bourinot, Sir John George	1837–1902
Bourke, Robert, Baron Connemara	1827–1902
Bourne, Francis Alphonsus	1861–1935
Bourne, Gilbert Charles	1861–1933
Bourne, Henry Richard Fox	1837–1909
Bourne, Robert Croft	1888–1938
Bousfield, Henry Brougham	1832–1902
Bowater, Sir Eric Vansittart	1895–1962
Bowden, Frank Philip	1903–1968
Bowen, Edward Ernest	1836–1901
Bower, Frederick Orpen	1855–1948
Bowes, Robert	1835–1919
Bowes-Lyon, Claude George, Earl of Strathmore and Kinghorne	1855–1944
Bowhill, Sir Frederick William	1880–1960
Bowlby, Sir Anthony Alfred	1855–1929
Bowler, Henry Alexander	1824–1903
Bowles, Thomas Gibson	1842–1922
Bowley, Sir Arthur Lyon	1869–1957
Boyce, Sir Rubert William	1863–1911
Boycott, Arthur Edwin	1877–1938
Boyd, Henry	1831–1922
Boyd, Sir Thomas Jamieson	1818–1902
Boyd Carpenter, William. See Carpenter	1841–1918
Boyle, Sir Courtenay Edmund	1845–1901
Boyle, Sir Edward	1848–1909
Boyle, George David	1828–1901
Boyle, Richard Vicars	1822–1908
Boyle, William Henry Dudley, Earl of Cork and Orrery	1873–1967
Boys, Sir Charles Vernon	1855–1944
Brabazon, Hercules Brabazon	1821–1906
Brabazon, John Theodore Cuthbert Moore-, Baron Brabazon of Tara	1884–1964
Brabazon, Reginald, Earl of Meath	1841–1929
Bracken, Brendan Rendall, Viscount	1901–1958
Brackenbury, Sir Henry	1837–1914
Brackley, Herbert George	1894–1948
Bradbury, John Swanwick, Baron	1872–1950
Braddon, Sir Edward Nicholas Coventry	1829–1904
Braddon, Mary Elizabeth. See Maxwell	1837–1915
Bradford, Sir Edward Ridley Colborne	1836–1911
Bradford, Sir John Rose	1863–1935
Bradley, Andrew Cecil	1851–1935
Bradley, Francis Herbert	1846–1924
Bradley, George Granville	1821–1903
Bradley, Henry	1845–1923
Bragg, Sir William Henry	1862–1942
Braid, James	1870–1950
Brailsford, Henry Noel	1873–1958
Brain, Dennis	1921–1957
Brain, Walter Russell, Baron	1895–1966
Braithwaite, Dame (Florence) Lilian	1873–1948
Braithwaite, Sir Walter Pipon	1865–1945
Brambell, Francis William Rogers	1901–1970
Brampton, Baron. See Hawkins, Henry	1817–1907
Bramwell, Sir Byrom	1847–1931
Bramwell, Sir Frederick Joseph	1818–1903
Brancker, Sir William Sefton	1877–1930
Brand, Henry Robert, Viscount Hampden	1841–1906
Brand, Herbert Charles Alexander	1839–1901
Brand, Robert Henry, Baron	1878–1963
Brandis, Sir Dietrich	1824–1907
Brangwyn, Sir Frank (François Guillaume)	1867–1956
Brassey, Thomas, Earl	1836–1918
Bray, Caroline	1814–1905
Bray, Sir Reginald More	1842–1923
Brazil, Angela	1868–1947

Buckmaster, Stanley Owen, Viscount	1861–1934
Buckton, George Bowdler	1818–1905
Budge, Sir Ernest Alfred Thompson Wallis	1857–1934
Bulfin, Sir Edward Stanislaus	1862–1939
Bullen, Arthur Henry	1857–1920
Buller, Arthur Henry Reginald	1874–1944
Buller, Sir Redvers Henry	1839–1908
Buller, Sir Walter Lawry	1838–1906
Bulloch, William	1868–1941
Bulwer, Sir Edward Earle Gascoyne	1829–1910
Bulwer-Lytton, Victor Alexander George Robert, Earl of Lytton	1876–1947
Bunsen, Ernest de	1819–1903
Bunsen, Sir Maurice William Ernest de. See de Bunsen	1852–1932
Bunting, Sir Percy William	1836–1911
Burbidge, Edward	1839–1903
Burbidge, Frederick William	1847–1905
Burbury, Samuel Hawksley	1831–1911
Burdett-Coutts, Angela Georgina, Baroness	1814–1906
Burdon, John Shaw	1826–1907
Burdon-Sanderson, Sir John Scott	1828–1905
Burge, Hubert Murray	1862–1925
Burgh Canning, Hubert George De, Marquess of Clanricarde	1832–1916
Burkitt, Francis Crawford	1864–1935
Burn, Robert	1829–1904
Burn-Murdoch, John	1852–1909
Burnand, Sir Francis Cowley	1836–1917
Burne, Sir Owen Tudor	1837–1909
Burnell, Charles Desborough	1876–1969
Burnet, John	1863–1928
Burnet, Sir John James	1857–1938
Burnett, Sir Charles Stuart	1882–1945
Burnett, Dame Ivy Compton-. See Compton-Burnett	1884–1969
Burnett, Sir Robert Lindsay	1887–1959
Burnett-Stuart, Sir John Theodosius	1875–1958
Burney, Sir (Charles) Dennistoun	1888–1968
Burney, Sir Cecil	1858–1929
Burnham, Baron. See Levy-Lawson, Edward	1833–1916
Burnham, Baron. See Lawson, Edward Frederick	1890–1963
Burnham, Viscount. See Lawson, Harry Lawson Webster Levy-	1862–1933
Burns, Dawson	1828–1909
Burns, John Elliot	1858–1943
Burnside, William	1852–1927
Burrell, Sir William	1861–1958
Burroughs (afterwards Traill-Burroughs), Sir Frederick William	1831–1905
Burrows, Christine Mary Elizabeth	1872–1959
Burrows, Montagu	1819–1905
Burt, Thomas	1837–1922
Burton, Baron. See Bass, Michael Arthur	1837–1909
Burton, Sir Montague Maurice	1885–1952
Bury, John Bagnell	1861–1927
Bushell, Stephen Wootton	1844–1908
Busk, Rachel Harriette	1831–1907
Butcher, Samuel Henry	1850–1910
Butler, Arthur Gray	1831–1909
Butler, Arthur John	1844–1910
Butler, Edward Joseph Aloysius (Dom Cuthbert)	1858–1934
Butler, Elizabeth Southerden, Lady	1846–1933
Butler, Frank Hedges	1855–1928

Butler, Sir (George) Geoffrey (Gilbert)	1887–1929
Butler, Sir Harold Beresford	1883–1951
Butler, Henry Montagu	1833–1918
Butler, Josephine Elizabeth	1828–1906
Butler, Sir Montagu Sherard Dawes	1873–1952
Butler, Sir Richard Harte Keatinge	1870–1935
Butler, Samuel	1835–1902
Butler, Sir (Spencer) Harcourt	1869–1938
Butler, Sir William Francis	1838–1910
Butlin, Sir Henry Trentham	1845–1912
Butt, Dame Clara Ellen	1872–1936
Butterworth, George Sainton Kaye	1885–1916
Buxton, Noel Edward Noel-, Baron Noel-Buxton. See Noel-Buxton	1869–1948
Buxton, Patrick Alfred	1892–1955
Buxton, Sydney Charles, Earl	1853–1934
Buxton, Sir Thomas Fowell	1837–1915
Buzzard, Sir (Edward) Farquhar	1871–1945
Byng, Julian Hedworth George, Viscount Byng of Vimy	1862–1935
Byrne, Sir Edmund Widdrington	1844–1904
Byron, Robert	1905–1941
Bywater, Ingram	1840–1914
Cable, (Alice) Mildred	1878–1952
Cadbury, George	1839–1922
Cadman, John, Baron	1877–1941
Cadogan, Sir Alexander George Montagu	1884–1968
Cadogan, George Henry, Earl	1840–1915
Caillard, Sir Vincent Henry Penalver	1856–1930
Caine, Sir (Thomas Henry) Hall	1853–1931
Caine, William Sproston	1842–1903
Caird, Edward	1835–1908
Caird, Sir James	1864–1954
Cairnes, William Elliot	1862–1902
Cairns, David Smith	1862–1946
Cairns, Sir Hugh William Bell	1896–1952
Caldecote, Viscount. See Inskip, Thomas Walker Hobart	1876–1947
Caldecott, Sir Andrew	1884–1951
Calderon, George	1868–1915
Calkin, John Baptiste	1827–1905
Callaghan, Sir George Astley	1852–1920
Callendar, Hugh Longbourne	1863–1930
Callender, Sir Geoffrey Arthur Romaine	1875–1946
Callow, William	1812–1908
Callwell, Sir Charles Edward	1859–1928
Calman, William Thomas	1871–1952
Calthorpe, Baron. See Gough-Calthorpe, Augustus Cholmondeley	1829–1910
Calthorpe, Sir Somerset Arthur Gough-	1864–1937
Cam, Helen Maud	1885–1968
Cambridge, Duke of. See George William Frederick Charles	1819–1904
Cambridge, Alexander Augustus Frederick William Alfred George, Earl of Athlone	1874–1957
Cameron, Sir David Young	1865–1945
Cameron, Sir Donald Charles	1872–1948
Cameron, Sir (Gordon) Roy	1899–1966
Camm, Sir Sydney	1893–1966
Campbell, Archibald Campbell, Baron Blythswood	1835–1908
Campbell, Beatrice Stella (Mrs Patrick Campbell)	1865–1940
Campbell, Frederick Archibald Vaughan, Earl Cawdor	1847–1911

Charlesworth, Martin Percival	1895–1950
Charley, Sir William Thomas	1833–1904
Charlot, André Eugene Maurice	1892–1956
Charnwood, Baron. See Benson, Godfrey Rathbone	1864–1945
Charoux, Siegfried Joseph	1896–1967
Charrington, Frederick Nicholas	1850–1936
Charteris, Archibald Hamilton	1835–1908
Chase, Drummond Percy	1820–1902
Chase, Frederic Henry	1853–1925
Chase, Marian Emma	1844–1905
Chase, William St. Lucian	1856–1908
Chatfield, Alfred Ernle Montacute, Baron	1873–1967
Chatterjee, Sir Atul Chandra	1874–1955
Chauvel, Sir Henry George	1865–1945
Chavasse, Christopher Maude	1884–1962
Chavasse, Francis James	1846–1928
Cheadle, Walter Butler	1835–1910
Cheatle, Arthur Henry	1866–1929
Cheesman, Robert Ernest	1878–1962
Cheetham, Samuel	1827–1908
Chelmsford, Baron. See Thesiger, Frederic Augustus	1827–1905
Chelmsford, Viscount. See Thesiger, Frederic John Napier	1868–1933
Chermside, Sir Herbert Charles	1850–1929
Cherry-Garrard, Apsley George Benet	1886–1959
Cherwell, Viscount. See Lindemann, Frederick Alexander	1886–1957
Chesterton, Gilbert Keith	1874–1936
Chetwode, Sir Philip Walhouse, Baron	1869–1950
Chevalier, Albert	1861–1923
Cheylesmore, Baron. See Eaton, Herbert Francis	1848–1925
Cheylesmore, Baron. See Eaton, William Meriton	1843–1902
Cheyne, Thomas Kelly	1841–1915
Cheyne, Sir (William) Watson	1852–1932
Chifley, Joseph Benedict	1885–1951
Child, Harold Hannyngton	1869–1945
Child, Thomas	1839–1906
Child-Villiers, Margaret Elizabeth, Countess of Jersey. See Villiers	1849–1945
Child-Villiers, Victor Albert George, Earl of Jersey. See Villiers	1845–1915
Childe, Vere Gordon	1892–1957
Childers, Robert Erskine	1870–1922
Childs, William Macbride	1869–1939
Chilston, Viscount. See Akers-Douglas, Aretas	1851–1926
Chilston, Viscount. See Akers-Douglas, Aretas	1876–1947
Chirol, Sir (Ignatius) Valentine	1852–1929
Chisholm, Hugh	1866–1924
Cholmondeley, Hugh, Baron Delamere	1870–1931
Christiansen, Arthur	1904–1963
Christie, John	1882–1962
Christie, Sir William Henry Mahoney	1845–1922
Chrystal, George	1851–1911
Chubb, Sir Lawrence Wensley	1873–1948
Church, Sir William Selby	1837–1928
Churchill, Sir Winston Leonard Spencer-	1874–1965
Chuter-Ede, James Chuter, Baron Chuter-Ede	1882–1965
Cilcennin, Viscount. See Thomas, James Purdon Lewes	1903–1960
Clanricarde, Marquess of. See Burgh Canning, Hubert George De	1832–1916

Clanwilliam, Earl of. See Meade, Richard James	1832–1907
Clapham, Sir Alfred William	1883–1950
Clapham, Sir John Harold	1873–1946
Clarendon, Earl of. See Villiers, George Herbert Hyde	1877–1955
Clark, Albert Curtis	1859–1937
Clark, Sir Allen George	1898–1962
Clark, James (Jim)	1936–1968
Clark, John Willis	1833–1910
Clark, Sir William Henry	1876–1952
Clark Kerr, Archibald John Kerr, Baron Inverchapel	1882–1951
Clarke, Sir Andrew	1824–1902
Clarke, Sir Caspar Purdon	1846–1911
Clarke, Charles Baron	1832–1906
Clarke, Sir Charles Noble Arden-. See Arden-Clarke	1898–1962
Clarke, Sir Edward George	1841–1931
Clarke, Sir Fred	1880–1952
Clarke, George Sydenham, Baron Sydenham of Combe	1848–1933
Clarke, Henry Butler	1863–1904
Clarke, Louis Colville Gray	1881–1960
Clarke, Sir Marshal James	1841–1909
Clarke, Maude Violet	1892–1935
Clarke, Thomas	1884–1957
Clasper, John Hawks	1836–1908
Clausen, Sir George	1852–1944
Clauson, Albert Charles, Baron	1870–1946
Claxton, Brooke	1898–1960
Clay, Sir Henry	1883–1954
Clayden, Peter William	1827–1902
Clayton, Sir Gilbert Falkingham	1875–1929
Clementi, Sir Cecil	1875–1947
Clerk, Sir Dugald	1854–1932
Clerk, Sir George Russell	1874–1951
Clerke, Agnes Mary	1842–1907
Clerke, Ellen Mary (1840–1906). See under Clerke, Agnes Mary	
Clery, Sir Cornelius Francis	1838–1926
Cleworth, Thomas Ebenezer	1854–1909
Clifford, Sir Bede Edmund Hugh	1890–1969
Clifford, Frederick	1828–1904
Clifford, Sir Hugh Charles	1866–1941
Clifford, John	1836–1923
Clive, Sir Robert Henry	1877–1948
Clodd, Edward	1840–1930
Close, Sir Charles Frederick Arden-. See Arden-Close	1865–1952
Close, Maxwell Henry	1822–1903
Clowes, Sir William Laird	1856–1905
Clunes, Alexander de Moro Sherriff (Alec)	1912–1970
Clunies-Ross, George	1842–1910
Clunies Ross, Sir Ian. See Ross	1899–1959
Clutton, Henry Hugh	1850–1909
Clutton-Brock, Arthur	1868–1924
Clyde, James Avon, Lord	1863–1944
Clydesmuir, Baron. See Colville, David John	1894–1954
Clynes, John Robert	1869–1949
Coade, Thorold Francis	1896–1963
Coatalen, Louis Hervé	1879–1962
Coates, Eric	1886–1957
Coates, Joseph Gordon	1878–1943
Cobb, Gerard Francis	1838–1904
Cobb, John Rhodes	1899–1952
Cobbe, Sir Alexander Stanhope	1870–1931
Cobbe, Frances Power	1822–1904

Costain, Sir Richard Rylandes 1902–1966
Cotton, Jack 1903–1964
Couch, Sir Arthur Thomas Quiller-,
('Q'). See Quiller-Couch 1863–1944
Couch, Sir Richard 1817–1905
Coulton, George Gordon 1858–1947
Couper, Sir George Ebenezer Wilson 1824–1908
Coupland, Sir Reginald 1884–1952
Court Brown, William Michael. See
Brown 1918–1968
Courtauld, Augustine 1904–1959
Courtauld, Samuel 1876–1947
Courthope, William John 1842–1917
Courtney, Leonard Henry, Baron
Courtney of Penwith 1832–1918
Courtney, William Leonard 1850–1928
Cousin, Anne Ross 1824–1906
Cowan, Sir Walter Henry 1871–1956
Cowans, Sir John Steven 1862–1921
Coward, Sir Henry 1849–1944
Cowdray, Viscount. See Pearson,
Weetman Dickinson 1856–1927
Cowell, Edward Byles 1826–1903
Cowen, Sir Frederic Hymen 1852–1935
Cowie, William Garden 1831–1902
Cowley, Sir Arthur Ernest 1861–1931
Cowper, Francis Thomas de Grey, Earl 1834–1905
Cox, Alfred 1866–1954
Cox, George (called Sir George) William 1827–1902
Cox, Harold 1859–1936
Cox, Leslie Reginald 1897–1965
Cox, Sir Percy Zachariah 1864–1937
Cozens-Hardy, Herbert Hardy, Baron 1838–1920
Craddock, Sir Reginald Henry 1864–1937
Cradock, Sir Christopher George
Francis Maurice 1862–1914
Craig, (Edward Henry) Gordon 1872–1966
Craig, Isa. See Knox 1831–1903
Craig, James, Viscount Craigavon 1871–1940
Craig, Sir John 1874–1957
Craig, William James 1843–1906
Craigavon, Viscount. See Craig, James 1871–1940
Craigie, Pearl Mary Teresa, 'John
Oliver Hobbes' 1867–1906
Craigie, Sir Robert Leslie 1883–1959
Craigie, Sir William Alexander 1867–1957
Craigmyle, Baron. See Shaw, Thomas 1850–1937
Craik, Sir Henry 1846–1927
Cranbrook, Earl of. See Gathorne-
Hardy, Gathorne 1814–1906
Crane, Walter 1845–1915
Craven, Hawes 1837–1910
Craven, Henry Thornton 1818–1905
Crawford, Earl of. See Lindsay, David
Alexander Edward 1871–1940
Crawford, Earl of. See Lindsay, James
Ludovic 1847–1913
Crawford, Osbert Guy Stanhope 1886–1957
Crawfurd, Oswald John Frederick 1834–1909
Crawfurd, Sir Raymond Henry Payne 1865–1938
Creagh, Sir Garrett O'Moore 1848–1923
Creagh, William 1828–1901
Creech Jones, Arthur. See Jones 1891–1964
Creed, John Martin 1889–1940
Creed, Sir Thomas Percival 1897–1969
Cremer, Robert Wyndham Ketton-.
See Ketton-Cremer 1906–1969
Cremer, Sir William Randal 1838–1908
Crew-Milnes, Robert Offley Ash-
burton, Marquess of Crewe 1858–1945

Crichton-Browne, Sir James. See
Browne 1840–1938
Cripps, Charles Alfred, Baron Parmoor 1852–1941
Cripps, Sir (Richard) Stafford 1889–1952
Cripps, Wilfred Joseph 1841–1903
Crocker, Henry Radcliffe-. See
Radcliffe-Crocker 1845–1909
Crockett, Samuel Rutherford 1860–1914
Croft, Henry Page, Baron 1881–1947
Croft, John 1833–1905
Crofts, Ernest 1847–1911
Croke, Thomas William 1824–1902
Cromer, Earl of. See Baring, Evelyn 1841–1917
Cromer, Earl of. See Baring, Rowland
Thomas 1877–1953
Crompton, Henry 1836–1904
Crompton, Richmal. See Lamburn,
Richmal Crompton 1890–1969
Crompton, Rookes Evelyn Bell 1845–1940
Crookes, Sir William 1832–1919
Crooks, William 1852–1921
Crookshank, Harry Frederick Comfort,
Viscount Crookshank 1893–1961
Cross, Charles Frederick 1855–1935
Cross, Kenneth Mervyn Baskerville 1890–1968
Cross, Richard Assheton, Viscount 1823–1914
Crossman, Sir William 1830–1901
Crosthwaite, Sir Charles Haukes Todd 1835–1915
Crowdy, Dame Rachel Eleanor 1884–1964
Crowe, Sir Edward Thomas Frederick 1877–1960
Crowe, Eyre 1824–1910
Crowe, Sir Eyre Alexander Barby
Wichart 1864–1925
Crozier, William Percival 1879–1944
Cruikshank, Robert James 1898–1956
Crum, Walter Ewing 1865–1944
Crump, Charles George 1862–1935
Cruttwell, Charles Robert Mowbray
Fraser 1887–1941
Cruttwell, Charles Thomas 1847–1911
Cubitt, William George 1835–1903
Cudlipp, Percival Thomas James 1905–1962
Cullen, William 1867–1948
Cullingworth, Charles James 1841–1908
Cullis, Winifred Clara 1875–1956
Cummings, Arthur John 1882–1957
Cummings, Bruce Frederick, 'W. N. P.
Barbellion' 1889–1919
Cuningham, James McNabb 1829–1905
Cunningham, Andrew Browne,
Viscount Cunningham of Hyndhope 1883–1963
Cunningham, Daniel John 1850–1909
Cunningham, Sir George 1888–1963
Cunningham, Sir John Henry Dacres 1885–1962
Cunningham, William 1849–1919
Cunninghame Graham, Robert
Bontine. See Graham 1852–1936
Currie, Sir Arthur William 1875–1933
Currie, Sir Donald 1825–1909
Currie, Sir James 1868–1937
Currie (formerly Singleton), Mary
Montgomerie, Lady, 'Violet Fane' 1843–1905
Currie, Philip Henry Wodehouse, Baron 1834–1906
Currie, Sir William Crawford 1884–1961
Curtin, John 1885–1945
Curtis, Edmund 1881–1943
Curtis, Lionel George 1872–1955
Curtis, William Edward 1889–1969
Curzon, George Nathaniel, Marquess
Curzon of Kedleston 1859–1925

Denniston, John Dewar	1887–1949		Dimock, Nathaniel	1825–1909
Denny, Sir Archibald	1860–1936		Dines, William Henry	1855–1927
Denny, Sir Maurice Edward	1886–1955		Dix, George Eglington Alston, Dom	
Dent, Edward Joseph	1876–1957		Gregory	1901–1952
Dent, Joseph Malaby	1849–1926		Dixie, Lady Florence Caroline	1857–1905
Derby, Earl of. See Stanley, Edward			Dixon, Sir Arthur Lewis	1881–1969
George Villiers	1865–1948		Dixon, Henry Horatio	1869–1953
Derby, Earl of. See Stanley, Frederick			Dixon, Sir Pierson John	1904–1965
Arthur	1841–1908		Dixon, Sir Robert Bland	1867–1939
D'Erlanger, Sir Gerard John Regis Leo	1906–1962		Dixon, Walter Ernest	1870–1931
De Robeck, Sir John Michael	1862–1928		Dobbs, Sir Henry Robert Conway	1871–1934
De Saulles, George William	1862–1903		Dobell, Bertram	1842–1914
Desborough, Baron. See Grenfell,			Dobson, Frank Owen	1886–1963
William Henry	1855–1945		Dobson, (Henry) Austin	1840–1921
De Selincourt, Ernest. See Selincourt	1870–1943		Dobson, Sir Roy Hardy	1891–1968
De Soissons, Louis Emmanuel Jean			Dodd, Francis	1874–1949
Guy de Savoie-Carignan	1890–1962		Dodgson, Campbell	1867–1948
De Stein, Sir Edward Sinauer	1887–1965		Dodgson, Frances Catharine	1883–1954
De Syllas, Stelios Messinesos (Leo)	1917–1964		Dods, Marcus	1834–1909
Des Voeux, Sir (George) William	1834–1909		Doherty, Hugh Lawrence	1875–1919
Detmold, Charles Maurice	1883–1908		Dolling, Robert William Radclyffe	1851–1902
De Vere, Aubrey Thomas	1814–1902		Dolmetsch, (Eugene) Arnold	1858–1940
De Vere, Sir Stephen Edward	1812–1904		Donald, Sir John Stewart	1861–1948
Deverell, Sir Cyril John	1874–1947		Donald, Sir Robert	1860–1933
De Villiers, John Henry, Baron	1842–1914		Donaldson, Sir James	1831–1915
Devine, George Alexander Cassady	1910–1966		Donaldson, St. Clair George Alfred	1863–1935
Devlin, Joseph	1871–1934		Donat, (Friederich) Robert	1905–1958
Devonport, Viscount. See Kearley,			Donkin, Bryan	1835–1902
Hudson Ewbanke	1856–1934		Donnan, Frederick George	1870–1956
Devons, Ely	1913–1967		Donnelly, Sir John Fretcheville Dykes	1834–1902
Devonshire, Duke of. See Cavendish,			Donnet, Sir James John Louis	1816–1905
Spencer Compton	1833–1908		Donoghue, Stephen	1884–1945
Devonshire, Duke of. See Cavendish,			Donoughmore, Earl of. See Hely-	
Victor Christian William	1868–1938		Hutchinson, Richard Walter John	1875–1948
Dewar, Sir James	1842–1923		Doodson, Arthur Thomas	1890–1968
De Wet, Christiaan Rudolph	1854–1922		Dorrien, Sir Horace Lockwood Smith-.	
De Wiart, Sir Adrian Carton. See			See Smith-Dorrien	1858–1930
Carton de Wiart	1880–1963		Doubleday, Herbert Arthur	1867–1941
De Winton, Sir Francis Walter	1835–1901		Doughty, Charles Montagu	1843–1926
De Worms, Henry, Baron Pirbright	1840–1903		Doughty-Wylie, Charles Hotham	
Dewrance, Sir John	1858–1937		Montagu	1868–1915
D'Eyncourt, Sir Eustace Henry			Douglas, Sir Adye	1815–1906
William Tennyson-. See Tennyson-			Douglas, Lord Alfred Bruce	1870–1945
d'Eyncourt	1868–1951		Douglas, Sir Charles Whittingham	
Dibbs, Sir George Richard	1834–1904		Horsley	1850–1914
Dibdin, Sir Lewis Tonna	1852–1938		Douglas, Claude Gordon	1882–1963
Dicey, Albert Venn	1835–1922		Douglas, Clifford (Hugh)	1879–1952
Dicey, Edward James Stephen	1832–1911		Douglas, George, pseudonym. See	
Dick, Sir William Reid	1878–1961		Brown, George Douglas	1869–1902
Dick-Read, Grantly	1890–1959		Douglas, George Cunninghame	
Dickinson, Goldsworthy Lowes	1862–1932		Monteath	1826–1904
Dickinson, Henry Winram	1870–1952		Douglas, (George) Norman	1868–1952
Dickinson, Hercules Henry	1827–1905		Douglas, Sir (Henry) Percy	1876–1939
Dickinson, Lowes (Cato)	1819–1908		Douglas, William Sholto, Baron	
Dicksee, Sir Francis Bernard (Frank)	1853–1928		Douglas of Kirtleside	1893–1969
Dickson, Sir Collingwood	1817–1904		Douglas, Sir William Scott	1890–1953
Dickson, William Purdie	1823–1901		Douglas-Pennant, George Sholto	
Dickson-Poynder, Sir John Poynder,			Gordon, Baron Penrhyn	1836–1907
Baron Islington. See Poynder	1866–1936		Douglas-Scott-Montagu, John Walter	
Digby, William	1849–1904		Edward, Baron Montagu of Beaulieu	1866–1929
Dilke, Sir Charles Wentworth	1843–1911		Dove, Dame (Jane) Frances	1847–1942
Dilke, Emilia Frances, Lady	1840–1904		Dove, John	1872–1934
Dill, Sir John Greer	1881–1944		Dover Wilson, John. See Wilson	1881–1969
Dill, Sir Samuel	1844–1924		Dowden, Edward	1843–1913
Dillon, Emile Joseph	1854–1933		Dowden, John	1840–1910
Dillon, Frank	1823–1909		Dowding, Hugh Caswall Tremenheere,	
Dillon, Harold Arthur Lee-, Viscount			Baron	1882–1970
Dillon	1844–1932		Dowie, John Alexander	1847–1907
Dillon, John	1851–1927		Downey, Richard Joseph	1881–1953
Dimbleby, Richard Frederick	1913–1965		Doyle, Sir Arthur Conan	1859–1930

Eliot, Sir Charles Norton Edgecumbe	1862-1931
Eliot, Sir John	1839-1908
Eliot, Thomas Stearns	1888-1963
Elkan, Benno	1877-1960
Ellerman, Sir John Reeves	1862-1933
Ellery, Robert Lewis John	1827-1908
Elles, Sir Hugh Jamieson	1880-1945
Ellicott, Charles John	1819-1905
Elliot, Arthur Ralph Douglas	1846-1923
Elliot, Sir George Augustus	1813-1901
Elliot, Gilbert John Murray Kynynmond, Earl of Minto	1845-1914
Elliot, Sir Henry George	1817-1907
Elliot, Walter Elliot	1888-1958
Elliott, Sir Charles Alfred	1835-1911
Elliott, Edwin Bailey	1851-1937
Elliott, Thomas Renton	1877-1961
Ellis, Sir Arthur William Mickle	1883-1966
Ellis, Frederick Startridge	1830-1901
Ellis, Henry Havelock	1859-1939
Ellis, John Devonshire	1824-1906
Ellis, Robinson	1834-1913
Ellis, Thomas Evelyn Scott-, Baron Howard de Walden. See Scott-Ellis	1880-1946
Ellis, Sir William Henry	1860-1945
Elphinstone, Sir (George) Keith (Buller)	1865-1941
Elsie, Lily	1886-1962
Elsmie, George Robert	1838-1909
Elton, Oliver	1861-1945
Elvin, Sir (James) Arthur	1899-1957
Elwes, Gervase Henry Cary-	1866-1921
Elwes, Henry John	1846-1922
Elworthy, Frederick Thomas	1830-1907
Emery, William	1825-1910
Emmott, Alfred, Baron	1858-1926
Ensor, Sir Robert Charles Kirkwood	1877-1958
Entwistle, William James	1895-1952
Epstein, Sir Jacob	1880-1959
Ernle, Baron. See Prothero, Rowland Edmund	1851-1937
Esdaile, Katharine Ada	1881-1950
Esher, Viscount. See Brett, Reginald Baliol	1852-1930
Esmond, Henry Vernon	1869-1922
Etheridge, Robert	1819-1903
Euan-Smith, Sir Charles Bean	1842-1910
Eumorfopoulos, George	1863-1939
Eva, pseudonym. See under O'Doherty, Kevin Izod	1823-1905
Evan-Thomas, Sir Hugh	1862-1928
Evans, Sir Arthur John	1851-1941
Evans, Sir Charles Arthur Lovatt	1884-1968
Evans, Daniel Silvan	1818-1903
Evans, Edmund	1826-1905
Evans, Edward Ratcliffe Garth Russell, Baron Mountevans	1880-1957
Evans, Sir (Evan) Vincent	1851-1934
Evans, George Essex	1863-1909
Evans, Sir Guildhaume Myrddin-. See Myrddin-Evans	1894-1964
Evans, Horace, Baron	1903-1963
Evans, Sir John	1823-1908
Evans, John Gwenogvryn	1852-1930
Evans, Meredith Gwynne	1904-1952
Evans, Sir Samuel Thomas	1859-1918
Evans, Sebastian	1830-1909
Evans, Sir (Worthington) Laming Worthington-	1868-1931
Evatt, Herbert Vere	1894-1965

Eve, Sir Harry Trelawney	1856-1940
Everard, Harry Stirling Crawfurd	1848-1909
Everett, Joseph David	1831-1904
Everett, Sir William	1844-1908
Evershed, (Francis) Raymond, Baron	1899-1966
Evershed, John	1864-1956
Eversley, Baron. See Shaw-Lefevre, George John	1831-1928
Eves, Reginald Grenville	1876-1941
Ewart, Alfred James	1872-1937
Ewart, Charles Brisbane	1827-1903
Ewart, Sir John Alexander	1821-1904
Ewart, Sir John Spencer	1861-1930
Ewing, Sir (James) Alfred	1855-1935
Ewins, Arthur James	1882-1957
Eyre, Edward John	1815-1901
Faber, Sir Geoffrey Cust	1889-1961
Faber, Oscar	1886-1956
Fachiri, Adila Adrienne Adalbertina Maria	1886-1962
Faed, John	1819-1902
Fagan, James Bernard	1873-1933
Fagan, Louis Alexander	1845-1903
Fairbairn, Andrew Martin	1838-1912
Fairbairn, Stephen	1862-1938
Fairbridge, Kingsley Ogilvie	1885-1924
Fairey, Sir (Charles) Richard	1887-1956
Fairfield, Baron. See Greer, (Frederick) Arthur	1863-1945
Fairley, Sir Neil Hamilton	1891-1966
Falcke, Isaac	1819-1909
Falconer, Lanoe, pseudonym. See Hawker, Mary Elizabeth	1848-1908
Falconer, Sir Robert Alexander	1867-1943
Falkiner, Caesar Litton	1863-1908
Falkiner, Sir Frederick Richard	1831-1908
Falkner, John Meade	1858-1932
Fane, Violet, pseudonym. See Currie, Mary Montgomerie, Lady	1843-1905
Fanshawe, Sir Edward Gennys	1814-1906
Farjeon, Benjamin Leopold	1838-1903
Farjeon, Eleanor	1881-1965
Farmer, Emily	1826-1905
Farmer, John	1835-1901
Farmer, Sir John Bretland	1865-1944
Farnell, Lewis Richard	1856-1934
Farningham, Marianne, pseudonym. See Hearn, Mary Anne	1834-1909
Farnol, (John) Jeffery	1878-1952
Farquhar, John Nicol	1861-1929
Farquharson, David	1840-1907
Farrar, Adam Storey	1826-1905
Farrar, Frederic William	1831-1903
Farren (afterwards Soutar), Ellen (Nellie)	1848-1904
Farren, William	1825-1908
Farren, Sir William Scott	1892-1970
Farrer, Austin Marsden	1904-1968
Farrer, William	1861-1924
Farwell, Sir George	1845-1915
Fausset, Andrew Robert	1821-1910
Fawcett, Dame Millicent	1847-1929
Fay, Sir Sam	1856-1953
Fay, William George	1872-1947
Fayrer, Sir Joseph	1824-1907
Fearnsides, William George	1879-1968
Feetham, Richard	1874-1965
Felkin, Ellen Thorneycroft	1860-1929

Foster, Sir Clement Le Neve	1841–1904	Freeman-Thomas, Freeman, Marquess	
Foster, Sir George Eulas	1847–1931	of Willingdon	1866–1941
Foster, Sir Harry Braustyn Hylton		Freeth, Francis Arthur	1884–1970
Hylton-. See Hylton-Foster	1905–1965	Fremantle, Sir Edmund Robert	1836–1929
Foster, Joseph	1844–1905	French, Evangeline Frances	1869–1960
Foster, Sir Michael	1836–1907	French, Francesca Law	1871–1960
Foster, Sir (Thomas) Gregory	1866–1931	French, Sir Henry Leon	1883–1966
Fotheringham, John Knight	1874–1936	French, John Denton Pinkstone, Earl of	
Fougasse, *pseudonym*. See Bird, (Cyril)		Ypres	1852–1925
Kenneth	1887–1965	Frere, Mary Eliza Isabella	1845–1911
Foulkes, Isaac	1836–1904	Frere, Walter Howard	1863–1938
Fowle, Thomas Welbank	1835–1903	Freshfield, Douglas William	1845–1934
Fowler, Alfred	1868–1940	Freyberg, Bernard Cyril, Baron	1889–1963
Fowler, Ellen Thorneycroft. See Felkin	1860–1929	Freyer, Sir Peter Johnston	1851–1921
Fowler, Henry Hartley, Viscount		Friese-Greene, William. See Greene	1855–1921
Wolverhampton	1830–1911	Frith, William Powell	1819–1909
Fowler, Henry Watson	1858–1933	Fritsch, Felix Eugen	1879–1954
Fowler, Sir James Kingston	1852–1934	Frowde, Henry	1841–1927
Fowler, Sir Ralph Howard	1889–1944	Fry, Charles Burgess	1872–1956
Fowler, Thomas	1832–1904	Fry, Danby Palmer	1818–1903
Fowler, William Warde	1847–1921	Fry, Sir Edward	1827–1918
Fox, Sir Cyril Fred	1882–1967	Fry, Joseph Storrs	1826–1913
Fox, Dame Evelyn Emily Marian	1874–1955	Fry, Roger Eliot	1866–1934
Fox, Sir Francis	1844–1927	Fry, Sara Margery	1874–1958
Fox, Harold Munro	1889–1967	Fry, Thomas Charles	1846–1930
Fox, Sir Lionel Wray	1895–1961	Fryatt, Charles Algernon	1872–1916
Fox, Samson	1838–1903	Fuller, Sir Cyril Thomas Moulden	1874–1942
Fox, Terence Robert Corelli	1912–1962	Fuller, John Frederick Charles	1878–1966
Fox Bourne, Henry Richard. See Bourne	1837–1909	Fuller, Sir (Joseph) Bampfylde	1854–1935
Fox Strangways, Arthur Henry. See		Fuller, Sir Thomas Ekins	1831–1910
Strangways	1859–1948	Fuller-Maitland, John Alexander. See	
Fox-Strangways, Giles Stephen		Maitland	1856–1936
Holland, Earl of Ilchester	1874–1959	Fulleylove, John	1845–1908
Foxwell, Arthur	1853–1909	Furneaux, William Mordaunt	1848–1928
Foxwell, Herbert Somerton	1849–1936	Furness, Christopher, Baron	1852–1912
Foyle, William Alfred	1885–1963	Furniss, Harry	1854–1925
Fraenkel, Eduard David Mortier	1888–1970	Furniss, Henry Sanderson, Baron	
Frampton, Sir George James	1860–1928	Sanderson	1868–1939
Francis-Williams, Baron. See Williams,		Furnivall, Frederick James	1825–1910
Edward Francis	1903–1970	Furse, Charles Wellington	1868–1904
Frankau, Gilbert	1884–1952	Furse, Dame Katharine	1875–1952
Frankfort de Montmorency, Viscount.		Fust, Herbert Jenner-. See Jenner-Fust	1806–1904
See de Montmorency, Raymond		Fyfe, David Patrick Maxwell, Earl of	
Harvey	1835–1902	Kilmuir	1900–1967
Frankland, Percy Faraday	1858–1946	Fyfe, Henry Hamilton	1869–1951
Franklin, Charles Samuel	1879–1964	Fyfe, Sir William Hamilton	1878–1965
Franks, Robert Sleightholme	1871–1964	Fyleman, Rose Amy	1877–1957
Fraser, Alexander Campbell	1819–1914		
Fraser, Sir Andrew Henderson Leith	1848–1919		
Fraser, Claud Lovat	1890–1921	Gaddum, Sir John Henry	1900–1965
Fraser, Donald	1870–1933	Gadsby, Henry Robert	1842–1907
Fraser, Sir Francis Richard	1885–1964	Gainford, Baron. See Pease, Joseph	
Fraser, Hugh, Baron Fraser of Allander	1903–1966	Albert	1860–1943
Fraser, Peter	1884–1950	Gairdner, James	1828–1912
Fraser, Simon Joseph, Baron Lovat	1871–1933	Gairdner, Sir William Tennant	1824–1907
Fraser, Sir Thomas Richard	1841–1920	Gaitskell, Hugh Todd Naylor	1906–1963
Fraser, William, Baron Strathalmond	1888–1970	Gale, Frederick	1823–1904
Frazer, Alastair Campbell	1909–1969	Gallacher, William	1881–1965
Frazer, Sir James George	1854–1941	Galloway, Sir William	1840–1927
Fream, William	1854–1906	Gallwey, Peter	1820–1906
Fréchette, Louis Honoré	1839–1908	Galsworthy, John	1867–1933
Freedman, Barnett	1901–1958	Galton, Sir Francis	1822–1911
Freeman, Gage Earle	1820–1903	Game, Sir Philip Woolcott	1876–1961
Freeman, John	1880–1929	Gamgee, Arthur	1841–1909
Freeman, John Peere Williams-. See		Gandhi, Mohandas Karamchand	1869–1948
Williams-Freeman	1858–1943	Gann, Thomas William Francis	1867–1938
Freeman, Sir Ralph	1880–1950	Garbett, Cyril Forster	1875–1955
Freeman, Sir Wilfrid Rhodes	1888–1953	García, Manuel Patricio Rodríguez	1805–1906
Freeman-Mitford, Algernon Bertram,		Gardiner, Sir Alan Henderson	1879–1963
Baron Redesdale. See Mitford	1837–1916	Gardiner, Alfred George	1865–1946

Gogarty, Oliver Joseph St. John	1878–1957
Gold, Sir Harcourt Gilbey	1876–1952
Goldie, Sir George Dashwood Taubman	1846–1925
Goldschmidt, Otto	1829–1907
Goldsmid, Sir Frederic John	1818–1908
Goldsmid-Montefiore, Claude Joseph. See Montefiore	1858–1938
Gollancz, Sir Hermann	1852–1930
Gollancz, Sir Israel	1863–1930
Gollancz, Sir Victor	1893–1967
Gooch, George Peabody	1873–1968
Goodall, Frederick	1822–1904
Goode, Sir William Athelstane Meredith	1875–1944
Gooden, Stephen Frederick	1892–1955
Goodenough, Frederick Craufurd	1866–1934
Goodenough, Sir William Edmund	1867–1945
Goodenough, Sir William Macnamara	1899–1951
Goodey, Tom	1885–1953
Goodhart-Rendel, Harry Stuart	1887–1959
Goodman (formerly Salaman), Julia	1812–1906
Goodrich, Edwin Stephen	1868–1946
Goossens, Sir Eugene	1893–1962
Gordon, Arthur Charles Hamilton-, Baron Stanmore	1829–1912
Gordon, Charles William, 'Ralph Connor'	1860–1937
Gordon, George Stuart	1881–1942
Gordon (formerly Marjoribanks), Ishbel Maria, Marchioness of Aberdeen and Temair (1857–1939). See under Gordon, John Campbell	
Gordon, James Frederick Skinner	1821–1904
Gordon, John Campbell, Marquess of Aberdeen and Temair	1847–1934
Gordon, Sir John James Hood	1832–1908
Gordon, Mervyn Henry	1872–1953
Gordon, Sir Thomas Edward	1832–1914
Gordon-Lennox, Charles Henry, Duke of Richmond and Gordon	1818–1903
Gordon-Taylor, Sir Gordon	1878–1960
Gore, Albert Augustus	1840–1901
Gore, Charles	1853–1932
Gore, George	1826–1908
Gore, John Ellard	1845–1910
Gore, William George Arthur Ormsby-, Baron Harlech. See Ormsby-Gore	1885–1964
Gore-Browne, Sir Stewart	1883–1967
Gorell, Baron. See Barnes, John Gorell	1848–1913
Gorer, Peter Alfred Isaac	1907–1961
Gorst, Sir John Eldon	1835–1916
Gorst, Sir (John) Eldon	1861–1911
Gort, Viscount. See Vereker, John Standish Surtees Prendergast	1886–1946
Goschen, George Joachim, Viscount	1831–1907
Gosling, Harry	1861–1930
Gossage, Sir (Ernest) Leslie	1891–1949
Gosse, Sir Edmund William	1849–1928
Gosselin, Sir Martin le Marchant Hadsley	1847–1905
Gosset, William Sealy, 'Student'	1876–1937
Gotch, John Alfred	1852–1942
Gott, John	1830–1906
Gott, William Henry Ewart	1897–1942
Gough, Sir Charles John Stanley	1832–1912
Gough, Herbert John	1890–1965
Gough, Sir Hubert de la Poer	1870–1963
Gough, Sir Hugh Henry	1833–1909
Gough, John Edmond	1871–1915

Gough-Calthorpe, Augustus Cholmondeley, Baron Calthorpe	1829–1910
Gough-Calthorpe, Sir Somerset Arthur. See Calthorpe	1864–1937
Gould, Sir Francis Carruthers	1844–1925
Gould, Nathaniel	1857–1919
Goulding, Frederick	1842–1909
Gower, (Edward) Frederick Leveson-. See Leveson-Gower	1819–1907
Gower, Sir Henry Dudley Gresham Leveson	1873–1954
Gowers, Sir Ernest Arthur	1880–1966
Gowers, Sir William Richard	1845–1915
Gowrie, Earl of. See Hore-Ruthven, Alexander Gore Arkwright	1872–1955
Grace, Edward Mills	1841–1911
Grace, William Gilbert	1848–1915
Graham, Henry Grey	1842–1906
Graham, Hugh, Baron Atholstan	1848–1938
Graham, John Anderson	1861–1942
Graham, Robert Bontine Cunninghame	1852–1936
Graham, Sir Ronald William	1870–1949
Graham, Thomas Alexander Ferguson	1840–1906
Graham, William	1839–1911
Graham, William	1887–1932
Graham Brown, Thomas. See Brown	1882–1965
Graham-Harrison, Sir William Montagu	1871–1949
Graham-Little, Sir Ernest Gordon Graham	1867–1950
Grahame, Kenneth	1859–1932
Grahame-White, Claude	1879–1959
Granet, Sir (William) Guy	1867–1943
Grant, Sir (Alfred) Hamilton	1872–1937
Grant, Sir Charles (1836–1903). See under Grant, Sir Robert	
Grant, George Monro	1835–1902
Grant, Sir Robert	1837–1904
Grant Duff, Sir Mountstuart Elphinstone	1829–1906
Grantham, Sir William	1835–1911
Granville-Barker, Harley Granville	1877–1946
Graves, Alfred Perceval	1846–1931
Graves, George Windsor	1873?–1949
Gray, Sir Alexander	1882–1968
Gray, Sir Archibald Montague Henry	1880–1967
Gray, Benjamin Kirkman	1862–1907
Gray, George Buchanan	1865–1922
Gray, George Edward Kruger	1880–1943
Gray, Herbert Branston	1851–1929
Gray, Louis Harold	1905–1965
Greaves, Walter	1846–1930
Green, Alice Sophia Amelia (Mrs Stopford Green)	1847–1929
Green, Charles Alfred Howell	1864–1944
Green, Frederick William Edridge-. See Edridge-Green	1863–1953
Green, Gustavus	1865–1964
Green, Samuel Gosnell	1822–1905
Green, William Curtis	1875–1960
Greenaway, Catherine (Kate)	1846–1901
Greene, Harry Plunket	1865–1936
Green, Wilfrid Arthur, Baron	1883–1952
Greene, William Friese-	1855–1921
Greene, Sir (William) Graham	1857–1950
Greenidge, Abel Hendy Jones	1865–1906
Greenwell, William	1820–1918
Greenwood, Arthur	1880–1954
Greenwood, Frederick	1830–1909
Greenwood, Hamar, Viscount	1870–1948

Hall, Sir (William) Reginald | 1870-**1943**
Hall, (William) Stephen (Richard) King-, Baron King-Hall. See King-Hall | 1893-**1966**
Hallé (formerly Norman-Neruda), Wilma Maria Francisca, Lady | 1839-**1911**
Halliburton, William Dobinson | 1860-**1931**
Halliday, Sir Frederick James | 1806-**1901**
Halsbury, Earl of. See Giffard, Hardinge Stanley | 1823-**1921**
Halsey, Sir Lionel | 1872-**1949**
Hambleden, Viscount. See Smith, William Frederick Danvers | 1868-**1928**
Hamblin Smith, James. See Smith | 1829-**1901**
Hambourg, Mark | 1879-**1960**
Hambro, Sir Charles Jocelyn | 1897-**1963**
Hamidullah, Nawab of Bhopal. See Bhopal | 1894-**1960**
Hamilton, Charles Harold St. John, 'Frank Richards' | 1876-**1961**
Hamilton, David James | 1849-**1909**
Hamilton, Sir Edward Walter | 1847-**1908**
Hamilton, Eugene Jacob Lee-. See Lee-Hamilton | 1845-**1907**
Hamilton, Lord George Francis | 1845-**1927**
Hamilton, Sir Ian Standish Monteith | 1853-**1947**
Hamilton, James, Duke of Abercorn | 1838-**1913**
Hamilton, John Andrew, Viscount Sumner | 1859-**1934**
Hamilton, Sir Richard Vesey | 1829-**1912**
Hamilton Fairley, Sir Neil. See Fairley | 1891-**1966**
Hamilton Fyfe, Sir William. See Fyfe | 1878-**1965**
Hammond, Sir John | 1889-**1964**
Hammond, John Lawrence Le Breton | 1872-**1949**
Hammond, Walter Reginald | 1903-**1965**
Hampden, Viscount. See Brand, Henry Robert | 1841-**1906**
Hamshaw Thomas, Hugh. See Thomas | 1885-**1962**
Hanbury, Charlotte (1830-1900). See under Hanbury, Elizabeth |
Hanbury, Elizabeth | 1793-**1901**
Hanbury, Sir James Arthur | 1832-**1908**
Hanbury, Robert William | 1845-**1903**
Hanbury-Williams, Sir John Coldbrook | 1892-**1965**
Hancock, Anthony John (Tony) | 1924-**1968**
Hancock, Sir Henry Drummond | 1895-**1965**
Handley, Thomas Reginald (Tommy) | 1892-**1949**
Handley Page, Sir Frederick. See Page | 1885-**1962**
Hankey, Maurice Pascal Alers, Baron | 1877-**1963**
Hankin, St. John Emile Clavering | 1869-**1909**
Hanlan (properly Hanlon), Edward | 1855-**1908**
Hannay, James Owen, 'George A. Birmingham' | 1865-**1950**
Hannay, Robert Kerr | 1867-**1940**
Hanworth, Viscount. See Pollock, Ernest Murray | 1861-**1936**
Harari, Manya | 1905-**1969**
Harari, Ralph Andrew | 1892-**1969**
Harben, Sir Henry | 1823-**1911**
Harcourt, Augustus George Vernon | 1834-**1919**
Harcourt, Leveson Francis Vernon-. See Vernon-Harcourt | 1839-**1907**
Harcourt, Lewis, Viscount | 1863-**1922**
Harcourt, Sir William George Granville Venables Vernon | 1827-**1904**
Harcourt-Smith, Sir Cecil | 1859-**1944**
Harden, Sir Arthur | 1865-**1940**
Hardie, James Keir | 1856-**1915**
Hardie, Martin | 1875-**1952**
Hardie, William Ross | 1862-**1916**

Hardiman, Alfred Frank | 1891-**1949**
Harding, Sir Edward John | 1880-**1954**
Harding, Gilbert Charles | 1907-**1960**
Hardinge, Alexander Henry Louis, Baron Hardinge of Penshurst | 1894-**1960**
Hardinge, Charles, Baron Hardinge of Penshurst | 1858-**1944**
Hardwicke, Sir Cedric Webster | 1893-**1964**
Hardwicke, Earl of. See Yorke, Albert Edward Philip Henry | 1867-**1904**
Hardy, Frederic Daniel | 1827-**1911**
Hardy, Gathorne Gathorne-, Earl of Cranbrook. See Gathorne-Hardy | 1814-**1906**
Hardy, Godfrey Harold | 1877-**1947**
Hardy, Herbert Hardy Cozens-, Baron Cozens-Hardy. See Cozens-Hardy | 1838-**1920**
Hardy, Sam | 1882-**1966**
Hardy, Thomas | 1840-**1928**
Hardy, Sir William Bate | 1864-**1934**
Hare, Augustus John Cuthbert | 1834-**1903**
Hare, Sir John | 1844-**1921**
Harewood, Earl of. See Lascelles, Henry George Charles | 1882-**1947**
Harington, Sir Charles ('Tim') | 1872-**1940**
Harker, Alfred | 1859-**1939**
Harland, Henry | 1861-**1905**
Harlech, Baron. See Ormsby-Gore, William George Arthur | 1885-**1964**
Harley, Robert | 1828-**1910**
Harman, Sir Charles Eustace | 1894-**1970**
Harmsworth, Alfred Charles William, Viscount Northcliffe | 1865-**1922**
Harmsworth, Harold Sidney, Viscount Rothermere | 1868-**1940**
Harper, Sir George Montague | 1865-**1922**
Harraden, Beatrice | 1864-**1936**
Harrel, Sir David | 1841-**1939**
Harrington, Timothy Charles | 1851-**1910**
Harris, Frederick Leverton | 1864-**1926**
Harris, George Robert Canning, Baron | 1851-**1932**
Harris, (Henry) Wilson | 1883-**1955**
Harris, James Rendel | 1852-**1941**
Harris, James Thomas ('Frank') | 1856-**1931**
Harris, John Wyndham Parkes Lucas Beynon, 'John Wyndham' | 1903-**1969**
Harris, Sir Percy Alfred | 1876-**1952**
Harris, Thomas Lake | 1823-**1906**
Harris, Tomás | 1908-**1964**
Harrison, Frederic | 1831-**1923**
Harrison, Henry | 1867-**1954**
Harrison, Jane Ellen | 1850-**1928**
Harrison, Mary St. Leger, 'Lucas Malet' | 1852-**1931**
Harrison, Reginald | 1837-**1908**
Harrison, Sir William Montagu Graham-. See Graham-Harrison | 1871-**1949**
Hart, Sir Basil Henry Liddell | 1895-**1970**
Hart, Sir Raymund George | 1899-**1960**
Hart, Sir Robert | 1835-**1911**
Hartington, Marquess of. See Cavendish, Spencer Compton | 1833-**1908**
Hartley, Arthur Clifford | 1889-**1960**
Hartley, Sir Charles Augustus | 1825-**1915**
Hartog, Sir Philip(pe) Joseph | 1864-**1947**
Hartree, Douglas Rayner | 1897-**1958**
Hartshorn, Vernon | 1872-**1931**
Hartshorne, Albert | 1839-**1910**
Harty, Sir (Herbert) Hamilton | 1879-**1941**
Harvey, Hildebrand Wolfe | 1887-**1970**
Harvey, Sir John Martin Martin-. See Martin-Harvey | 1863-**1944**

Hiles, Henry	1828–1904	Hofmeyr, Jan Hendrik	1845–1909
Hill, Alexander Staveley	1825–1905	Hofmeyr, Jan Hendrik	1894–1948
Hill, Alsager Hay	1839–1906	Hogarth, David George	1862–1927
Hill, Sir Arthur William	1875–1941	Hogg, Douglas McGarel, Viscount	
Hill, Sir (Edward) Maurice	1862–1934	Hailsham	1872–1950
Hill, Frank Harrison	1830–1910	Hogg, Quintin	1845–1903
Hill, George Birkbeck Norman	1835–1903	Holden, Charles Henry	1875–1960
Hill, Sir George Francis	1867–1948	Holden, Henry Smith	1887–1963
Hill, Sir Leonard Erskine	1866–1952	Holden, Luther	1815–1905
Hill, Leonard Raven-. See Raven-Hill	1867–1942	Holder, Sir Frederick William	1850–1909
Hill, Octavia	1838–1912	Holderness, Sir Thomas William	1849–1924
Hill, Sir Roderic Maxwell	1894–1954	Holdich, Sir Thomas Hungerford	1843–1929
Hill, Rosamund Davenport-	1825–1902	Holdsworth, Sir William Searle	1871–1944
Hills, Arnold Frank	1857–1927	Hole, Samuel Reynolds	1819–1904
Hills, Sir John	1834–1902	Holiday, Henry	1839–1927
Hilton, James	1900–1954	Hollams, Sir John	1820–1910
Hind, Arthur Mayger	1880–1957	Holland, Sir Eardley Lancelot	1879–1967
Hind, Henry Youle	1823–1908	Holland, Sir (Edward) Milner	1902–1969
Hind, Richard Dacre Archer-. See		Holland, Henry Scott	1847–1918
Archer-Hind	1849–1910	Holland, Sir Henry Thurstan, Viscount	
Hindley, Sir Clement Daniel Maggs	1874–1944	Knutsford	1825–1914
Hindley, John Scott, Viscount Hyndley	1883–1963	Holland, Sir Henry Tristram	1875–1965
Hingeston-Randolph (formerly Hing-		Holland, Sir Sidney George	1893–1961
ston), Francis Charles	1833–1910	Holland, Sydney George, Viscount	
Hingley, Sir Benjamin	1830–1905	Knutsford	1855–1931
Hingston, Sir William Hales	1829–1907	Holland, Sir Thomas Erskine	1835–1926
Hinks, Arthur Robert	1873–1945	Holland, Sir Thomas Henry	1868–1947
Hinkson (formerly Tynan), Katharine	1861–1931	Hollingshead, John	1827–1904
Hinshelwood, Sir Cyril Norman	1897–1967	Hollingworth, Sydney Ewart	1899–1966
Hinsley, Arthur	1865–1943	Hollis, Sir Leslie Chasemore	1897–1963
Hipkins, Alfred James	1826–1903	Hollowell, James Hirst	1851–1909
Hirst, Francis Wrigley	1873–1953	Holman Hunt, William. See Hunt	1827–1910
Hirst, George Herbert	1871–1954	Holme, Charles	1848–1923
Hirst, Hugo, Baron	1863–1943	Holmes, Arthur	1890–1965
Hitchcock, Sir Eldred Frederick	1887–1959	Holmes, Augusta Mary Anne	1847–1903
Hives, Ernest Walter, Baron	1886–1965	Holmes, Sir Charles John	1868–1936
Hoare, Joseph Charles	1851–1906	Holmes, Sir Gordon Morgan	1876–1965
Hoare, Sir Reginald Hervey	1882–1954	Holmes, Sir Richard Rivington	1835–1911
Hoare, Sir Samuel John Gurney, Vis-		Holmes, Thomas	1846–1918
count Templewood	1880–1959	Holmes, Thomas Rice Edward	1855–1933
Hobart, Sir Percy Cleghorn Stanley	1885–1957	Holmes, Timothy	1825–1907
Hobbes, John Oliver, *pseudonym*. See		Holmes, Sir Valentine	1888–1956
Craigie, Pearl Mary Teresa	1867–1906	Holmyard, Eric John	1891–1959
Hobbs, Sir John Berry (Jack)	1882–1963	Holroyd, Sir Charles	1861–1917
Hobday, Sir Frederick Thomas George	1869–1939	Holroyd, Henry North, Earl of Sheffield	1832–1909
Hobhouse, Arthur, Baron	1819–1904	Holst, Gustav Theodore	1874–1934
Hobhouse, Edmund	1817–1904	Holyoake, George Jacob	1817–1906
Hobhouse, Henry	1854–1937	Hone, Evie	1894–1955
Hobhouse, Sir John Richard	1893–1961	Hood, Arthur William Acland, Baron	1824–1901
Hobhouse, Leonard Trelawny	1864–1929	Hood, Sir Horace Lambert Alexander	1870–1916
Hobson, Ernest William	1856–1933	Hook, James Clarke	1819–1907
Hobson, Geoffrey Dudley	1882–1949	Hooke, Samuel Henry	1874–1968
Hobson, John Atkinson	1858–1940	Hooker, Sir Joseph Dalton	1817–1911
Hobson, Sir John Gardiner Sumner	1912–1967	Hooper, Sir Frederic Collins	1892–1963
Hocking, Joseph (1860–1937). See		Hope, Anthony, *pseudonym*. See	
under Hocking, Silas Kitto		Hawkins, Sir Anthony Hope	1863–1933
Hocking, Silas Kitto	1850–1935	Hope, James Fitzalan, Baron Rankeil-	
Hodge, John	1855–1937	lour	1870–1949
Hodgetts, James Frederick	1828–1906	Hope, John Adrian Louis, Earl of	
Hodgkin, Thomas	1831–1913	Hopetoun and Marquess of Lin-	
Hodgkins, Frances Mary	1869–1947	lithgow	1860–1908
Hodgson, Ralph Edwin	1871–1962	Hope, Laurence, *pseudonym*. See	
Hodgson, Richard Dacre. See Archer-		Nicolson, Adela Florence	1865–1904
Hind	1849–1910	Hope, Victor Alexander John,	
Hodgson, Sir Robert MacLeod	1874–1956	Marquess of Linlithgow	1887–1952
Hodgson, Shadworth Hollway	1832–1912	Hope, Sir William Henry St. John	1854–1919
Hodson (afterward Labouchere),		Hopetoun, Earl of. See Hope, John	
Henrietta	1841–1910	Adrian Louis	1860–1908
Hoey, Frances Sarah (Mrs Cashel		Hopkins, Edward John	1818–1901
Hoey)	1830–1908	Hopkins, Sir Frederick Gowland	1861–1947

Ibbetson, Henry John Selwin-, Baron Rookwood. See Selwin–Ibbetson	1826–1902
Ignatius, Father. See Lyne, Joseph Leycester	1837–1908
Ilbert, Sir Courtenay Peregrine	1841–1924
Ilchester, Earl of. See Fox-Strangways, Giles Stephen Holland	1874–1959
Iliffe, Edward Mauger, Baron	1877–1960
Illing, Vincent Charles	1890–1969
Image, Selwyn	1849–1930
Imms, Augustus Daniel	1880–1949
Ince, Sir Godfrey Herbert	1891–1960
Ince, William	1825–1910
Inchcape, Earl of. See Mackay, James Lyle	1852–1932
Inderwick, Frederick Andrew	1836–1904
Inge, William Ralph	1860–1954
Ingham, Albert Edward	1900–1967
Inglis, Sir Charles Edward	1875–1952
Inglis, Elsie Maud	1864–1917
Ingold, Sir Christopher Kelk	1893–1970
Ingram, Arthur Foley Winnington-. See Winnington-Ingram	1858–1946
Ingram, Sir Bruce Stirling	1877–1963
Ingram, John Kells	1823–1907
Ingram, Thomas Dunbar	1826–1901
Innes, James John McLeod	1830–1907
Innes, Sir James Rose-. See Rose-Innes	1855–1942
Inskip, Thomas Walker Hobart, Viscount Caldecote	1876–1947
Inverchapel, Baron. See Clark Kerr, Archibald John Kerr	1882–1951
Inverforth, Baron. See Weir, Andrew	1865–1955
Invernairn, Baron. See Beardmore, William	1856–1936
Iqbal, Sir Muhammad	1876–1938
Irby, Leonard Howard Loyd	1836–1905
Ireland, John Nicholson	1879–1962
Ireland, William Wotherspoon	1832–1909
Ironside, Robin Cunliffe	1912–1965
Ironside, William Edmund, Baron	1880–1959
Irvine, Sir James Colquhoun	1877–1952
Irvine, William	1840–1911
Irving, Sir Henry	1838–1905
Isaacs, Alick	1921–1967
Isaacs, Sir Isaac Alfred	1855–1948
Isaacs, Rufus Daniel, Marquess of Reading	1860–1935
Isherwood, Sir Joseph William	1870–1937
Isitt, Dame Adeline Genée-. See Genée	1878–1970
Islington, Baron. See Poynder, Sir John Poynder Dickson-	1866–1936
Ismail, Sir Mirza Mohammad	1883–1959
Ismay, Hastings Lionel, Baron	1887–1965
Ismay, Joseph Bruce	1862–1937
Iveagh, Countess of (1881–1966). See under Guinness, Rupert Edward Cecil Lee	
Iveagh, Earl of. See Guinness, Edward Cecil	1847–1927
Iveagh, Earl of. See Guinness, Rupert Edward Cecil Lee	1874–1967
Iwan-Müller, Ernest Bruce	1853–1910
Jacks, Lawrence Pearsall	1860–1955
Jacks, William	1841–1907
Jackson, Sir Barry Vincent	1879–1961
Jackson, Sir Cyril	1863–1924
Jackson, Sir (Francis) Stanley	1870–1947

Jackson, Frederick George	1860–1938
Jackson, Sir Frederick John	1860–1929
Jackson, Frederick John Foakes	1855–1941
Jackson, Henry	1839–1921
Jackson, Sir Henry Bradwardine	1855–1929
Jackson, Sir Herbert	1863–1936
Jackson, John	1833–1901
Jackson, John Hughlings	1835–1911
Jackson, Mason	1819–1903
Jackson, Samuel Phillips	1830–1904
Jackson, Sir Thomas Graham	1835–1924
Jackson, William Lawies, Baron Allerton	1840–1917
Jackson, Willis, Baron Jackson of Burnley	1904–1970
Jacob, Sir Claud William	1863–1948
Jacob, Edgar	1844–1920
Jacobs, William Wymark	1863–1943
Jagger, Charles Sargeant	1885–1934
James, Alexander Wilson	1901–1953
James, Arthur Lloyd	1884–1943
James, Henry, Baron James of Hereford	1828–1911
James, Henry	1843–1916
James, James	1832–1902
James, Montague Rhodes	1862–1936
James, Reginald William	1891–1964
James, Rolfe Arnold Scott-. See Scott-James	1878–1959
Jameson, Andrew, Lord Ardwall	1845–1911
Jameson, Sir Leander Starr	1853–1917
Jameson, Sir (William) Wilson	1885–1962
Japp, Alexander Hay, 'H. A. Page'	1837–1905
Jardine, Douglas Robert	1900–1958
Jardine, Sir Robert	1825–1905
Jarvis, Claude Scudamore	1879–1953
Jarvis, Sir John Layton (Jack)	1887–1968
Jayne, Francis John	1845–1921
Jeaffreson, John Cordy	1831–1901
Jeans, Sir James Hopwood	1877–1946
Jebb, Eglantyne	1876–1928
Jebb, Sir Richard Claverhouse	1841–1905
Jefferson, Sir Geoffrey	1886–1961
Jeffery, George Barker	1891–1957
Jelf, George Edward	1834–1908
Jellicoe, (John) Basil (Lee)	1899–1935
Jellicoe, John Rushworth, Earl	1859–1935
Jenkin, Charles Frewen	1865–1940
Jenkins, David Llewelyn, Baron	1899–1969
Jenkins, Ebenezer Evans	1820–1905
Jenkins, John Edward	1838–1910
Jenkins, Sir Lawrence Hugh	1857–1928
Jenkinson, Sir (Charles) Hilary	1882–1961
Jenkinson, Francis John Henry	1853–1923
Jenks, Edward	1861–1939
Jenner-Fust, Herbert	1806–1904
Jennings, Sir (William) Ivor	1903–1965
Jephson, Arthur Jermy Mounteney	1858–1908
Jerome, Jerome Klapka	1859–1927
Jerram, Sir (Thomas Henry) Martyn	1858–1933
Jerrold, Douglas Francis	1893–1964
Jersey, Countess of. See Villiers, Margaret Elizabeth Child-	1849–1945
Jersey, Earl of. See Villiers, Victor Albert George Child-	1845–1915
Jessop, Gilbert Laird	1874–1955
Jessopp, Augustus	1823–1914
Jeune, Francis Henry, Baron St. Helier	1843–1905
Jex-Blake, Sophia Louisa	1840–1912
Jex-Blake, Thomas William	1832–1915
Jinnah, Mahomed Ali	1876–1948
Joachim, Harold Henry	1868–1938

Ker, William Paton	1855-1923
Kermack, William Ogilvy	1898-1970
Kerr, Archibald John Kerr Clark, Baron Inverchapel. See Clark Kerr	1882-1951
Kerr, John	1824-1907
Kerr, Sir John Graham	1869-1957
Kerr, (John Martin) Munro	1868-1960
Kerr, Philip Henry, Marquess of Lothian	1882-1940
Kerr, Robert	1823-1904
Kerr, Lord Walter Talbot	1839-1927
Ketèlbey, Albert William	1875-1959
Kettle, Edgar Hartley	1882-1936
Ketton-Cremer, Robert Wyndham	1906-1969
Keyes, Roger John Brownlow, Baron	1872-1945
Keynes, John Maynard, Baron	1883-1946
Khan Sahib	1883-1958
Kidd, Benjamin	1858-1916
Kiggell, Sir Launcelot Edward	1862-1954
Kilbracken, Baron. See Godley, (John) Arthur	1847-1932
Killearn, Baron. See Lampson, Miles Wedderburn	1880-1964
Killen, William Dool	1806-1902
Kilmuir, Earl of. See Fyfe, David Patrick Maxwell	1900-1967
Kimberley, Earl of. See Wodehouse, John	1826-1902
Kimmins, Dame Grace Thyrza	1870-1954
Kinahan, George Henry	1829-1908
Kincairney, Lord. See Gloag, William Ellis	1828-1909
Kindersley, Robert Molesworth, Baron	1871-1954
King, Earl Judson	1901-1962
King, Edward	1829-1910
King, Sir (Frederic) Truby	1858-1938
King, Sir George	1840-1909
King, Harold	1887-1956
King, Haynes	1831-1904
King, William Bernard Robinson	1889-1963
King, William Lyon Mackenzie	1874-1950
King-Hall, (William) Stephen (Richard), Baron	1893-1966
Kingdon-Ward, Francis (Frank)	1885-1958
Kingsburgh, Lord. See Macdonald, John Hay Athole	1836-1919
Kingscote, Sir Robert Nigel Fitzhardinge	1830-1908
Kingsford, Charles Lethbridge	1862-1926
Kingston, Charles Cameron	1850-1908
Kinnear, Alexander Smith, Baron	1833-1917
Kinnear, Sir Norman Boyd	1882-1957
Kinns, Samuel	1826-1903
Kinross, Baron. See Balfour, John Blair	1837-1905
Kipling, (Joseph) Rudyard	1865-1936
Kipping, Frederic Stanley	1863-1949
Kirk, Sir John	1832-1922
Kirk, Sir John	1847-1922
Kirk, Kenneth Escott	1886-1954
Kirkpatrick, Sir Ivone Augustine	1897-1964
Kirkwood, David, Baron	1872-1955
Kitchener, Horatio Herbert, Earl	1850-1916
Kitchin, George William	1827-1912
Kitson, James, Baron Airedale	1835-1911
Kitton, Frederick George	1856-1904
Klein, Melanie	1882-1960
Knight, Harold	1874-1961
Knight, Joseph	1829-1907
Knight, Joseph	1837-1909

Knight, Dame Laura (1877-1970). See under Knight, Harold	
Knollys, Edward George William Tyrwhitt, Viscount	1895-1966
Knollys, Francis, Viscount	1837-1924
Knott, Ralph	1878-1929
Knowles, Sir James Thomas	1831-1908
Knox, Edmund Arbuthnott	1847-1937
Knox, Sir Geoffrey George	1884-1958
Knox, Sir George Edward	1845-1922
Knox (formerly Craig), Isa	1831-1903
Knox, Ronald Arbuthnott	1888-1957
Knox, Wilfred Lawrence	1886-1950
Knox-Little, William John	1839-1918
Knutsford, Viscount. See Holland, Sir Henry Thurstan	1825-1914
Knutsford, Viscount. See Holland, Sydney George	1855-1931
Komisarjevsky, Theodore	1882-1954
Korda, Sir Alexander	1893-1956
Kotzé, Sir John Gilbert	1849-1940
Kronberger, Hans	1920-1970
Kruger Gray, George Edward. See Gray	1880-1943
Kuczynski, Robert Rene	1876-1947
Kylsant, Baron. See Philipps, Owen Cosby	1863-1937
Kynaston (formerly Snow), Herbert	1835-1910
Labouchere, Henrietta. See Hodson	1841-1910
Labouchere, Henry Du Pré	1831-1912
Lacey, Thomas Alexander	1853-1931
Lachmann, Gustav Victor	1896-1966
Lafont, Eugène	1837-1908
Laidlaw, Anna Robena	1819-1901
Laidlaw, John	1832-1906
Laidlaw, Sir Patrick Playfair	1881-1940
Laird, John	1887-1946
Lake, Kirsopp	1872-1946
Lake, Sir Percy Henry Noel	1855-1940
Lamb, Henry Taylor	1883-1960
Lamb, Sir Horace	1849-1934
Lambart, Frederick Rudolph, Earl of Cavan	1865-1946
Lambe, Sir Charles Edward	1900-1960
Lambert, Brooke	1834-1901
Lambert, Constant	1905-1951
Lambert, George	1842-1915
Lambert, George, Viscount	1866-1958
Lambert, Maurice	1901-1964
Lambourne, Baron. See Lockwood, Amelius Mark Richard	1847-1928
Lamburn, Richmal Crompton	1890-1969
Lamington, Baron. See Baillie, Charles Wallace Alexander Napier Ross Cochrane-	1860-1940
Lampson, Miles Wedderburn, Baron Killearn	1880-1964
Lanchester, Frederick William	1868-1946
Lanchester, George Herbert	1874-1970
Lane, Sir Allen	1902-1970
Lane, Sir Hugh Percy	1875-1915
Lane, John	1854-1925
Lane, Lupino	1892-1959
Lane, Sir (William) Arbuthnot	1856-1943
Lane Poole, Reginald. See Poole	1857-1939
Lane-Poole, Stanley Edward. See Poole	1854-1931
Lang, (Alexander) Matheson	1877-1948
Lang, Andrew	1844-1912

Leveson Gower, Sir Henry Dudley Gresham. See Gower	1873–1954	Little, William John Knox-. See Knox-Little	1839–1918
Levick, George Murray	1876–1956	Littler, Sir Ralph Daniel Makinson	1835–1908
Levy-Lawson, Edward, Baron Burnham	1833–1916	Littlewood, Sir Sydney Charles Thomas	1895–1967
Levy-Lawson, Harry Lawson Webster, Viscount Burnham. See Lawson	1862–1933	Liveing, George Downing	1827–1924
Lewis, Agnes	1843–1926	Livens, William Howard	1889–1964
Lewis, Bunnell	1824–1908	Livesey, Sir George Thomas	1834–1908
Lewis, Clive Staples	1898–1963	Livingstone, Sir Richard Winn	1880–1960
Lewis, David (1814–1895). See under Lewis, Evan		Llandaff, Viscount. See Matthews, Henry	1826–1913
Lewis, Evan	1818–1901	Llewellin, John Jestyn, Baron	1893–1957
Lewis, Sir George Henry	1833–1911	Llewellyn, Sir (Samuel Henry) William	1858–1941
Lewis, John Spedan	1885–1963	Lloyd, Dorothy Jordan	1889–1946
Lewis, John Travers	1825–1901	Lloyd, Edward Mayow Hastings	1889–1968
Lewis, Percy Wyndham	1882–1957	Lloyd, George Ambrose, Baron	1879–1941
Lewis, Richard	1821–1905	Lloyd, Sir John Edward	1861–1947
Lewis, Rosa	1867–1952	Lloyd, Marie, pseudonym. See Wood, Matilda Alice Victoria	1870–1922
Lewis, Sir Thomas	1881–1945	Lloyd, Sir Thomas Ingram Kynaston	1896–1968
Lewis, Sir Wilfrid Hubert Poyer	1881–1950	Lloyd George, David, Earl Lloyd-George of Dwyfor	1863–1945
Lewis, William Cudmore McCullagh	1885–1956		
Lewis, William Thomas, Baron Merthyr	1837–1914	Lloyd-George, Gwilym, Viscount Tenby	1894–1967
Lewis, Sir Willmott Harsant	1877–1950	Lloyd George, Lady Megan	1902–1966
Ley, Henry George	1887–1962	Lloyd James, Arthur. See James	1884–1943
Leyel, Hilda Winifred Ivy (Mrs C. F. Leyel)	1880–1957	Loates, Thomas	1867–1910
		Loch, Sir Charles Stewart	1849–1923
Liaqat Ali Khan	1895–1951	Lock, Walter	1846–1933
Liberty, Sir Arthur Lasenby	1843–1917	Locke, William John	1863–1930
Liddell Hart, Sir Basil Henry. See Hart	1895–1970	Lockey, Charles	1820–1901
Lidderdale, William	1832–1902	Lockhart, Sir Robert Hamilton Bruce	1887–1970
Lidgett, John Scott	1854–1953	Lockwood, Amelius Mark Richard, Baron Lambourne	1847–1928
Lightwood, John Mason	1852–1947		
Lillicrap, Sir Charles Swift	1887–1966	Lockwood, Sir John Francis	1903–1965
Lincolnshire, Marquess of. See Wynn-Carrington, Charles Robert	1843–1928	Lockyer, Sir (Joseph) Norman	1836–1920
		Lodge, Eleanor Constance	1869–1936
Lindemann, Frederick Alexander, Viscount Cherwell	1886–1957	Lodge, Sir Oliver Joseph	1851–1940
		Lodge, Sir Richard	1855–1936
Lindley, Sir Francis Oswald	1872–1950	Loftie, William John	1839–1911
Lindley, Nathaniel, Baron	1828–1921	Loftus, Lord Augustus William Frederick Spencer	1817–1904
Lindrum, Walter Albert	1898–1960		
Lindsay, Alexander Dunlop, Baron Lindsay of Birker	1879–1952	Logue, Michael	1840–1924
		Lohmann, George Alfred	1865–1901
Lindsay, David	1856–1922	Lombard, Adrian Albert	1915–1967
Lindsay, David Alexander Edward, Earl of Crawford	1871–1940	London, Heinz	1907–1970
		Londonderry, Marquess of. See Vane-Tempest-Stewart, Charles Stewart	1852–1915
Lindsay, George Mackintosh	1880–1956		
Lindsay, James Gavin	1835–1903	Londonderry, Marquess of. See Vane-Tempest-Stewart, Charles Stewart Henry	1878–1949
Lindsay, James Ludovic, Earl of Crawford	1847–1913		
Lindsay, John Seymour	1882–1966	Long, Walter Hume, Viscount Long of Wraxall	1854–1924
Lindsay (afterwards Loyd-Lindsay), Robert James, Baron Wantage	1832–1901		
		Longhurst, William Henry	1819–1904
Lindsay, Sir Ronald Charles	1877–1945	Longmore, Sir Arthur Murray	1885–1970
Lindsay, Thomas Martin	1843–1914	Longstaff, Tom George	1875–1964
Lindsay, Wallace Martin	1858–1937	Lonsdale, Earl of. See Lowther, Hugh Cecil	1857–1944
Lingen, Ralph Robert Wheeler, Baron	1819–1905		
Linlithgow, Marquess of. See Hope, John Adrian Louis	1860–1908	Lonsdale, Frederick	1881–1954
		Lopes, Sir Lopes Massey	1818–1908
Linlithgow, Marquess of. See Hope, Victor Alexander John	1887–1952	Loraine, Sir Percy Lyham	1880–1961
		Loraine, Violet Mary	1886–1956
Linstead, Sir (Reginald) Patrick	1902–1966	Lord, Thomas	1808–1908
Lipson, Ephraim	1888–1960	Loreburn, Earl. See Reid, Robert Threshie	1846–1923
Lipton, Sir Thomas Johnstone	1850–1931		
Lister, Arthur	1830–1908	Lorimer, Sir Robert Stodart	1864–1929
Lister, Joseph, Baron	1827–1912	Lotbinière, Sir Henry Gustave Joly de. See Joly de Lotbinière	1829–1908
Lister, Samuel Cunliffe, Baron Masham	1815–1906		
Lithgow, Sir James	1883–1952	Lothian, Marquess of. See Kerr, Philip Henry	1882–1940
Little, Andrew George	1863–1945		
Little, Sir Ernest Gordon Graham Graham-. See Graham-Little	1867–1950	Louise Caroline Alberta, princess of Great Britain	1848–1939

Macdonald, John Hay Athole, Lord		Mackintosh, John	1833–1907
Kingsburgh	1836–1919	Mackworth-Young, Gerard	1884–1965
MacDonald, Sir Murdoch	1866–1957	McLachlan, Robert	1837–1904
Macdonell, Arthur Anthony	1854–1930	Maclagan, Christian	1811–1901
MacDonell, Sir Hugh Guion	1832–1904	Maclagan, Sir Eric Robert Dalrymple	1879–1951
Macdonell, Sir John	1845–1921	Maclagan, William Dalrymple	1826–1910
Macdonell, Sir Philip James	1873–1940	Maclaren, Alexander	1826–1910
MacDonnell, Antony Patrick, Baron	1844–1925	MacLaren, Archibald Campbell	1871–1944
McDonnell, Sir Schomberg Kerr	1861–1915	McLaren, Charles Benjamin Bright,	
McDougall, William	1871–1938	Baron Aberconway	1850–1934
Mace, James (Jem)	1831–1910	McLaren, Henry Duncan, Baron	
McEvoy, Arthur Ambrose	1878–1927	Aberconway	1879–1953
McEwen, Sir John Blackwood	1868–1948	Maclaren, Ian, *pseudonym*. See Watson,	
Macewen, Sir William	1848–1924	John	1850–1907
Macfadyen, Allan	1860–1907	McLaren, John, Lord	1831–1910
Macfadyen, Sir Eric	1879–1966	Maclay, Joseph Paton, Baron	1857–1951
M'Fadyen, John Edgar	1870–1933	Maclean, Sir Donald	1864–1932
MacFarlane, Sir (Frank) Noel Mason-.		Maclean, Sir Harry Aubrey de Vere	1848–1920
See Mason-MacFarlane	1889–1953	Maclean, James Mackenzie	1835–1906
Macfarren, Walter Cecil	1826–1905	McLean, Norman	1865–1947
MacGillivray, Sir Donald Charles	1906–1966	Maclear, George Frederick	1833–1902
McGowan, Harry Duncan, Baron	1874–1961	Maclear, John Fiot Lee Pearse	1838–1907
McGrath, Sir Patrick Thomas	1868–1929	McLennan, Sir John Cunningham	1867–1935
MacGregor, Sir Evan	1842–1926	Macleod, Fiona, *pseudonym*. See Sharp,	
MacGregor, James	1832–1910	William	1855–1905
MacGregor, Sir William	1846–1919	Macleod, Henry Dunning	1821–1902
McGrigor, Sir Rhoderick Robert	1893–1959	Macleod, Iain Norman	1913–1970
Machell, James Octavius	1837–1902	Macleod, John James Rickard	1876–1935
Machray, Robert	1831–1904	McLintock, Sir William	1873–1947
McIndoe, Sir Archibald Hector	1900–1960	McLintock, William Francis Porter	1887–1960
M'Intosh, William Carmichael	1838–1931	Maclure, Edward Craig	1833–1906
Macintyre, Donald	1831–1903	Maclure, Sir John William (1835–1901).	
MacIver, David Randall-. See Randall-		See under Maclure, Edward Craig	
MacIver	1873–1945	McMahon, Sir (Arthur) Henry	1862–1949
Mackail, John William	1859–1945	McMahon, Charles Alexander	1830–1904
Mackay, Æneas James George	1839–1911	MacMahon, Percy Alexander	1854–1929
Mackay, Alexander	1833–1902	MacMichael, Sir Harold Alfred	1882–1969
Mackay, Donald James, Baron Reay	1839–1921	Macmillan, Sir Frederick Orridge	1851–1936
Mackay, James Lyle, Earl of Inchcape	1852–1932	Macmillan, Hugh	1833–1903
Mackay, Mary, 'Marie Corelli'	1855–1924	Macmillan, Hugh Pattison, Baron	1873–1952
McKechnie, William Sharp	1863–1930	McMillan, Margaret	1860–1931
McKenna, Reginald	1863–1943	McMurrich, James Playfair	1859–1939
Mackennal, Alexander	1835–1904	Macnaghten, Sir Edward, Baron	1830–1913
Mackennal, Sir (Edgar) Bertram	1863–1931	McNair, John Frederick Adolphus	1828–1910
Mackenzie, Sir Alexander	1842–1902	MacNalty, Sir Arthur Salusbury	1880–1969
McKenzie, Alexander	1869–1951	Macnamara, Thomas James	1861–1931
Mackenzie, Sir Alexander Campbell	1847–1935	McNaughton, Andrew George Latta	1887–1966
Mackenzie, Sir George Sutherland	1844–1910	MacNeice, (Frederick) Louis	1907–1963
Mackenzie, Sir James	1853–1925	McNeil, Hector	1907–1955
M'Kenzie, Sir John	1836–1901	McNeile, (Herman) Cyril, 'Sapper'	1888–1937
MacKenzie, John Stuart	1860–1935	McNeill, James	1869–1938
McKenzie, (Robert) Tait	1867–1938	McNeill, Sir James McFadyen	1892–1964
Mackenzie, Sir Stephen	1844–1909	MacNeill, John (otherwise Eoin)	1867–1945
Mackenzie, Sir William	1849–1923	McNeill, Sir John Carstairs	1831–1904
Mackenzie, William Warrender, Baron		MacNeill, John Gordon Swift	1849–1926
Amulree	1860–1942	McNeill, Ronald John, Baron Cushen-	
Mackenzie King, William Lyon. See		dun	1861–1934
King	1874–1950	Macphail, Sir (John) Andrew	1864–1938
McKerrow, Ronald Brunlees	1872–1940	Macpherson, (James) Ian, Baron	
McKie, Douglas	1896–1967	Strathcarron	1880–1937
Mackinder, Sir Halford John	1861–1947	Macpherson, Sir John Molesworth	1853–1914
MacKinlay, Antionette. See Sterling	1843–1904	McQueen, Sir John Withers	1836–1909
Mackinnon, Sir Frank Douglas	1871–1946	Macqueen-Pope, Walter James	1888–1960
Mackinnon, Sir William Henry	1852–1929	Macready, Sir (Cecil Frederick) Nevil	1862–1946
Mackintosh, Sir Alexander	1858–1948	Macrorie, William Kenneth	1831–1905
Mackintosh, Charles Rennie	1868–1928	M'Taggart, John M'Taggart Ellis	1866–1925
Mackintosh, Harold Vincent, Viscount		McTaggart, William	1835–1910
Mackintosh of Halifax	1891–1964	MacWhirter, John	1839–1911
Mackintosh, Hugh Ross	1870–1936	Madden, Sir Charles Edward	1862–1935
Mackintosh, James Macalister	1891–1966	Madden, Frederic William	1839–1904

Maturin, Basil William	1847-1915	Mersey, Viscount. See Bigham, John	
Maud Charlotte Mary Victoria, Queen		Charles	1840-1929
of Norway	1869-1938	Merthyr, Baron. See Lewis, William	
Maude, Aylmer	1858-1938	Thomas	1837-1914
Maude, Sir (Frederick) Stanley	1864-1917	Merton, Sir Thomas Ralph	1888-1969
Maugham, Frederic Herbert, Viscount	1866-1958	Merz, Charles Hesterman	1874-1940
Maugham, William Somerset	1874-1965	Meston, James Scorgie, Baron	1865-1943
Maurice, Sir Frederick Barton	1871-1951	Metcalfe, Sir Charles Herbert	
Maurice, Sir John Frederick	1841-1912	Theophilus	1853-1928
Mavor, Osborne Henry, 'James Bridie'	1888-1951	Methuen, Sir Algernon Methuen	
Mawdsley, James	1848-1902	Marshall	1856-1924
Mawer, Sir Allen	1879-1942	Methuen, Paul Sanford, Baron	1845-1932
Mawson, Sir Douglas	1882-1958	Meux (formerly Lambton), Sir	
Maxim, Sir Hiram Stevens	1840-1916	Hedworth	1856-1929
Maxse, Sir (Frederick) Ivor	1862-1958	Mew, Charlotte Mary	1869-1928
Maxse, Leopold James	1864-1932	Meyer, Frederick Brotherton	1847-1929
Maxton, James	1885-1946	Meyer, Sir William Stevenson	1860-1922
Maxwell, Sir Alexander	1880-1963	Meynell, Alice Christiana Gertrude	1847-1922
Maxwell, Gavin	1914-1969	Meyrick, Edward	1854-1938
Maxwell, Sir Herbert Eustace	1845-1937	Meyrick, Frederick	1827-1906
Maxwell, Sir John Grenfell	1859-1929	Michell, Anthony George Maldon	1870-1959
Maxwell (formerly Braddon), Mary		Michell, Sir Lewis Loyd	1842-1928
Elizabeth	1837-1915	Michie, Alexander	1833-1902
Maxwell Fyfe, David Patrick, Earl of		Micklethwaite, John Thomas	1843-1906
Kilmuir. See Fyfe	1900-1967	Middleton, James Smith	1878-1962
Maxwell Lyte, Sir Henry Churchill. See		Midlane, Albert	1825-1909
Lyte	1848-1940	Midleton, Earl of. See Brodrick,	
May, George Ernest, Baron	1871-1946	(William) St. John (Fremantle)	1856-1942
May, Philip William (Phil)	1864-1903	Miers, Sir Henry Alexander	1858-1942
May, Sir William Henry	1849-1930	Milbanke, Ralph Gordon Noel King,	
Maybury, Sir Henry Percy	1864-1943	Earl of Lovelace	1839-1906
Mayor, John Eyton Bickersteth	1825-1910	Mildmay, Anthony Bingham, Baron	
Meade, Richard James, Earl of Clan-		Mildmay of Flete	1909-1950
william	1832-1907	Milford, Sir Humphrey Sumner	1877-1952
Meade-Fetherstonhaugh, Sir Herbert	1875-1964	Milford Haven, Marquess of. See	
Meakin, James Edward Budgett	1866-1906	Mountbatten, Louis Alexander	1854-1921
Meath, Earl of. See Brabazon, Reginald	1841-1929	Mill, Hugh Robert	1861-1950
Medd, Peter Goldsmith	1829-1908	Millar, Gertie	1879-1952
Medlicott, Henry Benedict	1829-1905	Miller, Sir James Percy	1864-1906
Mee, Arthur Henry	1875-1943	Miller, William	1864-1945
Meek, Charles Kingsley	1885-1965	Milligan, George	1860-1934
Meghnad Saha	1893-1956	Milligan, Sir William	1864-1929
Meighen, Arthur	1874-1960	Mills, Bertram Wagstaff	1873-1938
Meiklejohn, John Miller Dow	1836-1902	Mills, Percy Herbert, Viscount	1890-1968
Melba, Dame Nellie	1861-1931	Mills, Sir William	1856-1932
Melchett, Baron. See Mond, Alfred		Mills, William Hobson	1873-1959
Moritz	1868-1930	Milne, Alan Alexander	1882-1956
Meldrum, Charles	1821-1901	Milne, Sir (Archibald) Berkeley	1855-1938
Mellanby, Sir Edward	1884-1955	Milne, Edward Arthur	1896-1950
Mellanby, John	1878-1939	Milne, George Francis, Baron	1866-1948
Mellon (formerly Woolgar), Sarah Jane	1824-1909	Milne, John	1850-1913
Melville, Arthur	1855-1904	Milne-Watson, Sir David Milne	1869-1945
Mendelsohn, Eric	1887-1953	Milner, Alfred, Viscount	1854-1925
Mendl, Sir Charles Ferdinand	1871-1958	Milner, James, Baron Milner of Leeds	1889-1967
Menon, Vapal Pangunni	1894-1966	Milner, Violet Georgina, Viscountess	1872-1958
Menzies, Sir Frederick Norton Kay	1875-1949	Milner Holland, Sir Edward. See	
Menzies, Sir Stewart Graham	1890-1968	Holland	1902-1969
Mercer, Cecil William, 'Dornford Yates'	1885-1960	Milnes, Robert Offley Ashburton	
Mercer, James	1883-1932	Crewe-, Marquess of Crewe. See	
Meredith, George	1828-1909	Crewe-Milnes	1858-1945
Meredith, Sir William Ralph	1840-1923	Minett, Francis Colin	1890-1953
Merivale, Herman Charles	1839-1906	Minto, Earl of. See Elliot, Gilbert John	
Merriman, Frank Boyd, Baron	1880-1962	Murray Kynynmond	1845-1914
Merriman, Henry Seton, *pseudonym*.		Minton, Francis John	1917-1957
See Scott, Hugh Stowell	1862-1903	Mirza Mohammad Ismail, Sir. See	
Merriman, John Xavier	1841-1926	Ismail	1883-1959
Merrivale, Baron. See Duke, Henry		Mitchell, Sir Arthur	1826-1909
Edward	1885-1939	Mitchell, John Murray	1815-1904
Merry, William Walter	1835-1918	Mitchell, Sir Peter Chalmers	1864-1945
Merry del Val, Rafael	1865-1930	Mitchell, Sir Philip Euen	1890-1964

Moyne, Baron. See Guinness, Walter Edward	1880-1944
Moynihan, Berkeley George Andrew, Baron	1865-1936
Mozley, John Kenneth	1883-1946
Muddiman, Sir Alexander Phillips	1875-1928
Muir, Edwin	1887-1959
Muir, (John) Ramsay (Bryce)	1872-1941
Muir, Sir Robert	1864-1959
Muir, Sir William	1819-1905
Muirhead, John Henry	1855-1940
Müller, Ernest Bruce Iwan-. See Iwan-Müller	1853-1910
Mullins, Edwin Roscoe	1848-1907
Munby, Arthur Joseph	1828-1910
Munnings, Sir Alfred James	1878-1959
Munro, Hector Hugh	1870-1916
Munro, James	1832-1908
Munro–Ferguson, Ronald Crauford, Viscount Novar. See Ferguson	1860-1934
Murdoch, William Lloyd	1855-1911
Murison, Alexander Falconer	1847-1934
Murray, Alexander Stuart	1841-1904
Murray, Andrew Graham, Viscount Dunedin	1849-1942
Murray, Sir Archibald James	1860-1945
Murray, Charles Adolphus, Earl of Dunmore	1841-1907
Murray, David Christie	1847-1907
Murray, Sir (George) Evelyn (Pemberton)	1880-1947
Murray, George Gilbert Aimé	1866-1957
Murray, Sir George Herbert	1849-1936
Murray, George Redmayne	1865-1939
Murray, George Robert Milne	1858-1911
Murray, Sir James Augustus Henry	1837-1915
Murray, Sir James Wolfe	1853-1919
Murray, Sir John	1841-1914
Murray, Sir John	1851-1928
Murray, John	1879-1964
Murray, Sir (John) Hubert (Plunkett)	1861-1940
Murray, Margaret Alice	1863-1963
Murray, Sir Oswyn Alexander Ruthven	1873-1936
Murry, John Middleton	1889-1957
Murry, Kathleen, 'Katherine Mansfield'	1888-1923
Musgrave, Sir James	1826-1904
Muybridge, Eadweard	1830-1904
Myers, Charles Samuel	1873-1946
Myers, Ernest James	1844-1921
Myers, Leopold Hamilton	1881-1944
Myrddin–Evans, Sir Guildhaume	1894-1964
Myres, Sir John Linton	1869-1954
Mysore, Sir Shri Krishnaraja Wadiyar Bahadur, Maharaja of	1884-1940
Nair, Sir Chettur Sankaran. See Sankaran Nair	1857-1934
Nairne, Alexander	1863-1936
Namier, Sir Lewis Bernstein	1888-1960
Narbeth, John Harper	1863-1944
Nares, Sir George Strong	1831-1915
Nash, Paul	1889-1946
Nash, Sir Walter	1882-1968
Nathan, Harry Louis, Baron	1889-1963
Nathan, Sir Matthew	1862-1939
Nawanagar, Maharaja Shri Ranjitsinhji Vibhaji, Maharaja Jam Saheb of	1872-1933
Nehru, Jawaharlal	1889-1964
Nehru, Pandit Motilal	1861-1931

Neil, Robert Alexander	1852-1901
Neil, Samuel	1825-1901
Neilson, George	1858-1923
Neilson, Julia Emilie	1868-1957
Nelson, Eliza (1827-1908). See under Craven, Henry Thornton	1818-1905
Nelson, Sir Frank	1883-1966
Nelson, George Horatio, Baron Nelson of Stafford	1887-1962
Nelson, Sir Hugh Muir	1835-1906
Neruda, Wilma Maria Francisca. See Hallé, Lady	1839-1911
Nesbit, Edith. See Bland	1858-1924
Nettleship, Edward	1845-1913
Nettleship, John Trivett	1841-1902
Neubauer, Adolf	1832-1907
Neville, Henry	1837-1910
Nevinson, Christopher Richard Wynne	1889-1946
Nevinson, Henry Woodd	1856-1941
Newall (formerly Phillpotts), Dame Bertha Surtees	1877-1932
Newall, Cyril Louis Norton, Baron	1886-1963
Newall, Hugh Frank	1857-1944
Newberry, Percy Edward	1869-1949
Newbold, Sir Douglas	1894-1945
Newbolt, Sir Henry John	1862-1938
Newbolt, William Charles Edmund	1844-1930
Newman, Ernest	1868-1959
Newman, Sir George	1870-1948
Newman, William Lambert	1834-1923
Newmarch, Charles Henry	1824-1903
Newnes, Sir George	1851-1910
Newsam, Sir Frank Aubrey	1893-1964
Newsholme, Sir Arthur	1857-1943
Newton, Baron. See Legh, Thomas Wodehouse	1857-1942
Newton, Alfred	1829-1907
Newton, Ernest	1856-1922
Nichol Smith, David. See Smith	1875-1962
Nichols, Robert Malise Bowyer	1893-1944
Nicholson, Sir Charles	1808-1903
Nicholson, Sir Charles Archibald	1867-1949
Nicholson, Charles Ernest	1868-1954
Nicholson, Edward Williams Byron	1849-1912
Nicholson, George	1847-1908
Nicholson, Joseph Shield	1850-1927
Nicholson, Reynold Alleyne	1868-1945
Nicholson, Sir Sydney Hugo	1875-1947
Nicholson, William Gustavus, Baron	1845-1918
Nicholson, Sir William Newzam Prior	1872-1949
Nickalls, Guy	1866-1935
Nicol, Erskine	1825-1904
Nicoll, Sir William Robertson	1851-1923
Nicolson, Adela Florence, 'Laurence Hope'	1865-1904
Nicolson, Sir Arthur, Baron Carnock	1849-1928
Nicolson, Sir Harold George	1886-1968
Nicolson, Malcolm Hassels (1843-1904). See under Nicolson, Adela Florence	
Nicolson, Victoria Mary, Lady. See Sackville-West	1892-1962
Nightingale, Florence	1820-1910
Nixon, Sir John Eccles	1857-1921
Noble, Sir Andrew	1831-1915
Noble, Montagu Alfred	1873-1940
Noble, Sir Percy Lockhart Harnam	1880-1955
Nodal, John Howard	1831-1909
Noel-Buxton, Noel Edward, Baron	1869-1948
Norfolk, Duke of. See Howard, Henry FitzAlan-	1847-1917

Owen, Robert	1820–1902	Partridge, Sir Bernard	1861–1945
Oxford and Asquith, Countess of. See		Passfield, Baron. See Webb, Sidney	
Asquith, Emma Alice Margaret		James	1859–1947
(Margot)	1864–1945	Patel, Vallabhbhai Javerabhai	1875–1950
Oxford and Asquith, Earl of. See		Patel, Vithalbai Jhavabhai	1870–1933
Asquith, Herbert Henry	1852–1928	Paterson, Sir Alexander Henry	1884–1947
		Paterson, Sir William	1874–1956
		Paterson, William Paterson	1860–1939
Page, Sir Archibald	1875–1949	Patiala, Sir Bhupindra Singh, Maharaja	
Page, Sir Frederick Handley	1885–1962	of	1891–1938
Page, H. A., *pseudonym*. See Japp,		Paton, Diarmid Noël	1859–1928
Alexander Hay	1837–1905	Paton, John Brown	1830–1911
Page, Sir Leo Francis	1890–1951	Paton, John Gibson	1824–1907
Page, Thomas Ethelbert	1850–1936	Paton, John Lewis (Alexander)	1863–1946
Page, William	1861–1934	Paton, Sir Joseph Noël	1821–1901
Paget, Sir Bernard Charles Tolver	1887–1961	Paton, William	1886–1943
Paget, Francis	1851–1911	Pattison, Andrew Seth Pringle-	
Paget, Dame (Mary) Rosalind	1855–1948	(formerly Andrew Seth)	1856–1931
Paget, Lady Muriel Evelyn Vernon	1876–1938	Paul, Charles Kegan	1828–1902
Paget, Sir Richard Arthur Surtees	1869–1955	Paul, Herbert Woodfield	1853–1935
Paget, Sidney Edward	1860–1908	Paul, William	1822–1905
Paget, Stephen	1855–1926	Pauncefote, Julian, Baron	1828–1902
Paget, Violet, 'Vernon Lee'	1856–1935	Pavy, Frederick William	1829–1911
Pain, Barry Eric Odell	1864–1928	Payne, Edward John	1844–1904
Paine, Charles Hubert Scott-. See		Payne, Humfry Gilbert Garth	1902–1936
Scott-Paine	1891–1954	Payne, John Wesley Vivian (Jack)	1899–1969
Pakenham, Sir Francis John	1832–1905	Payne, Joseph Frank	1840–1910
Pakenham, Sir William Christopher	1861–1933	Peacock, Sir Edward Robert	1871–1962
Palairet, Sir (Charles) Michael	1882–1956	Peacocke, Joseph Ferguson	1835–1916
Palgrave, Sir Reginald Francis Douce	1829–1904	Peake, Arthur Samuel	1865–1929
Palles, Christopher	1831–1920	Peake, Sir Charles Brinsley Pemberton	1897–1958
Palmer, Sir Arthur Power	1840–1904	Peake, Frederick Gerard	1886–1970
Palmer, Sir Charles Mark	1822–1907	Peake, Harold John Edward	1867–1946
Palmer, Sir Elwin Mitford	1852–1906	Peake, Mervyn Laurence	1911–1968
Palmer, George Herbert	1846–1926	Pearce, Ernest Harold	1865–1930
Palmer, George William	1851–1913	Pearce, Sir George Foster	1870–1952
Palmer, William Waldegrave, Earl of		Pearce, Sir (Standen) Leonard	1873–1947
Selborne	1859–1942	Pearce, Stephen	1819–1904
Paneth, Friedrich Adolf	1887–1958	Pearce, Sir William George	1861–1907
Pankhurst, Dame Christabel Harriette	1880–1958	Pears, Sir Edwin	1835–1919
Pankhurst, Emmeline	1858–1928	Pearsall, William Harold	1891–1964
Pantin, Carl Frederick Abel	1899–1967	Pearsall Smith, (Lloyd) Logan. See	
Pares, Sir Bernard	1867–1949	Smith	1865–1946
Paris, Sir Archibald	1861–1937	Pearson, Alfred Chilton	1861–1935
Parish, William Douglas	1833–1904	Pearson, Charles John, Lord	1843–1910
Parker, Albert Edmund, Earl of Morley	1843–1905	Pearson, Sir Cyril Arthur	1866–1921
Parker, Charles Stuart	1829–1910	Pearson, Karl	1857–1936
Parker, Eric (Frederick Moore Searle)	1870–1955	Pearson, Weetman Dickinson, Viscount	
Parker, Sir (Horatio) Gilbert (George)	1862–1932	Cowdray	1856–1927
Parker, John	1875–1952	Pease, Sir Arthur Francis	1866–1927
Parker, Joseph	1830–1902	Pease, Edward Reynolds	1857–1955
Parker, Louis Napoleon	1852–1944	Pease, Joseph Albert, Baron Gainford	1860–1943
Parker, Robert John, Baron	1857–1918	Pease, Sir Joseph Whitwell	1828–1903
Parkin, Sir George Robert	1846–1922	Peat, Stanley	1902–1969
Parkinson, Sir (Arthur Charles) Cosmo	1884–1967	Peek, Sir Cuthbert Edgar	1855–1901
Parmoor, Baron. See Cripps, Charles		Peel, Arthur Wellesley, Viscount	1829–1912
Alfred	1852–1941	Peel, Sir Frederick	1823–1906
Parr (formerly Taylor), Louisa	*d*.1903	Peel, James	1811–1906
Parratt, Sir Walter	1841–1924	Peel, William Robert Wellesley, Earl	1867–1937
Parry, Sir Charles Hubert Hastings	1848–1918	Peers, Sir Charles Reed	1868–1952
Parry, Joseph	1841–1903	Peers, Edgar Allison	1891–1952
Parry, Joseph Haydn (1864–1894). See		Peet, Thomas Eric	1882–1934
under Parry, Joseph		Peile, Sir James Braithwaite	1833–1906
Parsons, Alfred William	1847–1920	Peile, John	1837–1910
Parsons, Sir Charles Algernon	1854–1931	Pelham, Henry Francis	1846–1907
Parsons, Sir John Herbert	1868–1957	Pélissier, Harry Gabriel	1874–1913
Parsons, Laurence, Earl of Rosse	1840–1908	Pell, Albert	1820–1907
Parsons, Sir Leonard Gregory	1879–1950	Pember, Edward Henry	1833–1911
Parsons, Richard Godfrey	1882–1948	Pemberton, Thomas Edgar	1849–1905
Partington, James Riddick	1886–1965	Pembrey, Marcus Seymour	1868–1934

Pope, Sir William Jackson	1870-1939	Pugh, Sir Arthur	1870-1955
Popham, Arthur Ewart	1889-1970	Pullen, Henry William	1836-1903
Popham, Sir (Henry) Robert (Moore)		Pumphrey, Richard Julius	1906-1967
Brooke-. See Brooke-Popham	1878-1953	Purcell, Albert Arthur William	1872-1935
Portal, Melville	1819-1904	Purse, Benjamin Ormond	1874-1950
Portal, Sir Wyndham Raymond,		Purser, Louis Claude	1854-1932
Viscount	1885-1949	Purvis, Arthur Blaikie	1890-1941
Porter, Sir Andrew Marshall	1837-1919	Pye, Sir David Randall	1886-1960
Porter, Samuel Lowry, Baron	1877-1956	Pyne, Louisa Fanny Bodda. See Bodda	
Postan (formerly Power), Eileen Edna le		Pyne	1832-1904
Poer	1889-1940		
Postgate, John Percival	1853-1926		
Pott, Alfred	1822-1908	Quarrier, William	1829-1903
Potter, (Helen) Beatrix (Mrs Heelis)	1866-1943	Quick, Sir John	1852-1932
Potter, Stephen Meredith	1900-1969	Quick, Oliver Chase	1885-1944
Poulton, Sir Edward Bagnall	1856-1943	Quickswood, Baron. See Cecil, Hugh	
Pound, Sir (Alfred) Dudley (Pickman		Richard Heathcote Gascoyne-	1869-1956
Rogers)	1877-1943	Quiller-Couch, Sir Arthur Thomas ('Q')	1863-1944
Powell, Cecil Frank	1903-1969	Quilter, Harry	1851-1907
Powell, Frederick York	1850-1904	Quilter, Roger Cuthbert	1877-1953
Powell, Sir (George) Allan	1876-1948	Quilter, Sir William Cuthbert	1841-1911
Powell, Sir Richard Douglas	1842-1925	Quin, Windham Thomas Wyndham-,	
Powell, Robert Stephenson Smyth		Earl of Dunraven and Mount-Earl	1841-1926
Baden-, Baron Baden-Powell. See			
Baden-Powell	1857-1941		
Power, Sir Arthur John	1889-1960	Rackham, Arthur	1867-1939
Power, Sir D'Arcy	1855-1941	Rackham, Bernard	1876-1964
Power, Eileen Edna le Poer. See Postan	1889-1940	Radcliffe-Crocker, Henry	1845-1909
Power, Sir John Cecil	1870-1950	Rae, William Fraser	1835-1905
Power, Sir William Henry	1842-1916	Raggi, Mario	1821-1907
Powicke, Sir (Frederick) Maurice	1879-1963	Raikes, Humphrey Rivaz	1891-1955
Pownall, Sir Henry Royds	1887-1961	Railton, Herbert	1858-1910
Powys, John Cowper	1872-1963	Raine, Allen, *pseudonym*. See	
Poynder, Sir John Poynder Dickson-,		Puddicombe, Anne Adalisa	1836-1908
Baron Islington	1866-1936	Raines, Sir Julius Augustus Robert	1827-1909
Poynter, Sir Edward John	1836-1919	Rainy, Adam Rolland (1862-1911). See	
Poynting, John Henry	1852-1914	under Rainy, Robert	
Prain, Sir David	1857-1944	Rainy, Robert	1826-1906
Pratt, Hodgson	1824-1907	Rait, Sir Robert Sangster	1874-1936
Pratt, Joseph Bishop	1854-1910	Raleigh, Sir Walter Alexander	1861-1922
Preece, Sir William Henry	1834-1913	Ralston, James Layton	1881-1948
Prendergast, Sir Harry North		Ram, Sir (Lucius Abel John) Granville	1885-1952
Dalrymple	1834-1913	Raman, Sir (Chandrasekhara) Venkata	1888-1970
Prestage, Edgar	1869-1951	Ramé, Marie Louise, 'Ouida'. See De la	
Previté-Orton, Charles William	1877-1947	Ramée	1839-1908
Price, Frederick George Hilton	1842-1909	Ramsay, Alexander	1822-1909
Price, Thomas	1852-1909	Ramsay, Sir Bertram Home	1883-1945
Prichard, Harold Arthur	1871-1947	Ramsay, Sir James Henry	1832-1925
Primrose, Archibald Philip, Earl of		Ramsay, Sir William	1852-1916
Rosebery	1847-1929	Ramsay, Sir William Mitchell	1851-1939
Primrose, Sir Henry William	1846-1923	Ramsay-Steel-Maitland, Sir Arthur	
Pringle, William Mather Rutherford	1874-1928	Herbert Drummond. See Steel-	
Pringle-Pattison, Andrew Seth. See		Maitland	1876-1935
Pattison	1856-1931	Ramsden, Omar	1873-1939
Prinsep, Valentine Cameron (Val)	1838-1904	Randall, Richard William	1824-1906
Prior, Melton	1845-1910	Randall-MacIver, David	1873-1945
Pritchard, Sir Charles Bradley	1837-1903	Randegger, Alberto	1832-1911
Pritchett, Robert Taylor	1828-1907	Randles, Marshall	1826-1904
Probert, Lewis	1841-1908	Randolph, Francis Charles Hingeston-.	
Procter, Francis	1812-1905	See Hingeston-Randolph	1833-1910
Proctor, Robert George Collier	1868-1903	Randolph, Sir George Granville	1818-1907
Propert, John Lumsden	1834-1902	Ranjitsinhji, Maharaja Jam Saheb of	
Prothero, Sir George Walter	1848-1922	Nawanagar. See Nawanagar	1872-1933
Prothero, Rowland Edmund, Baron		Rankeillour, Baron. See Hope, James	
Ernle	1851-1937	Fitzalan	1870-1949
Prout, Ebenezer	1835-1909	Rankin, Sir George Claus	1877-1946
Pryde, James Ferrier	1866-1941	Ransom, William Henry	1824-1907
Prynne, George Rundle	1818-1903	Ransome, Arthur Michell	1884-1967
Puddicombe, Anne Adalisa, 'Allen		Raper, Robert William	1842-1915
Raine'	1836-1908	Rapson, Edward James	1861-1937

Robertson, Douglas Moray Cooper Lamb Argyll	1837-1909
Robertson, George Matthew	1864-1932
Robertson, Sir George Scott	1852-1916
Robertson, Sir Howard Morley	1888-1963
Robertson, James Patrick Bannerman, Baron	1845-1909
Robertson, John Mackinnon	1856-1933
Robertson, Sir Johnston Forbes-	1853-1937
Robertson, Sir Robert	1869-1949
Robertson, Sir William Robert	1860-1933
Robertson Scott, John William	1866-1962
Robey, Sir George Edward	1869-1954
Robins, Thomas Ellis, Baron	1884-1962
Robinson, (Esmé Stuart) Lennox	1886-1958
Robinson, Frederick William	1830-1901
Robinson, George Frederick Samuel, Marquess of Ripon	1827-1909
Robinson, (George) Geoffrey. See Dawson	1874-1944
Robinson, Henry Wheeler	1872-1945
Robinson, Sir John	1839-1903
Robinson, Sir John Charles	1824-1913
Robinson, Sir John Richard	1828-1903
Robinson, Joseph Armitage	1858-1933
Robinson, Sir Joseph Benjamin	1840-1929
Robinson, Philip Stewart (Phil)	1847-1902
Robinson, Roy Lister, Baron	1883-1952
Robinson, Vincent Joseph	1829-1910
Robinson, Sir (William) Arthur	1874-1950
Robinson, William Heath	1872-1944
Robinson, William Leefe	1895-1918
Robison, Robert	1883-1941
Robson, William Snowdon, Baron	1852-1918
Roby, Henry John	1830-1915
Roche, Alexander Adair, Baron	1871-1956
Rodd, James Rennell, Baron Renell	1858-1941
Roe, Sir (Edwin) Alliott Verdon Verdon-. See Verdon-Roe	1877-1958
Rogers, Annie Mary Anne Henley	1856-1937
Rogers, Benjamin Bickley	1828-1919
Rogers, Edmund Dawson	1823-1910
Rogers, James Guinness	1822-1911
Rogers, Sir Leonard	1868-1962
Rogers, Leonard James	1862-1933
Rolleston, Sir Humphrey Davy	1862-1944
Rolls, Charles Stewart	1877-1910
Romer, Mark Lemon, Baron	1866-1944
Romer, Sir Robert	1840-1918
Ronald, Sir Landon	1873-1938
Ronan, Stephen	1848-1925
Rookwood, Baron. See Selwin-Ibbetson, Henry John	1826-1902
Rooper, Thomas Godolphin	1847-1903
Roos-Keppel, Sir George Olof	1866-1921
Roose, Edward Charles Robson	1848-1905
Rootes, William Edward, Baron	1894-1964
Ropes, Arthur Reed, 'Adrian Ross'	1859-1933
Roscoe, Sir Henry Enfield	1833-1915
Roscoe, Kenneth Harry	1914-1970
Rose, John Holland	1855-1942
Rose-Innes, Sir James	1855-1942
Rosebery, Earl of. See Primrose, Archibald Philip	1847-1929
Rosenhain, Walter	1875-1934
Rosenheim, (Sigmund) Otto	1871-1955
Ross, Adrian, pseudonym. See Ropes, Arthur Reed	1859-1933
Ross, Sir Alexander George	1840-1910
Ross, Sir (Edward) Denison	1871-1940

Ross, Sir Frederick William Leith-. See Leith-Ross	1887-1968
Ross, Sir Ian Clunies	1899-1959
Ross, Sir John	1829-1905
Ross, Sir John	1853-1935
Ross, Joseph Thorburn	1849-1903
Ross, Martin, pseudonym. See Martin, Violet Florence	1862-1915
Ross, Sir Ronald	1857-1932
Ross, William Stewart, 'Saladin'	1844-1906
Rosse, Earl of. See Parsons, Laurence	1840-1908
Rossetti, William Michael	1829-1919
Rothenstein, Sir William	1872-1945
Rothermere, Viscount. See Harms-worth, Harold Sidney	1868-1940
Rothery, William Hume-. See Hume-Rothery	1899-1968
Rothschild, Lionel Walter, Baron	1868-1937
Rothschild, Sir Nathan Meyer, Baron	1840-1915
Rotter, Godfrey	1879-1969
Round, Henry Joseph	1881-1966
Round, John Horace	1854-1928
Rousby, William Wybert	1835-1907
Rouse, William Henry Denham	1863-1950
Routh, Edward John	1831-1907
Rowe, Joshua Brooking	1837-1908
Rowlands, Sir Archibald	1892-1953
Rowlands, David, 'Dewi Môn'	1836-1907
Rowlatt, Sir Sidney Arthur Taylor	1862-1945
Rowley, Harold Henry	1890-1969
Rowntree, Benjamin Seebohm	1871-1954
Rowntree, Joseph	1836-1925
Rowton, Baron. See Corry, Montagu William Lowry	1838-1903
Roxburgh, John Fergusson	1888-1954
Roy, Camille Joseph	1870-1943
Royce, Sir (Frederick) Henry	1863-1933
Royden, (Agnes) Maude	1876-1956
Royden, Sir Thomas, Baron	1871-1950
Rudolf, Edward de Montjoie	1852-1933
Ruffside, Viscount. See Brown, Douglas Clifton	1879-1958
Rugby, Baron. See Maffey, John Loader	1877-1969
Ruggles-Brise, Sir Evelyn John	1857-1935
Ruggles Gates, Reginald. See Gates	1882-1962
Rumbold, Sir Horace	1829-1913
Rumbold, Sir Horace George Montagu	1869-1941
Runciman, Walter, Baron	1847-1937
Runciman, Walter, Viscount Runciman of Doxford	1870-1949
Rundall, Francis Hornblow	1823-1908
Rundle, Sir (Henry Macleod) Leslie	1856-1934
Rusden, George William	1819-1903
Rushbrooke, James Henry	1870-1947
Rushbury, Sir Henry George	1889-1968
Rushcliffe, Baron. See Betterton, Henry Bucknall	1872-1949
Russell, Arthur Oliver Villiers, Baron Ampthill	1869-1935
Russell, Bertrand Arthur William, Earl	1872-1970
Russell, Sir Charles	1863-1928
Russell, Sir (Edward) John	1872-1965
Russell, Edward Stuart	1887-1954
Russell, Francis Xavier Joseph (Frank), Baron Russell of Killowen	1867-1946
Russell, George William, 'AE'	1867-1935
Russell, Henry Chamberlaine	1836-1907
Russell, Herbrand Arthur, Duke of Bedford	1858-1940
Russell, Mary Annette, Countess	1866-1941

Schreiner, Olive Emilie Albertina (1855–1920). See under Schriener, William Philip	
Schreiner, William Philip	1857–1919
Schunck, Henry Edward	1820–1903
Schuster, Sir Arthur	1851–1934
Schuster, Claud, Baron	1869–1956
Schuster, Sir Felix Otto	1854–1936
Schwabe, Randolph	1885–1948
Scott, Archibald	1837–1909
Scott, Charles Prestwich	1846–1932
Scott, Lord Charles Thomas Montagu-Douglas-	1839–1911
Scott, Clement William	1841–1904
Scott, Cyril Meir	1879–1970
Scott, Dukinfield Henry	1854–1934
Scott, Lord Francis George Montagu-Douglas-	1879–1952
Scott, George Herbert	1888–1930
Scott, Sir Giles Gilbert	1880–1960
Scott, Hugh Stowell, 'Henry Seton Merriman'	1862–1903
Scott, Sir (James) George	1851–1935
Scott, John	1830–1903
Scott, Sir John	1841–1904
Scott, John William Robertson. See Robertson Scott	1866–1962
Scott, Kathleen. See Kennet, (Edith Agnes) Kathleen, Lady	1878–1947
Scott, Leader, pseudonym. See Baxter, Lucy	1837–1902
Scott, Sir Leslie Frederic	1869–1950
Scott, Sir Percy Moreton	1853–1924
Scott, Robert Falcon	1868–1912
Scott-Ellis, Thomas Evelyn, Baron Howard de Walden	1880–1946
Scott-James, Rolfe Arnold	1878–1959
Scott-Paine, Charles Hubert	1891–1954
Scrutton, Sir Thomas Edward	1856–1934
Seale-Hayne, Charles Hayne	1833–1903
Seaman, Sir Owen	1861–1936
Seccombe, Thomas	1866–1923
Seddon, Richard John	1845–1906
Sedgwick, Adam	1854–1913
See, Sir John	1844–1907
Seebohm, Frederic	1833–1912
Seeley, Harry Govier	1839–1909
Seely, John Edward Bernard, Baron Mottistone	1868–1947
Selbie, William Boothby	1862–1944
Selborne, Earl of. See Palmer, William Waldegrave	1859–1942
Selby, Viscount. See Gully, William Court	1835–1909
Selby, Thomas Gunn	1846–1910
Selfridge, Harry Gordon	1858–1947
Seligman, Charles Gabriel	1873–1940
Selincourt, Ernest de	1870–1943
Selous, Frederick Courteney	1851–1917
Selwin-Ibbetson, Henry John, Baron Rookwood	1826–1902
Selwyn, Alfred Richard Cecil	1824–1902
Semon, Sir Felix	1849–1921
Sempill, Baron. See Forbes-Sempill, William Francis	1893–1965
Senanayake, Don Stephen	1884–1952
Sendall, Sir Walter Joseph	1832–1904
Sequeira, James Harry	1865–1948
Sergeant, (Emily Frances) Adeline	1851–1904
Sergeant, Lewis	1841–1902

Service, Robert William	1874–1958
Seth, Andrew. See Pattison, Andrew Seth Pringle-	1856–1931
Seton, George	1822–1908
Seton-Watson, Robert William	1879–1951
Severn, Walter	1830–1904
Seward, Sir Albert Charles	1863–1941
Sewell, Elizabeth Missing	1815–1906
Sewell, James Edwards	1810–1903
Sewell, Robert Beresford Seymour	1880–1964
Sexton, Sir James	1856–1938
Sexton, Thomas	1848–1932
Seymour, Sir Edward Hobart	1840–1929
Shackleton, Sir David James	1863–1938
Shackleton, Sir Ernest Henry	1874–1922
Shadwell, Charles Lancelot	1840–1919
Shand, (afterwards Burns), Alexander, Baron	1828–1904
Shand, Alexander Innes	1832–1907
Shandon, Baron. See O'Brien, Ignatius John	1857–1930
Shannon, Charles Haslewood	1863–1937
Shannon, Sir James Jebusa	1862–1923
Sharp, Cecil James	1859–1924
Sharp, William, 'Fiona Macleod'	1855–1905
Sharpe, Richard Bowdler	1847–1909
Sharpey-Schafer, Sir Edward Albert. See Schafer	1850–1935
Shattock, Samuel George	1852–1924
Shaughnessy, Thomas George, Baron	1853–1923
Shaw, Alfred	1842–1907
Shaw, Sir Eyre Massey	1830–1908
Shaw, George Bernard	1856–1950
Shaw, Henry Selby Hele-. See Hele-Shaw	1854–1941
Shaw, James Johnston	1845–1910
Shaw, John Byam Lister	1872–1919
Shaw, Richard Norman	1831–1912
Shaw, Thomas, Baron Craigmyle	1850–1937
Shaw, Thomas	1872–1938
Shaw, William Arthur	1865–1943
Shaw, Sir (William) Napier	1854–1945
Shaw-Lefevre, George John, Baron Eversley	1831–1928
Shearman, Sir Montague	1857–1930
Sheepshanks, Sir Thomas Herbert	1895–1964
Sheffield, Earl of. See Holroyd, Henry North	1832–1909
Sheffield, Baron. See Stanley, Edward Lyulph	1839–1925
Shelford, Sir William	1834–1905
Shenstone, William Ashwell	1850–1908
Shepherd, George Robert, Baron	1881–1954
Sheppard, Hugh Richard Lawrie	1880–1937
Sherborn, Charles William	1831–1912
Sherek, (Jules) Henry	1900–1967
Sheridan, Clare Consuelo	1885–1970
Sherriff, George	1898–1967
Sherrington, Sir Charles Scott	1857–1952
Sherrington, Helen Lemmens-. See Lemmens-Sherrington	1834–1906
Shields, Frederic James	1833–1911
Shiels, Sir (Thomas) Drummond	1881–1953
Shipley, Sir Arthur Everett	1861–1927
Shippard, Sir Sidney Godolphin Alexander	1837–1902
Shirley, Frederick Joseph John	1890–1967
Shirreff, Maria Georgina. See Grey	1816–1906
Shoenberg, Sir Isaac	1880–1963
Shore, Thomas William	1840–1905

Somervell, Donald Bradley, Baron Somervell of Harrow	1889–1960
Somerville, Edith Anna Œnone	1858–1949
Somerville, Sir James Fownes	1882–1949
Somerville, Mary	1897–1963
Somerville, Sir William	1860–1932
Sonnenschein, Edward Adolf	1851–1929
Sorabji, Cornelia	1866–1954
Sorby, Henry Clifton	1826–1908
Sorley, William Ritchie	1855–1935
Sotheby, Sir Edward Southwell	1813–1902
Soutar, Ellen. See Farren	1848–1904
Southborough, Baron. See Hopwood, Francis John Stephens	1860–1947
Southesk, Earl of. See Carnegie, James	1827–1905
Southey, Sir Richard	1808–1901
Southward, John	1840–1902
Southwell, Sir Richard Vynne	1888–1970
Southwell, Thomas	1831–1909
Southwood, Viscount. See Elias, Julius Salter	1873–1946
Souttar, Sir Henry Sessions	1875–1964
Spare, Austin Osman	1886–1956
Spearman, Charles Edward	1863–1945
Spence, Sir James Calvert	1892–1954
Spencer, Sir Henry Francis	1892–1964
Spencer, Herbert	1820–1903
Spencer, John Poyntz, Earl Spencer	1835–1910
Spencer, Leonard James	1870–1959
Spencer, Sir Stanley	1891–1959
Spencer, Sir Walter Baldwin	1860–1929
Spender, John Alfred	1862–1942
Spens, Sir William (Will)	1882–1962
Speyer, Sir Edgar	1862–1932
Spiers, Richard Phené	1838–1916
Spilsbury, Sir Bernard Henry	1877–1947
Spofforth, Frederick Robert	1853–1926
Spooner, William Archibald	1844–1930
Sprengel, Hermann Johann Philipp	1834–1906
Sprigg, Sir John Gordon	1830–1913
Sprigge, Sir (Samuel) Squire	1860–1937
Spring, (Robert) Howard	1889–1965
Spring-Rice, Sir Cecil Arthur	1859–1918
Sprott, George Washington	1829–1909
Spry, Constance	1886–1960
Spy, *pseudonym*. See Ward, Sir Leslie	1851–1922
Squire, Sir John Collings	1884–1958
Squire, William Barclay	1855–1927
Stables, William Gordon	1840–1910
Stack, Sir Lee Oliver Fitzmaurice	1868–1924
Stacpoole, Frederick	1813–1907
Stacpoole, Henry de Vere	1863–1951
Stafford, Sir Edward William	1819–1901
Stainer, Sir John	1840–1901
Stalbridge, Baron. See Grosvenor, Richard de Aquila	1837–1912
Stallybrass, William Teulon Swan	1883–1948
Stamer, Sir Lovelace Tomlinson	1829–1908
Stamfordham, Baron. See Bigge, Arthur John	1849–1931
Stamp, Josiah Charles, Baron	1880–1941
Stamp, Sir (Laurence) Dudley	1898–1966
Stanford, Sir Charles Villiers	1852–1924
Stanier, Sir William Arthur	1876–1965
Stanley, Albert Henry, Baron Ashfield	1874–1948
Stanley, Sir Arthur	1869–1947
Stanley, Edward George Villiers, Earl of Derby	1865–1948
Stanley, Edward Lyulph, Baron Sheffield and Baron Stanley of Alderley	1839–1925
Stanley, Frederick Arthur, Earl of Derby	1841–1908
Stanley, Henry Edward John, Baron Stanley of Alderley	1827–1903
Stanley, Sir Henry Morton	1841–1904
Stanley, Sir Herbert James	1872–1955
Stanley, Oliver Frederick George	1896–1950
Stanley, William Ford Robinson	1829–1909
Stanmore, Baron. See Gordon, Arthur Charles Hamilton-	1829–1912
Stannard, Henrietta Eliza Vaughan, 'John Strange Winter'	1856–1911
Stannus, Hugh Hutton	1840–1908
Stansfeld, Margaret	1860–1951
Stansgate, Viscount. See Benn, William Wedgwood	1877–1960
Stanton, Arthur Henry	1839–1913
Stapledon, Sir (Reginald) George	1882–1960
Stark, Arthur James	1831–1902
Starling, Ernest Henry	1866–1927
Stead, William Thomas	1849–1912
Stebbing, (Lizzie) Susan	1885–1943
Steed, Henry Wickham	1871–1956
Steel, Allan Gibson	1858–1914
Steel, Flora Annie	1847–1929
Steel-Maitland, Sir Arthur Herbert Drummond Ramsay- (formerly Arthur Herbert Drummond Steel)	1876–1935
Steer, Philip Wilson	1860–1942
Steggall, Charles	1826–1905
Stein, Sir Edward Sinauer de. See de Stein	1887–1965
Stein, Sir (Mark) Aurel	1862–1943
Stenton, Sir Frank Merry	1880–1967
Stephen, Sir Alexander Condie	1850–1908
Stephen, Caroline Emelia (1834–1909). See under Stephen, Sir Leslie	
Stephen, George, Baron Mount Stephen	1829–1921
Stephen, Sir Leslie	1832–1904
Stephens, Frederic George	1828–1907
Stephens, James	1825–1901
Stephens, James	1880?–1950
Stephens, James Brunton	1835–1902
Stephens, William Richard Wood	1839–1902
Stephenson, Sir Frederick Charles Arthur	1821–1911
Stephenson, George Robert	1819–1905
Stephenson, (John) Cecil	1889–1965
Stephenson, Marjory	1885–1948
Stephenson, Thomas Alan	1898–1961
Sterling (afterwards MacKinlay), Antoinette	1843–1904
Stern, Sir Albert Gerald	1878–1966
Sterndale, Baron. See Pickford, William	1848–1923
Sterry, Charlotte	1870–1966
Stevens, Marshall	1852–1936
Stevenson, Sir Daniel Macaulay	1851–1944
Stevenson, David Watson	1842–1904
Stevenson, James, Baron	1873–1926
Stevenson, John James	1831–1908
Stevenson, Sir Thomas	1838–1908
Stevenson, William Henry	1858–1924
Stewart, Charles	1840–1907
Stewart, Sir Halley	1838–1937
Stewart, Isla	1855–1910
Stewart, James	1831–1905
Stewart, John Alexander	1846–1933
Stewart, Sir (Percy) Malcolm	1872–1951
Stewart, Sir (Samuel) Findlater	1879–1960
Stewart, William Downie	1878–1949

Tafawa Balewa, Alhaji Sir Abu Bakar	1912–1966
Tagore, Sir Rabindranath	1861–1941
Tait, Frederick Guthrie. See under Tait, Peter Guthrie	
Tait, James	1863–1944
Tait, Peter Guthrie	1831–1901
Tait, Sir (William Eric) Campbell	1886–1946
Talbot, Edward Stuart	1844–1934
Talbot, Sir George John	1861–1938
Tallack, William	1831–1908
Tallents, Sir Stephen George	1884–1958
Tangye, Sir Richard	1833–1906
Tanner, Joseph Robson	1860–1931
Tansley, Sir Arthur George	1871–1955
Tarn, Sir William Woodthorpe	1869–1957
Tarte, Joseph Israel	1848–1907
Taschereau, Sir Henri Elzéar	1836–1911
Taschereau, Sir Henri Thomas	1841–1909
Tata, Sir Dorabji Jamsetji	1859–1932
Tata, Jamsetji Nasarwanji	1839–1904
Tatlow, Tissington	1876–1957
Tattersfield, Frederick	1881–1959
Taunton, Ethelred Luke	1857–1907
Tawney, Richard Henry	1880–1962
Taylor, Alfred Edward	1869–1945
Taylor, Charles	1840–1908
Taylor, Charles Bell	1829–1909
Taylor, Eva Germaine Rimington	1879–1966
Taylor, Frank Sherwood	1897–1956
Taylor, Sir Gordon Gordon-. See Gordon-Taylor	1878–1960
Taylor, Helen	1831–1907
Taylor, Henry Martyn	1842–1927
Taylor, Isaac	1829–1901
Taylor, James Haward	1909–1968
Taylor, Sir John	1833–1912
Taylor, John Edward	1830–1905
Taylor, John Henry	1871–1963
Taylor, Louisa. See Parr	d. 1903
Taylor, Sir Thomas Murray	1897–1962
Taylor, Sir Thomas Weston Johns	1895–1953
Taylor, Walter Ross	1838–1907
Taylor, William	1865–1937
Teale, Thomas Pridgin	1831–1923
Teall, Sir Jethro Justinian Harris	1849–1924
Tearle, (George) Osmond	1852–1901
Tearle, Sir Godfrey Seymour	1884–1953
Tedder, Arthur William, Baron	1890–1967
Tegart, Sir Charles Augustus	1881–1946
Teichman, Sir Eric	1884–1944
Temperley, Harold William Vazeille	1879–1939
Tempest, Dame Marie	1864–1942
Temple, Frederick	1821–1902
Temple, Sir Richard	1826–1902
Temple, Sir Richard Carnac	1850–1931
Temple, William	1881–1944
Templewood, Viscount. See Hoare, Sir Samuel John Gurney	1880–1959
Tenby, Viscount. See Lloyd-George, Gwilym	1894–1967
Tennant, Sir Charles	1823–1906
Tennant, Sir David	1829–1905
Tennant, Margaret Mary Edith (May)	1869–1946
Tenniel, Sir John	1820–1914
Tennyson-d'Eyncourt, Sir Eustace Henry William	1868–1951
Terry, Dame (Alice) Ellen	1847–1928
Terry, Charles Sanford	1864–1936
Terry, Fred	1863–1933
Terry, Sir Richard Runciman	1865–1938

Thankerton, Baron. See Watson, William	1873–1948
Thesiger, Frederic Augustus, Baron Chelmsford	1827–1905
Thesiger, Frederic John Napier, Viscount Chelmsford	1868–1933
Thirkell, Angela Margaret	1890–1961
Thiselton-Dyer, Sir William Turner	1843–1928
Thoday, David	1883–1964
Thomas, Bertram Sidney	1892–1950
Thomas, David Alfred, Viscount Rhondda	1856–1918
Thomas, Dylan Marlais	1914–1953
Thomas, Forest Frederic Edward Yeo-. See Yeo-Thomas	1902–1964
Thomas, Frederick William	1867–1956
Thomas, Freeman Freeman-, Marquess of Willingdon. See Freeman-Thomas	1866–1941
Thomas, George Holt	1869–1929
Thomas, Sir Henry	1878–1952
Thomas, Herbert Henry	1876–1935
Thomas, Sir Hugh Evan-. See Evan-Thomas	1862–1928
Thomas, Hugh Hamshaw	1885–1962
Thomas, James Henry	1874–1949
Thomas, James Purdon Lewes, Viscount Cilcennin	1903–1960
Thomas, Margaret Haig, Viscountess Rhondda	1883–1958
Thomas, (Philip) Edward	1878–1917
Thomas, Sir (Thomas) Shenton (Whitelegge)	1879–1962
Thomas, Sir William Beach	1868–1957
Thomas, William Moy	1828–1910
Thompson, Alexander Hamilton	1873–1952
Thompson, D'Arcy Wentworth	1829–1902
Thompson, Sir D'Arcy Wentworth	1860–1948
Thompson, Edmund Symes-. See Symes-Thompson	1837–1906
Thompson, Edward John	1886–1946
Thompson, Sir Edward Maunde	1840–1929
Thompson, Francis	1859–1907
Thompson, Sir Henry	1820–1904
Thompson, Sir (Henry Francis) Herbert	1859–1944
Thompson, Henry Yates	1838–1928
Thompson, James Matthew	1878–1956
Thompson, Lydia	1836–1908
Thompson, Reginald Campbell	1876–1941
Thompson, Silvanus Phillips	1851–1916
Thompson, William Marcus	1857–1907
Thomson, Arthur	1858–1935
Thomson, Sir Basil Home	1861–1939
Thomson, Christopher Birdwood, Baron	1875–1930
Thomson, Sir George Pirie	1887–1965
Thomson, George Reid, Lord	1893–1962
Thomson, Hugh	1860–1920
Thomson, Jocelyn Home	1859–1908
Thomson, John	1856–1926
Thomson, Sir Joseph John	1856–1940
Thomson, William, Baron Kelvin	1824–1907
Thomson, Sir William	1843–1909
Thorne, William James (Will)	1857–1946
Thornton, Alfred Henry Robinson	1863–1939
Thornton, Sir Edward	1817–1906
Thornycroft, Sir John Isaac	1843–1928
Thornycroft, Sir (William) Hamo	1850–1925
Thorpe, Sir Thomas Edward	1845–1925
Threlfall, Sir Richard	1861–1932
Thring, Godfrey	1823–1903

Vane-Tempest-Stewart, Charles Stewart Henry, Marquess of Londonderry	1878-1949
Van Horne, Sir William Cornelius	1843-1915
Vansittart, Edward Westby	1818-1904
Vansittart, Robert Gilbert, Baron	1881-1957
Vaughan, Bernard John	1847-1922
Vaughan, David James	1825-1905
Vaughan, Dame Helen Charlotte Isabella Gwynne-. See Gwynne-Vaughan	1879-1967
Vaughan, Herbert Alfred	1832-1903
Vaughan, Kate	1852?-1903
Vaughan, William Wyamar	1865-1938
Vaughan Williams, Ralph	1872-1958
Veitch, Sir Harry James	1840-1924
Veitch, James Herbert	1868-1907
Venn, John	1834-1923
Ventris, Michael George Francis	1922-1956
Verdon-Roe, Sir (Edwin) Alliott Verdon	1877-1958
Vereker, John Standish Surtees Prendergast, Viscount Gort	1886-1946
Verney, Ernest Basil	1894-1967
Verney, Margaret Maria, Lady	1844-1930
Vernon-Harcourt, Leveson Francis	1839-1907
Verrall, Arthur Woollgar	1851-1912
Vestey, William, Baron	1859-1940
Vezin, Hermann	1829-1910
Vezin (formerly Mrs Charles Young), Jane Elizabeth	1827-1902
Vian, Sir Philip Louis	1894-1968
Vickers, Kenneth Hotham	1881-1958
Vicky. See Weisz, Victor	1913-1966
Victoria Adelaide Mary Louise, Princess Royal of Great Britain and German Empress	1840-1901
Victoria Alexandra Alice Mary, Princess Royal of Great Britain	1897-1965
Victoria Alexandra Olga Mary, princess of Great Britain	1868-1935
Victoria Eugénie Julia Ena, Queen of Spain	1887-1969
Villiers, George Herbert Hyde, Earl of Clarendon	1877-1955
Villiers, John Henry De, Baron. See De Villiers	1842-1914
Villiers, Margaret Elizabeth Child-, Countess of Jersey	1849-1945
Villiers, Victor Albert George Child-, Earl of Jersey	1845-1915
Vincent, Sir (Charles Edward) Howard	1849-1908
Vincent, Sir Edgar, Viscount D'Abernon	1857-1941
Vincent, James Edmund	1857-1909
Vines, Sydney Howard	1849-1934
Vinogradoff, Sir Paul Gavrilovitch	1854-1925
Voigt, Frederick Augustus	1892-1957
Von Hügel, Friedrich, Baron of the Holy Roman Empire	1852-1925
Voysey, Charles	1828-1912
Voysey, Charles Francis Annesley	1857-1941
Wace, Henry	1836-1924
Waddell, Helen Jane	1889-1965
Waddell, Lawrence Augustine (later Austine)	1854-1938
Wade, Sir Willoughby Francis	1827-1906
Wadsworth, Alfred Powell	1891-1956
Wadsworth, Edward Alexander	1889-1949

Wager, Lawrence Rickard	1904-1965
Waggett, Philip Napier	1862-1939
Wain, Louis William	1860-1939
Wake-Walker, Sir William Frederic	1888-1945
Wakefield, Charles Cheers, Viscount	1859-1941
Wakley, Thomas (1851-1909). See under Wakley, Thomas Henry	
Wakley, Thomas Henry	1821-1907
Walcot, William	1874-1943
Waley, Arthur David	1889-1966
Waley, Sir (Sigismund) David	1887-1962
Walkden, Alexander George, Baron	1873-1951
Walker, Sir Byron Edmund	1848-1924
Walker, Sir Emery	1851-1933
Walker, Ernest	1870-1949
Walker, Dame Ethel	1861-1951
Walker, Frederic John	1896-1944
Walker, Frederick William	1830-1910
Walker, Sir Frederick William Edward Forestier Forestier-. See Forestier-Walker	1844-1910
Walker, Sir Gilbert Thomas	1868-1958
Walker, Sir James	1863-1935
Walker, John	1900-1964
Walker, Sir Mark	1827-1902
Walker, Sir Norman Purvis	1862-1942
Walker, Sir Samuel	1832-1911
Walker, Vyell Edward	1837-1906
Walker, Sir William Frederic Wake-. See Wake-Walker	1888-1945
Walkley, Arthur Bingham	1855-1926
Wallace, Alfred Russel	1823-1913
Wallace, Sir Cuthbert Sidney	1867-1944
Wallace, Sir Donald Mackenzie	1841-1919
Wallace, (Richard Horatio) Edgar	1875-1932
Wallace, Thomas	1891-1965
Wallace, William Arthur James	1842-1902
Wallas, Graham	1858-1932
Waller, Charles Henry	1840-1910
Waller, Lewis	1860-1915
Waller, Samuel Edmund	1850-1903
Walls, Tom Kirby	1883-1949
Walpole, Sir Hugh Seymour	1884-1941
Walpole, Sir Spencer	1839-1907
Walsh, Stephen	1859-1929
Walsh, William Pakenham	1820-1902
Walsham, Sir John	1830-1905
Walsham, William Johnson	1847-1903
Walter, Sir Edward	1823-1904
Walter, John	1873-1968
Walton, Arthur	1897-1959
Walton, Frederick Parker	1858-1948
Walton, Sir John Lawson	1852-1908
Walton, Sir Joseph	1845-1910
Wanklyn, James Alfred	1834-1906
Wantage, Baron. See Lindsay (afterwards Loyd-Lindsay), Robert James	1832-1901
Warburg, Edmund Frederic	1908-1966
Warburton, Adrian	1918-1944
Ward, Sir Adolphus William	1837-1924
Ward, Sir Edward Willis Duncan	1853-1928
Ward, Francis (Frank) Kingdon-. See Kingdon-Ward	1885-1958
Ward, Harry Leigh Douglas	1825-1906
Ward, Harry Marshall	1854-1906
Ward, Henry Snowden	1865-1911
Ward, Ida Caroline	1880-1949
Ward, James	1843-1925
Ward, John	1866-1934
Ward, Sir Joseph George	1856-1930

Westland, Sir James	1842–1903	Wilde, Johannes (János)	1891–1970
Weston, Dame Agnes Elizabeth	1840–1918	Wilde, William James (Jimmy)	1892–1969
Weston, Sir Aylmer Gould Hunter-	1864–1940	Wilding, Anthony Frederick	1883–1915
Weston, Frank	1871–1924	Wilkie, Sir David Percival Dalbreck	1882–1938
Wet, Christiaan Rudolph De. See De		Wilkins, Augustus Samuel	1843–1905
Wet	1854–1922	Wilkins, Sir (George) Hubert	1888–1958
Weyman, Stanley John	1855–1928	Wilkins, William Henry	1860–1905
Weymouth, Richard Francis	1822–1902	Wilkinson, Ellen Cicely	1891–1947
Wharton, Sir William James Lloyd	1843–1905	Wilkinson, George Howard	1833–1907
Wheatley, John	1869–1930	Wilkinson, (Henry) Spenser	1853–1937
Wheeler, Sir William Ireland de Courcy	1879–1943	Wilkinson, Sir Nevile Rodwell	1869–1940
Wheelhouse, Claudius Galen	1826–1909	Wilkinson, Norman	1882–1934
Whetham, William Cecil Dampier. See		Wilks, Sir Samuel	1824–1911
Dampier	1867–1952	Will, John Shiress	1840–1910
Whibley, Charles	1859–1930	Willcocks, Sir James	1857–1926
Whibley, Leonard	1863–1941	Willcox, Sir William Henry	1870–1941
Whiddington, Richard	1885–1970	Willes, Sir George Ommanney	1823–1901
Whipple, Robert Stewart	1871–1953	Willett, William	1856–1915
Whistler, James Abbott McNeill	1834–1903	Williams, Alfred	1832–1905
Whistler, Reginald John (Rex)	1905–1944	Williams, Alwyn Terrell Petre	1888–1968
Whitaker, Sir (Frederick) Arthur	1893–1968	Williams, (Arthur Frederic) Basil	1867–1950
Whitby, Sir Lionel Ernest Howard	1895–1956	Williams, Charles	1838–1904
White, Claude Grahame-. See Grahame-		Williams, Charles Hanson Greville	1829–1910
White	1879–1959	Williams, Charles Walter Stansby	1886–1945
White, Sir (Cyril) Brudenell (Bingham)	1876–1940	Williams, Edward Francis, Baron	
White, Sir George Stuart	1835–1912	Francis-Williams	1903–1970
White, Henry Julian	1859–1934	Williams, Sir Edward Leader	1828–1910
White, John Campbell, Baron Overtoun	1843–1908	Williams, Sir George	1821–1905
White, Leonard Charles	1897–1955	Williams, Sir Harold Herbert	1880–1964
White, William Hale, 'Mark Rutherford'	1831–1913	Williams, Hugh	1843–1911
White, Sir William Hale-. See Hale-		Williams, Ivy	1877–1966
White	1857–1949	Williams, John Carvell	1821–1907
White, Sir William Henry	1845–1913	Williams, Sir John Coldbrook Han-	
Whitehead, Alfred North	1861–1947	bury-. See Hanbury-Williams	1892–1965
Whitehead, John Henry Constantine	1904–1960	Williams, Sir John Fischer	1870–1947
Whitehead, Robert	1823–1905	Williams, Norman Powell	1883–1943
Whiteing, Richard	1840–1928	Williams, Ralph Vaughan. See Vaughan	
Whiteley, William	1831–1907	Williams	1872–1958
Whiteley, William	1881–1955	Williams, Sir Roland Bowdler Vaughan	1838–1916
Whiteway, Sir William Vallance	1828–1908	Williams, Rowland, 'Hwfa Môn'	1823–1905
Whitfield, Ernest Albert, Baron		Williams, Thomas, Baron Williams of	
Kenswood	1887–1963	Barnburgh	1888–1967
Whitla, Sir William	1851–1933	Williams, Watkin Hezekiah, 'Watcyn	
Whitley, John Henry	1866–1935	Wyn'	1844–1905
Whitley, William Thomas	1858–1942	Williams-Freeman, John Peere	1858–1943
Whitman, Alfred Charles	1860–1910	Williamson, Alexander William	1824–1904
Whitmore, Sir George Stoddart	1830–1903	Williamson, John Thoburn	1907–1958
Whitney, James Pounder	1857–1939	Willingdon, Marquess of. See	
Whittaker, Sir Edmund Taylor	1873–1956	Freeman-Thomas, Freeman	1866–1941
Whittard, Walter Frederick	1902–1966	Willis, Henry	1821–1901
Whitten Brown, Sir Arthur. See Brown	1886–1948	Willis, William	1835–1911
Whitty, Dame Mary Louise (May)		Willock, Henry Davis	1830–1903
(1865–1948). See under Webster,		Willoughby, Digby	1845–1901
Benjamin	1864–1947	Wills, Sir George Alfred	1854–1928
Whitworth, Geoffrey Arundel	1883–1951	Wills, William Henry, Baron Winter-	
Whitworth, William Allen	1840–1905	stoke	1830–1911
Whymper, Edward	1840–1911	Wilmot, John, Baron Wilmot of	
Whymper, Josiah Wood	1813–1903	Selmeston	1895–1964
Whyte, Alexander	1836–1921	Wilmot, Sir Sainthill Eardley-	1852–1929
Wiart, Sir Adrian Carton de. See		Wilshaw, Sir Edward	1879–1968
Carton de Wiart	1880–1963	Wilson, Sir Arnold Talbot	1884–1940
Wickham, Edward Charles	1834–1910	Wilson, Arthur (1836–1909). See under	
Wiggins, Joseph	1832–1905	Wilson, Charles Henry, Baron	
Wigham, John Richardson	1829–1906	Nunburnholme	
Wigram, Clive, Baron	1873–1960	Wilson, Sir Arthur Knyvet	1842–1921
Wigram, Woolmore	1831–1907	Wilson, Charles Henry, Baron	
Wilberforce, Ernest Roland	1840–1907	Nunburnholme	1833–1907
Wilbraham, Sir Philip Wilbraham		Wilson, Sir Charles Rivers	1831–1916
Baker	1875–1957	Wilson, Charles Robert	1863–1904
Wild, (John Robert) Francis	1873–1939	Wilson, Charles Thomson Rees	1869–1959

Wyndham (formerly Moore), Mary, Lady 1861-1931

Wyndham-Quin, Windham Thomas, Earl of Dunraven and Mount-Earl. See Quin 1841-1926

Wynn-Carrington, Charles Robert, Baron Carrington and Marquess of Lincolnshire 1843-1928

Wynyard, Diana 1906-1964

Wyon, Allan 1843-1907

Yapp, Sir Arthur Keysall 1869-1936
Yarrow, Sir Alfred Fernandez 1842-1932
Yate, Sir Charles Edward 1849-1940
Yates, Dornford, *pseudonym.* See Mercer, Cecil William 1885-1960
Yeats, Jack Butler 1871-1957
Yeats, William Butler 1865-1939
Yeo, Gerald Francis 1845-1909
Yeo-Thomas, Forest Frederic Edward 1902-1964
Yerbury, Francis Rowland (Frank) 1885-1970
Yonge, Charlotte Mary 1823-1901
Yorke, Albert Edward Philip Henry, Earl of Hardwicke 1867-1904
Yorke, Francis Reginald Stevens 1906-1962
Yorke, Warrington 1883-1943
Youl, Sir James Arndell 1811-1904
Young, Sir Allen William 1827-1915

Young, Mrs Charles. See Vezin, Jane Elizabeth 1827-1902
Young, Edward Hilton, Baron Kennet 1879-1960
Young, Francis Brett 1884-1954
Young, Geoffrey Winthrop 1876-1958
Young, George, Lord 1819-1907
Young, Sir George 1837-1930
Young, George Malcolm 1883-1959
Young, Gerard Mackworth-. See Mackworth-Young 1884-1965
Young, Sir Hubert Winthrop 1885-1950
Young, Sir Robert Arthur 1871-1959
Young, Sydney 1857-1937
Young, William Henry 1863-1942
Young, Sir William Mackworth 1840-1924
Younger, George, Viscount Younger of Leckie 1851-1929
Younger, Robert, Baron Blanesburgh 1861-1946
Younghusband, Sir Francis Edward 1863-1942
Yoxall, Sir James Henry 1857-1925
Ypres, Earl of. See French, John Denton Pinkstone 1852-1925
Yule, George Udny 1871-1951

Zangwill, Israel 1864-1926
Zetland, Marquess of. See Dundas, Lawrence John Lumley 1876-1961
Zimmern, Sir Alfred Eckhard 1879-1957
Zulueta, Francis de (Francisco María José) 1878-1958